The

GOLFERS ENCYCLOPEDIA

The

GOLFERS ENCYCLOPEDIA

The Ultimate Guide to Modern Professional Golfers and Tournaments

Edited by
Sal Johnson and Dave Seanor

SKYHORSE PUBLISHING

Skyhorse Publishing books may be purchased in bulk at special discounts for sales promotion, corporate gifts, fund-raising, or educational purposes. Special editions can also be created to specifications. For details, contact the Special Sales Department, Skyhorse Publishing, 555 Eighth Avenue, Suite 903, New York, NY 10018 or info@skyhorsepublishing.com.

www.skyhorsepublishing.com

10 9 8 7 6 5 4 3 2 1

Library of Congress Cataloging-in-Publication Data

The USA TODAY golfer's encyclopedia : the ultimate guide to modern professional golfers and tournaments / edited by Sal Johnson and Dave Seanor.
   p. cm.
 ISBN 978-1-60239-302-8
1. Golf--Encyclopedias. 2. Golfers--Biography--Encyclopedias. I.
Johnson, Salvatore. II. Seanor, Dave. III. USA TODAY (Arlington, Va.)
 GV965.U93 2009
 796.352'64--dc22
                        2008052432

Printed in Canada

CONTENTS

Introduction   7

Part One: Player Statistics, A–Z   9

Part Two: Tournament Results, 1958–2008   601

INTRODUCTION

Welcome to *The USA TODAY Golfers Encyclopedia*. On the pages that follow, you'll find comprehensive statistics of PGA Tour players from the last 50 years—more than 1,500 golfers, listed alphabetically from Tommy Aaron to Richard Zokol—and Top 10 results from more than 2,300 tournaments contested during that period.

This project was born of frustration during a 30-year sports journalism career when I needed to find information about pro golfers from the past. Until this reference book was published, detailed information about golfers no longer active on the PGA Tour could be found only by combing through old media guides (if you happened to have collected them). There was no "go-to" source such as baseball enthusiasts enjoy with *The Baseball Encyclopedia*, or the *Ring Record Book and Boxing Encyclopedia*, which is indispensable to aficionados of the fight game. Hence *The USA TODAY Golfers Encyclopedia* is the first of its kind.

If you're curious as to how Dudley Wysong fared in 1968, after winning tournaments in 1966 and '67, you can turn to page 593 and learn that Wysong's best finish in 29 starts the following year was third place at the Philadelphia Golf Classic. Or you can look up a hometown hero—mine was Harry Toscano of New Castle, Pennsylvania—and learn the details of his career on the PGA Tour.

Golf statistics are sketchy before 1980, when the PGA Tour assiduously began to archive such data. Professional golf in the United States first became organized in 1916, with the founding of the PGA of America. The association conducted tournaments, but its priority was promoting the interests of club professionals who earned their living in golf shops and on lesson tees across the country. Tournament golf was loosely run and very local. Newspaper accounts often were incomplete; record keeping was haphazard; criteria varied.

Media guides appeared in the mid-1930s, but their publication through the '70s was sporadic and the data inconsistent. (The Masters, which has carefully archived player performance since the tournament began in 1934, is the exception.) Even in the Information Age, with answers to myriad questions accessible via the Internet, historical facts about golf are scarce. Statistics on PGATour.com go back only to 1980. If you search the Tour's Web site for details of Hale Irwin's career, you'll be hard-pressed to find anything about his first 14 years as a pro.

The prospect of compiling a comprehensive reference book was daunting. Fortunately, I'm friendly with Sal Johnson, who not only shared my desire to fill golf's information void, but also had the data to do it.

Sal worked for ABC Sports for 29 years, the last eight as a producer on golf telecasts. At various times he has been statistics editor for *Sports Illustrated, Golf Digest, Golfweek, Golf World,* and *Golf Magazine.* Each year he compiles player guides that are distributed to media at the four major championships. Like me, Johnson was frustrated by the absence of a reliable clearinghouse for golf statistics.

Twenty years ago, Sal began the task of acquiring media guides, tournament programs, newspaper clippings, magazines, and yearbooks, which he used to compile and cross-reference tournament results and player statistics. The resulting trove of data is now housed on a Web site Sal created called Golfstats.com, which is prominently featured on another Johnson venture, Golfobserver.com.

Sal's efforts caught my attention during my tenure as editor of *Golfweek* magazine. After several years of broken promises to co-produce an encyclopedia of golfers, Sal and I finally knuckled down and collaborated on this volume.

In order to keep the book manageable, we settled upon a 50-year history—roughly coinciding with the advent of televised golf—and a minimum of 25 career starts for a player to be included. Why 25 starts? Sal's database through 1958 includes more than 11,150 different players who completed nearly 862,000 rounds of golf. To include them all would have resulted in the death of far too many trees!

Drilling deeper into the database, Sal determined that nearly 5,300 players competed in only one tournament. Only about 2,300 teed it up more than ten times. Our 25-start threshold, which reflects the number of starts a typical full-time pro will make in a season, still yielded more than 1,500 players. The statistical breakdown of each player includes starts, rounds played, cuts made, wins, top-5 finishes, top 10s, top 25s, scoring average, and earnings. (For noteworthy figures such as Arnold Palmer, Ben Hogan, Sam Snead, and others whose careers bridged 1958, we added a line to account for results posted before the cutoff date.)

A note of caution when comparing prize money over the years: Three-time winner Arnold Palmer was leading money winner in 1958 with $42,511, which translates to $321,808 in today's dollars. Not a bad living, although it would have ranked No. 176 on the 2008 PGA Tour money list. But consider this: Comparable victories by Palmer alone in 1958 (including the Masters) would have been worth close to $3.6 million in 2008. Thanks to Tiger Woods, purse inflation in pro golf has far exceeded cost-of-living inflation.

Interesting, too, is the progression of tournament name changes owing to corporate sponsorship. The Buick Invitational in San Diego has had ten iterations in 50 years. Of the 48 events on the 2008 PGA Tour schedule, 17 have histories dating to 1958 or earlier.

The USA TODAY Golfers Encyclopedia does not reflect golf's international reach, nor does it include women's professional golf. Future volumes can cover that ground. After all, golf is a global game and it's a sport played with great skill by both sexes.

Meanwhile, Sal and I sincerely hope *The USA TODAY Golfers Encyclopedia*, supplemented by Golfstats.com, will be a valued resource for all who love the game and its history.

—Dave Seanor
November 15, 2008

PART ONE:
PLAYER STATISTICS, A–Z

Tommy Aaron

Year	Starts	Rounds Played	Cuts Made	Wins	Top-5s	Top-10s	Top-25s	Scoring Average	Money
1959	1	2	0	0	0	0	0	77.50	
1960	2	8	2	0	0	0	1	72.38	$150

Best finish for 1960: T-25th at the Masters

1961	21	84	21	0	0	4	14	70.50	$12,031

Best finish for 1961: T-7th at the Los Angles Open & St. Paul Open Invitational

1962	15	61	14	0	2	5	9	71.52	$9,257

Best finish for 1962: T-4th at the Palm Springs Golf Classic & Waco Turner Open Invitational

1963	23	93	23	0	6	9	12	71.19	$32,085

Best finish for 1963: T-2nd at the Memphis Open Invitational, Cleveland Open Invitational & Fig Garden Village Open Invitational

1964	36	123	25	0	3	6	12	72.03	$18,682

Best finish for 1964: T-4th at the Bing Crosby Pro-Am & Tucson Open

1965	32	125	29	0	4	9	18	71.50	$51,579

Best finish for 1965: T-2nd at the Bob Hope Classic & St. Paul Open

1966	32	113	24	0	4	7	13	72.00	$37,654

Best finish for 1966: T-2nd at the San Diego Open Invitational

1967	33	124	29	0	3	7	15	71.86	$39,732

Best finish for 1967: T-4th at the Cleveland Open

1968	31	119	29	0	3	12	19	70.88	$65,051

Best finish for 1968: 3rd at the Colonial National Invitational

1969	30	119	30	1	8	10	19	70.73	$112,529

Best finish for 1969: Win at the Canadian Open

1970	33	117	28	1	6	10	16	71.23	$95,518

Best finish for 1970: Win at the Atlanta Classic

1971	32	115	27	0	5	6	16	71.57	$63,836

Best finish for 1971: T-3rd at the Western Open, Kaiser International Open & Bahamas National Open

1972	28	103	24	0	5	8	15	71.44	$111,127

Best finish for 1972: T-2nd at the Glen Campbell Los Angles Open, Greater Greensboro Open, Houston Open & PGA Championship

1973	25	88	19	1	2	4	7	72.40	$60,619

Best finish for 1973: Win at the Masters

1974	33	110	22	0	0	2	6	72.25	$28,769

Best finish for 1974: T-6th at the Greater Milwaukee Open

1975	32	91	14	0	1	2	6	72.69	$29,613

Best finish for 1975: 3rd at the Phoenix Open

1976	29	94	18	0	1	1	6	72.60	$24,061

Best finish for 1976: T-4th at the Southern Open

1977	29	90	17	0	0	1	2	73.08	$14,270

Best finish for 1977: T-10th at the Joe Garagiola Tucson Open

1978	28	88	16	0	0	0	5	72.33	$24,560

Best finish for 1978: T-14th at the Greater Greensboro Open

1979	33	111	22	0	1	2	8	72.32	$62,814

Best finish for 1979: T-4th at the Jackie Gleason's Inverrary Classic

1980	28	72	10	0	0	0	0	73.35	$9,341

Best finish for 1980: T-34th at the Pleasant Valley Jimmy Fund Classic

1981	23	69	12	0	0	0	1	72.99	$16,747

Best finish for 1981: T-16th at the Canadian Open

1982	14	35	2	0	0	0	0	73.94	$2,775

Best finish for 1982: 26th at the Tallahassee Open

1983	7	18	0	0	0	0	0	74.22	$1,610
1984	5	13	2	0	0	0	0	74.62	$2,974

Best finish for 1984: T-57th at the Bing Crosby Pro-Am

1985	3	7	0	0	0	0	0	76.00	$1,500
1986	7	19	2	0	0	0	0	73.11	$3,122

Best finish for 1986: T-49th at the Hardee's Golf Classic

1987	2	7	1	0	0	0	0	76.43	$2,200

Best finish for 1987: T-50th at the Masters

1988	2	5	0	0	0	0	0	78.00	$1,500
1989	1	4	1	0	0	0	0	74.50	$4,900

Best finish for 1989: T-38th at the Masters

1990	1	2	0	0	0	0	0	75.50	$1,500
1991	1	4	1	0	0	0	0	72.75	$3,533

Best finish for 1991: T-49th at the Masters

1992	1	4	1	0	0	0	0	73.25	$3,440

Best finish for 1992: T-54th at the Masters

1993	1	2	0	0	0	0	0	75.50	$1,500
1994	1	2	0	0	0	0	0	78.00	$1,500
1996	1	2	0	0	0	0	0	73.50	$1,500
1997	1	2	0	0	0	0	0	77.00	$5,000
1998	1	2	0	0	0	0	0	80.00	$5,000
1999	1	2	0	0	0	0	0	79.50	$5,000
2000	1	4	1	0	0	0	0	78.25	$10,580

Best finish for 2000: 57th at the Masters

Year	Starts	Rounds Played	Cuts Made	Wins	Top-5s	Top-10s	Top-25s	Scoring Average	Money
2001	1	2	0	0	0	0	0	81.50	$5,000
2002	1	2	0	0	0	0	0	78.50	$5,000
2003	1	2	0	0	0	0	0	86.00	$5,000
2004	1	2	0	0	0	0	0	85.00	$5,000
2005	1	2	0	0	0	0	0	80.50	$5,000
Period Totals	Starts	Rounds Played	Cuts Made	Wins	Top-5s	Top-10s	Top-25s	Scoring Average	Money
	665	2263	466	3	54	105	220	72.09	$1,004,156

Bryan Abbott

Year	Starts	Rounds Played	Cuts Made	Wins	Top-5s	Top-10s	Top-25s	Scoring Average	Money
1972	1	2	0	0	0	0	0	76.50	
1973	1	4	1	0	0	0	0	74.25	

Best finish for 1973: T-71st at the Monsanto Open

1974	4	10	1	0	0	0	0	74.50	$357

Best finish for 1974: T-51st at the Monsanto Open

1975	12	31	4	0	0	0	0	73.94	$866

Best finish for 1975: T-52nd at the Pensacola Open

1976	3	6	0	0	0	0	0	75.00	$500
1977	2	4	0	0	0	0	0	76.00	$250
1978	2	4	0	0	0	0	0	76.25	$303
Period Totals	Starts	Rounds Played	Cuts Made	Wins	Top-5s	Top-10s	Top-25s	Scoring Average	Money
	25	61	6	0	0	0	0	74.52	$2,275

Jerry Abbott

Year	Starts	Rounds Played	Cuts Made	Wins	Top-5s	Top-10s	Top-25s	Scoring Average	Money
1968	19	54	8	0	0	0	0	73.67	$1,098

Best finish for 1968: T-28th at the AZALEA Open Invitational

1969	35	112	23	0	0	4	11	72.66	$19,346

Best finish for 1969: T-8th at the Phoenix Open & West End Classic

1970	24	72	12	0	0	1	5	72.54	$11,448

Best finish for 1970: 8th at the Byron Nelson Golf Classic

1971	22	71	13	0	0	0	4	72.25	$8,693

Best finish for 1971: T-16th at the Phoenix Open

1972	18	59	12	0	0	0	3	72.95	$8,574

Best finish for 1972: T-12th at the Glen Campbell Los Angles Open

1973	2	3	0	0	0	0	0	75.00	
Period Totals	Starts	Rounds Played	Cuts Made	Wins	Top-5s	Top-10s	Top-25s	Scoring Average	Money
	120	371	68	0	0	5	23	72.77	$49,159

Bob Ackerman

Year	Starts	Rounds Played	Cuts Made	Wins	Top-5s	Top-10s	Top-25s	Scoring Average	Money
1979	1	4	1	0	0	0	0	76.00	$573

Best finish for 1979: T-74th at the Western Open

1980	1	2	0	0	0	0	0	77.50	
1981	2	6	1	0	0	0	0	73.17	$1,453

Best finish for 1981: T-43rd at the U.S. Open

1982	10	20	1	0	0	0	0	74.25	$564

Best finish for 1982: T-67th at the USF&G Classic

1985	1	2	0	0	0	0	0	74.50	$1,000
1986	1	2	0	0	0	0	0	74.00	$1,000
1989	1	2	0	0	0	0	0	75.00	
1990	1	2	0	0	0	0	0	78.50	
1993	1	2	0	0	0	0	0	73.00	
1994	2	4	0	0	0	0	0	75.25	$1,200
2000	1	2	0	0	0	0	0	74.00	
2002	1	2	0	0	0	0	0	77.00	
2004	1	2	0	0	0	0	0	79.00	
2005	1	2	0	0	0	0	0	72.50	
Period Totals	Starts	Rounds Played	Cuts Made	Wins	Top-5s	Top-10s	Top-25s	Scoring Average	Money
	25	54	3	0	0	0	0	74.80	$5,790

Joe Acosta, Jr.

Year	Starts	Rounds Played	Cuts Made	Wins	Top-5s	Top-10s	Top-25s	Scoring Average	Money
1995	26	74	11	0	2	2	4	71.68	$147,745

Best finish for 1995: T-3rd at the Greater Milwaukee Open

1996	30	71	9	0	0	0	0	72.34	$37,632

Best finish for 1996: T-35th at the Phoenix Open

1997	1	4	1	0	0	0	0	71.25	$4,218

Best finish for 1997: T-58th at the AT&T Pebble Beach Pro-Am

1998	2	8	2	0	0	0	0	72.38	$16,898

Best finish for 1998: T-43rd at the U.S. Open

1999	1	3	0	0	0	0	0	73.67	

Year	Starts	Rounds Played	Cuts Made	Wins	Top-5s	Top-10s	Top-25s	Scoring Average	Money
2000	1	2	0	0	0	0	0	74.50	
2003	3	7	1	0	0	0	0	74.00	$9,765

Best finish for 2003: T-59th at the Nissan Open

Period Totals	Starts	Rounds Played	Cuts Made	Wins	Top-5s	Top-10s	Top-25s	Scoring Average	Money
	64	169	24	0	2	2	4	72.14	$216,258

Rick Acton

Year	Starts	Rounds Played	Cuts Made	Wins	Top-5s	Top-10s	Top-25s	Scoring Average	Money
1973	11	32	3	0	0	0	0	76.00	$210

Best finish for 1973: T-70th at the Andy Williams-San Diego Open

1974	16	44	5	0	0	0	0	74.57	$259

Best finish for 1974: T-65th at the IVB Philadelphia Golf Classic

1975	4	8	0	0	0	0	0	74.38	
1976	17	42	4	0	0	0	2	73.88	$6,779

Best finish for 1976: T-15th at the Andy Williams-San Diego Open & Florida Citrus Open Invitational

1977	11	26	2	0	0	0	0	74.35	$1,843

Best finish for 1977: T-39th at the Andy Williams-San Diego Open

1978	6	16	2	0	0	0	0	74.88	$1,631

Best finish for 1978: T-42nd at the Andy Williams-San Diego Open

1986	1	2	0	0	0	0	0	79.00	$1,000
1987	1	2	0	0	0	0	0	82.00	$1,000
1994	1	2	0	0	0	0	0	76.00	$1,200
1995	1	2	0	0	0	0	0	76.00	$1,200

Period Totals	Starts	Rounds Played	Cuts Made	Wins	Top-5s	Top-10s	Top-25s	Scoring Average	Money
	69	176	16	0	0	0	2	74.82	$15,123

Brad Adamonis

Year	Starts	Rounds Played	Cuts Made	Wins	Top-5s	Top-10s	Top-25s	Scoring Average	Money
2002	1	2	0	0	0	0	0	72.50	
2003	1	2	0	0	0	0	0	71.50	
2004	1	4	1	0	0	0	0	72.75	$9,712

Best finish for 2004: T-76th at the Buick Classic

2005	2	4	0	0	0	0	0	76.50	
2007	2	4	0	0	0	0	0	72.25	
2008	29	87	14	0	1	3	4	71.03	$862,413

Best finish for 2008: T-2nd at the John Deere Classic

Period Totals	Starts	Rounds Played	Cuts Made	Wins	Top-5s	Top-10s	Top-25s	Scoring Average	Money
	36	103	15	0	1	3	4	71.40	$872,126

Adam Adams

Year	Starts	Rounds Played	Cuts Made	Wins	Top-5s	Top-10s	Top-25s	Scoring Average	Money
1978	4	8	0	0	0	0	0	77.25	
1979	2	4	0	0	0	0	0	73.50	
1983	1	2	0	0	0	0	0	74.00	
1984	21	48	2	0	0	0	1	75.38	$4,304

Best finish for 1984: T-22nd at the Georgia-Pacific Atlanta Golf Classic

1987	1	2	0	0	0	0	0	80.50	$600
2006	1	2	0	0	0	0	0	75.50	

Period Totals	Starts	Rounds Played	Cuts Made	Wins	Top-5s	Top-10s	Top-25s	Scoring Average	Money
	30	66	2	0	0	0	1	75.61	$4,904

John Adams

Year	Starts	Rounds Played	Cuts Made	Wins	Top-5s	Top-10s	Top-25s	Scoring Average	Money
1969	1	2	0	0	0	0	0	75.50	
1972	1	2	0	0	0	0	0	73.00	
1973	13	28	1	0	0	0	0	74.57	$606

Best finish for 1973: T-42nd at the IVB Philadelphia Golf Classic

1978	10	23	2	0	0	0	1	74.13	$2,025

Best finish for 1978: T-17th at the Greater Milwaukee Open

1979	10	26	3	0	0	0	0	73.88	$1,784

Best finish for 1979: T-55th at the Houston Open

1980	24	61	10	0	0	1	3	72.92	$22,175

Best finish for 1980: 6th at the San Antonio Texas Open

1981	25	67	10	0	0	1	3	72.97	$18,498

Best finish for 1981: T-10th at the Greater Milwaukee Open

1982	26	79	15	0	2	2	5	72.22	$53,564

Best finish for 1982: 2nd at the Hall of Fame

1983	34	103	17	0	2	3	4	72.50	$59,887

Best finish for 1983: T-3rd at the B.C. Open

1984	28	91	18	0	1	2	8	71.73	$74,567

Best finish for 1984: T-3rd at the USF&G Classic

1985	24	67	9	0	0	0	0	73.21	$9,613

Best finish for 1985: T-38th at the Byron Nelson Golf Classic

Year	Starts	Rounds Played	Cuts Made	Wins	Top-5s	Top-10s	Top-25s	Scoring Average	Money
1986	30	93	18	0	1	2	6	72.06	$64,491

Best finish for 1986: 4th at the Deposit Guaranty Golf Classic

| 1987 | 33 | 101 | 20 | 0 | 0 | 0 | 4 | 71.84 | $51,972 |

Best finish for 1987: T-15th at the Pensacola Open

| 1988 | 19 | 68 | 15 | 0 | 1 | 1 | 4 | 70.54 | $64,341 |

Best finish for 1988: T-4th at the Deposit Guaranty Golf Classic

| 1989 | 30 | 87 | 14 | 0 | 0 | 2 | 6 | 71.44 | $107,824 |

Best finish for 1989: T-6th at the Hardee's Golf Classic

| 1990 | 31 | 87 | 13 | 0 | 0 | 2 | 4 | 71.87 | $127,733 |

Best finish for 1990: T-6th at the The International

| 1991 | 30 | 92 | 16 | 0 | 1 | 2 | 3 | 71.26 | $117,547 |

Best finish for 1991: T-5th at the Greater Milwaukee Open

| 1992 | 32 | 92 | 17 | 0 | 1 | 1 | 7 | 71.05 | $174,069 |

Best finish for 1992: T-3rd at the Las Vegas Invitational

| 1993 | 29 | 92 | 18 | 0 | 1 | 2 | 7 | 71.59 | $221,753 |

Best finish for 1993: T-4th at the Sprint Western Open

| 1994 | 32 | 82 | 11 | 0 | 0 | 1 | 3 | 72.45 | $109,189 |

Best finish for 1994: T-6th at the Sprint International

| 1995 | 25 | 81 | 16 | 0 | 1 | 3 | 7 | 70.62 | $243,366 |

Best finish for 1995: 4th at the Kmart Greater Greensboro Open

| 1996 | 25 | 78 | 15 | 0 | 1 | 1 | 3 | 71.22 | $257,840 |

Best finish for 1996: 2nd at the FedEx St. Jude Classic

| 1997 | 28 | 81 | 13 | 0 | 0 | 3 | 6 | 71.49 | $188,986 |

Best finish for 1997: T-6th at the Greater Vancouver Open

| 1998 | 25 | 62 | 7 | 0 | 0 | 0 | 1 | 72.39 | $56,467 |

Best finish for 1998: T-14th at the Kemper Open

2000	2	4	0	0	0	0	0	75.00	
2002	1	2	0	0	0	0	0	73.50	
2003	1	2	0	0	0	0	0	74.50	
2004	1	2	0	0	0	0	0	72.50	
Period Totals	Starts	Rounds Played	Cuts Made	Wins	Top-5s	Top-10s	Top-25s	Scoring Average	Money
	570	1655	278	0	12	29	85	71.96	$2,028,297

Sam Adams

Year	Starts	Rounds Played	Cuts Made	Wins	Top-5s	Top-10s	Top-25s	Scoring Average	Money
1971	1	4	1	0	0	0	0	74.25	

Best finish for 1971: 72nd at the Bahamas National Open

| 1972 | 25 | 68 | 9 | 0 | 1 | 1 | 4 | 73.60 | $18,774 |

Best finish for 1972: T-2nd at the Canadian Open

| 1973 | 25 | 55 | 3 | 1 | 2 | 2 | 2 | 73.53 | $24,888 |

Best finish for 1973: Win at the Quad Cities Open

| 1974 | 31 | 82 | 11 | 0 | 0 | 1 | 3 | 73.73 | $13,729 |

Best finish for 1974: T-8th at the B.C. Open

| 1975 | 15 | 38 | 4 | 0 | 0 | 1 | 3 | 73.95 | $5,150 |

Best finish for 1975: T-6th at the Tallahassee Open

| 1976 | 14 | 36 | 4 | 0 | 0 | 0 | 1 | 73.75 | $3,871 |

Best finish for 1976: T-13th at the B.C. Open

| 1977 | 22 | 64 | 10 | 0 | 0 | 0 | 4 | 72.53 | $10,037 |

Best finish for 1977: T-12th at the Ed McMahon Quad City Open & Pensacola Open

| 1978 | 15 | 36 | 4 | 0 | 0 | 0 | 0 | 74.64 | $2,026 |

Best finish for 1978: T-39th at the Tournament Players Championship

1979	1	2	0	0	0	0	0	73.00	
Period Totals	Starts	Rounds Played	Cuts Made	Wins	Top-5s	Top-10s	Top-25s	Scoring Average	Money
	149	385	46	1	3	5	17	73.59	$78,475

Bob Adamson

Year	Starts	Rounds Played	Cuts Made	Wins	Top-5s	Top-10s	Top-25s	Scoring Average	Money
1962	1	2	0	0	0	0	0	78.50	
1963	1	4	1	0	0	0	0	71.25	$195

Best finish for 1963: T-28th at the Cajun Classic Open Invitational

| 1964 | 25 | 62 | 8 | 0 | 0 | 0 | 2 | 73.53 | $1,918 |

Best finish for 1964: T-19th at the Almaden Open

1965	3	4	0	0	0	0	0	75.25	
Period Totals	Starts	Rounds Played	Cuts Made	Wins	Top-5s	Top-10s	Top-25s	Scoring Average	Money
	30	72	9	0	0	0	2	73.64	$2,113

Mitch Adcock

Year	Starts	Rounds Played	Cuts Made	Wins	Top-5s	Top-10s	Top-25s	Scoring Average	Money
1978	12	28	2	0	0	0	1	74.36	$2,730

Best finish for 1978: T-17th at the Sammy Davis, Jr. - Greater Hartford Open

| 1980 | 1 | 2 | 0 | 0 | 0 | 0 | 0 | 74.00 | |

Year	Starts	Rounds Played	Cuts Made	Wins	Top-5s	Top-10s	Top-25s	Scoring Average	Money
1984	1	4	1	0	0	0	0	74.50	$2,443

Best finish for 1984: 58th at the U.S. Open

Year	Starts	Rounds Played	Cuts Made	Wins	Top-5s	Top-10s	Top-25s	Scoring Average	Money
1987	1	2	0	0	0	0	0	74.00	$640
1990	21	61	11	0	0	0	2	71.70	$38,817

Best finish for 1990: T-13th at the Deposit Guaranty

Year	Starts	Rounds Played	Cuts Made	Wins	Top-5s	Top-10s	Top-25s	Scoring Average	Money
1991	3	10	2	0	0	0	1	69.10	$8,602

Best finish for 1991: T-22nd at the Chattanooga Classic

Year	Starts	Rounds Played	Cuts Made	Wins	Top-5s	Top-10s	Top-25s	Scoring Average	Money
1992	28	75	11	0	0	0	2	72.19	$58,394

Best finish for 1992: T-11th at the B.C. Open

Year	Starts	Rounds Played	Cuts Made	Wins	Top-5s	Top-10s	Top-25s	Scoring Average	Money
1993	1	2	0	0	0	0	0	72.50	
1994	1	2	0	0	0	0	0	73.50	
2008	1	2	0	0	0	0	0	73.50	
Period Totals	Starts	Rounds Played	Cuts Made	Wins	Top-5s	Top-10s	Top-25s	Scoring Average	Money
	70	188	27	0	0	0	6	72.31	$111,627

Jim Ahern

Year	Starts	Rounds Played	Cuts Made	Wins	Top-5s	Top-10s	Top-25s	Scoring Average	Money
1972	2	4	0	0	0	0	0	79.75	$500
1973	22	69	11	0	0	1	2	73.23	$7,083

Best finish for 1973: T-9th at the Quad Cities Open

1974	16	34	4	0	0	0	1	73.41	$2,532

Best finish for 1974: T-11th at the Tallahassee Open

1975	19	49	6	0	0	0	1	73.90	$3,771

Best finish for 1975: T-13th at the Phoenix Open

1978	1	2	0	0	0	0	0	78.00	$303
1979	2	4	0	0	0	0	0	75.00	
Period Totals	Starts	Rounds Played	Cuts Made	Wins	Top-5s	Top-10s	Top-25s	Scoring Average	Money
	62	162	21	0	0	1	4	73.73	$14,189

Rafael Alarcon

Year	Starts	Rounds Played	Cuts Made	Wins	Top-5s	Top-10s	Top-25s	Scoring Average	Money
1981	1	3	0	0	0	0	0	78.33	
1983	19	44	3	0	0	0	0	73.77	$3,153

Best finish for 1983: T-38th at the Hawaiian Open

1984	4	11	2	0	0	0	0	74.45	$3,145

Best finish for 1984: T-62nd at the Bing Crosby Pro-Am & U.S. Open

1985	5	17	3	0	0	0	0	73.18	$4,777

Best finish for 1985: T-52nd at the U.S. Open

1986	3	7	0	0	0	0	0	77.14	$600
1987	1	4	1	0	0	0	0	72.00	$856

Best finish for 1987: T-60th at the Southwest Golf Classic

1989	3	4	0	0	0	0	0	70.00	
1990	1	0	0	0	0	0	0		
1995	1	2	0	0	0	0	0	77.00	$1,000
1997	26	79	13	0	0	0	2	71.78	$79,928

Best finish for 1997: T-19th at the Kemper Open

Period Totals	Starts	Rounds Played	Cuts Made	Wins	Top-5s	Top-10s	Top-25s	Scoring Average	Money
	64	171	22	0	0	0	2	72.96	$93,459

Jim Albus

Year	Starts	Rounds Played	Cuts Made	Wins	Top-5s	Top-10s	Top-25s	Scoring Average	Money
1974	2	4	0	0	0	0	0	74.25	
1976	8	22	3	0	0	0	0	73.68	$1,110

Best finish for 1976: T-38th at the Greater Jacksonville Open

1977	4	12	2	0	0	0	0	72.92	$1,040

Best finish for 1977: T-45th at the Hawaiian Open

1978	1	4	1	0	0	0	0	71.75	$645

Best finish for 1978: T-55th at the American Express Westchester Classic

1979	2	4	0	0	0	0	0	77.50	
1980	1	2	0	0	0	0	0	75.00	$600
1981	3	4	1	0	0	0	1	76.25	$2,870

Best finish for 1981: T-23rd at the World Disney World National Team Championship

1982	5	14	2	0	0	0	0	73.00	$5,500

Best finish for 1982: T-26th at the Manufactures Hanover Westchester Classic

1983	3	8	1	0	0	0	0	74.75	$1,596

Best finish for 1983: T-68th at the Manufactures Hanover Westchester Classic

1984	3	12	3	0	0	0	0	73.58	$7,559

Best finish for 1984: T-30th at the U.S. Open

1985	2	6	1	0	0	0	0	75.33	$2,030

Best finish for 1985: T-66th at the Manufactures Hanover Westchester Classic

1986	1	2	0	0	0	0	0	77.50	$600
1988	2	4	0	0	0	0	0	74.50	$1,000
Period Totals	Starts	Rounds Played	Cuts Made	Wins	Top-5s	Top-10s	Top-25s	Scoring Average	Money
	37	98	14	0	0	0	1	74.01	$24,549

Steven Alker

Year	Starts	Rounds Played	Cuts Made	Wins	Top-5s	Top-10s	Top-25s	Scoring Average	Money
2001	1	4	1	0	0	0	0	70.25	$8,550
Best finish for 2001: T-55th at the Bell Canadian Open									
2003	30	85	13	0	0	0	3	71.88	$261,359
Best finish for 2003: 17th at the Buick Invitational									
2005	1	2	0	0	0	0	0	71.50	
2007	1	2	0	0	0	0	0	74.50	$4,882
Period Totals	Starts	Rounds Played	Cuts Made	Wins	Top-5s	Top-10s	Top-25s	Scoring Average	Money
	33	93	14	0	0	0	3	71.86	$274,790

Steve Allan

Year	Starts	Rounds Played	Cuts Made	Wins	Top-5s	Top-10s	Top-25s	Scoring Average	Money
1996	1	2	0	0	0	0	0	73.50	
1998	1	2	0	0	0	0	0	76.00	$1,152
1999	2	8	2	0	0	0	0	75.13	$26,343
Best finish for 1999: T-42nd at the U.S. Open									
2001	31	86	12	0	0	0	1	72.02	$156,686
Best finish for 2001: T-19th at the Buick Classic									
2002	30	91	16	0	0	0	5	70.88	$359,655
Best finish for 2002: T-14th at the Valero Texas Open									
2003	18	49	8	0	2	2	4	71.73	$616,325
Best finish for 2003: T-2nd at the Greater Milwaukee Open									
2004	33	99	18	0	1	1	5	71.04	$649,480
Best finish for 2004: T-2nd at the Reno-Tahoe Open									
2005	32	98	18	0	0	1	3	71.72	$418,428
Best finish for 2005: T-9th at the Reno-Tahoe Open									
2007	18	63	13	0	0	1	5	71.03	$568,059
Best finish for 2007: T-7th at the Canadian Open									
2008	21	58	9	0	2	4	5	71.40	$743,970
Best finish for 2008: T-3rd at the Turning Stone Resort Championship									
Period Totals	Starts	Rounds Played	Cuts Made	Wins	Top-5s	Top-10s	Top-25s	Scoring Average	Money
	187	556	96	0	5	9	28	71.47	$3,540,097

Bob Allard

Year	Starts	Rounds Played	Cuts Made	Wins	Top-5s	Top-10s	Top-25s	Scoring Average	Money
1972	1	2	0	0	0	0	0	81.00	
1973	18	49	5	0	0	1	1	73.82	$3,658
Best finish for 1973: T-7th at the B.C. Open									
1974	24	68	9	0	0	0	2	73.16	$5,113
Best finish for 1974: T-19th at the IVB Philadelphia Golf Classic									
1975	11	28	3	0	0	0	0	74.75	$975
Best finish for 1975: T-48th at the Andy Williams-San Diego Open									
1976	1	2	0	0	0	0	0	78.00	$500
Period Totals	Starts	Rounds Played	Cuts Made	Wins	Top-5s	Top-10s	Top-25s	Scoring Average	Money
	55	149	17	0	0	1	3	73.85	$10,246

Fulton Allem

Year	Starts	Rounds Played	Cuts Made	Wins	Top-5s	Top-10s	Top-25s	Scoring Average	Money
1986	3	6	0	0	0	0	0	76.17	$600
1987	7	19	4	0	1	1	1	72.11	$93,254
Best finish for 1987: 2nd at the NEC World Series of Golf									
1988	22	66	12	0	2	3	5	71.82	$164,910
Best finish for 1988: T-3rd at the Players Championship									
1989	25	85	18	0	0	0	10	71.20	$135,715
Best finish for 1989: T-12th at the Southwestern Bell Colonial									
1990	23	73	14	0	1	1	5	71.93	$132,493
Best finish for 1990: T-4th at the Nestle Invitational									
1991	24	73	14	1	1	2	5	71.27	$237,816
Best finish for 1991: Win at the Independent Insurance Agent Open									
1992	29	99	21	0	1	2	7	71.11	$209,982
Best finish for 1992: 4th at the Shell Houston Open									
1993	29	92	18	2	3	4	8	71.26	$852,269
Best finish for 1993: Win at the Southwestern Bell Colonial & NEC World Series of Golf									
1994	28	84	16	0	0	1	3	72.26	$167,116
Best finish for 1994: T-6th at the Bell Canadian Open									
1995	21	55	7	0	0	0	2	72.55	$55,227
Best finish for 1995: T-12th at the Doral-Ryder Open									
1996	18	54	10	0	1	1	3	71.13	$162,515
Best finish for 1996: T-4th at the Doral-Ryder Open									
1997	21	62	10	0	2	4	5	71.42	$237,051

Best finish for 1997: T-5th at the Doral-Ryder Open & Greater Milwaukee Open

Year	Starts	Rounds Played	Cuts Made	Wins	Top-5s	Top-10s	Top-25s	Scoring Average	Money
1998	21	59	9	0	1	1	1	72.39	$118,714

Best finish for 1998: 5th at the MCI Classic

| 1999 | 26 | 76 | 12 | 0 | 0 | 0 | 1 | 72.12 | $112,215 |

Best finish for 1999: T-15th at the Buick Open

| 2000 | 25 | 75 | 12 | 0 | 0 | 0 | 1 | 71.95 | $119,626 |

Best finish for 2000: T-21st at the Buick Invitational

| 2001 | 21 | 56 | 7 | 0 | 0 | 0 | 4 | 71.18 | $241,680 |

Best finish for 2001: T-11th at the Honda Classic

| 2002 | 26 | 64 | 6 | 0 | 0 | 0 | 1 | 72.59 | $92,379 |

Best finish for 2002: T-23rd at the COMPAQ Classic of New Orleans

| 2003 | 15 | 28 | 2 | 0 | 0 | 0 | 0 | 75.54 | $19,091 |

Best finish for 2003: T-49th at the Phoenix Open

| 2004 | 13 | 27 | 1 | 0 | 0 | 0 | 0 | 74.67 | $9,792 |

Best finish for 2004: 74th at the HP Classic of New Orleans

2005	3	6	0	0	0	0	0	73.00	
2006	2	2	0	0	0	0	0	75.00	
2007	1	2	0	0	0	0	0	73.50	
2008	1	3	1	0	0	0	0	71.33	$11,468

Best finish for 2008: T-74th at the Crowne Plaza Invitational at Colonial

Period Totals	Starts	Rounds Played	Cuts Made	Wins	Top-5s	Top-10s	Top-25s	Scoring Average	Money
	404	1166	194	3	13	20	62	71.92	$3,173,914

Michael Allen

Year	Starts	Rounds Played	Cuts Made	Wins	Top-5s	Top-10s	Top-25s	Scoring Average	Money
1988	2	5	0	0	0	0	0	76.80	$765
1989	1	4	1	0	0	0	0	72.75	$4,960

Best finish for 1989: T-52nd at the British Open

| 1990 | 31 | 96 | 17 | 0 | 0 | 0 | 4 | 72.22 | $101,609 |

Best finish for 1990: T-12th at the Nissan Los Angeles Open

| 1991 | 29 | 86 | 15 | 0 | 0 | 0 | 2 | 71.92 | $47,627 |

Best finish for 1991: T-18th at the Phoenix Open

| 1992 | 16 | 41 | 4 | 0 | 0 | 0 | 0 | 72.37 | $11,455 |

Best finish for 1992: T-43rd at the Buick Open & Hardee's Golf Classic

| 1993 | 27 | 84 | 15 | 0 | 2 | 3 | 6 | 71.79 | $231,072 |

Best finish for 1993: T-3rd at the Northern Telecom Open & Phoenix Open

| 1994 | 32 | 98 | 17 | 0 | 0 | 0 | 2 | 71.84 | $92,191 |

Best finish for 1994: T-13th at the Greater Milwaukee Open

| 1995 | 21 | 57 | 7 | 0 | 1 | 1 | 1 | 71.79 | $55,825 |

Best finish for 1995: T-5th at the Quad City Classic

| 1996 | 1 | 4 | 1 | 0 | 0 | 0 | 0 | 72.25 | $2,425 |

Best finish for 1996: T-72nd at the Nortel Open

| 1999 | 1 | 2 | 0 | 0 | 0 | 0 | 0 | 75.50 | |
| 2000 | 1 | 4 | 1 | 0 | 0 | 0 | 0 | 71.00 | $4,936 |

Best finish for 2000: T-49th at the B.C. Open

| 2001 | 1 | 4 | 1 | 0 | 0 | 0 | 1 | 70.75 | $91,734 |

Best finish for 2001: T-12th at the U.S. Open

| 2002 | 29 | 74 | 9 | 0 | 0 | 0 | 1 | 72.14 | $109,777 |

Best finish for 2002: T-25th at the Touchstone Energy Tucson Open

| 2004 | 28 | 85 | 15 | 0 | 1 | 2 | 4 | 71.07 | $882,872 |

Best finish for 2004: 2nd at the Chrysler Classic of Greensboro

| 2005 | 30 | 90 | 15 | 0 | 0 | 2 | 5 | 71.47 | $593,829 |

Best finish for 2005: T-6th at the B.C. Open

| 2006 | 25 | 84 | 17 | 0 | 0 | 0 | 3 | 71.06 | $470,946 |

Best finish for 2006: T-11th at the Booz Allen Classic

| 2007 | 22 | 74 | 15 | 0 | 1 | 2 | 4 | 71.12 | $1,016,952 |

Best finish for 2007: 2nd at the Turning Stone Resort Championship

| 2008 | 28 | 92 | 18 | 0 | 1 | 3 | 5 | 70.29 | $981,263 |

Best finish for 2008: T-3rd at the Justin Timberlake Shriners Hospitals for Children Classic

Period Totals	Starts	Rounds Played	Cuts Made	Wins	Top-5s	Top-10s	Top-25s	Scoring Average	Money
	325	984	168	0	6	13	38	71.58	$4,700,237

Ras Allen

Year	Starts	Rounds Played	Cuts Made	Wins	Top-5s	Top-10s	Top-25s	Scoring Average	Money
1964	1	2	0	0	0	0	0	74.00	
1966	2	4	0	0	0	0	0	77.50	
1968	3	6	0	0	0	0	0	76.00	
1969	16	40	4	0	0	0	0	74.00	$1,176

Best finish for 1969: T-31st at the Canadian Open

| 1971 | 1 | 2 | 0 | 0 | 0 | 0 | 0 | 79.00 | |
| 1972 | 17 | 40 | 3 | 0 | 0 | 0 | 1 | 74.30 | $2,559 |

Best finish for 1972: T-14th at the Tallahassee Open

1973	14	44	8	0	0	0	0	74.02	$2,814

Best finish for 1973: T-27th at the Greater Milwaukee Open

1974	24	56	4	0	0	0	1	73.68	$3,298

Best finish for 1974: T-20th at the Sammy Davis, Jr. - Greater Hartford Open

1975	8	20	2	0	0	0	0	73.85	$172

Best finish for 1975: T-64th at the Southern Open

Year	Starts	Rounds Played	Cuts Made	Wins	Top-5s	Top-10s	Top-25s	Scoring Average	Money
1976	2	4	0	0	0	0	0	75.75	
1980	1	2	0	0	0	0	0	77.50	
1983	1	2	0	0	0	0	0	77.50	
1985	1	2	0	0	0	0	0	75.50	$600
1991	1	2	0	0	0	0	0	78.50	
1992	1	1	0	0	0	0	0	74.00	
Period Totals	Starts	Rounds Played	Cuts Made	Wins	Top-5s	Top-10s	Top-25s	Scoring Average	Money
	93	227	21	0	0	0	2	74.27	$10,620

Robert Allenby

Year	Starts	Rounds Played	Cuts Made	Wins	Top-5s	Top-10s	Top-25s	Scoring Average	Money
1991	1	2	0	0	0	0	0	74.50	
1993	7	16	2	0	0	0	0	73.38	$13,176

Best finish for 1993: T-33rd at the U.S. Open

1994	1	4	1	0	0	0	0	71.00	$7,047

Best finish for 1994: T-60th at the British Open

1995	9	25	4	0	0	0	3	72.52	$74,488

Best finish for 1995: T-15th at the British Open

1996	7	18	2	0	0	0	0	73.17	$17,232

Best finish for 1996: T-31st at the Bay Hill Invitational

1997	8	22	3	0	0	1	2	73.77	$75,990

Best finish for 1997: T-10th at the British Open

1998	9	28	7	0	1	1	4	70.57	$191,867

Best finish for 1998: T-4th at the B.C. Open

1999	27	84	17	0	0	0	4	71.18	$323,256

Best finish for 1999: T-11th at the Bob Hope Chrysler Classic

2000	26	94	22	2	3	3	10	70.38	$1,968,685

Best finish for 2000: Win at the Shell Houston Open & Advil Western Open

2001	29	106	25	2	2	5	14	70.44	$2,310,029

Best finish for 2001: Win at the Nissan Open & Marconi Pennsylvania Classic

2002	27	95	22	0	4	8	14	70.25	$2,119,721

Best finish for 2002: T-2nd at the WGC-NEC Invitational & SEI Pennsylvania Classic

2003	24	80	21	0	4	9	13	70.11	$2,177,452

Best finish for 2003: 3rd at the EDS Byron Nelson Championship

2004	26	88	22	0	1	5	11	70.78	$1,523,218

Best finish for 2004: T-4th at the Honda Classic

2005	31	89	17	0	2	3	9	70.89	$1,193,458

Best finish for 2005: 4th at the Buick Open

2006	22	77	18	0	2	3	12	70.48	$1,503,581

Best finish for 2006: T-4th at the Bay Hill Invitational & Deutsche Bank Championship

2007	28	89	18	0	3	8	11	71.12	$2,228,354

Best finish for 2007: T-3rd at the Nissan Open & WGC-CA Championship

2008	28	107	27	0	5	9	17	70.64	$3,606,700

Best finish for 2008: T-2nd at the Stanford St. Jude Classic & Turning Stone Resort Championship

Period Totals	Starts	Rounds Played	Cuts Made	Wins	Top-5s	Top-10s	Top-25s	Scoring Average	Money
	310	1024	228	4	27	55	124	70.83	$19,334,253

Bud Allin

Year	Starts	Rounds Played	Cuts Made	Wins	Top-5s	Top-10s	Top-25s	Scoring Average	Money
1970	3	10	2	0	0	0	0	75.00	$335

Best finish for 1970: T-66th at the Coral Springs Open Invitational

1971	28	85	16	1	1	1	7	72.75	$54,548

Best finish for 1971: Win at the Greater Greensboro Open

1972	33	105	19	0	2	5	7	72.57	$42,654

Best finish for 1972: T-2nd at the Greater Milwaukee Open

1973	28	90	19	1	2	7	11	71.86	$74,933

Best finish for 1973: Win at the Florida Citrus Open Invitational

1974	25	88	19	2	3	8	15	71.31	$129,849

Best finish for 1974: Win at the Doral-Eastern Open & Byron Nelson Golf Classic

1975	28	97	21	0	4	5	14	71.91	$60,327

Best finish for 1975: T-3rd at the Pleasant Valley Classic

1976	24	79	16	1	3	7	10	71.76	$96,047

Best finish for 1976: Win at the Pleasant Valley Classic

1977	25	80	15	0	0	0	3	72.63	$20,357

Best finish for 1977: T-12th at the Anheuser-Busch Golf Classic

1979	7	18	2	0	0	0	0	72.94	$2,020

Best finish for 1979: T-26th at the Pensacola Open

Year	Starts	Rounds Played	Cuts Made	Wins	Top-5s	Top-10s	Top-25s	Scoring Average	Money
1980	28	89	17	0	0	2	6	72.20	$38,894

Best finish for 1980: T-7th at the Joe Garagiola Tucson Open

| 1981 | 18 | 59 | 12 | 0 | 0 | 1 | 3 | 72.05 | $30,171 |

Best finish for 1981: T-8th at the Doral-Eastern Open

| 1982 | 8 | 25 | 5 | 0 | 0 | 0 | 0 | 72.76 | $4,644 |

Best finish for 1982: T-33rd at the Honda Inverrary Classic

Period Totals	Starts	Rounds Played	Cuts Made	Wins	Top-5s	Top-10s	Top-25s	Scoring Average	Money
	255	825	163	5	15	36	76	72.19	$554,780

Peter Alliss

Year	Starts	Rounds Played	Cuts Made	Wins	Top-5s	Top-10s	Top-25s	Scoring Average	Money
1958	1	4	1	0	0	0	1	71.25	

Best finish for 1958: T-11th at the British Open

| 1959 | 1 | 4 | 1 | 0 | 0 | 0 | 1 | 72.75 | |

Best finish for 1959: T-16th at the British Open

| 1960 | 1 | 2 | 0 | 0 | 0 | 0 | 0 | 76.00 | |
| 1961 | 1 | 4 | 1 | 0 | 0 | 1 | 1 | 72.75 | |

Best finish for 1961: T-9th at the British Open

| 1962 | 1 | 4 | 1 | 0 | 0 | 1 | 1 | 73.25 | |

Best finish for 1962: T-8th at the British Open

| 1963 | 2 | 8 | 2 | 0 | 0 | 0 | 1 | 72.63 | $375 |

Best finish for 1963: T-18th at the British Open

| 1964 | 2 | 6 | 1 | 0 | 0 | 0 | 0 | 74.67 | $995 |

Best finish for 1964: T-33rd at the Carling World Open Championship

| 1965 | 2 | 6 | 1 | 0 | 0 | 0 | 0 | 76.50 | |

Best finish for 1965: T-47th at the British Open

| 1966 | 3 | 8 | 1 | 0 | 0 | 0 | 1 | 75.75 | $1,437 |

Best finish for 1966: T-20th at the British Open

| 1967 | 7 | 21 | 3 | 0 | 0 | 0 | 0 | 72.90 | $562 |

Best finish for 1967: T-30th at the Pensacola Open

| 1968 | 1 | 4 | 1 | 0 | 0 | 0 | 1 | 74.50 | $770 |

Best finish for 1968: T-13th at the British Open

| 1969 | 1 | 4 | 1 | 0 | 0 | 1 | 1 | 71.50 | $2,640 |

Best finish for 1969: 8th at the British Open

| 1970 | 1 | 4 | 1 | 0 | 0 | 0 | 0 | 74.25 | $420 |

Best finish for 1970: T-32nd at the British Open

| 1971 | 1 | 4 | 1 | 0 | 0 | 0 | 0 | 74.25 | $355 |

Best finish for 1971: T-47th at the British Open

| 1972 | 1 | 4 | 1 | 0 | 0 | 0 | 0 | 73.50 | $512 |

Best finish for 1972: T-31st at the British Open

| 1973 | 1 | 4 | 1 | 0 | 0 | 0 | 0 | 74.75 | $338 |

Best finish for 1973: T-51st at the British Open

| 1974 | 1 | 2 | 0 | 0 | 0 | 0 | 0 | 80.00 | $120 |

Period Totals	Starts	Rounds Played	Cuts Made	Wins	Top-5s	Top-10s	Top-25s	Scoring Average	Money
	28	93	18	0	0	3	8	73.85	$8,525

Jason Allred

Year	Starts	Rounds Played	Cuts Made	Wins	Top-5s	Top-10s	Top-25s	Scoring Average	Money
2003	2	4	0	0	0	0	0	75.25	
2005	29	73	8	0	0	0	1	72.53	$180,817

Best finish for 2005: T-17th at the Sony Open in Hawaii

| 2006 | 2 | 6 | 1 | 0 | 0 | 0 | 1 | 71.50 | $54,500 |

Best finish for 2006: T-14th at the Chrysler Classic of Tucson

| 2008 | 23 | 63 | 7 | 0 | 0 | 0 | 0 | 72.08 | $100,596 |

Best finish for 2008: T-28th at the U.S. Bank Championship in Milwaukee

Period Totals	Starts	Rounds Played	Cuts Made	Wins	Top-5s	Top-10s	Top-25s	Scoring Average	Money
	56	146	16	0	0	0	2	72.37	$335,913

Stanton Altgelt

Year	Starts	Rounds Played	Cuts Made	Wins	Top-5s	Top-10s	Top-25s	Scoring Average	Money
1975	1	4	1	0	0	0	0	78.00	$800

Best finish for 1975: 67th at the U.S. Open

| 1976 | 16 | 56 | 12 | 0 | 0 | 1 | 2 | 72.05 | $10,287 |

Best finish for 1976: T-8th at the Ed McMahon Quad City Open

| 1977 | 17 | 46 | 7 | 0 | 0 | 0 | 1 | 73.37 | $4,899 |

Best finish for 1977: T-14th at the Greater Milwaukee Open

| 1978 | 11 | 24 | 1 | 0 | 0 | 0 | 0 | 75.54 | $565 |

Best finish for 1978: T-47th at the Glen Campbell Los Angles Open

| 1979 | 4 | 10 | 1 | 0 | 0 | 0 | 0 | 74.30 | $663 |

Best finish for 1979: T-59th at the Byron Nelson Golf Classic

| 1980 | 22 | 68 | 14 | 0 | 0 | 0 | 1 | 72.53 | $12,871 |

Best finish for 1980: T-25th at the Greater New Orleans Open

Year	Starts	Rounds Played	Cuts Made	Wins	Top-5s	Top-10s	Top-25s	Scoring Average	Money
1981	18	48	8	0	0	0	0	72.83	$7,379

Best finish for 1981: T-29th at the Manufactures Hanover Westchester Classic

1982	5	14	2	0	0	0	0	73.07	$2,178

Best finish for 1982: T-31st at the Texas Open

1983	1	4	1	0	0	0	0	71.75	$597

Best finish for 1983: T-70th at the Texas Open

Period Totals	Starts	Rounds Played	Cuts Made	Wins	Top-5s	Top-10s	Top-25s	Scoring Average	Money
	95	274	47	0	0	1	4	73.05	$40,240

Stephen Ames

Year	Starts	Rounds Played	Cuts Made	Wins	Top-5s	Top-10s	Top-25s	Scoring Average	Money
1993	1	4	1	0	0	0	0	71.25	$6,709

Best finish for 1993: T-51st at the British Open

1996	1	4	1	0	0	0	0	71.50	$8,816

Best finish for 1996: T-55th at the British Open

1997	2	8	2	0	1	1	1	72.25	$110,461

Best finish for 1997: T-5th at the British Open

1998	16	52	10	0	1	3	7	71.25	$357,859

Best finish for 1998: 3rd at the Nissan Open

1999	18	55	11	0	2	4	5	70.42	$460,760

Best finish for 1999: 3rd at the Sprint International

2000	31	95	18	0	2	4	9	70.63	$747,312

Best finish for 2000: T-4th at the COMPAQ Classic of New Orleans

2001	26	84	18	0	0	2	8	70.45	$574,451

Best finish for 2001: T-6th at the B.C. Open

2002	28	88	16	0	1	4	9	70.75	$1,279,301

Best finish for 2002: 2nd at The Players Championship

2003	27	89	19	0	1	4	9	70.02	$1,007,959

Best finish for 2003: T-5th at the Chrysler Classic of Greensboro

2004	27	95	21	1	4	11	16	70.08	$3,307,419

Best finish for 2004: Win at the Cialis Western Open

2005	24	79	18	0	0	3	6	71.22	$963,607

Best finish for 2005: T-6th at the MCI Heritage

2006	21	62	13	1	2	3	9	70.79	$2,397,155

Best finish for 2006: Win at The Players Championship

2007	23	77	18	1	2	4	9	71.17	$2,107,742

Best finish for 2007: Win at the Children's Miracle network Classic

2008	24	82	19	0	4	7	10	70.67	$2,285,707

Best finish for 2008: 3rd at the Mercedes Championships

Period Totals	Starts	Rounds Played	Cuts Made	Wins	Top-5s	Top-10s	Top-25s	Scoring Average	Money
	269	874	185	3	20	50	98	70.66	$15,615,257

Brad Anderson

Year	Starts	Rounds Played	Cuts Made	Wins	Top-5s	Top-10s	Top-25s	Scoring Average	Money
1964	8	17	1	0	0	0	0	76.59	$061

Best finish for 1964: T-39th at the Greater Greensboro Open

1969	3	8	1	0	0	0	0	74.50	$200

Best finish for 1969: T-57th at the Kemper Insurance Open

1970	2	6	1	0	0	0	0	72.67	$300

Best finish for 1970: T-59th at the Greater Greensboro Open

1971	4	14	3	0	0	0	1	72.50	$2,630

Best finish for 1971: T-22nd at the PGA Championship

1972	11	30	4	0	1	1	1	73.60	$5,323

Best finish for 1972: T-4th at the San Antonio Texas Open

1973	2	4	0	0	0	0	0	74.50	

Period Totals	Starts	Rounds Played	Cuts Made	Wins	Top-5s	Top-10s	Top-25s	Scoring Average	Money
	30	79	10	0	1	1	2	74.11	$8,513

Chris M. Anderson

Year	Starts	Rounds Played	Cuts Made	Wins	Top-5s	Top-10s	Top-25s	Scoring Average	Money
2001	1	2	0	0	0	0	0	78.00	$1,000
2003	30	92	14	0	1	1	2	71.43	$333,153

Best finish for 2003: T-4th at the Southern Farm Bureau Classic

Period Totals	Starts	Rounds Played	Cuts Made	Wins	Top-5s	Top-10s	Top-25s	Scoring Average	Money
	31	94	14	0	1	1	2	71.57	$334,153

JC Anderson

Year	Starts	Rounds Played	Cuts Made	Wins	Top-5s	Top-10s	Top-25s	Scoring Average	Money
1988	1	2	0	0	0	0	0	77.00	$1,000
1991	26	62	7	0	0	0	3	72.16	$33,180

Best finish for 1991: T-20th at the Buick Open

1992	1	2	0	0	0	0	0	70.50	

1993	27	77	11	0	0	1	4	72.34	$89,782

Best finish for 1993: 6th at the Kemper Open

1994	11	31	4	0	0	1	1	71.35	$35,022

Best finish for 1994: T-8th at the Texas Open

| 1995 | 2 | 4 | 0 | 0 | 0 | 0 | 0 | 74.00 | |
| 2002 | 1 | 4 | 1 | 0 | 0 | 0 | 0 | 71.25 | $9,552 |

Best finish for 2002: T-67th at the Verizon Byron Nelson Classic

| 2003 | 2 | 4 | 0 | 0 | 0 | 0 | 0 | 74.75 | $2,000 |
| 2004 | 1 | 2 | 0 | 0 | 0 | 0 | 0 | 72.00 | |

Period Totals	Starts	Rounds Played	Cuts Made	Wins	Top-5s	Top-10s	Top-25s	Scoring Average	Money
	72	188	23	0	0	2	8	72.21	$170,536

Jeremy Anderson

Year	Starts	Rounds Played	Cuts Made	Wins	Top-5s	Top-10s	Top-25s	Scoring Average	Money
2000	1	3	0	0	0	0	0	70.00	
2001	27	69	7	0	0	0	1	71.97	$99,464

Best finish for 2001: T-23rd at the Michelob Championship at Kingsmill

| 2002 | 1 | 3 | 0 | 0 | 0 | 0 | 0 | 72.33 | |
| 2003 | 1 | 3 | 0 | 0 | 0 | 0 | 0 | 71.67 | |

Period Totals	Starts	Rounds Played	Cuts Made	Wins	Top-5s	Top-10s	Top-25s	Scoring Average	Money
	30	78	7	0	0	0	1	71.90	$99,464

Jerry Anderson

Year	Starts	Rounds Played	Cuts Made	Wins	Top-5s	Top-10s	Top-25s	Scoring Average	Money
1964	1	1	0	0	0	0	0	78.00	
1977	1	2	0	0	0	0	0	80.00	
1979	1	2	0	0	0	0	0	79.00	
1980	2	6	1	0	0	0	0	73.50	$798

Best finish for 1980: T-55th at the Canadian Open

| 1982 | 1 | 4 | 1 | 0 | 0 | 0 | 1 | 71.00 | $7,012 |

Best finish for 1982: T-15th at the Canadian Open

1983	1	2	0	0	0	0	0	76.00	
1984	1	2	0	0	0	0	0	73.50	
1985	3	8	1	0	0	0	0	76.13	$6,444

Best finish for 1985: 41st at the NEC World Series of Golf

1986	1	2	0	0	0	0	0	77.00	$600
1987	2	4	0	0	0	0	0	76.25	$640
1988	1	2	0	0	0	0	0	74.00	
1990	22	56	6	0	0	0	1	73.38	$28,037

Best finish for 1990: T-14th at the BellSouth Atlanta Golf Classic

| 1991 | 2 | 6 | 1 | 0 | 0 | 0 | 1 | 68.67 | $3,510 |

Best finish for 1991: T-19th at the Deposit Guaranty Classic

| 1992 | 33 | 87 | 8 | 0 | 0 | 0 | 0 | 72.92 | $20,312 |

Best finish for 1992: T-39th at the Greater Milwaukee Open

Period Totals	Starts	Rounds Played	Cuts Made	Wins	Top-5s	Top-10s	Top-25s	Scoring Average	Money
	72	184	18	0	0	0	3	73.38	$67,354

Billy Andrade

Year	Starts	Rounds Played	Cuts Made	Wins	Top-5s	Top-10s	Top-25s	Scoring Average	Money
1983	1	2	0	0	0	0	0	76.50	
1986	2	8	2	0	0	0	2	72.13	

Best finish for 1986: T-23rd at the Western Open

| 1987 | 6 | 15 | 4 | 0 | 0 | 0 | 0 | 73.33 | $7,761 |

Best finish for 1987: T-53rd at The International

| 1988 | 34 | 100 | 17 | 0 | 0 | 1 | 7 | 71.53 | $75,950 |

Best finish for 1988: T-9th at the Pensacola Open

| 1989 | 31 | 94 | 17 | 0 | 3 | 3 | 6 | 71.69 | $203,243 |

Best finish for 1989: T-2nd at the Buick Open

| 1990 | 28 | 103 | 25 | 0 | 0 | 1 | 12 | 71.07 | $231,345 |

Best finish for 1990: T-7th at the Federal Express St. Jude Classic

| 1991 | 29 | 99 | 19 | 2 | 4 | 4 | 10 | 70.86 | $616,765 |

Best finish for 1991: Win at the Kemper Open & Buick Classic

| 1992 | 29 | 90 | 17 | 0 | 1 | 2 | 9 | 71.68 | $217,910 |

Best finish for 1992: T-3rd at the Infiniti Tournament Of Champions

| 1993 | 30 | 94 | 18 | 0 | 2 | 7 | 10 | 71.55 | $367,883 |

Best finish for 1993: T-2nd at the Buick Southern Open

| 1994 | 26 | 87 | 18 | 0 | 3 | 3 | 5 | 71.21 | $342,208 |

Best finish for 1994: T-2nd at the Doral-Ryder Open

| 1995 | 29 | 90 | 16 | 0 | 0 | 3 | 8 | 71.52 | $278,730 |

Best finish for 1995: T-7th at the BellSouth Classic

| 1996 | 28 | 87 | 18 | 0 | 2 | 3 | 9 | 71.31 | $434,457 |

Best finish for 1996: T-2nd at the Motorola Western Open

| 1997 | 28 | 101 | 23 | 0 | 2 | 4 | 14 | 70.79 | $666,902 |

Best finish for 1997: T-4th at the Greater Greensboro Chrysler Classic

Year	Starts	Rounds Played	Cuts Made	Wins	Top-5s	Top-10s	Top-25s	Scoring Average	Money
1998	30	95	18	1	1	3	6	71.25	$711,434

Best finish for 1998: Win at the Bell Canadian Open

| 1999 | 29 | 88 | 17 | 0 | 0 | 0 | 7 | 71.88 | $348,957 |

Best finish for 1999: T-11th at the Mercedes Championships & Buick Invitational

| 2000 | 31 | 86 | 12 | 1 | 1 | 2 | 6 | 71.12 | $1,004,827 |

Best finish for 2000: Win at the Invensys Classic at Las Vegas

| 2001 | 27 | 79 | 14 | 0 | 3 | 6 | 8 | 70.76 | $1,314,047 |

Best finish for 2001: 2nd at the Canon Greater Hartford Open

| 2002 | 31 | 96 | 20 | 0 | 3 | 5 | 11 | 70.61 | $1,376,867 |

Best finish for 2002: T-2nd at the SEI Pennsylvania Classic

| 2003 | 29 | 100 | 19 | 0 | 0 | 3 | 5 | 70.77 | $660,694 |

Best finish for 2003: T-8th at the Las Vegas Invitational

| 2004 | 31 | 104 | 20 | 0 | 1 | 1 | 5 | 71.25 | $633,143 |

Best finish for 2004: T-4th at the U.S. Bank Championship in Milwaukee

| 2005 | 26 | 83 | 16 | 0 | 1 | 1 | 9 | 71.12 | $1,122,835 |

Best finish for 2005: T-2nd at the MCI Heritage

| 2006 | 24 | 74 | 15 | 0 | 2 | 3 | 4 | 71.09 | $1,059,137 |

Best finish for 2006: T-2nd at the Booz Allen Classic

| 2007 | 27 | 88 | 16 | 0 | 0 | 0 | 5 | 71.75 | $499,197 |

Best finish for 2007: T-14th at the PODS Championship

| 2008 | 24 | 71 | 10 | 0 | 0 | 0 | 2 | 72.15 | $243,490 |

Best finish for 2008: T-14th at the Verizon Heritage

Period Totals	Starts	Rounds Played	Cuts Made	Wins	Top-5s	Top-10s	Top-25s	Scoring Average	Money
	610	1934	371	4	29	55	160	71.30	$12,417,782

Terry Anton

Year	Starts	Rounds Played	Cuts Made	Wins	Top-5s	Top-10s	Top-25s	Scoring Average	Money
1973	1	2	0	0	0	0	0	79.00	
1974	1	2	0	0	0	0	0	77.00	
1977	1	2	0	0	0	0	0	75.00	
1981	10	20	1	0	0	0	0	74.25	$1,115

Best finish for 1981: T-65th at the Hall of Fame Tournament

| 1982 | 12 | 26 | 1 | 0 | 0 | 0 | 1 | 73.88 | $2,225 |

Best finish for 1982: T-23rd at the Southern Open

Period Totals	Starts	Rounds Played	Cuts Made	Wins	Top-5s	Top-10s	Top-25s	Scoring Average	Money
	25	52	2	0	0	0	1	74.38	$3,340

Isao Aoki

Year	Starts	Rounds Played	Cuts Made	Wins	Top-5s	Top-10s	Top-25s	Scoring Average	Money
1974	2	6	1	0	0	0	0	73.17	$2,214

Best finish for 1974: T-36th at the Hawaiian Open

| 1975 | 2 | 6 | 1 | 0 | 0 | 0 | 0 | 72.33 | $2,779 |

Best finish for 1975: T-27th at the Hawaiian Open

| 1977 | 4 | 13 | 2 | 0 | 0 | 0 | 1 | 73.31 | $7,840 |

Best finish for 1977: T-17th at the World Series Of Golf

| 1978 | 5 | 18 | 3 | 0 | 0 | 1 | 2 | 72.94 | $16,881 |

Best finish for 1978: T-7th at the British Open

| 1979 | 7 | 26 | 6 | 0 | 0 | 1 | 3 | 72.46 | $21,696 |

Best finish for 1979: T-7th at the British Open

| 1980 | 7 | 26 | 6 | 0 | 1 | 1 | 6 | 70.88 | $57,519 |

Best finish for 1980: 2nd at the U.S. Open

| 1981 | 14 | 54 | 13 | 0 | 3 | 3 | 9 | 71.26 | $102,918 |

Best finish for 1981: T-3rd at the Hawaiian Open & World Series Of Golf

| 1982 | 16 | 56 | 12 | 0 | 1 | 1 | 6 | 71.88 | $70,907 |

Best finish for 1982: 3rd at the World Series Of Golf

| 1983 | 15 | 57 | 13 | 1 | 3 | 5 | 7 | 71.16 | $146,567 |

Best finish for 1983: Win at the Hawaiian Open

| 1984 | 16 | 61 | 14 | 0 | 1 | 1 | 7 | 71.52 | $74,420 |

Best finish for 1984: T-4th at the Buick Open

| 1985 | 7 | 28 | 7 | 0 | 1 | 2 | 5 | 71.50 | $92,650 |

Best finish for 1985: T-2nd at the Greater Greensboro Open

| 1986 | 10 | 31 | 6 | 0 | 1 | 2 | 3 | 72.65 | $54,616 |

Best finish for 1986: T-3rd at the Greater Greensboro Open

| 1987 | 14 | 43 | 9 | 0 | 1 | 1 | 6 | 72.35 | $84,809 |

Best finish for 1987: T-5th at the Honda Classic

| 1988 | 15 | 50 | 12 | 0 | 1 | 2 | 5 | 72.16 | $137,386 |

Best finish for 1988: T-3rd at the Beatrice Western Open

| 1989 | 17 | 52 | 9 | 0 | 0 | 1 | 4 | 72.13 | $87,516 |

Best finish for 1989: T-8th at the Southwestern Bell Colonial

| 1990 | 11 | 36 | 7 | 0 | 0 | 0 | 3 | 73.00 | $50,043 |

Best finish for 1990: T-17th at the Nestle Invitational

Year	Starts	Rounds Played	Cuts Made	Wins	Top-5s	Top-10s	Top-25s	Scoring Average	Money
1992	1	4	1	0	0	0	0	72.50	$11,400

Best finish for 1992: T-31st at the NEC World Series of Golf

| 1993 | 1 | 4 | 1 | 0 | 0 | 0 | 1 | 72.00 | $32,500 |

Best finish for 1993: T-16th at the NEC World Series of Golf

1999	1	2	0	0	0	0	0	72.50	
Period Totals	Starts	Rounds Played	Cuts Made	Wins	Top-5s	Top-10s	Top-25s	Scoring Average	Money
	165	573	123	1	13	21	68	71.96	$1,054,658

Stuart Appleby

Year	Starts	Rounds Played	Cuts Made	Wins	Top-5s	Top-10s	Top-25s	Scoring Average	Money
1996	30	95	18	0	0	1	5	71.29	$164,483

Best finish for 1996: T-10th at the Freeport-McDermott Classic

| 1997 | 23 | 78 | 18 | 1 | 3 | 5 | 12 | 71.27 | $1,003,356 |

Best finish for 1997: Win at the Honda Classic

| 1998 | 22 | 65 | 12 | 1 | 2 | 5 | 7 | 71.83 | $725,531 |

Best finish for 1998: Win at the Kemper Open

| 1999 | 29 | 90 | 21 | 1 | 2 | 5 | 12 | 71.24 | $1,368,880 |

Best finish for 1999: Win at the Shell Houston Open

| 2000 | 24 | 81 | 20 | 0 | 3 | 5 | 15 | 70.32 | $1,648,221 |

Best finish for 2000: 2nd at the Sony Open in Hawaii

| 2001 | 29 | 98 | 23 | 0 | 1 | 4 | 8 | 70.40 | $1,005,528 |

Best finish for 2001: T-5th at the WGC-NEC Invitational

| 2002 | 28 | 94 | 21 | 0 | 3 | 4 | 10 | 70.51 | $1,734,459 |

Best finish for 2002: T-2nd at the British Open & Invensys Classic at Las Vegas

| 2003 | 27 | 85 | 19 | 1 | 4 | 5 | 13 | 70.53 | $2,668,538 |

Best finish for 2003: Win at the Las Vegas Invitational

| 2004 | 25 | 78 | 18 | 1 | 4 | 5 | 14 | 70.69 | $2,950,235 |

Best finish for 2004: Win at the Mercedes Championships

| 2005 | 25 | 80 | 19 | 1 | 1 | 4 | 8 | 70.83 | $2,204,506 |

Best finish for 2005: Win at the Mercedes Championships

| 2006 | 23 | 78 | 20 | 2 | 3 | 6 | 11 | 70.87 | $3,477,105 |

Best finish for 2006: Win at the Mercedes Championships & Shell Houston Open

| 2007 | 24 | 73 | 15 | 0 | 2 | 3 | 9 | 71.71 | $1,808,267 |

Best finish for 2007: T-2nd at the Shell Houston Open

| 2008 | 23 | 84 | 21 | 0 | 2 | 7 | 14 | 70.86 | $2,484,630 |

Best finish for 2008: T-2nd at the WGC-Bridgestone Invitational

Period Totals	Starts	Rounds Played	Cuts Made	Wins	Top-5s	Top-10s	Top-25s	Scoring Average	Money
	332	1079	245	8	30	59	138	70.92	$23,243,740

Alex Aragon

Year	Starts	Rounds Played	Cuts Made	Wins	Top-5s	Top-10s	Top-25s	Scoring Average	Money
2006	26	61	6	0	0	0	0	72.87	$94,504

Best finish for 2006: T-27th at the 84 Lumber Classic

2007	1	2	0	0	0	0	0	71.00	
2008	2	4	0	0	0	0	0	72.50	
Period Totals	Starts	Rounds Played	Cuts Made	Wins	Top-5s	Top-10s	Top-25s	Scoring Average	Money
	29	67	6	0	0	0	0	72.79	$94,504

Kikuo Arai

Year	Starts	Rounds Played	Cuts Made	Wins	Top-5s	Top-10s	Top-25s	Scoring Average	Money
1973	1	2	0	0	0	0	0	74.00	
1974	3	10	2	0	0	0	1	72.60	$2,298

Best finish for 1974: T-19th at the Ohio Kings Island Open

| 1977 | 2 | 7 | 1 | 0 | 0 | 0 | 0 | 73.57 | $576 |

Best finish for 1977: T-43rd at the Bob Hope Chrysler Classic

| 1978 | 1 | 5 | 1 | 0 | 0 | 0 | 0 | 71.40 | $854 |

Best finish for 1978: T-40th at the Bob Hope Chrysler Classic

| 1983 | 7 | 21 | 2 | 0 | 0 | 0 | 0 | 72.05 | $6,000 |

Best finish for 1983: T-36th at the World Series Of Golf

| 1984 | 8 | 21 | 3 | 0 | 0 | 0 | 0 | 73.24 | $5,078 |

Best finish for 1984: T-41st at the Seiko Tucson-Match Play Championship

| 1985 | 5 | 14 | 2 | 0 | 0 | 1 | 2 | 71.93 | $23,035 |

Best finish for 1985: T-6th at the USF&G Classic

| 1986 | 15 | 40 | 5 | 0 | 0 | 0 | 1 | 73.23 | $11,092 |

Best finish for 1986: T-17th at the AT&T Pebble Beach Pro-Am

| 1987 | 4 | 13 | 2 | 0 | 0 | 0 | 0 | 72.54 | $2,730 |

Best finish for 1987: T-45th at the Los Angeles Open

| 1988 | 4 | 9 | 1 | 0 | 0 | 0 | 0 | 73.67 | $1,710 |

Best finish for 1988: T-49th at the AT&T Pebble Beach Pro-Am

1989	1	2	0	0	0	0	0	76.50	
Period Totals	Starts	Rounds Played	Cuts Made	Wins	Top-5s	Top-10s	Top-25s	Scoring Average	Money
	51	144	19	0	0	1	4	72.86	$53,373

George Archer

Year	Starts	Rounds Played	Cuts Made	Wins	Top-5s	Top-10s	Top-25s	Scoring Average	Money
1962	2	8	2	0	0	0	0	73.62	

Best finish for 1961: T-T33rd at the Almaden Open

Year	Starts	Rounds Played	Cuts Made	Wins	Top-5s	Top-10s	Top-25s	Scoring Average	Money
1962	2	8	2	0	0	0	0	72.50	

Best finish for 1962: T-28th at the Lucky International Open

1963	1	4	1	0	0	0	0	71.75	

Best finish for 1963: T-32nd at the Lucky International Open

1964	34	110	21	0	2	2	11	72.08	$14,868

Best finish for 1964: T-4th at the San Diego Open

1965	34	120	25	1	3	4	14	72.09	$31,602

Best finish for 1965: Win at the Lucky International

1966	32	113	25	0	4	9	18	71.61	$71,280

Best finish for 1966: 3rd at the Lucky International Open Invitational, Insurance City Open Invitational & Houston Champions International

1967	30	111	26	1	9	11	18	71.31	$88,688

Best finish for 1967: Win at the Greater Greensboro Open

1968	29	112	27	2	9	13	23	70.48	$128,703

Best finish for 1968: Win at the Pensacola Open Invitational & Greater New Orleans Open Invitational

1969	29	107	26	2	4	8	18	71.61	$98,281

Best finish for 1969: Win at the Bing Crosby National Pro-Am & The Masters

1970	31	112	26	0	6	7	12	71.64	$61,371

Best finish for 1970: T-2nd at the National 4 Ball Championship PGA Players & Robinson Open Golf Classic

1971	32	118	29	2	7	9	18	71.32	$140,634

Best finish for 1971: Win at the Andy Williams-San Diego Open & Greater Hartford Open Invitational

1972	28	100	25	2	5	9	17	71.35	$136,604

Best finish for 1972: Win at the Glen Campbell Los Angles Open & Greater Greensboro Open

1973	31	115	26	0	3	7	10	72.19	$56,449

Best finish for 1973: T-2nd at the Dean Martin Tucson Open

1974	28	91	18	0	0	0	3	72.27	$16,527

Best finish for 1974: T-15th at the Glen Campbell Los Angles Open

1975	22	58	7	0	0	1	2	73.17	$11,028

Best finish for 1975: T-9th at the Sea Pines Heritage Classic

1976	31	82	12	1	3	3	5	72.95	$44,834

Best finish for 1976: Win at the Sahara Invitational

1977	33	118	28	0	3	6	15	71.44	$110,481

Best finish for 1977: 2nd at the American Express Westchester Classic & Anheuser-Busch Golf Classic

1978	23	58	7	0	0	0	1	73.29	$8,717

Best finish for 1978: T-22nd at the Phoenix Open

1979	9	28	5	0	0	0	2	71.04	$9,524

Best finish for 1979: T-13th at the American Optical Classic

1980	34	112	23	0	0	3	9	71.79	$68,664

Best finish for 1980: T-7th at the Glen Campbell Los Angles Open

1981	29	106	24	0	2	6	15	71.10	$111,643

Best finish for 1981: T-3rd at the Memorial Tournament

1982	32	118	27	0	1	3	9	71.45	$88,118

Best finish for 1982: T-3rd at the Buick Open

1983	28	104	22	0	1	1	7	72.18	$61,066

Best finish for 1983: 5th at the Glen Campbell Los Angles Open

1984	31	104	21	1	4	4	12	71.62	$207,543

Best finish for 1984: Win at the Bank of Boston Classic

1985	31	107	25	0	0	3	10	71.70	$109,096

Best finish for 1985: T-9th at the Kemper Open

1986	31	94	19	0	1	2	6	71.98	$83,200

Best finish for 1986: T-2nd at the Southern Open

1987	9	20	2	0	0	0	0	71.85	$3,861

Best finish for 1987: T-37th at the Buick Open

1988	30	94	18	0	1	3	5	71.36	$100,052

Best finish for 1988: T-3rd at the Southern Open

1989	20	64	12	0	0	0	4	72.13	$63,358

Best finish for 1989: T-14th at the Buick Open

1990	1	4	1	0	0	0	0	75.25	$3,400

Best finish for 1990: 49th at the Masters

1991	1	1	0	0	0	0	0	73.00	$1,500
1992	1	4	1	0	0	0	0	72.75	$3,700

Best finish for 1992: 51st at the Masters

Period Totals	Starts	Rounds Played	Cuts Made	Wins	Top-5s	Top-10s	Top-25s	Scoring Average	Money
	739	2505	533	12	68	114	264	71.76	$1,934,793

Ray Arinno

Year	Starts	Rounds Played	Cuts Made	Wins	Top-5s	Top-10s	Top-25s	Scoring Average	Money
1969	1	4	1	0	0	0	0	78.00	

Best finish for 1969: T-56th at the Alameda County Open

Year	Starts	Rounds Played	Cuts Made	Wins	Top-5s	Top-10s	Top-25s	Scoring Average	Money
1971	1	2	0	0	0	0	0	72.50	
1972	6	12	0	0	0	0	0	75.08	
1974	1	2	0	0	0	0	0	73.00	
1977	8	20	2	0	0	1	1	73.35	$4,240

Best finish for 1977: T-10th at the B.C. Open

1978	1	2	0	0	0	0	0	77.00	$600
1979	3	6	0	0	0	0	0	73.67	
1980	7	19	2	0	0	0	0	73.63	$1,811

Best finish for 1980: T-36th at the Phoenix Open

Period Totals	Starts	Rounds Played	Cuts Made	Wins	Top-5s	Top-10s	Top-25s	Scoring Average	Money
	28	67	5	0	0	1	1	74.12	$6,651

Ryan Armour

Year	Starts	Rounds Played	Cuts Made	Wins	Top-5s	Top-10s	Top-25s	Scoring Average	Money
2007	32	107	21	0	1	3	7	71.19	$862,979

Best finish for 2007: 4th at the Mayakoba Golf Classic

| 2008 | 32 | 87 | 13 | 0 | 0 | 0 | 4 | 71.78 | $354,508 |

Best finish for 2008: T-14th at the Shell Houston Open

Period Totals	Starts	Rounds Played	Cuts Made	Wins	Top-5s	Top-10s	Top-25s	Scoring Average	Money
	64	194	34	0	1	3	11	71.45	$1,217,487

Tommy Armour III

Year	Starts	Rounds Played	Cuts Made	Wins	Top-5s	Top-10s	Top-25s	Scoring Average	Money
1982	13	38	5	0	0	0	0	72.58	$4,254

Best finish for 1982: T-30th at the Tallahassee Open

| 1983 | 1 | 4 | 0 | 0 | 0 | 0 | 0 | 72.25 | |
| 1984 | 3 | 8 | 1 | 0 | 0 | 0 | 0 | 72.50 | $780 |

Best finish for 1984: T-55th at the Anheuser-Busch Golf Classic

| 1985 | 2 | 5 | 0 | 0 | 0 | 0 | 0 | 75.80 | |
| 1986 | 4 | 13 | 2 | 0 | 0 | 1 | 1 | 71.92 | $13,388 |

Best finish for 1986: T-7th at the Provident Classic

| 1987 | 3 | 9 | 1 | 0 | 0 | 0 | 0 | 72.22 | $970 |

Best finish for 1987: T-72nd at the Shearson Lehman/Andy Williams San Diego

| 1988 | 32 | 99 | 18 | 0 | 1 | 4 | 9 | 71.12 | $183,281 |

Best finish for 1988: 2nd at the Centel Classic

| 1989 | 33 | 111 | 22 | 0 | 1 | 2 | 7 | 71.15 | $192,578 |

Best finish for 1989: T-2nd at the Kemper Open

| 1990 | 32 | 95 | 16 | 1 | 2 | 2 | 6 | 71.80 | $352,154 |

Best finish for 1990: Win at the Phoenix Open

| 1991 | 31 | 87 | 15 | 0 | 0 | 1 | 3 | 71.83 | $90,514 |

Best finish for 1991: T-6th at the Infiniti Tournament Of Champions

| 1992 | 30 | 81 | 11 | 0 | 0 | 0 | 3 | 71.80 | $47,218 |

Best finish for 1992: T-20th at the Walt Disney World/Oldsmobile Classic

| 1993 | 20 | 56 | 7 | 0 | 0 | 1 | 2 | 72.32 | $52,011 |

Best finish for 1993: T-10th at the Kemper Open

| 1994 | 9 | 27 | 6 | 0 | 1 | 2 | 5 | 70.26 | $112,778 |

Best finish for 1994: T-3rd at the Deposit Guaranty Golf Classic

| 1995 | 30 | 92 | 16 | 0 | 0 | 1 | 5 | 71.39 | $134,407 |

Best finish for 1995: T-7th at the Bob Hope Chrysler Classic

| 1996 | 21 | 54 | 6 | 0 | 0 | 1 | 2 | 72.15 | $79,616 |

Best finish for 1996: T-7th at the Michelob Championship at Kingsmill

| 1997 | 30 | 94 | 18 | 0 | 0 | 0 | 7 | 71.27 | $163,664 |

Best finish for 1997: T-17th at the Buick Challenge & Walt Disney World/Oldsmobile Classic

| 1998 | 28 | 87 | 16 | 0 | 1 | 4 | 10 | 70.91 | $556,150 |

Best finish for 1998: T-2nd at the Phoenix Open

| 1999 | 27 | 88 | 16 | 0 | 2 | 5 | 6 | 71.35 | $783,935 |

Best finish for 1999: 2nd at the Touchstone Energy Tucson Open

| 2000 | 30 | 89 | 14 | 0 | 1 | 2 | 6 | 71.35 | $398,610 |

Best finish for 2000: T-5th at the Nissan Open

| 2001 | 32 | 91 | 13 | 0 | 0 | 0 | 3 | 71.38 | $238,091 |

Best finish for 2001: T-18th at the Greater Milwaukee Open

| 2002 | 30 | 81 | 13 | 0 | 0 | 3 | 3 | 71.60 | $379,191 |

Best finish for 2002: T-7th at the Sony Open in Hawaii

| 2003 | 23 | 64 | 11 | 1 | 1 | 1 | 4 | 71.02 | $933,984 |

Best finish for 2003: Win at the Valero Texas Open

| 2004 | 28 | 87 | 15 | 0 | 1 | 2 | 3 | 71.55 | $844,634 |

Best finish for 2004: T-2nd at the Chrysler Championship

| 2005 | 29 | 103 | 22 | 0 | 0 | 1 | 4 | 71.07 | $636,643 |

Best finish for 2005: T-7th at the Sony Open in Hawaii

| 2006 | 25 | 65 | 9 | 0 | 0 | 0 | 2 | 71.48 | $352,446 |

Best finish for 2006: T-11th at the Zurich Classic of New Orleans

Year	Starts	Rounds Played	Cuts Made	Wins	Top-5s	Top-10s	Top-25s	Scoring Average	Money
2007	24	81	16	0	2	2	8	70.86	$919,134

Best finish for 2007: 4th at the Shell Houston Open

| 2008 | 25 | 77 | 15 | 0 | 2 | 5 | 7 | 70.99 | $1,501,256 |

Best finish for 2008: T-2nd at the Travelers Championship

Period Totals	Starts	Rounds Played	Cuts Made	Wins	Top-5s	Top-10s	Top-25s	Scoring Average	Money
	595	1786	304	2	15	40	106	71.42	$8,971,686

Ty Armstrong

Year	Starts	Rounds Played	Cuts Made	Wins	Top-5s	Top-10s	Top-25s	Scoring Average	Money
1994	23	60	8	0	0	0	1	73.22	$30,181

Best finish for 1994: T-19th at the Anheuser-Busch Golf Classic

| 1996 | 1 | 2 | 0 | 0 | 0 | 0 | 0 | 75.00 | $1,000 |
| 1999 | 28 | 77 | 10 | 0 | 0 | 0 | 0 | 72.23 | $85,783 |

Best finish for 1999: T-27th at the Honda Classic

2004	1	2	0	0	0	0	0	76.00	
Period Totals	Starts	Rounds Played	Cuts Made	Wins	Top-5s	Top-10s	Top-25s	Scoring Average	Money
	53	141	18	0	0	0	1	72.74	$116,964

Wally Armstrong

Year	Starts	Rounds Played	Cuts Made	Wins	Top-5s	Top-10s	Top-25s	Scoring Average	Money
1966	1	2	0	0	0	0	0	80.50	
1968	1	2	0	0	0	0	0	75.00	
1973	5	18	2	0	0	0	1	73.67	$1,818

Best finish for 1973: T-22nd at the Shrine-Robinson Golf Classic

| 1974 | 26 | 87 | 16 | 0 | 2 | 2 | 7 | 72.75 | $31,374 |

Best finish for 1974: T-2nd at the Sahara Invitational

| 1975 | 31 | 98 | 17 | 0 | 2 | 4 | 9 | 72.33 | $44,078 |

Best finish for 1975: 2nd at the Pensacola Open

| 1976 | 34 | 123 | 27 | 0 | 3 | 7 | 8 | 71.83 | $60,576 |

Best finish for 1976: T-3rd at the Houston Open

| 1977 | 32 | 120 | 27 | 0 | 1 | 3 | 11 | 71.94 | $56,409 |

Best finish for 1977: T-2nd at the Western Open

| 1978 | 31 | 112 | 24 | 0 | 3 | 4 | 11 | 72.02 | $61,596 |

Best finish for 1978: T-5th at the Greater Greensboro Open, Masters & Kemper Open

| 1979 | 34 | 113 | 22 | 0 | 0 | 1 | 9 | 72.37 | $59,348 |

Best finish for 1979: 6th at the Atlanta Classic

| 1980 | 33 | 96 | 16 | 0 | 0 | 0 | 2 | 73.08 | $18,066 |

Best finish for 1980: T-16th at the Tallahassee Open

| 1981 | 24 | 63 | 9 | 0 | 0 | 0 | 2 | 73.14 | $12,759 |

Best finish for 1981: T-15th at the Bob Hope Chrysler Classic

| 1982 | 25 | 78 | 13 | 0 | 0 | 0 | 2 | 72.50 | $22,377 |

Best finish for 1982: T-14th at the Southern Open

| 1983 | 27 | 84 | 13 | 0 | 1 | 1 | 5 | 72.83 | $36,226 |

Best finish for 1983: 3rd at the Southern Open

| 1984 | 26 | 75 | 11 | 0 | 0 | 0 | 0 | 73.61 | $13,924 |

Best finish for 1984: T-38th at the Kemper Open

1985	2	4	0	0	0	0	0	78.50	
Period Totals	Starts	Rounds Played	Cuts Made	Wins	Top-5s	Top-10s	Top-25s	Scoring Average	Money
	332	1075	197	0	12	22	67	72.56	$418,551

Dewey Arnette

Year	Starts	Rounds Played	Cuts Made	Wins	Top-5s	Top-10s	Top-25s	Scoring Average	Money
1986	1	2	0	0	0	0	0	72.50	
1987	25	68	10	0	0	0	2	72.03	$18,181

Best finish for 1987: T-23rd at the Provident Classic

| 1988 | 7 | 20 | 3 | 0 | 0 | 0 | 0 | 71.90 | $3,345 |

Best finish for 1988: T-50th at the Anheuser-Busch Golf Classic

| 1989 | 6 | 15 | 2 | 0 | 0 | 0 | 0 | 71.93 | $6,362 |

Best finish for 1989: T-26th at the Deposit Guaranty Golf Classic

| 1990 | 25 | 64 | 7 | 0 | 0 | 0 | 0 | 73.20 | $14,746 |

Best finish for 1990: T-37th at the Shearson Lehman Hutton Open

Period Totals	Starts	Rounds Played	Cuts Made	Wins	Top-5s	Top-10s	Top-25s	Scoring Average	Money
	64	169	22	0	0	0	2	72.46	$42,635

Perry Arthur

Year	Starts	Rounds Played	Cuts Made	Wins	Top-5s	Top-10s	Top-25s	Scoring Average	Money
1978	13	32	3	0	0	0	1	73.19	$2,803

Best finish for 1978: T-22nd at the Anheuser-Busch Golf Classic

1979	1	2	0	0	0	0	0	77.50	
1980	1	2	0	0	0	0	0	74.50	
1981	12	25	1	0	0	0	0	74.08	$525

Best finish for 1981: 75th at the B.C. Open

Year	Starts	Rounds Played	Cuts Made	Wins	Top-5s	Top-10s	Top-25s	Scoring Average	Money
1982	13	36	6	0	0	0	0	72.56	$8,103

Best finish for 1982: T-27th at the Danny Thomas Memphis Classic

1986	1	2	0	0	0	0	0	81.00	$600
1987	29	74	9	0	0	1	1	72.54	$33,411

Best finish for 1987: T-6th at the Hardee's Golf Classic

1988	3	8	1	0	0	0	0	71.75	$463

Best finish for 1988: T-51st at the Deposit Guaranty Golf Classic

1989	2	5	1	0	0	1	1	69.20	$5,400

Best finish for 1989: 10th at the Deposit Guaranty Golf Classic

1990	1	4	1	0	0	0	1	69.25	$3,120

Best finish for 1990: T-21st at the Deposit Guaranty

1991	25	69	11	0	0	1	1	71.93	$49,396

Best finish for 1991: T-7th at the Chattanooga Classic

1992	1	2	0	0	0	0	0	71.00	
1994	1	2	1	0	0	0	0	68.50	$6,737

Best finish for 1994: T-28th at the GTE Byron Nelson Classic

1996	1	2	0	0	0	0	0	75.50	$1,300
1997	1	2	0	0	0	0	0	71.50	
1998	1	2	0	0	0	0	0	73.50	
1999	1	2	0	0	0	0	0	72.00	
2000	1	2	0	0	0	0	0	73.00	
2001	1	4	1	0	0	0	0	68.75	$10,317

Best finish for 2001: T-51st at the Verizon Byron Nelson Classic

2005	1	2	0	0	0	0	0	71.00	
2007	1	2	0	0	0	0	0	76.00	
Period Totals	Starts	Rounds Played	Cuts Made	Wins	Top-5s	Top-10s	Top-25s	Scoring Average	Money
	111	281	35	0	0	3	5	72.52	$122,176

Bruce Ashworth

Year	Starts	Rounds Played	Cuts Made	Wins	Top-5s	Top-10s	Top-25s	Scoring Average	Money
1970	2	6	1	0	0	0	0	75.83	

Best finish for 1970: 61st at the Houston Champions International

1971	1	2	0	0	0	0	0	77.50	
1972	2	4	0	0	0	0	0	75.75	
1973	25	68	9	0	0	0	1	73.13	$6,643

Best finish for 1973: T-13th at the Dean Martin Tucson Open

1974	19	42	4	0	0	0	1	74.57	$2,633

Best finish for 1974: T-25th at the Ohio Kings Island Open

1980	2	6	1	0	0	0	0	74.50	$606

Best finish for 1980: 69th at the Bing Crosby Pro-Am

1982	1	2	0	0	0	0	0	77.50	$650
1983	2	6	0	0	0	0	0	73.00	$100
Period Totals	Starts	Rounds Played	Cuts Made	Wins	Top-5s	Top-10s	Top-25s	Scoring Average	Money
	54	136	15	0	0	0	2	73.96	$10,632

Arjun Atwal

Year	Starts	Rounds Played	Cuts Made	Wins	Top-5s	Top-10s	Top-25s	Scoring Average	Money
1996	2	6	1	0	0	0	0	72.83	$3,506

Best finish for 1996: T-43rd at the Buick Classic

1999	2	4	0	0	0	0	0	70.50	
2002	1	2	0	0	0	0	0	73.00	
2003	1	4	1	0	0	0	0	73.50	$32,500

Best finish for 2003: T-48th at the American Express Championship

2004	30	83	12	0	0	1	4	71.71	$490,734

Best finish for 2004: 6th at the Chrysler Classic of Greensboro

2005	17	65	16	0	2	4	5	70.40	$965,768

Best finish for 2005: T-2nd at the BellSouth Classic

2006	33	95	15	0	1	1	6	71.27	$550,535

Best finish for 2006: T-4th at the Buick Invitational

2007	12	36	6	0	0	0	1	71.42	$135,015

Best finish for 2007: T-21st at the Frys.Com Open-Vegas

Period Totals	Starts	Rounds Played	Cuts Made	Wins	Top-5s	Top-10s	Top-25s	Scoring Average	Money
	98	295	51	0	3	6	16	71.28	$2,178,059

Emlyn Aubrey

Year	Starts	Rounds Played	Cuts Made	Wins	Top-5s	Top-10s	Top-25s	Scoring Average	Money
1988	2	4	0	0	0	0	0	73.75	$1,000
1989	2	8	2	0	0	0	0	73.00	$12,846

Best finish for 1989: T-29th at the U.S. Open

1990	30	99	19	0	0	2	4	71.90	$123,329

Best finish for 1990: T-7th at the H-E-B Texas Open

1991	32	105	21	0	0	0	4	70.97	$91,258

Best finish for 1991: T-15th at the Shearson Lehman Brothers Open

Year	Starts	Rounds Played	Cuts Made	Wins	Top-5s	Top-10s	Top-25s	Scoring Average	Money
1992	28	72	9	0	0	0	3	72.07	$58,087

Best finish for 1992: T-12th at the Chattanooga Classic

| 1993 | 1 | 4 | 1 | 0 | 0 | 0 | 1 | 71.00 | $18,125 |

Best finish for 1993: T-17th at the AT&T Pebble Beach Pro-Am

| 1994 | 1 | 4 | 1 | 0 | 0 | 0 | 0 | 75.50 | $3,800 |

Best finish for 1994: T-62nd at the U.S. Open

| 1995 | 30 | 86 | 15 | 0 | 0 | 1 | 6 | 71.26 | $137,020 |

Best finish for 1995: T-9th at the AT&T Pebble Beach Pro-Am

| 1996 | 17 | 58 | 13 | 0 | 2 | 2 | 7 | 71.14 | $297,005 |

Best finish for 1996: T-2nd at the Greater Vancouver Open

| 1997 | 27 | 72 | 10 | 0 | 0 | 0 | 3 | 72.14 | $70,383 |

Best finish for 1997: T-18th at the Quad City Classic

| 1999 | 17 | 51 | 10 | 0 | 0 | 3 | 3 | 71.20 | $290,806 |

Best finish for 1999: T-7th at the GTE Byron Nelson Classic

| 2000 | 26 | 64 | 7 | 0 | 0 | 0 | 2 | 72.08 | $110,221 |

Best finish for 2000: T-18th at the SEI Pennsylvania Classic

| 2001 | 1 | 2 | 0 | 0 | 0 | 0 | 0 | 72.00 | |

Period Totals	Starts	Rounds Played	Cuts Made	Wins	Top-5s	Top-10s	Top-25s	Scoring Average	Money
	214	629	108	0	2	8	33	71.64	$1,213,880

Hampton Auld

Year	Starts	Rounds Played	Cuts Made	Wins	Top-5s	Top-10s	Top-25s	Scoring Average	Money
1959	1	4	1	0	0	0	0	72.75	$130

Best finish for 1959: T-31st at the Oklahoma City Open Invitational

| 1964 | 2 | 4 | 0 | 0 | 0 | 0 | 0 | 75.50 | |
| 1965 | 3 | 10 | 2 | 0 | 0 | 0 | 0 | 75.30 | |

Best finish for 1965: T-65th at the Azalea Open

| 1966 | 10 | 24 | 2 | 0 | 0 | 0 | 1 | 74.38 | $532 |

Best finish for 1966: T-18th at the Azalea Open Invitational

| 1967 | 5 | 16 | 3 | 0 | 0 | 0 | 0 | 75.38 | |

Best finish for 1967: T-53rd at the Azalea Open

| 1968 | 1 | 4 | 1 | 0 | 0 | 0 | 0 | 70.50 | $088 |

Best finish for 1968: T-33rd at the AZALEA Open Invitational

| 1969 | 5 | 12 | 1 | 0 | 0 | 0 | 0 | 75.25 | |

Best finish for 1969: T-44th at the Azalea Open

| 1970 | 1 | 4 | 1 | 0 | 0 | 0 | 0 | 72.25 | $104 |

Best finish for 1970: 72nd at the Azalea Open Invitational

1971	1	2	0	0	0	0	0	76.50	
1972	2	3	0	0	0	0	0	77.00	
1973	2	4	0	0	0	0	0	82.00	

Period Totals	Starts	Rounds Played	Cuts Made	Wins	Top-5s	Top-10s	Top-25s	Scoring Average	Money
	33	87	11	0	0	0	1	74.98	$853

Woody Austin

Year	Starts	Rounds Played	Cuts Made	Wins	Top-5s	Top-10s	Top-25s	Scoring Average	Money
1992	1	2	0	0	0	0	0	73.00	
1995	34	114	22	1	4	7	12	70.95	$736,497

Best finish for 1995: Win at the Buick Open

| 1996 | 35 | 117 | 25 | 0 | 2 | 5 | 15 | 70.68 | $541,905 |

Best finish for 1996: T-3rd at the Buick Open

| 1997 | 35 | 87 | 7 | 0 | 0 | 1 | 2 | 72.44 | $75,151 |

Best finish for 1997: T-10th at the Deposit Guaranty Golf Classic

| 1998 | 10 | 29 | 4 | 0 | 0 | 0 | 1 | 70.97 | $51,628 |

Best finish for 1998: T-14th at the Greater Milwaukee Open

| 1999 | 30 | 97 | 20 | 0 | 0 | 1 | 5 | 71.23 | $338,045 |

Best finish for 1999: T-9th at the Reno-Tahoe Open

| 2000 | 32 | 101 | 19 | 0 | 1 | 3 | 5 | 71.27 | $485,589 |

Best finish for 2000: T-4th at the Buick Open

| 2001 | 34 | 95 | 14 | 0 | 0 | 2 | 5 | 71.49 | $406,352 |

Best finish for 2001: T-8th at the John Deere Classic & The International presented by Qwest

| 2002 | 36 | 99 | 14 | 0 | 0 | 1 | 3 | 71.67 | $308,348 |

Best finish for 2002: T-10th at the Reno-Tahoe Open

| 2003 | 31 | 104 | 23 | 0 | 1 | 4 | 10 | 70.62 | $1,518,706 |

Best finish for 2003: 2nd at the MCI Heritage

| 2004 | 29 | 94 | 18 | 1 | 2 | 3 | 8 | 70.98 | $1,495,980 |

Best finish for 2004: Win at the Buick Championship

| 2005 | 30 | 100 | 21 | 0 | 3 | 4 | 7 | 70.94 | $1,177,095 |

Best finish for 2005: T-3rd at the Valero Texas Open

| 2006 | 31 | 107 | 22 | 0 | 1 | 4 | 9 | 71.11 | $1,179,321 |

Best finish for 2006: T-5th at the Buick Championship

| 2007 | 27 | 95 | 20 | 1 | 3 | 3 | 6 | 70.84 | $2,889,596 |

Best finish for 2007: Win at the Stanford St. Jude Classic

Year	Starts	Rounds Played	Cuts Made	Wins	Top-5s	Top-10s	Top-25s	Scoring Average	Money
2008	30	105	24	0	4	6	11	71.10	$2,146,431

Best finish for 2008: T-2nd at the Buick Open

Period Totals	Starts	Rounds Played	Cuts Made	Wins	Top-5s	Top-10s	Top-25s	Scoring Average	Money
	425	1346	253	3	21	44	99	71.15	$13,350,644

Eric Axley

Year	Starts	Rounds Played	Cuts Made	Wins	Top-5s	Top-10s	Top-25s	Scoring Average	Money
2004	1	2	0	0	0	0	0	74.50	$1,000
2005	2	5	1	0	0	0	0	73.60	$13,100

Best finish for 2005: T-57th at the BellSouth Classic

2006	29	89	16	1	2	2	5	71.03	$1,274,580

Best finish for 2006: Win at the Valero Texas Open

2007	36	107	17	0	0	0	4	72.26	$445,411

Best finish for 2007: T-19th at the PODS Championship

2008	35	113	22	0	2	3	6	71.31	$899,215

Best finish for 2008: T-4th at the John Deere Classic & Reno-Tahoe Open

Period Totals	Starts	Rounds Played	Cuts Made	Wins	Top-5s	Top-10s	Top-25s	Scoring Average	Money
	103	316	56	1	4	5	15	71.61	$2,633,306

Tommy Aycock

Year	Starts	Rounds Played	Cuts Made	Wins	Top-5s	Top-10s	Top-25s	Scoring Average	Money
1965	1	2	0	0	0	0	0	76.50	
1968	2	6	1	0	0	0	0	74.83	$445

Best finish for 1968: T-51st at the PGA Championship

1969	7	20	3	0	0	0	1	72.95	$1,197

Best finish for 1969: T-23rd at the Texas Open

1970	18	56	12	0	0	0	0	73.21	$3,703

Best finish for 1970: T-31st at the AVCO Classic

1971	12	31	3	0	0	0	1	73.39	$2,424

Best finish for 1971: T-16th at the Monsanto Open

1973	2	8	2	0	0	0	1	71.88	$1,872

Best finish for 1973: T-22nd at the San Antonio Texas Open

1974	4	12	2	0	0	0	1	72.50	$5,378

Best finish for 1974: T-11th at the PGA Championship

1976	1	2	0	0	0	0	0	73.00	
1977	2	4	0	0	0	0	0	76.00	$250
1978	1	4	1	0	0	0	0	73.50	$512

Best finish for 1978: T-50th at the PGA Championship

1979	1	2	0	0	0	0	0	73.50	$350
1980	1	2	0	0	0	0	0	76.50	$500
1981	1	4	1	0	0	0	0	69.25	$1,155

Best finish for 1981: T-35th at the Texas Open

1982	2	6	1	0	0	0	0	72.33	$520

Best finish for 1982: T-64th at the Texas Open

1984	1	2	0	0	0	0	0	74.00	
1985	2	4	0	0	0	0	0	76.50	$1,000
1986	1	2	0	0	0	0	0	71.50	
1990	1	4	1	0	0	0	0	69.25	$1,894

Best finish for 1990: T-51st at the H-E-B Texas Open

1991	1	2	0	0	0	0	0	77.00	

Period Totals	Starts	Rounds Played	Cuts Made	Wins	Top-5s	Top-10s	Top-25s	Scoring Average	Money
	61	173	27	0	0	0	4	73.20	$21,200

Paul Azinger

Year	Starts	Rounds Played	Cuts Made	Wins	Top-5s	Top-10s	Top-25s	Scoring Average	Money
1982	20	57	9	0	0	0	0	73.05	$8,255

Best finish for 1982: T-31st at the Bay Hill Classic

1983	2	4	0	0	0	0	0	77.00	$600
1984	21	71	14	0	0	0	3	72.28	$27,821

Best finish for 1984: T-13th at the Greater Milwaukee Open

1985	33	105	18	0	1	3	6	71.69	$80,119

Best finish for 1985: T-5th at the Hertz Bay Hill Classic

1986	29	98	25	0	4	7	13	70.74	$255,019

Best finish for 1986: 2nd at the Hawaiian Open & Deposit Guaranty Golf Classic

1987	29	99	23	3	6	10	16	70.20	$903,281

Best finish for 1987: Win at the Phoenix Open, Panasonic Las Vegas Invitational & Canon Sammy Davis, Jr. - Greater Hartford Open

1988	29	96	22	1	6	10	16	70.48	$601,634

Best finish for 1988: Win at the Hertz Bay Hill Classic

1989	27	97	22	1	7	14	17	70.32	$986,249

Best finish for 1989: Win at the Canon Greater Hartford Open

1990	28	102	23	1	7	12	18	70.65	$952,964

Best finish for 1990: Win at the Infiniti Tournament Of Champions

Year	Starts	Rounds Played	Cuts Made	Wins	Top-5s	Top-10s	Top-25s	Scoring Average	Money
1991	21	76	18	1	5	6	13	70.58	$686,602

Best finish for 1991: Win at the AT&T Pebble Beach National Pro-Am

| 1992 | 24 | 90 | 21 | 1 | 5 | 10 | 14 | 70.18 | $936,765 |

Best finish for 1992: Win at The Tour Championship

| 1993 | 25 | 85 | 17 | 3 | 10 | 12 | 13 | 70.41 | $1,466,155 |

Best finish for 1993: Win at the Memorial Tournament, New England Classic & PGA Championship

| 1994 | 4 | 11 | 2 | 0 | 0 | 0 | 1 | 71.36 | $14,622 |

Best finish for 1994: T-19th at the Buick Southern Open

| 1995 | 23 | 76 | 15 | 0 | 1 | 1 | 5 | 71.34 | $184,632 |

Best finish for 1995: T-4th at the United Airlines Hawaiian Open

| 1996 | 22 | 77 | 17 | 0 | 0 | 1 | 8 | 70.95 | $233,048 |

Best finish for 1996: T-8th at the Las Vegas Invitational

| 1997 | 20 | 63 | 12 | 0 | 0 | 3 | 4 | 71.41 | $263,134 |

Best finish for 1997: T-7th at the AT&T Pebble Beach National Pro-Am

| 1998 | 22 | 70 | 14 | 0 | 2 | 3 | 11 | 70.94 | $565,549 |

Best finish for 1998: T-3rd at the AT&T Pebble Beach National Pro-Am

| 1999 | 24 | 73 | 14 | 0 | 0 | 4 | 10 | 71.49 | $567,053 |

Best finish for 1999: T-6th at the FedEx St. Jude Classic & Buick Challenge

| 2000 | 20 | 72 | 18 | 1 | 2 | 7 | 14 | 70.06 | $1,597,139 |

Best finish for 2000: Win at the Sony Open in Hawaii

| 2001 | 20 | 79 | 19 | 0 | 3 | 4 | 13 | 69.96 | $1,509,130 |

Best finish for 2001: T-2nd at the Memorial Tournament

| 2002 | 20 | 63 | 13 | 0 | 1 | 2 | 4 | 71.63 | $777,926 |

Best finish for 2002: 4th at the Accenture Match Play Championship

| 2003 | 26 | 73 | 10 | 0 | 0 | 0 | 1 | 71.75 | $227,822 |

Best finish for 2003: T-12th at the Buick Open

| 2004 | 23 | 75 | 14 | 0 | 0 | 3 | 4 | 71.17 | $601,438 |

Best finish for 2004: T-6th at the Shell Houston Open

| 2005 | 22 | 66 | 10 | 0 | 0 | 0 | 2 | 71.86 | $248,489 |

Best finish for 2005: T-17th at the Sony Open in Hawaii

| 2006 | 30 | 87 | 16 | 0 | 0 | 1 | 7 | 71.03 | $704,340 |

Best finish for 2006: 10th at the Memorial Tournament

| 2007 | 13 | 39 | 7 | 0 | 0 | 0 | 1 | 72.10 | $174,069 |

Best finish for 2007: T-13th at the Sony Open in Hawaii

| 2008 | 9 | 21 | 2 | 0 | 0 | 0 | 0 | 73.19 | $42,590 |

Best finish for 2008: T-32nd at the Sony Open in Hawaii

Period Totals	Starts	Rounds Played	Cuts Made	Wins	Top-5s	Top-10s	Top-25s	Scoring Average	Money
	586	1925	395	12	60	113	214	71.04	$14,616,447

Aaron Baddeley

Year	Starts	Rounds Played	Cuts Made	Wins	Top-5s	Top-10s	Top-25s	Scoring Average	Money
2000	9	20	1	0	0	0	0	73.45	

Best finish for 2000: T-57th at the Honda Classic

| 2001 | 9 | 22 | 2 | 0 | 0 | 0 | 0 | 72.64 | $26,008 |

Best finish for 2001: T-46th at the Memorial Tournament

| 2002 | 3 | 10 | 2 | 0 | 0 | 0 | 0 | 70.90 | $16,380 |

Best finish for 2002: T-44th at the Reno-Tahoe Open

| 2003 | 20 | 67 | 15 | 0 | 2 | 3 | 4 | 70.73 | $989,168 |

Best finish for 2003: 2nd at the Sony Open in Hawaii

| 2004 | 27 | 85 | 16 | 0 | 1 | 1 | 3 | 71.94 | $638,090 |

Best finish for 2004: 2nd at the Chrysler Classic of Tucson

| 2005 | 27 | 82 | 16 | 0 | 2 | 5 | 8 | 71.15 | $1,006,006 |

Best finish for 2005: T-4th at the Reno-Tahoe Open

| 2006 | 25 | 76 | 14 | 1 | 1 | 2 | 6 | 71.41 | $1,521,160 |

Best finish for 2006: Win at the Verizon Heritage

| 2007 | 23 | 80 | 19 | 1 | 3 | 7 | 13 | 70.96 | $3,447,935 |

Best finish for 2007: Win at the FBR Open

| 2008 | 22 | 73 | 17 | 0 | 1 | 3 | 9 | 70.86 | $1,665,587 |

Best finish for 2008: T-2nd at the Verizon Heritage

Period Totals	Starts	Rounds Played	Cuts Made	Wins	Top-5s	Top-10s	Top-25s	Scoring Average	Money
	165	515	102	2	10	21	43	71.34	$9,310,334

Briny Baird

Year	Starts	Rounds Played	Cuts Made	Wins	Top-5s	Top-10s	Top-25s	Scoring Average	Money
1999	28	78	12	0	0	0	0	72.12	$115,357

Best finish for 1999: T-28th at the Touchstone Energy Tucson Open

| 2001 | 31 | 103 | 22 | 0 | 2 | 2 | 6 | 70.39 | $812,000 |

Best finish for 2001: 2nd at the John Deere Classic

| 2002 | 33 | 108 | 22 | 0 | 2 | 2 | 6 | 70.76 | $817,514 |

Best finish for 2002: T-3rd at the Bob Hope Chrysler Classic

| 2003 | 33 | 109 | 24 | 0 | 3 | 7 | 16 | 69.91 | $2,202,519 |

Best finish for 2003: T-2nd at the Buick Open

Year	Starts	Rounds Played	Cuts Made	Wins	Top-5s	Top-10s	Top-25s	Scoring Average	Money
2004	30	97	21	0	2	3	9	70.69	$1,162,517

Best finish for 2004: T-2nd at the FUNAI Classic at the Walt Disney World Resort

2005	33	96	18	0	0	2	5	70.73	$624,191

Best finish for 2005: T-8th at the Bay Hill Invitational & Michelin Championship at Las Vegas

2006	25	77	16	0	1	3	8	70.51	$844,547

Best finish for 2006: T-5th at the FedEx St. Jude Classic

2007	31	115	26	0	0	1	7	70.66	$985,453

Best finish for 2007: T-9th at the AT&T Classic

2008	30	113	26	0	2	3	14	70.44	$2,039,808

Best finish for 2008: T-4th at the Puerto Rico Open & The Players

Period Totals	Starts	Rounds Played	Cuts Made	Wins	Top-5s	Top-10s	Top-25s	Scoring Average	Money
	274	896	187	0	12	23	71	70.65	$9,603,906

Butch Baird

Year	Starts	Rounds Played	Cuts Made	Wins	Top-5s	Top-10s	Top-25s	Scoring Average	Money
1958	1	4	1	0	0	0	0	73.25	

Best finish for 1958: T-44th at the Lafayette Open

1960	9	36	9	0	0	2	3	71.86	$2,767

Best finish for 1960: T-10th at the Tucson Open Invitational & Hesperia Open Invitational

1961	14	54	12	1	1	3	6	71.28	$6,489

Best finish for 1961: Win at the Waco Turner Open Invitational

1962	19	74	17	0	1	4	13	71.01	$13,384

Best finish for 1962: T-5th at the Thunderbird Classic Invitational

1963	10	41	10	0	0	0	2	71.76	$3,304

Best finish for 1963: T-11th at the Tucson Open Invitational

1964	17	52	9	0	1	2	3	73.46	$4,708

Best finish for 1964: T-4th at the Houston Classic

1965	25	83	17	0	1	2	7	72.52	$11,610

Best finish for 1965: T-5th at the Azalea Open

1966	29	102	20	0	0	0	3	73.00	$9,223

Best finish for 1966: T-18th at the Tournament of Champions

1967	22	77	16	0	0	0	4	72.78	$10,285

Best finish for 1967: T-11th at the "500" Festival Open

1968	18	58	12	0	0	0	4	71.98	$6,867

Best finish for 1968: T-11th at the "500" Festival Open Invitational

1969	20	69	15	0	0	1	4	73.07	$14,026

Best finish for 1969: 6th at the National Airlines Open

1970	12	40	8	0	0	0	0	72.95	$2,649

Best finish for 1970: T-32nd at the Greater New Orleans Open

1971	10	26	3	0	0	0	0	73.04	$835

Best finish for 1971: T-40th at the Walt Disney World Open

1972	23	80	17	0	0	0	3	72.50	$11,364

Best finish for 1972: T-17th at the Byron Nelson Golf Classic

1973	31	114	24	0	0	2	9	72.22	$31,686

Best finish for 1973: T-9th at the Bing Crosby Pro-Am & Southern Open

1974	25	86	19	0	1	2	7	71.94	$25,072

Best finish for 1974: T-5th at the Western Open

1975	26	89	18	0	0	2	6	72.19	$23,033

Best finish for 1975: T-7th at the Phoenix Open

1976	27	91	19	1	2	3	7	72.04	$58,441

Best finish for 1976: Win at the San Antonio Texas Open

1977	28	85	15	0	1	2	5	72.75	$32,072

Best finish for 1977: T-4th at the Pensacola Open

1978	10	29	4	0	0	0	1	73.79	$3,746

Best finish for 1978: T-20th at the Joe Garagiola Tucson Open

1979	17	51	9	0	0	0	2	72.25	$12,526

Best finish for 1979: T-14th at the Bob Hope Chrysler Classic

1980	22	70	14	0	1	1	4	71.96	$25,929

Best finish for 1980: T-5th at the Sammy Davis, Jr. - Greater Hartford Open

1981	16	37	4	0	0	0	1	72.73	$7,612

Best finish for 1981: T-13th at the B.C. Open

1982	14	40	6	0	0	0	0	73.03	$5,413

Best finish for 1982: T-31st at the Miller High-Life Quad Cities Open

1983	3	8	0	0	0	0	0	73.00	
1984	1	2	0	0	0	0	0	74.50	
1985	1	2	0	0	0	0	0	75.50	

Period Totals	Starts	Rounds Played	Cuts Made	Wins	Top-5s	Top-10s	Top-25s	Scoring Average	Money
	450	1500	298	2	9	26	94	72.39	$323,045

Bobby Baker

Year	Starts	Rounds Played	Cuts Made	Wins	Top-5s	Top-10s	Top-25s	Scoring Average	Money
1978	13	31	2	0	0	0	1	75.77	$1,459

Best finish for 1978: T-19th at the Buick Goodwrench Open

Year	Starts	Rounds Played	Cuts Made	Wins	Top-5s	Top-10s	Top-25s	Scoring Average	Money
1979	21	54	6	0	0	0	1	74.04	$7,660

Best finish for 1979: T-15th at the Colgate Hall Of Fame Classic

Period Totals	Starts	Rounds Played	Cuts Made	Wins	Top-5s	Top-10s	Top-25s	Scoring Average	Money
	34	85	8	0	0	0	2	74.67	$9,119

Don Baker

Year	Starts	Rounds Played	Cuts Made	Wins	Top-5s	Top-10s	Top-25s	Scoring Average	Money
1977	12	36	6	0	0	0	0	73.97	$1,872

Best finish for 1977: T-38th at the Southern Open

Year	Starts	Rounds Played	Cuts Made	Wins	Top-5s	Top-10s	Top-25s	Scoring Average	Money
1978	10	23	2	0	0	0	0	75.04	$710

Best finish for 1978: 66th at the B.C. Open

Year	Starts	Rounds Played	Cuts Made	Wins	Top-5s	Top-10s	Top-25s	Scoring Average	Money
1979	3	8	0	0	0	0	0	74.25	
Period Totals	Starts	Rounds Played	Cuts Made	Wins	Top-5s	Top-10s	Top-25s	Scoring Average	Money
	25	67	8	0	0	0	0	74.37	$2,582

Ralph Baker

Year	Starts	Rounds Played	Cuts Made	Wins	Top-5s	Top-10s	Top-25s	Scoring Average	Money
1971	9	26	3	0	0	0	0	72.96	$960

Best finish for 1971: T-31st at the Greater Hartford Open Invitational

Year	Starts	Rounds Played	Cuts Made	Wins	Top-5s	Top-10s	Top-25s	Scoring Average	Money
1972	20	51	4	0	0	0	1	73.82	$3,177

Best finish for 1972: T-25th at the Kemper Open

Year	Starts	Rounds Played	Cuts Made	Wins	Top-5s	Top-10s	Top-25s	Scoring Average	Money
1974	2	4	0	0	0	0	0	76.00	
Period Totals	Starts	Rounds Played	Cuts Made	Wins	Top-5s	Top-10s	Top-25s	Scoring Average	Money
	31	81	7	0	0	0	1	73.65	$4,137

Ian Baker-Finch

Year	Starts	Rounds Played	Cuts Made	Wins	Top-5s	Top-10s	Top-25s	Scoring Average	Money
1984	2	6	1	0	0	1	1	73.67	$14,643

Best finish for 1984: T-9th at the British Open

Year	Starts	Rounds Played	Cuts Made	Wins	Top-5s	Top-10s	Top-25s	Scoring Average	Money
1985	9	30	6	0	0	0	2	73.13	$23,452

Best finish for 1985: T-19th at the NEC World Series of Golf

Year	Starts	Rounds Played	Cuts Made	Wins	Top-5s	Top-10s	Top-25s	Scoring Average	Money
1986	1	2	0	0	0	0	0	77.50	$600
1987	1	2	0	0	0	0	0	75.00	$640
1988	5	14	4	0	1	2	3	69.93	$76,605

Best finish for 1988: T-3rd at the NEC World Series of Golf

Year	Starts	Rounds Played	Cuts Made	Wins	Top-5s	Top-10s	Top-25s	Scoring Average	Money
1989	19	63	14	1	1	1	5	71.24	$260,847

Best finish for 1989: Win at the Southwestern Bell Colonial

Year	Starts	Rounds Played	Cuts Made	Wins	Top-5s	Top-10s	Top-25s	Scoring Average	Money
1990	26	85	20	0	6	7	11	70.80	$664,577

Best finish for 1990: T-2nd at the Infiniti Tournament Of Champions, Kemper Open & Canadian Open

Year	Starts	Rounds Played	Cuts Made	Wins	Top-5s	Top-10s	Top-25s	Scoring Average	Money
1991	22	79	20	1	5	10	15	70.33	$801,713

Best finish for 1991: Win at the British Open

Year	Starts	Rounds Played	Cuts Made	Wins	Top-5s	Top-10s	Top-25s	Scoring Average	Money
1992	20	64	14	0	1	3	7	71.34	$283,950

Best finish for 1992: T-2nd at the Players Championship

Year	Starts	Rounds Played	Cuts Made	Wins	Top-5s	Top-10s	Top-25s	Scoring Average	Money
1993	21	65	13	0	1	1	4	72.09	$146,036

Best finish for 1993: T-3rd at the MCI Heritage Classic

Year	Starts	Rounds Played	Cuts Made	Wins	Top-5s	Top-10s	Top-25s	Scoring Average	Money
1994	21	51	6	0	0	1	1	73.45	$84,498

Best finish for 1994: T-10th at the Masters

Year	Starts	Rounds Played	Cuts Made	Wins	Top-5s	Top-10s	Top-25s	Scoring Average	Money
1995	18	32	0	0	0	0	0	77.06	$4,737
1996	11	22	0	0	0	0	0	77.00	$3,508
1997	1	1	0	0	0	0	0	92.00	$1,089
2001	1	2	0	0	0	0	0	75.50	
Period Totals	Starts	Rounds Played	Cuts Made	Wins	Top-5s	Top-10s	Top-25s	Scoring Average	Money
	178	518	98	2	15	26	49	72.17	$2,366,896

Al Balding

Year	Starts	Rounds Played	Cuts Made	Wins	Top-5s	Top-10s	Top-25s	Scoring Average	Money
1958	33	126	29	0	1	4	17	71.99	$10,836

Best finish for 1958: T-5th at the Los Angeles Open

Year	Starts	Rounds Played	Cuts Made	Wins	Top-5s	Top-10s	Top-25s	Scoring Average	Money
1959	12	47	11	0	1	2	5	71.85	$4,492

Best finish for 1959: T-3rd at the Memphis Open Invitational

Year	Starts	Rounds Played	Cuts Made	Wins	Top-5s	Top-10s	Top-25s	Scoring Average	Money
1960	19	77	19	0	2	5	12	71.57	$7,158

Best finish for 1960: T-5th at the Puerto Rico Open Invitational & Hot Springs Open Invitational

Year	Starts	Rounds Played	Cuts Made	Wins	Top-5s	Top-10s	Top-25s	Scoring Average	Money
1961	25	101	23	0	3	6	16	70.51	$17,994

Best finish for 1961: T-2nd at the San Diego Open & Texas Open Invitational

Year	Starts	Rounds Played	Cuts Made	Wins	Top-5s	Top-10s	Top-25s	Scoring Average	Money
1962	18	71	18	0	0	0	8	71.87	$6,771

Best finish for 1962: T-11th at the Insurance City Open Invitational

Year	Starts	Rounds Played	Cuts Made	Wins	Top-5s	Top-10s	Top-25s	Scoring Average	Money
1963	18	71	17	0	4	6	9	71.69	$21,765

Best finish for 1963: T-2nd at the Los Angles Open

Year	Starts	Rounds Played	Cuts Made	Wins	Top-5s	Top-10s	Top-25s	Scoring Average	Money
1964	28	105	23	0	1	2	12	72.16	$15,011

Best finish for 1964: 2nd at the Fresno Open

Year	Starts	Rounds Played	Cuts Made	Wins	Top-5s	Top-10s	Top-25s	Scoring Average	Money
1965	6	24	5	0	0	0	0	73.54	$449

Best finish for 1965: T-33rd at the Pensacola Open

Year	Starts	Rounds Played	Cuts Made	Wins	Top-5s	Top-10s	Top-25s	Scoring Average	Money
1966	9	27	4	0	0	0	1	73.52	$1,675

Best finish for 1966: T-17th at the Canadian Open

| 1967 | 10 | 34 | 8 | 0 | 0 | 3 | 7 | 71.65 | $12,400 |

Best finish for 1967: T-8th at the British Open

| 1968 | 18 | 66 | 15 | 0 | 0 | 2 | 9 | 71.58 | $18,792 |

Best finish for 1968: 9th at the British Open

| 1969 | 25 | 90 | 19 | 0 | 1 | 1 | 6 | 72.26 | $17,343 |

Best finish for 1969: T-5th at the Canadian Open

| 1970 | 20 | 70 | 14 | 0 | 0 | 1 | 5 | 72.33 | $12,972 |

Best finish for 1970: T-8th at the Azalea Open Invitational

| 1971 | 5 | 15 | 1 | 0 | 0 | 0 | 0 | 75.07 | |

Best finish for 1971: T-71st at the Canadian Open

1972	2	4	0	0	0	0	0	76.25	
1973	1	2	0	0	0	0	0	79.00	
1980	1	2	0	0	0	0	0	77.00	
Period Totals	Starts	Rounds Played	Cuts Made	Wins	Top-5s	Top-10s	Top-25s	Scoring Average	Money
	250	932	206	0	13	32	107	71.96	$147,658

PGA Tour career totals from 1951 to 1980

	Starts	Rounds Played	Cuts Made	Wins	Top-5s	Top-10s	Top-25s	Scoring Average	Money
	316	1193	272	1	17	44	133	N/A	$176,179

Seve Ballesteros

Year	Starts	Rounds Played	Cuts Made	Wins	Top-5s	Top-10s	Top-25s	Scoring Average	Money
1975	1	2	0	0	0	0	0	79.50	$220
1976	1	4	1	0	1	1	1	71.25	$9,450

Best finish for 1976: T-2nd at the British Open

| 1977 | 3 | 12 | 3 | 0 | 0 | 1 | 2 | 71.58 | $11,745 |

Best finish for 1977: 9th at the World Series Of Golf

| 1978 | 7 | 28 | 7 | 1 | 1 | 3 | 6 | 71.71 | $71,104 |

Best finish for 1978: Win at the Greater Greensboro Open

| 1979 | 6 | 18 | 3 | 1 | 1 | 1 | 3 | 73.61 | $40,590 |

Best finish for 1979: Win at the British Open

| 1980 | 7 | 23 | 5 | 1 | 2 | 2 | 5 | 71.09 | $93,347 |

Best finish for 1980: Win at the Masters

| 1981 | 10 | 34 | 7 | 0 | 0 | 0 | 1 | 73.18 | $12,979 |

Best finish for 1981: T-25th at the Sea Pines Heritage Classic

| 1982 | 10 | 36 | 9 | 0 | 2 | 4 | 7 | 71.72 | $115,608 |

Best finish for 1982: 2nd at the Kemper Open

| 1983 | 9 | 34 | 8 | 2 | 4 | 5 | 6 | 71.21 | $229,308 |

Best finish for 1983: Win at the Masters & Manufactures Hanover Westchester Classic

| 1984 | 16 | 56 | 12 | 1 | 4 | 4 | 8 | 71.52 | $212,410 |

Best finish for 1984: Win at the British Open

| 1985 | 10 | 35 | 8 | 1 | 4 | 4 | 5 | 71.74 | $210,408 |

Best finish for 1985: Win at the USF&G Classic

| 1986 | 5 | 16 | 3 | 0 | 1 | 2 | 3 | 72.19 | $78,862 |

Best finish for 1986: 4th at the Masters

| 1987 | 9 | 36 | 9 | 0 | 4 | 6 | 7 | 71.08 | $309,098 |

Best finish for 1987: T-2nd at the Doral-Ryder Open, Masters & Manufactures Hanover Westchester Classic

| 1988 | 8 | 26 | 5 | 2 | 2 | 2 | 4 | 70.96 | $302,202 |

Best finish for 1988: Win at the Manufactures Hanover Westchester Classic & British Open

| 1989 | 9 | 33 | 8 | 0 | 2 | 2 | 4 | 71.85 | $141,934 |

Best finish for 1989: T-3rd at the Independent Insurance Agent Open

| 1990 | 9 | 25 | 4 | 0 | 1 | 2 | 2 | 73.08 | $86,579 |

Best finish for 1990: T-3rd at the Independent Insurance Agent Open

| 1991 | 7 | 24 | 5 | 0 | 1 | 2 | 4 | 71.67 | $103,680 |

Best finish for 1991: T-5th at the Buick Classic

| 1992 | 6 | 18 | 3 | 0 | 0 | 0 | 2 | 72.33 | $40,406 |

Best finish for 1992: T-12th at the Freeport-McMoRan Classic

| 1993 | 4 | 12 | 2 | 0 | 0 | 0 | 1 | 72.17 | $46,976 |

Best finish for 1993: T-11th at the Masters

| 1994 | 6 | 20 | 4 | 0 | 0 | 0 | 2 | 72.50 | $60,327 |

Best finish for 1994: T-18th at the Masters & U.S. Open

| 1995 | 9 | 26 | 4 | 0 | 0 | 1 | 1 | 73.19 | $66,545 |

Best finish for 1995: T-8th at the Honda Classic

| 1996 | 3 | 8 | 1 | 0 | 0 | 0 | 0 | 75.88 | $10,308 |

Best finish for 1996: 43rd at the Masters

1997	2	4	0	0	0	0	0	75.75	$6,676
1998	3	6	0	0	0	0	0	75.83	$6,316
1999	4	8	0	0	0	0	0	78.88	$6,250
2000	2	4	0	0	0	0	0	77.25	$6,672

Year	Starts	Rounds Played	Cuts Made	Wins	Top-5s	Top-10s	Top-25s	Scoring Average	Money
2001	2	4	0	0	0	0	0	75.25	$6,430
2002	1	2	0	0	0	0	0	78.00	$5,000
2003	1	2	0	0	0	0	0	81.00	$5,000
2006	1	2	0	0	0	0	0	75.50	$3,718
2007	1	2	0	0	0	0	0	83.00	
Period Totals	Starts	Rounds Played	Cuts Made	Wins	Top-5s	Top-10s	Top-25s	Scoring Average	Money
	172	560	111	9	30	42	74	72.35	$2,300,145

Bob Barbarossa

Year	Starts	Rounds Played	Cuts Made	Wins	Top-5s	Top-10s	Top-25s	Scoring Average	Money
1964	1	4	1	0	0	0	0	75.50	

Best finish for 1964: 70th at the St. Paul Open

Year	Starts	Rounds Played	Cuts Made	Wins	Top-5s	Top-10s	Top-25s	Scoring Average	Money
1967	2	6	1	0	0	0	0	76.00	

Best finish for 1967: T-68th at the Houston Championship International

1968	2	6	1	0	0	0	0	72.50	$280

Best finish for 1968: T-45th at the Houston Champions International

1969	1	2	0	0	0	0	0	77.00	
1970	3	6	0	0	0	0	0	74.17	
1971	19	58	10	0	0	0	1	73.38	$4,309

Best finish for 1971: T-16th at the Western Open

1972	31	100	19	0	0	1	2	72.79	$15,678

Best finish for 1972: T-9th at the U.S. Professional Match Play Championship

1973	20	71	15	0	0	0	3	72.69	$13,187

Best finish for 1973: T-14th at the Phoenix Open

1974	1	2	0	0	0	0	0	74.50	
Period Totals	Starts	Rounds Played	Cuts Made	Wins	Top-5s	Top-10s	Top-25s	Scoring Average	Money
	80	255	47	0	0	1	6	73.09	$33,454

Aaron Barber

Year	Starts	Rounds Played	Cuts Made	Wins	Top-5s	Top-10s	Top-25s	Scoring Average	Money
2001	2	4	0	0	0	0	0	74.00	
2003	32	94	13	0	1	1	4	71.37	$425,277

Best finish for 2003: T-4th at the Chrysler Classic of Tucson

2004	17	47	6	0	0	1	2	71.36	$229,915

Best finish for 2004: T-9th at the Booz Allen Classic

2005	1	2	0	0	0	0	0	78.00	$2,000
Period Totals	Starts	Rounds Played	Cuts Made	Wins	Top-5s	Top-10s	Top-25s	Scoring Average	Money
	52	147	19	0	1	2	6	71.53	$657,192

Dave Barber

Year	Starts	Rounds Played	Cuts Made	Wins	Top-5s	Top-10s	Top-25s	Scoring Average	Money
1972	9	22	2	0	0	0	0	73.82	$727

Best finish for 1972: T-41st at the Greater Hartford Open Invitational

1973	23	67	10	0	0	1	1	72.93	$6,344

Best finish for 1973: T-9th at the IVB Philadelphia Golf Classic

1974	16	41	4	0	0	0	1	73.17	$2,600

Best finish for 1974: T-19th at the Greater Jacksonville Open

1975	5	15	1	0	0	0	0	74.27	$414

Best finish for 1975: T-47th at the Greater Jacksonville Open

1977	1	2	0	0	0	0	0	77.50	$250
1978	3	10	1	0	0	0	0	75.00	$668

Best finish for 1978: T-63rd at the Glen Campbell Los Angles Open

1979	4	13	2	0	0	0	0	73.77	$1,128

Best finish for 1979: T-54th at the PGA Championship

1980	1	2	0	0	0	0	0	77.00	$500
1981	1	2	0	0	0	0	0	80.00	$550
1982	1	2	0	0	0	0	0	74.50	$650
1983	1	2	0	0	0	0	0	75.50	$100
1987	2	6	0	0	0	0	0	75.00	
Period Totals	Starts	Rounds Played	Cuts Made	Wins	Top-5s	Top-10s	Top-25s	Scoring Average	Money
	67	184	20	0	0	1	2	73.65	$13,930

Jerry Barber

Year	Starts	Rounds Played	Cuts Made	Wins	Top-5s	Top-10s	Top-25s	Scoring Average	Money
1958	13	51	12	0	2	3	7	71.98	$3,856

Best finish for 1958: T-2nd at the Tijuana Open

1959	14	54	13	0	4	5	10	71.17	$12,795

Best finish for 1959: T-2nd at the PGA Championship

1960	19	77	15	2	6	9	13	70.88	$21,910

Best finish for 1960: Win at the Yorba Linda Open Invitational & Tournament of Champions

1961	18	73	18	1	1	2	9	70.90	$19,017

Best finish for 1961: Win at the PGA Championship

Year	Starts	Rounds Played	Cuts Made	Wins	Top-5s	Top-10s	Top-25s	Scoring Average	Money
1962	12	44	11	0	1	2	4	72.93	$8,534

Best finish for 1962: T-5th at the Masters

| 1963 | 18 | 71 | 17 | 1 | 1 | 1 | 4 | 71.99 | $8,996 |

Best finish for 1963: Win at the Azalea Open Invitational

| 1964 | 27 | 76 | 8 | 0 | 0 | 1 | 1 | 74.26 | $2,057 |

Best finish for 1964: T-9th at the San Diego Open

| 1965 | 21 | 70 | 13 | 0 | 0 | 0 | 1 | 73.33 | $3,777 |

Best finish for 1965: T-13th at the Bing Crosby Pro-Am

| 1966 | 8 | 23 | 2 | 0 | 0 | 1 | 1 | 77.57 | $2,200 |

Best finish for 1966: T-8th at the Azalea Open Invitational

| 1967 | 6 | 19 | 3 | 0 | 0 | 0 | 0 | 74.16 | $332 |

Best finish for 1967: T-38th at the Bob Hope Classic

| 1968 | 13 | 34 | 4 | 0 | 0 | 0 | 0 | 73.91 | $295 |

Best finish for 1968: T-46th at the American Golf Classic

| 1969 | 17 | 39 | 2 | 0 | 0 | 0 | 1 | 75.13 | $1,079 |

Best finish for 1969: T-23rd at the Canadian Open

| 1970 | 16 | 43 | 4 | 0 | 0 | 0 | 0 | 74.51 | $2,033 |

Best finish for 1970: T-43rd at the National Airlines Open

1971	10	19	0	0	0	0	0	75.00	
1972	8	18	0	0	0	0	0	75.22	
1973	9	24	1	0	0	0	0	75.63	

Best finish for 1973: T-78th at the Canadian Open

| 1974 | 10 | 25 | 2 | 0 | 0 | 0 | 0 | 76.08 | $1,025 |

Best finish for 1974: T-70th at the Phoenix Open & World Open

| 1975 | 8 | 19 | 1 | 0 | 0 | 0 | 0 | 75.32 | $426 |

Best finish for 1975: T-46th at the Bob Hope Chrysler Classic

1976	8	18	0	0	0	0	0	77.11	$750
1977	4	10	0	0	0	0	0	76.50	$250
1978	4	10	0	0	0	0	0	75.90	
1979	4	10	0	0	0	0	0	76.20	$350
1980	5	10	0	0	0	0	0	76.00	
1981	2	4	0	0	0	0	0	74.25	
1982	2	4	0	0	0	0	0	74.75	
1983	4	10	0	0	0	0	0	76.00	$100
1984	1	2	0	0	0	0	0	77.00	
1985	1	2	0	0	0	0	0	77.00	
1993	3	6	0	0	0	0	0	82.00	
1994	2	4	0	0	0	0	0	76.00	
Period Totals	Starts	Rounds Played	Cuts Made	Wins	Top-5s	Top-10s	Top-25s	Scoring Average	Money
	287	869	126	4	15	24	51	73.54	$89,780

PGA Tour career totals from 1948 to 1994

	Starts	Rounds Played	Cuts Made	Wins	Top-5s	Top-10s	Top-25s	Scoring Average	Money
	487	1637	326	6	34	95	189	N/A	$186,232

Jim Barber

Year	Starts	Rounds Played	Cuts Made	Wins	Top-5s	Top-10s	Top-25s	Scoring Average	Money
1972	21	60	8	0	0	0	0	74.25	$2,188

Best finish for 1972: T-48th at the Hawaiian Open

| 1973 | 25 | 73 | 11 | 0 | 1 | 1 | 3 | 72.90 | $22,306 |

Best finish for 1973: 2nd at the IVB Philadelphia Golf Classic

| 1974 | 28 | 75 | 10 | 0 | 0 | 0 | 1 | 73.64 | $4,664 |

Best finish for 1974: T-25th at the Tallahassee Open

| 1975 | 13 | 30 | 4 | 0 | 0 | 0 | 0 | 73.57 | $1,539 |

Best finish for 1975: T-35th at the Ed McMahon Quad City Open

| 1976 | 1 | 2 | 0 | 0 | 0 | 0 | 0 | 82.50 | $250 |
| 1980 | 10 | 26 | 4 | 0 | 0 | 0 | 0 | 72.54 | $2,872 |

Best finish for 1980: T-34th at the Quad Cities Open

| 1981 | 17 | 53 | 11 | 0 | 0 | 0 | 2 | 71.77 | $17,647 |

Best finish for 1981: T-11th at the USF&G New Orleans Open

| 1982 | 22 | 67 | 12 | 0 | 0 | 0 | 3 | 72.97 | $16,610 |

Best finish for 1982: T-12th at the Hall of Fame

| Period Totals | Starts | Rounds Played | Cuts Made | Wins | Top-5s | Top-10s | Top-25s | Scoring Average | Money |
| | 137 | 386 | 60 | 0 | 1 | 1 | 9 | 73.19 | $68,077 |

Miller Barber

Year	Starts	Rounds Played	Cuts Made	Wins	Top-5s	Top-10s	Top-25s	Scoring Average	Money
1959	5	20	5	0	0	1	4	70.95	$2,009

Best finish for 1959: T-8th at the Orange County Open Invitational

| 1960 | 8 | 32 | 7 | 0 | 0 | 1 | 4 | 71.97 | $2,594 |

Best finish for 1960: T-7th at the Hesperia Open Invitational

| 1961 | 14 | 54 | 12 | 0 | 0 | 0 | 6 | 71.33 | $3,398 |

Best finish for 1961: T-13th at the Denver Open Invitational

Year	Starts	Rounds Played	Cuts Made	Wins	Top-5s	Top-10s	Top-25s	Scoring Average	Money
1962	9	35	9	0	1	1	4	72.20	$3,330

Best finish for 1962: T-4th at the Carling Open Invitational

1963	28	111	26	0	2	5	19	71.46	$20,915

Best finish for 1963: T-4th at the Oklahoma City Open Invitational

1964	33	113	23	1	3	4	14	71.99	$18,782

Best finish for 1964: Win at the Cajun Classic

1965	35	125	26	0	0	10	14	72.06	$32,333

Best finish for 1965: T-6th at the Tournament of Champions & "500" Festival

1966	30	113	26	0	4	5	14	71.50	$45,668

Best finish for 1966: T-2nd at the Los Angles Open Invitational & Sahara Invitational

1967	32	118	26	1	5	8	16	71.86	$60,304

Best finish for 1967: Win at the Oklahoma City Open

1968	34	129	29	1	9	14	24	70.82	$99,629

Best finish for 1968: Win at the Byron Nelson Golf Classic

1969	34	127	31	1	5	8	18	71.20	$90,214

Best finish for 1969: Win at the Kaiser International Open

1970	33	110	24	1	5	6	18	71.75	$97,031

Best finish for 1970: Win at the Greater New Orleans Open

1971	31	105	25	1	6	9	13	71.43	$110,671

Best finish for 1971: Win at the Phoenix Open

1972	34	112	25	1	3	5	11	72.33	$69,610

Best finish for 1972: Win at the Tucson Open

1973	35	134	29	1	4	8	17	71.38	$178,133

Best finish for 1973: Win at the World Open

1974	34	122	27	1	4	5	17	71.66	$91,573

Best finish for 1974: Win at the Ohio Kings Island Open

1975	30	112	25	0	5	8	15	71.52	$81,994

Best finish for 1975: T-3rd at the Pensacola Open & Pleasant Valley Classic

1976	33	120	29	0	6	8	13	71.47	$106,925

Best finish for 1976: 2nd at the Greater Jacksonville Open & San Antonio Texas Open

1977	33	119	26	1	4	13	19	71.22	$148,515

Best finish for 1977: Win at the Anheuser-Busch Golf Classic

1978	31	107	23	1	3	5	12	71.99	$107,639

Best finish for 1978: Win at the Phoenix Open

1979	29	92	16	0	2	2	6	72.60	$68,438

Best finish for 1979: 2nd at the Memorial Tournament

1980	36	107	21	0	2	3	7	72.29	$64,505

Best finish for 1980: T-3rd at the Danny Thomas Memphis Classic

1981	29	81	13	0	2	2	6	72.21	$52,195

Best finish for 1981: T-3rd at the Glen Campbell Los Angles Open

1982	21	61	9	0	0	0	0	72.93	$9,020

Best finish for 1982: T-31st at the Miller High-Life Quad Cities Open

1983	13	38	5	0	0	1	2	73.00	$20,208

Best finish for 1983: T-10th at the Greater Greensboro Open

1984	6	17	2	0	0	0	0	73.65	$2,260

Best finish for 1984: T-42nd at the Bay Hill Classic

1985	5	15	2	0	0	0	0	73.93	$1,876

Best finish for 1985: T-60th at the Bob Hope Chrysler Classic

1986	3	10	1	0	0	0	0	72.40	$2,045

Best finish for 1986: T-44th at the Phoenix Open

1987	2	5	0	0	0	0	0	74.00	
1988	2	7	0	0	0	0	0	73.14	
1989	1	4	0	0	0	0	0	73.25	
1990	1	4	0	0	0	0	0	70.50	
Period Totals	Starts	Rounds Played	Cuts Made	Wins	Top-5s	Top-10s	Top-25s	Scoring Average	Money
	704	2459	522	11	75	132	293	71.78	$1,591,813

Rich Barcelo

Year	Starts	Rounds Played	Cuts Made	Wins	Top-5s	Top-10s	Top-25s	Scoring Average	Money
2004	26	65	8	0	0	0	2	71.85	$223,597

Best finish for 2004: T-16th at the Booz Allen Classic

2005	3	8	1	0	0	0	0	72.25	$10,887

Best finish for 2005: T-53rd at the Reno-Tahoe Open

2006	1	2	0	0	0	0	0	71.50	
2007	26	80	13	0	1	1	2	71.68	$334,244

Best finish for 2007: T-4th at the Reno-Tahoe Open

Period Totals	Starts	Rounds Played	Cuts Made	Wins	Top-5s	Top-10s	Top-25s	Scoring Average	Money
	56	155	22	0	1	1	4	71.77	$568,729

Jim Barker

Year	Starts	Rounds Played	Cuts Made	Wins	Top-5s	Top-10s	Top-25s	Scoring Average	Money
1970	3	6	1	0	0	0	0	73.83	$182

Best finish for 1970: T-62nd at the San Antonio Texas Open

Year	Starts	Rounds Played	Cuts Made	Wins	Top-5s	Top-10s	Top-25s	Scoring Average	Money
1972	18	40	3	0	0	0	0	74.80	$1,215

Best finish for 1972: T-34th at the Monsanto Open

Year	Starts	Rounds Played	Cuts Made	Wins	Top-5s	Top-10s	Top-25s	Scoring Average	Money
1974	1	2	0	0	0	0	0	75.50	
1975	1	2	0	0	0	0	0	73.50	
1976	1	2	0	0	0	0	0	72.50	$077
1977	12	34	5	0	0	0	0	72.50	$2,286

Best finish for 1977: T-29th at the B.C. Open

Year	Starts	Rounds Played	Cuts Made	Wins	Top-5s	Top-10s	Top-25s	Scoring Average	Money
1980	1	2	0	0	0	0	0	78.00	$600
1983	1	2	0	0	0	0	0	77.00	
1984	1	2	0	0	0	0	0	72.00	
1985	1	2	0	0	0	0	0	73.00	
1986	1	2	0	0	0	0	0	73.50	
1998	1	2	0	0	0	0	0	72.50	
Period Totals	Starts	Rounds Played	Cuts Made	Wins	Top-5s	Top-10s	Top-25s	Scoring Average	Money
	42	98	9	0	0	0	0	73.83	$4,360

Paul Barkhouse

Year	Starts	Rounds Played	Cuts Made	Wins	Top-5s	Top-10s	Top-25s	Scoring Average	Money
1969	3	8	1	0	0	0	0	72.75	$321

Best finish for 1969: T-30th at the Indian Ridge Hospital Open

Year	Starts	Rounds Played	Cuts Made	Wins	Top-5s	Top-10s	Top-25s	Scoring Average	Money
1970	17	48	7	0	0	0	1	73.75	$3,270

Best finish for 1970: T-15th at the Azalea Open Invitational

Year	Starts	Rounds Played	Cuts Made	Wins	Top-5s	Top-10s	Top-25s	Scoring Average	Money
1971	13	31	2	0	0	0	0	73.97	$428

Best finish for 1971: T-59th at the Glen Campbell Los Angles Open

Year	Starts	Rounds Played	Cuts Made	Wins	Top-5s	Top-10s	Top-25s	Scoring Average	Money
1972	4	9	0	0	0	0	0	74.44	
1973	1	2	0	0	0	0	0	76.00	
1974	2	4	0	0	0	0	0	75.50	
1975	1	2	0	0	0	0	0	74.50	
1976	1	2	0	0	0	0	0	73.50	
1977	3	6	0	0	0	0	0	73.83	
1978	3	6	0	0	0	0	0	77.83	$903
Period Totals	Starts	Rounds Played	Cuts Made	Wins	Top-5s	Top-10s	Top-25s	Scoring Average	Money
	48	118	10	0	0	0	1	74.11	$4,922

Craig Barlow

Year	Starts	Rounds Played	Cuts Made	Wins	Top-5s	Top-10s	Top-25s	Scoring Average	Money
1998	29	81	13	0	0	0	2	71.93	$98,111

Best finish for 1998: T-14th at the Kemper Open

| 1999 | 28 | 85 | 16 | 0 | 2 | 2 | 3 | 71.82 | $327,393 |

Best finish for 1999: T-3rd at the Buick Challenge

| 2000 | 31 | 96 | 18 | 0 | 0 | 1 | 4 | 70.96 | $297,672 |

Best finish for 2000: T-10th at the Tampa Bay Classic

| 2001 | 24 | 72 | 14 | 0 | 0 | 1 | 4 | 70.79 | $414,139 |

Best finish for 2001: T-6th at the AT&T Pebble Beach

| 2002 | 22 | 58 | 9 | 0 | 1 | 3 | 5 | 71.03 | $528,569 |

Best finish for 2002: T-3rd at the Air Canada Championship

| 2003 | 29 | 93 | 17 | 0 | 1 | 3 | 5 | 70.74 | $638,721 |

Best finish for 2003: T-4th at the Greater Hartford Open

| 2004 | 25 | 78 | 14 | 0 | 0 | 1 | 7 | 70.81 | $595,820 |

Best finish for 2004: T-8th at the Sony Open in Hawaii

| 2005 | 26 | 77 | 15 | 0 | 0 | 1 | 9 | 71.29 | $720,362 |

Best finish for 2005: T-8th at the Buick Open

| 2006 | 22 | 73 | 16 | 0 | 2 | 2 | 5 | 71.22 | $1,008,788 |

Best finish for 2006: 3rd at the Nissan Open

| 2007 | 16 | 52 | 10 | 0 | 0 | 0 | 1 | 71.25 | $154,214 |

Best finish for 2007: T-25th at the Reno-Tahoe Open

| 2008 | 15 | 43 | 6 | 0 | 0 | 0 | 1 | 72.79 | $129,732 |

Best finish for 2008: T-23rd at the Zurich Classic of New Orleans

Period Totals	Starts	Rounds Played	Cuts Made	Wins	Top-5s	Top-10s	Top-25s	Scoring Average	Money
	267	808	148	0	6	14	46	71.27	$4,913,521

Brian Barnes

Year	Starts	Rounds Played	Cuts Made	Wins	Top-5s	Top-10s	Top-25s	Scoring Average	Money
1965	1	2	0	0	0	0	0	76.00	
1966	1	2	0	0	0	0	0	77.50	
1967	2	6	1	0	0	0	1	74.67	$329

Best finish for 1967: T-25th at the British Open

| 1968 | 1 | 4 | 1 | 0 | 0 | 1 | 1 | 73.75 | $1,579 |

Best finish for 1968: T-6th at the British Open

| 1969 | 3 | 10 | 2 | 0 | 0 | 0 | 0 | 73.00 | $438 |

Best finish for 1969: T-40th at the British Open

Year	Starts	Rounds Played	Cuts Made	Wins	Top-5s	Top-10s	Top-25s	Scoring Average	Money
1970	14	46	9	0	1	1	3	72.93	$11,151

Best finish for 1970: T-3rd at the Doral-Eastern Open

| 1971 | 1 | 4 | 1 | 0 | 0 | 0 | 0 | 75.75 | $226 |

Best finish for 1971: 64th at the British Open

| 1972 | 2 | 6 | 1 | 0 | 1 | 1 | 1 | 74.67 | $7,125 |

Best finish for 1972: 5th at the British Open

| 1973 | 4 | 13 | 2 | 0 | 0 | 1 | 1 | 74.23 | $5,411 |

Best finish for 1973: T-10th at the British Open

| 1974 | 3 | 12 | 3 | 0 | 0 | 0 | 1 | 73.33 | $1,824 |

Best finish for 1974: T-24th at the Phoenix Open

| 1975 | 1 | 4 | 1 | 0 | 0 | 0 | 1 | 72.50 | $1,001 |

Best finish for 1975: T-23rd at the British Open

| 1976 | 1 | 4 | 1 | 0 | 0 | 0 | 1 | 72.50 | $2,880 |

Best finish for 1976: 14th at the British Open

| 1977 | 4 | 14 | 3 | 0 | 0 | 0 | 0 | 72.64 | $2,926 |

Best finish for 1977: T-26th at the Doral-Eastern Open

| 1978 | 4 | 11 | 3 | 0 | 0 | 0 | 0 | 72.91 | $2,451 |

Best finish for 1978: T-31st at the Jackie Gleason's Inverrary Classic

| 1979 | 4 | 10 | 1 | 0 | 0 | 0 | 0 | 74.70 | $971 |

Best finish for 1979: T-50th at the British Open

| 1980 | 1 | 4 | 1 | 0 | 0 | 0 | 0 | 73.50 | $1,320 |

Best finish for 1980: T-58th at the British Open

| 1981 | 1 | 4 | 1 | 0 | 0 | 0 | 1 | 72.00 | $6,480 |

Best finish for 1981: T-14th at the British Open

| 1982 | 1 | 4 | 1 | 0 | 0 | 0 | 0 | 74.50 | $1,417 |

Best finish for 1982: T-35th at the British Open

1989	1	2	0	0	0	0	0	74.00	$800
1990	1	2	0	0	0	0	0	72.00	$996
1996	1	4	1	0	0	0	0	71.75	$8,486

Best finish for 1996: T-59th at the British Open

Period Totals	Starts	Rounds Played	Cuts Made	Wins	Top-5s	Top-10s	Top-25s	Scoring Average	Money
	52	168	33	0	2	4	11	73.43	$57,810

John Barnum

Year	Starts	Rounds Played	Cuts Made	Wins	Top-5s	Top-10s	Top-25s	Scoring Average	Money
1958	14	46	8	0	1	1	3	72.76	$2,625

Best finish for 1958: 3rd at the Tucson Open

| 1959 | 5 | 19 | 5 | 0 | 0 | 1 | 3 | 72.58 | $1,568 |

Best finish for 1959: T-8th at the Mobile Sertoma Open Invitational

| 1960 | 12 | 45 | 12 | 0 | 0 | 2 | 6 | 70.73 | $3,079 |

Best finish for 1960: T-9th at the Coral Gables Open Invitational

| 1961 | 9 | 36 | 8 | 0 | 1 | 1 | 4 | 70.92 | $3,009 |

Best finish for 1961: T-5th at the West Palm Beach Open Invitational

| 1962 | 10 | 40 | 10 | 1 | 1 | 2 | 6 | 71.95 | $5,342 |

Best finish for 1962: Win at the Cajun Classic Open Invitational

| 1963 | 5 | 20 | 5 | 1 | 1 | 3 | 3 | 72.15 | $3,096 |

Best finish for 1963: Win at the Jamaica Open Invitational

| 1964 | 5 | 17 | 3 | 0 | 0 | 0 | 1 | 73.12 | $609 |

Best finish for 1964: T-18th at the Pensacola Open

| 1965 | 5 | 14 | 2 | 0 | 0 | 0 | 1 | 74.57 | $910 |

Best finish for 1965: T-12th at the Azalea Open

| 1966 | 3 | 8 | 1 | 0 | 0 | 0 | 0 | 75.50 | |

Best finish for 1966: T-62nd at the Doral Open Invitational

| 1967 | 1 | 2 | 0 | 0 | 0 | 0 | 0 | 76.50 | |

Period Totals	Starts	Rounds Played	Cuts Made	Wins	Top-5s	Top-10s	Top-25s	Scoring Average	Money
	69	247	54	2	4	10	27	72.17	$20,238

Dave Barr

Year	Starts	Rounds Played	Cuts Made	Wins	Top-5s	Top-10s	Top-25s	Scoring Average	Money
1976	1	2	0	0	0	0	0	72.50	
1977	1	2	0	0	0	0	0	76.50	*
1978	18	54	9	0	1	1	1	72.78	$11,087

Best finish for 1978: T-4th at the Greater Milwaukee Open

| 1979 | 23 | 62 | 8 | 0 | 0 | 1 | 1 | 72.97 | $13,022 |

Best finish for 1979: T-9th at the Joe Garagiola Tucson Open

| 1980 | 18 | 53 | 9 | 0 | 0 | 2 | 3 | 72.98 | $19,027 |

Best finish for 1980: T-8th at the World Disney World National Team Championship

| 1981 | 26 | 75 | 13 | 1 | 1 | 1 | 1 | 72.45 | $46,764 |

Best finish for 1981: Win at the Quad Cities Open

| 1982 | 24 | 72 | 11 | 0 | 0 | 0 | 0 | 73.22 | $13,974 |

Best finish for 1982: 28th at the MONY Tournament Of Champions

Year	Starts	Rounds Played	Cuts Made	Wins	Top-5s	Top-10s	Top-25s	Scoring Average	Money
1983	26	88	17	0	0	1	7	71.81	$53,400

Best finish for 1983: T-9th at the Walt Disney World Golf Classic

1984	28	89	18	0	2	4	7	71.65	$113,336

Best finish for 1984: T-4th at the Byron Nelson Golf Classic & Buick Open

1985	27	85	18	0	1	3	9	71.64	$125,215

Best finish for 1985: T-2nd at the U.S. Open

1986	27	82	17	0	1	3	6	72.00	$122,180

Best finish for 1986: T-2nd at the Greater Milwaukee Open

1987	27	94	20	1	1	1	7	71.21	$205,407

Best finish for 1987: Win at the Georgia-Pacific Atlanta Golf Classic

1988	27	95	20	0	4	7	14	70.37	$293,744

Best finish for 1988: T-2nd at the Southern Open & Canon Sammy Davis, Jr. - Greater Hartford Open

1989	25	93	20	0	0	2	10	71.10	$191,480

Best finish for 1989: T-8th at the Canadian Open

1990	26	95	23	0	1	3	7	71.27	$197,983

Best finish for 1990: T-3rd at the Hardee's Golf Classic

1991	26	86	17	0	1	3	5	71.06	$145,389

Best finish for 1991: T-5th at the Centel Western Open

1992	24	92	21	0	0	1	3	71.01	$118,859

Best finish for 1992: T-9th at the BellSouth Classic

1993	28	94	19	0	1	1	6	71.44	$180,263

Best finish for 1993: T-2nd at the Nissan Los Angeles Open

1994	28	94	18	0	2	4	9	70.72	$316,085

Best finish for 1994: T-3rd at the Canon Greater Hartford Open

1995	27	79	13	0	0	0	6	71.28	$118,218

Best finish for 1995: T-11th at the Canon Greater Hartford Open

1996	19	58	11	0	0	0	0	71.97	$31,810

Best finish for 1996: T-46th at the Greater Milwaukee Open

1997	4	11	1	0	0	0	0	72.82	$5,400

Best finish for 1997: T-38th at the United Airlines Hawaiian Open

1998	22	60	7	0	0	0	1	71.87	$44,130

Best finish for 1998: T-20th at the B.C. Open

1999	5	12	1	0	0	0	0	73.75	$5,375

Best finish for 1999: T-61st at the BellSouth Classic

2000	6	16	2	0	0	0	0	71.38	$15,600

Best finish for 2000: T-40th at the Westin Texas Open at LaCantera

2001	4	8	1	0	0	0	0	72.13	$3,760

Best finish for 2001: T-76th at the B.C. Open

2002	5	18	4	0	0	0	0	71.78	$28,395

Best finish for 2002: T-44th at the Valero Texas Open

Period Totals	Starts	Rounds Played	Cuts Made	Wins	Top-5s	Top-10s	Top-25s	Scoring Average	Money
	522	1669	318	2	16	38	103	71.66	$2,419,905

Ray Barr, Jr.

Year	Starts	Rounds Played	Cuts Made	Wins	Top-5s	Top-10s	Top-25s	Scoring Average	Money
1982	15	38	4	0	0	0	0	73.74	$2,436

Best finish for 1982: T-54th at the Sammy Davis, Jr. - Greater Hartford Open

1984	1	2	0	0	0	0	0	74.00	
1987	29	80	14	0	0	1	4	72.04	$51,385

Best finish for 1987: T-10th at the Byron Nelson Golf Classic

1988	19	64	13	0	0	1	7	71.02	$58,337

Best finish for 1988: T-9th at the Hardee's Golf Classic

1989	25	66	7	0	0	0	1	72.03	$16,827

Best finish for 1989: T-11th at the Deposit Guaranty Golf Classic

1990	24	61	5	0	0	0	0	73.89	$8,711

Best finish for 1990: T-55th at the Northern Telecom Tucson Open

Period Totals	Starts	Rounds Played	Cuts Made	Wins	Top-5s	Top-10s	Top-25s	Scoring Average	Money
	113	311	43	0	0	2	12	72.41	$137,696

Todd Barranger

Year	Starts	Rounds Played	Cuts Made	Wins	Top-5s	Top-10s	Top-25s	Scoring Average	Money
1994	27	71	11	0	0	0	1	72.32	$41,356

Best finish for 1994: T-13th at the B.C. Open

2000	5	16	3	0	0	0	1	70.38	$43,767

Best finish for 2000: T-18th at the B.C. Open

2001	1	4	1	0	0	0	0	71.25	$7,700

Best finish for 2001: T-59th at the WorldCom Classic

2002	1	4	1	0	0	0	1	71.00	$43,200

Best finish for 2002: T-22nd at the AT&T Pebble Beach

2003	31	75	8	0	0	0	1	72.80	$158,700

Best finish for 2003: T-19th at the Buick Open

2004	1	3	0	0	0	0	0	74.00	

2005	1	2	0	0	0	0	0	75.50	
Period Totals	Starts	Rounds Played	Cuts Made	Wins	Top-5s	Top-10s	Top-25s	Scoring Average	Money
	67	175	24	0	0	0	4	72.36	$294,723

Jerry Barrier

Year	Starts	Rounds Played	Cuts Made	Wins	Top-5s	Top-10s	Top-25s	Scoring Average	Money
1964	1	4	1	0	0	0	0	75.75	

Best finish for 1964: 67th at the Texas Open

Year	Starts	Rounds Played	Cuts Made	Wins	Top-5s	Top-10s	Top-25s	Scoring Average	Money
1969	19	50	6	0	0	0	2	73.96	$1,469

Best finish for 1969: T-12th at the West End Classic

1970	13	38	6	0	0	0	0	73.63	$1,138

Best finish for 1970: T-48th at the Cleveland Open

1971	13	39	7	0	0	0	0	73.56	$1,174

Best finish for 1971: T-38th at the Greater Milwaukee Open

1972	15	38	6	0	0	0	2	73.26	$3,324

Best finish for 1972: T-16th at the Southern Open

1973	13	38	5	0	0	0	0	73.50	$1,672

Best finish for 1973: T-49th at the Doral-Eastern Open & Westchester Classic

Period Totals	Starts	Rounds Played	Cuts Made	Wins	Top-5s	Top-10s	Top-25s	Scoring Average	Money
	74	207	31	0	0	0	4	73.65	$8,776

Doug Barron

Year	Starts	Rounds Played	Cuts Made	Wins	Top-5s	Top-10s	Top-25s	Scoring Average	Money
1996	1	2	0	0	0	0	0	71.00	
1997	31	103	21	0	0	2	5	71.18	$198,051

Best finish for 1997: T-6th at the LaCantera Texas Open

1998	30	89	16	0	0	2	5	71.57	$268,952

Best finish for 1998: 6th at the Greater Milwaukee Open

1999	32	89	14	0	1	1	7	71.60	$335,995

Best finish for 1999: T-5th at the Buick Classic

2000	27	82	16	0	2	3	7	70.98	$461,981

Best finish for 2000: T-4th at the Air Canada Championship

2001	25	62	8	0	0	0	0	71.95	$77,837

Best finish for 2001: T-27th at the BellSouth Classic

2002	6	17	2	0	0	0	0	72.35	$14,368

Best finish for 2002: T-60th at the FedEx St. Jude Classic

2003	32	88	12	0	0	0	2	71.40	$224,589

Best finish for 2003: T-21st at the Bob Hope Chrysler Classic & Honda Classic

2004	1	4	1	0	0	0	0	70.50	$23,291

Best finish for 2004: T-33rd at the FedEx St. Jude Classic

2005	24	70	11	0	2	2	5	71.00	$731,990

Best finish for 2005: T-3rd at the EDS Byron Nelson Championship

2006	28	73	10	0	0	2	2	71.89	$388,226

Best finish for 2006: T-7th at the Chrysler Classic of Tucson & BellSouth Classic

Period Totals	Starts	Rounds Played	Cuts Made	Wins	Top-5s	Top-10s	Top-25s	Scoring Average	Money
	237	679	111	0	5	12	33	71.44	$2,725,280

Rich Bassett

Year	Starts	Rounds Played	Cuts Made	Wins	Top-5s	Top-10s	Top-25s	Scoring Average	Money
1967	14	36	4	0	0	0	0	75.14	$931

Best finish for 1967: T-41st at the Buick Open

1968	22	61	8	0	0	0	1	73.95	$893

Best finish for 1968: T-22nd at the Minnesota Golf Classic

1969	21	59	9	0	0	0	3	73.88	$4,509

Best finish for 1969: T-12th at the Alameda County Open

1970	15	41	5	0	0	0	0	73.90	$809

Best finish for 1970: T-43rd at the Tallahassee Open

1971	5	10	0	0	0	0	0	74.30	
1972	9	24	3	0	0	0	1	74.13	$1,437

Best finish for 1972: T-17th at the Tallahassee Open

1973	3	8	1	0	0	0	0	72.75	$242

Best finish for 1973: T-41st at the Tallahassee Open

1974	4	10	1	0	0	0	1	73.80	$613

Best finish for 1974: T-25th at the Tallahassee Open

1975	4	10	1	0	0	0	0	73.90	$130

Best finish for 1975: T-56th at the Tallahassee Open

1976	2	4	0	0	0	0	0	77.00	
1977	2	4	0	0	0	0	0	74.75	
1978	3	6	0	0	0	0	0	76.33	
1979	3	6	0	0	0	0	0	76.67	
1980	1	2	0	0	0	0	0	74.00	
1982	1	2	0	0	0	0	0	74.50	$650
Period Totals	Starts	Rounds Played	Cuts Made	Wins	Top-5s	Top-10s	Top-25s	Scoring Average	Money
	109	283	32	0	0	0	6	74.23	$10,214

Bob Batdorff

Year	Starts	Rounds Played	Cuts Made	Wins	Top-5s	Top-10s	Top-25s	Scoring Average	Money
1959	1	4	1	0	0	0	0	75.75	

Best finish for 1959: T-46th at the U.S. Open

1963	4	16	4	0	0	0	1	71.94	$2,601

Best finish for 1963: T-23rd at the Whitemarsh Open Invitational

1964	18	51	6	0	1	2	4	72.63	$3,851

Best finish for 1964: T-5th at the Sunset-Camellia Open

1965	19	64	13	0	0	1	2	72.97	$3,808

Best finish for 1965: 8th at the Azalea Open

1966	14	32	2	0	0	0	0	74.81	$662

Best finish for 1966: T-30th at the Cleveland Open Invitational

1967	4	8	0	0	0	0	0	74.38	
1969	1	4	1	0	0	0	0	72.00	$150

Best finish for 1969: T-29th at the Azalea Open

Period Totals	Starts	Rounds Played	Cuts Made	Wins	Top-5s	Top-10s	Top-25s	Scoring Average	Money
	61	179	27	0	1	3	7	73.21	$11,073

Brian Bateman

Year	Starts	Rounds Played	Cuts Made	Wins	Top-5s	Top-10s	Top-25s	Scoring Average	Money
1991	1	2	0	0	0	0	0	72.50	
1997	1	2	0	0	0	0	0	72.50	
1998	1	2	0	0	0	0	0	72.50	
2002	31	91	16	0	0	0	4	71.40	$281,421

Best finish for 2002: T-15th at the SEI Pennsylvania Classic

2003	26	67	10	0	0	0	1	71.28	$217,150

Best finish for 2003: T-11th at the HP Classic of New Orleans

2004	24	80	18	0	1	2	6	70.88	$921,255

Best finish for 2004: 3rd at the Honda Classic

2005	32	94	18	0	0	0	4	71.31	$505,517

Best finish for 2005: T-14th at the Honda Classic

2006	26	65	10	0	1	1	2	71.57	$645,153

Best finish for 2006: 3rd at the Deutsche Bank Championship

2007	18	55	9	1	1	1	1	72.02	$1,022,763

Best finish for 2007: Win at the Buick Open

2008	17	46	6	0	0	0	2	72.28	$227,470

Best finish for 2008: T-20th at the Masters

Period Totals	Starts	Rounds Played	Cuts Made	Wins	Top-5s	Top-10s	Top-25s	Scoring Average	Money
	177	504	87	1	3	4	20	71.47	$3,820,729

Ben Bates

Year	Starts	Rounds Played	Cuts Made	Wins	Top-5s	Top-10s	Top-25s	Scoring Average	Money
1985	1	2	0	0	0	0	0	72.00	
1986	1	4	1	0	0	0	0	73.00	$432

Best finish for 1986: 63rd at the Tallahassee Open

1998	31	100	22	0	0	1	7	70.92	$260,225

Best finish for 1998: T-8th at the Buick Challenge

1999	34	99	16	0	0	1	1	71.93	$176,919

Best finish for 1999: T-10th at the Greater Milwaukee Open

2000	35	104	18	0	0	1	2	71.50	$248,087

Best finish for 2000: T-9th at the Westin Texas Open at LaCantera

2001	18	53	8	0	0	0	3	71.53	$198,191

Best finish for 2001: T-12th at the FedEx St. Jude Classic

Period Totals	Starts	Rounds Played	Cuts Made	Wins	Top-5s	Top-10s	Top-25s	Scoring Average	Money
	120	362	65	0	0	3	13	71.48	$883,854

Pat Bates

Year	Starts	Rounds Played	Cuts Made	Wins	Top-5s	Top-10s	Top-25s	Scoring Average	Money
1993	3	6	0	0	0	0	0	77.00	
1994	1	2	0	0	0	0	0	73.00	
1995	31	81	9	0	0	0	2	72.43	$48,048

Best finish for 1995: T-18th at the Canon Greater Hartford Open

1996	1	4	1	0	0	0	0	70.25	$5,714

Best finish for 1996: T-32nd at the CVS Charity Classic

1997	1	4	1	0	0	0	0	74.75	$3,582

Best finish for 1997: T-71st at the Doral-Ryder Open

2002	29	91	17	0	0	3	5	70.37	$537,284

Best finish for 2002: T-6th at the Buick Open

2003	35	108	19	0	1	1	3	70.77	$496,978

Best finish for 2003: T-5th at the Bank of America Colonial

2004	32	97	16	0	0	1	2	71.37	$299,384

Best finish for 2004: T-10th at the Southern Farm Bureau Classic

Period Totals	Starts	Rounds Played	Cuts Made	Wins	Top-5s	Top-10s	Top-25s	Scoring Average	Money
	133	393	63	0	1	5	12	71.31	$1,390,991

Eric Batten

Year	Starts	Rounds Played	Cuts Made	Wins	Top-5s	Top-10s	Top-25s	Scoring Average	Money
1979	1	4	1	0	0	0	0	76.25	$1,235

Best finish for 1979: T-59th at the U.S. Open

1981	2	5	0	0	0	0	0	76.80	$600
1982	23	71	13	0	0	1	3	72.55	$22,953

Best finish for 1982: T-8th at the Doral-Eastern Open

1983	16	40	4	0	0	0	0	72.98	$2,645

Best finish for 1983: T-39th at the Miller High-Life Quad Cities Open

1984	1	4	1	0	0	0	0	72.00	$780

Best finish for 1984: T-72nd at the Isuzu/Andy Williams San Diego Open

1985	1	3	0	0	0	0	0	76.33	

Period Totals	Starts	Rounds Played	Cuts Made	Wins	Top-5s	Top-10s	Top-25s	Scoring Average	Money
	44	127	19	0	0	1	3	73.04	$28,213

Gary Bauer

Year	Starts	Rounds Played	Cuts Made	Wins	Top-5s	Top-10s	Top-25s	Scoring Average	Money
1964	18	48	5	0	0	0	0	72.79	

Best finish for 1964: T-40th at the Fresno Open

1965	22	70	13	0	0	0	3	73.43	$4,518

Best finish for 1965: T-12th at the Almaden Open

1966	16	35	2	0	0	0	0	75.49	

Best finish for 1966: T-54th at the Pensacola Open Invitational

1980	1	3	0	0	0	0	0	79.00	
1981	1	3	0	0	0	0	0	79.67	

Period Totals	Starts	Rounds Played	Cuts Made	Wins	Top-5s	Top-10s	Top-25s	Scoring Average	Money
	58	159	20	0	0	0	3	73.91	$4,518

Beau Baugh

Year	Starts	Rounds Played	Cuts Made	Wins	Top-5s	Top-10s	Top-25s	Scoring Average	Money
1974	1	2	0	0	0	0	0	77.50	
1975	1	4	1	0	0	0	0	74.75	$905

Best finish for 1975: T-49th at the U.S. Open

1979	11	32	5	0	0	0	1	72.75	$5,444

Best finish for 1979: T-25th at the B.C. Open

1980	23	62	9	0	0	0	1	72.60	$8,366

Best finish for 1980: T-14th at the Tallahassee Open

1981	20	55	9	0	0	1	3	72.27	$21,720

Best finish for 1981: T-9th at the Kemper Open

1982	24	71	12	0	0	0	4	71.79	$22,772

Best finish for 1982: T-11th at the Sammy Davis, Jr. - Greater Hartford Open

1983	12	35	6	0	0	0	0	72.34	$4,180

Best finish for 1983: T-44th at the Buick Open

1988	1	4	1	0	0	0	1	70.00	$7,000

Best finish for 1988: T-17th at the Centel Classic

1989	1	3	1	0	0	0	0	71.33	$1,522

Best finish for 1989: T-67th at the Centel Classic

Period Totals	Starts	Rounds Played	Cuts Made	Wins	Top-5s	Top-10s	Top-25s	Scoring Average	Money
	94	268	44	0	0	1	10	72.32	$71,909

Rex Baxter

Year	Starts	Rounds Played	Cuts Made	Wins	Top-5s	Top-10s	Top-25s	Scoring Average	Money
1958	4	14	3	0	0	0	0	75.21	

Best finish for 1958: T-43rd at the Colonial Invitational

1959	1	4	1	0	0	0	0	76.25	$240

Best finish for 1959: T-51st at the U.S. Open

1960	3	12	2	0	0	1	1	72.50	$1,604

Best finish for 1960: T-6th at the Texas Open Invitational

1961	11	44	10	0	1	2	8	70.91	$6,694

Best finish for 1961: T-2nd at the Waco Turner Open Invitational

1962	22	88	20	0	1	4	15	71.36	$12,720

Best finish for 1962: T-5th at the Coral Gables Open Invitational

1963	22	88	21	1	2	5	12	71.55	$18,869

Best finish for 1963: Win at the Cajun Classic Open Invitational

1964	38	130	24	0	4	4	10	71.99	$19,725

Best finish for 1964: 2nd at the Tucson Open

1965	35	120	24	0	1	3	7	72.84	$14,475

Best finish for 1965: T-3rd at the Cajun Classic

1966	31	111	23	0	0	1	7	72.48	$14,954

Best finish for 1966: 9th at the Sahara Invitational

Year	Starts	Rounds Played	Cuts Made	Wins	Top-5s	Top-10s	Top-25s	Scoring Average	Money
1967	28	104	24	0	0	3	13	71.68	$27,884

Best finish for 1967: T-6th at the Texas Open

| 1968 | 28 | 75 | 10 | 0 | 0 | 1 | 1 | 73.68 | $4,058 |

Best finish for 1968: T-10th at the Jacksonville Open Invitational

| 1969 | 6 | 17 | 2 | 0 | 0 | 0 | 1 | 75.18 | $348 |

Best finish for 1969: T-24th at the West End Classic

| 1970 | 2 | 5 | 1 | 0 | 0 | 0 | 0 | 74.00 | $250 |

Best finish for 1970: T-67th at the Cleveland Open

| 1971 | 5 | 14 | 2 | 0 | 0 | 0 | 0 | 74.71 | $1,007 |

Best finish for 1971: T-59th at the Cleveland Open

| 1972 | 2 | 8 | 2 | 0 | 0 | 0 | 1 | 73.25 | $2,227 |

Best finish for 1972: T-24th at the Westchester Classic

1973	2	4	0	0	0	0	0	75.75	
1974	1	2	0	0	0	0	0	76.50	
1976	1	2	0	0	0	0	0	75.00	$250
1980	1	2	0	0	0	0	0	80.50	$500
Period Totals	Starts	Rounds Played	Cuts Made	Wins	Top-5s	Top-10s	Top-25s	Scoring Average	Money
	243	844	169	1	9	24	76	72.39	$125,805

George Bayer

Year	Starts	Rounds Played	Cuts Made	Wins	Top-5s	Top-10s	Top-25s	Scoring Average	Money
1958	35	130	30	2	5	6	18	71.50	$20,093

Best finish for 1958: Win at the Havana Invitational & Mayfair Inn Open

| 1959 | 25 | 98 | 23 | 0 | 3 | 4 | 16 | 71.46 | $11,537 |

Best finish for 1959: T-2nd at the Lafayette Open Invitational

| 1960 | 29 | 117 | 28 | 1 | 1 | 4 | 17 | 71.62 | $13,991 |

Best finish for 1960: Win at the St. Petersburg Open Invitational

| 1961 | 30 | 119 | 29 | 0 | 2 | 5 | 20 | 70.96 | $19,560 |

Best finish for 1961: T-2nd at the Ontario Open

| 1962 | 29 | 113 | 27 | 0 | 4 | 7 | 15 | 71.38 | $25,154 |

Best finish for 1962: T-2nd at the "500" Festival Open Invitational & Portland Open Invitational

| 1963 | 25 | 101 | 22 | 0 | 5 | 7 | 14 | 71.50 | $25,967 |

Best finish for 1963: T-2nd at the Insurance City Open Invitational

| 1964 | 30 | 111 | 24 | 0 | 3 | 4 | 13 | 71.95 | $21,917 |

Best finish for 1964: 4th at the "500" Festival Open & Sunset-Camellia Open

| 1965 | 21 | 71 | 15 | 0 | 0 | 1 | 7 | 72.58 | $8,491 |

Best finish for 1965: T-9th at the Azalea Open

| 1966 | 18 | 64 | 13 | 0 | 0 | 0 | 2 | 73.20 | $5,789 |

Best finish for 1966: T-21st at the Greater Greensboro Open Invitational

| 1967 | 12 | 38 | 6 | 0 | 0 | 0 | 0 | 73.34 | $1,027 |

Best finish for 1967: T-29th at the Greater Greensboro Open

| 1968 | 16 | 54 | 11 | 0 | 0 | 0 | 0 | 73.04 | $1,965 |

Best finish for 1968: T-30th at the Tucson Open Invitational

| 1969 | 7 | 17 | 2 | 0 | 0 | 0 | 1 | 74.35 | $635 |

Best finish for 1969: T-25th at the Kaiser International Open

1970	4	9	0	0	0	0	0	75.89	
1971	3	7	0	0	0	0	0	76.29	
1972	8	19	1	0	0	0	0	75.53	$240

Best finish for 1972: T-71st at the Tucson Open

| 1973 | 6 | 23 | 4 | 0 | 0 | 0 | 0 | 75.39 | $2,009 |

Best finish for 1973: T-45th at the Sahara Invitational

1974	3	4	0	0	0	0	0	77.25	
1975	2	4	0	0	0	0	0	74.25	
1976	2	4	0	0	0	0	0	73.25	
1977	1	2	0	0	0	0	0	79.00	
1978	2	4	0	0	0	0	0	76.00	
1979	1	2	0	0	0	0	0	75.00	
1981	1	4	0	0	0	0	0	77.50	
1983	1	3	0	0	0	0	0	78.33	
Period Totals	Starts	Rounds Played	Cuts Made	Wins	Top-5s	Top-10s	Top-25s	Scoring Average	Money
	311	1118	235	3	23	38	123	72.16	$158,374

PGA Tour career totals from 1953 to 1983

	Starts	Rounds Played	Cuts Made	Wins	Top-5s	Top-10s	Top-25s	Scoring Average	Money
	390	1497	314	4	29	55	162	N/A	$191,801

Andy Bean

Year	Starts	Rounds Played	Cuts Made	Wins	Top-5s	Top-10s	Top-25s	Scoring Average	Money
1973	1	2	0	0	0	0	0	76.50	
1974	1	4	1	0	0	0	0	78.50	

Best finish for 1974: T-63rd at the U.S. Open

Year	Starts	Rounds Played	Cuts Made	Wins	Top-5s	Top-10s	Top-25s	Scoring Average	Money
1976	18	56	10	0	0	0	2	72.89	$9,114

Best finish for 1976: T-17th at the Danny Thomas Memphis Classic

1977	33	109	22	1	4	8	19	71.61	$127,562

Best finish for 1977: Win at the Doral-Eastern Open

1978	33	112	26	3	6	13	18	71.04	$267,887

Best finish for 1978: Win at the Kemper Open, Danny Thomas Memphis Classic & Western Open

1979	30	102	21	1	6	10	16	71.54	$208,253

Best finish for 1979: Win at the Atlanta Classic

1980	29	108	27	1	5	10	22	70.72	$289,203

Best finish for 1980: Win at the Hawaiian Open

1981	15	50	12	1	2	5	7	70.82	$107,254

Best finish for 1981: Win at the Bay Hill Classic

1982	30	109	25	1	5	10	16	70.99	$209,877

Best finish for 1982: Win at the Doral-Eastern Open

1983	28	97	20	0	7	8	15	71.34	$217,296

Best finish for 1983: T-2nd at the Manufactures Hanover Westchester Classic & British Open

1984	31	111	26	1	6	10	19	70.94	$431,771

Best finish for 1984: Win at the Greater Greensboro Open

1985	28	100	24	0	3	8	15	71.34	$195,021

Best finish for 1985: T-3rd at the PGA Championship

1986	28	100	23	2	7	9	20	70.65	$510,688

Best finish for 1986: Win at the Doral-Eastern Open & Byron Nelson Golf Classic

1987	21	59	11	0	1	1	3	72.59	$79,248

Best finish for 1987: T-4th at the Bob Hope Chrysler Classic

1988	20	56	9	0	0	0	3	72.66	$69,311

Best finish for 1988: T-12th at the U.S. Open

1989	26	77	13	0	2	3	4	72.16	$237,897

Best finish for 1989: T-2nd at the PGA Championship & Greater Milwaukee Open

1990	22	67	11	0	0	2	4	72.28	$131,669

Best finish for 1990: 6th at the MCI Heritage Classic

1991	24	73	13	0	1	3	5	71.25	$194,609

Best finish for 1991: T-3rd at the Doral-Ryder Open

1992	18	45	4	0	0	1	1	72.60	$30,798

Best finish for 1992: T-7th at the Chattanooga Classic

1993	21	61	10	0	0	0	1	73.36	$37,292

Best finish for 1993: T-18th at the Northern Telecom Open

1994	19	46	3	0	0	0	0	73.17	$8,810

Best finish for 1994: T-44th at the Bob Hope Chrysler Classic

1995	14	35	3	0	0	0	0	73.06	$7,405

Best finish for 1995: T-47th at the United Airlines Hawaiian Open

1996	28	75	10	0	0	1	1	72.28	$80,849

Best finish for 1996: 8th at the Shell Houston Open

1997	15	41	5	0	0	0	0	72.07	$28,219

Best finish for 1997: T-31st at the LaCantera Texas Open

1998	20	48	6	0	0	0	1	72.79	$48,964

Best finish for 1998: T-17th at the Quad City Classic

1999	12	28	2	0	0	0	1	72.39	$33,200

Best finish for 1999: T-19th at the Doral-Ryder Open

2000	16	39	5	0	0	1	1	72.03	$70,028

Best finish for 2000: T-10th at the B.C. Open

2001	8	20	2	0	0	0	0	73.85	$12,490

Best finish for 2001: T-61st at the B.C. Open

2002	6	12	0	0	0	0	0	72.92	
2003	2	6	1	0	0	0	0	73.33	$8,550

Best finish for 2003: 75th at the FedEx St. Jude Classic

Period Totals	Starts	Rounds Played	Cuts Made	Wins	Top-5s	Top-10s	Top-25s	Scoring Average	Money
	597	1848	345	11	55	103	194	71.77	$3,653,265

Frank Beard

Year	Starts	Rounds Played	Cuts Made	Wins	Top-5s	Top-10s	Top-25s	Scoring Average	Money
1962	1	4	1	0	0	0	1	71.50	$270

Best finish for 1962: T-19th at the Mobile Sertoma Open Invitational

1963	16	64	16	1	3	4	8	71.50	$17,938

Best finish for 1963: Win at the Frank Sinatra Open Invitational

1964	33	120	24	0	1	7	12	71.88	$21,629

Best finish for 1964: T-3rd at the Fresno Open

1965	32	115	24	1	5	8	15	71.74	$44,545

Best finish for 1965: Win at the Texas Open

1966	31	119	28	1	4	7	22	71.39	$67,029

Best finish for 1966: Win at the Greater New Orleans Open Invitational

1967	34	122	28	3	5	11	15	71.43	$107,957

Best finish for 1967: Win at the Tournament of Champions, Houston Championship International & "500" Festival Open

Year	Starts	Rounds Played	Cuts Made	Wins	Top-5s	Top-10s	Top-25s	Scoring Average	Money
1968	31	118	27	0	7	16	20	71.03	$98,222

Best finish for 1968: T-2nd at the "500" Festival Open Invitational & American Golf Classic

1969	32	122	30	2	10	14	21	70.66	$158,032

Best finish for 1969: Win at the Minnesota Classic & Westchester Classic

1970	31	113	25	2	5	10	17	71.01	$122,599

Best finish for 1970: Win at the Tournament of Champions & American Golf Classic

1971	31	113	27	1	6	11	21	71.05	$109,077

Best finish for 1971: Win at the Greater New Orleans Open

1972	34	110	24	0	2	4	7	72.86	$52,195

Best finish for 1972: 2nd at the U.S. Professional Match Play Championship

1973	35	135	32	0	3	7	15	71.64	$68,547

Best finish for 1973: 2nd at the Monsanto Open

1974	34	111	22	0	1	2	11	72.43	$52,998

Best finish for 1974: 2nd at the World Open

1975	35	93	12	0	1	2	4	73.57	$23,683

Best finish for 1975: T-3rd at the U.S. Open

1976	35	93	14	0	1	1	2	74.18	$13,155

Best finish for 1976: T-3rd at the Pensacola Open

1977	31	97	16	0	1	1	2	72.75	$18,341

Best finish for 1977: T-5th at the Greater Milwaukee Open

1978	32	93	16	0	0	0	3	73.16	$14,824

Best finish for 1978: T-16th at the American Express Westchester Classic

1979	26	71	9	0	0	0	3	73.23	$10,285

Best finish for 1979: T-21st at the Joe Garagiola Tucson Open & Pensacola Open

1980	14	36	5	0	0	0	1	72.31	$7,081

Best finish for 1980: T-17th at the San Antonio Texas Open

1981	9	28	5	0	0	0	0	72.32	$2,936

Best finish for 1981: T-47th at the Wickes/Andy Williams San Diego Open

1989	1	4	0	0	0	0	0	73.25	
Period Totals	Starts	Rounds Played	Cuts Made	Wins	Top-5s	Top-10s	Top-25s	Scoring Average	Money
	558	1881	385	11	55	105	200	72.01	$1,011,342

Chip Beck

Year	Starts	Rounds Played	Cuts Made	Wins	Top-5s	Top-10s	Top-25s	Scoring Average	Money
1979	14	38	5	0	0	0	0	73.45	$4,166

Best finish for 1979: T-31st at the Colgate Hall Of Fame Classic

1980	26	76	14	0	0	1	2	73.07	$18,509

Best finish for 1980: T-10th at the Pensacola Open

1981	28	79	14	0	1	2	6	71.99	$53,834

Best finish for 1981: 2nd at the World Disney World National Team Championship

1982	29	89	15	0	1	2	6	72.65	$58,938

Best finish for 1982: 3rd at the Hawaiian Open

1983	32	117	25	0	3	5	12	71.56	$149,909

Best finish for 1983: T-2nd at the Georgia-Pacific Atlanta Golf Classic & Danny Thomas Memphis Classic

1984	31	102	20	0	5	7	10	71.60	$178,789

Best finish for 1984: T-3rd at the Isuzu/Andy Williams San Diego Open, Hawaiian Open, Walt Disney Memorial Tournament & World Golf Classic

1985	30	97	18	0	1	1	7	71.74	$77,038

Best finish for 1985: T-4th at the Los Angeles Open

1986	31	100	21	0	2	6	13	71.09	$215,140

Best finish for 1986: T-2nd at the Sea Pines Heritage Classic & U.S. Open

1987	29	92	19	0	5	7	14	70.83	$523,603

Best finish for 1987: T-2nd at the Seiko-Tucson Open & Nabisco Championship of Golf

1988	27	97	24	2	6	11	17	69.94	$924,638

Best finish for 1988: Win at the Los Angeles Open & USF&G Classic

1989	25	82	19	0	6	10	16	70.63	$703,347

Best finish for 1989: T-2nd at the Phoenix Open, The Players Championship & U.S. Open

1990	27	89	20	1	2	7	11	71.84	$572,830

Best finish for 1990: Win at the Buick Open

1991	27	97	23	0	5	7	16	70.16	$597,929

Best finish for 1991: 2nd at the Buick Open

1992	27	93	22	1	5	7	11	70.44	$728,171

Best finish for 1992: Win at the Freeport-McMoRan Classic

1993	28	90	19	0	2	5	13	71.34	$605,500

Best finish for 1993: 2nd at the Masters & Anheuser-Busch Golf Classic

1994	28	88	19	0	1	1	8	71.17	$282,103

Best finish for 1994: 3rd at the Nissan Los Angeles Open

1995	29	93	19	0	0	1	5	71.49	$171,080

Best finish for 1995: 9th at the United Airlines Hawaiian Open

1996	29	92	16	0	1	1	3	71.52	$228,127

Best finish for 1996: 2nd at the Buick Open

1997	32	71	3	0	0	0	0	73.79	$10,653

Best finish for 1997: T-45th at the Honda Classic

1998	29	62	2	0	0	0	0	73.92	$11,866

Best finish for 1998: T-42nd at the Greater Milwaukee Open

Year	Starts	Rounds Played	Cuts Made	Wins	Top-5s	Top-10s	Top-25s	Scoring Average	Money
1999	28	74	9	0	0	0	3	72.14	$137,423

Best finish for 1999: T-12th at the B.C. Open

| 2000 | 21 | 49 | 4 | 0 | 0 | 0 | 1 | 72.10 | $56,637 |

Best finish for 2000: T-21st at the Buick Invitational

2001	4	8	0	0	0	0	0	72.00	
2002	3	6	0	0	0	0	0	73.17	
2003	2	4	0	0	0	0	0	74.25	
2006	1	4	1	0	0	0	0	71.75	$6,180

Best finish for 2006: T-66th at the B.C. Open

Period Totals	Starts	Rounds Played	Cuts Made	Wins	Top-5s	Top-10s	Top-25s	Scoring Average	Money
	617	1889	351	4	46	81	174	71.62	$6,316,410

Cameron Beckman

Year	Starts	Rounds Played	Cuts Made	Wins	Top-5s	Top-10s	Top-25s	Scoring Average	Money
1993	1	2	0	0	0	0	0	72.00	
1997	1	4	1	0	0	0	0	70.75	$5,185

Best finish for 1997: T-38th at the LaCantera Texas Open

| 1998 | 1 | 2 | 0 | 0 | 0 | 0 | 0 | 74.00 | |
| 1999 | 28 | 81 | 12 | 0 | 0 | 0 | 3 | 72.00 | $147,036 |

Best finish for 1999: T-13th at the Buick Challenge

| 2000 | 26 | 81 | 14 | 0 | 0 | 0 | 6 | 71.09 | $292,514 |

Best finish for 2000: T-14th at the Westin Texas Open at LaCantera & Buick Challenge

| 2001 | 29 | 99 | 22 | 1 | 1 | 4 | 7 | 70.02 | $1,071,343 |

Best finish for 2001: Win at the Southern Farm Bureau Classic

| 2002 | 26 | 85 | 18 | 0 | 1 | 3 | 9 | 70.31 | $907,740 |

Best finish for 2002: T-3rd at the Bob Hope Chrysler Classic

| 2003 | 26 | 83 | 18 | 0 | 1 | 1 | 6 | 70.57 | $608,981 |

Best finish for 2003: T-5th at the 84 Lumber Classic of Pennsylvania

| 2004 | 30 | 96 | 20 | 0 | 1 | 2 | 4 | 70.56 | $783,402 |

Best finish for 2004: T-4th at the FUNAI Classic at the Walt Disney World Resort

| 2005 | 31 | 92 | 16 | 0 | 1 | 1 | 4 | 71.26 | $474,107 |

Best finish for 2005: T-5th at the 84 Lumber Classic

| 2006 | 16 | 48 | 8 | 0 | 0 | 1 | 4 | 70.71 | $288,427 |

Best finish for 2006: T-9th at the Chrysler Classic of Tucson

| 2007 | 29 | 96 | 19 | 0 | 2 | 3 | 7 | 70.78 | $902,259 |

Best finish for 2007: T-3rd at the Frys.Com Open-Vegas

| 2008 | 29 | 87 | 16 | 1 | 1 | 2 | 4 | 71.09 | $1,312,837 |

Best finish for 2008: Win at the Frys.Com Open

Period Totals	Starts	Rounds Played	Cuts Made	Wins	Top-5s	Top-10s	Top-25s	Scoring Average	Money
	273	856	164	2	8	17	54	70.83	$6,793,832

Rich Beem

Year	Starts	Rounds Played	Cuts Made	Wins	Top-5s	Top-10s	Top-25s	Scoring Average	Money
1999	24	66	9	1	2	2	3	72.33	$611,805

Best finish for 1999: Win at the Kemper Open

| 2000 | 29 | 81 | 12 | 0 | 0 | 0 | 2 | 71.96 | $249,881 |

Best finish for 2000: T-12th at the Bob Hope Chrysler Classic

| 2001 | 31 | 89 | 15 | 0 | 0 | 2 | 5 | 71.09 | $461,565 |

Best finish for 2001: T-7th at the Michelob Championship at Kingsmill

| 2002 | 30 | 95 | 19 | 2 | 4 | 5 | 8 | 70.56 | $2,938,365 |

Best finish for 2002: Win at The International presented by Qwest & PGA Championship

| 2003 | 26 | 77 | 14 | 0 | 1 | 2 | 5 | 71.75 | $1,016,950 |

Best finish for 2003: 2nd at the 100th Western Open

| 2004 | 28 | 77 | 14 | 0 | 0 | 0 | 0 | 71.99 | $238,499 |

Best finish for 2004: T-33rd at the WGC-Accenture Match Play Championship & FedEx St. Jude Classic

| 2005 | 26 | 62 | 8 | 0 | 2 | 2 | 4 | 72.32 | $713,747 |

Best finish for 2005: T-2nd at the BellSouth Classic

| 2006 | 27 | 83 | 15 | 0 | 0 | 1 | 5 | 71.54 | $665,802 |

Best finish for 2006: T-7th at the Ford Championship at Doral

| 2007 | 29 | 89 | 17 | 0 | 0 | 2 | 7 | 71.57 | $873,159 |

Best finish for 2007: T-7th at the Barclays Classic

| 2008 | 29 | 90 | 17 | 0 | 1 | 1 | 5 | 71.39 | $730,001 |

Best finish for 2008: 3rd at the Wyndham Championship

Period Totals	Starts	Rounds Played	Cuts Made	Wins	Top-5s	Top-10s	Top-25s	Scoring Average	Money
	279	809	140	3	10	17	44	71.59	$8,499,774

Notah Begay III

Year	Starts	Rounds Played	Cuts Made	Wins	Top-5s	Top-10s	Top-25s	Scoring Average	Money
1996	1	2	0	0	0	0	0	72.00	
1999	29	97	22	2	2	2	5	71.05	$1,256,314

Best finish for 1999: Win at the Reno-Tahoe Open & Michelob Championship at Kingsmill

2000	24	78	17	2	3	4	10	71.29	$1,819,323

Best finish for 2000: Win at the FedEx St. Jude Classic & Canon Greater Hartford Open

2001	12	32	4	0	0	0	0	73.44	$108,538

Best finish for 2001: T-31st at the WGC-NEC Invitational

| 2002 | 26 | 74 | 11 | 0 | 1 | 3 | 5 | 71.08 | $624,026 |

Best finish for 2002: 3rd at the FedEx St. Jude Classic

| 2003 | 30 | 90 | 15 | 0 | 1 | 2 | 6 | 71.38 | $565,572 |

Best finish for 2003: T-5th at the Honda Classic

| 2004 | 23 | 67 | 12 | 0 | 2 | 2 | 4 | 71.07 | $583,537 |

Best finish for 2004: T-3rd at the B.C. Open

| 2005 | 11 | 30 | 4 | 0 | 0 | 0 | 0 | 72.63 | $34,545 |

Best finish for 2005: T-56th at the Bell Canadian Open

| 2006 | 12 | 31 | 3 | 0 | 0 | 1 | 1 | 71.74 | $116,034 |

Best finish for 2006: T-9th at the Buick Championship

| 2007 | 7 | 18 | 2 | 0 | 0 | 0 | 0 | 73.11 | $19,245 |

Best finish for 2007: T-54th at the AT&T National

| 2008 | 9 | 24 | 3 | 0 | 0 | 0 | 0 | 72.38 | $27,872 |

Best finish for 2008: T-53rd at the Reno-Tahoe Open

Period Totals	Starts	Rounds Played	Cuts Made	Wins	Top-5s	Top-10s	Top-25s	Scoring Average	Money
	184	543	93	4	9	14	31	71.55	$5,155,004

Russell Beiersdorf

Year	Starts	Rounds Played	Cuts Made	Wins	Top-5s	Top-10s	Top-25s	Scoring Average	Money
1991	1	2	0	0	0	0	0	76.50	
1993	30	100	20	0	0	0	4	71.54	$111,750

Best finish for 1993: T-13th at the BellSouth Classic

| 1994 | 14 | 40 | 8 | 0 | 1 | 1 | 2 | 71.50 | $59,443 |

Best finish for 1994: T-5th at the B.C. Open

Period Totals	Starts	Rounds Played	Cuts Made	Wins	Top-5s	Top-10s	Top-25s	Scoring Average	Money
	45	142	28	0	1	1	6	71.60	$171,193

Brad Bell

Year	Starts	Rounds Played	Cuts Made	Wins	Top-5s	Top-10s	Top-25s	Scoring Average	Money
1988	1	2	0	0	0	0	0	77.50	$1,000
1991	24	57	4	0	0	0	1	72.70	$16,851

Best finish for 1991: T-23rd at the Greater Milwaukee Open

| 1992 | 21 | 54 | 6 | 0 | 0 | 0 | 1 | 72.63 | $21,414 |

Best finish for 1992: T-14th at the Buick Southern Open

1993	1	3	0	0	0	0	0	76.00	
1995	1	2	0	0	0	0	0	82.00	$1,000
1999	1	3	0	0	0	0	0	81.33	
2002	1	2	0	0	0	0	0	74.00	
Period Totals	Starts	Rounds Played	Cuts Made	Wins	Top-5s	Top-10s	Top-25s	Scoring Average	Money
	50	123	10	0	0	0	2	73.21	$40,264

George Bellino

Year	Starts	Rounds Played	Cuts Made	Wins	Top-5s	Top-10s	Top-25s	Scoring Average	Money
1959	1	2	0	0	0	0	0	78.50	
1960	1	4	1	0	0	0	0	75.00	$088

Best finish for 1960: T-118 at the Palm Springs Desert Golf Classic

| 1965 | 1 | 4 | 1 | 0 | 0 | 0 | 0 | 77.50 | |

Best finish for 1965: T-67th at the American Classic

1966	2	4	0	0	0	0	0	76.75	
1967	3	6	0	0	0	0	0	76.00	
1969	3	8	1	0	0	0	0	75.88	$191

Best finish for 1969: T-72nd at the Cleveland Open

| 1970 | 4 | 9 | 0 | 0 | 0 | 0 | 0 | 75.56 | $103 |
| 1971 | 3 | 8 | 1 | 0 | 0 | 0 | 0 | 74.50 | $446 |

Best finish for 1971: T-42nd at the Cleveland Open

| 1972 | 2 | 4 | 0 | 0 | 0 | 0 | 0 | 77.50 | |
| 1973 | 3 | 8 | 1 | 0 | 0 | 0 | 0 | 73.75 | $892 |

Best finish for 1973: 51st at the American Golf Classic

1974	1	2	0	0	0	0	0	75.00	
1976	2	4	0	0	0	0	0	76.50	$250
1977	1	2	0	0	0	0	0	80.00	$250
1978	1	2	0	0	0	0	0	76.00	$303
Period Totals	Starts	Rounds Played	Cuts Made	Wins	Top-5s	Top-10s	Top-25s	Scoring Average	Money
	28	67	5	0	0	0	0	75.84	$2,523

Deane Beman

Year	Starts	Rounds Played	Cuts Made	Wins	Top-5s	Top-10s	Top-25s	Scoring Average	Money
1958	2	6	1	0	0	0	0	74.50	

Best finish for 1958: T-27th at the Eastern Open

Year	Starts	Rounds Played	Cuts Made	Wins	Top-5s	Top-10s	Top-25s	Scoring Average	Money
1959	2	4	0	0	0	0	0	76.75	
1960	2	6	1	0	0	0	0	74.33	

Best finish for 1960: T-29th at the Masters

| 1961 | 4 | 14 | 3 | 0 | 0 | 0 | 1 | 72.71 | |

Best finish for 1961: T-12th at the U.S. Open

| 1962 | 2 | 6 | 1 | 0 | 0 | 0 | 1 | 74.67 | |

Best finish for 1962: T-14th at the U.S. Open

| 1963 | 1 | 2 | 0 | 0 | 0 | 0 | 0 | 79.00 | |
| 1964 | 4 | 12 | 2 | 0 | 0 | 0 | 1 | 74.25 | |

Best finish for 1964: T-25th at the Masters

| 1965 | 3 | 12 | 3 | 0 | 0 | 1 | 2 | 72.58 | |

Best finish for 1965: T-10th at the Memphis Open

| 1966 | 2 | 6 | 1 | 0 | 0 | 0 | 0 | 75.67 | |

Best finish for 1966: T-30th at the U.S. Open

| 1967 | 12 | 44 | 10 | 0 | 1 | 4 | 6 | 71.75 | $15,142 |

Best finish for 1967: T-3rd at the Hawaiian Open

| 1968 | 33 | 99 | 18 | 0 | 2 | 4 | 10 | 71.95 | $31,889 |

Best finish for 1968: 2nd at the Bob Hope Desert Classic

| 1969 | 29 | 98 | 21 | 1 | 4 | 10 | 15 | 71.19 | $77,895 |

Best finish for 1969: Win at the Texas Open

| 1970 | 28 | 95 | 20 | 1 | 1 | 5 | 10 | 71.81 | $49,326 |

Best finish for 1970: Win at the Greater Milwaukee Open

| 1971 | 35 | 123 | 29 | 0 | 3 | 6 | 13 | 71.61 | $72,282 |

Best finish for 1971: 2nd at the Southern Open & Walt Disney World Open

| 1972 | 31 | 103 | 23 | 1 | 4 | 7 | 14 | 71.67 | $83,134 |

Best finish for 1972: Win at the Quad Cities Open

| 1973 | 25 | 85 | 17 | 1 | 1 | 3 | 8 | 72.28 | $45,888 |

Best finish for 1973: Win at the Shrine-Robinson Golf Classic

1986	1	2	0	0	0	0	0	76.50	$600
1996	1	4	0	0	0	0	0	73.75	
1997	1	1	0	0	0	0	0	89.00	
Period Totals	Starts	Rounds Played	Cuts Made	Wins	Top-5s	Top-10s	Top-25s	Scoring Average	Money
	218	722	150	4	16	40	81	72.01	$376,156

Maurice Bembridge

Year	Starts	Rounds Played	Cuts Made	Wins	Top-5s	Top-10s	Top-25s	Scoring Average	Money
1966	1	2	0	0	0	0	0	78.00	
1967	1	2	0	0	0	0	0	76.00	
1968	1	4	1	0	1	1	1	73.25	$2,400

Best finish for 1968: 5th at the British Open

| 1969 | 1 | 3 | 0 | 0 | 0 | 0 | 0 | 74.67 | |
| 1970 | 5 | 18 | 4 | 0 | 0 | 0 | 2 | 72.61 | $6,288 |

Best finish for 1970: T-13th at the British Open

| 1971 | 1 | 4 | 1 | 0 | 0 | 0 | 0 | 75.25 | $226 |

Best finish for 1971: T-60th at the British Open

| 1972 | 4 | 13 | 2 | 0 | 0 | 0 | 1 | 73.31 | $1,938 |

Best finish for 1972: T-19th at the British Open

| 1973 | 1 | 2 | 0 | 0 | 0 | 0 | 0 | 76.50 | $130 |
| 1974 | 3 | 10 | 2 | 0 | 0 | 1 | 1 | 73.40 | $4,254 |

Best finish for 1974: T-9th at the Masters

| 1975 | 6 | 22 | 5 | 0 | 0 | 1 | 3 | 72.32 | $13,967 |

Best finish for 1975: 8th at the Greater Greensboro Open

| 1976 | 3 | 6 | 0 | 0 | 0 | 0 | 0 | 80.33 | $1,530 |
| 1977 | 1 | 4 | 1 | 0 | 0 | 0 | 0 | 74.25 | $425 |

Best finish for 1977: T-56th at the British Open

1979	1	2	0	0	0	0	0	79.00	$420
1980	1	3	0	0	0	0	0	73.33	$840
1981	1	3	0	0	0	0	0	76.33	$700
1982	1	2	0	0	0	0	0	77.50	$382
1984	1	2	0	0	0	0	0	76.00	$429
1985	1	2	0	0	0	0	0	80.50	$544
1986	1	2	0	0	0	0	0	77.00	$600
Period Totals	Starts	Rounds Played	Cuts Made	Wins	Top-5s	Top-10s	Top-25s	Scoring Average	Money
	35	106	16	0	1	3	8	74.26	$35,072

Mike Bender

Year	Starts	Rounds Played	Cuts Made	Wins	Top-5s	Top-10s	Top-25s	Scoring Average	Money
1981	2	6	1	0	0	0	0	73.83	$404

Best finish for 1981: T-67th at the Quad Cities Open

| 1983 | 1 | 2 | 0 | 0 | 0 | 0 | 0 | 71.00 | |
| 1987 | 31 | 81 | 11 | 0 | 0 | 0 | 1 | 72.54 | $26,464 |

Best finish for 1987: T-11th at the B.C. Open

Year	Starts	Rounds Played	Cuts Made	Wins	Top-5s	Top-10s	Top-25s	Scoring Average	Money
1988	28	82	12	0	0	0	2	71.68	$35,998

Best finish for 1988: T-12th at the Deposit Guaranty Golf Classic

| 1989 | 5 | 13 | 2 | 0 | 0 | 0 | 0 | 72.38 | $1,745 |

Best finish for 1989: T-41st at the Deposit Guaranty Golf Classic

Period Totals	Starts	Rounds Played	Cuts Made	Wins	Top-5s	Top-10s	Top-25s	Scoring Average	Money
	67	184	26	0	0	0	3	72.17	$64,611

Jim Benepe

Year	Starts	Rounds Played	Cuts Made	Wins	Top-5s	Top-10s	Top-25s	Scoring Average	Money
1988	13	37	6	1	1	1	1	71.78	$184,875

Best finish for 1988: Win at the Beatrice Western Open

| 1989 | 30 | 75 | 8 | 0 | 0 | 0 | 3 | 73.12 | $39,589 |

Best finish for 1989: T-12th at the Southern Open

| 1990 | 29 | 85 | 14 | 0 | 1 | 1 | 6 | 71.47 | $105,086 |

Best finish for 1990: T-3rd at the B.C. Open

| 1991 | 30 | 75 | 8 | 0 | 0 | 1 | 2 | 72.09 | $64,583 |

Best finish for 1991: 7th at the Canadian Open

1992	4	8	0	0	0	0	0	74.75	
1993	2	4	0	0	0	0	0	75.50	
1996	1	2	0	0	0	0	0	76.50	
1997	1	2	0	0	0	0	0	80.00	
1998	2	4	0	0	0	0	0	72.75	
1999	1	2	0	0	0	0	0	75.00	
2000	1	2	0	0	0	0	0	75.00	
2001	1	2	0	0	0	0	0	72.00	
2002	4	7	0	0	0	0	0	73.43	
2003	1	2	0	0	0	0	0	71.00	
2004	2	8	2	0	0	0	0	70.13	$13,900

Best finish for 2004: T-52nd at the Valero Texas Open

| 2005 | 2 | 4 | 0 | 0 | 0 | 0 | 0 | 74.75 | $2,000 |

Period Totals	Starts	Rounds Played	Cuts Made	Wins	Top-5s	Top-10s	Top-25s	Scoring Average	Money
	124	319	38	1	2	3	12	72.37	$410,034

Aaron Bengoechea

Year	Starts	Rounds Played	Cuts Made	Wins	Top-5s	Top-10s	Top-25s	Scoring Average	Money
1991	1	3	0	0	0	0	0	72.67	
2000	29	73	8	0	0	0	0	72.77	$60,429

Best finish for 2000: T-36th at the Michelob Championship at Kingsmill

| 2001 | 1 | 2 | 0 | 0 | 0 | 0 | 0 | 72.50 | |

Period Totals	Starts	Rounds Played	Cuts Made	Wins	Top-5s	Top-10s	Top-25s	Scoring Average	Money
	31	78	8	0	0	0	0	72.76	$60,429

David Berganio, Jr.

Year	Starts	Rounds Played	Cuts Made	Wins	Top-5s	Top-10s	Top-25s	Scoring Average	Money
1991	1	2	0	0	0	0	0	76.50	
1992	2	4	0	0	0	0	0	74.00	
1993	4	12	2	0	0	0	0	71.50	$2,486

Best finish for 1993: T-48th at the Hardee's Golf Classic

| 1994 | 4 | 9 | 1 | 0 | 0 | 0 | 0 | 73.44 | $5,105 |

Best finish for 1994: T-47th at the U.S. Open

| 1996 | 4 | 12 | 2 | 0 | 0 | 0 | 1 | 72.50 | $36,590 |

Best finish for 1996: T-16th at the U.S. Open

| 1997 | 30 | 84 | 14 | 0 | 0 | 1 | 3 | 71.36 | $123,289 |

Best finish for 1997: T-9th at the Buick Challenge

| 1998 | 3 | 7 | 1 | 0 | 0 | 0 | 0 | 71.71 | $6,487 |

Best finish for 1998: T-39th at the Buick Open

| 1999 | 5 | 18 | 4 | 0 | 0 | 0 | 0 | 72.11 | $48,015 |

Best finish for 1999: T-28th at the U.S. Open

| 2000 | 4 | 14 | 3 | 0 | 0 | 0 | 0 | 72.00 | $35,625 |

Best finish for 2000: T-29th at the Buick Classic

| 2001 | 25 | 73 | 16 | 0 | 2 | 4 | 6 | 70.52 | $686,082 |

Best finish for 2001: T-3rd at the Canon Greater Hartford Open

| 2002 | 30 | 79 | 13 | 0 | 1 | 1 | 2 | 70.85 | $573,151 |

Best finish for 2002: 2nd at the Bob Hope Chrysler Classic

| 2003 | 15 | 43 | 6 | 0 | 0 | 0 | 1 | 71.88 | $124,065 |

Best finish for 2003: T-19th at the EDS Byron Nelson Championship

2004	2	4	0	0	0	0	0	72.25	
2005	1	2	0	0	0	0	0	70.50	
2006	2	6	1	0	0	0	0	73.17	$8,060

Best finish for 2006: 69th at the Chrysler Classic of Tucson

| 2007 | 3 | 8 | 1 | 0 | 0 | 0 | 0 | 74.63 | $11,025 |

Best finish for 2007: T-82nd at the Wachovia Championship

Year	Starts	Rounds Played	Cuts Made	Wins	Top-5s	Top-10s	Top-25s	Scoring Average	Money
2008	1	2	0	0	0	0	0	72.50	
Period Totals	Starts	Rounds Played	Cuts Made	Wins	Top-5s	Top-10s	Top-25s	Scoring Average	Money
	136	379	64	0	3	6	13	71.47	$1,659,982

Bill Bergin

Year	Starts	Rounds Played	Cuts Made	Wins	Top-5s	Top-10s	Top-25s	Scoring Average	Money
1980	1	2	0	0	0	0	0	78.50	
1982	6	18	3	0	0	0	0	73.06	$3,082

Best finish for 1982: T-31st at the Texas Open

| 1983 | 1 | 3 | 1 | 0 | 0 | 0 | 0 | 73.33 | $957 |

Best finish for 1983: T-50th at the Georgia-Pacific Atlanta Golf Classic

| 1984 | 2 | 8 | 2 | 0 | 0 | 0 | 1 | 71.25 | $10,057 |

Best finish for 1984: T-14th at the British Open

| 1985 | 23 | 62 | 6 | 0 | 0 | 0 | 1 | 73.56 | $7,237 |

Best finish for 1985: T-25th at the Greater Milwaukee Open

| 1986 | 5 | 16 | 3 | 0 | 1 | 1 | 2 | 70.44 | $23,601 |

Best finish for 1986: T-4th at the Provident Classic

| 1987 | 7 | 16 | 1 | 0 | 0 | 0 | 0 | 73.94 | $1,384 |

Best finish for 1987: T-70th at the Southwest Golf Classic

| 1988 | 2 | 6 | 1 | 0 | 0 | 1 | 1 | 69.83 | $13,612 |

Best finish for 1988: T-6th at the Provident Classic

1989	2	4	0	0	0	0	0	75.50	
1994	1	2	0	0	0	0	0	81.50	
Period Totals	Starts	Rounds Played	Cuts Made	Wins	Top-5s	Top-10s	Top-25s	Scoring Average	Money
	50	137	17	0	1	2	5	73.12	$59,931

George Bernardin

Year	Starts	Rounds Played	Cuts Made	Wins	Top-5s	Top-10s	Top-25s	Scoring Average	Money
1958	17	53	9	0	0	0	2	72.36	$680

Best finish for 1958: T-21st at the Rubber City Open & Utah Open

| 1959 | 7 | 28 | 6 | 0 | 0 | 0 | 2 | 73.00 | $900 |

Best finish for 1959: T-12th at the Puerto Rico Open Invitational

| 1960 | 2 | 6 | 1 | 0 | 0 | 0 | 0 | 73.83 | $058 |

Best finish for 1960: T-32nd at the Coral Gables Open Invitational

Period Totals	Starts	Rounds Played	Cuts Made	Wins	Top-5s	Top-10s	Top-25s	Scoring Average	Money
	26	87	16	0	0	0	4	72.67	$1,638

Roberto Bernardini

Year	Starts	Rounds Played	Cuts Made	Wins	Top-5s	Top-10s	Top-25s	Scoring Average	Money
1966	1	4	1	0	0	0	0	75.00	$245

Best finish for 1966: T-38th at the British Open

| 1967 | 2 | 8 | 2 | 0 | 0 | 0 | 0 | 73.63 | $1,205 |

Best finish for 1967: T-30th at the Carling World Open

| 1968 | 1 | 3 | 0 | 0 | 0 | 0 | 0 | 78.33 | |
| 1969 | 4 | 16 | 3 | 0 | 0 | 0 | 1 | 74.25 | $2,466 |

Best finish for 1969: T-16th at the Alameda County Open

| 1970 | 7 | 21 | 3 | 0 | 0 | 0 | 1 | 74.05 | $2,498 |

Best finish for 1970: T-17th at the British Open

| 1971 | 12 | 31 | 2 | 0 | 0 | 0 | 1 | 74.19 | $1,590 |

Best finish for 1971: T-24th at the Bob Hope Chrysler Classic

| 1972 | 1 | 4 | 1 | 0 | 0 | 0 | 1 | 72.00 | $2,875 |

Best finish for 1972: T-13th at the British Open

| 1973 | 4 | 13 | 1 | 0 | 0 | 0 | 0 | 74.77 | $455 |

Best finish for 1973: T-67th at the Hawaiian Open

1974	1	2	0	0	0	0	0	73.50	
1975	1	3	0	0	0	0	0	76.33	$330
1977	1	2	0	0	0	0	0	77.50	$255
1980	1	2	0	0	0	0	0	76.00	$540
Period Totals	Starts	Rounds Played	Cuts Made	Wins	Top-5s	Top-10s	Top-25s	Scoring Average	Money
	36	109	13	0	0	0	4	74.40	$12,459

Shane Bertsch

Year	Starts	Rounds Played	Cuts Made	Wins	Top-5s	Top-10s	Top-25s	Scoring Average	Money
1993	1	3	1	0	0	0	0	71.33	$2,548

Best finish for 1993: T-72nd at the Shell Houston Open

| 1996 | 28 | 73 | 8 | 0 | 1 | 1 | 1 | 72.62 | $65,517 |

Best finish for 1996: T-5th at the Greater Vancouver Open

| 1997 | 30 | 83 | 11 | 0 | 0 | 0 | 2 | 72.28 | $73,450 |

Best finish for 1997: T-19th at the United Airlines Hawaiian Open

| 1998 | 2 | 2 | 0 | 0 | 0 | 0 | 0 | 77.00 | $1,000 |
| 2002 | 1 | 3 | 0 | 0 | 0 | 0 | 0 | 73.67 | |

Year	Starts	Rounds Played	Cuts Made	Wins	Top-5s	Top-10s	Top-25s	Scoring Average	Money
2006	34	102	19	0	0	1	6	71.29	$697,059

Best finish for 2006: T-7th at the BellSouth Classic

| 2007 | 4 | 12 | 2 | 0 | 0 | 0 | 0 | 71.08 | $39,760 |

Best finish for 2007: T-39th at the Bob Hope Chrysler Classic

| 2008 | 29 | 97 | 20 | 0 | 0 | 1 | 8 | 69.84 | $841,248 |

Best finish for 2008: T-9th at the Wyndham Championship

Period Totals	Starts	Rounds Played	Cuts Made	Wins	Top-5s	Top-10s	Top-25s	Scoring Average	Money
	129	375	61	0	1	3	17	71.43	$1,720,581

Scott Bess

Year	Starts	Rounds Played	Cuts Made	Wins	Top-5s	Top-10s	Top-25s	Scoring Average	Money
1979	13	32	3	0	0	0	0	74.66	$1,831

Best finish for 1979: T-65th at the PGA Championship

| 1980 | 12 | 30 | 3 | 0 | 0 | 0 | 0 | 73.13 | $1,548 |

Best finish for 1980: T-68th at the Quad Cities Open

| 1984 | 1 | 4 | 1 | 0 | 0 | 0 | 0 | 74.00 | $1,600 |

Best finish for 1984: T-62nd at the PGA Championship

1985	1	2	0	0	0	0	0	75.50	$1,000
1986	1	2	0	0	0	0	0	74.50	$1,000
1988	1	4	1	0	0	0	0	72.50	$2,092

Best finish for 1988: T-52nd at the PGA Championship

Period Totals	Starts	Rounds Played	Cuts Made	Wins	Top-5s	Top-10s	Top-25s	Scoring Average	Money
	29	74	8	0	0	0	0	73.91	$9,071

Al Besselink

Year	Starts	Rounds Played	Cuts Made	Wins	Top-5s	Top-10s	Top-25s	Scoring Average	Money
1958	25	92	20	0	0	2	7	72.74	$4,182

Best finish for 1958: T-8th at the Kentucky Derby Open

| 1959 | 19 | 76 | 18 | 0 | 1 | 3 | 12 | 71.28 | $7,786 |

Best finish for 1959: T-4th at the Sam Snead Festival

| 1960 | 19 | 77 | 16 | 0 | 3 | 6 | 12 | 71.48 | $11,581 |

Best finish for 1960: T-2nd at the Greater New Orleans Open Invitational

| 1961 | 2 | 8 | 2 | 0 | 0 | 0 | 0 | 73.38 | $388 |

Best finish for 1961: T-33rd at the Phoenix Open Invitational

| 1962 | 3 | 8 | 3 | 0 | 0 | 0 | 1 | 74.63 | $365 |

Best finish for 1962: T-20th at the West Palm Beach Open Invitational

| 1964 | 30 | 97 | 16 | 1 | 2 | 2 | 5 | 79.85 | $11,266 |

Best finish for 1964: Win at the Azalea Open

| 1965 | 26 | 89 | 16 | 0 | 1 | 1 | 5 | 72.55 | $11,301 |

Best finish for 1965: T-3rd at the Hawaiian Open

| 1966 | 25 | 79 | 16 | 0 | 1 | 4 | 11 | 72.75 | $18,438 |

Best finish for 1966: T-5th at the Azalea Open Invitational

| 1967 | 15 | 41 | 4 | 0 | 0 | 0 | 1 | 74.71 | $2,060 |

Best finish for 1967: T-11th at the Texas Open

| 1968 | 10 | 28 | 3 | 0 | 0 | 0 | 0 | 74.46 | $285 |

Best finish for 1968: T-45th at the Atlanta Classic

| 1969 | 6 | 18 | 3 | 0 | 1 | 1 | 2 | 73.44 | $3,806 |

Best finish for 1969: T-2nd at the West End Classic

1970	5	8	0	0	0	0	0	74.63	
1972	1	2	0	0	0	0	0	77.00	
1975	1	2	0	0	0	0	0	84.50	
1978	1	2	0	0	0	0	0	77.00	
1983	1	4	0	0	0	0	0	74.75	
Period Totals	Starts	Rounds Played	Cuts Made	Wins	Top-5s	Top-10s	Top-25s	Scoring Average	Money
	189	631	117	1	9	19	56	73.83	$71,459

PGA Tour career totals from 1945 to 1983

	Starts	Rounds Played	Cuts Made	Wins	Top-5s	Top-10s	Top-25s	Scoring Average	Money
	347	1224	275	4	18	49	139	N/A	$122,915

Bob Betley

Year	Starts	Rounds Played	Cuts Made	Wins	Top-5s	Top-10s	Top-25s	Scoring Average	Money
1972	1	2	0	0	0	0	0	74.50	
1978	1	2	0	0	0	0	0	77.50	
1979	9	26	4	0	0	0	0	73.27	$2,598

Best finish for 1979: T-43rd at the San Antonio Texas Open

| 1980 | 11 | 27 | 3 | 0 | 0 | 0 | 0 | 74.48 | $2,339 |

Best finish for 1980: T-36th at the Phoenix Open

| 1983 | 2 | 6 | 0 | 0 | 0 | 0 | 0 | 74.83 | $600 |
| 1984 | 2 | 2 | 0 | 0 | 0 | 0 | 0 | 74.00 | $750 |

Best finish for 1984: T-73rd at the Seiko Tucson-Match Play Championship

| 1985 | 1 | 2 | 0 | 0 | 0 | 0 | 0 | 79.00 | $600 |

Year	Starts	Rounds Played	Cuts Made	Wins	Top-5s	Top-10s	Top-25s	Scoring Average	Money
1986	1	3	0	0	0	0	0	71.33	
1987	1	4	1	0	0	0	0	75.00	$2,400

Best finish for 1987: T-47th at the PGA Championship

Year	Starts	Rounds Played	Cuts Made	Wins	Top-5s	Top-10s	Top-25s	Scoring Average	Money
1989	1	2	0	0	0	0	0	74.00	$1,000
Period Totals	**Starts**	**Rounds Played**	**Cuts Made**	**Wins**	**Top-5s**	**Top-10s**	**Top-25s**	**Scoring Average**	**Money**
	30	76	8	0	0	0	0	74.17	$10,287

Leo Biagetti

Year	Starts	Rounds Played	Cuts Made	Wins	Top-5s	Top-10s	Top-25s	Scoring Average	Money
1958	32	111	24	0	2	2	6	72.59	$5,606

Best finish for 1958: T-2nd at the Lafayette Open

Year	Starts	Rounds Played	Cuts Made	Wins	Top-5s	Top-10s	Top-25s	Scoring Average	Money
1959	1	4	1	0	0	0	0	71.50	$090

Best finish for 1959: T-28th at the Arlington Hotel Open Invitational

Year	Starts	Rounds Played	Cuts Made	Wins	Top-5s	Top-10s	Top-25s	Scoring Average	Money
1960	1	4	1	0	0	0	0	73.75	$088

Best finish for 1960: T-103 at the Palm Springs Desert Golf Classic

Year	Starts	Rounds Played	Cuts Made	Wins	Top-5s	Top-10s	Top-25s	Scoring Average	Money
1961	2	6	2	0	0	0	1	74.67	$525

Best finish for 1961: T-11th at the Mobile Sertoma Open Invitational

Year	Starts	Rounds Played	Cuts Made	Wins	Top-5s	Top-10s	Top-25s	Scoring Average	Money
1962	3	9	2	0	0	0	0	73.44	$090

Best finish for 1962: T-29th at the St Petersburg Open Invitational

Year	Starts	Rounds Played	Cuts Made	Wins	Top-5s	Top-10s	Top-25s	Scoring Average	Money
1964	5	7	0	0	0	0	0	76.57	
1965	2	4	0	0	0	0	0	77.50	
Period Totals	**Starts**	**Rounds Played**	**Cuts Made**	**Wins**	**Top-5s**	**Top-10s**	**Top-25s**	**Scoring Average**	**Money**
	46	145	30	0	2	2	7	73.06	$6,399

Roy Biancalana

Year	Starts	Rounds Played	Cuts Made	Wins	Top-5s	Top-10s	Top-25s	Scoring Average	Money
1981	1	2	0	0	0	0	0	78.00	
1983	1	2	0	0	0	0	0	74.00	
1984	2	6	1	0	0	0	0	74.67	$2,400

Best finish for 1984: T-38th at the Western Open

Year	Starts	Rounds Played	Cuts Made	Wins	Top-5s	Top-10s	Top-25s	Scoring Average	Money
1985	2	6	1	0	0	0	0	74.83	$1,030

Best finish for 1985: T-65th at the Western Open

Year	Starts	Rounds Played	Cuts Made	Wins	Top-5s	Top-10s	Top-25s	Scoring Average	Money
1986	2	4	0	0	0	0	0	75.50	$600
1987	6	15	2	0	0	0	1	72.80	$9,292

Best finish for 1987: T-25th at the Beatrice Western Open

Year	Starts	Rounds Played	Cuts Made	Wins	Top-5s	Top-10s	Top-25s	Scoring Average	Money
1988	27	75	10	0	0	0	3	72.04	$27,570

Best finish for 1988: T-18th at the AT&T Pebble Beach Pro-Am

Year	Starts	Rounds Played	Cuts Made	Wins	Top-5s	Top-10s	Top-25s	Scoring Average	Money
1989	23	63	9	0	0	0	0	72.24	$15,949

Best finish for 1989: T-35th at the Centel Classic

Year	Starts	Rounds Played	Cuts Made	Wins	Top-5s	Top-10s	Top-25s	Scoring Average	Money
1990	1	4	1	0	0	0	0	70.00	$1,386

Best finish for 1990: T-35th at the Deposit Guaranty

Year	Starts	Rounds Played	Cuts Made	Wins	Top-5s	Top-10s	Top-25s	Scoring Average	Money
2003	2	4	0	0	0	0	0	76.25	$1,000
2004	2	6	1	0	0	0	0	75.67	$11,900

Best finish for 2004: 71st at the PGA Championship

Year	Starts	Rounds Played	Cuts Made	Wins	Top-5s	Top-10s	Top-25s	Scoring Average	Money
2006	1	2	0	0	0	0	0	73.50	
Period Totals	**Starts**	**Rounds Played**	**Cuts Made**	**Wins**	**Top-5s**	**Top-10s**	**Top-25s**	**Scoring Average**	**Money**
	70	189	25	0	0	0	4	72.67	$71,127

Don Bies

Year	Starts	Rounds Played	Cuts Made	Wins	Top-5s	Top-10s	Top-25s	Scoring Average	Money
1960	1	2	0	0	0	0	0	75.00	
1961	1	4	1	0	0	0	0	69.75	$115

Best finish for 1961: T-33rd at the Greater Seattle Open Invitational

Year	Starts	Rounds Played	Cuts Made	Wins	Top-5s	Top-10s	Top-25s	Scoring Average	Money
1962	2	8	2	0	0	0	0	70.88	$076

Best finish for 1962: T-34th at the Seattle World's Fair Open Invitational

Year	Starts	Rounds Played	Cuts Made	Wins	Top-5s	Top-10s	Top-25s	Scoring Average	Money
1963	2	8	2	0	0	0	1	72.50	$999

Best finish for 1963: T-18th at the Seattle Open Invitational

Year	Starts	Rounds Played	Cuts Made	Wins	Top-5s	Top-10s	Top-25s	Scoring Average	Money
1964	4	14	3	0	0	0	0	72.79	$526

Best finish for 1964: T-39th at the PGA Championship

Year	Starts	Rounds Played	Cuts Made	Wins	Top-5s	Top-10s	Top-25s	Scoring Average	Money
1965	4	16	4	0	0	1	1	72.94	$2,241

Best finish for 1965: T-9th at the Seattle Open

Year	Starts	Rounds Played	Cuts Made	Wins	Top-5s	Top-10s	Top-25s	Scoring Average	Money
1966	3	12	3	0	1	1	2	70.42	$4,688

Best finish for 1966: T-3rd at the Greater Seattle-Everett Open Invitational

Year	Starts	Rounds Played	Cuts Made	Wins	Top-5s	Top-10s	Top-25s	Scoring Average	Money
1967	6	21	4	0	0	1	1	73.19	$7,591

Best finish for 1967: T-7th at the PGA Championship

Year	Starts	Rounds Played	Cuts Made	Wins	Top-5s	Top-10s	Top-25s	Scoring Average	Money
1968	16	54	11	0	2	2	7	72.19	$28,284

Best finish for 1968: T-4th at the American Golf Classic

Year	Starts	Rounds Played	Cuts Made	Wins	Top-5s	Top-10s	Top-25s	Scoring Average	Money
1969	31	110	24	0	1	4	9	71.87	$31,232

Best finish for 1969: T-4th at the Tucson Open

Year	Starts	Rounds Played	Cuts Made	Wins	Top-5s	Top-10s	Top-25s	Scoring Average	Money
1970	33	116	25	0	0	4	8	72.08	$28,597

Best finish for 1970: T-7th at the Bob Hope Chrysler Classic

Year	Starts	Rounds Played	Cuts Made	Wins	Top-5s	Top-10s	Top-25s	Scoring Average	Money
1971	31	102	20	0	0	0	8	72.59	$18,943

Best finish for 1971: T-11th at the Greater Milwaukee Open

Year	Starts	Rounds Played	Cuts Made	Wins	Top-5s	Top-10s	Top-25s	Scoring Average	Money
1972	30	99	21	0	3	7	10	71.91	$50,545

Best finish for 1972: T-3rd at the U.S. Professional Match Play Championship & Greater St. Louis Classic

| 1973 | 29 | 96 | 18 | 0 | 1 | 2 | 10 | 72.40 | $37,352 |

Best finish for 1973: T-2nd at the Glen Campbell Los Angles Open

| 1974 | 25 | 89 | 20 | 0 | 2 | 4 | 10 | 71.53 | $68,037 |

Best finish for 1974: 2nd at the Westchester Classic

| 1975 | 23 | 83 | 18 | 1 | 1 | 3 | 10 | 71.90 | $69,968 |

Best finish for 1975: Win at the Sammy Davis, Jr. - Greater Hartford Open

| 1976 | 22 | 82 | 19 | 0 | 3 | 4 | 12 | 71.62 | $73,780 |

Best finish for 1976: 2nd at the Andy Williams-San Diego Open & Byron Nelson Golf Classic

| 1977 | 26 | 93 | 20 | 0 | 0 | 2 | 5 | 72.78 | $26,606 |

Best finish for 1977: T-8th at the Joe Garagiola Tucson Open

| 1978 | 22 | 75 | 15 | 0 | 1 | 1 | 5 | 72.48 | $29,174 |

Best finish for 1978: T-4th at the Bing Crosby Pro-Am

| 1979 | 22 | 64 | 10 | 0 | 0 | 0 | 2 | 73.05 | $17,395 |

Best finish for 1979: T-14th at the Bob Hope Chrysler Classic

| 1980 | 13 | 37 | 4 | 0 | 0 | 0 | 2 | 72.81 | $13,114 |

Best finish for 1980: T-14th at the Hawaiian Open

| 1981 | 7 | 21 | 4 | 0 | 0 | 0 | 0 | 72.19 | $2,412 |

Best finish for 1981: T-47th at the Bing Crosby Pro-Am

| 1982 | 6 | 23 | 5 | 0 | 0 | 0 | 0 | 72.04 | $5,956 |

Best finish for 1982: T-30th at the U.S. Open

| 1983 | 3 | 10 | 2 | 0 | 0 | 0 | 0 | 71.00 | $1,488 |

Best finish for 1983: T-47th at the Hawaiian Open

| 1984 | 2 | 6 | 1 | 0 | 0 | 0 | 0 | 72.67 | $792 |

Best finish for 1984: T-70th at the Sammy Davis, Jr. - Greater Hartford Open

1985	2	5	0	0	0	0	0	75.60	
1987	1	2	0	0	0	0	0	74.50	$600
Period Totals	Starts	Rounds Played	Cuts Made	Wins	Top-5s	Top-10s	Top-25s	Scoring Average	Money
	367	1252	256	1	15	36	103	72.21	$520,510

Bill Bisdorf

Year	Starts	Rounds Played	Cuts Made	Wins	Top-5s	Top-10s	Top-25s	Scoring Average	Money
1958	3	8	1	0	1	1	1	71.63	$930

Best finish for 1958: T-5th at the Denver Open

| 1960 | 4 | 16 | 4 | 0 | 0 | 0 | 2 | 71.94 | $1,164 |

Best finish for 1960: T-23rd at the Los Angles Open Invitational & Utah Open Invitational

| 1961 | 4 | 12 | 3 | 0 | 0 | 0 | 0 | 72.75 | $195 |

Best finish for 1961: T-32nd at the Denver Open Invitational

| 1962 | 2 | 4 | 1 | 0 | 0 | 0 | 0 | 76.00 | |

Best finish for 1962: T-200 at the PGA Championship

| 1963 | 2 | 6 | 2 | 0 | 0 | 0 | 0 | 73.83 | $138 |

Best finish for 1963: T-38th at the Utah Open Invitational

| 1964 | 5 | 12 | 2 | 0 | 0 | 0 | 0 | 73.42 | $800 |

Best finish for 1964: T-28th at the PGA Championship

| 1965 | 3 | 8 | 1 | 0 | 0 | 0 | 0 | 74.75 | $478 |

Best finish for 1965: T-36th at the Sahara Invitational

| 1966 | 1 | 4 | 1 | 0 | 0 | 0 | 0 | 74.00 | $659 |

Best finish for 1966: T-37th at the PGA Championship

| 1967 | 4 | 13 | 2 | 0 | 0 | 0 | 1 | 73.00 | $1,600 |

Best finish for 1967: T-20th at the PGA Championship

| 1968 | 9 | 22 | 1 | 0 | 0 | 0 | 0 | 75.09 | $1,125 |

Best finish for 1968: T-30th at the Tucson Open Invitational

| 1969 | 1 | 4 | 1 | 0 | 0 | 0 | 0 | 74.25 | $147 |

Best finish for 1969: T-35th at the West End Classic

| 1971 | 5 | 13 | 2 | 0 | 0 | 0 | 0 | 73.00 | $1,008 |

Best finish for 1971: T-54th at the Phoenix Open

Period Totals	Starts	Rounds Played	Cuts Made	Wins	Top-5s	Top-10s	Top-25s	Scoring Average	Money
	43	122	21	0	1	1	4	73.49	$8,244

Vince Bizik

Year	Starts	Rounds Played	Cuts Made	Wins	Top-5s	Top-10s	Top-25s	Scoring Average	Money
1971	1	2	0	0	0	0	0	73.50	
1972	1	2	0	0	0	0	0	75.50	
1973	10	25	1	0	0	0	0	76.32	

Best finish for 1973: 75th at the Quad Cities Open

| 1977 | 13 | 30 | 2 | 0 | 0 | 0 | 0 | 75.47 | $2,108 |

Best finish for 1977: T-34th at the First NBC New Orleans Open

1982	1	2	0	0	0	0	0	78.50	$650
Period Totals	Starts	Rounds Played	Cuts Made	Wins	Top-5s	Top-10s	Top-25s	Scoring Average	Money
	26	61	3	0	0	0	0	75.85	$2,758

Thomas Bjorn

Year	Starts	Rounds Played	Cuts Made	Wins	Top-5s	Top-10s	Top-25s	Scoring Average	Money
1996	1	2	0	0	0	0	0	74.50	$1,008
1997	4	12	2	0	0	0	0	73.58	$14,458

Best finish for 1997: T-45th at the PGA Championship

| 1998 | 3 | 10 | 2 | 0 | 0 | 1 | 2 | 72.60 | $94,338 |

Best finish for 1998: T-9th at the British Open

| 1999 | 9 | 24 | 5 | 0 | 0 | 0 | 1 | 74.63 | $111,691 |

Best finish for 1999: T-17th at the Andersen Consulting Match Play Championship

| 2000 | 9 | 30 | 8 | 0 | 2 | 4 | 5 | 71.63 | $1,049,648 |

Best finish for 2000: T-2nd at the British Open

| 2001 | 7 | 22 | 4 | 0 | 0 | 0 | 2 | 72.18 | $170,210 |

Best finish for 2001: T-12th at the WorldCom Classic

| 2002 | 9 | 32 | 7 | 0 | 0 | 1 | 5 | 71.53 | $472,004 |

Best finish for 2002: T-8th at the British Open

| 2003 | 6 | 16 | 4 | 0 | 1 | 1 | 1 | 72.25 | $653,733 |

Best finish for 2003: T-2nd at the British Open

| 2004 | 12 | 34 | 7 | 0 | 2 | 2 | 4 | 72.74 | $1,060,548 |

Best finish for 2004: 2nd at the WGC-American Express Championship

| 2005 | 8 | 23 | 5 | 0 | 1 | 1 | 3 | 71.43 | $774,524 |

Best finish for 2005: T-2nd at the PGA Championship

| 2006 | 7 | 26 | 6 | 0 | 0 | 0 | 1 | 72.77 | $236,523 |

Best finish for 2006: T-18th at the WGC-NEC Invitational

| 2007 | 6 | 16 | 4 | 0 | 0 | 0 | 1 | 73.56 | $190,044 |

Best finish for 2007: T-11th at the WGC-CA Championship

Period Totals	Starts	Rounds Played	Cuts Made	Wins	Top-5s	Top-10s	Top-25s	Scoring Average	Money
	81	247	54	0	6	10	25	72.53	$4,828,728

Henrik Bjornstad

Year	Starts	Rounds Played	Cuts Made	Wins	Top-5s	Top-10s	Top-25s	Scoring Average	Money
2006	31	95	17	0	0	1	3	71.51	$491,043

Best finish for 2006: T-10th at the Buick Invitational

| 2008 | 1 | 2 | 0 | 0 | 0 | 0 | 0 | 72.50 | |

Period Totals	Starts	Rounds Played	Cuts Made	Wins	Top-5s	Top-10s	Top-25s	Scoring Average	Money
	32	97	17	0	0	1	3	71.53	$491,043

Doug Black

Year	Starts	Rounds Played	Cuts Made	Wins	Top-5s	Top-10s	Top-25s	Scoring Average	Money
1980	20	52	6	0	0	0	0	73.10	$4,565

Best finish for 1980: T-38th at the Buick Goodwrench Open

| 1981 | 14 | 39 | 7 | 0 | 0 | 1 | 4 | 72.36 | $14,928 |

Best finish for 1981: T-10th at the World Disney World National Team Championship

| 1982 | 19 | 44 | 3 | 0 | 0 | 1 | 2 | 73.48 | $12,840 |

Best finish for 1982: T-7th at the Greater Greensboro Open

| 1983 | 16 | 30 | 1 | 0 | 0 | 0 | 0 | 76.13 | $402 |

Best finish for 1983: T-69th at the Miller High-Life Quad Cities Open

Period Totals	Starts	Rounds Played	Cuts Made	Wins	Top-5s	Top-10s	Top-25s	Scoring Average	Money
	69	165	17	0	0	2	6	73.58	$32,735

Ronnie Black

Year	Starts	Rounds Played	Cuts Made	Wins	Top-5s	Top-10s	Top-25s	Scoring Average	Money
1982	20	54	7	0	0	0	0	72.93	$6,929

Best finish for 1982: T-34th at the Kemper Open

| 1983 | 24 | 82 | 17 | 1 | 1 | 1 | 7 | 71.29 | $87,524 |

Best finish for 1983: Win at the Southern Open

| 1984 | 33 | 111 | 22 | 1 | 2 | 4 | 9 | 71.93 | $173,236 |

Best finish for 1984: Win at the Anheuser-Busch Golf Classic

| 1985 | 30 | 101 | 19 | 0 | 0 | 0 | 4 | 72.03 | $62,684 |

Best finish for 1985: T-12th at the Hertz Bay Hill Classic & Kemper Open

| 1986 | 30 | 95 | 22 | 0 | 1 | 5 | 9 | 71.53 | $167,161 |

Best finish for 1986: T-3rd at the Vantage Championship

| 1987 | 30 | 100 | 22 | 0 | 1 | 3 | 9 | 70.97 | $144,158 |

Best finish for 1987: 3rd at the USF&G Classic

| 1988 | 25 | 86 | 19 | 0 | 1 | 1 | 4 | 71.64 | $100,603 |

Best finish for 1988: T-4th at the Canon Sammy Davis, Jr. - Greater Hartford Open

| 1989 | 28 | 86 | 16 | 0 | 2 | 3 | 6 | 71.62 | $264,988 |

Best finish for 1989: T-2nd at the Manufactures Hanover Westchester Classic & Centel Classic

| 1990 | 30 | 84 | 11 | 0 | 0 | 0 | 0 | 72.05 | $34,001 |

Best finish for 1990: T-26th at the Buick Southern Open

| 1991 | 25 | 76 | 14 | 0 | 1 | 1 | 6 | 70.61 | $135,865 |

Best finish for 1991: T-5th at the USF&G Classic

Year	Starts	Rounds Played	Cuts Made	Wins	Top-5s	Top-10s	Top-25s	Scoring Average	Money
1992	26	89	19	0	0	0	4	70.98	$129,386

Best finish for 1992: T-11th at the Shell Houston Open

| 1993 | 28 | 87 | 17 | 0 | 0 | 0 | 4 | 71.30 | $120,041 |

Best finish for 1993: T-12th at the Greater Milwaukee Open

| 1994 | 27 | 80 | 15 | 0 | 0 | 1 | 4 | 71.35 | $123,404 |

Best finish for 1994: T-8th at the GTE Byron Nelson Classic

| 1995 | 29 | 90 | 15 | 0 | 0 | 1 | 3 | 71.01 | $122,188 |

Best finish for 1995: T-9th at the Nissan Open

| 1996 | 26 | 85 | 20 | 0 | 1 | 3 | 7 | 70.69 | $247,320 |

Best finish for 1996: T-5th at the Las Vegas Invitational

| 1997 | 28 | 85 | 15 | 0 | 2 | 3 | 4 | 71.27 | $231,225 |

Best finish for 1997: T-5th at the Doral-Ryder Open & Honda Classic

| 1998 | 28 | 78 | 12 | 0 | 0 | 0 | 5 | 72.01 | $139,631 |

Best finish for 1998: T-14th at the Kemper Open

| 1999 | 18 | 56 | 11 | 0 | 2 | 3 | 4 | 71.30 | $306,636 |

Best finish for 1999: T-4th at the AT&T Pebble Beach Pro-Am & B.C. Open

| 2000 | 28 | 79 | 13 | 0 | 0 | 0 | 3 | 71.51 | $190,997 |

Best finish for 2000: T-12th at the John Deere Classic

| 2001 | 17 | 51 | 9 | 0 | 1 | 1 | 2 | 71.29 | $272,686 |

Best finish for 2001: 5th at the AT&T Pebble Beach

| 2002 | 12 | 28 | 2 | 0 | 0 | 0 | 0 | 72.75 | $14,219 |

Best finish for 2002: T-64th at the AT&T Pebble Beach

2003	4	8	0	0	0	0	0	73.25	
2007	1	2	0	0	0	0	0	71.50	
2008	2	6	1	0	0	0	0	73.17	$12,295

Best finish for 2008: T-39th at the Puerto Rico Open

Period Totals	Starts	Rounds Played	Cuts Made	Wins	Top-5s	Top-10s	Top-25s	Scoring Average	Money
	549	1699	318	2	15	30	94	71.49	$3,087,176

Mike Blackburn

Year	Starts	Rounds Played	Cuts Made	Wins	Top-5s	Top-10s	Top-25s	Scoring Average	Money
1980	1	0	1	0	0	0	0		$1,050

Best finish for 1980: T-35th at the World Disney World National Team Championship

1981	1	0	0	0	0	0			
1985	1	2	0	0	0	0	0	76.50	$600
1986	2	6	1	0	0	0	0	71.00	$901

Best finish for 1986: T-36th at the Deposit Guaranty Golf Classic

| 1987 | 2 | 4 | 0 | 0 | 0 | 0 | 0 | 74.00 | |
| 1988 | 29 | 83 | 12 | 0 | 0 | 0 | 0 | 72.60 | $20,928 |

Best finish for 1988: T-35th at the Independent Insurance Agent Open

| 1989 | 2 | 4 | 0 | 0 | 0 | 0 | 0 | 72.00 | |
| 1995 | 1 | 2 | 0 | 0 | 0 | 0 | 0 | 74.50 | |

Period Totals	Starts	Rounds Played	Cuts Made	Wins	Top-5s	Top-10s	Top-25s	Scoring Average	Money
	39	101	14	0	0	0	0	72.65	$23,479

Woody Blackburn

Year	Starts	Rounds Played	Cuts Made	Wins	Top-5s	Top-10s	Top-25s	Scoring Average	Money
1974	1	2	0	0	0	0	0	78.50	
1976	10	28	4	0	0	0	0	73.43	$1,638

Best finish for 1976: T-27th at the Ed McMahon Quad City Open

| 1977 | 34 | 87 | 8 | 0 | 0 | 0 | 2 | 74.66 | $9,350 |

Best finish for 1977: T-13th at the San Antonio Texas Open

| 1978 | 20 | 57 | 8 | 0 | 0 | 0 | 2 | 73.33 | $5,172 |

Best finish for 1978: T-14th at the Tallahassee Open

| 1979 | 12 | 32 | 3 | 0 | 0 | 0 | 0 | 74.47 | $1,837 |

Best finish for 1979: T-42nd at the First NBC New Orleans Open

| 1980 | 24 | 64 | 10 | 0 | 0 | 0 | 0 | 73.39 | $10,369 |

Best finish for 1980: T-31st at the B.C. Open

| 1981 | 27 | 82 | 15 | 0 | 1 | 1 | 1 | 72.73 | $24,167 |

Best finish for 1981: T-2nd at the Quad Cities Open

| 1982 | 31 | 102 | 20 | 0 | 1 | 1 | 7 | 72.32 | $54,165 |

Best finish for 1982: 4th at the Greater Greensboro Open

| 1983 | 31 | 84 | 10 | 0 | 0 | 0 | 3 | 73.99 | $18,105 |

Best finish for 1983: T-15th at the Sea Pines Heritage Classic

| 1984 | 18 | 57 | 11 | 0 | 0 | 1 | 4 | 71.72 | $29,074 |

Best finish for 1984: T-8th at the Miller High-Life Quad Cities Open

| 1985 | 29 | 93 | 19 | 1 | 1 | 2 | 5 | 72.38 | $140,401 |

Best finish for 1985: Win at the Isuzu/Andy Williams San Diego Open

| 1986 | 30 | 70 | 6 | 0 | 0 | 0 | 0 | 74.20 | $12,901 |

Best finish for 1986: T-28th at the Shearson Lehman/Andy Williams San Diego

| 1987 | 26 | 55 | 2 | 0 | 0 | 0 | 0 | 75.53 | $3,452 |

Best finish for 1987: T-68th at the Panasonic Las Vegas Invitational

Year	Starts	Rounds Played	Cuts Made	Wins	Top-5s	Top-10s	Top-25s	Scoring Average	Money
1988	10	24	3	0	0	0	0	74.46	$4,323

Best finish for 1988: T-58th at the Shearson Lehman/Andy Williams San Diego

Year	Starts	Rounds Played	Cuts Made	Wins	Top-5s	Top-10s	Top-25s	Scoring Average	Money
1989	7	14	0	0	0	0	0	75.14	
1990	3	6	0	0	0	0	0	73.50	
1991	1	2	0	0	0	0	0	74.50	
1992	3	6	0	0	0	0	0	73.67	
1993	1	2	0	0	0	0	0	84.50	
1994	1	2	0	0	0	0	0	73.50	
1995	1	2	0	0	0	0	0	75.00	
2002	1	2	0	0	0	0	0	76.00	
2003	1	2	0	0	0	0	0	77.50	
Period Totals	Starts	Rounds Played	Cuts Made	Wins	Top-5s	Top-10s	Top-25s	Scoring Average	Money
	322	875	119	1	3	5	24	73.53	$314,953

Phil Blackmar

Year	Starts	Rounds Played	Cuts Made	Wins	Top-5s	Top-10s	Top-25s	Scoring Average	Money
1984	1	4	1	0	0	0	0	73.50	$3,374

Best finish for 1984: T-43rd at the U.S. Open

Year	Starts	Rounds Played	Cuts Made	Wins	Top-5s	Top-10s	Top-25s	Scoring Average	Money
1985	27	84	16	1	2	4	7	72.42	$199,137

Best finish for 1985: Win at the Canon Sammy Davis, Jr. - Greater Hartford Open

1986	29	83	17	0	3	4	9	72.22	$191,228

Best finish for 1986: T-3rd at the Vantage Championship

1987	32	100	19	0	1	1	8	71.80	$99,581

Best finish for 1987: T-2nd at the Pensacola Open

1988	28	73	9	1	1	1	3	72.22	$108,403

Best finish for 1988: Win at the Provident Classic

1989	27	84	15	0	1	2	6	72.17	$140,949

Best finish for 1989: T-4th at the Nissan Los Angeles Open

1990	30	91	15	0	1	2	8	71.40	$201,796

Best finish for 1990: T-3rd at the Las Vegas Invitational

1991	27	82	13	0	2	3	6	71.49	$219,838

Best finish for 1991: T-3rd at the Players Championship

1992	24	80	17	0	1	3	5	71.13	$244,983

Best finish for 1992: T-2nd at the Players Championship

1993	30	88	17	0	1	2	6	71.89	$207,310

Best finish for 1993: 3rd at the International

1994	30	67	5	0	0	0	1	72.69	$28,159

Best finish for 1994: T-11th at the Buick Southern Open

1995	24	76	15	0	1	1	5	71.62	$154,801

Best finish for 1995: T-4th at the Las Vegas Invitational

1996	28	94	19	0	2	3	5	71.29	$230,274

Best finish for 1996: T-5th at the Deposit Guaranty Golf Classic & Quad City Classic

1997	27	92	19	1	1	3	9	71.02	$643,740

Best finish for 1997: Win at the Shell Houston Open

1998	27	80	14	0	0	1	3	72.24	$201,718

Best finish for 1998: T-8th at the Buick Open

1999	28	89	17	0	0	1	4	71.46	$261,853

Best finish for 1999: T-9th at the Greater Greensboro Chrysler Classic

2000	15	41	6	0	0	0	0	72.44	$48,778

Best finish for 2000: T-27th at the B.C. Open

2001	2	6	1	0	0	0	1	72.83	$49,300

Best finish for 2001: T-16th at the Shell Houston Open

2002	1	2	0	0	0	0	0	76.50	
2003	1	4	1	0	0	0	0	72.50	$9,225

Best finish for 2003: T-67th at the Shell Houston Open

2004	1	4	1	0	0	0	0	74.25	$10,100

Best finish for 2004: 69th at the Shell Houston Open

2005	1	2	0	0	0	0	0	76.00	
2006	1	2	0	0	0	0	0	77.00	
2007	1	2	0	0	0	0	0	78.50	
Period Totals	Starts	Rounds Played	Cuts Made	Wins	Top-5s	Top-10s	Top-25s	Scoring Average	Money
	442	1330	237	3	17	31	86	71.85	$3,254,549

Homero Blancas

Year	Starts	Rounds Played	Cuts Made	Wins	Top-5s	Top-10s	Top-25s	Scoring Average	Money
1959	1	4	1	0	0	0	0	72.75	

Best finish for 1959: T-39th at the Houston Classic

1960	1	4	1	0	0	0	0	73.75	

Best finish for 1960: T-47th at the Houston Classic

1961	1	4	1	0	0	0	0	73.50	

Best finish for 1961: T-65th at the Houston Classic

1962	1	4	1	0	0	0	0	72.25	

Best finish for 1962: T-47th at the Houston Classic

Year	Starts	Rounds Played	Cuts Made	Wins	Top-5s	Top-10s	Top-25s	Scoring Average	Money
1963	3	12	2	0	1	1	1	73.17	

Best finish for 1963: T-3rd at the Houston Classic

| 1964 | 2 | 8 | 2 | 0 | 0 | 0 | 1 | 72.63 | |

Best finish for 1964: T-17th at the Houston Classic

| 1965 | 17 | 62 | 14 | 0 | 1 | 5 | 11 | 71.24 | $26,162 |

Best finish for 1965: T-3rd at the Canadian Open

| 1966 | 30 | 104 | 21 | 1 | 3 | 5 | 8 | 72.19 | $26,333 |

Best finish for 1966: Win at the Greater Seattle-Everett Open Invitational

| 1967 | 27 | 98 | 22 | 0 | 1 | 2 | 10 | 72.03 | $27,810 |

Best finish for 1967: T-2nd at the Cleveland Open

| 1968 | 30 | 108 | 24 | 0 | 2 | 3 | 9 | 71.88 | $28,744 |

Best finish for 1968: 4th at the Thunderbird Classic

| 1969 | 31 | 110 | 24 | 0 | 5 | 8 | 12 | 71.45 | $54,710 |

Best finish for 1969: 2nd at the Michigan Golf Classic

| 1970 | 29 | 112 | 27 | 1 | 4 | 12 | 19 | 70.93 | $97,257 |

Best finish for 1970: Win at the Colonial National Invitational

| 1971 | 31 | 111 | 27 | 0 | 2 | 8 | 15 | 71.46 | $53,376 |

Best finish for 1971: T-4th at the Phoenix Open

| 1972 | 30 | 102 | 21 | 1 | 7 | 9 | 15 | 71.73 | $89,819 |

Best finish for 1972: Win at the Phoenix Open

| 1973 | 33 | 116 | 23 | 1 | 3 | 7 | 14 | 71.79 | $95,680 |

Best finish for 1973: Win at the Monsanto Open

| 1974 | 32 | 111 | 24 | 0 | 2 | 4 | 11 | 71.95 | $62,297 |

Best finish for 1974: T-2nd at the Florida Citrus Open Invitational & Byron Nelson Golf Classic

| 1975 | 32 | 96 | 16 | 0 | 1 | 2 | 3 | 72.75 | $22,919 |

Best finish for 1975: T-5th at the Ed McMahon Quad City Open

| 1976 | 32 | 99 | 18 | 0 | 1 | 2 | 5 | 72.84 | $21,642 |

Best finish for 1976: T-5th at the Greater Milwaukee Open

| 1977 | 26 | 77 | 13 | 0 | 0 | 1 | 3 | 72.78 | $12,452 |

Best finish for 1977: T-10th at the San Antonio Texas Open

| 1978 | 28 | 80 | 14 | 0 | 0 | 1 | 2 | 72.83 | $11,156 |

Best finish for 1978: T-7th at the Greater Milwaukee Open

| 1979 | 10 | 28 | 4 | 0 | 0 | 1 | 4 | 71.89 | $17,505 |

Best finish for 1979: T-7th at the Kemper Open

| 1980 | 9 | 24 | 4 | 0 | 0 | 0 | 0 | 72.79 | $3,451 |

Best finish for 1980: T-27th at the Phoenix Open

| 1981 | 5 | 12 | 2 | 0 | 0 | 0 | 0 | 72.08 | $993 |

Best finish for 1981: T-67th at the Pensacola Open

| 1982 | 3 | 8 | 1 | 0 | 0 | 0 | 0 | 71.25 | $2,085 |

Best finish for 1982: T-26th at the Phoenix Open

| 1983 | 5 | 14 | 1 | 0 | 0 | 0 | 0 | 73.50 | $2,042 |

Best finish for 1983: T-26th at the Joe Garagiola Tucson Open

| 1984 | 1 | 0 | 0 | 0 | 0 | 0 | 0 | | $750 |

Best finish for 1984: T-73rd at the Seiko Tucson-Match Play Championship

| 1987 | 2 | 4 | 0 | 0 | 0 | 0 | 0 | 73.25 | |
| 1988 | 1 | 4 | 1 | 0 | 0 | 0 | 0 | 70.50 | $2,820 |

Best finish for 1988: T-37th at the Northern Telecom Tucson Open

1990	1	2	0	0	0	0	0	71.50	
1991	1	2	0	0	0	0	0	73.50	
Period Totals	**Starts**	**Rounds Played**	**Cuts Made**	**Wins**	**Top-5s**	**Top-10s**	**Top-25s**	**Scoring Average**	**Money**
	455	1520	309	4	33	71	143	72.01	$660,003

Bill Blanton

Year	Starts	Rounds Played	Cuts Made	Wins	Top-5s	Top-10s	Top-25s	Scoring Average	Money
1959	4	16	4	0	0	0	0	71.56	$484

Best finish for 1959: T-29th at the Greater Greensboro Open Invitational & El Paso Open Invitational

| 1960 | 5 | 19 | 5 | 0 | 0 | 1 | 3 | 72.42 | $2,159 |

Best finish for 1960: T-9th at the Los Angles Open Invitational

| 1962 | 1 | 4 | 1 | 0 | 0 | 0 | 1 | 72.00 | $150 |

Best finish for 1962: T-25th at the Mobile Sertoma Open Invitational

| 1963 | 5 | 18 | 5 | 0 | 0 | 0 | 1 | 72.89 | $1,041 |

Best finish for 1963: T-18th at the Tucson Open Invitational

| 1964 | 1 | 2 | 0 | 0 | 0 | 0 | 0 | 74.00 | |
| 1966 | 8 | 26 | 5 | 0 | 0 | 0 | 0 | 74.65 | $469 |

Best finish for 1966: T-43rd at the Phoenix Open Invitational

| 1967 | 2 | 5 | 0 | 0 | 0 | 0 | 0 | 76.60 | |
| 1968 | 7 | 18 | 2 | 0 | 0 | 0 | 0 | 74.28 | $580 |

Best finish for 1968: T-43rd at the Robinson Open

| 1969 | 8 | 25 | 5 | 0 | 0 | 0 | 0 | 74.36 | $1,003 |

Best finish for 1969: T-33rd at the Alameda County Open

| 1970 | 2 | 2 | 0 | 0 | 0 | 0 | 0 | 73.50 | |

1971	2	5	0	0	0	0	0	77.00	
Period Totals	Starts	Rounds Played	Cuts Made	Wins	Top-5s	Top-10s	Top-25s	Scoring Average	Money
	45	140	27	0	0	1	5	73.72	$5,886

Chris Blocker

Year	Starts	Rounds Played	Cuts Made	Wins	Top-5s	Top-10s	Top-25s	Scoring Average	Money
1965	22	68	11	0	0	0	4	73.74	$3,818

Best finish for 1965: T-13th at the Los Angles Open

1966	29	97	20	0	0	1	6	72.97	$9,862

Best finish for 1966: 10th at the San Diego Open Invitational

1967	25	81	16	0	0	1	3	73.10	$6,097

Best finish for 1967: T-10th at the San Diego Open

1968	26	86	16	0	1	2	2	73.07	$6,702

Best finish for 1968: 2nd at the Rebel Yell Open

1969	23	67	11	0	0	0	2	72.90	$4,217

Best finish for 1969: T-19th at the San Francisco Open

1970	28	88	18	0	2	3	7	72.51	$32,906

Best finish for 1970: 2nd at the Green Island Open Invitational & Bahama Islands Open

1971	22	73	13	0	0	0	3	72.62	$8,196

Best finish for 1971: T-13th at the Monsanto Open

1972	31	103	21	0	3	4	7	72.38	$36,018

Best finish for 1972: 3rd at the Monsanto Open

1973	19	63	13	0	0	0	1	73.24	$8,463

Best finish for 1973: T-17th at the St. Louis Children's Hospital Golf Classic

1974	16	42	6	0	0	0	1	73.07	$3,052

Best finish for 1974: T-13th at the Southern Open

1975	4	13	2	0	0	0	1	72.46	$2,774

Best finish for 1975: T-20th at the Dean Martin Tucson Open

1976	2	4	0	0	0	0	0	76.50	
1977	1	2	0	0	0	0	0	74.00	
Period Totals	Starts	Rounds Played	Cuts Made	Wins	Top-5s	Top-10s	Top-25s	Scoring Average	Money
	248	787	147	0	6	11	37	72.93	$122,105

Steve Bogan

Year	Starts	Rounds Played	Cuts Made	Wins	Top-5s	Top-10s	Top-25s	Scoring Average	Money
1968	1	2	0	0	0	0	0	73.50	
1970	1	2	0	0	0	0	0	73.50	
1971	12	27	2	0	0	0	0	73.93	$719

Best finish for 1971: T-35th at the Robinson Open Golf Classic

1972	24	73	11	0	0	0	1	73.73	$5,205

Best finish for 1972: T-19th at the Robinson's Fall Golf Classic

1973	3	4	0	0	0	0	0	75.50	$500
1984	1	2	0	0	0	0	0	84.00	
Period Totals	Starts	Rounds Played	Cuts Made	Wins	Top-5s	Top-10s	Top-25s	Scoring Average	Money
	42	110	13	0	0	0	1	74.02	$6,424

Martin Bohen

Year	Starts	Rounds Played	Cuts Made	Wins	Top-5s	Top-10s	Top-25s	Scoring Average	Money
1965	1	4	1	0	0	0	0	76.25	

Best finish for 1965: 94th at the Los Angles Open

1967	1	2	0	0	0	0	0	79.50	
1969	2	6	1	0	0	0	0	75.17	$800

Best finish for 1969: 64th at the U.S. Open

1970	1	2	0	0	0	0	0	80.50	$500
1971	1	2	0	0	0	0	0	77.00	
1972	16	46	7	0	0	0	0	73.67	$3,361

Best finish for 1972: T-31st at the USI Classic

1973	29	96	18	0	0	0	2	72.56	$11,247

Best finish for 1973: T-15th at the Greater New Orleans Open

1974	22	62	9	0	0	0	1	73.52	$3,134

Best finish for 1974: T-17th at the Quad Cities Open

1975	2	4	0	0	0	0	0	74.75	
1976	1	2	0	0	0	0	0	79.00	$500
1977	4	8	0	0	0	0	0	75.25	
1978	1	2	0	0	0	0	0	75.00	
1982	1	2	0	0	0	0	0	74.00	
1983	1	2	0	0	0	0	0	76.50	
1984	1	2	0	0	0	0	0	79.00	$1,000
Period Totals	Starts	Rounds Played	Cuts Made	Wins	Top-5s	Top-10s	Top-25s	Scoring Average	Money
	84	242	36	0	0	0	3	73.60	$20,542

Jason Bohn

Year	Starts	Rounds Played	Cuts Made	Wins	Top-5s	Top-10s	Top-25s	Scoring Average	Money
2000	2	4	0	0	0	0	0	74.25	
2004	29	95	21	0	0	1	6	70.96	$567,930
Best finish for 2004: T-6th at the Buick Championship									
2005	28	91	18	1	3	3	6	70.44	$1,888,567
Best finish for 2005: Win at the B.C. Open									
2006	29	104	23	0	1	3	12	70.82	$1,679,143
Best finish for 2006: 2nd at the Chrysler Classic of Greensboro									
2007	17	57	12	0	0	0	4	71.26	$527,512
Best finish for 2007: T-11th at the FBR Open									
2008	15	45	8	0	1	2	5	71.76	$866,786
Best finish for 2008: 3rd at the Wachovia Championship									
Period Totals	Starts	Rounds Played	Cuts Made	Wins	Top-5s	Top-10s	Top-25s	Scoring Average	Money
	120	396	82	1	5	9	33	70.97	$5,529,938

Bob Boldt

Year	Starts	Rounds Played	Cuts Made	Wins	Top-5s	Top-10s	Top-25s	Scoring Average	Money
1965	2	6	0	0	0	0	0	75.00	
1966	2	6	1	0	0	0	0	73.83	
Best finish for 1966: T-65th at the Portland Open Invitational									
1967	22	54	5	0	0	0	0	74.30	$2,133
Best finish for 1967: T-28th at the Phoenix Open & Byron Nelson Dallas Open									
1968	16	38	3	0	0	0	0	74.26	
Best finish for 1968: T-61st at the Kemper Open Invitational									
1969	8	22	3	0	0	1	1	75.45	$1,396
Best finish for 1969: T-10th at the Tallahassee Open									
1970	3	6	0	0	0	0	0	76.33	
1973	3	6	0	0	0	0	0	76.50	
1974	2	5	0	0	0	0	0	76.80	
1975	2	5	0	0	0	0	0	77.40	
1977	2	4	0	0	0	0	0	78.50	$500
1978	3	7	0	0	0	0	0	76.57	$303
1979	3	7	0	0	0	0	0	77.57	
1980	2	5	0	0	0	0	0	75.00	
1984	1	3	0	0	0	0	0	80.67	
1986	1	3	0	0	0	0	0	74.67	
1989	1	3	0	0	0	0	0	76.00	
Period Totals	Starts	Rounds Played	Cuts Made	Wins	Top-5s	Top-10s	Top-25s	Scoring Average	Money
	73	180	12	0	0	1	1	75.21	$4,332

Rob Boldt

Year	Starts	Rounds Played	Cuts Made	Wins	Top-5s	Top-10s	Top-25s	Scoring Average	Money
1993	1	2	0	0	0	0	0	71.50	
1994	20	59	9	0	0	0	2	71.68	$52,992
Best finish for 1994: T-17th at the Motorola Western Open									
1995	5	10	0	0	0	0	0	72.50	
Period Totals	Starts	Rounds Played	Cuts Made	Wins	Top-5s	Top-10s	Top-25s	Scoring Average	Money
	26	71	9	0	0	0	2	71.79	$52,992

Justin Bolli

Year	Starts	Rounds Played	Cuts Made	Wins	Top-5s	Top-10s	Top-25s	Scoring Average	Money
2005	24	63	9	0	0	0	3	71.70	$207,400
Best finish for 2005: T-15th at the BellSouth Classic									
2007	1	2	0	0	0	0	0	72.50	
2008	28	87	16	0	1	1	2	72.00	$458,022
Best finish for 2008: T-5th at the AT&T Classic									
Period Totals	Starts	Rounds Played	Cuts Made	Wins	Top-5s	Top-10s	Top-25s	Scoring Average	Money
	53	152	25	0	1	1	5	71.88	$665,422

Charles Bolling

Year	Starts	Rounds Played	Cuts Made	Wins	Top-5s	Top-10s	Top-25s	Scoring Average	Money
1983	3	6	0	0	0	0	0	76.50	$975
1984	6	14	1	0	0	0	0	74.43	$1,788
Best finish for 1984: T-58th at the Texas Open									
1985	31	79	8	0	0	1	3	72.82	$25,446
Best finish for 1985: T-10th at the Southwest Golf Classic									
1986	34	110	23	0	0	2	10	71.47	$88,328
Best finish for 1986: T-9th at the Houston Open									
1987	35	102	17	0	0	1	2	72.47	$62,607
Best finish for 1987: T-10th at the Bob Hope Chrysler Classic									

Year	Starts	Rounds Played	Cuts Made	Wins	Top-5s	Top-10s	Top-25s	Scoring Average	Money
1988	20	43	2	0	0	0	0	73.72	$5,659

Best finish for 1988: T-34th at the Anheuser-Busch Golf Classic

1989	2	4	0	0	0	0	0	73.75	$800
1990	1	4	1	0	0	0	0	70.75	$684

Best finish for 1990: T-54th at the Deposit Guaranty

1996	2	4	0	0	0	0	0	72.50	
1997	2	4	0	0	0	0	0	76.50	
2001	1	2	0	0	0	0	0	76.50	
2003	1	2	0	0	0	0	0	75.00	
Period Totals	**Starts**	**Rounds Played**	**Cuts Made**	**Wins**	**Top-5s**	**Top-10s**	**Top-25s**	**Scoring Average**	**Money**
	138	374	52	0	0	4	15	72.61	$186,288

Dave Bollman

Year	Starts	Rounds Played	Cuts Made	Wins	Top-5s	Top-10s	Top-25s	Scoring Average	Money
1969	23	62	7	0	0	0	2	73.81	$4,134

Best finish for 1969: T-15th at the Robinson Open

1970	24	66	9	0	0	0	1	73.94	$3,054

Best finish for 1970: T-24th at the Greater Jacksonville Open

1971	12	28	2	0	0	0	0	74.71	$380

Best finish for 1971: T-58th at the Atlanta Classic

Period Totals	**Starts**	**Rounds Played**	**Cuts Made**	**Wins**	**Top-5s**	**Top-10s**	**Top-25s**	**Scoring Average**	**Money**
	59	156	18	0	0	0	3	74.03	$7,568

Tommy Bolt

Year	Starts	Rounds Played	Cuts Made	Wins	Top-5s	Top-10s	Top-25s	Scoring Average	Money
1958	27	97	22	2	5	13	19	71.08	$27,344

Best finish for 1958: Win at the Colonial Invitational & U.S. Open

1959	20	80	20	0	1	4	15	71.09	$12,468

Best finish for 1959: T-4th at the Rubber City Open Invitational

1960	22	86	20	1	2	6	18	70.62	$18,542

Best finish for 1960: Win at the Memphis Open Invitational

1961	14	54	12	1	4	6	11	70.43	$19,216

Best finish for 1961: Win at the Pensacola Open Invitational

1962	14	50	12	0	1	2	6	72.54	$6,490

Best finish for 1962: T-4th at the Azalea Open Invitational

1963	19	75	16	0	3	4	11	71.25	$15,551

Best finish for 1963: T-3rd at the Palm Springs Golf Classic

1964	22	74	15	0	0	4	7	71.97	$11,327

Best finish for 1964: T-6th at the Buick Open

1965	17	55	11	0	0	2	7	71.98	$12,920

Best finish for 1965: T-8th at the Masters

1966	16	52	10	0	1	3	8	71.48	$19,760

Best finish for 1966: T-4th at the Jacksonville Open Invitational

1967	19	60	12	0	2	2	7	71.95	$23,982

Best finish for 1967: T-2nd at the Atlanta Classic

1968	13	35	5	0	0	1	3	72.57	$5,748

Best finish for 1968: T-9th at the Colonial National Invitational

1969	13	42	9	0	0	2	5	71.48	$15,864

Best finish for 1969: 6th at the Doral Open

1970	13	33	4	0	0	0	1	73.12	$2,335

Best finish for 1970: T-17th at the Tallahassee Open

1971	5	15	3	0	1	1	1	71.80	$14,733

Best finish for 1971: 3rd at the PGA Championship

1972	6	8	1	0	0	0	0	74.13	$1,947

Best finish for 1972: T-28th at the Florida Citrus Open Invitational

1976	1	1	0	0	0	0	0	72.00	
1977	1	2	0	0	0	0	0	76.50	$500
1981	1	1	0	0	0	0	0	70.00	
Period Totals	**Starts**	**Rounds Played**	**Cuts Made**	**Wins**	**Top-5s**	**Top-10s**	**Top-25s**	**Scoring Average**	**Money**
	243	820	172	4	20	50	119	71.55	$208,726

PGA Tour career totals from 1946 to 1981

	Starts	Rounds Played	Cuts Made	Wins	Top-5s	Top-10s	Top-25s	Scoring Average	Money
	431	1510	359	15	56	128	254	N/A	$320,811

Paul Bondeson

Year	Starts	Rounds Played	Cuts Made	Wins	Top-5s	Top-10s	Top-25s	Scoring Average	Money
1962	10	40	8	0	1	2	3	71.73	$8,204

Best finish for 1962: T-2nd at the Doral Country Club Open Invitational

1963	19	75	17	0	0	3	8	71.28	$12,161

Best finish for 1963: T-6th at the Utah Open Invitational

1964	28	90	16	0	2	3	8	72.48	$13,417

Best finish for 1964: T-2nd at the Greater Hartford Open

Year	Starts	Rounds Played	Cuts Made	Wins	Top-5s	Top-10s	Top-25s	Scoring Average	Money
1965	28	87	14	0	0	1	4	73.17	$7,400

Best finish for 1965: T-9th at the Hawaiian Open

| 1966 | 30 | 93 | 18 | 0 | 2 | 5 | 10 | 72.00 | $20,596 |

Best finish for 1966: T-3rd at the Greater Seattle-Everett Open Invitational

| 1967 | 28 | 91 | 17 | 0 | 1 | 1 | 4 | 72.64 | $11,164 |

Best finish for 1967: T-5th at the Tucson Open

| 1968 | 20 | 58 | 9 | 0 | 1 | 1 | 2 | 73.66 | $7,540 |

Best finish for 1968: T-3rd at the Atlanta Classic

| 1969 | 9 | 26 | 4 | 0 | 0 | 0 | 0 | 73.69 | $622 |

Best finish for 1969: T-59th at the Los Angeles Open

| 1970 | 3 | 8 | 1 | 0 | 0 | 0 | 0 | 72.63 | $513 |

Best finish for 1970: T-35th at the Greater Milwaukee Open

| 1971 | 4 | 8 | 0 | 0 | 0 | 0 | 0 | 75.75 | |
| 1973 | 1 | 4 | 1 | 0 | 0 | 0 | 0 | 74.00 | |

Best finish for 1973: T-75th at the Walt Disney World Open

| 1974 | 2 | 5 | 1 | 0 | 0 | 0 | 0 | 74.20 | $376 |

Best finish for 1974: T-46th at the Bing Crosby Pro-Am

Period Totals	Starts	Rounds Played	Cuts Made	Wins	Top-5s	Top-10s	Top-25s	Scoring Average	Money
	182	585	106	0	7	16	39	72.57	$81,994

Gene Bone

Year	Starts	Rounds Played	Cuts Made	Wins	Top-5s	Top-10s	Top-25s	Scoring Average	Money
1958	14	41	6	0	0	0	3	73.71	$911

Best finish for 1958: T-12th at the Western Open

| 1959 | 3 | 9 | 2 | 0 | 0 | 0 | 1 | 73.67 | $270 |

Best finish for 1959: T-23rd at the Motor City Open Invitational

| 1960 | 1 | 4 | 1 | 0 | 0 | 0 | 1 | 72.50 | $1,125 |

Best finish for 1960: T-14th at the Buick Open Invitational

| 1961 | 3 | 8 | 2 | 0 | 0 | 0 | 0 | 75.75 | $085 |

Best finish for 1961: T-44th at the Buick Open Invitational

| 1963 | 4 | 14 | 4 | 0 | 0 | 1 | 2 | 71.64 | $2,395 |

Best finish for 1963: T-8th at the Texas Open Invitational

1964	1	2	0	0	0	0	0	77.50	
1965	1	2	0	0	0	0	0	79.00	
1966	3	8	1	0	0	0	0	75.75	$790

Best finish for 1966: T-36th at the U.S. Open

| 1967 | 2 | 6 | 1 | 0 | 0 | 0 | 0 | 75.67 | $300 |

Best finish for 1967: T-67th at the PGA Championship

1968	2	4	0	0	0	0	0	80.50	$500
1969	2	3	0	0	0	0	0	75.67	
1971	1	2	0	0	0	0	0	81.00	$500
1973	1	4	1	0	0	0	0	74.00	$360

Best finish for 1973: T-60th at the PGA Championship

1976	2	4	0	0	0	0	0	81.00	$250
Period Totals	Starts	Rounds Played	Cuts Made	Wins	Top-5s	Top-10s	Top-25s	Scoring Average	Money
	40	111	18	0	0	1	7	74.67	$7,487

Lee Bonse

Year	Starts	Rounds Played	Cuts Made	Wins	Top-5s	Top-10s	Top-25s	Scoring Average	Money
1965	1	2	0	0	0	0	0	79.00	
1968	1	2	0	0	0	0	0	76.50	
1970	6	12	1	0	0	0	0	75.92	$182

Best finish for 1970: T-68th at the Tucson Open

| 1971 | 13 | 34 | 3 | 0 | 0 | 0 | 0 | 74.32 | $497 |

Best finish for 1971: T-51st at the Canadian Open

| 1972 | 9 | 19 | 0 | 0 | 0 | 0 | 0 | 76.63 | $500 |
| 1973 | 7 | 16 | 1 | 0 | 0 | 0 | 0 | 74.06 | $296 |

Best finish for 1973: T-57th at the Phoenix Open

1975	2	4	0	0	0	0	0	73.75	
Period Totals	Starts	Rounds Played	Cuts Made	Wins	Top-5s	Top-10s	Top-25s	Scoring Average	Money
	39	89	5	0	0	0	0	75.11	$1,475

Eric Booker

Year	Starts	Rounds Played	Cuts Made	Wins	Top-5s	Top-10s	Top-25s	Scoring Average	Money
1991	1	2	0	0	0	0	0	77.50	$1,000
1993	1	2	0	0	0	0	0	76.50	
1994	1	2	0	0	0	0	0	73.50	
1995	1	2	0	0	0	0	0	70.50	
1996	2	6	1	0	0	0	0	72.50	$3,592

Best finish for 1996: T-73rd at the Buick Open

| 1997 | 1 | 4 | 1 | 0 | 0 | 0 | 0 | 71.75 | $3,240 |

Best finish for 1997: T-59th at the Buick Open

Year	Starts	Rounds Played	Cuts Made	Wins	Top-5s	Top-10s	Top-25s	Scoring Average	Money
1998	2	8	2	0	1	1	1	69.50	$84,288

Best finish for 1998: T-4th at the Buick Open

| 1999 | 31 | 90 | 14 | 0 | 2 | 2 | 3 | 71.69 | $320,753 |

Best finish for 1999: T-3rd at the Honda Classic

| 2000 | 31 | 85 | 12 | 0 | 0 | 0 | 0 | 72.36 | $88,615 |

Best finish for 2000: T-38th at the Bell Canadian Open

Period Totals	Starts	Rounds Played	Cuts Made	Wins	Top-5s	Top-10s	Top-25s	Scoring Average	Money
	71	201	30	0	3	3	4	72.02	$501,488

Jim Booros

Year	Starts	Rounds Played	Cuts Made	Wins	Top-5s	Top-10s	Top-25s	Scoring Average	Money
1977	18	45	5	0	0	0	0	73.64	$1,740

Best finish for 1977: T-31st at the Sammy Davis, Jr. - Greater Hartford Open

| 1980 | 1 | 2 | 0 | 0 | 0 | 0 | 0 | 78.50 | $600 |
| 1981 | 22 | 65 | 13 | 0 | 1 | 2 | 5 | 71.63 | $36,033 |

Best finish for 1981: T-4th at the Southern Open

| 1982 | 26 | 85 | 17 | 0 | 0 | 2 | 5 | 72.18 | $52,583 |

Best finish for 1982: T-7th at the Hawaiian Open

| 1983 | 31 | 95 | 14 | 0 | 0 | 1 | 4 | 72.80 | $34,980 |

Best finish for 1983: T-8th at the Isuzu/Andy Williams San Diego Open

| 1984 | 29 | 72 | 7 | 0 | 0 | 0 | 3 | 73.57 | $18,446 |

Best finish for 1984: T-15th at the Walt Disney World Golf Classic

| 1985 | 3 | 8 | 1 | 0 | 0 | 0 | 0 | 73.25 | $1,055 |

Best finish for 1985: T-62nd at the Kemper Open

| 1987 | 1 | 2 | 0 | 0 | 0 | 0 | 0 | 76.00 | $600 |
| 1988 | 30 | 85 | 11 | 0 | 0 | 0 | 3 | 71.92 | $25,970 |

Best finish for 1988: T-12th at the Deposit Guaranty Golf Classic

| 1989 | 28 | 86 | 16 | 1 | 2 | 3 | 5 | 71.12 | $119,824 |

Best finish for 1989: Win at the Deposit Guaranty Golf Classic

| 1990 | 30 | 88 | 13 | 0 | 1 | 2 | 6 | 71.64 | $121,948 |

Best finish for 1990: T-3rd at the Buick Southern Open

| 1991 | 30 | 96 | 16 | 0 | 0 | 0 | 3 | 71.69 | $53,682 |

Best finish for 1991: T-19th at the Deposit Guaranty Classic

| 1992 | 1 | 4 | 1 | 0 | 0 | 0 | 0 | 69.25 | $663 |

Best finish for 1992: T-57th at the Deposit Guaranty Classic

Period Totals	Starts	Rounds Played	Cuts Made	Wins	Top-5s	Top-10s	Top-25s	Scoring Average	Money
	250	733	114	1	4	10	34	72.18	$468,125

Gene Borek

Year	Starts	Rounds Played	Cuts Made	Wins	Top-5s	Top-10s	Top-25s	Scoring Average	Money
1958	1	2	0	0	0	0	0	76.50	
1963	3	10	2	0	0	0	0	74.50	$417

Best finish for 1963: T-39th at the Phoenix Open Invitational

| 1964 | 1 | 2 | 0 | 0 | 0 | 0 | 0 | 78.50 | |
| 1966 | 5 | 16 | 3 | 0 | 0 | 0 | 0 | 74.63 | $1,259 |

Best finish for 1966: T-37th at the PGA Championship

| 1967 | 2 | 4 | 0 | 0 | 0 | 0 | 0 | 75.25 | |
| 1968 | 2 | 6 | 1 | 0 | 0 | 0 | 0 | 75.33 | $740 |

Best finish for 1968: 56th at the U.S. Open

| 1969 | 3 | 8 | 1 | 0 | 0 | 1 | 1 | 73.63 | $681 |

Best finish for 1969: T-8th at the West End Classic

| 1970 | 3 | 8 | 1 | 0 | 0 | 0 | 0 | 75.88 | $800 |

Best finish for 1970: T-69th at the U.S. Open

| 1971 | 3 | 10 | 2 | 0 | 0 | 0 | 0 | 74.00 | $2,139 |

Best finish for 1971: T-30th at the PGA Championship

| 1972 | 2 | 4 | 0 | 0 | 0 | 0 | 0 | 75.25 | |
| 1973 | 3 | 10 | 2 | 0 | 0 | 0 | 0 | 73.60 | $1,604 |

Best finish for 1973: 38th at the U.S. Open

| 1974 | 2 | 6 | 1 | 0 | 0 | 0 | 0 | 72.67 | $1,260 |

Best finish for 1974: T-32nd at the PGA Championship

| 1975 | 3 | 4 | 0 | 0 | 0 | 0 | 0 | 73.50 | |
| 1976 | 2 | 8 | 2 | 0 | 0 | 0 | 0 | 75.50 | $1,450 |

Best finish for 1976: T-60th at the PGA Championship

| 1977 | 1 | 4 | 1 | 0 | 0 | 0 | 0 | 71.25 | $1,863 |

Best finish for 1977: T-30th at the American Express Westchester Classic

| 1978 | 2 | 6 | 1 | 0 | 0 | 0 | 0 | 73.00 | $1,233 |

Best finish for 1978: T-44th at the American Express Westchester Classic

1979	1	2	0	0	0	0	0	75.00	
1980	1	2	0	0	0	0	0	72.50	
1981	1	2	0	0	0	0	0	76.50	$550
1983	1	2	0	0	0	0	0	74.50	$100

Year	Starts	Rounds Played	Cuts Made	Wins	Top-5s	Top-10s	Top-25s	Scoring Average	Money
1985	1	2	0	0	0	0	0	77.50	$600
Period Totals	Starts	Rounds Played	Cuts Made	Wins	Top-5s	Top-10s	Top-25s	Scoring Average	Money
	43	118	17	0	0	1	1	74.44	$14,696

Ernie Boros

Year	Starts	Rounds Played	Cuts Made	Wins	Top-5s	Top-10s	Top-25s	Scoring Average	Money
1958	13	44	8	0	0	0	0	73.43	$230

Best finish for 1958: T-32nd at the Miller Open

1959	1	4	0	0	0	0	0	73.50	$097

Best finish for 1959: T-58th at the Western Open Championship

1962	1	2	1	0	0	0	0	75.00	$025

Best finish for 1962: T-106 at the Thunderbird Classic Invitational

1963	1	2	1	0	0	0	0	80.00	

Best finish for 1963: T-200 at the PGA Championship

1964	12	31	2	0	0	0	0	74.29	$717

Best finish for 1964: T-34th at the Whitemarsh Open

1965	4	10	1	0	0	0	0	74.80	

Best finish for 1965: T-62nd at the Buick Open

1967	3	6	0	0	0	0	0	75.17	
1968	1	2	0	0	0	0	0	77.50	
Period Totals	Starts	Rounds Played	Cuts Made	Wins	Top-5s	Top-10s	Top-25s	Scoring Average	Money
	36	101	13	0	0	0	0	74.18	$1,069

Guy Boros

Year	Starts	Rounds Played	Cuts Made	Wins	Top-5s	Top-10s	Top-25s	Scoring Average	Money
1990	1	2	0	0	0	0	0	77.50	
1991	1	2	0	0	0	0	0	74.50	
1994	30	93	19	0	1	4	8	71.02	$240,775

Best finish for 1994: T-3rd at the Deposit Guaranty Golf Classic

1995	34	97	14	0	2	4	9	71.11	$304,854

Best finish for 1995: T-4th at the BellSouth Classic & Buick Challenge

1996	31	93	17	1	1	1	5	71.47	$283,358

Best finish for 1996: Win at the Greater Vancouver Open

1997	27	79	13	0	1	1	2	72.01	$197,439

Best finish for 1997: 3rd at the Mercedes Championship

1998	35	88	11	0	0	0	2	72.59	$74,203

Best finish for 1998: T-22nd at the Shell Houston Open

1999	5	13	1	0	0	0	0	74.85	$4,500

Best finish for 1999: 80th at the Air Canada Championship

2000	4	10	1	0	0	0	0	72.60	$6,796

Best finish for 2000: T-52nd at the Air Canada Championship

2001	3	10	2	0	0	0	0	72.00	$15,088

Best finish for 2001: T-43rd at the Air Canada Championship

2002	11	28	3	0	0	0	1	71.71	$82,852

Best finish for 2002: T-13th at the SEI Pennsylvania Classic

2003	6	19	3	0	0	1	1	72.00	$95,612

Best finish for 2003: T-10th at the Reno-Tahoe Open

2004	24	65	8	0	0	0	1	72.51	$130,782

Best finish for 2004: T-18th at the Booz Allen Classic

2005	5	17	3	0	0	0	0	71.06	$27,765

Best finish for 2005: T-43rd at the B.C. Open

2006	5	14	2	0	0	0	0	72.36	$13,750

Best finish for 2006: T-71st at the B.C. Open & Valero Texas Open

2007	4	10	1	0	0	0	0	71.90	$7,269

Best finish for 2007: T-49th at the Reno-Tahoe Open

2008	6	17	2	0	0	0	0	72.71	$31,565

Best finish for 2008: T-32nd at the Viking Classic

Period Totals	Starts	Rounds Played	Cuts Made	Wins	Top-5s	Top-10s	Top-25s	Scoring Average	Money
	232	657	100	1	5	11	29	71.86	$1,516,610

Julius Boros

Year	Starts	Rounds Played	Cuts Made	Wins	Top-5s	Top-10s	Top-25s	Scoring Average	Money
1958	31	119	29	2	11	14	25	70.89	$37,032

Best finish for 1958: Win at the Arlington Hotel Open & Carling Open

1959	19	76	16	1	3	9	15	71.00	$17,932

Best finish for 1959: Win at the Dallas Open Invitational

1960	18	73	18	1	4	8	16	70.78	$24,558

Best finish for 1960: Win at the Colonial National Invitational

1961	26	99	22	0	1	4	16	71.12	$12,872

Best finish for 1961: T-5th at the Houston Classic

1962	28	112	28	0	1	7	22	70.96	$23,819

Best finish for 1962: T-3rd at the Insurance City Open Invitational

Year	Starts	Rounds Played	Cuts Made	Wins	Top-5s	Top-10s	Top-25s	Scoring Average	Money
1963	23	94	20	3	10	13	20	70.48	$141,857
Best finish for 1963: Win at the Colonial National Invitational, Buick Open Invitational & U.S. Open									
1964	24	93	22	1	3	5	14	70.86	$28,945
Best finish for 1964: Win at the Greater Greensboro Open									
1965	25	97	23	0	4	5	14	71.41	$40,508
Best finish for 1965: T-3rd at the Memphis Open & Buick Open									
1966	23	91	21	0	3	10	17	71.23	$46,398
Best finish for 1966: T-4th at the Cleveland Open Invitational & Houston Champions International									
1967	27	104	24	3	10	14	19	71.00	$128,841
Best finish for 1967: Win at the Phoenix Open, Florida Citrus Open & Buick Open									
1968	24	84	19	2	7	11	17	70.17	$145,192
Best finish for 1968: Win at the PGA Championship & Westchester Classic									
1969	25	95	22	0	2	4	13	71.67	$48,763
Best finish for 1969: T-2nd at the Greater Greensboro Open									
1970	25	88	20	0	1	3	9	71.72	$33,917
Best finish for 1970: 5th at the Coral Springs Open Invitational									
1971	21	72	17	0	2	4	6	71.99	$45,530
Best finish for 1971: 2nd at the Florida Citrus Open Invitational									
1972	17	56	12	0	1	2	4	72.27	$21,748
Best finish for 1972: T-5th at the Doral-Eastern Open									
1973	21	74	16	0	1	6	9	71.72	$40,262
Best finish for 1973: 5th at the Colonial National Invitational									
1974	14	35	5	0	2	2	3	72.46	$34,818
Best finish for 1974: 3rd at the Jackie Gleason's Inverrary Classic									
1975	17	62	14	0	1	1	1	72.68	$36,311
Best finish for 1975: 2nd at the Westchester Classic									
1976	15	43	6	0	0	0	0	73.63	$3,347
Best finish for 1976: T-31st at the Doral-Eastern Open									
1977	13	39	7	0	0	0	0	73.77	$4,289
Best finish for 1977: T-26th at the Colonial National Invitational									
1978	9	18	1	0	0	0	0	74.28	$822
Best finish for 1978: T-56th at the Colgate Hall Of Fame Classic									
1979	10	28	5	0	0	0	0	72.68	$3,471
Best finish for 1979: T-43rd at the Jackie Gleason's Inverrary Classic									
1980	5	10	0	0	0	0	0	76.10	$500
Period Totals	Starts	Rounds Played	Cuts Made	Wins	Top-5s	Top-10s	Top-25s	Scoring Average	Money
	460	1662	367	13	67	122	240	71.46	$921,731

PGA Tour career totals from 1950 to 1980

Starts	Rounds Played	Cuts Made	Wins	Top-5s	Top-10s	Top-25s	Scoring Average	Money
593	2175	499	18	80	168	333	N/A	$1,065,847

Rafe Botts

Year	Starts	Rounds Played	Cuts Made	Wins	Top-5s	Top-10s	Top-25s	Scoring Average	Money
1961	1	2	0	0	0	0	0	77.50	
1964	14	35	5	0	0	0	0	73.83	$2,100
Best finish for 1964: T-48th at the Cleveland Open									
1965	27	80	11	0	0	0	2	73.73	$2,148
Best finish for 1965: T-22nd at the Lucky International									
1966	21	62	8	0	0	0	0	74.18	
Best finish for 1966: T-42nd at the Azalea Open Invitational									
1967	14	37	4	0	0	0	0	73.84	$1,145
Best finish for 1967: T-47th at the Insurance City Open									
1968	20	56	7	0	0	1	2	73.32	$3,289
Best finish for 1968: T-8th at the Pensacola Open Invitational									
1969	15	45	7	0	0	0	0	73.87	$1,822
Best finish for 1969: T-30th at the Texas Open									
1970	25	69	8	0	0	0	1	73.91	$2,821
Best finish for 1970: T-25th at the IVB Philadelphia Golf Classic									
1971	8	21	2	0	0	0	0	73.43	$599
Best finish for 1971: T-39th at the Southern Open									
1972	13	38	6	0	0	0	0	73.18	$1,918
Best finish for 1972: T-26th at the Sahara Invitational									
1973	3	6	0	0	0	0	0	76.50	
1974	14	34	2	0	1	1	1	75.03	$4,100
Best finish for 1974: 5th at the Quad Cities Open									
1975	6	12	0	0	0	0	0	76.58	
1976	2	6	1	0	0	0	0	74.33	
Best finish for 1976: 73rd at the Glen Campbell Los Angles Open									
1977	6	14	0	0	0	0	0	75.00	
1978	1	2	0	0	0	0	0	79.00	
1979	3	8	0	0	0	0	0	75.13	

Year	Starts	Rounds Played	Cuts Made	Wins	Top-5s	Top-10s	Top-25s	Scoring Average	Money
1980	1	2	0	0	0	0	0	76.00	
1981	1	2	0	0	0	0	0	77.00	$450
1983	1	2	0	0	0	0	0	73.00	
1984	1	2	0	0	0	0	0	77.50	
1985	1	2	0	0	0	0	0	72.00	
1986	1	1	0	0	0	0	0	80.00	
Period Totals	Starts	Rounds Played	Cuts Made	Wins	Top-5s	Top-10s	Top-25s	Scoring Average	Money
	199	538	61	0	1	2	6	74.04	$20,393

Bob Bourne

Year	Starts	Rounds Played	Cuts Made	Wins	Top-5s	Top-10s	Top-25s	Scoring Average	Money
1970	2	6	1	0	0	0	0	76.17	$217

Best finish for 1970: T-66th at the Bahama Islands Open

| 1971 | 17 | 44 | 5 | 0 | 0 | 0 | 0 | 74.11 | $897 |

Best finish for 1971: T-47th at the Tucson Open

| 1972 | 15 | 40 | 5 | 0 | 0 | 0 | 1 | 74.38 | $2,595 |

Best finish for 1972: T-21st at the Greater Milwaukee Open

Period Totals	Starts	Rounds Played	Cuts Made	Wins	Top-5s	Top-10s	Top-25s	Scoring Average	Money
	34	90	11	0	0	0	1	74.37	$3,708

George Boutell

Year	Starts	Rounds Played	Cuts Made	Wins	Top-5s	Top-10s	Top-25s	Scoring Average	Money
1962	1	4	1	0	0	0	1	69.25	

Best finish for 1962: T-11th at the St. Paul Open Invitational

| 1963 | 1 | 2 | 0 | 0 | 0 | 0 | 0 | 83.00 | |
| 1964 | 3 | 9 | 1 | 0 | 0 | 0 | 0 | 72.78 | |

Best finish for 1964: T-58th at the St. Paul Open

1965	1	2	0	0	0	0	0	73.50	
1966	1	2	0	0	0	0	0	74.50	
1967	3	12	3	0	0	0	0	72.17	$612

Best finish for 1967: T-32nd at the Hawaiian Open

| 1968 | 21 | 60 | 10 | 0 | 0 | 0 | 0 | 73.20 | $1,022 |

Best finish for 1968: T-32nd at the Magnolia State Classic & Memphis Open Invitational

| 1969 | 20 | 64 | 12 | 0 | 0 | 0 | 2 | 72.67 | $4,064 |

Best finish for 1969: T-20th at the Buick Open

| 1970 | 19 | 49 | 6 | 0 | 0 | 0 | 0 | 72.80 | $2,537 |

Best finish for 1970: T-26th at the Phoenix Open

| 1971 | 17 | 54 | 10 | 0 | 0 | 1 | 2 | 72.65 | $11,012 |

Best finish for 1971: T-9th at the Westchester Classic

| 1972 | 22 | 55 | 6 | 0 | 0 | 0 | 2 | 74.15 | $5,033 |

Best finish for 1972: T-13th at the Phoenix Open

| 1973 | 4 | 14 | 2 | 0 | 0 | 0 | 0 | 74.71 | |

Best finish for 1973: 71st at the Bing Crosby Pro-Am

1988	1	0	0	0	0	0	0		
Period Totals	Starts	Rounds Played	Cuts Made	Wins	Top-5s	Top-10s	Top-25s	Scoring Average	Money
	114	327	51	0	0	1	7	73.14	$24,280

Craig Bowden

Year	Starts	Rounds Played	Cuts Made	Wins	Top-5s	Top-10s	Top-25s	Scoring Average	Money
1997	21	55	8	0	0	0	1	72.22	$40,118

Best finish for 1997: T-23rd at the Quad City Classic

| 1999 | 1 | 2 | 0 | 0 | 0 | 0 | 0 | 77.50 | $1,000 |
| 2000 | 25 | 54 | 4 | 0 | 0 | 0 | 0 | 73.24 | $34,280 |

Best finish for 2000: T-33rd at the Buick Invitational

| 2001 | 4 | 10 | 1 | 0 | 0 | 0 | 0 | 71.30 | $6,107 |

Best finish for 2001: T-69th at the Greater Milwaukee Open

| 2002 | 2 | 5 | 1 | 0 | 0 | 0 | 0 | 74.20 | $16,294 |

Best finish for 2002: T-50th at the U.S. Open

| 2003 | 2 | 4 | 0 | 0 | 0 | 0 | 0 | 74.00 | $1,000 |
| 2004 | 30 | 83 | 12 | 0 | 0 | 1 | 5 | 71.54 | $495,568 |

Best finish for 2004: T-9th at the FedEx St. Jude Classic

| 2005 | 15 | 41 | 6 | 0 | 0 | 0 | 2 | 71.59 | $199,911 |

Best finish for 2005: T-13th at the John Deere Classic

| 2007 | 25 | 78 | 13 | 0 | 0 | 1 | 1 | 71.22 | $333,970 |

Best finish for 2007: T-9th at the U.S. Bank Championship in Milwaukee

Period Totals	Starts	Rounds Played	Cuts Made	Wins	Top-5s	Top-10s	Top-25s	Scoring Average	Money
	125	332	45	0	0	2	9	71.96	$1,128,249

Steven Bowditch

Year	Starts	Rounds Played	Cuts Made	Wins	Top-5s	Top-10s	Top-25s	Scoring Average	Money
2003	1	2	0	0	0	0	0	76.50	$3,974
2005	1	4	1	0	0	0	0	71.75	$8,299

Best finish for 2005: T-73rd at the Buick Championship

Year	Starts	Rounds Played	Cuts Made	Wins	Top-5s	Top-10s	Top-25s	Scoring Average	Money
2006	22	41	2	0	0	0	0	74.90	$11,160

Best finish for 2006: 76th at the Reno-Tahoe Open

Year	Starts	Rounds Played	Cuts Made	Wins	Top-5s	Top-10s	Top-25s	Scoring Average	Money
2007	5	10	0	0	0	0	0	76.60	
Period Totals	Starts	Rounds Played	Cuts Made	Wins	Top-5s	Top-10s	Top-25s	Scoring Average	Money
	29	57	3	0	0	0	0	75.04	$23,433

Gary Bowerman

Year	Starts	Rounds Played	Cuts Made	Wins	Top-5s	Top-10s	Top-25s	Scoring Average	Money
1968	2	4	0	0	0	0	0	74.50	
1969	2	8	2	0	0	0	1	72.25	$769

Best finish for 1969: T-25th at the Azalea Open

| 1970 | 17 | 48 | 8 | 0 | 0 | 0 | 2 | 72.85 | $4,580 |

Best finish for 1970: T-12th at the Greater Milwaukee Open

| 1971 | 6 | 16 | 1 | 0 | 0 | 0 | 0 | 75.25 | $220 |

Best finish for 1971: T-58th at the Tucson Open

| 1972 | 22 | 58 | 7 | 0 | 0 | 0 | 1 | 74.31 | $2,263 |

Best finish for 1972: T-22nd at the Robinson's Fall Golf Classic

| 1973 | 3 | 8 | 1 | 0 | 0 | 0 | 0 | 75.63 | |

Best finish for 1973: 77th at the Canadian Open

1975	1	2	0	0	0	0	0	73.50	
1976	1	2	0	0	0	0	0	78.50	
Period Totals	Starts	Rounds Played	Cuts Made	Wins	Top-5s	Top-10s	Top-25s	Scoring Average	Money
	54	146	19	0	0	0	4	73.95	$7,832

Charles Bowles

Year	Starts	Rounds Played	Cuts Made	Wins	Top-5s	Top-10s	Top-25s	Scoring Average	Money
1986	1	3	1	0	0	0	0	71.33	$1,650

Best finish for 1986: T-43rd at the Hertz Bay Hill Classic

| 1988 | 1 | 2 | 0 | 0 | 0 | 0 | 0 | 82.50 | $1,000 |
| 1989 | 26 | 62 | 5 | 0 | 0 | 0 | 0 | 73.08 | $10,002 |

Best finish for 1989: T-28th at the Chattanooga Classic

| 1990 | 1 | 2 | 0 | 0 | 0 | 0 | 0 | 74.00 | |
| 1991 | 25 | 72 | 11 | 0 | 1 | 1 | 1 | 71.90 | $58,036 |

Best finish for 1991: T-5th at the New England Classic

1992	3	6	0	0	0	0	0	73.67	$1,000
Period Totals	Starts	Rounds Played	Cuts Made	Wins	Top-5s	Top-10s	Top-25s	Scoring Average	Money
	57	147	17	0	1	1	1	72.63	$71,687

Steve Bowman

Year	Starts	Rounds Played	Cuts Made	Wins	Top-5s	Top-10s	Top-25s	Scoring Average	Money
1985	21	61	10	0	0	1	3	72.30	$26,549

Best finish for 1985: T-8th at the Pensacola Open

| 1986 | 19 | 54 | 8 | 0 | 0 | 0 | 1 | 72.09 | $15,836 |

Best finish for 1986: T-14th at the Deposit Guaranty Golf Classic

| 1987 | 2 | 8 | 2 | 0 | 0 | 0 | 1 | 69.88 | $7,879 |

Best finish for 1987: T-13th at the Southwest Golf Classic

| 1988 | 2 | 8 | 2 | 0 | 0 | 0 | 0 | 72.75 | $5,274 |

Best finish for 1988: T-59th at the U.S. Open

1989	1	2	0	0	0	0	0	73.50	$1,000
2001	1	2	0	0	0	0	0	74.50	
Period Totals	Starts	Rounds Played	Cuts Made	Wins	Top-5s	Top-10s	Top-25s	Scoring Average	Money
	46	135	22	0	0	1	5	72.15	$56,537

Bob Boyd

Year	Starts	Rounds Played	Cuts Made	Wins	Top-5s	Top-10s	Top-25s	Scoring Average	Money
1980	1	4	1	0	0	0	0	72.75	$560

Best finish for 1980: T-57th at the Hall of Fame Tournament

| 1983 | 36 | 102 | 14 | 0 | 0 | 1 | 3 | 72.95 | $35,511 |

Best finish for 1983: T-6th at the Houston Coca-Cola Open

| 1984 | 33 | 93 | 13 | 0 | 0 | 0 | 1 | 73.31 | $20,235 |

Best finish for 1984: T-15th at the Walt Disney World Golf Classic

1985	3	6	0	0	0	0	0	76.00	
1987	1	2	0	0	0	0	0	76.50	
1988	2	4	0	0	0	0	0	77.25	$1,000
1989	5	12	1	0	0	0	0	73.83	$9,100

Best finish for 1989: 36th at the NEC World Series of Golf

| 1990 | 3 | 8 | 1 | 0 | 0 | 0 | 1 | 74.38 | $15,000 |

Best finish for 1990: T-19th at the PGA Championship

1991	2	4	0	0	0	0	0	73.25	$1,000
1993	1	2	0	0	0	0	0	73.50	$1,200
1994	3	8	1	0	0	0	0	72.50	$8,458

Best finish for 1994: T-30th at the PGA Championship

Year	Starts	Rounds Played	Cuts Made	Wins	Top-5s	Top-10s	Top-25s	Scoring Average	Money
1995	2	6	1	0	0	0	0	72.00	$5,400

Best finish for 1995: T-41st at the Kmart Greater Greensboro Open

| 1996 | 2 | 8 | 2 | 0 | 0 | 0 | 0 | 71.75 | $7,699 |

Best finish for 1996: T-52nd at the PGA Championship

1997	1	2	0	0	0	0	0	73.50	$1,300
1998	1	2	0	0	0	0	0	75.50	$1,500
1999	1	2	0	0	0	0	0	74.50	$1,750
2000	1	2	0	0	0	0	0	74.50	$2,000
2001	1	2	0	0	0	0	0	73.00	
2002	1	2	0	0	0	0	0	72.50	
2005	1	2	0	0	0	0	0	76.50	
Period Totals	Starts	Rounds Played	Cuts Made	Wins	Top-5s	Top-10s	Top-25s	Scoring Average	Money
	101	273	34	0	0	1	5	73.32	$111,713

Frank Boynton

Year	Starts	Rounds Played	Cuts Made	Wins	Top-5s	Top-10s	Top-25s	Scoring Average	Money
1958	15	45	7	0	0	0	0	73.51	$051

Best finish for 1958: T-29th at the Rubber City Open

| 1960 | 9 | 36 | 9 | 0 | 0 | 1 | 4 | 71.61 | $2,367 |

Best finish for 1960: T-10th at the Sam Snead Festival

| 1961 | 17 | 68 | 17 | 0 | 1 | 3 | 10 | 70.82 | $8,596 |

Best finish for 1961: T-5th at the Insurance City Open Invitational

| 1962 | 19 | 76 | 18 | 0 | 1 | 2 | 10 | 72.11 | $10,398 |

Best finish for 1962: T-2nd at the St Petersburg Open Invitational

| 1963 | 14 | 56 | 13 | 0 | 0 | 1 | 4 | 72.21 | $6,193 |

Best finish for 1963: T-7th at the Tucson Open Invitational

| 1964 | 1 | 4 | 1 | 0 | 0 | 0 | 0 | 70.75 | $235 |

Best finish for 1964: T-45th at the St. Paul Open

| 1965 | 3 | 8 | 1 | 0 | 0 | 0 | 0 | 74.50 | |

Best finish for 1965: T-46th at the Tucson Open

| 1966 | 4 | 12 | 2 | 0 | 0 | 0 | 1 | 72.08 | $1,731 |

Best finish for 1966: T-22nd at the PGA Championship

| 1967 | 16 | 59 | 13 | 0 | 0 | 0 | 4 | 72.49 | $8,615 |

Best finish for 1967: T-11th at the Bob Hope Classic

| 1968 | 31 | 105 | 21 | 0 | 2 | 4 | 11 | 71.83 | $34,483 |

Best finish for 1968: T-2nd at the Tucson Open Invitational

| 1969 | 30 | 99 | 20 | 0 | 0 | 0 | 7 | 72.09 | $13,611 |

Best finish for 1969: T-14th at the Greater Jacksonville Open

| 1970 | 1 | 4 | 1 | 0 | 0 | 0 | 0 | 73.00 | $250 |

Best finish for 1970: T-67th at the Cleveland Open

| 1972 | 1 | 4 | 1 | 0 | 0 | 0 | 0 | 74.00 | $240 |

Best finish for 1972: T-71st at the Tucson Open

1973	1	2	0	0	0	0	0	75.00	
1974	1	2	0	0	0	0	0	75.00	
1975	1	2	0	0	0	0	0	74.00	
1978	1	4	1	0	0	0	0	74.00	$350

Best finish for 1978: 65th at the Joe Garagiola Tucson Open

| Period Totals | Starts | Rounds Played | Cuts Made | Wins | Top-5s | Top-10s | Top-25s | Scoring Average | Money |
| | 165 | 586 | 125 | 0 | 4 | 11 | 51 | 72.11 | $87,120 |

Michael Bradley

Year	Starts	Rounds Played	Cuts Made	Wins	Top-5s	Top-10s	Top-25s	Scoring Average	Money
1988	2	6	1	0	0	0	0	71.50	$1,664

Best finish for 1988: T-50th at the Buick Open

1990	1	2	0	0	0	0	0	77.00	$1,000
1992	1	2	0	0	0	0	0	74.00	$1,000
1993	26	79	14	0	1	1	3	72.06	$126,160

Best finish for 1993: T-3rd at the Kemper Open

| 1994 | 29 | 89 | 15 | 0 | 1 | 3 | 4 | 71.00 | $176,137 |

Best finish for 1994: T-4th at the Anheuser-Busch Golf Classic

| 1995 | 27 | 88 | 18 | 0 | 0 | 2 | 6 | 70.97 | $214,469 |

Best finish for 1995: T-8th at the Honda Classic & Canon Greater Hartford Open

| 1996 | 26 | 87 | 20 | 1 | 4 | 6 | 11 | 70.34 | $820,825 |

Best finish for 1996: Win at the Buick Challenge

| 1997 | 28 | 88 | 17 | 0 | 2 | 3 | 8 | 71.20 | $471,887 |

Best finish for 1997: T-2nd at the Honda Classic

| 1998 | 22 | 70 | 13 | 1 | 1 | 2 | 5 | 71.59 | $576,501 |

Best finish for 1998: Win at the Doral-Ryder Open

| 1999 | 27 | 74 | 14 | 0 | 0 | 1 | 4 | 72.28 | $257,525 |

Best finish for 1999: T-10th at the Greater Milwaukee Open

| 2000 | 26 | 73 | 10 | 0 | 0 | 1 | 1 | 71.40 | $179,510 |

Best finish for 2000: T-9th at the Michelob Championship at Kingsmill

Year	Starts	Rounds Played	Cuts Made	Wins	Top-5s	Top-10s	Top-25s	Scoring Average	Money
2001	7	22	4	0	0	0	1	70.73	$47,885

Best finish for 2001: T-17th at the B.C. Open

| 2002 | 7 | 20 | 3 | 0 | 0 | 0 | 0 | 72.05 | $18,363 |

Best finish for 2002: T-59th at the Tampa Bay Classic presented by Buick

| 2003 | 4 | 10 | 1 | 0 | 0 | 0 | 1 | 72.70 | $49,500 |

Best finish for 2003: T-16th at the B.C. Open

| 2004 | 9 | 22 | 3 | 0 | 0 | 0 | 1 | 72.27 | $106,336 |

Best finish for 2004: T-13th at the FedEx St. Jude Classic

| 2005 | 4 | 12 | 2 | 0 | 0 | 0 | 0 | 71.00 | $25,254 |

Best finish for 2005: T-31st at the B.C. Open

| 2006 | 6 | 15 | 2 | 0 | 0 | 0 | 1 | 71.80 | $41,790 |

Best finish for 2006: T-20th at the B.C. Open

| 2007 | 8 | 22 | 3 | 0 | 0 | 0 | 0 | 72.05 | $31,889 |

Best finish for 2007: T-46th at the U.S. Bank Championship in Milwaukee

| 2008 | 14 | 40 | 6 | 0 | 0 | 0 | 1 | 71.08 | $138,454 |

Best finish for 2008: T-25th at the Children's Miracle Network Classic

Period Totals	Starts	Rounds Played	Cuts Made	Wins	Top-5s	Top-10s	Top-25s	Scoring Average	Money
	274	821	146	2	9	19	47	71.40	$3,286,150

Michael Brannan

Year	Starts	Rounds Played	Cuts Made	Wins	Top-5s	Top-10s	Top-25s	Scoring Average	Money
1978	1	2	0	0	0	0	0	81.00	$1,500
1979	27	81	13	0	2	5	6	72.36	$76,467

Best finish for 1979: 2nd at the Houston Open

| 1980 | 30 | 88 | 13 | 0 | 0 | 1 | 2 | 73.47 | $19,798 |

Best finish for 1980: T-9th at the Byron Nelson Golf Classic

| 1981 | 18 | 49 | 6 | 0 | 0 | 1 | 1 | 73.49 | $13,818 |

Best finish for 1981: 6th at the Joe Garagiola Tucson Open

| 1982 | 28 | 78 | 11 | 0 | 1 | 1 | 4 | 72.67 | $23,893 |

Best finish for 1982: T-5th at the B.C. Open

| 1983 | 26 | 74 | 9 | 0 | 0 | 0 | 0 | 72.97 | $9,334 |

Best finish for 1983: T-36th at the Houston Coca-Cola Open

1984	1	2	0	0	0	0	0	72.50	
Period Totals	Starts	Rounds Played	Cuts Made	Wins	Top-5s	Top-10s	Top-25s	Scoring Average	Money
	131	374	52	0	3	8	13	73.00	$144,810

David Branshaw

Year	Starts	Rounds Played	Cuts Made	Wins	Top-5s	Top-10s	Top-25s	Scoring Average	Money
2004	30	82	11	0	0	0	2	71.72	$293,617

Best finish for 2004: T-14th at the EDS Byron Nelson Championship & Bell Canadian Open

| 2006 | 29 | 98 | 20 | 0 | 1 | 2 | 7 | 70.79 | $706,346 |

Best finish for 2006: T-4th at the B.C. Open

| 2007 | 30 | 83 | 10 | 0 | 1 | 1 | 2 | 72.34 | $323,407 |

Best finish for 2007: T-5th at the Viking Classic

Period Totals	Starts	Rounds Played	Cuts Made	Wins	Top-5s	Top-10s	Top-25s	Scoring Average	Money
	89	263	41	0	2	3	11	71.57	$1,323,370

Bill Brask, Jr.

Year	Starts	Rounds Played	Cuts Made	Wins	Top-5s	Top-10s	Top-25s	Scoring Average	Money
1964	1	1	0	0	0	0	0	69.00	
1970	20	59	9	0	0	0	3	72.78	$4,257

Best finish for 1970: T-20th at the Green Island Open Invitational

| 1971 | 17 | 47 | 6 | 0 | 0 | 0 | 0 | 73.53 | $2,521 |

Best finish for 1971: T-32nd at the Bob Hope Chrysler Classic

| 1972 | 7 | 20 | 2 | 0 | 0 | 0 | 0 | 74.70 | $500 |

Best finish for 1972: T-53rd at the Hawaiian Open

1973	1	2	0	0	0	0	0	80.50	$500
1974	1	2	0	0	0	0	0	79.50	$500
1975	1	4	1	0	0	0	0	73.75	$407

Best finish for 1975: T-47th at the British Open

| 1976 | 8 | 23 | 3 | 0 | 0 | 0 | 0 | 73.39 | $1,200 |

Best finish for 1976: T-34th at the San Antonio Texas Open

| 1977 | 6 | 11 | 0 | 0 | 0 | 0 | 0 | 75.36 | |
| 1978 | 1 | 4 | 1 | 0 | 0 | 0 | 0 | 76.00 | $1,240 |

Best finish for 1978: T-57th at the U.S. Open

| 1980 | 1 | 4 | 1 | 0 | 0 | 0 | 0 | 72.75 | $1,440 |

Best finish for 1980: T-38th at the British Open

| 1984 | 1 | 4 | 1 | 0 | 0 | 0 | 0 | 75.50 | $5,800 |

Best finish for 1984: 41st at the NEC World Series of Golf

Period Totals	Starts	Rounds Played	Cuts Made	Wins	Top-5s	Top-10s	Top-25s	Scoring Average	Money
	65	181	24	0	0	0	3	73.71	$18,365

Alan Bratton

Year	Starts	Rounds Played	Cuts Made	Wins	Top-5s	Top-10s	Top-25s	Scoring Average	Money
1995	1	2	0	0	0	0	0	71.00	
1996	3	6	0	0	0	0	0	73.00	
1999	31	72	6	0	0	0	2	72.60	$80,998

Best finish for 1999: T-15th at the Nissan Open

Period Totals	Starts	Rounds Played	Cuts Made	Wins	Top-5s	Top-10s	Top-25s	Scoring Average	Money
	35	80	6	0	0	0	2	72.59	$80,998

Jeff Brehaut

Year	Starts	Rounds Played	Cuts Made	Wins	Top-5s	Top-10s	Top-25s	Scoring Average	Money
1999	28	77	12	0	0	1	1	72.29	$126,353

Best finish for 1999: T-8th at the Westin Texas Open

| 2000 | 1 | 2 | 0 | 0 | 0 | 0 | 0 | 74.00 | |
| 2001 | 26 | 77 | 14 | 0 | 0 | 0 | 2 | 71.57 | $175,046 |

Best finish for 2001: T-21st at the BellSouth Classic

| 2002 | 29 | 87 | 14 | 0 | 0 | 1 | 1 | 71.20 | $274,335 |

Best finish for 2002: T-7th at the SEI Pennsylvania Classic

| 2003 | 32 | 107 | 22 | 0 | 1 | 2 | 4 | 70.67 | $649,919 |

Best finish for 2003: T-5th at the Chrysler Classic of Greensboro

| 2004 | 34 | 104 | 17 | 0 | 0 | 1 | 4 | 71.53 | $448,914 |

Best finish for 2004: T-8th at the Chrysler Classic of Greensboro

| 2005 | 23 | 67 | 13 | 0 | 2 | 5 | 8 | 70.54 | $1,271,061 |

Best finish for 2005: 3rd at the International

| 2006 | 33 | 96 | 16 | 0 | 1 | 2 | 4 | 71.38 | $558,594 |

Best finish for 2006: T-5th at the Reno-Tahoe Open

| 2007 | 21 | 59 | 8 | 0 | 0 | 0 | 2 | 71.92 | $202,390 |

Best finish for 2007: T-17th at the U.S. Open

Period Totals	Starts	Rounds Played	Cuts Made	Wins	Top-5s	Top-10s	Top-25s	Scoring Average	Money
	227	676	116	0	4	12	26	71.36	$3,706,610

Gay Brewer

Year	Starts	Rounds Played	Cuts Made	Wins	Top-5s	Top-10s	Top-25s	Scoring Average	Money
1958	35	124	26	0	3	3	13	72.02	$8,670

Best finish for 1958: 3rd at the Los Angeles Open

| 1959 | 15 | 57 | 13 | 0 | 2 | 3 | 9 | 71.47 | $4,631 |

Best finish for 1959: T-2nd at the West Palm Beach Open Invitational

| 1960 | 17 | 68 | 15 | 0 | 2 | 5 | 13 | 71.29 | $12,024 |

Best finish for 1960: T-2nd at the Azalea Open Invitational

| 1961 | 23 | 90 | 19 | 3 | 11 | 12 | 19 | 69.84 | $31,150 |

Best finish for 1961: Win at the Carling Open Invitational, Mobile Sertoma Open Invitational & West Palm Beach Open Invitational

| 1962 | 24 | 94 | 23 | 0 | 2 | 6 | 20 | 70.94 | $21,987 |

Best finish for 1962: 2nd at the Cajun Classic Open Invitational

| 1963 | 22 | 84 | 19 | 1 | 2 | 3 | 12 | 71.51 | $20,568 |

Best finish for 1963: Win at the Waco Turner Open Invitational

| 1964 | 27 | 102 | 23 | 0 | 5 | 10 | 16 | 71.53 | $30,702 |

Best finish for 1964: T-2nd at the Bing Crosby Pro-Am & Cajun Classic

| 1965 | 30 | 96 | 16 | 2 | 2 | 3 | 8 | 72.81 | $27,738 |

Best finish for 1965: Win at the Seattle Open & Hawaiian Open

| 1966 | 29 | 114 | 27 | 1 | 6 | 10 | 18 | 71.48 | $77,099 |

Best finish for 1966: Win at the Pensacola Open Invitational

| 1967 | 24 | 93 | 22 | 2 | 5 | 5 | 14 | 71.26 | $78,995 |

Best finish for 1967: Win at the Pensacola Open & The Masters

| 1968 | 25 | 98 | 23 | 0 | 1 | 4 | 14 | 71.62 | $29,789 |

Best finish for 1968: T-5th at the Memphis Open Invitational

| 1969 | 28 | 97 | 21 | 0 | 4 | 7 | 13 | 71.53 | $59,738 |

Best finish for 1969: T-2nd at the Philadelphia Classic & Danny Thomas-Diplomat Classic

| 1970 | 29 | 92 | 17 | 0 | 0 | 2 | 7 | 72.50 | $21,690 |

Best finish for 1970: 6th at the Bahama Islands Open

| 1971 | 34 | 126 | 30 | 0 | 1 | 7 | 16 | 71.61 | $51,887 |

Best finish for 1971: T-3rd at the Robinson Open Golf Classic

| 1972 | 25 | 93 | 21 | 1 | 2 | 7 | 15 | 71.49 | $80,093 |

Best finish for 1972: Win at the Canadian Open

| 1973 | 27 | 100 | 20 | 0 | 6 | 10 | 16 | 71.34 | $103,606 |

Best finish for 1973: T-2nd at the Dean Martin Tucson Open & American Golf Classic

| 1974 | 24 | 75 | 14 | 0 | 1 | 2 | 7 | 72.39 | $46,051 |

Best finish for 1974: 2nd at the American Golf Classic

| 1975 | 26 | 75 | 10 | 0 | 1 | 2 | 2 | 73.28 | $24,748 |

Best finish for 1975: 3rd at the Canadian Open

| 1976 | 32 | 113 | 28 | 0 | 0 | 0 | 11 | 71.81 | $40,656 |

Best finish for 1976: T-11th at the World Open

Year	Starts	Rounds Played	Cuts Made	Wins	Top-5s	Top-10s	Top-25s	Scoring Average	Money
1977	28	81	12	0	0	0	1	73.37	$11,318

Best finish for 1977: T-13th at the Bob Hope Chrysler Classic

Year	Starts	Rounds Played	Cuts Made	Wins	Top-5s	Top-10s	Top-25s	Scoring Average	Money
1978	21	66	12	0	0	0	0	72.82	$10,740

Best finish for 1978: T-27th at the Hawaiian Open

1979	7	21	3	0	0	0	0	73.43	$3,792

Best finish for 1979: T-35th at the Bob Hope Chrysler Classic

1980	8	21	2	0	0	0	1	74.29	$3,865

Best finish for 1980: T-25th at the Glen Campbell Los Angles Open

1981	7	20	5	0	0	0	4	71.90	$13,758

Best finish for 1981: T-15th at the Masters

1982	5	17	2	0	0	0	0	73.76	$2,274

Best finish for 1982: 45th at the Masters

1983	5	19	3	0	0	0	1	72.32	$8,279

Best finish for 1983: T-12th at the Glen Campbell Los Angles Open

1984	3	7	0	0	0	0	0	75.29	$1,500
1985	3	9	1	0	0	0	0	76.56	$2,515

Best finish for 1985: T-64th at the Bing Crosby Pro-Am

Year	Starts	Rounds Played	Cuts Made	Wins	Top-5s	Top-10s	Top-25s	Scoring Average	Money
1986	2	6	0	0	0	0	0	74.17	$1,500
1987	1	2	0	0	0	0	0	80.50	$1,500
1988	1	2	0	0	0	0	0	79.50	$1,500
1989	1	1	0	0	0	0	0	83.00	$1,500
1990	1	2	0	0	0	0	0	76.50	$1,500
1991	1	2	0	0	0	0	0	76.00	$1,500
1992	1	2	0	0	0	0	0	79.00	$1,500
1993	1	2	0	0	0	0	0	81.50	$1,500
1994	1	2	0	0	0	0	0	81.50	$1,500
1995	1	2	0	0	0	0	0	74.50	$1,500
1996	1	2	0	0	0	0	0	76.00	$1,500
1997	1	2	0	0	0	0	0	81.50	$5,000
1998	1	2	0	0	0	0	0	79.00	$5,000
1999	1	1	0	0	0	0	0	80.00	$5,000
2000	1	2	0	0	0	0	0	81.00	$5,000
2001	1	1	0	0	0	0	0	84.00	$5,000
Period Totals	**600**	**2085**	**427**	**10**	**56**	**101**	**250**	**71.97**	**$871,364**

PGA Tour career totals from 1956 to 201

	Starts	Rounds Played	Cuts Made	Wins	Top-5s	Top-10s	Top-25s	Scoring Average	Money
	630	2205	457	10	56	105	260	N/A	$877,245

Danny Briggs

Year	Starts	Rounds Played	Cuts Made	Wins	Top-5s	Top-10s	Top-25s	Scoring Average	Money
1985	2	4	0	0	0	0	0	74.00	
1986	27	78	13	0	1	1	4	72.81	$35,308

Best finish for 1986: T-3rd at the Tallahassee Open

1987	5	18	4	0	0	0	0	70.44	$4,713

Best finish for 1987: T-41st at the Byron Nelson Golf Classic

1988	24	59	5	0	0	0	0	72.88	$11,417

Best finish for 1988: T-26th at the Provident Classic

1991	1	3	0	0	0	0	0	70.67	
1992	2	6	1	0	0	0	0	71.50	$2,265

Best finish for 1992: T-52nd at the Phoenix Open

1995	4	14	3	0	0	1	2	70.14	$46,415

Best finish for 1995: T-10th at the Freeport-McMoRan Classic

1996	3	8	1	0	0	0	0	71.38	$3,720

Best finish for 1996: T-45th at the Buick Invitational

1997	1	2	0	0	0	0	0	73.00	
1999	24	76	14	0	0	1	2	71.70	$182,245

Best finish for 1999: T-8th at the Doral-Ryder Open

2000	18	47	7	0	0	0	1	71.28	$72,354

Best finish for 2000: T-24th at the Buick Classic

2001	1	2	0	0	0	0	0	72.50	
2003	1	4	1	0	0	0	0	69.75	$11,712

Best finish for 2003: T-45th at the Buick Open

2004	28	81	15	0	0	1	4	71.20	$397,606

Best finish for 2004: T-7th at the U.S. Bank Championship in Milwaukee

2005	28	68	7	0	0	1	1	72.13	$148,836

Best finish for 2005: T-9th at the Chrysler Classic of Tucson

2008	1	2	0	0	0	0	0	75.00	
Period Totals	**170**	**472**	**71**	**0**	**1**	**5**	**14**	**71.88**	**$916,591**

Mike Bright

Year	Starts	Rounds Played	Cuts Made	Wins	Top-5s	Top-10s	Top-25s	Scoring Average	Money
1983	1	2	0	0	0	0	0	75.50	
1984	6	20	4	0	0	0	2	71.40	$10,944

Best finish for 1984: T-15th at the Southern Open

1985	30	80	9	0	0	0	2	73.14	$20,905

Best finish for 1985: T-17th at the Doral-Eastern Open

Period Totals	Starts	Rounds Played	Cuts Made	Wins	Top-5s	Top-10s	Top-25s	Scoring Average	Money
	37	102	13	0	0	0	4	72.84	$31,849

D.J. Brigman

Year	Starts	Rounds Played	Cuts Made	Wins	Top-5s	Top-10s	Top-25s	Scoring Average	Money
2004	27	76	12	0	0	0	3	71.66	$356,943

Best finish for 2004: T-11th at the Shell Houston Open & Bell Canadian Open

2005	26	72	12	0	0	0	3	72.14	$294,849

Best finish for 2005: T-12th at the FedEx St. Jude Classic

2007	22	67	11	0	0	0	2	71.69	$268,205

Best finish for 2007: T-20th at the Children's Miracle network Classic

2008	1	2	0	0	0	0	0	77.00	

Period Totals	Starts	Rounds Played	Cuts Made	Wins	Top-5s	Top-10s	Top-25s	Scoring Average	Money
	76	217	35	0	0	0	8	71.88	$919,998

Stan Brion

Year	Starts	Rounds Played	Cuts Made	Wins	Top-5s	Top-10s	Top-25s	Scoring Average	Money
1965	1	4	1	0	0	0	0	72.75	

Best finish for 1965: T-53rd at the Cajun Classic

1966	4	8	0	0	0	0	0	75.25	
1967	2	4	0	0	0	0	0	75.00	
1969	2	6	1	0	0	0	0	76.00	$070

Best finish for 1969: T-44th at the West End Classic

1970	6	12	0	0	0	0	0	75.33	
1971	10	21	1	0	0	0	0	75.38	

Best finish for 1971: T-49th at the Greater Milwaukee Open

1974	4	10	1	0	0	0	1	74.70	$2,182

Best finish for 1974: T-22nd at the PGA Championship

Period Totals	Starts	Rounds Played	Cuts Made	Wins	Top-5s	Top-10s	Top-25s	Scoring Average	Money
	29	65	4	0	0	0	1	75.12	$2,252

Mike Brisky

Year	Starts	Rounds Played	Cuts Made	Wins	Top-5s	Top-10s	Top-25s	Scoring Average	Money
1989	1	2	0	0	0	0	0	76.00	$1,000
1994	14	38	6	0	0	0	2	72.13	$38,713

Best finish for 1994: T-11th at the Deposit Guaranty Golf Classic & Buick Southern Open

1995	30	87	14	0	1	1	3	72.07	$194,874

Best finish for 1995: 2nd at the Buick Open

1996	27	83	14	0	1	3	5	71.82	$260,360

Best finish for 1996: T-4th at the Motorola Western Open

1997	30	100	20	0	2	6	7	71.20	$369,412

Best finish for 1997: 3rd at the Deposit Guaranty Golf Classic

1998	31	87	13	0	1	1	4	72.16	$221,388

Best finish for 1998: T-4th at the Doral-Ryder Open

1999	25	77	13	0	1	1	3	71.88	$361,084

Best finish for 1999: 2nd at the John Deere Classic

2000	31	86	12	0	0	0	3	71.86	$204,232

Best finish for 2000: T-12th at the Honda Classic

Period Totals	Starts	Rounds Played	Cuts Made	Wins	Top-5s	Top-10s	Top-25s	Scoring Average	Money
	189	560	92	0	6	12	27	71.85	$1,651,062

Bill Britton

Year	Starts	Rounds Played	Cuts Made	Wins	Top-5s	Top-10s	Top-25s	Scoring Average	Money
1979	1	2	0	0	0	0	0	76.50	
1980	10	26	4	0	0	1	2	71.38	$9,022

Best finish for 1980: T-9th at the Quad Cities Open

1981	27	86	18	0	0	2	6	71.69	$41,678

Best finish for 1981: T-6th at the Atlanta Classic

1982	33	97	16	0	1	1	6	71.94	$76,578

Best finish for 1982: 2nd at the Disney World

1983	32	97	14	0	0	0	3	73.64	$20,492

Best finish for 1983: T-18th at the Glen Campbell Los Angles Open

1984	31	94	15	0	0	0	3	73.26	$28,149

Best finish for 1984: T-15th at the B.C. Open

Year	Starts	Rounds Played	Cuts Made	Wins	Top-5s	Top-10s	Top-25s	Scoring Average	Money
1985	18	40	3	0	0	0	0	73.60	$3,245

Best finish for 1985: T-53rd at the Canadian Open

1987	30	86	16	0	0	0	4	71.74	$46,539

Best finish for 1987: T-16th at the Kemper Open

| 1988 | 31 | 96 | 19 | 0 | 0 | 1 | 9 | 71.30 | $111,781 |

Best finish for 1988: T-6th at the Provident Classic

| 1989 | 31 | 107 | 24 | 1 | 2 | 3 | 6 | 70.78 | $308,978 |

Best finish for 1989: Win at the Centel Classic

| 1990 | 30 | 99 | 20 | 0 | 2 | 3 | 9 | 71.59 | $278,977 |

Best finish for 1990: T-3rd at the Hardee's Golf Classic

| 1991 | 30 | 96 | 18 | 0 | 3 | 5 | 8 | 70.68 | $286,394 |

Best finish for 1991: T-3rd at the Kemper Open & H-E-B Texas Open

| 1992 | 26 | 84 | 18 | 0 | 2 | 6 | 9 | 70.68 | $391,700 |

Best finish for 1992: 2nd at the Northern Telecom Open

| 1993 | 30 | 89 | 14 | 0 | 0 | 0 | 3 | 71.54 | $75,748 |

Best finish for 1993: T-17th at the Shell Houston Open

| 1994 | 22 | 68 | 12 | 0 | 0 | 0 | 2 | 71.54 | $69,033 |

Best finish for 1994: T-13th at the Greater Milwaukee Open

| 1995 | 24 | 67 | 9 | 0 | 0 | 1 | 1 | 71.81 | $74,562 |

Best finish for 1995: 6th at the Honda Classic

| 1996 | 8 | 20 | 2 | 0 | 0 | 0 | 0 | 73.05 | $4,398 |

Best finish for 1996: T-51st at the Greater Vancouver Open

1997	2	4	0	0	0	0	0	74.50	
1999	1	2	0	0	0	0	0	73.50	
2004	2	4	0	0	0	0	0	72.75	$2,000
Period Totals	419	1264	222	1	10	23	71	71.81	$1,829,273

Steve Brodie

Year	Starts	Rounds Played	Cuts Made	Wins	Top-5s	Top-10s	Top-25s	Scoring Average	Money
1989	1	2	0	0	0	0	0	77.00	
1994	29	87	15	0	0	1	4	71.70	$112,081

Best finish for 1994: T-7th at the Freeport-McMoRan Classic

| 1995 | 8 | 21 | 3 | 0 | 0 | 0 | 0 | 72.76 | $11,461 |

Best finish for 1995: T-29th at the Buick Classic

Period Totals	Starts	Rounds Played	Cuts Made	Wins	Top-5s	Top-10s	Top-25s	Scoring Average	Money
	38	110	18	0	0	1	4	72.00	$123,542

Mark Brooks

Year	Starts	Rounds Played	Cuts Made	Wins	Top-5s	Top-10s	Top-25s	Scoring Average	Money
1983	7	18	2	0	0	0	1	72.33	$6,924

Best finish for 1983: T-12th at the B.C. Open

| 1984 | 35 | 104 | 16 | 0 | 0 | 1 | 4 | 72.93 | $41,038 |

Best finish for 1984: T-10th at the Danny Thomas Memphis Classic

| 1985 | 32 | 88 | 11 | 0 | 0 | 0 | 3 | 72.61 | $32,094 |

Best finish for 1985: T-12th at the Houston Open

| 1986 | 31 | 98 | 19 | 0 | 0 | 1 | 5 | 72.10 | $47,864 |

Best finish for 1986: T-8th at the Hardee's Golf Classic

| 1987 | 32 | 93 | 17 | 0 | 0 | 0 | 2 | 72.12 | $44,540 |

Best finish for 1987: T-13th at the Southwest Golf Classic

| 1988 | 30 | 101 | 22 | 1 | 2 | 2 | 11 | 70.63 | $282,636 |

Best finish for 1988: Win at the Canon Sammy Davis, Jr. - Greater Hartford Open

| 1989 | 30 | 87 | 15 | 0 | 1 | 1 | 3 | 72.09 | $115,338 |

Best finish for 1989: T-5th at the Canadian Open

| 1990 | 33 | 113 | 23 | 0 | 4 | 5 | 10 | 71.35 | $307,948 |

Best finish for 1990: T-3rd at the Honda Classic & Memorial Tournament

| 1991 | 31 | 112 | 25 | 2 | 4 | 5 | 11 | 70.94 | $673,301 |

Best finish for 1991: Win at the Kmart Greater Greensboro Open & Greater Milwaukee Open

| 1992 | 30 | 111 | 25 | 0 | 6 | 11 | 16 | 70.52 | $639,004 |

Best finish for 1992: T-3rd at the Honda Classic, The Nestle Invitational & Greater Milwaukee Open

| 1993 | 31 | 95 | 19 | 0 | 1 | 3 | 10 | 71.12 | $252,396 |

Best finish for 1993: T-2nd at the Buick Southern Open

| 1994 | 34 | 116 | 24 | 1 | 1 | 4 | 9 | 70.91 | $545,735 |

Best finish for 1994: Win at the Kemper Open

| 1995 | 29 | 93 | 17 | 0 | 1 | 3 | 10 | 70.80 | $368,360 |

Best finish for 1995: T-3rd at the British Open

| 1996 | 29 | 101 | 23 | 3 | 5 | 8 | 12 | 70.74 | $1,430,896 |

Best finish for 1996: Win at the Bob Hope Chrysler Classic, Shell Houston Open & PGA Championship

| 1997 | 30 | 89 | 15 | 0 | 0 | 1 | 3 | 71.88 | $222,156 |

Best finish for 1997: T-7th at the Players Championship

| 1998 | 30 | 92 | 18 | 0 | 0 | 0 | 5 | 71.82 | $224,570 |

Best finish for 1998: T-12th at the Canon Greater Hartford Open

Year	Starts	Rounds Played	Cuts Made	Wins	Top-5s	Top-10s	Top-25s	Scoring Average	Money
1999	33	113	24	0	0	3	7	71.84	$558,037

Best finish for 1999: T-9th at the Nissan Open & The Reno-Tahoe Open

| 2000 | 29 | 88 | 16 | 0 | 1 | 3 | 4 | 71.26 | $533,631 |

Best finish for 2000: T-5th at the Shell Houston Open

| 2001 | 27 | 88 | 16 | 0 | 1 | 2 | 5 | 71.09 | $903,017 |

Best finish for 2001: 2nd at the U.S. Open

| 2002 | 32 | 93 | 16 | 0 | 2 | 2 | 5 | 71.56 | $734,671 |

Best finish for 2002: 3rd at the International presented by Quest & Tampa Bay Classic presented by Buick

| 2003 | 31 | 87 | 14 | 0 | 0 | 0 | 2 | 71.74 | $238,489 |

Best finish for 2003: T-18th at the Las Vegas Invitational

| 2004 | 31 | 70 | 5 | 0 | 0 | 1 | 2 | 72.51 | $267,076 |

Best finish for 2004: T-9th at the Bank of America Colonial

| 2005 | 28 | 72 | 10 | 0 | 0 | 1 | 2 | 72.17 | $275,668 |

Best finish for 2005: T-10th at the EDS Byron Nelson Championship

| 2006 | 36 | 89 | 9 | 0 | 0 | 0 | 2 | 72.02 | $212,208 |

Best finish for 2006: T-15th at the B.C. Open

| 2007 | 18 | 53 | 7 | 0 | 0 | 0 | 1 | 71.62 | $165,339 |

Best finish for 2007: T-13th at the Mayakoba Golf Classic

| 2008 | 17 | 48 | 6 | 0 | 0 | 0 | 0 | 71.81 | $99,582 |

Best finish for 2008: T-30th at the Wyndham Championship

Period Totals	Starts	Rounds Played	Cuts Made	Wins	Top-5s	Top-10s	Top-25s	Scoring Average	Money
	756	2312	414	7	29	57	145	71.57	$9,222,518

Billy Ray Brown

Year	Starts	Rounds Played	Cuts Made	Wins	Top-5s	Top-10s	Top-25s	Scoring Average	Money
1983	1	2	0	0	0	0	0	77.00	
1986 Billy Ray Brown	1	2	0	0	0	0	0	76.00	
1987	2	2	1	0	0	0	0	73.00	$3,000

Best finish for 1987: T-43rd at the The International

| 1988 | 29 | 96 | 20 | 0 | 1 | 1 | 5 | 71.10 | $82,106 |

Best finish for 1988: T-3rd at the Provident Classic

| 1989 | 28 | 92 | 20 | 0 | 1 | 1 | 5 | 70.93 | $163,964 |

Best finish for 1989: T-2nd at the Kemper Open

| 1990 | 26 | 83 | 18 | 0 | 4 | 6 | 6 | 71.30 | $313,466 |

Best finish for 1990: T-3rd at the Phoenix Open, Honda Classic & U.S. Open

| 1991 | 29 | 94 | 19 | 1 | 2 | 2 | 8 | 71.76 | $348,082 |

Best finish for 1991: Win at the Canon Greater Hartford Open

| 1992 | 24 | 77 | 16 | 1 | 3 | 3 | 10 | 71.22 | $487,351 |

Best finish for 1992: Win at the GTE Byron Nelson Classic

| 1993 | 14 | 42 | 7 | 0 | 1 | 1 | 1 | 72.88 | $175,162 |

Best finish for 1993: 2nd at the AT&T Pebble Beach Pro-Am

| 1994 | 27 | 56 | 2 | 0 | 0 | 0 | 0 | 74.70 | $4,254 |

Best finish for 1994: T-65th at the GTE Byron Nelson Classic

| 1995 | 24 | 65 | 9 | 0 | 0 | 0 | 2 | 72.20 | $57,111 |

Best finish for 1995: T-15th at the Ideon Classic

| 1996 | 26 | 77 | 15 | 0 | 0 | 0 | 1 | 71.94 | $67,203 |

Best finish for 1996: T-22nd at the LaCantera Texas Open

| 1997 | 24 | 70 | 11 | 1 | 1 | 1 | 3 | 71.84 | $270,009 |

Best finish for 1997: Win at the Deposit Guaranty Golf Classic

| 1998 | 25 | 64 | 8 | 0 | 0 | 0 | 0 | 72.66 | $68,724 |

Best finish for 1998: T-27th at the Deposit Guaranty Golf Classic

| 1999 | 17 | 41 | 3 | 0 | 1 | 1 | 1 | 73.39 | $301,472 |

Best finish for 1999: 2nd at the Buick Invitational

2000	4	8	0	0	0	0	0	75.38	
2001	9	19	0	0	0	0	0	79.32	
2002	2	4	0	0	0	0	0	80.75	
Period Totals	Starts	Rounds Played	Cuts Made	Wins	Top-5s	Top-10s	Top-25s	Scoring Average	Money
	312	894	149	3	14	16	42	72.20	$2,341,905

Cliff Brown

Year	Starts	Rounds Played	Cuts Made	Wins	Top-5s	Top-10s	Top-25s	Scoring Average	Money
1964	19	54	7	0	1	1	1	73.02	$3,365

Best finish for 1964: T-5th at the "500" Festival Open

| 1965 | 12 | 29 | 3 | 0 | 0 | 0 | 1 | 74.93 | $895 |

Best finish for 1965: T-16th at the Azalea Open

| 1966 | 18 | 50 | 7 | 0 | 0 | 0 | 1 | 73.90 | $1,638 |

Best finish for 1966: T-18th at the Greater Seattle-Everett Open Invitational

| 1967 | 16 | 48 | 8 | 0 | 0 | 0 | 2 | 73.52 | $2,644 |

Best finish for 1967: T-19th at the Insurance City Open

| 1968 | 19 | 59 | 11 | 0 | 0 | 0 | 1 | 73.37 | $938 |

Best finish for 1968: T-21st at the Rebel Yell Open

| 1969 | 14 | 35 | 5 | 0 | 0 | 0 | 0 | 73.17 | $2,433 |

Best finish for 1969: T-27th at the Citrus Open

Year	Starts	Rounds Played	Cuts Made	Wins	Top-5s	Top-10s	Top-25s	Scoring Average	Money
1970	2	3	0	0	0	0	0	73.67	
1972	2	6	1	0	0	0	0	74.83	$200

Best finish for 1972: T-69th at the Greater Jacksonville Open

Period Totals	Starts	Rounds Played	Cuts Made	Wins	Top-5s	Top-10s	Top-25s	Scoring Average	Money
	102	284	42	0	1	1	6	73.59	$12,112

Ken Brown

Year	Starts	Rounds Played	Cuts Made	Wins	Top-5s	Top-10s	Top-25s	Scoring Average	Money
1976	1	2	0	0	0	0	0	78.50	$180
1977	1	4	1	0	0	0	0	72.50	$646

Best finish for 1977: T-34th at the British Open

| 1978 | 4 | 10 | 1 | 0 | 0 | 0 | 0 | 73.50 | $855 |

Best finish for 1978: T-34th at the British Open

| 1979 | 4 | 10 | 1 | 0 | 0 | 0 | 1 | 74.60 | $3,801 |

Best finish for 1979: T-19th at the British Open

| 1980 | 4 | 13 | 3 | 0 | 0 | 1 | 1 | 72.54 | $22,590 |

Best finish for 1980: T-6th at the British Open

| 1981 | 3 | 12 | 3 | 0 | 0 | 0 | 0 | 73.17 | $2,309 |

Best finish for 1981: T-44th at the British Open

| 1982 | 1 | 4 | 1 | 0 | 0 | 0 | 1 | 73.00 | $4,930 |

Best finish for 1982: 19th at the British Open

| 1983 | 1 | 2 | 0 | 0 | 0 | 0 | 0 | 74.00 | $375 |
| 1984 | 16 | 57 | 12 | 0 | 1 | 1 | 4 | 71.49 | $56,402 |

Best finish for 1984: T-2nd at the Pensacola Open

| 1985 | 24 | 82 | 16 | 0 | 0 | 0 | 7 | 71.70 | $59,682 |

Best finish for 1985: T-12th at the Texas Open & Pensacola Open

| 1986 | 25 | 78 | 18 | 0 | 0 | 2 | 6 | 71.83 | $79,928 |

Best finish for 1986: T-6th at the AT&T Pebble Beach Pro-Am

| 1987 | 20 | 67 | 15 | 1 | 2 | 6 | 9 | 71.37 | $246,287 |

Best finish for 1987: Win at the Southern Open

| 1988 | 21 | 70 | 15 | 0 | 1 | 1 | 3 | 71.77 | $87,986 |

Best finish for 1988: T-5th at the Phoenix Open

| 1989 | 7 | 16 | 0 | 0 | 0 | 0 | 0 | 73.88 | $800 |

Period Totals	Starts	Rounds Played	Cuts Made	Wins	Top-5s	Top-10s	Top-25s	Scoring Average	Money
	132	427	86	1	4	11	32	71.98	$566,771

Pete Brown

Year	Starts	Rounds Played	Cuts Made	Wins	Top-5s	Top-10s	Top-25s	Scoring Average	Money
1963	2	8	2	0	0	0	1	71.38	$920

Best finish for 1963: T-18th at the St. Paul Open Invitational

| 1964 | 31 | 105 | 21 | 0 | 3 | 3 | 9 | 72.28 | $18,978 |

Best finish for 1964: T-2nd at the Sunset-Camellia Open & Almaden Open

| 1965 | 22 | 74 | 16 | 0 | 0 | 3 | 3 | 72.50 | $10,454 |

Best finish for 1965: T-9th at the Texas Open, Thunderbird Classic & Hawaiian Open

| 1966 | 24 | 81 | 15 | 0 | 1 | 1 | 1 | 73.04 | $5,987 |

Best finish for 1966: 3rd at the Portland Open Invitational

| 1967 | 22 | 72 | 13 | 0 | 0 | 1 | 3 | 73.14 | $7,005 |

Best finish for 1967: T-6th at the San Diego Open

| 1968 | 23 | 61 | 9 | 0 | 1 | 1 | 2 | 73.44 | $7,527 |

Best finish for 1968: T-4th at the Minnesota Golf Classic

| 1969 | 34 | 109 | 22 | 0 | 1 | 2 | 6 | 72.35 | $19,486 |

Best finish for 1969: T-5th at the Atlanta Classic

| 1970 | 38 | 130 | 28 | 1 | 1 | 3 | 7 | 72.43 | $52,739 |

Best finish for 1970: Win at the Andy Williams-San Diego Open

| 1971 | 34 | 102 | 20 | 0 | 2 | 4 | 8 | 72.36 | $38,804 |

Best finish for 1971: T-2nd at the Monsanto Open

| 1972 | 19 | 45 | 4 | 0 | 0 | 0 | 0 | 74.69 | $1,639 |

Best finish for 1972: T-35th at the Greater Hartford Open Invitational

| 1973 | 32 | 110 | 21 | 0 | 0 | 0 | 5 | 72.44 | $16,845 |

Best finish for 1973: T-19th at the Westchester Classic

| 1974 | 23 | 57 | 5 | 0 | 0 | 0 | 1 | 73.47 | $2,138 |

Best finish for 1974: T-25th at the Tallahassee Open

| 1975 | 21 | 56 | 7 | 0 | 0 | 1 | 1 | 73.80 | $3,073 |

Best finish for 1975: T-8th at the Tallahassee Open

| 1976 | 18 | 41 | 4 | 0 | 0 | 0 | 1 | 73.20 | $5,345 |

Best finish for 1976: T-11th at the Glen Campbell Los Angles Open

| 1977 | 24 | 71 | 12 | 0 | 0 | 0 | 0 | 72.87 | $5,256 |

Best finish for 1977: T-28th at the Ohio Kings Island Open

| 1978 | 20 | 45 | 4 | 0 | 0 | 0 | 0 | 74.07 | $1,505 |

Best finish for 1978: T-45th at the Florida Citrus Open Invitational

| 1979 | 13 | 26 | 1 | 0 | 0 | 0 | 0 | 75.00 | $488 |

Best finish for 1979: T-72nd at the Andy Williams-San Diego Open

Year	Starts	Rounds Played	Cuts Made	Wins	Top-5s	Top-10s	Top-25s	Scoring Average	Money
1980	6	13	1	0	0	0	0	75.77	$495

Best finish for 1980: T-70th at the Andy Williams-San Diego Open

Year	Starts	Rounds Played	Cuts Made	Wins	Top-5s	Top-10s	Top-25s	Scoring Average	Money
1981	8	17	2	0	0	0	0	73.76	$1,044

Best finish for 1981: T-55th at the Tallahassee Open

Year	Starts	Rounds Played	Cuts Made	Wins	Top-5s	Top-10s	Top-25s	Scoring Average	Money
1983	3	6	0	0	0	0	0	75.00	
1984	1	2	0	0	0	0	0	76.00	
1985	1	2	0	0	0	0	0	77.00	
Period Totals	Starts	Rounds Played	Cuts Made	Wins	Top-5s	Top-10s	Top-25s	Scoring Average	Money
	419	1233	207	1	9	19	48	72.97	$199,727

Olin Browne

Year	Starts	Rounds Played	Cuts Made	Wins	Top-5s	Top-10s	Top-25s	Scoring Average	Money
1983	1	2	0	0	0	0	0	78.00	
1986	1	2	0	0	0	0	0	72.00	
1988	1	2	0	0	0	0	0	74.00	
1989	1	2	0	0	0	0	0	77.00	
1990	1	2	0	0	0	0	0	76.00	
1991	1	2	0	0	0	0	0	72.00	
1992	30	90	14	0	1	1	1	71.96	$84,153

Best finish for 1992: T-4th at the Northern Telecom Open

Year	Starts	Rounds Played	Cuts Made	Wins	Top-5s	Top-10s	Top-25s	Scoring Average	Money
1993	2	6	1	0	0	0	0	73.33	$2,738

Best finish for 1993: T-58th at the AT&T Pebble Beach National Pro-Am

Year	Starts	Rounds Played	Cuts Made	Wins	Top-5s	Top-10s	Top-25s	Scoring Average	Money
1994	31	91	15	0	0	1	2	72.09	$101,580

Best finish for 1994: 6th at the Northern Telecom Open

Year	Starts	Rounds Played	Cuts Made	Wins	Top-5s	Top-10s	Top-25s	Scoring Average	Money
1996	27	94	20	0	0	3	7	70.95	$223,703

Best finish for 1996: T-7th at the Buick Open & Greater Milwaukee Open

Year	Starts	Rounds Played	Cuts Made	Wins	Top-5s	Top-10s	Top-25s	Scoring Average	Money
1997	33	101	19	0	1	2	5	71.83	$261,810

Best finish for 1997: T-5th at the U.S. Open

Year	Starts	Rounds Played	Cuts Made	Wins	Top-5s	Top-10s	Top-25s	Scoring Average	Money
1998	25	77	15	1	1	2	7	71.48	$595,240

Best finish for 1998: Win at the Canon Greater Hartford Open

Year	Starts	Rounds Played	Cuts Made	Wins	Top-5s	Top-10s	Top-25s	Scoring Average	Money
1999	26	80	16	1	2	3	4	72.08	$835,331

Best finish for 1999: Win at the MasterCard Colonial

Year	Starts	Rounds Played	Cuts Made	Wins	Top-5s	Top-10s	Top-25s	Scoring Average	Money
2000	31	99	21	0	0	1	7	70.98	$494,307

Best finish for 2000: T-9th at the Greater Milwaukee Open

Year	Starts	Rounds Played	Cuts Made	Wins	Top-5s	Top-10s	Top-25s	Scoring Average	Money
2001	30	96	19	0	1	3	9	70.33	$817,636

Best finish for 2001: T-3rd at the AT&T Pebble Beach National Pro-Am

Year	Starts	Rounds Played	Cuts Made	Wins	Top-5s	Top-10s	Top-25s	Scoring Average	Money
2002	33	104	20	0	1	2	6	70.70	$616,828

Best finish for 2002: T-5th at the SEI Pennsylvania Classic

Year	Starts	Rounds Played	Cuts Made	Wins	Top-5s	Top-10s	Top-25s	Scoring Average	Money
2003	34	110	22	0	0	0	6	70.74	$479,592

Best finish for 2003: T-18th at the Bank of America Colonial

Year	Starts	Rounds Played	Cuts Made	Wins	Top-5s	Top-10s	Top-25s	Scoring Average	Money
2004	30	88	15	0	1	2	7	70.78	$597,034

Best finish for 2004: T-4th at the U.S. Bank Championship in Milwaukee

Year	Starts	Rounds Played	Cuts Made	Wins	Top-5s	Top-10s	Top-25s	Scoring Average	Money
2005	29	95	20	1	2	2	11	70.43	$2,171,928

Best finish for 2005: Win at the Deutsche Bank Championship

Year	Starts	Rounds Played	Cuts Made	Wins	Top-5s	Top-10s	Top-25s	Scoring Average	Money
2006	30	104	23	0	0	2	5	71.35	$756,061

Best finish for 2006: T-8th at the Bob Hope Chrysler Classic & Southern Farm Bureau Classic

Year	Starts	Rounds Played	Cuts Made	Wins	Top-5s	Top-10s	Top-25s	Scoring Average	Money
2007	15	44	7	0	0	1	3	71.36	$304,605

Best finish for 2007: T-9th at the AT&T Classic

Year	Starts	Rounds Played	Cuts Made	Wins	Top-5s	Top-10s	Top-25s	Scoring Average	Money
2008	27	77	11	0	0	0	0	71.81	$167,029

Best finish for 2008: T-29th at the Bob Hope Chrysler Classic

Period Totals	Starts	Rounds Played	Cuts Made	Wins	Top-5s	Top-10s	Top-25s	Scoring Average	Money
	439	1368	258	3	10	25	80	71.26	$8,509,575

Greg Bruckner

Year	Starts	Rounds Played	Cuts Made	Wins	Top-5s	Top-10s	Top-25s	Scoring Average	Money
1988	1	4	1	0	0	0	0	75.50	$3,698

Best finish for 1988: T-68th at the British Open

Year	Starts	Rounds Played	Cuts Made	Wins	Top-5s	Top-10s	Top-25s	Scoring Average	Money
1990	29	85	14	0	0	0	3	71.94	$57,132

Best finish for 1990: T-14th at the H-E-B Texas Open

Year	Starts	Rounds Played	Cuts Made	Wins	Top-5s	Top-10s	Top-25s	Scoring Average	Money
1991	32	99	17	0	0	0	4	71.64	$74,858

Best finish for 1991: T-14th at the Northern Telecom Open

Year	Starts	Rounds Played	Cuts Made	Wins	Top-5s	Top-10s	Top-25s	Scoring Average	Money
1992	9	20	1	0	0	0	0	72.95	$2,200

Best finish for 1992: T-69th at the Federal Express St. Jude Classic

Year	Starts	Rounds Played	Cuts Made	Wins	Top-5s	Top-10s	Top-25s	Scoring Average	Money
1995	1	4	1	0	0	0	0	73.25	$4,834

Best finish for 1995: T-56th at the U.S. Open

Period Totals	Starts	Rounds Played	Cuts Made	Wins	Top-5s	Top-10s	Top-25s	Scoring Average	Money
	72	212	34	0	0	0	7	71.99	$142,721

Bob Brue

Year	Starts	Rounds Played	Cuts Made	Wins	Top-5s	Top-10s	Top-25s	Scoring Average	Money
1958	1	4	1	0	0	0	0	71.75	

Best finish for 1958: T-62nd at the Miller Open

Year	Starts	Rounds Played	Cuts Made	Wins	Top-5s	Top-10s	Top-25s	Scoring Average	Money
1960	4	15	4	0	0	0	3	72.60	$1,057

Best finish for 1960: T-20th at the Coral Gables Open Invitational

| 1961 | 11 | 44 | 11 | 0 | 0 | 1 | 7 | 70.91 | $4,765 |

Best finish for 1961: T-10th at the St. Petersburg Open Invitational

| 1962 | 9 | 36 | 8 | 0 | 0 | 2 | 8 | 70.67 | $4,861 |

Best finish for 1962: T-9th at the Sahara Invitational & Cajun Classic Open Invitational

| 1963 | 7 | 28 | 7 | 0 | 1 | 1 | 4 | 71.39 | $2,361 |

Best finish for 1963: T-4th at the Jamaica Open Invitational

| 1964 | 11 | 33 | 5 | 0 | 1 | 1 | 2 | 73.27 | $5,100 |

Best finish for 1964: 2nd at the Phoenix Open

| 1965 | 4 | 10 | 1 | 0 | 0 | 0 | 0 | 73.90 | $051 |

Best finish for 1965: T-41st at the Almaden Open

| 1966 | 13 | 36 | 6 | 0 | 0 | 0 | 1 | 73.33 | $2,452 |

Best finish for 1966: T-22nd at the Western Open

1967	1	2	0	0	0	0	0	79.00	
1968	2	4	0	0	0	0	0	74.50	
1969	16	51	11	0	0	2	5	73.00	$10,008

Best finish for 1969: T-6th at the Kaiser International Open

| 1970 | 8 | 29 | 6 | 0 | 0 | 1 | 2 | 72.55 | $5,334 |

Best finish for 1970: T-9th at the Western Open

| 1971 | 5 | 14 | 2 | 0 | 0 | 0 | 0 | 73.79 | $980 |

Best finish for 1971: T-61st at the Tucson Open

| 1972 | 5 | 12 | 1 | 0 | 0 | 0 | 0 | 74.75 | $835 |

Best finish for 1972: T-55th at the U.S. Open

| 1973 | 3 | 10 | 2 | 0 | 0 | 0 | 1 | 71.70 | $4,554 |

Best finish for 1973: T-12th at the PGA Championship

1974	6	11	0	0	0	0	0	76.00	$500
1975	1	2	0	0	0	0	0	77.00	
1976	2	4	0	0	0	0	0	80.00	$250
1977	2	4	0	0	0	0	0	76.25	$500
1978	1	2	0	0	0	0	0	77.50	$303
1979	1	2	0	0	0	0	0	72.50	
1983	1	2	0	0	0	0	0	77.50	
Period Totals	Starts	Rounds Played	Cuts Made	Wins	Top-5s	Top-10s	Top-25s	Scoring Average	Money
	114	355	65	0	2	8	33	72.78	$43,911

Bob Bruno

Year	Starts	Rounds Played	Cuts Made	Wins	Top-5s	Top-10s	Top-25s	Scoring Average	Money
1958	1	2	0	0	0	0	0	75.50	
1961	3	12	3	0	0	0	0	72.83	$585

Best finish for 1961: T-30th at the Portland Open Invitational

| 1962 | 11 | 44 | 11 | 0 | 0 | 0 | 4 | 71.70 | $2,849 |

Best finish for 1962: T-14th at the Greater Greensboro Open Invitational

| 1963 | 4 | 16 | 4 | 0 | 0 | 0 | 1 | 71.94 | $1,485 |

Best finish for 1963: T-19th at the "500" Festival Open Invitational

| 1964 | 28 | 77 | 10 | 0 | 0 | 1 | 5 | 72.79 | $4,862 |

Best finish for 1964: T-10th at the St. Paul Open

| 1965 | 17 | 49 | 6 | 0 | 0 | 0 | 0 | 73.55 | $1,335 |

Best finish for 1965: T-28th at the Bing Crosby Pro-Am

| 1966 | 3 | 10 | 2 | 0 | 0 | 0 | 0 | 74.90 | |

Best finish for 1966: T-59th at the San Diego Open Invitational

1967	3	6	0	0	0	0	0	77.83	
1968	1	2	0	0	0	0	0	76.00	
1969	1	0	0	0	0	0	0		
1971	1	2	0	0	0	0	0	75.50	
1972	2	4	0	0	0	0	0	73.75	
1973	3	9	2	0	0	0	0	74.78	$360

Best finish for 1973: T-66th at the PGA Championship

1974	1	2	0	0	0	0	0	73.00	
1975	1	2	0	0	0	0	0	72.50	
1977	1	2	0	0	0	0	0	77.00	
1978	1	2	0	0	0	0	0	75.50	
1979	1	0	0	0	0	0	0		
Period Totals	Starts	Rounds Played	Cuts Made	Wins	Top-5s	Top-10s	Top-25s	Scoring Average	Money
	83	241	38	0	0	1	10	73.12	$11,477

Bart Bryant

Year	Starts	Rounds Played	Cuts Made	Wins	Top-5s	Top-10s	Top-25s	Scoring Average	Money
1986	1	4	1	0	0	0	0	69.50	$2,076

Best finish for 1986: T-32nd at the Hardee's Golf Classic

| 1987 | 1 | 2 | 0 | 0 | 0 | 0 | 0 | 75.00 | $600 |

Year	Starts	Rounds Played	Cuts Made	Wins	Top-5s	Top-10s	Top-25s	Scoring Average	Money
1991	30	92	17	0	0	2	5	71.50	$120,931

Best finish for 1991: 7th at the Honda Classic

1992	19	60	10	0	0	1	1	71.43	$52,075

Best finish for 1992: T-10th at the Hardee's Golf Classic

1993	2	5	0	0	0	0	0	70.60	
1994	1	2	0	0	0	0	0	79.00	$1,000
1995	27	82	13	0	0	0	5	71.28	$119,201

Best finish for 1995: T-11th at the LaCantera Texas Open

1996	26	77	14	0	0	0	3	71.45	$88,788

Best finish for 1996: T-18th at the Canon Greater Hartford Open

2000	25	73	11	0	0	0	0	71.88	$85,797

Best finish for 2000: T-37th at the B.C. Open

2001	10	34	7	0	0	0	1	71.18	$73,884

Best finish for 2001: T-25th at the John Deere Classic

2002	20	66	15	0	0	1	3	70.59	$309,880

Best finish for 2002: T-9th at the Kemper Insurance Open

2003	6	25	6	0	0	0	1	70.40	$78,966

Best finish for 2003: T-24th at the FUNAI Classic at the Walt Disney World Resort

2004	23	69	13	1	1	1	4	70.32	$962,167

Best finish for 2004: Win at the Valero Texas Open

2005	26	91	19	2	2	4	13	70.24	$3,253,136

Best finish for 2005: Win at the Memorial Tournament & The Tour Championship

2006	26	86	19	0	1	2	7	71.24	$1,323,381

Best finish for 2006: 2nd at the Canadian Open

2007	25	86	19	0	1	2	8	70.83	$1,167,874

Best finish for 2007: 4th at the FBR Open

2008	23	81	18	0	2	2	7	71.22	$1,719,153

Best finish for 2008: 2nd at the Arnold Palmer Invitational

Period Totals	Starts	Rounds Played	Cuts Made	Wins	Top-5s	Top-10s	Top-25s	Scoring Average	Money
	291	935	182	3	7	15	58	71.09	$9,358,909

Brad Bryant

Year	Starts	Rounds Played	Cuts Made	Wins	Top-5s	Top-10s	Top-25s	Scoring Average	Money
1978	11	36	7	0	0	0	1	72.06	$4,350

Best finish for 1978: T-16th at the Pensacola Open

1979	29	100	21	0	1	5	8	71.97	$63,013

Best finish for 1979: T-4th at the Bing Crosby Pro-Am

1980	33	113	25	0	0	3	11	71.99	$60,479

Best finish for 1980: 8th at the B.C. Open

1981	30	96	20	0	1	4	10	71.72	$59,340

Best finish for 1981: T-5th at the Bay Hill Classic

1982	29	97	18	0	4	4	5	72.51	$99,576

Best finish for 1982: T-2nd at the Tournament Players Championship & Miller High-Life Quad Cities Open

1983	30	102	20	0	2	2	8	71.80	$93,721

Best finish for 1983: T-2nd at the Byron Nelson Golf Classic

1984	31	92	16	0	0	0	3	72.45	$37,805

Best finish for 1984: T-17th at the Seiko Tucson-Match Play Championship

1985	16	37	2	0	0	0	0	74.49	$1,683

Best finish for 1985: T-61st at the Lite Quad Cities Open

1986	19	52	8	0	0	0	2	72.21	$11,290

Best finish for 1986: T-17th at the Tallahassee Open

1987	7	21	4	0	0	0	2	70.67	$17,090

Best finish for 1987: T-13th at the Bank of Boston Classic

1988	26	83	15	0	1	2	3	71.24	$62,614

Best finish for 1988: T-4th at the Gatlin Brothers - Southwest Golf Classic

1989	32	104	22	0	1	1	8	71.03	$174,393

Best finish for 1989: T-5th at the Las Vegas Invitational

1990	30	89	15	0	1	5	7	72.03	$191,795

Best finish for 1990: T-3rd at the Independent Insurance Agent Open

1991	29	76	9	0	1	1	3	71.75	$152,202

Best finish for 1991: 2nd at the Buick Classic

1992	33	113	25	0	1	3	8	71.04	$227,529

Best finish for 1992: T-4th at the Freeport-McMoRan Classic

1993	30	100	20	0	2	3	4	71.22	$230,139

Best finish for 1993: T-2nd at the Buick Southern Open

1994	32	109	25	0	4	6	11	70.72	$690,003

Best finish for 1994: T-2nd at the Doral-Ryder Open & Kmart Greater Greensboro Open

1995	31	95	19	1	2	5	14	70.85	$727,570

Best finish for 1995: Win at the Walt Disney World/Oldsmobile Classic

1996	27	84	17	0	2	3	8	71.30	$256,181

Best finish for 1996: T-4th at the Bob Hope Chrysler Classic

1997	24	78	15	0	2	3	5	71.23	$295,365

Best finish for 1997: T-3rd at the Tucson Chrysler Classic

Year	Starts	Rounds Played	Cuts Made	Wins	Top-5s	Top-10s	Top-25s	Scoring Average	Money
1998	1	2	0	0	0	0	0	76.50	
1999	19	45	4	0	0	0	0	72.56	$30,183

Best finish for 1999: T-36th at the Southern Farm Bureau Classic

| 2000 | 4 | 12 | 2 | 0 | 0 | 0 | 0 | 71.83 | $11,820 |

Best finish for 2000: T-66th at the National Car Rental Golf Classic/Disney

| 2001 | 2 | 6 | 1 | 0 | 0 | 0 | 0 | 69.67 | $12,760 |

Best finish for 2001: T-27th at the B.C. Open

| 2002 | 5 | 14 | 2 | 0 | 0 | 0 | 0 | 71.00 | $10,226 |

Best finish for 2002: T-53rd at the Tampa Bay Classic presented by Buick

| 2003 | 4 | 12 | 2 | 0 | 0 | 0 | 0 | 70.92 | $29,536 |

Best finish for 2003: T-30th at the FUNAI Classic at the Walt Disney World Resort

| 2004 | 4 | 14 | 3 | 0 | 0 | 0 | 0 | 70.14 | $32,210 |

Best finish for 2004: T-37th at the Valero Texas Open

2005	1	2	0	0	0	0	0	70.00	
2008	1	2	0	0	0	0	0	78.00	
Period Totals	Starts	Rounds Played	Cuts Made	Wins	Top-5s	Top-10s	Top-25s	Scoring Average	Money
	570	1786	337	1	25	50	121	71.64	$3,582,873

Howard Buchanan

Year	Starts	Rounds Played	Cuts Made	Wins	Top-5s	Top-10s	Top-25s	Scoring Average	Money
1966	3	6	0	0	0	0	0	75.83	
1967	4	8	0	0	0	0	0	78.25	
1968	1	2	0	0	0	0	0	76.50	
1970	9	18	0	0	0	0	0	75.56	
1971	10	19	1	0	0	0	0	74.37	

Best finish for 1971: T-42nd at the Greater Milwaukee Open

1974	1	2	0	0	0	0	0	74.00	
1977	1	1	0	0	0	0	0	79.00	
Period Totals	Starts	Rounds Played	Cuts Made	Wins	Top-5s	Top-10s	Top-25s	Scoring Average	Money
	29	56	1	0	0	0	0	75.61	

Andrew Buckle

Year	Starts	Rounds Played	Cuts Made	Wins	Top-5s	Top-10s	Top-25s	Scoring Average	Money
2004	1	2	0	0	0	0	0	79.00	$3,745
2006	2	6	1	0	0	0	0	72.67	$20,747

Best finish for 2006: T-61st at the British Open

| 2007 | 26 | 77 | 12 | 0 | 1 | 1 | 4 | 71.53 | $515,630 |

Best finish for 2007: T-4th at the Buick Invitational

| 2008 | 15 | 46 | 8 | 0 | 0 | 0 | 2 | 71.46 | $170,264 |

Best finish for 2008: T-14th at the Reno-Tahoe Open

| Period Totals | Starts | Rounds Played | Cuts Made | Wins | Top-5s | Top-10s | Top-25s | Scoring Average | Money |
| | 44 | 131 | 21 | 0 | 1 | 1 | 6 | 71.67 | $710,387 |

Jason Buha

Year	Starts	Rounds Played	Cuts Made	Wins	Top-5s	Top-10s	Top-25s	Scoring Average	Money
2000	29	82	12	0	0	0	3	71.70	$154,862

Best finish for 2000: T-18th at the Canon Greater Hartford Open

| 2003 | 25 | 58 | 7 | 0 | 0 | 0 | 0 | 72.14 | $72,833 |

Best finish for 2003: T-27th at the Reno-Tahoe Open

| Period Totals | Starts | Rounds Played | Cuts Made | Wins | Top-5s | Top-10s | Top-25s | Scoring Average | Money |
| | 54 | 140 | 19 | 0 | 0 | 0 | 3 | 71.88 | $227,696 |

Steve Bull

Year	Starts	Rounds Played	Cuts Made	Wins	Top-5s	Top-10s	Top-25s	Scoring Average	Money
1958	1	3	0	0	0	0	0	72.33	
1961	1	1	0	0	0	0	0	78.00	
1963	1	2	1	0	0	0	0	78.50	

Best finish for 1963: T-200 at the PGA Championship

1964	1	3	0	0	0	0	0	74.33	
1965	3	6	0	0	0	0	0	79.33	
1966	2	4	0	0	0	0	0	76.50	
1967	5	16	3	0	0	0	0	73.25	$396

Best finish for 1967: T-39th at the Jacksonville Open

| 1968 | 2 | 4 | 0 | 0 | 0 | 0 | 0 | 75.50 | |
| 1969 | 1 | 4 | 1 | 0 | 0 | 0 | 0 | 74.75 | $200 |

Best finish for 1969: T-64th at the Greater Milwaukee Open

| 1970 | 1 | 4 | 1 | 0 | 0 | 0 | 0 | 72.75 | $152 |

Best finish for 1970: T-71st at the Greater Milwaukee Open

1971	1	2	0	0	0	0	0	71.50	
1974	1	2	0	0	0	0	0	78.00	
1975	1	1	0	0	0	0	0	78.00	

Year	Starts	Rounds Played	Cuts Made	Wins	Top-5s	Top-10s	Top-25s	Scoring Average	Money
1976	1	0	0	0	0	0	0		
1977	1	2	0	0	0	0	0	77.00	
1978	1	2	0	0	0	0	0	74.00	
1979	1	2	0	0	0	0	0	75.50	
1980	1	2	0	0	0	0	0	74.50	
Period Totals	Starts	Rounds Played	Cuts Made	Wins	Top-5s	Top-10s	Top-25s	Scoring Average	Money
	26	60	6	0	0	0	0	75.00	$748

Johnny Bulla

Year	Starts	Rounds Played	Cuts Made	Wins	Top-5s	Top-10s	Top-25s	Scoring Average	Money
1958	6	20	4	0	0	0	0	71.95	$420

Best finish for 1958: T-29th at the Canadian Open

1959	4	14	4	0	0	0	1	73.64	$993

Best finish for 1959: T-14th at the Los Angles Open Invitational

1960	5	19	4	0	0	0	1	72.68	$1,270

Best finish for 1960: T-13th at the Los Angles Open Invitational

1961	1	4	1	0	0	0	0	75.00	$225

Best finish for 1961: T-57th at the PGA Championship

1962	2	6	1	0	0	0	0	75.50	$200

Best finish for 1962: T-49th at the Western Open Championship

1964	10	30	5	0	0	0	2	73.17	$3,370

Best finish for 1964: T-15th at the Cleveland Open

1965	3	8	1	0	0	0	0	73.88	

Best finish for 1965: T-78th at the Cleveland Open

1966	6	20	4	0	0	0	0	74.25	$793

Best finish for 1966: T-45th at the Los Angles Open Invitational

1967	4	10	1	0	0	0	0	74.60	$300

Best finish for 1967: 63rd at the PGA Championship

1968	3	6	0	0	0	0	0	76.00	
1969	3	8	1	0	0	0	0	73.25	$361

Best finish for 1969: T-40th at the Los Angeles Open

1970	2	6	1	0	0	0	0	71.83	$190

Best finish for 1970: T-58th at the Los Angles Open

1971	2	8	2	0	0	0	0	71.25	$470

Best finish for 1971: T-63rd at the Phoenix Open

1972	2	4	0	0	0	0	0	75.75	
1973	1	2	0	0	0	0	0	78.00	
1974	1	2	0	0	0	0	0	75.50	
1975	1	2	0	0	0	0	0	78.00	
1976	1	2	0	0	0	0	0	80.50	
1985	1	2	0	0	0	0	0	78.50	
Period Totals	Starts	Rounds Played	Cuts Made	Wins	Top-5s	Top-10s	Top-25s	Scoring Average	Money
	58	173	29	0	0	0	4	73.69	$8,592

PGA Tour career totals from 1936 to 1985

	Starts	Rounds Played	Cuts Made	Wins	Top-5s	Top-10s	Top-25s	Scoring Average	Money
	233	622	224	1	N/A	81	153	N/A	$67,875

Jim Bullard

Year	Starts	Rounds Played	Cuts Made	Wins	Top-5s	Top-10s	Top-25s	Scoring Average	Money
1969	10	27	4	0	0	0	2	74.22	$1,078

Best finish for 1969: T-23rd at the Alameda County Open

1970	9	24	3	0	0	0	0	74.17	$498

Best finish for 1970: T-58th at the Western Open

1975	12	28	2	0	0	0	0	74.61	$800

Best finish for 1975: T-41st at the Canadian Open

1977	2	4	0	0	0	0	0	75.75	
Period Totals	Starts	Rounds Played	Cuts Made	Wins	Top-5s	Top-10s	Top-25s	Scoring Average	Money
	33	83	9	0	0	0	2	74.41	$2,376

Patrick Burke

Year	Starts	Rounds Played	Cuts Made	Wins	Top-5s	Top-10s	Top-25s	Scoring Average	Money
1990	23	53	3	0	0	0	0	73.43	$5,228

Best finish for 1990: T-43rd at the B.C. Open

1992	28	90	18	0	0	1	2	71.29	$102,513

Best finish for 1992: T-6th at the BellSouth Classic

1993	18	59	11	0	0	1	5	71.71	$100,717

Best finish for 1993: T-9th at the Buick Invitational of California

1994	10	20	2	0	0	0	0	73.05	$5,034

Best finish for 1994: T-37th at the Deposit Guaranty Golf Classic

1995	24	75	15	0	0	1	5	71.16	$162,892

Best finish for 1995: T-7th at the Walt Disney World/Oldsmobile Classic

| 1996 | 24 | 72 | 14 | 0 | 1 | 2 | 7 | 71.01 | $265,083 |

Best finish for 1996: T-3rd at the B.C. Open

| 1997 | 23 | 65 | 11 | 0 | 0 | 0 | 3 | 71.43 | $89,117 |

Best finish for 1997: T-17th at the Bob Hope Chrysler Classic

| 1998 | 1 | 0 | 0 | 0 | 0 | 0 | 0 | | |

Period Totals	Starts	Rounds Played	Cuts Made	Wins	Top-5s	Top-10s	Top-25s	Scoring Average	Money
	151	434	74	0	1	5	22	71.64	$730,584

Jack Burke, Jr.

Year	Starts	Rounds Played	Cuts Made	Wins	Top-5s	Top-10s	Top-25s	Scoring Average	Money
1958	17	64	15	1	7	8	12	70.70	$17,377

Best finish for 1958: Win at the Insurance City Open

| 1959 | 16 | 64 | 16 | 1 | 3 | 5 | 9 | 71.11 | $12,344 |

Best finish for 1959: Win at the Houston Classic

| 1960 | 14 | 57 | 14 | 0 | 0 | 1 | 9 | 71.68 | $7,546 |

Best finish for 1960: T-10th at the Eastern Open Invitational

| 1961 | 15 | 61 | 13 | 1 | 1 | 6 | 11 | 71.03 | $22,225 |

Best finish for 1961: Win at the Buick Open Invitational

| 1962 | 16 | 63 | 13 | 0 | 1 | 4 | 10 | 71.22 | $14,103 |

Best finish for 1962: T-4th at the Los Angles Open

| 1963 | 13 | 50 | 12 | 1 | 1 | 3 | 9 | 71.86 | $21,506 |

Best finish for 1963: Win at the Lucky International Open

| 1964 | 13 | 44 | 8 | 0 | 0 | 1 | 1 | 73.68 | $2,872 |

Best finish for 1964: T-9th at the Cajun Classic

| 1965 | 12 | 37 | 6 | 0 | 0 | 1 | 2 | 72.95 | $7,948 |

Best finish for 1965: T-8th at the PGA Championship

| 1966 | 7 | 27 | 6 | 0 | 0 | 0 | 3 | 72.96 | $5,897 |

Best finish for 1966: 11th at the Greater New Orleans Open Invitational

| 1967 | 10 | 37 | 7 | 0 | 1 | 1 | 2 | 73.62 | $7,049 |

Best finish for 1967: T-4th at the Bing Crosby Pro-Am

| 1968 | 3 | 8 | 1 | 0 | 0 | 0 | 0 | 75.38 | $1,000 |

Best finish for 1968: T-61st at the Bing Crosby National Professional-Amateur

| 1969 | 5 | 16 | 2 | 0 | 0 | 0 | 1 | 73.94 | $2,041 |

Best finish for 1969: T-24th at the Masters

Period Totals	Starts	Rounds Played	Cuts Made	Wins	Top-5s	Top-10s	Top-25s	Scoring Average	Money
	141	528	113	4	14	30	69	71.96	$121,908

PGA Tour career totals from 1947 to 1969

	Starts	Rounds Played	Cuts Made	Wins	Top-5s	Top-10s	Top-25s	Scoring Average	Money
	325	1138	297	16	55	123	209	N/A	$263,440

Walter Burkemo

Year	Starts	Rounds Played	Cuts Made	Wins	Top-5s	Top-10s	Top-25s	Scoring Average	Money
1958	21	75	16	0	3	5	13	72.20	$9,388

Best finish for 1958: T-2nd at the Phoenix Open

| 1959 | 13 | 51 | 12 | 0 | 1 | 2 | 9 | 71.59 | $5,569 |

Best finish for 1959: T-5th at the Mobile Sertoma Open Invitational

| 1960 | 13 | 52 | 13 | 0 | 0 | 1 | 6 | 72.67 | $6,777 |

Best finish for 1960: T-6th at the Masters

| 1961 | 4 | 14 | 3 | 0 | 0 | 0 | 3 | 72.29 | $3,640 |

Best finish for 1961: T-11th at the Masters

| 1962 | 2 | 6 | 1 | 0 | 0 | 0 | 0 | 73.83 | $800 |

Best finish for 1962: T-39th at the PGA Championship

| 1963 | 4 | 14 | 4 | 0 | 0 | 1 | 1 | 74.64 | $3,300 |

Best finish for 1963: T-8th at the U.S. Open

| 1964 | 7 | 21 | 2 | 0 | 0 | 0 | 1 | 74.00 | $1,527 |

Best finish for 1964: T-17th at the PGA Championship

| 1965 | 9 | 29 | 4 | 0 | 0 | 0 | 0 | 74.10 | $2,331 |

Best finish for 1965: T-26th at the Carling Open

| 1966 | 8 | 24 | 3 | 0 | 0 | 0 | 1 | 74.17 | $1,175 |

Best finish for 1966: T-22nd at the U.S. Open

1967	3	6	0	0	0	0	0	75.50	
1968	2	4	0	0	0	0	0	75.50	
1969	2	4	0	0	0	0	0	79.00	
1970	3	6	0	0	0	0	0	76.50	
1971	1	2	0	0	0	0	0	81.00	

Period Totals	Starts	Rounds Played	Cuts Made	Wins	Top-5s	Top-10s	Top-25s	Scoring Average	Money
	92	308	58	0	4	9	34	73.12	$34,508

PGA Tour career totals from 1940 to 1971

	Starts	Rounds Played	Cuts Made	Wins	Top-5s	Top-10s	Top-25s	Scoring Average	Money
	198	703	183	2	12	41	115	N/A	$89,593

Bob Burns

Year	Starts	Rounds Played	Cuts Made	Wins	Top-5s	Top-10s	Top-25s	Scoring Average	Money
1992	1	2	0	0	0	0	0	75.50	$1,000
1994	24	69	11	0	1	3	6	71.58	$178,168

Best finish for 1994: T-5th at the Buick Classic

1995	30	83	11	0	0	0	1	72.33	$59,243

Best finish for 1995: T-12th at the Buick Challenge

1999	31	89	13	0	0	0	2	72.16	$138,118

Best finish for 1999: T-18th at the Buick Invitational

2000	29	89	16	0	0	2	4	71.73	$391,075

Best finish for 2000: T-6th at the COMPAQ Classic of New Orleans

2001	29	89	16	0	0	1	5	71.01	$353,046

Best finish for 2001: T-8th at the Texas Open at LaCantera

2002	30	96	19	1	2	2	5	70.68	$1,199,802

Best finish for 2002: Win at the Disney Golf Classic

2003	28	84	15	0	0	0	1	71.93	$294,974

Best finish for 2003: T-21st at the John Deere Classic

2004	30	86	13	0	0	1	4	71.35	$581,421

Best finish for 2004: T-10th at the Players Championship

2005	15	40	5	0	0	0	0	71.80	$44,407

Best finish for 2005: T-46th at the Chrysler Classic of Tucson

2006	9	23	3	0	0	0	0	71.65	$49,170

Best finish for 2006: T-28th at the FedEx St. Jude Classic

2007	5	14	2	0	0	0	0	74.21	$18,153

Best finish for 2007: T-66th at the Viking Classic

2008	7	17	1	0	0	0	0	74.71	$6,650

Best finish for 2008: 75th at the Mayakoba Golf Classic

Period Totals	Starts	Rounds Played	Cuts Made	Wins	Top-5s	Top-10s	Top-25s	Scoring Average	Money
	268	781	125	1	3	9	28	71.72	$3,315,226

George Burns

Year	Starts	Rounds Played	Cuts Made	Wins	Top-5s	Top-10s	Top-25s	Scoring Average	Money
1974	2	4	0	0	0	0	0	74.25	
1975	6	22	5	0	0	2	3	71.45	$11,020

Best finish for 1975: T-7th at the Southern Open

1976	32	106	21	0	4	8	14	71.45	$89,538

Best finish for 1976: T-3rd at the Bing Crosby Pro-Am, Houston Open & World Open

1977	30	110	25	0	5	6	14	71.75	$108,526

Best finish for 1977: T-2nd at the Greater Greensboro Open & Kemper Open

1978	34	125	30	0	2	4	14	71.31	$71,925

Best finish for 1978: T-5th at the Canadian Open & San Antonio Texas Open

1979	34	109	23	0	1	6	13	72.13	$107,830

Best finish for 1979: T-2nd at the Greater Greensboro Open

1980	31	108	24	1	6	13	21	71.23	$226,831

Best finish for 1980: Win at the Bing Crosby Pro-Am

1981	30	99	21	0	4	6	11	71.47	$105,395

Best finish for 1981: T-2nd at the U.S. Open

1982	32	120	29	0	5	7	17	71.21	$181,864

Best finish for 1982: T-2nd at the Honda Inverrary Classic

1983	29	83	14	0	1	2	6	72.24	$64,061

Best finish for 1983: 3rd at the Doral-Eastern Open

1984	30	105	23	0	3	6	14	71.24	$168,848

Best finish for 1984: 2nd at the Bay Hill Classic

1985	29	101	24	1	4	5	10	71.37	$224,352

Best finish for 1985: Win at the Bank of Boston Classic

1986	28	83	15	0	0	1	7	72.54	$80,574

Best finish for 1986: T-10th at the Western Open

1987	32	102	19	1	1	3	9	71.50	$218,757

Best finish for 1987: Win at the Shearson Lehman/Andy Williams San Diego

1988	22	54	7	0	0	0	2	73.17	$31,130

Best finish for 1988: T-16th at the MONY Tournament Of Champions

1989	25	56	3	0	0	0	0	73.34	$5,646

Best finish for 1989: T-39th at the Bank of Boston Classic

1990	28	93	19	0	0	1	4	72.10	$97,443

Best finish for 1990: T-8th at the Honda Classic

1991	6	10	0	0	0	0	0	74.10	
1992	15	36	3	0	0	0	0	73.61	$6,864

Best finish for 1992: T-50th at the Doral-Ryder Open

1993	9	18	1	0	0	0	0	74.89	$2,550

Best finish for 1993: T-67th at the AT&T Pebble Beach Pro-Am

1994	8	16	0	0	0	0	0	74.94	

Year	Starts	Rounds Played	Cuts Made	Wins	Top-5s	Top-10s	Top-25s	Scoring Average	Money
1995	7	17	1	0	0	0	0	72.35	$2,462

Best finish for 1995: T-48th at the Ideon Classic

| 1996 | 9 | 19 | 1 | 0 | 0 | 0 | 0 | 73.32 | $3,456 |

Best finish for 1996: T-53rd at the Kemper Open

| 1997 | 8 | 21 | 2 | 0 | 0 | 0 | 0 | 72.52 | $5,618 |

Best finish for 1997: T-70th at the Greater Vancouver Open

1998	7	14	0	0	0	0	0	75.79	
1999	4	9	0	0	0	0	0	75.22	
2000	1	2	0	0	0	0	0	75.50	
2002	1	2	0	0	0	0	0	81.00	
2003	1	3	0	0	0	0	0	78.67	
2004	1	3	0	0	0	0	0	77.67	
2005	1	3	0	0	0	0	0	74.00	
Period Totals	Starts	Rounds Played	Cuts Made	Wins	Top-5s	Top-10s	Top-25s	Scoring Average	Money
	532	1653	310	3	36	70	159	72.00	$1,814,691

Clark Burroughs

Year	Starts	Rounds Played	Cuts Made	Wins	Top-5s	Top-10s	Top-25s	Scoring Average	Money
1984	1	4	1	0	0	0	0	74.25	

Best finish for 1984: T-46th at the Masters

| 1985 | 3 | 8 | 1 | 0 | 0 | 0 | 1 | 71.88 | $4,800 |

Best finish for 1985: T-15th at the Greater Milwaukee Open

| 1986 | 2 | 8 | 2 | 0 | 0 | 0 | 0 | 71.25 | $1,664 |

Best finish for 1986: T-63rd at the Greater Milwaukee Open

| 1987 | 2 | 6 | 1 | 0 | 0 | 0 | 0 | 71.00 | $1,296 |

Best finish for 1987: T-59th at the Greater Milwaukee Open

| 1988 | 30 | 90 | 15 | 0 | 0 | 0 | 1 | 72.03 | $33,671 |

Best finish for 1988: T-19th at the Canon Sammy Davis, Jr. - Greater Hartford Open

| 1989 | 26 | 70 | 11 | 0 | 1 | 2 | 4 | 71.26 | $124,715 |

Best finish for 1989: T-2nd at the Canadian Open

| 1990 | 29 | 96 | 19 | 0 | 0 | 2 | 3 | 71.70 | $115,923 |

Best finish for 1990: T-7th at the Kemper Open

| 1991 | 19 | 54 | 6 | 0 | 0 | 0 | 1 | 71.93 | $29,377 |

Best finish for 1991: T-14th at the Canadian Open

| 1992 | 2 | 4 | 0 | 0 | 0 | 0 | 0 | 75.50 | |
| 1995 | 15 | 35 | 2 | 0 | 0 | 0 | 0 | 73.20 | $5,206 |

Best finish for 1995: T-65th at the Buick Classic

| Period Totals | Starts | Rounds Played | Cuts Made | Wins | Top-5s | Top-10s | Top-25s | Scoring Average | Money |
| | 129 | 375 | 58 | 0 | 1 | 4 | 10 | 71.92 | $316,651 |

Kevin Burton

Year	Starts	Rounds Played	Cuts Made	Wins	Top-5s	Top-10s	Top-25s	Scoring Average	Money
1993	2	6	1	0	0	0	0	73.33	$3,512

Best finish for 1993: T-71st at the PGA Championship

| 1995 | 1 | 4 | 1 | 0 | 0 | 0 | 0 | 72.75 | $2,232 |

Best finish for 1995: 77th at the Nissan Open

| 1997 | 26 | 74 | 10 | 0 | 0 | 1 | 1 | 72.20 | $78,534 |

Best finish for 1997: T-6th at the CVS Charity Classic

2000	1	2	0	0	0	0	0	79.50	$2,000
2003	1	2	0	0	0	0	0	75.50	$2,000
2007	1	2	0	0	0	0	0	77.50	$2,500
Period Totals	Starts	Rounds Played	Cuts Made	Wins	Top-5s	Top-10s	Top-25s	Scoring Average	Money
	32	90	12	0	0	1	1	72.66	$90,778

Dick Bury

Year	Starts	Rounds Played	Cuts Made	Wins	Top-5s	Top-10s	Top-25s	Scoring Average	Money
1958	1	2	0	0	0	0	0	78.50	
1960	1	2	0	0	0	0	0	77.50	
1962	1	3	1	0	0	0	0	74.67	
1964	28	56	3	0	0	0	0	75.75	

Best finish for 1964: T-34th at the Cajun Classic

| 1966 | 1 | 2 | 0 | 0 | 0 | 0 | 0 | 77.00 | |
| 1970 | 1 | 4 | 1 | 0 | 0 | 0 | 0 | 76.00 | $400 |

Best finish for 1970: 64th at the PGA Championship

| Period Totals | Starts | Rounds Played | Cuts Made | Wins | Top-5s | Top-10s | Top-25s | Scoring Average | Money |
| | 33 | 69 | 5 | 0 | 0 | 0 | 0 | 75.88 | $400 |

Peter Butler

Year	Starts	Rounds Played	Cuts Made	Wins	Top-5s	Top-10s	Top-25s	Scoring Average	Money
1958	1	2	0	0	0	0	0	76.00	
1960	1	4	1	0	0	0	0	73.50	$140

Best finish for 1960: 35th at the British Open

Year	Starts	Rounds Played	Cuts Made	Wins	Top-5s	Top-10s	Top-25s	Scoring Average	Money
1961	1	4	1	0	0	0	1	75.00	

Best finish for 1961: T-22nd at the British Open

Year	Starts	Rounds Played	Cuts Made	Wins	Top-5s	Top-10s	Top-25s	Scoring Average	Money
1962	1	2	0	0	0	0	0	77.00	
1963	1	2	0	0	0	0	0	75.50	
1964	14	52	11	0	0	0	6	72.63	$6,156

Best finish for 1964: T-11th at the San Diego Open

1965	8	22	3	0	0	0	0	74.59	

Best finish for 1965: T-42nd at the Azalea Open

1966	7	24	5	0	0	0	4	73.42	$6,507

Best finish for 1966: T-11th at the Greater Greensboro Open Invitational

1967	4	12	2	0	0	0	2	72.33	$2,184

Best finish for 1967: T-23rd at the Pensacola Open

1968	3	9	1	0	0	0	0	74.00	$1,446

Best finish for 1968: T-42nd at the Greater Greensboro Open Invitational

1969	2	4	0	0	0	0	0	78.00	
1970	4	9	0	0	0	0	0	75.33	$1,103
1971	3	12	3	0	0	0	1	72.75	$1,143

Best finish for 1971: T-25th at the British Open

1972	1	4	1	0	0	0	1	72.25	$2,125

Best finish for 1972: T-15th at the British Open

1973	2	8	1	0	0	1	1	74.63	$5,590

Best finish for 1973: 6th at the British Open

1974	1	4	1	0	0	0	0	75.25	$510

Best finish for 1974: T-31st at the British Open

1976	1	4	1	0	0	1	1	72.25	$3,555

Best finish for 1976: T-10th at the British Open

1977	1	4	1	0	0	0	1	71.75	$2,295

Best finish for 1977: T-15th at the British Open

1978	1	4	1	0	0	0	0	74.25	$570

Best finish for 1978: 59th at the British Open

1979	1	3	0	0	0	0	0	77.00	$630
1983	1	2	0	0	0	0	0	82.00	$375
Period Totals	Starts	Rounds Played	Cuts Made	Wins	Top-5s	Top-10s	Top-25s	Scoring Average	Money
	59	191	33	0	0	2	18	73.73	$34,330

Bill Buttner

Year	Starts	Rounds Played	Cuts Made	Wins	Top-5s	Top-10s	Top-25s	Scoring Average	Money
1980	2	4	0	0	0	0	0	78.25	$600
1982	15	35	3	0	0	0	0	72.91	$2,796

Best finish for 1982: T-39th at the Bank of Boston Classic

1983	2	6	1	0	0	0	0	74.50	$1,236

Best finish for 1983: T-61st at the Doral-Eastern Open

1985	18	50	8	0	0	0	1	72.84	$13,486

Best finish for 1985: T-12th at the Southwest Golf Classic

1986	1	2	0	0	0	0	0	74.50	
1987	4	8	0	0	0	0	0	75.00	$600
1988	30	89	13	0	0	0	1	72.06	$28,928

Best finish for 1988: T-22nd at the Honda Classic

1989	28	87	17	0	1	1	4	71.18	$96,601

Best finish for 1989: T-4th at the Centel Classic

1990	31	87	14	0	0	0	6	71.93	$108,621

Best finish for 1990: 11th at the Northern Telecom Tucson Open

1991	27	76	11	0	0	0	1	71.91	$40,373

Best finish for 1991: T-19th at the Federal Express St. Jude Classic

1992	3	10	2	0	0	0	0	71.20	$6,187

Best finish for 1992: T-33rd at the Anheuser-Busch Golf Classic

1993	1	4	1	0	0	1	1	67.75	$6,650

Best finish for 1993: T-10th at the Deposit Guaranty Classic

1994	1	2	0	0	0	0	0	72.50	
Period Totals	Starts	Rounds Played	Cuts Made	Wins	Top-5s	Top-10s	Top-25s	Scoring Average	Money
	163	460	70	0	1	2	14	72.09	$306,078

Bob Byman

Year	Starts	Rounds Played	Cuts Made	Wins	Top-5s	Top-10s	Top-25s	Scoring Average	Money
1972	1	2	0	0	0	0	0	82.50	
1975	1	2	0	0	0	0	0	77.50	
1976	1	2	0	0	0	0	0	81.00	
1978	12	36	7	0	0	1	4	71.50	$18,478

Best finish for 1978: T-10th at the B.C. Open

1979	30	98	21	1	1	3	12	72.53	$104,764

Best finish for 1979: Win at the Bay Hill Citrus Classic

1980	27	72	12	0	0	0	1	73.61	$15,677

Best finish for 1980: T-17th at the World Disney World National Team Championship

Year	Starts	Rounds Played	Cuts Made	Wins	Top-5s	Top-10s	Top-25s	Scoring Average	Money
1981	27	77	12	0	0	0	0	73.22	$10,829

Best finish for 1981: 26th at the Tallahassee Open

| 1982 | 21 | 73 | 14 | 0 | 0 | 1 | 4 | 71.42 | $29,006 |

Best finish for 1982: T-9th at the Tallahassee Open

| 1983 | 24 | 51 | 1 | 0 | 0 | 0 | 0 | 75.53 | $1,140 |

Best finish for 1983: 80th at the Joe Garagiola Tucson Open

1984	1	2	0	0	0	0	0	76.50	
1985	1	2	0	0	0	0	0	75.00	$544
1986	2	5	1	0	0	0	0	73.20	$970

Best finish for 1986: T-72nd at the Hertz Bay Hill Classic

1987	2	4	0	0	0	0	0	76.75	
1988	4	8	0	0	0	0	0	75.00	
1990	2	4	0	0	0	0	0	74.50	
2002	1	1	0	0	0	0	0	80.00	
2003	1	1	0	0	0	0	0	82.00	
2004	1	1	0	0	0	0	0	79.00	
Period Totals	Starts	Rounds Played	Cuts Made	Wins	Top-5s	Top-10s	Top-25s	Scoring Average	Money
	159	441	68	1	1	5	21	73.20	$181,409

Ed Byman

Year	Starts	Rounds Played	Cuts Made	Wins	Top-5s	Top-10s	Top-25s	Scoring Average	Money
1973	1	2	0	0	0	0	0	82.00	
1978	10	26	3	0	0	0	0	73.27	$914

Best finish for 1978: T-55th at the Pensacola Open

| 1979 | 18 | 46 | 4 | 0 | 0 | 0 | 0 | 74.33 | $3,410 |

Best finish for 1979: T-30th at the Western Open

| 1980 | 11 | 26 | 1 | 0 | 0 | 0 | 0 | 74.69 | $538 |

Best finish for 1980: T-62nd at the Andy Williams-San Diego Open

1983	1	2	0	0	0	0	0	78.00	
Period Totals	Starts	Rounds Played	Cuts Made	Wins	Top-5s	Top-10s	Top-25s	Scoring Average	Money
	41	102	8	0	0	0	0	74.37	$4,862

Jonathan Byrd

Year	Starts	Rounds Played	Cuts Made	Wins	Top-5s	Top-10s	Top-25s	Scoring Average	Money
2000	1	4	1	0	0	0	0	70.50	$14,130

Best finish for 2000: T-36th at the Michelob Championship at Kingsmill

| 2001 | 1 | 4 | 1 | 0 | 0 | 0 | 0 | 69.75 | $8,400 |

Best finish for 2001: T-37th at the B.C. Open

| 2002 | 32 | 94 | 15 | 1 | 3 | 4 | 10 | 70.39 | $1,462,713 |

Best finish for 2002: Win at the Buick Challenge

| 2003 | 29 | 101 | 21 | 0 | 3 | 5 | 9 | 70.94 | $1,432,538 |

Best finish for 2003: T-2nd at the John Deere Classic

| 2004 | 27 | 83 | 15 | 1 | 2 | 3 | 5 | 71.02 | $1,141,165 |

Best finish for 2004: Win at the B.C. Open

| 2005 | 31 | 99 | 22 | 0 | 1 | 1 | 5 | 71.14 | $726,022 |

Best finish for 2005: T-5th at the 84 Lumber Classic

| 2006 | 20 | 66 | 12 | 0 | 3 | 5 | 9 | 69.97 | $1,408,418 |

Best finish for 2006: T-3rd at the AT&T Pebble Beach National Pro-Am

| 2007 | 23 | 73 | 13 | 1 | 1 | 4 | 11 | 70.56 | $1,857,406 |

Best finish for 2007: Win at the John Deere Classic

| 2008 | 27 | 85 | 18 | 0 | 1 | 2 | 6 | 71.36 | $1,039,584 |

Best finish for 2008: 4th at the AT&T Classic

Period Totals	Starts	Rounds Played	Cuts Made	Wins	Top-5s	Top-10s	Top-25s	Scoring Average	Money
	191	609	118	3	14	24	55	70.80	$9,090,376

Curt Byrum

Year	Starts	Rounds Played	Cuts Made	Wins	Top-5s	Top-10s	Top-25s	Scoring Average	Money
1982	4	12	2	0	0	0	0	73.25	$1,247

Best finish for 1982: T-62nd at the Western Open

| 1983 | 31 | 99 | 17 | 0 | 1 | 1 | 2 | 72.57 | $30,772 |

Best finish for 1983: 4th at the Texas Open

| 1984 | 27 | 79 | 13 | 0 | 1 | 1 | 2 | 72.76 | $27,836 |

Best finish for 1984: T-5th at the Miller High-Life Quad Cities Open

| 1985 | 14 | 38 | 6 | 0 | 0 | 0 | 0 | 72.87 | $6,943 |

Best finish for 1985: T-44th at the Isuzu/Andy Williams San Diego Open

| 1986 | 9 | 26 | 6 | 0 | 2 | 2 | 2 | 70.81 | $79,454 |

Best finish for 1986: 2nd at the Hardee's Golf Classic

| 1987 | 33 | 111 | 24 | 0 | 1 | 5 | 9 | 71.18 | $212,449 |

Best finish for 1987: 2nd at the Memorial Tournament

| 1988 | 31 | 99 | 19 | 0 | 2 | 3 | 8 | 71.21 | $209,853 |

Best finish for 1988: T-3rd at the Players Championship

Year	Starts	Rounds Played	Cuts Made	Wins	Top-5s	Top-10s	Top-25s	Scoring Average	Money
1989	33	98	15	1	1	1	5	72.22	$221,703

Best finish for 1989: Win at the Hardee's Golf Classic

Year	Starts	Rounds Played	Cuts Made	Wins	Top-5s	Top-10s	Top-25s	Scoring Average	Money
1990	31	89	16	0	0	0	5	71.90	$118,635

Best finish for 1990: 12th at the USF&G Classic

| 1991 | 31 | 97 | 18 | 0 | 0 | 1 | 1 | 71.55 | $78,725 |

Best finish for 1991: T-8th at the USF&G Classic

| 1992 | 14 | 43 | 7 | 0 | 0 | 0 | 1 | 71.23 | $31,450 |

Best finish for 1992: T-16th at the Northern Telecom Open

| 1994 | 28 | 81 | 12 | 0 | 1 | 2 | 5 | 71.15 | $137,586 |

Best finish for 1994: T-5th at the B.C. Open

| 1995 | 33 | 106 | 21 | 0 | 0 | 1 | 4 | 71.38 | $173,838 |

Best finish for 1995: T-8th at the Quad City Classic

| 1996 | 17 | 56 | 10 | 0 | 0 | 1 | 2 | 71.52 | $104,226 |

Best finish for 1996: T-6th at the Phoenix Open

| 1997 | 15 | 42 | 5 | 0 | 0 | 0 | 2 | 72.10 | $39,704 |

Best finish for 1997: T-20th at the Honda Classic

| 1998 | 9 | 28 | 5 | 0 | 1 | 1 | 2 | 70.64 | $88,734 |

Best finish for 1998: T-4th at the B.C. Open

| 1999 | 1 | 4 | 1 | 0 | 0 | 0 | 0 | 69.25 | $3,840 |

Best finish for 1999: T-73rd at the John Deere Classic

| 2000 | 4 | 12 | 2 | 0 | 0 | 0 | 0 | 70.83 | $12,041 |

Best finish for 2000: T-44th at the John Deere Classic

| 2001 | 1 | 2 | 0 | 0 | 0 | 0 | 0 | 71.50 | |
| 2002 | 2 | 5 | 0 | 0 | 0 | 0 | 0 | 74.40 | |

Period Totals	Starts	Rounds Played	Cuts Made	Wins	Top-5s	Top-10s	Top-25s	Scoring Average	Money
	368	1127	199	1	10	19	50	71.72	$1,579,036

Tom Byrum

Year	Starts	Rounds Played	Cuts Made	Wins	Top-5s	Top-10s	Top-25s	Scoring Average	Money
1985	1	4	1	0	0	0	0	74.00	$935

Best finish for 1985: T-76th at the Byron Nelson Golf Classic

| 1986 | 34 | 99 | 18 | 0 | 2 | 4 | 5 | 72.45 | $90,339 |

Best finish for 1986: 2nd at the Southwest Golf Classic

| 1987 | 33 | 108 | 23 | 0 | 1 | 5 | 8 | 71.59 | $146,384 |

Best finish for 1987: T-3rd at the Greater Greensboro Open

| 1988 | 34 | 112 | 23 | 0 | 2 | 2 | 11 | 70.99 | $175,378 |

Best finish for 1988: T-2nd at the Pensacola Open

| 1989 | 32 | 101 | 17 | 1 | 2 | 4 | 7 | 72.03 | $321,939 |

Best finish for 1989: Win at the Kemper Open

| 1990 | 31 | 89 | 14 | 0 | 1 | 1 | 3 | 72.56 | $138,410 |

Best finish for 1990: 3rd at the Shearson Lehman Hutton Open

| 1991 | 33 | 100 | 16 | 0 | 0 | 0 | 3 | 71.91 | $69,871 |

Best finish for 1991: T-15th at the Shearson Lehman Brothers Open

| 1992 | 29 | 76 | 10 | 0 | 1 | 1 | 2 | 71.75 | $94,399 |

Best finish for 1992: T-3rd at the Kmart Greater Greensboro Open

| 1993 | 26 | 75 | 12 | 0 | 0 | 1 | 2 | 72.19 | $82,355 |

Best finish for 1993: T-8th at the Anheuser-Busch Golf Classic

| 1994 | 12 | 33 | 7 | 0 | 1 | 1 | 3 | 70.67 | $112,259 |

Best finish for 1994: T-2nd at the GTE Byron Nelson Classic

| 1995 | 14 | 47 | 10 | 0 | 2 | 2 | 3 | 69.94 | $145,427 |

Best finish for 1995: T-3rd at the Buick Open

| 1996 | 26 | 76 | 12 | 0 | 1 | 2 | 4 | 71.13 | $166,500 |

Best finish for 1996: T-3rd at the Bell Canadian Open

| 1997 | 27 | 98 | 21 | 0 | 2 | 5 | 11 | 70.62 | $525,161 |

Best finish for 1997: T-2nd at the Canon Greater Hartford Open & Buick Open

| 1998 | 30 | 92 | 15 | 0 | 1 | 2 | 5 | 71.43 | $252,832 |

Best finish for 1998: T-5th at the Buick Classic

| 1999 | 27 | 89 | 17 | 0 | 1 | 2 | 5 | 71.47 | $495,319 |

Best finish for 1999: 2nd at the Michelob Championship at Kingsmill

| 2000 | 27 | 89 | 18 | 0 | 0 | 3 | 6 | 70.56 | $514,193 |

Best finish for 2000: T-6th at the Southern Farm Bureau Classic

| 2001 | 27 | 85 | 15 | 0 | 0 | 1 | 5 | 70.93 | $391,924 |

Best finish for 2001: T-10th at the Sony Open in Hawaii

| 2002 | 23 | 77 | 15 | 0 | 0 | 3 | 8 | 70.79 | $620,280 |

Best finish for 2002: T-6th at the Buick Open

| 2003 | 31 | 97 | 17 | 0 | 0 | 0 | 7 | 71.11 | $595,720 |

Best finish for 2003: T-13th at the Chrysler Classic of Tucson

| 2004 | 25 | 83 | 17 | 0 | 1 | 2 | 7 | 70.70 | $874,139 |

Best finish for 2004: T-4th at the Buick Classic

| 2005 | 27 | 83 | 14 | 0 | 0 | 0 | 3 | 71.37 | $328,334 |

Best finish for 2005: T-17th at the Southern Farm Bureau Classic

| 2006 | 11 | 28 | 3 | 0 | 0 | 0 | 1 | 72.57 | $101,094 |

Best finish for 2006: T-16th at the Sony Open in Hawaii

Year	Starts	Rounds Played	Cuts Made	Wins	Top-5s	Top-10s	Top-25s	Scoring Average	Money
2007	20	50	5	0	0	0	2	72.08	$203,508

Best finish for 2007: T-13th at the U.S. Bank Championship in Milwaukee

Year	Starts	Rounds Played	Cuts Made	Wins	Top-5s	Top-10s	Top-25s	Scoring Average	Money
2008	12	36	6	0	0	0	0	71.03	$87,782

Best finish for 2008: T-34th at the AT&T Classic

Period Totals	Starts	Rounds Played	Cuts Made	Wins	Top-5s	Top-10s	Top-25s	Scoring Average	Money
	592	1827	326	1	18	41	111	71.41	$6,534,482

Angel Cabrera

Year	Starts	Rounds Played	Cuts Made	Wins	Top-5s	Top-10s	Top-25s	Scoring Average	Money
1997	1	4	1	0	0	0	0	72.75	$10,315

Best finish for 1997: T-51st at the British Open

Year	Starts	Rounds Played	Cuts Made	Wins	Top-5s	Top-10s	Top-25s	Scoring Average	Money
1999	3	12	3	0	1	1	2	72.75	$209,230

Best finish for 1999: T-4th at the British Open

| 2000 | 6 | 16 | 4 | 0 | 0 | 0 | 2 | 72.69 | $166,178 |

Best finish for 2000: T-17th at the American Express Championship

| 2001 | 8 | 24 | 6 | 0 | 0 | 2 | 2 | 71.13 | $338,392 |

Best finish for 2001: T-7th at the U.S. Open

| 2002 | 13 | 46 | 12 | 0 | 1 | 4 | 6 | 71.37 | $753,606 |

Best finish for 2002: T-5th at the Genuity Championship

| 2003 | 14 | 38 | 8 | 0 | 0 | 0 | 5 | 72.42 | $372,252 |

Best finish for 2003: T-15th at the Masters

| 2004 | 8 | 26 | 5 | 0 | 1 | 1 | 5 | 70.81 | $606,339 |

Best finish for 2004: T-4th at the WGC-NEC Invitational

| 2005 | 11 | 30 | 7 | 0 | 0 | 1 | 4 | 71.80 | $459,970 |

Best finish for 2005: T-10th at the Ford Championship at Doral

| 2006 | 12 | 38 | 9 | 0 | 1 | 3 | 5 | 70.92 | $1,023,671 |

Best finish for 2006: T-4th at the WGC-NEC Invitational

| 2007 | 14 | 42 | 9 | 1 | 1 | 1 | 4 | 72.24 | $1,663,606 |

Best finish for 2007: Win at the U.S. Open

| 2008 | 17 | 51 | 11 | 0 | 1 | 1 | 7 | 71.94 | $868,182 |

Best finish for 2008: T-5th at the WGC-Accenture Match Play Championship

Period Totals	Starts	Rounds Played	Cuts Made	Wins	Top-5s	Top-10s	Top-25s	Scoring Average	Money
	107	327	75	1	6	14	42	71.75	$6,471,741

George Cadle

Year	Starts	Rounds Played	Cuts Made	Wins	Top-5s	Top-10s	Top-25s	Scoring Average	Money
1974	2	6	0	0	0	0	0	77.83	
1975	23	77	15	0	1	2	4	72.03	$18,417

Best finish for 1975: T-5th at the Sahara Invitational

| 1976 | 34 | 109 | 22 | 0 | 2 | 3 | 8 | 72.28 | $36,382 |

Best finish for 1976: T-4th at the San Antonio Texas Open

| 1977 | 28 | 91 | 18 | 0 | 0 | 3 | 9 | 72.30 | $40,278 |

Best finish for 1977: T-6th at the Phoenix Open & Sea Pines Heritage Classic

| 1978 | 30 | 86 | 13 | 0 | 1 | 1 | 2 | 73.42 | $17,237 |

Best finish for 1978: T-5th at the Southern Open

| 1979 | 22 | 63 | 9 | 0 | 1 | 1 | 2 | 72.51 | $27,433 |

Best finish for 1979: T-3rd at the Sammy Davis, Jr. - Greater Hartford Open

| 1980 | 30 | 97 | 20 | 0 | 3 | 5 | 8 | 71.89 | $76,665 |

Best finish for 1980: T-3rd at the Greater Milwaukee Open

| 1981 | 30 | 90 | 15 | 0 | 1 | 2 | 5 | 72.07 | $37,312 |

Best finish for 1981: T-5th at the Pensacola Open

| 1982 | 26 | 85 | 15 | 0 | 0 | 0 | 4 | 71.87 | $28,050 |

Best finish for 1982: T-12th at the Georgia-Pacific Atlanta Golf Classic

| 1983 | 18 | 54 | 11 | 0 | 2 | 2 | 4 | 71.67 | $51,458 |

Best finish for 1983: 2nd at the Greater Milwaukee Open

| 1984 | 30 | 81 | 11 | 0 | 0 | 0 | 0 | 72.69 | $18,441 |

Best finish for 1984: T-30th at the Texas Open

| 1985 | 3 | 5 | 0 | 0 | 0 | 0 | 0 | 75.80 | |
| 1986 | 8 | 22 | 3 | 0 | 0 | 0 | 1 | 71.59 | $4,967 |

Best finish for 1986: T-20th at the Provident Classic

| 1987 | 1 | 2 | 0 | 0 | 0 | 0 | 0 | 76.50 | |
| 1989 | 9 | 24 | 4 | 0 | 0 | 0 | 0 | 71.67 | $6,444 |

Best finish for 1989: T-41st at the Federal Express St. Jude Classic

| 1990 | 1 | 4 | 1 | 0 | 0 | 0 | 0 | 71.25 | $648 |

Best finish for 1990: T-61st at the Deposit Guaranty

| 1991 | 1 | 4 | 1 | 0 | 0 | 0 | 0 | 69.75 | $633 |

Best finish for 1991: T-63rd at the Deposit Guaranty Classic

Period Totals	Starts	Rounds Played	Cuts Made	Wins	Top-5s	Top-10s	Top-25s	Scoring Average	Money
	296	900	158	0	11	19	47	72.30	$364,366

Steve Cain

Year	Starts	Rounds Played	Cuts Made	Wins	Top-5s	Top-10s	Top-25s	Scoring Average	Money
1973	16	37	3	0	0	0	0	74.30	$906

Best finish for 1973: T-45th at the Quad Cities Open

| 1974 | 14 | 36 | 4 | 0 | 0 | 0 | 0 | 74.08 | $1,018 |

Best finish for 1974: T-35th at the San Antonio Texas Open

| 1975 | 7 | 18 | 2 | 0 | 0 | 0 | 0 | 74.06 | $364 |

Best finish for 1975: T-66th at the Phoenix Open

| 1976 | 1 | 2 | 0 | 0 | 0 | 0 | 0 | 72.50 | $077 |
| 1977 | 9 | 22 | 4 | 0 | 0 | 0 | 0 | 73.91 | $1,532 |

Best finish for 1977: T-35th at the Danny Thomas Memphis Classic

1985	1	2	0	0	0	0	0	75.50	
1986	1	2	0	0	0	0	0	75.00	
1990	1	2	0	0	0	0	0	75.50	
Period Totals	Starts	Rounds Played	Cuts Made	Wins	Top-5s	Top-10s	Top-25s	Scoring Average	Money
	50	121	13	0	0	0	0	74.15	$3,898

Mark Calcavecchia

Year	Starts	Rounds Played	Cuts Made	Wins	Top-5s	Top-10s	Top-25s	Scoring Average	Money
1981	8	16	1	0	0	0	0	73.94	$404

Best finish for 1981: T-67th at the Quad Cities Open

| 1982 | 24 | 75 | 13 | 0 | 0 | 0 | 4 | 72.91 | $22,664 |

Best finish for 1982: T-11th at the B.C. Open

| 1983 | 20 | 57 | 9 | 0 | 0 | 1 | 2 | 72.98 | $16,313 |

Best finish for 1983: T-6th at the Greater Milwaukee Open

| 1984 | 25 | 75 | 13 | 0 | 1 | 1 | 1 | 72.91 | $29,660 |

Best finish for 1984: T-4th at the Greater Milwaukee Open

| 1985 | 15 | 43 | 7 | 0 | 0 | 0 | 2 | 72.65 | $15,957 |

Best finish for 1985: T-20th at the Kemper Open

| 1986 | 16 | 43 | 8 | 1 | 1 | 5 | 8 | 70.88 | $155,012 |

Best finish for 1986: Win at the Southwest Golf Classic

| 1987 | 28 | 93 | 21 | 1 | 8 | 9 | 13 | 70.85 | $544,998 |

Best finish for 1987: Win at the Honda Classic

| 1988 | 35 | 120 | 28 | 1 | 9 | 12 | 18 | 70.77 | $752,684 |

Best finish for 1988: Win at the Bank of Boston Classic

| 1989 | 27 | 91 | 19 | 3 | 9 | 11 | 14 | 70.40 | $935,741 |

Best finish for 1989: Win at the Phoenix Open, Nissan Los Angeles Open & British Open

| 1990 | 29 | 95 | 22 | 0 | 6 | 9 | 14 | 71.02 | $841,027 |

Best finish for 1990: T-2nd at the Northern Telecom Tucson Open, Doral-Ryder Open, Honda Classic, The Players Championship & Canon Greater Hartford Open

| 1991 | 25 | 80 | 17 | 0 | 3 | 6 | 8 | 71.03 | $324,629 |

Best finish for 1991: T-3rd at the Nestle Invitational

| 1992 | 28 | 99 | 22 | 1 | 1 | 4 | 6 | 71.14 | $390,152 |

Best finish for 1992: Win at the Phoenix Open

| 1993 | 31 | 99 | 21 | 0 | 3 | 6 | 14 | 71.04 | $653,796 |

Best finish for 1993: T-2nd at the BellSouth Classic, The International & Greater Milwaukee Open

| 1994 | 28 | 88 | 19 | 0 | 3 | 6 | 14 | 70.47 | $568,221 |

Best finish for 1994: 2nd at the Bell Canadian Open

| 1995 | 29 | 105 | 25 | 1 | 4 | 6 | 13 | 70.74 | $845,752 |

Best finish for 1995: Win at the BellSouth Classic

| 1996 | 29 | 103 | 23 | 0 | 4 | 6 | 12 | 70.65 | $629,851 |

Best finish for 1996: T-3rd at the Canon Greater Hartford Open & Las Vegas Invitational

| 1997 | 27 | 97 | 23 | 1 | 6 | 7 | 17 | 70.15 | $1,118,365 |

Best finish for 1997: Win at the Greater Vancouver Open

| 1998 | 27 | 96 | 22 | 1 | 5 | 7 | 13 | 70.48 | $1,369,554 |

Best finish for 1998: Win at the Honda Classic

| 1999 | 29 | 95 | 22 | 0 | 1 | 4 | 10 | 71.57 | $741,378 |

Best finish for 1999: T-3rd at the Canon Greater Hartford Open

| 2000 | 28 | 92 | 21 | 0 | 4 | 9 | 14 | 70.34 | $1,702,317 |

Best finish for 2000: T-2nd at the Canon Greater Hartford Open & SEI Pennsylvania Classic

| 2001 | 23 | 79 | 16 | 1 | 5 | 5 | 8 | 70.27 | $1,991,576 |

Best finish for 2001: Win at the Phoenix Open

| 2002 | 25 | 79 | 16 | 0 | 2 | 5 | 8 | 71.37 | $1,170,169 |

Best finish for 2002: 2nd at the Greater Greensboro Chrysler Classic

| 2003 | 24 | 84 | 19 | 0 | 1 | 3 | 8 | 70.40 | $1,125,838 |

Best finish for 2003: T-2nd at the Shell Houston Open

| 2004 | 24 | 79 | 16 | 0 | 0 | 2 | 6 | 71.19 | $717,876 |

Best finish for 2004: T-6th at the FUNAI Classic at the Walt Disney World Resort

| 2005 | 27 | 90 | 19 | 1 | 2 | 5 | 9 | 70.76 | $2,185,310 |

Best finish for 2005: Win at the Bell Canadian Open

| 2006 | 27 | 93 | 22 | 0 | 0 | 1 | 5 | 72.04 | $712,315 |

Best finish for 2006: T-9th at the FUNAI Classic at the Walt Disney World Resort

2007	28	93	19	1	5	6	11	71.11	$2,995,832

Best finish for 2007: Win at the PODS Championship

2008	25	66	11	0	1	2	5	71.86	$784,810

Best finish for 2008: T-4th at the Honda Classic

Period Totals	Starts	Rounds Played	Cuts Made	Wins	Top-5s	Top-10s	Top-25s	Scoring Average	Money
	711	2325	494	13	84	138	257	71.11	$23,342,197

Rex Caldwell

Year	Starts	Rounds Played	Cuts Made	Wins	Top-5s	Top-10s	Top-25s	Scoring Average	Money
1975	17	44	5	0	0	0	0	74.30	$2,867

Best finish for 1975: T-27th at the Greater Milwaukee Open

1976	24	75	14	0	1	2	4	72.57	$24,513

Best finish for 1976: 3rd at the Ed McMahon Quad City Open

1977	25	72	11	0	0	0	2	73.81	$9,581

Best finish for 1977: T-13th at the Ohio Kings Island Open

1978	30	107	23	0	3	7	14	71.52	$68,191

Best finish for 1978: T-3rd at the Buick Goodwrench Open

1979	32	112	23	0	4	5	13	71.77	$98,169

Best finish for 1979: 3rd at the PGA Championship

1980	36	120	25	0	1	4	11	71.97	$65,909

Best finish for 1980: T-4th at the Buick Goodwrench Open

1981	27	79	15	0	2	2	5	72.54	$57,745

Best finish for 1981: 2nd at the World Disney World National Team Championship

1982	31	102	19	0	2	2	5	72.04	$65,370

Best finish for 1982: T-3rd at the Bob Hope Chrysler Classic & Bing Crosby Pro-Am

1983	32	108	23	1	5	6	10	71.34	$284,434

Best finish for 1983: Win at the LaJet Coors Classic

1984	30	108	23	0	2	3	10	71.80	$127,000

Best finish for 1984: T-2nd at the Southern Open

1985	29	87	14	0	2	2	4	72.70	$60,289

Best finish for 1985: T-4th at the Isuzu/Andy Williams San Diego Open

1986	31	90	16	0	0	1	2	72.61	$39,674

Best finish for 1986: T-9th at the Georgia-Pacific Atlanta Golf Classic

1987	21	67	13	0	1	2	5	71.76	$50,054

Best finish for 1987: 5th at the Southern Open

1988	17	47	7	0	0	0	1	72.06	$15,271

Best finish for 1988: T-15th at the Bank of Boston Classic

1989	29	72	10	0	0	1	4	72.11	$55,066

Best finish for 1989: 7th at the Hawaiian Open

1990	2	4	0	0	0	0	0	75.75	
1991	1	2	0	0	0	0	0	70.00	
1992	5	14	2	0	0	0	0	71.29	$3,865

Best finish for 1992: T-39th at the Deposit Guaranty Classic

1993	2	6	1	0	0	0	1	69.67	$4,350

Best finish for 1993: T-16th at the Deposit Guaranty Classic

1994	2	4	0	0	0	0	0	75.75	
1995	6	18	3	0	0	0	0	72.06	$8,694

Best finish for 1995: T-38th at the LaCantera Texas Open

1996	9	24	4	0	0	0	1	71.83	$25,271

Best finish for 1996: T-17th at the Michelob Championship at Kingsmill

1997	3	8	1	0	0	0	0	74.00	$1,890

Best finish for 1997: T-75th at the Deposit Guaranty Golf Classic

1998	2	3	0	0	0	0	0	79.67	
2003	1	2	0	0	0	0	0	71.50	

Period Totals	Starts	Rounds Played	Cuts Made	Wins	Top-5s	Top-10s	Top-25s	Scoring Average	Money
	444	1375	252	1	23	37	92	72.21	$1,068,202

Bill Calfee

Year	Starts	Rounds Played	Cuts Made	Wins	Top-5s	Top-10s	Top-25s	Scoring Average	Money
1976	11	30	4	0	0	0	0	73.13	$1,712

Best finish for 1976: T-38th at the Kaiser International Open

1977	22	63	9	0	0	1	2	73.00	$11,052

Best finish for 1977: T-6th at the Kemper Open

1978	26	83	16	0	0	1	4	72.23	$21,840

Best finish for 1978: T-7th at the Hawaiian Open

1979	25	70	9	0	0	0	2	72.76	$14,202

Best finish for 1979: T-17th at the Hawaiian Open

1980	29	90	17	0	1	1	3	72.51	$33,463

Best finish for 1980: T-5th at the Bay Hill Classic

1981	28	82	14	0	0	1	4	72.46	$27,322

Best finish for 1981: T-8th at the Pleasant Valley Jimmy Fund Classic

1982	24	70	10	0	0	1	2	71.97	$22,257

Best finish for 1982: T-7th at the Texas Open

Year	Starts	Rounds Played	Cuts Made	Wins	Top-5s	Top-10s	Top-25s	Scoring Average	Money
1983	15	46	8	0	0	0	3	71.78	$20,442

Best finish for 1983: T-12th at the Southern Open

1984	11	36	8	0	0	1	5	70.78	$27,379

Best finish for 1984: T-8th at the Miller High-Life Quad Cities Open

1985	15	38	5	0	0	1	1	72.61	$13,859

Best finish for 1985: T-8th at the Lite Quad Cities Open

Period Totals	Starts	Rounds Played	Cuts Made	Wins	Top-5s	Top-10s	Top-25s	Scoring Average	Money
	206	608	100	0	1	7	26	72.36	$193,529

Roger Calvin

Year	Starts	Rounds Played	Cuts Made	Wins	Top-5s	Top-10s	Top-25s	Scoring Average	Money
1977	1	2	0	0	0	0	0	77.00	$255
1979	17	47	7	0	0	0	1	72.30	$7,451

Best finish for 1979: T-17th at the First NBC New Orleans Open

1980	20	62	11	0	0	0	2	72.85	$14,835

Best finish for 1980: T-13th at the Buick Goodwrench Open

1981	28	81	15	0	0	0	2	72.98	$15,506

Best finish for 1981: T-20th at the World Disney World National Team Championship

1982	16	42	5	0	0	0	1	72.90	$4,413

Best finish for 1982: T-14th at the Tallahassee Open

Period Totals	Starts	Rounds Played	Cuts Made	Wins	Top-5s	Top-10s	Top-25s	Scoring Average	Money
	82	234	38	0	0	0	6	72.83	$42,459

Chad Campbell

Year	Starts	Rounds Played	Cuts Made	Wins	Top-5s	Top-10s	Top-25s	Scoring Average	Money
1998	1	4	1	0	0	0	0	71.50	$4,332

Best finish for 1998: T-54th at the Michelob Championship at Kingsmill

1999	2	6	1	0	0	0	0	73.17	$12,038

Best finish for 1999: T-35th at the Michelob Championship at Kingsmill

2000	1	2	0	0	0	0	0	75.50	$1,000
2001	3	8	1	0	1	1	1	69.63	$260,200

Best finish for 2001: 2nd at the Southern Farm Bureau Classic

2002	34	109	21	0	2	2	7	70.54	$827,474

Best finish for 2002: T-3rd at the Greater Greensboro Chrysler Classic

2003	27	102	25	1	5	9	15	69.91	$3,917,064

Best finish for 2003: Win at The Tour Championship

2004	28	93	22	1	2	4	9	71.03	$2,276,602

Best finish for 2004: Win at the Bay Hill Invitational

2005	27	92	22	0	3	5	11	70.67	$2,395,374

Best finish for 2005: 2nd at the Nissan Open & Chrysler Championship

2006	25	87	20	1	5	5	10	70.90	$2,813,067

Best finish for 2006: Win at the Bob Hope Chrysler Classic

2007	28	90	18	1	2	2	6	72.01	$1,706,124

Best finish for 2007: Win at the Viking Classic

2008	28	94	19	0	3	7	14	70.37	$2,404,770

Best finish for 2008: T-2nd at the Shell Houston Open

Period Totals	Starts	Rounds Played	Cuts Made	Wins	Top-5s	Top-10s	Top-25s	Scoring Average	Money
	204	687	150	4	23	35	73	70.78	$16,618,045

Doug Campbell

Year	Starts	Rounds Played	Cuts Made	Wins	Top-5s	Top-10s	Top-25s	Scoring Average	Money
1979	9	22	2	0	0	0	0	72.68	$804

Best finish for 1979: T-60th at the Southern Open

1980	18	44	6	0	0	1	2	73.57	$13,053

Best finish for 1980: T-6th at the World Disney World National Team Championship

1981	6	13	1	0	0	0	0	74.15	$463

Best finish for 1981: T-53rd at the Southern Open

1982	14	32	2	0	0	0	0	73.78	$1,547

Best finish for 1982: T-45th at the Hawaiian Open

1984	1	2	0	0	0	0	0	74.50	
1986	1	2	0	0	0	0	0	81.00	$600

Period Totals	Starts	Rounds Played	Cuts Made	Wins	Top-5s	Top-10s	Top-25s	Scoring Average	Money
	49	115	11	0	0	1	2	73.67	$16,468

Joe Campbell

Year	Starts	Rounds Played	Cuts Made	Wins	Top-5s	Top-10s	Top-25s	Scoring Average	Money
1958	6	22	5	0	0	0	1	74.14	$200

Best finish for 1958: T-16th at the Pensacola Open

1959	22	88	18	0	2	6	19	71.15	$11,911

Best finish for 1959: T-2nd at the Tucson Open Invitational

1960	17	64	15	0	0	4	8	71.88	$6,212

Best finish for 1960: T-6th at the Tucson Open Invitational & Pensacola Open Invitational

Year	Starts	Rounds Played	Cuts Made	Wins	Top-5s	Top-10s	Top-25s	Scoring Average	Money
1961	12	48	11	1	3	4	8	70.35	$10,161

Best finish for 1961: Win at the Beaumont Open Invitational

| 1962 | 21 | 84 | 20 | 1 | 4 | 6 | 12 | 71.25 | $19,076 |

Best finish for 1962: Win at the Baton Rouge Open Invitational

| 1963 | 17 | 67 | 16 | 0 | 0 | 1 | 7 | 71.78 | $9,841 |

Best finish for 1963: T-10th at the Thunderbird Classic Invitational

| 1964 | 21 | 73 | 14 | 0 | 1 | 2 | 2 | 72.47 | $6,294 |

Best finish for 1964: T-4th at the St. Petersburg Open

| 1965 | 24 | 87 | 19 | 0 | 5 | 7 | 11 | 71.70 | $42,960 |

Best finish for 1965: T-2nd at the Philadelphia Classic

| 1966 | 23 | 82 | 19 | 1 | 2 | 5 | 9 | 71.74 | $32,674 |

Best finish for 1966: Win at the Tucson Open Invitational

| 1967 | 19 | 69 | 15 | 0 | 2 | 2 | 7 | 72.07 | $20,364 |

Best finish for 1967: 2nd at the Azalea Open

| 1968 | 5 | 20 | 5 | 0 | 0 | 0 | 1 | 71.05 | $2,035 |

Best finish for 1968: T-19th at the AZALEA Open Invitational

| 1969 | 7 | 20 | 3 | 0 | 0 | 1 | 3 | 71.75 | $4,058 |

Best finish for 1969: T-6th at the Azalea Open

| 1970 | 3 | 12 | 3 | 0 | 1 | 2 | 2 | 69.58 | $6,507 |

Best finish for 1970: T-5th at the Danny Thomas Memphis Classic

| 1971 | 2 | 6 | 1 | 0 | 0 | 0 | 0 | 74.00 | $258 |

Best finish for 1971: T-63rd at the PGA Championship

| 1972 | 8 | 25 | 4 | 0 | 0 | 0 | 0 | 72.92 | $2,880 |

Best finish for 1972: T-26th at the Greater Hartford Open Invitational

| 1973 | 2 | 6 | 1 | 0 | 0 | 0 | 0 | 75.67 | $930 |

Best finish for 1973: T-45th at the U.S. Open

1974	1	2	0	0	0	0	0	75.00	
1978	1	2	0	0	0	0	0	79.00	$600
Period Totals	Starts	Rounds Played	Cuts Made	Wins	Top-5s	Top-10s	Top-25s	Scoring Average	Money
	211	777	169	3	20	40	90	71.77	$176,961

Michael Campbell

Year	Starts	Rounds Played	Cuts Made	Wins	Top-5s	Top-10s	Top-25s	Scoring Average	Money
1994	1	2	0	0	0	0	0	72.50	$972
1995	2	4	2	0	1	1	1	70.75	$115,388

Best finish for 1995: T-3rd at the British Open

| 1996 | 10 | 27 | 4 | 0 | 0 | 1 | 1 | 72.56 | $70,146 |

Best finish for 1996: T-7th at the Honda Classic

| 1998 | 1 | 4 | 1 | 0 | 0 | 0 | 0 | 74.75 | $9,541 |

Best finish for 1998: T-66th at the British Open

| 1999 | 1 | 2 | 0 | 0 | 0 | 0 | 0 | 78.00 | $1,719 |
| 2000 | 6 | 16 | 4 | 0 | 0 | 1 | 3 | 72.13 | $325,699 |

Best finish for 2000: 9th at the American Express Championship

| 2001 | 10 | 28 | 6 | 0 | 0 | 1 | 4 | 72.61 | $334,192 |

Best finish for 2001: T-9th at the Accenture Match Play Championship

| 2002 | 11 | 30 | 6 | 0 | 1 | 2 | 5 | 71.60 | $842,241 |

Best finish for 2002: 2nd at the Bay Hill Invitational

| 2003 | 14 | 31 | 5 | 0 | 0 | 0 | 0 | 75.32 | $113,814 |

Best finish for 2003: T-33rd at the WGC-Accenture Match Play Championship

| 2004 | 6 | 16 | 4 | 0 | 0 | 0 | 1 | 73.38 | $158,506 |

Best finish for 2004: T-20th at the British Open

| 2005 | 5 | 20 | 5 | 1 | 2 | 3 | 3 | 71.25 | $1,661,810 |

Best finish for 2005: Win at the U.S. Open

| 2006 | 10 | 26 | 5 | 0 | 1 | 1 | 3 | 72.12 | $525,233 |

Best finish for 2006: T-4th at the Mercedes Championships

| 2007 | 9 | 24 | 5 | 0 | 0 | 0 | 0 | 75.38 | $162,332 |

Best finish for 2007: T-33rd at the WGC-Accenture Match Play Championship

| 2008 | 6 | 16 | 2 | 0 | 0 | 0 | 0 | 75.94 | $48,054 |

Best finish for 2008: T-42nd at the PGA Championship

| Period Totals | Starts | Rounds Played | Cuts Made | Wins | Top-5s | Top-10s | Top-25s | Scoring Average | Money |
| | 92 | 246 | 49 | 1 | 5 | 10 | 21 | 73.21 | $4,369,646 |

David Canipe

Year	Starts	Rounds Played	Cuts Made	Wins	Top-5s	Top-10s	Top-25s	Scoring Average	Money
1974	1	2	0	0	0	0	0	75.00	
1976	12	28	2	0	0	0	0	74.61	$790

Best finish for 1976: T-51st at the Southern Open

| 1977 | 14 | 34 | 3 | 0 | 0 | 0 | 0 | 74.82 | $1,654 |

Best finish for 1977: T-47th at the U.S. Open

| 1979 | 8 | 22 | 3 | 0 | 0 | 0 | 0 | 73.41 | $1,581 |

Best finish for 1979: T-41st at the Ed McMahon Quad City Open

Year	Starts	Rounds Played	Cuts Made	Wins	Top-5s	Top-10s	Top-25s	Scoring Average	Money
1980	7	17	1	0	0	0	0	74.88	$1,050

Best finish for 1980: T-42nd at the Joe Garagiola Tucson Open

Year	Starts	Rounds Played	Cuts Made	Wins	Top-5s	Top-10s	Top-25s	Scoring Average	Money
1981	1	0	1	0	0	1	1		$4,577

Best finish for 1981: T-10th at the World Disney World National Team Championship

Year	Starts	Rounds Played	Cuts Made	Wins	Top-5s	Top-10s	Top-25s	Scoring Average	Money
1984	1	4	1	0	0	0	0	75.50	$2,325

Best finish for 1984: T-62nd at the U.S. Open

Year	Starts	Rounds Played	Cuts Made	Wins	Top-5s	Top-10s	Top-25s	Scoring Average	Money
1986	1	4	1	0	0	0	0	68.25	$2,265

Best finish for 1986: T-26th at the Provident Classic

Year	Starts	Rounds Played	Cuts Made	Wins	Top-5s	Top-10s	Top-25s	Scoring Average	Money
1987	33	88	15	0	0	1	2	71.92	$37,527

Best finish for 1987: T-8th at the Pensacola Open

Year	Starts	Rounds Played	Cuts Made	Wins	Top-5s	Top-10s	Top-25s	Scoring Average	Money
1988	30	89	15	0	1	2	5	71.69	$114,180

Best finish for 1988: T-4th at the Panasonic Las Vegas Invitational

Year	Starts	Rounds Played	Cuts Made	Wins	Top-5s	Top-10s	Top-25s	Scoring Average	Money
1989	30	90	15	0	1	1	4	71.52	$93,077

Best finish for 1989: T-5th at the BellSouth Atlanta Golf Classic

Year	Starts	Rounds Played	Cuts Made	Wins	Top-5s	Top-10s	Top-25s	Scoring Average	Money
1990	28	88	15	0	1	2	6	72.14	$150,015

Best finish for 1990: 3rd at the Federal Express St. Jude Classic

Year	Starts	Rounds Played	Cuts Made	Wins	Top-5s	Top-10s	Top-25s	Scoring Average	Money
1991	30	90	14	0	1	2	3	71.78	$126,520

Best finish for 1991: T-3rd at the Federal Express St. Jude Classic

Year	Starts	Rounds Played	Cuts Made	Wins	Top-5s	Top-10s	Top-25s	Scoring Average	Money
1992	29	77	9	0	0	0	1	72.78	$40,894

Best finish for 1992: T-14th at the Shell Houston Open

Year	Starts	Rounds Played	Cuts Made	Wins	Top-5s	Top-10s	Top-25s	Scoring Average	Money
1993	2	6	1	0	0	0	0	72.00	$1,557

Best finish for 1993: T-32nd at the Deposit Guaranty Classic

Period Totals	Starts	Rounds Played	Cuts Made	Wins	Top-5s	Top-10s	Top-25s	Scoring Average	Money
	227	639	96	0	4	9	22	72.36	$578,014

Joe Cardenas

Year	Starts	Rounds Played	Cuts Made	Wins	Top-5s	Top-10s	Top-25s	Scoring Average	Money
1964	7	14	1	0	0	0	0	75.21	

Best finish for 1964: T-52nd at the Greater Greensboro Open

Year	Starts	Rounds Played	Cuts Made	Wins	Top-5s	Top-10s	Top-25s	Scoring Average	Money
1966	1	2	0	0	0	0	0	80.00	
1967	1	2	0	0	0	0	0	79.50	
1968	1	4	1	0	0	0	0	75.50	$365

Best finish for 1968: T-67th at the PGA Championship

Year	Starts	Rounds Played	Cuts Made	Wins	Top-5s	Top-10s	Top-25s	Scoring Average	Money
1969	7	14	0	0	0	0	0	75.79	
1970	11	19	1	0	0	0	0	75.53	$167

Best finish for 1970: T-40th at the National 4 Ball Championship PGA Players

Year	Starts	Rounds Played	Cuts Made	Wins	Top-5s	Top-10s	Top-25s	Scoring Average	Money
1971	3	11	2	0	0	0	0	73.45	$529

Best finish for 1971: T-64th at the Hawaiian Open

Year	Starts	Rounds Played	Cuts Made	Wins	Top-5s	Top-10s	Top-25s	Scoring Average	Money
1973	1	0	0	0	0	0	0		
1977	1	2	0	0	0	0	0	76.50	

Period Totals	Starts	Rounds Played	Cuts Made	Wins	Top-5s	Top-10s	Top-25s	Scoring Average	Money
	33	68	5	0	0	0	0	75.46	$1,061

Sam Carmichael

Year	Starts	Rounds Played	Cuts Made	Wins	Top-5s	Top-10s	Top-25s	Scoring Average	Money
1959	1	2	0	0	0	0	0	80.00	
1960	1	2	0	0	0	0	0	75.50	
1961	1	4	1	0	0	0	0	70.00	

Best finish for 1961: T-34th at the Milwaukee Open Invitational

Year	Starts	Rounds Played	Cuts Made	Wins	Top-5s	Top-10s	Top-25s	Scoring Average	Money
1962	4	12	2	0	0	0	1	72.83	$432

Best finish for 1962: T-18th at the Mobile Sertoma Open Invitational

Year	Starts	Rounds Played	Cuts Made	Wins	Top-5s	Top-10s	Top-25s	Scoring Average	Money
1963	14	56	14	0	0	1	5	72.16	$5,387

Best finish for 1963: T-10th at the "500" Festival Open Invitational

Year	Starts	Rounds Played	Cuts Made	Wins	Top-5s	Top-10s	Top-25s	Scoring Average	Money
1964	33	92	13	0	1	2	4	73.67	$8,240

Best finish for 1964: T-2nd at the Greater Hartford Open

Year	Starts	Rounds Played	Cuts Made	Wins	Top-5s	Top-10s	Top-25s	Scoring Average	Money
1965	24	74	13	0	0	0	2	73.49	$3,539

Best finish for 1965: T-20th at the Pensacola Open & New Orleans Open

Year	Starts	Rounds Played	Cuts Made	Wins	Top-5s	Top-10s	Top-25s	Scoring Average	Money
1966	9	31	6	0	0	0	0	74.29	$2,044

Best finish for 1966: T-28th at the Florida Citrus Open Invitational

Year	Starts	Rounds Played	Cuts Made	Wins	Top-5s	Top-10s	Top-25s	Scoring Average	Money
1967	14	38	6	0	0	1	3	73.45	$7,089

Best finish for 1967: T-9th at the Buick Open

Year	Starts	Rounds Played	Cuts Made	Wins	Top-5s	Top-10s	Top-25s	Scoring Average	Money
1968	28	93	18	0	2	2	5	72.33	$16,105

Best finish for 1968: T-2nd at the Phoenix Open Invitational

Year	Starts	Rounds Played	Cuts Made	Wins	Top-5s	Top-10s	Top-25s	Scoring Average	Money
1969	4	9	1	0	0	0	0	72.11	$570

Best finish for 1969: T-33rd at the Phoenix Open

Year	Starts	Rounds Played	Cuts Made	Wins	Top-5s	Top-10s	Top-25s	Scoring Average	Money
1970	4	12	2	0	0	1	1	73.58	$2,280

Best finish for 1970: T-6th at the Tallahassee Open

Year	Starts	Rounds Played	Cuts Made	Wins	Top-5s	Top-10s	Top-25s	Scoring Average	Money
1971	2	4	0	0	0	0	0	77.50	$500
1972	1	4	1	0	0	0	0	73.50	$1,147

Best finish for 1972: T-36th at the PGA Championship

Year	Starts	Rounds Played	Cuts Made	Wins	Top-5s	Top-10s	Top-25s	Scoring Average	Money
1973	1	2	0	0	0	0	0	77.50	

Period Totals	Starts	Rounds Played	Cuts Made	Wins	Top-5s	Top-10s	Top-25s	Scoring Average	Money
	141	435	77	0	3	7	21	73.18	$47,332

Dick Carmody

Year	Starts	Rounds Played	Cuts Made	Wins	Top-5s	Top-10s	Top-25s	Scoring Average	Money
1967	1	4	1	0	0	0	0	72.50	

Best finish for 1967: T-53rd at the Cajun Classic

| 1968 | 21 | 63 | 9 | 0 | 0 | 0 | 0 | 73.70 | $996 |

Best finish for 1968: T-29th at the Minnesota Golf Classic

| 1969 | 3 | 6 | 0 | 0 | 0 | 0 | 0 | 77.17 | |
| 1970 | 18 | 47 | 6 | 0 | 0 | 0 | 0 | 73.91 | $1,909 |

Best finish for 1970: T-36th at the Kemper Open

| 1971 | 19 | 54 | 7 | 0 | 0 | 0 | 0 | 74.02 | $3,353 |

Best finish for 1971: T-32nd at the Bob Hope Chrysler Classic

1980	1	2	0	0	0	0	0	76.00	
Period Totals	Starts	Rounds Played	Cuts Made	Wins	Top-5s	Top-10s	Top-25s	Scoring Average	Money
	63	176	23	0	0	0	0	73.97	$6,258

Mark Carnevale

Year	Starts	Rounds Played	Cuts Made	Wins	Top-5s	Top-10s	Top-25s	Scoring Average	Money
1983	1	2	0	0	0	0	0	78.50	
1984	1	2	0	0	0	0	0	74.00	
1985	1	2	0	0	0	0	0	73.00	
1986	2	8	2	0	0	0	0	72.75	$2,584

Best finish for 1986: T-40th at the Bank of Boston Classic

1987	2	4	0	0	0	0	0	72.75	
1988	1	2	0	0	0	0	0	71.50	
1989	1	2	0	0	0	0	0	73.50	
1991	1	2	0	0	0	0	0	72.50	
1992	27	83	14	1	1	1	3	71.60	$222,122

Best finish for 1992: Win at the Chattanooga Classic

| 1993 | 32 | 94 | 15 | 0 | 0 | 0 | 3 | 72.29 | $101,546 |

Best finish for 1993: T-13th at the Buick Southern Open

| 1994 | 31 | 86 | 13 | 0 | 2 | 2 | 4 | 72.17 | $192,653 |

Best finish for 1994: T-2nd at the GTE Byron Nelson Classic

| 1995 | 29 | 77 | 11 | 0 | 0 | 0 | 1 | 72.74 | $62,206 |

Best finish for 1995: T-17th at the Sprint International

| 1996 | 13 | 31 | 3 | 0 | 0 | 0 | 0 | 72.68 | $17,485 |

Best finish for 1996: T-26th at the B.C. Open

| 1997 | 3 | 8 | 1 | 0 | 0 | 0 | 0 | 72.88 | $3,162 |

Best finish for 1997: 68th at the Michelob Championship at Kingsmill

| 1998 | 32 | 93 | 15 | 0 | 0 | 1 | 4 | 71.52 | $174,470 |

Best finish for 1998: T-7th at the Greater Milwaukee Open

| 1999 | 11 | 32 | 5 | 0 | 1 | 1 | 1 | 71.66 | $92,799 |

Best finish for 1999: T-4th at the B.C. Open

| 2000 | 7 | 16 | 1 | 0 | 0 | 0 | 0 | 71.69 | $6,210 |

Best finish for 2000: T-65th at the Kemper Insurance Open

| 2001 | 3 | 12 | 3 | 0 | 0 | 0 | 0 | 70.17 | $25,016 |

Best finish for 2001: T-37th at the B.C. Open

| 2002 | 5 | 14 | 2 | 0 | 0 | 0 | 0 | 72.64 | $9,372 |

Best finish for 2002: T-77th at the John Deere Classic

2003	5	7	0	0	0	0	0	75.43	
2005	1	2	0	0	0	0	0	77.50	
Period Totals	Starts	Rounds Played	Cuts Made	Wins	Top-5s	Top-10s	Top-25s	Scoring Average	Money
	209	579	85	1	4	5	16	72.15	$909,625

Jason Caron

Year	Starts	Rounds Played	Cuts Made	Wins	Top-5s	Top-10s	Top-25s	Scoring Average	Money
2000	29	75	9	0	0	0	1	72.35	$87,110

Best finish for 2000: T-19th at the Honda Classic

| 2002 | 1 | 4 | 1 | 0 | 0 | 0 | 0 | 73.00 | $35,639 |

Best finish for 2002: T-30th at the U.S. Open

| 2003 | 29 | 71 | 9 | 0 | 0 | 0 | 1 | 72.34 | $172,262 |

Best finish for 2003: T-15th at the AT&T Pebble Beach

| 2004 | 1 | 2 | 0 | 0 | 0 | 0 | 0 | 73.00 | |
| 2006 | 1 | 4 | 1 | 0 | 0 | 0 | 0 | 72.25 | $29,260 |

Best finish for 2006: T-31st at the Honda Classic

| Period Totals | Starts | Rounds Played | Cuts Made | Wins | Top-5s | Top-10s | Top-25s | Scoring Average | Money |
| | 61 | 156 | 20 | 0 | 0 | 0 | 2 | 72.37 | $324,270 |

Joe Carr

Year	Starts	Rounds Played	Cuts Made	Wins	Top-5s	Top-10s	Top-25s	Scoring Average	Money
1958	1	4	1	0	0	0	0	74.50	

Best finish for 1958: 37th at the British Open

Year	Starts	Rounds Played	Cuts Made	Wins	Top-5s	Top-10s	Top-25s	Scoring Average	Money
1959	1	4	1	0	0	0	0	74.50	

Best finish for 1959: T-38th at the British Open

1960	1	4	1	0	0	1	1	71.25	

Best finish for 1960: 8th at the British Open

1961	1	2	0	0	0	0	0	80.50	
1962	1	2	0	0	0	0	0	76.50	
1963	2	6	1	0	0	0	1	74.00	$530

Best finish for 1963: T-18th at the Fig Garden Village Open Invitational

1964	24	61	7	0	0	0	1	74.10	$2,032

Best finish for 1964: T-13th at the Portland Open

1965	17	49	7	0	0	0	1	73.47	$2,520

Best finish for 1965: T-11th at the Tucson Open

1966	20	51	6	0	0	0	0	74.76	$450

Best finish for 1966: T-37th at the Bing Crosby National Professional-Amateur

1967	25	78	14	0	0	0	1	74.17	$2,255

Best finish for 1967: T-23rd at the Greater Greensboro Open

1968	9	28	5	0	0	0	1	73.50	$1,578

Best finish for 1968: T-21st at the Kemper Open Invitational

1969	19	52	7	0	0	0	3	73.83	$3,883

Best finish for 1969: T-21st at the Kemper Insurance Open & West End Classic

1970	19	56	8	0	0	1	3	72.39	$6,636

Best finish for 1970: T-10th at the Danny Thomas Memphis Classic

1971	10	33	6	0	0	0	0	72.91	$2,550

Best finish for 1971: T-28th at the Bing Crosby Pro-Am

1972	3	6	0	0	0	0	0	73.67	
1973	6	21	3	0	0	0	2	72.62	$4,423

Best finish for 1973: T-14th at the Liggett Meyers Open

1974	4	8	0	0	0	0	0	78.38	
1975	10	23	1	0	0	0	0	74.74	$910

Best finish for 1975: T-43rd at the Jackie Gleason's Inverrary Classic

1976	3	6	0	0	0	0	0	75.17	
1978	1	2	0	0	0	0	0	76.50	
1979	1	4	1	0	0	0	0	75.25	$502

Best finish for 1979: T-69th at the American Optical Classic

1980	3	6	1	0	0	0	0	75.17	$558

Best finish for 1980: T-76th at the Pleasant Valley Jimmy Fund Classic

1981	1	0	0	0	0	0	0		
1983	1	4	1	0	0	0	0	72.25	$654

Best finish for 1983: T-75th at the Bank of Boston Classic

1984	2	4	0	0	0	0	0	81.25	$1,000
1986	1	2	0	0	0	0	0	77.00	
1987	1	2	0	0	0	0	0	72.50	
Period Totals	Starts	Rounds Played	Cuts Made	Wins	Top-5s	Top-10s	Top-25s	Scoring Average	Money
	187	518	71	0	0	2	14	73.93	$30,482

Jim Carter

Year	Starts	Rounds Played	Cuts Made	Wins	Top-5s	Top-10s	Top-25s	Scoring Average	Money
1985	1	2	0	0	0	0	0	76.00	
1987	33	102	20	0	0	1	5	71.64	$60,102

Best finish for 1987: T-10th at the Provident Classic

1988	30	96	19	0	2	5	10	71.85	$191,488

Best finish for 1988: T-4th at the AT&T Pebble Beach Pro-Am & Independent Insurance Agent Open

1989	32	106	22	0	3	6	13	70.74	$321,719

Best finish for 1989: T-3rd at the AT&T Pebble Beach Pro-Am

1990	32	89	12	0	0	0	2	72.52	$54,392

Best finish for 1990: T-14th at the Shearson Lehman Hutton Open

1991	7	16	1	0	0	0	0	72.06	$2,450

Best finish for 1991: T-43rd at the Chattanooga Classic

1993	1	4	1	0	0	0	0	71.25	$2,752

Best finish for 1993: T-45th at the Phoenix Open

1994	1	2	0	0	0	0	0	72.00	
1995	30	96	19	0	1	1	3	71.03	$180,664

Best finish for 1995: T-3rd at the Anheuser-Busch Golf Classic

1996	31	107	25	0	1	2	5	70.98	$223,696

Best finish for 1996: T-3rd at the Buick Open

1997	29	98	21	0	1	2	7	71.00	$281,134

Best finish for 1997: 5th at the Buick Classic

1998	32	106	22	0	1	3	8	71.05	$407,184

Best finish for 1998: T-3rd at the Freeport-McDermott Classic

1999	28	96	19	0	1	1	8	71.10	$460,776

Best finish for 1999: T-5th at the Buick Classic

2000	30	94	17	1	1	1	5	71.27	$967,322

Best finish for 2000: Win at the Touchstone Energy Tucson Open

Year	Starts	Rounds Played	Cuts Made	Wins	Top-5s	Top-10s	Top-25s	Scoring Average	Money
2001	28	101	23	0	0	0	1	70.84	$345,926

Best finish for 2001: T-22nd at the MasterCard Colonial

| 2002 | 29 | 98 | 19 | 0 | 2 | 4 | 7 | 71.07 | $814,610 |

Best finish for 2002: T-5th at the Canon Greater Hartford Open & FedEx St. Jude Classic

| 2003 | 33 | 93 | 14 | 0 | 0 | 0 | 0 | 71.68 | $217,961 |

Best finish for 2003: T-28th at the BellSouth Classic & Shell Houston Open

| 2004 | 18 | 47 | 5 | 0 | 0 | 0 | 1 | 71.60 | $111,105 |

Best finish for 2004: T-18th at the Buick Open

| 2005 | 25 | 60 | 6 | 0 | 0 | 0 | 0 | 72.38 | $104,138 |

Best finish for 2005: T-26th at the Chrysler Classic of Tucson

2006	3	7	0	0	0	0	0	74.29	
Period Totals	Starts	Rounds Played	Cuts Made	Wins	Top-5s	Top-10s	Top-25s	Scoring Average	Money
	453	1420	265	1	13	26	75	71.36	$4,747,419

Tom Carter

Year	Starts	Rounds Played	Cuts Made	Wins	Top-5s	Top-10s	Top-25s	Scoring Average	Money
1976	1	2	0	0	0	0	0	82.50	
1993	1	2	0	0	0	0	0	73.50	
1998	1	2	0	0	0	0	0	74.00	
2003	8	21	2	0	0	0	1	71.00	$105,143

Best finish for 2003: T-12th at the FUNAI Classic at the Walt Disney World Resort

| 2004 | 35 | 110 | 20 | 0 | 0 | 0 | 3 | 71.94 | $395,780 |

Best finish for 2004: T-13th at the Chrysler Championship

| Period Totals | Starts | Rounds Played | Cuts Made | Wins | Top-5s | Top-10s | Top-25s | Scoring Average | Money |
| | 46 | 137 | 22 | 0 | 0 | 0 | 4 | 72.00 | $500,923 |

Paul Casey

Year	Starts	Rounds Played	Cuts Made	Wins	Top-5s	Top-10s	Top-25s	Scoring Average	Money
2001	3	9	1	0	0	0	0	72.00	$8,580

Best finish for 2001: T-45th at the Texas Open at LaCantera

| 2002 | 9 | 27 | 4 | 0 | 0 | 0 | 1 | 71.67 | $61,476 |

Best finish for 2002: T-22nd at the Buick Invitational

| 2003 | 7 | 16 | 5 | 0 | 0 | 2 | 3 | 72.50 | $368,027 |

Best finish for 2003: T-8th at the American Express Championship

| 2004 | 11 | 31 | 7 | 0 | 0 | 2 | 6 | 71.26 | $707,272 |

Best finish for 2004: T-6th at the Masters

| 2005 | 10 | 23 | 4 | 0 | 0 | 0 | 2 | 73.00 | $206,135 |

Best finish for 2005: T-16th at the Ford Championship at Doral

| 2006 | 8 | 22 | 7 | 0 | 1 | 1 | 3 | 72.09 | $531,401 |

Best finish for 2006: T-4th at the WGC-NEC Invitational

| 2007 | 10 | 34 | 9 | 0 | 1 | 4 | 5 | 72.21 | $1,012,770 |

Best finish for 2007: T-5th at the WGC-Accenture Match Play Championship

| 2008 | 16 | 52 | 12 | 0 | 0 | 4 | 7 | 71.75 | $1,156,414 |

Best finish for 2008: T-7th at the British Open & Barclays Classic

| Period Totals | Starts | Rounds Played | Cuts Made | Wins | Top-5s | Top-10s | Top-25s | Scoring Average | Money |
| | 74 | 214 | 49 | 0 | 2 | 13 | 27 | 71.98 | $4,052,077 |

Billy Casper

Year	Starts	Rounds Played	Cuts Made	Wins	Top-5s	Top-10s	Top-25s	Scoring Average	Money
1958	28	108	26	3	12	16	23	70.72	$43,674

Best finish for 1958: Win at the Bing Crosby Pro-Am, New Orleans Open & Buick Open

| 1959 | 23 | 90 | 21 | 4 | 7 | 14 | 20 | 70.27 | $34,108 |

Best finish for 1959: Win at the Portland Centennial Open Invitational, Lafayette Open Invitational, Mobile Sertoma Open Invitational & U.S. Open

| 1960 | 23 | 93 | 21 | 3 | 10 | 13 | 20 | 69.32 | $31,061 |

Best finish for 1960: Win at the Portland Open Invitational, Hesperia Open Invitational & Orange County Open Invitational

| 1961 | 23 | 93 | 19 | 1 | 9 | 15 | 22 | 69.94 | $36,127 |

Best finish for 1961: Win at the Portland Open Invitational

| 1962 | 22 | 87 | 15 | 4 | 13 | 13 | 18 | 69.59 | $57,182 |

Best finish for 1962: Win at the Doral Country Club Open Invitational, Greater Greensboro Open Invitational, "500" Festival Open Invitational & Bakersfield Open

| 1963 | 19 | 77 | 15 | 2 | 4 | 8 | 19 | 70.64 | $32,726 |

Best finish for 1963: Win at the Bing Crosby National & Insurance City Open Invitational

| 1964 | 32 | 126 | 30 | 4 | 15 | 24 | 26 | 70.46 | $93,582 |

Best finish for 1964: Win at the Doral Open, Colonial National Invitational, Seattle Open & Almaden Open

| 1965 | 31 | 124 | 30 | 4 | 13 | 17 | 23 | 70.70 | $121,782 |

Best finish for 1965: Win at the Bob Hope Classic, Western Open, Greater Hartford Open & Sahara Invitational

| 1966 | 25 | 101 | 24 | 4 | 11 | 16 | 24 | 70.43 | $144,833 |

Best finish for 1966: Win at the San Diego Open Invitational, U.S. Open, Western Open & "500" Festival Open Invitational

| 1967 | 25 | 101 | 25 | 2 | 10 | 16 | 20 | 71.00 | $151,677 |

Best finish for 1967: Win at the Canadian Open & Carling World Open

| 1968 | 24 | 97 | 24 | 6 | 12 | 16 | 22 | 70.02 | $196,828 |

Best finish for 1968: Win at the Los Angeles Open Invitational, Greater Greensboro Open, Colonial National Invitational, "500" Festival Open Invitational, Greater

Hartford Open Invitational & Lucky International Open Invitational

Year	Starts	Rounds Played	Cuts Made	Wins	Top-5s	Top-10s	Top-25s	Scoring Average	Money
1969	23	87	21	2	6	10	16	71.10	$108,571

Best finish for 1969: Win at the Bob Hope Desert Classic & Western Open

| 1970 | 20 | 73 | 17 | 4 | 5 | 9 | 14 | 69.88 | $145,381 |

Best finish for 1970: Win at the Los Angles Open, Masters, IVB Philadelphia Golf Classic & AVCO Classic

| 1971 | 21 | 78 | 18 | 1 | 5 | 7 | 15 | 70.68 | $107,667 |

Best finish for 1971: Win at the Kaiser International Open

| 1972 | 20 | 74 | 16 | 0 | 2 | 4 | 12 | 71.53 | $52,526 |

Best finish for 1972: 2nd at the Byron Nelson Golf Classic

| 1973 | 18 | 73 | 16 | 2 | 5 | 7 | 11 | 71.33 | $136,115 |

Best finish for 1973: Win at the Western Open & Sammy Davis, Jr. - Greater Hartford Open

| 1974 | 20 | 74 | 17 | 0 | 4 | 5 | 10 | 71.54 | $62,373 |

Best finish for 1974: T-2nd at the Kaiser International Open

| 1975 | 19 | 71 | 16 | 1 | 3 | 8 | 11 | 71.20 | $102,277 |

Best finish for 1975: Win at the First NBC New Orleans Open

| 1976 | 23 | 80 | 17 | 0 | 1 | 6 | 9 | 71.73 | $48,432 |

Best finish for 1976: T-4th at the First NBC New Orleans Open

| 1977 | 22 | 77 | 16 | 0 | 0 | 1 | 5 | 72.22 | $27,579 |

Best finish for 1977: T-10th at the Joe Garagiola Tucson Open

| 1978 | 18 | 56 | 9 | 0 | 0 | 0 | 3 | 73.34 | $15,113 |

Best finish for 1978: T-12th at the Colgate Hall Of Fame Classic

| 1979 | 19 | 54 | 7 | 0 | 1 | 1 | 3 | 73.63 | $12,190 |

Best finish for 1979: T-5th at the Tallahassee Open

1980	9	20	0	0	0	0	0	78.50	$2,000
1981	5	12	0	0	0	0	0	75.92	$1,500
1982	5	13	1	0	0	0	0	75.23	$2,610

Best finish for 1982: T-67th at the PGA Championship

1983	3	6	0	0	0	0	0	73.83	$1,920
1984	1	2	0	0	0	0	0	75.50	$1,500
1985	3	11	1	0	0	0	0	75.00	$1,730

Best finish for 1985: T-57th at the Masters

| 1986 | 1 | 2 | 0 | 0 | 0 | 0 | 0 | 76.50 | $1,500 |
| 1987 | 2 | 6 | 1 | 0 | 0 | 0 | 0 | 75.17 | $2,200 |

Best finish for 1987: T-50th at the Masters

| 1988 | 2 | 4 | 0 | 0 | 0 | 0 | 0 | 79.25 | $1,500 |
| 1989 | 2 | 6 | 1 | 0 | 0 | 0 | 0 | 74.00 | $4,425 |

Best finish for 1989: T-56th at the Doral-Ryder Open

1990	2	4	0	0	0	0	0	75.00	$1,500
1991	2	4	0	0	0	0	0	75.25	$1,500
1992	1	2	0	0	0	0	0	75.00	
1993	2	4	0	0	0	0	0	76.50	$1,500
1994	2	4	0	0	0	0	0	77.25	$1,500
1995	2	4	0	0	0	0	0	81.00	$1,500
1996	2	4	0	0	0	0	0	77.75	$1,500
1997	1	2	0	0	0	0	0	80.00	$5,000
1998	1	2	0	0	0	0	0	83.50	$5,000
1999	1	1	0	0	0	0	0	86.00	$5,000
2000	1	1	0	0	0	0	0	84.00	$5,000
2001	1	2	0	0	0	0	0	83.50	$5,000
2005	1	0	0	0	0	0	0		$5,000
Period Totals	Starts	Rounds Played	Cuts Made	Wins	Top-5s	Top-10s	Top-25s	Scoring Average	Money
	550	2010	424	47	148	226	346	71.18	$1,821,489

PGA Tour career totals from 1940 to 2005

	Starts	Rounds Played	Cuts Made	Wins	Top-5s	Top-10s	Top-25s	Scoring Average	Money
	627	2301	495	51	154	248	401	N/A	$1,864,284

Alex Cejka

Year	Starts	Rounds Played	Cuts Made	Wins	Top-5s	Top-10s	Top-25s	Scoring Average	Money
1996	10	30	5	0	0	1	2	72.83	$134,961

Best finish for 1996: T-6th at the NEC World Series of Golf

| 1997 | 1 | 2 | 0 | 0 | 0 | 0 | 0 | 80.50 | $1,089 |
| 1999 | 2 | 8 | 2 | 0 | 0 | 0 | 0 | 74.50 | $33,300 |

Best finish for 1999: T-55th at the American Express Championship

| 2000 | 1 | 2 | 0 | 0 | 0 | 0 | 0 | 74.00 | $1,520 |
| 2001 | 1 | 4 | 1 | 0 | 0 | 0 | 1 | 70.00 | $57,310 |

Best finish for 2001: T-13th at the British Open

| 2002 | 1 | 2 | 0 | 0 | 0 | 0 | 0 | 73.00 | $3,950 |
| 2003 | 30 | 91 | 20 | 0 | 2 | 4 | 7 | 70.80 | $1,182,883 |

Best finish for 2003: T-2nd at the B.C. Open

| 2004 | 24 | 70 | 15 | 0 | 1 | 3 | 7 | 71.56 | $1,315,483 |

Best finish for 2004: 2nd at The International

Year	Starts	Rounds Played	Cuts Made	Wins	Top-5s	Top-10s	Top-25s	Scoring Average	Money
2005	31	81	14	0	0	0	5	71.59	$517,339

Best finish for 2005: T-12th at The Players Championship

2006	30	91	16	0	1	2	3	70.97	$525,484

Best finish for 2006: T-3rd at the John Deere Classic

2007	25	80	16	0	0	4	6	70.29	$868,304

Best finish for 2007: T-6th at the Fry's Electronics Open

2008	25	75	13	0	1	4	5	71.69	$893,998

Best finish for 2008: T-4th at the Stanford St. Jude Classic

Period Totals	Starts	Rounds Played	Cuts Made	Wins	Top-5s	Top-10s	Top-25s	Scoring Average	Money
	181	536	102	0	5	18	36	71.32	$5,535,621

Antonio Cerda

Year	Starts	Rounds Played	Cuts Made	Wins	Top-5s	Top-10s	Top-25s	Scoring Average	Money
1958	1	4	1	0	0	0	0	73.00	

Best finish for 1958: T-26th at the British Open

1959	1	4	1	0	0	0	1	72.75	

Best finish for 1959: T-16th at the British Open

1960	3	12	3	0	0	1	3	72.67	$900

Best finish for 1960: T-8th at the Jamaica Open Invitational

1961	2	8	2	0	0	0	1	73.00	$1,035

Best finish for 1961: T-24th at the Masters

1962	2	8	2	0	0	0	1	73.00	$775

Best finish for 1962: T-13th at the Puerto Rico Open Invitational

1963	3	12	3	0	0	1	2	73.08	$1,460

Best finish for 1963: T-9th at the Puerto Rico Open Invitational

1964	1	2	0	0	0	0	0	79.50	
1969	1	2	0	0	0	0	0	78.50	
1971	1	2	0	0	0	0	0	78.00	
1975	5	14	2	0	0	2	2	72.00	$7,594

Best finish for 1975: T-7th at the Kaiser International Open

1976	22	71	16	0	0	0	1	73.15	$8,409

Best finish for 1976: T-14th at the Western Open

1977	20	56	8	0	0	1	2	73.96	$8,769

Best finish for 1977: T-6th at the Ohio Kings Island Open

1978	22	61	9	0	0	0	1	73.26	$4,915

Best finish for 1978: T-22nd at the Buick Goodwrench Open

1979	19	53	8	0	0	0	1	72.89	$9,261

Best finish for 1979: T-23rd at the Glen Campbell Los Angles Open

1980	20	56	9	0	0	0	1	73.02	$8,911

Best finish for 1980: T-17th at the Sammy Davis, Jr. - Greater Hartford Open

1981	15	40	5	0	0	0	3	73.05	$15,018

Best finish for 1981: T-15th at the Hawaiian Open & Glen Campbell Los Angles Open

1982	23	73	15	0	0	1	4	72.05	$31,980

Best finish for 1982: T-7th at the B.C. Open

1983	31	90	14	0	0	0	0	72.74	$13,965

Best finish for 1983: T-31st at the Honda Inverrary Classic

1984	2	6	1	0	0	0	0	72.00	$444

Best finish for 1984: T-57th at the Miller High-Life Quad Cities Open

1986	30	94	19	0	0	2	6	71.70	$61,980

Best finish for 1986: T-6th at the Los Angeles Open

1987	34	95	15	0	0	0	3	71.83	$45,299

Best finish for 1987: T-11th at the B.C. Open

1988	25	67	10	0	0	0	1	72.40	$24,444

Best finish for 1988: T-20th at the Provident Classic

1989	2	7	2	0	0	0	0	70.57	$1,935

Best finish for 1989: T-34th at the Deposit Guaranty Golf Classic

Period Totals	Starts	Rounds Played	Cuts Made	Wins	Top-5s	Top-10s	Top-25s	Scoring Average	Money
	285	837	145	0	0	8	33	72.65	$247,096

Ron Cerrudo

Year	Starts	Rounds Played	Cuts Made	Wins	Top-5s	Top-10s	Top-25s	Scoring Average	Money
1965	1	4	1	0	0	0	1	70.25	$935

Best finish for 1965: T-17th at the Almaden Open

1966	1	4	1	0	0	0	0	76.75	

Best finish for 1966: T-54th at the Masters

1967	6	22	4	0	0	0	3	72.23	$1,100

Best finish for 1967: 11th at the Cajun Classic

1968	34	126	29	1	4	4	14	71.33	$35,424

Best finish for 1968: Win at the Cajun Classic

1969	37	132	30	0	0	4	14	71.77	$30,993

Best finish for 1969: T-7th at the Tucson Open

1970	19	56	11	1	1	2	8	71.82	$35,617

Best finish for 1970: Win at the San Antonio Texas Open

Year	Starts	Rounds Played	Cuts Made	Wins	Top-5s	Top-10s	Top-25s	Scoring Average	Money
1971	34	112	21	0	1	2	7	72.22	$21,310

Best finish for 1971: 5th at the Sahara Invitational

| 1972 | 36 | 129 | 28 | 0 | 0 | 1 | 9 | 72.50 | $24,913 |

Best finish for 1972: T-6th at the Greater New Orleans Open

| 1973 | 31 | 106 | 19 | 0 | 0 | 1 | 5 | 72.73 | $20,432 |

Best finish for 1973: T-8th at the Byron Nelson Golf Classic

| 1974 | 26 | 84 | 15 | 0 | 0 | 0 | 1 | 73.40 | $8,792 |

Best finish for 1974: T-13th at the American Golf Classic

| 1975 | 26 | 90 | 18 | 0 | 0 | 0 | 1 | 72.76 | $9,863 |

Best finish for 1975: T-21st at the Greater Milwaukee Open

| 1976 | 26 | 89 | 21 | 0 | 1 | 2 | 8 | 72.24 | $23,387 |

Best finish for 1976: T-5th at the Tallahassee Open

| 1977 | 26 | 82 | 16 | 0 | 0 | 0 | 3 | 73.26 | $16,428 |

Best finish for 1977: T-11th at the Hawaiian Open

| 1978 | 10 | 24 | 1 | 0 | 0 | 0 | 0 | 74.83 | $190 |

Best finish for 1978: T-61st at the Buick Goodwrench Open

1979	1	2	0	0	0	0	0	72.50	
1980	1	2	0	0	0	0	0	75.00	
1981	1	0	0	0	0	0	0		
Period Totals	Starts	Rounds Played	Cuts Made	Wins	Top-5s	Top-10s	Top-25s	Scoring Average	Money
	316	1064	215	2	7	16	74	72.42	$229,384

Greg Cesario

Year	Starts	Rounds Played	Cuts Made	Wins	Top-5s	Top-10s	Top-25s	Scoring Average	Money
1989	1	3	0	0	0	0	0	75.33	
1991	1	2	0	0	0	0	0	73.00	
1993	25	62	7	0	0	0	0	73.55	$15,333

Best finish for 1993: T-54th at the International

Period Totals	Starts	Rounds Played	Cuts Made	Wins	Top-5s	Top-10s	Top-25s	Scoring Average	Money
	27	67	7	0	0	0	0	73.61	$15,333

Jon Chaffee

Year	Starts	Rounds Played	Cuts Made	Wins	Top-5s	Top-10s	Top-25s	Scoring Average	Money
1980	21	58	9	0	0	1	1	72.50	$11,660

Best finish for 1980: T-10th at the Pensacola Open

| 1981 | 20 | 55 | 8 | 0 | 0 | 0 | 2 | 72.75 | $10,788 |

Best finish for 1981: T-16th at the Pensacola Open

| 1982 | 2 | 4 | 0 | 0 | 0 | 0 | 0 | 76.50 | $600 |
| 1983 | 22 | 66 | 11 | 0 | 0 | 2 | 3 | 72.32 | $26,410 |

Best finish for 1983: T-7th at the Pensacola Open

| 1984 | 14 | 35 | 5 | 0 | 0 | 0 | 0 | 72.86 | $6,135 |

Best finish for 1984: T-31st at the Miller High-Life Quad Cities Open

| 1985 | 3 | 8 | 1 | 0 | 0 | 0 | 0 | 72.38 | $1,065 |

Best finish for 1985: T-63rd at the Anheuser-Busch Golf Classic

1988	1	2	0	0	0	0	0	72.50	
1990	1	2	0	0	0	0	0	73.50	$1,000
1991	1	2	0	0	0	0	0	74.50	$1,000
1992	29	66	4	0	0	0	1	73.05	$18,245

Best finish for 1992: T-23rd at the Northern Telecom Open

1995	2	4	0	0	0	0	0	77.00	$1,000
2000	1	2	0	0	0	0	0	75.00	
Period Totals	Starts	Rounds Played	Cuts Made	Wins	Top-5s	Top-10s	Top-25s	Scoring Average	Money
	117	304	38	0	0	3	7	72.81	$77,904

Tom Chain

Year	Starts	Rounds Played	Cuts Made	Wins	Top-5s	Top-10s	Top-25s	Scoring Average	Money
1979	16	40	4	0	0	0	1	73.70	$4,694

Best finish for 1979: T-21st at the Hawaiian Open

| 1981 | 8 | 16 | 1 | 0 | 0 | 0 | 0 | 72.88 | $398 |

Best finish for 1981: T-70th at the Pensacola Open

| 1982 | 15 | 41 | 6 | 0 | 0 | 0 | 1 | 73.27 | $5,721 |

Best finish for 1982: T-24th at the Anheuser-Busch Golf Classic

Period Totals	Starts	Rounds Played	Cuts Made	Wins	Top-5s	Top-10s	Top-25s	Scoring Average	Money
	39	97	11	0	0	0	2	73.38	$10,813

Greg Chalmers

Year	Starts	Rounds Played	Cuts Made	Wins	Top-5s	Top-10s	Top-25s	Scoring Average	Money
1998	2	6	1	0	0	0	0	74.17	$11,805

Best finish for 1998: T-57th at the British Open

| 1999 | 34 | 106 | 20 | 0 | 0 | 1 | 7 | 71.21 | $362,635 |

Best finish for 1999: T-10th at the Doral-Ryder Open

Year	Starts	Rounds Played	Cuts Made	Wins	Top-5s	Top-10s	Top-25s	Scoring Average	Money
2000	28	92	19	0	3	5	10	70.11	$1,063,456

Best finish for 2000: T-2nd at the Kemper Insurance Open

2001	27	89	20	0	1	1	7	70.43	$697,170

Best finish for 2001: T-5th at the Sony Open in Hawaii

2002	31	91	15	0	2	2	7	71.24	$641,898

Best finish for 2002: T-4th at the Bell Canadian Open

2003	32	96	17	0	0	1	3	70.57	$403,254

Best finish for 2003: T-7th at the Wachovia Championship

2004	22	70	13	0	1	2	3	71.06	$402,380

Best finish for 2004: T-4th at the John Deere Classic

2006	28	67	8	0	0	0	0	72.24	$151,265

Best finish for 2006: T-32nd at the B.C. Open & The International

Period Totals	Starts	Rounds Played	Cuts Made	Wins	Top-5s	Top-10s	Top-25s	Scoring Average	Money
	204	617	113	0	7	12	37	70.96	$3,733,862

Brandel Chamblee

Year	Starts	Rounds Played	Cuts Made	Wins	Top-5s	Top-10s	Top-25s	Scoring Average	Money
1983	1	4	1	0	0	0	0	72.00	

Best finish for 1983: T-42nd at the Colonial National Invitational

1984	2	4	0	0	0	0	0	76.00	
1985	1	4	1	0	0	0	0	70.75	$1,190

Best finish for 1985: T-42nd at the Texas Open

1987	5	13	1	0	0	0	0	74.54	$3,400

Best finish for 1987: T-66th at the British Open

1988	28	75	10	0	0	1	1	72.13	$33,617

Best finish for 1988: T-6th at the Manufactures Hanover Westchester Classic

1989	4	8	0	0	0	0	0	70.63	
1991	30	83	12	0	1	1	3	71.82	$64,141

Best finish for 1991: T-5th at the Deposit Guaranty Classic

1992	28	85	15	0	0	0	6	71.62	$98,921

Best finish for 1992: T-14th at the Shell Houston Open

1993	28	82	13	0	0	2	4	71.38	$126,941

Best finish for 1993: T-9th at the AT&T Pebble Beach Pro-Am

1994	27	86	20	0	1	1	3	71.67	$161,018

Best finish for 1994: 3rd at the Honda Classic

1995	25	75	13	0	1	3	8	71.40	$216,033

Best finish for 1995: T-5th at the FedEx St. Jude Classic

1996	23	70	10	0	1	2	3	71.87	$234,564

Best finish for 1996: 2nd at the BellSouth Classic

1997	26	79	15	0	2	3	5	71.24	$335,964

Best finish for 1997: T-2nd at the Quad City Classic & Canon Greater Hartford Open

1998	25	80	17	1	2	4	9	70.70	$756,936

Best finish for 1998: Win at the Greater Vancouver Open

1999	24	76	13	0	1	2	7	71.87	$416,744

Best finish for 1999: T-5th at the Bay Hill Invitational

2000	21	70	14	0	0	3	6	70.84	$493,906

Best finish for 2000: T-7th at the GTE Byron Nelson Classic

2001	23	77	14	0	2	2	3	71.18	$582,085

Best finish for 2001: T-2nd at the Nissan Open

2002	30	84	13	0	0	1	5	71.20	$372,263

Best finish for 2002: T-6th at the Bob Hope Chrysler Classic

2003	15	43	6	0	0	0	1	71.37	$126,092

Best finish for 2003: T-21st at the Bank of America Colonial

2004	1	4	1	0	0	0	0	71.25	$6,580

Best finish for 2004: 76th at the Valero Texas Open

2007	1	2	0	0	0	0	0	71.50	
2008	1	3	0	0	0	0	0	74.00	

Period Totals	Starts	Rounds Played	Cuts Made	Wins	Top-5s	Top-10s	Top-25s	Scoring Average	Money
	369	1107	189	1	11	25	64	71.51	$4,030,396

Warren Chancellor

Year	Starts	Rounds Played	Cuts Made	Wins	Top-5s	Top-10s	Top-25s	Scoring Average	Money
1973	1	4	0	0	0	0	0	77.25	
1974	13	25	1	0	0	0	0	75.40	

Best finish for 1974: T-71st at the Western Open

1977	11	24	1	0	0	0	0	75.83	$350

Best finish for 1977: T-64th at the Danny Thomas Memphis Classic

1978	4	9	0	0	0	0	0	76.00	
1980	1	2	0	0	0	0	0	71.50	
1983	1	2	0	0	0	0	0	73.50	
1985	1	2	0	0	0	0	0	76.00	
1986	1	2	0	0	0	0	0	72.50	

Year	Starts	Rounds Played	Cuts Made	Wins	Top-5s	Top-10s	Top-25s	Scoring Average	Money
1988	1	2	0	0	0	0	0	70.00	
1989	1	2	0	0	0	0	0	73.50	
1990	1	2	0	0	0	0	0	74.00	
1991	1	2	0	0	0	0	0	78.00	
1992	1	2	0	0	0	0	0	75.00	
1993	1	2	0	0	0	0	0	71.50	
1994	1	2	0	0	0	0	0	72.00	
Period Totals	Starts	Rounds Played	Cuts Made	Wins	Top-5s	Top-10s	Top-25s	Scoring Average	Money
	40	84	2	0	0	0	0	75.15	$350

Jim Chancey

Year	Starts	Rounds Played	Cuts Made	Wins	Top-5s	Top-10s	Top-25s	Scoring Average	Money
1977	6	12	1	0	0	0	0	73.50	

Best finish for 1977: 72nd at the Ed McMahon Quad City Open

1978	23	75	15	0	0	1	3	72.67	$15,117

Best finish for 1978: T-9th at the Hawaiian Open

1979	25	67	9	0	0	0	2	73.21	$10,542

Best finish for 1979: T-17th at the Tallahassee Open

1980	26	66	9	0	0	0	1	73.44	$9,920

Best finish for 1980: T-25th at the Glen Campbell Los Angles Open

1981	17	44	6	0	0	0	1	73.18	$7,387

Best finish for 1981: T-19th at the Western Open

1987	1	2	0	0	0	0	0	74.50	
Period Totals	Starts	Rounds Played	Cuts Made	Wins	Top-5s	Top-10s	Top-25s	Scoring Average	Money
	98	266	40	0	0	1	7	73.13	$42,966

Bob Charles

Year	Starts	Rounds Played	Cuts Made	Wins	Top-5s	Top-10s	Top-25s	Scoring Average	Money
1958	2	4	0	0	0	0	0	76.75	
1961	1	2	0	0	0	0	0	78.00	
1962	4	16	4	0	1	1	3	72.81	$1,215

Best finish for 1962: 5th at the British Open

1963	21	84	21	2	3	6	13	71.65	$27,837

Best finish for 1963: Win at the Houston Classic & British Open

1964	33	122	27	0	6	7	16	71.83	$32,969

Best finish for 1964: T-2nd at the Texas Open

1965	27	95	19	1	4	4	11	72.29	$30,601

Best finish for 1965: Win at the Tucson Open

1966	24	78	15	0	0	2	6	73.37	$13,435

Best finish for 1966: T-8th at the Philadelphia Golf Classic & Carling World Open

1967	28	99	20	1	5	9	16	71.53	$75,084

Best finish for 1967: Win at the Atlanta Classic

1968	22	84	20	1	3	8	14	71.19	$71,825

Best finish for 1968: Win at the Canadian Open

1969	26	101	24	0	6	14	19	71.03	$72,367

Best finish for 1969: 2nd at the British Open

1970	24	88	22	0	5	7	14	71.20	$70,163

Best finish for 1970: T-2nd at the Greater New Orleans Open & Danny Thomas Memphis Classic

1971	25	90	22	0	0	6	15	71.56	$46,436

Best finish for 1971: T-7th at the Greater Greensboro Open

1972	23	84	19	0	0	1	5	72.40	$22,178

Best finish for 1972: T-10th at the Greater Greensboro Open

1973	16	56	12	0	1	2	7	72.29	$23,963

Best finish for 1973: T-5th at the Monsanto Open

1974	16	51	10	1	1	4	5	72.55	$65,297

Best finish for 1974: Win at the Greater Greensboro Open

1975	16	51	9	0	1	1	4	72.82	$12,326

Best finish for 1975: 5th at the Tallahassee Open

1976	13	41	8	0	0	0	0	72.63	$4,039

Best finish for 1976: T-34th at the Tallahassee Open

1977	4	14	3	0	0	0	0	72.64	$2,022

Best finish for 1977: T-27th at the First NBC New Orleans Open

1978	1	4	1	0	0	0	0	73.75	$646

Best finish for 1978: T-48th at the British Open

1979	5	18	4	0	0	1	1	72.22	$11,510

Best finish for 1979: T-10th at the British Open

1980	1	4	1	0	0	0	0	73.75	$1,320

Best finish for 1980: T-60th at the British Open

1981	1	4	1	0	0	0	0	73.00	$1,388

Best finish for 1981: T-35th at the British Open

1982	4	8	0	0	0	0	0	75.75	$382
1983	5	14	2	0	0	0	1	72.71	$4,458

Best finish for 1983: T-12th at the Miller High-Life Quad Cities Open

Year	Starts	Rounds Played	Cuts Made	Wins	Top-5s	Top-10s	Top-25s	Scoring Average	Money
1984	3	10	2	0	0	0	0	73.60	$3,265

Best finish for 1984: T-47th at the British Open

| 1985 | 1 | 3 | 0 | 0 | 0 | 0 | 0 | 71.67 | $2,030 |
| 1986 | 1 | 4 | 1 | 0 | 0 | 0 | 1 | 73.25 | $10,875 |

Best finish for 1986: T-19th at the British Open

| 1988 | 1 | 4 | 1 | 0 | 0 | 0 | 1 | 71.75 | $11,900 |

Best finish for 1988: T-20th at the British Open

1990	1	2	0	0	0	0	0	75.50	$996
1994	1	2	0	0	0	0	0	76.50	$972
1995	1	2	0	0	0	0	0	74.50	$1,037
1996	1	4	1	0	0	0	0	72.75	$7,750

Best finish for 1996: 70th at the British Open

1999	1	2	0	0	0	0	0	82.00	$1,250
2000	1	2	0	0	0	0	0	73.50	$1,672
2001	1	2	0	0	0	0	0	74.50	$1,430
Period Totals	Starts	Rounds Played	Cuts Made	Wins	Top-5s	Top-10s	Top-25s	Scoring Average	Money
	355	1249	269	6	36	73	152	72.08	$634,638

Barry Cheesman

Year	Starts	Rounds Played	Cuts Made	Wins	Top-5s	Top-10s	Top-25s	Scoring Average	Money
1988	29	71	6	0	0	0	2	72.86	$26,476

Best finish for 1988: T-11th at the Greater Milwaukee Open

| 1989 | 8 | 19 | 2 | 0 | 0 | 0 | 2 | 71.42 | $11,155 |

Best finish for 1989: T-16th at the Deposit Guaranty Golf Classic

| 1990 | 1 | 2 | 0 | 0 | 0 | 0 | 0 | 72.50 | |
| 1991 | 27 | 67 | 6 | 0 | 0 | 0 | 1 | 72.60 | $25,156 |

Best finish for 1991: T-21st at the United Hawaiian Open

| 1992 | 1 | 4 | 1 | 0 | 0 | 0 | 0 | 69.00 | $722 |

Best finish for 1992: T-49th at the Deposit Guaranty Classic

| 1993 | 30 | 87 | 13 | 0 | 0 | 1 | 2 | 72.07 | $67,748 |

Best finish for 1993: T-10th at the New England Classic

| 1994 | 1 | 2 | 0 | 0 | 0 | 0 | 0 | 74.50 | |
| 1995 | 1 | 3 | 1 | 0 | 0 | 0 | 0 | 71.33 | $1,960 |

Best finish for 1995: T-67th at the Quad City Classic

| 1998 | 32 | 93 | 15 | 0 | 1 | 2 | 5 | 71.23 | $310,535 |

Best finish for 1998: 3rd at the Michelob Championship at Kingsmill

| 1999 | 34 | 97 | 17 | 0 | 2 | 3 | 3 | 72.24 | $418,728 |

Best finish for 1999: 4th at the Michelob Championship at Kingsmill

| 2000 | 35 | 93 | 13 | 0 | 0 | 0 | 6 | 71.78 | $277,918 |

Best finish for 2000: T-13th at the Greater Greensboro Chrysler Classic

| 2001 | 16 | 45 | 6 | 0 | 0 | 1 | 1 | 71.73 | $109,635 |

Best finish for 2001: T-10th at the John Deere Classic

| 2002 | 1 | 4 | 1 | 0 | 0 | 0 | 0 | 70.50 | $4,263 |

Best finish for 2002: T-66th at the B.C. Open

| 2003 | 2 | 6 | 1 | 0 | 0 | 0 | 1 | 70.00 | $32,910 |

Best finish for 2003: T-18th at the B.C. Open

| Period Totals | Starts | Rounds Played | Cuts Made | Wins | Top-5s | Top-10s | Top-25s | Scoring Average | Money |
| | 218 | 593 | 82 | 0 | 3 | 7 | 23 | 71.98 | $1,287,205 |

T.C. Chen

Year	Starts	Rounds Played	Cuts Made	Wins	Top-5s	Top-10s	Top-25s	Scoring Average	Money
1983	27	86	16	0	1	3	7	72.05	$79,030

Best finish for 1983: T-2nd at the Kemper Open

| 1984 | 22 | 67 | 11 | 0 | 0 | 4 | 5 | 72.60 | $55,570 |

Best finish for 1984: 6th at the Western Open

| 1985 | 18 | 62 | 12 | 0 | 1 | 1 | 5 | 71.31 | $75,862 |

Best finish for 1985: T-2nd at the U.S. Open

| 1986 | 19 | 61 | 12 | 0 | 0 | 1 | 6 | 71.98 | $86,590 |

Best finish for 1986: T-6th at the Anheuser-Busch Golf Classic

| 1987 | 16 | 55 | 11 | 1 | 1 | 2 | 6 | 71.91 | $205,216 |

Best finish for 1987: Win at the Los Angeles Open

| 1988 | 15 | 49 | 9 | 0 | 0 | 2 | 5 | 72.59 | $83,924 |

Best finish for 1988: T-9th at the Phoenix Open

| 1989 | 12 | 37 | 5 | 0 | 0 | 0 | 1 | 73.46 | $24,457 |

Best finish for 1989: T-19th at the Doral-Ryder Open

| 1993 | 1 | 3 | 1 | 0 | 0 | 0 | 0 | 71.33 | $5,800 |

Best finish for 1993: T-31st at the Nissan Los Angeles Open

| 1994 | 1 | 2 | 0 | 0 | 0 | 0 | 0 | 74.00 | |
| 1997 | 1 | 4 | 1 | 0 | 0 | 0 | 0 | 71.75 | $3,094 |

Best finish for 1997: T-57th at the Nissan Open

| Period Totals | Starts | Rounds Played | Cuts Made | Wins | Top-5s | Top-10s | Top-25s | Scoring Average | Money |
| | 132 | 426 | 78 | 1 | 3 | 13 | 35 | 72.19 | $619,543 |

Don Cherry

Year	Starts	Rounds Played	Cuts Made	Wins	Top-5s	Top-10s	Top-25s	Scoring Average	Money
1958	3	10	2	0	0	0	0	76.50	$300

Best finish for 1958: T-59th at the Buick Open

1959	4	16	3	0	0	0	1	73.94	

Best finish for 1959: T-25th at the Masters

1960	2	8	2	0	0	1	1	73.13	$072

Best finish for 1960: T-9th at the U.S. Open

1961	3	8	1	0	0	0	0	75.25	

Best finish for 1961: T-61st at the Houston Classic

1962	3	10	2	0	0	0	0	74.30	

Best finish for 1962: 42nd at the Masters

1963	2	6	0	0	0	0	0	73.83	$340
1964	18	50	1	0	0	1	1	73.76	$1,300

Best finish for 1964: T-9th at the Dallas Open

1965	19	63	12	0	0	0	0	73.56	$1,764

Best finish for 1965: T-26th at the Seattle Open

1966	13	40	7	0	0	0	1	73.43	$1,360

Best finish for 1966: T-24th at the Bing Crosby National Professional-Amateur

1967	14	41	5	0	0	0	0	74.17	$535

Best finish for 1967: T-37th at the Cajun Classic

1968	10	26	4	0	0	0	0	74.50	$1,133

Best finish for 1968: T-26th at the Sahara Invitational

1969	9	26	3	0	0	0	0	74.69	$475

Best finish for 1969: T-50th at the Canadian Open

1970	4	11	1	0	0	0	0	73.27	$114

Best finish for 1970: T-56th at the Sahara Invitational

1971	7	16	2	0	0	0	0	74.06	$442

Best finish for 1971: T-65th at the Phoenix Open

1972	5	12	1	0	0	0	0	73.75	$227

Best finish for 1972: T-65th at the Phoenix Open

1973	4	11	1	0	0	0	0	76.18	$210

Best finish for 1973: T-68th at the Sahara Invitational

1974	1	2	0	0	0	0	0	73.00	
1975	1	2	0	0	0	0	0	77.50	
1976	1	1	0	0	0	0	0	73.00	
1983	1	4	0	0	0	0	0	77.50	
Period Totals	Starts	Rounds Played	Cuts Made	Wins	Top-5s	Top-10s	Top-25s	Scoring Average	Money
	124	363	47	0	0	2	4	74.10	$8,272

K.J. Choi

Year	Starts	Rounds Played	Cuts Made	Wins	Top-5s	Top-10s	Top-25s	Scoring Average	Money
1998	1	2	0	0	0	0	0	75.00	$1,316
1999	2	8	2	0	0	0	1	73.63	$31,457

Best finish for 1999: T-24th at the Memorial Tournament

2000	30	89	16	0	0	1	4	71.19	$305,745

Best finish for 2000: T-8th at the Air Canada Championship

2001	29	92	19	0	3	5	8	70.60	$802,326

Best finish for 2001: T-4th at the Greater Greensboro Chrysler Classic

2002	27	89	19	2	2	7	11	70.56	$2,210,858

Best finish for 2002: Win at the COMPAQ Classic of New Orleans & Tampa Bay Classic presented by Buick

2003	32	106	25	0	4	6	13	70.81	$2,000,663

Best finish for 2003: T-2nd at the Mercedes Championships

2004	24	82	19	0	4	7	10	71.12	$2,077,775

Best finish for 2004: 3rd at the Masters

2005	24	73	18	1	1	3	7	71.12	$1,765,374

Best finish for 2005: Win at the Chrysler Classic of Greensboro

2006	26	92	22	1	1	4	10	70.65	$2,388,195

Best finish for 2006: Win at the Chrysler Championship

2007	25	85	20	2	4	7	17	70.40	$4,589,859

Best finish for 2007: Win at the Memorial Tournament & AT&T National

2008	21	70	16	1	3	5	12	71.01	$2,683,442

Best finish for 2008: Win at the Sony Open in Hawaii

Period Totals	Starts	Rounds Played	Cuts Made	Wins	Top-5s	Top-10s	Top-25s	Scoring Average	Money
	241	788	176	7	22	45	93	70.86	$18,857,010

Daniel Chopra

Year	Starts	Rounds Played	Cuts Made	Wins	Top-5s	Top-10s	Top-25s	Scoring Average	Money
2004	33	106	20	0	1	3	5	70.81	$763,253

Best finish for 2004: T-4th at the Deutsche Bank Championship

2005	34	104	19	0	0	2	9	70.96	$898,624

Best finish for 2005: T-9th at the Zurich Classic of New Orleans

Year	Starts	Rounds Played	Cuts Made	Wins	Top-5s	Top-10s	Top-25s	Scoring Average	Money
2006	33	107	22	0	3	6	9	70.65	$1,530,455

Best finish for 2006: T-2nd at the Frys.Com Open-Vegas

| 2007 | 34 | 106 | 20 | 1 | 2 | 3 | 6 | 70.84 | $1,757,610 |

Best finish for 2007: Win at the Ginn sur Mer Classic at Tesoro

| 2008 | 27 | 83 | 15 | 1 | 1 | 1 | 4 | 71.51 | $1,630,690 |

Best finish for 2008: Win at the Mercedes Championships

Period Totals	Starts	Rounds Played	Cuts Made	Wins	Top-5s	Top-10s	Top-25s	Scoring Average	Money
	161	506	96	2	7	15	33	70.93	$6,580,632

Michael Christie

Year	Starts	Rounds Played	Cuts Made	Wins	Top-5s	Top-10s	Top-25s	Scoring Average	Money
1993	1	4	1	0	0	0	0	71.50	$6,526

Best finish for 1993: T-52nd at the U.S. Open

| 1996 | 1 | 4 | 1 | 0 | 0 | 0 | 0 | 73.25 | $5,505 |

Best finish for 1996: T-79th at the U.S. Open

| 1997 | 33 | 95 | 17 | 0 | 0 | 2 | 8 | 71.54 | $204,882 |

Best finish for 1997: T-6th at the Greater Vancouver Open

| 1998 | 20 | 44 | 3 | 0 | 0 | 0 | 0 | 73.93 | $16,559 |

Best finish for 1998: T-41st at the Doral-Ryder Open

| 1999 | 3 | 6 | 0 | 0 | 0 | 0 | 0 | 75.33 | |
| 2000 | 5 | 9 | 0 | 0 | 0 | 0 | 0 | 75.22 | |

Period Totals	Starts	Rounds Played	Cuts Made	Wins	Top-5s	Top-10s	Top-25s	Scoring Average	Money
	63	162	22	0	0	2	8	72.57	$233,472

Stewart Cink

Year	Starts	Rounds Played	Cuts Made	Wins	Top-5s	Top-10s	Top-25s	Scoring Average	Money
1995	6	22	5	0	1	1	2	70.64	$58,426

Best finish for 1995: T-5th at the B.C. Open

| 1996 | 5 | 19 | 5 | 0 | 0 | 1 | 4 | 69.68 | $108,710 |

Best finish for 1996: T-9th at the Buick Challenge

| 1997 | 31 | 99 | 19 | 1 | 2 | 4 | 13 | 70.82 | $815,880 |

Best finish for 1997: Win at the Canon Greater Hartford Open

| 1998 | 28 | 97 | 23 | 0 | 3 | 6 | 15 | 70.49 | $835,148 |

Best finish for 1998: T-2nd at the Canon Greater Hartford Open

| 1999 | 27 | 92 | 21 | 0 | 3 | 8 | 14 | 70.80 | $1,256,350 |

Best finish for 1999: 2nd at the BellSouth Classic

| 2000 | 27 | 95 | 22 | 1 | 4 | 9 | 15 | 70.00 | $2,169,727 |

Best finish for 2000: Win at the MCI Classic

| 2001 | 29 | 97 | 22 | 0 | 3 | 6 | 14 | 70.10 | $1,748,028 |

Best finish for 2001: T-3rd at the U.S. Open & Buick Classic

| 2002 | 27 | 88 | 20 | 0 | 1 | 4 | 8 | 70.76 | $895,212 |

Best finish for 2002: T-5th at the Buick Classic

| 2003 | 28 | 100 | 23 | 0 | 2 | 6 | 14 | 70.03 | $1,783,885 |

Best finish for 2003: T-2nd at the Bay Hill Invitational & FUNAI Classic at the Walt Disney World Resort

| 2004 | 28 | 97 | 24 | 2 | 6 | 10 | 20 | 70.10 | $4,451,270 |

Best finish for 2004: Win at the MCI Heritage & WGC-NEC Invitational

| 2005 | 26 | 90 | 23 | 0 | 4 | 5 | 10 | 70.62 | $1,736,991 |

Best finish for 2005: T-3rd at the Chrysler Championship

| 2006 | 26 | 88 | 22 | 0 | 5 | 7 | 16 | 70.30 | $2,757,122 |

Best finish for 2006: 2nd at the WGC-NEC Invitational

| 2007 | 25 | 88 | 21 | 0 | 3 | 6 | 13 | 70.80 | $2,485,146 |

Best finish for 2007: T-3rd at The Players

| 2008 | 22 | 77 | 18 | 1 | 5 | 7 | 12 | 70.71 | $3,963,661 |

Best finish for 2008: Win at the Travelers Championship

Period Totals	Starts	Rounds Played	Cuts Made	Wins	Top-5s	Top-10s	Top-25s	Scoring Average	Money
	335	1149	268	5	42	80	170	70.44	$25,065,557

Brian Claar

Year	Starts	Rounds Played	Cuts Made	Wins	Top-5s	Top-10s	Top-25s	Scoring Average	Money
1986	27	86	20	0	0	4	12	71.22	$117,354

Best finish for 1986: T-6th at the Canadian Open

| 1987 | 37 | 107 | 18 | 0 | 0 | 0 | 2 | 72.01 | $43,111 |

Best finish for 1987: 11th at the Greater Greensboro Open

| 1988 | 11 | 36 | 7 | 0 | 0 | 0 | 5 | 70.31 | $30,276 |

Best finish for 1988: T-16th at the Hardee's Golf Classic

| 1989 | 13 | 44 | 9 | 0 | 1 | 1 | 4 | 70.91 | $88,010 |

Best finish for 1989: 5th at the U.S. Open

| 1990 | 25 | 84 | 19 | 0 | 0 | 2 | 5 | 71.26 | $162,856 |

Best finish for 1990: 7th at the BellSouth Atlanta Golf Classic

| 1991 | 31 | 104 | 21 | 0 | 3 | 3 | 5 | 70.90 | $252,306 |

Best finish for 1991: T-2nd at the AT&T Pebble Beach Pro-Am

Year	Starts	Rounds Played	Cuts Made	Wins	Top-5s	Top-10s	Top-25s	Scoring Average	Money
1992	29	99	20	0	0	3	5	70.90	$193,255

Best finish for 1992: T-8th at the Bob Hope Chrysler Classic

1993	32	108	23	0	0	1	5	71.19	$203,824

Best finish for 1993: T-7th at the BellSouth Classic

1994	31	99	19	0	1	2	3	71.30	$165,370

Best finish for 1994: T-3rd at the B.C. Open

1995	30	96	17	0	0	3	5	71.43	$241,107

Best finish for 1995: T-6th at the Shell Houston Open

1996	33	104	20	0	1	1	4	71.30	$165,511

Best finish for 1996: 5th at the B.C. Open

1997	18	59	11	0	1	1	4	70.93	$121,258

Best finish for 1997: T-4th at the Deposit Guaranty Golf Classic

1998	18	49	7	0	1	1	4	70.94	$161,630

Best finish for 1998: 4th at the Greater Vancouver Open

1999	7	21	4	0	0	0	0	71.90	$32,927

Best finish for 1999: T-39th at the AT&T Pebble Beach Pro-Am

2000	8	28	6	0	0	0	1	70.21	$90,959

Best finish for 2000: T-14th at the Westin Texas Open at LaCantera

2001	8	23	3	0	0	1	2	70.91	$129,519

Best finish for 2001: T-8th at the John Deere Classic

2002	9	23	2	0	0	0	0	71.48	$13,757

Best finish for 2002: T-48th at the John Deere Classic

2003	2	6	1	0	0	0	0	72.00	$17,500

Best finish for 2003: T-42nd at the AT&T Pebble Beach

Period Totals	Starts	Rounds Played	Cuts Made	Wins	Top-5s	Top-10s	Top-25s	Scoring Average	Money
	369	1176	227	0	8	23	66	71.19	$2,230,531

Bobby Clampett

Year	Starts	Rounds Played	Cuts Made	Wins	Top-5s	Top-10s	Top-25s	Scoring Average	Money
1978	1	4	1	0	0	0	0	74.25	

Best finish for 1978: T-30th at the U.S. Open

1979	4	14	3	0	0	0	2	72.93	

Best finish for 1979: T-20th at the Colonial National Invitational

1980	13	40	8	0	0	1	3	71.73	$19,800

Best finish for 1980: T-8th at the Buick Goodwrench Open

1981	25	94	22	0	6	8	16	70.77	$184,710

Best finish for 1981: T-2nd at the Bing Crosby Pro-Am, Manufactures Hanover Westchester Classic, Sammy Davis, Jr. - Greater Hartford Open & Buick Open

1982	27	97	22	1	7	8	14	71.13	$197,745

Best finish for 1982: Win at the Southern Open

1983	27	84	14	0	2	3	7	72.31	$90,113

Best finish for 1983: T-5th at the Greater Greensboro Open & MONY Tournament Of Champions

1984	29	91	15	0	0	0	5	72.89	$41,837

Best finish for 1984: T-16th at the Sammy Davis, Jr. - Greater Hartford Open

1985	30	104	21	0	1	2	6	71.74	$81,121

Best finish for 1985: T-4th at the Western Open

1986	32	101	22	0	1	1	4	72.11	$97,778

Best finish for 1986: T-3rd at the Vantage Championship

1987	26	82	16	0	1	2	3	71.78	$124,872

Best finish for 1987: 2nd at the Anheuser-Busch Golf Classic

1988	30	90	16	0	0	2	6	71.92	$88,067

Best finish for 1988: T-9th at the Independent Insurance Agent Open

1989	29	88	14	0	0	0	3	71.70	$68,809

Best finish for 1989: T-11th at the Beatrice Western Open

1990	19	57	9	0	0	0	0	72.14	$29,268

Best finish for 1990: T-29th at the BellSouth Atlanta Golf Classic

1991	30	81	12	0	1	2	5	71.60	$127,815

Best finish for 1991: T-5th at The International

1992	16	39	4	0	0	0	1	72.64	$29,175

Best finish for 1992: T-14th at the Walt Disney World/Oldsmobile Classic

1993	16	54	11	0	1	3	3	71.48	$112,363

Best finish for 1993: T-4th at the New England Classic

1994	16	47	8	0	0	2	4	71.62	$105,710

Best finish for 1994: T-7th at the Freeport-McMoRan Classic

1995	9	25	2	0	0	0	0	72.96	$5,472

Best finish for 1995: T-35th at the Deposit Guaranty Golf Classic

1996	1	2	0	0	0	0	0	71.50	
1997	5	16	3	0	0	0	0	70.88	$10,092

Best finish for 1997: T-34th at the Deposit Guaranty Golf Classic

1998	4	10	1	0	0	0	0	72.80	$3,488

Best finish for 1998: T-54th at the Quad City Classic

2000	2	6	1	0	0	0	0	74.00	$22,056

Best finish for 2000: T-37th at the U.S. Open

Year	Starts	Rounds Played	Cuts Made	Wins	Top-5s	Top-10s	Top-25s	Scoring Average	Money
2002	1	2	0	0	0	0	0	71.50	
2006	1	3	0	0	0	0	0	74.33	
2007	1	3	0	0	0	0	0	73.33	
2008	1	2	0	0	0	0	0	74.00	
Period Totals	Starts	Rounds Played	Cuts Made	Wins	Top-5s	Top-10s	Top-25s	Scoring Average	Money
	395	1236	225	1	20	34	82	71.87	$1,440,291

Chris Clark

Year	Starts	Rounds Played	Cuts Made	Wins	Top-5s	Top-10s	Top-25s	Scoring Average	Money
1977	2	2	0	0	0	0	0	75.00	
1978	10	27	4	0	0	0	0	74.96	$621

Best finish for 1978: T-48th at the Southern Open

Year	Starts	Rounds Played	Cuts Made	Wins	Top-5s	Top-10s	Top-25s	Scoring Average	Money
1979	14	29	2	0	0	0	0	74.10	$1,641

Best finish for 1979: T-39th at the Colgate Hall Of Fame Classic

Year	Starts	Rounds Played	Cuts Made	Wins	Top-5s	Top-10s	Top-25s	Scoring Average	Money
1980	1	2	0	0	0	0	0	75.00	
Period Totals	Starts	Rounds Played	Cuts Made	Wins	Top-5s	Top-10s	Top-25s	Scoring Average	Money
	27	60	6	0	0	0	0	74.55	$2,262

Howard Clark

Year	Starts	Rounds Played	Cuts Made	Wins	Top-5s	Top-10s	Top-25s	Scoring Average	Money
1972	1	2	0	0	0	0	0	78.50	$125
1976	1	2	0	0	0	0	0	80.00	$180
1977	1	4	1	0	0	0	1	71.50	$3,740

Best finish for 1977: T-13th at the British Open

| 1978 | 1 | 4 | 1 | 0 | 0 | 0 | 0 | 73.50 | $703 |

Best finish for 1978: T-44th at the British Open

| 1979 | 4 | 12 | 2 | 0 | 0 | 0 | 0 | 74.92 | $2,428 |

Best finish for 1979: T-30th at the Doral-Eastern Open

| 1980 | 1 | 4 | 1 | 0 | 0 | 0 | 0 | 72.50 | $1,870 |

Best finish for 1980: T-32nd at the British Open

| 1981 | 1 | 4 | 1 | 0 | 0 | 1 | 1 | 71.50 | $13,000 |

Best finish for 1981: T-8th at the British Open

| 1982 | 3 | 8 | 1 | 0 | 0 | 0 | 1 | 73.63 | $4,582 |

Best finish for 1982: T-18th at the Bay Hill Classic

| 1983 | 1 | 4 | 1 | 0 | 0 | 0 | 0 | 71.00 | $3,225 |

Best finish for 1983: T-26th at the British Open

| 1984 | 2 | 8 | 2 | 0 | 0 | 0 | 0 | 73.63 | $7,933 |

Best finish for 1984: 39th at the NEC World Series of Golf

| 1985 | 1 | 4 | 1 | 0 | 0 | 0 | 0 | 73.50 | $3,086 |

Best finish for 1985: T-47th at the British Open

| 1986 | 2 | 4 | 0 | 0 | 0 | 0 | 0 | 75.75 | $1,600 |
| 1987 | 4 | 15 | 3 | 0 | 0 | 0 | 0 | 73.93 | $10,127 |

Best finish for 1987: T-35th at the Masters

| 1988 | 2 | 8 | 2 | 0 | 0 | 0 | 1 | 72.13 | $13,962 |

Best finish for 1988: T-22nd at the AT&T Pebble Beach Pro-Am

| 1989 | 3 | 12 | 3 | 0 | 0 | 0 | 2 | 71.92 | $34,642 |

Best finish for 1989: T-13th at the British Open

| 1990 | 3 | 7 | 1 | 0 | 0 | 0 | 0 | 74.71 | $3,156 |

Best finish for 1990: 62nd at the AT&T Pebble Beach Pro-Am

| 1991 | 2 | 8 | 2 | 0 | 0 | 0 | 0 | 72.00 | $10,463 |

Best finish for 1991: T-35th at the AT&T Pebble Beach Pro-Am

| 1992 | 4 | 9 | 0 | 0 | 0 | 0 | 0 | 74.44 | $2,200 |
| 1993 | 1 | 4 | 1 | 0 | 0 | 0 | 1 | 69.75 | $15,400 |

Best finish for 1993: T-21st at the British Open

1994	2	5	0	0	0	0	0	72.60	$972
1995	1	2	0	0	0	0	0	74.50	$1,037
1996	2	8	2	0	0	0	0	73.50	$11,390

Best finish for 1996: 69th at the British Open

| 1997 | 2 | 7 | 1 | 0 | 0 | 0 | 0 | 71.43 | $4,290 |

Best finish for 1997: T-45th at the Buick Invitational

1998	1	2	0	0	0	0	0	76.00	$1,152
Period Totals	Starts	Rounds Played	Cuts Made	Wins	Top-5s	Top-10s	Top-25s	Scoring Average	Money
	46	147	26	0	0	1	7	73.33	$151,262

Jimmy Clark

Year	Starts	Rounds Played	Cuts Made	Wins	Top-5s	Top-10s	Top-25s	Scoring Average	Money
1958	17	55	10	0	0	1	2	73.44	$261

Best finish for 1958: 19th at the Hesperia Open

| 1959 | 3 | 11 | 3 | 0 | 1 | 1 | 2 | 70.82 | $1,528 |

Best finish for 1959: T-3rd at the Phoenix Open Invitational

| 1960 | 15 | 58 | 13 | 0 | 0 | 3 | 8 | 71.83 | $4,905 |

Best finish for 1960: T-10th at the Baton Rouge Open Invitational & Oklahoma City Open Invitational

Year	Starts	Rounds Played	Cuts Made	Wins	Top-5s	Top-10s	Top-25s	Scoring Average	Money
1961	6	24	6	0	0	1	5	71.00	$2,533

Best finish for 1961: T-7th at the Waco Turner Open Invitational

| 1963 | 10 | 40 | 9 | 0 | 1 | 1 | 5 | 71.70 | $7,137 |

Best finish for 1963: T-2nd at the Greensboro Open Invitational

| 1964 | 20 | 59 | 8 | 0 | 0 | 0 | 2 | 73.66 | $2,220 |

Best finish for 1964: T-11th at the Los Angles Open

| 1965 | 6 | 14 | 2 | 0 | 0 | 0 | 0 | 75.07 | |

Best finish for 1965: T-72nd at the San Diego Open

1966	3	5	0	0	0	0	0	76.00	
1967	1	4	0	0	0	0	0	78.50	
1968	14	30	1	0	0	0	0	74.80	$650

Best finish for 1968: T-29th at the Los Angeles Open Invitational

| 1969 | 3 | 8 | 1 | 0 | 0 | 0 | 0 | 75.63 | $133 |

Best finish for 1969: T-74th at the Los Angeles Open

| 1970 | 6 | 12 | 1 | 0 | 0 | 0 | 0 | 75.25 | $250 |

Best finish for 1970: 73rd at the Cleveland Open

1973	1	1	0	0	0	0	0	79.00	
1974	1	1	0	0	0	0	0	80.00	
1976	1	2	0	0	0	0	0	79.00	

Period Totals	Starts	Rounds Played	Cuts Made	Wins	Top-5s	Top-10s	Top-25s	Scoring Average	Money
	107	324	54	0	2	5	21	73.20	$19,618

PGA Tour career totals from 1948 to 1976

	Starts	Rounds Played	Cuts Made	Wins	Top-5s	Top-10s	Top-25s	Scoring Average	Money
	265	930	211	2	12	45	102	N/A	$61,252

Tim Clark

Year	Starts	Rounds Played	Cuts Made	Wins	Top-5s	Top-10s	Top-25s	Scoring Average	Money
1998	1	2	0	0	0	0	0	79.00	$5,000
2001	3	7	1	0	0	0	0	71.43	$21,750

Best finish for 2001: T-26th at the Touchstone Energy Tucson Open

| 2002 | 23 | 73 | 15 | 0 | 0 | 3 | 7 | 70.93 | $636,560 |

Best finish for 2002: T-6th at the Michelob Championship at Kingsmill & Disney Golf Classic

| 2003 | 25 | 78 | 16 | 0 | 1 | 3 | 10 | 71.10 | $1,254,690 |

Best finish for 2003: 3rd at the PGA Championship

| 2004 | 26 | 84 | 16 | 0 | 1 | 6 | 9 | 70.75 | $1,120,808 |

Best finish for 2004: T-5th at the Valero Texas Open

| 2005 | 26 | 87 | 22 | 0 | 3 | 6 | 16 | 70.49 | $2,310,037 |

Best finish for 2005: T-2nd at the Bob Hope Chrysler Classic

| 2006 | 22 | 79 | 19 | 0 | 2 | 4 | 11 | 71.04 | $1,976,931 |

Best finish for 2006: 2nd at the Masters

| 2007 | 19 | 64 | 15 | 0 | 4 | 6 | 12 | 70.55 | $2,617,652 |

Best finish for 2007: T-2nd at the John Deere Classic, U.S. Bank Championship in Milwaukee & Children's Miracle Network Classic

| 2008 | 27 | 89 | 19 | 0 | 1 | 3 | 9 | 70.87 | $1,722,030 |

Best finish for 2008: T-2nd at the Crowne Plaza Invitational at Colonial

Period Totals	Starts	Rounds Played	Cuts Made	Wins	Top-5s	Top-10s	Top-25s	Scoring Average	Money
	172	563	123	0	12	31	74	70.86	$11,665,458

Michael Clark II

Year	Starts	Rounds Played	Cuts Made	Wins	Top-5s	Top-10s	Top-25s	Scoring Average	Money
1993	1	2	0	0	0	0	0	72.50	$1,000
1994	1	2	0	0	0	0	0	73.50	
1997	1	2	0	0	0	0	0	74.00	$1,000
2000	28	80	13	1	2	2	7	71.45	$854,822

Best finish for 2000: Win at the John Deere Classic

| 2001 | 30 | 85 | 12 | 0 | 0 | 1 | 2 | 71.26 | $238,990 |

Best finish for 2001: T-8th at the Mercedes Championships

| 2002 | 33 | 95 | 14 | 0 | 0 | 0 | 3 | 71.26 | $240,422 |

Best finish for 2002: T-14th at the Air Canada Championship

| 2003 | 21 | 54 | 5 | 0 | 0 | 1 | 2 | 71.89 | $210,177 |

Best finish for 2003: T-7th at the FUNAI Classic at the Walt Disney World Resort

| 2004 | 14 | 39 | 5 | 0 | 0 | 0 | 1 | 71.79 | $101,639 |

Best finish for 2004: T-15th at the Chrysler Classic of Tucson

| 2005 | 2 | 4 | 0 | 0 | 0 | 0 | 0 | 72.00 | |
| 2006 | 4 | 10 | 1 | 0 | 0 | 0 | 0 | 72.80 | $6,390 |

Best finish for 2006: T-62nd at the B.C. Open

| 2007 | 1 | 2 | 0 | 0 | 0 | 0 | 0 | 71.50 | |
| 2008 | 1 | 2 | 0 | 0 | 0 | 0 | 0 | 75.50 | |

Period Totals	Starts	Rounds Played	Cuts Made	Wins	Top-5s	Top-10s	Top-25s	Scoring Average	Money
	137	377	50	1	2	4	15	71.55	$1,654,440

Darren Clarke

Year	Starts	Rounds Played	Cuts Made	Wins	Top-5s	Top-10s	Top-25s	Scoring Average	Money
1991	1	4	1	0	0	0	0	71.75	$5,301

Best finish for 1991: T-64th at the British Open

1992	1	2	0	0	0	0	0	74.00	$1,200
1993	1	4	1	0	0	0	0	70.75	$8,205

Best finish for 1993: T-39th at the British Open

1994	2	6	1	0	0	0	0	72.17	$10,882

Best finish for 1994: T-38th at the British Open

1995	1	4	1	0	0	0	0	72.50	$12,955

Best finish for 1995: T-31st at the British Open

1996	2	6	1	0	0	0	1	71.33	$42,850

Best finish for 1996: T-11th at the British Open

1997	4	14	3	0	1	1	2	71.86	$284,116

Best finish for 1997: T-2nd at the British Open

1998	6	19	4	0	0	1	2	72.58	$122,944

Best finish for 1998: T-8th at the Masters

1999	10	26	7	0	0	1	2	74.15	$234,618

Best finish for 1999: T-10th at the U.S. Open

2000	10	32	8	1	1	3	5	72.09	$1,393,364

Best finish for 2000: Win at the Andersen Consulting Match Play Championship

2001	7	24	5	0	2	2	3	71.21	$707,870

Best finish for 2001: 3rd at the WGC-NEC Invitational

2002	11	34	8	0	1	2	5	71.44	$771,811

Best finish for 2002: 2nd at the Shell Houston Open

2003	16	54	14	1	2	5	6	70.85	$2,015,931

Best finish for 2003: Win at the WGC-NEC Invitational

2004	16	48	10	0	3	4	9	70.81	$2,015,819

Best finish for 2004: 3rd at the Mercedes Championships & WGC-Accenture Match Play Championship

2005	12	40	11	0	3	5	7	70.73	$1,467,921

Best finish for 2005: T-2nd at the MCI Heritage

2006	10	26	6	0	1	1	3	72.08	$664,616

Best finish for 2006: 3rd at the Bay Hill Invitational

2007	10	21	4	0	0	0	0	73.38	$113,427

Best finish for 2007: T-33rd at the WGC-Accenture Match Play Championship

2008	2	6	1	0	0	1	1	70.67	$220,000

Best finish for 2008: T-6th at the WGC-Bridgestone Invitational

Period Totals	Starts	Rounds Played	Cuts Made	Wins	Top-5s	Top-10s	Top-25s	Scoring Average	Money
	122	370	86	2	14	26	46	71.68	$10,093,830

Paul Claxton

Year	Starts	Rounds Played	Cuts Made	Wins	Top-5s	Top-10s	Top-25s	Scoring Average	Money
1997	23	66	10	0	0	0	2	71.97	$79,118

Best finish for 1997: 12th at the CVS Charity Classic

1998	1	2	0	0	0	0	0	72.00	
2002	29	83	13	0	0	0	2	71.54	$156,696

Best finish for 2002: T-23rd at the Reno-Tahoe Open

2005	29	79	11	0	0	0	3	71.66	$269,700

Best finish for 2005: T-15th at the Valero Texas Open

2008	23	63	8	0	0	0	1	71.78	$116,678

Best finish for 2008: T-21st at the Puerto Rico Open

Period Totals	Starts	Rounds Played	Cuts Made	Wins	Top-5s	Top-10s	Top-25s	Scoring Average	Money
	105	293	42	0	0	0	8	71.72	$622,191

Keith Clearwater

Year	Starts	Rounds Played	Cuts Made	Wins	Top-5s	Top-10s	Top-25s	Scoring Average	Money
1980	1	2	0	0	0	0	0	78.00	
1982	2	4	0	0	0	0	0	73.25	
1983	1	3	0	0	0	0	0	75.00	
1986	3	10	2	0	0	0	0	73.00	$2,221

Best finish for 1986: T-52nd at the Buick Open

1987	35	118	25	2	3	3	11	71.52	$321,006

Best finish for 1987: Win at the Colonial National Invitational & Centel Classic

1988	34	85	10	0	1	2	5	72.04	$85,376

Best finish for 1988: T-5th at the MONY Tournament Of Champions

1989	33	100	18	0	0	0	5	71.64	$88,490

Best finish for 1989: T-14th at the Greater Milwaukee Open

1990	25	75	14	0	1	1	2	72.35	$130,103

Best finish for 1990: T-2nd at the BellSouth Atlanta Golf Classic

1991	29	104	24	0	0	2	12	70.91	$239,727

Best finish for 1991: T-8th at the Anheuser-Busch Golf Classic

Year	Starts	Rounds Played	Cuts Made	Wins	Top-5s	Top-10s	Top-25s	Scoring Average	Money
1992	33	109	23	0	4	10	13	70.52	$610,473

Best finish for 1992: T-2nd at the Doral-Ryder Open

| 1993 | 31 | 104 | 23 | 0 | 2 | 6 | 10 | 70.75 | $348,763 |

Best finish for 1993: T-4th at the United Airlines Hawaiian Open & Bob Hope Chrysler Classic

| 1994 | 27 | 89 | 18 | 0 | 0 | 3 | 5 | 71.33 | $203,549 |

Best finish for 1994: T-6th at the Bob Hope Chrysler Classic & Buick Open

| 1995 | 28 | 69 | 8 | 0 | 0 | 0 | 1 | 72.86 | $34,354 |

Best finish for 1995: T-25th at the Nissan Open

| 1996 | 25 | 78 | 14 | 0 | 0 | 0 | 5 | 71.68 | $137,617 |

Best finish for 1996: T-12th at the Michelob Championship at Kingsmill

| 1997 | 14 | 42 | 7 | 0 | 0 | 0 | 2 | 71.60 | $51,043 |

Best finish for 1997: T-20th at the B.C. Open

| 1998 | 13 | 31 | 4 | 0 | 0 | 0 | 0 | 72.39 | $18,465 |

Best finish for 1998: T-40th at the United Airlines Hawaiian Open

| 1999 | 7 | 15 | 0 | 0 | 0 | 0 | 0 | 73.67 | $1,000 |
| 2000 | 13 | 31 | 4 | 0 | 0 | 0 | 0 | 72.29 | $34,032 |

Best finish for 2000: T-46th at the MasterCard Colonial

| 2001 | 23 | 62 | 7 | 0 | 0 | 0 | 0 | 72.32 | $66,178 |

Best finish for 2001: T-27th at the B.C. Open

2002	7	12	0	0	0	0	0	73.92	
2003	3	6	0	0	0	0	0	76.00	
2004	5	11	0	0	0	0	0	73.73	
2005	2	5	0	0	0	0	0	73.00	
2006	2	4	0	0	0	0	0	75.75	
2007	2	4	0	0	0	0	0	74.25	
2008	2	5	0	0	0	0	0	77.60	
Period Totals	Starts	Rounds Played	Cuts Made	Wins	Top-5s	Top-10s	Top-25s	Scoring Average	Money
	400	1178	201	2	11	27	71	71.76	$2,372,397

John Cleary

Year	Starts	Rounds Played	Cuts Made	Wins	Top-5s	Top-10s	Top-25s	Scoring Average	Money
1958	18	51	7	0	0	0	0	75.51	$203

Best finish for 1958: T-28th at the Denver Open

| 1963 | 2 | 6 | 1 | 0 | 0 | 0 | 0 | 76.17 | $350 |

Best finish for 1963: 68th at the PGA Championship

1964	6	8	0	0	0	0	0	75.75	
1965	2	4	0	0	0	0	0	78.00	
1967	2	6	1	0	0	0	0	74.83	

Best finish for 1967: T-71st at the Insurance City Open

2000	1	2	0	0	0	0	0	77.00	
Period Totals	Starts	Rounds Played	Cuts Made	Wins	Top-5s	Top-10s	Top-25s	Scoring Average	Money
	31	77	9	0	0	0	0	75.70	$553

Lennie Clements

Year	Starts	Rounds Played	Cuts Made	Wins	Top-5s	Top-10s	Top-25s	Scoring Average	Money
1979	2	4	0	0	0	0	0	78.75	
1980	1	4	1	0	0	0	0	71.25	$1,695

Best finish for 1980: T-33rd at the Joe Garagiola Tucson Open

| 1981 | 23 | 66 | 11 | 0 | 0 | 0 | 2 | 72.88 | $16,669 |

Best finish for 1981: T-13th at the Michelob Houston Open

| 1982 | 22 | 66 | 11 | 0 | 2 | 2 | 5 | 72.55 | $43,109 |

Best finish for 1982: T-4th at the Glen Campbell Los Angles Open

| 1983 | 29 | 92 | 14 | 0 | 1 | 1 | 6 | 72.78 | $44,455 |

Best finish for 1983: T-3rd at the Miller High-Life Quad Cities Open

| 1984 | 31 | 87 | 12 | 0 | 0 | 0 | 2 | 73.44 | $27,212 |

Best finish for 1984: T-15th at the Southern Open

| 1985 | 24 | 81 | 16 | 0 | 0 | 1 | 6 | 72.10 | $49,383 |

Best finish for 1985: T-7th at the Bank of Boston Classic

| 1986 | 28 | 83 | 18 | 0 | 0 | 4 | 11 | 71.60 | $111,627 |

Best finish for 1986: T-9th at the Bob Hope Chrysler Classic, Houston Open & Seiko Tucson-Match Play Championship

| 1987 | 25 | 78 | 15 | 0 | 1 | 3 | 7 | 71.77 | $125,989 |

Best finish for 1987: T-4th at the Beatrice Western Open

| 1988 | 33 | 110 | 21 | 0 | 0 | 3 | 3 | 71.74 | $88,832 |

Best finish for 1988: T-8th at the Canon Sammy Davis, Jr. - Greater Hartford Open

| 1989 | 29 | 82 | 13 | 0 | 0 | 1 | 4 | 71.40 | $69,399 |

Best finish for 1989: T-9th at the Chattanooga Classic

| 1990 | 29 | 82 | 12 | 0 | 0 | 1 | 4 | 71.90 | $80,096 |

Best finish for 1990: T-10th at the Kmart Greater Greensboro Open

| 1991 | 15 | 52 | 10 | 0 | 0 | 0 | 3 | 70.40 | $62,827 |

Best finish for 1991: T-13th at the B.C. Open

| 1992 | 10 | 37 | 8 | 0 | 0 | 0 | 0 | 70.86 | $30,121 |

Best finish for 1992: T-30th at the Kemper Open

Year	Starts	Rounds Played	Cuts Made	Wins	Top-5s	Top-10s	Top-25s	Scoring Average	Money
1993	25	80	16	0	0	2	6	70.89	$141,526

Best finish for 1993: T-8th at the Northern Telecom Open & Anheuser-Busch Golf Classic

1994	23	88	22	0	2	6	11	70.28	$423,441

Best finish for 1994: T-2nd at the Bob Hope Chrysler Classic

1995	24	93	21	0	2	4	12	70.24	$355,130

Best finish for 1995: T-3rd at the Anheuser-Busch Golf Classic

1996	24	83	17	0	3	5	9	70.64	$326,466

Best finish for 1996: T-3rd at the Buick Invitational

1997	28	88	15	0	1	1	4	71.35	$189,958

Best finish for 1997: T-4th at the MCI Classic

1998	28	70	7	0	0	1	1	72.24	$99,839

Best finish for 1998: T-8th at the Greater Greensboro Chrysler Classic

Period Totals	Starts	Rounds Played	Cuts Made	Wins	Top-5s	Top-10s	Top-25s	Scoring Average	Money
	453	1426	260	0	12	35	96	71.65	$2,287,775

Jose Coceres

Year	Starts	Rounds Played	Cuts Made	Wins	Top-5s	Top-10s	Top-25s	Scoring Average	Money
1992	1	4	1	0	0	0	0	72.00	$9,350

Best finish for 1992: T-45th at the British Open

1995	1	4	1	0	0	0	0	74.75	$6,380

Best finish for 1995: T-96th at the British Open

1996	1	2	0	0	0	0	0	72.50	$1,008
1997	1	4	1	0	0	0	0	72.25	$11,812

Best finish for 1997: T-44th at the British Open

2000	3	10	2	0	0	0	1	72.50	$91,756

Best finish for 2000: T-14th at the American Express Championship

2001	19	57	12	2	2	2	5	70.39	$1,534,462

Best finish for 2001: Win at the WorldCom Classic & National Car Rental Golf Classic/Disney

2002	16	51	9	0	0	1	2	71.96	$296,107

Best finish for 2002: T-10th at the PGA Championship

2003	21	62	11	0	0	1	3	72.35	$337,682

Best finish for 2003: T-7th at the Southern Farm Bureau Classic

2004	20	64	14	0	1	2	6	70.84	$779,196

Best finish for 2004: 3rd at the John Deere Classic

2005	22	54	7	0	0	0	3	72.00	$269,705

Best finish for 2005: T-13th at the Nissan Open

2006	13	38	7	0	1	3	4	70.39	$522,592

Best finish for 2006: T-5th at the Reno-Tahoe Open

2007	17	50	9	0	3	3	4	71.22	$1,290,343

Best finish for 2007: T-2nd at the Mayakoba Golf Classic & Honda Classic

2008	13	37	6	0	0	0	2	72.27	$240,392

Best finish for 2008: T-12th at the Honda Classic

Period Totals	Starts	Rounds Played	Cuts Made	Wins	Top-5s	Top-10s	Top-25s	Scoring Average	Money
	148	437	80	2	7	12	30	71.50	$5,390,785

Bobby Cochran

Year	Starts	Rounds Played	Cuts Made	Wins	Top-5s	Top-10s	Top-25s	Scoring Average	Money
1994	1	2	0	0	0	0	0	73.50	
2000	30	76	9	0	0	0	1	72.08	$127,342

Best finish for 2000: T-13th at the Southern Farm Bureau Classic

2001	1	4	1	0	0	0	0	70.75	$7,455

Best finish for 2001: T-63rd at the FedEx St. Jude Classic

2002	1	2	0	0	0	0	0	73.00	
2003	1	2	0	0	0	0	0	71.50	
2004	1	2	0	0	0	0	0	77.50	
Period Totals	Starts	Rounds Played	Cuts Made	Wins	Top-5s	Top-10s	Top-25s	Scoring Average	Money
	35	88	10	0	0	0	1	72.18	$134,797

Russ Cochran

Year	Starts	Rounds Played	Cuts Made	Wins	Top-5s	Top-10s	Top-25s	Scoring Average	Money
1981	3	8	1	0	0	0	1	72.00	$1,307

Best finish for 1981: T-17th at the Tallahassee Open

1983	18	48	6	0	0	0	0	72.63	$7,968

Best finish for 1983: T-27th at the Isuzu/Andy Williams San Diego Open

1984	30	110	24	0	1	4	12	71.33	$133,342

Best finish for 1984: T-2nd at the B.C. Open

1985	27	81	14	0	2	3	5	72.09	$88,331

Best finish for 1985: T-3rd at the St. Jude Memphis Classic

1986	32	101	20	0	1	2	10	71.57	$89,817

Best finish for 1986: 2nd at the Tallahassee Open

1987	33	112	22	0	1	3	7	71.22	$148,110

Best finish for 1987: T-2nd at the Federal Express St. Jude Classic

Year	Starts	Rounds Played	Cuts Made	Wins	Top-5s	Top-10s	Top-25s	Scoring Average	Money
1988	33	106	20	0	0	4	9	71.05	$149,960

Best finish for 1988: T-6th at the Provident Classic

Year	Starts	Rounds Played	Cuts Made	Wins	Top-5s	Top-10s	Top-25s	Scoring Average	Money
1989	29	90	16	0	2	2	6	71.39	$133,679

Best finish for 1989: T-5th at the Las Vegas Invitational & Chattanooga Classic

1990	31	96	17	0	2	2	8	71.05	$232,278

Best finish for 1990: 3rd at the USF&G Classic

1991	29	98	20	1	5	6	12	70.28	$685,851

Best finish for 1991: Win at the Centel Western Open

1992	30	100	20	0	2	5	11	71.02	$340,708

Best finish for 1992: T-3rd at the BellSouth Classic

1993	27	93	19	0	1	2	9	70.85	$294,868

Best finish for 1993: T-2nd at the Freeport-McMoRan Classic

1994	28	94	20	0	2	4	6	71.24	$241,027

Best finish for 1994: T-5th at the Federal Express St. Jude Classic & Hardee's Golf Classic

1995	26	81	16	0	0	1	4	70.98	$145,663

Best finish for 1995: T-7th at the Walt Disney World/Oldsmobile Classic

1996	28	83	14	0	2	2	10	70.90	$330,183

Best finish for 1996: 2nd at the CVS Charity Classic

1997	29	103	21	0	2	5	8	70.68	$471,929

Best finish for 1997: T-2nd at the Buick Open

1998	27	88	16	0	1	3	8	71.09	$332,889

Best finish for 1998: T-5th at the Greater Vancouver Open

1999	29	83	14	0	0	3	5	71.30	$314,423

Best finish for 1999: T-7th at the National Car Rental Golf Classic/Disney

2000	25	71	10	0	2	4	8	70.79	$585,605

Best finish for 2000: T-4th at the Nissan Open & FedEx St. Jude Classic

2001	24	73	15	0	0	1	4	70.58	$362,556

Best finish for 2001: T-8th at the Buick Classic

2002	24	67	12	0	0	1	1	71.45	$176,110

Best finish for 2002: T-6th at the Touchstone Energy Tucson Open

2003	4	13	2	0	0	1	1	69.23	$103,400

Best finish for 2003: T-10th at the Southern Farm Bureau Classic

2004	25	62	8	0	0	0	2	70.19	$185,108

Best finish for 2004: T-24th at the Nissan Open & Ford Championship at Doral

| 2006 | 1 | 2 | 0 | 0 | 0 | 0 | 0 | 71.50 | |
2007	1	4	1	0	0	0	0	71.25	$31,275

Best finish for 2007: T-26th at the Ginn sur Mer Classic at Tesoro

2008	1	2	0	0	0	0	0	78.00	
Period Totals	**Starts**	**Rounds Played**	**Cuts Made**	**Wins**	**Top-5s**	**Top-10s**	**Top-25s**	**Scoring Average**	**Money**
	594	1869	348	1	26	58	147	71.10	$5,586,388

Mike Colandro

Year	Starts	Rounds Played	Cuts Made	Wins	Top-5s	Top-10s	Top-25s	Scoring Average	Money
1979	13	26	1	0	0	0	0	75.15	$498

Best finish for 1979: T-70th at the San Antonio Texas Open

1980	7	16	1	0	0	0	0	74.19	$1,102

Best finish for 1980: T-42nd at the Hawaiian Open

| 1984 | 1 | 2 | 0 | 0 | 0 | 0 | 0 | 76.00 | $429 |
| 1985 | 1 | 2 | 0 | 0 | 0 | 0 | 0 | 75.50 | |
1986	3	8	1	0	0	0	0	74.38	$1,392

Best finish for 1986: 71st at the B.C. Open

1987	1	2	0	0	0	0	0	76.50	
1988	1	2	0	0	0	0	0	72.00	
1993	1	2	0	0	0	0	0	72.50	$1,000
Period Totals	**Starts**	**Rounds Played**	**Cuts Made**	**Wins**	**Top-5s**	**Top-10s**	**Top-25s**	**Scoring Average**	**Money**
	28	60	3	0	0	0	0	74.68	$4,421

Jim Colbert

Year	Starts	Rounds Played	Cuts Made	Wins	Top-5s	Top-10s	Top-25s	Scoring Average	Money
1966	21	65	11	0	0	0	1	73.88	$2,938

Best finish for 1966: T-15th at the Portland Open Invitational

1967	30	105	22	0	2	4	8	72.52	$26,199

Best finish for 1967: T-3rd at the Jacksonville Open

1968	34	99	16	0	0	0	4	72.81	$8,537

Best finish for 1968: T-13th at the Minnesota Golf Classic

1969	38	122	24	1	1	4	11	72.30	$41,901

Best finish for 1969: Win at the Monsanto Open

1970	34	114	25	0	1	4	11	72.16	$46,494

Best finish for 1970: 2nd at the Doral-Eastern Open

1971	37	117	23	0	2	5	8	71.91	$38,453

Best finish for 1971: T-3rd at the U.S. Open & Robinson Open Golf Classic

1972	33	103	19	1	3	5	10	72.28	$83,535

Best finish for 1972: Win at the Greater Milwaukee Open

Year	Starts	Rounds Played	Cuts Made	Wins	Top-5s	Top-10s	Top-25s	Scoring Average	Money
1973	34	103	19	1	2	4	9	72.33	$66,776

Best finish for 1973: Win at the Greater Jacksonville Open

| 1974 | 31 | 103 | 21 | 1 | 4 | 6 | 15 | 71.44 | $93,974 |

Best finish for 1974: Win at the American Golf Classic

| 1975 | 31 | 101 | 19 | 0 | 3 | 3 | 9 | 72.34 | $51,861 |

Best finish for 1975: T-2nd at the B.C. Open

| 1976 | 31 | 114 | 26 | 0 | 3 | 5 | 10 | 71.49 | $53,023 |

Best finish for 1976: T-4th at the Bob Hope Chrysler Classic, First NBC New Orleans Open & Southern Open

| 1977 | 20 | 69 | 13 | 0 | 0 | 1 | 5 | 72.45 | $20,103 |

Best finish for 1977: T-8th at the Greater Greensboro Open

| 1978 | 34 | 116 | 25 | 0 | 0 | 3 | 8 | 72.13 | $46,860 |

Best finish for 1978: 7th at the Atlanta Classic

| 1979 | 30 | 105 | 24 | 0 | 2 | 5 | 14 | 71.74 | $90,561 |

Best finish for 1979: 4th at the Colonial National Invitational & Buick Goodwrench Open

| 1980 | 27 | 93 | 20 | 1 | 3 | 3 | 10 | 71.84 | $150,411 |

Best finish for 1980: Win at the Joe Garagiola Tucson Open

| 1981 | 29 | 102 | 23 | 0 | 4 | 4 | 11 | 71.30 | $100,847 |

Best finish for 1981: T-2nd at the Western Open

| 1982 | 28 | 95 | 20 | 0 | 1 | 3 | 11 | 71.08 | $80,804 |

Best finish for 1982: 4th at the Greater Milwaukee Open

| 1983 | 29 | 104 | 22 | 2 | 3 | 5 | 11 | 71.43 | $224,410 |

Best finish for 1983: Win at the Colonial National Invitational & Texas Open

| 1984 | 27 | 97 | 21 | 0 | 1 | 3 | 11 | 71.85 | $113,168 |

Best finish for 1984: T-5th at the Georgia-Pacific Atlanta Golf Classic

| 1985 | 24 | 80 | 15 | 0 | 1 | 3 | 9 | 71.59 | $87,214 |

Best finish for 1985: 5th at the Texas Open

| 1986 | 24 | 75 | 16 | 0 | 0 | 2 | 9 | 71.72 | $109,502 |

Best finish for 1986: T-9th at the Seiko Tucson-Match Play Championship

| 1987 | 10 | 28 | 5 | 0 | 0 | 0 | 1 | 71.43 | $16,541 |

Best finish for 1987: T-24th at the USF&G Classic

| 1990 | 1 | 3 | 0 | 0 | 0 | 0 | 0 | 73.00 | |

Period Totals	Starts	Rounds Played	Cuts Made	Wins	Top-5s	Top-10s	Top-25s	Scoring Average	Money
	637	2113	429	7	36	72	196	71.99	$1,554,111

Bobby Cole

Year	Starts	Rounds Played	Cuts Made	Wins	Top-5s	Top-10s	Top-25s	Scoring Average	Money
1966	2	8	2	0	0	0	0	72.38	

Best finish for 1966: T-30th at the British Open

| 1967 | 6 | 16 | 2 | 0 | 0 | 1 | 1 | 74.69 | $2,150 |

Best finish for 1967: T-10th at the Insurance City Open

| 1968 | 23 | 82 | 18 | 0 | 1 | 2 | 5 | 72.49 | $14,654 |

Best finish for 1968: T-3rd at the Greater New Orleans Open Invitational

| 1969 | 26 | 92 | 20 | 0 | 1 | 2 | 8 | 72.04 | $20,753 |

Best finish for 1969: T-5th at the Greater Jacksonville Open

| 1970 | 18 | 58 | 13 | 0 | 0 | 1 | 3 | 72.53 | $8,599 |

Best finish for 1970: T-10th at the Green Island Open Invitational

| 1971 | 15 | 42 | 8 | 0 | 0 | 1 | 3 | 71.90 | $8,793 |

Best finish for 1971: T-9th at the Cleveland Open

| 1972 | 18 | 64 | 14 | 0 | 0 | 1 | 4 | 72.42 | $17,434 |

Best finish for 1972: T-8th at the American Golf Classic

| 1973 | 22 | 75 | 17 | 0 | 1 | 2 | 4 | 72.00 | $27,538 |

Best finish for 1973: 3rd at the Canadian Open

| 1974 | 19 | 66 | 14 | 0 | 4 | 6 | 8 | 71.41 | $56,651 |

Best finish for 1974: T-2nd at the Greater New Orleans Open

| 1975 | 22 | 74 | 16 | 0 | 2 | 4 | 7 | 72.07 | $50,949 |

Best finish for 1975: 2nd at the Western Open

| 1976 | 25 | 88 | 19 | 0 | 0 | 0 | 5 | 72.63 | $19,415 |

Best finish for 1976: T-11th at the Sahara Invitational

| 1977 | 20 | 68 | 14 | 0 | 0 | 2 | 6 | 72.06 | $23,596 |

Best finish for 1977: T-6th at the Tallahassee Open

| 1978 | 25 | 86 | 19 | 0 | 1 | 1 | 6 | 71.93 | $32,541 |

Best finish for 1978: T-3rd at the Buick Goodwrench Open

| 1979 | 15 | 46 | 8 | 0 | 0 | 0 | 1 | 72.85 | $6,525 |

Best finish for 1979: T-24th at the Ed McMahon Quad City Open

| 1980 | 19 | 54 | 9 | 0 | 1 | 1 | 4 | 71.76 | $22,202 |

Best finish for 1980: T-4th at the Tallahassee Open

| 1981 | 15 | 44 | 9 | 0 | 0 | 1 | 1 | 71.55 | $13,559 |

Best finish for 1981: T-10th at the Greater Milwaukee Open

| 1982 | 22 | 72 | 14 | 0 | 1 | 1 | 4 | 72.00 | $38,743 |

Best finish for 1982: T-3rd at the LaJet Classic

| 1983 | 21 | 60 | 7 | 0 | 0 | 0 | 2 | 73.02 | $16,753 |

Best finish for 1983: T-12th at the Joe Garagiola Tucson Open

Year	Starts	Rounds Played	Cuts Made	Wins	Top-5s	Top-10s	Top-25s	Scoring Average	Money
1984	1	2	0	0	0	0	0	73.50	
1985	9	30	6	0	0	0	0	71.73	$5,211

Best finish for 1985: T-31st at the Anheuser-Busch Golf Classic

| 1986 | 14 | 50 | 12 | 0 | 1 | 2 | 6 | 70.74 | $88,472 |

Best finish for 1986: 3rd at the NEC World Series of Golf

| 1987 | 29 | 97 | 19 | 0 | 0 | 0 | 3 | 71.92 | $46,309 |

Best finish for 1987: T-23rd at the Bob Hope Chrysler Classic & Shearson Lehman/Andy Williams San Diego

| 1988 | 7 | 5 | 0 | 0 | 0 | 0 | 0 | 74.00 | |
| 1989 | 7 | 16 | 1 | 0 | 0 | 0 | 0 | 72.44 | $980 |

Best finish for 1989: T-70th at the Chattanooga Classic

| 1990 | 1 | 4 | 1 | 0 | 0 | 0 | 0 | 71.75 | $612 |

Best finish for 1990: T-67th at the Deposit Guaranty

| 1991 | 4 | 10 | 1 | 0 | 0 | 0 | 0 | 73.30 | $1,400 |

Best finish for 1991: T-69th at the Buick Southern Open

1992	2	4	0	0	0	0	0	74.50	
1993	4	8	0	0	0	0	0	73.13	
1994	2	4	0	0	0	0	0	75.00	
1995	2	4	0	0	0	0	0	74.25	
1996	1	2	0	0	0	0	0	73.50	
1998	4	10	1	0	0	0	0	73.70	$2,970

Best finish for 1998: 71st at the B.C. Open

1999	1	2	0	0	0	0	0	74.50	
2001	1	2	0	0	0	0	0	77.50	
2003	1	2	0	0	0	0	0	73.00	
Period Totals	Starts	Rounds Played	Cuts Made	Wins	Top-5s	Top-10s	Top-25s	Scoring Average	Money
	423	1347	264	0	13	28	81	72.19	$526,805

Gavin Coles

Year	Starts	Rounds Played	Cuts Made	Wins	Top-5s	Top-10s	Top-25s	Scoring Average	Money
2003	28	66	7	0	0	0	0	72.59	$55,350

Best finish for 2003: T-56th at The International

| 2005 | 22 | 70 | 13 | 0 | 0 | 1 | 2 | 71.50 | $359,523 |

Best finish for 2005: T-7th at the Shell Houston Open

| 2006 | 5 | 17 | 3 | 0 | 0 | 0 | 0 | 71.59 | $34,674 |

Best finish for 2006: T-44th at the Shell Houston Open

| 2007 | 28 | 87 | 16 | 0 | 0 | 2 | 4 | 71.32 | $511,353 |

Best finish for 2007: T-9th at the Mayakoba Golf Classic

| 2008 | 16 | 54 | 11 | 0 | 0 | 1 | 4 | 70.65 | $455,003 |

Best finish for 2008: T-8th at the Stanford St. Jude Classic

| Period Totals | Starts | Rounds Played | Cuts Made | Wins | Top-5s | Top-10s | Top-25s | Scoring Average | Money |
| | 99 | 294 | 50 | 0 | 0 | 4 | 10 | 71.54 | $1,415,902 |

Neil Coles

Year	Starts	Rounds Played	Cuts Made	Wins	Top-5s	Top-10s	Top-25s	Scoring Average	Money
1959	3	12	3	0	0	0	1	73.08	$180

Best finish for 1959: T-21st at the British Open

| 1960 | 1 | 2 | 0 | 0 | 0 | 0 | 0 | 75.00 | |
| 1961 | 1 | 4 | 1 | 0 | 1 | 1 | 1 | 72.00 | |

Best finish for 1961: T-3rd at the British Open

| 1962 | 1 | 5 | 1 | 0 | 0 | 1 | 1 | 69.40 | $1,350 |

Best finish for 1962: T-8th at the Palm Springs Golf Classic

| 1963 | 1 | 4 | 1 | 0 | 0 | 0 | 1 | 73.25 | $217 |

Best finish for 1963: T-20th at the British Open

| 1964 | 1 | 2 | 0 | 0 | 0 | 0 | 0 | 82.00 | |
| 1965 | 1 | 4 | 1 | 0 | 0 | 0 | 1 | 73.50 | $371 |

Best finish for 1965: T-12th at the British Open

| 1966 | 12 | 39 | 6 | 0 | 1 | 1 | 1 | 73.33 | $10,976 |

Best finish for 1966: 3rd at the Carling World Open

| 1967 | 1 | 4 | 1 | 0 | 0 | 0 | 0 | 74.25 | $220 |

Best finish for 1967: T-36th at the British Open

| 1968 | 1 | 4 | 1 | 0 | 0 | 1 | 1 | 73.75 | $1,579 |

Best finish for 1968: T-6th at the British Open

| 1969 | 1 | 4 | 1 | 0 | 0 | 0 | 1 | 72.25 | $1,577 |

Best finish for 1969: T-11th at the British Open

| 1970 | 1 | 4 | 1 | 0 | 0 | 1 | 1 | 71.75 | $4,200 |

Best finish for 1970: T-6th at the British Open

| 1971 | 1 | 4 | 1 | 0 | 0 | 0 | 1 | 72.75 | $871 |

Best finish for 1971: T-22nd at the British Open

| 1972 | 1 | 3 | 0 | 0 | 0 | 0 | 0 | 76.00 | $188 |
| 1973 | 1 | 4 | 1 | 0 | 1 | 1 | 1 | 69.75 | $9,425 |

Best finish for 1973: T-2nd at the British Open

Year	Starts	Rounds Played	Cuts Made	Wins	Top-5s	Top-10s	Top-25s	Scoring Average	Money
1974	1	4	1	0	0	0	1	74.00	$2,400

Best finish for 1974: T-13th at the British Open

Year	Starts	Rounds Played	Cuts Made	Wins	Top-5s	Top-10s	Top-25s	Scoring Average	Money
1975	1	4	1	0	0	1	1	70.50	$5,940

Best finish for 1975: 7th at the British Open

1976	1	4	1	0	0	0	0	73.50	$603

Best finish for 1976: T-28th at the British Open

1977	1	4	1	0	0	0	0	73.00	$527

Best finish for 1977: T-41st at the British Open

1978	1	4	1	0	0	0	0	73.75	$646

Best finish for 1978: T-48th at the British Open

1979	1	0	0	0	0	0	0		$420
1980	1	4	1	0	0	0	0	72.25	$2,400

Best finish for 1980: T-29th at the British Open

1981	1	4	1	0	0	0	0	73.25	$1,180

Best finish for 1981: T-39th at the British Open

1982	1	4	1	0	0	0	0	75.00	$1,105

Best finish for 1982: T-42nd at the British Open

1983	1	3	0	0	0	0	0	73.00	$638
1984	1	3	0	0	0	0	0	74.67	$793
1985	1	2	0	0	0	0	0	75.50	$544
Period Totals	40	139	27	0	3	7	13	73.19	$48,349

Bill Collins

Year	Starts	Rounds Played	Cuts Made	Wins	Top-5s	Top-10s	Top-25s	Scoring Average	Money
1958	32	115	25	0	3	4	16	71.70	$10,669

Best finish for 1958: 3rd at the Carling Open

1959	21	81	18	1	2	6	11	71.17	$11,745

Best finish for 1959: Win at the Greater New Orleans Open Invitational

1960	24	96	23	2	7	10	21	70.67	$26,496

Best finish for 1960: Win at the Houston Classic & Hot Springs Open Invitational

1961	21	80	19	0	0	7	17	70.51	$17,450

Best finish for 1961: T-7th at the Denver Open Invitational

1962	17	67	17	1	4	5	9	70.99	$20,668

Best finish for 1962: Win at the Buick Open Invitational

1963	10	38	8	0	1	1	7	71.74	$10,902

Best finish for 1963: T-5th at the Thunderbird Classic Invitational

1964	29	97	18	0	1	4	9	72.61	$15,783

Best finish for 1964: T-5th at the Canadian Open

1965	12	32	3	0	0	0	1	74.38	$1,517

Best finish for 1965: T-18th at the Bing Crosby Pro-Am

1966	5	15	2	0	0	0	1	73.27	$1,411

Best finish for 1966: T-22nd at the Insurance City Open Invitational

1967	18	67	15	0	1	1	6	72.19	$22,218

Best finish for 1967: 2nd at the Jacksonville Open

1968	18	66	15	0	1	1	4	71.82	$17,973

Best finish for 1968: 3rd at the Haig Open Invitational

1969	12	40	8	0	0	1	3	72.80	$6,409

Best finish for 1969: T-8th at the Bing Crosby National Pro-Am

1970	12	29	5	0	0	0	2	73.79	$4,841

Best finish for 1970: T-17th at the Monsanto Open & National 4 Ball Championship PGA Players

1971	5	13	2	0	0	0	1	73.46	$2,240

Best finish for 1971: T-22nd at the Westchester Classic

1972	3	6	0	0	0	0	0	74.17	
1973	5	14	2	0	0	0	0	74.14	$1,025

Best finish for 1973: T-39th at the Westchester Classic

1974	5	11	1	0	0	0	0	74.00	$337

Best finish for 1974: T-54th at the Doral-Eastern Open

1975	2	6	1	0	0	0	0	74.17	$413

Best finish for 1975: 67th at the Westchester Classic

1976	3	8	1	0	0	0	0	73.50	$1,225

Best finish for 1976: T-34th at the PGA Championship

1977	3	6	0	0	0	0	0	74.67	$500
Period Totals	257	887	183	4	20	40	108	71.93	$173,820

Chad Collins

Year	Starts	Rounds Played	Cuts Made	Wins	Top-5s	Top-10s	Top-25s	Scoring Average	Money
2006	1	4	1	0	0	0	0	74.00	$29,459

Best finish for 2006: T-40th at the U.S. Open

2008	24	72	12	0	0	0	4	71.43	$339,959

Best finish for 2008: T-11th at the U.S. Bank Championship in Milwaukee

Period Totals	Starts	Rounds Played	Cuts Made	Wins	Top-5s	Top-10s	Top-25s	Scoring Average	Money
	25	76	13	0	0	0	4	71.57	$369,418

Tim Collins

Year	Starts	Rounds Played	Cuts Made	Wins	Top-5s	Top-10s	Top-25s	Scoring Average	Money
1972	2	6	1	0	0	0	0	76.33	$835

Best finish for 1972: T-55th at the U.S. Open

1973	22	69	12	0	0	0	2	73.12	$8,340

Best finish for 1973: T-11th at the Tallahassee Open

1974	21	51	6	0	1	2	2	73.78	$10,748

Best finish for 1974: T-5th at the Kaiser International Open

1975	13	30	3	0	0	0	0	75.27	$1,826

Best finish for 1975: T-29th at the Sammy Davis, Jr. - Greater Hartford Open

1976	1	4	1	0	0	0	0	74.50	$1,150

Best finish for 1976: T-44th at the U.S. Open

1977	4	8	0	0	0	0	0	76.38	$250
1978	3	8	1	0	0	0	0	75.13	$387

Best finish for 1978: T-68th at the Colgate Hall Of Fame Classic

1979	3	8	1	0	0	0	0	74.13	$850

Best finish for 1979: T-70th at the Colgate Hall Of Fame Classic

1981	1	2	0	0	0	0	0	74.50	$550
1982	2	4	0	0	0	0	0	74.50	
1983	2	4	0	0	0	0	0	78.00	$100
1984	2	4	0	0	0	0	0	82.25	$1,000
1985	2	4	0	0	0	0	0	76.00	$1,000
Period Totals	Starts	Rounds Played	Cuts Made	Wins	Top-5s	Top-10s	Top-25s	Scoring Average	Money
	78	202	25	0	1	2	4	74.35	$27,036

Andrew Coltart

Year	Starts	Rounds Played	Cuts Made	Wins	Top-5s	Top-10s	Top-25s	Scoring Average	Money
1991	1	2	0	0	0	0	0	76.50	
1992	1	2	0	0	0	0	0	76.00	$1,200
1994	1	4	1	0	0	0	0	69.50	$12,916

Best finish for 1994: T-32nd at the British Open

1995	3	10	2	0	0	0	1	72.80	$36,682

Best finish for 1995: T-20th at the British Open

1996	2	6	1	0	0	0	0	72.67	$5,369

Best finish for 1996: T-49th at the Memorial Tournament

1997	2	6	1	0	0	0	0	74.67	$7,143

Best finish for 1997: T-75th at the U.S. Open

1998	4	12	3	0	0	0	0	73.00	$37,971

Best finish for 1998: T-30th at the NEC World Series of Golf

1999	3	12	3	0	0	0	1	73.50	$72,827

Best finish for 1999: T-18th at the British Open

2000	4	16	4	0	0	0	2	71.56	$162,057

Best finish for 2000: T-17th at the American Express Championship

2001	3	8	3	0	0	1	1	70.75	$119,317

Best finish for 2001: T-9th at the Accenture Match Play Championship

2002	1	4	1	0	0	0	0	71.25	$26,732

Best finish for 2002: T-37th at the British Open

Period Totals	Starts	Rounds Played	Cuts Made	Wins	Top-5s	Top-10s	Top-25s	Scoring Average	Money
	25	82	19	0	0	1	5	72.55	$482,214

Ron Commans

Year	Starts	Rounds Played	Cuts Made	Wins	Top-5s	Top-10s	Top-25s	Scoring Average	Money
1978	2	6	1	0	0	0	0	75.00	$600

Best finish for 1978: T-34th at the Glen Campbell Los Angles Open

1979	1	2	0	0	0	0	0	74.00	
1981	1	4	1	0	0	0	1	69.75	

Best finish for 1981: T-20th at the Glen Campbell Los Angles Open

1982	23	62	7	0	0	0	0	73.63	$6,061

Best finish for 1982: T-34th at the Kemper Open

1983	6	19	2	0	0	0	0	74.89	$1,851

Best finish for 1983: T-68th at the Glen Campbell Los Angles Open

1984	2	4	0	0	0	0	0	77.75	$600
1985	24	59	5	0	0	0	0	74.44	$4,534

Best finish for 1985: T-44th at the St. Jude Memphis Classic

1986	1	4	1	0	0	0	0	74.00	$4,752

Best finish for 1986: T-35th at the British Open

1988	1	2	0	0	0	0	0	76.50	$765
Period Totals	Starts	Rounds Played	Cuts Made	Wins	Top-5s	Top-10s	Top-25s	Scoring Average	Money
	61	162	17	0	0	0	1	74.18	$19,163

Byron Comstock

Year	Starts	Rounds Played	Cuts Made	Wins	Top-5s	Top-10s	Top-25s	Scoring Average	Money
1966	1	2	0	0	0	0	0	78.00	
1968	10	30	5	0	0	0	0	74.07	

Best finish for 1968: T-51st at the "500" Festival Open Invitational

Year	Starts	Rounds Played	Cuts Made	Wins	Top-5s	Top-10s	Top-25s	Scoring Average	Money
1970	15	39	4	0	0	0	0	74.54	$566

Best finish for 1970: T-47th at the Green Island Open Invitational

Year	Starts	Rounds Played	Cuts Made	Wins	Top-5s	Top-10s	Top-25s	Scoring Average	Money
1971	7	18	1	0	0	0	1	74.11	$577

Best finish for 1971: T-22nd at the Tallahassee Open

Year	Starts	Rounds Played	Cuts Made	Wins	Top-5s	Top-10s	Top-25s	Scoring Average	Money
1972	19	49	6	0	0	0	2	73.98	$3,428

Best finish for 1972: T-13th at the Liggett Meyers Open

Year	Starts	Rounds Played	Cuts Made	Wins	Top-5s	Top-10s	Top-25s	Scoring Average	Money
1973	21	58	8	0	0	0	0	74.14	$1,865

Best finish for 1973: T-39th at the Liggett Meyers Open

Year	Starts	Rounds Played	Cuts Made	Wins	Top-5s	Top-10s	Top-25s	Scoring Average	Money
1974	6	16	2	0	0	0	0	73.75	$581

Best finish for 1974: T-45th at the Monsanto Open

Year	Starts	Rounds Played	Cuts Made	Wins	Top-5s	Top-10s	Top-25s	Scoring Average	Money
1975	5	11	1	0	0	0	0	77.18	$116

Best finish for 1975: 69th at the Ed McMahon Quad City Open

Period Totals	Starts	Rounds Played	Cuts Made	Wins	Top-5s	Top-10s	Top-25s	Scoring Average	Money
	84	223	27	0	0	0	3	74.32	$7,133

Tim Conley

Year	Starts	Rounds Played	Cuts Made	Wins	Top-5s	Top-10s	Top-25s	Scoring Average	Money
1992	1	2	0	0	0	0	0	76.50	$1,000
1993	22	63	10	0	0	0	2	72.21	$66,593

Best finish for 1993: T-14th at the Kemper Open & H-E-B Texas Open

Year	Starts	Rounds Played	Cuts Made	Wins	Top-5s	Top-10s	Top-25s	Scoring Average	Money
1994	2	6	1	0	0	0	1	69.50	$13,040

Best finish for 1994: T-18th at the Hardee's Golf Classic

Year	Starts	Rounds Played	Cuts Made	Wins	Top-5s	Top-10s	Top-25s	Scoring Average	Money
1997	1	2	0	0	0	0	0	74.50	
1998	26	70	10	0	1	1	3	72.33	$140,355

Best finish for 1998: 5th at the FedEx St. Jude Classic

Year	Starts	Rounds Played	Cuts Made	Wins	Top-5s	Top-10s	Top-25s	Scoring Average	Money
1999	1	4	1	0	0	0	0	72.25	$3,676

Best finish for 1999: T-52nd at the B.C. Open

Year	Starts	Rounds Played	Cuts Made	Wins	Top-5s	Top-10s	Top-25s	Scoring Average	Money
2000	1	2	0	0	0	0	0	73.00	
2001	1	4	1	0	0	0	0	72.00	$3,680

Best finish for 2001: 79th at the B.C. Open

Year	Starts	Rounds Played	Cuts Made	Wins	Top-5s	Top-10s	Top-25s	Scoring Average	Money
2002	1	2	0	0	0	0	0	72.50	
2003	1	2	0	0	0	0	0	71.50	
2004	1	4	1	0	0	0	0	70.50	$6,420

Best finish for 2004: T-60th at the B.C. Open

Year	Starts	Rounds Played	Cuts Made	Wins	Top-5s	Top-10s	Top-25s	Scoring Average	Money
2005	1	2	0	0	0	0	0	72.00	
Period Totals	Starts	Rounds Played	Cuts Made	Wins	Top-5s	Top-10s	Top-25s	Scoring Average	Money
	59	163	24	0	1	1	6	72.20	$234,764

Michael Connell

Year	Starts	Rounds Played	Cuts Made	Wins	Top-5s	Top-10s	Top-25s	Scoring Average	Money
2001	1	2	0	0	0	0	0	70.00	
2002	2	6	1	0	0	0	0	74.17	$8,976

Best finish for 2002: T-76th at the Verizon Byron Nelson Classic

Year	Starts	Rounds Played	Cuts Made	Wins	Top-5s	Top-10s	Top-25s	Scoring Average	Money
2006	22	48	4	0	0	0	1	72.52	$97,771

Best finish for 2006: T-17th at the John Deere Classic

Period Totals	Starts	Rounds Played	Cuts Made	Wins	Top-5s	Top-10s	Top-25s	Scoring Average	Money
	25	56	5	0	0	0	1	72.61	$106,747

Frank Conner

Year	Starts	Rounds Played	Cuts Made	Wins	Top-5s	Top-10s	Top-25s	Scoring Average	Money
1971	1	2	0	0	0	0	0	76.00	
1973	2	4	0	0	0	0	0	76.00	$500
1975	21	61	10	0	0	0	1	73.26	$4,418

Best finish for 1975: T-24th at the Tallahassee Open

Year	Starts	Rounds Played	Cuts Made	Wins	Top-5s	Top-10s	Top-25s	Scoring Average	Money
1976	24	70	12	0	0	1	1	72.90	$8,245

Best finish for 1976: T-9th at the San Antonio Texas Open

Year	Starts	Rounds Played	Cuts Made	Wins	Top-5s	Top-10s	Top-25s	Scoring Average	Money
1977	19	63	14	0	0	0	5	71.94	$14,630

Best finish for 1977: T-11th at the Byron Nelson Golf Classic

Year	Starts	Rounds Played	Cuts Made	Wins	Top-5s	Top-10s	Top-25s	Scoring Average	Money
1978	24	72	12	0	0	0	1	72.83	$9,054

Best finish for 1978: T-17th at the Southern Open

Year	Starts	Rounds Played	Cuts Made	Wins	Top-5s	Top-10s	Top-25s	Scoring Average	Money
1979	31	93	17	0	1	1	6	72.72	$46,020

Best finish for 1979: T-2nd at the First NBC New Orleans Open

Year	Starts	Rounds Played	Cuts Made	Wins	Top-5s	Top-10s	Top-25s	Scoring Average	Money
1980	32	91	14	0	0	1	8	72.15	$38,110

Best finish for 1980: T-8th at the Hawaiian Open

Year	Starts	Rounds Played	Cuts Made	Wins	Top-5s	Top-10s	Top-25s	Scoring Average	Money
1981	30	91	17	0	1	5	9	72.03	$82,809

Best finish for 1981: T-2nd at the Quad Cities Open

Year	Starts	Rounds Played	Cuts Made	Wins	Top-5s	Top-10s	Top-25s	Scoring Average	Money
1982	36	122	23	0	1	1	5	72.39	$74,931

Best finish for 1982: 2nd at the Sea Pines Heritage Classic

1983	34	103	18	0	1	3	8	72.40	$71,320

Best finish for 1983: T-5th at the Buick Open

1984	34	97	14	0	1	1	3	72.77	$55,405

Best finish for 1984: T-2nd at the Bank of Boston Classic

1985	32	108	20	0	0	2	5	72.23	$68,804

Best finish for 1985: T-7th at the Anheuser-Busch Golf Classic

1986	34	98	16	0	0	0	3	72.48	$35,729

Best finish for 1986: T-14th at the Deposit Guaranty Golf Classic

1987	18	58	13	0	0	0	5	71.10	$52,074

Best finish for 1987: T-13th at the Big I Houston Open & Southern Open

1988	24	62	8	1	1	1	1	72.65	$44,802

Best finish for 1988: Win at the Deposit Guaranty Golf Classic

1989	19	44	3	0	0	0	0	72.73	$3,052

Best finish for 1989: T-41st at the Deposit Guaranty Golf Classic

1990	6	17	2	0	0	0	0	71.88	$3,461

Best finish for 1990: T-48th at the Buick Southern Open

1991	5	15	2	0	0	1	2	70.87	$18,319

Best finish for 1991: T-7th at the Deposit Guaranty Classic

1992	32	87	13	0	0	1	3	71.86	$74,835

Best finish for 1992: T-6th at the Deposit Guaranty Classic

1993	7	21	3	0	0	0	2	71.90	$34,154

Best finish for 1993: T-11th at the Canon Greater Hartford Open

1994	2	4	1	0	0	0	0	72.50	$1,435

Best finish for 1994: T-62nd at the Deposit Guaranty Golf Classic

1995	2	6	1	0	0	0	0	72.17	$7,480

Best finish for 1995: T-28th at the LaCantera Texas Open

Period Totals	Starts	Rounds Played	Cuts Made	Wins	Top-5s	Top-10s	Top-25s	Scoring Average	Money
	469	1389	233	1	6	18	68	72.38	$749,586

Joe Conrad

Year	Starts	Rounds Played	Cuts Made	Wins	Top-5s	Top-10s	Top-25s	Scoring Average	Money
1958	29	95	17	0	0	1	5	72.87	$3,403

Best finish for 1958: T-8th at the Baton Rouge Open

1959	6	22	4	0	1	1	4	71.64	$2,470

Best finish for 1959: T-3rd at the Puerto Rico Open Invitational

1964	4	11	2	0	0	0	0	74.09	$402

Best finish for 1964: T-44th at the PGA Championship

1965	1	4	1	0	0	1	1	69.00	$1,300

Best finish for 1965: T-9th at the Texas Open

1966	3	10	2	0	0	0	0	73.70	$592

Best finish for 1966: T-43rd at the Texas Open Invitational

1967	2	6	1	0	0	0	0	72.83	$550

Best finish for 1967: T-34th at the Texas Open

1968	1	2	0	0	0	0	0	77.50	
1970	1	2	0	0	0	0	0	77.00	
1972	1	2	0	0	0	0	0	81.50	

Period Totals	Starts	Rounds Played	Cuts Made	Wins	Top-5s	Top-10s	Top-25s	Scoring Average	Money
	48	154	27	0	1	3	10	72.96	$8,718

Charles Coody

Year	Starts	Rounds Played	Cuts Made	Wins	Top-5s	Top-10s	Top-25s	Scoring Average	Money
1960	2	6	1	0	0	0	1	73.67	

Best finish for 1960: T-25th at the Texas Open Invitational

1961	1	2	0	0	0	0	0	80.50	
1962	1	4	1	0	0	0	0	70.25	

Best finish for 1962: T-27th at the Texas Open Invitational

1963	6	20	4	0	0	0	2	73.65	$1,367

Best finish for 1963: T-19th at the Denver Open Invitational

1964	31	94	14	1	2	2	3	73.03	$10,284

Best finish for 1964: Win at the Dallas Open

1965	35	125	27	0	1	4	12	72.30	$21,427

Best finish for 1965: T-3rd at the Seattle Open

1966	33	121	27	0	1	5	10	72.12	$30,367

Best finish for 1966: T-2nd at the Florida Citrus Open Invitational

1967	32	125	29	0	3	5	17	71.84	$62,438

Best finish for 1967: T-2nd at the Colonial National Invitational & Thunderbird Classic

1968	32	114	24	0	3	8	15	71.72	$47,239

Best finish for 1968: T-4th at the Doral Open Invitational & Philadelphia Golf Classic

1969	30	109	25	1	5	6	10	72.21	$77,252

Best finish for 1969: Win at the Cleveland Open

Year	Starts	Rounds Played	Cuts Made	Wins	Top-5s	Top-10s	Top-25s	Scoring Average	Money
1970	30	103	24	0	3	5	16	71.78	$57,915

Best finish for 1970: 3rd at the Tucson Open

1971	29	96	21	1	7	10	13	71.83	$94,266

Best finish for 1971: Win at the Masters

1972	30	102	21	0	4	4	12	71.98	$54,226

Best finish for 1972: T-3rd at the Hawaiian Open & Byron Nelson Golf Classic

1973	30	115	27	0	2	3	11	71.77	$61,116

Best finish for 1973: 2nd at the Florida Citrus Open Invitational

1974	31	114	26	0	2	5	10	71.50	$58,826

Best finish for 1974: T-2nd at the Byron Nelson Golf Classic

1975	27	96	20	0	4	7	15	71.22	$87,312

Best finish for 1975: 3rd at the Sea Pines Heritage Classic & Atlanta Classic

1976	29	107	24	0	4	8	15	71.53	$85,586

Best finish for 1976: T-3rd at the Western Open

1977	28	107	25	0	2	7	13	71.69	$75,537

Best finish for 1977: T-4th at the Canadian Open & PGA Championship

1978	32	110	22	0	3	3	7	72.12	$52,709

Best finish for 1978: T-4th at the Joe Garagiola Tucson Open & Glen Campbell Los Angles Open

1979	30	105	22	0	1	2	8	72.09	$59,803

Best finish for 1979: T-4th at the Hawaiian Open

1980	26	86	18	0	2	2	7	71.69	$73,918

Best finish for 1980: T-2nd at the Jackie Gleason's Inverrary Classic

1981	27	89	19	0	0	1	2	72.25	$32,628

Best finish for 1981: T-6th at the American Motors Inverrary Classic

1982	25	86	18	0	1	1	8	71.81	$65,395

Best finish for 1982: T-3rd at the Canadian Open

1983	25	77	11	0	0	0	1	72.65	$19,056

Best finish for 1983: T-12th at the Joe Garagiola Tucson Open

1984	20	61	11	0	0	0	1	72.97	$18,340

Best finish for 1984: T-22nd at the Byron Nelson Golf Classic

1985	26	77	11	0	0	0	1	72.21	$26,953

Best finish for 1985: T-12th at the Georgia-Pacific Atlanta Golf Classic

1986	16	42	6	0	0	0	1	72.88	$12,740

Best finish for 1986: T-19th at the Southern Open

1987	7	15	1	0	0	0	0	74.07	$2,796

Best finish for 1987: 63rd at the Colonial National Invitational

1988	1	2	0	0	0	0	0	77.00	$1,500
1989	1	4	1	0	0	0	0	74.50	$4,900

Best finish for 1989: T-38th at the Masters

1990	1	2	0	0	0	0	0	76.00	$1,500
1991	1	2	0	0	0	0	0	77.00	$1,500
1993	1	4	1	0	0	0	0	74.75	$3,800

Best finish for 1993: T-57th at the Masters

1994	1	2	0	0	0	0	0	77.00	$1,500
1995	1	2	0	0	0	0	0	73.50	$1,500
1996	1	2	0	0	0	0	0	80.00	$1,500
1997	1	2	0	0	0	0	0	80.00	$5,000
1998	1	2	0	0	0	0	0	82.00	$5,000
1999	1	2	0	0	0	0	0	75.50	$5,000
2000	1	2	0	0	0	0	0	77.50	$5,000
2001	1	2	0	0	0	0	0	76.00	$5,000
2002	1	2	0	0	0	0	0	83.00	$5,000
2003	1	2	0	0	0	0	0	82.00	$5,000
2004	1	2	0	0	0	0	0	83.50	$5,000
2005	1	2	0	0	0	0	0	85.50	$5,000
2006	1	2	0	0	0	0	0	81.50	$5,000
Period Totals	Starts	Rounds Played	Cuts Made	Wins	Top-5s	Top-10s	Top-25s	Scoring Average	Money
	689	2348	481	3	50	88	211	72.14	$1,257,195

Jeff Cook

Year	Starts	Rounds Played	Cuts Made	Wins	Top-5s	Top-10s	Top-25s	Scoring Average	Money
1989	1	2	0	0	0	0	0	72.50	
1990	1	2	0	0	0	0	0	70.50	
1991	1	2	0	0	0	0	0	73.00	
1993	29	83	13	0	0	0	3	72.11	$72,398

Best finish for 1993: T-17th at the Anheuser-Busch Golf Classic

1994	1	2	0	0	0	0	0	73.50	
Period Totals	Starts	Rounds Played	Cuts Made	Wins	Top-5s	Top-10s	Top-25s	Scoring Average	Money
	33	91	13	0	0	0	3	72.13	$72,398

John Cook

Year	Starts	Rounds Played	Cuts Made	Wins	Top-5s	Top-10s	Top-25s	Scoring Average	Money
1977	1	2	0	0	0	0	0	78.00	
1978	1	4	1	0	0	0	1	75.25	

Best finish for 1978: T-22nd at the World Series Of Golf

| 1979 | 5 | 16 | 3 | 0 | 0 | 0 | 0 | 75.31 | |

Best finish for 1979: 39th at the Masters

| 1980 | 31 | 99 | 19 | 0 | 1 | 2 | 6 | 72.24 | $43,856 |

Best finish for 1980: T-4th at the Pleasant Valley Jimmy Fund Classic

| 1981 | 31 | 101 | 24 | 1 | 3 | 3 | 13 | 71.42 | $130,648 |

Best finish for 1981: Win at the Bing Crosby Pro-Am

| 1982 | 28 | 97 | 21 | 0 | 1 | 3 | 6 | 71.79 | $59,583 |

Best finish for 1982: T-5th at the Bank of Boston Classic

| 1983 | 28 | 112 | 27 | 1 | 4 | 7 | 12 | 71.14 | $216,868 |

Best finish for 1983: Win at the Canadian Open

| 1984 | 28 | 94 | 19 | 0 | 1 | 1 | 5 | 72.05 | $68,810 |

Best finish for 1984: T-5th at the Canadian Open

| 1985 | 29 | 96 | 17 | 0 | 0 | 1 | 5 | 72.06 | $64,173 |

Best finish for 1985: T-10th at the Canon Sammy Davis, Jr. - Greater Hartford Open

| 1986 | 29 | 88 | 19 | 0 | 3 | 6 | 13 | 70.97 | $249,956 |

Best finish for 1986: T-2nd at the Bob Hope Chrysler Classic & Southern Open

| 1987 | 32 | 98 | 19 | 1 | 2 | 6 | 10 | 71.39 | $332,834 |

Best finish for 1987: Win at the International

| 1988 | 29 | 100 | 21 | 0 | 1 | 2 | 9 | 71.25 | $141,416 |

Best finish for 1988: T-5th at the GTE Byron Nelson Classic

| 1989 | 12 | 36 | 6 | 0 | 0 | 1 | 2 | 72.33 | $39,444 |

Best finish for 1989: T-9th at the Shearson Lehman Hutton Open

| 1990 | 28 | 95 | 20 | 0 | 2 | 4 | 10 | 70.88 | $448,111 |

Best finish for 1990: T-2nd at the Federal Express St. Jude Classic & Las Vegas Invitational

| 1991 | 25 | 92 | 21 | 0 | 5 | 8 | 12 | 70.22 | $549,484 |

Best finish for 1991: 2nd at the United Hawaiian Open

| 1992 | 22 | 83 | 19 | 3 | 8 | 9 | 14 | 69.87 | $1,315,606 |

Best finish for 1992: Win at the Bob Hope Chrysler Classic, United Airlines Hawaiian Open & Las Vegas Invitational

| 1993 | 24 | 86 | 18 | 0 | 1 | 5 | 13 | 70.84 | $343,245 |

Best finish for 1993: T-5th at the Infiniti Tournament Of Champions

| 1994 | 25 | 84 | 17 | 0 | 3 | 6 | 11 | 70.62 | $437,339 |

Best finish for 1994: 3rd at the Memorial Tournament

| 1995 | 27 | 84 | 16 | 0 | 1 | 1 | 5 | 71.37 | $189,677 |

Best finish for 1995: T-5th at the FedEx St. Jude Classic

| 1996 | 26 | 89 | 19 | 2 | 2 | 5 | 10 | 70.53 | $831,260 |

Best finish for 1996: Win at the FedEx St. Jude Classic & CVS Charity Classic

| 1997 | 28 | 99 | 21 | 1 | 2 | 6 | 11 | 70.75 | $822,244 |

Best finish for 1997: Win at the Bob Hope Chrysler Classic

| 1998 | 26 | 92 | 19 | 1 | 4 | 6 | 12 | 70.75 | $1,146,511 |

Best finish for 1998: Win at the GTE Byron Nelson Classic

| 1999 | 26 | 81 | 16 | 0 | 2 | 2 | 5 | 71.77 | $573,918 |

Best finish for 1999: T-2nd at the Shell Houston Open

| 2000 | 28 | 88 | 15 | 0 | 2 | 3 | 6 | 70.73 | $538,105 |

Best finish for 2000: T-5th at the Buick Classic & Invensys Classic at Las Vegas

| 2001 | 25 | 88 | 21 | 1 | 2 | 2 | 3 | 70.13 | $1,022,778 |

Best finish for 2001: Win at the Reno-Tahoe Open

| 2002 | 25 | 82 | 16 | 0 | 4 | 6 | 7 | 70.84 | $1,630,651 |

Best finish for 2002: T-2nd at the Sony Open in Hawaii & Memorial Tournament

| 2003 | 10 | 28 | 4 | 0 | 0 | 0 | 0 | 71.50 | $83,830 |

Best finish for 2003: T-33rd at the WGC-Accenture Match Play Championship

| 2004 | 19 | 53 | 9 | 0 | 0 | 0 | 2 | 71.34 | $210,448 |

Best finish for 2004: T-19th at the Memorial Tournament

| 2005 | 26 | 70 | 9 | 0 | 1 | 1 | 4 | 71.39 | $374,185 |

Best finish for 2005: T-5th at the Southern Farm Bureau Classic

| 2006 | 22 | 67 | 11 | 0 | 2 | 2 | 4 | 71.04 | $644,505 |

Best finish for 2006: T-3rd at the FedEx St. Jude Classic

| 2007 | 13 | 34 | 5 | 0 | 0 | 0 | 0 | 71.65 | $119,756 |

Best finish for 2007: T-26th at the Mayakoba Golf Classic

Period Totals	Starts	Rounds Played	Cuts Made	Wins	Top-5s	Top-10s	Top-25s	Scoring Average	Money
	709	2338	472	11	57	98	211	71.18	$12,629,242

John-H. Cook

Year	Starts	Rounds Played	Cuts Made	Wins	Top-5s	Top-10s	Top-25s	Scoring Average	Money
1958	3	6	0	0	0	0	0	76.50	
1959	1	2	0	0	0	0	0	77.00	
1960	2	7	2	0	0	0	0	75.57	$100

Best finish for 1960: T-39th at the Bing Crosby National

Year	Starts	Rounds Played	Cuts Made	Wins	Top-5s	Top-10s	Top-25s	Scoring Average	Money
1962	1	2	1	0	0	0	0	76.00	

Best finish for 1962: T-200 at the PGA Championship

1963	2	8	2	0	0	0	0	73.88	$270

Best finish for 1963: T-39th at the St. Paul Open Invitational

1964	12	39	7	0	0	1	3	72.51	$3,852

Best finish for 1964: T-10th at the St. Paul Open

1965	25	76	14	0	0	0	2	73.21	$2,855

Best finish for 1965: T-19th at the Azalea Open

1966	25	75	13	0	0	0	4	83.29	$4,835

Best finish for 1966: T-17th at the Greater New Orleans Open Invitational

1967	20	58	9	0	1	1	4	73.14	$5,413

Best finish for 1967: T-4th at the Azalea Open

1968	8	25	3	0	0	0	0	74.36	$531

Best finish for 1968: T-42nd at the Pensacola Open Invitational

1969	1	4	1	0	0	0	0	74.75	$241

Best finish for 1969: T-76th at the PGA Championship

1970	2	6	1	0	0	0	0	76.33	$850

Best finish for 1970: T-54th at the U.S. Open

1971	2	4	0	0	0	0	0	76.25	
1972	11	26	2	0	0	0	0	74.04	$622

Best finish for 1972: T-34th at the Tallahassee Open

1974	1	4	1	0	0	0	0	75.75	$432

Best finish for 1974: T-39th at the British Open

1975	1	2	0	0	0	0	0	77.50	$220
1977	1	2	0	0	0	0	0	78.50	$250
Period Totals	Starts	Rounds Played	Cuts Made	Wins	Top-5s	Top-10s	Top-25s	Scoring Average	Money
	118	346	56	0	1	2	13	75.80	$20,473

Ross Coon

Year	Starts	Rounds Played	Cuts Made	Wins	Top-5s	Top-10s	Top-25s	Scoring Average	Money
1963	1	4	1	0	0	0	0	78.50	$300

Best finish for 1963: T-47th at the U.S. Open

1964	1	1	0	0	0	0	0	77.00	
1965	6	14	1	0	0	0	0	74.14	$449

Best finish for 1965: T-33rd at the Pensacola Open

1966	2	6	1	0	0	0	0	74.83	

Best finish for 1966: 71st at the Hawaiian Open Invitational

1967	2	6	1	0	0	0	0	72.33	

Best finish for 1967: T-52nd at the Insurance City Open

1968	3	12	3	0	0	0	0	72.92	$1,192

Best finish for 1968: T-33rd at the Kemper Open Invitational

1969	12	31	4	0	0	1	2	72.61	$2,546

Best finish for 1969: 8th at the Indian Ridge Hospital Open

1970	6	19	2	0	0	0	0	74.63	$700

Best finish for 1970: 54th at the PGA Championship

1971	1	2	0	0	0	0	0	75.00	
1972	2	4	0	0	0	0	0	77.75	
1973	2	4	0	0	0	0	0	78.00	
1974	1	2	0	0	0	0	0	76.50	
1975	1	2	0	0	0	0	0	76.50	
Period Totals	Starts	Rounds Played	Cuts Made	Wins	Top-5s	Top-10s	Top-25s	Scoring Average	Money
	40	107	13	0	0	1	2	74.16	$5,187

Carl Cooper

Year	Starts	Rounds Played	Cuts Made	Wins	Top-5s	Top-10s	Top-25s	Scoring Average	Money
1990	23	57	5	0	0	0	2	73.53	$28,755

Best finish for 1990: T-12th at the Federal Express St. Jude Classic

1991	26	71	9	0	0	0	1	72.55	$37,387

Best finish for 1991: T-14th at the Hardee's Golf Classic

1992	29	76	8	0	0	0	1	72.04	$38,401

Best finish for 1992: T-15th at the Canadian Open

1993	19	47	4	0	0	0	0	72.89	$10,774

Best finish for 1993: T-30th at the New England Classic

2000	1	2	0	0	0	0	0	76.00	
Period Totals	Starts	Rounds Played	Cuts Made	Wins	Top-5s	Top-10s	Top-25s	Scoring Average	Money
	98	253	26	0	0	0	4	72.71	$115,317

Pete Cooper

Year	Starts	Rounds Played	Cuts Made	Wins	Top-5s	Top-10s	Top-25s	Scoring Average	Money
1958	7	26	6	1	2	2	4	72.19	$3,970

Best finish for 1958: Win at the West Palm Beach Open

Year	Starts	Rounds Played	Cuts Made	Wins	Top-5s	Top-10s	Top-25s	Scoring Average	Money
1959	22	86	19	1	5	8	15	71.24	$13,214

Best finish for 1959: Win at the Puerto Rico Open Invitational

| 1960 | 13 | 50 | 10 | 1 | 4 | 5 | 9 | 71.46 | $9,286 |

Best finish for 1960: Win at the Jamaica Open Invitational

| 1961 | 8 | 30 | 7 | 0 | 0 | 1 | 2 | 72.30 | $2,564 |

Best finish for 1961: T-9th at the Mobile Sertoma Open Invitational

| 1962 | 10 | 40 | 9 | 0 | 0 | 2 | 3 | 72.45 | $4,751 |

Best finish for 1962: T-8th at the Puerto Rico Open Invitational

| 1963 | 2 | 8 | 2 | 0 | 1 | 1 | 2 | 71.50 | $1,044 |

Best finish for 1963: T-4th at the Puerto Rico Open Invitational

| 1964 | 13 | 37 | 5 | 0 | 0 | 0 | 2 | 73.11 | $1,665 |

Best finish for 1964: T-22nd at the Doral Open

| 1965 | 5 | 13 | 2 | 0 | 0 | 0 | 1 | 74.15 | $750 |

Best finish for 1965: T-23rd at the Doral Open

| 1966 | 2 | 6 | 1 | 0 | 0 | 0 | 0 | 74.33 | |

Best finish for 1966: T-56th at the Doral Open Invitational

| 1967 | 4 | 14 | 3 | 0 | 0 | 0 | 0 | 73.21 | $501 |

Best finish for 1967: T-44th at the PGA Championship

| 1968 | 6 | 16 | 2 | 0 | 0 | 0 | 0 | 73.81 | $183 |

Best finish for 1968: T-46th at the Doral Open Invitational

| 1969 | 1 | 2 | 0 | 0 | 0 | 0 | 0 | 76.00 | |
| 1970 | 3 | 10 | 2 | 0 | 0 | 0 | 0 | 73.80 | $343 |

Best finish for 1970: T-69th at the Greater Jacksonville Open

| 1971 | 3 | 8 | 1 | 0 | 0 | 0 | 0 | 73.88 | $171 |

Best finish for 1971: T-66th at the Walt Disney World Open

1972	1	2	0	0	0	0	0	76.00	
1975	2	4	0	0	0	0	0	74.00	
1976	1	2	0	0	0	0	0	78.50	$180
Period Totals	Starts	Rounds Played	Cuts Made	Wins	Top-5s	Top-10s	Top-25s	Scoring Average	Money
	103	354	69	3	12	19	38	72.38	$38,622

PGA Tour career totals from 1944 to 1976

	Starts	Rounds Played	Cuts Made	Wins	Top-5s	Top-10s	Top-25s	Scoring Average	Money
	226	756	191	6	22	60	120	N/A	$85,823

Jeff Coston

Year	Starts	Rounds Played	Cuts Made	Wins	Top-5s	Top-10s	Top-25s	Scoring Average	Money
1977	1	2	0	0	0	0	0	79.00	$500
1978	1	2	0	0	0	0	0	86.50	$600
1981	1	0	0	0	0	0	0		
1985	23	50	2	0	0	0	1	74.42	$6,090

Best finish for 1985: T-20th at the Honda Classic

| 1988 | 27 | 69 | 8 | 0 | 0 | 1 | 1 | 73.06 | $28,685 |

Best finish for 1988: T-7th at the Anheuser-Busch Golf Classic

| 1989 | 4 | 11 | 2 | 0 | 0 | 0 | 0 | 70.18 | $1,770 |

Best finish for 1989: T-46th at the Chattanooga Classic

| 2000 | 2 | 8 | 2 | 0 | 0 | 0 | 0 | 73.38 | $17,967 |

Best finish for 2000: T-53rd at the U.S. Open

| 2002 | 1 | 2 | 0 | 0 | 0 | 0 | 0 | 72.50 | |
| 2004 | 1 | 4 | 1 | 0 | 0 | 0 | 0 | 75.25 | $11,800 |

Best finish for 2004: 72nd at the PGA Championship

2005	1	2	0	0	0	0	0	74.00	$2,000
Period Totals	Starts	Rounds Played	Cuts Made	Wins	Top-5s	Top-10s	Top-25s	Scoring Average	Money
	62	150	15	0	0	1	2	73.64	$69,412

Kawika Cotner

Year	Starts	Rounds Played	Cuts Made	Wins	Top-5s	Top-10s	Top-25s	Scoring Average	Money
1994	1	2	0	0	0	0	0	71.00	
1995	26	82	14	0	0	0	1	71.99	$56,625

Best finish for 1995: T-14th at the Bell Canadian Open

| 1996 | 2 | 4 | 0 | 0 | 0 | 0 | 0 | 75.00 | |
| 1997 | 2 | 6 | 1 | 0 | 0 | 0 | 0 | 72.67 | $3,392 |

Best finish for 1997: T-49th at the LaCantera Texas Open

1998	1	2	0	0	0	0	0	74.00	
Period Totals	Starts	Rounds Played	Cuts Made	Wins	Top-5s	Top-10s	Top-25s	Scoring Average	Money
	32	96	15	0	0	0	1	72.18	$60,017

Chris Couch

Year	Starts	Rounds Played	Cuts Made	Wins	Top-5s	Top-10s	Top-25s	Scoring Average	Money
1990	1	2	0	0	0	0	0	79.50	
1999	30	72	6	0	0	1	1	72.85	$121,752

Best finish for 1999: T-7th at the Sony Open in Hawaii

Year	Starts	Rounds Played	Cuts Made	Wins	Top-5s	Top-10s	Top-25s	Scoring Average	Money
2004	24	55	4	0	0	1	1	73.16	$100,282

Best finish for 2004: T-10th at the Southern Farm Bureau Classic

2005	1	4	1	0	0	0	1	70.00	$96,667

Best finish for 2005: T-13th at the Cialis Western Open

2006	27	75	10	1	1	1	4	71.56	$1,358,981

Best finish for 2006: Win at the Zurich Classic of New Orleans

2007	30	76	10	0	0	0	4	72.00	$355,386

Best finish for 2007: T-13th at the U.S. Bank Championship in Milwaukee

Period Totals	Starts	Rounds Played	Cuts Made	Wins	Top-5s	Top-10s	Top-25s	Scoring Average	Money
	113	284	31	1	1	3	11	72.35	$2,033,068

Richie Coughlan

Year	Starts	Rounds Played	Cuts Made	Wins	Top-5s	Top-10s	Top-25s	Scoring Average	Money
1998	31	94	18	0	0	1	4	71.44	$174,035

Best finish for 1998: T-9th at the B.C. Open

1999	1	2	0	0	0	0	0	73.50	
2000	1	2	0	0	0	0	0	73.50	
2001	26	66	8	0	0	0	1	71.94	$80,222

Best finish for 2001: T-25th at the Greater Milwaukee Open

2002	5	15	2	0	0	0	0	72.87	$13,955

Best finish for 2002: T-53rd at the Buick Open

2003	1	2	0	0	0	0	0	74.00	

Period Totals	Starts	Rounds Played	Cuts Made	Wins	Top-5s	Top-10s	Top-25s	Scoring Average	Money
	65	181	28	0	0	1	5	71.81	$268,212

Fred Couples

Year	Starts	Rounds Played	Cuts Made	Wins	Top-5s	Top-10s	Top-25s	Scoring Average	Money
1979	1	4	1	0	0	0	0	75.50	

Best finish for 1979: T-48th at the U.S. Open

1981	25	84	18	0	3	4	9	71.56	$78,519

Best finish for 1981: T-2nd at the Sammy Davis, Jr. - Greater Hartford Open

1982	28	92	18	0	1	2	9	71.82	$78,206

Best finish for 1982: T-3rd at the PGA Championship

1983	30	108	23	1	3	7	15	71.40	$210,333

Best finish for 1983: Win at the Kemper Open

1984	27	102	25	1	4	9	20	71.11	$360,313

Best finish for 1984: Win at the Tournament Players Championship

1985	26	97	23	0	2	7	10	71.58	$171,272

Best finish for 1985: T-4th at the Honda Classic & Panasonic Las Vegas Invitational

1986	27	85	17	0	1	1	6	72.46	$119,778

Best finish for 1986: T-2nd at the Western Open

1987	30	95	22	1	3	9	15	70.52	$446,864

Best finish for 1987: Win at the Byron Nelson Golf Classic

1988	29	105	26	0	5	11	20	70.10	$547,772

Best finish for 1988: 2nd at the Phoenix Open

1989	26	93	22	0	6	10	18	70.39	$696,504

Best finish for 1989: 2nd at the Doral-Ryder Open

1990	24	79	18	1	8	9	13	71.16	$770,553

Best finish for 1990: Win at the Nissan Los Angeles Open

1991	22	86	21	2	9	10	13	70.07	$884,149

Best finish for 1991: Win at the Federal Express St. Jude Classic & B.C. Open

1992	23	86	20	3	9	12	19	69.81	$1,345,388

Best finish for 1992: Win at the Nissan Los Angeles Open, The Nestle Invitational & Masters

1993	20	75	18	1	5	10	16	70.33	$835,849

Best finish for 1993: Win at the Honda Classic

1994	14	51	13	1	3	4	7	69.94	$625,654

Best finish for 1994: Win at the Buick Open

1995	15	54	12	0	1	4	7	70.83	$300,259

Best finish for 1995: T-5th at the Mercedes Championships

1996	18	66	16	1	5	9	12	69.71	$1,248,694

Best finish for 1996: Win at The Players Championship

1997	15	57	13	0	1	7	7	70.93	$448,385

Best finish for 1997: T-4th at the Mercedes Championship

1998	17	68	16	2	5	5	10	70.56	$1,650,389

Best finish for 1998: Win at the Bob Hope Chrysler Classic & Memorial Tournament

1999	16	56	13	0	2	6	7	71.14	$770,192

Best finish for 1999: T-4th at the AT&T Pebble Beach National Pro-Am & The Players Championship

2000	19	70	17	0	2	5	11	70.37	$992,215

Best finish for 2000: T-5th at the Buick Invitational & Nissan Open

2001	19	68	14	0	0	0	4	70.82	$388,414

Best finish for 2001: T-11th at the Verizon Byron Nelson Classic

2002	18	60	13	0	1	2	7	70.47	$646,703

Best finish for 2002: T-2nd at the Valero Texas Open

Year	Starts	Rounds Played	Cuts Made	Wins	Top-5s	Top-10s	Top-25s	Scoring Average	Money
2003	18	67	17	1	1	4	9	70.70	$1,820,495

Best finish for 2003: Win at the Shell Houston Open

| 2004 | 16 | 52 | 12 | 0 | 2 | 3 | 8 | 71.46 | $1,397,109 |

Best finish for 2004: 2nd at the Memorial Tournament

| 2005 | 22 | 68 | 15 | 0 | 2 | 4 | 9 | 70.94 | $1,804,179 |

Best finish for 2005: 2nd at the Memorial Tournament

| 2006 | 17 | 50 | 10 | 0 | 2 | 2 | 4 | 71.72 | $787,258 |

Best finish for 2006: T-3rd at the Masters

| 2007 | 3 | 6 | 1 | 0 | 0 | 0 | 0 | 73.83 | $43,085 |

Best finish for 2007: T-30th at the Masters

| 2008 | 18 | 60 | 12 | 0 | 1 | 3 | 6 | 71.22 | $949,281 |

Best finish for 2008: T-4th at the Shell Houston Open

Period Totals	Starts	Rounds Played	Cuts Made	Wins	Top-5s	Top-10s	Top-25s	Scoring Average	Money
	583	2044	466	15	87	159	291	70.88	$20,417,814

Chuck Courtney

Year	Starts	Rounds Played	Cuts Made	Wins	Top-5s	Top-10s	Top-25s	Scoring Average	Money
1960	1	2	0	0	0	0	0	74.50	
1962	1	2	0	0	0	0	0	75.50	
1964	33	106	18	1	4	4	9	72.65	$22,088

Best finish for 1964: Win at the St. Paul Open

| 1965 | 32 | 98 | 16 | 0 | 0 | 0 | 4 | 73.88 | $6,501 |

Best finish for 1965: T-14th at the Tournament of Champions

| 1966 | 29 | 99 | 21 | 0 | 0 | 1 | 9 | 72.13 | $15,997 |

Best finish for 1966: T-6th at the Philadelphia Golf Classic

| 1967 | 30 | 110 | 25 | 0 | 2 | 5 | 8 | 72.30 | $26,387 |

Best finish for 1967: 2nd at the Tucson Open

| 1968 | 33 | 100 | 17 | 0 | 0 | 0 | 4 | 72.95 | $10,318 |

Best finish for 1968: T-16th at the Greater Greensboro Open Invitational & Memphis Open Invitational

| 1969 | 32 | 89 | 14 | 1 | 1 | 2 | 6 | 72.82 | $18,674 |

Best finish for 1969: Win at the Tallahassee Open

| 1970 | 35 | 112 | 22 | 0 | 0 | 2 | 10 | 72.20 | $22,475 |

Best finish for 1970: T-7th at the Atlanta Classic & Greater Milwaukee Open

| 1971 | 34 | 114 | 24 | 0 | 0 | 2 | 6 | 72.32 | $22,358 |

Best finish for 1971: T-6th at the Robinson Open Golf Classic

| 1972 | 33 | 114 | 25 | 0 | 3 | 5 | 11 | 71.67 | $48,151 |

Best finish for 1972: T-2nd at the Southern Open

| 1973 | 36 | 129 | 26 | 0 | 2 | 5 | 10 | 71.96 | $46,909 |

Best finish for 1973: 4th at the Shrine-Robinson Golf Classic

| 1974 | 34 | 114 | 23 | 0 | 2 | 3 | 7 | 72.05 | $46,415 |

Best finish for 1974: T-3rd at the Colonial National Invitational & Greater Milwaukee Open

| 1975 | 28 | 85 | 16 | 0 | 0 | 1 | 6 | 72.29 | $23,341 |

Best finish for 1975: T-9th at the Sahara Invitational

| 1976 | 11 | 25 | 4 | 0 | 0 | 0 | 0 | 74.72 | |

Best finish for 1976: T-71st at the Andy Williams-San Diego Open

| 1978 | 1 | 2 | 0 | 0 | 0 | 0 | 0 | 77.50 | |
| 1983 | 1 | 2 | 0 | 0 | 0 | 0 | 0 | 75.50 | |

Period Totals	Starts	Rounds Played	Cuts Made	Wins	Top-5s	Top-10s	Top-25s	Scoring Average	Money
	404	1303	251	2	14	30	90	72.47	$309,614

Kris Cox

Year	Starts	Rounds Played	Cuts Made	Wins	Top-5s	Top-10s	Top-25s	Scoring Average	Money
2001	1	2	0	0	0	0	0	72.50	
2004	26	71	10	0	0	0	2	72.13	$205,171

Best finish for 2004: T-18th at the FedEx St. Jude Classic

| 2006 | 28 | 81 | 12 | 0 | 1 | 1 | 3 | 71.15 | $517,836 |

Best finish for 2006: T-3rd at the FedEx St. Jude Classic

| 2007 | 8 | 16 | 1 | 0 | 0 | 0 | 0 | 72.25 | $36,729 |

Best finish for 2007: T-29th at the EDS Byron Nelson Championship

| 2008 | 8 | 17 | 0 | 0 | 0 | 0 | 0 | 73.76 | |

Period Totals	Starts	Rounds Played	Cuts Made	Wins	Top-5s	Top-10s	Top-25s	Scoring Average	Money
	71	187	23	0	1	1	5	71.87	$759,736

Rick Cramer

Year	Starts	Rounds Played	Cuts Made	Wins	Top-5s	Top-10s	Top-25s	Scoring Average	Money
1983	1	2	0	0	0	0	0	74.50	
1985	2	4	0	0	0	0	0	74.25	$600
1986	27	75	10	0	0	0	0	73.40	$9,745

Best finish for 1986: T-37th at the Buick Open

| 1993 | 2 | 4 | 0 | 0 | 0 | 0 | 0 | 74.00 | $1,000 |
| 1995 | 1 | 2 | 0 | 0 | 0 | 0 | 0 | 77.00 | $1,000 |

Year	Starts	Rounds Played	Cuts Made	Wins	Top-5s	Top-10s	Top-25s	Scoring Average	Money
1997	1	2	0	0	0	0	0	76.50	$1,000
Period Totals	Starts	Rounds Played	Cuts Made	Wins	Top-5s	Top-10s	Top-25s	Scoring Average	Money
	34	89	10	0	0	0	0	73.64	$13,345

Bruce Crampton

Year	Starts	Rounds Played	Cuts Made	Wins	Top-5s	Top-10s	Top-25s	Scoring Average	Money
1958	12	46	11	0	0	1	4	72.85	$2,954

Best finish for 1958: T-8th at the Dallas Open

1959	13	48	11	0	1	3	6	71.52	$5,334

Best finish for 1959: T-5th at the Canadian Open Championship

1960	11	44	10	0	0	1	6	71.59	$4,302

Best finish for 1960: T-9th at the Greater Greensboro Open Invitational

1961	11	42	9	1	1	2	6	71.12	$8,300

Best finish for 1961: Win at the Milwaukee Open Invitational

1962	26	104	24	1	4	9	17	71.18	$28,281

Best finish for 1962: Win at the Motor City Open Invitational

1963	31	125	31	0	7	8	15	71.30	$31,018

Best finish for 1963: T-3rd at the Memphis Open Invitational & PGA Championship

1964	33	119	24	1	2	3	10	72.47	$18,448

Best finish for 1964: Win at the Texas Open

1965	34	130	30	3	3	7	16	71.97	$66,679

Best finish for 1965: Win at the Bing Crosby Pro-Am, Colonial National Invitational & "500" Festival

1966	32	120	27	0	3	4	8	72.58	$23,648

Best finish for 1966: T-4th at the Portland Open Invitational

1967	33	123	29	0	2	5	17	71.98	$38,718

Best finish for 1967: 3rd at the Tucson Open

1968	32	121	27	0	5	10	19	71.09	$94,099

Best finish for 1968: T-2nd at the Thunderbird Classic, Greater Hartford Open Invitational & Kemper Open Invitational

1969	30	110	25	1	6	12	19	70.92	$115,844

Best finish for 1969: Win at the Hawaiian Open

1970	30	114	29	1	4	12	20	70.97	$139,455

Best finish for 1970: Win at the Westchester Classic

1971	29	105	26	1	6	7	17	71.58	$170,590

Best finish for 1971: Win at the Western Open

1972	28	105	25	0	9	13	21	71.18	$106,370

Best finish for 1972: T-2nd at the Masters & U.S. Open

1973	28	106	24	4	12	15	21	70.72	$272,798

Best finish for 1973: Win at the Phoenix Open, Dean Martin Tucson Open, Houston Open & American Golf Classic

1974	32	122	29	0	5	12	21	71.18	$123,641

Best finish for 1974: T-2nd at the B.C. Open & Southern Open

1975	24	92	21	1	9	11	15	70.61	$134,582

Best finish for 1975: Win at the Houston Open

1976	25	88	20	0	2	3	7	72.05	$52,064

Best finish for 1976: T-3rd at the Andy Williams-San Diego Open & MONY Tournament Of Champions

1977	4	13	2	0	0	0	0	73.62	$800

Best finish for 1977: T-41st at the Phoenix Open

1985	2	4	0	0	0	0	0	74.75	
1987	1	5	1	0	0	0	0	72.40	$1,899

Best finish for 1987: T-62nd at the Bob Hope Chrysler Classic

Period Totals	Starts	Rounds Played	Cuts Made	Wins	Top-5s	Top-10s	Top-25s	Scoring Average	Money
	501	1886	435	14	81	138	265	71.52	$1,439,826

Ben Crane

Year	Starts	Rounds Played	Cuts Made	Wins	Top-5s	Top-10s	Top-25s	Scoring Average	Money
2002	30	89	16	0	1	2	7	70.66	$922,076

Best finish for 2002: 2nd at the Verizon Byron Nelson Classic

2003	27	92	19	1	1	3	8	70.76	$1,422,647

Best finish for 2003: Win at the BellSouth Classic

2004	27	92	19	0	1	5	7	70.78	$1,036,958

Best finish for 2004: T-5th at the Bob Hope Chrysler Classic

2005	21	74	18	1	4	6	8	69.89	$2,457,329

Best finish for 2005: Win at the U.S. Bank Championship in Milwaukee

2006	26	80	19	0	2	3	9	71.23	$1,496,343

Best finish for 2006: T-2nd at the Frys.Com Open-Vegas

2007	9	27	6	0	0	0	4	71.04	$278,252

Best finish for 2007: T-17th at the WGC-Accenture Match Play Championship

2008	25	86	19	0	2	4	8	70.38	$1,488,505

Best finish for 2008: T-4th at the FBR Open

Period Totals	Starts	Rounds Played	Cuts Made	Wins	Top-5s	Top-10s	Top-25s	Scoring Average	Money
	165	540	116	2	11	23	51	70.65	$9,102,109

Richard Crawford

Year	Starts	Rounds Played	Cuts Made	Wins	Top-5s	Top-10s	Top-25s	Scoring Average	Money
1960	2	8	2	0	0	1	1	72.75	

Best finish for 1960: T-6th at the Houston Classic

Year	Starts	Rounds Played	Cuts Made	Wins	Top-5s	Top-10s	Top-25s	Scoring Average	Money
1961	1	4	1	0	0	0	0	73.50	

Best finish for 1961: T-64th at the Houston Classic

Year	Starts	Rounds Played	Cuts Made	Wins	Top-5s	Top-10s	Top-25s	Scoring Average	Money
1962	1	4	1	0	0	0	0	72.75	

Best finish for 1962: T-59th at the Houston Classic

Year	Starts	Rounds Played	Cuts Made	Wins	Top-5s	Top-10s	Top-25s	Scoring Average	Money
1963	1	4	1	0	0	0	0	72.00	$305

Best finish for 1963: T-53rd at the Thunderbird Classic Invitational

Year	Starts	Rounds Played	Cuts Made	Wins	Top-5s	Top-10s	Top-25s	Scoring Average	Money
1964	19	62	11	0	0	1	5	72.79	$6,427

Best finish for 1964: T-8th at the Greater Hartford Open

Year	Starts	Rounds Played	Cuts Made	Wins	Top-5s	Top-10s	Top-25s	Scoring Average	Money
1965	24	77	15	0	0	0	5	72.60	$8,513

Best finish for 1965: T-11th at the Thunderbird Classic

Year	Starts	Rounds Played	Cuts Made	Wins	Top-5s	Top-10s	Top-25s	Scoring Average	Money
1966	26	96	22	0	0	1	6	72.59	$13,062

Best finish for 1966: T-9th at the Phoenix Open Invitational

Year	Starts	Rounds Played	Cuts Made	Wins	Top-5s	Top-10s	Top-25s	Scoring Average	Money
1967	29	95	18	0	2	3	8	72.73	$23,297

Best finish for 1967: T-2nd at the Atlanta Classic

Year	Starts	Rounds Played	Cuts Made	Wins	Top-5s	Top-10s	Top-25s	Scoring Average	Money
1968	32	108	23	0	0	1	8	72.28	$20,071

Best finish for 1968: T-6th at the Kaiser International Open Invitational

Year	Starts	Rounds Played	Cuts Made	Wins	Top-5s	Top-10s	Top-25s	Scoring Average	Money
1969	36	122	25	0	1	5	12	72.41	$38,333

Best finish for 1969: T-2nd at the Heritage Golf Classic

Year	Starts	Rounds Played	Cuts Made	Wins	Top-5s	Top-10s	Top-25s	Scoring Average	Money
1970	38	122	24	0	4	5	9	72.25	$43,341

Best finish for 1970: T-2nd at the Greater Milwaukee Open

Year	Starts	Rounds Played	Cuts Made	Wins	Top-5s	Top-10s	Top-25s	Scoring Average	Money
1971	32	105	20	0	0	0	6	72.35	$16,207

Best finish for 1971: T-11th at the Sahara Invitational

Year	Starts	Rounds Played	Cuts Made	Wins	Top-5s	Top-10s	Top-25s	Scoring Average	Money
1972	32	102	19	0	0	0	6	72.47	$18,066

Best finish for 1972: T-11th at the USI Classic & Quad Cities Open

Year	Starts	Rounds Played	Cuts Made	Wins	Top-5s	Top-10s	Top-25s	Scoring Average	Money
1973	31	118	25	0	1	1	8	71.83	$29,562

Best finish for 1973: T-5th at the Tallahassee Open

Year	Starts	Rounds Played	Cuts Made	Wins	Top-5s	Top-10s	Top-25s	Scoring Average	Money
1974	28	87	15	0	1	1	4	72.25	$27,333

Best finish for 1974: 3rd at the Sea Pines Heritage Classic

Year	Starts	Rounds Played	Cuts Made	Wins	Top-5s	Top-10s	Top-25s	Scoring Average	Money
1975	27	85	15	0	0	2	7	72.25	$21,630

Best finish for 1975: T-7th at the Hawaiian Open

Year	Starts	Rounds Played	Cuts Made	Wins	Top-5s	Top-10s	Top-25s	Scoring Average	Money
1976	28	80	13	0	1	3	5	72.45	$21,917

Best finish for 1976: T-4th at the Southern Open

Year	Starts	Rounds Played	Cuts Made	Wins	Top-5s	Top-10s	Top-25s	Scoring Average	Money
1977	15	35	3	0	0	0	0	73.91	$1,292

Best finish for 1977: T-31st at the San Antonio Texas Open

Year	Starts	Rounds Played	Cuts Made	Wins	Top-5s	Top-10s	Top-25s	Scoring Average	Money
1981	1	4	1	0	0	0	0	71.25	$463

Best finish for 1981: T-53rd at the Southern Open

Year	Starts	Rounds Played	Cuts Made	Wins	Top-5s	Top-10s	Top-25s	Scoring Average	Money
1982	2	4	0	0	0	0	0	74.00	$650
1983	2	4	0	0	0	0	0	73.25	
1984	2	4	0	0	0	0	0	73.75	
1985	1	2	0	0	0	0	0	72.00	
1986	1	2	0	0	0	0	0	72.50	
1987	1	2	0	0	0	0	0	76.00	
1988	1	2	0	0	0	0	0	72.00	
1989	1	4	1	0	0	0	0	70.00	$994

Best finish for 1989: T-48th at the Southern Open

Year	Starts	Rounds Played	Cuts Made	Wins	Top-5s	Top-10s	Top-25s	Scoring Average	Money
1990	1	2	0	0	0	0	0	70.00	
1996	1	2	0	0	0	0	0	78.50	
Period Totals	Starts	Rounds Played	Cuts Made	Wins	Top-5s	Top-10s	Top-25s	Scoring Average	Money
	416	1346	255	0	10	24	90	72.43	$291,464

Ben Crenshaw

Year	Starts	Rounds Played	Cuts Made	Wins	Top-5s	Top-10s	Top-25s	Scoring Average	Money
1970	1	4	1	0	0	0	0	75.25	

Best finish for 1970: T-36th at the U.S. Open

Year	Starts	Rounds Played	Cuts Made	Wins	Top-5s	Top-10s	Top-25s	Scoring Average	Money
1971	3	12	3	0	0	1	2	71.75	

Best finish for 1971: T-7th at the Houston Champions International

Year	Starts	Rounds Played	Cuts Made	Wins	Top-5s	Top-10s	Top-25s	Scoring Average	Money
1972	5	18	4	0	1	1	4	72.44	

Best finish for 1972: T-3rd at the Sea Pines Heritage Classic

Year	Starts	Rounds Played	Cuts Made	Wins	Top-5s	Top-10s	Top-25s	Scoring Average	Money
1973	10	40	8	1	2	4	7	71.63	$76,374

Best finish for 1973: Win at the San Antonio Texas Open

Year	Starts	Rounds Played	Cuts Made	Wins	Top-5s	Top-10s	Top-25s	Scoring Average	Money
1974	28	101	23	0	3	6	11	71.97	$67,413

Best finish for 1974: T-2nd at the Dean Martin Tucson Open & Greater New Orleans Open

Year	Starts	Rounds Played	Cuts Made	Wins	Top-5s	Top-10s	Top-25s	Scoring Average	Money
1975	28	97	20	0	3	6	8	71.82	$63,528

Best finish for 1975: T-3rd at the Florida Citrus Open Invitational, U.S. Open & Pleasant Valley Classic

Year	Starts	Rounds Played	Cuts Made	Wins	Top-5s	Top-10s	Top-25s	Scoring Average	Money
1976	28	110	27	3	9	14	17	71.00	$257,959

Best finish for 1976: Win at the Bing Crosby Pro-Am, Hawaiian Open & Ohio Kings Island Open

Year	Starts	Rounds Played	Cuts Made	Wins	Top-5s	Top-10s	Top-25s	Scoring Average	Money
1977	26	88	20	1	6	7	12	71.81	$131,066

Best finish for 1977: Win at the Colonial National Invitational

Year	Starts	Rounds Played	Cuts Made	Wins	Top-5s	Top-10s	Top-25s	Scoring Average	Money
1978	28	106	25	0	6	6	14	71.52	$122,799

Best finish for 1978: T-2nd at the Bing Crosby Pro-Am & British Open

1979	27	97	21	1	7	9	17	71.23	$261,896

Best finish for 1979: Win at the Phoenix Open

1980	28	105	26	1	7	12	15	70.87	$274,490

Best finish for 1980: Win at the Anheuser-Busch Golf Classic

1981	26	91	21	0	6	10	15	70.98	$164,588

Best finish for 1981: T-2nd at the Bing Crosby Pro-Am & Texas Open

1982	22	77	16	0	2	2	9	72.30	$61,557

Best finish for 1982: T-4th at the Hawaiian Open

1983	22	81	18	1	5	9	14	71.01	$276,369

Best finish for 1983: Win at the Byron Nelson Golf Classic

1984	25	90	21	1	4	8	14	71.43	$277,594

Best finish for 1984: Win at the Masters

1985	23	64	9	0	0	0	2	73.64	$30,564

Best finish for 1985: T-12th at the Southwest Golf Classic

1986	27	92	23	2	2	5	13	71.47	$395,702

Best finish for 1986: Win at the Buick Open & Vantage Championship

1987	26	87	20	1	9	15	16	70.34	$687,794

Best finish for 1987: Win at the USF&G Classic

1988	28	102	26	1	5	8	22	70.19	$714,745

Best finish for 1988: Win at the Doral-Ryder Open

1989	25	82	19	0	2	5	12	71.27	$449,055

Best finish for 1989: 2nd at the NEC World Series of Golf

1990	22	72	16	1	2	2	8	71.63	$361,469

Best finish for 1990: Win at the Southwestern Bell Colonial

1991	22	64	11	0	3	4	7	71.13	$229,603

Best finish for 1991: T-3rd at the Masters & H-E-B Texas Open

1992	24	82	19	1	2	4	7	70.70	$439,071

Best finish for 1992: Win at the Centel Western Open

1993	23	73	15	1	1	1	7	71.63	$321,029

Best finish for 1993: Win at the Nestle Invitational

1994	25	90	21	1	1	6	13	70.91	$665,165

Best finish for 1994: Win at the Freeport-McMoRan Classic

1995	23	80	17	1	4	4	7	71.45	$737,475

Best finish for 1995: Win at the Masters

1996	19	59	11	0	0	1	5	71.85	$179,357

Best finish for 1996: T-6th at the MasterCard Colonial

1997	17	44	5	0	0	0	1	73.86	$43,813

Best finish for 1997: T-19th at the Kemper Open

1998	15	33	2	0	0	0	0	74.42	$20,044

Best finish for 1998: T-43rd at the GTE Byron Nelson Classic

1999	13	27	0	0	0	0	0	74.74	$7,750
2000	13	27	1	0	0	0	0	75.26	$12,400

Best finish for 2000: T-77th at the GTE Byron Nelson Classic

2001	11	24	1	0	0	0	0	74.13	$12,770

Best finish for 2001: 59th at the Kemper Insurance Open

2002	2	4	0	0	0	0	0	76.00	$5,000
2003	1	2	0	0	0	0	0	77.50	$5,000
2004	1	2	0	0	0	0	0	74.50	$5,000
2005	1	2	0	0	0	0	0	78.00	$5,000
2006	2	8	2	0	0	0	0	73.13	$32,060

Best finish for 2006: 47th at the Masters

2007	1	4	1	0	0	0	0	77.25	$16,530

Best finish for 2007: T-55th at the Masters

Year	Starts	Rounds Played	Cuts Made	Wins	Top-5s	Top-10s	Top-25s	Scoring Average	Money
2008	1	2	0	0	0	0	0	76.00	
Period Totals	672	2243	473	18	92	150	279	71.63	$7,412,030

Richard Cromwell

Year	Starts	Rounds Played	Cuts Made	Wins	Top-5s	Top-10s	Top-25s	Scoring Average	Money
1988	28	75	9	0	0	0	0	73.15	$13,660

Best finish for 1988: T-35th at the Centel Classic

2000	1	2	0	0	0	0	0	79.00	
Period Totals	29	77	9	0	0	0	0	73.30	$13,660

Jay Cudd

Year	Starts	Rounds Played	Cuts Made	Wins	Top-5s	Top-10s	Top-25s	Scoring Average	Money
1982	25	78	14	0	0	0	1	72.78	$14,633

Best finish for 1982: T-23rd at the Byron Nelson Golf Classic

Year	Starts	Rounds Played	Cuts Made	Wins	Top-5s	Top-10s	Top-25s	Scoring Average	Money
1983	11	29	4	0	0	0	0	72.72	$2,688

Best finish for 1983: T-52nd at the Danny Thomas Memphis Classic

1984	26	69	9	0	0	0	0	73.19	$9,417

Best finish for 1984: T-33rd at the Honda Classic

Period Totals	Starts	Rounds Played	Cuts Made	Wins	Top-5s	Top-10s	Top-25s	Scoring Average	Money
	62	176	27	0	0	0	1	72.93	$26,738

Guy Cullins

Year	Starts	Rounds Played	Cuts Made	Wins	Top-5s	Top-10s	Top-25s	Scoring Average	Money
1976	11	22	0	0	0	0	0	74.59	$500
1977	1	2	0	0	0	0	0	78.00	$500
1979	14	33	3	0	0	0	0	74.73	$1,872

Best finish for 1979: T-60th at the Western Open

Period Totals	Starts	Rounds Played	Cuts Made	Wins	Top-5s	Top-10s	Top-25s	Scoring Average	Money
	26	57	3	0	0	0	0	74.79	$2,872

Michael Cunning

Year	Starts	Rounds Played	Cuts Made	Wins	Top-5s	Top-10s	Top-25s	Scoring Average	Money
1984	16	34	1	0	0	0	0	75.65	$400

Best finish for 1984: 70th at the Miller High-Life Quad Cities Open

1992	30	82	11	0	0	1	3	72.28	$58,732

Best finish for 1992: T-10th at the Deposit Guaranty Classic

1993	1	2	0	0	0	0	0	71.00	
1995	1	2	0	0	0	0	0	74.00	

Period Totals	Starts	Rounds Played	Cuts Made	Wins	Top-5s	Top-10s	Top-25s	Scoring Average	Money
	48	120	12	0	0	1	3	73.24	$59,132

Buster Cupit

Year	Starts	Rounds Played	Cuts Made	Wins	Top-5s	Top-10s	Top-25s	Scoring Average	Money
1958	2	8	2	0	0	1	1	72.25	$1,300

Best finish for 1958: T-8th at the PGA Championship

1959	2	6	1	0	0	0	1	73.67	$1,075

Best finish for 1959: T-17th at the PGA Championship

1960	4	12	2	0	0	0	1	74.42	$590

Best finish for 1960: T-16th at the Hot Springs Open Invitational

1961	9	36	7	0	4	5	5	71.08	$9,530

Best finish for 1961: T-2nd at the St. Paul Open Invitational

1962	9	36	8	0	2	2	6	71.31	$6,511

Best finish for 1962: T-3rd at the Waco Turner Open Invitational & Hot Springs Open Invitational

1963	6	22	5	0	1	2	3	71.86	$3,202

Best finish for 1963: T-5th at the Fig Garden Village Open Invitational

1964	12	39	8	0	0	1	4	73.08	$4,202

Best finish for 1964: T-7th at the Houston Classic

1965	3	8	1	0	0	0	0	73.25	

Best finish for 1965: T-31st at the Cajun Classic

1966	16	57	12	0	0	0	5	72.65	$7,560

Best finish for 1966: T-11th at the San Diego Open Invitational

1967	5	14	1	0	0	0	0	74.50	$105
1971	1	2	0	0	0	0	0	79.00	
1972	1	1	0	0	0	0	0	84.00	

Period Totals	Starts	Rounds Played	Cuts Made	Wins	Top-5s	Top-10s	Top-25s	Scoring Average	Money
	70	241	47	0	7	11	26	72.54	$34,074

Jacky Cupit

Year	Starts	Rounds Played	Cuts Made	Wins	Top-5s	Top-10s	Top-25s	Scoring Average	Money
1958	2	8	2	0	0	0	0	75.25	

Best finish for 1958: T-45th at the Baton Rouge Open

1961	23	92	22	1	4	12	17	70.34	$22,814

Best finish for 1961: Win at the Canadian Open Invitational

1962	18	72	17	1	2	2	11	71.71	$20,603

Best finish for 1962: Win at the Western Open Championship

1963	18	71	17	0	2	4	12	71.44	$22,298

Best finish for 1963: T-2nd at the U.S. Open

1964	35	134	31	1	2	4	11	72.08	$21,302

Best finish for 1964: Win at the Tucson Open

1965	27	102	21	0	4	10	15	71.84	$43,251

Best finish for 1965: T-2nd at the "500" Festival

1966	31	108	22	1	6	9	15	72.06	$51,075

Best finish for 1966: Win at the Cajun Classic

1967	22	80	18	0	0	2	11	72.14	$19,738

Best finish for 1967: T-8th at the Los Angles Open

1968	29	90	16	0	0	0	4	72.98	$7,968

Best finish for 1968: T-12th at the Cajun Classic

Year	Starts	Rounds Played	Cuts Made	Wins	Top-5s	Top-10s	Top-25s	Scoring Average	Money
1969	27	85	17	0	1	3	9	72.33	$18,625

Best finish for 1969: T-2nd at the Tallahassee Open

1970	23	66	10	0	0	0	2	73.44	$4,067

Best finish for 1970: 19th at the Green Island Open Invitational

1971	19	58	11	0	0	2	2	72.86	$8,462

Best finish for 1971: T-6th at the Tucson Open

1972	11	34	6	0	0	1	1	73.29	$4,450

Best finish for 1972: T-9th at the Quad Cities Open

1973	1	2	0	0	0	0	0	76.00	
Period Totals	Starts	Rounds Played	Cuts Made	Wins	Top-5s	Top-10s	Top-25s	Scoring Average	Money
	286	1002	210	4	21	49	110	72.14	$244,653

Rod Curl

Year	Starts	Rounds Played	Cuts Made	Wins	Top-5s	Top-10s	Top-25s	Scoring Average	Money
1966	1	2	0	0	0	0	0	82.00	
1969	14	42	7	0	0	0	0	73.19	$2,347

Best finish for 1969: T-27th at the Kemper Insurance Open

1970	17	48	7	0	0	1	1	73.54	$4,999

Best finish for 1970: T-6th at the Greater New Orleans Open

1971	27	88	16	0	1	1	2	72.99	$11,953

Best finish for 1971: T-4th at the Phoenix Open

1972	31	98	18	0	0	1	5	72.94	$13,733

Best finish for 1972: T-9th at the Quad Cities Open

1973	38	143	33	0	2	5	14	71.54	$48,938

Best finish for 1973: T-4th at the Doral-Eastern Open

1974	27	90	18	1	6	7	10	71.42	$117,253

Best finish for 1974: Win at the Colonial National Invitational

1975	32	105	20	0	2	4	9	72.09	$60,320

Best finish for 1975: 2nd at the Kaiser International Open

1976	29	92	17	0	1	2	5	72.15	$34,003

Best finish for 1976: T-3rd at the Phoenix Open

1977	30	102	21	0	1	5	10	71.71	$55,495

Best finish for 1977: T-5th at the IVB Philadelphia Golf Classic

1978	32	107	22	0	0	4	9	72.12	$47,274

Best finish for 1978: T-8th at the Atlanta Classic

1979	29	99	20	0	3	6	12	71.38	$95,460

Best finish for 1979: 3rd at the Doral-Eastern Open

1980	30	99	19	0	1	2	8	71.85	$53,481

Best finish for 1980: T-4th at the Phoenix Open

1981	29	89	14	0	0	2	6	72.65	$39,846

Best finish for 1981: T-9th at the USF&G New Orleans Open & Colonial National Invitational

1982	30	88	14	0	0	1	2	71.94	$19,302

Best finish for 1982: T-8th at the Miller High-Life Quad Cities Open

1983	12	34	5	0	0	1	1	71.97	$11,410

Best finish for 1983: T-8th at the Southern Open

1984	6	18	3	0	0	0	0	72.44	$2,760

Best finish for 1984: T-45th at the Sammy Davis, Jr. - Greater Hartford Open

1985	11	33	5	0	0	0	0	72.30	$4,780

Best finish for 1985: T-31st at the Anheuser-Busch Golf Classic

1986	30	92	16	0	0	0	1	71.90	$27,572

Best finish for 1986: T-25th at the Manufactures Hanover Westchester Classic

1987	9	23	2	0	0	0	0	72.78	$2,250

Best finish for 1987: T-32nd at the Deposit Guaranty Golf Classic

1988	13	40	7	0	0	0	0	71.68	$12,119

Best finish for 1988: T-26th at the Hardee's Golf Classic

1989	14	32	1	0	0	0	0	73.53	$2,180

Best finish for 1989: T-60th at the Southwestern Bell Colonial

1990	7	16	1	0	0	0	0	73.44	$1,176

Best finish for 1990: T-72nd at the Buick Southern Open

1991	6	13	0	0	0	0	0	73.54	
1992	4	7	0	0	0	0	0	74.00	
1993	2	4	0	0	0	0	0	74.00	
1994	1	2	0	0	0	0	0	76.50	
1995	1	2	0	0	0	0	0	77.00	
1996	1	2	0	0	0	0	0	78.50	
1997	1	2	0	0	0	0	0	78.00	
1998	1	2	0	0	0	0	0	78.00	
1999	1	2	0	0	0	0	0	76.00	
2000	1	1	0	0	0	0	0	74.00	
2001	1	2	0	0	0	0	0	76.00	
2002	2	3	0	0	0	0	0	81.33	

Year	Starts	Rounds Played	Cuts Made	Wins	Top-5s	Top-10s	Top-25s	Scoring Average	Money
2003	2	4	0	0	0	0	0	77.25	
2004	1	2	0	0	0	0	0	80.00	
2005	1	2	0	0	0	0	0	80.50	
2007	1	1	0	0	0	0	0	86.00	
Period Totals	Starts	Rounds Played	Cuts Made	Wins	Top-5s	Top-10s	Top-25s	Scoring Average	Money
	525	1631	286	1	17	42	95	72.30	$668,651

Paul Curry

Year	Starts	Rounds Played	Cuts Made	Wins	Top-5s	Top-10s	Top-25s	Scoring Average	Money
1980	1	0	0	0	0	0	0		
1981	1	0	0	0	0	0	0		
1990	1	2	0	0	0	0	0	73.00	$996
1994	1	2	0	0	0	0	0	73.50	$972
1997	1	2	0	0	0	0	0	74.00	$1,676
2000	25	64	7	0	0	0	3	71.88	$128,701

Best finish for 2000: T-12th at the John Deere Classic

| 2001 | 1 | 4 | 1 | 0 | 0 | 0 | 0 | 72.25 | $12,793 |

Best finish for 2001: T-54th at the British Open

Period Totals	Starts	Rounds Played	Cuts Made	Wins	Top-5s	Top-10s	Top-25s	Scoring Average	Money
	31	74	8	0	0	0	3	72.03	$145,137

Ben Curtis

Year	Starts	Rounds Played	Cuts Made	Wins	Top-5s	Top-10s	Top-25s	Scoring Average	Money
2000	1	2	0	0	0	0	0	74.50	
2001	1	4	1	0	0	0	0	70.00	$6,020

Best finish for 2001: T-46th at the B.C. Open

| 2003 | 21 | 69 | 13 | 1 | 1 | 1 | 3 | 71.83 | $1,436,911 |

Best finish for 2003: Win at the British Open

| 2004 | 20 | 52 | 9 | 0 | 0 | 1 | 4 | 72.00 | $512,031 |

Best finish for 2004: T-8th at the Memorial Tournament

| 2005 | 24 | 65 | 8 | 0 | 2 | 2 | 2 | 72.63 | $606,050 |

Best finish for 2005: 3rd at the Cialis Western Open

| 2006 | 26 | 86 | 17 | 2 | 2 | 2 | 7 | 71.59 | $2,260,973 |

Best finish for 2006: Win at the Booz Allen Classic & 84 Lumber Classic

| 2007 | 25 | 80 | 15 | 0 | 1 | 2 | 2 | 72.50 | $774,821 |

Best finish for 2007: 4th at the Arnold Palmer Invitational

| 2008 | 22 | 80 | 18 | 0 | 4 | 5 | 8 | 70.96 | $2,615,798 |

Best finish for 2008: T-2nd at the Wachovia Championship & PGA Championship

Period Totals	Starts	Rounds Played	Cuts Made	Wins	Top-5s	Top-10s	Top-25s	Scoring Average	Money
	140	438	81	3	10	13	26	71.88	$8,212,604

Archie Dadian

Year	Starts	Rounds Played	Cuts Made	Wins	Top-5s	Top-10s	Top-25s	Scoring Average	Money
1958	1	4	1	0	0	0	0	73.25	

Best finish for 1958: T-66th at the Miller Open

| 1961 | 1 | 4 | 1 | 0 | 0 | 0 | 0 | 70.00 | |

Best finish for 1961: T-33rd at the Milwaukee Open Invitational

| 1964 | 18 | 43 | 4 | 0 | 0 | 0 | 0 | 73.86 | $1,241 |

Best finish for 1964: T-27th at the "500" Festival Open

| 1965 | 9 | 23 | 3 | 0 | 0 | 0 | 1 | 75.00 | $744 |

Best finish for 1965: T-25th at the Houston Classic

Period Totals	Starts	Rounds Played	Cuts Made	Wins	Top-5s	Top-10s	Top-25s	Scoring Average	Money
	29	74	9	0	0	0	1	73.97	$1,984

Jess Daley

Year	Starts	Rounds Played	Cuts Made	Wins	Top-5s	Top-10s	Top-25s	Scoring Average	Money
2001	2	4	0	0	0	0	0	74.25	$1,000
2002	27	76	10	0	0	0	2	71.49	$154,675

Best finish for 2002: T-17th at the Greater Milwaukee Open

Period Totals	Starts	Rounds Played	Cuts Made	Wins	Top-5s	Top-10s	Top-25s	Scoring Average	Money
	29	80	10	0	0	0	2	71.63	$155,675

Joe Daley

Year	Starts	Rounds Played	Cuts Made	Wins	Top-5s	Top-10s	Top-25s	Scoring Average	Money
1994	1	4	1	0	0	0	0	70.00	$6,239

Best finish for 1994: T-31st at the Anheuser-Busch Golf Classic

| 1995 | 1 | 2 | 0 | 0 | 0 | 0 | 0 | 73.50 | |
| 1996 | 27 | 77 | 13 | 0 | 0 | 1 | 2 | 72.08 | $96,287 |

Best finish for 1996: T-6th at the B.C. Open

| 1998 | 27 | 68 | 8 | 0 | 0 | 0 | 0 | 72.59 | $42,092 |

Best finish for 1998: T-27th at the BellSouth Classic

| 2000 | 1 | 2 | 0 | 0 | 0 | 0 | 0 | 76.00 | $1,000 |

Year	Starts	Rounds Played	Cuts Made	Wins	Top-5s	Top-10s	Top-25s	Scoring Average	Money
2007	2	6	1	0	0	0	0	72.83	$12,920

Best finish for 2007: T-65th at the Sony Open in Hawaii

Period Totals	Starts	Rounds Played	Cuts Made	Wins	Top-5s	Top-10s	Top-25s	Scoring Average	Money
	59	159	23	0	0	1	2	72.34	$158,537

Rick Dalpos

Year	Starts	Rounds Played	Cuts Made	Wins	Top-5s	Top-10s	Top-25s	Scoring Average	Money
1982	1	2	0	0	0	0	0	76.50	
1983	20	46	3	0	0	0	0	74.20	$4,048

Best finish for 1983: T-30th at the Western Open

| 1984 | 19 | 50 | 5 | 0 | 0 | 0 | 2 | 73.80 | $10,002 |

Best finish for 1984: T-21st at the LaJet Golf Classic

| 1985 | 5 | 16 | 3 | 0 | 0 | 0 | 0 | 72.63 | $2,904 |

Best finish for 1985: T-48th at the Greater Milwaukee Open

| 1986 | 29 | 87 | 14 | 0 | 0 | 0 | 2 | 72.52 | $25,446 |

Best finish for 1986: T-15th at the Kemper Open

| 1987 | 36 | 95 | 15 | 0 | 0 | 1 | 3 | 72.51 | $44,843 |

Best finish for 1987: T-10th at the Los Angeles Open

| 1988 | 6 | 12 | 1 | 0 | 0 | 0 | 0 | 72.50 | $2,602 |

Best finish for 1988: T-45th at the Hardee's Golf Classic

| 1989 | 24 | 69 | 11 | 0 | 0 | 0 | 1 | 71.67 | $28,821 |

Best finish for 1989: T-19th at the USF&G Classic

| 1990 | 3 | 6 | 0 | 0 | 0 | 0 | 0 | 72.00 | |
| 1991 | 1 | 4 | 1 | 0 | 0 | 0 | 0 | 71.75 | $6,075 |

Best finish for 1991: T-30th at the Centel Western Open

| 1992 | 2 | 6 | 1 | 0 | 0 | 0 | 0 | 73.00 | $3,398 |

Best finish for 1992: T-59th at the Centel Western Open

| 1993 | 28 | 70 | 8 | 0 | 0 | 0 | 0 | 73.10 | $31,585 |

Best finish for 1993: T-31st at the Nissan Los Angeles Open

Period Totals	Starts	Rounds Played	Cuts Made	Wins	Top-5s	Top-10s	Top-25s	Scoring Average	Money
	174	463	62	0	0	1	8	72.79	$159,724

John Daly

Year	Starts	Rounds Played	Cuts Made	Wins	Top-5s	Top-10s	Top-25s	Scoring Average	Money
1986	1	2	0	0	0	0	0	82.00	
1989	6	18	3	0	0	0	1	71.89	$14,689

Best finish for 1989: T-14th at the Chattanooga Classic

| 1990 | 2 | 8 | 2 | 0 | 0 | 0 | 1 | 70.75 | $10,000 |

Best finish for 1990: T-21st at the Federal Express St. Jude Classic

| 1991 | 33 | 105 | 21 | 1 | 4 | 4 | 11 | 71.30 | $574,783 |

Best finish for 1991: Win at the PGA Championship

| 1992 | 26 | 82 | 16 | 1 | 3 | 5 | 8 | 71.66 | $394,855 |

Best finish for 1992: Win at the B.C. Open

| 1993 | 25 | 74 | 16 | 0 | 1 | 1 | 6 | 72.35 | $249,021 |

Best finish for 1993: T-3rd at the Masters

| 1994 | 18 | 53 | 9 | 1 | 2 | 3 | 4 | 72.81 | $347,904 |

Best finish for 1994: Win at the BellSouth Classic

| 1995 | 23 | 75 | 15 | 1 | 1 | 1 | 4 | 72.07 | $322,948 |

Best finish for 1995: Win at the British Open

| 1996 | 23 | 72 | 14 | 0 | 0 | 1 | 3 | 72.15 | $174,857 |

Best finish for 1996: T-10th at the Kemper Open

| 1997 | 17 | 50 | 9 | 0 | 0 | 1 | 2 | 72.16 | $107,762 |

Best finish for 1997: 7th at the Bob Hope Chrysler Classic

| 1998 | 25 | 77 | 13 | 0 | 2 | 2 | 6 | 71.95 | $396,391 |

Best finish for 1998: T-4th at the Nissan Open & Honda Classic

| 1999 | 22 | 63 | 11 | 0 | 0 | 0 | 3 | 72.56 | $186,215 |

Best finish for 1999: T-14th at the Phoenix Open

| 2000 | 26 | 71 | 10 | 0 | 0 | 0 | 1 | 72.82 | $124,980 |

Best finish for 2000: T-16th at the Honda Classic

| 2001 | 25 | 82 | 16 | 0 | 2 | 4 | 8 | 70.70 | $832,487 |

Best finish for 2001: 4th at the Bell Canadian Open

| 2002 | 21 | 62 | 12 | 0 | 2 | 2 | 4 | 71.85 | $598,755 |

Best finish for 2002: T-4th at the Phoenix Open & Buick Invitational

| 2003 | 22 | 56 | 7 | 0 | 0 | 1 | 1 | 72.68 | $222,647 |

Best finish for 2003: T-7th at the Shell Houston Open

| 2004 | 22 | 79 | 17 | 1 | 3 | 5 | 8 | 70.81 | $2,371,188 |

Best finish for 2004: Win at the Buick Invitational

| 2005 | 25 | 76 | 16 | 0 | 2 | 2 | 6 | 71.83 | $1,764,921 |

Best finish for 2005: 2nd at the Shell Houston Open & WGC-American Express Championship

| 2006 | 21 | 49 | 8 | 0 | 0 | 0 | 1 | 72.82 | $204,032 |

Best finish for 2006: T-17th at the WGC-Accenture Match Play Championship

| 2007 | 24 | 59 | 8 | 0 | 0 | 0 | 2 | 72.39 | $252,818 |

Best finish for 2007: T-16th at the Buick Open

Year	Starts	Rounds Played	Cuts Made	Wins	Top-5s	Top-10s	Top-25s	Scoring Average	Money
2008	17	43	5	0	0	0	0	73.28	$56,017

Best finish for 2008: T-40th at the Viking Classic

Period Totals	Starts	Rounds Played	Cuts Made	Wins	Top-5s	Top-10s	Top-25s	Scoring Average	Money
	424	1256	228	5	22	32	80	72.02	$9,207,269

Robert Damron

Year	Starts	Rounds Played	Cuts Made	Wins	Top-5s	Top-10s	Top-25s	Scoring Average	Money
1994	1	2	0	0	0	0	0	73.50	
1997	32	98	17	0	4	4	8	71.20	$458,244

Best finish for 1997: T-3rd at the Buick Classic & FedEx St. Jude Classic

1998	28	88	18	0	0	1	8	70.89	$371,711

Best finish for 1998: T-7th at the FedEx St. Jude Classic

1999	30	109	24	0	1	3	4	71.37	$434,157

Best finish for 1999: 4th at the Bay Hill Invitational

2000	28	91	17	0	1	3	6	71.13	$724,580

Best finish for 2000: T-3rd at the Players Championship

2001	27	91	18	1	1	1	4	71.15	$1,060,187

Best finish for 2001: Win at the Verizon Byron Nelson Classic

2002	28	82	15	0	0	1	4	71.76	$391,867

Best finish for 2002: T-10th at the Disney Golf Classic

2003	32	96	16	0	0	2	6	71.35	$580,087

Best finish for 2003: T-7th at the Greater Hartford Open

2004	28	92	17	0	1	2	5	71.42	$933,388

Best finish for 2004: T-2nd at the EDS Byron Nelson Championship

2005	28	89	16	0	1	1	4	71.56	$739,836

Best finish for 2005: T-2nd at the John Deere Classic

2006	31	91	13	0	0	1	5	71.55	$451,299

Best finish for 2006: T-8th at the Southern Farm Bureau Classic

2007	10	22	1	0	0	0	0	72.36	$18,060

Best finish for 2007: T-34th at the Viking Classic

2008	8	22	4	0	0	0	1	71.77	$94,612

Best finish for 2008: T-22nd at the Mayakoba Golf Classic

Period Totals	Starts	Rounds Played	Cuts Made	Wins	Top-5s	Top-10s	Top-25s	Scoring Average	Money
	311	973	176	1	9	19	55	71.37	$6,258,028

Brian Davis

Year	Starts	Rounds Played	Cuts Made	Wins	Top-5s	Top-10s	Top-25s	Scoring Average	Money
1998	1	2	0	0	0	0	0	73.50	$1,645
1999	1	4	1	0	0	0	0	77.50	$9,491

Best finish for 1999: T-68th at the British Open

2000	1	2	0	0	0	0	0	74.50	$1,520
2003	4	14	3	0	0	1	1	72.71	$272,111

Best finish for 2003: T-6th at the British Open

2004	7	12	2	0	0	0	1	73.75	$155,463

Best finish for 2004: T-13th at the PGA Championship

2005	23	75	15	0	1	2	6	71.07	$860,840

Best finish for 2005: T-3rd at the Nissan Open

2006	28	90	18	0	0	2	5	71.11	$762,281

Best finish for 2006: T-7th at the AT&T Pebble Beach National Pro-Am

2007	28	101	22	0	1	3	5	70.90	$1,289,208

Best finish for 2007: 2nd at the Stanford St. Jude Classic

2008	34	108	22	0	1	2	9	70.73	$1,151,558

Best finish for 2008: T-2nd at the Reno-Tahoe Open

Period Totals	Starts	Rounds Played	Cuts Made	Wins	Top-5s	Top-10s	Top-25s	Scoring Average	Money
	127	408	83	0	3	10	27	71.17	$4,504,119

Ed Davis

Year	Starts	Rounds Played	Cuts Made	Wins	Top-5s	Top-10s	Top-25s	Scoring Average	Money
1964	25	55	5	0	0	0	1	74.85	$1,017

Best finish for 1964: T-14th at the Azalea Open

1965	7	24	3	0	0	0	0	73.88	

Best finish for 1965: T-50th at the Portland Open

1966	3	6	0	0	0	0	0	75.50	
1968	5	18	4	0	0	0	0	73.17	

Best finish for 1968: 56th at the Hawaiian Open Invitational

1969	15	36	3	0	0	0	0	75.06	$187

Best finish for 1969: T-44th at the Azalea Open

1970	5	8	0	0	0	0	0	76.38	

Period Totals	Starts	Rounds Played	Cuts Made	Wins	Top-5s	Top-10s	Top-25s	Scoring Average	Money
	60	147	15	0	0	0	1	74.65	$1,204

Mike Davis

Year	Starts	Rounds Played	Cuts Made	Wins	Top-5s	Top-10s	Top-25s	Scoring Average	Money
1966	1	2	0	0	0	0	0	77.00	
1968	1	2	0	0	0	0	0	77.50	
1969	1	2	0	0	0	0	0	76.00	
1974	9	22	2	0	0	0	0	74.95	$224

Best finish for 1974: T-63rd at the Greater Milwaukee Open

| 1976 | 12 | 33 | 5 | 0 | 0 | 0 | 0 | 74.79 | $997 |

Best finish for 1976: T-44th at the Pensacola Open

| 1977 | 6 | 15 | 2 | 0 | 0 | 0 | 0 | 74.27 | $244 |

Best finish for 1977: T-63rd at the Bing Crosby Pro-Am

1979	1	2	0	0	0	0	0	78.00	$350
1989	1	2	0	0	0	0	0	84.00	
1992	1	2	0	0	0	0	0	89.50	$1,000
Period Totals	Starts	Rounds Played	Cuts Made	Wins	Top-5s	Top-10s	Top-25s	Scoring Average	Money
	33	82	9	0	0	0	0	75.55	$2,815

Rodger Davis

Year	Starts	Rounds Played	Cuts Made	Wins	Top-5s	Top-10s	Top-25s	Scoring Average	Money
1977	1	4	1	0	0	0	0	74.00	$425

Best finish for 1977: T-52nd at the British Open

| 1978 | 1 | 4 | 1 | 0 | 0 | 0 | 0 | 74.00 | $580 |

Best finish for 1978: T-52nd at the British Open

| 1979 | 1 | 4 | 1 | 0 | 1 | 1 | 1 | 72.00 | $13,650 |

Best finish for 1979: 5th at the British Open

| 1980 | 1 | 4 | 1 | 0 | 0 | 0 | 0 | 72.75 | $1,440 |

Best finish for 1980: T-38th at the British Open

| 1981 | 1 | 4 | 1 | 0 | 0 | 0 | 0 | 73.25 | $1,180 |

Best finish for 1981: T-39th at the British Open

| 1982 | 1 | 2 | 0 | 0 | 0 | 0 | 0 | 79.00 | $382 |
| 1983 | 1 | 4 | 1 | 0 | 0 | 0 | 0 | 71.00 | $3,225 |

Best finish for 1983: T-26th at the British Open

| 1985 | 1 | 2 | 0 | 0 | 0 | 0 | 0 | 76.50 | $544 |
| 1986 | 3 | 6 | 2 | 0 | 1 | 1 | 1 | 72.67 | $27,150 |

Best finish for 1986: T-5th at the NEC World Series of Golf

| 1987 | 9 | 26 | 6 | 0 | 1 | 1 | 3 | 72.69 | $114,659 |

Best finish for 1987: T-2nd at the British Open

| 1988 | 6 | 22 | 5 | 0 | 0 | 0 | 1 | 73.00 | $28,044 |

Best finish for 1988: T-20th at the British Open

1989	1	2	0	0	0	0	0	78.50	$800
1990	2	4	0	0	0	0	0	78.00	$1,996
1991	2	8	2	0	0	0	1	72.13	$35,604

Best finish for 1991: T-12th at the British Open

| 1992 | 5 | 12 | 1 | 0 | 0 | 0 | 0 | 74.58 | $5,400 |

Best finish for 1992: 63rd at the Masters

| 1993 | 2 | 6 | 1 | 0 | 0 | 0 | 1 | 71.33 | $14,136 |

Best finish for 1993: T-24th at the British Open

| 1994 | 1 | 2 | 0 | 0 | 0 | 0 | 0 | 76.50 | $972 |
| 1997 | 1 | 4 | 1 | 0 | 0 | 0 | 0 | 71.50 | $13,879 |

Best finish for 1997: T-33rd at the British Open

| 1998 | 1 | 4 | 1 | 0 | 0 | 0 | 0 | 73.75 | $12,471 |

Best finish for 1998: T-44th at the British Open

| Period Totals | Starts | Rounds Played | Cuts Made | Wins | Top-5s | Top-10s | Top-25s | Scoring Average | Money |
| | 41 | 124 | 25 | 0 | 3 | 3 | 8 | 73.34 | $276,536 |

Marco Dawson

Year	Starts	Rounds Played	Cuts Made	Wins	Top-5s	Top-10s	Top-25s	Scoring Average	Money
1986	1	4	1	0	0	0	1	70.75	$2,080

Best finish for 1986: T-21st at the Tallahassee Open

| 1990 | 2 | 6 | 1 | 0 | 0 | 0 | 0 | 71.33 | $2,154 |

Best finish for 1990: T-50th at the Bank of Boston Classic

| 1991 | 29 | 82 | 12 | 0 | 0 | 2 | 3 | 71.20 | $96,756 |

Best finish for 1991: T-9th at the Kmart Greater Greensboro Open

| 1992 | 28 | 80 | 14 | 0 | 1 | 2 | 4 | 71.09 | $113,465 |

Best finish for 1992: T-5th at the GTE Byron Nelson Classic

| 1993 | 32 | 105 | 21 | 0 | 1 | 1 | 4 | 72.09 | $120,462 |

Best finish for 1993: T-5th at the H-E-B Texas Open

| 1994 | 30 | 85 | 13 | 0 | 0 | 1 | 4 | 71.87 | $121,025 |

Best finish for 1994: T-7th at the Greater Milwaukee Open

| 1995 | 25 | 82 | 14 | 0 | 1 | 2 | 7 | 70.94 | $261,214 |

Best finish for 1995: 2nd at the Greater Milwaukee Open

1996	27	87	17	0	2	3	7	71.23	$261,661

Best finish for 1996: T-3rd at the Buick Invitational

1997	30	85	13	0	0	0	2	72.02	$100,110

Best finish for 1997: T-11th at the Freeport-McDermott Classic

1998	1	4	1	0	0	0	0	70.50	$3,173

Best finish for 1998: T-48th at the Deposit Guaranty Golf Classic

2000	11	33	5	0	0	0	0	71.76	$44,290

Best finish for 2000: T-31st at the Touchstone Energy Tucson Open

2001	19	57	10	0	0	0	2	71.23	$172,738

Best finish for 2001: T-16th at the Shell Houston Open

2002	1	2	0	0	0	0	0	72.00	
2003	31	84	11	0	0	2	6	70.82	$601,729

Best finish for 2003: T-7th at the Buick Invitational

2004	6	19	3	0	0	0	0	70.95	$59,550

Best finish for 2004: T-27th at the FBR Open

2005	23	82	18	0	0	1	5	70.77	$526,264

Best finish for 2005: T-10th at the Deutsche Bank Championship

2006	27	87	16	0	1	1	5	71.01	$545,076

Best finish for 2006: T-5th at the FUNAI Classic at the Walt Disney World Resort

2007	23	73	13	0	1	1	5	71.21	$521,432

Best finish for 2007: T-5th at the Buick Open

2008	21	64	12	0	0	2	4	71.42	$439,964

Best finish for 2008: T-6th at the Puerto Rico Open

Period Totals	Starts	Rounds Played	Cuts Made	Wins	Top-5s	Top-10s	Top-25s	Scoring Average	Money
	367	1121	195	0	7	18	59	71.32	$3,993,141

Glen Day

Year	Starts	Rounds Played	Cuts Made	Wins	Top-5s	Top-10s	Top-25s	Scoring Average	Money
1993	1	2	0	0	0	0	0	72.00	$924
1994	30	94	18	0	1	4	10	71.00	$358,236

Best finish for 1994: 2nd at the Anheuser-Busch Golf Classic

1995	32	91	15	0	0	1	8	71.51	$204,009

Best finish for 1995: T-7th at the Las Vegas Invitational

1996	27	89	19	0	1	2	9	70.48	$298,131

Best finish for 1996: T-4th at the Motorola Western Open

1997	29	82	14	0	0	4	6	71.79	$250,964

Best finish for 1997: T-9th at the AT&T Pebble Beach National Pro-Am

1998	26	92	21	0	5	6	13	70.48	$1,284,732

Best finish for 1998: T-2nd at The Players Championship & MCI Classic

1999	29	93	20	1	2	7	10	71.25	$1,118,669

Best finish for 1999: Win at the MCI Classic

2000	28	92	19	0	0	2	9	70.85	$618,242

Best finish for 2000: 6th at the National Car Rental Golf Classic/Disney

2001	28	84	17	0	1	2	7	70.37	$718,780

Best finish for 2001: 4th at the MasterCard Colonial

2002	31	103	22	0	2	2	7	70.60	$859,930

Best finish for 2002: 2nd at the Tampa Bay Classic presented by Buick

2003	31	101	19	0	1	3	8	70.39	$788,557

Best finish for 2003: T-5th at the B.C. Open

2004	33	99	17	0	1	1	5	71.13	$524,617

Best finish for 2004: T-3rd at the Southern Farm Bureau Classic

2005	27	78	13	0	0	1	4	71.21	$370,221

Best finish for 2005: T-9th at the U.S. Bank Championship in Milwaukee

2006	12	30	3	0	1	1	1	71.27	$134,580

Best finish for 2006: T-5th at the Southern Farm Bureau Classic

2007	27	85	16	0	0	0	3	71.25	$397,491

Best finish for 2007: T-15th at the Canadian Open

2008	19	64	13	0	0	1	4	70.61	$435,263

Best finish for 2008: T-8th at the RBC Canadian Open

Period Totals	Starts	Rounds Played	Cuts Made	Wins	Top-5s	Top-10s	Top-25s	Scoring Average	Money
	410	1279	246	1	15	37	104	70.93	$8,363,346

Jason Day

Year	Starts	Rounds Played	Cuts Made	Wins	Top-5s	Top-10s	Top-25s	Scoring Average	Money
2006	7	20	5	0	0	0	2	70.20	$174,508

Best finish for 2006: T-11th at the Reno-Tahoe Open

2008	28	81	13	0	0	2	6	71.06	$767,393

Best finish for 2008: 6th at the AT&T Pebble Beach National Pro-Am

Period Totals	Starts	Rounds Played	Cuts Made	Wins	Top-5s	Top-10s	Top-25s	Scoring Average	Money
	35	101	18	0	0	2	8	70.89	$941,901

Brendon de Jonge

Year	Starts	Rounds Played	Cuts Made	Wins	Top-5s	Top-10s	Top-25s	Scoring Average	Money
2007	26	76	12	0	0	2	3	71.45	$447,172

Best finish for 2007: T-6th at the Reno-Tahoe Open

Period Totals	Starts	Rounds Played	Cuts Made	Wins	Top-5s	Top-10s	Top-25s	Scoring Average	Money
	26	76	12	0	0	2	3	71.45	$447,172

Manuel De La Torre

Year	Starts	Rounds Played	Cuts Made	Wins	Top-5s	Top-10s	Top-25s	Scoring Average	Money
1958	10	36	8	0	0	0	0	72.39	$014

Best finish for 1958: T-30th at the Tucson Open

| 1959 | 1 | 2 | 0 | 0 | 0 | 0 | 0 | 76.00 | |
| 1960 | 3 | 11 | 3 | 0 | 0 | 1 | 2 | 72.09 | $1,098 |

Best finish for 1960: T-8th at the Puerto Rico Open Invitational

| 1961 | 1 | 4 | 1 | 0 | 0 | 0 | 0 | 73.25 | $225 |

Best finish for 1961: T-41st at the PGA Championship

| 1963 | 3 | 12 | 2 | 0 | 1 | 1 | 3 | 71.67 | $2,130 |

Best finish for 1963: T-3rd at the Puerto Rico Open Invitational

| 1964 | 8 | 22 | 1 | 0 | 0 | 0 | 0 | 74.64 | |

Best finish for 1964: T-42nd at the Phoenix Open

| 1965 | 2 | 6 | 1 | 0 | 0 | 0 | 0 | 74.00 | $738 |

Best finish for 1965: T-33rd at the PGA Championship

| 1966 | 6 | 19 | 3 | 0 | 0 | 0 | 0 | 74.16 | $542 |

Best finish for 1966: T-37th at the PGA Championship

| 1967 | 2 | 5 | 0 | 0 | 0 | 0 | 0 | 76.00 | |
| 1968 | 3 | 10 | 1 | 0 | 0 | 0 | 0 | 75.70 | $365 |

Best finish for 1968: T-73rd at the PGA Championship

| 1969 | 3 | 9 | 1 | 0 | 0 | 0 | 0 | 74.33 | $167 |

Best finish for 1969: T-69th at the Bob Hope Desert Classic

| 1970 | 3 | 6 | 0 | 0 | 0 | 0 | 0 | 77.50 | |
| 1971 | 3 | 8 | 1 | 0 | 0 | 0 | 0 | 74.13 | $258 |

Best finish for 1971: T-75th at the PGA Championship

| 1972 | 1 | 4 | 1 | 0 | 0 | 0 | 0 | 72.75 | $192 |

Best finish for 1972: 75th at the Greater Milwaukee Open

| 1974 | 1 | 2 | 0 | 0 | 0 | 0 | 0 | 79.00 | |
| 1977 | 1 | 2 | 0 | 0 | 0 | 0 | 0 | 79.00 | |

Period Totals	Starts	Rounds Played	Cuts Made	Wins	Top-5s	Top-10s	Top-25s	Scoring Average	Money
	51	158	23	0	1	2	5	73.86	$5,729

Roberto De Vicenzo

Year	Starts	Rounds Played	Cuts Made	Wins	Top-5s	Top-10s	Top-25s	Scoring Average	Money
1958	14	52	12	0	2	2	10	72.13	$7,432

Best finish for 1958: T-2nd at the Houston Open

| 1959 | 1 | 4 | 1 | 0 | 0 | 0 | 0 | 75.25 | $100 |

Best finish for 1959: T-40th at the Colonial National Invitational

| 1960 | 2 | 8 | 2 | 0 | 1 | 1 | 1 | 72.38 | $1,593 |

Best finish for 1960: T-3rd at the British Open

| 1961 | 4 | 16 | 4 | 0 | 1 | 1 | 2 | 72.31 | $4,405 |

Best finish for 1961: T-3rd at the Bing Crosby National

| 1962 | 1 | 4 | 1 | 0 | 0 | 0 | 0 | 74.00 | $500 |

Best finish for 1962: T-33rd at the Masters

| 1963 | 1 | 4 | 1 | 0 | 0 | 0 | 1 | 71.50 | $219 |

Best finish for 1963: T-16th at the Jamaica Open Invitational

| 1964 | 4 | 16 | 3 | 0 | 1 | 1 | 1 | 72.13 | $2,996 |

Best finish for 1964: 3rd at the British Open

| 1965 | 3 | 12 | 3 | 0 | 1 | 1 | 2 | 72.75 | $4,616 |

Best finish for 1965: 4th at the British Open

| 1966 | 8 | 32 | 8 | 1 | 2 | 4 | 6 | 71.78 | $27,626 |

Best finish for 1966: Win at the Dallas Open Invitational

| 1967 | 11 | 42 | 10 | 1 | 3 | 6 | 8 | 71.10 | $48,167 |

Best finish for 1967: Win at the British Open

| 1968 | 10 | 40 | 10 | 1 | 3 | 4 | 7 | 70.90 | $47,014 |

Best finish for 1968: Win at the Houston Champions International

| 1969 | 5 | 18 | 4 | 0 | 1 | 3 | 4 | 72.33 | $16,546 |

Best finish for 1969: T-3rd at the British Open

| 1970 | 5 | 16 | 3 | 0 | 0 | 0 | 3 | 72.50 | $5,079 |

Best finish for 1970: T-15th at the Houston Champions International

| 1971 | 3 | 12 | 3 | 0 | 0 | 1 | 2 | 72.25 | $7,053 |

Best finish for 1971: T-9th at the Masters

| 1972 | 1 | 4 | 1 | 0 | 0 | 0 | 1 | 74.00 | $2,160 |

Best finish for 1972: T-22nd at the Masters

Year	Starts	Rounds Played	Cuts Made	Wins	Top-5s	Top-10s	Top-25s	Scoring Average	Money
1973	3	12	2	0	0	0	0	74.33	$2,237

Best finish for 1973: T-28th at the British Open

| 1974 | 2 | 6 | 1 | 0 | 0 | 0 | 0 | 75.83 | $300 |

Best finish for 1974: T-51st at the British Open

| 1975 | 2 | 6 | 1 | 0 | 0 | 0 | 0 | 73.33 | $1,987 |

Best finish for 1975: T-28th at the British Open

| 1976 | 1 | 4 | 1 | 0 | 0 | 0 | 0 | 74.00 | $513 |

Best finish for 1976: T-32nd at the British Open

| 1977 | 1 | 4 | 1 | 0 | 0 | 0 | 0 | 73.75 | $440 |

Best finish for 1977: T-48th at the British Open

1978	1	2	0	0	0	0	0	75.00	$332
1979	3	6	0	0	0	0	0	76.50	$420
1983	1	4	0	0	0	0	0	73.00	
1986	1	2	0	0	0	0	0	77.50	
Period Totals	88	326	72	3	15	24	48	72.28	$181,736

PGA Tour career totals from 1947 to 1986

	Starts	Rounds Played	Cuts Made	Wins	Top-5s	Top-10s	Top-25s	Scoring Average	Money
	150	567	134	5	21	48	90	N/A	$224,642

Tim Debaufre

Year	Starts	Rounds Played	Cuts Made	Wins	Top-5s	Top-10s	Top-25s	Scoring Average	Money
1965	10	24	2	0	0	0	0	75.21	

Best finish for 1965: T-53rd at the Portland Open

| 1966 | 15 | 38 | 3 | 0 | 0 | 0 | 0 | 74.66 | $351 |

Best finish for 1966: T-36th at the Lucky International Open Invitational

| 1968 | 4 | 12 | 2 | 0 | 0 | 0 | 0 | 74.42 | $586 |

Best finish for 1968: T-41st at the PGA Championship

| 1969 | 5 | 12 | 1 | 0 | 0 | 0 | 1 | 74.67 | $215 |

Best finish for 1969: T-24th at the West End Classic

1974	1	2	0	0	0	0	0	77.00	
1975	1	2	0	0	0	0	0	81.50	
1976	1	2	0	0	0	0	0	77.00	
1977	1	2	0	0	0	0	0	75.50	
Period Totals	38	94	8	0	0	0	1	75.03	$1,152

John Deforest

Year	Starts	Rounds Played	Cuts Made	Wins	Top-5s	Top-10s	Top-25s	Scoring Average	Money
1982	3	8	1	0	0	0	0	74.13	$618

Best finish for 1982: T-67th at the Doral-Eastern Open

1983	1	2	0	0	0	0	0	75.00	
1984	1	2	0	0	0	0	0	79.50	$600
1985	24	54	3	0	0	0	0	74.81	$3,674

Best finish for 1985: T-35th at the Doral-Eastern Open

1986	1	2	0	0	0	0	0	73.00	
1988	1	2	0	0	0	0	0	73.50	
1989	2	4	0	0	0	0	0	77.50	
1993	1	2	0	0	0	0	0	74.00	
1994	2	4	0	0	0	0	0	73.75	$1,200
1996	2	4	0	0	0	0	0	75.50	$1,300
Period Totals	38	84	4	0	0	0	0	74.88	$7,392

Jay Delsing

Year	Starts	Rounds Played	Cuts Made	Wins	Top-5s	Top-10s	Top-25s	Scoring Average	Money
1985	27	83	14	0	0	2	3	72.30	$46,480

Best finish for 1985: T-7th at the B.C. Open

| 1986 | 32 | 93 | 17 | 0 | 1 | 2 | 5 | 72.23 | $65,850 |

Best finish for 1986: T-4th at the Los Angeles Open

| 1987 | 35 | 96 | 13 | 0 | 0 | 1 | 4 | 72.07 | $58,575 |

Best finish for 1987: T-7th at the USF&G Classic

| 1988 | 30 | 82 | 10 | 0 | 0 | 1 | 3 | 72.28 | $45,504 |

Best finish for 1988: T-7th at the Canadian Open

| 1989 | 23 | 64 | 10 | 0 | 0 | 0 | 1 | 71.44 | $26,565 |

Best finish for 1989: T-14th at the Chattanooga Classic

| 1990 | 29 | 96 | 20 | 0 | 2 | 4 | 7 | 71.53 | $207,740 |

Best finish for 1990: T-3rd at the Hardee's Golf Classic

| 1991 | 31 | 93 | 15 | 0 | 0 | 0 | 7 | 71.20 | $151,775 |

Best finish for 1991: T-11th at the MCI Heritage Classic

| 1992 | 29 | 93 | 19 | 0 | 3 | 5 | 9 | 70.92 | $296,342 |

Best finish for 1992: T-4th at the Phoenix Open, Canadian Open & Hardee's Golf Classic

Year	Starts	Rounds Played	Cuts Made	Wins	Top-5s	Top-10s	Top-25s	Scoring Average	Money
1993	29	100	20	0	1	3	6	71.48	$234,684

Best finish for 1993: T-2nd at the New England Classic

| 1994 | 27 | 88 | 15 | 0 | 0 | 2 | 3 | 71.31 | $143,738 |

Best finish for 1994: T-7th at the AT&T Pebble Beach Pro-Am

| 1995 | 28 | 77 | 11 | 0 | 2 | 2 | 3 | 71.99 | $230,769 |

Best finish for 1995: T-2nd at the FedEx St. Jude Classic

| 1996 | 31 | 86 | 14 | 0 | 0 | 0 | 3 | 71.47 | $117,246 |

Best finish for 1996: T-12th at the FedEx St. Jude Classic & B.C. Open

| 1997 | 28 | 84 | 14 | 0 | 0 | 1 | 1 | 71.74 | $102,592 |

Best finish for 1997: T-7th at the Motorola Western Open

| 1998 | 24 | 75 | 13 | 0 | 0 | 1 | 3 | 71.41 | $154,683 |

Best finish for 1998: T-9th at the Bell Canadian Open

| 1999 | 27 | 76 | 11 | 0 | 1 | 4 | 8 | 70.99 | $431,879 |

Best finish for 1999: T-3rd at the Buick Challenge

| 2000 | 33 | 93 | 14 | 0 | 0 | 0 | 1 | 71.83 | $132,842 |

Best finish for 2000: T-22nd at the BellSouth Classic

| 2001 | 5 | 13 | 1 | 0 | 0 | 0 | 0 | 72.38 | $4,887 |

Best finish for 2001: T-50th at the B.C. Open

| 2002 | 6 | 18 | 3 | 0 | 0 | 0 | 0 | 72.00 | $22,430 |

Best finish for 2002: T-53rd at the Air Canada Championship

| 2003 | 9 | 29 | 6 | 0 | 0 | 0 | 2 | 70.83 | $159,654 |

Best finish for 2003: T-11th at the Greater Hartford Open

| 2004 | 26 | 73 | 11 | 0 | 0 | 0 | 2 | 71.47 | $190,184 |

Best finish for 2004: T-19th at the Chrysler Classic of Greensboro

| 2005 | 11 | 37 | 7 | 0 | 0 | 2 | 2 | 70.03 | $230,851 |

Best finish for 2005: T-8th at the Valero Texas Open

| 2006 | 14 | 36 | 6 | 0 | 1 | 1 | 2 | 71.58 | $278,447 |

Best finish for 2006: T-5th at the FedEx St. Jude Classic

| 2007 | 12 | 37 | 6 | 0 | 0 | 0 | 2 | 71.35 | $181,809 |

Best finish for 2007: T-13th at the U.S. Bank Championship in Milwaukee & Viking Classic

| 2008 | 8 | 19 | 1 | 0 | 0 | 0 | 1 | 73.00 | $48,000 |

Best finish for 2008: T-14th at the Reno-Tahoe Open

Period Totals	Starts	Rounds Played	Cuts Made	Wins	Top-5s	Top-10s	Top-25s	Scoring Average	Money
	554	1641	271	0	11	31	78	71.60	$3,563,526

Jimmy Demaret

Year	Starts	Rounds Played	Cuts Made	Wins	Top-5s	Top-10s	Top-25s	Scoring Average	Money
1958	10	36	8	0	3	3	8	71.11	$6,663

Best finish for 1958: T-2nd at the Thunderbird Invitational

| 1959 | 6 | 22 | 5 | 0 | 2 | 2 | 4 | 72.05 | $2,870 |

Best finish for 1959: T-2nd at the Thunderbird Invitational

| 1960 | 4 | 14 | 2 | 0 | 0 | 0 | 1 | 73.14 | $1,432 |

Best finish for 1960: T-19th at the Houston Classic

| 1961 | 4 | 14 | 3 | 0 | 0 | 0 | 0 | 72.57 | $1,015 |

Best finish for 1961: T-28th at the Bing Crosby National

| 1962 | 5 | 21 | 5 | 0 | 1 | 1 | 2 | 71.62 | $5,043 |

Best finish for 1962: T-5th at the Masters

| 1963 | 5 | 20 | 5 | 0 | 0 | 0 | 2 | 72.05 | $3,716 |

Best finish for 1963: T-19th at the Houston Classic

| 1964 | 8 | 26 | 4 | 0 | 1 | 1 | 2 | 72.62 | $6,050 |

Best finish for 1964: 2nd at the Palm Springs Classic

| 1965 | 5 | 14 | 1 | 0 | 0 | 0 | 0 | 74.71 | $1,050 |

Best finish for 1965: T-34th at the Masters

| 1966 | 2 | 7 | 1 | 0 | 0 | 0 | 0 | 75.71 | $210 |

Best finish for 1966: T-48th at the Houston Champions International

| 1967 | 1 | 2 | 0 | 0 | 0 | 0 | 0 | 77.00 | |

Period Totals	Starts	Rounds Played	Cuts Made	Wins	Top-5s	Top-10s	Top-25s	Scoring Average	Money
	50	176	34	0	7	7	19	72.43	$28,050

PGA Tour career totals from 1934 to 1967

	Starts	Rounds Played	Cuts Made	Wins	Top-5s	Top-10s	Top-25s	Scoring Average	Money
	330	905	312	31	85	172	256	N/A	$210,275

Rolf Deming

Year	Starts	Rounds Played	Cuts Made	Wins	Top-5s	Top-10s	Top-25s	Scoring Average	Money
1969	20	63	11	0	0	0	2	73.32	$12,696

Best finish for 1969: T-11th at the Indian Ridge Hospital Open

| 1970 | 23 | 68 | 10 | 0 | 0 | 1 | 2 | 73.47 | $7,126 |

Best finish for 1970: T-6th at the Azalea Open Invitational

| 1971 | 22 | 70 | 13 | 0 | 0 | 0 | 2 | 72.59 | $6,093 |

Best finish for 1971: T-12th at the Southern Open

Year	Starts	Rounds Played	Cuts Made	Wins	Top-5s	Top-10s	Top-25s	Scoring Average	Money
1972	21	60	8	0	0	0	2	73.30	$4,191

Best finish for 1972: T-16th at the IVB Philadelphia Golf Classic

1973	4	14	2	0	0	0	0	74.07	

Best finish for 1973: T-76th at the Dean Martin Tucson Open

1975	1	4	1	0	0	0	0	75.00	$429

Best finish for 1975: T-67th at the PGA Championship

1980	1	2	0	0	0	0	0	79.50	$600
1981	1	2	0	0	0	0	0	77.00	$600
Period Totals	Starts	Rounds Played	Cuts Made	Wins	Top-5s	Top-10s	Top-25s	Scoring Average	Money
	93	283	45	0	0	1	8	73.30	$31,734

Todd Demsey

Year	Starts	Rounds Played	Cuts Made	Wins	Top-5s	Top-10s	Top-25s	Scoring Average	Money
1993	1	2	0	0	0	0	0	77.00	
1994	1	4	1	0	0	0	0	70.00	

Best finish for 1994: T-31st at the Buick Invitational of California

1996	4	10	1	0	0	0	0	73.50	$3,512

Best finish for 1996: T-68th at the Nortel Open

1997	27	74	9	0	0	0	1	72.23	$41,774

Best finish for 1997: T-24th at the Greater Vancouver Open

2007	1	4	1	0	0	0	0	73.50	$12,411

Best finish for 2007: T-69th at the Wachovia Championship

2008	25	80	14	0	0	0	1	71.24	$217,417

Best finish for 2008: T-19th at the U.S. Bank Championship in Milwaukee

Period Totals	Starts	Rounds Played	Cuts Made	Wins	Top-5s	Top-10s	Top-25s	Scoring Average	Money
	59	174	26	0	0	0	2	71.88	$275,114

Clark Dennis

Year	Starts	Rounds Played	Cuts Made	Wins	Top-5s	Top-10s	Top-25s	Scoring Average	Money
1987	1	4	1	0	0	0	0	70.75	$1,040

Best finish for 1987: T-64th at the Hardee's Golf Classic

1988	3	8	1	0	0	0	0	73.25	$2,027

Best finish for 1988: T-47th at the Gatlin Brothers - Southwest Golf Classic

1989	3	9	1	0	0	0	0	73.89	$6,281

Best finish for 1989: T-43rd at the U.S. Open

1990	33	86	11	0	1	1	3	72.19	$103,711

Best finish for 1990: T-3rd at the Hawaiian Open

1991	30	80	10	0	0	0	5	71.88	$57,720

Best finish for 1991: T-20th at the AT&T Pebble Beach Pro-Am

1992	6	17	2	0	0	0	0	71.29	$12,935

Best finish for 1992: T-30th at the Southwestern Bell Colonial

1993	2	8	2	0	0	0	0	71.38	$6,050

Best finish for 1993: T-45th at the Southwestern Bell Colonial

1994	30	98	21	0	0	3	9	70.99	$289,065

Best finish for 1994: T-6th at the U.S. Open

1995	33	92	12	0	0	0	3	71.95	$94,577

Best finish for 1995: T-12th at the Shell Houston Open & Quad City Classic

1996	4	10	1	0	0	0	0	73.30	$2,775

Best finish for 1996: T-77th at the Kemper Open

1997	1	2	0	0	0	0	0	70.50	
1998	26	75	14	0	1	4	8	71.20	$402,940

Best finish for 1998: T-3rd at the Kemper Open

1999	33	89	11	0	1	1	2	72.31	$180,843

Best finish for 1999: T-5th at the Shell Houston Open

2000	1	2	0	0	0	0	0	74.50	
2001	1	2	0	0	0	0	0	78.00	$1,000
2005	2	4	0	0	0	0	0	71.50	
2006	1	2	0	0	0	0	0	76.00	
2007	1	2	0	0	0	0	0	75.50	
Period Totals	Starts	Rounds Played	Cuts Made	Wins	Top-5s	Top-10s	Top-25s	Scoring Average	Money
	211	590	87	0	3	9	30	71.86	$1,160,965

Jim Dent

Year	Starts	Rounds Played	Cuts Made	Wins	Top-5s	Top-10s	Top-25s	Scoring Average	Money
1970	1	2	0	0	0	0	0	78.00	$500
1971	21	55	8	0	0	0	2	73.44	$3,432

Best finish for 1971: T-17th at the Tallahassee Open

1972	31	86	14	0	1	1	6	72.62	$23,001

Best finish for 1972: T-2nd at the Walt Disney World Open

1973	27	91	16	0	0	0	7	72.86	$23,505

Best finish for 1973: T-11th at the Doral-Eastern Open & San Antonio Texas Open

1974	37	128	29	0	2	5	11	71.95	$46,597

Best finish for 1974: T-5th at the Tallahassee Open

Year	Starts	Rounds Played	Cuts Made	Wins	Top-5s	Top-10s	Top-25s	Scoring Average	Money
1975	33	113	23	0	1	3	10	72.44	$33,649

Best finish for 1975: T-4th at the Atlanta Classic

1976	30	93	18	0	0	0	4	72.35	$20,042

Best finish for 1976: T-12th at the Kemper Open

1977	28	102	23	0	1	6	8	71.88	$45,936

Best finish for 1977: T-3rd at the Ohio Kings Island Open

1978	30	112	25	0	0	1	6	72.43	$30,063

Best finish for 1978: T-8th at the Byron Nelson Golf Classic

1979	30	98	20	0	0	0	4	72.29	$30,709

Best finish for 1979: T-9th at the Greater Milwaukee Open

1980	22	64	12	0	0	1	4	72.78	$20,261

Best finish for 1980: T-8th at the World Disney World National Team Championship

1981	22	71	16	0	1	1	5	71.86	$35,223

Best finish for 1981: 5th at the World Disney World National Team Championship

1982	30	99	21	0	0	3	7	71.69	$52,394

Best finish for 1982: T-8th at the Doral-Eastern Open & Miller High-Life Quad Cities Open

1983	31	95	16	0	0	1	5	72.38	$40,423

Best finish for 1983: T-10th at the Miller High-Life Quad Cities Open

1984	30	95	18	0	0	1	5	72.73	$50,941

Best finish for 1984: T-9th at the Seiko Tucson-Match Play Championship

1985	29	86	12	0	0	0	2	72.71	$30,012

Best finish for 1985: T-17th at the Tournament Players Championship

1986	28	77	10	0	0	0	3	72.56	$34,342

Best finish for 1986: T-18th at the Manufactures Hanover Westchester Classic & Canon Sammy Davis, Jr. - Greater Hartford Open

1987	6	13	1	0	0	0	0	72.15	$1,322

Best finish for 1987: T-36th at the Pensacola Open

1988	10	31	6	0	1	2	2	70.84	$44,365

Best finish for 1988: T-3rd at the Provident Classic

1989	2	3	1	0	0	0	1	68.67	$3,000

Best finish for 1989: T-16th at the Deposit Guaranty Golf Classic

Period Totals	Starts	Rounds Played	Cuts Made	Wins	Top-5s	Top-10s	Top-25s	Scoring Average	Money
	478	1514	289	0	7	25	92	72.35	$569,716

Bruce Devlin

Year	Starts	Rounds Played	Cuts Made	Wins	Top-5s	Top-10s	Top-25s	Scoring Average	Money
1962	6	18	3	0	0	0	2	73.89	$2,416

Best finish for 1962: T-16th at the Eastern Open Invitational

1963	7	28	7	0	0	2	4	71.54	$5,492

Best finish for 1963: T-7th at the St. Paul Open Invitational

1964	30	115	27	1	5	10	20	71.63	$37,242

Best finish for 1964: Win at the St. Petersburg Open

1965	25	99	24	0	6	13	19	70.31	$68,656

Best finish for 1965: T-2nd at the Doral Open, Jacksonville Open, Houston Classic & New Orleans Open

1966	18	72	18	2	6	8	11	71.24	$86,119

Best finish for 1966: Win at the Colonial National Invitation & Carling World Open

1967	18	60	12	0	0	3	6	73.08	$12,726

Best finish for 1967: T-8th at the British Open

1968	28	99	21	0	3	8	10	71.90	$36,666

Best finish for 1968: T-2nd at the Bing Crosby National Professional-Amateur

1969	21	79	19	1	4	9	15	71.08	$76,362

Best finish for 1969: Win at the Byron Nelson

1970	20	77	20	2	5	9	14	71.13	$111,530

Best finish for 1970: Win at the Bob Hope Chrysler Classic & Cleveland Open

1971	21	73	18	0	2	3	8	72.07	$39,891

Best finish for 1971: T-2nd at the Tournament of Champions

1972	21	78	18	2	5	7	10	71.99	$118,482

Best finish for 1972: Win at the Houston Open & USI Classic

1973	22	72	16	0	2	4	8	72.21	$57,260

Best finish for 1973: 2nd at the Sammy Davis, Jr. - Greater Hartford Open

1974	21	76	16	0	1	2	8	72.05	$36,959

Best finish for 1974: T-3rd at the Doral-Eastern Open

1975	24	82	17	0	1	2	5	72.44	$26,628

Best finish for 1975: T-5th at the Florida Citrus Open Invitational

1976	22	73	17	0	0	1	5	73.15	$18,188

Best finish for 1976: T-10th at the Houston Open

1977	20	63	12	0	2	2	6	72.79	$41,101

Best finish for 1977: T-3rd at the Tournament Players Championship

1978	15	48	9	0	0	0	1	73.04	$9,173

Best finish for 1978: T-14th at the Andy Williams-San Diego Open

1979	21	69	14	0	1	2	7	72.52	$30,597

Best finish for 1979: T-5th at the American Optical Classic

1980	16	55	11	0	0	1	6	72.35	$34,818

Best finish for 1980: T-9th at the San Antonio Texas Open

1981	16	50	11	0	1	2	4	72.60	$46,970

Best finish for 1981: T-2nd at the Sea Pines Heritage Classic

1982	20	68	14	0	0	2	3	72.34	$33,537

Best finish for 1982: 6th at the LaJet Classic

1983	15	43	6	0	0	0	1	74.42	$13,646

Best finish for 1983: T-18th at the Colonial National Invitational

1984	4	9	1	0	0	0	0	74.67	$924

Best finish for 1984: T-54th at the Bing Crosby Pro-Am

1987	1	0	0	0	0	0	0		
1988	1	4	0	0	0	0	0	73.75	

Period Totals	Starts	Rounds Played	Cuts Made	Wins	Top-5s	Top-10s	Top-25s	Scoring Average	Money
	433	1510	331	8	44	90	173	72.10	$945,382

Bubba Dickerson

Year	Starts	Rounds Played	Cuts Made	Wins	Top-5s	Top-10s	Top-25s	Scoring Average	Money
2002	10	27	5	0	0	0	0	73.22	$44,141

Best finish for 2002: T-42nd at the COMPAQ Classic of New Orleans

2003	1	2	0	0	0	0	0	72.50	
2005	1	3	0	0	0	0	0	71.33	
2006	32	96	18	0	1	3	6	71.36	$650,314

Best finish for 2006: T-5th at the Buick Championship

2007	19	51	6	0	0	0	0	72.59	$87,430

Best finish for 2007: T-27th at the Buick Open

2008	1	4	1	0	0	0	0	71.75	$13,640

Best finish for 2008: T-57th at the Zurich Classic of New Orleans

Period Totals	Starts	Rounds Played	Cuts Made	Wins	Top-5s	Top-10s	Top-25s	Scoring Average	Money
	64	183	30	0	1	3	6	72.00	$795,525

Gardner Dickinson

Year	Starts	Rounds Played	Cuts Made	Wins	Top-5s	Top-10s	Top-25s	Scoring Average	Money
1958	12	46	11	0	1	3	5	71.72	$4,733

Best finish for 1958: T-3rd at the Colonial Invitational

1959	20	80	19	0	0	2	13	71.30	$8,527

Best finish for 1959: T-6th at the Dallas Open Invitational

1960	9	36	8	0	1	2	7	70.22	$5,642

Best finish for 1960: T-3rd at the Sam Snead Festival

1961	19	77	19	0	2	6	15	70.92	$17,093

Best finish for 1961: T-3rd at the Memphis Open Invitational

1962	21	85	20	1	2	2	12	71.75	$13,324

Best finish for 1962: Win at the Coral Gables Open Invitational

1963	23	91	21	0	3	9	16	71.15	$24,349

Best finish for 1963: T-4th at the Phoenix Open Invitational

1964	29	103	20	0	0	4	9	72.12	$13,146

Best finish for 1964: T-6th at the Bing Crosby Pro-Am & Fresno Open

1965	28	106	23	0	6	9	15	71.45	$47,485

Best finish for 1965: 2nd at the Texas Open

1966	26	99	22	0	4	7	14	71.70	$54,156

Best finish for 1966: 2nd at the Phoenix Open Invitational, Greater New Orleans Open Invitational & Houston Champions International

1967	30	108	23	1	4	9	18	71.44	$70,272

Best finish for 1967: Win at the Cleveland Open

1968	29	104	24	1	3	6	16	71.09	$67,428

Best finish for 1968: Win at the Doral Open Invitational

1969	24	85	17	1	2	5	7	71.94	$51,304

Best finish for 1969: Win at the Colonial National Invitational

1970	20	63	13	0	1	4	8	72.57	$27,021

Best finish for 1970: T-2nd at the National 4 Ball Championship PGA Players

1971	27	89	19	1	2	5	5	72.12	$58,100

Best finish for 1971: Win at the Atlanta Classic

1972	14	39	6	0	1	2	4	72.72	$19,717

Best finish for 1972: 3rd at the Andy Williams-San Diego Open

1973	19	51	8	0	0	1	3	72.90	$10,561

Best finish for 1973: T-10th at the Masters

1974	12	26	2	0	0	0	0	74.50	$1,850

Best finish for 1974: T-48th at the Jackie Gleason's Inverrary Classic

1975	18	48	6	0	0	0	0	74.08	$1,976

Best finish for 1975: T-45th at the Sea Pines Heritage Classic

1976	8	18	0	0	0	0	0	75.56	
1977	6	14	1	0	0	0	0	75.14	

Best finish for 1977: T-77th at the Andy Williams-San Diego Open

1978	5	12	0	0	0	0	0	74.17	

Year	Starts	Rounds Played	Cuts Made	Wins	Top-5s	Top-10s	Top-25s	Scoring Average	Money
1979	3	5	0	0	0	0	0	75.60	
1980	4	13	1	0	0	0	0	74.31	$552

Best finish for 1980: T-59th at the Doral-Eastern Open

1981	1	3	0	0	0	0	0	78.33	
Period Totals	Starts	Rounds Played	Cuts Made	Wins	Top-5s	Top-10s	Top-25s	Scoring Average	Money
	407	1401	283	5	32	76	167	71.95	$497,238

PGA Tour career totals from 1948 to 1981

	Starts	Rounds Played	Cuts Made	Wins	Top-5s	Top-10s	Top-25s	Scoring Average	Money
	505	567	1782	7	40	95	221	N/A	$536,855

Bob Dickson

Year	Starts	Rounds Played	Cuts Made	Wins	Top-5s	Top-10s	Top-25s	Scoring Average	Money
1965	2	6	1	0	0	0	0	75.67	

Best finish for 1965: T-41st at the Oklahoma City Open

1966	2	6	1	0	0	0	0	76.00	

Best finish for 1966: T-50th at the Masters

1967	1	4	1	0	0	0	0	73.50	

Best finish for 1967: 69th at the Cajun Classic

1968	21	68	13	1	3	3	3	72.29	$42,683

Best finish for 1968: Win at the Haig Open Invitational

1969	32	106	21	0	1	1	13	72.25	$32,666

Best finish for 1969: T-2nd at the Bing Crosby National Pro-Am

1970	27	88	17	0	0	0	2	72.90	$10,392

Best finish for 1970: T-11th at the Greater New Orleans Open

1971	20	63	12	0	1	1	6	72.30	$21,060

Best finish for 1971: 3rd at the Sahara Invitational

1972	29	92	16	0	0	2	4	72.65	$15,474

Best finish for 1972: T-6th at the Danny Thomas Memphis Classic

1973	32	111	23	1	3	6	10	72.02	$87,244

Best finish for 1973: Win at the Andy Williams-San Diego Open

1974	30	85	12	0	0	1	5	73.02	$15,982

Best finish for 1974: T-8th at the Southern Open

1975	25	83	17	0	1	2	5	72.72	$24,409

Best finish for 1975: T-4th at the Tournament Players Championship

1976	31	97	22	0	1	2	6	72.52	$36,649

Best finish for 1976: T-3rd at the Western Open

1977	15	47	8	0	0	0	1	73.15	$7,623

Best finish for 1977: T-17th at the Hawaiian Open

1978	13	31	3	0	0	0	0	73.97	$1,271

Best finish for 1978: T-33rd at the Ed McMahon Quad City Open

Period Totals	Starts	Rounds Played	Cuts Made	Wins	Top-5s	Top-10s	Top-25s	Scoring Average	Money
	280	887	167	2	10	18	55	72.64	$295,453

Terry Diehl

Year	Starts	Rounds Played	Cuts Made	Wins	Top-5s	Top-10s	Top-25s	Scoring Average	Money
1970	1	2	0	0	0	0	0	80.50	
1973	1	4	0	0	0	0	0	76.75	
1974	17	47	7	1	1	1	1	73.13	$26,912

Best finish for 1974: Win at the San Antonio Texas Open

1975	31	97	18	0	1	1	7	72.91	$31,583

Best finish for 1975: 4th at the B.C. Open

1976	27	81	14	0	2	4	7	72.22	$55,803

Best finish for 1976: 2nd at the IVB - Bicentennial Golf Classic

1977	28	93	19	0	0	2	6	72.40	$32,114

Best finish for 1977: T-7th at the U.S. Open

1978	24	78	16	0	0	2	4	72.26	$25,270

Best finish for 1978: T-6th at the Ed McMahon Quad City Open

1979	26	83	16	0	2	2	4	72.75	$40,771

Best finish for 1979: 3rd at the American Optical Classic

1980	31	102	20	0	1	4	5	72.46	$67,636

Best finish for 1980: 2nd at the San Antonio Texas Open

1981	33	94	15	0	1	3	5	72.22	$53,317

Best finish for 1981: T-3rd at the Hawaiian Open

1982	27	77	11	0	1	1	4	72.30	$38,037

Best finish for 1982: 3rd at the Greater Milwaukee Open

1983	32	85	9	0	0	1	3	73.82	$33,914

Best finish for 1983: T-9th at the Sammy Davis, Jr. - Greater Hartford Open

1991	2	6	1	0	0	0	0	75.17	$1,488

Best finish for 1991: 77th at the B.C. Open

1992	2	4	0	0	0	0	0	74.50	
1993	1	2	0	0	0	0	0	77.50	
Period Totals	Starts	Rounds Played	Cuts Made	Wins	Top-5s	Top-10s	Top-25s	Scoring Average	Money
	283	855	146	1	9	21	46	72.70	$406,846

Mike Dietz

Year	Starts	Rounds Played	Cuts Made	Wins	Top-5s	Top-10s	Top-25s	Scoring Average	Money
1958	17	56	10	0	0	1	1	73.57	$1,098

Best finish for 1958: T-7th at the St. Petersburg Open

1959	5	18	4	0	0	0	1	73.56	$618

Best finish for 1959: T-19th at the St. Petersburg Open Invitational

1960	3	11	3	0	0	0	1	73.45	$705

Best finish for 1960: T-22nd at the De Soto Open Invitational

1961	1	2	1	0	0	0	0	77.50	

Best finish for 1961: T-200 at the PGA Championship

1964	1	2	0	0	0	0	0	79.00	
1965	1	4	1	0	0	0	0	76.75	

Best finish for 1965: T-70th at the Hawaiian Open

Period Totals	Starts	Rounds Played	Cuts Made	Wins	Top-5s	Top-10s	Top-25s	Scoring Average	Money
	28	93	19	0	0	1	3	73.89	$2,421

Terry Dill

Year	Starts	Rounds Played	Cuts Made	Wins	Top-5s	Top-10s	Top-25s	Scoring Average	Money
1962	4	16	4	0	1	1	4	71.56	$3,443

Best finish for 1962: T-4th at the Oklahoma City Open Invitational

1963	5	20	5	0	0	0	1	72.25	$2,552

Best finish for 1963: T-12th at the Hot Springs Open Invitational

1964	24	73	11	0	1	3	6	73.18	$16,290

Best finish for 1964: T-3rd at the Cleveland Open

1965	27	99	22	0	1	1	6	72.53	$12,320

Best finish for 1965: 4th at the Doral Open

1966	26	90	19	0	2	4	9	72.33	$22,862

Best finish for 1966: T-3rd at the Minnesota Golf Classic

1967	30	93	18	0	1	2	7	72.61	$18,882

Best finish for 1967: T-4th at the Sahara Open

1968	30	108	24	0	0	1	10	71.63	$21,309

Best finish for 1968: T-10th at the Phoenix Open Invitational

1969	29	99	22	0	1	6	13	71.43	$37,508

Best finish for 1969: 5th at the Buick Open

1970	35	125	27	0	3	4	10	71.94	$37,541

Best finish for 1970: T-2nd at the Sahara Invitational

1971	23	66	14	0	2	2	8	72.35	$29,469

Best finish for 1971: T-5th at the Doral-Eastern Open & Greater Greensboro Open

1972	3	8	1	0	0	0	1	74.00	$1,191

Best finish for 1972: T-23rd at the IVB Philadelphia Golf Classic

1974	6	18	3	0	0	0	1	72.83	$3,256

Best finish for 1974: T-11th at the Ohio Kings Island Open

1975	24	76	14	0	2	3	7	72.12	$26,036

Best finish for 1975: 3rd at the Southern Open

1976	10	30	7	0	0	1	4	72.53	$13,655

Best finish for 1976: T-8th at the Ed McMahon Quad City Open

1980	1	2	0	0	0	0	0	73.50	$600
1981	1	2	0	0	0	0	0	80.50	$600
1988	10	22	1	0	0	0	0	73.77	$1,760

Best finish for 1988: T-37th at the Gatlin Brothers - Southwest Golf Classic

1990	1	2	0	0	0	0	0	72.00	

Period Totals	Starts	Rounds Played	Cuts Made	Wins	Top-5s	Top-10s	Top-25s	Scoring Average	Money
	289	949	192	0	14	28	87	72.27	$249,273

Andy Dillard

Year	Starts	Rounds Played	Cuts Made	Wins	Top-5s	Top-10s	Top-25s	Scoring Average	Money
1984	1	4	1	0	0	0	0	73.25	$707

Best finish for 1984: T-66th at the LaJet Golf Classic

1985	2	4	0	0	0	0	0	73.75	
1986	27	79	15	0	1	2	3	72.03	$73,798

Best finish for 1986: T-5th at the Hawaiian Open

1987	28	81	14	0	0	0	3	72.32	$63,033

Best finish for 1987: T-12th at the Federal Express St. Jude Classic

1988	17	46	5	0	0	0	0	72.83	$5,740

Best finish for 1988: T-40th at the Southern Open

1989	1	2	0	0	0	0	0	71.50	
1990	1	2	0	0	0	0	0	73.50	
1991	1	4	1	0	0	0	0	68.25	$1,644

Best finish for 1991: T-50th at the Chattanooga Classic

1992	4	16	4	0	0	0	2	70.88	$38,567

Best finish for 1992: T-12th at the Chattanooga Classic

Year	Starts	Rounds Played	Cuts Made	Wins	Top-5s	Top-10s	Top-25s	Scoring Average	Money
1994	1	3	0	0	0	0	0	75.33	
Period Totals	Starts	Rounds Played	Cuts Made	Wins	Top-5s	Top-10s	Top-25s	Scoring Average	Money
	83	241	40	0	1	2	8	72.24	$183,488

Joey Dills

Year	Starts	Rounds Played	Cuts Made	Wins	Top-5s	Top-10s	Top-25s	Scoring Average	Money
1974	1	2	0	0	0	0	0	76.00	
1975	4	8	0	0	0	0	0	75.50	
1976	18	52	7	0	0	0	2	73.88	$6,554

Best finish for 1976: T-12th at the Ed McMahon Quad City Open

Year	Starts	Rounds Played	Cuts Made	Wins	Top-5s	Top-10s	Top-25s	Scoring Average	Money
1977	5	12	1	0	0	0	0	75.25	

Best finish for 1977: T-77th at the Danny Thomas Memphis Classic

Period Totals	Starts	Rounds Played	Cuts Made	Wins	Top-5s	Top-10s	Top-25s	Scoring Average	Money
	28	74	8	0	0	0	2	74.34	$6,554

Chris DiMarco

Year	Starts	Rounds Played	Cuts Made	Wins	Top-5s	Top-10s	Top-25s	Scoring Average	Money
1989	1	4	1	0	0	0	0	71.50	

Best finish for 1989: T-43rd at the Beatrice Western Open

Year	Starts	Rounds Played	Cuts Made	Wins	Top-5s	Top-10s	Top-25s	Scoring Average	Money
1990	1	2	0	0	0	0	0	73.00	
1992	1	2	0	0	0	0	0	75.50	
1994	29	86	16	0	2	4	5	71.51	$216,839

Best finish for 1994: T-3rd at the Deposit Guaranty Golf Classic

Year	Starts	Rounds Played	Cuts Made	Wins	Top-5s	Top-10s	Top-25s	Scoring Average	Money
1995	33	88	13	0	0	0	3	72.19	$74,698

Best finish for 1995: T-19th at the Kmart Greater Greensboro Open

Year	Starts	Rounds Played	Cuts Made	Wins	Top-5s	Top-10s	Top-25s	Scoring Average	Money
1996	5	14	3	0	0	0	0	72.07	$18,678

Best finish for 1996: T-26th at the B.C. Open

Year	Starts	Rounds Played	Cuts Made	Wins	Top-5s	Top-10s	Top-25s	Scoring Average	Money
1998	31	96	17	0	0	2	5	71.31	$260,334

Best finish for 1998: T-9th at the Bell Canadian Open & B.C. Open

Year	Starts	Rounds Played	Cuts Made	Wins	Top-5s	Top-10s	Top-25s	Scoring Average	Money
1999	31	99	20	0	2	3	8	71.48	$672,503

Best finish for 1999: 2nd at the Southern Farm Bureau Classic

Year	Starts	Rounds Played	Cuts Made	Wins	Top-5s	Top-10s	Top-25s	Scoring Average	Money
2000	33	114	25	1	5	5	13	70.41	$1,843,741

Best finish for 2000: Win at the SEI Pennsylvania Classic

Year	Starts	Rounds Played	Cuts Made	Wins	Top-5s	Top-10s	Top-25s	Scoring Average	Money
2001	29	103	26	1	5	10	18	69.70	$2,595,201

Best finish for 2001: Win at the Buick Challenge

Year	Starts	Rounds Played	Cuts Made	Wins	Top-5s	Top-10s	Top-25s	Scoring Average	Money
2002	29	106	27	1	4	7	16	70.03	$2,606,430

Best finish for 2002: Win at the Phoenix Open

Year	Starts	Rounds Played	Cuts Made	Wins	Top-5s	Top-10s	Top-25s	Scoring Average	Money
2003	27	93	23	0	4	10	14	70.02	$2,359,604

Best finish for 2003: T-2nd at the Buick Open

Year	Starts	Rounds Played	Cuts Made	Wins	Top-5s	Top-10s	Top-25s	Scoring Average	Money
2004	27	98	25	0	3	9	17	70.53	$2,971,842

Best finish for 2004: T-2nd at the FBR Open & PGA Championship

Year	Starts	Rounds Played	Cuts Made	Wins	Top-5s	Top-10s	Top-25s	Scoring Average	Money
2005	24	75	17	0	6	6	10	70.77	$3,566,548

Best finish for 2005: 2nd at the WGC-Accenture Match Play Championship, Masters & WGC-NEC Invitational

Year	Starts	Rounds Played	Cuts Made	Wins	Top-5s	Top-10s	Top-25s	Scoring Average	Money
2006	26	78	16	0	1	2	7	71.04	$1,544,926

Best finish for 2006: 2nd at the British Open

Year	Starts	Rounds Played	Cuts Made	Wins	Top-5s	Top-10s	Top-25s	Scoring Average	Money
2007	24	77	17	0	1	1	5	72.10	$952,914

Best finish for 2007: T-4th at the WGC-Bridgestone Invitational

Year	Starts	Rounds Played	Cuts Made	Wins	Top-5s	Top-10s	Top-25s	Scoring Average	Money
2008	29	87	14	0	0	1	5	71.70	$590,744

Best finish for 2008: T-10th at the Justin Timberlake Shriners Hospitals for Children Open

Period Totals	Starts	Rounds Played	Cuts Made	Wins	Top-5s	Top-10s	Top-25s	Scoring Average	Money
	380	1222	260	3	33	60	126	70.96	$20,275,001

Trevor Dodds

Year	Starts	Rounds Played	Cuts Made	Wins	Top-5s	Top-10s	Top-25s	Scoring Average	Money
1985	1	2	0	0	0	0	0	73.00	
1986	20	56	9	0	0	0	0	72.68	$13,536

Best finish for 1986: T-26th at the Byron Nelson Golf Classic

Year	Starts	Rounds Played	Cuts Made	Wins	Top-5s	Top-10s	Top-25s	Scoring Average	Money
1987	30	83	12	0	0	1	3	72.00	$46,646

Best finish for 1987: T-8th at the Buick Open

Year	Starts	Rounds Played	Cuts Made	Wins	Top-5s	Top-10s	Top-25s	Scoring Average	Money
1988	5	14	2	0	0	0	1	70.93	$16,179

Best finish for 1988: T-16th at the Federal Express St. Jude Classic

Year	Starts	Rounds Played	Cuts Made	Wins	Top-5s	Top-10s	Top-25s	Scoring Average	Money
1989	21	61	12	0	0	0	3	71.30	$47,066

Best finish for 1989: T-19th at the Bank of Boston Classic

Year	Starts	Rounds Played	Cuts Made	Wins	Top-5s	Top-10s	Top-25s	Scoring Average	Money
1990	8	26	6	0	0	2	3	70.12	$75,544

Best finish for 1990: T-8th at the NEC World Series of Golf

Year	Starts	Rounds Played	Cuts Made	Wins	Top-5s	Top-10s	Top-25s	Scoring Average	Money
1991	28	86	15	0	0	0	2	71.62	$57,786

Best finish for 1991: T-14th at the Hardee's Golf Classic

Year	Starts	Rounds Played	Cuts Made	Wins	Top-5s	Top-10s	Top-25s	Scoring Average	Money
1993	30	84	13	0	1	1	2	72.48	$119,436

Best finish for 1993: T-3rd at the AT&T Pebble Beach Pro-Am

Year	Starts	Rounds Played	Cuts Made	Wins	Top-5s	Top-10s	Top-25s	Scoring Average	Money
1994	29	90	10	0	1	1	1	71.71	$93,734

Best finish for 1994: T-4th at the Walt Disney World/Oldsmobile Classic

Year	Starts	Rounds Played	Cuts Made	Wins	Top-5s	Top-10s	Top-25s	Scoring Average	Money
1995	3	10	2	0	0	0	1	71.70	$20,122

Best finish for 1995: T-24th at the Bell Canadian Open

Year	Starts	Rounds Played	Cuts Made	Wins	Top-5s	Top-10s	Top-25s	Scoring Average	Money
1996	2	5	1	0	0	0	0	71.60	$6,638

Best finish for 1996: T-34th at the Bell Canadian Open

Year	Starts	Rounds Played	Cuts Made	Wins	Top-5s	Top-10s	Top-25s	Scoring Average	Money
1998	29	91	18	1	2	4	7	71.53	$792,340

Best finish for 1998: Win at the Greater Greensboro Chrysler Classic

Year	Starts	Rounds Played	Cuts Made	Wins	Top-5s	Top-10s	Top-25s	Scoring Average	Money
1999	30	97	18	0	0	2	5	71.86	$316,311

Best finish for 1999: 8th at the Greater Greensboro Chrysler Classic

Year	Starts	Rounds Played	Cuts Made	Wins	Top-5s	Top-10s	Top-25s	Scoring Average	Money
2000	29	84	14	0	0	0	3	71.92	$191,044

Best finish for 2000: T-15th at the BellSouth Classic

Year	Starts	Rounds Played	Cuts Made	Wins	Top-5s	Top-10s	Top-25s	Scoring Average	Money
2001	2	8	2	0	0	1	1	69.50	$66,366

Best finish for 2001: T-10th at the B.C. Open

Year	Starts	Rounds Played	Cuts Made	Wins	Top-5s	Top-10s	Top-25s	Scoring Average	Money
2002	6	18	3	0	0	0	0	72.61	$28,352

Best finish for 2002: T-39th at the AT&T Pebble Beach

Year	Starts	Rounds Played	Cuts Made	Wins	Top-5s	Top-10s	Top-25s	Scoring Average	Money
2003	3	9	1	0	0	0	0	72.89	$6,720

Best finish for 2003: T-54th at the B.C. Open

Year	Starts	Rounds Played	Cuts Made	Wins	Top-5s	Top-10s	Top-25s	Scoring Average	Money
2004	20	48	4	0	0	0	0	73.15	$45,015

Best finish for 2004: T-29th at the Reno-Tahoe Open

Year	Starts	Rounds Played	Cuts Made	Wins	Top-5s	Top-10s	Top-25s	Scoring Average	Money
2005	2	6	1	0	0	0	0	70.83	$5,820

Best finish for 2005: T-71st at the B.C. Open

Year	Starts	Rounds Played	Cuts Made	Wins	Top-5s	Top-10s	Top-25s	Scoring Average	Money
2006	2	4	0	0	0	0	0	73.75	
2007	1	2	0	0	0	0	0	77.50	
2008	2	4	0	0	0	0	0	75.00	
Period Totals	Starts	Rounds Played	Cuts Made	Wins	Top-5s	Top-10s	Top-25s	Scoring Average	Money
	303	877	143	1	4	12	32	71.91	$1,948,656

Art Doering

Year	Starts	Rounds Played	Cuts Made	Wins	Top-5s	Top-10s	Top-25s	Scoring Average	Money
1958	14	43	7	0	0	0	1	72.93	$427

Best finish for 1958: T-24th at the Baton Rouge Open

Year	Starts	Rounds Played	Cuts Made	Wins	Top-5s	Top-10s	Top-25s	Scoring Average	Money
1959	2	6	1	0	0	0	1	73.83	$352

Best finish for 1959: T-25th at the Bing Crosby National

Year	Starts	Rounds Played	Cuts Made	Wins	Top-5s	Top-10s	Top-25s	Scoring Average	Money
1960	1	3	0	0	0	0	0	77.00	$042
1961	1	2	0	0	0	0	0	76.00	
1963	1	2	0	0	0	0	0	84.50	$150
1964	5	7	0	0	0	0	0	77.14	
1965	3	6	0	0	0	0	0	78.33	
Period Totals	Starts	Rounds Played	Cuts Made	Wins	Top-5s	Top-10s	Top-25s	Scoring Average	Money
	27	69	8	0	0	0	2	74.51	$971

Jay Dolan

Year	Starts	Rounds Played	Cuts Made	Wins	Top-5s	Top-10s	Top-25s	Scoring Average	Money
1962	3	10	2	0	0	0	0	73.10	$221

Best finish for 1962: T-28th at the Denver Open Invitational

Year	Starts	Rounds Played	Cuts Made	Wins	Top-5s	Top-10s	Top-25s	Scoring Average	Money
1963	2	8	1	0	0	0	2	70.75	$1,270

Best finish for 1963: T-17th at the Insurance City Open Invitational

Year	Starts	Rounds Played	Cuts Made	Wins	Top-5s	Top-10s	Top-25s	Scoring Average	Money
1964	16	47	7	0	0	0	2	72.70	$2,523

Best finish for 1964: T-16th at the Buick Open & Cajun Classic

Year	Starts	Rounds Played	Cuts Made	Wins	Top-5s	Top-10s	Top-25s	Scoring Average	Money
1965	20	62	10	0	1	1	5	72.85	$7,129

Best finish for 1965: T-5th at the San Diego Open

Year	Starts	Rounds Played	Cuts Made	Wins	Top-5s	Top-10s	Top-25s	Scoring Average	Money
1966	29	95	18	0	1	2	6	72.96	$18,823

Best finish for 1966: T-2nd at the Doral Open Invitational

Year	Starts	Rounds Played	Cuts Made	Wins	Top-5s	Top-10s	Top-25s	Scoring Average	Money
1967	33	91	12	0	0	0	2	74.02	$3,103

Best finish for 1967: T-18th at the Carling World Open

Year	Starts	Rounds Played	Cuts Made	Wins	Top-5s	Top-10s	Top-25s	Scoring Average	Money
1968	19	51	7	0	0	0	0	73.63	$1,325

Best finish for 1968: T-39th at the Phoenix Open Invitational

Year	Starts	Rounds Played	Cuts Made	Wins	Top-5s	Top-10s	Top-25s	Scoring Average	Money
1969	7	17	1	0	0	0	0	75.35	$179

Best finish for 1969: T-67th at the Bing Crosby National Pro-Am

Year	Starts	Rounds Played	Cuts Made	Wins	Top-5s	Top-10s	Top-25s	Scoring Average	Money
1970	2	5	1	0	0	0	0	75.40	$206

Best finish for 1970: 78th at the AVCO Classic

Year	Starts	Rounds Played	Cuts Made	Wins	Top-5s	Top-10s	Top-25s	Scoring Average	Money
1971	4	12	2	0	0	0	0	73.25	$1,119

Best finish for 1971: T-36th at the National Airlines Open

Year	Starts	Rounds Played	Cuts Made	Wins	Top-5s	Top-10s	Top-25s	Scoring Average	Money
1972	1	2	0	0	0	0	0	72.50	
1974	2	6	1	0	0	0	0	74.67	

Best finish for 1974: T-74th at the Pleasant Valley Classic

Year	Starts	Rounds Played	Cuts Made	Wins	Top-5s	Top-10s	Top-25s	Scoring Average	Money
1975	1	2	0	0	0	0	0	78.00	
1977	1	2	0	0	0	0	0	77.50	
Period Totals	Starts	Rounds Played	Cuts Made	Wins	Top-5s	Top-10s	Top-25s	Scoring Average	Money
	140	410	62	0	2	3	17	73.40	$35,898

Jay Don Blake

Year	Starts	Rounds Played	Cuts Made	Wins	Top-5s	Top-10s	Top-25s	Scoring Average	Money
1980	1	2	0	0	0	0	0	75.50	

Year	Starts	Rounds Played	Cuts Made	Wins	Top-5s	Top-10s	Top-25s	Scoring Average	Money
1984	2	6	0	0	0	0	0	71.17	
1985	2	5	0	0	0	0	0	74.80	
1987	31	97	19	0	0	1	9	71.20	$87,634

Best finish for 1987: T-10th at the Provident Classic

| 1988 | 33 | 113 | 25 | 0 | 0 | 2 | 8 | 71.35 | $133,428 |

Best finish for 1988: T-9th at the Pensacola Open

| 1989 | 28 | 87 | 16 | 0 | 1 | 3 | 9 | 70.93 | $201,499 |

Best finish for 1989: T-3rd at the BellSouth Atlanta Golf Classic

| 1990 | 30 | 91 | 16 | 0 | 0 | 0 | 9 | 71.29 | $149,384 |

Best finish for 1990: T-11th at the Las Vegas Invitational

| 1991 | 28 | 104 | 24 | 1 | 2 | 6 | 14 | 70.18 | $569,155 |

Best finish for 1991: Win at the Shearson Lehman Brothers Open

| 1992 | 24 | 78 | 15 | 0 | 2 | 4 | 8 | 71.01 | $300,799 |

Best finish for 1992: 2nd at the BellSouth Classic

| 1993 | 25 | 77 | 15 | 0 | 2 | 3 | 6 | 71.16 | $202,482 |

Best finish for 1993: T-4th at the Buick Invitational of California & Buick Open

| 1994 | 25 | 87 | 20 | 0 | 2 | 2 | 9 | 70.46 | $310,351 |

Best finish for 1994: T-2nd at the Northern Telecom Open

| 1995 | 26 | 86 | 17 | 0 | 2 | 3 | 9 | 70.70 | $334,750 |

Best finish for 1995: T-2nd at the Nissan Open

| 1996 | 26 | 91 | 20 | 0 | 1 | 1 | 6 | 70.69 | $348,628 |

Best finish for 1996: T-2nd at the Motorola Western Open

| 1997 | 28 | 91 | 18 | 0 | 2 | 3 | 10 | 70.79 | $380,784 |

Best finish for 1997: T-4th at the United Airlines Hawaiian Open

| 1998 | 24 | 78 | 17 | 0 | 1 | 1 | 6 | 70.72 | $405,305 |

Best finish for 1998: 2nd at the BellSouth Classic

| 1999 | 29 | 92 | 18 | 0 | 1 | 2 | 6 | 71.08 | $389,765 |

Best finish for 1999: T-5th at the Michelob Championship at Kingsmill

| 2000 | 29 | 93 | 18 | 0 | 1 | 3 | 8 | 71.03 | $592,109 |

Best finish for 2000: T-5th at the BellSouth Classic

| 2001 | 31 | 96 | 20 | 0 | 0 | 1 | 4 | 70.75 | $437,576 |

Best finish for 2001: T-7th at the Buick Invitational

| 2002 | 34 | 105 | 19 | 0 | 1 | 1 | 2 | 70.92 | $496,066 |

Best finish for 2002: 3rd at the Sony Open in Hawaii

| 2003 | 27 | 75 | 10 | 0 | 0 | 0 | 1 | 71.44 | $194,293 |

Best finish for 2003: T-14th at the Bell Canadian Open

| 2004 | 14 | 37 | 4 | 0 | 0 | 0 | 0 | 72.54 | $41,555 |

Best finish for 2004: T-41st at the AT&T Pebble Beach National Pro-Am

2005	1	2	0	0	0	0	0	72.50	
Period Totals	Starts	Rounds Played	Cuts Made	Wins	Top-5s	Top-10s	Top-25s	Scoring Average	Money
	498	1593	311	1	18	36	124	70.98	$5,575,563

Luke Donald

Year	Starts	Rounds Played	Cuts Made	Wins	Top-5s	Top-10s	Top-25s	Scoring Average	Money
1999	2	4	0	0	0	0	0	76.25	
2000	3	8	1	0	0	0	0	72.88	

Best finish for 2000: T-51st at the Memorial Tournament

| 2001 | 7 | 20 | 3 | 0 | 0 | 0 | 1 | 71.05 | $80,747 |

Best finish for 2001: T-18th at the Bell Canadian Open

| 2002 | 30 | 104 | 23 | 1 | 1 | 1 | 11 | 70.66 | $1,092,155 |

Best finish for 2002: Win at the Southern Farm Bureau Classic

| 2003 | 27 | 88 | 17 | 0 | 0 | 2 | 8 | 71.02 | $709,095 |

Best finish for 2003: T-7th at the Buick Invitational

| 2004 | 21 | 72 | 15 | 0 | 2 | 4 | 12 | 70.58 | $1,651,886 |

Best finish for 2004: T-2nd at the Buick Invitational

| 2005 | 18 | 60 | 17 | 0 | 3 | 5 | 12 | 70.27 | $2,480,562 |

Best finish for 2005: T-2nd at the Buick Invitational & The Players Championship

| 2006 | 18 | 63 | 16 | 1 | 4 | 10 | 14 | 70.06 | $3,177,408 |

Best finish for 2006: Win at the Honda Classic

| 2007 | 20 | 67 | 15 | 0 | 2 | 5 | 8 | 71.36 | $2,192,053 |

Best finish for 2007: T-2nd at the Sony Open in Hawaii & EDS Byron Nelson Championship

| 2008 | 11 | 33 | 7 | 0 | 2 | 3 | 6 | 71.18 | $1,456,650 |

Best finish for 2008: 2nd at the Honda Classic

| Period Totals | Starts | Rounds Played | Cuts Made | Wins | Top-5s | Top-10s | Top-25s | Scoring Average | Money |
| | 157 | 519 | 114 | 2 | 14 | 30 | 72 | 70.81 | $12,840,556 |

Mike Donald

Year	Starts	Rounds Played	Cuts Made	Wins	Top-5s	Top-10s	Top-25s	Scoring Average	Money
1980	18	50	8	0	0	0	3	72.48	$12,269

Best finish for 1980: T-23rd at the Anheuser-Busch Golf Classic

| 1981 | 34 | 98 | 16 | 0 | 1 | 4 | 7 | 72.39 | $51,595 |

Best finish for 1981: T-5th at the Bay Hill Classic

Year	Starts	Rounds Played	Cuts Made	Wins	Top-5s	Top-10s	Top-25s	Scoring Average	Money
1982	31	97	17	0	0	0	5	72.06	$39,033

Best finish for 1982: T-11th at the Sea Pines Heritage Classic & Buick Open

| 1983 | 34 | 118 | 23 | 0 | 2 | 2 | 7 | 71.93 | $72,343 |

Best finish for 1983: T-3rd at the Honda Inverrary Classic

| 1984 | 35 | 121 | 26 | 0 | 3 | 4 | 12 | 71.83 | $146,324 |

Best finish for 1984: T-3rd at the Kemper Open & Georgia-Pacific Atlanta Golf Classic

| 1985 | 32 | 111 | 23 | 0 | 1 | 1 | 5 | 72.23 | $91,888 |

Best finish for 1985: T-2nd at the Walt Disney World/Oldsmobile Classic

| 1986 | 35 | 111 | 22 | 0 | 1 | 2 | 9 | 71.95 | $108,772 |

Best finish for 1986: T-3rd at the Canadian Open

| 1987 | 34 | 116 | 24 | 0 | 2 | 2 | 6 | 71.75 | $138,334 |

Best finish for 1987: T-2nd at the Federal Express St. Jude Classic

| 1988 | 37 | 112 | 19 | 0 | 2 | 4 | 6 | 71.57 | $119,509 |

Best finish for 1988: T-5th at the Walt Disney World/Oldsmobile Classic & Centel Classic

| 1989 | 36 | 118 | 24 | 1 | 3 | 5 | 13 | 71.11 | $432,232 |

Best finish for 1989: Win at the Anheuser-Busch Golf Classic

| 1990 | 32 | 114 | 24 | 0 | 3 | 3 | 8 | 71.28 | $349,328 |

Best finish for 1990: T-2nd at the U.S. Open & Buick Open

| 1991 | 34 | 103 | 18 | 0 | 0 | 1 | 2 | 71.90 | $90,748 |

Best finish for 1991: T-8th at the Anheuser-Busch Golf Classic

| 1992 | 31 | 101 | 19 | 0 | 1 | 1 | 5 | 71.45 | $117,252 |

Best finish for 1992: T-2nd at the Deposit Guaranty Classic

| 1993 | 34 | 92 | 11 | 0 | 0 | 1 | 1 | 72.16 | $51,313 |

Best finish for 1993: T-10th at the Deposit Guaranty Classic

| 1994 | 16 | 48 | 8 | 0 | 1 | 1 | 5 | 71.25 | $119,065 |

Best finish for 1994: T-3rd at the Hardee's Golf Classic

| 1995 | 15 | 35 | 2 | 0 | 0 | 0 | 0 | 72.89 | $5,760 |

Best finish for 1995: T-40th at the Anheuser-Busch Golf Classic

| 1996 | 17 | 41 | 3 | 0 | 0 | 0 | 0 | 73.61 | $7,829 |

Best finish for 1996: T-49th at the Bob Hope Chrysler Classic

| 1997 | 9 | 22 | 2 | 0 | 0 | 0 | 0 | 72.18 | $4,684 |

Best finish for 1997: T-63rd at the Quad City Classic

| 1998 | 11 | 26 | 2 | 0 | 0 | 0 | 0 | 73.42 | $7,590 |

Best finish for 1998: T-39th at the Deposit Guaranty Golf Classic

| 1999 | 5 | 12 | 2 | 0 | 0 | 0 | 0 | 72.83 | $7,472 |

Best finish for 1999: T-67th at the B.C. Open

| 2000 | 6 | 14 | 1 | 0 | 0 | 0 | 0 | 73.21 | $3,920 |

Best finish for 2000: 72nd at the B.C. Open

2001	3	6	0	0	0	0	0	73.33	
2002	3	6	0	0	0	0	0	74.67	
2003	3	6	0	0	0	0	0	74.33	
2004	1	2	0	0	0	0	0	74.50	
2006	1	2	0	0	0	0	0	80.00	
Period Totals	Starts	Rounds Played	Cuts Made	Wins	Top-5s	Top-10s	Top-25s	Scoring Average	Money
	547	1682	294	1	20	31	94	71.96	$1,977,260

Robert Donald

Year	Starts	Rounds Played	Cuts Made	Wins	Top-5s	Top-10s	Top-25s	Scoring Average	Money
1979	15	33	2	0	0	0	1	74.79	$2,860

Best finish for 1979: T-21st at the Pensacola Open

| 1980 | 11 | 26 | 1 | 0 | 0 | 0 | 0 | 74.77 | $630 |

Best finish for 1980: 65th at the Joe Garagiola Tucson Open

1983	1	2	0	0	0	0	0	77.00	
1984	2	4	0	0	0	0	0	72.50	
1986	1	2	0	0	0	0	0	73.50	
Period Totals	Starts	Rounds Played	Cuts Made	Wins	Top-5s	Top-10s	Top-25s	Scoring Average	Money
	30	67	3	0	0	0	1	74.67	$3,490

Ed Dougherty

Year	Starts	Rounds Played	Cuts Made	Wins	Top-5s	Top-10s	Top-25s	Scoring Average	Money
1974	1	2	0	0	0	0	0	77.50	
1975	16	50	9	0	0	0	4	72.74	$9,374

Best finish for 1975: T-18th at the Westchester Classic

| 1976 | 26 | 78 | 14 | 0 | 1 | 1 | 1 | 73.14 | $16,717 |

Best finish for 1976: T-3rd at the Greater Jacksonville Open

| 1977 | 24 | 80 | 16 | 0 | 0 | 2 | 4 | 73.15 | $16,702 |

Best finish for 1977: T-6th at the Tallahassee Open

| 1978 | 19 | 53 | 7 | 0 | 1 | 1 | 3 | 73.75 | $9,590 |

Best finish for 1978: 5th at the Tallahassee Open

| 1979 | 25 | 74 | 12 | 0 | 0 | 2 | 3 | 72.84 | $24,802 |

Best finish for 1979: T-5th at the Greater Milwaukee Open

| 1980 | 25 | 62 | 8 | 0 | 0 | 1 | 2 | 73.47 | $13,476 |

Best finish for 1980: T-8th at the World Disney World National Team Championship

Year	Starts	Rounds Played	Cuts Made	Wins	Top-5s	Top-10s	Top-25s	Scoring Average	Money
1981	22	66	12	0	0	1	3	72.68	$21,582

Best finish for 1981: T-8th at the Pleasant Valley Jimmy Fund Classic

1982	25	79	15	0	0	1	3	72.38	$27,948

Best finish for 1982: T-10th at the Anheuser-Busch Golf Classic

1983	18	51	8	0	0	0	1	72.45	$9,422

Best finish for 1983: T-21st at the Bank of Boston Classic

1984	1	2	0	0	0	0	0	73.50	
1985	1	2	0	0	0	0	0	74.00	$1,000
1986	9	23	3	0	0	0	1	72.83	$13,343

Best finish for 1986: 19th at the NEC World Series of Golf

1987	28	88	17	0	0	1	6	71.08	$82,524

Best finish for 1987: T-6th at the Deposit Guaranty Golf Classic

1988	35	93	10	0	0	0	0	72.29	$23,455

Best finish for 1988: T-26th at the Provident Classic

1989	3	8	1	0	0	0	0	71.00	$1,800

Best finish for 1989: T-41st at the B.C. Open

1990	27	76	12	0	1	1	3	71.87	$125,505

Best finish for 1990: T-2nd at the Greater Milwaukee Open

1991	36	114	20	0	2	2	5	71.43	$202,958

Best finish for 1991: 3rd at the United Hawaiian Open

1992	36	108	19	0	2	2	4	71.35	$238,725

Best finish for 1992: T-2nd at the Chattanooga Classic

1993	34	111	22	0	0	3	5	71.68	$167,651

Best finish for 1993: T-6th at the Honda Classic

1994	33	98	18	0	0	0	4	71.71	$96,987

Best finish for 1994: T-15th at the Freeport-McMoRan Classic

1995	15	43	7	1	1	1	1	72.37	$154,007

Best finish for 1995: Win at the Deposit Guaranty Golf Classic

1996	15	33	1	0	0	0	0	74.18	$16,750

Best finish for 1996: 27th at the Mercedes Championship

1997	28	65	6	0	0	1	3	72.72	$65,504

Best finish for 1997: T-10th at the Quad City Classic

1998	1	2	0	0	0	0	0	73.50	
1999	1	2	0	0	0	0	0	71.50	
2003	1	2	0	0	0	0	0	73.50	

Period Totals	Starts	Rounds Played	Cuts Made	Wins	Top-5s	Top-10s	Top-25s	Scoring Average	Money
	505	1465	237	1	8	20	56	72.32	$1,339,824

Bruce Douglass

Year	Starts	Rounds Played	Cuts Made	Wins	Top-5s	Top-10s	Top-25s	Scoring Average	Money
1976	1	4	1	0	0	0	0	76.25	

Best finish for 1976: T-62nd at the U.S. Open

1979	1	4	1	0	1	1	1	71.75	$17,400

Best finish for 1979: T-3rd at the Western Open

1980	20	51	7	0	0	0	1	73.00	$6,399

Best finish for 1980: T-23rd at the Sammy Davis, Jr. - Greater Hartford Open

1981	27	89	20	0	0	1	5	72.17	$39,085

Best finish for 1981: T-7th at the World Disney World National Team Championship

1982	28	86	14	0	0	0	1	72.70	$15,903

Best finish for 1982: T-16th at the Hawaiian Open

1983	6	16	2	0	0	0	1	72.31	$3,798

Best finish for 1983: T-22nd at the Texas Open

1984	1	4	1	0	0	0	0	73.00	$1,065

Best finish for 1984: T-63rd at the Manufactures Hanover Westchester Classic

Period Totals	Starts	Rounds Played	Cuts Made	Wins	Top-5s	Top-10s	Top-25s	Scoring Average	Money
	84	254	46	0	1	2	9	72.59	$83,649

Dale Douglass

Year	Starts	Rounds Played	Cuts Made	Wins	Top-5s	Top-10s	Top-25s	Scoring Average	Money
1963	2	8	2	0	0	0	1	71.50	$938

Best finish for 1963: T-11th at the Almaden Open Invitational

1964	31	81	8	0	0	0	1	73.44	$2,708

Best finish for 1964: T-17th at the Texas Open

1965	29	98	18	0	0	1	6	72.85	$11,248

Best finish for 1965: T-9th at the "500" Festival

1966	33	117	24	0	0	3	7	72.49	$17,993

Best finish for 1966: T-6th at the Memphis Open Invitational & "500" Festival Open Invitational

1967	37	130	26	0	0	3	9	72.63	$21,543

Best finish for 1967: T-8th at the Bob Hope Classic

1968	35	122	25	0	3	7	14	71.53	$53,207

Best finish for 1968: 2nd at the Sahara Invitational

Year	Starts	Rounds Played	Cuts Made	Wins	Top-5s	Top-10s	Top-25s	Scoring Average	Money
1969	37	136	31	2	4	8	18	71.35	$87,650

Best finish for 1969: Win at the Azalea Open & Kemper Insurance Open

1970	36	122	26	1	3	7	11	71.79	$76,397

Best finish for 1970: Win at the Phoenix Open

1971	35	122	27	0	4	6	11	71.94	$72,482

Best finish for 1971: 2nd at the Tucson Open, Kemper Open & American Golf Classic

1972	36	110	18	0	1	1	7	72.72	$24,357

Best finish for 1972: T-4th at the Tucson Open

1973	34	101	14	0	0	0	2	73.42	$6,921

Best finish for 1973: T-19th at the Greater Milwaukee Open

1974	33	123	27	0	2	4	10	71.89	$47,692

Best finish for 1974: T-4th at the Canadian Open & Pleasant Valley Classic

1975	30	108	24	0	0	3	8	72.33	$34,583

Best finish for 1975: T-9th at the Hawaiian Open & Andy Williams-San Diego Open

1976	35	92	15	0	0	1	4	73.35	$17,010

Best finish for 1976: T-9th at the Greater Jacksonville Open

1977	33	94	12	0	0	1	2	73.64	$11,993

Best finish for 1977: T-9th at the Florida Citrus Open Invitational

1978	20	50	5	0	1	1	2	72.94	$20,739

Best finish for 1978: T-2nd at the Sammy Davis, Jr. - Greater Hartford Open

1979	27	80	13	0	0	0	3	73.56	$17,737

Best finish for 1979: T-14th at the Southern Open

1980	24	68	10	0	0	0	1	73.16	$10,291

Best finish for 1980: T-16th at the Quad Cities Open

1981	13	30	3	0	0	0	0	73.67	$2,067

Best finish for 1981: T-50th at the Quad Cities Open

1982	14	41	6	0	0	0	0	72.93	$5,360

Best finish for 1982: T-29th at the Greater Milwaukee Open

1983	14	44	6	0	0	1	2	72.36	$15,454

Best finish for 1983: T-8th at the Bank of Boston Classic

1984	15	42	7	0	0	0	0	72.86	$7,575

Best finish for 1984: T-37th at the USF&G Classic & Greater Milwaukee Open

1985	8	21	3	0	0	0	0	72.86	$2,662

Best finish for 1985: T-47th at the Lite Quad Cities Open

1986	3	8	2	0	0	0	0	72.13	$2,030

Best finish for 1986: T-54th at the Hawaiian Open

1987	2	6	1	0	0	0	0	72.83	$6,555

Best finish for 1987: T-31st at the U.S. Open

1988	2	2	0	0	0	0	0	72.00	
1989	1	4	1	0	0	0	0	73.75	$1,204

Best finish for 1989: 84th at the Phoenix Open

1990	1	2	0	0	0	0	0	74.50	
Period Totals	Starts	Rounds Played	Cuts Made	Wins	Top-5s	Top-10s	Top-25s	Scoring Average	Money
	620	1962	354	3	18	47	119	72.56	$578,392

John Dowdall

Year	Starts	Rounds Played	Cuts Made	Wins	Top-5s	Top-10s	Top-25s	Scoring Average	Money
1990	22	55	6	0	0	0	2	72.47	$22,215

Best finish for 1990: T-17th at the Chattanooga Classic

1992	1	2	0	0	0	0	0	75.00	
1993	22	54	6	0	0	0	0	73.43	$20,380

Best finish for 1993: T-26th at the Shell Houston Open

1994	2	4	0	0	0	0	0	77.25	
1995	1	2	0	0	0	0	0	73.00	
1997	24	61	6	0	0	0	0	73.10	$27,389

Best finish for 1997: T-31st at the United Airlines Hawaiian Open & CVS Charity Classic

Period Totals	Starts	Rounds Played	Cuts Made	Wins	Top-5s	Top-10s	Top-25s	Scoring Average	Money
	72	178	18	0	0	0	2	73.12	$69,984

Allen Doyle

Year	Starts	Rounds Played	Cuts Made	Wins	Top-5s	Top-10s	Top-25s	Scoring Average	Money
1991	2	6	1	0	0	0	0	74.17	

Best finish for 1991: T-64th at the Memorial Tournament

1992	1	2	0	0	0	0	0	76.00	
1993	1	2	0	0	0	0	0	74.50	
1994	1	4	1	0	0	0	0	73.75	

Best finish for 1994: T-64th at the Memorial Tournament

1995	2	6	1	0	0	0	0	74.67	$3,264

Best finish for 1995: 74th at the Memorial Tournament

1996	28	88	16	0	0	1	7	71.26	$136,789

Best finish for 1996: T-10th at the GTE Byron Nelson Classic

1997	28	85	13	0	0	0	0	71.80	$66,555

Best finish for 1997: T-26th at the Phoenix Open & Walt Disney World/Oldsmobile Classic

Year	Starts	Rounds Played	Cuts Made	Wins	Top-5s	Top-10s	Top-25s	Scoring Average	Money
1998	2	8	2	0	0	1	1	69.75	$39,315

Best finish for 1998: T-7th at the Deposit Guaranty Golf Classic

Year	Starts	Rounds Played	Cuts Made	Wins	Top-5s	Top-10s	Top-25s	Scoring Average	Money
2006	1	2	0	0	0	0	0	75.00	$2,000
2007	1	2	0	0	0	0	0	83.50	$2,000
Period Totals	Starts	Rounds Played	Cuts Made	Wins	Top-5s	Top-10s	Top-25s	Scoring Average	Money
	67	205	34	0	0	2	8	71.89	$249,923

James Driscoll

Year	Starts	Rounds Played	Cuts Made	Wins	Top-5s	Top-10s	Top-25s	Scoring Average	Money
1998	1	4	1	0	0	0	0	72.00	

Best finish for 1998: T-74th at the CVS Charity Classic

| 2001 | 4 | 11 | 1 | 0 | 0 | 0 | 0 | 73.36 | $7,208 |

Best finish for 2001: T-62nd at the Air Canada Championship

| 2002 | 6 | 21 | 4 | 0 | 0 | 0 | 0 | 71.29 | $34,293 |

Best finish for 2002: T-40th at the B.C. Open

| 2005 | 26 | 71 | 11 | 0 | 1 | 1 | 4 | 71.51 | $851,891 |

Best finish for 2005: 2nd at the Zurich Classic of New Orleans

| 2006 | 29 | 80 | 11 | 0 | 0 | 0 | 0 | 72.31 | $219,904 |

Best finish for 2006: T-27th at The Players Championship & Deutsche Bank Championship

| 2007 | 2 | 4 | 0 | 0 | 0 | 0 | 0 | 72.00 | |
| 2008 | 28 | 85 | 15 | 0 | 1 | 1 | 7 | 71.60 | $708,549 |

Best finish for 2008: T-5th at the AT&T Classic

Period Totals	Starts	Rounds Played	Cuts Made	Wins	Top-5s	Top-10s	Top-25s	Scoring Average	Money
	96	276	43	0	2	2	11	71.84	$1,821,846

Stan Dudas

Year	Starts	Rounds Played	Cuts Made	Wins	Top-5s	Top-10s	Top-25s	Scoring Average	Money
1958	8	26	5	0	0	0	1	73.38	$578

Best finish for 1958: T-20th at the Greenbrier Invitational

| 1959 | 3 | 10 | 2 | 0 | 0 | 0 | 1 | 73.40 | $428 |

Best finish for 1959: T-12th at the Sam Snead Festival

| 1960 | 5 | 18 | 3 | 0 | 0 | 3 | 3 | 72.83 | $1,725 |

Best finish for 1960: T-7th at the Panama Open Invitational

1964	2	5	0	0	0	0	0	74.00	
1965	1	2	0	0	0	0	0	75.00	
1966	2	4	0	0	0	0	0	77.25	
1967	2	4	0	0	0	0	0	76.75	
1968	1	2	0	0	0	0	0	75.50	
1969	3	10	2	0	0	0	0	74.90	$472

Best finish for 1969: T-69th at the PGA Championship

1973	2	5	0	0	0	0	0	76.40	
1976	1	2	0	0	0	0	0	75.00	
Period Totals	Starts	Rounds Played	Cuts Made	Wins	Top-5s	Top-10s	Top-25s	Scoring Average	Money
	30	88	12	0	0	3	5	74.10	$3,202

Bob Duden

Year	Starts	Rounds Played	Cuts Made	Wins	Top-5s	Top-10s	Top-25s	Scoring Average	Money
1958	9	31	6	0	0	1	1	73.00	$1,070

Best finish for 1958: 10th at the Tucson Open

| 1959 | 11 | 44 | 11 | 0 | 2 | 3 | 7 | 70.82 | $5,897 |

Best finish for 1959: T-2nd at the Portland Centennial Open Invitational & Hesperia Open Invitational

| 1960 | 6 | 24 | 6 | 0 | 0 | 1 | 3 | 71.17 | $2,203 |

Best finish for 1960: T-7th at the Carling Open Invitational

| 1961 | 6 | 22 | 6 | 0 | 0 | 2 | 3 | 71.41 | $2,124 |

Best finish for 1961: T-10th at the Western Open Championship & Ontario Open

| 1962 | 4 | 16 | 3 | 0 | 1 | 2 | 3 | 69.19 | $3,269 |

Best finish for 1962: T-4th at the Denver Open Invitational

| 1963 | 19 | 76 | 18 | 0 | 0 | 5 | 10 | 71.16 | $12,353 |

Best finish for 1963: T-6th at the Texas Open Invitational

| 1964 | 27 | 86 | 17 | 0 | 0 | 0 | 7 | 72.42 | $7,304 |

Best finish for 1964: T-11th at the Thunderbird Classic

| 1965 | 14 | 33 | 5 | 0 | 0 | 1 | 5 | 72.97 | $4,302 |

Best finish for 1965: T-8th at the Almaden Open

| 1966 | 14 | 37 | 7 | 0 | 0 | 0 | 0 | 73.54 | $1,836 |

Best finish for 1966: T-28th at the Portland Open Invitational

| 1967 | 6 | 14 | 1 | 0 | 0 | 0 | 0 | 75.21 | $229 |

Best finish for 1967: T-43rd at the Bing Crosby Pro-Am

| 1968 | 4 | 11 | 1 | 0 | 0 | 0 | 1 | 73.91 | $1,525 |

Best finish for 1968: T-20th at the Lucky International Open Invitational

| 1969 | 9 | 24 | 4 | 0 | 0 | 1 | 1 | 72.54 | $2,047 |

Best finish for 1969: T-9th at the Azalea Open

| 1971 | 1 | 4 | 1 | 0 | 0 | 0 | 0 | 74.75 | $258 |

Best finish for 1971: T-66th at the PGA Championship

| 1975 | 1 | 2 | 0 | 0 | 0 | 0 | 0 | 75.50 | |
| 1977 | 1 | 4 | 1 | 0 | 0 | 0 | 0 | 75.25 | $488 |

Best finish for 1977: T-54th at the PGA Championship

1978	4	6	0	0	0	0	0	75.83	$303
Period Totals	Starts	Rounds Played	Cuts Made	Wins	Top-5s	Top-10s	Top-25s	Scoring Average	Money
	136	434	87	0	3	16	41	72.22	$45,209

Jason Dufner

Year	Starts	Rounds Played	Cuts Made	Wins	Top-5s	Top-10s	Top-25s	Scoring Average	Money
2001	1	2	0	0	0	0	0	76.00	$1,000
2004	28	79	11	0	0	1	2	71.20	$317,770

Best finish for 2004: T-8th at the Chrysler Classic of Greensboro

| 2006 | 2 | 6 | 1 | 0 | 0 | 0 | 0 | 73.17 | $29,459 |

Best finish for 2006: T-40th at the U.S. Open

| 2007 | 32 | 100 | 18 | 0 | 0 | 1 | 5 | 71.45 | $574,992 |

Best finish for 2007: T-6th at the John Deere Classic

| 2008 | 16 | 49 | 8 | 0 | 0 | 0 | 2 | 70.96 | $284,138 |

Best finish for 2008: T-11th at the U.S. Bank Championship in Milwaukee

| Period Totals | Starts | Rounds Played | Cuts Made | Wins | Top-5s | Top-10s | Top-25s | Scoring Average | Money |
| | 79 | 236 | 38 | 0 | 0 | 2 | 9 | 71.35 | $1,207,358 |

Ken Duke

Year	Starts	Rounds Played	Cuts Made	Wins	Top-5s	Top-10s	Top-25s	Scoring Average	Money
1986	1	2	0	0	0	0	0	81.00	
1996	1	4	1	0	0	0	1	69.75	$8,900

Best finish for 1996: T-23rd at the Greater Vancouver Open

1997	1	2	0	0	0	0	0	78.00	$1,089
1999	2	4	0	0	0	0	0	74.50	
2002	4	12	2	0	0	0	0	72.83	$24,162

Best finish for 2002: T-31st at the Tampa Bay Classic presented by Buick

| 2004 | 30 | 87 | 14 | 0 | 0 | 1 | 2 | 72.01 | $301,309 |

Best finish for 2004: T-9th at the Reno-Tahoe Open

| 2006 | 2 | 8 | 2 | 0 | 0 | 0 | 1 | 70.50 | $138,231 |

Best finish for 2006: T-14th at the Wachovia Championship

| 2007 | 31 | 112 | 24 | 0 | 2 | 5 | 10 | 70.93 | $1,927,102 |

Best finish for 2007: 2nd at the Zurich Classic of New Orleans

| 2008 | 33 | 116 | 24 | 0 | 3 | 5 | 13 | 70.61 | $2,238,885 |

Best finish for 2008: T-2nd at the U.S. Bank Championship in Milwaukee & Ginn sur Mer Classic

| Period Totals | Starts | Rounds Played | Cuts Made | Wins | Top-5s | Top-10s | Top-25s | Scoring Average | Money |
| | 105 | 347 | 67 | 0 | 5 | 11 | 27 | 71.28 | $4,639,677 |

Doug Dunakey

Year	Starts	Rounds Played	Cuts Made	Wins	Top-5s	Top-10s	Top-25s	Scoring Average	Money
1995	1	3	1	0	0	0	0	70.67	$2,309

Best finish for 1995: T-52nd at the Quad City Classic

| 1996 | 1 | 4 | 1 | 0 | 0 | 0 | 0 | 71.00 | $2,030 |

Best finish for 1996: T-66th at the Deposit Guaranty Golf Classic

| 1997 | 1 | 2 | 0 | 0 | 0 | 0 | 0 | 72.00 | |
| 1998 | 1 | 4 | 1 | 0 | 0 | 0 | 0 | 70.00 | $6,045 |

Best finish for 1998: T-35th at the Deposit Guaranty Golf Classic

| 1999 | 32 | 87 | 12 | 0 | 1 | 1 | 4 | 72.07 | $298,069 |

Best finish for 1999: T-3rd at the Honda Classic

| 2000 | 27 | 80 | 14 | 0 | 2 | 2 | 5 | 71.40 | $393,059 |

Best finish for 2000: T-4th at the Reno-Tahoe Open

| 2001 | 32 | 81 | 9 | 0 | 0 | 0 | 0 | 72.01 | $77,793 |

Best finish for 2001: T-36th at the Canon Greater Hartford Open

2003	1	2	0	0	0	0	0	73.50	$1,000
Period Totals	Starts	Rounds Played	Cuts Made	Wins	Top-5s	Top-10s	Top-25s	Scoring Average	Money
	96	263	38	0	3	3	9	71.79	$780,305

Skip Dunaway

Year	Starts	Rounds Played	Cuts Made	Wins	Top-5s	Top-10s	Top-25s	Scoring Average	Money
1977	8	20	2	0	0	0	0	74.05	$985

Best finish for 1977: T-43rd at the Western Open

| 1978 | 5 | 16 | 2 | 0 | 0 | 0 | 0 | 73.19 | $405 |

Best finish for 1978: T-57th at the Atlanta Classic

| 1979 | 14 | 42 | 7 | 0 | 0 | 0 | 2 | 73.00 | $7,697 |

Best finish for 1979: T-25th at the Anheuser-Busch Golf Classic & Southern Open

| 1980 | 22 | 60 | 8 | 0 | 0 | 1 | 2 | 72.60 | $13,784 |

Best finish for 1980: T-9th at the Quad Cities Open

| 1981 | 21 | 54 | 7 | 0 | 0 | 0 | 0 | 73.74 | $5,033 |

Best finish for 1981: T-49th at the Kemper Open

| 1982 | 19 | 50 | 6 | 0 | 0 | 0 | 0 | 73.70 | $5,340 |

Best finish for 1982: T-36th at the Glen Campbell Los Angles Open

Period Totals	Starts	Rounds Played	Cuts Made	Wins	Top-5s	Top-10s	Top-25s	Scoring Average	Money
	89	242	32	0	0	1	4	73.31	$33,243

Billy Dunk

Year	Starts	Rounds Played	Cuts Made	Wins	Top-5s	Top-10s	Top-25s	Scoring Average	Money
1962	7	26	6	0	0	0	4	72.08	$2,668

Best finish for 1962: T-14th at the Insurance City Open Invitational

| 1963 | 7 | 28 | 6 | 0 | 1 | 2 | 3 | 71.18 | $4,495 |

Best finish for 1963: T-3rd at the Waco Turner Open Invitational

| 1964 | 12 | 35 | 6 | 0 | 0 | 1 | 2 | 73.14 | $2,188 |

Best finish for 1964: T-8th at the Greater Greensboro Open

| 1967 | 1 | 4 | 1 | 0 | 0 | 0 | 0 | 72.25 | $1,140 |

Best finish for 1967: T-26th at the Carling World Open

| 1976 | 1 | 4 | 1 | 0 | 0 | 0 | 1 | 73.00 | $6,100 |

Best finish for 1976: T-14th at the World Series Of Golf

| 1981 | 1 | 4 | 1 | 0 | 0 | 0 | 0 | 73.00 | $1,388 |

Best finish for 1981: T-35th at the British Open

Period Totals	Starts	Rounds Played	Cuts Made	Wins	Top-5s	Top-10s	Top-25s	Scoring Average	Money
	29	101	21	0	1	3	10	72.28	$17,978

Scott Dunlap

Year	Starts	Rounds Played	Cuts Made	Wins	Top-5s	Top-10s	Top-25s	Scoring Average	Money
1992	1	2	0	0	0	0	0	74.00	$1,000
1995	2	8	2	0	0	1	1	70.25	$44,000

Best finish for 1995: 8th at the Bell Canadian Open

| 1996 | 28 | 80 | 13 | 0 | 1 | 2 | 3 | 71.39 | $169,682 |

Best finish for 1996: T-3rd at the Bell Canadian Open

| 1997 | 32 | 92 | 14 | 0 | 0 | 0 | 3 | 71.88 | $121,807 |

Best finish for 1997: T-13th at the Bell Canadian Open

| 1998 | 1 | 4 | 1 | 0 | 0 | 0 | 0 | 73.00 | $16,499 |

Best finish for 1998: T-29th at the British Open

| 1999 | 24 | 86 | 19 | 0 | 1 | 3 | 7 | 71.43 | $533,027 |

Best finish for 1999: T-3rd at the Doral-Ryder Open

| 2000 | 30 | 106 | 23 | 0 | 1 | 5 | 12 | 70.52 | $1,041,916 |

Best finish for 2000: T-3rd at the Players Championship

| 2001 | 28 | 79 | 14 | 0 | 0 | 0 | 4 | 71.16 | $420,777 |

Best finish for 2001: T-11th at the BellSouth Classic

| 2002 | 30 | 72 | 7 | 0 | 0 | 1 | 1 | 72.54 | $145,454 |

Best finish for 2002: T-10th at the Michelob Championship at Kingsmill

| 2003 | 1 | 4 | 1 | 0 | 0 | 0 | 0 | 74.25 | $7,600 |

Best finish for 2003: T-74th at the BellSouth Classic

| 2004 | 1 | 2 | 0 | 0 | 0 | 0 | 0 | 73.50 | |
| 2005 | 3 | 9 | 2 | 0 | 0 | 1 | 2 | 71.22 | $204,500 |

Best finish for 2005: T-6th at the BellSouth Classic

2006	1	2	0	0	0	0	0	73.00	
2007	1	2	0	0	0	0	0	73.00	
2008	1	2	0	0	0	0	0	72.50	

Period Totals	Starts	Rounds Played	Cuts Made	Wins	Top-5s	Top-10s	Top-25s	Scoring Average	Money
	184	550	96	0	3	13	33	71.47	$2,706,263

Joe Durant

Year	Starts	Rounds Played	Cuts Made	Wins	Top-5s	Top-10s	Top-25s	Scoring Average	Money
1987	1	2	0	0	0	0	0	72.50	
1993	18	43	2	0	0	0	0	74.19	$4,055

Best finish for 1993: T-47th at the Buick Invitational of California

| 1997 | 31 | 98 | 19 | 0 | 1 | 3 | 7 | 71.23 | $240,921 |

Best finish for 1997: T-5th at the Honda Classic

| 1998 | 24 | 79 | 15 | 1 | 1 | 2 | 6 | 71.30 | $653,119 |

Best finish for 1998: Win at the Motorola Western Open

| 1999 | 26 | 79 | 13 | 0 | 0 | 0 | 2 | 72.05 | $193,062 |

Best finish for 1999: T-12th at the John Deere Classic

| 2000 | 28 | 94 | 18 | 0 | 1 | 4 | 7 | 70.48 | $612,882 |

Best finish for 2000: 5th at the Tampa Bay Classic

| 2001 | 25 | 80 | 14 | 2 | 4 | 6 | 9 | 70.31 | $2,388,544 |

Best finish for 2001: Win at the Bob Hope Chrysler Classic & Genuity Championship

| 2002 | 28 | 86 | 16 | 0 | 0 | 0 | 5 | 71.01 | $433,217 |

Best finish for 2002: T-11th at the Honda Classic

| 2003 | 28 | 96 | 19 | 0 | 1 | 4 | 7 | 70.41 | $1,123,976 |

Best finish for 2003: T-2nd at the FBR Capital Open

Year	Starts	Rounds Played	Cuts Made	Wins	Top-5s	Top-10s	Top-25s	Scoring Average	Money
2004	26	85	16	0	2	3	7	70.40	$954,547

Best finish for 2004: 4th at the Ford Championship at Doral & Chrysler Championship

2005	25	81	15	0	2	3	5	71.01	$1,044,956

Best finish for 2005: T-3rd at the Bank of America Colonial

2006	28	101	22	1	6	7	7	70.75	$2,811,139

Best finish for 2006: Win at the FUNAI Classic at the Walt Disney World Resort

2007	28	87	17	0	0	0	7	71.76	$732,176

Best finish for 2007: T-14th at the WGC-Bridgestone Invitational

2008	28	92	18	0	1	2	6	71.24	$802,568

Best finish for 2008: 5th at the Children's Miracle Network Classic

Period Totals	Starts	Rounds Played	Cuts Made	Wins	Top-5s	Top-10s	Top-25s	Scoring Average	Money
	344	1103	204	4	19	34	75	71.11	$11,995,161

David Duval

Year	Starts	Rounds Played	Cuts Made	Wins	Top-5s	Top-10s	Top-25s	Scoring Average	Money
1990	1	4	1	0	0	0	0	73.25	

Best finish for 1990: T-56th at the U.S. Open

1992	5	14	2	0	0	0	2	72.14	

Best finish for 1992: T-13th at the BellSouth Classic

1993	5	18	4	0	0	0	1	71.06	$27,181

Best finish for 1993: T-19th at the Federal Express St. Jude Classic

1994	6	20	4	0	0	1	1	72.20	$44,006

Best finish for 1994: T-8th at the Motorola Western Open

1995	26	89	20	0	5	8	14	70.76	$882,636

Best finish for 1995: T-2nd at the AT&T Pebble Beach National Pro-Am, Bob Hope Chrysler Classic & Memorial Tournament

1996	23	75	16	0	6	6	11	70.45	$977,079

Best finish for 1996: 2nd at the Memorial Tournament & Bell Canadian Open

1997	29	98	21	3	6	7	14	70.37	$1,890,308

Best finish for 1997: Win at the Michelob Championship at Kingsmill, Walt Disney World/Oldsmobile Classic & The Tour Championship

1998	23	83	19	4	7	12	17	69.60	$2,592,531

Best finish for 1998: Win at the Tucson Chrysler Classic, Shell Houston Open, NEC World Series of Golf & Michelob Championship at Kingsmill

1999	21	74	20	4	7	12	17	70.24	$3,641,906

Best finish for 1999: Win at the Mercedes Championships, Bob Hope Chrysler Classic, The Players Championship & BellSouth Classic

2000	19	67	17	1	7	9	14	69.90	$2,462,846

Best finish for 2000: Win at the Buick Challenge

2001	20	74	18	1	4	7	11	69.58	$2,801,760

Best finish for 2001: Win at the British Open

2002	24	75	15	0	1	2	7	70.60	$844,045

Best finish for 2002: T-4th at the Memorial Tournament

2003	20	44	4	0	0	0	0	74.57	$94,284

Best finish for 2003: T-28th at the FBR Capital Open

2004	9	22	3	0	0	0	1	72.91	$124,044

Best finish for 2004: T-13th at the Deutsche Bank Championship

2005	20	42	1	0	0	0	0	75.62	$20,134

Best finish for 2005: T-60th at the Valero Texas Open

2006	24	69	11	0	0	0	3	72.10	$325,526

Best finish for 2006: T-16th at the U.S. Open

2007	7	23	4	0	0	0	0	71.52	$71,945

Best finish for 2007: T-36th at the AT&T Pebble Beach National Pro-Am

2008	20	51	5	0	0	0	1	73.73	$114,974

Best finish for 2008: T-22nd at the Viking Classic

Period Totals	Starts	Rounds Played	Cuts Made	Wins	Top-5s	Top-10s	Top-25s	Scoring Average	Money
	302	942	185	13	43	64	114	71.18	$16,915,205

R.W. Eaks

Year	Starts	Rounds Played	Cuts Made	Wins	Top-5s	Top-10s	Top-25s	Scoring Average	Money
1980	8	13	1	0	0	1	1	74.00	$4,363

Best finish for 1980: T-8th at the World Disney World National Team Championship

1981	9	21	2	0	0	0	1	73.81	$2,443

Best finish for 1981: T-15th at the Tallahassee Open

1986	1	2	0	0	0	0	0	85.50	$600
1988	1	2	0	0	0	0	0	76.50	
1990	2	4	0	0	0	0	0	74.50	$1,000
1991	1	3	0	0	0	0	0	71.33	
1993	1	4	1	0	0	0	0	70.75	$5,414

Best finish for 1993: T-32nd at the Phoenix Open

1994	1	4	1	0	0	0	0	72.25	$2,352

Best finish for 1994: 73rd at the Phoenix Open

1995	1	2	0	0	0	0	0	72.00	
1998	33	80	11	0	0	2	4	71.86	$199,499

Best finish for 1998: T-7th at the United Airlines Hawaiian Open

Year	Starts	Rounds Played	Cuts Made	Wins	Top-5s	Top-10s	Top-25s	Scoring Average	Money
1999	16	41	6	0	0	0	1	71.51	$77,524

Best finish for 1999: T-20th at the Touchstone Energy Tucson Open

| 2000 | 1 | 4 | 1 | 0 | 0 | 0 | 0 | 71.75 | $4,180 |

Best finish for 2000: T-63rd at the B.C. Open

Period Totals	Starts	Rounds Played	Cuts Made	Wins	Top-5s	Top-10s	Top-25s	Scoring Average	Money
	75	180	23	0	0	3	7	72.40	$297,376

Bob Eastwood

Year	Starts	Rounds Played	Cuts Made	Wins	Top-5s	Top-10s	Top-25s	Scoring Average	Money
1969	7	20	3	0	0	0	0	76.10	$340

Best finish for 1969: T-56th at the Alameda County Open

| 1972 | 29 | 83 | 13 | 0 | 1 | 1 | 1 | 74.25 | $8,583 |

Best finish for 1972: T-5th at the Sahara Invitational

| 1973 | 28 | 75 | 11 | 0 | 0 | 0 | 4 | 73.35 | $8,742 |

Best finish for 1973: T-17th at the Shrine-Robinson Golf Classic

| 1974 | 31 | 91 | 17 | 0 | 0 | 1 | 4 | 72.37 | $13,835 |

Best finish for 1974: T-9th at the Bing Crosby Pro-Am

| 1975 | 25 | 88 | 19 | 0 | 0 | 1 | 4 | 72.33 | $16,511 |

Best finish for 1975: T-8th at the Byron Nelson Golf Classic

| 1976 | 22 | 64 | 11 | 0 | 2 | 2 | 2 | 72.72 | $14,992 |

Best finish for 1976: T-5th at the Tallahassee Open & Canadian Open

| 1977 | 23 | 76 | 16 | 0 | 0 | 0 | 3 | 72.63 | $18,877 |

Best finish for 1977: T-11th at the Houston Open & Sammy Davis, Jr. - Greater Hartford Open

| 1978 | 23 | 73 | 13 | 0 | 0 | 2 | 5 | 72.21 | $21,443 |

Best finish for 1978: T-9th at the Ed McMahon Quad City Open & Sammy Davis, Jr. - Greater Hartford Open

| 1979 | 21 | 63 | 11 | 0 | 2 | 2 | 6 | 72.79 | $29,630 |

Best finish for 1979: T-5th at the Tallahassee Open & Buick Goodwrench Open

| 1980 | 26 | 84 | 16 | 0 | 0 | 0 | 4 | 72.05 | $36,751 |

Best finish for 1980: T-11th at the Greater Greensboro Open & Pleasant Valley Jimmy Fund Classic

| 1981 | 33 | 108 | 22 | 0 | 0 | 2 | 9 | 71.67 | $66,617 |

Best finish for 1981: T-6th at the LaJet Classic

| 1982 | 31 | 109 | 23 | 0 | 1 | 5 | 11 | 71.37 | $92,283 |

Best finish for 1982: T-5th at the Colonial National Invitational

| 1983 | 33 | 109 | 23 | 0 | 2 | 4 | 8 | 71.87 | $157,640 |

Best finish for 1983: 2nd at the Tournament Players Championship

| 1984 | 32 | 97 | 17 | 2 | 3 | 3 | 4 | 72.43 | $235,842 |

Best finish for 1984: Win at the USF&G Classic & Danny Thomas Memphis Classic

| 1985 | 29 | 88 | 17 | 1 | 1 | 1 | 8 | 72.35 | $153,839 |

Best finish for 1985: Win at the Byron Nelson Golf Classic

| 1986 | 29 | 78 | 15 | 0 | 0 | 1 | 5 | 71.92 | $72,934 |

Best finish for 1986: T-6th at the AT&T Pebble Beach Pro-Am

| 1987 | 28 | 93 | 19 | 0 | 1 | 2 | 7 | 71.22 | $114,897 |

Best finish for 1987: T-2nd at the Southwest Golf Classic

| 1988 | 30 | 93 | 17 | 0 | 0 | 2 | 4 | 72.08 | $97,004 |

Best finish for 1988: T-6th at the Hawaiian Open & Manufactures Hanover Westchester Classic

| 1989 | 30 | 84 | 12 | 0 | 1 | 2 | 3 | 71.86 | $84,088 |

Best finish for 1989: T-5th at the Buick Open

| 1990 | 29 | 86 | 15 | 0 | 0 | 1 | 6 | 72.02 | $123,908 |

Best finish for 1990: T-8th at the Honda Classic

| 1991 | 28 | 75 | 10 | 0 | 0 | 0 | 2 | 72.52 | $65,215 |

Best finish for 1991: T-15th at the Kmart Greater Greensboro Open

| 1992 | 16 | 49 | 8 | 0 | 1 | 1 | 5 | 70.90 | $83,818 |

Best finish for 1992: T-2nd at the Deposit Guaranty Classic

| 1993 | 16 | 38 | 3 | 0 | 0 | 0 | 1 | 73.03 | $24,289 |

Best finish for 1993: T-18th at the United Airlines Hawaiian Open

| 1994 | 6 | 12 | 1 | 0 | 0 | 0 | 0 | 73.33 | $6,737 |

Best finish for 1994: T-28th at the GTE Byron Nelson Classic

1995	4	8	0	0	0	0	0	74.88	
Period Totals	Starts	Rounds Played	Cuts Made	Wins	Top-5s	Top-10s	Top-25s	Scoring Average	Money
	609	1844	332	3	15	33	106	72.29	$1,548,817

Danny Edwards

Year	Starts	Rounds Played	Cuts Made	Wins	Top-5s	Top-10s	Top-25s	Scoring Average	Money
1973	1	4	1	0	0	0	0	74.00	

Best finish for 1973: T-39th at the British Open

| 1974 | 1 | 4 | 1 | 0 | 1 | 1 | 1 | 73.00 | $5,520 |

Best finish for 1974: T-5th at the British Open

| 1975 | 30 | 108 | 23 | 0 | 0 | 0 | 11 | 72.25 | $28,260 |

Best finish for 1975: T-13th at the Byron Nelson Golf Classic

| 1976 | 31 | 96 | 17 | 0 | 1 | 1 | 8 | 72.49 | $26,175 |

Best finish for 1976: T-4th at the Ohio Kings Island Open

| 1977 | 26 | 94 | 22 | 1 | 1 | 2 | 15 | 71.79 | $92,336 |

Best finish for 1977: Win at the Greater Greensboro Open

Year	Starts	Rounds Played	Cuts Made	Wins	Top-5s	Top-10s	Top-25s	Scoring Average	Money
1978	29	100	21	0	1	3	11	71.93	$57,443

Best finish for 1978: 5th at the Colgate Hall Of Fame Classic

| 1979 | 16 | 52 | 9 | 0 | 1 | 1 | 2 | 72.31 | $21,238 |

Best finish for 1979: 4th at the Colgate Hall Of Fame Classic

| 1980 | 26 | 94 | 23 | 1 | 3 | 4 | 11 | 71.38 | $104,696 |

Best finish for 1980: Win at the World Disney World National Team Championship

| 1981 | 26 | 80 | 16 | 0 | 2 | 4 | 9 | 72.10 | $82,567 |

Best finish for 1981: 3rd at the World Disney World National Team Championship

| 1982 | 22 | 76 | 15 | 1 | 2 | 4 | 8 | 71.96 | $124,655 |

Best finish for 1982: Win at the Greater Greensboro Open

| 1983 | 23 | 81 | 17 | 1 | 2 | 3 | 9 | 71.35 | $105,542 |

Best finish for 1983: Win at the Miller High-Life Quad Cities Open

| 1984 | 26 | 88 | 19 | 0 | 1 | 1 | 5 | 72.23 | $54,472 |

Best finish for 1984: T-5th at the Pensacola Open

| 1985 | 28 | 99 | 24 | 1 | 3 | 6 | 9 | 71.34 | $206,891 |

Best finish for 1985: Win at the Pensacola Open

| 1986 | 30 | 95 | 21 | 0 | 1 | 4 | 11 | 71.69 | $135,272 |

Best finish for 1986: T-4th at the MONY Tournament Of Champions

| 1987 | 25 | 81 | 16 | 0 | 2 | 3 | 7 | 71.53 | $154,408 |

Best finish for 1987: T-2nd at the Pensacola Open

| 1988 | 20 | 61 | 12 | 0 | 0 | 0 | 0 | 71.92 | $36,637 |

Best finish for 1988: T-27th at the Anheuser-Busch Golf Classic

| 1989 | 12 | 28 | 3 | 0 | 0 | 0 | 1 | 72.61 | $12,917 |

Best finish for 1989: T-19th at the Hawaiian Open

| 1990 | 3 | 10 | 2 | 0 | 0 | 0 | 0 | 73.40 | $9,343 |

Best finish for 1990: T-33rd at the AT&T Pebble Beach Pro-Am

| 1991 | 3 | 8 | 1 | 0 | 0 | 0 | 0 | 72.88 | $5,423 |

Best finish for 1991: T-35th at the AT&T Pebble Beach Pro-Am

| 1992 | 8 | 19 | 3 | 0 | 0 | 0 | 0 | 71.84 | $10,852 |

Best finish for 1992: T-36th at the Kmart Greater Greensboro Open

| 1993 | 3 | 8 | 1 | 0 | 0 | 0 | 0 | 72.25 | $1,557 |

Best finish for 1993: T-32nd at the Deposit Guaranty Classic

1994	3	6	0	0	0	0	0	72.67	
1995	2	4	0	0	0	0	0	74.00	
1996	2	4	0	0	0	0	0	74.25	
1997	6	14	1	0	0	0	0	73.50	$2,688

Best finish for 1997: T-72nd at the LaCantera Texas Open

| 1998 | 13 | 27 | 1 | 0 | 0 | 0 | 0 | 73.26 | $4,422 |

Best finish for 1998: T-67th at the Bell Canadian Open

1999	7	14	0	0	0	0	0	74.64	
2000	1	2	0	0	0	0	0	77.00	
Period Totals	Starts	Rounds Played	Cuts Made	Wins	Top-5s	Top-10s	Top-25s	Scoring Average	Money
	423	1357	269	5	21	37	118	72.01	$1,283,313

David Edwards

Year	Starts	Rounds Played	Cuts Made	Wins	Top-5s	Top-10s	Top-25s	Scoring Average	Money
1978	2	6	1	0	0	0	0	73.67	

Best finish for 1978: T-31st at the Greater Greensboro Open

| 1979 | 27 | 89 | 18 | 0 | 0 | 4 | 5 | 71.94 | $43,456 |

Best finish for 1979: T-6th at the Bay Hill Citrus Classic

| 1980 | 29 | 79 | 13 | 1 | 1 | 4 | 6 | 72.34 | $67,310 |

Best finish for 1980: Win at the World Disney World National Team Championship

| 1981 | 29 | 91 | 18 | 0 | 3 | 5 | 6 | 72.15 | $84,661 |

Best finish for 1981: 3rd at the Bob Hope Chrysler Classic & World Disney World National Team Championship

| 1982 | 21 | 68 | 13 | 0 | 1 | 4 | 5 | 71.96 | $49,896 |

Best finish for 1982: T-5th at the Georgia-Pacific Atlanta Golf Classic

| 1983 | 25 | 88 | 18 | 0 | 2 | 5 | 9 | 71.53 | $114,137 |

Best finish for 1983: T-2nd at the USF&G Classic

| 1984 | 19 | 67 | 14 | 1 | 4 | 5 | 9 | 71.22 | $236,061 |

Best finish for 1984: Win at the Los Angeles Open

| 1985 | 26 | 80 | 12 | 0 | 0 | 0 | 0 | 72.16 | $22,106 |

Best finish for 1985: T-30th at the Bank of Boston Classic

| 1986 | 23 | 66 | 15 | 0 | 2 | 4 | 7 | 72.35 | $122,079 |

Best finish for 1986: T-4th at the Houston Open

| 1987 | 21 | 66 | 14 | 0 | 2 | 3 | 8 | 71.30 | $148,217 |

Best finish for 1987: T-2nd at the Southwest Golf Classic

| 1988 | 23 | 81 | 16 | 0 | 1 | 1 | 4 | 71.56 | $151,558 |

Best finish for 1988: 2nd at the Bob Hope Chrysler Classic

| 1989 | 27 | 91 | 17 | 0 | 1 | 2 | 8 | 71.13 | $239,728 |

Best finish for 1989: 2nd at the Southwestern Bell Colonial

| 1990 | 22 | 73 | 13 | 0 | 0 | 4 | 7 | 71.49 | $166,028 |

Best finish for 1990: T-7th at the USF&G Classic

Year	Starts	Rounds Played	Cuts Made	Wins	Top-5s	Top-10s	Top-25s	Scoring Average	Money
1991	27	97	20	0	2	5	11	70.23	$396,694

Best finish for 1991: T-2nd at the Southwestern Bell Colonial & Canadian Open

| 1992 | 26 | 94 | 21 | 1 | 3 | 4 | 9 | 70.40 | $515,070 |

Best finish for 1992: Win at the Memorial Tournament

| 1993 | 22 | 80 | 18 | 1 | 3 | 6 | 11 | 70.46 | $655,210 |

Best finish for 1993: Win at the MCI Heritage Classic

| 1994 | 24 | 86 | 21 | 0 | 3 | 6 | 12 | 70.73 | $467,674 |

Best finish for 1994: T-2nd at the GTE Byron Nelson Classic

| 1995 | 22 | 74 | 15 | 0 | 0 | 2 | 7 | 70.77 | $225,857 |

Best finish for 1995: T-7th at the MCI Classic & Las Vegas Invitational

| 1996 | 24 | 82 | 16 | 0 | 1 | 2 | 6 | 71.15 | $204,474 |

Best finish for 1996: T-5th at the Deposit Guaranty Golf Classic

| 1997 | 23 | 70 | 11 | 0 | 1 | 1 | 5 | 71.07 | $292,096 |

Best finish for 1997: T-2nd at the Las Vegas Invitational

| 1998 | 24 | 76 | 13 | 0 | 0 | 0 | 2 | 71.89 | $97,252 |

Best finish for 1998: T-18th at the Greater Milwaukee Open

| 1999 | 10 | 29 | 5 | 0 | 0 | 0 | 2 | 71.21 | $70,249 |

Best finish for 1999: T-17th at the Michelob Championship at Kingsmill

| 2000 | 15 | 36 | 4 | 0 | 0 | 0 | 0 | 72.28 | $44,194 |

Best finish for 2000: T-35th at the AT&T Pebble Beach

| 2001 | 1 | 2 | 0 | 0 | 0 | 0 | 0 | 79.50 | |
| 2002 | 11 | 33 | 6 | 0 | 0 | 0 | 1 | 70.82 | $89,285 |

Best finish for 2002: T-19th at the FedEx St. Jude Classic

| 2003 | 13 | 42 | 8 | 0 | 0 | 0 | 1 | 71.45 | $129,370 |

Best finish for 2003: T-23rd at the Bell Canadian Open

| 2004 | 13 | 43 | 9 | 0 | 0 | 0 | 0 | 71.35 | $123,681 |

Best finish for 2004: T-29th at the Reno-Tahoe Open

| 2005 | 9 | 25 | 3 | 0 | 0 | 0 | 1 | 71.76 | $62,459 |

Best finish for 2005: T-20th at the B.C. Open

| 2006 | 3 | 9 | 1 | 0 | 0 | 0 | 0 | 72.11 | $16,364 |

Best finish for 2006: T-30th at the Chrysler Classic of Tucson

Period Totals	Starts	Rounds Played	Cuts Made	Wins	Top-5s	Top-10s	Top-25s	Scoring Average	Money
	561	1823	353	4	30	67	142	71.40	$4,835,166

Jerry Edwards

Year	Starts	Rounds Played	Cuts Made	Wins	Top-5s	Top-10s	Top-25s	Scoring Average	Money
1962	2	6	1	0	0	0	1	75.00	$803

Best finish for 1962: T-16th at the Oklahoma City Open Invitational

| 1963 | 10 | 40 | 10 | 0 | 0 | 2 | 4 | 72.35 | $6,023 |

Best finish for 1963: T-6th at the Colonial National Invitational

| 1964 | 30 | 106 | 22 | 0 | 1 | 3 | 11 | 72.57 | $14,355 |

Best finish for 1964: 2nd at the Dallas Open

| 1965 | 20 | 56 | 8 | 0 | 0 | 0 | 3 | 73.41 | $3,515 |

Best finish for 1965: T-15th at the Colonial National Invitational

| 1966 | 13 | 41 | 7 | 0 | 0 | 0 | 1 | 73.56 | $1,515 |

Best finish for 1966: T-15th at the Texas Open Invitational

| 1967 | 22 | 70 | 10 | 0 | 1 | 1 | 2 | 73.53 | $8,304 |

Best finish for 1967: T-4th at the Cleveland Open

| 1968 | 7 | 20 | 2 | 0 | 0 | 0 | 0 | 74.55 | $200 |

Best finish for 1968: T-53rd at the Colonial National Invitational

| 1969 | 13 | 35 | 5 | 0 | 0 | 0 | 1 | 73.83 | $1,598 |

Best finish for 1969: T-25th at the Indian Ridge Hospital Open

| 1970 | 3 | 8 | 1 | 0 | 0 | 0 | 0 | 75.13 | $143 |

Best finish for 1970: T-61st at the Byron Nelson Golf Classic

Period Totals	Starts	Rounds Played	Cuts Made	Wins	Top-5s	Top-10s	Top-25s	Scoring Average	Money
	120	382	66	0	2	6	23	73.26	$36,456

Joel Edwards

Year	Starts	Rounds Played	Cuts Made	Wins	Top-5s	Top-10s	Top-25s	Scoring Average	Money
1984	1	2	0	0	0	0	0	75.50	$600
1985	2	4	0	0	0	0	0	74.50	
1987	2	4	0	0	0	0	0	75.75	$600
1988	1	2	0	0	0	0	0	72.00	
1989	27	71	10	0	0	0	3	71.59	$46,851

Best finish for 1989: T-14th at the Buick Open & Chattanooga Classic

| 1990 | 32 | 86 | 11 | 0 | 0 | 2 | 4 | 72.05 | $109,809 |

Best finish for 1990: T-7th at the Kemper Open

| 1991 | 30 | 86 | 13 | 0 | 1 | 1 | 5 | 71.36 | $106,820 |

Best finish for 1991: T-5th at the USF&G Classic

| 1992 | 19 | 54 | 8 | 0 | 1 | 2 | 3 | 71.26 | $107,264 |

Best finish for 1992: T-2nd at the B.C. Open

Year	Starts	Rounds Played	Cuts Made	Wins	Top-5s	Top-10s	Top-25s	Scoring Average	Money
1993	30	90	16	0	0	0	5	71.88	$151,823

Best finish for 1993: T-11th at the Players Championship

| 1994 | 28 | 85 | 13 | 0 | 0 | 2 | 3 | 72.20 | $139,141 |

Best finish for 1994: 6th at the Kemper Open

| 1995 | 31 | 95 | 16 | 0 | 0 | 1 | 2 | 71.72 | $114,285 |

Best finish for 1995: 7th at the Buick Open

| 1996 | 27 | 94 | 20 | 0 | 1 | 2 | 6 | 71.23 | $248,450 |

Best finish for 1996: T-4th at the Freeport-McDermott Classic

| 1997 | 31 | 92 | 14 | 0 | 0 | 0 | 3 | 71.80 | $114,856 |

Best finish for 1997: T-11th at the Freeport-McDermott Classic

| 1998 | 2 | 4 | 0 | 0 | 0 | 0 | 0 | 73.00 | |
| 2000 | 29 | 99 | 19 | 0 | 2 | 2 | 9 | 70.45 | $638,422 |

Best finish for 2000: T-3rd at the Shell Houston Open

| 2001 | 30 | 99 | 19 | 1 | 2 | 3 | 8 | 70.09 | $1,193,528 |

Best finish for 2001: Win at the Air Canada Championship

| 2002 | 28 | 101 | 22 | 0 | 2 | 4 | 10 | 70.14 | $1,077,651 |

Best finish for 2002: T-5th at the Canon Greater Hartford Open & Valero Texas Open

| 2003 | 23 | 60 | 7 | 0 | 0 | 0 | 2 | 71.73 | $143,382 |

Best finish for 2003: T-18th at the B.C. Open

| 2004 | 11 | 32 | 5 | 0 | 0 | 0 | 0 | 71.47 | $83,572 |

Best finish for 2004: T-29th at the Valero Texas Open

| 2005 | 1 | 2 | 0 | 0 | 0 | 0 | 0 | 72.00 | |
| 2006 | 3 | 10 | 2 | 0 | 0 | 0 | 0 | 72.40 | $11,760 |

Best finish for 2006: T-66th at the B.C. Open

2007	4	8	0	0	0	0	0	75.50	
2008	1	2	0	0	0	0	0	76.50	
Period Totals	Starts	Rounds Played	Cuts Made	Wins	Top-5s	Top-10s	Top-25s	Scoring Average	Money
	393	1182	195	1	9	19	63	71.39	$4,288,814

David Eger

Year	Starts	Rounds Played	Cuts Made	Wins	Top-5s	Top-10s	Top-25s	Scoring Average	Money
1978	15	39	5	0	0	0	0	73.77	$1,633

Best finish for 1978: T-32nd at the Greater Milwaukee Open

| 1979 | 12 | 36 | 6 | 0 | 1 | 1 | 1 | 72.47 | $12,804 |

Best finish for 1979: T-5th at the American Optical Classic

| 1980 | 27 | 75 | 12 | 0 | 0 | 0 | 0 | 72.85 | $12,359 |

Best finish for 1980: T-26th at the Hawaiian Open & Pleasant Valley Jimmy Fund Classic

| 1981 | 18 | 48 | 6 | 0 | 0 | 0 | 0 | 73.29 | $4,007 |

Best finish for 1981: T-37th at the Quad Cities Open

1989	1	2	0	0	0	0	0	81.00	
1992	1	2	0	0	0	0	0	75.50	
1998	1	2	0	0	0	0	0	74.50	
Period Totals	Starts	Rounds Played	Cuts Made	Wins	Top-5s	Top-10s	Top-25s	Scoring Average	Money
	75	204	29	0	1	1	1	73.19	$30,803

Bill Eggers

Year	Starts	Rounds Played	Cuts Made	Wins	Top-5s	Top-10s	Top-25s	Scoring Average	Money
1958	2	5	0	0	0	0	0	76.60	
1959	2	6	2	0	0	0	0	75.50	$043

Best finish for 1959: T-108 at the Bing Crosby National

| 1960 | 6 | 21 | 6 | 0 | 0 | 1 | 2 | 71.67 | $1,251 |

Best finish for 1960: T-9th at the Orange County Open Invitational

| 1962 | 5 | 20 | 5 | 0 | 0 | 0 | 1 | 70.80 | $1,432 |

Best finish for 1962: T-18th at the Seattle World's Fair Open Invitational

| 1963 | 10 | 39 | 8 | 0 | 1 | 2 | 6 | 71.54 | $9,880 |

Best finish for 1963: T-2nd at the Denver Open Invitational

1964	10	18	0	0	0	0	0	75.61	
1965	2	4	0	0	0	0	0	75.75	
1966	2	7	1	0	0	0	0	74.71	$412

Best finish for 1966: T-28th at the Portland Open Invitational

1971	1	4	0	0	0	0	0	74.25	
Period Totals	Starts	Rounds Played	Cuts Made	Wins	Top-5s	Top-10s	Top-25s	Scoring Average	Money
	40	124	22	0	1	3	9	72.83	$13,018

Dave Eichelberger

Year	Starts	Rounds Played	Cuts Made	Wins	Top-5s	Top-10s	Top-25s	Scoring Average	Money
1965	1	2	0	0	0	0	0	78.50	
1966	1	2	0	0	0	0	0	78.00	
1967	11	38	8	0	0	0	0	73.42	$2,798

Best finish for 1967: T-29th at the Atlanta Classic

| 1968 | 33 | 115 | 24 | 0 | 0 | 1 | 9 | 72.15 | $13,071 |

Best finish for 1968: T-7th at the Rebel Yell Open

Year	Starts	Rounds Played	Cuts Made	Wins	Top-5s	Top-10s	Top-25s	Scoring Average	Money
1969	28	96	20	0	0	0	2	72.61	$9,338

Best finish for 1969: T-20th at the Philadelphia Classic

1970	33	107	21	0	0	3	8	72.04	$21,999

Best finish for 1970: T-9th at the National 4 Ball Championship PGA Players & Robinson Open Golf Classic

1971	34	122	29	1	3	8	17	71.96	$103,946

Best finish for 1971: Win at the Greater Milwaukee Open

1972	37	120	23	0	2	2	6	72.89	$34,587

Best finish for 1972: T-2nd at the Greater New Orleans Open

1973	35	126	26	0	3	6	13	71.98	$58,439

Best finish for 1973: 2nd at the Sahara Invitational

1974	35	117	25	0	0	3	7	72.44	$27,002

Best finish for 1974: T-7th at the Bing Crosby Pro-Am

1975	23	67	10	0	1	1	2	73.09	$12,780

Best finish for 1975: 2nd at the Ed McMahon Quad City Open

1976	29	90	19	0	1	2	8	72.52	$25,814

Best finish for 1976: T-3rd at the Greater Milwaukee Open

1977	30	104	22	1	1	4	7	72.22	$59,742

Best finish for 1977: Win at the Greater Milwaukee Open

1978	33	116	25	0	3	5	10	71.78	$64,905

Best finish for 1978: T-5th at the Greater Greensboro Open, Kemper Open & American Express Westchester Classic

1979	36	108	19	0	1	2	7	72.44	$43,787

Best finish for 1979: 3rd at the Buick Goodwrench Open

1980	34	110	22	1	3	5	10	71.83	$123,852

Best finish for 1980: Win at the Bay Hill Classic

1981	35	118	23	1	1	2	5	71.97	$61,077

Best finish for 1981: Win at the Tallahassee Open

1982	31	106	22	0	0	1	8	71.58	$57,784

Best finish for 1982: T-8th at the Miller High-Life Quad Cities Open

1983	33	104	18	0	0	2	4	72.50	$43,093

Best finish for 1983: T-8th at the Hawaiian Open & Southern Open

1984	33	85	9	0	0	0	0	74.41	$9,934

Best finish for 1984: T-31st at the Southern Open

1985	30	78	8	0	0	0	1	73.60	$14,060

Best finish for 1985: T-11th at the B.C. Open

1986	26	72	14	0	0	0	3	72.46	$31,991

Best finish for 1986: T-23rd at the Federal Express St. Jude Classic & Pensacola Open

1987	33	99	18	0	0	0	5	72.05	$55,247

Best finish for 1987: T-13th at the Beatrice Western Open

1988	30	94	18	0	0	2	7	71.53	$110,510

Best finish for 1988: T-6th at the Hertz Bay Hill Classic

1989	34	99	16	0	2	2	4	72.29	$106,434

Best finish for 1989: T-4th at the Kmart Greater Greensboro Open & B.C. Open

1990	35	100	15	0	0	1	4	72.24	$80,692

Best finish for 1990: T-8th at the Chattanooga Classic

1991	15	31	0	0	0	0	0	74.13	
1992	10	16	0	0	0	0	0	78.13	
1993	5	11	1	0	0	0	0	77.64	$1,640

Best finish for 1993: T-87th at the Buick Invitational of California

1995	1	3	0	0	0	0	0	75.33	
2000	1	4	1	0	0	0	0	75.75	$11,760

Best finish for 2000: T-57th at the U.S. Open

2004	1	2	0	0	0	0	0	78.50	
Period Totals	Starts	Rounds Played	Cuts Made	Wins	Top-5s	Top-10s	Top-25s	Scoring Average	Money
	786	2462	456	4	21	52	147	72.45	$1,186,282

Steve Eichstaedt

Year	Starts	Rounds Played	Cuts Made	Wins	Top-5s	Top-10s	Top-25s	Scoring Average	Money
1968	5	18	3	0	0	0	1	73.78	$1,150

Best finish for 1968: T-19th at the Los Angeles Open Invitational

1970	14	40	6	0	1	1	1	73.30	$18,439

Best finish for 1970: 2nd at the Cleveland Open

1971	16	41	4	0	0	0	0	74.22	$1,494

Best finish for 1971: T-38th at the Glen Campbell Los Angles Open

1977	1	2	0	0	0	0	0	77.50	$500
Period Totals	Starts	Rounds Played	Cuts Made	Wins	Top-5s	Top-10s	Top-25s	Scoring Average	Money
	36	101	13	0	1	1	2	73.84	$21,583

Brad Elder

Year	Starts	Rounds Played	Cuts Made	Wins	Top-5s	Top-10s	Top-25s	Scoring Average	Money
1998	7	20	3	0	0	0	0	72.45	$14,842

Best finish for 1998: T-42nd at the Kemper Open

1999	2	4	0	0	0	0	0	74.50	

2000	34	110	20	0	1	2	9	71.11	$701,738

Best finish for 2000: T-2nd at the SEI Pennsylvania Classic

2001	35	109	20	0	0	0	5	71.20	$396,967

Best finish for 2001: T-11th at the Bob Hope Chrysler Classic

2002	26	74	11	0	1	1	3	71.31	$362,892

Best finish for 2002: 3rd at the Southern Farm Bureau Classic

2003	20	49	5	0	0	0	0	71.80	$75,341

Best finish for 2003: T-28th at the FBR Capital Open

2004	1	2	0	0	0	0	0	72.50	
2006	1	2	0	0	0	0	0	76.00	
2008	23	67	9	0	0	1	3	71.25	$270,365

Best finish for 2008: T-8th at the Viking Classic

Period Totals	Starts	Rounds Played	Cuts Made	Wins	Top-5s	Top-10s	Top-25s	Scoring Average	Money
	149	437	68	0	2	4	20	71.39	$1,822,145

Lee Elder

Year	Starts	Rounds Played	Cuts Made	Wins	Top-5s	Top-10s	Top-25s	Scoring Average	Money
1958	1	2	0	0	0	0	0	76.50	
1964	1	2	0	0	0	0	0	75.00	
1966	1	4	1	0	0	0	0	76.00	$565

Best finish for 1966: T-57th at the U.S. Open

1967	2	6	1	0	0	0	0	73.00	

Best finish for 1967: T-47th at the Cajun Classic

1968	29	101	22	0	1	2	9	71.85	$31,269

Best finish for 1968: T-2nd at the American Golf Classic

1969	34	104	19	0	2	7	11	72.24	$49,459

Best finish for 1969: 2nd at the Memphis Open

1970	36	102	18	0	0	1	8	72.35	$18,023

Best finish for 1970: T-10th at the Bahama Islands Open

1971	27	93	22	0	2	4	12	71.44	$46,782

Best finish for 1971: T-2nd at the Danny Thomas Memphis Classic

1972	30	98	21	0	2	4	12	71.67	$67,060

Best finish for 1972: 2nd at the USI Classic & Greater Hartford Open Invitational

1973	26	91	20	0	4	8	16	71.32	$80,305

Best finish for 1973: T-2nd at the USI Classic

1974	28	96	20	1	2	3	10	72.19	$68,277

Best finish for 1974: Win at the Monsanto Open

1975	27	81	13	0	0	3	7	72.60	$28,060

Best finish for 1975: T-8th at the Greater Milwaukee Open

1976	26	94	21	1	4	7	11	71.11	$113,263

Best finish for 1976: Win at the Houston Open

1977	26	93	20	0	2	3	11	71.94	$76,695

Best finish for 1977: 2nd at the B.C. Open

1978	25	96	23	2	4	5	11	71.61	$152,198

Best finish for 1978: Win at the Greater Milwaukee Open & American Express Westchester Classic

1979	25	85	19	0	1	3	9	72.42	$66,454

Best finish for 1979: T-4th at the Jackie Gleason's Inverrary Classic

1980	27	84	16	0	0	0	0	72.65	$19,793

Best finish for 1980: T-26th at the PGA Championship

1981	33	109	23	0	1	2	6	71.90	$62,739

Best finish for 1981: T-3rd at the Atlanta Classic

1982	32	100	18	0	0	0	5	72.16	$33,602

Best finish for 1982: T-12th at the Anheuser-Busch Golf Classic

1983	26	87	16	0	1	3	7	71.75	$72,718

Best finish for 1983: T-2nd at the Houston Coca-Cola Open

1984	21	65	13	0	0	1	4	72.91	$37,458

Best finish for 1984: T-9th at the Bob Hope Chrysler Classic

1985	3	11	2	0	0	0	0	73.00	$2,365

Best finish for 1985: T-48th at the Bing Crosby Pro-Am

1986	1	4	0	0	0	0	0	71.50	
1987	1	1	0	0	0	0	0	73.00	

Period Totals	Starts	Rounds Played	Cuts Made	Wins	Top-5s	Top-10s	Top-25s	Scoring Average	Money
	488	1609	328	4	26	56	149	72.01	$1,027,087

Steve Elkington

Year	Starts	Rounds Played	Cuts Made	Wins	Top-5s	Top-10s	Top-25s	Scoring Average	Money
1984	1	4	1	0	0	0	0	72.00	

Best finish for 1984: T-59th at the Colonial National Invitational

1985	7	28	7	0	0	0	1	71.21	$9,896

Best finish for 1985: T-15th at the Greater Milwaukee Open

1986	5	17	3	0	0	0	1	71.47	$12,705

Best finish for 1986: T-12th at the USF&G Classic

Year	Starts	Rounds Played	Cuts Made	Wins	Top-5s	Top-10s	Top-25s	Scoring Average	Money
1987	35	105	19	0	0	2	7	71.52	$75,738

Best finish for 1987: T-8th at the Honda Classic

| 1988 | 29 | 92 | 19 | 0 | 1 | 2 | 9 | 71.07 | $149,972 |

Best finish for 1988: 5th at the Manufactures Hanover Westchester Classic

| 1989 | 29 | 99 | 21 | 0 | 2 | 3 | 9 | 70.94 | $231,062 |

Best finish for 1989: T-2nd at the Shearson Lehman Hutton Open

| 1990 | 28 | 97 | 23 | 1 | 2 | 4 | 14 | 70.84 | $550,560 |

Best finish for 1990: Win at the Kmart Greater Greensboro Open

| 1991 | 29 | 95 | 18 | 1 | 2 | 4 | 10 | 70.98 | $556,234 |

Best finish for 1991: Win at The Players Championship

| 1992 | 25 | 90 | 22 | 1 | 7 | 9 | 14 | 70.01 | $758,872 |

Best finish for 1992: Win at the Infiniti Tournament Of Champions

| 1993 | 24 | 92 | 24 | 0 | 2 | 8 | 14 | 70.34 | $682,852 |

Best finish for 1993: 2nd at the Kmart Greater Greensboro Open

| 1994 | 20 | 66 | 15 | 1 | 1 | 2 | 5 | 71.41 | $303,004 |

Best finish for 1994: Win at the Buick Southern Open

| 1995 | 21 | 72 | 15 | 2 | 6 | 7 | 11 | 70.25 | $1,254,352 |

Best finish for 1995: Win at the Mercedes Championships & PGA Championship

| 1996 | 19 | 64 | 15 | 0 | 2 | 5 | 9 | 70.77 | $462,145 |

Best finish for 1996: T-2nd at the Buick Classic

| 1997 | 17 | 62 | 14 | 2 | 3 | 3 | 9 | 71.08 | $1,322,057 |

Best finish for 1997: Win at the Doral-Ryder Open & The Players Championship

| 1998 | 16 | 45 | 10 | 1 | 2 | 4 | 5 | 71.49 | $697,844 |

Best finish for 1998: Win at the Buick Challenge

| 1999 | 21 | 68 | 17 | 1 | 1 | 3 | 7 | 71.74 | $1,087,782 |

Best finish for 1999: Win at the Doral-Ryder Open

| 2000 | 17 | 58 | 14 | 0 | 0 | 1 | 2 | 71.60 | $232,785 |

Best finish for 2000: T-10th at the Buick Challenge

| 2001 | 20 | 61 | 14 | 0 | 0 | 2 | 4 | 71.02 | $438,630 |

Best finish for 2001: T-6th at the Marconi Pennsylvania Classic & Texas Open at LaCantera

| 2002 | 23 | 79 | 17 | 0 | 3 | 3 | 5 | 71.20 | $1,084,535 |

Best finish for 2002: T-2nd at the British Open

| 2003 | 14 | 40 | 6 | 0 | 0 | 0 | 2 | 71.85 | $162,303 |

Best finish for 2003: T-17th at the Nissan Open

| 2004 | 20 | 61 | 13 | 0 | 0 | 0 | 1 | 71.36 | $243,238 |

Best finish for 2004: T-18th at the Reno-Tahoe Open

| 2005 | 20 | 67 | 15 | 0 | 2 | 3 | 5 | 70.64 | $1,410,350 |

Best finish for 2005: T-2nd at the PGA Championship

| 2006 | 17 | 51 | 10 | 0 | 0 | 0 | 3 | 70.86 | $259,844 |

Best finish for 2006: T-17th at the John Deere Classic

| 2007 | 25 | 87 | 17 | 0 | 1 | 2 | 8 | 71.00 | $916,375 |

Best finish for 2007: T-5th at the Buick Open

| 2008 | 25 | 84 | 17 | 0 | 2 | 3 | 9 | 70.67 | $1,291,114 |

Best finish for 2008: T-4th at the FBR Open

Period Totals	Starts	Rounds Played	Cuts Made	Wins	Top-5s	Top-10s	Top-25s	Scoring Average	Money
	507	1684	366	10	39	70	164	70.99	$14,194,250

John Elliott

Year	Starts	Rounds Played	Cuts Made	Wins	Top-5s	Top-10s	Top-25s	Scoring Average	Money
1971	1	1	0	0	0	0	0	78.00	
1972	1	0	0	0	0	0	0		
1973	1	2	0	0	0	0	0	75.00	
1975	2	6	1	0	0	0	0	74.83	

Best finish for 1975: 76th at the Jackie Gleason's Inverrary Classic

1983	1	2	0	0	0	0	0	76.00	$100
1984	1	2	0	0	0	0	0	74.50	$1,000
1992	24	58	5	0	0	0	0	73.57	$9,857

Best finish for 1992: T-46th at the B.C. Open

| 1993 | 28 | 77 | 13 | 0 | 0 | 0 | 1 | 72.87 | $60,378 |

Best finish for 1993: T-11th at the H-E-B Texas Open

| 1994 | 2 | 6 | 2 | 0 | 0 | 0 | 0 | 71.00 | $4,480 |

Best finish for 1994: T-50th at the Deposit Guaranty Golf Classic

| 1996 | 22 | 51 | 5 | 0 | 0 | 0 | 1 | 72.71 | $26,926 |

Best finish for 1996: T-14th at the Greater Vancouver Open

| 1997 | 1 | 2 | 0 | 0 | 0 | 0 | 0 | 72.50 | |
| 1999 | 28 | 79 | 11 | 0 | 0 | 0 | 3 | 71.46 | $120,083 |

Best finish for 1999: T-20th at the Touchstone Energy Tucson Open

| 2004 | 1 | 2 | 0 | 0 | 0 | 0 | 0 | 74.50 | $1,000 |
| 2005 | 25 | 56 | 6 | 0 | 0 | 0 | 0 | 72.59 | $67,819 |

Best finish for 2005: T-39th at the BellSouth Classic

Period Totals	Starts	Rounds Played	Cuts Made	Wins	Top-5s	Top-10s	Top-25s	Scoring Average	Money
	138	344	43	0	0	0	5	72.66	$291,643

Danny Ellis

Year	Starts	Rounds Played	Cuts Made	Wins	Top-5s	Top-10s	Top-25s	Scoring Average	Money
1994	1	2	0	0	0	0	0	76.00	
2001	27	76	10	0	0	1	3	71.36	$242,487

Best finish for 2001: T-6th at the National Car Rental Golf Classic/Disney

2002	17	44	5	0	0	0	1	71.73	$73,340

Best finish for 2002: T-21st at the Honda Classic

2003	10	34	7	0	0	0	0	70.76	$101,443

Best finish for 2003: T-27th at the Greater Milwaukee Open

2004	26	77	14	0	0	2	3	71.19	$490,413

Best finish for 2004: T-7th at the Michelin Championship at Las Vegas

2005	7	22	4	0	0	0	0	71.82	$36,956

Best finish for 2005: T-50th at the Southern Farm Bureau Classic

2006	23	64	11	0	0	1	2	71.59	$382,500

Best finish for 2006: T-7th at the Zurich Classic of New Orleans

2007	2	8	2	0	0	0	0	70.63	$28,771

Best finish for 2007: T-41st at the Mayakoba Golf Classic

Period Totals	Starts	Rounds Played	Cuts Made	Wins	Top-5s	Top-10s	Top-25s	Scoring Average	Money
	113	327	53	0	0	4	9	71.39	$1,355,910

Wes Ellis

Year	Starts	Rounds Played	Cuts Made	Wins	Top-5s	Top-10s	Top-25s	Scoring Average	Money
1958	33	124	29	1	5	8	19	71.07	$16,176

Best finish for 1958: Win at the Canadian Open

1959	30	117	26	0	2	7	20	71.25	$15,163

Best finish for 1959: T-2nd at the Mobile Sertoma Open Invitational

1960	12	46	8	0	1	7	8	70.89	$9,022

Best finish for 1960: T-4th at the Texas Open Invitational

1961	11	43	9	0	2	2	8	71.16	$8,926

Best finish for 1961: T-2nd at the Baton Rouge Open Invitational

1962	12	47	10	0	2	2	7	71.47	$10,908

Best finish for 1962: T-4th at the Thunderbird Classic Invitational

1963	12	47	9	0	1	1	10	71.66	$11,509

Best finish for 1963: T-3rd at the Insurance City Open Invitational

1964	13	42	7	0	0	1	4	73.12	$5,636

Best finish for 1964: 7th at the New Orleans Open

1965	10	40	9	1	1	1	7	72.40	$13,800

Best finish for 1965: Win at the San Diego Open

1966	11	44	11	0	2	3	5	72.20	$24,447

Best finish for 1966: T-2nd at the Texas Open Invitational & Insurance City Open Invitational

1967	11	42	10	0	0	1	5	72.33	$11,040

Best finish for 1967: T-7th at the Bing Crosby Pro-Am

1968	11	36	7	0	0	0	2	72.78	$5,048

Best finish for 1968: T-14th at the Bing Crosby National Professional-Amateur

1969	4	12	2	0	0	0	1	72.75	$960

Best finish for 1969: T-15th at the Azalea Open

1970	3	6	0	0	0	0	0	75.50	$500
1971	2	6	1	0	0	0	0	75.17	$333

Best finish for 1971: T-75th at the Westchester Classic

1972	2	6	1	0	0	0	0	72.83	$705

Best finish for 1972: T-43rd at the Westchester Classic

1973	1	2	0	0	0	0	0	77.00	

Period Totals	Starts	Rounds Played	Cuts Made	Wins	Top-5s	Top-10s	Top-25s	Scoring Average	Money
	178	660	139	2	16	33	96	71.77	$134,173

Bob Ellsworth

Year	Starts	Rounds Played	Cuts Made	Wins	Top-5s	Top-10s	Top-25s	Scoring Average	Money
1958	8	19	1	0	0	0	0	81.26	

Best finish for 1958: 60th at the West Palm Beach Open

1964	14	27	0	0	0	0	0	76.37	
1966	1	2	0	0	0	0	0	85.50	
1969	2	6	0	0	0	0	0	78.33	
1973	1	2	0	0	0	0	0	80.50	

Period Totals	Starts	Rounds Played	Cuts Made	Wins	Top-5s	Top-10s	Top-25s	Scoring Average	Money
	26	56	1	0	0	0	0	78.71	

Ken Ellsworth

Year	Starts	Rounds Played	Cuts Made	Wins	Top-5s	Top-10s	Top-25s	Scoring Average	Money
1968	2	8	2	0	0	0	1	72.38	$1,281

Best finish for 1968: T-20th at the Hawaiian Open Invitational

1969	18	54	9	0	0	0	1	73.59	$4,032

Best finish for 1969: T-11th at the Los Angeles Open

Year	Starts	Rounds Played	Cuts Made	Wins	Top-5s	Top-10s	Top-25s	Scoring Average	Money
1970	17	45	8	0	0	0	1	73.51	$3,641

Best finish for 1970: T-14th at the National 4 Ball Championship PGA Players

1971	9	24	3	0	0	0	0	73.88	$683

Best finish for 1971: T-55th at the Monsanto Open

1972	12	31	4	0	0	0	0	74.03	$660

Best finish for 1972: T-50th at the Liggett Meyers Open

1974	1	2	0	0	0	0	0	78.00	$500
1976	1	2	0	0	0	0	0	76.00	
1977	4	8	0	0	0	0	0	74.75	
Period Totals	Starts	Rounds Played	Cuts Made	Wins	Top-5s	Top-10s	Top-25s	Scoring Average	Money
	64	174	26	0	0	0	3	73.76	$10,797

Ernie Els

Year	Starts	Rounds Played	Cuts Made	Wins	Top-5s	Top-10s	Top-25s	Scoring Average	Money
1989	1	2	0	0	0	0	0	74.00	
1990	1	2	0	0	0	0	0	72.50	
1991	1	0	1	0	0	0	0		$2,647

Best finish for 1991: T-51st at the International

1992	4	10	3	0	1	1	1	72.80	$79,763

Best finish for 1992: T-5th at the British Open

1993	7	16	3	0	0	2	2	72.25	$90,462

Best finish for 1993: T-6th at the British Open

1994	12	43	11	1	3	4	7	70.81	$697,355

Best finish for 1994: Win at the U.S. Open

1995	18	60	14	1	5	6	10	70.53	$845,090

Best finish for 1995: Win at the GTE Byron Nelson Classic

1996	18	65	17	1	3	6	11	70.63	$906,944

Best finish for 1996: Win at the Buick Classic

1997	19	62	15	2	3	7	11	70.92	$1,243,008

Best finish for 1997: Win at the U.S. Open & Buick Classic

1998	15	48	12	1	1	4	8	71.00	$763,783

Best finish for 1998: Win at the Bay Hill Invitational

1999	18	60	16	1	5	7	10	71.08	$1,713,506

Best finish for 1999: Win at the Nissan Open

2000	20	68	19	1	10	10	15	69.90	$3,469,405

Best finish for 2000: Win at the International presented by Quest

2001	19	60	15	0	7	9	11	70.50	$2,336,456

Best finish for 2001: T-2nd at the Tour Championship

2002	18	62	17	2	5	7	14	70.27	$3,291,895

Best finish for 2002: Win at the Genuity Championship & British Open

2003	17	60	17	2	4	7	14	69.90	$3,371,237

Best finish for 2003: Win at the Mercedes Championships & Sony Open in Hawaii

2004	16	58	15	3	7	10	12	69.69	$5,787,225

Best finish for 2004: Win at the Sony Open in Hawaii, Memorial Tournament & WGC-American Express Championship

2005	11	44	11	0	2	5	8	70.48	$1,627,184

Best finish for 2005: 2nd at the Sony Open in Hawaii

2006	18	64	18	0	2	8	11	70.63	$2,326,220

Best finish for 2006: 3rd at the British Open

2007	16	58	15	0	5	5	10	70.50	$2,705,715

Best finish for 2007: 2nd at the Verizon Heritage

2008	16	50	11	1	2	5	7	71.44	$2,537,290

Best finish for 2008: Win at the Honda Classic

Period Totals	Starts	Rounds Played	Cuts Made	Wins	Top-5s	Top-10s	Top-25s	Scoring Average	Money
	265	892	230	16	65	103	162	70.60	$33,795,186

Billy Emmons

Year	Starts	Rounds Played	Cuts Made	Wins	Top-5s	Top-10s	Top-25s	Scoring Average	Money
1964	15	27	0	0	0	0	0	76.04	
1965	10	28	4	0	0	0	0	74.25	

Best finish for 1965: T-50th at the Almaden Open

1966	10	26	3	0	0	0	0	76.50	$400

Best finish for 1966: T-59th at the Insurance City Open Invitational

1967	7	20	3	0	0	0	0	74.60	

Best finish for 1967: T-58th at the Cajun Classic

1968	2	6	0	0	0	0	0	75.67	
1970	4	12	1	0	0	0	0	74.50	$182

Best finish for 1970: 68th at the San Antonio Texas Open

1971	4	10	1	0	0	0	0	73.60	

Best finish for 1971: T-55th at the Greater Milwaukee Open

1972	3	6	0	0	0	0	0	76.17	
Period Totals	Starts	Rounds Played	Cuts Made	Wins	Top-5s	Top-10s	Top-25s	Scoring Average	Money
	55	135	12	0	0	0	0	75.21	$582

John Engler, Jr.

Year	Starts	Rounds Played	Cuts Made	Wins	Top-5s	Top-10s	Top-25s	Scoring Average	Money
2006	27	67	7	0	0	0	0	72.79	$72,694

Best finish for 2006: T-39th at the Southern Farm Bureau Classic

Period Totals	Starts	Rounds Played	Cuts Made	Wins	Top-5s	Top-10s	Top-25s	Scoring Average	Money
	27	67	7	0	0	0	0	72.79	$72,694

Bob Erickson

Year	Starts	Rounds Played	Cuts Made	Wins	Top-5s	Top-10s	Top-25s	Scoring Average	Money
1962	2	8	2	0	0	0	0	73.25	$093

Best finish for 1962: T-31st at the Beaumont Open Invitational

| 1964 | 4 | 7 | 0 | 0 | 0 | 0 | 0 | 75.71 | |
| 1965 | 2 | 8 | 2 | 0 | 0 | 0 | 0 | 71.88 | $200 |

Best finish for 1965: T-36th at the Cajun Classic

| 1966 | 5 | 12 | 1 | 0 | 0 | 0 | 0 | 75.33 | $640 |

Best finish for 1966: T-58th at the PGA Championship

| 1967 | 4 | 12 | 2 | 0 | 0 | 0 | 0 | 74.42 | $300 |

Best finish for 1967: T-63rd at the Cajun Classic

| 1968 | 27 | 75 | 10 | 0 | 0 | 0 | 3 | 73.03 | $3,266 |

Best finish for 1968: T-13th at the Robinson Open

| 1969 | 23 | 69 | 12 | 0 | 1 | 2 | 3 | 73.07 | $9,742 |

Best finish for 1969: 3rd at the Alameda County Open

| 1970 | 17 | 48 | 7 | 0 | 0 | 0 | 1 | 73.23 | $2,857 |

Best finish for 1970: T-17th at the Tallahassee Open

| 1971 | 17 | 50 | 8 | 0 | 0 | 1 | 1 | 72.96 | $7,124 |

Best finish for 1971: 7th at the Greater Jacksonville Open

| 1972 | 17 | 48 | 7 | 0 | 0 | 0 | 1 | 73.15 | $2,797 |

Best finish for 1972: T-20th at the Quad Cities Open

| 1973 | 10 | 28 | 3 | 0 | 0 | 0 | 1 | 74.00 | $3,188 |

Best finish for 1973: T-18th at the San Antonio Texas Open

| 1974 | 2 | 6 | 1 | 0 | 0 | 0 | 0 | 70.50 | $794 |

Best finish for 1974: T-29th at the San Antonio Texas Open

| 1975 | 8 | 22 | 3 | 0 | 0 | 0 | 0 | 74.00 | $1,109 |

Best finish for 1975: T-53rd at the Sammy Davis, Jr. - Greater Hartford Open

| 1976 | 21 | 60 | 9 | 0 | 0 | 0 | 1 | 73.38 | $3,893 |

Best finish for 1976: T-24th at the Pleasant Valley Classic

| 1977 | 13 | 30 | 2 | 0 | 0 | 0 | 0 | 75.67 | |

Best finish for 1977: 76th at the Danny Thomas Memphis Classic

1978	3	6	0	0	0	0	0	73.83	
1980	2	2	0	0	0	0	0	78.50	
1983	2	6	0	0	0	0	0	75.67	

Period Totals	Starts	Rounds Played	Cuts Made	Wins	Top-5s	Top-10s	Top-25s	Scoring Average	Money
	179	497	69	0	1	3	11	73.50	$36,004

Randy Erskine

Year	Starts	Rounds Played	Cuts Made	Wins	Top-5s	Top-10s	Top-25s	Scoring Average	Money
1973	2	8	1	0	0	0	0	73.50	$356

Best finish for 1973: T-51st at the Walt Disney World Open

| 1974 | 23 | 61 | 7 | 0 | 0 | 0 | 0 | 73.28 | $4,540 |

Best finish for 1974: T-27th at the World Open

| 1975 | 27 | 84 | 15 | 0 | 0 | 0 | 5 | 72.81 | $14,496 |

Best finish for 1975: T-12th at the IVB Philadelphia Golf Classic

| 1976 | 24 | 69 | 13 | 0 | 0 | 0 | 1 | 73.48 | $7,373 |

Best finish for 1976: T-13th at the Canadian Open

| 1977 | 20 | 58 | 9 | 0 | 0 | 0 | 1 | 73.50 | $4,898 |

Best finish for 1977: T-25th at the Kemper Open

| 1978 | 19 | 52 | 8 | 0 | 0 | 0 | 3 | 72.62 | $9,576 |

Best finish for 1978: T-12th at the Kemper Open

| 1979 | 19 | 55 | 9 | 0 | 0 | 0 | 1 | 73.40 | $9,872 |

Best finish for 1979: T-14th at the Andy Williams-San Diego Open

| 1980 | 3 | 6 | 1 | 0 | 0 | 0 | 0 | 74.17 | $508 |

Best finish for 1980: T-64th at the Buick Goodwrench Open

| 1981 | 1 | 0 | 1 | 0 | 0 | 0 | 0 | | $1,410 |

Best finish for 1981: T-32nd at the World Disney World National Team Championship

| 1982 | 1 | 4 | 1 | 0 | 0 | 0 | 0 | 72.25 | $766 |

Best finish for 1982: T-58th at the Buick Open

1983	1	2	0	0	0	0	0	72.50	
1984	1	2	0	0	0	0	0	72.50	
1985	1	2	0	0	0	0	0	74.50	$600

Period Totals	Starts	Rounds Played	Cuts Made	Wins	Top-5s	Top-10s	Top-25s	Scoring Average	Money
	142	403	65	0	0	0	11	73.18	$54,396

Bob Estes

Year	Starts	Rounds Played	Cuts Made	Wins	Top-5s	Top-10s	Top-25s	Scoring Average	Money
1988	5	18	4	0	0	0	0	71.17	$5,968

Best finish for 1988: T-30th at the Southern Open

1989	26	76	14	0	2	2	5	71.20	$135,628

Best finish for 1989: 2nd at the B.C. Open

1990	29	95	18	0	1	4	9	71.27	$214,085

Best finish for 1990: T-4th at the Federal Express St. Jude Classic

1991	32	100	19	0	0	1	7	71.32	$148,364

Best finish for 1991: T-7th at the H-E-B Texas Open

1992	28	89	18	0	1	2	4	71.43	$190,778

Best finish for 1992: T-3rd at the Las Vegas Invitational

1993	28	98	23	0	4	5	12	70.66	$447,187

Best finish for 1993: T-2nd at the Buick Southern Open

1994	28	99	24	1	4	8	18	69.77	$779,776

Best finish for 1994: Win at the Texas Open

1995	24	91	21	0	0	5	12	70.52	$434,992

Best finish for 1995: T-6th at the Motorola Western Open & PGA Championship

1996	26	64	7	0	1	1	2	72.38	$125,408

Best finish for 1996: T-3rd at the Nortel Open

1997	19	69	15	0	1	3	8	69.94	$340,057

Best finish for 1997: 3rd at the Greater Vancouver Open

1998	29	104	23	0	4	7	14	70.52	$987,930

Best finish for 1998: T-2nd at the Bay Hill Invitational

1999	28	108	27	0	4	9	15	70.83	$1,357,618

Best finish for 1999: T-4th at the Bob Hope Chrysler Classic & Masters

2000	21	63	12	0	0	3	7	71.27	$541,706

Best finish for 2000: T-6th at the GTE Byron Nelson Classic & MasterCard Colonial

2001	26	88	20	2	5	8	12	69.55	$2,795,477

Best finish for 2001: Win at the FedEx St. Jude Classic & Invensys Classic at Las Vegas

2002	26	87	20	1	3	8	14	70.37	$1,937,600

Best finish for 2002: Win at the Kemper Insurance Open

2003	25	91	22	0	2	6	10	70.21	$1,825,414

Best finish for 2003: 2nd at the HP Classic of New Orleans

2004	23	71	14	0	1	1	7	70.65	$1,049,064

Best finish for 2004: 2nd at the FedEx St. Jude Classic

2005	25	92	22	0	0	1	7	70.41	$891,477

Best finish for 2005: T-8th at the FedEx St. Jude Classic

2006	25	85	17	0	2	2	6	70.68	$1,344,494

Best finish for 2006: 2nd at the Shell Houston Open & The Reno-Tahoe Open

2007	28	88	16	0	0	3	6	71.14	$878,051

Best finish for 2007: T-6th at the AT&T Classic

2008	28	90	17	0	0	2	6	70.69	$829,395

Best finish for 2008: T-6th at the Shell Houston Open

Period Totals	Starts	Rounds Played	Cuts Made	Wins	Top-5s	Top-10s	Top-25s	Scoring Average	Money
	529	1766	373	4	35	81	181	70.72	$17,260,470

Jim Estes

Year	Starts	Rounds Played	Cuts Made	Wins	Top-5s	Top-10s	Top-25s	Scoring Average	Money
1990	1	2	0	0	0	0	0	73.50	$1,000
1994	1	2	0	0	0	0	0	76.00	
1995	2	4	0	0	0	0	0	76.75	$1,000
1996	1	2	0	0	0	0	0	76.50	
1997	1	2	0	0	0	0	0	74.50	$1,000
1998	26	64	8	0	0	0	1	72.27	$74,438

Best finish for 1998: T-16th at the Greater Greensboro Chrysler Classic

2008	1	2	0	0	0	0	0	77.50	

Period Totals	Starts	Rounds Played	Cuts Made	Wins	Top-5s	Top-10s	Top-25s	Scoring Average	Money
	33	78	8	0	0	0	1	72.92	$77,438

Tom Eubank

Year	Starts	Rounds Played	Cuts Made	Wins	Top-5s	Top-10s	Top-25s	Scoring Average	Money
1986	1	2	0	0	0	0	0	79.50	
1988	2	4	0	0	0	0	0	75.50	$1,000
1990	24	59	7	0	0	1	1	72.41	$27,345

Best finish for 1990: T-10th at the Buick Southern Open

1991	4	10	1	0	0	0	0	72.00	$7,310

Best finish for 1991: T-36th at the Doral-Ryder Open

2000	1	2	0	0	0	0	0	75.00	

Period Totals	Starts	Rounds Played	Cuts Made	Wins	Top-5s	Top-10s	Top-25s	Scoring Average	Money
	32	77	8	0	0	1	1	72.77	$35,655

Chick Evans

Year	Starts	Rounds Played	Cuts Made	Wins	Top-5s	Top-10s	Top-25s	Scoring Average	Money
1959	1	2	0	0	0	0	0	88.50	
1960	1	2	0	0	0	0	0	90.00	
1963	2	8	2	0	0	0	1	72.13	$569

Best finish for 1963: T-24th at the Utah Open Invitational

| 1964 | 7 | 14 | 1 | 0 | 0 | 0 | 1 | 75.64 | $650 |

Best finish for 1964: T-21st at the Phoenix Open

| 1965 | 6 | 15 | 1 | 0 | 0 | 0 | 0 | 75.60 | |

Best finish for 1965: T-62nd at the Tucson Open

| 1966 | 4 | 12 | 2 | 0 | 0 | 0 | 0 | 78.42 | $659 |

Best finish for 1966: T-37th at the PGA Championship

| 1967 | 2 | 4 | 0 | 0 | 0 | 0 | 0 | 81.50 | |
| 1968 | 25 | 68 | 9 | 0 | 0 | 1 | 1 | 73.44 | $2,024 |

Best finish for 1968: T-8th at the Robinson Open

| 1969 | 15 | 40 | 6 | 0 | 0 | 0 | 1 | 73.65 | $10,519 |

Best finish for 1969: T-25th at the Azalea Open

| 1970 | 2 | 6 | 1 | 0 | 0 | 0 | 0 | 74.33 | $1,289 |

Best finish for 1970: T-30th at the Canadian Open

| 1971 | 3 | 7 | 1 | 0 | 0 | 0 | 0 | 76.00 | $258 |

Best finish for 1971: T-66th at the PGA Championship

1972	1	2	0	0	0	0	0	78.00	
1973	2	4	0	0	0	0	0	74.50	$500
1974	2	4	0	0	0	0	0	76.25	
1980	1	2	0	0	0	0	0	78.50	$600
Period Totals	Starts	Rounds Played	Cuts Made	Wins	Top-5s	Top-10s	Top-25s	Scoring Average	Money
	74	190	23	0	0	1	4	74.88	$17,068

Tom Evans

Year	Starts	Rounds Played	Cuts Made	Wins	Top-5s	Top-10s	Top-25s	Scoring Average	Money
1972	1	2	0	0	0	0	0	74.00	
1973	20	57	7	0	0	0	1	73.72	$3,456

Best finish for 1973: T-23rd at the Sammy Davis, Jr. - Greater Hartford Open

| 1974 | 16 | 45 | 8 | 0 | 0 | 0 | 0 | 73.36 | $4,213 |

Best finish for 1974: T-26th at the Houston Open

| 1975 | 24 | 73 | 12 | 0 | 0 | 0 | 2 | 73.19 | $5,588 |

Best finish for 1975: T-17th at the Ed McMahon Quad City Open

| 1976 | 16 | 46 | 7 | 0 | 0 | 0 | 2 | 73.30 | $6,815 |

Best finish for 1976: T-11th at the First NBC New Orleans Open

| 1977 | 16 | 44 | 6 | 0 | 0 | 0 | 0 | 74.36 | $2,016 |

Best finish for 1977: T-41st at the Phoenix Open

1978	2	4	0	0	0	0	0	76.25	$600
Period Totals	Starts	Rounds Played	Cuts Made	Wins	Top-5s	Top-10s	Top-25s	Scoring Average	Money
	95	271	40	0	0	0	5	73.59	$22,687

Tony Evans

Year	Starts	Rounds Played	Cuts Made	Wins	Top-5s	Top-10s	Top-25s	Scoring Average	Money
1964	18	42	4	0	0	0	0	74.86	

Best finish for 1964: T-33rd at the Sunset-Camellia Open

| 1965 | 19 | 54 | 11 | 0 | 0 | 0 | 2 | 73.94 | $2,304 |

Best finish for 1965: T-14th at the Sahara Invitational

| 1966 | 13 | 34 | 4 | 0 | 0 | 0 | 0 | 74.35 | $858 |

Best finish for 1966: T-27th at the "500" Festival Open Invitational

| 1967 | 3 | 8 | 1 | 0 | 0 | 0 | 1 | 73.63 | $350 |

Best finish for 1967: T-23rd at the Azalea Open

| 1968 | 2 | 8 | 2 | 0 | 0 | 0 | 0 | 72.75 | |

Best finish for 1968: T-52nd at the Atlanta Classic

| 1969 | 1 | 4 | 1 | 0 | 0 | 0 | 0 | 71.75 | $275 |

Best finish for 1969: T-29th at the Azalea Open

| 1970 | 2 | 6 | 1 | 0 | 0 | 0 | 0 | 75.17 | $1,031 |

Best finish for 1970: T-36th at the U.S. Open

1971	2	4	0	0	0	0	0	77.00	
Period Totals	Starts	Rounds Played	Cuts Made	Wins	Top-5s	Top-10s	Top-25s	Scoring Average	Money
	60	160	24	0	0	0	3	74.26	$4,817

Jack Ewing

Year	Starts	Rounds Played	Cuts Made	Wins	Top-5s	Top-10s	Top-25s	Scoring Average	Money
1964	1	1	1	0	0	0	0	84.00	

Best finish for 1964: 100 at the Fresno Open

| 1966 | 2 | 4 | 0 | 0 | 0 | 0 | 0 | 73.25 | |
| 1968 | 10 | 24 | 2 | 0 | 0 | 0 | 0 | 72.88 | $1,239 |

Best finish for 1968: T-30th at the Canadian Open

Year	Starts	Rounds Played	Cuts Made	Wins	Top-5s	Top-10s	Top-25s	Scoring Average	Money
1969	26	87	18	0	2	4	6	72.40	$20,451

Best finish for 1969: T-5th at the Phoenix Open & Tallahassee Open

Year	Starts	Rounds Played	Cuts Made	Wins	Top-5s	Top-10s	Top-25s	Scoring Average	Money
1970	23	74	13	0	0	0	2	72.85	$6,685

Best finish for 1970: T-11th at the Los Angles Open

Year	Starts	Rounds Played	Cuts Made	Wins	Top-5s	Top-10s	Top-25s	Scoring Average	Money
1971	23	68	12	0	2	4	4	72.07	$16,863

Best finish for 1971: T-4th at the Tallahassee Open & Greater Hartford Open Invitational

Year	Starts	Rounds Played	Cuts Made	Wins	Top-5s	Top-10s	Top-25s	Scoring Average	Money
1972	27	85	16	0	1	2	3	72.76	$13,445

Best finish for 1972: T-5th at the Houston Open

Year	Starts	Rounds Played	Cuts Made	Wins	Top-5s	Top-10s	Top-25s	Scoring Average	Money
1973	17	61	11	0	1	1	4	72.36	$14,552

Best finish for 1973: T-5th at the San Antonio Texas Open

Year	Starts	Rounds Played	Cuts Made	Wins	Top-5s	Top-10s	Top-25s	Scoring Average	Money
1974	29	92	18	0	1	2	6	72.05	$23,372

Best finish for 1974: T-5th at the Tallahassee Open

Year	Starts	Rounds Played	Cuts Made	Wins	Top-5s	Top-10s	Top-25s	Scoring Average	Money
1975	25	82	16	0	2	2	4	72.90	$20,727

Best finish for 1975: 3rd at the Byron Nelson Golf Classic

Year	Starts	Rounds Played	Cuts Made	Wins	Top-5s	Top-10s	Top-25s	Scoring Average	Money
1976	22	72	17	0	1	1	2	72.60	$14,880

Best finish for 1976: T-5th at the Kaiser International Open

Year	Starts	Rounds Played	Cuts Made	Wins	Top-5s	Top-10s	Top-25s	Scoring Average	Money
1977	11	33	5	0	1	1	1	73.55	$4,971

Best finish for 1977: T-4th at the Tallahassee Open

Year	Starts	Rounds Played	Cuts Made	Wins	Top-5s	Top-10s	Top-25s	Scoring Average	Money
1978	1	3	0	0	0	0	0	74.67	
1979	6	17	3	0	0	0	0	72.47	$2,139

Best finish for 1979: T-40th at the Joe Garagiola Tucson Open

Period Totals	Starts	Rounds Played	Cuts Made	Wins	Top-5s	Top-10s	Top-25s	Scoring Average	Money
	223	703	132	0	11	17	32	72.59	$139,325

Bill Ezinicki

Year	Starts	Rounds Played	Cuts Made	Wins	Top-5s	Top-10s	Top-25s	Scoring Average	Money
1958	15	46	9	0	1	2	3	73.13	$1,821

Best finish for 1958: 5th at the Jackson Open

Year	Starts	Rounds Played	Cuts Made	Wins	Top-5s	Top-10s	Top-25s	Scoring Average	Money
1959	2	8	2	0	0	1	1	72.88	$850

Best finish for 1959: T-10th at the Baton Rouge Open Invitational

Year	Starts	Rounds Played	Cuts Made	Wins	Top-5s	Top-10s	Top-25s	Scoring Average	Money
1960	8	28	7	0	0	0	2	73.18	$670

Best finish for 1960: T-22nd at the Tucson Open Invitational

Year	Starts	Rounds Played	Cuts Made	Wins	Top-5s	Top-10s	Top-25s	Scoring Average	Money
1961	3	10	2	0	0	0	0	72.10	$217

Best finish for 1961: T-28th at the Coral Gables Open Invitational

Year	Starts	Rounds Played	Cuts Made	Wins	Top-5s	Top-10s	Top-25s	Scoring Average	Money
1962	1	3	1	0	0	0	0	75.33	
1963	2	6	1	0	0	0	0	77.33	$300

Best finish for 1963: 78th at the PGA Championship

Year	Starts	Rounds Played	Cuts Made	Wins	Top-5s	Top-10s	Top-25s	Scoring Average	Money
1964	1	2	0	0	0	0	0	77.00	
1965	1	2	0	0	0	0	0	73.50	
1966	11	33	4	0	0	1	1	73.88	$2,121

Best finish for 1966: T-9th at the Phoenix Open Invitational

Year	Starts	Rounds Played	Cuts Made	Wins	Top-5s	Top-10s	Top-25s	Scoring Average	Money
1967	13	40	6	0	0	2	2	73.25	$2,774

Best finish for 1967: T-8th at the Azalea Open

Year	Starts	Rounds Played	Cuts Made	Wins	Top-5s	Top-10s	Top-25s	Scoring Average	Money
1968	9	24	3	0	0	0	0	74.21	$500

Best finish for 1968: 61st at the Florida Citrus Open Invitational

Year	Starts	Rounds Played	Cuts Made	Wins	Top-5s	Top-10s	Top-25s	Scoring Average	Money
1969	13	33	4	0	0	0	0	74.42	$1,096

Best finish for 1969: T-34th at the Citrus Open

Period Totals	Starts	Rounds Played	Cuts Made	Wins	Top-5s	Top-10s	Top-25s	Scoring Average	Money
	79	235	39	0	1	6	9	73.67	$10,350

Brad Fabel

Year	Starts	Rounds Played	Cuts Made	Wins	Top-5s	Top-10s	Top-25s	Scoring Average	Money
1984	1	2	0	0	0	0	0	74.00	
1985	30	89	13	0	2	3	5	72.04	$74,425

Best finish for 1985: T-3rd at the Lite Quad Cities Open & Greater Milwaukee Open

Year	Starts	Rounds Played	Cuts Made	Wins	Top-5s	Top-10s	Top-25s	Scoring Average	Money
1986	34	94	13	0	0	1	1	72.65	$26,234

Best finish for 1986: 9th at the Southern Open

Year	Starts	Rounds Played	Cuts Made	Wins	Top-5s	Top-10s	Top-25s	Scoring Average	Money
1987	25	73	13	0	1	2	5	71.93	$90,024

Best finish for 1987: 5th at the Hardee's Golf Classic

Year	Starts	Rounds Played	Cuts Made	Wins	Top-5s	Top-10s	Top-25s	Scoring Average	Money
1988	30	100	20	0	1	2	6	71.22	$112,093

Best finish for 1988: T-4th at the Hardee's Golf Classic

Year	Starts	Rounds Played	Cuts Made	Wins	Top-5s	Top-10s	Top-25s	Scoring Average	Money
1989	29	84	14	0	0	0	4	71.71	$69,757

Best finish for 1989: T-14th at the International & Chattanooga Classic

Year	Starts	Rounds Played	Cuts Made	Wins	Top-5s	Top-10s	Top-25s	Scoring Average	Money
1990	26	87	17	0	1	1	5	71.14	$166,876

Best finish for 1990: T-2nd at the Canon Greater Hartford Open

Year	Starts	Rounds Played	Cuts Made	Wins	Top-5s	Top-10s	Top-25s	Scoring Average	Money
1991	30	93	16	0	0	4	6	70.66	$147,563

Best finish for 1991: T-7th at the Deposit Guaranty Classic, Anheuser-Busch Golf Classic, Chattanooga Classic & Hardee's Golf Classic

Year	Starts	Rounds Played	Cuts Made	Wins	Top-5s	Top-10s	Top-25s	Scoring Average	Money
1992	27	94	19	0	1	3	10	70.91	$220,495

Best finish for 1992: T-4th at the Chattanooga Classic

Year	Starts	Rounds Played	Cuts Made	Wins	Top-5s	Top-10s	Top-25s	Scoring Average	Money
1993	27	82	14	0	0	0	1	72.12	$60,672

Best finish for 1993: T-15th at the Freeport-McMoRan Classic

Year	Starts	Rounds Played	Cuts Made	Wins	Top-5s	Top-10s	Top-25s	Scoring Average	Money
1994	12	36	7	0	0	0	0	71.72	$33,812

Best finish for 1994: T-26th at the Deposit Guaranty Golf Classic

1996	27	86	18	0	0	2	9	70.81	$228,667

Best finish for 1996: 7th at the Kemper Open

1997	30	94	18	0	2	4	10	71.06	$375,122

Best finish for 1997: T-2nd at the Buick Open

1998	30	92	15	0	2	3	5	71.41	$286,474

Best finish for 1998: T-3rd at the Kemper Open

1999	26	88	17	0	0	1	7	71.48	$380,441

Best finish for 1999: T-10th at the Air Canada Championship

2000	30	88	12	0	1	1	1	71.83	$219,924

Best finish for 2000: T-5th at the Shell Houston Open

2001	10	31	5	0	0	1	2	70.61	$140,940

Best finish for 2001: T-10th at the B.C. Open

2002	7	14	0	0	0	0	0	73.50	
2003	2	4	0	0	0	0	0	74.50	
2004	1	2	0	0	0	0	0	73.00	
2005	1	4	1	0	0	0	0	69.00	$6,926

Best finish for 2005: T-52nd at the B.C. Open

Period Totals	Starts	Rounds Played	Cuts Made	Wins	Top-5s	Top-10s	Top-25s	Scoring Average	Money
	435	1337	232	0	11	28	77	71.50	$2,640,445

Don Fairfield

Year	Starts	Rounds Played	Cuts Made	Wins	Top-5s	Top-10s	Top-25s	Scoring Average	Money
1958	36	132	30	0	3	8	16	71.64	$13,358

Best finish for 1958: 3rd at the Pepsi Open

1959	28	111	25	0	1	7	19	71.13	$13,287

Best finish for 1959: T-2nd at the Kansas City Open Invitational

1960	26	104	23	1	2	6	16	71.07	$14,968

Best finish for 1960: Win at the St. Paul Open Invitational

1961	26	101	23	0	1	7	17	70.56	$18,248

Best finish for 1961: T-3rd at the American Golf Classic

1962	24	95	23	0	3	6	17	71.45	$17,742

Best finish for 1962: T-2nd at the Pensacola Open Invitational

1963	21	81	19	1	1	3	8	71.79	$15,448

Best finish for 1963: Win at the Oklahoma City Open Invitational

1964	29	110	25	0	1	5	13	71.77	$22,839

Best finish for 1964: T-4th at the Tournament of Champions

1965	12	41	8	0	0	0	3	72.59	$5,537

Best finish for 1965: T-17th at the Western Open

1966	10	31	5	0	0	0	2	73.39	$2,592

Best finish for 1966: T-16th at the Buick Open Invitational

1967	7	15	0	0	0	0	0	76.53	
1968	9	30	5	0	0	0	0	74.00	$126

Best finish for 1968: T-46th at the Bing Crosby National Professional-Amateur

1969	6	15	0	0	0	0	0	75.93	
1970	1	4	0	0	0	0	0	73.50	
1971	1	2	0	0	0	0	0	75.50	
1973	1	4	0	0	0	0	0	74.75	
1974	1	4	0	0	0	0	0	74.75	
1975	1	4	0	0	0	0	0	75.00	
1976	1	4	0	0	0	0	0	78.50	

Period Totals	Starts	Rounds Played	Cuts Made	Wins	Top-5s	Top-10s	Top-25s	Scoring Average	Money
	240	888	186	2	12	42	111	71.83	$124,144

PGA Tour career totals from 1949 to 1976

	Starts	Rounds Played	Cuts Made	Wins	Top-5s	Top-10s	Top-25s	Scoring Average	Money
	301	1118	237	3	15	56	172	N/A	$148,261

Nick Faldo

Year	Starts	Rounds Played	Cuts Made	Wins	Top-5s	Top-10s	Top-25s	Scoring Average	Money
1976	2	6	1	0	0	0	0	73.67	$603

Best finish for 1976: T-28th at the British Open

1977	1	4	1	0	0	0	0	74.75	$425

Best finish for 1977: T-62nd at the British Open

1978	1	4	1	0	0	1	1	71.25	$7,481

Best finish for 1978: T-7th at the British Open

1979	3	12	3	0	0	0	1	73.83	$6,414

Best finish for 1979: T-19th at the British Open

1980	1	4	1	0	0	0	1	71.00	$10,200

Best finish for 1980: T-12th at the British Open

1981	12	42	10	0	1	2	4	71.52	$49,674

Best finish for 1981: 3rd at the Greater Greensboro Open

Year	Starts	Rounds Played	Cuts Made	Wins	Top-5s	Top-10s	Top-25s	Scoring Average	Money
1982	15	55	14	0	2	3	9	71.80	$74,067

Best finish for 1982: T-4th at the British Open

| 1983 | 14 | 47 | 9 | 0 | 1 | 3 | 6 | 71.55 | $82,388 |

Best finish for 1983: T-2nd at the Walt Disney World Golf Classic

| 1984 | 20 | 71 | 15 | 1 | 2 | 5 | 10 | 71.38 | $188,152 |

Best finish for 1984: Win at the Sea Pines Heritage Classic

| 1985 | 18 | 63 | 14 | 0 | 1 | 2 | 5 | 72.59 | $56,597 |

Best finish for 1985: T-4th at the Phoenix Open

| 1986 | 17 | 53 | 10 | 0 | 2 | 2 | 6 | 71.89 | $91,465 |

Best finish for 1986: T-3rd at the USF&G Classic

| 1987 | 7 | 26 | 6 | 1 | 2 | 2 | 3 | 71.46 | $156,281 |

Best finish for 1987: Win at the British Open

| 1988 | 10 | 36 | 8 | 0 | 4 | 4 | 4 | 71.72 | $259,020 |

Best finish for 1988: 2nd at the U.S. Open

| 1989 | 17 | 65 | 15 | 1 | 1 | 2 | 10 | 71.26 | $355,141 |

Best finish for 1989: Win at the Masters

| 1990 | 8 | 31 | 8 | 2 | 3 | 3 | 7 | 70.48 | $499,112 |

Best finish for 1990: Win at the Masters & British Open

| 1991 | 8 | 31 | 8 | 0 | 0 | 2 | 6 | 70.87 | $144,050 |

Best finish for 1991: T-6th at the Buick Open

| 1992 | 8 | 30 | 7 | 1 | 4 | 5 | 7 | 70.40 | $535,168 |

Best finish for 1992: Win at the British Open

| 1993 | 7 | 27 | 7 | 0 | 2 | 3 | 4 | 70.52 | $312,086 |

Best finish for 1993: 2nd at the British Open

| 1994 | 10 | 34 | 7 | 0 | 2 | 3 | 4 | 71.38 | $270,746 |

Best finish for 1994: T-4th at the PGA Championship

| 1995 | 19 | 72 | 17 | 1 | 5 | 6 | 12 | 70.47 | $790,961 |

Best finish for 1995: Win at the Doral-Ryder Open

| 1996 | 16 | 56 | 14 | 1 | 3 | 7 | 10 | 70.48 | $942,621 |

Best finish for 1996: Win at the Masters

| 1997 | 15 | 49 | 11 | 1 | 2 | 2 | 4 | 71.82 | $437,626 |

Best finish for 1997: Win at the Nissan Open

| 1998 | 15 | 49 | 11 | 0 | 0 | 0 | 2 | 72.35 | $152,703 |

Best finish for 1998: T-18th at the Players Championship

| 1999 | 15 | 41 | 7 | 0 | 1 | 2 | 2 | 72.95 | $228,951 |

Best finish for 1999: T-5th at the Michelob Championship at Kingsmill

| 2000 | 15 | 49 | 11 | 0 | 0 | 1 | 2 | 72.08 | $276,583 |

Best finish for 2000: 7th at the U.S. Open

| 2001 | 13 | 45 | 10 | 0 | 0 | 1 | 2 | 71.56 | $222,535 |

Best finish for 2001: T-10th at the FedEx St. Jude Classic

| 2002 | 5 | 20 | 5 | 0 | 1 | 1 | 2 | 72.65 | $321,208 |

Best finish for 2002: T-5th at the U.S. Open

| 2003 | 7 | 26 | 6 | 0 | 0 | 1 | 2 | 72.50 | $284,383 |

Best finish for 2003: T-8th at the British Open

| 2004 | 6 | 18 | 3 | 0 | 0 | 0 | 0 | 73.94 | $50,205 |

Best finish for 2004: T-49th at the PGA Championship

| 2005 | 5 | 14 | 3 | 0 | 0 | 0 | 1 | 72.07 | $189,649 |

Best finish for 2005: T-11th at the British Open

2006	6	13	0	0	0	0	0	74.38	$6,210
2007	1	2	0	0	0	0	0	76.00	$4,316
Period Totals	Starts	Rounds Played	Cuts Made	Wins	Top-5s	Top-10s	Top-25s	Scoring Average	Money
	317	1095	243	9	39	63	127	71.68	$7,007,025

Sam Farlow

Year	Starts	Rounds Played	Cuts Made	Wins	Top-5s	Top-10s	Top-25s	Scoring Average	Money
1973	1	3	0	0	0	0	0	78.67	
1974	16	36	4	0	0	0	0	74.44	$1,697

Best finish for 1974: T-38th at the IVB Philadelphia Golf Classic

| 1976 | 7 | 20 | 3 | 0 | 0 | 0 | 0 | 74.20 | $431 |

Best finish for 1976: T-57th at the Sammy Davis, Jr. - Greater Hartford Open

| 1977 | 15 | 41 | 6 | 0 | 0 | 0 | 0 | 73.76 | $3,880 |

Best finish for 1977: T-33rd at the Jackie Gleason's Inverrary Classic

1983	1	2	0	0	0	0	0	82.50	
Period Totals	Starts	Rounds Played	Cuts Made	Wins	Top-5s	Top-10s	Top-25s	Scoring Average	Money
	40	102	13	0	0	0	0	74.40	$6,007

Billy Farrell

Year	Starts	Rounds Played	Cuts Made	Wins	Top-5s	Top-10s	Top-25s	Scoring Average	Money
1958	2	4	0	0	0	0	0	76.00	
1960	1	4	1	0	0	0	1	72.00	$263

Best finish for 1960: T-18th at the Hesperia Open Invitational

Year	Starts	Rounds Played	Cuts Made	Wins	Top-5s	Top-10s	Top-25s	Scoring Average	Money
1961	8	32	8	0	0	0	3	72.31	$1,802

Best finish for 1961: T-16th at the Cajun Classic Open Invitational

Year	Starts	Rounds Played	Cuts Made	Wins	Top-5s	Top-10s	Top-25s	Scoring Average	Money
1962	7	28	7	0	0	0	2	71.93	$2,586

Best finish for 1962: T-17th at the Carling Open Invitational

1963	8	30	7	0	0	0	2	72.37	$4,013

Best finish for 1963: T-19th at the Whitemarsh Open Invitational

1964	6	16	2	0	0	0	2	73.00	$2,124

Best finish for 1964: T-15th at the St. Petersburg Open

1965	12	35	6	0	0	0	0	74.89	$1,772

Best finish for 1965: T-33rd at the Pensacola Open

1966	4	14	3	0	0	0	3	72.93	$3,391

Best finish for 1966: T-21st at the Greater Greensboro Open Invitational

1967	14	44	7	0	0	0	5	72.61	$9,524

Best finish for 1967: T-11th at the PGA Championship

1968	13	42	7	0	0	1	3	72.55	$6,962

Best finish for 1968: T-9th at the Kaiser International Open Invitational

1969	7	15	1	0	0	0	1	74.93	$375

Best finish for 1969: 18th at the West End Classic

1970	3	6	0	0	0	0	0	77.17	
1971	4	9	0	0	0	0	0	75.89	$500
Period Totals	Starts	Rounds Played	Cuts Made	Wins	Top-5s	Top-10s	Top-25s	Scoring Average	Money
	89	279	49	0	0	1	22	73.16	$33,312

Greg Farrow

Year	Starts	Rounds Played	Cuts Made	Wins	Top-5s	Top-10s	Top-25s	Scoring Average	Money
1984	9	20	1	0	0	0	0	74.95	$590

Best finish for 1984: T-44th at the Miller High-Life Quad Cities Open

1986	1	2	0	0	0	0	0	77.50	$600
1988	14	32	2	0	0	0	0	73.78	$2,110

Best finish for 1988: 73rd at the Centel Classic

1991	1	2	0	0	0	0	0	76.00	$1,000
1992	1	2	0	0	0	0	0	78.00	$1,000
Period Totals	Starts	Rounds Played	Cuts Made	Wins	Top-5s	Top-10s	Top-25s	Scoring Average	Money
	26	58	3	0	0	0	0	74.53	$5,300

Niclas Fasth

Year	Starts	Rounds Played	Cuts Made	Wins	Top-5s	Top-10s	Top-25s	Scoring Average	Money
1998	15	35	3	0	0	0	0	73.26	$20,360

Best finish for 1998: T-30th at the Freeport-McDermott Classic

2001	3	12	3	0	1	1	2	69.75	$610,418

Best finish for 2001: 2nd at the British Open

2002	9	26	6	0	0	1	2	72.77	$279,378

Best finish for 2002: T-9th at the Accenture Match Play Championship

2003	14	42	10	0	0	2	7	71.67	$649,751

Best finish for 2003: T-7th at the FBR Capital Open

2004	22	60	10	0	0	0	2	72.20	$265,423

Best finish for 2004: T-16th at the Buick Invitational

2005	3	10	2	0	0	0	0	71.60	$109,500

Best finish for 2005: T-33rd at the WGC-NEC Invitational

2006	4	6	1	0	0	0	0	74.33	$44,827

Best finish for 2006: T-33rd at the WGC-Accenture Match Play Championship

2007	10	30	7	0	1	3	4	73.00	$813,405

Best finish for 2007: 4th at the U.S. Open

2008	10	30	7	0	0	1	2	73.03	$391,690

Best finish for 2008: T-8th at the Arnold Palmer Invitational

Period Totals	Starts	Rounds Played	Cuts Made	Wins	Top-5s	Top-10s	Top-25s	Scoring Average	Money
	90	251	49	0	2	8	19	72.42	$3,184,752

Brad Faxon

Year	Starts	Rounds Played	Cuts Made	Wins	Top-5s	Top-10s	Top-25s	Scoring Average	Money
1981	2	6	1	0	0	0	0	73.00	

Best finish for 1981: T-56th at the Pleasant Valley Jimmy Fund Classic

1982	1	2	0	0	0	0	0	76.50	
1983	9	30	6	0	0	1	2	71.67	$16,526

Best finish for 1983: T-7th at the Buick Open

1984	33	104	19	0	1	2	6	72.36	$71,688

Best finish for 1984: T-3rd at the Walt Disney World Golf Classic

1985	32	96	15	0	0	1	6	72.49	$48,356

Best finish for 1985: T-10th at the Greater Greensboro Open

1986	34	96	16	1	1	1	2	72.81	$93,716

Best finish for 1986: Win at the Provident Classic

Year	Starts	Rounds Played	Cuts Made	Wins	Top-5s	Top-10s	Top-25s	Scoring Average	Money
1987	28	91	19	0	0	2	10	71.42	$114,184

Best finish for 1987: T-7th at the Canadian Open

1988	30	94	16	0	2	3	9	71.46	$192,706

Best finish for 1988: T-3rd at the Beatrice Western Open

1989	29	97	21	0	2	2	5	71.59	$226,916

Best finish for 1989: T-2nd at the Shearson Lehman Hutton Open & Bank of Boston Classic

1990	28	89	16	0	2	3	8	71.90	$198,118

Best finish for 1990: T-3rd at the Memorial Tournament

1991	28	98	23	1	3	4	11	70.84	$423,088

Best finish for 1991: Win at the Buick Open

1992	26	89	20	2	4	8	12	71.04	$813,093

Best finish for 1992: Win at the New England Classic & The International

1993	26	87	19	0	2	4	11	71.23	$312,947

Best finish for 1993: T-4th at the Memorial Tournament

1994	26	96	24	0	4	7	11	70.72	$671,167

Best finish for 1994: T-3rd at the Buick Classic & NEC World Series of Golf

1995	25	87	19	0	3	5	8	70.70	$471,887

Best finish for 1995: 2nd at The Nestle Invitational

1996	22	82	22	0	4	9	14	70.33	$1,055,050

Best finish for 1996: T-2nd at the United Airlines Hawaiian Open, Kemper Open, Sprint International & The Tour Championship

1997	23	75	17	1	5	6	10	70.68	$1,239,804

Best finish for 1997: Win at the Freeport-McDermott Classic

1998	25	82	19	0	0	1	8	71.66	$401,496

Best finish for 1998: T-6th at the Sprint International

1999	21	63	15	1	1	1	7	71.67	$582,691

Best finish for 1999: Win at the B.C. Open

2000	29	96	20	1	2	5	9	70.79	$1,000,460

Best finish for 2000: Win at the B.C. Open

2001	26	87	21	1	3	6	12	70.36	$1,952,412

Best finish for 2001: Win at the Sony Open in Hawaii

2002	25	85	21	0	4	5	10	70.88	$1,819,412

Best finish for 2002: T-2nd at the Nissan Open & Honda Classic

2003	27	95	22	0	4	8	15	70.76	$2,721,445

Best finish for 2003: T-2nd at the Bay Hill Invitational, Bell Canadian Open & Chrysler Classic of Greensboro

2004	28	89	20	0	0	2	8	71.25	$1,017,898

Best finish for 2004: 8th at the Honda Classic

2005	23	71	14	1	2	4	8	70.94	$1,702,535

Best finish for 2005: Win at the Buick Championship

2006	26	78	13	0	0	0	5	72.23	$545,931

Best finish for 2006: T-16th at The Players Championship & Southern Farm Bureau Classic

2007	18	46	5	0	0	0	0	72.89	$84,645

Best finish for 2007: T-33rd at the Travelers Championship

2008	3	6	0	0	0	0	0	74.50	
Period Totals	Starts	Rounds Played	Cuts Made	Wins	Top-5s	Top-10s	Top-25s	Scoring Average	Money
	653	2117	443	9	49	90	207	71.38	$17,778,172

David Feherty

Year	Starts	Rounds Played	Cuts Made	Wins	Top-5s	Top-10s	Top-25s	Scoring Average	Money
1979	1	3	0	0	0	0	0	77.67	$630
1980	1	0	0	0	0	0	0		
1981	1	0	0	0	0	0	0		
1982	1	2	0	0	0	0	0	78.00	$382
1986	1	2	0	0	0	0	0	80.50	$600
1987	1	4	1	0	0	0	0	72.00	$7,733

Best finish for 1987: T-26th at the British Open

1988	2	4	1	0	0	0	0	73.25	$8,400

Best finish for 1988: 33rd at the NEC World Series of Golf

1989	1	4	1	0	0	1	1	69.75	$41,600

Best finish for 1989: T-6th at the British Open

1990	1	4	1	0	0	0	0	72.50	$5,023

Best finish for 1990: T-68th at the British Open

1991	2	6	1	0	0	1	1	72.83	$39,008

Best finish for 1991: T-7th at the PGA Championship

1992	8	22	4	0	0	0	0	72.23	$21,618

Best finish for 1992: T-28th at the B.C. Open

1993	1	2	0	0	0	0	0	74.50	$924
1994	23	72	14	0	2	3	4	71.60	$260,581

Best finish for 1994: 2nd at the New England Classic

1995	26	71	12	0	0	0	2	72.93	$90,274

Best finish for 1995: T-11th at the Sprint International

1996	3	6	1	0	0	0	0	70.50	$4,068

Best finish for 1996: T-64th at the GTE Byron Nelson Classic

Period Totals	Starts	Rounds Played	Cuts Made	Wins	Top-5s	Top-10s	Top-25s	Scoring Average	Money
	73	202	36	0	2	5	8	72.43	$480,840

Rick Fehr

Year	Starts	Rounds Played	Cuts Made	Wins	Top-5s	Top-10s	Top-25s	Scoring Average	Money
1983	2	6	1	0	0	0	0	75.67	

Best finish for 1983: T-64th at the Western Open

| 1984 | 2 | 8 | 2 | 0 | 0 | 0 | 1 | 72.75 | |

Best finish for 1984: T-25th at the Masters

| 1985 | 15 | 52 | 11 | 0 | 0 | 1 | 4 | 71.38 | $40,101 |

Best finish for 1985: T-9th at the U.S. Open

| 1986 | 27 | 83 | 20 | 1 | 1 | 4 | 7 | 71.83 | $151,182 |

Best finish for 1986: Win at the B.C. Open

| 1987 | 24 | 62 | 8 | 0 | 1 | 3 | 4 | 72.55 | $109,308 |

Best finish for 1987: 2nd at the MONY Tournament Of Champions

| 1988 | 28 | 77 | 11 | 0 | 1 | 1 | 2 | 72.35 | $79,080 |

Best finish for 1988: T-4th at the Panasonic Las Vegas Invitational

| 1989 | 21 | 74 | 16 | 0 | 0 | 1 | 4 | 70.49 | $93,142 |

Best finish for 1989: T-6th at the Federal Express St. Jude Classic

| 1990 | 28 | 90 | 17 | 0 | 1 | 2 | 4 | 71.74 | $150,866 |

Best finish for 1990: T-3rd at the Bank of Boston Classic

| 1991 | 26 | 82 | 14 | 0 | 2 | 3 | 5 | 71.17 | $288,983 |

Best finish for 1991: T-2nd at the Federal Express St. Jude Classic & Canon Greater Hartford Open

| 1992 | 26 | 85 | 18 | 0 | 3 | 4 | 12 | 70.12 | $434,003 |

Best finish for 1992: 2nd at the Bob Hope Chrysler Classic & Memorial Tournament

| 1993 | 26 | 98 | 23 | 0 | 2 | 6 | 13 | 70.38 | $556,322 |

Best finish for 1993: T-2nd at the Bob Hope Chrysler Classic & Federal Express St. Jude Classic

| 1994 | 25 | 77 | 16 | 1 | 2 | 4 | 9 | 71.08 | $577,663 |

Best finish for 1994: Win at the Walt Disney World/Oldsmobile Classic

| 1995 | 24 | 76 | 14 | 0 | 1 | 2 | 3 | 71.24 | $148,766 |

Best finish for 1995: T-5th at the Mercedes Championships

| 1996 | 22 | 74 | 14 | 0 | 3 | 3 | 7 | 70.42 | $273,186 |

Best finish for 1996: T-3rd at the Buick Open

| 1997 | 22 | 69 | 14 | 0 | 2 | 2 | 7 | 70.68 | $328,504 |

Best finish for 1997: T-2nd at the LaCantera Texas Open

| 1998 | 21 | 62 | 12 | 0 | 0 | 1 | 4 | 71.00 | $196,745 |

Best finish for 1998: T-8th at the Las Vegas Invitational

| 1999 | 26 | 71 | 12 | 0 | 0 | 2 | 5 | 71.77 | $275,865 |

Best finish for 1999: T-6th at the FedEx St. Jude Classic

| 2000 | 24 | 71 | 12 | 0 | 1 | 2 | 4 | 71.10 | $313,701 |

Best finish for 2000: T-5th at the Touchstone Energy Tucson Open

| 2001 | 9 | 16 | 1 | 0 | 0 | 0 | 0 | 73.19 | $5,400 |

Best finish for 2001: 80th at the Touchstone Energy Tucson Open

2002	1	2	0	0	0	0	0	71.00	
2003	1	2	0	0	0	0	0	70.50	
2004	3	6	0	0	0	0	0	71.67	
2005	1	2	0	0	0	0	0	72.00	
2008	1	4	1	0	0	0	0	75.50	$5,940

Best finish for 2008: 71st at the Reno-Tahoe Open

Period Totals	Starts	Rounds Played	Cuts Made	Wins	Top-5s	Top-10s	Top-25s	Scoring Average	Money
	405	1249	237	2	20	41	95	71.25	$4,028,759

John Felus

Year	Starts	Rounds Played	Cuts Made	Wins	Top-5s	Top-10s	Top-25s	Scoring Average	Money
1966	11	36	7	0	0	0	0	74.31	$828

Best finish for 1966: T-27th at the Canadian Open

| 1967 | 19 | 45 | 5 | 0 | 0 | 0 | 0 | 74.96 | $485 |

Best finish for 1967: T-37th at the Cajun Classic

| 1968 | 15 | 37 | 4 | 0 | 0 | 0 | 0 | 73.95 | $638 |

Best finish for 1968: T-33rd at the AZALEA Open Invitational

| 1969 | 2 | 6 | 1 | 0 | 0 | 0 | 0 | 76.83 | $300 |

Best finish for 1969: T-33rd at the Alameda County Open

Period Totals	Starts	Rounds Played	Cuts Made	Wins	Top-5s	Top-10s	Top-25s	Scoring Average	Money
	47	124	17	0	0	0	0	74.56	$2,250

Jack Ferenz

Year	Starts	Rounds Played	Cuts Made	Wins	Top-5s	Top-10s	Top-25s	Scoring Average	Money
1979	18	54	9	0	0	0	1	72.39	$8,272

Best finish for 1979: T-19th at the Greater Milwaukee Open

| 1980 | 19 | 49 | 6 | 0 | 0 | 0 | 0 | 72.69 | $5,603 |

Best finish for 1980: T-31st at the Quad Cities Open

| 1981 | 16 | 39 | 5 | 0 | 0 | 0 | 1 | 72.82 | $7,841 |

Best finish for 1981: T-18th at the Atlanta Classic

| 1982 | 21 | 57 | 7 | 0 | 0 | 1 | 2 | 73.51 | $15,155 |

Best finish for 1982: T-10th at the Glen Campbell Los Angles Open

Year	Starts	Rounds Played	Cuts Made	Wins	Top-5s	Top-10s	Top-25s	Scoring Average	Money
1983	1	2	0	0	0	0	0	78.50	$600
1984	13	31	3	0	0	0	0	73.10	$2,598

Best finish for 1984: 42nd at the B.C. Open

1985	1	2	0	0	0	0	0	73.00	
1989	1	2	0	0	0	0	0	74.00	$1,000
1990	21	51	5	0	1	1	1	72.33	$39,596

Best finish for 1990: T-2nd at the Deposit Guaranty

| 1991 | 3 | 8 | 1 | 0 | 0 | 0 | 0 | 71.38 | $2,984 |

Best finish for 1991: T-46th at the Chattanooga Classic

| 1994 | 1 | 2 | 0 | 0 | 0 | 0 | 0 | 75.50 | $1,000 |
| 1997 | 1 | 4 | 1 | 0 | 0 | 0 | 0 | 75.75 | $5,110 |

Best finish for 1997: 82nd at the U.S. Open

2002	1	2	0	0	0	0	0	74.50	
Period Totals	**Starts**	**Rounds Played**	**Cuts Made**	**Wins**	**Top-5s**	**Top-10s**	**Top-25s**	**Scoring Average**	**Money**
	117	303	37	0	1	2	5	72.87	$89,759

Keith Fergus

Year	Starts	Rounds Played	Cuts Made	Wins	Top-5s	Top-10s	Top-25s	Scoring Average	Money
1976	3	8	1	0	0	0	0	73.13	$1,995

Best finish for 1976: T-34th at the San Antonio Texas Open

| 1977 | 26 | 91 | 19 | 0 | 1 | 2 | 9 | 72.04 | $27,750 |

Best finish for 1977: T-5th at the Greater Milwaukee Open

| 1978 | 33 | 117 | 27 | 0 | 1 | 4 | 10 | 71.81 | $55,773 |

Best finish for 1978: T-4th at the Joe Garagiola Tucson Open

| 1979 | 29 | 106 | 24 | 0 | 3 | 7 | 12 | 71.26 | $97,045 |

Best finish for 1979: 3rd at the Colgate Hall Of Fame Classic

| 1980 | 24 | 91 | 24 | 0 | 4 | 5 | 16 | 70.75 | $122,694 |

Best finish for 1980: T-3rd at the Bing Crosby Pro-Am, Doral-Eastern Open & U.S. Open

| 1981 | 26 | 93 | 23 | 1 | 4 | 6 | 10 | 71.10 | $155,369 |

Best finish for 1981: Win at the Memorial Tournament

| 1982 | 28 | 94 | 18 | 1 | 2 | 3 | 9 | 71.89 | $123,515 |

Best finish for 1982: Win at the Georgia-Pacific Atlanta Golf Classic

| 1983 | 25 | 92 | 20 | 1 | 1 | 3 | 10 | 71.70 | $155,922 |

Best finish for 1983: Win at the Bob Hope Chrysler Classic

| 1984 | 26 | 81 | 15 | 0 | 1 | 3 | 7 | 72.21 | $80,258 |

Best finish for 1984: 3rd at the Greater Milwaukee Open

| 1985 | 26 | 92 | 21 | 0 | 2 | 3 | 11 | 71.10 | $137,352 |

Best finish for 1985: T-4th at the Houston Open & Memorial Tournament

| 1986 | 28 | 77 | 14 | 0 | 0 | 0 | 4 | 72.09 | $44,533 |

Best finish for 1986: T-16th at the Los Angeles Open

| 1987 | 7 | 23 | 3 | 0 | 0 | 0 | 0 | 72.22 | $4,033 |

Best finish for 1987: T-45th at the Big I Houston Open

| 1988 | 3 | 10 | 1 | 0 | 0 | 0 | 0 | 73.30 | $2,002 |

Best finish for 1988: T-45th at the Georgia-Pacific Atlanta Golf Classic

| 1989 | 2 | 6 | 0 | 0 | 0 | 0 | 0 | 74.50 | |
| 1991 | 1 | 4 | 1 | 0 | 0 | 0 | 0 | 70.25 | $2,532 |

Best finish for 1991: T-41st at the Independent Insurance Agent Open

1992	1	4	0	0	0	0	0	71.00	
1993	1	2	0	0	0	0	0	76.50	
1994	5	14	3	0	0	0	1	72.00	$16,749

Best finish for 1994: T-22nd at the Anheuser-Busch Golf Classic

| 1995 | 26 | 82 | 17 | 0 | 0 | 1 | 4 | 71.17 | $146,358 |

Best finish for 1995: T-8th at the Honda Classic

| 1996 | 29 | 84 | 13 | 0 | 0 | 1 | 4 | 71.40 | $164,640 |

Best finish for 1996: T-6th at the LaCantera Texas Open

| 1997 | 17 | 58 | 12 | 0 | 0 | 0 | 5 | 70.81 | $96,025 |

Best finish for 1997: T-14th at the BellSouth Classic

| 1998 | 17 | 53 | 9 | 0 | 0 | 0 | 3 | 71.09 | $77,098 |

Best finish for 1998: T-21st at the Deposit Guaranty Golf Classic

| 1999 | 7 | 19 | 3 | 0 | 0 | 0 | 0 | 72.89 | $17,644 |

Best finish for 1999: T-44th at the Bell Canadian Open

| 2000 | 7 | 18 | 1 | 0 | 0 | 0 | 0 | 72.22 | $6,169 |

Best finish for 2000: T-68th at the Memorial Tournament

2001	3	8	0	0	0	0	0	73.50	
2002	2	6	0	0	0	0	0	70.67	
2003	5	16	2	0	0	0	0	71.81	$20,455

Best finish for 2003: T-58th at the Memorial Tournament

2004	1	4	0	0	0	0	0	69.75	
2006	1	4	0	0	0	0	0	71.75	
2007	1	4	0	0	0	0	0	72.50	
Period Totals	**Starts**	**Rounds Played**	**Cuts Made**	**Wins**	**Top-5s**	**Top-10s**	**Top-25s**	**Scoring Average**	**Money**
	410	1361	271	3	19	38	115	71.58	$1,555,913

Ben Ferguson

Year	Starts	Rounds Played	Cuts Made	Wins	Top-5s	Top-10s	Top-25s	Scoring Average	Money
2001	30	74	7	0	0	1	2	72.46	$187,970

Best finish for 2001: T-9th at the Shell Houston Open

Year	Starts	Rounds Played	Cuts Made	Wins	Top-5s	Top-10s	Top-25s	Scoring Average	Money
2007	1	2	0	0	0	0	0	73.00	
Period Totals	31	76	7	0	0	1	2	72.47	$187,970

Vicente Fernandez

Year	Starts	Rounds Played	Cuts Made	Wins	Top-5s	Top-10s	Top-25s	Scoring Average	Money
1971	1	4	1	0	0	0	1	73.00	$638

Best finish for 1971: T-25th at the British Open

Year	Starts	Rounds Played	Cuts Made	Wins	Top-5s	Top-10s	Top-25s	Scoring Average	Money
1972	1	4	1	0	0	0	0	73.50	$512

Best finish for 1972: T-31st at the British Open

Year	Starts	Rounds Played	Cuts Made	Wins	Top-5s	Top-10s	Top-25s	Scoring Average	Money
1973	1	2	0	0	0	0	0	77.00	$130
1974	1	4	1	0	0	0	0	75.25	$462

Best finish for 1974: T-31st at the British Open

Year	Starts	Rounds Played	Cuts Made	Wins	Top-5s	Top-10s	Top-25s	Scoring Average	Money
1975	1	4	1	0	0	0	0	74.25	$385

Best finish for 1975: T-53rd at the British Open

Year	Starts	Rounds Played	Cuts Made	Wins	Top-5s	Top-10s	Top-25s	Scoring Average	Money
1976	1	4	1	0	0	1	1	72.25	$3,555

Best finish for 1976: T-10th at the British Open

Year	Starts	Rounds Played	Cuts Made	Wins	Top-5s	Top-10s	Top-25s	Scoring Average	Money
1977	13	37	6	0	0	0	2	73.00	$7,734

Best finish for 1977: T-11th at the Houston Open

Year	Starts	Rounds Played	Cuts Made	Wins	Top-5s	Top-10s	Top-25s	Scoring Average	Money
1978	12	32	4	0	0	0	0	74.06	$1,372

Best finish for 1978: T-58th at the Doral-Eastern Open

Year	Starts	Rounds Played	Cuts Made	Wins	Top-5s	Top-10s	Top-25s	Scoring Average	Money
1979	1	2	0	0	0	0	0	77.00	$420
1980	1	4	1	0	0	0	0	73.00	$1,380

Best finish for 1980: T-45th at the British Open

Year	Starts	Rounds Played	Cuts Made	Wins	Top-5s	Top-10s	Top-25s	Scoring Average	Money
1981	1	3	0	0	0	0	0	74.33	$700
1983	1	4	1	0	0	0	0	71.50	$1,450

Best finish for 1983: T-39th at the British Open

Year	Starts	Rounds Played	Cuts Made	Wins	Top-5s	Top-10s	Top-25s	Scoring Average	Money
1984	1	2	0	0	0	0	0	74.50	$429
1985	1	2	0	0	0	0	0	77.50	$544
1986	1	4	1	0	0	0	1	73.50	$7,533

Best finish for 1986: T-21st at the British Open

Year	Starts	Rounds Played	Cuts Made	Wins	Top-5s	Top-10s	Top-25s	Scoring Average	Money
1987	1	2	0	0	0	0	0	74.50	$640
1989	1	2	0	0	0	0	0	75.50	$800
1990	1	4	1	0	0	0	0	71.00	$9,276

Best finish for 1990: T-31st at the British Open

Year	Starts	Rounds Played	Cuts Made	Wins	Top-5s	Top-10s	Top-25s	Scoring Average	Money
1993	1	2	0	0	0	0	0	72.50	$924
Period Totals	42	122	19	0	0	1	5	73.61	$38,885

Jim Ferree

Year	Starts	Rounds Played	Cuts Made	Wins	Top-5s	Top-10s	Top-25s	Scoring Average	Money
1958	32	115	25	1	2	3	8	76.86	$11,641

Best finish for 1958: Win at the Vancouver Open

Year	Starts	Rounds Played	Cuts Made	Wins	Top-5s	Top-10s	Top-25s	Scoring Average	Money
1959	27	106	23	0	3	6	21	70.96	$16,888

Best finish for 1959: T-2nd at the Arlington Hotel Open Invitational & Kentucky Derby Open Invitational

Year	Starts	Rounds Played	Cuts Made	Wins	Top-5s	Top-10s	Top-25s	Scoring Average	Money
1960	16	64	15	0	0	0	8	71.83	$5,031

Best finish for 1960: T-12th at the Western Open Championship, Utah Open Invitational & Portland Open Invitational

Year	Starts	Rounds Played	Cuts Made	Wins	Top-5s	Top-10s	Top-25s	Scoring Average	Money
1961	16	65	15	0	1	4	12	70.98	$11,108

Best finish for 1961: T-3rd at the Bakersfield Open

Year	Starts	Rounds Played	Cuts Made	Wins	Top-5s	Top-10s	Top-25s	Scoring Average	Money
1962	21	82	21	0	2	2	10	71.73	$11,584

Best finish for 1962: T-5th at the Colonial National Invitational & Mobile Sertoma Open Invitational

Year	Starts	Rounds Played	Cuts Made	Wins	Top-5s	Top-10s	Top-25s	Scoring Average	Money
1963	25	98	24	0	0	4	9	71.93	$10,529

Best finish for 1963: T-6th at the Jamaica Open Invitational

Year	Starts	Rounds Played	Cuts Made	Wins	Top-5s	Top-10s	Top-25s	Scoring Average	Money
1964	31	105	19	0	1	2	7	72.50	$10,884

Best finish for 1964: T-4th at the Portland Open

Year	Starts	Rounds Played	Cuts Made	Wins	Top-5s	Top-10s	Top-25s	Scoring Average	Money
1965	33	116	24	0	1	3	9	72.58	$18,219

Best finish for 1965: T-3rd at the Almaden Open

Year	Starts	Rounds Played	Cuts Made	Wins	Top-5s	Top-10s	Top-25s	Scoring Average	Money
1966	24	82	17	0	0	0	2	72.85	$6,993

Best finish for 1966: T-19th at the Houston Champions International

Year	Starts	Rounds Played	Cuts Made	Wins	Top-5s	Top-10s	Top-25s	Scoring Average	Money
1967	9	24	3	0	0	0	0	74.00	

Best finish for 1967: T-58th at the Atlanta Classic

Year	Starts	Rounds Played	Cuts Made	Wins	Top-5s	Top-10s	Top-25s	Scoring Average	Money
1968	5	10	0	0	0	0	0	76.20	
1969	5	14	2	0	0	0	0	74.93	$182

Best finish for 1969: T-52nd at the Heritage Golf Classic

Year	Starts	Rounds Played	Cuts Made	Wins	Top-5s	Top-10s	Top-25s	Scoring Average	Money
1971	1	2	0	0	0	0	0	74.00	
1972	2	4	0	0	0	0	0	75.00	
1973	1	4	0	0	0	0	0	75.75	

Year	Starts	Rounds Played	Cuts Made	Wins	Top-5s	Top-10s	Top-25s	Scoring Average	Money
1974	1	2	0	0	0	0	0	76.00	
1975	2	6	1	0	0	0	0	75.83	$203

Best finish for 1975: T-70th at the Sea Pines Heritage Classic

1976	4	10	1	0	0	0	0	77.40	$1,000

Best finish for 1976: 66th at the U.S. Open

1977	6	15	2	0	0	0	0	74.40	$619

Best finish for 1977: T-63rd at the Bing Crosby Pro-Am

1979	2	4	0	0	0	0	0	75.50	$350
Period Totals	Starts	Rounds Played	Cuts Made	Wins	Top-5s	Top-10s	Top-25s	Scoring Average	Money
	265	932	192	1	10	24	86	72.89	$105,231

PGA Tour career totals from 1953 to 1979

	Starts	Rounds Played	Cuts Made	Wins	Top-5s	Top-10s	Top-25s	Scoring Average	Money
	293	1048	222	1	11	25	90	N/A	$107,707

Gene Ferrell

Year	Starts	Rounds Played	Cuts Made	Wins	Top-5s	Top-10s	Top-25s	Scoring Average	Money
1968	3	8	1	0	0	0	0	75.13	$500

Best finish for 1968: 72nd at the Lucky International Open Invitational

1969	13	40	7	0	0	0	0	73.68	$1,531

Best finish for 1969: T-38th at the Monsanto Open

1970	19	63	13	0	0	0	0	73.32	$4,640

Best finish for 1970: T-26th at the Bahama Islands Open

1971	19	50	7	0	0	0	1	73.70	$3,194

Best finish for 1971: T-16th at the Glen Campbell Los Angles Open

1972	1	0	0	0	0	0	0		
1975	1	2	0	0	0	0	0	77.00	
1981	1	2	0	0	0	0	0	76.50	$550
1982	1	2	0	0	0	0	0	78.00	$650
1987	1	2	0	0	0	0	0	72.50	
Period Totals	Starts	Rounds Played	Cuts Made	Wins	Top-5s	Top-10s	Top-25s	Scoring Average	Money
	59	169	28	0	0	0	1	73.73	$11,065

Kenneth Ferrie

Year	Starts	Rounds Played	Cuts Made	Wins	Top-5s	Top-10s	Top-25s	Scoring Average	Money
2003	1	2	0	0	0	0	0	77.50	$3,974
2004	1	4	1	0	0	0	0	72.50	$27,714

Best finish for 2004: T-42nd at the British Open

2005	3	10	2	0	0	0	1	71.70	$124,192

Best finish for 2005: T-19th at the WGC-NEC Invitational

2006	3	7	1	0	0	1	1	73.14	$189,223

Best finish for 2006: T-6th at the U.S. Open

2007	2	6	1	0	0	0	0	76.17	$31,084

Best finish for 2007: T-42nd at the U.S. Open

2008	25	72	11	0	0	0	3	71.81	$288,772

Best finish for 2008: T-13th at the Buick Invitational

Period Totals	Starts	Rounds Played	Cuts Made	Wins	Top-5s	Top-10s	Top-25s	Scoring Average	Money
	35	101	16	0	0	1	5	72.29	$664,960

Jim Ferriell

Year	Starts	Rounds Played	Cuts Made	Wins	Top-5s	Top-10s	Top-25s	Scoring Average	Money
1965	18	52	9	0	0	0	4	72.94	$4,268

Best finish for 1965: T-16th at the Texas Open & Oklahoma City Open

1966	20	63	12	0	0	0	2	73.59	$3,192

Best finish for 1966: T-12th at the Portland Open Invitational

1968	2	4	0	0	0	0	0	76.00	
1969	4	12	2	0	0	0	1	74.75	$579

Best finish for 1969: T-16th at the West End Classic

1970	19	60	11	0	0	0	3	72.82	$6,899

Best finish for 1970: T-12th at the Tallahassee Open & Sahara Invitational

1971	11	34	6	0	0	0	1	73.24	$4,059

Best finish for 1971: T-16th at the Sahara Invitational

1972	27	91	17	0	0	1	5	72.86	$16,179

Best finish for 1972: T-10th at the Sahara Invitational

1973	31	111	22	0	2	5	9	71.98	$40,924

Best finish for 1973: T-3rd at the Sahara Invitational

1974	27	71	10	0	1	1	4	73.49	$13,102

Best finish for 1974: T-5th at the Southern Open

1975	4	9	0	0	0	0	0	74.89	
1977	2	6	1	0	0	0	0	76.17	$488

Best finish for 1977: T-66th at the PGA Championship

1980	3	6	0	0	0	0	0	84.33	

Year	Starts	Rounds Played	Cuts Made	Wins	Top-5s	Top-10s	Top-25s	Scoring Average	Money
1981	3	5	0	0	0	0	0	84.20	$550
1982	1	2	0	0	0	0	0	86.00	
1983	1	2	0	0	0	0	0	80.50	
Period Totals	Starts	Rounds Played	Cuts Made	Wins	Top-5s	Top-10s	Top-25s	Scoring Average	Money
	173	528	90	0	3	7	29	73.33	$90,240

Jim Ferrier

Year	Starts	Rounds Played	Cuts Made	Wins	Top-5s	Top-10s	Top-25s	Scoring Average	Money
1958	5	20	5	0	0	0	2	72.65	$512

Best finish for 1958: T-13th at the Tijuana Open

1959	5	20	4	0	0	0	3	71.10	$2,287

Best finish for 1959: T-12th at the Carling Open Invitational

1960	5	19	4	0	1	1	3	71.63	$7,400

Best finish for 1960: 2nd at the PGA Championship

1961	13	52	13	1	1	3	7	71.25	$6,388

Best finish for 1961: Win at the Almaden Open

1962	17	67	15	0	1	3	12	71.55	$12,530

Best finish for 1962: T-2nd at the Tucson Open Invitational

1963	17	69	16	0	0	2	8	71.39	$9,819

Best finish for 1963: 7th at the PGA Championship

1964	28	84	16	0	1	2	5	72.96	$10,121

Best finish for 1964: T-5th at the Masters

1965	22	59	7	0	0	0	2	73.61	$3,000

Best finish for 1965: T-20th at the Greater Greensboro Open

1966	12	30	2	0	0	0	0	74.73	$436

Best finish for 1966: T-49th at the PGA Championship

1967	21	52	4	0	0	0	0	74.56	$1,113

Best finish for 1967: T-33rd at the Los Angles Open

1968	28	79	10	0	0	0	1	73.48	$2,693

Best finish for 1968: T-24th at the Greater Milwaukee Open Invitational

1969	19	51	7	0	0	0	0	73.76	$1,172

Best finish for 1969: T-52nd at the Sahara Invitational

1970	12	27	1	0	0	0	0	74.56	$114

Best finish for 1970: 79th at the Sahara Invitational

1971	16	34	1	0	0	0	0	75.62	$220

Best finish for 1971: 68th at the Tucson Open

1972	15	34	1	0	0	0	0	75.91	$240

Best finish for 1972: T-74th at the Tucson Open

1973	10	24	1	0	0	0	0	75.92	

Best finish for 1973: T-76th at the Phoenix Open

1974	11	22	0	0	0	0	0	76.36	
1975	7	14	0	0	0	0	0	77.71	
1976	6	14	0	0	0	0	0	77.93	
1977	10	16	0	0	0	0	0	79.38	
1978	8	17	0	0	0	0	0	78.71	
1979	5	12	0	0	0	0	0	77.75	
Period Totals	Starts	Rounds Played	Cuts Made	Wins	Top-5s	Top-10s	Top-25s	Scoring Average	Money
	292	911	107	1	4	11	43	73.78	$58,043

PGA Tour career totals from 1940 to 1979

	Starts	Rounds Played	Cuts Made	Wins	Top-5s	Top-10s	Top-25s	Scoring Average	Money
	600	1156	368	18	N/A	162	271	N/A	$211,560

Mike Fetchick

Year	Starts	Rounds Played	Cuts Made	Wins	Top-5s	Top-10s	Top-25s	Scoring Average	Money
1958	36	122	24	0	1	1	9	72.61	$6,126

Best finish for 1958: T-5th at the Eastern Open

1959	6	20	3	0	1	2	3	72.55	$2,043

Best finish for 1959: T-4th at the Tijuana Open Invitational

1960	1	5	1	0	0	0	0	71.40	$182

Best finish for 1960: T-49th at the Palm Springs Desert Golf Classic

1961	2	6	1	0	0	0	1	72.17	$353

Best finish for 1961: T-21st at the Baton Rouge Open Invitational

1962	3	12	3	0	0	0	0	72.08	$789

Best finish for 1962: T-29th at the Phoenix Open Invitational

1963	8	30	8	0	0	0	3	72.57	$3,273

Best finish for 1963: T-14th at the U.S. Open

1964	13	35	5	0	0	0	1	74.23	$1,025

Best finish for 1964: T-23rd at the PGA Championship

1965	14	47	7	0	0	1	2	73.62	$2,637

Best finish for 1965: T-10th at the Bing Crosby Pro-Am

1966	8	24	3	0	0	0	0	73.54	$1,156

Best finish for 1966: T-44th at the Cajun Classic

Year	Starts	Rounds Played	Cuts Made	Wins	Top-5s	Top-10s	Top-25s	Scoring Average	Money
1967	10	33	6	0	0	0	0	72.94	$2,547

Best finish for 1967: T-27th at the Bob Hope Classic

| 1968 | 18 | 63 | 13 | 0 | 0 | 0 | 3 | 72.57 | $4,609 |

Best finish for 1968: T-14th at the Greater Hartford Open Invitational

| 1969 | 12 | 37 | 5 | 0 | 0 | 0 | 1 | 73.92 | $2,452 |

Best finish for 1969: T-23rd at the Andy Williams-San Diego Open

| 1970 | 4 | 12 | 1 | 0 | 0 | 0 | 0 | 72.33 | $174 |

Best finish for 1970: T-59th at the Greater Hartford Open Invitational

| 1971 | 7 | 20 | 3 | 0 | 0 | 0 | 0 | 74.55 | $894 |

Best finish for 1971: T-51st at the National Airlines Open

| 1975 | 2 | 3 | 0 | 0 | 0 | 0 | 0 | 80.67 | $500 |
| 1981 | 1 | 0 | 0 | 0 | 0 | 0 | 0 | | |

Period Totals	Starts	Rounds Played	Cuts Made	Wins	Top-5s	Top-10s	Top-25s	Scoring Average	Money
	145	469	83	0	2	4	23	73.09	$28,760

PGA Tour career totals from 1952 to 1981

	Starts	Rounds Played	Cuts Made	Wins	Top-5s	Top-10s	Top-25s	Scoring Average	Money
	242	847	180	3	7	15	63	N/A	$57,022

Forrest Fezler

Year	Starts	Rounds Played	Cuts Made	Wins	Top-5s	Top-10s	Top-25s	Scoring Average	Money
1969	1	4	1	0	0	0	0	76.25	

Best finish for 1969: T-33rd at the Alameda County Open

1970	2	6	0	0	0	0	0	75.33	$500
1971	1	2	0	0	0	0	0	74.00	
1972	30	104	21	0	0	3	10	72.33	$24,603

Best finish for 1972: T-8th at the Glen Campbell Los Angles Open

| 1973 | 36 | 129 | 26 | 0 | 5 | 7 | 12 | 71.85 | $104,353 |

Best finish for 1973: 2nd at the Jackie Gleason's Inverrary Classic, Canadian Open & Southern Open

| 1974 | 32 | 110 | 24 | 1 | 3 | 6 | 13 | 71.75 | $87,198 |

Best finish for 1974: Win at the Southern Open

| 1975 | 29 | 87 | 17 | 0 | 3 | 4 | 9 | 72.41 | $52,158 |

Best finish for 1975: T-2nd at the Doral-Eastern Open

| 1976 | 31 | 109 | 25 | 0 | 2 | 2 | 8 | 72.20 | $59,793 |

Best finish for 1976: T-2nd at the Houston Open & Danny Thomas Memphis Classic

| 1977 | 32 | 95 | 17 | 0 | 0 | 1 | 10 | 72.14 | $30,569 |

Best finish for 1977: 9th at the Southern Open

| 1978 | 30 | 93 | 17 | 0 | 1 | 1 | 3 | 72.99 | $31,115 |

Best finish for 1978: 3rd at the Glen Campbell Los Angles Open

| 1979 | 25 | 72 | 11 | 0 | 0 | 0 | 1 | 72.93 | $11,427 |

Best finish for 1979: T-22nd at the IVB Philadelphia Golf Classic

| 1980 | 24 | 64 | 8 | 0 | 0 | 2 | 2 | 72.97 | $18,943 |

Best finish for 1980: T-7th at the Andy Williams-San Diego Open

| 1981 | 25 | 66 | 11 | 0 | 0 | 1 | 4 | 72.02 | $17,641 |

Best finish for 1981: T-10th at the World Disney World National Team Championship

| 1982 | 29 | 85 | 14 | 0 | 0 | 1 | 7 | 71.55 | $38,983 |

Best finish for 1982: 10th at the Bob Hope Chrysler Classic

| 1983 | 30 | 89 | 13 | 0 | 0 | 1 | 1 | 72.82 | $24,452 |

Best finish for 1983: T-7th at the Buick Open

| 1984 | 12 | 36 | 6 | 0 | 0 | 0 | 2 | 73.00 | $14,152 |

Best finish for 1984: T-12th at the Canadian Open

| 1985 | 2 | 6 | 1 | 0 | 0 | 0 | 0 | 71.50 | $1,400 |

Best finish for 1985: T-41st at the Southern Open

| 1986 | 4 | 10 | 1 | 0 | 0 | 0 | 1 | 73.30 | $2,080 |

Best finish for 1986: T-21st at the Tallahassee Open

| 1987 | 6 | 17 | 2 | 0 | 0 | 0 | 0 | 74.00 | $1,784 |

Best finish for 1987: 70th at the Centel Classic

| 1988 | 9 | 26 | 4 | 0 | 0 | 0 | 0 | 72.88 | $3,477 |

Best finish for 1988: T-60th at the Hardee's Golf Classic

| 1989 | 7 | 15 | 2 | 0 | 0 | 0 | 0 | 72.47 | $1,853 |

Best finish for 1989: T-47th at the Deposit Guaranty Golf Classic

1991	7	15	0	0	0	0	0	73.93	
1992	3	6	0	0	0	0	0	74.83	
1993	7	17	2	0	0	0	0	73.53	$2,610

Best finish for 1993: T-41st at the Deposit Guaranty Classic

1994	2	4	0	0	0	0	0	72.25	
1995	1	2	0	0	0	0	0	74.50	
1996	2	4	0	0	0	0	0	75.25	

Period Totals	Starts	Rounds Played	Cuts Made	Wins	Top-5s	Top-10s	Top-25s	Scoring Average	Money
	419	1273	223	1	14	29	83	72.44	$529,090

Dow Finsterwald

Year	Starts	Rounds Played	Cuts Made	Wins	Top-5s	Top-10s	Top-25s	Scoring Average	Money
1958	34	135	33	3	15	19	29	70.29	$36,731

Best finish for 1958: Win at the Rubber City Open, Utah Open & PGA Championship

| 1959 | 26 | 104 | 24 | 3 | 10 | 13 | 21 | 70.94 | $33,907 |

Best finish for 1959: Win at the Greater Greensboro Open Invitational, Carling Open Invitational & Kansas City Open Invitational

| 1960 | 23 | 93 | 19 | 2 | 10 | 13 | 19 | 70.18 | $39,642 |

Best finish for 1960: Win at the Los Angles Open Invitational & Greater New Orleans Open Invitational

| 1961 | 19 | 75 | 16 | 0 | 2 | 5 | 11 | 71.27 | $15,018 |

Best finish for 1961: T-2nd at the Canadian Open Invitational

| 1962 | 28 | 114 | 24 | 0 | 7 | 12 | 20 | 71.20 | $33,709 |

Best finish for 1962: T-3rd at the Masters, Thunderbird Classic Invitational, Beaumont Open Invitational, Carling Open Invitational & West Palm Beach Open Invitational

| 1963 | 28 | 113 | 25 | 1 | 8 | 11 | 22 | 71.04 | $49,888 |

Best finish for 1963: Win at the "500" Festival Open Invitational

| 1964 | 26 | 96 | 22 | 0 | 3 | 8 | 16 | 71.46 | $27,423 |

Best finish for 1964: 2nd at the Buick Open

| 1965 | 22 | 67 | 12 | 0 | 0 | 0 | 3 | 73.99 | $5,079 |

Best finish for 1965: T-19th at the Azalea Open

| 1966 | 20 | 68 | 13 | 0 | 0 | 1 | 7 | 73.10 | $13,827 |

Best finish for 1966: T-8th at the Dallas Open Invitational

| 1967 | 20 | 60 | 9 | 0 | 0 | 0 | 2 | 74.30 | $4,055 |

Best finish for 1967: T-12th at the Oklahoma City Open

| 1968 | 21 | 70 | 13 | 0 | 0 | 2 | 5 | 73.01 | $13,015 |

Best finish for 1968: T-6th at the Kemper Open Invitational

| 1969 | 26 | 89 | 19 | 0 | 1 | 1 | 5 | 72.58 | $16,082 |

Best finish for 1969: 5th at the Andy Williams-San Diego Open

| 1970 | 20 | 54 | 7 | 0 | 0 | 0 | 4 | 73.00 | $8,355 |

Best finish for 1970: T-14th at the Doral-Eastern Open

| 1971 | 17 | 44 | 6 | 0 | 0 | 1 | 2 | 73.68 | $7,905 |

Best finish for 1971: T-9th at the Andy Williams-San Diego Open

| 1972 | 15 | 42 | 6 | 0 | 0 | 0 | 3 | 73.48 | $7,957 |

Best finish for 1972: T-11th at the Kaiser International Open

| 1973 | 16 | 44 | 5 | 0 | 0 | 0 | 1 | 74.02 | $3,013 |

Best finish for 1973: T-21st at the Kaiser International Open

| 1974 | 12 | 27 | 3 | 0 | 0 | 0 | 0 | 74.74 | $618 |

Best finish for 1974: T-50th at the Andy Williams-San Diego Open

| 1975 | 11 | 26 | 2 | 0 | 0 | 0 | 0 | 76.35 | $638 |

Best finish for 1975: T-66th at the Sahara Invitational

| 1976 | 5 | 13 | 3 | 0 | 0 | 0 | 0 | 77.46 | |
| 1977 | 7 | 19 | 1 | 0 | 0 | 0 | 0 | 75.74 | $488 |

Best finish for 1977: 70th at the PGA Championship

1978	6	15	0	0	0	0	0	76.40	$303
1979	3	7	0	0	0	0	0	75.29	$941
1980	4	9	0	0	0	0	0	76.78	$1,100
1981	1	2	0	0	0	0	0	73.50	
1982	2	5	0	0	0	0	0	76.80	
1983	1	2	0	0	0	0	0	77.50	
1984	2	4	0	0	0	0	0	79.75	$1,000
1985	1	2	0	0	0	0	0	80.00	
1990	1	2	0	0	0	0	0	76.50	
1991	1	2	0	0	0	0	0	74.50	
Period Totals	**Starts**	**Rounds Played**	**Cuts Made**	**Wins**	**Top-5s**	**Top-10s**	**Top-25s**	**Scoring Average**	**Money**
	418	1403	262	9	56	86	170	72.35	$320,695

PGA Tour career totals from 1950 to 1991

	Starts	Rounds Played	Cuts Made	Wins	Top-5s	Top-10s	Top-25s	Scoring Average	Money
	535	1866	379	13	75	135	253	N/A	$402,102

Ed Fiori

Year	Starts	Rounds Played	Cuts Made	Wins	Top-5s	Top-10s	Top-25s	Scoring Average	Money
1978	25	70	11	0	1	1	4	72.73	$19,546

Best finish for 1978: T-4th at the Doral-Eastern Open

| 1979 | 27 | 87 | 17 | 1 | 1 | 1 | 5 | 72.52 | $61,737 |

Best finish for 1979: Win at the Southern Open

| 1980 | 31 | 105 | 23 | 0 | 1 | 5 | 12 | 71.80 | $84,352 |

Best finish for 1980: T-5th at the Doral-Eastern Open

| 1981 | 34 | 98 | 17 | 1 | 1 | 4 | 8 | 72.48 | $107,010 |

Best finish for 1981: Win at the Western Open

| 1982 | 31 | 109 | 23 | 1 | 1 | 2 | 6 | 72.17 | $93,099 |

Best finish for 1982: Win at the Bob Hope Chrysler Classic

| 1983 | 29 | 105 | 23 | 0 | 3 | 5 | 10 | 71.30 | $175,619 |

Best finish for 1983: 2nd at the Doral-Eastern Open

Year	Starts	Rounds Played	Cuts Made	Wins	Top-5s	Top-10s	Top-25s	Scoring Average	Money
1984	32	92	16	0	0	0	5	72.74	$44,682

Best finish for 1984: T-14th at the Isuzu/Andy Williams San Diego Open

| 1985 | 29 | 94 | 19 | 0 | 2 | 5 | 8 | 71.54 | $116,002 |

Best finish for 1985: T-3rd at the Hawaiian Open

| 1986 | 32 | 96 | 16 | 0 | 1 | 2 | 6 | 71.77 | $70,828 |

Best finish for 1986: 4th at the Buick Open

| 1987 | 28 | 87 | 17 | 0 | 0 | 2 | 5 | 71.13 | $104,570 |

Best finish for 1987: T-6th at the Bob Hope Chrysler Classic

| 1988 | 29 | 109 | 25 | 0 | 2 | 2 | 9 | 70.81 | $193,765 |

Best finish for 1988: T-2nd at the Honda Classic

| 1989 | 29 | 100 | 22 | 0 | 1 | 2 | 7 | 71.11 | $189,637 |

Best finish for 1989: 3rd at the Kmart Greater Greensboro Open

| 1990 | 33 | 108 | 22 | 0 | 0 | 0 | 4 | 71.85 | $108,816 |

Best finish for 1990: T-11th at the H-E-B Texas Open

| 1991 | 29 | 100 | 21 | 0 | 0 | 0 | 7 | 70.69 | $120,722 |

Best finish for 1991: T-11th at the Buick Southern Open

| 1992 | 30 | 95 | 18 | 0 | 0 | 2 | 5 | 71.39 | $124,536 |

Best finish for 1992: T-7th at the Phoenix Open

| 1993 | 31 | 95 | 16 | 0 | 0 | 2 | 4 | 71.62 | $117,617 |

Best finish for 1993: T-10th at the Freeport-McMoRan Classic & Kemper Open

| 1994 | 14 | 46 | 8 | 0 | 1 | 1 | 1 | 71.24 | $108,259 |

Best finish for 1994: 3rd at the New England Classic

| 1995 | 15 | 49 | 10 | 0 | 0 | 0 | 3 | 71.31 | $83,852 |

Best finish for 1995: T-12th at the Shell Houston Open

| 1996 | 21 | 61 | 10 | 1 | 1 | 1 | 2 | 72.21 | $261,292 |

Best finish for 1996: Win at the Quad City Classic

| 1997 | 21 | 50 | 7 | 0 | 0 | 0 | 1 | 72.66 | $60,155 |

Best finish for 1997: T-24th at the Mercedes Championship

| 1998 | 3 | 8 | 1 | 0 | 0 | 0 | 0 | 73.38 | $4,080 |

Best finish for 1998: T-67th at the Doral-Ryder Open

| 1999 | 7 | 16 | 1 | 0 | 0 | 0 | 0 | 73.94 | $5,610 |

Best finish for 1999: T-76th at the Doral-Ryder Open

| 2000 | 15 | 37 | 3 | 0 | 0 | 0 | 0 | 72.54 | $16,925 |

Best finish for 2000: T-53rd at the Phoenix Open

| 2001 | 6 | 14 | 1 | 0 | 0 | 0 | 0 | 72.79 | $12,760 |

Best finish for 2001: T-27th at the B.C. Open

2002	6	14	0	0	0	0	0	73.14	
2004	1	4	0	0	0	0	0	73.75	
Period Totals	**Starts**	**Rounds Played**	**Cuts Made**	**Wins**	**Top-5s**	**Top-10s**	**Top-25s**	**Scoring Average**	**Money**
	588	1849	347	4	16	37	112	71.79	$2,285,469

Todd Fischer

Year	Starts	Rounds Played	Cuts Made	Wins	Top-5s	Top-10s	Top-25s	Scoring Average	Money
1993	1	2	0	0	0	0	0	78.50	
1995	1	2	0	0	0	0	0	75.00	
2000	1	2	0	0	0	0	0	75.00	$1,000
2001	1	2	0	0	0	0	0	75.50	$1,000
2002	1	4	1	0	0	0	1	70.75	$60,000

Best finish for 2002: T-15th at the AT&T Pebble Beach

| 2003 | 32 | 95 | 15 | 0 | 1 | 2 | 4 | 71.17 | $621,398 |

Best finish for 2003: 3rd at the Greater Hartford Open

| 2004 | 33 | 102 | 18 | 0 | 2 | 4 | 7 | 71.04 | $847,996 |

Best finish for 2004: T-3rd at the B.C. Open & Valero Texas Open

| 2005 | 35 | 97 | 15 | 0 | 1 | 2 | 6 | 71.25 | $664,098 |

Best finish for 2005: 3rd at the Reno-Tahoe Open

| 2006 | 35 | 99 | 16 | 0 | 0 | 0 | 3 | 71.43 | $395,817 |

Best finish for 2006: T-15th at the BellSouth Classic

| 2007 | 4 | 13 | 2 | 0 | 0 | 1 | 1 | 72.31 | $94,000 |

Best finish for 2007: T-9th at the Reno-Tahoe Open

| **Period Totals** | **Starts** | **Rounds Played** | **Cuts Made** | **Wins** | **Top-5s** | **Top-10s** | **Top-25s** | **Scoring Average** | **Money** |
| | 144 | 418 | 67 | 0 | 4 | 9 | 22 | 71.34 | $2,685,310 |

Marvin Fitts

Year	Starts	Rounds Played	Cuts Made	Wins	Top-5s	Top-10s	Top-25s	Scoring Average	Money
1958	7	23	4	0	0	0	1	72.39	$721

Best finish for 1958: T-15th at the Kentucky Derby Open

| 1965 | 8 | 22 | 3 | 0 | 0 | 0 | 0 | 74.64 | $222 |

Best finish for 1965: T-38th at the Portland Open

| 1966 | 19 | 53 | 9 | 0 | 0 | 1 | 3 | 73.49 | $3,442 |

Best finish for 1966: T-8th at the Azalea Open Invitational

| 1967 | 10 | 34 | 7 | 0 | 0 | 0 | 0 | 73.44 | $517 |

Best finish for 1967: T-39th at the Memphis Open

Year	Starts	Rounds Played	Cuts Made	Wins	Top-5s	Top-10s	Top-25s	Scoring Average	Money
1968	2	7	1	0	0	0	0	72.00	

Best finish for 1968: T-44th at the Magnolia State Classic

Year	Starts	Rounds Played	Cuts Made	Wins	Top-5s	Top-10s	Top-25s	Scoring Average	Money
1969	1	2	0	0	0	0	0	76.00	
Period Totals	Starts	Rounds Played	Cuts Made	Wins	Top-5s	Top-10s	Top-25s	Scoring Average	Money
	47	141	24	0	0	1	4	73.44	$4,904

Woody Fitzhugh

Year	Starts	Rounds Played	Cuts Made	Wins	Top-5s	Top-10s	Top-25s	Scoring Average	Money
1980	20	46	4	0	0	0	1	73.63	$5,185

Best finish for 1980: T-18th at the Buick Goodwrench Open

Year	Starts	Rounds Played	Cuts Made	Wins	Top-5s	Top-10s	Top-25s	Scoring Average	Money
1981	2	6	1	0	0	0	0	76.00	$752

Best finish for 1981: 76th at the Kemper Open

Year	Starts	Rounds Played	Cuts Made	Wins	Top-5s	Top-10s	Top-25s	Scoring Average	Money
1982	12	32	3	0	0	0	0	73.50	$3,011

Best finish for 1982: T-30th at the Joe Garagiola Tucson Open

Year	Starts	Rounds Played	Cuts Made	Wins	Top-5s	Top-10s	Top-25s	Scoring Average	Money
1983	2	4	0	0	0	0	0	79.50	
1984	1	2	0	0	0	0	0	74.00	
1985	1	2	0	0	0	0	0	74.00	
1986	2	3	0	0	0	0	0	76.67	
1987	1	2	0	0	0	0	0	73.00	
1988	2	4	0	0	0	0	0	75.50	$1,000
1993	2	4	0	0	0	0	0	75.00	
1994	1	2	0	0	0	0	0	72.00	
Period Totals	Starts	Rounds Played	Cuts Made	Wins	Top-5s	Top-10s	Top-25s	Scoring Average	Money
	46	107	8	0	0	0	1	74.12	$9,948

Pat Fitzsimons

Year	Starts	Rounds Played	Cuts Made	Wins	Top-5s	Top-10s	Top-25s	Scoring Average	Money
1972	2	6	1	0	0	1	1	72.17	$2,901

Best finish for 1972: T-9th at the Sea Pines Heritage Classic

Year	Starts	Rounds Played	Cuts Made	Wins	Top-5s	Top-10s	Top-25s	Scoring Average	Money
1973	26	84	14	0	0	1	4	72.73	$15,228

Best finish for 1973: T-9th at the Atlanta Classic

Year	Starts	Rounds Played	Cuts Made	Wins	Top-5s	Top-10s	Top-25s	Scoring Average	Money
1974	14	36	4	0	0	0	3	73.56	$8,325

Best finish for 1974: T-11th at the Monsanto Open

Year	Starts	Rounds Played	Cuts Made	Wins	Top-5s	Top-10s	Top-25s	Scoring Average	Money
1975	23	83	18	1	4	6	12	71.59	$86,182

Best finish for 1975: Win at the Glen Campbell Los Angles Open

Year	Starts	Rounds Played	Cuts Made	Wins	Top-5s	Top-10s	Top-25s	Scoring Average	Money
1976	24	77	14	0	1	1	3	73.03	$20,096

Best finish for 1976: T-4th at the NBC Tucson Open

Year	Starts	Rounds Played	Cuts Made	Wins	Top-5s	Top-10s	Top-25s	Scoring Average	Money
1977	14	41	7	0	0	2	2	73.41	$11,978

Best finish for 1977: T-7th at the San Antonio Texas Open

Year	Starts	Rounds Played	Cuts Made	Wins	Top-5s	Top-10s	Top-25s	Scoring Average	Money
1978	10	23	2	0	0	0	0	73.30	$1,429

Best finish for 1978: T-32nd at the American Optical Classic

Year	Starts	Rounds Played	Cuts Made	Wins	Top-5s	Top-10s	Top-25s	Scoring Average	Money
1979	2	4	0	0	0	0	0	78.00	
1980	9	23	3	0	0	0	0	73.26	$3,202

Best finish for 1980: T-38th at the Buick Goodwrench Open

Year	Starts	Rounds Played	Cuts Made	Wins	Top-5s	Top-10s	Top-25s	Scoring Average	Money
1981	3	8	1	0	0	0	0	72.75	$875

Best finish for 1981: T-42nd at the Wickes/Andy Williams San Diego Open

Year	Starts	Rounds Played	Cuts Made	Wins	Top-5s	Top-10s	Top-25s	Scoring Average	Money
1982	1	4	1	0	0	0	0	74.25	$597

Best finish for 1982: T-71st at the Glen Campbell Los Angles Open

Year	Starts	Rounds Played	Cuts Made	Wins	Top-5s	Top-10s	Top-25s	Scoring Average	Money
1984	2	4	0	0	0	0	0	77.50	$600
1985	1	2	0	0	0	0	0	75.50	$600
1986	2	4	0	0	0	0	0	73.75	$1,000
1989	1	4	1	0	0	0	0	72.25	$756

Best finish for 1989: T-75th at the Southern Open

Year	Starts	Rounds Played	Cuts Made	Wins	Top-5s	Top-10s	Top-25s	Scoring Average	Money
1990	11	24	1	0	0	0	0	75.50	$3,080

Best finish for 1990: 66th at the Nissan Los Angeles Open

Year	Starts	Rounds Played	Cuts Made	Wins	Top-5s	Top-10s	Top-25s	Scoring Average	Money
1996	3	8	1	0	0	0	0	71.50	$2,240

Best finish for 1996: T-56th at the Greater Vancouver Open

Year	Starts	Rounds Played	Cuts Made	Wins	Top-5s	Top-10s	Top-25s	Scoring Average	Money
1997	3	6	0	0	0	0	0	72.83	
1998	4	8	0	0	0	0	0	76.25	
1999	1	2	0	0	0	0	0	76.00	
2000	1	2	0	0	0	0	0	79.00	
Period Totals	Starts	Rounds Played	Cuts Made	Wins	Top-5s	Top-10s	Top-25s	Scoring Average	Money
	157	453	68	1	5	11	25	73.10	$159,089

Nick Flanagan

Year	Starts	Rounds Played	Cuts Made	Wins	Top-5s	Top-10s	Top-25s	Scoring Average	Money
2004	10	21	1	0	0	0	0	73.67	$6,180

Best finish for 2004: T-66th at the Reno-Tahoe Open

Year	Starts	Rounds Played	Cuts Made	Wins	Top-5s	Top-10s	Top-25s	Scoring Average	Money
2005	1	4	1	0	0	0	1	71.00	$56,946

Best finish for 2005: T-23rd at the British Open

Year	Starts	Rounds Played	Cuts Made	Wins	Top-5s	Top-10s	Top-25s	Scoring Average	Money
2007	4	12	2	0	0	0	2	70.42	$122,029

Best finish for 2007: T-17th at the Viking Classic

Year	Starts	Rounds Played	Cuts Made	Wins	Top-5s	Top-10s	Top-25s	Scoring Average	Money
2008	29	89	16	0	0	1	3	71.63	$379,036

Best finish for 2008: T-9th at the Mayakoba Golf Classic

Period Totals	Starts	Rounds Played	Cuts Made	Wins	Top-5s	Top-10s	Top-25s	Scoring Average	Money
	44	126	20	0	0	1	6	71.83	$564,191

John Flannery

Year	Starts	Rounds Played	Cuts Made	Wins	Top-5s	Top-10s	Top-25s	Scoring Average	Money
1988	1	3	0	0	0	0	0	74.67	
1989	1	2	0	0	0	0	0	71.00	
1990	1	2	0	0	0	0	0	77.50	$1,000
1992	1	2	0	0	0	0	0	75.00	$1,000
1993	31	104	23	0	0	1	4	71.66	$161,234

Best finish for 1993: T-9th at the AT&T Pebble Beach Pro-Am

1994	33	94	14	0	0	0	4	71.88	$94,105

Best finish for 1994: T-12th at the Freeport-McMoRan Classic

1995	3	7	0	0	0	0	0	75.43	
1996	1	2	0	0	0	0	0	75.50	$1,000

Period Totals	Starts	Rounds Played	Cuts Made	Wins	Top-5s	Top-10s	Top-25s	Scoring Average	Money
	72	216	37	0	0	1	8	72.04	$258,338

Jack Fleck

Year	Starts	Rounds Played	Cuts Made	Wins	Top-5s	Top-10s	Top-25s	Scoring Average	Money
1958	21	69	13	0	0	2	2	72.71	$3,823

Best finish for 1958: 6th at the Rubber City Open

1959	17	68	16	0	3	5	12	70.81	$11,776

Best finish for 1959: T-3rd at the Orange County Open Invitational

1960	18	72	17	1	5	8	13	71.43	$19,798

Best finish for 1960: Win at the Phoenix Open

1961	21	84	19	1	2	4	11	70.71	$15,026

Best finish for 1961: Win at the Bakersfield Open

1962	11	45	11	0	1	2	7	71.27	$9,845

Best finish for 1962: T-2nd at the Denver Open Invitational

1963	22	84	19	0	1	3	12	71.48	$15,950

Best finish for 1963: T-3rd at the Texas Open Invitational

1964	11	36	5	0	0	0	2	73.53	$2,722

Best finish for 1964: T-17th at the Mountain View Open

1965	12	31	6	0	0	0	2	73.00	$3,460

Best finish for 1965: T-20th at the PGA Championship

1966	10	34	7	0	0	0	0	73.82	$1,644

Best finish for 1966: T-28th at the Los Angles Open Invitational

1967	18	55	8	0	0	0	2	73.18	$3,916

Best finish for 1967: T-17th at the Cleveland Open

1968	21	60	10	0	0	0	3	72.15	$5,534

Best finish for 1968: T-12th at the Sahara Invitational

1969	4	7	1	0	0	0	0	74.14	$167

Best finish for 1969: T-64th at the Bob Hope Desert Classic

1970	14	44	8	0	0	0	1	73.18	$3,578

Best finish for 1970: T-15th at the Houston Champions International

1971	11	27	4	0	0	0	0	73.67	$442

Best finish for 1971: T-38th at the Greater Milwaukee Open

1972	2	4	0	0	0	0	0	73.00	
1973	5	15	1	0	0	0	0	74.40	

Best finish for 1973: T-71st at the Quad Cities Open

1974	4	10	1	0	0	0	0	74.40	$907

Best finish for 1974: T-32nd at the Bob Hope Chrysler Classic

1975	5	13	0	0	0	0	0	76.08	
1976	3	8	1	0	0	0	0	74.38	$325

Best finish for 1976: T-67th at the Danny Thomas Memphis Classic

1977	7	15	1	0	0	0	0	74.93	$910

Best finish for 1977: T-58th at the Phoenix Open

1978	6	15	2	0	0	0	0	73.67	$640

Best finish for 1978: T-44th at the Buick Goodwrench Open

1979	8	18	0	0	0	0	0	75.28	
1980	4	7	0	0	0	0	0	75.71	
1981	3	6	0	0	0	0	0	73.83	
1983	1	3	0	0	0	0	0	74.33	

Period Totals	Starts	Rounds Played	Cuts Made	Wins	Top-5s	Top-10s	Top-25s	Scoring Average	Money
	259	830	150	2	12	24	67	72.46	$100,463

PGA Tour career totals from 1949 to 1983

	Starts	Rounds Played	Cuts Made	Wins	Top-5s	Top-10s	Top-25s	Scoring Average	Money
	341	1124	231	3	14	35	105	N/A	$126,647

Marty Fleckman

Year	Starts	Rounds Played	Cuts Made	Wins	Top-5s	Top-10s	Top-25s	Scoring Average	Money
1966	1	4	1	0	0	0	0	73.00	

Best finish for 1966: T-54th at the Houston Champions International

1967	5	20	5	1	1	1	3	72.15	$5,000

Best finish for 1967: Win at the Cajun Classic

1968	36	119	23	0	1	2	5	72.82	$25,261

Best finish for 1968: T-4th at the PGA Championship

1969	33	82	10	0	0	0	1	74.11	$3,929

Best finish for 1969: T-16th at the Buick Open

1970	22	63	8	0	1	1	2	73.79	$10,296

Best finish for 1970: T-5th at the National Airlines Open

1971	21	58	9	0	0	1	1	73.62	$7,990

Best finish for 1971: 9th at the Bob Hope Chrysler Classic

1972	26	70	11	0	2	3	4	73.23	$26,741

Best finish for 1972: 3rd at the Phoenix Open

1973	16	39	5	0	0	0	1	74.72	$3,109

Best finish for 1973: T-13th at the Dean Martin Tucson Open

1974	15	42	5	0	0	0	0	73.60	$2,936

Best finish for 1974: T-33rd at the Sammy Davis, Jr. - Greater Hartford Open

1975	19	46	5	0	1	1	2	73.96	$13,122

Best finish for 1975: T-3rd at the Kaiser International Open

1976	23	72	13	0	0	1	6	72.50	$18,206

Best finish for 1976: T-9th at the Tallahassee Open

1977	17	40	3	0	0	0	0	74.55	$1,567

Best finish for 1977: T-39th at the Andy Williams-San Diego Open

1978	18	52	8	0	0	1	3	72.79	$15,442

Best finish for 1978: T-8th at the Western Open

1979	24	75	13	0	1	1	3	73.19	$24,388

Best finish for 1979: T-5th at the Joe Garagiola Tucson Open

1980	7	12	0	0	0	0	0	74.92	
Period Totals	**Starts**	**Rounds Played**	**Cuts Made**	**Wins**	**Top-5s**	**Top-10s**	**Top-25s**	**Scoring Average**	**Money**
	283	794	119	1	7	12	31	73.43	$157,988

Bruce Fleisher

Year	Starts	Rounds Played	Cuts Made	Wins	Top-5s	Top-10s	Top-25s	Scoring Average	Money
1968	1	2	0	0	0	0	0	81.00	
1969	6	17	2	0	0	0	1	74.24	

Best finish for 1969: T-18th at the Western Open

1970	3	10	2	0	0	0	0	75.20	$479

Best finish for 1970: T-65th at the American Golf Classic

1971	5	14	2	0	1	1	1	73.21	$5,950

Best finish for 1971: T-5th at the Doral-Eastern Open

1972	25	74	13	0	0	0	0	72.91	$6,035

Best finish for 1972: T-27th at the San Antonio Texas Open

1973	25	75	12	0	0	0	2	72.76	$9,484

Best finish for 1973: T-14th at the Sahara Invitational & San Antonio Texas Open

1974	29	88	16	0	2	2	6	72.13	$33,303

Best finish for 1974: 2nd at the Quad Cities Open

1975	28	82	12	0	0	0	2	73.45	$7,774

Best finish for 1975: T-15th at the Glen Campbell Los Angles Open

1976	22	70	16	0	0	0	3	73.00	$11,796

Best finish for 1976: T-11th at the Sahara Invitational

1977	21	55	7	0	0	0	3	72.85	$7,900

Best finish for 1977: T-14th at the Southern Open

1978	13	36	5	0	0	0	1	73.47	$5,109

Best finish for 1978: T-12th at the San Antonio Texas Open

1979	19	58	10	0	0	0	0	73.38	$8,728

Best finish for 1979: T-30th at the Doral-Eastern Open

1980	7	24	6	0	0	1	3	71.96	$16,309

Best finish for 1980: T-10th at the Jackie Gleason's Inverrary Classic

1981	23	67	13	0	1	3	8	72.00	$72,198

Best finish for 1981: 2nd at the USF&G New Orleans Open

1982	28	87	14	0	0	1	6	72.23	$36,160

Best finish for 1982: T-9th at the USF&G Classic

1983	28	103	22	0	0	0	5	72.20	$50,285

Best finish for 1983: T-14th at the USF&G Classic

1984	27	72	9	0	0	1	1	73.26	$30,186

Best finish for 1984: T-10th at the Panasonic Las Vegas Invitational

1985	1	2	0	0	0	0	0	78.50	
1986	2	8	2	0	0	0	1	70.63	$7,866

Best finish for 1986: T-14th at the Deposit Guaranty Golf Classic

Year	Starts	Rounds Played	Cuts Made	Wins	Top-5s	Top-10s	Top-25s	Scoring Average	Money
1987	1	4	1	0	0	0	0	72.75	$2,405

Best finish for 1987: T-49th at the Doral-Ryder Open

| 1988 | 2 | 6 | 1 | 0 | 0 | 0 | 0 | 72.50 | $2,198 |

Best finish for 1988: T-42nd at the Honda Classic

| 1989 | 2 | 4 | 0 | 0 | 0 | 0 | 0 | 75.00 | |
| 1990 | 5 | 15 | 2 | 0 | 0 | 0 | 0 | 72.80 | $11,626 |

Best finish for 1990: T-38th at the NEC World Series of Golf

| 1991 | 10 | 31 | 6 | 1 | 1 | 1 | 3 | 70.45 | $220,335 |

Best finish for 1991: Win at the New England Classic

| 1992 | 29 | 102 | 22 | 0 | 0 | 4 | 10 | 70.70 | $236,516 |

Best finish for 1992: T-9th at the Centel Western Open

| 1993 | 28 | 90 | 16 | 0 | 1 | 1 | 6 | 71.28 | $214,279 |

Best finish for 1993: T-2nd at the New England Classic

| 1994 | 29 | 82 | 13 | 0 | 0 | 1 | 2 | 71.61 | $88,680 |

Best finish for 1994: T-9th at the Honda Classic

| 1995 | 22 | 69 | 13 | 0 | 0 | 2 | 4 | 71.25 | $108,830 |

Best finish for 1995: T-8th at the Buick Classic

| 1996 | 14 | 43 | 9 | 0 | 1 | 1 | 3 | 70.91 | $143,380 |

Best finish for 1996: 3rd at the CVS Charity Classic

| 1997 | 17 | 61 | 13 | 0 | 1 | 2 | 4 | 70.48 | $151,902 |

Best finish for 1997: T-5th at the B.C. Open

| 1998 | 25 | 77 | 13 | 0 | 1 | 2 | 3 | 71.32 | $201,086 |

Best finish for 1998: 4th at the Buick Classic

Period Totals	Starts	Rounds Played	Cuts Made	Wins	Top-5s	Top-10s	Top-25s	Scoring Average	Money
	497	1528	272	1	9	23	78	72.16	$1,690,800

Pete Fleming

Year	Starts	Rounds Played	Cuts Made	Wins	Top-5s	Top-10s	Top-25s	Scoring Average	Money
1958	1	4	1	0	0	0	1	71.00	$490

Best finish for 1958: T-16th at the Arlington Hotel Open

| 1961 | 3 | 12 | 3 | 0 | 0 | 0 | 1 | 70.25 | $1,005 |

Best finish for 1961: T-16th at the St. Paul Open Invitational

| 1962 | 1 | 3 | 1 | 0 | 0 | 0 | 0 | 75.00 | |
| 1963 | 4 | 16 | 4 | 0 | 0 | 0 | 2 | 71.75 | $1,748 |

Best finish for 1963: T-13th at the Seattle Open Invitational

| 1964 | 12 | 33 | 4 | 0 | 0 | 0 | 3 | 72.61 | $2,590 |

Best finish for 1964: T-16th at the Oklahoma City Open

| 1965 | 6 | 12 | 0 | 0 | 0 | 0 | 0 | 75.42 | |
| 1966 | 12 | 38 | 6 | 0 | 0 | 0 | 0 | 74.00 | $463 |

Best finish for 1966: T-33rd at the Azalea Open Invitational & Oklahoma City Open Invitational

| 1968 | 5 | 16 | 3 | 0 | 1 | 1 | 1 | 71.13 | $2,050 |

Best finish for 1968: 2nd at the Magnolia State Classic

| 1969 | 1 | 4 | 1 | 0 | 0 | 0 | 0 | 70.75 | $422 |

Best finish for 1969: T-32nd at the Robinson Open

| 1971 | 3 | 8 | 1 | 0 | 0 | 0 | 0 | 74.38 | $222 |

Best finish for 1971: T-74th at the Monsanto Open

Period Totals	Starts	Rounds Played	Cuts Made	Wins	Top-5s	Top-10s	Top-25s	Scoring Average	Money
	48	146	24	0	1	1	8	72.80	$8,991

Steve Flesch

Year	Starts	Rounds Played	Cuts Made	Wins	Top-5s	Top-10s	Top-25s	Scoring Average	Money
1998	29	99	23	0	2	5	14	70.23	$777,186

Best finish for 1998: 2nd at the Freeport-McDermott Classic

| 1999 | 31 | 98 | 20 | 0 | 1 | 3 | 6 | 71.28 | $553,346 |

Best finish for 1999: T-2nd at the COMPAQ Classic of New Orleans

| 2000 | 32 | 121 | 29 | 0 | 4 | 13 | 21 | 69.64 | $2,027,781 |

Best finish for 2000: 2nd at the National Car Rental Golf Classic/Disney

| 2001 | 32 | 107 | 24 | 0 | 1 | 6 | 14 | 70.46 | $1,215,412 |

Best finish for 2001: 5th at the National Car Rental Golf Classic/Disney

| 2002 | 32 | 105 | 22 | 0 | 1 | 7 | 11 | 70.65 | $1,192,341 |

Best finish for 2002: T-4th at the Bell Canadian Open

| 2003 | 33 | 108 | 21 | 1 | 1 | 9 | 12 | 70.44 | $2,276,206 |

Best finish for 2003: Win at the HP Classic of New Orleans

| 2004 | 31 | 105 | 24 | 1 | 3 | 4 | 11 | 71.03 | $2,461,787 |

Best finish for 2004: Win at the Bank of America Colonial

| 2005 | 30 | 85 | 16 | 0 | 1 | 2 | 5 | 72.00 | $869,106 |

Best finish for 2005: T-4th at the FBR Open

| 2006 | 33 | 115 | 26 | 0 | 2 | 4 | 8 | 70.79 | $1,417,615 |

Best finish for 2006: T-3rd at The International & Chrysler Classic of Greensboro

Year	Starts	Rounds Played	Cuts Made	Wins	Top-5s	Top-10s	Top-25s	Scoring Average	Money
2007	31	100	19	2	3	3	6	71.25	$2,288,899

Best finish for 2007: Win at the Reno-Tahoe Open & Turning Stone Resort Championship

2008	29	95	19	0	1	2	10	71.17	$1,265,059

Best finish for 2008: T-5th at the Masters

Period Totals	Starts	Rounds Played	Cuts Made	Wins	Top-5s	Top-10s	Top-25s	Scoring Average	Money
	343	1138	243	4	20	58	118	70.77	$16,344,738

Gary Floan

Year	Starts	Rounds Played	Cuts Made	Wins	Top-5s	Top-10s	Top-25s	Scoring Average	Money
1963	3	12	3	0	0	0	0	71.67	$492

Best finish for 1963: T-35th at the Memphis Open Invitational

1964	16	40	6	0	0	0	0	73.70	

Best finish for 1964: T-36th at the Almaden Open

1965	13	34	4	0	0	0	1	74.21	$1,108

Best finish for 1965: T-12th at the Azalea Open

Period Totals	Starts	Rounds Played	Cuts Made	Wins	Top-5s	Top-10s	Top-25s	Scoring Average	Money
	32	86	13	0	0	0	1	73.62	$1,600

Ray Floyd

Year	Starts	Rounds Played	Cuts Made	Wins	Top-5s	Top-10s	Top-25s	Scoring Average	Money
1963	11	44	11	1	2	2	4	72.14	$9,067

Best finish for 1963: Win at the St. Petersburg Open Invitational

1964	30	105	22	0	3	4	11	71.91	$21,282

Best finish for 1964: T-3rd at the Lucky International Open & Canadian Open

1965	28	96	18	1	1	3	9	72.29	$37,141

Best finish for 1965: Win at the St. Paul Open

1966	27	90	18	0	3	6	12	72.08	$31,213

Best finish for 1966: T-2nd at the Dallas Open Invitational

1967	30	103	22	0	1	3	8	72.20	$25,225

Best finish for 1967: T-3rd at the Insurance City Open

1968	31	98	21	0	5	7	16	71.04	$61,757

Best finish for 1968: T-2nd at the Lucky International Open Invitational

1969	30	101	22	3	5	6	10	71.74	$107,949

Best finish for 1969: Win at the Greater Jacksonville Open, American Classic & PGA Championship

1970	26	83	17	0	2	3	10	72.11	$44,306

Best finish for 1970: 3rd at the Monsanto Open

1971	30	94	20	0	3	5	11	72.14	$67,314

Best finish for 1971: 2nd at the Bob Hope Chrysler Classic & Massachusetts Classic

1972	25	79	15	0	2	4	7	72.43	$34,079

Best finish for 1972: T-4th at the PGA Championship

1973	26	81	17	0	1	2	7	72.00	$38,601

Best finish for 1973: 2nd at the Bing Crosby Pro-Am

1974	26	94	22	0	6	8	14	70.93	$116,385

Best finish for 1974: 2nd at the Greater Greensboro Open, American Golf Classic & Sammy Davis, Jr. - Greater Hartford Open

1975	27	95	20	1	2	5	14	71.80	$104,629

Best finish for 1975: Win at the Kemper Open

1976	24	92	22	2	7	10	17	70.90	$185,158

Best finish for 1976: Win at the Masters & World Open

1977	25	97	23	2	5	9	16	71.40	$169,366

Best finish for 1977: Win at the Byron Nelson Golf Classic & Pleasant Valley Classic

1978	27	94	21	0	3	5	15	71.27	$91,489

Best finish for 1978: T-2nd at the American Optical Classic & British Open

1979	28	95	20	1	3	6	10	72.73	$124,679

Best finish for 1979: Win at the Greater Greensboro Open

1980	27	103	24	1	2	9	15	71.53	$192,993

Best finish for 1980: Win at the Doral-Eastern Open

1981	24	94	23	3	7	15	19	70.22	$382,860

Best finish for 1981: Win at the Doral-Eastern Open, Tournament Players Championship & Manufactures Hanover Westchester Classic

1982	24	87	19	3	6	9	17	70.80	$393,438

Best finish for 1982: Win at the Memorial Tournament, Danny Thomas Memphis Classic & PGA Championship

1983	23	93	23	0	5	8	19	70.60	$215,913

Best finish for 1983: 2nd at the MONY Tournament Of Champions

1984	24	83	18	0	0	2	8	71.84	$103,606

Best finish for 1984: T-6th at the Bay Hill Classic

1985	22	86	20	1	7	9	15	70.53	$379,989

Best finish for 1985: Win at the Houston Open

1986	24	81	20	2	3	5	16	70.78	$396,508

Best finish for 1986: Win at the U.S. Open & Walt Disney World/Oldsmobile Classic

1987	21	69	13	0	0	2	10	71.46	$136,299

Best finish for 1987: T-6th at the Shearson Lehman/Andy Williams San Diego

1988	20	70	15	0	1	3	8	71.34	$170,314

Best finish for 1988: 4th at the Doral-Ryder Open

Year	Starts	Rounds Played	Cuts Made	Wins	Top-5s	Top-10s	Top-25s	Scoring Average	Money
1989	18	59	13	0	0	1	2	72.22	$80,659

Best finish for 1989: T-8th at the Memorial Tournament

Year	Starts	Rounds Played	Cuts Made	Wins	Top-5s	Top-10s	Top-25s	Scoring Average	Money
1990	18	58	12	0	2	3	6	72.33	$272,710

Best finish for 1990: T-2nd at the Masters

Year	Starts	Rounds Played	Cuts Made	Wins	Top-5s	Top-10s	Top-25s	Scoring Average	Money
1991	18	62	15	0	2	5	10	70.85	$287,905

Best finish for 1991: T-3rd at the GTE Byron Nelson Classic

Year	Starts	Rounds Played	Cuts Made	Wins	Top-5s	Top-10s	Top-25s	Scoring Average	Money
1992	16	64	16	1	4	5	12	70.08	$776,685

Best finish for 1992: Win at the Doral-Ryder Open

Year	Starts	Rounds Played	Cuts Made	Wins	Top-5s	Top-10s	Top-25s	Scoring Average	Money
1993	7	26	7	0	0	2	4	70.54	$137,233

Best finish for 1993: T-7th at the U.S. Open

Year	Starts	Rounds Played	Cuts Made	Wins	Top-5s	Top-10s	Top-25s	Scoring Average	Money
1994	4	16	4	0	0	1	3	71.63	$95,017

Best finish for 1994: T-10th at the Masters

Year	Starts	Rounds Played	Cuts Made	Wins	Top-5s	Top-10s	Top-25s	Scoring Average	Money
1995	4	16	4	0	0	0	2	71.75	$65,031

Best finish for 1995: T-17th at the Doral-Ryder Open & Masters

Year	Starts	Rounds Played	Cuts Made	Wins	Top-5s	Top-10s	Top-25s	Scoring Average	Money
1996	2	8	2	0	0	1	2	71.13	$67,800

Best finish for 1996: T-8th at the Doral-Ryder Open

Year	Starts	Rounds Played	Cuts Made	Wins	Top-5s	Top-10s	Top-25s	Scoring Average	Money
1997	3	9	2	0	0	0	0	73.33	$12,811

Best finish for 1997: T-56th at the Doral-Ryder Open

Year	Starts	Rounds Played	Cuts Made	Wins	Top-5s	Top-10s	Top-25s	Scoring Average	Money
1998	2	6	1	0	0	0	1	72.67	$36,000

Best finish for 1998: T-15th at the Doral-Ryder Open

Year	Starts	Rounds Played	Cuts Made	Wins	Top-5s	Top-10s	Top-25s	Scoring Average	Money
1999	2	8	2	0	0	0	0	73.88	$22,480

Best finish for 1999: T-38th at the Masters

Year	Starts	Rounds Played	Cuts Made	Wins	Top-5s	Top-10s	Top-25s	Scoring Average	Money
2000	3	6	0	0	0	0	0	74.33	$5,000
2001	2	4	0	0	0	0	0	75.50	$5,000
2002	2	4	0	0	0	0	0	74.25	$5,000
2003	1	2	0	0	0	0	0	78.50	$5,000
2004	2	4	0	0	0	0	0	74.75	$6,000
2005	1	2	0	0	0	0	0	76.00	$5,000
2006	1	2	0	0	0	0	0	76.00	$5,000
2007	2	4	0	0	0	0	0	77.25	
2008	1	2	0	0	0	0	0	77.00	
Period Totals	769	2669	584	22	93	168	360	71.57	$5,531,893

Ken Folkes

Year	Starts	Rounds Played	Cuts Made	Wins	Top-5s	Top-10s	Top-25s	Scoring Average	Money
1965	17	44	5	0	0	0	0	73.77	$1,325

Best finish for 1965: T-28th at the Memphis Open

Year	Starts	Rounds Played	Cuts Made	Wins	Top-5s	Top-10s	Top-25s	Scoring Average	Money
1966	12	36	6	0	0	0	0	74.36	$619

Best finish for 1966: T-40th at the Greater Greensboro Open Invitational

Year	Starts	Rounds Played	Cuts Made	Wins	Top-5s	Top-10s	Top-25s	Scoring Average	Money
1971	1	2	0	0	0	0	0	74.00	
1972	3	6	0	0	0	0	0	77.83	
1973	1	2	0	0	0	0	0	75.50	
1977	1	2	0	0	0	0	0	76.00	$250
1978	3	6	0	0	0	0	0	76.00	
Period Totals	38	98	11	0	0	0	0	74.46	$2,194

Bob Ford

Year	Starts	Rounds Played	Cuts Made	Wins	Top-5s	Top-10s	Top-25s	Scoring Average	Money
1964	6	18	3	0	0	0	0	74.72	$500

Best finish for 1964: T-29th at the Canadian Open

Year	Starts	Rounds Played	Cuts Made	Wins	Top-5s	Top-10s	Top-25s	Scoring Average	Money
1965	17	43	4	0	0	0	0	74.70	$266

Best finish for 1965: T-44th at the Pensacola Open

Year	Starts	Rounds Played	Cuts Made	Wins	Top-5s	Top-10s	Top-25s	Scoring Average	Money
1966	6	12	0	0	0	0	0	77.75	
1967	9	26	4	0	0	0	1	73.73	$1,044

Best finish for 1967: T-15th at the Tucson Open

Year	Starts	Rounds Played	Cuts Made	Wins	Top-5s	Top-10s	Top-25s	Scoring Average	Money
1970	1	2	0	0	0	0	0	79.50	
Period Totals	39	101	11	0	0	0	1	74.91	$1,810

Doug Ford

Year	Starts	Rounds Played	Cuts Made	Wins	Top-5s	Top-10s	Top-25s	Scoring Average	Money
1958	35	138	34	1	5	10	22	71.09	$24,324

Best finish for 1958: Win at the Pensacola Open

Year	Starts	Rounds Played	Cuts Made	Wins	Top-5s	Top-10s	Top-25s	Scoring Average	Money
1959	35	140	31	1	7	15	30	70.66	$30,164

Best finish for 1959: Win at the Canadian Open Championship

Year	Starts	Rounds Played	Cuts Made	Wins	Top-5s	Top-10s	Top-25s	Scoring Average	Money
1960	29	117	28	1	2	11	22	71.06	$27,792

Best finish for 1960: Win at the "500" Festival Open Invitational

Year	Starts	Rounds Played	Cuts Made	Wins	Top-5s	Top-10s	Top-25s	Scoring Average	Money
1961	23	92	23	1	3	7	13	70.83	$24,577

Best finish for 1961: Win at the "500" Festival Open Invitational

Year	Starts	Rounds Played	Cuts Made	Wins	Top-5s	Top-10s	Top-25s	Scoring Average	Money
1962	21	85	20	2	3	6	15	71.54	$25,365

Best finish for 1962: Win at the Bing Crosby National & Eastern Open Invitational

1963	23	90	21	1	3	4	12	71.54	$24,995

Best finish for 1963: Win at the Canadian Open

1964	31	106	19	0	0	1	6	73.27	$8,115

Best finish for 1964: T-6th at the Azalea Open

1965	27	93	17	0	0	1	9	73.02	$11,659

Best finish for 1965: T-6th at the Pensacola Open

1966	28	81	11	0	0	1	5	73.52	$7,986

Best finish for 1966: T-8th at the Texas Open Invitational

1967	33	100	16	0	3	3	3	73.39	$21,247

Best finish for 1967: T-3rd at the Insurance City Open

1968	27	80	15	0	0	0	0	73.08	$4,566

Best finish for 1968: T-26th at the Buick Open Invitational

1969	26	69	8	0	1	1	2	73.86	$7,294

Best finish for 1969: 4th at the Heritage Golf Classic

1970	23	60	8	0	0	0	1	73.77	$7,918

Best finish for 1970: T-12th at the Dow Jones Open Invitational

1971	20	43	3	0	0	0	1	74.86	$3,947

Best finish for 1971: T-15th at the Greater Jacksonville Open

1972	20	50	6	0	0	0	1	74.40	$3,616

Best finish for 1972: T-23rd at the IVB Philadelphia Golf Classic

1973	22	51	4	0	0	0	0	74.33	$3,238

Best finish for 1973: T-35th at the Western Open

1974	22	59	8	0	0	0	0	74.83	$4,088

Best finish for 1974: T-38th at the IVB Philadelphia Golf Classic

1975	17	36	3	0	0	0	1	74.78	$3,603

Best finish for 1975: T-23rd at the Sea Pines Heritage Classic

1976	17	29	0	0	0	0	0	76.83	$1,600
1977	16	28	0	0	0	0	0	77.32	$1,750
1978	15	31	1	0	0	0	0	77.10	$1,973

Best finish for 1978: T-70th at the B.C. Open

1979	11	18	0	0	0	0	0	78.33	$1,850
1980	11	18	0	0	0	0	0	77.06	$2,000
1981	7	12	1	0	0	0	0	74.58	$2,109

Best finish for 1981: T-67th at the Sammy Davis, Jr. - Greater Hartford Open

1982	3	6	0	0	0	0	0	79.33	$1,500
1983	1	1	0	0	0	0	0	85.00	$1,500
1984	2	3	0	0	0	0	0	80.33	$1,500
1985	1	1	0	0	0	0	0	76.00	$1,500
1986	1	2	0	0	0	0	0	78.00	$1,500
1987	1	2	0	0	0	0	0	80.00	$1,500
1988	1	2	0	0	0	0	0	81.00	$1,500
1989	1	2	0	0	0	0	0	81.50	$1,500
1990	1	2	0	0	0	0	0	81.50	$1,500
1991	1	0	0	0	0	0	0		$1,500
1992	1	2	0	0	0	0	0	82.00	$1,500
1993	1	2	0	0	0	0	0	80.50	$1,500
1994	1	1	0	0	0	0	0	85.00	$1,500
1995	1	1	0	0	0	0	0	88.00	$1,500
1996	1	2	0	0	0	0	0	84.50	$1,500
1997	1	2	0	0	0	0	0	89.50	$5,000
1998	1	1	0	0	0	0	0	86.00	$5,000
1999	1	1	0	0	0	0	0	88.00	$5,000
2000	1	1	0	0	0	0	0	94.00	$5,000
2001	1	0	0	0	0	0	0		$5,000

Period Totals	Starts	Rounds Played	Cuts Made	Wins	Top-5s	Top-10s	Top-25s	Scoring Average	Money
	562	1660	277	7	27	60	143	73.12	$303,277

PGA Tour career totals from 1941 to 2001

	Starts	Rounds Played	Cuts Made	Wins	Top-5s	Top-10s	Top-25s	Scoring Average	Money
	814	3453	532	19	68	162	332	N/A	$473,273

Anders Forsbrand

Year	Starts	Rounds Played	Cuts Made	Wins	Top-5s	Top-10s	Top-25s	Scoring Average	Money
1984	1	3	0	0	0	0	0	73.33	$793
1985	1	4	1	0	0	1	1	71.25	$22,571

Best finish for 1985: T-8th at the British Open

1986	3	9	2	0	0	0	1	72.11	$14,683

Best finish for 1986: T-16th at the British Open

1987	2	8	2	0	0	0	0	72.13	$9,510

Best finish for 1987: T-29th at the British Open

Year	Starts	Rounds Played	Cuts Made	Wins	Top-5s	Top-10s	Top-25s	Scoring Average	Money
1988	3	6	2	0	0	0	1	73.67	$18,815

Best finish for 1988: T-14th at the NEC World Series of Golf

1989	1	3	0	0	0	0	0	73.67	
1991	1	4	1	0	0	0	0	71.00	$8,366

Best finish for 1991: T-38th at the British Open

1992	3	12	3	0	0	1	1	72.17	$61,653

Best finish for 1992: T-9th at the PGA Championship

1993	6	14	2	0	0	0	1	73.36	$37,974

Best finish for 1993: T-11th at the Masters

1994	3	8	1	0	1	1	1	71.75	$84,780

Best finish for 1994: T-4th at the British Open

1995	1	4	1	0	0	0	0	73.00	$10,128

Best finish for 1995: T-49th at the British Open

1996	8	21	5	0	0	0	0	72.05	$44,198

Best finish for 1996: T-31st at the NEC World Series of Golf

Period Totals	Starts	Rounds Played	Cuts Made	Wins	Top-5s	Top-10s	Top-25s	Scoring Average	Money
	33	96	20	0	1	3	6	72.40	$313,472

Dan Forsman

Year	Starts	Rounds Played	Cuts Made	Wins	Top-5s	Top-10s	Top-25s	Scoring Average	Money
1982	1	2	0	0	0	0	0	78.50	$600
1983	30	93	14	0	0	1	5	72.63	$37,859

Best finish for 1983: T-10th at the Honda Inverrary Classic

1984	32	95	16	0	0	2	6	72.77	$52,152

Best finish for 1984: T-7th at the LaJet Golf Classic & Texas Open

1985	26	84	16	1	2	4	8	72.06	$151,334

Best finish for 1985: Win at the Lite Quad Cities Open

1986	28	72	15	1	2	2	6	72.42	$169,945

Best finish for 1986: Win at the Hertz Bay Hill Classic

1987	33	121	29	0	1	1	7	71.53	$158,728

Best finish for 1987: T-2nd at the Canon Sammy Davis, Jr. - Greater Hartford Open

1988	35	122	26	0	4	4	10	71.01	$269,441

Best finish for 1988: 2nd at the Hardee's Golf Classic

1989	30	85	15	0	0	4	5	72.14	$142,174

Best finish for 1989: T-6th at the Shearson Lehman Hutton Open & Hardee's Golf Classic

1990	26	86	19	1	2	3	7	71.33	$322,664

Best finish for 1990: Win at the Shearson Lehman Hutton Open

1991	26	88	19	0	1	2	7	70.93	$214,175

Best finish for 1991: 3rd at the Shearson Lehman Brothers Open

1992	29	109	28	1	4	7	14	70.29	$763,220

Best finish for 1992: Win at the Buick Open

1993	26	91	20	0	2	6	11	70.75	$415,540

Best finish for 1993: T-2nd at the Canon Greater Hartford Open

1994	23	68	13	0	0	0	6	71.46	$160,805

Best finish for 1994: T-12th at the AT&T Pebble Beach Pro-Am

1995	23	77	17	0	0	2	6	71.18	$194,539

Best finish for 1995: T-8th at the Ideon Classic & Sprint International

1996	22	65	12	0	0	0	6	71.69	$170,198

Best finish for 1996: T-13th at the Kemper Open, U.S. Open & FedEx St. Jude Classic

1997	27	84	16	0	2	4	6	71.31	$449,085

Best finish for 1997: 2nd at the Walt Disney World/Oldsmobile Classic

1998	22	77	17	0	0	3	8	70.64	$312,058

Best finish for 1998: T-6th at the Shell Houston Open

1999	27	92	19	0	1	3	8	70.86	$439,571

Best finish for 1999: T-4th at the Greater Milwaukee Open

2000	27	88	17	0	1	2	4	70.92	$379,349

Best finish for 2000: T-3rd at the MCI Classic

2001	25	78	16	0	1	3	5	70.92	$456,195

Best finish for 2001: 4th at the Southern Farm Bureau Classic

2002	25	81	16	1	2	4	7	70.26	$1,305,790

Best finish for 2002: Win at the SEI Pennsylvania Classic

2003	27	98	21	0	0	4	10	70.03	$1,142,209

Best finish for 2003: T-6th at the Valero Texas Open & Chrysler Championship

2004	28	77	10	0	0	0	4	71.71	$316,540

Best finish for 2004: T-16th at the FUNAI Classic at the Walt Disney World Resort

2005	17	50	9	0	0	0	2	70.58	$214,135

Best finish for 2005: T-20th at the Chrysler Championship

2006	15	43	6	0	0	0	1	71.33	$117,126

Best finish for 2006: T-17th at the John Deere Classic

2007	12	33	5	0	0	1	1	71.85	$185,522

Best finish for 2007: T-6th at the Valero Texas Open

Year	Starts	Rounds Played	Cuts Made	Wins	Top-5s	Top-10s	Top-25s	Scoring Average	Money
2008	11	36	7	0	0	0	2	71.50	$169,106

Period Totals	Starts	Rounds Played	Cuts Made	Wins	Top-5s	Top-10s	Top-25s	Scoring Average	Money
	653	2095	418	5	25	62	162	71.29	$8,710,058

John Fought

Year	Starts	Rounds Played	Cuts Made	Wins	Top-5s	Top-10s	Top-25s	Scoring Average	Money
1976	1	4	1	0	0	0	0	75.00	

Best finish for 1976: T-50th at the U.S. Open

1977	4	12	2	0	0	0	0	75.67	

Best finish for 1977: 50th at the Masters

1978	4	11	1	0	0	0	0	74.91	$1,020

Best finish for 1978: T-58th at the Colonial National Invitational

1979	26	79	13	2	2	2	8	72.41	$109,027

Best finish for 1979: Win at the Buick Goodwrench Open & Anheuser-Busch Golf Classic

1980	30	102	21	0	1	3	7	72.08	$61,822

Best finish for 1980: T-5th at the Sammy Davis, Jr. - Greater Hartford Open

1981	28	86	14	0	0	0	2	72.74	$21,861

Best finish for 1981: T-13th at the Glen Campbell Los Angles Open

1982	18	56	10	0	1	2	5	71.68	$28,596

Best finish for 1982: T-4th at the Pensacola Open

1983	30	102	21	0	3	4	11	71.88	$105,809

Best finish for 1983: T-4th at the Bob Hope Chrysler Classic

1984	25	70	10	0	0	1	5	72.61	$43,603

Best finish for 1984: T-8th at the Bing Crosby Pro-Am

1985	26	75	11	0	0	0	2	72.96	$18,770

Best finish for 1985: T-21st at the Bank of Boston Classic

1986	3	6	0	0	0	0	0	74.33	
1987	11	21	0	0	0	0	0	74.67	
1989	1	4	1	0	0	0	0	71.00	$828

Best finish for 1989: T-65th at the Southern Open

Period Totals	Starts	Rounds Played	Cuts Made	Wins	Top-5s	Top-10s	Top-25s	Scoring Average	Money
	207	628	105	2	7	12	40	72.55	$391,336

Carlos Franco

Year	Starts	Rounds Played	Cuts Made	Wins	Top-5s	Top-10s	Top-25s	Scoring Average	Money
1994	2	4	0	0	0	0	0	75.75	$972
1997	2	8	2	0	0	1	1	71.75	$74,950

Best finish for 1997: T-7th at the NEC World Series of Golf

1998	2	8	2	0	0	0	0	73.13	$21,079

Best finish for 1998: T-40th at the PGA Championship

1999	22	69	15	2	5	7	10	71.09	$1,866,302

Best finish for 1999: Win at the COMPAQ Classic of New Orleans & Greater Milwaukee Open

2000	24	84	20	1	1	6	11	71.14	$1,552,112

Best finish for 2000: Win at the COMPAQ Classic of New Orleans

2001	27	87	17	0	0	0	8	71.24	$487,665

Best finish for 2001: T-14th at the Buick Challenge

2002	31	105	22	0	0	2	8	70.67	$652,147

Best finish for 2002: T-10th at the Disney Golf Classic & Buick Challenge

2003	30	97	19	0	0	1	7	70.58	$672,022

Best finish for 2003: T-10th at the Chrysler Classic of Tucson

2004	27	99	23	1	3	4	10	70.53	$1,956,395

Best finish for 2004: Win at the U.S. Bank Championship in Milwaukee

2005	25	76	14	0	2	2	4	71.07	$1,036,267

Best finish for 2005: 2nd at the 84 Lumber Classic

2006	29	86	13	0	0	1	3	71.87	$454,385

Best finish for 2006: T-7th at the Ford Championship at Doral

2007	12	34	5	0	0	0	1	71.56	$108,021

Best finish for 2007: T-21st at the Reno-Tahoe Open

2008	25	73	12	0	0	0	5	71.16	$378,768

Best finish for 2008: T-14th at the RBC Canadian Open & Reno-Tahoe Open

Period Totals	Starts	Rounds Played	Cuts Made	Wins	Top-5s	Top-10s	Top-25s	Scoring Average	Money
	258	830	164	4	11	24	68	71.08	$9,261,085

Howell Fraser

Year	Starts	Rounds Played	Cuts Made	Wins	Top-5s	Top-10s	Top-25s	Scoring Average	Money
1965	19	44	3	0	0	0	1	74.89	$1,850

Best finish for 1965: T-14th at the Cleveland Open

1966	22	62	9	0	0	0	0	74.19	$1,672

Best finish for 1966: T-27th at the "500" Festival Open Invitational

1967	14	40	6	0	1	1	1	74.23	$2,699

Best finish for 1967: T-4th at the Azalea Open

Year	Starts	Rounds Played	Cuts Made	Wins	Top-5s	Top-10s	Top-25s	Scoring Average	Money
1968	7	23	4	0	0	0	0	74.74	

Best finish for 1968: T-53rd at the Bing Crosby National Professional-Amateur

1969	34	102	17	0	1	2	3	72.89	$12,609

Best finish for 1969: T-4th at the Robinson Open

1970	16	44	8	0	0	1	2	72.41	$4,272

Best finish for 1970: T-8th at the Azalea Open Invitational

1971	16	51	9	0	0	0	0	72.69	$3,249

Best finish for 1971: T-30th at the Kemper Open

1972	1	2	0	0	0	0	0	74.00	
1974	2	6	1	0	0	0	0	75.00	$321

Best finish for 1974: T-67th at the PGA Championship

1975	2	4	0	0	0	0	0	74.75	
1976	1	2	0	0	0	0	0	73.50	
1977	1	2	0	0	0	0	0	77.50	
1978	1	2	0	0	0	0	0	75.00	$303
1979	1	2	0	0	0	0	0	75.00	$350
1980	1	2	0	0	0	0	0	77.50	$500
1981	1	2	0	0	0	0	0	76.50	$550
Period Totals	Starts	Rounds Played	Cuts Made	Wins	Top-5s	Top-10s	Top-25s	Scoring Average	Money
	139	390	57	0	2	4	7	73.64	$28,376

Harrison Frazar

Year	Starts	Rounds Played	Cuts Made	Wins	Top-5s	Top-10s	Top-25s	Scoring Average	Money
1997	1	2	0	0	0	0	0	74.00	
1998	26	81	16	0	2	3	5	71.28	$463,133

Best finish for 1998: T-2nd at the GTE Byron Nelson Classic

1999	29	96	19	0	1	2	6	71.33	$532,721

Best finish for 1999: T-2nd at the COMPAQ Classic of New Orleans

2000	24	70	11	0	2	2	5	70.99	$610,535

Best finish for 2000: T-3rd at the BellSouth Classic & COMPAQ Classic of New Orleans

2001	25	84	18	0	2	4	9	70.75	$794,456

Best finish for 2001: 4th at the COMPAQ Classic of New Orleans

2002	28	88	15	0	1	5	6	71.20	$731,295

Best finish for 2002: T-4th at the Memorial Tournament

2003	27	85	17	0	2	4	5	70.60	$776,876

Best finish for 2003: T-3rd at the Phoenix Open

2004	25	82	17	0	3	4	7	70.45	$1,448,764

Best finish for 2004: T-2nd at the Sony Open in Hawaii & Michelin Championship at Las Vegas

2005	31	101	21	0	2	4	7	70.54	$999,083

Best finish for 2005: T-3rd at the Michelin Championship at Las Vegas & FUNAI Classic at the Walt Disney World Resort

2006	29	91	18	0	0	2	11	70.77	$889,022

Best finish for 2006: T-7th at the Buick Open

2007	32	88	11	0	0	2	5	71.75	$698,534

Best finish for 2007: T-7th at the Crowne Plaza Invitational at Colonial

2008	23	73	13	0	1	1	4	71.48	$444,059

Best finish for 2008: T-4th at the Reno-Tahoe Open

Period Totals	Starts	Rounds Played	Cuts Made	Wins	Top-5s	Top-10s	Top-25s	Scoring Average	Money
	300	941	176	0	16	33	70	71.01	$8,388,478

Cody Freeman

Year	Starts	Rounds Played	Cuts Made	Wins	Top-5s	Top-10s	Top-25s	Scoring Average	Money
2002	1	2	0	0	0	0	0	71.50	
2006	1	2	0	0	0	0	0	73.00	
2008	26	66	6	0	0	0	0	72.52	$68,673

Best finish for 2008: T-45th at the Viking Classic

Period Totals	Starts	Rounds Played	Cuts Made	Wins	Top-5s	Top-10s	Top-25s	Scoring Average	Money
	28	70	6	0	0	0	0	72.50	$68,673

Robin Freeman

Year	Starts	Rounds Played	Cuts Made	Wins	Top-5s	Top-10s	Top-25s	Scoring Average	Money
1983	1	2	0	0	0	0	0	80.00	
1988	1	4	1	0	0	0	0	71.50	$1,508

Best finish for 1988: T-69th at the USF&G Classic

1989	30	78	9	0	0	0	1	72.12	$26,517

Best finish for 1989: T-24th at the GTE Byron Nelson Classic

1990	2	4	0	0	0	0	0	71.75	
1992	31	83	10	0	1	1	3	72.41	$101,642

Best finish for 1992: T-4th at the Buick Open

1993	30	87	14	0	1	1	1	72.11	$92,096

Best finish for 1993: T-3rd at the Northern Telecom Open

Year	Starts	Rounds Played	Cuts Made	Wins	Top-5s	Top-10s	Top-25s	Scoring Average	Money
1994	29	91	20	0	0	3	7	71.10	$177,044

Best finish for 1994: T-6th at the Buick Invitational of California

| 1995 | 30 | 97 | 19 | 0 | 2 | 2 | 4 | 71.20 | $283,756 |

Best finish for 1995: T-2nd at the GTE Byron Nelson Classic

| 1996 | 35 | 102 | 17 | 0 | 0 | 1 | 4 | 72.03 | $133,605 |

Best finish for 1996: 9th at the Deposit Guaranty Golf Classic

| 1997 | 20 | 65 | 14 | 0 | 0 | 1 | 3 | 71.15 | $135,702 |

Best finish for 1997: T-6th at the Nissan Open

| 1998 | 12 | 33 | 4 | 0 | 0 | 0 | 1 | 71.64 | $32,960 |

Best finish for 1998: T-21st at the Deposit Guaranty Golf Classic

| 1999 | 29 | 79 | 10 | 0 | 0 | 0 | 0 | 72.11 | $63,495 |

Best finish for 1999: T-38th at the Westin Texas Open

| 2000 | 32 | 98 | 17 | 0 | 1 | 1 | 4 | 71.29 | $415,430 |

Best finish for 2000: 3rd at the Nissan Open

| 2001 | 34 | 103 | 17 | 0 | 0 | 0 | 2 | 71.55 | $248,543 |

Best finish for 2001: T-16th at the Michelob Championship at Kingsmill

| 2002 | 27 | 75 | 13 | 0 | 1 | 1 | 1 | 71.63 | $227,179 |

Best finish for 2002: T-5th at the Southern Farm Bureau Classic

| 2003 | 12 | 34 | 4 | 0 | 0 | 0 | 0 | 71.97 | $54,651 |

Best finish for 2003: T-26th at the Greater Hartford Open

| 2004 | 13 | 29 | 1 | 0 | 1 | 1 | 1 | 72.62 | $144,000 |

Best finish for 2004: T-3rd at the B.C. Open

| 2005 | 8 | 21 | 2 | 0 | 0 | 0 | 0 | 71.76 | $17,258 |

Best finish for 2005: T-52nd at the FedEx St. Jude Classic

2006	2	4	0	0	0	0	0	75.00	
2007	1	2	0	0	0	0	0	74.00	
2008	2	4	0	0	0	0	0	75.25	
Period Totals	Starts	Rounds Played	Cuts Made	Wins	Top-5s	Top-10s	Top-25s	Scoring Average	Money
	381	1095	172	0	7	12	32	71.77	$2,155,387

Bob Friend

Year	Starts	Rounds Played	Cuts Made	Wins	Top-5s	Top-10s	Top-25s	Scoring Average	Money
1987	1	2	0	0	0	0	0	76.50	
1988	1	2	0	0	0	0	0	77.00	$1,000
1989	1	2	0	0	0	0	0	77.50	
1992	31	97	19	0	0	0	3	71.46	$93,317

Best finish for 1992: T-11th at the Buick Southern Open

| 1993 | 10 | 26 | 3 | 0 | 0 | 0 | 0 | 73.77 | $5,647 |

Best finish for 1993: T-52nd at the AT&T Pebble Beach Pro-Am

| 1994 | 2 | 4 | 0 | 0 | 0 | 0 | 0 | 74.50 | $1,000 |
| 1998 | 30 | 85 | 14 | 0 | 1 | 3 | 4 | 71.40 | $492,188 |

Best finish for 1998: 2nd at the Bell Canadian Open

| 1999 | 38 | 114 | 19 | 0 | 0 | 0 | 2 | 72.12 | $173,732 |

Best finish for 1999: T-17th at the Shell Houston Open

| 2000 | 32 | 92 | 15 | 0 | 0 | 0 | 2 | 71.52 | $202,973 |

Best finish for 2000: T-21st at the Doral Ryder Open

2002	1	2	0	0	0	0	0	73.50	
2003	1	2	0	0	0	0	0	71.00	
Period Totals	Starts	Rounds Played	Cuts Made	Wins	Top-5s	Top-10s	Top-25s	Scoring Average	Money
	148	428	70	0	1	3	11	71.89	$969,858

David Frost

Year	Starts	Rounds Played	Cuts Made	Wins	Top-5s	Top-10s	Top-25s	Scoring Average	Money
1983	2	6	1	0	0	0	0	72.67	$5,325

Best finish for 1983: T-32nd at the World Series Of Golf

| 1984 | 1 | 4 | 1 | 0 | 0 | 0 | 0 | 72.75 | $2,220 |

Best finish for 1984: T-47th at the British Open

| 1985 | 29 | 92 | 19 | 0 | 2 | 3 | 8 | 71.88 | $124,963 |

Best finish for 1985: T-2nd at the Houston Open

| 1986 | 29 | 90 | 20 | 0 | 2 | 6 | 14 | 71.61 | $188,544 |

Best finish for 1986: T-2nd at the Western Open

| 1987 | 29 | 102 | 25 | 0 | 6 | 13 | 20 | 70.11 | $559,672 |

Best finish for 1987: T-2nd at the Hertz Bay Hill Classic, Canadian Open & Southern Open

| 1988 | 27 | 90 | 19 | 2 | 8 | 12 | 14 | 70.32 | $729,180 |

Best finish for 1988: Win at the Southern Open & Northern Telecom Tucson Open

| 1989 | 28 | 93 | 22 | 1 | 3 | 8 | 12 | 71.10 | $621,230 |

Best finish for 1989: Win at the NEC World Series of Golf

| 1990 | 27 | 84 | 15 | 1 | 3 | 4 | 8 | 71.52 | $374,981 |

Best finish for 1990: Win at the USF&G Classic

| 1991 | 29 | 92 | 18 | 0 | 0 | 2 | 8 | 71.27 | $173,270 |

Best finish for 1991: T-8th at the Memorial Tournament

Year	Starts	Rounds Played	Cuts Made	Wins	Top-5s	Top-10s	Top-25s	Scoring Average	Money
1992	25	81	16	2	3	6	11	70.80	$717,883

Best finish for 1992: Win at the Buick Classic & Hardee's Golf Classic

| 1993 | 23 | 77 | 16 | 2 | 7 | 9 | 16 | 70.12 | $1,047,353 |

Best finish for 1993: Win at the Canadian Open & Hardee's Golf Classic

| 1994 | 23 | 82 | 20 | 1 | 5 | 6 | 10 | 70.60 | $680,661 |

Best finish for 1994: Win at the Canon Greater Hartford Open

| 1995 | 21 | 72 | 15 | 0 | 3 | 3 | 5 | 71.35 | $358,658 |

Best finish for 1995: T-2nd at the MCI Classic

| 1996 | 22 | 71 | 14 | 0 | 1 | 4 | 7 | 71.15 | $385,247 |

Best finish for 1996: T-3rd at the Memorial Tournament

| 1997 | 24 | 69 | 12 | 1 | 1 | 2 | 5 | 72.00 | $461,089 |

Best finish for 1997: Win at the MasterCard Colonial

| 1998 | 23 | 72 | 12 | 0 | 0 | 0 | 2 | 71.90 | $175,621 |

Best finish for 1998: T-14th at the MasterCard Colonial

| 1999 | 24 | 83 | 17 | 0 | 0 | 1 | 7 | 71.64 | $360,452 |

Best finish for 1999: T-7th at the British Open

| 2000 | 25 | 63 | 8 | 0 | 0 | 1 | 1 | 71.92 | $152,123 |

Best finish for 2000: T-8th at the John Deere Classic

| 2001 | 27 | 87 | 15 | 0 | 0 | 1 | 6 | 70.86 | $505,950 |

Best finish for 2001: T-8th at the Texas Open at LaCantera

| 2002 | 29 | 90 | 15 | 0 | 0 | 2 | 6 | 71.31 | $510,845 |

Best finish for 2002: T-8th at the Verizon Byron Nelson Classic

| 2003 | 26 | 80 | 16 | 0 | 1 | 2 | 5 | 70.74 | $583,177 |

Best finish for 2003: T-5th at the Las Vegas Invitational

| 2004 | 26 | 78 | 13 | 0 | 0 | 1 | 3 | 71.60 | $402,589 |

Best finish for 2004: T-7th at the Michelin Championship at Las Vegas

| 2005 | 10 | 24 | 3 | 0 | 0 | 0 | 1 | 72.79 | $111,258 |

Best finish for 2005: T-15th at the British Open

| 2006 | 7 | 23 | 4 | 0 | 0 | 0 | 0 | 71.35 | $56,960 |

Best finish for 2006: T-37th at the Valero Texas Open

| 2007 | 3 | 7 | 0 | 0 | 0 | 0 | 0 | 74.14 | $4,882 |
| 2008 | 3 | 9 | 1 | 0 | 0 | 0 | 0 | 73.00 | $23,554 |

Best finish for 2008: T-51st at the British Open

Period Totals	Starts	Rounds Played	Cuts Made	Wins	Top-5s	Top-10s	Top-25s	Scoring Average	Money
	542	1721	337	10	45	86	169	71.22	$9,317,688

Bob Fry

Year	Starts	Rounds Played	Cuts Made	Wins	Top-5s	Top-10s	Top-25s	Scoring Average	Money
1960	1	3	1	0	0	0	0	75.67	
1963	1	2	1	0	0	0	0	76.00	

Best finish for 1963: T-200 at the PGA Championship

| 1964 | 4 | 9 | 1 | 0 | 0 | 0 | 0 | 75.22 | |

Best finish for 1964: T-55th at the Cajun Classic

1965	1	2	0	0	0	0	0	75.00	
1966	1	2	0	0	0	0	0	76.50	
1967	1	2	0	0	0	0	0	73.50	
1968	1	2	0	0	0	0	0	74.00	
1969	3	6	0	0	0	0	0	76.50	
1970	2	4	0	0	0	0	0	76.25	
1971	1	1	0	0	0	0	0	77.00	
1972	2	6	1	0	0	0	0	74.83	$118

Best finish for 1972: T-69th at the Quad Cities Open

1973	1	2	0	0	0	0	0	74.50	
1974	1	2	0	0	0	0	0	77.00	
1975	2	4	0	0	0	0	0	76.00	
1976	1	2	0	0	0	0	0	75.50	
1977	1	1	0	0	0	0	0	74.00	
1978	1	2	0	0	0	0	0	78.00	
Period Totals	Starts	Rounds Played	Cuts Made	Wins	Top-5s	Top-10s	Top-25s	Scoring Average	Money
	25	52	4	0	0	0	0	75.62	$118

Edward Fryatt

Year	Starts	Rounds Played	Cuts Made	Wins	Top-5s	Top-10s	Top-25s	Scoring Average	Money
1994	1	3	0	0	0	0	0	72.67	
1997	2	9	2	0	0	0	2	70.56	$65,574

Best finish for 1997: T-11th at the Las Vegas Invitational

| 1998 | 2 | 6 | 1 | 0 | 0 | 0 | 0 | 72.33 | $10,240 |

Best finish for 1998: T-38th at the Memorial Tournament

| 1999 | 1 | 5 | 1 | 0 | 0 | 0 | 0 | 69.60 | $17,375 |

Best finish for 1999: T-28th at the Las Vegas Invitational

| 2000 | 32 | 97 | 17 | 0 | 2 | 5 | 5 | 71.33 | $614,209 |

Best finish for 2000: T-3rd at the MCI Classic

Year	Starts	Rounds Played	Cuts Made	Wins	Top-5s	Top-10s	Top-25s	Scoring Average	Money
2001	31	89	16	0	0	2	8	70.79	$572,820

Best finish for 2001: T-8th at the Air Canada Championship

Year	Starts	Rounds Played	Cuts Made	Wins	Top-5s	Top-10s	Top-25s	Scoring Average	Money
2002	34	92	11	0	0	0	2	71.83	$225,823

Best finish for 2002: T-14th at the Greater Greensboro Chrysler Classic

Year	Starts	Rounds Played	Cuts Made	Wins	Top-5s	Top-10s	Top-25s	Scoring Average	Money
2003	1	5	1	0	0	0	0	71.20	$7,280

Best finish for 2003: T-79th at the Las Vegas Invitational

Year	Starts	Rounds Played	Cuts Made	Wins	Top-5s	Top-10s	Top-25s	Scoring Average	Money
2004	1	3	0	0	0	0	0	70.33	
Period Totals	Starts	Rounds Played	Cuts Made	Wins	Top-5s	Top-10s	Top-25s	Scoring Average	Money
	105	309	49	0	2	7	17	71.29	$1,513,321

Frank Fuhrer

Year	Starts	Rounds Played	Cuts Made	Wins	Top-5s	Top-10s	Top-25s	Scoring Average	Money
1982	2	4	0	0	0	0	0	80.50	$1,500
1983	2	4	0	0	0	0	0	75.50	
1984	21	54	4	0	0	0	0	74.65	$4,370

Best finish for 1984: T-38th at the Georgia-Pacific Atlanta Golf Classic

Year	Starts	Rounds Played	Cuts Made	Wins	Top-5s	Top-10s	Top-25s	Scoring Average	Money
1985	1	2	0	0	0	0	0	71.50	
Period Totals	Starts	Rounds Played	Cuts Made	Wins	Top-5s	Top-10s	Top-25s	Scoring Average	Money
	26	64	4	0	0	0	0	74.97	$5,870

Ken Fulton

Year	Starts	Rounds Played	Cuts Made	Wins	Top-5s	Top-10s	Top-25s	Scoring Average	Money
1966	1	2	0	0	0	0	0	80.00	
1968	6	14	1	0	0	0	0	73.57	$172

Best finish for 1968: T-43rd at the Greater Hartford Open Invitational

| 1969 | 12 | 27 | 2 | 0 | 0 | 0 | 1 | 74.96 | $2,242 |

Best finish for 1969: T-15th at the Canadian Open

| 1970 | 5 | 12 | 1 | 0 | 0 | 0 | 0 | 74.00 | $152 |

Best finish for 1970: T-54th at the Greater Milwaukee Open

| 1971 | 14 | 43 | 7 | 0 | 0 | 0 | 1 | 73.35 | $2,111 |

Best finish for 1971: T-24th at the Robinson Open Golf Classic

| 1972 | 11 | 25 | 2 | 0 | 0 | 0 | 0 | 74.00 | $795 |

Best finish for 1972: T-29th at the Liggett Meyers Open

| 1973 | 2 | 4 | 0 | 0 | 0 | 0 | 0 | 76.25 | |
| 1976 | 1 | 4 | 1 | 0 | 0 | 0 | 0 | 73.50 | |

Best finish for 1976: 77th at the Canadian Open

1979	1	2	0	0	0	0	0	78.50	
1984	1	2	0	0	0	0	0	79.00	
Period Totals	Starts	Rounds Played	Cuts Made	Wins	Top-5s	Top-10s	Top-25s	Scoring Average	Money
	54	135	14	0	0	0	2	74.22	$5,472

Fred Funk

Year	Starts	Rounds Played	Cuts Made	Wins	Top-5s	Top-10s	Top-25s	Scoring Average	Money
1982	3	9	2	0	0	0	0	74.22	$1,779

Best finish for 1982: T-50th at the Anheuser-Busch Golf Classic

| 1985 | 1 | 4 | 1 | 0 | 0 | 0 | 1 | 71.75 | $6,345 |

Best finish for 1985: T-23rd at the U.S. Open

| 1986 | 3 | 5 | 0 | 0 | 0 | 0 | 0 | 76.40 | $600 |
| 1987 | 2 | 6 | 1 | 0 | 0 | 0 | 0 | 74.83 | $3,000 |

Best finish for 1987: T-47th at the PGA Championship

| 1988 | 2 | 6 | 1 | 0 | 0 | 0 | 0 | 73.50 | $1,552 |

Best finish for 1988: 73rd at the Kemper Open

| 1989 | 29 | 89 | 17 | 0 | 1 | 2 | 3 | 71.51 | $60,695 |

Best finish for 1989: T-3rd at the Deposit Guaranty Golf Classic

| 1990 | 29 | 83 | 13 | 0 | 2 | 3 | 7 | 71.64 | $179,346 |

Best finish for 1990: T-3rd at the Chattanooga Classic

| 1991 | 31 | 97 | 17 | 0 | 2 | 5 | 9 | 71.13 | $227,915 |

Best finish for 1991: 4th at the Deposit Guaranty Classic

| 1992 | 33 | 113 | 25 | 1 | 2 | 3 | 9 | 71.31 | $424,132 |

Best finish for 1992: Win at the Shell Houston Open

| 1993 | 34 | 115 | 24 | 0 | 0 | 5 | 11 | 71.08 | $310,935 |

Best finish for 1993: T-6th at the Federal Express St. Jude Classic & Buick Open

| 1994 | 30 | 105 | 23 | 0 | 0 | 4 | 8 | 71.17 | $281,905 |

Best finish for 1994: T-6th at the New England Classic

| 1995 | 32 | 112 | 26 | 2 | 3 | 4 | 11 | 70.84 | $718,232 |

Best finish for 1995: Win at the Ideon Classic & Buick Challenge

| 1996 | 31 | 108 | 23 | 1 | 4 | 8 | 13 | 70.66 | $815,334 |

Best finish for 1996: Win at the B.C. Open

| 1997 | 33 | 115 | 24 | 0 | 3 | 3 | 10 | 71.09 | $544,419 |

Best finish for 1997: T-3rd at the NEC World Series of Golf

| 1998 | 32 | 114 | 25 | 1 | 5 | 8 | 17 | 70.53 | $1,126,988 |

Best finish for 1998: Win at the Deposit Guaranty Golf Classic

Year	Starts	Rounds Played	Cuts Made	Wins	Top-5s	Top-10s	Top-25s	Scoring Average	Money
1999	34	118	27	0	7	8	14	70.49	$1,645,975

Best finish for 1999: T-2nd at the MasterCard Colonial, Air Canada Championship & B.C. Open

2000	32	109	24	0	1	4	10	70.65	$830,667

Best finish for 2000: T-4th at the National Car Rental Golf Classic/Disney

2001	33	117	27	0	3	4	13	70.15	$1,237,004

Best finish for 2001: T-3rd at the Air Canada Championship & Southern Farm Bureau Classic

2002	29	106	24	0	6	7	19	69.64	$2,383,071

Best finish for 2002: T-2nd at the B.C. Open, Buick Open, WGC-NEC Invitational & Valero Texas Open

2003	33	109	25	0	3	9	12	70.30	$2,153,627

Best finish for 2003: T-2nd at the FBR Capital Open

2004	29	96	20	1	3	6	8	70.58	$2,110,731

Best finish for 2004: Win at the Southern Farm Bureau Classic

2005	30	101	23	1	2	3	11	70.89	$2,839,426

Best finish for 2005: Win at the Players Championship

2006	29	105	25	0	1	3	9	70.90	$1,584,837

Best finish for 2006: T-2nd at the Zurich Classic of New Orleans

2007	22	65	12	1	2	2	6	71.51	$1,241,876

Best finish for 2007: Win at the Mayakoba Golf Classic

2008	14	42	7	0	0	1	2	71.31	$257,283

Best finish for 2008: T-10th at the Sony Open in Hawaii

Period Totals	Starts	Rounds Played	Cuts Made	Wins	Top-5s	Top-10s	Top-25s	Scoring Average	Money
	610	2049	436	8	50	92	203	70.87	$20,987,675

Rod Funseth

Year	Starts	Rounds Played	Cuts Made	Wins	Top-5s	Top-10s	Top-25s	Scoring Average	Money
1961	3	12	3	0	0	0	2	69.75	$1,495

Best finish for 1961: T-12th at the Carling Open Invitational

1962	4	16	4	0	0	0	1	71.69	$1,492

Best finish for 1962: T-14th at the Coral Gables Open Invitational

1963	14	56	14	0	0	0	5	71.57	$5,479

Best finish for 1963: T-11th at the Seattle Open Invitational

1964	22	67	11	0	1	1	7	72.93	$10,264

Best finish for 1964: T-2nd at the St. Paul Open

1965	31	120	29	1	2	4	10	72.15	$34,172

Best finish for 1965: Win at the Phoenix Open

1966	34	117	25	0	1	1	11	72.45	$20,721

Best finish for 1966: T-3rd at the Canadian Open

1967	30	99	20	0	3	3	3	72.83	$23,282

Best finish for 1967: T-2nd at the "500" Festival Open

1968	32	110	22	0	0	1	8	71.96	$20,255

Best finish for 1968: T-6th at the Florida Citrus Open Invitational

1969	34	119	27	0	0	4	12	71.73	$27,380

Best finish for 1969: T-8th at the Bing Crosby National Pro-Am & Sahara Invitational

1970	29	105	23	0	2	4	10	71.76	$42,524

Best finish for 1970: T-2nd at the AVCO Classic

1971	32	110	24	0	5	6	9	71.94	$58,094

Best finish for 1971: 2nd at the Greater Greensboro Open

1972	33	118	27	0	3	4	12	71.79	$43,180

Best finish for 1972: T-3rd at the Greater Jacksonville Open & Tallahassee Open

1973	28	99	20	1	4	7	13	71.88	$85,627

Best finish for 1973: Win at the Glen Campbell Los Angles Open

1974	27	80	15	0	1	1	7	72.31	$24,901

Best finish for 1974: T-3rd at the Bing Crosby Pro-Am

1975	26	90	20	0	2	4	11	71.71	$48,454

Best finish for 1975: T-4th at the Andy Williams-San Diego Open & Byron Nelson Golf Classic

1976	29	102	22	0	0	2	6	72.04	$33,710

Best finish for 1976: T-7th at the Andy Williams-San Diego Open

1977	26	81	14	0	0	2	8	72.58	$25,400

Best finish for 1977: T-9th at the Andy Williams-San Diego Open

1978	24	74	12	1	3	3	3	72.20	$84,331

Best finish for 1978: Win at the Sammy Davis, Jr. - Greater Hartford Open

1979	21	69	14	0	0	1	6	72.84	$34,935

Best finish for 1979: T-8th at the Phoenix Open

1980	16	51	10	0	0	0	2	72.63	$9,997

Best finish for 1980: T-25th at the Glen Campbell Los Angles Open & Tallahassee Open

1981	4	9	0	0	0	0	0	73.00	
1982	4	11	2	0	0	0	1	74.45	$4,422

Best finish for 1982: T-21st at the Glen Campbell Los Angles Open

1983	3	9	1	0	0	0	1	70.89	$2,430

Best finish for 1983: T-24th at the Glen Campbell Los Angles Open

1984	1	3	0	0	0	0	0	74.33	

Period Totals	Starts	Rounds Played	Cuts Made	Wins	Top-5s	Top-10s	Top-25s	Scoring Average	Money
	507	1727	359	3	27	48	148	72.14	$642,544

Ed Furgol

Year	Starts	Rounds Played	Cuts Made	Wins	Top-5s	Top-10s	Top-25s	Scoring Average	Money
1958	27	79	11	0	0	0	2	74.24	$1,450

Best finish for 1958: T-11th at the Jackson Open

| 1959 | 7 | 22 | 4 | 0 | 0 | 0 | 1 | 76.05 | $593 |

Best finish for 1959: T-15th at the Puerto Rico Open Invitational

| 1960 | 6 | 19 | 3 | 0 | 1 | 1 | 2 | 74.47 | $1,355 |

Best finish for 1960: T-4th at the Jamaica Open Invitational

| 1961 | 4 | 12 | 2 | 0 | 0 | 1 | 1 | 74.00 | $1,388 |

Best finish for 1961: T-7th at the Coral Gables Open Invitational

| 1962 | 5 | 16 | 3 | 0 | 0 | 0 | 2 | 73.75 | $1,457 |

Best finish for 1962: T-23rd at the Doral Country Club Open Invitational

| 1963 | 10 | 39 | 10 | 0 | 1 | 1 | 4 | 73.00 | $8,389 |

Best finish for 1963: T-5th at the Masters

| 1964 | 14 | 43 | 5 | 0 | 0 | 0 | 2 | 73.56 | $3,275 |

Best finish for 1964: T-13th at the PGA Championship

| 1965 | 15 | 50 | 7 | 0 | 0 | 0 | 1 | 73.32 | $3,652 |

Best finish for 1965: T-13th at the Los Angles Open

| 1966 | 27 | 76 | 10 | 0 | 0 | 0 | 0 | 73.97 | $1,582 |

Best finish for 1966: T-32nd at the Cajun Classic

| 1967 | 10 | 29 | 4 | 0 | 0 | 0 | 0 | 74.59 | $575 |

Best finish for 1967: T-34th at the Jacksonville Open

| 1968 | 8 | 20 | 1 | 0 | 0 | 0 | 0 | 75.20 | |

Best finish for 1968: T-68th at the Los Angeles Open Invitational

1969	3	6	0	0	0	0	0	76.17	
1970	5	8	0	0	0	0	0	75.38	
1971	11	26	2	0	0	0	0	74.50	$479

Best finish for 1971: T-68th at the Greater New Orleans Open

| 1972 | 14 | 31 | 2 | 0 | 0 | 0 | 0 | 75.65 | $237 |

Best finish for 1972: T-58th at the Tallahassee Open

1973	12	20	0	0	0	0	0	76.45	
1974	4	7	0	0	0	0	0	77.14	
1975	7	14	1	0	0	0	0	76.64	$500

Best finish for 1975: T-57th at the Kemper Open

1976	4	8	0	0	0	0	0	76.88	
1977	5	10	0	0	0	0	0	78.40	
1978	3	6	0	0	0	0	0	79.67	
1979	3	3	0	0	0	0	0	80.67	
1980	2	4	0	0	0	0	0	80.25	
1981	1	1	0	0	0	0	0	85.00	
1983	1	4	0	0	0	0	0	80.00	
Period Totals	Starts	Rounds Played	Cuts Made	Wins	Top-5s	Top-10s	Top-25s	Scoring Average	Money
	208	553	65	0	2	3	15	74.71	$24,931

PGA Tour career totals from 1944 to 1983

	Starts	Rounds Played	Cuts Made	Wins	Top-5s	Top-10s	Top-25s	Scoring Average	Money
	502	1441	359	5	24	111	243	N/A	$146,725

Marty Furgol

Year	Starts	Rounds Played	Cuts Made	Wins	Top-5s	Top-10s	Top-25s	Scoring Average	Money
1958	31	114	26	0	2	5	15	71.90	$11,644

Best finish for 1958: T-4th at the Houston Open & Memphis Invitational

| 1959 | 18 | 71 | 17 | 2 | 3 | 4 | 9 | 70.93 | $10,719 |

Best finish for 1959: Win at the San Diego Open Invitational & El Paso Open Invitational

| 1960 | 4 | 16 | 4 | 0 | 0 | 1 | 4 | 70.50 | $1,673 |

Best finish for 1960: T-6th at the Coral Gables Open Invitational

| 1961 | 32 | 129 | 32 | 0 | 2 | 6 | 20 | 70.94 | $15,709 |

Best finish for 1961: T-5th at the Pensacola Open Invitational & Orange County Open

| 1962 | 11 | 44 | 11 | 0 | 0 | 1 | 4 | 71.70 | $4,463 |

Best finish for 1962: T-8th at the Waco Turner Open Invitational

| 1963 | 6 | 25 | 6 | 0 | 0 | 0 | 0 | 71.56 | $913 |

Best finish for 1963: T-27th at the Tucson Open Invitational

| 1964 | 11 | 32 | 5 | 0 | 0 | 0 | 1 | 73.06 | $806 |

Best finish for 1964: T-21st at the Oklahoma City Open

| 1965 | 12 | 30 | 3 | 0 | 0 | 0 | 0 | 72.93 | $750 |

Best finish for 1965: T-30th at the Greater Hartford Open

| 1966 | 3 | 10 | 2 | 0 | 0 | 0 | 0 | 75.00 | |

Best finish for 1966: T-63rd at the Florida Citrus Open Invitational

| 1967 | 2 | 5 | 0 | 0 | 0 | 0 | 0 | 71.20 | |
| 1971 | 3 | 6 | 0 | 0 | 0 | 0 | 0 | 74.50 | |

Period Totals	Starts	Rounds Played	Cuts Made	Wins	Top-5s	Top-10s	Top-25s	Scoring Average	Money
	133	482	106	2	7	17	53	71.65	$46,677

PGA Tour career totals from 1938 to 1971

	Starts	Rounds Played	Cuts Made	Wins	Top-5s	Top-10s	Top-25s	Scoring Average	Money
	402	1468	372	5	23	101	243	N/A	$153,788

Jim Furyk

Year	Starts	Rounds Played	Cuts Made	Wins	Top-5s	Top-10s	Top-25s	Scoring Average	Money
1988	1	2	0	0	0	0	0	75.50	
1990	1	2	0	0	0	0	0	73.00	
1991	1	2	0	0	0	0	0	74.50	
1993	1	2	0	0	0	0	0	76.00	
1994	31	95	17	0	1	3	7	71.15	$236,603

Best finish for 1994: T-5th at the Las Vegas Invitational

| 1995 | 31 | 102 | 22 | 1 | 2 | 3 | 10 | 70.81 | $535,380 |

Best finish for 1995: Win at the Las Vegas Invitational

| 1996 | 28 | 100 | 24 | 1 | 2 | 3 | 13 | 70.83 | $738,950 |

Best finish for 1996: Win at the United Airlines Hawaiian Open

| 1997 | 27 | 98 | 24 | 0 | 8 | 13 | 17 | 70.09 | $1,619,480 |

Best finish for 1997: 2nd at the United Airlines Hawaiian Open, Memorial Tournament & The Tour Championship

| 1998 | 28 | 101 | 24 | 1 | 8 | 12 | 19 | 69.98 | $2,055,834 |

Best finish for 1998: Win at the Las Vegas Invitational

| 1999 | 25 | 96 | 24 | 1 | 2 | 8 | 17 | 70.75 | $1,827,593 |

Best finish for 1999: Win at the Las Vegas Invitational

| 2000 | 25 | 95 | 24 | 1 | 6 | 8 | 15 | 70.36 | $1,940,519 |

Best finish for 2000: Win at the Doral Ryder Open

| 2001 | 24 | 88 | 19 | 1 | 3 | 8 | 16 | 69.65 | $2,542,022 |

Best finish for 2001: Win at the Mercedes Championships

| 2002 | 25 | 85 | 19 | 1 | 3 | 9 | 14 | 70.15 | $2,373,200 |

Best finish for 2002: Win at the Memorial Tournament

| 2003 | 27 | 101 | 25 | 2 | 10 | 15 | 22 | 69.28 | $5,187,633 |

Best finish for 2003: Win at the U.S. Open & Buick Open

| 2004 | 14 | 44 | 8 | 0 | 0 | 2 | 5 | 70.95 | $699,293 |

Best finish for 2004: T-6th at the Buick Open

| 2005 | 26 | 93 | 23 | 1 | 5 | 10 | 14 | 69.68 | $4,259,749 |

Best finish for 2005: Win at the Cialis Western Open

| 2006 | 24 | 88 | 22 | 2 | 12 | 13 | 19 | 69.45 | $7,213,316 |

Best finish for 2006: Win at the Wachovia Championship & Canadian Open

| 2007 | 23 | 82 | 20 | 1 | 7 | 8 | 16 | 70.21 | $4,156,546 |

Best finish for 2007: Win at the Canadian Open

| 2008 | 26 | 94 | 23 | 0 | 6 | 9 | 13 | 70.56 | $3,455,714 |

Best finish for 2008: T-2nd at the WGC-CA Championship

Period Totals	Starts	Rounds Played	Cuts Made	Wins	Top-5s	Top-10s	Top-25s	Scoring Average	Money
	388	1370	318	13	75	124	217	70.27	$38,841,832

Bobby Gage

Year	Starts	Rounds Played	Cuts Made	Wins	Top-5s	Top-10s	Top-25s	Scoring Average	Money
1989	1	2	0	0	0	0	0	73.50	
1993	1	2	0	0	0	0	0	79.50	
1998	23	52	5	0	0	0	1	72.37	$33,881

Best finish for 1998: T-22nd at the Shell Houston Open

| 2000 | 3 | 8 | 1 | 0 | 0 | 0 | 0 | 71.38 | $6,210 |

Best finish for 2000: T-65th at the Doral Ryder Open

Period Totals	Starts	Rounds Played	Cuts Made	Wins	Top-5s	Top-10s	Top-25s	Scoring Average	Money
	28	64	6	0	0	0	1	72.50	$40,091

Tommy Gainey

Year	Starts	Rounds Played	Cuts Made	Wins	Top-5s	Top-10s	Top-25s	Scoring Average	Money
2007	1	2	0	0	0	0	0	77.50	
2008	24	60	6	0	1	1	1	71.95	$562,205

Best finish for 2008: 2nd at the Children's Miracle Network Classic

Period Totals	Starts	Rounds Played	Cuts Made	Wins	Top-5s	Top-10s	Top-25s	Scoring Average	Money
	25	62	6	0	1	1	1	72.13	$562,205

Bob Gajda

Year	Starts	Rounds Played	Cuts Made	Wins	Top-5s	Top-10s	Top-25s	Scoring Average	Money
1958	12	37	6	0	0	0	2	74.51	$622

Best finish for 1958: T-18th at the St. Petersburg Open

| 1959 | 3 | 11 | 3 | 0 | 0 | 0 | 1 | 72.36 | $738 |

Best finish for 1959: T-15th at the Phoenix Open Invitational

| 1960 | 4 | 15 | 4 | 0 | 0 | 0 | 2 | 73.00 | $383 |

Best finish for 1960: T-14th at the Panama Open Invitational

Year	Starts	Rounds Played	Cuts Made	Wins	Top-5s	Top-10s	Top-25s	Scoring Average	Money
1961	2	8	2	0	0	0	0	70.88	$795

Best finish for 1961: T-28th at the Lucky International Open

| 1962 | 3 | 10 | 2 | 0 | 0 | 0 | 1 | 73.80 | $600 |

Best finish for 1962: T-14th at the Puerto Rico Open Invitational

| 1963 | 3 | 12 | 3 | 0 | 0 | 0 | 0 | 75.83 | $966 |

Best finish for 1963: 46th at the U.S. Open

| 1964 | 5 | 17 | 3 | 0 | 0 | 1 | 2 | 73.88 | $2,485 |

Best finish for 1964: T-6th at the Azalea Open

1965	3	6	0	0	0	0	0	77.17	
1966	1	2	0	0	0	0	0	75.00	
1967	5	16	3	0	0	0	0	72.31	$325

Best finish for 1967: T-42nd at the Florida Citrus Open

| 1968 | 1 | 2 | 0 | 0 | 0 | 0 | 0 | 75.00 | |
| 1969 | 1 | 4 | 1 | 0 | 0 | 0 | 0 | 76.00 | $054 |

Best finish for 1969: T-48th at the West End Classic

Period Totals	Starts	Rounds Played	Cuts Made	Wins	Top-5s	Top-10s	Top-25s	Scoring Average	Money
	43	140	27	0	0	1	8	73.88	$6,968

Sandy Galbraith

Year	Starts	Rounds Played	Cuts Made	Wins	Top-5s	Top-10s	Top-25s	Scoring Average	Money
1974	1	2	0	0	0	0	0	82.00	$120
1976	14	37	7	0	1	1	1	73.49	$5,651

Best finish for 1976: T-4th at the San Antonio Texas Open

| 1977 | 12 | 29 | 2 | 0 | 0 | 0 | 0 | 74.72 | $370 |

Best finish for 1977: T-60th at the Anheuser-Busch Golf Classic

Period Totals	Starts	Rounds Played	Cuts Made	Wins	Top-5s	Top-10s	Top-25s	Scoring Average	Money
	27	68	9	0	1	1	1	74.26	$6,141

Jeff Gallagher

Year	Starts	Rounds Played	Cuts Made	Wins	Top-5s	Top-10s	Top-25s	Scoring Average	Money
1989	1	2	0	0	0	0	0	73.00	
1994	1	2	0	0	0	0	0	72.50	
1996	31	84	11	0	0	2	4	71.83	$114,001

Best finish for 1996: T-10th at the Freeport-McDermott Classic & MasterCard Colonial

| 1997 | 2 | 6 | 1 | 0 | 0 | 0 | 0 | 71.50 | $3,376 |

Best finish for 1997: T-63rd at the MasterCard Colonial

| 1998 | 29 | 89 | 18 | 0 | 0 | 2 | 4 | 71.69 | $259,769 |

Best finish for 1998: T-6th at the Nissan Open

| 1999 | 34 | 92 | 12 | 0 | 0 | 1 | 3 | 72.40 | $190,847 |

Best finish for 1999: T-9th at the Southern Farm Bureau Classic

| 2000 | 4 | 15 | 3 | 0 | 0 | 0 | 0 | 71.87 | $40,855 |

Best finish for 2000: T-28th at the Greater Greensboro Chrysler Classic

| 2001 | 7 | 21 | 3 | 0 | 0 | 0 | 0 | 73.33 | $20,984 |

Best finish for 2001: T-48th at the Touchstone Energy Tucson Open

| 2002 | 16 | 37 | 3 | 0 | 0 | 0 | 0 | 72.46 | $21,711 |

Best finish for 2002: T-67th at the COMPAQ Classic of New Orleans

| 2003 | 10 | 31 | 5 | 0 | 1 | 1 | 1 | 70.81 | $163,900 |

Best finish for 2003: T-5th at the Greater Milwaukee Open

Period Totals	Starts	Rounds Played	Cuts Made	Wins	Top-5s	Top-10s	Top-25s	Scoring Average	Money
	135	379	56	0	1	6	12	72.00	$815,443

Jim Gallagher, Jr.

Year	Starts	Rounds Played	Cuts Made	Wins	Top-5s	Top-10s	Top-25s	Scoring Average	Money
1984	25	80	13	0	0	1	2	72.91	$22,249

Best finish for 1984: T-8th at the Miller High-Life Quad Cities Open

| 1985 | 16 | 48 | 8 | 0 | 0 | 0 | 2 | 72.19 | $19,061 |

Best finish for 1985: T-12th at the Manufactures Hanover Westchester Classic

| 1986 | 36 | 111 | 21 | 0 | 2 | 3 | 6 | 72.08 | $79,967 |

Best finish for 1986: T-3rd at the Tallahassee Open

| 1987 | 36 | 104 | 16 | 0 | 0 | 1 | 2 | 72.52 | $37,978 |

Best finish for 1987: T-8th at the Hardee's Golf Classic

| 1988 | 18 | 62 | 13 | 0 | 1 | 1 | 1 | 70.68 | $81,080 |

Best finish for 1988: T-2nd at the Greater Milwaukee Open

| 1989 | 34 | 118 | 24 | 0 | 2 | 3 | 13 | 70.59 | $266,809 |

Best finish for 1989: T-4th at the Beatrice Western Open & Hardee's Golf Classic

| 1990 | 35 | 115 | 25 | 1 | 3 | 5 | 10 | 71.61 | $477,706 |

Best finish for 1990: Win at the Greater Milwaukee Open

| 1991 | 32 | 112 | 25 | 0 | 6 | 6 | 11 | 70.79 | $570,627 |

Best finish for 1991: T-2nd at the NEC World Series of Golf

| 1992 | 29 | 107 | 25 | 0 | 6 | 7 | 14 | 70.47 | $639,514 |

Best finish for 1992: 2nd at the Anheuser-Busch Golf Classic, PGA Championship & Buick Southern Open

Year	Starts	Rounds Played	Cuts Made	Wins	Top-5s	Top-10s	Top-25s	Scoring Average	Money
1993	28	91	18	2	5	6	8	71.37	$1,083,494

Best finish for 1993: Win at the Anheuser-Busch Golf Classic & The Tour Championship

1994	27	87	16	0	1	4	8	71.02	$337,505

Best finish for 1994: T-2nd at the Bob Hope Chrysler Classic

1995	27	99	22	2	5	6	12	70.81	$1,057,241

Best finish for 1995: Win at the Kmart Greater Greensboro Open & FedEx St. Jude Classic

1996	24	73	15	0	1	2	8	71.38	$277,740

Best finish for 1996: T-4th at the Motorola Western Open

1997	28	87	14	0	0	1	4	71.91	$137,624

Best finish for 1997: T-7th at the Michelob Championship at Kingsmill

1998	28	72	8	0	0	1	3	72.04	$153,992

Best finish for 1998: T-6th at the MasterCard Colonial

1999	30	82	11	0	0	0	2	72.15	$131,758

Best finish for 1999: T-15th at the Honda Classic

2000	16	48	8	0	1	1	2	70.90	$240,514

Best finish for 2000: T-3rd at the Westin Texas Open at LaCantera

2001	15	35	3	0	0	0	1	72.37	$47,424

Best finish for 2001: T-17th at the Southern Farm Bureau Classic

2002	15	45	7	0	1	1	1	71.29	$192,403

Best finish for 2002: T-5th at the Greater Greensboro Chrysler Classic

2003	9	22	3	0	0	0	0	72.23	$22,245

Best finish for 2003: T-54th at the B.C. Open

2004	9	22	2	0	0	1	1	71.86	$82,385

Best finish for 2004: T-10th at the B.C. Open

2005	5	10	0	0	0	0	0	73.20	
2006	4	10	1	0	0	0	0	72.10	$6,390

Best finish for 2006: T-62nd at the B.C. Open

2007	9	26	4	0	0	0	0	73.08	$38,635

Best finish for 2007: T-55th at the Stanford St. Jude Classic

2008	7	17	1	0	0	0	0	74.82	$7,520

Best finish for 2008: 76th at the U.S. Bank Championship in Milwaukee

Period Totals	Starts	Rounds Played	Cuts Made	Wins	Top-5s	Top-10s	Top-25s	Scoring Average	Money
	542	1683	303	5	34	50	111	71.57	$6,011,863

Bill Galloway

Year	Starts	Rounds Played	Cuts Made	Wins	Top-5s	Top-10s	Top-25s	Scoring Average	Money
1974	6	11	0	0	0	0	0	76.55	
1976	1	2	0	0	0	0	0	73.00	
1977	1	2	0	0	0	0	0	72.50	
1978	17	39	4	0	0	0	0	74.36	$633

Best finish for 1978: T-60th at the Bob Hope Chrysler Classic

1979	2	4	0	0	0	0	0	74.50	
1980	13	32	4	0	0	0	0	73.66	$2,149

Best finish for 1980: T-46th at the Tallahassee Open

1981	1	2	0	0	0	0	0	76.50	
1982	1	2	0	0	0	0	0	76.50	
1983	1	2	0	0	0	0	0	77.00	
1984	1	2	0	0	0	0	0	79.00	
1985	1	2	0	0	0	0	0	77.00	
1986	1	2	0	0	0	0	0	75.00	
1987	1	2	0	0	0	0	0	77.50	
1988	1	2	0	0	0	0	0	75.00	
1989	1	2	0	0	0	0	0	76.00	

Period Totals	Starts	Rounds Played	Cuts Made	Wins	Top-5s	Top-10s	Top-25s	Scoring Average	Money
	49	108	8	0	0	0	0	74.69	$2,782

Bob Galloway

Year	Starts	Rounds Played	Cuts Made	Wins	Top-5s	Top-10s	Top-25s	Scoring Average	Money
1965	12	28	2	0	0	0	1	74.36	$1,550

Best finish for 1965: T-12th at the Memphis Open

1966	1	2	0	0	0	0	0	78.00	
1968	1	1	0	0	0	0	0	80.00	
1971	2	4	0	0	0	0	0	76.25	
1972	6	12	0	0	0	0	0	75.50	
1973	6	14	0	0	0	0	0	74.64	
1974	4	9	1	0	0	0	0	74.33	$321

Best finish for 1974: T-63rd at the PGA Championship

1975	3	6	0	0	0	0	0	76.33	
1976	2	3	0	0	0	0	0	76.33	
1977	5	11	1	0	0	0	0	76.55	$250

Best finish for 1977: T-81st at the Colgate Hall Of Fame Golf Classic

1978	1	2	0	0	0	0	0	74.50	$303

1979	1	2	0	0	0	0	0	78.50	$350
Period Totals	Starts	Rounds Played	Cuts Made	Wins	Top-5s	Top-10s	Top-25s	Scoring Average	Money
	44	94	4	0	0	0	1	75.30	$2,774

Robert Gamez

Year	Starts	Rounds Played	Cuts Made	Wins	Top-5s	Top-10s	Top-25s	Scoring Average	Money
1988	1	4	1	0	0	0	0	71.00	

Best finish for 1988: T-46th at the Northern Telecom Tucson Open

| 1989 | 3 | 8 | 1 | 0 | 0 | 0 | 1 | 70.63 | $4,827 |

Best finish for 1989: T-20th at the Southern Open

| 1990 | 27 | 83 | 17 | 2 | 2 | 2 | 7 | 72.12 | $492,545 |

Best finish for 1990: Win at the Northern Telecom Tucson Open & The Nestle Invitational

| 1991 | 28 | 83 | 14 | 0 | 2 | 3 | 7 | 71.49 | $289,963 |

Best finish for 1991: 2nd at the Greater Milwaukee Open & Buick Southern Open

| 1992 | 25 | 79 | 13 | 0 | 1 | 3 | 3 | 71.33 | $215,648 |

Best finish for 1992: T-2nd at the Federal Express St. Jude Classic

| 1993 | 24 | 79 | 16 | 0 | 1 | 3 | 4 | 71.81 | $237,658 |

Best finish for 1993: 2nd at the Honda Classic

| 1994 | 23 | 76 | 15 | 0 | 1 | 5 | 7 | 71.62 | $381,353 |

Best finish for 1994: 2nd at the Las Vegas Invitational

| 1995 | 27 | 82 | 13 | 0 | 1 | 3 | 5 | 71.72 | $208,788 |

Best finish for 1995: T-5th at the Memorial Tournament

| 1996 | 25 | 75 | 12 | 0 | 2 | 2 | 6 | 71.25 | $249,227 |

Best finish for 1996: 3rd at the Walt Disney World/Oldsmobile Classic

| 1997 | 28 | 82 | 12 | 0 | 3 | 3 | 5 | 71.57 | $284,734 |

Best finish for 1997: T-2nd at the Quad City Classic

| 1998 | 24 | 69 | 9 | 0 | 0 | 0 | 1 | 72.13 | $76,148 |

Best finish for 1998: T-16th at the United Airlines Hawaiian Open

| 1999 | 19 | 59 | 11 | 0 | 0 | 0 | 0 | 71.98 | $71,236 |

Best finish for 1999: T-39th at the Greater Milwaukee Open

| 2000 | 26 | 76 | 11 | 0 | 0 | 0 | 5 | 71.04 | $260,305 |

Best finish for 2000: T-12th at the Honda Classic

| 2001 | 22 | 59 | 6 | 0 | 0 | 0 | 2 | 71.81 | $194,525 |

Best finish for 2001: T-11th at the Bob Hope Chrysler Classic & Marconi Pennsylvania Classic

| 2002 | 21 | 69 | 13 | 0 | 2 | 4 | 5 | 70.58 | $809,892 |

Best finish for 2002: 2nd at the John Deere Classic

| 2003 | 31 | 114 | 25 | 0 | 2 | 2 | 12 | 70.16 | $1,519,804 |

Best finish for 2003: T-2nd at the Wachovia Championship

| 2004 | 31 | 103 | 20 | 0 | 1 | 2 | 6 | 70.92 | $725,368 |

Best finish for 2004: T-5th at the Bank of America Colonial

| 2005 | 28 | 91 | 17 | 1 | 1 | 2 | 4 | 71.04 | $1,117,364 |

Best finish for 2005: Win at the Valero Texas Open

| 2006 | 30 | 94 | 16 | 0 | 0 | 0 | 6 | 71.51 | $495,891 |

Best finish for 2006: T-17th at the Mercedes Championships

| 2007 | 30 | 88 | 14 | 0 | 1 | 3 | 4 | 71.73 | $693,464 |

Best finish for 2007: T-3rd at the Children's Miracle network Classic

| 2008 | 26 | 79 | 13 | 0 | 0 | 0 | 1 | 71.70 | $249,944 |

Best finish for 2008: T-16th at the Bob Hope Chrysler Classic

| Period Totals | Starts | Rounds Played | Cuts Made | Wins | Top-5s | Top-10s | Top-25s | Scoring Average | Money |
| | 499 | 1552 | 269 | 3 | 20 | 37 | 91 | 71.40 | $8,578,684 |

Stephen Gangluff

Year	Starts	Rounds Played	Cuts Made	Wins	Top-5s	Top-10s	Top-25s	Scoring Average	Money
2001	1	4	1	0	0	0	0	75.25	$8,105

Best finish for 2001: 79th at the U.S. Open

| 2002 | 27 | 75 | 10 | 0 | 0 | 0 | 3 | 71.28 | $187,804 |

Best finish for 2002: T-19th at the FedEx St. Jude Classic

| 2005 | 1 | 4 | 1 | 0 | 0 | 0 | 0 | 70.50 | $14,161 |

Best finish for 2005: T-44th at the FedEx St. Jude Classic

| 2006 | 2 | 8 | 2 | 0 | 0 | 0 | 0 | 71.75 | $53,584 |

Best finish for 2006: T-35th at the Canadian Open

2008	1	2	0	0	0	0	0	73.00	
Period Totals	Starts	Rounds Played	Cuts Made	Wins	Top-5s	Top-10s	Top-25s	Scoring Average	Money
	32	93	14	0	0	0	3	71.49	$263,654

Sergio Garcia

Year	Starts	Rounds Played	Cuts Made	Wins	Top-5s	Top-10s	Top-25s	Scoring Average	Money
1996	1	2	0	0	0	0	0	74.50	
1998	1	4	1	0	0	0	0	73.00	

Best finish for 1998: T-29th at the British Open

| 1999 | 9 | 28 | 7 | 0 | 2 | 4 | 6 | 71.64 | $921,010 |

Best finish for 1999: 2nd at the PGA Championship

Year	Starts	Rounds Played	Cuts Made	Wins	Top-5s	Top-10s	Top-25s	Scoring Average	Money
2000	16	52	14	0	4	5	8	71.12	$1,054,338

Best finish for 2000: 3rd at the Buick Classic & Bell Canadian Open

2001	18	60	14	2	6	8	12	69.60	$2,905,635

Best finish for 2001: Win at the MasterCard Colonial & Buick Classic

2002	21	72	19	1	3	9	14	70.57	$2,401,993

Best finish for 2002: Win at the Mercedes Championships

2003	20	57	12	0	1	2	4	71.07	$668,386

Best finish for 2003: T-4th at the Buick Classic

2004	18	64	16	2	4	5	10	70.56	$3,245,897

Best finish for 2004: Win at the EDS Byron Nelson Championship & Buick Classic

2005	20	68	17	1	5	8	13	70.24	$3,218,375

Best finish for 2005: Win at the Booz Allen Classic

2006	17	55	14	0	3	6	9	71.45	$1,562,733

Best finish for 2006: T-3rd at the PGA Championship

2007	19	66	16	0	5	7	13	70.45	$3,723,185

Best finish for 2007: 2nd at The Players & British Open

2008	19	70	18	1	6	6	11	70.60	$4,858,224

Best finish for 2008: Win at The Players

Period Totals	Starts	Rounds Played	Cuts Made	Wins	Top-5s	Top-10s	Top-25s	Scoring Average	Money
	179	598	148	7	39	60	100	70.68	$24,559,776

Buddy Gardner

Year	Starts	Rounds Played	Cuts Made	Wins	Top-5s	Top-10s	Top-25s	Scoring Average	Money
1977	1	1	0	0	0	0	0	80.00	$255
1978	21	59	8	0	0	0	1	73.12	$3,260

Best finish for 1978: T-22nd at the Buick Goodwrench Open

1979	29	93	18	0	2	2	6	72.34	$67,018

Best finish for 1979: T-2nd at the Joe Garagiola Tucson Open & Anheuser-Busch Golf Classic

1980	35	108	22	0	0	1	7	72.31	$35,270

Best finish for 1980: T-8th at the World Disney World National Team Championship

1981	25	67	10	0	0	0	1	73.19	$14,635

Best finish for 1981: T-12th at the Hawaiian Open

1982	16	45	6	0	0	0	0	73.51	$4,914

Best finish for 1982: T-35th at the Southern Open

1983	30	105	22	0	0	1	8	72.02	$56,529

Best finish for 1983: T-9th at the Kemper Open

1984	33	97	16	0	2	2	7	72.77	$119,945

Best finish for 1984: 2nd at the Houston Coca-Cola Open

1985	30	103	23	0	2	4	8	71.29	$122,409

Best finish for 1985: T-5th at the Bob Hope Chrysler Classic & Hawaiian Open

1986	38	104	18	0	1	2	8	72.10	$94,106

Best finish for 1986: T-4th at the Greater Milwaukee Open

1987	31	108	24	0	2	3	6	71.32	$173,047

Best finish for 1987: T-2nd at the Big I Houston Open

1988	35	114	23	0	2	2	7	71.25	$130,859

Best finish for 1988: 3rd at the Gatlin Brothers - Southwest Golf Classic

1989	33	111	22	0	0	1	5	71.12	$136,488

Best finish for 1989: T-9th at the Doral-Ryder Open

1990	32	104	21	0	1	1	8	71.24	$159,737

Best finish for 1990: T-5th at the Canadian Open

1991	30	106	22	0	1	2	10	70.62	$202,700

Best finish for 1991: T-5th at the Buick Southern Open

1992	32	89	12	0	1	1	3	71.72	$113,394

Best finish for 1992: T-4th at the Northern Telecom Open

1993	25	65	7	0	0	0	0	72.58	$13,722

Best finish for 1993: T-48th at the Buick Open & Hardee's Golf Classic

1994	11	28	3	0	1	1	1	72.86	$37,609

Best finish for 1994: T-4th at the Buick Southern Open

1995	6	16	2	0	0	0	0	72.31	$5,610

Best finish for 1995: T-35th at the Deposit Guaranty Golf Classic

1996	6	14	1	0	0	0	0	73.21	$2,616

Best finish for 1996: T-58th at the CVS Charity Classic

1997	2	4	0	0	0	0	0	71.75	
2002	1	2	0	0	0	0	0	74.50	

Period Totals	Starts	Rounds Played	Cuts Made	Wins	Top-5s	Top-10s	Top-25s	Scoring Average	Money
	502	1543	280	0	15	23	86	71.92	$1,494,122

Tom Garner

Year	Starts	Rounds Played	Cuts Made	Wins	Top-5s	Top-10s	Top-25s	Scoring Average	Money
1985	1	2	0	0	0	0	0	76.50	
1987	31	82	10	0	0	0	0	73.01	$12,228

Best finish for 1987: T-44th at the Georgia-Pacific Atlanta Golf Classic

Year	Starts	Rounds Played	Cuts Made	Wins	Top-5s	Top-10s	Top-25s	Scoring Average	Money
1988	7	19	2	0	0	0	0	72.26	$5,148

Best finish for 1988: T-37th at the Georgia-Pacific Atlanta Golf Classic

1989	3	9	2	0	0	0	0	72.33	$2,437

Best finish for 1989: T-47th at the Deposit Guaranty Golf Classic

1990	2	6	1	0	0	0	0	74.17	$3,486

Best finish for 1990: T-48th at the Honda Classic

1991	1	2	0	0	0	0	0	74.50	
1994	23	56	6	0	0	0	0	72.80	$19,904

Best finish for 1994: T-28th at the GTE Byron Nelson Classic

1998	1	2	0	0	0	0	0	78.00	
Period Totals	Starts	Rounds Played	Cuts Made	Wins	Top-5s	Top-10s	Top-25s	Scoring Average	Money
	69	178	21	0	0	0	0	72.98	$43,203

Bill Garrett

Year	Starts	Rounds Played	Cuts Made	Wins	Top-5s	Top-10s	Top-25s	Scoring Average	Money
1964	13	41	8	0	0	0	3	72.68	$1,994

Best finish for 1964: T-12th at the Sunset-Camellia Open

1965	24	77	12	0	0	0	1	73.08	$2,417

Best finish for 1965: T-24th at the Western Open

1966	17	42	4	0	0	0	1	74.81	$1,371

Best finish for 1966: T-24th at the Phoenix Open Invitational

1967	5	16	3	0	0	0	2	73.00	$2,778

Best finish for 1967: T-12th at the Cajun Classic

1968	26	86	16	0	0	0	7	72.49	$10,796

Best finish for 1968: T-12th at the Sahara Invitational

1969	29	97	19	0	0	1	6	72.58	$11,634

Best finish for 1969: T-7th at the Robinson Open

1970	27	88	16	1	1	1	4	72.42	$31,899

Best finish for 1970: Win at the Coral Springs Open Invitational

1971	35	106	19	0	0	1	5	73.25	$16,976

Best finish for 1971: T-10th at the Glen Campbell Los Angles Open

1972	15	47	7	0	0	0	0	73.70	$1,612

Best finish for 1972: T-39th at the Tallahassee Open

1973	5	16	2	0	0	0	0	74.38	$219

Best finish for 1973: T-64th at the Ohio Kings Island Open

1974	12	35	6	0	0	0	0	73.51	$1,802

Best finish for 1974: T-39th at the Sahara Invitational

1975	12	29	2	0	0	0	0	75.21	$1,227

Best finish for 1975: T-47th at the British Open

1976	12	39	10	0	0	0	0	73.00	$3,539

Best finish for 1976: T-28th at the Pensacola Open

1977	16	51	9	0	0	2	2	72.84	$13,564

Best finish for 1977: T-6th at the Phoenix Open

1978	17	41	3	0	0	0	0	73.73	$1,487

Best finish for 1978: T-35th at the Phoenix Open

1979	9	21	2	0	0	0	0	74.05	$1,008

Best finish for 1979: T-63rd at the Houston Open

1980	2	4	0	0	0	0	0	76.00	
1981	5	8	0	0	0	0	0	76.63	$600
1982	3	6	0	0	0	0	0	74.67	
1983	1	2	0	0	0	0	0	74.00	
1984	1	4	0	0	0	0	0	73.75	
1985	1	3	0	0	0	0	0	75.67	
1990	1	2	0	0	0	0	0	75.00	
Period Totals	Starts	Rounds Played	Cuts Made	Wins	Top-5s	Top-10s	Top-25s	Scoring Average	Money
	288	861	138	1	1	5	31	73.24	$104,922

Wright Garrett

Year	Starts	Rounds Played	Cuts Made	Wins	Top-5s	Top-10s	Top-25s	Scoring Average	Money
1963	1	4	1	0	0	0	0	71.25	

Best finish for 1963: T-51st at the Houston Classic

1964	2	8	2	0	0	0	1	72.38	$975

Best finish for 1964: T-18th at the Western Open

1965	12	40	8	0	0	0	0	73.53	$2,158

Best finish for 1965: T-33rd at the Buick Open

1966	26	88	18	0	2	3	5	72.77	$12,257

Best finish for 1966: T-4th at the Portland Open Invitational

1967	14	35	4	0	0	1	2	73.80	$2,338

Best finish for 1967: T-10th at the Azalea Open

1971	3	5	0	0	0	0	0	74.80	
Period Totals	Starts	Rounds Played	Cuts Made	Wins	Top-5s	Top-10s	Top-25s	Scoring Average	Money
	58	180	33	0	2	4	8	73.14	$17,728

Robert Garrigus

Year	Starts	Rounds Played	Cuts Made	Wins	Top-5s	Top-10s	Top-25s	Scoring Average	Money
2004	1	2	0	0	0	0	0	74.00	$1,000
2006	28	83	15	0	1	1	4	71.53	$537,595

Best finish for 2006: T-4th at the 84 Lumber Classic

| 2007 | 28 | 95 | 18 | 0 | 2 | 4 | 7 | 71.28 | $1,260,010 |

Best finish for 2007: T-3rd at the Frys.Com Open-Vegas

| 2008 | 29 | 90 | 18 | 0 | 1 | 2 | 6 | 71.02 | $756,732 |

Best finish for 2008: T-3rd at the Turning Stone Resort Championship

Period Totals	Starts	Rounds Played	Cuts Made	Wins	Top-5s	Top-10s	Top-25s	Scoring Average	Money
	86	270	51	0	4	7	17	71.29	$2,555,337

Brian Gay

Year	Starts	Rounds Played	Cuts Made	Wins	Top-5s	Top-10s	Top-25s	Scoring Average	Money
1996	1	2	0	0	0	0	0	76.00	$1,000
1999	26	69	8	0	0	0	1	72.39	$74,329

Best finish for 1999: T-24th at the Reno-Tahoe Open

| 2000 | 33 | 99 | 17 | 0 | 1 | 1 | 8 | 70.93 | $483,028 |

Best finish for 2000: T-4th at the Honda Classic

| 2001 | 33 | 112 | 23 | 0 | 2 | 5 | 12 | 70.10 | $1,300,935 |

Best finish for 2001: T-2nd at the MasterCard Colonial

| 2002 | 34 | 115 | 24 | 0 | 2 | 4 | 10 | 70.58 | $927,735 |

Best finish for 2002: T-2nd at the Buick Open

| 2003 | 34 | 97 | 15 | 0 | 0 | 1 | 4 | 71.23 | $448,647 |

Best finish for 2003: T-8th at the Honda Classic

| 2004 | 32 | 94 | 16 | 0 | 1 | 1 | 6 | 70.84 | $646,194 |

Best finish for 2004: T-5th at the FedEx St. Jude Classic

| 2005 | 33 | 99 | 19 | 0 | 1 | 1 | 5 | 71.21 | $689,862 |

Best finish for 2005: T-3rd at the Barclays Classic

| 2006 | 31 | 107 | 22 | 0 | 0 | 2 | 10 | 70.32 | $1,037,600 |

Best finish for 2006: T-9th at the Verizon Heritage & Chrysler Championship

| 2007 | 32 | 107 | 21 | 0 | 2 | 2 | 8 | 70.89 | $1,114,571 |

Best finish for 2007: T-4th at the PODS Championship & Stanford St. Jude Classic

| 2008 | 31 | 102 | 20 | 1 | 2 | 6 | 12 | 70.11 | $2,205,513 |

Best finish for 2008: Win at the Mayakoba Golf Classic

Period Totals	Starts	Rounds Played	Cuts Made	Wins	Top-5s	Top-10s	Top-25s	Scoring Average	Money
	320	1003	185	1	11	23	76	70.80	$8,929,414

Al Geiberger

Year	Starts	Rounds Played	Cuts Made	Wins	Top-5s	Top-10s	Top-25s	Scoring Average	Money
1958	1	2	0	0	0	0	0	79.00	
1959	1	4	1	0	0	1	1	70.75	

Best finish for 1959: T-8th at the Los Angles Open Invitational

| 1960 | 21 | 84 | 19 | 0 | 2 | 6 | 14 | 71.13 | $10,511 |

Best finish for 1960: T-4th at the Pensacola Open Invitational

| 1961 | 24 | 97 | 22 | 0 | 4 | 6 | 18 | 70.59 | $19,307 |

Best finish for 1961: T-3rd at the Orange County Open

| 1962 | 22 | 84 | 16 | 0 | 4 | 8 | 16 | 70.95 | $20,757 |

Best finish for 1962: T-3rd at the Puerto Rico Open Invitational

| 1963 | 22 | 87 | 17 | 1 | 7 | 9 | 17 | 71.25 | $33,276 |

Best finish for 1963: Win at the Almaden Open Invitational

| 1964 | 31 | 123 | 29 | 0 | 7 | 10 | 18 | 71.39 | $38,355 |

Best finish for 1964: T-2nd at the Tournament of Champions

| 1965 | 26 | 101 | 24 | 1 | 5 | 12 | 18 | 71.06 | $62,075 |

Best finish for 1965: Win at the American Classic

| 1966 | 29 | 111 | 26 | 1 | 3 | 11 | 16 | 71.46 | $69,890 |

Best finish for 1966: Win at the PGA Championship

| 1967 | 25 | 97 | 24 | 0 | 4 | 9 | 18 | 71.34 | $65,895 |

Best finish for 1967: 2nd at the Carling World Open

| 1968 | 24 | 90 | 21 | 0 | 3 | 10 | 15 | 70.83 | $63,955 |

Best finish for 1968: 2nd at the Andy Williams-San Diego Open Invitational

| 1969 | 17 | 60 | 14 | 0 | 1 | 2 | 6 | 71.68 | $25,934 |

Best finish for 1969: T-2nd at the U.S. Open

| 1970 | 20 | 75 | 17 | 0 | 1 | 1 | 5 | 72.08 | $20,418 |

Best finish for 1970: T-5th at the San Antonio Texas Open

| 1971 | 20 | 69 | 14 | 0 | 0 | 2 | 5 | 72.28 | $19,056 |

Best finish for 1971: T-7th at the Greater Greensboro Open

| 1972 | 22 | 80 | 18 | 0 | 0 | 0 | 10 | 71.99 | $25,361 |

Best finish for 1972: T-11th at the USI Classic

| 1973 | 27 | 108 | 25 | 0 | 2 | 2 | 11 | 71.69 | $62,260 |

Best finish for 1973: 3rd at the Atlanta Classic

Year	Starts	Rounds Played	Cuts Made	Wins	Top-5s	Top-10s	Top-25s	Scoring Average	Money
1974	26	95	21	1	3	8	16	71.49	$88,748

Best finish for 1974: Win at the Sahara Invitational

1975	26	92	20	2	4	7	12	71.47	$177,163

Best finish for 1975: Win at the MONY Tournament Of Champions & Tournament Players Championship

1976	26	97	25	2	7	10	17	70.96	$195,072

Best finish for 1976: Win at the Greater Greensboro Open & Western Open

1977	24	82	17	1	2	5	12	71.76	$90,145

Best finish for 1977: Win at the Danny Thomas Memphis Classic

1978	17	60	13	0	0	0	2	72.12	$20,780

Best finish for 1978: T-14th at the B.C. Open

1979	20	69	14	1	1	1	4	72.88	$70,046

Best finish for 1979: Win at the Colonial National Invitational

1980	18	55	9	0	0	0	2	73.45	$16,894

Best finish for 1980: T-11th at the Greater Greensboro Open

1981	13	36	7	0	0	0	1	72.75	$8,508

Best finish for 1981: T-15th at the Pleasant Valley Jimmy Fund Classic

1982	18	57	10	0	0	0	2	72.35	$21,739

Best finish for 1982: T-11th at the Hawaiian Open

1983	21	67	10	0	0	0	0	73.04	$13,577

Best finish for 1983: T-28th at the Colonial National Invitational

1984	16	46	5	0	0	0	1	73.41	$10,807

Best finish for 1984: T-17th at the Phoenix Open

1985	14	40	5	0	0	0	1	72.63	$11,001

Best finish for 1985: T-19th at the Isuzu/Andy Williams San Diego Open

1986	13	38	5	0	0	0	0	71.71	$8,212

Best finish for 1986: T-34th at the Bank of Boston Classic

1987	5	14	1	0	0	0	1	72.36	$8,640

Best finish for 1987: T-23rd at the Bob Hope Chrysler Classic

1998	1	2	0	0	0	0	0	79.00	$1,500
Period Totals	Starts	Rounds Played	Cuts Made	Wins	Top-5s	Top-10s	Top-25s	Scoring Average	Money
	590	2122	449	10	60	120	259	71.70	$1,279,883

Brent Geiberger

Year	Starts	Rounds Played	Cuts Made	Wins	Top-5s	Top-10s	Top-25s	Scoring Average	Money
1997	29	93	19	0	1	1	11	70.58	$395,472

Best finish for 1997: T-2nd at the LaCantera Texas Open

1998	26	89	18	0	2	4	7	70.85	$569,698

Best finish for 1998: T-2nd at the Phoenix Open

1999	30	103	21	1	5	6	11	70.88	$1,543,159

Best finish for 1999: Win at the Canon Greater Hartford Open

2000	24	75	17	0	1	4	7	70.85	$572,918

Best finish for 2000: T-5th at the Buick Challenge

2001	25	79	18	0	3	3	7	70.51	$711,194

Best finish for 2001: T-5th at the Buick Invitational, Greater Milwaukee Open & Air Canada Championship

2002	29	92	18	0	0	2	8	70.68	$583,592

Best finish for 2002: T-7th at the SEI Pennsylvania Classic

2003	16	51	9	0	1	1	2	70.73	$588,533

Best finish for 2003: T-2nd at the Wachovia Championship

2004	31	91	18	1	1	1	4	70.64	$1,259,779

Best finish for 2004: Win at the Chrysler Classic of Greensboro

2005	21	59	10	0	0	1	1	71.58	$311,559

Best finish for 2005: T-6th at the Chrysler Classic of Tucson

2006	30	97	19	0	0	1	6	70.96	$590,478

Best finish for 2006: T-10th at the FedEx St. Jude Classic

2007	17	45	6	0	0	0	0	71.62	$91,750

Best finish for 2007: T-27th at the Wyndham Championship

2008	12	26	3	0	0	1	1	73.31	$165,600

Best finish for 2008: T-9th at the AT&T Pebble Beach National Pro-Am

Period Totals	Starts	Rounds Played	Cuts Made	Wins	Top-5s	Top-10s	Top-25s	Scoring Average	Money
	290	900	176	2	14	25	65	70.92	$7,383,732

John Gentile

Year	Starts	Rounds Played	Cuts Made	Wins	Top-5s	Top-10s	Top-25s	Scoring Average	Money
1971	2	6	1	0	0	0	0	75.33	

Best finish for 1971: T-62nd at the Bahamas National Open

1972	14	38	5	0	0	0	0	73.61	$1,536

Best finish for 1972: T-40th at the Robinson's Fall Golf Classic

1973	1	4	1	0	0	0	0	75.75	$820

Best finish for 1973: T-58th at the U.S. Open

1975	1	2	0	0	0	0	0	78.00	$500
1976	16	48	8	0	0	0	0	73.21	$4,546

Best finish for 1976: T-26th at the Houston Open

Year	Starts	Rounds Played	Cuts Made	Wins	Top-5s	Top-10s	Top-25s	Scoring Average	Money
1977	17	51	9	0	0	0	0	73.55	$2,629

Best finish for 1977: T-33rd at the Greater Milwaukee Open

Year	Starts	Rounds Played	Cuts Made	Wins	Top-5s	Top-10s	Top-25s	Scoring Average	Money
1978	2	4	0	0	0	0	0	74.25	$600
1979	3	8	1	0	0	0	0	75.75	$1,570

Best finish for 1979: 61st at the U.S. Open

Year	Starts	Rounds Played	Cuts Made	Wins	Top-5s	Top-10s	Top-25s	Scoring Average	Money
1982	1	2	0	0	0	0	0	76.50	
1983	1	2	0	0	0	0	0	77.50	$100
1984	1	2	0	0	0	0	0	72.50	
1985	1	1	0	0	0	0	0	85.00	
Period Totals	60	168	25	0	0	0	0	73.89	$12,302

Ernie George

Year	Starts	Rounds Played	Cuts Made	Wins	Top-5s	Top-10s	Top-25s	Scoring Average	Money
1959	1	3	1	0	0	0	0	76.67	$043

Best finish for 1959: T-116 at the Bing Crosby National

Year	Starts	Rounds Played	Cuts Made	Wins	Top-5s	Top-10s	Top-25s	Scoring Average	Money
1964	2	4	0	0	0	0	0	75.75	
1965	1	2	0	0	0	0	0	76.50	
1966	1	2	0	0	0	0	0	73.50	
1967	1	2	0	0	0	0	0	78.50	
1968	2	4	0	0	0	0	0	77.50	$500
1969	4	11	1	0	0	0	0	75.64	$185

Best finish for 1969: T-62nd at the Canadian Open

Year	Starts	Rounds Played	Cuts Made	Wins	Top-5s	Top-10s	Top-25s	Scoring Average	Money
1970	3	9	1	0	0	0	0	74.22	$366

Best finish for 1970: T-55th at the Bing Crosby Pro-Am

Year	Starts	Rounds Played	Cuts Made	Wins	Top-5s	Top-10s	Top-25s	Scoring Average	Money
1971	2	5	0	0	0	0	0	76.60	
1972	1	3	0	0	0	0	0	79.33	
1973	1	2	0	0	0	0	0	80.00	
1974	2	5	0	0	0	0	0	77.60	
1975	1	2	0	0	0	0	0	75.50	
1976	2	6	1	0	0	0	0	74.67	$370

Best finish for 1976: T-59th at the Bing Crosby Pro-Am

Year	Starts	Rounds Played	Cuts Made	Wins	Top-5s	Top-10s	Top-25s	Scoring Average	Money
1977	2	5	0	0	0	0	0	77.80	
1978	1	3	0	0	0	0	0	75.00	
1979	2	5	0	0	0	0	0	77.80	
1980	1	3	0	0	0	0	0	80.00	
1981	1	3	0	0	0	0	0	79.67	
1983	1	3	0	0	0	0	0	74.67	
1984	1	3	0	0	0	0	0	80.33	
Period Totals	33	85	4	0	0	0	0	76.65	$1,464

Chris Gers

Year	Starts	Rounds Played	Cuts Made	Wins	Top-5s	Top-10s	Top-25s	Scoring Average	Money
1958	7	16	1	0	0	0	0	75.94	

Best finish for 1958: T-58th at the Pensacola Open

Year	Starts	Rounds Played	Cuts Made	Wins	Top-5s	Top-10s	Top-25s	Scoring Average	Money
1962	1	4	1	0	0	0	0	74.25	$096

Best finish for 1962: T-37th at the Oklahoma City Open Invitational

Year	Starts	Rounds Played	Cuts Made	Wins	Top-5s	Top-10s	Top-25s	Scoring Average	Money
1964	12	28	2	0	0	0	0	74.46	$227

Best finish for 1964: T-29th at the Dallas Open

Year	Starts	Rounds Played	Cuts Made	Wins	Top-5s	Top-10s	Top-25s	Scoring Average	Money
1965	3	6	0	0	0	0	0	75.17	
1966	4	10	1	0	0	0	0	75.80	

Best finish for 1966: 64th at the Dallas Open Invitational

Year	Starts	Rounds Played	Cuts Made	Wins	Top-5s	Top-10s	Top-25s	Scoring Average	Money
1967	4	8	0	0	0	0	0	76.13	
1968	4	8	0	0	0	0	0	74.50	
1969	7	18	2	0	0	0	0	74.06	$160

Best finish for 1969: T-57th at the Robinson Open

Year	Starts	Rounds Played	Cuts Made	Wins	Top-5s	Top-10s	Top-25s	Scoring Average	Money
1970	1	2	0	0	0	0	0	74.50	
1971	5	12	1	0	0	0	0	75.83	

Best finish for 1971: 53rd at the Tallahassee Open

Year	Starts	Rounds Played	Cuts Made	Wins	Top-5s	Top-10s	Top-25s	Scoring Average	Money
1972	4	8	0	0	0	0	0	74.88	
1973	4	8	0	0	0	0	0	77.50	
1974	1	2	0	0	0	0	0	78.50	
Period Totals	57	130	8	0	0	0	0	75.22	$483

Vic Ghezzi

Year	Starts	Rounds Played	Cuts Made	Wins	Top-5s	Top-10s	Top-25s	Scoring Average	Money
1958	10	32	6	0	0	0	1	74.38	$942

Best finish for 1958: 11th at the Greenbrier Invitational

Year	Starts	Rounds Played	Cuts Made	Wins	Top-5s	Top-10s	Top-25s	Scoring Average	Money
1959	3	10	2	0	0	0	1	74.50	$1,070

Best finish for 1959: T-21st at the Bing Crosby National

Year	Starts	Rounds Played	Cuts Made	Wins	Top-5s	Top-10s	Top-25s	Scoring Average	Money
1960	2	4	1	0	0	0	0	77.00	$350

Best finish for 1960: T-200 at the PGA Championship

| 1961 | 2 | 4 | 1 | 0 | 0 | 0 | 0 | 77.50 | $400 |

Best finish for 1961: T-200 at the PGA Championship

| 1962 | 3 | 8 | 1 | 0 | 0 | 0 | 0 | 76.75 | $622 |

Best finish for 1962: T-57th at the PGA Championship

| 1963 | 2 | 4 | 1 | 0 | 0 | 0 | 0 | 77.75 | $150 |

Best finish for 1963: T-200 at the PGA Championship

| 1964 | 3 | 5 | 0 | 0 | 0 | 0 | 0 | 75.40 | |
| 1965 | 4 | 10 | 1 | 0 | 0 | 0 | 0 | 75.40 | $467 |

Best finish for 1965: T-49th at the PGA Championship

| 1966 | 2 | 5 | 1 | 0 | 0 | 0 | 0 | 74.80 | |

Best finish for 1966: T-72nd at the Doral Open Invitational

1967	2	3	0	0	0	0	0	74.33	
1968	1	2	0	0	0	0	0	76.00	
1969	1	2	0	0	0	0	0	79.00	
1970	1	1	0	0	0	0	0	79.00	
1973	1	1	0	0	0	0	0	84.00	
Period Totals	Starts	Rounds Played	Cuts Made	Wins	Top-5s	Top-10s	Top-25s	Scoring Average	Money
	37	91	14	0	0	0	2	75.48	$4,001

PGA Tour career totals from 1928 to 1973

	Starts	Rounds Played	Cuts Made	Wins	Top-5s	Top-10s	Top-25s	Scoring Average	Money
	321	690	N/A	11	N/A	135	220	N/A	N/A

Charlie Gibson

Year	Starts	Rounds Played	Cuts Made	Wins	Top-5s	Top-10s	Top-25s	Scoring Average	Money
1978	7	20	3	0	0	0	0	73.00	$912

Best finish for 1978: T-36th at the Pensacola Open

| 1979 | 9 | 21 | 0 | 0 | 0 | 0 | 0 | 75.19 | $600 |
| 1980 | 15 | 42 | 7 | 0 | 0 | 0 | 1 | 72.93 | $7,790 |

Best finish for 1980: T-20th at the Pleasant Valley Jimmy Fund Classic

| 1981 | 25 | 65 | 9 | 0 | 0 | 0 | 0 | 73.29 | $8,210 |

Best finish for 1981: T-30th at the Tallahassee Open

| 1982 | 12 | 29 | 2 | 0 | 0 | 0 | 0 | 74.48 | $1,391 |

Best finish for 1982: T-57th at the Hawaiian Open

1985	1	3	0	0	0	0	0	77.33	
1987	1	3	0	0	0	0	0	79.33	
1995	1	3	0	0	0	0	0	76.00	
1997	1	3	0	0	0	0	0	73.00	
Period Totals	Starts	Rounds Played	Cuts Made	Wins	Top-5s	Top-10s	Top-25s	Scoring Average	Money
	72	189	21	0	0	0	1	73.77	$18,903

Kelly Gibson

Year	Starts	Rounds Played	Cuts Made	Wins	Top-5s	Top-10s	Top-25s	Scoring Average	Money
1989	1	3	1	0	0	0	0	70.67	$502

Best finish for 1989: T-47th at the Deposit Guaranty Golf Classic

| 1990 | 2 | 4 | 0 | 0 | 0 | 0 | 0 | 74.75 | $1,000 |
| 1991 | 2 | 6 | 1 | 0 | 0 | 0 | 0 | 73.50 | $2,140 |

Best finish for 1991: T-62nd at the Canadian Open

| 1992 | 33 | 93 | 14 | 0 | 1 | 3 | 5 | 71.27 | $137,984 |

Best finish for 1992: T-4th at the Buick Southern Open

| 1993 | 33 | 102 | 20 | 0 | 0 | 0 | 6 | 71.94 | $149,003 |

Best finish for 1993: T-12th at the Bob Hope Chrysler Classic

| 1994 | 33 | 93 | 13 | 0 | 0 | 2 | 4 | 72.01 | $134,841 |

Best finish for 1994: T-6th at the Motorola Western Open

| 1995 | 33 | 101 | 19 | 0 | 0 | 1 | 6 | 71.37 | $173,425 |

Best finish for 1995: T-7th at the Bob Hope Chrysler Classic

| 1996 | 35 | 114 | 24 | 0 | 1 | 2 | 7 | 71.06 | $307,228 |

Best finish for 1996: T-3rd at the Las Vegas Invitational

| 1997 | 36 | 121 | 24 | 0 | 0 | 1 | 7 | 71.12 | $268,530 |

Best finish for 1997: T-6th at the Canon Greater Hartford Open

| 1998 | 34 | 107 | 19 | 0 | 0 | 0 | 3 | 71.50 | $194,574 |

Best finish for 1998: T-15th at the CVS Charity Classic & Greater Vancouver Open

| 1999 | 11 | 32 | 6 | 0 | 0 | 0 | 0 | 72.06 | $38,105 |

Best finish for 1999: T-39th at the Greater Milwaukee Open

| 2000 | 30 | 82 | 11 | 0 | 0 | 0 | 0 | 71.88 | $103,304 |

Best finish for 2000: T-30th at the John Deere Classic

| 2001 | 3 | 7 | 0 | 0 | 0 | 0 | 0 | 72.29 | |
| 2002 | 14 | 40 | 6 | 0 | 0 | 0 | 3 | 71.03 | $155,459 |

Best finish for 2002: T-14th at the Valero Texas Open

Year	Starts	Rounds Played	Cuts Made	Wins	Top-5s	Top-10s	Top-25s	Scoring Average	Money
2003	13	37	5	0	0	0	0	71.97	$55,651

Best finish for 2003: T-32nd at the Bell Canadian Open

2004	10	29	4	0	0	0	0	71.86	$34,510

Best finish for 2004: T-50th at the HP Classic of New Orleans

2005	2	4	0	0	0	0	0	72.75	
2006	2	4	0	0	0	0	0	75.25	
2007	2	2	0	0	0	0	0	75.50	
Period Totals	**Starts**	**Rounds Played**	**Cuts Made**	**Wins**	**Top-5s**	**Top-10s**	**Top-25s**	**Scoring Average**	**Money**
	329	981	167	0	2	9	41	71.58	$1,756,257

Gibby Gilbert

Year	Starts	Rounds Played	Cuts Made	Wins	Top-5s	Top-10s	Top-25s	Scoring Average	Money
1964	10	24	2	0	0	0	0	74.21	$125

Best finish for 1964: T-37th at the Canadian Open

1965	8	20	2	0	0	0	0	74.90	$240

Best finish for 1965: T-45th at the Greater Greensboro Open

1966	1	2	0	0	0	0	0	75.50	
1967	1	4	0	0	0	0	0	72.00	
1968	17	50	8	0	0	0	0	73.42	$1,753

Best finish for 1968: T-36th at the Buick Open Invitational

1969	14	39	6	0	0	0	1	73.13	$3,775

Best finish for 1969: T-16th at the Buick Open

1970	31	108	26	1	2	3	11	71.88	$62,359

Best finish for 1970: Win at the Houston Champions International

1971	31	92	20	0	3	6	8	72.14	$59,544

Best finish for 1971: T-2nd at the Westchester Classic

1972	36	110	22	0	1	2	5	72.99	$24,600

Best finish for 1972: T-5th at the Quad Cities Open

1973	33	119	25	0	1	4	13	71.71	$58,209

Best finish for 1973: T-5th at the Westchester Classic

1974	32	107	24	0	1	5	9	71.71	$64,728

Best finish for 1974: 2nd at the Sea Pines Heritage Classic

1975	33	111	24	0	3	6	14	71.81	$56,279

Best finish for 1975: T-4th at the Western Open & Greater Milwaukee Open

1976	30	107	24	1	4	5	7	71.61	$97,276

Best finish for 1976: Win at the Danny Thomas Memphis Classic

1977	23	78	16	0	0	0	6	71.97	$23,139

Best finish for 1977: T-12th at the Southern Open

1978	27	94	19	0	3	6	10	71.70	$73,061

Best finish for 1978: T-2nd at the First NBC New Orleans Open

1979	29	103	23	0	2	4	10	71.76	$76,807

Best finish for 1979: T-4th at the Doral-Eastern Open

1980	27	92	20	0	3	6	7	72.03	$123,903

Best finish for 1980: T-2nd at the Masters, Manufactures Hanover Westchester Classic & World Disney World National Team Championship

1981	30	88	16	0	2	3	8	72.00	$73,638

Best finish for 1981: T-2nd at the Manufactures Hanover Westchester Classic

1982	23	74	15	0	1	1	5	72.14	$39,639

Best finish for 1982: T-5th at the Georgia-Pacific Atlanta Golf Classic

1983	17	65	15	0	1	1	6	71.55	$57,117

Best finish for 1983: T-2nd at the Glen Campbell Los Angles Open

1984	21	74	17	0	1	4	4	71.95	$68,246

Best finish for 1984: T-5th at the Pensacola Open

1985	17	53	9	0	0	0	4	71.96	$34,082

Best finish for 1985: T-11th at the USF&G Classic

1986	8	25	5	0	0	1	1	71.72	$16,406

Best finish for 1986: T-9th at the Deposit Guaranty Golf Classic

1987	9	25	4	0	0	0	3	71.92	$17,634

Best finish for 1987: T-16th at the Southern Open

1988	7	24	5	0	0	0	0	71.21	$7,141

Best finish for 1988: T-30th at the Southern Open

1989	7	15	1	0	0	0	0	73.47	$1,318

Best finish for 1989: T-46th at the Chattanooga Classic

1990	7	18	3	0	0	0	1	71.61	$12,618

Best finish for 1990: T-13th at the Deposit Guaranty

1992	1	2	0	0	0	0	0	74.50	
Period Totals	**Starts**	**Rounds Played**	**Cuts Made**	**Wins**	**Top-5s**	**Top-10s**	**Top-25s**	**Scoring Average**	**Money**
	530	1723	351	2	28	57	133	72.07	$1,053,637

Larry Gilbert

Year	Starts	Rounds Played	Cuts Made	Wins	Top-5s	Top-10s	Top-25s	Scoring Average	Money
1972	11	30	4	0	0	0	0	74.97	$935

Best finish for 1972: T-59th at the Southern Open

Year	Starts	Rounds Played	Cuts Made	Wins	Top-5s	Top-10s	Top-25s	Scoring Average	Money
1975	1	2	0	0	0	0	0	79.50	
1976	2	4	0	0	0	0	0	76.50	$750
1977	1	2	0	0	0	0	0	76.00	$250
1978	1	2	0	0	0	0	0	76.00	$600
1979	1	2	0	0	0	0	0	76.50	$600
1981	1	2	0	0	0	0	0	75.50	$550
1982	3	10	2	0	0	0	1	75.10	$5,638

Best finish for 1982: 25th at the World Series Of Golf

Year	Starts	Rounds Played	Cuts Made	Wins	Top-5s	Top-10s	Top-25s	Scoring Average	Money
1983	4	14	2	0	0	0	0	73.57	$7,050

Best finish for 1983: T-27th at the World Series Of Golf

Year	Starts	Rounds Played	Cuts Made	Wins	Top-5s	Top-10s	Top-25s	Scoring Average	Money
1985	1	2	0	0	0	0	0	74.50	$1,000
1986	1	2	0	0	0	0	0	74.50	$1,000
1987	1	2	0	0	0	0	0	77.50	$1,000
1990	1	2	0	0	0	0	0	81.00	$1,000
1991	1	2	0	0	0	0	0	76.00	$1,000
1992	5	13	1	0	0	0	0	72.92	$12,900

Best finish for 1992: T-28th at the NEC World Series of Golf

Period Totals	Starts	Rounds Played	Cuts Made	Wins	Top-5s	Top-10s	Top-25s	Scoring Average	Money
	35	91	9	0	0	0	1	74.92	$34,273

Bob Gilder

Year	Starts	Rounds Played	Cuts Made	Wins	Top-5s	Top-10s	Top-25s	Scoring Average	Money
1973	1	2	0	0	0	0	0	79.00	
1975	3	10	2	0	0	0	0	74.40	$1,385

Best finish for 1975: T-40th at the British Open

| 1976 | 32 | 112 | 26 | 1 | 4 | 5 | 6 | 72.68 | $101,263 |

Best finish for 1976: Win at the Phoenix Open

| 1977 | 31 | 107 | 24 | 0 | 2 | 2 | 5 | 72.42 | $36,827 |

Best finish for 1977: 4th at the IVB Philadelphia Golf Classic

| 1978 | 29 | 103 | 23 | 0 | 2 | 8 | 11 | 71.79 | $72,475 |

Best finish for 1978: T-4th at the Doral-Eastern Open & Anheuser-Busch Golf Classic

| 1979 | 30 | 107 | 23 | 0 | 3 | 8 | 17 | 71.37 | $134,428 |

Best finish for 1979: T-3rd at the Houston Open & Memorial Tournament

| 1980 | 30 | 97 | 20 | 1 | 3 | 5 | 8 | 72.06 | $157,595 |

Best finish for 1980: Win at the Canadian Open

| 1981 | 31 | 108 | 23 | 0 | 1 | 3 | 10 | 71.81 | $75,356 |

Best finish for 1981: T-4th at the PGA Championship

| 1982 | 28 | 105 | 24 | 3 | 5 | 7 | 16 | 71.01 | $308,648 |

Best finish for 1982: Win at the Byron Nelson Golf Classic, Manufactures Hanover Westchester Classic & Bank of Boston Classic

| 1983 | 29 | 105 | 22 | 1 | 2 | 4 | 6 | 72.30 | $140,575 |

Best finish for 1983: Win at the Phoenix Open

| 1984 | 31 | 93 | 16 | 0 | 0 | 0 | 1 | 73.17 | $25,742 |

Best finish for 1984: T-25th at the Sea Pines Heritage Classic

| 1985 | 29 | 99 | 20 | 0 | 0 | 0 | 4 | 72.23 | $48,999 |

Best finish for 1985: T-18th at the PGA Championship

| 1986 | 30 | 88 | 18 | 0 | 0 | 3 | 10 | 72.09 | $98,781 |

Best finish for 1986: T-6th at the Pensacola Open

| 1987 | 32 | 101 | 19 | 0 | 0 | 1 | 7 | 71.61 | $94,307 |

Best finish for 1987: T-6th at the Centel Classic

| 1988 | 29 | 91 | 17 | 0 | 1 | 3 | 8 | 71.02 | $144,523 |

Best finish for 1988: T-5th at the Kemper Open

| 1989 | 27 | 86 | 17 | 0 | 1 | 3 | 4 | 71.77 | $188,910 |

Best finish for 1989: T-3rd at the Federal Express St. Jude Classic

| 1990 | 27 | 81 | 16 | 0 | 0 | 1 | 7 | 72.19 | $154,934 |

Best finish for 1990: 7th at the Walt Disney World/Oldsmobile Classic

| 1991 | 26 | 78 | 14 | 0 | 3 | 4 | 8 | 70.95 | $251,683 |

Best finish for 1991: 4th at the Centel Western Open

| 1992 | 30 | 94 | 18 | 0 | 0 | 2 | 6 | 71.27 | $171,961 |

Best finish for 1992: T-6th at the U.S. Open

| 1993 | 27 | 78 | 13 | 0 | 0 | 2 | 4 | 71.71 | $148,496 |

Best finish for 1993: T-7th at the Buick Classic

| 1994 | 28 | 82 | 15 | 0 | 1 | 2 | 5 | 71.33 | $154,868 |

Best finish for 1994: T-5th at the Shell Houston Open

| 1995 | 30 | 85 | 13 | 0 | 0 | 3 | 4 | 71.75 | $139,361 |

Best finish for 1995: T-8th at the Buick Classic, Deposit Guaranty Golf Classic & Quad City Classic

| 1996 | 27 | 85 | 17 | 0 | 0 | 0 | 3 | 71.45 | $114,844 |

Best finish for 1996: T-12th at the Canon Greater Hartford Open

| 1997 | 5 | 16 | 2 | 0 | 0 | 0 | 0 | 72.25 | $14,590 |

Best finish for 1997: T-27th at the Buick Classic

| 1998 | 31 | 81 | 12 | 0 | 0 | 1 | 3 | 72.07 | $186,913 |

Best finish for 1998: T-9th at the AT&T Pebble Beach Pro-Am

| 1999 | 11 | 27 | 2 | 0 | 0 | 0 | 0 | 73.07 | $11,052 |

Best finish for 1999: T-55th at the Greater Milwaukee Open

| 2000 | 14 | 44 | 8 | 0 | 0 | 0 | 0 | 71.43 | $70,236 |

Best finish for 2000: T-33rd at the John Deere Classic & SEI Pennsylvania Classic

Period Totals	Starts	Rounds Played	Cuts Made	Wins	Top-5s	Top-10s	Top-25s	Scoring Average	Money
	678	2165	424	6	28	67	153	71.87	$3,048,753

Ron Gillespie

Year	Starts	Rounds Played	Cuts Made	Wins	Top-5s	Top-10s	Top-25s	Scoring Average	Money
1965	1	4	1	0	0	0	0	72.75	

Best finish for 1965: T-53rd at the Cajun Classic

| 1966 | 20 | 61 | 10 | 0 | 0 | 0 | 3 | 73.67 | $2,717 |

Best finish for 1966: T-15th at the Greater New Orleans Open Invitational

| 1967 | 16 | 43 | 5 | 0 | 0 | 0 | 1 | 74.63 | $822 |

Best finish for 1967: T-25th at the Hawaiian Open

1968	2	4	0	0	0	0	0	73.50	
Period Totals	Starts	Rounds Played	Cuts Made	Wins	Top-5s	Top-10s	Top-25s	Scoring Average	Money
	39	112	16	0	0	0	4	74.00	$3,538

Tom Gillis

Year	Starts	Rounds Played	Cuts Made	Wins	Top-5s	Top-10s	Top-25s	Scoring Average	Money
1993	1	2	0	0	0	0	0	77.00	
1995	1	2	0	0	0	0	0	70.50	
1996	1	4	1	0	0	0	0	70.75	$2,775

Best finish for 1996: T-56th at the Michelob Championship at Kingsmill

| 1997 | 2 | 8 | 2 | 0 | 0 | 0 | 0 | 69.88 | $13,330 |

Best finish for 1997: T-28th at the Buick Challenge

| 1999 | 1 | 1 | 0 | 0 | 0 | 0 | 0 | 90.00 | $1,094 |
| 2002 | 2 | 8 | 2 | 0 | 0 | 0 | 0 | 73.38 | $18,414 |

Best finish for 2002: T-53rd at the Buick Open

| 2003 | 25 | 68 | 11 | 0 | 0 | 1 | 5 | 71.04 | $433,100 |

Best finish for 2003: T-7th at the FBR Capital Open

| 2005 | 28 | 75 | 12 | 0 | 0 | 0 | 3 | 71.71 | $421,050 |

Best finish for 2005: T-11th at the Buick Invitational

| 2006 | 1 | 2 | 0 | 0 | 0 | 0 | 0 | 73.00 | |
| 2007 | 3 | 8 | 1 | 0 | 0 | 0 | 0 | 72.38 | $13,152 |

Best finish for 2007: T-52nd at the Buick Open

| 2008 | 3 | 10 | 2 | 0 | 0 | 0 | 0 | 72.80 | $38,915 |

Best finish for 2008: T-35th at the Puerto Rico Open

| Period Totals | Starts | Rounds Played | Cuts Made | Wins | Top-5s | Top-10s | Top-25s | Scoring Average | Money |
| | 68 | 188 | 31 | 0 | 0 | 1 | 8 | 71.68 | $941,830 |

Roger Ginsberg

Year	Starts	Rounds Played	Cuts Made	Wins	Top-5s	Top-10s	Top-25s	Scoring Average	Money
1963	8	32	8	0	0	0	5	71.75	$5,351

Best finish for 1963: T-11th at the Cajun Classic Open Invitational

| 1964 | 23 | 65 | 9 | 0 | 0 | 0 | 3 | 73.12 | $2,514 |

Best finish for 1964: T-16th at the Fresno Open

| 1965 | 13 | 30 | 2 | 0 | 0 | 0 | 1 | 73.37 | $2,342 |

Best finish for 1965: T-12th at the Western Open

| 1966 | 26 | 92 | 20 | 0 | 0 | 2 | 5 | 72.52 | $14,237 |

Best finish for 1966: T-8th at the Azalea Open Invitational

| 1967 | 19 | 58 | 10 | 0 | 0 | 2 | 6 | 72.95 | $9,370 |

Best finish for 1967: T-8th at the Phoenix Open

| 1972 | 1 | 4 | 1 | 0 | 0 | 0 | 0 | 74.75 | $417 |

Best finish for 1972: 73rd at the Westchester Classic

| 1973 | 1 | 4 | 1 | 0 | 0 | 0 | 0 | 74.75 | $930 |

Best finish for 1973: T-45th at the U.S. Open

1979	2	3	0	0	0	0	0	78.00	$350
1984	1	2	0	0	0	0	0	77.00	$1,000
Period Totals	Starts	Rounds Played	Cuts Made	Wins	Top-5s	Top-10s	Top-25s	Scoring Average	Money
	94	290	51	0	0	4	20	72.89	$36,512

Bill Glasson

Year	Starts	Rounds Played	Cuts Made	Wins	Top-5s	Top-10s	Top-25s	Scoring Average	Money
1984	19	52	6	0	0	0	3	72.54	$17,845

Best finish for 1984: T-13th at the Buick Open

| 1985 | 29 | 94 | 20 | 1 | 3 | 4 | 6 | 71.82 | $195,449 |

Best finish for 1985: Win at the Kemper Open

Year	Starts	Rounds Played	Cuts Made	Wins	Top-5s	Top-10s	Top-25s	Scoring Average	Money
1986	28	89	24	0	2	3	8	71.64	$122,516

Best finish for 1986: 4th at the Hardee's Golf Classic

| 1987 | 29 | 96 | 19 | 0 | 3 | 4 | 6 | 71.33 | $152,301 |

Best finish for 1987: T-2nd at the Provident Classic & Centel Classic

| 1988 | 29 | 91 | 19 | 2 | 3 | 6 | 11 | 70.82 | $380,651 |

Best finish for 1988: Win at the B.C. Open & Centel Classic

| 1989 | 24 | 80 | 19 | 1 | 2 | 5 | 9 | 71.03 | $476,010 |

Best finish for 1989: Win at the Doral-Ryder Open

| 1990 | 24 | 67 | 11 | 0 | 0 | 4 | 6 | 72.45 | $157,787 |

Best finish for 1990: T-6th at the Bank of Boston Classic

| 1991 | 11 | 35 | 5 | 0 | 0 | 0 | 1 | 71.34 | $46,995 |

Best finish for 1991: T-12th at the Las Vegas Invitational

| 1992 | 19 | 52 | 11 | 1 | 1 | 2 | 4 | 71.63 | $283,765 |

Best finish for 1992: Win at the Kemper Open

| 1993 | 22 | 77 | 16 | 0 | 1 | 6 | 10 | 70.47 | $302,299 |

Best finish for 1993: 3rd at the B.C. Open

| 1994 | 21 | 75 | 16 | 1 | 4 | 7 | 14 | 70.12 | $689,110 |

Best finish for 1994: Win at the Phoenix Open

| 1995 | 22 | 73 | 14 | 0 | 4 | 5 | 11 | 70.63 | $414,794 |

Best finish for 1995: 3rd at the Mercedes Championships

| 1996 | 8 | 22 | 3 | 0 | 1 | 1 | 1 | 72.77 | $51,528 |

Best finish for 1996: T-4th at the Bay Hill Invitational

| 1997 | 19 | 68 | 16 | 1 | 4 | 6 | 8 | 70.26 | $926,552 |

Best finish for 1997: Win at the Las Vegas Invitational

| 1998 | 12 | 42 | 9 | 0 | 2 | 3 | 6 | 70.19 | $358,222 |

Best finish for 1998: 3rd at the Buick Challenge

| 1999 | 23 | 76 | 16 | 0 | 3 | 5 | 8 | 71.38 | $839,788 |

Best finish for 1999: T-2nd at the Kemper Open

| 2000 | 26 | 93 | 20 | 0 | 1 | 2 | 8 | 70.53 | $552,795 |

Best finish for 2000: T-3rd at the B.C. Open

| 2001 | 26 | 65 | 9 | 0 | 0 | 0 | 2 | 71.26 | $180,441 |

Best finish for 2001: T-15th at the John Deere Classic

| 2002 | 13 | 29 | 1 | 0 | 0 | 0 | 0 | 72.41 | $4,599 |

Best finish for 2002: T-56th at the B.C. Open

| 2003 | 13 | 41 | 7 | 0 | 0 | 0 | 2 | 71.20 | $193,579 |

Best finish for 2003: T-11th at the Greater Hartford Open

| 2004 | 17 | 48 | 7 | 0 | 0 | 2 | 3 | 71.04 | $346,030 |

Best finish for 2004: T-6th at the Chrysler Classic of Tucson

| 2005 | 21 | 52 | 7 | 0 | 0 | 0 | 1 | 71.90 | $108,426 |

Best finish for 2005: T-18th at the Reno-Tahoe Open

| 2006 | 17 | 45 | 6 | 0 | 0 | 0 | 1 | 71.38 | $127,932 |

Best finish for 2006: T-22nd at the Deutsche Bank Championship

2007	4	7	0	0	0	0	0	74.57	
Period Totals	Starts	Rounds Played	Cuts Made	Wins	Top-5s	Top-10s	Top-25s	Scoring Average	Money
	476	1469	281	7	34	65	129	71.23	$6,929,414

Tom Gleeton

Year	Starts	Rounds Played	Cuts Made	Wins	Top-5s	Top-10s	Top-25s	Scoring Average	Money
1980	1	2	0	0	0	0	0	80.50	
1986	25	72	11	0	0	0	0	73.69	$12,344

Best finish for 1986: T-29th at the Deposit Guaranty Golf Classic

1989	1	2	0	0	0	0	0	78.50	
1991	1	2	0	0	0	0	0	76.50	
1992	1	2	0	0	0	0	0	75.00	
2004	1	2	0	0	0	0	0	75.50	
2005	1	2	0	0	0	0	0	76.50	
Period Totals	Starts	Rounds Played	Cuts Made	Wins	Top-5s	Top-10s	Top-25s	Scoring Average	Money
	31	84	11	0	0	0	0	74.18	$12,344

David Glenz

Year	Starts	Rounds Played	Cuts Made	Wins	Top-5s	Top-10s	Top-25s	Scoring Average	Money
1971	1	2	0	0	0	0	0	74.00	
1972	28	93	19	0	0	0	1	72.96	$7,710

Best finish for 1972: T-14th at the Greater St. Louis Classic

| 1973 | 34 | 116 | 22 | 0 | 1 | 4 | 6 | 72.28 | $37,019 |

Best finish for 1973: T-4th at the Danny Thomas Memphis Classic

| 1974 | 27 | 79 | 14 | 0 | 0 | 1 | 1 | 73.25 | $9,235 |

Best finish for 1974: T-7th at the Bing Crosby Pro-Am

| 1975 | 29 | 83 | 13 | 0 | 0 | 0 | 4 | 72.96 | $11,776 |

Best finish for 1975: T-13th at the Sammy Davis, Jr. - Greater Hartford Open

| 1976 | 16 | 41 | 6 | 0 | 0 | 0 | 0 | 74.29 | $1,294 |

Best finish for 1976: T-40th at the Hawaiian Open

Year	Starts	Rounds Played	Cuts Made	Wins	Top-5s	Top-10s	Top-25s	Scoring Average	Money
1977	10	22	1	0	0	0	0	74.50	$950

Best finish for 1977: T-39th at the Jackie Gleason's Inverrary Classic

Year	Starts	Rounds Played	Cuts Made	Wins	Top-5s	Top-10s	Top-25s	Scoring Average	Money
1979	2	4	0	0	0	0	0	78.75	$600
1981	1	4	1	0	0	0	0	76.50	$750

Best finish for 1981: 78th at the PGA Championship

Year	Starts	Rounds Played	Cuts Made	Wins	Top-5s	Top-10s	Top-25s	Scoring Average	Money
1984	2	4	0	0	0	0	0	76.25	$1,429
1985	1	4	1	0	0	0	0	75.50	$1,500

Best finish for 1985: T-73rd at the PGA Championship

Year	Starts	Rounds Played	Cuts Made	Wins	Top-5s	Top-10s	Top-25s	Scoring Average	Money
1987	1	2	0	0	0	0	0	78.50	$1,000
1988	1	2	0	0	0	0	0	78.50	$1,000
1989	1	2	0	0	0	0	0	78.00	$1,000
1992	1	2	0	0	0	0	0	76.00	$1,200
Period Totals	Starts	Rounds Played	Cuts Made	Wins	Top-5s	Top-10s	Top-25s	Scoring Average	Money
	155	460	77	0	1	5	12	73.25	$76,463

Billy Glisson

Year	Starts	Rounds Played	Cuts Made	Wins	Top-5s	Top-10s	Top-25s	Scoring Average	Money
1981	8	14	0	0	0	0	0	75.00	
1982	20	51	5	0	0	0	1	73.75	$7,154

Best finish for 1982: T-18th at the Western Open

Year	Starts	Rounds Played	Cuts Made	Wins	Top-5s	Top-10s	Top-25s	Scoring Average	Money
1983	1	2	0	0	0	0	0	77.50	
Period Totals	Starts	Rounds Played	Cuts Made	Wins	Top-5s	Top-10s	Top-25s	Scoring Average	Money
	29	67	5	0	0	0	1	74.12	$7,154

Lucas Glover

Year	Starts	Rounds Played	Cuts Made	Wins	Top-5s	Top-10s	Top-25s	Scoring Average	Money
2001	2	6	1	0	0	0	0	71.00	$6,180

Best finish for 2001: T-66th at the Texas Open at LaCantera

Year	Starts	Rounds Played	Cuts Made	Wins	Top-5s	Top-10s	Top-25s	Scoring Average	Money
2002	6	17	2	0	0	0	0	71.82	$17,349

Best finish for 2002: T-40th at the John Deere Classic

Year	Starts	Rounds Played	Cuts Made	Wins	Top-5s	Top-10s	Top-25s	Scoring Average	Money
2004	30	91	17	0	0	2	5	71.26	$557,454

Best finish for 2004: T-10th at the Wachovia Championship & FUNAI Classic at the Walt Disney World Resort

Year	Starts	Rounds Played	Cuts Made	Wins	Top-5s	Top-10s	Top-25s	Scoring Average	Money
2005	28	86	16	1	2	7	9	70.94	$2,052,068

Best finish for 2005: Win at the FUNAI Classic at the Walt Disney World Resort

Year	Starts	Rounds Played	Cuts Made	Wins	Top-5s	Top-10s	Top-25s	Scoring Average	Money
2006	31	101	23	0	4	9	17	70.56	$2,599,630

Best finish for 2006: T-4th at the Buick Invitational, Wachovia Championship & WGC-NEC Invitational

Year	Starts	Rounds Played	Cuts Made	Wins	Top-5s	Top-10s	Top-25s	Scoring Average	Money
2007	29	97	22	0	1	3	13	70.85	$1,666,168

Best finish for 2007: T-4th at the PODS Championship

Year	Starts	Rounds Played	Cuts Made	Wins	Top-5s	Top-10s	Top-25s	Scoring Average	Money
2008	26	91	20	0	0	2	8	70.95	$998,491

Best finish for 2008: T-7th at the Verizon Heritage & Buick Open

Period Totals	Starts	Rounds Played	Cuts Made	Wins	Top-5s	Top-10s	Top-25s	Scoring Average	Money
	152	489	101	1	7	23	52	70.94	$7,897,339

Randy Glover

Year	Starts	Rounds Played	Cuts Made	Wins	Top-5s	Top-10s	Top-25s	Scoring Average	Money
1962	2	8	2	0	0	0	0	72.63	$217

Best finish for 1962: T-36th at the Denver Open Invitational

Year	Starts	Rounds Played	Cuts Made	Wins	Top-5s	Top-10s	Top-25s	Scoring Average	Money
1963	6	24	6	0	1	1	4	70.88	$4,183

Best finish for 1963: T-4th at the Fig Garden Village Open Invitational

Year	Starts	Rounds Played	Cuts Made	Wins	Top-5s	Top-10s	Top-25s	Scoring Average	Money
1964	17	54	9	0	0	1	2	73.43	$2,245

Best finish for 1964: T-9th at the Sunset-Camellia Open

Year	Starts	Rounds Played	Cuts Made	Wins	Top-5s	Top-10s	Top-25s	Scoring Average	Money
1965	34	118	25	0	5	9	14	71.63	$43,335

Best finish for 1965: T-3rd at the Doral Open, Canadian Open & Oklahoma City Open

Year	Starts	Rounds Played	Cuts Made	Wins	Top-5s	Top-10s	Top-25s	Scoring Average	Money
1966	35	118	23	0	4	4	10	72.55	$25,911

Best finish for 1966: T-3rd at the Canadian Open

Year	Starts	Rounds Played	Cuts Made	Wins	Top-5s	Top-10s	Top-25s	Scoring Average	Money
1967	27	93	18	1	3	5	11	71.87	$31,041

Best finish for 1967: Win at the Azalea Open

Year	Starts	Rounds Played	Cuts Made	Wins	Top-5s	Top-10s	Top-25s	Scoring Average	Money
1968	18	51	9	0	1	1	3	72.08	$16,408

Best finish for 1968: 3rd at the Tournament of Champions

Year	Starts	Rounds Played	Cuts Made	Wins	Top-5s	Top-10s	Top-25s	Scoring Average	Money
1969	10	25	3	0	0	0	0	74.28	$463

Best finish for 1969: T-55th at the Tucson Open

Year	Starts	Rounds Played	Cuts Made	Wins	Top-5s	Top-10s	Top-25s	Scoring Average	Money
1970	1	4	1	0	0	0	0	71.00	$104

Best finish for 1970: T-60th at the Azalea Open Invitational

Year	Starts	Rounds Played	Cuts Made	Wins	Top-5s	Top-10s	Top-25s	Scoring Average	Money
1971	4	10	1	0	0	0	0	74.90	

Best finish for 1971: T-65th at the Sea Pines Heritage Classic

Year	Starts	Rounds Played	Cuts Made	Wins	Top-5s	Top-10s	Top-25s	Scoring Average	Money
1973	1	2	0	0	0	0	0	73.00	
1974	3	7	1	0	0	0	0	74.43	$425

Best finish for 1974: T-54th at the Sea Pines Heritage Classic

Year	Starts	Rounds Played	Cuts Made	Wins	Top-5s	Top-10s	Top-25s	Scoring Average	Money
1975	2	4	0	0	0	0	0	77.25	
1976	5	16	3	0	0	0	1	73.69	$2,942

Best finish for 1976: T-19th at the U.S. Open

Year	Starts	Rounds Played	Cuts Made	Wins	Top-5s	Top-10s	Top-25s	Scoring Average	Money
1977	2	6	1	0	0	0	0	72.83	$190

Best finish for 1977: T-69th at the Colgate Hall Of Fame Golf Classic

Year	Starts	Rounds Played	Cuts Made	Wins	Top-5s	Top-10s	Top-25s	Scoring Average	Money
1978	3	6	0	0	0	0	0	77.17	$600
1979	2	4	0	0	0	0	0	75.25	
1980	1	2	0	0	0	0	0	76.50	$500
Period Totals	Starts	Rounds Played	Cuts Made	Wins	Top-5s	Top-10s	Top-25s	Scoring Average	Money
	173	552	102	1	14	21	45	72.50	$128,566

Bob Goalby

Year	Starts	Rounds Played	Cuts Made	Wins	Top-5s	Top-10s	Top-25s	Scoring Average	Money
1958	38	135	29	1	4	6	15	72.19	$11,332

Best finish for 1958: Win at the Greater Greensboro Open

1959	31	124	25	0	7	14	22	70.93	$24,455

Best finish for 1959: T-2nd at the Oklahoma City Open Invitational & Insurance City Open Invitational

1960	27	107	24	1	6	10	21	70.64	$24,724

Best finish for 1960: Win at the Coral Gables Open Invitational

1961	24	97	24	2	5	6	15	70.78	$29,879

Best finish for 1961: Win at the Los Angles Open & St. Petersburg Open Invitational

1962	25	101	21	2	6	12	21	71.03	$42,866

Best finish for 1962: Win at the Insurance City Open Invitational & Denver Open Invitational

1963	19	72	16	0	1	6	13	71.39	$16,529

Best finish for 1963: T-5th at the Hot Springs Open Invitational

1964	30	99	17	0	2	2	9	72.67	$13,924

Best finish for 1964: T-3rd at the Los Angles Open

1965	32	114	24	0	2	2	13	72.35	$24,477

Best finish for 1965: 2nd at the Hawaiian Open

1966	35	132	31	0	3	7	19	71.77	$52,310

Best finish for 1966: 2nd at the Cleveland Open Invitational

1967	29	104	24	1	5	10	19	71.38	$79,108

Best finish for 1967: Win at the San Diego Open

1968	28	96	20	1	2	3	10	72.05	$52,705

Best finish for 1968: Win at the Masters

1969	32	107	22	1	1	2	5	72.23	$32,940

Best finish for 1969: Win at the Robinson Open

1970	31	109	23	1	2	4	10	71.96	$54,496

Best finish for 1970: Win at the Heritage Classic

1971	34	102	20	1	1	2	4	72.64	$44,149

Best finish for 1971: Win at the Bahamas National Open

1972	32	111	24	0	3	3	12	71.84	$43,985

Best finish for 1972: T-3rd at the Greater St. Louis Classic

1973	32	109	21	0	3	4	10	72.07	$47,539

Best finish for 1973: T-3rd at the St. Louis Children's Hospital Golf Classic

1974	27	83	14	0	0	0	5	72.78	$14,465

Best finish for 1974: T-14th at the Doral-Eastern Open

1975	22	69	12	0	0	0	2	73.48	$9,409

Best finish for 1975: T-19th at the Glen Campbell Los Angles Open

1976	12	37	6	0	0	0	0	73.59	$4,000

Best finish for 1976: T-32nd at the Greater Greensboro Open

1977	21	55	5	0	0	0	3	74.27	$9,109

Best finish for 1977: T-16th at the San Antonio Texas Open

1978	6	13	1	0	0	0	0	75.38	$1,700

Best finish for 1978: 52nd at the Masters

1979	2	4	0	0	0	0	0	78.75	$1,500
1980	4	8	1	0	0	0	0	75.38	$2,172

Best finish for 1980: 58th at the Sea Pines Heritage Classic

1981	3	6	2	0	0	0	0	74.33	$4,334

Best finish for 1981: T-32nd at the World Disney World National Team Championship

1982	1	4	1	0	0	0	0	77.00	$1,500

Best finish for 1982: 46th at the Masters

1983	1	2	0	0	0	0	0	77.50	$1,500
1984	1	2	0	0	0	0	0	76.00	$1,500
1985	1	2	0	0	0	0	0	79.50	$1,500
1986	1	2	0	0	0	0	0	79.50	$1,500
Period Totals	Starts	Rounds Played	Cuts Made	Wins	Top-5s	Top-10s	Top-25s	Scoring Average	Money
	581	2006	407	11	53	93	228	72.06	$649,606

Bob Goetz

Year	Starts	Rounds Played	Cuts Made	Wins	Top-5s	Top-10s	Top-25s	Scoring Average	Money
1958	18	59	11	0	1	1	5	72.32	$2,625

Best finish for 1958: T-4th at the Canadian Open

1959	14	54	11	0	0	0	8	72.35	$3,815

Best finish for 1959: T-11th at the Greater Greensboro Open Invitational

1960	15	61	15	0	0	2	8	71.54	$6,499

Best finish for 1960: T-8th at the Oklahoma City Open Invitational

1961	18	70	17	0	1	2	11	70.79	$8,696

Best finish for 1961: T-4th at the St. Petersburg Open Invitational

Year	Starts	Rounds Played	Cuts Made	Wins	Top-5s	Top-10s	Top-25s	Scoring Average	Money
1962	13	50	11	0	0	1	4	72.80	$4,843

Best finish for 1962: T-7th at the Cajun Classic Open Invitational

Year	Starts	Rounds Played	Cuts Made	Wins	Top-5s	Top-10s	Top-25s	Scoring Average	Money
1963	15	60	14	0	0	2	6	72.22	$6,680

Best finish for 1963: T-6th at the Cajun Classic Open Invitational

Year	Starts	Rounds Played	Cuts Made	Wins	Top-5s	Top-10s	Top-25s	Scoring Average	Money
1964	7	23	4	0	0	0	1	73.65	$521

Best finish for 1964: T-22nd at the Dallas Open

Year	Starts	Rounds Played	Cuts Made	Wins	Top-5s	Top-10s	Top-25s	Scoring Average	Money
1965	4	12	2	0	0	0	1	73.83	$760

Best finish for 1965: T-19th at the Cajun Classic

Year	Starts	Rounds Played	Cuts Made	Wins	Top-5s	Top-10s	Top-25s	Scoring Average	Money
1966	4	12	2	0	0	0	0	72.50	

Best finish for 1966: T-55th at the Texas Open Invitational

Year	Starts	Rounds Played	Cuts Made	Wins	Top-5s	Top-10s	Top-25s	Scoring Average	Money
1967	9	28	5	0	0	0	1	74.29	$2,642

Best finish for 1967: T-16th at the Thunderbird Classic

Year	Starts	Rounds Played	Cuts Made	Wins	Top-5s	Top-10s	Top-25s	Scoring Average	Money
1968	3	8	1	0	0	0	0	74.50	

Best finish for 1968: T-74th at the Cajun Classic

Year	Starts	Rounds Played	Cuts Made	Wins	Top-5s	Top-10s	Top-25s	Scoring Average	Money
1969	1	4	1	0	0	0	0	73.00	$133

Best finish for 1969: T-71st at the Los Angeles Open

Year	Starts	Rounds Played	Cuts Made	Wins	Top-5s	Top-10s	Top-25s	Scoring Average	Money
1974	2	4	0	0	0	0	0	76.75	
1976	1	2	0	0	0	0	0	76.50	
1978	1	2	0	0	0	0	0	78.50	
1979	1	2	0	0	0	0	0	75.50	
Period Totals	Starts	Rounds Played	Cuts Made	Wins	Top-5s	Top-10s	Top-25s	Scoring Average	Money
	126	451	94	0	2	8	45	72.40	$37,215

Dick Goetz

Year	Starts	Rounds Played	Cuts Made	Wins	Top-5s	Top-10s	Top-25s	Scoring Average	Money
1964	1	4	1	0	0	0	0	73.00	

Best finish for 1964: T-36th at the Almaden Open

Year	Starts	Rounds Played	Cuts Made	Wins	Top-5s	Top-10s	Top-25s	Scoring Average	Money
1969	4	10	1	0	0	0	0	76.40	

Best finish for 1969: 52nd at the Tallahassee Open

Year	Starts	Rounds Played	Cuts Made	Wins	Top-5s	Top-10s	Top-25s	Scoring Average	Money
1970	7	13	0	0	0	0	0	76.31	
1971	7	14	0	0	0	0	0	75.57	
1974	2	4	0	0	0	0	0	75.25	
1975	3	7	0	0	0	0	0	76.14	
1976	1	2	0	0	0	0	0	77.50	$250
1978	1	2	0	0	0	0	0	76.50	
1979	1	2	0	0	0	0	0	76.00	
1980	2	4	0	0	0	0	0	78.75	$500
1986	1	2	0	0	0	0	0	80.00	
1987	1	2	0	0	0	0	0	86.50	$1,000
Period Totals	Starts	Rounds Played	Cuts Made	Wins	Top-5s	Top-10s	Top-25s	Scoring Average	Money
	31	66	2	0	0	0	0	76.48	$1,750

Matt Gogel

Year	Starts	Rounds Played	Cuts Made	Wins	Top-5s	Top-10s	Top-25s	Scoring Average	Money
1992	1	2	0	0	0	0	0	80.50	
1995	1	4	1	0	0	0	0	73.00	$5,843

Best finish for 1995: T-51st at the U.S. Open

Year	Starts	Rounds Played	Cuts Made	Wins	Top-5s	Top-10s	Top-25s	Scoring Average	Money
1997	1	2	0	0	0	0	0	75.50	$1,000
2000	30	84	12	0	1	2	4	71.67	$605,199

Best finish for 2000: T-2nd at the AT&T Pebble Beach

Year	Starts	Rounds Played	Cuts Made	Wins	Top-5s	Top-10s	Top-25s	Scoring Average	Money
2001	26	81	14	0	1	4	7	71.04	$729,784

Best finish for 2001: T-5th at the John Deere Classic

Year	Starts	Rounds Played	Cuts Made	Wins	Top-5s	Top-10s	Top-25s	Scoring Average	Money
2002	25	76	14	1	1	3	4	71.43	$1,090,482

Best finish for 2002: Win at the AT&T Pebble Beach

Year	Starts	Rounds Played	Cuts Made	Wins	Top-5s	Top-10s	Top-25s	Scoring Average	Money
2003	25	73	13	0	1	3	6	71.25	$897,410

Best finish for 2003: 3rd at the Chrysler Classic of Greensboro

Year	Starts	Rounds Played	Cuts Made	Wins	Top-5s	Top-10s	Top-25s	Scoring Average	Money
2004	25	84	16	0	0	2	7	71.01	$818,117

Best finish for 2004: T-6th at the Buick Championship

Year	Starts	Rounds Played	Cuts Made	Wins	Top-5s	Top-10s	Top-25s	Scoring Average	Money
2005	28	76	10	0	0	1	3	71.59	$344,151

Best finish for 2005: T-7th at the Booz Allen Classic

Year	Starts	Rounds Played	Cuts Made	Wins	Top-5s	Top-10s	Top-25s	Scoring Average	Money
2006	14	34	3	0	0	1	1	71.35	$108,230

Best finish for 2006: T-6th at the B.C. Open

Year	Starts	Rounds Played	Cuts Made	Wins	Top-5s	Top-10s	Top-25s	Scoring Average	Money
2007	1	3	0	0	0	0	0	82.00	
Period Totals	Starts	Rounds Played	Cuts Made	Wins	Top-5s	Top-10s	Top-25s	Scoring Average	Money
	177	519	83	1	4	16	32	71.46	$4,600,216

Mathew Goggin

Year	Starts	Rounds Played	Cuts Made	Wins	Top-5s	Top-10s	Top-25s	Scoring Average	Money
2000	31	89	12	0	1	2	5	71.42	$414,123

Best finish for 2000: T-3rd at the Greater Milwaukee Open

Year	Starts	Rounds Played	Cuts Made	Wins	Top-5s	Top-10s	Top-25s	Scoring Average	Money
2001	33	93	15	0	0	1	3	72.18	$283,165

Best finish for 2001: T-6th at the BellSouth Classic

Year	Starts	Rounds Played	Cuts Made	Wins	Top-5s	Top-10s	Top-25s	Scoring Average	Money
2002	20	64	12	0	0	1	5	71.14	$391,852

Best finish for 2002: T-8th at the AT&T Pebble Beach National Pro-Am

Year	Starts	Rounds Played	Cuts Made	Wins	Top-5s	Top-10s	Top-25s	Scoring Average	Money
2003	28	86	16	0	0	0	2	71.65	$299,238

Best finish for 2003: T-20th at The International

Year	Starts	Rounds Played	Cuts Made	Wins	Top-5s	Top-10s	Top-25s	Scoring Average	Money
2004	1	2	0	0	0	0	0	73.00	$5,618
2006	26	70	10	0	1	3	6	71.57	$1,083,719

Best finish for 2006: T-2nd at the Cialis Western Open

Year	Starts	Rounds Played	Cuts Made	Wins	Top-5s	Top-10s	Top-25s	Scoring Average	Money
2007	30	97	20	0	1	1	6	71.04	$969,488

Best finish for 2007: T-5th at the Turning Stone Resort Championship

Year	Starts	Rounds Played	Cuts Made	Wins	Top-5s	Top-10s	Top-25s	Scoring Average	Money
2008	27	91	18	0	4	5	11	70.73	$1,969,962

Best finish for 2008: T-2nd at the Memorial Tournament

Period Totals	Starts	Rounds Played	Cuts Made	Wins	Top-5s	Top-10s	Top-25s	Scoring Average	Money
	196	592	103	0	7	13	38	71.40	$5,417,164

Ted Goin

Year	Starts	Rounds Played	Cuts Made	Wins	Top-5s	Top-10s	Top-25s	Scoring Average	Money
1976	11	30	4	0	0	0	0	73.77	$1,291

Best finish for 1976: T-39th at the San Antonio Texas Open

Year	Starts	Rounds Played	Cuts Made	Wins	Top-5s	Top-10s	Top-25s	Scoring Average	Money
1979	1	2	0	0	0	0	0	76.50	$600
1980	15	34	3	0	0	0	1	74.24	$5,847

Best finish for 1980: T-18th at the Atlanta Classic

Year	Starts	Rounds Played	Cuts Made	Wins	Top-5s	Top-10s	Top-25s	Scoring Average	Money
1981	12	30	3	0	0	0	0	73.33	$2,705

Best finish for 1981: T-36th at the Buick Open

Year	Starts	Rounds Played	Cuts Made	Wins	Top-5s	Top-10s	Top-25s	Scoring Average	Money
1987	1	2	0	0	0	0	0	81.00	$1,000
1990	1	2	0	0	0	0	0	85.00	$1,000
1994	1	4	1	0	0	0	0	73.50	$2,575

Best finish for 1994: T-66th at the AT&T Pebble Beach Pro-Am

Period Totals	Starts	Rounds Played	Cuts Made	Wins	Top-5s	Top-10s	Top-25s	Scoring Average	Money
	42	104	11	0	0	0	1	74.19	$15,018

Joel Goldstrand

Year	Starts	Rounds Played	Cuts Made	Wins	Top-5s	Top-10s	Top-25s	Scoring Average	Money
1965	8	16	1	0	0	0	0	74.75	$362

Best finish for 1965: T-35th at the Hawaiian Open

Year	Starts	Rounds Played	Cuts Made	Wins	Top-5s	Top-10s	Top-25s	Scoring Average	Money
1966	26	81	13	0	0	0	0	74.07	$2,236

Best finish for 1966: T-27th at the Carling World Open

Year	Starts	Rounds Played	Cuts Made	Wins	Top-5s	Top-10s	Top-25s	Scoring Average	Money
1967	19	55	7	0	0	0	1	74.22	$2,180

Best finish for 1967: T-24th at the San Diego Open

Year	Starts	Rounds Played	Cuts Made	Wins	Top-5s	Top-10s	Top-25s	Scoring Average	Money
1968	27	82	13	0	0	0	0	73.07	$3,049

Best finish for 1968: T-33rd at the Kemper Open Invitational

Year	Starts	Rounds Played	Cuts Made	Wins	Top-5s	Top-10s	Top-25s	Scoring Average	Money
1969	30	101	19	0	3	4	6	72.42	$21,142

Best finish for 1969: T-3rd at the Greater New Orleans Open

Year	Starts	Rounds Played	Cuts Made	Wins	Top-5s	Top-10s	Top-25s	Scoring Average	Money
1970	24	79	17	0	0	0	4	72.66	$12,436

Best finish for 1970: T-12th at the Andy Williams-San Diego Open & U.S. Open

Year	Starts	Rounds Played	Cuts Made	Wins	Top-5s	Top-10s	Top-25s	Scoring Average	Money
1971	24	70	11	0	0	0	0	73.69	$4,984

Best finish for 1971: T-31st at the Greater Hartford Open Invitational

Year	Starts	Rounds Played	Cuts Made	Wins	Top-5s	Top-10s	Top-25s	Scoring Average	Money
1972	13	39	6	0	0	0	0	73.28	$2,749

Best finish for 1972: T-30th at the Glen Campbell Los Angles Open

Year	Starts	Rounds Played	Cuts Made	Wins	Top-5s	Top-10s	Top-25s	Scoring Average	Money
1973	5	16	2	0	0	0	0	72.31	$1,893

Best finish for 1973: T-28th at the Hawaiian Open

Period Totals	Starts	Rounds Played	Cuts Made	Wins	Top-5s	Top-10s	Top-25s	Scoring Average	Money
	176	539	89	0	3	4	11	73.28	$51,032

Jaime Gomez

Year	Starts	Rounds Played	Cuts Made	Wins	Top-5s	Top-10s	Top-25s	Scoring Average	Money
1990	2	4	0	0	0	0	0	74.25	$1,000
1992	1	2	0	0	0	0	0	74.00	
1993	30	85	14	0	0	1	3	71.95	$76,495

Best finish for 1993: T-10th at the Freeport-McMoRan Classic

Year	Starts	Rounds Played	Cuts Made	Wins	Top-5s	Top-10s	Top-25s	Scoring Average	Money
1994	1	2	0	0	0	0	0	75.50	
1997	1	2	0	0	0	0	0	74.00	
1998	1	2	0	0	0	0	0	76.00	
2002	1	2	0	0	0	0	0	71.00	
2005	1	2	0	0	0	0	0	74.50	

Period Totals	Starts	Rounds Played	Cuts Made	Wins	Top-5s	Top-10s	Top-25s	Scoring Average	Money
	38	101	14	0	0	1	3	72.31	$77,495

Ernie Gonzalez

Year	Starts	Rounds Played	Cuts Made	Wins	Top-5s	Top-10s	Top-25s	Scoring Average	Money
1985	25	66	7	0	0	0	1	73.94	$12,729

Best finish for 1985: T-16th at the Buick Open

Year	Starts	Rounds Played	Cuts Made	Wins	Top-5s	Top-10s	Top-25s	Scoring Average	Money
1986	24	69	13	1	2	3	6	71.93	$124,548

Best finish for 1986: Win at the Pensacola Open

| 1987 | 36 | 105 | 17 | 0 | 0 | 0 | 3 | 72.92 | $51,512 |

Best finish for 1987: T-20th at the Phoenix Open

| 1988 | 32 | 81 | 9 | 0 | 0 | 0 | 0 | 72.69 | $14,135 |

Best finish for 1988: T-41st at the Hawaiian Open

| 1989 | 13 | 40 | 8 | 0 | 0 | 0 | 1 | 72.10 | $13,840 |

Best finish for 1989: T-24th at the Hardee's Golf Classic

| 1990 | 7 | 21 | 3 | 0 | 0 | 0 | 1 | 71.71 | $13,540 |

Best finish for 1990: T-21st at the Bank of Boston Classic

| 1991 | 4 | 10 | 1 | 0 | 0 | 0 | 0 | 71.50 | $5,550 |

Best finish for 1991: T-31st at the New England Classic

| 1992 | 5 | 16 | 3 | 0 | 0 | 0 | 0 | 71.75 | $5,485 |

Best finish for 1992: T-39th at the Deposit Guaranty Classic

| 1993 | 2 | 6 | 1 | 0 | 0 | 0 | 0 | 70.00 | $2,175 |

Best finish for 1993: T-26th at the Deposit Guaranty Classic

| 1994 | 3 | 8 | 2 | 0 | 0 | 0 | 1 | 70.50 | $16,860 |

Best finish for 1994: T-11th at the Deposit Guaranty Golf Classic

| 1995 | 3 | 9 | 2 | 0 | 0 | 0 | 0 | 73.67 | $4,227 |

Best finish for 1995: T-44th at the Quad City Classic

1996	6	12	0	0	0	0	0	74.83	
1997	3	6	0	0	0	0	0	73.83	
1998	5	10	0	0	0	0	0	74.20	
1999	1	2	0	0	0	0	0	76.50	
2000	1	2	0	0	0	0	0	75.00	
2001	1	4	1	0	0	0	0	75.00	$3,440

Best finish for 2001: 85th at the B.C. Open

2002	1	2	0	0	0	0	0	71.50	
2003	1	3	0	0	0	0	0	69.33	
2006	1	2	0	0	0	0	0	75.50	
Period Totals	Starts	Rounds Played	Cuts Made	Wins	Top-5s	Top-10s	Top-25s	Scoring Average	Money
	174	474	67	1	2	3	13	72.73	$268,040

Jaime Gonzalez

Year	Starts	Rounds Played	Cuts Made	Wins	Top-5s	Top-10s	Top-25s	Scoring Average	Money
1977	1	4	1	0	0	0	0	73.25	$487

Best finish for 1977: T-43rd at the British Open

| 1978 | 9 | 18 | 1 | 0 | 0 | 0 | 0 | 74.44 | $420 |

Best finish for 1978: T-38th at the Buick Goodwrench Open

| 1980 | 20 | 51 | 7 | 0 | 1 | 1 | 3 | 72.67 | $19,895 |

Best finish for 1980: T-5th at the Sammy Davis, Jr. - Greater Hartford Open

| 1981 | 16 | 36 | 2 | 0 | 0 | 0 | 0 | 74.08 | $1,470 |

Best finish for 1981: T-47th at the British Open

1982	1	2	0	0	0	0	0	77.00	$382
1983	1	2	0	0	0	0	0	76.50	$375
1984	1	4	1	0	0	0	0	71.75	$3,861

Best finish for 1984: T-28th at the British Open

| 1985 | 1 | 4 | 1 | 0 | 0 | 0 | 1 | 72.00 | $7,627 |

Best finish for 1985: T-20th at the British Open

1986	1	2	0	0	0	0	0	83.50	$600
Period Totals	Starts	Rounds Played	Cuts Made	Wins	Top-5s	Top-10s	Top-25s	Scoring Average	Money
	51	123	13	0	1	1	4	73.62	$35,117

Lan Gooch

Year	Starts	Rounds Played	Cuts Made	Wins	Top-5s	Top-10s	Top-25s	Scoring Average	Money
1988	1	2	0	0	0	0	0	78.50	
1992	1	2	0	0	0	0	0	73.50	
1997	1	2	0	0	0	0	0	75.50	
1998	22	45	1	0	0	0	0	73.64	$3,173

Best finish for 1998: T-48th at the Deposit Guaranty Golf Classic

| Period Totals | Starts | Rounds Played | Cuts Made | Wins | Top-5s | Top-10s | Top-25s | Scoring Average | Money |
| | 25 | 51 | 1 | 0 | 0 | 0 | 0 | 73.90 | $3,173 |

Retief Goosen

Year	Starts	Rounds Played	Cuts Made	Wins	Top-5s	Top-10s	Top-25s	Scoring Average	Money
1993	1	2	0	0	0	0	0	72.50	$924
1995	3	8	3	0	0	0	0	74.88	$20,652

Best finish for 1995: T-37th at the NEC World Series of Golf

| 1996 | 1 | 4 | 1 | 0 | 0 | 0 | 0 | 73.25 | $7,362 |

Best finish for 1996: 75th at the British Open

| 1997 | 5 | 12 | 2 | 0 | 0 | 1 | 1 | 71.58 | $45,048 |

Best finish for 1997: T-10th at the British Open

Year	Starts	Rounds Played	Cuts Made	Wins	Top-5s	Top-10s	Top-25s	Scoring Average	Money
1998	6	12	0	0	0	0	0	74.58	$8,816
1999	4	12	2	0	0	1	2	74.08	$98,868

Best finish for 1999: T-10th at the British Open

2000	13	40	9	0	0	0	4	71.90	$339,926

Best finish for 2000: T-12th at the U.S. Open

2001	10	28	6	1	1	2	4	70.96	$1,181,985

Best finish for 2001: Win at the U.S. Open

2002	15	54	14	1	3	5	13	70.13	$2,618,004

Best finish for 2002: Win at the BellSouth Classic

2003	19	64	17	1	6	9	14	69.73	$3,168,373

Best finish for 2003: Win at the Chrysler Championship

2004	16	55	13	2	4	9	11	69.58	$3,885,572

Best finish for 2004: Win at the U.S. Open & The Tour Championship

2005	18	61	17	1	6	8	12	70.54	$3,494,106

Best finish for 2005: Win at the International

2006	18	60	16	0	5	6	9	70.98	$2,619,453

Best finish for 2006: 2nd at the Players Championship

2007	14	48	12	0	1	1	5	72.08	$1,046,386

Best finish for 2007: T-2nd at the Masters

2008	18	58	13	0	2	2	6	71.71	$1,431,965

Best finish for 2008: T-2nd at the WGC-CA Championship

Period Totals	Starts	Rounds Played	Cuts Made	Wins	Top-5s	Top-10s	Top-25s	Scoring Average	Money
	161	518	125	6	28	44	81	71.04	$19,967,442

J.C. Goosie

Year	Starts	Rounds Played	Cuts Made	Wins	Top-5s	Top-10s	Top-25s	Scoring Average	Money
1958	36	120	24	0	1	2	11	72.48	$6,352

Best finish for 1958: T-4th at the Gleneagles-Chicago Open

1959	8	32	8	0	0	1	2	71.84	$1,642

Best finish for 1959: T-9th at the Kentucky Derby Open Invitational

1960	9	35	9	0	1	1	5	71.49	$4,215

Best finish for 1960: T-5th at the Memphis Open Invitational

1961	3	12	3	0	0	0	3	70.00	$840

Best finish for 1961: T-20th at the Beaumont Open Invitational

1962	3	12	3	0	0	2	2	71.75	$2,505

Best finish for 1962: T-6th at the West Palm Beach Open Invitational

1963	3	12	3	0	0	0	2	72.17	$2,075

Best finish for 1963: T-18th at the St. Petersburg Open Invitational

1964	7	22	3	0	0	0	2	72.41	$1,245

Best finish for 1964: T-22nd at the Memphis Open

1965	2	6	1	0	0	0	0	73.50	$050

Best finish for 1965: T-45th at the Jacksonville Open

1966	5	12	1	0	0	0	0	73.92	

Best finish for 1966: T-48th at the Memphis Open Invitational

1967	4	14	3	0	0	0	0	73.79	

Best finish for 1967: T-56th at the Atlanta Classic

1968	10	33	7	0	0	1	4	71.42	$7,275

Best finish for 1968: T-6th at the Robinson Open

1969	25	75	14	0	0	1	4	72.43	$8,990

Best finish for 1969: T-9th at the Cleveland Open

1970	13	40	9	0	0	1	5	71.95	$12,638

Best finish for 1970: T-9th at the National 4 Ball Championship PGA Players

1971	10	22	2	0	0	0	1	73.55	$3,958

Best finish for 1971: T-11th at the IVB Philadelphia Golf Classic

1972	7	24	5	0	0	0	1	72.50	$2,281

Best finish for 1972: T-19th at the Greater St. Louis Classic

1973	1	2	0	0	0	0	0	74.50	
1977	1	2	0	0	0	0	0	74.50	
1980	1	2	0	0	0	0	0	77.00	

Period Totals	Starts	Rounds Played	Cuts Made	Wins	Top-5s	Top-10s	Top-25s	Scoring Average	Money
	148	477	95	0	2	9	42	72.32	$54,066

Jason Gore

Year	Starts	Rounds Played	Cuts Made	Wins	Top-5s	Top-10s	Top-25s	Scoring Average	Money
1998	1	2	0	0	0	0	0	76.50	$1,000
1999	2	6	1	0	0	0	0	71.00	$20,385

Best finish for 1999: T-26th at the Buick Invitational

2000	1	2	0	0	0	0	0	72.50	
2001	30	80	12	0	0	0	2	71.49	$180,451

Best finish for 2001: T-18th at the Invensys Classic at Las Vegas

2002	1	2	0	0	0	0	0	73.50	
2003	30	83	12	0	0	0	2	71.66	$208,801

Best finish for 2003: T-20th at the Sony Open in Hawaii & Greater Milwaukee Open

2004	1	3	0	0	0	0	0	72.33	

Year	Starts	Rounds Played	Cuts Made	Wins	Top-5s	Top-10s	Top-25s	Scoring Average	Money
2005	8	28	6	1	1	1	1	70.68	$871,135

Best finish for 2005: Win at the 84 Lumber Classic

2006	29	84	14	0	0	4	5	72.20	$717,005

Best finish for 2006: T-7th at the Chrysler Classic of Tucson

2007	27	86	16	0	1	3	8	71.02	$1,105,985

Best finish for 2007: T-2nd at the Buick Open

2008	33	94	17	0	0	3	8	71.03	$779,664

Best finish for 2008: T-8th at the Reno-Tahoe Open & Viking Classic

Period Totals	Starts	Rounds Played	Cuts Made	Wins	Top-5s	Top-10s	Top-25s	Scoring Average	Money
	163	470	78	1	2	11	26	71.46	$3,884,427

Bryan Gorman

Year	Starts	Rounds Played	Cuts Made	Wins	Top-5s	Top-10s	Top-25s	Scoring Average	Money
1992	1	2	0	0	0	0	0	78.50	$1,000
1994	1	2	0	0	0	0	0	72.00	
1996	24	69	11	0	0	0	0	72.28	$47,713

Best finish for 1996: T-28th at the FedEx St. Jude Classic

Period Totals	Starts	Rounds Played	Cuts Made	Wins	Top-5s	Top-10s	Top-25s	Scoring Average	Money
	26	73	11	0	0	0	0	72.44	$48,713

David Gossett

Year	Starts	Rounds Played	Cuts Made	Wins	Top-5s	Top-10s	Top-25s	Scoring Average	Money
1998	2	6	1	0	0	0	0	71.17	

Best finish for 1998: T-71st at the FedEx St. Jude Classic

1999	4	9	1	0	0	0	1	73.44	

Best finish for 1999: T-23rd at the Southern Farm Bureau Classic

2000	10	20	1	0	0	0	0	74.40	

Best finish for 2000: T-54th at the Masters

2001	15	47	8	1	2	2	5	69.96	$750,126

Best finish for 2001: Win at the John Deere Classic

2002	29	93	18	0	1	3	3	70.81	$678,308

Best finish for 2002: T-2nd at the Buick Classic

2003	28	92	17	0	2	2	6	70.87	$769,740

Best finish for 2003: T-3rd at the MCI Heritage

2004	25	57	2	0	0	0	0	74.95	$21,250

Best finish for 2004: T-59th at the Honda Classic

2005	1	2	0	0	0	0	0	82.50	
2006	7	19	1	0	0	0	0	72.79	$7,480

Best finish for 2006: T-75th at the John Deere Classic

2007	2	4	0	0	0	0	0	77.00	

Period Totals	Starts	Rounds Played	Cuts Made	Wins	Top-5s	Top-10s	Top-25s	Scoring Average	Money
	123	349	49	1	5	7	15	71.91	$2,226,904

Steve Gotsche

Year	Starts	Rounds Played	Cuts Made	Wins	Top-5s	Top-10s	Top-25s	Scoring Average	Money
1985	1	2	0	0	0	0	0	76.50	$600
1986	1	2	0	0	0	0	0	79.50	$600
1987	1	2	0	0	0	0	0	74.00	$600
1991	1	4	1	0	0	0	0	75.00	$5,164

Best finish for 1991: T-55th at the U.S. Open

1992	1	2	0	0	0	0	0	77.50	$1,000
1993	1	4	1	0	0	0	0	72.00	$5,657

Best finish for 1993: T-68th at the U.S. Open

1994	21	56	7	0	1	1	1	72.25	$59,227

Best finish for 1994: 5th at the New England Classic

1995	28	81	13	0	0	0	1	71.36	$70,425

Best finish for 1995: T-19th at the Kmart Greater Greensboro Open

1996	1	4	1	0	0	0	0	72.00	$14,070

Best finish for 1996: T-32nd at the U.S. Open

2000	32	89	13	0	0	0	2	71.60	$164,203

Best finish for 2000: T-12th at the John Deere Classic

2003	1	2	0	0	0	0	0	76.00	$1,000
2004	1	2	0	0	0	0	0	77.00	$1,000

Period Totals	Starts	Rounds Played	Cuts Made	Wins	Top-5s	Top-10s	Top-25s	Scoring Average	Money
	90	250	36	0	1	1	4	71.98	$323,548

Jeff Gove

Year	Starts	Rounds Played	Cuts Made	Wins	Top-5s	Top-10s	Top-25s	Scoring Average	Money
2000	31	82	11	0	0	0	2	71.83	$153,753

Best finish for 2000: T-16th at the Kemper Insurance Open

2001	1	1	0	0	0	0	0	74.00	
2002	30	89	14	0	0	1	3	71.25	$271,652

Best finish for 2002: T-10th at the Canon Greater Hartford Open

Year	Starts	Rounds Played	Cuts Made	Wins	Top-5s	Top-10s	Top-25s	Scoring Average	Money
2003	1	2	0	0	0	0	0	74.00	
2004	1	2	0	0	0	0	0	76.00	$1,000
2006	29	87	16	0	0	2	7	70.74	$793,477

Best finish for 2006: T-6th at the Booz Allen Classic

2007	30	103	20	0	0	1	3	71.19	$526,644

Best finish for 2007: T-6th at the John Deere Classic

2008	18	50	7	0	0	1	2	71.54	$290,410

Best finish for 2008: T-9th at the John Deere Classic

Period Totals	Starts	Rounds Played	Cuts Made	Wins	Top-5s	Top-10s	Top-25s	Scoring Average	Money
	141	416	68	0	0	5	17	71.32	$2,036,936

Mike Gove

Year	Starts	Rounds Played	Cuts Made	Wins	Top-5s	Top-10s	Top-25s	Scoring Average	Money
1980	16	48	10	0	1	2	3	72.17	$24,358

Best finish for 1980: T-4th at the Pensacola Open

1981	25	71	9	0	0	0	0	73.18	$8,264

Best finish for 1981: T-29th at the Hawaiian Open

1982	11	26	2	0	0	0	0	73.73	$2,132

Best finish for 1982: T-41st at the Danny Thomas Memphis Classic

1983	24	69	9	0	0	1	3	72.75	$26,555

Best finish for 1983: T-8th at the Western Open

1984	22	60	10	0	0	0	2	72.82	$30,716

Best finish for 1984: T-15th at the Panasonic Las Vegas Invitational

1985	16	39	4	0	0	0	0	72.59	$4,201

Best finish for 1985: T-34th at the Greater Milwaukee Open

1986	18	42	4	0	0	0	1	73.69	$12,052

Best finish for 1986: T-18th at the Manufactures Hanover Westchester Classic

1990	1	2	0	0	0	0	0	81.00	$1,000
1994	1	2	0	0	0	0	0	73.50	$1,200
Period Totals	Starts	Rounds Played	Cuts Made	Wins	Top-5s	Top-10s	Top-25s	Scoring Average	Money
	134	359	48	0	1	3	9	72.98	$110,479

Paul Gow

Year	Starts	Rounds Played	Cuts Made	Wins	Top-5s	Top-10s	Top-25s	Scoring Average	Money
2000	2	6	1	0	0	0	0	71.67	$14,627

Best finish for 2000: T-32nd at the Canon Greater Hartford Open

2001	27	75	12	0	2	3	5	71.17	$608,382

Best finish for 2001: 2nd at the B.C. Open

2002	35	96	14	0	0	2	6	71.59	$449,752

Best finish for 2002: 6th at the Tampa Bay Classic presented by Buick

2003	21	62	9	0	0	1	2	71.00	$264,927

Best finish for 2003: T-8th at the Buick Open

2005	27	74	13	0	0	0	3	71.65	$324,459

Best finish for 2005: T-12th at the International

2007	26	70	10	0	0	1	2	71.81	$264,149

Best finish for 2007: T-10th at the Canadian Open

Period Totals	Starts	Rounds Played	Cuts Made	Wins	Top-5s	Top-10s	Top-25s	Scoring Average	Money
	138	383	59	0	2	7	18	71.47	$1,926,296

Paul Goydos

Year	Starts	Rounds Played	Cuts Made	Wins	Top-5s	Top-10s	Top-25s	Scoring Average	Money
1993	30	95	18	0	0	0	4	71.84	$87,804

Best finish for 1993: T-13th at the Buick Classic

1994	31	104	22	0	0	3	9	71.44	$241,107

Best finish for 1994: T-7th at the B.C. Open

1995	35	109	21	0	0	0	6	71.24	$146,423

Best finish for 1995: T-15th at the Las Vegas Invitational

1996	29	84	15	1	1	4	7	71.81	$440,611

Best finish for 1996: Win at the Bay Hill Invitational

1997	30	100	21	0	3	5	9	70.95	$396,241

Best finish for 1997: T-4th at the Mercedes Championship & MasterCard Colonial

1998	31	100	20	0	1	2	5	70.83	$368,413

Best finish for 1998: T-2nd at the Deposit Guaranty Golf Classic

1999	29	95	20	0	1	4	8	71.21	$695,052

Best finish for 1999: T-2nd at the MasterCard Colonial

2000	30	97	19	0	0	3	5	70.92	$399,393

Best finish for 2000: T-10th at the Bay Hill Invitational, B.C. Open & Buick Challenge

2001	29	84	12	0	1	2	3	71.31	$376,557

Best finish for 2001: T-5th at the FedEx St. Jude Classic

2002	20	66	13	0	0	2	4	71.38	$408,345

Best finish for 2002: T-8th at the AT&T Pebble Beach National Pro-Am

Year	Starts	Rounds Played	Cuts Made	Wins	Top-5s	Top-10s	Top-25s	Scoring Average	Money
2003	25	83	18	0	0	2	7	70.47	$734,284

Best finish for 2003: T-6th at the Buick Open

2004	2	8	2	0	0	0	0	69.25	$19,366

Best finish for 2004: T-49th at the FUNAI Classic at the Walt Disney World Resort

2005	15	48	9	0	1	1	3	71.04	$486,362

Best finish for 2005: T-4th at the AT&T Pebble Beach National Pro-Am

2006	24	72	11	0	1	2	4	71.24	$890,392

Best finish for 2006: T-2nd at the Chrysler Championship

2007	19	59	12	1	1	1	1	71.80	$1,233,855

Best finish for 2007: Win at the Sony Open in Hawaii

2008	25	78	14	0	1	3	5	71.60	$1,640,737

Best finish for 2008: 2nd at The Players

Period Totals	Starts	Rounds Played	Cuts Made	Wins	Top-5s	Top-10s	Top-25s	Scoring Average	Money
	404	1282	247	2	11	34	80	71.25	$8,564,942

Wayne Grady

Year	Starts	Rounds Played	Cuts Made	Wins	Top-5s	Top-10s	Top-25s	Scoring Average	Money
1979	2	5	0	0	0	0	0	78.60	$420
1983	1	3	0	0	0	0	0	73.33	$638
1984	10	26	3	0	0	0	0	74.19	$3,486

Best finish for 1984: T-50th at the Byron Nelson Golf Classic

1985	30	110	26	0	2	4	11	71.12	$167,497

Best finish for 1985: 2nd at the Buick Open

1986	33	88	14	0	0	1	5	72.38	$49,417

Best finish for 1986: T-10th at the Bank of Boston Classic

1987	17	54	12	0	1	2	4	71.63	$85,472

Best finish for 1987: T-2nd at the Bank of Boston Classic

1988	23	70	12	0	1	3	6	71.29	$119,410

Best finish for 1988: T-5th at the Honda Classic

1989	28	86	17	1	2	5	11	71.27	$491,364

Best finish for 1989: Win at the Manufactures Hanover Westchester Classic

1990	24	85	19	1	2	5	10	71.68	$529,181

Best finish for 1990: Win at the PGA Championship

1991	20	68	14	0	0	3	4	71.40	$139,490

Best finish for 1991: T-7th at the Southwestern Bell Colonial

1992	22	74	15	0	0	1	9	71.58	$194,727

Best finish for 1992: T-6th at the MCI Heritage Classic

1993	21	56	10	0	0	1	2	72.63	$87,928

Best finish for 1993: T-9th at the British Open

1994	20	60	11	0	1	1	4	71.60	$128,948

Best finish for 1994: T-5th at the Federal Express St. Jude Classic

1995	16	48	7	0	0	0	2	72.25	$48,454

Best finish for 1995: T-21st at the Kemper Open

1996	20	64	12	0	0	0	3	71.80	$94,338

Best finish for 1996: T-19th at the Players Championship

1997	10	24	3	0	0	0	0	74.21	$10,555

Best finish for 1997: T-58th at the Freeport-McDermott Classic

1998	18	47	6	0	0	0	0	74.40	$23,544

Best finish for 1998: T-54th at the Buick Classic

1999	15	38	4	0	0	0	0	73.89	$25,413

Best finish for 1999: T-40th at the Greater Greensboro Chrysler Classic

2000	15	35	6	0	0	0	0	72.74	$49,406

Best finish for 2000: T-38th at the Bay Hill Invitational

2002	5	12	1	0	0	0	0	74.08	$21,880

Best finish for 2002: T-31st at the Kemper Insurance Open

2005	1	2	0	0	0	0	0	78.00	$2,000

Period Totals	Starts	Rounds Played	Cuts Made	Wins	Top-5s	Top-10s	Top-25s	Scoring Average	Money
	351	1055	192	2	9	26	71	72.10	$2,273,569

David Graham

Year	Starts	Rounds Played	Cuts Made	Wins	Top-5s	Top-10s	Top-25s	Scoring Average	Money
1970	5	16	3	0	0	0	0	73.25	$1,612

Best finish for 1970: T-32nd at the British Open

1971	7	19	2	0	0	0	0	74.58	$2,836

Best finish for 1971: T-36th at the Masters

1972	23	72	13	1	2	3	6	73.01	$54,637

Best finish for 1972: Win at the Cleveland Open

1973	35	119	24	0	1	2	10	72.68	$40,619

Best finish for 1973: T-2nd at the Glen Campbell Los Angles Open

1974	30	108	23	0	0	6	17	71.58	$63,075

Best finish for 1974: T-6th at the Sahara Invitational

1975	31	109	23	0	1	4	11	72.05	$52,380

Best finish for 1975: T-2nd at the B.C. Open

Year	Starts	Rounds Played	Cuts Made	Wins	Top-5s	Top-10s	Top-25s	Scoring Average	Money
1976	26	97	22	2	6	9	14	71.40	$177,614

Best finish for 1976: Win at the American Express Westchester Classic & The American Golf Classic

1977	19	65	14	0	1	4	10	71.74	$73,187

Best finish for 1977: 2nd at the Doral-Eastern Open

1978	23	83	18	0	1	5	11	71.93	$68,581

Best finish for 1978: 2nd at the Florida Citrus Open Invitational

1979	24	86	19	1	4	9	10	71.98	$179,184

Best finish for 1979: Win at the PGA Championship

1980	20	75	18	1	3	5	10	71.55	$140,219

Best finish for 1980: Win at the Memorial Tournament

1981	19	63	13	2	4	7	8	71.60	$194,766

Best finish for 1981: Win at the Phoenix Open & U.S. Open

1982	23	81	17	0	3	6	8	71.37	$106,336

Best finish for 1982: T-2nd at the MONY Tournament Of Champions

1983	24	92	21	1	5	10	14	71.25	$252,484

Best finish for 1983: Win at the Houston Coca-Cola Open

1984	21	79	18	0	2	3	5	71.75	$117,420

Best finish for 1984: T-2nd at the Manufactures Hanover Westchester Classic

1985	22	79	17	0	1	3	7	71.92	$107,022

Best finish for 1985: T-3rd at the British Open

1986	21	71	16	0	0	3	6	71.73	$116,109

Best finish for 1986: T-7th at the PGA Championship

1987	22	64	11	0	0	0	4	72.38	$61,974

Best finish for 1987: T-11th at the Buick Open

1988	16	48	8	0	1	2	3	71.77	$97,852

Best finish for 1988: T-3rd at the GTE Byron Nelson Classic

1989	11	37	7	0	0	0	1	73.78	$27,555

Best finish for 1989: T-19th at the USF&G Classic

1990	11	33	6	0	0	1	2	73.58	$64,312

Best finish for 1990: T-8th at the British Open

1991	9	26	4	0	0	0	0	73.92	$14,241

Best finish for 1991: T-50th at the Phoenix Open

1992	2	4	0	0	0	0	0	75.25	
1993	3	6	0	0	0	0	0	76.67	$1,200
1994	2	4	0	0	0	0	0	76.75	$1,200
1995	5	13	1	0	0	0	0	75.15	$4,396

Best finish for 1995: 76th at the Memorial Tournament

Period Totals	Starts	Rounds Played	Cuts Made	Wins	Top-5s	Top-10s	Top-25s	Scoring Average	Money
	454	1549	318	8	35	82	157	72.10	$2,020,810

Lou Graham

Year	Starts	Rounds Played	Cuts Made	Wins	Top-5s	Top-10s	Top-25s	Scoring Average	Money
1958	1	4	1	0	0	0	0	74.00	

Best finish for 1958: 63rd at the Memphis Invitational

1963	1	2	0	0	0	0	0	81.50	$150
1964	9	29	5	0	0	0	2	73.28	$2,322

Best finish for 1964: T-11th at the Mountain View Open

1965	28	101	21	0	1	2	6	72.90	$11,093

Best finish for 1965: T-3rd at the Memphis Open

1966	28	87	15	0	1	2	5	73.30	$11,196

Best finish for 1966: T-3rd at the Canadian Open

1967	34	118	24	1	3	4	11	72.46	$44,023

Best finish for 1967: Win at the Minnesota Golf Classic

1968	24	73	15	0	4	6	8	71.85	$34,545

Best finish for 1968: T-3rd at the Memphis Open Invitational & Atlanta Classic

1969	31	94	16	0	1	4	6	72.50	$22,608

Best finish for 1969: 5th at the Kaiser International Open

1970	31	117	27	0	4	4	13	71.49	$51,046

Best finish for 1970: T-2nd at the Kemper Open

1971	35	124	29	0	4	10	23	71.15	$76,281

Best finish for 1971: 2nd at the Greater Hartford Open Invitational

1972	34	130	31	1	4	7	18	71.51	$91,461

Best finish for 1972: Win at the Liggett Meyers Open

1973	32	109	24	0	7	9	16	71.43	$92,320

Best finish for 1973: T-2nd at the Greater Jacksonville Open & Greater Greensboro Open

1974	31	101	20	0	4	6	9	71.75	$73,071

Best finish for 1974: T-2nd at the Danny Thomas Memphis Classic

1975	27	105	25	1	4	6	11	71.10	$95,962

Best finish for 1975: Win at the U.S. Open

1976	29	105	25	0	5	7	18	71.22	$107,007

Best finish for 1976: 2nd at the American Golf Classic

| 1977 | 29 | 109 | 25 | 0 | 6 | 9 | 17 | 71.29 | $128,836 |

Best finish for 1977: 2nd at the U.S. Open

| 1978 | 30 | 106 | 22 | 0 | 4 | 9 | 10 | 71.49 | $107,420 |

Best finish for 1978: T-2nd at the Tournament Players Championship & Atlanta Classic

| 1979 | 30 | 107 | 23 | 3 | 4 | 5 | 12 | 72.16 | $190,827 |

Best finish for 1979: Win at the IVB Philadelphia Golf Classic, American Optical Classic & San Antonio Texas Open

| 1980 | 27 | 86 | 17 | 0 | 2 | 3 | 6 | 72.03 | $58,595 |

Best finish for 1980: T-3rd at the IVB Golf Classic

| 1981 | 28 | 81 | 15 | 0 | 0 | 1 | 6 | 72.52 | $35,108 |

Best finish for 1981: T-7th at the Tallahassee Open

| 1982 | 33 | 99 | 16 | 0 | 1 | 1 | 3 | 72.91 | $37,864 |

Best finish for 1982: T-5th at the Canadian Open

| 1983 | 30 | 101 | 19 | 0 | 0 | 0 | 3 | 72.36 | $34,723 |

Best finish for 1983: T-15th at the Sea Pines Heritage Classic

| 1984 | 26 | 76 | 10 | 0 | 0 | 1 | 1 | 73.38 | $21,240 |

Best finish for 1984: T-8th at the Bank of Boston Classic

| 1985 | 26 | 65 | 6 | 0 | 0 | 0 | 1 | 74.11 | $9,996 |

Best finish for 1985: T-23rd at the Georgia-Pacific Atlanta Golf Classic

| 1986 | 28 | 77 | 11 | 0 | 0 | 0 | 1 | 72.91 | $15,371 |

Best finish for 1986: T-20th at the Provident Classic

| 1987 | 15 | 46 | 8 | 0 | 0 | 0 | 1 | 72.54 | $16,088 |

Best finish for 1987: T-18th at the Honda Classic

Period Totals	Starts	Rounds Played	Cuts Made	Wins	Top-5s	Top-10s	Top-25s	Scoring Average	Money
	677	2252	450	6	59	96	207	72.11	$1,369,155

Jim Grant

Year	Starts	Rounds Played	Cuts Made	Wins	Top-5s	Top-10s	Top-25s	Scoring Average	Money
1958	1	4	1	0	0	0	0	75.50	

Best finish for 1958: 70th at the Insurance City Open

| 1963 | 1 | 4 | 1 | 0 | 0 | 0 | 0 | 71.50 | |

Best finish for 1963: T-27th at the Insurance City Open Invitational

| 1964 | 1 | 4 | 1 | 0 | 1 | 1 | 1 | 68.50 | |

Best finish for 1964: T-2nd at the Greater Hartford Open

| 1965 | 2 | 6 | 1 | 0 | 0 | 0 | 0 | 72.00 | |

Best finish for 1965: T-58th at the Texas Open

| 1966 | 2 | 8 | 2 | 0 | 0 | 1 | 1 | 71.25 | |

Best finish for 1966: T-6th at the Insurance City Open Invitational

| 1967 | 5 | 16 | 3 | 0 | 1 | 1 | 2 | 71.94 | $3,850 |

Best finish for 1967: T-3rd at the Cajun Classic

| 1968 | 26 | 86 | 17 | 0 | 1 | 1 | 2 | 72.47 | $5,017 |

Best finish for 1968: T-3rd at the Robinson Open

| 1969 | 26 | 78 | 13 | 0 | 0 | 0 | 3 | 73.05 | $4,951 |

Best finish for 1969: T-17th at the Indian Ridge Hospital Open

| 1970 | 22 | 62 | 11 | 0 | 1 | 1 | 4 | 72.53 | $12,753 |

Best finish for 1970: T-4th at the Greater Hartford Open Invitational

| 1971 | 17 | 46 | 6 | 0 | 0 | 0 | 0 | 73.35 | $1,457 |

Best finish for 1971: T-39th at the Atlanta Classic

| 1972 | 20 | 57 | 8 | 0 | 0 | 0 | 2 | 73.81 | $3,177 |

Best finish for 1972: T-17th at the Tallahassee Open

| 1973 | 12 | 27 | 2 | 0 | 0 | 0 | 1 | 74.48 | $1,040 |

Best finish for 1973: T-23rd at the Quad Cities Open

1974	1	2	0	0	0	0	0	72.50	
1976	1	2	0	0	0	0	0	79.00	
1983	1	2	0	0	0	0	0	70.00	
Period Totals	Starts	Rounds Played	Cuts Made	Wins	Top-5s	Top-10s	Top-25s	Scoring Average	Money
	138	404	66	0	4	5	16	72.96	$32,246

Thomas Gray

Year	Starts	Rounds Played	Cuts Made	Wins	Top-5s	Top-10s	Top-25s	Scoring Average	Money
1980	1	2	0	0	0	0	0	74.50	
1981	17	53	10	0	0	0	4	72.68	$21,608

Best finish for 1981: T-16th at the Kemper Open

| 1982 | 22 | 69 | 12 | 0 | 1 | 1 | 3 | 72.71 | $52,574 |

Best finish for 1982: 2nd at the LaJet Classic

| 1983 | 35 | 105 | 16 | 0 | 0 | 0 | 4 | 72.76 | $35,510 |

Best finish for 1983: T-12th at the Colonial National Invitational & Miller High-Life Quad Cities Open

| 1984 | 32 | 89 | 13 | 0 | 0 | 0 | 1 | 73.47 | $21,484 |

Best finish for 1984: T-21st at the Panasonic Las Vegas Invitational

1988	1	2	0	0	0	0	0	74.00	
1994	1	2	0	0	0	0	0	76.50	$1,200
Period Totals	Starts	Rounds Played	Cuts Made	Wins	Top-5s	Top-10s	Top-25s	Scoring Average	Money
	109	322	51	0	1	1	12	72.98	$132,376

Hubert Green

Year	Starts	Rounds Played	Cuts Made	Wins	Top-5s	Top-10s	Top-25s	Scoring Average	Money
1969	2	4	0	0	0	0	0	75.00	
1970	1	4	1	0	0	0	1	71.50	$1,150

Best finish for 1970: T-23rd at the Bahama Islands Open

1971	33	107	22	1	5	5	9	72.27	$70,254

Best finish for 1971: Win at the Houston Champions International

1972	34	121	25	0	0	3	9	72.71	$40,568

Best finish for 1972: T-6th at the IVB Philadelphia Golf Classic

1973	36	132	27	2	6	11	17	71.29	$112,517

Best finish for 1973: Win at the Tallahassee Open & B.C. Open

1974	28	100	22	3	8	12	18	70.89	$185,609

Best finish for 1974: Win at the Bob Hope Chrysler Classic, Greater Jacksonville Open & IVB Philadelphia Golf Classic

1975	27	101	23	1	5	6	12	71.44	$114,155

Best finish for 1975: Win at the Southern Open

1976	27	105	25	3	7	10	19	70.81	$232,958

Best finish for 1976: Win at the Doral-Eastern Open, Greater Jacksonville Open & Sea Pines Heritage Classic

1977	24	95	22	1	4	10	16	71.27	$150,455

Best finish for 1977: Win at the U.S. Open

1978	23	87	20	2	8	9	13	70.89	$249,007

Best finish for 1978: Win at the Hawaiian Open & Sea Pines Heritage Classic

1979	24	92	21	2	2	6	16	71.60	$184,115

Best finish for 1979: Win at the Hawaiian Open & First NBC New Orleans Open

1980	25	89	21	0	3	6	12	71.64	$108,687

Best finish for 1980: T-4th at the Masters & Greater New Orleans Open

1981	29	95	21	1	2	2	11	71.82	$116,090

Best finish for 1981: Win at the Sammy Davis, Jr. - Greater Hartford Open

1982	29	90	14	0	1	2	7	72.30	$79,336

Best finish for 1982: T-2nd at the Sammy Davis, Jr. - Greater Hartford Open

1983	28	91	16	0	0	0	4	72.68	$33,706

Best finish for 1983: T-13th at the Bob Hope Chrysler Classic

1984	27	96	20	1	3	5	8	71.39	$182,378

Best finish for 1984: Win at the Southern Open

1985	26	83	16	1	2	2	10	71.71	$235,627

Best finish for 1985: Win at the PGA Championship

1986	26	83	16	0	2	2	5	72.86	$115,622

Best finish for 1986: T-2nd at the Doral-Eastern Open

1987	24	71	12	0	0	1	4	72.59	$63,949

Best finish for 1987: T-6th at the Centel Classic

1988	23	73	12	0	0	0	5	72.23	$58,028

Best finish for 1988: T-18th at the Texas Open

1989	20	74	16	0	1	3	4	71.64	$161,190

Best finish for 1989: T-3rd at the Federal Express St. Jude Classic

1990	19	61	11	0	0	0	3	72.41	$69,448

Best finish for 1990: T-12th at the Hawaiian Open

1991	17	46	4	0	0	0	1	72.65	$19,031

Best finish for 1991: T-19th at the Northern Telecom Open

1992	19	50	4	0	0	0	1	72.78	$24,802

Best finish for 1992: T-17th at the H-E-B Texas Open

1993	19	54	7	0	0	0	1	72.63	$29,786

Best finish for 1993: T-20th at the Canon Greater Hartford Open

1994	15	36	2	0	0	0	0	73.67	$6,054

Best finish for 1994: T-65th at the GTE Byron Nelson Classic

1995	17	38	2	0	0	0	0	74.00	$7,400

Best finish for 1995: T-59th at the Memorial Tournament

1996	12	25	1	0	0	0	0	74.28	$3,520

Best finish for 1996: T-76th at the CVS Charity Classic

1997	1	5	1	0	0	0	0	69.80	$3,195

Best finish for 1997: T-61st at the Bob Hope Chrysler Classic

1998	1	4	0	0	0	0	0	72.25	

Period Totals	Starts	Rounds Played	Cuts Made	Wins	Top-5s	Top-10s	Top-25s	Scoring Average	Money
	636	2112	404	18	59	95	206	71.96	$2,658,639

Jimmy Green

Year	Starts	Rounds Played	Cuts Made	Wins	Top-5s	Top-10s	Top-25s	Scoring Average	Money
1993	1	2	0	0	0	0	0	77.50	
1994	1	2	0	0	0	0	0	74.50	$1,000
1995	1	4	1	0	0	0	0	70.50	$3,162

Best finish for 1995: T-35th at the Deposit Guaranty Golf Classic

1997	31	82	12	0	0	0	2	71.96	$61,136

Best finish for 1997: T-19th at the Deposit Guaranty Golf Classic

Year	Starts	Rounds Played	Cuts Made	Wins	Top-5s	Top-10s	Top-25s	Scoring Average	Money
1998	2	4	0	0	0	0	0	74.50	$1,000
1999	28	75	10	0	0	1	3	72.48	$152,091

Best finish for 1999: T-7th at the Sony Open in Hawaii

2000	27	83	16	0	1	1	3	71.42	$414,509

Best finish for 2000: T-4th at the AT&T Pebble Beach

2001	33	92	12	0	0	1	1	71.78	$213,942

Best finish for 2001: T-7th at the Michelob Championship at Kingsmill

2002	2	6	1	0	0	0	0	71.17	$4,599

Best finish for 2002: T-56th at the B.C. Open

2004	2	4	0	0	0	0	0	76.25	$4,745
Period Totals	Starts	Rounds Played	Cuts Made	Wins	Top-5s	Top-10s	Top-25s	Scoring Average	Money
	128	354	52	0	1	3	9	71.99	$856,184

Ken Green

Year	Starts	Rounds Played	Cuts Made	Wins	Top-5s	Top-10s	Top-25s	Scoring Average	Money
1981	1	0	0	0	0	0	0		
1982	21	54	7	0	0	0	1	73.74	$12,499

Best finish for 1982: T-14th at the Disney World

1983	33	103	19	0	0	1	4	72.72	$40,263

Best finish for 1983: T-7th at the Bing Crosby Pro-Am

1984	34	90	11	0	0	1	2	73.34	$20,760

Best finish for 1984: T-7th at the Anheuser-Busch Golf Classic

1985	30	100	24	1	1	2	6	71.67	$151,355

Best finish for 1985: Win at the Buick Open

1986	31	87	19	1	2	3	7	72.16	$318,435

Best finish for 1986: Win at the International

1987	29	97	23	0	3	4	9	71.37	$283,185

Best finish for 1987: 2nd at the International

1988	31	96	21	2	8	10	15	70.25	$780,181

Best finish for 1988: Win at the Canadian Open & Greater Milwaukee Open

1989	28	84	17	1	1	1	6	71.89	$309,034

Best finish for 1989: Win at the Kmart Greater Greensboro Open

1990	25	85	18	0	2	5	7	71.51	$269,667

Best finish for 1990: 4th at the Buick Classic

1991	29	93	19	0	1	5	8	71.11	$264,924

Best finish for 1991: T-3rd at the Canadian Open

1992	26	86	18	0	4	6	9	70.79	$361,397

Best finish for 1992: T-2nd at the Kemper Open & B.C. Open

1993	21	58	10	0	1	3	6	71.64	$229,750

Best finish for 1993: T-3rd at the Walt Disney World/Oldsmobile Classic

1994	29	86	18	0	0	2	5	71.52	$156,156

Best finish for 1994: T-9th at the Canon Greater Hartford Open & New England Classic

1995	22	69	12	0	1	1	2	71.80	$173,577

Best finish for 1995: T-2nd at the FedEx St. Jude Classic

1996	30	81	12	0	0	1	3	71.96	$161,663

Best finish for 1996: T-7th at the U.S. Open

1997	20	53	8	0	0	0	2	71.92	$65,602

Best finish for 1997: T-12th at the Greater Milwaukee Open

1998	17	34	4	0	1	1	1	72.82	$16,858

Best finish for 1998: T-35th at the Greater Milwaukee Open

1999	11	22	3	0	0	0	0	73.23	$19,922

Best finish for 1999: T-37th at the Bell Canadian Open

2000	3	5	1	0	0	0	0	72.60	$14,512

Best finish for 2000: T-34th at the Greater Greensboro Chrysler Classic

2001	5	6	0	0	0	0	0	72.17	
2002	4	5	1	0	0	0	0	71.40	$10,995

Best finish for 2002: T-49th at the International presented by Quest

2003	7	16	3	0	0	0	1	71.56	$70,633

Best finish for 2003: T-25th at the AT&T Pebble Beach

2004	18	35	4	0	0	0	0	72.74	$43,356

Best finish for 2004: T-37th at the Deutsche Bank Championship

2005	5	7	0	0	0	0	0	72.86	
2006	1	0	0	0	0	0	0		
Period Totals	Starts	Rounds Played	Cuts Made	Wins	Top-5s	Top-10s	Top-25s	Scoring Average	Money
	511	1452	272	5	25	46	94	71.86	$3,774,725

Nathan Green

Year	Starts	Rounds Played	Cuts Made	Wins	Top-5s	Top-10s	Top-25s	Scoring Average	Money
2001	1	2	0	0	0	0	0	75.00	$1,431
2006	30	104	24	0	4	6	8	70.96	$1,702,803

Best finish for 2006: T-2nd at the Buick Invitational

2007	29	103	22	0	2	2	9	70.81	$1,382,317

Best finish for 2007: T-3rd at the John Deere Classic

Year	Starts	Rounds Played	Cuts Made	Wins	Top-5s	Top-10s	Top-25s	Scoring Average	Money
2008	30	95	17	0	1	1	6	71.33	$912,867

Best finish for 2008: 3rd at the Honda Classic

Period Totals	Starts	Rounds Played	Cuts Made	Wins	Top-5s	Top-10s	Top-25s	Scoring Average	Money
	90	304	63	0	7	9	23	71.05	$3,999,418

Richard Green

Year	Starts	Rounds Played	Cuts Made	Wins	Top-5s	Top-10s	Top-25s	Scoring Average	Money
1997	3	7	1	0	1	1	1	73.43	$48,623

Best finish for 1997: T-5th at the B.C. Open

| 1999 | 1 | 2 | 0 | 0 | 0 | 0 | 0 | 79.00 | $1,406 |
| 2001 | 1 | 4 | 1 | 0 | 0 | 0 | 0 | 71.75 | $19,312 |

Best finish for 2001: T-42nd at the British Open

| 2002 | 1 | 4 | 1 | 0 | 0 | 0 | 0 | 72.25 | $14,696 |

Best finish for 2002: T-59th at the British Open

| 2004 | 2 | 6 | 1 | 0 | 0 | 0 | 0 | 72.67 | $58,838 |

Best finish for 2004: T-28th at the WGC-American Express Championship

| 2005 | 11 | 36 | 9 | 0 | 0 | 1 | 1 | 72.22 | $367,807 |

Best finish for 2005: T-8th at the Memorial Tournament

| 2006 | 4 | 8 | 2 | 0 | 0 | 0 | 0 | 73.50 | $70,898 |

Best finish for 2006: T-33rd at the WGC-Accenture Match Play Championship

| 2007 | 5 | 16 | 5 | 0 | 1 | 1 | 1 | 71.50 | $544,070 |

Best finish for 2007: T-4th at the British Open

| 2008 | 9 | 28 | 7 | 0 | 0 | 0 | 0 | 73.11 | $224,310 |

Best finish for 2008: T-32nd at the British Open

Period Totals	Starts	Rounds Played	Cuts Made	Wins	Top-5s	Top-10s	Top-25s	Scoring Average	Money
	37	111	27	0	2	3	3	72.64	$1,349,959

Bert Greene

Year	Starts	Rounds Played	Cuts Made	Wins	Top-5s	Top-10s	Top-25s	Scoring Average	Money
1965	1	2	0	0	0	0	0	78.50	
1967	20	59	8	0	0	0	0	74.20	$1,318

Best finish for 1967: T-33rd at the Los Angles Open

| 1968 | 34 | 102 | 18 | 0 | 1 | 2 | 11 | 72.08 | $19,926 |

Best finish for 1968: 5th at the Kaiser International Open Invitational

| 1969 | 36 | 130 | 29 | 0 | 5 | 5 | 13 | 72.00 | $72,765 |

Best finish for 1969: T-2nd at the Tallahassee Open & Westchester Classic

| 1970 | 34 | 114 | 25 | 0 | 1 | 4 | 10 | 71.89 | $31,508 |

Best finish for 1970: 3rd at the Houston Champions International

| 1971 | 34 | 104 | 24 | 0 | 0 | 3 | 8 | 71.85 | $31,107 |

Best finish for 1971: 6th at the Western Open

| 1972 | 21 | 59 | 10 | 0 | 0 | 4 | 5 | 72.88 | $19,655 |

Best finish for 1972: T-6th at the Colonial National Invitational & Greater Milwaukee Open

| 1973 | 26 | 83 | 15 | 1 | 3 | 5 | 9 | 71.96 | $49,823 |

Best finish for 1973: Win at the Liggett Meyers Open

| 1974 | 27 | 82 | 14 | 0 | 0 | 0 | 2 | 73.09 | $14,212 |

Best finish for 1974: T-11th at the Kaiser International Open

| 1975 | 20 | 58 | 11 | 0 | 0 | 0 | 0 | 72.98 | $4,248 |

Best finish for 1975: T-32nd at the Southern Open

1976	1	2	0	0	0	0	0	79.00	
1993	1	2	0	0	0	0	0	80.50	
1994	1	2	0	0	0	0	0	80.00	
1995	1	2	0	0	0	0	0	80.00	

Period Totals	Starts	Rounds Played	Cuts Made	Wins	Top-5s	Top-10s	Top-25s	Scoring Average	Money
	257	801	154	1	10	23	58	72.48	$244,560

Bobby Greenwood

Year	Starts	Rounds Played	Cuts Made	Wins	Top-5s	Top-10s	Top-25s	Scoring Average	Money
1966	1	2	0	0	0	0	0	73.50	
1967	2	4	0	0	0	0	0	81.50	
1968	1	4	1	0	0	0	0	73.75	

Best finish for 1968: T-65th at the Rebel Yell Open

| 1969 | 13 | 36 | 5 | 0 | 0 | 1 | 1 | 73.08 | $2,568 |

Best finish for 1969: 6th at the West End Classic

| 1970 | 24 | 74 | 13 | 0 | 0 | 1 | 4 | 72.43 | $9,733 |

Best finish for 1970: T-10th at the Tallahassee Open

| 1971 | 28 | 89 | 16 | 0 | 1 | 1 | 3 | 73.26 | $11,086 |

Best finish for 1971: T-4th at the Glen Campbell Los Angles Open

| 1972 | 28 | 87 | 16 | 0 | 0 | 2 | 3 | 73.32 | $13,838 |

Best finish for 1972: T-8th at the USI Classic & Liggett Meyers Open

| 1973 | 24 | 66 | 9 | 0 | 0 | 0 | 2 | 73.21 | $4,066 |

Best finish for 1973: T-18th at the Sahara Invitational

Year	Starts	Rounds Played	Cuts Made	Wins	Top-5s	Top-10s	Top-25s	Scoring Average	Money
1974	15	47	9	0	0	1	2	72.77	$7,557

Best finish for 1974: T-7th at the San Antonio Texas Open

Year	Starts	Rounds Played	Cuts Made	Wins	Top-5s	Top-10s	Top-25s	Scoring Average	Money
1975	15	34	3	0	0	0	0	75.50	$700

Best finish for 1975: T-49th at the Greater Milwaukee Open

Period Totals	Starts	Rounds Played	Cuts Made	Wins	Top-5s	Top-10s	Top-25s	Scoring Average	Money
	151	443	72	0	1	6	15	73.31	$49,548

Brad Greer

Year	Starts	Rounds Played	Cuts Made	Wins	Top-5s	Top-10s	Top-25s	Scoring Average	Money
1986	2	6	1	0	0	0	0	76.50	$2,791

Best finish for 1986: 70th at the U.S. Open

Year	Starts	Rounds Played	Cuts Made	Wins	Top-5s	Top-10s	Top-25s	Scoring Average	Money
1987	30	79	12	0	0	0	3	72.68	$33,392

Best finish for 1987: T-16th at the Walt Disney World/Oldsmobile Classic

Year	Starts	Rounds Played	Cuts Made	Wins	Top-5s	Top-10s	Top-25s	Scoring Average	Money
1988	3	10	2	0	0	0	0	70.90	$1,486

Best finish for 1988: T-51st at the Provident Classic

Period Totals	Starts	Rounds Played	Cuts Made	Wins	Top-5s	Top-10s	Top-25s	Scoring Average	Money
	35	95	15	0	0	0	3	72.74	$37,668

Malcolm Gregson

Year	Starts	Rounds Played	Cuts Made	Wins	Top-5s	Top-10s	Top-25s	Scoring Average	Money
1964	1	4	1	0	0	0	1	74.50	$241

Best finish for 1964: T-19th at the British Open

Year	Starts	Rounds Played	Cuts Made	Wins	Top-5s	Top-10s	Top-25s	Scoring Average	Money
1965	4	8	0	0	0	0	0	77.00	
1966	1	4	1	0	0	0	0	75.75	$218

Best finish for 1966: T-47th at the British Open

| 1967 | 3 | 6 | 1 | 0 | 0 | 0 | 0 | 74.50 | $130 |

Best finish for 1967: T-51st at the British Open

| 1968 | 8 | 22 | 2 | 0 | 0 | 0 | 0 | 74.14 | $1,778 |

Best finish for 1968: T-27th at the British Open

| 1969 | 15 | 50 | 8 | 0 | 0 | 1 | 2 | 73.24 | $5,399 |

Best finish for 1969: 7th at the West End Classic

| 1971 | 1 | 4 | 1 | 0 | 0 | 0 | 1 | 73.00 | $638 |

Best finish for 1971: T-25th at the British Open

1972	1	2	0	0	0	0	0	78.00	$125
1973	1	2	0	0	0	0	0	77.00	$130
1974	1	4	1	0	0	0	0	76.50	$300

Best finish for 1974: T-51st at the British Open

| 1975 | 1 | 3 | 0 | 0 | 0 | 0 | 0 | 74.00 | $330 |
| 1976 | 1 | 4 | 1 | 0 | 0 | 0 | 0 | 74.50 | $374 |

Best finish for 1976: T-42nd at the British Open

1977	1	2	0	0	0	0	0	77.00	$255
1978	1	2	0	0	0	0	0	75.00	$332
1979	1	2	0	0	0	0	0	77.00	$420
1980	1	2	0	0	0	0	0	76.00	$540
1983	1	2	0	0	0	0	0	76.50	$375

Period Totals	Starts	Rounds Played	Cuts Made	Wins	Top-5s	Top-10s	Top-25s	Scoring Average	Money
	43	123	16	0	0	1	4	74.37	$11,587

Ed Griffiths

Year	Starts	Rounds Played	Cuts Made	Wins	Top-5s	Top-10s	Top-25s	Scoring Average	Money
1958	7	26	6	0	0	1	1	72.85	$725

Best finish for 1958: T-7th at the Texas Open

1960	1	3	1	0	0	0	0	75.33	
1962	1	2	0	0	0	0	0	80.00	
1963	1	2	0	0	0	0	0	80.50	$150
1964	3	9	2	0	1	1	1	71.56	$3,650

Best finish for 1964: T-5th at the Cleveland Open

| 1965 | 23 | 70 | 12 | 0 | 0 | 0 | 2 | 73.63 | $3,137 |

Best finish for 1965: T-23rd at the Oklahoma City Open

| 1966 | 29 | 89 | 15 | 0 | 0 | 0 | 2 | 73.61 | $5,781 |

Best finish for 1966: T-15th at the Texas Open Invitational

| 1967 | 16 | 43 | 5 | 0 | 0 | 0 | 1 | 74.47 | $1,320 |

Best finish for 1967: T-24th at the Jacksonville Open

| 1968 | 3 | 8 | 1 | 0 | 0 | 0 | 0 | 73.25 | |

Best finish for 1968: 66th at the Jacksonville Open Invitational

| 1973 | 1 | 1 | 0 | 0 | 0 | 0 | 0 | 76.00 | |

Period Totals	Starts	Rounds Played	Cuts Made	Wins	Top-5s	Top-10s	Top-25s	Scoring Average	Money
	85	253	42	0	1	2	7	73.73	$14,763

Tony Grimes

Year	Starts	Rounds Played	Cuts Made	Wins	Top-5s	Top-10s	Top-25s	Scoring Average	Money
1984	1	2	0	0	0	0	0	73.50	

Year	Starts	Rounds Played	Cuts Made	Wins	Top-5s	Top-10s	Top-25s	Scoring Average	Money
1985	1	2	0	0	0	0	0	77.00	$600
1986	1	4	1	0	0	0	0	70.25	$880

Best finish for 1986: T-58th at the Hardee's Golf Classic

1987	27	67	8	0	0	0	0	72.58	$12,390

Best finish for 1987: T-35th at the Byron Nelson Golf Classic

1988	3	10	2	0	0	0	0	71.50	$1,696

Best finish for 1988: T-38th at the Deposit Guaranty Golf Classic

1989	28	69	7	0	0	0	1	72.67	$26,688

Best finish for 1989: T-14th at the USF&G Classic

1990	2	6	1	0	0	0	0	70.83	$1,020

Best finish for 1990: T-43rd at the Deposit Guaranty

Period Totals	Starts	Rounds Played	Cuts Made	Wins	Top-5s	Top-10s	Top-25s	Scoring Average	Money
	63	160	19	0	0	0	1	72.49	$43,274

Mike Grob

Year	Starts	Rounds Played	Cuts Made	Wins	Top-5s	Top-10s	Top-25s	Scoring Average	Money
1996	2	6	1	0	0	0	0	72.50	$4,100

Best finish for 1996: T-37th at the Greater Vancouver Open

1997	2	4	0	0	0	0	0	72.00	
1998	2	4	0	0	0	0	0	73.50	
2002	1	2	0	0	0	0	0	74.00	
2003	27	82	14	0	1	2	3	71.41	$354,286

Best finish for 2003: T-5th at the B.C. Open

2004	13	37	5	0	0	0	0	71.68	$60,103

Best finish for 2004: T-33rd at the FedEx St. Jude Classic

2007	1	4	1	0	0	0	0	71.25	$10,200

Best finish for 2007: T-66th at the Canadian Open

Period Totals	Starts	Rounds Played	Cuts Made	Wins	Top-5s	Top-10s	Top-25s	Scoring Average	Money
	48	139	21	0	1	2	3	71.64	$428,690

Gary Groh

Year	Starts	Rounds Played	Cuts Made	Wins	Top-5s	Top-10s	Top-25s	Scoring Average	Money
1969	12	31	4	0	0	0	1	73.97	$776

Best finish for 1969: T-21st at the West End Classic

1970	6	12	0	0	0	0	0	74.33	
1971	5	14	2	0	0	0	0	73.36	$1,777

Best finish for 1971: T-27th at the Florida Citrus Open Invitational

1972	22	61	8	0	0	0	0	74.18	$3,567

Best finish for 1972: T-29th at the Byron Nelson Golf Classic

1973	32	102	19	0	0	0	5	72.84	$11,426

Best finish for 1973: T-15th at the Tallahassee Open & Ohio Kings Island Open

1974	29	94	19	0	0	1	3	72.20	$16,810

Best finish for 1974: T-10th at the Danny Thomas Memphis Classic

1975	30	92	16	1	1	2	7	72.79	$68,296

Best finish for 1975: Win at the Hawaiian Open

1976	31	99	18	0	0	0	2	73.07	$13,611

Best finish for 1976: T-12th at the Kemper Open

1977	21	66	12	0	0	1	2	73.41	$11,255

Best finish for 1977: T-9th at the Ohio Kings Island Open

1978	26	77	12	0	0	0	1	73.30	$8,455

Best finish for 1978: T-19th at the Buick Goodwrench Open

1979	1	2	0	0	0	0	0	73.50	
1980	1	2	0	0	0	0	0	76.00	
1981	3	6	0	0	0	0	0	76.17	$550
1982	1	2	0	0	0	0	0	80.50	
1983	2	6	1	0	0	0	0	73.83	$548

Best finish for 1983: T-58th at the Greater Milwaukee Open

1984	2	4	0	0	0	0	0	75.50	
1985	2	6	1	0	0	0	0	74.33	$657

Best finish for 1985: T-60th at the Greater Milwaukee Open

1986	1	4	1	0	0	0	0	75.75	$900

Best finish for 1986: T-80th at the Western Open

1987	1	1	0	0	0	0	0	73.00	
1988	1	2	0	0	0	0	0	77.00	
1990	1	2	0	0	0	0	0	79.50	
1991	1	2	0	0	0	0	0	77.50	
1992	2	4	0	0	0	0	0	76.00	
1993	1	2	0	0	0	0	0	74.50	$1,200
2002	1	2	0	0	0	0	0	79.00	

Period Totals	Starts	Rounds Played	Cuts Made	Wins	Top-5s	Top-10s	Top-25s	Scoring Average	Money
	235	695	113	1	1	4	21	73.29	$139,828

Mathias Gronberg

Year	Starts	Rounds Played	Cuts Made	Wins	Top-5s	Top-10s	Top-25s	Scoring Average	Money
1995	1	2	0	0	0	0	0	76.50	$1,037
1999	3	8	1	0	0	0	0	73.50	$8,367

Best finish for 1999: T-51st at the COMPAQ Classic of New Orleans

Year	Starts	Rounds Played	Cuts Made	Wins	Top-5s	Top-10s	Top-25s	Scoring Average	Money
2000	2	6	1	0	0	0	0	74.33	$35,000

Best finish for 2000: T-42nd at the American Express Championship

Year	Starts	Rounds Played	Cuts Made	Wins	Top-5s	Top-10s	Top-25s	Scoring Average	Money
2001	4	8	2	0	0	0	0	73.75	$37,723

Best finish for 2001: T-33rd at the Accenture Match Play Championship

Year	Starts	Rounds Played	Cuts Made	Wins	Top-5s	Top-10s	Top-25s	Scoring Average	Money
2002	2	4	0	0	0	0	0	74.25	$3,950
2003	4	12	2	0	0	0	2	71.75	$130,013

Best finish for 2003: T-15th at the John Deere Classic

Year	Starts	Rounds Played	Cuts Made	Wins	Top-5s	Top-10s	Top-25s	Scoring Average	Money
2004	32	87	12	0	0	2	5	71.70	$565,014

Best finish for 2004: T-9th at the Wachovia Championship & The International

Year	Starts	Rounds Played	Cuts Made	Wins	Top-5s	Top-10s	Top-25s	Scoring Average	Money
2005	19	58	11	0	0	1	2	70.60	$401,140

Best finish for 2005: T-6th at the B.C. Open

Year	Starts	Rounds Played	Cuts Made	Wins	Top-5s	Top-10s	Top-25s	Scoring Average	Money
2006	30	89	16	0	1	1	6	71.07	$674,002

Best finish for 2006: 4th at the Shell Houston Open

Year	Starts	Rounds Played	Cuts Made	Wins	Top-5s	Top-10s	Top-25s	Scoring Average	Money
2007	31	95	16	0	1	2	5	71.19	$785,180

Best finish for 2007: T-3rd at the Valero Texas Open

Year	Starts	Rounds Played	Cuts Made	Wins	Top-5s	Top-10s	Top-25s	Scoring Average	Money
2008	30	87	14	0	0	0	1	71.68	$245,281

Best finish for 2008: T-14th at the Reno-Tahoe Open

Period Totals	Starts	Rounds Played	Cuts Made	Wins	Top-5s	Top-10s	Top-25s	Scoring Average	Money
	158	456	75	0	2	6	21	71.47	$2,886,707

John Gross

Year	Starts	Rounds Played	Cuts Made	Wins	Top-5s	Top-10s	Top-25s	Scoring Average	Money
1964	5	16	3	0	0	0	0	74.50	$350

Best finish for 1964: T-27th at the Mountain View Open

Year	Starts	Rounds Played	Cuts Made	Wins	Top-5s	Top-10s	Top-25s	Scoring Average	Money
1965	17	54	8	0	0	0	0	74.22	$550

Best finish for 1965: T-30th at the Greater Hartford Open

Year	Starts	Rounds Played	Cuts Made	Wins	Top-5s	Top-10s	Top-25s	Scoring Average	Money
1966	12	30	3	0	0	0	0	73.77	$040

Best finish for 1966: T-48th at the Azalea Open Invitational

Period Totals	Starts	Rounds Played	Cuts Made	Wins	Top-5s	Top-10s	Top-25s	Scoring Average	Money
	34	100	14	0	0	0	0	74.13	$940

Kelly Grunewald

Year	Starts	Rounds Played	Cuts Made	Wins	Top-5s	Top-10s	Top-25s	Scoring Average	Money
1995	1	2	0	0	0	0	0	72.00	
1997	1	2	0	0	0	0	0	71.50	
1999	1	2	0	0	0	0	0	73.50	
2001	27	66	6	0	0	0	0	72.23	$59,244

Best finish for 2001: T-34th at the BellSouth Classic

Year	Starts	Rounds Played	Cuts Made	Wins	Top-5s	Top-10s	Top-25s	Scoring Average	Money
2005	1	4	1	0	0	0	0	72.25	$11,935

Best finish for 2005: T-59th at the Zurich Classic of New Orleans

Period Totals	Starts	Rounds Played	Cuts Made	Wins	Top-5s	Top-10s	Top-25s	Scoring Average	Money
	31	76	7	0	0	0	0	72.24	$71,179

Jeff Grygiel

Year	Starts	Rounds Played	Cuts Made	Wins	Top-5s	Top-10s	Top-25s	Scoring Average	Money
1982	1	2	0	0	0	0	0	79.50	$600
1983	1	2	0	0	0	0	0	73.50	
1984	1	4	1	0	0	0	0	72.75	$2,000

Best finish for 1984: T-38th at the Honda Classic

Year	Starts	Rounds Played	Cuts Made	Wins	Top-5s	Top-10s	Top-25s	Scoring Average	Money
1985	5	14	2	0	0	0	0	73.14	$5,877

Best finish for 1985: T-27th at the Honda Classic

Year	Starts	Rounds Played	Cuts Made	Wins	Top-5s	Top-10s	Top-25s	Scoring Average	Money
1986	26	81	14	0	0	1	1	72.58	$23,451

Best finish for 1986: T-10th at the Tallahassee Open

Year	Starts	Rounds Played	Cuts Made	Wins	Top-5s	Top-10s	Top-25s	Scoring Average	Money
1987	4	16	4	0	1	1	1	70.75	$14,052

Best finish for 1987: T-3rd at the Deposit Guaranty Golf Classic

Year	Starts	Rounds Played	Cuts Made	Wins	Top-5s	Top-10s	Top-25s	Scoring Average	Money
1988	2	4	0	0	0	0	0	72.50	
1993	1	2	0	0	0	0	0	76.50	

Period Totals	Starts	Rounds Played	Cuts Made	Wins	Top-5s	Top-10s	Top-25s	Scoring Average	Money
	41	125	21	0	1	2	2	72.60	$45,980

Joey Gullion

Year	Starts	Rounds Played	Cuts Made	Wins	Top-5s	Top-10s	Top-25s	Scoring Average	Money
1995	1	4	1	0	0	0	0	75.25	$2,574

Best finish for 1995: 73rd at the U.S. Open

Year	Starts	Rounds Played	Cuts Made	Wins	Top-5s	Top-10s	Top-25s	Scoring Average	Money
1996	30	87	13	0	1	1	2	71.99	$99,849

Best finish for 1996: T-5th at the Greater Vancouver Open

| 2000 | 7 | 20 | 3 | 0 | 0 | 0 | 2 | 70.60 | $84,651 |

Best finish for 2000: T-14th at the Greater Milwaukee Open

| 2001 | 3 | 8 | 1 | 0 | 0 | 0 | 0 | 71.75 | $16,200 |

Best finish for 2001: T-37th at the Advil Western Open

Period Totals	Starts	Rounds Played	Cuts Made	Wins	Top-5s	Top-10s	Top-25s	Scoring Average	Money
	41	119	18	0	1	1	4	71.85	$203,274

Dave Gumlia

Year	Starts	Rounds Played	Cuts Made	Wins	Top-5s	Top-10s	Top-25s	Scoring Average	Money
1964	1	4	1	0	0	0	0	72.00	

Best finish for 1964: T-60th at the St. Paul Open

| 1966 | 2 | 8 | 2 | 0 | 0 | 0 | 0 | 71.63 | |

Best finish for 1966: T-48th at the Cajun Classic

| 1967 | 20 | 55 | 11 | 0 | 0 | 0 | 1 | 73.51 | $1,842 |

Best finish for 1967: T-25th at the Texas Open

| 1968 | 23 | 67 | 10 | 0 | 0 | 1 | 1 | 73.12 | $2,596 |

Best finish for 1968: T-9th at the AZALEA Open Invitational

| 1969 | 10 | 26 | 3 | 0 | 0 | 0 | 1 | 74.58 | $1,366 |

Best finish for 1969: T-18th at the Minnesota Classic

| 1970 | 8 | 24 | 3 | 0 | 0 | 0 | 0 | 73.29 | $804 |

Best finish for 1970: T-41st at the Phoenix Open

| 1971 | 5 | 19 | 4 | 0 | 0 | 0 | 1 | 72.68 | $3,662 |

Best finish for 1971: T-16th at the Hawaiian Open

Period Totals	Starts	Rounds Played	Cuts Made	Wins	Top-5s	Top-10s	Top-25s	Scoring Average	Money
	69	203	34	0	0	1	4	73.31	$10,270

Scott Gump

Year	Starts	Rounds Played	Cuts Made	Wins	Top-5s	Top-10s	Top-25s	Scoring Average	Money
1988	2	6	1	0	0	0	0	77.17	

Best finish for 1988: 74th at the Honda Classic

| 1989 | 1 | 2 | 0 | 0 | 0 | 0 | 0 | 70.50 | |
| 1991 | 29 | 92 | 18 | 0 | 2 | 2 | 7 | 71.11 | $208,809 |

Best finish for 1991: T-2nd at the International

| 1992 | 33 | 111 | 24 | 0 | 0 | 1 | 5 | 71.38 | $148,695 |

Best finish for 1992: T-6th at the Federal Express St. Jude Classic

| 1993 | 31 | 92 | 17 | 0 | 0 | 0 | 4 | 71.88 | $96,822 |

Best finish for 1993: T-11th at the Canon Greater Hartford Open

| 1994 | 3 | 11 | 2 | 0 | 0 | 0 | 0 | 71.73 | $4,181 |

Best finish for 1994: T-52nd at the Buick Southern Open

| 1995 | 29 | 93 | 18 | 0 | 0 | 1 | 5 | 71.11 | $184,828 |

Best finish for 1995: T-10th at the Motorola Western Open

| 1996 | 31 | 97 | 20 | 0 | 0 | 0 | 6 | 71.21 | $178,332 |

Best finish for 1996: T-15th at the CVS Charity Classic

| 1997 | 33 | 108 | 22 | 0 | 0 | 0 | 6 | 71.34 | $209,672 |

Best finish for 1997: T-13th at the Tucson Chrysler Classic

| 1998 | 31 | 97 | 20 | 0 | 1 | 2 | 7 | 71.23 | $402,092 |

Best finish for 1998: 2nd at the Quad City Classic

| 1999 | 30 | 95 | 19 | 0 | 1 | 4 | 7 | 71.39 | $958,888 |

Best finish for 1999: 2nd at the Players Championship

| 2000 | 36 | 105 | 18 | 0 | 0 | 0 | 2 | 71.82 | $194,460 |

Best finish for 2000: T-19th at the Tampa Bay Classic

| 2001 | 6 | 20 | 4 | 0 | 0 | 0 | 0 | 71.20 | $31,902 |

Best finish for 2001: T-35th at the John Deere Classic

| 2002 | 8 | 23 | 3 | 0 | 0 | 0 | 0 | 72.09 | $23,610 |

Best finish for 2002: T-33rd at the B.C. Open

| 2005 | 2 | 4 | 0 | 0 | 0 | 0 | 0 | 71.00 | |
| 2006 | 10 | 28 | 4 | 0 | 0 | 0 | 1 | 71.96 | $72,248 |

Best finish for 2006: T-17th at the B.C. Open

| 2007 | 12 | 27 | 1 | 0 | 0 | 0 | 0 | 74.07 | $7,805 |

Best finish for 2007: T-55th at the Mayakoba Golf Classic

2008	2	4	0	0	0	0	0	74.50	
Period Totals	Starts	Rounds Played	Cuts Made	Wins	Top-5s	Top-10s	Top-25s	Scoring Average	Money
	329	1015	191	0	4	10	50	71.53	$2,722,345

Jon Gustin

Year	Starts	Rounds Played	Cuts Made	Wins	Top-5s	Top-10s	Top-25s	Scoring Average	Money
1958	3	6	1	0	0	0	0	74.67	
1959	10	38	8	0	2	2	6	71.42	$3,803

Best finish for 1959: T-4th at the Mobile Sertoma Open Invitational

| 1960 | 18 | 71 | 16 | 0 | 1 | 4 | 7 | 71.24 | $6,315 |

Best finish for 1960: T-3rd at the Cajun Classic Open Invitational

| 1961 | 16 | 64 | 15 | 0 | 1 | 2 | 9 | 71.11 | $7,507 |

Best finish for 1961: T-4th at the Ontario Open

Year	Starts	Rounds Played	Cuts Made	Wins	Top-5s	Top-10s	Top-25s	Scoring Average	Money
1962	22	83	21	0	1	3	10	71.72	$9,701

Best finish for 1962: T-4th at the West Palm Beach Open Invitational

| 1963 | 1 | 4 | 0 | 0 | 0 | 0 | 1 | 69.75 | $450 |

Best finish for 1963: T-20th at the San Diego Open Invitational

| 1964 | 11 | 36 | 6 | 0 | 0 | 2 | 2 | 72.86 | $3,990 |

Best finish for 1964: T-9th at the Lucky International Open & PGA Championship

| 1965 | 9 | 30 | 4 | 0 | 0 | 1 | 1 | 74.30 | $2,025 |

Best finish for 1965: T-10th at the Bing Crosby Pro-Am

1966	3	6	0	0	0	0	0	75.33	
1967	3	6	0	0	0	0	0	73.17	
1970	2	4	0	0	0	0	0	78.50	
1971	1	2	0	0	0	0	0	74.00	
1972	1	1	0	0	0	0	0	82.00	
1973	1	2	0	0	0	0	0	77.00	
1974	2	4	0	0	0	0	0	76.25	
1975	2	6	1	0	0	0	0	74.83	

Best finish for 1975: T-76th at the Pensacola Open

1976	1	2	0	0	0	0	0	81.00	$500
1977	1	2	0	0	0	0	0	74.50	
Period Totals	Starts	Rounds Played	Cuts Made	Wins	Top-5s	Top-10s	Top-25s	Scoring Average	Money
	107	367	72	0	5	14	36	72.23	$34,291

Scott Gutschewski

Year	Starts	Rounds Played	Cuts Made	Wins	Top-5s	Top-10s	Top-25s	Scoring Average	Money
2004	1	3	1	0	0	0	0	72.00	$9,858

Best finish for 2004: T-69th at the AT&T Pebble Beach National Pro-Am

| 2005 | 27 | 82 | 16 | 0 | 0 | 0 | 6 | 70.79 | $485,487 |

Best finish for 2005: T-13th at the Chrysler Classic of Greensboro

| 2006 | 19 | 51 | 7 | 0 | 0 | 2 | 4 | 71.39 | $379,488 |

Best finish for 2006: T-6th at the B.C. Open

| 2007 | 22 | 67 | 11 | 0 | 0 | 0 | 2 | 71.76 | $252,179 |

Best finish for 2007: T-21st at the Stanford St. Jude Classic

Period Totals	Starts	Rounds Played	Cuts Made	Wins	Top-5s	Top-10s	Top-25s	Scoring Average	Money
	69	203	35	0	0	2	12	71.28	$1,127,012

Bill Haas

Year	Starts	Rounds Played	Cuts Made	Wins	Top-5s	Top-10s	Top-25s	Scoring Average	Money
2002	1	2	0	0	0	0	0	72.50	
2003	2	4	0	0	0	0	0	75.00	
2004	10	34	9	0	0	1	3	70.85	$315,259

Best finish for 2004: T-9th at the Deutsche Bank Championship

| 2005 | 6 | 21 | 4 | 0 | 0 | 0 | 2 | 71.81 | $159,586 |

Best finish for 2005: T-18th at the Buick Invitational

| 2006 | 30 | 96 | 19 | 0 | 1 | 1 | 7 | 70.96 | $887,024 |

Best finish for 2006: T-4th at the Wachovia Championship

| 2007 | 30 | 93 | 16 | 0 | 2 | 3 | 7 | 70.83 | $967,443 |

Best finish for 2007: T-3rd at the Viking Classic

| 2008 | 31 | 99 | 18 | 0 | 1 | 2 | 10 | 70.66 | $1,000,939 |

Best finish for 2008: T-4th at the Viking Classic

Period Totals	Starts	Rounds Played	Cuts Made	Wins	Top-5s	Top-10s	Top-25s	Scoring Average	Money
	110	349	66	0	4	7	29	70.93	$3,330,252

Fred Haas

Year	Starts	Rounds Played	Cuts Made	Wins	Top-5s	Top-10s	Top-25s	Scoring Average	Money
1958	14	48	10	0	1	3	5	72.02	$3,978

Best finish for 1958: 4th at the Baton Rouge Open

| 1959 | 9 | 36 | 9 | 0 | 0 | 2 | 6 | 71.28 | $4,385 |

Best finish for 1959: T-6th at the Pensacola Open Invitational & Houston Classic

| 1960 | 11 | 42 | 8 | 0 | 2 | 4 | 9 | 69.33 | $6,171 |

Best finish for 1960: T-3rd at the Pensacola Open Invitational

| 1961 | 9 | 34 | 8 | 0 | 0 | 2 | 6 | 71.32 | $4,935 |

Best finish for 1961: T-7th at the Houston Classic

| 1962 | 8 | 32 | 8 | 0 | 0 | 0 | 3 | 72.31 | $2,392 |

Best finish for 1962: T-18th at the Cajun Classic Open Invitational

| 1963 | 5 | 20 | 5 | 0 | 0 | 0 | 1 | 72.35 | $2,877 |

Best finish for 1963: T-16th at the Cajun Classic Open Invitational

| 1964 | 14 | 43 | 7 | 0 | 1 | 1 | 2 | 72.67 | $4,317 |

Best finish for 1964: T-3rd at the Dallas Open

| 1965 | 6 | 18 | 3 | 0 | 0 | 1 | 2 | 71.56 | $1,883 |

Best finish for 1965: T-9th at the Cajun Classic

| 1966 | 15 | 46 | 8 | 0 | 0 | 0 | 0 | 72.89 | $2,790 |

Best finish for 1966: T-35th at the Thunderbird Classic

Year	Starts	Rounds Played	Cuts Made	Wins	Top-5s	Top-10s	Top-25s	Scoring Average	Money
1967	7	26	6	0	0	0	2	72.23	$2,922

Best finish for 1967: T-12th at the Cajun Classic

| 1968 | 7 | 18 | 2 | 0 | 0 | 0 | 1 | 72.50 | $1,440 |

Best finish for 1968: T-14th at the Pensacola Open Invitational

| 1969 | 6 | 18 | 3 | 0 | 0 | 0 | 0 | 72.94 | $1,358 |

Best finish for 1969: T-33rd at the Western Open

| 1970 | 6 | 16 | 2 | 0 | 0 | 0 | 0 | 73.75 | $993 |

Best finish for 1970: T-27th at the Greater New Orleans Open

| 1971 | 3 | 6 | 0 | 0 | 0 | 0 | 0 | 73.83 | |
| 1975 | 3 | 8 | 1 | 0 | 0 | 0 | 0 | 74.38 | |

Best finish for 1975: 76th at the First NBC New Orleans Open

| 1976 | 2 | 4 | 0 | 0 | 0 | 0 | 0 | 75.75 | |
| 1977 | 2 | 5 | 1 | 0 | 0 | 0 | 0 | 74.40 | $325 |

Best finish for 1977: T-66th at the Houston Open

1978	1	2	0	0	0	0	0	74.50	
1980	1	0	0	0	0	0	0		
1984	1	2	0	0	0	0	0	76.00	
1985	1	2	0	0	0	0	0	76.50	
1986	1	2	0	0	0	0	0	77.00	
Period Totals	Starts	Rounds Played	Cuts Made	Wins	Top-5s	Top-10s	Top-25s	Scoring Average	Money
	132	428	81	0	4	13	37	72.16	$40,764

PGA Tour career totals from 1935 to 1986

	Starts	Rounds Played	Cuts Made	Wins	Top-5s	Top-10s	Top-25s	Scoring Average	Money
	381	N/A	N/A	5	N/A	116	224	N/A	N/A

Hunter Haas

Year	Starts	Rounds Played	Cuts Made	Wins	Top-5s	Top-10s	Top-25s	Scoring Average	Money
2000	6	10	1	0	0	0	0	75.30	$6,685

Best finish for 2000: T-74th at the International presented by Quest

| 2001 | 30 | 76 | 8 | 0 | 0 | 0 | 1 | 72.34 | $109,110 |

Best finish for 2001: T-15th at the Touchstone Energy Tucson Open

| 2002 | 1 | 0 | 1 | 0 | 0 | 0 | 0 | | $13,545 |

Best finish for 2002: T-45th at the International presented by Quest

| 2005 | 28 | 79 | 14 | 0 | 0 | 1 | 3 | 71.16 | $371,925 |

Best finish for 2005: T-10th at the BellSouth Classic

2008	1	2	0	0	0	0	0	75.00	
Period Totals	Starts	Rounds Played	Cuts Made	Wins	Top-5s	Top-10s	Top-25s	Scoring Average	Money
	66	167	24	0	0	1	4	71.99	$501,265

Jay Haas

Year	Starts	Rounds Played	Cuts Made	Wins	Top-5s	Top-10s	Top-25s	Scoring Average	Money
1973	2	6	1	0	0	0	0	71.50	

Best finish for 1973: 61st at the Greater Greensboro Open

| 1974 | 2 | 6 | 1 | 0 | 0 | 0 | 0 | 74.83 | |

Best finish for 1974: T-54th at the U.S. Open

| 1975 | 2 | 6 | 1 | 0 | 0 | 0 | 1 | 74.50 | |

Best finish for 1975: T-18th at the U.S. Open

| 1976 | 4 | 14 | 3 | 0 | 0 | 0 | 0 | 73.36 | $3,232 |

Best finish for 1976: T-33rd at the Sammy Davis, Jr. - Greater Hartford Open

| 1977 | 29 | 97 | 18 | 0 | 1 | 2 | 5 | 72.73 | $32,326 |

Best finish for 1977: T-5th at the U.S. Open

| 1978 | 29 | 99 | 20 | 1 | 1 | 4 | 9 | 72.35 | $77,776 |

Best finish for 1978: Win at the Andy Williams-San Diego Open

| 1979 | 28 | 96 | 20 | 0 | 1 | 7 | 12 | 71.82 | $102,515 |

Best finish for 1979: 2nd at the Phoenix Open

| 1980 | 31 | 112 | 26 | 0 | 1 | 7 | 14 | 71.34 | $114,102 |

Best finish for 1980: 3rd at the Sammy Davis, Jr. - Greater Hartford Open

| 1981 | 31 | 108 | 26 | 2 | 4 | 6 | 13 | 71.25 | $183,904 |

Best finish for 1981: Win at the Greater Milwaukee Open & B.C. Open

| 1982 | 30 | 116 | 28 | 2 | 5 | 10 | 15 | 71.02 | $232,466 |

Best finish for 1982: Win at the Hall of Fame & Texas Open

| 1983 | 29 | 110 | 26 | 0 | 4 | 8 | 16 | 71.14 | $196,090 |

Best finish for 1983: T-2nd at the USF&G Classic & Sammy Davis, Jr. - Greater Hartford Open

| 1984 | 28 | 99 | 21 | 0 | 3 | 3 | 12 | 71.51 | $149,413 |

Best finish for 1984: T-2nd at the Manufactures Hanover Westchester Classic

| 1985 | 29 | 96 | 20 | 0 | 1 | 3 | 7 | 71.92 | $121,488 |

Best finish for 1985: 5th at the Masters

| 1986 | 29 | 86 | 17 | 0 | 2 | 7 | 12 | 71.24 | $189,804 |

Best finish for 1986: T-4th at the Houston Open

| 1987 | 30 | 108 | 25 | 1 | 1 | 5 | 10 | 70.94 | $275,946 |

Best finish for 1987: Win at the Big I Houston Open

| 1988 | 31 | 104 | 23 | 1 | 2 | 6 | 12 | 70.83 | $497,783 |

Best finish for 1988: Win at the Bob Hope Chrysler Classic

Year	Starts	Rounds Played	Cuts Made	Wins	Top-5s	Top-10s	Top-25s	Scoring Average	Money
1989	30	91	17	0	2	5	8	71.57	$250,831

Best finish for 1989: T-2nd at the MONY Tournament Of Champions & Southern Open

1990	28	92	17	0	1	1	5	71.74	$182,023

Best finish for 1990: T-2nd at the Northern Telecom Tucson Open

1991	29	93	18	0	1	3	8	70.66	$200,637

Best finish for 1991: T-3rd at the Federal Express St. Jude Classic

1992	28	104	24	1	4	5	16	70.21	$632,627

Best finish for 1992: Win at the Federal Express St. Jude Classic

1993	29	112	27	1	4	6	15	70.67	$601,603

Best finish for 1993: Win at the H-E-B Texas Open

1994	29	102	24	0	3	5	14	70.36	$594,386

Best finish for 1994: T-3rd at the Buick Classic

1995	27	88	18	0	7	11	14	70.50	$822,259

Best finish for 1995: T-2nd at the Motorola Western Open

1996	26	89	21	0	2	4	11	70.48	$523,019

Best finish for 1996: 2nd at the LaCantera Texas Open

1997	24	80	18	0	3	4	11	70.86	$437,895

Best finish for 1997: T-5th at the U.S. Open, Sprint International & Buick Challenge

1998	25	79	17	0	1	4	7	71.15	$516,454

Best finish for 1998: T-2nd at the Westin Texas Open

1999	24	76	16	0	3	5	7	71.63	$696,861

Best finish for 1999: T-3rd at the Doral-Ryder Open & PGA Championship

2000	26	77	13	0	0	0	4	71.86	$265,755

Best finish for 2000: T-12th at the Nissan Open

2001	21	72	16	0	1	2	8	70.04	$566,141

Best finish for 2001: 4th at the B.C. Open

2002	24	79	18	0	1	1	9	70.65	$724,782

Best finish for 2002: T-4th at the Shell Houston Open

2003	25	83	19	0	7	8	13	70.30	$2,574,314

Best finish for 2003: T-2nd at the Bob Hope Chrysler Classic & The Players Championship

2004	23	79	20	0	2	8	11	70.37	$2,077,244

Best finish for 2004: 3rd at the Bob Hope Chrysler Classic

2005	16	51	12	0	0	1	5	71.90	$489,109

Best finish for 2005: T-9th at the WGC-Accenture Match Play Championship

2006	7	25	5	0	0	0	1	72.72	$163,398

Best finish for 2006: T-22nd at the Wachovia Championship

	Starts	Rounds Played	Cuts Made	Wins	Top-5s	Top-10s	Top-25s	Scoring Average	Money
2008	1	2	0	0	0	0	0	75.00	
Period Totals	806	2737	596	9	68	141	305	71.18	$14,496,182

Jerry Haas

Year	Starts	Rounds Played	Cuts Made	Wins	Top-5s	Top-10s	Top-25s	Scoring Average	Money
1985	2	6	1	0	0	0	0	74.83	

Best finish for 1985: T-31st at the Masters

1986	2	4	0	0	0	0	0	74.50	$600
1987	2	4	0	0	0	0	0	73.75	$600
1988	1	4	1	0	0	0	0	74.75	$3,691

Best finish for 1988: 65th at the U.S. Open

1990	31	89	13	0	0	1	3	72.21	$74,702

Best finish for 1990: T-10th at the Anheuser-Busch Golf Classic

1991	32	98	17	0	1	2	5	71.09	$103,104

Best finish for 1991: T-5th at the Deposit Guaranty Classic

1992	18	59	10	0	0	1	4	71.78	$60,794

Best finish for 1992: T-10th at the Hardee's Golf Classic

1993	3	7	0	0	0	0	0	75.71	
1995	29	82	13	0	0	0	4	71.49	$78,769

Best finish for 1995: T-18th at the Buick Classic & Canon Greater Hartford Open

2002	1	2	0	0	0	0	0	79.00	$1,000
2004	1	2	0	0	0	0	0	74.00	
2005	1	2	0	0	0	0	0	77.50	
2006	1	2	0	0	0	0	0	76.50	$2,250
Period Totals	124	361	55	0	1	4	16	71.96	$325,509

Dave Haberle

Year	Starts	Rounds Played	Cuts Made	Wins	Top-5s	Top-10s	Top-25s	Scoring Average	Money
1972	13	28	1	0	0	0	0	75.64	$200

Best finish for 1972: T-70th at the Greater New Orleans Open

1977	10	25	3	0	0	0	0	74.52	$962

Best finish for 1977: T-38th at the Greater Milwaukee Open

1978	2	8	1	0	0	0	0	75.75	$519

Best finish for 1978: T-56th at the Hawaiian Open

1981	1	2	0	0	0	0	0	74.50	$550

Period Totals	Starts	Rounds Played	Cuts Made	Wins	Top-5s	Top-10s	Top-25s	Scoring Average	Money
	26	63	5	0	0	0	0	75.17	$2,231

Mike Hadlock

Year	Starts	Rounds Played	Cuts Made	Wins	Top-5s	Top-10s	Top-25s	Scoring Average	Money
1967	4	10	1	0	0	0	0	75.50	

Best finish for 1967: T-52nd at the Memphis Open

1968	11	30	4	0	0	0	1	74.57	$305

Best finish for 1968: T-20th at the Magnolia State Classic

1969	3	8	1	0	0	0	0	73.88	$220

Best finish for 1969: T-47th at the Los Angeles Open

1974	2	6	1	0	0	0	0	74.33	$289

Best finish for 1974: T-66th at the Andy Williams-San Diego Open

1976	4	8	0	0	0	0	0	77.13	$500
1977	2	4	0	0	0	0	0	81.00	$500

Period Totals	Starts	Rounds Played	Cuts Made	Wins	Top-5s	Top-10s	Top-25s	Scoring Average	Money
	26	66	7	0	0	0	1	75.30	$1,814

Joe Hager

Year	Starts	Rounds Played	Cuts Made	Wins	Top-5s	Top-10s	Top-25s	Scoring Average	Money
1978	3	8	1	0	0	0	0	73.13	$602

Best finish for 1978: T-36th at the Pensacola Open

1979	23	74	13	0	0	0	2	72.88	$16,643

Best finish for 1979: T-15th at the Bay Hill Citrus Classic

1980	25	73	13	0	0	1	6	72.33	$28,474

Best finish for 1980: T-10th at the Greater Milwaukee Open

1981	24	62	9	0	0	1	2	73.27	$20,781

Best finish for 1981: T-7th at the World Disney World National Team Championship

1982	19	52	6	0	0	1	3	72.65	$17,322

Best finish for 1982: T-6th at the Joe Garagiola Tucson Open

1983	1	2	0	0	0	0	0	75.00	
1984	1	4	1	0	0	0	1	72.50	$5,718

Best finish for 1984: T-25th at the U.S. Open

1986	1	2	0	0	0	0	0	71.00	
1992	1	2	0	0	0	0	0	75.50	
1995	1	2	0	0	0	0	0	74.00	
1997	1	2	0	0	0	0	0	74.00	

Period Totals	Starts	Rounds Played	Cuts Made	Wins	Top-5s	Top-10s	Top-25s	Scoring Average	Money
	100	283	43	0	0	3	14	72.82	$89,540

Gary Hallberg

Year	Starts	Rounds Played	Cuts Made	Wins	Top-5s	Top-10s	Top-25s	Scoring Average	Money
1976	2	4	0	0	0	0	0	76.00	
1977	2	8	2	0	0	0	0	74.88	

Best finish for 1977: T-63rd at the Greater Greensboro Open

1978	3	7	1	0	0	0	0	76.71	

Best finish for 1978: T-47th at the Masters

1979	1	2	0	0	0	0	0	78.00	
1980	15	54	12	0	4	6	8	70.83	$75,844

Best finish for 1980: T-2nd at the Pensacola Open

1981	33	101	20	0	1	3	7	72.67	$49,383

Best finish for 1981: T-4th at the Wickes/Andy Williams San Diego Open

1982	31	93	16	0	0	2	4	72.72	$36,842

Best finish for 1982: T-6th at the Southern Open

1983	30	99	18	1	2	3	7	72.35	$120,170

Best finish for 1983: Win at the Isuzu/Andy Williams San Diego Open

1984	32	113	26	0	5	6	12	71.42	$187,885

Best finish for 1984: 2nd at the Isuzu/Andy Williams San Diego Open

1985	29	83	11	0	2	3	5	72.59	$109,472

Best finish for 1985: T-4th at the Tournament Players Championship & Buick Open

1986	32	96	17	0	0	1	5	72.20	$69,979

Best finish for 1986: T-6th at the Shearson Lehman/Andy Williams San Diego

1987	31	94	17	1	2	4	6	71.78	$206,353

Best finish for 1987: Win at the Greater Milwaukee Open

1988	24	64	7	0	0	0	1	73.88	$29,551

Best finish for 1988: T-19th at the Greater Milwaukee Open

1989	28	86	17	0	1	1	6	71.47	$146,833

Best finish for 1989: 3rd at the Centel Classic

1990	29	81	11	0	1	1	2	72.15	$128,954

Best finish for 1990: T-2nd at the H-E-B Texas Open

Year	Starts	Rounds Played	Cuts Made	Wins	Top-5s	Top-10s	Top-25s	Scoring Average	Money
1991	26	88	18	0	2	3	9	70.51	$284,010

Best finish for 1991: 2nd at the H-E-B Texas Open

1992	28	87	17	1	1	2	4	71.77	$236,630

Best finish for 1992: Win at the Buick Southern Open

1993	26	90	19	0	0	0	4	71.99	$147,706

Best finish for 1993: T-11th at the Phoenix Open

1994	27	78	14	0	1	2	7	72.26	$227,165

Best finish for 1994: T-5th at the Southwestern Bell Colonial

1995	28	78	11	0	0	0	3	72.45	$99,332

Best finish for 1995: T-14th at the Kmart Greater Greensboro Open

1996	19	35	1	0	0	0	0	74.63	$2,544

Best finish for 1996: T-63rd at the United Airlines Hawaiian Open

1997	13	37	7	0	0	0	1	72.22	$40,132

Best finish for 1997: T-20th at the LaCantera Texas Open

1998	20	61	12	0	0	1	4	71.16	$168,540

Best finish for 1998: T-6th at the Michelob Championship at Kingsmill

1999	15	33	4	0	1	1	1	73.24	$24,110

Best finish for 1999: T-42nd at the U.S. Open

2000	10	21	3	0	0	0	0	72.95	$19,212

Best finish for 2000: T-48th at the International presented by Quest

2001	9	19	2	0	0	0	0	72.26	$15,296

Best finish for 2001: T-53rd at the AT&T Pebble Beach

2002	3	7	0	0	0	0	0	74.14	
2003	8	20	3	0	0	0	0	73.65	$24,417

Best finish for 2003: T-47th at the AT&T Pebble Beach

2004	2	2	0	0	0	0	0	74.50	
2005	1	4	1	0	0	0	0	72.75	$7,160

Best finish for 2005: T-80th at the Michelin Championship at Las Vegas

2006	4	12	2	0	0	0	1	71.83	$35,692

Best finish for 2006: T-24th at the B.C. Open

2007	7	15	0	0	0	0	0	74.13	
Period Totals	Starts	Rounds Played	Cuts Made	Wins	Top-5s	Top-10s	Top-25s	Scoring Average	Money
	568	1672	289	3	23	39	97	72.22	$2,493,210

Dan Halldorson

Year	Starts	Rounds Played	Cuts Made	Wins	Top-5s	Top-10s	Top-25s	Scoring Average	Money
1974	2	6	0	0	0	0	0	74.67	
1975	9	22	2	0	0	0	0	75.27	$618

Best finish for 1975: T-60th at the B.C. Open

1976	3	8	1	0	0	0	0	73.13	$430

Best finish for 1976: T-52nd at the Canadian Open

1977	1	2	0	0	0	0	0	81.00	
1978	1	2	0	0	0	0	0	79.50	
1979	21	65	12	0	0	2	3	72.03	$24,559

Best finish for 1979: T-6th at the Hawaiian Open

1980	28	95	22	1	3	4	9	71.48	$126,753

Best finish for 1980: Win at the Pensacola Open

1981	27	81	15	0	3	5	7	71.83	$91,564

Best finish for 1981: T-2nd at the Quad Cities Open

1982	25	95	22	0	2	4	9	71.42	$93,705

Best finish for 1982: T-2nd at the Pensacola Open

1983	25	72	10	0	0	1	2	72.44	$21,558

Best finish for 1983: T-10th at the Manufactures Hanover Westchester Classic

1984	31	97	18	0	1	2	4	72.49	$55,815

Best finish for 1984: T-3rd at the LaJet Golf Classic

1985	27	89	19	0	3	3	6	71.85	$113,702

Best finish for 1985: T-4th at the Western Open

1986	26	77	13	1	1	2	4	71.71	$84,876

Best finish for 1986: Win at the Deposit Guaranty Golf Classic

1987	31	91	17	0	1	1	4	71.70	$69,094

Best finish for 1987: T-2nd at the Southwest Golf Classic

1988	30	97	18	0	0	0	4	71.56	$96,079

Best finish for 1988: T-11th at the Beatrice Western Open

1989	27	88	15	0	0	1	5	71.44	$86,607

Best finish for 1989: T-10th at the Canadian Open

1990	16	51	8	0	0	0	0	71.65	$18,155

Best finish for 1990: T-29th at the Buick Southern Open

1991	27	86	17	0	1	2	3	71.34	$159,743

Best finish for 1991: T-3rd at the Honda Classic

1992	30	86	14	0	0	2	5	71.48	$120,002

Best finish for 1992: T-10th at the Federal Express St. Jude Classic & Hardee's Golf Classic

Year	Starts	Rounds Played	Cuts Made	Wins	Top-5s	Top-10s	Top-25s	Scoring Average	Money
1993	29	77	9	0	0	0	0	72.91	$24,284

Best finish for 1993: T-31st at the Hardee's Golf Classic

1994	5	11	1	0	0	0	0	73.18	$7,215

Best finish for 1994: T-31st at the Bell Canadian Open

1995	3	6	0	0	0	0	0	76.17	
1996	6	12	1	0	0	0	0	71.92	$4,100

Best finish for 1996: T-37th at the Greater Vancouver Open

1997	4	8	0	0	0	0	0	74.13	
1998	6	18	3	0	0	0	0	72.44	$11,056

Best finish for 1998: T-52nd at the Greater Milwaukee Open

1999	1	2	0	0	0	0	0	71.00	
2000	4	8	0	0	0	0	0	73.88	
2001	2	4	0	0	0	0	0	76.25	
2003	5	11	1	0	0	0	0	74.36	$5,640

Best finish for 2003: 76th at the B.C. Open

2004	1	2	0	0	0	0	0	74.00	
Period Totals	Starts	Rounds Played	Cuts Made	Wins	Top-5s	Top-10s	Top-25s	Scoring Average	Money
	453	1369	238	2	15	29	65	72.01	$1,215,555

Jim Hallet

Year	Starts	Rounds Played	Cuts Made	Wins	Top-5s	Top-10s	Top-25s	Scoring Average	Money
1983	2	6	1	0	0	0	0	74.50	

Best finish for 1983: T-40th at the Masters

1984	4	16	4	0	0	0	1	71.19	$7,285

Best finish for 1984: T-15th at the Bank of Boston Classic

1985	6	22	5	0	0	0	1	71.23	$12,844

Best finish for 1985: T-11th at the Greater Milwaukee Open

1986	3	8	1	0	0	0	0	71.88	$1,105

Best finish for 1986: T-57th at the Buick Open

1987	4	10	1	0	0	0	1	74.70	$6,615

Best finish for 1987: T-21st at the PGA Championship

1988	34	114	23	0	2	4	9	71.17	$170,993

Best finish for 1988: T-5th at the Kemper Open & Buick Open

1989	35	111	22	0	0	2	8	71.54	$157,658

Best finish for 1989: T-6th at the Federal Express St. Jude Classic

1990	35	115	23	0	1	3	7	71.59	$204,060

Best finish for 1990: T-2nd at the Buick Southern Open

1991	31	107	24	0	2	3	9	70.89	$333,010

Best finish for 1991: 2nd at the USF&G Classic

1992	35	112	22	0	0	0	4	71.05	$135,064

Best finish for 1992: T-11th at the Honda Classic

1993	34	90	10	0	0	1	2	72.63	$81,367

Best finish for 1993: T-6th at the Anheuser-Busch Golf Classic

1995	3	8	1	0	0	0	0	71.50	$4,956

Best finish for 1995: T-33rd at the Ideon Classic

Period Totals	Starts	Rounds Played	Cuts Made	Wins	Top-5s	Top-10s	Top-25s	Scoring Average	Money
	226	719	137	0	5	13	42	71.51	$1,114,956

John Hamarik

Year	Starts	Rounds Played	Cuts Made	Wins	Top-5s	Top-10s	Top-25s	Scoring Average	Money
1984	24	59	4	0	0	0	1	74.15	$6,626

Best finish for 1984: T-22nd at the Canadian Open

1985	1	2	0	0	0	0	0	78.50	
Period Totals	Starts	Rounds Played	Cuts Made	Wins	Top-5s	Top-10s	Top-25s	Scoring Average	Money
	25	61	4	0	0	0	1	74.30	$6,626

Todd Hamilton

Year	Starts	Rounds Played	Cuts Made	Wins	Top-5s	Top-10s	Top-25s	Scoring Average	Money
1986	1	2	0	0	0	0	0	71.00	
1987	3	6	0	0	0	0	0	73.00	
1988	2	6	1	0	0	0	0	73.33	$2,074

Best finish for 1988: T-80th at the Hardee's Golf Classic

1992	2	4	0	0	0	0	0	75.25	$1,200
1993	1	2	0	0	0	0	0	72.00	
1994	1	0	0	0	0	0	0		
1996	1	4	1	0	0	0	0	71.25	$9,920

Best finish for 1996: T-44th at the British Open

2003	3	10	2	0	0	0	0	74.50	$66,574

Best finish for 2003: T-29th at the PGA Championship

2004	27	88	19	2	2	3	8	71.42	$3,064,778

Best finish for 2004: Win at the Honda Classic & British Open

2005	31	91	17	0	0	0	4	71.79	$565,875

Best finish for 2005: T-13th at the John Deere Classic

Year	Starts	Rounds Played	Cuts Made	Wins	Top-5s	Top-10s	Top-25s	Scoring Average	Money
2006	27	72	8	0	0	1	1	73.21	$174,402

Best finish for 2006: T-10th at the John Deere Classic

Year	Starts	Rounds Played	Cuts Made	Wins	Top-5s	Top-10s	Top-25s	Scoring Average	Money
2007	28	76	9	0	0	0	0	73.58	$116,092

Best finish for 2007: T-37th at the Reno-Tahoe Open

Year	Starts	Rounds Played	Cuts Made	Wins	Top-5s	Top-10s	Top-25s	Scoring Average	Money
2008	28	92	17	0	0	0	4	71.83	$537,958

Best finish for 2008: T-18th at the Ginn sur Mer Classic

Period Totals	Starts	Rounds Played	Cuts Made	Wins	Top-5s	Top-10s	Top-25s	Scoring Average	Money
	155	453	74	2	2	4	17	72.37	$4,538,874

Laurie Hammer

Year	Starts	Rounds Played	Cuts Made	Wins	Top-5s	Top-10s	Top-25s	Scoring Average	Money
1965	1	2	0	0	0	0	0	78.50	
1966	18	46	5	0	0	1	1	74.48	$1,617

Best finish for 1966: T-6th at the Portland Open Invitational

Year	Starts	Rounds Played	Cuts Made	Wins	Top-5s	Top-10s	Top-25s	Scoring Average	Money
1967	21	60	10	0	1	1	3	73.57	$5,205

Best finish for 1967: T-3rd at the Cajun Classic

Year	Starts	Rounds Played	Cuts Made	Wins	Top-5s	Top-10s	Top-25s	Scoring Average	Money
1968	30	89	15	0	0	0	2	73.26	$6,947

Best finish for 1968: T-16th at the Buick Open Invitational

Year	Starts	Rounds Played	Cuts Made	Wins	Top-5s	Top-10s	Top-25s	Scoring Average	Money
1969	20	59	9	0	0	1	1	73.22	$3,706

Best finish for 1969: 7th at the Indian Ridge Hospital Open

Year	Starts	Rounds Played	Cuts Made	Wins	Top-5s	Top-10s	Top-25s	Scoring Average	Money
1973	1	1	0	0	0	0	0	77.00	
1975	4	16	4	0	0	0	1	71.88	$2,595

Best finish for 1975: T-25th at the Pensacola Open

Year	Starts	Rounds Played	Cuts Made	Wins	Top-5s	Top-10s	Top-25s	Scoring Average	Money
1976	1	2	0	0	0	0	0	77.00	
1977	3	10	2	0	0	0	0	74.20	$1,159

Best finish for 1977: T-55th at the Jackie Gleason's Inverrary Classic

Year	Starts	Rounds Played	Cuts Made	Wins	Top-5s	Top-10s	Top-25s	Scoring Average	Money
1978	5	20	5	0	0	1	1	72.20	$6,149

Best finish for 1978: T-9th at the Sammy Davis, Jr. - Greater Hartford Open

Year	Starts	Rounds Played	Cuts Made	Wins	Top-5s	Top-10s	Top-25s	Scoring Average	Money
1979	3	6	0	0	0	0	0	75.00	
1980	1	0	0	0	0	0	0		
1981	2	2	0	0	0	0	0	74.50	$550
1984	1	2	0	0	0	0	0	74.50	$1,000
1985	1	2	0	0	0	0	0	77.00	$1,000
Period Totals	Starts	Rounds Played	Cuts Made	Wins	Top-5s	Top-10s	Top-25s	Scoring Average	Money
	112	317	50	0	1	4	9	73.52	$29,927

Donnie Hammond

Year	Starts	Rounds Played	Cuts Made	Wins	Top-5s	Top-10s	Top-25s	Scoring Average	Money
1981	2	2	0	0	0	0	0	78.50	$600
1982	1	2	0	0	0	0	0	76.50	$600
1983	28	96	19	0	0	0	5	72.17	$41,336

Best finish for 1983: T-14th at the Bing Crosby Pro-Am

Year	Starts	Rounds Played	Cuts Made	Wins	Top-5s	Top-10s	Top-25s	Scoring Average	Money
1984	27	96	22	0	0	0	5	71.82	$67,874

Best finish for 1984: 14th at the Byron Nelson Golf Classic

Year	Starts	Rounds Played	Cuts Made	Wins	Top-5s	Top-10s	Top-25s	Scoring Average	Money
1985	28	99	20	0	0	4	9	71.43	$102,719

Best finish for 1985: T-7th at the Anheuser-Busch Golf Classic

Year	Starts	Rounds Played	Cuts Made	Wins	Top-5s	Top-10s	Top-25s	Scoring Average	Money
1986	22	75	19	1	2	4	12	71.16	$258,052

Best finish for 1986: Win at the Bob Hope Chrysler Classic

Year	Starts	Rounds Played	Cuts Made	Wins	Top-5s	Top-10s	Top-25s	Scoring Average	Money
1987	26	85	17	0	1	5	7	71.51	$157,497

Best finish for 1987: T-4th at the Byron Nelson Golf Classic

Year	Starts	Rounds Played	Cuts Made	Wins	Top-5s	Top-10s	Top-25s	Scoring Average	Money
1988	28	100	23	0	1	6	10	70.66	$256,010

Best finish for 1988: T-2nd at the Greater Milwaukee Open

Year	Starts	Rounds Played	Cuts Made	Wins	Top-5s	Top-10s	Top-25s	Scoring Average	Money
1989	26	90	21	1	3	4	8	70.72	$459,741

Best finish for 1989: Win at the Texas Open

Year	Starts	Rounds Played	Cuts Made	Wins	Top-5s	Top-10s	Top-25s	Scoring Average	Money
1990	25	78	14	0	1	3	8	71.85	$192,631

Best finish for 1990: 4th at the NEC World Series of Golf

Year	Starts	Rounds Played	Cuts Made	Wins	Top-5s	Top-10s	Top-25s	Scoring Average	Money
1991	25	80	15	0	0	1	5	71.40	$109,782

Best finish for 1991: T-7th at the Independent Insurance Agent Open

Year	Starts	Rounds Played	Cuts Made	Wins	Top-5s	Top-10s	Top-25s	Scoring Average	Money
1992	22	70	14	0	2	3	6	70.90	$257,227

Best finish for 1992: T-2nd at the Canon Greater Hartford Open

Year	Starts	Rounds Played	Cuts Made	Wins	Top-5s	Top-10s	Top-25s	Scoring Average	Money
1993	24	85	20	0	2	3	10	70.87	$341,357

Best finish for 1993: T-2nd at the Nissan Los Angeles Open

Year	Starts	Rounds Played	Cuts Made	Wins	Top-5s	Top-10s	Top-25s	Scoring Average	Money
1994	25	83	19	0	1	3	10	70.45	$295,436

Best finish for 1994: 4th at the Memorial Tournament

Year	Starts	Rounds Played	Cuts Made	Wins	Top-5s	Top-10s	Top-25s	Scoring Average	Money
1995	24	80	17	0	0	1	4	70.89	$141,150

Best finish for 1995: T-7th at the Bob Hope Chrysler Classic

Year	Starts	Rounds Played	Cuts Made	Wins	Top-5s	Top-10s	Top-25s	Scoring Average	Money
1996	21	61	11	0	0	1	3	71.36	$98,455

Best finish for 1996: T-9th at the Michelob Championship at Kingsmill

Year	Starts	Rounds Played	Cuts Made	Wins	Top-5s	Top-10s	Top-25s	Scoring Average	Money
1997	21	68	12	0	2	2	5	71.40	$224,799

Best finish for 1997: T-2nd at the Buick Invitational

Year	Starts	Rounds Played	Cuts Made	Wins	Top-5s	Top-10s	Top-25s	Scoring Average	Money
1998	27	87	18	0	0	0	3	71.48	$141,843

Best finish for 1998: T-22nd at the Shell Houston Open

Year	Starts	Rounds Played	Cuts Made	Wins	Top-5s	Top-10s	Top-25s	Scoring Average	Money
1999	8	28	6	0	0	0	1	71.25	$68,952

Best finish for 1999: T-17th at the Greater Greensboro Chrysler Classic

Year	Starts	Rounds Played	Cuts Made	Wins	Top-5s	Top-10s	Top-25s	Scoring Average	Money
2000	6	18	2	0	0	1	2	70.78	$96,938

Best finish for 2000: T-10th at the Kemper Insurance Open

Year	Starts	Rounds Played	Cuts Made	Wins	Top-5s	Top-10s	Top-25s	Scoring Average	Money
2001	14	51	11	0	0	0	2	70.57	$153,698

Best finish for 2001: T-19th at the Greater Greensboro Chrysler Classic

Year	Starts	Rounds Played	Cuts Made	Wins	Top-5s	Top-10s	Top-25s	Scoring Average	Money
2002	17	60	12	0	0	1	4	70.43	$263,366

Best finish for 2002: T-9th at the Tampa Bay Classic presented by Buick

Year	Starts	Rounds Played	Cuts Made	Wins	Top-5s	Top-10s	Top-25s	Scoring Average	Money
2003	27	92	19	0	0	0	1	71.29	$255,384

Best finish for 2003: T-23rd at the BellSouth Classic

Year	Starts	Rounds Played	Cuts Made	Wins	Top-5s	Top-10s	Top-25s	Scoring Average	Money
2004	13	37	5	0	0	0	0	71.24	$65,024

Best finish for 2004: T-35th at the Wachovia Championship

Year	Starts	Rounds Played	Cuts Made	Wins	Top-5s	Top-10s	Top-25s	Scoring Average	Money
2005	3	10	1	0	0	0	0	69.80	$20,150

Best finish for 2005: T-35th at the Michelin Championship at Las Vegas

Year	Starts	Rounds Played	Cuts Made	Wins	Top-5s	Top-10s	Top-25s	Scoring Average	Money
2006	11	33	5	0	0	0	0	71.70	$52,693

Best finish for 2006: T-39th at the John Deere Classic

Year	Starts	Rounds Played	Cuts Made	Wins	Top-5s	Top-10s	Top-25s	Scoring Average	Money
2007	1	4	0	0	0	0	0	71.75	
Period Totals	Starts	Rounds Played	Cuts Made	Wins	Top-5s	Top-10s	Top-25s	Scoring Average	Money
	502	1670	342	2	15	42	120	71.22	$4,123,313

Mike Hammond

Year	Starts	Rounds Played	Cuts Made	Wins	Top-5s	Top-10s	Top-25s	Scoring Average	Money
1988	24	76	14	0	0	0	1	72.54	$23,195

Best finish for 1988: T-23rd at the B.C. Open

Year	Starts	Rounds Played	Cuts Made	Wins	Top-5s	Top-10s	Top-25s	Scoring Average	Money
1989	3	6	0	0	0	0	0	71.33	
Period Totals	Starts	Rounds Played	Cuts Made	Wins	Top-5s	Top-10s	Top-25s	Scoring Average	Money
	27	82	14	0	0	0	1	72.45	$23,195

Phil Hancock

Year	Starts	Rounds Played	Cuts Made	Wins	Top-5s	Top-10s	Top-25s	Scoring Average	Money
1974	1	2	0	0	0	0	0	77.50	$500
1976	3	8	1	0	0	0	0	74.38	$617

Best finish for 1976: T-35th at the Pensacola Open

Year	Starts	Rounds Played	Cuts Made	Wins	Top-5s	Top-10s	Top-25s	Scoring Average	Money
1977	16	54	11	0	1	2	6	71.39	$28,931

Best finish for 1977: T-2nd at the Southern Open

Year	Starts	Rounds Played	Cuts Made	Wins	Top-5s	Top-10s	Top-25s	Scoring Average	Money
1978	30	102	22	0	2	3	10	71.97	$66,460

Best finish for 1978: 2nd at the Southern Open

Year	Starts	Rounds Played	Cuts Made	Wins	Top-5s	Top-10s	Top-25s	Scoring Average	Money
1979	25	78	14	0	1	2	2	72.58	$38,566

Best finish for 1979: 4th at the Tournament Players Championship

Year	Starts	Rounds Played	Cuts Made	Wins	Top-5s	Top-10s	Top-25s	Scoring Average	Money
1980	29	89	18	1	2	3	8	71.99	$108,569

Best finish for 1980: Win at the Hall of Fame Tournament

Year	Starts	Rounds Played	Cuts Made	Wins	Top-5s	Top-10s	Top-25s	Scoring Average	Money
1981	31	77	11	0	0	2	2	73.57	$25,406

Best finish for 1981: T-9th at the Bay Hill Classic

Year	Starts	Rounds Played	Cuts Made	Wins	Top-5s	Top-10s	Top-25s	Scoring Average	Money
1982	25	83	17	0	0	1	2	72.01	$35,386

Best finish for 1982: T-6th at the Byron Nelson Golf Classic

Year	Starts	Rounds Played	Cuts Made	Wins	Top-5s	Top-10s	Top-25s	Scoring Average	Money
1983	28	97	21	0	0	2	5	72.20	$55,888

Best finish for 1983: T-7th at the Greater Greensboro Open

Year	Starts	Rounds Played	Cuts Made	Wins	Top-5s	Top-10s	Top-25s	Scoring Average	Money
1984	27	81	12	0	0	1	4	72.78	$51,938

Best finish for 1984: T-10th at the Honda Classic

Year	Starts	Rounds Played	Cuts Made	Wins	Top-5s	Top-10s	Top-25s	Scoring Average	Money
1985	28	66	5	0	0	0	0	73.27	$8,579

Best finish for 1985: T-27th at the Honda Classic

Year	Starts	Rounds Played	Cuts Made	Wins	Top-5s	Top-10s	Top-25s	Scoring Average	Money
1986	13	33	4	0	0	0	0	72.88	$5,674

Best finish for 1986: T-36th at the Federal Express St. Jude Classic

Year	Starts	Rounds Played	Cuts Made	Wins	Top-5s	Top-10s	Top-25s	Scoring Average	Money
1987	7	22	4	0	0	0	1	70.86	$5,882

Best finish for 1987: T-24th at the Deposit Guaranty Golf Classic

Year	Starts	Rounds Played	Cuts Made	Wins	Top-5s	Top-10s	Top-25s	Scoring Average	Money
1988	7	20	3	0	0	0	0	71.90	$4,416

Best finish for 1988: T-43rd at the Provident Classic

Year	Starts	Rounds Played	Cuts Made	Wins	Top-5s	Top-10s	Top-25s	Scoring Average	Money
1989	2	4	0	0	0	0	0	70.75	
1990	1	2	0	0	0	0	0	78.50	$1,000
Period Totals	Starts	Rounds Played	Cuts Made	Wins	Top-5s	Top-10s	Top-25s	Scoring Average	Money
	273	818	143	1	6	16	40	72.41	$437,812

Dick Hanscom

Year	Starts	Rounds Played	Cuts Made	Wins	Top-5s	Top-10s	Top-25s	Scoring Average	Money
1964	1	2	0	0	0	0	0	72.50	
1967	3	6	0	0	0	0	0	75.67	
1968	17	43	4	0	0	0	1	74.26	$390

Best finish for 1968: 19th at the Magnolia State Classic

Year	Starts	Rounds Played	Cuts Made	Wins	Top-5s	Top-10s	Top-25s	Scoring Average	Money
1969	2	8	2	0	0	0	1	72.50	$762

Best finish for 1969: T-17th at the Indian Ridge Hospital Open

Year	Starts	Rounds Played	Cuts Made	Wins	Top-5s	Top-10s	Top-25s	Scoring Average	Money
1970	1	2	0	0	0	0	0	76.50	
1971	1	2	0	0	0	0	0	75.50	
1972	1	2	0	0	0	0	0	75.00	
1973	1	2	0	0	0	0	0	73.50	
1974	2	6	1	0	0	0	0	73.67	$405

Best finish for 1974: T-58th at the Pleasant Valley Classic

Year	Starts	Rounds Played	Cuts Made	Wins	Top-5s	Top-10s	Top-25s	Scoring Average	Money
1975	1	2	0	0	0	0	0	75.00	
1976	1	2	0	0	0	0	0	78.50	
1979	1	2	0	0	0	0	0	75.00	
Period Totals	Starts	Rounds Played	Cuts Made	Wins	Top-5s	Top-10s	Top-25s	Scoring Average	Money
	32	79	7	0	0	0	2	74.33	$1,557

Anders Hansen

Year	Starts	Rounds Played	Cuts Made	Wins	Top-5s	Top-10s	Top-25s	Scoring Average	Money
1999	1	2	0	0	0	0	0	83.00	$1,250
2002	4	14	3	0	0	0	0	73.14	$73,432

Best finish for 2002: T-57th at the American Express Championship

| 2003 | 3 | 4 | 1 | 0 | 0 | 0 | 0 | 76.50 | $36,769 |

Best finish for 2003: T-33rd at the WGC-Accenture Match Play Championship

| 2004 | 1 | 2 | 0 | 0 | 0 | 0 | 0 | 75.00 | $4,213 |
| 2006 | 1 | 4 | 1 | 0 | 0 | 0 | 1 | 71.00 | $53,100 |

Best finish for 2006: T-24th at the PGA Championship

| 2007 | 17 | 55 | 10 | 0 | 0 | 0 | 4 | 71.64 | $461,216 |

Best finish for 2007: T-11th at the Wyndham Championship

| 2008 | 6 | 16 | 4 | 0 | 0 | 0 | 2 | 72.63 | $251,892 |

Best finish for 2008: T-12th at the WGC-CA Championship

Period Totals	Starts	Rounds Played	Cuts Made	Wins	Top-5s	Top-10s	Top-25s	Scoring Average	Money
	33	97	19	0	0	0	7	72.49	$881,871

Matt Hansen

Year	Starts	Rounds Played	Cuts Made	Wins	Top-5s	Top-10s	Top-25s	Scoring Average	Money
2006	25	66	9	0	0	0	1	71.77	$187,252

Best finish for 2006: T-18th at the Deutsche Bank Championship

Period Totals	Starts	Rounds Played	Cuts Made	Wins	Top-5s	Top-10s	Top-25s	Scoring Average	Money
	25	66	9	0	0	0	1	71.77	$187,252

Chick Harbert

Year	Starts	Rounds Played	Cuts Made	Wins	Top-5s	Top-10s	Top-25s	Scoring Average	Money
1958	20	74	17	0	2	4	11	72.27	$9,714

Best finish for 1958: T-2nd at the Kentucky Derby Open & Mayfair Inn Open

| 1959 | 7 | 28 | 7 | 0 | 2 | 3 | 5 | 71.50 | $6,360 |

Best finish for 1959: T-4th at the West Palm Beach Open Invitational

| 1960 | 10 | 40 | 10 | 0 | 0 | 2 | 4 | 72.70 | $4,215 |

Best finish for 1960: T-7th at the Insurance City Open Invitational

| 1961 | 5 | 20 | 5 | 0 | 0 | 0 | 1 | 72.90 | $1,895 |

Best finish for 1961: T-13th at the Coral Gables Open Invitational

| 1962 | 3 | 12 | 3 | 0 | 0 | 0 | 1 | 72.50 | $1,972 |

Best finish for 1962: T-11th at the PGA Championship

| 1963 | 4 | 10 | 2 | 0 | 0 | 0 | 1 | 75.80 | $1,675 |

Best finish for 1963: T-20th at the Doral Country Club Open Invitational

| 1964 | 5 | 16 | 3 | 0 | 0 | 1 | 1 | 74.06 | $2,502 |

Best finish for 1964: 8th at the Doral Open

| 1965 | 3 | 10 | 2 | 0 | 0 | 0 | 0 | 73.20 | $496 |

Best finish for 1965: T-42nd at the Canadian Open

| 1966 | 3 | 8 | 1 | 0 | 0 | 0 | 0 | 75.13 | $300 |

Best finish for 1966: 51st at the Doral Open Invitational

| 1967 | 3 | 10 | 2 | 0 | 0 | 0 | 0 | 74.00 | $988 |

Best finish for 1967: T-27th at the Doral Open

| 1968 | 1 | 4 | 1 | 0 | 0 | 0 | 0 | 74.00 | |

Best finish for 1968: T-70th at the Doral Open Invitational

1969	1	2	0	0	0	0	0	77.00	
1971	1	0	0	0	0	0	0		
1973	1	1	0	0	0	0	0	82.00	
1975	1	2	0	0	0	0	0	77.00	
Period Totals	Starts	Rounds Played	Cuts Made	Wins	Top-5s	Top-10s	Top-25s	Scoring Average	Money
	68	237	53	0	4	10	24	72.95	$30,117

PGA Tour career totals from 1937 to 1975

	Starts	Rounds Played	Cuts Made	Wins	Top-5s	Top-10s	Top-25s	Scoring Average	Money
	244	N/A	N/A	6	N/A	80	227	N/A	N/A

Jack Harden, Jr.

Year	Starts	Rounds Played	Cuts Made	Wins	Top-5s	Top-10s	Top-25s	Scoring Average	Money
1968	3	10	2	0	0	0	0	74.60	

Best finish for 1968: T-46th at the Kemper Open Invitational

1969	14	37	4	0	0	0	1	74.14	$1,292

Best finish for 1969: T-25th at the Greater New Orleans Open

1970	15	40	4	0	0	0	0	74.25	$1,093

Best finish for 1970: T-34th at the IVB Philadelphia Golf Classic

1971	12	31	3	0	0	0	0	74.03	$917

Best finish for 1971: T-39th at the Atlanta Classic

1972	5	12	1	0	0	0	0	74.08	$200

Best finish for 1972: T-57th at the Greater New Orleans Open

Period Totals	Starts	Rounds Played	Cuts Made	Wins	Top-5s	Top-10s	Top-25s	Scoring Average	Money
	49	130	14	0	0	0	1	74.18	$3,502

Gary Hardin

Year	Starts	Rounds Played	Cuts Made	Wins	Top-5s	Top-10s	Top-25s	Scoring Average	Money
1977	6	15	2	0	0	0	0	76.53	

Best finish for 1977: 76th at the Atlanta Classic

1980	12	26	2	0	0	0	0	72.92	$981

Best finish for 1980: T-56th at the Southern Open

1981	7	18	2	0	0	0	0	73.78	$1,111

Best finish for 1981: T-53rd at the USF&G New Orleans Open

1986	1	2	0	0	0	0	0	75.00	$1,000

Period Totals	Starts	Rounds Played	Cuts Made	Wins	Top-5s	Top-10s	Top-25s	Scoring Average	Money
	26	61	6	0	0	0	0	74.13	$3,092

Jim Hardy

Year	Starts	Rounds Played	Cuts Made	Wins	Top-5s	Top-10s	Top-25s	Scoring Average	Money
1969	16	38	4	0	0	0	0	74.11	$770

Best finish for 1969: T-37th at the Minnesota Classic

1970	4	10	1	0	0	0	0	75.70	$152

Best finish for 1970: 80th at the Greater Milwaukee Open

1971	14	36	3	0	0	0	0	74.42	$1,784

Best finish for 1971: T-28th at the IVB Philadelphia Golf Classic

1972	18	53	8	0	0	0	2	74.06	$4,615

Best finish for 1972: T-19th at the Robinson's Fall Golf Classic

1973	21	58	6	0	0	0	1	74.09	$2,708

Best finish for 1973: T-22nd at the Phoenix Open

1974	3	9	2	0	0	0	1	72.67	$1,385

Best finish for 1974: T-24th at the Phoenix Open

1975	7	17	3	0	0	0	0	74.82	$1,336

Best finish for 1975: T-36th at the Dean Martin Tucson Open

Period Totals	Starts	Rounds Played	Cuts Made	Wins	Top-5s	Top-10s	Top-25s	Scoring Average	Money
	83	221	27	0	0	0	4	74.21	$12,749

Claude Harmon

Year	Starts	Rounds Played	Cuts Made	Wins	Top-5s	Top-10s	Top-25s	Scoring Average	Money
1958	12	42	9	0	0	1	3	73.90	$2,588

Best finish for 1958: T-9th at the Masters

1959	3	10	2	0	1	1	1	72.70	$4,100

Best finish for 1959: T-3rd at the U.S. Open

1960	4	15	4	0	0	0	1	74.20	$1,547

Best finish for 1960: T-16th at the Masters

1961	2	4	1	0	0	0	0	76.75	$400

Best finish for 1961: T-200 at the PGA Championship

1962	4	10	2	0	0	0	0	76.10	$785

Best finish for 1962: T-44th at the PGA Championship

1963	1	1	0	0	0	0	0	82.00	$500
1964	5	14	0	0	0	0	0	77.43	
1965	1	2	0	0	0	0	0	76.50	
1966	1	0	0	0	0	0	0		$1,008
1967	2	1	0	0	0	0	0	80.00	
1968	2	2	0	0	0	0	0	80.50	$1,000
1969	16	41	6	0	0	0	0	74.41	$2,166

Best finish for 1969: T-33rd at the AVCO Classic

Period Totals	Starts	Rounds Played	Cuts Made	Wins	Top-5s	Top-10s	Top-25s	Scoring Average	Money
	53	142	24	0	1	2	5	74.81	$14,094

PGA Tour career totals from 1933 to 1969

	Starts	Rounds Played	Cuts Made	Wins	Top-5s	Top-10s	Top-25s	Scoring Average	Money
	135	N/A	N/A	1	N/A	30	67	N/A	N/A

Butch Harmon

Year	Starts	Rounds Played	Cuts Made	Wins	Top-5s	Top-10s	Top-25s	Scoring Average	Money
1970	18	56	9	0	0	0	0	73.64	$3,832

Best finish for 1970: T-27th at the San Antonio Texas Open

| 1971 | 13 | 33 | 2 | 0 | 0 | 0 | 0 | 74.67 | $659 |

Best finish for 1971: T-39th at the Atlanta Classic

| 1974 | 2 | 8 | 1 | 0 | 0 | 0 | 0 | 73.13 | $338 |

Best finish for 1974: T-53rd at the B.C. Open

| 1975 | 1 | 2 | 0 | 0 | 0 | 0 | 0 | 76.00 | $500 |
| 1981 | 1 | 4 | 1 | 0 | 0 | 0 | 0 | 72.50 | $344 |

Best finish for 1981: T-84th at the Quad Cities Open

1983	1	2	0	0	0	0	0	73.50	
Period Totals	Starts	Rounds Played	Cuts Made	Wins	Top-5s	Top-10s	Top-25s	Scoring Average	Money
	36	105	13	0	0	0	0	73.92	$5,673

Paul Harney

Year	Starts	Rounds Played	Cuts Made	Wins	Top-5s	Top-10s	Top-25s	Scoring Average	Money
1958	26	96	22	0	2	5	18	71.47	$12,019

Best finish for 1958: T-4th at the Memphis Invitational

| 1959 | 28 | 112 | 26 | 1 | 5 | 11 | 22 | 70.67 | $22,247 |

Best finish for 1959: Win at the Pensacola Open Invitational

| 1960 | 23 | 93 | 20 | 0 | 3 | 6 | 18 | 70.81 | $17,006 |

Best finish for 1960: T-2nd at the Carling Open Invitational & Portland Open Invitational

| 1961 | 23 | 93 | 20 | 0 | 4 | 8 | 18 | 70.83 | $25,541 |

Best finish for 1961: T-3rd at the Texas Open Invitational & Carling Open Invitational

| 1962 | 25 | 100 | 24 | 0 | 2 | 8 | 18 | 71.47 | $21,875 |

Best finish for 1962: T-4th at the Pensacola Open Invitational

| 1963 | 9 | 36 | 8 | 0 | 3 | 4 | 6 | 71.86 | $22,477 |

Best finish for 1963: T-2nd at the Thunderbird Classic Invitational

| 1964 | 10 | 38 | 9 | 1 | 3 | 4 | 7 | 72.11 | $18,091 |

Best finish for 1964: Win at the Los Angles Open

| 1965 | 9 | 32 | 8 | 1 | 1 | 1 | 3 | 71.94 | $18,616 |

Best finish for 1965: Win at the Los Angles Open

| 1966 | 11 | 35 | 5 | 0 | 1 | 3 | 5 | 72.34 | $13,870 |

Best finish for 1966: T-2nd at the Los Angles Open Invitational

| 1967 | 13 | 50 | 11 | 0 | 1 | 3 | 5 | 72.00 | $16,513 |

Best finish for 1967: T-4th at the Bob Hope Classic

| 1968 | 9 | 35 | 8 | 0 | 0 | 1 | 2 | 72.14 | $10,355 |

Best finish for 1968: T-7th at the Andy Williams-San Diego Open Invitational

| 1969 | 14 | 53 | 13 | 0 | 0 | 0 | 5 | 71.66 | $10,230 |

Best finish for 1969: T-14th at the Westchester Classic

| 1970 | 15 | 59 | 14 | 0 | 2 | 4 | 10 | 71.03 | $39,178 |

Best finish for 1970: 2nd at the Greater Hartford Open Invitational

| 1971 | 14 | 55 | 13 | 0 | 1 | 2 | 7 | 71.38 | $21,150 |

Best finish for 1971: T-3rd at the Andy Williams-San Diego Open

| 1972 | 14 | 52 | 12 | 1 | 1 | 2 | 7 | 71.92 | $49,018 |

Best finish for 1972: Win at the Andy Williams-San Diego Open

| 1973 | 11 | 44 | 10 | 0 | 1 | 1 | 4 | 72.20 | $15,588 |

Best finish for 1973: T-4th at the Phoenix Open

1974	1	2	0	0	0	0	0	76.50	$1,200
1975	1	3	0	0	0	0	0	74.67	
1977	2	6	0	0	0	0	0	73.50	
Period Totals	Starts	Rounds Played	Cuts Made	Wins	Top-5s	Top-10s	Top-25s	Scoring Average	Money
	258	994	223	4	30	63	155	71.46	$334,973

PGA Tour career totals from 1944 to 1977

	Starts	Rounds Played	Cuts Made	Wins	Top-5s	Top-10s	Top-25s	Scoring Average	Money
	335	1292	296	7	33	80	194	N/A	$366,476

Chandler Harper

Year	Starts	Rounds Played	Cuts Made	Wins	Top-5s	Top-10s	Top-25s	Scoring Average	Money
1958	5	9	0	0	0	0	0	77.11	$300
1959	4	14	3	0	1	1	2	72.21	$2,689

Best finish for 1959: T-4th at the Pensacola Open Invitational

| 1960 | 6 | 20 | 5 | 0 | 0 | 0 | 1 | 72.90 | $927 |

Best finish for 1960: T-24th at the Pensacola Open Invitational

| 1961 | 3 | 9 | 2 | 0 | 0 | 0 | 1 | 70.67 | $1,397 |

Best finish for 1961: T-12th at the Pensacola Open Invitational

Year	Starts	Rounds Played	Cuts Made	Wins	Top-5s	Top-10s	Top-25s	Scoring Average	Money
1962	4	15	4	0	0	0	0	73.00	$1,083

Best finish for 1962: T-26th at the Texas Open Invitational

1963	1	4	1	0	0	0	0	71.00	$135

Best finish for 1963: T-29th at the Pensacola Open Invitational

| 1964 | 1 | 4 | 1 | 0 | 0 | 0 | 0 | 72.25 | |

Best finish for 1964: T-54th at the Texas Open

| 1965 | 2 | 6 | 1 | 0 | 0 | 0 | 0 | 73.17 | $200 |

Best finish for 1965: T-58th at the Western Open

1967	1	0	0	0	0	0	0		
1970	1	2	0	0	0	0	0	77.00	
1971	1	3	0	0	0	0	0	76.33	
Period Totals	Starts	Rounds Played	Cuts Made	Wins	Top-5s	Top-10s	Top-25s	Scoring Average	Money
	29	86	17	0	1	1	4	73.13	$6,731

PGA Tour career totals from 1933 to 1971

	Starts	Rounds Played	Cuts Made	Wins	Top-5s	Top-10s	Top-25s	Scoring Average	Money
	231	N/A	N/A	7	N/A	60	141	N/A	N/A

Dennis Harrington

Year	Starts	Rounds Played	Cuts Made	Wins	Top-5s	Top-10s	Top-25s	Scoring Average	Money
1990	28	75	10	0	0	0	0	72.72	$19,215

Best finish for 1990: T-53rd at the B.C. Open

| 1991 | 2 | 6 | 1 | 0 | 0 | 0 | 0 | 70.67 | $2,328 |

Best finish for 1991: T-51st at the Federal Express St. Jude Classic

| 1993 | 1 | 2 | 0 | 0 | 0 | 0 | 0 | 73.00 | |
| 1996 | 1 | 4 | 1 | 0 | 0 | 0 | 0 | 72.75 | $5,825 |

Best finish for 1996: T-60th at the U.S. Open

| Period Totals | Starts | Rounds Played | Cuts Made | Wins | Top-5s | Top-10s | Top-25s | Scoring Average | Money |
| | 32 | 87 | 12 | 0 | 0 | 0 | 0 | 72.59 | $27,367 |

Padraig Harrington

Year	Starts	Rounds Played	Cuts Made	Wins	Top-5s	Top-10s	Top-25s	Scoring Average	Money
1996	1	4	1	0	0	0	1	70.00	$24,025

Best finish for 1996: T-18th at the British Open

| 1997 | 3 | 8 | 1 | 0 | 1 | 1 | 1 | 72.50 | $107,019 |

Best finish for 1997: T-5th at the British Open

| 1998 | 3 | 10 | 2 | 0 | 0 | 0 | 0 | 73.70 | $24,668 |

Best finish for 1998: T-32nd at the U.S. Open

| 1999 | 4 | 16 | 4 | 0 | 0 | 0 | 2 | 71.81 | $198,241 |

Best finish for 1999: T-12th at the WGC-NEC Invitational & B.C. Open

| 2000 | 8 | 26 | 7 | 0 | 2 | 2 | 4 | 71.65 | $491,813 |

Best finish for 2000: T-5th at the U.S. Open & American Express Championship

| 2001 | 9 | 30 | 8 | 0 | 0 | 1 | 2 | 71.07 | $350,426 |

Best finish for 2001: T-6th at the Buick Open

| 2002 | 9 | 32 | 9 | 0 | 2 | 4 | 7 | 70.91 | $924,847 |

Best finish for 2002: T-5th at the Masters & British Open

| 2003 | 11 | 36 | 9 | 0 | 1 | 3 | 7 | 71.22 | $1,244,235 |

Best finish for 2003: T-2nd at the Players Championship

| 2004 | 12 | 42 | 11 | 0 | 4 | 5 | 7 | 71.17 | $2,338,958 |

Best finish for 2004: T-2nd at the Players Championship & Buick Classic

| 2005 | 15 | 48 | 11 | 2 | 2 | 4 | 6 | 71.52 | $2,624,731 |

Best finish for 2005: Win at the Honda Classic & Barclays Classic

| 2006 | 15 | 50 | 12 | 0 | 3 | 3 | 6 | 70.92 | $1,343,136 |

Best finish for 2006: T-2nd at the Booz Allen Classic

| 2007 | 18 | 62 | 15 | 1 | 1 | 3 | 9 | 71.05 | $2,660,283 |

Best finish for 2007: Win at the British Open

| 2008 | 15 | 50 | 12 | 2 | 6 | 6 | 9 | 70.70 | $4,313,551 |

Best finish for 2008: Win at the British Open & PGA Championship

| Period Totals | Starts | Rounds Played | Cuts Made | Wins | Top-5s | Top-10s | Top-25s | Scoring Average | Money |
| | 123 | 414 | 102 | 5 | 22 | 32 | 61 | 71.21 | $16,645,931 |

Bob Harris

Year	Starts	Rounds Played	Cuts Made	Wins	Top-5s	Top-10s	Top-25s	Scoring Average	Money
1958	7	28	7	0	0	2	5	70.96	$3,728

Best finish for 1958: T-7th at the Bing Crosby Pro-Am

| 1959 | 5 | 18 | 3 | 0 | 0 | 1 | 2 | 71.72 | $1,310 |

Best finish for 1959: T-7th at the San Diego Open Invitational

| 1960 | 8 | 31 | 7 | 0 | 1 | 1 | 4 | 71.68 | $4,082 |

Best finish for 1960: T-2nd at the Tucson Open Invitational

| 1961 | 4 | 12 | 3 | 0 | 0 | 0 | 0 | 74.33 | $1,350 |

Best finish for 1961: T-26th at the "500" Festival Open Invitational

| 1962 | 4 | 16 | 4 | 0 | 0 | 0 | 0 | 72.75 | $1,243 |

Best finish for 1962: T-29th at the Western Open Championship

Year	Starts	Rounds Played	Cuts Made	Wins	Top-5s	Top-10s	Top-25s	Scoring Average	Money
1963	4	16	4	0	0	0	2	73.25	$2,860

Best finish for 1963: T-11th at the Western Open Championship

| 1965 | 6 | 20 | 3 | 0 | 0 | 0 | 2 | 72.70 | $1,980 |

Best finish for 1965: T-13th at the Bing Crosby Pro-Am

| 1966 | 2 | 5 | 0 | 0 | 0 | 0 | 0 | 78.40 | |
| 1967 | 2 | 6 | 1 | 0 | 0 | 1 | 1 | 71.50 | $1,635 |

Best finish for 1967: T-8th at the Tucson Open

1968	1	2	0	0	0	0	0	77.50	$500
Period Totals	Starts	Rounds Played	Cuts Made	Wins	Top-5s	Top-10s	Top-25s	Scoring Average	Money
	43	154	32	0	1	5	16	72.45	$18,688

John Harris

Year	Starts	Rounds Played	Cuts Made	Wins	Top-5s	Top-10s	Top-25s	Scoring Average	Money
1968	1	2	0	0	0	0	0	75.00	
1976	18	45	6	0	0	0	0	74.87	$2,347

Best finish for 1976: T-26th at the Hawaiian Open

| 1977 | 1 | 2 | 0 | 0 | 0 | 0 | 0 | 77.00 | $500 |
| 1994 | 5 | 16 | 3 | 0 | 0 | 0 | 0 | 73.56 | |

Best finish for 1994: T-50th at the Masters & Southwestern Bell Colonial

1996	1	2	0	0	0	0	0	75.50	
2001	1	2	0	0	0	0	0	76.50	
Period Totals	Starts	Rounds Played	Cuts Made	Wins	Top-5s	Top-10s	Top-25s	Scoring Average	Money
	27	69	9	0	0	0	0	74.70	$2,847

Labron Harris, Jr.

Year	Starts	Rounds Played	Cuts Made	Wins	Top-5s	Top-10s	Top-25s	Scoring Average	Money
1960	1	2	0	0	0	0	0	75.50	
1961	1	2	1	0	0	0	0	77.00	

Best finish for 1961: T-200 at the PGA Championship

| 1962 | 1 | 2 | 0 | 0 | 0 | 0 | 0 | 77.50 | |
| 1963 | 4 | 14 | 3 | 0 | 0 | 0 | 1 | 74.36 | |

Best finish for 1963: T-25th at the Waco Turner Open Invitational

| 1964 | 19 | 66 | 13 | 0 | 1 | 2 | 5 | 72.39 | $7,738 |

Best finish for 1964: T-5th at the St. Paul Open

| 1965 | 20 | 60 | 10 | 0 | 1 | 1 | 5 | 73.38 | $7,674 |

Best finish for 1965: 5th at the Greater Greensboro Open

| 1966 | 10 | 32 | 6 | 0 | 0 | 1 | 2 | 72.91 | $5,932 |

Best finish for 1966: T-8th at the Cleveland Open Invitational

| 1967 | 26 | 92 | 19 | 0 | 0 | 1 | 6 | 72.80 | $14,551 |

Best finish for 1967: T-6th at the Memphis Open

| 1968 | 27 | 88 | 17 | 0 | 1 | 1 | 4 | 72.33 | $18,578 |

Best finish for 1968: 2nd at the Philadelphia Golf Classic

| 1969 | 33 | 112 | 22 | 0 | 1 | 2 | 5 | 72.71 | $13,760 |

Best finish for 1969: T-4th at the Minnesota Classic

| 1970 | 30 | 104 | 21 | 0 | 2 | 3 | 6 | 72.17 | $52,661 |

Best finish for 1970: 2nd at the Dow Jones Open Invitational

| 1971 | 34 | 114 | 23 | 1 | 1 | 2 | 9 | 72.31 | $41,553 |

Best finish for 1971: Win at the Robinson Open Golf Classic

| 1972 | 37 | 120 | 23 | 0 | 3 | 5 | 12 | 72.23 | $57,971 |

Best finish for 1972: 2nd at the Western Open

| 1973 | 35 | 119 | 24 | 0 | 1 | 3 | 10 | 72.29 | $34,752 |

Best finish for 1973: T-2nd at the Dean Martin Tucson Open

| 1974 | 33 | 99 | 16 | 0 | 0 | 2 | 4 | 72.90 | $17,461 |

Best finish for 1974: T-8th at the Greater Jacksonville Open

| 1975 | 22 | 66 | 11 | 0 | 0 | 0 | 0 | 73.83 | $4,939 |

Best finish for 1975: T-30th at the Bing Crosby Pro-Am

| 1976 | 14 | 40 | 5 | 0 | 0 | 0 | 0 | 74.30 | $1,208 |

Best finish for 1976: T-53rd at the Sammy Davis, Jr. - Greater Hartford Open

Period Totals	Starts	Rounds Played	Cuts Made	Wins	Top-5s	Top-10s	Top-25s	Scoring Average	Money
	347	1132	214	1	11	23	69	72.70	$278,778

Bob Harrison

Year	Starts	Rounds Played	Cuts Made	Wins	Top-5s	Top-10s	Top-25s	Scoring Average	Money
1961	6	24	5	0	1	2	4	70.58	$3,005

Best finish for 1961: T-4th at the Portland Open Invitational

| 1962 | 10 | 39 | 8 | 0 | 1 | 1 | 6 | 71.28 | $4,970 |

Best finish for 1962: T-4th at the Seattle World's Fair Open Invitational

| 1963 | 14 | 56 | 14 | 0 | 0 | 0 | 2 | 71.91 | $4,623 |

Best finish for 1963: T-15th at the Azalea Open Invitational

| 1964 | 29 | 83 | 11 | 0 | 0 | 0 | 4 | 73.60 | $4,339 |

Best finish for 1964: T-13th at the Canadian Open

Year	Starts	Rounds Played	Cuts Made	Wins	Top-5s	Top-10s	Top-25s	Scoring Average	Money
1965	6	17	3	0	0	0	0	74.12	$500

Best finish for 1965: T-28th at the Bing Crosby Pro-Am

Year	Starts	Rounds Played	Cuts Made	Wins	Top-5s	Top-10s	Top-25s	Scoring Average	Money
1966	1	2	0	0	0	0	0	78.00	
1967	3	8	0	0	0	0	0	77.25	
1968	2	4	0	0	0	0	0	78.75	
1969	1	2	0	0	0	0	0	78.00	
1970	1	2	0	0	0	0	0	77.50	
1971	2	6	0	0	0	0	0	77.50	
1972	1	2	0	0	0	0	0	78.50	
1973	1	2	0	0	0	0	0	80.00	
1974	1	2	0	0	0	0	0	81.50	
1975	1	2	0	0	0	0	0	80.00	
1977	1	2	0	0	0	0	0	77.50	
Period Totals	Starts	Rounds Played	Cuts Made	Wins	Top-5s	Top-10s	Top-25s	Scoring Average	Money
	80	253	41	0	2	3	16	73.24	$17,437

Dutch Harrison

Year	Starts	Rounds Played	Cuts Made	Wins	Top-5s	Top-10s	Top-25s	Scoring Average	Money
1958	13	50	12	1	2	2	5	72.10	$6,693

Best finish for 1958: Win at the Tijuana Open

1959	8	32	6	0	2	4	5	70.66	$5,612

Best finish for 1959: T-3rd at the Sam Snead Festival & Kansas City Open Invitational

1960	5	21	5	0	2	2	5	70.29	$6,948

Best finish for 1960: T-3rd at the Tucson Open Invitational

1961	7	28	5	0	0	1	5	71.54	$4,821

Best finish for 1961: T-10th at the American Golf Classic

1962	3	12	3	0	0	1	2	70.67	$1,838

Best finish for 1962: T-10th at the Portland Open Invitational

1963	16	65	16	0	1	2	7	71.52	$9,645

Best finish for 1963: T-3rd at the Almaden Open Invitational

1964	19	56	8	0	0	1	3	73.02	$4,488

Best finish for 1964: T-8th at the Texas Open

1965	8	22	3	0	0	0	0	74.09	$630

Best finish for 1965: T-28th at the U.S. Open

1966	9	28	5	0	0	0	0	73.71	$894

Best finish for 1966: T-29th at the Bing Crosby National Professional-Amateur

1967	10	36	7	0	0	0	2	72.69	$4,179

Best finish for 1967: T-16th at the U.S. Open

1968	6	16	2	0	1	1	1	73.94	$5,420

Best finish for 1968: T-4th at the "500" Festival Open Invitational

1969	7	26	5	0	0	0	1	72.73	$9,869

Best finish for 1969: T-12th at the West End Classic

1970	1	2	0	0	0	0	0	74.50	
1971	1	2	0	0	0	0	0	77.00	$500
1972	3	6	0	0	0	0	0	76.33	
1973	1	3	0	0	0	0	0	80.67	
Period Totals	Starts	Rounds Played	Cuts Made	Wins	Top-5s	Top-10s	Top-25s	Scoring Average	Money
	117	405	77	1	8	14	36	72.39	$61,536

PGA Tour career totals from 1934 to 1973

	Starts	Rounds Played	Cuts Made	Wins	Top-5s	Top-10s	Top-25s	Scoring Average	Money
	459	N/A	N/A	18	N/A	191	322	N/A	N/A

Dick Hart

Year	Starts	Rounds Played	Cuts Made	Wins	Top-5s	Top-10s	Top-25s	Scoring Average	Money
1958	9	19	0	0	0	0	0	75.74	
1959	2	6	2	0	0	0	0	76.83	$043

Best finish for 1959: T-119 at the Bing Crosby National

1960	1	4	1	0	0	0	1	68.75	$670

Best finish for 1960: T-17th at the St. Paul Open Invitational

1961	1	2	1	0	0	0	0	75.00	

Best finish for 1961: T-200 at the PGA Championship

1962	7	26	6	0	0	0	1	72.54	$1,180

Best finish for 1962: T-25th at the Los Angles Open

1963	7	28	7	0	0	0	1	71.96	$2,249

Best finish for 1963: T-17th at the PGA Championship

1964	16	54	9	0	0	0	2	72.67	$3,672

Best finish for 1964: T-16th at the Pensacola Open

1965	16	59	12	1	1	2	6	72.64	$11,733

Best finish for 1965: Win at the Azalea Open

1966	17	56	10	0	0	1	2	73.00	$5,119

Best finish for 1966: T-8th at the Pensacola Open Invitational

Year	Starts	Rounds Played	Cuts Made	Wins	Top-5s	Top-10s	Top-25s	Scoring Average	Money
1967	12	41	8	0	0	1	1	72.54	$3,880

Best finish for 1967: 7th at the Tucson Open

1968	8	22	3	0	0	0	0	73.32	$219

Best finish for 1968: T-42nd at the Pensacola Open Invitational

1969	7	26	6	0	0	0	0	72.54	$3,468

Best finish for 1969: T-27th at the Greater Jacksonville Open & National Airlines Open

1970	7	22	4	0	0	0	1	72.77	$1,745

Best finish for 1970: T-23rd at the Western Open

1971	1	2	0	0	0	0	0	75.50	
1972	2	4	0	0	0	0	0	75.75	
1973	1	2	0	0	0	0	0	77.00	$500
1975	2	4	0	0	0	0	0	77.25	
1976	1	2	0	0	0	0	0	82.00	$250
1977	4	8	0	0	0	0	0	76.63	
1978	1	2	0	0	0	0	0	77.50	
1979	2	4	0	0	0	0	0	79.00	
1982	1	2	0	0	0	0	0	81.50	
1983	1	2	0	0	0	0	0	83.00	
Period Totals	Starts	Rounds Played	Cuts Made	Wins	Top-5s	Top-10s	Top-25s	Scoring Average	Money
	126	397	69	1	1	4	15	73.28	$34,727

Dudley Hart

Year	Starts	Rounds Played	Cuts Made	Wins	Top-5s	Top-10s	Top-25s	Scoring Average	Money
1991	31	95	17	0	1	2	8	71.52	$126,217

Best finish for 1991: T-5th at the Buick Southern Open

1992	29	94	19	0	2	3	10	71.27	$256,103

Best finish for 1992: T-3rd at the Greater Milwaukee Open

1993	30	91	16	0	2	4	8	71.55	$316,750

Best finish for 1993: T-3rd at the Northern Telecom Open & Kmart Greater Greensboro Open

1994	31	81	11	0	0	2	3	72.07	$127,813

Best finish for 1994: T-7th at the AT&T Pebble Beach Pro-Am

1995	30	96	18	0	0	0	4	71.59	$116,334

Best finish for 1995: T-15th at the Ideon Classic

1996	13	46	10	1	1	3	7	69.57	$422,198

Best finish for 1996: Win at the Bell Canadian Open

1997	28	79	14	0	2	3	6	71.80	$417,661

Best finish for 1997: 2nd at the FedEx St. Jude Classic

1998	25	83	19	0	2	3	8	71.42	$554,729

Best finish for 1998: T-3rd at the Motorola Western Open

1999	26	88	23	0	4	8	12	70.97	$1,269,744

Best finish for 1999: T-3rd at the Bell Canadian Open, Las Vegas Invitational & American Express Championship

2000	24	73	15	1	2	3	6	70.86	$1,059,794

Best finish for 2000: Win at the Honda Classic

2001	25	74	16	0	2	5	11	70.14	$1,035,711

Best finish for 2001: T-3rd at the Canon Greater Hartford Open

2002	26	84	18	0	2	3	7	70.90	$1,166,241

Best finish for 2002: T-2nd at the COMPAQ Classic of New Orleans

2003	22	66	13	0	0	1	1	71.12	$386,709

Best finish for 2003: T-8th at the 100th Western Open

2004	23	58	8	0	2	2	2	71.14	$854,638

Best finish for 2004: T-2nd at the EDS Byron Nelson Championship

2005	29	84	18	0	1	3	9	70.54	$1,051,339

Best finish for 2005: 5th at the Buick Open

2006	29	83	15	0	0	3	7	71.07	$762,736

Best finish for 2006: 6th at the Honda Classic

2007	12	37	7	0	0	1	3	71.38	$299,249

Best finish for 2007: T-8th at the Bob Hope Chrysler Classic

2008	21	70	14	0	3	6	9	70.81	$2,209,203

Best finish for 2008: 2nd at the BMW Championship

Period Totals	Starts	Rounds Played	Cuts Made	Wins	Top-5s	Top-10s	Top-25s	Scoring Average	Money
	454	1382	271	2	26	55	121	71.14	$12,433,168

Jeff Hart

Year	Starts	Rounds Played	Cuts Made	Wins	Top-5s	Top-10s	Top-25s	Scoring Average	Money
1979	1	2	0	0	0	0	0	76.00	
1985	25	68	9	0	0	0	0	72.63	$11,066

Best finish for 1985: T-27th at the Southern Open

1988	1	4	1	0	1	1	1	68.50	$7,875

Best finish for 1988: T-4th at the Deposit Guaranty Golf Classic

1989	22	59	9	0	0	0	3	71.56	$44,650

Best finish for 1989: T-11th at the Kemper Open

1990	26	82	16	0	0	0	2	71.88	$57,189

Best finish for 1990: T-21st at the Bank of Boston Classic

Year	Starts	Rounds Played	Cuts Made	Wins	Top-5s	Top-10s	Top-25s	Scoring Average	Money
1991	2	6	1	0	0	0	0	68.67	$1,866

Best finish for 1991: T-30th at the Deposit Guaranty Classic

1992	1	2	0	0	0	0	0	78.50	$1,000
1994	1	2	0	0	0	0	0	71.50	
1996	23	65	11	0	0	0	3	71.62	$66,450

Best finish for 1996: T-20th at the Buick Challenge

1997	28	79	12	0	0	0	1	71.75	$67,829

Best finish for 1997: T-21st at the Buick Classic

2001	28	85	16	0	0	0	1	71.39	$220,386

Best finish for 2001: T-11th at the Marconi Pennsylvania Classic

2005	23	61	9	0	0	0	1	71.92	$135,165

Best finish for 2005: T-25th at the Buick Championship

Period Totals	Starts	Rounds Played	Cuts Made	Wins	Top-5s	Top-10s	Top-25s	Scoring Average	Money
	181	515	84	0	1	1	12	71.79	$613,476

Steve Hart

Year	Starts	Rounds Played	Cuts Made	Wins	Top-5s	Top-10s	Top-25s	Scoring Average	Money
1982	15	39	4	0	0	0	0	73.74	$2,762

Best finish for 1982: T-57th at the Disney World

1983	30	84	11	0	0	0	4	73.00	$19,314

Best finish for 1983: T-19th at the Canadian Open

1984	2	7	1	0	0	0	0	73.71	$4,060

Best finish for 1984: T-38th at the U.S. Open

1985	2	4	0	0	0	0	0	72.00	
1986	2	6	1	0	0	0	0	72.33	$1,440

Best finish for 1986: T-41st at the B.C. Open

1989	29	78	11	0	0	0	4	71.96	$41,079

Best finish for 1989: T-16th at the Deposit Guaranty Golf Classic

1990	27	67	10	0	0	0	0	72.58	$28,577

Best finish for 1990: T-35th at the Deposit Guaranty & Hardee's Golf Classic

1991	2	4	0	0	0	0	0	70.25	
1992	31	90	13	0	0	0	3	72.03	$69,124

Best finish for 1992: T-14th at the Shell Houston Open

1993	1	4	1	0	0	0	0	68.50	$2,175

Best finish for 1993: T-26th at the Deposit Guaranty Classic

1994	2	4	0	0	0	0	0	75.00	
1995	17	37	1	0	0	0	0	72.78	$2,748

Best finish for 1995: T-54th at the Buick Invitational of California

1996	1	4	1	0	0	0	0	73.75	$2,325

Best finish for 1996: 77th at the Nortel Open

1997	25	69	9	0	0	0	0	72.62	$38,714

Best finish for 1997: T-36th at the Bell Canadian Open

1998	1	4	1	0	0	0	0	72.25	$3,971

Best finish for 1998: T-63rd at the Michelob Championship at Kingsmill

1999	1	2	0	0	0	0	0	76.00	
2000	30	70	7	0	0	0	1	72.54	$107,949

Best finish for 2000: T-13th at the COMPAQ Classic of New Orleans

Period Totals	Starts	Rounds Played	Cuts Made	Wins	Top-5s	Top-10s	Top-25s	Scoring Average	Money
	218	573	71	0	0	0	12	72.56	$324,239

Sam Harvey

Year	Starts	Rounds Played	Cuts Made	Wins	Top-5s	Top-10s	Top-25s	Scoring Average	Money
1962	1	4	1	0	0	0	1	71.50	$256

Best finish for 1962: T-22nd at the Cajun Classic Open Invitational

1964	12	23	1	0	0	0	0	76.17	

Best finish for 1964: T-61st at the Greater Greensboro Open

1965	7	14	0	0	0	0	0	75.86	
1966	7	15	1	0	0	0	0	75.33	$028

Best finish for 1966: T-51st at the Jacksonville Open Invitational

1967	6	13	1	0	0	0	0	75.69	

Best finish for 1967: T-58th at the Azalea Open

1968	4	9	1	0	0	0	0	74.78	

Best finish for 1968: 76th at the Doral Open Invitational

1969	3	6	0	0	0	0	0	76.17	
1970	1	2	0	0	0	0	0	73.00	
1971	4	10	1	0	0	0	0	76.00	$172

Best finish for 1971: T-67th at the Byron Nelson Golf Classic

1972	4	12	2	0	0	0	0	75.42	$250

Best finish for 1972: T-68th at the Byron Nelson Golf Classic

1974	1	2	0	0	0	0	0	78.50	

Period Totals	Starts	Rounds Played	Cuts Made	Wins	Top-5s	Top-10s	Top-25s	Scoring Average	Money
	50	110	8	0	0	0	1	75.56	$706

Barry Harwell

Year	Starts	Rounds Played	Cuts Made	Wins	Top-5s	Top-10s	Top-25s	Scoring Average	Money
1980	8	18	3	0	1	1	1	72.83	$16,450

Best finish for 1980: T-2nd at the World Disney World National Team Championship

| 1981 | 20 | 50 | 7 | 0 | 0 | 0 | 2 | 73.48 | $8,759 |

Best finish for 1981: T-23rd at the World Disney World National Team Championship

| 1982 | 14 | 41 | 6 | 0 | 0 | 0 | 2 | 71.85 | $14,638 |

Best finish for 1982: T-13th at the Bob Hope Chrysler Classic

| 1991 | 1 | 2 | 0 | 0 | 0 | 0 | 0 | 73.50 | |

Period Totals	Starts	Rounds Played	Cuts Made	Wins	Top-5s	Top-10s	Top-25s	Scoring Average	Money
	43	111	16	0	1	1	5	72.77	$39,847

Morris Hatalsky

Year	Starts	Rounds Played	Cuts Made	Wins	Top-5s	Top-10s	Top-25s	Scoring Average	Money
1976	7	16	1	0	0	0	0	74.69	$250

Best finish for 1976: T-57th at the Southern Open

| 1977 | 30 | 101 | 20 | 0 | 1 | 1 | 9 | 72.21 | $31,513 |

Best finish for 1977: T-2nd at the Greater Milwaukee Open

| 1978 | 26 | 76 | 13 | 0 | 0 | 1 | 1 | 73.03 | $16,940 |

Best finish for 1978: T-7th at the Memorial Tournament

| 1979 | 32 | 107 | 21 | 0 | 2 | 3 | 8 | 72.38 | $61,962 |

Best finish for 1979: T-3rd at the Pensacola Open

| 1980 | 27 | 86 | 17 | 0 | 0 | 4 | 7 | 72.52 | $51,471 |

Best finish for 1980: 6th at the Danny Thomas Memphis Classic

| 1981 | 28 | 85 | 15 | 1 | 1 | 1 | 4 | 72.48 | $70,186 |

Best finish for 1981: Win at the Hall of Fame Tournament

| 1982 | 28 | 97 | 20 | 0 | 3 | 3 | 7 | 72.20 | $66,728 |

Best finish for 1982: T-4th at the Phoenix Open & Hall of Fame

| 1983 | 26 | 78 | 12 | 1 | 3 | 4 | 5 | 72.09 | $104,177 |

Best finish for 1983: Win at the Greater Milwaukee Open

| 1984 | 29 | 90 | 16 | 0 | 0 | 0 | 6 | 72.94 | $52,386 |

Best finish for 1984: T-16th at the Bay Hill Classic

| 1985 | 24 | 76 | 13 | 0 | 1 | 2 | 3 | 72.37 | $76,059 |

Best finish for 1985: T-2nd at the Phoenix Open

| 1986 | 29 | 92 | 20 | 0 | 2 | 3 | 11 | 71.50 | $105,543 |

Best finish for 1986: T-3rd at the Southwest Golf Classic

| 1987 | 26 | 78 | 16 | 0 | 2 | 3 | 7 | 71.90 | $150,654 |

Best finish for 1987: T-2nd at the Walt Disney World/Oldsmobile Classic

| 1988 | 22 | 72 | 15 | 1 | 1 | 2 | 4 | 71.17 | $240,019 |

Best finish for 1988: Win at the Kemper Open

| 1989 | 24 | 69 | 11 | 0 | 0 | 1 | 3 | 72.68 | $68,077 |

Best finish for 1989: T-6th at the MONY Tournament Of Champions

| 1990 | 25 | 83 | 17 | 1 | 1 | 1 | 4 | 72.02 | $253,639 |

Best finish for 1990: Win at the Bank of Boston Classic

| 1991 | 26 | 83 | 14 | 0 | 1 | 1 | 2 | 71.82 | $107,265 |

Best finish for 1991: T-5th at the Buick Southern Open

| 1992 | 27 | 75 | 10 | 0 | 0 | 1 | 2 | 72.47 | $55,042 |

Best finish for 1992: T-7th at the H-E-B Texas Open

| 1993 | 18 | 60 | 13 | 0 | 1 | 2 | 2 | 71.05 | $111,057 |

Best finish for 1993: T-2nd at the Deposit Guaranty Classic

| 1994 | 25 | 76 | 15 | 0 | 0 | 0 | 2 | 71.50 | $81,902 |

Best finish for 1994: T-22nd at the Northern Telecom Open

| 1995 | 5 | 14 | 2 | 0 | 0 | 0 | 1 | 72.29 | $9,833 |

Best finish for 1995: T-20th at the Deposit Guaranty Golf Classic

1999	4	8	0	0	0	0	0	74.88	
2000	2	4	0	0	0	0	0	73.25	
2001	1	4	1	0	0	0	0	71.25	$4,000

Best finish for 2001: T-70th at the B.C. Open

Period Totals	Starts	Rounds Played	Cuts Made	Wins	Top-5s	Top-10s	Top-25s	Scoring Average	Money
	491	1530	282	4	19	33	88	72.19	$1,718,702

Jerry Hatfield

Year	Starts	Rounds Played	Cuts Made	Wins	Top-5s	Top-10s	Top-25s	Scoring Average	Money
1968	3	8	1	0	0	0	0	74.88	$010

Best finish for 1968: T-50th at the Robinson Open

| 1969 | 14 | 38 | 5 | 0 | 0 | 0 | 2 | 73.61 | $2,355 |

Best finish for 1969: T-15th at the Texas Open

| 1970 | 8 | 20 | 2 | 0 | 0 | 0 | 0 | 73.90 | $351 |

Best finish for 1970: T-38th at the Tallahassee Open

Period Totals	Starts	Rounds Played	Cuts Made	Wins	Top-5s	Top-10s	Top-25s	Scoring Average	Money
	25	66	8	0	0	0	2	73.85	$2,716

Jeff Hawkes

Year	Starts	Rounds Played	Cuts Made	Wins	Top-5s	Top-10s	Top-25s	Scoring Average	Money
1977	1	3	0	0	0	0	0	74.33	$340
1978	10	40	10	0	0	1	4	71.65	$13,340

Best finish for 1978: T-8th at the Canadian Open

Year	Starts	Rounds Played	Cuts Made	Wins	Top-5s	Top-10s	Top-25s	Scoring Average	Money
1980	9	20	2	0	0	0	1	72.05	$2,584

Best finish for 1980: T-24th at the B.C. Open

Year	Starts	Rounds Played	Cuts Made	Wins	Top-5s	Top-10s	Top-25s	Scoring Average	Money
1981	2	3	0	0	0	0	0	77.00	
1982	1	3	0	0	0	0	0	75.67	$748
1984	1	2	0	0	0	0	0	75.00	$429
1986	1	4	1	0	0	0	0	74.50	$3,712

Best finish for 1986: T-46th at the British Open

Year	Starts	Rounds Played	Cuts Made	Wins	Top-5s	Top-10s	Top-25s	Scoring Average	Money
1987	1	4	1	0	0	0	0	75.75	$2,560

Best finish for 1987: 74th at the British Open

Year	Starts	Rounds Played	Cuts Made	Wins	Top-5s	Top-10s	Top-25s	Scoring Average	Money
1989	1	4	1	0	0	0	0	71.50	$7,538

Best finish for 1989: T-30th at the British Open

Year	Starts	Rounds Played	Cuts Made	Wins	Top-5s	Top-10s	Top-25s	Scoring Average	Money
1990	1	2	0	0	0	0	0	74.00	$996
1992	1	4	1	0	0	0	0	74.25	$10,550

Best finish for 1992: T-40th at the NEC World Series of Golf

Period Totals	Starts	Rounds Played	Cuts Made	Wins	Top-5s	Top-10s	Top-25s	Scoring Average	Money
	29	89	16	0	0	1	5	72.70	$42,796

Fred Hawkins

Year	Starts	Rounds Played	Cuts Made	Wins	Top-5s	Top-10s	Top-25s	Scoring Average	Money
1958	34	132	33	1	7	9	23	71.24	$21,114

Best finish for 1958: Win at the Jackson Open

Year	Starts	Rounds Played	Cuts Made	Wins	Top-5s	Top-10s	Top-25s	Scoring Average	Money
1959	29	116	28	0	3	7	20	70.98	$17,315

Best finish for 1959: T-2nd at the Colonial National Invitational

Year	Starts	Rounds Played	Cuts Made	Wins	Top-5s	Top-10s	Top-25s	Scoring Average	Money
1960	29	114	26	0	5	14	18	71.02	$24,900

Best finish for 1960: T-2nd at the Palm Springs Desert Golf Classic

Year	Starts	Rounds Played	Cuts Made	Wins	Top-5s	Top-10s	Top-25s	Scoring Average	Money
1961	17	67	16	0	0	0	7	72.00	$5,702

Best finish for 1961: T-13th at the Eastern Open Invitational

Year	Starts	Rounds Played	Cuts Made	Wins	Top-5s	Top-10s	Top-25s	Scoring Average	Money
1962	17	65	16	0	2	6	8	71.55	$16,082

Best finish for 1962: T-3rd at the Los Angles Open & Western Open Championship

Year	Starts	Rounds Played	Cuts Made	Wins	Top-5s	Top-10s	Top-25s	Scoring Average	Money
1963	20	78	16	0	3	6	13	70.79	$25,444

Best finish for 1963: T-2nd at the Houston Classic & St. Paul Open Invitational

Year	Starts	Rounds Played	Cuts Made	Wins	Top-5s	Top-10s	Top-25s	Scoring Average	Money
1964	23	66	7	0	0	0	3	73.39	$4,300

Best finish for 1964: T-14th at the Pensacola Open & St. Paul Open

Year	Starts	Rounds Played	Cuts Made	Wins	Top-5s	Top-10s	Top-25s	Scoring Average	Money
1965	23	73	14	0	0	0	1	73.00	$5,456

Best finish for 1965: T-21st at the Greater Hartford Open

Year	Starts	Rounds Played	Cuts Made	Wins	Top-5s	Top-10s	Top-25s	Scoring Average	Money
1966	1	2	0	0	0	0	0	75.00	
1967	1	2	0	0	0	0	0	74.50	
1968	1	2	0	0	0	0	0	82.00	
1969	1	2	0	0	0	0	0	75.00	
1973	1	2	0	0	0	0	0	81.50	

Period Totals	Starts	Rounds Played	Cuts Made	Wins	Top-5s	Top-10s	Top-25s	Scoring Average	Money
	197	721	156	1	20	42	93	71.68	$120,313

PGA Tour career totals from 1947 to 1965

	Starts	Rounds Played	Cuts Made	Wins	Top-5s	Top-10s	Top-25s	Scoring Average	Money
	449	1663	403	2	36	104	222	N/A	$205,228

Dale Hayes

Year	Starts	Rounds Played	Cuts Made	Wins	Top-5s	Top-10s	Top-25s	Scoring Average	Money
1969	1	2	0	0	0	0	0	77.50	
1971	1	4	1	0	0	0	1	72.00	$1,920

Best finish for 1971: 17th at the British Open

Year	Starts	Rounds Played	Cuts Made	Wins	Top-5s	Top-10s	Top-25s	Scoring Average	Money
1972	1	3	0	0	0	0	0	77.00	$188
1973	2	12	2	0	0	0	0	74.00	$1,634

Best finish for 1973: T-39th at the British Open

Year	Starts	Rounds Played	Cuts Made	Wins	Top-5s	Top-10s	Top-25s	Scoring Average	Money
1974	1	2	0	0	0	0	0	79.00	$120
1975	5	16	3	0	0	0	1	73.44	$4,283

Best finish for 1975: T-23rd at the Sea Pines Heritage Classic

Year	Starts	Rounds Played	Cuts Made	Wins	Top-5s	Top-10s	Top-25s	Scoring Average	Money
1976	18	66	15	0	0	0	3	72.79	$13,676

Best finish for 1976: T-14th at the Doral-Eastern Open

Year	Starts	Rounds Played	Cuts Made	Wins	Top-5s	Top-10s	Top-25s	Scoring Average	Money
1977	23	74	14	0	1	2	6	72.59	$39,944

Best finish for 1977: T-2nd at the Florida Citrus Open Invitational

Year	Starts	Rounds Played	Cuts Made	Wins	Top-5s	Top-10s	Top-25s	Scoring Average	Money
1978	7	17	1	0	0	0	1	74.88	$5,732

Best finish for 1978: T-11th at the British Open

Year	Starts	Rounds Played	Cuts Made	Wins	Top-5s	Top-10s	Top-25s	Scoring Average	Money
1979	2	6	1	0	0	0	1	73.33	$4,270

Best finish for 1979: T-23rd at the World Series Of Golf

| 1980 | 1 | 4 | 1 | 0 | 0 | 0 | 0 | 72.75 | $1,440 |

Best finish for 1980: T-38th at the British Open

1981	1	2	0	0	0	0	0	76.00	$450
Period Totals	Starts	Rounds Played	Cuts Made	Wins	Top-5s	Top-10s	Top-25s	Scoring Average	Money
	63	208	38	0	1	2	13	73.21	$73,656

J.P. Hayes

Year	Starts	Rounds Played	Cuts Made	Wins	Top-5s	Top-10s	Top-25s	Scoring Average	Money
1992	28	75	10	0	0	1	4	72.27	$73,830

Best finish for 1992: T-6th at the Anheuser-Busch Golf Classic

| 1993 | 1 | 4 | 1 | 0 | 0 | 1 | 1 | 67.75 | $6,650 |

Best finish for 1993: T-10th at the Deposit Guaranty Classic

| 1995 | 27 | 81 | 13 | 0 | 0 | 0 | 5 | 71.98 | $111,696 |

Best finish for 1995: T-12th at the Quad City Classic

| 1996 | 4 | 8 | 0 | 0 | 0 | 0 | 0 | 74.00 | |
| 1997 | 29 | 95 | 18 | 0 | 0 | 1 | 6 | 71.48 | $160,692 |

Best finish for 1997: T-8th at the Shell Houston Open

| 1998 | 22 | 67 | 12 | 1 | 2 | 2 | 4 | 71.55 | $558,088 |

Best finish for 1998: Win at the Buick Classic

| 1999 | 28 | 90 | 18 | 0 | 1 | 2 | 5 | 71.59 | $441,302 |

Best finish for 1999: T-5th at the Shell Houston Open

| 2000 | 26 | 89 | 18 | 0 | 2 | 5 | 9 | 71.11 | $839,054 |

Best finish for 2000: T-2nd at the Honda Classic

| 2001 | 23 | 76 | 14 | 0 | 2 | 3 | 4 | 71.22 | $622,964 |

Best finish for 2001: T-3rd at the Buick Classic & Greater Milwaukee Open

| 2002 | 24 | 76 | 14 | 1 | 2 | 3 | 5 | 70.88 | $955,271 |

Best finish for 2002: Win at the John Deere Classic

| 2003 | 25 | 79 | 14 | 0 | 0 | 1 | 7 | 70.87 | $585,331 |

Best finish for 2003: 8th at the Reno-Tahoe Open

| 2004 | 27 | 75 | 11 | 0 | 0 | 0 | 2 | 71.55 | $261,816 |

Best finish for 2004: T-18th at the Buick Open

| 2005 | 22 | 63 | 10 | 0 | 2 | 2 | 4 | 71.13 | $531,704 |

Best finish for 2005: T-2nd at the B.C. Open

| 2006 | 19 | 55 | 8 | 0 | 2 | 2 | 4 | 71.24 | $701,433 |

Best finish for 2006: 2nd at the John Deere Classic

| 2007 | 28 | 89 | 15 | 0 | 0 | 3 | 7 | 71.18 | $890,815 |

Best finish for 2007: T-6th at The Players

| 2008 | 26 | 67 | 7 | 0 | 0 | 1 | 3 | 72.09 | $312,152 |

Best finish for 2008: T-9th at the John Deere Classic

| Period Totals | Starts | Rounds Played | Cuts Made | Wins | Top-5s | Top-10s | Top-25s | Scoring Average | Money |
| | 359 | 1089 | 183 | 2 | 13 | 27 | 70 | 71.44 | $7,052,796 |

Mark Hayes

Year	Starts	Rounds Played	Cuts Made	Wins	Top-5s	Top-10s	Top-25s	Scoring Average	Money
1973	3	12	1	0	0	0	1	73.83	$8,637

Best finish for 1973: T-11th at the World Open

| 1974 | 32 | 116 | 26 | 0 | 1 | 4 | 13 | 71.94 | $39,415 |

Best finish for 1974: T-4th at the Bob Hope Chrysler Classic

| 1975 | 32 | 114 | 24 | 0 | 1 | 4 | 17 | 71.83 | $50,098 |

Best finish for 1975: 3rd at the Ed McMahon Quad City Open

| 1976 | 31 | 115 | 27 | 2 | 4 | 9 | 18 | 71.18 | $151,699 |

Best finish for 1976: Win at the Byron Nelson Golf Classic & Pensacola Open

| 1977 | 31 | 114 | 26 | 1 | 2 | 4 | 12 | 71.82 | $120,636 |

Best finish for 1977: Win at the Tournament Players Championship

| 1978 | 31 | 114 | 25 | 0 | 4 | 7 | 16 | 71.31 | $151,319 |

Best finish for 1978: 2nd at the Kemper Open, American Express Westchester Classic & B.C. Open

| 1979 | 29 | 99 | 21 | 0 | 4 | 7 | 11 | 71.95 | $132,974 |

Best finish for 1979: T-2nd at the Bing Crosby Pro-Am

| 1980 | 29 | 101 | 22 | 0 | 1 | 5 | 9 | 72.26 | $69,905 |

Best finish for 1980: 5th at the Bob Hope Chrysler Classic

| 1981 | 33 | 109 | 22 | 0 | 2 | 3 | 8 | 71.95 | $93,124 |

Best finish for 1981: 2nd at the Greater Greensboro Open

| 1982 | 31 | 107 | 23 | 0 | 0 | 1 | 5 | 72.34 | $48,377 |

Best finish for 1982: T-10th at the Masters

| 1983 | 28 | 98 | 19 | 0 | 2 | 3 | 7 | 72.17 | $63,531 |

Best finish for 1983: T-4th at the Byron Nelson Golf Classic

| 1984 | 32 | 92 | 14 | 0 | 1 | 1 | 1 | 72.76 | $43,707 |

Best finish for 1984: T-5th at the Seiko Tucson-Match Play Championship

| 1985 | 29 | 95 | 17 | 0 | 1 | 1 | 6 | 72.27 | $61,988 |

Best finish for 1985: T-3rd at the Texas Open

| 1986 | 29 | 91 | 19 | 1 | 2 | 2 | 8 | 71.40 | $118,837 |

Best finish for 1986: Win at the Tallahassee Open

Year	Starts	Rounds Played	Cuts Made	Wins	Top-5s	Top-10s	Top-25s	Scoring Average	Money
1987	33	104	19	0	0	2	3	71.95	$77,585

Best finish for 1987: T-8th at the MCI Heritage Classic & Beatrice Western Open

1988	33	100	17	0	1	1	4	71.90	$78,072

Best finish for 1988: T-3rd at the Provident Classic

1989	29	85	15	0	1	2	4	71.61	$87,689

Best finish for 1989: 4th at the USF&G Classic

1990	27	76	12	0	0	1	3	72.32	$77,743

Best finish for 1990: T-7th at the Kemper Open

1991	22	59	8	0	0	0	2	71.69	$36,370

Best finish for 1991: T-21st at the Hardee's Golf Classic

1992	13	35	4	0	0	1	3	71.80	$50,324

Best finish for 1992: T-10th at the Buick Open

1993	9	27	3	0	0	0	0	72.52	$6,942

Best finish for 1993: T-54th at the B.C. Open

1994	4	9	0	0	0	0	0	73.78	
1995	6	17	1	0	0	0	1	72.06	$7,061

Best finish for 1995: T-20th at the Deposit Guaranty Golf Classic

1996	8	18	0	0	0	0	0	73.28	
1997	6	13	0	0	0	0	0	73.85	
1998	8	18	0	0	0	0	0	75.11	
1999	3	11	1	0	0	0	0	73.91	$3,841

Best finish for 1999: T-86th at the Greater Milwaukee Open

2000	1	4	0	0	0	0	0	69.75	
2002	1	4	0	0	0	0	0	73.00	
2003	1	4	0	0	0	0	0	72.50	
2004	1	4	0	0	0	0	0	75.75	
Period Totals	Starts	Rounds Played	Cuts Made	Wins	Top-5s	Top-10s	Top-25s	Scoring Average	Money
	605	1965	366	4	27	58	152	72.02	$1,579,874

Ted Hayes, Jr.

Year	Starts	Rounds Played	Cuts Made	Wins	Top-5s	Top-10s	Top-25s	Scoring Average	Money
1970	29	94	18	0	1	2	9	72.40	$25,816

Best finish for 1970: T-2nd at the Greater Milwaukee Open

1971	33	113	23	0	0	2	7	72.09	$22,656

Best finish for 1971: T-8th at the Tallahassee Open

1972	18	51	7	0	0	0	0	73.59	$2,908

Best finish for 1972: T-32nd at the Atlanta Classic

1973	1	2	0	0	0	0	0	79.00	
Period Totals	Starts	Rounds Played	Cuts Made	Wins	Top-5s	Top-10s	Top-25s	Scoring Average	Money
	81	260	48	0	1	4	16	72.55	$51,381

Don Headings

Year	Starts	Rounds Played	Cuts Made	Wins	Top-5s	Top-10s	Top-25s	Scoring Average	Money
1965	1	2	0	0	0	0	0	82.50	
1967	17	47	5	0	0	0	0	75.04	$534

Best finish for 1967: T-33rd at the Los Angles Open

1968	9	24	3	0	0	0	1	74.04	$275

Best finish for 1968: T-21st at the Rebel Yell Open

1970	7	16	1	0	0	0	0	74.31	$152

Best finish for 1970: T-62nd at the Greater Milwaukee Open

1971	5	11	1	0	0	0	0	75.00	

Best finish for 1971: T-49th at the Greater Milwaukee Open

1972	4	10	1	0	0	0	0	74.50	$143

Best finish for 1972: 75th at the Liggett Meyers Open

1976	4	8	0	0	0	0	0	76.50	
1977	1	2	0	0	0	0	0	74.00	
1978	2	6	1	0	0	0	0	74.83	

Best finish for 1978: T-74th at the Jackie Gleason's Inverrary Classic

Period Totals	Starts	Rounds Played	Cuts Made	Wins	Top-5s	Top-10s	Top-25s	Scoring Average	Money
	50	126	12	0	0	0	1	74.90	$1,104

Vance Heafner

Year	Starts	Rounds Played	Cuts Made	Wins	Top-5s	Top-10s	Top-25s	Scoring Average	Money
1978	4	12	2	0	0	0	0	74.25	

Best finish for 1978: T-45th at the Masters

1979	4	14	3	0	0	0	1	74.64	$4,573

Best finish for 1979: T-22nd at the Bing Crosby Pro-Am

1980	21	69	14	0	0	0	2	72.71	$15,463

Best finish for 1980: T-22nd at the Danny Thomas Memphis Classic

1981	36	126	28	1	1	4	13	71.52	$109,244

Best finish for 1981: Win at the World Disney World National Team Championship

1982	35	121	25	0	3	6	10	71.53	$113,717

Best finish for 1982: T-2nd at the Joe Garagiola Tucson Open

Year	Starts	Rounds Played	Cuts Made	Wins	Top-5s	Top-10s	Top-25s	Scoring Average	Money
1983	33	107	20	0	1	2	6	72.19	$86,810

Best finish for 1983: T-2nd at the USF&G Classic

Year	Starts	Rounds Played	Cuts Made	Wins	Top-5s	Top-10s	Top-25s	Scoring Average	Money
1984	30	82	14	0	3	3	9	71.89	$90,702

Best finish for 1984: T-2nd at the Miller High-Life Quad Cities Open

Year	Starts	Rounds Played	Cuts Made	Wins	Top-5s	Top-10s	Top-25s	Scoring Average	Money
1985	28	86	15	0	0	1	3	72.72	$32,964

Best finish for 1985: T-8th at the Isuzu/Andy Williams San Diego Open

Year	Starts	Rounds Played	Cuts Made	Wins	Top-5s	Top-10s	Top-25s	Scoring Average	Money
1986	21	66	14	0	1	1	1	71.62	$28,763

Best finish for 1986: T-5th at the Deposit Guaranty Golf Classic

Year	Starts	Rounds Played	Cuts Made	Wins	Top-5s	Top-10s	Top-25s	Scoring Average	Money
1987	30	86	15	0	0	3	7	71.79	$74,490

Best finish for 1987: T-8th at the Southwest Golf Classic

Year	Starts	Rounds Played	Cuts Made	Wins	Top-5s	Top-10s	Top-25s	Scoring Average	Money
1988	12	20	2	0	0	0	0	73.30	$2,117

Best finish for 1988: T-42nd at the Deposit Guaranty Golf Classic

Year	Starts	Rounds Played	Cuts Made	Wins	Top-5s	Top-10s	Top-25s	Scoring Average	Money
1989	2	5	1	0	0	0	0	72.00	$1,624

Best finish for 1989: T-74th at the Anheuser-Busch Golf Classic

Year	Starts	Rounds Played	Cuts Made	Wins	Top-5s	Top-10s	Top-25s	Scoring Average	Money
1993	3	8	1	0	0	0	0	72.13	$6,526

Best finish for 1993: T-52nd at the U.S. Open

Year	Starts	Rounds Played	Cuts Made	Wins	Top-5s	Top-10s	Top-25s	Scoring Average	Money
1994	2	8	2	0	0	0	0	70.63	$5,297

Best finish for 1994: T-44th at the Hardee's Golf Classic

Year	Starts	Rounds Played	Cuts Made	Wins	Top-5s	Top-10s	Top-25s	Scoring Average	Money
1995	2	5	1	0	0	0	0	72.40	$1,690

Best finish for 1995: T-85th at the Quad City Classic

Year	Starts	Rounds Played	Cuts Made	Wins	Top-5s	Top-10s	Top-25s	Scoring Average	Money
1996	1	2	0	0	0	0	0	73.00	
1998	1	2	0	0	0	0	0	70.50	
1999	1	2	0	0	0	0	0	70.00	
Period Totals	266	821	157	1	9	20	52	72.05	$573,977

Jerry Heard

Year	Starts	Rounds Played	Cuts Made	Wins	Top-5s	Top-10s	Top-25s	Scoring Average	Money
1966	1	2	0	0	0	0	0	78.00	
1968	4	14	3	0	0	0	0	72.50	

Best finish for 1968: T-38th at the Cajun Classic

Year	Starts	Rounds Played	Cuts Made	Wins	Top-5s	Top-10s	Top-25s	Scoring Average	Money
1969	23	67	11	0	0	1	4	72.78	$9,220

Best finish for 1969: T-6th at the San Francisco Open

Year	Starts	Rounds Played	Cuts Made	Wins	Top-5s	Top-10s	Top-25s	Scoring Average	Money
1970	32	111	25	0	2	4	12	72.13	$42,335

Best finish for 1970: T-4th at the Westchester Classic & Kaiser International Open

Year	Starts	Rounds Played	Cuts Made	Wins	Top-5s	Top-10s	Top-25s	Scoring Average	Money
1971	32	106	25	1	5	10	16	71.44	$102,101

Best finish for 1971: Win at the American Golf Classic

Year	Starts	Rounds Played	Cuts Made	Wins	Top-5s	Top-10s	Top-25s	Scoring Average	Money
1972	30	113	28	2	6	11	16	71.42	$133,705

Best finish for 1972: Win at the Florida Citrus Open Invitational & Colonial National Invitational

Year	Starts	Rounds Played	Cuts Made	Wins	Top-5s	Top-10s	Top-25s	Scoring Average	Money
1973	32	112	26	0	2	9	16	71.41	$91,350

Best finish for 1973: T-2nd at the Colonial National Invitational & Sea Pines Heritage Classic

Year	Starts	Rounds Played	Cuts Made	Wins	Top-5s	Top-10s	Top-25s	Scoring Average	Money
1974	27	99	23	1	7	8	15	71.40	$144,096

Best finish for 1974: Win at the Florida Citrus Open Invitational

Year	Starts	Rounds Played	Cuts Made	Wins	Top-5s	Top-10s	Top-25s	Scoring Average	Money
1975	26	102	24	0	4	6	11	71.72	$81,688

Best finish for 1975: 2nd at the Phoenix Open

Year	Starts	Rounds Played	Cuts Made	Wins	Top-5s	Top-10s	Top-25s	Scoring Average	Money
1976	19	63	15	0	1	2	7	71.87	$29,007

Best finish for 1976: T-4th at the Bob Hope Chrysler Classic

Year	Starts	Rounds Played	Cuts Made	Wins	Top-5s	Top-10s	Top-25s	Scoring Average	Money
1977	11	36	7	0	0	0	1	72.50	$5,438

Best finish for 1977: T-15th at the B.C. Open

Year	Starts	Rounds Played	Cuts Made	Wins	Top-5s	Top-10s	Top-25s	Scoring Average	Money
1978	27	92	18	1	2	2	7	72.16	$78,611

Best finish for 1978: Win at the Atlanta Classic

Year	Starts	Rounds Played	Cuts Made	Wins	Top-5s	Top-10s	Top-25s	Scoring Average	Money
1979	28	73	8	0	0	0	1	74.47	$13,612

Best finish for 1979: T-16th at the Bing Crosby Pro-Am

Year	Starts	Rounds Played	Cuts Made	Wins	Top-5s	Top-10s	Top-25s	Scoring Average	Money
1980	12	26	2	0	0	0	0	73.08	$2,694

Best finish for 1980: T-32nd at the Anheuser-Busch Golf Classic

Year	Starts	Rounds Played	Cuts Made	Wins	Top-5s	Top-10s	Top-25s	Scoring Average	Money
1981	21	58	8	0	0	2	4	72.52	$19,295

Best finish for 1981: T-9th at the Colonial National Invitational

Year	Starts	Rounds Played	Cuts Made	Wins	Top-5s	Top-10s	Top-25s	Scoring Average	Money
1982	23	63	7	0	0	0	1	73.35	$8,438

Best finish for 1982: T-19th at the Hall of Fame

Year	Starts	Rounds Played	Cuts Made	Wins	Top-5s	Top-10s	Top-25s	Scoring Average	Money
1983	5	11	1	0	0	0	0	75.45	$820

Best finish for 1983: T-68th at the Colonial National Invitational

Year	Starts	Rounds Played	Cuts Made	Wins	Top-5s	Top-10s	Top-25s	Scoring Average	Money
1985	1	2	0	0	0	0	0	83.00	
1987	1	2	0	0	0	0	0	79.00	
Period Totals	355	1152	231	5	29	55	111	72.20	$762,409

David Hearn

Year	Starts	Rounds Played	Cuts Made	Wins	Top-5s	Top-10s	Top-25s	Scoring Average	Money
2002	2	4	0	0	0	0	0	72.00	
2003	1	2	0	0	0	0	0	72.00	
2004	1	2	0	0	0	0	0	76.50	

Year	Starts	Rounds Played	Cuts Made	Wins	Top-5s	Top-10s	Top-25s	Scoring Average	Money
2005	24	68	10	0	0	0	2	71.40	$199,453

Best finish for 2005: T-13th at the B.C. Open

| 2006 | 1 | 4 | 1 | 0 | 0 | 0 | 1 | 68.75 | $50,438 |

Best finish for 2006: T-20th at the Canadian Open

| 2007 | 1 | 4 | 1 | 0 | 0 | 0 | 0 | 71.00 | $10,850 |

Best finish for 2007: T-58th at the Canadian Open

| 2008 | 2 | 6 | 1 | 0 | 0 | 0 | 0 | 72.50 | $11,100 |

Best finish for 2008: T-58th at the RBC Canadian Open

Period Totals	Starts	Rounds Played	Cuts Made	Wins	Top-5s	Top-10s	Top-25s	Scoring Average	Money
	32	90	13	0	0	0	3	71.49	$271,840

Skeeter Heath

Year	Starts	Rounds Played	Cuts Made	Wins	Top-5s	Top-10s	Top-25s	Scoring Average	Money
1978	14	33	4	0	0	0	0	74.39	$946

Best finish for 1978: T-38th at the Sammy Davis, Jr. - Greater Hartford Open

| 1980 | 20 | 56 | 8 | 0 | 0 | 0 | 1 | 73.14 | $8,290 |

Best finish for 1980: T-18th at the Buick Goodwrench Open

| 1981 | 14 | 41 | 9 | 0 | 0 | 0 | 2 | 71.93 | $15,116 |

Best finish for 1981: T-13th at the Greater Milwaukee Open & Texas Open

| 1982 | 27 | 78 | 11 | 0 | 0 | 0 | 0 | 72.83 | $12,579 |

Best finish for 1982: T-28th at the Greater Greensboro Open

| 1983 | 6 | 20 | 4 | 0 | 1 | 1 | 1 | 72.45 | $18,442 |

Best finish for 1983: T-3rd at the Greater Milwaukee Open

| 1984 | 2 | 4 | 0 | 0 | 0 | 0 | 0 | 73.25 | |
| 1985 | 30 | 81 | 10 | 0 | 0 | 0 | 0 | 73.33 | $15,720 |

Best finish for 1985: T-34th at the U.S. Open

1986	1	2	0	0	0	0	0	75.50	
1987	1	2	0	0	0	0	0	77.00	
1988	1	3	0	0	0	0	0	76.00	
1990	1	2	0	0	0	0	0	75.50	
1991	1	3	0	0	0	0	0	79.33	
1993	1	2	0	0	0	0	0	78.50	
1994	2	4	0	0	0	0	0	78.00	
Period Totals	Starts	Rounds Played	Cuts Made	Wins	Top-5s	Top-10s	Top-25s	Scoring Average	Money
	121	331	46	0	1	1	4	73.27	$71,094

Jay Hebert

Year	Starts	Rounds Played	Cuts Made	Wins	Top-5s	Top-10s	Top-25s	Scoring Average	Money
1958	39	152	36	1	8	17	28	70.98	$29,662.83

Best finish for 1958: Win at the Lafayette Open

| 1959 | 34 | 136 | 30 | 1 | 6 | 13 | 29 | 70.58 | $26,134.27 |

Best finish for 1959: Win at the Orange County Open Invitational

| 1960 | 25 | 98 | 22 | 1 | 7 | 9 | 19 | 70.84 | $29,748.37 |

Best finish for 1960: Win at the PGA Championship

| 1961 | 28 | 113 | 28 | 2 | 3 | 8 | 19 | 70.48 | $33,823.22 |

Best finish for 1961: Win at the Houston Classic & American Golf Classic

| 1962 | 24 | 93 | 22 | 0 | 2 | 5 | 17 | 71.19 | $19,708.97 |

Best finish for 1962: T-3rd at the Palm Springs Golf Classic

| 1963 | 27 | 109 | 26 | 0 | 2 | 9 | 15 | 71.58 | $25,133.74 |

Best finish for 1963: T-4th at the Denver Open Invitational & Almaden Open Invitational

| 1964 | 33 | 124 | 27 | 0 | 3 | 5 | 14 | 72.07 | $24,934.97 |

Best finish for 1964: T-3rd at the Fresno Open

| 1965 | 27 | 97 | 21 | 0 | 0 | 2 | 10 | 72.40 | $16,448.21 |

Best finish for 1965: T-9th at the Tucson Open

| 1966 | 25 | 84 | 17 | 0 | 2 | 4 | 10 | 72.48 | $21,404.35 |

Best finish for 1966: T-3rd at the Tucson Open Invitational

| 1967 | 24 | 77 | 14 | 0 | 0 | 0 | 3 | 73.42 | $5,268.00 |

Best finish for 1967: T-21st at the Florida Citrus Open & The Masters

| 1968 | 21 | 60 | 10 | 0 | 0 | 0 | 2 | 73.02 | $5,516.70 |

Best finish for 1968: T-18th at the Haig Open Invitational

| 1969 | 22 | 60 | 8 | 0 | 0 | 0 | 0 | 73.10 | $2,287.27 |

Best finish for 1969: 35th at the Greater Jacksonville Open

1970	1	2	0	0	0	0	0	76.00	$0.00
1971	1	2	0	0	0	0	0	76.50	$0.00
1974	2	6	1	0	0	0	0	72.83	$281.11

Best finish for 1974: T-50th at the San Antonio Texas Open

1975	2	6	0	0	0	0	0	77.00	$0.00
1976	3	6	0	0	0	0	0	76.50	$250.00
1977	1	2	0	0	0	0	0	79.50	$250.00
1978	2	6	0	0	0	0	0	77.33	$0.00
Period Totals	Starts	Rounds Played	Cuts Made	Wins	Top-5s	Top-10s	Top-25s	Scoring Average	Money
	341	1233	262	5	33	72	166	71.75	$240,852

PGA Tour career totals from 1949 to 1978

	Starts	Rounds Played	Cuts Made	Wins	Top-5s	Top-10s	Top-25s	Scoring Average	Money
	453	1667	374	6	38	104	241	N/A	$290,034

Lionel Hebert

Year	Starts	Rounds Played	Cuts Made	Wins	Top-5s	Top-10s	Top-25s	Scoring Average	Money
1958	36	140	34	1	4	8	20	71.76	$15,566.22
Best finish for 1958: Win at the Tucson Open									
1959	24	95	22	0	1	5	12	71.52	$11,259.31
Best finish for 1959: T-5th at the Memphis Open Invitational									
1960	26	103	23	1	4	8	19	70.74	$18,249.05
Best finish for 1960: Win at the Cajun Classic Open Invitational									
1961	21	80	19	0	2	6	12	71.08	$13,769.58
Best finish for 1961: T-4th at the Houston Classic									
1962	23	90	20	1	3	5	16	71.56	$20,743.43
Best finish for 1962: Win at the Memphis Open Invitational									
1963	24	94	21	0	1	4	12	71.94	$27,490.95
Best finish for 1963: T-2nd at the Whitemarsh Open Invitational									
1964	34	128	29	0	2	7	17	71.74	$26,848.80
Best finish for 1964: 2nd at the Azalea Open & Oklahoma City Open									
1965	32	108	21	0	1	3	9	72.67	$20,693.61
Best finish for 1965: T-2nd at the "500" Festival									
1966	32	112	22	1	3	4	11	72.89	$46,533.21
Best finish for 1966: Win at the Florida Citrus Open Invitational									
1967	29	99	20	0	1	2	9	72.52	$20,250.63
Best finish for 1967: T-5th at the Doral Open									
1968	27	101	23	0	0	1	9	71.57	$19,569.57
Best finish for 1968: T-7th at the Masters									
1969	29	93	17	0	0	3	7	72.68	$23,403.20
Best finish for 1969: T-7th at the National Airlines Open & Greater New Orleans Open									
1970	29	92	18	0	0	3	9	72.59	$28,944.04
Best finish for 1970: T-6th at the Kemper Open									
1971	34	103	19	0	1	3	9	73.22	$26,182.00
Best finish for 1971: T-5th at the Massachusetts Classic									
1972	32	100	17	0	0	1	6	73.18	$16,811.99
Best finish for 1972: T-7th at the Sahara Invitational									
1973	35	100	13	0	0	1	1	73.53	$9,631.10
Best finish for 1973: 7th at the Liggett Meyers Open									
1974	27	85	15	0	0	1	3	72.89	$28,390.50
Best finish for 1974: T-9th at the Canadian Open									
1975	27	72	8	0	1	2	2	73.60	$10,647.50
Best finish for 1975: T-5th at the Houston Open									
1976	28	66	5	0	0	0	0	74.14	$2,630.92
Best finish for 1976: T-34th at the Byron Nelson Golf Classic									
1977	19	46	4	0	0	0	0	75.46	$1,078.00
Best finish for 1977: T-47th at the Doral-Eastern Open									
1978	7	17	0	0	0	0	0	77.53	$0.00
1981	1	2	0	0	0	0	0	75.00	$550.00
Period Totals	Starts	Rounds Played	Cuts Made	Wins	Top-5s	Top-10s	Top-25s	Scoring Average	Money
	576	1926	370	4	24	67	183	72.48	$389,244

PGA Tour career totals from 1951 to 1981

	Starts	Rounds Played	Cuts Made	Wins	Top-5s	Top-10s	Top-25s	Scoring Average	Money
	643	2178	437	5	27	80	210	N/A	$412,365

Marion Heck

Year	Starts	Rounds Played	Cuts Made	Wins	Top-5s	Top-10s	Top-25s	Scoring Average	Money
1964	1	2	0	0	0	0	0	76.00	
1966	1	2	0	0	0	0	0	79.00	
1971	4	8	0	0	0	0	0	74.25	
1972	11	30	4	0	0	0	0	74.97	$833
Best finish for 1972: T-54th at the Canadian Open									
1973	12	30	3	0	0	0	1	73.57	$1,256
Best finish for 1973: T-22nd at the Shrine-Robinson Golf Classic									
1974	16	41	5	0	0	1	1	74.05	$5,728
Best finish for 1974: 7th at the Monsanto Open									
1975	10	34	7	0	0	0	0	73.41	$3,122
Best finish for 1975: T-31st at the IVB Philadelphia Golf Classic									
1976	13	38	7	0	0	0	1	73.37	$3,820
Best finish for 1976: T-21st at the Tallahassee Open									
1977	5	9	0	0	0	0	0	74.78	
Period Totals	Starts	Rounds Played	Cuts Made	Wins	Top-5s	Top-10s	Top-25s	Scoring Average	Money
	73	194	26	0	0	1	3	73.98	$14,759

Mike Heinen

Year	Starts	Rounds Played	Cuts Made	Wins	Top-5s	Top-10s	Top-25s	Scoring Average	Money
1990	1	2	0	0	0	0	0	76.50	
1991	1	2	0	0	0	0	0	75.50	
1994	27	79	12	1	1	3	5	71.39	$392,163

Best finish for 1994: Win at the Shell Houston Open

1995	29	87	16	0	2	3	6	71.23	$354,620

Best finish for 1995: T-2nd at the Freeport-McMoRan Classic & GTE Byron Nelson Classic

1996	32	95	16	0	0	0	2	71.67	$103,588

Best finish for 1996: T-21st at the Freeport-McDermott Classic

1997	10	25	1	0	0	0	0	72.28	$3,000

Best finish for 1997: T-69th at the Freeport-McDermott Classic

1998	15	40	5	0	1	1	1	71.60	$93,134

Best finish for 1998: T-4th at the CVS Charity Classic

1999	2	4	0	0	0	0	0	74.00	
2000	3	8	1	0	0	0	0	71.75	$5,018

Best finish for 2000: T-72nd at the Westin Texas Open at LaCantera

2001	8	24	4	0	0	0	1	71.58	$50,838

Best finish for 2001: T-22nd at the Kemper Insurance Open

2002	15	49	9	0	1	1	3	71.14	$246,853

Best finish for 2002: T-5th at the John Deere Classic

2003	29	88	16	0	0	0	4	70.80	$432,417

Best finish for 2003: T-11th at the Greater Hartford Open

2004	17	53	9	0	0	1	1	72.09	$166,185

Best finish for 2004: T-8th at the Chrysler Classic of Tucson

2005	7	17	1	0	0	0	0	71.94	$6,300

Best finish for 2005: T-64th at the B.C. Open

2006	5	10	0	0	0	0	0	73.20	
2007	1	2	0	0	0	0	0	72.50	
2008	7	15	0	0	0	0	0	75.13	
Period Totals	Starts	Rounds Played	Cuts Made	Wins	Top-5s	Top-10s	Top-25s	Scoring Average	Money
	209	600	90	1	5	9	23	71.62	$1,854,116

Bobby Heins

Year	Starts	Rounds Played	Cuts Made	Wins	Top-5s	Top-10s	Top-25s	Scoring Average	Money
1974	21	57	7	0	0	0	1	73.04	$5,117

Best finish for 1974: T-11th at the Tallahassee Open

1975	12	32	3	0	0	0	0	75.03	$895

Best finish for 1975: 56th at the Bing Crosby Pro-Am

1976	2	4	0	0	0	0	0	74.75	
1979	16	34	1	0	0	0	0	73.71	$922

Best finish for 1979: T-36th at the Southern Open

1980	7	16	1	0	0	0	0	74.69	$532

Best finish for 1980: T-62nd at the Doral-Eastern Open

1982	2	4	0	0	0	0	0	73.75	$600
1983	2	6	1	0	0	0	0	75.50	$2,100

Best finish for 1983: T-77th at the PGA Championship

1984	1	4	1	0	0	0	0	71.00	$2,355

Best finish for 1984: T-36th at the Manufactures Hanover Westchester Classic

1985	2	4	0	0	0	0	0	79.50	$1,000
1987	1	4	1	0	0	0	0	75.75	$1,164

Best finish for 1987: 73rd at the Manufactures Hanover Westchester Classic

1988	1	2	0	0	0	0	0	74.00	
1989	1	2	0	0	0	0	0	74.50	$1,000
1990	1	4	1	0	0	0	0	72.75	$1,740

Best finish for 1990: T-82nd at the Buick Classic

1992	1	2	0	0	0	0	0	74.50	
Period Totals	Starts	Rounds Played	Cuts Made	Wins	Top-5s	Top-10s	Top-25s	Scoring Average	Money
	70	175	16	0	0	0	1	74.02	$17,425

Bob Heintz

Year	Starts	Rounds Played	Cuts Made	Wins	Top-5s	Top-10s	Top-25s	Scoring Average	Money
1999	1	2	0	0	0	0	0	75.00	$1,000
2000	34	85	9	0	0	1	2	72.02	$127,412

Best finish for 2000: T-10th at the B.C. Open

2002	28	68	6	0	0	0	2	72.18	$127,346

Best finish for 2002: T-14th at the Southern Farm Bureau Classic

2004	1	2	0	0	0	0	0	74.50	
2005	24	67	9	0	1	1	3	71.45	$355,488

Best finish for 2005: T-5th at the Valero Texas Open

2007	27	85	15	0	2	2	3	71.08	$649,342

Best finish for 2007: T-5th at the U.S. Bank Championship in Milwaukee & Canadian Open

Year	Starts	Rounds Played	Cuts Made	Wins	Top-5s	Top-10s	Top-25s	Scoring Average	Money
2008	17	48	7	0	0	0	2	71.35	$301,015

Best finish for 2008: T-11th at the Stanford St. Jude Classic & Reno-Tahoe Open

Period Totals	Starts	Rounds Played	Cuts Made	Wins	Top-5s	Top-10s	Top-25s	Scoring Average	Money
	132	357	46	0	3	4	12	71.66	$1,561,603

Webb Heintzelman

Year	Starts	Rounds Played	Cuts Made	Wins	Top-5s	Top-10s	Top-25s	Scoring Average	Money
1987	1	2	0	0	0	0	0	75.00	
1988	4	12	2	0	0	0	0	72.42	$5,427

Best finish for 1988: T-39th at the Kemper Open

| 1989 | 33 | 105 | 19 | 0 | 0 | 1 | 7 | 71.15 | $102,994 |

Best finish for 1989: T-10th at the Bank of Boston Classic

| 1990 | 34 | 96 | 14 | 0 | 0 | 0 | 3 | 72.02 | $67,376 |

Best finish for 1990: T-11th at the AT&T Pebble Beach Pro-Am

| 1991 | 1 | 4 | 1 | 0 | 0 | 0 | 0 | 68.50 | $1,292 |

Best finish for 1991: T-37th at the Deposit Guaranty Classic

| 1992 | 2 | 4 | 0 | 0 | 0 | 0 | 0 | 76.00 | $1,000 |
| 1993 | 2 | 6 | 1 | 0 | 0 | 0 | 0 | 70.83 | $4,290 |

Best finish for 1993: T-39th at the Anheuser-Busch Golf Classic

1997	1	2	0	0	0	0	0	75.00	
1998	1	2	0	0	0	0	0	75.50	
Period Totals	Starts	Rounds Played	Cuts Made	Wins	Top-5s	Top-10s	Top-25s	Scoring Average	Money
	79	233	37	0	0	1	10	71.71	$182,379

Scott Hend

Year	Starts	Rounds Played	Cuts Made	Wins	Top-5s	Top-10s	Top-25s	Scoring Average	Money
2004	29	79	11	0	1	1	3	72.22	$532,263

Best finish for 2004: 3rd at the BellSouth Classic

| 2005 | 28 | 73 | 9 | 0 | 0 | 1 | 3 | 72.45 | $360,190 |

Best finish for 2005: T-6th at the Bank of America Colonial

| 2006 | 6 | 16 | 2 | 0 | 0 | 0 | 0 | 73.25 | $61,162 |

Best finish for 2006: T-32nd at the U.S. Open

Period Totals	Starts	Rounds Played	Cuts Made	Wins	Top-5s	Top-10s	Top-25s	Scoring Average	Money
	63	168	22	0	1	2	6	72.42	$953,614

Dick Hendrickson

Year	Starts	Rounds Played	Cuts Made	Wins	Top-5s	Top-10s	Top-25s	Scoring Average	Money
1958	2	6	1	0	0	0	0	74.67	

Best finish for 1958: T-38th at the Eastern Open

| 1962 | 1 | 3 | 1 | 0 | 0 | 0 | 0 | 73.67 | $080 |

Best finish for 1962: T-84th at the Thunderbird Classic Invitational

| 1964 | 7 | 14 | 1 | 0 | 0 | 0 | 0 | 74.43 | |

Best finish for 1964: T-43rd at the San Diego Open

| 1965 | 6 | 20 | 4 | 0 | 0 | 0 | 0 | 74.65 | $558 |

Best finish for 1965: T-40th at the U.S. Open

| 1966 | 2 | 4 | 0 | 0 | 0 | 0 | 0 | 76.25 | |
| 1967 | 4 | 11 | 2 | 0 | 0 | 0 | 0 | 73.64 | $554 |

Best finish for 1967: T-44th at the Philadelphia Classic

| 1968 | 3 | 8 | 1 | 0 | 0 | 0 | 0 | 73.88 | $500 |

Best finish for 1968: T-65th at the Philadelphia Golf Classic

1969	1	2	0	0	0	0	0	75.50	
1970	2	4	0	0	0	0	0	76.25	
1972	19	46	6	0	0	0	2	74.91	$4,351

Best finish for 1972: T-13th at the Quad Cities Open

| 1973 | 12 | 31 | 5 | 0 | 0 | 0 | 1 | 73.32 | $4,841 |

Best finish for 1973: T-14th at the Liggett Meyers Open

1974	1	2	0	0	0	0	0	76.00	
1975	1	2	0	0	0	0	0	78.50	
1976	1	2	0	0	0	0	0	76.50	
1978	1	2	0	0	0	0	0	74.00	
1979	1	2	0	0	0	0	0	75.00	
1982	1	2	0	0	0	0	0	77.50	$650
Period Totals	Starts	Rounds Played	Cuts Made	Wins	Top-5s	Top-10s	Top-25s	Scoring Average	Money
	65	161	21	0	0	0	3	74.53	$11,534

Matt Hendrix

Year	Starts	Rounds Played	Cuts Made	Wins	Top-5s	Top-10s	Top-25s	Scoring Average	Money
2004	3	8	1	0	0	0	0	71.25	$6,750

Best finish for 2004: T-56th at the B.C. Open

| 2005 | 1 | 4 | 1 | 0 | 0 | 0 | 1 | 67.25 | $51,429 |

Best finish for 2005: T-13th at the B.C. Open

Year	Starts	Rounds Played	Cuts Made	Wins	Top-5s	Top-10s	Top-25s	Scoring Average	Money
2007	24	63	7	0	0	0	0	72.27	$108,269

Best finish for 2007: T-31st at the Shell Houston Open

Period Totals	Starts	Rounds Played	Cuts Made	Wins	Top-5s	Top-10s	Top-25s	Scoring Average	Money
	28	75	9	0	0	0	1	71.89	$166,448

Nolan Henke

Year	Starts	Rounds Played	Cuts Made	Wins	Top-5s	Top-10s	Top-25s	Scoring Average	Money
1986	1	4	1	0	0	0	0	71.50	

Best finish for 1986: T-37th at the Tallahassee Open

Year	Starts	Rounds Played	Cuts Made	Wins	Top-5s	Top-10s	Top-25s	Scoring Average	Money
1987	2	8	2	0	0	0	1	70.88	$9,072

Best finish for 1987: T-16th at the Centel Classic

| 1989 | 25 | 73 | 13 | 0 | 0 | 1 | 3 | 71.26 | $57,464 |

Best finish for 1989: 8th at the B.C. Open

| 1990 | 29 | 88 | 16 | 1 | 2 | 4 | 9 | 70.97 | $294,592 |

Best finish for 1990: Win at the B.C. Open

| 1991 | 28 | 99 | 21 | 1 | 3 | 6 | 13 | 71.06 | $527,174 |

Best finish for 1991: Win at the Phoenix Open

| 1992 | 27 | 86 | 16 | 0 | 3 | 4 | 11 | 70.84 | $328,637 |

Best finish for 1992: T-2nd at the B.C. Open

| 1993 | 26 | 93 | 20 | 1 | 1 | 4 | 9 | 71.32 | $502,375 |

Best finish for 1993: Win at the BellSouth Classic

| 1994 | 26 | 79 | 11 | 0 | 2 | 3 | 5 | 71.33 | $282,119 |

Best finish for 1994: T-2nd at the BellSouth Classic

| 1995 | 25 | 81 | 14 | 0 | 1 | 2 | 5 | 71.63 | $237,141 |

Best finish for 1995: T-2nd at the MCI Classic

| 1996 | 24 | 80 | 15 | 0 | 3 | 3 | 6 | 71.15 | $302,726 |

Best finish for 1996: T-3rd at the Greater Milwaukee Open

| 1997 | 24 | 82 | 16 | 0 | 0 | 1 | 6 | 71.35 | $205,859 |

Best finish for 1997: T-8th at the Shell Houston Open

| 1998 | 25 | 88 | 18 | 0 | 3 | 4 | 6 | 70.92 | $444,561 |

Best finish for 1998: T-3rd at the Greater Milwaukee Open & B.C. Open

| 1999 | 28 | 83 | 13 | 0 | 1 | 3 | 4 | 71.70 | $337,554 |

Best finish for 1999: T-5th at the MCI Classic

| 2000 | 32 | 79 | 7 | 0 | 0 | 0 | 0 | 72.87 | $47,722 |

Best finish for 2000: T-64th at the John Deere Classic

| 2001 | 8 | 22 | 4 | 0 | 0 | 0 | 0 | 71.86 | $25,420 |

Best finish for 2001: T-49th at the Phoenix Open

| 2002 | 3 | 8 | 1 | 0 | 0 | 0 | 0 | 73.13 | $6,240 |

Best finish for 2002: T-64th at the John Deere Classic

| 2003 | 6 | 16 | 2 | 0 | 0 | 0 | 0 | 72.63 | $13,970 |

Best finish for 2003: T-69th at the BellSouth Classic

2004	1	2	0	0	0	0	0	72.50	
2006	1	2	0	0	0	0	0	75.50	
2007	1	2	0	0	0	0	0	73.50	
2008	1	2	0	0	0	0	0	77.50	

Period Totals	Starts	Rounds Played	Cuts Made	Wins	Top-5s	Top-10s	Top-25s	Scoring Average	Money
	343	1077	190	3	19	35	78	71.42	$3,622,626

Allan Henning

Year	Starts	Rounds Played	Cuts Made	Wins	Top-5s	Top-10s	Top-25s	Scoring Average	Money
1963	2	8	2	0	0	0	1	71.38	$510

Best finish for 1963: T-22nd at the Pensacola Open Invitational

| 1964 | 1 | 2 | 0 | 0 | 0 | 0 | 0 | 76.00 | |
| 1966 | 2 | 6 | 1 | 0 | 0 | 0 | 0 | 75.50 | $286 |

Best finish for 1966: T-30th at the British Open

| 1967 | 18 | 57 | 10 | 0 | 1 | 2 | 7 | 72.54 | $14,342 |

Best finish for 1967: T-4th at the Cleveland Open

| 1968 | 13 | 38 | 6 | 0 | 0 | 1 | 1 | 73.08 | $1,341 |

Best finish for 1968: 7th at the Magnolia State Classic

| 1969 | 17 | 54 | 10 | 0 | 0 | 0 | 2 | 72.78 | $4,149 |

Best finish for 1969: T-15th at the Greater Milwaukee Open

| 1970 | 11 | 30 | 7 | 0 | 0 | 0 | 1 | 73.00 | $2,779 |

Best finish for 1970: T-23rd at the National 4 Ball Championship PGA Players

| 1975 | 1 | 2 | 0 | 0 | 0 | 0 | 0 | 75.00 | $220 |
| 1976 | 2 | 6 | 1 | 0 | 0 | 0 | 1 | 76.50 | $5,000 |

Best finish for 1976: 20th at the World Series Of Golf

Period Totals	Starts	Rounds Played	Cuts Made	Wins	Top-5s	Top-10s	Top-25s	Scoring Average	Money
	67	203	37	0	1	3	13	72.99	$28,627

Harold Henning

Year	Starts	Rounds Played	Cuts Made	Wins	Top-5s	Top-10s	Top-25s	Scoring Average	Money
1958	1	4	1	0	0	0	1	71.50	

Best finish for 1958: 13th at the British Open

Year	Starts	Rounds Played	Cuts Made	Wins	Top-5s	Top-10s	Top-25s	Scoring Average	Money
1959	1	4	1	0	0	0	1	73.50	

Best finish for 1959: T-23rd at the British Open

Year	Starts	Rounds Played	Cuts Made	Wins	Top-5s	Top-10s	Top-25s	Scoring Average	Money
1960	5	18	4	0	1	1	3	71.72	$3,543

Best finish for 1960: T-3rd at the British Open

| 1961 | 1 | 4 | 1 | 0 | 0 | 0 | 1 | 73.25 | |

Best finish for 1961: T-11th at the British Open

| 1962 | 7 | 28 | 7 | 0 | 0 | 0 | 3 | 73.04 | $3,528 |

Best finish for 1962: T-11th at the Masters

| 1963 | 1 | 4 | 1 | 0 | 0 | 0 | 1 | 73.25 | $217 |

Best finish for 1963: T-20th at the British Open

| 1964 | 7 | 15 | 1 | 0 | 0 | 1 | 1 | 74.67 | $520 |

Best finish for 1964: T-8th at the British Open

| 1965 | 2 | 6 | 1 | 0 | 0 | 0 | 1 | 73.00 | $2,062 |

Best finish for 1965: T-13th at the Carling Open

| 1966 | 12 | 46 | 11 | 1 | 3 | 3 | 9 | 71.87 | $33,644 |

Best finish for 1966: Win at the Texas Open Invitational

| 1967 | 28 | 99 | 23 | 0 | 4 | 8 | 16 | 71.59 | $59,561 |

Best finish for 1967: T-2nd at the Doral Open

| 1968 | 30 | 112 | 26 | 0 | 3 | 6 | 17 | 71.08 | $53,852 |

Best finish for 1968: 3rd at the Bob Hope Desert Classic & Byron Nelson Golf Classic

| 1969 | 25 | 88 | 21 | 0 | 2 | 3 | 13 | 71.74 | $42,631 |

Best finish for 1969: 2nd at the Los Angeles Open

| 1970 | 16 | 42 | 9 | 1 | 2 | 3 | 5 | 71.62 | $25,837 |

Best finish for 1970: Win at the Tallahassee Open

| 1971 | 9 | 34 | 8 | 0 | 0 | 0 | 1 | 73.09 | $7,745 |

Best finish for 1971: T-16th at the Monsanto Open

| 1972 | 5 | 8 | 0 | 0 | 0 | 0 | 0 | 73.13 | |
| 1973 | 1 | 4 | 1 | 0 | 0 | 1 | 1 | 72.25 | $3,510 |

Best finish for 1973: T-10th at the British Open

| 1980 | 1 | 4 | 1 | 0 | 0 | 0 | 0 | 73.25 | $1,329 |

Best finish for 1980: T-51st at the British Open

| 1981 | 1 | 2 | 0 | 0 | 0 | 0 | 0 | 77.50 | $450 |
| 1982 | 2 | 6 | 1 | 0 | 0 | 0 | 0 | 75.83 | $1,105 |

Best finish for 1982: 41st at the British Open

| 1983 | 1 | 4 | 1 | 0 | 0 | 1 | 1 | 69.75 | $18,375 |

Best finish for 1983: T-6th at the British Open

| 1984 | 1 | 3 | 0 | 0 | 0 | 0 | 0 | 73.67 | $793 |

Period Totals	Starts	Rounds Played	Cuts Made	Wins	Top-5s	Top-10s	Top-25s	Scoring Average	Money
	157	535	119	2	15	27	75	71.96	$258,701

PGA Tour career totals from 1955 to 1984

	Starts	Rounds Played	Cuts Made	Wins	Top-5s	Top-10s	Top-25s	Scoring Average	Money
	167	575	129	2	15	28	77	N/A	$260,673

Brian Henninger

Year	Starts	Rounds Played	Cuts Made	Wins	Top-5s	Top-10s	Top-25s	Scoring Average	Money
1993	29	88	16	0	1	1	3	71.86	$112,811

Best finish for 1993: T-4th at the Sprint Western Open

| 1994 | 21 | 69 | 16 | 1 | 2 | 2 | 2 | 71.26 | $294,075 |

Best finish for 1994: Win at the Deposit Guaranty Golf Classic

| 1995 | 28 | 79 | 11 | 0 | 1 | 2 | 3 | 72.00 | $167,930 |

Best finish for 1995: T-5th at the Canon Greater Hartford Open

| 1996 | 28 | 84 | 15 | 0 | 0 | 1 | 5 | 71.58 | $138,180 |

Best finish for 1996: T-9th at the CVS Charity Classic

| 1997 | 25 | 77 | 15 | 0 | 2 | 3 | 6 | 70.92 | $329,864 |

Best finish for 1997: T-2nd at the BellSouth Classic

| 1998 | 29 | 95 | 19 | 0 | 0 | 2 | 5 | 71.09 | $256,714 |

Best finish for 1998: T-8th at the MasterCard Colonial

| 1999 | 29 | 96 | 19 | 1 | 3 | 4 | 6 | 71.47 | $774,486 |

Best finish for 1999: Win at the Southern Farm Bureau Classic

| 2000 | 29 | 89 | 16 | 0 | 1 | 2 | 6 | 71.22 | $528,741 |

Best finish for 2000: T-4th at the Reno-Tahoe Open

| 2001 | 29 | 79 | 10 | 0 | 0 | 0 | 2 | 71.70 | $161,814 |

Best finish for 2001: T-17th at the Buick Challenge

| 2002 | 20 | 66 | 12 | 0 | 1 | 1 | 3 | 70.95 | $281,614 |

Best finish for 2002: T-3rd at the B.C. Open

| 2003 | 17 | 56 | 12 | 0 | 0 | 0 | 2 | 71.11 | $166,003 |

Best finish for 2003: T-18th at the B.C. Open

| 2004 | 9 | 21 | 1 | 0 | 0 | 0 | 0 | 72.90 | $6,240 |

Best finish for 2004: T-65th at the Chrysler Classic of Tucson

| 2005 | 2 | 7 | 1 | 0 | 0 | 0 | 0 | 71.29 | $7,236 |

Best finish for 2005: T-50th at the Southern Farm Bureau Classic

Year	Starts	Rounds Played	Cuts Made	Wins	Top-5s	Top-10s	Top-25s	Scoring Average	Money
2006	12	39	7	0	0	0	1	71.21	$96,453

Best finish for 2006: T-24th at the Chrysler Classic of Tucson

Year	Starts	Rounds Played	Cuts Made	Wins	Top-5s	Top-10s	Top-25s	Scoring Average	Money
2007	2	5	0	0	0	0	0	74.00	
Period Totals	Starts	Rounds Played	Cuts Made	Wins	Top-5s	Top-10s	Top-25s	Scoring Average	Money
	309	950	170	2	11	18	44	71.43	$3,322,160

Bunky Henry

Year	Starts	Rounds Played	Cuts Made	Wins	Top-5s	Top-10s	Top-25s	Scoring Average	Money
1965	1	2	0	0	0	0	0	75.50	
1966	1	2	0	0	0	0	0	78.50	
1967	2	6	1	0	0	0	0	73.83	

Best finish for 1967: T-47th at the Cajun Classic

| 1968 | 19 | 58 | 10 | 0 | 0 | 0 | 1 | 73.10 | $524 |

Best finish for 1968: T-15th at the Rebel Yell Open

| 1969 | 30 | 95 | 18 | 1 | 1 | 2 | 5 | 73.13 | $53,331 |

Best finish for 1969: Win at the National Airlines Open

| 1970 | 35 | 105 | 16 | 0 | 1 | 2 | 4 | 73.01 | $17,813 |

Best finish for 1970: T-3rd at the IVB Philadelphia Golf Classic

| 1971 | 22 | 65 | 10 | 0 | 0 | 0 | 2 | 74.06 | $4,487 |

Best finish for 1971: T-20th at the Bahamas National Open

| 1972 | 31 | 90 | 14 | 0 | 0 | 2 | 3 | 73.84 | $16,766 |

Best finish for 1972: T-6th at the Hawaiian Open

| 1973 | 26 | 76 | 11 | 0 | 1 | 1 | 2 | 73.17 | $15,612 |

Best finish for 1973: T-2nd at the Shrine-Robinson Golf Classic

| 1974 | 19 | 62 | 12 | 0 | 0 | 0 | 1 | 73.06 | $6,908 |

Best finish for 1974: T-22nd at the San Antonio Texas Open

| 1975 | 8 | 18 | 1 | 0 | 0 | 0 | 0 | 74.44 | $210 |

Best finish for 1975: T-40th at the Tallahassee Open

| 1977 | 6 | 12 | 0 | 0 | 0 | 0 | 0 | 74.92 | $500 |
| 1978 | 19 | 59 | 10 | 0 | 0 | 1 | 3 | 73.22 | $11,465 |

Best finish for 1978: T-8th at the Canadian Open

| 1979 | 3 | 8 | 1 | 0 | 0 | 0 | 0 | 75.63 | $582 |

Best finish for 1979: 73rd at the Atlanta Classic

| 1980 | 8 | 21 | 5 | 0 | 0 | 0 | 1 | 71.67 | $5,394 |

Best finish for 1980: T-21st at the Pensacola Open

| 1981 | 14 | 34 | 3 | 0 | 0 | 0 | 0 | 72.41 | $3,396 |

Best finish for 1981: T-30th at the USF&G New Orleans Open

1986	1	2	0	0	0	0	0	77.50	
1987	1	1	0	0	0	0	0	81.00	
1988	5	10	0	0	0	0	0	75.10	
1991	3	6	0	0	0	0	0	77.17	
1992	2	4	0	0	0	0	0	75.00	
1993	2	4	0	0	0	0	0	74.50	
1994	1	2	0	0	0	0	0	75.50	
1995	3	6	0	0	0	0	0	77.50	
1997	1	2	0	0	0	0	0	73.50	
1998	2	6	1	0	0	0	0	74.50	$2,376

Best finish for 1998: 72nd at the Deposit Guaranty Golf Classic

Period Totals	Starts	Rounds Played	Cuts Made	Wins	Top-5s	Top-10s	Top-25s	Scoring Average	Money
	265	756	113	1	3	8	22	73.47	$139,363

J.J. Henry

Year	Starts	Rounds Played	Cuts Made	Wins	Top-5s	Top-10s	Top-25s	Scoring Average	Money
1998	3	12	3	0	0	0	0	70.92	$6,871

Best finish for 1998: T-56th at the Canon Greater Hartford Open

| 1999 | 2 | 4 | 0 | 0 | 0 | 0 | 0 | 72.00 | |
| 2001 | 28 | 84 | 15 | 0 | 2 | 5 | 6 | 70.63 | $1,073,847 |

Best finish for 2001: T-2nd at the Kemper Insurance Open & Texas Open at LaCantera

| 2002 | 34 | 108 | 21 | 0 | 1 | 2 | 5 | 70.98 | $569,875 |

Best finish for 2002: T-3rd at the Reno-Tahoe Open

| 2003 | 31 | 96 | 18 | 0 | 0 | 1 | 7 | 70.73 | $660,341 |

Best finish for 2003: T-9th at the BellSouth Classic

| 2004 | 30 | 103 | 21 | 0 | 2 | 3 | 7 | 70.94 | $848,823 |

Best finish for 2004: T-3rd at the Southern Farm Bureau Classic

| 2005 | 32 | 100 | 20 | 0 | 3 | 4 | 6 | 70.69 | $942,347 |

Best finish for 2005: T-4th at the Reno-Tahoe Open

| 2006 | 28 | 93 | 20 | 1 | 3 | 5 | 9 | 70.84 | $2,308,128 |

Best finish for 2006: Win at the Buick Championship

| 2007 | 26 | 85 | 18 | 0 | 0 | 2 | 7 | 71.39 | $1,091,160 |

Best finish for 2007: T-6th at the Valero Texas Open

| 2008 | 34 | 108 | 19 | 0 | 2 | 2 | 4 | 71.07 | $931,162 |

Best finish for 2008: T-4th at the Wyndham Championship & Frys.Com Open

Period Totals	Starts	Rounds Played	Cuts Made	Wins	Top-5s	Top-10s	Top-25s	Scoring Average	Money
	248	793	155	1	13	24	51	70.92	$8,432,553

Mark Hensby

Year	Starts	Rounds Played	Cuts Made	Wins	Top-5s	Top-10s	Top-25s	Scoring Average	Money
1995	1	2	0	0	0	0	0	73.50	
1996	1	4	1	0	0	0	0	69.75	$3,799

Best finish for 1996: T-41st at the Quad City Classic

Year	Starts	Rounds Played	Cuts Made	Wins	Top-5s	Top-10s	Top-25s	Scoring Average	Money
1997	1	2	0	0	0	0	0	76.00	
2001	29	70	7	0	0	1	2	71.93	$155,629

Best finish for 2001: T-9th at the Touchstone Energy Tucson Open

Year	Starts	Rounds Played	Cuts Made	Wins	Top-5s	Top-10s	Top-25s	Scoring Average	Money
2003	1	4	1	0	0	0	0	69.50	$8,880

Best finish for 2003: T-58th at the Phoenix Open

Year	Starts	Rounds Played	Cuts Made	Wins	Top-5s	Top-10s	Top-25s	Scoring Average	Money
2004	29	93	19	1	5	8	12	70.77	$2,718,766

Best finish for 2004: Win at the John Deere Classic

Year	Starts	Rounds Played	Cuts Made	Wins	Top-5s	Top-10s	Top-25s	Scoring Average	Money
2005	21	68	16	0	3	3	9	71.79	$1,312,637

Best finish for 2005: T-3rd at the U.S. Open

Year	Starts	Rounds Played	Cuts Made	Wins	Top-5s	Top-10s	Top-25s	Scoring Average	Money
2006	16	44	8	0	0	0	2	72.98	$253,883

Best finish for 2006: T-22nd at the Masters & British Open

Year	Starts	Rounds Played	Cuts Made	Wins	Top-5s	Top-10s	Top-25s	Scoring Average	Money
2007	25	81	16	0	1	1	4	71.48	$974,049

Best finish for 2007: 2nd at the Fry's Electronics Open

Year	Starts	Rounds Played	Cuts Made	Wins	Top-5s	Top-10s	Top-25s	Scoring Average	Money
2008	26	71	9	0	1	1	3	71.85	$480,483

Best finish for 2008: T-4th at the EDS Byron Nelson Championship

Period Totals	Starts	Rounds Played	Cuts Made	Wins	Top-5s	Top-10s	Top-25s	Scoring Average	Money
	150	439	77	1	10	14	32	71.66	$5,908,124

Denny Hepler

Year	Starts	Rounds Played	Cuts Made	Wins	Top-5s	Top-10s	Top-25s	Scoring Average	Money
1979	1	2	0	0	0	0	0	73.00	
1982	2	4	0	0	0	0	0	75.50	$382
1983	2	6	1	0	0	0	1	71.83	$3,024

Best finish for 1983: T-19th at the Miller High-Life Quad Cities Open

Year	Starts	Rounds Played	Cuts Made	Wins	Top-5s	Top-10s	Top-25s	Scoring Average	Money
1984	1	2	0	0	0	0	0	77.50	$600
1986	25	65	9	0	0	0	1	73.46	$13,921

Best finish for 1986: T-16th at the Provident Classic

Year	Starts	Rounds Played	Cuts Made	Wins	Top-5s	Top-10s	Top-25s	Scoring Average	Money
1987	25	60	7	0	0	0	1	72.60	$13,748

Best finish for 1987: T-21st at the Kemper Open

Year	Starts	Rounds Played	Cuts Made	Wins	Top-5s	Top-10s	Top-25s	Scoring Average	Money
1988	3	8	1	0	0	0	0	73.25	$1,050

Best finish for 1988: T-64th at the Centel Classic

Year	Starts	Rounds Played	Cuts Made	Wins	Top-5s	Top-10s	Top-25s	Scoring Average	Money
1989	3	7	0	0	0	0	0	74.43	$1,000
1990	1	2	0	0	0	0	0	77.50	$1,000
1991	1	4	1	0	0	0	0	74.25	$2,225

Best finish for 1991: T-70th at the PGA Championship

Year	Starts	Rounds Played	Cuts Made	Wins	Top-5s	Top-10s	Top-25s	Scoring Average	Money
1992	1	2	0	0	0	0	0	75.00	$1,200
1994	1	2	0	0	0	0	0	75.50	$1,200
1995	1	2	0	0	0	0	0	78.50	$1,200

Period Totals	Starts	Rounds Played	Cuts Made	Wins	Top-5s	Top-10s	Top-25s	Scoring Average	Money
	67	166	19	0	0	0	3	73.39	$40,551

Eduardo Herrera

Year	Starts	Rounds Played	Cuts Made	Wins	Top-5s	Top-10s	Top-25s	Scoring Average	Money
1986	1	2	0	0	0	0	0	77.00	
1994	1	2	0	0	0	0	0	78.00	$972
1995	1	4	1	0	0	0	0	73.50	$8,733

Best finish for 1995: T-58th at the British Open

Year	Starts	Rounds Played	Cuts Made	Wins	Top-5s	Top-10s	Top-25s	Scoring Average	Money
1997	3	10	2	0	0	0	0	70.80	$7,778

Best finish for 1997: T-40th at the Canon Greater Hartford Open

Year	Starts	Rounds Played	Cuts Made	Wins	Top-5s	Top-10s	Top-25s	Scoring Average	Money
1998	2	6	1	0	0	0	0	72.17	$7,757

Best finish for 1998: T-33rd at the B.C. Open

Year	Starts	Rounds Played	Cuts Made	Wins	Top-5s	Top-10s	Top-25s	Scoring Average	Money
1999	1	2	0	0	0	0	0	83.50	$1,094
2002	23	59	7	0	0	1	1	72.64	$109,953

Best finish for 2002: 8th at the B.C. Open

Period Totals	Starts	Rounds Played	Cuts Made	Wins	Top-5s	Top-10s	Top-25s	Scoring Average	Money
	32	85	11	0	0	1	1	72.92	$136,286

Tim Herron

Year	Starts	Rounds Played	Cuts Made	Wins	Top-5s	Top-10s	Top-25s	Scoring Average	Money
1995	1	2	0	0	0	0	0	75.00	$1,000
1996	31	100	22	1	1	3	7	71.32	$479,178

Best finish for 1996: Win at the Honda Classic

Year	Starts	Rounds Played	Cuts Made	Wins	Top-5s	Top-10s	Top-25s	Scoring Average	Money
1997	31	101	21	1	1	6	11	70.99	$640,997

Best finish for 1997: Win at the LaCantera Texas Open

Year	Starts	Rounds Played	Cuts Made	Wins	Top-5s	Top-10s	Top-25s	Scoring Average	Money
1998	29	94	20	0	1	4	10	71.10	$525,973

Best finish for 1998: T-4th at the Tucson Chrysler Classic

| 1999 | 29 | 96 | 21 | 1 | 3 | 7 | 11 | 70.83 | $1,512,952 |

Best finish for 1999: Win at the Bay Hill Invitational

| 2000 | 28 | 94 | 20 | 0 | 0 | 4 | 10 | 70.83 | $741,445 |

Best finish for 2000: T-7th at the Kemper Insurance Open & John Deere Classic

| 2001 | 29 | 91 | 20 | 0 | 1 | 3 | 10 | 70.60 | $947,440 |

Best finish for 2001: T-3rd at the Greater Milwaukee Open

| 2002 | 30 | 99 | 21 | 0 | 2 | 3 | 7 | 70.59 | $956,917 |

Best finish for 2002: T-2nd at the Greater Milwaukee Open

| 2003 | 29 | 100 | 21 | 0 | 6 | 6 | 9 | 70.31 | $2,176,390 |

Best finish for 2003: T-2nd at the Reno-Tahoe Open & American Express Championship

| 2004 | 26 | 83 | 17 | 0 | 4 | 4 | 10 | 71.17 | $1,739,258 |

Best finish for 2004: 2nd at the Buick Championship

| 2005 | 28 | 99 | 23 | 0 | 3 | 7 | 13 | 70.36 | $2,105,550 |

Best finish for 2005: T-3rd at the Chrysler Championship

| 2006 | 27 | 81 | 15 | 1 | 1 | 2 | 4 | 71.70 | $1,777,352 |

Best finish for 2006: Win at the Bank of America Colonial

| 2007 | 27 | 98 | 22 | 0 | 1 | 1 | 5 | 71.10 | $951,200 |

Best finish for 2007: T-2nd at the U.S. Bank Championship in Milwaukee

| 2008 | 28 | 97 | 20 | 0 | 1 | 3 | 9 | 70.66 | $1,164,999 |

Best finish for 2008: T-5th at the Deutsche Bank Championship

Period Totals	Starts	Rounds Played	Cuts Made	Wins	Top-5s	Top-10s	Top-25s	Scoring Average	Money
	373	1235	263	4	25	53	116	70.88	$15,720,650

Pete Hessemer

Year	Starts	Rounds Played	Cuts Made	Wins	Top-5s	Top-10s	Top-25s	Scoring Average	Money
1958	6	16	2	0	0	0	0	74.31	

Best finish for 1958: T-45th at the Dallas Open

| 1961 | 1 | 4 | 1 | 0 | 0 | 0 | 1 | 70.50 | $610 |

Best finish for 1961: T-12th at the Beaumont Open Invitational

| 1962 | 1 | 4 | 1 | 0 | 0 | 0 | 0 | 73.25 | $150 |

Best finish for 1962: T-67th at the Houston Classic

1964	1	2	0	0	0	0	0	75.00	
1965	2	4	0	0	0	0	0	76.00	
1966	1	2	0	0	0	0	0	76.50	
1967	11	24	1	0	0	0	0	76.54	

Best finish for 1967: 76th at the Florida Citrus Open

| 1968 | 6 | 16 | 2 | 0 | 0 | 0 | 0 | 74.75 | |

Best finish for 1968: T-50th at the Magnolia State Classic

1975	2	4	0	0	0	0	0	79.25	
1977	4	8	0	0	0	0	0	75.25	
1980	2	4	0	0	0	0	0	75.50	
1983	1	4	0	0	0	0	0	74.25	
1985	1	2	0	0	0	0	0	77.50	

Period Totals	Starts	Rounds Played	Cuts Made	Wins	Top-5s	Top-10s	Top-25s	Scoring Average	Money
	39	94	7	0	0	0	1	75.29	$760

Jeff Hewes

Year	Starts	Rounds Played	Cuts Made	Wins	Top-5s	Top-10s	Top-25s	Scoring Average	Money
1973	8	20	2	0	0	0	0	72.85	$699

Best finish for 1973: T-51st at the Shrine-Robinson Golf Classic

| 1976 | 5 | 12 | 1 | 0 | 0 | 0 | 0 | 74.33 | $250 |

Best finish for 1976: T-57th at the Southern Open

| 1977 | 10 | 28 | 3 | 0 | 0 | 0 | 0 | 74.00 | $1,330 |

Best finish for 1977: T-50th at the Joe Garagiola Tucson Open & Atlanta Classic

| 1978 | 15 | 37 | 3 | 0 | 0 | 0 | 0 | 74.03 | $2,059 |

Best finish for 1978: T-37th at the Kemper Open

| 1979 | 24 | 57 | 5 | 0 | 0 | 0 | 0 | 74.07 | $3,180 |

Best finish for 1979: T-36th at the Phoenix Open

| 1980 | 1 | 0 | 0 | 0 | 0 | 0 | 0 | | |
| 1981 | 14 | 31 | 3 | 0 | 0 | 0 | 0 | 73.81 | $2,707 |

Best finish for 1981: T-40th at the Danny Thomas Memphis Classic

Period Totals	Starts	Rounds Played	Cuts Made	Wins	Top-5s	Top-10s	Top-25s	Scoring Average	Money
	77	185	17	0	0	0	0	73.89	$10,225

Greg Hickman

Year	Starts	Rounds Played	Cuts Made	Wins	Top-5s	Top-10s	Top-25s	Scoring Average	Money
1980	1	2	0	0	0	0	0	76.00	$600
1984	1	2	0	0	0	0	0	76.50	$600
1985	1	2	0	0	0	0	0	82.50	

Year	Starts	Rounds Played	Cuts Made	Wins	Top-5s	Top-10s	Top-25s	Scoring Average	Money
1988	1	2	0	0	0	0	0	71.50	
1990	25	62	7	0	0	0	1	73.00	$19,927

Best finish for 1990: T-13th at the Deposit Guaranty

1992	27	64	7	0	0	0	1	72.92	$39,941

Best finish for 1992: T-11th at the Honda Classic

1993	2	4	0	0	0	0	0	74.50	
Period Totals	Starts	Rounds Played	Cuts Made	Wins	Top-5s	Top-10s	Top-25s	Scoring Average	Money
	58	138	14	0	0	0	2	73.22	$61,069

Darrell Hickok

Year	Starts	Rounds Played	Cuts Made	Wins	Top-5s	Top-10s	Top-25s	Scoring Average	Money
1958	6	18	2	0	0	0	0	74.61	$100

Best finish for 1958: 47th at the Greenbrier Invitational

1959	2	8	2	0	0	0	0	73.13	$327

Best finish for 1959: T-29th at the San Diego Open Invitational

1961	1	4	1	0	0	0	1	69.75	$550

Best finish for 1961: T-15th at the San Diego Open

1962	1	2	0	0	0	0	0	78.00	
1964	1	2	0	0	0	0	0	74.50	
1965	2	6	1	0	0	0	1	74.00	$576

Best finish for 1965: T-21st at the Tucson Open

1966	2	6	1	0	0	0	0	73.33	$067

Best finish for 1966: T-46th at the Tucson Open Invitational

1967	3	8	1	0	0	0	0	73.38	$390

Best finish for 1967: 34th at the Tucson Open

1968	12	34	5	0	0	0	2	73.44	$2,305

Best finish for 1968: T-16th at the Tucson Open Invitational

1969	4	12	2	0	0	0	0	74.00	$346

Best finish for 1969: T-52nd at the Tucson Open

1970	1	2	0	0	0	0	0	75.00	
1971	1	2	0	0	0	0	0	76.00	
1972	1	2	0	0	0	0	0	82.00	$500
1975	1	1	0	0	0	0	0	85.00	
Period Totals	Starts	Rounds Played	Cuts Made	Wins	Top-5s	Top-10s	Top-25s	Scoring Average	Money
	38	107	15	0	0	0	4	74.01	$5,160

Mike Higgins

Year	Starts	Rounds Played	Cuts Made	Wins	Top-5s	Top-10s	Top-25s	Scoring Average	Money
1968	18	55	10	0	0	0	3	72.82	$2,816

Best finish for 1968: T-15th at the "500" Festival Open Invitational

1971	2	6	1	0	0	0	0	72.33	$904

Best finish for 1971: T-28th at the Bahamas National Open

1972	19	43	2	0	0	0	0	75.14	$345

Best finish for 1972: T-70th at the Phoenix Open

1973	11	28	3	0	0	0	0	74.21	$567

Best finish for 1973: T-57th at the Quad Cities Open

1974	6	12	1	0	0	0	0	73.75	$289

Best finish for 1974: T-59th at the Houston Open

1975	3	6	0	0	0	0	0	75.33	
1980	1	2	0	0	0	0	0	77.50	
Period Totals	Starts	Rounds Played	Cuts Made	Wins	Top-5s	Top-10s	Top-25s	Scoring Average	Money
	60	152	17	0	0	0	3	73.95	$4,921

Bob Hill

Year	Starts	Rounds Played	Cuts Made	Wins	Top-5s	Top-10s	Top-25s	Scoring Average	Money
1958	14	45	8	0	0	1	2	73.49	$1,094

Best finish for 1958: T-6th at the Baton Rouge Open

1959	2	8	2	0	0	0	0	70.38	$168

Best finish for 1959: T-27th at the Tucson Open Invitational

1960	4	14	3	0	0	1	3	73.50	$791

Best finish for 1960: T-7th at the Puerto Rico Open Invitational

1961	1	2	0	0	0	0	0	75.50	
1962	2	5	1	0	0	0	0	77.40	
1963	1	2	1	0	0	0	0	78.50	

Best finish for 1963: T-200 at the PGA Championship

1964	1	4	1	0	0	0	0	73.00	$319

Best finish for 1964: T-52nd at the PGA Championship

1965	1	2	0	0	0	0	0	76.50	
1966	1	2	0	0	0	0	0	76.00	
1967	1	2	0	0	0	0	0	80.50	
1968	1	2	0	0	0	0	0	76.00	
Period Totals	Starts	Rounds Played	Cuts Made	Wins	Top-5s	Top-10s	Top-25s	Scoring Average	Money
	29	88	16	0	0	2	5	73.91	$2,372

Dave Hill

Year	Starts	Rounds Played	Cuts Made	Wins	Top-5s	Top-10s	Top-25s	Scoring Average	Money
1959	2	8	2	0	0	0	2	71.13	$875

Best finish for 1959: T-12th at the Coral Gables Open Invitational

| 1960 | 13 | 51 | 12 | 0 | 3 | 4 | 7 | 71.41 | $7,550 |

Best finish for 1960: T-3rd at the Mobile Sertoma Open Invitational

| 1961 | 21 | 85 | 18 | 2 | 4 | 8 | 13 | 70.53 | $20,160 |

Best finish for 1961: Win at the Home Of The Sun Open Invitational & Denver Open Invitational

| 1962 | 27 | 103 | 22 | 0 | 4 | 9 | 14 | 71.08 | $19,669 |

Best finish for 1962: T-2nd at the Motor City Open Invitational & St. Paul Open Invitational

| 1963 | 15 | 60 | 13 | 1 | 6 | 6 | 11 | 70.72 | $18,906 |

Best finish for 1963: Win at the Hot Springs Open Invitational

| 1964 | 30 | 107 | 23 | 0 | 1 | 2 | 10 | 72.59 | $13,332 |

Best finish for 1964: T-4th at the Tucson Open

| 1965 | 27 | 93 | 19 | 0 | 0 | 3 | 10 | 72.22 | $14,674 |

Best finish for 1965: T-7th at the Oklahoma City Open

| 1966 | 25 | 93 | 21 | 0 | 2 | 6 | 16 | 72.45 | $26,587 |

Best finish for 1966: 4th at the Cajun Classic

| 1967 | 27 | 96 | 23 | 1 | 2 | 6 | 14 | 71.49 | $51,864 |

Best finish for 1967: Win at the Memphis Open

| 1968 | 29 | 97 | 22 | 0 | 0 | 4 | 11 | 71.95 | $28,840 |

Best finish for 1968: 7th at the Los Angeles Open Invitational

| 1969 | 27 | 99 | 23 | 3 | 10 | 12 | 19 | 70.34 | $154,092 |

Best finish for 1969: Win at the Memphis Open, Buick Open & Philadelphia Classic

| 1970 | 27 | 96 | 24 | 1 | 8 | 13 | 20 | 70.81 | $114,727 |

Best finish for 1970: Win at the Danny Thomas Memphis Classic

| 1971 | 23 | 75 | 16 | 0 | 2 | 5 | 13 | 71.47 | $55,924 |

Best finish for 1971: 2nd at the IVB Philadelphia Golf Classic

| 1972 | 20 | 72 | 15 | 1 | 6 | 8 | 11 | 71.46 | $92,859 |

Best finish for 1972: Win at the Monsanto Open

| 1973 | 21 | 78 | 18 | 1 | 5 | 9 | 14 | 71.08 | $94,985 |

Best finish for 1973: Win at the Danny Thomas Memphis Classic

| 1974 | 26 | 89 | 18 | 1 | 6 | 9 | 16 | 71.10 | $125,474 |

Best finish for 1974: Win at the Houston Open

| 1975 | 27 | 91 | 19 | 1 | 3 | 6 | 12 | 71.62 | $80,533 |

Best finish for 1975: Win at the Sahara Invitational

| 1976 | 26 | 101 | 24 | 1 | 6 | 8 | 15 | 71.08 | $116,365 |

Best finish for 1976: Win at the Greater Milwaukee Open

| 1977 | 16 | 54 | 11 | 0 | 0 | 1 | 3 | 72.81 | $16,878 |

Best finish for 1977: T-10th at the Phoenix Open

| 1978 | 17 | 42 | 4 | 0 | 0 | 0 | 0 | 73.83 | $4,381 |

Best finish for 1978: T-32nd at the Pensacola Open

| 1979 | 18 | 45 | 5 | 0 | 0 | 0 | 1 | 73.93 | $6,949 |

Best finish for 1979: T-23rd at the Bob Hope Chrysler Classic

| 1980 | 26 | 85 | 17 | 0 | 0 | 1 | 7 | 72.33 | $43,287 |

Best finish for 1980: T-6th at the Bob Hope Chrysler Classic

| 1981 | 18 | 46 | 5 | 0 | 0 | 0 | 2 | 73.39 | $8,838 |

Best finish for 1981: T-17th at the Buick Open

| 1982 | 7 | 19 | 3 | 0 | 0 | 0 | 1 | 72.42 | $7,824 |

Best finish for 1982: T-16th at the Danny Thomas Memphis Classic

| 1983 | 4 | 12 | 2 | 0 | 0 | 0 | 0 | 72.33 | $2,276 |

Best finish for 1983: T-64th at the Buick Open

| 1984 | 2 | 4 | 0 | 0 | 0 | 0 | 0 | 74.50 | |
| 1985 | 2 | 8 | 2 | 0 | 0 | 0 | 0 | 73.00 | $1,812 |

Best finish for 1985: T-71st at the Buick Open

1987	1	2	0	0	0	0	0	71.50	
1992	1	2	0	0	0	0	0	75.00	
Period Totals	Starts	Rounds Played	Cuts Made	Wins	Top-5s	Top-10s	Top-25s	Scoring Average	Money
	525	1813	381	13	68	120	242	71.69	$1,129,661

Guy Hill

Year	Starts	Rounds Played	Cuts Made	Wins	Top-5s	Top-10s	Top-25s	Scoring Average	Money
1995	1	2	0	0	0	0	0	73.50	
1996	2	5	1	0	0	0	1	71.20	$24,000

Best finish for 1996: T-15th at the Bell Canadian Open

| 1998 | 26 | 71 | 10 | 0 | 0 | 0 | 1 | 72.86 | $71,495 |

Best finish for 1998: T-24th at the Nissan Open

| 1999 | 3 | 10 | 2 | 0 | 0 | 1 | 1 | 71.40 | $74,616 |

Best finish for 1999: T-10th at the Doral-Ryder Open

| Period Totals | Starts | Rounds Played | Cuts Made | Wins | Top-5s | Top-10s | Top-25s | Scoring Average | Money |
| | 32 | 88 | 13 | 0 | 0 | 1 | 3 | 72.61 | $170,111 |

Jason Hill

Year	Starts	Rounds Played	Cuts Made	Wins	Top-5s	Top-10s	Top-25s	Scoring Average	Money
1996	1	2	0	0	0	0	0	73.00	
1997	1	2	0	0	0	0	0	70.50	
1998	1	2	0	0	0	0	0	71.50	
2002	24	59	6	0	0	0	2	72.42	$150,860

Best finish for 2002: T-14th at the FedEx St. Jude Classic & Michelob Championship at Kingsmill

Period Totals	Starts	Rounds Played	Cuts Made	Wins	Top-5s	Top-10s	Top-25s	Scoring Average	Money
	27	65	6	0	0	0	2	72.35	$150,860

Mike Hill

Year	Starts	Rounds Played	Cuts Made	Wins	Top-5s	Top-10s	Top-25s	Scoring Average	Money
1968	13	42	8	0	3	3	3	71.64	$28,438

Best finish for 1968: T-2nd at the "500" Festival Open Invitational, Buick Open Invitational & Robinson Open

1969	33	103	18	0	2	2	5	71.77	$14,677

Best finish for 1969: T-3rd at the Indian Ridge Hospital Open

1970	32	111	26	1	2	2	8	72.15	$54,841

Best finish for 1970: Win at the Doral-Eastern Open

1971	33	112	25	0	2	5	13	72.37	$41,096

Best finish for 1971: T-5th at the Massachusetts Classic & Kaiser International Open

1972	32	110	24	1	1	5	11	72.16	$59,420

Best finish for 1972: Win at the San Antonio Texas Open

1973	29	104	20	0	1	1	12	72.04	$41,333

Best finish for 1973: T-5th at the Sahara Invitational

1974	31	112	25	0	4	8	12	71.40	$70,407

Best finish for 1974: T-2nd at the Sahara Invitational & San Antonio Texas Open

1975	23	86	20	0	2	3	9	71.62	$41,797

Best finish for 1975: T-4th at the Phoenix Open & Dean Martin Tucson Open

1976	29	101	26	0	3	4	11	71.50	$58,478

Best finish for 1976: T-3rd at the Greater Jacksonville Open

1977	26	84	17	1	1	1	5	72.23	$49,933

Best finish for 1977: Win at the Ohio Kings Island Open

1978	28	85	14	0	0	0	2	72.59	$17,951

Best finish for 1978: T-17th at the First NBC New Orleans Open

1979	29	94	18	0	0	0	8	71.97	$38,088

Best finish for 1979: T-13th at the Manufactures Hanover Westchester Classic

1980	28	87	18	0	0	1	3	72.45	$28,841

Best finish for 1980: T-6th at the Jackie Gleason's Inverrary Classic

1981	12	24	1	0	0	0	0	74.25	$627

Best finish for 1981: T-66th at the Sea Pines Heritage Classic

1982	14	36	4	0	0	0	1	73.33	$4,753

Best finish for 1982: T-22nd at the Greater Milwaukee Open

1983	4	12	1	0	0	0	0	72.67	$384

Best finish for 1983: T-73rd at the Miller High-Life Quad Cities Open

1984	3	6	0	0	0	0	0	74.50	
1985	3	10	2	0	0	0	0	72.50	$2,898

Best finish for 1985: T-35th at the Doral-Eastern Open

1986	2	6	1	0	0	0	1	71.17	$4,800

Best finish for 1986: T-22nd at the Buick Open

1987	2	4	0	0	0	0	0	73.50	
1988	1	2	0	0	0	0	0	76.00	

Period Totals	Starts	Rounds Played	Cuts Made	Wins	Top-5s	Top-10s	Top-25s	Scoring Average	Money
	407	1331	268	3	21	35	104	72.10	$558,762

Lon Hinkle

Year	Starts	Rounds Played	Cuts Made	Wins	Top-5s	Top-10s	Top-25s	Scoring Average	Money
1972	3	8	1	0	1	1	1	72.63	$7,350

Best finish for 1972: T-3rd at the Sea Pines Heritage Classic

1973	15	55	10	0	0	0	1	73.40	$6,735

Best finish for 1973: T-13th at the Walt Disney World Open

1974	19	54	10	0	0	0	2	72.89	$5,779

Best finish for 1974: T-11th at the Quad Cities Open

1975	11	37	7	0	0	1	3	72.35	$10,112

Best finish for 1975: T-8th at the Byron Nelson Golf Classic

1976	19	62	12	0	0	0	2	72.77	$10,198

Best finish for 1976: T-18th at the Kemper Open

1977	27	91	19	0	1	6	10	72.16	$133,055

Best finish for 1977: 2nd at the Tallahassee Open

1978	29	97	21	1	2	6	14	71.35	$117,688

Best finish for 1978: Win at the First NBC New Orleans Open

Year	Starts	Rounds Played	Cuts Made	Wins	Top-5s	Top-10s	Top-25s	Scoring Average	Money
1979	28	93	19	2	5	9	12	72.06	$249,613

Best finish for 1979: Win at the Bing Crosby Pro-Am & World Series Of Golf

Year	Starts	Rounds Played	Cuts Made	Wins	Top-5s	Top-10s	Top-25s	Scoring Average	Money
1980	25	80	16	0	6	9	11	71.50	$141,316

Best finish for 1980: T-3rd at the Andy Williams-San Diego Open, Sea Pines Heritage Classic, U.S. Open & PGA Championship

Year	Starts	Rounds Played	Cuts Made	Wins	Top-5s	Top-10s	Top-25s	Scoring Average	Money
1981	30	101	22	0	3	4	12	71.65	$144,307

Best finish for 1981: 2nd at the Joe Garagiola Tucson Open & Phoenix Open

Year	Starts	Rounds Played	Cuts Made	Wins	Top-5s	Top-10s	Top-25s	Scoring Average	Money
1982	22	63	10	0	1	3	7	72.59	$56,906

Best finish for 1982: T-5th at the USF&G Classic

Year	Starts	Rounds Played	Cuts Made	Wins	Top-5s	Top-10s	Top-25s	Scoring Average	Money
1983	29	100	23	0	2	5	12	71.13	$116,822

Best finish for 1983: T-2nd at the Pensacola Open

Year	Starts	Rounds Played	Cuts Made	Wins	Top-5s	Top-10s	Top-25s	Scoring Average	Money
1984	28	80	14	0	1	4	5	72.81	$89,850

Best finish for 1984: T-5th at the Seiko Tucson-Match Play Championship

Year	Starts	Rounds Played	Cuts Made	Wins	Top-5s	Top-10s	Top-25s	Scoring Average	Money
1985	27	87	18	0	0	3	8	71.91	$102,839

Best finish for 1985: T-6th at the Canon Sammy Davis, Jr. - Greater Hartford Open

Year	Starts	Rounds Played	Cuts Made	Wins	Top-5s	Top-10s	Top-25s	Scoring Average	Money
1986	28	78	15	0	1	1	6	72.35	$97,610

Best finish for 1986: T-2nd at the Walt Disney World/Oldsmobile Classic

Year	Starts	Rounds Played	Cuts Made	Wins	Top-5s	Top-10s	Top-25s	Scoring Average	Money
1987	23	68	11	0	0	0	6	72.40	$45,751

Best finish for 1987: T-15th at the Canadian Open

Year	Starts	Rounds Played	Cuts Made	Wins	Top-5s	Top-10s	Top-25s	Scoring Average	Money
1988	13	25	0	0	0	0	0	74.80	
1989	28	90	18	0	1	4	6	71.20	$151,828

Best finish for 1989: T-5th at the Southwestern Bell Colonial

Year	Starts	Rounds Played	Cuts Made	Wins	Top-5s	Top-10s	Top-25s	Scoring Average	Money
1990	25	67	9	0	0	0	1	73.18	$26,072

Best finish for 1990: T-25th at the Nissan Los Angeles Open

Year	Starts	Rounds Played	Cuts Made	Wins	Top-5s	Top-10s	Top-25s	Scoring Average	Money
1991	15	46	9	0	0	0	3	70.89	$49,692

Best finish for 1991: T-17th at the New England Classic

Year	Starts	Rounds Played	Cuts Made	Wins	Top-5s	Top-10s	Top-25s	Scoring Average	Money
1992	19	58	11	0	0	1	5	71.09	$91,854

Best finish for 1992: T-7th at the New England Classic

Year	Starts	Rounds Played	Cuts Made	Wins	Top-5s	Top-10s	Top-25s	Scoring Average	Money
1993	13	36	5	0	0	0	0	74.14	$8,620

Best finish for 1993: T-58th at the AT&T Pebble Beach Pro-Am

Year	Starts	Rounds Played	Cuts Made	Wins	Top-5s	Top-10s	Top-25s	Scoring Average	Money
1994	7	18	2	0	0	0	0	72.89	$4,411

Best finish for 1994: T-66th at the AT&T Pebble Beach Pro-Am

Year	Starts	Rounds Played	Cuts Made	Wins	Top-5s	Top-10s	Top-25s	Scoring Average	Money
1995	1	3	0	0	0	0	0	76.00	
1996	3	6	0	0	0	0	0	79.00	
1997	6	17	2	0	0	0	0	72.71	$5,398

Best finish for 1997: T-63rd at the Quad City Classic

Year	Starts	Rounds Played	Cuts Made	Wins	Top-5s	Top-10s	Top-25s	Scoring Average	Money
1998	7	17	1	0	0	0	0	72.47	$2,760

Best finish for 1998: 79th at the CVS Charity Classic

Year	Starts	Rounds Played	Cuts Made	Wins	Top-5s	Top-10s	Top-25s	Scoring Average	Money
1999	1	3	0	0	0	0	0	74.00	
2000	1	3	0	0	0	0	0	75.00	
2001	1	3	0	0	0	0	0	75.33	
2002	1	3	0	0	0	0	0	75.00	
2003	1	3	0	0	0	0	0	76.67	
2006	1	3	0	0	0	0	0	75.67	
2007	1	0	0	0	0	0	0		
Period Totals	Starts	Rounds Played	Cuts Made	Wins	Top-5s	Top-10s	Top-25s	Scoring Average	Money
	507	1555	285	3	24	57	127	72.21	$1,676,566

Larry Hinson

Year	Starts	Rounds Played	Cuts Made	Wins	Top-5s	Top-10s	Top-25s	Scoring Average	Money
1967	1	4	1	0	0	0	1	72.25	

Best finish for 1967: T-12th at the Atlanta Classic

Year	Starts	Rounds Played	Cuts Made	Wins	Top-5s	Top-10s	Top-25s	Scoring Average	Money
1968	18	58	11	0	0	0	2	72.84	$1,983

Best finish for 1968: T-14th at the Memphis Open Invitational

Year	Starts	Rounds Played	Cuts Made	Wins	Top-5s	Top-10s	Top-25s	Scoring Average	Money
1969	33	113	23	1	4	6	11	71.95	$48,720

Best finish for 1969: Win at the Greater New Orleans Open

Year	Starts	Rounds Played	Cuts Made	Wins	Top-5s	Top-10s	Top-25s	Scoring Average	Money
1970	31	123	30	0	9	10	19	70.98	$115,397

Best finish for 1970: T-2nd at the Kemper Open & Westchester Classic

Year	Starts	Rounds Played	Cuts Made	Wins	Top-5s	Top-10s	Top-25s	Scoring Average	Money
1971	30	101	22	0	1	4	14	71.68	$40,876

Best finish for 1971: T-3rd at the Robinson Open Golf Classic

Year	Starts	Rounds Played	Cuts Made	Wins	Top-5s	Top-10s	Top-25s	Scoring Average	Money
1972	35	121	26	0	1	5	11	72.22	$41,191

Best finish for 1972: 3rd at the Cleveland Open

Year	Starts	Rounds Played	Cuts Made	Wins	Top-5s	Top-10s	Top-25s	Scoring Average	Money
1973	33	120	26	0	2	4	9	71.86	$52,175

Best finish for 1973: T-2nd at the Western Open

Year	Starts	Rounds Played	Cuts Made	Wins	Top-5s	Top-10s	Top-25s	Scoring Average	Money
1974	31	118	27	0	1	4	11	71.94	$41,951

Best finish for 1974: T-4th at the Greater New Orleans Open

Year	Starts	Rounds Played	Cuts Made	Wins	Top-5s	Top-10s	Top-25s	Scoring Average	Money
1975	26	79	14	0	2	3	9	71.97	$42,342

Best finish for 1975: 2nd at the San Antonio Texas Open

Year	Starts	Rounds Played	Cuts Made	Wins	Top-5s	Top-10s	Top-25s	Scoring Average	Money
1976	19	52	7	0	0	0	1	73.85	$4,773

Best finish for 1976: T-19th at the Doral-Eastern Open

Year	Starts	Rounds Played	Cuts Made	Wins	Top-5s	Top-10s	Top-25s	Scoring Average	Money
1977	3	6	0	0	0	0	0	76.83	
1978	2	4	0	0	0	0	0	75.00	
1979	3	6	0	0	0	0	0	75.33	

Year	Starts	Rounds Played	Cuts Made	Wins	Top-5s	Top-10s	Top-25s	Scoring Average	Money
1980	3	4	0	0	0	0	0	75.50	
1981	1	0	0	0	0	0	0		
1982	2	4	0	0	0	0	0	76.25	
1983	1	2	0	0	0	0	0	74.00	
1985	2	5	1	0	0	0	0	72.00	$962

Best finish for 1985: T-50th at the USF&G Classic

Year	Starts	Rounds Played	Cuts Made	Wins	Top-5s	Top-10s	Top-25s	Scoring Average	Money
1986	1	2	0	0	0	0	0	76.50	
1988	1	2	0	0	0	0	0	74.50	
1991	1	2	0	0	0	0	0	79.50	
1998	1	1	0	0	0	0	0	81.00	
Period Totals	**Starts**	**Rounds Played**	**Cuts Made**	**Wins**	**Top-5s**	**Top-10s**	**Top-25s**	**Scoring Average**	**Money**
	278	927	188	1	20	36	88	72.13	$390,370

Babe Hiskey

Year	Starts	Rounds Played	Cuts Made	Wins	Top-5s	Top-10s	Top-25s	Scoring Average	Money
1958	1	4	1	0	0	0	0	74.25	

Best finish for 1958: T-59th at the Utah Open

Year	Starts	Rounds Played	Cuts Made	Wins	Top-5s	Top-10s	Top-25s	Scoring Average	Money
1963	1	4	1	0	0	0	0	71.50	$395

Best finish for 1963: T-29th at the Utah Open Invitational

| 1964 | 29 | 77 | 9 | 0 | 0 | 0 | 3 | 73.90 | $3,445 |

Best finish for 1964: T-12th at the Sunset-Camellia Open

| 1965 | 25 | 85 | 17 | 1 | 1 | 1 | 4 | 72.82 | $8,985 |

Best finish for 1965: Win in the Cajun Classic

| 1966 | 32 | 105 | 20 | 0 | 0 | 1 | 9 | 72.48 | $16,677 |

Best finish for 1966: T-9th at the Minnesota Golf Classic

| 1967 | 28 | 97 | 20 | 0 | 1 | 2 | 6 | 72.21 | $16,042 |

Best finish for 1967: T-3rd at the Hawaiian Open

| 1968 | 18 | 48 | 6 | 0 | 0 | 0 | 1 | 73.60 | $2,775 |

Best finish for 1968: T-19th at the Kaiser International Open Invitational

| 1969 | 22 | 63 | 10 | 0 | 0 | 0 | 3 | 73.35 | $12,102 |

Best finish for 1969: T-18th at the Michigan Golf Classic

| 1970 | 22 | 69 | 14 | 1 | 1 | 1 | 4 | 72.45 | $26,587 |

Best finish for 1970: Win at the Sahara Invitational

| 1971 | 35 | 105 | 19 | 0 | 0 | 2 | 5 | 73.25 | $19,470 |

Best finish for 1971: T-7th at the Western Open

| 1972 | 30 | 96 | 20 | 0 | 1 | 2 | 6 | 72.53 | $27,329 |

Best finish for 1972: T-3rd at the U.S. Professional Match Play Championship

| 1973 | 33 | 109 | 20 | 0 | 0 | 0 | 11 | 72.57 | $25,938 |

Best finish for 1973: T-13th at the IVB Philadelphia Golf Classic

| 1974 | 25 | 79 | 15 | 0 | 0 | 0 | 2 | 72.65 | $9,415 |

Best finish for 1974: T-21st at the Southern Open

| 1975 | 22 | 61 | 7 | 0 | 0 | 0 | 2 | 73.00 | $5,913 |

Best finish for 1975: T-14th at the First NBC New Orleans Open

| 1976 | 21 | 60 | 12 | 0 | 0 | 0 | 1 | 73.35 | $4,834 |

Best finish for 1976: T-14th at the Sahara Invitational

| 1977 | 18 | 53 | 8 | 0 | 0 | 0 | 0 | 73.42 | $4,333 |

Best finish for 1977: T-31st at the IVB Philadelphia Golf Classic

| 1978 | 16 | 37 | 3 | 0 | 0 | 0 | 0 | 73.89 | $705 |

Best finish for 1978: T-38th at the Buick Goodwrench Open

| 1979 | 9 | 18 | 1 | 0 | 0 | 0 | 0 | 74.50 | $358 |

Best finish for 1979: T-74th at the Phoenix Open

1980	3	4	0	0	0	0	0	73.25	
1981	1	0	0	0	0	0	0		
1982	3	6	0	0	0	0	0	75.17	
1983	2	6	1	0	0	0	0	72.17	$384

Best finish for 1983: T-73rd at the Miller High-Life Quad Cities Open

1984	1	2	0	0	0	0	0	75.50	
1985	4	8	0	0	0	0	0	75.50	
1986	3	8	1	0	0	0	0	74.13	$416

Best finish for 1986: T-65th at the Deposit Guaranty Golf Classic

| 1987 | 1 | 4 | 1 | 0 | 0 | 0 | 0 | 71.00 | $398 |

Best finish for 1987: T-70th at the Deposit Guaranty Golf Classic

1988	1	2	0	0	0	0	0	73.50	
1989	3	6	0	0	0	0	0	76.50	$800
1990	1	4	1	0	0	0	0	71.50	$630

Best finish for 1990: T-64th at the Deposit Guaranty

1991	1	2	0	0	0	0	0	71.50	
1992	1	1	0	0	0	0	0	72.00	
1997	1	1	0	0	0	0	0	80.00	
Period Totals	**Starts**	**Rounds Played**	**Cuts Made**	**Wins**	**Top-5s**	**Top-10s**	**Top-25s**	**Scoring Average**	**Money**
	413	1224	207	2	4	9	57	73.00	$187,931

George Hixon

Year	Starts	Rounds Played	Cuts Made	Wins	Top-5s	Top-10s	Top-25s	Scoring Average	Money
1962	1	4	1	0	0	0	0	73.25	

Best finish for 1962: T-26th at the Oklahoma City Open Invitational

Year	Starts	Rounds Played	Cuts Made	Wins	Top-5s	Top-10s	Top-25s	Scoring Average	Money
1965	1	2	0	0	0	0	0	81.00	
1968	1	4	1	0	0	0	0	72.50	

Best finish for 1968: 67th at the Cajun Classic

Year	Starts	Rounds Played	Cuts Made	Wins	Top-5s	Top-10s	Top-25s	Scoring Average	Money
1969	7	22	4	0	0	0	0	75.23	$1,047

Best finish for 1969: T-35th at the Cleveland Open

Year	Starts	Rounds Played	Cuts Made	Wins	Top-5s	Top-10s	Top-25s	Scoring Average	Money
1970	11	34	5	0	0	0	2	73.06	$2,958

Best finish for 1970: T-20th at the Sahara Invitational

Year	Starts	Rounds Played	Cuts Made	Wins	Top-5s	Top-10s	Top-25s	Scoring Average	Money
1971	16	47	7	0	0	1	1	73.55	$4,792

Best finish for 1971: T-10th at the Bob Hope Chrysler Classic

Year	Starts	Rounds Played	Cuts Made	Wins	Top-5s	Top-10s	Top-25s	Scoring Average	Money
1972	21	62	9	0	1	1	1	73.56	$12,825

Best finish for 1972: T-3rd at the Danny Thomas Memphis Classic

Year	Starts	Rounds Played	Cuts Made	Wins	Top-5s	Top-10s	Top-25s	Scoring Average	Money
1973	14	36	4	0	0	0	1	74.28	$3,455

Best finish for 1973: T-13th at the Dean Martin Tucson Open

Period Totals	Starts	Rounds Played	Cuts Made	Wins	Top-5s	Top-10s	Top-25s	Scoring Average	Money
	72	211	31	0	1	2	5	73.82	$25,077

Gabriel Hjertstedt

Year	Starts	Rounds Played	Cuts Made	Wins	Top-5s	Top-10s	Top-25s	Scoring Average	Money
1994	1	2	0	0	0	0	0	73.50	$972
1997	23	72	11	1	1	1	1	72.00	$279,624

Best finish for 1997: Win at the B.C. Open

Year	Starts	Rounds Played	Cuts Made	Wins	Top-5s	Top-10s	Top-25s	Scoring Average	Money
1998	26	72	10	0	0	2	3	72.86	$173,572

Best finish for 1998: T-6th at the Mercedes Championship

Year	Starts	Rounds Played	Cuts Made	Wins	Top-5s	Top-10s	Top-25s	Scoring Average	Money
1999	31	98	18	1	2	3	7	71.77	$939,439

Best finish for 1999: Win at the Touchstone Energy Tucson Open

Year	Starts	Rounds Played	Cuts Made	Wins	Top-5s	Top-10s	Top-25s	Scoring Average	Money
2000	29	83	14	0	0	0	3	71.63	$301,189

Best finish for 2000: T-14th at the Canon Greater Hartford Open

Year	Starts	Rounds Played	Cuts Made	Wins	Top-5s	Top-10s	Top-25s	Scoring Average	Money
2001	30	76	8	0	1	1	3	71.66	$296,273

Best finish for 2001: T-4th at the Greater Greensboro Chrysler Classic

Year	Starts	Rounds Played	Cuts Made	Wins	Top-5s	Top-10s	Top-25s	Scoring Average	Money
2002	17	43	5	0	0	0	1	72.56	$69,186

Best finish for 2002: T-25th at the Valero Texas Open

Year	Starts	Rounds Played	Cuts Made	Wins	Top-5s	Top-10s	Top-25s	Scoring Average	Money
2003	9	20	2	0	0	0	0	74.40	$12,720

Best finish for 2003: T-69th at the 84 Lumber Classic of Pennsylvania

Year	Starts	Rounds Played	Cuts Made	Wins	Top-5s	Top-10s	Top-25s	Scoring Average	Money
2004	5	14	2	0	0	0	0	71.71	$23,870

Best finish for 2004: T-35th at the B.C. Open

Year	Starts	Rounds Played	Cuts Made	Wins	Top-5s	Top-10s	Top-25s	Scoring Average	Money
2005	3	6	0	0	0	0	0	73.17	
2006	16	46	7	0	0	2	2	71.02	$251,235

Best finish for 2006: T-6th at the B.C. Open

Year	Starts	Rounds Played	Cuts Made	Wins	Top-5s	Top-10s	Top-25s	Scoring Average	Money
2007	9	19	0	0	0	0	0	73.63	
2008	4	10	1	0	0	0	0	73.30	$11,495

Best finish for 2008: T-63rd at the AT&T Classic

Period Totals	Starts	Rounds Played	Cuts Made	Wins	Top-5s	Top-10s	Top-25s	Scoring Average	Money
	203	561	78	2	4	9	20	72.11	$2,359,574

Glen Hnatiuk

Year	Starts	Rounds Played	Cuts Made	Wins	Top-5s	Top-10s	Top-25s	Scoring Average	Money
1997	2	8	2	0	0	0	0	70.75	$8,625

Best finish for 1997: T-44th at the Bell Canadian Open

Year	Starts	Rounds Played	Cuts Made	Wins	Top-5s	Top-10s	Top-25s	Scoring Average	Money
1998	29	83	15	0	0	0	3	71.54	$148,098

Best finish for 1998: T-14th at the Tucson Chrysler Classic

Year	Starts	Rounds Played	Cuts Made	Wins	Top-5s	Top-10s	Top-25s	Scoring Average	Money
2000	30	90	16	0	1	2	5	71.00	$482,744

Best finish for 2000: T-3rd at the B.C. Open

Year	Starts	Rounds Played	Cuts Made	Wins	Top-5s	Top-10s	Top-25s	Scoring Average	Money
2001	31	101	23	0	0	1	5	70.68	$434,524

Best finish for 2001: 9th at the Marconi Pennsylvania Classic

Year	Starts	Rounds Played	Cuts Made	Wins	Top-5s	Top-10s	Top-25s	Scoring Average	Money
2002	28	93	19	0	0	1	8	70.20	$558,940

Best finish for 2002: T-8th at the WorldCom Classic

Year	Starts	Rounds Played	Cuts Made	Wins	Top-5s	Top-10s	Top-25s	Scoring Average	Money
2003	29	89	18	0	0	2	4	71.39	$488,429

Best finish for 2003: T-7th at the Valero Texas Open

Year	Starts	Rounds Played	Cuts Made	Wins	Top-5s	Top-10s	Top-25s	Scoring Average	Money
2004	9	26	4	0	0	0	1	72.04	$103,500

Best finish for 2004: T-20th at the BellSouth Classic

Year	Starts	Rounds Played	Cuts Made	Wins	Top-5s	Top-10s	Top-25s	Scoring Average	Money
2005	21	55	8	0	0	0	2	71.53	$185,162

Best finish for 2005: T-21st at the Zurich Classic of New Orleans

Period Totals	Starts	Rounds Played	Cuts Made	Wins	Top-5s	Top-10s	Top-25s	Scoring Average	Money
	179	545	105	0	1	6	28	71.05	$2,410,023

David Hobby

Year	Starts	Rounds Played	Cuts Made	Wins	Top-5s	Top-10s	Top-25s	Scoring Average	Money
1985	1	2	0	0	0	0	0	77.00	$600
1986	2	6	1	0	0	0	0	72.67	$3,427

Best finish for 1986: T-50th at the U.S. Open

1987	27	68	9	0	0	0	0	73.18	$13,134

Best finish for 1987: T-47th at the Shearson Lehman/Andy Williams San Diego

1988	3	10	2	0	0	0	0	71.30	$1,294

Best finish for 1988: T-58th at the Gatlin Brothers - Southwest Golf Classic

Period Totals	Starts	Rounds Played	Cuts Made	Wins	Top-5s	Top-10s	Top-25s	Scoring Average	Money
	33	86	12	0	0	0	0	73.01	$18,455

Scott Hoch

Year	Starts	Rounds Played	Cuts Made	Wins	Top-5s	Top-10s	Top-25s	Scoring Average	Money
1975	1	2	0	0	0	0	0	78.50	
1979	1	4	1	0	0	0	0	73.25	

Best finish for 1979: T-34th at the Masters

1980	19	47	6	1	1	1	4	72.62	$46,100

Best finish for 1980: Win at the Quad Cities Open

1981	32	103	20	0	1	3	8	72.33	$61,956

Best finish for 1981: 4th at the World Disney World National Team Championship

1982	28	101	23	1	4	8	17	70.75	$194,462

Best finish for 1982: Win at the USF&G Classic

1983	25	92	20	0	5	7	11	71.21	$144,605

Best finish for 1983: T-3rd at the Miller High-Life Quad Cities Open

1984	25	91	21	1	6	7	13	71.03	$224,345

Best finish for 1984: Win at the Miller High-Life Quad Cities Open

1985	30	105	24	0	2	6	13	71.28	$186,020

Best finish for 1985: T-2nd at the Walt Disney World/Oldsmobile Classic

1986	28	90	23	0	5	6	13	70.08	$222,077

Best finish for 1986: 2nd at the Provident Classic

1987	28	101	23	0	5	8	12	70.44	$391,746

Best finish for 1987: T-3rd at the Memorial Tournament, Anheuser-Busch Golf Classic, Buick Open & PGA Championship

1988	32	111	26	0	2	10	18	70.34	$397,099

Best finish for 1988: T-4th at the Kmart Greater Greensboro Open & Hardee's Golf Classic

1989	28	98	21	1	3	6	12	70.63	$670,680

Best finish for 1989: Win at the Las Vegas Invitational

1990	27	88	18	0	4	7	13	70.94	$334,974

Best finish for 1990: T-3rd at the Kemper Open

1991	31	115	26	0	3	9	14	70.18	$520,035

Best finish for 1991: T-2nd at the Southwestern Bell Colonial

1992	17	59	13	0	0	0	3	71.29	$86,997

Best finish for 1992: T-11th at the Anheuser-Busch Golf Classic

1993	28	93	18	0	2	6	15	70.46	$403,742

Best finish for 1993: T-3rd at the Kemper Open

1994	27	94	20	1	4	7	14	70.40	$807,259

Best finish for 1994: Win at the Bob Hope Chrysler Classic

1995	28	100	23	1	4	8	14	70.56	$793,843

Best finish for 1995: Win at the Greater Milwaukee Open

1996	27	96	23	1	7	8	14	70.09	$1,039,564

Best finish for 1996: Win at the Michelob Championship at Kingsmill

1997	22	87	22	1	6	11	15	70.03	$1,393,788

Best finish for 1997: Win at the Greater Milwaukee Open

1998	27	100	22	0	3	9	17	70.43	$1,239,369

Best finish for 1998: T-2nd at the Kemper Open & CVS Charity Classic

1999	27	99	24	0	2	6	17	70.65	$1,173,692

Best finish for 1999: 4th at the Buick Classic

2000	29	104	24	0	3	7	17	70.40	$1,373,888

Best finish for 2000: T-2nd at the SEI Pennsylvania Classic

2001	24	84	17	2	3	10	14	69.87	$2,876,892

Best finish for 2001: Win at the Greater Greensboro Chrysler Classic & Advil Western Open

2002	21	70	16	0	3	7	11	70.51	$1,472,173

Best finish for 2002: T-2nd at the Michelob Championship at Kingsmill

2003	16	43	8	1	2	2	2	72.88	$1,204,250

Best finish for 2003: Win at the Ford Championship at Doral

2004	17	51	11	0	1	4	6	70.84	$1,239,360

Best finish for 2004: 2nd at the Shell Houston Open

2005	2	5	1	0	0	0	0	71.40	$31,130

Best finish for 2005: T-32nd at the Ford Championship at Doral

2008	1	4	1	0	0	0	0	72.00	$11,385

Best finish for 2008: T-65th at the Honda Classic

Period Totals	Starts	Rounds Played	Cuts Made	Wins	Top-5s	Top-10s	Top-25s	Scoring Average	Money
	648	2237	495	11	81	163	307	70.73	$18,541,430

Charley Hoffman

Year	Starts	Rounds Played	Cuts Made	Wins	Top-5s	Top-10s	Top-25s	Scoring Average	Money
1994	1	2	0	0	0	0	0	75.00	
1996	1	4	1	0	0	0	0	73.25	

Best finish for 1996: 76th at the Buick Invitational

Year	Starts	Rounds Played	Cuts Made	Wins	Top-5s	Top-10s	Top-25s	Scoring Average	Money
1998	1	2	0	0	0	0	0	74.00	
1999	1	3	0	0	0	0	0	68.67	
2000	1	2	0	0	0	0	0	72.50	
2001	2	4	0	0	0	0	0	75.50	
2002	1	2	0	0	0	0	0	76.00	
2003	1	2	0	0	0	0	0	76.00	
2004	1	4	1	0	0	0	0	70.50	$11,296

Best finish for 2004: T-51st at the Booz Allen Classic

Year	Starts	Rounds Played	Cuts Made	Wins	Top-5s	Top-10s	Top-25s	Scoring Average	Money
2005	1	4	1	0	0	0	0	72.00	$10,656

Best finish for 2005: T-56th at the Buick Invitational

Year	Starts	Rounds Played	Cuts Made	Wins	Top-5s	Top-10s	Top-25s	Scoring Average	Money
2006	29	98	21	0	1	5	10	70.62	$1,115,193

Best finish for 2006: T-5th at the Frys.Com Open-Vegas

Year	Starts	Rounds Played	Cuts Made	Wins	Top-5s	Top-10s	Top-25s	Scoring Average	Money
2007	30	97	18	1	2	2	7	71.54	$1,691,866

Best finish for 2007: Win at the Bob Hope Chrysler Classic

Year	Starts	Rounds Played	Cuts Made	Wins	Top-5s	Top-10s	Top-25s	Scoring Average	Money
2008	29	94	19	0	0	3	6	71.16	$945,702

Best finish for 2008: T-6th at the Shell Houston Open

Period Totals	Starts	Rounds Played	Cuts Made	Wins	Top-5s	Top-10s	Top-25s	Scoring Average	Money
	99	318	61	1	3	10	23	71.28	$3,774,713

Ben Hogan

Year	Starts	Rounds Played	Cuts Made	Wins	Top-5s	Top-10s	Top-25s	Scoring Average	Money
1958	4	16	4	0	2	3	4	70.94	$3,733

Best finish for 1958: 3rd at the Greenbrier Invitational

Year	Starts	Rounds Played	Cuts Made	Wins	Top-5s	Top-10s	Top-25s	Scoring Average	Money
1959	5	20	5	1	1	2	3	71.80	$7,528

Best finish for 1959: Win at the Colonial National Invitational

Year	Starts	Rounds Played	Cuts Made	Wins	Top-5s	Top-10s	Top-25s	Scoring Average	Money
1960	5	19	4	0	1	4	4	71.37	$5,950

Best finish for 1960: T-2nd at the Memphis Open Invitational

Year	Starts	Rounds Played	Cuts Made	Wins	Top-5s	Top-10s	Top-25s	Scoring Average	Money
1961	3	12	3	0	0	0	2	73.17	$1,950

Best finish for 1961: T-14th at the U.S. Open

Year	Starts	Rounds Played	Cuts Made	Wins	Top-5s	Top-10s	Top-25s	Scoring Average	Money
1962	3	12	3	0	1	1	2	72.67	$3,825

Best finish for 1962: T-4th at the Doral Country Club Open Invitational

Year	Starts	Rounds Played	Cuts Made	Wins	Top-5s	Top-10s	Top-25s	Scoring Average	Money
1963	1	4	1	0	0	0	0	71.25	$827

Best finish for 1963: T-26th at the Thunderbird Classic Invitational

Year	Starts	Rounds Played	Cuts Made	Wins	Top-5s	Top-10s	Top-25s	Scoring Average	Money
1964	4	16	4	0	2	4	4	71.13	$14,010

Best finish for 1964: T-4th at the Colonial National Invitational & Carling World Open Championship

Year	Starts	Rounds Played	Cuts Made	Wins	Top-5s	Top-10s	Top-25s	Scoring Average	Money
1965	5	20	5	0	0	1	3	72.45	$6,823

Best finish for 1965: T-10th at the Colonial National Invitational

Year	Starts	Rounds Played	Cuts Made	Wins	Top-5s	Top-10s	Top-25s	Scoring Average	Money
1966	4	16	4	0	1	2	4	71.69	$10,400

Best finish for 1966: T-5th at the Colonial National Invitation

Year	Starts	Rounds Played	Cuts Made	Wins	Top-5s	Top-10s	Top-25s	Scoring Average	Money
1967	4	16	4	0	2	3	3	71.31	$18,035

Best finish for 1967: T-3rd at the Houston Championship International & Colonial National Invitational

Year	Starts	Rounds Played	Cuts Made	Wins	Top-5s	Top-10s	Top-25s	Scoring Average	Money
1970	3	9	2	0	0	1	1	72.89	$2,792

Best finish for 1970: T-9th at the Houston Champions International

Year	Starts	Rounds Played	Cuts Made	Wins	Top-5s	Top-10s	Top-25s	Scoring Average	Money
1971	1	0	0	0	0	0	0		

Period Totals	Starts	Rounds Played	Cuts Made	Wins	Top-5s	Top-10s	Top-25s	Scoring Average	Money
	42	160	39	1	10	21	30	71.83	$75,873

PGA Tour career totals from 1932 to 1971

	Starts	Rounds Played	Cuts Made	Wins	Top-5s	Top-10s	Top-25s	Scoring Average	Money
	297	705	294	64	N/A	229	277	N/A	$332,516

Mike Holland

Year	Starts	Rounds Played	Cuts Made	Wins	Top-5s	Top-10s	Top-25s	Scoring Average	Money
1980	11	24	2	0	0	0	0	73.29	$1,961

Best finish for 1980: T-30th at the San Antonio Texas Open

Year	Starts	Rounds Played	Cuts Made	Wins	Top-5s	Top-10s	Top-25s	Scoring Average	Money
1981	26	82	18	1	1	3	6	72.10	$66,646

Best finish for 1981: Win at the World Disney World National Team Championship

Year	Starts	Rounds Played	Cuts Made	Wins	Top-5s	Top-10s	Top-25s	Scoring Average	Money
1982	34	97	15	0	1	1	4	72.59	$66,310

Best finish for 1982: 2nd at the Danny Thomas Memphis Classic

Year	Starts	Rounds Played	Cuts Made	Wins	Top-5s	Top-10s	Top-25s	Scoring Average	Money
1983	27	70	7	0	0	0	0	73.34	$9,306

Best finish for 1983: T-31st at the Canadian Open

Year	Starts	Rounds Played	Cuts Made	Wins	Top-5s	Top-10s	Top-25s	Scoring Average	Money
1984	25	64	6	0	0	0	0	73.55	$7,556

Best finish for 1984: T-33rd at the Buick Open

Year	Starts	Rounds Played	Cuts Made	Wins	Top-5s	Top-10s	Top-25s	Scoring Average	Money
1985	14	36	3	0	0	0	1	74.14	$7,289

Best finish for 1985: T-23rd at the Byron Nelson Golf Classic

Year	Starts	Rounds Played	Cuts Made	Wins	Top-5s	Top-10s	Top-25s	Scoring Average	Money
1989	2	4	0	0	0	0	0	77.00	

Year	Starts	Rounds Played	Cuts Made	Wins	Top-5s	Top-10s	Top-25s	Scoring Average	Money
1990	6	21	4	0	0	0	1	69.86	$21,262

Best finish for 1990: T-11th at the Chattanooga Classic

Year	Starts	Rounds Played	Cuts Made	Wins	Top-5s	Top-10s	Top-25s	Scoring Average	Money
1991	4	12	2	0	0	0	0	71.67	$2,741

Best finish for 1991: T-44th at the Buick Southern Open

Year	Starts	Rounds Played	Cuts Made	Wins	Top-5s	Top-10s	Top-25s	Scoring Average	Money
1992	2	4	0	0	0	0	0	72.25	
1995	1	2	0	0	0	0	0	72.00	
Period Totals	Starts	Rounds Played	Cuts Made	Wins	Top-5s	Top-10s	Top-25s	Scoring Average	Money
	152	416	57	1	2	4	12	72.81	$183,070

Tony Hollifield

Year	Starts	Rounds Played	Cuts Made	Wins	Top-5s	Top-10s	Top-25s	Scoring Average	Money
1975	1	2	0	0	0	0	0	78.50	
1979	16	33	2	0	0	0	0	73.94	$1,333

Best finish for 1979: T-30th at the Tallahassee Open

Year	Starts	Rounds Played	Cuts Made	Wins	Top-5s	Top-10s	Top-25s	Scoring Average	Money
1980	20	46	4	0	0	1	1	73.37	$8,747

Best finish for 1980: T-10th at the Sammy Davis, Jr. - Greater Hartford Open

Period Totals	Starts	Rounds Played	Cuts Made	Wins	Top-5s	Top-10s	Top-25s	Scoring Average	Money
	37	81	6	0	0	1	1	73.73	$10,080

J.B. Holmes

Year	Starts	Rounds Played	Cuts Made	Wins	Top-5s	Top-10s	Top-25s	Scoring Average	Money
2003	1	2	0	0	0	0	0	72.50	
2005	1	2	0	0	0	0	0	72.50	
2006	26	77	16	1	1	2	4	71.44	$1,488,814

Best finish for 2006: Win at the FBR Open

Year	Starts	Rounds Played	Cuts Made	Wins	Top-5s	Top-10s	Top-25s	Scoring Average	Money
2007	24	71	12	0	1	3	5	71.66	$874,216

Best finish for 2007: T-4th at the Mercedes Championships

Year	Starts	Rounds Played	Cuts Made	Wins	Top-5s	Top-10s	Top-25s	Scoring Average	Money
2008	26	85	19	1	1	3	9	71.39	$2,166,130

Best finish for 2008: Win at the FBR Open

Period Totals	Starts	Rounds Played	Cuts Made	Wins	Top-5s	Top-10s	Top-25s	Scoring Average	Money
	78	237	47	2	3	8	18	71.51	$4,529,160

Bud Holscher

Year	Starts	Rounds Played	Cuts Made	Wins	Top-5s	Top-10s	Top-25s	Scoring Average	Money
1958	6	23	5	0	0	0	2	72.96	$396

Best finish for 1958: T-16th at the Thunderbird Invitational

Year	Starts	Rounds Played	Cuts Made	Wins	Top-5s	Top-10s	Top-25s	Scoring Average	Money
1959	1	3	1	0	0	0	0	74.33	$043

Best finish for 1959: T-70th at the Bing Crosby National

Year	Starts	Rounds Played	Cuts Made	Wins	Top-5s	Top-10s	Top-25s	Scoring Average	Money
1960	4	15	2	0	0	0	0	74.00	$475

Best finish for 1960: T-26th at the Orange County Open Invitational

Year	Starts	Rounds Played	Cuts Made	Wins	Top-5s	Top-10s	Top-25s	Scoring Average	Money
1961	6	24	6	0	0	0	2	71.54	$1,065

Best finish for 1961: T-21st at the San Diego Open

Year	Starts	Rounds Played	Cuts Made	Wins	Top-5s	Top-10s	Top-25s	Scoring Average	Money
1962	2	6	2	0	0	0	1	72.67	$700

Best finish for 1962: T-20th at the Los Angles Open

Year	Starts	Rounds Played	Cuts Made	Wins	Top-5s	Top-10s	Top-25s	Scoring Average	Money
1963	2	6	1	0	0	0	1	72.83	$1,125

Best finish for 1963: T-19th at the Los Angles Open

Year	Starts	Rounds Played	Cuts Made	Wins	Top-5s	Top-10s	Top-25s	Scoring Average	Money
1964	9	31	5	0	0	1	2	72.68	$2,750

Best finish for 1964: T-8th at the Mountain View Open

Year	Starts	Rounds Played	Cuts Made	Wins	Top-5s	Top-10s	Top-25s	Scoring Average	Money
1965	11	36	6	0	2	2	2	72.75	$5,648

Best finish for 1965: T-5th at the San Diego Open & Lucky International

Year	Starts	Rounds Played	Cuts Made	Wins	Top-5s	Top-10s	Top-25s	Scoring Average	Money
1966	7	23	4	0	0	0	0	74.26	$364

Best finish for 1966: T-47th at the Bing Crosby National Professional-Amateur & Bob Hope Desert Classic

Year	Starts	Rounds Played	Cuts Made	Wins	Top-5s	Top-10s	Top-25s	Scoring Average	Money
1967	3	10	1	0	0	0	0	73.20	

Best finish for 1967: T-43rd at the San Diego Open

Year	Starts	Rounds Played	Cuts Made	Wins	Top-5s	Top-10s	Top-25s	Scoring Average	Money
1968	3	10	1	0	0	0	0	75.50	

Best finish for 1968: T-63rd at the Bing Crosby National Professional-Amateur

Year	Starts	Rounds Played	Cuts Made	Wins	Top-5s	Top-10s	Top-25s	Scoring Average	Money
1969	1	4	0	0	0	0	0	78.75	
Period Totals	Starts	Rounds Played	Cuts Made	Wins	Top-5s	Top-10s	Top-25s	Scoring Average	Money
	55	191	34	0	2	3	10	73.21	$12,565

Mike Homa

Year	Starts	Rounds Played	Cuts Made	Wins	Top-5s	Top-10s	Top-25s	Scoring Average	Money
1958	9	29	5	0	0	0	1	74.03	

Best finish for 1958: T-25th at the Greenbrier Invitational

Year	Starts	Rounds Played	Cuts Made	Wins	Top-5s	Top-10s	Top-25s	Scoring Average	Money
1959	12	45	9	0	0	1	5	72.84	$3,659

Best finish for 1959: T-9th at the Sam Snead Festival

Year	Starts	Rounds Played	Cuts Made	Wins	Top-5s	Top-10s	Top-25s	Scoring Average	Money
1960	3	10	2	0	0	0	0	74.00	$174

Best finish for 1960: T-33rd at the Texas Open Invitational

Year	Starts	Rounds Played	Cuts Made	Wins	Top-5s	Top-10s	Top-25s	Scoring Average	Money
1963	2	6	2	0	0	0	0	73.00	$365

Best finish for 1963: T-26th at the Insurance City Open Invitational

Year	Starts	Rounds Played	Cuts Made	Wins	Top-5s	Top-10s	Top-25s	Scoring Average	Money
1964	3	7	1	0	0	0	0	74.14	

Best finish for 1964: T-53rd at the Thunderbird Classic

Year	Starts	Rounds Played	Cuts Made	Wins	Top-5s	Top-10s	Top-25s	Scoring Average	Money
1966	1	2	0	0	0	0	0	76.50	
1967	1	2	0	0	0	0	0	81.00	
Period Totals	Starts	Rounds Played	Cuts Made	Wins	Top-5s	Top-10s	Top-25s	Scoring Average	Money
	31	101	19	0	0	1	6	73.63	$4,199

Wilf Homenuik

Year	Starts	Rounds Played	Cuts Made	Wins	Top-5s	Top-10s	Top-25s	Scoring Average	Money
1962	1	4	1	0	0	0	0	72.00	$150

Best finish for 1962: T-26th at the Mobile Sertoma Open Invitational

| 1963 | 2 | 8 | 2 | 0 | 0 | 0 | 0 | 72.13 | $232 |

Best finish for 1963: T-37th at the St. Paul Open Invitational

| 1964 | 13 | 32 | 4 | 0 | 0 | 0 | 0 | 74.44 | |

Best finish for 1964: T-42nd at the Greater Hartford Open

| 1965 | 2 | 6 | 1 | 0 | 0 | 0 | 0 | 74.33 | $795 |

Best finish for 1965: T-54th at the Carling Open

| 1966 | 3 | 10 | 2 | 0 | 0 | 0 | 0 | 74.30 | $1,195 |

Best finish for 1966: T-37th at the Carling World Open

| 1967 | 13 | 46 | 10 | 0 | 0 | 0 | 0 | 73.63 | $1,521 |

Best finish for 1967: T-38th at the Azalea Open

| 1968 | 12 | 34 | 6 | 0 | 0 | 1 | 1 | 72.35 | $1,685 |

Best finish for 1968: T-9th at the AZALEA Open Invitational

| 1969 | 18 | 59 | 12 | 0 | 0 | 0 | 4 | 71.92 | $6,940 |

Best finish for 1969: T-12th at the Azalea Open

| 1970 | 17 | 50 | 10 | 0 | 0 | 1 | 5 | 72.10 | $11,958 |

Best finish for 1970: T-10th at the Azalea Open Invitational

| 1971 | 20 | 60 | 10 | 0 | 0 | 1 | 5 | 72.55 | $12,420 |

Best finish for 1971: T-10th at the Tallahassee Open

| 1972 | 23 | 70 | 13 | 0 | 1 | 1 | 3 | 72.93 | $14,062 |

Best finish for 1972: T-3rd at the Byron Nelson Golf Classic

| 1973 | 17 | 44 | 5 | 0 | 1 | 1 | 1 | 73.18 | $4,179 |

Best finish for 1973: T-5th at the Tallahassee Open

| 1974 | 13 | 35 | 5 | 0 | 0 | 1 | 1 | 72.60 | $7,534 |

Best finish for 1974: T-7th at the Greater Greensboro Open

| 1975 | 8 | 18 | 1 | 0 | 0 | 0 | 0 | 74.44 | $292 |

Best finish for 1975: T-59th at the Phoenix Open

1976	1	2	0	0	0	0	0	76.00	
Period Totals	Starts	Rounds Played	Cuts Made	Wins	Top-5s	Top-10s	Top-25s	Scoring Average	Money
	163	478	82	0	2	6	20	72.89	$62,964

Herb Hooper

Year	Starts	Rounds Played	Cuts Made	Wins	Top-5s	Top-10s	Top-25s	Scoring Average	Money
1963	2	8	2	0	0	0	1	72.00	$715

Best finish for 1963: T-21st at the Greater New Orleans Open Invitational

| 1964 | 10 | 25 | 2 | 0 | 0 | 0 | 0 | 74.92 | $125 |

Best finish for 1964: T-37th at the Canadian Open

| 1966 | 1 | 4 | 1 | 0 | 0 | 0 | 0 | 76.50 | $530 |

Best finish for 1966: 63rd at the U.S. Open

| 1968 | 16 | 46 | 7 | 0 | 0 | 1 | 3 | 72.17 | $2,255 |

Best finish for 1968: T-7th at the Rebel Yell Open

| 1969 | 27 | 84 | 16 | 0 | 0 | 2 | 4 | 72.25 | $14,042 |

Best finish for 1969: T-6th at the Buick Open

| 1970 | 32 | 105 | 22 | 0 | 1 | 2 | 10 | 71.63 | $22,767 |

Best finish for 1970: T-4th at the Green Island Open Invitational

| 1971 | 37 | 115 | 20 | 0 | 0 | 0 | 7 | 72.51 | $24,277 |

Best finish for 1971: T-11th at the Westchester Classic

| 1972 | 17 | 45 | 6 | 0 | 0 | 0 | 3 | 73.67 | $5,284 |

Best finish for 1972: T-14th at the Bing Crosby Pro-Am

| 1973 | 8 | 19 | 1 | 0 | 0 | 0 | 0 | 75.05 | $1,065 |

Best finish for 1973: T-27th at the Walt Disney World Open

1974	3	6	0	0	0	0	0	74.00	
Period Totals	Starts	Rounds Played	Cuts Made	Wins	Top-5s	Top-10s	Top-25s	Scoring Average	Money
	153	457	77	0	1	5	28	72.62	$71,060

P.H. Horgan III

Year	Starts	Rounds Played	Cuts Made	Wins	Top-5s	Top-10s	Top-25s	Scoring Average	Money
1983	1	2	0	0	0	0	0	74.00	
1984	1	2	0	0	0	0	0	75.00	
1986	1	2	0	0	0	0	0	75.00	
1987	1	2	0	0	0	0	0	74.50	$600
1989	31	85	11	0	1	2	3	72.04	$64,787

Best finish for 1989: T-5th at the USF&G Classic

| 1990 | 30 | 85 | 14 | 0 | 0 | 0 | 2 | 72.39 | $72,898 |

Best finish for 1990: T-12th at the Bank of Boston Classic

Year	Starts	Rounds Played	Cuts Made	Wins	Top-5s	Top-10s	Top-25s	Scoring Average	Money
1991	7	19	2	0	0	0	0	72.58	$2,912

Best finish for 1991: T-53rd at the Buick Classic

| 1992 | 30 | 75 | 11 | 0 | 0 | 2 | 4 | 71.56 | $123,684 |

Best finish for 1992: T-6th at the Anheuser-Busch Golf Classic & Hardee's Golf Classic

| 1993 | 31 | 87 | 12 | 0 | 0 | 3 | 3 | 72.32 | $105,571 |

Best finish for 1993: T-7th at the Sprint Western Open

| 1994 | 17 | 47 | 9 | 0 | 0 | 1 | 1 | 71.40 | $54,734 |

Best finish for 1994: T-10th at the B.C. Open

| 1995 | 2 | 6 | 1 | 0 | 0 | 0 | 0 | 72.33 | $2,462 |

Best finish for 1995: T-48th at the Ideon Classic

| 1997 | 30 | 89 | 15 | 0 | 1 | 3 | 5 | 71.35 | $226,249 |

Best finish for 1997: 5th at the Greater Vancouver Open

| 1998 | 34 | 105 | 19 | 0 | 1 | 1 | 4 | 71.21 | $224,100 |

Best finish for 1998: T-5th at the Deposit Guaranty Golf Classic

| 1999 | 31 | 98 | 20 | 0 | 0 | 1 | 2 | 71.42 | $265,956 |

Best finish for 1999: T-8th at the Doral-Ryder Open

| 2000 | 25 | 65 | 7 | 0 | 0 | 0 | 1 | 71.92 | $80,612 |

Best finish for 2000: T-25th at the Canon Greater Hartford Open

| 2005 | 2 | 6 | 1 | 0 | 0 | 0 | 0 | 70.67 | $6,540 |

Best finish for 2005: T-59th at the B.C. Open

2006	1	2	0	0	0	0	0	73.50	
2008	1	2	0	0	0	0	0	72.00	
Period Totals	Starts	Rounds Played	Cuts Made	Wins	Top-5s	Top-10s	Top-25s	Scoring Average	Money
	276	779	122	0	3	13	25	71.78	$1,231,105

Rod Horn

Year	Starts	Rounds Played	Cuts Made	Wins	Top-5s	Top-10s	Top-25s	Scoring Average	Money
1966	2	4	0	0	0	0	0	78.75	
1968	18	47	7	0	1	1	2	72.62	$12,867

Best finish for 1968: 3rd at the Buick Open Invitational

1969	7	13	0	0	0	0	0	76.08	
Period Totals	Starts	Rounds Played	Cuts Made	Wins	Top-5s	Top-10s	Top-25s	Scoring Average	Money
	27	64	7	0	1	1	2	73.70	$12,867

John Horne

Year	Starts	Rounds Played	Cuts Made	Wins	Top-5s	Top-10s	Top-25s	Scoring Average	Money
1984	1	4	1	0	0	0	0	70.00	$471

Best finish for 1984: T-51st at the Miller High-Life Quad Cities Open

| 1986 | 2 | 4 | 0 | 0 | 0 | 0 | 0 | 76.75 | |
| 1987 | 30 | 63 | 4 | 0 | 0 | 0 | 0 | 73.29 | $4,490 |

Best finish for 1987: T-48th at the Provident Classic

| Period Totals | Starts | Rounds Played | Cuts Made | Wins | Top-5s | Top-10s | Top-25s | Scoring Average | Money |
| | 33 | 71 | 5 | 0 | 0 | 0 | 0 | 73.30 | $4,960 |

Tommy Horton

Year	Starts	Rounds Played	Cuts Made	Wins	Top-5s	Top-10s	Top-25s	Scoring Average	Money
1965	2	6	1	0	0	0	1	74.33	$287

Best finish for 1965: T-17th at the British Open

| 1966 | 1 | 2 | 0 | 0 | 0 | 0 | 0 | 76.00 | |
| 1967 | 2 | 6 | 1 | 0 | 0 | 1 | 1 | 72.83 | $927 |

Best finish for 1967: T-8th at the British Open

| 1968 | 2 | 6 | 1 | 0 | 0 | 0 | 1 | 75.17 | $1,770 |

Best finish for 1968: T-13th at the British Open

| 1969 | 2 | 6 | 1 | 0 | 0 | 0 | 1 | 73.50 | $1,577 |

Best finish for 1969: T-11th at the British Open

| 1970 | 1 | 4 | 1 | 0 | 0 | 1 | 1 | 72.25 | $2,880 |

Best finish for 1970: T-9th at the British Open

| 1971 | 2 | 6 | 1 | 0 | 0 | 0 | 0 | 75.50 | $1,468 |

Best finish for 1971: T-37th at the British Open

| 1972 | 1 | 4 | 1 | 0 | 0 | 0 | 0 | 73.75 | $420 |

Best finish for 1972: T-40th at the British Open

| 1973 | 2 | 8 | 1 | 0 | 0 | 0 | 0 | 74.13 | $552 |

Best finish for 1973: T-31st at the British Open

| 1974 | 1 | 4 | 1 | 0 | 0 | 0 | 0 | 75.25 | $510 |

Best finish for 1974: T-31st at the British Open

| 1975 | 2 | 8 | 2 | 0 | 0 | 0 | 1 | 72.75 | $2,168 |

Best finish for 1975: T-19th at the British Open

| 1976 | 1 | 4 | 1 | 0 | 1 | 1 | 1 | 72.00 | $5,076 |

Best finish for 1976: 5th at the British Open

| 1977 | 6 | 17 | 3 | 0 | 0 | 1 | 1 | 73.59 | $6,758 |

Best finish for 1977: T-9th at the British Open

Year	Starts	Rounds Played	Cuts Made	Wins	Top-5s	Top-10s	Top-25s	Scoring Average	Money
1978	3	7	0	0	0	0	0	76.00	$332
1979	1	3	0	0	0	0	0	76.67	$630
1980	1	4	1	0	0	0	0	72.50	$1,870

Best finish for 1980: T-32nd at the British Open

1981	1	4	1	0	0	0	0	73.00	$1,388

Best finish for 1981: T-35th at the British Open

1982	1	3	0	0	0	0	0	76.33	$638
1985	1	2	0	0	0	0	0	76.00	$544
1986	1	4	1	0	0	0	0	76.50	$2,250

Best finish for 1986: 74th at the British Open

Period Totals	Starts	Rounds Played	Cuts Made	Wins	Top-5s	Top-10s	Top-25s	Scoring Average	Money
	34	108	18	0	1	4	8	74.17	$32,045

Kazuhiko Hosokawa

Year	Starts	Rounds Played	Cuts Made	Wins	Top-5s	Top-10s	Top-25s	Scoring Average	Money
1997	4	12	2	0	0	0	1	71.67	$20,804

Best finish for 1997: T-22nd at the MasterCard Colonial

1998	5	14	1	0	0	0	0	73.50	$8,883

Best finish for 1998: 77th at the British Open

1999	3	8	1	0	0	0	0	75.88	$28,375

Best finish for 1999: T-53rd at the American Express Championship

2000	14	34	5	0	1	1	2	72.38	$227,588

Best finish for 2000: T-2nd at the Kemper Insurance Open

2001	2	6	1	0	0	0	1	70.50	$29,944

Best finish for 2001: T-22nd at the Kemper Insurance Open

2005	1	4	1	0	0	0	0	73.50	$34,500

Best finish for 2005: 65th at the WGC-NEC Invitational

Period Totals	Starts	Rounds Played	Cuts Made	Wins	Top-5s	Top-10s	Top-25s	Scoring Average	Money
	29	78	11	0	1	1	4	72.74	$350,095

Charles Houts

Year	Starts	Rounds Played	Cuts Made	Wins	Top-5s	Top-10s	Top-25s	Scoring Average	Money
1968	15	34	4	0	0	0	1	73.59	$233

Best finish for 1968: T-21st at the Robinson Open

1969	10	27	4	0	0	0	0	74.44	$462

Best finish for 1969: T-32nd at the Tallahassee Open

1973	1	2	0	0	0	0	0	78.00	

Period Totals	Starts	Rounds Played	Cuts Made	Wins	Top-5s	Top-10s	Top-25s	Scoring Average	Money
	26	63	8	0	0	0	1	74.10	$695

David Howell

Year	Starts	Rounds Played	Cuts Made	Wins	Top-5s	Top-10s	Top-25s	Scoring Average	Money
1997	1	2	0	0	0	0	0	74.00	$1,676
1998	1	4	1	0	0	0	0	73.75	$12,471

Best finish for 1998: T-44th at the British Open

1999	2	6	1	0	0	0	0	76.33	$12,675

Best finish for 1999: T-45th at the British Open

2001	1	2	0	0	0	0	0	73.50	$1,574
2002	2	4	0	0	0	0	0	76.50	$4,950
2003	2	6	1	0	0	0	0	74.00	$49,648

Best finish for 2003: T-28th at the American Express Championship

2004	3	10	2	0	1	1	1	71.80	$472,245

Best finish for 2004: 3rd at the WGC-American Express Championship

2005	12	32	6	0	0	2	4	71.53	$700,950

Best finish for 2005: T-6th at the WGC-NEC Invitational & WGC-American Express Championship

2006	14	45	12	0	1	1	7	71.67	$916,155

Best finish for 2006: T-5th at the WGC-Accenture Match Play Championship

2007	10	27	7	0	0	0	0	73.26	$216,083

Best finish for 2007: T-29th at the Nissan Open

2008	3	10	2	0	0	1	1	72.80	$226,243

Best finish for 2008: T-7th at the British Open

Period Totals	Starts	Rounds Played	Cuts Made	Wins	Top-5s	Top-10s	Top-25s	Scoring Average	Money
	51	148	32	0	2	5	13	72.54	$2,614,669

Dick Howell

Year	Starts	Rounds Played	Cuts Made	Wins	Top-5s	Top-10s	Top-25s	Scoring Average	Money
1962	1	2	1	0	0	0	0	80.50	

Best finish for 1962: T-200 at the PGA Championship

1964	26	48	2	0	0	1	1	75.04	$1,017

Best finish for 1964: T-8th at the St. Petersburg Open

1965	1	2	0	0	0	0	0	73.50	

	Starts	Rounds Played	Cuts Made	Wins	Top-5s	Top-10s	Top-25s	Scoring Average	Money
1966	2	3	0	0	0	0	0	80.67	
Period Totals	Starts	Rounds Played	Cuts Made	Wins	Top-5s	Top-10s	Top-25s	Scoring Average	Money
	30	55	3	0	0	1	1	75.49	$1,017

Charles Howell III

Year	Starts	Rounds Played	Cuts Made	Wins	Top-5s	Top-10s	Top-25s	Scoring Average	Money
1996	1	2	0	0	0	0	0	77.50	
1997	1	2	0	0	0	0	0	73.50	
2000	13	39	7	0	1	1	2	70.41	$263,533

Best finish for 2000: 3rd at the John Deere Classic

2001	24	85	20	0	3	5	14	69.59	$1,521,632

Best finish for 2001: 2nd at the Greater Milwaukee Open

2002	32	112	27	1	4	7	16	69.99	$2,702,747

Best finish for 2002: Win at the Michelob Championship at Kingsmill

2003	31	115	29	0	2	6	16	70.30	$2,568,955

Best finish for 2003: 2nd at the Nissan Open & The Tour Championship

2004	30	101	22	0	2	5	10	71.09	$1,703,485

Best finish for 2004: 2nd at the Booz Allen Classic

2005	29	90	21	0	5	6	13	70.72	$2,084,586

Best finish for 2005: T-2nd at the Buick Invitational

2006	30	93	20	0	2	3	5	71.46	$1,560,355

Best finish for 2006: T-2nd at the Zurich Classic of New Orleans & 84 Lumber Classic

2007	26	86	18	1	3	5	8	71.47	$2,836,972

Best finish for 2007: Win at the Nissan Open

2008	31	99	22	0	1	4	12	71.15	$1,449,232

Best finish for 2008: T-3rd at the Turning Stone Resort Championship

Period Totals	Starts	Rounds Played	Cuts Made	Wins	Top-5s	Top-10s	Top-25s	Scoring Average	Money
	248	824	186	2	23	42	96	70.71	$16,691,496

Ryan Howison

Year	Starts	Rounds Played	Cuts Made	Wins	Top-5s	Top-10s	Top-25s	Scoring Average	Money
1995	19	46	4	0	0	0	0	72.91	$11,078

Best finish for 1995: T-38th at the Canon Greater Hartford Open

1998	1	4	1	0	0	0	0	71.50	$3,996

Best finish for 1998: T-57th at the Honda Classic

2000	30	81	11	0	0	0	0	72.37	$99,149

Best finish for 2000: T-29th at the Shell Houston Open

2007	1	2	0	0	0	0	0	73.50	
Period Totals	Starts	Rounds Played	Cuts Made	Wins	Top-5s	Top-10s	Top-25s	Scoring Average	Money
	51	133	16	0	0	0	0	72.55	$114,222

Brian Huggett

Year	Starts	Rounds Played	Cuts Made	Wins	Top-5s	Top-10s	Top-25s	Scoring Average	Money
1961	1	4	1	0	0	0	0	75.25	

Best finish for 1961: T-27th at the British Open

1962	1	4	1	0	1	1	1	72.25	

Best finish for 1962: T-3rd at the British Open

1963	1	4	1	0	0	0	1	72.75	$322

Best finish for 1963: T-14th at the British Open

1964	2	4	0	0	0	0	0	77.50	
1965	1	4	1	0	1	1	1	71.75	$3,150

Best finish for 1965: T-2nd at the British Open

1966	2	6	1	0	0	0	0	75.67	$227

Best finish for 1966: T-43rd at the British Open

1967	2	6	1	0	0	0	1	74.00	$329

Best finish for 1967: T-25th at the British Open

1968	1	4	1	0	0	0	1	74.50	$770

Best finish for 1968: T-13th at the British Open

1969	4	12	2	0	0	0	1	73.17	$1,051

Best finish for 1969: T-16th at the British Open

1970	2	8	2	0	0	0	0	73.50	$792

Best finish for 1970: T-28th at the British Open

1971	1	4	1	0	0	0	1	73.00	$638

Best finish for 1971: T-25th at the British Open

1972	1	4	1	0	0	0	0	73.00	$675

Best finish for 1972: T-26th at the British Open

1973	1	3	0	0	0	0	0	75.67	$195
1974	1	3	0	0	0	0	0	78.00	$180
1975	1	4	1	0	0	0	0	73.25	$480

Best finish for 1975: T-40th at the British Open

1976	1	2	0	0	0	0	0	77.50	$180
1977	1	4	1	0	0	0	0	73.75	$440

Best finish for 1977: T-48th at the British Open

Year	Starts	Rounds Played	Cuts Made	Wins	Top-5s	Top-10s	Top-25s	Scoring Average	Money
1978	1	3	0	0	0	0	0	74.33	$428
1979	1	2	0	0	0	0	0	77.50	$420
Period Totals	Starts	Rounds Played	Cuts Made	Wins	Top-5s	Top-10s	Top-25s	Scoring Average	Money
	26	85	15	0	2	2	7	74.19	$10,277

Bradley Hughes

Year	Starts	Rounds Played	Cuts Made	Wins	Top-5s	Top-10s	Top-25s	Scoring Average	Money
1989	1	0	0	0	0	0	0		
1993	2	4	1	0	0	0	1	72.25	$28,125

Best finish for 1993: T-19th at the NEC World Series of Golf

1994	7	18	4	0	0	0	1	73.00	$30,863

Best finish for 1994: 22nd at the Sprint International

1995	6	14	1	0	0	0	0	73.21	$7,146

Best finish for 1995: T-45th at the U.S. Open

1996	5	15	3	0	0	2	2	71.40	$74,420

Best finish for 1996: T-9th at the Shell Houston Open & B.C. Open

1997	27	78	12	0	0	1	3	71.90	$142,793

Best finish for 1997: T-8th at the B.C. Open

1998	23	63	10	0	3	3	4	71.86	$375,767

Best finish for 1998: T-2nd at the CVS Charity Classic

1999	31	100	18	0	1	2	5	72.11	$474,071

Best finish for 1999: T-2nd at the Kemper Open

2000	33	90	13	0	2	3	5	71.54	$469,590

Best finish for 2000: T-5th at the Nissan Open & Michelob Championship at Kingsmill

2001	33	94	14	0	1	2	3	71.28	$406,258

Best finish for 2001: T-3rd at the Kemper Insurance Open

2002	22	60	8	0	0	0	0	72.13	$85,450

Best finish for 2002: T-27th at the Advil Western Open

2003	2	4	0	0	0	0	0	72.25	
2004	1	2	0	0	0	0	0	71.00	
2005	20	52	6	0	0	0	0	72.04	$76,819

Best finish for 2005: T-29th at the U.S. Bank Championship in Milwaukee

2006	1	2	0	0	0	0	0	73.50	$1,210
Period Totals	Starts	Rounds Played	Cuts Made	Wins	Top-5s	Top-10s	Top-25s	Scoring Average	Money
	214	596	90	0	7	13	24	71.87	$2,172,513

Mike Hulbert

Year	Starts	Rounds Played	Cuts Made	Wins	Top-5s	Top-10s	Top-25s	Scoring Average	Money
1983	1	2	0	0	0	0	0	72.50	
1985	26	78	12	0	0	0	1	72.64	$18,368

Best finish for 1985: T-22nd at the Anheuser-Busch Golf Classic

1986	36	112	26	1	4	5	13	71.61	$277,287

Best finish for 1986: Win at the Federal Express St. Jude Classic

1987	36	114	23	0	2	6	10	71.89	$205,794

Best finish for 1987: T-2nd at the Southern Open

1988	35	112	21	0	0	1	9	71.22	$129,751

Best finish for 1988: 6th at the Southern Open

1989	34	114	25	1	3	7	12	70.92	$424,221

Best finish for 1989: Win at the B.C. Open

1990	32	119	27	0	2	3	7	71.98	$223,634

Best finish for 1990: T-4th at the Kmart Greater Greensboro Open

1991	31	110	24	1	5	5	13	70.65	$551,750

Best finish for 1991: Win at the Anheuser-Busch Golf Classic

1992	32	110	24	0	0	4	11	70.84	$279,578

Best finish for 1992: T-6th at the U.S. Open

1993	31	100	21	0	0	0	6	71.74	$195,334

Best finish for 1993: T-11th at the The Players Championship

1994	31	103	20	0	1	2	5	71.11	$222,007

Best finish for 1994: T-3rd at the B.C. Open

1995	31	102	22	0	1	3	8	70.82	$312,255

Best finish for 1995: T-2nd at the Buick Invitational of California

1996	31	94	18	0	1	2	6	71.18	$236,431

Best finish for 1996: T-3rd at the Nortel Open

1997	30	98	20	0	1	4	6	71.52	$318,547

Best finish for 1997: T-2nd at the Buick Invitational

1998	31	89	14	0	1	1	5	71.63	$331,954

Best finish for 1998: 3rd at the Bell Canadian Open

1999	34	101	17	0	0	1	6	71.55	$264,524

Best finish for 1999: T-9th at the Southern Farm Bureau Classic

2000	34	80	5	0	0	0	1	72.60	$59,878

Best finish for 2000: T-19th at the Honda Classic

| 2001 | 19 | 44 | 4 | 0 | 0 | 0 | 0 | 72.73 | $28,999 |

Best finish for 2001: T-47th at the Michelob Championship at Kingsmill

| 2002 | 20 | 53 | 6 | 0 | 0 | 0 | 0 | 72.08 | $46,148 |

Best finish for 2002: T-39th at the Canon Greater Hartford Open

| 2003 | 14 | 31 | 1 | 0 | 0 | 0 | 0 | 74.48 | $6,300 |

Best finish for 2003: 80th at the Greater Milwaukee Open

| 2004 | 8 | 16 | 0 | 0 | 0 | 0 | 0 | 72.44 | |
| 2005 | 4 | 11 | 1 | 0 | 0 | 0 | 0 | 74.09 | $6,030 |

Best finish for 2005: T-69th at the B.C. Open

| 2006 | 6 | 15 | 1 | 0 | 0 | 0 | 0 | 73.87 | $6,540 |

Best finish for 2006: 61st at the B.C. Open

2007	3	6	0	0	0	0	0	73.33	
2008	1	2	0	0	0	0	0	77.00	
Period Totals	Starts	Rounds Played	Cuts Made	Wins	Top-5s	Top-10s	Top-25s	Scoring Average	Money
	591	1816	332	3	21	44	119	71.62	$4,145,329

Ed Humenik

Year	Starts	Rounds Played	Cuts Made	Wins	Top-5s	Top-10s	Top-25s	Scoring Average	Money
1987	1	2	0	0	0	0	0	77.50	
1989	30	81	11	0	0	0	3	71.91	$46,384

Best finish for 1989: T-14th at the Anheuser-Busch Golf Classic

| 1990 | 2 | 4 | 0 | 0 | 0 | 0 | 0 | 72.25 | |
| 1991 | 33 | 92 | 14 | 0 | 0 | 2 | 3 | 71.60 | $125,497 |

Best finish for 1991: T-7th at the Las Vegas Invitational

| 1992 | 32 | 100 | 18 | 0 | 1 | 1 | 7 | 71.11 | $149,337 |

Best finish for 1992: T-4th at the Buick Southern Open

| 1993 | 31 | 93 | 17 | 0 | 1 | 3 | 4 | 71.63 | $152,562 |

Best finish for 1993: 5th at the The Nestle Invitational

| 1994 | 31 | 89 | 13 | 0 | 1 | 1 | 2 | 72.29 | $168,331 |

Best finish for 1994: T-2nd at the Kmart Greater Greensboro Open

| 1995 | 32 | 87 | 11 | 0 | 0 | 0 | 3 | 71.94 | $78,150 |

Best finish for 1995: T-11th at the Deposit Guaranty Golf Classic

| 1996 | 6 | 14 | 1 | 0 | 0 | 0 | 1 | 73.07 | $13,508 |

Best finish for 1996: T-23rd at the Greater Greensboro Chrysler Classic

1997	1	2	0	0	0	0	0	78.50	$1,000
Period Totals	Starts	Rounds Played	Cuts Made	Wins	Top-5s	Top-10s	Top-25s	Scoring Average	Money
	199	564	85	0	3	7	23	71.81	$734,767

Bernard Hunt

Year	Starts	Rounds Played	Cuts Made	Wins	Top-5s	Top-10s	Top-25s	Scoring Average	Money
1958	1	4	1	0	0	0	0	73.75	

Best finish for 1958: T-30th at the British Open

| 1959 | 1 | 4 | 1 | 0 | 0 | 0 | 1 | 72.50 | |

Best finish for 1959: T-11th at the British Open

| 1960 | 1 | 4 | 1 | 0 | 1 | 1 | 1 | 70.50 | $1,493 |

Best finish for 1960: T-3rd at the British Open

| 1961 | 1 | 2 | 0 | 0 | 0 | 0 | 0 | 77.50 | |
| 1962 | 4 | 16 | 4 | 0 | 0 | 0 | 2 | 73.38 | $1,278 |

Best finish for 1962: T-12th at the Bing Crosby National

| 1963 | 2 | 8 | 2 | 0 | 0 | 0 | 1 | 72.25 | $487 |

Best finish for 1963: T-11th at the British Open

| 1964 | 9 | 33 | 6 | 0 | 1 | 1 | 3 | 73.24 | $4,080 |

Best finish for 1964: 4th at the British Open

| 1965 | 6 | 24 | 6 | 0 | 1 | 1 | 3 | 72.58 | $3,871 |

Best finish for 1965: T-5th at the British Open

| 1966 | 7 | 18 | 2 | 0 | 0 | 0 | 1 | 75.11 | $2,558 |

Best finish for 1966: T-19th at the Carling World Open

| 1967 | 2 | 8 | 2 | 0 | 0 | 0 | 0 | 74.00 | $220 |

Best finish for 1967: T-36th at the British Open

| 1968 | 1 | 2 | 0 | 0 | 0 | 0 | 0 | 78.00 | |
| 1969 | 1 | 4 | 1 | 0 | 0 | 0 | 1 | 73.00 | $540 |

Best finish for 1969: T-23rd at the British Open

| 1970 | 1 | 3 | 0 | 0 | 0 | 0 | 0 | 75.67 | $079 |
| 1971 | 1 | 4 | 1 | 0 | 0 | 0 | 1 | 72.50 | $1,080 |

Best finish for 1971: T-20th at the British Open

| 1972 | 1 | 3 | 0 | 0 | 0 | 0 | 0 | 76.00 | $188 |
| 1973 | 1 | 4 | 1 | 0 | 0 | 0 | 0 | 74.50 | $358 |

Best finish for 1973: T-49th at the British Open

| 1974 | 1 | 4 | 1 | 0 | 0 | 0 | 0 | 76.00 | $402 |

Best finish for 1974: T-42nd at the British Open

Period Totals	Starts	Rounds Played	Cuts Made	Wins	Top-5s	Top-10s	Top-25s	Scoring Average	Money
	41	145	29	0	3	3	14	73.60	$16,633

Mac Hunter, Jr.

Year	Starts	Rounds Played	Cuts Made	Wins	Top-5s	Top-10s	Top-25s	Scoring Average	Money
1970	4	11	1	0	0	0	0	74.18	$890

Best finish for 1970: T-39th at the Los Angles Open

Year	Starts	Rounds Played	Cuts Made	Wins	Top-5s	Top-10s	Top-25s	Scoring Average	Money
1971	2	5	0	0	0	0	0	75.20	
1972	6	16	2	0	0	1	1	75.19	$3,943

Best finish for 1972: T-10th at the Bing Crosby Pro-Am

| 1973 | 5 | 16 | 3 | 0 | 0 | 0 | 0 | 73.75 | $2,224 |

Best finish for 1973: T-35th at the Bing Crosby Pro-Am

| 1974 | 5 | 15 | 2 | 0 | 0 | 0 | 0 | 76.13 | $504 |

Best finish for 1974: T-59th at the Bing Crosby Pro-Am

1978	3	6	0	0	0	0	0	77.00	
1980	1	2	0	0	0	0	0	78.00	
Period Totals	Starts	Rounds Played	Cuts Made	Wins	Top-5s	Top-10s	Top-25s	Scoring Average	Money
	26	71	8	0	0	1	1	75.14	$7,561

John Huston

Year	Starts	Rounds Played	Cuts Made	Wins	Top-5s	Top-10s	Top-25s	Scoring Average	Money
1987	1	4	1	0	0	0	0	73.25	$1,055

Best finish for 1987: T-63rd at the Centel Classic

| 1988 | 31 | 93 | 17 | 0 | 2 | 2 | 6 | 71.31 | $150,300 |

Best finish for 1988: 3rd at the Hawaiian Open

| 1989 | 29 | 85 | 14 | 0 | 1 | 3 | 5 | 72.21 | $205,207 |

Best finish for 1989: 2nd at the Kmart Greater Greensboro Open

| 1990 | 27 | 81 | 16 | 1 | 2 | 3 | 7 | 72.53 | $436,686 |

Best finish for 1990: Win at the Honda Classic

| 1991 | 27 | 97 | 23 | 0 | 3 | 5 | 13 | 70.37 | $396,853 |

Best finish for 1991: T-3rd at the Kmart Greater Greensboro Open

| 1992 | 32 | 104 | 23 | 1 | 4 | 4 | 15 | 70.36 | $515,453 |

Best finish for 1992: Win at the Walt Disney World/Oldsmobile Classic

| 1993 | 31 | 116 | 27 | 0 | 3 | 6 | 15 | 70.72 | $689,910 |

Best finish for 1993: T-2nd at the Shell Houston Open & The Tour Championship

| 1994 | 25 | 86 | 18 | 1 | 3 | 8 | 11 | 70.41 | $734,671 |

Best finish for 1994: Win at the Doral-Ryder Open

| 1995 | 27 | 81 | 14 | 0 | 0 | 5 | 7 | 71.31 | $295,574 |

Best finish for 1995: T-6th at the Motorola Western Open

| 1996 | 25 | 84 | 18 | 0 | 3 | 6 | 9 | 70.95 | $507,473 |

Best finish for 1996: 2nd at the Bob Hope Chrysler Classic

| 1997 | 28 | 75 | 11 | 0 | 0 | 1 | 3 | 71.81 | $151,840 |

Best finish for 1997: 9th at the MasterCard Colonial

| 1998 | 25 | 93 | 21 | 2 | 4 | 8 | 16 | 70.16 | $1,544,109 |

Best finish for 1998: Win at the United Airlines Hawaiian Open & Walt Disney World/Oldsmobile Classic

| 1999 | 23 | 76 | 17 | 0 | 6 | 7 | 11 | 71.20 | $1,521,137 |

Best finish for 1999: T-3rd at the Bob Hope Chrysler Classic, Andersen Consulting Match Play Championship & BellSouth Classic

| 2000 | 23 | 80 | 19 | 1 | 5 | 8 | 11 | 70.40 | $1,633,367 |

Best finish for 2000: Win at the Tampa Bay Classic

| 2001 | 20 | 60 | 14 | 0 | 1 | 1 | 7 | 70.88 | $507,683 |

Best finish for 2001: 5th at the Mercedes Championships

| 2002 | 26 | 96 | 23 | 0 | 3 | 5 | 12 | 70.00 | $1,300,053 |

Best finish for 2002: T-3rd at the Bay Hill Invitational

| 2003 | 23 | 75 | 17 | 1 | 2 | 2 | 8 | 70.08 | $1,570,119 |

Best finish for 2003: Win at the Southern Farm Bureau Classic

| 2004 | 20 | 56 | 11 | 0 | 1 | 4 | 5 | 71.14 | $880,961 |

Best finish for 2004: 3rd at the Shell Houston Open

| 2005 | 31 | 86 | 15 | 0 | 1 | 2 | 6 | 71.13 | $657,970 |

Best finish for 2005: T-5th at the 84 Lumber Classic

| 2006 | 27 | 72 | 12 | 0 | 1 | 1 | 2 | 71.33 | $431,025 |

Best finish for 2006: 4th at the Bob Hope Chrysler Classic

| 2007 | 16 | 46 | 7 | 0 | 0 | 0 | 2 | 71.74 | $170,570 |

Best finish for 2007: T-20th at the Wyndham Championship

| 2008 | 18 | 56 | 11 | 0 | 0 | 1 | 5 | 70.48 | $496,876 |

Best finish for 2008: T-7th at the Ginn sur Mer Classic

Period Totals	Starts	Rounds Played	Cuts Made	Wins	Top-5s	Top-10s	Top-25s	Scoring Average	Money
	535	1702	349	7	45	82	176	70.94	$14,798,891

Ryuji Imada

Year	Starts	Rounds Played	Cuts Made	Wins	Top-5s	Top-10s	Top-25s	Scoring Average	Money
1996	1	2	0	0	0	0	0	77.50	
1999	3	6	0	0	0	0	0	72.67	
2000	1	2	0	0	0	0	0	75.00	$1,000
2001	1	2	0	0	0	0	0	70.50	

Year	Starts	Rounds Played	Cuts Made	Wins	Top-5s	Top-10s	Top-25s	Scoring Average	Money
2003	1	4	1	0	0	0	0	74.25	$7,600

Best finish for 2003: T-74th at the BellSouth Classic

| 2005 | 25 | 78 | 14 | 0 | 1 | 1 | 4 | 70.92 | $650,221 |

Best finish for 2005: 5th at the Booz Allen Classic

| 2006 | 31 | 102 | 22 | 0 | 0 | 1 | 10 | 70.76 | $1,018,140 |

Best finish for 2006: T-10th at the BellSouth Classic

| 2007 | 32 | 104 | 20 | 0 | 1 | 2 | 8 | 70.97 | $1,419,364 |

Best finish for 2007: 2nd at the AT&T Classic

| 2008 | 25 | 80 | 16 | 1 | 5 | 5 | 11 | 71.13 | $3,029,363 |

Best finish for 2008: Win at the AT&T Classic

Period Totals	Starts	Rounds Played	Cuts Made	Wins	Top-5s	Top-10s	Top-25s	Scoring Average	Money
	120	380	73	1	7	9	33	71.05	$6,125,689

Trevor Immelman

Year	Starts	Rounds Played	Cuts Made	Wins	Top-5s	Top-10s	Top-25s	Scoring Average	Money
1999	1	4	1	0	0	0	0	76.25	

Best finish for 1999: 56th at the Masters

| 2001 | 1 | 2 | 0 | 0 | 0 | 0 | 0 | 74.00 | |
| 2002 | 2 | 8 | 2 | 0 | 0 | 0 | 0 | 70.50 | $70,228 |

Best finish for 2002: T-27th at the American Express Championship

| 2003 | 12 | 34 | 7 | 0 | 0 | 1 | 2 | 72.15 | $308,150 |

Best finish for 2003: T-9th at the WGC-NEC Invitational

| 2004 | 12 | 36 | 9 | 0 | 0 | 0 | 2 | 72.50 | $305,560 |

Best finish for 2004: T-17th at the WGC-Accenture Match Play Championship

| 2005 | 14 | 40 | 10 | 0 | 1 | 2 | 5 | 71.05 | $726,867 |

Best finish for 2005: T-5th at the Masters

| 2006 | 24 | 86 | 19 | 1 | 5 | 8 | 15 | 69.93 | $3,849,189 |

Best finish for 2006: Win at the Cialis Western Open

| 2007 | 21 | 68 | 15 | 0 | 2 | 4 | 6 | 71.79 | $1,803,647 |

Best finish for 2007: 3rd at the Mercedes Championships & WGC-Accenture Match Play Championship

| 2008 | 22 | 68 | 14 | 1 | 2 | 3 | 6 | 71.85 | $2,566,199 |

Best finish for 2008: Win at the Masters

Period Totals	Starts	Rounds Played	Cuts Made	Wins	Top-5s	Top-10s	Top-25s	Scoring Average	Money
	109	346	77	2	10	18	36	71.40	$9,629,840

Stu Ingraham

Year	Starts	Rounds Played	Cuts Made	Wins	Top-5s	Top-10s	Top-25s	Scoring Average	Money
1986	29	74	8	0	0	0	1	74.08	$11,878

Best finish for 1986: T-14th at the Pensacola Open

1989	1	2	0	0	0	0	0	73.00	$1,000
1990	1	2	0	0	0	0	0	78.00	$1,000
1991	1	2	0	0	0	0	0	75.50	$1,000
1993	1	4	1	0	0	0	0	70.75	$7,058

Best finish for 1993: T-31st at the PGA Championship

| 1996 | 1 | 4 | 1 | 0 | 0 | 0 | 0 | 74.25 | $3,612 |

Best finish for 1996: T-78th at the PGA Championship

| 2002 | 1 | 4 | 1 | 0 | 0 | 0 | 0 | 73.00 | $6,270 |

Best finish for 2002: 75th at the SEI Pennsylvania Classic

Period Totals	Starts	Rounds Played	Cuts Made	Wins	Top-5s	Top-10s	Top-25s	Scoring Average	Money
	35	92	11	0	0	0	1	73.99	$31,819

Joe Inman

Year	Starts	Rounds Played	Cuts Made	Wins	Top-5s	Top-10s	Top-25s	Scoring Average	Money
1966	1	2	0	0	0	0	0	81.50	
1970	2	4	0	0	0	0	0	75.75	
1972	2	6	1	0	0	0	0	72.33	

Best finish for 1972: T-54th at the Greater Greensboro Open

| 1973 | 2 | 12 | 2 | 0 | 0 | 0 | 0 | 74.00 | $1,332 |

Best finish for 1973: T-40th at the Walt Disney World Open

| 1974 | 31 | 115 | 26 | 0 | 2 | 4 | 13 | 71.62 | $46,264 |

Best finish for 1974: T-2nd at the Tallahassee Open

| 1975 | 30 | 107 | 23 | 0 | 2 | 4 | 11 | 71.84 | $53,226 |

Best finish for 1975: T-3rd at the Houston Open & Sahara Invitational

| 1976 | 29 | 93 | 19 | 1 | 1 | 1 | 5 | 72.67 | $69,892 |

Best finish for 1976: Win at the Kemper Open

| 1977 | 27 | 97 | 21 | 0 | 1 | 4 | 11 | 71.97 | $68,564 |

Best finish for 1977: T-2nd at the Florida Citrus Open Invitational

| 1978 | 28 | 98 | 20 | 0 | 1 | 4 | 12 | 71.94 | $62,034 |

Best finish for 1978: T-3rd at the Byron Nelson Golf Classic

| 1979 | 29 | 97 | 19 | 0 | 1 | 2 | 9 | 72.49 | $75,385 |

Best finish for 1979: 2nd at the Atlanta Classic

| 1980 | 32 | 107 | 22 | 0 | 0 | 1 | 4 | 72.51 | $35,014 |

Best finish for 1980: T-9th at the Southern Open

Year	Starts	Rounds Played	Cuts Made	Wins	Top-5s	Top-10s	Top-25s	Scoring Average	Money
1981	25	81	16	0	0	1	7	71.63	$52,568

Best finish for 1981: T-6th at the LaJet Classic

| 1982 | 25 | 78 | 14 | 0 | 2 | 3 | 6 | 71.97 | $53,723 |

Best finish for 1982: T-3rd at the Bing Crosby Pro-Am

| 1983 | 27 | 88 | 16 | 0 | 1 | 3 | 6 | 71.77 | $60,513 |

Best finish for 1983: T-4th at the Southern Open

| 1984 | 26 | 83 | 15 | 0 | 0 | 3 | 4 | 72.36 | $55,094 |

Best finish for 1984: T-7th at the Western Open & Anheuser-Busch Golf Classic

| 1985 | 22 | 73 | 14 | 0 | 0 | 1 | 8 | 71.70 | $62,562 |

Best finish for 1985: T-6th at the USF&G Classic

| 1986 | 29 | 76 | 11 | 0 | 0 | 1 | 2 | 72.62 | $23,829 |

Best finish for 1986: T-10th at the Southern Open

| 1987 | 5 | 16 | 3 | 0 | 0 | 0 | 0 | 72.81 | $7,013 |

Best finish for 1987: T-26th at the MCI Heritage Classic

| 1988 | 2 | 8 | 2 | 0 | 0 | 0 | 0 | 71.25 | $11,699 |

Best finish for 1988: T-27th at the Kmart Greater Greensboro Open

| 1994 | 2 | 4 | 1 | 0 | 0 | 0 | 0 | 71.75 | $1,618 |

Best finish for 1994: T-50th at the Deposit Guaranty Golf Classic

1995	1	2	0	0	0	0	0	74.00	
1997	2	4	0	0	0	0	0	75.75	
Period Totals	Starts	Rounds Played	Cuts Made	Wins	Top-5s	Top-10s	Top-25s	Scoring Average	Money
	379	1251	245	1	11	32	98	72.15	$740,330

John Inman

Year	Starts	Rounds Played	Cuts Made	Wins	Top-5s	Top-10s	Top-25s	Scoring Average	Money
1984	1	2	0	0	0	0	0	76.50	
1985	7	18	2	0	0	0	0	74.28	$1,444

Best finish for 1985: 59th at the Masters

| 1986 | 2 | 4 | 0 | 0 | 0 | 0 | 0 | 74.50 | |
| 1987 | 32 | 95 | 17 | 1 | 1 | 3 | 5 | 71.51 | $148,385 |

Best finish for 1987: Win at the Provident Classic

| 1988 | 34 | 98 | 14 | 0 | 0 | 0 | 2 | 72.54 | $62,006 |

Best finish for 1988: T-11th at the Colonial National Invitational

| 1989 | 29 | 87 | 16 | 0 | 1 | 1 | 4 | 70.95 | $99,318 |

Best finish for 1989: T-5th at the Chattanooga Classic

| 1990 | 32 | 102 | 18 | 0 | 0 | 0 | 4 | 71.95 | $85,289 |

Best finish for 1990: T-14th at the U.S. Open

| 1991 | 32 | 99 | 17 | 0 | 0 | 0 | 2 | 71.51 | $86,001 |

Best finish for 1991: T-11th at the AT&T Pebble Beach Pro-Am

| 1992 | 31 | 98 | 19 | 0 | 0 | 2 | 6 | 71.24 | $173,808 |

Best finish for 1992: T-6th at the Freeport-McMoRan Classic

| 1993 | 32 | 98 | 18 | 1 | 1 | 2 | 4 | 71.65 | $242,140 |

Best finish for 1993: Win at the Buick Southern Open

| 1994 | 34 | 101 | 14 | 0 | 0 | 0 | 5 | 72.17 | $118,856 |

Best finish for 1994: T-13th at the Greater Milwaukee Open

| 1995 | 3 | 5 | 0 | 0 | 0 | 0 | 0 | 73.80 | |
| 1996 | 28 | 79 | 13 | 0 | 0 | 0 | 1 | 72.28 | $62,806 |

Best finish for 1996: T-25th at the Sprint International

| 1997 | 1 | 4 | 1 | 0 | 0 | 0 | 0 | 70.75 | $2,100 |

Best finish for 1997: T-61st at the Deposit Guaranty Golf Classic

| 2000 | 1 | 4 | 1 | 0 | 0 | 0 | 0 | 71.75 | $5,014 |

Best finish for 2000: T-60th at the Buick Challenge

2002	1	2	0	0	0	0	0	73.00	
Period Totals	Starts	Rounds Played	Cuts Made	Wins	Top-5s	Top-10s	Top-25s	Scoring Average	Money
	300	896	150	2	3	8	33	71.84	$1,087,167

Walker Inman, Jr.

Year	Starts	Rounds Played	Cuts Made	Wins	Top-5s	Top-10s	Top-25s	Scoring Average	Money
1958	16	57	11	0	0	0	2	72.75	$974

Best finish for 1958: T-15th at the Texas Open

| 1959 | 8 | 30 | 6 | 0 | 0 | 0 | 5 | 71.63 | $1,756 |

Best finish for 1959: T-18th at the Rubber City Open Invitational

| 1960 | 4 | 13 | 3 | 0 | 0 | 0 | 0 | 75.92 | $204 |

Best finish for 1960: T-27th at the Pensacola Open Invitational

| 1961 | 1 | 4 | 1 | 0 | 0 | 0 | 0 | 70.50 | $260 |

Best finish for 1961: T-30th at the Canadian Open Invitational

| 1964 | 7 | 16 | 2 | 0 | 0 | 0 | 0 | 73.69 | $056 |

Best finish for 1964: T-29th at the San Diego Open

| 1965 | 2 | 4 | 0 | 0 | 0 | 0 | 0 | 76.25 | |
| 1966 | 5 | 16 | 3 | 0 | 0 | 0 | 0 | 73.88 | $842 |

Best finish for 1966: T-43rd at the PGA Championship

Year	Starts	Rounds Played	Cuts Made	Wins	Top-5s	Top-10s	Top-25s	Scoring Average	Money
1968	2	4	0	0	0	0	0	76.50	
Period Totals	45	144	26	0	0	0	7	73.17	$4,093

Hale Irwin

Year	Starts	Rounds Played	Cuts Made	Wins	Top-5s	Top-10s	Top-25s	Scoring Average	Money
1966	1	4	1	0	0	0	0	76.25	

Best finish for 1966: T-61st at the U.S. Open

Year	Starts	Rounds Played	Cuts Made	Wins	Top-5s	Top-10s	Top-25s	Scoring Average	Money
1967	1	4	1	0	0	0	0	78.00	

Best finish for 1967: 73rd at the Houston Championship International

| 1968 | 17 | 56 | 11 | 0 | 0 | 0 | 4 | 72.30 | $5,129 |

Best finish for 1968: T-21st at the Robinson Open

| 1969 | 31 | 105 | 21 | 0 | 0 | 1 | 7 | 72.11 | $18,597 |

Best finish for 1969: T-10th at the Memphis Open

| 1970 | 33 | 112 | 24 | 0 | 2 | 4 | 14 | 71.63 | $44,596 |

Best finish for 1970: 2nd at the Los Angles Open

| 1971 | 36 | 122 | 28 | 1 | 5 | 7 | 13 | 71.52 | $97,072 |

Best finish for 1971: Win at the Sea Pines Heritage Classic

| 1972 | 33 | 117 | 26 | 0 | 7 | 10 | 16 | 71.66 | $104,490 |

Best finish for 1972: T-2nd at the Andy Williams-San Diego Open, Liggett Meyers Open & Kaiser International Open

| 1973 | 31 | 112 | 24 | 1 | 5 | 11 | 17 | 71.38 | $123,062 |

Best finish for 1973: Win at the Sea Pines Heritage Classic

| 1974 | 21 | 83 | 21 | 1 | 6 | 7 | 15 | 71.23 | $147,317 |

Best finish for 1974: Win at the U.S. Open

| 1975 | 23 | 90 | 22 | 2 | 9 | 15 | 18 | 70.90 | $210,660 |

Best finish for 1975: Win at the Atlanta Classic & Western Open

| 1976 | 22 | 88 | 22 | 2 | 10 | 12 | 17 | 70.81 | $253,232 |

Best finish for 1976: Win at the Glen Campbell Los Angles Open & Florida Citrus Open Invitational

| 1977 | 24 | 96 | 24 | 3 | 6 | 8 | 13 | 71.15 | $222,079 |

Best finish for 1977: Win at the Atlanta Classic, Colgate Hall Of Fame Golf Classic & San Antonio Texas Open

| 1978 | 23 | 92 | 23 | 0 | 10 | 13 | 19 | 70.73 | $193,367 |

Best finish for 1978: T-2nd at the Sea Pines Heritage Classic & Colgate Hall Of Fame Classic

| 1979 | 23 | 81 | 17 | 1 | 5 | 7 | 13 | 71.49 | $167,119 |

Best finish for 1979: Win at the U.S. Open

| 1980 | 25 | 87 | 18 | 0 | 3 | 9 | 14 | 71.07 | $130,910 |

Best finish for 1980: T-3rd at the Western Open

| 1981 | 23 | 86 | 21 | 2 | 7 | 8 | 12 | 71.29 | $276,499 |

Best finish for 1981: Win at the Hawaiian Open & Buick Open

| 1982 | 23 | 85 | 20 | 1 | 2 | 4 | 11 | 71.39 | $175,219 |

Best finish for 1982: Win at the Honda Inverrary Classic

| 1983 | 21 | 86 | 21 | 1 | 7 | 10 | 16 | 70.73 | $267,067 |

Best finish for 1983: Win at the Memorial Tournament

| 1984 | 21 | 78 | 17 | 1 | 1 | 6 | 12 | 71.55 | $192,161 |

Best finish for 1984: Win at the Bing Crosby Pro-Am

| 1985 | 20 | 68 | 14 | 1 | 2 | 2 | 8 | 71.57 | $195,007 |

Best finish for 1985: Win at the Memorial Tournament

| 1986 | 25 | 74 | 15 | 0 | 0 | 1 | 3 | 72.45 | $62,083 |

Best finish for 1986: T-10th at the Anheuser-Busch Golf Classic

| 1987 | 22 | 70 | 14 | 0 | 0 | 2 | 7 | 71.16 | $101,425 |

Best finish for 1987: 7th at the Southern Open

| 1988 | 23 | 74 | 14 | 0 | 1 | 2 | 7 | 71.31 | $164,976 |

Best finish for 1988: T-2nd at the Memorial Tournament

| 1989 | 19 | 63 | 14 | 0 | 1 | 2 | 6 | 71.54 | $150,977 |

Best finish for 1989: 3rd at the Nissan Los Angeles Open

| 1990 | 19 | 65 | 16 | 2 | 6 | 6 | 11 | 70.95 | $844,540 |

Best finish for 1990: Win at the U.S. Open & Buick Classic

| 1991 | 18 | 64 | 16 | 0 | 5 | 6 | 7 | 71.08 | $428,616 |

Best finish for 1991: 2nd at the Memorial Tournament

| 1992 | 21 | 69 | 14 | 0 | 0 | 1 | 3 | 71.41 | $120,341 |

Best finish for 1992: T-7th at the Doral-Ryder Open

| 1993 | 21 | 67 | 14 | 0 | 0 | 2 | 9 | 70.66 | $252,686 |

Best finish for 1993: T-6th at the PGA Championship

| 1994 | 21 | 74 | 18 | 1 | 4 | 6 | 11 | 70.49 | $814,436 |

Best finish for 1994: Win at the MCI Heritage Classic

| 1995 | 14 | 49 | 10 | 0 | 0 | 2 | 5 | 70.98 | $191,961 |

Best finish for 1995: T-7th at the Phoenix Open & Doral-Ryder Open

| 1996 | 3 | 12 | 3 | 0 | 0 | 0 | 0 | 72.25 | $31,550 |

Best finish for 1996: T-29th at the Masters

| 1997 | 3 | 10 | 2 | 0 | 0 | 0 | 0 | 73.00 | $20,764 |

Best finish for 1997: T-29th at the PGA Championship

| 1998 | 2 | 6 | 1 | 0 | 0 | 0 | 0 | 72.17 | $6,244 |

Best finish for 1998: T-47th at the BellSouth Classic

Year	Starts	Rounds Played	Cuts Made	Wins	Top-5s	Top-10s	Top-25s	Scoring Average	Money
1999	2	5	1	0	0	0	0	73.60	$12,250

Best finish for 1999: T-41st at the PGA Championship

2000	1	4	1	0	0	0	0	74.00	$34,066

Best finish for 2000: T-27th at the U.S. Open

2001	1	4	1	0	0	0	0	73.00	$13,164

Best finish for 2001: T-52nd at the U.S. Open

2002	1	2	0	0	0	0	0	81.50	$1,000
2003	1	0	0	0	0	0	0		$1,000
2004	1	2	0	0	0	0	0	73.00	$2,000
Period Totals	Starts	Rounds Played	Cuts Made	Wins	Top-5s	Top-10s	Top-25s	Scoring Average	Money
	670	2366	530	20	104	164	308	71.37	$6,077,661

Tripp Isenhour

Year	Starts	Rounds Played	Cuts Made	Wins	Top-5s	Top-10s	Top-25s	Scoring Average	Money
1994	1	4	1	0	0	0	0	72.50	$2,604

Best finish for 1994: T-59th at the BellSouth Classic

2001	30	89	16	0	0	1	4	71.25	$300,452

Best finish for 2001: T-7th at the Canon Greater Hartford Open

2002	21	68	14	0	1	1	3	70.96	$319,210

Best finish for 2002: T-5th at the FedEx St. Jude Classic

2004	22	53	8	0	0	0	0	72.23	$91,699

Best finish for 2004: T-37th at the Buick Invitational

2005	7	18	2	0	0	0	0	71.78	$14,448

Best finish for 2005: T-69th at the Valero Texas Open

2007	32	86	14	0	1	1	3	71.66	$473,980

Best finish for 2007: T-5th at the Honda Classic

2008	1	2	0	0	0	0	0	73.00	
Period Totals	Starts	Rounds Played	Cuts Made	Wins	Top-5s	Top-10s	Top-25s	Scoring Average	Money
	114	320	55	0	2	3	10	71.52	$1,202,393

David Ishii

Year	Starts	Rounds Played	Cuts Made	Wins	Top-5s	Top-10s	Top-25s	Scoring Average	Money
1978	1	2	0	0	0	0	0	73.50	
1983	1	4	1	0	0	0	1	69.50	$3,786

Best finish for 1983: T-20th at the Hawaiian Open

1985	1	4	1	0	0	0	0	71.25	$2,309

Best finish for 1985: T-35th at the Honda Classic

1986	2	6	1	0	0	1	1	72.83	$16,800

Best finish for 1986: T-9th at the NEC World Series of Golf

1987	2	4	0	0	0	0	0	76.00	
1988	9	26	6	0	0	1	2	72.50	$45,454

Best finish for 1988: T-10th at the Hawaiian Open

1989	2	4	0	0	0	0	0	72.00	
1990	4	12	2	1	1	1	1	73.92	$190,500

Best finish for 1990: Win at the Hawaiian Open

1991	2	8	2	0	0	0	1	71.50	$17,615

Best finish for 1991: T-18th at the Infiniti Tournament Of Champions

1992	1	4	1	0	0	0	0	71.25	$2,604

Best finish for 1992: T-61st at the United Airlines Hawaiian Open

1993	1	2	0	0	0	0	0	73.00	
1994	1	4	1	0	0	1	1	69.00	$31,200

Best finish for 1994: T-8th at the United Airlines Hawaiian Open

1995	3	8	1	0	0	1	1	71.88	$31,200

Best finish for 1995: T-10th at the United Airlines Hawaiian Open

1996	1	4	1	0	0	0	1	70.75	$11,606

Best finish for 1996: T-21st at the United Airlines Hawaiian Open

1997	1	4	1	0	0	0	0	72.00	$2,520

Best finish for 1997: 65th at the United Airlines Hawaiian Open

1998	1	4	1	0	0	0	0	70.75	$3,330

Best finish for 1998: T-77th at the United Airlines Hawaiian Open

1999	1	4	1	0	0	0	0	70.75	$6,614

Best finish for 1999: T-48th at the Sony Open in Hawaii

2000	1	4	1	0	0	0	0	73.00	$5,568

Best finish for 2000: 74th at the Sony Open in Hawaii

2001	1	2	0	0	0	0	0	73.00	
2002	1	4	1	0	0	0	0	70.25	$8,520

Best finish for 2002: T-60th at the Sony Open in Hawaii

2004	1	4	1	0	0	0	0	69.75	$10,464

Best finish for 2004: T-59th at the Sony Open in Hawaii

2005	1	2	0	0	0	0	0	72.50	
2006	1	2	0	0	0	0	0	72.00	
Period Totals	Starts	Rounds Played	Cuts Made	Wins	Top-5s	Top-10s	Top-25s	Scoring Average	Money
	40	122	23	1	1	5	9	72.04	$390,090

Bill Israelson

Year	Starts	Rounds Played	Cuts Made	Wins	Top-5s	Top-10s	Top-25s	Scoring Average	Money
1982	3	10	2	0	0	0	0	74.40	$2,700

Best finish for 1982: T-42nd at the Manufactures Hanover Westchester Classic

Year	Starts	Rounds Played	Cuts Made	Wins	Top-5s	Top-10s	Top-25s	Scoring Average	Money
1985	1	4	1	0	0	0	0	73.25	$2,887

Best finish for 1985: T-52nd at the U.S. Open

| 1986 | 33 | 93 | 16 | 0 | 0 | 1 | 5 | 72.57 | $55,321 |

Best finish for 1986: T-7th at the USF&G Classic

| 1987 | 16 | 32 | 1 | 0 | 0 | 0 | 0 | 73.88 | $680 |

Best finish for 1987: T-43rd at the Deposit Guaranty Golf Classic

| 1996 | 1 | 2 | 0 | 0 | 0 | 0 | 0 | 74.00 | $1,300 |

Period Totals	Starts	Rounds Played	Cuts Made	Wins	Top-5s	Top-10s	Top-25s	Scoring Average	Money
	54	141	20	0	0	1	5	73.04	$62,888

Don Iverson

Year	Starts	Rounds Played	Cuts Made	Wins	Top-5s	Top-10s	Top-25s	Scoring Average	Money
1964	1	4	1	0	0	0	0	77.75	

Best finish for 1964: 71st at the St. Paul Open

| 1971 | 14 | 43 | 7 | 0 | 0 | 0 | 0 | 73.14 | $1,606 |

Best finish for 1971: T-31st at the Greater Hartford Open Invitational

| 1972 | 35 | 117 | 24 | 0 | 1 | 2 | 8 | 72.44 | $30,158 |

Best finish for 1972: 3rd at the Quad Cities Open

| 1973 | 35 | 111 | 20 | 0 | 0 | 2 | 7 | 72.25 | $30,294 |

Best finish for 1973: T-6th at the PGA Championship

| 1974 | 30 | 100 | 19 | 0 | 0 | 0 | 5 | 72.86 | $20,200 |

Best finish for 1974: T-11th at the Ohio Kings Island Open

| 1975 | 30 | 94 | 16 | 1 | 2 | 2 | 8 | 72.67 | $56,737 |

Best finish for 1975: Win at the B.C. Open

| 1976 | 35 | 110 | 21 | 0 | 0 | 0 | 4 | 73.04 | $20,977 |

Best finish for 1976: T-14th at the MONY Tournament Of Champions

| 1977 | 23 | 71 | 12 | 0 | 0 | 0 | 5 | 73.20 | $11,200 |

Best finish for 1977: T-15th at the B.C. Open

| 1978 | 19 | 56 | 8 | 0 | 1 | 1 | 3 | 73.14 | $16,000 |

Best finish for 1978: T-3rd at the Ed McMahon Quad City Open

| 1979 | 17 | 44 | 5 | 0 | 0 | 0 | 2 | 73.64 | $6,314 |

Best finish for 1979: T-19th at the Tallahassee Open

1980	2	4	0	0	0	0	0	74.25	
1981	1	2	0	0	0	0	0	74.50	
1982	2	4	0	0	0	0	0	75.75	
1983	1	2	0	0	0	0	0	78.00	

Period Totals	Starts	Rounds Played	Cuts Made	Wins	Top-5s	Top-10s	Top-25s	Scoring Average	Money
	245	762	133	1	4	7	42	72.89	$193,484

Toshi Izawa

Year	Starts	Rounds Played	Cuts Made	Wins	Top-5s	Top-10s	Top-25s	Scoring Average	Money
1999	1	2	0	0	0	0	0	74.00	$1,750
2000	1	4	1	0	0	0	0	71.50	$20,500

Best finish for 2000: T-39th at the PGA Championship

| 2001 | 5 | 14 | 4 | 0 | 2 | 2 | 3 | 70.57 | $519,180 |

Best finish for 2001: T-2nd at the Nissan Open

| 2002 | 7 | 19 | 5 | 0 | 0 | 0 | 3 | 72.68 | $175,204 |

Best finish for 2002: T-17th at the Accenture Match Play Championship

| 2003 | 6 | 16 | 4 | 0 | 0 | 1 | 4 | 72.00 | $301,000 |

Best finish for 2003: T-9th at the WGC-Accenture Match Play Championship

| 2004 | 3 | 4 | 1 | 0 | 0 | 0 | 0 | 75.00 | $41,000 |

Best finish for 2004: T-33rd at the WGC-Accenture Match Play Championship

| 2005 | 1 | 2 | 0 | 0 | 0 | 0 | 0 | 71.50 | |
| 2007 | 1 | 2 | 0 | 0 | 0 | 0 | 0 | 74.00 | $5,447 |

Period Totals	Starts	Rounds Played	Cuts Made	Wins	Top-5s	Top-10s	Top-25s	Scoring Average	Money
	25	63	15	0	2	3	10	72.16	$1,064,081

Tony Jacklin

Year	Starts	Rounds Played	Cuts Made	Wins	Top-5s	Top-10s	Top-25s	Scoring Average	Money
1963	1	4	1	0	0	0	0	73.75	$159

Best finish for 1963: T-30th at the British Open

| 1965 | 2 | 8 | 2 | 0 | 0 | 0 | 1 | 73.50 | $1,005 |

Best finish for 1965: T-25th at the British Open

| 1966 | 2 | 6 | 1 | 0 | 0 | 0 | 0 | 75.33 | $286 |

Best finish for 1966: T-30th at the British Open

| 1967 | 8 | 28 | 6 | 0 | 1 | 2 | 5 | 72.39 | $14,787 |

Best finish for 1967: 5th at the British Open

Year	Starts	Rounds Played	Cuts Made	Wins	Top-5s	Top-10s	Top-25s	Scoring Average	Money
1968	26	95	21	1	3	7	12	71.87	$56,840

Best finish for 1968: Win at the Jacksonville Open Invitational

1969	26	87	19	1	4	5	11	70.98	$41,561

Best finish for 1969: Win at the British Open

| 1970 | 22 | 75 | 15 | 1 | 6 | 7 | 10 | 71.80 | $91,262 |

Best finish for 1970: Win at the U.S. Open

| 1971 | 17 | 62 | 14 | 0 | 1 | 2 | 5 | 71.90 | $26,275 |

Best finish for 1971: 3rd at the British Open

| 1972 | 21 | 74 | 17 | 1 | 4 | 6 | 11 | 72.16 | $72,603 |

Best finish for 1972: Win at the Greater Jacksonville Open

| 1973 | 8 | 26 | 5 | 0 | 0 | 0 | 1 | 73.12 | $5,332 |

Best finish for 1973: T-14th at the British Open

| 1974 | 6 | 15 | 2 | 0 | 0 | 0 | 1 | 74.93 | $3,341 |

Best finish for 1974: T-18th at the British Open

| 1975 | 16 | 52 | 10 | 0 | 0 | 0 | 2 | 72.58 | $12,575 |

Best finish for 1975: T-12th at the Greater Greensboro Open

| 1976 | 18 | 68 | 18 | 0 | 0 | 1 | 4 | 72.28 | $18,446 |

Best finish for 1976: T-7th at the Canadian Open

| 1977 | 15 | 48 | 10 | 0 | 1 | 1 | 3 | 72.88 | $30,212 |

Best finish for 1977: 2nd at the Bing Crosby Pro-Am

| 1978 | 6 | 14 | 2 | 0 | 0 | 1 | 1 | 73.29 | $6,999 |

Best finish for 1978: T-8th at the Bing Crosby Pro-Am

| 1979 | 1 | 4 | 1 | 0 | 0 | 0 | 1 | 74.00 | $2,415 |

Best finish for 1979: T-24th at the British Open

| 1980 | 1 | 4 | 1 | 0 | 0 | 0 | 0 | 72.50 | $1,870 |

Best finish for 1980: T-32nd at the British Open

| 1981 | 1 | 4 | 1 | 0 | 0 | 0 | 1 | 72.50 | $2,438 |

Best finish for 1981: T-23rd at the British Open

| 1982 | 1 | 2 | 0 | 0 | 0 | 0 | 0 | 76.50 | $382 |
| 1983 | 1 | 4 | 1 | 0 | 0 | 0 | 0 | 71.50 | $1,450 |

Best finish for 1983: T-39th at the British Open

1984	1	2	0	0	0	0	0	78.00	$429
1985	1	2	0	0	0	0	0	77.00	$544
1988	1	2	0	0	0	0	0	79.50	$765
1989	1	2	0	0	0	0	0	78.50	$800
1993	1	2	0	0	0	0	0	74.50	$924
1994	1	3	0	0	0	0	0	77.33	
1999	1	2	0	0	0	0	0	83.50	$1,094
2001	1	2	0	0	0	0	0	74.50	$1,430
2005	1	2	0	0	0	0	0	77.50	$3,504
2007	1	2	0	0	0	0	0	80.50	$4,316
Period Totals	Starts	Rounds Played	Cuts Made	Wins	Top-5s	Top-10s	Top-25s	Scoring Average	Money
	209	701	147	4	20	32	69	72.38	$404,044

David Jackson

Year	Starts	Rounds Played	Cuts Made	Wins	Top-5s	Top-10s	Top-25s	Scoring Average	Money
1986	1	4	1	0	0	0	1	70.25	$3,600

Best finish for 1986: T-14th at the Tallahassee Open

| 1987 | 2 | 6 | 1 | 0 | 0 | 0 | 0 | 73.83 | $1,257 |

Best finish for 1987: T-48th at the Centel Classic

| 1988 | 3 | 10 | 2 | 0 | 0 | 0 | 1 | 71.20 | $7,433 |

Best finish for 1988: T-23rd at the Federal Express St. Jude Classic

| 1989 | 21 | 57 | 7 | 0 | 0 | 0 | 1 | 72.35 | $14,112 |

Best finish for 1989: T-24th at the Hardee's Golf Classic

| 1990 | 4 | 10 | 1 | 0 | 0 | 0 | 0 | 72.10 | $2,220 |

Best finish for 1990: T-26th at the Deposit Guaranty

| 1991 | 1 | 2 | 0 | 0 | 0 | 0 | 0 | 75.50 | $1,000 |
| 1993 | 31 | 87 | 13 | 0 | 0 | 0 | 1 | 72.48 | $53,562 |

Best finish for 1993: T-16th at the Phoenix Open

1996	1	2	0	0	0	0	0	71.00	
2001	1	2	0	0	0	0	0	78.50	
Period Totals	Starts	Rounds Played	Cuts Made	Wins	Top-5s	Top-10s	Top-25s	Scoring Average	Money
	65	180	25	0	0	0	4	72.43	$83,185

John Jackson

Year	Starts	Rounds Played	Cuts Made	Wins	Top-5s	Top-10s	Top-25s	Scoring Average	Money
1974	2	4	0	0	0	0	0	75.75	
1976	8	24	4	0	0	0	2	72.71	$4,367

Best finish for 1976: T-19th at the Ed McMahon Quad City Open & Pleasant Valley Classic

| 1977 | 15 | 42 | 5 | 0 | 0 | 0 | 0 | 72.90 | $2,759 |

Best finish for 1977: T-47th at the San Antonio Texas Open

Year	Starts	Rounds Played	Cuts Made	Wins	Top-5s	Top-10s	Top-25s	Scoring Average	Money
1979	2	4	0	0	0	0	0	71.25	
1980	2	6	1	0	0	0	0	73.67	$1,731

Best finish for 1980: T-36th at the Phoenix Open

1981	2	8	2	0	0	0	0	71.63	$1,416

Best finish for 1981: T-55th at the Sammy Davis, Jr. - Greater Hartford Open

1982	3	8	1	0	0	1	1	70.38	$9,414

Best finish for 1982: T-6th at the Joe Garagiola Tucson Open

1983	2	4	0	0	0	0	0	72.75	$100
1984	2	4	0	0	0	0	0	75.25	$600
1985	1	2	0	0	0	0	0	76.50	$1,000
1986	1	2	0	0	0	0	0	72.50	
1987	2	6	1	0	0	0	0	76.50	$1,600

Best finish for 1987: 72nd at the PGA Championship

1988	1	2	0	0	0	0	0	71.50	
1989	1	2	0	0	0	0	0	75.50	$1,000
Period Totals	Starts	Rounds Played	Cuts Made	Wins	Top-5s	Top-10s	Top-25s	Scoring Average	Money
	44	118	14	0	0	1	3	73.02	$23,988

John Jacobs

Year	Starts	Rounds Played	Cuts Made	Wins	Top-5s	Top-10s	Top-25s	Scoring Average	Money
1958	1	2	0	0	0	0	0	75.00	
1959	1	2	0	0	0	0	0	75.50	
1960	1	4	1	0	0	0	0	73.25	$140

Best finish for 1960: T-32nd at the British Open

1961	1	4	1	0	0	0	1	75.00	

Best finish for 1961: T-20th at the British Open

1962	1	2	0	0	0	0	0	77.00	
1963	1	2	0	0	0	0	0	75.00	
1964	2	4	0	0	0	0	0	77.25	
1968	8	19	3	0	0	0	0	73.05	$305

Best finish for 1968: T-41st at the Memphis Open Invitational

1969	27	89	19	0	1	4	8	72.13	$18,734

Best finish for 1969: T-5th at the Tallahassee Open

1970	24	74	13	0	1	1	4	72.73	$11,550

Best finish for 1970: T-5th at the Bing Crosby Pro-Am

1971	14	41	7	0	0	0	0	72.73	$2,924

Best finish for 1971: T-28th at the Glen CampbellLos Angeles Open

1972	25	63	9	0	1	1	5	72.71	$20,359

Best finish for 1972: 2nd at the Greater Jacksonville Open

1973	19	61	12	0	0	0	2	72.72	$7,508

Best finish for 1973: T-23rd at the Quad Cities Open

1974	19	52	10	0	1	1	4	72.37	$18,170

Best finish for 1974: T-3rd at the Bing Crosby Pro-Am

1975	18	55	10	0	0	0	1	72.96	$5,760

Best finish for 1975: T-25th at the Pensacola Open

1976	18	60	11	0	1	1	4	72.72	$27,338

Best finish for 1976: 2nd at the Greater Milwaukee Open

1977	13	25	0	0	0	0	0	75.36	
1978	4	8	0	0	0	0	0	74.75	
1979	6	14	1	0	0	0	0	72.79	$406

Best finish for 1979: T-68th at the Greater Milwaukee Open

1981	4	7	0	0	0	0	0	73.43	
1984	2	4	0	0	0	0	0	74.50	
1985	2	4	0	0	0	0	0	73.50	$600
2003	1	1	0	0	0	0	0	87.00	
Period Totals	Starts	Rounds Played	Cuts Made	Wins	Top-5s	Top-10s	Top-25s	Scoring Average	Money
	212	597	97	0	5	8	29	72.91	$113,794

Tommy Jacobs

Year	Starts	Rounds Played	Cuts Made	Wins	Top-5s	Top-10s	Top-25s	Scoring Average	Money
1958	30	110	24	1	3	7	15	71.61	$12,392

Best finish for 1958: Win at the Denver Open

1959	21	81	17	0	2	6	13	70.99	$11,507

Best finish for 1959: T-3rd at the Oklahoma City Open Invitational

1960	20	80	18	0	1	3	12	71.23	$8,822

Best finish for 1960: T-2nd at the Bing Crosby National

1961	15	58	14	0	0	2	11	71.03	$7,852

Best finish for 1961: T-7th at the Greater Greensboro Open Invitational

1962	23	93	22	0	0	5	16	71.33	$17,967

Best finish for 1962: T-6th at the U.S. Open

1963	21	85	20	1	2	7	12	71.66	$26,011

Best finish for 1963: Win at the Utah Open Invitational

Year	Starts	Rounds Played	Cuts Made	Wins	Top-5s	Top-10s	Top-25s	Scoring Average	Money
1964	27	100	21	1	6	10	16	71.55	$44,572

Best finish for 1964: Win at the Palm Springs Classic

Year	Starts	Rounds Played	Cuts Made	Wins	Top-5s	Top-10s	Top-25s	Scoring Average	Money
1965	25	86	15	0	0	3	5	72.91	$13,191

Best finish for 1965: T-6th at the Tucson Open

1966	24	79	15	0	2	2	6	72.62	$23,459

Best finish for 1966: 2nd at the Masters

1967	28	92	17	0	1	2	6	73.17	$12,224

Best finish for 1967: T-5th at the Pensacola Open

1968	22	56	6	0	0	0	3	72.96	$7,098

Best finish for 1968: T-11th at the Tucson Open Invitational

1969	26	86	17	0	2	2	3	72.57	$20,247

Best finish for 1969: T-2nd at the Philadelphia Classic

1970	28	99	21	0	0	0	7	72.44	$17,416

Best finish for 1970: T-11th at the Tucson Open

1971	7	26	5	0	0	0	1	72.04	$2,618

Best finish for 1971: T-24th at the Tucson Open

| 1972 | 5 | 13 | 0 | 0 | 0 | 0 | 0 | 74.69 | |
| 1973 | 6 | 22 | 4 | 0 | 0 | 1 | 1 | 72.23 | $7,312 |

Best finish for 1973: T-6th at the Andy Williams-San Diego Open

1974	5	16	2	0	0	0	1	73.88	$1,360

Best finish for 1974: T-25th at the Dean Martin Tucson Open

1975	2	4	0	0	0	0	0	77.00	
1976	4	10	0	0	0	0	0	74.80	$250
1977	2	6	0	0	0	0	0	77.00	
1979	2	4	0	0	0	0	0	80.25	

Best finish for 1979: 100 at the Andy Williams-San Diego Open

1991	1	2	0	0	0	0	0	76.00	
Period Totals	Starts	Rounds Played	Cuts Made	Wins	Top-5s	Top-10s	Top-25s	Scoring Average	Money
	344	1208	238	3	19	50	128	72.16	$234,296

Peter Jacobsen

Year	Starts	Rounds Played	Cuts Made	Wins	Top-5s	Top-10s	Top-25s	Scoring Average	Money
1977	22	62	9	0	0	0	3	72.56	$12,492

Best finish for 1977: T-12th at the Ed McMahon Quad City Open

1978	25	79	14	0	1	2	4	72.37	$34,188

Best finish for 1978: 3rd at the B.C. Open

1979	33	112	22	0	0	1	6	72.06	$49,439

Best finish for 1979: T-8th at the Danny Thomas Memphis Classic

1980	29	102	23	1	3	5	12	71.54	$139,377

Best finish for 1980: Win at the Buick Goodwrench Open

1981	23	81	17	0	3	3	7	72.06	$85,624

Best finish for 1981: T-2nd at the Buick Open

1982	24	95	23	0	5	7	10	71.04	$145,832

Best finish for 1982: T-2nd at the Memorial Tournament & Manufactures Hanover Westchester Classic

1983	27	100	23	0	3	5	13	71.36	$169,640

Best finish for 1983: 3rd at the PGA Championship

1984	24	89	20	2	4	6	13	71.21	$300,030

Best finish for 1984: Win at the Colonial National Invitational & Sammy Davis, Jr. - Greater Hartford Open

1985	22	75	17	0	3	7	14	71.48	$232,989

Best finish for 1985: T-2nd at the Honda Classic & USF&G Classic

1986	24	79	17	0	1	1	5	71.68	$113,564

Best finish for 1986: 3rd at the PGA Championship

1987	27	85	19	0	0	1	5	71.55	$81,983

Best finish for 1987: T-6th at the Shearson Lehman/Andy Williams San Diego

1988	26	88	19	0	3	6	11	70.81	$526,765

Best finish for 1988: T-2nd at the Panasonic Las Vegas Invitational, Beatrice Western Open & Federal Express St. Jude Classic

1989	25	90	21	0	1	3	9	70.98	$274,778

Best finish for 1989: 2nd at the Beatrice Western Open

1990	24	85	21	1	3	5	13	70.87	$568,461

Best finish for 1990: Win at the Bob Hope Chrysler Classic

1991	24	76	14	0	2	2	5	71.42	$268,217

Best finish for 1991: T-2nd at the Hardee's Golf Classic & B.C. Open

1992	27	93	18	0	0	0	4	71.49	$106,277

Best finish for 1992: T-18th at the Anheuser-Busch Golf Classic & Canadian Open

1993	23	80	17	0	0	3	9	70.90	$223,291

Best finish for 1993: T-6th at the Nissan Los Angeles Open & New England Classic

1994	20	72	16	0	0	3	7	70.63	$224,678

Best finish for 1994: T-6th at the Nissan Los Angeles Open

1995	25	93	22	2	5	5	13	70.44	$1,075,057

Best finish for 1995: Win at the AT&T Pebble Beach Pro-Am & Buick Invitational of California

1996	19	65	14	0	0	1	3	71.43	$127,197

Best finish for 1996: T-10th at the Nissan Open

Year	Starts	Rounds Played	Cuts Made	Wins	Top-5s	Top-10s	Top-25s	Scoring Average	Money
1997	25	87	19	0	1	2	9	70.70	$294,931

Best finish for 1997: 3rd at the CVS Charity Classic

1998	22	65	12	0	1	1	5	70.74	$327,336

Best finish for 1998: 2nd at the B.C. Open

1999	22	73	15	0	0	1	5	71.33	$285,460

Best finish for 1999: 9th at the B.C. Open

2000	22	65	10	0	0	0	1	71.08	$141,484

Best finish for 2000: T-16th at the Bob Hope Chrysler Classic

2001	17	49	7	0	0	0	0	71.45	$64,297

Best finish for 2001: T-37th at the Air Canada Championship

2002	21	67	11	0	0	3	5	70.79	$389,123

Best finish for 2002: T-8th at the Honda Classic & John Deere Classic

2003	22	75	14	1	1	3	5	70.95	$1,164,726

Best finish for 2003: Win at the Greater Hartford Open

2004	10	31	6	0	0	0	2	71.35	$232,851

Best finish for 2004: T-14th at the AT&T Pebble Beach National Pro-Am

2005	11	31	5	0	0	0	2	71.71	$180,583

Best finish for 2005: T-15th at the U.S. Open

2006	4	12	2	0	0	0	0	72.25	$48,256

Best finish for 2006: T-27th at the Verizon Heritage

2007	1	3	0	0	0	0	0	76.00	
2008	1	3	0	0	0	0	0	75.33	

Period Totals	Starts	Rounds Played	Cuts Made	Wins	Top-5s	Top-10s	Top-25s	Scoring Average	Money
	671	2262	467	7	40	76	200	71.32	$7,888,927

Fredrik Jacobson

Year	Starts	Rounds Played	Cuts Made	Wins	Top-5s	Top-10s	Top-25s	Scoring Average	Money
1998	1	4	1	0	0	0	0	76.25	$8,965

Best finish for 1998: 76th at the British Open

2000	1	2	0	0	0	0	0	77.50	$1,064
2001	1	2	0	0	0	0	0	72.50	$1,860
2002	1	2	0	0	0	0	0	75.50	$3,160
2003	8	30	7	0	2	4	4	70.90	$855,592

Best finish for 2003: T-3rd at the FedEx St. Jude Classic

2004	24	80	18	0	2	5	9	70.81	$1,265,666

Best finish for 2004: T-4th at the Honda Classic

2005	23	71	14	0	0	3	7	71.44	$873,525

Best finish for 2005: T-6th at the FedEx St. Jude Classic

2006	18	56	10	0	2	2	5	71.32	$788,764

Best finish for 2006: 4th at the Ford Championship at Doral

2007	20	70	15	0	2	5	9	70.30	$1,469,541

Best finish for 2007: T-2nd at the Ginn sur Mer Classic at Tesoro

2008	23	76	16	0	1	3	9	71.28	$1,597,423

Best finish for 2008: 2nd at the AT&T National

Period Totals	Starts	Rounds Played	Cuts Made	Wins	Top-5s	Top-10s	Top-25s	Scoring Average	Money
	120	393	81	0	9	22	43	71.12	$6,865,561

Barry Jaeckel

Year	Starts	Rounds Played	Cuts Made	Wins	Top-5s	Top-10s	Top-25s	Scoring Average	Money
1969	1	2	0	0	0	0	0	75.50	
1970	1	4	1	0	0	0	0	71.75	

Best finish for 1970: T-58th at the Los Angeles Open

1972	1	4	1	0	0	0	0	76.50	$1,090

Best finish for 1972: T-36th at the U.S. Open

1973	4	8	0	0	0	0	0	75.25	$130
1974	2	5	0	0	0	0	0	75.80	
1975	10	33	7	0	0	0	3	72.18	$4,858

Best finish for 1975: T-24th at the San Antonio Texas Open

1976	30	100	23	0	1	3	7	72.12	$36,889

Best finish for 1976: T-5th at the Sammy Davis, Jr. - Greater Hartford Open

1977	27	88	17	0	0	1	6	72.39	$20,004

Best finish for 1977: T-6th at the Ohio Kings Island Open

1978	29	105	23	1	3	5	11	71.59	$73,378

Best finish for 1978: Win at the Tallahassee Open

1979	34	110	21	0	0	1	6	72.48	$47,462

Best finish for 1979: T-10th at the Atlanta Classic

1980	29	96	20	0	0	0	5	72.45	$28,161

Best finish for 1980: T-14th at the Sammy Davis, Jr. - Greater Hartford Open

1981	27	86	19	0	3	3	7	71.95	$91,451

Best finish for 1981: 2nd at the Tournament Players Championship

1982	31	100	20	0	1	1	11	71.56	$62,940

Best finish for 1982: T-5th at the Miller High-Life Quad Cities Open

Year	Starts	Rounds Played	Cuts Made	Wins	Top-5s	Top-10s	Top-25s	Scoring Average	Money
1983	27	83	13	0	1	2	6	72.55	$64,472

Best finish for 1983: T-2nd at the Kemper Open

| 1984 | 30 | 96 | 17 | 0 | 0 | 0 | 5 | 72.80 | $50,308 |

Best finish for 1984: T-11th at the Houston Coca-Cola Open

| 1985 | 30 | 106 | 22 | 0 | 0 | 2 | 7 | 71.88 | $81,765 |

Best finish for 1985: T-7th at the Manufactures Hanover Westchester Classic

| 1986 | 31 | 93 | 17 | 0 | 0 | 2 | 5 | 72.43 | $81,646 |

Best finish for 1986: T-6th at the Los Angeles Open & Honda Classic

| 1987 | 35 | 98 | 16 | 0 | 0 | 0 | 3 | 72.14 | $53,839 |

Best finish for 1987: T-14th at the Greater Milwaukee Open

| 1988 | 28 | 77 | 10 | 0 | 0 | 0 | 2 | 71.78 | $30,227 |

Best finish for 1988: T-17th at the Canadian Open

| 1989 | 24 | 66 | 11 | 0 | 1 | 2 | 3 | 71.52 | $64,782 |

Best finish for 1989: T-4th at the Hardee's Golf Classic

| 1990 | 19 | 57 | 10 | 0 | 1 | 1 | 2 | 71.63 | $63,590 |

Best finish for 1990: T-3rd at the B.C. Open

| 1991 | 12 | 41 | 8 | 0 | 1 | 1 | 3 | 70.73 | $59,216 |

Best finish for 1991: T-5th at the New England Classic

| 1992 | 12 | 38 | 6 | 0 | 0 | 0 | 1 | 72.08 | $13,351 |

Best finish for 1992: T-22nd at the Deposit Guaranty Classic

| 1993 | 10 | 29 | 3 | 0 | 1 | 1 | 1 | 72.31 | $15,584 |

Best finish for 1993: T-4th at the Deposit Guaranty Classic

| 1994 | 9 | 21 | 1 | 0 | 0 | 0 | 1 | 72.43 | $15,750 |

Best finish for 1994: T-18th at the MCI Heritage Classic

| 1995 | 8 | 21 | 1 | 0 | 0 | 0 | 0 | 72.86 | $1,540 |

Best finish for 1995: T-57th at the Deposit Guaranty Golf Classic

| 1996 | 8 | 23 | 4 | 0 | 0 | 0 | 0 | 72.04 | $10,779 |

Best finish for 1996: T-43rd at the B.C. Open

| 1997 | 4 | 12 | 2 | 0 | 0 | 0 | 1 | 71.33 | $12,906 |

Best finish for 1997: T-23rd at the B.C. Open

| 1998 | 4 | 10 | 1 | 0 | 0 | 0 | 0 | 72.40 | $2,883 |

Best finish for 1998: T-76th at the Quad City Classic

2000	1	2	0	0	0	0	0	73.00	
2001	1	0	0	0	0	0	0		
2002	1	2	0	0	0	0	0	72.50	
2003	1	2	0	0	0	0	0	75.50	
2008	1	2	0	0	0	0	0	78.00	
Period Totals	Starts	Rounds Played	Cuts Made	Wins	Top-5s	Top-10s	Top-25s	Scoring Average	Money
	522	1620	294	1	13	25	96	72.14	$989,001

Mark James

Year	Starts	Rounds Played	Cuts Made	Wins	Top-5s	Top-10s	Top-25s	Scoring Average	Money
1973	1	2	0	0	0	0	0	84.00	
1976	1	4	1	0	1	1	1	72.00	$5,076

Best finish for 1976: T-5th at the British Open

1977	1	3	0	0	0	0	0	77.67	$340
1978	3	7	0	0	0	0	0	76.00	$428
1979	4	16	4	0	1	1	1	72.88	$18,733

Best finish for 1979: 4th at the British Open

| 1980 | 5 | 14 | 2 | 0 | 0 | 0 | 0 | 74.36 | $4,468 |

Best finish for 1980: T-30th at the Doral-Eastern Open

| 1981 | 1 | 4 | 1 | 0 | 1 | 1 | 1 | 70.75 | $23,500 |

Best finish for 1981: T-3rd at the British Open

| 1982 | 4 | 14 | 3 | 0 | 0 | 0 | 0 | 73.57 | $2,685 |

Best finish for 1982: T-49th at the Honda Inverrary Classic

| 1983 | 1 | 4 | 1 | 0 | 0 | 0 | 0 | 71.25 | $2,198 |

Best finish for 1983: T-29th at the British Open

| 1984 | 2 | 6 | 1 | 0 | 0 | 0 | 0 | 72.83 | $2,505 |

Best finish for 1984: T-44th at the British Open

| 1985 | 1 | 4 | 1 | 0 | 0 | 0 | 1 | 72.00 | $7,627 |

Best finish for 1985: T-20th at the British Open

| 1986 | 1 | 4 | 1 | 0 | 0 | 0 | 0 | 74.00 | $4,752 |

Best finish for 1986: T-35th at the British Open

| 1987 | 1 | 2 | 0 | 0 | 0 | 0 | 0 | 74.00 | $640 |
| 1988 | 1 | 4 | 1 | 0 | 0 | 0 | 0 | 74.50 | $4,080 |

Best finish for 1988: T-63rd at the British Open

| 1989 | 1 | 4 | 1 | 0 | 0 | 0 | 1 | 70.50 | $20,800 |

Best finish for 1989: T-13th at the British Open

| 1990 | 4 | 10 | 1 | 0 | 0 | 0 | 0 | 74.70 | $11,276 |

Best finish for 1990: T-31st at the British Open

| 1991 | 1 | 4 | 1 | 0 | 0 | 0 | 0 | 70.50 | $11,340 |

Best finish for 1991: T-26th at the British Open

Year	Starts	Rounds Played	Cuts Made	Wins	Top-5s	Top-10s	Top-25s	Scoring Average	Money
1992	2	6	1	0	0	0	0	72.83	$6,362

Best finish for 1992: T-40th at the PGA Championship

| 1993 | 2 | 6 | 1 | 0 | 0 | 0 | 0 | 71.17 | $12,326 |

Best finish for 1993: T-27th at the British Open

| 1994 | 2 | 6 | 1 | 0 | 1 | 1 | 1 | 70.00 | $83,280 |

Best finish for 1994: T-4th at the British Open

| 1995 | 1 | 4 | 1 | 0 | 0 | 1 | 1 | 71.25 | $53,167 |

Best finish for 1995: T-8th at the British Open

| 1996 | 3 | 8 | 1 | 0 | 0 | 0 | 1 | 72.88 | $20,706 |

Best finish for 1996: T-22nd at the British Open

| 1997 | 1 | 4 | 1 | 0 | 0 | 0 | 1 | 70.75 | $24,295 |

Best finish for 1997: T-20th at the British Open

| 1998 | 1 | 4 | 1 | 0 | 0 | 0 | 1 | 72.50 | $28,327 |

Best finish for 1998: T-19th at the British Open

| 1999 | 3 | 12 | 3 | 0 | 0 | 0 | 1 | 73.50 | $75,342 |

Best finish for 1999: T-25th at the American Express Championship

2000	1	2	0	0	0	0	0	75.50	$1,064
Period Totals	Starts	Rounds Played	Cuts Made	Wins	Top-5s	Top-10s	Top-25s	Scoring Average	Money
	49	158	29	0	4	5	11	73.18	$425,316

Jim Jamieson

Year	Starts	Rounds Played	Cuts Made	Wins	Top-5s	Top-10s	Top-25s	Scoring Average	Money
1964	1	2	0	0	0	0	0	76.00	
1966	1	4	1	0	0	0	0	72.00	

Best finish for 1966: T-51st at the Cajun Classic

| 1967 | 1 | 2 | 0 | 0 | 0 | 0 | 0 | 79.00 | |
| 1968 | 2 | 6 | 1 | 0 | 0 | 0 | 0 | 72.17 | |

Best finish for 1968: T-38th at the Cajun Classic

| 1969 | 24 | 65 | 9 | 0 | 0 | 1 | 2 | 73.48 | $6,125 |

Best finish for 1969: T-8th at the Danny Thomas-Diplomat Classic

| 1970 | 29 | 107 | 23 | 0 | 2 | 3 | 8 | 71.68 | $30,396 |

Best finish for 1970: T-3rd at the Western Open & Green Island Open Invitational

| 1971 | 35 | 125 | 27 | 0 | 0 | 4 | 9 | 71.86 | $33,599 |

Best finish for 1971: T-6th at the PGA Championship & Robinson Open Golf Classic

| 1972 | 36 | 125 | 27 | 1 | 5 | 8 | 13 | 71.69 | $106,609 |

Best finish for 1972: Win at the Western Open

| 1973 | 36 | 130 | 28 | 0 | 2 | 4 | 10 | 72.13 | $63,802 |

Best finish for 1973: T-3rd at the Masters

| 1974 | 30 | 91 | 17 | 0 | 2 | 4 | 6 | 72.21 | $45,189 |

Best finish for 1974: T-2nd at the Florida Citrus Open Invitational

| 1975 | 26 | 72 | 10 | 0 | 0 | 0 | 2 | 73.89 | $4,998 |

Best finish for 1975: T-16th at the Pensacola Open

| 1976 | 15 | 41 | 5 | 0 | 0 | 0 | 0 | 73.17 | $2,231 |

Best finish for 1976: T-35th at the Bob Hope Chrysler Classic

| 1977 | 12 | 36 | 6 | 0 | 0 | 0 | 0 | 74.39 | $1,860 |

Best finish for 1977: T-43rd at the Bing Crosby Pro-Am

| 1978 | 4 | 10 | 2 | 0 | 0 | 0 | 0 | 72.80 | $1,390 |

Best finish for 1978: T-30th at the Ed McMahon Quad City Open

| 1979 | 2 | 8 | 2 | 0 | 0 | 0 | 0 | 74.13 | $887 |

Best finish for 1979: T-76th at the Ed McMahon Quad City Open

| 1980 | 3 | 4 | 0 | 0 | 0 | 0 | 0 | 75.00 | |
| 1981 | 4 | 8 | 1 | 0 | 0 | 0 | 0 | 73.38 | $374 |

Best finish for 1981: T-75th at the Quad Cities Open

1982	2	4	0	0	0	0	0	78.50	
1983	3	8	0	0	0	0	0	76.38	
1984	2	6	0	0	0	0	0	76.17	
1988	1	2	0	0	0	0	0	80.00	
1996	1	2	0	0	0	0	0	80.50	
1997	1	2	0	0	0	0	0	80.00	
Period Totals	Starts	Rounds Played	Cuts Made	Wins	Top-5s	Top-10s	Top-25s	Scoring Average	Money
	271	860	159	1	11	24	50	72.60	$297,460

Don January

Year	Starts	Rounds Played	Cuts Made	Wins	Top-5s	Top-10s	Top-25s	Scoring Average	Money
1958	28	104	24	0	4	8	17	71.44	$14,277

Best finish for 1958: T-2nd at the Tucson Open & Greater Greensboro Open

| 1959 | 21 | 84 | 21 | 0 | 0 | 8 | 16 | 71.05 | $12,832 |

Best finish for 1959: T-6th at the Bing Crosby National & Rubber City Open Invitational

| 1960 | 21 | 85 | 16 | 1 | 6 | 13 | 18 | 70.34 | $23,325 |

Best finish for 1960: Win at the Tucson Open Invitational

| 1961 | 16 | 62 | 13 | 1 | 6 | 6 | 10 | 70.56 | $23,809 |

Best finish for 1961: Win at the St. Paul Open Invitational

| 1962 | 23 | 89 | 20 | 0 | 2 | 8 | 17 | 71.11 | $20,572 |

Best finish for 1962: T-2nd at the Sahara Invitational

Year	Starts	Rounds Played	Cuts Made	Wins	Top-5s	Top-10s	Top-25s	Scoring Average	Money
1963	22	85	19	1	4	8	14	70.98	$32,730

Best finish for 1963: Win at the Tucson Open Invitational

Year	Starts	Rounds Played	Cuts Made	Wins	Top-5s	Top-10s	Top-25s	Scoring Average	Money
1964	23	87	19	0	4	6	14	71.47	$25,910

Best finish for 1964: 2nd at the Lucky International Open

| 1965 | 27 | 94 | 19 | 0 | 4 | 7 | 11 | 71.81 | $32,240 |

Best finish for 1965: T-2nd at the Tucson Open

| 1966 | 23 | 84 | 20 | 1 | 3 | 7 | 12 | 71.37 | $55,280 |

Best finish for 1966: Win at the Philadelphia Golf Classic

| 1967 | 22 | 80 | 19 | 1 | 2 | 5 | 12 | 72.30 | $61,397 |

Best finish for 1967: Win at the PGA Championship

| 1968 | 21 | 78 | 18 | 1 | 3 | 4 | 12 | 71.42 | $60,655 |

Best finish for 1968: Win at the Tournament of Champions

| 1969 | 24 | 88 | 21 | 0 | 5 | 7 | 14 | 71.03 | $63,698 |

Best finish for 1969: T-2nd at the Kaiser International Open

| 1970 | 20 | 65 | 14 | 1 | 2 | 4 | 10 | 71.94 | $46,191 |

Best finish for 1970: Win at the Greater Jacksonville Open

| 1971 | 20 | 70 | 17 | 0 | 4 | 6 | 8 | 71.13 | $53,767 |

Best finish for 1971: 2nd at the Houston Champions International

| 1972 | 17 | 60 | 13 | 0 | 0 | 0 | 10 | 72.23 | $23,251 |

Best finish for 1972: T-11th at the U.S. Open

| 1973 | 4 | 14 | 3 | 0 | 0 | 1 | 1 | 73.93 | $3,755 |

Best finish for 1973: T-10th at the Masters

| 1975 | 26 | 98 | 23 | 1 | 3 | 7 | 11 | 71.56 | $69,035 |

Best finish for 1975: Win at the San Antonio Texas Open

| 1976 | 24 | 96 | 24 | 1 | 6 | 10 | 19 | 70.56 | $163,622 |

Best finish for 1976: Win at the MONY Tournament Of Champions

| 1977 | 24 | 80 | 16 | 0 | 2 | 6 | 11 | 71.65 | $73,715 |

Best finish for 1977: T-2nd at the Hawaiian Open

| 1978 | 26 | 91 | 21 | 0 | 2 | 2 | 9 | 71.58 | $52,703 |

Best finish for 1978: T-3rd at the Byron Nelson Golf Classic & Southern Open

| 1979 | 26 | 92 | 20 | 0 | 2 | 5 | 7 | 71.71 | $81,220 |

Best finish for 1979: T-2nd at the Colonial National Invitational

| 1980 | 16 | 48 | 8 | 0 | 1 | 2 | 3 | 72.46 | $43,070 |

Best finish for 1980: T-2nd at the Glen CampbellLos Angeles Open

| 1981 | 8 | 29 | 7 | 0 | 1 | 2 | 4 | 71.10 | $53,747 |

Best finish for 1981: 2nd at the Hawaiian Open

| 1982 | 10 | 34 | 7 | 0 | 0 | 0 | 3 | 71.41 | $19,491 |

Best finish for 1982: T-19th at the Tournament Players Championship

| 1983 | 5 | 14 | 2 | 0 | 0 | 0 | 0 | 71.00 | $2,316 |

Best finish for 1983: T-35th at the Joe Garagiola Tucson Open

| 1984 | 1 | 2 | 0 | 0 | 0 | 0 | 0 | 73.50 | |

Period Totals	Starts	Rounds Played	Cuts Made	Wins	Top-5s	Top-10s	Top-25s	Scoring Average	Money
	498	1813	404	9	66	132	263	71.40	$1,112,610

PGA Tour career totals from 1954 to 1984

	Starts	Rounds Played	Cuts Made	Wins	Top-5s	Top-10s	Top-25s	Scoring Average	Money
	543	1991	449	10	70	145	288	N/A	$1,134,883

Lee Janzen

Year	Starts	Rounds Played	Cuts Made	Wins	Top-5s	Top-10s	Top-25s	Scoring Average	Money
1985	1	2	0	0	0	0	0	80.50	
1988	2	6	1	0	0	0	1	70.17	$3,686

Best finish for 1988: T-12th at the Deposit Guaranty Golf Classic

| 1989 | 2 | 6 | 1 | 0 | 0 | 0 | 0 | 70.67 | $5,100 |

Best finish for 1989: T-31st at the Buick Open

| 1990 | 30 | 97 | 20 | 0 | 1 | 2 | 6 | 71.25 | $132,986 |

Best finish for 1990: 5th at the Deposit Guaranty

| 1991 | 33 | 109 | 23 | 0 | 0 | 2 | 11 | 70.40 | $229,243 |

Best finish for 1991: 6th at the B.C. Open

| 1992 | 33 | 108 | 22 | 1 | 4 | 6 | 15 | 70.69 | $806,446 |

Best finish for 1992: Win at the Northern Telecom Open

| 1993 | 27 | 97 | 24 | 2 | 3 | 7 | 15 | 70.92 | $939,804 |

Best finish for 1993: Win at the Phoenix Open & U.S. Open

| 1994 | 27 | 92 | 20 | 1 | 2 | 2 | 8 | 71.22 | $454,442 |

Best finish for 1994: Win at the Buick Classic

| 1995 | 28 | 96 | 22 | 3 | 3 | 4 | 14 | 71.19 | $1,378,877 |

Best finish for 1995: Win at The Players Championship, Kemper Open & Sprint International

| 1996 | 27 | 92 | 21 | 0 | 2 | 7 | 13 | 70.83 | $541,924 |

Best finish for 1996: T-2nd at the Greater Vancouver Open

| 1997 | 27 | 99 | 24 | 0 | 5 | 7 | 15 | 70.45 | $879,172 |

Best finish for 1997: T-2nd at the Buick Invitational & BellSouth Classic

| 1998 | 24 | 82 | 19 | 1 | 3 | 3 | 12 | 70.85 | $1,152,814 |

Best finish for 1998: Win at the U.S. Open

Year	Starts	Rounds Played	Cuts Made	Wins	Top-5s	Top-10s	Top-25s	Scoring Average	Money
1999	26	85	18	0	2	5	11	71.45	$851,744

Best finish for 1999: T-3rd at the GTE Byron Nelson Classic & Bell Canadian Open

| 2000 | 27 | 91 | 20 | 0 | 0 | 2 | 9 | 70.78 | $760,381 |

Best finish for 2000: T-6th at the Tampa Bay Classic

| 2001 | 29 | 92 | 18 | 0 | 1 | 2 | 9 | 70.66 | $908,628 |

Best finish for 2001: T-2nd at the Shell Houston Open

| 2002 | 29 | 96 | 22 | 0 | 2 | 4 | 9 | 70.79 | $1,135,399 |

Best finish for 2002: T-3rd at the AT&T Pebble Beach National Pro-Am

| 2003 | 25 | 80 | 16 | 0 | 1 | 2 | 6 | 70.99 | $1,141,770 |

Best finish for 2003: 2nd at the Memorial Tournament

| 2004 | 25 | 82 | 17 | 0 | 0 | 3 | 6 | 70.82 | $837,482 |

Best finish for 2004: T-6th at the BellSouth Classic

| 2005 | 26 | 73 | 11 | 0 | 0 | 1 | 4 | 71.56 | $424,748 |

Best finish for 2005: T-7th at the U.S. Bank Championship in Milwaukee

| 2006 | 28 | 79 | 11 | 0 | 2 | 2 | 2 | 71.95 | $526,198 |

Best finish for 2006: 3rd at the Southern Farm Bureau Classic

| 2007 | 24 | 66 | 8 | 0 | 0 | 0 | 4 | 71.97 | $409,188 |

Best finish for 2007: T-13th at the U.S. Open

| 2008 | 28 | 89 | 17 | 0 | 0 | 1 | 4 | 71.46 | $500,155 |

Best finish for 2008: T-10th at the PODS Championship

Period Totals	Starts	Rounds Played	Cuts Made	Wins	Top-5s	Top-10s	Top-25s	Scoring Average	Money
	528	1719	355	8	31	62	174	71.03	$14,020,187

Tom Jenkins

Year	Starts	Rounds Played	Cuts Made	Wins	Top-5s	Top-10s	Top-25s	Scoring Average	Money
1970	1	4	1	0	0	0	0	77.25	

Best finish for 1970: T-62nd at the Houston Champions International

| 1972 | 3 | 12 | 3 | 0 | 0 | 0 | 0 | 74.75 | $1,317 |

Best finish for 1972: T-52nd at the U.S. Open

| 1973 | 33 | 119 | 24 | 0 | 1 | 3 | 6 | 72.43 | $36,640 |

Best finish for 1973: T-2nd at the USI Classic

| 1974 | 28 | 81 | 12 | 0 | 1 | 1 | 6 | 72.69 | $25,566 |

Best finish for 1974: T-3rd at the IVB Philadelphia Golf Classic

| 1975 | 30 | 94 | 16 | 1 | 1 | 2 | 5 | 72.65 | $45,267 |

Best finish for 1975: Win at the IVB Philadelphia Golf Classic

| 1976 | 34 | 110 | 23 | 0 | 1 | 4 | 6 | 72.80 | $44,341 |

Best finish for 1976: 3rd at the American Golf Classic

| 1977 | 31 | 91 | 16 | 0 | 0 | 0 | 2 | 73.41 | $15,700 |

Best finish for 1977: T-16th at the Bing Crosby Pro-Am

| 1978 | 15 | 38 | 4 | 0 | 0 | 0 | 0 | 74.18 | $2,353 |

Best finish for 1978: T-38th at the Jackie Gleason's Inverrary Classic

| 1979 | 19 | 49 | 5 | 0 | 0 | 0 | 1 | 73.80 | $6,689 |

Best finish for 1979: T-17th at the Western Open

| 1980 | 25 | 69 | 10 | 0 | 0 | 1 | 3 | 72.51 | $18,512 |

Best finish for 1980: T-9th at the B.C. Open

| 1981 | 35 | 123 | 29 | 0 | 1 | 2 | 10 | 71.79 | $82,704 |

Best finish for 1981: T-2nd at the Wickes/Andy Williams San Diego Open

| 1982 | 31 | 105 | 21 | 0 | 0 | 3 | 8 | 71.63 | $65,353 |

Best finish for 1982: T-8th at the Bay Hill Classic & Western Open

| 1983 | 31 | 108 | 24 | 0 | 1 | 1 | 5 | 71.89 | $52,564 |

Best finish for 1983: T-5th at the Sammy Davis, Jr. - Greater Hartford Open

| 1984 | 29 | 96 | 20 | 0 | 0 | 1 | 6 | 72.26 | $54,200 |

Best finish for 1984: T-8th at the Bank of Boston Classic

| 1985 | 26 | 71 | 9 | 0 | 0 | 0 | 0 | 73.51 | $9,347 |

Best finish for 1985: T-42nd at the Walt Disney World/Oldsmobile Classic

| 1986 | 4 | 10 | 1 | 0 | 0 | 0 | 0 | 74.70 | $995 |

Best finish for 1986: T-47th at the Southwest Golf Classic

| 1989 | 1 | 0 | 0 | 0 | 0 | 0 | 0 | | |
| 1992 | 8 | 18 | 2 | 0 | 0 | 0 | 0 | 72.00 | $7,963 |

Best finish for 1992: T-41st at the New England Classic

| 1993 | 4 | 12 | 2 | 0 | 0 | 0 | 0 | 70.83 | $4,302 |

Best finish for 1993: T-38th at the B.C. Open

1994	4	8	0	0	0	0	0	73.75	
1995	3	6	0	0	0	0	0	75.00	
1996	1	4	1	0	0	0	0	73.25	$2,312

Best finish for 1996: T-77th at the Michelob Championship at Kingsmill

| 1997 | 1 | 2 | 0 | 0 | 0 | 0 | 0 | 74.50 | |

Period Totals	Starts	Rounds Played	Cuts Made	Wins	Top-5s	Top-10s	Top-25s	Scoring Average	Money
	397	1230	223	1	6	18	58	72.61	$476,126

Rick Jetter

Year	Starts	Rounds Played	Cuts Made	Wins	Top-5s	Top-10s	Top-25s	Scoring Average	Money
1961	1	4	1	0	0	0	1	73.50	$125

Best finish for 1961: T-22nd at the Almaden Open

Year	Starts	Rounds Played	Cuts Made	Wins	Top-5s	Top-10s	Top-25s	Scoring Average	Money
1964	6	11	0	0	0	0	0	78.82	
1965	4	9	0	0	0	0	0	76.67	
1966	3	9	1	0	0	0	0	76.11	

Best finish for 1966: T-55th at the Hawaiian Open Invitational

Year	Starts	Rounds Played	Cuts Made	Wins	Top-5s	Top-10s	Top-25s	Scoring Average	Money
1967	1	3	0	0	0	0	0	80.00	
1968	3	6	0	0	0	0	0	74.50	
1969	6	17	2	0	0	0	0	76.94	$455

Best finish for 1969: T-38th at the Alameda County Open

Year	Starts	Rounds Played	Cuts Made	Wins	Top-5s	Top-10s	Top-25s	Scoring Average	Money
1970	2	5	0	0	0	0	0	75.40	
1973	2	5	0	0	0	0	0	78.00	
1974	1	3	0	0	0	0	0	80.33	
Period Totals	Starts	Rounds Played	Cuts Made	Wins	Top-5s	Top-10s	Top-25s	Scoring Average	Money
	29	72	4	0	0	0	1	76.93	$580

Jim Jewell

Year	Starts	Rounds Played	Cuts Made	Wins	Top-5s	Top-10s	Top-25s	Scoring Average	Money
1970	3	8	1	0	0	0	0	72.88	$161

Best finish for 1970: T-61st at the Coral Springs Open Invitational

Year	Starts	Rounds Played	Cuts Made	Wins	Top-5s	Top-10s	Top-25s	Scoring Average	Money
1971	16	46	6	0	0	0	0	73.93	$1,492

Best finish for 1971: T-26th at the Massachusetts Classic

Year	Starts	Rounds Played	Cuts Made	Wins	Top-5s	Top-10s	Top-25s	Scoring Average	Money
1972	21	53	5	0	0	0	1	74.08	$4,396

Best finish for 1972: T-14th at the Greater St. Louis Classic

Year	Starts	Rounds Played	Cuts Made	Wins	Top-5s	Top-10s	Top-25s	Scoring Average	Money
1973	24	65	7	0	0	0	0	73.98	$2,094

Best finish for 1973: T-38th at the Byron Nelson Golf Classic

Year	Starts	Rounds Played	Cuts Made	Wins	Top-5s	Top-10s	Top-25s	Scoring Average	Money
1974	10	27	4	0	0	0	0	73.30	$2,411

Best finish for 1974: T-32nd at the Southern Open

Year	Starts	Rounds Played	Cuts Made	Wins	Top-5s	Top-10s	Top-25s	Scoring Average	Money
1976	1	2	0	0	0	0	0	75.50	

Best finish for 1976: T-100 at the B.C. Open

Period Totals	Starts	Rounds Played	Cuts Made	Wins	Top-5s	Top-10s	Top-25s	Scoring Average	Money
	75	201	23	0	0	0	1	73.88	$10,554

David Jimenez

Year	Starts	Rounds Played	Cuts Made	Wins	Top-5s	Top-10s	Top-25s	Scoring Average	Money
1963	1	4	1	0	0	0	1	73.50	$140

Best finish for 1963: T-18th at the Puerto Rico Open Invitational

Year	Starts	Rounds Played	Cuts Made	Wins	Top-5s	Top-10s	Top-25s	Scoring Average	Money
1964	1	2	0	0	0	0	0	78.00	
1966	1	4	1	0	0	0	0	76.00	$565

Best finish for 1966: T-57th at the U.S. Open

Year	Starts	Rounds Played	Cuts Made	Wins	Top-5s	Top-10s	Top-25s	Scoring Average	Money
1967	17	47	6	0	0	1	1	74.21	$4,709

Best finish for 1967: T-7th at the Minnesota Golf Classic

Year	Starts	Rounds Played	Cuts Made	Wins	Top-5s	Top-10s	Top-25s	Scoring Average	Money
1968	18	49	8	0	0	0	2	73.43	$2,475

Best finish for 1968: T-13th at the Magnolia State Classic

Year	Starts	Rounds Played	Cuts Made	Wins	Top-5s	Top-10s	Top-25s	Scoring Average	Money
1973	1	4	0	0	0	0	0	76.75	
1974	5	17	3	0	0	0	0	73.29	$1,147

Best finish for 1974: T-49th at the Bob Hope Chrysler Classic

Year	Starts	Rounds Played	Cuts Made	Wins	Top-5s	Top-10s	Top-25s	Scoring Average	Money
1976	1	2	0	0	0	0	0	79.00	$250
1979	2	4	0	0	0	0	0	76.25	$350
1981	1	2	0	0	0	0	0	79.50	$550
1986	1	2	0	0	0	0	0	79.00	
Period Totals	Starts	Rounds Played	Cuts Made	Wins	Top-5s	Top-10s	Top-25s	Scoring Average	Money
	49	137	19	0	0	1	4	74.26	$10,186

Miguel-A. Jimenez

Year	Starts	Rounds Played	Cuts Made	Wins	Top-5s	Top-10s	Top-25s	Scoring Average	Money
1991	1	4	1	0	0	0	0	72.25	$5,040

Best finish for 1991: T-80th at the British Open

Year	Starts	Rounds Played	Cuts Made	Wins	Top-5s	Top-10s	Top-25s	Scoring Average	Money
1993	1	4	1	0	0	0	0	71.25	$6,709

Best finish for 1993: T-51st at the British Open

Year	Starts	Rounds Played	Cuts Made	Wins	Top-5s	Top-10s	Top-25s	Scoring Average	Money
1994	1	2	0	0	0	0	0	72.50	$972
1995	5	18	4	0	0	0	1	71.78	$58,696

Best finish for 1995: T-13th at the PGA Championship

Year	Starts	Rounds Played	Cuts Made	Wins	Top-5s	Top-10s	Top-25s	Scoring Average	Money
1996	3	6	2	0	0	0	1	72.17	$27,638

Best finish for 1996: T-24th at the PGA Championship

Year	Starts	Rounds Played	Cuts Made	Wins	Top-5s	Top-10s	Top-25s	Scoring Average	Money
1997	1	2	0	0	0	0	0	76.00	$1,173
1998	1	1	0	0	0	0	0	73.00	$1,069
1999	11	32	8	0	1	3	4	71.72	$667,240

Best finish for 1999: 2nd at the American Express Championship

Year	Starts	Rounds Played	Cuts Made	Wins	Top-5s	Top-10s	Top-25s	Scoring Average	Money
2000	11	35	9	0	2	2	4	72.46	$716,348
Best finish for 2000: T-2nd at the U.S. Open									
2001	15	44	6	0	1	2	4	71.57	$467,457
Best finish for 2001: T-3rd at the British Open									
2002	19	58	10	0	0	1	3	71.69	$284,123
Best finish for 2002: T-9th at the Masters									
2003	1	2	0	0	0	0	0	76.50	$5,000
2004	7	22	6	0	0	0	1	71.82	$239,367
Best finish for 2004: T-16th at the WGC-American Express Championship									
2005	9	28	7	0	0	0	1	72.64	$283,398
Best finish for 2005: T-17th at the WGC-Accenture Match Play Championship									
2006	8	26	7	0	0	0	3	72.65	$458,511
Best finish for 2006: T-11th at the Masters									
2007	5	12	3	0	0	0	1	73.50	$185,491
Best finish for 2007: T-12th at the British Open									
2008	8	24	6	0	0	3	3	72.04	$725,946
Best finish for 2008: T-6th at the U.S. Open									
Period Totals	**Starts**	**Rounds Played**	**Cuts Made**	**Wins**	**Top-5s**	**Top-10s**	**Top-25s**	**Scoring Average**	**Money**
	107	320	70	0	4	11	26	72.11	$4,134,178

Brandt Jobe

Year	Starts	Rounds Played	Cuts Made	Wins	Top-5s	Top-10s	Top-25s	Scoring Average	Money
1987	1	2	0	0	0	0	0	77.50	
1990	1	2	0	0	0	0	0	75.00	$1,000
1991	27	63	5	0	0	0	2	72.56	$37,502
Best finish for 1991: T-11th at the Buick Southern Open									
1992	2	2	1	0	0	0	0	74.50	$7,340
Best finish for 1992: T-33rd at The International									
1993	1	2	0	0	0	0	0	76.50	
1994	1	4	1	0	0	0	0	73.50	$8,006
Best finish for 1994: T-39th at the U.S. Open									
1995	4	8	1	0	0	0	0	74.25	$5,006
Best finish for 1995: T-62nd at the U.S. Open									
1996	2	2	0	0	0	0	0	75.50	$1,000
1997	1	0	0	0	0	0	0		
1998	4	10	3	0	0	1	2	72.50	$115,785
Best finish for 1998: T-6th at the Sprint International									
1999	13	37	10	0	1	1	4	72.49	$323,819
Best finish for 1999: T-4th at the Reno-Tahoe Open									
2000	32	88	14	0	1	2	5	71.36	$403,017
Best finish for 2000: T-4th at the Phoenix Open									
2001	30	94	17	0	0	0	5	70.86	$407,065
Best finish for 2001: T-11th at the BellSouth Classic									
2002	28	94	18	0	2	3	6	70.66	$972,479
Best finish for 2002: T-2nd at the Michelob Championship at Kingsmill									
2003	22	77	16	0	1	1	4	70.48	$691,604
Best finish for 2003: 4th at the Bank of America Colonial									
2004	9	30	5	0	0	1	2	71.20	$247,911
Best finish for 2004: T-10th at the Buick Invitational									
2005	27	92	22	0	3	6	10	70.73	$2,133,149
Best finish for 2005: T-2nd at the BellSouth Classic & The International									
2006	28	88	18	0	1	2	4	71.20	$806,682
Best finish for 2006: T-4th at the Memorial Tournament									
2007	5	10	1	0	0	0	0	74.00	$11,016
Best finish for 2007: 68th at the Verizon Heritage									
2008	19	52	7	0	0	0	2	71.48	$293,214
Best finish for 2008: T-11th at the U.S. Bank Championship in Milwaukee									
Period Totals	**Starts**	**Rounds Played**	**Cuts Made**	**Wins**	**Top-5s**	**Top-10s**	**Top-25s**	**Scoring Average**	**Money**
	257	757	139	0	9	17	46	71.33	$6,465,594

Per-Ulrik Johansson

Year	Starts	Rounds Played	Cuts Made	Wins	Top-5s	Top-10s	Top-25s	Scoring Average	Money
1990	1	2	0	0	0	0	0	74.00	
1992	2	8	2	0	0	0	0	71.63	$8,740
Best finish for 1992: T-52nd at the Phoenix Open									
1993	2	4	0	0	0	0	0	74.25	$924
1994	1	4	1	0	0	0	0	71.00	$7,047
Best finish for 1994: T-60th at the British Open									
1995	3	10	2	0	0	0	1	71.90	$33,659
Best finish for 1995: T-15th at the British Open									
1996	4	8	2	0	0	1	2	72.63	$80,108
Best finish for 1996: T-8th at the PGA Championship									

Year	Starts	Rounds Played	Cuts Made	Wins	Top-5s	Top-10s	Top-25s	Scoring Average	Money
1997	4	14	3	0	0	0	1	73.43	$66,151

Best finish for 1997: T-12th at the Masters
| 1998 | 8 | 28 | 6 | 0 | 0 | 0 | 3 | 72.36 | $150,508 |

Best finish for 1998: T-12th at the Masters
| 1999 | 8 | 26 | 5 | 0 | 0 | 0 | 1 | 73.08 | $74,073 |

Best finish for 1999: T-24th at the Masters
| 2000 | 1 | 4 | 1 | 0 | 0 | 0 | 0 | 72.75 | $10,970 |

Best finish for 2000: T-64th at the British Open
| 2001 | 29 | 80 | 13 | 0 | 0 | 2 | 6 | 70.91 | $510,488 |

Best finish for 2001: T-6th at the Kemper Insurance Open
| 2002 | 27 | 87 | 16 | 0 | 0 | 2 | 5 | 70.76 | $557,064 |

Best finish for 2002: T-6th at the Nissan Open
| 2003 | 31 | 96 | 16 | 0 | 0 | 1 | 5 | 70.89 | $484,577 |

Best finish for 2003: T-6th at the EDS Byron Nelson Championship
| 2004 | 12 | 36 | 5 | 0 | 0 | 1 | 1 | 72.03 | $146,733 |

Best finish for 2004: T-6th at the Chrysler Classic of Tucson
| 2005 | 7 | 23 | 3 | 0 | 0 | 0 | 1 | 71.04 | $126,640 |

Best finish for 2005: T-16th at the Wachovia Championship
| Period Totals | Starts | Rounds Played | Cuts Made | Wins | Top-5s | Top-10s | Top-25s | Scoring Average | Money |
| | 140 | 430 | 75 | 0 | 0 | 7 | 26 | 71.41 | $2,257,682 |

Bob Johnson
Year	Starts	Rounds Played	Cuts Made	Wins	Top-5s	Top-10s	Top-25s	Scoring Average	Money
1963	1	4	1	0	0	0	0	72.50	

Best finish for 1963: T-38th at the Seattle Open Invitational
| 1964 | 20 | 42 | 4 | 0 | 0 | 0 | 0 | 74.74 | $150 |

Best finish for 1964: T-29th at the Azalea Open
| 1965 | 21 | 63 | 10 | 0 | 0 | 1 | 2 | 73.76 | $2,688 |

Best finish for 1965: T-6th at the Tucson Open
| 1966 | 19 | 49 | 6 | 0 | 1 | 1 | 2 | 73.20 | $3,860 |

Best finish for 1966: 2nd at the Azalea Open Invitational
| 1967 | 11 | 34 | 6 | 0 | 0 | 0 | 0 | 73.47 | $446 |

Best finish for 1967: T-39th at the Jacksonville Open
| 1968 | 5 | 12 | 1 | 0 | 0 | 0 | 1 | 74.25 | $1,425 |

Best finish for 1968: T-24th at the Greater Milwaukee Open Invitational
| 1969 | 2 | 6 | 1 | 0 | 0 | 0 | 0 | 75.00 | $184 |

Best finish for 1969: 75th at the Atlanta Classic
| 1970 | 1 | 2 | 0 | 0 | 0 | 0 | 0 | 77.00 | $500 |
| 1972 | 8 | 24 | 4 | 0 | 0 | 0 | 1 | 74.38 | $3,082 |

Best finish for 1972: T-19th at the IVB Philadelphia Golf Classic
1973	1	2	0	0	0	0	0	79.00	$500
Period Totals	Starts	Rounds Played	Cuts Made	Wins	Top-5s	Top-10s	Top-25s	Scoring Average	Money
	89	238	33	0	1	2	6	73.95	$12,835

Clayton Johnson
Year	Starts	Rounds Played	Cuts Made	Wins	Top-5s	Top-10s	Top-25s	Scoring Average	Money
1958	1	2	0	0	0	0	0	74.50	
1964	12	26	1	0	0	0	1	74.85	$332

Best finish for 1964: T-23rd at the Tucson Open
| 1965 | 6 | 18 | 3 | 0 | 0 | 0 | 0 | 74.78 | |

Best finish for 1965: 71st at the Phoenix Open
| 1966 | 2 | 6 | 1 | 0 | 0 | 0 | 0 | 74.33 | |

Best finish for 1966: T-69th at the Minnesota Golf Classic
| 1967 | 2 | 4 | 0 | 0 | 0 | 0 | 0 | 78.75 | |
| 1968 | 3 | 10 | 2 | 0 | 0 | 0 | 0 | 73.00 | |

Best finish for 1968: T-71st at the Minnesota Golf Classic
| Period Totals | Starts | Rounds Played | Cuts Made | Wins | Top-5s | Top-10s | Top-25s | Scoring Average | Money |
| | 26 | 66 | 7 | 0 | 0 | 0 | 1 | 74.73 | $332 |

Doug Johnson
Year	Starts	Rounds Played	Cuts Made	Wins	Top-5s	Top-10s	Top-25s	Scoring Average	Money
1980	8	16	1	0	0	1	1	73.31	$9,175

Best finish for 1980: 7th at the B.C. Open
| 1981 | 12 | 29 | 3 | 0 | 0 | 0 | 0 | 74.97 | $1,594 |

Best finish for 1981: 71st at the Hawaiian Open
| 1986 | 30 | 73 | 6 | 0 | 0 | 0 | 0 | 74.04 | $5,036 |

Best finish for 1986: T-43rd at the Tallahassee Open
| 1987 | 29 | 75 | 9 | 0 | 0 | 0 | 0 | 73.67 | $11,540 |

Best finish for 1987: T-50th at the Southwest Golf Classic
| 1988 | 2 | 6 | 1 | 0 | 0 | 0 | 0 | 72.83 | $1,017 |

Best finish for 1988: T-56th at the Provident Classic
1990	1	2	0	0	0	0	0	77.00	
Period Totals	Starts	Rounds Played	Cuts Made	Wins	Top-5s	Top-10s	Top-25s	Scoring Average	Money
	82	201	20	0	0	1	1	73.97	$28,363

Dustin Johnson

Year	Starts	Rounds Played	Cuts Made	Wins	Top-5s	Top-10s	Top-25s	Scoring Average	Money
2007	1	2	0	0	0	0	0	72.50	
2008	30	92	17	1	1	3	6	71.50	$1,789,895

Best finish for 2008: Win at the Turning Stone Resort Championship

Period Totals	Starts	Rounds Played	Cuts Made	Wins	Top-5s	Top-10s	Top-25s	Scoring Average	Money
	31	94	17	1	1	3	6	71.52	$1,789,895

Eric Johnson

Year	Starts	Rounds Played	Cuts Made	Wins	Top-5s	Top-10s	Top-25s	Scoring Average	Money
1991	1	2	0	0	0	0	0	74.00	$1,000
1993	2	6	1	0	0	0	0	75.00	$1,880

Best finish for 1993: T-75th at the Freeport-McMoRan Classic

1994	1	2	0	0	0	0	0	74.50	$1,000
1997	30	83	11	0	0	0	2	71.93	$92,091

Best finish for 1997: T-12th at the GTE Byron Nelson Classic

Period Totals	Starts	Rounds Played	Cuts Made	Wins	Top-5s	Top-10s	Top-25s	Scoring Average	Money
	34	93	12	0	0	0	2	72.23	$95,971

George Johnson

Year	Starts	Rounds Played	Cuts Made	Wins	Top-5s	Top-10s	Top-25s	Scoring Average	Money
1968	3	10	2	0	0	0	0	73.30	

Best finish for 1968: T-84th at the Cajun Classic

1969	22	59	7	0	0	0	1	74.29	$2,539

Best finish for 1969: T-25th at the Greater Milwaukee Open

1970	25	74	14	0	0	0	1	73.28	$5,614

Best finish for 1970: T-20th at the Green Island Open Invitational

1971	32	104	19	0	3	4	5	72.54	$28,833

Best finish for 1971: T-3rd at the Greater New Orleans Open

1972	34	104	21	0	1	3	9	72.40	$30,910

Best finish for 1972: T-2nd at the Greater Milwaukee Open

1973	30	98	18	0	0	0	4	72.44	$11,000

Best finish for 1973: T-22nd at the Shrine-Robinson Golf Classic & Sea Pines Heritage Classic

1974	27	85	15	0	3	3	6	72.60	$36,815

Best finish for 1974: 2nd at the Ohio Kings Island Open

1975	27	79	13	0	0	2	3	73.09	$16,837

Best finish for 1975: T-7th at the Western Open

1976	29	89	16	0	0	0	4	72.76	$12,825

Best finish for 1976: T-15th at the Tallahassee Open

1977	23	65	9	0	0	0	1	73.45	$6,229

Best finish for 1977: T-13th at the IVB Philadelphia Golf Classic

1978	20	52	7	0	0	0	0	73.48	$2,666

Best finish for 1978: T-35th at the Southern Open

1979	19	47	4	0	0	0	1	73.19	$6,682

Best finish for 1979: T-22nd at the Danny Thomas Memphis Classic

1980	1	2	0	0	0	0	0	73.50	
1981	3	6	1	0	0	0	0	72.00	$420

Best finish for 1981: T-64th at the Southern Open

1985	1	2	0	0	0	0	0	75.50	

Period Totals	Starts	Rounds Played	Cuts Made	Wins	Top-5s	Top-10s	Top-25s	Scoring Average	Money
	296	876	146	0	7	12	35	72.94	$161,368

Howie Johnson

Year	Starts	Rounds Played	Cuts Made	Wins	Top-5s	Top-10s	Top-25s	Scoring Average	Money
1958	34	119	26	1	2	3	15	71.71	$9,556

Best finish for 1958: Win at the Azalea Open

1959	20	80	19	1	1	3	11	70.95	$8,048

Best finish for 1959: Win at the Baton Rouge Open Invitational

1960	18	72	17	0	0	1	9	71.57	$5,562

Best finish for 1960: T-8th at the Cajun Classic Open Invitational

1961	18	72	17	0	0	0	8	71.28	$5,899

Best finish for 1961: T-12th at the Greater Seattle Open Invitational

1962	16	64	16	0	0	4	4	72.16	$6,764

Best finish for 1962: T-6th at the Azalea Open Invitational

1963	3	10	2	0	0	0	1	74.10	$1,035

Best finish for 1963: T-24th at the Western Open Championship

1964	22	77	17	0	2	2	8	71.66	$11,935

Best finish for 1964: T-5th at the St. Paul Open & Mountain View Open

1965	32	102	18	0	1	4	7	72.65	$15,351

Best finish for 1965: T-5th at the Seattle Open

1966	31	105	22	0	0	2	6	72.68	$11,674

Best finish for 1966: T-8th at the Los Angeles Open Invitational

Year	Starts	Rounds Played	Cuts Made	Wins	Top-5s	Top-10s	Top-25s	Scoring Average	Money
1967	28	107	25	0	0	1	8	72.49	$18,568

Best finish for 1967: T-7th at the Bing Crosby Pro-Am

| 1968 | 31 | 111 | 26 | 0 | 0 | 4 | 10 | 71.67 | $22,446 |

Best finish for 1968: T-7th at the Greater Hartford Open Invitational & Sahara Invitational

| 1969 | 35 | 133 | 32 | 0 | 2 | 5 | 15 | 71.29 | $48,969 |

Best finish for 1969: T-2nd at the Bing Crosby National Pro-Am

| 1970 | 30 | 115 | 29 | 0 | 3 | 5 | 16 | 71.50 | $60,625 |

Best finish for 1970: T-2nd at the Phoenix Open & Greater New Orleans Open

| 1971 | 13 | 38 | 6 | 0 | 1 | 1 | 2 | 73.71 | $10,267 |

Best finish for 1971: T-4th at the Bing Crosby Pro-Am

| 1972 | 30 | 101 | 20 | 0 | 0 | 0 | 2 | 73.23 | $10,197 |

Best finish for 1972: T-13th at the Doral-Eastern Open

| 1973 | 28 | 89 | 15 | 0 | 0 | 1 | 4 | 72.79 | $13,667 |

Best finish for 1973: T-9th at the Bing Crosby Pro-Am

| 1974 | 5 | 13 | 2 | 0 | 0 | 0 | 0 | 74.85 | $1,013 |

Best finish for 1974: T-44th at the Andy Williams-San Diego Open

1975	3	5	0	0	0	0	0	75.80	
1976	1	2	0	0	0	0	0	73.50	
Period Totals	Starts	Rounds Played	Cuts Made	Wins	Top-5s	Top-10s	Top-25s	Scoring Average	Money
	398	1415	309	2	12	36	126	72.09	$271,958

PGA Tour career totals from 1952 to 1976

	Starts	Rounds Played	Cuts Made	Wins	Top-5s	Top-10s	Top-25s	Scoring Average	Money
	439	1578	350	2	13	40	145	N/A	$332,516

Kevin Johnson

Year	Starts	Rounds Played	Cuts Made	Wins	Top-5s	Top-10s	Top-25s	Scoring Average	Money
1989	1	2	0	0	0	0	0	79.50	
1990	1	2	0	0	0	0	0	72.50	
1992	2	6	1	0	0	0	0	71.83	$2,050

Best finish for 1992: T-66th at the New England Classic

1993	1	2	0	0	0	0	0	73.00	
1996	1	2	0	0	0	0	0	74.00	
2000	1	2	0	0	0	0	0	75.00	$1,000
2001	32	91	14	0	0	0	1	71.42	$206,242

Best finish for 2001: T-11th at the Bob Hope Chrysler Classic

| 2002 | 1 | 4 | 1 | 0 | 0 | 0 | 1 | 68.75 | $37,100 |

Best finish for 2002: T-13th at the B.C. Open

| 2005 | 1 | 4 | 1 | 0 | 0 | 0 | 0 | 72.25 | $11,330 |

Best finish for 2005: T-65th at the Honda Classic

| Period Totals | Starts | Rounds Played | Cuts Made | Wins | Top-5s | Top-10s | Top-25s | Scoring Average | Money |
| | 41 | 115 | 17 | 0 | 0 | 0 | 2 | 71.67 | $257,722 |

Richard Johnson

Year	Starts	Rounds Played	Cuts Made	Wins	Top-5s	Top-10s	Top-25s	Scoring Average	Money
2001	1	4	1	0	0	0	0	71.00	$18,029

Best finish for 2001: T-36th at the AT&T Pebble Beach National Pro-Am

| 2006 | 1 | 2 | 0 | 0 | 0 | 0 | 0 | 76.00 | |
| 2008 | 29 | 77 | 9 | 0 | 0 | 0 | 0 | 71.96 | $200,210 |

Best finish for 2008: T-27th at the Turning Stone Resort Championship

| Period Totals | Starts | Rounds Played | Cuts Made | Wins | Top-5s | Top-10s | Top-25s | Scoring Average | Money |
| | 31 | 83 | 10 | 0 | 0 | 0 | 0 | 72.01 | $218,238 |

Richard S. Johnson

Year	Starts	Rounds Played	Cuts Made	Wins	Top-5s	Top-10s	Top-25s	Scoring Average	Money
2002	1	0	0	0	0	0	0		
2003	28	89	16	0	1	2	3	70.99	$560,021

Best finish for 2003: T-3rd at the FedEx St. Jude Classic

| 2004 | 32 | 102 | 18 | 0 | 0 | 1 | 3 | 71.03 | $461,183 |

Best finish for 2004: T-8th at the Chrysler Classic of Greensboro

| 2005 | 16 | 50 | 9 | 0 | 0 | 4 | 5 | 70.28 | $691,364 |

Best finish for 2005: T-6th at the FedEx St. Jude Classic

| 2006 | 29 | 94 | 17 | 0 | 1 | 3 | 10 | 70.85 | $1,557,626 |

Best finish for 2006: 2nd at the Bank of America Colonial

| 2007 | 32 | 93 | 15 | 0 | 0 | 0 | 3 | 71.61 | $377,951 |

Best finish for 2007: T-15th at the Valero Texas Open

| 2008 | 21 | 60 | 9 | 1 | 1 | 1 | 2 | 71.13 | $884,367 |

Best finish for 2008: Win at the U.S. Bank Championship in Milwaukee

| Period Totals | Starts | Rounds Played | Cuts Made | Wins | Top-5s | Top-10s | Top-25s | Scoring Average | Money |
| | 159 | 488 | 84 | 1 | 3 | 11 | 26 | 71.03 | $4,532,512 |

Tom Johnson

Year	Starts	Rounds Played	Cuts Made	Wins	Top-5s	Top-10s	Top-25s	Scoring Average	Money
2007	27	74	11	0	0	0	1	71.85	$190,926

Best finish for 2007: T-18th at the Bob Hope Chrysler Classic

Period Totals	Starts	Rounds Played	Cuts Made	Wins	Top-5s	Top-10s	Top-25s	Scoring Average	Money
	27	74	11	0	0	0	1	71.85	$190,926

Zach Johnson

Year	Starts	Rounds Played	Cuts Made	Wins	Top-5s	Top-10s	Top-25s	Scoring Average	Money
2001	1	2	0	0	0	0	0	71.50	
2002	2	6	1	0	0	0	1	71.50	$57,000

Best finish for 2002: T-17th at the AT&T Classic

| 2003 | 1 | 2 | 0 | 0 | 0 | 0 | 0 | 73.50 | |
| 2004 | 30 | 107 | 24 | 1 | 3 | 5 | 15 | 70.49 | $2,421,898 |

Best finish for 2004: Win at the AT&T Classic

| 2005 | 30 | 95 | 21 | 0 | 2 | 5 | 11 | 70.81 | $1,807,821 |

Best finish for 2005: T-2nd at the Buick Open

| 2006 | 27 | 88 | 21 | 0 | 4 | 4 | 9 | 70.85 | $2,461,148 |

Best finish for 2006: T-2nd at the AT&T Classic & Memorial Tournament

| 2007 | 23 | 75 | 18 | 2 | 3 | 5 | 10 | 70.95 | $2,619,968 |

Best finish for 2007: Win at the Masters & AT&T Classic

| 2008 | 25 | 84 | 19 | 1 | 1 | 3 | 7 | 71.06 | $1,615,123 |

Best finish for 2008: Win at the Valero Texas Open

Period Totals	Starts	Rounds Played	Cuts Made	Wins	Top-5s	Top-10s	Top-25s	Scoring Average	Money
	139	459	104	4	13	22	53	70.83	$10,982,958

Al Johnston

Year	Starts	Rounds Played	Cuts Made	Wins	Top-5s	Top-10s	Top-25s	Scoring Average	Money
1958	1	2	0	0	0	0	0	77.50	
1959	1	3	1	0	0	0	0	76.00	$043

Best finish for 1959: T-106 at the Bing Crosby National

| 1960 | 5 | 19 | 5 | 0 | 0 | 0 | 1 | 73.26 | $713 |

Best finish for 1960: T-24th at the West Palm Beach Open Invitational

| 1961 | 6 | 24 | 5 | 0 | 0 | 1 | 4 | 71.04 | $1,368 |

Best finish for 1961: T-6th at the Greater Greensboro Open Invitational

| 1962 | 11 | 43 | 10 | 1 | 1 | 2 | 5 | 70.30 | $7,313 |

Best finish for 1962: Win at the Hot Springs Open Invitational

| 1963 | 10 | 38 | 8 | 0 | 1 | 2 | 4 | 72.24 | $7,441 |

Best finish for 1963: T-4th at the Hot Springs Open Invitational

| 1964 | 18 | 48 | 7 | 0 | 0 | 1 | 3 | 73.96 | $3,350 |

Best finish for 1964: T-7th at the Tucson Open

| 1965 | 13 | 35 | 4 | 0 | 0 | 0 | 0 | 73.94 | $657 |

Best finish for 1965: T-33rd at the Canadian Open

| 1966 | 2 | 3 | 0 | 0 | 0 | 0 | 0 | 78.00 | |
| 1967 | 9 | 23 | 3 | 0 | 0 | 0 | 0 | 75.30 | $325 |

Best finish for 1967: T-42nd at the Florida Citrus Open

| 1968 | 11 | 28 | 3 | 0 | 0 | 0 | 0 | 74.82 | |

Best finish for 1968: T-68th at the Florida Citrus Open Invitational & Pensacola Open Invitational

| 1969 | 2 | 7 | 1 | 0 | 0 | 0 | 0 | 72.29 | $615 |

Best finish for 1969: T-30th at the Bob Hope Desert Classic

1970	1	2	0	0	0	0	0	74.50	
1971	4	7	0	0	0	0	0	75.71	
1973	1	3	0	0	0	0	0	80.33	

Period Totals	Starts	Rounds Played	Cuts Made	Wins	Top-5s	Top-10s	Top-25s	Scoring Average	Money
	95	285	47	1	2	6	17	73.24	$21,824

Bill Johnston

Year	Starts	Rounds Played	Cuts Made	Wins	Top-5s	Top-10s	Top-25s	Scoring Average	Money
1958	21	81	19	1	1	2	10	72.01	$6,602

Best finish for 1958: Win at the Texas Open

| 1959 | 15 | 58 | 13 | 0 | 1 | 3 | 10 | 71.38 | $6,082 |

Best finish for 1959: T-4th at the Tucson Open Invitational

| 1960 | 11 | 44 | 11 | 1 | 1 | 2 | 5 | 71.59 | $7,690 |

Best finish for 1960: Win at the Utah Open Invitational

| 1961 | 9 | 31 | 7 | 0 | 0 | 0 | 3 | 71.29 | $1,872 |

Best finish for 1961: T-19th at the Home Of The Sun Open Invitational & Eastern Open Invitational

| 1962 | 6 | 22 | 5 | 0 | 1 | 1 | 2 | 71.82 | $2,954 |

Best finish for 1962: T-5th at the Denver Open Invitational

| 1963 | 7 | 28 | 7 | 0 | 0 | 2 | 3 | 72.21 | $4,785 |

Best finish for 1963: T-8th at the PGA Championship

| 1964 | 11 | 33 | 3 | 0 | 0 | 1 | 1 | 73.76 | $2,033 |

Best finish for 1964: T-9th at the Sahara Invitational

Year	Starts	Rounds Played	Cuts Made	Wins	Top-5s	Top-10s	Top-25s	Scoring Average	Money
1965	6	15	1	0	0	0	0	74.00	$478

Best finish for 1965: T-36th at the Sahara Invitational

| 1966 | 7 | 20 | 3 | 0 | 0 | 0 | 0 | 75.30 | $629 |

Best finish for 1966: T-29th at the Bing Crosby National Professional-Amateur

| 1967 | 5 | 14 | 1 | 0 | 0 | 0 | 0 | 74.71 | |

Best finish for 1967: T-57th at the Sahara Open

| 1968 | 9 | 26 | 4 | 0 | 0 | 0 | 1 | 72.42 | $811 |

Best finish for 1968: T-25th at the Cajun Classic

| 1969 | 7 | 18 | 2 | 0 | 0 | 0 | 0 | 74.28 | $300 |

Best finish for 1969: T-55th at the Tucson Open

| 1970 | 7 | 22 | 3 | 0 | 0 | 0 | 0 | 73.23 | $1,210 |

Best finish for 1970: T-26th at the Phoenix Open

| 1971 | 10 | 27 | 3 | 0 | 0 | 0 | 0 | 74.48 | $756 |

Best finish for 1971: T-45th at the Bing Crosby Pro-Am

| 1972 | 11 | 34 | 6 | 0 | 0 | 1 | 2 | 72.82 | $4,280 |

Best finish for 1972: T-8th at the Robinson's Fall Golf Classic

| 1973 | 12 | 37 | 3 | 0 | 0 | 0 | 0 | 74.73 | $1,540 |

Best finish for 1973: T-45th at the San Antonio Texas Open

| 1974 | 9 | 26 | 4 | 0 | 0 | 0 | 0 | 73.31 | $1,154 |

Best finish for 1974: T-50th at the Andy Williams-San Diego Open

1975	5	10	0	0	0	0	0	75.00	
1976	3	6	0	0	0	0	0	75.33	
1977	2	6	1	0	0	0	0	75.67	

Best finish for 1977: T-73rd at the Phoenix Open

1978	2	3	0	0	0	0	0	76.33	
1979	4	8	0	0	0	0	0	74.38	
1980	3	8	1	0	0	0	0	73.50	$612

Best finish for 1980: T-67th at the Joe Garagiola Tucson Open

1982	1	2	0	0	0	0	0	75.00	
1983	1	2	0	0	0	0	0	77.00	
Period Totals	Starts	Rounds Played	Cuts Made	Wins	Top-5s	Top-10s	Top-25s	Scoring Average	Money
	184	581	97	2	4	12	37	72.96	$43,789

Jimmy Johnston

Year	Starts	Rounds Played	Cuts Made	Wins	Top-5s	Top-10s	Top-25s	Scoring Average	Money
1975	1	2	0	0	0	0	0	81.00	
1992	1	2	0	0	0	0	0	78.50	$1,000
1993	27	68	7	0	0	1	2	72.90	$54,419

Best finish for 1993: T-7th at the BellSouth Classic

| 1994 | 1 | 2 | 0 | 0 | 0 | 0 | 0 | 77.00 | |
| 1997 | 30 | 85 | 12 | 0 | 1 | 1 | 2 | 71.94 | $163,202 |

Best finish for 1997: T-2nd at the Quad City Classic

| 1998 | 21 | 58 | 9 | 0 | 0 | 0 | 0 | 72.31 | $45,391 |

Best finish for 1998: T-36th at the BellSouth Classic

| Period Totals | Starts | Rounds Played | Cuts Made | Wins | Top-5s | Top-10s | Top-25s | Scoring Average | Money |
| | 81 | 217 | 28 | 0 | 1 | 2 | 4 | 72.53 | $264,012 |

Ralph Johnston

Year	Starts	Rounds Played	Cuts Made	Wins	Top-5s	Top-10s	Top-25s	Scoring Average	Money
1965	1	4	1	0	0	0	0	72.50	

Best finish for 1965: T-50th at the Cajun Classic

| 1970 | 2 | 6 | 1 | 0 | 0 | 0 | 0 | 72.17 | $661 |

Best finish for 1970: T-33rd at the Coral Springs Open Invitational

| 1971 | 24 | 85 | 18 | 0 | 2 | 2 | 6 | 71.92 | $29,558 |

Best finish for 1971: T-2nd at the Greater Milwaukee Open

| 1972 | 30 | 112 | 25 | 0 | 1 | 2 | 5 | 73.14 | $22,085 |

Best finish for 1972: T-3rd at the Greater Hartford Open Invitational

| 1973 | 23 | 73 | 13 | 0 | 1 | 1 | 3 | 72.88 | $14,135 |

Best finish for 1973: T-4th at the Doral-Eastern Open

| 1974 | 20 | 58 | 10 | 0 | 0 | 0 | 5 | 72.76 | $11,578 |

Best finish for 1974: T-13th at the Greater Milwaukee Open

| 1975 | 23 | 79 | 16 | 0 | 2 | 3 | 7 | 71.92 | $20,846 |

Best finish for 1975: T-4th at the Tallahassee Open & San Antonio Texas Open

| 1976 | 15 | 34 | 3 | 0 | 0 | 0 | 0 | 75.53 | $1,600 |

Best finish for 1976: 60th at the San Antonio Texas Open

| 1977 | 7 | 18 | 2 | 0 | 0 | 0 | 0 | 74.06 | $600 |

Best finish for 1977: T-46th at the Canadian Open

| 1978 | 2 | 6 | 1 | 0 | 0 | 0 | 0 | 72.33 | $508 |

Best finish for 1978: T-30th at the Tallahassee Open

| Period Totals | Starts | Rounds Played | Cuts Made | Wins | Top-5s | Top-10s | Top-25s | Scoring Average | Money |
| | 147 | 475 | 90 | 0 | 6 | 8 | 26 | 72.81 | $101,570 |

Tony Johnstone

Year	Starts	Rounds Played	Cuts Made	Wins	Top-5s	Top-10s	Top-25s	Scoring Average	Money
1982	1	3	0	0	0	0	0	77.33	$638
1983	1	2	0	0	0	0	0	73.50	$375
1984	4	12	2	0	0	0	1	72.33	$13,779

Best finish for 1984: T-12th at the B.C. Open

1985	1	4	1	0	0	0	0	73.00	$3,770

Best finish for 1985: T-39th at the British Open

1986	1	2	0	0	0	0	0	80.00	$600
1988	1	2	0	0	0	0	0	75.50	$765
1989	4	12	3	0	0	0	0	73.42	$17,052

Best finish for 1989: T-34th at the NEC World Series of Golf

1991	1	4	1	0	0	0	0	72.00	$5,040

Best finish for 1991: T-73rd at the British Open

1992	4	10	3	0	0	0	1	74.60	$38,520

Best finish for 1992: 20th at the International

1993	5	14	2	0	0	0	0	73.00	$14,517

Best finish for 1993: T-52nd at the Players Championship

1994	3	6	0	0	0	0	0	73.83	$2,172
1995	1	2	0	0	0	0	0	75.00	$1,037
1996	1	2	0	0	0	0	0	73.00	$1,008
1998	2	6	1	0	0	0	0	75.00	$20,220

Best finish for 1998: 42nd at the NEC World Series of Golf

2000	1	2	0	0	0	0	0	77.00	$1,064
Period Totals	Starts	Rounds Played	Cuts Made	Wins	Top-5s	Top-10s	Top-25s	Scoring Average	Money
	31	83	13	0	0	0	2	73.86	$120,556

Philip Jonas

Year	Starts	Rounds Played	Cuts Made	Wins	Top-5s	Top-10s	Top-25s	Scoring Average	Money
1986	3	6	0	0	0	0	0	73.50	
1987	28	64	7	0	0	0	0	73.39	$8,989

Best finish for 1987: T-43rd at the Hawaiian Open & Deposit Guaranty Golf Classic

1988	2	4	0	0	0	0	0	73.75	
1991	1	2	0	0	0	0	0	77.50	
1993	1	2	0	0	0	0	0	78.50	
1996	2	4	0	0	0	0	0	73.00	
1997	2	8	2	0	0	0	0	70.75	$9,498

Best finish for 1997: T-39th at the Greater Vancouver Open

1998	2	8	2	0	0	0	0	72.00	$9,075

Best finish for 1998: T-53rd at the Greater Vancouver Open

1999	1	2	0	0	0	0	0	72.50	
2000	2	4	0	0	0	0	0	73.25	
Period Totals	Starts	Rounds Played	Cuts Made	Wins	Top-5s	Top-10s	Top-25s	Scoring Average	Money
	44	104	11	0	0	0	0	73.24	$27,562

Brendan Jones

Year	Starts	Rounds Played	Cuts Made	Wins	Top-5s	Top-10s	Top-25s	Scoring Average	Money
2004	3	6	0	0	0	0	0	74.50	$7,682
2005	28	79	14	0	1	1	3	71.34	$498,817

Best finish for 2005: T-2nd at the B.C. Open

2006	9	22	3	0	0	0	1	71.41	$68,760

Best finish for 2006: T-18th at the Chrysler Classic of Tucson

2008	5	14	4	0	0	0	0	72.50	$163,186

Best finish for 2008: T-33rd at the WGC-Accenture Match Play Championship

Period Totals	Starts	Rounds Played	Cuts Made	Wins	Top-5s	Top-10s	Top-25s	Scoring Average	Money
	45	121	21	0	1	1	4	71.64	$738,444

Gordon Jones

Year	Starts	Rounds Played	Cuts Made	Wins	Top-5s	Top-10s	Top-25s	Scoring Average	Money
1958	29	89	15	0	0	0	2	73.39	$1,106

Best finish for 1958: T-11th at the Memphis Invitational

1959	1	4	1	0	0	0	1	71.25	$375

Best finish for 1959: T-14th at the Lafayette Open Invitational

1960	10	40	8	0	0	1	4	71.68	$8,090

Best finish for 1960: T-7th at the St. Paul Open Invitational

1961	12	48	10	0	1	1	6	71.04	$5,238

Best finish for 1961: T-3rd at the Beaumont Open Invitational

1962	6	23	5	0	0	0	1	71.48	$1,094

Best finish for 1962: T-18th at the West Palm Beach Open Invitational

1963	9	36	9	0	0	0	3	72.00	$2,936

Best finish for 1963: T-16th at the Waco Turner Open Invitational

Year	Starts	Rounds Played	Cuts Made	Wins	Top-5s	Top-10s	Top-25s	Scoring Average	Money
1964	31	96	16	0	1	2	6	72.80	$7,408

Best finish for 1964: 5th at the Cajun Classic

1965	31	101	19	0	0	2	10	72.89	$12,843

Best finish for 1965: T-8th at the Jacksonville Open

1966	34	100	14	0	1	1	3	73.68	$7,677

Best finish for 1966: T-5th at the Pensacola Open Invitational

1967	13	33	3	0	0	0	2	73.58	$2,417

Best finish for 1967: T-18th at the Jacksonville Open & Azalea Open

1968	9	24	3	0	0	0	0	73.25	$377

Best finish for 1968: T-39th at the Pensacola Open Invitational

1969	20	56	8	0	0	1	1	73.25	$4,903

Best finish for 1969: T-9th at the Cleveland Open

1970	21	47	5	0	0	0	0	74.09	$1,135

Best finish for 1970: T-43rd at the National 4 Ball Championship PGA Players

1971	10	30	5	0	0	0	0	73.20	$1,199

Best finish for 1971: T-31st at the Greater Hartford Open Invitational

1972	8	24	4	0	0	0	1	72.92	$2,471

Best finish for 1972: T-17th at the Tallahassee Open

Year	Starts	Rounds Played	Cuts Made	Wins	Top-5s	Top-10s	Top-25s	Scoring Average	Money
1973	3	6	0	0	0	0	0	73.17	
1976	2	4	0	0	0	0	0	76.00	
1977	1	2	0	0	0	0	0	73.50	
1979	1	2	0	0	0	0	0	79.00	
1984	1	2	0	0	0	0	0	76.50	
1985	1	2	0	0	0	0	0	77.00	
Period Totals	Starts	Rounds Played	Cuts Made	Wins	Top-5s	Top-10s	Top-25s	Scoring Average	Money
	253	769	125	0	3	8	40	72.98	$59,269

Grier Jones

Year	Starts	Rounds Played	Cuts Made	Wins	Top-5s	Top-10s	Top-25s	Scoring Average	Money
1967	1	2	0	0	0	0	0	76.50	
1968	5	20	5	0	0	0	2	71.50	$1,424

Best finish for 1968: T-18th at the Haig Open Invitational

1969	34	118	26	0	3	6	14	71.75	$35,382

Best finish for 1969: T-5th at the Atlanta Classic, Michigan Golf Classic & Sahara Invitational

1970	34	118	28	0	3	5	13	71.38	$51,399

Best finish for 1970: T-2nd at the Kemper Open

1971	35	112	22	0	0	1	8	71.94	$25,435

Best finish for 1971: T-6th at the Bahamas National Open

1972	34	123	29	2	5	12	17	71.24	$124,101

Best finish for 1972: Win at the Hawaiian Open & Robinson's Fall Golf Classic

1973	32	109	25	0	4	7	11	71.48	$74,536

Best finish for 1973: T-2nd at the Andy Williams-San Diego Open & Sea Pines Heritage Classic

1974	31	91	16	0	2	4	8	71.91	$49,207

Best finish for 1974: 2nd at the Bing Crosby Pro-Am & Greater Milwaukee Open

1975	31	95	18	0	0	0	6	72.45	$15,719

Best finish for 1975: T-17th at the Greater Jacksonville Open

1976	32	113	28	0	1	5	13	71.52	$68,006

Best finish for 1976: T-2nd at the Kemper Open

1977	30	109	24	0	4	7	12	71.61	$80,021

Best finish for 1977: T-2nd at the Sammy Davis, Jr. - Greater Hartford Open

1978	22	80	18	0	2	6	12	70.83	$76,930

Best finish for 1978: 2nd at the Jackie Gleason's Inverrary Classic

1979	20	73	17	0	3	6	13	70.75	$111,851

Best finish for 1979: 2nd at the Jackie Gleason's Inverrary Classic

1980	17	47	10	0	1	3	4	72.43	$41,269

Best finish for 1980: T-2nd at the World Disney World National Team Championship

1981	22	63	12	0	0	0	2	72.10	$20,801

Best finish for 1981: T-12th at the Tournament Players Championship

1982	9	20	1	0	0	0	0	73.00	$690

Best finish for 1982: T-54th at the Georgia-Pacific Atlanta Golf Classic

1983	6	21	4	0	0	0	0	70.48	$4,599

Best finish for 1983: T-31st at the Pensacola Open

1984	13	43	6	0	0	0	1	72.16	$8,594

Best finish for 1984: T-22nd at the Bank of Boston Classic

1994	2	4	0	0	0	0	0	75.50	
Period Totals	Starts	Rounds Played	Cuts Made	Wins	Top-5s	Top-10s	Top-25s	Scoring Average	Money
	410	1361	289	2	28	62	136	71.65	$789,965

Kent Jones

Year	Starts	Rounds Played	Cuts Made	Wins	Top-5s	Top-10s	Top-25s	Scoring Average	Money
1996	1	4	1	0	0	0	0	73.50	$5,415

Best finish for 1996: T-82nd at the U.S. Open

Year	Starts	Rounds Played	Cuts Made	Wins	Top-5s	Top-10s	Top-25s	Scoring Average	Money
1997	1	2	0	0	0	0	0	76.00	$1,000
1998	29	87	17	0	0	0	2	71.99	$133,339

Best finish for 1998: T-12th at the Buick Open

Year	Starts	Rounds Played	Cuts Made	Wins	Top-5s	Top-10s	Top-25s	Scoring Average	Money
1999	26	67	7	0	0	0	1	72.85	$64,217

Best finish for 1999: T-19th at the Doral-Ryder Open

| 2001 | 28 | 74 | 7 | 0 | 0 | 0 | 1 | 72.05 | $87,308 |

Best finish for 2001: T-15th at the John Deere Classic

| 2002 | 33 | 103 | 19 | 0 | 0 | 1 | 6 | 71.07 | $489,879 |

Best finish for 2002: T-8th at the AT&T Pebble Beach National Pro-Am

| 2003 | 23 | 70 | 13 | 0 | 0 | 0 | 7 | 70.64 | $540,737 |

Best finish for 2003: T-13th at the Chrysler Classic of Tucson, Deutsche Bank Championship, Valero Texas Open & Southern Farm Bureau Classic

| 2004 | 32 | 97 | 17 | 0 | 0 | 2 | 6 | 70.81 | $674,909 |

Best finish for 2004: T-9th at the Bob Hope Chrysler Classic

| 2005 | 32 | 97 | 17 | 0 | 0 | 2 | 4 | 71.15 | $629,944 |

Best finish for 2005: T-7th at the Shell Houston Open

| 2006 | 32 | 101 | 18 | 0 | 0 | 2 | 8 | 71.05 | $860,766 |

Best finish for 2006: T-6th at the 84 Lumber Classic

| 2007 | 30 | 97 | 17 | 0 | 0 | 2 | 6 | 71.16 | $651,108 |

Best finish for 2007: T-8th at the Viking Classic

| 2008 | 23 | 68 | 11 | 0 | 0 | 0 | 4 | 70.96 | $304,432 |

Best finish for 2008: T-19th at the U.S. Bank Championship in Milwaukee

Period Totals	Starts	Rounds Played	Cuts Made	Wins	Top-5s	Top-10s	Top-25s	Scoring Average	Money
	290	867	144	0	0	9	45	71.35	$4,443,055

Matt Jones

Year	Starts	Rounds Played	Cuts Made	Wins	Top-5s	Top-10s	Top-25s	Scoring Average	Money
2008	31	95	17	0	2	2	5	71.40	$775,899

Best finish for 2008: T-4th at the Honda Classic & Buick Open

Period Totals	Starts	Rounds Played	Cuts Made	Wins	Top-5s	Top-10s	Top-25s	Scoring Average	Money
	31	95	17	0	2	2	5	71.40	$775,899

Steve Jones

Year	Starts	Rounds Played	Cuts Made	Wins	Top-5s	Top-10s	Top-25s	Scoring Average	Money
1982	11	30	3	0	0	0	0	73.73	$1,986

Best finish for 1982: T-59th at the USF&G Classic

| 1984 | 1 | 4 | 1 | 0 | 0 | 0 | 0 | 75.50 | $788 |

Best finish for 1984: T-71st at the Los Angeles Open

| 1985 | 21 | 67 | 12 | 0 | 0 | 1 | 7 | 71.69 | $43,379 |

Best finish for 1985: T-6th at the Texas Open

| 1986 | 23 | 71 | 14 | 0 | 0 | 2 | 5 | 71.49 | $51,473 |

Best finish for 1986: T-6th at the Tallahassee Open

| 1987 | 30 | 96 | 19 | 0 | 1 | 2 | 6 | 71.47 | $154,917 |

Best finish for 1987: 2nd at the MCI Heritage Classic

| 1988 | 25 | 87 | 19 | 1 | 2 | 3 | 6 | 71.55 | $241,877 |

Best finish for 1988: Win at the AT&T Pebble Beach Pro-Am

| 1989 | 28 | 94 | 21 | 3 | 3 | 6 | 11 | 70.94 | $746,378 |

Best finish for 1989: Win at the MONY Tournament Of Champions, Bob Hope Chrysler Classic & Canadian Open

| 1990 | 23 | 75 | 16 | 0 | 2 | 5 | 13 | 70.87 | $372,163 |

Best finish for 1990: T-2nd at the MCI Heritage Classic

| 1991 | 28 | 95 | 20 | 0 | 1 | 4 | 11 | 70.63 | $302,762 |

Best finish for 1991: 3rd at the Greater Milwaukee Open

| 1994 | 2 | 8 | 2 | 0 | 0 | 0 | 0 | 69.50 | $8,740 |

Best finish for 1994: T-31st at the Hardee's Golf Classic

| 1995 | 24 | 80 | 16 | 0 | 2 | 2 | 9 | 70.43 | $234,748 |

Best finish for 1995: T-4th at the Phoenix Open

| 1996 | 25 | 83 | 18 | 1 | 2 | 6 | 10 | 71.00 | $812,952 |

Best finish for 1996: Win at the U.S. Open

| 1997 | 24 | 78 | 16 | 2 | 3 | 6 | 9 | 71.10 | $964,108 |

Best finish for 1997: Win at the Phoenix Open & Bell Canadian Open

| 1998 | 23 | 80 | 19 | 1 | 2 | 2 | 11 | 70.41 | $742,544 |

Best finish for 1998: Win at the Quad City Classic

| 1999 | 19 | 55 | 11 | 0 | 1 | 3 | 8 | 71.76 | $368,456 |

Best finish for 1999: T-5th at the John Deere Classic

| 2000 | 21 | 71 | 16 | 0 | 2 | 2 | 7 | 71.59 | $548,070 |

Best finish for 2000: T-5th at the Touchstone Energy Tucson Open & BellSouth Classic

| 2001 | 25 | 71 | 12 | 0 | 0 | 0 | 2 | 71.58 | $265,886 |

Best finish for 2001: T-15th at the John Deere Classic

| 2002 | 24 | 68 | 12 | 0 | 0 | 0 | 0 | 71.57 | $170,315 |

Best finish for 2002: T-35th at the Touchstone Energy Tucson Open & Tampa Bay Classic presented by Buick

| 2003 | 11 | 32 | 5 | 0 | 0 | 0 | 0 | 71.84 | $68,756 |

Best finish for 2003: T-33rd at the BellSouth Classic

| 2005 | 20 | 54 | 8 | 0 | 0 | 0 | 0 | 72.37 | $124,144 |

Best finish for 2005: T-36th at the FBR Open

Year	Starts	Rounds Played	Cuts Made	Wins	Top-5s	Top-10s	Top-25s	Scoring Average	Money
2006	27	82	15	0	0	0	2	71.79	$308,360

Best finish for 2006: T-17th at the John Deere Classic

Year	Starts	Rounds Played	Cuts Made	Wins	Top-5s	Top-10s	Top-25s	Scoring Average	Money
2007	9	26	3	0	0	0	0	71.69	$34,922

Best finish for 2007: T-44th at the Canadian Open

Period Totals	Starts	Rounds Played	Cuts Made	Wins	Top-5s	Top-10s	Top-25s	Scoring Average	Money
	444	1407	278	8	21	44	117	71.34	$6,567,722

Tom Jones

Year	Starts	Rounds Played	Cuts Made	Wins	Top-5s	Top-10s	Top-25s	Scoring Average	Money
1970	1	4	1	0	0	0	0	76.25	

Best finish for 1970: 72nd at the Greater Jacksonville Open

Year	Starts	Rounds Played	Cuts Made	Wins	Top-5s	Top-10s	Top-25s	Scoring Average	Money
1980	17	51	9	0	0	0	2	71.86	$10,376

Best finish for 1980: 13th at the Tallahassee Open

Year	Starts	Rounds Played	Cuts Made	Wins	Top-5s	Top-10s	Top-25s	Scoring Average	Money
1981	15	36	4	0	0	0	0	72.58	$2,368

Best finish for 1981: T-44th at the Quad Cities Open

Year	Starts	Rounds Played	Cuts Made	Wins	Top-5s	Top-10s	Top-25s	Scoring Average	Money
1982	16	41	4	0	0	0	1	72.98	$5,039

Best finish for 1982: T-23rd at the Byron Nelson Golf Classic

Year	Starts	Rounds Played	Cuts Made	Wins	Top-5s	Top-10s	Top-25s	Scoring Average	Money
1983	17	39	1	0	0	0	0	74.59	$522

Best finish for 1983: T-65th at the Pensacola Open

Period Totals	Starts	Rounds Played	Cuts Made	Wins	Top-5s	Top-10s	Top-25s	Scoring Average	Money
	66	171	19	0	0	0	3	73.01	$18,306

Pete Jordan

Year	Starts	Rounds Played	Cuts Made	Wins	Top-5s	Top-10s	Top-25s	Scoring Average	Money
1985	1	2	0	0	0	0	0	79.50	
1988	1	2	0	0	0	0	0	75.50	
1990	2	6	1	0	0	0	0	71.83	$2,034

Best finish for 1990: T-55th at the Northern Telecom Tucson Open

1993	1	4	1	0	0	0	0	72.25	$5,405

Best finish for 1993: T-72nd at the U.S. Open

1994	30	88	13	0	1	1	2	71.56	$128,960

Best finish for 1994: 4th at the Southwestern Bell Colonial

1995	18	59	12	0	1	1	6	70.63	$143,936

Best finish for 1995: 3rd at the Deposit Guaranty Golf Classic

1996	26	73	10	0	1	1	4	71.64	$191,240

Best finish for 1996: 2nd at the B.C. Open

1997	33	101	18	0	0	1	6	71.49	$209,020

Best finish for 1997: T-9th at the Buick Classic

1998	34	89	12	0	0	0	3	72.06	$176,807

Best finish for 1998: T-12th at the Walt Disney World/Oldsmobile Classic

1999	30	90	14	0	1	2	5	71.41	$295,419

Best finish for 1999: T-5th at the John Deere Classic

2000	31	102	19	0	2	2	6	71.01	$464,480

Best finish for 2000: T-4th at the FedEx St. Jude Classic & Southern Farm Bureau Classic

2001	36	103	16	0	1	1	2	71.17	$387,088

Best finish for 2001: 3rd at the John Deere Classic

2002	30	78	9	0	0	0	0	72.28	$102,330

Best finish for 2002: T-28th at the Bell Canadian Open

2003	1	4	1	0	0	0	0	70.00	$6,720

Best finish for 2003: T-54th at the B.C. Open

2004	2	6	1	0	0	0	0	71.83	$24,280

Best finish for 2004: T-33rd at the Booz Allen Classic

2006	1	2	0	0	0	0	0	74.00	
2008	1	4	1	0	0	0	0	72.75	$10,725

Best finish for 2008: T-72nd at the Honda Classic

Period Totals	Starts	Rounds Played	Cuts Made	Wins	Top-5s	Top-10s	Top-25s	Scoring Average	Money
	278	813	128	0	7	9	34	71.52	$2,148,444

John Joseph

Year	Starts	Rounds Played	Cuts Made	Wins	Top-5s	Top-10s	Top-25s	Scoring Average	Money
1963	1	4	1	0	0	0	1	70.75	$610

Best finish for 1963: T-19th at the Almaden Open Invitational

1964	1	4	1	0	0	0	0	73.50	

Best finish for 1964: 48th at the Almaden Open

1967	13	31	1	0	0	0	0	75.90	

Best finish for 1967: T-53rd at the Cajun Classic

1969	7	18	2	0	0	0	0	73.67	$465

Best finish for 1969: T-29th at the Azalea Open

1985	1	3	0	0	0	0	0	78.67	
1989	1	3	0	0	0	0	0	78.33	
1990	1	3	0	0	0	0	0	75.33	

Year	Starts	Rounds Played	Cuts Made	Wins	Top-5s	Top-10s	Top-25s	Scoring Average	Money
1991	1	4	1	0	0	0	0	71.50	$7,322

Best finish for 1991: T-27th at the AT&T Pebble Beach Pro-Am

Year	Starts	Rounds Played	Cuts Made	Wins	Top-5s	Top-10s	Top-25s	Scoring Average	Money
1992	1	3	0	0	0	0	0	76.00	
Period Totals	Starts	Rounds Played	Cuts Made	Wins	Top-5s	Top-10s	Top-25s	Scoring Average	Money
	27	73	6	0	0	0	1	74.89	$8,398

John Josephson

Year	Starts	Rounds Played	Cuts Made	Wins	Top-5s	Top-10s	Top-25s	Scoring Average	Money
1965	1	2	0	0	0	0	0	74.50	
1966	18	48	7	0	0	1	1	74.02	$1,967

Best finish for 1966: T-8th at the Cajun Classic

1967	6	16	2	0	0	0	0	74.63	$105

Best finish for 1967: T-30th at the Azalea Open

1968	7	16	2	0	0	0	0	73.06	

Best finish for 1968: T-38th at the Magnolia State Classic

Period Totals	Starts	Rounds Played	Cuts Made	Wins	Top-5s	Top-10s	Top-25s	Scoring Average	Money
	32	82	11	0	0	1	1	73.96	$2,072

Tom Joyce

Year	Starts	Rounds Played	Cuts Made	Wins	Top-5s	Top-10s	Top-25s	Scoring Average	Money
1968	2	6	1	0	0	0	0	74.33	

Best finish for 1968: T-69th at the Thunderbird Classic

1969	1	2	0	0	0	0	0	75.00	
1970	4	10	1	0	0	0	0	75.80	$182

Best finish for 1970: T-67th at the Greater Jacksonville Open

1972	4	10	1	0	0	0	1	74.90	$1,077

Best finish for 1972: T-25th at the Tallahassee Open

1973	1	4	1	0	0	0	0	76.25	$800

Best finish for 1973: T-63rd at the U.S. Open

1974	2	4	0	0	0	0	0	75.75	$500
1975	2	4	0	0	0	0	0	73.50	
1976	3	8	1	0	0	0	0	74.75	$250

Best finish for 1976: 83rd at the American Express Westchester Classic

1977	5	14	2	0	0	0	0	73.21	$2,172

Best finish for 1977: T-34th at the Doral-Eastern Open

1978	1	2	0	0	0	0	0	76.50	
1979	1	2	0	0	0	0	0	76.50	$350
1980	1	2	0	0	0	0	0	72.50	
1992	1	2	0	0	0	0	0	78.50	$1,200
1993	1	2	0	0	0	0	0	79.00	$1,200
Period Totals	Starts	Rounds Played	Cuts Made	Wins	Top-5s	Top-10s	Top-25s	Scoring Average	Money
	29	72	7	0	0	0	1	74.92	$7,731

Jeff Julian

Year	Starts	Rounds Played	Cuts Made	Wins	Top-5s	Top-10s	Top-25s	Scoring Average	Money
1988	1	2	0	0	0	0	0	72.50	
1990	1	2	0	0	0	0	0	79.00	$1,000
1995	1	2	0	0	0	0	0	74.50	$1,000
1996	26	69	9	0	0	0	2	72.38	$56,602

Best finish for 1996: T-16th at the Buick Classic

2001	22	55	6	0	0	0	0	73.13	$55,132

Best finish for 2001: T-34th at the Bell Canadian Open

2002	7	15	0	0	0	0	0	75.40	
Period Totals	Starts	Rounds Played	Cuts Made	Wins	Top-5s	Top-10s	Top-25s	Scoring Average	Money
	58	145	15	0	0	0	2	73.10	$113,734

Steve Jurgensen

Year	Starts	Rounds Played	Cuts Made	Wins	Top-5s	Top-10s	Top-25s	Scoring Average	Money
1987	1	1	0	0	0	0	0	73.00	
1991	1	2	0	0	0	0	0	75.50	
1994	1	4	1	0	0	0	0	71.25	$2,544

Best finish for 1994: T-63rd at the United Airlines Hawaiian Open

1996	31	87	15	0	0	1	4	71.82	$119,049

Best finish for 1996: T-10th at the Deposit Guaranty Golf Classic

1997	4	16	4	0	1	1	1	70.63	$50,258

Best finish for 1997: T-4th at the Deposit Guaranty Golf Classic

1998	29	72	8	0	0	1	1	72.64	$88,783

Best finish for 1998: T-6th at the Buick Invitational

1999	23	55	4	0	0	0	0	73.75	$28,136

Best finish for 1999: T-33rd at the Sony Open in Hawaii

2000	2	5	0	0	0	0	0	73.60	
2001	1	2	0	0	0	0	0	79.00	
Period Totals	Starts	Rounds Played	Cuts Made	Wins	Top-5s	Top-10s	Top-25s	Scoring Average	Money
	93	244	32	0	1	3	6	72.54	$288,770

Mike Kallam

Year	Starts	Rounds Played	Cuts Made	Wins	Top-5s	Top-10s	Top-25s	Scoring Average	Money
1972	1	2	0	0	0	0	0	75.00	
1973	26	76	11	0	0	1	2	73.62	$6,013

Best finish for 1973: T-10th at the Monsanto Open

Year	Starts	Rounds Played	Cuts Made	Wins	Top-5s	Top-10s	Top-25s	Scoring Average	Money
1974	16	37	3	0	0	0	0	74.86	$1,162

Best finish for 1974: T-41st at the B.C. Open

Year	Starts	Rounds Played	Cuts Made	Wins	Top-5s	Top-10s	Top-25s	Scoring Average	Money
1985	1	2	0	0	0	0	0	78.00	
1987	1	2	0	0	0	0	0	79.50	
1988	1	2	0	0	0	0	0	76.00	
1991	1	2	0	0	0	0	0	76.00	$1,000
Period Totals	Starts	Rounds Played	Cuts Made	Wins	Top-5s	Top-10s	Top-25s	Scoring Average	Money
	47	123	14	0	0	1	2	74.26	$8,175

Brian Kamm

Year	Starts	Rounds Played	Cuts Made	Wins	Top-5s	Top-10s	Top-25s	Scoring Average	Money
1986	1	4	1	0	0	0	0	72.25	$538

Best finish for 1986: T-48th at the Tallahassee Open

Year	Starts	Rounds Played	Cuts Made	Wins	Top-5s	Top-10s	Top-25s	Scoring Average	Money
1988	1	4	1	0	0	0	0	70.00	$1,162

Best finish for 1988: T-30th at the Deposit Guaranty Golf Classic

Year	Starts	Rounds Played	Cuts Made	Wins	Top-5s	Top-10s	Top-25s	Scoring Average	Money
1990	21	50	5	0	0	0	0	73.00	$8,775

Best finish for 1990: T-47th at the USF&G Classic

Year	Starts	Rounds Played	Cuts Made	Wins	Top-5s	Top-10s	Top-25s	Scoring Average	Money
1991	27	74	11	0	0	1	4	71.59	$81,932

Best finish for 1991: T-8th at the Canadian Open

Year	Starts	Rounds Played	Cuts Made	Wins	Top-5s	Top-10s	Top-25s	Scoring Average	Money
1992	4	10	1	0	0	0	1	72.00	$20,020

Best finish for 1992: T-13th at the Kemper Open

Year	Starts	Rounds Played	Cuts Made	Wins	Top-5s	Top-10s	Top-25s	Scoring Average	Money
1993	27	86	17	0	0	3	7	71.14	$183,185

Best finish for 1993: T-7th at the Canon Greater Hartford Open

Year	Starts	Rounds Played	Cuts Made	Wins	Top-5s	Top-10s	Top-25s	Scoring Average	Money
1994	32	94	16	0	0	3	5	71.64	$182,884

Best finish for 1994: T-6th at the Bell Canadian Open

Year	Starts	Rounds Played	Cuts Made	Wins	Top-5s	Top-10s	Top-25s	Scoring Average	Money
1995	30	90	17	0	0	2	6	71.94	$165,235

Best finish for 1995: T-9th at the Nissan Open & Bell Canadian Open

Year	Starts	Rounds Played	Cuts Made	Wins	Top-5s	Top-10s	Top-25s	Scoring Average	Money
1996	31	87	13	0	0	0	1	72.78	$64,988

Best finish for 1996: T-16th at the Greater Greensboro Chrysler Classic

Year	Starts	Rounds Played	Cuts Made	Wins	Top-5s	Top-10s	Top-25s	Scoring Average	Money
1998	28	70	10	0	0	0	2	72.40	$87,326

Best finish for 1998: 13th at the Greater Milwaukee Open

Period Totals	Starts	Rounds Played	Cuts Made	Wins	Top-5s	Top-10s	Top-25s	Scoring Average	Money
	202	569	92	0	0	9	26	71.99	$796,047

Craig Kanada

Year	Starts	Rounds Played	Cuts Made	Wins	Top-5s	Top-10s	Top-25s	Scoring Average	Money
1991	1	2	0	0	0	0	0	78.50	
1992	1	3	0	0	0	0	0	70.67	
1993	1	2	0	0	0	0	0	74.00	
1994	1	2	0	0	0	0	0	73.50	
1995	1	4	1	0	0	0	0	72.25	$2,220

Best finish for 1995: T-77th at the Buick Invitational of California

Year	Starts	Rounds Played	Cuts Made	Wins	Top-5s	Top-10s	Top-25s	Scoring Average	Money
1997	23	54	5	0	0	0	0	72.87	$25,125

Best finish for 1997: T-28th at the BellSouth Classic

Year	Starts	Rounds Played	Cuts Made	Wins	Top-5s	Top-10s	Top-25s	Scoring Average	Money
2001	28	78	11	0	0	0	1	71.68	$132,163

Best finish for 2001: T-20th at the Touchstone Energy Tucson Open

Year	Starts	Rounds Played	Cuts Made	Wins	Top-5s	Top-10s	Top-25s	Scoring Average	Money
2003	2	4	0	0	0	0	0	74.00	
2007	34	109	20	0	0	1	5	71.13	$745,305

Best finish for 2007: T-10th at the Sony Open in Hawaii

Year	Starts	Rounds Played	Cuts Made	Wins	Top-5s	Top-10s	Top-25s	Scoring Average	Money
2008	23	65	11	0	0	0	3	71.05	$363,597

Best finish for 2008: T-11th at the AT&T Classic

Period Totals	Starts	Rounds Played	Cuts Made	Wins	Top-5s	Top-10s	Top-25s	Scoring Average	Money
	115	323	48	0	0	1	9	71.66	$1,268,410

Jim Kane

Year	Starts	Rounds Played	Cuts Made	Wins	Top-5s	Top-10s	Top-25s	Scoring Average	Money
1983	1	3	0	0	0	0	0	74.67	
1984	24	74	12	0	0	0	2	72.93	$18,035

Best finish for 1984: T-20th at the Western Open

Year	Starts	Rounds Played	Cuts Made	Wins	Top-5s	Top-10s	Top-25s	Scoring Average	Money
1985	1	3	0	0	0	0	0	75.33	
1992	2	8	2	0	0	0	1	73.75	$16,481

Best finish for 1992: T-23rd at the U.S. Open

Year	Starts	Rounds Played	Cuts Made	Wins	Top-5s	Top-10s	Top-25s	Scoring Average	Money
1993	2	7	1	0	0	0	0	70.86	$5,660

Best finish for 1993: T-32nd at the H-E-B Texas Open

Year	Starts	Rounds Played	Cuts Made	Wins	Top-5s	Top-10s	Top-25s	Scoring Average	Money
1994	1	3	0	0	0	0	0	74.67	
2006	1	4	1	0	0	0	0	75.25	$12,725

Best finish for 2006: 70th at the PGA Championship

Period Totals	Starts	Rounds Played	Cuts Made	Wins	Top-5s	Top-10s	Top-25s	Scoring Average	Money
	32	102	16	0	0	0	3	73.12	$52,901

Richie Karl

Year	Starts	Rounds Played	Cuts Made	Wins	Top-5s	Top-10s	Top-25s	Scoring Average	Money
1971	9	24	3	0	0	0	0	73.50	$749

Best finish for 1971: T-32nd at the Tallahassee Open

1972	14	45	8	0	0	0	2	73.09	$5,822

Best finish for 1972: T-13th at the Phoenix Open

1973	15	43	6	0	1	1	3	73.37	$8,614

Best finish for 1973: T-5th at the Dean Martin Tucson Open

1974	16	38	3	1	1	1	1	74.29	$30,578

Best finish for 1974: Win at the B.C. Open

1975	19	52	7	0	0	0	0	75.21	$5,497

Best finish for 1975: 30th at the MONY Tournament Of Champions

1976	6	15	2	0	0	0	0	73.80	$652

Best finish for 1976: T-52nd at the Ed McMahon Quad City Open

1977	2	4	0	0	0	0	0	74.75	
1978	3	4	0	0	0	0	0	75.75	
1979	3	5	0	0	0	0	0	75.80	
1980	3	4	0	0	0	0	0	76.00	$600
1981	3	4	0	0	0	0	0	72.75	
1982	3	10	2	0	0	0	0	72.50	$1,024

Best finish for 1982: T-52nd at the B.C. Open

1983	2	4	0	0	0	0	0	72.25	
1984	3	6	0	0	0	0	0	76.83	
1985	3	8	1	0	0	0	0	74.00	$582

Best finish for 1985: T-71st at the B.C. Open

1986	2	4	0	0	0	0	0	76.75	
1987	2	4	0	0	0	0	0	72.50	
1988	2	6	1	0	0	0	0	71.67	$970

Best finish for 1988: T-71st at the B.C. Open

1989	2	6	1	0	0	0	0	72.83	$1,060

Best finish for 1989: 64th at the B.C. Open

1990	1	2	0	0	0	0	0	72.00	
1992	1	2	0	0	0	0	0	73.50	
1993	1	4	1	0	0	0	0	73.00	$1,464

Best finish for 1993: T-78th at the B.C. Open

1994	1	2	0	0	0	0	0	72.00	
1995	1	2	0	0	0	0	0	73.50	
1996	1	1	0	0	0	0	0	79.00	
1998	1	2	0	0	0	0	0	76.50	
2000	1	2	0	0	0	0	0	74.50	
2001	1	2	0	0	0	0	0	78.00	

Period Totals	Starts	Rounds Played	Cuts Made	Wins	Top-5s	Top-10s	Top-25s	Scoring Average	Money
	121	305	35	1	2	2	6	73.99	$57,612

Robert Karlsson

Year	Starts	Rounds Played	Cuts Made	Wins	Top-5s	Top-10s	Top-25s	Scoring Average	Money
1989	1	4	1	0	0	0	0	74.75	

Best finish for 1989: T-77th at the British Open

1992	1	4	1	0	1	1	1	69.75	$60,143

Best finish for 1992: T-5th at the British Open

1993	1	2	0	0	0	0	0	73.00	$924
1995	1	2	0	0	0	0	0	75.50	$1,037
1997	1	2	0	0	0	0	0	74.00	$1,676
1998	5	12	1	0	0	0	0	74.83	$7,902

Best finish for 1998: T-65th at the PGA Championship

1999	7	24	5	0	0	1	2	72.88	$131,396

Best finish for 1999: T-9th at the Nissan Open

2000	3	6	0	0	0	0	0	74.33	$1,064
2001	2	4	0	0	0	0	0	73.25	$3,574
2002	2	6	1	0	0	0	0	73.50	$24,022

Best finish for 2002: T-45th at the U.S. Open

2003	3	6	2	0	0	0	0	74.67	$54,000

Best finish for 2003: T-33rd at the WGC-Accenture Match Play Championship

2005	1	2	0	0	0	0	0	74.50	$2,000
2006	5	20	5	0	0	0	1	71.30	$234,283

Best finish for 2006: 21st at the WGC-American Express Championship

2007	13	42	10	0	0	1	3	73.29	$615,686

Best finish for 2007: T-6th at The Players

| 2008 | 8 | 28 | 8 | 0 | 1 | 3 | 5 | 71.43 | $985,685 |

Best finish for 2008: T-4th at the U.S. Open

Period Totals	Starts	Rounds Played	Cuts Made	Wins	Top-5s	Top-10s	Top-25s	Scoring Average	Money
	54	164	34	0	2	6	12	72.87	$2,123,391

Hideki Kase

Year	Starts	Rounds Played	Cuts Made	Wins	Top-5s	Top-10s	Top-25s	Scoring Average	Money
1991	1	4	1	0	0	0	0	73.00	$7,875

Best finish for 1991: T-40th at the NEC World Series of Golf

| 1992 | 4 | 12 | 2 | 0 | 0 | 0 | 0 | 73.92 | $4,868 |

Best finish for 1992: T-59th at the Honda Classic

| 1997 | 30 | 85 | 14 | 0 | 0 | 0 | 2 | 72.58 | $120,478 |

Best finish for 1997: 15th at the Sprint International

| 2005 | 1 | 2 | 0 | 0 | 0 | 0 | 0 | 73.00 | |

Period Totals	Starts	Rounds Played	Cuts Made	Wins	Top-5s	Top-10s	Top-25s	Scoring Average	Money
	36	103	17	0	0	0	2	72.76	$133,221

Monty Kaser

Year	Starts	Rounds Played	Cuts Made	Wins	Top-5s	Top-10s	Top-25s	Scoring Average	Money
1967	24	69	10	0	0	1	2	74.17	$4,338

Best finish for 1967: 9th at the Azalea Open

| 1968 | 31 | 92 | 15 | 0 | 1 | 1 | 5 | 73.25 | $15,699 |

Best finish for 1968: 2nd at the Memphis Open Invitational

| 1969 | 27 | 80 | 14 | 1 | 1 | 1 | 3 | 72.78 | $11,819 |

Best finish for 1969: Win at the Indian Ridge Hospital Open

| 1970 | 12 | 30 | 3 | 0 | 0 | 0 | 0 | 74.77 | $1,390 |

Best finish for 1970: T-38th at the Azalea Open Invitational

| 1971 | 6 | 12 | 0 | 0 | 0 | 0 | 0 | 76.17 | $500 |
| 1972 | 8 | 24 | 3 | 0 | 0 | 1 | 1 | 73.67 | $2,153 |

Best finish for 1972: T-10th at the Tallahassee Open

| 1973 | 6 | 16 | 1 | 0 | 0 | 0 | 1 | 74.44 | $887 |

Best finish for 1973: T-25th at the San Antonio Texas Open

| 1974 | 17 | 53 | 9 | 0 | 0 | 0 | 3 | 72.94 | $9,759 |

Best finish for 1974: T-14th at the IVB Philadelphia Golf Classic

| 1975 | 20 | 53 | 6 | 0 | 0 | 0 | 0 | 73.75 | $2,360 |

Best finish for 1975: T-33rd at the Tallahassee Open

| 1976 | 14 | 39 | 8 | 0 | 0 | 1 | 1 | 73.10 | $6,436 |

Best finish for 1976: T-8th at the Byron Nelson Golf Classic

| 1977 | 14 | 40 | 5 | 0 | 0 | 0 | 0 | 74.13 | $3,940 |

Best finish for 1977: T-28th at the Jackie Gleason's Inverrary Classic

1978	3	8	0	0	0	0	0	75.13	
1983	1	4	0	0	0	0	0	76.50	
Period Totals	Starts	Rounds Played	Cuts Made	Wins	Top-5s	Top-10s	Top-25s	Scoring Average	Money
	183	520	74	1	2	5	16	73.64	$59,281

Shingo Katayama

Year	Starts	Rounds Played	Cuts Made	Wins	Top-5s	Top-10s	Top-25s	Scoring Average	Money
1995	1	2	0	0	0	0	0	72.00	
1999	1	4	1	0	0	0	0	78.00	$9,374

Best finish for 1999: 71st at the British Open

| 2000 | 4 | 8 | 0 | 0 | 0 | 0 | 0 | 74.88 | $3,520 |
| 2001 | 6 | 18 | 3 | 0 | 1 | 1 | 1 | 72.28 | $257,116 |

Best finish for 2001: T-4th at the PGA Championship

| 2002 | 8 | 20 | 4 | 0 | 0 | 0 | 0 | 73.10 | $100,777 |

Best finish for 2002: T-33rd at the Accenture Match Play Championship

| 2003 | 5 | 12 | 3 | 0 | 0 | 0 | 0 | 74.17 | $93,499 |

Best finish for 2003: T-33rd at the WGC-Accenture Match Play Championship

| 2004 | 3 | 8 | 3 | 0 | 0 | 0 | 0 | 74.88 | $78,650 |

Best finish for 2004: T-33rd at the WGC-Accenture Match Play Championship

| 2005 | 5 | 11 | 3 | 0 | 0 | 0 | 1 | 73.09 | $133,020 |

Best finish for 2005: T-23rd at the PGA Championship

| 2006 | 6 | 16 | 4 | 0 | 0 | 1 | 1 | 73.81 | $210,472 |

Best finish for 2006: T-9th at the WGC-Accenture Match Play Championship

| 2007 | 7 | 22 | 6 | 0 | 0 | 0 | 0 | 74.41 | $194,928 |

Best finish for 2007: T-33rd at the WGC-Accenture Match Play Championship

| 2008 | 5 | 10 | 2 | 0 | 0 | 0 | 0 | 74.80 | $76,375 |

Best finish for 2008: T-33rd at the WGC-Accenture Match Play Championship

Period Totals	Starts	Rounds Played	Cuts Made	Wins	Top-5s	Top-10s	Top-25s	Scoring Average	Money
	51	131	29	0	1	2	3	73.87	$1,157,731

Jack Kay Jr.

Year	Starts	Rounds Played	Cuts Made	Wins	Top-5s	Top-10s	Top-25s	Scoring Average	Money
1970	1	2	0	0	0	0	0	78.50	
1971	1	2	0	0	0	0	0	76.50	
1986	2	4	0	0	0	0	0	75.50	
1987	1	2	0	0	0	0	0	77.50	
1988	1	2	0	0	0	0	0	77.50	
1989	27	71	9	0	0	0	1	72.18	$20,309

Best finish for 1989: T-25th at the Independent Insurance Agent Open

1990	2	6	1	0	0	0	0	72.50	$1,020

Best finish for 1990: T-43rd at the Deposit Guaranty

1991	2	4	0	0	0	0	0	78.00	$1,000
Period Totals	Starts	Rounds Played	Cuts Made	Wins	Top-5s	Top-10s	Top-25s	Scoring Average	Money
	37	93	10	0	0	0	1	73.05	$22,329

Jonathan Kaye

Year	Starts	Rounds Played	Cuts Made	Wins	Top-5s	Top-10s	Top-25s	Scoring Average	Money
1995	25	65	8	0	1	2	4	71.51	$191,883

Best finish for 1995: 2nd at the Quad City Classic

1996	3	9	1	0	0	0	0	71.11	$5,070

Best finish for 1996: T-41st at the Bob Hope Chrysler Classic

1997	2	6	1	0	0	0	1	71.33	$10,692

Best finish for 1997: T-23rd at the B.C. Open

1998	21	63	12	0	0	0	1	71.24	$86,496

Best finish for 1998: T-18th at the Deposit Guaranty Golf Classic

1999	32	108	24	0	3	5	10	70.55	$845,051

Best finish for 1999: 2nd at the Las Vegas Invitational

2000	34	112	24	0	3	4	11	70.46	$1,097,131

Best finish for 2000: T-2nd at the SEI Pennsylvania Classic

2001	33	112	26	0	1	1	6	70.60	$683,210

Best finish for 2001: 3rd at the B.C. Open

2002	27	80	15	0	3	4	5	70.98	$1,087,963

Best finish for 2002: T-2nd at the Canon Greater Hartford Open & The Reno-Tahoe Open

2003	27	88	18	1	2	8	9	70.77	$2,478,414

Best finish for 2003: Win at the Buick Classic

2004	25	76	15	1	2	2	6	71.49	$1,707,546

Best finish for 2004: Win at the FBR Open

2005	24	74	16	0	2	3	5	71.14	$1,418,109

Best finish for 2005: 2nd at the Mercedes Championships & The Reno-Tahoe Open

2006	32	92	17	0	1	1	5	71.25	$578,714

Best finish for 2006: T-4th at the Buick Invitational

2008	8	22	3	0	0	0	0	72.41	$41,375

Best finish for 2008: T-44th at the AT&T Classic

Period Totals	Starts	Rounds Played	Cuts Made	Wins	Top-5s	Top-10s	Top-25s	Scoring Average	Money
	293	907	180	2	18	30	63	70.97	$10,231,654

Dan Keefe

Year	Starts	Rounds Played	Cuts Made	Wins	Top-5s	Top-10s	Top-25s	Scoring Average	Money
1963	2	8	2	0	0	1	1	72.63	$1,933

Best finish for 1963: T-8th at the Canadian Open

1964	13	24	0	0	0	0	0	75.08	
1965	5	13	1	0	0	0	0	74.23	

Best finish for 1965: T-67th at the Doral Open

1966	12	37	7	0	0	0	0	74.16	$2,116

Best finish for 1966: 28th at the Lucky International Open Invitational

1967	6	20	3	0	0	0	0	74.00	

Best finish for 1967: T-56th at the San Diego Open

1968	8	20	1	0	0	0	0	74.00	$830

Best finish for 1968: T-38th at the Bing Crosby National Professional-Amateur

1969	6	12	0	0	0	0	0	76.00	
1970	4	11	1	0	0	0	0	74.82	$182

Best finish for 1970: T-62nd at the Tucson Open

1973	1	2	0	0	0	0	0	79.50	
Period Totals	Starts	Rounds Played	Cuts Made	Wins	Top-5s	Top-10s	Top-25s	Scoring Average	Money
	57	147	15	0	0	1	1	74.46	$5,061

Herman Keiser

Year	Starts	Rounds Played	Cuts Made	Wins	Top-5s	Top-10s	Top-25s	Scoring Average	Money
1958	2	6	1	0	0	0	0	74.17	$300

Best finish for 1958: T-54th at the Rubber City Open

1959	1	2	0	0	0	0	0	77.50	$300

Year	Starts	Rounds Played	Cuts Made	Wins	Top-5s	Top-10s	Top-25s	Scoring Average	Money
1960	1	2	0	0	0	0	0	78.00	$350
1961	1	2	0	0	0	0	0	81.00	$400
1962	1	1	0	0	0	0	0	75.00	$400
1963	3	12	3	0	0	1	1	72.33	$2,612

Best finish for 1963: T-9th at the Canadian Open

Year	Starts	Rounds Played	Cuts Made	Wins	Top-5s	Top-10s	Top-25s	Scoring Average	Money
1964	1	2	0	0	0	0	0	77.50	
1965	2	3	0	0	0	0	0	78.67	
1966	3	6	0	0	0	0	0	76.00	$1,000
1967	4	10	1	0	0	0	0	75.50	

Best finish for 1967: T-61st at the American Golf Classic

1968	3	8	1	0	0	0	0	73.88	$1,000

Best finish for 1968: T-64th at the American Golf Classic

1969	4	11	1	0	0	0	0	74.73	$167

Best finish for 1969: T-76th at the American Classic

1970	2	3	0	0	0	0	0	78.00	$1,000
1971	1	1	0	0	0	0	0	81.00	$1,000
1972	1	2	0	0	0	0	0	79.50	$1,000
1974	1	2	0	0	0	0	0	77.50	$1,200

Period Totals	Starts	Rounds Played	Cuts Made	Wins	Top-5s	Top-10s	Top-25s	Scoring Average	Money
	31	73	7	0	0	1	1	75.41	$10,728

PGA Tour career totals from 1934 to 1974

	Starts	Rounds Played	Cuts Made	Wins	Top-5s	Top-10s	Top-25s	Scoring Average	Money
	182	N/A	N/A	5	N/A	68	118	N/A	N/A

Bob Keller

Year	Starts	Rounds Played	Cuts Made	Wins	Top-5s	Top-10s	Top-25s	Scoring Average	Money
1958	14	47	9	0	0	1	4	72.62	$1,509

Best finish for 1958: T-8th at the Kentucky Derby Open

1959	1	4	1	0	0	0	0	73.25	$017

Best finish for 1959: T-31st at the Baton Rouge Open Invitational

1960	2	8	2	0	0	0	1	72.13	$260

Best finish for 1960: T-23rd at the Pensacola Open Invitational

1961	3	10	2	0	0	0	0	72.90	$490

Best finish for 1961: T-29th at the PGA Championship

1962	5	19	4	0	0	0	1	71.58	$914

Best finish for 1962: T-18th at the Pensacola Open Invitational

1963	2	4	1	0	0	0	0	78.75	$150

Best finish for 1963: T-200 at the PGA Championship

1964	3	10	2	0	0	0	0	73.40	$526

Best finish for 1964: T-39th at the PGA Championship

1965	2	6	1	0	0	0	0	75.00	$449

Best finish for 1965: T-33rd at the Pensacola Open

1966	3	8	1	0	0	0	0	74.00	$436

Best finish for 1966: T-49th at the PGA Championship

1967	4	10	1	0	1	1	1	71.80	$9,000

Best finish for 1967: 2nd at the Pensacola Open

1968	2	4	0	0	0	0	0	73.50	
1969	3	10	2	0	0	0	0	73.70	$664

Best finish for 1969: T-34th at the Monsanto Open

1970	3	8	1	0	0	0	0	72.88	$263

Best finish for 1970: T-32nd at the Green Island Open Invitational

1971	1	2	0	0	0	0	0	73.50	
1972	1	2	0	0	0	0	0	75.00	
1973	2	4	0	0	0	0	0	75.75	

Period Totals	Starts	Rounds Played	Cuts Made	Wins	Top-5s	Top-10s	Top-25s	Scoring Average	Money
	51	156	27	0	1	2	7	73.04	$14,679

Al Kelley

Year	Starts	Rounds Played	Cuts Made	Wins	Top-5s	Top-10s	Top-25s	Scoring Average	Money
1962	1	4	1	0	0	0	1	70.25	$490

Best finish for 1962: T-17th at the Coral Gables Open Invitational

1963	10	40	9	0	0	0	3	72.10	$3,061

Best finish for 1963: T-16th at the Portland Open Invitational

1964	33	85	8	0	0	0	1	74.08	$1,465

Best finish for 1964: T-22nd at the San Diego Open

1965	7	16	1	0	0	0	0	74.56	

Best finish for 1965: T-36th at the Cajun Classic

1966	10	32	5	0	0	0	0	74.09	$711

Best finish for 1966: T-35th at the Los Angeles Open Invitational

1967	18	42	3	0	0	0	0	94.14	

Best finish for 1967: T-62nd at the Byron Nelson Dallas Open

Year	Starts	Rounds Played	Cuts Made	Wins	Top-5s	Top-10s	Top-25s	Scoring Average	Money
1968	5	11	0	0	0	0	0	75.82	
1969	3	6	0	0	0	0	0	74.50	
1970	2	6	1	0	0	0	0	75.00	$250

Best finish for 1970: T-52nd at the Doral-Eastern Open

1971	6	16	2	0	0	0	0	74.25	$472

Best finish for 1971: T-55th at the PGA Championship

1972	4	8	0	0	0	0	0	74.75	
1973	4	8	0	0	0	0	0	75.13	
1974	2	4	0	0	0	0	0	73.50	
1975	4	10	1	0	0	0	0	75.10	

Best finish for 1975: 72nd at the Jackie Gleason's Inverrary Classic

1976	2	4	0	0	0	0	0	74.25	
1977	1	2	0	0	0	0	0	74.50	
1978	2	6	1	0	0	0	1	72.67	$1,465

Best finish for 1978: T-18th at the Tallahassee Open

1981	1	0	0	0	0	0	0		
1983	1	2	0	0	0	0	0	78.50	
1984	1	2	0	0	0	0	0	74.50	
1985	1	2	0	0	0	0	0	76.00	
Period Totals	Starts	Rounds Played	Cuts Made	Wins	Top-5s	Top-10s	Top-25s	Scoring Average	Money
	118	306	32	0	0	0	6	76.74	$7,914

Ken Kelley

Year	Starts	Rounds Played	Cuts Made	Wins	Top-5s	Top-10s	Top-25s	Scoring Average	Money
1983	20	42	1	0	0	0	0	75.52	$1,590

Best finish for 1983: T-29th at the Southern Open

1984	21	50	3	0	0	0	0	75.04	$2,950

Best finish for 1984: T-38th at the B.C. Open

1999	2	4	0	0	0	0	0	75.50	
2004	1	2	0	0	0	0	0	77.50	
Period Totals	Starts	Rounds Played	Cuts Made	Wins	Top-5s	Top-10s	Top-25s	Scoring Average	Money
	44	98	4	0	0	0	0	75.32	$4,540

Spike Kelley

Year	Starts	Rounds Played	Cuts Made	Wins	Top-5s	Top-10s	Top-25s	Scoring Average	Money
1973	2	8	1	0	0	0	0	76.13	$112

Best finish for 1973: T-70th at the Walt Disney World Open

1974	21	60	9	0	0	0	1	73.32	$3,984

Best finish for 1974: T-25th at the B.C. Open

1975	17	43	4	0	1	1	1	73.98	$6,461

Best finish for 1975: T-2nd at the Tallahassee Open

1976	13	30	3	0	0	0	0	73.60	$2,019

Best finish for 1976: T-27th at the Florida Citrus Open Invitational

1977	3	6	0	0	0	0	0	76.50	
1978	3	6	0	0	0	0	0	74.83	
Period Totals	Starts	Rounds Played	Cuts Made	Wins	Top-5s	Top-10s	Top-25s	Scoring Average	Money
	59	153	17	0	1	1	2	73.89	$12,576

Jerry Kelly

Year	Starts	Rounds Played	Cuts Made	Wins	Top-5s	Top-10s	Top-25s	Scoring Average	Money
1991	1	2	0	0	0	0	0	73.00	
1992	1	2	0	0	0	0	0	73.00	
1993	2	5	0	0	0	0	0	74.00	
1995	2	6	1	0	0	0	0	71.67	$4,733

Best finish for 1995: T-34th at the Greater Milwaukee Open

1996	31	91	17	0	2	4	5	71.42	$336,748

Best finish for 1996: 2nd at the Greater Milwaukee Open

1997	34	92	13	0	0	3	7	71.90	$235,557

Best finish for 1997: T-6th at the Shell Houston Open

1998	31	93	16	0	0	2	8	71.71	$335,744

Best finish for 1998: T-6th at the Shell Houston Open

1999	34	108	22	0	1	2	8	71.28	$533,702

Best finish for 1999: 3rd at the Greater Milwaukee Open

2000	32	111	23	0	2	3	12	70.69	$786,754

Best finish for 2000: T-4th at the AT&T Pebble Beach National Pro-Am

2001	31	101	21	0	4	7	11	70.34	$1,494,037

Best finish for 2001: 2nd at the Reno-Tahoe Open

2002	29	98	21	2	5	8	14	70.41	$2,949,889

Best finish for 2002: Win at the Sony Open in Hawaii & Advil Western Open

2003	30	104	23	0	4	10	16	70.46	$2,164,521

Best finish for 2003: T-3rd at the 100th Western Open

2004	29	109	27	0	5	8	15	70.23	$2,498,222

Best finish for 2004: 3rd at The Tour Championship

Year	Starts	Rounds Played	Cuts Made	Wins	Top-5s	Top-10s	Top-25s	Scoring Average	Money
2005	31	99	21	0	2	4	11	70.99	$1,356,867

Best finish for 2005: T-4th at the Buick Championship

| 2006 | 31 | 100 | 18 | 0 | 3 | 5 | 8 | 70.80 | $1,737,800 |

Best finish for 2006: 2nd at the Chrysler Classic of Tucson & U.S. Bank Championship in Milwaukee

| 2007 | 28 | 101 | 21 | 0 | 2 | 7 | 10 | 71.08 | $1,980,534 |

Best finish for 2007: T-3rd at the EDS Byron Nelson Championship

| 2008 | 31 | 88 | 15 | 0 | 3 | 4 | 8 | 71.49 | $1,652,400 |

Best finish for 2008: T-2nd at the Puerto Rico Open & Memorial Tournament

Period Totals	Starts	Rounds Played	Cuts Made	Wins	Top-5s	Top-10s	Top-25s	Scoring Average	Money
	408	1310	259	2	33	67	133	70.98	$18,067,509

Skip Kendall

Year	Starts	Rounds Played	Cuts Made	Wins	Top-5s	Top-10s	Top-25s	Scoring Average	Money
1987	1	2	0	0	0	0	0	77.00	
1988	1	2	0	0	0	0	0	76.00	
1990	1	4	1	0	0	0	0	70.50	$2,118

Best finish for 1990: T-51st at the Greater Milwaukee Open

1991	1	2	0	0	0	0	0	73.50	
1992	1	2	0	0	0	0	0	76.00	$1,000
1993	32	97	18	0	0	1	3	72.15	$115,189

Best finish for 1993: 8th at the International

| 1994 | 4 | 12 | 2 | 0 | 0 | 0 | 0 | 71.83 | $8,392 |

Best finish for 1994: T-32nd at the United Airlines Hawaiian Open

| 1995 | 31 | 96 | 18 | 0 | 0 | 1 | 1 | 71.47 | $93,606 |

Best finish for 1995: T-7th at the B.C. Open

| 1996 | 2 | 6 | 1 | 0 | 0 | 0 | 0 | 73.33 | $5,415 |

Best finish for 1996: T-82nd at the U.S. Open

| 1997 | 31 | 102 | 22 | 0 | 1 | 2 | 7 | 70.94 | $320,800 |

Best finish for 1997: 3rd at the Sprint International

| 1998 | 30 | 104 | 22 | 0 | 2 | 5 | 13 | 70.47 | $797,715 |

Best finish for 1998: 2nd at the Buick Invitational

| 1999 | 31 | 105 | 24 | 0 | 1 | 4 | 13 | 70.83 | $962,642 |

Best finish for 1999: 2nd at the Canon Greater Hartford Open

| 2000 | 32 | 112 | 24 | 0 | 2 | 3 | 7 | 70.63 | $947,118 |

Best finish for 2000: 2nd at the Southern Farm Bureau Classic

| 2001 | 33 | 108 | 23 | 0 | 0 | 1 | 12 | 70.40 | $754,701 |

Best finish for 2001: T-6th at the National Car Rental Golf Classic/Disney

| 2002 | 31 | 101 | 20 | 0 | 0 | 2 | 8 | 70.78 | $655,594 |

Best finish for 2002: T-7th at the Canon Greater Hartford Open

| 2003 | 30 | 110 | 24 | 0 | 1 | 2 | 12 | 70.48 | $1,024,244 |

Best finish for 2003: T-4th at the Buick Classic

| 2004 | 29 | 99 | 20 | 0 | 2 | 2 | 7 | 71.12 | $1,206,438 |

Best finish for 2004: 2nd at the Bob Hope Chrysler Classic

| 2005 | 32 | 78 | 7 | 0 | 0 | 0 | 1 | 71.96 | $180,561 |

Best finish for 2005: T-14th at the EDS Byron Nelson Championship

| 2006 | 22 | 72 | 14 | 0 | 0 | 1 | 5 | 71.10 | $439,934 |

Best finish for 2006: T-9th at the Buick Championship

| 2007 | 5 | 15 | 2 | 0 | 0 | 1 | 1 | 71.27 | $116,346 |

Best finish for 2007: T-9th at the Mayakoba Golf Classic

| 2008 | 6 | 15 | 1 | 0 | 0 | 0 | 0 | 72.93 | $7,910 |

Best finish for 2008: T-54th at the Puerto Rico Open

Period Totals	Starts	Rounds Played	Cuts Made	Wins	Top-5s	Top-10s	Top-25s	Scoring Average	Money
	386	1244	243	0	9	25	90	71.06	$7,639,723

Bill Kennedy

Year	Starts	Rounds Played	Cuts Made	Wins	Top-5s	Top-10s	Top-25s	Scoring Average	Money
1962	1	4	1	0	0	0	0	71.75	$212

Best finish for 1962: T-34th at the Carling Open Invitational

| 1964 | 5 | 8 | 0 | 0 | 0 | 0 | 0 | 75.13 | |
| 1970 | 4 | 10 | 2 | 0 | 0 | 0 | 0 | 73.70 | $503 |

Best finish for 1970: T-46th at the Doral-Eastern Open

| 1971 | 3 | 8 | 1 | 0 | 0 | 0 | 0 | 74.75 | $214 |

Best finish for 1971: T-63rd at the Doral-Eastern Open

| 1972 | 4 | 8 | 1 | 0 | 0 | 0 | 0 | 74.63 | $188 |

Best finish for 1972: T-68th at the Doral-Eastern Open

1973	4	8	0	0	0	0	0	75.75	
1974	1	2	0	0	0	0	0	76.00	
1975	3	6	0	0	0	0	0	75.83	
1976	1	2	0	0	0	0	0	73.50	
1977	1	2	0	0	0	0	0	80.00	
1995	1	2	0	0	0	0	0	77.50	

Period Totals	Starts	Rounds Played	Cuts Made	Wins	Top-5s	Top-10s	Top-25s	Scoring Average	Money
	28	60	5	0	0	0	0	74.92	$1,116

John Kennedy

Year	Starts	Rounds Played	Cuts Made	Wins	Top-5s	Top-10s	Top-25s	Scoring Average	Money
1969	14	41	7	0	0	0	1	73.12	$1,951

Best finish for 1969: T-14th at the Indian Ridge Hospital Open

1970	12	29	3	0	0	0	0	73.69	$936

Best finish for 1970: T-42nd at the Kemper Open

1971	11	34	6	0	0	0	0	73.35	$1,756

Best finish for 1971: T-54th at the IVB Philadelphia Golf Classic

1972	9	21	1	0	0	0	0	76.00	$227

Best finish for 1972: T-68th at the Houston Open

1973	4	14	3	0	0	0	0	72.50	$790

Best finish for 1973: T-57th at the Quad Cities Open

1974	5	14	2	0	0	0	0	75.86	$656

Best finish for 1974: T-60th at the Western Open

1975	2	4	0	0	0	0	0	75.25	
1977	1	2	0	0	0	0	0	74.00	
Period Totals	Starts	Rounds Played	Cuts Made	Wins	Top-5s	Top-10s	Top-25s	Scoring Average	Money
	58	159	22	0	0	0	1	73.91	$6,317

Roger Kennedy

Year	Starts	Rounds Played	Cuts Made	Wins	Top-5s	Top-10s	Top-25s	Scoring Average	Money
1973	1	2	0	0	0	0	0	75.50	
1974	2	4	0	0	0	0	0	76.50	
1976	1	2	0	0	0	0	0	73.50	
1977	2	4	0	0	0	0	0	78.50	
1978	1	2	0	0	0	0	0	73.50	
1979	3	6	0	0	0	0	0	78.33	
1980	3	8	1	0	0	0	0	76.75	$1,020

Best finish for 1980: 66th at the Doral-Eastern Open

1981	1	2	0	0	0	0	0	79.50	$550
1982	2	4	0	0	0	0	0	75.75	$650
1983	2	4	0	0	0	0	0	76.00	
1984	1	2	0	0	0	0	0	77.50	
1985	2	4	0	0	0	0	0	75.75	
1986	1	2	0	0	0	0	0	78.00	
1989	1	2	0	0	0	0	0	77.00	
1990	1	2	0	0	0	0	0	74.00	
1994	1	2	0	0	0	0	0	74.00	
Period Totals	Starts	Rounds Played	Cuts Made	Wins	Top-5s	Top-10s	Top-25s	Scoring Average	Money
	25	52	1	0	0	0	0	76.52	$2,220

Ben Kern

Year	Starts	Rounds Played	Cuts Made	Wins	Top-5s	Top-10s	Top-25s	Scoring Average	Money
1968	1	4	1	0	0	0	0	77.25	

Best finish for 1968: 73rd at the Houston Champions International

1969	1	2	0	0	0	0	0	78.50	
1970	16	42	5	0	0	0	0	73.60	$1,055

Best finish for 1970: T-41st at the Cleveland Open

1971	19	50	6	0	0	0	0	73.46	$2,439

Best finish for 1971: T-26th at the Andy Williams-San Diego Open

1972	27	66	7	0	1	1	1	73.33	$7,377

Best finish for 1972: T-4th at the San Antonio Texas Open

1973	33	106	18	0	0	1	4	72.59	$13,653

Best finish for 1973: T-10th at the Sahara Invitational

1974	30	90	15	0	0	0	3	73.14	$10,066

Best finish for 1974: T-15th at the Greater Jacksonville Open

1975	21	56	8	0	0	0	0	74.34	$3,242

Best finish for 1975: T-42nd at the Phoenix Open

1980	1	2	0	0	0	0	0	81.50	
Period Totals	Starts	Rounds Played	Cuts Made	Wins	Top-5s	Top-10s	Top-25s	Scoring Average	Money
	149	418	60	0	1	2	8	73.38	$37,833

Darrell Kestner

Year	Starts	Rounds Played	Cuts Made	Wins	Top-5s	Top-10s	Top-25s	Scoring Average	Money
1979	1	2	0	0	0	0	0	82.50	$600
1981	9	18	1	0	0	0	0	74.17	$649

Best finish for 1981: T-30th at the Tallahassee Open

1982	1	2	0	0	0	0	0	73.00	
1983	26	70	7	0	0	0	0	74.29	$4,759

Best finish for 1983: T-56th at the Kemper Open

1987	1	2	0	0	0	0	0	75.00	$600

Year	Starts	Rounds Played	Cuts Made	Wins	Top-5s	Top-10s	Top-25s	Scoring Average	Money
1988	3	6	0	0	0	0	0	78.00	$2,000
1989	1	4	1	0	0	0	0	74.75	$2,030

Best finish for 1989: T-68th at the Manufactures Hanover Westchester Classic

Year	Starts	Rounds Played	Cuts Made	Wins	Top-5s	Top-10s	Top-25s	Scoring Average	Money
1991	2	4	0	0	0	0	0	78.25	$2,000
1993	1	2	1	0	0	0	0	72.50	$1,200
1994	1	2	0	0	0	0	0	73.50	$1,200
1995	3	6	0	0	0	0	0	73.83	$2,200
1996	2	4	0	0	0	0	0	74.75	$1,000
1997	6	15	2	0	0	0	0	74.27	$19,880

Best finish for 1997: 43rd at the NEC World Series of Golf

Year	Starts	Rounds Played	Cuts Made	Wins	Top-5s	Top-10s	Top-25s	Scoring Average	Money
1998	1	3	1	0	0	0	0	71.67	$4,623

Best finish for 1998: T-47th at the Buick Classic

Year	Starts	Rounds Played	Cuts Made	Wins	Top-5s	Top-10s	Top-25s	Scoring Average	Money
1999	1	2	0	0	0	0	0	77.50	$1,750
2000	2	4	0	0	0	0	0	76.00	$1,000
2001	1	2	0	0	0	0	0	75.00	$2,000
2002	1	2	0	0	0	0	0	81.50	$1,000
2004	1	2	0	0	0	0	0	73.50	
2005	1	4	1	0	0	0	0	74.75	$11,700

Best finish for 2005: 78th at the PGA Championship

Year	Starts	Rounds Played	Cuts Made	Wins	Top-5s	Top-10s	Top-25s	Scoring Average	Money
2006	1	2	0	0	0	0	0	75.00	
Period Totals	Starts	Rounds Played	Cuts Made	Wins	Top-5s	Top-10s	Top-25s	Scoring Average	Money
	66	158	14	0	0	0	0	74.73	$60,191

Richard Killian

Year	Starts	Rounds Played	Cuts Made	Wins	Top-5s	Top-10s	Top-25s	Scoring Average	Money
1965	1	2	0	0	0	0	0	72.50	
1966	12	30	3	0	0	0	0	74.93	

Best finish for 1966: T-70th at the Oklahoma City Open Invitational

Year	Starts	Rounds Played	Cuts Made	Wins	Top-5s	Top-10s	Top-25s	Scoring Average	Money
1972	4	8	0	0	0	0	0	74.00	
1973	3	6	0	0	0	0	0	76.33	
1974	1	2	0	0	0	0	0	78.50	
1975	1	2	0	0	0	0	0	77.50	
1976	1	2	0	0	0	0	0	77.50	
1977	1	2	0	0	0	0	0	77.00	
1979	1	1	0	0	0	0	0	83.00	
Period Totals	Starts	Rounds Played	Cuts Made	Wins	Top-5s	Top-10s	Top-25s	Scoring Average	Money
	25	55	3	0	0	0	0	75.40	

Anthony Kim

Year	Starts	Rounds Played	Cuts Made	Wins	Top-5s	Top-10s	Top-25s	Scoring Average	Money
2006	2	8	2	0	1	1	2	68.63	$338,067

Best finish for 2006: T-2nd at the Valero Texas Open

Year	Starts	Rounds Played	Cuts Made	Wins	Top-5s	Top-10s	Top-25s	Scoring Average	Money
2007	26	93	20	0	3	4	10	70.69	$1,545,195

Best finish for 2007: T-3rd at the Zurich Classic of New Orleans

Year	Starts	Rounds Played	Cuts Made	Wins	Top-5s	Top-10s	Top-25s	Scoring Average	Money
2008	22	81	19	2	6	8	10	70.22	$4,656,265

Best finish for 2008: Win at the Wachovia Championship & AT&T National

Period Totals	Starts	Rounds Played	Cuts Made	Wins	Top-5s	Top-10s	Top-25s	Scoring Average	Money
	50	182	41	2	10	13	22	70.39	$6,539,527

Karl Kimball

Year	Starts	Rounds Played	Cuts Made	Wins	Top-5s	Top-10s	Top-25s	Scoring Average	Money
1985	1	2	0	0	0	0	0	78.50	
1986	1	1	0	0	0	0	0	76.00	
1989	23	52	3	0	0	0	0	72.62	$3,745

Best finish for 1989: T-47th at the Deposit Guaranty Golf Classic

Year	Starts	Rounds Played	Cuts Made	Wins	Top-5s	Top-10s	Top-25s	Scoring Average	Money
1991	25	69	9	0	0	0	0	72.14	$19,703

Best finish for 1991: T-30th at the Deposit Guaranty Classic

Year	Starts	Rounds Played	Cuts Made	Wins	Top-5s	Top-10s	Top-25s	Scoring Average	Money
1998	1	2	0	0	0	0	0	77.50	$1,500
2000	1	2	0	0	0	0	0	76.00	$2,000
Period Totals	Starts	Rounds Played	Cuts Made	Wins	Top-5s	Top-10s	Top-25s	Scoring Average	Money
	52	128	12	0	0	0	0	72.61	$26,948

Claude King

Year	Starts	Rounds Played	Cuts Made	Wins	Top-5s	Top-10s	Top-25s	Scoring Average	Money
1958	1	4	1	0	0	0	0	77.50	

Best finish for 1958: T-56th at the Azalea Open

Year	Starts	Rounds Played	Cuts Made	Wins	Top-5s	Top-10s	Top-25s	Scoring Average	Money
1962	6	21	5	0	0	0	3	72.29	$1,129

Best finish for 1962: T-15th at the Mobile Sertoma Open Invitational

Year	Starts	Rounds Played	Cuts Made	Wins	Top-5s	Top-10s	Top-25s	Scoring Average	Money
1963	14	56	14	0	0	0	6	71.63	$7,497

Best finish for 1963: T-11th at the St. Paul Open Invitational & Sahara Invitational

Year	Starts	Rounds Played	Cuts Made	Wins	Top-5s	Top-10s	Top-25s	Scoring Average	Money
1964	29	94	17	0	1	1	2	72.80	$4,317

Best finish for 1964: T-5th at the Sunset-Camellia Open

| 1965 | 31 | 106 | 20 | 0 | 0 | 4 | 7 | 72.70 | $15,351 |

Best finish for 1965: T-7th at the Houston Classic

| 1966 | 20 | 62 | 11 | 0 | 0 | 0 | 2 | 73.47 | $5,510 |

Best finish for 1966: T-13th at the Philadelphia Golf Classic

| 1967 | 1 | 2 | 0 | 0 | 0 | 0 | 0 | 75.50 | |
| 1968 | 2 | 5 | 1 | 0 | 0 | 1 | 1 | 71.60 | $1,500 |

Best finish for 1968: T-6th at the AZALEA Open Invitational

| 1969 | 1 | 4 | 1 | 0 | 0 | 0 | 0 | 72.75 | |

Best finish for 1969: T-50th at the Azalea Open

| 1970 | 1 | 2 | 0 | 0 | 0 | 0 | 0 | 77.00 | |
| 1972 | 1 | 2 | 0 | 0 | 0 | 0 | 0 | 77.50 | |

Period Totals	Starts	Rounds Played	Cuts Made	Wins	Top-5s	Top-10s	Top-25s	Scoring Average	Money
	107	358	70	0	1	6	21	72.77	$35,305

Jim King

Year	Starts	Rounds Played	Cuts Made	Wins	Top-5s	Top-10s	Top-25s	Scoring Average	Money
1960	1	3	1	0	0	0	0	80.67	$042

Best finish for 1960: T-132 at the Bing Crosby National

| 1962 | 1 | 4 | 1 | 0 | 0 | 0 | 0 | 72.00 | $274 |

Best finish for 1962: T-28th at the Phoenix Open Invitational

| 1968 | 16 | 51 | 10 | 0 | 0 | 0 | 1 | 73.16 | $315 |

Best finish for 1968: T-21st at the Robinson Open

| 1969 | 16 | 34 | 2 | 0 | 0 | 0 | 0 | 74.44 | $340 |

Best finish for 1969: T-55th at the Western Open

| 1970 | 11 | 25 | 2 | 0 | 0 | 0 | 0 | 74.28 | $378 |

Best finish for 1970: 60th at the Bahama Islands Open

| 1971 | 11 | 28 | 3 | 0 | 0 | 0 | 1 | 72.93 | $1,660 |

Best finish for 1971: T-21st at the Greater Milwaukee Open

| 1972 | 6 | 12 | 1 | 0 | 0 | 0 | 0 | 73.75 | $167 |

Best finish for 1972: T-62nd at the Robinson's Fall Golf Classic

| 1973 | 16 | 37 | 5 | 0 | 0 | 0 | 0 | 73.78 | $1,557 |

Best finish for 1973: T-35th at the B.C. Open

| 1974 | 1 | 2 | 0 | 0 | 0 | 0 | 0 | 77.50 | |
| 1975 | 10 | 24 | 2 | 0 | 0 | 0 | 0 | 73.54 | $370 |

Best finish for 1975: T-56th at the Southern Open

1976	3	6	0	0	0	0	0	76.00	
1977	4	8	0	0	0	0	0	74.63	$500
1978	8	20	2	0	0	0	0	75.60	$528

Best finish for 1978: T-62nd at the Pensacola Open

| 1979 | 3 | 8 | 1 | 0 | 0 | 0 | 1 | 73.75 | $5,775 |

Best finish for 1979: T-11th at the Jackie Gleason's Inverrary Classic

| 1981 | 2 | 6 | 1 | 0 | 0 | 0 | 0 | 72.67 | $1,444 |

Best finish for 1981: T-36th at the American Motors Inverrary Classic

| 1982 | 10 | 24 | 2 | 0 | 0 | 0 | 0 | 74.67 | $2,354 |

Best finish for 1982: T-62nd at the U.S. Open

| 1983 | 3 | 8 | 1 | 0 | 0 | 0 | 0 | 75.88 | $1,500 |

Best finish for 1983: 87th at the PGA Championship

1984	1	2	0	0	0	0	0	77.50	$1,000
1985	1	2	0	0	0	0	0	72.50	
1986	1	2	0	0	0	0	0	78.00	
1990	2	4	0	0	0	0	0	77.50	

Period Totals	Starts	Rounds Played	Cuts Made	Wins	Top-5s	Top-10s	Top-25s	Scoring Average	Money
	127	310	34	0	0	0	3	74.14	$18,204

Eddie Kirby

Year	Starts	Rounds Played	Cuts Made	Wins	Top-5s	Top-10s	Top-25s	Scoring Average	Money
1984	1	2	0	0	0	0	0	79.00	
1985	1	2	0	0	0	0	0	78.50	
1987	1	4	1	0	0	0	0	73.25	$3,178

Best finish for 1987: T-58th at the U.S. Open

| 1988 | 1 | 2 | 0 | 0 | 0 | 0 | 0 | 72.00 | |
| 1989 | 3 | 8 | 1 | 0 | 0 | 0 | 0 | 73.38 | $7,577 |

Best finish for 1989: T-33rd at the U.S. Open

| 1992 | 1 | 2 | 0 | 0 | 0 | 0 | 0 | 73.00 | |
| 1993 | 2 | 6 | 1 | 0 | 0 | 0 | 0 | 71.50 | $6,526 |

Best finish for 1993: T-52nd at the U.S. Open

| 1994 | 18 | 52 | 8 | 0 | 0 | 0 | 1 | 72.40 | $26,744 |

Best finish for 1994: T-22nd at the B.C. Open

Period Totals	Starts	Rounds Played	Cuts Made	Wins	Top-5s	Top-10s	Top-25s	Scoring Average	Money
	28	78	11	0	0	0	1	72.81	$44,024

Joe Kirkwood, Jr.

Year	Starts	Rounds Played	Cuts Made	Wins	Top-5s	Top-10s	Top-25s	Scoring Average	Money
1958	3	8	1	0	0	0	0	74.63	$041

Best finish for 1958: T-28th at the Mayfair Inn Open

| 1959 | 5 | 18 | 5 | 0 | 0 | 1 | 2 | 72.39 | $893 |

Best finish for 1959: T-9th at the Hesperia Open Invitational

| 1960 | 3 | 10 | 3 | 0 | 0 | 0 | 2 | 72.30 | $663 |

Best finish for 1960: T-13th at the Orange County Open Invitational

| 1961 | 1 | 4 | 1 | 0 | 0 | 0 | 1 | 70.75 | $307 |

Best finish for 1961: T-20th at the Hot Springs Open Invitational

| 1964 | 4 | 7 | 0 | 0 | 0 | 0 | 0 | 75.00 | |
| 1965 | 9 | 26 | 3 | 0 | 0 | 0 | 1 | 74.35 | $778 |

Best finish for 1965: T-21st at the Greater Hartford Open

| 1968 | 3 | 7 | 1 | 0 | 0 | 0 | 0 | 73.57 | |

Best finish for 1968: T-41st at the Rebel Yell Open

| 1970 | 3 | 5 | 0 | 0 | 0 | 0 | 0 | 79.60 | |
| 1971 | 2 | 6 | 1 | 0 | 0 | 0 | 0 | 73.67 | $594 |

Best finish for 1971: T-33rd at the Tucson Open

1972	2	4	0	0	0	0	0	77.25	
1973	2	1	0	0	0	0	0	77.00	
Period Totals	Starts	Rounds Played	Cuts Made	Wins	Top-5s	Top-10s	Top-25s	Scoring Average	Money
	37	96	15	0	0	1	6	74.01	$3,276

PGA Tour career totals from 1941 to 1973

	Starts	Rounds Played	Cuts Made	Wins	Top-5s	Top-10s	Top-25s	Scoring Average	Money
	114	N/A	N/A	2	N/A	13	55	N/A	N/A

Chris Kite

Year	Starts	Rounds Played	Cuts Made	Wins	Top-5s	Top-10s	Top-25s	Scoring Average	Money
1987	6	10	0	0	0	0	0	75.80	
1988	4	14	3	0	0	0	2	70.36	$23,252

Best finish for 1988: T-11th at the Anheuser-Busch Golf Classic

| 1989 | 6 | 13 | 1 | 0 | 0 | 0 | 1 | 72.15 | $2,080 |

Best finish for 1989: T-21st at the Deposit Guaranty Golf Classic

| 1994 | 19 | 46 | 5 | 0 | 0 | 0 | 0 | 73.09 | $13,983 |

Best finish for 1994: T-35th at the Freeport-McMoRan Classic

| Period Totals | Starts | Rounds Played | Cuts Made | Wins | Top-5s | Top-10s | Top-25s | Scoring Average | Money |
| | 35 | 83 | 9 | 0 | 0 | 0 | 3 | 72.81 | $39,315 |

Tom Kite

Year	Starts	Rounds Played	Cuts Made	Wins	Top-5s	Top-10s	Top-25s	Scoring Average	Money
1970	1	2	0	0	0	0	0	79.00	
1971	1	4	1	0	0	0	0	75.00	

Best finish for 1971: T-42nd at the Masters

| 1972 | 7 | 28 | 7 | 0 | 0 | 0 | 2 | 72.75 | $2,418 |

Best finish for 1972: T-19th at the U.S. Open

| 1973 | 34 | 135 | 31 | 0 | 1 | 2 | 15 | 71.58 | $51,219 |

Best finish for 1973: 5th at the Ohio Kings Island Open

| 1974 | 27 | 106 | 26 | 0 | 1 | 7 | 17 | 71.29 | $71,913 |

Best finish for 1974: 4th at the Sea Pines Heritage Classic

| 1975 | 26 | 92 | 21 | 0 | 6 | 9 | 14 | 71.43 | $87,546 |

Best finish for 1975: 2nd at the Glen CampbellLos Angeles Open

| 1976 | 28 | 107 | 26 | 1 | 4 | 9 | 16 | 71.17 | $121,757 |

Best finish for 1976: Win at the IVB - Bicentennial Golf Classic

| 1977 | 29 | 113 | 27 | 0 | 5 | 7 | 16 | 71.08 | $125,204 |

Best finish for 1977: 2nd at the Ohio Kings Island Open

| 1978 | 29 | 111 | 26 | 1 | 7 | 9 | 16 | 71.17 | $175,567 |

Best finish for 1978: Win at the B.C. Open

| 1979 | 29 | 109 | 25 | 0 | 6 | 11 | 15 | 71.46 | $168,974 |

Best finish for 1979: T-3rd at the Phoenix Open, Sea Pines Heritage Classic & Danny Thomas Memphis Classic

| 1980 | 28 | 100 | 24 | 0 | 5 | 10 | 19 | 71.00 | $158,450 |

Best finish for 1980: 2nd at the IVB Golf Classic

| 1981 | 26 | 103 | 26 | 1 | 10 | 21 | 24 | 69.80 | $375,699 |

Best finish for 1981: Win at the American Motors Inverrary Classic

| 1982 | 26 | 102 | 24 | 1 | 10 | 15 | 17 | 70.38 | $341,761 |

Best finish for 1982: Win at the Bay Hill Classic

| 1983 | 26 | 97 | 22 | 1 | 5 | 8 | 16 | 71.05 | $259,263 |

Best finish for 1983: Win at the Bing Crosby Pro-Am

| 1984 | 26 | 95 | 22 | 2 | 5 | 10 | 15 | 70.86 | $354,245 |

Best finish for 1984: Win at the Doral-Eastern Open & Georgia-Pacific Atlanta Golf Classic

| 1985 | 25 | 91 | 22 | 1 | 3 | 7 | 12 | 71.02 | $282,864 |

Best finish for 1985: Win at the MONY Tournament Of Champions

Year	Starts	Rounds Played	Cuts Made	Wins	Top-5s	Top-10s	Top-25s	Scoring Average	Money
1986	27	94	24	1	4	9	13	71.10	$394,764

Best finish for 1986: Win at the Western Open

| 1987 | 26 | 94 | 22 | 1 | 3 | 11 | 18 | 70.60 | $528,076 |

Best finish for 1987: Win at the Kemper Open

| 1988 | 27 | 90 | 22 | 0 | 7 | 10 | 17 | 70.18 | $772,304 |

Best finish for 1988: T-2nd at the Hertz Bay Hill Classic, Kemper Open & Nabisco Golf Championship

| 1989 | 25 | 93 | 24 | 3 | 5 | 10 | 15 | 70.43 | $1,408,999 |

Best finish for 1989: Win at the Nestle Invitational, The Players Championship & Nabisco Championships

| 1990 | 24 | 88 | 21 | 1 | 6 | 9 | 15 | 70.82 | $659,198 |

Best finish for 1990: Win at the Federal Express St. Jude Classic

| 1991 | 26 | 93 | 20 | 1 | 3 | 4 | 9 | 70.74 | $404,585 |

Best finish for 1991: Win at the Infiniti Tournament Of Champions

| 1992 | 24 | 95 | 23 | 2 | 4 | 9 | 18 | 70.06 | $979,578 |

Best finish for 1992: Win at the BellSouth Classic & U.S. Open

| 1993 | 21 | 72 | 15 | 2 | 4 | 8 | 11 | 70.10 | $913,741 |

Best finish for 1993: Win at the Bob Hope Chrysler Classic & Nissan Los Angeles Open

| 1994 | 24 | 82 | 19 | 0 | 4 | 9 | 13 | 70.61 | $707,289 |

Best finish for 1994: T-2nd at the Shell Houston Open

| 1995 | 25 | 87 | 21 | 0 | 0 | 1 | 4 | 71.23 | $180,080 |

Best finish for 1995: T-6th at the Northern Telecom Open

| 1996 | 21 | 69 | 15 | 0 | 1 | 1 | 5 | 71.32 | $322,126 |

Best finish for 1996: 2nd at the Canon Greater Hartford Open

| 1997 | 22 | 74 | 15 | 0 | 3 | 5 | 8 | 71.34 | $631,252 |

Best finish for 1997: 2nd at the Masters

| 1998 | 22 | 66 | 12 | 0 | 0 | 0 | 3 | 72.36 | $162,795 |

Best finish for 1998: T-22nd at the Buick Invitational

| 1999 | 21 | 58 | 7 | 0 | 0 | 0 | 1 | 72.67 | $87,380 |

Best finish for 1999: T-17th at the Canon Greater Hartford Open

| 2000 | 6 | 25 | 6 | 0 | 0 | 0 | 1 | 72.00 | $121,605 |

Best finish for 2000: T-19th at the PGA Championship

| 2001 | 5 | 16 | 3 | 0 | 1 | 1 | 1 | 71.50 | $213,252 |

Best finish for 2001: T-5th at the U.S. Open

| 2002 | 5 | 14 | 2 | 0 | 0 | 0 | 1 | 72.64 | $60,350 |

Best finish for 2002: T-25th at the Valero Texas Open

| 2003 | 1 | 2 | 0 | 0 | 0 | 0 | 0 | 74.00 | $1,000 |
| 2004 | 1 | 4 | 1 | 0 | 0 | 0 | 0 | 75.50 | $17,304 |

Best finish for 2004: T-57th at the U.S. Open

| 2005 | 12 | 31 | 3 | 0 | 0 | 0 | 1 | 72.77 | $103,429 |

Best finish for 2005: T-13th at the Booz Allen Classic

2006	1	2	0	0	0	0	0	74.50	
2008	1	2	0	0	0	0	0	75.50	
Period Totals	Starts	Rounds Played	Cuts Made	Wins	Top-5s	Top-10s	Top-25s	Scoring Average	Money
	735	2646	605	19	113	212	368	71.06	$11,245,988

Jeff Klein

Year	Starts	Rounds Played	Cuts Made	Wins	Top-5s	Top-10s	Top-25s	Scoring Average	Money
1983	1	2	0	0	0	0	0	78.50	$600
1989	1	2	0	0	0	0	0	71.00	
1990	2	6	1	0	0	0	0	71.17	$1,608

Best finish for 1990: T-70th at the H-E-B Texas Open

| 1991 | 2 | 4 | 0 | 0 | 0 | 0 | 0 | 71.75 | |
| 2003 | 25 | 58 | 4 | 0 | 0 | 0 | 0 | 73.40 | $40,680 |

Best finish for 2003: T-31st at the Chrysler Classic of Tucson

| Period Totals | Starts | Rounds Played | Cuts Made | Wins | Top-5s | Top-10s | Top-25s | Scoring Average | Money |
| | 31 | 72 | 5 | 0 | 0 | 0 | 0 | 73.19 | $42,888 |

Harold Kneece

Year	Starts	Rounds Played	Cuts Made	Wins	Top-5s	Top-10s	Top-25s	Scoring Average	Money
1960	4	16	4	0	0	0	1	72.25	$922

Best finish for 1960: T-15th at the Mobile Sertoma Open Invitational

| 1961 | 4 | 16 | 4 | 0 | 1 | 1 | 2 | 71.13 | $2,943 |

Best finish for 1961: T-3rd at the Eastern Open Invitational

| 1962 | 7 | 26 | 7 | 0 | 0 | 3 | 4 | 72.35 | $4,612 |

Best finish for 1962: T-8th at the Lucky International Open, Western Open Championship & Mobile Sertoma Open Invitational

| 1963 | 23 | 93 | 23 | 0 | 2 | 6 | 15 | 71.31 | $19,057 |

Best finish for 1963: T-2nd at the Pensacola Open Invitational

| 1964 | 27 | 89 | 17 | 0 | 1 | 2 | 8 | 72.04 | $10,019 |

Best finish for 1964: T-4th at the San Diego Open

| 1965 | 25 | 96 | 21 | 0 | 1 | 3 | 10 | 72.00 | $17,577 |

Best finish for 1965: T-5th at the Bing Crosby Pro-Am

| 1966 | 24 | 77 | 14 | 0 | 1 | 2 | 4 | 72.84 | $9,267 |

Best finish for 1966: T-3rd at the Bob Hope Desert Classic

Year	Starts	Rounds Played	Cuts Made	Wins	Top-5s	Top-10s	Top-25s	Scoring Average	Money
1967	16	49	8	0	0	0	2	73.51	$2,025

Best finish for 1967: T-24th at the Jacksonville Open & Greater New Orleans Open

1968	13	43	9	0	0	0	2	71.70	$3,474

Best finish for 1968: T-11th at the "500" Festival Open Invitational

| 1969 | 5 | 17 | 4 | 0 | 0 | 0 | 2 | 68.00 | $3,893 |

Best finish for 1969: T-11th at the Greater Greensboro Open

1970	1	2	0	0	0	0	0	75.00	
Period Totals	Starts	Rounds Played	Cuts Made	Wins	Top-5s	Top-10s	Top-25s	Scoring Average	Money
	149	524	111	0	6	17	50	72.01	$73,790

Dick Knight

Year	Starts	Rounds Played	Cuts Made	Wins	Top-5s	Top-10s	Top-25s	Scoring Average	Money
1958	2	7	1	0	0	0	1	72.14	$350

Best finish for 1958: T-14th at the Hesperia Open

| 1959 | 23 | 91 | 23 | 0 | 1 | 5 | 13 | 71.35 | $8,863 |

Best finish for 1959: T-4th at the Kentucky Derby Open Invitational

| 1960 | 13 | 48 | 9 | 0 | 0 | 1 | 5 | 72.44 | $4,744 |

Best finish for 1960: T-8th at the Greater New Orleans Open Invitational

Period Totals	Starts	Rounds Played	Cuts Made	Wins	Top-5s	Top-10s	Top-25s	Scoring Average	Money
	38	146	33	0	1	6	19	71.75	$13,956

Dwaine Knight

Year	Starts	Rounds Played	Cuts Made	Wins	Top-5s	Top-10s	Top-25s	Scoring Average	Money
1972	2	4	0	0	0	0	0	75.00	
1973	17	42	4	0	0	0	0	74.55	$966

Best finish for 1973: T-26th at the Quad Cities Open

1974	10	20	0	0	0	0	0	74.40	
1975	4	9	0	0	0	0	0	77.67	
1976	3	6	0	0	0	0	0	76.33	
Period Totals	Starts	Rounds Played	Cuts Made	Wins	Top-5s	Top-10s	Top-25s	Scoring Average	Money
	36	81	4	0	0	0	0	75.01	$966

Jim Knoll

Year	Starts	Rounds Played	Cuts Made	Wins	Top-5s	Top-10s	Top-25s	Scoring Average	Money
1975	1	2	0	0	0	0	0	81.50	
1976	4	8	0	0	0	0	0	74.00	
1977	9	24	3	0	0	0	1	73.96	$3,751

Best finish for 1977: T-20th at the Greater Greensboro Open

1978	7	13	0	0	0	0	0	75.46	
1979	10	27	3	0	0	0	0	74.96	$1,693

Best finish for 1979: T-38th at the Tallahassee Open

Period Totals	Starts	Rounds Played	Cuts Made	Wins	Top-5s	Top-10s	Top-25s	Scoring Average	Money
	31	74	6	0	0	0	1	74.80	$5,444

Kenny Knox

Year	Starts	Rounds Played	Cuts Made	Wins	Top-5s	Top-10s	Top-25s	Scoring Average	Money
1978	1	2	0	0	0	0	0	72.50	
1980	6	20	4	0	0	0	0	71.95	$3,082

Best finish for 1980: T-31st at the Tallahassee Open

1981	1	2	0	0	0	0	0	73.00	
1982	21	57	7	0	0	0	0	73.33	$6,919

Best finish for 1982: T-30th at the Hall of Fame

1983	1	2	0	0	0	0	0	72.50	
1984	25	71	9	0	0	0	2	73.18	$15,606

Best finish for 1984: T-15th at the Southern Open

| 1985 | 26 | 75 | 12 | 0 | 0 | 1 | 2 | 72.72 | $27,568 |

Best finish for 1985: T-8th at the Pensacola Open

| 1986 | 31 | 106 | 26 | 1 | 2 | 7 | 12 | 71.38 | $263,908 |

Best finish for 1986: Win at the Honda Classic

| 1987 | 33 | 107 | 23 | 1 | 2 | 2 | 9 | 71.79 | $201,691 |

Best finish for 1987: Win at the Hardee's Golf Classic

| 1988 | 36 | 113 | 20 | 0 | 1 | 4 | 9 | 71.35 | $169,599 |

Best finish for 1988: T-3rd at the Anheuser-Busch Golf Classic

| 1989 | 32 | 109 | 24 | 0 | 3 | 5 | 8 | 71.06 | $231,012 |

Best finish for 1989: T-3rd at the Walt Disney World/Oldsmobile Classic

| 1990 | 31 | 96 | 19 | 1 | 2 | 2 | 4 | 71.73 | $210,657 |

Best finish for 1990: Win at the Buick Southern Open

| 1991 | 33 | 116 | 25 | 0 | 3 | 5 | 13 | 70.58 | $424,525 |

Best finish for 1991: 2nd at the Anheuser-Busch Golf Classic

| 1992 | 32 | 82 | 9 | 0 | 0 | 0 | 0 | 72.90 | $27,589 |

Best finish for 1992: T-32nd at the Federal Express St. Jude Classic

Year	Starts	Rounds Played	Cuts Made	Wins	Top-5s	Top-10s	Top-25s	Scoring Average	Money
1993	21	48	2	0	0	0	0	75.46	$3,630
Best finish for 1993: 74th at the Freeport-McMoRan Classic									
1994	15	38	5	0	0	0	1	72.45	$23,872
Best finish for 1994: T-20th at the Buick Open									
1995	11	24	2	0	0	0	0	73.79	$9,010
Best finish for 1995: T-27th at the Quad City Classic									
1996	4	7	0	0	0	0	0	76.00	
1997	4	8	0	0	0	0	0	75.25	
1998	1	2	0	0	0	0	0	77.50	
1999	6	11	0	0	0	0	0	75.55	
2000	2	3	0	0	0	0	0	77.00	
2002	1	1	0	0	0	0	0	79.00	
2004	1	2	0	0	0	0	0	73.50	
2005	1	2	0	0	0	0	0	72.00	
2006	1	2	0	0	0	0	0	78.00	
2008	1	2	0	0	0	0	0	73.50	
Period Totals	Starts	Rounds Played	Cuts Made	Wins	Top-5s	Top-10s	Top-25s	Scoring Average	Money
	378	1108	187	3	13	26	60	72.19	$1,618,666

George Knudson

Year	Starts	Rounds Played	Cuts Made	Wins	Top-5s	Top-10s	Top-25s	Scoring Average	Money
1958	1	4	1	0	0	0	0	70.00	
Best finish for 1958: T-39th at the Canadian Open									
1959	1	4	1	0	0	0	0	75.50	$100
Best finish for 1959: T-64th at the Bing Crosby National									
1960	1	4	1	0	0	0	1	72.75	$240
Best finish for 1960: T-16th at the West Palm Beach Open Invitational									
1961	7	28	6	1	2	3	4	70.46	$5,682
Best finish for 1961: Win at the Coral Gables Open Invitational									
1962	13	52	12	1	3	4	9	71.62	$12,954
Best finish for 1962: Win at the Puerto Rico Open Invitational									
1963	17	68	15	1	4	7	10	70.81	$20,081
Best finish for 1963: Win at the Portland Open Invitational									
1964	23	84	18	1	2	6	11	72.05	$22,112
Best finish for 1964: Win at the Fresno Open									
1965	22	79	15	0	5	10	13	71.84	$42,193
Best finish for 1965: 2nd at the Colonial National Invitational									
1966	22	80	18	0	0	5	12	72.20	$25,224
Best finish for 1966: T-6th at the Masters, Philadelphia Golf Classic & Portland Open Invitational									
1967	19	62	12	1	3	4	8	72.31	$43,742
Best finish for 1967: Win at the Greater New Orleans Open									
1968	21	73	17	2	3	8	13	70.93	$70,935
Best finish for 1968: Win at the Phoenix Open Invitational & Tucson Open Invitational									
1969	18	67	15	0	4	7	10	71.46	$44,531
Best finish for 1969: T-2nd at the Masters									
1970	24	81	18	1	1	5	8	72.31	$44,279
Best finish for 1970: Win at the Robinson Open Golf Classic									
1971	29	88	17	0	3	4	10	72.47	$39,154
Best finish for 1971: T-3rd at the Colonial National Invitational									
1972	28	96	19	1	3	7	13	71.74	$72,161
Best finish for 1972: Win at the Kaiser International Open									
1973	25	91	21	0	1	1	4	72.53	$25,899
Best finish for 1973: 4th at the Greater Milwaukee Open									
1974	20	54	7	0	0	1	1	73.83	$7,844
Best finish for 1974: T-9th at the Bob Hope Chrysler Classic									
1975	31	101	19	0	0	2	9	72.55	$32,554
Best finish for 1975: T-7th at the Pleasant Valley Classic									
1976	24	74	15	0	1	1	1	73.16	$14,870
Best finish for 1976: T-3rd at the B.C. Open									
1977	12	35	5	0	0	1	2	73.14	$11,466
Best finish for 1977: T-6th at the Houston Open									
1978	13	39	6	0	0	1	3	72.59	$10,791
Best finish for 1978: T-6th at the Phoenix Open									
1979	9	28	4	0	0	0	0	72.71	$4,243
Best finish for 1979: T-33rd at the Bing Crosby Pro-Am									
1980	4	12	1	0	0	0	0	74.42	$543
Best finish for 1980: T-79th at the Phoenix Open									
1981	1	2	0	0	0	0	0	80.50	
Period Totals	Starts	Rounds Played	Cuts Made	Wins	Top-5s	Top-10s	Top-25s	Scoring Average	Money
	385	1306	263	9	35	77	142	72.18	$551,599

Gary Koch

Year	Starts	Rounds Played	Cuts Made	Wins	Top-5s	Top-10s	Top-25s	Scoring Average	Money
1973	1	4	1	0	0	0	0	75.50	

Best finish for 1973: 57th at the U.S. Open

1974	3	8	1	0	0	0	0	75.00	$1,700

Best finish for 1974: T-61st at the Greater Jacksonville Open

1975	2	4	0	0	0	0	0	75.25	$1,470
1976	32	108	22	1	2	2	5	72.40	$38,130

Best finish for 1976: Win at the Tallahassee Open

1977	31	94	16	1	1	2	4	73.32	$59,133

Best finish for 1977: Win at the Florida Citrus Open Invitational

1978	31	109	23	0	1	6	12	71.77	$59,260

Best finish for 1978: T-4th at the Danny Thomas Memphis Classic

1979	32	107	21	0	1	2	9	72.21	$46,809

Best finish for 1979: T-5th at the Tallahassee Open

1980	30	93	18	0	0	3	8	72.08	$46,562

Best finish for 1980: T-6th at the World Disney World National Team Championship

1981	27	77	12	0	0	0	0	72.58	$12,599

Best finish for 1981: T-28th at the Bay Hill Classic

1982	26	85	17	0	1	2	4	71.96	$43,449

Best finish for 1982: 5th at the LaJet Classic

1983	30	111	24	1	4	7	12	71.38	$177,510

Best finish for 1983: Win at the Doral-Eastern Open

1984	29	108	24	2	2	6	13	71.23	$264,109

Best finish for 1984: Win at the Isuzu/Andy Williams San Diego Open & Bay Hill Classic

1985	27	98	21	0	2	4	11	71.21	$139,696

Best finish for 1985: T-4th at the Los Angeles Open & Walt Disney World/Oldsmobile Classic

1986	27	92	22	0	3	7	15	70.99	$213,693

Best finish for 1986: T-4th at the Walt Disney World/Oldsmobile Classic

1987	26	71	9	0	0	0	3	72.52	$34,344

Best finish for 1987: T-15th at the Provident Classic

1988	26	85	17	1	2	4	8	71.44	$472,644

Best finish for 1988: Win at the Panasonic Las Vegas Invitational

1989	22	69	11	0	0	2	3	72.14	$96,385

Best finish for 1989: T-8th at the Players Championship

1990	19	57	10	0	0	0	1	72.18	$36,469

Best finish for 1990: T-21st at the USF&G Classic

1991	10	26	3	0	0	0	0	71.12	$7,189

Best finish for 1991: T-42nd at the Nestle Invitational

1992	4	12	2	0	0	0	0	74.17	$4,690

Best finish for 1992: 77th at the Nestle Invitational

1993	4	10	1	0	0	0	0	72.50	$702

Best finish for 1993: T-51st at the Deposit Guaranty Classic

1994	2	4	0	0	0	0	0	73.75	
1995	2	4	0	0	0	0	0	75.25	$1,000
1996	2	4	0	0	0	0	0	73.25	
1997	1	3	0	0	0	0	0	71.33	
1998	2	5	0	0	0	0	0	72.20	
1999	1	4	1	0	0	0	0	73.25	$5,250

Best finish for 1999: T-64th at the Bay Hill Invitational

2001	2	6	1	0	0	0	0	73.83	$7,825

Best finish for 2001: T-71st at the Bay Hill Invitational

2002	1	2	0	0	0	0	0	75.00	

Period Totals	Starts	Rounds Played	Cuts Made	Wins	Top-5s	Top-10s	Top-25s	Scoring Average	Money
	452	1460	277	6	19	47	108	72.00	$1,770,618

Mike Korich

Year	Starts	Rounds Played	Cuts Made	Wins	Top-5s	Top-10s	Top-25s	Scoring Average	Money
1964	18	27	0	0	0	0	0	76.59	
1967	14	30	1	0	0	0	0	76.07	

Best finish for 1967: 71st at the Azalea Open

Period Totals	Starts	Rounds Played	Cuts Made	Wins	Top-5s	Top-10s	Top-25s	Scoring Average	Money
	32	57	1	0	0	0	0	76.32	

Brian Kortan

Year	Starts	Rounds Played	Cuts Made	Wins	Top-5s	Top-10s	Top-25s	Scoring Average	Money
2004	24	62	8	0	0	0	1	72.19	$159,939

Best finish for 2004: T-13th at the FedEx St. Jude Classic

2008	1	2	0	0	0	0	0	81.00	

Period Totals	Starts	Rounds Played	Cuts Made	Wins	Top-5s	Top-10s	Top-25s	Scoring Average	Money
	25	64	8	0	0	0	1	72.47	$159,939

Greg Kraft

Year	Starts	Rounds Played	Cuts Made	Wins	Top-5s	Top-10s	Top-25s	Scoring Average	Money
1992	30	81	11	0	0	1	3	71.78	$88,824

Best finish for 1992: T-6th at the Kemper Open

1993	24	72	13	1	3	4	5	71.60	$290,581

Best finish for 1993: Win at the Deposit Guaranty Classic

1994	31	90	14	0	2	3	5	71.59	$288,730

Best finish for 1994: 2nd at the Motorola Western Open

1995	35	100	15	0	0	1	7	71.78	$138,855

Best finish for 1995: T-8th at the Ideon Classic

1996	27	81	15	0	3	5	9	71.07	$333,008

Best finish for 1996: T-3rd at the Deposit Guaranty Golf Classic

1997	35	104	18	0	0	0	5	71.63	$152,109

Best finish for 1997: T-12th at the Greater Vancouver Open

1998	25	83	17	0	2	2	6	71.07	$326,571

Best finish for 1998: T-4th at the United Airlines Hawaiian Open

1999	28	95	19	0	2	3	6	71.66	$810,777

Best finish for 1999: T-2nd at the Doral-Ryder Open & MasterCard Colonial

2000	29	106	23	0	1	2	6	70.61	$597,021

Best finish for 2000: T-3rd at the Advil Western Open

2001	33	102	19	0	1	2	5	71.10	$503,605

Best finish for 2001: T-5th at the Touchstone Energy Tucson Open

2002	31	84	12	0	0	1	2	71.51	$222,614

Best finish for 2002: T-6th at the Touchstone Energy Tucson Open

2003	9	30	6	0	0	0	0	71.57	$71,756

Best finish for 2003: T-28th at the AT&T Pebble Beach National Pro-Am

2004	4	8	0	0	0	0	0	72.38	
2006	26	75	14	0	0	0	2	71.60	$275,734

Best finish for 2006: T-19th at The International

2007	10	30	5	0	0	1	3	71.00	$278,590

Best finish for 2007: 6th at the Wyndham Championship

2008	21	63	11	1	1	3	5	71.56	$1,204,559

Best finish for 2008: Win at the Puerto Rico Open

Period Totals	Starts	Rounds Played	Cuts Made	Wins	Top-5s	Top-10s	Top-25s	Scoring Average	Money
	398	1204	212	2	15	28	69	71.41	$5,583,334

Mike Krak

Year	Starts	Rounds Played	Cuts Made	Wins	Top-5s	Top-10s	Top-25s	Scoring Average	Money
1958	16	50	10	0	2	2	5	72.96	$2,563

Best finish for 1958: T-2nd at the Jackson Open

1959	2	7	2	0	0	0	1	71.71	$188

Best finish for 1959: T-13th at the Sam Snead Festival

1960	3	11	2	0	0	0	0	74.64	$292

Best finish for 1960: T-46th at the Palm Springs Desert Golf Classic

1961	2	6	1	0	0	0	0	76.50	$225

Best finish for 1961: T-57th at the PGA Championship

1962	6	24	6	0	0	0	1	72.04	$1,397

Best finish for 1962: T-19th at the Phoenix Open Invitational

1963	1	4	1	0	0	0	0	72.75	$480

Best finish for 1963: T-34th at the PGA Championship

1964	3	9	1	0	0	0	0	75.00	

Best finish for 1964: T-55th at the St. Petersburg Open

1965	1	4	1	0	0	0	0	76.50	$300

Best finish for 1965: T-73rd at the PGA Championship

1966	1	2	0	0	0	0	0	77.50	$300
1967	1	4	1	0	0	0	0	74.50	

Best finish for 1967: 78th at the Westchester Classic

1969	3	8	1	0	0	0	0	75.25	$231

Best finish for 1969: T-75th at the Doral Open

1971	1	2	0	0	0	0	0	73.50	
1972	1	2	0	0	0	0	0	75.00	
1973	1	2	0	0	0	0	0	74.50	

Period Totals	Starts	Rounds Played	Cuts Made	Wins	Top-5s	Top-10s	Top-25s	Scoring Average	Money
	42	135	26	0	2	2	7	73.57	$5,976

Bill Kratzert

Year	Starts	Rounds Played	Cuts Made	Wins	Top-5s	Top-10s	Top-25s	Scoring Average	Money
1962	1	2	1	0	0	0	0	77.00	

Best finish for 1962: T-200 at the PGA Championship

1974	1	2	0	0	0	0	0	76.00	$1,200
1975	1	2	0	0	0	0	0	76.00	$500

| 1976 | 13 | 46 | 10 | 0 | 0 | 3 | 6 | 70.98 | $19,558 |

Best finish for 1976: T-7th at the Greater Milwaukee Open

| 1977 | 33 | 122 | 27 | 1 | 6 | 12 | 19 | 71.32 | $134,758 |

Best finish for 1977: Win at the Sammy Davis, Jr. - Greater Hartford Open

| 1978 | 31 | 112 | 26 | 0 | 7 | 12 | 20 | 71.02 | $184,016 |

Best finish for 1978: T-2nd at the Hawaiian Open, Memorial Tournament & Sammy Davis, Jr. - Greater Hartford Open

| 1979 | 32 | 108 | 22 | 0 | 4 | 6 | 11 | 72.07 | $101,978 |

Best finish for 1979: T-2nd at the Andy Williams-San Diego Open & Pensacola Open

| 1980 | 31 | 115 | 27 | 1 | 5 | 9 | 15 | 71.10 | $175,771 |

Best finish for 1980: Win at the Greater Milwaukee Open

| 1981 | 33 | 103 | 20 | 0 | 1 | 2 | 9 | 72.17 | $57,563 |

Best finish for 1981: T-5th at the Greater Milwaukee Open

| 1982 | 28 | 84 | 15 | 0 | 0 | 0 | 2 | 72.94 | $23,429 |

Best finish for 1982: T-15th at the Pensacola Open

| 1983 | 23 | 64 | 9 | 0 | 0 | 0 | 2 | 73.28 | $14,744 |

Best finish for 1983: T-12th at the Joe Garagiola Tucson Open

| 1984 | 28 | 93 | 20 | 1 | 2 | 4 | 10 | 71.33 | $149,827 |

Best finish for 1984: Win at the Pensacola Open

| 1985 | 28 | 99 | 23 | 0 | 3 | 6 | 15 | 71.20 | $180,331 |

Best finish for 1985: 3rd at the Memorial Tournament

| 1986 | 31 | 83 | 14 | 0 | 0 | 1 | 3 | 72.63 | $47,421 |

Best finish for 1986: T-8th at the Doral-Eastern Open

| 1987 | 29 | 86 | 14 | 0 | 1 | 2 | 3 | 72.06 | $78,231 |

Best finish for 1987: T-2nd at the Centel Classic

| 1988 | 33 | 90 | 12 | 0 | 0 | 0 | 1 | 72.23 | $43,519 |

Best finish for 1988: T-12th at the Manufactures Hanover Westchester Classic

| 1989 | 18 | 43 | 3 | 0 | 0 | 0 | 0 | 73.51 | $7,773 |

Best finish for 1989: T-32nd at the Bank of Boston Classic

| 1990 | 12 | 33 | 4 | 0 | 0 | 0 | 1 | 71.79 | $14,630 |

Best finish for 1990: T-17th at the Chattanooga Classic

| 1991 | 14 | 39 | 6 | 0 | 0 | 0 | 1 | 71.97 | $19,819 |

Best finish for 1991: T-23rd at the Greater Milwaukee Open

| 1992 | 11 | 35 | 6 | 0 | 0 | 0 | 1 | 71.94 | $16,439 |

Best finish for 1992: T-23rd at the Chattanooga Classic

| 1993 | 15 | 52 | 11 | 0 | 0 | 1 | 2 | 70.83 | $78,992 |

Best finish for 1993: T-10th at the Nestle Invitational

| 1994 | 25 | 69 | 8 | 0 | 0 | 0 | 1 | 72.71 | $42,127 |

Best finish for 1994: T-15th at the Kmart Greater Greensboro Open

| 1995 | 10 | 25 | 2 | 0 | 0 | 0 | 0 | 72.80 | $4,548 |

Best finish for 1995: T-59th at the B.C. Open

| 1996 | 7 | 16 | 1 | 0 | 0 | 0 | 0 | 73.00 | $3,030 |

Best finish for 1996: T-67th at the Canon Greater Hartford Open

| 1997 | 1 | 3 | 0 | 0 | 0 | 0 | 0 | 76.00 | |

Period Totals	Starts	Rounds Played	Cuts Made	Wins	Top-5s	Top-10s	Top-25s	Scoring Average	Money
	489	1526	281	3	29	58	122	71.93	$1,400,205

Charlie Krenkel

Year	Starts	Rounds Played	Cuts Made	Wins	Top-5s	Top-10s	Top-25s	Scoring Average	Money
1975	1	2	0	0	0	0	0	75.50	
1981	12	34	5	0	0	0	1	72.44	$3,702

Best finish for 1981: T-25th at the Southern Open

| 1982 | 22 | 61 | 8 | 0 | 0 | 0 | 0 | 73.11 | $7,341 |

Best finish for 1982: T-29th at the Greater Milwaukee Open

| 1987 | 1 | 2 | 0 | 0 | 0 | 0 | 0 | 72.50 | |

Period Totals	Starts	Rounds Played	Cuts Made	Wins	Top-5s	Top-10s	Top-25s	Scoring Average	Money
	36	99	13	0	0	0	1	72.92	$11,043

Cliff Kresge

Year	Starts	Rounds Played	Cuts Made	Wins	Top-5s	Top-10s	Top-25s	Scoring Average	Money
1994	1	2	0	0	0	0	0	77.50	
1995	3	6	0	0	0	0	0	72.17	
1996	1	2	0	0	0	0	0	75.00	
1998	1	2	0	0	0	0	0	72.50	
1999	2	6	1	0	0	0	0	71.17	$4,876

Best finish for 1999: T-62nd at the Greater Milwaukee Open

| 2000 | 1 | 2 | 0 | 0 | 0 | 0 | 0 | 73.00 | |
| 2001 | 31 | 82 | 12 | 0 | 1 | 1 | 2 | 71.59 | $220,649 |

Best finish for 2001: T-5th at the Touchstone Energy Tucson Open

| 2002 | 2 | 8 | 2 | 0 | 1 | 1 | 1 | 68.75 | $101,370 |

Best finish for 2002: T-3rd at the B.C. Open

| 2003 | 32 | 100 | 18 | 0 | 0 | 3 | 5 | 71.07 | $738,641 |

Best finish for 2003: T-6th at the 100th Western Open

Year	Starts	Rounds Played	Cuts Made	Wins	Top-5s	Top-10s	Top-25s	Scoring Average	Money
2004	33	87	10	0	0	0	2	72.17	$258,062

Best finish for 2004: T-14th at the Bell Canadian Open

2007	30	107	23	0	0	1	7	70.88	$901,549

Best finish for 2007: T-6th at the Bob Hope Chrysler Classic

2008	28	84	13	0	3	4	6	71.54	$1,068,207

Best finish for 2008: T-3rd at the Arnold Palmer Invitational

Period Totals	Starts	Rounds Played	Cuts Made	Wins	Top-5s	Top-10s	Top-25s	Scoring Average	Money
	165	488	79	0	5	10	23	71.42	$3,293,355

Joel Kribel

Year	Starts	Rounds Played	Cuts Made	Wins	Top-5s	Top-10s	Top-25s	Scoring Average	Money
1997	2	4	0	0	0	0	0	74.00	
1998	2	6	1	0	0	0	0	76.50	

Best finish for 1998: 45th at the Masters

1999	7	18	2	0	0	0	0	71.44	$10,519

Best finish for 1999: T-46th at the Westin Texas Open

2000	2	5	0	0	0	0	0	74.20	
2001	1	2	0	0	0	0	0	75.50	$1,000
2003	16	39	3	0	0	0	0	72.95	$39,120

Best finish for 2003: T-37th at the Buick Invitational

2004	13	36	6	0	1	1	2	71.75	$276,862

Best finish for 2004: T-4th at the John Deere Classic

2005	2	6	1	0	0	0	1	71.17	$112,360

Best finish for 2005: T-11th at the AT&T Pebble Beach National Pro-Am

2006	2	5	1	0	0	0	0	72.00	$10,476

Best finish for 2006: T-68th at the AT&T Pebble Beach National Pro-Am

2007	1	3	0	0	0	0	0	73.00	
2008	1	3	0	0	0	0	0	73.33	

Period Totals	Starts	Rounds Played	Cuts Made	Wins	Top-5s	Top-10s	Top-25s	Scoring Average	Money
	49	127	14	0	1	1	3	72.57	$450,336

Phil Krick

Year	Starts	Rounds Played	Cuts Made	Wins	Top-5s	Top-10s	Top-25s	Scoring Average	Money
1964	9	13	0	0	0	0	0	77.46	
1965	6	14	1	0	0	0	0	77.64	

Best finish for 1965: T-67th at the Cajun Classic

1966	4	6	0	0	0	0	0	78.67	
1967	1	2	0	0	0	0	0	75.00	
1968	2	4	0	0	0	0	0	77.50	$500
1970	1	2	0	0	0	0	0	74.50	
1971	1	2	0	0	0	0	0	79.00	
1972	3	6	0	0	0	0	0	78.00	
1973	10	16	0	0	0	0	0	76.06	$095

Period Totals	Starts	Rounds Played	Cuts Made	Wins	Top-5s	Top-10s	Top-25s	Scoring Average	Money
	37	65	1	0	0	0	0	77.20	$595

Ed Kroll

Year	Starts	Rounds Played	Cuts Made	Wins	Top-5s	Top-10s	Top-25s	Scoring Average	Money
1958	8	22	4	0	0	0	1	73.77	$080

Best finish for 1958: T-17th at the Jackson Open

1959	1	4	1	0	0	0	1	72.25	$350

Best finish for 1959: T-15th at the Baton Rouge Open Invitational

1962	1	2	0	0	0	0	0	78.00	$025

Best finish for 1962: T-128 at the Thunderbird Classic Invitational

1963	1	2	0	0	0	0	0	84.50	$150
1964	6	14	2	0	0	0	1	74.07	$930

Best finish for 1964: T-23rd at the PGA Championship

1965	10	24	1	0	0	0	0	76.04	

Best finish for 1965: T-64th at the San Diego Open

1966	1	4	1	0	0	0	0	75.50	$300

Best finish for 1966: T-66th at the PGA Championship

1967	1	2	0	0	0	0	0	77.50	
1968	3	9	2	0	0	0	1	71.22	$934

Best finish for 1968: T-17th at the Pensacola Open Invitational

1969	3	10	2	0	0	0	0	75.80	$341

Best finish for 1969: T-66th at the Alameda County Open

1971	1	2	0	0	0	0	0	76.50	
1975	1	2	0	0	0	0	0	79.50	

Period Totals	Starts	Rounds Played	Cuts Made	Wins	Top-5s	Top-10s	Top-25s	Scoring Average	Money
	37	97	13	0	0	0	4	74.92	$3,110

Ted Kroll

Year	Starts	Rounds Played	Cuts Made	Wins	Top-5s	Top-10s	Top-25s	Scoring Average	Money
1958	21	82	20	0	4	8	16	71.60	$17,760

Best finish for 1958: T-2nd at the Buick Open

| 1959 | 14 | 56 | 13 | 0 | 4 | 5 | 10 | 70.82 | $12,970 |

Best finish for 1959: T-4th at the Western Open Championship & Miller Open Invitational

| 1960 | 16 | 64 | 12 | 0 | 5 | 7 | 13 | 70.92 | $18,472 |

Best finish for 1960: T-3rd at the U.S. Open, Dallas Open Invitational & Coral Gables Open Invitational

| 1961 | 18 | 73 | 17 | 0 | 3 | 8 | 15 | 70.66 | $22,198 |

Best finish for 1961: T-2nd at the St. Petersburg Open Invitational & Insurance City Open Invitational

| 1962 | 12 | 48 | 11 | 0 | 3 | 3 | 7 | 72.15 | $11,159 |

Best finish for 1962: T-4th at the Eastern Open Invitational

| 1963 | 8 | 30 | 7 | 0 | 0 | 0 | 2 | 73.10 | $3,213 |

Best finish for 1963: T-22nd at the American Golf Classic

| 1964 | 6 | 22 | 4 | 0 | 0 | 0 | 1 | 73.36 | $2,102 |

Best finish for 1964: T-23rd at the PGA Championship

| 1965 | 7 | 21 | 2 | 0 | 0 | 0 | 1 | 75.19 | $1,032 |

Best finish for 1965: T-24th at the U.S. Open

| 1966 | 1 | 4 | 1 | 0 | 0 | 0 | 0 | 78.75 | |

Best finish for 1966: 73rd at the Buick Open Invitational

| 1967 | 3 | 8 | 1 | 0 | 0 | 0 | 0 | 76.00 | $715 |

Best finish for 1967: T-48th at the U.S. Open

1969	1	2	0	0	0	0	0	78.50	
1975	1	2	0	0	0	0	0	73.50	
1976	2	4	0	0	0	0	0	75.50	
1983	1	4	0	0	0	0	0	79.50	
Period Totals	**Starts**	**Rounds Played**	**Cuts Made**	**Wins**	**Top-5s**	**Top-10s**	**Top-25s**	**Scoring Average**	**Money**
	111	420	88	0	19	31	65	71.98	$89,622

PGA Tour career totals from 1946 to 1983

	Starts	Rounds Played	Cuts Made	Wins	Top-5s	Top-10s	Top-25s	Scoring Average	Money
	306	N/A	N/A/	8	N/A	117	210	N/A	$254,286

Gary Krueger

Year	Starts	Rounds Played	Cuts Made	Wins	Top-5s	Top-10s	Top-25s	Scoring Average	Money
1984	24	75	12	0	0	0	2	73.13	$15,334

Best finish for 1984: T-18th at the B.C. Open

| 1985 | 2 | 6 | 1 | 0 | 0 | 0 | 0 | 72.50 | $1,248 |

Best finish for 1985: T-61st at the Lite Quad Cities Open

| 1986 | 2 | 4 | 0 | 0 | 0 | 0 | 0 | 77.00 | $600 |
| 1987 | 28 | 73 | 9 | 0 | 0 | 0 | 1 | 72.64 | $20,366 |

Best finish for 1987: T-19th at the Beatrice Western Open

1988	3	6	0	0	0	0	0	73.17	
Period Totals	**Starts**	**Rounds Played**	**Cuts Made**	**Wins**	**Top-5s**	**Top-10s**	**Top-25s**	**Scoring Average**	**Money**
	59	164	22	0	0	0	3	72.99	$37,548

Kenichi Kuboya

Year	Starts	Rounds Played	Cuts Made	Wins	Top-5s	Top-10s	Top-25s	Scoring Average	Money
1998	1	2	0	0	0	0	0	76.50	
2002	2	8	2	0	0	0	0	73.38	$40,196

Best finish for 2002: T-59th at the British Open

| 2003 | 31 | 89 | 14 | 0 | 0 | 0 | 2 | 71.71 | $257,282 |

Best finish for 2003: T-13th at the 84 Lumber Classic of Pennsylvania

| 2004 | 1 | 4 | 1 | 0 | 0 | 0 | 0 | 69.50 | $10,944 |

Best finish for 2004: T-54th at the Sony Open in Hawaii

| **Period Totals** | **Starts** | **Rounds Played** | **Cuts Made** | **Wins** | **Top-5s** | **Top-10s** | **Top-25s** | **Scoring Average** | **Money** |
| | 35 | 103 | 17 | 0 | 0 | 0 | 2 | 71.84 | $308,422 |

Matt Kuchar

Year	Starts	Rounds Played	Cuts Made	Wins	Top-5s	Top-10s	Top-25s	Scoring Average	Money
1998	6	20	4	0	0	0	2	72.00	

Best finish for 1998: T-14th at the U.S. Open

| 1999 | 4 | 12 | 2 | 0 | 0 | 0 | 0 | 74.33 | |

Best finish for 1999: T-50th at the Masters

| 2000 | 1 | 2 | 0 | 0 | 0 | 0 | 0 | 73.00 | |
| 2001 | 11 | 35 | 6 | 0 | 2 | 2 | 4 | 70.00 | $572,669 |

Best finish for 2001: T-2nd at the Texas Open at LaCantera

| 2002 | 27 | 82 | 14 | 1 | 3 | 4 | 6 | 71.00 | $1,250,466 |

Best finish for 2002: Win at the Honda Classic

| 2003 | 23 | 61 | 8 | 0 | 0 | 0 | 2 | 72.02 | $176,047 |

Best finish for 2003: T-20th at the FedEx St. Jude Classic

| 2004 | 28 | 83 | 13 | 0 | 0 | 1 | 4 | 71.48 | $509,257 |

Best finish for 2004: T-10th at the HP Classic of New Orleans

Year	Starts	Rounds Played	Cuts Made	Wins	Top-5s	Top-10s	Top-25s	Scoring Average	Money
2005	21	60	9	0	0	1	3	71.38	$404,786

Best finish for 2005: T-10th at the MCI Heritage

2006	8	21	2	0	0	0	0	73.14	$32,297

Best finish for 2006: T-38th at the FedEx St. Jude Classic

2007	26	85	16	0	1	2	4	70.79	$890,462

Best finish for 2007: T-3rd at the AT&T Classic

2008	27	88	16	0	2	5	8	71.03	$1,447,638

Best finish for 2008: 2nd at the Justin Timberlake Shriners Hospitals for Children Open

Period Totals	Starts	Rounds Played	Cuts Made	Wins	Top-5s	Top-10s	Top-25s	Scoring Average	Money
	182	549	90	1	8	15	33	71.34	$5,283,622

Hank Kuehne

Year	Starts	Rounds Played	Cuts Made	Wins	Top-5s	Top-10s	Top-25s	Scoring Average	Money
1999	8	20	3	0	0	0	0	74.50	$19,869

Best finish for 1999: T-29th at the Bell Canadian Open

2000	6	14	2	0	0	0	1	72.29	$85,656

Best finish for 2000: T-13th at the GTE Byron Nelson Classic

2002	6	16	4	0	0	0	2	69.63	$80,840

Best finish for 2002: T-19th at the B.C. Open

2003	23	71	14	0	3	4	5	70.92	$874,139

Best finish for 2003: T-2nd at the Shell Houston Open

2004	30	89	15	0	1	2	8	71.26	$816,889

Best finish for 2004: 5th at the Nissan Open

2005	30	80	12	0	2	2	3	72.08	$786,817

Best finish for 2005: T-2nd at the John Deere Classic

2006	9	25	2	0	0	0	0	73.76	$24,677

Best finish for 2006: T-49th at the Buick Invitational

2007	3	6	0	0	0	0	0	74.50	

Period Totals	Starts	Rounds Played	Cuts Made	Wins	Top-5s	Top-10s	Top-25s	Scoring Average	Money
	115	321	52	0	6	8	19	71.81	$2,688,886

Joe Kunes

Year	Starts	Rounds Played	Cuts Made	Wins	Top-5s	Top-10s	Top-25s	Scoring Average	Money
1977	16	44	6	0	0	0	1	73.25	$4,543

Best finish for 1977: T-14th at the Greater Milwaukee Open

1978	22	62	9	0	0	0	1	72.76	$7,340

Best finish for 1978: T-22nd at the IVB Philadelphia Golf Classic

1979	22	60	8	0	0	0	0	73.05	$6,862

Best finish for 1979: T-36th at the Jackie Gleason's Inverrary Classic & Ed McMahon Quad City Open

1980	4	15	3	0	0	0	0	74.53	$2,281

Best finish for 1980: T-36th at the Phoenix Open

Period Totals	Starts	Rounds Played	Cuts Made	Wins	Top-5s	Top-10s	Top-25s	Scoring Average	Money
	64	181	26	0	0	0	2	73.12	$21,026

Massy Kuramoto

Year	Starts	Rounds Played	Cuts Made	Wins	Top-5s	Top-10s	Top-25s	Scoring Average	Money
1978	1	2	0	0	0	0	0	75.00	
1982	8	28	6	0	1	1	2	73.36	$27,812

Best finish for 1982: T-4th at the British Open

1983	8	30	7	0	0	1	2	72.13	$25,793

Best finish for 1983: T-6th at the Doral-Eastern Open

1984	6	17	2	0	0	0	1	73.29	$16,687

Best finish for 1984: T-13th at the Hawaiian Open

1985	2	4	0	0	0	0	0	75.25	
1986	6	16	3	0	0	1	2	72.31	$21,350

Best finish for 1986: T-10th at the Los Angeles Open

1987	1	4	1	0	0	0	0	72.75	$1,212

Best finish for 1987: T-68th at the Los Angeles Open

1989	1	2	0	0	0	0	0	78.00	
1993	21	61	11	0	1	1	3	72.75	$75,133

Best finish for 1993: T-4th at the Deposit Guaranty Classic

1994	1	2	0	0	0	0	0	75.50	$1,000
1995	2	6	1	0	0	0	0	72.00	$3,660

Best finish for 1995: T-65th at the United Airlines Hawaiian Open

1996	3	12	3	0	0	0	0	72.25	$13,214

Best finish for 1996: T-31st at the Bay Hill Invitational

1997	2	5	0	0	0	0	0	74.20	

Period Totals	Starts	Rounds Played	Cuts Made	Wins	Top-5s	Top-10s	Top-25s	Scoring Average	Money
	62	189	34	0	2	4	10	72.90	$185,861

Huston La Clair

Year	Starts	Rounds Played	Cuts Made	Wins	Top-5s	Top-10s	Top-25s	Scoring Average	Money
1958	22	73	13	0	0	1	1	73.70	$862

Best finish for 1958: T-10th at the Rubber City Open

1959	9	34	8	0	1	2	3	71.71	$3,483

Best finish for 1959: T-4th at the Greater New Orleans Open Invitational

1960	9	36	8	0	1	2	4	71.81	$4,830

Best finish for 1960: T-4th at the Greater New Orleans Open Invitational

1961	13	52	12	0	0	0	7	71.42	$4,194

Best finish for 1961: T-15th at the Waco Turner Open Invitational & Cajun Classic Open Invitational

1962	6	22	4	0	0	0	2	72.59	$1,546

Best finish for 1962: T-14th at the Carling Open Invitational

1963	3	10	2	0	0	0	1	72.40	$1,265

Best finish for 1963: T-17th at the Los Angeles Open

1964	7	21	4	0	0	0	0	73.10	$270

Best finish for 1964: T-42nd at the Greater Hartford Open

1965	1	4	1	0	0	0	0	76.25	$300

Best finish for 1965: T-71st at the PGA Championship

Period Totals	Starts	Rounds Played	Cuts Made	Wins	Top-5s	Top-10s	Top-25s	Scoring Average	Money
	70	252	52	0	2	5	18	72.53	$16,749

Doug LaBelle II

Year	Starts	Rounds Played	Cuts Made	Wins	Top-5s	Top-10s	Top-25s	Scoring Average	Money
1997	1	2	0	0	0	0	0	74.50	
1999	1	2	0	0	0	0	0	73.50	
2003	1	2	0	0	0	0	0	74.00	$1,000
2007	33	104	18	0	1	1	2	71.32	$604,633

Best finish for 2007: T-4th at the Sony Open in Hawaii

2008	22	65	11	0	0	1	3	71.37	$338,132

Best finish for 2008: T-10th at the Sony Open in Hawaii

Period Totals	Starts	Rounds Played	Cuts Made	Wins	Top-5s	Top-10s	Top-25s	Scoring Average	Money
	58	175	29	0	1	2	5	71.43	$943,765

Martin Laird

Year	Starts	Rounds Played	Cuts Made	Wins	Top-5s	Top-10s	Top-25s	Scoring Average	Money
2007	1	2	0	0	0	0	0	77.50	$2,000
2008	29	98	20	0	2	3	5	70.81	$852,752

Best finish for 2008: T-4th at the Reno-Tahoe Open & Wyndham Championship

Period Totals	Starts	Rounds Played	Cuts Made	Wins	Top-5s	Top-10s	Top-25s	Scoring Average	Money
	30	100	20	0	2	3	5	70.94	$854,752

Greg Ladehoff

Year	Starts	Rounds Played	Cuts Made	Wins	Top-5s	Top-10s	Top-25s	Scoring Average	Money
1985	1	2	0	0	0	0	0	73.50	
1986	33	84	11	0	1	1	3	73.25	$45,382

Best finish for 1986: T-3rd at the USF&G Classic

1987	18	48	6	0	0	0	0	72.17	$9,198

Best finish for 1987: T-34th at the Greater Milwaukee Open

1988	33	99	17	0	0	1	2	71.79	$73,056

Best finish for 1988: 6th at the USF&G Classic

1989	28	81	15	0	0	1	3	71.52	$62,270

Best finish for 1989: T-8th at the Hardee's Golf Classic

1990	8	22	3	0	0	0	0	72.27	$10,795

Best finish for 1990: T-35th at the Buick Open & Chattanooga Classic

1991	26	72	11	0	0	2	3	71.36	$75,659

Best finish for 1991: T-7th at the Deposit Guaranty Classic

1992	5	14	2	0	0	0	0	71.93	$2,682

Best finish for 1992: T-49th at the Deposit Guaranty Classic

1994	1	2	0	0	0	0	0	71.00	

Period Totals	Starts	Rounds Played	Cuts Made	Wins	Top-5s	Top-10s	Top-25s	Scoring Average	Money
	153	424	65	0	1	5	11	72.03	$279,042

Steve Lamontagne

Year	Starts	Rounds Played	Cuts Made	Wins	Top-5s	Top-10s	Top-25s	Scoring Average	Money
1989	1	2	0	0	0	0	0	74.50	$1,000
1990	29	84	15	0	0	0	2	72.02	$67,598

Best finish for 1990: T-12th at the Hawaiian Open

1991	2	6	1	0	0	0	1	68.50	$4,950

Best finish for 1991: T-15th at the Deposit Guaranty Classic

1992	29	88	18	0	1	1	7	71.07	$132,498

Best finish for 1992: T-4th at the Chattanooga Classic

Year	Starts	Rounds Played	Cuts Made	Wins	Top-5s	Top-10s	Top-25s	Scoring Average	Money
1993	33	98	16	0	0	1	4	71.73	$107,077

Best finish for 1993: T-6th at the Buick Open

Year	Starts	Rounds Played	Cuts Made	Wins	Top-5s	Top-10s	Top-25s	Scoring Average	Money
1994	26	79	15	0	0	0	4	71.63	$91,643

Best finish for 1994: T-11th at the Buick Southern Open

Year	Starts	Rounds Played	Cuts Made	Wins	Top-5s	Top-10s	Top-25s	Scoring Average	Money
1995	2	6	1	0	0	0	0	71.33	$2,176

Best finish for 1995: T-44th at the Deposit Guaranty Golf Classic

Period Totals	Starts	Rounds Played	Cuts Made	Wins	Top-5s	Top-10s	Top-25s	Scoring Average	Money
	122	363	66	0	1	2	18	71.57	$406,942

Tom Lamore

Year	Starts	Rounds Played	Cuts Made	Wins	Top-5s	Top-10s	Top-25s	Scoring Average	Money
1982	1	2	0	0	0	0	0	76.50	
1984	26	62	5	0	0	0	0	74.90	$4,174

Best finish for 1984: T-60th at the Los Angeles Open

Year	Starts	Rounds Played	Cuts Made	Wins	Top-5s	Top-10s	Top-25s	Scoring Average	Money
1986	1	4	1	0	0	0	0	75.25	$2,888

Best finish for 1986: T-59th at the British Open

Period Totals	Starts	Rounds Played	Cuts Made	Wins	Top-5s	Top-10s	Top-25s	Scoring Average	Money
	28	68	6	0	0	0	0	74.97	$7,062

Neal Lancaster

Year	Starts	Rounds Played	Cuts Made	Wins	Top-5s	Top-10s	Top-25s	Scoring Average	Money
1989	1	2	0	0	0	0	0	79.50	
1990	26	74	11	0	0	2	7	71.18	$85,769

Best finish for 1990: T-10th at the Deposit Guaranty & Federal Express St. Jude Classic

| 1991 | 33 | 110 | 22 | 0 | 1 | 3 | 5 | 71.12 | $180,037 |

Best finish for 1991: T-5th at the Greater Milwaukee Open

| 1992 | 35 | 115 | 23 | 0 | 0 | 1 | 4 | 71.65 | $146,867 |

Best finish for 1992: T-6th at the Freeport-McMoRan Classic

| 1993 | 32 | 100 | 19 | 0 | 0 | 2 | 5 | 71.50 | $149,382 |

Best finish for 1993: T-6th at the Freeport-McMoRan Classic

| 1994 | 29 | 95 | 19 | 1 | 1 | 1 | 2 | 71.51 | $305,038 |

Best finish for 1994: Win at the GTE Byron Nelson Classic

| 1995 | 29 | 90 | 18 | 0 | 1 | 1 | 4 | 71.86 | $183,719 |

Best finish for 1995: T-4th at the U.S. Open

| 1996 | 32 | 102 | 22 | 0 | 1 | 2 | 6 | 71.43 | $211,500 |

Best finish for 1996: T-5th at the Deposit Guaranty Golf Classic

| 1997 | 34 | 101 | 19 | 0 | 0 | 0 | 4 | 71.49 | $179,273 |

Best finish for 1997: T-12th at the GTE Byron Nelson Classic

| 1998 | 28 | 86 | 18 | 0 | 1 | 2 | 7 | 71.19 | $348,063 |

Best finish for 1998: 4th at the Greater Greensboro Chrysler Classic

| 1999 | 35 | 92 | 13 | 0 | 0 | 1 | 3 | 72.04 | $283,140 |

Best finish for 1999: T-8th at the AT&T Pebble Beach Pro-Am

| 2000 | 31 | 95 | 19 | 0 | 1 | 2 | 5 | 71.41 | $466,712 |

Best finish for 2000: T-4th at the Bay Hill Invitational

| 2001 | 36 | 105 | 18 | 0 | 1 | 3 | 6 | 70.58 | $657,580 |

Best finish for 2001: T-3rd at the Buick Challenge

| 2002 | 31 | 101 | 20 | 0 | 2 | 3 | 4 | 71.10 | $813,230 |

Best finish for 2002: T-2nd at the Bell Canadian Open

| 2003 | 35 | 107 | 21 | 0 | 0 | 1 | 6 | 70.80 | $591,627 |

Best finish for 2003: T-6th at the Buick Open

| 2004 | 33 | 103 | 21 | 0 | 0 | 2 | 6 | 71.19 | $701,239 |

Best finish for 2004: T-7th at the B.C. Open

| 2005 | 31 | 95 | 17 | 0 | 0 | 1 | 4 | 71.06 | $532,185 |

Best finish for 2005: T-8th at the FedEx St. Jude Classic

| 2006 | 19 | 43 | 5 | 0 | 0 | 0 | 0 | 71.84 | $54,680 |

Best finish for 2006: T-41st at the Zurich Classic of New Orleans

| 2007 | 13 | 41 | 7 | 0 | 0 | 1 | 2 | 71.44 | $229,052 |

Best finish for 2007: T-6th at the John Deere Classic

| 2008 | 9 | 28 | 5 | 0 | 0 | 0 | 0 | 70.96 | $70,138 |

Best finish for 2008: T-28th at the Mayakoba Golf Classic & Puerto Rico Open

Period Totals	Starts	Rounds Played	Cuts Made	Wins	Top-5s	Top-10s	Top-25s	Scoring Average	Money
	552	1685	317	1	9	28	80	71.33	$6,189,232

Ralph Landrum

Year	Starts	Rounds Played	Cuts Made	Wins	Top-5s	Top-10s	Top-25s	Scoring Average	Money
1978	1	2	0	0	0	0	0	78.00	$1,500
1981	1	2	0	0	0	0	0	74.00	$600
1982	2	4	0	0	0	0	0	77.25	$600
1983	14	45	8	0	2	3	4	71.96	$46,808

Best finish for 1983: T-4th at the Canadian Open

| 1984 | 34 | 86 | 8 | 0 | 2 | 3 | 4 | 73.49 | $73,431 |

Best finish for 1984: T-2nd at the Danny Thomas Memphis Classic

| 1985 | 34 | 98 | 15 | 0 | 0 | 0 | 1 | 72.85 | $25,244 |

Best finish for 1985: T-25th at the Phoenix Open

Year	Starts	Rounds Played	Cuts Made	Wins	Top-5s	Top-10s	Top-25s	Scoring Average	Money
1986	1	2	0	0	0	0	0	77.00	
1987	1	4	1	0	0	0	0	72.75	$4,240

Best finish for 1987: T-46th at the U.S. Open

Year	Starts	Rounds Played	Cuts Made	Wins	Top-5s	Top-10s	Top-25s	Scoring Average	Money
1988	1	2	0	0	0	0	0	74.50	$1,000
1989	1	2	0	0	0	0	0	80.50	$1,000
Period Totals	Starts	Rounds Played	Cuts Made	Wins	Top-5s	Top-10s	Top-25s	Scoring Average	Money
	90	247	32	0	4	6	9	73.14	$154,423

Barry Lane

Year	Starts	Rounds Played	Cuts Made	Wins	Top-5s	Top-10s	Top-25s	Scoring Average	Money
1987	1	2	0	0	0	0	0	73.50	$640
1988	1	2	0	0	0	0	0	81.50	$765
1989	1	2	0	0	0	0	0	73.50	$800
1991	1	4	1	0	0	0	1	70.25	$16,893

Best finish for 1991: T-17th at the British Open

Year	Starts	Rounds Played	Cuts Made	Wins	Top-5s	Top-10s	Top-25s	Scoring Average	Money
1992	1	4	1	0	0	0	0	72.25	$8,150

Best finish for 1992: T-51st at the British Open

Year	Starts	Rounds Played	Cuts Made	Wins	Top-5s	Top-10s	Top-25s	Scoring Average	Money
1993	3	12	3	0	0	0	2	71.00	$55,659

Best finish for 1993: 13th at the British Open

Year	Starts	Rounds Played	Cuts Made	Wins	Top-5s	Top-10s	Top-25s	Scoring Average	Money
1994	5	14	2	0	0	0	1	73.93	$20,577

Best finish for 1994: T-25th at the PGA Championship

Year	Starts	Rounds Played	Cuts Made	Wins	Top-5s	Top-10s	Top-25s	Scoring Average	Money
1995	3	12	3	0	0	0	1	71.92	$33,080

Best finish for 1995: T-20th at the British Open

Year	Starts	Rounds Played	Cuts Made	Wins	Top-5s	Top-10s	Top-25s	Scoring Average	Money
1996	5	12	1	0	0	0	1	71.83	$20,858

Best finish for 1996: T-17th at the Phoenix Open

Year	Starts	Rounds Played	Cuts Made	Wins	Top-5s	Top-10s	Top-25s	Scoring Average	Money
1998	1	2	0	0	0	0	0	73.50	$1,645
2001	1	4	1	0	0	0	0	71.00	$35,762

Best finish for 2001: 29th at the British Open

Year	Starts	Rounds Played	Cuts Made	Wins	Top-5s	Top-10s	Top-25s	Scoring Average	Money
2002	1	4	1	0	0	0	0	72.00	$16,223

Best finish for 2002: T-50th at the British Open

Year	Starts	Rounds Played	Cuts Made	Wins	Top-5s	Top-10s	Top-25s	Scoring Average	Money
2004	3	12	3	0	0	0	2	71.42	$206,802

Best finish for 2004: T-14th at the British Open

Year	Starts	Rounds Played	Cuts Made	Wins	Top-5s	Top-10s	Top-25s	Scoring Average	Money
2006	1	2	0	0	0	0	0	75.00	$3,718
Period Totals	Starts	Rounds Played	Cuts Made	Wins	Top-5s	Top-10s	Top-25s	Scoring Average	Money
	28	88	16	0	0	0	8	72.33	$421,573

Bernhard Langer

Year	Starts	Rounds Played	Cuts Made	Wins	Top-5s	Top-10s	Top-25s	Scoring Average	Money
1976	1	2	0	0	0	0	0	80.50	$180
1978	1	2	0	0	0	0	0	75.50	$332
1980	1	4	1	0	0	0	0	73.25	$1,329

Best finish for 1980: T-51st at the British Open

Year	Starts	Rounds Played	Cuts Made	Wins	Top-5s	Top-10s	Top-25s	Scoring Average	Money
1981	2	8	2	0	1	2	2	70.13	$49,500

Best finish for 1981: 2nd at the British Open

Year	Starts	Rounds Played	Cuts Made	Wins	Top-5s	Top-10s	Top-25s	Scoring Average	Money
1982	7	20	3	0	0	0	1	75.00	$12,636

Best finish for 1982: T-13th at the British Open

Year	Starts	Rounds Played	Cuts Made	Wins	Top-5s	Top-10s	Top-25s	Scoring Average	Money
1983	4	10	1	0	0	0	0	73.90	$1,088

Best finish for 1983: T-56th at the British Open

Year	Starts	Rounds Played	Cuts Made	Wins	Top-5s	Top-10s	Top-25s	Scoring Average	Money
1984	9	36	9	0	3	4	6	70.81	$123,935

Best finish for 1984: T-2nd at the British Open

Year	Starts	Rounds Played	Cuts Made	Wins	Top-5s	Top-10s	Top-25s	Scoring Average	Money
1985	17	63	13	2	3	5	8	71.46	$305,864

Best finish for 1985: Win at the Masters & Sea Pines Heritage Classic

Year	Starts	Rounds Played	Cuts Made	Wins	Top-5s	Top-10s	Top-25s	Scoring Average	Money
1986	22	71	19	0	6	9	16	70.27	$433,299

Best finish for 1986: T-2nd at the Shearson Lehman/Andy Williams San Diego & The International

Year	Starts	Rounds Played	Cuts Made	Wins	Top-5s	Top-10s	Top-25s	Scoring Average	Money
1987	17	62	14	0	4	7	13	70.58	$378,350

Best finish for 1987: T-2nd at the Bob Hope Chrysler Classic & Honda Classic

Year	Starts	Rounds Played	Cuts Made	Wins	Top-5s	Top-10s	Top-25s	Scoring Average	Money
1988	16	50	9	0	1	3	4	72.24	$106,205

Best finish for 1988: T-4th at the AT&T Pebble Beach Pro-Am

Year	Starts	Rounds Played	Cuts Made	Wins	Top-5s	Top-10s	Top-25s	Scoring Average	Money
1989	15	59	14	0	2	3	5	72.10	$199,813

Best finish for 1989: T-3rd at the MCI Heritage Classic & Federal Express St. Jude Classic

Year	Starts	Rounds Played	Cuts Made	Wins	Top-5s	Top-10s	Top-25s	Scoring Average	Money
1990	6	17	2	0	0	1	1	73.24	$43,883

Best finish for 1990: T-7th at the Masters

Year	Starts	Rounds Played	Cuts Made	Wins	Top-5s	Top-10s	Top-25s	Scoring Average	Money
1991	8	27	6	0	0	3	4	71.56	$152,899

Best finish for 1991: T-6th at the Players Championship

Year	Starts	Rounds Played	Cuts Made	Wins	Top-5s	Top-10s	Top-25s	Scoring Average	Money
1992	6	24	6	0	0	0	1	72.58	$48,510

Best finish for 1992: T-23rd at the U.S. Open

Year	Starts	Rounds Played	Cuts Made	Wins	Top-5s	Top-10s	Top-25s	Scoring Average	Money
1993	7	24	6	1	3	4	5	69.88	$732,318

Best finish for 1993: Win at the Masters

Year	Starts	Rounds Played	Cuts Made	Wins	Top-5s	Top-10s	Top-25s	Scoring Average	Money
1994	7	28	7	0	1	1	5	71.29	$125,288

Best finish for 1994: T-4th at the Honda Classic

Year	Starts	Rounds Played	Cuts Made	Wins	Top-5s	Top-10s	Top-25s	Scoring Average	Money
1995	7	28	7	0	1	1	3	71.46	$394,877

Best finish for 1995: 2nd at the Players Championship

Year	Starts	Rounds Played	Cuts Made	Wins	Top-5s	Top-10s	Top-25s	Scoring Average	Money
1996	7	18	3	0	0	0	1	73.22	$36,190

Best finish for 1996: T-13th at the Bay Hill Invitational

1997	7	26	6	0	0	1	3	71.54	$159,508

Best finish for 1997: T-7th at the Masters

1998	8	24	4	0	1	1	3	72.63	$144,031

Best finish for 1998: T-4th at the Bay Hill Invitational

1999	9	30	8	0	0	1	3	73.33	$265,757

Best finish for 1999: T-9th at the Andersen Consulting Match Play Championship

2000	10	34	9	0	0	0	2	71.85	$255,455

Best finish for 2000: T-11th at the British Open

2001	17	61	15	0	4	7	9	69.80	$1,812,363

Best finish for 2001: 2nd at the FedEx St. Jude Classic

2002	16	54	13	0	1	1	3	71.48	$559,395

Best finish for 2002: 4th at the WorldCom Classic

2003	21	64	13	0	1	2	4	71.73	$565,750

Best finish for 2003: T-5th at the FBR Capital Open

2004	15	55	14	0	2	4	5	71.22	$943,589

Best finish for 2004: T-4th at the Masters

2005	19	67	14	0	2	3	6	71.09	$952,451

Best finish for 2005: T-5th at the Buick Invitational & British Open

2006	24	72	15	0	0	1	7	71.13	$569,973

Best finish for 2006: T-10th at the Bob Hope Chrysler Classic

2007	14	47	9	0	1	4	6	70.79	$1,153,603

Best finish for 2007: T-2nd at the Crowne Plaza Invitational at Colonial

2008	2	6	1	0	0	0	1	73.67	$147,250

Best finish for 2008: T-15th at The Players

Period Totals	Starts	Rounds Played	Cuts Made	Wins	Top-5s	Top-10s	Top-25s	Scoring Average	Money
	322	1093	243	3	37	68	127	71.48	$10,675,621

Franklin Langham

Year	Starts	Rounds Played	Cuts Made	Wins	Top-5s	Top-10s	Top-25s	Scoring Average	Money
1992	1	2	0	0	0	0	0	76.00	
1994	1	2	0	0	0	0	0	76.50	
1996	33	92	15	0	0	0	1	71.98	$83,632

Best finish for 1996: T-15th at the Freeport-McDermott Classic

1997	1	2	0	0	0	0	0	74.50	
1998	30	92	17	0	1	1	4	71.45	$244,412

Best finish for 1998: T-2nd at the Deposit Guaranty Golf Classic

1999	29	99	20	0	2	3	5	71.18	$535,652

Best finish for 1999: T-3rd at the National Car Rental Golf Classic/Disney

2000	28	91	18	0	3	7	12	70.56	$1,604,952

Best finish for 2000: T-2nd at the Doral Ryder Open, Kemper Insurance Open & Greater Milwaukee Open

2001	22	60	11	0	0	1	2	72.07	$334,538

Best finish for 2001: T-8th at the AT&T Pebble Beach

2002	25	69	11	0	0	0	2	71.87	$238,461

Best finish for 2002: T-13th at the Kemper Insurance Open

2003	2	4	0	0	0	0	0	72.00	
2004	1	4	1	0	0	0	0	72.50	$18,450

Best finish for 2004: T-38th at the BellSouth Classic

2005	31	87	14	0	0	0	3	71.83	$382,436

Best finish for 2005: T-19th at the FBR Open & Barclays Classic

2006	1	4	1	0	0	0	0	71.00	$16,642

Best finish for 2006: T-42nd at the BellSouth Classic

2007	1	4	1	0	0	0	0	70.75	$30,720

Best finish for 2007: T-30th at the AT&T Classic

2008	1	0	0	0	0	0	0		
Period Totals	Starts	Rounds Played	Cuts Made	Wins	Top-5s	Top-10s	Top-25s	Scoring Average	Money
	207	612	109	0	6	12	29	71.56	$3,489,894

Jim Langley

Year	Starts	Rounds Played	Cuts Made	Wins	Top-5s	Top-10s	Top-25s	Scoring Average	Money
1964	1	4	1	0	0	0	0	83.25	

Best finish for 1964: 67th at the Fresno Open

1966	13	31	3	0	0	0	0	74.74	$301

Best finish for 1966: T-39th at the Hawaiian Open Invitational

1967	3	4	1	0	0	0	0	73.75	
1968	19	54	8	0	0	0	0	74.33	$322

Best finish for 1968: T-33rd at the Robinson Open

1969	13	34	4	0	1	1	1	73.82	$2,970

Best finish for 1969: T-2nd at the Azalea Open

1970	11	24	1	0	0	0	1	74.04	$1,206

Best finish for 1970: T-24th at the Cleveland Open

1971	2	4	0	0	0	0	0	76.50	

Year	Starts	Rounds Played	Cuts Made	Wins	Top-5s	Top-10s	Top-25s	Scoring Average	Money
1973	1	3	0	0	0	0	0	75.00	
1974	3	11	1	0	0	0	0	74.73	$289

Best finish for 1974: T-61st at the Kaiser International Open

| 1975 | 3 | 10 | 1 | 0 | 0 | 0 | 0 | 74.30 | $256 |

Best finish for 1975: T-66th at the Bob Hope Chrysler Classic

1976	1	3	3	0	0	0	0	79.33	
1977	1	3	0	0	0	0	0	74.67	
1978	1	3	0	0	0	0	0	78.00	
1979	1	3	0	0	0	0	0	78.00	
1980	1	3	0	0	0	0	0	78.00	
1981	1	3	0	0	0	0	0	77.00	
1983	1	3	0	0	0	0	0	75.00	
1984	1	3	0	0	0	0	0	77.00	
1985	1	3	0	0	0	0	0	77.67	
1986	1	3	0	0	0	0	0	77.67	
1987	1	3	0	0	0	0	0	79.00	
Period Totals	Starts	Rounds Played	Cuts Made	Wins	Top-5s	Top-10s	Top-25s	Scoring Average	Money
	80	212	23	0	1	1	2	74.98	$5,344

Jeffrey Lankford

Year	Starts	Rounds Played	Cuts Made	Wins	Top-5s	Top-10s	Top-25s	Scoring Average	Money
1987	1	4	1	0	0	0	0	72.00	$864

Best finish for 1987: 74th at the Provident Classic

| 1988 | 21 | 41 | 1 | 0 | 0 | 0 | 0 | 75.34 | $661 |

Best finish for 1988: T-42nd at the Deposit Guaranty Golf Classic

1997	2	4	0	0	0	0	0	73.25	$1,300
1998	1	2	0	0	0	0	0	79.50	$1,500
1999	1	2	0	0	0	0	0	74.50	$1,750
2001	2	6	1	0	0	0	0	72.00	$23,775

Best finish for 2001: T-29th at the Greater Greensboro Chrysler Classic

2002	3	6	0	0	0	0	0	76.67	$2,000
2003	2	4	0	0	0	0	0	76.00	$2,000
2004	4	8	0	0	0	0	0	76.88	$2,000
Period Totals	Starts	Rounds Played	Cuts Made	Wins	Top-5s	Top-10s	Top-25s	Scoring Average	Money
	37	77	3	0	0	0	0	75.18	$35,850

Brad Lardon

Year	Starts	Rounds Played	Cuts Made	Wins	Top-5s	Top-10s	Top-25s	Scoring Average	Money
1991	23	62	8	0	0	0	1	72.89	$20,926

Best finish for 1991: T-18th at the Independent Insurance Agent Open

| 1992 | 1 | 2 | 0 | 0 | 0 | 0 | 0 | 75.50 | |
| 1994 | 21 | 55 | 8 | 0 | 0 | 0 | 0 | 72.60 | $21,429 |

Best finish for 1994: T-37th at the Deposit Guaranty Golf Classic

| 1997 | 1 | 4 | 1 | 0 | 0 | 0 | 0 | 72.25 | $6,880 |

Best finish for 1997: T-38th at the Shell Houston Open

| 2002 | 22 | 59 | 8 | 0 | 0 | 0 | 0 | 72.78 | $71,511 |

Best finish for 2002: T-38th at the Bell Canadian Open

| 2003 | 8 | 19 | 1 | 0 | 0 | 0 | 0 | 73.32 | $16,400 |

Best finish for 2003: T-39th at the BellSouth Classic

| 2004 | 17 | 43 | 5 | 0 | 0 | 0 | 0 | 72.40 | $41,253 |

Best finish for 2004: T-51st at the Southern Farm Bureau Classic

| 2005 | 4 | 12 | 2 | 0 | 0 | 0 | 0 | 71.67 | $25,332 |

Best finish for 2005: T-33rd at the Valero Texas Open

2006	1	1	0	0	0	0	0	74.00	
2007	3	6	0	0	0	0	0	74.17	$2,500
Period Totals	Starts	Rounds Played	Cuts Made	Wins	Top-5s	Top-10s	Top-25s	Scoring Average	Money
	101	263	33	0	0	0	1	72.74	$206,231

Duff Lawrence

Year	Starts	Rounds Played	Cuts Made	Wins	Top-5s	Top-10s	Top-25s	Scoring Average	Money
1958	1	4	1	0	0	0	0	74.25	

Best finish for 1958: 64th at the Phoenix Open

| 1963 | 5 | 18 | 4 | 0 | 0 | 0 | 1 | 73.56 | $834 |

Best finish for 1963: T-22nd at the Hot Springs Open Invitational

| 1964 | 30 | 86 | 11 | 0 | 0 | 0 | 0 | 73.70 | $982 |

Best finish for 1964: T-26th at the St. Paul Open

| 1965 | 9 | 28 | 4 | 0 | 0 | 0 | 2 | 73.18 | $2,411 |

Best finish for 1965: T-15th at the Jacksonville Open

| 1966 | 11 | 35 | 6 | 0 | 0 | 0 | 1 | 72.94 | $1,666 |

Best finish for 1966: T-12th at the Tucson Open Invitational

| 1967 | 3 | 7 | 0 | 0 | 0 | 0 | 0 | 75.86 | |
| 1968 | 3 | 6 | 0 | 0 | 0 | 0 | 0 | 73.17 | |

Year	Starts	Rounds Played	Cuts Made	Wins	Top-5s	Top-10s	Top-25s	Scoring Average	Money
1970	1	2	0	0	0	0	0	78.00	
1971	1	2	0	0	0	0	0	74.00	
1973	2	4	0	0	0	0	0	81.00	
Period Totals	Starts	Rounds Played	Cuts Made	Wins	Top-5s	Top-10s	Top-25s	Scoring Average	Money
	66	192	26	0	0	0	4	73.74	$5,892

Paul Lawrie

Year	Starts	Rounds Played	Cuts Made	Wins	Top-5s	Top-10s	Top-25s	Scoring Average	Money
1992	1	4	1	0	0	0	1	70.75	$17,900

Best finish for 1992: T-22nd at the British Open

1993	1	4	1	0	0	1	1	68.50	$51,077

Best finish for 1993: T-6th at the British Open

1994	1	4	1	0	0	0	1	69.50	$12,916

Best finish for 1994: T-24th at the British Open

1995	1	4	1	0	0	0	0	73.50	$8,733

Best finish for 1995: T-58th at the British Open

1996	1	2	0	0	0	0	0	77.50	$1,008
1998	1	2	0	0	0	0	0	74.50	$1,316
1999	4	16	4	1	1	1	2	72.31	$662,734

Best finish for 1999: Win at the British Open

2000	8	20	4	0	1	2	2	74.10	$255,799

Best finish for 2000: T-5th at the Andersen Consulting Match Play Championship

2001	6	12	2	0	0	0	1	73.50	$77,312

Best finish for 2001: T-17th at the Accenture Match Play Championship

2002	8	22	5	0	0	0	0	73.18	$142,960

Best finish for 2002: T-30th at the U.S. Open

2003	7	20	5	0	0	1	2	72.55	$260,948

Best finish for 2003: T-9th at the BellSouth Classic

2004	5	12	1	0	0	0	0	75.42	$37,408

Best finish for 2004: T-37th at the Masters

2005	1	4	1	0	0	0	0	72.00	$19,154

Best finish for 2005: T-52nd at the British Open

2006	2	4	0	0	0	0	0	75.25	$3,718
2007	1	2	0	0	0	0	0	73.50	$6,577
2008	1	2	0	0	0	0	0	75.00	
Period Totals	Starts	Rounds Played	Cuts Made	Wins	Top-5s	Top-10s	Top-25s	Scoring Average	Money
	49	134	26	1	2	5	10	73.18	$1,559,558

Scott Laycock

Year	Starts	Rounds Played	Cuts Made	Wins	Top-5s	Top-10s	Top-25s	Scoring Average	Money
2002	5	12	1	0	0	0	0	73.92	$33,450

Best finish for 2002: 60th at the American Express Championship

2003	25	69	10	0	0	1	3	71.07	$300,342

Best finish for 2003: T-10th at the FBR Capital Open

2007	1	2	0	0	0	0	0	77.00	$4,316
Period Totals	Starts	Rounds Played	Cuts Made	Wins	Top-5s	Top-10s	Top-25s	Scoring Average	Money
	31	83	11	0	0	1	3	71.63	$338,109

Stephen Leaney

Year	Starts	Rounds Played	Cuts Made	Wins	Top-5s	Top-10s	Top-25s	Scoring Average	Money
1995	1	2	0	0	0	0	0	75.00	$1,037
1998	2	6	1	0	0	0	0	74.00	$6,802

Best finish for 1998: 68th at the PGA Championship

1999	4	6	1	0	0	0	0	76.00	$29,469

Best finish for 1999: T-33rd at the Andersen Consulting Match Play Championship

2000	1	2	0	0	0	0	0	72.50	$1,976
2001	1	2	0	0	0	0	0	72.50	$1,860
2002	2	8	2	0	0	0	1	70.25	$79,232

Best finish for 2002: T-23rd at the American Express Championship

2003	9	24	6	0	1	2	3	72.83	$844,361

Best finish for 2003: 2nd at the U.S. Open

2004	24	75	17	0	1	2	6	71.44	$1,173,241

Best finish for 2004: 4th at the WGC-Accenture Match Play Championship

2005	29	86	17	0	0	0	7	70.93	$773,807

Best finish for 2005: T-11th at the Wachovia Championship

2006	27	84	14	0	1	2	5	70.79	$746,747

Best finish for 2006: T-4th at the Cialis Western Open

2007	26	82	15	0	1	2	8	70.94	$1,017,700

Best finish for 2007: 3rd at the Verizon Heritage

2008	17	53	9	0	0	0	0	72.23	$157,963

Best finish for 2008: T-30th at the FBR Open

Period Totals	Starts	Rounds Played	Cuts Made	Wins	Top-5s	Top-10s	Top-25s	Scoring Average	Money
	143	430	82	0	4	8	30	71.39	$4,834,194

Bob Leaver

Year	Starts	Rounds Played	Cuts Made	Wins	Top-5s	Top-10s	Top-25s	Scoring Average	Money
1971	2	6	1	0	0	0	0	75.67	

Best finish for 1971: 52nd at the Tallahassee Open

1972	3	6	0	0	0	0	0	77.83	
1974	1	2	0	0	0	0	0	76.50	
1975	2	4	0	0	0	0	0	75.75	
1976	5	9	0	0	0	0	0	78.33	
1978	3	4	0	0	0	0	0	78.75	$303
1979	5	14	2	0	0	0	0	75.00	$1,086

Best finish for 1979: T-74th at the Greater Greensboro Open

1984	1	2	0	0	0	0	0	82.50	
1985	2	4	0	0	0	0	0	77.00	$1,000
1986	1	2	0	0	0	0	0	80.50	$1,000
Period Totals	Starts	Rounds Played	Cuts Made	Wins	Top-5s	Top-10s	Top-25s	Scoring Average	Money
	25	53	3	0	0	0	0	77.00	$3,390

David Lee

Year	Starts	Rounds Played	Cuts Made	Wins	Top-5s	Top-10s	Top-25s	Scoring Average	Money
1969	1	2	0	0	0	0	0	80.00	
1970	6	12	0	0	0	0	0	74.50	
1971	9	17	1	0	0	0	0	74.71	$190

Best finish for 1971: T-60th at the Southern Open

1972	7	13	0	0	0	0	0	78.31	
1973	1	2	0	0	0	0	0	79.00	
1977	5	14	2	0	0	0	0	74.71	$125

Best finish for 1977: T-71st at the Pleasant Valley Classic

1984	1	2	0	0	0	0	0	80.50	$600
1988	1	2	0	0	0	0	0	74.00	
2001	1	2	0	0	0	0	0	76.50	
Period Totals	Starts	Rounds Played	Cuts Made	Wins	Top-5s	Top-10s	Top-25s	Scoring Average	Money
	32	66	3	0	0	0	0	75.88	$915

Stan Lee

Year	Starts	Rounds Played	Cuts Made	Wins	Top-5s	Top-10s	Top-25s	Scoring Average	Money
1976	12	36	7	0	0	1	1	72.89	$6,601

Best finish for 1976: T-10th at the Greater Greensboro Open

1977	18	52	9	0	1	1	2	72.87	$24,967

Best finish for 1977: 2nd at the First NBC New Orleans Open

1978	24	81	16	0	0	1	2	72.54	$14,465

Best finish for 1978: T-9th at the Sammy Davis, Jr. - Greater Hartford Open

1979	4	16	4	0	0	0	1	71.44	$6,555

Best finish for 1979: T-16th at the Danny Thomas Memphis Classic

1980	23	59	8	0	0	0	1	73.25	$7,738

Best finish for 1980: T-20th at the IVB Golf Classic

Period Totals	Starts	Rounds Played	Cuts Made	Wins	Top-5s	Top-10s	Top-25s	Scoring Average	Money
	81	244	44	0	1	3	7	72.76	$60,326

Ian Leggatt

Year	Starts	Rounds Played	Cuts Made	Wins	Top-5s	Top-10s	Top-25s	Scoring Average	Money
1992	1	2	0	0	0	0	0	76.50	
1994	1	2	0	0	0	0	0	78.50	
1995	1	2	0	0	0	0	0	76.50	
1996	2	7	2	0	0	0	0	73.14	$4,780

Best finish for 1996: T-73rd at the Greater Vancouver Open

1998	2	6	1	0	0	0	0	71.83	$4,420

Best finish for 1998: T-56th at the Greater Vancouver Open

1999	2	6	1	0	0	0	0	73.83	$4,725

Best finish for 1999: T-75th at the Bell Canadian Open

2000	2	4	0	0	0	0	0	73.25	
2001	29	84	12	0	1	2	3	70.92	$368,862

Best finish for 2001: T-5th at the John Deere Classic

2002	29	93	20	1	2	3	8	70.75	$1,247,048

Best finish for 2002: Win at the Touchstone Energy Tucson Open

2003	25	68	11	0	0	0	3	71.32	$271,014

Best finish for 2003: T-20th at the U.S. Open

2004	5	13	1	0	0	0	0	72.54	$8,280

Best finish for 2004: 78th at the Bob Hope Chrysler Classic

2005	12	28	3	0	0	0	0	72.18	$65,283

Best finish for 2005: T-32nd at the Barclays Classic

2006	29	76	10	0	0	1	3	71.89	$377,903

Best finish for 2006: T-6th at the International

Year	Starts	Rounds Played	Cuts Made	Wins	Top-5s	Top-10s	Top-25s	Scoring Average	Money
2007	4	8	0	0	0	0	0	73.25	
2008	5	17	4	0	0	0	0	72.06	$62,481

Best finish for 2008: T-33rd at the Reno-Tahoe Open

Period Totals	Starts	Rounds Played	Cuts Made	Wins	Top-5s	Top-10s	Top-25s	Scoring Average	Money
	149	416	65	1	3	6	17	71.56	$2,414,796

Cobie Legrange

Year	Starts	Rounds Played	Cuts Made	Wins	Top-5s	Top-10s	Top-25s	Scoring Average	Money
1964	1	2	0	0	0	0	0	81.50	
1965	11	34	6	0	0	0	1	73.41	$1,754

Best finish for 1965: T-17th at the British Open

| 1966 | 10 | 32 | 6 | 0 | 0 | 0 | 3 | 73.13 | $5,421 |

Best finish for 1966: T-17th at the Memphis Open Invitational

| 1967 | 22 | 70 | 13 | 0 | 1 | 2 | 5 | 73.14 | $11,934 |

Best finish for 1967: T-4th at the Greater New Orleans Open

| 1968 | 20 | 68 | 14 | 0 | 0 | 0 | 1 | 72.57 | $4,008 |

Best finish for 1968: T-24th at the Greater Milwaukee Open Invitational

| 1969 | 1 | 4 | 1 | 0 | 0 | 0 | 1 | 72.25 | $1,577 |

Best finish for 1969: T-11th at the British Open

Period Totals	Starts	Rounds Played	Cuts Made	Wins	Top-5s	Top-10s	Top-25s	Scoring Average	Money
	65	210	40	0	1	2	11	73.06	$24,695

Tom Lehman

Year	Starts	Rounds Played	Cuts Made	Wins	Top-5s	Top-10s	Top-25s	Scoring Average	Money
1983	22	65	9	0	0	0	1	73.22	$9,413

Best finish for 1983: T-24th at the Miller High-Life Quad Cities Open

| 1984 | 26 | 75 | 9 | 0 | 0 | 0 | 0 | 73.23 | $9,382 |

Best finish for 1984: T-31st at the Miller High-Life Quad Cities Open

| 1985 | 26 | 70 | 10 | 0 | 0 | 0 | 2 | 72.44 | $20,232 |

Best finish for 1985: T-11th at the Lite Quad Cities Open

1986	2	4	0	0	0	0	0	76.25	$600
1987	1	2	0	0	0	0	0	74.50	$600
1990	1	2	0	0	0	0	0	73.00	$1,000
1992	29	103	25	0	5	9	15	70.10	$579,094

Best finish for 1992: T-2nd at the Hardee's Golf Classic

| 1993 | 28 | 99 | 21 | 0 | 3 | 6 | 12 | 70.65 | $430,159 |

Best finish for 1993: T-3rd at the Masters

| 1994 | 23 | 85 | 21 | 1 | 4 | 9 | 16 | 69.87 | $1,044,060 |

Best finish for 1994: Win at the Memorial Tournament

| 1995 | 18 | 65 | 16 | 1 | 4 | 5 | 12 | 70.68 | $831,431 |

Best finish for 1995: Win at the Colonial National Invitational

| 1996 | 22 | 79 | 20 | 2 | 7 | 13 | 19 | 69.96 | $1,780,158 |

Best finish for 1996: Win at the British Open & The Tour Championship

| 1997 | 21 | 72 | 18 | 0 | 3 | 9 | 14 | 70.26 | $960,584 |

Best finish for 1997: 2nd at the Mercedes Championship

| 1998 | 23 | 79 | 18 | 0 | 3 | 5 | 12 | 70.82 | $1,039,989 |

Best finish for 1998: T-2nd at the Players Championship

| 1999 | 23 | 80 | 19 | 0 | 5 | 5 | 9 | 70.83 | $1,437,283 |

Best finish for 1999: T-2nd at the FedEx St. Jude Classic, Greater Milwaukee Open & Buick Open

| 2000 | 21 | 69 | 17 | 1 | 3 | 7 | 13 | 70.62 | $2,068,499 |

Best finish for 2000: Win at the Phoenix Open

| 2001 | 23 | 79 | 17 | 0 | 3 | 5 | 12 | 69.75 | $1,911,233 |

Best finish for 2001: T-2nd at the Sony Open in Hawaii & Invensys Classic at Las Vegas

| 2002 | 22 | 70 | 17 | 0 | 1 | 3 | 8 | 71.00 | $877,582 |

Best finish for 2002: T-5th at the Accenture Match Play Championship

| 2003 | 25 | 82 | 19 | 0 | 1 | 2 | 9 | 70.46 | $1,180,237 |

Best finish for 2003: 2nd at the AT&T Pebble Beach

| 2004 | 19 | 66 | 16 | 0 | 3 | 4 | 11 | 69.97 | $1,347,490 |

Best finish for 2004: T-2nd at the Michelin Championship at Las Vegas

| 2005 | 20 | 67 | 15 | 0 | 2 | 4 | 7 | 71.07 | $1,659,416 |

Best finish for 2005: T-2nd at the Buick Invitational & The Players Championship

| 2006 | 20 | 60 | 14 | 0 | 2 | 4 | 6 | 71.60 | $1,705,978 |

Best finish for 2006: 2nd at the International

| 2007 | 19 | 62 | 12 | 0 | 2 | 3 | 5 | 71.08 | $880,824 |

Best finish for 2007: T-5th at the Crowne Plaza Invitational at Colonial

| 2008 | 17 | 51 | 8 | 0 | 0 | 2 | 3 | 71.98 | $676,651 |

Best finish for 2008: T-6th at The Players

Period Totals	Starts	Rounds Played	Cuts Made	Wins	Top-5s	Top-10s	Top-25s	Scoring Average	Money
	451	1486	321	5	51	95	186	70.93	$20,451,897

Ted Lehmann

Year	Starts	Rounds Played	Cuts Made	Wins	Top-5s	Top-10s	Top-25s	Scoring Average	Money
1987	28	66	5	0	0	0	0	74.30	$5,111

Best finish for 1987: T-53rd at the Hardee's Golf Classic

| 1996 | 1 | 2 | 0 | 0 | 0 | 0 | 0 | 75.00 | |

Period Totals	Starts	Rounds Played	Cuts Made	Wins	Top-5s	Top-10s	Top-25s	Scoring Average	Money
	29	68	5	0	0	0	0	74.32	$5,111

Tony Lema

Year	Starts	Rounds Played	Cuts Made	Wins	Top-5s	Top-10s	Top-25s	Scoring Average	Money
1958	37	138	31	0	2	4	18	71.72	$12,043

Best finish for 1958: T-2nd at the Greater Greensboro Open

| 1959 | 15 | 57 | 13 | 0 | 0 | 1 | 8 | 70.89 | $5,484 |

Best finish for 1959: T-6th at the Portland Centennial Open Invitational

| 1960 | 15 | 61 | 15 | 0 | 0 | 0 | 6 | 71.67 | $3,061 |

Best finish for 1960: T-16th at the Portland Open Invitational

| 1961 | 25 | 100 | 24 | 0 | 0 | 3 | 13 | 70.89 | $11,643 |

Best finish for 1961: T-6th at the Milwaukee Open Invitational

| 1962 | 26 | 100 | 22 | 2 | 6 | 8 | 18 | 71.00 | $25,174 |

Best finish for 1962: Win at the Sahara Invitational & Mobile Sertoma Open Invitational

| 1963 | 24 | 97 | 22 | 1 | 10 | 13 | 20 | 70.90 | $61,813 |

Best finish for 1963: Win at the Memphis Open Invitational

| 1964 | 28 | 107 | 25 | 5 | 7 | 14 | 22 | 71.21 | $84,130 |

Best finish for 1964: Win at the Bing Crosby Pro-Am, Thunderbird Classic, Buick Open, Cleveland Open & British Open

| 1965 | 26 | 97 | 23 | 2 | 10 | 12 | 20 | 78.01 | $108,945 |

Best finish for 1965: Win at the Buick Open & Carling Open

| 1966 | 20 | 74 | 17 | 1 | 6 | 8 | 13 | 71.77 | $49,707 |

Best finish for 1966: Win at the Oklahoma City Open Invitational

Period Totals	Starts	Rounds Played	Cuts Made	Wins	Top-5s	Top-10s	Top-25s	Scoring Average	Money
	216	831	192	11	41	63	138	72.05	$362,001

Jeff Leonard

Year	Starts	Rounds Played	Cuts Made	Wins	Top-5s	Top-10s	Top-25s	Scoring Average	Money
1995	26	72	9	0	0	1	1	72.33	$53,444

Best finish for 1995: T-7th at the B.C. Open

Period Totals	Starts	Rounds Played	Cuts Made	Wins	Top-5s	Top-10s	Top-25s	Scoring Average	Money
	26	72	9	0	0	1	1	72.33	$53,444

Justin Leonard

Year	Starts	Rounds Played	Cuts Made	Wins	Top-5s	Top-10s	Top-25s	Scoring Average	Money
1993	8	25	5	0	0	0	1	71.92	

Best finish for 1993: T-25th at the Sprint Western Open

| 1994 | 13 | 33 | 5 | 0 | 1 | 2 | 4 | 70.61 | $140,413 |

Best finish for 1994: 3rd at the Anheuser-Busch Golf Classic

| 1995 | 31 | 110 | 25 | 0 | 5 | 7 | 13 | 70.45 | $748,793 |

Best finish for 1995: T-2nd at the Motorola Western Open & LaCantera Texas Open

| 1996 | 29 | 101 | 23 | 1 | 5 | 8 | 13 | 70.67 | $944,148 |

Best finish for 1996: Win at the Buick Open

| 1997 | 29 | 101 | 25 | 2 | 5 | 8 | 13 | 70.44 | $1,587,532 |

Best finish for 1997: Win at the Kemper Open & British Open

| 1998 | 28 | 100 | 22 | 1 | 4 | 8 | 13 | 70.70 | $1,673,323 |

Best finish for 1998: Win at The Players Championship

| 1999 | 28 | 104 | 26 | 0 | 6 | 7 | 25 | 70.42 | $2,022,741 |

Best finish for 1999: T-2nd at the Phoenix Open & British Open

| 2000 | 28 | 93 | 22 | 1 | 4 | 4 | 14 | 70.43 | $2,023,465 |

Best finish for 2000: Win at the Westin Texas Open at LaCantera

| 2001 | 30 | 99 | 22 | 1 | 4 | 9 | 12 | 70.43 | $1,786,702 |

Best finish for 2001: Win at the Texas Open at LaCantera

| 2002 | 26 | 94 | 23 | 1 | 4 | 7 | 17 | 69.91 | $2,738,235 |

Best finish for 2002: Win at the WorldCom Classic

| 2003 | 23 | 75 | 18 | 1 | 2 | 4 | 13 | 70.29 | $2,462,294 |

Best finish for 2003: Win at the Honda Classic

| 2004 | 25 | 85 | 21 | 0 | 1 | 3 | 9 | 70.75 | $1,532,023 |

Best finish for 2004: T-2nd at the PGA Championship

| 2005 | 24 | 75 | 17 | 2 | 2 | 4 | 8 | 70.53 | $2,667,131 |

Best finish for 2005: Win at the Bob Hope Chrysler Classic & FedEx St. Jude Classic

| 2006 | 26 | 79 | 17 | 0 | 0 | 2 | 5 | 71.28 | $786,006 |

Best finish for 2006: T-7th at the FBR Open

| 2007 | 29 | 95 | 17 | 1 | 2 | 5 | 9 | 71.05 | $2,090,325 |

Best finish for 2007: Win at the Valero Texas Open

Year	Starts	Rounds Played	Cuts Made	Wins	Top-5s	Top-10s	Top-25s	Scoring Average	Money
2008	25	95	24	1	4	8	15	70.41	$3,943,542

Best finish for 2008: Win at the Stanford St. Jude Classic

Period Totals	Starts	Rounds Played	Cuts Made	Wins	Top-5s	Top-10s	Top-25s	Scoring Average	Money
	402	1364	312	12	49	86	184	70.58	$27,146,673

Stan Leonard

Year	Starts	Rounds Played	Cuts Made	Wins	Top-5s	Top-10s	Top-25s	Scoring Average	Money
1958	15	58	14	1	6	9	12	70.81	$20,956

Best finish for 1958: Win at Tournament of Champions,

1959	12	48	10	0	1	2	9	70.67	$7,083

Best finish for 1959: T-4th at the Masters

1960	14	55	13	1	3	6	10	71.40	$13,349

Best finish for 1960: Win at the Western Open Championship

1961	16	65	16	0	1	6	13	70.55	$14,097

Best finish for 1961: T-4th at the Greater Greensboro Open Invitational

1962	13	51	10	0	0	1	9	71.82	$9,914

Best finish for 1962: T-8th at the Eastern Open Invitational

1963	13	51	11	0	1	1	5	71.90	$8,157

Best finish for 1963: T-2nd at the Seattle Open Invitational

1964	12	41	8	0	1	2	3	72.29	$5,210

Best finish for 1964: T-2nd at the Sunset-Camellia Open

1965	11	31	5	0	0	0	3	73.16	$2,692

Best finish for 1965: T-16th at the Bob Hope Classic

1966	4	10	0	0	0	0	0	76.10	
1967	2	7	0	0	0	0	0	77.86	
1968	1	3	0	0	0	0	0	78.33	
1970	1	2	0	0	0	0	0	76.00	
Period Totals	Starts	Rounds Played	Cuts Made	Wins	Top-5s	Top-10s	Top-25s	Scoring Average	Money
	114	422	87	2	13	27	64	71.73	$81,458

PGA Tour career totals from 1938 to 1970

	Starts	Rounds Played	Cuts Made	Wins	Top-5s	Top-10s	Top-25s	Scoring Average	Money
	199	729	169	4	18	57	116	N/A	$124,380

Greg Lesher

Year	Starts	Rounds Played	Cuts Made	Wins	Top-5s	Top-10s	Top-25s	Scoring Average	Money
1989	1	4	1	0	0	0	0	74.00	

Best finish for 1989: T-63rd at the U.S. Open

| 1991 | 1 | 2 | 0 | 0 | 0 | 0 | 0 | 72.00 | |
| 1992 | 27 | 76 | 12 | 0 | 0 | 1 | 4 | 71.68 | $84,818 |

Best finish for 1992: T-6th at the Buick Open

1993	13	31	3	0	0	0	1	72.97	$23,171

Best finish for 1993: T-14th at the Anheuser-Busch Golf Classic

1996	2	4	0	0	0	0	0	75.75	$1,000
Period Totals	Starts	Rounds Played	Cuts Made	Wins	Top-5s	Top-10s	Top-25s	Scoring Average	Money
	44	117	16	0	0	1	5	72.25	$108,988

Perry Leslie

Year	Starts	Rounds Played	Cuts Made	Wins	Top-5s	Top-10s	Top-25s	Scoring Average	Money
1974	8	20	2	0	0	0	0	73.65	$1,512

Best finish for 1974: T-29th at the Canadian Open

1975	18	51	8	0	0	0	2	73.65	$5,118

Best finish for 1975: T-24th at the B.C. Open

1976	23	65	12	0	0	0	1	73.57	$5,428

Best finish for 1976: T-23rd at the Ohio Kings Island Open

1977	15	47	9	0	0	0	0	73.09	$3,735

Best finish for 1977: T-31st at the Sammy Davis, Jr. - Greater Hartford Open

1978	20	50	6	0	0	0	0	73.90	$2,409

Best finish for 1978: T-41st at the Greater Milwaukee Open

1980	1	2	0	0	0	0	0	80.00	$500
Period Totals	Starts	Rounds Played	Cuts Made	Wins	Top-5s	Top-10s	Top-25s	Scoring Average	Money
	85	235	37	0	0	0	3	73.62	$18,702

Ron Letellier

Year	Starts	Rounds Played	Cuts Made	Wins	Top-5s	Top-10s	Top-25s	Scoring Average	Money
1963	3	12	3	0	0	0	1	71.08	$1,324

Best finish for 1963: T-23rd at the "500" Festival Open Invitational

1964	25	68	10	0	0	0	1	73.43	$1,406

Best finish for 1964: T-23rd at the Tucson Open

1965	3	9	1	0	0	0	0	72.67	$552

Best finish for 1965: T-27th at the Almaden Open

Year	Starts	Rounds Played	Cuts Made	Wins	Top-5s	Top-10s	Top-25s	Scoring Average	Money
1966	2	6	1	0	0	0	0	72.50	$362

Best finish for 1966: T-37th at the Tucson Open Invitational

1967	2	6	0	0	0	0	0	77.33	
1968	2	4	0	0	0	0	0	76.25	
1971	1	2	0	0	0	0	0	73.00	
1972	3	10	2	0	0	0	0	76.10	$1,263

Best finish for 1972: T-47th at the U.S. Open

1975	3	8	1	0	0	0	0	75.38	$429

Best finish for 1975: T-65th at the PGA Championship

Period Totals	Starts	Rounds Played	Cuts Made	Wins	Top-5s	Top-10s	Top-25s	Scoring Average	Money
	44	125	18	0	0	0	2	73.71	$5,336

Michael Letzig

Year	Starts	Rounds Played	Cuts Made	Wins	Top-5s	Top-10s	Top-25s	Scoring Average	Money
2008	29	88	15	0	1	5	7	71.01	$1,166,976

Best finish for 2008: T-2nd at the Ginn sur Mer Classic

Period Totals	Starts	Rounds Played	Cuts Made	Wins	Top-5s	Top-10s	Top-25s	Scoring Average	Money
	29	88	15	0	1	5	7	71.01	$1,166,976

Gavin Levenson

Year	Starts	Rounds Played	Cuts Made	Wins	Top-5s	Top-10s	Top-25s	Scoring Average	Money
1979	1	2	0	0	0	0	0	78.00	$420
1980	1	2	0	0	0	0	0	75.50	$540
1981	10	29	5	0	0	0	1	73.45	$4,892

Best finish for 1981: T-22nd at the Pleasant Valley Jimmy Fund Classic

1982	20	62	11	0	1	1	3	72.10	$28,411

Best finish for 1982: T-4th at the Sammy Davis, Jr. - Greater Hartford Open

1983	19	62	12	0	0	0	1	72.60	$15,568

Best finish for 1983: T-17th at the Sammy Davis, Jr. - Greater Hartford Open

1984	25	79	13	0	0	0	1	73.04	$26,458

Best finish for 1984: T-24th at the Greater Greensboro Open

1985	1	4	1	0	0	0	0	71.00	$7,700

Best finish for 1985: T-26th at the NEC World Series of Golf

1987	1	2	0	0	0	0	0	73.50	$640
1989	1	4	1	0	0	0	0	75.25	$3,840

Best finish for 1989: 79th at the British Open

1990	1	2	0	0	0	0	0	74.50	$996
1991	1	4	1	0	0	0	0	71.50	$5,964

Best finish for 1991: T-57th at the British Open

Period Totals	Starts	Rounds Played	Cuts Made	Wins	Top-5s	Top-10s	Top-25s	Scoring Average	Money
	81	252	44	0	1	1	6	72.80	$95,428

Thomas Levet

Year	Starts	Rounds Played	Cuts Made	Wins	Top-5s	Top-10s	Top-25s	Scoring Average	Money
1994	10	25	1	0	0	0	0	74.24	$2,200

Best finish for 1994: T-69th at the Buick Invitational of California

1998	1	2	0	0	0	0	0	73.50	$1,645
1999	1	4	1	0	0	0	0	76.00	$11,275

Best finish for 1999: T-49th at the British Open

2001	1	4	1	0	0	0	0	74.00	$11,766

Best finish for 2001: T-66th at the British Open

2002	3	12	3	0	1	1	2	73.17	$532,186

Best finish for 2002: T-2nd at the British Open

2003	26	83	16	0	0	1	4	71.55	$475,021

Best finish for 2003: T-6th at the Chrysler Championship

2004	5	16	3	0	1	1	1	71.50	$407,305

Best finish for 2004: T-5th at the British Open

2005	20	53	9	0	0	1	2	72.89	$487,343

Best finish for 2005: T-6th at the MCI Heritage

2006	19	51	9	0	0	0	0	72.04	$168,110

Best finish for 2006: T-33rd at the FBR Open

2007	5	10	0	0	0	0	0	72.90	
2008	1	2	0	0	0	0	0	75.00	

Period Totals	Starts	Rounds Played	Cuts Made	Wins	Top-5s	Top-10s	Top-25s	Scoring Average	Money
	92	262	43	0	2	4	9	72.44	$2,096,851

Wayne Levi

Year	Starts	Rounds Played	Cuts Made	Wins	Top-5s	Top-10s	Top-25s	Scoring Average	Money
1975	1	2	0	0	0	0	0	76.50	$500
1976	1	4	1	0	0	0	0	73.50	$1,412

Best finish for 1976: T-28th at the U.S. Open

1977	13	40	7	0	0	0	3	72.20	$8,636

Best finish for 1977: T-12th at the Ed McMahon Quad City Open

Year	Starts	Rounds Played	Cuts Made	Wins	Top-5s	Top-10s	Top-25s	Scoring Average	Money
1978	23	78	16	0	1	1	5	72.53	$25,039

Best finish for 1978: 3rd at the Pensacola Open

| 1979 | 29 | 103 | 24 | 1 | 3 | 6 | 14 | 71.97 | $141,034 |

Best finish for 1979: Win at the Houston Open

| 1980 | 33 | 102 | 19 | 1 | 2 | 5 | 10 | 72.00 | $122,145 |

Best finish for 1980: Win at the Pleasant Valley Jimmy Fund Classic

| 1981 | 31 | 107 | 24 | 0 | 0 | 2 | 11 | 72.06 | $62,177 |

Best finish for 1981: T-9th at the Anheuser-Busch Golf Classic

| 1982 | 27 | 98 | 22 | 2 | 5 | 9 | 18 | 70.68 | $281,331 |

Best finish for 1982: Win at the Hawaiian Open & LaJet Classic

| 1983 | 22 | 84 | 20 | 1 | 2 | 6 | 13 | 70.98 | $193,252 |

Best finish for 1983: Win at the Buick Open

| 1984 | 28 | 98 | 22 | 1 | 3 | 7 | 16 | 71.07 | $254,521 |

Best finish for 1984: Win at the B.C. Open

| 1985 | 23 | 86 | 21 | 1 | 1 | 5 | 14 | 71.00 | $221,425 |

Best finish for 1985: Win at the Georgia-Pacific Atlanta Golf Classic

| 1986 | 28 | 89 | 20 | 0 | 2 | 5 | 9 | 71.40 | $154,776 |

Best finish for 1986: T-4th at the Hertz Bay Hill Classic & Bank of Boston Classic

| 1987 | 27 | 83 | 16 | 0 | 4 | 5 | 7 | 71.18 | $204,322 |

Best finish for 1987: T-2nd at the Canon Sammy Davis, Jr. - Greater Hartford Open & Greater Milwaukee Open

| 1988 | 22 | 79 | 17 | 0 | 1 | 4 | 8 | 70.68 | $190,073 |

Best finish for 1988: T-2nd at the B.C. Open

| 1989 | 27 | 86 | 17 | 0 | 4 | 7 | 11 | 70.63 | $499,272 |

Best finish for 1989: 2nd at the Canon Greater Hartford Open

| 1990 | 24 | 73 | 13 | 4 | 5 | 5 | 6 | 71.78 | $1,027,147 |

Best finish for 1990: Win at the BellSouth Atlanta Golf Classic, Centel Western Open, Canon Greater Hartford Open & Canadian Open

| 1991 | 25 | 75 | 12 | 0 | 2 | 3 | 6 | 71.37 | $195,861 |

Best finish for 1991: T-3rd at the Infiniti Tournament Of Champions

| 1992 | 25 | 83 | 16 | 0 | 1 | 4 | 7 | 71.05 | $239,135 |

Best finish for 1992: 4th at the United Airlines Hawaiian Open

| 1993 | 22 | 75 | 14 | 0 | 0 | 2 | 6 | 71.09 | $179,521 |

Best finish for 1993: T-9th at the United Airlines Hawaiian Open & Bob Hope Chrysler Classic

| 1994 | 24 | 83 | 17 | 0 | 0 | 4 | 7 | 71.23 | $200,476 |

Best finish for 1994: T-7th at the Canon Greater Hartford Open

| 1995 | 20 | 52 | 6 | 0 | 0 | 0 | 2 | 72.12 | $46,095 |

Best finish for 1995: T-20th at the MCI Classic & B.C. Open

| 1996 | 20 | 71 | 14 | 0 | 0 | 2 | 6 | 71.07 | $194,999 |

Best finish for 1996: T-7th at the Greater Greensboro Chrysler Classic & Buick Open

| 1997 | 20 | 67 | 12 | 0 | 0 | 3 | 4 | 70.84 | $195,820 |

Best finish for 1997: T-6th at the Canon Greater Hartford Open

| 1998 | 9 | 24 | 1 | 0 | 0 | 0 | 0 | 72.38 | $4,900 |

Best finish for 1998: 72nd at the Phoenix Open

| 1999 | 17 | 47 | 7 | 0 | 0 | 0 | 0 | 73.02 | $36,138 |

Best finish for 1999: T-48th at the Greater Greensboro Chrysler Classic

| 2000 | 4 | 14 | 3 | 0 | 0 | 0 | 0 | 73.00 | $14,144 |

Best finish for 2000: T-70th at the B.C. Open

| 2001 | 2 | 6 | 1 | 0 | 0 | 0 | 0 | 71.50 | $3,880 |

Best finish for 2001: T-73rd at the B.C. Open

| 2003 | 1 | 2 | 0 | 0 | 0 | 0 | 0 | 70.50 | |
| 2004 | 1 | 4 | 1 | 0 | 0 | 0 | 1 | 68.75 | $28,162 |

Best finish for 2004: T-21st at the B.C. Open

| 2005 | 1 | 4 | 1 | 0 | 0 | 0 | 0 | 69.00 | $6,926 |

Best finish for 2005: T-52nd at the B.C. Open

| 2006 | 1 | 4 | 1 | 0 | 0 | 0 | 0 | 71.50 | $6,390 |

Best finish for 2006: T-62nd at the B.C. Open

Period Totals	Starts	Rounds Played	Cuts Made	Wins	Top-5s	Top-10s	Top-25s	Scoring Average	Money
	551	1823	365	11	36	85	184	71.43	$4,739,509

Don Levin

Year	Starts	Rounds Played	Cuts Made	Wins	Top-5s	Top-10s	Top-25s	Scoring Average	Money
1981	21	58	8	0	0	1	2	72.81	$16,973

Best finish for 1981: T-6th at the Texas Open

| 1982 | 18 | 42 | 3 | 0 | 0 | 0 | 0 | 73.90 | $1,862 |

Best finish for 1982: T-67th at the Manufactures Hanover Westchester Classic

| 1983 | 2 | 6 | 1 | 0 | 0 | 0 | 0 | 74.00 | $1,342 |

Best finish for 1983: T-60th at the Bank of Boston Classic

Period Totals	Starts	Rounds Played	Cuts Made	Wins	Top-5s	Top-10s	Top-25s	Scoring Average	Money
	41	106	12	0	0	1	2	73.31	$20,177

John Levinson

Year	Starts	Rounds Played	Cuts Made	Wins	Top-5s	Top-10s	Top-25s	Scoring Average	Money
1958	1	4	1	0	0	0	0	73.25	

Best finish for 1958: T-65th at the Insurance City Open

Year	Starts	Rounds Played	Cuts Made	Wins	Top-5s	Top-10s	Top-25s	Scoring Average	Money
1964	1	1	0	0	0	0	0	79.00	
1966	1	2	0	0	0	0	0	79.50	
1967	1	2	0	0	0	0	0	73.50	
1968	2	4	0	0	0	0	0	73.75	
1969	14	36	4	0	0	1	1	74.17	$4,449

Best finish for 1969: T-7th at the Cleveland Open

Year	Starts	Rounds Played	Cuts Made	Wins	Top-5s	Top-10s	Top-25s	Scoring Average	Money
1970	13	27	3	0	0	0	0	74.15	$798

Best finish for 1970: T-34th at the Western Open

Period Totals	Starts	Rounds Played	Cuts Made	Wins	Top-5s	Top-10s	Top-25s	Scoring Average	Money
	33	76	8	0	0	1	1	74.28	$5,246

Bob Lewis, Jr.

Year	Starts	Rounds Played	Cuts Made	Wins	Top-5s	Top-10s	Top-25s	Scoring Average	Money
1971	10	26	3	0	0	0	2	72.92	$2,917

Best finish for 1971: T-19th at the Massachusetts Classic

Year	Starts	Rounds Played	Cuts Made	Wins	Top-5s	Top-10s	Top-25s	Scoring Average	Money
1972	21	59	9	0	0	0	1	73.85	$3,590

Best finish for 1972: T-17th at the Houston Open

Year	Starts	Rounds Played	Cuts Made	Wins	Top-5s	Top-10s	Top-25s	Scoring Average	Money
1973	18	47	6	0	0	1	1	73.70	$5,821

Best finish for 1973: T-6th at the Shrine-Robinson Golf Classic

Year	Starts	Rounds Played	Cuts Made	Wins	Top-5s	Top-10s	Top-25s	Scoring Average	Money
1974	7	13	0	0	0	0	0	74.38	

Period Totals	Starts	Rounds Played	Cuts Made	Wins	Top-5s	Top-10s	Top-25s	Scoring Average	Money
	56	145	18	0	0	1	4	73.68	$12,327

J.L. Lewis

Year	Starts	Rounds Played	Cuts Made	Wins	Top-5s	Top-10s	Top-25s	Scoring Average	Money
1985	1	2	0	0	0	0	0	75.00	
1989	20	48	4	0	0	0	0	72.17	$9,087

Best finish for 1989: T-28th at the Texas Open

Year	Starts	Rounds Played	Cuts Made	Wins	Top-5s	Top-10s	Top-25s	Scoring Average	Money
1992	2	4	0	0	0	0	0	72.75	
1993	3	9	2	0	0	0	0	71.89	$7,165

Best finish for 1993: T-41st at the Shell Houston Open

Year	Starts	Rounds Played	Cuts Made	Wins	Top-5s	Top-10s	Top-25s	Scoring Average	Money
1994	3	9	1	0	0	0	0	71.78	$4,499

Best finish for 1994: T-47th at the Shell Houston Open

Year	Starts	Rounds Played	Cuts Made	Wins	Top-5s	Top-10s	Top-25s	Scoring Average	Money
1995	28	85	13	0	0	0	1	71.55	$59,750

Best finish for 1995: T-17th at the Buick Open

Year	Starts	Rounds Played	Cuts Made	Wins	Top-5s	Top-10s	Top-25s	Scoring Average	Money
1996	3	10	2	0	0	0	1	72.60	$26,118

Best finish for 1996: T-18th at the LaCantera Texas Open

Year	Starts	Rounds Played	Cuts Made	Wins	Top-5s	Top-10s	Top-25s	Scoring Average	Money
1998	32	94	15	0	1	2	6	71.34	$287,753

Best finish for 1998: 4th at the Buick Challenge

Year	Starts	Rounds Played	Cuts Made	Wins	Top-5s	Top-10s	Top-25s	Scoring Average	Money
1999	31	95	17	1	1	2	6	71.73	$622,883

Best finish for 1999: Win at the John Deere Classic

Year	Starts	Rounds Played	Cuts Made	Wins	Top-5s	Top-10s	Top-25s	Scoring Average	Money
2000	30	102	21	0	1	2	5	70.88	$611,432

Best finish for 2000: T-3rd at the Bob Hope Chrysler Classic

Year	Starts	Rounds Played	Cuts Made	Wins	Top-5s	Top-10s	Top-25s	Scoring Average	Money
2001	31	106	23	0	0	1	5	70.84	$508,618

Best finish for 2001: T-8th at the Texas Open at LaCantera

Year	Starts	Rounds Played	Cuts Made	Wins	Top-5s	Top-10s	Top-25s	Scoring Average	Money
2002	31	98	17	0	3	4	9	70.63	$959,182

Best finish for 2002: T-2nd at the Buick Invitational

Year	Starts	Rounds Played	Cuts Made	Wins	Top-5s	Top-10s	Top-25s	Scoring Average	Money
2003	31	97	18	1	4	6	9	71.12	$2,039,259

Best finish for 2003: Win at the 84 Lumber Classic of Pennsylvania

Year	Starts	Rounds Played	Cuts Made	Wins	Top-5s	Top-10s	Top-25s	Scoring Average	Money
2004	32	107	21	0	0	2	9	71.04	$813,345

Best finish for 2004: T-9th at the Bob Hope Chrysler Classic

Year	Starts	Rounds Played	Cuts Made	Wins	Top-5s	Top-10s	Top-25s	Scoring Average	Money
2005	30	98	19	0	2	4	5	71.00	$1,031,159

Best finish for 2005: T-4th at the John Deere Classic

Year	Starts	Rounds Played	Cuts Made	Wins	Top-5s	Top-10s	Top-25s	Scoring Average	Money
2006	17	57	11	0	0	1	3	72.00	$438,669

Best finish for 2006: T-6th at the Shell Houston Open

Year	Starts	Rounds Played	Cuts Made	Wins	Top-5s	Top-10s	Top-25s	Scoring Average	Money
2007	4	12	1	0	0	0	0	73.17	$12,915

Best finish for 2007: T-67th at the EDS Byron Nelson Championship

Year	Starts	Rounds Played	Cuts Made	Wins	Top-5s	Top-10s	Top-25s	Scoring Average	Money
2008	16	40	3	0	0	0	0	73.78	$34,003

Best finish for 2008: T-47th at the Shell Houston Open

Period Totals	Starts	Rounds Played	Cuts Made	Wins	Top-5s	Top-10s	Top-25s	Scoring Average	Money
	345	1073	188	2	12	24	59	71.37	$7,465,838

Jack Lewis

Year	Starts	Rounds Played	Cuts Made	Wins	Top-5s	Top-10s	Top-25s	Scoring Average	Money
1966	1	2	0	0	0	0	0	81.00	
1967	3	8	1	0	0	0	0	75.25	

Best finish for 1967: T-53rd at the American Golf Classic

Year	Starts	Rounds Played	Cuts Made	Wins	Top-5s	Top-10s	Top-25s	Scoring Average	Money
1968	2	8	2	0	0	0	0	74.63	

Best finish for 1968: T-45th at the Masters

Year	Starts	Rounds Played	Cuts Made	Wins	Top-5s	Top-10s	Top-25s	Scoring Average	Money
1969	5	10	0	0	0	0	0	74.50	
1970	20	60	12	0	1	2	3	72.80	$12,178

Best finish for 1970: T-5th at the Greater Milwaukee Open

| 1971 | 22 | 72 | 14 | 0 | 0 | 0 | 2 | 72.57 | $7,949 |

Best finish for 1971: T-12th at the Greater New Orleans Open

| 1972 | 23 | 64 | 9 | 0 | 0 | 0 | 2 | 73.97 | $4,778 |

Best finish for 1972: T-19th at the Greater St. Louis Classic

| 1973 | 23 | 56 | 4 | 0 | 0 | 0 | 1 | 73.61 | $2,006 |

Best finish for 1973: T-23rd at the B.C. Open

1975	1	1	0	0	0	0	0	80.00	
1977	1	0	0	0	0	0	0		
1978	2	4	0	0	0	0	0	78.00	$600
1979	1	2	0	0	0	0	0	77.00	
1980	3	6	0	0	0	0	0	77.17	$500
1981	3	10	2	0	0	0	0	74.70	$1,990

Best finish for 1981: T-44th at the Sea Pines Heritage Classic

1984	1	2	0	0	0	0	0	75.50	
1985	1	2	0	0	0	0	0	76.50	$1,000
1986	2	4	0	0	0	0	0	75.50	$600
1987	1	2	0	0	0	0	0	73.50	
1989	1	2	0	0	0	0	0	74.50	$1,000
Period Totals	**Starts**	**Rounds Played**	**Cuts Made**	**Wins**	**Top-5s**	**Top-10s**	**Top-25s**	**Scoring Average**	**Money**
	116	315	44	0	1	2	8	73.69	$32,600

Jeff Lewis

Year	Starts	Rounds Played	Cuts Made	Wins	Top-5s	Top-10s	Top-25s	Scoring Average	Money
1984	1	2	0	0	0	0	0	75.50	$600
1986	28	76	11	0	0	0	2	72.96	$20,009

Best finish for 1986: T-17th at the Pensacola Open

| 1987 | 28 | 61 | 5 | 0 | 0 | 0 | 2 | 73.16 | $23,412 |

Best finish for 1987: T-15th at the Bank of Boston Classic

| **Period Totals** | **Starts** | **Rounds Played** | **Cuts Made** | **Wins** | **Top-5s** | **Top-10s** | **Top-25s** | **Scoring Average** | **Money** |
| | 57 | 139 | 16 | 0 | 0 | 0 | 4 | 73.09 | $44,021 |

Babe Lichardus

Year	Starts	Rounds Played	Cuts Made	Wins	Top-5s	Top-10s	Top-25s	Scoring Average	Money
1958	9	28	5	0	0	0	1	73.07	$909

Best finish for 1958: T-12th at the Los Angeles Open

| 1959 | 4 | 14 | 3 | 0 | 0 | 0 | 2 | 71.86 | $1,471 |

Best finish for 1959: T-17th at the PGA Championship

| 1960 | 6 | 21 | 4 | 0 | 1 | 1 | 2 | 72.29 | $2,619 |

Best finish for 1960: T-2nd at the Sam Snead Festival

| 1963 | 2 | 8 | 2 | 0 | 0 | 0 | 0 | 73.63 | $412 |

Best finish for 1963: T-41st at the Insurance City Open Invitational

| 1964 | 4 | 11 | 1 | 0 | 0 | 0 | 0 | 73.27 | $402 |

Best finish for 1964: T-44th at the PGA Championship

| 1965 | 2 | 6 | 1 | 0 | 0 | 0 | 0 | 72.50 | $688 |

Best finish for 1965: T-32nd at the Philadelphia Classic

| 1966 | 5 | 18 | 4 | 0 | 0 | 0 | 1 | 73.33 | $1,797 |

Best finish for 1966: T-22nd at the Thunderbird Classic

| 1967 | 5 | 13 | 2 | 0 | 0 | 0 | 0 | 74.15 | $681 |

Best finish for 1967: T-44th at the PGA Championship

| 1968 | 4 | 10 | 1 | 0 | 0 | 0 | 0 | 74.60 | |

Best finish for 1968: T-66th at the Tucson Open Invitational

| 1969 | 6 | 19 | 4 | 0 | 0 | 0 | 1 | 74.05 | $1,016 |

Best finish for 1969: T-25th at the Kaiser International Open

| 1972 | 1 | 2 | 0 | 0 | 0 | 0 | 0 | 79.00 | |
| 1973 | 1 | 4 | 1 | 0 | 0 | 0 | 0 | 75.75 | $360 |

Best finish for 1973: T-73rd at the PGA Championship

1975	1	2	0	0	0	0	0	75.50	
1977	1	2	0	0	0	0	0	77.50	$250
1978	1	2	0	0	0	0	0	82.00	$303
1979	1	2	0	0	0	0	0	77.00	$350
Period Totals	**Starts**	**Rounds Played**	**Cuts Made**	**Wins**	**Top-5s**	**Top-10s**	**Top-25s**	**Scoring Average**	**Money**
	53	162	28	0	1	1	7	73.59	$11,257

Frank Lickliter II

Year	Starts	Rounds Played	Cuts Made	Wins	Top-5s	Top-10s	Top-25s	Scoring Average	Money
1994	1	2	0	0	0	0	0	77.50	$1,000
1996	29	84	15	0	0	1	4	71.68	$138,847

Best finish for 1996: T-7th at the BellSouth Classic

Year	Starts	Rounds Played	Cuts Made	Wins	Top-5s	Top-10s	Top-25s	Scoring Average	Money
1997	30	85	14	0	2	3	5	71.29	$222,049

Best finish for 1997: T-4th at the Bell Canadian Open

| 1998 | 32 | 106 | 22 | 0 | 1 | 5 | 12 | 71.09 | $600,847 |

Best finish for 1998: T-4th at the PGA Championship

| 1999 | 31 | 104 | 23 | 0 | 1 | 4 | 12 | 70.71 | $879,172 |

Best finish for 1999: 2nd at the AT&T Pebble Beach National Pro-Am

| 2000 | 31 | 105 | 22 | 0 | 3 | 6 | 9 | 70.70 | $890,153 |

Best finish for 2000: T-3rd at the Michelob Championship at Kingsmill & Tampa Bay Classic

| 2001 | 29 | 102 | 21 | 1 | 2 | 8 | 11 | 70.14 | $1,941,911 |

Best finish for 2001: Win at the Kemper Insurance Open

| 2002 | 30 | 89 | 19 | 0 | 0 | 2 | 8 | 71.08 | $751,016 |

Best finish for 2002: T-7th at The International presented by Qwest

| 2003 | 30 | 91 | 17 | 1 | 2 | 3 | 7 | 71.08 | $1,340,436 |

Best finish for 2003: Win at the Chrysler Classic of Tucson

| 2004 | 27 | 86 | 19 | 0 | 2 | 4 | 7 | 71.12 | $1,262,979 |

Best finish for 2004: T-3rd at The Players Championship

| 2005 | 33 | 96 | 19 | 0 | 0 | 1 | 3 | 71.52 | $486,581 |

Best finish for 2005: T-6th at the BellSouth Classic

| 2006 | 29 | 97 | 19 | 0 | 4 | 6 | 10 | 70.47 | $1,655,678 |

Best finish for 2006: T-2nd at the FUNAI Classic at the Walt Disney World Resort

| 2007 | 30 | 95 | 18 | 0 | 0 | 0 | 4 | 71.32 | $584,084 |

Best finish for 2007: T-13th at the Honda Classic & Wyndham Championship

| 2008 | 32 | 107 | 22 | 0 | 0 | 0 | 3 | 71.22 | $548,113 |

Best finish for 2008: T-13th at the EDS Byron Nelson Championship

Period Totals	Starts	Rounds Played	Cuts Made	Wins	Top-5s	Top-10s	Top-25s	Scoring Average	Money
	394	1249	250	2	17	43	95	71.03	$11,302,866

Steven Liebler

Year	Starts	Rounds Played	Cuts Made	Wins	Top-5s	Top-10s	Top-25s	Scoring Average	Money
1982	23	60	7	0	0	2	2	72.68	$19,885

Best finish for 1982: T-7th at the LaJet Classic

| 1983 | 13 | 38 | 6 | 0 | 0 | 1 | 2 | 72.26 | $13,954 |

Best finish for 1983: T-8th at the B.C. Open

| 1984 | 32 | 97 | 16 | 0 | 0 | 1 | 1 | 72.69 | $32,730 |

Best finish for 1984: T-8th at the Greater Greensboro Open

| 1985 | 20 | 58 | 9 | 0 | 0 | 0 | 1 | 73.02 | $13,483 |

Best finish for 1985: T-20th at the Manufactures Hanover Westchester Classic

Period Totals	Starts	Rounds Played	Cuts Made	Wins	Top-5s	Top-10s	Top-25s	Scoring Average	Money
	88	253	38	0	0	4	6	72.70	$80,052

Bruce Lietzke

Year	Starts	Rounds Played	Cuts Made	Wins	Top-5s	Top-10s	Top-25s	Scoring Average	Money
1972	1	2	0	0	0	0	0	79.50	
1975	14	44	8	0	2	5	6	71.61	$31,280

Best finish for 1975: T-4th at the Westchester Classic & San Antonio Texas Open

| 1976 | 31 | 114 | 28 | 0 | 3 | 6 | 13 | 71.68 | $68,329 |

Best finish for 1976: 3rd at the San Antonio Texas Open

| 1977 | 27 | 102 | 25 | 2 | 6 | 7 | 18 | 71.23 | $202,156 |

Best finish for 1977: Win at the Joe Garagiola Tucson Open & Hawaiian Open

| 1978 | 27 | 94 | 19 | 1 | 3 | 7 | 11 | 71.83 | $113,904 |

Best finish for 1978: Win at the Canadian Open

| 1979 | 27 | 100 | 23 | 1 | 6 | 10 | 17 | 71.28 | $198,439 |

Best finish for 1979: Win at the Joe Garagiola Tucson Open

| 1980 | 25 | 91 | 20 | 1 | 3 | 6 | 16 | 71.29 | $170,214 |

Best finish for 1980: Win at the Colonial National Invitational

| 1981 | 25 | 96 | 23 | 3 | 10 | 14 | 19 | 70.06 | $358,946 |

Best finish for 1981: Win at the Bob Hope Chrysler Classic, Wickes/Andy Williams San Diego Open & Byron Nelson Golf Classic

| 1982 | 25 | 89 | 20 | 1 | 3 | 6 | 14 | 71.35 | $218,430 |

Best finish for 1982: Win at the Canadian Open

| 1983 | 20 | 77 | 18 | 0 | 3 | 6 | 11 | 71.30 | $153,855 |

Best finish for 1983: T-3rd at the Tournament Players Championship & Colonial National Invitational

| 1984 | 21 | 80 | 18 | 1 | 5 | 7 | 12 | 71.00 | $342,853 |

Best finish for 1984: Win at the Honda Classic

| 1985 | 18 | 63 | 13 | 0 | 2 | 5 | 9 | 71.27 | $136,992 |

Best finish for 1985: T-4th at the Western Open & B.C. Open

| 1986 | 22 | 75 | 20 | 0 | 3 | 5 | 10 | 70.88 | $183,761 |

Best finish for 1986: T-4th at the Houston Open

| 1987 | 21 | 69 | 15 | 0 | 1 | 2 | 9 | 71.23 | $154,382 |

Best finish for 1987: 4th at the Honda Classic

| 1988 | 26 | 87 | 20 | 1 | 4 | 10 | 12 | 70.45 | $500,814 |

Best finish for 1988: Win at the GTE Byron Nelson Classic

Year	Starts	Rounds Played	Cuts Made	Wins	Top-5s	Top-10s	Top-25s	Scoring Average	Money
1989	20	74	18	0	3	4	9	70.81	$305,987

Best finish for 1989: T-3rd at the Doral-Ryder Open & The Players Championship

1990	18	61	16	0	3	4	11	70.80	$330,294

Best finish for 1990: T-3rd at the Honda Classic, Independent Insurance Agent Open & GTE Byron Nelson Classic

1991	19	71	16	0	5	7	13	70.04	$566,272

Best finish for 1991: 2nd at the PGA Championship

1992	18	66	17	1	3	7	12	70.08	$703,805

Best finish for 1992: Win at the Southwestern Bell Colonial

1993	16	50	10	0	2	2	4	70.88	$164,440

Best finish for 1993: T-4th at the Greater Milwaukee Open & Canadian Open

1994	18	59	13	1	2	4	10	69.95	$564,926

Best finish for 1994: Win at the Las Vegas Invitational

1995	16	53	12	0	2	2	5	71.43	$269,394

Best finish for 1995: 2nd at the Mercedes Championships

1996	16	49	10	0	0	1	4	71.00	$122,941

Best finish for 1996: T-9th at the Nortel Open

1997	9	33	7	0	0	0	1	71.61	$42,880

Best finish for 1997: T-22nd at the MasterCard Colonial

1998	10	34	6	0	1	1	3	71.06	$377,188

Best finish for 1998: 2nd at the Bob Hope Chrysler Classic

1999	9	29	4	0	0	0	0	72.59	$59,487

Best finish for 1999: T-27th at the Shell Houston Open

2000	9	30	5	0	0	1	2	70.33	$149,196

Best finish for 2000: T-9th at the Doral Ryder Open

2001	2	8	1	0	0	0	0	71.38	$8,840

Best finish for 2001: T-58th at the MasterCard Colonial

Period Totals	Starts	Rounds Played	Cuts Made	Wins	Top-5s	Top-10s	Top-25s	Scoring Average	Money
	510	1800	405	13	75	129	251	71.04	$6,500,005

Craig Lile

Year	Starts	Rounds Played	Cuts Made	Wins	Top-5s	Top-10s	Top-25s	Scoring Average	Money
2000	1	2	0	0	0	0	0	78.00	
2007	24	77	15	0	0	0	2	71.29	$255,659

Best finish for 2007: T-22nd at the Viking Classic

Period Totals	Starts	Rounds Played	Cuts Made	Wins	Top-5s	Top-10s	Top-25s	Scoring Average	Money
	25	79	15	0	0	0	2	71.46	$255,659

David Lind

Year	Starts	Rounds Played	Cuts Made	Wins	Top-5s	Top-10s	Top-25s	Scoring Average	Money
1975	8	18	1	0	0	0	0	74.33	

Best finish for 1975: T-75th at the Southern Open

1976	9	20	1	0	0	0	0	74.85	

Best finish for 1976: T-78th at the Southern Open

1977	11	30	4	0	0	0	0	74.60	$832

Best finish for 1977: T-61st at the Ed McMahon Quad City Open

Period Totals	Starts	Rounds Played	Cuts Made	Wins	Top-5s	Top-10s	Top-25s	Scoring Average	Money
	28	68	6	0	0	0	0	74.60	$832

Pat Lindsey

Year	Starts	Rounds Played	Cuts Made	Wins	Top-5s	Top-10s	Top-25s	Scoring Average	Money
1979	10	28	4	0	0	0	0	73.71	$1,900

Best finish for 1979: T-60th at the Colgate Hall Of Fame Classic

1980	26	63	6	0	0	0	1	73.29	$11,204

Best finish for 1980: T-18th at the Byron Nelson Golf Classic

1981	21	57	9	0	0	1	2	72.68	$17,433

Best finish for 1981: T-9th at the Atlanta Classic

1982	27	88	18	0	0	3	6	72.23	$45,979

Best finish for 1982: T-7th at the Disney World

1983	31	99	18	1	1	2	4	72.28	$83,405

Best finish for 1983: Win at the B.C. Open

1984	32	98	16	0	0	1	4	73.11	$59,417

Best finish for 1984: 7th at the NEC World Series of Golf

1985	29	95	18	0	0	2	5	71.78	$51,253

Best finish for 1985: 6th at the B.C. Open

1986	31	90	14	0	1	1	2	72.36	$48,197

Best finish for 1986: 3rd at the Hardee's Golf Classic

1987	7	18	2	0	0	0	0	72.61	$2,492

Best finish for 1987: T-61st at the Anheuser-Busch Golf Classic

1992	1	2	0	0	0	0	0	78.00	

Period Totals	Starts	Rounds Played	Cuts Made	Wins	Top-5s	Top-10s	Top-25s	Scoring Average	Money
	215	638	105	1	2	10	24	72.56	$321,280

John Lister

Year	Starts	Rounds Played	Cuts Made	Wins	Top-5s	Top-10s	Top-25s	Scoring Average	Money
1970	2	4	0	0	0	0	0	74.25	
1971	20	74	17	0	0	0	7	72.26	$18,043

Best finish for 1971: T-11th at the Kaiser International Open

| 1972 | 28 | 81 | 12 | 0 | 1 | 1 | 7 | 73.14 | $23,914 |

Best finish for 1972: T-4th at the Greater New Orleans Open

| 1973 | 23 | 72 | 13 | 0 | 1 | 3 | 6 | 72.01 | $23,973 |

Best finish for 1973: T-5th at the B.C. Open

| 1974 | 28 | 82 | 13 | 0 | 0 | 0 | 4 | 72.73 | $16,534 |

Best finish for 1974: T-11th at the Hawaiian Open

| 1975 | 21 | 69 | 13 | 0 | 2 | 4 | 4 | 72.75 | $22,448 |

Best finish for 1975: T-4th at the Western Open

| 1976 | 23 | 72 | 13 | 1 | 2 | 3 | 6 | 72.01 | $53,173 |

Best finish for 1976: Win at the Ed McMahon Quad City Open

| 1977 | 28 | 91 | 18 | 0 | 1 | 1 | 4 | 73.38 | $36,061 |

Best finish for 1977: T-2nd at the IVB Philadelphia Golf Classic

| 1978 | 22 | 76 | 16 | 0 | 1 | 3 | 5 | 72.54 | $29,084 |

Best finish for 1978: T-4th at the Danny Thomas Memphis Classic

| 1979 | 26 | 71 | 9 | 0 | 1 | 1 | 3 | 72.90 | $19,247 |

Best finish for 1979: T-5th at the Greater Milwaukee Open

| 1980 | 12 | 35 | 5 | 0 | 0 | 0 | 0 | 72.66 | $4,846 |

Best finish for 1980: T-26th at the Hawaiian Open

| 1981 | 7 | 13 | 0 | 0 | 0 | 0 | 0 | 75.77 | |
| 1982 | 6 | 18 | 3 | 0 | 0 | 0 | 1 | 73.50 | $5,803 |

Best finish for 1982: T-16th at the Wickes/Andy Williams San Diego Open

Period Totals	Starts	Rounds Played	Cuts Made	Wins	Top-5s	Top-10s	Top-25s	Scoring Average	Money
	246	758	132	1	9	16	47	72.74	$253,126

Gene Littler

Year	Starts	Rounds Played	Cuts Made	Wins	Top-5s	Top-10s	Top-25s	Scoring Average	Money
1958	26	103	25	0	3	9	16	71.29	$13,772

Best finish for 1958: T-2nd at the Thunderbird Invitational & Hesperia Open

| 1959 | 27 | 108 | 25 | 5 | 11 | 14 | 26 | 70.01 | $36,991 |

Best finish for 1959: Win at the Phoenix Open Invitational, Tucson Open Invitational, Arlington Hotel Open Invitational, Insurance City Open Invitational & Miller Open Invitational

| 1960 | 23 | 89 | 21 | 2 | 5 | 9 | 17 | 77.67 | $24,338 |

Best finish for 1960: Win at the Oklahoma City Open Invitational & Eastern Open Invitational

| 1961 | 15 | 60 | 15 | 1 | 4 | 6 | 13 | 70.88 | $27,746 |

Best finish for 1961: Win at the U.S. Open

| 1962 | 20 | 79 | 19 | 2 | 8 | 12 | 16 | 70.75 | $60,781 |

Best finish for 1962: Win at the Lucky International Open & Thunderbird Classic Invitational

| 1963 | 20 | 81 | 19 | 0 | 3 | 11 | 15 | 71.22 | $30,716 |

Best finish for 1963: T-3rd at the Tucson Open Invitational & Thunderbird Classic Invitational

| 1964 | 29 | 115 | 28 | 0 | 5 | 7 | 20 | 71.27 | $34,424 |

Best finish for 1964: T-3rd at the Phoenix Open & Colonial National Invitational

| 1965 | 25 | 99 | 24 | 1 | 3 | 9 | 15 | 71.29 | $59,399 |

Best finish for 1965: Win at the Canadian Open

| 1966 | 26 | 102 | 24 | 0 | 8 | 10 | 17 | 71.35 | $68,815 |

Best finish for 1966: T-2nd at the Tucson Open Invitational, Texas Open Invitational & Memphis Open Invitational

| 1967 | 26 | 95 | 21 | 0 | 2 | 5 | 11 | 71.84 | $40,434 |

Best finish for 1967: 5th at the Colonial National Invitational & "500" Festival Open

| 1968 | 22 | 85 | 20 | 0 | 3 | 7 | 11 | 70.98 | $57,821 |

Best finish for 1968: T-2nd at the Greater Greensboro Open Invitational & Colonial National Invitational

| 1969 | 19 | 69 | 16 | 2 | 7 | 10 | 14 | 70.93 | $105,612 |

Best finish for 1969: Win at the Phoenix Open & Greater Greensboro Open

| 1970 | 20 | 77 | 19 | 0 | 6 | 7 | 11 | 69.87 | $76,564 |

Best finish for 1970: T-2nd at the Masters & Colonial National Invitational

| 1971 | 20 | 73 | 19 | 2 | 4 | 6 | 12 | 71.11 | $93,041 |

Best finish for 1971: Win at the Monsanto Open & Colonial National Invitational

| 1972 | 11 | 35 | 6 | 0 | 1 | 1 | 2 | 72.03 | $10,262 |

Best finish for 1972: T-4th at the Phoenix Open

| 1973 | 22 | 82 | 19 | 1 | 3 | 7 | 14 | 71.46 | $93,928 |

Best finish for 1973: Win at the St. Louis Children's Hospital Golf Classic

| 1974 | 25 | 93 | 22 | 0 | 5 | 9 | 16 | 71.28 | $100,483 |

Best finish for 1974: T-2nd at the Andy Williams-San Diego Open

| 1975 | 23 | 90 | 22 | 3 | 4 | 8 | 16 | 71.10 | $183,103 |

Best finish for 1975: Win at the Bing Crosby Pro-Am, Danny Thomas Memphis Classic & Westchester Classic

| 1976 | 26 | 90 | 22 | 0 | 1 | 7 | 13 | 71.58 | $61,984 |

Best finish for 1976: T-4th at the First NBC New Orleans Open

| 1977 | 21 | 76 | 16 | 1 | 4 | 6 | 8 | 72.00 | $119,799 |

Best finish for 1977: Win at the Houston Open

Year	Starts	Rounds Played	Cuts Made	Wins	Top-5s	Top-10s	Top-25s	Scoring Average	Money
1978	23	83	19	0	1	2	10	71.45	$55,879

Best finish for 1978: T-2nd at the Andy Williams-San Diego Open

| 1979 | 25 | 88 | 20 | 0 | 1 | 3 | 8 | 71.57 | $70,543 |

Best finish for 1979: T-2nd at the Colonial National Invitational

| 1980 | 21 | 69 | 13 | 0 | 0 | 1 | 4 | 72.86 | $27,831 |

Best finish for 1980: T-10th at the Greater New Orleans Open

| 1981 | 17 | 52 | 8 | 0 | 0 | 0 | 1 | 73.10 | $9,431 |

Best finish for 1981: T-24th at the Byron Nelson Golf Classic

| 1982 | 14 | 50 | 10 | 0 | 0 | 1 | 3 | 72.34 | $23,237 |

Best finish for 1982: T-8th at the Bing Crosby Pro-Am

| 1983 | 10 | 29 | 3 | 0 | 0 | 0 | 1 | 71.86 | $7,643 |

Best finish for 1983: T-12th at the Glen CampbellLos Angeles Open

| 1984 | 7 | 18 | 1 | 0 | 0 | 0 | 0 | 74.22 | $995 |

Best finish for 1984: T-69th at the Hawaiian Open

| 1985 | 4 | 13 | 1 | 0 | 0 | 0 | 0 | 73.46 | $768 |

Best finish for 1985: 74th at the Isuzu/Andy Williams San Diego Open

1986	1	3	0	0	0	0	0	78.33	
Period Totals	Starts	Rounds Played	Cuts Made	Wins	Top-5s	Top-10s	Top-25s	Scoring Average	Money
	568	2106	477	20	92	167	310	71.65	$1,496,341

PGA Tour career totals from 1950 to 1986

	Starts	Rounds Played	Cuts Made	Wins	Top-5s	Top-10s	Top-25s	Scoring Average	Money
	658	2455	566	29	116	209	379	N/A	$1,552,655

John Lively

Year	Starts	Rounds Played	Cuts Made	Wins	Top-5s	Top-10s	Top-25s	Scoring Average	Money
1959	1	2	0	0	0	0	0	77.00	
1964	1	1	0	0	0	0	0	79.00	
1967	19	56	9	0	0	0	0	74.32	$612

Best finish for 1967: T-33rd at the "500" Festival Open

| 1968 | 25 | 78 | 13 | 0 | 1 | 1 | 2 | 73.46 | $10,328 |

Best finish for 1968: T-4th at the Kemper Open Invitational

| 1969 | 23 | 59 | 7 | 0 | 0 | 0 | 0 | 74.03 | $1,343 |

Best finish for 1969: T-43rd at the Memphis Open

1987	1	2	0	0	0	0	0	77.00	
Period Totals	Starts	Rounds Played	Cuts Made	Wins	Top-5s	Top-10s	Top-25s	Scoring Average	Money
	70	198	29	0	1	1	2	73.97	$12,284

Bill Loeffler

Year	Starts	Rounds Played	Cuts Made	Wins	Top-5s	Top-10s	Top-25s	Scoring Average	Money
1979	1	2	0	0	0	0	0	81.50	$600
1980	11	26	4	0	0	0	0	73.15	$3,245

Best finish for 1980: T-33rd at the World Disney World National Team Championship

| 1981 | 19 | 46 | 5 | 0 | 0 | 0 | 0 | 73.80 | $3,336 |

Best finish for 1981: T-32nd at the Quad Cities Open

1982	1	2	0	0	0	0	0	76.00	
1987	1	0	0	0	0	0	0		
1988	1	2	0	0	0	0	0	78.00	
1991	1	0	0	0	0	0	0		
1993	1	0	0	0	0	0	0		
2001	1	2	0	0	0	0	0	79.50	$2,000
2004	1	0	0	0	0	0	0		
Period Totals	Starts	Rounds Played	Cuts Made	Wins	Top-5s	Top-10s	Top-25s	Scoring Average	Money
	38	80	9	0	0	0	0	74.09	$9,181

Bob Lohr

Year	Starts	Rounds Played	Cuts Made	Wins	Top-5s	Top-10s	Top-25s	Scoring Average	Money
1985	30	98	18	0	1	2	7	72.33	$94,651

Best finish for 1985: T-2nd at the Houston Open

| 1986 | 34 | 105 | 18 | 0 | 1 | 3 | 6 | 72.15 | $87,549 |

Best finish for 1986: T-5th at the Hardee's Golf Classic

| 1987 | 33 | 103 | 18 | 0 | 2 | 3 | 7 | 72.02 | $138,108 |

Best finish for 1987: T-2nd at the Centel Classic

| 1988 | 32 | 110 | 23 | 1 | 4 | 5 | 10 | 70.79 | $317,536 |

Best finish for 1988: Win at the Walt Disney World/Oldsmobile Classic

| 1989 | 31 | 97 | 19 | 0 | 1 | 3 | 7 | 71.99 | $144,242 |

Best finish for 1989: T-3rd at the Texas Open

| 1990 | 30 | 96 | 20 | 0 | 0 | 2 | 3 | 71.86 | $142,260 |

Best finish for 1990: T-6th at the Canon Greater Hartford Open

| 1991 | 26 | 81 | 15 | 0 | 3 | 7 | 9 | 70.89 | $387,759 |

Best finish for 1991: T-2nd at the Southwestern Bell Colonial & The International

1992	30	89	16	0	0	2	5	71.34	$129,507
Best finish for 1992: T-6th at the Buick Invitational of California									
1993	26	85	17	0	3	3	6	71.02	$316,182
Best finish for 1993: 2nd at the H-E-B Texas Open									
1994	28	88	16	0	1	2	7	71.18	$226,248
Best finish for 1994: 5th at the Kmart Greater Greensboro Open									
1995	28	95	22	0	2	2	6	71.18	$314,947
Best finish for 1995: 2nd at the Bell Canadian Open									
1996	30	90	15	0	0	0	5	71.76	$123,763
Best finish for 1996: T-13th at the Nortel Open									
1997	8	15	0	0	0	0	0	76.80	
1998	8	18	1	0	0	0	0	73.78	$2,508
Best finish for 1998: T-65th at the Deposit Guaranty Golf Classic									
1999	4	7	0	0	0	0	0	73.14	
2000	1	2	0	0	0	0	0	73.00	
2001	1	4	1	0	0	0	0	70.75	$4,300
Best finish for 2001: T-61st at the B.C. Open									
2002	2	4	0	0	0	0	0	77.75	
2003	1	2	0	0	0	0	0	76.00	
2004	1	2	0	0	0	0	0	82.50	
Period Totals	Starts	Rounds Played	Cuts Made	Wins	Top-5s	Top-10s	Top-25s	Scoring Average	Money
	384	1191	219	1	18	34	78	71.71	$2,429,560

Carl Lohren

Year	Starts	Rounds Played	Cuts Made	Wins	Top-5s	Top-10s	Top-25s	Scoring Average	Money
1958	2	4	0	0	0	0	0	78.75	
1963	1	4	1	0	0	0	1	73.50	$140
Best finish for 1963: T-19th at the Puerto Rico Open Invitational									
1967	1	2	0	0	0	0	0	75.00	
1968	3	5	0	0	0	0	0	74.80	
1969	5	12	2	0	0	1	2	74.67	$1,128
Best finish for 1969: T-8th at the West End Classic									
1970	2	6	1	0	0	0	0	73.33	$430
Best finish for 1970: T-43rd at the Bahama Islands Open									
1971	5	11	0	0	0	0	0	74.82	
1972	3	10	1	0	0	0	0	73.30	$286
Best finish for 1972: T-61st at the Hawaiian Open									
1973	2	5	1	0	0	0	0	76.00	$375
Best finish for 1973: 70th at the Westchester Classic									
1974	1	2	0	0	0	0	0	76.50	
1975	2	4	0	0	0	0	0	76.50	
1976	1	2	0	0	0	0	0	74.50	
1977	1	2	0	0	0	0	0	77.00	
1983	1	2	0	0	0	0	0	84.50	$600
Period Totals	Starts	Rounds Played	Cuts Made	Wins	Top-5s	Top-10s	Top-25s	Scoring Average	Money
	30	71	6	0	0	1	3	75.15	$2,959

Peter Lonard

Year	Starts	Rounds Played	Cuts Made	Wins	Top-5s	Top-10s	Top-25s	Scoring Average	Money
1996	1	0	0	0	0	0	0		
1997	5	13	3	0	0	0	1	73.38	$38,837
Best finish for 1997: T-24th at the British Open									
1998	1	2	0	0	0	0	0	76.50	$1,500
1999	1	4	1	0	0	0	0	76.00	$11,275
Best finish for 1999: T-49th at the British Open									
2001	7	20	3	0	0	0	1	71.90	$91,173
Best finish for 2001: T-15th at the Memorial Tournament									
2002	24	93	23	0	2	4	14	70.11	$1,413,113
Best finish for 2002: 3rd at the Genuity Championship									
2003	26	90	21	0	1	3	11	71.06	$1,328,594
Best finish for 2003: 4th at the WGC-Accenture Match Play Championship									
2004	23	66	12	0	1	1	5	71.74	$686,871
Best finish for 2004: 5th at the BellSouth Classic									
2005	27	84	17	1	3	3	6	71.31	$1,904,998
Best finish for 2005: Win at the MCI Heritage									
2006	22	76	18	0	1	3	4	71.79	$844,267
Best finish for 2006: T-4th at the Bank of America Colonial									
2007	27	85	15	0	2	3	6	70.93	$1,259,881
Best finish for 2007: 3rd at the Mayakoba Golf Classic									
2008	30	92	17	0	1	3	7	70.93	$1,462,894
Best finish for 2008: 2nd at the Zurich Classic of New Orleans									
Period Totals	Starts	Rounds Played	Cuts Made	Wins	Top-5s	Top-10s	Top-25s	Scoring Average	Money
	194	625	130	1	11	20	55	71.20	$9,043,403

Michael Long

Year	Starts	Rounds Played	Cuts Made	Wins	Top-5s	Top-10s	Top-25s	Scoring Average	Money
1997	1	2	0	0	0	0	0	74.00	$1,676
1998	1	4	1	0	0	0	0	74.75	$9,541
Best finish for 1998: T-66th at the British Open									
1999	1	2	0	0	0	0	0	78.00	$1,719
2002	27	71	9	0	0	0	2	71.58	$157,723
Best finish for 2002: T-15th at the SEI Pennsylvania Classic									
2005	26	70	11	0	0	0	1	71.71	$180,418
Best finish for 2005: T-22nd at the Barclays Classic									
Period Totals	Starts	Rounds Played	Cuts Made	Wins	Top-5s	Top-10s	Top-25s	Scoring Average	Money
	56	149	21	0	0	0	3	71.85	$351,076

Francisco Lopez

Year	Starts	Rounds Played	Cuts Made	Wins	Top-5s	Top-10s	Top-25s	Scoring Average	Money
1959	1	2	0	0	0	0	0	77.00	
1960	1	2	1	0	0	0	0	81.50	
Best finish for 1960: T-200 at the PGA Championship									
1964	5	13	1	0	0	0	1	76.15	$413
Best finish for 1964: T-19th at the Almaden Open									
1965	2	8	2	0	0	0	0	74.38	
Best finish for 1965: 60th at the Hawaiian Open									
1966	3	12	2	0	0	0	0	75.08	
Best finish for 1966: 66th at the Lucky International Open Invitational									
1967	1	3	0	0	0	0	0	75.33	
1968	3	8	1	0	0	0	0	76.25	
Best finish for 1968: T-73rd at the Bing Crosby National Professional-Amateur									
1969	5	11	0	0	0	0	0	75.45	
1971	2	5	0	0	0	0	0	76.20	
1973	2	5	0	0	0	0	0	77.60	
1974	1	2	0	0	0	0	0	78.00	
1975	1	2	0	0	0	0	0	76.50	
Period Totals	Starts	Rounds Played	Cuts Made	Wins	Top-5s	Top-10s	Top-25s	Scoring Average	Money
	27	73	7	0	0	0	1	75.99	$413

Joe Lopez, Jr.

Year	Starts	Rounds Played	Cuts Made	Wins	Top-5s	Top-10s	Top-25s	Scoring Average	Money
1961	1	4	1	0	0	0	1	70.75	$145
Best finish for 1961: T-22nd at the Cajun Classic Open Invitational									
1962	6	22	6	0	0	0	1	72.05	$1,645
Best finish for 1962: T-12th at the Carling Open Invitational									
1963	1	2	1	0	0	0	0	79.00	
Best finish for 1963: T-200 at the PGA Championship									
1964	1	2	0	0	0	0	0	76.50	
1965	2	6	1	0	0	0	0	74.67	
Best finish for 1965: T-57th at the Doral Open									
1966	2	4	0	0	0	0	0	74.25	
1967	4	7	0	0	0	0	0	77.14	
1968	4	12	2	0	0	0	0	74.75	
Best finish for 1968: T-64th at the Doral Open Invitational									
1969	1	2	0	0	0	0	0	78.00	
1971	2	4	0	0	0	0	0	77.25	
1972	2	4	0	0	0	0	0	74.25	
1973	2	4	0	0	0	0	0	77.00	
1974	2	4	0	0	0	0	0	74.75	
Period Totals	Starts	Rounds Played	Cuts Made	Wins	Top-5s	Top-10s	Top-25s	Scoring Average	Money
	30	77	11	0	0	0	2	74.42	$1,790

Lyn Lott

Year	Starts	Rounds Played	Cuts Made	Wins	Top-5s	Top-10s	Top-25s	Scoring Average	Money
1967	1	2	0	0	0	0	0	81.00	
1973	2	4	0	0	0	0	0	77.00	
1974	26	83	15	0	0	0	3	72.83	$11,344
Best finish for 1974: T-11th at the Kaiser International Open									
1975	29	95	18	0	0	0	4	72.34	$19,023
Best finish for 1975: T-12th at the Sahara Invitational									
1976	36	128	27	0	2	4	10	71.78	$57,358
Best finish for 1976: 3rd at the Canadian Open									
1977	33	123	28	0	2	6	16	71.72	$76,875
Best finish for 1977: T-3rd at the Byron Nelson Golf Classic									
1978	27	88	17	0	1	2	5	72.91	$28,831

Best finish for 1978: T-4th at the Glen CampbellLos Angeles Open

Year	Starts	Rounds Played	Cuts Made	Wins	Top-5s	Top-10s	Top-25s	Scoring Average	Money
1979	10	29	4	0	0	1	1	72.45	$6,217

Best finish for 1979: T-9th at the Colgate Hall Of Fame Classic

| 1980 | 28 | 85 | 16 | 0 | 1 | 2 | 4 | 72.48 | $31,391 |

Best finish for 1980: T-4th at the Pensacola Open

| 1981 | 28 | 82 | 14 | 0 | 1 | 2 | 6 | 71.91 | $41,938 |

Best finish for 1981: T-3rd at the Greater Milwaukee Open

| 1982 | 28 | 86 | 14 | 0 | 0 | 1 | 2 | 72.91 | $21,290 |

Best finish for 1982: T-8th at the Miller High-Life Quad Cities Open

| 1983 | 29 | 79 | 9 | 0 | 2 | 2 | 2 | 73.41 | $32,664 |

Best finish for 1983: T-5th at the Pensacola Open

1984	22	47	2	0	0	0	0	74.96	$2,386
1985	1	2	0	0	0	0	0	72.00	
1988	2	4	0	0	0	0	0	73.50	
1989	1	2	0	0	0	0	0	75.00	
Period Totals	Starts	Rounds Played	Cuts Made	Wins	Top-5s	Top-10s	Top-25s	Scoring Average	Money
	303	939	164	0	9	20	53	72.58	$329,318

Dick Lotz

Year	Starts	Rounds Played	Cuts Made	Wins	Top-5s	Top-10s	Top-25s	Scoring Average	Money
1963	1	4	1	0	1	1	1	69.50	

Best finish for 1963: T-2nd at the Almaden Open Invitational

| 1964 | 11 | 35 | 6 | 0 | 0 | 2 | 2 | 72.83 | $2,224 |

Best finish for 1964: T-6th at the Cajun Classic

| 1965 | 24 | 67 | 8 | 0 | 0 | 0 | 0 | 73.99 | $200 |

Best finish for 1965: T-44th at the Cajun Classic

| 1966 | 18 | 50 | 8 | 0 | 0 | 0 | 2 | 73.54 | $3,018 |

Best finish for 1966: T-22nd at the Pensacola Open Invitational

| 1967 | 20 | 65 | 11 | 0 | 0 | 0 | 3 | 73.12 | $5,519 |

Best finish for 1967: T-15th at the Minnesota Golf Classic

| 1968 | 32 | 113 | 25 | 0 | 2 | 3 | 12 | 71.51 | $21,842 |

Best finish for 1968: 4th at the Magnolia State Classic

| 1969 | 30 | 102 | 21 | 1 | 1 | 5 | 6 | 72.59 | $35,611 |

Best finish for 1969: Win at the Alameda County Open

| 1970 | 32 | 108 | 24 | 2 | 5 | 8 | 15 | 71.42 | $120,864 |

Best finish for 1970: Win at the Monsanto Open, Kemper Open

| 1971 | 33 | 114 | 26 | 0 | 1 | 3 | 10 | 72.07 | $37,348 |

Best finish for 1971: 5th at the Western Open

| 1972 | 27 | 86 | 16 | 0 | 0 | 1 | 5 | 72.64 | $17,743 |

Best finish for 1972: T-9th at the Jackie Gleason's Inverrary Classic

| 1973 | 33 | 104 | 18 | 0 | 0 | 0 | 3 | 73.15 | $12,879 |

Best finish for 1973: T-11th at the Andy Williams-San Diego Open

| 1974 | 24 | 71 | 11 | 0 | 0 | 1 | 2 | 73.30 | $8,788 |

Best finish for 1974: T-9th at the Houston Open

| 1975 | 19 | 56 | 8 | 0 | 0 | 1 | 1 | 73.55 | $7,461 |

Best finish for 1975: T-7th at the Phoenix Open

| 1976 | 23 | 71 | 12 | 0 | 0 | 0 | 2 | 72.62 | $8,958 |

Best finish for 1976: T-15th at the Andy Williams-San Diego Open & Greater Jacksonville Open

| 1977 | 2 | 4 | 0 | 0 | 0 | 0 | 0 | 73.75 | |
| 1978 | 8 | 24 | 4 | 0 | 0 | 0 | 0 | 73.71 | $1,648 |

Best finish for 1978: T-53rd at the Phoenix Open

| 1980 | 1 | 4 | 1 | 0 | 0 | 0 | 0 | 73.00 | $710 |

Best finish for 1980: T-51st at the Anheuser-Busch Golf Classic

| 1985 | 1 | 3 | 1 | 0 | 0 | 0 | 0 | 74.33 | $1,015 |

Best finish for 1985: T-64th at the Bing Crosby Pro-Am

1986	1	3	0	0	0	0	0	78.00	
1989	1	0	0	0	0	0	0		
1992	4	8	0	0	0	0	0	74.13	
Period Totals	Starts	Rounds Played	Cuts Made	Wins	Top-5s	Top-10s	Top-25s	Scoring Average	Money
	345	1092	201	3	10	25	64	72.68	$285,826

John Lotz

Year	Starts	Rounds Played	Cuts Made	Wins	Top-5s	Top-10s	Top-25s	Scoring Average	Money
1961	1	4	1	0	1	1	1	70.25	

Best finish for 1961: T-4th at the Almaden Open

| 1963 | 1 | 4 | 1 | 0 | 0 | 0 | 1 | 71.00 | $470 |

Best finish for 1963: T-24th at the Almaden Open Invitational

| 1964 | 10 | 27 | 3 | 0 | 0 | 0 | 1 | 73.85 | $831 |

Best finish for 1964: T-17th at the Mountain View Open

| 1965 | 18 | 52 | 7 | 0 | 0 | 1 | 3 | 74.00 | $3,568 |

Best finish for 1965: T-7th at the Lucky International

| 1966 | 32 | 102 | 18 | 0 | 1 | 2 | 4 | 73.20 | $9,331 |

Best finish for 1966: T-5th at the Dallas Open Invitational

Year	Starts	Rounds Played	Cuts Made	Wins	Top-5s	Top-10s	Top-25s	Scoring Average	Money
1967	24	72	13	0	0	0	2	73.51	$5,361

Best finish for 1967: T-13th at the Western Open

| 1968 | 30 | 102 | 21 | 0 | 1 | 2 | 10 | 71.78 | $20,186 |

Best finish for 1968: T-5th at the Rebel Yell Open

| 1969 | 28 | 85 | 16 | 0 | 1 | 3 | 6 | 72.74 | $16,098 |

Best finish for 1969: 5th at the Bing Crosby National Pro-Am

| 1970 | 20 | 47 | 6 | 0 | 1 | 1 | 1 | 73.94 | $6,126 |

Best finish for 1970: 5th at the Tucson Open

| 1971 | 23 | 72 | 13 | 0 | 0 | 2 | 3 | 72.94 | $13,055 |

Best finish for 1971: T-6th at the Greater New Orleans Open

| 1972 | 12 | 28 | 3 | 0 | 0 | 1 | 1 | 73.46 | $3,828 |

Best finish for 1972: T-9th at the Andy Williams-San Diego Open

| 1973 | 15 | 37 | 6 | 0 | 0 | 0 | 0 | 73.78 | $2,718 |

Best finish for 1973: T-40th at the Atlanta Classic

1974	2	2	0	0	0	0	0	78.50	
1976	3	7	3	0	0	0	0	76.00	
1977	1	4	1	0	0	0	0	72.00	$924

Best finish for 1977: T-35th at the Bing Crosby Pro-Am

1980	1	3	0	0	0	0	0	78.33	
Period Totals	Starts	Rounds Played	Cuts Made	Wins	Top-5s	Top-10s	Top-25s	Scoring Average	Money
	221	648	112	0	5	13	33	73.14	$82,497

Tim Loustalot

Year	Starts	Rounds Played	Cuts Made	Wins	Top-5s	Top-10s	Top-25s	Scoring Average	Money
1988	1	2	0	0	0	0	0	79.00	
1993	1	4	1	0	0	0	0	73.25	$2,550

Best finish for 1993: T-67th at the AT&T Pebble Beach Pro-Am

| 1995 | 22 | 55 | 5 | 0 | 0 | 0 | 0 | 72.13 | $17,077 |

Best finish for 1995: T-32nd at the Freeport-McMoRan Classic

| 1998 | 24 | 64 | 11 | 0 | 1 | 1 | 2 | 71.73 | $172,918 |

Best finish for 1998: T-2nd at the Deposit Guaranty Golf Classic

| 1999 | 26 | 66 | 7 | 0 | 0 | 0 | 1 | 73.14 | $68,679 |

Best finish for 1999: T-18th at the FedEx St. Jude Classic

2000	1	1	0	0	0	0	0	81.00	
Period Totals	Starts	Rounds Played	Cuts Made	Wins	Top-5s	Top-10s	Top-25s	Scoring Average	Money
	75	192	24	0	1	1	3	72.48	$261,224

Davis Love III

Year	Starts	Rounds Played	Cuts Made	Wins	Top-5s	Top-10s	Top-25s	Scoring Average	Money
1985	1	2	0	0	0	0	0	76.00	
1986	31	97	22	0	2	2	7	72.25	$113,245

Best finish for 1986: T-3rd at the Canadian Open

| 1987 | 27 | 91 | 18 | 1 | 2 | 4 | 9 | 71.11 | $299,018 |

Best finish for 1987: Win at the MCI Heritage Classic

| 1988 | 30 | 91 | 17 | 0 | 1 | 3 | 9 | 71.55 | $159,333 |

Best finish for 1988: 4th at the Phoenix Open

| 1989 | 25 | 87 | 18 | 0 | 2 | 4 | 11 | 70.93 | $289,533 |

Best finish for 1989: 2nd at The Nestle Invitational

| 1990 | 29 | 93 | 20 | 1 | 3 | 4 | 12 | 71.57 | $538,168 |

Best finish for 1990: Win at The International

| 1991 | 29 | 103 | 24 | 1 | 6 | 8 | 14 | 70.66 | $693,475 |

Best finish for 1991: Win at the MCI Heritage Classic

| 1992 | 26 | 94 | 22 | 3 | 6 | 9 | 15 | 70.15 | $1,192,859 |

Best finish for 1992: Win at The Players Championship, MCI Heritage Classic & Kmart Greater Greensboro Open

| 1993 | 27 | 102 | 23 | 2 | 3 | 5 | 12 | 70.56 | $777,983 |

Best finish for 1993: Win at the Infiniti Tournament of Champions & Las Vegas Invitational

| 1994 | 28 | 95 | 21 | 0 | 3 | 4 | 9 | 70.99 | $486,801 |

Best finish for 1994: 2nd at the United Airlines Hawaiian Open

| 1995 | 24 | 89 | 22 | 1 | 6 | 9 | 15 | 70.56 | $1,113,199 |

Best finish for 1995: Win at the Freeport-McMoRan Classic

| 1996 | 23 | 80 | 19 | 1 | 7 | 11 | 14 | 70.00 | $1,213,446 |

Best finish for 1996: Win at the Buick Invitational

| 1997 | 25 | 90 | 22 | 2 | 3 | 13 | 17 | 70.13 | $1,635,953 |

Best finish for 1997: Win at the PGA Championship & Buick Challenge

| 1998 | 21 | 74 | 19 | 1 | 6 | 10 | 16 | 70.11 | $1,542,152 |

Best finish for 1998: Win at the MCI Classic

| 1999 | 23 | 78 | 20 | 0 | 6 | 13 | 17 | 70.22 | $2,475,328 |

Best finish for 1999: T-2nd at the Sony Open in Hawaii, Nissan Open, Masters & The Tour Championship

| 2000 | 25 | 92 | 22 | 0 | 6 | 9 | 16 | 69.89 | $2,338,765 |

Best finish for 2000: T-2nd at the Bay Hill Invitational, GTE Byron Nelson Classic & MasterCard Colonial

| 2001 | 20 | 75 | 17 | 1 | 7 | 12 | 15 | 69.03 | $3,174,463 |

Best finish for 2001: Win at the AT&T Pebble Beach National Pro-Am

Year	Starts	Rounds Played	Cuts Made	Wins	Top-5s	Top-10s	Top-25s	Scoring Average	Money
2002	26	87	21	0	5	6	14	70.21	$2,056,160

Best finish for 2002: T-2nd at the Canon Greater Hartford Open & Advil Western Open

| 2003 | 23 | 79 | 20 | 4 | 9 | 11 | 16 | 69.78 | $6,084,896 |

Best finish for 2003: Win at the AT&T Pebble Beach National Pro-Am, The Players Championship, MCI Heritage & The International

| 2004 | 24 | 75 | 18 | 0 | 5 | 8 | 11 | 70.76 | $3,078,092 |

Best finish for 2004: 2nd at the WGC-Accenture Match Play Championship & Honda Classic

| 2005 | 24 | 75 | 16 | 0 | 5 | 9 | 14 | 70.45 | $2,667,722 |

Best finish for 2005: T-2nd at the MCI Heritage & Booz Allen Classic

| 2006 | 23 | 76 | 18 | 1 | 4 | 4 | 9 | 71.11 | $2,750,416 |

Best finish for 2006: Win at the Chrysler Classic of Greensboro

| 2007 | 21 | 65 | 13 | 0 | 2 | 3 | 4 | 72.02 | $1,025,306 |

Best finish for 2007: T-4th at the Mercedes Championships & AT&T Pebble Beach National Pro-Am

| 2008 | 23 | 78 | 16 | 1 | 2 | 3 | 7 | 71.21 | $1,695,237 |

Best finish for 2008: Win at the Children's Miracle Network Classic

Period Totals	Starts	Rounds Played	Cuts Made	Wins	Top-5s	Top-10s	Top-25s	Scoring Average	Money
	578	1968	448	20	101	164	283	70.68	$37,401,550

Davis Love, Jr.

Year	Starts	Rounds Played	Cuts Made	Wins	Top-5s	Top-10s	Top-25s	Scoring Average	Money
1958	14	41	5	0	0	0	0	73.80	$077

Best finish for 1958: T-27th at the Utah Open

| 1959 | 8 | 31 | 8 | 0 | 0 | 0 | 4 | 72.55 | $1,296 |

Best finish for 1959: T-19th at the Azalea Open Invitational

| 1960 | 2 | 6 | 1 | 0 | 0 | 0 | 1 | 72.17 | $232 |

Best finish for 1960: T-24th at the Coral Gables Open Invitational

| 1961 | 2 | 8 | 2 | 0 | 0 | 0 | 1 | 70.00 | $254 |

Best finish for 1961: T-22nd at the Home Of The Sun Open Invitational

| 1962 | 1 | 2 | 1 | 0 | 0 | 0 | 0 | 77.00 | |

Best finish for 1962: T-200 at the PGA Championship

| 1963 | 3 | 12 | 3 | 0 | 0 | 0 | 2 | 72.50 | $2,443 |

Best finish for 1963: T-14th at the U.S. Open

| 1964 | 5 | 16 | 3 | 0 | 0 | 0 | 1 | 74.38 | $1,812 |

Best finish for 1964: T-23rd at the American Classic

| 1965 | 2 | 6 | 1 | 0 | 0 | 0 | 0 | 74.83 | |

Best finish for 1965: T-53rd at the American Classic

| 1967 | 3 | 12 | 3 | 0 | 0 | 0 | 0 | 73.33 | $704 |

Best finish for 1967: T-44th at the Atlanta Classic

| 1968 | 3 | 6 | 0 | 0 | 0 | 0 | 0 | 74.67 | $500 |
| 1969 | 6 | 22 | 5 | 0 | 0 | 1 | 1 | 73.45 | $4,383 |

Best finish for 1969: T-6th at the British Open

Period Totals	Starts	Rounds Played	Cuts Made	Wins	Top-5s	Top-10s	Top-25s	Scoring Average	Money
	49	162	32	0	0	1	10	73.30	$11,701

Steve Lowery

Year	Starts	Rounds Played	Cuts Made	Wins	Top-5s	Top-10s	Top-25s	Scoring Average	Money
1983	2	4	0	0	0	0	0	74.25	
1984	1	2	0	0	0	0	0	74.00	
1986	1	4	1	0	0	0	0	70.25	$666

Best finish for 1986: T-56th at the Provident Classic

| 1987 | 4 | 12 | 2 | 0 | 0 | 0 | 0 | 70.83 | $4,190 |

Best finish for 1987: T-30th at the Provident Classic

| 1988 | 33 | 102 | 17 | 0 | 0 | 0 | 2 | 71.97 | $45,334 |

Best finish for 1988: T-14th at the Canon Sammy Davis, Jr. - Greater Hartford Open

| 1989 | 11 | 35 | 7 | 0 | 0 | 3 | 3 | 70.60 | $38,699 |

Best finish for 1989: T-7th at the Deposit Guaranty Golf Classic

| 1990 | 8 | 28 | 6 | 0 | 1 | 2 | 2 | 70.18 | $68,524 |

Best finish for 1990: T-4th at the Greater Milwaukee Open

| 1991 | 10 | 34 | 7 | 0 | 1 | 2 | 3 | 69.76 | $87,597 |

Best finish for 1991: T-3rd at the Chattanooga Classic

| 1992 | 7 | 22 | 4 | 0 | 0 | 0 | 2 | 71.64 | $22,608 |

Best finish for 1992: T-18th at the Kemper Open

| 1993 | 32 | 110 | 25 | 0 | 0 | 1 | 8 | 71.27 | $188,286 |

Best finish for 1993: T-10th at the New England Classic

| 1994 | 30 | 94 | 20 | 1 | 3 | 5 | 9 | 71.17 | $795,248 |

Best finish for 1994: Win at the Sprint International

| 1995 | 30 | 107 | 25 | 0 | 0 | 6 | 15 | 70.54 | $465,358 |

Best finish for 1995: T-6th at the Motorola Western Open & Greater Milwaukee Open

| 1996 | 31 | 100 | 21 | 0 | 1 | 2 | 7 | 71.30 | $264,805 |

Best finish for 1996: T-4th at the Freeport-McDermott Classic

| 1997 | 30 | 99 | 20 | 0 | 3 | 5 | 9 | 70.57 | $480,467 |

Best finish for 1997: T-3rd at the Motorola Western Open & Buick Challenge

Year	Starts	Rounds Played	Cuts Made	Wins	Top-5s	Top-10s	Top-25s	Scoring Average	Money
1998	28	86	15	0	3	4	8	71.08	$409,940

Best finish for 1998: T-3rd at the Freeport-McDermott Classic

| 1999 | 30 | 99 | 19 | 0 | 1 | 2 | 6 | 71.39 | $386,937 |

Best finish for 1999: T-4th at the Greater Milwaukee Open

| 2000 | 30 | 104 | 23 | 1 | 4 | 9 | 14 | 70.14 | $1,543,818 |

Best finish for 2000: Win at the Southern Farm Bureau Classic

| 2001 | 28 | 97 | 23 | 0 | 4 | 6 | 11 | 70.36 | $1,738,820 |

Best finish for 2001: 2nd at the Air Canada Championship

| 2002 | 28 | 92 | 21 | 0 | 3 | 5 | 10 | 70.76 | $1,883,553 |

Best finish for 2002: T-2nd at the Greater Milwaukee Open, The International presented by Qwest & Air Canada Championship

| 2003 | 29 | 80 | 15 | 0 | 2 | 2 | 5 | 71.20 | $939,293 |

Best finish for 2003: T-2nd at the B.C. Open

| 2004 | 28 | 89 | 17 | 0 | 2 | 2 | 5 | 71.45 | $1,193,245 |

Best finish for 2004: 2nd at the Cialis Western Open

| 2005 | 32 | 96 | 17 | 0 | 1 | 3 | 8 | 71.17 | $952,274 |

Best finish for 2005: T-3rd at the Chrysler Championship

| 2006 | 31 | 97 | 19 | 0 | 2 | 3 | 6 | 71.22 | $1,126,950 |

Best finish for 2006: T-2nd at the FBR Open

| 2007 | 22 | 74 | 14 | 0 | 0 | 1 | 3 | 71.35 | $502,622 |

Best finish for 2007: T-10th at the Sony Open in Hawaii

| 2008 | 25 | 74 | 13 | 1 | 1 | 2 | 4 | 71.96 | $1,524,275 |

Best finish for 2008: Win at the AT&T Pebble Beach National Pro-Am

Period Totals	Starts	Rounds Played	Cuts Made	Wins	Top-5s	Top-10s	Top-25s	Scoring Average	Money
	541	1741	351	3	32	65	140	71.05	$14,663,510

Bobby Loy

Year	Starts	Rounds Played	Cuts Made	Wins	Top-5s	Top-10s	Top-25s	Scoring Average	Money
1964	9	21	1	0	0	0	0	75.19	

Best finish for 1964: 67th at the Greater Greensboro Open

| 1965 | 10 | 22 | 1 | 0 | 0 | 0 | 0 | 75.73 | |

Best finish for 1965: T-73rd at the Pensacola Open

| 1972 | 5 | 11 | 1 | 0 | 0 | 0 | 0 | 75.82 | $222 |

Best finish for 1972: T-50th at the San Antonio Texas Open

1973	2	6	0	0	0	0	0	75.67	
1974	3	6	0	0	0	0	0	74.67	
1979	1	2	0	0	0	0	0	79.00	
1980	1	2	0	0	0	0	0	79.00	
Period Totals	Starts	Rounds Played	Cuts Made	Wins	Top-5s	Top-10s	Top-25s	Scoring Average	Money
	31	70	3	0	0	0	0	75.67	$222

Frank Luke

Year	Starts	Rounds Played	Cuts Made	Wins	Top-5s	Top-10s	Top-25s	Scoring Average	Money
1963	1	4	1	0	0	0	1	69.50	$800

Best finish for 1963: T-13th at the Texas Open Invitational

| 1964 | 11 | 25 | 2 | 0 | 0 | 0 | 0 | 75.60 | |

Best finish for 1964: 62nd at the New Orleans Open

| 1965 | 13 | 34 | 4 | 0 | 0 | 0 | 0 | 75.12 | |

Best finish for 1965: T-53rd at the Texas Open

Period Totals	Starts	Rounds Played	Cuts Made	Wins	Top-5s	Top-10s	Top-25s	Scoring Average	Money
	25	63	7	0	0	0	1	74.95	$800

Wren Lum

Year	Starts	Rounds Played	Cuts Made	Wins	Top-5s	Top-10s	Top-25s	Scoring Average	Money
1977	4	10	1	0	0	0	0	74.30	

Best finish for 1977: T-76th at the Sammy Davis, Jr. - Greater Hartford Open

| 1978 | 10 | 26 | 3 | 0 | 0 | 0 | 0 | 74.04 | $1,026 |

Best finish for 1978: T-40th at the Pensacola Open

| 1979 | 10 | 30 | 4 | 0 | 0 | 0 | 0 | 72.90 | $3,811 |

Best finish for 1979: T-26th at the Joe Garagiola Tucson Open

| 1980 | 7 | 18 | 2 | 0 | 0 | 0 | 0 | 72.61 | $898 |

Best finish for 1980: T-54th at the Quad Cities Open

| 1981 | 2 | 4 | 0 | 0 | 0 | 0 | 0 | 73.00 | |
| 1983 | 1 | 4 | 1 | 0 | 0 | 0 | 0 | 71.50 | $560 |

Best finish for 1983: T-57th at the Pensacola Open

| 1986 | 1 | 2 | 1 | 0 | 0 | 0 | 0 | 69.50 | $536 |

Best finish for 1986: T-47th at the Pensacola Open

1987	1	2	0	0	0	0	0	74.50	
Period Totals	Starts	Rounds Played	Cuts Made	Wins	Top-5s	Top-10s	Top-25s	Scoring Average	Money
	36	96	12	0	0	0	0	73.21	$6,831

David Lundstrom

Year	Starts	Rounds Played	Cuts Made	Wins	Top-5s	Top-10s	Top-25s	Scoring Average	Money
1972	1	2	0	0	0	0	0	79.00	
1976	15	39	8	0	0	0	0	74.67	$1,698

Best finish for 1976: T-58th at the Ed McMahon Quad City Open

1977	10	29	4	0	0	0	0	74.21	$1,573

Best finish for 1977: T-31st at the Tallahassee Open

1978	2	4	0	0	0	0	0	74.50	
1979	20	46	4	0	0	0	0	73.67	$2,540

Best finish for 1979: T-40th at the Buick Goodwrench Open

1980	2	4	0	0	0	0	0	73.50	
1981	15	41	6	0	0	0	0	72.49	$4,472

Best finish for 1981: T-36th at the Pleasant Valley Jimmy Fund Classic

1982	1	2	0	0	0	0	0	75.50	
1983	2	4	0	0	0	0	0	78.25	$600
1985	27	76	11	0	1	1	2	72.59	$34,368

Best finish for 1985: T-4th at the B.C. Open

1986	28	70	8	0	0	0	2	72.96	$23,454

Best finish for 1986: T-12th at the Canon Sammy Davis, Jr. - Greater Hartford Open

1987	3	8	1	0	0	0	0	71.38	$434

Best finish for 1987: T-59th at the Deposit Guaranty Golf Classic

1988	4	8	0	0	0	0	0	75.00	
1992	1	2	0	0	0	0	0	72.50	
1993	1	2	0	0	0	0	0	72.00	
1994	2	4	0	0	0	0	0	78.00	$1,000
1997	1	2	0	0	0	0	0	74.00	
2003	1	2	0	0	0	0	0	73.50	
2004	2	4	0	0	0	0	0	72.25	
2005	2	6	1	0	0	0	0	71.17	$7,000

Best finish for 2005: T-69th at the Valero Texas Open

2006	2	4	0	0	0	0	0	75.00	
Period Totals	Starts	Rounds Played	Cuts Made	Wins	Top-5s	Top-10s	Top-25s	Scoring Average	Money
	142	359	43	0	1	1	4	73.39	$77,138

Bob Lunn

Year	Starts	Rounds Played	Cuts Made	Wins	Top-5s	Top-10s	Top-25s	Scoring Average	Money
1964	1	4	1	0	0	0	0	76.25	

Best finish for 1964: T-67th at the Lucky International Open

1967	22	73	13	0	0	0	0	74.15	$2,132

Best finish for 1967: T-32nd at the Minnesota Golf Classic

1968	33	122	27	2	7	9	20	71.11	$101,012

Best finish for 1968: Win at the Memphis Open Invitational & Atlanta Classic

1969	35	124	28	1	4	8	20	71.61	$68,277

Best finish for 1969: Win at the Greater Hartford Open

1970	34	125	30	1	5	9	22	71.17	$97,992

Best finish for 1970: Win at the Florida Citrus Open Invitational

1971	34	122	29	1	3	5	16	71.58	$77,889

Best finish for 1971: Win at the Glen CampbellLos Angeles Open

1972	30	94	17	1	2	3	5	72.71	$47,137

Best finish for 1972: Win at the Atlanta Classic

1973	31	107	21	0	0	0	3	72.81	$17,846

Best finish for 1973: T-12th at the Greater Milwaukee Open

1974	21	47	6	0	0	0	0	73.81	$2,409

Best finish for 1974: T-29th at the Andy Williams-San Diego Open

1975	6	12	0	0	0	0	0	76.92	
1976	22	54	8	0	0	0	1	73.91	$2,839

Best finish for 1976: T-23rd at the Greater Milwaukee Open

1977	19	56	9	0	0	0	0	72.73	$6,155

Best finish for 1977: T-26th at the Joe Garagiola Tucson Open & Florida Citrus Open Invitational

1978	17	54	10	0	0	0	3	72.65	$10,114

Best finish for 1978: T-15th at the Canadian Open

1979	17	47	6	0	0	0	1	72.91	$7,074

Best finish for 1979: T-22nd at the Canadian Open

1980	5	10	0	0	0	0	0	74.50	
1982	1	3	1	0	0	0	0	73.33	$633

Best finish for 1982: T-61st at the Bing Crosby Pro-Am

1983	1	3	0	0	0	0	0	74.33	
1987	18	41	2	0	0	0	0	72.80	$3,378

Best finish for 1987: T-32nd at the Deposit Guaranty Golf Classic

1988	15	35	3	0	0	0	0	73.20	$3,037

Best finish for 1988: T-51st at the Deposit Guaranty Golf Classic

Year	Starts	Rounds Played	Cuts Made	Wins	Top-5s	Top-10s	Top-25s	Scoring Average	Money
1989	1	3	0	0	0	0	0	75.00	
1990	1	1	0	0	0	0	0	79.00	
Period Totals	Starts	Rounds Played	Cuts Made	Wins	Top-5s	Top-10s	Top-25s	Scoring Average	Money
	364	1137	211	6	21	34	91	72.45	$447,923

Mark Lye

Year	Starts	Rounds Played	Cuts Made	Wins	Top-5s	Top-10s	Top-25s	Scoring Average	Money
1972	1	2	0	0	0	0	0	77.50	
1973	1	2	0	0	0	0	0	76.00	
1977	28	91	18	0	0	0	5	72.91	$22,289

Best finish for 1977: T-13th at the Bob Hope Chrysler Classic

| 1978 | 25 | 81 | 15 | 0 | 0 | 0 | 3 | 72.58 | $11,713 |

Best finish for 1978: T-14th at the Greater Milwaukee Open

| 1979 | 29 | 98 | 21 | 0 | 0 | 1 | 9 | 71.68 | $50,763 |

Best finish for 1979: T-6th at the Anheuser-Busch Golf Classic

| 1980 | 31 | 104 | 22 | 0 | 4 | 5 | 14 | 71.74 | $109,954 |

Best finish for 1980: T-2nd at the Tallahassee Open & Buick Goodwrench Open

| 1981 | 37 | 122 | 27 | 0 | 2 | 4 | 11 | 71.57 | $80,621 |

Best finish for 1981: T-5th at the Phoenix Open & Pleasant Valley Jimmy Fund Classic

| 1982 | 33 | 105 | 19 | 0 | 2 | 3 | 6 | 72.21 | $67,460 |

Best finish for 1982: T-5th at the Tallahassee Open & Danny Thomas Memphis Classic

| 1983 | 31 | 104 | 21 | 1 | 3 | 6 | 9 | 71.38 | $164,506 |

Best finish for 1983: Win at the Bank of Boston Classic

| 1984 | 34 | 123 | 27 | 0 | 1 | 5 | 12 | 71.73 | $152,956 |

Best finish for 1984: T-5th at the Danny Thomas Memphis Classic

| 1985 | 31 | 107 | 23 | 0 | 2 | 2 | 7 | 71.75 | $112,735 |

Best finish for 1985: 3rd at the Hertz Bay Hill Classic

| 1986 | 29 | 86 | 18 | 0 | 1 | 2 | 3 | 72.00 | $78,961 |

Best finish for 1986: T-3rd at the Shearson Lehman/Andy Williams San Diego

| 1987 | 34 | 104 | 19 | 0 | 0 | 1 | 5 | 71.89 | $74,222 |

Best finish for 1987: 6th at the Southern Open

| 1988 | 30 | 94 | 19 | 0 | 0 | 1 | 7 | 71.38 | $106,972 |

Best finish for 1988: T-9th at the USF&G Classic

| 1989 | 28 | 90 | 18 | 0 | 2 | 5 | 10 | 71.01 | $242,884 |

Best finish for 1989: T-3rd at the Greater Milwaukee Open

| 1990 | 28 | 90 | 20 | 0 | 0 | 1 | 11 | 71.26 | $202,011 |

Best finish for 1990: T-8th at the Hardee's Golf Classic

| 1991 | 29 | 91 | 19 | 0 | 0 | 2 | 7 | 71.22 | $147,530 |

Best finish for 1991: T-7th at the B.C. Open

| 1992 | 15 | 38 | 4 | 0 | 0 | 0 | 0 | 71.47 | $9,921 |

Best finish for 1992: T-45th at the Phoenix Open

| 1993 | 23 | 65 | 13 | 0 | 1 | 1 | 4 | 71.80 | $106,936 |

Best finish for 1993: T-4th at the B.C. Open

| 1994 | 15 | 44 | 7 | 0 | 0 | 1 | 1 | 71.84 | $64,394 |

Best finish for 1994: T-7th at the Kemper Open

1995	2	4	0	0	0	0	0	71.25	
Period Totals	Starts	Rounds Played	Cuts Made	Wins	Top-5s	Top-10s	Top-25s	Scoring Average	Money
	514	1645	330	1	18	40	124	71.75	$1,806,828

Jarrod Lyle

Year	Starts	Rounds Played	Cuts Made	Wins	Top-5s	Top-10s	Top-25s	Scoring Average	Money
2006	1	2	0	0	0	0	0	72.00	$5,577
2007	24	77	14	0	0	0	3	71.10	$390,303

Best finish for 2007: T-12th at the Reno-Tahoe Open & Fry's Electronics Open

| 2008 | 1 | 4 | 1 | 0 | 0 | 0 | 0 | 73.50 | $23,985 |

Best finish for 2008: T-48th at the U.S. Open

| Period Totals | Starts | Rounds Played | Cuts Made | Wins | Top-5s | Top-10s | Top-25s | Scoring Average | Money |
| | 26 | 83 | 15 | 0 | 0 | 0 | 3 | 71.24 | $419,865 |

Sandy Lyle

Year	Starts	Rounds Played	Cuts Made	Wins	Top-5s	Top-10s	Top-25s	Scoring Average	Money
1974	1	3	0	0	0	0	0	78.67	
1977	1	2	0	0	0	0	0	77.50	
1978	1	2	0	0	0	0	0	75.00	$332
1979	1	4	1	0	0	0	1	73.75	$3,801

Best finish for 1979: T-19th at the British Open

| 1980 | 6 | 19 | 4 | 0 | 0 | 0 | 3 | 72.68 | $19,750 |

Best finish for 1980: T-12th at the British Open

| 1981 | 5 | 15 | 2 | 0 | 0 | 0 | 1 | 73.53 | $9,980 |

Best finish for 1981: T-14th at the British Open

| 1982 | 4 | 12 | 2 | 0 | 0 | 1 | 1 | 72.67 | $15,679 |

Best finish for 1982: T-8th at the British Open

Year	Starts	Rounds Played	Cuts Made	Wins	Top-5s	Top-10s	Top-25s	Scoring Average	Money
1983	2	5	0	0	0	0	0	73.20	$2,458
1984	7	24	5	0	0	0	4	71.58	$24,309

Best finish for 1984: T-14th at the British Open

1985	14	52	12	1	1	1	6	71.98	$134,702

Best finish for 1985: Win at the British Open

1986	14	47	10	1	1	1	4	71.60	$149,114

Best finish for 1986: Win at the Greater Greensboro Open

1987	16	57	12	1	1	4	8	71.70	$298,096

Best finish for 1987: Win at the Tournament Players Championship

1988	19	67	15	3	5	6	14	70.45	$762,634

Best finish for 1988: Win at the Phoenix Open, Kmart Greater Greensboro Open & Masters

1989	18	57	10	0	3	4	4	71.91	$300,473

Best finish for 1989: T-2nd at the Bob Hope Chrysler Classic & Nissan Los Angeles Open

1990	16	48	8	0	0	1	3	72.58	$73,961

Best finish for 1990: T-10th at the Phoenix Open

1991	9	27	5	0	0	0	3	72.37	$62,302

Best finish for 1991: T-12th at the Phoenix Open

1992	10	31	6	0	0	1	3	71.48	$109,425

Best finish for 1992: 6th at the Nissan Los Angeles Open

1993	8	26	5	0	1	1	2	71.58	$87,045

Best finish for 1993: 5th at the Doral-Ryder Open

1994	8	28	6	0	0	1	1	72.79	$53,774

Best finish for 1994: T-9th at the Honda Classic

1995	7	22	4	0	0	0	0	73.05	$24,408

Best finish for 1995: T-32nd at the Freeport-McMoRan Classic

1996	15	43	8	0	0	1	3	71.72	$95,990

Best finish for 1996: T-10th at the Phoenix Open

1997	21	63	9	0	0	0	2	72.49	$73,033

Best finish for 1997: T-18th at the Buick Invitational

1998	23	61	8	0	0	1	5	72.36	$176,954

Best finish for 1998: T-7th at the Bell Canadian Open

1999	15	44	7	0	0	0	3	73.48	$114,254

Best finish for 1999: T-13th at the Touchstone Energy Tucson Open

2000	18	48	5	0	0	2	2	72.04	$205,510

Best finish for 2000: 7th at the SEI Pennsylvania Classic

2001	5	15	1	0	0	0	0	72.80	$16,551

Best finish for 2001: T-69th at the British Open

2002	9	23	2	0	0	0	0	73.04	$34,032

Best finish for 2002: T-40th at the Bay Hill Invitational

2003	5	13	0	0	0	0	0	74.46	$9,769
2004	2	8	2	0	0	0	0	75.00	$49,142

Best finish for 2004: T-37th at the Masters

2005	4	13	1	0	0	0	0	72.38	$51,433

Best finish for 2005: T-32nd at the British Open

2006	3	6	0	0	0	0	0	77.50	$9,648
2007	2	8	2	0	0	0	0	75.13	$47,494

Best finish for 2007: 43rd at the Masters

2008	2	4	1	0	0	0	0	75.50	$24,750

Best finish for 2008: 45th at the Masters

Period Totals	Starts	Rounds Played	Cuts Made	Wins	Top-5s	Top-10s	Top-25s	Scoring Average	Money
	291	897	153	6	12	25	73	72.30	$3,040,803

Denny Lyons

Year	Starts	Rounds Played	Cuts Made	Wins	Top-5s	Top-10s	Top-25s	Scoring Average	Money
1967	1	2	0	0	0	0	0	80.00	
1969	16	43	5	0	0	0	0	74.47	$1,088

Best finish for 1969: T-36th at the Tallahassee Open & Indian Ridge Hospital Open

1971	1	2	0	0	0	0	0	75.50	$500
1972	5	16	4	0	0	0	0	73.69	$1,394

Best finish for 1972: T-40th at the PGA Championship

1973	3	10	2	0	0	0	2	72.90	$5,575

Best finish for 1973: T-12th at the PGA Championship

1974	3	6	0	0	0	0	0	77.50	$500
1975	2	4	0	0	0	0	0	74.25	
1976	1	2	0	0	0	0	0	76.00	$250
1978	1	2	0	0	0	0	0	79.50	$303
1980	1	2	0	0	0	0	0	76.00	$500
Period Totals	Starts	Rounds Played	Cuts Made	Wins	Top-5s	Top-10s	Top-25s	Scoring Average	Money
	34	89	11	0	0	0	2	74.67	$10,109

Dick Lytle

Year	Starts	Rounds Played	Cuts Made	Wins	Top-5s	Top-10s	Top-25s	Scoring Average	Money
1964	1	4	1	0	0	0	0	75.75	

Best finish for 1964: 68th at the San Diego Open

1965	13	36	5	0	0	0	0	73.61	$1,124

Best finish for 1965: T-30th at the Almaden Open

1966	24	76	13	0	2	2	2	73.51	$12,649

Best finish for 1966: T-2nd at the Florida Citrus Open Invitational

1967	22	66	10	0	0	0	0	74.15	$813

Best finish for 1967: T-42nd at the San Diego Open

1968	7	22	3	0	0	0	0	74.55	$275

Best finish for 1968: T-28th at the AZALEA Open Invitational

Period Totals	Starts	Rounds Played	Cuts Made	Wins	Top-5s	Top-10s	Top-25s	Scoring Average	Money
	67	204	32	0	2	2	2	73.89	$14,861

Will MacKenzie

Year	Starts	Rounds Played	Cuts Made	Wins	Top-5s	Top-10s	Top-25s	Scoring Average	Money
2005	25	73	12	0	0	1	2	71.62	$275,529

Best finish for 2005: T-8th at the Michelin Championship at Las Vegas

2006	29	88	16	1	1	1	3	71.14	$879,965

Best finish for 2006: Win at the Reno-Tahoe Open

2007	30	100	20	0	1	3	6	71.02	$1,116,507

Best finish for 2007: T-4th at the Mercedes Championships

2008	21	62	10	1	2	2	2	71.63	$911,194

Best finish for 2008: Win at the Viking Classic

Period Totals	Starts	Rounds Played	Cuts Made	Wins	Top-5s	Top-10s	Top-25s	Scoring Average	Money
	105	323	58	2	4	7	13	71.30	$3,183,195

Andrew Magee

Year	Starts	Rounds Played	Cuts Made	Wins	Top-5s	Top-10s	Top-25s	Scoring Average	Money
1981	1	2	0	0	0	0	0	78.50	
1984	3	8	1	0	0	0	0	72.75	$1,701

Best finish for 1984: T-31st at the B.C. Open

1985	30	97	18	0	0	4	5	71.67	$72,933

Best finish for 1985: T-6th at the Canon Sammy Davis, Jr. - Greater Hartford Open & Texas Open

1986	33	99	17	0	0	1	5	72.41	$71,078

Best finish for 1986: T-6th at the Manufactures Hanover Westchester Classic

1987	33	98	18	0	0	2	7	71.50	$94,517

Best finish for 1987: T-9th at the Big I Houston Open

1988	31	95	17	1	3	4	8	71.22	$263,719

Best finish for 1988: Win at the Pensacola Open

1989	33	102	18	0	0	3	5	71.82	$129,270

Best finish for 1989: T-6th at the Kemper Open

1990	30	98	22	0	1	3	8	71.50	$211,507

Best finish for 1990: T-5th at the GTE Byron Nelson Classic

1991	29	96	20	2	3	7	12	70.90	$757,046

Best finish for 1991: Win at the Nestle Invitational & Las Vegas Invitational

1992	29	100	22	0	1	4	13	70.88	$346,089

Best finish for 1992: T-5th at the British Open

1993	26	78	15	0	1	2	7	71.32	$278,191

Best finish for 1993: 2nd at the Phoenix Open

1994	26	91	19	1	1	3	9	70.97	$432,013

Best finish for 1994: Win at the Northern Telecom Open

1995	27	86	18	0	2	3	5	70.92	$257,918

Best finish for 1995: 4th at the Honda Classic

1996	26	76	13	0	2	3	7	71.14	$332,504

Best finish for 1996: 2nd at the Quad City Classic

1997	29	102	23	0	4	7	15	70.64	$752,007

Best finish for 1997: T-2nd at the Greater Vancouver Open & B.C. Open

1998	29	94	19	0	4	6	12	70.90	$966,454

Best finish for 1998: 2nd at the Memorial Tournament

1999	27	84	17	0	2	2	8	71.58	$914,283

Best finish for 1999: 2nd at the Andersen Consulting Match Play Championship

2000	26	73	14	0	1	4	8	71.12	$870,372

Best finish for 2000: 2nd at the Greater Greensboro Chrysler Classic

2001	31	94	16	0	0	0	1	71.39	$175,108

Best finish for 2001: T-25th at the Invensys Classic at Las Vegas

2002	28	88	17	0	1	2	6	71.11	$543,035

Best finish for 2002: T-3rd at the AT&T Pebble Beach

2003	26	89	19	0	0	3	4	70.64	$578,558

Best finish for 2003: T-6th at the Chrysler Classic of Tucson

| 2005 | 29 | 78 | 13 | 0 | 0 | 2 | 3 | 71.88 | $488,779 |

Best finish for 2005: T-7th at the Sony Open in Hawaii

| 2006 | 19 | 47 | 5 | 0 | 0 | 0 | 0 | 72.43 | $52,711 |

Best finish for 2006: T-32nd at the B.C. Open

| 2007 | 1 | 3 | 0 | 0 | 0 | 0 | 0 | 76.67 | |
| 2008 | 3 | 9 | 1 | 0 | 0 | 0 | 0 | 72.44 | $12,238 |

Best finish for 2008: T-64th at the Arnold Palmer Invitational

Period Totals	Starts	Rounds Played	Cuts Made	Wins	Top-5s	Top-10s	Top-25s	Scoring Average	Money
	605	1887	362	4	26	65	148	71.34	$8,602,030

Jerry Magee

Year	Starts	Rounds Played	Cuts Made	Wins	Top-5s	Top-10s	Top-25s	Scoring Average	Money
1958	28	91	15	0	0	1	5	72.57	$2,779

Best finish for 1958: T-7th at the Texas Open

| 1959 | 9 | 36 | 8 | 0 | 1 | 1 | 6 | 71.67 | $3,687 |

Best finish for 1959: T-2nd at the Orange County Open Invitational

| 1960 | 9 | 35 | 9 | 0 | 0 | 0 | 3 | 71.97 | $2,249 |

Best finish for 1960: T-20th at the Dallas Open Invitational

| 1961 | 5 | 20 | 5 | 0 | 0 | 1 | 1 | 72.75 | $1,010 |

Best finish for 1961: T-6th at the Almaden Open

| 1962 | 5 | 20 | 4 | 0 | 0 | 1 | 2 | 71.25 | $1,608 |

Best finish for 1962: T-7th at the Azalea Open Invitational

| 1963 | 1 | 4 | 1 | 0 | 0 | 0 | 0 | 70.25 | $024 |

Best finish for 1963: T-54th at the "500" Festival Open Invitational

| 1964 | 16 | 39 | 5 | 0 | 0 | 0 | 0 | 73.05 | $1,561 |

Best finish for 1964: T-27th at the New Orleans Open

| 1965 | 1 | 4 | 1 | 0 | 0 | 0 | 0 | 71.00 | $275 |

Best finish for 1965: T-28th at the Cajun Classic

| 1966 | 3 | 12 | 3 | 0 | 0 | 0 | 0 | 72.58 | |

Best finish for 1966: T-59th at the Los Angeles Open Invitational

| 1967 | 1 | 2 | 0 | 0 | 0 | 0 | 0 | 77.50 | |

Period Totals	Starts	Rounds Played	Cuts Made	Wins	Top-5s	Top-10s	Top-25s	Scoring Average	Money
	78	263	51	0	1	4	17	72.33	$13,194

Jeff Maggert

Year	Starts	Rounds Played	Cuts Made	Wins	Top-5s	Top-10s	Top-25s	Scoring Average	Money
1986	4	10	1	0	0	1	1	73.40	$14,000

Best finish for 1986: 7th at the Southwest Golf Classic

| 1987 | 4 | 10 | 1 | 0 | 0 | 0 | 0 | 73.60 | $1,536 |

Best finish for 1987: T-65th at the Provident Classic

| 1990 | 2 | 5 | 1 | 0 | 0 | 0 | 0 | 73.60 | $2,060 |

Best finish for 1990: T-64th at the Independent Insurance Agent Open

| 1991 | 29 | 90 | 17 | 0 | 2 | 2 | 9 | 71.12 | $240,940 |

Best finish for 1991: 4th at the Greater Milwaukee Open

| 1992 | 27 | 91 | 19 | 0 | 3 | 4 | 9 | 70.46 | $378,608 |

Best finish for 1992: T-3rd at the United Airlines Hawaiian Open & H-E-B Texas Open

| 1993 | 29 | 92 | 17 | 1 | 5 | 6 | 13 | 70.72 | $793,947 |

Best finish for 1993: Win at the Walt Disney World/Oldsmobile Classic

| 1994 | 26 | 92 | 22 | 0 | 5 | 11 | 15 | 70.58 | $828,590 |

Best finish for 1994: T-2nd at the AT&T Pebble Beach National Pro-Am & Shell Houston Open

| 1995 | 23 | 81 | 17 | 0 | 4 | 5 | 10 | 70.96 | $529,452 |

Best finish for 1995: T-2nd at the Motorola Western Open

| 1996 | 26 | 91 | 20 | 0 | 5 | 9 | 12 | 70.73 | $804,955 |

Best finish for 1996: T-2nd at the Bay Hill Invitational, Shell Houston Open & Buick Classic

| 1997 | 27 | 93 | 19 | 0 | 5 | 6 | 10 | 71.02 | $840,884 |

Best finish for 1997: T-2nd at the Buick Classic & Canon Greater Hartford Open

| 1998 | 24 | 83 | 18 | 0 | 5 | 8 | 12 | 70.72 | $994,609 |

Best finish for 1998: T-2nd at the Bay Hill Invitational & Shell Houston Open

| 1999 | 23 | 82 | 20 | 1 | 3 | 6 | 10 | 70.99 | $2,023,219 |

Best finish for 1999: Win at the Andersen Consulting Match Play Championship

| 2000 | 27 | 82 | 17 | 0 | 2 | 6 | 11 | 71.18 | $1,146,749 |

Best finish for 2000: T-2nd at the Buick Challenge

| 2001 | 27 | 84 | 15 | 0 | 1 | 4 | 7 | 70.86 | $717,180 |

Best finish for 2001: T-4th at the Greater Greensboro Chrysler Classic

| 2002 | 27 | 83 | 14 | 0 | 1 | 2 | 5 | 71.51 | $735,198 |

Best finish for 2002: 3rd at the U.S. Open

| 2003 | 24 | 81 | 16 | 0 | 1 | 2 | 5 | 71.26 | $750,106 |

Best finish for 2003: 5th at the Masters

| 2004 | 20 | 60 | 10 | 0 | 3 | 5 | 5 | 71.08 | $1,532,884 |

Best finish for 2004: 2nd at the AT&T Pebble Beach National Pro-Am

| 2005 | 25 | 74 | 17 | 0 | 0 | 2 | 7 | 71.27 | $745,780 |

Best finish for 2005: T-7th at the Shell Houston Open

Year	Starts	Rounds Played	Cuts Made	Wins	Top-5s	Top-10s	Top-25s	Scoring Average	Money
2006	26	81	14	1	1	2	4	71.65	$1,435,953

Best finish for 2006: Win at the FedEx St. Jude Classic

| 2007 | 26 | 79 | 15 | 0 | 1 | 1 | 7 | 71.30 | $845,585 |

Best finish for 2007: T-5th at the U.S. Bank Championship in Milwaukee

| 2008 | 28 | 86 | 16 | 0 | 0 | 0 | 6 | 71.29 | $444,484 |

Best finish for 2008: T-15th at the Valero Texas Open

Period Totals	Starts	Rounds Played	Cuts Made	Wins	Top-5s	Top-10s	Top-25s	Scoring Average	Money
	474	1530	306	3	47	82	158	71.07	$15,806,719

John Maginnes

Year	Starts	Rounds Played	Cuts Made	Wins	Top-5s	Top-10s	Top-25s	Scoring Average	Money
1992	1	2	0	0	0	0	0	76.00	
1995	1	4	1	0	0	0	0	74.25	$2,806

Best finish for 1995: T-71st at the U.S. Open

| 1996 | 28 | 81 | 14 | 0 | 1 | 1 | 6 | 71.21 | $184,065 |

Best finish for 1996: T-2nd at the Buick Challenge

| 1997 | 35 | 101 | 14 | 0 | 0 | 1 | 3 | 72.15 | $110,136 |

Best finish for 1997: T-10th at the Quad City Classic

| 1998 | 8 | 32 | 8 | 0 | 1 | 1 | 6 | 69.66 | $172,165 |

Best finish for 1998: T-5th at the Deposit Guaranty Golf Classic

| 1999 | 29 | 91 | 16 | 0 | 0 | 4 | 6 | 70.95 | $426,666 |

Best finish for 1999: T-6th at the Motorola Western Open & Buick Challenge

| 2000 | 32 | 99 | 16 | 0 | 0 | 0 | 3 | 71.73 | $211,749 |

Best finish for 2000: T-16th at the Bob Hope Chrysler Classic

| 2001 | 2 | 4 | 0 | 0 | 0 | 0 | 0 | 74.75 | $1,000 |
| 2002 | 2 | 8 | 2 | 0 | 0 | 0 | 0 | 73.75 | $21,701 |

Best finish for 2002: T-59th at the U.S. Open

| 2003 | 29 | 87 | 13 | 0 | 1 | 1 | 3 | 71.67 | $308,928 |

Best finish for 2003: T-5th at the B.C. Open

| 2004 | 12 | 29 | 2 | 0 | 0 | 0 | 0 | 73.28 | $26,420 |

Best finish for 2004: T-41st at the Sony Open in Hawaii

| 2005 | 17 | 37 | 1 | 0 | 0 | 0 | 0 | 73.41 | $10,080 |

Best finish for 2005: T-46th at the John Deere Classic

Period Totals	Starts	Rounds Played	Cuts Made	Wins	Top-5s	Top-10s	Top-25s	Scoring Average	Money
	196	575	87	0	3	8	27	71.75	$1,475,717

John Mahaffey

Year	Starts	Rounds Played	Cuts Made	Wins	Top-5s	Top-10s	Top-25s	Scoring Average	Money
1970	1	4	1	0	0	0	0	75.25	

Best finish for 1970: T-36th at the U.S. Open

| 1971 | 2 | 6 | 1 | 0 | 0 | 0 | 1 | 72.50 | $1,950 |

Best finish for 1971: T-12th at the Colonial National Invitational

| 1972 | 32 | 111 | 24 | 0 | 2 | 4 | 6 | 72.05 | $51,286 |

Best finish for 1972: 2nd at the Danny Thomas Memphis Classic

| 1973 | 36 | 140 | 32 | 1 | 3 | 12 | 21 | 71.22 | $107,115 |

Best finish for 1973: Win at the Sahara Invitational

| 1974 | 26 | 103 | 25 | 0 | 5 | 7 | 17 | 71.02 | $116,627 |

Best finish for 1974: T-2nd at the Glen CampbellLos Angeles Open, Greater Jacksonville Open & Tournament of Champions

| 1975 | 27 | 96 | 21 | 0 | 6 | 11 | 17 | 70.26 | $146,946 |

Best finish for 1975: 2nd at the Dean Martin Tucson Open, Danny Thomas Memphis Classic, Kemper Open & U.S. Open

| 1976 | 26 | 97 | 23 | 0 | 6 | 6 | 12 | 71.30 | $77,643 |

Best finish for 1976: 2nd at the Tallahassee Open

| 1977 | 13 | 36 | 5 | 0 | 0 | 0 | 4 | 72.72 | $9,847 |

Best finish for 1977: T-12th at the Pensacola Open

| 1978 | 28 | 103 | 23 | 2 | 4 | 5 | 12 | 71.43 | $153,574 |

Best finish for 1978: Win at the PGA Championship & American Optical Classic

| 1979 | 20 | 69 | 15 | 1 | 2 | 2 | 5 | 71.46 | $90,193 |

Best finish for 1979: Win at the Bob Hope Chrysler Classic

| 1980 | 26 | 93 | 22 | 1 | 4 | 5 | 13 | 71.15 | $170,357 |

Best finish for 1980: Win at the Kemper Open

| 1981 | 26 | 80 | 15 | 1 | 2 | 5 | 10 | 71.29 | $129,945 |

Best finish for 1981: Win at the Anheuser-Busch Golf Classic

| 1982 | 26 | 92 | 20 | 0 | 1 | 2 | 9 | 71.75 | $78,547 |

Best finish for 1982: T-2nd at the Joe Garagiola Tucson Open

| 1983 | 28 | 99 | 20 | 0 | 3 | 4 | 9 | 71.65 | $127,015 |

Best finish for 1983: T-2nd at the Bank of Boston Classic

| 1984 | 30 | 98 | 21 | 1 | 3 | 8 | 15 | 71.11 | $254,048 |

Best finish for 1984: Win at the Bob Hope Chrysler Classic

| 1985 | 29 | 107 | 26 | 1 | 6 | 9 | 18 | 70.44 | $341,595 |

Best finish for 1985: Win at the Texas Open

| 1986 | 29 | 94 | 24 | 1 | 4 | 6 | 13 | 70.90 | $385,472 |

Best finish for 1986: Win at the Tournament Players Championship

| 1987 | 28 | 102 | 23 | 0 | 1 | 6 | 13 | 70.89 | $193,938 |

Best finish for 1987: T-5th at the Bank of Boston Classic

Year	Starts	Rounds Played	Cuts Made	Wins	Top-5s	Top-10s	Top-25s	Scoring Average	Money
1988	30	102	21	0	2	3	15	70.59	$266,415

Best finish for 1988: T-3rd at the Bank of Boston Classic

| 1989 | 32 | 106 | 24 | 1 | 1 | 2 | 8 | 71.02 | $401,367 |

Best finish for 1989: Win at the Federal Express St. Jude Classic

| 1990 | 28 | 96 | 20 | 0 | 2 | 3 | 8 | 71.48 | $326,115 |

Best finish for 1990: T-2nd at the Southwestern Bell Colonial & Walt Disney World/Oldsmobile Classic

| 1991 | 21 | 70 | 13 | 0 | 0 | 0 | 2 | 71.43 | $65,403 |

Best finish for 1991: T-12th at the Independent Insurance Agent Open

| 1992 | 28 | 76 | 8 | 0 | 0 | 2 | 4 | 71.99 | $102,712 |

Best finish for 1992: T-7th at the Chattanooga Classic

| 1993 | 26 | 73 | 11 | 0 | 0 | 0 | 0 | 72.68 | $39,113 |

Best finish for 1993: T-27th at the Kmart Greater Greensboro Open

| 1994 | 26 | 75 | 10 | 0 | 0 | 0 | 2 | 72.31 | $67,580 |

Best finish for 1994: T-17th at the Motorola Western Open

| 1995 | 25 | 81 | 15 | 0 | 1 | 2 | 2 | 71.40 | $158,808 |

Best finish for 1995: T-3rd at the LaCantera Texas Open

| 1996 | 28 | 65 | 4 | 0 | 0 | 0 | 1 | 72.85 | $30,016 |

Best finish for 1996: T-17th at the Honda Classic

| 1997 | 21 | 43 | 1 | 0 | 0 | 0 | 0 | 73.58 | $2,850 |

Best finish for 1997: T-73rd at the Bob Hope Chrysler Classic

| 1998 | 3 | 12 | 2 | 0 | 0 | 0 | 0 | 73.50 | $7,779 |

Best finish for 1998: T-59th at the Shell Houston Open

1999	1	4	0	0	0	0	0	73.00	
2002	1	4	0	0	0	0	0	72.00	
Period Totals	Starts	Rounds Played	Cuts Made	Wins	Top-5s	Top-10s	Top-25s	Scoring Average	Money
	703	2337	470	10	58	104	237	71.43	$3,904,257

Hunter Mahan

Year	Starts	Rounds Played	Cuts Made	Wins	Top-5s	Top-10s	Top-25s	Scoring Average	Money
2000	1	2	0	0	0	0	0	70.00	
2002	1	2	0	0	0	0	0	69.50	
2003	9	28	5	0	0	0	2	71.36	$106,300

Best finish for 2003: T-17th at the Valero Texas Open

| 2004 | 30 | 94 | 16 | 0 | 3 | 3 | 6 | 71.38 | $813,089 |

Best finish for 2004: T-2nd at the Reno-Tahoe Open

| 2005 | 34 | 101 | 18 | 0 | 0 | 2 | 5 | 71.21 | $591,567 |

Best finish for 2005: T-7th at the John Deere Classic

| 2006 | 29 | 98 | 21 | 0 | 1 | 2 | 6 | 70.70 | $1,107,457 |

Best finish for 2006: T-2nd at the Buick Championship

| 2007 | 27 | 91 | 18 | 1 | 4 | 6 | 12 | 70.78 | $2,858,995 |

Best finish for 2007: Win at the Travelers Championship

| 2008 | 27 | 85 | 18 | 0 | 2 | 5 | 13 | 70.78 | $2,208,855 |

Best finish for 2008: T-2nd at the Travelers Championship

Period Totals	Starts	Rounds Played	Cuts Made	Wins	Top-5s	Top-10s	Top-25s	Scoring Average	Money
	158	501	96	1	10	18	44	70.99	$7,686,262

Mac Main

Year	Starts	Rounds Played	Cuts Made	Wins	Top-5s	Top-10s	Top-25s	Scoring Average	Money
1958	5	12	1	0	0	0	0	75.42	$112

Best finish for 1958: T-32nd at the Carling Open

| 1959 | 3 | 12 | 3 | 0 | 0 | 0 | 1 | 73.67 | $535 |

Best finish for 1959: T-19th at the Greater Greensboro Open Invitational

| 1960 | 11 | 38 | 9 | 0 | 0 | 0 | 4 | 72.39 | $6,630 |

Best finish for 1960: T-15th at the Milwaukee Open Invitational

| 1961 | 12 | 46 | 10 | 0 | 2 | 4 | 4 | 70.70 | $7,361 |

Best finish for 1961: T-3rd at the Greater New Orleans Open Invitational

| 1962 | 7 | 27 | 6 | 0 | 0 | 0 | 4 | 72.04 | $3,446 |

Best finish for 1962: T-14th at the Waco Turner Open Invitational

| 1963 | 2 | 6 | 1 | 0 | 0 | 0 | 0 | 75.50 | $312 |

Best finish for 1963: T-37th at the American Golf Classic

| 1964 | 1 | 2 | 0 | 0 | 0 | 0 | 0 | 78.00 | |
| 1966 | 3 | 8 | 1 | 0 | 0 | 0 | 0 | 76.75 | $300 |

Best finish for 1966: T-69th at the Azalea Open Invitational

| 1968 | 1 | 4 | 1 | 0 | 0 | 0 | 0 | 70.75 | |

Best finish for 1968: T-39th at the AZALEA Open Invitational

| 1969 | 1 | 4 | 1 | 0 | 0 | 0 | 0 | 72.50 | |

Best finish for 1969: T-44th at the Azalea Open

1970	1	2	0	0	0	0	0	73.00	
1973	1	2	0	0	0	0	0	72.00	
1974	1	2	0	0	0	0	0	73.00	
1975	1	2	0	0	0	0	0	76.00	
1978	1	2	0	0	0	0	0	83.50	$303

Year	Starts	Rounds Played	Cuts Made	Wins	Top-5s	Top-10s	Top-25s	Scoring Average	Money
1979	1	2	0	0	0	0	0	81.50	
1980	1	0	0	0	0	0	0		
1991	1	2	0	0	0	0	0	77.50	
Period Totals	Starts	Rounds Played	Cuts Made	Wins	Top-5s	Top-10s	Top-25s	Scoring Average	Money
	54	173	33	0	2	4	13	72.87	$18,999

Ted Makalena

Year	Starts	Rounds Played	Cuts Made	Wins	Top-5s	Top-10s	Top-25s	Scoring Average	Money
1958	2	5	0	0	0	0	0	78.00	
1959	1	3	1	0	0	0	0	79.67	$043

Best finish for 1959: T-135 at the Bing Crosby National

| 1963 | 1 | 4 | 1 | 0 | 0 | 0 | 0 | 76.25 | $400 |

Best finish for 1963: T-27th at the U.S. Open

| 1964 | 5 | 16 | 4 | 0 | 0 | 0 | 1 | 73.00 | $720 |

Best finish for 1964: T-23rd at the U.S. Open

| 1965 | 5 | 15 | 1 | 0 | 0 | 0 | 0 | 75.27 | |

Best finish for 1965: T-61st at the Hawaiian Open

| 1966 | 5 | 21 | 5 | 1 | 1 | 1 | 2 | 71.81 | $10,432 |

Best finish for 1966: Win at the Hawaiian Open Invitational

| 1967 | 26 | 91 | 19 | 0 | 0 | 1 | 4 | 73.19 | $12,148 |

Best finish for 1967: T-7th at the Hawaiian Open

| 1968 | 18 | 50 | 6 | 0 | 0 | 1 | 2 | 73.28 | $5,132 |

Best finish for 1968: T-8th at the Bob Hope Desert Classic

Period Totals	Starts	Rounds Played	Cuts Made	Wins	Top-5s	Top-10s	Top-25s	Scoring Average	Money
	63	205	37	1	1	3	9	73.48	$28,876

John Mallinger

Year	Starts	Rounds Played	Cuts Made	Wins	Top-5s	Top-10s	Top-25s	Scoring Average	Money
2005	1	4	1	0	0	0	0	74.25	$13,553

Best finish for 2005: T-67th at the U.S. Open

| 2006 | 3 | 8 | 1 | 0 | 0 | 0 | 0 | 73.13 | $18,354 |

Best finish for 2006: T-43rd at the Buick Invitational

| 2007 | 29 | 96 | 18 | 0 | 3 | 4 | 7 | 71.25 | $1,681,764 |

Best finish for 2007: T-3rd at the AT&T Pebble Beach National Pro-Am, Zurich Classic of New Orleans & Turning Stone Resort Championship

| 2008 | 29 | 95 | 20 | 0 | 2 | 4 | 8 | 71.02 | $1,201,433 |

Best finish for 2008: T-3rd at the AT&T Pebble Beach National Pro-Am & Justin Timberlake Shriners Hospitals for Children Open

Period Totals	Starts	Rounds Played	Cuts Made	Wins	Top-5s	Top-10s	Top-25s	Scoring Average	Money
	62	203	40	0	5	8	15	71.28	$2,915,104

Bill Mallon

Year	Starts	Rounds Played	Cuts Made	Wins	Top-5s	Top-10s	Top-25s	Scoring Average	Money
1976	20	67	14	0	0	2	3	72.63	$20,595

Best finish for 1976: 6th at the Western Open

| 1977 | 28 | 89 | 18 | 0 | 1 | 1 | 5 | 72.78 | $23,204 |

Best finish for 1977: T-5th at the Joe Garagiola Tucson Open

| 1978 | 17 | 38 | 2 | 0 | 0 | 0 | 0 | 75.87 | $310 |

Best finish for 1978: T-44th at the Buick Goodwrench Open

Period Totals	Starts	Rounds Played	Cuts Made	Wins	Top-5s	Top-10s	Top-25s	Scoring Average	Money
	65	194	34	0	1	3	8	73.33	$44,109

Roger Maltbie

Year	Starts	Rounds Played	Cuts Made	Wins	Top-5s	Top-10s	Top-25s	Scoring Average	Money
1975	29	94	18	2	2	5	9	72.19	$81,035

Best finish for 1975: Win at the Ed McMahon Quad City Open & Pleasant Valley Classic

| 1976 | 27 | 91 | 20 | 1 | 4 | 5 | 9 | 72.00 | $117,951 |

Best finish for 1976: Win at the Memorial Tournament

| 1977 | 28 | 94 | 20 | 0 | 0 | 5 | 9 | 72.09 | $54,490 |

Best finish for 1977: 6th at the Bob Hope Chrysler Classic

| 1978 | 25 | 79 | 13 | 0 | 0 | 0 | 4 | 72.75 | $12,441 |

Best finish for 1978: T-19th at the Greater Greensboro Open

| 1979 | 19 | 52 | 7 | 0 | 0 | 0 | 1 | 73.08 | $9,796 |

Best finish for 1979: T-15th at the Ed McMahon Quad City Open

| 1980 | 25 | 72 | 12 | 0 | 0 | 3 | 7 | 72.08 | $38,489 |

Best finish for 1980: T-7th at the Manufactures Hanover Westchester Classic

| 1981 | 31 | 103 | 21 | 0 | 2 | 3 | 10 | 71.73 | $75,009 |

Best finish for 1981: T-2nd at the Sammy Davis, Jr. - Greater Hartford Open

| 1982 | 30 | 97 | 18 | 0 | 2 | 3 | 7 | 71.97 | $77,067 |

Best finish for 1982: T-2nd at the Memorial Tournament

| 1983 | 30 | 106 | 22 | 0 | 0 | 2 | 7 | 71.81 | $75,751 |

Best finish for 1983: T-6th at the Kemper Open

| 1984 | 32 | 109 | 23 | 0 | 1 | 3 | 11 | 71.61 | $118,128 |

Best finish for 1984: T-3rd at the Memorial Tournament

Year	Starts	Rounds Played	Cuts Made	Wins	Top-5s	Top-10s	Top-25s	Scoring Average	Money
1985	29	105	24	2	3	7	10	70.84	$360,554

Best finish for 1985: Win at the Manufactures Hanover Westchester Classic & NEC World Series of Golf

1986	28	92	21	0	3	4	9	71.48	$217,406

Best finish for 1986: T-2nd at the Sea Pines Heritage Classic & Canon Sammy Davis, Jr. - Greater Hartford Open

1987	23	84	20	0	2	3	6	71.26	$157,023

Best finish for 1987: 3rd at the Manufactures Hanover Westchester Classic

1988	26	84	16	0	2	4	7	71.20	$152,103

Best finish for 1988: T-5th at the Shearson Lehman/Andy Williams San Diego & Texas Open

1989	24	77	14	0	0	3	6	71.18	$135,334

Best finish for 1989: T-6th at the Anheuser-Busch Golf Classic

1990	21	64	14	0	0	0	2	72.52	$58,540

Best finish for 1990: 20th at the AT&T Pebble Beach Pro-Am

1991	25	66	8	0	0	0	1	72.11	$37,962

Best finish for 1991: T-17th at the Buick Classic

1992	21	64	11	0	0	1	5	71.25	$110,742

Best finish for 1992: T-7th at the New England Classic

1993	20	59	9	0	1	2	2	71.22	$156,454

Best finish for 1993: T-2nd at the Canon Greater Hartford Open

1994	15	42	8	0	0	0	1	72.05	$67,686

Best finish for 1994: T-15th at the Kmart Greater Greensboro Open

1995	11	31	6	0	1	1	2	71.48	$61,664

Best finish for 1995: T-4th at the Ideon Classic

1996	4	11	2	0	0	1	1	72.36	$48,800

Best finish for 1996: T-9th at the Canon Greater Hartford Open

Year	Starts	Rounds Played	Cuts Made	Wins	Top-5s	Top-10s	Top-25s	Scoring Average	Money
1997	3	7	0	0	0	0	0	73.57	
1998	2	5	0	0	0	0	0	74.40	
1999	4	11	0	0	0	0	0	76.45	
2000	2	4	0	0	0	0	0	79.75	
2001	2	5	0	0	0	0	0	75.20	
2002	2	5	0	0	0	0	0	76.00	
2003	1	3	0	0	0	0	0	81.67	
2004	1	3	0	0	0	0	0	78.00	
2005	1	3	0	0	0	0	0	73.33	
2006	1	3	0	0	0	0	0	77.33	
Period Totals	Starts	Rounds Played	Cuts Made	Wins	Top-5s	Top-10s	Top-25s	Scoring Average	Money
	542	1725	327	5	23	55	126	71.90	$2,224,426

Larry Mancour

Year	Starts	Rounds Played	Cuts Made	Wins	Top-5s	Top-10s	Top-25s	Scoring Average	Money
1961	1	4	1	0	0	0	0	73.75	$108

Best finish for 1961: T-26th at the Almaden Open

1962	1	4	1	0	0	0	0	73.00	$190

Best finish for 1962: T-36th at the Dallas Open Invitational

1963	1	4	1	0	0	0	0	73.00	$039

Best finish for 1963: T-33rd at the Fig Garden Village Open Invitational

1964	7	23	4	0	0	0	1	74.61	$650

Best finish for 1964: T-14th at the Almaden Open

1965	1	2	0	0	0	0	0	74.00	
1966	4	12	1	0	0	0	1	73.58	$1,158

Best finish for 1966: T-13th at the Lucky International Open Invitational

1967	4	12	2	0	0	0	0	75.58	$674

Best finish for 1967: T-44th at the PGA Championship

1968	3	6	0	0	0	0	0	74.00	
1969	4	12	1	0	0	0	0	76.50	$167

Best finish for 1969: 73rd at the Tucson Open

1971	2	6	1	0	0	0	0	75.67	$258

Best finish for 1971: T-71st at the PGA Championship

1972	1	2	0	0	0	0	0	81.00	
1973	5	14	1	0	0	0	0	73.14	$508

Best finish for 1973: T-48th at the Bob Hope Chrysler Classic

1974	8	24	3	0	0	0	0	74.75	$1,639

Best finish for 1974: T-34th at the Florida Citrus Open Invitational

1975	4	12	1	0	0	0	1	75.08	$1,277

Best finish for 1975: T-23rd at the Doral-Eastern Open

1976	2	4	0	0	0	0	0	78.00	
1977	3	7	0	0	0	0	0	75.71	
1978	1	4	1	0	0	0	0	73.25	$210

Best finish for 1978: T-57th at the Buick Goodwrench Open

1979	1	2	0	0	0	0	0	76.50	
1983	1	2	0	0	0	0	0	76.00	
Period Totals	Starts	Rounds Played	Cuts Made	Wins	Top-5s	Top-10s	Top-25s	Scoring Average	Money
	54	156	18	0	0	0	3	74.81	$6,879

Mark Maness

Year	Starts	Rounds Played	Cuts Made	Wins	Top-5s	Top-10s	Top-25s	Scoring Average	Money
1988	25	59	4	0	0	0	1	73.17	$10,532

Best finish for 1988: T-22nd at the Deposit Guaranty Golf Classic

Year	Starts	Rounds Played	Cuts Made	Wins	Top-5s	Top-10s	Top-25s	Scoring Average	Money
1992	1	2	0	0	0	0	0	73.50	
2003	1	2	0	0	0	0	0	78.50	
Period Totals	Starts	Rounds Played	Cuts Made	Wins	Top-5s	Top-10s	Top-25s	Scoring Average	Money
	27	63	4	0	0	0	1	73.35	$10,532

Lloyd Mangrum

Year	Starts	Rounds Played	Cuts Made	Wins	Top-5s	Top-10s	Top-25s	Scoring Average	Money
1958	13	47	10	0	1	2	6	72.23	$3,875

Best finish for 1958: T-5th at the Colonial Invitational

1959	12	46	9	0	1	4	8	71.04	$5,857

Best finish for 1959: T-4th at the Thunderbird Invitational

1960	7	29	6	0	0	1	2	73.10	$2,479

Best finish for 1960: T-10th at the Phoenix Open

1961	4	14	2	0	0	0	1	73.79	$1,388

Best finish for 1961: T-12th at the Ontario Open

1962	2	8	2	0	0	0	0	74.75	$600

Best finish for 1962: T-33rd at the Masters

Period Totals	Starts	Rounds Played	Cuts Made	Wins	Top-5s	Top-10s	Top-25s	Scoring Average	Money
	38	144	29	0	2	7	17	72.32	$14,199

PGA Tour career totals from 1934 to 1962

	Starts	Rounds Played	Cuts Made	Wins	Top-5s	Top-10s	Top-25s	Scoring Average	Money
	383	N/A	N/A	36	N/A	218	309	N/A	N/A

Bob Mann

Year	Starts	Rounds Played	Cuts Made	Wins	Top-5s	Top-10s	Top-25s	Scoring Average	Money
1974	1	2	0	0	0	0	0	80.00	$500
1977	11	26	2	0	0	0	0	73.96	$438

Best finish for 1977: T-50th at the Tallahassee Open

1978	20	57	8	0	0	0	1	73.07	$6,398

Best finish for 1978: T-22nd at the Phoenix Open

1979	34	100	15	0	1	1	3	73.11	$19,388

Best finish for 1979: T-5th at the Tallahassee Open

1980	22	62	9	0	0	1	3	72.79	$16,901

Best finish for 1980: T-10th at the Pensacola Open

1981	1	2	0	0	0	0	0	76.00	
1982	4	10	1	0	0	0	0	72.80	$1,734

Best finish for 1982: T-31st at the Miller High-Life Quad Cities Open

1984	1	2	0	0	0	0	0	79.00	$600
1985	1	2	0	0	0	0	0	73.50	$600
1988	1	2	0	0	0	0	0	75.50	$1,000
1989	3	4	0	0	0	0	0	74.50	$2,000
Period Totals	Starts	Rounds Played	Cuts Made	Wins	Top-5s	Top-10s	Top-25s	Scoring Average	Money
	99	269	35	0	1	2	7	73.26	$49,559

Dave Marad

Year	Starts	Rounds Played	Cuts Made	Wins	Top-5s	Top-10s	Top-25s	Scoring Average	Money
1964	14	34	2	0	0	0	0	75.12	$041

Best finish for 1964: T-43rd at the Almaden Open

1966	21	58	8	0	1	1	3	73.10	$5,468

Best finish for 1966: 3rd at the Azalea Open Invitational

1967	16	51	9	0	0	1	2	73.73	$1,809

Best finish for 1967: T-10th at the Azalea Open

1968	15	41	5	0	0	0	0	73.93	$544

Best finish for 1968: T-39th at the Tucson Open Invitational

1971	5	14	1	0	0	0	0	74.07	$333

Best finish for 1971: T-66th at the Westchester Classic

1972	23	74	13	0	1	1	2	73.20	$17,611

Best finish for 1972: 2nd at the Robinson's Fall Golf Classic

1973	18	58	11	0	0	0	2	72.71	$6,738

Best finish for 1973: T-20th at the Greater Jacksonville Open

1974	1	3	0	0	0	0	0	77.00	
1978	2	6	1	0	0	0	0	74.33	$693

Best finish for 1978: T-63rd at the American Optical Classic

Period Totals	Starts	Rounds Played	Cuts Made	Wins	Top-5s	Top-10s	Top-25s	Scoring Average	Money
	115	339	50	0	2	3	9	73.55	$33,237

Steve Marino

Year	Starts	Rounds Played	Cuts Made	Wins	Top-5s	Top-10s	Top-25s	Scoring Average	Money
2003	1	2	0	0	0	0	0	71.50	
2005	1	4	1	0	0	0	0	70.50	$14,542

Best finish for 2005: T-47th at the Deutsche Bank Championship

Year	Starts	Rounds Played	Cuts Made	Wins	Top-5s	Top-10s	Top-25s	Scoring Average	Money
2007	31	106	21	0	0	4	10	71.03	$1,181,166

Best finish for 2007: T-6th at the AT&T Classic

Year	Starts	Rounds Played	Cuts Made	Wins	Top-5s	Top-10s	Top-25s	Scoring Average	Money
2008	32	119	27	0	4	6	13	70.29	$2,094,267

Best finish for 2008: 2nd at the Mayakoba Golf Classic

Period Totals	Starts	Rounds Played	Cuts Made	Wins	Top-5s	Top-10s	Top-25s	Scoring Average	Money
	65	231	49	0	4	10	23	70.64	$3,289,975

Gary Marlowe

Year	Starts	Rounds Played	Cuts Made	Wins	Top-5s	Top-10s	Top-25s	Scoring Average	Money
1982	1	2	0	0	0	0	0	76.00	
1983	2	4	0	0	0	0	0	78.25	$600
1984	18	44	3	0	0	0	0	75.16	$3,104

Best finish for 1984: T-39th at the Canadian Open

Year	Starts	Rounds Played	Cuts Made	Wins	Top-5s	Top-10s	Top-25s	Scoring Average	Money
1985	2	4	0	0	0	0	0	76.50	$600
1986	1	2	0	0	0	0	0	74.50	
1988	1	2	0	0	0	0	0	73.50	
Period Totals	Starts	Rounds Played	Cuts Made	Wins	Top-5s	Top-10s	Top-25s	Scoring Average	Money
	25	58	3	0	0	0	0	75.41	$4,304

Dave Marr

Year	Starts	Rounds Played	Cuts Made	Wins	Top-5s	Top-10s	Top-25s	Scoring Average	Money
1958	17	62	14	0	2	3	7	71.85	$5,217

Best finish for 1958: 2nd at the Bing Crosby Pro-Am

| 1959 | 4 | 16 | 4 | 0 | 1 | 1 | 3 | 72.00 | $1,395 |

Best finish for 1959: T-5th at the Sam Snead Festival

| 1960 | 20 | 81 | 19 | 1 | 1 | 5 | 14 | 71.25 | $13,466 |

Best finish for 1960: Win at the Sam Snead Festival

| 1961 | 23 | 90 | 22 | 1 | 1 | 3 | 16 | 70.73 | $15,570 |

Best finish for 1961: Win at the Greater Seattle Open Invitational

| 1962 | 19 | 74 | 17 | 1 | 1 | 5 | 9 | 71.58 | $13,818 |

Best finish for 1962: Win at the Azalea Open Invitational

| 1963 | 24 | 94 | 23 | 0 | 2 | 7 | 12 | 71.51 | $18,018 |

Best finish for 1963: T-2nd at the St. Petersburg Open Invitational

| 1964 | 25 | 95 | 22 | 0 | 2 | 10 | 19 | 71.23 | $40,472 |

Best finish for 1964: T-2nd at the Masters

| 1965 | 28 | 108 | 25 | 1 | 6 | 10 | 18 | 71.13 | $70,042 |

Best finish for 1965: Win at the PGA Championship

| 1966 | 26 | 93 | 19 | 0 | 4 | 8 | 15 | 71.67 | $40,148 |

Best finish for 1966: T-3rd at the Bob Hope Desert Classic

| 1967 | 29 | 106 | 23 | 0 | 0 | 3 | 10 | 72.20 | $24,651 |

Best finish for 1967: T-6th at the Atlanta Classic

| 1968 | 24 | 91 | 21 | 0 | 4 | 8 | 14 | 71.35 | $61,884 |

Best finish for 1968: T-2nd at the Kaiser International Open Invitational & Pensacola Open Invitational

| 1969 | 23 | 70 | 13 | 0 | 0 | 1 | 7 | 72.20 | $15,682 |

Best finish for 1969: T-10th at the U.S. Open

| 1970 | 24 | 78 | 16 | 0 | 1 | 1 | 6 | 72.44 | $19,306 |

Best finish for 1970: T-4th at the Phoenix Open

| 1971 | 14 | 45 | 9 | 0 | 0 | 1 | 5 | 72.04 | $12,463 |

Best finish for 1971: 9th at the Sea Pines Heritage Classic

| 1972 | 23 | 70 | 11 | 0 | 0 | 2 | 4 | 73.10 | $15,100 |

Best finish for 1972: T-8th at the Walt Disney World Open

| 1973 | 19 | 52 | 6 | 0 | 1 | 1 | 1 | 73.65 | $11,437 |

Best finish for 1973: 4th at the Bing Crosby Pro-Am

| 1974 | 7 | 18 | 2 | 0 | 0 | 0 | 1 | 74.00 | $1,839 |

Best finish for 1974: T-19th at the Houston Open

| 1975 | 4 | 12 | 2 | 0 | 0 | 0 | 0 | 73.92 | $628 |

Best finish for 1975: T-61st at the Sea Pines Heritage Classic

| 1976 | 1 | 2 | 1 | 0 | 0 | 0 | 0 | 72.50 | $197 |

Best finish for 1976: T-57th at the Houston Open

| 1977 | 4 | 12 | 2 | 0 | 0 | 0 | 0 | 73.33 | $760 |

Best finish for 1977: T-38th at the Houston Open

1978	2	4	0	0	0	0	0	74.00	
1979	2	6	0	0	0	0	0	73.67	
1980	1	2	0	0	0	0	0	73.50	
1981	1	2	0	0	0	0	0	72.00	
Period Totals	Starts	Rounds Played	Cuts Made	Wins	Top-5s	Top-10s	Top-25s	Scoring Average	Money
	364	1283	271	4	26	69	161	71.85	$382,093

Graham Marsh

Year	Starts	Rounds Played	Cuts Made	Wins	Top-5s	Top-10s	Top-25s	Scoring Average	Money
1970	1	4	1	0	0	0	0	73.75	$600

Best finish for 1970: T-25th at the British Open

1971	1	4	1	0	0	0	0	74.75	$226

Best finish for 1971: 57th at the British Open

1972	1	4	1	0	0	0	0	74.50	$325

Best finish for 1972: T-50th at the British Open

1973	1	4	1	0	0	0	0	73.50	$552

Best finish for 1973: T-31st at the British Open

1974	4	16	4	0	1	1	1	72.94	$9,778

Best finish for 1974: T-5th at the Ohio Kings Island Open

1975	4	16	4	0	0	2	4	70.88	$16,438

Best finish for 1975: 6th at the British Open

1976	5	18	4	0	0	2	3	72.28	$14,490

Best finish for 1976: T-6th at the Sea Pines Heritage Classic

1977	18	68	15	1	5	7	9	71.69	$110,060

Best finish for 1977: Win at the Sea Pines Heritage Classic

1978	18	66	15	0	0	2	9	71.70	$47,075

Best finish for 1978: T-6th at the Sea Pines Heritage Classic

1979	19	68	15	0	0	3	7	72.93	$56,570

Best finish for 1979: T-4th at the Danny Thomas Memphis Classic

1980	5	18	4	0	0	0	0	73.11	$5,238

Best finish for 1980: T-33rd at the Masters

1981	1	4	1	0	0	0	1	72.25	$4,025

Best finish for 1981: T-19th at the British Open

1982	1	4	1	0	0	0	1	73.75	$3,315

Best finish for 1982: T-25th at the British Open

1983	2	8	2	0	1	1	2	69.75	$30,625

Best finish for 1983: 4th at the British Open

1984	1	4	1	0	0	1	1	71.00	$14,643

Best finish for 1984: T-9th at the British Open

1985	1	4	1	0	0	0	1	72.00	$7,627

Best finish for 1985: T-20th at the British Open

1986	1	4	1	0	0	0	0	75.00	$3,225

Best finish for 1986: T-56th at the British Open

1987	1	4	1	0	0	0	1	71.25	$21,600

Best finish for 1987: T-11th at the British Open

1988	1	4	1	0	0	0	0	73.25	$5,874

Best finish for 1988: T-38th at the British Open

1991	1	4	1	0	0	0	0	71.25	$7,114

Best finish for 1991: T-44th at the British Open

1998	1	2	0	0	0	0	0	76.00	$1,000
Period Totals	Starts	Rounds Played	Cuts Made	Wins	Top-5s	Top-10s	Top-25s	Scoring Average	Money
	88	328	75	1	7	19	40	72.25	$360,399

Jim Marshall

Year	Starts	Rounds Played	Cuts Made	Wins	Top-5s	Top-10s	Top-25s	Scoring Average	Money
1971	12	30	3	0	0	0	0	74.43	$495

Best finish for 1971: 50th at the Tallahassee Open

1972	17	45	5	0	0	0	0	74.11	$1,058

Best finish for 1972: T-44th at the San Antonio Texas Open

1973	15	35	3	0	0	0	0	73.77	$1,510

Best finish for 1973: T-32nd at the Liggett Meyers Open

1974	21	62	10	0	0	0	2	73.35	$5,934

Best finish for 1974: T-20th at the Quad Cities Open

1975	23	64	8	0	0	0	1	73.91	$4,911

Best finish for 1975: T-17th at the Bob Hope Chrysler Classic

1976	3	6	0	0	0	0	0	74.00	$250
1977	1	2	0	0	0	0	0	79.50	$500
1978	1	2	0	0	0	0	0	74.00	$650
1982	1	2	0	0	0	0	0	76.50	$650
Period Totals	Starts	Rounds Played	Cuts Made	Wins	Top-5s	Top-10s	Top-25s	Scoring Average	Money
	94	248	29	0	0	0	3	73.92	$15,308

Elroy Marti

Year	Starts	Rounds Played	Cuts Made	Wins	Top-5s	Top-10s	Top-25s	Scoring Average	Money
1958	5	11	1	0	0	0	0	75.55	

Best finish for 1958: T-34th at the Lafayette Open

1959	1	4	1	0	0	0	0	75.75	$050

Best finish for 1959: T-64th at the Houston Classic

Year	Starts	Rounds Played	Cuts Made	Wins	Top-5s	Top-10s	Top-25s	Scoring Average	Money
1960	1	2	1	0	0	0	0	78.00	

Best finish for 1960: T-200 at the PGA Championship

| 1961 | 1 | 4 | 1 | 0 | 0 | 0 | 0 | 74.25 | $150 |

Best finish for 1961: T-67th at the Houston Classic

1964	1	2	0	0	0	0	0	82.50	
1965	1	2	0	0	0	0	0	75.50	
1969	1	2	0	0	0	0	0	78.50	
1976	5	12	1	0	0	0	0	75.50	

Best finish for 1976: T-63rd at the Greater Milwaukee Open

| 1977 | 3 | 10 | 1 | 0 | 0 | 0 | 0 | 74.20 | |

Best finish for 1977: T-71st at the Houston Open

1978	5	10	0	0	0	0	0	76.30	
1979	5	11	0	0	0	0	0	76.36	
1991	1	2	0	0	0	0	0	76.00	
Period Totals	Starts	Rounds Played	Cuts Made	Wins	Top-5s	Top-10s	Top-25s	Scoring Average	Money
	30	72	6	0	0	0	0	75.88	$200

Fred Marti

Year	Starts	Rounds Played	Cuts Made	Wins	Top-5s	Top-10s	Top-25s	Scoring Average	Money
1961	1	4	1	0	0	0	0	73.00	

Best finish for 1961: T-60th at the Houston Classic

| 1962 | 1 | 4 | 1 | 0 | 0 | 0 | 0 | 72.00 | |

Best finish for 1962: T-40th at the Houston Classic

| 1963 | 2 | 8 | 2 | 0 | 0 | 0 | 0 | 73.00 | |

Best finish for 1963: T-46th at the Colonial National Invitational

| 1964 | 22 | 77 | 16 | 0 | 0 | 1 | 9 | 71.92 | $8,728 |

Best finish for 1964: T-8th at the Seattle Open

| 1965 | 23 | 71 | 11 | 0 | 1 | 1 | 1 | 73.51 | $5,456 |

Best finish for 1965: T-5th at the Doral Open

| 1966 | 24 | 79 | 15 | 0 | 1 | 1 | 5 | 72.72 | $10,832 |

Best finish for 1966: T-4th at the Buick Open Invitational

| 1967 | 26 | 89 | 17 | 0 | 0 | 0 | 6 | 72.66 | $16,289 |

Best finish for 1967: T-12th at the Westchester Classic & Atlanta Classic

| 1968 | 28 | 102 | 22 | 0 | 1 | 4 | 11 | 71.28 | $34,529 |

Best finish for 1968: T-4th at the "500" Festival Open Invitational

| 1969 | 32 | 117 | 26 | 0 | 1 | 3 | 12 | 71.56 | $32,171 |

Best finish for 1969: T-4th at the AVCO Classic

| 1970 | 36 | 112 | 22 | 0 | 1 | 3 | 6 | 72.67 | $23,545 |

Best finish for 1970: T-3rd at the Tallahassee Open

| 1971 | 28 | 93 | 21 | 0 | 2 | 4 | 11 | 71.48 | $50,540 |

Best finish for 1971: 2nd at the Kaiser International Open

| 1972 | 33 | 100 | 19 | 0 | 2 | 3 | 10 | 72.21 | $43,825 |

Best finish for 1972: 2nd at the Colonial National Invitational

| 1973 | 36 | 121 | 24 | 0 | 0 | 1 | 9 | 72.34 | $27,162 |

Best finish for 1973: T-10th at the Monsanto Open

| 1974 | 20 | 57 | 10 | 0 | 0 | 0 | 2 | 72.82 | $6,708 |

Best finish for 1974: T-21st at the Hawaiian Open

| 1975 | 19 | 57 | 10 | 0 | 0 | 0 | 4 | 72.37 | $10,702 |

Best finish for 1975: T-14th at the San Antonio Texas Open

| 1976 | 27 | 85 | 17 | 0 | 0 | 2 | 7 | 72.09 | $28,130 |

Best finish for 1976: T-6th at the Danny Thomas Memphis Classic

| 1977 | 26 | 82 | 15 | 0 | 1 | 1 | 4 | 72.72 | $20,168 |

Best finish for 1977: 5th at the Ohio Kings Island Open

| 1978 | 25 | 73 | 12 | 0 | 1 | 2 | 4 | 72.26 | $33,307 |

Best finish for 1978: 2nd at the Ed McMahon Quad City Open

| 1979 | 23 | 69 | 13 | 0 | 0 | 0 | 2 | 72.36 | $19,064 |

Best finish for 1979: T-12th at the Kemper Open

| 1980 | 16 | 50 | 9 | 0 | 0 | 0 | 1 | 72.96 | $8,394 |

Best finish for 1980: T-24th at the Tournament Players Championship

1981	2	4	0	0	0	0	0	73.75	
1982	1	2	0	0	0	0	0	72.50	
1983	1	1	0	0	0	0	0	77.00	
1984	1	0	0	0	0	0	0		$750

Best finish for 1984: T-73rd at the Seiko Tucson-Match Play Championship

1987	1	2	0	0	0	0	0	77.50	
Period Totals	Starts	Rounds Played	Cuts Made	Wins	Top-5s	Top-10s	Top-25s	Scoring Average	Money
	454	1459	283	0	11	26	104	72.30	$380,300

Casey Martin

Year	Starts	Rounds Played	Cuts Made	Wins	Top-5s	Top-10s	Top-25s	Scoring Average	Money
1998	3	10	2	0	0	0	1	71.10	$37,220

Best finish for 1998: T-23rd at the U.S. Open

Year	Starts	Rounds Played	Cuts Made	Wins	Top-5s	Top-10s	Top-25s	Scoring Average	Money
2000	29	88	14	0	0	0	1	71.41	$143,248

Best finish for 2000: T-17th at the Touchstone Energy Tucson Open

2001	2	5	0	0	0	0	0	73.40	
2002	3	6	0	0	0	0	0	73.67	
2003	1	3	0	0	0	0	0	77.00	
2004	2	7	2	0	0	0	0	72.29	$15,858

Best finish for 2004: T-69th at the Chrysler Classic of Tucson

| 2005 | 1 | 3 | 0 | 0 | 0 | 0 | 0 | 71.00 | $10,547 |

Best finish for 2005: T-65th at the AT&T Pebble Beach National Pro-Am

Period Totals	Starts	Rounds Played	Cuts Made	Wins	Top-5s	Top-10s	Top-25s	Scoring Average	Money
	41	122	18	0	0	0	2	71.75	$206,874

Doug Martin

Year	Starts	Rounds Played	Cuts Made	Wins	Top-5s	Top-10s	Top-25s	Scoring Average	Money
1989	1	4	1	0	0	0	0	70.50	$1,234

Best finish for 1989: T-47th at the B.C. Open

| 1990 | 2 | 6 | 1 | 0 | 0 | 0 | 0 | 71.67 | $1,819 |

Best finish for 1990: T-31st at the Deposit Guaranty

| 1992 | 32 | 85 | 12 | 0 | 0 | 1 | 2 | 72.19 | $77,184 |

Best finish for 1992: 7th at the Nissan Los Angeles Open

| 1993 | 5 | 18 | 4 | 0 | 1 | 1 | 1 | 70.61 | $21,381 |

Best finish for 1993: T-4th at the Deposit Guaranty Classic

| 1994 | 33 | 81 | 8 | 0 | 0 | 1 | 4 | 72.43 | $81,201 |

Best finish for 1994: T-9th at the Buick Invitational of California

| 1995 | 29 | 92 | 18 | 0 | 1 | 1 | 2 | 71.11 | $229,663 |

Best finish for 1995: 2nd at the Buick Classic

| 1996 | 29 | 92 | 17 | 0 | 1 | 1 | 6 | 71.09 | $211,967 |

Best finish for 1996: T-5th at the Shell Houston Open

| 1997 | 30 | 102 | 22 | 0 | 1 | 3 | 10 | 70.68 | $383,593 |

Best finish for 1997: T-5th at the Honda Classic

| 1998 | 33 | 110 | 23 | 0 | 0 | 1 | 8 | 71.03 | $302,718 |

Best finish for 1998: T-7th at the Walt Disney World/Oldsmobile Classic

| 1999 | 33 | 96 | 17 | 0 | 0 | 0 | 4 | 71.56 | $179,610 |

Best finish for 1999: T-22nd at the Buick Challenge & Greater Milwaukee Open

Period Totals	Starts	Rounds Played	Cuts Made	Wins	Top-5s	Top-10s	Top-25s	Scoring Average	Money
	227	686	123	0	4	9	37	71.37	$1,490,369

Bill Martindale

Year	Starts	Rounds Played	Cuts Made	Wins	Top-5s	Top-10s	Top-25s	Scoring Average	Money
1964	33	102	17	0	0	0	4	73.24	$4,774

Best finish for 1964: T-16th at the Dallas Open

| 1965 | 32 | 119 | 27 | 0 | 5 | 8 | 12 | 71.71 | $45,315 |

Best finish for 1965: T-2nd at the New Orleans Open, Sahara Invitational & Almaden Open

| 1966 | 31 | 108 | 21 | 0 | 2 | 3 | 7 | 72.82 | $22,845 |

Best finish for 1966: T-3rd at the Bing Crosby National Professional-Amateur & Thunderbird Classic

| 1967 | 32 | 107 | 21 | 0 | 0 | 0 | 6 | 72.49 | $13,496 |

Best finish for 1967: T-12th at the Phoenix Open

| 1968 | 12 | 37 | 6 | 0 | 0 | 0 | 1 | 73.16 | $1,540 |

Best finish for 1968: T-19th at the AZALEA Open Invitational

| 1969 | 3 | 6 | 1 | 0 | 0 | 0 | 0 | 75.33 | $160 |

Best finish for 1969: T-61st at the Byron Nelson

Period Totals	Starts	Rounds Played	Cuts Made	Wins	Top-5s	Top-10s	Top-25s	Scoring Average	Money
	143	479	93	0	7	11	30	72.62	$88,130

Richard Martinez

Year	Starts	Rounds Played	Cuts Made	Wins	Top-5s	Top-10s	Top-25s	Scoring Average	Money
1964	7	13	1	0	0	0	0	75.23	

Best finish for 1964: T-52nd at the Tucson Open

| 1965 | 1 | 2 | 0 | 0 | 0 | 0 | 0 | 78.50 | |
| 1966 | 2 | 6 | 1 | 0 | 0 | 0 | 0 | 74.67 | $300 |

Best finish for 1966: T-67th at the Cajun Classic

| 1967 | 13 | 44 | 8 | 0 | 0 | 0 | 3 | 73.25 | $3,769 |

Best finish for 1967: T-12th at the Cajun Classic

| 1968 | 25 | 78 | 14 | 0 | 0 | 2 | 6 | 72.14 | $9,021 |

Best finish for 1968: 7th at the Pensacola Open Invitational

| 1969 | 24 | 78 | 16 | 0 | 0 | 1 | 5 | 72.91 | $8,351 |

Best finish for 1969: T-7th at the Robinson Open

| 1970 | 20 | 57 | 8 | 0 | 0 | 0 | 2 | 73.42 | $5,488 |

Best finish for 1970: T-14th at the Greater New Orleans Open

| 1971 | 6 | 15 | 2 | 0 | 0 | 0 | 0 | 74.53 | $470 |

Best finish for 1971: T-62nd at the Andy Williams-San Diego Open

| 1977 | 6 | 14 | 1 | 0 | 0 | 0 | 0 | 75.79 | |

Best finish for 1977: T-82nd at the Western Open

Year	Starts	Rounds Played	Cuts Made	Wins	Top-5s	Top-10s	Top-25s	Scoring Average	Money
1978	1	2	0	0	0	0	0	75.00	
1979	2	3	0	0	0	0	0	76.67	$350
1980	1	2	0	0	0	0	0	75.50	
1985	1	2	0	0	0	0	0	76.50	
1986	1	2	0	0	0	0	0	75.50	
1989	1	2	0	0	0	0	0	74.00	
1990	1	1	0	0	0	0	0	82.00	
Period Totals	Starts	Rounds Played	Cuts Made	Wins	Top-5s	Top-10s	Top-25s	Scoring Average	Money
	112	321	51	0	0	3	16	73.36	$27,749

Daisuke Maruyama

Year	Starts	Rounds Played	Cuts Made	Wins	Top-5s	Top-10s	Top-25s	Scoring Average	Money
2004	1	2	0	0	0	0	0	73.50	
2006	25	79	16	0	2	4	6	71.01	$956,874

Best finish for 2006: T-3rd at the International

2007	28	86	15	0	0	1	4	71.57	$499,206

Best finish for 2007: T-6th at the Fry's Electronics Open

2008	4	12	2	0	0	0	1	71.75	$98,596

Best finish for 2008: T-14th at the AT&T Pebble Beach National Pro-Am

Period Totals	Starts	Rounds Played	Cuts Made	Wins	Top-5s	Top-10s	Top-25s	Scoring Average	Money
	58	179	33	0	2	5	11	71.36	$1,554,676

Shigeki Maruyama

Year	Starts	Rounds Played	Cuts Made	Wins	Top-5s	Top-10s	Top-25s	Scoring Average	Money
1994	1	2	0	0	0	0	0	74.00	
1995	1	2	0	0	0	0	0	77.00	
1996	2	8	2	0	0	0	1	70.88	$50,588

Best finish for 1996: T-14th at the British Open

1997	6	22	5	0	0	1	3	71.00	$111,781

Best finish for 1997: T-10th at the British Open

1998	6	20	4	0	0	0	1	72.75	$83,556

Best finish for 1998: T-11th at the NEC World Series of Golf

1999	9	22	4	0	1	3	3	73.00	$411,293

Best finish for 1999: T-5th at the Andersen Consulting Match Play Championship

2000	26	85	19	0	3	7	11	71.11	$1,208,104

Best finish for 2000: T-2nd at the Buick Invitational

2001	27	94	22	1	3	4	13	70.32	$1,448,028

Best finish for 2001: Win at the Greater Milwaukee Open

2002	24	87	20	1	4	5	13	70.68	$2,214,794

Best finish for 2002: Win at the Verizon Byron Nelson Classic

2003	28	85	17	1	2	4	9	70.96	$1,678,868

Best finish for 2003: Win at the Chrysler Classic of Greensboro

2004	26	92	22	0	3	6	13	70.62	$2,308,692

Best finish for 2004: 2nd at the Nissan Open

2005	29	98	22	0	2	5	8	70.55	$1,943,991

Best finish for 2005: 2nd at the Chrysler Classic of Greensboro

2006	30	92	19	0	2	4	9	70.72	$1,161,365

Best finish for 2006: 3rd at the B.C. Open

2007	31	84	13	0	1	2	6	71.29	$951,288

Best finish for 2007: T-2nd at the Ginn sur Mer Classic at Tesoro

2008	18	50	8	0	0	0	1	71.78	$160,175

Best finish for 2008: T-25th at the Sony Open in Hawaii

Period Totals	Starts	Rounds Played	Cuts Made	Wins	Top-5s	Top-10s	Top-25s	Scoring Average	Money
	264	843	177	3	21	41	91	70.96	$13,732,523

Don Massengale

Year	Starts	Rounds Played	Cuts Made	Wins	Top-5s	Top-10s	Top-25s	Scoring Average	Money
1960	6	24	6	0	0	0	4	71.08	$1,902

Best finish for 1960: T-12th at the Coral Gables Open Invitational

1961	15	60	15	0	2	4	9	69.43	$7,272

Best finish for 1961: T-4th at the Cajun Classic Open Invitational

1962	17	68	16	0	3	7	8	71.94	$11,981

Best finish for 1962: T-2nd at the Beaumont Open Invitational

1963	16	65	16	0	0	0	4	72.46	$5,114

Best finish for 1963: T-13th at the Utah Open Invitational

1964	22	71	12	0	1	6	7	72.04	$11,024

Best finish for 1964: T-3rd at the Western Open

1965	27	92	18	0	1	3	4	72.68	$12,054

Best finish for 1965: T-3rd at the Seattle Open

1966	31	108	22	2	3	4	12	72.18	$53,000

Best finish for 1966: Win at the Bing Crosby National Professional-Amateur & Canadian Open

Year	Starts	Rounds Played	Cuts Made	Wins	Top-5s	Top-10s	Top-25s	Scoring Average	Money
1967	29	109	23	0	2	2	8	73.72	$34,091

Best finish for 1967: T-2nd at the PGA Championship

1968	29	86	13	0	2	2	4	73.09	$18,129

Best finish for 1968: T-2nd at the Lucky International Open Invitational

1969	30	86	13	0	0	1	3	73.45	$8,091

Best finish for 1969: T-8th at the Bing Crosby National Pro-Am

1970	27	93	19	0	2	3	7	71.95	$25,574

Best finish for 1970: T-2nd at the Greater Milwaukee Open

1971	5	18	4	0	0	1	2	72.06	$5,181

Best finish for 1971: T-7th at the Phoenix Open

1972	6	20	4	0	0	1	3	72.35	$7,150

Best finish for 1972: T-9th at the Tucson Open

1973	9	28	5	0	0	1	1	74.14	$8,270

Best finish for 1973: 6th at the Greater Jacksonville Open

1974	5	15	2	0	0	0	1	73.87	$2,250

Best finish for 1974: T-24th at the PGA Championship

1975	6	17	3	0	0	0	0	74.41	$846

Best finish for 1975: T-48th at the Greater Greensboro Open

1976	12	42	9	0	1	1	2	72.64	$11,773

Best finish for 1976: T-5th at the Kaiser International Open

1977	9	24	2	0	0	0	0	74.54	$385

Best finish for 1977: T-58th at the Bob Hope Chrysler Classic

1978	6	15	0	0	0	0	0	76.13	
1979	2	5	1	0	0	0	0	76.20	$648

Best finish for 1979: 62nd at the Bing Crosby Pro-Am

1980	2	3	0	0	0	0	0	79.00	
1982	1	2	0	0	0	0	0	75.50	$650
1983	1	3	0	0	0	0	0	75.33	
1985	1	2	0	0	0	0	0	78.00	
Period Totals	Starts	Rounds Played	Cuts Made	Wins	Top-5s	Top-10s	Top-25s	Scoring Average	Money
	314	1056	203	2	17	36	79	72.66	$225,384

Rik Massengale

Year	Starts	Rounds Played	Cuts Made	Wins	Top-5s	Top-10s	Top-25s	Scoring Average	Money
1969	1	2	0	0	0	0	0	75.50	
1970	1	2	0	0	0	0	0	74.50	
1971	21	68	13	0	0	0	1	72.41	$6,960

Best finish for 1971: T-17th at the Danny Thomas Memphis Classic

1972	25	68	11	0	0	1	3	73.49	$14,708

Best finish for 1972: 6th at the USI Classic

1973	33	122	26	0	1	2	8	72.20	$40,922

Best finish for 1973: T-2nd at the USI Classic

1974	29	93	16	0	0	0	1	72.83	$11,441

Best finish for 1974: T-16th at the Southern Open

1975	28	95	21	1	3	6	16	71.64	$77,080

Best finish for 1975: Win at the Tallahassee Open

1976	30	111	25	1	4	7	15	71.35	$124,965

Best finish for 1976: Win at the Sammy Davis, Jr. - Greater Hartford Open

1977	26	103	25	1	3	7	15	71.33	$127,249

Best finish for 1977: Win at the Bob Hope Chrysler Classic

1978	29	80	11	0	0	0	4	73.61	$15,991

Best finish for 1978: T-13th at the Bob Hope Chrysler Classic

1979	27	76	11	0	0	0	2	73.70	$16,389

Best finish for 1979: T-12th at the Bay Hill Citrus Classic

1980	19	55	10	0	1	2	4	72.00	$54,167

Best finish for 1980: 2nd at the Phoenix Open

1981	23	64	8	0	0	0	1	73.05	$13,881

Best finish for 1981: T-12th at the Western Open

1982	22	57	5	0	2	2	2	73.04	$25,727

Best finish for 1982: T-3rd at the Anheuser-Busch Golf Classic

1983	2	6	1	0	0	0	0	72.67	$704

Best finish for 1983: T-69th at the Buick Open

1990	1	4	0	0	0	0	0	74.50	
1992	1	4	0	0	0	0	0	74.25	
1993	1	2	0	0	0	0	0	76.50	
1994	2	6	0	0	0	0	0	75.83	
1995	3	8	0	0	0	0	0	74.50	
1996	8	18	0	0	0	0	0	75.22	
1997	2	6	0	0	0	0	0	75.33	
1998	1	1	0	0	0	0	0	77.00	
1999	1	1	0	0	0	0	0	72.00	
Period Totals	Starts	Rounds Played	Cuts Made	Wins	Top-5s	Top-10s	Top-25s	Scoring Average	Money
	336	1052	183	3	14	27	72	72.58	$530,181

Jim Masserio

Year	Starts	Rounds Played	Cuts Made	Wins	Top-5s	Top-10s	Top-25s	Scoring Average	Money
1971	1	4	1	0	0	0	0	75.50	

Best finish for 1971: T-63rd at the U.S. Open

Year	Starts	Rounds Played	Cuts Made	Wins	Top-5s	Top-10s	Top-25s	Scoring Average	Money
1973	2	8	1	0	0	0	0	73.38	$356

Best finish for 1973: T-51st at the Walt Disney World Open

| 1974 | 25 | 71 | 10 | 0 | 0 | 0 | 1 | 73.54 | $6,550 |

Best finish for 1974: T-25th at the B.C. Open

| 1975 | 26 | 80 | 14 | 0 | 1 | 1 | 4 | 72.69 | $22,687 |

Best finish for 1975: T-5th at the Kemper Open

| 1976 | 30 | 95 | 20 | 0 | 1 | 1 | 3 | 72.86 | $29,376 |

Best finish for 1976: T-3rd at the Tournament Players Championship

| 1977 | 21 | 62 | 10 | 0 | 0 | 1 | 3 | 73.71 | $12,601 |

Best finish for 1977: T-9th at the Glen CampbellLos Angeles Open

| 1978 | 1 | 2 | 0 | 0 | 0 | 0 | 0 | 76.00 | $600 |
| 1979 | 4 | 12 | 2 | 0 | 0 | 0 | 0 | 73.33 | $3,040 |

Best finish for 1979: T-35th at the Buick Goodwrench Open

1980	1	0	0	0	0	0	0		
1981	1	2	0	0	0	0	0	75.50	$600
1983	1	2	0	0	0	0	0	74.50	$100
1991	1	2	0	0	0	0	0	76.50	$1,000
Period Totals	Starts	Rounds Played	Cuts Made	Wins	Top-5s	Top-10s	Top-25s	Scoring Average	Money
	114	340	58	0	2	3	11	73.24	$76,911

Dick Mast

Year	Starts	Rounds Played	Cuts Made	Wins	Top-5s	Top-10s	Top-25s	Scoring Average	Money
1974	19	54	8	0	0	0	3	74.04	$6,549

Best finish for 1974: T-16th at the Andy Williams-San Diego Open

| 1975 | 18 | 38 | 2 | 0 | 0 | 0 | 0 | 75.21 | $158 |

Best finish for 1975: T-68th at the Southern Open

| 1977 | 20 | 54 | 6 | 0 | 0 | 0 | 2 | 73.37 | $4,207 |

Best finish for 1977: T-23rd at the Hawaiian Open & Ed McMahon Quad City Open

| 1979 | 14 | 36 | 4 | 0 | 0 | 0 | 1 | 73.97 | $5,715 |

Best finish for 1979: T-18th at the Doral-Eastern Open

| 1981 | 5 | 12 | 2 | 0 | 0 | 0 | 0 | 73.33 | $2,595 |

Best finish for 1981: T-30th at the Bay Hill Classic

| 1982 | 5 | 18 | 4 | 0 | 0 | 0 | 0 | 73.06 | $3,647 |

Best finish for 1982: T-28th at the Southern Open

| 1983 | 1 | 2 | 0 | 0 | 0 | 0 | 0 | 77.00 | |
| 1985 | 2 | 6 | 1 | 0 | 0 | 0 | 0 | 73.83 | $2,887 |

Best finish for 1985: T-52nd at the U.S. Open

| 1986 | 28 | 84 | 14 | 0 | 1 | 3 | 7 | 71.82 | $79,419 |

Best finish for 1986: T-5th at the Western Open

| 1987 | 30 | 99 | 21 | 0 | 1 | 1 | 8 | 71.44 | $90,767 |

Best finish for 1987: T-4th at the USF&G Classic

| 1988 | 29 | 100 | 21 | 0 | 0 | 2 | 5 | 71.52 | $128,567 |

Best finish for 1988: T-6th at the Manufactures Hanover Westchester Classic

| 1989 | 30 | 90 | 15 | 0 | 0 | 0 | 0 | 71.61 | $38,955 |

Best finish for 1989: T-26th at the BellSouth Atlanta Golf Classic

| 1990 | 4 | 11 | 1 | 0 | 0 | 0 | 1 | 71.09 | $4,200 |

Best finish for 1990: T-18th at the Deposit Guaranty

| 1991 | 28 | 68 | 7 | 0 | 0 | 0 | 0 | 72.37 | $17,273 |

Best finish for 1991: T-31st at the Independent Insurance Agent Open

| 1992 | 26 | 70 | 9 | 0 | 1 | 2 | 2 | 72.10 | $150,847 |

Best finish for 1992: 2nd at the Greater Milwaukee Open

| 1993 | 28 | 87 | 17 | 0 | 1 | 4 | 6 | 71.62 | $209,325 |

Best finish for 1993: 4th at the Honda Classic

| 1994 | 27 | 84 | 14 | 0 | 0 | 1 | 4 | 71.68 | $129,822 |

Best finish for 1994: T-7th at the Freeport-McMoRan Classic

| 1995 | 13 | 37 | 5 | 0 | 0 | 0 | 1 | 72.11 | $26,622 |

Best finish for 1995: T-12th at the Quad City Classic

| 1996 | 6 | 15 | 2 | 0 | 0 | 0 | 0 | 71.67 | $6,560 |

Best finish for 1996: T-37th at the B.C. Open

| 1997 | 8 | 28 | 6 | 0 | 0 | 1 | 1 | 71.43 | $62,822 |

Best finish for 1997: T-8th at the B.C. Open

| 1998 | 8 | 22 | 3 | 0 | 0 | 0 | 0 | 72.64 | $10,893 |

Best finish for 1998: T-48th at the Deposit Guaranty Golf Classic

| 1999 | 3 | 8 | 1 | 0 | 0 | 1 | 1 | 69.00 | $60,000 |

Best finish for 1999: T-8th at the John Deere Classic

| 2000 | 17 | 47 | 7 | 0 | 0 | 0 | 1 | 72.38 | $58,834 |

Best finish for 2000: T-18th at the B.C. Open

Year	Starts	Rounds Played	Cuts Made	Wins	Top-5s	Top-10s	Top-25s	Scoring Average	Money
2001	3	8	2	0	0	0	0	71.63	$10,171

Best finish for 2001: T-68th at the BellSouth Classic

Year	Starts	Rounds Played	Cuts Made	Wins	Top-5s	Top-10s	Top-25s	Scoring Average	Money
2003	1	1	0	0	0	0	0	78.00	
2005	3	8	1	0	0	0	0	72.50	$12,053

Best finish for 2005: T-47th at the Sony Open in Hawaii

Year	Starts	Rounds Played	Cuts Made	Wins	Top-5s	Top-10s	Top-25s	Scoring Average	Money
2008	1	2	0	0	0	0	0	74.00	
Period Totals	Starts	Rounds Played	Cuts Made	Wins	Top-5s	Top-10s	Top-25s	Scoring Average	Money
	377	1089	173	0	4	15	43	72.22	$1,122,890

Chuck Matlack

Year	Starts	Rounds Played	Cuts Made	Wins	Top-5s	Top-10s	Top-25s	Scoring Average	Money
1958	1	0	0	0	0	0	0		
1963	1	2	0	0	0	0	0	78.00	$150
1964	1	2	0	0	0	0	0	75.00	
1966	14	36	3	0	0	0	0	75.92	$300

Best finish for 1966: T-55th at the Cajun Classic

1967	9	22	2	0	0	0	0	74.36	

Best finish for 1967: T-56th at the San Diego Open

1968	4	12	2	0	0	0	0	75.17	

Best finish for 1968: 72nd at the Pensacola Open Invitational

1969	3	6	1	0	0	0	0	77.00	$200

Best finish for 1969: 81st at the Kemper Insurance Open

Period Totals	Starts	Rounds Played	Cuts Made	Wins	Top-5s	Top-10s	Top-25s	Scoring Average	Money
	33	80	8	0	0	0	0	75.49	$650

Troy Matteson

Year	Starts	Rounds Played	Cuts Made	Wins	Top-5s	Top-10s	Top-25s	Scoring Average	Money
2003	3	10	2	0	0	0	0	72.20	$18,135

Best finish for 2003: T-59th at the FBR Capital Open

2006	32	101	18	1	2	5	7	71.21	$1,778,597

Best finish for 2006: Win at the Frys.Com Open-Vegas

2007	26	87	17	0	2	3	7	71.41	$1,282,421

Best finish for 2007: T-3rd at the AT&T Classic & John Deere Classic

2008	30	94	16	0	1	5	7	71.40	$1,212,018

Best finish for 2008: T-2nd at the PODS Championship

Period Totals	Starts	Rounds Played	Cuts Made	Wins	Top-5s	Top-10s	Top-25s	Scoring Average	Money
	91	292	53	1	5	13	21	71.37	$4,291,172

Duke Matthews

Year	Starts	Rounds Played	Cuts Made	Wins	Top-5s	Top-10s	Top-25s	Scoring Average	Money
1963	3	12	3	0	0	0	0	73.17	$583

Best finish for 1963: T-35th at the Almaden Open Invitational

1964	21	51	6	0	0	0	0	74.37	$754

Best finish for 1964: T-31st at the Memphis Open

1965	4	12	2	0	0	0	0	74.17	$280

Best finish for 1965: T-44th at the Sahara Invitational

1966	7	19	2	0	0	0	0	75.95	

Best finish for 1966: T-63rd at the Canadian Open

1967	1	2	0	0	0	0	0	76.50	
1970	1	2	0	0	0	0	0	76.00	
1973	1	2	0	0	0	0	0	73.50	
Period Totals	Starts	Rounds Played	Cuts Made	Wins	Top-5s	Top-10s	Top-25s	Scoring Average	Money
	38	100	13	0	0	0	0	74.56	$1,618

Len Mattiace

Year	Starts	Rounds Played	Cuts Made	Wins	Top-5s	Top-10s	Top-25s	Scoring Average	Money
1988	1	2	0	0	0	0	0	78.00	
1991	1	2	0	0	0	0	0	73.00	
1993	26	78	13	0	1	2	3	72.64	$74,521

Best finish for 1993: T-4th at the Deposit Guaranty Classic

1996	30	85	15	0	2	2	6	71.51	$238,977

Best finish for 1996: T-2nd at the Buick Challenge

1997	35	107	18	0	1	1	12	71.19	$316,956

Best finish for 1997: T-3rd at the Walt Disney World/Oldsmobile Classic

1998	31	103	22	0	1	3	5	70.89	$415,916

Best finish for 1998: T-5th at the Players Championship

1999	31	97	17	0	1	2	4	72.06	$403,115

Best finish for 1999: T-2nd at the Sony Open in Hawaii

2000	31	107	22	0	1	5	8	70.67	$762,979

Best finish for 2000: T-3rd at the Tampa Bay Classic

2001	30	96	19	0	1	2	6	70.70	$594,781

Best finish for 2001: 5th at the Michelob Championship at Kingsmill

Year	Starts	Rounds Played	Cuts Made	Wins	Top-5s	Top-10s	Top-25s	Scoring Average	Money
2002	28	106	25	2	3	4	9	70.63	$2,194,327

Best finish for 2002: Win at the Nissan Open & FedEx St. Jude Classic

Year	Starts	Rounds Played	Cuts Made	Wins	Top-5s	Top-10s	Top-25s	Scoring Average	Money
2003	27	93	21	0	1	2	4	71.44	$1,221,476

Best finish for 2003: 2nd at the Masters

2004	25	75	12	0	0	0	1	72.31	$218,707

Best finish for 2004: T-20th at the John Deere Classic

2005	34	84	9	0	0	0	1	72.79	$211,638

Best finish for 2005: T-12th at the Barclays Classic

2006	22	59	6	0	0	0	0	72.44	$66,540

Best finish for 2006: T-38th at the U.S. Bank Championship in Milwaukee

2007	10	21	0	0	0	0	0	73.95	
2008	11	31	4	0	0	0	0	72.19	$35,333

Best finish for 2008: T-49th at the Reno-Tahoe Open

Period Totals	Starts	Rounds Played	Cuts Made	Wins	Top-5s	Top-10s	Top-25s	Scoring Average	Money
	373	1146	203	2	12	23	59	71.59	$6,755,266

Terry Mauney

Year	Starts	Rounds Played	Cuts Made	Wins	Top-5s	Top-10s	Top-25s	Scoring Average	Money
1977	4	8	0	0	0	0	0	75.75	
1978	8	23	5	0	0	0	0	73.87	$863

Best finish for 1978: T-63rd at the Florida Citrus Open Invitational

1979	12	38	7	0	0	0	0	72.29	$6,321

Best finish for 1979: T-27th at the San Antonio Texas Open

1980	31	99	19	0	0	2	6	72.34	$39,084

Best finish for 1980: T-6th at the Tallahassee Open

1981	25	71	11	0	0	1	3	72.63	$15,341

Best finish for 1981: T-7th at the Tallahassee Open

1982	18	56	9	0	0	0	3	72.38	$13,652

Best finish for 1982: T-16th at the Phoenix Open

Period Totals	Starts	Rounds Played	Cuts Made	Wins	Top-5s	Top-10s	Top-25s	Scoring Average	Money
	98	295	51	0	0	3	12	72.62	$75,260

John Maurycy

Year	Starts	Rounds Played	Cuts Made	Wins	Top-5s	Top-10s	Top-25s	Scoring Average	Money
1963	1	2	0	0	0	0	0	77.00	$150
1964	1	2	0	0	0	0	0	75.50	
1965	1	2	0	0	0	0	0	81.50	
1966	15	38	4	0	0	0	0	75.42	

Best finish for 1966: T-62nd at the Greater Seattle-Everett Open Invitational

1967	11	26	2	0	0	0	0	74.50	$275

Best finish for 1967: T-43rd at the Memphis Open

1971	1	2	0	0	0	0	0	82.00	

Period Totals	Starts	Rounds Played	Cuts Made	Wins	Top-5s	Top-10s	Top-25s	Scoring Average	Money
	30	72	6	0	0	0	0	75.49	$425

Billy Maxwell

Year	Starts	Rounds Played	Cuts Made	Wins	Top-5s	Top-10s	Top-25s	Scoring Average	Money
1958	32	126	30	1	3	11	24	71.43	$19,487

Best finish for 1958: Win at the Memphis Invitational

1959	29	116	27	0	4	15	24	71.04	$22,785

Best finish for 1959: T-3rd at the Los Angeles Open Invitational & Colonial National Invitational

1960	18	71	16	0	2	6	15	71.55	$13,010

Best finish for 1960: T-2nd at the Yorba Linda Open Invitational

1961	22	89	20	2	4	8	15	70.74	$26,835

Best finish for 1961: Win at the Palm Springs Golf Classic & Insurance City Open Invitational

1962	24	93	22	1	7	10	16	71.11	$29,634

Best finish for 1962: Win at the Dallas Open Invitational

1963	28	113	25	0	3	5	14	71.88	$21,240

Best finish for 1963: T-5th at the St. Petersburg Open Invitational, U.S. Open & PGA Championship

1964	27	98	21	0	0	1	12	71.97	$14,045

Best finish for 1964: T-10th at the Whitemarsh Open

1965	30	108	23	0	3	5	10	72.10	$24,997

Best finish for 1965: 3rd at the Portland Open

1966	29	109	25	0	1	2	12	72.00	$23,950

Best finish for 1966: T-5th at the Florida Citrus Open Invitational

1967	31	114	24	0	0	3	7	72.38	$20,137

Best finish for 1967: T-6th at the Atlanta Classic

1968	34	125	28	0	0	3	11	71.76	$24,799

Best finish for 1968: T-7th at the Minnesota Golf Classic

1969	35	123	27	0	2	2	6	72.08	$25,095

Best finish for 1969: T-2nd at the Phoenix Open

1970	34	113	25	0	2	6	11	71.48	$40,866

Best finish for 1970: T-3rd at the Heritage Classic

Year	Starts	Rounds Played	Cuts Made	Wins	Top-5s	Top-10s	Top-25s	Scoring Average	Money
1971	28	82	13	0	0	1	4	72.71	$13,178

Best finish for 1971: T-9th at the Monsanto Open

| 1972 | 16 | 53 | 10 | 0 | 0 | 0 | 0 | 72.89 | $3,773 |

Best finish for 1972: T-34th at the American Golf Classic

1974	2	4	0	0	0	0	0	78.00	
Period Totals	Starts	Rounds Played	Cuts Made	Wins	Top-5s	Top-10s	Top-25s	Scoring Average	Money
	419	1537	336	4	31	78	181	71.79	$323,829

PGA Tour career totals from 1950 to 1974

	Starts	Rounds Played	Cuts Made	Wins	Top-5s	Top-10s	Top-25s	Scoring Average	Money
	504	1780	420	7	43	110	243	N/A	$374,761

Bob May

Year	Starts	Rounds Played	Cuts Made	Wins	Top-5s	Top-10s	Top-25s	Scoring Average	Money
1985	1	2	0	0	0	0	0	74.50	
1987	1	2	0	0	0	0	0	75.00	
1993	3	6	0	0	0	0	0	72.33	
1994	31	78	7	0	0	0	1	72.33	$31,079

Best finish for 1994: T-18th at the Kemper Open

| 1998 | 2 | 9 | 2 | 0 | 0 | 0 | 1 | 72.11 | $40,130 |

Best finish for 1998: T-16th at the Las Vegas Invitational

| 1999 | 2 | 9 | 2 | 0 | 0 | 0 | 2 | 70.33 | $102,800 |

Best finish for 1999: T-13th at the Las Vegas Invitational

| 2000 | 26 | 91 | 21 | 0 | 3 | 3 | 10 | 70.32 | $1,557,720 |

Best finish for 2000: T-2nd at the FedEx St. Jude Classic & PGA Championship

| 2001 | 25 | 80 | 18 | 0 | 0 | 0 | 6 | 70.46 | $536,367 |

Best finish for 2001: T-11th at the COMPAQ Classic of New Orleans

| 2002 | 30 | 89 | 15 | 0 | 0 | 0 | 6 | 70.58 | $407,778 |

Best finish for 2002: T-15th at the John Deere Classic

| 2003 | 7 | 26 | 6 | 0 | 0 | 0 | 1 | 71.35 | $134,248 |

Best finish for 2003: T-21st at the Shell Houston Open

| 2006 | 21 | 62 | 12 | 0 | 1 | 1 | 3 | 70.81 | $548,712 |

Best finish for 2006: 2nd at the B.C. Open

| 2007 | 16 | 49 | 9 | 0 | 1 | 1 | 1 | 71.10 | $244,970 |

Best finish for 2007: T-5th at the Frys.Com Open-Vegas

| 2008 | 4 | 15 | 3 | 0 | 0 | 0 | 1 | 70.73 | $114,085 |

Best finish for 2008: T-12th at the Mayakoba Golf Classic

Period Totals	Starts	Rounds Played	Cuts Made	Wins	Top-5s	Top-10s	Top-25s	Scoring Average	Money
	169	518	95	0	5	5	32	70.97	$3,717,888

Dick Mayer

Year	Starts	Rounds Played	Cuts Made	Wins	Top-5s	Top-10s	Top-25s	Scoring Average	Money
1958	26	85	16	0	0	3	8	73.58	$4,922

Best finish for 1958: T-7th at the Rubber City Open

| 1959 | 16 | 60 | 15 | 0 | 1 | 2 | 10 | 71.80 | $7,692 |

Best finish for 1959: T-4th at the Masters

| 1960 | 1 | 4 | 1 | 0 | 0 | 0 | 0 | 72.75 | $088 |

Best finish for 1960: T-79th at the Palm Springs Desert Golf Classic

| 1961 | 8 | 33 | 8 | 0 | 0 | 0 | 2 | 72.42 | $2,826 |

Best finish for 1961: T-13th at the Hot Springs Open Invitational

| 1962 | 3 | 11 | 2 | 0 | 0 | 1 | 1 | 71.64 | $1,600 |

Best finish for 1962: T-10th at the Palm Springs Golf Classic

| 1963 | 16 | 63 | 15 | 0 | 0 | 0 | 6 | 71.76 | $7,913 |

Best finish for 1963: T-14th at the Memphis Open Invitational

| 1964 | 9 | 29 | 4 | 0 | 0 | 0 | 1 | 73.24 | $2,127 |

Best finish for 1964: T-13th at the Sahara Invitational

| 1965 | 19 | 61 | 12 | 1 | 1 | 1 | 2 | 73.16 | $24,656 |

Best finish for 1965: Win at the New Orleans Open

| 1966 | 14 | 36 | 5 | 0 | 0 | 0 | 1 | 74.17 | $3,886 |

Best finish for 1966: T-18th at the Tucson Open Invitational

| 1967 | 16 | 50 | 11 | 0 | 0 | 0 | 1 | 73.30 | $3,249 |

Best finish for 1967: T-19th at the Sahara Open

| 1968 | 23 | 77 | 16 | 0 | 0 | 0 | 3 | 72.22 | $7,203 |

Best finish for 1968: T-12th at the Pensacola Open Invitational & Magnolia State Classic

| 1969 | 9 | 30 | 5 | 0 | 0 | 0 | 1 | 72.40 | $3,383 |

Best finish for 1969: T-19th at the San Francisco Open

| 1970 | 6 | 16 | 3 | 0 | 0 | 0 | 1 | 72.56 | $1,294 |

Best finish for 1970: T-22nd at the Greater Jacksonville Open

| 1971 | 7 | 16 | 1 | 0 | 0 | 0 | 0 | 75.19 | $300 |

Best finish for 1971: T-38th at the Andy Williams-San Diego Open

| 1972 | 9 | 26 | 3 | 0 | 0 | 0 | 0 | 74.00 | $762 |

Best finish for 1972: T-62nd at the Greater New Orleans Open & Greater Greensboro Open

	Starts	Rounds Played	Cuts Made	Wins	Top-5s	Top-10s	Top-25s	Scoring Average	Money
1976	1	4	0	0	0	0	0	75.25	
Period Totals	183	601	117	1	2	7	37	72.87	$71,899

PGA Tour career totals from 1948 to 1976

	Starts	Rounds Played	Cuts Made	Wins	Top-5s	Top-10s	Top-25s	Scoring Average	Money
	353	1253	286	7	N/A	49	132	N/A	$202,001

Billy Mayfair

Year	Starts	Rounds Played	Cuts Made	Wins	Top-5s	Top-10s	Top-25s	Scoring Average	Money
1987	3	8	1	0	0	0	0	71.00	

Best finish for 1987: T-46th at the Seiko-Tucson Open

Year	Starts	Rounds Played	Cuts Made	Wins	Top-5s	Top-10s	Top-25s	Scoring Average	Money
1988	8	26	5	0	0	0	2	71.81	$8,433

Best finish for 1988: T-19th at the B.C. Open

| 1989 | 33 | 99 | 17 | 0 | 0 | 0 | 6 | 71.53 | $111,998 |

Best finish for 1989: T-12th at the Doral-Ryder Open

| 1990 | 33 | 109 | 23 | 0 | 4 | 7 | 15 | 70.44 | $694,658 |

Best finish for 1990: T-2nd at the Greater Milwaukee Open & Nabisco Championships

| 1991 | 33 | 106 | 20 | 0 | 0 | 1 | 7 | 71.04 | $187,558 |

Best finish for 1991: T-7th at the MCI Heritage Classic

| 1992 | 33 | 114 | 23 | 0 | 0 | 1 | 9 | 70.82 | $193,078 |

Best finish for 1992: T-8th at the Canon Greater Hartford Open

| 1993 | 32 | 110 | 22 | 1 | 2 | 5 | 8 | 71.17 | $513,072 |

Best finish for 1993: Win at the Greater Milwaukee Open

| 1994 | 32 | 99 | 18 | 0 | 0 | 1 | 7 | 71.67 | $160,659 |

Best finish for 1994: T-9th at the Northern Telecom Open

| 1995 | 28 | 99 | 21 | 2 | 5 | 6 | 9 | 70.48 | $1,543,192 |

Best finish for 1995: Win at the Motorola Western Open & The Tour Championship

| 1996 | 28 | 93 | 18 | 0 | 1 | 1 | 8 | 71.03 | $359,154 |

Best finish for 1996: T-2nd at the NEC World Series of Golf

| 1997 | 30 | 90 | 16 | 0 | 1 | 1 | 5 | 71.29 | $304,083 |

Best finish for 1997: T-2nd at the Las Vegas Invitational

| 1998 | 27 | 90 | 19 | 2 | 3 | 5 | 9 | 70.93 | $1,282,285 |

Best finish for 1998: Win at the Nissan Open & Buick Open

| 1999 | 29 | 83 | 16 | 0 | 2 | 4 | 10 | 71.48 | $747,983 |

Best finish for 1999: T-2nd at the Mercedes Championships

| 2000 | 29 | 88 | 17 | 0 | 0 | 2 | 6 | 71.43 | $467,345 |

Best finish for 2000: T-10th at the Phoenix Open & Bay Hill Invitational

| 2001 | 29 | 100 | 21 | 0 | 3 | 5 | 15 | 70.01 | $1,718,002 |

Best finish for 2001: 2nd at the WorldCom Classic

| 2002 | 31 | 94 | 19 | 0 | 3 | 3 | 6 | 71.06 | $870,696 |

Best finish for 2002: T-5th at the WorldCom Classic, U.S. Open & Michelob Championship at Kingsmill

| 2003 | 31 | 105 | 20 | 0 | 2 | 3 | 7 | 70.91 | $842,186 |

Best finish for 2003: T-5th at the Honda Classic & Greater Milwaukee Open

| 2004 | 32 | 105 | 22 | 0 | 0 | 1 | 3 | 71.80 | $503,251 |

Best finish for 2004: T-10th at the Buick Invitational

| 2005 | 31 | 110 | 27 | 0 | 2 | 6 | 13 | 70.36 | $2,238,455 |

Best finish for 2005: 2nd at the Bank of America Colonial

| 2006 | 29 | 94 | 18 | 0 | 2 | 4 | 8 | 71.00 | $1,369,998 |

Best finish for 2006: T-3rd at the Honda Classic & Verizon Heritage

| 2007 | 30 | 98 | 18 | 0 | 3 | 6 | 10 | 70.69 | $1,814,518 |

Best finish for 2007: T-2nd at the Wyndham Championship

| 2008 | 29 | 103 | 22 | 0 | 3 | 4 | 7 | 70.76 | $1,750,683 |

Best finish for 2008: T-2nd at the PODS Championship & RBC Canadian Open

Period Totals	Starts	Rounds Played	Cuts Made	Wins	Top-5s	Top-10s	Top-25s	Scoring Average	Money
	620	2023	403	5	36	66	170	70.99	$17,681,287

Shelley Mayfield

Year	Starts	Rounds Played	Cuts Made	Wins	Top-5s	Top-10s	Top-25s	Scoring Average	Money
1958	13	47	10	0	0	0	4	72.60	$1,820

Best finish for 1958: T-15th at the Phoenix Open & Texas Open

| 1959 | 3 | 12 | 3 | 0 | 0 | 0 | 2 | 73.92 | $705 |

Best finish for 1959: T-18th at the Azalea Open Invitational

| 1960 | 2 | 6 | 1 | 0 | 0 | 0 | 0 | 75.00 | $247 |

Best finish for 1960: T-32nd at the PGA Championship

| 1961 | 1 | 4 | 1 | 0 | 0 | 0 | 1 | 72.00 | $780 |

Best finish for 1961: T-22nd at the PGA Championship

| 1962 | 3 | 8 | 2 | 0 | 0 | 0 | 0 | 75.25 | $495 |

Best finish for 1962: T-30th at the PGA Championship

| 1963 | 1 | 4 | 1 | 0 | 0 | 0 | 0 | 74.00 | $319 |

Best finish for 1963: T-53rd at the PGA Championship

| 1964 | 3 | 12 | 3 | 0 | 0 | 0 | 0 | 72.92 | $155 |

Best finish for 1964: T-46th at the Texas Open

Year	Starts	Rounds Played	Cuts Made	Wins	Top-5s	Top-10s	Top-25s	Scoring Average	Money
1965	2	3	0	0	0	0	0	74.33	
1966	2	6	1	0	0	0	0	73.50	$050

Best finish for 1966: T-47th at the Hawaiian Open Invitational

Year	Starts	Rounds Played	Cuts Made	Wins	Top-5s	Top-10s	Top-25s	Scoring Average	Money
1967	1	2	0	0	0	0	0	75.00	
Period Totals	Starts	Rounds Played	Cuts Made	Wins	Top-5s	Top-10s	Top-25s	Scoring Average	Money
	31	104	22	0	0	0	7	73.31	$4,571

Pete Mazur

Year	Starts	Rounds Played	Cuts Made	Wins	Top-5s	Top-10s	Top-25s	Scoring Average	Money
1958	23	70	12	0	0	0	1	74.34	$345

Best finish for 1958: T-25th at the Kansas City Open

| 1961 | 3 | 11 | 2 | 0 | 0 | 0 | 0 | 71.09 | $248 |

Best finish for 1961: T-32nd at the St. Petersburg Open Invitational

| 1962 | 2 | 7 | 1 | 0 | 0 | 0 | 0 | 75.00 | $127 |

Best finish for 1962: T-52nd at the Doral Country Club Open Invitational

| 1964 | 6 | 14 | 1 | 0 | 0 | 0 | 0 | 75.07 | |

Best finish for 1964: T-55th at the Tucson Open

1967	3	5	0	0	0	0	0	74.80	
1968	1	2	0	0	0	0	0	77.00	
Period Totals	Starts	Rounds Played	Cuts Made	Wins	Top-5s	Top-10s	Top-25s	Scoring Average	Money
	38	109	16	0	0	0	1	74.22	$720

John Mazza

Year	Starts	Rounds Played	Cuts Made	Wins	Top-5s	Top-10s	Top-25s	Scoring Average	Money
1979	10	28	4	0	0	0	1	72.71	$5,832

Best finish for 1979: T-15th at the B.C. Open

| 1980 | 22 | 54 | 6 | 0 | 0 | 0 | 1 | 73.43 | $5,966 |

Best finish for 1980: T-25th at the Greater New Orleans Open

| 1981 | 22 | 53 | 6 | 0 | 0 | 1 | 2 | 73.57 | $15,388 |

Best finish for 1981: T-8th at the Sammy Davis, Jr. - Greater Hartford Open

| 1982 | 15 | 38 | 4 | 0 | 0 | 0 | 0 | 74.79 | $2,894 |

Best finish for 1982: T-48th at the Greater Greensboro Open

| 1983 | 4 | 12 | 2 | 0 | 0 | 0 | 0 | 72.42 | $1,443 |

Best finish for 1983: T-51st at the B.C. Open

1989	1	2	0	0	0	0	0	75.50	$1,000
1997	2	4	0	0	0	0	0	74.50	$2,300
2001	2	4	0	0	0	0	0	74.75	$2,000
2006	1	2	0	0	0	0	0	77.50	
Period Totals	Starts	Rounds Played	Cuts Made	Wins	Top-5s	Top-10s	Top-25s	Scoring Average	Money
	79	197	22	0	0	1	4	73.68	$36,823

Rives McBee

Year	Starts	Rounds Played	Cuts Made	Wins	Top-5s	Top-10s	Top-25s	Scoring Average	Money
1966	2	6	1	0	0	0	1	73.00	$1,900

Best finish for 1966: T-13th at the U.S. Open

| 1967 | 27 | 88 | 17 | 0 | 2 | 2 | 2 | 73.34 | $18,375 |

Best finish for 1967: T-2nd at the "500" Festival Open

| 1968 | 24 | 70 | 13 | 0 | 0 | 1 | 4 | 72.57 | $15,003 |

Best finish for 1968: T-6th at the Westchester Classic

| 1969 | 24 | 60 | 7 | 0 | 0 | 0 | 2 | 73.63 | $6,048 |

Best finish for 1969: T-12th at the Monsanto Open

| 1970 | 25 | 75 | 13 | 0 | 1 | 2 | 4 | 72.88 | $16,942 |

Best finish for 1970: 2nd at the Tallahassee Open

| 1971 | 5 | 10 | 0 | 0 | 0 | 0 | 0 | 75.40 | |
| 1972 | 2 | 8 | 2 | 0 | 0 | 0 | 0 | 73.50 | $794 |

Best finish for 1972: T-37th at the San Antonio Texas Open

| 1973 | 3 | 9 | 1 | 0 | 0 | 0 | 0 | 75.00 | $441 |

Best finish for 1973: T-44th at the Byron Nelson Golf Classic

1974	5	10	0	0	0	0	0	75.60	$500
1975	2	4	0	0	0	0	0	75.00	$500
1976	2	4	0	0	0	0	0	75.50	$250
1977	1	4	1	0	0	0	0	72.50	$520

Best finish for 1977: T-47th at the Byron Nelson Golf Classic

1978	2	4	0	0	0	0	0	75.50	$303
1979	1	2	0	0	0	0	0	74.50	
1980	2	4	0	0	0	0	0	76.25	$500
1981	1	4	1	0	0	0	0	72.75	$1,830

Best finish for 1981: T-28th at the Byron Nelson Golf Classic

| 1982 | 1 | 2 | 0 | 0 | 0 | 0 | 0 | 77.50 | |
| 1983 | 2 | 6 | 1 | 0 | 0 | 0 | 0 | 76.00 | $696 |

Best finish for 1983: T-70th at the LaJet Coors Classic

| 1984 | 1 | 2 | 0 | 0 | 0 | 0 | 0 | 75.00 | |

Year	Starts	Rounds Played	Cuts Made	Wins	Top-5s	Top-10s	Top-25s	Scoring Average	Money
1985	1	4	1	0	0	0	0	72.75	$1,011

Best finish for 1985: T-49th at the Southwest Golf Classic

Year	Starts	Rounds Played	Cuts Made	Wins	Top-5s	Top-10s	Top-25s	Scoring Average	Money
1986	1	2	0	0	0	0	0	77.50	$1,000
Period Totals	134	378	58	0	3	5	13	73.48	$66,613

Blaine McCallister

Year	Starts	Rounds Played	Cuts Made	Wins	Top-5s	Top-10s	Top-25s	Scoring Average	Money
1982	21	54	6	0	0	0	1	72.69	$7,501

Best finish for 1982: T-24th at the Bank of Boston Classic

Year	Starts	Rounds Played	Cuts Made	Wins	Top-5s	Top-10s	Top-25s	Scoring Average	Money
1983	24	63	6	0	0	0	0	74.25	$5,218

Best finish for 1983: T-32nd at the Isuzu/Andy Williams San Diego Open

Year	Starts	Rounds Played	Cuts Made	Wins	Top-5s	Top-10s	Top-25s	Scoring Average	Money
1984	1	2	0	0	0	0	0	76.50	$600
1986	34	100	17	0	1	1	3	72.10	$88,732

Best finish for 1986: T-2nd at the Bank of Boston Classic

Year	Starts	Rounds Played	Cuts Made	Wins	Top-5s	Top-10s	Top-25s	Scoring Average	Money
1987	35	106	19	0	1	2	6	71.83	$120,924

Best finish for 1987: T-5th at the Provident Classic

Year	Starts	Rounds Played	Cuts Made	Wins	Top-5s	Top-10s	Top-25s	Scoring Average	Money
1988	34	115	23	1	1	3	11	71.42	$226,660

Best finish for 1988: Win at the Hardee's Golf Classic

Year	Starts	Rounds Played	Cuts Made	Wins	Top-5s	Top-10s	Top-25s	Scoring Average	Money
1989	32	103	20	2	2	5	11	70.95	$525,391

Best finish for 1989: Win at the Honda Classic & Bank of Boston Classic

Year	Starts	Rounds Played	Cuts Made	Wins	Top-5s	Top-10s	Top-25s	Scoring Average	Money
1990	31	99	19	0	1	2	5	71.95	$159,385

Best finish for 1990: T-5th at the Buick Classic

Year	Starts	Rounds Played	Cuts Made	Wins	Top-5s	Top-10s	Top-25s	Scoring Average	Money
1991	26	98	22	1	2	4	11	70.51	$412,974

Best finish for 1991: Win at the H-E-B Texas Open

Year	Starts	Rounds Played	Cuts Made	Wins	Top-5s	Top-10s	Top-25s	Scoring Average	Money
1992	28	96	19	0	3	4	7	71.07	$261,187

Best finish for 1992: T-3rd at the Honda Classic & Centel Western Open

Year	Starts	Rounds Played	Cuts Made	Wins	Top-5s	Top-10s	Top-25s	Scoring Average	Money
1993	27	88	16	1	2	2	5	70.98	$290,434

Best finish for 1993: Win at the B.C. Open

Year	Starts	Rounds Played	Cuts Made	Wins	Top-5s	Top-10s	Top-25s	Scoring Average	Money
1994	27	95	20	0	1	7	11	70.78	$353,054

Best finish for 1994: T-3rd at the Phoenix Open

Year	Starts	Rounds Played	Cuts Made	Wins	Top-5s	Top-10s	Top-25s	Scoring Average	Money
1995	26	90	18	0	1	2	8	71.13	$241,047

Best finish for 1995: 5th at the Honda Classic

Year	Starts	Rounds Played	Cuts Made	Wins	Top-5s	Top-10s	Top-25s	Scoring Average	Money
1996	28	91	18	0	1	2	4	71.49	$180,727

Best finish for 1996: T-4th at the Freeport-McDermott Classic

Year	Starts	Rounds Played	Cuts Made	Wins	Top-5s	Top-10s	Top-25s	Scoring Average	Money
1997	30	85	11	0	1	1	4	71.66	$140,966

Best finish for 1997: T-4th at the Deposit Guaranty Golf Classic

Year	Starts	Rounds Played	Cuts Made	Wins	Top-5s	Top-10s	Top-25s	Scoring Average	Money
1998	30	104	22	0	0	0	2	70.88	$228,304

Best finish for 1998: T-11th at the Kemper Open

Year	Starts	Rounds Played	Cuts Made	Wins	Top-5s	Top-10s	Top-25s	Scoring Average	Money
1999	30	94	17	0	0	1	5	71.44	$295,932

Best finish for 1999: T-9th at the Southern Farm Bureau Classic

Year	Starts	Rounds Played	Cuts Made	Wins	Top-5s	Top-10s	Top-25s	Scoring Average	Money
2000	30	104	21	0	2	3	7	70.41	$963,974

Best finish for 2000: 2nd at the COMPAQ Classic of New Orleans

Year	Starts	Rounds Played	Cuts Made	Wins	Top-5s	Top-10s	Top-25s	Scoring Average	Money
2001	28	80	11	0	1	1	4	71.20	$280,589

Best finish for 2001: T-5th at the Greater Milwaukee Open

Year	Starts	Rounds Played	Cuts Made	Wins	Top-5s	Top-10s	Top-25s	Scoring Average	Money
2002	27	75	9	0	0	0	2	71.56	$124,349

Best finish for 2002: T-23rd at the Kemper Insurance Open & Air Canada Championship

Year	Starts	Rounds Played	Cuts Made	Wins	Top-5s	Top-10s	Top-25s	Scoring Average	Money
2003	8	25	4	0	0	0	0	71.44	$65,820

Best finish for 2003: T-29th at the Wachovia Championship

Year	Starts	Rounds Played	Cuts Made	Wins	Top-5s	Top-10s	Top-25s	Scoring Average	Money
2004	27	68	6	0	0	0	3	72.19	$162,700

Best finish for 2004: T-20th at the Chrysler Classic of Tucson & BellSouth Classic

Year	Starts	Rounds Played	Cuts Made	Wins	Top-5s	Top-10s	Top-25s	Scoring Average	Money
2005	9	29	5	0	0	0	0	71.34	$64,253

Best finish for 2005: T-33rd at the FedEx St. Jude Classic

Year	Starts	Rounds Played	Cuts Made	Wins	Top-5s	Top-10s	Top-25s	Scoring Average	Money
2006	10	29	4	0	0	0	0	73.38	$32,190

Best finish for 2006: T-54th at the Shell Houston Open

Year	Starts	Rounds Played	Cuts Made	Wins	Top-5s	Top-10s	Top-25s	Scoring Average	Money
2007	8	19	1	0	0	0	0	74.21	$11,330

Best finish for 2007: T-66th at the Shell Houston Open

Year	Starts	Rounds Played	Cuts Made	Wins	Top-5s	Top-10s	Top-25s	Scoring Average	Money
2008	2	4	0	0	0	0	0	78.75	
Period Totals	613	1916	334	5	20	40	110	71.51	$5,244,241

Bob McCallister

Year	Starts	Rounds Played	Cuts Made	Wins	Top-5s	Top-10s	Top-25s	Scoring Average	Money
1958	1	4	1	0	0	0	0	72.75	$094

Best finish for 1958: T-38th at the Los Angeles Open

Year	Starts	Rounds Played	Cuts Made	Wins	Top-5s	Top-10s	Top-25s	Scoring Average	Money
1960	4	16	4	0	0	0	2	70.38	$2,119

Best finish for 1960: T-12th at the Oklahoma City Open Invitational & Insurance City Open Invitational

Year	Starts	Rounds Played	Cuts Made	Wins	Top-5s	Top-10s	Top-25s	Scoring Average	Money
1961	10	40	10	1	1	2	5	70.50	$5,404

Best finish for 1961: Win at the Orange County Open

Year	Starts	Rounds Played	Cuts Made	Wins	Top-5s	Top-10s	Top-25s	Scoring Average	Money
1962	20	81	20	0	1	1	9	71.89	$10,293

Best finish for 1962: T-2nd at the Phoenix Open Invitational

Year	Starts	Rounds Played	Cuts Made	Wins	Top-5s	Top-10s	Top-25s	Scoring Average	Money
1963	20	81	17	0	0	2	8	71.78	$9,893

Best finish for 1963: T-9th at the San Diego Open Invitational

Year	Starts	Rounds Played	Cuts Made	Wins	Top-5s	Top-10s	Top-25s	Scoring Average	Money
1964	28	90	15	1	2	3	6	72.53	$9,925

Best finish for 1964: Win at the Sunset-Camellia Open

Year	Starts	Rounds Played	Cuts Made	Wins	Top-5s	Top-10s	Top-25s	Scoring Average	Money
1965	25	89	19	0	1	4	9	72.27	$18,620

Best finish for 1965: T-3rd at the Memphis Open

Year	Starts	Rounds Played	Cuts Made	Wins	Top-5s	Top-10s	Top-25s	Scoring Average	Money
1966	21	65	11	0	0	1	1	73.74	$5,964

Best finish for 1966: T-7th at the Sahara Invitational

Year	Starts	Rounds Played	Cuts Made	Wins	Top-5s	Top-10s	Top-25s	Scoring Average	Money
1967	16	56	11	0	0	1	3	73.04	$7,867

Best finish for 1967: T-7th at the Bing Crosby Pro-Am

Year	Starts	Rounds Played	Cuts Made	Wins	Top-5s	Top-10s	Top-25s	Scoring Average	Money
1968	32	113	23	0	1	2	11	71.72	$28,836

Best finish for 1968: T-5th at the Memphis Open Invitational

Year	Starts	Rounds Played	Cuts Made	Wins	Top-5s	Top-10s	Top-25s	Scoring Average	Money
1969	20	71	16	0	0	1	3	72.08	$9,629

Best finish for 1969: T-6th at the Kaiser International Open

	Starts	Rounds Played	Cuts Made	Wins	Top-5s	Top-10s	Top-25s	Scoring Average	Money
1978	1	2	0	0	0	0	0	76.50	
Period Totals	198	708	147	2	6	17	57	72.16	$108,644

Ronnie McCann

Year	Starts	Rounds Played	Cuts Made	Wins	Top-5s	Top-10s	Top-25s	Scoring Average	Money
1987	2	5	0	0	0	0	0	74.40	
1988	1	3	0	0	0	0	0	72.00	
1989	23	62	9	0	0	0	1	71.31	$25,423

Best finish for 1989: T-19th at the BellSouth Atlanta Golf Classic

Year	Starts	Rounds Played	Cuts Made	Wins	Top-5s	Top-10s	Top-25s	Scoring Average	Money
1990	4	9	0	0	0	0	0	73.89	
1991	1	2	0	0	0	0	0	72.50	
1992	2	5	0	0	0	0	0	75.00	
Period Totals	33	86	9	0	0	0	1	72.02	$25,423

Scott McCarron

Year	Starts	Rounds Played	Cuts Made	Wins	Top-5s	Top-10s	Top-25s	Scoring Average	Money
1995	25	77	12	0	1	1	2	71.48	$147,371

Best finish for 1995: 3rd at the Las Vegas Invitational

Year	Starts	Rounds Played	Cuts Made	Wins	Top-5s	Top-10s	Top-25s	Scoring Average	Money
1996	27	86	17	1	1	2	5	71.27	$404,329

Best finish for 1996: Win at the Freeport-McDermott Classic

Year	Starts	Rounds Played	Cuts Made	Wins	Top-5s	Top-10s	Top-25s	Scoring Average	Money
1997	26	81	16	1	2	7	13	71.01	$853,800

Best finish for 1997: Win at the BellSouth Classic

Year	Starts	Rounds Played	Cuts Made	Wins	Top-5s	Top-10s	Top-25s	Scoring Average	Money
1998	28	83	14	0	1	3	7	71.24	$415,746

Best finish for 1998: T-5th at the Quad City Classic

Year	Starts	Rounds Played	Cuts Made	Wins	Top-5s	Top-10s	Top-25s	Scoring Average	Money
1999	27	88	18	0	1	1	7	70.93	$400,678

Best finish for 1999: T-4th at the Air Canada Championship

Year	Starts	Rounds Played	Cuts Made	Wins	Top-5s	Top-10s	Top-25s	Scoring Average	Money
2000	30	98	19	0	2	2	4	70.98	$495,975

Best finish for 2000: T-4th at the Reno-Tahoe Open

Year	Starts	Rounds Played	Cuts Made	Wins	Top-5s	Top-10s	Top-25s	Scoring Average	Money
2001	25	94	23	1	3	4	15	69.57	$1,793,506

Best finish for 2001: Win at the BellSouth Classic

Year	Starts	Rounds Played	Cuts Made	Wins	Top-5s	Top-10s	Top-25s	Scoring Average	Money
2002	28	98	23	0	4	5	10	70.62	$1,901,714

Best finish for 2002: T-2nd at the Nissan Open & Accenture Match Play Championship

Year	Starts	Rounds Played	Cuts Made	Wins	Top-5s	Top-10s	Top-25s	Scoring Average	Money
2003	27	81	16	0	1	2	11	70.85	$1,251,749

Best finish for 2003: 2nd at the Las Vegas Invitational

Year	Starts	Rounds Played	Cuts Made	Wins	Top-5s	Top-10s	Top-25s	Scoring Average	Money
2004	27	86	17	0	1	2	7	71.01	$792,720

Best finish for 2004: T-2nd at the Reno-Tahoe Open

Year	Starts	Rounds Played	Cuts Made	Wins	Top-5s	Top-10s	Top-25s	Scoring Average	Money
2005	24	74	15	0	1	3	4	71.54	$979,517

Best finish for 2005: T-2nd at the FBR Open

Year	Starts	Rounds Played	Cuts Made	Wins	Top-5s	Top-10s	Top-25s	Scoring Average	Money
2006	15	47	7	0	0	0	1	71.85	$175,727

Best finish for 2006: T-15th at the Zurich Classic of New Orleans

Year	Starts	Rounds Played	Cuts Made	Wins	Top-5s	Top-10s	Top-25s	Scoring Average	Money
2008	22	63	9	0	2	2	3	71.22	$952,070

Best finish for 2008: 2nd at the Wyndham Championship

Period Totals	Starts	Rounds Played	Cuts Made	Wins	Top-5s	Top-10s	Top-25s	Scoring Average	Money
	331	1056	206	3	20	34	89	70.99	$10,564,902

Dick McClean

Year	Starts	Rounds Played	Cuts Made	Wins	Top-5s	Top-10s	Top-25s	Scoring Average	Money
1975	1	3	0	0	0	0	0	76.67	
1977	8	18	1	0	0	0	0	74.50	$345

Best finish for 1977: T-64th at the IVB Philadelphia Golf Classic

Year	Starts	Rounds Played	Cuts Made	Wins	Top-5s	Top-10s	Top-25s	Scoring Average	Money
1978	4	10	1	0	0	0	0	76.40	$1,255

Best finish for 1978: T-55th at the U.S. Open

Year	Starts	Rounds Played	Cuts Made	Wins	Top-5s	Top-10s	Top-25s	Scoring Average	Money
1981	1	3	0	0	0	0	0	77.00	
1985	1	2	0	0	0	0	0	71.50	
1986	1	2	0	0	0	0	0	75.50	
1987	1	2	0	0	0	0	0	77.50	
1988	2	4	0	0	0	0	0	77.00	

Year	Starts	Rounds Played	Cuts Made	Wins	Top-5s	Top-10s	Top-25s	Scoring Average	Money
1989	1	3	1	0	0	0	0	72.33	$1,350

Best finish for 1989: 80th at the Hawaiian Open

Year	Starts	Rounds Played	Cuts Made	Wins	Top-5s	Top-10s	Top-25s	Scoring Average	Money
1990	1	2	0	0	0	0	0	76.50	
1992	1	2	0	0	0	0	0	75.50	
1993	2	5	0	0	0	0	0	76.80	
1994	2	4	0	0	0	0	0	75.50	
1995	1	2	0	0	0	0	0	75.50	
Period Totals	Starts	Rounds Played	Cuts Made	Wins	Top-5s	Top-10s	Top-25s	Scoring Average	Money
	27	62	3	0	0	0	0	75.50	$2,950

John McComish

Year	Starts	Rounds Played	Cuts Made	Wins	Top-5s	Top-10s	Top-25s	Scoring Average	Money
1983	27	81	13	0	0	0	2	73.01	$18,963

Best finish for 1983: T-21st at the Panasonic Las Vegas Pro Celebrity

| 1986 | 24 | 65 | 9 | 0 | 0 | 0 | 3 | 72.23 | $27,645 |

Best finish for 1986: T-13th at the AT&T Pebble Beach Pro-Am & Provident Classic

| 1987 | 23 | 74 | 14 | 0 | 0 | 1 | 2 | 71.84 | $34,319 |

Best finish for 1987: T-9th at the Deposit Guaranty Golf Classic

| 1989 | 27 | 80 | 13 | 0 | 0 | 1 | 4 | 71.64 | $76,495 |

Best finish for 1989: T-6th at the Shearson Lehman Hutton Open

| 1990 | 6 | 17 | 2 | 0 | 0 | 0 | 1 | 70.59 | $9,992 |

Best finish for 1990: T-19th at the B.C. Open

Period Totals	Starts	Rounds Played	Cuts Made	Wins	Top-5s	Top-10s	Top-25s	Scoring Average	Money
	107	317	51	0	0	2	12	72.10	$167,414

Gary McCord

Year	Starts	Rounds Played	Cuts Made	Wins	Top-5s	Top-10s	Top-25s	Scoring Average	Money
1973	1	4	1	0	0	0	0	71.75	$499

Best finish for 1973: T-40th at the Walt Disney World Open

| 1974 | 26 | 86 | 17 | 0 | 0 | 3 | 8 | 72.01 | $32,067 |

Best finish for 1974: T-6th at the Quad Cities Open

| 1975 | 30 | 98 | 20 | 0 | 2 | 4 | 8 | 72.21 | $42,751 |

Best finish for 1975: 2nd at the Greater Milwaukee Open

| 1976 | 31 | 105 | 21 | 0 | 0 | 1 | 6 | 72.44 | $27,730 |

Best finish for 1976: T-9th at the Phoenix Open

| 1977 | 27 | 100 | 22 | 0 | 2 | 4 | 8 | 72.25 | $43,718 |

Best finish for 1977: T-2nd at the Greater Milwaukee Open

| 1978 | 24 | 77 | 15 | 0 | 0 | 0 | 3 | 73.01 | $15,280 |

Best finish for 1978: T-12th at the Joe Garagiola Tucson Open

| 1979 | 26 | 88 | 17 | 0 | 1 | 1 | 4 | 72.30 | $36,843 |

Best finish for 1979: T-5th at the San Antonio Texas Open

| 1980 | 23 | 60 | 9 | 0 | 0 | 0 | 2 | 73.35 | $16,680 |

Best finish for 1980: T-12th at the Byron Nelson Golf Classic

| 1981 | 23 | 68 | 14 | 0 | 0 | 1 | 5 | 71.78 | $24,242 |

Best finish for 1981: T-10th at the Tallahassee Open

| 1982 | 23 | 68 | 10 | 0 | 0 | 3 | 3 | 72.43 | $27,380 |

Best finish for 1982: T-7th at the Texas Open

| 1983 | 29 | 92 | 16 | 0 | 1 | 1 | 6 | 72.24 | $55,856 |

Best finish for 1983: T-4th at the Byron Nelson Golf Classic

| 1984 | 29 | 95 | 19 | 0 | 0 | 2 | 5 | 72.34 | $68,213 |

Best finish for 1984: T-6th at the Houston Coca-Cola Open & Manufactures Hanover Westchester Classic

| 1985 | 28 | 79 | 13 | 0 | 0 | 1 | 1 | 72.92 | $32,198 |

Best finish for 1985: 6th at the Walt Disney World/Oldsmobile Classic

| 1986 | 20 | 58 | 10 | 0 | 1 | 1 | 2 | 71.95 | $27,747 |

Best finish for 1986: T-4th at the Provident Classic

| 1987 | 11 | 27 | 2 | 0 | 0 | 0 | 0 | 72.30 | $3,689 |

Best finish for 1987: T-28th at the B.C. Open

| 1988 | 6 | 20 | 4 | 0 | 0 | 0 | 1 | 70.55 | $15,502 |

Best finish for 1988: T-14th at the Texas Open

| 1989 | 9 | 28 | 5 | 0 | 0 | 0 | 1 | 71.18 | $29,629 |

Best finish for 1989: T-11th at the Kemper Open

| 1990 | 6 | 23 | 5 | 0 | 0 | 0 | 1 | 71.65 | $32,249 |

Best finish for 1990: T-18th at the Honda Classic

| 1991 | 8 | 24 | 3 | 0 | 0 | 0 | 0 | 72.46 | $7,365 |

Best finish for 1991: T-59th at the Las Vegas Invitational

| 1992 | 11 | 35 | 6 | 0 | 0 | 1 | 3 | 70.80 | $64,502 |

Best finish for 1992: T-10th at the Northern Telecom Open

| 1993 | 8 | 25 | 5 | 0 | 0 | 0 | 0 | 71.88 | $16,456 |

Best finish for 1993: T-32nd at the Phoenix Open

| 1994 | 7 | 26 | 5 | 0 | 0 | 0 | 1 | 71.54 | $25,602 |

Best finish for 1994: T-18th at the Phoenix Open

| 1995 | 5 | 14 | 1 | 0 | 0 | 0 | 1 | 71.29 | $15,812 |

Best finish for 1995: T-17th at the Northern Telecom Open

Year	Starts	Rounds Played	Cuts Made	Wins	Top-5s	Top-10s	Top-25s	Scoring Average	Money
1996	4	11	1	0	0	0	0	72.27	$2,548

Best finish for 1996: T-71st at the Bob Hope Chrysler Classic

1997	4	12	1	0	0	0	0	72.83	$2,880

Best finish for 1997: 74th at the Buick Invitational

1998	3	8	0	0	0	0	0	71.25	
1999	1	4	0	0	0	0	0	72.75	
Period Totals	Starts	Rounds Played	Cuts Made	Wins	Top-5s	Top-10s	Top-25s	Scoring Average	Money
	423	1335	242	0	7	23	69	72.24	$667,439

Mike McCullough

Year	Starts	Rounds Played	Cuts Made	Wins	Top-5s	Top-10s	Top-25s	Scoring Average	Money
1969	2	6	1	0	0	0	0	74.50	

Best finish for 1969: T-75th at the Canadian Open

| 1970 | 1 | 2 | 0 | 0 | 0 | 0 | 0 | 75.50 | |
| 1972 | 2 | 6 | 1 | 0 | 0 | 0 | 0 | 74.83 | $227 |

Best finish for 1972: T-59th at the Sea Pines Heritage Classic

| 1973 | 30 | 88 | 12 | 0 | 0 | 1 | 2 | 73.41 | $15,248 |

Best finish for 1973: T-9th at the World Open

| 1974 | 30 | 95 | 18 | 0 | 1 | 2 | 7 | 72.48 | $27,044 |

Best finish for 1974: T-4th at the Bob Hope Chrysler Classic

| 1975 | 24 | 78 | 16 | 0 | 0 | 1 | 4 | 72.67 | $15,221 |

Best finish for 1975: 7th at the San Antonio Texas Open

| 1976 | 32 | 107 | 22 | 0 | 1 | 2 | 6 | 72.13 | $29,382 |

Best finish for 1976: T-4th at the Sahara Invitational

| 1977 | 31 | 110 | 24 | 0 | 2 | 3 | 8 | 72.19 | $72,413 |

Best finish for 1977: 2nd at the Tournament Players Championship

| 1978 | 28 | 94 | 19 | 0 | 1 | 5 | 12 | 72.24 | $57,566 |

Best finish for 1978: T-5th at the Canadian Open

| 1979 | 33 | 100 | 17 | 0 | 1 | 1 | 6 | 73.24 | $46,114 |

Best finish for 1979: T-4th at the Doral-Eastern Open

| 1980 | 18 | 56 | 11 | 0 | 0 | 0 | 4 | 72.05 | $19,588 |

Best finish for 1980: T-13th at the Southern Open

| 1981 | 25 | 82 | 19 | 0 | 0 | 1 | 4 | 72.13 | $33,932 |

Best finish for 1981: T-7th at the World Disney World National Team Championship

| 1982 | 26 | 76 | 12 | 0 | 1 | 1 | 4 | 72.24 | $43,207 |

Best finish for 1982: T-3rd at the Bank of Boston Classic

| 1983 | 30 | 90 | 13 | 0 | 0 | 2 | 4 | 72.57 | $40,957 |

Best finish for 1983: T-9th at the Bing Crosby Pro-Am

| 1984 | 32 | 102 | 18 | 0 | 0 | 0 | 1 | 72.88 | $21,631 |

Best finish for 1984: T-24th at the Greater Greensboro Open

| 1985 | 18 | 51 | 8 | 0 | 0 | 0 | 4 | 72.29 | $24,597 |

Best finish for 1985: T-11th at the Lite Quad Cities Open

| 1986 | 30 | 89 | 19 | 0 | 0 | 1 | 7 | 71.61 | $61,147 |

Best finish for 1986: T-10th at the Southern Open

| 1987 | 23 | 74 | 15 | 0 | 2 | 2 | 4 | 71.73 | $75,890 |

Best finish for 1987: T-3rd at the B.C. Open

| 1988 | 32 | 87 | 13 | 0 | 0 | 1 | 1 | 72.59 | $27,561 |

Best finish for 1988: T-9th at the Pensacola Open

| 1989 | 11 | 29 | 5 | 0 | 0 | 0 | 1 | 71.14 | $22,081 |

Best finish for 1989: T-15th at the AT&T Pebble Beach Pro-Am

| 1990 | 5 | 16 | 3 | 0 | 1 | 1 | 1 | 71.00 | $20,870 |

Best finish for 1990: T-3rd at the Deposit Guaranty

| 1991 | 4 | 12 | 2 | 0 | 0 | 1 | 1 | 70.25 | $24,600 |

Best finish for 1991: T-9th at the B.C. Open

| 1992 | 3 | 9 | 1 | 0 | 0 | 0 | 0 | 71.33 | $722 |

Best finish for 1992: T-49th at the Deposit Guaranty Classic

| 1993 | 3 | 9 | 1 | 0 | 0 | 0 | 0 | 72.67 | $2,011 |

Best finish for 1993: T-48th at the B.C. Open

| 1994 | 3 | 7 | 0 | 0 | 0 | 0 | 0 | 75.14 | |
| 1995 | 2 | 5 | 1 | 0 | 0 | 0 | 0 | 75.40 | $2,376 |

Best finish for 1995: 71st at the Buick Classic

1996	2	2	0	0	0	0	0	74.00	
Period Totals	Starts	Rounds Played	Cuts Made	Wins	Top-5s	Top-10s	Top-25s	Scoring Average	Money
	480	1482	271	0	10	25	81	72.41	$684,386

Mark McCumber

Year	Starts	Rounds Played	Cuts Made	Wins	Top-5s	Top-10s	Top-25s	Scoring Average	Money
1978	8	28	6	0	0	1	1	71.04	$6,948

Best finish for 1978: T-7th at the Pensacola Open

| 1979 | 31 | 90 | 15 | 1 | 1 | 1 | 4 | 73.11 | $69,386 |

Best finish for 1979: Win at the Doral-Eastern Open

Year	Starts	Rounds Played	Cuts Made	Wins	Top-5s	Top-10s	Top-25s	Scoring Average	Money
1980	31	91	15	0	0	2	6	72.63	$36,985

Best finish for 1980: T-9th at the San Antonio Texas Open

1981	26	79	15	0	0	2	4	72.71	$33,963

Best finish for 1981: T-6th at the Quad Cities Open & Anheuser-Busch Golf Classic

1982	26	88	18	0	0	1	5	72.08	$32,934

Best finish for 1982: T-9th at the Pensacola Open

1983	29	99	20	2	7	8	13	71.15	$268,394

Best finish for 1983: Win at the Western Open & Pensacola Open

1984	27	92	20	0	3	6	11	71.76	$152,035

Best finish for 1984: T-4th at the Los Angeles Open & Honda Classic

1985	25	74	14	1	3	3	8	71.86	$193,296

Best finish for 1985: Win at the Doral-Eastern Open

1986	27	85	21	0	0	1	10	71.54	$110,442

Best finish for 1986: T-8th at the U.S. Open

1987	30	103	24	1	5	5	14	70.76	$390,885

Best finish for 1987: Win at the Anheuser-Busch Golf Classic

1988	24	85	22	1	3	5	12	70.65	$565,296

Best finish for 1988: Win at the Players Championship

1989	22	72	16	1	3	8	13	71.17	$552,267

Best finish for 1989: Win at the Beatrice Western Open

1990	25	87	21	0	0	3	6	71.79	$172,689

Best finish for 1990: T-9th at the Players Championship & The International

1991	23	79	17	0	0	1	5	71.13	$174,850

Best finish for 1991: T-7th at the Las Vegas Invitational

1992	24	80	16	0	0	1	4	71.20	$137,853

Best finish for 1992: T-8th at the Nissan Los Angeles Open

1993	21	78	18	0	2	3	11	70.62	$364,768

Best finish for 1993: T-2nd at the Doral-Ryder Open

1994	20	76	18	3	4	6	13	69.86	$1,208,209

Best finish for 1994: Win at the Anheuser-Busch Golf Classic, Hardee's Golf Classic & The Tour Championship

1995	19	66	14	0	3	3	12	71.08	$378,160

Best finish for 1995: T-4th at the MCI Classic

1996	15	51	10	0	2	4	7	71.27	$491,026

Best finish for 1996: T-2nd at the Honda Classic & British Open

1997	4	9	1	0	0	0	0	73.56	$3,870

Best finish for 1997: T-48th at the Honda Classic

1998	3	6	0	0	0	0	0	75.67	
1999	4	9	1	0	0	0	0	74.11	$5,434

Best finish for 1999: T-65th at the Honda Classic

2000	10	22	1	0	0	0	0	73.91	$6,180

Best finish for 2000: T-66th at the MCI Classic

2001	11	22	1	0	0	0	0	72.41	$7,276

Best finish for 2001: T-59th at the National Car Rental Golf Classic/Disney

2002	1	2	0	0	0	0	0	71.00	
2005	1	4	0	0	0	0	0	72.50	
Period Totals	Starts	Rounds Played	Cuts Made	Wins	Top-5s	Top-10s	Top-25s	Scoring Average	Money
	487	1577	324	10	36	64	159	71.57	$5,363,148

Graeme McDowell

Year	Starts	Rounds Played	Cuts Made	Wins	Top-5s	Top-10s	Top-25s	Scoring Average	Money
2001	1	2	0	0	0	0	0	75.50	
2002	3	12	3	0	0	0	0	70.83	$63,160

Best finish for 2002: T-30th at the Air Canada Championship

2003	3	11	1	0	0	0	0	71.55	$9,620

Best finish for 2003: T-44th at the Chrysler Classic of Tucson

2004	3	8	1	0	0	0	0	74.13	$47,745

Best finish for 2004: T-43rd at the WGC-American Express Championship

2005	14	42	10	0	1	3	5	71.98	$1,093,859

Best finish for 2005: T-2nd at the Bay Hill Invitational

2006	15	43	8	0	0	0	3	71.72	$357,902

Best finish for 2006: 12th at the Barclays Classic

2007	3	10	2	0	0	0	0	72.90	$57,084

Best finish for 2007: T-30th at the U.S. Open

2008	4	16	4	0	0	0	2	72.00	$269,545

Best finish for 2008: T-15th at the PGA Championship

Period Totals	Starts	Rounds Played	Cuts Made	Wins	Top-5s	Top-10s	Top-25s	Scoring Average	Money
	46	144	29	0	1	3	10	72.01	$1,898,915

Jerry McGee

Year	Starts	Rounds Played	Cuts Made	Wins	Top-5s	Top-10s	Top-25s	Scoring Average	Money
1966	1	4	0	0	0	0	0	74.00	
1967	22	62	8	0	0	1	1	73.76	$4,213

Best finish for 1967: T-6th at the Memphis Open

Year	Starts	Rounds Played	Cuts Made	Wins	Top-5s	Top-10s	Top-25s	Scoring Average	Money
1968	32	99	17	0	0	2	6	72.74	$7,918

Best finish for 1968: T-8th at the Cajun Classic

| 1969 | 31 | 94 | 17 | 0 | 0 | 1 | 6 | 72.88 | $12,660 |

Best finish for 1969: T-9th at the Michigan Golf Classic

| 1970 | 28 | 97 | 20 | 0 | 0 | 1 | 8 | 72.11 | $20,637 |

Best finish for 1970: T-10th at the Bahama Islands Open

| 1971 | 24 | 88 | 20 | 0 | 3 | 4 | 13 | 71.26 | $53,324 |

Best finish for 1971: T-2nd at the Byron Nelson Golf Classic

| 1972 | 39 | 144 | 32 | 0 | 1 | 3 | 16 | 72.33 | $43,460 |

Best finish for 1972: T-5th at the Masters

| 1973 | 42 | 151 | 31 | 0 | 1 | 3 | 8 | 72.20 | $44,720 |

Best finish for 1973: 3rd at the Southern Open

| 1974 | 34 | 118 | 25 | 0 | 3 | 5 | 10 | 71.87 | $51,452 |

Best finish for 1974: 4th at the Westchester Classic

| 1975 | 30 | 110 | 25 | 1 | 3 | 6 | 16 | 71.26 | $94,066 |

Best finish for 1975: Win at the Pensacola Open

| 1976 | 32 | 114 | 26 | 0 | 8 | 11 | 17 | 71.19 | $130,986 |

Best finish for 1976: 2nd at the Sea Pines Heritage Classic & World Open

| 1977 | 31 | 111 | 24 | 1 | 3 | 7 | 14 | 71.49 | $124,584 |

Best finish for 1977: Win at the IVB Philadelphia Golf Classic

| 1978 | 28 | 100 | 23 | 0 | 1 | 2 | 11 | 71.55 | $71,228 |

Best finish for 1978: 2nd at the Bob Hope Chrysler Classic

| 1979 | 26 | 95 | 21 | 2 | 3 | 4 | 8 | 71.62 | $168,235 |

Best finish for 1979: Win at the Kemper Open & Sammy Davis, Jr. - Greater Hartford Open

| 1980 | 27 | 83 | 16 | 0 | 0 | 0 | 2 | 73.16 | $22,714 |

Best finish for 1980: T-24th at the MONY Tournament Of Champions & Kemper Open

| 1981 | 19 | 65 | 14 | 0 | 0 | 0 | 2 | 72.08 | $22,590 |

Best finish for 1981: T-13th at the Kemper Open

1983	2	7	0	0	0	0	0	72.14	
Period Totals	Starts	Rounds Played	Cuts Made	Wins	Top-5s	Top-10s	Top-25s	Scoring Average	Money
	448	1542	319	4	26	50	138	72.05	$872,786

Paul McGinley

Year	Starts	Rounds Played	Cuts Made	Wins	Top-5s	Top-10s	Top-25s	Scoring Average	Money
1992	1	2	0	0	0	0	0	72.50	$1,200
1993	2	2	0	0	0	0	0	72.50	$924
1994	1	2	0	0	0	0	0	72.00	$972
1996	1	4	1	0	0	0	1	69.75	$31,388

Best finish for 1996: T-14th at the British Open

| 1997 | 2 | 6 | 1 | 0 | 0 | 0 | 0 | 73.83 | $10,131 |

Best finish for 1997: T-66th at the British Open

1998	1	2	0	0	0	0	0	73.50	$1,645
1999	1	2	0	0	0	0	0	80.00	$1,250
2000	4	14	3	0	0	0	2	71.57	$140,217

Best finish for 2000: T-20th at the British Open

| 2001 | 4 | 12 | 4 | 0 | 0 | 0 | 1 | 70.92 | $133,079 |

Best finish for 2001: T-22nd at the PGA Championship

| 2002 | 10 | 26 | 5 | 0 | 0 | 0 | 3 | 73.08 | $210,523 |

Best finish for 2002: T-17th at the Accenture Match Play Championship

| 2003 | 3 | 10 | 2 | 0 | 0 | 0 | 0 | 73.00 | $70,330 |

Best finish for 2003: T-28th at the British Open

| 2004 | 5 | 19 | 4 | 0 | 0 | 1 | 1 | 71.95 | $310,476 |

Best finish for 2004: T-6th at the PGA Championship

| 2005 | 6 | 24 | 6 | 0 | 1 | 1 | 2 | 71.04 | $547,184 |

Best finish for 2005: T-3rd at the WGC-NEC Invitational

| 2006 | 8 | 20 | 4 | 0 | 0 | 0 | 1 | 72.30 | $207,561 |

Best finish for 2006: T-12th at the AT&T Pebble Beach National Pro-Am

| 2007 | 5 | 20 | 5 | 0 | 0 | 0 | 1 | 71.65 | $195,152 |

Best finish for 2007: 19th at the British Open

| 2008 | 1 | 4 | 1 | 0 | 0 | 0 | 0 | 70.00 | $60,000 |

Best finish for 2008: T-27th at the WGC-Bridgestone Invitational

| Period Totals | Starts | Rounds Played | Cuts Made | Wins | Top-5s | Top-10s | Top-25s | Scoring Average | Money |
| | 55 | 169 | 36 | 0 | 1 | 2 | 12 | 72.05 | $1,922,030 |

Tommy McGinnis

Year	Starts	Rounds Played	Cuts Made	Wins	Top-5s	Top-10s	Top-25s	Scoring Average	Money
1973	23	69	10	0	0	1	2	73.74	$6,974

Best finish for 1973: T-7th at the B.C. Open

| 1974 | 16 | 43 | 6 | 0 | 0 | 0 | 0 | 73.02 | $1,447 |

Best finish for 1974: T-37th at the Bob Hope Chrysler Classic

| 1976 | 19 | 57 | 9 | 0 | 1 | 1 | 1 | 73.25 | $8,780 |

Best finish for 1976: 5th at the Ed McMahon Quad City Open

Year	Starts	Rounds Played	Cuts Made	Wins	Top-5s	Top-10s	Top-25s	Scoring Average	Money
1977	13	37	6	0	0	0	0	73.38	$1,850

Best finish for 1977: T-43rd at the IVB Philadelphia Golf Classic

1978	4	12	2	0	0	0	0	73.75	$1,800

Best finish for 1978: T-29th at the Bing Crosby Pro-Am

1979	10	26	3	0	0	0	0	73.88	$2,279

Best finish for 1979: T-41st at the Danny Thomas Memphis Classic

1980	3	10	2	0	0	0	0	73.10	$2,225

Best finish for 1980: T-49th at the Canadian Open

1982	5	15	3	0	0	0	0	73.00	$3,088

Best finish for 1982: T-30th at the Tallahassee Open

Period Totals	Starts	Rounds Played	Cuts Made	Wins	Top-5s	Top-10s	Top-25s	Scoring Average	Money
	93	269	41	0	1	2	3	73.42	$28,443

Jim McGovern

Year	Starts	Rounds Played	Cuts Made	Wins	Top-5s	Top-10s	Top-25s	Scoring Average	Money
1989	2	4	0	0	0	0	0	75.00	$1,000
1991	34	98	14	0	0	1	4	71.68	$89,869

Best finish for 1991: T-10th at the Bob Hope Chrysler Classic

1992	33	101	19	0	1	1	8	70.92	$170,888

Best finish for 1992: 4th at the Federal Express St. Jude Classic

1993	34	119	27	1	2	3	14	71.18	$588,419

Best finish for 1993: Win at the Shell Houston Open

1994	31	97	18	0	1	1	6	71.78	$229,936

Best finish for 1994: T-5th at the Masters

1995	31	97	18	0	3	3	8	70.95	$405,287

Best finish for 1995: 2nd at the Ideon Classic & B.C. Open

1996	31	87	15	0	0	0	4	71.67	$118,027

Best finish for 1996: T-13th at the Walt Disney World/Oldsmobile Classic

1997	32	89	13	0	0	1	4	71.83	$141,756

Best finish for 1997: T-7th at the Kemper Open

1998	28	85	18	0	0	0	2	71.29	$106,726

Best finish for 1998: T-25th at the Kemper Open & CVS Charity Classic

1999	6	13	1	0	0	0	0	73.54	$8,940

Best finish for 1999: T-44th at the AT&T Pebble Beach National Pro-Am

2000	18	53	9	0	0	2	4	71.15	$267,647

Best finish for 2000: T-10th at the John Deere Classic & Bell Canadian Open

2001	21	63	13	0	0	2	2	70.94	$271,494

Best finish for 2001: T-6th at the B.C. Open

2002	15	44	7	0	0	0	1	71.07	$86,862

Best finish for 2002: T-25th at the Valero Texas Open

2003	11	31	4	0	0	0	2	70.87	$115,148

Best finish for 2003: T-13th at the Southern Farm Bureau Classic

2004	11	30	4	0	0	0	1	72.47	$72,377

Best finish for 2004: T-20th at the John Deere Classic

2005	2	7	1	0	0	0	0	70.86	$7,932

Best finish for 2005: T-47th at the B.C. Open

2006	8	20	2	0	0	0	0	72.05	$26,070

Best finish for 2006: T-38th at the FedEx St. Jude Classic

2007	5	16	3	0	0	0	0	72.13	$27,333

Best finish for 2007: T-49th at the Viking Classic

2008	26	75	11	0	0	0	0	71.44	$136,088

Best finish for 2008: T-36th at the Mayakoba Golf Classic

Period Totals	Starts	Rounds Played	Cuts Made	Wins	Top-5s	Top-10s	Top-25s	Scoring Average	Money
	379	1129	197	1	7	14	60	71.42	$2,871,799

Jack McGowan

Year	Starts	Rounds Played	Cuts Made	Wins	Top-5s	Top-10s	Top-25s	Scoring Average	Money
1960	1	4	1	0	0	1	1	72.50	$760

Best finish for 1960: T-8th at the Baton Rouge Open Invitational

1961	2	8	2	0	0	0	1	70.50	$915

Best finish for 1961: T-12th at the St. Petersburg Open Invitational

1962	10	38	9	0	0	2	5	72.21	$4,513

Best finish for 1962: T-9th at the Azalea Open Invitational & Hot Springs Open Invitational

1963	11	44	11	0	0	1	6	71.64	$5,298

Best finish for 1963: T-7th at the Greensboro Open Invitational

1964	27	98	19	1	4	6	11	71.94	$22,460

Best finish for 1964: Win at the Mountain View Open

1965	31	110	23	0	3	7	13	72.01	$30,597

Best finish for 1965: T-2nd at the Greater Greensboro Open & Western Open

1966	27	89	18	0	3	6	12	71.66	$28,226

Best finish for 1966: T-4th at the Doral Open Invitational

Year	Starts	Rounds Played	Cuts Made	Wins	Top-5s	Top-10s	Top-25s	Scoring Average	Money
1967	23	79	17	0	1	4	9	72.03	$21,451

Best finish for 1967: T-3rd at the American Golf Classic

1968	27	83	18	0	0	2	7	71.61	$17,724

Best finish for 1968: T-6th at the Byron Nelson Golf Classic

1969	28	101	23	0	2	2	5	72.18	$36,241

Best finish for 1969: 2nd at the Texas Open

1970	17	55	13	0	0	1	5	71.62	$16,964

Best finish for 1970: 6th at the Doral-Eastern Open

1971	3	6	0	0	0	0	0	73.33	
1980	1	2	0	0	0	0	0	77.50	
Period Totals	**Starts**	**Rounds Played**	**Cuts Made**	**Wins**	**Top-5s**	**Top-10s**	**Top-25s**	**Scoring Average**	**Money**
	208	717	154	1	13	32	75	71.91	$185,148

Pat McGowan

Year	Starts	Rounds Played	Cuts Made	Wins	Top-5s	Top-10s	Top-25s	Scoring Average	Money
1978	24	72	13	0	1	2	5	72.46	$46,833

Best finish for 1978: 2nd at the Canadian Open

1979	32	104	21	0	1	2	4	72.95	$37,018

Best finish for 1979: T-4th at the Phoenix Open

1980	30	90	15	0	1	1	3	72.63	$28,008

Best finish for 1980: T-3rd at the Quad Cities Open

1981	25	73	14	0	0	1	2	73.10	$21,465

Best finish for 1981: T-10th at the World Disney World National Team Championship

1982	26	88	17	0	1	2	7	71.60	$58,673

Best finish for 1982: T-2nd at the Miller High-Life Quad Cities Open

1983	32	115	24	0	1	3	10	71.74	$100,508

Best finish for 1983: 4th at the PGA Championship

1984	30	99	20	0	0	0	7	72.42	$55,508

Best finish for 1984: T-11th at the Bing Crosby Pro-Am

1985	29	101	20	0	1	1	8	71.71	$87,032

Best finish for 1985: T-3rd at the Greater Milwaukee Open

1986	30	93	20	0	2	2	7	71.45	$138,664

Best finish for 1986: 2nd at the USF&G Classic

1987	29	90	14	0	1	3	4	72.30	$79,728

Best finish for 1987: T-4th at the Shearson Lehman/Andy Williams San Diego

1988	32	92	13	0	1	1	3	72.13	$74,156

Best finish for 1988: 3rd at the Texas Open

1989	26	91	19	0	0	1	6	70.90	$99,454

Best finish for 1989: T-9th at the USF&G Classic

1990	29	86	13	0	0	1	2	72.09	$66,738

Best finish for 1990: T-7th at the Kemper Open

1991	23	64	8	0	0	0	0	71.75	$21,098

Best finish for 1991: T-26th at the Walt Disney World/Oldsmobile Classic

1992	11	27	2	0	0	0	1	72.30	$4,065

Best finish for 1992: T-22nd at the Deposit Guaranty Classic

1993	4	11	1	0	0	1	1	72.00	$6,650

Best finish for 1993: T-10th at the Deposit Guaranty Classic

1994	1	2	0	0	0	0	0	74.50	
2002	1	2	0	0	0	0	0	72.50	
Period Totals	**Starts**	**Rounds Played**	**Cuts Made**	**Wins**	**Top-5s**	**Top-10s**	**Top-25s**	**Scoring Average**	**Money**
	414	1300	234	0	10	21	70	72.09	$925,600

Paul McGuire

Year	Starts	Rounds Played	Cuts Made	Wins	Top-5s	Top-10s	Top-25s	Scoring Average	Money
1958	3	6	0	0	0	0	0	77.50	
1961	2	8	2	0	0	0	1	69.50	$522

Best finish for 1961: T-18th at the Home Of The Sun Open Invitational

1962	2	8	2	0	0	0	0	72.88	$489

Best finish for 1962: T-28th at the Greater New Orleans Open Invitational

1963	3	13	3	0	0	0	0	71.46	$801

Best finish for 1963: T-28th at the Phoenix Open Invitational

1964	11	24	2	0	0	0	0	75.17	

Best finish for 1964: T-45th at the Los Angeles Open

1966	2	5	0	0	0	0	0	76.20	
1972	2	5	0	0	0	0	0	79.60	
1973	2	6	0	0	0	0	0	74.17	
1974	2	4	0	0	0	0	0	76.50	
1975	4	10	0	0	0	0	0	78.20	
1978	2	6	0	0	0	0	0	80.00	
Period Totals	**Starts**	**Rounds Played**	**Cuts Made**	**Wins**	**Top-5s**	**Top-10s**	**Top-25s**	**Scoring Average**	**Money**
	35	95	9	0	0	0	1	75.04	$1,813

David McKenzie

Year	Starts	Rounds Played	Cuts Made	Wins	Top-5s	Top-10s	Top-25s	Scoring Average	Money
1998	1	4	1	0	0	0	0	72.50	$5,210

Best finish for 1998: T-51st at the Bell Canadian Open

2006	28	80	12	0	0	2	4	71.20	$425,228

Best finish for 2006: 7th at the Valero Texas Open

Period Totals	Starts	Rounds Played	Cuts Made	Wins	Top-5s	Top-10s	Top-25s	Scoring Average	Money
	29	84	13	0	0	2	4	71.26	$430,437

Parker McLachlin

Year	Starts	Rounds Played	Cuts Made	Wins	Top-5s	Top-10s	Top-25s	Scoring Average	Money
2000	1	2	0	0	0	0	0	74.50	
2004	1	2	0	0	0	0	0	74.50	$1,000
2006	2	8	2	0	0	0	0	70.88	$34,674

Best finish for 2006: T-38th at the AT&T Pebble Beach National Pro-Am

2007	28	83	13	0	1	1	6	71.52	$627,582

Best finish for 2007: T-5th at the Turning Stone Resort Championship

2008	27	88	17	1	2	3	6	71.07	$1,311,839

Best finish for 2008: Win at the Reno-Tahoe Open

Period Totals	Starts	Rounds Played	Cuts Made	Wins	Top-5s	Top-10s	Top-25s	Scoring Average	Money
	59	183	32	1	3	4	12	71.34	$1,975,096

Andrew McLardy

Year	Starts	Rounds Played	Cuts Made	Wins	Top-5s	Top-10s	Top-25s	Scoring Average	Money
1998	1	4	1	0	0	0	0	76.00	$9,048

Best finish for 1998: 75th at the British Open

2001	26	75	10	0	0	0	1	71.31	$130,160

Best finish for 2001: T-15th at the John Deere Classic

2004	3	12	3	0	0	0	0	72.33	$79,026

Best finish for 2004: T-50th at the WGC-American Express Championship

2008	2	6	1	0	0	0	0	70.67	$47,000

Best finish for 2008: T-48th at the WGC-CA Championship

Period Totals	Starts	Rounds Played	Cuts Made	Wins	Top-5s	Top-10s	Top-25s	Scoring Average	Money
	32	97	15	0	0	0	1	71.59	$265,233

James H. McLean

Year	Starts	Rounds Played	Cuts Made	Wins	Top-5s	Top-10s	Top-25s	Scoring Average	Money
2003	19	49	5	0	0	0	1	71.78	$117,182

Best finish for 2003: T-18th at the Chrysler Classic of Tucson

2004	1	4	1	0	0	0	1	69.00	$57,324

Best finish for 2004: T-20th at the HP Classic of New Orleans

2005	5	12	1	0	0	0	0	73.42	$18,000

Best finish for 2005: T-40th at the Bell Canadian Open

2006	4	12	2	0	0	0	0	72.17	$16,760

Best finish for 2006: T-55th at the B.C. Open

Period Totals	Starts	Rounds Played	Cuts Made	Wins	Top-5s	Top-10s	Top-25s	Scoring Average	Money
	29	77	9	0	0	0	2	71.95	$209,266

Mac McLendon

Year	Starts	Rounds Played	Cuts Made	Wins	Top-5s	Top-10s	Top-25s	Scoring Average	Money
1968	21	80	19	1	4	9	14	70.91	$40,013

Best finish for 1968: Win at the Magnolia State Classic

1969	38	130	27	0	0	4	10	72.23	$28,878

Best finish for 1969: T-6th at the Philadelphia Classic

1970	34	98	17	0	1	1	5	72.79	$16,484

Best finish for 1970: T-4th at the AVCO Classic

1971	19	65	14	0	0	1	6	72.06	$19,094

Best finish for 1971: T-7th at the Sea Pines Heritage Classic

1972	34	115	23	0	2	2	6	72.77	$36,295

Best finish for 1972: 3rd at the Jackie Gleason's Inverrary Classic

1973	30	94	17	0	0	2	5	71.98	$22,380

Best finish for 1973: T-6th at the Kemper Open

1974	23	71	12	0	0	0	1	72.90	$6,977

Best finish for 1974: T-15th at the B.C. Open

1975	30	105	22	0	3	6	15	71.69	$78,722

Best finish for 1975: T-2nd at the Greater Jacksonville Open & Pleasant Valley Classic

1976	32	111	23	1	1	5	13	71.46	$72,389

Best finish for 1976: Win at the Southern Open

1977	31	114	26	0	3	7	17	71.64	$86,135

Best finish for 1977: T-2nd at the Southern Open

1978	28	93	18	2	4	5	8	72.13	$107,299

Best finish for 1978: Win at the Florida Citrus Open Invitational & Pensacola Open

1979	26	73	11	0	0	0	1	74.10	$15,841

Best finish for 1979: T-20th at the MONY Tournament Of Champions

Year	Starts	Rounds Played	Cuts Made	Wins	Top-5s	Top-10s	Top-25s	Scoring Average	Money
1980	17	35	3	0	0	1	1	74.37	$5,397

Best finish for 1980: T-8th at the World Disney World National Team Championship

Year	Starts	Rounds Played	Cuts Made	Wins	Top-5s	Top-10s	Top-25s	Scoring Average	Money
1981	2	4	1	0	0	0	0	73.00	$378

Best finish for 1981: T-75th at the Pensacola Open

Period Totals	Starts	Rounds Played	Cuts Made	Wins	Top-5s	Top-10s	Top-25s	Scoring Average	Money
	365	1188	233	4	18	43	102	72.25	$536,281

John McMullin

Year	Starts	Rounds Played	Cuts Made	Wins	Top-5s	Top-10s	Top-25s	Scoring Average	Money
1958	28	100	20	1	3	5	7	71.89	$8,275

Best finish for 1958: Win at the Hesperia Open

Year	Starts	Rounds Played	Cuts Made	Wins	Top-5s	Top-10s	Top-25s	Scoring Average	Money
1959	15	58	12	0	4	5	11	71.09	$10,038

Best finish for 1959: T-2nd at the Tijuana Open Invitational

Year	Starts	Rounds Played	Cuts Made	Wins	Top-5s	Top-10s	Top-25s	Scoring Average	Money
1960	20	80	18	0	0	2	14	71.23	$9,386

Best finish for 1960: T-8th at the Milwaukee Open Invitational & Orange County Open Invitational

Year	Starts	Rounds Played	Cuts Made	Wins	Top-5s	Top-10s	Top-25s	Scoring Average	Money
1961	5	21	5	0	0	0	3	70.62	$1,786

Best finish for 1961: T-11th at the St. Petersburg Open Invitational

Year	Starts	Rounds Played	Cuts Made	Wins	Top-5s	Top-10s	Top-25s	Scoring Average	Money
1963	2	8	2	0	0	0	0	72.25	$172

Best finish for 1963: T-38th at the Almaden Open Invitational

Year	Starts	Rounds Played	Cuts Made	Wins	Top-5s	Top-10s	Top-25s	Scoring Average	Money
1964	2	4	0	0	0	0	0	75.00	
1965	3	7	0	0	0	0	0	76.14	
1967	1	3	0	0	0	0	0	77.67	
1968	4	11	1	0	0	0	1	73.64	$650

Best finish for 1968: T-17th at the Cajun Classic

Year	Starts	Rounds Played	Cuts Made	Wins	Top-5s	Top-10s	Top-25s	Scoring Average	Money
1969	1	2	0	0	0	0	0	74.50	
Period Totals	Starts	Rounds Played	Cuts Made	Wins	Top-5s	Top-10s	Top-25s	Scoring Average	Money
	81	294	58	1	7	12	36	71.76	$30,307

George McNeill

Year	Starts	Rounds Played	Cuts Made	Wins	Top-5s	Top-10s	Top-25s	Scoring Average	Money
2000	1	2	0	0	0	0	0	72.50	
2002	1	2	0	0	0	0	0	79.00	$1,000
2003	1	2	0	0	0	0	0	71.50	
2006	1	2	0	0	0	0	0	79.50	$2,000
2007	30	95	18	1	2	2	6	71.12	$1,504,627

Best finish for 2007: Win at the Frys.Com Open-Vegas

Year	Starts	Rounds Played	Cuts Made	Wins	Top-5s	Top-10s	Top-25s	Scoring Average	Money
2008	29	97	19	0	2	3	9	70.94	$1,361,532

Best finish for 2008: T-2nd at the PODS Championship & Ginn sur Mer Classic

Period Totals	Starts	Rounds Played	Cuts Made	Wins	Top-5s	Top-10s	Top-25s	Scoring Average	Money
	63	200	37	1	4	5	15	71.21	$2,869,158

Artie McNickle

Year	Starts	Rounds Played	Cuts Made	Wins	Top-5s	Top-10s	Top-25s	Scoring Average	Money
1971	1	2	0	0	0	0	0	81.00	
1972	1	2	0	0	0	0	0	77.50	
1973	20	51	8	0	1	1	2	72.96	$10,707

Best finish for 1973: T-5th at the U.S. Professional Match Play Championship

Year	Starts	Rounds Played	Cuts Made	Wins	Top-5s	Top-10s	Top-25s	Scoring Average	Money
1974	19	52	8	0	0	0	3	72.40	$6,413

Best finish for 1974: T-16th at the Greater New Orleans Open

Year	Starts	Rounds Played	Cuts Made	Wins	Top-5s	Top-10s	Top-25s	Scoring Average	Money
1975	19	53	7	0	0	0	0	73.81	$2,022

Best finish for 1975: T-54th at the Pleasant Valley Classic & B.C. Open

Year	Starts	Rounds Played	Cuts Made	Wins	Top-5s	Top-10s	Top-25s	Scoring Average	Money
1976	14	41	10	0	0	0	0	73.17	$2,615

Best finish for 1976: T-34th at the San Antonio Texas Open

Year	Starts	Rounds Played	Cuts Made	Wins	Top-5s	Top-10s	Top-25s	Scoring Average	Money
1977	24	74	13	0	0	0	2	72.62	$9,855

Best finish for 1977: T-22nd at the B.C. Open

Year	Starts	Rounds Played	Cuts Made	Wins	Top-5s	Top-10s	Top-25s	Scoring Average	Money
1978	24	86	20	0	0	1	5	71.83	$26,407

Best finish for 1978: T-7th at the B.C. Open

Year	Starts	Rounds Played	Cuts Made	Wins	Top-5s	Top-10s	Top-25s	Scoring Average	Money
1979	30	85	14	0	2	3	4	73.04	$46,167

Best finish for 1979: T-2nd at the Andy Williams-San Diego Open

Year	Starts	Rounds Played	Cuts Made	Wins	Top-5s	Top-10s	Top-25s	Scoring Average	Money
1980	29	87	17	0	0	3	4	72.05	$41,636

Best finish for 1980: T-8th at the World Disney World National Team Championship

Year	Starts	Rounds Played	Cuts Made	Wins	Top-5s	Top-10s	Top-25s	Scoring Average	Money
1981	18	49	7	0	0	0	0	73.12	$6,393

Best finish for 1981: T-33rd at the Canadian Open

Period Totals	Starts	Rounds Played	Cuts Made	Wins	Top-5s	Top-10s	Top-25s	Scoring Average	Money
	199	582	104	0	3	8	20	72.72	$152,217

Mark McNulty

Year	Starts	Rounds Played	Cuts Made	Wins	Top-5s	Top-10s	Top-25s	Scoring Average	Money
1980	1	4	1	0	0	0	1	71.75	$4,830

Best finish for 1980: T-23rd at the British Open

Year	Starts	Rounds Played	Cuts Made	Wins	Top-5s	Top-10s	Top-25s	Scoring Average	Money
1981	3	12	3	0	0	0	2	72.08	$13,788

Best finish for 1981: 12th at the World Series Of Golf

Year	Starts	Rounds Played	Cuts Made	Wins	Top-5s	Top-10s	Top-25s	Scoring Average	Money
1982	18	66	15	0	2	2	5	72.03	$116,942

Best finish for 1982: T-4th at the Danny Thomas Memphis Classic & Sammy Davis, Jr. - Greater Hartford Open

Year	Starts	Rounds Played	Cuts Made	Wins	Top-5s	Top-10s	Top-25s	Scoring Average	Money
1983	23	76	15	0	1	1	4	72.76	$41,248

Best finish for 1983: T-5th at the Colonial National Invitational

1984	18	53	7	0	0	0	0	73.70	$5,982

Best finish for 1984: T-49th at the Southern Open

1985	5	14	2	0	0	0	0	75.50	$4,144

Best finish for 1985: T-70th at the PGA Championship

1986	3	10	2	0	0	0	0	73.90	$9,058

Best finish for 1986: T-35th at the U.S. Open

1987	3	11	2	0	0	0	1	72.73	$24,765

Best finish for 1987: T-11th at the British Open

1988	5	16	4	0	0	0	3	71.81	$47,301

Best finish for 1988: T-16th at the Masters

1989	4	10	1	0	0	0	1	73.10	$29,700

Best finish for 1989: T-11th at the British Open

1990	2	8	2	0	1	2	2	70.88	$142,975

Best finish for 1990: T-2nd at the British Open

1991	5	19	5	0	0	0	1	71.68	$39,622

Best finish for 1991: T-23rd at the Players Championship

1992	4	16	4	0	0	0	1	72.50	$59,090

Best finish for 1992: T-13th at the Players Championship

1993	2	6	2	0	0	0	1	70.33	$24,630

Best finish for 1993: T-14th at the British Open

1994	6	18	5	0	2	2	5	69.28	$189,020

Best finish for 1994: T-5th at the Texas Open

1995	10	26	3	0	0	0	2	72.50	$67,295

Best finish for 1995: T-11th at the Nestle Invitational

1996	2	6	1	0	0	0	1	70.83	$32,688

Best finish for 1996: T-14th at the British Open

1997	4	14	3	0	0	0	0	72.64	$48,654

Best finish for 1997: T-28th at the U.S. Open

1998	1	2	0	0	0	0	0	75.50	$1,152
1999	1	4	1	0	0	0	0	75.25	$14,842

Best finish for 1999: T-37th at the British Open

2000	1	4	1	0	0	0	1	70.25	$56,346

Best finish for 2000: T-11th at the British Open

2001	3	4	1	0	0	1	1	75.00	$78,430

Best finish for 2001: T-9th at the Accenture Match Play Championship

Period Totals	Starts	Rounds Played	Cuts Made	Wins	Top-5s	Top-10s	Top-25s	Scoring Average	Money
	124	399	80	0	6	8	32	72.52	$1,052,499

Spike McRoy

Year	Starts	Rounds Played	Cuts Made	Wins	Top-5s	Top-10s	Top-25s	Scoring Average	Money
1997	27	68	7	0	0	0	2	71.87	$67,274

Best finish for 1997: T-19th at the Deposit Guaranty Golf Classic

1998	32	87	12	0	0	1	3	71.68	$179,770

Best finish for 1998: T-6th at the Buick Invitational

1999	11	27	3	0	0	0	1	73.19	$49,701

Best finish for 1999: T-17th at the Greater Milwaukee Open

2001	31	91	15	0	1	1	2	70.91	$401,654

Best finish for 2001: T-3rd at the Kemper Insurance Open

2002	25	67	9	1	2	3	3	71.58	$618,814

Best finish for 2002: Win at the B.C. Open

2003	35	101	17	0	0	1	5	71.19	$481,773

Best finish for 2003: T-10th at the Greater Milwaukee Open

2004	33	91	13	0	0	1	2	71.76	$378,400

Best finish for 2004: T-8th at the Chrysler Championship

2005	12	33	4	0	0	1	2	71.39	$173,919

Best finish for 2005: T-9th at the Reno-Tahoe Open

2006	9	20	1	0	0	0	0	71.95	$18,225

Best finish for 2006: T-30th at the Reno-Tahoe Open

2007	6	16	2	0	0	0	0	71.94	$18,280

Best finish for 2007: T-67th at the Wyndham Championship

2008	4	13	2	0	0	0	0	72.62	$15,641

Best finish for 2008: T-45th at the Viking Classic

Period Totals	Starts	Rounds Played	Cuts Made	Wins	Top-5s	Top-10s	Top-25s	Scoring Average	Money
	225	614	85	1	3	8	20	71.59	$2,403,450

Rocco Mediate

Year	Starts	Rounds Played	Cuts Made	Wins	Top-5s	Top-10s	Top-25s	Scoring Average	Money
1984	1	2	0	0	0	0	0	75.50	

Year	Starts	Rounds Played	Cuts Made	Wins	Top-5s	Top-10s	Top-25s	Scoring Average	Money
1985	2	4	0	0	0	0	0	75.75	
1986	27	69	10	0	0	1	4	72.68	$20,670

Best finish for 1986: T-9th at the Deposit Guaranty Golf Classic

| 1987 | 31 | 95 | 19 | 0 | 1 | 1 | 7 | 71.55 | $112,095 |

Best finish for 1987: T-2nd at the Provident Classic

| 1988 | 31 | 109 | 25 | 0 | 0 | 1 | 9 | 71.04 | $129,829 |

Best finish for 1988: T-8th at the Deposit Guaranty Golf Classic

| 1989 | 30 | 104 | 23 | 0 | 0 | 0 | 8 | 71.11 | $132,501 |

Best finish for 1989: T-11th at The Players Championship & Deposit Guaranty Golf Classic

| 1990 | 27 | 85 | 17 | 0 | 2 | 3 | 5 | 71.95 | $240,625 |

Best finish for 1990: T-2nd at the Canon Greater Hartford Open

| 1991 | 26 | 86 | 19 | 1 | 2 | 7 | 14 | 70.74 | $600,336 |

Best finish for 1991: Win at the Doral-Ryder Open

| 1992 | 26 | 85 | 18 | 0 | 3 | 6 | 8 | 71.06 | $311,246 |

Best finish for 1992: T-3rd at the Infiniti Tournament Of Champions & Phoenix Open

| 1993 | 24 | 87 | 22 | 1 | 2 | 6 | 10 | 71.09 | $688,828 |

Best finish for 1993: Win at the Kmart Greater Greensboro Open

| 1994 | 6 | 18 | 3 | 0 | 0 | 1 | 2 | 71.94 | $46,940 |

Best finish for 1994: T-9th at the Northern Telecom Open

| 1995 | 18 | 51 | 8 | 0 | 1 | 2 | 2 | 71.98 | $105,618 |

Best finish for 1995: T-5th at the FedEx St. Jude Classic

| 1996 | 21 | 69 | 15 | 0 | 2 | 4 | 10 | 70.71 | $475,255 |

Best finish for 1996: 3rd at the MasterCard Colonial

| 1997 | 24 | 80 | 18 | 0 | 0 | 2 | 7 | 71.05 | $240,520 |

Best finish for 1997: T-8th at the Buick Open

| 1998 | 24 | 82 | 20 | 0 | 2 | 2 | 9 | 70.96 | $391,496 |

Best finish for 1998: T-4th at the Walt Disney World/Oldsmobile Classic

| 1999 | 25 | 81 | 18 | 1 | 1 | 3 | 8 | 71.22 | $964,793 |

Best finish for 1999: Win at the Phoenix Open

| 2000 | 24 | 76 | 17 | 1 | 3 | 3 | 7 | 71.01 | $1,320,278 |

Best finish for 2000: Win at the Buick Open

| 2001 | 21 | 69 | 14 | 0 | 3 | 5 | 10 | 69.97 | $1,475,722 |

Best finish for 2001: T-2nd at the Phoenix Open & Marconi Pennsylvania Classic

| 2002 | 23 | 75 | 17 | 1 | 3 | 4 | 11 | 70.40 | $2,040,676 |

Best finish for 2002: Win at the Greater Greensboro Chrysler Classic

| 2003 | 24 | 78 | 18 | 0 | 4 | 5 | 8 | 70.65 | $1,833,656 |

Best finish for 2003: T-2nd at the Mercedes Championships & Deutsche Bank Championship

| 2004 | 19 | 48 | 8 | 0 | 0 | 0 | 2 | 71.67 | $264,692 |

Best finish for 2004: T-15th at The International

| 2005 | 24 | 73 | 16 | 0 | 0 | 1 | 8 | 71.03 | $696,250 |

Best finish for 2005: T-6th at the U.S. Open

| 2006 | 18 | 49 | 8 | 0 | 0 | 0 | 1 | 72.10 | $147,899 |

Best finish for 2006: T-16th at the Southern Farm Bureau Classic

| 2007 | 22 | 72 | 14 | 0 | 1 | 3 | 4 | 71.19 | $1,166,294 |

Best finish for 2007: 2nd at the Arnold Palmer Invitational

| 2008 | 27 | 87 | 16 | 0 | 1 | 2 | 4 | 71.61 | $1,420,875 |

Best finish for 2008: 2nd at the U.S. Open

Period Totals	Starts	Rounds Played	Cuts Made	Wins	Top-5s	Top-10s	Top-25s	Scoring Average	Money
	545	1734	363	5	31	62	158	71.21	$14,827,094

Scott Medlin

Year	Starts	Rounds Played	Cuts Made	Wins	Top-5s	Top-10s	Top-25s	Scoring Average	Money
1994	2	4	0	0	0	0	0	78.50	$1,000
1996	23	53	5	0	0	0	0	73.21	$23,276

Best finish for 1996: T-26th at the Bell Canadian Open

| 1997 | 1 | 4 | 1 | 0 | 0 | 0 | 0 | 73.25 | $3,800 |

Best finish for 1997: 70th at the Greater Greensboro Chrysler Classic

| 2000 | 1 | 2 | 0 | 0 | 0 | 0 | 0 | 73.50 | |

Period Totals	Starts	Rounds Played	Cuts Made	Wins	Top-5s	Top-10s	Top-25s	Scoring Average	Money
	27	63	6	0	0	0	0	73.56	$28,076

Steve Melnyk

Year	Starts	Rounds Played	Cuts Made	Wins	Top-5s	Top-10s	Top-25s	Scoring Average	Money
1969	1	2	0	0	0	0	0	75.00	
1970	8	26	5	0	0	0	2	73.65	

Best finish for 1970: T-11th at the Heritage Classic

| 1971 | 6 | 22 | 5 | 0 | 1 | 1 | 2 | 73.18 | $657 |

Best finish for 1971: T-5th at the Greater Jacksonville Open

| 1972 | 30 | 95 | 18 | 0 | 1 | 4 | 9 | 72.48 | $28,927 |

Best finish for 1972: T-3rd at the Tallahassee Open

| 1973 | 36 | 115 | 22 | 0 | 1 | 3 | 9 | 72.36 | $43,662 |

Best finish for 1973: T-2nd at the Phoenix Open

Year	Starts	Rounds Played	Cuts Made	Wins	Top-5s	Top-10s	Top-25s	Scoring Average	Money
1974	34	120	27	0	1	3	7	71.98	$44,509

Best finish for 1974: T-2nd at the Houston Open

| 1975 | 34 | 104 | 19 | 0 | 1 | 4 | 12 | 72.19 | $44,716 |

Best finish for 1975: T-5th at the First NBC New Orleans Open

| 1976 | 34 | 92 | 17 | 0 | 0 | 0 | 1 | 73.46 | $10,336 |

Best finish for 1976: T-20th at the Sahara Invitational

| 1977 | 30 | 96 | 18 | 0 | 2 | 4 | 8 | 72.55 | $42,616 |

Best finish for 1977: 4th at the Florida Citrus Open Invitational

| 1978 | 30 | 93 | 16 | 0 | 2 | 3 | 6 | 73.05 | $44,690 |

Best finish for 1978: T-4th at the Colonial National Invitational & Kemper Open

| 1979 | 25 | 64 | 8 | 0 | 1 | 1 | 3 | 73.16 | $26,276 |

Best finish for 1979: T-2nd at the First NBC New Orleans Open

| 1980 | 26 | 75 | 12 | 0 | 0 | 1 | 3 | 72.85 | $17,675 |

Best finish for 1980: T-6th at the Tallahassee Open

| 1981 | 28 | 77 | 12 | 0 | 1 | 2 | 5 | 72.30 | $50,325 |

Best finish for 1981: 2nd at the Pensacola Open

| 1982 | 23 | 83 | 19 | 0 | 2 | 3 | 11 | 70.82 | $91,122 |

Best finish for 1982: 4th at the USF&G Classic

| 1983 | 30 | 92 | 14 | 0 | 0 | 0 | 3 | 72.38 | $29,208 |

Best finish for 1983: 13th at the Buick Open

| 1984 | 8 | 19 | 2 | 0 | 0 | 0 | 0 | 73.79 | $2,281 |

Best finish for 1984: T-36th at the Anheuser-Busch Golf Classic

Period Totals	Starts	Rounds Played	Cuts Made	Wins	Top-5s	Top-10s	Top-25s	Scoring Average	Money
	383	1175	214	0	13	29	81	72.51	$477,000

Al Mengert

Year	Starts	Rounds Played	Cuts Made	Wins	Top-5s	Top-10s	Top-25s	Scoring Average	Money
1958	8	28	6	0	1	3	5	71.68	$3,931

Best finish for 1958: T-5th at the Greenbrier Invitational

| 1959 | 3 | 10 | 2 | 0 | 0 | 0 | 1 | 73.60 | $600 |

Best finish for 1959: T-19th at the Pensacola Open Invitational

| 1960 | 2 | 8 | 2 | 0 | 0 | 0 | 1 | 71.88 | $608 |

Best finish for 1960: T-22nd at the Phoenix Open

| 1961 | 2 | 9 | 2 | 0 | 0 | 1 | 1 | 71.33 | $1,625 |

Best finish for 1961: T-10th at the Palm Springs Golf Classic

| 1962 | 2 | 8 | 2 | 0 | 0 | 0 | 1 | 71.63 | $505 |

Best finish for 1962: T-22nd at the Tucson Open Invitational

| 1963 | 5 | 20 | 5 | 0 | 0 | 0 | 1 | 72.25 | $1,266 |

Best finish for 1963: T-23rd at the Tucson Open Invitational

| 1964 | 4 | 14 | 2 | 0 | 0 | 0 | 0 | 73.86 | |

Best finish for 1964: T-37th at the Sunset-Camellia Open

| 1965 | 6 | 22 | 4 | 0 | 1 | 1 | 3 | 72.77 | $4,578 |

Best finish for 1965: T-5th at the Bing Crosby Pro-Am

| 1966 | 8 | 31 | 6 | 0 | 0 | 0 | 2 | 73.26 | $5,507 |

Best finish for 1966: T-11th at the Greater Seattle-Everett Open Invitational

| 1967 | 3 | 11 | 2 | 0 | 0 | 0 | 1 | 72.91 | $800 |

Best finish for 1967: T-23rd at the Los Angeles Open

| 1968 | 5 | 17 | 3 | 0 | 0 | 0 | 2 | 72.88 | $4,036 |

Best finish for 1968: T-16th at the Hawaiian Open Invitational

| 1969 | 27 | 85 | 16 | 0 | 0 | 1 | 3 | 73.13 | $12,432 |

Best finish for 1969: T-10th at the Westchester Classic

| 1970 | 17 | 49 | 8 | 0 | 0 | 0 | 3 | 72.73 | $8,644 |

Best finish for 1970: T-16th at the Western Open

| 1971 | 12 | 37 | 6 | 0 | 1 | 2 | 3 | 72.16 | $11,607 |

Best finish for 1971: T-3rd at the Tucson Open

| 1972 | 6 | 20 | 3 | 0 | 0 | 1 | 2 | 73.15 | $4,568 |

Best finish for 1972: T-9th at the Tucson Open

| 1973 | 6 | 16 | 2 | 0 | 0 | 0 | 0 | 74.69 | $842 |

Best finish for 1973: T-38th at the Kaiser International Open

1975	2	4	0	0	0	0	0	74.50	
1977	1	2	0	0	0	0	0	78.50	$250
1979	1	2	0	0	0	0	0	73.50	$350

Period Totals	Starts	Rounds Played	Cuts Made	Wins	Top-5s	Top-10s	Top-25s	Scoring Average	Money
	120	393	71	0	3	9	29	72.86	$62,149

Bob Menne

Year	Starts	Rounds Played	Cuts Made	Wins	Top-5s	Top-10s	Top-25s	Scoring Average	Money
1969	18	55	9	0	0	0	3	72.67	$3,739

Best finish for 1969: T-12th at the West End Classic

| 1970 | 33 | 97 | 17 | 0 | 1 | 1 | 4 | 73.04 | $32,432 |

Best finish for 1970: 2nd at the National Airlines Open

| 1971 | 16 | 34 | 1 | 0 | 0 | 0 | 0 | 75.26 | $208 |

Best finish for 1971: T-57th at the Greater New Orleans Open

Year	Starts	Rounds Played	Cuts Made	Wins	Top-5s	Top-10s	Top-25s	Scoring Average	Money
1972	23	72	13	0	0	1	3	72.78	$9,555

Best finish for 1972: T-8th at the Robinson's Fall Golf Classic

1973	19	56	8	0	0	1	4	71.05	$9,338

Best finish for 1973: T-9th at the Southern Open

| 1974 | 30 | 86 | 14 | 1 | 1 | 1 | 1 | 72.66 | $60,070 |

Best finish for 1974: Win at the Kemper Open

| 1975 | 25 | 64 | 7 | 0 | 0 | 0 | 2 | 74.09 | $9,273 |

Best finish for 1975: T-15th at the B.C. Open

| 1976 | 22 | 67 | 14 | 0 | 1 | 2 | 2 | 73.22 | $21,733 |

Best finish for 1976: T-3rd at the Pleasant Valley Classic

| 1977 | 23 | 61 | 8 | 0 | 0 | 1 | 1 | 74.51 | $9,651 |

Best finish for 1977: T-7th at the B.C. Open

| 1978 | 1 | 4 | 1 | 0 | 0 | 0 | 0 | 74.25 | $500 |

Best finish for 1978: T-58th at the Jackie Gleason's Inverrary Classic

| 1979 | 2 | 6 | 1 | 0 | 0 | 0 | 0 | 73.83 | $562 |

Best finish for 1979: T-56th at the American Optical Classic

1980	1	2	0	0	0	0	0	72.00	
1981	2	4	0	0	0	0	0	75.50	
1982	2	4	0	0	0	0	0	77.00	$650
1986	1	2	0	0	0	0	0	74.50	
1988	1	2	0	0	0	0	0	77.00	$1,000
1989	1	2	0	0	0	0	0	75.00	
1991	3	6	0	0	0	0	0	72.67	
1992	1	2	0	0	0	0	0	72.00	
1993	1	0	0	0	0	0	0		
1996	2	4	0	0	0	0	0	75.00	
Period Totals	Starts	Rounds Played	Cuts Made	Wins	Top-5s	Top-10s	Top-25s	Scoring Average	Money
	227	630	93	1	3	7	20	73.22	$158,713

John Merrick

Year	Starts	Rounds Played	Cuts Made	Wins	Top-5s	Top-10s	Top-25s	Scoring Average	Money
2005	1	2	0	0	0	0	0	75.00	$2,000
2007	29	92	16	0	1	1	8	71.05	$649,439

Best finish for 2007: T-4th at the Reno-Tahoe Open

| 2008 | 28 | 98 | 22 | 0 | 1 | 4 | 7 | 70.97 | $1,312,005 |

Best finish for 2008: T-3rd at the Mayakoba Golf Classic

Period Totals	Starts	Rounds Played	Cuts Made	Wins	Top-5s	Top-10s	Top-25s	Scoring Average	Money
	58	192	38	0	2	5	15	71.05	$1,963,444

Eddie Merrins

Year	Starts	Rounds Played	Cuts Made	Wins	Top-5s	Top-10s	Top-25s	Scoring Average	Money
1958	15	43	6	0	0	0	1	74.23	$258

Best finish for 1958: T-15th at the Lafayette Open

| 1959 | 1 | 4 | 1 | 0 | 0 | 0 | 0 | 70.50 | $203 |

Best finish for 1959: T-27th at the Rubber City Open Invitational

| 1960 | 1 | 4 | 1 | 0 | 0 | 0 | 0 | 72.50 | $088 |

Best finish for 1960: T-76th at the Palm Springs Desert Golf Classic

| 1961 | 4 | 14 | 3 | 0 | 1 | 1 | 2 | 71.29 | $1,617 |

Best finish for 1961: T-4th at the Beaumont Open Invitational

| 1962 | 3 | 8 | 3 | 0 | 0 | 0 | 1 | 75.38 | $1,150 |

Best finish for 1962: T-15th at the Western Open Championship

| 1963 | 1 | 4 | 1 | 0 | 0 | 0 | 0 | 72.75 | $480 |

Best finish for 1963: T-34th at the PGA Championship

| 1964 | 6 | 17 | 1 | 0 | 0 | 0 | 0 | 74.53 | $079 |

Best finish for 1964: T-34th at the Mountain View Open

| 1965 | 5 | 15 | 1 | 0 | 0 | 0 | 0 | 75.67 | $200 |

Best finish for 1965: T-53rd at the Western Open

| 1966 | 5 | 13 | 0 | 0 | 0 | 0 | 0 | 77.15 | $300 |
| 1967 | 7 | 21 | 2 | 0 | 0 | 0 | 0 | 74.67 | $278 |

Best finish for 1967: T-45th at the Minnesota Golf Classic

| 1968 | 8 | 19 | 0 | 0 | 0 | 0 | 0 | 75.00 | $500 |
| 1969 | 10 | 31 | 4 | 0 | 0 | 0 | 0 | 73.65 | $1,026 |

Best finish for 1969: T-40th at the Los Angeles Open

| 1970 | 5 | 13 | 0 | 0 | 0 | 0 | 0 | 74.85 | |
| 1971 | 7 | 19 | 1 | 0 | 0 | 0 | 1 | 73.95 | $1,910 |

Best finish for 1971: T-14th at the Andy Williams-San Diego Open

1972	4	11	0	0	0	0	0	77.09	
1973	5	8	0	0	0	0	0	77.88	$500
1974	3	7	0	0	0	0	0	76.71	
1975	1	2	0	0	0	0	0	78.50	
1976	3	7	3	0	0	0	0	76.00	

Year	Starts	Rounds Played	Cuts Made	Wins	Top-5s	Top-10s	Top-25s	Scoring Average	Money
1977	3	7	0	0	0	0	0	79.14	
1978	1	3	0	0	0	0	0	81.00	
1979	2	5	0	0	0	0	0	82.80	
1980	1	2	0	0	0	0	0	80.00	
Period Totals	Starts	Rounds Played	Cuts Made	Wins	Top-5s	Top-10s	Top-25s	Scoring Average	Money
	101	277	27	0	1	1	5	75.03	$8,589

Sonny Methvin

Year	Starts	Rounds Played	Cuts Made	Wins	Top-5s	Top-10s	Top-25s	Scoring Average	Money
1964	28	68	9	0	0	0	2	74.35	$1,870

Best finish for 1964: T-16th at the Cajun Classic

1965	20	57	8	0	0	0	0	74.00	$892

Best finish for 1965: T-28th at the St. Paul Open

1966	16	41	5	0	0	0	0	74.32	

Best finish for 1966: T-33rd at the Azalea Open Invitational

Period Totals	Starts	Rounds Played	Cuts Made	Wins	Top-5s	Top-10s	Top-25s	Scoring Average	Money
	64	166	22	0	0	0	2	74.22	$2,762

Craig Metz

Year	Starts	Rounds Played	Cuts Made	Wins	Top-5s	Top-10s	Top-25s	Scoring Average	Money
1966	6	14	1	0	0	0	0	75.93	

Best finish for 1966: T-43rd at the Oklahoma City Open Invitational

1970	2	4	0	0	0	0	0	75.75	
1971	6	12	0	0	0	0	0	75.00	
1972	9	26	4	0	0	0	0	73.62	$1,162

Best finish for 1972: T-30th at the Tallahassee Open

1975	1	2	0	0	0	0	0	75.00	
1981	3	6	0	0	0	0	0	75.17	
Period Totals	Starts	Rounds Played	Cuts Made	Wins	Top-5s	Top-10s	Top-25s	Scoring Average	Money
	27	64	5	0	0	0	0	74.70	$1,162

Dennis Meyer

Year	Starts	Rounds Played	Cuts Made	Wins	Top-5s	Top-10s	Top-25s	Scoring Average	Money
1964	1	4	1	0	0	0	0	82.75	

Best finish for 1964: 76th at the Los Angeles Open

1968	2	6	1	0	0	0	0	73.17	

Best finish for 1968: 76th at the Minnesota Golf Classic

1969	7	16	1	0	0	0	0	75.63	$154

Best finish for 1969: T-67th at the Texas Open

1970	6	19	3	0	0	0	0	72.89	$424

Best finish for 1970: T-49th at the Green Island Open Invitational

1971	1	2	0	0	0	0	0	75.00	
1972	1	2	0	0	0	0	0	74.50	
1973	3	8	0	0	0	0	0	76.13	$500
1974	3	9	1	0	0	0	0	74.56	$820

Best finish for 1974: T-57th at the Bob Hope Chrysler Classic

1975	6	21	4	0	0	0	1	72.52	$3,695

Best finish for 1975: T-18th at the Sammy Davis, Jr. - Greater Hartford Open

1976	24	72	15	0	0	0	2	73.44	$9,737

Best finish for 1976: T-21st at the Hawaiian Open

1977	13	32	3	0	0	0	0	73.63	$1,519

Best finish for 1977: T-31st at the Tallahassee Open

1978	8	24	4	0	0	0	0	73.13	$1,970

Best finish for 1978: T-45th at the Atlanta Classic

1985	1	2	0	0	0	0	0	75.50	
1987	1	4	1	0	0	0	0	73.75	$368

Best finish for 1987: 78th at the Deposit Guaranty Golf Classic

1992	1	2	0	0	0	0	0	70.50	
Period Totals	Starts	Rounds Played	Cuts Made	Wins	Top-5s	Top-10s	Top-25s	Scoring Average	Money
	78	223	34	0	0	0	3	73.78	$19,187

Shaun Micheel

Year	Starts	Rounds Played	Cuts Made	Wins	Top-5s	Top-10s	Top-25s	Scoring Average	Money
1989	1	2	0	0	0	0	0	77.00	
1991	1	2	0	0	0	0	0	76.50	
1994	19	45	4	0	0	0	0	72.89	$12,252

Best finish for 1994: T-26th at the Deposit Guaranty Golf Classic

1997	21	53	5	0	0	0	0	73.19	$14,518

Best finish for 1997: T-49th at the Buick Open

1998	2	8	2	0	0	0	0	69.63	$8,918

Best finish for 1998: T-43rd at the FedEx St. Jude Classic

1999	1	2	0	0	0	0	0	75.00	$1,000

Year	Starts	Rounds Played	Cuts Made	Wins	Top-5s	Top-10s	Top-25s	Scoring Average	Money
2000	31	91	15	0	2	3	4	71.05	$467,431

Best finish for 2000: T-5th at the John Deere Classic & Invensys Classic at Las Vegas

2001	34	100	18	0	0	0	3	71.33	$351,095

Best finish for 2001: T-11th at the BellSouth Classic

2002	30	97	21	0	2	2	8	70.56	$641,450

Best finish for 2002: T-3rd at the B.C. Open

2003	28	94	21	1	1	4	7	70.56	$1,827,000

Best finish for 2003: Win at the PGA Championship

2004	27	91	20	0	0	1	8	71.22	$949,919

Best finish for 2004: 9th at the Players Championship

2005	29	79	12	0	1	2	3	71.72	$500,782

Best finish for 2005: T-5th at the Southern Farm Bureau Classic

2006	29	93	19	0	1	2	8	70.91	$1,641,052

Best finish for 2006: 2nd at the PGA Championship

2007	29	88	17	0	1	3	7	71.58	$950,195

Best finish for 2007: T-5th at the Viking Classic

2008	16	45	6	0	0	0	1	72.89	$157,828

Best finish for 2008: T-21st at the Puerto Rico Open

Period Totals	Starts	Rounds Played	Cuts Made	Wins	Top-5s	Top-10s	Top-25s	Scoring Average	Money
	298	890	160	1	8	17	49	71.43	$7,523,440

Phil Mickelson

Year	Starts	Rounds Played	Cuts Made	Wins	Top-5s	Top-10s	Top-25s	Scoring Average	Money
1988	2	4	0	0	0	0	0	73.25	
1989	1	2	0	0	0	0	0	73.50	
1990	2	8	2	0	0	0	1	71.00	

Best finish for 1990: T-19th at the Northern Telecom Tucson Open

1991	8	30	7	1	1	1	1	71.53	

Best finish for 1991: Win at the Northern Telecom Open

1992	17	46	8	0	1	2	4	71.46	$172,714

Best finish for 1992: 2nd at the New England Classic

1993	24	73	14	2	2	4	7	71.64	$628,735

Best finish for 1993: Win at the Buick Invitational of California & The International

1994	18	67	16	1	5	9	10	70.04	$749,288

Best finish for 1994: Win at the Mercedes Championship

1995	24	78	15	1	3	4	9	71.17	$656,977

Best finish for 1995: Win at the Northern Telecom Open

1996	21	77	19	4	6	8	10	70.29	$1,697,799

Best finish for 1996: Win at the Nortel Open, Phoenix Open, GTE Byron Nelson Classic & NEC World Series of Golf

1997	21	76	19	2	3	5	15	70.41	$1,230,390

Best finish for 1997: Win at the Bay Hill Invitational & Sprint International

1998	24	79	18	2	5	9	11	71.19	$1,833,246

Best finish for 1998: Win at the Mercedes Championship & AT&T Pebble Beach Pro-Am

1999	23	78	20	0	3	6	14	71.06	$1,724,400

Best finish for 1999: 2nd at the U.S. Open & WGC-NEC Invitational

2000	23	80	20	4	9	12	18	69.35	$4,746,457

Best finish for 2000: Win at the Buick Invitational, BellSouth Classic, MasterCard Colonial & The Tour Championship

2001	23	82	20	2	10	13	13	69.16	$4,403,883

Best finish for 2001: Win at the Buick Invitational & Canon Greater Hartford Open

2002	26	94	23	2	9	12	18	69.71	$4,311,971

Best finish for 2002: Win at the Bob Hope Chrysler Classic & Canon Greater Hartford Open

2003	23	80	20	0	2	7	10	70.64	$1,623,137

Best finish for 2003: 3rd at the Masters

2004	22	79	19	2	10	13	16	69.63	$5,784,822

Best finish for 2004: Win at the Bob Hope Chrysler Classic & Masters

2005	21	74	20	4	5	9	11	69.86	$5,699,604

Best finish for 2005: Win at the FBR Open, AT&T Pebble Beach National Pro-Am, BellSouth Classic & PGA Championship

2006	19	69	18	2	5	8	14	70.07	$4,256,505

Best finish for 2006: Win at the BellSouth Classic & Masters

2007	22	71	16	3	6	7	11	70.39	$5,827,435

Best finish for 2007: Win at the AT&T Pebble Beach National Pro-Am, The Players & Deutsche Bank Championship

2008	21	78	20	2	6	8	19	70.28	$5,188,875

Best finish for 2008: Win at the Northern Trust & Crowne Plaza Invitational at Colonial

Period Totals	Starts	Rounds Played	Cuts Made	Wins	Top-5s	Top-10s	Top-25s	Scoring Average	Money
	385	1325	314	34	91	137	212	70.38	$50,536,239

Cary Middlecoff

Year	Starts	Rounds Played	Cuts Made	Wins	Top-5s	Top-10s	Top-25s	Scoring Average	Money
1958	14	56	14	1	4	6	11	70.57	$16,050

Best finish for 1958: Win at the Miller Open

1959	10	40	9	1	3	6	9	70.88	$17,660

Best finish for 1959: Win at the St. Petersburg Open Invitational

Year	Starts	Rounds Played	Cuts Made	Wins	Top-5s	Top-10s	Top-25s	Scoring Average	Money
1960	13	47	10	0	0	0	3	72.60	$3,905

Best finish for 1960: T-12th at the Memphis Open Invitational & Dallas Open Invitational

1961	14	53	12	1	1	1	6	71.64	$9,728

Best finish for 1961: Win at the Memphis Open Invitational

1962	10	38	9	0	0	0	5	72.79	$5,240

Best finish for 1962: T-12th at the Doral Country Club Open Invitational

1963	9	32	7	0	0	0	1	73.84	$2,768

Best finish for 1963: T-12th at the Memphis Open Invitational

1964	8	26	3	0	0	0	0	73.85	$155

Best finish for 1964: T-34th at the St. Petersburg Open

1965	7	20	3	0	0	0	0	73.80	$368

Best finish for 1965: T-46th at the Thunderbird Classic

1966	9	23	2	0	0	0	1	74.17	$3,700

Best finish for 1966: 11th at the Minnesota Golf Classic

1967	6	16	1	0	0	0	0	74.06	

Best finish for 1967: T-74th at the Pensacola Open

1968	4	8	0	0	0	0	0	75.88	$1,000
1969	6	11	0	0	0	0	0	76.36	
1970	2	4	0	0	0	0	0	75.00	$1,000
1971	2	3	0	0	0	0	0	76.67	$1,000
Period Totals	Starts	Rounds Played	Cuts Made	Wins	Top-5s	Top-10s	Top-25s	Scoring Average	Money
	114	377	70	3	8	13	36	72.65	$62,574

PGA Tour career totals from 1945 to 1971

	Starts	Rounds Played	Cuts Made	Wins	Top-5s	Top-10s	Top-25s	Scoring Average	Money
	337	N/A	N/A	35	N/A	146	235	N/A	$298,941

Danny Mijovic

Year	Starts	Rounds Played	Cuts Made	Wins	Top-5s	Top-10s	Top-25s	Scoring Average	Money
1983	1	2	0	0	0	0	0	73.00	
1984	2	4	0	0	0	0	0	74.50	
1985	4	10	1	0	0	0	0	74.40	$1,400

Best finish for 1985: T-69th at the Southwest Golf Classic

1986	2	6	1	0	0	0	0	74.83	$995

Best finish for 1986: T-47th at the Southwest Golf Classic

1987	1	2	0	0	0	0	0	75.00	
1988	2	4	0	0	0	0	0	76.25	
1989	2	4	0	0	0	0	0	75.75	$1,000
1990	3	6	1	0	0	0	0	73.00	$5,837

Best finish for 1990: T-57th at the British Open

1991	1	4	1	0	0	0	0	72.25	$5,040

Best finish for 1991: T-80th at the British Open

1992	1	4	1	0	0	0	0	73.00	$6,850

Best finish for 1992: T-64th at the British Open

1993	1	2	0	0	0	0	0	71.00	
1994	4	8	0	0	0	0	0	73.00	
1996	1	2	0	0	0	0	0	76.00	
1997	1	2	0	0	0	0	0	76.00	
1998	2	6	1	0	0	0	0	72.33	$4,420

Best finish for 1998: T-56th at the Greater Vancouver Open

1999	2	4	0	0	0	0	0	75.75	
Period Totals	Starts	Rounds Played	Cuts Made	Wins	Top-5s	Top-10s	Top-25s	Scoring Average	Money
	30	70	6	0	0	0	0	74.01	$25,542

Lee Mikles

Year	Starts	Rounds Played	Cuts Made	Wins	Top-5s	Top-10s	Top-25s	Scoring Average	Money
1978	23	66	11	0	0	0	3	72.29	$12,483

Best finish for 1978: T-17th at the First NBC New Orleans Open & Southern Open

1979	14	34	3	0	0	0	0	73.97	$1,603

Best finish for 1979: T-53rd at the Doral-Eastern Open

Period Totals	Starts	Rounds Played	Cuts Made	Wins	Top-5s	Top-10s	Top-25s	Scoring Average	Money
	37	100	14	0	0	0	3	72.86	$14,087

Ron Milanovich

Year	Starts	Rounds Played	Cuts Made	Wins	Top-5s	Top-10s	Top-25s	Scoring Average	Money
1976	1	2	0	0	0	0	0	78.50	
1977	5	10	0	0	0	0	0	73.80	
1978	4	8	0	0	0	0	0	73.88	
1980	19	44	4	0	0	0	0	73.73	$4,274

Best finish for 1980: T-34th at the Pleasant Valley Jimmy Fund Classic

Period Totals	Starts	Rounds Played	Cuts Made	Wins	Top-5s	Top-10s	Top-25s	Scoring Average	Money
	29	64	4	0	0	0	0	73.91	$4,274

Eldridge Miles

Year	Starts	Rounds Played	Cuts Made	Wins	Top-5s	Top-10s	Top-25s	Scoring Average	Money
1967	1	2	0	0	0	0	0	77.00	
1968	18	57	11	0	0	1	2	72.67	$5,291
Best finish for 1968: T-9th at the Kaiser International Open Invitational									
1969	1	2	0	0	0	0	0	75.00	
1970	3	8	1	0	0	0	0	73.75	$143
Best finish for 1970: T-58th at the Byron Nelson Golf Classic									
1971	1	2	0	0	0	0	0	75.50	
1972	1	2	0	0	0	0	0	73.00	
1973	1	2	0	0	0	0	0	78.50	
1974	1	2	0	0	0	0	0	73.00	
1976	1	2	0	0	0	0	0	74.00	
1977	2	4	0	0	0	0	0	80.75	$250
1983	1	4	0	0	0	0	0	75.75	
Period Totals	Starts	Rounds Played	Cuts Made	Wins	Top-5s	Top-10s	Top-25s	Scoring Average	Money
	31	87	12	0	0	1	2	73.68	$5,683

Mike Miles

Year	Starts	Rounds Played	Cuts Made	Wins	Top-5s	Top-10s	Top-25s	Scoring Average	Money
1986	23	55	4	0	0	0	1	74.24	$4,492
Best finish for 1986: T-23rd at the Deposit Guaranty Golf Classic									
1987	1	2	0	0	0	0	0	77.50	$600
1988	2	4	0	0	0	0	0	72.50	
1989	25	66	8	0	0	1	1	72.08	$33,475
Best finish for 1989: T-10th at the BellSouth Atlanta Golf Classic									
1990	1	2	0	0	0	0	0	72.00	
1991	1	2	0	0	0	0	0	73.00	
Period Totals	Starts	Rounds Played	Cuts Made	Wins	Top-5s	Top-10s	Top-25s	Scoring Average	Money
	53	131	12	0	0	1	2	73.09	$38,567

Allen Miller

Year	Starts	Rounds Played	Cuts Made	Wins	Top-5s	Top-10s	Top-25s	Scoring Average	Money
1969	1	2	0	0	0	0	0	75.50	
1970	2	6	1	0	0	0	0	74.83	
Best finish for 1970: T-55th at the Monsanto Open									
1971	3	10	2	0	0	0	0	74.00	
Best finish for 1971: T-42nd at the Masters									
1972	35	107	18	0	0	1	8	72.77	$19,610
Best finish for 1972: T-6th at the Sea Pines Heritage Classic									
1973	39	127	25	0	3	4	6	72.95	$46,432
Best finish for 1973: T-2nd at the Danny Thomas Memphis Classic									
1974	36	108	19	1	1	2	3	72.70	$34,476
Best finish for 1974: Win at the Tallahassee Open									
1975	34	119	25	0	0	2	8	72.51	$31,641
Best finish for 1975: T-9th at the Hawaiian Open									
1976	33	107	22	0	0	0	6	72.39	$22,918
Best finish for 1976: T-16th at the B.C. Open									
1977	26	81	13	0	0	1	4	72.99	$16,804
Best finish for 1977: T-6th at the Kemper Open									
1978	28	93	18	0	1	2	5	72.42	$24,523
Best finish for 1978: T-4th at the Pensacola Open									
1979	29	94	17	0	0	0	5	72.56	$22,899
Best finish for 1979: T-13th at the Tallahassee Open									
1980	26	72	11	0	1	1	2	73.01	$28,713
Best finish for 1980: 3rd at the Joe Garagiola Tucson Open									
1981	23	64	9	0	0	0	3	72.27	$11,210
Best finish for 1981: T-17th at the Quad Cities Open									
1982	31	111	24	0	2	2	6	71.73	$47,626
Best finish for 1982: T-4th at the Hall of Fame									
1983	30	101	19	0	0	1	6	72.33	$45,658
Best finish for 1983: T-10th at the Honda Inverrary Classic									
1984	27	87	18	0	0	2	5	72.30	$58,840
Best finish for 1984: T-9th at the Los Angeles Open									
1985	27	69	7	0	0	0	1	72.77	$12,971
Best finish for 1985: T-20th at the Canadian Open									
1986	3	7	1	0	0	0	0	72.86	$735
Best finish for 1986: T-62nd at the Southern Open									
Period Totals	Starts	Rounds Played	Cuts Made	Wins	Top-5s	Top-10s	Top-25s	Scoring Average	Money
	433	1365	249	1	8	18	68	72.57	$425,055

Andy Miller

Year	Starts	Rounds Played	Cuts Made	Wins	Top-5s	Top-10s	Top-25s	Scoring Average	Money
2000	2	6	1	0	0	0	0	71.67	$5,640

Best finish for 2000: T-73rd at the Air Canada Championship

2001	1	3	0	0	0	0	0	74.67	
2002	2	6	1	0	0	0	0	75.00	$12,794

Best finish for 2002: T-62nd at the U.S. Open

2003	25	75	13	0	0	0	0	71.69	$134,930

Best finish for 2003: T-31st at the B.C. Open

Period Totals	Starts	Rounds Played	Cuts Made	Wins	Top-5s	Top-10s	Top-25s	Scoring Average	Money
	30	90	15	0	0	0	0	72.01	$153,364

Johnny Miller

Year	Starts	Rounds Played	Cuts Made	Wins	Top-5s	Top-10s	Top-25s	Scoring Average	Money
1966	1	4	1	0	0	1	1	72.50	

Best finish for 1966: T-8th at the U.S. Open

1967	2	6	1	0	0	0	0	76.33	

Best finish for 1967: T-53rd at the Masters

1969	21	68	14	0	0	0	3	72.44	$8,428

Best finish for 1969: T-15th at the Greater Milwaukee Open

1970	35	121	27	0	0	7	16	71.60	$48,653

Best finish for 1970: T-6th at the Monsanto Open, Tallahassee Open & Dow Jones Open Invitational

1971	33	117	27	1	5	9	14	71.50	$87,007

Best finish for 1971: Win at the Southern Open

1972	30	110	25	1	3	6	15	72.05	$86,475

Best finish for 1972: Win at the Sea Pines Heritage Classic

1973	26	95	22	1	5	11	18	70.97	$134,191

Best finish for 1973: Win at the U.S. Open

1974	22	82	20	8	11	13	15	70.29	$349,902

Best finish for 1974: Win at the Bing Crosby Pro-Am, Phoenix Open, Dean Martin Tucson Open, Sea Pines Heritage Classic, Tournament of Champions, Westchester Classic, World Open & Kaiser International Open

1975	22	85	20	4	9	12	16	70.22	$234,626

Best finish for 1975: Win at the Phoenix Open, Dean Martin Tucson Open, Bob Hope Chrysler Classic, & Kaiser International Open

1976	18	71	17	3	4	8	13	71.31	$149,388

Best finish for 1976: Win at the NBC Tucson Open, Bob Hope Chrysler Classic & British Open

1977	23	79	15	0	3	5	8	71.87	$66,072

Best finish for 1977: T-2nd at the Western Open & Southern Open

1978	16	48	8	0	0	1	2	73.23	$17,772

Best finish for 1978: T-6th at the U.S. Open

1979	21	67	12	0	1	2	4	72.28	$52,311

Best finish for 1979: 2nd at the Colgate Hall Of Fame Classic

1980	17	65	15	1	2	6	11	71.14	$128,557

Best finish for 1980: Win at the Jackie Gleason's Inverrary Classic

1981	18	66	16	2	3	5	11	70.94	$194,896

Best finish for 1981: Win at the Joe Garagiola Tucson Open & Glen CampbellLos Angeles Open

1982	18	66	15	1	5	6	9	70.95	$174,305

Best finish for 1982: Win at the Wickes/Andy Williams San Diego Open

1983	19	71	16	1	4	5	11	70.96	$230,786

Best finish for 1983: Win at the Honda Inverrary Classic

1984	16	56	12	0	3	5	8	71.18	$144,300

Best finish for 1984: 3rd at the Bob Hope Chrysler Classic

1985	19	70	17	0	1	5	10	71.36	$127,616

Best finish for 1985: T-4th at the Canadian Open

1986	16	51	10	0	1	1	4	71.31	$73,044

Best finish for 1986: T-3rd at the Memorial Tournament

1987	17	49	8	1	1	1	1	71.98	$139,998

Best finish for 1987: Win at the AT&T Pebble Beach Pro-Am

1988	15	44	9	0	0	0	2	71.95	$36,748

Best finish for 1988: T-17th at the Canadian Open

1989	12	37	8	0	0	1	2	71.32	$71,614

Best finish for 1989: T-9th at the Nissan Los Angeles Open

1990	1	4	1	0	0	0	1	72.75	$8,900

Best finish for 1990: T-21st at the AT&T Pebble Beach Pro-Am

1991	2	6	1	0	0	0	0	73.83	$3,872

Best finish for 1991: T-47th at the AT&T Pebble Beach Pro-Am

1992	2	7	1	0	0	0	0	71.86	$4,312

Best finish for 1992: T-67th at the Northern Telecom Open

1993	1	3	0	0	0	0	0	74.33	
1994	4	10	1	1	1	1	1	75.40	$227,500

Best finish for 1994: Win at the AT&T Pebble Beach Pro-Am

1995	2	6	0	0	0	0	0	73.00	

Year	Starts	Rounds Played	Cuts Made	Wins	Top-5s	Top-10s	Top-25s	Scoring Average	Money
1997	1	3	0	0	0	0	0	73.67	
Period Totals	Starts	Rounds Played	Cuts Made	Wins	Top-5s	Top-10s	Top-25s	Scoring Average	Money
	450	1567	339	25	62	111	196	71.51	$2,801,275

Lindy Miller

Year	Starts	Rounds Played	Cuts Made	Wins	Top-5s	Top-10s	Top-25s	Scoring Average	Money
1975	1	2	0	0	0	0	0	78.50	
1977	2	8	2	0	0	0	0	73.50	

Best finish for 1977: T-48th at the Colonial National Invitational

1978	3	10	2	0	0	0	1	72.50	

Best finish for 1978: T-16th at the Masters

1979	32	101	19	0	1	3	6	72.58	$45,454

Best finish for 1979: 2nd at the Tallahassee Open

1980	30	86	14	0	1	1	3	72.49	$33,946

Best finish for 1980: 4th at the Sammy Davis, Jr. - Greater Hartford Open

1981	18	47	5	0	0	0	2	72.94	$7,533

Best finish for 1981: T-17th at the Tallahassee Open

1982	25	80	15	0	0	0	3	72.13	$21,678

Best finish for 1982: T-16th at the Southern Open

1983	28	89	16	0	0	0	3	72.30	$25,399

Best finish for 1983: T-17th at the Hawaiian Open

1984	12	36	6	0	0	1	3	71.94	$16,442

Best finish for 1984: T-8th at the Miller High-Life Quad Cities Open

1985	3	8	1	0	0	0	1	71.50	$7,750

Best finish for 1985: T-12th at the Southwest Golf Classic

1986	2	4	0	0	0	0	0	74.00	
1987	1	4	1	0	0	0	0	77.75	$1,600

Best finish for 1987: 71st at the PGA Championship

1988	1	2	0	0	0	0	0	75.50	
1989	1	2	0	0	0	0	0	75.00	$1,000
1991	3	10	2	0	0	0	0	72.10	$7,378

Best finish for 1991: T-37th at the GTE Byron Nelson Classic

1999	1	2	0	0	0	0	0	73.00	
2005	1	2	0	0	0	0	0	75.50	
Period Totals	Starts	Rounds Played	Cuts Made	Wins	Top-5s	Top-10s	Top-25s	Scoring Average	Money
	164	493	83	0	2	5	22	72.53	$168,180

Jon Mills

Year	Starts	Rounds Played	Cuts Made	Wins	Top-5s	Top-10s	Top-25s	Scoring Average	Money
2001	2	4	0	0	0	0	0	74.50	
2002	1	2	0	0	0	0	0	73.00	
2003	1	4	1	0	0	0	0	71.50	$8,988

Best finish for 2003: T-60th at the Bell Canadian Open

2004	1	2	0	0	0	0	0	74.00	
2005	1	2	0	0	0	0	0	73.50	
2006	27	66	6	0	0	0	0	72.09	$65,494

Best finish for 2006: T-42nd at the AT&T Pebble Beach National Pro-Am

2007	1	2	0	0	0	0	0	75.50	$2,000
2008	32	95	16	0	0	0	4	71.62	$489,510

Best finish for 2008: T-13th at the Puerto Rico Open

Period Totals	Starts	Rounds Played	Cuts Made	Wins	Top-5s	Top-10s	Top-25s	Scoring Average	Money
	66	177	23	0	0	0	4	71.97	$565,993

Bobby Mitchell

Year	Starts	Rounds Played	Cuts Made	Wins	Top-5s	Top-10s	Top-25s	Scoring Average	Money
1965	1	2	0	0	0	0	0	75.00	
1966	10	22	1	0	0	0	1	75.86	$1,194

Best finish for 1966: T-23rd at the Canadian Open

1967	19	58	10	0	0	0	0	73.55	$3,274

Best finish for 1967: T-28th at the "500" Festival Open

1968	26	93	21	0	3	4	9	71.91	$19,754

Best finish for 1968: T-2nd at the Cajun Classic

1969	37	131	29	0	3	4	10	72.30	$33,437

Best finish for 1969: T-3rd at the Greater New Orleans Open

1970	36	124	26	0	1	3	10	72.24	$31,982

Best finish for 1970: 2nd at the Azalea Open Invitational

1971	32	111	26	1	2	3	13	71.73	$67,240

Best finish for 1971: Win at the Cleveland Open

1972	30	108	24	1	5	7	14	72.10	$110,151

Best finish for 1972: Win at the Tournament of Champions

1973	36	108	17	0	1	3	8	72.81	$41,396

Best finish for 1973: T-5th at the USI Classic

Year	Starts	Rounds Played	Cuts Made	Wins	Top-5s	Top-10s	Top-25s	Scoring Average	Money
1974	35	122	26	0	0	4	12	72.09	$41,222

Best finish for 1974: T-6th at the Dean Martin Tucson Open

1975	28	95	20	0	1	3	7	72.28	$29,362

Best finish for 1975: T-3rd at the Sahara Invitational

1976	27	76	14	0	1	1	3	73.42	$16,829

Best finish for 1976: T-5th at the Doral-Eastern Open

1977	18	46	6	0	0	0	1	74.43	$2,615

Best finish for 1977: T-25th at the Southern Open

1978	16	35	2	0	0	0	1	74.09	$1,802

Best finish for 1978: T-14th at the Buick Goodwrench Open

1979	12	25	1	0	0	0	0	74.40	$386

Best finish for 1979: T-73rd at the Southern Open

1980	4	7	1	0	0	0	1	73.29	$1,760

Best finish for 1980: T-24th at the Pensacola Open

1981	9	17	1	0	0	0	0	75.12	$370

Best finish for 1981: T-52nd at the Tallahassee Open

1982	11	27	3	0	0	0	0	73.74	$1,550

Best finish for 1982: T-55th at the Southern Open

1983	3	6	0	0	0	0	0	74.50	
1984	7	15	1	0	0	0	0	76.27	$1,581

Best finish for 1984: 88th at the LaJet Golf Classic

1985	7	15	0	0	0	0	0	76.20	$544
1986	9	20	2	0	0	0	0	74.20	$1,648

Best finish for 1986: T-51st at the Deposit Guaranty Golf Classic

1987	9	23	3	0	0	0	0	73.65	$2,385

Best finish for 1987: T-64th at the Southern Open

1988	11	24	1	0	0	0	0	75.38	$1,020

Best finish for 1988: T-67th at the Centel Classic

1989	8	14	0	0	0	0	0	76.29	
1990	5	9	0	0	0	0	0	76.11	
1991	3	6	0	0	0	0	0	77.83	
1992	2	4	0	0	0	0	0	74.25	
1994	2	4	0	0	0	0	0	77.25	
1996	2	2	0	0	0	0	0	80.50	
1998	1	2	0	0	0	0	0	81.50	
1999	1	2	0	0	0	0	0	77.00	
Period Totals	Starts	Rounds Played	Cuts Made	Wins	Top-5s	Top-10s	Top-25s	Scoring Average	Money
	457	1353	235	2	17	32	90	72.98	$411,503

Jeff Mitchell

Year	Starts	Rounds Played	Cuts Made	Wins	Top-5s	Top-10s	Top-25s	Scoring Average	Money
1977	21	68	12	0	1	1	2	72.85	$23,796

Best finish for 1977: 3rd at the Colgate Hall Of Fame Golf Classic

1978	24	69	10	0	0	0	2	73.09	$9,148

Best finish for 1978: T-16th at the Ed McMahon Quad City Open

1979	22	71	13	0	1	1	7	72.25	$38,032

Best finish for 1979: 4th at the American Optical Classic

1980	30	90	16	1	2	4	6	72.26	$111,717

Best finish for 1980: Win at the Phoenix Open

1981	32	103	21	0	3	4	9	71.74	$73,864

Best finish for 1981: 3rd at the Southern Open

1982	28	89	16	0	1	1	3	72.11	$31,591

Best finish for 1982: T-5th at the Miller High-Life Quad Cities Open

1983	27	73	7	0	0	0	0	73.32	$5,927

Best finish for 1983: T-28th at the Miller High-Life Quad Cities Open

1984	28	82	12	0	0	0	4	72.99	$21,995

Best finish for 1984: T-18th at the B.C. Open

1985	2	4	0	0	0	0	0	74.25	
1986	2	4	0	0	0	0	0	76.00	
1987	1	2	0	0	0	0	0	74.00	
1988	1	2	0	0	0	0	0	74.50	
Period Totals	Starts	Rounds Played	Cuts Made	Wins	Top-5s	Top-10s	Top-25s	Scoring Average	Money
	218	657	107	1	8	11	33	72.56	$316,071

Mike Mitchell

Year	Starts	Rounds Played	Cuts Made	Wins	Top-5s	Top-10s	Top-25s	Scoring Average	Money
1967	1	4	1	0	0	0	0	75.75	

Best finish for 1967: T-71st at the Houston Championship International

1969	2	6	1	0	0	0	1	73.83	$494

Best finish for 1969: T-12th at the West End Classic

1970	2	5	0	0	0	0	0	75.80	
1972	11	24	0	0	0	0	0	76.08	

Year	Starts	Rounds Played	Cuts Made	Wins	Top-5s	Top-10s	Top-25s	Scoring Average	Money
1973	1	2	0	0	0	0	0	76.00	
1974	13	27	2	0	0	0	0	74.04	$820

Best finish for 1974: T-55th at the Monsanto Open

1975	20	59	8	0	0	0	0	73.58	$2,198

Best finish for 1975: T-42nd at the Phoenix Open

1976	13	35	4	0	0	0	0	73.17	$2,001

Best finish for 1976: T-42nd at the Bob Hope Chrysler Classic & Canadian Open

Period Totals	Starts	Rounds Played	Cuts Made	Wins	Top-5s	Top-10s	Top-25s	Scoring Average	Money
	63	162	16	0	0	0	1	74.10	$5,513

Gene Mitchell, Jr.

Year	Starts	Rounds Played	Cuts Made	Wins	Top-5s	Top-10s	Top-25s	Scoring Average	Money
1960	1	4	1	0	0	0	0	72.00	$077

Best finish for 1960: T-30th at the Orange County Open Invitational

1964	20	42	3	0	0	0	0	75.24	$250

Best finish for 1964: T-33rd at the Oklahoma City Open

1965	15	43	6	0	0	0	0	73.42	$518

Best finish for 1965: T-40th at the Texas Open

1966	1	2	0	0	0	0	0	73.00	
1967	2	6	0	0	0	0	0	74.33	
1968	2	6	1	0	0	0	0	76.00	$365

Best finish for 1968: T-70th at the PGA Championship

1970	1	2	0	0	0	0	0	78.00	

Period Totals	Starts	Rounds Played	Cuts Made	Wins	Top-5s	Top-10s	Top-25s	Scoring Average	Money
	42	105	11	0	0	0	0	74.37	$1,210

Katsumasa Miyamoto

Year	Starts	Rounds Played	Cuts Made	Wins	Top-5s	Top-10s	Top-25s	Scoring Average	Money
1995	1	4	1	0	0	0	0	73.00	$3,075

Best finish for 1995: T-65th at the Kmart Greater Greensboro Open

1999	22	60	7	0	0	0	3	72.02	$154,402

Best finish for 1999: T-11th at the Buick Invitational

2002	2	4	0	0	0	0	0	74.50	

Period Totals	Starts	Rounds Played	Cuts Made	Wins	Top-5s	Top-10s	Top-25s	Scoring Average	Money
	25	68	8	0	0	0	3	72.22	$157,477

Hirofumi Miyase

Year	Starts	Rounds Played	Cuts Made	Wins	Top-5s	Top-10s	Top-25s	Scoring Average	Money
1994	2	4	0	0	0	0	0	77.00	
1997	1	2	0	0	0	0	0	77.00	$1,173
2000	1	2	0	0	0	0	0	72.50	$1,976
2001	1	0	1	0	0	0	0		$25,000

Best finish for 2001: T-33rd at the Accenture Match Play Championship

2003	1	2	0	0	0	0	0	77.00	$3,974
2004	27	63	5	0	0	1	1	72.95	$162,120

Best finish for 2004: T-9th at the FedEx St. Jude Classic

Period Totals	Starts	Rounds Played	Cuts Made	Wins	Top-5s	Top-10s	Top-25s	Scoring Average	Money
	33	73	6	0	0	1	1	73.38	$194,242

Larry Mize

Year	Starts	Rounds Played	Cuts Made	Wins	Top-5s	Top-10s	Top-25s	Scoring Average	Money
1980	2	6	1	0	0	0	0	71.17	$1,189

Best finish for 1980: T-30th at the Southern Open

1981	2	4	0	0	0	0	0	73.50	$600
1982	27	79	13	0	0	1	4	72.66	$29,387

Best finish for 1982: T-9th at the Pensacola Open

1983	35	124	25	1	2	3	7	71.81	$146,325

Best finish for 1983: Win at the Danny Thomas Memphis Classic

1984	32	116	26	0	2	6	13	71.33	$173,331

Best finish for 1984: T-3rd at the Phoenix Open

1985	29	104	25	0	3	8	17	70.59	$231,041

Best finish for 1985: T-2nd at the Kemper Open

1986	25	90	23	0	4	6	11	70.87	$317,763

Best finish for 1986: T-2nd at the Tournament Players Championship, Kemper Open & B.C. Open

1987	25	84	17	1	6	9	15	70.75	$570,140

Best finish for 1987: Win at the Masters

1988	25	84	17	0	2	3	10	71.21	$189,587

Best finish for 1988: T-4th at the Federal Express St. Jude Classic

1989	26	99	23	0	2	7	12	71.09	$292,108

Best finish for 1989: T-5th at the GTE Byron Nelson Classic & NEC World Series of Golf

1990	25	91	21	0	6	7	16	70.23	$677,475

Best finish for 1990: T-2nd at the MCI Heritage Classic, BellSouth Atlanta Golf Classic & Anheuser-Busch Golf Classic

Year	Starts	Rounds Played	Cuts Made	Wins	Top-5s	Top-10s	Top-25s	Scoring Average	Money
1991	26	93	22	0	1	4	12	70.60	$281,069

Best finish for 1991: T-5th at the International

| 1992 | 25 | 83 | 18 | 0 | 1 | 5 | 10 | 70.69 | $318,628 |

Best finish for 1992: T-3rd at the BellSouth Classic

| 1993 | 23 | 80 | 18 | 2 | 3 | 7 | 11 | 70.54 | $737,986 |

Best finish for 1993: Win at the Northern Telecom Open & Buick Open

| 1994 | 23 | 79 | 18 | 0 | 2 | 4 | 10 | 70.84 | $418,349 |

Best finish for 1994: 3rd at the Masters

| 1995 | 22 | 70 | 15 | 0 | 1 | 3 | 7 | 70.93 | $294,313 |

Best finish for 1995: T-5th at the FedEx St. Jude Classic

| 1996 | 23 | 73 | 15 | 0 | 1 | 3 | 7 | 71.15 | $318,468 |

Best finish for 1996: T-4th at the United Airlines Hawaiian Open

| 1997 | 21 | 69 | 15 | 0 | 0 | 1 | 6 | 71.38 | $246,773 |

Best finish for 1997: T-7th at the Sprint International

| 1998 | 24 | 81 | 17 | 0 | 1 | 2 | 6 | 70.86 | $470,794 |

Best finish for 1998: T-2nd at the Canon Greater Hartford Open

| 1999 | 21 | 70 | 15 | 0 | 0 | 2 | 9 | 71.03 | $386,554 |

Best finish for 1999: T-10th at the Shell Houston Open & Westin Texas Open

| 2000 | 21 | 69 | 15 | 0 | 1 | 1 | 5 | 70.99 | $425,624 |

Best finish for 2000: T-3rd at the MCI Classic

| 2001 | 24 | 74 | 13 | 0 | 1 | 1 | 2 | 71.05 | $445,179 |

Best finish for 2001: T-2nd at the Marconi Pennsylvania Classic

| 2002 | 10 | 22 | 1 | 0 | 0 | 0 | 0 | 73.09 | $12,634 |

Best finish for 2002: T-48th at the Greater Milwaukee Open

| 2003 | 19 | 46 | 5 | 0 | 0 | 0 | 1 | 72.63 | $99,713 |

Best finish for 2003: T-24th at the Wachovia Championship

| 2004 | 13 | 37 | 6 | 0 | 0 | 0 | 1 | 71.76 | $141,020 |

Best finish for 2004: T-21st at the Honda Classic

| 2005 | 18 | 50 | 9 | 0 | 0 | 0 | 2 | 71.60 | $211,969 |

Best finish for 2005: T-18th at the Buick Open

| 2006 | 18 | 51 | 8 | 0 | 0 | 1 | 2 | 71.80 | $217,971 |

Best finish for 2006: T-6th at the B.C. Open

| 2007 | 12 | 31 | 3 | 0 | 0 | 1 | 1 | 72.74 | $105,740 |

Best finish for 2007: T-9th at the Mayakoba Golf Classic

| 2008 | 16 | 46 | 7 | 0 | 0 | 1 | 2 | 72.17 | $190,804 |

Best finish for 2008: T-10th at the Puerto Rico Open

Period Totals	Starts	Rounds Played	Cuts Made	Wins	Top-5s	Top-10s	Top-25s	Scoring Average	Money
	612	2005	411	4	39	86	199	71.20	$7,952,532

Yoshinori Mizumaki

Year	Starts	Rounds Played	Cuts Made	Wins	Top-5s	Top-10s	Top-25s	Scoring Average	Money
1992	2	2	0	0	0	0	0	73.00	
1993	3	10	2	0	0	0	0	73.00	$12,836

Best finish for 1993: T-27th at the British Open

| 1994 | 18 | 61 | 13 | 0 | 1 | 2 | 3 | 71.15 | $168,450 |

Best finish for 1994: T-2nd at the GTE Byron Nelson Classic

| 1995 | 15 | 43 | 7 | 0 | 0 | 0 | 1 | 72.21 | $28,292 |

Best finish for 1995: T-22nd at the United Airlines Hawaiian Open

| 1996 | 4 | 12 | 2 | 0 | 0 | 0 | 0 | 73.50 | $5,232 |

Best finish for 1996: T-57th at the Nissan Open

| 1997 | 2 | 6 | 1 | 0 | 0 | 0 | 0 | 73.50 | $16,888 |

Best finish for 1997: T-36th at the NEC World Series of Golf

| 1998 | 3 | 8 | 1 | 0 | 0 | 0 | 0 | 72.25 | $5,924 |

Best finish for 1998: T-54th at the Tucson Chrysler Classic

| 2000 | 4 | 14 | 3 | 0 | 0 | 0 | 0 | 71.36 | $20,848 |

Best finish for 2000: T-51st at the Reno-Tahoe Open

| 2001 | 1 | 4 | 1 | 0 | 0 | 0 | 0 | 73.00 | $5,520 |

Best finish for 2001: 78th at the Touchstone Energy Tucson Open

Period Totals	Starts	Rounds Played	Cuts Made	Wins	Top-5s	Top-10s	Top-25s	Scoring Average	Money
	52	160	30	0	1	2	4	71.96	$263,990

Kris Moe

Year	Starts	Rounds Played	Cuts Made	Wins	Top-5s	Top-10s	Top-25s	Scoring Average	Money
1985	1	4	1	0	0	0	1	72.25	$5,426

Best finish for 1985: T-25th at the British Open

| 1986 | 22 | 54 | 6 | 0 | 0 | 0 | 0 | 74.26 | $7,104 |

Best finish for 1986: T-43rd at the Deposit Guaranty Golf Classic

2002	2	5	0	0	0	0	0	77.60	
2003	1	3	0	0	0	0	0	76.33	
2004	1	3	0	0	0	0	0	73.33	

Period Totals	Starts	Rounds Played	Cuts Made	Wins	Top-5s	Top-10s	Top-25s	Scoring Average	Money
	27	69	7	0	0	0	1	74.43	$12,530

Ed Moehling

Year	Starts	Rounds Played	Cuts Made	Wins	Top-5s	Top-10s	Top-25s	Scoring Average	Money
1963	2	8	2	0	0	0	0	72.13	$260

Best finish for 1963: T-31st at the Waco Turner Open Invitational

1964	15	37	4	0	0	0	1	74.05	$1,783

Best finish for 1964: T-15th at the Seattle Open

1965	6	16	2	0	0	0	0	75.75	

Best finish for 1965: T-61st at the Pensacola Open

1966	5	11	0	0	0	0	0	75.45	$300
1968	4	10	1	0	0	0	0	73.20	$1,050

Best finish for 1968: T-36th at the Phoenix Open Invitational

1969	7	20	3	0	0	0	2	72.20	$3,037

Best finish for 1969: 12th at the Michigan Golf Classic

1970	4	8	0	0	0	0	0	73.50	
1972	9	24	3	0	0	0	0	74.63	$928

Best finish for 1972: T-29th at the Liggett Meyers Open

1973	6	10	0	0	0	0	0	75.30	
Period Totals	**Starts**	**Rounds Played**	**Cuts Made**	**Wins**	**Top-5s**	**Top-10s**	**Top-25s**	**Scoring Average**	**Money**
	58	144	15	0	0	0	3	74.08	$7,358

Brian Mogg

Year	Starts	Rounds Played	Cuts Made	Wins	Top-5s	Top-10s	Top-25s	Scoring Average	Money
1986	30	75	7	0	0	0	0	73.44	$9,352

Best finish for 1986: T-28th at the Shearson Lehman/Andy Williams San Diego

1987	3	6	0	0	0	0	0	73.17	
1988	27	69	7	0	1	1	2	72.46	$34,092

Best finish for 1988: 2nd at the Deposit Guaranty Golf Classic

1989	4	10	1	0	0	0	0	71.20	$1,800

Best finish for 1989: T-42nd at the Chattanooga Classic

1990	2	6	1	0	0	0	0	70.83	$1,386

Best finish for 1990: T-35th at the Deposit Guaranty

1994	1	2	0	0	0	0	0	73.00	
1995	1	2	0	0	0	0	0	75.00	$1,000
Period Totals	**Starts**	**Rounds Played**	**Cuts Made**	**Wins**	**Top-5s**	**Top-10s**	**Top-25s**	**Scoring Average**	**Money**
	68	170	16	0	1	1	2	72.82	$47,630

Bryce Molder

Year	Starts	Rounds Played	Cuts Made	Wins	Top-5s	Top-10s	Top-25s	Scoring Average	Money
1999	1	2	0	0	0	0	0	75.50	
2000	1	2	0	0	0	0	0	72.00	
2001	7	20	3	0	1	1	1	71.35	$211,105

Best finish for 2001: 3rd at the Reno-Tahoe Open

2002	22	63	10	0	0	1	4	71.14	$348,028

Best finish for 2002: T-9th at the COMPAQ Classic of New Orleans

2003	3	7	0	0	0	0	0	75.29	$1,000
2004	3	9	1	0	0	0	0	73.33	$10,716

Best finish for 2004: T-54th at the FedEx St. Jude Classic

2007	21	56	7	0	0	1	2	72.64	$257,593

Best finish for 2007: T-6th at the Children's Miracle network Classic

2008	1	2	0	0	0	0	0	71.50	
Period Totals	**Starts**	**Rounds Played**	**Cuts Made**	**Wins**	**Top-5s**	**Top-10s**	**Top-25s**	**Scoring Average**	**Money**
	59	161	21	0	1	3	7	72.06	$828,442

John Molenda

Year	Starts	Rounds Played	Cuts Made	Wins	Top-5s	Top-10s	Top-25s	Scoring Average	Money
1967	14	31	3	0	0	0	0	74.90	

Best finish for 1967: T-55th at the "500" Festival Open

1968	10	23	1	0	0	0	0	74.43	

Best finish for 1968: T-58th at the Rebel Yell Open

1969	1	4	1	0	0	0	0	71.00	$240

Best finish for 1969: T-47th at the Michigan Golf Classic

Period Totals	**Starts**	**Rounds Played**	**Cuts Made**	**Wins**	**Top-5s**	**Top-10s**	**Top-25s**	**Scoring Average**	**Money**
	25	58	5	0	0	0	0	74.45	$240

Florentino Molina

Year	Starts	Rounds Played	Cuts Made	Wins	Top-5s	Top-10s	Top-25s	Scoring Average	Money
1964	1	2	0	0	0	0	0	77.00	
1970	1	4	1	0	0	0	0	74.25	$420

Best finish for 1970: T-32nd at the British Open

1971	1	2	0	0	0	0	0	77.00	
1974	5	12	1	0	0	0	1	74.42	$1,753

Best finish for 1974: T-22nd at the Pleasant Valley Classic

Year	Starts	Rounds Played	Cuts Made	Wins	Top-5s	Top-10s	Top-25s	Scoring Average	Money
1975	16	52	10	0	0	1	1	72.88	$8,497

Best finish for 1975: T-7th at the Western Open

| 1976 | 15 | 44 | 7 | 0 | 0 | 0 | 2 | 72.80 | $6,895 |

Best finish for 1976: T-12th at the IVB - Bicentennial Golf Classic

| 1977 | 16 | 48 | 8 | 0 | 1 | 1 | 1 | 72.85 | $13,040 |

Best finish for 1977: 4th at the B.C. Open

| 1978 | 14 | 41 | 6 | 0 | 1 | 1 | 3 | 73.34 | $15,788 |

Best finish for 1978: T-5th at the Greater Greensboro Open

| 1979 | 8 | 20 | 2 | 0 | 0 | 0 | 0 | 72.95 | $1,923 |

Best finish for 1979: T-34th at the Greater Greensboro Open

| 1980 | 3 | 6 | 0 | 0 | 0 | 0 | 0 | 74.17 | |
| 1981 | 1 | 4 | 1 | 0 | 0 | 0 | 0 | 73.25 | $1,180 |

Best finish for 1981: T-39th at the British Open

Period Totals	Starts	Rounds Played	Cuts Made	Wins	Top-5s	Top-10s	Top-25s	Scoring Average	Money
	81	235	36	0	2	3	8	73.16	$49,496

Lloyd Monroe

Year	Starts	Rounds Played	Cuts Made	Wins	Top-5s	Top-10s	Top-25s	Scoring Average	Money
1963	1	4	1	0	0	0	0	72.00	

Best finish for 1963: T-46th at the Insurance City Open Invitational

| 1965 | 1 | 2 | 0 | 0 | 0 | 0 | 0 | 76.00 | |
| 1968 | 2 | 6 | 1 | 0 | 0 | 0 | 0 | 72.50 | $994 |

Best finish for 1968: T-28th at the Thunderbird Classic

| 1969 | 3 | 10 | 2 | 0 | 0 | 0 | 0 | 74.70 | $367 |

Best finish for 1969: T-62nd at the Heritage Golf Classic

| 1970 | 3 | 10 | 2 | 0 | 0 | 0 | 0 | 71.80 | $2,158 |

Best finish for 1970: T-31st at the AVCO Classic

| 1972 | 11 | 28 | 2 | 0 | 0 | 1 | 1 | 73.96 | $4,150 |

Best finish for 1972: T-10th at the Monsanto Open

| 1973 | 12 | 33 | 3 | 0 | 0 | 0 | 0 | 74.21 | $1,430 |

Best finish for 1973: T-43rd at the Bob Hope Chrysler Classic

1974	2	4	0	0	0	0	0	77.50	$500
1975	2	4	0	0	0	0	0	75.00	$500
1976	1	4	1	0	0	0	0	72.75	$330

Best finish for 1976: T-65th at the Pleasant Valley Classic

| 1979 | 1 | 2 | 0 | 0 | 0 | 0 | 0 | 75.00 | $350 |
| 1982 | 2 | 6 | 1 | 0 | 0 | 0 | 0 | 74.83 | $1,300 |

Best finish for 1982: T-62nd at the U.S. Open

Period Totals	Starts	Rounds Played	Cuts Made	Wins	Top-5s	Top-10s	Top-25s	Scoring Average	Money
	41	113	13	0	0	1	1	73.98	$12,079

Colin Montgomerie

Year	Starts	Rounds Played	Cuts Made	Wins	Top-5s	Top-10s	Top-25s	Scoring Average	Money
1990	1	4	1	0	0	0	0	71.50	$6,733

Best finish for 1990: T-48th at the British Open

| 1991 | 1 | 4 | 1 | 0 | 0 | 0 | 0 | 70.50 | $11,340 |

Best finish for 1991: T-26th at the British Open

| 1992 | 7 | 20 | 3 | 0 | 1 | 1 | 1 | 73.10 | $99,245 |

Best finish for 1992: 3rd at the U.S. Open

| 1993 | 5 | 16 | 4 | 0 | 0 | 0 | 0 | 72.50 | $20,116 |

Best finish for 1993: T-33rd at the U.S. Open

| 1994 | 6 | 21 | 4 | 0 | 1 | 3 | 3 | 70.95 | $263,928 |

Best finish for 1994: T-2nd at the U.S. Open

| 1995 | 8 | 30 | 7 | 0 | 1 | 1 | 4 | 71.17 | $336,654 |

Best finish for 1995: 2nd at the PGA Championship

| 1996 | 7 | 24 | 5 | 0 | 1 | 3 | 4 | 71.25 | $423,318 |

Best finish for 1996: T-2nd at the Players Championship

| 1997 | 9 | 36 | 9 | 0 | 2 | 3 | 8 | 70.86 | $578,991 |

Best finish for 1997: 2nd at the U.S. Open

| 1998 | 8 | 26 | 5 | 0 | 1 | 3 | 4 | 71.62 | $323,468 |

Best finish for 1998: 3rd at the Honda Classic

| 1999 | 12 | 44 | 12 | 0 | 0 | 1 | 6 | 72.25 | $484,451 |

Best finish for 1999: T-6th at the PGA Championship

| 2000 | 9 | 32 | 9 | 0 | 1 | 2 | 5 | 71.56 | $653,044 |

Best finish for 2000: T-3rd at the Players Championship

| 2001 | 7 | 25 | 5 | 0 | 1 | 1 | 2 | 71.56 | $407,762 |

Best finish for 2001: 4th at the WGC-NEC Invitational

| 2002 | 10 | 29 | 7 | 0 | 0 | 0 | 2 | 72.55 | $265,992 |

Best finish for 2002: T-14th at the Masters

| 2003 | 12 | 28 | 5 | 0 | 0 | 0 | 1 | 72.96 | $169,786 |

Best finish for 2003: T-23rd at the WGC-NEC Invitational

Year	Starts	Rounds Played	Cuts Made	Wins	Top-5s	Top-10s	Top-25s	Scoring Average	Money
2004	6	18	5	0	0	1	2	72.94	$250,979

Best finish for 2004: T-9th at the WGC-Accenture Match Play Championship

| 2005 | 6 | 20 | 5 | 0 | 3 | 4 | 4 | 70.25 | $1,452,736 |

Best finish for 2005: 2nd at the British Open

| 2006 | 8 | 18 | 3 | 0 | 1 | 1 | 2 | 72.89 | $647,209 |

Best finish for 2006: T-2nd at the U.S. Open

| 2007 | 9 | 24 | 5 | 0 | 0 | 0 | 1 | 73.79 | $225,566 |

Best finish for 2007: T-17th at the WGC-Accenture Match Play Championship

| 2008 | 7 | 18 | 4 | 0 | 0 | 1 | 1 | 74.67 | $221,534 |

Best finish for 2008: T-9th at the WGC-Accenture Match Play Championship

Period Totals	Starts	Rounds Played	Cuts Made	Wins	Top-5s	Top-10s	Top-25s	Scoring Average	Money
	138	437	99	0	13	25	50	72.05	$6,842,851

Jack Montgomery

Year	Starts	Rounds Played	Cuts Made	Wins	Top-5s	Top-10s	Top-25s	Scoring Average	Money
1964	1	4	1	0	0	0	0	74.50	

Best finish for 1964: T-51st at the Cajun Classic

| 1965 | 26 | 85 | 15 | 0 | 0 | 0 | 4 | 73.18 | $6,206 |

Best finish for 1965: T-14th at the Buick Open

| 1966 | 16 | 46 | 7 | 0 | 0 | 0 | 2 | 73.87 | $2,524 |

Best finish for 1966: T-17th at the Greater New Orleans Open Invitational

| 1967 | 19 | 56 | 9 | 0 | 1 | 1 | 2 | 73.48 | $7,018 |

Best finish for 1967: 2nd at the Cajun Classic

| 1968 | 29 | 101 | 21 | 0 | 3 | 6 | 15 | 71.59 | $41,673 |

Best finish for 1968: T-2nd at the Phoenix Open Invitational

| 1969 | 30 | 113 | 27 | 0 | 2 | 2 | 8 | 72.09 | $23,509 |

Best finish for 1969: 3rd at the Bob Hope Desert Classic

| 1970 | 24 | 77 | 13 | 0 | 1 | 1 | 6 | 72.18 | $17,613 |

Best finish for 1970: T-4th at the Kaiser International Open

| 1971 | 23 | 67 | 10 | 0 | 0 | 0 | 3 | 73.43 | $6,431 |

Best finish for 1971: T-16th at the Hawaiian Open

| 1972 | 21 | 55 | 6 | 0 | 0 | 1 | 2 | 74.07 | $6,012 |

Best finish for 1972: T-9th at the Tucson Open

| 1973 | 19 | 45 | 5 | 0 | 0 | 0 | 1 | 73.93 | $2,600 |

Best finish for 1973: T-23rd at the Dean Martin Tucson Open

| 1976 | 1 | 2 | 0 | 0 | 0 | 0 | 0 | 77.00 | |
| 1978 | 1 | 2 | 0 | 0 | 0 | 0 | 0 | 79.00 | |

Period Totals	Starts	Rounds Played	Cuts Made	Wins	Top-5s	Top-10s	Top-25s	Scoring Average	Money
	210	653	114	0	7	11	43	72.89	$113,586

Ray Montgomery

Year	Starts	Rounds Played	Cuts Made	Wins	Top-5s	Top-10s	Top-25s	Scoring Average	Money
1964	9	13	0	0	0	0	0	75.46	
1965	4	11	1	0	0	0	0	76.18	

Best finish for 1965: T-63rd at the Cajun Classic

1966	4	8	0	0	0	0	0	76.00	
1967	1	2	0	0	0	0	0	75.00	
1969	1	4	1	0	0	0	0	75.25	$070

Best finish for 1969: T-44th at the West End Classic

1970	3	6	0	0	0	0	0	77.33	$500
1971	1	2	0	0	0	0	0	72.50	
1974	3	6	0	0	0	0	0	75.00	

Period Totals	Starts	Rounds Played	Cuts Made	Wins	Top-5s	Top-10s	Top-25s	Scoring Average	Money
	26	52	2	0	0	0	0	75.71	$570

Eric Monti

Year	Starts	Rounds Played	Cuts Made	Wins	Top-5s	Top-10s	Top-25s	Scoring Average	Money
1958	4	14	3	0	0	0	1	72.71	$891

Best finish for 1958: T-20th at the PGA Championship

| 1959 | 5 | 19 | 5 | 1 | 1 | 1 | 2 | 71.42 | $3,421 |

Best finish for 1959: Win at the Hesperia Open Invitational

| 1960 | 5 | 18 | 4 | 0 | 0 | 2 | 2 | 73.94 | $2,464 |

Best finish for 1960: T-6th at the Hesperia Open Invitational

| 1961 | 8 | 33 | 8 | 1 | 2 | 3 | 7 | 70.42 | $9,326 |

Best finish for 1961: Win at the Ontario Open

| 1962 | 8 | 28 | 6 | 0 | 0 | 0 | 1 | 73.46 | $2,643 |

Best finish for 1962: T-12th at the Lucky International Open

| 1963 | 2 | 6 | 2 | 0 | 0 | 0 | 0 | 74.33 | $050 |

Best finish for 1963: T-47th at the Los Angeles Open

| 1964 | 6 | 21 | 3 | 0 | 0 | 0 | 0 | 73.81 | |

Best finish for 1964: T-49th at the Fresno Open

| 1965 | 4 | 13 | 2 | 0 | 0 | 0 | 1 | 74.38 | $925 |

Best finish for 1965: T-21st at the U.S. Open

Year	Starts	Rounds Played	Cuts Made	Wins	Top-5s	Top-10s	Top-25s	Scoring Average	Money
1966	1	2	0	0	0	0	0	79.50	
1967	2	7	0	0	0	0	0	77.00	
1968	1	1	0	0	0	0	0	79.00	
Period Totals	Starts	Rounds Played	Cuts Made	Wins	Top-5s	Top-10s	Top-25s	Scoring Average	Money
	46	162	33	2	3	6	14	73.01	$19,720

Griff Moody

Year	Starts	Rounds Played	Cuts Made	Wins	Top-5s	Top-10s	Top-25s	Scoring Average	Money
1982	3	8	1	0	0	0	0	74.25	$1,098

Best finish for 1982: T-68th at the Southern Open

1983	3	10	2	0	0	0	1	72.40	$6,787

Best finish for 1983: T-20th at the U.S. Open

1984	30	86	11	0	0	0	1	72.86	$21,084

Best finish for 1984: T-19th at the Honda Classic

1985	2	4	0	0	0	0	0	73.50	$600
Period Totals	Starts	Rounds Played	Cuts Made	Wins	Top-5s	Top-10s	Top-25s	Scoring Average	Money
	38	108	14	0	0	0	2	72.94	$29,568

Orville Moody

Year	Starts	Rounds Played	Cuts Made	Wins	Top-5s	Top-10s	Top-25s	Scoring Average	Money
1962	1	2	0	0	0	0	0	76.50	
1967	1	2	0	0	0	0	0	74.00	
1968	27	84	15	0	1	2	5	72.44	$11,587

Best finish for 1968: T-4th at the Kemper Open Invitational

1969	32	111	26	1	4	7	15	73.16	$76,552

Best finish for 1969: Win at the U.S. Open

1970	33	113	25	0	2	6	7	72.11	$46,955

Best finish for 1970: T-2nd at the National 4 Ball Championship PGA Players

1971	31	100	19	0	1	3	5	72.42	$22,972

Best finish for 1971: T-3rd at the Colonial National Invitational

1972	21	63	11	0	0	1	4	73.46	$10,711

Best finish for 1972: T-8th at the Robinson's Fall Golf Classic

1973	26	93	19	0	3	3	8	71.92	$71,822

Best finish for 1973: 2nd at the Bing Crosby Pro-Am, Hawaiian Open & San Antonio Texas Open

1974	17	56	11	0	0	0	4	72.75	$12,680

Best finish for 1974: T-15th at the Bing Crosby Pro-Am & Colonial National Invitational

1975	12	32	4	0	0	0	1	73.69	$3,314

Best finish for 1975: T-25th at the Bob Hope Chrysler Classic

1976	6	20	6	0	0	0	0	73.20	$2,867

Best finish for 1976: T-27th at the Glen CampbellLos Angeles Open

1977	27	81	13	0	0	0	2	72.86	$12,283

Best finish for 1977: T-16th at the Danny Thomas Memphis Classic

1978	29	95	17	0	2	2	10	71.85	$49,936

Best finish for 1978: T-3rd at the Sea Pines Heritage Classic

1979	30	94	19	0	2	2	6	72.44	$52,634

Best finish for 1979: T-3rd at the Houston Open

1980	27	70	9	0	0	0	1	73.60	$14,459

Best finish for 1980: T-13th at the Danny Thomas Memphis Classic

1981	7	21	2	0	0	0	0	73.57	$1,534

Best finish for 1981: T-49th at the LaJet Classic

1982	2	4	0	0	0	0	0	75.25	
1983	20	52	4	0	0	0	1	73.56	$5,928

Best finish for 1983: T-25th at the Bob Hope Chrysler Classic

1984	3	7	0	0	0	0	0	77.29	
1985	3	9	1	0	0	0	0	73.78	$980

Best finish for 1985: 72nd at the Bob Hope Chrysler Classic

Period Totals	Starts	Rounds Played	Cuts Made	Wins	Top-5s	Top-10s	Top-25s	Scoring Average	Money
	355	1109	201	1	15	26	69	72.75	$397,213

Parker Moore

Year	Starts	Rounds Played	Cuts Made	Wins	Top-5s	Top-10s	Top-25s	Scoring Average	Money
1977	2	4	0	0	0	0	0	78.25	$1,500
1978	16	42	5	0	0	0	2	73.40	$7,329

Best finish for 1978: T-15th at the Colgate Hall Of Fame Classic

1979	15	36	3	0	0	1	1	74.08	$8,818

Best finish for 1979: T-9th at the B.C. Open

Period Totals	Starts	Rounds Played	Cuts Made	Wins	Top-5s	Top-10s	Top-25s	Scoring Average	Money
	33	82	8	0	0	1	3	73.94	$17,647

Ryan Moore

Year	Starts	Rounds Played	Cuts Made	Wins	Top-5s	Top-10s	Top-25s	Scoring Average	Money
2002	1	2	0	0	0	0	0	77.50	
2003	1	4	1	0	0	0	0	75.25	

Best finish for 2003: T-45th at the Masters

Year	Starts	Rounds Played	Cuts Made	Wins	Top-5s	Top-10s	Top-25s	Scoring Average	Money
2004	1	4	1	0	0	0	1	70.25	

Best finish for 2004: T-24th at the Chrysler Classic of Greensboro

Year	Starts	Rounds Played	Cuts Made	Wins	Top-5s	Top-10s	Top-25s	Scoring Average	Money
2005	14	48	10	0	1	1	5	70.69	$686,250

Best finish for 2005: T-2nd at the Bell Canadian Open

Year	Starts	Rounds Played	Cuts Made	Wins	Top-5s	Top-10s	Top-25s	Scoring Average	Money
2006	22	65	13	0	1	4	5	71.03	$1,122,118

Best finish for 2006: T-2nd at the Buick Championship

Year	Starts	Rounds Played	Cuts Made	Wins	Top-5s	Top-10s	Top-25s	Scoring Average	Money
2007	28	92	17	0	1	3	8	71.01	$1,559,401

Best finish for 2007: 2nd at the Memorial Tournament

Year	Starts	Rounds Played	Cuts Made	Wins	Top-5s	Top-10s	Top-25s	Scoring Average	Money
2008	24	72	12	0	2	3	5	71.50	$1,214,900

Best finish for 2008: 2nd at the EDS Byron Nelson Championship

Period Totals	Starts	Rounds Played	Cuts Made	Wins	Top-5s	Top-10s	Top-25s	Scoring Average	Money
	91	287	54	0	5	11	24	71.18	$4,582,669

Tommy Moore

Year	Starts	Rounds Played	Cuts Made	Wins	Top-5s	Top-10s	Top-25s	Scoring Average	Money
1981	2	6	1	0	0	0	0	73.17	

Best finish for 1981: T-47th at the USF&G New Orleans Open

Year	Starts	Rounds Played	Cuts Made	Wins	Top-5s	Top-10s	Top-25s	Scoring Average	Money
1982	1	3	1	0	0	0	0	71.33	

Best finish for 1982: T-28th at the USF&G Classic

Year	Starts	Rounds Played	Cuts Made	Wins	Top-5s	Top-10s	Top-25s	Scoring Average	Money
1983	1	4	1	0	0	0	0	72.50	

Best finish for 1983: T-61st at the USF&G Classic

Year	Starts	Rounds Played	Cuts Made	Wins	Top-5s	Top-10s	Top-25s	Scoring Average	Money
1985	1	2	0	0	0	0	0	73.00	
1986	2	4	0	0	0	0	0	72.25	
1987	2	4	0	0	0	0	0	73.25	
1988	1	2	0	0	0	0	0	73.50	
1990	33	88	10	0	1	3	4	71.85	$100,276

Best finish for 1990: T-5th at the Buick Southern Open

Year	Starts	Rounds Played	Cuts Made	Wins	Top-5s	Top-10s	Top-25s	Scoring Average	Money
1991	20	59	9	0	0	0	1	71.12	$35,409

Best finish for 1991: T-25th at the BellSouth Atlanta Golf Classic

Year	Starts	Rounds Played	Cuts Made	Wins	Top-5s	Top-10s	Top-25s	Scoring Average	Money
1992	1	4	1	0	0	0	0	69.50	$630

Best finish for 1992: T-63rd at the Deposit Guaranty Classic

Year	Starts	Rounds Played	Cuts Made	Wins	Top-5s	Top-10s	Top-25s	Scoring Average	Money
1993	1	2	0	0	0	0	0	73.50	
1994	20	49	4	0	0	0	0	73.04	$12,601

Best finish for 1994: T-37th at the Kemper Open

Period Totals	Starts	Rounds Played	Cuts Made	Wins	Top-5s	Top-10s	Top-25s	Scoring Average	Money
	85	227	27	0	1	3	5	71.99	$148,916

Paul Moran

Year	Starts	Rounds Played	Cuts Made	Wins	Top-5s	Top-10s	Top-25s	Scoring Average	Money
1966	1	2	0	0	0	0	0	73.00	
1968	6	18	3	0	0	0	0	73.28	$750

Best finish for 1968: T-38th at the Thunderbird Classic

Year	Starts	Rounds Played	Cuts Made	Wins	Top-5s	Top-10s	Top-25s	Scoring Average	Money
1969	16	48	8	0	0	0	0	73.60	$2,070

Best finish for 1969: T-31st at the Heritage Golf Classic

Year	Starts	Rounds Played	Cuts Made	Wins	Top-5s	Top-10s	Top-25s	Scoring Average	Money
1970	22	62	9	0	0	0	1	73.94	$4,030

Best finish for 1970: T-20th at the Sahara Invitational

Year	Starts	Rounds Played	Cuts Made	Wins	Top-5s	Top-10s	Top-25s	Scoring Average	Money
1971	16	50	9	0	0	1	1	72.60	$5,191

Best finish for 1971: T-6th at the Greater Milwaukee Open

Year	Starts	Rounds Played	Cuts Made	Wins	Top-5s	Top-10s	Top-25s	Scoring Average	Money
1972	30	93	18	0	1	2	4	73.11	$18,172

Best finish for 1972: T-4th at the Phoenix Open

Year	Starts	Rounds Played	Cuts Made	Wins	Top-5s	Top-10s	Top-25s	Scoring Average	Money
1973	24	77	13	0	0	0	1	72.92	$7,807

Best finish for 1973: T-21st at the Canadian Open

Year	Starts	Rounds Played	Cuts Made	Wins	Top-5s	Top-10s	Top-25s	Scoring Average	Money
1974	19	50	7	0	0	0	1	73.48	$3,918

Best finish for 1974: T-17th at the Monsanto Open

Year	Starts	Rounds Played	Cuts Made	Wins	Top-5s	Top-10s	Top-25s	Scoring Average	Money
1975	6	18	3	0	0	0	0	73.50	$1,261

Best finish for 1975: T-39th at the Atlanta Classic

Year	Starts	Rounds Played	Cuts Made	Wins	Top-5s	Top-10s	Top-25s	Scoring Average	Money
1976	14	38	5	0	0	0	0	73.24	$2,543

Best finish for 1976: T-35th at the Sahara Invitational

Year	Starts	Rounds Played	Cuts Made	Wins	Top-5s	Top-10s	Top-25s	Scoring Average	Money
1977	20	56	8	0	0	0	3	73.07	$6,527

Best finish for 1977: T-24th at the Tallahassee Open & San Antonio Texas Open

Year	Starts	Rounds Played	Cuts Made	Wins	Top-5s	Top-10s	Top-25s	Scoring Average	Money
1978	10	31	5	0	0	0	0	73.48	$1,498

Best finish for 1978: T-51st at the Glen CampbellLos Angeles Open

Period Totals	Starts	Rounds Played	Cuts Made	Wins	Top-5s	Top-10s	Top-25s	Scoring Average	Money
	184	543	88	0	1	3	11	73.25	$53,767

Bob Moreland

Year	Starts	Rounds Played	Cuts Made	Wins	Top-5s	Top-10s	Top-25s	Scoring Average	Money
1967	1	1	0	0	0	0	0	75.00	
1968	15	40	5	0	0	0	0	73.70	$010

Best finish for 1968: T-44th at the AZALEA Open Invitational & Magnolia State Classic

Year	Starts	Rounds Played	Cuts Made	Wins	Top-5s	Top-10s	Top-25s	Scoring Average	Money
1973	1	4	1	0	0	0	0	72.50	$053

Best finish for 1973: T-70th at the Western Open

Year	Starts	Rounds Played	Cuts Made	Wins	Top-5s	Top-10s	Top-25s	Scoring Average	Money
1976	1	2	0	0	0	0	0	75.00	
1977	3	6	0	0	0	0	0	73.83	$250
1978	1	2	0	0	0	0	0	73.00	
1980	1	2	0	0	0	0	0	75.00	
1981	1	2	0	0	0	0	0	78.00	$550
1982	2	4	0	0	0	0	0	76.00	$650
1983	1	2	0	0	0	0	0	73.00	
1986	1	2	0	0	0	0	0	75.00	
Period Totals	Starts	Rounds Played	Cuts Made	Wins	Top-5s	Top-10s	Top-25s	Scoring Average	Money
	28	67	6	0	0	0	0	74.00	$1,513

Joe Moresco

Year	Starts	Rounds Played	Cuts Made	Wins	Top-5s	Top-10s	Top-25s	Scoring Average	Money
1958	5	11	0	0	0	0	0	76.64	
1959	2	8	2	0	0	0	0	72.25	$148

Best finish for 1959: T-30th at the Lafayette Open Invitational

Year	Starts	Rounds Played	Cuts Made	Wins	Top-5s	Top-10s	Top-25s	Scoring Average	Money
1960	1	3	1	0	0	0	0	76.67	$042

Best finish for 1960: T-87th at the Bing Crosby National

Year	Starts	Rounds Played	Cuts Made	Wins	Top-5s	Top-10s	Top-25s	Scoring Average	Money
1961	1	4	1	0	0	0	0	71.25	$150

Best finish for 1961: T-26th at the Beaumont Open Invitational

Year	Starts	Rounds Played	Cuts Made	Wins	Top-5s	Top-10s	Top-25s	Scoring Average	Money
1962	2	6	1	0	0	0	0	74.33	$350

Best finish for 1962: T-42nd at the Thunderbird Classic Invitational

Year	Starts	Rounds Played	Cuts Made	Wins	Top-5s	Top-10s	Top-25s	Scoring Average	Money
1963	2	8	1	0	0	0	0	72.88	$485

Best finish for 1963: T-31st at the Cajun Classic Open Invitational

Year	Starts	Rounds Played	Cuts Made	Wins	Top-5s	Top-10s	Top-25s	Scoring Average	Money
1964	13	31	4	0	0	0	0	74.55	$388

Best finish for 1964: T-33rd at the Tucson Open

Year	Starts	Rounds Played	Cuts Made	Wins	Top-5s	Top-10s	Top-25s	Scoring Average	Money
1965	3	6	0	0	0	0	0	74.67	
1966	4	12	2	0	0	0	0	75.25	

Best finish for 1966: T-67th at the Pensacola Open Invitational

Year	Starts	Rounds Played	Cuts Made	Wins	Top-5s	Top-10s	Top-25s	Scoring Average	Money
1967	3	8	1	0	0	0	0	75.50	

Best finish for 1967: 77th at the Westchester Classic

Year	Starts	Rounds Played	Cuts Made	Wins	Top-5s	Top-10s	Top-25s	Scoring Average	Money
1968	3	8	1	0	0	0	0	73.25	

Best finish for 1968: 66th at the Pensacola Open Invitational

Year	Starts	Rounds Played	Cuts Made	Wins	Top-5s	Top-10s	Top-25s	Scoring Average	Money
1969	2	4	0	0	0	0	0	76.50	
1970	2	4	0	0	0	0	0	75.50	
1971	2	4	0	0	0	0	0	76.50	
1981	1	2	0	0	0	0	0	79.00	$550
Period Totals	Starts	Rounds Played	Cuts Made	Wins	Top-5s	Top-10s	Top-25s	Scoring Average	Money
	46	119	14	0	0	0	0	74.70	$2,112

Gil Morgan

Year	Starts	Rounds Played	Cuts Made	Wins	Top-5s	Top-10s	Top-25s	Scoring Average	Money
1973	3	10	1	0	0	0	1	73.80	$3,300

Best finish for 1973: T-11th at the Walt Disney World Open

Year	Starts	Rounds Played	Cuts Made	Wins	Top-5s	Top-10s	Top-25s	Scoring Average	Money
1974	31	98	17	0	2	3	6	72.56	$20,855

Best finish for 1974: T-5th at the Tallahassee Open & San Antonio Texas Open

Year	Starts	Rounds Played	Cuts Made	Wins	Top-5s	Top-10s	Top-25s	Scoring Average	Money
1975	26	87	17	0	2	2	7	72.10	$41,971

Best finish for 1975: 2nd at the Houston Open

Year	Starts	Rounds Played	Cuts Made	Wins	Top-5s	Top-10s	Top-25s	Scoring Average	Money
1976	32	113	24	0	2	6	10	71.95	$61,373

Best finish for 1976: T-2nd at the Danny Thomas Memphis Classic

Year	Starts	Rounds Played	Cuts Made	Wins	Top-5s	Top-10s	Top-25s	Scoring Average	Money
1977	33	118	25	1	4	5	10	71.81	$106,317

Best finish for 1977: Win at the B.C. Open

Year	Starts	Rounds Played	Cuts Made	Wins	Top-5s	Top-10s	Top-25s	Scoring Average	Money
1978	28	105	24	2	6	11	18	70.89	$268,059

Best finish for 1978: Win at the Glen CampbellLos Angeles Open & World Series Of Golf

Year	Starts	Rounds Played	Cuts Made	Wins	Top-5s	Top-10s	Top-25s	Scoring Average	Money
1979	26	91	19	1	1	2	11	72.63	$117,087

Best finish for 1979: Win at the Danny Thomas Memphis Classic

Year	Starts	Rounds Played	Cuts Made	Wins	Top-5s	Top-10s	Top-25s	Scoring Average	Money
1980	27	92	20	0	3	8	11	71.60	$149,108

Best finish for 1980: 2nd at the Pleasant Valley Jimmy Fund Classic

Year	Starts	Rounds Played	Cuts Made	Wins	Top-5s	Top-10s	Top-25s	Scoring Average	Money
1981	25	85	19	0	6	6	12	70.96	$171,784

Best finish for 1981: T-2nd at the Sea Pines Heritage Classic, Buick Open & LaJet Classic

Year	Starts	Rounds Played	Cuts Made	Wins	Top-5s	Top-10s	Top-25s	Scoring Average	Money
1982	26	96	20	0	3	8	14	71.34	$141,789

Best finish for 1982: T-2nd at the Memorial Tournament

Year	Starts	Rounds Played	Cuts Made	Wins	Top-5s	Top-10s	Top-25s	Scoring Average	Money
1983	25	98	23	2	6	10	16	71.04	$306,133

Best finish for 1983: Win at the Joe Garagiola Tucson Open & Glen CampbellLos Angeles Open

Year	Starts	Rounds Played	Cuts Made	Wins	Top-5s	Top-10s	Top-25s	Scoring Average	Money
1984	24	88	20	0	6	8	17	71.15	$287,953

Best finish for 1984: 2nd at the Seiko Tucson-Match Play Championship

Year	Starts	Rounds Played	Cuts Made	Wins	Top-5s	Top-10s	Top-25s	Scoring Average	Money
1985	25	84	18	0	2	3	10	71.58	$135,441

Best finish for 1985: T-2nd at the Pensacola Open

| 1986 | 15 | 46 | 9 | 0 | 1 | 3 | 5 | 71.46 | $99,770 |

Best finish for 1986: T-3rd at the Manufactures Hanover Westchester Classic

| 1987 | 16 | 50 | 10 | 0 | 2 | 3 | 7 | 71.18 | $133,979 |

Best finish for 1987: 2nd at the Hardee's Golf Classic

| 1988 | 23 | 76 | 14 | 0 | 4 | 7 | 7 | 70.68 | $290,002 |

Best finish for 1988: T-2nd at the MCI Heritage Classic

| 1989 | 25 | 85 | 19 | 0 | 2 | 6 | 9 | 70.61 | $322,395 |

Best finish for 1989: T-3rd at the Las Vegas Invitational

| 1990 | 25 | 85 | 18 | 1 | 4 | 5 | 12 | 70.95 | $702,629 |

Best finish for 1990: Win at the Kemper Open

| 1991 | 25 | 86 | 17 | 0 | 2 | 2 | 8 | 70.88 | $240,714 |

Best finish for 1991: T-2nd at the Phoenix Open

| 1992 | 23 | 87 | 19 | 0 | 1 | 3 | 11 | 70.37 | $272,939 |

Best finish for 1992: T-5th at the Canon Greater Hartford Open & Hardee's Golf Classic

| 1993 | 25 | 90 | 21 | 0 | 4 | 9 | 15 | 70.01 | $635,942 |

Best finish for 1993: T-3rd at the Players Championship & Kmart Greater Greensboro Open

| 1994 | 20 | 67 | 14 | 0 | 1 | 3 | 9 | 70.22 | $313,162 |

Best finish for 1994: 2nd at the Texas Open

| 1995 | 21 | 71 | 14 | 0 | 2 | 3 | 5 | 70.66 | $255,565 |

Best finish for 1995: 2nd at the Deposit Guaranty Golf Classic

| 1996 | 18 | 61 | 12 | 0 | 1 | 2 | 7 | 70.39 | $259,776 |

Best finish for 1996: T-4th at the FedEx St. Jude Classic

| 1997 | 1 | 4 | 1 | 0 | 0 | 0 | 0 | 73.50 | $7,954 |

Best finish for 1997: T-53rd at the Players Championship

Period Totals	Starts	Rounds Played	Cuts Made	Wins	Top-5s	Top-10s	Top-25s	Scoring Average	Money
	568	1973	415	7	67	118	238	71.24	$5,345,999

John E. Morgan

Year	Starts	Rounds Played	Cuts Made	Wins	Top-5s	Top-10s	Top-25s	Scoring Average	Money
2003	29	79	11	0	2	3	4	71.85	$422,917

Best finish for 2003: T-5th at the B.C. Open & Chrysler Classic of Greensboro

| 2004 | 16 | 37 | 4 | 0 | 1 | 1 | 2 | 71.70 | $487,032 |

Best finish for 2004: 2nd at the John Deere Classic

| 2005 | 11 | 27 | 2 | 0 | 0 | 0 | 0 | 72.04 | $21,030 |

Best finish for 2005: T-39th at the Valero Texas Open

2006	1	2	0	0	0	0	0	70.50	
Period Totals	Starts	Rounds Played	Cuts Made	Wins	Top-5s	Top-10s	Top-25s	Scoring Average	Money
	57	145	17	0	3	4	6	71.83	$930,979

John Morgan

Year	Starts	Rounds Played	Cuts Made	Wins	Top-5s	Top-10s	Top-25s	Scoring Average	Money
1958	1	2	0	0	0	0	0	79.50	
1968	1	2	0	0	0	0	0	86.50	
1972	3	6	0	0	0	0	0	78.67	
1973	16	35	2	0	0	0	0	75.00	$130

Best finish for 1973: 72nd at the Walt Disney World Open

| 1974 | 3 | 9 | 1 | 0 | 0 | 0 | 1 | 75.78 | $2,400 |

Best finish for 1974: T-13th at the British Open

| 1975 | 2 | 5 | 0 | 0 | 0 | 0 | 0 | 76.00 | $330 |
| 1977 | 1 | 4 | 1 | 0 | 0 | 0 | 0 | 72.75 | $586 |

Best finish for 1977: T-36th at the British Open

| 1978 | 1 | 4 | 1 | 0 | 0 | 0 | 0 | 72.75 | $1,001 |

Best finish for 1978: T-29th at the British Open

| 1979 | 1 | 2 | 0 | 0 | 0 | 0 | 0 | 78.50 | $420 |
| 1981 | 1 | 4 | 1 | 0 | 0 | 0 | 0 | 72.75 | $1,750 |

Best finish for 1981: T-31st at the British Open

1988	1	2	0	0	0	0	0	77.00	$765
1990	1	2	0	0	0	0	0	72.00	$996
Period Totals	Starts	Rounds Played	Cuts Made	Wins	Top-5s	Top-10s	Top-25s	Scoring Average	Money
	32	77	6	0	0	0	1	75.57	$8,378

David Morland IV

Year	Starts	Rounds Played	Cuts Made	Wins	Top-5s	Top-10s	Top-25s	Scoring Average	Money
1995	1	2	0	0	0	0	0	74.50	$1,000
1996	1	3	1	0	0	0	0	71.67	$4,500

Best finish for 1996: T-46th at the Bell Canadian Open

1997	1	2	0	0	0	0	0	73.00	
1998	2	4	0	0	0	0	0	75.00	
1999	4	10	1	0	0	0	0	74.20	$10,750

Best finish for 1999: T-37th at the Bell Canadian Open

Year	Starts	Rounds Played	Cuts Made	Wins	Top-5s	Top-10s	Top-25s	Scoring Average	Money
2000	31	86	12	0	0	1	4	71.71	$218,648

Best finish for 2000: T-10th at the National Car Rental Golf Classic/Disney

| 2001 | 29 | 86 | 15 | 0 | 1 | 1 | 1 | 71.52 | $279,877 |

Best finish for 2001: T-5th at the Bell Canadian Open

| 2002 | 21 | 58 | 8 | 0 | 0 | 1 | 1 | 71.50 | $154,115 |

Best finish for 2002: T-10th at the Michelob Championship at Kingsmill

| 2003 | 1 | 4 | 1 | 0 | 0 | 0 | 0 | 72.00 | $8,022 |

Best finish for 2003: T-73rd at the Bell Canadian Open

| 2004 | 27 | 73 | 9 | 0 | 0 | 0 | 1 | 72.29 | $165,435 |

Best finish for 2004: T-21st at the Booz Allen Classic

2005	1	2	0	0	0	0	0	77.00	
2006	1	2	0	0	0	0	0	72.00	
2007	1	2	0	0	0	0	0	76.00	
2008	1	2	0	0	0	0	0	71.50	
Period Totals	Starts	Rounds Played	Cuts Made	Wins	Top-5s	Top-10s	Top-25s	Scoring Average	Money
	122	336	47	0	1	3	7	71.95	$842,347

Mike Morley

Year	Starts	Rounds Played	Cuts Made	Wins	Top-5s	Top-10s	Top-25s	Scoring Average	Money
1967	1	2	0	0	0	0	0	77.00	
1968	1	2	0	0	0	0	0	75.00	
1969	1	2	0	0	0	0	0	71.50	
1970	11	31	4	0	0	0	0	73.03	$1,789

Best finish for 1970: T-26th at the Bahama Islands Open

| 1971 | 6 | 14 | 1 | 0 | 0 | 0 | 1 | 72.71 | $836 |

Best finish for 1971: T-24th at the Robinson Open Golf Classic

| 1972 | 19 | 59 | 10 | 0 | 0 | 0 | 1 | 73.27 | $4,729 |

Best finish for 1972: T-19th at the Tucson Open

| 1973 | 21 | 82 | 18 | 0 | 0 | 0 | 5 | 72.37 | $17,983 |

Best finish for 1973: T-15th at the Greater Milwaukee Open

| 1974 | 23 | 80 | 18 | 0 | 0 | 3 | 5 | 72.15 | $25,200 |

Best finish for 1974: T-6th at the Quad Cities Open

| 1975 | 26 | 90 | 20 | 0 | 1 | 2 | 8 | 72.07 | $37,112 |

Best finish for 1975: T-2nd at the Greater Jacksonville Open

| 1976 | 23 | 76 | 16 | 0 | 4 | 4 | 12 | 71.53 | $86,696 |

Best finish for 1976: 2nd at the Bing Crosby Pro-Am & Colonial National Invitational

| 1977 | 26 | 91 | 20 | 1 | 5 | 5 | 9 | 72.03 | $86,719 |

Best finish for 1977: Win at the Ed McMahon Quad City Open

| 1978 | 26 | 90 | 19 | 0 | 2 | 2 | 6 | 72.29 | $48,271 |

Best finish for 1978: T-3rd at the Hawaiian Open

| 1979 | 21 | 71 | 14 | 0 | 1 | 2 | 7 | 71.58 | $47,118 |

Best finish for 1979: T-3rd at the Sea Pines Heritage Classic

| 1980 | 25 | 87 | 19 | 0 | 0 | 1 | 6 | 72.01 | $40,641 |

Best finish for 1980: T-8th at the U.S. Open

| 1981 | 25 | 84 | 17 | 0 | 1 | 2 | 6 | 72.12 | $55,209 |

Best finish for 1981: T-3rd at the Atlanta Classic

| 1982 | 21 | 61 | 9 | 0 | 1 | 2 | 3 | 72.34 | $27,808 |

Best finish for 1982: T-3rd at the Bing Crosby Pro-Am

| 1983 | 7 | 24 | 5 | 0 | 0 | 0 | 2 | 70.58 | $10,167 |

Best finish for 1983: T-12th at the Miller High-Life Quad Cities Open

| 1984 | 2 | 4 | 1 | 0 | 0 | 0 | 1 | 68.75 | $3,950 |

Best finish for 1984: T-14th at the Miller High-Life Quad Cities Open

| 1985 | 2 | 8 | 2 | 0 | 0 | 0 | 1 | 70.25 | $7,005 |

Best finish for 1985: T-11th at the Lite Quad Cities Open

| 1986 | 3 | 11 | 2 | 0 | 0 | 0 | 0 | 70.36 | $1,886 |

Best finish for 1986: T-41st at the Hardee's Golf Classic

| 1987 | 3 | 10 | 2 | 0 | 0 | 0 | 0 | 69.90 | $6,295 |

Best finish for 1987: T-26th at the Hardee's Golf Classic

1991	1	2	0	0	0	0	0	70.00	
Period Totals	Starts	Rounds Played	Cuts Made	Wins	Top-5s	Top-10s	Top-25s	Scoring Average	Money
	294	981	197	1	15	23	73	72.07	$509,415

Tommy Morrow

Year	Starts	Rounds Played	Cuts Made	Wins	Top-5s	Top-10s	Top-25s	Scoring Average	Money
1963	1	4	1	0	0	0	0	72.75	$057

Best finish for 1963: T-44th at the Seattle Open Invitational

| 1964 | 20 | 65 | 11 | 0 | 0 | 0 | 1 | 73.45 | $1,161 |

Best finish for 1964: T-23rd at the Whitemarsh Open

| 1965 | 9 | 20 | 1 | 0 | 0 | 0 | 0 | 74.70 | $338 |

Best finish for 1965: T-39th at the Houston Classic

| 1971 | 1 | 4 | 1 | 0 | 0 | 0 | 0 | 72.25 | $325 |

Best finish for 1971: T-45th at the Greater New Orleans Open

Period Totals	Starts	Rounds Played	Cuts Made	Wins	Top-5s	Top-10s	Top-25s	Scoring Average	Money
	31	93	14	0	0	0	1	73.63	$1,880

John Morse

Year	Starts	Rounds Played	Cuts Made	Wins	Top-5s	Top-10s	Top-25s	Scoring Average	Money
1984	2	4	0	0	0	0	0	76.25	$600
1987	1	2	0	0	0	0	0	74.00	$600
1988	1	2	0	0	0	0	0	70.50	
1991	4	10	2	0	0	0	0	73.50	$14,157

Best finish for 1991: T-27th at the NEC World Series of Golf

| 1994 | 26 | 76 | 12 | 0 | 0 | 1 | 4 | 71.58 | $147,137 |

Best finish for 1994: T-6th at the Kmart Greater Greensboro Open

| 1995 | 24 | 71 | 12 | 1 | 3 | 3 | 4 | 71.75 | $420,540 |

Best finish for 1995: Win at the United Airlines Hawaiian Open

| 1996 | 27 | 94 | 20 | 0 | 1 | 2 | 8 | 71.11 | $322,090 |

Best finish for 1996: 4th at the U.S. Open

| 1997 | 30 | 92 | 15 | 0 | 0 | 1 | 3 | 71.68 | $166,363 |

Best finish for 1997: T-8th at the Shell Houston Open

| 1998 | 23 | 59 | 7 | 0 | 0 | 0 | 1 | 72.10 | $43,140 |

Best finish for 1998: T-17th at the Quad City Classic

| 2001 | 1 | 4 | 1 | 0 | 0 | 0 | 0 | 71.50 | $3,880 |

Best finish for 2001: T-73rd at the B.C. Open

| 2002 | 8 | 18 | 2 | 0 | 1 | 1 | 1 | 70.50 | $125,260 |

Best finish for 2002: T-4th at the Tampa Bay Classic presented by Buick

| 2003 | 8 | 21 | 3 | 0 | 0 | 0 | 0 | 72.57 | $22,361 |

Best finish for 2003: T-52nd at the Greater Milwaukee Open

| 2004 | 3 | 9 | 1 | 0 | 0 | 0 | 0 | 73.11 | $6,420 |

Best finish for 2004: T-60th at the B.C. Open

2005	2	4	0	0	0	0	0	71.75	
2006	1	2	0	0	0	0	0	72.00	
2007	1	2	0	0	0	0	0	71.50	
2008	7	21	3	0	0	0	0	73.19	$25,705

Best finish for 2008: T-63rd at the AT&T Classic

Period Totals	Starts	Rounds Played	Cuts Made	Wins	Top-5s	Top-10s	Top-25s	Scoring Average	Money
	169	491	78	1	5	8	21	71.78	$1,298,252

Stan Mosel

Year	Starts	Rounds Played	Cuts Made	Wins	Top-5s	Top-10s	Top-25s	Scoring Average	Money
1958	15	45	8	0	1	1	4	73.27	$886

Best finish for 1958: T-5th at the Greenbrier Invitational

1959	1	2	0	0	0	0	0	81.00	
1960	1	2	0	0	0	0	0	74.00	
1961	1	2	0	0	0	0	0	76.00	
1962	1	3	1	0	0	0	0	73.67	$080

Best finish for 1962: T-85th at the Thunderbird Classic Invitational

| 1963 | 2 | 8 | 2 | 0 | 0 | 0 | 0 | 72.88 | $630 |

Best finish for 1963: 39th at the PGA Championship

| 1964 | 2 | 4 | 0 | 0 | 0 | 0 | 0 | 75.75 | |
| 1965 | 7 | 20 | 3 | 0 | 0 | 0 | 0 | 73.95 | $230 |

Best finish for 1965: T-37th at the Azalea Open

| 1966 | 2 | 6 | 1 | 0 | 0 | 0 | 0 | 73.33 | |

Best finish for 1966: T-64th at the Thunderbird Classic

| 1967 | 2 | 4 | 0 | 0 | 0 | 0 | 0 | 75.50 | |
| 1968 | 2 | 6 | 1 | 0 | 0 | 0 | 0 | 74.67 | $915 |

Best finish for 1968: T-54th at the PGA Championship

Period Totals	Starts	Rounds Played	Cuts Made	Wins	Top-5s	Top-10s	Top-25s	Scoring Average	Money
	36	102	16	0	1	1	4	73.87	$2,741

Perry Moss

Year	Starts	Rounds Played	Cuts Made	Wins	Top-5s	Top-10s	Top-25s	Scoring Average	Money
1993	29	86	16	0	0	0	3	72.21	$63,565

Best finish for 1993: T-21st at the B.C. Open

| 1998 | 1 | 2 | 0 | 0 | 0 | 0 | 0 | 77.00 | $1,000 |
| 1999 | 22 | 71 | 14 | 0 | 1 | 1 | 4 | 71.24 | $238,986 |

Best finish for 1999: T-3rd at the Southern Farm Bureau Classic

| 2000 | 21 | 53 | 6 | 0 | 0 | 0 | 1 | 71.62 | $104,735 |

Best finish for 2000: T-15th at the Michelob Championship at Kingsmill

Period Totals	Starts	Rounds Played	Cuts Made	Wins	Top-5s	Top-10s	Top-25s	Scoring Average	Money
	73	212	36	0	1	1	8	71.78	$408,286

Jerry Mowlds

Year	Starts	Rounds Played	Cuts Made	Wins	Top-5s	Top-10s	Top-25s	Scoring Average	Money
1964	22	47	5	0	0	0	1	75.47	$877

Best finish for 1964: T-17th at the Mountain View Open

1965	13	36	4	0	0	0	0	74.36	$815

Best finish for 1965: T-32nd at the Lucky International

1966	4	12	2	0	0	0	0	74.25	$360

Best finish for 1966: T-42nd at the Canadian Open

1967	13	38	6	0	0	1	3	72.39	$4,756

Best finish for 1967: T-8th at the Phoenix Open

1968	7	20	2	0	0	0	0	74.15	$575

Best finish for 1968: T-35th at the Bob Hope Desert Classic

1969	3	8	0	0	0	0	0	74.50	
Period Totals	**Starts**	**Rounds Played**	**Cuts Made**	**Wins**	**Top-5s**	**Top-10s**	**Top-25s**	**Scoring Average**	**Money**
	62	161	19	0	0	1	4	74.19	$7,383

Larry Mowry

Year	Starts	Rounds Played	Cuts Made	Wins	Top-5s	Top-10s	Top-25s	Scoring Average	Money
1960	1	4	1	0	0	0	0	73.00	$145

Best finish for 1960: T-26th at the Hesperia Open Invitational

1961	5	18	4	0	0	0	2	71.67	$644

Best finish for 1961: T-15th at the Almaden Open

1962	13	51	12	0	0	0	7	71.67	$4,659

Best finish for 1962: T-12th at the Seattle World's Fair Open Invitational

1963	3	12	2	0	1	1	1	71.08	$2,362

Best finish for 1963: T-5th at the Seattle Open Invitational

1964	30	100	17	0	1	1	7	72.58	$8,332

Best finish for 1964: T-4th at the Azalea Open

1965	22	69	12	0	0	1	4	72.43	$7,635

Best finish for 1965: T-6th at the Texas Open

1966	10	37	8	0	0	0	2	72.00	$4,796

Best finish for 1966: T-14th at the Phoenix Open Invitational

1967	22	70	14	0	0	1	1	73.23	$2,439

Best finish for 1967: T-8th at the Azalea Open

1968	22	77	18	1	1	2	6	71.51	$18,256

Best finish for 1968: Win at the Rebel Yell Open

1969	19	63	13	0	1	1	5	72.24	$14,493

Best finish for 1969: T-2nd at the Azalea Open

1970	11	25	3	0	0	1	2	72.52	$2,602

Best finish for 1970: T-6th at the Tallahassee Open

1971	18	61	12	0	0	1	2	73.20	$8,236

Best finish for 1971: T-7th at the Western Open

1972	8	20	3	0	0	0	0	74.25	$1,232

Best finish for 1972: T-30th at the Glen Campbell-Los Angeles Open

1977	1	2	0	0	0	0	0	76.00	$250
1980	5	9	1	0	0	0	1	72.78	$1,317

Best finish for 1980: T-16th at the Tallahassee Open

1981	1	0	0	0	0	0	0		
Period Totals	**Starts**	**Rounds Played**	**Cuts Made**	**Wins**	**Top-5s**	**Top-10s**	**Top-25s**	**Scoring Average**	**Money**
	191	618	120	1	4	9	40	72.43	$77,398

Jodie Mudd

Year	Starts	Rounds Played	Cuts Made	Wins	Top-5s	Top-10s	Top-25s	Scoring Average	Money
1980	1	2	0	0	0	0	0	78.00	
1981	1	2	0	0	0	0	0	77.50	
1982	23	72	13	0	1	1	6	72.03	$34,216

Best finish for 1982: T-5th at the USF&G Classic

1983	33	99	16	0	0	0	1	72.53	$22,115

Best finish for 1983: T-18th at the Glen Campbell-Los Angeles Open

1984	26	83	16	0	0	0	4	72.04	$42,244

Best finish for 1984: T-14th at the Danny Thomas Memphis Classic

1985	31	102	21	0	3	6	10	71.56	$186,648

Best finish for 1985: T-2nd at the Canon Sammy Davis, Jr. - Greater Hartford Open, Bank of Boston Classic & Texas Open

1986	19	71	16	0	3	4	7	71.07	$178,884

Best finish for 1986: T-2nd at the Honda Classic & Anheuser-Busch Golf Classic

1987	30	97	19	0	3	4	10	71.39	$204,923

Best finish for 1987: T-2nd at the Canadian Open

1988	32	104	23	1	2	4	15	71.13	$422,022

Best finish for 1988: Win at the Federal Express St. Jude Classic

1989	30	99	20	1	2	4	9	71.62	$452,860

Best finish for 1989: Win at the GTE Byron Nelson Classic

Year	Starts	Rounds Played	Cuts Made	Wins	Top-5s	Top-10s	Top-25s	Scoring Average	Money
1990	25	87	19	2	4	4	8	71.10	$985,146

Best finish for 1990: Win at the Players Championship & Nabisco Championships

1991	19	64	12	0	1	4	5	71.61	$205,853

Best finish for 1991: T-5th at the British Open

1992	21	70	14	0	0	1	3	71.34	$102,898

Best finish for 1992: T-6th at the Buick Invitational of California

1993	20	57	9	0	0	1	4	71.65	$89,366

Best finish for 1993: T-6th at the Nissan Los Angeles Open

1994	15	46	7	0	0	0	0	71.63	$27,868

Best finish for 1994: T-32nd at the Federal Express St. Jude Classic

1995	9	18	1	0	0	1	1	73.00	$43,200

Best finish for 1995: 6th at the Nissan Open

1996	4	10	0	0	0	0	0	73.40	
Period Totals	Starts	Rounds Played	Cuts Made	Wins	Top-5s	Top-10s	Top-25s	Scoring Average	Money
	339	1083	206	4	19	34	83	71.66	$2,998,243

Michael Muehr

Year	Starts	Rounds Played	Cuts Made	Wins	Top-5s	Top-10s	Top-25s	Scoring Average	Money
1995	1	2	0	0	0	0	0	77.50	$1,000
1997	1	2	0	0	0	0	0	75.50	
1998	1	4	1	0	0	0	0	71.50	$5,913

Best finish for 1998: T-42nd at the Kemper Open

1999	2	4	0	0	0	0	0	74.25	$1,000
2000	1	2	0	0	0	0	0	74.50	
2001	32	92	16	0	0	2	4	70.76	$409,250

Best finish for 2001: T-7th at the Michelob Championship at Kingsmill

2002	27	71	9	0	0	0	1	72.15	$98,530

Best finish for 2002: T-25th at the Buick Classic

2003	7	19	3	0	0	0	0	72.68	$35,376

Best finish for 2003: T-32nd at the Greater Milwaukee Open

Period Totals	Starts	Rounds Played	Cuts Made	Wins	Top-5s	Top-10s	Top-25s	Scoring Average	Money
	72	196	29	0	0	2	5	71.69	$551,070

Moon Mullins

Year	Starts	Rounds Played	Cuts Made	Wins	Top-5s	Top-10s	Top-25s	Scoring Average	Money
1958	1	2	0	0	0	0	0	77.50	
1961	1	4	1	0	0	0	0	71.75	$020

Best finish for 1961: T-33rd at the Orange County Open

1962	9	33	9	0	0	0	1	72.88	$1,750

Best finish for 1962: T-17th at the Eastern Open Invitational

1963	9	37	8	0	0	1	2	71.59	$2,706

Best finish for 1963: T-8th at the Waco Turner Open Invitational

1964	7	20	2	0	0	0	0	73.45	$438

Best finish for 1964: T-26th at the Texas Open

1965	4	10	0	0	0	0	0	73.50	
1966	2	3	0	0	0	0	0	76.67	
1967	2	5	0	0	0	0	0	76.00	
1968	4	12	1	0	0	0	0	73.58	

Best finish for 1968: T-74th at the Haig Open Invitational

1969	5	14	1	0	0	0	0	74.29	$231

Best finish for 1969: T-74th at the Philadelphia Classic

1970	2	6	1	0	0	0	0	73.33	$200

Best finish for 1970: T-68th at the Bob Hope Chrysler Classic

1971	5	14	1	0	0	0	0	74.43	$254

Best finish for 1971: 70th at the Bob Hope Chrysler Classic

1972	5	13	1	0	0	0	0	73.85	$232

Best finish for 1972: T-68th at the Bob Hope Chrysler Classic

1973	1	2	0	0	0	0	0	77.00	
1978	1	3	0	0	0	0	0	82.33	
Period Totals	Starts	Rounds Played	Cuts Made	Wins	Top-5s	Top-10s	Top-25s	Scoring Average	Money
	58	178	25	0	0	1	3	73.46	$5,830

Bill Murchison

Year	Starts	Rounds Played	Cuts Made	Wins	Top-5s	Top-10s	Top-25s	Scoring Average	Money
1978	3	6	0	0	0	0	0	74.50	
1979	7	16	1	0	0	0	0	74.13	$455

Best finish for 1979: T-43rd at the Tallahassee Open

1980	14	31	3	0	0	0	1	72.81	$6,434

Best finish for 1980: T-12th at the B.C. Open

1981	2	2	0	0	0	0	0	73.50	
1983	27	81	12	0	0	0	2	73.19	$14,427

Best finish for 1983: T-22nd at the Georgia-Pacific Atlanta Golf Classic

Year	Starts	Rounds Played	Cuts Made	Wins	Top-5s	Top-10s	Top-25s	Scoring Average	Money
1987	1	2	0	0	0	0	0	74.00	
1990	1	2	0	0	0	0	0	75.00	
1991	1	3	0	0	0	0	0	73.33	
1992	1	4	1	0	0	0	0	73.00	$2,170

Best finish for 1992: T-58th at the Nestle Invitational

1993	19	54	8	0	0	0	3	72.11	$45,402

Best finish for 1993: T-17th at the B.C. Open

1995	1	2	0	0	0	0	0	76.50	$1,000
1996	1	4	1	0	0	0	0	72.75	$5,825

Best finish for 1996: T-60th at the U.S. Open

Period Totals	Starts	Rounds Played	Cuts Made	Wins	Top-5s	Top-10s	Top-25s	Scoring Average	Money
	78	207	26	0	0	0	6	73.01	$75,712

Bob Murphy

Year	Starts	Rounds Played	Cuts Made	Wins	Top-5s	Top-10s	Top-25s	Scoring Average	Money
1966	2	8	2	0	0	0	1	75.63	

Best finish for 1966: T-15th at the U.S. Open

1967	5	16	3	0	0	0	1	72.81	

Best finish for 1967: T-23rd at the U.S. Open

1968	31	112	24	2	4	6	18	71.06	$101,598

Best finish for 1968: Win at the Philadelphia Golf Classic & Thunderbird Classic

1969	32	113	24	0	3	5	14	71.50	$55,222

Best finish for 1969: T-2nd at the National Airlines Open

1970	32	115	27	1	7	12	15	71.29	$117,424

Best finish for 1970: Win at the Greater Hartford Open Invitational

1971	33	109	23	0	5	8	15	71.53	$72,827

Best finish for 1971: T-3rd at the Bing Crosby Pro-Am, Houston Champions International & American Golf Classic

1972	30	106	23	0	6	10	12	71.99	$78,433

Best finish for 1972: 2nd at the Hawaiian Open

1973	34	129	29	0	4	5	14	71.98	$88,709

Best finish for 1973: T-2nd at the American Golf Classic & Westchester Classic

1974	19	68	15	0	3	4	8	71.87	$55,762

Best finish for 1974: 2nd at the World Open

1975	23	87	20	1	5	6	10	71.54	$127,471

Best finish for 1975: Win at the Jackie Gleason's Inverrary Classic

1976	24	87	20	0	0	6	10	71.93	$48,701

Best finish for 1976: T-6th at the Sea Pines Heritage Classic

1977	27	88	18	0	2	5	9	72.24	$47,649

Best finish for 1977: T-2nd at the Ed McMahon Quad City Open

1978	30	105	22	0	4	6	11	71.63	$74,198

Best finish for 1978: T-2nd at the Atlanta Classic

1979	32	103	19	0	0	4	11	72.07	$67,266

Best finish for 1979: T-7th at the Sea Pines Heritage Classic & Manufactures Hanover Westchester Classic

1980	29	105	24	0	2	8	13	71.10	$107,474

Best finish for 1980: T-3rd at the B.C. Open

1981	29	98	21	0	2	3	14	71.09	$87,192

Best finish for 1981: T-2nd at the Tallahassee Open

1982	24	74	13	0	1	2	4	72.07	$30,952

Best finish for 1982: T-5th at the Tallahassee Open

1983	27	94	19	0	1	3	6	72.00	$63,403

Best finish for 1983: T-5th at the Colonial National Invitational

1984	26	85	15	0	0	1	3	72.89	$36,344

Best finish for 1984: T-10th at the Memorial Tournament

1985	21	71	13	0	2	2	3	72.38	$99,031

Best finish for 1985: 2nd at the Colonial National Invitational

1986	26	74	16	1	1	3	6	72.19	$183,273

Best finish for 1986: Win at the Canadian Open

1987	25	78	14	0	1	1	4	72.51	$65,518

Best finish for 1987: T-5th at the MCI Heritage Classic

1988	28	74	9	0	0	0	1	73.15	$23,875

Best finish for 1988: T-18th at the Kmart Greater Greensboro Open

1989	8	16	0	0	0	0	0	75.00	
1990	1	2	0	0	0	0	0	70.50	
1992	4	8	0	0	0	0	0	73.25	
Period Totals	Starts	Rounds Played	Cuts Made	Wins	Top-5s	Top-10s	Top-25s	Scoring Average	Money
	602	2025	413	5	53	100	203	71.90	$1,632,321

Sean Murphy

Year	Starts	Rounds Played	Cuts Made	Wins	Top-5s	Top-10s	Top-25s	Scoring Average	Money
1990	24	59	6	0	0	0	1	72.86	$19,705

Best finish for 1990: T-24th at the B.C. Open

1991	24	64	8	0	0	0	0	72.84	$22,147

Best finish for 1991: T-29th at the Greater Milwaukee Open

Year	Starts	Rounds Played	Cuts Made	Wins	Top-5s	Top-10s	Top-25s	Scoring Average	Money
1993	1	2	0	0	0	0	0	73.00	$1,000
1994	30	85	14	0	0	1	2	71.61	$97,597

Best finish for 1994: T-8th at the Las Vegas Invitational

1995	3	12	3	0	0	0	2	71.00	$40,115

Best finish for 1995: T-18th at the United Airlines Hawaiian Open

1996	26	81	15	0	0	0	1	71.90	$87,401

Best finish for 1996: T-14th at the Nissan Open

1997	2	6	1	0	0	0	1	71.33	$25,700

Best finish for 1997: T-12th at the B.C. Open

1999	28	83	15	0	0	0	3	72.05	$185,299

Best finish for 1999: T-13th at the Greater Greensboro Chrysler Classic

2000	35	100	15	0	1	2	4	71.13	$339,242

Best finish for 2000: T-5th at the Michelob Championship at Kingsmill

2001	27	70	8	0	0	0	0	72.59	$51,744

Best finish for 2001: T-58th at the FedEx St. Jude Classic

2002	2	6	1	0	0	0	0	71.00	$8,284

Best finish for 2002: T-60th at the FedEx St. Jude Classic

2003	3	6	0	0	0	0	0	73.33	$1,000
2004	2	4	0	0	0	0	0	71.75	
2005	3	8	1	0	0	0	0	71.25	$21,120

Best finish for 2005: T-38th at the Sony Open in Hawaii

2006	1	2	0	0	0	0	0	74.50	
Period Totals	Starts	Rounds Played	Cuts Made	Wins	Top-5s	Top-10s	Top-25s	Scoring Average	Money
	211	588	87	0	1	3	14	72.01	$900,354

Kevin Na

Year	Starts	Rounds Played	Cuts Made	Wins	Top-5s	Top-10s	Top-25s	Scoring Average	Money
2001	1	2	0	0	0	0	0	72.50	
2003	2	6	1	0	0	0	0	73.50	$23,375

Best finish for 2003: T-71st at the WGC-NEC Invitational

2004	32	96	19	0	2	2	7	70.91	$901,158

Best finish for 2004: T-3rd at the Southern Farm Bureau Classic

2005	32	86	14	0	2	2	7	71.40	$1,097,204

Best finish for 2005: T-2nd at the FBR Open & Chrysler Classic of Tucson

2006	11	31	5	0	0	0	2	71.45	$146,099

Best finish for 2006: T-23rd at the Honda Classic

2007	27	84	16	0	1	3	5	70.70	$856,670

Best finish for 2007: T-4th at the Verizon Heritage

2008	29	97	20	0	2	3	6	70.81	$1,041,059

Best finish for 2008: T-4th at the Sony Open in Hawaii & FBR Open

Period Totals	Starts	Rounds Played	Cuts Made	Wins	Top-5s	Top-10s	Top-25s	Scoring Average	Money
	134	402	75	0	7	10	27	71.03	$4,065,565

Kel Nagle

Year	Starts	Rounds Played	Cuts Made	Wins	Top-5s	Top-10s	Top-25s	Scoring Average	Money
1960	8	30	6	1	2	2	5	71.10	$7,967

Best finish for 1960: Win at the British Open

1961	7	26	5	0	1	2	4	69.58	$5,424

Best finish for 1961: T-2nd at the Colonial National Invitational

1962	10	38	8	0	1	1	7	71.11	$6,256

Best finish for 1962: 2nd at the British Open

1963	11	42	9	0	2	2	4	71.64	$7,802

Best finish for 1963: 3rd at the Greensboro Open Invitational

1964	17	66	16	1	1	5	11	71.67	$24,770

Best finish for 1964: Win at the Canadian Open

1965	26	98	22	0	3	4	17	71.09	$41,098

Best finish for 1965: T-2nd at the U.S. Open

1966	18	60	12	0	3	5	7	72.48	$22,057

Best finish for 1966: T-4th at the British Open & Carling World Open

1967	22	84	20	0	0	4	8	72.07	$19,945

Best finish for 1967: T-7th at the Insurance City Open

1968	18	68	16	0	0	1	3	72.10	$11,117

Best finish for 1968: T-9th at the Cleveland Open Invitational

1969	11	30	4	0	0	1	1	73.10	$3,650

Best finish for 1969: 9th at the British Open

1970	9	30	6	0	1	1	1	72.40	$9,670

Best finish for 1970: 4th at the Colonial National Invitational

1971	1	4	1	0	0	0	1	71.75	$2,760

Best finish for 1971: T-11th at the British Open

1972	1	4	1	0	0	0	0	73.50	$512

Best finish for 1972: T-31st at the British Open

Year	Starts	Rounds Played	Cuts Made	Wins	Top-5s	Top-10s	Top-25s	Scoring Average	Money
1973	1	4	1	0	0	0	0	74.00	$448

Best finish for 1973: T-39th at the British Open

1974	1	3	0	0	0	0	0	79.67	$180
1975	1	4	1	0	0	0	0	73.25	$480

Best finish for 1975: T-40th at the British Open

1976	1	2	0	0	0	0	0	77.50	$180
1978	1	2	0	0	0	0	0	79.50	$332
1984	1	2	0	0	0	0	0	79.50	$429
Period Totals	**Starts**	**Rounds Played**	**Cuts Made**	**Wins**	**Top-5s**	**Top-10s**	**Top-25s**	**Scoring Average**	**Money**
	165	597	128	2	14	28	69	71.86	$165,080

Tommy Nakajima

Year	Starts	Rounds Played	Cuts Made	Wins	Top-5s	Top-10s	Top-25s	Scoring Average	Money
1978	3	9	1	0	0	0	1	75.56	$4,540

Best finish for 1978: T-17th at the British Open

1979	1	2	0	0	0	0	0	77.00	$420
1982	1	4	1	0	0	0	1	72.50	$8,750

Best finish for 1982: T-13th at the World Series Of Golf

1983	8	30	7	0	1	1	4	71.93	$54,576

Best finish for 1983: 4th at the Greater Greensboro Open

1984	15	59	14	0	0	3	8	71.46	$82,295

Best finish for 1984: T-6th at the Honda Classic

1985	7	22	4	0	0	0	0	74.64	$7,167

Best finish for 1985: T-46th at the Colonial National Invitational

1986	9	27	6	0	0	2	2	72.81	$62,832

Best finish for 1986: T-8th at the Masters & British Open

1987	14	42	9	0	0	2	7	71.64	$88,051

Best finish for 1987: T-6th at the Hertz Bay Hill Classic

1988	16	55	12	0	1	1	5	71.55	$148,304

Best finish for 1988: 3rd at the PGA Championship

1989	7	20	3	0	0	0	0	73.75	$8,020

Best finish for 1989: T-52nd at the Doral-Ryder Open

1991	2	6	1	0	0	1	1	71.50	$36,150

Best finish for 1991: T-10th at the Masters

1992	4	12	2	0	0	0	1	71.92	$19,651

Best finish for 1992: T-21st at the PGA Championship

1993	4	10	3	0	0	0	2	72.90	$51,778

Best finish for 1993: T-15th at the International

1994	4	12	3	0	0	0	1	71.08	$28,814

Best finish for 1994: T-24th at the NEC World Series of Golf

1995	3	8	1	0	0	0	0	73.25	$12,828

Best finish for 1995: T-49th at the British Open

1996	2	8	2	0	0	0	0	71.63	$7,165

Best finish for 1996: T-52nd at the PGA Championship

2002	1	2	0	0	0	0	0	73.50	$3,950
Period Totals	**Starts**	**Rounds Played**	**Cuts Made**	**Wins**	**Top-5s**	**Top-10s**	**Top-25s**	**Scoring Average**	**Money**
	101	328	69	0	2	10	33	72.27	$625,292

Bill Nary

Year	Starts	Rounds Played	Cuts Made	Wins	Top-5s	Top-10s	Top-25s	Scoring Average	Money
1958	17	61	13	0	0	1	4	73.28	$1,843

Best finish for 1958: T-10th at the Azalea Open

1959	1	3	1	0	0	0	0	74.67	$043

Best finish for 1959: T-81st at the Bing Crosby National

1960	1	3	0	0	0	0	0	77.33	$042
1964	5	14	2	0	0	0	0	74.50	

Best finish for 1964: T-48th at the Mountain View Open

1965	1	2	0	0	0	0	0	72.50	
1966	2	5	0	0	0	0	0	77.40	
1969	1	2	0	0	0	0	0	77.00	
Period Totals	**Starts**	**Rounds Played**	**Cuts Made**	**Wins**	**Top-5s**	**Top-10s**	**Top-25s**	**Scoring Average**	**Money**
	28	90	16	0	0	1	4	73.94	$1,928

Jim Nelford

Year	Starts	Rounds Played	Cuts Made	Wins	Top-5s	Top-10s	Top-25s	Scoring Average	Money
1976	1	2	0	0	0	0	0	73.50	
1977	1	4	1	0	0	0	0	77.75	

Best finish for 1977: T-69th at the Canadian Open

1978	26	84	16	0	2	3	5	72.05	$29,613

Best finish for 1978: T-3rd at the Tallahassee Open & Southern Open

1979	27	81	14	0	0	2	5	73.05	$40,524

Best finish for 1979: T-6th at the Bing Crosby Pro-Am

Year	Starts	Rounds Played	Cuts Made	Wins	Top-5s	Top-10s	Top-25s	Scoring Average	Money
1980	32	100	20	0	0	0	5	72.31	$33,769

Best finish for 1980: T-11th at the Pleasant Valley Jimmy Fund Classic

1981	26	77	15	0	0	1	3	72.34	$24,852

Best finish for 1981: T-10th at the World Disney World National Team Championship

1982	24	80	16	0	0	2	5	72.11	$48,088

Best finish for 1982: T-7th at the Glen CampbellLos Angeles Open & Kemper Open

1983	31	115	26	0	1	3	11	71.94	$111,932

Best finish for 1983: 2nd at the Sea Pines Heritage Classic

1984	26	82	15	0	1	2	5	72.70	$82,070

Best finish for 1984: 2nd at the Bing Crosby Pro-Am

1985	24	74	13	0	0	0	6	72.14	$60,276

Best finish for 1985: T-11th at the Honda Classic

1986	3	7	0	0	0	0	0	72.71	
1987	31	81	11	0	0	0	2	72.86	$24,097

Best finish for 1987: T-18th at the Canadian Open

1988	28	70	8	0	0	0	1	73.07	$20,910

Best finish for 1988: T-15th at the Independent Insurance Agent Open

1989	5	13	1	0	0	0	0	74.62	$1,225

Best finish for 1989: T-82nd at the Phoenix Open

1990	6	18	3	0	0	0	0	71.94	$4,132

Best finish for 1990: 60th at the AT&T Pebble Beach Pro-Am

1991	4	11	1	0	0	0	1	72.36	$3,510

Best finish for 1991: T-19th at the Deposit Guaranty Classic

1992	2	4	0	0	0	0	0	73.75	
1994	2	6	1	0	0	0	0	72.83	$4,435

Best finish for 1994: T-37th at the AT&T Pebble Beach Pro-Am

1995	1	3	0	0	0	0	0	72.33	
1996	3	8	1	0	0	0	0	72.50	$1,860

Best finish for 1996: T-74th at the Deposit Guaranty Golf Classic

1998	3	6	0	0	0	0	0	77.17	
Period Totals	Starts	Rounds Played	Cuts Made	Wins	Top-5s	Top-10s	Top-25s	Scoring Average	Money
	306	926	162	0	4	13	49	72.51	$491,293

Byron Nelson

Year	Starts	Rounds Played	Cuts Made	Wins	Top-5s	Top-10s	Top-25s	Scoring Average	Money
1958	4	14	4	0	1	1	2	73.57	$1,573

Best finish for 1958: T-2nd at the Jackson Open

1959	4	14	1	0	0	0	1	72.36	$820

Best finish for 1959: T-25th at the Colonial National Invitational

1960	4	13	3	0	0	0	0	74.69	$580

Best finish for 1960: T-37th at the Colonial National Invitational

1961	2	8	1	0	0	0	0	74.63	$600

Best finish for 1961: T-32nd at the Masters

1962	3	12	3	0	0	0	2	73.25	$2,010

Best finish for 1962: T-15th at the Bing Crosby National

1963	2	6	1	0	0	0	0	76.00	$750

Best finish for 1963: T-48th at the Colonial National Invitational

1964	3	6	1	0	0	0	0	75.50	
1965	3	11	2	0	0	0	1	74.64	$1,450

Best finish for 1965: T-15th at the Masters

1966	2	3	0	0	0	0	0	76.33	$1,165
Period Totals	Starts	Rounds Played	Cuts Made	Wins	Top-5s	Top-10s	Top-25s	Scoring Average	Money
	27	87	16	0	1	1	6	74.13	$8,947

PGA Tour career totals from 1933 to 1966

	Starts	Rounds Played	Cuts Made	Wins	Top-5s	Top-10s	Top-25s	Scoring Average	Money
	287	N/A	N/A	52	N/A	207	277	N/A	N/A

Larry Nelson

Year	Starts	Rounds Played	Cuts Made	Wins	Top-5s	Top-10s	Top-25s	Scoring Average	Money
1973	3	10	1	0	0	0	0	75.30	$356

Best finish for 1973: T-51st at the Walt Disney World Open

1974	23	77	15	0	1	2	6	72.39	$22,559

Best finish for 1974: T-5th at the Western Open

1975	28	94	19	0	3	5	8	72.19	$39,811

Best finish for 1975: T-4th at the Byron Nelson Golf Classic & Sammy Davis, Jr. - Greater Hartford Open

1976	34	123	27	0	2	4	11	72.06	$66,482

Best finish for 1976: T-2nd at the Hawaiian Open

1977	32	111	24	0	4	6	10	72.29	$104,856

Best finish for 1977: T-2nd at the Andy Williams-San Diego Open, Greater Greensboro Open & Sammy Davis, Jr. - Greater Hartford Open

1978	31	108	22	0	2	4	12	71.65	$66,286

Best finish for 1978: T-3rd at the Sea Pines Heritage Classic

Year	Starts	Rounds Played	Cuts Made	Wins	Top-5s	Top-10s	Top-25s	Scoring Average	Money
1979	27	98	22	2	8	9	14	71.30	$281,022

Best finish for 1979: Win at the Jackie Gleason's Inverrary Classic & Western Open

1980	31	107	23	1	5	9	17	71.27	$193,415

Best finish for 1980: Win at the Atlanta Classic

1981	29	95	21	2	3	4	14	71.31	$194,842

Best finish for 1981: Win at the Greater Greensboro Open & PGA Championship

1982	27	93	19	0	5	8	13	71.23	$161,824

Best finish for 1982: 2nd at the Western Open

1983	24	77	14	1	2	3	7	72.05	$141,276

Best finish for 1983: Win at the U.S. Open

1984	21	64	11	1	2	4	8	72.05	$157,082

Best finish for 1984: Win at the Walt Disney World Golf Classic

1985	22	82	20	0	1	5	13	71.56	$146,349

Best finish for 1985: T-5th at the Hertz Bay Hill Classic

1986	24	70	10	0	2	3	3	72.13	$125,938

Best finish for 1986: T-3rd at the Panasonic Las Vegas Invitational

1987	24	76	15	2	4	7	9	71.26	$507,671

Best finish for 1987: Win at the PGA Championship & Walt Disney World/Oldsmobile Classic

1988	20	72	17	1	4	6	11	70.89	$435,084

Best finish for 1988: Win at the Georgia-Pacific Atlanta Golf Classic

1989	18	60	12	0	1	2	5	71.82	$189,169

Best finish for 1989: T-2nd at the GTE Byron Nelson Classic

1990	15	48	10	0	1	2	5	71.75	$125,260

Best finish for 1990: T-4th at the Buick Southern Open

1991	16	49	8	0	2	3	4	71.73	$161,543

Best finish for 1991: T-3rd at the U.S. Open & Buick Southern Open

1992	15	46	9	0	0	1	3	71.96	$97,430

Best finish for 1992: T-7th at the Doral-Ryder Open

1993	18	55	9	0	0	0	2	72.02	$54,870

Best finish for 1993: T-13th at the Sprint Western Open

1994	17	55	8	0	0	1	1	72.67	$69,030

Best finish for 1994: T-10th at the Doral-Ryder Open

1995	21	56	6	0	0	1	1	72.38	$41,889

Best finish for 1995: T-8th at the Buick Challenge

1996	21	76	16	0	0	3	12	70.42	$305,083

Best finish for 1996: T-8th at the Doral-Ryder Open & MCI Classic

1997	18	54	8	0	1	1	2	72.44	$197,951

Best finish for 1997: T-2nd at the Doral-Ryder Open

1998	4	13	2	0	0	0	0	71.38	$11,400

Best finish for 1998: T-43rd at the Walt Disney World/Oldsmobile Classic

1999	1	2	0	0	0	0	0	78.00	$1,750
2001	1	2	0	0	0	0	0	71.00	$2,000
2002	1	2	0	0	0	0	0	74.50	$2,000
2006	1	2	0	0	0	0	0	76.00	$2,250
2007	1	2	0	0	0	0	0	76.50	
Period Totals	Starts	Rounds Played	Cuts Made	Wins	Top-5s	Top-10s	Top-25s	Scoring Average	Money
	568	1879	368	10	53	93	191	71.78	$3,906,477

Dwight Nevil

Year	Starts	Rounds Played	Cuts Made	Wins	Top-5s	Top-10s	Top-25s	Scoring Average	Money
1971	18	53	8	0	0	0	4	72.49	$8,926

Best finish for 1971: T-12th at the Robinson Open Golf Classic & Walt Disney World Open

1972	29	95	18	0	1	2	4	72.75	$31,610

Best finish for 1972: 3rd at the Westchester Classic

1973	39	145	32	0	2	2	6	72.15	$40,193

Best finish for 1973: T-2nd at the B.C. Open & Quad Cities Open

1974	35	121	25	0	2	5	9	72.30	$41,768

Best finish for 1974: T-4th at the Hawaiian Open

1975	34	101	18	0	2	3	5	72.96	$19,920

Best finish for 1975: T-3rd at the Pensacola Open

1976	27	86	16	0	0	0	1	72.85	$10,613

Best finish for 1976: T-12th at the Bob Hope Chrysler Classic

1977	28	91	17	0	0	0	3	72.51	$17,471

Best finish for 1977: T-13th at the Bob Hope Chrysler Classic

1978	18	45	4	0	0	0	0	73.64	$2,243

Best finish for 1978: T-30th at the Sea Pines Heritage Classic

1979	6	12	0	0	0	0	0	74.92	
1981	3	10	1	0	0	0	0	72.60	$675

Best finish for 1981: T-55th at the Joe Garagiola Tucson Open

1982	2	4	0	0	0	0	0	78.00	$650
1983	1	2	0	0	0	0	0	77.50	
1985	1	2	0	0	0	0	0	76.50	

Year	Starts	Rounds Played	Cuts Made	Wins	Top-5s	Top-10s	Top-25s	Scoring Average	Money
1986	4	14	3	0	0	0	0	74.14	$2,626

Best finish for 1986: T-59th at the Deposit Guaranty Golf Classic

1987	1	2	0	0	0	0	0	81.00	$1,000
1988	3	8	1	0	0	0	0	76.25	$1,434

Best finish for 1988: T-60th at the Deposit Guaranty Golf Classic

1989	1	3	1	0	0	0	0	72.00	$398

Best finish for 1989: T-69th at the Deposit Guaranty Golf Classic

1990	5	11	1	0	0	0	0	74.45	$612

Best finish for 1990: T-67th at the Deposit Guaranty

1991	1	2	0	0	0	0	0	71.50	
1993	1	2	0	0	0	0	0	71.00	
1994	1	2	0	0	0	0	0	76.50	
1995	1	2	0	0	0	0	0	75.00	
1996	1	2	0	0	0	0	0	73.00	
Period Totals	Starts	Rounds Played	Cuts Made	Wins	Top-5s	Top-10s	Top-25s	Scoring Average	Money
	260	815	145	0	7	12	32	72.80	$180,140

Dave Newquist

Year	Starts	Rounds Played	Cuts Made	Wins	Top-5s	Top-10s	Top-25s	Scoring Average	Money
1975	23	71	11	0	0	0	0	73.45	$6,745

Best finish for 1975: T-27th at the Kaiser International Open

1976	21	62	12	0	1	2	3	73.08	$15,260

Best finish for 1976: T-4th at the Bob Hope Chrysler Classic

1977	20	55	8	0	0	0	2	73.45	$6,125

Best finish for 1977: T-16th at the San Antonio Texas Open

1978	11	26	2	0	0	0	0	73.65	$645

Best finish for 1978: T-59th at the Anheuser-Busch Golf Classic

Period Totals	Starts	Rounds Played	Cuts Made	Wins	Top-5s	Top-10s	Top-25s	Scoring Average	Money
	75	214	33	0	1	2	5	73.37	$28,774

Jack Newton

Year	Starts	Rounds Played	Cuts Made	Wins	Top-5s	Top-10s	Top-25s	Scoring Average	Money
1971	1	4	1	0	0	0	0	74.50	$310

Best finish for 1971: T-49th at the British Open

1972	1	4	1	0	0	0	0	73.75	$420

Best finish for 1972: T-40th at the British Open

1973	1	3	0	0	0	0	0	76.33	$195
1974	1	3	0	0	0	0	0	77.67	$180
1975	1	4	1	0	1	1	1	69.75	$13,200

Best finish for 1975: 2nd at the British Open

1976	2	6	1	0	0	0	1	75.17	$3,083

Best finish for 1976: T-17th at the British Open

1977	14	43	7	0	0	1	1	73.19	$10,274

Best finish for 1977: T-10th at the Colgate Hall Of Fame Golf Classic

1978	19	59	11	1	1	1	3	72.71	$29,129

Best finish for 1978: Win at the Buick Goodwrench Open

1979	23	77	16	0	0	1	6	73.19	$39,849

Best finish for 1979: T-9th at the Tournament Players Championship

1980	18	60	12	0	3	4	7	72.02	$99,981

Best finish for 1980: T-2nd at the Greater Greensboro Open & Masters

1981	19	53	8	0	0	0	0	73.53	$10,404

Best finish for 1981: T-33rd at the Doral-Eastern Open & Kemper Open

1982	19	59	11	0	0	1	4	71.76	$27,313

Best finish for 1982: T-10th at the Byron Nelson Golf Classic

Period Totals	Starts	Rounds Played	Cuts Made	Wins	Top-5s	Top-10s	Top-25s	Scoring Average	Money
	119	375	69	1	5	9	23	72.83	$234,338

Bobby Nichols

Year	Starts	Rounds Played	Cuts Made	Wins	Top-5s	Top-10s	Top-25s	Scoring Average	Money
1958	2	6	2	0	0	0	0	77.83	

Best finish for 1958: T-52nd at the U.S. Open

1960	15	60	14	0	2	2	6	71.23	$5,001

Best finish for 1960: T-4th at the West Palm Beach Open Invitational

1961	23	93	22	0	3	9	18	70.68	$15,616

Best finish for 1961: T-3rd at the Ontario Open

1962	25	101	22	2	4	8	17	71.46	$32,762

Best finish for 1962: Win at the St Petersburg Open Invitational & Houston Classic

1963	27	108	24	1	4	7	22	71.19	$32,605

Best finish for 1963: Win at the Seattle Open Invitational

1964	29	112	25	2	4	6	18	71.47	$75,115

Best finish for 1964: Win at the PGA Championship & Carling World Open Championship

1965	28	103	23	1	6	8	16	71.92	$55,299

Best finish for 1965: Win at the Houston Classic

Year	Starts	Rounds Played	Cuts Made	Wins	Top-5s	Top-10s	Top-25s	Scoring Average	Money
1966	29	111	25	1	2	6	16	71.83	$54,412

Best finish for 1966: Win at the Minnesota Golf Classic

1967	28	106	25	0	4	7	19	71.64	$51,557

Best finish for 1967: 2nd at the Masters

1968	28	101	22	0	3	5	10	71.87	$44,705

Best finish for 1968: T-2nd at the Greater Greensboro Open Invitational

1969	24	79	15	0	1	3	6	72.09	$33,297

Best finish for 1969: 2nd at the American Classic

1970	25	85	20	1	4	4	10	71.41	$100,470

Best finish for 1970: Win at the Dow Jones Open Invitational

1971	33	107	23	0	2	7	14	71.59	$68,298

Best finish for 1971: 2nd at the Western Open

1972	33	119	27	0	4	8	12	71.87	$69,351

Best finish for 1972: T-2nd at the Kaiser International Open

1973	26	100	22	1	2	4	11	71.86	$88,223

Best finish for 1973: Win at the Westchester Classic

1974	26	86	18	2	3	6	10	71.57	$116,032

Best finish for 1974: Win at the Andy Williams-San Diego Open & Canadian Open

1975	23	75	14	0	2	3	6	72.40	$50,332

Best finish for 1975: T-2nd at the Andy Williams-San Diego Open

1976	23	61	8	0	0	0	2	73.57	$11,921

Best finish for 1976: T-16th at the Greater Greensboro Open

1977	19	58	9	0	0	0	2	73.34	$9,255

Best finish for 1977: T-25th at the Jackie Gleason's Inverrary Classic & Canadian Open

1978	20	54	8	0	0	0	2	73.50	$8,335

Best finish for 1978: T-19th at the PGA Championship

1979	18	55	10	0	0	0	2	72.93	$11,367

Best finish for 1979: T-18th at the Greater Greensboro Open

1980	23	62	9	0	0	0	3	73.23	$21,613

Best finish for 1980: T-12th at the Bay Hill Classic

1981	21	58	9	0	0	0	1	72.86	$9,169

Best finish for 1981: T-23rd at the World Disney World National Team Championship

1982	18	49	5	0	0	0	0	73.71	$7,635

Best finish for 1982: T-28th at the Greater Greensboro Open

1983	10	26	3	0	0	0	0	74.04	$4,609

Best finish for 1983: T-36th at the PGA Championship

1984	10	27	2	0	0	0	0	72.67	$2,675

Best finish for 1984: T-52nd at the Isuzu/Andy Williams San Diego Open

1985	13	39	7	0	0	0	0	73.21	$8,824

Best finish for 1985: T-40th at the PGA Championship

1986	5	13	0	0	0	0	0	74.46	
1987	3	7	0	0	0	0	0	73.14	
1989	1	2	0	0	0	0	0	75.50	
1990	1	2	0	0	0	0	0	82.50	
Period Totals	Starts	Rounds Played	Cuts Made	Wins	Top-5s	Top-10s	Top-25s	Scoring Average	Money
	609	2065	413	11	50	93	223	72.08	$988,476

Gary Nicklaus

Year	Starts	Rounds Played	Cuts Made	Wins	Top-5s	Top-10s	Top-25s	Scoring Average	Money
1992	5	9	0	0	0	0	0	76.11	
1993	6	13	2	0	0	0	0	73.31	$5,427

Best finish for 1993: T-58th at the Honda Classic

1994	5	9	0	0	0	0	0	74.44	
1995	2	2	0	0	0	0	0	73.50	
1996	1	2	0	0	0	0	0	73.00	
1997	4	7	0	0	0	0	0	73.00	$1,000
1998	2	4	0	0	0	0	0	73.25	
1999	1	2	0	0	0	0	0	76.50	
2000	30	82	11	0	1	1	2	71.99	$403,982

Best finish for 2000: 2nd at the BellSouth Classic

2001	34	94	12	0	0	0	3	72.21	$210,893

Best finish for 2001: T-15th at the Memorial Tournament

2002	26	66	6	0	0	0	0	72.58	$41,969

Best finish for 2002: T-52nd at the Reno-Tahoe Open

2003	6	16	2	0	0	0	0	72.44	$32,300

Best finish for 2003: T-31st at the Chrysler Classic of Tucson

Period Totals	Starts	Rounds Played	Cuts Made	Wins	Top-5s	Top-10s	Top-25s	Scoring Average	Money
	122	306	33	0	1	1	5	72.54	$695,571

Jack Nicklaus

Year	Starts	Rounds Played	Cuts Made	Wins	Top-5s	Top-10s	Top-25s	Scoring Average	Money
1958	2	8	2	0	0	0	1	72.63	

Best finish for 1958: T-15th at the Rubber City Open

Year	Starts	Rounds Played	Cuts Made	Wins	Top-5s	Top-10s	Top-25s	Scoring Average	Money
1959	5	16	3	0	0	0	1	73.06	

Best finish for 1959: T-14th at the Buick Open Invitational

| 1960 | 3 | 12 | 3 | 0 | 1 | 1 | 2 | 72.75 | |

Best finish for 1960: 2nd at the U.S. Open

| 1961 | 6 | 24 | 5 | 0 | 1 | 3 | 3 | 72.25 | |

Best finish for 1961: T-4th at the U.S. Open

| 1962 | 24 | 98 | 21 | 3 | 11 | 15 | 19 | 70.99 | $61,819 |

Best finish for 1962: Win at the U.S. Open, Seattle World's Fair Open Invitational & Portland Open Invitational

| 1963 | 21 | 91 | 17 | 5 | 12 | 16 | 22 | 70.33 | $102,430 |

Best finish for 1963: Win at the Palm Springs Golf Classic, Masters, Tournament of Champions, PGA Championship & Sahara Invitational

| 1964 | 27 | 108 | 26 | 4 | 18 | 18 | 26 | 70.21 | $116,678 |

Best finish for 1964: Win at the Phoenix Open, Tournament of Champions, Whitemarsh Open & Portland Open

| 1965 | 24 | 97 | 24 | 5 | 16 | 19 | 21 | 70.43 | $150,040 |

Best finish for 1965: Win at the Masters, Memphis Open, Thunderbird Classic, Philadelphia Classic & Portland Open

| 1966 | 19 | 77 | 19 | 3 | 11 | 13 | 18 | 70.74 | $118,090 |

Best finish for 1966: Win at the Masters, British Open & Sahara Invitational

| 1967 | 23 | 91 | 22 | 5 | 14 | 16 | 17 | 70.30 | $214,487 |

Best finish for 1967: Win at the Bing Crosby Pro-Am, U.S. Open, Western Open, Westchester Classic & Sahara Open

| 1968 | 22 | 84 | 20 | 2 | 12 | 14 | 20 | 70.21 | $154,820 |

Best finish for 1968: Win at the Western Open & American Golf Classic

| 1969 | 24 | 93 | 22 | 3 | 6 | 12 | 18 | 71.06 | $141,140 |

Best finish for 1969: Win at the Andy Williams-San Diego Open, Sahara Invitational, Kaiser International Open

| 1970 | 22 | 78 | 19 | 3 | 9 | 13 | 17 | 70.81 | $152,129 |

Best finish for 1970: Win at the Byron Nelson Golf Classic, British Open & National 4 Ball Championship PGA Players

| 1971 | 18 | 69 | 18 | 5 | 12 | 15 | 15 | 69.10 | $241,035 |

Best finish for 1971: Win at the PGA Championship, Tournament of Champions, Byron Nelson Golf Classic, National Team Championship & Walt Disney World Open

| 1972 | 20 | 77 | 20 | 7 | 12 | 15 | 17 | 70.21 | $326,916 |

Best finish for 1972: Win at the Bing Crosby Pro-Am, Doral-Eastern Open, Masters, U.S. Open, Westchester Classic, U.S. Professional Match Play Championship & Walt Disney World Open

| 1973 | 19 | 73 | 19 | 7 | 13 | 17 | 18 | 69.82 | $312,613 |

Best finish for 1973: Win at the Bing Crosby Pro-Am, Greater New Orleans Open, Tournament of Champions, Atlanta Classic, PGA Championship, Ohio Kings Island Open & Walt Disney World Open

| 1974 | 18 | 71 | 18 | 2 | 9 | 13 | 18 | 70.15 | $242,255 |

Best finish for 1974: Win at the Hawaiian Open & Tournament Players Championship

| 1975 | 17 | 68 | 17 | 5 | 11 | 15 | 17 | 69.88 | $306,656 |

Best finish for 1975: Win at the Doral-Eastern Open, Sea Pines Heritage Classic, Masters, PGA Championship, World Open

| 1976 | 17 | 67 | 16 | 2 | 8 | 12 | 16 | 70.24 | $276,799 |

Best finish for 1976: Win at the Tournament Players Championship & World Series Of Golf

| 1977 | 19 | 72 | 17 | 3 | 11 | 15 | 17 | 70.19 | $298,109 |

Best finish for 1977: Win at the Jackie Gleason's Inverrary Classic, MONY Tournament Of Champions & Memorial Tournament

| 1978 | 16 | 60 | 14 | 4 | 7 | 11 | 13 | 71.02 | $280,725 |

Best finish for 1978: Win at the Jackie Gleason's Inverrary Classic, Tournament Players Championship, IVB Philadelphia Golf Classic & British Open

| 1979 | 13 | 53 | 13 | 0 | 3 | 5 | 7 | 72.42 | $83,059 |

Best finish for 1979: T-2nd at the British Open

| 1980 | 14 | 53 | 12 | 2 | 4 | 4 | 9 | 70.79 | $194,586 |

Best finish for 1980: Win at the U.S. Open & PGA Championship

| 1981 | 17 | 66 | 16 | 0 | 4 | 8 | 14 | 70.82 | $180,650 |

Best finish for 1981: T-2nd at the American Motors Inverrary Classic, Masters & Canadian Open

| 1982 | 16 | 56 | 13 | 1 | 6 | 8 | 12 | 70.98 | $245,140 |

Best finish for 1982: Win at the Colonial National Invitational

| 1983 | 16 | 62 | 15 | 0 | 5 | 8 | 11 | 70.90 | $259,856 |

Best finish for 1983: 2nd at the Honda Inverrary Classic, PGA Championship & World Series Of Golf

| 1984 | 14 | 56 | 14 | 1 | 4 | 6 | 12 | 70.84 | $275,972 |

Best finish for 1984: Win at the Memorial Tournament

| 1985 | 16 | 60 | 14 | 0 | 3 | 4 | 8 | 71.95 | $166,600 |

Best finish for 1985: T-2nd at the Canadian Open & Greater Milwaukee Open

| 1986 | 16 | 52 | 12 | 1 | 2 | 4 | 7 | 71.79 | $229,727 |

Best finish for 1986: Win at the Masters

| 1987 | 12 | 40 | 10 | 0 | 0 | 1 | 5 | 73.15 | $67,246 |

Best finish for 1987: T-7th at the Masters

| 1988 | 10 | 27 | 6 | 0 | 0 | 0 | 3 | 72.67 | $40,193 |

Best finish for 1988: T-21st at the Masters

| 1989 | 11 | 38 | 10 | 0 | 0 | 2 | 4 | 72.26 | $104,132 |

Best finish for 1989: 9th at the International

| 1990 | 10 | 28 | 7 | 0 | 0 | 1 | 1 | 73.50 | $74,389 |

Best finish for 1990: 6th at the Masters

| 1991 | 9 | 35 | 8 | 0 | 1 | 1 | 4 | 71.57 | $130,911 |

Best finish for 1991: T-5th at the Doral-Ryder Open

Year	Starts	Rounds Played	Cuts Made	Wins	Top-5s	Top-10s	Top-25s	Scoring Average	Money
1992	9	23	3	0	0	0	0	72.43	$18,268

Best finish for 1992: T-29th at the Honda Classic

| 1993 | 11 | 29 | 5 | 0 | 0 | 1 | 1 | 72.90 | $53,656 |

Best finish for 1993: T-10th at the Doral-Ryder Open

| 1994 | 9 | 21 | 1 | 0 | 0 | 0 | 0 | 74.57 | $15,186 |

Best finish for 1994: T-28th at the U.S. Open

| 1995 | 11 | 28 | 4 | 0 | 0 | 1 | 1 | 73.57 | $69,180 |

Best finish for 1995: T-6th at the AT&T Pebble Beach Pro-Am

| 1996 | 6 | 18 | 3 | 0 | 0 | 0 | 0 | 73.00 | $39,079 |

Best finish for 1996: T-27th at the U.S. Open

| 1997 | 7 | 22 | 4 | 0 | 0 | 1 | 1 | 72.91 | $86,683 |

Best finish for 1997: T-8th at the Memorial Tournament

| 1998 | 5 | 16 | 3 | 0 | 0 | 1 | 1 | 72.81 | $128,157 |

Best finish for 1998: T-6th at the Masters

| 1999 | 2 | 6 | 1 | 0 | 0 | 0 | 0 | 75.00 | $6,074 |

Best finish for 1999: T-70th at the Memorial Tournament

| 2000 | 8 | 21 | 2 | 0 | 0 | 0 | 0 | 74.67 | $21,308 |

Best finish for 2000: T-54th at the Masters

| 2001 | 4 | 8 | 0 | 0 | 0 | 0 | 0 | 73.00 | $5,000 |
| 2002 | 1 | 4 | 1 | 0 | 0 | 0 | 0 | 73.75 | $8,910 |

Best finish for 2002: 71st at the Memorial Tournament

| 2003 | 4 | 8 | 0 | 0 | 0 | 0 | 0 | 76.75 | $5,000 |
| 2004 | 2 | 6 | 1 | 0 | 0 | 0 | 0 | 74.17 | $16,130 |

Best finish for 2004: T-63rd at the Memorial Tournament

| 2005 | 3 | 6 | 0 | 0 | 0 | 0 | 0 | 75.33 | $9,380 |

Period Totals	Starts	Rounds Played	Cuts Made	Wins	Top-5s	Top-10s	Top-25s	Scoring Average	Money
	623	2272	519	73	225	308	416	71.08	$6,021,213

Mike Nicolette

Year	Starts	Rounds Played	Cuts Made	Wins	Top-5s	Top-10s	Top-25s	Scoring Average	Money
1979	8	24	4	0	0	0	2	72.17	$9,140

Best finish for 1979: T-13th at the Pensacola Open

| 1980 | 22 | 52 | 6 | 0 | 0 | 1 | 1 | 73.46 | $12,871 |

Best finish for 1980: 8th at the Atlanta Classic

| 1981 | 9 | 18 | 1 | 0 | 0 | 0 | 0 | 74.06 | $589 |

Best finish for 1981: T-72nd at the Michelob Houston Open

| 1982 | 21 | 63 | 11 | 0 | 1 | 1 | 2 | 72.56 | $38,084 |

Best finish for 1982: T-2nd at the Doral-Eastern Open

| 1983 | 27 | 94 | 19 | 1 | 2 | 3 | 5 | 72.57 | $127,868 |

Best finish for 1983: Win at the Bay Hill Classic

| 1984 | 27 | 79 | 14 | 0 | 0 | 2 | 6 | 72.27 | $62,894 |

Best finish for 1984: T-7th at the Texas Open

| 1985 | 30 | 92 | 17 | 0 | 0 | 0 | 4 | 72.60 | $41,750 |

Best finish for 1985: T-12th at the Pensacola Open

| 1986 | 22 | 59 | 9 | 0 | 0 | 0 | 0 | 72.90 | $12,197 |

Best finish for 1986: T-33rd at the Doral-Eastern Open

| 1987 | 18 | 55 | 10 | 0 | 1 | 1 | 3 | 71.47 | $43,007 |

Best finish for 1987: T-5th at the B.C. Open

| 1988 | 16 | 47 | 7 | 0 | 0 | 0 | 1 | 71.17 | $24,342 |

Best finish for 1988: T-19th at the Greater Milwaukee Open

| 1989 | 5 | 10 | 1 | 0 | 0 | 0 | 0 | 73.50 | $1,881 |

Best finish for 1989: T-65th at the BellSouth Atlanta Golf Classic

| 1990 | 2 | 6 | 1 | 0 | 0 | 0 | 1 | 71.50 | $4,200 |

Best finish for 1990: T-18th at the Deposit Guaranty

| 1991 | 5 | 15 | 3 | 0 | 1 | 1 | 1 | 70.60 | $33,222 |

Best finish for 1991: T-2nd at the Deposit Guaranty Classic

| 1992 | 4 | 12 | 2 | 0 | 1 | 1 | 1 | 70.67 | $22,065 |

Best finish for 1992: T-2nd at the Deposit Guaranty Classic

| 1993 | 2 | 6 | 1 | 0 | 0 | 0 | 0 | 72.50 | $1,557 |

Best finish for 1993: T-32nd at the Deposit Guaranty Classic

1994	2	4	0	0	0	0	0	74.75	
1995	1	2	0	0	0	0	0	77.00	
1996	1	2	0	0	0	0	0	74.50	
1999	1	4	1	0	0	0	0	72.00	$7,225

Best finish for 1999: T-44th at the Bay Hill Invitational

| 2000 | 1 | 4 | 1 | 0 | 0 | 0 | 0 | 72.25 | $6,996 |

Best finish for 2000: T-52nd at the Bay Hill Invitational

| 2002 | 1 | 2 | 0 | 0 | 0 | 0 | 0 | 77.00 | |

Period Totals	Starts	Rounds Played	Cuts Made	Wins	Top-5s	Top-10s	Top-25s	Scoring Average	Money
	225	650	108	1	6	10	27	72.43	$449,889

Lanny Nielsen

Year	Starts	Rounds Played	Cuts Made	Wins	Top-5s	Top-10s	Top-25s	Scoring Average	Money
1964	13	19	0	0	0	0	0	77.37	
1965	6	11	0	0	0	0	0	77.45	
1966	7	14	0	0	0	0	0	78.00	
1968	2	4	0	0	0	0	0	76.25	
Period Totals	Starts	Rounds Played	Cuts Made	Wins	Top-5s	Top-10s	Top-25s	Scoring Average	Money
	28	48	0	0	0	0	0	77.48	

Lonnie Nielsen

Year	Starts	Rounds Played	Cuts Made	Wins	Top-5s	Top-10s	Top-25s	Scoring Average	Money
1977	2	4	0	0	0	0	0	74.25	$500
1978	18	53	9	0	0	0	2	72.58	$8,292

Best finish for 1978: T-16th at the American Express Westchester Classic

Year	Starts	Rounds Played	Cuts Made	Wins	Top-5s	Top-10s	Top-25s	Scoring Average	Money
1979	22	60	7	0	1	1	1	72.42	$13,328

Best finish for 1979: T-5th at the Ed McMahon Quad City Open

| 1980 | 29 | 87 | 15 | 0 | 0 | 1 | 3 | 72.76 | $29,014 |

Best finish for 1980: T-8th at the Danny Thomas Memphis Classic

| 1981 | 20 | 60 | 10 | 0 | 0 | 0 | 3 | 72.57 | $18,625 |

Best finish for 1981: T-12th at the Western Open

| 1982 | 21 | 65 | 11 | 0 | 0 | 0 | 1 | 72.72 | $11,041 |

Best finish for 1982: T-23rd at the Southern Open

| 1983 | 21 | 66 | 11 | 0 | 0 | 0 | 0 | 72.74 | $11,215 |

Best finish for 1983: T-30th at the Sammy Davis, Jr. - Greater Hartford Open

| 1985 | 1 | 4 | 1 | 0 | 0 | 0 | 1 | 70.25 | $5,957 |

Best finish for 1985: T-11th at the B.C. Open

| 1986 | 2 | 8 | 2 | 0 | 0 | 0 | 1 | 70.63 | $14,722 |

Best finish for 1986: T-11th at the PGA Championship

| 1987 | 3 | 10 | 2 | 0 | 0 | 0 | 0 | 74.20 | $3,776 |

Best finish for 1987: T-56th at the PGA Championship

| 1988 | 2 | 6 | 1 | 0 | 0 | 0 | 0 | 74.00 | $1,920 |

Best finish for 1988: 78th at the B.C. Open

1989	1	2	0	0	0	0	0	80.00	$1,000
1990	1	2	0	0	0	0	0	76.50	$1,000
1991	1	4	1	0	0	0	0	74.25	$2,225

Best finish for 1991: T-70th at the PGA Championship

1994	1	2	0	0	0	0	0	75.00	$1,200
1996	1	2	0	0	0	0	0	75.50	$1,300
Period Totals	Starts	Rounds Played	Cuts Made	Wins	Top-5s	Top-10s	Top-25s	Scoring Average	Money
	146	435	70	0	1	2	12	72.74	$125,115

Tom Nieporte

Year	Starts	Rounds Played	Cuts Made	Wins	Top-5s	Top-10s	Top-25s	Scoring Average	Money
1958	38	137	31	0	3	4	16	71.66	$9,534

Best finish for 1958: T-4th at the Kentucky Derby Open & Mayfair Inn Open

| 1959 | 26 | 101 | 24 | 1 | 4 | 5 | 16 | 71.40 | $15,399 |

Best finish for 1959: Win at the Rubber City Open Invitational

| 1960 | 26 | 103 | 21 | 1 | 4 | 6 | 17 | 71.47 | $13,862 |

Best finish for 1960: Win at the Azalea Open Invitational

| 1961 | 16 | 64 | 15 | 0 | 0 | 2 | 8 | 71.39 | $6,913 |

Best finish for 1961: T-7th at the Milwaukee Open Invitational

| 1962 | 6 | 22 | 5 | 0 | 0 | 1 | 2 | 72.91 | $2,001 |

Best finish for 1962: T-8th at the Azalea Open Invitational

| 1963 | 6 | 22 | 4 | 0 | 1 | 2 | 2 | 72.77 | $4,824 |

Best finish for 1963: T-4th at the Tucson Open Invitational

| 1964 | 13 | 44 | 9 | 0 | 1 | 1 | 3 | 72.89 | $7,065 |

Best finish for 1964: T-5th at the PGA Championship

| 1965 | 16 | 53 | 9 | 0 | 0 | 1 | 2 | 73.51 | $3,522 |

Best finish for 1965: T-9th at the Cajun Classic

| 1966 | 10 | 32 | 5 | 0 | 0 | 0 | 1 | 74.88 | $2,290 |

Best finish for 1966: T-24th at the Bing Crosby National Professional-Amateur

| 1967 | 14 | 48 | 10 | 1 | 1 | 1 | 3 | 72.63 | $26,960 |

Best finish for 1967: Win at the Bob Hope Classic

| 1968 | 12 | 38 | 6 | 0 | 0 | 1 | 3 | 72.58 | $7,092 |

Best finish for 1968: T-9th at the Florida Citrus Open Invitational

| 1969 | 7 | 23 | 4 | 0 | 0 | 0 | 0 | 72.57 | $2,158 |

Best finish for 1969: T-30th at the Bob Hope Desert Classic & Greater Greensboro Open

| 1970 | 7 | 22 | 3 | 0 | 0 | 0 | 0 | 73.91 | $1,357 |

Best finish for 1970: T-50th at the National Airlines Open

| 1971 | 3 | 10 | 1 | 0 | 0 | 0 | 0 | 73.80 | $254 |

Best finish for 1971: T-50th at the Bob Hope Chrysler Classic

Year	Starts	Rounds Played	Cuts Made	Wins	Top-5s	Top-10s	Top-25s	Scoring Average	Money
1972	4	12	1	0	0	0	0	74.75	$280

Best finish for 1972: T-63rd at the Bing Crosby Pro-Am

1973	2	6	0	0	0	0	0	73.83	
1974	5	15	1	0	0	0	0	76.73	$321

Best finish for 1974: T-60th at the PGA Championship

1975	9	29	4	0	0	0	1	73.48	$4,718

Best finish for 1975: T-17th at the Florida Citrus Open Invitational

1976	4	13	4	0	0	0	0	74.62	

Best finish for 1976: T-72nd at the Florida Citrus Open Invitational

1977	3	9	1	0	0	0	0	75.56	$635

Best finish for 1977: T-58th at the Bob Hope Chrysler Classic

1978	4	11	1	0	0	0	0	75.45	$854

Best finish for 1978: T-40th at the Bob Hope Chrysler Classic

1979	1	4	0	0	0	0	0	77.75	
1980	2	6	0	0	0	0	0	75.83	
1981	1	4	0	0	0	0	0	74.25	
1982	1	4	0	0	0	0	0	76.00	
1983	1	4	0	0	0	0	0	74.75	
1984	1	4	0	0	0	0	0	75.75	
1985	1	4	0	0	0	0	0	78.00	
1986	1	4	0	0	0	0	0	76.50	
1987	1	4	0	0	0	0	0	76.50	
1988	1	4	0	0	0	0	0	76.75	
1989	1	4	0	0	0	0	0	76.25	
Period Totals	Starts	Rounds Played	Cuts Made	Wins	Top-5s	Top-10s	Top-25s	Scoring Average	Money
	243	860	159	3	14	24	74	72.73	$110,039

PGA Tour career totals from 1951 to 1989

	Starts	Rounds Played	Cuts Made	Wins	Top-5s	Top-10s	Top-25s	Scoring Average	Money
	274	984	190	3	14	27	84	N/A	$115,854

Frank Nobilo

Year	Starts	Rounds Played	Cuts Made	Wins	Top-5s	Top-10s	Top-25s	Scoring Average	Money
1986	1	4	1	0	0	0	0	75.25	$2,888

Best finish for 1986: T-59th at the British Open

1990	1	4	1	0	0	0	1	70.25	$20,182

Best finish for 1990: T-16th at the British Open

1991	1	4	1	0	0	0	0	72.00	$5,040

Best finish for 1991: T-73rd at the British Open

1992	1	4	1	0	0	0	0	72.50	$7,000

Best finish for 1992: T-33rd at the PGA Championship

1993	2	8	2	0	0	0	1	70.75	$21,209

Best finish for 1993: T-22nd at the PGA Championship

1994	3	12	3	0	0	1	2	70.67	$72,612

Best finish for 1994: T-9th at the U.S. Open

1995	5	14	2	0	0	1	1	73.43	$54,819

Best finish for 1995: T-10th at the U.S. Open

1996	8	29	7	0	1	2	4	71.00	$262,292

Best finish for 1996: 4th at the Masters

1997	19	64	14	1	2	4	9	71.50	$891,315

Best finish for 1997: Win at the Greater Greensboro Chrysler Classic

1998	21	62	13	0	1	2	4	72.15	$276,786

Best finish for 1998: 5th at the Greater Greensboro Chrysler Classic

1999	29	85	15	0	0	0	3	72.18	$191,734

Best finish for 1999: T-18th at the British Open

2000	28	95	20	0	0	0	2	71.23	$237,476

Best finish for 2000: T-13th at the Southern Farm Bureau Classic

2001	28	89	17	0	0	1	8	70.69	$462,650

Best finish for 2001: T-8th at the AT&T Pebble Beach

2002	30	94	16	0	0	1	6	71.15	$447,324

Best finish for 2002: T-10th at the WorldCom Classic

Period Totals	Starts	Rounds Played	Cuts Made	Wins	Top-5s	Top-10s	Top-25s	Scoring Average	Money
	177	568	113	1	4	12	41	71.46	$2,953,325

Keith Nolan

Year	Starts	Rounds Played	Cuts Made	Wins	Top-5s	Top-10s	Top-25s	Scoring Average	Money
1998	25	54	3	0	0	0	0	72.93	$13,203

Best finish for 1998: T-47th at the Shell Houston Open

2000	23	57	5	0	0	0	1	72.46	$46,006

Best finish for 2000: T-20th at the Southern Farm Bureau Classic

Period Totals	Starts	Rounds Played	Cuts Made	Wins	Top-5s	Top-10s	Top-25s	Scoring Average	Money
	48	111	8	0	0	0	1	72.68	$59,209

Greg Norman

Year	Starts	Rounds Played	Cuts Made	Wins	Top-5s	Top-10s	Top-25s	Scoring Average	Money
1977	2	5	0	0	0	0	0	76.00	$340
1978	1	4	1	0	0	0	0	72.75	$1,001

Best finish for 1978: T-29th at the British Open

1979	3	12	3	0	0	1	1	73.75	$12,052

Best finish for 1979: T-10th at the British Open

1980	1	3	0	0	0	0	0	74.67	$840
1981	10	38	9	0	2	3	5	71.68	$56,022

Best finish for 1981: T-4th at the Masters & PGA Championship

1982	5	18	4	0	1	1	2	72.83	$25,391

Best finish for 1982: T-5th at the PGA Championship

1983	10	40	10	0	2	2	5	72.38	$75,847

Best finish for 1983: 2nd at the Bay Hill Classic

1984	17	67	16	2	4	8	11	69.76	$331,537

Best finish for 1984: Win at the Kemper Open & Canadian Open

1985	17	63	14	0	2	6	10	71.29	$198,313

Best finish for 1985: T-2nd at the Canadian Open & Bank of Boston Classic

1986	21	76	18	3	10	11	13	70.21	$758,296

Best finish for 1986: Win at the Panasonic Las Vegas Invitational, Kemper Open & British Open

1987	20	71	19	0	7	9	13	70.79	$541,050

Best finish for 1987: T-2nd at the Masters & Beatrice Western Open

1988	15	51	12	1	5	7	11	70.61	$515,854

Best finish for 1988: Win at the MCI Heritage Classic

1989	19	66	17	2	9	9	15	70.47	$923,097

Best finish for 1989: Win at the International & Greater Milwaukee Open

1990	19	64	17	2	8	12	16	70.23	$1,218,562

Best finish for 1990: Win at the Doral-Ryder Open & Memorial Tournament

1991	18	67	16	0	3	7	8	70.66	$361,056

Best finish for 1991: 2nd at the Centel Western Open

1992	17	62	16	1	3	8	11	70.39	$702,842

Best finish for 1992: Win at the Canadian Open

1993	16	58	15	2	11	13	14	69.29	$1,514,653

Best finish for 1993: Win at the Doral-Ryder Open & British Open

1994	17	67	17	1	5	11	15	69.31	$1,361,627

Best finish for 1994: Win at the Players Championship

1995	16	58	15	3	7	9	14	69.88	$1,654,959

Best finish for 1995: Win at the Memorial Tournament, Canon Greater Hartford Open & NEC World Series of Golf

1996	17	51	11	1	3	5	10	70.61	$891,237

Best finish for 1996: Win at the Doral-Ryder Open

1997	15	51	13	2	6	7	10	70.41	$1,351,856

Best finish for 1997: Win at the FedEx St. Jude Classic & NEC World Series of Golf

1998	3	8	1	0	0	0	0	73.63	$30,925

Best finish for 1998: 27th at the Mercedes Championship

1999	12	33	8	0	1	2	6	72.33	$573,629

Best finish for 1999: 3rd at the Masters

2000	12	34	9	0	2	2	4	72.03	$583,510

Best finish for 2000: 4th at the Buick Classic & The International presented by Quest

2001	11	32	7	0	1	1	1	72.19	$261,310

Best finish for 2001: T-4th at the Bay Hill Invitational

2002	13	41	10	0	1	1	4	72.05	$498,488

Best finish for 2002: T-4th at the International presented by Quest

2003	7	17	3	0	0	0	2	71.94	$121,799

Best finish for 2003: T-18th at the British Open

2004	7	13	1	0	0	0	0	74.69	$18,373

Best finish for 2004: T-81st at the Players Championship

2005	2	4	1	0	0	0	0	72.25	$17,522

Best finish for 2005: T-60th at the British Open

2006	1	0	0	0	0	0	0		
2008	4	11	1	0	1	1	1	74.00	$509,618

Best finish for 2008: T-3rd at the British Open

Period Totals	Starts	Rounds Played	Cuts Made	Wins	Top-5s	Top-10s	Top-25s	Scoring Average	Money
	348	1185	284	20	94	136	202	70.87	$15,111,607

Tim Norris

Year	Starts	Rounds Played	Cuts Made	Wins	Top-5s	Top-10s	Top-25s	Scoring Average	Money
1981	27	85	18	0	0	2	5	72.24	$41,024

Best finish for 1981: 6th at the World Disney World National Team Championship

1982	17	47	7	1	1	1	4	71.74	$66,243

Best finish for 1982: Win at the Sammy Davis, Jr. - Greater Hartford Open

1983	18	51	8	0	1	1	2	73.25	$55,601

Best finish for 1983: 2nd at the Anheuser-Busch Golf Classic

Year	Starts	Rounds Played	Cuts Made	Wins	Top-5s	Top-10s	Top-25s	Scoring Average	Money
1984	36	108	17	0	1	4	5	72.56	$62,789

Best finish for 1984: T-5th at the Pensacola Open

1985	31	99	17	0	1	1	8	71.93	$82,835

Best finish for 1985: T-3rd at the Sea Pines Heritage Classic

1986	31	99	20	0	0	0	2	71.97	$40,412

Best finish for 1986: T-19th at the Byron Nelson Golf Classic

1987	30	94	19	0	0	0	6	72.02	$61,912

Best finish for 1987: T-15th at the Byron Nelson Golf Classic & Provident Classic

1988	27	85	16	0	1	1	4	70.93	$85,331

Best finish for 1988: 4th at the Buick Open

1989	30	88	14	0	0	1	2	71.76	$58,124

Best finish for 1989: T-7th at the Centel Classic

1990	1	2	0	0	0	0	0	70.00	
1992	2	6	1	0	0	0	0	72.17	$1,624

Best finish for 1992: T-68th at the Chattanooga Classic

Period Totals	Starts	Rounds Played	Cuts Made	Wins	Top-5s	Top-10s	Top-25s	Scoring Average	Money
	250	764	137	1	5	11	38	72.01	$555,896

Andy North

Year	Starts	Rounds Played	Cuts Made	Wins	Top-5s	Top-10s	Top-25s	Scoring Average	Money
1971	1	2	0	0	0	0	0	73.00	
1972	1	4	1	0	0	0	0	70.75	$922

Best finish for 1972: T-30th at the Walt Disney World Open

1973	36	120	22	0	2	4	8	72.31	$43,833

Best finish for 1973: T-3rd at the Monsanto Open & Ohio Kings Island Open

1974	33	117	27	0	3	4	8	72.05	$53,355

Best finish for 1974: T-2nd at the Houston Open

1975	32	109	23	0	2	4	9	72.08	$44,830

Best finish for 1975: 4th at the PGA Championship

1976	33	119	27	0	1	6	13	71.71	$71,267

Best finish for 1976: 2nd at the Ohio Kings Island Open

1977	30	101	21	1	3	5	11	72.02	$117,544

Best finish for 1977: Win at the American Express Westchester Classic

1978	27	100	23	1	4	6	12	72.01	$150,399

Best finish for 1978: Win at the U.S. Open

1979	28	96	20	0	1	3	11	72.33	$74,643

Best finish for 1979: 5th at the Colgate Hall Of Fame Classic

1980	24	85	19	0	1	2	8	71.72	$56,592

Best finish for 1980: T-4th at the Andy Williams-San Diego Open

1981	27	93	19	0	2	3	8	72.18	$112,901

Best finish for 1981: T-2nd at the Anheuser-Busch Golf Classic & Canadian Open

1982	23	77	15	0	2	2	6	72.44	$84,198

Best finish for 1982: 2nd at the Colonial National Invitational

1983	23	77	16	0	0	2	6	72.25	$52,516

Best finish for 1983: T-6th at the Glen CampbellLos Angeles Open

1984	26	83	16	0	0	0	1	73.06	$22,731

Best finish for 1984: T-24th at the Bob Hope Chrysler Classic

1985	24	78	16	1	2	5	8	71.83	$213,268

Best finish for 1985: Win at the U.S. Open

1986	23	65	10	0	0	1	3	72.42	$42,682

Best finish for 1986: T-7th at the Walt Disney World/Oldsmobile Classic

1987	20	60	10	0	0	1	3	72.25	$45,976

Best finish for 1987: T-9th at the Phoenix Open

1988	19	49	5	0	0	0	0	74.16	$17,944

Best finish for 1988: T-36th at the Masters

1989	15	32	3	0	0	0	0	73.97	$16,120

Best finish for 1989: T-27th at the Honda Classic

1990	24	69	12	0	1	1	3	72.75	$107,283

Best finish for 1990: 4th at the Canadian Open

1991	21	53	5	0	0	0	0	73.04	$24,653

Best finish for 1991: T-27th at the Players Championship

1992	20	48	3	0	0	0	0	72.63	$17,360

Best finish for 1992: T-28th at the Bob Hope Chrysler Classic

1993	4	10	1	0	0	0	1	73.20	$15,500

Best finish for 1993: T-16th at the Buick Classic

1994	6	13	1	0	0	0	0	74.85	$4,165

Best finish for 1994: T-64th at the Memorial Tournament

1995	9	18	0	0	0	0	0	75.56	$1,000
1996	1	2	0	0	0	0	0	73.00	
1997	1	2	0	0	0	0	0	72.50	
1998	1	2	0	0	0	0	0	72.50	

Year	Starts	Rounds Played	Cuts Made	Wins	Top-5s	Top-10s	Top-25s	Scoring Average	Money
1999	3	8	1	0	0	0	0	72.25	$3,841

Best finish for 1999: T-86th at the Greater Milwaukee Open

Year	Starts	Rounds Played	Cuts Made	Wins	Top-5s	Top-10s	Top-25s	Scoring Average	Money
2000	1	3	0	0	0	0	0	75.33	
2006	1	2	0	0	0	0	0	72.00	
Period Totals	Starts	Rounds Played	Cuts Made	Wins	Top-5s	Top-10s	Top-25s	Scoring Average	Money
	537	1697	316	3	24	49	119	72.38	$1,395,521

Bryan Norton

Year	Starts	Rounds Played	Cuts Made	Wins	Top-5s	Top-10s	Top-25s	Scoring Average	Money
1980	1	2	0	0	0	0	0	78.00	
1981	1	2	0	0	0	0	0	74.00	
1984	1	4	1	0	0	0	0	70.50	$430

Best finish for 1984: T-62nd at the Miller High-Life Quad Cities Open

Year	Starts	Rounds Played	Cuts Made	Wins	Top-5s	Top-10s	Top-25s	Scoring Average	Money
1990	2	8	1	0	0	0	0	71.88	$9,276

Best finish for 1990: T-31st at the British Open

Year	Starts	Rounds Played	Cuts Made	Wins	Top-5s	Top-10s	Top-25s	Scoring Average	Money
1991	25	64	9	0	0	1	1	72.08	$51,226

Best finish for 1991: T-7th at the Independent Insurance Agent Open

Year	Starts	Rounds Played	Cuts Made	Wins	Top-5s	Top-10s	Top-25s	Scoring Average	Money
1992	2	4	0	0	0	0	0	75.00	$1,000
Period Totals	Starts	Rounds Played	Cuts Made	Wins	Top-5s	Top-10s	Top-25s	Scoring Average	Money
	32	84	11	0	0	1	1	72.31	$61,933

Vern Novak

Year	Starts	Rounds Played	Cuts Made	Wins	Top-5s	Top-10s	Top-25s	Scoring Average	Money
1968	1	4	1	0	0	0	0	71.50	

Best finish for 1968: T-46th at the Cajun Classic

Year	Starts	Rounds Played	Cuts Made	Wins	Top-5s	Top-10s	Top-25s	Scoring Average	Money
1969	17	45	6	0	0	0	2	73.96	$2,691

Best finish for 1969: T-21st at the West End Classic

Year	Starts	Rounds Played	Cuts Made	Wins	Top-5s	Top-10s	Top-25s	Scoring Average	Money
1970	13	36	5	0	0	0	0	74.00	$1,098

Best finish for 1970: T-38th at the San Antonio Texas Open

Year	Starts	Rounds Played	Cuts Made	Wins	Top-5s	Top-10s	Top-25s	Scoring Average	Money
1972	2	4	0	0	0	0	0	74.25	
1973	23	60	6	0	0	0	0	73.97	$1,945

Best finish for 1973: T-32nd at the Ohio Kings Island Open

Year	Starts	Rounds Played	Cuts Made	Wins	Top-5s	Top-10s	Top-25s	Scoring Average	Money
1974	16	46	7	0	0	0	0	73.46	$2,207

Best finish for 1974: T-38th at the Greater New Orleans Open

Year	Starts	Rounds Played	Cuts Made	Wins	Top-5s	Top-10s	Top-25s	Scoring Average	Money
1976	1	2	0	0	0	0	0	74.50	
1979	1	2	0	0	0	0	0	75.50	
1986	1	2	0	0	0	0	0	78.50	
Period Totals	Starts	Rounds Played	Cuts Made	Wins	Top-5s	Top-10s	Top-25s	Scoring Average	Money
	75	201	25	0	0	0	2	73.88	$7,941

Rod Nuckolls

Year	Starts	Rounds Played	Cuts Made	Wins	Top-5s	Top-10s	Top-25s	Scoring Average	Money
1981	24	70	13	0	0	0	2	72.43	$12,648

Best finish for 1981: T-20th at the World Disney World National Team Championship

Year	Starts	Rounds Played	Cuts Made	Wins	Top-5s	Top-10s	Top-25s	Scoring Average	Money
1982	24	63	7	0	0	0	1	73.22	$8,636

Best finish for 1982: T-20th at the Miller High-Life Quad Cities Open

Year	Starts	Rounds Played	Cuts Made	Wins	Top-5s	Top-10s	Top-25s	Scoring Average	Money
1983	30	88	13	0	0	0	3	72.85	$22,839

Best finish for 1983: T-13th at the Western Open

Year	Starts	Rounds Played	Cuts Made	Wins	Top-5s	Top-10s	Top-25s	Scoring Average	Money
1984	13	36	6	0	0	0	1	72.67	$7,884

Best finish for 1984: T-14th at the Miller High-Life Quad Cities Open

Year	Starts	Rounds Played	Cuts Made	Wins	Top-5s	Top-10s	Top-25s	Scoring Average	Money
1985	1	2	0	0	0	0	0	73.50	$600
1994	1	2	0	0	0	0	0	75.50	$1,200
Period Totals	Starts	Rounds Played	Cuts Made	Wins	Top-5s	Top-10s	Top-25s	Scoring Average	Money
	93	261	39	0	0	0	7	72.83	$53,807

Christy O'Connor

Year	Starts	Rounds Played	Cuts Made	Wins	Top-5s	Top-10s	Top-25s	Scoring Average	Money
1958	1	4	1	0	1	1	1	69.75	

Best finish for 1958: T-3rd at the British Open

Year	Starts	Rounds Played	Cuts Made	Wins	Top-5s	Top-10s	Top-25s	Scoring Average	Money
1959	1	4	1	0	1	1	1	72.00	

Best finish for 1959: T-5th at the British Open

Year	Starts	Rounds Played	Cuts Made	Wins	Top-5s	Top-10s	Top-25s	Scoring Average	Money
1960	1	4	1	0	0	0	0	73.75	$140

Best finish for 1960: T-36th at the British Open

Year	Starts	Rounds Played	Cuts Made	Wins	Top-5s	Top-10s	Top-25s	Scoring Average	Money
1961	1	4	1	0	1	1	1	72.00	

Best finish for 1961: T-4th at the British Open

Year	Starts	Rounds Played	Cuts Made	Wins	Top-5s	Top-10s	Top-25s	Scoring Average	Money
1962	1	4	1	0	0	0	1	74.25	

Best finish for 1962: T-16th at the British Open

Year	Starts	Rounds Played	Cuts Made	Wins	Top-5s	Top-10s	Top-25s	Scoring Average	Money
1963	2	8	2	0	0	1	1	71.88	$1,082

Best finish for 1963: 6th at the British Open

Year	Starts	Rounds Played	Cuts Made	Wins	Top-5s	Top-10s	Top-25s	Scoring Average	Money
1964	10	36	6	0	0	1	2	73.36	$1,543

Best finish for 1964: T-6th at the British Open

Year	Starts	Rounds Played	Cuts Made	Wins	Top-5s	Top-10s	Top-25s	Scoring Average	Money
1965	2	8	2	0	1	2	2	71.63	$6,500

Best finish for 1965: T-2nd at the British Open

Year	Starts	Rounds Played	Cuts Made	Wins	Top-5s	Top-10s	Top-25s	Scoring Average	Money
1966	2	8	2	0	0	0	1	73.88	$1,608

Best finish for 1966: T-13th at the British Open

| 1967 | 2 | 6 | 1 | 0 | 0 | 0 | 1 | 73.83 | $406 |

Best finish for 1967: 21st at the British Open

| 1968 | 1 | 2 | 0 | 0 | 0 | 0 | 0 | 78.50 | |
| 1969 | 1 | 4 | 1 | 0 | 1 | 1 | 1 | 71.00 | $4,200 |

Best finish for 1969: 5th at the British Open

| 1970 | 2 | 6 | 1 | 0 | 0 | 0 | 1 | 73.67 | $679 |

Best finish for 1970: T-17th at the British Open

| 1971 | 1 | 4 | 1 | 0 | 0 | 0 | 0 | 73.50 | $499 |

Best finish for 1971: T-35th at the British Open

| 1972 | 1 | 4 | 1 | 0 | 0 | 0 | 1 | 72.75 | $812 |

Best finish for 1972: T-23rd at the British Open

| 1973 | 1 | 4 | 1 | 0 | 0 | 1 | 1 | 72.00 | $4,463 |

Best finish for 1973: T-7th at the British Open

| 1974 | 1 | 4 | 1 | 0 | 0 | 0 | 0 | 77.25 | $300 |

Best finish for 1974: T-56th at the British Open

1976	1	2	0	0	0	0	0	77.50	$180
1977	1	3	0	0	0	0	0	75.33	$340
1979	1	4	1	0	0	0	0	74.75	$1,208

Best finish for 1979: T-36th at the British Open

Period Totals	Starts	Rounds Played	Cuts Made	Wins	Top-5s	Top-10s	Top-25s	Scoring Average	Money
	34	123	25	0	5	9	15	73.29	$23,960

Christy O'Connor, Jr.

Year	Starts	Rounds Played	Cuts Made	Wins	Top-5s	Top-10s	Top-25s	Scoring Average	Money
1970	1	2	0	0	0	0	0	77.50	
1974	1	4	1	0	0	0	1	74.75	$699

Best finish for 1974: T-24th at the British Open

| 1975 | 2 | 6 | 1 | 0 | 0 | 0 | 0 | 74.67 | $407 |

Best finish for 1975: T-47th at the British Open

| 1976 | 1 | 4 | 1 | 0 | 1 | 1 | 1 | 72.00 | $5,076 |

Best finish for 1976: T-5th at the British Open

| 1977 | 2 | 6 | 1 | 0 | 0 | 0 | 0 | 75.50 | $1,925 |

Best finish for 1977: T-52nd at the British Open

1978	1	2	0	0	0	0	0	75.00	$332
1980	1	2	0	0	0	0	0	75.50	$540
1982	1	2	0	0	0	0	0	77.50	$382
1983	1	4	1	0	0	1	1	70.00	$14,438

Best finish for 1983: T-8th at the British Open

| 1984 | 1 | 3 | 0 | 0 | 0 | 0 | 0 | 73.67 | $793 |
| 1985 | 1 | 4 | 1 | 0 | 1 | 1 | 1 | 71.00 | $34,220 |

Best finish for 1985: T-3rd at the British Open

| 1986 | 2 | 6 | 1 | 0 | 0 | 0 | 1 | 72.67 | $21,000 |

Best finish for 1986: T-11th at the British Open

| 1987 | 1 | 2 | 0 | 0 | 0 | 0 | 0 | 73.50 | $640 |
| 1988 | 2 | 6 | 1 | 0 | 0 | 0 | 0 | 73.83 | $2,256 |

Best finish for 1988: T-61st at the Manufactures Hanover Westchester Classic

| 1989 | 1 | 4 | 1 | 0 | 0 | 0 | 0 | 72.50 | $5,440 |

Best finish for 1989: T-49th at the British Open

| 1990 | 1 | 4 | 1 | 0 | 0 | 0 | 1 | 70.75 | $11,554 |

Best finish for 1990: T-25th at the British Open

| 1991 | 1 | 4 | 1 | 0 | 0 | 0 | 0 | 70.75 | $9,464 |

Best finish for 1991: T-32nd at the British Open

| 1992 | 2 | 4 | 1 | 0 | 0 | 0 | 1 | 71.50 | $21,020 |

Best finish for 1992: T-16th at the NEC World Series of Golf

| 1993 | 1 | 4 | 1 | 0 | 0 | 0 | 0 | 70.75 | $8,205 |

Best finish for 1993: T-39th at the British Open

| 1994 | 1 | 4 | 1 | 0 | 0 | 0 | 0 | 71.00 | $7,047 |

Best finish for 1994: T-60th at the British Open

| 2000 | 1 | 4 | 1 | 0 | 0 | 0 | 0 | 72.50 | $11,273 |

Best finish for 2000: T-60th at the British Open

Period Totals	Starts	Rounds Played	Cuts Made	Wins	Top-5s	Top-10s	Top-25s	Scoring Average	Money
	26	81	15	0	2	3	7	72.95	$156,711

Mac O'Grady

Year	Starts	Rounds Played	Cuts Made	Wins	Top-5s	Top-10s	Top-25s	Scoring Average	Money
1981	3	9	1	0	0	0	0	74.00	$645

Best finish for 1981: T-62nd at the Glen CampbellLos Angeles Open

| 1983 | 24 | 76 | 15 | 0 | 1 | 1 | 2 | 72.42 | $50,379 |

Best finish for 1983: T-3rd at the Sea Pines Heritage Classic

Year	Starts	Rounds Played	Cuts Made	Wins	Top-5s	Top-10s	Top-25s	Scoring Average	Money
1984	36	108	17	0	0	0	4	72.91	$42,143

Best finish for 1984: T-13th at the Hawaiian Open & Greater Greensboro Open

1985	26	79	15	0	5	6	9	71.35	$224,808

Best finish for 1985: T-3rd at the Panasonic Las Vegas Invitational, Byron Nelson Golf Classic & Buick Open

1986	24	77	17	1	3	5	8	71.51	$262,556

Best finish for 1986: Win at the Canon Sammy Davis, Jr. - Greater Hartford Open

1987	27	87	17	1	3	4	9	71.39	$285,109

Best finish for 1987: Win at the MONY Tournament Of Champions

1988	24	65	8	0	1	1	3	72.51	$118,153

Best finish for 1988: T-2nd at the Los Angeles Open

1989	24	53	6	0	0	1	1	72.45	$41,090

Best finish for 1989: T-10th at the International

1990	1	0	0	0	0	0	0		
1991	8	23	4	0	0	0	0	72.78	$14,102

Best finish for 1991: T-27th at the AT&T Pebble Beach Pro-Am

1992	2	8	1	0	0	0	0	70.75	$2,030

Best finish for 1992: T-68th at the Nissan Los Angeles Open

1993	4	12	1	0	0	0	1	72.58	$10,429

Best finish for 1993: T-20th at the Hardee's Golf Classic

1994	2	7	1	0	0	0	0	70.86	$2,409

Best finish for 1994: T-58th at the Bob Hope Chrysler Classic

1995	5	11	1	0	0	0	0	72.91	$1,540

Best finish for 1995: T-57th at the Deposit Guaranty Golf Classic

1996	10	19	0	0	0	0	0	75.63	
1997	9	19	1	0	0	0	0	73.53	$3,078

Best finish for 1997: T-51st at the B.C. Open

1998	8	16	0	0	0	0	0	74.00	
1999	1	4	1	0	0	0	0	71.75	$3,520

Best finish for 1999: 82nd at the John Deere Classic

2004	1	2	0	0	0	0	0	74.00	
2006	1	2	0	0	0	0	0	76.00	
Period Totals	Starts	Rounds Played	Cuts Made	Wins	Top-5s	Top-10s	Top-25s	Scoring Average	Money
	240	677	106	2	13	18	37	72.33	$1,061,991

Sean O'Hair

Year	Starts	Rounds Played	Cuts Made	Wins	Top-5s	Top-10s	Top-25s	Scoring Average	Money
2005	29	99	24	1	2	4	9	70.85	$2,461,482

Best finish for 2005: Win at the John Deere Classic

2006	30	98	20	0	2	2	7	71.62	$1,416,387

Best finish for 2006: 3rd at the Canadian Open

2007	28	98	21	0	3	5	14	70.64	$1,923,226

Best finish for 2007: T-4th at the Fry's Electronics Open

2008	25	81	16	1	3	3	6	71.25	$2,089,857

Best finish for 2008: Win at the PODS Championship

Period Totals	Starts	Rounds Played	Cuts Made	Wins	Top-5s	Top-10s	Top-25s	Scoring Average	Money
	112	376	81	2	10	14	36	71.08	$7,890,952

Nick O'Hern

Year	Starts	Rounds Played	Cuts Made	Wins	Top-5s	Top-10s	Top-25s	Scoring Average	Money
2000	1	4	1	0	0	0	0	71.75	$15,707

Best finish for 2000: T-41st at the British Open

2001	4	6	1	0	1	1	1	72.33	$152,000

Best finish for 2001: T-5th at the Accenture Match Play Championship

2003	1	2	0	0	0	0	0	76.00	$4,769
2004	2	8	2	0	0	0	0	71.63	$88,875

Best finish for 2004: T-28th at the WGC-American Express Championship

2005	13	40	10	0	1	3	5	72.08	$891,202

Best finish for 2005: T-5th at the WGC-Accenture Match Play Championship

2006	15	46	10	0	1	2	6	70.65	$1,002,133

Best finish for 2006: T-2nd at the Booz Allen Classic

2007	22	68	14	0	2	3	7	71.72	$1,347,272

Best finish for 2007: 3rd at the Travelers Championship

2008	26	80	18	0	1	4	9	70.89	$1,370,771

Best finish for 2008: T-3rd at the AT&T National

Period Totals	Starts	Rounds Played	Cuts Made	Wins	Top-5s	Top-10s	Top-25s	Scoring Average	Money
	84	254	56	0	6	13	28	71.37	$4,872,729

Jack O'Keefe

Year	Starts	Rounds Played	Cuts Made	Wins	Top-5s	Top-10s	Top-25s	Scoring Average	Money
1961	1	4	1	0	0	1	1	71.25	$550

Best finish for 1961: T-10th at the Almaden Open

1963	4	16	4	0	0	0	0	71.25	$969

Best finish for 1963: T-28th at the St. Paul Open Invitational

Year	Starts	Rounds Played	Cuts Made	Wins	Top-5s	Top-10s	Top-25s	Scoring Average	Money
1964	7	17	0	0	0	0	0	76.18	
1996	1	4	1	0	0	0	0	73.75	$5,305

Best finish for 1996: T-90th at the U.S. Open

1997	27	75	10	0	0	0	2	71.85	$85,220

Best finish for 1997: T-13th at the Deposit Guaranty Golf Classic

1998	1	4	1	0	0	0	0	71.50	$2,592

Best finish for 1998: T-62nd at the Deposit Guaranty Golf Classic

Period Totals	Starts	Rounds Played	Cuts Made	Wins	Top-5s	Top-10s	Top-25s	Scoring Average	Money
	41	120	17	0	0	1	3	72.42	$94,636

Paul O'Leary

Year	Starts	Rounds Played	Cuts Made	Wins	Top-5s	Top-10s	Top-25s	Scoring Average	Money
1958	27	94	20	0	0	2	3	72.33	$2,329

Best finish for 1958: T-9th at the Los Angeles Open

1959	3	12	3	0	0	1	3	70.17	$1,360

Best finish for 1959: T-7th at the Tucson Open Invitational

1960	1	4	1	0	0	0	0	75.25	$100

Best finish for 1960: T-40th at the Bing Crosby National

Period Totals	Starts	Rounds Played	Cuts Made	Wins	Top-5s	Top-10s	Top-25s	Scoring Average	Money
	31	110	24	0	0	3	6	72.20	$3,789

Peter O'Malley

Year	Starts	Rounds Played	Cuts Made	Wins	Top-5s	Top-10s	Top-25s	Scoring Average	Money
1988	2	2	0	0	0	0	0	75.00	
1991	1	4	1	0	0	0	0	71.00	$8,366

Best finish for 1991: T-38th at the British Open

1992	2	6	1	0	0	0	0	74.33	$6,475

Best finish for 1992: T-68th at the British Open

1993	3	10	2	0	0	0	0	74.50	$9,220

Best finish for 1993: T-26th at the Freeport-McMoRan Classic

1995	1	4	1	0	0	0	0	73.25	$9,410

Best finish for 1995: T-55th at the British Open

1996	5	14	4	0	0	0	1	71.43	$34,560

Best finish for 1996: T-16th at the FedEx St. Jude Classic

1997	1	4	1	0	0	1	1	70.25	$68,137

Best finish for 1997: T-7th at the British Open

1998	5	16	4	0	0	0	1	71.81	$39,094

Best finish for 1998: T-24th at the British Open

1999	2	6	1	0	0	0	1	74.33	$25,653

Best finish for 1999: T-24th at the British Open

2000	1	2	0	0	0	0	0	74.00	$2,000
2001	1	2	0	0	0	0	0	72.50	$1,860
2002	6	16	4	0	0	1	2	72.81	$215,266

Best finish for 2002: T-8th at the British Open

2003	3	10	2	0	0	0	0	74.60	$49,274

Best finish for 2003: T-44th at the American Express Championship

2004	1	2	0	0	0	0	0	73.50	$4,682

Period Totals	Starts	Rounds Played	Cuts Made	Wins	Top-5s	Top-10s	Top-25s	Scoring Average	Money
	34	98	21	0	0	2	6	72.91	$473,996

Mark O'Meara

Year	Starts	Rounds Played	Cuts Made	Wins	Top-5s	Top-10s	Top-25s	Scoring Average	Money
1979	1	4	1	0	0	0	0	73.00	

Best finish for 1979: T-32nd at the World Series Of Golf

1980	3	8	1	0	0	0	1	76.00	$1,500

Best finish for 1980: T-25th at the World Series Of Golf

1981	36	116	23	0	2	4	9	71.84	$77,813

Best finish for 1981: T-2nd at the Tallahassee Open

1982	35	108	19	0	0	1	4	72.41	$31,733

Best finish for 1982: T-6th at the Bob Hope Chrysler Classic

1983	32	100	17	0	2	2	6	72.11	$69,454

Best finish for 1983: T-2nd at the Phoenix Open

1984	32	111	23	1	10	15	19	70.77	$465,873

Best finish for 1984: Win at the Greater Milwaukee Open

1985	26	90	20	2	6	7	14	70.97	$375,060

Best finish for 1985: Win at the Bing Crosby Pro-Am & Hawaiian Open

1986	26	92	23	0	5	5	12	71.14	$258,027

Best finish for 1986: 2nd at the MONY Tournament Of Champions

1987	28	91	21	0	3	7	11	71.05	$331,650

Best finish for 1987: T-2nd at the Southwest Golf Classic & Walt Disney World/Oldsmobile Classic

1988	29	95	21	0	4	7	12	71.12	$447,149

Best finish for 1988: T-2nd at the Panasonic Las Vegas Invitational & Northern Telecom Tucson Open

Year	Starts	Rounds Played	Cuts Made	Wins	Top-5s	Top-10s	Top-25s	Scoring Average	Money
1989	28	94	20	1	5	7	13	70.88	$623,764

Best finish for 1989: Win at the AT&T Pebble Beach Pro-Am

| 1990 | 27 | 89 | 21 | 2 | 5 | 6 | 14 | 71.06 | $716,409 |

Best finish for 1990: Win at the AT&T Pebble Beach Pro-Am & H-E-B Texas Open

| 1991 | 26 | 85 | 16 | 1 | 5 | 6 | 13 | 70.40 | $658,296 |

Best finish for 1991: Win at the Walt Disney World/Oldsmobile Classic

| 1992 | 24 | 85 | 19 | 1 | 5 | 9 | 16 | 70.08 | $796,615 |

Best finish for 1992: Win at the AT&T Pebble Beach Pro-Am

| 1993 | 27 | 88 | 18 | 0 | 2 | 4 | 9 | 71.31 | $352,640 |

Best finish for 1993: T-3rd at the Infiniti Tournament Of Champions

| 1994 | 29 | 91 | 17 | 0 | 0 | 3 | 8 | 71.49 | $215,070 |

Best finish for 1994: T-8th at the Texas Open

| 1995 | 27 | 96 | 21 | 2 | 4 | 8 | 12 | 70.34 | $914,129 |

Best finish for 1995: Win at the Honda Classic & Bell Canadian Open

| 1996 | 21 | 80 | 19 | 2 | 7 | 8 | 14 | 69.93 | $1,255,749 |

Best finish for 1996: Win at the Mercedes Championship & Greater Greensboro Chrysler Classic

| 1997 | 22 | 78 | 19 | 2 | 4 | 6 | 11 | 70.92 | $1,124,559 |

Best finish for 1997: Win at the AT&T Pebble Beach Pro-Am & Buick Invitational

| 1998 | 19 | 68 | 15 | 2 | 5 | 7 | 11 | 70.40 | $1,786,699 |

Best finish for 1998: Win at the Masters & British Open

| 1999 | 19 | 59 | 15 | 0 | 2 | 3 | 8 | 71.51 | $871,202 |

Best finish for 1999: T-2nd at the Mercedes Championships

| 2000 | 19 | 55 | 12 | 0 | 0 | 1 | 5 | 71.91 | $429,309 |

Best finish for 2000: T-9th at The Players Championship

| 2001 | 21 | 65 | 13 | 0 | 0 | 1 | 5 | 71.09 | $439,620 |

Best finish for 2001: T-9th at the International presented by Quest

| 2002 | 24 | 66 | 9 | 0 | 2 | 2 | 5 | 71.44 | $737,132 |

Best finish for 2002: T-2nd at the Buick Invitational & Buick Open

| 2003 | 25 | 67 | 11 | 0 | 0 | 1 | 2 | 72.34 | $390,349 |

Best finish for 2003: T-8th at the Masters

| 2004 | 17 | 58 | 12 | 0 | 0 | 1 | 4 | 71.52 | $545,866 |

Best finish for 2004: T-10th at the Buick Open

| 2005 | 21 | 66 | 11 | 0 | 0 | 0 | 0 | 72.17 | $196,226 |

Best finish for 2005: T-27th at the EDS Byron Nelson Championship

| 2006 | 18 | 50 | 7 | 0 | 0 | 0 | 2 | 72.38 | $208,667 |

Best finish for 2006: T-16th at the Buick Invitational

| 2007 | 4 | 14 | 2 | 0 | 0 | 0 | 0 | 72.86 | $42,914 |

Best finish for 2007: T-39th at the Buick Invitational

| 2008 | 5 | 14 | 1 | 0 | 0 | 0 | 0 | 74.07 | $10,920 |

Best finish for 2008: 66th at the Buick Invitational

Period Totals	Starts	Rounds Played	Cuts Made	Wins	Top-5s	Top-10s	Top-25s	Scoring Average	Money
	671	2183	447	16	78	121	240	71.27	$14,374,393

Arron Oberholser

Year	Starts	Rounds Played	Cuts Made	Wins	Top-5s	Top-10s	Top-25s	Scoring Average	Money
2000	1	2	0	0	0	0	0	71.00	
2001	1	3	0	0	0	0	0	72.33	
2003	25	80	15	0	1	2	4	70.36	$619,765

Best finish for 2003: T-4th at the Buick Invitational

| 2004 | 23 | 73 | 16 | 0 | 3 | 3 | 5 | 71.16 | $1,355,433 |

Best finish for 2004: 2nd at the Wachovia Championship

| 2005 | 21 | 63 | 13 | 0 | 0 | 4 | 6 | 70.68 | $921,796 |

Best finish for 2005: T-6th at the Buick Invitational, AT&T Pebble Beach National Pro-Am & BellSouth Classic

| 2006 | 23 | 79 | 19 | 1 | 2 | 4 | 13 | 70.37 | $2,471,232 |

Best finish for 2006: Win at the AT&T Pebble Beach National Pro-Am

| 2007 | 21 | 68 | 17 | 0 | 2 | 5 | 8 | 71.04 | $1,799,458 |

Best finish for 2007: T-2nd at the Deutsche Bank Championship

| 2008 | 10 | 31 | 8 | 0 | 1 | 1 | 3 | 71.16 | $454,881 |

Best finish for 2008: T-4th at the Frys.Com Open

Period Totals	Starts	Rounds Played	Cuts Made	Wins	Top-5s	Top-10s	Top-25s	Scoring Average	Money
	125	399	88	1	9	19	39	70.76	$7,622,566

Alvin Odom

Year	Starts	Rounds Played	Cuts Made	Wins	Top-5s	Top-10s	Top-25s	Scoring Average	Money
1964	5	9	0	0	0	0	0	75.11	
1965	1	2	0	0	0	0	0	78.00	
1969	8	20	2	0	0	0	0	74.20	$185

Best finish for 1969: 66th at the Azalea Open

| 1970 | 6 | 12 | 0 | 0 | 0 | 0 | 0 | 75.33 | |
| 1971 | 5 | 14 | 2 | 0 | 0 | 0 | 0 | 75.07 | $334 |

Best finish for 1971: 49th at the Tallahassee Open

Year	Starts	Rounds Played	Cuts Made	Wins	Top-5s	Top-10s	Top-25s	Scoring Average	Money
1973	1	2	0	0	0	0	0	79.00	
Period Totals	Starts	Rounds Played	Cuts Made	Wins	Top-5s	Top-10s	Top-25s	Scoring Average	Money
	26	59	4	0	0	0	0	75.07	$519

Bill Ogden

Year	Starts	Rounds Played	Cuts Made	Wins	Top-5s	Top-10s	Top-25s	Scoring Average	Money
1958	12	46	11	0	0	1	2	72.76	$1,486

Best finish for 1958: T-8th at the Baton Rouge Open

1959	4	14	3	0	0	0	0	72.93	$386

Best finish for 1959: T-31st at the Tucson Open Invitational

1960	2	8	2	0	0	0	0	72.88	$250

Best finish for 1960: T-45th at the Palm Springs Desert Golf Classic

1961	1	2	1	0	0	0	0	77.00	

Best finish for 1961: T-200 at the PGA Championship

1963	2	8	2	0	0	0	1	74.00	$1,738

Best finish for 1963: T-12th at the Western Open Championship

1964	8	30	7	0	0	0	2	72.53	$2,258

Best finish for 1964: T-17th at the Tucson Open

1965	8	31	6	0	0	0	2	72.74	$2,274

Best finish for 1965: T-13th at the Bing Crosby Pro-Am

1966	8	21	2	0	0	0	1	74.38	$1,550

Best finish for 1966: T-14th at the Phoenix Open Invitational

1967	5	21	5	0	0	0	1	71.19	$2,000

Best finish for 1967: T-15th at the Tucson Open

1968	7	23	4	0	1	1	1	72.78	$4,962

Best finish for 1968: T-4th at the Tucson Open Invitational

1969	7	24	6	0	1	1	1	73.92	$3,517

Best finish for 1969: T-5th at the Alameda County Open

1970	8	23	4	0	0	0	0	73.17	$2,094

Best finish for 1970: T-26th at the Andy Williams-San Diego Open

1971	4	10	1	0	0	0	0	74.30	$754

Best finish for 1971: T-50th at the Bob Hope Chrysler Classic

1972	3	6	0	0	0	0	0	77.33	$500
1973	3	8	0	0	0	0	0	74.63	
1975	1	4	0	0	0	0	0	75.50	
1976	1	4	0	0	0	0	0	74.25	
1977	2	6	0	0	0	0	0	76.17	
1978	2	6	0	0	0	0	0	75.67	
1979	1	4	0	0	0	0	0	73.50	
Period Totals	Starts	Rounds Played	Cuts Made	Wins	Top-5s	Top-10s	Top-25s	Scoring Average	Money
	89	299	54	0	2	3	11	73.32	$23,768

Joe Ogilvie

Year	Starts	Rounds Played	Cuts Made	Wins	Top-5s	Top-10s	Top-25s	Scoring Average	Money
1996	1	2	0	0	0	0	0	73.00	
1998	1	2	0	0	0	0	0	70.50	
1999	31	92	14	0	0	2	5	71.79	$287,346

Best finish for 1999: T-9th at the Motorola Western Open

2000	30	91	17	0	1	3	7	71.01	$519,740

Best finish for 2000: T-4th at the FedEx St. Jude Classic

2001	34	108	20	0	0	0	4	71.12	$343,189

Best finish for 2001: T-17th at the Canon Greater Hartford Open

2002	20	50	5	0	0	0	1	72.36	$47,696

Best finish for 2002: T-25th at the B.C. Open

2003	1	2	0	0	0	0	0	72.00	$1,000
2004	32	102	20	0	2	4	9	71.02	$1,443,363

Best finish for 2004: T-2nd at the HP Classic of New Orleans

2005	30	99	21	0	2	5	10	71.31	$1,821,547

Best finish for 2005: T-2nd at the Bob Hope Chrysler Classic & Honda Classic

2006	29	91	18	0	1	3	9	70.84	$1,078,111

Best finish for 2006: 3rd at the Reno-Tahoe Open

2007	31	102	19	1	1	2	7	70.90	$1,341,653

Best finish for 2007: Win at the U.S. Bank Championship in Milwaukee

2008	29	100	22	0	0	4	7	70.92	$1,035,831

Best finish for 2008: T-6th at the U.S. Bank Championship in Milwaukee

Period Totals	Starts	Rounds Played	Cuts Made	Wins	Top-5s	Top-10s	Top-25s	Scoring Average	Money
	269	841	156	1	7	23	59	71.19	$7,919,476

Geoff Ogilvy

Year	Starts	Rounds Played	Cuts Made	Wins	Top-5s	Top-10s	Top-25s	Scoring Average	Money
1999	1	2	0	0	0	0	0	79.50	$1,406
2001	23	60	7	0	2	2	4	71.58	$526,768

Best finish for 2001: T-2nd at the Honda Classic

Year	Starts	Rounds Played	Cuts Made	Wins	Top-5s	Top-10s	Top-25s	Scoring Average	Money
2002	27	86	17	0	2	3	4	70.86	$957,184

Best finish for 2002: T-2nd at the COMPAQ Classic of New Orleans

2003	26	82	16	0	3	7	10	70.85	$1,478,246

Best finish for 2003: T-2nd at the Buick Open

| 2004 | 26 | 87 | 19 | 0 | 1 | 4 | 14 | 70.51 | $1,236,910 |

Best finish for 2004: T-5th at the Cialis Western Open

| 2005 | 26 | 93 | 22 | 1 | 3 | 5 | 9 | 70.51 | $1,931,676 |

Best finish for 2005: Win at the Chrysler Classic of Tucson

| 2006 | 20 | 70 | 17 | 2 | 3 | 5 | 13 | 71.19 | $4,354,969 |

Best finish for 2006: Win at the WGC-Accenture Match Play Championship & U.S. Open

| 2007 | 22 | 78 | 19 | 0 | 3 | 7 | 13 | 71.17 | $2,948,085 |

Best finish for 2007: 2nd at the WGC-Accenture Match Play Championship

| 2008 | 20 | 64 | 14 | 1 | 2 | 6 | 8 | 71.38 | $2,880,099 |

Best finish for 2008: Win at the WGC-CA Championship

Period Totals	Starts	Rounds Played	Cuts Made	Wins	Top-5s	Top-10s	Top-25s	Scoring Average	Money
	191	622	131	4	19	39	75	70.98	$16,315,343

Brett Ogle

Year	Starts	Rounds Played	Cuts Made	Wins	Top-5s	Top-10s	Top-25s	Scoring Average	Money
1986	1	0	1	0	0	0	1		$6,000

Best finish for 1986: T-13th at the International

| 1987 | 1 | 0 | 0 | 0 | 0 | 0 | 0 | | |
| 1989 | 1 | 4 | 1 | 0 | 0 | 0 | 0 | 72.75 | $4,960 |

Best finish for 1989: T-52nd at the British Open

| 1990 | 1 | 2 | 0 | 0 | 0 | 0 | 0 | 74.00 | $996 |
| 1991 | 3 | 8 | 2 | 0 | 0 | 0 | 1 | 71.88 | $15,215 |

Best finish for 1991: T-25th at the NEC World Series of Golf

| 1993 | 18 | 56 | 12 | 1 | 2 | 2 | 3 | 72.21 | $338,574 |

Best finish for 1993: Win at the AT&T Pebble Beach Pro-Am

| 1994 | 21 | 58 | 8 | 1 | 1 | 1 | 3 | 71.93 | $287,195 |

Best finish for 1994: Win at the United Airlines Hawaiian Open

| 1995 | 20 | 64 | 14 | 0 | 1 | 2 | 10 | 70.95 | $328,132 |

Best finish for 1995: 4th at the Northern Telecom Open

| 1996 | 18 | 48 | 7 | 0 | 0 | 1 | 1 | 72.33 | $77,622 |

Best finish for 1996: T-10th at the GTE Byron Nelson Classic

Period Totals	Starts	Rounds Played	Cuts Made	Wins	Top-5s	Top-10s	Top-25s	Scoring Average	Money
	84	240	45	2	4	6	19	71.85	$1,058,693

David Ogrin

Year	Starts	Rounds Played	Cuts Made	Wins	Top-5s	Top-10s	Top-25s	Scoring Average	Money
1979	1	2	0	0	0	0	0	77.50	
1983	29	97	19	0	0	0	4	72.06	$36,003

Best finish for 1983: T-13th at the U.S. Open

| 1984 | 35 | 110 | 19 | 0 | 0 | 0 | 5 | 72.84 | $46,461 |

Best finish for 1984: T-15th at the Western Open

| 1985 | 31 | 95 | 15 | 0 | 1 | 1 | 3 | 72.71 | $76,294 |

Best finish for 1985: 2nd at the St. Jude Memphis Classic

| 1986 | 31 | 87 | 12 | 0 | 1 | 3 | 6 | 72.77 | $72,525 |

Best finish for 1986: T-5th at the Hawaiian Open

| 1987 | 33 | 96 | 15 | 1 | 2 | 2 | 3 | 72.02 | $80,149 |

Best finish for 1987: Win at the Deposit Guaranty Golf Classic

| 1988 | 27 | 96 | 22 | 0 | 2 | 3 | 6 | 71.03 | $138,807 |

Best finish for 1988: 3rd at the Deposit Guaranty Golf Classic

| 1989 | 28 | 96 | 21 | 0 | 1 | 2 | 8 | 71.24 | $235,196 |

Best finish for 1989: 2nd at the Hawaiian Open

| 1990 | 31 | 85 | 9 | 0 | 1 | 1 | 2 | 72.61 | $64,190 |

Best finish for 1990: T-3rd at the Deposit Guaranty

| 1991 | 15 | 41 | 4 | 0 | 0 | 0 | 0 | 71.80 | $8,024 |

Best finish for 1991: T-47th at the H-E-B Texas Open

| 1992 | 28 | 80 | 11 | 0 | 0 | 0 | 0 | 72.19 | $33,971 |

Best finish for 1992: T-28th at the H-E-B Texas Open

| 1993 | 28 | 92 | 18 | 0 | 2 | 3 | 6 | 71.43 | $155,015 |

Best finish for 1993: T-4th at the B.C. Open

| 1994 | 29 | 90 | 17 | 0 | 1 | 2 | 7 | 71.30 | $200,199 |

Best finish for 1994: T-2nd at the GTE Byron Nelson Classic

| 1995 | 30 | 91 | 14 | 0 | 0 | 3 | 4 | 71.48 | $151,419 |

Best finish for 1995: 7th at the Buick Challenge

| 1996 | 30 | 102 | 21 | 1 | 3 | 5 | 11 | 70.56 | $537,225 |

Best finish for 1996: Win at the LaCantera Texas Open

| 1997 | 28 | 96 | 20 | 0 | 3 | 7 | 11 | 70.54 | $598,683 |

Best finish for 1997: T-2nd at the Buick Invitational & MasterCard Colonial

Year	Starts	Rounds Played	Cuts Made	Wins	Top-5s	Top-10s	Top-25s	Scoring Average	Money
1998	29	100	21	0	0	0	5	71.12	$221,123

Best finish for 1998: T-14th at the Greater Milwaukee Open

1999	18	57	10	0	0	0	4	71.98	$141,082

Best finish for 1999: T-17th at the Greater Milwaukee Open

2000	7	20	3	0	0	0	1	70.95	$40,522

Best finish for 2000: T-22nd at the Greater Milwaukee Open

2001	2	6	1	0	0	0	0	71.33	$6,030

Best finish for 2001: T-69th at the Texas Open at LaCantera

2002	3	6	0	0	0	0	0	72.00	
2003	4	10	1	0	0	0	0	72.90	$5,700

Best finish for 2003: T-74th at the Reno-Tahoe Open

2004	2	6	1	0	0	0	0	70.50	$6,420

Best finish for 2004: T-60th at the B.C. Open

2005	2	4	0	0	0	0	0	74.25	
2006	1	2	0	0	0	0	0	73.50	
2007	1	2	0	0	0	0	0	73.50	
2008	1	2	0	0	0	0	0	70.00	
Period Totals	Starts	Rounds Played	Cuts Made	Wins	Top-5s	Top-10s	Top-25s	Scoring Average	Money
	504	1571	274	2	17	32	86	71.74	$2,855,039

Aki Ohmachi

Year	Starts	Rounds Played	Cuts Made	Wins	Top-5s	Top-10s	Top-25s	Scoring Average	Money
1987	29	82	13	0	0	3	5	71.90	$65,695

Best finish for 1987: T-6th at the Big I Houston Open

1988	33	91	12	0	0	0	0	72.64	$29,552

Best finish for 1988: T-28th at the Independent Insurance Agent Open

1989	1	2	0	0	0	0	0	73.50	
1990	2	8	2	0	0	0	0	72.75	$9,630

Best finish for 1990: 44th at the NEC World Series of Golf

1991	2	6	1	0	0	0	0	72.50	$2,002

Best finish for 1991: 79th at the United Hawaiian Open

1992	4	11	2	0	0	0	0	71.36	$7,384

Best finish for 1992: T-32nd at the Nissan Los Angeles Open

1993	1	2	0	0	0	0	0	74.00	
1999	1	3	0	0	0	0	0	80.00	
Period Totals	Starts	Rounds Played	Cuts Made	Wins	Top-5s	Top-10s	Top-25s	Scoring Average	Money
	73	205	30	0	0	3	5	72.40	$114,264

Jose Maria Olazabal

Year	Starts	Rounds Played	Cuts Made	Wins	Top-5s	Top-10s	Top-25s	Scoring Average	Money
1984	1	2	0	0	0	0	0	74.50	
1985	2	6	1	0	0	0	1	74.33	

Best finish for 1985: T-25th at the British Open

1986	1	4	1	0	0	0	1	73.00	$13,500

Best finish for 1986: T-16th at the British Open

1987	6	20	4	0	0	0	1	73.75	$31,570

Best finish for 1987: T-11th at the British Open

1988	1	4	1	0	0	0	0	73.00	$6,715

Best finish for 1988: T-36th at the British Open

1989	5	18	4	0	0	2	3	71.78	$67,811

Best finish for 1989: T-8th at the Masters

1990	9	30	8	1	1	4	8	70.60	$358,018

Best finish for 1990: Win at the NEC World Series of Golf

1991	8	24	6	1	2	3	3	72.08	$388,164

Best finish for 1991: Win at the International

1992	9	26	6	0	1	2	2	71.31	$193,629

Best finish for 1992: 3rd at the British Open

1993	7	18	3	0	0	1	1	73.00	$62,084

Best finish for 1993: T-7th at the Masters

1994	9	28	7	2	3	4	6	70.14	$980,782

Best finish for 1994: Win at the Masters & NEC World Series of Golf

1995	10	32	8	0	0	2	4	71.53	$213,415

Best finish for 1995: T-6th at the Sprint International

1997	6	22	5	0	0	1	4	71.23	$174,889

Best finish for 1997: T-7th at the Freeport-McDermott Classic

1998	7	25	6	0	0	0	6	71.92	$209,986

Best finish for 1998: T-12th at the Masters

1999	13	33	8	1	3	3	4	72.06	$1,140,323

Best finish for 1999: Win at the Masters

2000	12	31	7	0	1	2	5	71.87	$557,221

Best finish for 2000: T-4th at the PGA Championship

Year	Starts	Rounds Played	Cuts Made	Wins	Top-5s	Top-10s	Top-25s	Scoring Average	Money
2001	15	47	10	0	0	0	5	70.96	$459,678

Best finish for 2001: T-12th at the Players Championship

| 2002 | 20 | 64 | 16 | 1 | 5 | 7 | 7 | 71.13 | $1,991,768 |

Best finish for 2002: Win at the Buick Invitational

| 2003 | 16 | 42 | 9 | 0 | 0 | 2 | 3 | 72.76 | $484,924 |

Best finish for 2003: T-8th at the Masters

| 2004 | 17 | 52 | 11 | 0 | 0 | 1 | 4 | 71.44 | $497,050 |

Best finish for 2004: T-9th at the 84 Lumber Classic

| 2005 | 16 | 53 | 14 | 0 | 3 | 6 | 8 | 70.66 | $1,769,227 |

Best finish for 2005: T-2nd at the BellSouth Classic

| 2006 | 18 | 58 | 14 | 0 | 3 | 4 | 10 | 71.09 | $2,120,422 |

Best finish for 2006: T-2nd at the Buick Invitational & BellSouth Classic

| 2007 | 16 | 50 | 11 | 0 | 1 | 1 | 4 | 72.92 | $981,749 |

Best finish for 2007: T-3rd at The Players

| 2008 | 4 | 12 | 2 | 0 | 0 | 0 | 0 | 73.33 | $60,200 |

Best finish for 2008: T-26th at the Shell Houston Open

Period Totals	Starts	Rounds Played	Cuts Made	Wins	Top-5s	Top-10s	Top-25s	Scoring Average	Money
	228	701	162	6	23	45	90	71.67	$12,763,124

Ed Oliver

Year	Starts	Rounds Played	Cuts Made	Wins	Top-5s	Top-10s	Top-25s	Scoring Average	Money
1958	32	119	26	1	2	8	14	71.74	$15,173

Best finish for 1958: Win at the Houston Open

| 1959 | 14 | 55 | 11 | 0 | 2 | 3 | 10 | 71.35 | $7,916 |

Best finish for 1959: T-2nd at the Puerto Rico Open Invitational

| 1960 | 8 | 32 | 7 | 0 | 1 | 3 | 5 | 72.94 | $4,781 |

Best finish for 1960: T-4th at the Bing Crosby National

Period Totals	Starts	Rounds Played	Cuts Made	Wins	Top-5s	Top-10s	Top-25s	Scoring Average	Money
	54	206	44	1	5	14	29	71.82	$27,870

PGA Tour career totals from 1936 to 1960

	Starts	Rounds Played	Cuts Made	Wins	Top-5s	Top-10s	Top-25s	Scoring Average	Money
	322	N/A	N/A	8	N/A	138	242	N/A	$159,966

Dan Olsen

Year	Starts	Rounds Played	Cuts Made	Wins	Top-5s	Top-10s	Top-25s	Scoring Average	Money
1989	1	2	0	0	0	0	0	72.50	
1991	1	2	0	0	0	0	0	76.00	
1994	1	2	0	0	0	0	0	72.00	$2,101
2004	31	74	8	0	0	0	1	72.20	$136,731

Best finish for 2004: T-12th at the Chrysler Classic of Tucson

Period Totals	Starts	Rounds Played	Cuts Made	Wins	Top-5s	Top-10s	Top-25s	Scoring Average	Money
	34	80	8	0	0	0	1	72.30	$138,832

Doug Olson

Year	Starts	Rounds Played	Cuts Made	Wins	Top-5s	Top-10s	Top-25s	Scoring Average	Money
1964	1	2	0	0	0	0	0	77.00	
1968	2	6	1	0	0	0	0	74.83	

Best finish for 1968: T-62nd at the Houston Champions International

| 1969 | 2 | 4 | 0 | 0 | 0 | 0 | 0 | 77.50 | |
| 1970 | 19 | 52 | 7 | 0 | 0 | 0 | 1 | 73.27 | $2,259 |

Best finish for 1970: T-25th at the IVB Philadelphia Golf Classic

| 1971 | 12 | 30 | 3 | 0 | 0 | 0 | 0 | 73.03 | $1,225 |

Best finish for 1971: T-34th at the Greater Milwaukee Open

| 1972 | 16 | 40 | 5 | 0 | 1 | 1 | 1 | 73.68 | $5,753 |

Best finish for 1972: T-5th at the Quad Cities Open

| 1973 | 16 | 39 | 2 | 0 | 0 | 0 | 0 | 74.49 | $678 |

Best finish for 1973: T-42nd at the Greater Jacksonville Open

| 1974 | 1 | 3 | 0 | 0 | 0 | 0 | 0 | 79.00 | |
| 1977 | 3 | 8 | 1 | 0 | 0 | 0 | 0 | 75.88 | |

Best finish for 1977: 79th at the Tallahassee Open

Period Totals	Starts	Rounds Played	Cuts Made	Wins	Top-5s	Top-10s	Top-25s	Scoring Average	Money
	72	184	19	0	1	1	2	73.97	$9,915

Peter Oosterhuis

Year	Starts	Rounds Played	Cuts Made	Wins	Top-5s	Top-10s	Top-25s	Scoring Average	Money
1968	1	2	0	0	0	0	0	80.00	
1969	1	2	0	0	0	0	0	77.00	
1970	1	4	1	0	0	1	1	71.75	$4,200

Best finish for 1970: T-6th at the British Open

| 1971 | 3 | 8 | 1 | 0 | 0 | 0 | 1 | 73.88 | $2,560 |

Best finish for 1971: T-18th at the British Open

| 1972 | 4 | 12 | 2 | 0 | 0 | 0 | 0 | 73.92 | $2,288 |

Best finish for 1972: T-28th at the British Open

Year	Starts	Rounds Played	Cuts Made	Wins	Top-5s	Top-10s	Top-25s	Scoring Average	Money
1973	7	26	5	0	1	1	4	72.65	$17,333

Best finish for 1973: T-3rd at the Masters

| 1974 | 6 | 24 | 6 | 0 | 2 | 2 | 3 | 71.75 | $31,514 |

Best finish for 1974: 2nd at the British Open & Monsanto Open

| 1975 | 32 | 115 | 25 | 0 | 2 | 4 | 11 | 71.92 | $67,926 |

Best finish for 1975: 2nd at the First NBC New Orleans Open

| 1976 | 31 | 115 | 26 | 0 | 1 | 3 | 11 | 72.05 | $41,692 |

Best finish for 1976: T-4th at the Southern Open

| 1977 | 26 | 85 | 16 | 0 | 1 | 3 | 8 | 72.27 | $54,178 |

Best finish for 1977: 2nd at the Canadian Open

| 1978 | 27 | 95 | 21 | 0 | 1 | 4 | 7 | 72.01 | $59,980 |

Best finish for 1978: 3rd at the Bob Hope Chrysler Classic

| 1979 | 26 | 78 | 12 | 0 | 1 | 2 | 4 | 72.88 | $42,108 |

Best finish for 1979: T-4th at the Manufactures Hanover Westchester Classic

| 1980 | 30 | 99 | 20 | 0 | 0 | 1 | 4 | 72.37 | $35,527 |

Best finish for 1980: T-10th at the Greater New Orleans Open

| 1981 | 28 | 89 | 17 | 1 | 1 | 1 | 7 | 71.87 | $116,437 |

Best finish for 1981: Win in the Canadian Open

| 1982 | 32 | 110 | 23 | 0 | 1 | 5 | 14 | 71.53 | $127,848 |

Best finish for 1982: T-2nd at the British Open

| 1983 | 28 | 99 | 21 | 0 | 0 | 2 | 6 | 72.00 | $69,268 |

Best finish for 1983: T-7th at the Greater Greensboro Open & Canadian Open

| 1984 | 27 | 95 | 21 | 0 | 0 | 2 | 6 | 71.79 | $76,814 |

Best finish for 1984: T-7th at the Isuzu/Andy Williams San Diego Open & Southern Open

| 1985 | 30 | 96 | 17 | 0 | 0 | 1 | 2 | 71.95 | $41,805 |

Best finish for 1985: T-10th at the Doral-Eastern Open

| 1986 | 23 | 56 | 7 | 0 | 0 | 0 | 2 | 72.88 | $15,394 |

Best finish for 1986: T-20th at the Greater Milwaukee Open

| 1987 | 5 | 13 | 1 | 0 | 0 | 0 | 0 | 73.77 | $969 |

Best finish for 1987: T-49th at the Southern Open

1988	2	4	0	0	0	0	0	75.00	
1989	1	1	0	0	0	0	0	81.00	
Period Totals	Starts	Rounds Played	Cuts Made	Wins	Top-5s	Top-10s	Top-25s	Scoring Average	Money
	371	1228	242	1	11	32	91	72.17	$807,840

Steve Oppermann

Year	Starts	Rounds Played	Cuts Made	Wins	Top-5s	Top-10s	Top-25s	Scoring Average	Money
1961	1	4	1	0	0	0	0	73.75	

Best finish for 1961: T-27th at the Almaden Open

| 1963 | 1 | 4 | 1 | 0 | 0 | 0 | 0 | 71.25 | |

Best finish for 1963: T-30th at the Almaden Open Invitational

| 1964 | 2 | 6 | 1 | 0 | 0 | 0 | 0 | 73.83 | |

Best finish for 1964: T-43rd at the Almaden Open

| 1965 | 21 | 63 | 10 | 0 | 1 | 1 | 3 | 72.67 | $7,030 |

Best finish for 1965: T-3rd at the Texas Open

| 1966 | 34 | 116 | 23 | 0 | 0 | 0 | 7 | 73.15 | $12,290 |

Best finish for 1966: T-12th at the Portland Open Invitational

| 1967 | 28 | 100 | 21 | 0 | 2 | 2 | 5 | 72.61 | $31,340 |

Best finish for 1967: 2nd at the Insurance City Open

| 1968 | 28 | 84 | 13 | 0 | 0 | 2 | 7 | 72.73 | $13,768 |

Best finish for 1968: T-7th at the Minnesota Golf Classic

| 1969 | 19 | 61 | 12 | 0 | 1 | 1 | 3 | 72.82 | $10,398 |

Best finish for 1969: 2nd at the Indian Ridge Hospital Open

| 1970 | 25 | 77 | 15 | 0 | 1 | 1 | 4 | 72.57 | $12,957 |

Best finish for 1970: T-4th at the Greater Hartford Open Invitational

| 1971 | 13 | 31 | 3 | 0 | 0 | 0 | 0 | 73.74 | $1,076 |

Best finish for 1971: T-36th at the IVB Philadelphia Golf Classic

| 1972 | 14 | 42 | 7 | 0 | 0 | 0 | 2 | 73.40 | $5,870 |

Best finish for 1972: T-11th at the Western Open

| 1973 | 13 | 31 | 3 | 0 | 0 | 0 | 0 | 73.94 | $1,671 |

Best finish for 1973: T-36th at the Atlanta Classic

| 1977 | 1 | 2 | 0 | 0 | 0 | 0 | 0 | 77.00 | |
| 1980 | 1 | 4 | 1 | 0 | 0 | 0 | 0 | 72.50 | $648 |

Best finish for 1980: T-60th at the Atlanta Classic

1981	1	0	0	0	0	0	0		
1986	1	2	0	0	0	0	0	78.00	
Period Totals	Starts	Rounds Played	Cuts Made	Wins	Top-5s	Top-10s	Top-25s	Scoring Average	Money
	203	627	111	0	5	7	31	72.96	$97,047

Jay Overton

Year	Starts	Rounds Played	Cuts Made	Wins	Top-5s	Top-10s	Top-25s	Scoring Average	Money
1977	1	2	0	0	0	0	0	73.50	
1979	2	4	0	0	0	0	0	74.75	$350
1980	4	8	0	0	0	0	0	77.50	$500
1981	2	2	0	0	0	0	0	73.50	
1982	2	4	0	0	0	0	0	75.25	
1984	2	6	1	0	0	0	0	73.50	$784

Best finish for 1984: T-71st at the Walt Disney World Golf Classic

Year	Starts	Rounds Played	Cuts Made	Wins	Top-5s	Top-10s	Top-25s	Scoring Average	Money
1985	2	4	0	0	0	0	0	77.25	$600
1986	3	5	0	0	0	0	0	74.80	$1,000
1987	4	12	2	0	0	0	1	74.33	$6,815

Best finish for 1987: T-23rd at the Centel Classic

Year	Starts	Rounds Played	Cuts Made	Wins	Top-5s	Top-10s	Top-25s	Scoring Average	Money
1988	3	10	2	0	0	1	2	70.70	$26,000

Best finish for 1988: T-8th at the Centel Classic

Year	Starts	Rounds Played	Cuts Made	Wins	Top-5s	Top-10s	Top-25s	Scoring Average	Money
1990	1	2	0	0	0	0	0	78.00	$1,000
1991	1	2	0	0	0	0	0	77.00	$1,000
1992	2	8	2	0	0	0	0	71.75	$4,755

Best finish for 1992: T-62nd at the PGA Championship

Year	Starts	Rounds Played	Cuts Made	Wins	Top-5s	Top-10s	Top-25s	Scoring Average	Money
1993	13	32	4	0	0	0	0	74.03	$9,568

Best finish for 1993: T-38th at the Canon Greater Hartford Open

Year	Starts	Rounds Played	Cuts Made	Wins	Top-5s	Top-10s	Top-25s	Scoring Average	Money
1997	1	2	0	0	0	0	0	74.50	$1,300
1998	1	2	0	0	0	0	0	74.50	$1,500
1999	1	2	0	0	0	0	0	75.00	$1,750
2000	1	2	0	0	0	0	0	72.50	
2004	1	2	0	0	0	0	0	74.00	
2005	1	2	0	0	0	0	0	74.50	
Period Totals	Starts	Rounds Played	Cuts Made	Wins	Top-5s	Top-10s	Top-25s	Scoring Average	Money
	48	113	11	0	0	1	3	74.16	$56,922

Jeff Overton

Year	Starts	Rounds Played	Cuts Made	Wins	Top-5s	Top-10s	Top-25s	Scoring Average	Money
2006	28	93	19	0	0	2	5	70.98	$577,132

Best finish for 2006: T-9th at the 84 Lumber Classic

Year	Starts	Rounds Played	Cuts Made	Wins	Top-5s	Top-10s	Top-25s	Scoring Average	Money
2007	19	60	11	0	1	3	6	70.10	$1,009,630

Best finish for 2007: T-2nd at the Wyndham Championship

Year	Starts	Rounds Played	Cuts Made	Wins	Top-5s	Top-10s	Top-25s	Scoring Average	Money
2008	32	103	20	0	1	3	7	71.29	$890,489

Best finish for 2008: 5th at the Valero Texas Open

Period Totals	Starts	Rounds Played	Cuts Made	Wins	Top-5s	Top-10s	Top-25s	Scoring Average	Money
	79	256	50	0	2	8	18	70.90	$2,477,250

Greg Owen

Year	Starts	Rounds Played	Cuts Made	Wins	Top-5s	Top-10s	Top-25s	Scoring Average	Money
1999	1	2	0	0	0	0	0	79.50	$1,406
2000	1	4	1	0	0	0	0	72.25	$11,843

Best finish for 2000: T-55th at the British Open

Year	Starts	Rounds Played	Cuts Made	Wins	Top-5s	Top-10s	Top-25s	Scoring Average	Money
2001	1	4	1	0	0	0	1	70.50	$43,630

Best finish for 2001: T-23rd at the British Open

Year	Starts	Rounds Played	Cuts Made	Wins	Top-5s	Top-10s	Top-25s	Scoring Average	Money
2002	2	4	0	0	0	0	0	74.25	$5,555
2003	2	4	0	0	0	0	0	76.50	$5,577
2005	24	80	19	0	2	3	9	71.14	$1,352,878

Best finish for 2005: 3rd at the AT&T Pebble Beach National Pro-Am

Year	Starts	Rounds Played	Cuts Made	Wins	Top-5s	Top-10s	Top-25s	Scoring Average	Money
2006	24	77	15	0	1	2	9	71.00	$1,318,935

Best finish for 2006: 2nd at the Bay Hill Invitational

Year	Starts	Rounds Played	Cuts Made	Wins	Top-5s	Top-10s	Top-25s	Scoring Average	Money
2007	29	81	11	0	1	1	2	71.99	$426,601

Best finish for 2007: T-4th at the AT&T Pebble Beach National Pro-Am

Year	Starts	Rounds Played	Cuts Made	Wins	Top-5s	Top-10s	Top-25s	Scoring Average	Money
2008	1	3	0	0	0	0	0	72.67	
Period Totals	Starts	Rounds Played	Cuts Made	Wins	Top-5s	Top-10s	Top-25s	Scoring Average	Money
	85	259	47	0	4	6	21	71.58	$3,166,425

Charles Owens

Year	Starts	Rounds Played	Cuts Made	Wins	Top-5s	Top-10s	Top-25s	Scoring Average	Money
1971	14	40	6	0	0	0	1	73.43	$2,943

Best finish for 1971: T-16th at the Monsanto Open

Year	Starts	Rounds Played	Cuts Made	Wins	Top-5s	Top-10s	Top-25s	Scoring Average	Money
1972	17	39	3	0	0	0	0	75.26	$919

Best finish for 1972: T-40th at the IVB Philadelphia Golf Classic

Year	Starts	Rounds Played	Cuts Made	Wins	Top-5s	Top-10s	Top-25s	Scoring Average	Money
1973	10	25	4	0	0	0	0	74.00	$1,312

Best finish for 1973: T-34th at the Greater Jacksonville Open

Year	Starts	Rounds Played	Cuts Made	Wins	Top-5s	Top-10s	Top-25s	Scoring Average	Money
1974	12	32	4	0	0	0	0	73.94	$1,844

Best finish for 1974: T-33rd at the Danny Thomas Memphis Classic

Year	Starts	Rounds Played	Cuts Made	Wins	Top-5s	Top-10s	Top-25s	Scoring Average	Money
1975	1	2	0	0	0	0	0	73.50	

Year	Starts	Rounds Played	Cuts Made	Wins	Top-5s	Top-10s	Top-25s	Scoring Average	Money
1977	4	9	0	0	0	0	0	74.44	
1980	1	1	0	0	0	0	0	79.00	
Period Totals	Starts	Rounds Played	Cuts Made	Wins	Top-5s	Top-10s	Top-25s	Scoring Average	Money
	59	148	17	0	0	0	1	74.22	$7,018

Jet Ozaki

Year	Starts	Rounds Played	Cuts Made	Wins	Top-5s	Top-10s	Top-25s	Scoring Average	Money
1981	7	20	3	0	0	0	2	71.70	$5,757

Best finish for 1981: T-21st at the B.C. Open

| 1982 | 10 | 33 | 6 | 0 | 0 | 0 | 1 | 72.18 | $5,919 |

Best finish for 1982: T-24th at the Bob Hope Chrysler Classic

| 1983 | 1 | 4 | 1 | 0 | 0 | 0 | 0 | 71.50 | $663 |

Best finish for 1983: T-59th at the Isuzu/Andy Williams San Diego Open

| 1985 | 2 | 4 | 0 | 0 | 0 | 0 | 0 | 75.75 | $544 |
| 1986 | 5 | 15 | 4 | 0 | 0 | 0 | 0 | 72.13 | $9,471 |

Best finish for 1986: T-32nd at the NEC World Series of Golf

| 1987 | 4 | 9 | 1 | 0 | 0 | 0 | 0 | 73.89 | $2,800 |

Best finish for 1987: T-66th at the British Open

| 1988 | 3 | 8 | 1 | 0 | 0 | 0 | 0 | 73.25 | $4,355 |

Best finish for 1988: T-29th at the Honda Classic

| 1989 | 3 | 8 | 1 | 0 | 0 | 0 | 0 | 73.38 | $4,960 |

Best finish for 1989: T-52nd at the British Open

1990	1	2	0	0	0	0	0	75.00	
1998	3	6	0	0	0	0	0	74.67	
Period Totals	Starts	Rounds Played	Cuts Made	Wins	Top-5s	Top-10s	Top-25s	Scoring Average	Money
	39	109	17	0	0	0	3	72.69	$34,468

Joe Ozaki

Year	Starts	Rounds Played	Cuts Made	Wins	Top-5s	Top-10s	Top-25s	Scoring Average	Money
1984	1	4	1	0	0	0	0	74.00	$1,430

Best finish for 1984: T-62nd at the British Open

| 1985 | 3 | 8 | 1 | 0 | 0 | 0 | 0 | 74.13 | $1,424 |

Best finish for 1985: T-59th at the Los Angeles Open

| 1989 | 3 | 9 | 2 | 0 | 0 | 0 | 0 | 71.89 | $8,285 |

Best finish for 1989: T-46th at the British Open

| 1990 | 9 | 26 | 6 | 0 | 0 | 0 | 1 | 72.58 | $45,945 |

Best finish for 1990: T-13th at the NEC World Series of Golf

| 1991 | 2 | 6 | 1 | 0 | 0 | 1 | 1 | 71.33 | $38,850 |

Best finish for 1991: T-6th at the NEC World Series of Golf

| 1992 | 9 | 26 | 5 | 0 | 0 | 1 | 2 | 71.88 | $78,646 |

Best finish for 1992: T-6th at the Federal Express St. Jude Classic

| 1993 | 13 | 42 | 8 | 0 | 0 | 1 | 3 | 72.69 | $140,708 |

Best finish for 1993: T-6th at the Players Championship

| 1994 | 17 | 61 | 15 | 0 | 0 | 1 | 5 | 71.13 | $147,308 |

Best finish for 1994: T-8th at the Buick Classic

| 1995 | 20 | 62 | 13 | 0 | 0 | 4 | 8 | 70.58 | $290,001 |

Best finish for 1995: T-6th at the Northern Telecom Open

| 1996 | 22 | 68 | 13 | 0 | 0 | 1 | 7 | 71.50 | $229,063 |

Best finish for 1996: T-6th at the Doral-Ryder Open

| 1997 | 19 | 66 | 14 | 0 | 1 | 2 | 3 | 71.80 | $201,596 |

Best finish for 1997: T-2nd at the Buick Open

| 1998 | 17 | 57 | 12 | 0 | 0 | 1 | 6 | 71.35 | $240,551 |

Best finish for 1998: T-9th at the Motorola Western Open

| 1999 | 15 | 53 | 13 | 0 | 0 | 1 | 3 | 72.64 | $318,485 |

Best finish for 1999: T-10th at the Players Championship

| 2000 | 18 | 53 | 11 | 0 | 0 | 1 | 5 | 71.81 | $401,836 |

Best finish for 2000: T-6th at the Buick Open

| 2001 | 17 | 45 | 7 | 0 | 1 | 1 | 2 | 72.04 | $274,632 |

Best finish for 2001: T-5th at the Sony Open in Hawaii

Period Totals	Starts	Rounds Played	Cuts Made	Wins	Top-5s	Top-10s	Top-25s	Scoring Average	Money
	185	586	122	0	2	15	46	71.76	$2,418,761

Jumbo Ozaki

Year	Starts	Rounds Played	Cuts Made	Wins	Top-5s	Top-10s	Top-25s	Scoring Average	Money
1972	2	4	0	0	0	0	0	76.75	$1,000
1973	2	8	2	0	0	1	2	71.38	$7,450

Best finish for 1973: T-8th at the Masters

| 1974 | 4 | 12 | 2 | 0 | 0 | 0 | 1 | 71.83 | $3,774 |

Best finish for 1974: T-20th at the Andy Williams-San Diego Open

| 1975 | 3 | 12 | 3 | 0 | 0 | 0 | 0 | 72.58 | $3,574 |

Best finish for 1975: T-33rd at the Jackie Gleason's Inverrary Classic

| 1976 | 1 | 4 | 1 | 0 | 0 | 0 | 0 | 74.00 | $1,900 |

Best finish for 1976: T-33rd at the Masters

Year	Starts	Rounds Played	Cuts Made	Wins	Top-5s	Top-10s	Top-25s	Scoring Average	Money
1977	1	2	0	0	0	0	0	73.50	
1978	3	8	1	0	0	0	1	73.13	$6,060

Best finish for 1978: T-14th at the British Open

| 1979 | 4 | 14 | 3 | 0 | 0 | 1 | 2 | 72.36 | $15,018 |

Best finish for 1979: T-10th at the British Open

| 1980 | 4 | 16 | 4 | 0 | 0 | 0 | 1 | 74.19 | $5,306 |

Best finish for 1980: T-20th at the Glen CampbellLos Angeles Open

| 1981 | 7 | 24 | 5 | 0 | 0 | 0 | 0 | 72.38 | $7,241 |

Best finish for 1981: T-26th at the Glen CampbellLos Angeles Open

1983	1	2	0	0	0	0	0	73.50	
1986	1	2	0	0	0	0	0	73.50	
1987	6	20	4	0	0	0	3	72.00	$44,827

Best finish for 1987: T-11th at the British Open

| 1988 | 4 | 10 | 1 | 0 | 0 | 0 | 1 | 73.20 | $7,321 |

Best finish for 1988: T-23rd at the Los Angeles Open

| 1989 | 6 | 22 | 5 | 0 | 0 | 1 | 2 | 72.14 | $55,293 |

Best finish for 1989: T-6th at the U.S. Open

| 1990 | 9 | 28 | 5 | 0 | 0 | 0 | 2 | 73.25 | $32,829 |

Best finish for 1990: 23rd at the Masters

| 1991 | 3 | 10 | 2 | 0 | 0 | 0 | 0 | 72.60 | $16,765 |

Best finish for 1991: T-27th at the Players Championship

| 1992 | 2 | 6 | 1 | 0 | 0 | 0 | 1 | 74.17 | $15,106 |

Best finish for 1992: T-23rd at the U.S. Open

| 1993 | 4 | 13 | 3 | 0 | 1 | 1 | 1 | 71.54 | $66,742 |

Best finish for 1993: T-4th at the Memorial Tournament

| 1994 | 6 | 22 | 5 | 0 | 0 | 0 | 0 | 72.23 | $36,939 |

Best finish for 1994: T-28th at the U.S. Open

| 1995 | 6 | 22 | 5 | 0 | 0 | 0 | 0 | 71.91 | $61,329 |

Best finish for 1995: T-28th at the U.S. Open

| 1996 | 4 | 12 | 2 | 0 | 0 | 0 | 0 | 72.83 | $31,720 |

Best finish for 1996: T-29th at the Players Championship

| 1997 | 3 | 10 | 2 | 0 | 0 | 0 | 0 | 74.50 | $20,140 |

Best finish for 1997: 42nd at the Masters

1998	4	8	0	0	0	0	0	75.38	$7,500
1999	3	6	0	0	0	0	0	75.83	$6,000
2000	3	10	2	0	0	0	0	74.00	$37,673

Best finish for 2000: T-28th at the Masters

Period Totals	Starts	Rounds Played	Cuts Made	Wins	Top-5s	Top-10s	Top-25s	Scoring Average	Money
	96	307	58	0	1	4	17	72.86	$491,508

Roy Pace

Year	Starts	Rounds Played	Cuts Made	Wins	Top-5s	Top-10s	Top-25s	Scoring Average	Money
1964	28	70	7	0	0	0	1	73.93	$1,110

Best finish for 1964: T-12th at the Sunset-Camellia Open

| 1965 | 23 | 60 | 7 | 0 | 0 | 0 | 0 | 74.17 | $1,743 |

Best finish for 1965: T-34th at the Cleveland Open

| 1966 | 7 | 18 | 2 | 0 | 0 | 0 | 0 | 74.83 | $830 |

Best finish for 1966: T-48th at the Greater Greensboro Open Invitational

| 1967 | 6 | 18 | 2 | 0 | 0 | 0 | 0 | 73.89 | $049 |

Best finish for 1967: T-50th at the Tucson Open

| 1968 | 22 | 66 | 11 | 0 | 0 | 0 | 4 | 72.44 | $4,923 |

Best finish for 1968: T-13th at the Robinson Open

| 1969 | 24 | 67 | 10 | 0 | 0 | 2 | 3 | 73.07 | $9,434 |

Best finish for 1969: T-8th at the Los Angeles Open

| 1970 | 21 | 70 | 14 | 0 | 0 | 0 | 4 | 72.60 | $11,403 |

Best finish for 1970: T-12th at the Greater Milwaukee Open

| 1971 | 33 | 103 | 18 | 0 | 0 | 2 | 6 | 72.99 | $17,230 |

Best finish for 1971: T-6th at the Greater Milwaukee Open

| 1972 | 28 | 93 | 18 | 0 | 0 | 1 | 7 | 72.44 | $16,692 |

Best finish for 1972: T-9th at the Greater Milwaukee Open

| 1973 | 35 | 128 | 26 | 0 | 0 | 3 | 8 | 72.43 | $26,488 |

Best finish for 1973: T-7th at the USI Classic

| 1974 | 34 | 119 | 25 | 0 | 0 | 3 | 9 | 72.36 | $33,330 |

Best finish for 1974: T-8th at the Jackie Gleason's Inverrary Classic

| 1975 | 29 | 92 | 17 | 0 | 1 | 2 | 3 | 73.26 | $18,119 |

Best finish for 1975: 5th at the Phoenix Open

| 1976 | 4 | 11 | 4 | 0 | 0 | 0 | 0 | 74.09 | $660 |

Best finish for 1976: 44th at the American Golf Classic

1977	1	4	0	0	0	0	0	74.50	
1978	1	2	0	0	0	0	0	74.00	
1991	1	2	0	0	0	0	0	75.00	

Period Totals	Starts	Rounds Played	Cuts Made	Wins	Top-5s	Top-10s	Top-25s	Scoring Average	Money
	297	923	161	0	1	13	45	72.97	$142,011

Don Padgett

Year	Starts	Rounds Played	Cuts Made	Wins	Top-5s	Top-10s	Top-25s	Scoring Average	Money
1972	1	4	1	0	0	0	0	71.00	$707

Best finish for 1972: T-36th at the Walt Disney World Open

Year	Starts	Rounds Played	Cuts Made	Wins	Top-5s	Top-10s	Top-25s	Scoring Average	Money
1973	27	85	13	0	0	0	2	73.06	$8,862

Best finish for 1973: T-15th at the Hawaiian Open

Year	Starts	Rounds Played	Cuts Made	Wins	Top-5s	Top-10s	Top-25s	Scoring Average	Money
1974	21	52	7	0	0	0	0	73.25	$2,638

Best finish for 1974: T-38th at the Kaiser International Open

Year	Starts	Rounds Played	Cuts Made	Wins	Top-5s	Top-10s	Top-25s	Scoring Average	Money
1976	1	4	1	0	0	0	0	73.25	$725

Best finish for 1976: T-43rd at the PGA Championship

Year	Starts	Rounds Played	Cuts Made	Wins	Top-5s	Top-10s	Top-25s	Scoring Average	Money
1977	1	4	1	0	0	0	0	72.50	$1,412

Best finish for 1977: T-27th at the U.S. Open

Year	Starts	Rounds Played	Cuts Made	Wins	Top-5s	Top-10s	Top-25s	Scoring Average	Money
1978	1	2	0	0	0	0	0	75.50	$600
1979	2	6	1	0	0	0	0	74.33	$1,304

Best finish for 1979: T-46th at the PGA Championship

Year	Starts	Rounds Played	Cuts Made	Wins	Top-5s	Top-10s	Top-25s	Scoring Average	Money
1981	1	4	1	0	0	0	0	73.00	$782

Best finish for 1981: T-61st at the PGA Championship

Year	Starts	Rounds Played	Cuts Made	Wins	Top-5s	Top-10s	Top-25s	Scoring Average	Money
1982	1	4	1	0	0	0	0	73.75	$1,100

Best finish for 1982: 72nd at the PGA Championship

Year	Starts	Rounds Played	Cuts Made	Wins	Top-5s	Top-10s	Top-25s	Scoring Average	Money
1983	1	2	0	0	0	0	0	74.50	$100
1984	1	2	0	0	0	0	0	75.50	$1,000
1987	1	2	0	0	0	0	0	80.50	$1,000
Period Totals	Starts	Rounds Played	Cuts Made	Wins	Top-5s	Top-10s	Top-25s	Scoring Average	Money
	59	171	26	0	0	0	2	73.28	$20,231

Anthony Painter

Year	Starts	Rounds Played	Cuts Made	Wins	Top-5s	Top-10s	Top-25s	Scoring Average	Money
1997	3	10	2	0	0	1	1	69.10	$31,548

Best finish for 1997: T-10th at the Quad City Classic

Year	Starts	Rounds Played	Cuts Made	Wins	Top-5s	Top-10s	Top-25s	Scoring Average	Money
2001	1	2	0	0	0	0	0	74.00	
2003	31	85	12	0	0	0	2	72.39	$220,714

Best finish for 2003: T-14th at the EDS Byron Nelson Championship

Period Totals	Starts	Rounds Played	Cuts Made	Wins	Top-5s	Top-10s	Top-25s	Scoring Average	Money
	35	97	14	0	0	1	3	72.08	$252,263

Arnold Palmer

Year	Starts	Rounds Played	Cuts Made	Wins	Top-5s	Top-10s	Top-25s	Scoring Average	Money
1958	31	118	28	3	10	14	23	70.66	$42,511

Best finish for 1958: Win at the St. Petersburg Open, Pepsi Open & Masters

Year	Starts	Rounds Played	Cuts Made	Wins	Top-5s	Top-10s	Top-25s	Scoring Average	Money
1959	27	108	26	3	11	16	26	70.20	$33,962

Best finish for 1959: Win at the Thunderbird Invitational, Oklahoma City Open Invitational & West Palm Beach Open Invitational

Year	Starts	Rounds Played	Cuts Made	Wins	Top-5s	Top-10s	Top-25s	Scoring Average	Money
1960	26	105	24	8	14	19	24	69.94	$77,783

Best finish for 1960: Win at the Palm Springs Desert Golf Classic, Texas Open Invitational, Baton Rouge Open Invitational, Pensacola Open Invitational, Masters, U.S. Open, Insurance City Open Invitational & Mobile Sertoma Open Invitational

Year	Starts	Rounds Played	Cuts Made	Wins	Top-5s	Top-10s	Top-25s	Scoring Average	Money
1961	24	97	19	6	16	19	23	69.64	$59,931

Best finish for 1961: Win at the Phoenix Open Invitational, Baton Rouge Open Invitational, Texas Open Invitational, Western Open Championship & British Open

Year	Starts	Rounds Played	Cuts Made	Wins	Top-5s	Top-10s	Top-25s	Scoring Average	Money
1962	21	87	20	8	11	13	19	70.27	$83,673

Best finish for 1962: Win at the Palm Springs Golf Classic, Phoenix Open Invitational, Texas Open Invitational, Masters, Tournament of Champions, Colonial National Invitational, British Open, American Golf Classic

Year	Starts	Rounds Played	Cuts Made	Wins	Top-5s	Top-10s	Top-25s	Scoring Average	Money
1963	19	78	18	7	9	13	15	70.94	$114,608

Best finish for 1963: Win at the Los Angeles Open, Phoenix Open Invitational, Pensacola Open Invitational, Tournament of Champions, Thunderbird Classic Invitational, Cleveland Open Invitational , Western Open Championship & Whitemarsh Open Invitational

Year	Starts	Rounds Played	Cuts Made	Wins	Top-5s	Top-10s	Top-25s	Scoring Average	Money
1964	26	104	25	2	15	18	24	70.23	$113,203

Best finish for 1964: Win at the Masters & Oklahoma City Open

Year	Starts	Rounds Played	Cuts Made	Wins	Top-5s	Top-10s	Top-25s	Scoring Average	Money
1965	22	85	20	1	5	9	16	71.53	$78,693

Best finish for 1965: Win at the Tournament of Champions

Year	Starts	Rounds Played	Cuts Made	Wins	Top-5s	Top-10s	Top-25s	Scoring Average	Money
1966	22	88	21	3	11	16	18	70.77	$127,092

Best finish for 1966: Win at the Los Angeles Open Invitational, Tournament of Champions & Houston Champions International

Year	Starts	Rounds Played	Cuts Made	Wins	Top-5s	Top-10s	Top-25s	Scoring Average	Money
1967	25	94	22	4	12	17	20	70.41	$191,072

Best finish for 1967: Win at the Los Angeles Open, Tucson Open, American Golf Classic, Thunderbird Classic

Year	Starts	Rounds Played	Cuts Made	Wins	Top-5s	Top-10s	Top-25s	Scoring Average	Money
1968	24	91	21	2	5	10	16	71.12	$110,083

Best finish for 1968: Win at the Bob Hope Desert Classic & Kemper Open Invitational

Year	Starts	Rounds Played	Cuts Made	Wins	Top-5s	Top-10s	Top-25s	Scoring Average	Money
1969	26	100	25	2	6	11	17	71.04	$101,364

Best finish for 1969: Win at the Heritage Golf Classic & Danny Thomas-Diplomat Classic

Year	Starts	Rounds Played	Cuts Made	Wins	Top-5s	Top-10s	Top-25s	Scoring Average	Money
1970	23	89	23	1	9	13	17	71.01	$129,520

Best finish for 1970: Win at the National 4 Ball Championship PGA Players

Year	Starts	Rounds Played	Cuts Made	Wins	Top-5s	Top-10s	Top-25s	Scoring Average	Money
1971	23	89	23	4	8	11	21	71.36	$186,294

Best finish for 1971: Win at the Bob Hope Chrysler Classic, Florida Citrus Open Invitational, National Team Championship & Westchester Classic

Year	Starts	Rounds Played	Cuts Made	Wins	Top-5s	Top-10s	Top-25s	Scoring Average	Money
1972	22	79	19	0	3	11	16	71.42	$84,887

Best finish for 1972: 2nd at the Sahara Invitational

Year	Starts	Rounds Played	Cuts Made	Wins	Top-5s	Top-10s	Top-25s	Scoring Average	Money
1973	23	93	21	1	3	7	16	71.35	$89,745

Best finish for 1973: Win at the Bob Hope Chrysler Classic

Year	Starts	Rounds Played	Cuts Made	Wins	Top-5s	Top-10s	Top-25s	Scoring Average	Money
1974	18	63	13	0	2	2	7	72.27	$32,627

Best finish for 1974: T-5th at the U.S. Open & Western Open

| 1975 | 20 | 73 | 16 | 0 | 2 | 5 | 13 | 71.78 | $61,548 |

Best finish for 1975: 3rd at the Hawaiian Open

| 1976 | 19 | 65 | 14 | 0 | 0 | 0 | 6 | 72.23 | $18,683 |

Best finish for 1976: T-15th at the Tallahassee Open & PGA Championship

| 1977 | 21 | 77 | 16 | 0 | 0 | 1 | 8 | 72.39 | $28,325 |

Best finish for 1977: 7th at the British Open

| 1978 | 16 | 58 | 12 | 0 | 1 | 2 | 4 | 72.88 | $28,831 |

Best finish for 1978: 5th at the Phoenix Open

| 1979 | 16 | 53 | 9 | 0 | 0 | 0 | 1 | 73.74 | $11,126 |

Best finish for 1979: T-25th at the Southern Open

| 1980 | 15 | 49 | 9 | 0 | 0 | 0 | 3 | 73.14 | $17,139 |

Best finish for 1980: T-13th at the Southern Open

| 1981 | 14 | 40 | 7 | 0 | 0 | 0 | 1 | 73.70 | $8,702 |

Best finish for 1981: T-23rd at the British Open

| 1982 | 12 | 36 | 5 | 0 | 0 | 0 | 1 | 74.19 | $10,591 |

Best finish for 1982: T-22nd at the Hawaiian Open

| 1983 | 12 | 42 | 7 | 0 | 0 | 1 | 1 | 73.69 | $17,992 |

Best finish for 1983: T-10th at the Glen CampbellLos Angeles Open

| 1984 | 9 | 25 | 2 | 0 | 0 | 0 | 0 | 74.64 | $5,381 |

Best finish for 1984: T-66th at the Tournament Players Championship

| 1985 | 6 | 18 | 2 | 0 | 0 | 0 | 0 | 74.17 | $4,827 |

Best finish for 1985: T-65th at the PGA Championship

| 1986 | 6 | 11 | 0 | 0 | 0 | 0 | 0 | 75.09 | $2,500 |
| 1987 | 5 | 14 | 1 | 0 | 0 | 0 | 0 | 76.14 | $3,790 |

Best finish for 1987: T-65th at the PGA Championship

| 1988 | 5 | 12 | 0 | 0 | 0 | 0 | 0 | 73.67 | $2,500 |
| 1989 | 5 | 14 | 1 | 0 | 0 | 0 | 0 | 76.86 | $4,590 |

Best finish for 1989: T-63rd at the PGA Championship

| 1990 | 5 | 12 | 0 | 0 | 0 | 0 | 0 | 74.67 | $3,496 |
| 1991 | 5 | 14 | 1 | 0 | 0 | 0 | 1 | 74.50 | $10,238 |

Best finish for 1991: T-24th at the Nestle Invitational

| 1992 | 5 | 13 | 0 | 0 | 0 | 0 | 0 | 74.46 | $2,700 |
| 1993 | 5 | 14 | 1 | 0 | 0 | 0 | 0 | 75.50 | $4,670 |

Best finish for 1993: T-71st at the Nestle Invitational

1994	6	15	0	0	0	0	0	75.47	$3,700
1995	5	13	0	0	0	0	0	75.31	$2,537
1996	3	8	0	0	0	0	0	74.50	$1,500
1997	2	4	0	0	0	0	0	83.75	$5,000
1998	3	8	0	0	0	0	0	78.13	$5,000
1999	3	8	0	0	0	0	0	77.25	$5,000
2000	3	8	0	0	0	0	0	79.00	$5,000
2001	4	8	0	0	0	0	0	78.38	$5,000
2002	3	7	0	0	0	0	0	83.29	$5,000
2003	2	4	0	0	0	0	0	84.50	$5,000
2004	2	4	0	0	0	0	0	83.75	$5,000
Period Totals	Starts	Rounds Played	Cuts Made	Wins	Top-5s	Top-10s	Top-25s	Scoring Average	Money
	639	2295	471	55	153	228	357	71.78	$2,051,412

PGA Tour career totals from 1949 to 2004

	Starts	Rounds Played	Cuts Made	Wins	Top-5s	Top-10s	Top-25s	Scoring Average	Money
	737	2636	559	62	174	258	408	N/A	$2,103,318

Johnny Palmer

Year	Starts	Rounds Played	Cuts Made	Wins	Top-5s	Top-10s	Top-25s	Scoring Average	Money
1958	7	21	4	0	0	0	1	73.95	$258

Best finish for 1958: T-24th at the Arlington Hotel Open

| 1959 | 3 | 12 | 3 | 0 | 1 | 1 | 1 | 71.92 | $1,290 |

Best finish for 1959: T-4th at the Arlington Hotel Open Invitational

| 1960 | 7 | 27 | 6 | 0 | 1 | 1 | 5 | 71.48 | $5,040 |

Best finish for 1960: T-3rd at the Palm Springs Desert Golf Classic

| 1961 | 1 | 4 | 1 | 0 | 0 | 0 | 0 | 75.50 | $100 |

Best finish for 1961: T-49th at the Colonial National Invitational

| 1962 | 1 | 4 | 1 | 0 | 0 | 0 | 0 | 74.75 | $091 |

Best finish for 1962: T-39th at the Bing Crosby National

| 1964 | 3 | 9 | 1 | 0 | 0 | 0 | 0 | 79.00 | $155 |

Best finish for 1964: 69th at the Colonial National Invitational

| 1965 | 1 | 3 | 0 | 0 | 0 | 0 | 0 | 80.33 | $150 |
| 1966 | 1 | 4 | 1 | 0 | 0 | 0 | 0 | 78.00 | $165 |

Best finish for 1966: 67th at the Colonial National Invitation

1970	1	2	0	0	0	0	0	77.50	
Period Totals	Starts	Rounds Played	Cuts Made	Wins	Top-5s	Top-10s	Top-25s	Scoring Average	Money
	25	86	17	0	2	2	7	74.02	$7,250

PGA Tour career totals from 1941 to 1970

	Starts	Rounds Played	Cuts Made	Wins	Top-5s	Top-10s	Top-25s	Scoring Average	Money
	290	N/A	N/A	7	N/A	113	227	N/A	N/A

Ryan Palmer

Year	Starts	Rounds Played	Cuts Made	Wins	Top-5s	Top-10s	Top-25s	Scoring Average	Money
1998	1	2	0	0	0	0	0	77.50	
2002	1	2	0	0	0	0	0	71.00	
2004	33	100	18	1	2	2	6	71.02	$1,592,344

Best finish for 2004: Win at the FUNAI Classic at the Walt Disney World Resort

| 2005 | 32 | 97 | 18 | 0 | 3 | 3 | 7 | 71.02 | $1,280,002 |

Best finish for 2005: T-2nd at the B.C. Open

| 2006 | 30 | 99 | 20 | 0 | 2 | 4 | 8 | 70.95 | $1,092,853 |

Best finish for 2006: T-2nd at the FBR Open

| 2007 | 30 | 91 | 14 | 0 | 1 | 1 | 1 | 71.78 | $526,988 |

Best finish for 2007: T-3rd at the Canadian Open

| 2008 | 22 | 69 | 12 | 1 | 2 | 3 | 7 | 70.48 | $1,453,183 |

Best finish for 2008: Win at the Ginn sur Mer Classic

| Period Totals | Starts | Rounds Played | Cuts Made | Wins | Top-5s | Top-10s | Top-25s | Scoring Average | Money |
| | 149 | 460 | 82 | 2 | 10 | 13 | 29 | 71.10 | $5,945,370 |

Rod Pampling

Year	Starts	Rounds Played	Cuts Made	Wins	Top-5s	Top-10s	Top-25s	Scoring Average	Money
1999	6	16	3	0	0	0	0	72.63	$53,382

Best finish for 1999: T-37th at the Reno-Tahoe Open & American Express Championship

| 2001 | 1 | 2 | 0 | 0 | 0 | 0 | 0 | 75.00 | |
| 2002 | 29 | 94 | 19 | 0 | 1 | 3 | 11 | 70.50 | $776,903 |

Best finish for 2002: T-4th at the Tampa Bay Classic presented by Buick

| 2003 | 27 | 83 | 16 | 0 | 2 | 5 | 9 | 70.19 | $1,065,974 |

Best finish for 2003: T-3rd at the Reno-Tahoe Open

| 2004 | 26 | 94 | 22 | 1 | 1 | 2 | 10 | 70.66 | $1,737,725 |

Best finish for 2004: Win at The International

| 2005 | 26 | 84 | 21 | 0 | 1 | 6 | 10 | 71.15 | $1,617,815 |

Best finish for 2005: T-5th at the Masters

| 2006 | 24 | 84 | 21 | 1 | 2 | 6 | 9 | 70.98 | $2,666,923 |

Best finish for 2006: Win at the Bay Hill Invitational

| 2007 | 25 | 90 | 22 | 0 | 1 | 2 | 9 | 71.08 | $1,477,970 |

Best finish for 2007: T-3rd at the Memorial Tournament

| 2008 | 28 | 80 | 14 | 0 | 2 | 5 | 10 | 71.39 | $1,702,952 |

Best finish for 2008: T-2nd at the Crowne Plaza Invitational at Colonial

| Period Totals | Starts | Rounds Played | Cuts Made | Wins | Top-5s | Top-10s | Top-25s | Scoring Average | Money |
| | 192 | 627 | 138 | 2 | 10 | 29 | 68 | 70.90 | $11,099,645 |

Bob Panasiuk

Year	Starts	Rounds Played	Cuts Made	Wins	Top-5s	Top-10s	Top-25s	Scoring Average	Money
1961	2	8	2	0	0	0	1	71.75	$190

Best finish for 1961: T-23rd at the Mobile Sertoma Open Invitational

| 1964 | 13 | 41 | 7 | 0 | 0 | 0 | 1 | 74.10 | $1,817 |

Best finish for 1964: T-20th at the Buick Open

| 1965 | 10 | 22 | 1 | 0 | 0 | 0 | 0 | 75.55 | |

Best finish for 1965: T-58th at the Azalea Open

| 1968 | 1 | 2 | 0 | 0 | 0 | 0 | 0 | 75.00 | $500 |
| 1969 | 13 | 32 | 3 | 0 | 0 | 0 | 2 | 73.75 | $2,738 |

Best finish for 1969: T-18th at the Minnesota Classic

| 1970 | 2 | 4 | 0 | 0 | 0 | 0 | 0 | 76.50 | $500 |
| 1972 | 3 | 8 | 1 | 0 | 0 | 0 | 1 | 73.50 | $2,750 |

Best finish for 1972: T-16th at the Canadian Open

| 1973 | 2 | 6 | 1 | 0 | 0 | 0 | 0 | 74.00 | $1,094 |

Best finish for 1973: T-42nd at the Canadian Open

| 1974 | 4 | 14 | 3 | 0 | 0 | 1 | 1 | 71.79 | $5,626 |

Best finish for 1974: T-7th at the Ohio Kings Island Open

| 1975 | 3 | 12 | 3 | 0 | 0 | 1 | 1 | 72.58 | $2,828 |

Best finish for 1975: T-8th at the Tallahassee Open

1977	1	2	0	0	0	0	0	77.00	
1978	1	2	0	0	0	0	0	81.50	
1979	1	2	0	0	0	0	0	76.00	
1980	1	2	0	0	0	0	0	78.00	
1981	1	0	0	0	0	0	0		

Year	Starts	Rounds Played	Cuts Made	Wins	Top-5s	Top-10s	Top-25s	Scoring Average	Money
1983	1	2	0	0	0	0	0	79.50	$600
1986	1	2	0	0	0	0	0	76.00	
1987	1	2	0	0	0	0	0	78.00	
Period Totals	Starts	Rounds Played	Cuts Made	Wins	Top-5s	Top-10s	Top-25s	Scoring Average	Money
	61	163	21	0	0	2	7	74.17	$18,643

Bobby Pancratz

Year	Starts	Rounds Played	Cuts Made	Wins	Top-5s	Top-10s	Top-25s	Scoring Average	Money
1980	8	18	3	0	0	0	0	73.83	$2,068

Best finish for 1980: T-35th at the World Disney World National Team Championship

1981	8	21	3	0	0	0	0	73.76	$1,678

Best finish for 1981: T-60th at the Byron Nelson Golf Classic

1982	10	22	1	0	0	0	0	74.68	$597

Best finish for 1982: T-70th at the Bank of Boston Classic

1985	1	2	0	0	0	0	0	79.00	$600
1986	19	48	6	0	0	0	0	74.21	$4,999

Best finish for 1986: T-41st at the Tallahassee Open

1987	1	2	0	0	0	0	0	75.50	
1988	1	2	0	0	0	0	0	73.50	
1993	1	2	0	0	0	0	0	75.00	
Period Totals	Starts	Rounds Played	Cuts Made	Wins	Top-5s	Top-10s	Top-25s	Scoring Average	Money
	49	117	13	0	0	0	0	74.26	$9,942

Brenden Pappas

Year	Starts	Rounds Played	Cuts Made	Wins	Top-5s	Top-10s	Top-25s	Scoring Average	Money
2002	25	62	6	0	0	0	0	72.58	$83,519

Best finish for 2002: T-27th at the Tampa Bay Classic presented by Buick

2003	33	103	18	0	4	5	8	70.60	$1,307,809

Best finish for 2003: 2nd at the Southern Farm Bureau Classic

2004	34	108	21	0	0	0	6	71.16	$526,905

Best finish for 2004: T-12th at the Buick Open

2005	15	51	10	0	0	0	3	71.00	$279,340

Best finish for 2005: T-12th at the FedEx St. Jude Classic

2008	24	66	9	0	0	1	4	70.80	$384,072

Best finish for 2008: 9th at the Puerto Rico Open

Period Totals	Starts	Rounds Played	Cuts Made	Wins	Top-5s	Top-10s	Top-25s	Scoring Average	Money
	131	390	64	0	4	6	21	71.16	$2,581,645

Deane Pappas

Year	Starts	Rounds Played	Cuts Made	Wins	Top-5s	Top-10s	Top-25s	Scoring Average	Money
1992	2	4	0	0	0	0	0	74.50	
1993	3	8	1	0	0	0	0	71.63	$4,537

Best finish for 1993: T-31st at the B.C. Open

1994	1	2	0	0	0	0	0	77.50	
1999	29	82	11	0	0	0	2	72.27	$113,380

Best finish for 1999: T-12th at the B.C. Open

2002	34	88	11	0	1	2	2	72.07	$494,404

Best finish for 2002: 2nd at the Southern Farm Bureau Classic

2003	24	73	13	0	0	0	1	70.97	$189,955

Best finish for 2003: T-19th at the BellSouth Classic

2004	22	70	14	0	0	0	2	71.27	$346,633

Best finish for 2004: T-11th at the EDS Byron Nelson Championship

2006	1	2	0	0	0	0	0	74.50	
2008	3	8	1	0	0	0	0	71.13	$9,573

Best finish for 2008: T-50th at the U.S. Bank Championship in Milwaukee

Period Totals	Starts	Rounds Played	Cuts Made	Wins	Top-5s	Top-10s	Top-25s	Scoring Average	Money
	119	337	51	0	1	2	7	71.76	$1,158,482

Jin Park

Year	Starts	Rounds Played	Cuts Made	Wins	Top-5s	Top-10s	Top-25s	Scoring Average	Money
1996	1	2	0	0	0	0	0	78.00	
2002	1	2	0	0	0	0	0	82.50	
2003	2	5	0	0	0	0	0	79.80	
2004	2	5	0	0	0	0	0	74.20	
2006	1	4	1	0	0	0	0	70.00	$6,450

Best finish for 2006: T-60th at the Chrysler Classic of Tucson

2007	1	2	0	0	0	0	0	74.00	
2008	30	85	13	0	0	0	1	72.07	$227,102

Best finish for 2008: T-18th at the John Deere Classic

Period Totals	Starts	Rounds Played	Cuts Made	Wins	Top-5s	Top-10s	Top-25s	Scoring Average	Money
	38	105	14	0	0	0	1	72.81	$233,552

Bill Parker

Year	Starts	Rounds Played	Cuts Made	Wins	Top-5s	Top-10s	Top-25s	Scoring Average	Money
1958	31	102	20	0	0	1	5	73.03	$1,555

Best finish for 1958: T-7th at the Texas Open

1959	11	43	10	0	0	0	2	72.33	$1,374

Best finish for 1959: T-18th at the El Paso Open Invitational

1960	2	8	2	0	0	0	0	71.88	$312

Best finish for 1960: T-26th at the Dallas Open Invitational

1962	1	4	1	0	0	0	1	71.25	$475

Best finish for 1962: T-11th at the Mobile Sertoma Open Invitational

1963	2	8	2	0	0	0	0	71.50	$166

Best finish for 1963: T-36th at the San Diego Open Invitational

1964	20	54	5	0	0	0	2	74.07	$978

Best finish for 1964: T-20th at the Cajun Classic

1965	5	14	1	0	0	0	0	74.71	

Best finish for 1965: T-63rd at the Cajun Classic

1966	6	16	2	0	0	0	0	74.63	

Best finish for 1966: T-55th at the Cajun Classic

1967	18	52	7	0	1	1	1	74.37	$5,076

Best finish for 1967: T-4th at the Bing Crosby Pro-Am

1968	6	18	3	0	0	0	0	73.22	$1,781

Best finish for 1968: T-33rd at the Bing Crosby National Professional-Amateur & Kemper Open Invitational

1969	2	6	1	0	0	0	0	72.00	$240

Best finish for 1969: T-67th at the Memphis Open

1970	1	2	0	0	0	0	0	78.00	
1971	2	6	1	0	0	0	0	73.83	$192

Best finish for 1971: T-72nd at the Bing Crosby Pro-Am

1972	1	2	0	0	0	0	0	75.00	
1973	2	4	0	0	0	0	0	76.25	
Period Totals	Starts	Rounds Played	Cuts Made	Wins	Top-5s	Top-10s	Top-25s	Scoring Average	Money
	110	339	55	0	1	2	11	73.46	$12,150

Roger Parker

Year	Starts	Rounds Played	Cuts Made	Wins	Top-5s	Top-10s	Top-25s	Scoring Average	Money
1973	3	10	1	0	0	0	0	75.00	$216

Best finish for 1973: T-64th at the San Antonio Texas Open

1974	15	34	1	0	0	0	0	75.35	

Best finish for 1974: 72nd at the Colonial National Invitational

1975	7	13	1	0	0	0	0	74.38	$124

Best finish for 1975: 67th at the Ed McMahon Quad City Open

1976	14	30	4	0	0	0	0	74.70	$500

Best finish for 1976: T-73rd at the Pleasant Valley Classic

1977	13	27	2	0	0	0	0	75.26	

Best finish for 1977: T-72nd at the Florida Citrus Open Invitational

1979	1	2	0	0	0	0	0	72.00	
1983	1	2	0	0	0	0	0	71.00	
1984	1	2	0	0	0	0	0	77.50	
Period Totals	Starts	Rounds Played	Cuts Made	Wins	Top-5s	Top-10s	Top-25s	Scoring Average	Money
	55	120	9	0	0	0	0	74.94	$840

Philip Parkin

Year	Starts	Rounds Played	Cuts Made	Wins	Top-5s	Top-10s	Top-25s	Scoring Average	Money
1983	2	6	1	0	0	0	0	73.83	

Best finish for 1983: 39th at the World Series Of Golf

1984	3	8	1	0	0	0	0	73.13	$3,377

Best finish for 1984: T-31st at the British Open

1985	2	8	2	0	0	0	2	71.63	$9,476

Best finish for 1985: T-24th at the Houston Open

1986	4	15	4	0	0	0	2	71.73	$17,354

Best finish for 1986: T-15th at the Houston Open

1987	19	47	6	0	0	0	2	73.19	$12,998

Best finish for 1987: T-22nd at the Southern Open

1989	1	2	0	0	0	0	0	75.00	$800
Period Totals	Starts	Rounds Played	Cuts Made	Wins	Top-5s	Top-10s	Top-25s	Scoring Average	Money
	31	86	14	0	0	0	6	72.87	$44,004

Jesper Parnevik

Year	Starts	Rounds Played	Cuts Made	Wins	Top-5s	Top-10s	Top-25s	Scoring Average	Money
1993	1	4	1	0	0	0	1	69.75	$15,400

Best finish for 1993: T-21st at the British Open

1994	18	60	13	0	2	3	5	71.38	$292,576

Best finish for 1994: 2nd at the British Open

Year	Starts	Rounds Played	Cuts Made	Wins	Top-5s	Top-10s	Top-25s	Scoring Average	Money
1995	19	65	15	0	1	2	7	70.92	$222,458

Best finish for 1995: T-5th at The Nestle Invitational

1996	19	68	17	0	2	5	9	70.29	$389,266

Best finish for 1996: T-3rd at the Greater Milwaukee Open

1997	19	70	16	0	8	9	11	70.24	$1,217,587

Best finish for 1997: T-2nd at the Phoenix Open, Buick Invitational, Freeport-McDermott Classic, MCI Classic & British Open

1998	20	69	17	1	4	5	13	70.77	$1,292,322

Best finish for 1998: Win at the Phoenix Open

1999	20	67	17	1	1	4	10	71.43	$1,060,368

Best finish for 1999: Win at the Greater Greensboro Chrysler Classic

2000	20	68	16	2	5	9	11	70.34	$2,414,345

Best finish for 2000: Win at the Bob Hope Chrysler Classic & GTE Byron Nelson Classic

2001	24	91	21	1	1	4	13	70.02	$1,574,208

Best finish for 2001: Win at the Honda Classic

2002	26	84	17	0	1	2	4	71.42	$966,304

Best finish for 2002: 2nd at the BellSouth Classic

2003	31	99	18	0	1	1	5	71.02	$584,701

Best finish for 2003: T-5th at the 84 Lumber Classic of Pennsylvania

2004	24	86	18	0	3	5	9	70.16	$1,552,135

Best finish for 2004: T-2nd at the Chrysler Championship

2005	24	82	17	0	1	2	4	71.09	$737,845

Best finish for 2005: 4th at the Bell Canadian Open

2006	24	84	17	0	1	4	7	70.64	$1,310,560

Best finish for 2006: T-2nd at the Bob Hope Chrysler Classic

2007	27	88	16	0	1	1	7	70.70	$1,075,216

Best finish for 2007: 2nd at the Valero Texas Open

2008	29	88	16	0	0	0	5	71.25	$635,819

Best finish for 2008: T-12th at the Wachovia Championship & Ginn sur Mer Classic

Period Totals	Starts	Rounds Played	Cuts Made	Wins	Top-5s	Top-10s	Top-25s	Scoring Average	Money
	345	1173	252	5	32	56	121	70.77	$15,341,110

Craig Parry

Year	Starts	Rounds Played	Cuts Made	Wins	Top-5s	Top-10s	Top-25s	Scoring Average	Money
1987	2	4	0	0	0	0	0	80.25	$640
1988	2	6	1	0	0	0	0	73.00	$2,415

Best finish for 1988: T-58th at the Canadian Open

1990	9	27	7	0	0	0	3	72.44	$59,193

Best finish for 1990: T-15th at the Independent Insurance Agent Open

1991	7	27	7	0	0	1	4	71.15	$109,967

Best finish for 1991: 8th at the British Open

1992	14	52	12	0	1	4	6	71.38	$254,819

Best finish for 1992: T-3rd at the Kmart Greater Greensboro Open

1993	24	77	17	0	2	6	7	71.44	$329,267

Best finish for 1993: T-3rd at the U.S. Open

1994	20	66	15	0	1	3	8	71.26	$360,515

Best finish for 1994: 2nd at the Honda Classic

1995	24	76	16	0	2	2	5	71.17	$295,650

Best finish for 1995: 2nd at the Colonial National Invitational

1996	24	81	19	0	3	3	7	71.04	$455,211

Best finish for 1996: T-2nd at the GTE Byron Nelson Classic & Buick Classic

1997	20	71	16	0	3	4	7	70.90	$390,243

Best finish for 1997: T-3rd at the FedEx St. Jude Classic

1998	16	47	10	0	0	4	6	71.21	$314,355

Best finish for 1998: T-6th at the Bay Hill Invitational

1999	19	64	15	0	3	5	8	71.63	$964,126

Best finish for 1999: T-3rd at the WGC-NEC Invitational

2000	22	69	16	0	0	1	5	71.03	$509,308

Best finish for 2000: T-7th at the FedEx St. Jude Classic

2001	22	63	13	0	0	1	6	70.71	$503,923

Best finish for 2001: T-7th at the Invensys Classic at Las Vegas

2002	21	69	13	1	2	2	6	70.97	$1,473,185

Best finish for 2002: Win at the WGC-NEC Invitational

2003	16	48	10	0	0	0	1	72.63	$260,281

Best finish for 2003: T-25th at the Mercedes Championships

2004	16	50	10	1	1	1	4	72.14	$1,318,267

Best finish for 2004: Win at the Ford Championship at Doral

2005	15	46	10	0	0	2	4	72.22	$637,391

Best finish for 2005: T-6th at the Ford Championship at Doral

2006	15	44	7	0	0	0	2	72.09	$283,282

Best finish for 2006: T-14th at the Memorial Tournament

2008	4	14	3	0	0	0	0	74.93	$86,311

Best finish for 2008: T-70th at the British Open

Period Totals	Starts	Rounds Played	Cuts Made	Wins	Top-5s	Top-10s	Top-25s	Scoring Average	Money
	312	1001	217	2	18	39	89	71.50	$8,608,350

Don Parson

Year	Starts	Rounds Played	Cuts Made	Wins	Top-5s	Top-10s	Top-25s	Scoring Average	Money
1969	13	38	7	0	0	0	0	72.97	$2,434

Best finish for 1969: T-32nd at the Robinson Open

Year	Starts	Rounds Played	Cuts Made	Wins	Top-5s	Top-10s	Top-25s	Scoring Average	Money
1970	10	22	1	0	0	0	0	74.73	$168

Best finish for 1970: T-58th at the Western Open

Year	Starts	Rounds Played	Cuts Made	Wins	Top-5s	Top-10s	Top-25s	Scoring Average	Money
1975	1	2	0	0	0	0	0	73.50	
1976	1	2	0	0	0	0	0	76.50	
1977	1	2	0	0	0	0	0	73.00	
Period Totals	26	66	8	0	0	0	0	73.68	$2,602

Lucas Parsons

Year	Starts	Rounds Played	Cuts Made	Wins	Top-5s	Top-10s	Top-25s	Scoring Average	Money
1996	24	56	4	0	0	0	0	73.41	$21,233

Best finish for 1996: T-35th at the FedEx St. Jude Classic

Year	Starts	Rounds Played	Cuts Made	Wins	Top-5s	Top-10s	Top-25s	Scoring Average	Money
2000	2	8	2	0	0	0	0	72.75	$45,873

Best finish for 2000: T-41st at the British Open

Period Totals	Starts	Rounds Played	Cuts Made	Wins	Top-5s	Top-10s	Top-25s	Scoring Average	Money
	26	64	6	0	0	0	0	73.33	$67,106

Jimmy Paschal

Year	Starts	Rounds Played	Cuts Made	Wins	Top-5s	Top-10s	Top-25s	Scoring Average	Money
1977	1	2	0	0	0	0	0	74.50	
1978	1	2	0	0	0	0	0	75.50	
1979	10	22	1	0	0	0	0	75.05	$1,490

Best finish for 1979: T-39th at the Sammy Davis, Jr. - Greater Hartford Open

Year	Starts	Rounds Played	Cuts Made	Wins	Top-5s	Top-10s	Top-25s	Scoring Average	Money
1980	1	2	0	0	0	0	0	78.50	
1981	8	16	1	0	0	0	0	74.19	$860

Best finish for 1981: T-62nd at the Manufactures Hanover Westchester Classic

Year	Starts	Rounds Played	Cuts Made	Wins	Top-5s	Top-10s	Top-25s	Scoring Average	Money
1982	1	4	1	0	0	0	0	75.75	$800

Best finish for 1982: 71st at the Danny Thomas Memphis Classic

Year	Starts	Rounds Played	Cuts Made	Wins	Top-5s	Top-10s	Top-25s	Scoring Average	Money
1983	1	1	0	0	0	0	0	79.00	
1988	1	2	0	0	0	0	0	73.50	
1990	1	2	0	0	0	0	0	75.50	
Period Totals	25	53	3	0	0	0	0	75.00	$3,150

Alan Pate

Year	Starts	Rounds Played	Cuts Made	Wins	Top-5s	Top-10s	Top-25s	Scoring Average	Money
1977	8	20	2	0	0	0	0	73.00	$100

Best finish for 1977: T-69th at the IVB Philadelphia Golf Classic

Year	Starts	Rounds Played	Cuts Made	Wins	Top-5s	Top-10s	Top-25s	Scoring Average	Money
1978	11	31	4	0	1	1	1	74.26	$11,131

Best finish for 1978: T-5th at the Kemper Open

Year	Starts	Rounds Played	Cuts Made	Wins	Top-5s	Top-10s	Top-25s	Scoring Average	Money
1979	18	39	1	0	0	0	0	75.97	$450

Best finish for 1979: 80th at the Andy Williams-San Diego Open

Year	Starts	Rounds Played	Cuts Made	Wins	Top-5s	Top-10s	Top-25s	Scoring Average	Money
1980	1	2	0	0	0	0	0	73.50	$600
1981	1	2	0	0	0	0	0	72.50	
1983	3	8	1	0	0	0	0	71.75	$679

Best finish for 1983: T-72nd at the Bank of Boston Classic

Year	Starts	Rounds Played	Cuts Made	Wins	Top-5s	Top-10s	Top-25s	Scoring Average	Money
1984	1	2	0	0	0	0	0	75.00	
1985	1	2	0	0	0	0	0	79.00	
1988	3	8	1	0	0	0	0	74.63	$1,528

Best finish for 1988: T-74th at the Kemper Open

Year	Starts	Rounds Played	Cuts Made	Wins	Top-5s	Top-10s	Top-25s	Scoring Average	Money
1989	2	4	0	0	0	0	0	74.00	
1990	1	2	0	0	0	0	0	74.50	
1991	1	4	1	0	0	0	0	70.50	$588

Best finish for 1991: 73rd at the Deposit Guaranty Classic

Year	Starts	Rounds Played	Cuts Made	Wins	Top-5s	Top-10s	Top-25s	Scoring Average	Money
1995	3	8	1	0	0	0	0	74.13	$4,160

Best finish for 1995: 67th at the Motorola Western Open

Period Totals	Starts	Rounds Played	Cuts Made	Wins	Top-5s	Top-10s	Top-25s	Scoring Average	Money
	54	132	11	0	1	1	1	74.36	$19,236

Jerry Pate

Year	Starts	Rounds Played	Cuts Made	Wins	Top-5s	Top-10s	Top-25s	Scoring Average	Money
1975	7	26	6	0	0	1	4	71.69	$3,250

Best finish for 1975: 6th at the Pensacola Open

Year	Starts	Rounds Played	Cuts Made	Wins	Top-5s	Top-10s	Top-25s	Scoring Average	Money
1976	29	100	21	2	5	8	15	71.43	$153,373

Best finish for 1976: Win at the U.S. Open & Canadian Open

Year	Starts	Rounds Played	Cuts Made	Wins	Top-5s	Top-10s	Top-25s	Scoring Average	Money
1977	18	62	15	2	3	6	9	71.13	$100,947

Best finish for 1977: Win at the Phoenix Open & Southern Open

| 1978 | 26 | 98 | 22 | 1 | 6 | 9 | 16 | 71.35 | $173,426 |

Best finish for 1978: Win at the Southern Open

| 1979 | 28 | 99 | 22 | 0 | 6 | 12 | 15 | 71.41 | $195,570 |

Best finish for 1979: T-2nd at the MONY Tournament Of Champions, Kemper Open & U.S. Open

| 1980 | 28 | 99 | 23 | 0 | 5 | 12 | 23 | 70.74 | $232,706 |

Best finish for 1980: T-2nd at the Sea Pines Heritage Classic, Greater Greensboro Open & Canadian Open

| 1981 | 25 | 99 | 25 | 2 | 7 | 11 | 21 | 70.55 | $284,652 |

Best finish for 1981: Win at the Danny Thomas Memphis Classic & Pensacola Open

| 1982 | 23 | 81 | 18 | 1 | 6 | 10 | 15 | 70.91 | $281,124 |

Best finish for 1982: Win at the Tournament Players Championship

| 1983 | 17 | 53 | 8 | 0 | 0 | 1 | 3 | 72.15 | $29,490 |

Best finish for 1983: T-8th at the Manufactures Hanover Westchester Classic

| 1984 | 18 | 50 | 7 | 0 | 1 | 1 | 3 | 72.74 | $42,746 |

Best finish for 1984: 4th at the Bank of Boston Classic

| 1985 | 19 | 56 | 7 | 0 | 0 | 0 | 0 | 73.88 | $8,392 |

Best finish for 1985: T-46th at the Phoenix Open

| 1986 | 8 | 18 | 1 | 0 | 0 | 0 | 0 | 72.67 | $2,045 |

Best finish for 1986: T-44th at the Phoenix Open

| 1987 | 6 | 19 | 2 | 0 | 0 | 0 | 0 | 73.47 | $2,116 |

Best finish for 1987: T-69th at the Shearson Lehman/Andy Williams San Diego

| 1988 | 9 | 19 | 1 | 0 | 0 | 0 | 1 | 73.37 | $10,075 |

Best finish for 1988: T-14th at the Anheuser-Busch Golf Classic

| 1989 | 20 | 51 | 5 | 0 | 0 | 0 | 0 | 73.49 | $10,168 |

Best finish for 1989: T-53rd at the Canadian Open

| 1990 | 17 | 53 | 8 | 0 | 0 | 0 | 1 | 73.00 | $27,953 |

Best finish for 1990: T-21st at the AT&T Pebble Beach Pro-Am

| 1991 | 18 | 44 | 3 | 0 | 0 | 0 | 0 | 73.64 | $7,249 |

Best finish for 1991: T-35th at the Southwestern Bell Colonial

| 1992 | 14 | 40 | 5 | 0 | 0 | 0 | 0 | 72.68 | $10,971 |

Best finish for 1992: T-48th at the Centel Western Open

| 1993 | 2 | 7 | 0 | 0 | 0 | 0 | 0 | 73.29 | |
| 1994 | 8 | 24 | 3 | 0 | 0 | 0 | 0 | 73.46 | $6,513 |

Best finish for 1994: T-55th at the MCI Heritage Classic

| 1995 | 22 | 71 | 12 | 0 | 0 | 0 | 1 | 72.01 | $62,001 |

Best finish for 1995: T-15th at the BellSouth Classic

1998	2	7	0	0	0	0	0	71.71	
2000	1	3	0	0	0	0	0	76.67	
2001	3	6	0	0	0	0	0	73.50	$2,000
2002	5	15	2	0	0	0	0	72.53	$15,372

Best finish for 2002: 66th at the Buick Challenge

2003	3	9	0	0	0	0	0	73.78	
Period Totals	Starts	Rounds Played	Cuts Made	Wins	Top-5s	Top-10s	Top-25s	Scoring Average	Money
	376	1209	216	8	39	71	127	71.95	$1,662,140

Steve Pate

Year	Starts	Rounds Played	Cuts Made	Wins	Top-5s	Top-10s	Top-25s	Scoring Average	Money
1985	27	81	12	0	1	3	3	72.25	$89,358

Best finish for 1985: 2nd at the Georgia-Pacific Atlanta Golf Classic

| 1986 | 33 | 108 | 26 | 0 | 1 | 3 | 10 | 71.69 | $176,100 |

Best finish for 1986: T-3rd at the Panasonic Las Vegas Invitational

| 1987 | 34 | 116 | 27 | 1 | 5 | 6 | 13 | 70.78 | $335,729 |

Best finish for 1987: Win at the Southwest Golf Classic

| 1988 | 33 | 108 | 24 | 2 | 4 | 7 | 17 | 70.91 | $583,237 |

Best finish for 1988: Win at the MONY Tournament Of Champions & Shearson Lehman/Andy Williams San Diego

| 1989 | 32 | 114 | 26 | 0 | 2 | 5 | 15 | 70.80 | $327,334 |

Best finish for 1989: T-3rd at the Honda Classic

| 1990 | 30 | 104 | 23 | 0 | 2 | 6 | 12 | 71.21 | $374,324 |

Best finish for 1990: T-2nd at the International

| 1991 | 27 | 100 | 24 | 1 | 6 | 8 | 15 | 70.33 | $733,298 |

Best finish for 1991: Win at the Honda Classic

| 1992 | 32 | 109 | 25 | 1 | 2 | 6 | 11 | 70.93 | $579,626 |

Best finish for 1992: Win at the Buick Invitational of California

| 1993 | 29 | 91 | 19 | 0 | 0 | 4 | 9 | 71.31 | $257,265 |

Best finish for 1993: T-6th at the Honda Classic & The International

| 1994 | 29 | 93 | 20 | 0 | 3 | 5 | 9 | 71.08 | $291,651 |

Best finish for 1994: T-3rd at the Buick Open

| 1995 | 32 | 95 | 15 | 0 | 0 | 0 | 3 | 71.64 | $90,758 |

Best finish for 1995: T-17th at the Greater Milwaukee Open & B.C. Open

| 1996 | 3 | 13 | 3 | 0 | 0 | 0 | 0 | 70.62 | $10,403 |

Best finish for 1996: T-40th at the Nortel Open

Year	Starts	Rounds Played	Cuts Made	Wins	Top-5s	Top-10s	Top-25s	Scoring Average	Money
1997	28	83	15	0	0	4	6	71.05	$261,436

Best finish for 1997: T-7th at the Motorola Western Open

| 1998 | 26 | 85 | 18 | 1 | 2 | 4 | 9 | 70.78 | $784,004 |

Best finish for 1998: Win at the CVS Charity Classic

| 1999 | 28 | 96 | 24 | 0 | 4 | 5 | 11 | 71.34 | $1,755,960 |

Best finish for 1999: 2nd at the Bob Hope Chrysler Classic & GTE Byron Nelson Classic

| 2000 | 28 | 92 | 21 | 0 | 1 | 1 | 7 | 71.20 | $650,674 |

Best finish for 2000: T-3rd at the Greater Milwaukee Open

| 2001 | 30 | 86 | 15 | 0 | 1 | 1 | 3 | 71.27 | $271,967 |

Best finish for 2001: 5th at the B.C. Open

| 2002 | 21 | 60 | 10 | 0 | 0 | 0 | 3 | 71.08 | $221,183 |

Best finish for 2002: T-14th at the FedEx St. Jude Classic

| 2003 | 16 | 42 | 5 | 0 | 1 | 1 | 1 | 71.90 | $192,518 |

Best finish for 2003: T-4th at the Greater Hartford Open

| 2004 | 24 | 69 | 10 | 0 | 0 | 0 | 1 | 71.57 | $199,569 |

Best finish for 2004: T-15th at the HP Classic of New Orleans

| 2005 | 9 | 18 | 1 | 0 | 0 | 0 | 0 | 72.72 | $12,402 |

Best finish for 2005: T-51st at the AT&T Pebble Beach National Pro-Am

2006	2	4	0	0	0	0	0	73.50	
2008	3	7	0	0	0	0	0	74.00	
Period Totals	Starts	Rounds Played	Cuts Made	Wins	Top-5s	Top-10s	Top-25s	Scoring Average	Money
	556	1774	363	6	35	69	158	71.20	$8,198,798

Carl Paulson

Year	Starts	Rounds Played	Cuts Made	Wins	Top-5s	Top-10s	Top-25s	Scoring Average	Money
1995	21	62	10	0	0	1	2	71.89	$64,501

Best finish for 1995: T-7th at the Walt Disney World/Oldsmobile Classic

| 1996 | 30 | 87 | 14 | 0 | 0 | 0 | 4 | 71.84 | $117,071 |

Best finish for 1996: T-12th at the Bell Canadian Open

| 1999 | 1 | 2 | 0 | 0 | 0 | 0 | 0 | 73.50 | |
| 2000 | 33 | 103 | 19 | 0 | 2 | 4 | 7 | 70.66 | $741,995 |

Best finish for 2000: 2nd at the Tampa Bay Classic

| 2001 | 31 | 93 | 16 | 0 | 1 | 2 | 4 | 71.54 | $512,638 |

Best finish for 2001: T-3rd at the WorldCom Classic

| 2002 | 28 | 82 | 14 | 0 | 2 | 2 | 4 | 71.57 | $570,924 |

Best finish for 2002: T-4th at the Players Championship

| 2003 | 31 | 101 | 18 | 0 | 0 | 0 | 3 | 70.84 | $365,177 |

Best finish for 2003: T-15th at the Sony Open in Hawaii

| 2004 | 13 | 29 | 2 | 0 | 0 | 0 | 1 | 71.79 | $71,088 |

Best finish for 2004: T-14th at the John Deere Classic

| 2005 | 13 | 36 | 6 | 0 | 0 | 0 | 2 | 71.75 | $198,214 |

Best finish for 2005: T-13th at the Shell Houston Open

| Period Totals | Starts | Rounds Played | Cuts Made | Wins | Top-5s | Top-10s | Top-25s | Scoring Average | Money |
| | 201 | 595 | 99 | 0 | 5 | 9 | 27 | 71.38 | $2,641,609 |

Dennis Paulson

Year	Starts	Rounds Played	Cuts Made	Wins	Top-5s	Top-10s	Top-25s	Scoring Average	Money
1985	1	2	0	0	0	0	0	72.50	
1986	1	2	0	0	0	0	0	76.50	
1994	27	77	12	0	1	1	5	71.38	$142,515

Best finish for 1994: T-4th at the Freeport-McMoRan Classic

| 1995 | 30 | 82 | 11 | 0 | 1 | 1 | 4 | 71.79 | $103,411 |

Best finish for 1995: T-5th at the Quad City Classic

| 1998 | 1 | 4 | 1 | 0 | 0 | 0 | 0 | 72.50 | $4,557 |

Best finish for 1998: T-59th at the Nissan Open

| 1999 | 28 | 103 | 25 | 0 | 3 | 7 | 9 | 71.01 | $1,315,564 |

Best finish for 1999: 2nd at the Buick Classic & Bell Canadian Open

| 2000 | 26 | 81 | 15 | 1 | 1 | 1 | 5 | 71.79 | $897,098 |

Best finish for 2000: Win at the Buick Classic

| 2001 | 25 | 74 | 13 | 0 | 2 | 3 | 7 | 71.12 | $820,679 |

Best finish for 2001: T-2nd at the Nissan Open

| 2002 | 30 | 87 | 13 | 0 | 0 | 0 | 4 | 71.16 | $344,121 |

Best finish for 2002: T-11th at the B.C. Open

| 2003 | 15 | 49 | 9 | 0 | 2 | 2 | 3 | 70.45 | $452,648 |

Best finish for 2003: T-3rd at the Reno-Tahoe Open

| 2004 | 21 | 71 | 15 | 0 | 0 | 2 | 9 | 71.10 | $678,035 |

Best finish for 2004: T-9th at the Reno-Tahoe Open

| 2005 | 24 | 63 | 8 | 0 | 0 | 1 | 2 | 72.41 | $232,147 |

Best finish for 2005: T-10th at the BellSouth Classic

| 2007 | 3 | 6 | 0 | 0 | 0 | 0 | 0 | 72.00 | |
| 2008 | 1 | 4 | 1 | 0 | 0 | 0 | 0 | 72.75 | $6,420 |

Best finish for 2008: T-62nd at the Reno-Tahoe Open

Period Totals	Starts	Rounds Played	Cuts Made	Wins	Top-5s	Top-10s	Top-25s	Scoring Average	Money
	233	705	123	1	10	18	48	71.40	$4,997,194

Corey Pavin

Year	Starts	Rounds Played	Cuts Made	Wins	Top-5s	Top-10s	Top-25s	Scoring Average	Money
1979	1	2	0	0	0	0	0	74.00	
1980	1	4	1	0	0	0	0	72.50	

Best finish for 1980: T-45th at the Glen Campbell Los Angeles Open

1981	1	2	0	0	0	0	0	74.50	
1982	2	6	1	0	0	0	0	77.00	$1,500

Best finish for 1982: T-60th at the U.S. Open

1983	3	8	1	0	0	0	1	75.00	$4,809

Best finish for 1983: T-19th at the Greater Greensboro Open

1984	30	117	27	1	4	5	15	71.26	$265,541

Best finish for 1984: Win at the Houston Coca-Cola Open

1985	28	101	24	1	7	13	19	70.59	$371,276

Best finish for 1985: Win at the Colonial National Invitational

1986	29	94	23	2	2	6	14	71.22	$305,758

Best finish for 1986: Win at the Hawaiian Open & Greater Milwaukee Open

1987	29	86	17	2	3	7	10	71.21	$500,646

Best finish for 1987: Win at the Bob Hope Chrysler Classic & Hawaiian Open

1988	27	88	18	1	1	3	7	71.26	$223,642

Best finish for 1988: Win at the Texas Open

1989	28	99	23	0	0	1	10	71.04	$178,084

Best finish for 1989: T-10th at the Canadian Open

1990	31	109	27	0	4	7	14	70.92	$508,651

Best finish for 1990: T-2nd at the Southwestern Bell Colonial

1991	26	101	24	2	6	10	18	69.91	$980,438

Best finish for 1991: Win at the Bob Hope Chrysler Classic & BellSouth Atlanta Golf Classic

1992	26	93	21	1	7	7	13	70.37	$993,454

Best finish for 1992: Win at the Honda Classic

1993	25	95	23	0	5	7	14	70.18	$754,057

Best finish for 1993: 2nd at the Memorial Tournament

1994	20	70	15	1	6	9	11	70.44	$908,277

Best finish for 1994: Win at the Nissan Los Angeles Open

1995	22	79	17	2	5	6	11	70.51	$1,341,279

Best finish for 1995: Win at the Nissan Open & U.S. Open

1996	22	81	21	1	2	9	14	70.43	$851,320

Best finish for 1996: Win at the MasterCard Colonial

1997	22	63	11	0	0	1	1	71.89	$100,304

Best finish for 1997: T-8th at the Mercedes Championship

1998	23	67	12	0	0	2	3	71.69	$172,301

Best finish for 1998: T-10th at the Westin Texas Open & Michelob Championship at Kingsmill

1999	25	82	18	0	1	3	10	71.46	$575,764

Best finish for 1999: T-5th at the MCI Classic

2000	25	74	11	0	0	1	3	72.11	$219,403

Best finish for 2000: T-9th at the Westin Texas Open at LaCantera

2001	22	70	14	0	0	1	6	70.81	$459,975

Best finish for 2001: T-8th at the MasterCard Colonial

2002	24	76	14	0	0	1	2	71.17	$362,012

Best finish for 2002: T-6th at the Michelob Championship at Kingsmill

2003	26	86	18	0	0	0	2	71.06	$364,680

Best finish for 2003: T-15th at the Sony Open in Hawaii

2004	23	79	18	0	0	2	8	70.66	$881,938

Best finish for 2004: T-6th at the Buick Championship

2005	23	73	15	0	1	2	6	70.81	$736,506

Best finish for 2005: T-5th at the Bay Hill Invitational

2006	23	70	13	1	1	1	7	70.91	$1,310,084

Best finish for 2006: Win at the U.S. Bank Championship in Milwaukee

2007	25	81	15	0	0	1	3	71.60	$498,252

Best finish for 2007: T-6th at the AT&T Pebble Beach National Pro-Am

2008	20	69	14	0	1	2	6	70.67	$924,282

Best finish for 2008: T-3rd at the AT&T Pebble Beach National Pro-Am

Period Totals	Starts	Rounds Played	Cuts Made	Wins	Top-5s	Top-10s	Top-25s	Scoring Average	Money
	632	2125	456	15	56	107	228	70.99	$14,794,232

Bob Payne

Year	Starts	Rounds Played	Cuts Made	Wins	Top-5s	Top-10s	Top-25s	Scoring Average	Money
1968	1	4	1	0	0	0	0	71.75	

Best finish for 1968: T-53rd at the Cajun Classic

1969	22	67	11	0	1	1	2	73.10	$8,011

Best finish for 1969: T-4th at the Robinson Open

Year	Starts	Rounds Played	Cuts Made	Wins	Top-5s	Top-10s	Top-25s	Scoring Average	Money
1970	26	71	10	0	0	1	3	73.42	$7,406

Best finish for 1970: T-10th at the Bahama Islands Open

| 1971 | 22 | 68 | 12 | 0 | 0 | 0 | 2 | 73.19 | $6,999 |

Best finish for 1971: T-12th at the Greater New Orleans Open

| 1972 | 24 | 72 | 11 | 0 | 0 | 0 | 3 | 73.13 | $8,960 |

Best finish for 1972: T-13th at the Danny Thomas Memphis Classic

| 1973 | 33 | 113 | 22 | 0 | 0 | 2 | 8 | 71.98 | $24,819 |

Best finish for 1973: T-7th at the Sammy Davis, Jr. - Greater Hartford Open

| 1974 | 31 | 99 | 18 | 0 | 0 | 0 | 7 | 72.41 | $16,545 |

Best finish for 1974: T-11th at the Quad Cities Open

| 1975 | 20 | 53 | 7 | 0 | 0 | 0 | 2 | 73.25 | $7,873 |

Best finish for 1975: T-12th at the Greater Milwaukee Open

| 1976 | 21 | 59 | 9 | 0 | 0 | 0 | 0 | 72.88 | $7,501 |

Best finish for 1976: T-26th at the Hawaiian Open

| 1977 | 20 | 60 | 10 | 0 | 0 | 1 | 1 | 72.88 | $11,502 |

Best finish for 1977: 6th at the B.C. Open

| 1978 | 13 | 39 | 6 | 0 | 0 | 0 | 1 | 73.33 | $6,432 |

Best finish for 1978: T-14th at the Greater Greensboro Open

| 1979 | 3 | 8 | 1 | 0 | 0 | 0 | 0 | 74.00 | $424 |

Best finish for 1979: T-63rd at the Southern Open

| 1980 | 5 | 10 | 1 | 0 | 0 | 0 | 0 | 73.00 | $749 |

Best finish for 1980: T-61st at the Michelob Houston Open

1981	1	2	0	0	0	0	0	75.50	
1983	1	2	0	0	0	0	0	76.00	
1985	1	2	0	0	0	0	0	76.50	
Period Totals	Starts	Rounds Played	Cuts Made	Wins	Top-5s	Top-10s	Top-25s	Scoring Average	Money
	244	729	119	0	1	5	29	72.89	$107,220

Eddie Pearce

Year	Starts	Rounds Played	Cuts Made	Wins	Top-5s	Top-10s	Top-25s	Scoring Average	Money
1968	1	2	0	0	0	0	0	78.00	
1971	2	6	1	0	0	0	0	71.50	

Best finish for 1971: T-28th at the Greater Greensboro Open

| 1972 | 5 | 12 | 1 | 0 | 0 | 0 | 0 | 74.58 | $200 |

Best finish for 1972: T-55th at the Walt Disney World Open

| 1973 | 4 | 14 | 1 | 0 | 0 | 0 | 0 | 73.79 | $2,166 |

Best finish for 1973: 40th at the World Open

| 1974 | 28 | 88 | 17 | 0 | 2 | 4 | 8 | 72.32 | $55,206 |

Best finish for 1974: T-2nd at the Hawaiian Open & Tallahassee Open

| 1975 | 28 | 88 | 17 | 0 | 2 | 3 | 8 | 72.70 | $54,980 |

Best finish for 1975: 2nd at the Jackie Gleason's Inverrary Classic

| 1976 | 28 | 87 | 17 | 0 | 0 | 1 | 2 | 72.36 | $24,126 |

Best finish for 1976: T-6th at the Greater Greensboro Open

| 1977 | 25 | 54 | 4 | 0 | 0 | 0 | 0 | 74.59 | $4,408 |

Best finish for 1977: T-27th at the American Express Westchester Classic

| 1978 | 23 | 75 | 15 | 0 | 1 | 1 | 4 | 72.20 | $26,542 |

Best finish for 1978: T-4th at the Doral-Eastern Open

| 1979 | 28 | 80 | 11 | 0 | 1 | 2 | 5 | 72.85 | $43,120 |

Best finish for 1979: T-2nd at the San Antonio Texas Open

| 1980 | 11 | 26 | 2 | 0 | 0 | 0 | 0 | 75.12 | $2,344 |

Best finish for 1980: T-28th at the Buick Goodwrench Open

| 1981 | 14 | 34 | 4 | 0 | 0 | 0 | 0 | 73.82 | $2,654 |

Best finish for 1981: T-60th at the Canadian Open

| 1993 | 27 | 62 | 6 | 0 | 0 | 0 | 0 | 73.76 | $18,741 |

Best finish for 1993: T-39th at the Freeport-McMoRan Classic

| 1995 | 1 | 4 | 1 | 0 | 0 | 0 | 0 | 75.00 | $2,280 |

Best finish for 1995: 75th at the Nestle Invitational

| Period Totals | Starts | Rounds Played | Cuts Made | Wins | Top-5s | Top-10s | Top-25s | Scoring Average | Money |
| | 225 | 632 | 97 | 0 | 6 | 11 | 27 | 73.06 | $236,766 |

Rick Pearson

Year	Starts	Rounds Played	Cuts Made	Wins	Top-5s	Top-10s	Top-25s	Scoring Average	Money
1981	1	2	0	0	0	0	0	78.00	$600
1982	13	29	1	0	0	0	1	73.90	$4,200

Best finish for 1982: T-17th at the Doral-Eastern Open

| 1983 | 19 | 48 | 5 | 0 | 0 | 0 | 0 | 73.98 | $3,964 |

Best finish for 1983: T-38th at the Hawaiian Open

| 1985 | 1 | 2 | 0 | 0 | 0 | 0 | 0 | 77.50 | |
| 1986 | 1 | 4 | 1 | 0 | 0 | 0 | 1 | 70.50 | $2,900 |

Best finish for 1986: T-17th at the Tallahassee Open

| 1987 | 3 | 10 | 2 | 0 | 0 | 0 | 0 | 72.50 | $3,156 |

Best finish for 1987: T-37th at the Georgia-Pacific Atlanta Golf Classic

Year	Starts	Rounds Played	Cuts Made	Wins	Top-5s	Top-10s	Top-25s	Scoring Average	Money
1988	29	91	17	0	0	1	5	71.32	$58,881

Best finish for 1988: T-8th at the Deposit Guaranty Golf Classic

Year	Starts	Rounds Played	Cuts Made	Wins	Top-5s	Top-10s	Top-25s	Scoring Average	Money
1989	29	77	11	0	0	0	4	71.57	$53,226

Best finish for 1989: T-19th at the Hawaiian Open & Chattanooga Classic

Year	Starts	Rounds Played	Cuts Made	Wins	Top-5s	Top-10s	Top-25s	Scoring Average	Money
1990	1	2	0	0	0	0	0	71.00	
1992	1	4	1	0	0	0	0	72.00	$3,333

Best finish for 1992: T-40th at the Freeport-McMoRan Classic

Period Totals	Starts	Rounds Played	Cuts Made	Wins	Top-5s	Top-10s	Top-25s	Scoring Average	Money
	98	269	38	0	0	1	11	72.28	$130,259

Mike Peck

Year	Starts	Rounds Played	Cuts Made	Wins	Top-5s	Top-10s	Top-25s	Scoring Average	Money
1979	1	2	0	0	0	0	0	76.50	
1980	24	59	6	0	0	1	1	73.24	$8,866

Best finish for 1980: T-10th at the Greater New Orleans Open

Year	Starts	Rounds Played	Cuts Made	Wins	Top-5s	Top-10s	Top-25s	Scoring Average	Money
1981	20	49	6	0	0	0	1	73.59	$7,819

Best finish for 1981: T-25th at the Western Open

Year	Starts	Rounds Played	Cuts Made	Wins	Top-5s	Top-10s	Top-25s	Scoring Average	Money
1982	3	10	2	0	0	0	0	73.70	$1,289

Best finish for 1982: T-56th at the Bing Crosby Pro-Am

Year	Starts	Rounds Played	Cuts Made	Wins	Top-5s	Top-10s	Top-25s	Scoring Average	Money
1983	32	84	8	0	0	0	2	73.65	$12,703

Best finish for 1983: T-21st at the Bing Crosby Pro-Am & Isuzu/Andy Williams San Diego Open

Year	Starts	Rounds Played	Cuts Made	Wins	Top-5s	Top-10s	Top-25s	Scoring Average	Money
1984	17	54	9	0	0	0	0	73.30	$10,044

Best finish for 1984: T-30th at the Canadian Open

Year	Starts	Rounds Played	Cuts Made	Wins	Top-5s	Top-10s	Top-25s	Scoring Average	Money
1985	1	4	1	0	0	0	0	72.25	$1,025

Best finish for 1985: T-66th at the Byron Nelson Golf Classic

Period Totals	Starts	Rounds Played	Cuts Made	Wins	Top-5s	Top-10s	Top-25s	Scoring Average	Money
	98	262	32	0	0	1	4	73.48	$41,747

Wayne Peddy

Year	Starts	Rounds Played	Cuts Made	Wins	Top-5s	Top-10s	Top-25s	Scoring Average	Money
1971	1	2	0	0	0	0	0	77.50	$500
1972	14	38	4	0	0	0	0	73.97	$849

Best finish for 1972: T-41st at the Greater Milwaukee Open

Year	Starts	Rounds Played	Cuts Made	Wins	Top-5s	Top-10s	Top-25s	Scoring Average	Money
1977	7	20	3	0	0	0	0	73.10	$1,740

Best finish for 1977: T-35th at the Colgate Hall Of Fame Golf Classic

Year	Starts	Rounds Played	Cuts Made	Wins	Top-5s	Top-10s	Top-25s	Scoring Average	Money
1978	7	16	2	0	0	0	0	74.13	$443

Best finish for 1978: T-64th at the Tallahassee Open

Period Totals	Starts	Rounds Played	Cuts Made	Wins	Top-5s	Top-10s	Top-25s	Scoring Average	Money
	29	76	9	0	0	0	0	73.87	$3,532

Dave Peege

Year	Starts	Rounds Played	Cuts Made	Wins	Top-5s	Top-10s	Top-25s	Scoring Average	Money
1985	1	4	1	0	0	0	0	71.75	$793

Best finish for 1985: T-47th at the B.C. Open

Year	Starts	Rounds Played	Cuts Made	Wins	Top-5s	Top-10s	Top-25s	Scoring Average	Money
1992	27	69	7	0	0	0	1	72.83	$22,747

Best finish for 1992: T-23rd at the Hardee's Golf Classic

Year	Starts	Rounds Played	Cuts Made	Wins	Top-5s	Top-10s	Top-25s	Scoring Average	Money
1993	22	57	8	0	0	0	1	72.89	$33,531

Best finish for 1993: T-16th at the Canon Greater Hartford Open

Period Totals	Starts	Rounds Played	Cuts Made	Wins	Top-5s	Top-10s	Top-25s	Scoring Average	Money
	50	130	16	0	0	0	2	72.82	$57,071

Calvin Peete

Year	Starts	Rounds Played	Cuts Made	Wins	Top-5s	Top-10s	Top-25s	Scoring Average	Money
1975	3	6	0	0	0	0	0	74.67	
1976	26	79	14	0	0	1	6	72.59	$19,250

Best finish for 1976: T-10th at the IVB - Bicentennial Golf Classic

Year	Starts	Rounds Played	Cuts Made	Wins	Top-5s	Top-10s	Top-25s	Scoring Average	Money
1977	26	77	15	0	0	1	4	72.36	$19,590

Best finish for 1977: T-6th at the Sammy Davis, Jr. - Greater Hartford Open

Year	Starts	Rounds Played	Cuts Made	Wins	Top-5s	Top-10s	Top-25s	Scoring Average	Money
1978	20	59	10	0	1	2	3	72.02	$20,270

Best finish for 1978: T-5th at the First NBC New Orleans Open

Year	Starts	Rounds Played	Cuts Made	Wins	Top-5s	Top-10s	Top-25s	Scoring Average	Money
1979	25	81	16	1	4	6	10	71.58	$122,481

Best finish for 1979: Win at the Greater Milwaukee Open

Year	Starts	Rounds Played	Cuts Made	Wins	Top-5s	Top-10s	Top-25s	Scoring Average	Money
1980	27	96	23	0	3	6	15	71.13	$105,716

Best finish for 1980: T-3rd at the IVB Golf Classic

Year	Starts	Rounds Played	Cuts Made	Wins	Top-5s	Top-10s	Top-25s	Scoring Average	Money
1981	30	101	23	0	3	6	11	71.35	$104,443

Best finish for 1981: T-3rd at the Phoenix Open & Atlanta Classic

Year	Starts	Rounds Played	Cuts Made	Wins	Top-5s	Top-10s	Top-25s	Scoring Average	Money
1982	26	98	23	4	7	10	17	70.33	$318,470

Best finish for 1982: Win at the Greater Milwaukee Open, Anheuser-Busch Golf Classic, B.C. Open & Pensacola Open

Year	Starts	Rounds Played	Cuts Made	Wins	Top-5s	Top-10s	Top-25s	Scoring Average	Money
1983	24	87	20	2	9	11	14	70.62	$313,845

Best finish for 1983: Win at the Georgia-Pacific Atlanta Golf Classic & Anheuser-Busch Golf Classic

Year	Starts	Rounds Played	Cuts Made	Wins	Top-5s	Top-10s	Top-25s	Scoring Average	Money
1984	24	82	18	1	3	9	15	70.56	$232,124

Best finish for 1984: Win at the Texas Open

Year	Starts	Rounds Played	Cuts Made	Wins	Top-5s	Top-10s	Top-25s	Scoring Average	Money
1985	21	72	17	2	5	8	12	70.56	$384,488

Best finish for 1985: Win at the Phoenix Open & Tournament Players Championship

| 1986 | 26 | 85 | 21 | 2 | 6 | 7 | 10 | 70.48 | $374,953 |

Best finish for 1986: Win at the MONY Tournament Of Champions & USF&G Classic

| 1987 | 20 | 64 | 12 | 0 | 0 | 1 | 3 | 71.69 | $57,441 |

Best finish for 1987: T-9th at the Phoenix Open

| 1988 | 23 | 76 | 15 | 0 | 1 | 2 | 6 | 70.84 | $138,310 |

Best finish for 1988: 4th at the USF&G Classic

| 1989 | 17 | 51 | 8 | 0 | 0 | 0 | 2 | 72.45 | $38,584 |

Best finish for 1989: T-16th at the Independent Insurance Agent Open

| 1990 | 25 | 64 | 6 | 0 | 0 | 1 | 2 | 72.70 | $54,469 |

Best finish for 1990: T-9th at the MCI Heritage Classic

| 1991 | 11 | 27 | 2 | 0 | 0 | 0 | 0 | 74.33 | $4,978 |

Best finish for 1991: T-70th at the Kemper Open

1992	5	10	0	0	0	0	0	76.40	
1993	3	4	0	0	0	0	0	73.50	
1994	1	1	0	0	0	0	0	85.00	
Period Totals	Starts	Rounds Played	Cuts Made	Wins	Top-5s	Top-10s	Top-25s	Scoring Average	Money
	383	1220	243	12	42	71	130	71.47	$2,309,413

Bill Pelham

Year	Starts	Rounds Played	Cuts Made	Wins	Top-5s	Top-10s	Top-25s	Scoring Average	Money
1976	9	23	3	0	0	0	0	74.26	$677

Best finish for 1976: T-60th at the Sahara Invitational

| 1977 | 13 | 34 | 4 | 0 | 0 | 0 | 1 | 73.44 | $4,342 |

Best finish for 1977: T-13th at the Ohio Kings Island Open

| 1978 | 17 | 42 | 4 | 0 | 0 | 0 | 0 | 73.57 | $3,494 |

Best finish for 1978: T-29th at the Canadian Open

1979	1	2	0	0	0	0	0	77.50	$600
1980	9	16	0	0	0	0	0	75.81	$1,040
1981	1	4	1	0	0	0	0	73.50	$1,300

Best finish for 1981: T-65th at the U.S. Open

1982	1	2	0	0	0	0	0	78.50	$382
Period Totals	Starts	Rounds Played	Cuts Made	Wins	Top-5s	Top-10s	Top-25s	Scoring Average	Money
	51	123	12	0	0	0	1	74.10	$11,835

David Peoples

Year	Starts	Rounds Played	Cuts Made	Wins	Top-5s	Top-10s	Top-25s	Scoring Average	Money
1983	32	91	13	0	1	1	2	72.93	$28,446

Best finish for 1983: T-5th at the Miller High-Life Quad Cities Open

| 1984 | 27 | 71 | 8 | 0 | 0 | 1 | 1 | 73.82 | $18,124 |

Best finish for 1984: T-8th at the Greater Greensboro Open

| 1986 | 31 | 89 | 15 | 0 | 0 | 0 | 5 | 72.72 | $37,668 |

Best finish for 1986: T-14th at the Walt Disney World/Oldsmobile Classic

| 1987 | 31 | 75 | 10 | 0 | 0 | 0 | 3 | 72.81 | $31,234 |

Best finish for 1987: T-16th at the Centel Classic

| 1988 | 36 | 100 | 16 | 0 | 0 | 0 | 7 | 71.78 | $65,567 |

Best finish for 1988: T-11th at the Southern Open

| 1989 | 20 | 64 | 12 | 0 | 2 | 2 | 5 | 70.94 | $82,624 |

Best finish for 1989: T-3rd at the Deposit Guaranty Golf Classic

| 1990 | 32 | 111 | 26 | 0 | 2 | 4 | 10 | 71.05 | $259,366 |

Best finish for 1990: T-3rd at the Independent Insurance Agent Open

| 1991 | 28 | 96 | 21 | 1 | 4 | 4 | 9 | 70.42 | $414,346 |

Best finish for 1991: Win at the Buick Southern Open

| 1992 | 28 | 99 | 21 | 1 | 4 | 5 | 10 | 70.72 | $539,531 |

Best finish for 1992: Win at the Anheuser-Busch Golf Classic

| 1993 | 29 | 83 | 15 | 0 | 0 | 2 | 3 | 71.99 | $106,309 |

Best finish for 1993: T-9th at the Buick Invitational of California

| 1994 | 30 | 88 | 17 | 0 | 1 | 1 | 4 | 71.35 | $126,918 |

Best finish for 1994: T-4th at the BellSouth Classic

| 1995 | 15 | 51 | 11 | 0 | 1 | 1 | 2 | 71.02 | $86,679 |

Best finish for 1995: T-5th at the Freeport-McMoRan Classic

| 1996 | 22 | 56 | 7 | 0 | 0 | 0 | 1 | 72.73 | $32,384 |

Best finish for 1996: T-25th at the FedEx St. Jude Classic

| 1997 | 8 | 24 | 4 | 0 | 0 | 0 | 0 | 71.83 | $13,740 |

Best finish for 1997: T-39th at the Greater Vancouver Open

| 1998 | 9 | 23 | 3 | 0 | 0 | 0 | 1 | 71.22 | $24,994 |

Best finish for 1998: T-20th at the Buick Challenge

| 1999 | 7 | 25 | 6 | 0 | 0 | 0 | 3 | 70.48 | $112,965 |

Best finish for 1999: T-12th at the John Deere Classic

| 2000 | 28 | 99 | 21 | 0 | 0 | 1 | 6 | 70.36 | $459,812 |

Best finish for 2000: T-7th at the Kemper Insurance Open

Year	Starts	Rounds Played	Cuts Made	Wins	Top-5s	Top-10s	Top-25s	Scoring Average	Money
2001	31	93	19	0	1	2	7	70.61	$712,657

Best finish for 2001: T-3rd at the National Car Rental Golf Classic/Disney

2002	30	105	22	0	2	4	9	70.19	$1,245,774

Best finish for 2002: T-2nd at the Touchstone Energy Tucson Open & Memorial Tournament

2003	30	96	18	0	0	1	8	70.32	$674,222

Best finish for 2003: 8th at the FedEx St. Jude Classic

2004	26	80	15	0	0	0	3	70.90	$479,464

Best finish for 2004: T-11th at the BellSouth Classic & Shell Houston Open

2005	12	31	4	0	0	0	2	70.94	$127,907

Best finish for 2005: T-21st at the Shell Houston Open

2006	4	9	1	0	0	0	0	72.44	$13,988

Best finish for 2006: T-47th at the FedEx St. Jude Classic

2007	2	4	0	0	0	0	0	74.25	
2008	2	4	0	0	0	0	0	73.25	
Period Totals	Starts	Rounds Played	Cuts Made	Wins	Top-5s	Top-10s	Top-25s	Scoring Average	Money
	550	1667	305	2	18	29	101	71.40	$5,694,720

Pat Perez

Year	Starts	Rounds Played	Cuts Made	Wins	Top-5s	Top-10s	Top-25s	Scoring Average	Money
2002	30	87	14	0	4	6	10	71.06	$1,452,726

Best finish for 2002: T-2nd at the AT&T Pebble Beach National Pro-Am & Buick Classic

2003	33	93	16	0	0	2	5	71.62	$578,141

Best finish for 2003: T-6th at the Bob Hope Chrysler Classic

2004	32	100	18	0	1	1	7	71.27	$723,724

Best finish for 2004: T-3rd at the 84 Lumber Classic

2005	28	89	18	0	2	4	9	71.11	$1,258,087

Best finish for 2005: 4th at the Honda Classic

2006	19	50	9	0	1	1	4	71.62	$721,757

Best finish for 2006: T-3rd at The Players Championship

2007	27	84	16	0	2	6	11	70.76	$1,680,295

Best finish for 2007: T-3rd at the AT&T National

2008	27	92	21	0	1	6	12	70.70	$1,756,038

Best finish for 2008: T-4th at the Sony Open in Hawaii

Period Totals	Starts	Rounds Played	Cuts Made	Wins	Top-5s	Top-10s	Top-25s	Scoring Average	Money
	196	595	112	0	11	26	58	71.14	$8,170,769

Craig Perks

Year	Starts	Rounds Played	Cuts Made	Wins	Top-5s	Top-10s	Top-25s	Scoring Average	Money
1993	1	2	0	0	0	0	0	76.50	
2000	28	82	12	0	1	1	3	71.68	$297,912

Best finish for 2000: T-4th at the Bell Canadian Open

2001	30	76	9	0	1	2	3	71.13	$457,127

Best finish for 2001: T-2nd at the Honda Classic

2002	28	87	17	1	2	3	4	71.72	$1,638,042

Best finish for 2002: Win at the Players Championship

2003	28	79	12	0	0	0	3	71.92	$377,137

Best finish for 2003: T-13th at the Buick Invitational

2004	27	72	11	0	1	1	1	71.75	$432,961

Best finish for 2004: 4th at the Bank of America Colonial

2005	27	65	6	0	0	0	1	72.89	$171,379

Best finish for 2005: T-13th at the Cialis Western Open

2006	18	37	1	0	0	0	0	75.43	$11,880

Best finish for 2006: 71st at the Zurich Classic of New Orleans

2007	15	28	0	0	0	0	0	75.93	
Period Totals	Starts	Rounds Played	Cuts Made	Wins	Top-5s	Top-10s	Top-25s	Scoring Average	Money
	202	528	68	1	5	7	15	72.31	$3,386,439

Tom Pernice, Jr.

Year	Starts	Rounds Played	Cuts Made	Wins	Top-5s	Top-10s	Top-25s	Scoring Average	Money
1983	1	3	0	0	0	0	0	75.67	
1986	32	91	12	0	0	0	5	72.71	$40,772

Best finish for 1986: T-16th at the B.C. Open & Greater Milwaukee Open

1987	20	50	5	0	0	1	1	72.64	$15,431

Best finish for 1987: T-6th at the Deposit Guaranty Golf Classic

1988	31	91	14	0	1	1	2	71.81	$47,108

Best finish for 1988: T-5th at the Texas Open

1989	22	65	10	0	1	2	5	71.06	$81,863

Best finish for 1989: T-4th at the Centel Classic

1990	20	54	7	0	0	0	1	72.78	$22,004

Best finish for 1990: T-25th at the Chattanooga Classic

1991	3	8	1	0	0	0	0	71.75	$1,824

Best finish for 1991: T-54th at the B.C. Open

Year	Starts	Rounds Played	Cuts Made	Wins	Top-5s	Top-10s	Top-25s	Scoring Average	Money
1992	1	2	0	0	0	0	0	73.00	
1993	1	4	1	0	0	0	0	72.00	$5,660

Best finish for 1993: T-66th at the British Open

1994	1	2	0	0	0	0	0	72.00	
1996	1	4	1	0	0	0	0	74.00	$5,235

Best finish for 1996: T-94th at the U.S. Open

1997	30	85	12	0	1	1	5	71.52	$173,012

Best finish for 1997: 4th at the Greater Milwaukee Open

1998	27	79	15	0	1	1	8	71.03	$520,400

Best finish for 1998: 2nd at the AT&T Pebble Beach National Pro-Am

1999	31	89	14	1	1	1	5	71.40	$657,890

Best finish for 1999: Win at the Buick Open

2000	32	96	16	0	1	2	5	71.21	$387,716

Best finish for 2000: T-5th at the BellSouth Classic

2001	33	102	19	1	2	4	6	70.83	$1,319,762

Best finish for 2001: Win at The International presented by Qwest

2002	31	99	19	0	0	2	8	71.24	$646,110

Best finish for 2002: T-6th at the Shell Houston Open & The Reno-Tahoe Open

2003	31	102	21	0	1	4	9	70.59	$1,210,541

Best finish for 2003: 3rd at the Bell Canadian Open

2004	31	99	20	0	2	5	9	70.85	$1,478,274

Best finish for 2004: T-3rd at The International & Buick Championship

2005	32	107	23	0	2	2	11	70.95	$1,611,561

Best finish for 2005: 2nd at the FUNAI Classic at the Walt Disney World Resort

2006	33	104	20	0	4	7	14	70.65	$2,404,375

Best finish for 2006: 2nd at the FedEx St. Jude Classic

2007	31	104	20	0	0	2	7	71.29	$936,486

Best finish for 2007: T-10th at the Verizon Heritage & Canadian Open

2008	30	104	22	0	0	6	8	70.54	$1,336,277

Best finish for 2008: T-8th at the Sony Open in Hawaii, Arnold Palmer Invitational, Stanford St. Jude Classic & Justin Timberlake Shriners Hospitals for Children Open

Period Totals	Starts	Rounds Played	Cuts Made	Wins	Top-5s	Top-10s	Top-25s	Scoring Average	Money
	505	1544	272	2	17	41	109	71.29	$12,902,296

Chris Perry

Year	Starts	Rounds Played	Cuts Made	Wins	Top-5s	Top-10s	Top-25s	Scoring Average	Money
1982	1	2	0	0	0	0	0	78.50	
1984	7	20	3	0	0	0	1	72.60	$5,086

Best finish for 1984: T-14th at the Miller High-Life Quad Cities Open

1985	30	102	22	0	0	1	5	71.82	$61,401

Best finish for 1985: T-10th at the Bank of Boston Classic

1986	33	106	22	0	0	1	5	71.93	$75,812

Best finish for 1986: T-10th at the Walt Disney World/Oldsmobile Classic

1987	32	100	21	0	2	4	10	71.18	$197,593

Best finish for 1987: T-2nd at the Kemper Open

1988	32	104	21	0	1	1	3	71.63	$85,546

Best finish for 1988: T-3rd at the Centel Classic

1989	31	107	24	0	2	3	7	71.13	$206,932

Best finish for 1989: T-3rd at the Bank of Boston Classic

1990	30	96	20	0	2	3	8	71.36	$259,108

Best finish for 1990: T-2nd at the Canon Greater Hartford Open

1991	33	103	20	0	0	2	5	71.19	$116,103

Best finish for 1991: T-7th at the Deposit Guaranty Classic

1992	29	78	11	0	0	0	3	71.72	$53,943

Best finish for 1992: T-17th at the H-E-B Texas Open

1993	9	28	5	0	0	0	3	70.54	$25,332

Best finish for 1993: T-21st at the B.C. Open

1994	2	4	1	0	0	0	1	71.50	$15,840

Best finish for 1994: T-11th at the Deposit Guaranty Golf Classic

1995	30	87	17	0	0	0	2	71.43	$113,632

Best finish for 1995: T-12th at the Buick Classic & Quad City Classic

1996	20	68	15	0	1	2	5	70.65	$184,171

Best finish for 1996: T-3rd at the Quad City Classic

1997	32	106	22	0	2	2	11	70.95	$462,073

Best finish for 1997: T-2nd at the B.C. Open

1998	31	107	24	1	2	4	12	70.79	$730,171

Best finish for 1998: Win at the B.C. Open

1999	31	120	30	0	9	14	21	70.19	$2,145,707

Best finish for 1999: T-2nd at the Sony Open in Hawaii & The Reno-Tahoe Open

2000	31	105	25	0	4	7	15	70.40	$1,564,635

Best finish for 2000: T-2nd at the Buick Open & SEI Pennsylvania Classic

2001	26	78	15	0	0	2	8	71.00	$571,679

Best finish for 2001: T-8th at the Nissan Open & Bay Hill Invitational

Year	Starts	Rounds Played	Cuts Made	Wins	Top-5s	Top-10s	Top-25s	Scoring Average	Money
2002	5	8	0	0	0	0	0	74.00	
2003	3	6	0	0	0	0	0	72.33	
2004	1	2	0	0	0	0	0	75.00	
2005	1	2	0	0	0	0	0	78.00	
2006	3	6	0	0	0	0	0	75.00	
Period Totals	Starts	Rounds Played	Cuts Made	Wins	Top-5s	Top-10s	Top-25s	Scoring Average	Money
	483	1545	318	1	25	46	125	71.21	$6,874,766

Kenny Perry

Year	Starts	Rounds Played	Cuts Made	Wins	Top-5s	Top-10s	Top-25s	Scoring Average	Money
1984	1	2	0	0	0	0	0	73.50	
1985	1	2	0	0	0	0	0	76.00	
1987	27	79	15	0	1	1	5	71.65	$107,239

Best finish for 1987: T-4th at the Panasonic Las Vegas Invitational

Year	Starts	Rounds Played	Cuts Made	Wins	Top-5s	Top-10s	Top-25s	Scoring Average	Money
1988	32	101	20	0	1	3	7	71.25	$139,421

Best finish for 1988: T-5th at the Centel Classic

| 1989 | 26 | 83 | 15 | 0 | 1 | 3 | 7 | 71.18 | $202,099 |

Best finish for 1989: 2nd at the MCI Heritage Classic

| 1990 | 23 | 74 | 17 | 0 | 2 | 2 | 9 | 71.46 | $279,881 |

Best finish for 1990: 2nd at the AT&T Pebble Beach Pro-Am

| 1991 | 25 | 81 | 16 | 1 | 1 | 3 | 7 | 71.28 | $369,792 |

Best finish for 1991: Win at the Memorial Tournament

| 1992 | 26 | 82 | 17 | 0 | 0 | 3 | 9 | 70.87 | $191,955 |

Best finish for 1992: T-6th at the MCI Heritage Classic & BellSouth Classic

| 1993 | 28 | 90 | 18 | 0 | 1 | 3 | 8 | 71.17 | $196,863 |

Best finish for 1993: T-5th at the Canon Greater Hartford Open

| 1994 | 30 | 99 | 22 | 1 | 3 | 4 | 10 | 70.88 | $585,941 |

Best finish for 1994: Win at the New England Classic

| 1995 | 25 | 94 | 21 | 1 | 4 | 5 | 13 | 70.53 | $774,388 |

Best finish for 1995: Win at the Bob Hope Chrysler Classic

| 1996 | 25 | 81 | 17 | 0 | 6 | 9 | 13 | 70.67 | $926,578 |

Best finish for 1996: 2nd at the PGA Championship

| 1997 | 26 | 81 | 17 | 0 | 1 | 2 | 8 | 71.15 | $276,081 |

Best finish for 1997: T-4th at the Phoenix Open

| 1998 | 25 | 82 | 16 | 0 | 1 | 5 | 7 | 70.38 | $487,551 |

Best finish for 1998: 3rd at the Quad City Classic

| 1999 | 26 | 82 | 16 | 0 | 0 | 1 | 7 | 71.01 | $426,184 |

Best finish for 1999: T-6th at the Phoenix Open

| 2000 | 20 | 76 | 18 | 0 | 3 | 4 | 9 | 69.96 | $889,381 |

Best finish for 2000: T-3rd at the BellSouth Classic, Greater Milwaukee Open & Southern Farm Bureau Classic

| 2001 | 26 | 89 | 22 | 1 | 3 | 6 | 13 | 69.60 | $1,786,066 |

Best finish for 2001: Win at the Buick Open

| 2002 | 27 | 95 | 23 | 0 | 4 | 6 | 13 | 70.02 | $1,933,598 |

Best finish for 2002: T-2nd at the Phoenix Open & MasterCard Colonial

| 2003 | 26 | 97 | 24 | 3 | 7 | 11 | 14 | 70.02 | $4,400,122 |

Best finish for 2003: Win at the Bank of America Colonial, Memorial Tournament & Greater Milwaukee Open

| 2004 | 23 | 76 | 17 | 0 | 2 | 7 | 13 | 70.51 | $1,960,043 |

Best finish for 2004: T-3rd at the Players Championship

| 2005 | 23 | 80 | 19 | 2 | 3 | 7 | 14 | 70.04 | $3,607,155 |

Best finish for 2005: Win at the Bay Hill Invitational & Bank of America Colonial

| 2006 | 22 | 72 | 16 | 0 | 0 | 0 | 6 | 70.94 | $819,908 |

Best finish for 2006: T-11th at the Buick Open

| 2007 | 24 | 83 | 17 | 0 | 2 | 3 | 9 | 70.60 | $1,197,618 |

Best finish for 2007: T-3rd at the Memorial Tournament

| 2008 | 26 | 97 | 24 | 3 | 5 | 7 | 13 | 70.21 | $4,663,794 |

Best finish for 2008: Win at the Memorial Tournament, Buick Open & John Deere Classic

Period Totals	Starts	Rounds Played	Cuts Made	Wins	Top-5s	Top-10s	Top-25s	Scoring Average	Money
	563	1878	407	12	51	95	214	70.69	$26,221,660

Peter Persons

Year	Starts	Rounds Played	Cuts Made	Wins	Top-5s	Top-10s	Top-25s	Scoring Average	Money
1985	1	4	1	0	0	0	0	72.25	

Best finish for 1985: 71st at the Southern Open

1986	3	6	0	0	0	0	0	73.33	
1987	3	6	0	0	0	0	0	73.00	
1988	3	8	1	0	0	0	0	72.50	$1,526

Best finish for 1988: T-59th at the Georgia-Pacific Atlanta Golf Classic

| 1989 | 1 | 2 | 0 | 0 | 0 | 0 | 0 | 73.50 | |
| 1990 | 33 | 100 | 17 | 1 | 1 | 2 | 5 | 71.92 | $218,505 |

Best finish for 1990: Win at the Chattanooga Classic

| 1991 | 31 | 104 | 20 | 0 | 0 | 1 | 5 | 71.30 | $131,447 |

Best finish for 1991: T-10th at the Federal Express St. Jude Classic

Year	Starts	Rounds Played	Cuts Made	Wins	Top-5s	Top-10s	Top-25s	Scoring Average	Money
1992	28	95	21	0	0	1	6	70.95	$168,013

Best finish for 1992: T-6th at the Federal Express St. Jude Classic

| 1993 | 30 | 90 | 16 | 0 | 0 | 0 | 2 | 72.09 | $73,092 |

Best finish for 1993: T-20th at the Shell Houston Open & The International

| 1994 | 4 | 12 | 2 | 0 | 0 | 0 | 0 | 70.83 | $10,986 |

Best finish for 1994: T-31st at the Hardee's Golf Classic

| 1995 | 1 | 2 | 0 | 0 | 0 | 0 | 0 | 74.00 | |
| 1996 | 7 | 18 | 2 | 0 | 0 | 0 | 0 | 72.61 | $4,815 |

Best finish for 1996: T-70th at the Kemper Open

Period Totals	Starts	Rounds Played	Cuts Made	Wins	Top-5s	Top-10s	Top-25s	Scoring Average	Money
	145	447	80	1	1	4	18	71.66	$608,384

Les Peterson

Year	Starts	Rounds Played	Cuts Made	Wins	Top-5s	Top-10s	Top-25s	Scoring Average	Money
1969	19	56	9	0	0	0	4	73.89	$4,779

Best finish for 1969: T-14th at the Indian Ridge Hospital Open

| 1970 | 29 | 76 | 10 | 0 | 0 | 0 | 1 | 73.80 | $4,490 |

Best finish for 1970: T-23rd at the National 4 Ball Championship PGA Players

| 1971 | 18 | 48 | 5 | 0 | 0 | 0 | 0 | 73.71 | $1,579 |

Best finish for 1971: T-31st at the Kaiser International Open

| 1972 | 21 | 53 | 5 | 0 | 0 | 0 | 1 | 73.62 | $4,453 |

Best finish for 1972: T-12th at the Florida Citrus Open Invitational

| 1973 | 14 | 36 | 4 | 0 | 0 | 0 | 0 | 74.31 | $1,122 |

Best finish for 1973: T-41st at the Dean Martin Tucson Open

Period Totals	Starts	Rounds Played	Cuts Made	Wins	Top-5s	Top-10s	Top-25s	Scoring Average	Money
	101	269	33	0	0	0	6	73.84	$16,424

Matt Peterson

Year	Starts	Rounds Played	Cuts Made	Wins	Top-5s	Top-10s	Top-25s	Scoring Average	Money
1990	2	4	0	0	0	0	0	73.50	
2002	27	80	13	0	0	1	3	71.14	$266,543

Best finish for 2002: T-10th at the Valero Texas Open

| 2003 | 2 | 6 | 1 | 0 | 0 | 0 | 0 | 71.50 | $29,962 |

Best finish for 2003: T-27th at the Ford Championship at Doral

Period Totals	Starts	Rounds Played	Cuts Made	Wins	Top-5s	Top-10s	Top-25s	Scoring Average	Money
	31	90	14	0	0	1	3	71.27	$296,504

Randy Petri

Year	Starts	Rounds Played	Cuts Made	Wins	Top-5s	Top-10s	Top-25s	Scoring Average	Money
1964	1	4	1	0	0	0	0	71.50	

Best finish for 1964: T-99th at the Dallas Open

| 1965 | 2 | 4 | 0 | 0 | 0 | 0 | 0 | 76.75 | |
| 1966 | 15 | 47 | 8 | 0 | 0 | 0 | 1 | 73.53 | $1,696 |

Best finish for 1966: T-21st at the Minnesota Golf Classic

| 1967 | 25 | 75 | 11 | 0 | 0 | 0 | 3 | 73.51 | $7,037 |

Best finish for 1967: T-13th at the Buick Open

| 1968 | 20 | 61 | 11 | 0 | 0 | 0 | 1 | 72.77 | $1,930 |

Best finish for 1968: T-14th at the AZALEA Open Invitational

| 1969 | 18 | 55 | 11 | 0 | 0 | 1 | 4 | 72.62 | $7,770 |

Best finish for 1969: T-6th at the Azalea Open

| 1970 | 7 | 18 | 3 | 0 | 0 | 0 | 0 | 73.00 | $1,096 |

Best finish for 1970: T-30th at the Canadian Open

| 1971 | 3 | 10 | 2 | 0 | 0 | 0 | 0 | 72.50 | $305 |

Best finish for 1971: T-60th at the Southern Open

| 1972 | 4 | 12 | 1 | 0 | 0 | 0 | 0 | 76.00 | $227 |

Best finish for 1972: 73rd at the Phoenix Open

| 1978 | 1 | 2 | 0 | 0 | 0 | 0 | 0 | 72.00 | |
| 1980 | 1 | 2 | 0 | 0 | 0 | 0 | 0 | 78.00 | $600 |

Period Totals	Starts	Rounds Played	Cuts Made	Wins	Top-5s	Top-10s	Top-25s	Scoring Average	Money
	97	290	48	0	0	1	9	73.26	$20,661

Tim Petrovic

Year	Starts	Rounds Played	Cuts Made	Wins	Top-5s	Top-10s	Top-25s	Scoring Average	Money
1988	1	2	0	0	0	0	0	75.50	
1989	1	4	1	0	0	0	0	69.75	$2,569

Best finish for 1989: T-47th at the Canon Greater Hartford Open

1990	2	4	0	0	0	0	0	73.00	
1991	2	4	0	0	0	0	0	74.25	
1992	2	4	0	0	0	0	0	74.75	
1996	2	6	1	0	0	0	0	74.50	$2,088

Best finish for 1996: 83rd at the Buick Classic

Year	Starts	Rounds Played	Cuts Made	Wins	Top-5s	Top-10s	Top-25s	Scoring Average	Money
2001	1	4	1	0	0	0	0	73.25	$11,443

Best finish for 2001: T-62nd at the U.S. Open

Year	Starts	Rounds Played	Cuts Made	Wins	Top-5s	Top-10s	Top-25s	Scoring Average	Money
2002	31	89	15	0	1	1	5	70.66	$801,157

Best finish for 2002: 2nd at the FedEx St. Jude Classic

2003	32	104	21	0	4	4	14	70.21	$1,741,289

Best finish for 2003: T-2nd at the 84 Lumber Classic of Pennsylvania

2004	32	107	23	0	1	3	11	71.19	$1,195,354

Best finish for 2004: T-5th at the Bank of America Colonial

2005	32	93	16	1	1	3	6	71.25	$1,716,733

Best finish for 2005: Win at the Zurich Classic of New Orleans

2006	30	91	16	0	0	0	5	71.68	$601,928

Best finish for 2006: T-11th at the Mercedes Championships

2007	32	106	20	0	1	1	9	70.92	$1,054,447

Best finish for 2007: T-2nd at the Wyndham Championship

2008	32	97	17	0	0	3	8	71.23	$958,577

Best finish for 2008: T-7th at the Mayakoba Golf Classic & Zurich Classic of New Orleans

Period Totals	Starts	Rounds Played	Cuts Made	Wins	Top-5s	Top-10s	Top-25s	Scoring Average	Money
	232	715	131	1	8	15	58	71.11	$8,085,584

Carl Pettersson

Year	Starts	Rounds Played	Cuts Made	Wins	Top-5s	Top-10s	Top-25s	Scoring Average	Money
2002	3	10	2	0	0	0	0	72.40	$53,728

Best finish for 2002: T-43rd at the British Open

2003	26	79	15	0	1	1	6	71.23	$979,076

Best finish for 2003: 2nd at the Buick Invitational

2004	28	97	22	0	3	7	11	70.46	$1,367,962

Best finish for 2004: T-3rd at the MCI Heritage

2005	34	105	20	1	3	3	9	70.70	$1,995,851

Best finish for 2005: Win at the Chrysler Championship

2006	28	93	20	1	2	6	12	71.31	$2,652,232

Best finish for 2006: Win at the Memorial Tournament

2007	31	110	25	0	4	6	13	70.97	$2,040,938

Best finish for 2007: T-4th at the Fry's Electronics Open

2008	29	110	25	1	2	5	14	70.84	$2,512,538

Best finish for 2008: Win at the Wyndham Championship

Period Totals	Starts	Rounds Played	Cuts Made	Wins	Top-5s	Top-10s	Top-25s	Scoring Average	Money
	179	604	129	3	15	28	65	70.93	$11,602,324

Mark Pfeil

Year	Starts	Rounds Played	Cuts Made	Wins	Top-5s	Top-10s	Top-25s	Scoring Average	Money
1973	1	4	1	0	0	0	0	71.75	

Best finish for 1973: T-27th at the Glen CampbellLos Angeles Open

1974	2	6	1	0	0	0	0	76.17	$1,200

Best finish for 1974: T-78th at the Glen CampbellLos Angeles Open

1975	1	3	0	0	0	0	0	74.33	$330
1976	11	27	5	0	0	0	0	74.89	$198

Best finish for 1976: T-48th at the Tallahassee Open

1977	24	74	13	0	0	0	3	72.70	$9,243

Best finish for 1977: T-14th at the Tallahassee Open

1978	24	74	13	0	0	1	1	72.81	$13,943

Best finish for 1978: T-6th at the Andy Williams-San Diego Open

1979	25	73	12	0	0	0	2	72.89	$19,563

Best finish for 1979: T-11th at the Bing Crosby Pro-Am

1980	24	81	16	1	1	1	8	72.09	$52,704

Best finish for 1980: Win at the Tallahassee Open

1981	29	89	15	0	0	0	4	72.57	$30,450

Best finish for 1981: T-12th at the Sammy Davis, Jr. - Greater Hartford Open

1982	28	101	22	0	0	1	10	71.45	$62,633

Best finish for 1982: 7th at the Western Open

1983	29	102	22	0	1	2	7	71.79	$85,477

Best finish for 1983: 2nd at the Texas Open

1984	25	85	18	0	2	3	5	72.02	$101,878

Best finish for 1984: T-3rd at the Canadian Open

1985	29	89	14	0	1	2	3	72.27	$54,098

Best finish for 1985: T-5th at the Doral-Eastern Open

1986	28	81	14	0	0	2	5	72.43	$68,088

Best finish for 1986: T-6th at the AT&T Pebble Beach Pro-Am

1987	19	53	8	0	0	0	0	73.21	$11,882

Best finish for 1987: T-45th at the Los Angeles Open

1988	20	48	3	0	0	0	0	73.85	$6,057

Best finish for 1988: T-31st at the Centel Classic

1989	14	30	0	0	0	0	0	74.37	

Year	Starts	Rounds Played	Cuts Made	Wins	Top-5s	Top-10s	Top-25s	Scoring Average	Money
1990	5	13	2	0	0	0	0	72.62	$3,383

Best finish for 1990: T-63rd at the AT&T Pebble Beach Pro-Am

1991	5	10	0	0	0	0	0	72.90	
1992	2	6	1	0	0	0	0	71.17	$2,495

Best finish for 1992: T-49th at the Hardee's Golf Classic

1993	5	15	2	0	0	0	1	73.27	$10,100

Best finish for 1993: T-21st at the B.C. Open

1994	3	6	1	0	0	0	0	71.83	$1,435

Best finish for 1994: T-62nd at the Deposit Guaranty Golf Classic

1995	4	11	1	0	0	0	0	71.82	$2,890

Best finish for 1995: T-44th at the Quad City Classic

1996	7	20	3	0	0	0	1	71.05	$23,510

Best finish for 1996: T-19th at the Quad City Classic

1997	3	8	1	0	0	0	1	71.00	$9,912

Best finish for 1997: T-23rd at the Quad City Classic

1998	5	14	2	0	0	0	0	72.21	$6,225

Best finish for 1998: T-58th at the B.C. Open

1999	1	2	0	0	0	0	0	75.00	
2000	1	2	0	0	0	0	0	75.00	
2001	1	2	0	0	0	0	0	71.50	
Period Totals	Starts	Rounds Played	Cuts Made	Wins	Top-5s	Top-10s	Top-25s	Scoring Average	Money
	375	1129	190	1	5	12	51	72.50	$577,694

E.J. Pfister

Year	Starts	Rounds Played	Cuts Made	Wins	Top-5s	Top-10s	Top-25s	Scoring Average	Money
1988	3	8	1	0	0	0	0	71.63	$1,436

Best finish for 1988: T-57th at the Anheuser-Busch Golf Classic

1989	2	4	0	0	0	0	0	74.00	
1992	24	58	6	0	0	0	0	73.36	$12,616

Best finish for 1992: T-38th at the Shell Houston Open

1999	1	2	0	0	0	0	0	78.00	$1,000
Period Totals	Starts	Rounds Played	Cuts Made	Wins	Top-5s	Top-10s	Top-25s	Scoring Average	Money
	30	72	7	0	0	0	0	73.33	$15,052

Bobby Phillips

Year	Starts	Rounds Played	Cuts Made	Wins	Top-5s	Top-10s	Top-25s	Scoring Average	Money
1972	2	6	1	0	0	0	0	74.83	$217

Best finish for 1972: 71st at the San Antonio Texas Open

1973	15	36	2	0	0	0	0	74.72	$623

Best finish for 1973: T-40th at the Sahara Invitational

1975	1	2	0	0	0	0	0	78.00	
1976	1	2	0	0	0	0	0	76.50	
1978	2	6	1	0	0	0	0	72.00	$440

Best finish for 1978: T-53rd at the Phoenix Open

1979	3	6	0	0	0	0	0	74.33	$350
1980	1	2	0	0	0	0	0	75.00	
Period Totals	Starts	Rounds Played	Cuts Made	Wins	Top-5s	Top-10s	Top-25s	Scoring Average	Money
	25	60	4	0	0	0	0	74.60	$1,630

Frank Phillips

Year	Starts	Rounds Played	Cuts Made	Wins	Top-5s	Top-10s	Top-25s	Scoring Average	Money
1958	16	60	13	0	0	1	5	71.73	$3,475

Best finish for 1958: T-10th at the Greater Greensboro Open

1961	2	8	2	0	0	0	1	73.00	$651

Best finish for 1961: T-15th at the Texas Open Invitational

1962	7	24	5	0	0	0	1	72.33	$1,935

Best finish for 1962: T-11th at the Waco Turner Open Invitational

1963	1	4	1	0	0	0	1	73.00	$217

Best finish for 1963: T-18th at the British Open

1964	1	4	1	0	0	0	1	73.50	$378

Best finish for 1964: 12th at the British Open

1965	1	2	0	0	0	0	0	77.00	
1966	1	4	1	0	0	0	1	74.25	$1,558

Best finish for 1966: T-19th at the Carling World Open

1968	1	3	0	0	0	0	0	77.33	
Period Totals	Starts	Rounds Played	Cuts Made	Wins	Top-5s	Top-10s	Top-25s	Scoring Average	Money
	30	109	23	0	0	1	10	72.41	$8,215

Jimmy Picard

Year	Starts	Rounds Played	Cuts Made	Wins	Top-5s	Top-10s	Top-25s	Scoring Average	Money
1964	6	16	2	0	0	0	0	74.94	

Best finish for 1964: T-49th at the St. Petersburg Open

1967	2	6	1	0	0	1	1	72.67	$1,550

Best finish for 1967: T-6th at the Cajun Classic

Year	Starts	Rounds Played	Cuts Made	Wins	Top-5s	Top-10s	Top-25s	Scoring Average	Money
1968	17	44	4	0	0	0	0	74.48	$515

Best finish for 1968: T-33rd at the Robinson Open

Year	Starts	Rounds Played	Cuts Made	Wins	Top-5s	Top-10s	Top-25s	Scoring Average	Money
1969	16	48	8	0	0	0	1	74.10	$3,021

Best finish for 1969: T-22nd at the Azalea Open

Year	Starts	Rounds Played	Cuts Made	Wins	Top-5s	Top-10s	Top-25s	Scoring Average	Money
1970	12	33	3	0	0	0	0	74.21	$518

Best finish for 1970: T-48th at the Tucson Open

Year	Starts	Rounds Played	Cuts Made	Wins	Top-5s	Top-10s	Top-25s	Scoring Average	Money
1971	13	33	3	0	0	0	0	73.21	$1,684

Best finish for 1971: T-27th at the Bob Hope Chrysler Classic

Year	Starts	Rounds Played	Cuts Made	Wins	Top-5s	Top-10s	Top-25s	Scoring Average	Money
1977	1	2	0	0	0	0	0	78.00	$250
1978	2	6	1	0	0	0	0	75.33	$303

Best finish for 1978: 71st at the Buick Goodwrench Open

Year	Starts	Rounds Played	Cuts Made	Wins	Top-5s	Top-10s	Top-25s	Scoring Average	Money
1979	1	2	0	0	0	0	0	76.00	
Period Totals	**Starts**	**Rounds Played**	**Cuts Made**	**Wins**	**Top-5s**	**Top-10s**	**Top-25s**	**Scoring Average**	**Money**
	70	190	22	0	0	1	2	74.18	$7,841

Billy Pierot

Year	Starts	Rounds Played	Cuts Made	Wins	Top-5s	Top-10s	Top-25s	Scoring Average	Money
1985	3	10	2	0	0	0	0	71.40	$1,680

Best finish for 1985: T-43rd at the Southern Open

Year	Starts	Rounds Played	Cuts Made	Wins	Top-5s	Top-10s	Top-25s	Scoring Average	Money
1986	32	93	16	0	0	0	3	72.24	$38,469

Best finish for 1986: T-18th at the International

Year	Starts	Rounds Played	Cuts Made	Wins	Top-5s	Top-10s	Top-25s	Scoring Average	Money
1987	17	57	12	0	0	0	5	71.04	$34,972

Best finish for 1987: T-15th at the Deposit Guaranty Golf Classic & Bank of Boston Classic

Year	Starts	Rounds Played	Cuts Made	Wins	Top-5s	Top-10s	Top-25s	Scoring Average	Money
1988	4	14	3	0	0	0	1	70.07	$6,515

Best finish for 1988: T-19th at the Deposit Guaranty Golf Classic

Year	Starts	Rounds Played	Cuts Made	Wins	Top-5s	Top-10s	Top-25s	Scoring Average	Money
1989	24	65	9	0	0	0	1	72.34	$28,028

Best finish for 1989: T-12th at the Hawaiian Open

Year	Starts	Rounds Played	Cuts Made	Wins	Top-5s	Top-10s	Top-25s	Scoring Average	Money
1990	2	4	0	0	0	0	0	71.50	
1991	1	2	0	0	0	0	0	71.00	
1992	1	2	0	0	0	0	0	75.50	
Period Totals	**Starts**	**Rounds Played**	**Cuts Made**	**Wins**	**Top-5s**	**Top-10s**	**Top-25s**	**Scoring Average**	**Money**
	84	247	42	0	0	0	10	71.83	$109,664

Manuel Pinero

Year	Starts	Rounds Played	Cuts Made	Wins	Top-5s	Top-10s	Top-25s	Scoring Average	Money
1973	1	4	0	0	0	0	0	79.00	
1975	1	2	0	0	0	0	0	76.00	
1977	3	11	2	0	0	0	0	72.55	$1,412

Best finish for 1977: T-36th at the British Open

Year	Starts	Rounds Played	Cuts Made	Wins	Top-5s	Top-10s	Top-25s	Scoring Average	Money
1978	4	10	0	0	0	0	0	74.60	$1,928
1979	1	2	0	0	0	0	0	78.00	$420
1980	1	4	1	0	0	0	0	73.50	$1,320

Best finish for 1980: T-58th at the British Open

Year	Starts	Rounds Played	Cuts Made	Wins	Top-5s	Top-10s	Top-25s	Scoring Average	Money
1981	1	4	1	0	0	1	1	71.25	$15,500

Best finish for 1981: T-6th at the British Open

Year	Starts	Rounds Played	Cuts Made	Wins	Top-5s	Top-10s	Top-25s	Scoring Average	Money
1982	4	16	4	0	0	0	1	73.25	$8,659

Best finish for 1982: T-11th at the Bay Hill Classic

Year	Starts	Rounds Played	Cuts Made	Wins	Top-5s	Top-10s	Top-25s	Scoring Average	Money
1983	1	4	1	0	0	0	0	71.75	$1,186

Best finish for 1983: T-45th at the British Open

Year	Starts	Rounds Played	Cuts Made	Wins	Top-5s	Top-10s	Top-25s	Scoring Average	Money
1984	1	4	1	0	0	0	0	72.25	$2,899

Best finish for 1984: T-36th at the British Open

Year	Starts	Rounds Played	Cuts Made	Wins	Top-5s	Top-10s	Top-25s	Scoring Average	Money
1985	2	8	2	0	0	0	0	71.75	$12,526

Best finish for 1985: T-28th at the British Open

Year	Starts	Rounds Played	Cuts Made	Wins	Top-5s	Top-10s	Top-25s	Scoring Average	Money
1986	3	6	2	0	0	0	1	73.67	$17,875

Best finish for 1986: T-19th at the British Open

Year	Starts	Rounds Played	Cuts Made	Wins	Top-5s	Top-10s	Top-25s	Scoring Average	Money
1988	1	4	1	0	0	0	0	74.75	$2,210

Best finish for 1988: 66th at the British Open

Year	Starts	Rounds Played	Cuts Made	Wins	Top-5s	Top-10s	Top-25s	Scoring Average	Money
1991	1	2	0	0	0	0	0	76.50	$1,008
1993	1	4	1	0	0	0	0	71.25	$6,709

Best finish for 1993: T-51st at the British Open

Period Totals	Starts	Rounds Played	Cuts Made	Wins	Top-5s	Top-10s	Top-25s	Scoring Average	Money
	26	85	16	0	0	1	3	73.51	$73,650

Gary Pinns

Year	Starts	Rounds Played	Cuts Made	Wins	Top-5s	Top-10s	Top-25s	Scoring Average	Money
1980	1	4	1	0	0	0	0	75.25	

Best finish for 1980: T-76th at the Greater Greensboro Open

Year	Starts	Rounds Played	Cuts Made	Wins	Top-5s	Top-10s	Top-25s	Scoring Average	Money
1982	3	6	0	0	0	0	0	75.33	$600
1983	1	2	0	0	0	0	0	73.50	
1984	14	41	6	0	0	1	2	72.32	$19,560

Best finish for 1984: T-10th at the Greater Milwaukee Open

Year	Starts	Rounds Played	Cuts Made	Wins	Top-5s	Top-10s	Top-25s	Scoring Average	Money
1985	23	57	5	0	0	0	0	73.54	$5,033

Best finish for 1985: T-51st at the Texas Open

| 1986 | 2 | 6 | 1 | 0 | 0 | 0 | 0 | 72.17 | $3,190 |

Best finish for 1986: T-27th at the Buick Open

| 1987 | 3 | 9 | 2 | 0 | 0 | 0 | 0 | 73.22 | $3,624 |

Best finish for 1987: T-49th at the Greater Milwaukee Open

1988	1	2	0	0	0	0	0	74.50	
1989	1	2	0	0	0	0	0	78.00	
1993	1	2	0	0	0	0	0	73.50	
Period Totals	Starts	Rounds Played	Cuts Made	Wins	Top-5s	Top-10s	Top-25s	Scoring Average	Money
	50	131	15	0	0	1	2	73.29	$32,008

Jerry Pittman

Year	Starts	Rounds Played	Cuts Made	Wins	Top-5s	Top-10s	Top-25s	Scoring Average	Money
1958	1	4	1	0	0	0	1	74.25	

Best finish for 1958: T-17th at the U.S. Open

| 1959 | 5 | 20 | 5 | 0 | 0 | 0 | 4 | 71.55 | $1,286 |

Best finish for 1959: T-19th at the Coral Gables Open Invitational

| 1960 | 16 | 65 | 16 | 0 | 0 | 3 | 12 | 70.86 | $7,965 |

Best finish for 1960: T-10th at the "500" Festival Open Invitational & St. Paul Open Invitational

| 1961 | 12 | 48 | 12 | 0 | 0 | 1 | 7 | 71.02 | $4,435 |

Best finish for 1961: T-10th at the Greater New Orleans Open Invitational

| 1962 | 9 | 36 | 8 | 0 | 1 | 4 | 7 | 71.56 | $5,813 |

Best finish for 1962: T-5th at the West Palm Beach Open Invitational

| 1963 | 20 | 76 | 15 | 0 | 0 | 2 | 9 | 71.82 | $10,605 |

Best finish for 1963: T-9th at the Buick Open Invitational

| 1964 | 24 | 66 | 10 | 0 | 0 | 0 | 3 | 73.17 | $4,661 |

Best finish for 1964: T-13th at the Buick Open

| 1965 | 15 | 42 | 5 | 0 | 0 | 0 | 0 | 74.60 | |

Best finish for 1965: T-37th at the Azalea Open

| 1966 | 11 | 35 | 6 | 0 | 0 | 0 | 3 | 72.94 | $4,351 |

Best finish for 1966: T-11th at the Thunderbird Classic

| 1967 | 10 | 38 | 8 | 0 | 0 | 0 | 2 | 72.61 | $4,537 |

Best finish for 1967: T-16th at the U.S. Open

| 1968 | 7 | 24 | 5 | 0 | 0 | 2 | 2 | 72.92 | $8,891 |

Best finish for 1968: T-7th at the Masters & U.S. Open

| 1969 | 7 | 19 | 2 | 0 | 0 | 1 | 1 | 73.37 | $7,988 |

Best finish for 1969: T-8th at the Westchester Classic

| 1970 | 8 | 22 | 3 | 0 | 0 | 0 | 1 | 72.86 | $1,744 |

Best finish for 1970: T-22nd at the Phoenix Open

| 1971 | 4 | 9 | 0 | 0 | 0 | 0 | 0 | 75.00 | |
| 1973 | 1 | 4 | 1 | 0 | 0 | 0 | 0 | 72.50 | $1,054 |

Best finish for 1973: T-35th at the PGA Championship

1976	1	3	3	0	0	0	0	76.33	
Period Totals	Starts	Rounds Played	Cuts Made	Wins	Top-5s	Top-10s	Top-25s	Scoring Average	Money
	151	511	100	0	1	13	52	72.39	$63,329

Greg Pitzer

Year	Starts	Rounds Played	Cuts Made	Wins	Top-5s	Top-10s	Top-25s	Scoring Average	Money
1964	2	5	1	0	0	0	0	74.20	

Best finish for 1964: 64th at the Cleveland Open

1965	4	9	0	0	0	0	0	73.78	
1968	1	2	0	0	0	0	0	74.00	
1972	1	2	0	0	0	0	0	78.00	
1973	1	2	0	0	0	0	0	75.50	
1977	4	12	2	0	0	0	0	74.00	$545

Best finish for 1977: T-67th at the Ohio Kings Island Open

| 1978 | 5 | 12 | 1 | 0 | 0 | 0 | 0 | 74.25 | $340 |

Best finish for 1978: 69th at the American Optical Classic

| 1979 | 7 | 19 | 3 | 0 | 0 | 0 | 0 | 74.05 | $2,253 |

Best finish for 1979: T-31st at the San Antonio Texas Open

| Period Totals | Starts | Rounds Played | Cuts Made | Wins | Top-5s | Top-10s | Top-25s | Scoring Average | Money |
| | 25 | 63 | 7 | 0 | 0 | 0 | 0 | 74.22 | $3,138 |

Gary Player

Year	Starts	Rounds Played	Cuts Made	Wins	Top-5s	Top-10s	Top-25s	Scoring Average	Money
1956	1	4	1	0	1	1	1	72.75	

Best finish for 1956: T4th at the British Open

| 1957 | 9 | 36 | 9 | 0 | 1 | 1 | 6 | 72.28 | $3683 |

Best finish for 1957: T3rd at the Greater Greensboro Open

| 1958 | 17 | 66 | 16 | 1 | 7 | 12 | 14 | 70.03 | $20,581 |

Best finish for 1958: Win at the Kentucky Derby Open

1959	8	32	8	1	2	3	6	71.47	$8,494

Best finish for 1959: Win at the British Open

1960	15	60	12	0	3	7	14	70.53	$14,929

Best finish for 1960: T-2nd at the Eastern Open Invitational

1961	28	111	22	3	12	17	24	69.79	$62,780

Best finish for 1961: Win at the Masters, Lucky International Open & Sunshine Open Invitational

1962	16	64	14	1	6	9	14	70.56	$44,938

Best finish for 1962: Win at the PGA Championship

1963	22	89	15	1	10	18	21	70.42	$54,692

Best finish for 1963: Win at the San Diego Open Invitational

1964	19	75	18	2	8	10	15	71.19	$61,970

Best finish for 1964: Win at the Pensacola Open & "500" Festival Open

1965	14	53	12	1	5	7	10	70.09	$70,964

Best finish for 1965: Win at the U.S. Open

1966	12	46	11	0	3	5	8	71.80	$28,365

Best finish for 1966: T-3rd at the Jacksonville Open Invitational & PGA Championship

1967	15	60	15	0	5	9	13	70.47	$59,001

Best finish for 1967: 2nd at the Oklahoma City Open

1968	17	66	16	1	6	13	15	70.20	$56,957

Best finish for 1968: Win at the British Open

1969	16	64	16	1	9	9	13	70.73	$118,149

Best finish for 1969: Win at the Tournament of Champions

1970	18	67	15	1	5	8	12	71.18	$99,391

Best finish for 1970: Win at the Greater Greensboro Open

1971	15	56	15	2	6	9	9	70.91	$123,269

Best finish for 1971: Win at the Greater Jacksonville Open & National Airlines Open

1972	14	55	13	2	4	9	13	71.07	$153,341

Best finish for 1972: Win at the Greater New Orleans Open & PGA Championship

1973	12	48	10	1	2	3	8	71.00	$50,222

Best finish for 1973: Win at the Southern Open

1974	16	59	14	3	3	6	11	70.92	$119,186

Best finish for 1974: Win at the Masters, Danny Thomas Memphis Classic & British Open

1975	16	62	15	0	2	4	8	71.55	$74,548

Best finish for 1975: T-2nd at the MONY Tournament Of Champions & Kemper Open

1976	18	68	16	0	1	4	10	71.34	$54,272

Best finish for 1976: 3rd at the Glen CampbellLos Angeles Open

1977	19	75	18	0	4	8	13	71.32	$113,653

Best finish for 1977: T-2nd at the Danny Thomas Memphis Classic

1978	20	76	18	3	5	7	10	71.49	$178,191

Best finish for 1978: Win at the Masters, MONY Tournament Of Champions & Houston Open

1979	13	42	8	0	3	3	7	72.12	$78,283

Best finish for 1979: T-2nd at the Greater Greensboro Open & U.S. Open

1980	12	45	10	0	1	3	4	72.09	$56,911

Best finish for 1980: T-3rd at the Sea Pines Heritage Classic

1981	16	51	9	0	0	0	3	72.80	$23,183

Best finish for 1981: T-15th at the Masters

1982	12	38	7	0	0	0	3	73.47	$24,414

Best finish for 1982: T-11th at the Sea Pines Heritage Classic

1983	12	42	9	0	0	0	2	73.57	$22,552

Best finish for 1983: T-20th at the U.S. Open

1984	14	47	10	0	1	1	5	72.30	$93,687

Best finish for 1984: T-2nd at the PGA Championship

1985	9	27	4	0	0	0	1	72.15	$13,047

Best finish for 1985: T-24th at the Houston Open

1986	2	6	1	0	0	0	0	74.33	$6,252

Best finish for 1986: T-35th at the British Open

1987	2	8	2	0	0	0	0	74.63	$7,057

Best finish for 1987: T-35th at the Masters

1988	3	8	1	0	0	0	0	74.88	$6,792

Best finish for 1988: T-61st at the British Open

1989	3	6	0	0	0	0	0	75.33	$3,300
1990	2	6	1	0	0	0	1	72.67	$11,996

Best finish for 1990: T-24th at the Masters

1991	2	6	1	0	0	0	0	72.17	$7,464

Best finish for 1991: T-57th at the British Open

1992	2	4	0	0	0	0	0	73.50	$2,700
1993	2	6	1	0	0	0	0	74.33	$4,624

Best finish for 1993: 60th at the Masters

1994	2	4	0	0	0	0	0	73.75	$2,472
1995	2	6	1	0	0	0	0	74.00	$9,435

Best finish for 1995: T-68th at the British Open

1996	2	4	0	0	0	0	0	74.00	$2,508

Year	Starts	Rounds Played	Cuts Made	Wins	Top-5s	Top-10s	Top-25s	Scoring Average	Money
1997	2	4	0	0	0	0	0	75.00	$6,340
1998	2	6	1	0	0	0	0	75.50	$12,352

Best finish for 1998: 46th at the Masters

Year	Starts	Rounds Played	Cuts Made	Wins	Top-5s	Top-10s	Top-25s	Scoring Average	Money
1999	2	4	0	0	0	0	0	80.50	$6,250
2000	2	4	0	0	0	0	0	76.50	$6,064
2001	2	4	0	0	0	0	0	77.00	$6,287
2002	1	2	0	0	0	0	0	79.00	$5,000
2003	1	2	0	0	0	0	0	81.00	$5,000
2004	1	2	0	0	0	0	0	81.00	$5,000
2005	1	2	0	0	0	0	0	83.50	$5,000
2006	1	2	0	0	0	0	0	80.00	$5,000
2007	1	2	0	0	0	0	0	80.00	
2008	1	2	0	0	0	0	0	80.50	
Period Totals	Starts	Rounds Played	Cuts Made	Wins	Top-5s	Top-10s	Top-25s	Scoring Average	Money
	486	1784	385	24	116	182	294	71.39	$2,010,548

Dan Pohl

Year	Starts	Rounds Played	Cuts Made	Wins	Top-5s	Top-10s	Top-25s	Scoring Average	Money
1978	11	30	4	0	0	0	0	73.37	$1,047

Best finish for 1978: T-59th at the Greater Milwaukee Open

1979	20	65	11	0	1	3	5	72.29	$38,076

Best finish for 1979: T-3rd at the Western Open

1980	29	96	20	0	2	5	11	71.71	$105,608

Best finish for 1980: 2nd at the Bing Crosby Pro-Am

1981	29	96	21	0	2	7	9	71.59	$98,880

Best finish for 1981: 3rd at the PGA Championship

1982	31	104	21	0	2	4	7	71.80	$97,213

Best finish for 1982: 2nd at the Masters

1983	27	96	20	0	0	6	8	71.67	$90,430

Best finish for 1983: T-6th at the Greater Milwaukee Open

1984	28	105	26	0	4	7	15	71.05	$182,653

Best finish for 1984: T-3rd at the Isuzu/Andy Williams San Diego Open

1985	27	95	22	0	3	7	17	70.94	$199,429

Best finish for 1985: T-2nd at the Canon Sammy Davis, Jr. - Greater Hartford Open

1986	25	76	19	2	4	5	11	70.70	$464,830

Best finish for 1986: Win at the Colonial National Invitational & NEC World Series of Golf

1987	27	96	24	0	4	9	19	70.25	$467,019

Best finish for 1987: 2nd at the Buick Open

1988	27	91	21	0	5	7	13	70.66	$396,400

Best finish for 1988: T-2nd at the International & Greater Milwaukee Open

1989	19	69	15	0	2	4	5	71.52	$195,789

Best finish for 1989: T-5th at the Honda Classic & Las Vegas Invitational

1991	21	67	16	0	0	2	8	70.12	$164,328

Best finish for 1991: T-7th at the Canon Greater Hartford Open

1992	19	60	12	0	1	1	6	70.93	$131,486

Best finish for 1992: T-3rd at the Nestle Invitational

1993	19	52	8	0	0	2	4	71.44	$97,830

Best finish for 1993: T-10th at the Nestle Invitational & Federal Express St. Jude Classic

1994	15	43	6	0	0	0	0	71.79	$21,734

Best finish for 1994: T-27th at the Nissan Los Angeles Open

1995	15	46	9	0	1	2	4	70.67	$166,219

Best finish for 1995: T-4th at the United Airlines Hawaiian Open

1996	18	58	11	0	0	0	3	71.29	$100,562

Best finish for 1996: T-12th at the Las Vegas Invitational

1997	5	14	2	0	0	0	0	71.50	$12,047

Best finish for 1997: T-38th at the AT&T Pebble Beach Pro-Am & LaCantera Texas Open

1998	8	23	3	0	0	0	0	72.04	$11,523

Best finish for 1998: T-53rd at the MasterCard Colonial

1999	3	12	3	0	0	0	0	69.92	$15,008

Best finish for 1999: T-62nd at the MasterCard Colonial & Greater Milwaukee Open

2000	5	15	3	0	0	0	0	70.60	$28,776

Best finish for 2000: T-30th at the John Deere Classic

2001	3	6	0	0	0	0	0	72.67	
2002	3	8	1	0	0	0	1	70.50	$24,570

Best finish for 2002: T-19th at the B.C. Open

2003	2	4	0	0	0	0	0	73.00	
2004	3	8	1	0	0	0	0	71.75	$10,706

Best finish for 2004: T-68th at the Bank of America Colonial

Period Totals	Starts	Rounds Played	Cuts Made	Wins	Top-5s	Top-10s	Top-25s	Scoring Average	Money
	439	1435	299	2	31	71	146	71.25	$3,122,162

D.A. Points

Year	Starts	Rounds Played	Cuts Made	Wins	Top-5s	Top-10s	Top-25s	Scoring Average	Money
2004	2	5	0	0	0	0	0	73.20	
2005	33	90	15	0	0	0	4	71.37	$400,540

Best finish for 2005: T-13th at the Nissan Open & B.C. Open

| 2006 | 28 | 80 | 12 | 0 | 0 | 1 | 3 | 71.50 | $405,984 |

Best finish for 2006: T-10th at the Honda Classic

| 2008 | 3 | 12 | 3 | 0 | 0 | 0 | 1 | 72.00 | $126,918 |

Best finish for 2008: T-14th at the AT&T Pebble Beach National Pro-Am

Period Totals	Starts	Rounds Played	Cuts Made	Wins	Top-5s	Top-10s	Top-25s	Scoring Average	Money
	66	187	30	0	0	1	8	71.51	$933,442

Don Pooley

Year	Starts	Rounds Played	Cuts Made	Wins	Top-5s	Top-10s	Top-25s	Scoring Average	Money
1976	16	45	6	0	0	0	1	72.91	$2,004

Best finish for 1976: T-25th at the Southern Open

| 1977 | 26 | 78 | 13 | 0 | 1 | 3 | 3 | 72.55 | $21,850 |

Best finish for 1977: T-4th at the Ed McMahon Quad City Open

| 1978 | 29 | 90 | 15 | 0 | 0 | 1 | 9 | 72.17 | $32,248 |

Best finish for 1978: T-8th at the Bing Crosby Pro-Am

| 1979 | 26 | 67 | 8 | 0 | 0 | 0 | 0 | 73.34 | $6,932 |

Best finish for 1979: T-24th at the Greater Milwaukee Open

| 1980 | 28 | 98 | 23 | 1 | 4 | 8 | 13 | 71.44 | $162,336 |

Best finish for 1980: Win at the B.C. Open

| 1981 | 32 | 108 | 22 | 0 | 1 | 5 | 9 | 71.88 | $76,330 |

Best finish for 1981: T-5th at the Pleasant Valley Jimmy Fund Classic

| 1982 | 29 | 93 | 18 | 0 | 3 | 5 | 10 | 71.67 | $90,062 |

Best finish for 1982: T-4th at the Manufactures Hanover Westchester Classic & Disney World

| 1983 | 29 | 107 | 24 | 0 | 3 | 7 | 14 | 70.80 | $145,979 |

Best finish for 1983: T-2nd at the Georgia-Pacific Atlanta Golf Classic

| 1984 | 24 | 84 | 19 | 0 | 2 | 3 | 9 | 71.44 | $120,699 |

Best finish for 1984: 2nd at the Georgia-Pacific Atlanta Golf Classic

| 1985 | 26 | 97 | 24 | 0 | 1 | 5 | 15 | 70.36 | $159,434 |

Best finish for 1985: T-4th at the Phoenix Open

| 1986 | 27 | 93 | 24 | 0 | 4 | 9 | 13 | 70.81 | $268,274 |

Best finish for 1986: 2nd at the Memorial Tournament

| 1987 | 26 | 91 | 20 | 1 | 5 | 8 | 11 | 70.62 | $450,006 |

Best finish for 1987: Win at the Memorial Tournament

| 1988 | 25 | 83 | 18 | 0 | 4 | 7 | 10 | 71.07 | $258,385 |

Best finish for 1988: 2nd at the Bank of Boston Classic

| 1989 | 24 | 80 | 16 | 0 | 2 | 4 | 10 | 71.25 | $228,382 |

Best finish for 1989: T-3rd at the Bank of Boston Classic

| 1990 | 25 | 79 | 15 | 0 | 1 | 3 | 6 | 71.70 | $201,202 |

Best finish for 1990: T-3rd at the Memorial Tournament

| 1991 | 15 | 47 | 8 | 0 | 0 | 0 | 3 | 71.19 | $67,549 |

Best finish for 1991: T-13th at the MCI Heritage Classic

| 1992 | 16 | 57 | 12 | 0 | 0 | 1 | 5 | 70.72 | $135,683 |

Best finish for 1992: T-8th at the Canadian Open

| 1993 | 15 | 44 | 8 | 0 | 1 | 2 | 3 | 72.11 | $123,105 |

Best finish for 1993: T-3rd at the MCI Heritage Classic

| 1994 | 5 | 15 | 3 | 0 | 1 | 1 | 1 | 70.80 | $76,978 |

Best finish for 1994: 3rd at the Texas Open

| 1995 | 22 | 77 | 15 | 0 | 2 | 3 | 5 | 71.06 | $228,004 |

Best finish for 1995: 3rd at the Ideon Classic

| 1996 | 21 | 63 | 12 | 0 | 0 | 0 | 3 | 71.46 | $94,351 |

Best finish for 1996: T-17th at the Nissan Open

| 1997 | 19 | 72 | 17 | 0 | 2 | 4 | 9 | 70.25 | $312,660 |

Best finish for 1997: T-5th at the Bob Hope Chrysler Classic & Tucson Chrysler Classic

| 1998 | 20 | 60 | 9 | 0 | 0 | 0 | 0 | 71.72 | $49,547 |

Best finish for 1998: T-31st at the MCI Classic

| 1999 | 8 | 20 | 2 | 0 | 0 | 0 | 0 | 72.15 | $19,062 |

Best finish for 1999: T-37th at the Touchstone Energy Tucson Open

| 2000 | 7 | 18 | 2 | 0 | 0 | 0 | 0 | 72.83 | $11,872 |

Best finish for 2000: 73rd at the John Deere Classic

2001	3	6	0	0	0	0	0	72.83	
2003	1	2	0	0	0	0	0	78.50	$1,000
2004	1	2	0	0	0	0	0	70.50	
2006	1	2	0	0	0	0	0	71.50	
Period Totals	Starts	Rounds Played	Cuts Made	Wins	Top-5s	Top-10s	Top-25s	Scoring Average	Money
	546	1778	353	2	37	79	162	71.45	$3,343,933

Adolph Popp

Year	Starts	Rounds Played	Cuts Made	Wins	Top-5s	Top-10s	Top-25s	Scoring Average	Money
1964	1	2	0	0	0	0	0	77.00	
1967	3	6	0	0	0	0	0	77.00	
1968	1	2	0	0	0	0	0	78.50	
1969	1	2	0	0	0	0	0	74.50	
1970	4	8	0	0	0	0	0	75.13	
1971	2	3	0	0	0	0	0	80.33	
1972	3	8	1	0	0	0	1	73.00	$1,159

Best finish for 1972: T-24th at the Doral-Eastern Open

Year	Starts	Rounds Played	Cuts Made	Wins	Top-5s	Top-10s	Top-25s	Scoring Average	Money
1973	2	4	0	0	0	0	0	74.00	
1975	2	4	0	0	0	0	0	74.75	
1976	1	2	0	0	0	0	0	73.00	
1979	1	2	0	0	0	0	0	80.00	
1980	1	2	0	0	0	0	0	79.00	
1981	2	2	0	0	0	0	0	76.50	
1982	2	4	0	0	0	0	0	74.50	
1983	1	2	0	0	0	0	0	79.50	
Period Totals	Starts	Rounds Played	Cuts Made	Wins	Top-5s	Top-10s	Top-25s	Scoring Average	Money
	27	53	1	0	0	0	1	75.79	$1,159

Bill Porter

Year	Starts	Rounds Played	Cuts Made	Wins	Top-5s	Top-10s	Top-25s	Scoring Average	Money
1990	1	4	1	0	0	0	0	72.00	$1,930

Best finish for 1990: T-73rd at the Nissan Los Angeles Open

Year	Starts	Rounds Played	Cuts Made	Wins	Top-5s	Top-10s	Top-25s	Scoring Average	Money
1995	25	76	12	0	0	0	2	72.07	$68,390

Best finish for 1995: T-11th at the Deposit Guaranty Golf Classic

Year	Starts	Rounds Played	Cuts Made	Wins	Top-5s	Top-10s	Top-25s	Scoring Average	Money
1996	1	4	1	0	0	0	0	72.75	$5,825

Best finish for 1996: T-60th at the U.S. Open

Year	Starts	Rounds Played	Cuts Made	Wins	Top-5s	Top-10s	Top-25s	Scoring Average	Money
1997	1	2	0	0	0	0	0	75.00	$1,000
1998	1	3	0	0	0	0	0	73.00	
2002	1	1	0	0	0	0	0	86.00	
Period Totals	Starts	Rounds Played	Cuts Made	Wins	Top-5s	Top-10s	Top-25s	Scoring Average	Money
	30	90	14	0	0	0	2	72.34	$77,145

Joe Porter

Year	Starts	Rounds Played	Cuts Made	Wins	Top-5s	Top-10s	Top-25s	Scoring Average	Money
1968	12	34	6	0	0	0	0	73.65	

Best finish for 1968: T-48th at the Tucson Open Invitational

Year	Starts	Rounds Played	Cuts Made	Wins	Top-5s	Top-10s	Top-25s	Scoring Average	Money
1969	11	24	1	0	0	0	0	74.83	$214

Best finish for 1969: T-58th at the AVCO Classic

Year	Starts	Rounds Played	Cuts Made	Wins	Top-5s	Top-10s	Top-25s	Scoring Average	Money
1970	19	59	10	0	1	1	1	73.42	$5,811

Best finish for 1970: T-3rd at the Tallahassee Open

Year	Starts	Rounds Played	Cuts Made	Wins	Top-5s	Top-10s	Top-25s	Scoring Average	Money
1971	10	30	5	0	0	0	2	73.20	$3,411

Best finish for 1971: T-19th at the Sahara Invitational

Year	Starts	Rounds Played	Cuts Made	Wins	Top-5s	Top-10s	Top-25s	Scoring Average	Money
1972	15	41	6	0	0	0	1	73.29	$4,182

Best finish for 1972: T-13th at the Liggett Meyers Open

Year	Starts	Rounds Played	Cuts Made	Wins	Top-5s	Top-10s	Top-25s	Scoring Average	Money
1973	20	56	9	0	0	1	2	72.80	$10,795

Best finish for 1973: T-9th at the U.S. Professional Match Play Championship

Year	Starts	Rounds Played	Cuts Made	Wins	Top-5s	Top-10s	Top-25s	Scoring Average	Money
1974	29	92	17	0	0	0	3	72.92	$11,088

Best finish for 1974: T-17th at the Western Open

Year	Starts	Rounds Played	Cuts Made	Wins	Top-5s	Top-10s	Top-25s	Scoring Average	Money
1975	26	78	14	0	0	3	4	72.68	$19,819

Best finish for 1975: T-8th at the First NBC New Orleans Open & Tournament Players Championship

Year	Starts	Rounds Played	Cuts Made	Wins	Top-5s	Top-10s	Top-25s	Scoring Average	Money
1976	31	96	19	0	2	4	4	72.53	$42,782

Best finish for 1976: 2nd at the Western Open

Year	Starts	Rounds Played	Cuts Made	Wins	Top-5s	Top-10s	Top-25s	Scoring Average	Money
1977	28	75	11	0	0	0	3	73.19	$7,799

Best finish for 1977: T-24th at the San Antonio Texas Open

Year	Starts	Rounds Played	Cuts Made	Wins	Top-5s	Top-10s	Top-25s	Scoring Average	Money
1978	30	85	12	0	0	0	2	73.22	$9,039

Best finish for 1978: T-20th at the Jackie Gleason's Inverrary Classic

Year	Starts	Rounds Played	Cuts Made	Wins	Top-5s	Top-10s	Top-25s	Scoring Average	Money
1979	15	32	4	0	0	0	0	74.25	$2,127

Best finish for 1979: T-42nd at the First NBC New Orleans Open

Year	Starts	Rounds Played	Cuts Made	Wins	Top-5s	Top-10s	Top-25s	Scoring Average	Money
1980	1	2	0	0	0	0	0	77.00	
Period Totals	Starts	Rounds Played	Cuts Made	Wins	Top-5s	Top-10s	Top-25s	Scoring Average	Money
	247	704	114	0	3	9	22	73.14	$117,069

Lee Porter

Year	Starts	Rounds Played	Cuts Made	Wins	Top-5s	Top-10s	Top-25s	Scoring Average	Money
1989	1	2	0	0	0	0	0	76.00	
1990	1	4	1	0	0	0	0	72.25	$2,255

Best finish for 1990: T-52nd at the BellSouth Atlanta Golf Classic

Year	Starts	Rounds Played	Cuts Made	Wins	Top-5s	Top-10s	Top-25s	Scoring Average	Money
1992	1	2	0	0	0	0	0	75.50	

Year	Starts	Rounds Played	Cuts Made	Wins	Top-5s	Top-10s	Top-25s	Scoring Average	Money
1993	19	51	6	0	0	0	0	73.04	$14,908

Best finish for 1993: T-32nd at the H-E-B Texas Open

| 1994 | 1 | 3 | 1 | 0 | 0 | 0 | 0 | 70.67 | $4,256 |

Best finish for 1994: T-31st at the Buick Southern Open

1995	1	2	0	0	0	0	0	72.00	
1996	1	2	0	0	0	0	0	77.00	
1997	32	81	8	0	0	1	1	72.65	$62,121

Best finish for 1997: T-7th at the United Airlines Hawaiian Open

| 1998 | 30 | 91 | 17 | 0 | 1 | 1 | 5 | 71.41 | $325,415 |

Best finish for 1998: 3rd at the Greater Vancouver Open

| 1999 | 34 | 88 | 10 | 0 | 0 | 0 | 1 | 72.26 | $110,247 |

Best finish for 1999: T-22nd at the Las Vegas Invitational

| 2000 | 2 | 6 | 1 | 0 | 0 | 0 | 0 | 74.33 | $28,247 |

Best finish for 2000: T-32nd at the U.S. Open

| 2001 | 30 | 90 | 16 | 0 | 0 | 1 | 3 | 71.14 | $346,462 |

Best finish for 2001: T-8th at the Genuity Championship

| 2002 | 32 | 88 | 13 | 0 | 0 | 0 | 1 | 71.72 | $179,396 |

Best finish for 2002: T-14th at the Greater Greensboro Chrysler Classic

Period Totals	Starts	Rounds Played	Cuts Made	Wins	Top-5s	Top-10s	Top-25s	Scoring Average	Money
	185	510	73	0	1	3	11	72.02	$1,073,306

Johnny Pott

Year	Starts	Rounds Played	Cuts Made	Wins	Top-5s	Top-10s	Top-25s	Scoring Average	Money
1957	16	64	16	0	0	1	6	N/A	$2391

Best finish for 1957: T-7th at the Houston Open

| 1958 | 35 | 130 | 29 | 0 | 0 | 2 | 13 | 72.15 | $5,416 |

Best finish for 1958: T-7th at the Houston Open

| 1959 | 26 | 103 | 22 | 0 | 2 | 3 | 15 | 71.84 | $11,716 |

Best finish for 1959: T-2nd at the Gleneagles-Chicago Open Invitational

| 1960 | 23 | 92 | 18 | 2 | 7 | 11 | 19 | 70.43 | $25,555 |

Best finish for 1960: Win at the Dallas Open Invitational & West Palm Beach Open Invitational

| 1961 | 31 | 123 | 26 | 0 | 9 | 16 | 25 | 70.33 | $32,027 |

Best finish for 1961: T-2nd at the Mobile Sertoma Open Invitational

| 1962 | 26 | 102 | 24 | 1 | 4 | 9 | 17 | 71.53 | $26,583 |

Best finish for 1962: Win at the Waco Turner Open Invitational

| 1963 | 22 | 85 | 20 | 1 | 2 | 4 | 10 | 71.84 | $22,479 |

Best finish for 1963: Win at the American Golf Classic

| 1964 | 31 | 110 | 22 | 0 | 1 | 6 | 12 | 71.95 | $20,213 |

Best finish for 1964: T-4th at the Pensacola Open

| 1965 | 27 | 103 | 24 | 0 | 6 | 9 | 14 | 71.41 | $52,552 |

Best finish for 1965: T-2nd at the Buick Open & Greater Hartford Open

| 1966 | 25 | 94 | 22 | 0 | 4 | 9 | 15 | 71.26 | $48,943 |

Best finish for 1966: T-2nd at the Buick Open Invitational

| 1967 | 31 | 109 | 24 | 0 | 1 | 3 | 15 | 77.52 | $40,188 |

Best finish for 1967: 2nd at the Memphis Open

| 1968 | 28 | 99 | 23 | 1 | 1 | 2 | 8 | 72.46 | $35,663 |

Best finish for 1968: Win at the Bing Crosby National Professional-Amateur

| 1969 | 29 | 99 | 21 | 0 | 2 | 4 | 10 | 71.73 | $31,833 |

Best finish for 1969: T-2nd at the West End Classic

| 1970 | 24 | 70 | 14 | 0 | 0 | 0 | 3 | 72.97 | $6,319 |

Best finish for 1970: T-22nd at the Byron Nelson Golf Classic

| 1971 | 17 | 53 | 9 | 0 | 0 | 4 | 6 | 72.02 | $20,563 |

Best finish for 1971: T-6th at the National Airlines Open & Monsanto Open

| 1972 | 17 | 52 | 9 | 0 | 0 | 0 | 1 | 73.13 | $5,275 |

Best finish for 1972: T-25th at the Tallahassee Open

| 1973 | 5 | 13 | 1 | 0 | 0 | 0 | 0 | 75.62 | $260 |

Best finish for 1973: T-67th at the American Golf Classic

| 1974 | 3 | 5 | 0 | 0 | 0 | 0 | 0 | 76.40 | |
| 1975 | 2 | 6 | 1 | 0 | 0 | 0 | 0 | 77.00 | $370 |

Best finish for 1975: 60th at the Bing Crosby Pro-Am

1976	1	1	0	0	0	0	0	75.00	
1980	1	3	0	0	0	0	0	82.33	
1981	1	0	0	0	0	0	0		
1982	1	3	0	0	0	0	0	78.67	

Period Totals	Starts	Rounds Played	Cuts Made	Wins	Top-5s	Top-10s	Top-25s	Scoring Average	Money
	424	1519	325	5	39	83	189	72.25	$388,346

Ian Poulter

Year	Starts	Rounds Played	Cuts Made	Wins	Top-5s	Top-10s	Top-25s	Scoring Average	Money
2000	1	4	1	0	0	0	0	72.75	$10,970

Best finish for 2000: T-64th at the British Open

| 2001 | 2 | 6 | 1 | 0 | 0 | 0 | 1 | 70.67 | $102,500 |

Best finish for 2001: T-13th at the WGC-NEC Invitational

Year	Starts	Rounds Played	Cuts Made	Wins	Top-5s	Top-10s	Top-25s	Scoring Average	Money
2002	1	4	1	0	0	0	0	72.00	$16,223

Best finish for 2002: T-50th at the British Open

2003	4	16	4	0	0	0	0	73.06	$103,693

Best finish for 2003: T-33rd at the WGC-NEC Invitational

2004	9	26	6	0	1	1	2	72.38	$402,318

Best finish for 2004: T-5th at the WGC-Accenture Match Play Championship

2005	20	56	10	0	1	2	4	72.09	$946,890

Best finish for 2005: 4th at the WGC-Accenture Match Play Championship

2006	15	52	13	0	1	4	7	71.04	$1,557,624

Best finish for 2006: T-2nd at the WGC-American Express Championship

2007	18	60	14	0	1	5	8	71.35	$1,431,390

Best finish for 2007: T-3rd at the EDS Byron Nelson Championship

2008	15	49	12	0	1	1	7	71.84	$1,488,214

Best finish for 2008: 2nd at the British Open

Period Totals	Starts	Rounds Played	Cuts Made	Wins	Top-5s	Top-10s	Top-25s	Scoring Average	Money
	85	273	62	0	5	13	29	71.74	$6,059,823

Jimmy Powell

Year	Starts	Rounds Played	Cuts Made	Wins	Top-5s	Top-10s	Top-25s	Scoring Average	Money
1959	2	6	1	0	0	0	1	73.17	$165

Best finish for 1959: T-23rd at the Lafayette Open Invitational

1960	5	19	4	0	0	0	2	73.95	$762

Best finish for 1960: T-20th at the Baton Rouge Open Invitational

1961	3	10	2	0	0	0	1	73.00	$540

Best finish for 1961: T-12th at the Almaden Open

1962	7	28	7	0	0	1	2	71.57	$2,825

Best finish for 1962: T-8th at the St. Paul Open Invitational

1963	2	8	2	0	0	0	0	70.88	$480

Best finish for 1963: T-35th at the Texas Open Invitational

1964	2	2	0	0	0	0	0	77.50	
1966	1	4	1	0	0	0	0	72.50	

Best finish for 1966: T-71st at the San Diego Open Invitational

1968	5	17	3	0	0	1	2	71.71	$6,648

Best finish for 1968: 6th at the Andy Williams-San Diego Open Invitational

1969	6	20	4	0	0	1	3	73.05	$5,278

Best finish for 1969: T-8th at the Bing Crosby National Pro-Am

1970	6	17	1	0	0	0	0	74.12	$300

Best finish for 1970: T-61st at the Andy Williams-San Diego Open

1971	7	23	4	0	0	0	1	72.00	$2,319

Best finish for 1971: T-17th at the Andy Williams-San Diego Open

1972	7	26	5	0	0	0	1	73.54	$3,172

Best finish for 1972: T-23rd at the Glen CampbellLos Angeles Open

1973	5	17	3	0	0	0	0	73.29	$1,335

Best finish for 1973: T-27th at the Glen CampbellLos Angeles Open

1974	3	8	1	0	0	0	0	73.88	$274

Best finish for 1974: T-62nd at the Dean Martin Tucson Open

1975	3	12	2	0	0	0	0	74.33	$1,830

Best finish for 1975: T-33rd at the PGA Championship

1976	6	17	5	0	0	0	0	73.41	$1,832

Best finish for 1976: T-26th at the Bob Hope Chrysler Classic

1979	1	2	0	0	0	0	0	76.00	
1980	10	26	5	0	0	0	1	73.50	$4,822

Best finish for 1980: T-23rd at the World Disney World National Team Championship

1981	8	21	2	0	0	0	0	72.52	$1,264

Best finish for 1981: T-53rd at the Bob Hope Chrysler Classic

1982	1	2	0	0	0	0	0	78.50	
1983	2	4	0	0	0	0	0	76.50	

Period Totals	Starts	Rounds Played	Cuts Made	Wins	Top-5s	Top-10s	Top-25s	Scoring Average	Money
	91	289	52	0	0	3	14	73.09	$33,846

Greg Powers

Year	Starts	Rounds Played	Cuts Made	Wins	Top-5s	Top-10s	Top-25s	Scoring Average	Money
1969	2	4	0	0	0	0	0	74.00	
1970	2	6	1	0	0	0	0	72.67	

Best finish for 1970: 70th at the Danny Thomas Memphis Classic

1971	2	6	1	0	0	0	0	73.50	$171

Best finish for 1971: T-72nd at the Walt Disney World Open

1972	11	30	4	0	0	0	0	74.37	$705

Best finish for 1972: T-54th at the Sea Pines Heritage Classic

1973	7	22	3	0	0	0	0	74.82	$1,337

Best finish for 1973: T-39th at the Andy Williams-San Diego Open

Year	Starts	Rounds Played	Cuts Made	Wins	Top-5s	Top-10s	Top-25s	Scoring Average	Money
1975	2	4	0	0	0	0	0	75.00	
1976	19	54	8	0	0	0	0	73.35	$4,164

Best finish for 1976: T-26th at the World Open

1977	2	6	0	0	0	0	0	74.00	
1978	29	92	17	0	1	2	6	72.09	$27,269

Best finish for 1978: T-3rd at the Buick Goodwrench Open

1979	29	81	12	0	0	0	1	73.22	$14,079

Best finish for 1979: T-17th at the Manufactures Hanover Westchester Classic

1980	25	71	12	0	0	0	3	72.31	$20,393

Best finish for 1980: T-14th at the Byron Nelson Golf Classic

1981	31	97	20	0	3	6	9	71.55	$85,887

Best finish for 1981: T-2nd at the Western Open

1982	35	108	19	0	0	1	3	72.46	$40,678

Best finish for 1982: T-6th at the Joe Garagiola Tucson Open

1983	32	85	10	0	1	1	2	73.09	$29,803

Best finish for 1983: 5th at the Georgia-Pacific Atlanta Golf Classic

1984	28	81	13	0	0	0	3	73.14	$31,845

Best finish for 1984: 11th at the Texas Open

1985	21	55	7	0	0	0	1	73.45	$10,092

Best finish for 1985: T-18th at the B.C. Open

1986	5	14	2	0	0	0	0	75.00	$3,328

Best finish for 1986: T-55th at the U.S. Open

1987	8	25	5	0	1	3	3	71.12	$59,558

Best finish for 1987: T-4th at the Beatrice Western Open

1988	23	59	7	0	0	0	2	72.41	$30,676

Best finish for 1988: T-12th at the Buick Open

1989	2	7	1	0	0	0	0	72.86	$1,234

Best finish for 1989: T-47th at the B.C. Open

1990	6	18	3	0	0	0	0	72.33	$13,082

Best finish for 1990: T-31st at the British Open

1991	6	18	3	0	0	0	0	72.72	$6,464

Best finish for 1991: T-43rd at the Centel Western Open

1992	5	17	3	0	0	0	1	71.18	$10,473

Best finish for 1992: T-13th at the Deposit Guaranty Classic

1994	2	4	0	0	0	0	0	74.75	
1995	4	11	1	0	0	0	0	74.82	$2,712

Best finish for 1995: T-55th at the Buick Classic

1996	3	8	1	0	0	0	0	74.88	$1,720

Best finish for 1996: 84th at the Deposit Guaranty Golf Classic

1997	2	4	0	0	0	0	0	72.25	
1998	2	5	1	0	0	0	0	74.40	$2,508

Best finish for 1998: T-65th at the Deposit Guaranty Golf Classic

2000	1	2	0	0	0	0	0	75.00	
2001	1	2	0	0	0	0	0	75.00	
Period Totals	Starts	Rounds Played	Cuts Made	Wins	Top-5s	Top-10s	Top-25s	Scoring Average	Money
	347	996	154	0	6	13	34	72.80	$398,176

Nick Price

Year	Starts	Rounds Played	Cuts Made	Wins	Top-5s	Top-10s	Top-25s	Scoring Average	Money
1975	1	2	0	0	0	0	0	77.00	
1978	1	4	1	0	0	0	0	73.25	$770

Best finish for 1978: T-39th at the British Open

1980	1	4	1	0	0	0	0	72.00	$2,700

Best finish for 1980: T-28th at the British Open

1981	1	4	1	0	0	0	1	72.50	$2,438

Best finish for 1981: T-23rd at the British Open

1982	1	4	1	0	1	1	1	71.25	$32,810

Best finish for 1982: T-2nd at the British Open

1983	22	70	14	1	1	2	5	72.50	$149,810

Best finish for 1983: Win at the World Series Of Golf

1984	20	73	16	0	2	4	6	72.40	$113,484

Best finish for 1984: T-3rd at the Canadian Open

1985	21	69	14	0	2	2	5	72.16	$97,212

Best finish for 1985: T-4th at the Colonial National Invitational

1986	25	72	16	0	3	6	11	71.76	$226,373

Best finish for 1986: T-2nd at the Western Open

1987	26	84	20	0	3	8	15	70.87	$364,035

Best finish for 1987: T-2nd at the Canadian Open

1988	25	88	21	0	2	5	11	70.92	$368,300

Best finish for 1988: T-2nd at the Federal Express St. Jude Classic & British Open

1989	28	96	22	0	2	7	12	70.74	$299,470

Best finish for 1989: T-3rd at the AT&T Pebble Beach Pro-Am

Year	Starts	Rounds Played	Cuts Made	Wins	Top-5s	Top-10s	Top-25s	Scoring Average	Money
1990	30	102	23	0	4	6	14	70.88	$532,331

Best finish for 1990: T-2nd at the Southwestern Bell Colonial & BellSouth Atlanta Golf Classic

1991	24	87	19	2	4	9	11	70.44	$721,503

Best finish for 1991: Win at the GTE Byron Nelson Classic & Canadian Open

1992	27	103	25	2	7	13	19	69.89	$1,143,923

Best finish for 1992: Win at the PGA Championship & H-E-B Texas Open

1993	19	73	18	4	6	9	13	69.68	$1,531,134

Best finish for 1993: Win at the Players Championship, Canon Greater Hartford Open, Sprint Western Open & Federal Express St. Jude Classic

1994	19	64	14	6	8	9	11	69.86	$1,679,127

Best finish for 1994: Win at the Honda Classic, Southwestern Bell Colonial, Motorola Western Open, British Open, PGA Championship & Bell Canadian Open

1995	18	66	15	0	2	5	11	70.77	$613,200

Best finish for 1995: T-2nd at the NEC World Series of Golf

1996	15	52	12	0	4	5	7	70.65	$402,467

Best finish for 1996: T-3rd at the Honda Classic & BellSouth Classic

1997	16	58	15	1	6	8	14	70.00	$1,055,185

Best finish for 1997: Win at the MCI Classic

1998	18	62	15	1	4	6	9	70.82	$1,024,404

Best finish for 1998: Win at the FedEx St. Jude Classic

1999	18	62	17	0	5	7	12	70.79	$1,572,402

Best finish for 1999: T-3rd at the Players Championship & WGC-NEC Invitational

2000	18	62	15	0	6	6	11	70.21	$1,808,105

Best finish for 2000: T-2nd at the Advil Western Open & Buick Challenge

2001	20	74	17	0	2	6	12	69.69	$1,292,756

Best finish for 2001: T-3rd at the Verizon Byron Nelson Classic

2002	18	66	17	1	2	8	14	70.05	$2,172,912

Best finish for 2002: Win at the MasterCard Colonial

2003	17	62	16	0	5	6	9	70.50	$2,271,111

Best finish for 2003: 2nd at the EDS Byron Nelson Championship & FedEx St. Jude Classic

2004	15	50	12	0	0	2	6	71.18	$796,086

Best finish for 2004: T-6th at the Masters

2005	16	48	11	0	0	2	4	71.29	$636,116

Best finish for 2005: T-6th at the EDS Byron Nelson Championship

2006	16	43	5	0	0	0	1	72.40	$213,188

Best finish for 2006: T-16th at the FedEx St. Jude Classic

2008	1	4	1	0	0	0	0	70.00	$11,900

Best finish for 2008: T-42nd at the Mayakoba Golf Classic

Period Totals	Starts	Rounds Played	Cuts Made	Wins	Top-5s	Top-10s	Top-25s	Scoring Average	Money
	497	1708	394	18	81	142	245	70.83	$21,135,251

Phillip Price

Year	Starts	Rounds Played	Cuts Made	Wins	Top-5s	Top-10s	Top-25s	Scoring Average	Money
1992	1	2	0	0	0	0	0	73.50	$1,200
1998	1	2	0	0	0	0	0	73.50	$1,645
1999	2	8	2	0	0	0	0	75.63	$19,815

Best finish for 1999: T-53rd at the U.S. Open

2000	4	12	2	0	1	1	2	71.33	$497,422

Best finish for 2000: T-2nd at the WGC-NEC Invitational

2001	6	14	4	0	0	0	0	71.50	$114,406

Best finish for 2001: 28th at the WGC-NEC Invitational

2002	7	19	4	0	0	0	1	72.37	$113,814

Best finish for 2002: T-24th at the AT&T Pebble Beach

2003	9	29	6	0	0	1	2	71.69	$282,551

Best finish for 2003: T-10th at the British Open

2004	12	32	7	0	0	0	1	73.09	$230,430

Best finish for 2004: T-17th at the AT&T Pebble Beach National Pro-Am

2005	25	73	13	0	0	0	3	70.84	$419,415

Best finish for 2005: 11th at the FedEx St. Jude Classic

2006	1	2	0	0	0	0	0	72.00	$5,577

Period Totals	Starts	Rounds Played	Cuts Made	Wins	Top-5s	Top-10s	Top-25s	Scoring Average	Money
	68	193	38	0	1	2	9	71.83	$1,686,275

Dicky Pride

Year	Starts	Rounds Played	Cuts Made	Wins	Top-5s	Top-10s	Top-25s	Scoring Average	Money
1992	1	2	0	0	0	0	0	85.50	
1994	27	74	12	1	1	2	3	72.43	$305,769

Best finish for 1994: Win at the Federal Express St. Jude Classic

1995	31	83	12	0	0	1	4	72.54	$99,212

Best finish for 1995: T-8th at the Deposit Guaranty Golf Classic

1996	27	81	14	0	1	2	2	71.91	$167,852

Best finish for 1996: T-3rd at the Canon Greater Hartford Open

1997	32	76	7	0	0	0	2	72.70	$45,813

Best finish for 1997: T-16th at the CVS Charity Classic

Year	Starts	Rounds Played	Cuts Made	Wins	Top-5s	Top-10s	Top-25s	Scoring Average	Money
1998	26	59	4	0	0	0	0	72.85	$27,680

Best finish for 1998: T-27th at the BellSouth Classic

| 1999 | 29 | 84 | 14 | 0 | 2 | 2 | 5 | 71.46 | $381,040 |

Best finish for 1999: T-5th at the Bay Hill Invitational & Motorola Western Open

| 2000 | 35 | 94 | 14 | 0 | 0 | 1 | 2 | 72.09 | $233,720 |

Best finish for 2000: T-10th at the BellSouth Classic

| 2001 | 27 | 78 | 12 | 0 | 0 | 1 | 2 | 71.91 | $207,022 |

Best finish for 2001: T-6th at the Southern Farm Bureau Classic

| 2002 | 16 | 51 | 9 | 0 | 0 | 0 | 3 | 71.27 | $142,556 |

Best finish for 2002: T-15th at the John Deere Classic

| 2003 | 23 | 73 | 14 | 0 | 0 | 1 | 6 | 70.58 | $483,923 |

Best finish for 2003: T-10th at the Reno-Tahoe Open

| 2004 | 23 | 63 | 10 | 0 | 1 | 1 | 1 | 72.71 | $230,329 |

Best finish for 2004: T-5th at the Michelin Championship at Las Vegas

| 2005 | 4 | 12 | 2 | 0 | 0 | 0 | 0 | 71.58 | $36,931 |

Best finish for 2005: T-30th at the AT&T Pebble Beach National Pro-Am

| 2006 | 9 | 30 | 6 | 0 | 0 | 1 | 1 | 70.90 | $174,674 |

Best finish for 2006: T-9th at the U.S. Bank Championship in Milwaukee

| 2007 | 25 | 71 | 10 | 0 | 1 | 1 | 3 | 71.38 | $415,792 |

Best finish for 2007: 4th at the Ginn sur Mer Classic at Tesoro

| 2008 | 14 | 39 | 5 | 0 | 0 | 1 | 2 | 72.05 | $182,890 |

Best finish for 2008: T-8th at the Viking Classic

Period Totals	Starts	Rounds Played	Cuts Made	Wins	Top-5s	Top-10s	Top-25s	Scoring Average	Money
	349	970	145	1	6	14	36	71.98	$3,135,201

Bob Proben

Year	Starts	Rounds Played	Cuts Made	Wins	Top-5s	Top-10s	Top-25s	Scoring Average	Money
1979	7	18	2	0	0	0	0	73.22	$1,682

Best finish for 1979: T-36th at the Southern Open

| 1980 | 9 | 27 | 3 | 0 | 0 | 0 | 1 | 73.93 | $4,017 |

Best finish for 1980: T-20th at the Andy Williams-San Diego Open

| 1981 | 6 | 16 | 2 | 0 | 0 | 0 | 0 | 72.88 | $1,438 |

Best finish for 1981: T-57th at the Canadian Open

| 1982 | 11 | 27 | 3 | 0 | 0 | 0 | 1 | 73.74 | $4,191 |

Best finish for 1982: T-22nd at the Hawaiian Open

| 1985 | 1 | 2 | 0 | 0 | 0 | 0 | 0 | 74.00 | $600 |
| 1988 | 30 | 80 | 10 | 0 | 0 | 0 | 2 | 72.54 | $34,180 |

Best finish for 1988: T-15th at the Independent Insurance Agent Open & Bank of Boston Classic

| 1989 | 5 | 12 | 2 | 0 | 0 | 0 | 0 | 71.58 | $3,208 |

Best finish for 1989: T-47th at the Hardee's Golf Classic

| 1992 | 1 | 4 | 1 | 0 | 0 | 0 | 0 | 71.75 | $2,442 |

Best finish for 1992: T-48th at the Buick Open

Period Totals	Starts	Rounds Played	Cuts Made	Wins	Top-5s	Top-10s	Top-25s	Scoring Average	Money
	70	186	23	0	0	0	4	72.95	$51,758

Dillard Pruitt

Year	Starts	Rounds Played	Cuts Made	Wins	Top-5s	Top-10s	Top-25s	Scoring Average	Money
1988	29	86	13	0	0	0	1	71.97	$33,889

Best finish for 1988: T-17th at the Kemper Open

| 1989 | 4 | 14 | 3 | 0 | 0 | 0 | 0 | 71.79 | $6,830 |

Best finish for 1989: T-46th at the Chattanooga Classic

| 1990 | 30 | 79 | 12 | 0 | 0 | 1 | 3 | 72.15 | $76,352 |

Best finish for 1990: T-9th at the International

| 1991 | 27 | 85 | 18 | 1 | 1 | 2 | 7 | 71.01 | $271,860 |

Best finish for 1991: Win at the Chattanooga Classic

| 1992 | 30 | 90 | 18 | 0 | 0 | 2 | 6 | 71.67 | $189,605 |

Best finish for 1992: T-6th at the Southwestern Bell Colonial

| 1993 | 26 | 86 | 20 | 0 | 0 | 2 | 5 | 71.16 | $169,553 |

Best finish for 1993: T-7th at the BellSouth Classic

| 1994 | 29 | 88 | 18 | 0 | 0 | 2 | 6 | 71.31 | $171,866 |

Best finish for 1994: T-8th at the Texas Open

| 1995 | 25 | 77 | 16 | 0 | 2 | 3 | 4 | 71.10 | $210,453 |

Best finish for 1995: T-3rd at the Bob Hope Chrysler Classic

| 1996 | 27 | 74 | 12 | 0 | 0 | 0 | 0 | 72.01 | $55,954 |

Best finish for 1996: T-27th at the Nortel Open

Period Totals	Starts	Rounds Played	Cuts Made	Wins	Top-5s	Top-10s	Top-25s	Scoring Average	Money
	227	679	130	1	3	12	32	71.54	$1,186,362

Ted Purdy

Year	Starts	Rounds Played	Cuts Made	Wins	Top-5s	Top-10s	Top-25s	Scoring Average	Money
1998	1	2	0	0	0	0	0	72.50	
1999	27	64	7	0	0	0	0	73.70	$46,660

Best finish for 1999: T-35th at the Buick Invitational

Year	Starts	Rounds Played	Cuts Made	Wins	Top-5s	Top-10s	Top-25s	Scoring Average	Money
2000	1	4	1	0	0	0	1	68.50	$72,000

Best finish for 2000: T-11th at the Touchstone Energy Tucson Open

Year	Starts	Rounds Played	Cuts Made	Wins	Top-5s	Top-10s	Top-25s	Scoring Average	Money
2003	2	4	0	0	0	0	0	73.50	
2004	35	112	22	0	3	4	12	70.53	$1,638,876

Best finish for 2004: 2nd at the MCI Heritage & B.C. Open

Year	Starts	Rounds Played	Cuts Made	Wins	Top-5s	Top-10s	Top-25s	Scoring Average	Money
2005	34	122	27	1	2	3	7	71.23	$2,203,368

Best finish for 2005: Win at the EDS Byron Nelson Championship

Year	Starts	Rounds Played	Cuts Made	Wins	Top-5s	Top-10s	Top-25s	Scoring Average	Money
2006	33	101	17	0	3	3	10	71.50	$1,223,326

Best finish for 2006: T-4th at the 84 Lumber Classic

Year	Starts	Rounds Played	Cuts Made	Wins	Top-5s	Top-10s	Top-25s	Scoring Average	Money
2007	33	102	19	0	0	1	8	71.32	$761,234

Best finish for 2007: T-9th at the AT&T Pebble Beach National Pro-Am

Year	Starts	Rounds Played	Cuts Made	Wins	Top-5s	Top-10s	Top-25s	Scoring Average	Money
2008	25	68	10	0	0	1	1	71.71	$248,207

Best finish for 2008: T-10th at the Puerto Rico Open

Period Totals	Starts	Rounds Played	Cuts Made	Wins	Top-5s	Top-10s	Top-25s	Scoring Average	Money
	191	579	103	1	8	12	39	71.49	$6,193,672

Paul Purtzer

Year	Starts	Rounds Played	Cuts Made	Wins	Top-5s	Top-10s	Top-25s	Scoring Average	Money
1971	1	2	0	0	0	0	0	77.00	
1972	2	6	1	0	0	0	0	74.17	

Best finish for 1972: T-60th at the Phoenix Open

Year	Starts	Rounds Played	Cuts Made	Wins	Top-5s	Top-10s	Top-25s	Scoring Average	Money
1973	20	54	5	0	0	0	1	74.04	$3,210

Best finish for 1973: T-20th at the San Antonio Texas Open

Year	Starts	Rounds Played	Cuts Made	Wins	Top-5s	Top-10s	Top-25s	Scoring Average	Money
1974	9	24	3	0	0	0	0	73.71	$1,768

Best finish for 1974: T-28th at the Phoenix Open

Year	Starts	Rounds Played	Cuts Made	Wins	Top-5s	Top-10s	Top-25s	Scoring Average	Money
1975	5	10	0	0	0	0	0	75.60	
1976	3	8	1	0	0	0	0	76.13	

Best finish for 1976: T-75th at the Southern Open

Year	Starts	Rounds Played	Cuts Made	Wins	Top-5s	Top-10s	Top-25s	Scoring Average	Money
1977	11	30	4	0	0	0	0	73.37	$1,454

Best finish for 1977: T-38th at the Tallahassee Open

Year	Starts	Rounds Played	Cuts Made	Wins	Top-5s	Top-10s	Top-25s	Scoring Average	Money
1978	3	10	2	0	0	0	0	73.20	$1,460

Best finish for 1978: T-53rd at the Phoenix Open

Year	Starts	Rounds Played	Cuts Made	Wins	Top-5s	Top-10s	Top-25s	Scoring Average	Money
1979	4	8	0	0	0	0	0	73.75	$350
1980	4	8	0	0	0	0	0	76.38	$600
1981	1	2	0	0	0	0	0	71.50	
1982	1	2	0	0	0	0	0	74.50	
1983	2	4	0	0	0	0	0	74.25	
1985	1	2	0	0	0	0	0	75.00	
1988	1	2	0	0	0	0	0	77.50	
Period Totals	Starts	Rounds Played	Cuts Made	Wins	Top-5s	Top-10s	Top-25s	Scoring Average	Money
	68	172	16	0	0	0	1	74.18	$8,842

Tom Purtzer

Year	Starts	Rounds Played	Cuts Made	Wins	Top-5s	Top-10s	Top-25s	Scoring Average	Money
1972	1	2	0	0	0	0	0	74.50	
1975	9	28	5	0	0	0	0	72.89	$2,093

Best finish for 1975: T-28th at the San Antonio Texas Open

Year	Starts	Rounds Played	Cuts Made	Wins	Top-5s	Top-10s	Top-25s	Scoring Average	Money
1976	21	66	12	0	1	1	6	72.50	$23,445

Best finish for 1976: T-3rd at the Pensacola Open

Year	Starts	Rounds Played	Cuts Made	Wins	Top-5s	Top-10s	Top-25s	Scoring Average	Money
1977	30	89	13	1	3	4	7	72.89	$81,087

Best finish for 1977: Win at the Glen CampbellLos Angeles Open

Year	Starts	Rounds Played	Cuts Made	Wins	Top-5s	Top-10s	Top-25s	Scoring Average	Money
1978	31	112	24	0	1	6	12	72.00	$58,618

Best finish for 1978: T-4th at the Danny Thomas Memphis Classic

Year	Starts	Rounds Played	Cuts Made	Wins	Top-5s	Top-10s	Top-25s	Scoring Average	Money
1979	30	109	24	0	1	5	16	71.39	$113,620

Best finish for 1979: 2nd at the B.C. Open

Year	Starts	Rounds Played	Cuts Made	Wins	Top-5s	Top-10s	Top-25s	Scoring Average	Money
1980	30	93	18	0	4	5	10	71.46	$119,285

Best finish for 1980: T-2nd at the Bob Hope Chrysler Classic & Danny Thomas Memphis Classic

Year	Starts	Rounds Played	Cuts Made	Wins	Top-5s	Top-10s	Top-25s	Scoring Average	Money
1981	31	106	25	0	3	7	14	71.22	$130,132

Best finish for 1981: T-3rd at the Byron Nelson Golf Classic, Memorial Tournament & Anheuser-Busch Golf Classic

Year	Starts	Rounds Played	Cuts Made	Wins	Top-5s	Top-10s	Top-25s	Scoring Average	Money
1982	30	112	26	0	2	5	16	71.17	$119,418

Best finish for 1982: T-4th at the British Open

Year	Starts	Rounds Played	Cuts Made	Wins	Top-5s	Top-10s	Top-25s	Scoring Average	Money
1983	28	98	20	0	1	4	12	71.70	$103,736

Best finish for 1983: T-4th at the Byron Nelson Golf Classic

Year	Starts	Rounds Played	Cuts Made	Wins	Top-5s	Top-10s	Top-25s	Scoring Average	Money
1984	29	96	20	1	1	2	10	72.14	$165,244

Best finish for 1984: Win at the Phoenix Open

Year	Starts	Rounds Played	Cuts Made	Wins	Top-5s	Top-10s	Top-25s	Scoring Average	Money
1985	26	91	18	0	0	0	3	71.88	$51,479

Best finish for 1985: T-12th at the Southwest Golf Classic

Year	Starts	Rounds Played	Cuts Made	Wins	Top-5s	Top-10s	Top-25s	Scoring Average	Money
1986	31	101	25	0	1	10	17	70.72	$217,280

Best finish for 1986: T-4th at the Greater Milwaukee Open

Year	Starts	Rounds Played	Cuts Made	Wins	Top-5s	Top-10s	Top-25s	Scoring Average	Money
1987	26	93	21	0	0	1	8	71.40	$123,206

Best finish for 1987: T-9th at the Tournament Players Championship

Year	Starts	Rounds Played	Cuts Made	Wins	Top-5s	Top-10s	Top-25s	Scoring Average	Money
1988	24	80	17	1	1	3	7	70.90	$198,740

Best finish for 1988: Win at the Gatlin Brothers - Southwest Golf Classic

1989	24	78	15	0	1	2	7	71.63	$154,868

Best finish for 1989: T-5th at the Greater Milwaukee Open

1990	24	77	15	0	2	3	10	71.36	$285,176

Best finish for 1990: T-3rd at the Players Championship

1991	25	88	19	2	3	4	11	70.80	$750,568

Best finish for 1991: Win at the Southwestern Bell Colonial & NEC World Series of Golf

1992	25	83	18	0	0	1	7	71.41	$184,224

Best finish for 1992: T-7th at the Centel Western Open

1993	21	59	11	0	0	1	5	71.95	$112,986

Best finish for 1993: T-8th at the Walt Disney World/Oldsmobile Classic

1994	22	68	13	0	1	2	7	70.94	$187,307

Best finish for 1994: T-3rd at the Greater Milwaukee Open

1995	19	58	11	0	0	0	4	70.66	$120,717

Best finish for 1995: T-12th at the Northern Telecom Open & Phoenix Open

1996	23	83	18	0	2	3	8	70.52	$397,744

Best finish for 1996: 2nd at the Michelob Championship at Kingsmill

1997	23	66	11	0	1	1	3	71.91	$161,393

Best finish for 1997: T-4th at the Nissan Open

1998	16	35	3	0	1	1	1	72.60	$97,589

Best finish for 1998: T-4th at the Walt Disney World/Oldsmobile Classic

1999	21	52	6	0	0	0	0	73.15	$30,782

Best finish for 1999: T-49th at the Phoenix Open

2000	21	56	8	0	0	0	2	71.71	$170,683

Best finish for 2000: T-12th at the SEI Pennsylvania Classic

2001	16	38	3	0	0	0	0	72.24	$21,904

Best finish for 2001: T-47th at the Greater Milwaukee Open

2005	1	4	1	0	0	0	1	68.50	$58,240

Best finish for 2005: T-21st at the Bank of America Colonial

Period Totals	Starts	Rounds Played	Cuts Made	Wins	Top-5s	Top-10s	Top-25s	Scoring Average	Money
	658	2121	420	5	30	71	204	71.57	$4,241,563

Michael Putnam

Year	Starts	Rounds Played	Cuts Made	Wins	Top-5s	Top-10s	Top-25s	Scoring Average	Money
2005	4	14	3	0	1	1	2	69.29	$229,733

Best finish for 2005: T-4th at the Buick Championship

2007	29	96	19	0	0	0	2	71.55	$426,675

Best finish for 2007: T-16th at the Buick Invitational

2008	1	2	0	0	0	0	0	75.00	

Period Totals	Starts	Rounds Played	Cuts Made	Wins	Top-5s	Top-10s	Top-25s	Scoring Average	Money
	34	112	22	0	1	1	4	71.33	$656,409

Brett Quigley

Year	Starts	Rounds Played	Cuts Made	Wins	Top-5s	Top-10s	Top-25s	Scoring Average	Money
1991	2	6	1	0	0	0	0	71.83	$1,990

Best finish for 1991: T-70th at the New England Classic

1992	1	2	0	0	0	0	0	73.50	
1997	34	111	21	0	0	0	4	71.42	$172,023

Best finish for 1997: T-12th at the Greater Vancouver Open

1998	29	88	16	0	1	2	5	71.23	$224,076

Best finish for 1998: T-4th at the United Airlines Hawaiian Open

1999	22	60	12	0	0	2	3	71.58	$209,318

Best finish for 1999: T-10th at the AT&T Pebble Beach National Pro-Am & FedEx St. Jude Classic

2000	21	63	10	0	0	1	4	71.08	$248,037

Best finish for 2000: T-5th at the B.C. Open

2001	21	63	13	0	3	6	8	70.14	$959,934

Best finish for 2001: T-2nd at the Greater Greensboro Chrysler Classic

2002	32	92	15	0	1	1	5	71.55	$404,422

Best finish for 2002: T-4th at the Honda Classic

2003	27	88	19	0	1	2	7	70.58	$786,294

Best finish for 2003: 4th at the Greater Milwaukee Open

2004	31	98	20	0	1	1	5	71.12	$836,380

Best finish for 2004: T-2nd at the U.S. Bank Championship in Milwaukee

2005	31	92	18	0	2	2	9	70.85	$1,000,155

Best finish for 2005: T-5th at the Sony Open in Hawaii & Cialis Western Open

2006	33	105	22	0	5	10	15	70.31	$2,625,387

Best finish for 2006: T-3rd at the Barclays Classic & 84 Lumber Classic

2007	25	78	16	0	0	1	5	72.03	$724,858

Best finish for 2007: T-10th at the Wachovia Championship

2008	25	80	15	0	0	2	7	71.28	$878,216

Best finish for 2008: T-6th at The Players

Period Totals	Starts	Rounds Played	Cuts Made	Wins	Top-5s	Top-10s	Top-25s	Scoring Average	Money
	334	1026	198	0	15	30	77	71.10	$9,071,088

Dana Quigley

Year	Starts	Rounds Played	Cuts Made	Wins	Top-5s	Top-10s	Top-25s	Scoring Average	Money
1973	1	2	0	0	0	0	0	76.00	
1978	16	43	5	0	0	0	0	73.51	$2,615
Best finish for 1978: T-28th at the Buick Goodwrench Open									
1979	25	76	13	0	0	1	3	73.29	$17,486
Best finish for 1979: T-8th at the Buick Goodwrench Open									
1980	27	84	17	0	1	3	5	72.15	$46,070
Best finish for 1980: T-2nd at the World Disney World National Team Championship									
1981	23	67	12	0	0	1	2	72.37	$14,005
Best finish for 1981: T-10th at the Tallahassee Open									
1982	12	33	3	0	0	1	1	71.94	$11,798
Best finish for 1982: T-9th at the Sammy Davis, Jr. - Greater Hartford Open									
1983	1	4	1	0	0	0	1	70.00	$5,425
Best finish for 1983: T-15th at the Bank of Boston Classic									
1984	1	2	0	0	0	0	0	76.00	
1986	1	2	0	0	0	0	0	74.00	
1987	1	2	0	0	0	0	0	79.00	$1,000
1988	1	2	0	0	0	0	0	76.50	$1,000
1990	2	4	0	0	0	0	0	77.50	$1,000
1991	1	4	1	0	0	0	0	71.00	$2,140
Best finish for 1991: T-62nd at the New England Classic									
1992	1	2	0	0	0	0	0	73.50	
1993	2	6	1	0	0	0	0	71.83	$3,553
Best finish for 1993: T-51st at the New England Classic									
1994	1	4	1	0	0	0	0	72.25	$1,920
Best finish for 1994: 74th at the New England Classic									
1995	3	6	0	0	0	0	0	72.83	$2,200
1996	1	2	0	0	0	0	0	71.00	
Period Totals	Starts	Rounds Played	Cuts Made	Wins	Top-5s	Top-10s	Top-25s	Scoring Average	Money
	120	345	54	0	1	6	12	72.75	$110,212

Fran Quinn

Year	Starts	Rounds Played	Cuts Made	Wins	Top-5s	Top-10s	Top-25s	Scoring Average	Money
1988	2	4	0	0	0	0	0	75.25	
1989	1	2	0	0	0	0	0	73.00	
1990	2	8	2	0	0	0	1	70.00	$16,824
Best finish for 1990: T-12th at the Bank of Boston Classic									
1991	2	6	1	0	0	0	0	72.33	$2,569
Best finish for 1991: T-47th at the New England Classic									
1992	25	61	6	0	0	0	1	73.30	$37,155
Best finish for 1992: T-12th at the Canadian Open									
1993	4	8	0	0	0	0	0	73.88	
1994	4	12	2	0	0	1	1	71.50	$30,365
Best finish for 1994: T-9th at the New England Classic									
1996	3	8	1	0	0	0	0	72.50	$3,616
Best finish for 1996: T-58th at the CVS Charity Classic									
1997	1	2	0	0	0	0	0	72.50	
1998	1	4	1	0	0	0	0	70.50	$3,463
Best finish for 1998: T-52nd at the CVS Charity Classic									
1999	1	2	0	0	0	0	0	75.00	
2008	1	2	0	0	0	0	0	69.50	
Period Totals	Starts	Rounds Played	Cuts Made	Wins	Top-5s	Top-10s	Top-25s	Scoring Average	Money
	47	119	13	0	0	1	3	72.75	$93,992

Jeff Quinney

Year	Starts	Rounds Played	Cuts Made	Wins	Top-5s	Top-10s	Top-25s	Scoring Average	Money
2000	1	2	0	0	0	0	0	71.50	
2001	7	17	1	0	0	0	0	73.00	$11,400
Best finish for 2001: T-41st at the Texas Open at LaCantera									
2002	5	10	2	0	0	0	0	71.90	$40,310
Best finish for 2002: 29th at The International presented by Qwest									
2003	2	7	1	0	0	0	0	73.29	$14,550
Best finish for 2003: T-34th at the Chrysler Classic of Tucson									
2005	1	3	0	0	0	0	0	73.67	
2007	29	95	18	0	2	5	9	71.23	$1,614,556
Best finish for 2007: 3rd at the FBR Open									
2008	28	87	16	0	2	3	6	71.39	$1,999,371
Best finish for 2008: 2nd at the Northern Trust Open									
Period Totals	Starts	Rounds Played	Cuts Made	Wins	Top-5s	Top-10s	Top-25s	Scoring Average	Money
	73	221	38	0	4	8	15	71.56	$3,680,187

Sammy Rachels

Year	Starts	Rounds Played	Cuts Made	Wins	Top-5s	Top-10s	Top-25s	Scoring Average	Money
1975	13	44	9	0	0	0	2	72.25	$8,534

Best finish for 1975: T-12th at the B.C. Open

| 1976 | 17 | 49 | 10 | 0 | 0 | 0 | 1 | 72.76 | $4,900 |

Best finish for 1976: T-18th at the Southern Open

| 1977 | 4 | 14 | 3 | 0 | 0 | 0 | 1 | 71.14 | $6,057 |

Best finish for 1977: T-11th at the Pleasant Valley Classic

| 1978 | 7 | 17 | 2 | 0 | 0 | 1 | 2 | 72.71 | $5,865 |

Best finish for 1978: T-9th at the Florida Citrus Open Invitational

| 1979 | 13 | 33 | 5 | 0 | 1 | 1 | 1 | 72.61 | $17,095 |

Best finish for 1979: T-3rd at the Houston Open

| 1980 | 16 | 40 | 6 | 0 | 0 | 1 | 2 | 72.78 | $13,011 |

Best finish for 1980: T-9th at the Atlanta Classic

| 1981 | 15 | 38 | 5 | 0 | 0 | 2 | 5 | 72.21 | $19,880 |

Best finish for 1981: T-6th at the U.S. Open

| 1982 | 3 | 7 | 1 | 0 | 0 | 0 | 0 | 72.71 | $621 |

Best finish for 1982: T-48th at the Southern Open

| 1983 | 15 | 43 | 8 | 0 | 2 | 4 | 5 | 71.00 | $75,238 |

Best finish for 1983: T-2nd at the Danny Thomas Memphis Classic & Bank of Boston Classic

| 1984 | 21 | 67 | 13 | 0 | 1 | 2 | 7 | 71.58 | $64,119 |

Best finish for 1984: 5th at the Bay Hill Classic

| 1985 | 16 | 35 | 2 | 0 | 0 | 0 | 1 | 72.71 | $4,774 |

Best finish for 1985: T-16th at the Lite Quad Cities Open

| 1989 | 1 | 2 | 0 | 0 | 0 | 0 | 0 | 75.00 | $1,000 |
| 1990 | 1 | 4 | 1 | 0 | 0 | 0 | 0 | 74.75 | $3,700 |

Best finish for 1990: T-45th at the PGA Championship

1993	1	2	1	0	0	0	0	72.50	$1,200
1995	2	4	0	0	0	0	0	75.00	
Period Totals	Starts	Rounds Played	Cuts Made	Wins	Top-5s	Top-10s	Top-25s	Scoring Average	Money
	145	399	66	0	4	11	27	72.24	$225,995

Ronan Rafferty

Year	Starts	Rounds Played	Cuts Made	Wins	Top-5s	Top-10s	Top-25s	Scoring Average	Money
1980	1	2	0	0	0	0	0	75.50	$540
1983	1	4	1	0	0	0	0	72.75	$1,088

Best finish for 1983: 61st at the British Open

| 1984 | 1 | 4 | 1 | 0 | 0 | 1 | 1 | 71.00 | $14,643 |

Best finish for 1984: T-9th at the British Open

| 1985 | 1 | 4 | 1 | 0 | 0 | 0 | 0 | 73.25 | $3,480 |

Best finish for 1985: T-44th at the British Open

| 1986 | 1 | 4 | 1 | 0 | 0 | 0 | 1 | 73.50 | $7,533 |

Best finish for 1986: T-21st at the British Open

| 1987 | 1 | 2 | 0 | 0 | 0 | 0 | 0 | 76.50 | $640 |
| 1988 | 2 | 4 | 1 | 0 | 0 | 0 | 0 | 73.25 | $5,874 |

Best finish for 1988: T-38th at the British Open

| 1989 | 2 | 8 | 2 | 0 | 0 | 0 | 1 | 72.88 | $14,047 |

Best finish for 1989: T-24th at the NEC World Series of Golf

| 1990 | 7 | 21 | 6 | 0 | 0 | 0 | 1 | 72.86 | $44,306 |

Best finish for 1990: T-14th at the Masters

| 1991 | 2 | 4 | 0 | 0 | 0 | 0 | 0 | 77.00 | $2,500 |
| 1992 | 7 | 22 | 4 | 0 | 0 | 0 | 0 | 72.59 | $23,035 |

Best finish for 1992: T-30th at the Kmart Greater Greensboro Open

| 1994 | 1 | 4 | 1 | 0 | 0 | 0 | 1 | 69.00 | $31,320 |

Best finish for 1994: T-11th at the British Open

1995	1	2	0	0	0	0	0	76.50	$1,037
Period Totals	Starts	Rounds Played	Cuts Made	Wins	Top-5s	Top-10s	Top-25s	Scoring Average	Money
	28	85	18	0	0	1	5	73.01	$150,041

Dave Ragan

Year	Starts	Rounds Played	Cuts Made	Wins	Top-5s	Top-10s	Top-25s	Scoring Average	Money
1958	27	97	21	0	1	7	10	72.31	$8,189

Best finish for 1958: T-4th at the Houston Open

| 1959 | 22 | 87 | 21 | 1 | 5 | 7 | 13 | 71.07 | $13,490 |

Best finish for 1959: Win at the Eastern Open Invitational

| 1960 | 24 | 97 | 23 | 0 | 1 | 2 | 18 | 71.71 | $13,952 |

Best finish for 1960: T-2nd at the Los Angeles Open Invitational

| 1961 | 26 | 105 | 25 | 0 | 6 | 10 | 19 | 70.53 | $21,641 |

Best finish for 1961: T-2nd at the Bing Crosby National

| 1962 | 32 | 128 | 27 | 2 | 9 | 14 | 26 | 70.83 | $37,327 |

Best finish for 1962: Win at the Beaumont Open Invitational & West Palm Beach Open Invitational

Year	Starts	Rounds Played	Cuts Made	Wins	Top-5s	Top-10s	Top-25s	Scoring Average	Money
1963	20	81	20	0	2	3	10	71.75	$19,296

Best finish for 1963: 2nd at the PGA Championship

| 1964 | 30 | 102 | 19 | 0 | 1 | 3 | 6 | 72.70 | $10,066 |

Best finish for 1964: T-4th at the St. Petersburg Open

| 1965 | 27 | 98 | 21 | 0 | 0 | 1 | 2 | 72.91 | $8,497 |

Best finish for 1965: 8th at the Cajun Classic

| 1966 | 27 | 101 | 23 | 0 | 2 | 3 | 11 | 72.02 | $23,420 |

Best finish for 1966: T-3rd at the Greater Greensboro Open Invitational

| 1967 | 24 | 65 | 8 | 0 | 0 | 0 | 1 | 74.37 | $1,529 |

Best finish for 1967: T-23rd at the Oklahoma City Open

| 1968 | 13 | 41 | 7 | 0 | 0 | 0 | 1 | 72.83 | $3,822 |

Best finish for 1968: T-12th at the Florida Citrus Open Invitational

| 1969 | 17 | 57 | 11 | 0 | 1 | 1 | 2 | 73.40 | $5,694 |

Best finish for 1969: 4th at the Alameda County Open

| 1970 | 14 | 35 | 3 | 0 | 0 | 0 | 2 | 73.34 | $2,374 |

Best finish for 1970: T-17th at the Greater Milwaukee Open

1971	1	2	0	0	0	0	0	72.50	
1982	1	2	0	0	0	0	0	79.00	$650
1983	2	4	0	0	0	0	0	74.50	
Period Totals	Starts	Rounds Played	Cuts Made	Wins	Top-5s	Top-10s	Top-25s	Scoring Average	Money
	307	1102	229	3	28	51	121	72.09	$169,947

PGA Tour career totals from 1956 to 1983

	Starts	Rounds Played	Cuts Made	Wins	Top-5s	Top-10s	Top-25s	Scoring Average	Money
	325	1173	247	3	28	51	125	N/A	$170,851

Ross Randall

Year	Starts	Rounds Played	Cuts Made	Wins	Top-5s	Top-10s	Top-25s	Scoring Average	Money
1965	1	2	0	0	0	0	0	74.00	
1967	1	2	0	0	0	0	0	76.50	
1968	1	2	0	0	0	0	0	78.50	
1969	18	45	4	0	0	0	1	74.09	$1,796

Best finish for 1969: T-16th at the Alameda County Open

| 1970 | 23 | 63 | 9 | 0 | 0 | 0 | 1 | 73.65 | $3,898 |

Best finish for 1970: T-20th at the San Antonio Texas Open

| 1971 | 25 | 71 | 10 | 0 | 0 | 0 | 3 | 72.94 | $6,622 |

Best finish for 1971: T-18th at the Greater Milwaukee Open

| 1972 | 23 | 63 | 8 | 0 | 0 | 0 | 2 | 73.86 | $5,149 |

Best finish for 1972: T-12th at the Greater New Orleans Open

| 1973 | 26 | 74 | 10 | 0 | 0 | 0 | 1 | 73.19 | $6,880 |

Best finish for 1973: T-11th at the Shrine-Robinson Golf Classic

| 1974 | 27 | 80 | 13 | 0 | 0 | 0 | 0 | 73.44 | $4,869 |

Best finish for 1974: T-41st at the Tallahassee Open

| 1975 | 19 | 54 | 8 | 0 | 0 | 0 | 1 | 73.54 | $2,914 |

Best finish for 1975: T-25th at the Southern Open

| 1976 | 4 | 12 | 2 | 0 | 0 | 0 | 1 | 72.83 | $1,175 |

Best finish for 1976: T-22nd at the Southern Open

1977	1	2	0	0	0	0	0	75.00	
1978	2	5	0	0	0	0	0	76.00	
1982	1	2	0	0	0	0	0	77.00	$650
1985	1	2	0	0	0	0	0	83.00	$1,000
Period Totals	Starts	Rounds Played	Cuts Made	Wins	Top-5s	Top-10s	Top-25s	Scoring Average	Money
	173	479	64	0	0	0	10	73.59	$34,953

Sam Randolph

Year	Starts	Rounds Played	Cuts Made	Wins	Top-5s	Top-10s	Top-25s	Scoring Average	Money
1982	1	4	1	0	0	0	0	72.50	

Best finish for 1982: T-61st at the Glen CampbellLos Angeles Open

| 1985 | 2 | 6 | 1 | 0 | 0 | 0 | 1 | 72.83 | |

Best finish for 1985: T-18th at the Masters

| 1986 | 8 | 26 | 7 | 0 | 0 | 0 | 1 | 72.54 | $15,201 |

Best finish for 1986: T-25th at the International

| 1987 | 23 | 77 | 18 | 1 | 2 | 2 | 6 | 71.79 | $180,378 |

Best finish for 1987: Win at the Bank of Boston Classic

| 1988 | 26 | 79 | 14 | 0 | 1 | 1 | 7 | 72.08 | $119,633 |

Best finish for 1988: 3rd at the Hardee's Golf Classic

| 1989 | 21 | 54 | 6 | 0 | 0 | 1 | 1 | 72.39 | $35,561 |

Best finish for 1989: T-6th at the Shearson Lehman Hutton Open

| 1990 | 8 | 27 | 5 | 0 | 0 | 0 | 1 | 71.07 | $27,529 |

Best finish for 1990: T-12th at the Bank of Boston Classic

| 1991 | 27 | 69 | 9 | 0 | 0 | 1 | 4 | 72.04 | $69,668 |

Best finish for 1991: T-6th at the Nissan Los Angeles Open

| 1992 | 14 | 44 | 8 | 0 | 0 | 0 | 3 | 71.41 | $49,085 |

Best finish for 1992: T-15th at the Buick Invitational of California

| 1993 | 4 | 10 | 1 | 0 | 0 | 0 | 0 | 72.30 | $4,460 |

Best finish for 1993: T-63rd at the New England Classic

| 1994 | 3 | 8 | 1 | 0 | 0 | 0 | 0 | 72.63 | $4,513 |

Best finish for 1994: T-39th at the New England Classic

| 1995 | 1 | 4 | 1 | 0 | 0 | 0 | 0 | 69.50 | $4,956 |

Best finish for 1995: T-33rd at the Ideon Classic

| 1996 | 7 | 25 | 6 | 0 | 0 | 0 | 1 | 71.08 | $22,166 |

Best finish for 1996: T-23rd at the CVS Charity Classic

| 1997 | 3 | 8 | 1 | 0 | 0 | 0 | 0 | 71.63 | $2,484 |

Best finish for 1997: T-65th at the CVS Charity Classic

| 1998 | 5 | 13 | 2 | 0 | 0 | 0 | 1 | 70.92 | $25,779 |

Best finish for 1998: T-25th at the AT&T Pebble Beach Pro-Am

| 1999 | 1 | 3 | 0 | 0 | 0 | 0 | 0 | 74.33 | |
| 2000 | 1 | 4 | 1 | 0 | 0 | 0 | 0 | 70.50 | $7,200 |

Best finish for 2000: T-42nd at the B.C. Open

| 2001 | 5 | 15 | 2 | 0 | 0 | 0 | 0 | 71.27 | $14,988 |

Best finish for 2001: T-46th at the B.C. Open

2002	6	13	0	0	0	0	0	73.85	
2003	2	4	0	0	0	0	0	75.25	
2004	1	2	0	0	0	0	0	74.00	
2006	1	2	0	0	0	0	0	76.00	
Period Totals	Starts	Rounds Played	Cuts Made	Wins	Top-5s	Top-10s	Top-25s	Scoring Average	Money
	170	497	84	1	3	5	26	71.96	$583,602

Henry Ransom

Year	Starts	Rounds Played	Cuts Made	Wins	Top-5s	Top-10s	Top-25s	Scoring Average	Money
1958	12	42	9	0	0	1	1	72.43	$2,525

Best finish for 1958: T-7th at the Pepsi Open

| 1959 | 7 | 28 | 7 | 0 | 1 | 1 | 2 | 71.68 | $2,876 |

Best finish for 1959: T-3rd at the Eastern Open Invitational

| 1960 | 5 | 20 | 5 | 0 | 0 | 0 | 0 | 72.45 | $719 |

Best finish for 1960: T-29th at the Cajun Classic Open Invitational

| 1961 | 5 | 18 | 4 | 0 | 0 | 2 | 2 | 72.28 | $2,655 |

Best finish for 1961: T-6th at the Houston Classic

| 1962 | 4 | 15 | 4 | 0 | 0 | 0 | 1 | 73.00 | $1,231 |

Best finish for 1962: T-21st at the Houston Classic

| 1963 | 2 | 8 | 2 | 0 | 0 | 0 | 1 | 71.25 | $675 |

Best finish for 1963: T-19th at the Texas Open Invitational

| 1964 | 2 | 8 | 2 | 0 | 0 | 0 | 0 | 72.00 | $475 |

Best finish for 1964: T-31st at the Houston Classic

| 1965 | 2 | 6 | 1 | 0 | 0 | 0 | 0 | 71.17 | |

Best finish for 1965: T-44th at the Texas Open

1966	3	6	0	0	0	0	0	74.50	
1975	1	2	0	0	0	0	0	78.50	
Period Totals	Starts	Rounds Played	Cuts Made	Wins	Top-5s	Top-10s	Top-25s	Scoring Average	Money
	43	153	34	0	1	4	7	72.36	$11,155

PGA Tour career totals from 1936 to 1975

	Starts	Rounds Played	Cuts Made	Wins	Top-5s	Top-10s	Top-25s	Scoring Average	Money
	225	N/A	N/A	4	N/A	65	218	N/A	N/A

Joey Rassett

Year	Starts	Rounds Played	Cuts Made	Wins	Top-5s	Top-10s	Top-25s	Scoring Average	Money
1979	1	4	1	0	0	0	0	76.00	

Best finish for 1979: T-53rd at the U.S. Open

| 1980 | 2 | 4 | 0 | 0 | 0 | 0 | 0 | 75.00 | $1,500 |
| 1981 | 5 | 16 | 3 | 0 | 0 | 0 | 2 | 72.00 | $7,366 |

Best finish for 1981: T-13th at the Hall of Fame Tournament

| 1982 | 3 | 8 | 0 | 0 | 0 | 0 | 0 | 74.75 | $680 |
| 1983 | 33 | 102 | 16 | 0 | 0 | 0 | 3 | 72.39 | $30,797 |

Best finish for 1983: T-19th at the Greater Greensboro Open

| 1984 | 14 | 37 | 6 | 0 | 0 | 0 | 0 | 73.00 | $11,221 |

Best finish for 1984: T-27th at the Hawaiian Open

| 1985 | 2 | 8 | 2 | 0 | 0 | 0 | 0 | 73.38 | $3,451 |

Best finish for 1985: T-41st at the Bing Crosby Pro-Am

| 1987 | 2 | 6 | 1 | 0 | 0 | 0 | 0 | 71.83 | $2,915 |

Best finish for 1987: T-32nd at the Southwest Golf Classic

| 1988 | 27 | 72 | 9 | 0 | 0 | 0 | 2 | 72.11 | $27,555 |

Best finish for 1988: T-16th at the Provident Classic

| 1993 | 1 | 2 | 0 | 0 | 0 | 0 | 0 | 75.00 | |

Year	Starts	Rounds Played	Cuts Made	Wins	Top-5s	Top-10s	Top-25s	Scoring Average	Money
1994	24	72	12	0	0	0	2	71.88	$62,826

Best finish for 1994: T-17th at the B.C. Open

1995	22	55	5	0	0	0	1	72.20	$34,132

Best finish for 1995: T-11th at the Anheuser-Busch Golf Classic

Period Totals	Starts	Rounds Played	Cuts Made	Wins	Top-5s	Top-10s	Top-25s	Scoring Average	Money
	136	386	55	0	0	0	10	72.40	$182,442

Charles Raulerson

Year	Starts	Rounds Played	Cuts Made	Wins	Top-5s	Top-10s	Top-25s	Scoring Average	Money
1994	24	62	9	0	0	0	0	72.63	$33,919

Best finish for 1994: T-29th at the AT&T Pebble Beach Pro-Am & Greater Milwaukee Open

1995	1	1	0	0	0	0	0	77.00	
1996	1	1	0	0	0	0	0	83.00	$1,000
1999	32	102	20	0	0	2	5	71.52	$326,893

Best finish for 1999: 7th at the Air Canada Championship

2000	32	98	17	0	0	0	2	71.86	$210,093

Best finish for 2000: T-11th at the Shell Houston Open

2001	2	4	0	0	0	0	0	74.00	$1,000
2002	1	2	0	0	0	0	0	79.50	$1,000

Period Totals	Starts	Rounds Played	Cuts Made	Wins	Top-5s	Top-10s	Top-25s	Scoring Average	Money
	93	270	46	0	0	2	7	72.06	$573,905

Dick Rautmann

Year	Starts	Rounds Played	Cuts Made	Wins	Top-5s	Top-10s	Top-25s	Scoring Average	Money
1969	10	26	3	0	0	0	0	73.96	$1,206

Best finish for 1969: T-31st at the Canadian Open

1970	10	26	2	0	0	0	0	73.54	$459

Best finish for 1970: T-53rd at the Canadian Open

1974	1	3	0	0	0	0	0	77.67	
1975	2	7	1	0	0	0	0	77.43	$267

Best finish for 1975: T-68th at the Kaiser International Open

1976	2	4	3	0	0	0	0	77.75	
1979	2	4	0	0	0	0	0	79.25	

Period Totals	Starts	Rounds Played	Cuts Made	Wins	Top-5s	Top-10s	Top-25s	Scoring Average	Money
	27	70	9	0	0	0	0	74.83	$1,932

D-Lee Raymond

Year	Starts	Rounds Played	Cuts Made	Wins	Top-5s	Top-10s	Top-25s	Scoring Average	Money
1959	1	2	0	0	0	0	0	79.00	
1960	6	22	3	0	0	0	3	72.45	$980

Best finish for 1960: T-11th at the Sam Snead Festival

1961	3	12	3	0	0	0	3	70.83	$1,618

Best finish for 1961: T-20th at the Buick Open Invitational

1962	1	2	0	0	0	0	0	79.00	
1964	17	43	7	0	0	0	1	73.40	$872

Best finish for 1964: T-15th at the Greater Hartford Open

1965	11	34	4	0	0	0	1	73.24	$892

Best finish for 1965: T-24th at the Bing Crosby Pro-Am

1966	2	6	1	0	0	0	0	75.00	$096

Best finish for 1966: T-47th at the Bing Crosby National Professional-Amateur

Period Totals	Starts	Rounds Played	Cuts Made	Wins	Top-5s	Top-10s	Top-25s	Scoring Average	Money
	41	121	18	0	0	0	8	73.19	$4,457

Mike Reasor

Year	Starts	Rounds Played	Cuts Made	Wins	Top-5s	Top-10s	Top-25s	Scoring Average	Money
1966	1	4	1	0	0	0	0	72.00	

Best finish for 1966: T-46th at the Portland Open Invitational

1969	17	48	8	0	1	1	2	73.48	$3,139

Best finish for 1969: 4th at the West End Classic

1970	31	88	12	0	0	0	1	73.19	$6,216

Best finish for 1970: T-13th at the Canadian Open

1971	24	68	9	0	1	1	1	73.49	$8,337

Best finish for 1971: T-5th at the Massachusetts Classic

1972	29	85	13	0	0	1	3	72.87	$14,496

Best finish for 1972: T-6th at the Greater New Orleans Open

1973	28	88	14	0	0	0	2	73.06	$9,040

Best finish for 1973: T-13th at the Walt Disney World Open

1974	23	70	12	0	1	1	2	74.56	$22,603

Best finish for 1974: T-5th at the Kaiser International Open

1975	26	79	14	0	0	1	4	72.84	$11,446

Best finish for 1975: T-9th at the Ed McMahon Quad City Open

1976	21	55	6	0	0	0	3	73.11	$5,977

Best finish for 1976: T-15th at the Bob Hope Chrysler Classic & Tallahassee Open

Year	Starts	Rounds Played	Cuts Made	Wins	Top-5s	Top-10s	Top-25s	Scoring Average	Money
1977	23	66	9	0	0	0	1	73.80	$6,226

Best finish for 1977: T-22nd at the Glen CampbellLos Angeles Open

| 1978 | 20 | 56 | 7 | 0 | 0 | 0 | 2 | 73.18 | $9,328 |

Best finish for 1978: T-12th at the Glen CampbellLos Angeles Open

1979	12	26	0	0	0	0	0	76.42	
1990	1	2	0	0	0	0	0	76.00	
Period Totals	Starts	Rounds Played	Cuts Made	Wins	Top-5s	Top-10s	Top-25s	Scoring Average	Money
	256	735	105	0	3	5	21	73.44	$96,808

Chez Reavie

Year	Starts	Rounds Played	Cuts Made	Wins	Top-5s	Top-10s	Top-25s	Scoring Average	Money
2002	1	2	0	0	0	0	0	80.00	
2003	1	2	0	0	0	0	0	76.50	
2004	2	8	2	0	0	0	0	74.25	$7,840

Best finish for 2004: T-62nd at the U.S. Open

2005	1	3	0	0	0	0	0	74.33	
2006	1	2	0	0	0	0	0	76.00	
2008	30	102	21	1	2	2	2	71.03	$1,444,102

Best finish for 2008: Win at the RBC Canadian Open

| Period Totals | Starts | Rounds Played | Cuts Made | Wins | Top-5s | Top-10s | Top-25s | Scoring Average | Money |
| | 36 | 119 | 23 | 1 | 2 | 2 | 2 | 71.66 | $1,451,942 |

Don Reese

Year	Starts	Rounds Played	Cuts Made	Wins	Top-5s	Top-10s	Top-25s	Scoring Average	Money
1981	6	10	0	0	0	0	0	74.10	
1982	18	46	5	0	0	0	0	74.26	$4,804

Best finish for 1982: T-31st at the Byron Nelson Golf Classic

1986	2	4	0	0	0	0	0	78.00	$600
1987	1	2	0	0	0	0	0	73.50	
1988	1	2	0	0	0	0	0	76.00	
1989	34	91	12	0	1	1	3	72.35	$61,838

Best finish for 1989: T-5th at the Hawaiian Open

| 1990 | 8 | 22 | 3 | 0 | 0 | 0 | 0 | 71.86 | $6,927 |

Best finish for 1990: T-31st at the Deposit Guaranty

| 1994 | 17 | 42 | 5 | 0 | 0 | 0 | 1 | 72.24 | $19,760 |

Best finish for 1994: T-19th at the Buick Southern Open

| 1995 | 26 | 75 | 10 | 0 | 0 | 0 | 1 | 72.12 | $38,905 |

Best finish for 1995: T-20th at the Deposit Guaranty Golf Classic

1996	1	2	0	0	0	0	0	74.00	
Period Totals	Starts	Rounds Played	Cuts Made	Wins	Top-5s	Top-10s	Top-25s	Scoring Average	Money
	114	296	35	0	1	1	5	72.72	$132,835

Dean Refram

Year	Starts	Rounds Played	Cuts Made	Wins	Top-5s	Top-10s	Top-25s	Scoring Average	Money
1958	1	4	1	0	0	0	0	76.25	

Best finish for 1958: 65th at the Gleneagles-Chicago Open

| 1961 | 2 | 8 | 2 | 0 | 0 | 0 | 1 | 70.13 | $770 |

Best finish for 1961: T-21st at the St. Paul Open Invitational

| 1962 | 3 | 12 | 3 | 0 | 0 | 0 | 1 | 71.92 | $1,160 |

Best finish for 1962: T-16th at the Coral Gables Open Invitational

| 1963 | 10 | 41 | 10 | 0 | 0 | 0 | 1 | 72.71 | $2,782 |

Best finish for 1963: T-14th at the U.S. Open

| 1964 | 32 | 94 | 16 | 0 | 0 | 0 | 1 | 73.01 | $4,659 |

Best finish for 1964: T-25th at the Fresno Open

| 1965 | 28 | 96 | 19 | 0 | 2 | 2 | 7 | 72.82 | $13,931 |

Best finish for 1965: 4th at the St. Paul Open

| 1966 | 25 | 78 | 15 | 0 | 0 | 0 | 3 | 73.21 | $6,151 |

Best finish for 1966: T-11th at the San Diego Open Invitational

| 1967 | 30 | 101 | 20 | 0 | 2 | 2 | 3 | 73.03 | $13,827 |

Best finish for 1967: 4th at the Florida Citrus Open

| 1968 | 26 | 79 | 14 | 1 | 1 | 2 | 4 | 72.70 | $12,639 |

Best finish for 1968: Win at the Robinson Open

| 1969 | 29 | 94 | 19 | 0 | 0 | 1 | 4 | 72.82 | $12,391 |

Best finish for 1969: T-10th at the Citrus Open

| 1970 | 23 | 59 | 8 | 0 | 0 | 1 | 2 | 73.80 | $8,097 |

Best finish for 1970: T-9th at the National 4 Ball Championship PGA Players

| 1971 | 23 | 68 | 11 | 0 | 0 | 1 | 3 | 72.51 | $8,122 |

Best finish for 1971: T-6th at the Greater Milwaukee Open

| 1972 | 13 | 35 | 5 | 0 | 0 | 0 | 1 | 73.46 | $2,382 |

Best finish for 1972: T-21st at the Greater Jacksonville Open

| 1973 | 8 | 19 | 3 | 0 | 0 | 0 | 0 | 72.89 | $1,580 |

Best finish for 1973: T-36th at the Tallahassee Open

Year	Starts	Rounds Played	Cuts Made	Wins	Top-5s	Top-10s	Top-25s	Scoring Average	Money
1974	3	8	1	0	0	0	0	73.75	$500

Best finish for 1974: T-60th at the Jackie Gleason's Inverrary Classic

Year	Starts	Rounds Played	Cuts Made	Wins	Top-5s	Top-10s	Top-25s	Scoring Average	Money
1975	3	8	1	0	0	0	0	74.00	$395

Best finish for 1975: T-57th at the Florida Citrus Open Invitational

Year	Starts	Rounds Played	Cuts Made	Wins	Top-5s	Top-10s	Top-25s	Scoring Average	Money
1976	22	53	4	0	0	0	0	74.89	$3,922

Best finish for 1976: T-33rd at the American Golf Classic

Year	Starts	Rounds Played	Cuts Made	Wins	Top-5s	Top-10s	Top-25s	Scoring Average	Money
1978	3	8	1	0	0	0	0	74.00	$094

Best finish for 1978: T-70th at the Jackie Gleason's Inverrary Classic

Year	Starts	Rounds Played	Cuts Made	Wins	Top-5s	Top-10s	Top-25s	Scoring Average	Money
1979	4	10	1	0	0	0	0	74.30	$500

Best finish for 1979: 72nd at the PGA Championship

Year	Starts	Rounds Played	Cuts Made	Wins	Top-5s	Top-10s	Top-25s	Scoring Average	Money
1980	4	6	0	0	0	0	0	75.33	$500
1981	1	0	0	0	0	0	0		
Period Totals	Starts	Rounds Played	Cuts Made	Wins	Top-5s	Top-10s	Top-25s	Scoring Average	Money
	293	881	154	1	5	9	31	73.12	$94,403

Victor Regalado

Year	Starts	Rounds Played	Cuts Made	Wins	Top-5s	Top-10s	Top-25s	Scoring Average	Money
1971	2	6	1	0	0	0	0	73.67	

Best finish for 1971: T-58th at the Andy Williams-San Diego Open

Year	Starts	Rounds Played	Cuts Made	Wins	Top-5s	Top-10s	Top-25s	Scoring Average	Money
1972	2	5	0	0	0	0	0	77.80	
1973	22	69	12	0	0	0	4	72.84	$8,335

Best finish for 1973: T-14th at the B.C. Open

Year	Starts	Rounds Played	Cuts Made	Wins	Top-5s	Top-10s	Top-25s	Scoring Average	Money
1974	27	89	17	1	2	2	6	72.61	$60,469

Best finish for 1974: Win at the Pleasant Valley Classic

Year	Starts	Rounds Played	Cuts Made	Wins	Top-5s	Top-10s	Top-25s	Scoring Average	Money
1975	35	109	19	0	2	2	5	72.71	$25,833

Best finish for 1975: T-4th at the Sammy Davis, Jr. - Greater Hartford Open

Year	Starts	Rounds Played	Cuts Made	Wins	Top-5s	Top-10s	Top-25s	Scoring Average	Money
1976	32	109	24	0	2	4	8	71.94	$53,186

Best finish for 1976: 2nd at the First NBC New Orleans Open

Year	Starts	Rounds Played	Cuts Made	Wins	Top-5s	Top-10s	Top-25s	Scoring Average	Money
1977	32	117	26	0	4	6	14	71.76	$77,941

Best finish for 1977: T-2nd at the Ed McMahon Quad City Open

Year	Starts	Rounds Played	Cuts Made	Wins	Top-5s	Top-10s	Top-25s	Scoring Average	Money
1978	31	110	23	1	1	3	6	72.04	$62,621

Best finish for 1978: Win at the Ed McMahon Quad City Open

Year	Starts	Rounds Played	Cuts Made	Wins	Top-5s	Top-10s	Top-25s	Scoring Average	Money
1979	27	94	19	0	3	6	10	72.32	$83,314

Best finish for 1979: T-2nd at the Greater Milwaukee Open

Year	Starts	Rounds Played	Cuts Made	Wins	Top-5s	Top-10s	Top-25s	Scoring Average	Money
1980	31	95	18	0	1	1	6	72.25	$44,457

Best finish for 1980: T-4th at the Buick Goodwrench Open

Year	Starts	Rounds Played	Cuts Made	Wins	Top-5s	Top-10s	Top-25s	Scoring Average	Money
1981	26	76	14	0	1	1	3	72.41	$31,831

Best finish for 1981: T-2nd at the Quad Cities Open

Year	Starts	Rounds Played	Cuts Made	Wins	Top-5s	Top-10s	Top-25s	Scoring Average	Money
1982	24	73	12	0	1	2	4	72.03	$53,172

Best finish for 1982: 2nd at the Greater Milwaukee Open

Year	Starts	Rounds Played	Cuts Made	Wins	Top-5s	Top-10s	Top-25s	Scoring Average	Money
1983	33	111	22	0	0	1	5	71.98	$50,495

Best finish for 1983: T-8th at the B.C. Open

Year	Starts	Rounds Played	Cuts Made	Wins	Top-5s	Top-10s	Top-25s	Scoring Average	Money
1984	26	77	13	0	0	2	4	72.96	$48,412

Best finish for 1984: T-9th at the Seiko Tucson-Match Play Championship

Year	Starts	Rounds Played	Cuts Made	Wins	Top-5s	Top-10s	Top-25s	Scoring Average	Money
1985	31	89	12	0	0	0	0	72.91	$23,299

Best finish for 1985: T-27th at the Lite Quad Cities Open

Year	Starts	Rounds Played	Cuts Made	Wins	Top-5s	Top-10s	Top-25s	Scoring Average	Money
1986	11	30	4	0	0	0	1	72.13	$5,558

Best finish for 1986: T-23rd at the Deposit Guaranty Golf Classic

Year	Starts	Rounds Played	Cuts Made	Wins	Top-5s	Top-10s	Top-25s	Scoring Average	Money
1987	8	18	1	0	0	0	1	73.44	$1,548

Best finish for 1987: T-24th at the Deposit Guaranty Golf Classic

Year	Starts	Rounds Played	Cuts Made	Wins	Top-5s	Top-10s	Top-25s	Scoring Average	Money
1988	6	14	1	0	0	0	0	71.93	$1,248

Best finish for 1988: T-49th at the Centel Classic

Year	Starts	Rounds Played	Cuts Made	Wins	Top-5s	Top-10s	Top-25s	Scoring Average	Money
1989	3	5	0	0	0	0	0	75.80	
Period Totals	Starts	Rounds Played	Cuts Made	Wins	Top-5s	Top-10s	Top-25s	Scoring Average	Money
	409	1296	238	2	17	30	77	72.38	$631,718

Clyde Rego

Year	Starts	Rounds Played	Cuts Made	Wins	Top-5s	Top-10s	Top-25s	Scoring Average	Money
1982	8	19	1	0	0	0	0	73.32	$597

Best finish for 1982: T-70th at the Phoenix Open

Year	Starts	Rounds Played	Cuts Made	Wins	Top-5s	Top-10s	Top-25s	Scoring Average	Money
1983	1	2	0	0	0	0	0	78.00	$600
1984	21	57	7	0	0	0	2	72.96	$18,154

Best finish for 1984: T-13th at the Georgia-Pacific Atlanta Golf Classic

Period Totals	Starts	Rounds Played	Cuts Made	Wins	Top-5s	Top-10s	Top-25s	Scoring Average	Money
	30	78	8	0	0	0	2	73.18	$19,351

Mike Reid

Year	Starts	Rounds Played	Cuts Made	Wins	Top-5s	Top-10s	Top-25s	Scoring Average	Money
1975	1	2	0	0	0	0	0	75.50	
1976	1	4	1	0	0	0	0	75.00	

Best finish for 1976: T-50th at the U.S. Open

Year	Starts	Rounds Played	Cuts Made	Wins	Top-5s	Top-10s	Top-25s	Scoring Average	Money
1977	32	108	21	0	0	1	6	72.57	$24,440

Best finish for 1977: T-9th at the Florida Citrus Open Invitational

| 1978 | 26 | 82 | 16 | 0 | 2 | 2 | 4 | 72.04 | $37,474 |

Best finish for 1978: 2nd at the Pensacola Open

| 1979 | 31 | 113 | 25 | 0 | 1 | 1 | 13 | 71.88 | $64,396 |

Best finish for 1979: T-3rd at the Southern Open

| 1980 | 29 | 111 | 28 | 0 | 8 | 13 | 17 | 70.78 | $208,267 |

Best finish for 1980: T-3rd at the Michelob Houston Open, Memorial Tournament & Pleasant Valley Jimmy Fund Classic

| 1981 | 27 | 90 | 20 | 0 | 2 | 5 | 12 | 71.48 | $95,947 |

Best finish for 1981: T-3rd at the Phoenix Open

| 1982 | 26 | 95 | 22 | 0 | 1 | 3 | 9 | 71.56 | $80,766 |

Best finish for 1982: 3rd at the Phoenix Open

| 1983 | 24 | 84 | 17 | 0 | 3 | 4 | 10 | 71.79 | $99,055 |

Best finish for 1983: T-4th at the Manufactures Hanover Westchester Classic

| 1984 | 26 | 94 | 21 | 0 | 2 | 4 | 12 | 71.35 | $134,672 |

Best finish for 1984: T-3rd at the Kemper Open & Texas Open

| 1985 | 26 | 93 | 22 | 0 | 2 | 3 | 11 | 71.13 | $169,871 |

Best finish for 1985: 2nd at the B.C. Open & Southwest Golf Classic

| 1986 | 25 | 81 | 20 | 0 | 2 | 3 | 10 | 71.12 | $135,143 |

Best finish for 1986: T-3rd at the Kemper Open

| 1987 | 31 | 99 | 20 | 1 | 5 | 6 | 13 | 70.84 | $365,934 |

Best finish for 1987: Win at the Seiko-Tucson Open

| 1988 | 25 | 80 | 18 | 1 | 4 | 5 | 10 | 71.44 | $536,606 |

Best finish for 1988: Win at the NEC World Series of Golf

| 1989 | 24 | 79 | 18 | 0 | 4 | 7 | 9 | 71.41 | $406,945 |

Best finish for 1989: T-2nd at the PGA Championship

| 1990 | 20 | 70 | 15 | 0 | 2 | 3 | 5 | 71.41 | $258,281 |

Best finish for 1990: T-2nd at the Kmart Greater Greensboro Open

| 1991 | 21 | 73 | 16 | 0 | 0 | 2 | 5 | 71.04 | $164,018 |

Best finish for 1991: T-7th at the Canon Greater Hartford Open & Independent Insurance Agent Open

| 1992 | 25 | 77 | 15 | 0 | 1 | 1 | 3 | 71.26 | $125,376 |

Best finish for 1992: T-3rd at the Kmart Greater Greensboro Open

| 1993 | 5 | 12 | 1 | 0 | 0 | 0 | 0 | 74.17 | $5,125 |

Best finish for 1993: T-67th at the Players Championship

| 1994 | 22 | 67 | 13 | 0 | 0 | 2 | 6 | 71.19 | $154,441 |

Best finish for 1994: T-9th at the Canon Greater Hartford Open

| 1995 | 23 | 62 | 8 | 0 | 1 | 2 | 2 | 71.94 | $102,809 |

Best finish for 1995: T-4th at the Walt Disney World/Oldsmobile Classic

| 1996 | 23 | 72 | 14 | 0 | 1 | 1 | 4 | 71.33 | $162,584 |

Best finish for 1996: T-4th at the CVS Charity Classic

| 1997 | 25 | 81 | 15 | 0 | 1 | 3 | 6 | 70.85 | $326,551 |

Best finish for 1997: T-2nd at the United Airlines Hawaiian Open

| 1998 | 26 | 78 | 13 | 0 | 2 | 2 | 3 | 71.74 | $238,505 |

Best finish for 1998: T-4th at the United Airlines Hawaiian Open & Westin Texas Open

| 1999 | 22 | 75 | 17 | 0 | 2 | 3 | 5 | 70.83 | $482,867 |

Best finish for 1999: T-3rd at the Touchstone Energy Tucson Open

| 2000 | 23 | 72 | 14 | 0 | 1 | 1 | 4 | 71.00 | $299,138 |

Best finish for 2000: T-5th at the Michelob Championship at Kingsmill

| 2001 | 13 | 35 | 5 | 0 | 0 | 0 | 0 | 72.17 | $47,608 |

Best finish for 2001: T-32nd at the Touchstone Energy Tucson Open

2002	4	9	0	0	0	0	0	73.33	
2003	2	5	0	0	0	0	0	75.40	
2005	1	2	0	0	0	0	0	78.50	$2,000
Period Totals	Starts	Rounds Played	Cuts Made	Wins	Top-5s	Top-10s	Top-25s	Scoring Average	Money
	609	2005	415	2	47	77	179	71.47	$4,728,819

Steve Reid

Year	Starts	Rounds Played	Cuts Made	Wins	Top-5s	Top-10s	Top-25s	Scoring Average	Money
1964	9	16	2	0	0	0	0	75.63	

Best finish for 1964: T-49th at the Almaden Open

| 1965 | 25 | 74 | 10 | 0 | 0 | 1 | 3 | 73.54 | $4,139 |

Best finish for 1965: T-8th at the Almaden Open

| 1966 | 20 | 58 | 9 | 0 | 0 | 0 | 0 | 74.31 | $928 |

Best finish for 1966: T-28th at the Portland Open Invitational

| 1967 | 22 | 61 | 9 | 0 | 1 | 1 | 2 | 74.02 | $13,322 |

Best finish for 1967: T-3rd at the Canadian Open

| 1968 | 37 | 118 | 21 | 1 | 1 | 2 | 3 | 72.33 | $14,724 |

Best finish for 1968: Win at the AZALEA Open Invitational

| 1969 | 36 | 121 | 25 | 0 | 1 | 5 | 10 | 72.01 | $32,464 |

Best finish for 1969: 5th at the Memphis Open

| 1970 | 38 | 108 | 19 | 0 | 0 | 3 | 8 | 72.72 | $24,329 |

Best finish for 1970: T-6th at the Kemper Open

1971	29	78	12	0	2	3	5	72.90	$16,332

Best finish for 1971: T-5th at the Atlanta Classic & American Golf Classic

1972	20	55	8	0	0	0	0	74.36	$2,714

Best finish for 1972: T-27th at the Monsanto Open

1973	7	15	0	0	0	0	0	76.40	$060
1974	1	2	0	0	0	0	0	81.50	
1978	1	2	0	0	0	0	0	74.50	
Period Totals	Starts	Rounds Played	Cuts Made	Wins	Top-5s	Top-10s	Top-25s	Scoring Average	Money
	245	708	115	1	5	15	31	73.18	$109,012

Ronnie Reif

Year	Starts	Rounds Played	Cuts Made	Wins	Top-5s	Top-10s	Top-25s	Scoring Average	Money
1960	1	2	0	0	0	0	0	77.50	
1964	6	19	2	0	0	0	0	75.37	

Best finish for 1964: T-40th at the Mountain View Open

1967	3	12	2	0	0	1	1	72.33	$2,162

Best finish for 1967: T-6th at the San Diego Open

1968	5	21	5	0	0	0	1	71.90	$4,304

Best finish for 1968: T-12th at the Andy Williams-San Diego Open Invitational

1969	2	6	1	0	0	0	0	74.33	$184

Best finish for 1969: T-62nd at the Atlanta Classic

1970	15	40	5	0	0	0	0	73.90	$1,064

Best finish for 1970: T-38th at the San Antonio Texas Open

1971	21	64	11	0	0	0	0	72.88	$3,583

Best finish for 1971: T-35th at the Robinson Open Golf Classic

1972	5	9	0	0	0	0	0	75.78	
1973	20	48	5	0	0	0	0	74.15	$904

Best finish for 1973: T-30th at the Tallahassee Open

1974	5	11	1	0	0	0	0	75.09	$497

Best finish for 1974: T-41st at the Dean Martin Tucson Open

Period Totals	Starts	Rounds Played	Cuts Made	Wins	Top-5s	Top-10s	Top-25s	Scoring Average	Money
	83	232	32	0	0	1	2	73.70	$12,697

Kyle Reifers

Year	Starts	Rounds Played	Cuts Made	Wins	Top-5s	Top-10s	Top-25s	Scoring Average	Money
2006	1	2	0	0	0	0	0	75.50	
2007	27	71	9	0	0	0	2	72.46	$276,369

Best finish for 2007: T-12th at the Arnold Palmer Invitational

2008	1	1	0	0	0	0	0	74.00	
Period Totals	Starts	Rounds Played	Cuts Made	Wins	Top-5s	Top-10s	Top-25s	Scoring Average	Money
	29	74	9	0	0	0	2	72.57	$276,369

Bob Reith

Year	Starts	Rounds Played	Cuts Made	Wins	Top-5s	Top-10s	Top-25s	Scoring Average	Money
1958	1	2	0	0	0	0	0	77.50	
1959	1	2	0	0	0	0	0	79.00	
1964	6	13	1	0	0	0	0	74.62	

Best finish for 1964: T-58th at the St. Paul Open

1965	19	57	9	0	0	0	0	73.84	$599

Best finish for 1965: T-45th at the Memphis Open

1969	1	2	0	0	0	0	0	75.00	
1970	1	2	0	0	0	0	0	78.00	
1973	1	2	0	0	0	0	0	76.50	
Period Totals	Starts	Rounds Played	Cuts Made	Wins	Top-5s	Top-10s	Top-25s	Scoring Average	Money
	30	80	10	0	0	0	0	74.39	$599

Jack Renner

Year	Starts	Rounds Played	Cuts Made	Wins	Top-5s	Top-10s	Top-25s	Scoring Average	Money
1974	1	4	1	0	0	0	0	73.00	

Best finish for 1974: T-66th at the Andy Williams-San Diego Open

1976	1	2	0	0	0	0	0	74.00	
1977	8	28	6	0	0	1	3	70.93	$12,837

Best finish for 1977: T-6th at the Ed McMahon Quad City Open

1978	28	95	21	0	2	5	13	71.34	$74,300

Best finish for 1978: T-2nd at the Greater Greensboro Open

1979	27	102	23	1	3	6	9	71.59	$182,808

Best finish for 1979: Win at the Manufactures Hanover Westchester Classic

1980	28	87	15	0	4	5	7	71.64	$98,016

Best finish for 1980: 2nd at the Anheuser-Busch Golf Classic

1981	29	104	24	1	2	9	14	71.08	$193,292

Best finish for 1981: Win at the Pleasant Valley Jimmy Fund Classic

1982	26	96	21	0	1	3	12	71.63	$96,239

Best finish for 1982: 3rd at the Greater Greensboro Open

Year	Starts	Rounds Played	Cuts Made	Wins	Top-5s	Top-10s	Top-25s	Scoring Average	Money
1983	26	94	20	0	2	4	12	71.28	$133,290

Best finish for 1983: T-2nd at the Hawaiian Open & Sammy Davis, Jr. - Greater Hartford Open

Year	Starts	Rounds Played	Cuts Made	Wins	Top-5s	Top-10s	Top-25s	Scoring Average	Money
1984	25	89	19	1	3	6	11	71.31	$260,153

Best finish for 1984: Win at the Hawaiian Open

Year	Starts	Rounds Played	Cuts Made	Wins	Top-5s	Top-10s	Top-25s	Scoring Average	Money
1985	25	81	17	0	2	7	9	71.43	$203,761

Best finish for 1985: 2nd at the Seiko Tucson-Match Play Championship

Year	Starts	Rounds Played	Cuts Made	Wins	Top-5s	Top-10s	Top-25s	Scoring Average	Money
1986	26	77	14	0	1	3	7	71.35	$86,128

Best finish for 1986: T-4th at the Bank of Boston Classic

Year	Starts	Rounds Played	Cuts Made	Wins	Top-5s	Top-10s	Top-25s	Scoring Average	Money
1987	26	87	20	0	0	1	8	70.95	$92,289

Best finish for 1987: T-6th at the Hardee's Golf Classic

Year	Starts	Rounds Played	Cuts Made	Wins	Top-5s	Top-10s	Top-25s	Scoring Average	Money
1988	29	93	18	0	0	2	3	71.42	$82,047

Best finish for 1988: T-7th at the Buick Open

Year	Starts	Rounds Played	Cuts Made	Wins	Top-5s	Top-10s	Top-25s	Scoring Average	Money
1989	4	7	0	0	0	0	0	74.00	
1990	5	14	2	0	0	0	0	72.00	$7,451

Best finish for 1990: T-33rd at the Hawaiian Open

Year	Starts	Rounds Played	Cuts Made	Wins	Top-5s	Top-10s	Top-25s	Scoring Average	Money
1991	8	28	6	0	0	0	0	71.25	$13,612

Best finish for 1991: T-36th at the Chattanooga Classic

Year	Starts	Rounds Played	Cuts Made	Wins	Top-5s	Top-10s	Top-25s	Scoring Average	Money
1992	5	14	2	0	0	1	1	70.57	$13,512

Best finish for 1992: T-6th at the Deposit Guaranty Classic

Year	Starts	Rounds Played	Cuts Made	Wins	Top-5s	Top-10s	Top-25s	Scoring Average	Money
1993	3	6	0	0	0	0	0	74.33	
1994	4	10	1	0	0	0	0	72.60	$2,819

Best finish for 1994: T-50th at the United Airlines Hawaiian Open

Year	Starts	Rounds Played	Cuts Made	Wins	Top-5s	Top-10s	Top-25s	Scoring Average	Money
1995	1	2	0	0	0	0	0	74.00	
1996	5	12	1	0	0	0	1	73.00	$17,500

Best finish for 1996: T-14th at the Greater Vancouver Open

Year	Starts	Rounds Played	Cuts Made	Wins	Top-5s	Top-10s	Top-25s	Scoring Average	Money
1997	1	2	0	0	0	0	0	72.50	
1998	3	8	1	0	0	0	0	71.88	$2,697

Best finish for 1998: 83rd at the Quad City Classic

Year	Starts	Rounds Played	Cuts Made	Wins	Top-5s	Top-10s	Top-25s	Scoring Average	Money
1999	4	10	1	0	0	0	0	72.10	$10,909

Best finish for 1999: T-30th at the John Deere Classic

Year	Starts	Rounds Played	Cuts Made	Wins	Top-5s	Top-10s	Top-25s	Scoring Average	Money
2000	3	6	0	0	0	0	0	72.17	
2001	1	2	0	0	0	0	0	72.00	
2002	1	2	0	0	0	0	0	72.50	
2003	1	2	0	0	0	0	0	75.50	
Period Totals	Starts	Rounds Played	Cuts Made	Wins	Top-5s	Top-10s	Top-25s	Scoring Average	Money
	354	1164	233	3	20	53	110	71.45	$1,583,660

John Restino

Year	Starts	Rounds Played	Cuts Made	Wins	Top-5s	Top-10s	Top-25s	Scoring Average	Money
2000	17	43	5	0	0	0	0	72.79	$34,242

Best finish for 2000: T-53rd at the Greater Greensboro Chrysler Classic

Year	Starts	Rounds Played	Cuts Made	Wins	Top-5s	Top-10s	Top-25s	Scoring Average	Money
2001	11	25	2	0	0	0	0	72.92	$13,808

Best finish for 2001: T-62nd at the Air Canada Championship

Year	Starts	Rounds Played	Cuts Made	Wins	Top-5s	Top-10s	Top-25s	Scoring Average	Money
Period Totals	Starts	Rounds Played	Cuts Made	Wins	Top-5s	Top-10s	Top-25s	Scoring Average	Money
	28	68	7	0	0	0	0	72.84	$48,050

Sam Reynolds

Year	Starts	Rounds Played	Cuts Made	Wins	Top-5s	Top-10s	Top-25s	Scoring Average	Money
1958	2	8	2	0	0	0	0	74.75	

Best finish for 1958: 51st at the Kansas City Open

Year	Starts	Rounds Played	Cuts Made	Wins	Top-5s	Top-10s	Top-25s	Scoring Average	Money
1960	3	12	2	0	0	0	2	73.00	$1,224

Best finish for 1960: T-14th at the Bing Crosby National

Year	Starts	Rounds Played	Cuts Made	Wins	Top-5s	Top-10s	Top-25s	Scoring Average	Money
1961	1	2	1	0	0	0	0	76.00	

Best finish for 1961: T-200 at the PGA Championship

Year	Starts	Rounds Played	Cuts Made	Wins	Top-5s	Top-10s	Top-25s	Scoring Average	Money
1963	1	4	1	0	0	0	1	71.00	$375

Best finish for 1963: T-21st at the Cajun Classic Open Invitational

Year	Starts	Rounds Played	Cuts Made	Wins	Top-5s	Top-10s	Top-25s	Scoring Average	Money
1964	9	23	3	0	0	0	0	75.00	

Best finish for 1964: T-41st at the Tucson Open

Year	Starts	Rounds Played	Cuts Made	Wins	Top-5s	Top-10s	Top-25s	Scoring Average	Money
1965	5	12	1	0	0	0	0	75.25	

Best finish for 1965: T-53rd at the Cajun Classic

Year	Starts	Rounds Played	Cuts Made	Wins	Top-5s	Top-10s	Top-25s	Scoring Average	Money
1966	6	18	2	0	0	0	0	75.06	

Best finish for 1966: T-61st at the Lucky International Open Invitational

Year	Starts	Rounds Played	Cuts Made	Wins	Top-5s	Top-10s	Top-25s	Scoring Average	Money
1967	1	2	0	0	0	0	0	73.50	
1969	2	6	1	0	0	0	0	75.83	$178

Best finish for 1969: T-29th at the West End Classic

Year	Starts	Rounds Played	Cuts Made	Wins	Top-5s	Top-10s	Top-25s	Scoring Average	Money
1972	2	4	0	0	0	0	0	76.00	
Period Totals	Starts	Rounds Played	Cuts Made	Wins	Top-5s	Top-10s	Top-25s	Scoring Average	Money
	32	91	13	0	0	0	3	74.67	$1,777

Rick Rhoads

Year	Starts	Rounds Played	Cuts Made	Wins	Top-5s	Top-10s	Top-25s	Scoring Average	Money
1964	1	4	1	0	0	0	0	79.00	

Best finish for 1964: 74th at the Los Angeles Open

Year	Starts	Rounds Played	Cuts Made	Wins	Top-5s	Top-10s	Top-25s	Scoring Average	Money
1967	1	4	1	0	0	0	1	71.00	$417

Best finish for 1967: T-22nd at the Cajun Classic

| 1968 | 11 | 33 | 5 | 0 | 0 | 0 | 1 | 73.00 | $1,414 |

Best finish for 1968: T-25th at the Cajun Classic

| 1969 | 21 | 56 | 7 | 0 | 0 | 0 | 1 | 73.23 | $2,216 |

Best finish for 1969: T-16th at the West End Classic

| 1970 | 17 | 48 | 6 | 0 | 0 | 0 | 2 | 72.73 | $6,027 |

Best finish for 1970: T-12th at the Bob Hope Chrysler Classic

| 1971 | 24 | 82 | 16 | 0 | 0 | 0 | 1 | 72.52 | $6,586 |

Best finish for 1971: T-18th at the IVB Philadelphia Golf Classic

| 1972 | 23 | 74 | 13 | 0 | 0 | 0 | 3 | 72.92 | $9,224 |

Best finish for 1972: T-11th at the Greater Hartford Open Invitational

| 1973 | 27 | 89 | 15 | 0 | 0 | 0 | 5 | 72.61 | $14,217 |

Best finish for 1973: T-14th at the Sahara Invitational

| 1974 | 32 | 93 | 14 | 0 | 0 | 0 | 1 | 73.23 | $8,695 |

Best finish for 1974: T-25th at the Greater Milwaukee Open

| 1975 | 11 | 29 | 4 | 0 | 0 | 0 | 1 | 73.38 | $1,714 |

Best finish for 1975: T-24th at the Ed McMahon Quad City Open

Year	Starts	Rounds Played	Cuts Made	Wins	Top-5s	Top-10s	Top-25s	Scoring Average	Money
1976	2	4	0	0	0	0	0	77.00	$500
1978	1	3	0	0	0	0	0	78.67	
1979	1	3	0	0	0	0	0	77.67	
1980	1	3	0	0	0	0	0	77.67	
1981	1	3	0	0	0	0	0	78.00	
1983	1	3	0	0	0	0	0	75.33	
1984	1	3	0	0	0	0	0	75.67	
1985	1	3	0	0	0	0	0	81.67	
1986	1	3	0	0	0	0	0	76.00	
1987	1	3	0	0	0	0	0	76.67	
1988	1	3	0	0	0	0	0	78.67	
1989	1	3	0	0	0	0	0	80.67	
1990	1	3	0	0	0	0	0	80.00	
1991	1	3	0	0	0	0	0	74.00	
1992	1	3	0	0	0	0	0	75.67	
1994	1	3	0	0	0	0	0	74.67	
Period Totals	Starts	Rounds Played	Cuts Made	Wins	Top-5s	Top-10s	Top-25s	Scoring Average	Money
	185	561	82	0	0	0	16	73.32	$51,009

Dick Rhyan

Year	Starts	Rounds Played	Cuts Made	Wins	Top-5s	Top-10s	Top-25s	Scoring Average	Money
1964	21	48	2	0	0	0	1	74.85	$930

Best finish for 1964: T-23rd at the PGA Championship

| 1965 | 28 | 84 | 13 | 0 | 0 | 0 | 1 | 73.73 | $3,098 |

Best finish for 1965: T-15th at the Jacksonville Open

| 1967 | 5 | 11 | 0 | 0 | 0 | 0 | 0 | 75.27 | |

| 1968 | 29 | 99 | 20 | 0 | 0 | 1 | 3 | 72.38 | $5,387 |

Best finish for 1968: T-6th at the AZALEA Open Invitational

| 1969 | 35 | 105 | 18 | 0 | 1 | 1 | 1 | 73.02 | $9,919 |

Best finish for 1969: T-5th at the Western Open

| 1970 | 25 | 77 | 13 | 0 | 0 | 1 | 1 | 72.97 | $5,304 |

Best finish for 1970: T-10th at the Greater Jacksonville Open

| 1971 | 23 | 73 | 13 | 0 | 0 | 0 | 3 | 72.64 | $9,749 |

Best finish for 1971: T-15th at the Bob Hope Chrysler Classic

| 1972 | 24 | 73 | 12 | 0 | 2 | 2 | 3 | 72.59 | $18,493 |

Best finish for 1972: T-3rd at the IVB Philadelphia Golf Classic

| 1973 | 30 | 100 | 18 | 0 | 0 | 1 | 3 | 73.10 | $10,471 |

Best finish for 1973: T-6th at the Southern Open

| 1974 | 26 | 83 | 16 | 0 | 0 | 0 | 5 | 72.67 | $13,014 |

Best finish for 1974: T-15th at the B.C. Open

| 1975 | 26 | 79 | 15 | 0 | 0 | 0 | 2 | 72.87 | $8,302 |

Best finish for 1975: T-18th at the First NBC New Orleans Open

| 1976 | 23 | 66 | 9 | 0 | 0 | 0 | 1 | 73.56 | $5,983 |

Best finish for 1976: T-24th at the Danny Thomas Memphis Classic

Period Totals	Starts	Rounds Played	Cuts Made	Wins	Top-5s	Top-10s	Top-25s	Scoring Average	Money
	295	898	149	0	3	6	24	73.08	$90,649

Tad Rhyan

Year	Starts	Rounds Played	Cuts Made	Wins	Top-5s	Top-10s	Top-25s	Scoring Average	Money
1993	32	79	7	0	1	1	2	72.95	$51,524

Best finish for 1993: T-2nd at the Deposit Guaranty Classic

Year	Starts	Rounds Played	Cuts Made	Wins	Top-5s	Top-10s	Top-25s	Scoring Average	Money
1994	1	2	0	0	0	0	0	76.00	
Period Totals	Starts	Rounds Played	Cuts Made	Wins	Top-5s	Top-10s	Top-25s	Scoring Average	Money
	33	81	7	0	1	1	2	73.02	$51,524

Tag Ridings

Year	Starts	Rounds Played	Cuts Made	Wins	Top-5s	Top-10s	Top-25s	Scoring Average	Money
2003	6	14	1	0	0	0	0	72.93	$31,275

Best finish for 2003: T-27th at the Sony Open in Hawaii

Year	Starts	Rounds Played	Cuts Made	Wins	Top-5s	Top-10s	Top-25s	Scoring Average	Money
2004	18	50	9	0	1	1	4	71.24	$623,262

Best finish for 2004: T-2nd at the Michelin Championship at Las Vegas

| 2005 | 31 | 91 | 17 | 0 | 2 | 5 | 6 | 71.04 | $891,812 |

Best finish for 2005: T-3rd at the Chrysler Championship

| 2006 | 33 | 100 | 18 | 0 | 1 | 1 | 2 | 71.77 | $500,242 |

Best finish for 2006: T-5th at the Ford Championship at Doral

| 2007 | 18 | 52 | 9 | 0 | 1 | 1 | 1 | 71.15 | $351,590 |

Best finish for 2007: T-3rd at the Children's Miracle network Classic

| 2008 | 29 | 88 | 14 | 0 | 0 | 2 | 3 | 71.34 | $568,494 |

Best finish for 2008: T-9th at the AT&T Pebble Beach National Pro-Am

Period Totals	Starts	Rounds Played	Cuts Made	Wins	Top-5s	Top-10s	Top-25s	Scoring Average	Money
	135	395	68	0	5	10	16	71.40	$2,966,675

Skee Riegel

Year	Starts	Rounds Played	Cuts Made	Wins	Top-5s	Top-10s	Top-25s	Scoring Average	Money
1958	4	14	3	0	0	0	0	75.07	$220

Best finish for 1958: T-40th at the PGA Championship

| 1959 | 4 | 11 | 2 | 0 | 0 | 0 | 1 | 73.36 | $155 |

Best finish for 1959: T-16th at the Sam Snead Festival

| 1960 | 2 | 7 | 2 | 0 | 0 | 0 | 0 | 73.86 | $130 |

Best finish for 1960: T-67th at the Bing Crosby National

| 1962 | 1 | 3 | 1 | 0 | 0 | 0 | 0 | 75.00 | |
| 1963 | 4 | 14 | 3 | 0 | 0 | 0 | 0 | 74.93 | $690 |

Best finish for 1963: T-50th at the Canadian Open

| 1964 | 15 | 39 | 5 | 0 | 0 | 0 | 1 | 74.21 | $1,370 |

Best finish for 1964: T-18th at the Western Open

| 1965 | 15 | 42 | 6 | 0 | 0 | 0 | 2 | 72.98 | $2,870 |

Best finish for 1965: T-14th at the Lucky International

| 1967 | 8 | 18 | 1 | 0 | 0 | 0 | 0 | 74.56 | $430 |

Best finish for 1967: T-51st at the PGA Championship

| 1968 | 6 | 10 | 1 | 0 | 0 | 0 | 0 | 73.50 | $172 |

Best finish for 1968: T-43rd at the Greater Hartford Open Invitational

| 1969 | 5 | 10 | 1 | 0 | 0 | 0 | 0 | 74.30 | $150 |

Best finish for 1969: T-29th at the Azalea Open

1970	1	2	0	0	0	0	0	77.50	
1973	1	2	0	0	0	0	0	80.00	
Period Totals	Starts	Rounds Played	Cuts Made	Wins	Top-5s	Top-10s	Top-25s	Scoring Average	Money
	66	172	25	0	0	0	4	74.09	$6,186

John Riegger

Year	Starts	Rounds Played	Cuts Made	Wins	Top-5s	Top-10s	Top-25s	Scoring Average	Money
1987	23	58	6	0	0	0	0	73.21	$8,760

Best finish for 1987: T-34th at the Federal Express St. Jude Classic

1988	1	2	0	0	0	0	0	72.50	
1990	1	2	0	0	0	0	0	74.50	
1992	28	70	10	0	0	0	1	72.94	$33,981

Best finish for 1992: T-22nd at the GTE Byron Nelson Classic

| 1993 | 1 | 4 | 1 | 0 | 0 | 0 | 1 | 68.75 | $22,275 |

Best finish for 1993: T-12th at the Federal Express St. Jude Classic

| 1995 | 1 | 2 | 0 | 0 | 0 | 0 | 0 | 72.50 | |
| 1998 | 29 | 83 | 16 | 0 | 0 | 0 | 3 | 71.73 | $150,874 |

Best finish for 1998: T-20th at the Canon Greater Hartford Open & Westin Texas Open

| 2001 | 27 | 84 | 17 | 0 | 0 | 0 | 5 | 70.68 | $342,221 |

Best finish for 2001: 14th at the John Deere Classic

| 2002 | 29 | 86 | 16 | 0 | 0 | 1 | 4 | 70.63 | $393,835 |

Best finish for 2002: T-8th at the Honda Classic

| 2003 | 17 | 52 | 12 | 0 | 0 | 0 | 3 | 70.63 | $318,102 |

Best finish for 2003: T-13th at the Shell Houston Open

| 2004 | 17 | 53 | 10 | 0 | 0 | 1 | 3 | 71.23 | $423,263 |

Best finish for 2004: 7th at the Sony Open in Hawaii

Year	Starts	Rounds Played	Cuts Made	Wins	Top-5s	Top-10s	Top-25s	Scoring Average	Money
2005	4	13	2	0	0	0	0	71.54	$23,328

Best finish for 2005: T-47th at the Sony Open in Hawaii

| 2006 | 20 | 49 | 5 | 0 | 1 | 1 | 2 | 71.43 | $230,765 |

Best finish for 2006: T-5th at the John Deere Classic

| 2008 | 24 | 73 | 13 | 0 | 0 | 0 | 3 | 70.92 | $289,501 |

Best finish for 2008: T-18th at the John Deere Classic

Period Totals	Starts	Rounds Played	Cuts Made	Wins	Top-5s	Top-10s	Top-25s	Scoring Average	Money
	222	631	108	0	1	3	25	71.45	$2,236,907

Chris Riley

Year	Starts	Rounds Played	Cuts Made	Wins	Top-5s	Top-10s	Top-25s	Scoring Average	Money
1995	1	2	0	0	0	0	0	75.50	
1996	1	3	0	0	0	0	0	71.33	
1999	28	84	15	0	0	3	6	71.19	$368,805

Best finish for 1999: T-7th at the Sony Open in Hawaii & Buick Invitational

| 2000 | 28 | 94 | 20 | 0 | 2 | 4 | 7 | 70.62 | $660,707 |

Best finish for 2000: T-4th at the John Deere Classic & Air Canada Championship

| 2001 | 30 | 100 | 21 | 0 | 1 | 4 | 11 | 70.50 | $1,198,225 |

Best finish for 2001: 2nd at The International presented by Qwest

| 2002 | 28 | 100 | 23 | 1 | 4 | 5 | 14 | 69.90 | $2,032,979 |

Best finish for 2002: Win at the Reno-Tahoe Open

| 2003 | 29 | 90 | 19 | 0 | 5 | 7 | 13 | 70.31 | $2,185,107 |

Best finish for 2003: T-2nd at the Greater Hartford Open & John Deere Classic

| 2004 | 23 | 74 | 17 | 0 | 2 | 3 | 6 | 71.07 | $1,297,413 |

Best finish for 2004: T-2nd at the Buick Invitational

| 2005 | 25 | 64 | 11 | 0 | 0 | 0 | 1 | 72.45 | $268,735 |

Best finish for 2005: T-18th at the Bob Hope Chrysler Classic

| 2006 | 27 | 82 | 16 | 0 | 1 | 1 | 4 | 71.07 | $495,314 |

Best finish for 2006: T-5th at the Valero Texas Open

| 2007 | 17 | 59 | 12 | 0 | 0 | 0 | 5 | 70.85 | $403,199 |

Best finish for 2007: T-11th at the Valero Texas Open

| 2008 | 17 | 51 | 9 | 0 | 1 | 1 | 4 | 70.92 | $388,850 |

Best finish for 2008: T-3rd at the U.S. Bank Championship in Milwaukee

Period Totals	Starts	Rounds Played	Cuts Made	Wins	Top-5s	Top-10s	Top-25s	Scoring Average	Money
	254	803	163	1	16	28	71	70.82	$9,299,335

Larry Rinker

Year	Starts	Rounds Played	Cuts Made	Wins	Top-5s	Top-10s	Top-25s	Scoring Average	Money
1978	1	2	0	0	0	0	0	75.00	$303
1980	2	4	0	0	0	0	0	76.00	$600
1981	13	33	4	0	0	0	0	72.97	$2,279

Best finish for 1981: T-40th at the Pensacola Open

| 1982 | 26 | 74 | 13 | 0 | 0 | 1 | 5 | 71.99 | $26,993 |

Best finish for 1982: T-8th at the Southern Open

| 1983 | 29 | 94 | 18 | 0 | 0 | 0 | 4 | 72.64 | $33,494 |

Best finish for 1983: T-16th at the Isuzu/Andy Williams San Diego Open

| 1984 | 25 | 85 | 19 | 0 | 1 | 3 | 9 | 71.95 | $116,494 |

Best finish for 1984: 2nd at the USF&G Classic

| 1985 | 30 | 104 | 24 | 0 | 3 | 6 | 10 | 71.44 | $196,390 |

Best finish for 1985: T-2nd at the Bing Crosby Pro-Am

| 1986 | 32 | 98 | 18 | 0 | 0 | 2 | 8 | 71.87 | $83,135 |

Best finish for 1986: T-6th at the Shearson Lehman/Andy Williams San Diego

| 1987 | 31 | 96 | 19 | 0 | 0 | 2 | 3 | 71.74 | $72,103 |

Best finish for 1987: T-9th at the Bank of Boston Classic

| 1988 | 29 | 100 | 21 | 0 | 0 | 1 | 9 | 71.18 | $125,471 |

Best finish for 1988: T-7th at the Canadian Open

| 1989 | 27 | 89 | 17 | 0 | 1 | 3 | 6 | 71.58 | $110,105 |

Best finish for 1989: T-4th at the Southern Open

| 1990 | 30 | 98 | 18 | 0 | 0 | 0 | 6 | 71.54 | $133,432 |

Best finish for 1990: T-11th at the GTE Byron Nelson Classic

| 1991 | 26 | 81 | 13 | 0 | 1 | 2 | 3 | 71.25 | $115,956 |

Best finish for 1991: T-5th at the Buick Classic

| 1992 | 25 | 86 | 18 | 0 | 0 | 3 | 6 | 70.95 | $198,721 |

Best finish for 1992: T-6th at the Freeport-McMoRan Classic

| 1993 | 29 | 76 | 11 | 0 | 0 | 2 | 4 | 71.88 | $131,537 |

Best finish for 1993: T-8th at the GTE Byron Nelson Classic & Hardee's Golf Classic

| 1994 | 28 | 74 | 10 | 0 | 0 | 0 | 1 | 72.20 | $47,435 |

Best finish for 1994: T-18th at the Phoenix Open

| 1995 | 8 | 20 | 2 | 0 | 0 | 0 | 0 | 72.10 | $9,975 |

Best finish for 1995: T-36th at the Buick Classic

| 1996 | 10 | 27 | 4 | 0 | 0 | 0 | 0 | 72.26 | $12,770 |

Best finish for 1996: T-37th at the Greater Vancouver Open

Year	Starts	Rounds Played	Cuts Made	Wins	Top-5s	Top-10s	Top-25s	Scoring Average	Money
1997	33	98	15	0	0	2	4	71.63	$189,281

Best finish for 1997: T-8th at the Shell Houston Open

| 1998 | 31 | 93 | 17 | 0 | 0 | 0 | 5 | 71.24 | $240,743 |

Best finish for 1998: T-12th at the CVS Charity Classic & Walt Disney World/Oldsmobile Classic

| 1999 | 31 | 88 | 13 | 0 | 0 | 0 | 2 | 72.24 | $114,890 |

Best finish for 1999: T-22nd at the Las Vegas Invitational

| 2000 | 16 | 46 | 7 | 0 | 0 | 0 | 1 | 71.48 | $76,731 |

Best finish for 2000: T-15th at the B.C. Open

| 2001 | 7 | 17 | 1 | 0 | 0 | 0 | 0 | 73.00 | $9,270 |

Best finish for 2001: T-63rd at the Genuity Championship

| 2002 | 5 | 12 | 1 | 0 | 0 | 0 | 0 | 74.33 | $4,628 |

Best finish for 2002: 81st at the Tampa Bay Classic presented by Buick

2003	3	7	0	0	0	0	0	75.14	
2004	2	4	0	0	0	0	0	73.50	
2006	1	2	0	0	0	0	0	76.00	
2007	1	2	0	0	0	0	0	82.00	
Period Totals	Starts	Rounds Played	Cuts Made	Wins	Top-5s	Top-10s	Top-25s	Scoring Average	Money
	531	1610	283	0	6	27	86	71.82	$2,052,738

Lee Rinker

Year	Starts	Rounds Played	Cuts Made	Wins	Top-5s	Top-10s	Top-25s	Scoring Average	Money
1983	1	2	0	0	0	0	0	78.50	
1984	17	50	6	0	0	0	0	72.66	$6,002

Best finish for 1984: T-31st at the Miller High-Life Quad Cities Open

| 1985 | 2 | 8 | 2 | 0 | 0 | 0 | 0 | 73.75 | $3,197 |

Best finish for 1985: T-58th at the U.S. Open

| 1991 | 1 | 2 | 0 | 0 | 0 | 0 | 0 | 74.50 | $1,000 |
| 1992 | 1 | 4 | 1 | 0 | 0 | 0 | 0 | 73.25 | $3,000 |

Best finish for 1992: T-56th at the PGA Championship

| 1993 | 1 | 4 | 1 | 0 | 0 | 0 | 0 | 71.00 | $11,052 |

Best finish for 1993: T-33rd at the U.S. Open

| 1995 | 29 | 91 | 18 | 0 | 0 | 3 | 5 | 71.14 | $187,065 |

Best finish for 1995: T-6th at the Greater Milwaukee Open

| 1996 | 32 | 100 | 20 | 0 | 1 | 1 | 3 | 71.58 | $185,530 |

Best finish for 1996: T-3rd at the Honda Classic

| 1997 | 31 | 95 | 17 | 0 | 3 | 3 | 3 | 71.65 | $416,442 |

Best finish for 1997: T-2nd at the GTE Byron Nelson Classic & B.C. Open

| 1998 | 32 | 104 | 21 | 0 | 0 | 1 | 5 | 71.49 | $264,164 |

Best finish for 1998: T-8th at the Freeport-McDermott Classic

| 1999 | 32 | 91 | 13 | 0 | 0 | 0 | 2 | 71.86 | $145,678 |

Best finish for 1999: T-12th at the Westin Texas Open

2003	1	2	0	0	0	0	0	73.00	
2004	1	2	0	0	0	0	0	75.50	
2005	2	4	0	0	0	0	0	75.75	$2,000
2006	2	4	0	0	0	0	0	74.50	$2,250
2007	2	5	0	0	0	0	0	77.40	
2008	1	2	0	0	0	0	0	75.50	
Period Totals	Starts	Rounds Played	Cuts Made	Wins	Top-5s	Top-10s	Top-25s	Scoring Average	Money
	188	570	99	0	4	8	18	71.85	$1,227,379

Steve Rintoul

Year	Starts	Rounds Played	Cuts Made	Wins	Top-5s	Top-10s	Top-25s	Scoring Average	Money
1988	1	2	0	0	0	0	0	79.00	
1994	27	80	15	0	1	1	4	71.13	$157,618

Best finish for 1994: 2nd at the Buick Southern Open

| 1995 | 34 | 96 | 17 | 0 | 1 | 2 | 2 | 71.82 | $114,077 |

Best finish for 1995: T-4th at the Deposit Guaranty Golf Classic

| 1996 | 27 | 75 | 10 | 0 | 0 | 0 | 0 | 72.40 | $33,965 |

Best finish for 1996: T-35th at the Kemper Open

| 1997 | 6 | 15 | 1 | 0 | 0 | 0 | 0 | 72.73 | $6,123 |

Best finish for 1997: T-36th at the B.C. Open

Period Totals	Starts	Rounds Played	Cuts Made	Wins	Top-5s	Top-10s	Top-25s	Scoring Average	Money
	95	268	43	0	2	3	6	71.88	$311,783

Bob Risch

Year	Starts	Rounds Played	Cuts Made	Wins	Top-5s	Top-10s	Top-25s	Scoring Average	Money
1971	1	4	1	0	0	0	0	73.50	$915

Best finish for 1971: T-49th at the U.S. Open

| 1975 | 17 | 46 | 6 | 0 | 0 | 0 | 0 | 73.72 | $3,386 |

Best finish for 1975: T-26th at the First NBC New Orleans Open

| 1976 | 14 | 37 | 7 | 0 | 0 | 0 | 0 | 73.57 | $2,307 |

Best finish for 1976: T-26th at the NBC Tucson Open

Year	Starts	Rounds Played	Cuts Made	Wins	Top-5s	Top-10s	Top-25s	Scoring Average	Money
1977	1	2	0	0	0	0	0	77.50	$500
Period Totals	Starts	Rounds Played	Cuts Made	Wins	Top-5s	Top-10s	Top-25s	Scoring Average	Money
	33	89	14	0	0	0	0	73.73	$7,108

Loren Roberts

Year	Starts	Rounds Played	Cuts Made	Wins	Top-5s	Top-10s	Top-25s	Scoring Average	Money
1981	19	53	7	0	0	0	2	73.34	$8,421

Best finish for 1981: T-22nd at the Danny Thomas Memphis Classic & Texas Open

1982	2	4	0	0	0	0	0	76.00	
1983	24	66	8	0	0	0	0	73.27	$7,724

Best finish for 1983: T-26th at the Southern Open

1984	26	82	14	0	1	3	7	72.63	$67,515

Best finish for 1984: T-5th at the Danny Thomas Memphis Classic

1985	32	108	22	0	3	3	5	72.14	$93,761

Best finish for 1985: 3rd at the Isuzu/Andy Williams San Diego Open

1986	32	99	19	0	1	2	5	71.77	$52,640

Best finish for 1986: T-4th at the Provident Classic

1987	31	86	13	0	0	0	4	72.07	$58,089

Best finish for 1987: T-12th at the Federal Express St. Jude Classic

1988	28	92	19	0	0	3	13	70.76	$136,890

Best finish for 1988: T-6th at the Hawaiian Open & Manufactures Hanover Westchester Classic

1989	30	113	28	0	2	5	11	70.82	$276,882

Best finish for 1989: T-4th at the Nestle Invitational & GTE Byron Nelson Classic

1990	31	112	26	0	3	7	14	70.78	$478,522

Best finish for 1990: T-3rd at the Centel Western Open

1991	29	107	23	0	1	4	12	70.45	$282,671

Best finish for 1991: T-4th at the Canon Greater Hartford Open

1992	28	102	23	0	2	3	13	70.18	$338,673

Best finish for 1992: T-2nd at the Hardee's Golf Classic

1993	28	95	19	0	2	4	9	70.84	$316,506

Best finish for 1993: T-3rd at the Walt Disney World/Oldsmobile Classic

1994	22	82	19	1	6	9	13	69.89	$1,028,587

Best finish for 1994: Win at the Nestle Invitational

1995	23	83	19	1	3	5	10	70.59	$680,372

Best finish for 1995: Win at the Nestle Invitational

1996	24	81	19	2	2	3	11	70.49	$726,531

Best finish for 1996: Win at the MCI Classic & Greater Milwaukee Open

1997	24	82	17	1	3	9	14	70.45	$1,095,480

Best finish for 1997: Win at the CVS Charity Classic

1998	22	80	18	0	2	3	10	70.53	$467,285

Best finish for 1998: T-4th at the Westin Texas Open

1999	26	89	20	1	3	7	10	70.58	$1,265,495

Best finish for 1999: Win at the GTE Byron Nelson Classic

2000	24	86	21	1	4	9	15	70.36	$1,932,280

Best finish for 2000: Win at the Greater Milwaukee Open

2001	25	84	17	0	1	2	6	70.68	$586,072

Best finish for 2001: T-5th at the Sony Open in Hawaii

2002	25	93	21	1	3	5	11	69.98	$1,919,047

Best finish for 2002: Win at the Valero Texas Open

2003	24	86	21	0	1	3	10	70.45	$1,297,739

Best finish for 2003: T-2nd at the Valero Texas Open

2004	22	79	19	0	1	2	12	70.09	$998,677

Best finish for 2004: T-3rd at the Southern Farm Bureau Classic

2005	18	53	11	0	2	2	6	70.55	$876,330

Best finish for 2005: T-2nd at the Southern Farm Bureau Classic

2006	4	14	3	0	0	0	1	70.79	$134,572

Best finish for 2006: T-18th at the Sony Open in Hawaii

2007	3	8	1	0	0	0	0	72.63	$17,542

Best finish for 2007: T-63rd at the Stanford St. Jude Classic

Period Totals	Starts	Rounds Played	Cuts Made	Wins	Top-5s	Top-10s	Top-25s	Scoring Average	Money
	626	2119	447	8	46	93	224	70.95	$15,144,302

Bill Robinson

Year	Starts	Rounds Played	Cuts Made	Wins	Top-5s	Top-10s	Top-25s	Scoring Average	Money
1968	8	20	3	0	0	0	0	73.50	

Best finish for 1968: T-41st at the Rebel Yell Open

1969	5	12	1	0	0	0	0	74.33	$160

Best finish for 1969: T-50th at the Texas Open

1971	4	7	1	0	0	0	0	74.29	$782

Best finish for 1971: T-31st at the Greater Jacksonville Open

1972	6	14	2	0	0	0	0	77.07	$388

Best finish for 1972: T-68th at the Doral-Eastern Open

Year	Starts	Rounds Played	Cuts Made	Wins	Top-5s	Top-10s	Top-25s	Scoring Average	Money
1973	3	6	0	0	0	0	0	73.67	
1974	7	16	1	0	0	0	0	74.00	$510

Best finish for 1974: T-41st at the Greater Jacksonville Open

1979	2	4	0	0	0	0	0	75.25	
1980	1	0	0	0	0	0	0		
1982	2	6	1	0	0	0	0	73.50	$824

Best finish for 1982: 67th at the Honda Inverrary Classic

1985	1	2	0	0	0	0	0	76.50	
1991	2	4	0	0	0	0	0	76.00	
1992	1	2	0	0	0	0	0	78.00	
1993	1	2	0	0	0	0	0	77.50	
Period Totals	Starts	Rounds Played	Cuts Made	Wins	Top-5s	Top-10s	Top-25s	Scoring Average	Money
	43	95	9	0	0	0	0	74.71	$2,664

Costantino Rocca

Year	Starts	Rounds Played	Cuts Made	Wins	Top-5s	Top-10s	Top-25s	Scoring Average	Money
1991	1	4	1	0	0	0	0	71.25	$7,114

Best finish for 1991: T-44th at the British Open

1992	1	4	1	0	0	0	0	72.50	$7,750

Best finish for 1992: T-55th at the British Open

1993	1	2	0	0	0	0	0	72.00	$924
1994	6	19	3	0	0	0	0	72.37	$19,522

Best finish for 1994: T-31st at the Bob Hope Chrysler Classic

1995	2	8	2	0	1	1	2	69.75	$185,500

Best finish for 1995: 2nd at the British Open

1996	8	26	5	0	0	0	0	72.96	$42,816

Best finish for 1996: T-27th at the NEC World Series of Golf

1997	5	16	3	0	1	1	1	73.06	$119,365

Best finish for 1997: T-5th at the Masters

1998	6	16	2	0	0	1	1	73.94	$78,540

Best finish for 1998: T-9th at the British Open

1999	1	4	1	0	0	0	1	74.25	$32,027

Best finish for 1999: T-18th at the British Open

Period Totals	Starts	Rounds Played	Cuts Made	Wins	Top-5s	Top-10s	Top-25s	Scoring Average	Money
	31	99	18	0	2	3	5	72.71	$493,559

Phil Rodgers

Year	Starts	Rounds Played	Cuts Made	Wins	Top-5s	Top-10s	Top-25s	Scoring Average	Money
1958	2	8	2	0	0	0	1	74.00	

Best finish for 1958: 22nd at the Masters

1959	3	8	1	0	0	0	0	74.75	

Best finish for 1959: T-34th at the Los Angeles Open Invitational

1960	2	8	2	0	0	0	2	70.88	

Best finish for 1960: T-24th at the San Diego Open Invitational

1961	13	52	13	0	1	4	10	70.27	$8,734

Best finish for 1961: T-2nd at the Orange County Open

1962	23	90	21	2	6	8	17	71.30	$30,279

Best finish for 1962: Win at the Los Angeles Open & Tucson Open Invitational

1963	25	96	24	1	3	5	17	71.56	$25,809

Best finish for 1963: Win at the Texas Open Invitational

1964	29	109	22	0	2	3	13	72.33	$18,725

Best finish for 1964: T-3rd at the Sahara Invitational

1965	33	117	25	0	4	6	10	72.19	$25,665

Best finish for 1965: T-2nd at the Azalea Open & Greater Greensboro Open

1966	30	110	25	2	4	7	18	71.78	$74,480

Best finish for 1966: Win at the Doral Open Invitational & Buick Open Invitational

1967	28	90	17	0	2	4	7	72.89	$21,267

Best finish for 1967: T-4th at the Cleveland Open

1968	33	107	20	0	0	2	6	72.65	$16,013

Best finish for 1968: T-6th at the Kemper Open Invitational

1969	33	109	23	0	1	4	10	71.61	$30,894

Best finish for 1969: T-3rd at the Michigan Golf Classic

1970	35	111	23	0	0	4	12	72.50	$36,349

Best finish for 1970: T-6th at the Canadian Open, Westchester Classic & Heritage Classic

1971	35	124	30	0	4	6	13	71.41	$68,615

Best finish for 1971: 2nd at the U.S. Professional Match Play Championship

1972	34	110	21	0	3	6	12	72.19	$49,414

Best finish for 1972: 3rd at the San Antonio Texas Open

1973	32	93	16	0	1	1	4	73.15	$21,960

Best finish for 1973: T-2nd at the Andy Williams-San Diego Open

1974	30	86	14	0	1	2	3	73.09	$15,956

Best finish for 1974: T-5th at the Southern Open

Year	Starts	Rounds Played	Cuts Made	Wins	Top-5s	Top-10s	Top-25s	Scoring Average	Money
1975	29	73	8	0	0	0	0	74.37	$4,723

Best finish for 1975: T-35th at the Andy Williams-San Diego Open

| 1976 | 31 | 95 | 17 | 0 | 1 | 1 | 5 | 72.46 | $19,653 |

Best finish for 1976: T-5th at the Pensacola Open

| 1977 | 21 | 56 | 7 | 0 | 0 | 1 | 1 | 73.63 | $8,761 |

Best finish for 1977: T-10th at the Joe Garagiola Tucson Open

| 1978 | 10 | 31 | 4 | 0 | 0 | 0 | 0 | 73.90 | $2,716 |

Best finish for 1978: T-29th at the Canadian Open & Greater Milwaukee Open

| 1979 | 7 | 16 | 1 | 0 | 0 | 0 | 0 | 73.50 | $518 |

Best finish for 1979: T-64th at the Joe Garagiola Tucson Open

| 1980 | 7 | 16 | 1 | 0 | 0 | 0 | 0 | 75.44 | $475 |

Best finish for 1980: 75th at the Buick Goodwrench Open

| 1981 | 3 | 8 | 1 | 0 | 0 | 0 | 0 | 73.50 | $642 |

Best finish for 1981: T-47th at the Wickes/Andy Williams San Diego Open

1982	2	4	0	0	0	0	0	75.25	
1983	1	2	0	0	0	0	0	72.50	
Period Totals	Starts	Rounds Played	Cuts Made	Wins	Top-5s	Top-10s	Top-25s	Scoring Average	Money
	531	1729	338	5	33	64	161	72.38	$481,648

Anthony Rodriguez

Year	Starts	Rounds Played	Cuts Made	Wins	Top-5s	Top-10s	Top-25s	Scoring Average	Money
1995	4	10	3	0	0	0	0	72.00	$12,847

Best finish for 1995: T-28th at the B.C. Open

| 1996 | 3 | 10 | 2 | 0 | 0 | 0 | 0 | 73.00 | $7,965 |

Best finish for 1996: 79th at the GTE Byron Nelson Classic

| 1997 | 25 | 61 | 6 | 0 | 0 | 0 | 1 | 72.90 | $45,319 |

Best finish for 1997: T-13th at the Bell Canadian Open

1998	2	6	0	0	0	0	0	74.17	
1999	1	2	0	0	0	0	0	72.50	
2000	1	2	0	0	0	0	0	72.00	
Period Totals	Starts	Rounds Played	Cuts Made	Wins	Top-5s	Top-10s	Top-25s	Scoring Average	Money
	36	91	11	0	0	0	1	72.87	$66,130

Chi Chi Rodriguez

Year	Starts	Rounds Played	Cuts Made	Wins	Top-5s	Top-10s	Top-25s	Scoring Average	Money
1959	1	4	0	0	0	1	1	73.75	$300
1960	5	20	5	0	1	1	2	71.90	$2,262

Best finish for 1960: T-4th at the Eastern Open Invitational

| 1961 | 9 | 34 | 7 | 0 | 0 | 0 | 4 | 71.12 | $2,469 |

Best finish for 1961: T-16th at the Almaden Open

| 1962 | 10 | 39 | 10 | 0 | 1 | 3 | 6 | 71.49 | $6,864 |

Best finish for 1962: T-4th at the Dallas Open Invitational

| 1963 | 16 | 62 | 15 | 1 | 1 | 3 | 12 | 71.15 | $18,968 |

Best finish for 1963: Win at the Denver Open Invitational

| 1964 | 26 | 91 | 19 | 2 | 8 | 8 | 13 | 71.22 | $49,470 |

Best finish for 1964: Win at the Lucky International Open & Western Open

| 1965 | 23 | 79 | 15 | 0 | 5 | 5 | 10 | 71.99 | $34,568 |

Best finish for 1965: T-2nd at the Houston Classic, Tournament of Champions & Western Open

| 1966 | 27 | 95 | 20 | 0 | 3 | 5 | 10 | 71.98 | $36,636 |

Best finish for 1966: 2nd at the Canadian Open & Cajun Classic

| 1967 | 27 | 95 | 19 | 1 | 2 | 3 | 12 | 71.79 | $55,309 |

Best finish for 1967: Win at the Texas Open

| 1968 | 28 | 92 | 19 | 1 | 3 | 5 | 9 | 71.76 | $55,267 |

Best finish for 1968: Win at the Sahara Invitational

| 1969 | 30 | 108 | 24 | 0 | 2 | 5 | 14 | 71.41 | $49,912 |

Best finish for 1969: 2nd at the San Francisco Open

| 1970 | 29 | 97 | 19 | 0 | 3 | 7 | 11 | 71.79 | $47,451 |

Best finish for 1970: T-3rd at the Canadian Open

| 1971 | 32 | 106 | 20 | 0 | 0 | 3 | 6 | 72.27 | $26,045 |

Best finish for 1971: T-6th at the American Golf Classic

| 1972 | 32 | 119 | 27 | 1 | 6 | 10 | 17 | 71.31 | $109,157 |

Best finish for 1972: Win at the Byron Nelson Golf Classic

| 1973 | 23 | 91 | 20 | 1 | 3 | 5 | 13 | 71.54 | $89,487 |

Best finish for 1973: Win at the Greater Greensboro Open

| 1974 | 26 | 95 | 21 | 0 | 1 | 5 | 11 | 71.43 | $51,482 |

Best finish for 1974: T-4th at the Canadian Open

| 1975 | 26 | 75 | 12 | 0 | 0 | 0 | 3 | 72.64 | $15,216 |

Best finish for 1975: T-12th at the Greater Greensboro Open

| 1976 | 28 | 89 | 16 | 0 | 2 | 3 | 7 | 72.42 | $30,371 |

Best finish for 1976: T-5th at the Sammy Davis, Jr. - Greater Hartford Open & Pensacola Open

| 1977 | 28 | 88 | 16 | 0 | 2 | 4 | 10 | 72.32 | $56,288 |

Best finish for 1977: 3rd at the Houston Open

Year	Starts	Rounds Played	Cuts Made	Wins	Top-5s	Top-10s	Top-25s	Scoring Average	Money
1978	29	95	18	0	1	2	8	72.18	$39,619

Best finish for 1978: T-5th at the Southern Open

1979	23	80	17	1	1	2	7	71.63	$58,225

Best finish for 1979: Win at the Tallahassee Open

| 1980 | 28 | 82 | 13 | 0 | 0 | 3 | 4 | 72.32 | $36,506 |

Best finish for 1980: T-10th at the Hawaiian Open, Jackie Gleason's Inverrary Classic & Greater Milwaukee Open

| 1981 | 23 | 70 | 13 | 0 | 2 | 3 | 6 | 71.66 | $65,152 |

Best finish for 1981: 2nd at the Greater Milwaukee Open

| 1982 | 23 | 63 | 7 | 0 | 0 | 0 | 0 | 73.59 | $7,719 |

Best finish for 1982: T-35th at the Manufactures Hanover Westchester Classic

| 1983 | 21 | 57 | 8 | 0 | 0 | 0 | 1 | 73.60 | $8,190 |

Best finish for 1983: T-22nd at the Buick Open

| 1984 | 23 | 75 | 13 | 0 | 0 | 1 | 1 | 71.95 | $30,989 |

Best finish for 1984: T-9th at the Sammy Davis, Jr. - Greater Hartford Open

| 1985 | 21 | 58 | 8 | 0 | 1 | 1 | 4 | 72.38 | $38,956 |

Best finish for 1985: T-5th at the Byron Nelson Golf Classic

| 1986 | 2 | 7 | 2 | 0 | 0 | 1 | 1 | 73.57 | $16,145 |

Best finish for 1986: T-10th at the AT&T Pebble Beach Pro-Am

1987	1	2	0	0	0	0	0	76.00	
1991	1	2	0	0	0	0	0	75.00	
1997	1	4	0	0	0	0	0	73.50	
Period Totals	Starts	Rounds Played	Cuts Made	Wins	Top-5s	Top-10s	Top-25s	Scoring Average	Money
	622	2074	403	8	48	89	203	71.95	$1,039,019

Martin Roesink

Year	Starts	Rounds Played	Cuts Made	Wins	Top-5s	Top-10s	Top-25s	Scoring Average	Money
1967	1	2	0	0	0	0	0	78.50	
1969	19	60	10	0	0	0	3	73.40	$4,579

Best finish for 1969: T-14th at the Phoenix Open

| 1970 | 14 | 38 | 4 | 0 | 0 | 0 | 0 | 74.24 | $1,209 |

Best finish for 1970: T-28th at the Azalea Open Invitational

| 1971 | 11 | 31 | 4 | 0 | 0 | 0 | 0 | 73.42 | $2,283 |

Best finish for 1971: T-27th at the Southern Open

| 1972 | 16 | 46 | 7 | 0 | 0 | 0 | 1 | 73.22 | $3,280 |

Best finish for 1972: T-21st at the Greater Jacksonville Open

| 1973 | 12 | 31 | 3 | 0 | 0 | 0 | 0 | 74.16 | $660 |

Best finish for 1973: T-46th at the Ohio Kings Island Open

| 1974 | 1 | 2 | 0 | 0 | 0 | 0 | 0 | 75.50 | |
| 1976 | 1 | 4 | 1 | 0 | 0 | 0 | 0 | 74.50 | $320 |

Best finish for 1976: T-66th at the American Golf Classic

Period Totals	Starts	Rounds Played	Cuts Made	Wins	Top-5s	Top-10s	Top-25s	Scoring Average	Money
	75	214	29	0	0	0	4	73.71	$12,331

Bill Rogers

Year	Starts	Rounds Played	Cuts Made	Wins	Top-5s	Top-10s	Top-25s	Scoring Average	Money
1961	1	4	1	0	0	0	1	71.75	$400

Best finish for 1961: T-13th at the Almaden Open

| 1971 | 1 | 2 | 0 | 0 | 0 | 0 | 0 | 79.00 | $500 |
| 1973 | 2 | 6 | 1 | 0 | 0 | 0 | 0 | 76.17 | |

Best finish for 1973: T-65th at the Houston Open

| 1974 | 1 | 4 | 1 | 0 | 0 | 0 | 1 | 70.50 | $925 |

Best finish for 1974: T-21st at the Southern Open

| 1975 | 26 | 92 | 19 | 0 | 1 | 2 | 6 | 72.33 | $29,302 |

Best finish for 1975: 4th at the Southern Open

| 1976 | 27 | 89 | 19 | 0 | 0 | 2 | 7 | 72.72 | $24,376 |

Best finish for 1976: T-8th at the Byron Nelson Golf Classic

| 1977 | 28 | 97 | 21 | 0 | 2 | 8 | 14 | 71.56 | $81,229 |

Best finish for 1977: T-2nd at the Kemper Open

| 1978 | 29 | 101 | 21 | 1 | 3 | 5 | 9 | 72.07 | $114,206 |

Best finish for 1978: Win at the Bob Hope Chrysler Classic

| 1979 | 28 | 108 | 26 | 0 | 8 | 12 | 16 | 70.76 | $230,500 |

Best finish for 1979: T-2nd at the Doral-Eastern Open, Byron Nelson Golf Classic, World Series Of Golf & San Antonio Texas Open

| 1980 | 26 | 101 | 24 | 0 | 5 | 9 | 17 | 70.95 | $151,713 |

Best finish for 1980: T-2nd at the Tallahassee Open & Byron Nelson Golf Classic

| 1981 | 27 | 95 | 21 | 4 | 8 | 10 | 15 | 70.91 | $365,411 |

Best finish for 1981: Win at the Sea Pines Heritage Classic, British Open, World Series Of Golf & Texas Open

| 1982 | 24 | 89 | 22 | 0 | 5 | 7 | 12 | 71.56 | $132,422 |

Best finish for 1982: T-3rd at the U.S. Open

| 1983 | 22 | 72 | 13 | 1 | 2 | 4 | 9 | 72.15 | $146,931 |

Best finish for 1983: Win at the USF&G Classic

| 1984 | 19 | 59 | 12 | 0 | 0 | 0 | 3 | 72.75 | $36,675 |

Best finish for 1984: T-11th at the Houston Coca-Cola Open

Year	Starts	Rounds Played	Cuts Made	Wins	Top-5s	Top-10s	Top-25s	Scoring Average	Money
1985	19	52	6	0	0	1	2	73.21	$46,823

Best finish for 1985: 7th at the Memorial Tournament

| 1986 | 23 | 58 | 11 | 0 | 1 | 1 | 4 | 73.00 | $59,943 |

Best finish for 1986: T-3rd at the Colonial National Invitational

| 1987 | 23 | 75 | 15 | 0 | 0 | 0 | 1 | 72.27 | $33,965 |

Best finish for 1987: T-19th at the Byron Nelson Golf Classic

| 1988 | 15 | 36 | 3 | 0 | 0 | 0 | 0 | 74.14 | $5,482 |

Best finish for 1988: T-51st at the Doral-Ryder Open

1989	2	1	0	0	0	0	0	78.00	
1991	1	2	0	0	0	0	0	74.00	
Period Totals	Starts	Rounds Played	Cuts Made	Wins	Top-5s	Top-10s	Top-25s	Scoring Average	Money
	344	1143	236	6	35	61	117	71.99	$1,460,803

Mark Rohde

Year	Starts	Rounds Played	Cuts Made	Wins	Top-5s	Top-10s	Top-25s	Scoring Average	Money
1980	10	23	4	0	0	1	4	71.57	$14,057

Best finish for 1980: T-8th at the World Disney World National Team Championship

| 1981 | 15 | 37 | 4 | 0 | 0 | 0 | 0 | 74.11 | $3,293 |

Best finish for 1981: T-35th at the Bay Hill Classic

1990	1	2	0	0	0	0	0	71.50	
Period Totals	Starts	Rounds Played	Cuts Made	Wins	Top-5s	Top-10s	Top-25s	Scoring Average	Money
	26	62	8	0	0	1	4	73.08	$17,350

John Rollins

Year	Starts	Rounds Played	Cuts Made	Wins	Top-5s	Top-10s	Top-25s	Scoring Average	Money
1998	1	2	0	0	0	0	0	73.00	
2000	27	72	8	0	0	1	2	72.29	$169,570

Best finish for 2000: T-9th at the Greater Milwaukee Open

| 2002 | 34 | 120 | 27 | 1 | 2 | 6 | 15 | 70.22 | $1,958,565 |

Best finish for 2002: Win at the Bell Canadian Open

| 2003 | 27 | 85 | 17 | 0 | 3 | 5 | 8 | 71.12 | $1,614,314 |

Best finish for 2003: 2nd at the Buick Classic

| 2004 | 29 | 85 | 17 | 0 | 1 | 2 | 7 | 71.47 | $742,956 |

Best finish for 2004: T-4th at the Deutsche Bank Championship

| 2005 | 30 | 95 | 18 | 0 | 1 | 1 | 8 | 71.09 | $854,147 |

Best finish for 2005: T-2nd at the B.C. Open

| 2006 | 28 | 91 | 18 | 1 | 3 | 4 | 7 | 71.12 | $1,503,078 |

Best finish for 2006: Win at the B.C. Open

| 2007 | 29 | 101 | 23 | 0 | 4 | 4 | 13 | 70.97 | $2,496,837 |

Best finish for 2007: 2nd at the Bob Hope Chrysler Classic & FBR Open

| 2008 | 28 | 94 | 18 | 0 | 1 | 2 | 6 | 71.54 | $1,016,032 |

Best finish for 2008: T-2nd at the Reno-Tahoe Open

Period Totals	Starts	Rounds Played	Cuts Made	Wins	Top-5s	Top-10s	Top-25s	Scoring Average	Money
	233	745	146	2	15	25	66	71.16	$10,355,500

Andres Romero

Year	Starts	Rounds Played	Cuts Made	Wins	Top-5s	Top-10s	Top-25s	Scoring Average	Money
2006	2	6	1	0	0	1	1	71.17	$179,475

Best finish for 2006: T-8th at the British Open

| 2007 | 3 | 10 | 2 | 0 | 1 | 2 | 2 | 71.30 | $800,914 |

Best finish for 2007: 3rd at the British Open

| 2008 | 20 | 67 | 15 | 1 | 1 | 3 | 4 | 71.85 | $2,064,612 |

Best finish for 2008: Win at the Zurich Classic of New Orleans

Period Totals	Starts	Rounds Played	Cuts Made	Wins	Top-5s	Top-10s	Top-25s	Scoring Average	Money
	25	83	18	1	2	6	7	71.73	$3,045,001

Eduardo Romero

Year	Starts	Rounds Played	Cuts Made	Wins	Top-5s	Top-10s	Top-25s	Scoring Average	Money
1985	1	2	0	0	0	0	0	76.50	$544
1986	29	80	11	0	1	1	2	72.38	$21,748

Best finish for 1986: T-5th at the Deposit Guaranty Golf Classic

| 1987 | 1 | 0 | 0 | 0 | 0 | 0 | 0 | | |
| 1988 | 1 | 4 | 1 | 0 | 0 | 0 | 1 | 71.25 | $23,800 |

Best finish for 1988: T-13th at the British Open

| 1989 | 1 | 4 | 1 | 0 | 0 | 1 | 1 | 70.00 | $33,600 |

Best finish for 1989: T-8th at the British Open

| 1990 | 3 | 6 | 2 | 0 | 1 | 1 | 1 | 74.33 | $81,956 |

Best finish for 1990: T-2nd at the International

| 1991 | 4 | 10 | 3 | 0 | 0 | 0 | 0 | 72.80 | $17,519 |

Best finish for 1991: T-26th at the British Open

| 1992 | 3 | 6 | 0 | 0 | 0 | 0 | 0 | 74.83 | $3,400 |

Year	Starts	Rounds Played	Cuts Made	Wins	Top-5s	Top-10s	Top-25s	Scoring Average	Money
1993	2	6	1	0	0	0	1	70.67	$19,424
Best finish for 1993: T-20th at the PGA Championship									
1994	1	2	0	0	0	0	0	72.50	$972
1995	15	39	4	0	0	0	1	72.33	$24,942
Best finish for 1995: T-24th at the Honda Classic									
1996	1	4	1	0	0	0	0	70.75	$12,158
Best finish for 1996: T-32nd at the British Open									
1997	2	8	2	0	0	1	1	71.00	$76,512
Best finish for 1997: T-7th at the British Open									
1998	3	10	2	0	0	0	1	73.70	$37,445
Best finish for 1998: T-25th at the U.S. Open									
1999	4	4	2	0	1	2	2	73.75	$216,750
Best finish for 1999: T-5th at the Andersen Consulting Match Play Championship									
2000	3	10	2	0	0	0	1	72.70	$72,034
Best finish for 2000: T-25th at the American Express Championship									
2001	6	14	2	0	0	0	1	73.14	$61,374
Best finish for 2001: T-25th at the British Open									
2002	4	12	2	0	0	0	0	71.92	$79,291
Best finish for 2002: T-36th at the American Express Championship									
2003	12	30	7	0	0	0	4	73.00	$317,867
Best finish for 2003: T-15th at the U.S. Open									
2004	6	14	3	0	0	0	0	73.64	$83,495
Best finish for 2004: T-33rd at the WGC-Accenture Match Play Championship									
Period Totals	102	265	46	0	3	6	17	72.60	$1,184,830

Bob Rosburg

Year	Starts	Rounds Played	Cuts Made	Wins	Top-5s	Top-10s	Top-25s	Scoring Average	Money
1958	34	124	29	0	10	14	22	71.06	$26,960
Best finish for 1958: T-2nd at the Texas Open, Lafayette Open, Eastern Open & Miller Open									
1959	23	92	21	1	5	10	21	70.59	$31,842
Best finish for 1959: Win at the PGA Championship									
1960	18	70	16	0	2	5	11	71.23	$10,611
Best finish for 1960: T-2nd at the Hesperia Open Invitational									
1961	24	97	21	1	6	8	16	70.73	$25,348
Best finish for 1961: Win at the Bing Crosby National									
1962	19	75	16	0	3	4	10	71.17	$14,858
Best finish for 1962: T-2nd at the Greater New Orleans Open Invitational & Baton Rouge Open Invitational									
1963	22	85	17	0	3	7	14	71.56	$22,639
Best finish for 1963: T-2nd at the Bing Crosby National & Greater New Orleans Open Invitational									
1964	30	109	22	0	2	5	13	71.74	$21,864
Best finish for 1964: T-2nd at the San Diego Open									
1965	27	83	12	0	0	1	4	73.41	$8,625
Best finish for 1965: 9th at the Cleveland Open									
1966	26	77	11	0	0	5	5	73.27	$12,236
Best finish for 1966: T-8th at the Texas Open Invitational & Greater Seattle-Everett Open Invitational									
1967	21	67	12	0	1	1	5	73.04	$11,329
Best finish for 1967: T-4th at the Bing Crosby Pro-Am									
1968	11	34	6	0	0	0	1	72.53	$3,537
Best finish for 1968: T-19th at the Bob Hope Desert Classic									
1969	19	64	12	0	1	2	3	72.31	$19,407
Best finish for 1969: T-2nd at the U.S. Open									
1970	24	85	20	0	0	0	3	72.59	$15,103
Best finish for 1970: T-14th at the Greater New Orleans Open & IVB Philadelphia Golf Classic									
1971	28	85	18	0	3	6	12	71.88	$51,555
Best finish for 1971: T-3rd at the U.S. Open									
1972	28	83	17	1	3	6	7	72.40	$74,874
Best finish for 1972: Win at the Bob Hope Chrysler Classic									
1973	22	43	3	0	0	0	0	74.14	$1,068
Best finish for 1973: T-48th at the Canadian Open									
1974	22	52	6	0	0	1	2	73.35	$21,007
Best finish for 1974: T-7th at the Houston Open									
1975	13	20	0	0	0	0	0	75.40	
1976	4	10	0	0	0	0	0	74.60	
1977	3	8	0	0	0	0	0	74.38	
1978	3	9	1	0	0	0	0	72.67	$385
Best finish for 1978: T-60th at the Phoenix Open									
1979	2	6	0	0	0	0	0	76.67	
1980	1	5	1	0	0	0	0	72.40	$562
Best finish for 1980: T-66th at the Bob Hope Chrysler Classic									
1982	1	4	0	0	0	0	0	77.25	
1983	1	4	0	0	0	0	0	73.75	

Period Totals	Starts	Rounds Played	Cuts Made	Wins	Top-5s	Top-10s	Top-25s	Scoring Average	Money
	426	1391	261	3	39	75	149	72.13	$373,810

PGA Tour career totals from 1944 to 1983

	Starts	Rounds Played	Cuts Made	Wins	Top-5s	Top-10s	Top-25s	Scoring Average	Money
	528	1784	362	6	51	112	214	N/A	$431,211

Clarence Rose

Year	Starts	Rounds Played	Cuts Made	Wins	Top-5s	Top-10s	Top-25s	Scoring Average	Money
1981	9	18	3	0	1	1	1	73.78	$10,085

Best finish for 1981: 5th at the World Disney World National Team Championship

Year	Starts	Rounds Played	Cuts Made	Wins	Top-5s	Top-10s	Top-25s	Scoring Average	Money
1982	26	83	16	0	0	0	8	72.12	$41,075

Best finish for 1982: T-11th at the Sammy Davis, Jr. - Greater Hartford Open

| 1983 | 35 | 109 | 18 | 0 | 0 | 1 | 4 | 72.50 | $45,971 |

Best finish for 1983: T-6th at the Western Open

| 1984 | 32 | 103 | 18 | 0 | 1 | 2 | 5 | 72.14 | $63,278 |

Best finish for 1984: T-5th at the Canadian Open

| 1985 | 35 | 113 | 22 | 0 | 1 | 3 | 10 | 71.73 | $134,610 |

Best finish for 1985: 2nd at the Southern Open

| 1986 | 33 | 98 | 20 | 0 | 3 | 5 | 9 | 71.53 | $189,387 |

Best finish for 1986: T-2nd at the Los Angeles Open & Honda Classic

| 1987 | 36 | 114 | 21 | 0 | 3 | 4 | 6 | 71.55 | $174,154 |

Best finish for 1987: 2nd at the Greater Greensboro Open

| 1988 | 33 | 114 | 24 | 0 | 2 | 4 | 8 | 71.22 | $229,976 |

Best finish for 1988: T-2nd at the GTE Byron Nelson Classic

| 1989 | 32 | 106 | 21 | 0 | 2 | 2 | 8 | 71.56 | $267,141 |

Best finish for 1989: 2nd at the International

| 1990 | 34 | 87 | 9 | 0 | 0 | 0 | 0 | 73.56 | $25,908 |

Best finish for 1990: T-30th at the Bank of Boston Classic

| 1991 | 21 | 52 | 4 | 0 | 0 | 0 | 0 | 72.63 | $9,564 |

Best finish for 1991: T-36th at the Buick Southern Open

| 1992 | 8 | 22 | 3 | 0 | 0 | 0 | 0 | 72.50 | $10,488 |

Best finish for 1992: T-26th at the Anheuser-Busch Golf Classic

| 1993 | 4 | 14 | 3 | 0 | 0 | 0 | 0 | 71.50 | $6,823 |

Best finish for 1993: T-39th at the Anheuser-Busch Golf Classic

| 1994 | 4 | 11 | 1 | 0 | 0 | 0 | 0 | 72.18 | $2,992 |

Best finish for 1994: T-46th at the Anheuser-Busch Golf Classic

| 1995 | 2 | 6 | 1 | 0 | 0 | 0 | 1 | 70.67 | $7,061 |

Best finish for 1995: T-20th at the Deposit Guaranty Golf Classic

| 1996 | 27 | 85 | 17 | 1 | 1 | 2 | 8 | 70.88 | $461,899 |

Best finish for 1996: Win at the Sprint International

| 1997 | 32 | 92 | 14 | 0 | 2 | 3 | 5 | 71.87 | $257,781 |

Best finish for 1997: T-5th at the Tucson Chrysler Classic & Greater Milwaukee Open

| 1998 | 33 | 98 | 17 | 0 | 0 | 0 | 4 | 71.53 | $191,343 |

Best finish for 1998: T-12th at the BellSouth Classic

| 1999 | 22 | 48 | 4 | 0 | 0 | 0 | 0 | 72.60 | $36,451 |

Best finish for 1999: T-27th at the Shell Houston Open

| 2000 | 7 | 14 | 1 | 0 | 0 | 0 | 0 | 71.79 | $5,512 |

Best finish for 2000: T-61st at the Westin Texas Open at LaCantera

Year	Starts	Rounds Played	Cuts Made	Wins	Top-5s	Top-10s	Top-25s	Scoring Average	Money
2001	1	0	0	0	0	0	0		
2002	1	0	0	0	0	0	0		
2003	1	0	0	0	0	0	0		
2004	1	0	0	0	0	0	0		
2005	1	0	0	0	0	0	0		
2006	1	0	0	0	0	0	0		
Period Totals	471	1387	237	1	16	27	77	71.92	$2,171,500

Justin Rose

Year	Starts	Rounds Played	Cuts Made	Wins	Top-5s	Top-10s	Top-25s	Scoring Average	Money
1998	1	4	1	0	1	1	1	70.50	

Best finish for 1998: T-4th at the British Open

| 1999 | 1 | 2 | 0 | 0 | 0 | 0 | 0 | 78.00 | $1,719 |
| 2001 | 1 | 4 | 1 | 0 | 0 | 0 | 0 | 71.25 | $30,756 |

Best finish for 2001: T-30th at the British Open

| 2002 | 4 | 16 | 4 | 0 | 1 | 1 | 3 | 70.81 | $316,316 |

Best finish for 2002: 5th at the WGC-NEC Invitational

| 2003 | 11 | 36 | 9 | 0 | 2 | 2 | 3 | 71.83 | $750,105 |

Best finish for 2003: 3rd at the Deutsche Bank Championship

| 2004 | 22 | 72 | 18 | 0 | 3 | 4 | 10 | 70.63 | $1,239,764 |

Best finish for 2004: T-4th at the Memorial Tournament & Bell Canadian Open

| 2005 | 28 | 95 | 22 | 0 | 2 | 3 | 11 | 70.48 | $1,365,191 |

Best finish for 2005: T-3rd at the Buick Championship & FUNAI Classic at the Walt Disney World Resort

Year	Starts	Rounds Played	Cuts Made	Wins	Top-5s	Top-10s	Top-25s	Scoring Average	Money
2006	28	95	21	0	3	5	11	70.35	$1,629,288

Best finish for 2006: T-2nd at the Valero Texas Open

| 2007 | 16 | 59 | 15 | 0 | 5 | 7 | 11 | 70.24 | $2,705,875 |

Best finish for 2007: T-2nd at the WGC-Bridgestone Invitational

| 2008 | 15 | 45 | 10 | 0 | 1 | 2 | 6 | 71.80 | $1,047,854 |

Best finish for 2008: T-2nd at the Memorial Tournament

Period Totals	Starts	Rounds Played	Cuts Made	Wins	Top-5s	Top-10s	Top-25s	Scoring Average	Money
	127	428	101	0	18	25	56	70.75	$9,086,868

Bob Ross

Year	Starts	Rounds Played	Cuts Made	Wins	Top-5s	Top-10s	Top-25s	Scoring Average	Money
1961	1	2	0	0	0	0	0	75.50	
1962	3	10	2	0	0	0	0	74.50	$426

Best finish for 1962: T-26th at the Azalea Open Invitational

| 1963 | 1 | 4 | 1 | 0 | 0 | 0 | 1 | 72.25 | $104 |

Best finish for 1963: T-22nd at the Jamaica Open Invitational

1964	1	2	0	0	0	0	0	77.00	
1965	1	2	0	0	0	0	0	77.00	
1966	3	10	2	0	0	0	0	75.30	

Best finish for 1966: 64th at the Philadelphia Golf Classic

| 1967 | 6 | 16 | 2 | 0 | 0 | 0 | 0 | 73.50 | |

Best finish for 1967: T-51st at the Philadelphia Classic

| 1968 | 3 | 8 | 1 | 0 | 0 | 0 | 0 | 73.88 | |

Best finish for 1968: T-62nd at the Philadelphia Golf Classic

| 1969 | 1 | 2 | 0 | 0 | 0 | 0 | 0 | 74.50 | |
| 1970 | 5 | 16 | 3 | 0 | 0 | 0 | 0 | 73.44 | $682 |

Best finish for 1970: T-59th at the Greater Jacksonville Open, Greater Greensboro Open & Greater New Orleans Open

1971	1	2	0	0	0	0	0	77.50	
1972	1	2	0	0	0	0	0	75.50	
1973	2	6	1	0	0	0	0	75.17	

Best finish for 1973: T-78th at the Canadian Open

| 1974 | 3 | 6 | 0 | 0 | 0 | 0 | 0 | 75.67 | |
| 1975 | 3 | 8 | 1 | 0 | 0 | 0 | 0 | 73.63 | $360 |

Best finish for 1975: T-63rd at the Canadian Open

Period Totals	Starts	Rounds Played	Cuts Made	Wins	Top-5s	Top-10s	Top-25s	Scoring Average	Money
	35	96	13	0	0	0	1	74.34	$1,572

John Ross

Year	Starts	Rounds Played	Cuts Made	Wins	Top-5s	Top-10s	Top-25s	Scoring Average	Money
1989	1	2	0	0	0	0	0	71.50	
1991	3	8	1	0	0	0	1	73.75	$18,500

Best finish for 1991: T-17th at the Kmart Greater Greensboro Open

| 1992 | 29 | 86 | 16 | 0 | 0 | 0 | 4 | 71.27 | $85,541 |

Best finish for 1992: T-16th at the Buick Open

| 1993 | 15 | 45 | 7 | 0 | 0 | 0 | 1 | 72.42 | $23,412 |

Best finish for 1993: T-22nd at the Deposit Guaranty Classic

Period Totals	Starts	Rounds Played	Cuts Made	Wins	Top-5s	Top-10s	Top-25s	Scoring Average	Money
	48	141	24	0	0	0	6	71.78	$127,453

Chuck Rotar

Year	Starts	Rounds Played	Cuts Made	Wins	Top-5s	Top-10s	Top-25s	Scoring Average	Money
1959	4	16	3	0	0	1	2	70.69	$1,114

Best finish for 1959: T-10th at the Hesperia Open Invitational

| 1960 | 3 | 12 | 3 | 0 | 0 | 0 | 1 | 70.58 | $838 |

Best finish for 1960: T-16th at the San Diego Open Invitational

| 1961 | 2 | 8 | 2 | 0 | 0 | 0 | 1 | 71.38 | $608 |

Best finish for 1961: T-14th at the Ontario Open

| 1962 | 3 | 10 | 2 | 0 | 0 | 0 | 1 | 71.50 | $590 |

Best finish for 1962: T-20th at the Seattle World's Fair Open Invitational

| 1964 | 19 | 49 | 5 | 0 | 0 | 0 | 3 | 73.57 | $2,563 |

Best finish for 1964: T-13th at the Greater Greensboro Open

| 1965 | 12 | 30 | 3 | 0 | 0 | 1 | 1 | 74.90 | $2,200 |

Best finish for 1965: T-7th at the Oklahoma City Open

| 1966 | 9 | 20 | 1 | 0 | 0 | 0 | 0 | 75.25 | |

Best finish for 1966: T-66th at the Buick Open Invitational

1967	3	8	0	0	0	0	0	75.88	
1968	1	2	0	0	0	0	0	72.50	
1970	2	4	0	0	0	0	0	75.75	
1971	1	2	0	0	0	0	0	74.50	
1972	1	2	0	0	0	0	0	82.50	

Period Totals	Starts	Rounds Played	Cuts Made	Wins	Top-5s	Top-10s	Top-25s	Scoring Average	Money
	60	163	19	0	0	2	9	73.56	$7,913

Dennis Rouse

Year	Starts	Rounds Played	Cuts Made	Wins	Top-5s	Top-10s	Top-25s	Scoring Average	Money
1966	1	2	0	0	0	0	0	75.50	
1968	6	14	1	0	0	0	0	73.50	$178

Best finish for 1968: T-29th at the Robinson Open

1969	8	19	2	0	0	0	0	75.53	$309

Best finish for 1969: 56th at the Indian Ridge Hospital Open

1970	5	12	1	0	0	0	0	75.17	$161

Best finish for 1970: T-73rd at the Coral Springs Open Invitational

1971	11	28	3	0	0	0	0	74.14	$872

Best finish for 1971: T-41st at the Greater Jacksonville Open

1972	7	15	1	0	0	0	0	76.33	$345

Best finish for 1972: T-47th at the Doral-Eastern Open

1973	3	8	1	0	0	0	0	74.00	$270

Best finish for 1973: T-62nd at the Walt Disney World Open

1974	4	9	0	0	0	0	0	76.22	
Period Totals	Starts	Rounds Played	Cuts Made	Wins	Top-5s	Top-10s	Top-25s	Scoring Average	Money
	45	107	9	0	0	0	0	74.92	$2,135

Jimmy Roy

Year	Starts	Rounds Played	Cuts Made	Wins	Top-5s	Top-10s	Top-25s	Scoring Average	Money
1983	27	75	9	0	0	0	0	73.75	$8,301

Best finish for 1983: T-40th at the Bing Crosby Pro-Am

1984	2	6	1	0	0	0	0	73.67	$1,018

Best finish for 1984: T-48th at the Bing Crosby Pro-Am

1985	1	2	0	0	0	0	0	74.50	
1989	1	2	0	0	0	0	0	76.00	$1,000
1992	1	2	0	0	0	0	0	74.50	
1993	1	2	0	0	0	0	0	74.50	
Period Totals	Starts	Rounds Played	Cuts Made	Wins	Top-5s	Top-10s	Top-25s	Scoring Average	Money
	33	89	10	0	0	0	0	73.84	$10,319

Hugh Royer III

Year	Starts	Rounds Played	Cuts Made	Wins	Top-5s	Top-10s	Top-25s	Scoring Average	Money
1985	1	4	1	0	0	0	0	71.25	

Best finish for 1985: T-60th at the Southern Open

1994	1	4	1	0	0	0	0	74.50	$4,325

Best finish for 1994: T-55th at the U.S. Open

1996	31	91	16	0	1	3	5	71.51	$183,066

Best finish for 1996: T-5th at the Quad City Classic

1997	33	83	7	0	0	0	0	72.63	$23,377

Best finish for 1997: T-43rd at the GTE Byron Nelson Classic

1998	31	82	11	0	1	1	2	72.05	$143,963

Best finish for 1998: T-5th at the Greater Vancouver Open

1999	1	2	0	0	0	0	0	76.50	
Period Totals	Starts	Rounds Played	Cuts Made	Wins	Top-5s	Top-10s	Top-25s	Scoring Average	Money
	98	266	36	0	2	4	7	72.10	$354,731

Hugh Royer, Jr.

Year	Starts	Rounds Played	Cuts Made	Wins	Top-5s	Top-10s	Top-25s	Scoring Average	Money
1958	1	4	1	0	0	0	0	79.00	

Best finish for 1958: T-66th at the Carling Open

1960	2	8	2	0	0	1	1	72.13	$841

Best finish for 1960: T-10th at the Texas Open Invitational

1963	1	2	0	0	0	0	0	79.00	$150
1964	1	2	0	0	0	0	0	78.50	
1965	1	2	0	0	0	0	0	76.00	
1966	7	26	6	0	0	0	3	72.19	$5,483

Best finish for 1966: T-12th at the Canadian Open

1967	24	82	17	0	1	2	5	72.35	$16,786

Best finish for 1967: 3rd at the Sahara Open

1968	27	92	19	0	0	2	5	71.86	$10,833

Best finish for 1968: T-7th at the Rebel Yell Open

1969	32	109	23	0	0	2	8	72.14	$20,087

Best finish for 1969: T-8th at the Doral Open & Sahara Invitational

1970	36	129	30	1	2	2	8	72.11	$49,528

Best finish for 1970: Win at the Western Open

1971	35	111	21	0	0	1	6	72.83	$20,756

Best finish for 1971: T-8th at the Byron Nelson Golf Classic

1972	5	14	2	0	0	0	1	73.64	$1,246

Best finish for 1972: T-21st at the Greater Jacksonville Open

Year	Starts	Rounds Played	Cuts Made	Wins	Top-5s	Top-10s	Top-25s	Scoring Average	Money
1974	1	4	1	0	0	0	0	73.00	

Best finish for 1974: 71st at the Southern Open

1975	1	4	1	0	0	0	0	70.50	$341

Best finish for 1975: T-40th at the Southern Open

1976	1	2	0	0	0	0	0	77.00	
1977	1	4	1	0	0	0	0	71.75	$284

Best finish for 1977: T-50th at the Southern Open

1978	1	2	0	0	0	0	0	72.00	
1980	1	2	0	0	0	0	0	73.50	
1983	1	2	0	0	0	0	0	74.50	
1984	1	2	0	0	0	0	0	77.00	
1985	1	2	0	0	0	0	0	72.50	
1987	3	8	1	0	0	0	0	73.00	$687

Best finish for 1987: T-54th at the Pensacola Open

1988	2	6	1	0	0	0	0	72.67	$744

Best finish for 1988: T-76th at the Southern Open

1989	1	4	1	0	0	0	0	69.50	$1,893

Best finish for 1989: T-34th at the Southern Open

1990	1	2	0	0	0	0	0	71.00	
Period Totals	**Starts**	**Rounds Played**	**Cuts Made**	**Wins**	**Top-5s**	**Top-10s**	**Top-25s**	**Scoring Average**	**Money**
	188	625	127	1	3	10	37	72.41	$129,660

Edward Rubis

Year	Starts	Rounds Played	Cuts Made	Wins	Top-5s	Top-10s	Top-25s	Scoring Average	Money
1958	1	4	1	0	0	0	0	72.00	

Best finish for 1958: 54th at the Insurance City Open

1959	1	2	0	0	0	0	0	76.50	
1961	1	2	0	0	0	0	0	78.50	
1962	2	7	2	0	0	0	0	76.00	$312

Best finish for 1962: T-50th at the U.S. Open

1963	5	18	4	0	1	1	2	73.11	$1,372

Best finish for 1963: T-3rd at the Jamaica Open Invitational

1964	10	29	6	0	0	0	2	73.34	$443

Best finish for 1964: T-23rd at the Azalea Open

1965	4	9	1	0	0	0	0	73.89	

Best finish for 1965: T-51st at the Greater Hartford Open

1966	5	15	3	0	0	0	0	74.00	$300

Best finish for 1966: T-39th at the Azalea Open Invitational

1967	1	2	0	0	0	0	0	74.00	
1968	1	2	0	0	0	0	0	74.00	
Period Totals	**Starts**	**Rounds Played**	**Cuts Made**	**Wins**	**Top-5s**	**Top-10s**	**Top-25s**	**Scoring Average**	**Money**
	31	90	17	0	1	1	4	73.82	$2,428

Craig Rudolph

Year	Starts	Rounds Played	Cuts Made	Wins	Top-5s	Top-10s	Top-25s	Scoring Average	Money
1989	1	2	0	0	0	0	0	72.00	
1990	1	2	0	0	0	0	0	74.00	
1991	26	67	7	0	0	0	0	72.88	$14,765

Best finish for 1991: T-42nd at the USF&G Classic

Period Totals	**Starts**	**Rounds Played**	**Cuts Made**	**Wins**	**Top-5s**	**Top-10s**	**Top-25s**	**Scoring Average**	**Money**
	28	71	7	0	0	0	0	72.89	$14,765

Mason Rudolph

Year	Starts	Rounds Played	Cuts Made	Wins	Top-5s	Top-10s	Top-25s	Scoring Average	Money
1958	2	6	1	0	1	1	1	70.17	

Best finish for 1958: 3rd at the Memphis Invitational

1959	14	56	13	1	2	3	10	70.57	$12,710

Best finish for 1959: Win at the Golden Gate Championship

1960	26	101	22	0	1	7	21	71.04	$14,170

Best finish for 1960: T-5th at the Texas Open Invitational

1961	27	108	25	0	4	9	19	70.92	$19,105

Best finish for 1961: T-5th at the St. Petersburg Open Invitational, "500" Festival Open Invitational, Buick Open Invitational & Eastern Open Invitational

1962	27	109	21	0	5	10	18	71.11	$24,996

Best finish for 1962: T-2nd at the Texas Open Invitational, Waco Turner Open Invitational & American Golf Classic

1963	31	125	31	1	5	10	27	70.87	$39,130

Best finish for 1963: Win at the Fig Garden Village Open Invitational

1964	28	112	27	1	9	14	23	70.83	$53,556

Best finish for 1964: Win at the New Orleans Open

1965	25	99	24	0	2	5	15	71.74	$34,079

Best finish for 1965: T-3rd at the Canadian Open

1966	25	92	21	1	4	7	14	71.65	$50,469

Best finish for 1966: Win at the Thunderbird Classic

Year	Starts	Rounds Played	Cuts Made	Wins	Top-5s	Top-10s	Top-25s	Scoring Average	Money
1967	29	105	23	0	2	4	11	72.18	$36,692

Best finish for 1967: T-3rd at the Philadelphia Classic

1968	28	98	21	0	1	2	11	72.14	$24,429

Best finish for 1968: T-5th at the Greater Hartford Open Invitational

1969	32	106	22	0	0	0	7	72.45	$17,246

Best finish for 1969: T-11th at the Los Angeles Open & The Masters

1970	32	110	25	1	1	5	8	71.89	$41,613

Best finish for 1970: Win at the Green Island Open Invitational

1971	25	86	20	0	0	2	14	71.71	$37,918

Best finish for 1971: T-6th at the Monsanto Open & Westchester Classic

1972	25	83	18	0	1	4	7	72.69	$24,309

Best finish for 1972: T-5th at the Liggett Meyers Open

1973	29	106	22	0	2	3	11	71.96	$56,920

Best finish for 1973: 2nd at the Walt Disney World Open

1974	26	88	18	0	0	1	5	72.63	$22,891

Best finish for 1974: T-10th at the American Golf Classic

1975	19	53	8	0	1	2	4	72.98	$21,711

Best finish for 1975: T-4th at the Tournament Players Championship

1976	25	77	14	0	0	1	4	72.48	$15,594

Best finish for 1976: T-9th at the San Antonio Texas Open

1977	21	56	7	0	0	0	0	73.52	$4,237

Best finish for 1977: T-33rd at the Jackie Gleason's Inverrary Classic

1978	13	34	4	0	0	0	0	73.35	$1,566

Best finish for 1978: T-55th at the Danny Thomas Memphis Classic

1979	10	22	1	0	0	0	0	74.91	$480

Best finish for 1979: 75th at the Colgate Hall Of Fame Classic

1980	4	8	0	0	0	0	0	74.38	
1981	1	2	0	0	0	0	0	76.50	
1983	1	2	0	0	0	0	0	77.00	
Period Totals	Starts	Rounds Played	Cuts Made	Wins	Top-5s	Top-10s	Top-25s	Scoring Average	Money
	525	1844	388	5	41	90	230	71.86	$553,822

Jack Rule

Year	Starts	Rounds Played	Cuts Made	Wins	Top-5s	Top-10s	Top-25s	Scoring Average	Money
1962	8	32	8	0	0	0	3	72.28	$2,172

Best finish for 1962: T-17th at the Oklahoma City Open Invitational

1963	27	109	26	1	5	5	15	71.28	$22,131

Best finish for 1963: Win at the St. Paul Open Invitational

1964	35	115	22	0	3	5	10	72.38	$18,232

Best finish for 1964: 3rd at the Mountain View Open

1965	30	89	13	1	2	5	6	73.19	$24,558

Best finish for 1965: Win at the Oklahoma City Open

1966	32	113	24	0	0	2	10	72.59	$21,172

Best finish for 1966: T-7th at the Bing Crosby National Professional-Amateur

1967	26	84	16	0	0	1	4	72.96	$7,785

Best finish for 1967: T-8th at the Phoenix Open

1968	6	19	3	0	0	1	1	73.05	$2,240

Best finish for 1968: 9th at the Bing Crosby National Professional-Amateur

1969	4	11	1	0	0	0	0	76.09	$114

Best finish for 1969: 83rd at the Minnesota Classic

1970	2	4	0	0	0	0	0	76.75	
1972	2	6	1	0	0	0	0	74.67	$118

Best finish for 1972: T-72nd at the Quad Cities Open

1974	1	4	1	0	0	0	0	76.75	$845

Best finish for 1974: T-54th at the U.S. Open

1976	1	2	0	0	0	0	0	78.00	$500
1978	1	2	0	0	0	0	0	77.50	$600
1987	1	0	0	0	0	0	0		
Period Totals	Starts	Rounds Played	Cuts Made	Wins	Top-5s	Top-10s	Top-25s	Scoring Average	Money
	176	590	115	2	10	19	49	72.63	$100,467

Brett Rumford

Year	Starts	Rounds Played	Cuts Made	Wins	Top-5s	Top-10s	Top-25s	Scoring Average	Money
2001	1	2	0	0	0	0	0	75.50	$1,431
2004	1	4	1	0	0	0	0	70.50	$58,000

Best finish for 2004: T-27th at the WGC-NEC Invitational

2005	1	2	0	0	0	0	0	75.50	
2006	1	4	1	0	0	0	1	70.50	$83,655

Best finish for 2006: T-16th at the British Open

2008	26	72	9	0	0	1	3	71.89	$386,419

Best finish for 2008: T-8th at the Bob Hope Chrysler Classic

Period Totals	Starts	Rounds Played	Cuts Made	Wins	Top-5s	Top-10s	Top-25s	Scoring Average	Money
	30	84	11	0	0	1	4	71.93	$529,504

Dave Rummells

Year	Starts	Rounds Played	Cuts Made	Wins	Top-5s	Top-10s	Top-25s	Scoring Average	Money
1981	1	0	0	0	0	0	0		
1986	32	91	15	0	0	2	5	72.74	$81,827

Best finish for 1986: T-9th at the Hawaiian Open

| 1987 | 30 | 110 | 25 | 0 | 0 | 1 | 10 | 70.94 | $149,286 |

Best finish for 1987: T-9th at the Doral-Ryder Open

| 1988 | 32 | 111 | 24 | 0 | 3 | 7 | 12 | 70.49 | $275,799 |

Best finish for 1988: T-3rd at the Bank of Boston Classic

| 1989 | 31 | 98 | 21 | 0 | 3 | 5 | 14 | 70.55 | $419,979 |

Best finish for 1989: 3rd at the Hawaiian Open & Canon Greater Hartford Open

| 1990 | 30 | 83 | 14 | 0 | 0 | 1 | 5 | 71.99 | $113,039 |

Best finish for 1990: 7th at the Honda Classic

| 1991 | 31 | 102 | 20 | 0 | 1 | 3 | 8 | 70.84 | $214,627 |

Best finish for 1991: T-3rd at the Chattanooga Classic

| 1992 | 32 | 96 | 18 | 0 | 0 | 1 | 2 | 71.41 | $95,182 |

Best finish for 1992: T-8th at the Buick Open

| 1993 | 27 | 77 | 11 | 0 | 2 | 2 | 5 | 71.45 | $249,163 |

Best finish for 1993: 2nd at the Buick Invitational of California

| 1994 | 31 | 100 | 20 | 0 | 0 | 0 | 4 | 71.46 | $122,872 |

Best finish for 1994: T-13th at the BellSouth Classic

| 1995 | 10 | 31 | 6 | 0 | 0 | 0 | 1 | 71.39 | $26,095 |

Best finish for 1995: T-20th at the Deposit Guaranty Golf Classic

| 1996 | 1 | 4 | 1 | 0 | 0 | 0 | 0 | 71.75 | $3,045 |

Best finish for 1996: T-47th at the United Airlines Hawaiian Open

| 1997 | 11 | 39 | 7 | 0 | 0 | 1 | 3 | 70.15 | $90,345 |

Best finish for 1997: T-7th at the Quad City Classic

| 1998 | 18 | 45 | 5 | 0 | 0 | 0 | 0 | 72.11 | $18,746 |

Best finish for 1998: T-54th at the Tucson Chrysler Classic

1999	2	4	0	0	0	0	0	71.75	
2000	1	2	0	0	0	0	0	72.00	
2001	2	4	0	0	0	0	0	75.00	
2002	4	12	2	0	0	0	0	71.00	$27,349

Best finish for 2002: T-29th at the Valero Texas Open

| 2003 | 7 | 16 | 1 | 0 | 0 | 0 | 0 | 72.69 | $14,280 |

Best finish for 2003: T-42nd at the Bell Canadian Open

| 2004 | 1 | 2 | 0 | 0 | 0 | 0 | 0 | 72.00 | |
| 2005 | 2 | 6 | 1 | 0 | 0 | 0 | 0 | 72.00 | $5,640 |

Best finish for 2005: 76th at the B.C. Open

2006	1	2	0	0	0	0	0	72.50	
2007	1	2	0	0	0	0	0	75.50	
2008	2	4	0	0	0	0	0	76.25	
Period Totals	**Starts**	**Rounds Played**	**Cuts Made**	**Wins**	**Top-5s**	**Top-10s**	**Top-25s**	**Scoring Average**	**Money**
	340	1041	191	0	9	23	69	71.34	$1,907,275

Paul Runyan

Year	Starts	Rounds Played	Cuts Made	Wins	Top-5s	Top-10s	Top-25s	Scoring Average	Money
1958	4	16	4	0	0	0	1	73.50	$470

Best finish for 1958: T-23rd at the Tijuana Open

| 1959 | 3 | 12 | 3 | 0 | 0 | 1 | 1 | 71.83 | $953 |

Best finish for 1959: T-9th at the Tijuana Open Invitational

| 1960 | 4 | 11 | 2 | 0 | 0 | 0 | 0 | 76.00 | $546 |

Best finish for 1960: T-38th at the Los Angeles Open Invitational

| 1961 | 1 | 4 | 1 | 0 | 0 | 0 | 1 | 74.75 | |

Best finish for 1961: T-18th at the British Open

| 1962 | 1 | 2 | 0 | 0 | 0 | 0 | 0 | 78.00 | |
| 1963 | 1 | 4 | 1 | 0 | 0 | 0 | 0 | 71.25 | $050 |

Best finish for 1963: T-50th at the Los Angeles Open

| 1964 | 3 | 9 | 1 | 0 | 0 | 0 | 0 | 74.67 | |

Best finish for 1964: T-48th at the San Diego Open

| 1965 | 5 | 12 | 1 | 0 | 0 | 0 | 0 | 76.42 | |

Best finish for 1965: 71st at the Sahara Invitational

1966	2	6	0	0	0	0	0	75.17	
1967	2	3	0	0	0	0	0	79.33	
1968	3	7	0	0	0	0	0	76.14	
1969	2	8	1	0	0	0	0	76.38	$214

Best finish for 1969: T-74th at the Andy Williams-San Diego Open

1970	2	7	0	0	0	0	0	78.57	
1971	1	4	0	0	0	0	0	73.25	
1972	2	6	0	0	0	0	0	76.17	
1973	1	2	0	0	0	0	0	85.50	

Year	Starts	Rounds Played	Cuts Made	Wins	Top-5s	Top-10s	Top-25s	Scoring Average	Money
1974	3	8	0	0	0	0	0	80.38	
1975	2	6	0	0	0	0	0	77.83	
1976	2	6	0	0	0	0	0	74.33	
1979	1	4	0	0	0	0	0	78.00	
1980	1	4	0	0	0	0	0	75.75	
Period Totals	Starts	Rounds Played	Cuts Made	Wins	Top-5s	Top-10s	Top-25s	Scoring Average	Money
	46	141	14	0	0	1	3	75.73	$2,233

PGA Tour career totals from 1928 to 1980

	Starts	Rounds Played	Cuts Made	Wins	Top-5s	Top-10s	Top-25s	Scoring Average	Money
	303	N/A	N/A	27	N/A	161	233	N/A	N/A

Gary Rusnak

Year	Starts	Rounds Played	Cuts Made	Wins	Top-5s	Top-10s	Top-25s	Scoring Average	Money
1986	1	2	0	0	0	0	0	73.00	
1987	1	2	0	0	0	0	0	72.50	
1988	1	4	1	0	0	0	0	71.75	$1,136

Best finish for 1988: T-53rd at the Centel Classic

1989	1	2	0	0	0	0	0	71.50	
1991	1	4	1	0	0	0	0	68.75	$858

Best finish for 1991: T-46th at the Deposit Guaranty Classic

1996	26	78	14	0	0	0	3	71.92	$74,209

Best finish for 1996: T-20th at the B.C. Open & Buick Challenge

Period Totals	Starts	Rounds Played	Cuts Made	Wins	Top-5s	Top-10s	Top-25s	Scoring Average	Money
	31	92	16	0	0	0	3	71.80	$76,203

Jim Rutledge

Year	Starts	Rounds Played	Cuts Made	Wins	Top-5s	Top-10s	Top-25s	Scoring Average	Money
1980	1	2	0	0	0	0	0	77.50	
1982	2	6	1	0	0	0	0	72.50	$3,081

Best finish for 1982: T-26th at the Canadian Open

1983	1	2	0	0	0	0	0	79.50	
1984	3	6	0	0	0	0	0	75.50	
1985	6	18	3	0	0	0	0	71.72	$3,913

Best finish for 1985: T-28th at the Texas Open

1986	5	16	3	0	0	0	0	72.19	$3,785

Best finish for 1986: T-41st at the Hardee's Golf Classic

1987	3	4	0	0	0	0	0	72.75	
1989	1	2	0	0	0	0	0	72.50	
1990	1	4	1	0	0	0	0	72.00	$5,837

Best finish for 1990: T-57th at the British Open

1991	1	2	0	0	0	0	0	75.00	$1,008
1993	1	2	0	0	0	0	0	76.50	
1994	1	2	0	0	0	0	0	74.00	
1996	1	2	0	0	0	0	0	72.00	
1997	1	2	0	0	0	0	0	71.00	
1998	1	2	0	0	0	0	0	72.50	
2002	1	2	0	0	0	0	0	72.50	
2003	1	2	0	0	0	0	0	74.00	
2004	1	4	1	0	0	0	0	72.25	$11,898

Best finish for 2004: T-47th at the Bell Canadian Open

2005	1	2	0	0	0	0	0	72.50	
2006	1	2	0	0	0	0	0	73.50	
2007	23	59	5	0	0	0	0	72.41	$62,242

Best finish for 2007: T-31st at the Mayakoba Golf Classic

2008	1	2	0	0	0	0	0	73.00	
Period Totals	Starts	Rounds Played	Cuts Made	Wins	Top-5s	Top-10s	Top-25s	Scoring Average	Money
	58	145	14	0	0	0	0	72.73	$91,764

Charlie Rymer

Year	Starts	Rounds Played	Cuts Made	Wins	Top-5s	Top-10s	Top-25s	Scoring Average	Money
1988	1	2	0	0	0	0	0	80.00	
1992	2	6	1	0	0	0	0	71.83	$2,832

Best finish for 1992: T-54th at the Chattanooga Classic

1993	1	2	0	0	0	0	0	73.50	
1995	28	75	11	0	1	2	4	71.47	$180,401

Best finish for 1995: 3rd at the Shell Houston Open

1996	29	90	16	0	1	1	3	71.63	$132,076

Best finish for 1996: T-4th at the CVS Charity Classic

1997	16	46	9	0	0	0	1	71.07	$69,110

Best finish for 1997: T-13th at the CVS Charity Classic

1998	2	4	0	0	0	0	0	72.50	

Year	Starts	Rounds Played	Cuts Made	Wins	Top-5s	Top-10s	Top-25s	Scoring Average	Money
1999	1	2	0	0	0	0	0	72.50	
2000	3	6	0	0	0	0	0	75.83	
2001	1	1	0	0	0	0	0	73.00	
Period Totals	Starts	Rounds Played	Cuts Made	Wins	Top-5s	Top-10s	Top-25s	Scoring Average	Money
	84	234	37	0	2	3	8	71.70	$384,419

Rory Sabbatini

Year	Starts	Rounds Played	Cuts Made	Wins	Top-5s	Top-10s	Top-25s	Scoring Average	Money
1999	27	78	13	0	2	2	5	72.01	$381,322

Best finish for 1999: T-3rd at the BellSouth Classic & B.C. Open

2000	26	83	16	1	2	3	7	71.22	$1,263,534

Best finish for 2000: Win at the Air Canada Championship

2001	23	69	13	0	3	3	3	71.28	$1,045,590

Best finish for 2001: T-2nd at the Mercedes Championships & Invensys Classic at Las Vegas

2002	23	64	13	0	3	4	6	70.94	$943,664

Best finish for 2002: T-2nd at the Nissan Open

2003	27	93	20	1	2	5	6	71.15	$1,605,701

Best finish for 2003: Win at the FBR Capital Open

2004	26	86	19	0	4	7	13	70.88	$2,503,397

Best finish for 2004: T-2nd at the Buick Classic & WGC-NEC Invitational

2005	26	78	15	0	0	3	6	71.41	$929,930

Best finish for 2005: T-6th at the Bank of America Colonial & Booz Allen Classic

2006	24	83	19	1	4	5	10	70.80	$2,866,001

Best finish for 2006: Win at the Nissan Open

2007	23	79	18	1	6	10	13	70.49	$4,556,856

Best finish for 2007: Win at the Crowne Plaza Invitational at Colonial

2008	23	76	17	0	2	3	6	71.05	$1,559,277

Best finish for 2008: 2nd at the Sony Open in Hawaii

Period Totals	Starts	Rounds Played	Cuts Made	Wins	Top-5s	Top-10s	Top-25s	Scoring Average	Money
	248	789	163	4	28	45	75	71.12	$17,655,272

Ed Sabo

Year	Starts	Rounds Played	Cuts Made	Wins	Top-5s	Top-10s	Top-25s	Scoring Average	Money
1975	2	4	0	0	0	0	0	75.50	
1976	14	44	7	0	1	1	2	72.64	$10,601

Best finish for 1976: T-4th at the Ohio Kings Island Open

1977	27	81	14	0	0	0	2	73.31	$10,368

Best finish for 1977: T-16th at the Ed McMahon Quad City Open

1978	24	78	16	0	0	0	3	72.74	$11,792

Best finish for 1978: T-18th at the Tallahassee Open

1979	22	63	10	0	1	1	1	72.97	$13,446

Best finish for 1979: T-5th at the Ed McMahon Quad City Open

1981	7	17	1	0	0	0	0	73.18	$733

Best finish for 1981: T-56th at the Hawaiian Open

1983	1	1	0	0	0	0	0	74.00	
1992	1	2	0	0	0	0	0	77.50	$1,200
2000	1	2	0	0	0	0	0	75.00	$2,000
Period Totals	Starts	Rounds Played	Cuts Made	Wins	Top-5s	Top-10s	Top-25s	Scoring Average	Money
	99	292	48	0	2	2	8	73.05	$50,140

Akio Sadakata

Year	Starts	Rounds Played	Cuts Made	Wins	Top-5s	Top-10s	Top-25s	Scoring Average	Money
2003	29	81	11	0	0	0	0	71.77	$107,730

Best finish for 2003: T-39th at the B.C. Open

2004	1	2	0	0	0	0	0	72.50	
2005	2	6	1	0	0	0	0	71.83	$7,315

Best finish for 2005: T-63rd at the Valero Texas Open

Period Totals	Starts	Rounds Played	Cuts Made	Wins	Top-5s	Top-10s	Top-25s	Scoring Average	Money
	32	89	12	0	0	0	0	71.79	$115,045

Jarmo Sandelin

Year	Starts	Rounds Played	Cuts Made	Wins	Top-5s	Top-10s	Top-25s	Scoring Average	Money
1995	1	4	1	0	0	0	0	74.00	$7,178

Best finish for 1995: T-79th at the British Open

1996	14	29	1	0	0	0	0	74.31	$2,509

Best finish for 1996: T-72nd at the Honda Classic

1999	5	14	3	0	0	0	1	73.71	$101,314

Best finish for 1999: T-20th at the American Express Championship

2000	3	10	2	0	0	0	1	72.30	$67,432

Best finish for 2000: T-24th at the PGA Championship

2001	2	3	0	0	0	0	0	73.67	$1,000
Period Totals	Starts	Rounds Played	Cuts Made	Wins	Top-5s	Top-10s	Top-25s	Scoring Average	Money
	25	60	7	0	0	0	2	73.78	$179,432

Bill Sander

Year	Starts	Rounds Played	Cuts Made	Wins	Top-5s	Top-10s	Top-25s	Scoring Average	Money
1977	5	14	2	0	0	0	0	75.29	

Best finish for 1977: 49th at the Masters

1978	9	22	2	0	0	0	1	72.64	$3,167

Best finish for 1978: T-17th at the Western Open

1979	22	64	10	0	0	0	1	72.88	$9,631

Best finish for 1979: T-21st at the Joe Garagiola Tucson Open

1980	23	66	11	0	0	0	2	72.79	$13,644

Best finish for 1980: T-20th at the Glen Campbell Los Angeles Open

1981	16	48	7	0	0	0	2	72.40	$10,359

Best finish for 1981: T-11th at the Quad Cities Open

1982	16	44	6	0	0	0	1	73.09	$7,648

Best finish for 1982: T-22nd at the Greater Milwaukee Open

1983	26	73	8	0	0	0	1	73.12	$9,416

Best finish for 1983: T-21st at the Kemper Open

1984	30	91	14	0	1	2	3	72.90	$36,357

Best finish for 1984: T-5th at the Phoenix Open

1985	18	57	11	0	1	2	6	72.02	$55,307

Best finish for 1985: T-4th at the Canadian Open

1986	31	93	16	0	0	0	3	72.26	$38,564

Best finish for 1986: T-17th at the Tallahassee Open

1987	32	96	18	0	0	4	6	71.70	$93,154

Best finish for 1987: T-6th at the Shearson Lehman/Andy Williams San Diego

1988	30	86	14	0	1	1	3	71.67	$104,323

Best finish for 1988: T-2nd at the Los Angeles Open

1989	33	98	17	0	1	2	4	71.50	$106,074

Best finish for 1989: T-5th at the USF&G Classic

1990	30	99	22	0	1	2	6	71.45	$174,886

Best finish for 1990: T-4th at the Northern Telecom Tucson Open

1991	20	58	11	0	1	1	2	71.97	$139,442

Best finish for 1991: 2nd at the Shearson Lehman Brothers Open

1992	22	52	7	0	0	0	1	73.44	$23,248

Best finish for 1992: T-14th at the Buick Southern Open

1993	1	4	1	0	0	0	0	73.00	$582

Best finish for 1993: 73rd at the Deposit Guaranty Classic

Period Totals	Starts	Rounds Played	Cuts Made	Wins	Top-5s	Top-10s	Top-25s	Scoring Average	Money
	364	1065	177	0	6	14	42	72.32	$825,802

Doug Sanders

Year	Starts	Rounds Played	Cuts Made	Wins	Top-5s	Top-10s	Top-25s	Scoring Average	Money
1955	2	16	4	0	0	1	3	69.00	

Best finish for 1955: T8th at the Mayfair Inn Open

1956	4	16	4	1	1	1	3	69.75	N/A

Best finish for 1956: Win at the Canadian Open

1957	8	32	8	0	1	1	3	72.22	$2,894

Best finish for 1957: T4th at Carling Open

1958	25	93	21	1	2	6	15	70.96	$14,650

Best finish for 1958: Win at the Western Open

1959	23	91	20	1	4	13	20	70.04	$21,392

Best finish for 1959: Win at the Coral Gables Open Invitational

1960	27	108	25	0	8	12	21	70.79	$26,591

Best finish for 1960: T-2nd at the Pensacola Open Invitational

1961	32	129	29	5	15	16	28	70.07	$55,788

Best finish for 1961: Win at the Greater New Orleans Open Invitational, Colonial National Invitational, Hot Springs Open Invitational, Eastern Open Invitational & Cajun Classic Open Invitational

1962	29	117	27	3	11	16	22	70.91	$39,940

Best finish for 1962: Win at the Pensacola Open Invitational, St. Paul Open Invitational & Oklahoma City Open Invitational

1963	19	74	18	1	3	9	16	71.27	$25,952

Best finish for 1963: Win at the Greensboro Open Invitational

1964	33	125	29	0	5	7	21	71.52	$35,503

Best finish for 1964: T-2nd at the Greater Greensboro Open, Tournament of Champions & "500" Festival Open

1965	31	112	26	2	7	11	22	71.04	$79,601

Best finish for 1965: Win at the Pensacola Open & Doral Open

1966	33	122	27	3	8	17	21	71.29	$103,111

Best finish for 1966: Win at the Bob Hope Desert Classic, Jacksonville Open Invitational & Greater Greensboro Open Invitational

1967	33	122	27	1	9	14	22	71.21	$123,586

Best finish for 1967: Win at the Doral Open

1968	32	116	26	0	2	4	13	72.09	$36,438

Best finish for 1968: T-2nd at the Jacksonville Open Invitational

1969	35	109	24	0	0	4	9	72.06	$28,876

Best finish for 1969: T-7th at the Canadian Open

Year	Starts	Rounds Played	Cuts Made	Wins	Top-5s	Top-10s	Top-25s	Scoring Average	Money
1970	31	98	19	1	2	3	8	72.00	$54,363

Best finish for 1970: Win at the Bahama Islands Open

| 1971 | 30 | 98 | 20 | 0 | 0 | 1 | 9 | 72.52 | $26,845 |

Best finish for 1971: T-9th at the British Open

| 1972 | 27 | 97 | 22 | 1 | 5 | 8 | 16 | 71.41 | $103,985 |

Best finish for 1972: Win at the Kemper Open

| 1973 | 24 | 81 | 16 | 0 | 1 | 4 | 9 | 72.58 | $36,070 |

Best finish for 1973: T-4th at the Atlanta Classic

| 1974 | 9 | 25 | 2 | 0 | 0 | 0 | 0 | 73.04 | $1,447 |

Best finish for 1974: T-32nd at the Bob Hope Chrysler Classic

| 1975 | 21 | 69 | 12 | 0 | 0 | 1 | 1 | 72.68 | $9,093 |

Best finish for 1975: T-10th at the Pensacola Open

| 1976 | 11 | 37 | 9 | 0 | 0 | 0 | 0 | 73.14 | $3,875 |

Best finish for 1976: T-28th at the British Open

1977	4	7	0	0	0	0	0	75.86	
1978	10	22	0	0	0	0	0	77.09	
1979	7	18	1	0	0	0	0	75.00	$578

Best finish for 1979: T-63rd at the Bob Hope Chrysler Classic

| 1980 | 5 | 13 | 0 | 0 | 0 | 0 | 0 | 75.38 | |
| 1981 | 6 | 18 | 2 | 0 | 0 | 0 | 0 | 73.39 | $1,050 |

Best finish for 1981: 70th at the Wickes/Andy Williams San Diego Open

| 1982 | 4 | 11 | 0 | 0 | 0 | 0 | 0 | 75.09 | |
| 1983 | 5 | 15 | 1 | 0 | 0 | 0 | 0 | 73.67 | $659 |

Best finish for 1983: T-62nd at the Bing Crosby Pro-Am

1984	3	9	0	0	0	0	0	75.00	
1985	2	6	0	0	0	0	0	74.67	
1986	1	4	0	0	0	0	0	72.50	
1989	1	4	0	0	0	0	0	75.00	
2000	1	4	0	0	0	0	0	75.25	
2001	1	4	0	0	0	0	0	78.25	
2002	1	4	0	0	0	0	0	77.50	
Period Totals	**Starts**	**Rounds Played**	**Cuts Made**	**Wins**	**Top-5s**	**Top-10s**	**Top-25s**	**Scoring Average**	**Money**
	570	2009	417	20	84	149	282	71.71	$846,030

Gary Sanders

Year	Starts	Rounds Played	Cuts Made	Wins	Top-5s	Top-10s	Top-25s	Scoring Average	Money
1972	1	2	0	0	0	0	0	73.00	
1973	21	53	6	0	0	0	0	74.06	$1,136

Best finish for 1973: T-44th at the USI Classic

| 1974 | 21 | 67 | 13 | 0 | 0 | 2 | 5 | 72.43 | $17,209 |

Best finish for 1974: T-6th at the Quad Cities Open

| 1975 | 17 | 52 | 9 | 0 | 0 | 0 | 1 | 73.17 | $5,451 |

Best finish for 1975: T-13th at the Phoenix Open

| **Period Totals** | **Starts** | **Rounds Played** | **Cuts Made** | **Wins** | **Top-5s** | **Top-10s** | **Top-25s** | **Scoring Average** | **Money** |
| | 60 | 174 | 28 | 0 | 0 | 2 | 6 | 73.16 | $23,796 |

Jeff Sanders

Year	Starts	Rounds Played	Cuts Made	Wins	Top-5s	Top-10s	Top-25s	Scoring Average	Money
1981	10	27	4	0	0	0	1	72.81	$4,222

Best finish for 1981: T-22nd at the Pleasant Valley Jimmy Fund Classic

| 1982 | 23 | 65 | 9 | 0 | 0 | 0 | 1 | 72.45 | $17,670 |

Best finish for 1982: T-11th at the Hawaiian Open

| 1983 | 24 | 68 | 9 | 0 | 0 | 1 | 2 | 72.68 | $17,959 |

Best finish for 1983: T-9th at the Texas Open

| 1985 | 18 | 47 | 6 | 0 | 0 | 0 | 3 | 72.55 | $22,955 |

Best finish for 1985: T-11th at the B.C. Open

1998	1	2	0	0	0	0	0	75.00	
Period Totals	**Starts**	**Rounds Played**	**Cuts Made**	**Wins**	**Top-5s**	**Top-10s**	**Top-25s**	**Scoring Average**	**Money**
	76	209	28	0	0	1	7	72.62	$62,806

Monte Sanders

Year	Starts	Rounds Played	Cuts Made	Wins	Top-5s	Top-10s	Top-25s	Scoring Average	Money
1958	1	2	0	0	0	0	0	78.00	
1964	2	4	0	0	0	0	0	77.75	
1965	1	1	1	0	0	0	0	83.00	

Best finish for 1965: 101 at the Bing Crosby Pro-Am

1966	1	2	0	0	0	0	0	77.50	
1967	1	2	0	0	0	0	0	78.00	
1968	8	22	3	0	0	0	1	73.05	$1,365

Best finish for 1968: T-18th at the Haig Open Invitational

| 1969 | 5 | 14 | 2 | 0 | 0 | 0 | 0 | 73.93 | $133 |

Best finish for 1969: T-54th at the Robinson Open

Year	Starts	Rounds Played	Cuts Made	Wins	Top-5s	Top-10s	Top-25s	Scoring Average	Money
1970	1	2	0	0	0	0	0	75.00	
1971	6	17	2	0	0	1	1	74.65	$2,940

Best finish for 1971: T-10th at the Glen Campbell Los Angeles Open

Year	Starts	Rounds Played	Cuts Made	Wins	Top-5s	Top-10s	Top-25s	Scoring Average	Money
1972	2	4	0	0	0	0	0	74.75	
1974	3	6	0	0	0	0	0	77.83	
1976	12	29	3	0	0	0	0	74.00	$1,082

Best finish for 1976: T-52nd at the Ed McMahon Quad City Open & Canadian Open

Year	Starts	Rounds Played	Cuts Made	Wins	Top-5s	Top-10s	Top-25s	Scoring Average	Money
1984	1	2	0	0	0	0	0	79.00	
Period Totals	Starts	Rounds Played	Cuts Made	Wins	Top-5s	Top-10s	Top-25s	Scoring Average	Money
	44	107	11	0	0	1	2	74.69	$5,521

Tom Sanderson

Year	Starts	Rounds Played	Cuts Made	Wins	Top-5s	Top-10s	Top-25s	Scoring Average	Money
1968	1	2	0	0	0	0	0	78.00	
1969	3	8	1	0	0	0	0	77.38	$166

Best finish for 1969: T-43rd at the Alameda County Open

| 1970 | 12 | 28 | 1 | 0 | 0 | 0 | 0 | 75.71 | $104 |

Best finish for 1970: T-58th at the Azalea Open Invitational

| 1971 | 14 | 33 | 2 | 0 | 0 | 0 | 0 | 73.88 | $390 |

Best finish for 1971: T-64th at the Hawaiian Open

| 1972 | 17 | 45 | 6 | 0 | 0 | 0 | 0 | 73.87 | $4,050 |

Best finish for 1972: T-27th at the Canadian Open

| 1973 | 16 | 48 | 7 | 0 | 0 | 0 | 0 | 73.90 | $2,578 |

Best finish for 1973: T-34th at the Kemper Open

| 1974 | 5 | 16 | 2 | 0 | 0 | 0 | 1 | 73.00 | $2,850 |

Best finish for 1974: T-21st at the Hawaiian Open

1976	1	2	0	0	0	0	0	78.50	
Period Totals	Starts	Rounds Played	Cuts Made	Wins	Top-5s	Top-10s	Top-25s	Scoring Average	Money
	69	182	19	0	0	0	1	74.34	$10,138

Cesar Sanudo

Year	Starts	Rounds Played	Cuts Made	Wins	Top-5s	Top-10s	Top-25s	Scoring Average	Money
1966	1	2	0	0	0	0	0	79.50	
1969	29	93	17	0	0	0	4	73.29	$7,972

Best finish for 1969: T-15th at the AVCO Classic

| 1970 | 28 | 81 | 13 | 1 | 1 | 1 | 3 | 72.73 | $17,746 |

Best finish for 1970: Win at the Azalea Open Invitational

| 1971 | 32 | 81 | 13 | 0 | 0 | 1 | 4 | 72.98 | $15,804 |

Best finish for 1971: T-6th at the National Airlines Open

| 1972 | 29 | 85 | 14 | 0 | 1 | 5 | 8 | 72.87 | $28,763 |

Best finish for 1972: T-4th at the Kemper Open

| 1973 | 28 | 91 | 18 | 0 | 0 | 1 | 4 | 72.63 | $21,021 |

Best finish for 1973: T-6th at the Kemper Open

| 1974 | 16 | 47 | 8 | 0 | 0 | 0 | 1 | 73.51 | $5,722 |

Best finish for 1974: 12th at the Greater Milwaukee Open

| 1975 | 13 | 32 | 4 | 0 | 0 | 0 | 0 | 73.84 | $2,130 |

Best finish for 1975: T-37th at the Bing Crosby Pro-Am

| 1976 | 16 | 41 | 8 | 0 | 0 | 0 | 1 | 73.93 | $4,494 |

Best finish for 1976: T-17th at the Greater Milwaukee Open

| 1977 | 9 | 28 | 5 | 0 | 0 | 0 | 1 | 73.82 | $4,475 |

Best finish for 1977: T-13th at the Phoenix Open

| 1978 | 19 | 50 | 6 | 0 | 0 | 1 | 1 | 72.70 | $9,836 |

Best finish for 1978: T-6th at the Western Open

| 1979 | 29 | 95 | 18 | 0 | 0 | 0 | 3 | 72.79 | $25,986 |

Best finish for 1979: T-8th at the Danny Thomas Memphis Classic

| 1980 | 17 | 43 | 5 | 0 | 0 | 0 | 1 | 73.02 | $5,688 |

Best finish for 1980: T-21st at the Greater Milwaukee Open

| 1981 | 19 | 60 | 10 | 0 | 0 | 1 | 3 | 72.72 | $18,015 |

Best finish for 1981: T-6th at the Byron Nelson Golf Classic

1982	8	16	0	0	0	0	0	73.13	
1983	2	4	0	0	0	0	0	74.75	
1984	1	2	0	0	0	0	0	71.50	
1985	2	6	1	0	0	0	0	73.00	$792

Best finish for 1985: T-70th at the Isuzu/Andy Williams San Diego Open

1987	1	2	0	0	0	0	0	72.00	
1988	1	2	0	0	0	0	0	75.00	
1989	1	2	0	0	0	0	0	77.50	
Period Totals	Starts	Rounds Played	Cuts Made	Wins	Top-5s	Top-10s	Top-25s	Scoring Average	Money
	301	863	140	1	2	10	34	73.06	$168,445

Gene Sarazen

Year	Starts	Rounds Played	Cuts Made	Wins	Top-5s	Top-10s	Top-25s	Scoring Average	Money
1958	5	12	1	0	0	0	1	76.42	$300

Best finish for 1958: T-16th at the British Open

1959	3	7	1	0	0	0	0	75.14	$343

Best finish for 1959: T-72nd at the Bing Crosby National

1960	2	3	0	0	0	0	0	79.67	$350
1961	1	2	0	0	0	0	0	78.00	$400
1962	1	2	0	0	0	0	0	74.00	$400
1963	1	4	1	0	0	0	0	77.00	$750

Best finish for 1963: 49th at the Masters

1964	1	1	0	0	0	0	0	73.00	
1965	2	4	0	0	0	0	0	75.75	
1966	1	2	0	0	0	0	0	81.00	$1,000
1967	2	1	0	0	0	0	0	76.00	
1968	1	0	0	0	0	0	0		$1,000
1969	1	2	0	0	0	0	0	79.00	
1970	3	6	0	0	0	0	0	79.67	$1,000
1971	2	4	0	0	0	0	0	80.75	$1,000
1972	2	3	0	0	0	0	0	79.00	$1,000
1973	2	4	0	0	0	0	0	83.50	$1,130
1976	1	0	0	0	0	0	0		$270
Period Totals	Starts	Rounds Played	Cuts Made	Wins	Top-5s	Top-10s	Top-25s	Scoring Average	Money
	31	57	3	0	0	0	1	77.86	$8,943

PGA Tour career totals from 1920 to 1976

	Starts	Rounds Played	Cuts Made	Wins	Top-5s	Top-10s	Top-25s	Scoring Average	Money
	315	N/A	N/A	37	N/A	185	249	N/A	N/A

Hisayuki Sasaki

Year	Starts	Rounds Played	Cuts Made	Wins	Top-5s	Top-10s	Top-25s	Scoring Average	Money
1995	2	8	2	0	0	0	0	73.25	$27,855

Best finish for 1995: T-31st at the British Open

1996	19	64	13	0	0	0	3	71.52	$105,651

Best finish for 1996: T-11th at the Greater Greensboro Chrysler Classic

1997	5	12	1	0	0	0	0	72.25	$11,566

Best finish for 1997: T-29th at the Greater Greensboro Chrysler Classic

1998	2	4	0	0	0	0	0	76.25	
Period Totals	Starts	Rounds Played	Cuts Made	Wins	Top-5s	Top-10s	Top-25s	Scoring Average	Money
	28	88	16	0	0	0	3	71.99	$145,072

Gene Sauers

Year	Starts	Rounds Played	Cuts Made	Wins	Top-5s	Top-10s	Top-25s	Scoring Average	Money
1984	23	74	13	0	1	1	4	72.66	$37,137

Best finish for 1984: T-5th at the Pensacola Open

1985	21	66	12	0	1	1	5	71.86	$48,526

Best finish for 1985: T-4th at the Buick Open

1986	34	116	28	1	2	4	9	71.51	$199,044

Best finish for 1986: Win at the Bank of Boston Classic

1987	32	104	22	0	3	5	12	71.32	$244,655

Best finish for 1987: T-2nd at the Bank of Boston Classic

1988	30	102	23	0	3	6	11	70.34	$281,719

Best finish for 1988: T-3rd at the Anheuser-Busch Golf Classic

1989	26	86	19	1	2	5	7	71.06	$310,129

Best finish for 1989: Win at the Hawaiian Open

1990	27	97	21	1	2	5	13	70.66	$375,485

Best finish for 1990: Win at the Deposit Guaranty

1991	25	83	17	0	2	5	10	70.22	$400,535

Best finish for 1991: 2nd at the Kmart Greater Greensboro Open

1992	24	78	16	0	5	5	9	70.67	$434,566

Best finish for 1992: T-2nd at the Bob Hope Chrysler Classic, The Nestle Invitational & PGA Championship

1993	28	95	19	0	0	0	3	71.66	$117,608

Best finish for 1993: T-12th at the Kmart Greater Greensboro Open

1994	26	82	18	0	2	2	4	71.11	$250,654

Best finish for 1994: T-2nd at the Federal Express St. Jude Classic

1995	23	75	15	0	2	2	5	71.05	$311,578

Best finish for 1995: T-3rd at the Players Championship

1996	25	78	16	0	0	1	2	71.56	$123,904

Best finish for 1996: T-8th at the MCI Classic

1997	16	53	10	0	0	2	2	71.17	$116,445

Best finish for 1997: T-6th at the LaCantera Texas Open

| 1998 | 11 | 38 | 8 | 0 | 0 | 0 | 1 | 71.29 | $47,917 |

Best finish for 1998: T-20th at the Canon Greater Hartford Open

| 1999 | 6 | 13 | 1 | 0 | 0 | 0 | 0 | 72.08 | $9,720 |

Best finish for 1999: T-30th at the B.C. Open

| 2000 | 8 | 20 | 2 | 0 | 0 | 0 | 1 | 71.85 | $28,217 |

Best finish for 2000: T-18th at the B.C. Open

| 2001 | 2 | 6 | 1 | 0 | 0 | 0 | 0 | 70.83 | $8,400 |

Best finish for 2001: T-37th at the B.C. Open

| 2002 | 11 | 33 | 5 | 1 | 1 | 1 | 2 | 69.91 | $715,605 |

Best finish for 2002: Win at the Air Canada Championship

| 2003 | 30 | 85 | 12 | 0 | 0 | 1 | 1 | 72.20 | $280,644 |

Best finish for 2003: T-10th at the Mercedes Championships

| 2004 | 30 | 81 | 10 | 0 | 1 | 1 | 1 | 72.11 | $287,151 |

Best finish for 2004: T-5th at the Ford Championship at Doral

| 2005 | 7 | 18 | 2 | 0 | 0 | 0 | 0 | 71.72 | $29,091 |

Best finish for 2005: T-40th at the Chrysler Classic of Tucson

Period Totals	Starts	Rounds Played	Cuts Made	Wins	Top-5s	Top-10s	Top-25s	Scoring Average	Money
	465	1483	290	4	27	47	102	71.29	$4,658,728

Ken Schall

Year	Starts	Rounds Played	Cuts Made	Wins	Top-5s	Top-10s	Top-25s	Scoring Average	Money
1988	1	4	1	0	0	0	0	69.75	$1,296

Best finish for 1988: T-60th at the Hardee's Golf Classic

1989	2	4	0	0	0	0	0	72.50	$1,000
1990	2	4	0	0	0	0	0	76.25	$1,000
1991	30	79	10	0	0	0	2	71.68	$42,248

Best finish for 1991: T-11th at the Chattanooga Classic

1992	2	4	0	0	0	0	0	72.50	
1993	1	2	0	0	0	0	0	70.00	
1995	1	3	1	0	0	0	0	71.33	$1,960

Best finish for 1995: T-67th at the Quad City Classic

| 1996 | 2 | 6 | 1 | 0 | 0 | 0 | 1 | 71.83 | $21,700 |

Best finish for 1996: T-14th at the Quad City Classic

1997	2	4	0	0	0	0	0	73.25	$1,000
1998	1	2	0	0	0	0	0	79.50	$1,500
1999	1	2	0	0	0	0	0	75.00	$1,750
2001	1	2	0	0	0	0	0	75.50	$2,000
2003	1	2	0	0	0	0	0	77.00	$2,000
Period Totals	Starts	Rounds Played	Cuts Made	Wins	Top-5s	Top-10s	Top-25s	Scoring Average	Money
	47	118	13	0	0	0	3	72.19	$77,454

Tom Scherrer

Year	Starts	Rounds Played	Cuts Made	Wins	Top-5s	Top-10s	Top-25s	Scoring Average	Money
1992	1	2	0	0	0	0	0	76.00	
1996	34	89	12	0	1	1	1	72.27	$136,323

Best finish for 1996: 3rd at the Phoenix Open

| 1997 | 3 | 10 | 2 | 0 | 0 | 0 | 0 | 72.40 | $6,372 |

Best finish for 1997: T-45th at the United Airlines Hawaiian Open

| 1999 | 29 | 93 | 20 | 0 | 1 | 2 | 8 | 70.81 | $427,849 |

Best finish for 1999: T-5th at the Michelob Championship at Kingsmill

| 2000 | 33 | 101 | 19 | 1 | 3 | 4 | 7 | 70.94 | $1,264,649 |

Best finish for 2000: Win at the Kemper Insurance Open

| 2001 | 28 | 66 | 9 | 0 | 0 | 0 | 2 | 72.50 | $212,091 |

Best finish for 2001: T-17th at the Texas Open at LaCantera

| 2002 | 33 | 95 | 15 | 0 | 0 | 1 | 4 | 71.46 | $356,657 |

Best finish for 2002: 6th at the Air Canada Championship

| 2003 | 16 | 45 | 7 | 0 | 0 | 0 | 2 | 71.67 | $122,431 |

Best finish for 2003: T-16th at the 84 Lumber Classic of Pennsylvania

| 2004 | 1 | 2 | 0 | 0 | 0 | 0 | 0 | 71.00 | |
| 2005 | 2 | 8 | 2 | 0 | 0 | 0 | 0 | 70.50 | $27,333 |

Best finish for 2005: T-33rd at the Chrysler Classic of Tucson

2006	4	9	0	0	0	0	0	73.44	
2007	1	3	0	0	0	0	0	78.67	
2008	20	56	8	0	0	1	2	71.64	$288,390

Best finish for 2008: T-7th at the Ginn sur Mer Classic

| Period Totals | Starts | Rounds Played | Cuts Made | Wins | Top-5s | Top-10s | Top-25s | Scoring Average | Money |
| | 205 | 579 | 94 | 1 | 5 | 9 | 26 | 71.63 | $2,842,094 |

Marty Schiene

Year	Starts	Rounds Played	Cuts Made	Wins	Top-5s	Top-10s	Top-25s	Scoring Average	Money
1987	2	4	0	0	0	0	0	74.00	
1988	1	2	0	0	0	0	0	74.00	

Year	Starts	Rounds Played	Cuts Made	Wins	Top-5s	Top-10s	Top-25s	Scoring Average	Money
1989	1	2	0	0	0	0	0	77.00	$1,000
1991	1	4	1	0	0	0	0	72.50	$2,050

Best finish for 1991: T-65th at the Canadian Open

1992	1	4	1	0	0	0	0	71.75	$2,791

Best finish for 1992: T-48th at the Centel Western Open

1993	25	62	7	0	0	0	0	73.21	$20,857

Best finish for 1993: T-33rd at the Kmart Greater Greensboro Open

1994	1	2	0	0	0	0	0	76.50	$1,000
1996	1	2	0	0	0	0	0	78.50	
1997	1	2	0	0	0	0	0	79.50	$1,000
1998	1	2	0	0	0	0	0	70.50	
2001	1	2	0	0	0	0	0	78.50	$1,000
2003	1	2	0	0	0	0	0	80.50	
Period Totals	Starts	Rounds Played	Cuts Made	Wins	Top-5s	Top-10s	Top-25s	Scoring Average	Money
	37	90	9	0	0	0	0	73.80	$29,699

John Schlee

Year	Starts	Rounds Played	Cuts Made	Wins	Top-5s	Top-10s	Top-25s	Scoring Average	Money
1964	3	4	0	0	0	0	0	76.75	
1965	1	4	1	0	0	0	1	70.25	$850

Best finish for 1965: T-12th at the Cajun Classic

1966	25	77	13	0	1	1	8	72.61	$21,605

Best finish for 1966: 2nd at the Minnesota Golf Classic

1967	32	100	18	0	1	3	8	72.82	$16,112

Best finish for 1967: 4th at the Tucson Open

1968	32	105	20	0	1	2	9	72.16	$19,624

Best finish for 1968: T-4th at the Los Angeles Open Invitational

1969	33	94	13	0	0	1	5	73.21	$12,125

Best finish for 1969: 6th at the Cleveland Open

1970	31	100	20	0	2	4	8	72.09	$25,227

Best finish for 1970: 3rd at the Azalea Open Invitational

1971	33	100	20	0	0	5	9	72.14	$39,020

Best finish for 1971: T-7th at the Andy Williams-San Diego Open, Kaiser International Open & Walt Disney World Open

1972	34	121	26	0	1	7	10	72.34	$43,817

Best finish for 1972: 5th at the USI Classic

1973	26	97	21	1	5	6	13	71.87	$114,026

Best finish for 1973: Win at the Hawaiian Open

1974	30	96	20	0	2	3	9	72.03	$54,925

Best finish for 1974: T-2nd at the Canadian Open

1975	25	75	14	0	0	5	11	71.95	$44,338

Best finish for 1975: T-6th at the World Open

1976	28	96	21	0	1	1	11	71.56	$46,876

Best finish for 1976: T-4th at the PGA Championship

1977	19	68	15	0	0	1	2	73.13	$17,897

Best finish for 1977: T-8th at the Masters

1978	9	30	6	0	0	0	1	73.70	$6,154

Best finish for 1978: T-20th at the Tournament Players Championship

Period Totals	Starts	Rounds Played	Cuts Made	Wins	Top-5s	Top-10s	Top-25s	Scoring Average	Money
	361	1167	228	1	14	39	105	72.35	$462,597

Willie Scholl

Year	Starts	Rounds Played	Cuts Made	Wins	Top-5s	Top-10s	Top-25s	Scoring Average	Money
1964	26	59	4	0	0	0	0	74.86	

Best finish for 1964: T-47th at the Azalea Open

1965	7	16	1	0	0	0	0	74.38	

Best finish for 1965: T-65th at the Azalea Open

1968	1	2	0	0	0	0	0	75.00	
1969	3	5	0	0	0	0	0	76.40	
1970	5	14	1	0	0	0	0	75.79	$182

Best finish for 1970: 70th at the San Antonio Texas Open

1972	1	2	0	0	0	0	0	81.50	
Period Totals	Starts	Rounds Played	Cuts Made	Wins	Top-5s	Top-10s	Top-25s	Scoring Average	Money
	43	98	6	0	0	0	0	75.13	$182

Dave Schreyer

Year	Starts	Rounds Played	Cuts Made	Wins	Top-5s	Top-10s	Top-25s	Scoring Average	Money
1988	1	2	0	0	0	0	0	77.00	
1992	23	53	3	0	0	0	0	73.72	$10,215

Best finish for 1992: T-32nd at the Federal Express St. Jude Classic

1996	1	2	0	0	0	0	0	77.50	
1997	1	4	1	0	0	0	0	74.25	$6,000

Best finish for 1997: T-65th at the U.S. Open

Period Totals	Starts	Rounds Played	Cuts Made	Wins	Top-5s	Top-10s	Top-25s	Scoring Average	Money
	26	61	4	0	0	0	0	73.98	$16,215

John Schroeder

Year	Starts	Rounds Played	Cuts Made	Wins	Top-5s	Top-10s	Top-25s	Scoring Average	Money
1967	1	2	0	0	0	0	0	77.50	
1968	1	2	0	0	0	0	0	77.50	
1969	17	58	12	0	1	1	1	73.07	$9,219
Best finish for 1969: T-3rd at the Hawaiian Open									
1970	34	113	22	0	1	3	9	71.96	$31,570
Best finish for 1970: T-3rd at the Byron Nelson Golf Classic									
1971	34	112	22	0	0	2	6	72.73	$19,330
Best finish for 1971: T-9th at the Southern Open									
1972	32	108	21	0	0	3	8	72.64	$25,280
Best finish for 1972: 6th at the Greater St. Louis Classic									
1973	31	104	21	1	1	4	9	72.21	$65,315
Best finish for 1973: Win at the U.S. Professional Match Play Championship									
1974	32	91	15	0	1	1	3	73.34	$22,350
Best finish for 1974: T-3rd at the Phoenix Open									
1975	24	73	12	0	2	2	4	72.66	$25,520
Best finish for 1975: 2nd at the Southern Open									
1976	25	80	16	0	0	0	4	72.39	$17,206
Best finish for 1976: T-16th at the NBC Tucson Open									
1977	29	98	20	0	3	4	10	72.00	$74,220
Best finish for 1977: T-2nd at the Andy Williams-San Diego Open & Colonial National Invitational									
1978	29	103	23	0	2	6	12	71.66	$78,188
Best finish for 1978: T-2nd at the Andy Williams-San Diego Open									
1979	28	87	16	0	1	4	7	72.82	$80,114
Best finish for 1979: 2nd at the Bay Hill Citrus Classic									
1980	26	83	15	0	0	2	4	72.42	$30,681
Best finish for 1980: T-8th at the Hawaiian Open									
1981	26	85	17	0	1	3	6	72.08	$56,276
Best finish for 1981: T-4th at the U.S. Open									
1982	24	69	10	0	0	0	2	72.57	$15,378
Best finish for 1982: T-24th at the Masters									
1983	1	2	0	0	0	0	0	79.00	$1,500
1995	6	18	2	0	0	0	0	71.44	$5,122
Best finish for 1995: T-35th at the Deposit Guaranty Golf Classic									
Period Totals	Starts	Rounds Played	Cuts Made	Wins	Top-5s	Top-10s	Top-25s	Scoring Average	Money
	400	1288	244	1	13	35	85	72.45	$557,269

Mike Schuchart

Year	Starts	Rounds Played	Cuts Made	Wins	Top-5s	Top-10s	Top-25s	Scoring Average	Money
1983	1	2	0	0	0	0	0	80.50	$600
1987	1	2	0	0	0	0	0	83.00	$1,000
1990	28	68	7	0	0	0	0	72.72	$22,501
Best finish for 1990: T-30th at the Buick Open									
1992	1	2	0	0	0	0	0	74.50	$1,200
1993	24	72	11	0	1	1	1	72.08	$61,493
Best finish for 1993: T-5th at the Hardee's Golf Classic									
1995	1	2	0	0	0	0	0	75.50	$1,000
2003	1	2	0	0	0	0	0	79.00	$2,000
2004	1	2	0	0	0	0	0	79.00	$2,000
Period Totals	Starts	Rounds Played	Cuts Made	Wins	Top-5s	Top-10s	Top-25s	Scoring Average	Money
	58	152	18	0	1	1	1	72.88	$91,794

Jason Schultz

Year	Starts	Rounds Played	Cuts Made	Wins	Top-5s	Top-10s	Top-25s	Scoring Average	Money
1999	1	2	0	0	0	0	0	73.50	
2006	28	75	10	0	0	0	2	71.72	$147,424
Best finish for 2006: T-24th at the B.C. Open									
2007	22	63	9	0	0	0	0	71.63	$163,245
Best finish for 2007: T-28th at the Zurich Classic of New Orleans									
Period Totals	Starts	Rounds Played	Cuts Made	Wins	Top-5s	Top-10s	Top-25s	Scoring Average	Money
	51	140	19	0	0	0	2	71.71	$310,668

Ted Schulz

Year	Starts	Rounds Played	Cuts Made	Wins	Top-5s	Top-10s	Top-25s	Scoring Average	Money
1987	30	76	8	0	0	0	2	72.70	$17,838
Best finish for 1987: T-22nd at the Buick Open									
1988	5	14	2	0	0	0	0	70.86	$2,854
Best finish for 1988: T-43rd at the Provident Classic									
1989	35	114	24	1	2	6	13	70.79	$392,855
Best finish for 1989: Win at the Southern Open									

Year	Starts	Rounds Played	Cuts Made	Wins	Top-5s	Top-10s	Top-25s	Scoring Average	Money
1990	34	116	24	0	1	1	7	71.63	$195,627

Best finish for 1990: T-4th at the Bob Hope Chrysler Classic

1991	31	99	18	1	4	5	12	70.89	$510,558

Best finish for 1991: Win at the Nissan Los Angeles Open

1992	32	106	24	0	1	2	10	71.23	$259,204

Best finish for 1992: 3rd at the Walt Disney World/Oldsmobile Classic

1993	31	95	17	0	1	1	2	72.43	$164,260

Best finish for 1993: T-2nd at the Greater Milwaukee Open

1994	30	78	8	0	0	0	1	72.65	$37,537

Best finish for 1994: T-20th at the Northern Telecom Open

1995	16	44	5	0	0	0	1	72.43	$29,290

Best finish for 1995: 16th at the Greater Milwaukee Open

1996	14	34	3	0	0	0	0	72.71	$10,259

Best finish for 1996: T-41st at the Deposit Guaranty Golf Classic

1997	7	13	0	0	0	0	0	73.92	
1998	11	23	1	0	0	0	0	73.48	$4,137

Best finish for 1998: T-70th at the Nissan Open

1999	5	16	3	0	0	0	0	71.50	$20,377

Best finish for 1999: T-30th at the John Deere Classic

2000	6	11	0	0	0	0	0	74.00	
2001	1	2	0	0	0	0	0	74.50	
2008	1	4	1	0	0	0	0	72.75	$6,420

Best finish for 2008: T-62nd at the Reno-Tahoe Open

Period Totals	Starts	Rounds Played	Cuts Made	Wins	Top-5s	Top-10s	Top-25s	Scoring Average	Money
	289	845	138	2	9	15	48	71.86	$1,651,215

Pat Schwab

Year	Starts	Rounds Played	Cuts Made	Wins	Top-5s	Top-10s	Top-25s	Scoring Average	Money
1958	16	54	11	0	0	0	2	73.61	$787

Best finish for 1958: T-16th at the Greenbrier Invitational

1960	2	6	1	0	0	0	1	75.00	$263

Best finish for 1960: T-16th at the Mobile Sertoma Open Invitational

1961	1	4	1	0	0	0	1	72.00	$350

Best finish for 1961: T-16th at the Mobile Sertoma Open Invitational

1962	4	16	4	0	0	0	1	72.31	$766

Best finish for 1962: T-22nd at the Mobile Sertoma Open Invitational

1964	1	3	0	0	0	0	0	73.00	
1965	3	12	3	0	0	0	0	72.92	$025

Best finish for 1965: T-50th at the Thunderbird Classic

1966	8	22	3	0	0	0	0	73.86	$435

Best finish for 1966: T-45th at the Los Angeles Open Invitational & Thunderbird Classic

1967	4	14	3	0	0	1	2	72.86	$6,388

Best finish for 1967: T-10th at the Thunderbird Classic

1968	3	12	3	0	0	0	2	71.42	$3,863

Best finish for 1968: T-24th at the U.S. Open & Westchester Classic

1969	2	6	1	0	0	0	0	74.00	$241

Best finish for 1969: T-59th at the PGA Championship

1970	2	4	0	0	0	0	0	74.50	
1971	1	2	0	0	0	0	0	78.00	
1972	2	6	1	0	0	0	0	74.17	$333

Best finish for 1972: T-58th at the PGA Championship

1973	1	2	0	0	0	0	0	76.00	
1976	1	2	0	0	0	0	0	79.00	$250

Period Totals	Starts	Rounds Played	Cuts Made	Wins	Top-5s	Top-10s	Top-25s	Scoring Average	Money
	51	165	31	0	0	1	9	73.45	$13,702

Brent Schwarzrock

Year	Starts	Rounds Played	Cuts Made	Wins	Top-5s	Top-10s	Top-25s	Scoring Average	Money
1999	1	1	0	0	0	0	0	80.00	
2000	18	48	6	0	0	0	2	71.46	$94,347

Best finish for 2000: T-18th at the Southern Farm Bureau Classic

2001	20	63	11	0	0	2	5	71.06	$322,336

Best finish for 2001: T-8th at the Air Canada Championship

2002	11	28	6	0	0	0	2	71.68	$160,673

Best finish for 2002: T-11th at the Honda Classic

2003	20	58	10	0	0	0	2	71.26	$216,561

Best finish for 2003: T-12th at the FUNAI Classic at the Walt Disney World Resort

2004	1	2	0	0	0	0	0	72.50	

Period Totals	Starts	Rounds Played	Cuts Made	Wins	Top-5s	Top-10s	Top-25s	Scoring Average	Money
	71	200	33	0	0	2	11	71.36	$793,917

Paul Scodeller

Year	Starts	Rounds Played	Cuts Made	Wins	Top-5s	Top-10s	Top-25s	Scoring Average	Money
1958	2	4	0	0	0	0	0	76.75	
1964	4	11	2	0	0	0	1	74.09	$1,081

Best finish for 1964: T-21st at the Lucky International Open

| 1965 | 3 | 8 | 1 | 0 | 0 | 0 | 1 | 73.88 | $750 |

Best finish for 1965: T-21st at the Hawaiian Open

| 1966 | 2 | 6 | 1 | 0 | 0 | 0 | 0 | 76.00 | |

Best finish for 1966: T-63rd at the Hawaiian Open Invitational

| 1967 | 4 | 13 | 1 | 0 | 0 | 0 | 1 | 73.92 | $800 |

Best finish for 1967: T-23rd at the Los Angeles Open

| 1968 | 4 | 8 | 0 | 0 | 0 | 0 | 0 | 75.00 | |
| 1969 | 3 | 8 | 1 | 0 | 0 | 0 | 0 | 73.63 | $121 |

Best finish for 1969: T-62nd at the Sahara Invitational

1971	2	4	0	0	0	0	0	75.75	
1973	3	8	0	0	0	0	0	75.00	
1975	2	6	0	0	0	0	0	78.33	
Period Totals	Starts	Rounds Played	Cuts Made	Wins	Top-5s	Top-10s	Top-25s	Scoring Average	Money
	29	76	6	0	0	0	3	74.89	$2,752

Adam Scott

Year	Starts	Rounds Played	Cuts Made	Wins	Top-5s	Top-10s	Top-25s	Scoring Average	Money
2000	6	12	1	0	0	0	0	72.25	$11,872

Best finish for 2000: T-44th at the Air Canada Championship

| 2001 | 6 | 20 | 4 | 0 | 0 | 0 | 1 | 72.05 | $95,026 |

Best finish for 2001: T-11th at the Honda Classic

| 2002 | 10 | 30 | 7 | 0 | 0 | 2 | 4 | 72.63 | $437,148 |

Best finish for 2002: T-6th at the Shell Houston Open

| 2003 | 14 | 46 | 11 | 1 | 2 | 2 | 6 | 71.61 | $1,748,813 |

Best finish for 2003: Win at the Deutsche Bank Championship

| 2004 | 16 | 52 | 12 | 2 | 4 | 7 | 8 | 70.67 | $3,730,984 |

Best finish for 2004: Win at the Players Championship & Booz Allen Classic

| 2005 | 19 | 68 | 18 | 1 | 4 | 6 | 8 | 70.87 | $2,592,255 |

Best finish for 2005: Win at the Nissan Open

| 2006 | 19 | 68 | 17 | 1 | 8 | 10 | 14 | 70.01 | $4,978,858 |

Best finish for 2006: Win at the Tour Championship

| 2007 | 19 | 68 | 17 | 1 | 4 | 6 | 10 | 70.96 | $3,415,185 |

Best finish for 2007: Win at the Shell Houston Open

| 2008 | 15 | 49 | 12 | 1 | 1 | 3 | 7 | 71.45 | $1,979,160 |

Best finish for 2008: Win at the EDS Byron Nelson Championship

Period Totals	Starts	Rounds Played	Cuts Made	Wins	Top-5s	Top-10s	Top-25s	Scoring Average	Money
	124	413	99	7	23	36	58	71.09	$18,989,300

Larry Sears

Year	Starts	Rounds Played	Cuts Made	Wins	Top-5s	Top-10s	Top-25s	Scoring Average	Money
1968	2	4	0	0	0	0	0	78.25	$500
1969	14	36	4	0	0	0	0	73.44	$1,124

Best finish for 1969: T-40th at the Canadian Open

| 1970 | 10 | 22 | 1 | 0 | 0 | 0 | 0 | 74.95 | $168 |

Best finish for 1970: T-67th at the Western Open

1971	2	4	0	0	0	0	0	77.75	
Period Totals	Starts	Rounds Played	Cuts Made	Wins	Top-5s	Top-10s	Top-25s	Scoring Average	Money
	28	66	5	0	0	0	0	74.50	$1,791

Ed Selser

Year	Starts	Rounds Played	Cuts Made	Wins	Top-5s	Top-10s	Top-25s	Scoring Average	Money
1980	1	2	0	0	0	0	0	75.00	
1981	4	8	1	0	0	0	0	72.00	$465

Best finish for 1981: T-41st at the Tallahassee Open

| 1982 | 12 | 28 | 2 | 0 | 0 | 0 | 0 | 73.86 | $1,107 |

Best finish for 1982: T-66th at the Joe Garagiola Tucson Open

1984	1	2	0	0	0	0	0	74.50	
1985	1	2	0	0	0	0	0	75.50	
1986	1	2	0	0	0	0	0	78.50	
1987	2	4	0	0	0	0	0	73.50	
1988	1	2	0	0	0	0	0	71.00	
1991	2	4	0	0	0	0	0	74.00	
1992	1	2	0	0	0	0	0	77.00	
1993	1	4	1	0	0	0	0	70.50	$624

Best finish for 1993: T-65th at the Deposit Guaranty Classic

Period Totals	Starts	Rounds Played	Cuts Made	Wins	Top-5s	Top-10s	Top-25s	Scoring Average	Money
	27	60	4	0	0	0	0	73.65	$2,196

John Senden

Year	Starts	Rounds Played	Cuts Made	Wins	Top-5s	Top-10s	Top-25s	Scoring Average	Money
2002	30	93	18	0	0	1	8	70.55	$582,563

Best finish for 2002: T-9th at the Air Canada Championship

| 2003 | 33 | 107 | 21 | 0 | 0 | 0 | 5 | 70.46 | $601,570 |

Best finish for 2003: T-13th at the Deutsche Bank Championship

| 2004 | 28 | 96 | 21 | 0 | 0 | 2 | 7 | 70.48 | $699,203 |

Best finish for 2004: T-9th at the Bank of America Colonial

| 2005 | 29 | 99 | 21 | 0 | 0 | 3 | 6 | 70.60 | $855,325 |

Best finish for 2005: T-6th at the Bob Hope Chrysler Classic

| 2006 | 28 | 93 | 20 | 1 | 2 | 3 | 10 | 70.51 | $1,652,924 |

Best finish for 2006: Win at the John Deere Classic

| 2007 | 27 | 97 | 21 | 0 | 4 | 5 | 8 | 70.93 | $1,899,558 |

Best finish for 2007: T-2nd at the PODS Championship

| 2008 | 28 | 92 | 20 | 0 | 1 | 3 | 8 | 70.90 | $1,269,083 |

Best finish for 2008: T-2nd at the PODS Championship

Period Totals	Starts	Rounds Played	Cuts Made	Wins	Top-5s	Top-10s	Top-25s	Scoring Average	Money
	203	677	142	1	7	17	52	70.63	$7,560,225

Peter Senior

Year	Starts	Rounds Played	Cuts Made	Wins	Top-5s	Top-10s	Top-25s	Scoring Average	Money
1979	1	3	0	0	0	0	0	76.00	$630
1984	1	4	1	0	0	0	1	71.25	$8,777

Best finish for 1984: T-14th at the British Open

| 1985 | 1 | 4 | 1 | 0 | 0 | 0 | 0 | 73.25 | $3,480 |

Best finish for 1985: T-44th at the British Open

| 1986 | 13 | 33 | 2 | 0 | 0 | 0 | 0 | 73.73 | $3,098 |

Best finish for 1986: T-56th at the Los Angeles Open

| 1987 | 1 | 2 | 0 | 0 | 0 | 0 | 0 | 76.00 | $640 |
| 1988 | 4 | 12 | 3 | 0 | 0 | 1 | 1 | 71.67 | $50,974 |

Best finish for 1988: 6th at the British Open

| 1989 | 1 | 2 | 0 | 0 | 0 | 0 | 0 | 73.50 | $800 |
| 1990 | 9 | 25 | 5 | 0 | 1 | 1 | 2 | 72.68 | $96,238 |

Best finish for 1990: T-2nd at the International

| 1991 | 5 | 12 | 3 | 0 | 0 | 0 | 2 | 72.58 | $50,110 |

Best finish for 1991: T-12th at the International

| 1992 | 2 | 8 | 2 | 0 | 0 | 0 | 1 | 72.00 | $19,088 |

Best finish for 1992: T-25th at the British Open

| 1993 | 4 | 11 | 2 | 0 | 1 | 1 | 1 | 71.09 | $81,370 |

Best finish for 1993: T-4th at the British Open

| 1994 | 4 | 10 | 2 | 0 | 0 | 0 | 1 | 71.50 | $22,762 |

Best finish for 1994: T-20th at the British Open

| 1995 | 4 | 12 | 4 | 0 | 0 | 0 | 0 | 72.75 | $33,391 |

Best finish for 1995: T-42nd at the Sprint International & NEC World Series of Golf

| 1996 | 3 | 4 | 0 | 0 | 0 | 0 | 0 | 74.50 | $2,308 |
| 1997 | 2 | 8 | 2 | 0 | 0 | 0 | 0 | 72.63 | $29,215 |

Best finish for 1997: T-26th at the NEC World Series of Golf

| 1998 | 1 | 2 | 0 | 0 | 0 | 0 | 0 | 74.00 | $1,316 |
| 2000 | 2 | 8 | 2 | 0 | 0 | 0 | 0 | 73.63 | $43,628 |

Best finish for 2000: T-42nd at the American Express Championship

| 2004 | 2 | 8 | 2 | 0 | 0 | 0 | 0 | 73.13 | $69,750 |

Best finish for 2004: T-43rd at the WGC-American Express Championship

Period Totals	Starts	Rounds Played	Cuts Made	Wins	Top-5s	Top-10s	Top-25s	Scoring Average	Money
	60	168	31	0	2	3	9	72.82	$517,574

Bob Shave, Jr.

Year	Starts	Rounds Played	Cuts Made	Wins	Top-5s	Top-10s	Top-25s	Scoring Average	Money
1958	1	4	1	0	0	0	0	73.25	

Best finish for 1958: T-61st at the Rubber City Open

| 1959 | 3 | 12 | 3 | 0 | 0 | 0 | 1 | 71.08 | |

Best finish for 1959: T-11th at the Rubber City Open Invitational

| 1960 | 6 | 24 | 5 | 0 | 1 | 1 | 2 | 71.33 | $2,596 |

Best finish for 1960: T-4th at the Canadian Open Invitational

| 1961 | 13 | 52 | 12 | 0 | 1 | 3 | 9 | 71.31 | $8,366 |

Best finish for 1961: T-4th at the Memphis Open Invitational

| 1962 | 14 | 54 | 13 | 0 | 0 | 1 | 8 | 71.91 | $6,325 |

Best finish for 1962: T-7th at the Waco Turner Open Invitational

| 1963 | 6 | 25 | 5 | 0 | 1 | 1 | 4 | 70.76 | $5,295 |

Best finish for 1963: T-2nd at the Cajun Classic Open Invitational

| 1964 | 30 | 104 | 17 | 0 | 0 | 1 | 7 | 72.61 | $6,530 |

Best finish for 1964: T-6th at the Doral Open

Year	Starts	Rounds Played	Cuts Made	Wins	Top-5s	Top-10s	Top-25s	Scoring Average	Money
1965	10	32	6	0	0	0	1	73.34	$1,592

Best finish for 1965: T-18th at the Doral Open

1966	13	40	7	0	1	1	1	73.75	$7,736

Best finish for 1966: T-5th at the Florida Citrus Open Invitational

1967	17	44	6	0	0	1	1	73.95	$3,002

Best finish for 1967: T-10th at the Western Open

1968	2	4	0	0	0	0	0	74.75	
1969	2	6	1	0	0	0	0	74.67	$134

Best finish for 1969: T-37th at the West End Classic

Period Totals	Starts	Rounds Played	Cuts Made	Wins	Top-5s	Top-10s	Top-25s	Scoring Average	Money
	117	401	76	0	4	9	34	72.49	$41,577

Bob Shaw

Year	Starts	Rounds Played	Cuts Made	Wins	Top-5s	Top-10s	Top-25s	Scoring Average	Money
1964	1	4	1	0	0	0	0	73.50	

Best finish for 1964: T-58th at the Portland Open

1968	2	6	1	0	0	0	0	75.83	$403

Best finish for 1968: T-27th at the British Open

1969	22	66	11	0	1	1	3	73.26	$6,070

Best finish for 1969: T-2nd at the Tallahassee Open

1970	12	29	4	0	0	0	2	73.59	$3,957

Best finish for 1970: T-18th at the Doral-Eastern Open

1971	13	36	5	0	1	1	2	73.00	$14,282

Best finish for 1971: T-2nd at the Greater Milwaukee Open

1972	25	57	7	1	1	1	4	73.46	$23,794

Best finish for 1972: Win at the Tallahassee Open

1973	22	57	8	0	0	0	4	73.63	$13,300

Best finish for 1973: T-14th at the Phoenix Open

1974	10	25	3	0	0	0	1	73.64	$1,564

Best finish for 1974: T-16th at the Tallahassee Open

1975	16	44	8	0	0	1	1	72.30	$7,033

Best finish for 1975: T-8th at the San Antonio Texas Open

1976	9	25	4	0	0	0	0	73.80	$473

Best finish for 1976: T-63rd at the Sammy Davis, Jr. - Greater Hartford Open

1977	3	5	0	0	0	0	0	72.20	
1978	9	23	3	0	0	0	0	74.43	$1,142

Best finish for 1978: T-40th at the Ed McMahon Quad City Open

Period Totals	Starts	Rounds Played	Cuts Made	Wins	Top-5s	Top-10s	Top-25s	Scoring Average	Money
	144	377	55	1	3	4	17	73.40	$72,020

Tom Shaw

Year	Starts	Rounds Played	Cuts Made	Wins	Top-5s	Top-10s	Top-25s	Scoring Average	Money
1963	4	16	4	0	0	0	1	71.56	$711

Best finish for 1963: T-25th at the Portland Open Invitational

1964	29	69	6	0	0	1	1	74.58	$4,782

Best finish for 1964: T-6th at the Whitemarsh Open

1965	25	79	15	0	0	0	4	72.91	$6,636

Best finish for 1965: T-11th at the Tucson Open

1966	24	79	15	0	0	0	1	73.90	$2,849

Best finish for 1966: T-23rd at the Canadian Open

1967	4	13	1	0	0	0	0	75.23	

Best finish for 1967: T-56th at the San Diego Open

1968	25	86	18	0	0	2	3	72.57	$9,550

Best finish for 1968: 6th at the Pensacola Open Invitational

1969	34	106	19	2	2	3	10	72.59	$78,835

Best finish for 1969: Win at the Doral Open & AVCO Classic

1970	36	117	22	0	1	5	7	72.44	$31,684

Best finish for 1970: T-5th at the Florida Citrus Open Invitational

1971	33	103	21	2	2	4	10	72.43	$92,865

Best finish for 1971: Win at the Bing Crosby Pro-Am & Hawaiian Open

1972	37	122	23	0	0	2	8	72.75	$26,072

Best finish for 1972: T-7th at the Kemper Open & Greater Hartford Open Invitational

1973	36	120	22	0	0	2	8	72.73	$27,948

Best finish for 1973: T-6th at the St. Louis Children's Hospital Golf Classic

1974	30	100	19	0	0	0	4	73.05	$13,926

Best finish for 1974: T-20th at the Jackie Gleason's Inverrary Classic

1975	29	96	18	0	2	5	6	72.34	$39,964

Best finish for 1975: 4th at the Bob Hope Chrysler Classic

1976	24	69	12	0	1	1	2	73.67	$12,133

Best finish for 1976: T-4th at the Glen Campbell Los Angeles Open

1977	25	80	15	0	0	1	3	72.45	$17,127

Best finish for 1977: 10th at the Canadian Open

Year	Starts	Rounds Played	Cuts Made	Wins	Top-5s	Top-10s	Top-25s	Scoring Average	Money
1978	15	53	11	0	0	0	1	72.89	$8,355

Best finish for 1978: T-12th at the Tallahassee Open

1979	17	45	4	0	0	0	0	73.60	$2,265

Best finish for 1979: T-27th at the Tallahassee Open

1980	21	55	7	0	0	1	3	73.62	$17,108

Best finish for 1980: T-9th at the Atlanta Classic

1981	16	38	4	0	0	0	0	73.00	$3,082

Best finish for 1981: T-42nd at the Buick Open & B.C. Open

1982	18	48	6	0	0	0	1	73.56	$7,114

Best finish for 1982: T-24th at the Bank of Boston Classic

1983	8	18	1	0	0	0	0	74.89	$957

Best finish for 1983: T-50th at the Georgia-Pacific Atlanta Golf Classic

1984	4	12	2	0	0	0	0	73.50	$1,778

Best finish for 1984: T-63rd at the Doral-Eastern Open

1985	5	10	0	0	0	0	0	74.70	
1986	9	26	4	0	0	0	0	73.23	$4,250

Best finish for 1986: T-49th at the Hardee's Golf Classic

1987	6	14	1	0	0	1	1	72.36	$13,000

Best finish for 1987: T-8th at the Hardee's Golf Classic

1988	9	22	2	0	0	0	1	72.86	$4,760

Best finish for 1988: T-12th at the Deposit Guaranty Golf Classic

1989	1	2	0	0	0	0	0	75.00	
1991	1	2	0	0	0	0	0	76.00	
1992	1	2	0	0	0	0	0	74.00	
1993	2	6	1	0	0	0	0	72.17	$2,716

Best finish for 1993: T-72nd at the Doral-Ryder Open

1994	1	2	0	0	0	0	0	78.00	
1997	1	3	0	0	0	0	0	73.33	
Period Totals	Starts	Rounds Played	Cuts Made	Wins	Top-5s	Top-10s	Top-25s	Scoring Average	Money
	530	1613	273	4	8	28	75	73.00	$430,467

Mike Shea

Year	Starts	Rounds Played	Cuts Made	Wins	Top-5s	Top-10s	Top-25s	Scoring Average	Money
1966	1	2	0	0	0	0	0	76.50	
1974	2	6	1	0	0	0	0	73.33	

Best finish for 1974: T-73rd at the Greater New Orleans Open

1975	11	28	3	0	0	0	0	74.75	$591

Best finish for 1975: T-35th at the San Antonio Texas Open

1976	15	42	8	0	0	0	1	74.00	$3,982

Best finish for 1976: T-21st at the Hawaiian Open

1977	1	2	0	0	0	0	0	73.50	
1978	17	44	5	0	0	0	0	73.61	$3,923

Best finish for 1978: T-26th at the Tallahassee Open

Period Totals	Starts	Rounds Played	Cuts Made	Wins	Top-5s	Top-10s	Top-25s	Scoring Average	Money
	47	124	17	0	0	0	1	74.03	$8,495

Bob Shearer

Year	Starts	Rounds Played	Cuts Made	Wins	Top-5s	Top-10s	Top-25s	Scoring Average	Money
1972	1	4	1	0	0	0	0	73.50	$512

Best finish for 1972: T-31st at the British Open

1974	1	4	1	0	0	0	0	77.50	$300

Best finish for 1974: T-59th at the British Open

1975	2	6	1	0	0	0	0	73.50	$605

Best finish for 1975: T-32nd at the British Open

1976	7	22	5	0	0	0	1	73.64	$5,069

Best finish for 1976: T-21st at the British Open

1977	19	64	12	0	3	3	8	71.97	$56,046

Best finish for 1977: T-2nd at the IVB Philadelphia Golf Classic

1978	25	95	22	0	2	4	12	72.16	$69,359

Best finish for 1978: T-4th at the American Optical Classic

1979	24	63	9	0	0	0	2	73.48	$19,037

Best finish for 1979: T-12th at the First NBC New Orleans Open

1980	16	56	12	0	1	1	2	72.23	$27,236

Best finish for 1980: T-5th at the Atlanta Classic

1981	20	63	12	0	0	1	4	72.21	$32,336

Best finish for 1981: T-7th at the Greater Greensboro Open

1982	17	58	13	1	5	6	6	72.33	$133,311

Best finish for 1982: Win at the Tallahassee Open

1983	21	74	16	0	0	1	2	72.97	$39,999

Best finish for 1983: T-10th at the USF&G Classic

1984	19	61	12	0	0	1	4	72.97	$42,940

Best finish for 1984: T-6th at the Doral-Eastern Open

Year	Starts	Rounds Played	Cuts Made	Wins	Top-5s	Top-10s	Top-25s	Scoring Average	Money
1985	1	4	1	0	0	0	0	72.75	$4,150

Best finish for 1985: T-35th at the British Open

Period Totals	Starts	Rounds Played	Cuts Made	Wins	Top-5s	Top-10s	Top-25s	Scoring Average	Money
	173	574	117	1	11	17	41	72.62	$430,900

Patrick Sheehan

Year	Starts	Rounds Played	Cuts Made	Wins	Top-5s	Top-10s	Top-25s	Scoring Average	Money
2002	1	2	0	0	0	0	0	74.00	
2003	32	99	20	0	0	0	7	70.48	$618,019

Best finish for 2003: T-11th at the HP Classic of New Orleans

| 2004 | 33 | 111 | 23 | 0 | 3 | 3 | 7 | 70.98 | $1,234,344 |

Best finish for 2004: 2nd at the Valero Texas Open

| 2005 | 35 | 110 | 22 | 0 | 1 | 1 | 3 | 71.45 | $675,038 |

Best finish for 2005: T-5th at the Bay Hill Invitational

| 2006 | 34 | 100 | 17 | 0 | 0 | 1 | 3 | 71.40 | $386,797 |

Best finish for 2006: T-7th at the John Deere Classic

| 2008 | 35 | 124 | 27 | 0 | 0 | 2 | 5 | 70.93 | $805,897 |

Best finish for 2008: T-6th at the Mayakoba Golf Classic & U.S. Bank Championship in Milwaukee

Period Totals	Starts	Rounds Played	Cuts Made	Wins	Top-5s	Top-10s	Top-25s	Scoring Average	Money
	170	546	109	0	4	7	25	71.06	$3,720,095

Don Shirley, Jr.

Year	Starts	Rounds Played	Cuts Made	Wins	Top-5s	Top-10s	Top-25s	Scoring Average	Money
1987	31	88	14	0	0	1	3	71.85	$45,991

Best finish for 1987: T-9th at the Walt Disney World/Oldsmobile Classic

| 1988 | 5 | 12 | 1 | 0 | 0 | 0 | 0 | 73.08 | $768 |

Best finish for 1988: 74th at the Gatlin Brothers - Southwest Golf Classic

| 1989 | 27 | 85 | 16 | 0 | 1 | 2 | 4 | 71.00 | $123,307 |

Best finish for 1989: T-3rd at the Chattanooga Classic

| 1990 | 34 | 92 | 13 | 0 | 0 | 0 | 1 | 72.38 | $51,423 |

Best finish for 1990: T-23rd at the Buick Open

| 1991 | 6 | 16 | 2 | 0 | 0 | 0 | 2 | 70.94 | $8,703 |

Best finish for 1991: T-22nd at the Chattanooga Classic

| 1992 | 5 | 14 | 2 | 0 | 0 | 0 | 0 | 72.00 | $3,341 |

Best finish for 1992: T-39th at the Deposit Guaranty Classic

| 1993 | 3 | 8 | 1 | 0 | 0 | 0 | 0 | 72.88 | $597 |

Best finish for 1993: T-70th at the Deposit Guaranty Classic

Period Totals	Starts	Rounds Played	Cuts Made	Wins	Top-5s	Top-10s	Top-25s	Scoring Average	Money
	111	315	49	0	1	3	10	71.81	$234,130

Wes Short, Jr.

Year	Starts	Rounds Played	Cuts Made	Wins	Top-5s	Top-10s	Top-25s	Scoring Average	Money
2002	1	2	0	0	0	0	0	74.50	
2004	12	31	4	0	0	0	1	71.10	$75,536

Best finish for 2004: T-24th at the Buick Open

| 2005 | 16 | 44 | 7 | 1 | 2 | 2 | 3 | 70.39 | $1,029,640 |

Best finish for 2005: Win at the Michelin Championship at Las Vegas

| 2006 | 33 | 94 | 14 | 0 | 0 | 0 | 3 | 72.28 | $424,756 |

Best finish for 2006: T-11th at the Mercedes Championships

| 2007 | 12 | 31 | 3 | 0 | 0 | 0 | 0 | 72.71 | $42,119 |

Best finish for 2007: T-44th at the Zurich Classic of New Orleans

Period Totals	Starts	Rounds Played	Cuts Made	Wins	Top-5s	Top-10s	Top-25s	Scoring Average	Money
	74	202	28	1	2	2	7	71.77	$1,572,051

George Shortridge

Year	Starts	Rounds Played	Cuts Made	Wins	Top-5s	Top-10s	Top-25s	Scoring Average	Money
1965	6	14	1	0	0	0	0	74.93	

Best finish for 1965: T-72nd at the "500" Festival

| 1966 | 1 | 4 | 1 | 0 | 0 | 0 | 0 | 71.00 | $040 |

Best finish for 1966: T-50th at the Minnesota Golf Classic

| 1967 | 1 | 4 | 1 | 0 | 0 | 0 | 0 | 75.25 | |

Best finish for 1967: T-53rd at the Minnesota Golf Classic

1968	2	4	0	0	0	0	0	74.50	
1969	3	6	0	0	0	0	0	77.50	
1972	20	66	13	0	1	1	1	73.56	$8,849

Best finish for 1972: T-5th at the Doral-Eastern Open

1973	5	9	0	0	0	0	0	73.56	$168
1979	1	2	0	0	0	0	0	75.00	$350
1980	2	2	0	0	0	0	0	76.00	$500
1982	3	6	0	0	0	0	0	78.67	
1988	1	2	0	0	0	0	0	74.00	$1,000

Period Totals	Starts	Rounds Played	Cuts Made	Wins	Top-5s	Top-10s	Top-25s	Scoring Average	Money
	45	119	16	0	1	1	1	74.25	$10,907

David Shuster

Year	Starts	Rounds Played	Cuts Made	Wins	Top-5s	Top-10s	Top-25s	Scoring Average	Money
1968	1	2	0	0	0	0	0	74.50	
1969	3	12	3	0	0	0	0	73.50	

Best finish for 1969: T-44th at the Greater Milwaukee Open

1974	5	12	1	0	0	0	0	73.25	$273

Best finish for 1974: T-56th at the Greater Milwaukee Open

1975	10	22	1	0	0	0	0	75.18	$094

Best finish for 1975: T-70th at the San Antonio Texas Open

1976	7	22	4	0	0	0	0	73.09	$1,004

Best finish for 1976: T-56th at the Tallahassee Open

Period Totals	Starts	Rounds Played	Cuts Made	Wins	Top-5s	Top-10s	Top-25s	Scoring Average	Money
	26	70	9	0	0	0	0	73.89	$1,371

Denny Shute

Year	Starts	Rounds Played	Cuts Made	Wins	Top-5s	Top-10s	Top-25s	Scoring Average	Money
1958	3	9	2	0	0	0	0	75.00	$300

Best finish for 1958: 41st at the Greenbrier Invitational

1959	2	6	1	0	0	0	0	74.83	$500

Best finish for 1959: T-44th at the PGA Championship

1960	2	4	1	0	0	0	0	78.25	$350

Best finish for 1960: T-200 at the PGA Championship

1961	2	4	1	0	0	0	0	79.50	$400

Best finish for 1961: T-200 at the PGA Championship

1962	2	4	1	0	0	0	0	77.50	$425

Best finish for 1962: T-125 at the Thunderbird Classic Invitational

1964	3	6	0	0	0	0	0	78.83	
1965	2	4	0	0	0	0	0	81.00	
1966	2	4	0	0	0	0	0	78.75	
1968	1	2	0	0	0	0	0	82.00	
1969	2	4	0	0	0	0	0	81.25	
1970	2	4	0	0	0	0	0	80.25	
1971	2	4	0	0	0	0	0	82.75	
1972	1	2	0	0	0	0	0	88.00	

Period Totals	Starts	Rounds Played	Cuts Made	Wins	Top-5s	Top-10s	Top-25s	Scoring Average	Money
	26	57	6	0	0	0	0	78.84	$1,975

PGA Tour career totals from 1925 to 1972

	Starts	Rounds Played	Cuts Made	Wins	Top-5s	Top-10s	Top-25s	Scoring Average	Money
	286	N/A	N/A	15	N/A	125	204	N/A	N/A

Dick Siderowf

Year	Starts	Rounds Played	Cuts Made	Wins	Top-5s	Top-10s	Top-25s	Scoring Average	Money
1958	1	4	1	0	0	0	0	72.25	

Best finish for 1958: T-55th at the Insurance City Open

1959	1	4	1	0	0	0	1	71.00	

Best finish for 1959: T-24th at the Insurance City Open Invitational

1960	1	4	1	0	0	0	0	70.75	

Best finish for 1960: T-33rd at the Insurance City Open Invitational

1961	1	2	0	0	0	0	0	75.00	
1963	1	4	1	0	0	0	0	72.00	

Best finish for 1963: T-43rd at the Insurance City Open Invitational

1964	2	3	0	0	0	0	0	76.00	
1966	1	0	0	0	0	0	0		
1967	2	4	0	0	0	0	0	78.25	
1968	1	4	1	0	0	0	0	75.00	

Best finish for 1968: T-57th at the U.S. Open

1969	2	6	1	0	0	0	0	76.17	

Best finish for 1969: 46th at the Masters

1970	3	6	0	0	0	0	0	78.33	
1971	1	4	1	0	0	0	0	73.50	

Best finish for 1971: T-65th at the Doral-Eastern Open

1972	1	2	0	0	0	0	0	78.50	
1973	1	2	0	0	0	0	0	76.00	
1974	3	6	0	0	0	0	0	73.83	$1,200
1975	2	4	0	0	0	0	0	75.75	$1,250
1976	3	10	2	0	0	0	0	74.90	

Best finish for 1976: 46th at the Masters

1977	2	4	0	0	0	0	0	76.25	$1,500
1978	1	4	1	0	0	0	0	74.50	

Best finish for 1978: 49th at the Masters

Year	Starts	Rounds Played	Cuts Made	Wins	Top-5s	Top-10s	Top-25s	Scoring Average	Money
1981	1	4	1	0	0	0	0	72.50	

Best finish for 1981: T-55th at the Doral-Eastern Open

| 1982 | 1 | 4 | 1 | 0 | 0 | 0 | 0 | 73.50 | |

Best finish for 1982: T-58th at the Doral-Eastern Open

1983	1	2	0	0	0	0	0	75.50	
1984	1	2	0	0	0	0	0	75.50	
1986	1	2	0	0	0	0	0	74.50	
Period Totals	**Starts**	**Rounds Played**	**Cuts Made**	**Wins**	**Top-5s**	**Top-10s**	**Top-25s**	**Scoring Average**	**Money**
	35	91	12	0	0	0	1	74.70	$3,950

Tom Sieckmann

Year	Starts	Rounds Played	Cuts Made	Wins	Top-5s	Top-10s	Top-25s	Scoring Average	Money
1979	1	2	0	0	0	0	0	80.50	$600
1980	1	2	0	0	0	0	0	73.00	
1982	1	4	1	0	0	0	0	75.25	$1,358

Best finish for 1982: T-56th at the U.S. Open

| 1984 | 1 | 2 | 0 | 0 | 0 | 0 | 0 | 81.00 | $600 |
| 1985 | 30 | 82 | 9 | 0 | 0 | 0 | 3 | 72.68 | $30,052 |

Best finish for 1985: T-12th at the Byron Nelson Golf Classic

| 1986 | 34 | 96 | 14 | 0 | 2 | 2 | 3 | 72.99 | $63,995 |

Best finish for 1986: T-3rd at the USF&G Classic & Tallahassee Open

| 1987 | 35 | 90 | 10 | 0 | 0 | 1 | 4 | 72.37 | $52,597 |

Best finish for 1987: T-9th at the Anheuser-Busch Golf Classic

| 1988 | 28 | 78 | 11 | 1 | 2 | 3 | 7 | 71.73 | $210,151 |

Best finish for 1988: Win at the Anheuser-Busch Golf Classic

| 1989 | 28 | 81 | 13 | 0 | 0 | 1 | 7 | 72.25 | $98,965 |

Best finish for 1989: T-8th at the Hardee's Golf Classic

| 1990 | 27 | 84 | 17 | 0 | 1 | 3 | 5 | 71.57 | $139,383 |

Best finish for 1990: T-4th at the Shearson Lehman Hutton Open

| 1991 | 28 | 85 | 16 | 0 | 2 | 3 | 7 | 71.39 | $280,096 |

Best finish for 1991: 2nd at the Nestle Invitational

| 1992 | 29 | 93 | 19 | 0 | 0 | 1 | 6 | 70.92 | $174,424 |

Best finish for 1992: T-6th at the Players Championship

| 1993 | 31 | 96 | 18 | 0 | 1 | 2 | 4 | 71.63 | $201,429 |

Best finish for 1993: T-2nd at the BellSouth Classic

| 1994 | 29 | 79 | 10 | 0 | 0 | 0 | 2 | 72.38 | $55,304 |

Best finish for 1994: T-13th at the Greater Milwaukee Open

| 1996 | 3 | 5 | 0 | 0 | 0 | 0 | 0 | 74.20 | |
| 1997 | 2 | 6 | 1 | 0 | 0 | 0 | 0 | 72.33 | $3,224 |

Best finish for 1997: T-65th at the Michelob Championship at Kingsmill

| 1998 | 2 | 4 | 0 | 0 | 0 | 0 | 0 | 75.00 | |
| 1999 | 2 | 6 | 1 | 0 | 0 | 0 | 0 | 73.50 | $3,408 |

Best finish for 1999: T-63rd at the B.C. Open

2000	1	2	0	0	0	0	0	77.00	
Period Totals	**Starts**	**Rounds Played**	**Cuts Made**	**Wins**	**Top-5s**	**Top-10s**	**Top-25s**	**Scoring Average**	**Money**
	313	897	140	1	8	16	48	72.09	$1,315,587

Charles Sifford

Year	Starts	Rounds Played	Cuts Made	Wins	Top-5s	Top-10s	Top-25s	Scoring Average	Money
1958	9	30	5	0	0	1	2	72.60	$1,478

Best finish for 1958: T-10th at the Rubber City Open

| 1959 | 8 | 32 | 7 | 0 | 0 | 1 | 5 | 71.78 | $2,781 |

Best finish for 1959: T-8th at the Portland Centennial Open Invitational

| 1960 | 12 | 48 | 11 | 0 | 1 | 3 | 6 | 70.98 | $6,313 |

Best finish for 1960: T-2nd at the Orange County Open Invitational

| 1961 | 18 | 73 | 18 | 0 | 3 | 3 | 14 | 70.53 | $10,233 |

Best finish for 1961: T-3rd at the Almaden Open

| 1962 | 17 | 68 | 17 | 0 | 2 | 3 | 7 | 71.29 | $9,009 |

Best finish for 1962: T-3rd at the Dallas Open Invitational

| 1963 | 18 | 72 | 17 | 1 | 5 | 7 | 13 | 70.49 | $18,615 |

Best finish for 1963: Win at the Puerto Rico Open Invitational

| 1964 | 33 | 115 | 23 | 0 | 2 | 5 | 7 | 72.13 | $17,963 |

Best finish for 1964: T-2nd at the St. Paul Open

| 1965 | 31 | 112 | 25 | 0 | 0 | 5 | 10 | 72.22 | $19,286 |

Best finish for 1965: T-8th at the Canadian Open

| 1966 | 33 | 126 | 29 | 0 | 0 | 2 | 11 | 72.30 | $19,237 |

Best finish for 1966: T-8th at the Los Angeles Open Invitational & Lucky International Open Invitational

| 1967 | 30 | 108 | 23 | 1 | 2 | 5 | 11 | 71.97 | $47,404 |

Best finish for 1967: Win at the Insurance City Open

| 1968 | 35 | 123 | 27 | 0 | 1 | 1 | 13 | 71.93 | $28,419 |

Best finish for 1968: T-2nd at the Cajun Classic

| 1969 | 36 | 112 | 20 | 1 | 1 | 1 | 7 | 72.52 | $34,301 |

Best finish for 1969: Win at the Los Angeles Open

Year	Starts	Rounds Played	Cuts Made	Wins	Top-5s	Top-10s	Top-25s	Scoring Average	Money
1970	36	103	19	0	0	1	2	72.91	$8,876

Best finish for 1970: T-6th at the Robinson Open Golf Classic

| 1971 | 28 | 94 | 18 | 0 | 0 | 1 | 2 | 72.35 | $10,985 |

Best finish for 1971: T-10th at the Tallahassee Open

| 1972 | 37 | 120 | 24 | 0 | 0 | 1 | 12 | 72.47 | $28,294 |

Best finish for 1972: T-7th at the Westchester Classic

| 1973 | 33 | 98 | 16 | 0 | 2 | 3 | 8 | 72.43 | $27,753 |

Best finish for 1973: T-4th at the Danny Thomas Memphis Classic

| 1974 | 32 | 101 | 20 | 0 | 0 | 2 | 6 | 72.44 | $20,284 |

Best finish for 1974: T-9th at the Sahara Invitational

| 1975 | 6 | 12 | 1 | 0 | 0 | 0 | 0 | 74.83 | $1,018 |

Best finish for 1975: T-48th at the PGA Championship

| 1976 | 6 | 18 | 3 | 0 | 0 | 0 | 0 | 73.56 | $1,991 |

Best finish for 1976: T-39th at the Florida Citrus Open Invitational

| 1977 | 7 | 18 | 3 | 0 | 0 | 0 | 0 | 74.28 | $1,625 |

Best finish for 1977: T-43rd at the Doral-Eastern Open

| 1978 | 3 | 6 | 0 | 0 | 0 | 0 | 0 | 76.17 | $600 |
| 1979 | 4 | 10 | 1 | 0 | 0 | 0 | 0 | 73.10 | $550 |

Best finish for 1979: T-58th at the Glen Campbell Los Angeles Open

1980	3	6	0	0	0	0	0	74.33	$500
1981	2	4	0	0	0	0	0	73.50	
1982	1	2	0	0	0	0	0	78.00	
1983	1	4	1	0	0	0	0	71.00	$636

Best finish for 1983: T-61st at the Glen Campbell Los Angeles Open

| 1984 | 1 | 4 | 1 | 0 | 0 | 0 | 0 | 76.75 | $748 |

Best finish for 1984: T-76th at the Los Angeles Open

Period Totals	Starts	Rounds Played	Cuts Made	Wins	Top-5s	Top-10s	Top-25s	Scoring Average	Money
	480	1619	329	3	19	45	136	72.17	$318,898

PGA Tour career totals from 1949 to 1984

	Starts	Rounds Played	Cuts Made	Wins	Top-5s	Top-10s	Top-25s	Scoring Average	Money
	517	1765	366	3	20	48	147	N/A	$324,407

Curtis Sifford

Year	Starts	Rounds Played	Cuts Made	Wins	Top-5s	Top-10s	Top-25s	Scoring Average	Money
1966	1	2	0	0	0	0	0	78.50	
1967	1	2	0	0	0	0	0	75.50	
1969	19	51	6	0	0	0	0	73.90	$1,562

Best finish for 1969: T-33rd at the Western Open

| 1970 | 15 | 37 | 5 | 0 | 0 | 0 | 1 | 73.59 | $1,552 |

Best finish for 1970: T-23rd at the Robinson Open Golf Classic

| 1971 | 21 | 68 | 12 | 0 | 0 | 0 | 1 | 72.72 | $5,464 |

Best finish for 1971: T-19th at the Greater Hartford Open Invitational

| 1972 | 26 | 74 | 11 | 0 | 1 | 3 | 4 | 73.04 | $18,426 |

Best finish for 1972: T-5th at the Greater Hartford Open Invitational

| 1973 | 29 | 87 | 15 | 0 | 1 | 2 | 6 | 72.56 | $19,752 |

Best finish for 1973: T-4th at the Southern Open

| 1974 | 28 | 82 | 14 | 0 | 1 | 1 | 5 | 72.94 | $19,348 |

Best finish for 1974: T-5th at the B.C. Open

| 1975 | 26 | 82 | 15 | 0 | 0 | 0 | 1 | 73.33 | $7,564 |

Best finish for 1975: 13th at the Bob Hope Chrysler Classic

| 1976 | 20 | 51 | 9 | 0 | 0 | 0 | 1 | 73.41 | $3,410 |

Best finish for 1976: T-20th at the Sahara Invitational

| 1977 | 21 | 55 | 6 | 0 | 0 | 0 | 0 | 74.44 | $1,598 |

Best finish for 1977: T-47th at the Jackie Gleason's Inverrary Classic

| 1978 | 1 | 4 | 1 | 0 | 0 | 0 | 0 | 73.00 | $552 |

Best finish for 1978: T-46th at the Andy Williams-San Diego Open

| 1981 | 19 | 48 | 5 | 0 | 0 | 0 | 0 | 73.33 | $4,841 |

Best finish for 1981: T-31st at the LaJet Classic

| 1983 | 3 | 10 | 1 | 0 | 0 | 0 | 0 | 73.10 | $576 |

Best finish for 1983: 74th at the Isuzu/Andy Williams San Diego Open

| 1984 | 2 | 6 | 1 | 0 | 0 | 0 | 0 | 73.50 | $2,064 |

Best finish for 1984: T-34th at the Los Angeles Open

Period Totals	Starts	Rounds Played	Cuts Made	Wins	Top-5s	Top-10s	Top-25s	Scoring Average	Money
	232	659	101	0	3	6	19	73.26	$86,710

Dan Sikes

Year	Starts	Rounds Played	Cuts Made	Wins	Top-5s	Top-10s	Top-25s	Scoring Average	Money
1961	14	56	13	0	1	3	7	71.27	$6,616

Best finish for 1961: T-3rd at the Coral Gables Open Invitational

| 1962 | 22 | 88 | 20 | 0 | 1 | 4 | 12 | 71.75 | $13,764 |

Best finish for 1962: T-2nd at the Houston Classic

Year	Starts	Rounds Played	Cuts Made	Wins	Top-5s	Top-10s	Top-25s	Scoring Average	Money
1963	25	101	24	1	1	6	12	71.80	$24,568

Best finish for 1963: Win at the Doral Country Club Open Invitational

| 1964 | 28 | 99 | 23 | 0 | 2 | 5 | 13 | 71.72 | $21,739 |

Best finish for 1964: 2nd at the St. Petersburg Open

| 1965 | 27 | 96 | 20 | 1 | 4 | 7 | 9 | 72.23 | $55,809 |

Best finish for 1965: Win at the Cleveland Open

| 1966 | 25 | 96 | 23 | 0 | 1 | 5 | 13 | 71.71 | $27,549 |

Best finish for 1966: 3rd at the Cajun Classic

| 1967 | 23 | 81 | 20 | 2 | 7 | 11 | 15 | 70.89 | $111,530 |

Best finish for 1967: Win at the Jacksonville Open & Philadelphia Classic

| 1968 | 25 | 92 | 21 | 2 | 5 | 8 | 14 | 71.51 | $110,240 |

Best finish for 1968: Win at the Florida Citrus Open Invitational & Minnesota Golf Classic

| 1969 | 27 | 101 | 23 | 0 | 4 | 10 | 19 | 71.09 | $87,160 |

Best finish for 1969: T-2nd at the National Airlines Open

| 1970 | 27 | 93 | 22 | 0 | 4 | 7 | 12 | 71.51 | $74,357 |

Best finish for 1970: 2nd at the Atlanta Classic

| 1971 | 26 | 88 | 21 | 0 | 2 | 5 | 11 | 71.13 | $47,359 |

Best finish for 1971: T-2nd at the Phoenix Open

| 1972 | 28 | 106 | 25 | 0 | 0 | 5 | 10 | 71.82 | $37,782 |

Best finish for 1972: T-6th at the Bing Crosby Pro-Am & Monsanto Open

| 1973 | 27 | 87 | 20 | 0 | 4 | 7 | 17 | 71.13 | $101,945 |

Best finish for 1973: T-2nd at the Greater Jacksonville Open & Byron Nelson Golf Classic

| 1974 | 26 | 90 | 19 | 0 | 1 | 3 | 12 | 71.63 | $37,913 |

Best finish for 1974: T-2nd at the Tallahassee Open

| 1975 | 23 | 75 | 16 | 0 | 0 | 2 | 6 | 72.11 | $23,348 |

Best finish for 1975: T-7th at the Pensacola Open

| 1976 | 22 | 71 | 16 | 0 | 1 | 2 | 6 | 71.82 | $26,830 |

Best finish for 1976: T-5th at the American Express Westchester Classic

| 1977 | 21 | 64 | 12 | 0 | 0 | 0 | 2 | 73.14 | $12,086 |

Best finish for 1977: T-13th at the IVB Philadelphia Golf Classic

| 1978 | 15 | 46 | 8 | 0 | 0 | 0 | 0 | 72.50 | $6,151 |

Best finish for 1978: T-29th at the American Express Westchester Classic

| 1979 | 5 | 12 | 1 | 0 | 0 | 0 | 0 | 74.83 | $532 |

Best finish for 1979: T-63rd at the Bay Hill Citrus Classic

1980	5	8	0	0	0	0	0	75.25	
1981	1	2	0	0	0	0	0	76.00	
Period Totals	Starts	Rounds Played	Cuts Made	Wins	Top-5s	Top-10s	Top-25s	Scoring Average	Money
	442	1552	347	6	38	90	190	71.72	$827,279

R.H. Sikes

Year	Starts	Rounds Played	Cuts Made	Wins	Top-5s	Top-10s	Top-25s	Scoring Average	Money
1962	1	2	0	0	0	0	0	80.00	
1963	1	4	1	0	0	0	0	76.50	

Best finish for 1963: T-46th at the Masters

| 1964 | 14 | 49 | 10 | 1 | 3 | 4 | 5 | 71.61 | $22,453 |

Best finish for 1964: Win at the Sahara Invitational

| 1965 | 20 | 68 | 13 | 0 | 1 | 3 | 9 | 72.29 | $23,318 |

Best finish for 1965: T-5th at the Cleveland Open

| 1966 | 31 | 118 | 27 | 1 | 5 | 9 | 15 | 71.64 | $70,450 |

Best finish for 1966: Win at the Cleveland Open Invitational

| 1967 | 32 | 110 | 22 | 0 | 1 | 6 | 14 | 72.39 | $42,780 |

Best finish for 1967: T-2nd at the Buick Open

| 1968 | 33 | 112 | 23 | 0 | 2 | 4 | 16 | 71.51 | $38,003 |

Best finish for 1968: T-4th at the "500" Festival Open Invitational & Canadian Open

| 1969 | 34 | 120 | 26 | 0 | 1 | 7 | 13 | 71.68 | $50,483 |

Best finish for 1969: T-2nd at the Philadelphia Classic

| 1970 | 31 | 106 | 24 | 0 | 1 | 2 | 10 | 71.90 | $37,485 |

Best finish for 1970: 3rd at the Greater Greensboro Open

| 1971 | 36 | 108 | 19 | 0 | 1 | 2 | 8 | 72.56 | $24,038 |

Best finish for 1971: 4th at the Canadian Open

| 1972 | 26 | 66 | 8 | 0 | 0 | 0 | 2 | 73.86 | $5,444 |

Best finish for 1972: T-18th at the Western Open

| 1973 | 10 | 21 | 2 | 0 | 0 | 0 | 1 | 73.86 | $1,512 |

Best finish for 1973: T-22nd at the Shrine-Robinson Golf Classic

| 1974 | 4 | 10 | 1 | 0 | 0 | 0 | 0 | 75.90 | $224 |

Best finish for 1974: T-63rd at the Greater Milwaukee Open

| 1975 | 3 | 10 | 2 | 0 | 0 | 0 | 0 | 72.20 | $634 |

Best finish for 1975: T-51st at the Sahara Invitational

| 1976 | 12 | 35 | 6 | 0 | 0 | 0 | 1 | 73.51 | $5,602 |

Best finish for 1976: T-11th at the Florida Citrus Open Invitational

| 1977 | 4 | 10 | 1 | 0 | 0 | 0 | 0 | 75.90 | |

Best finish for 1977: T-79th at the Jackie Gleason's Inverrary Classic

Year	Starts	Rounds Played	Cuts Made	Wins	Top-5s	Top-10s	Top-25s	Scoring Average	Money
1981	6	10	0	0	0	0	0	75.00	
1982	10	26	2	0	0	0	0	73.77	$1,203

Best finish for 1982: T-51st at the Greater Milwaukee Open

Year	Starts	Rounds Played	Cuts Made	Wins	Top-5s	Top-10s	Top-25s	Scoring Average	Money
1983	2	4	0	0	0	0	0	74.75	
1984	1	2	0	0	0	0	0	77.00	
1985	2	4	0	0	0	0	0	78.00	
1990	1	2	0	0	0	0	0	76.50	
Period Totals	**Starts**	**Rounds Played**	**Cuts Made**	**Wins**	**Top-5s**	**Top-10s**	**Top-25s**	**Scoring Average**	**Money**
	314	997	187	2	15	37	94	72.42	$323,628

Tony Sills

Year	Starts	Rounds Played	Cuts Made	Wins	Top-5s	Top-10s	Top-25s	Scoring Average	Money
1976	2	4	0	0	0	0	0	76.00	
1977	1	2	0	0	0	0	0	74.00	
1983	27	85	13	0	1	2	3	72.60	$47,488

Best finish for 1983: 3rd at the Texas Open

Year	Starts	Rounds Played	Cuts Made	Wins	Top-5s	Top-10s	Top-25s	Scoring Average	Money
1984	33	114	23	0	1	3	6	72.46	$90,055

Best finish for 1984: T-4th at the Colonial National Invitational

Year	Starts	Rounds Played	Cuts Made	Wins	Top-5s	Top-10s	Top-25s	Scoring Average	Money
1985	33	101	19	0	4	6	9	71.85	$126,255

Best finish for 1985: T-4th at the USF&G Classic & Southern Open

Year	Starts	Rounds Played	Cuts Made	Wins	Top-5s	Top-10s	Top-25s	Scoring Average	Money
1986	29	103	26	0	2	5	13	70.73	$216,881

Best finish for 1986: T-2nd at the Phoenix Open

Year	Starts	Rounds Played	Cuts Made	Wins	Top-5s	Top-10s	Top-25s	Scoring Average	Money
1987	30	92	18	0	1	2	7	71.79	$101,059

Best finish for 1987: T-3rd at the B.C. Open

Year	Starts	Rounds Played	Cuts Made	Wins	Top-5s	Top-10s	Top-25s	Scoring Average	Money
1988	33	97	17	0	0	0	4	71.78	$76,654

Best finish for 1988: T-11th at the Panasonic Las Vegas Invitational

Year	Starts	Rounds Played	Cuts Made	Wins	Top-5s	Top-10s	Top-25s	Scoring Average	Money
1989	31	90	15	0	0	1	2	72.12	$77,181

Best finish for 1989: T-9th at the Las Vegas Invitational

Year	Starts	Rounds Played	Cuts Made	Wins	Top-5s	Top-10s	Top-25s	Scoring Average	Money
1990	18	51	8	1	1	2	2	72.31	$244,850

Best finish for 1990: Win at the Independent Insurance Agent Open

Year	Starts	Rounds Played	Cuts Made	Wins	Top-5s	Top-10s	Top-25s	Scoring Average	Money
1991	11	28	2	0	0	0	0	73.14	$13,490

Best finish for 1991: 31st at the Infiniti Tournament Of Champions

Year	Starts	Rounds Played	Cuts Made	Wins	Top-5s	Top-10s	Top-25s	Scoring Average	Money
1992	26	66	5	0	0	0	0	72.73	$10,575

Best finish for 1992: T-41st at the United Airlines Hawaiian Open

Year	Starts	Rounds Played	Cuts Made	Wins	Top-5s	Top-10s	Top-25s	Scoring Average	Money
1993	5	14	2	0	0	0	0	71.86	$11,686

Best finish for 1993: T-26th at the United Airlines Hawaiian Open

Year	Starts	Rounds Played	Cuts Made	Wins	Top-5s	Top-10s	Top-25s	Scoring Average	Money
1994	9	28	6	0	0	0	0	70.46	$22,807

Best finish for 1994: T-27th at the New England Classic

Year	Starts	Rounds Played	Cuts Made	Wins	Top-5s	Top-10s	Top-25s	Scoring Average	Money
1995	24	73	12	0	0	1	3	71.60	$113,186

Best finish for 1995: 7th at the Bell Canadian Open

Year	Starts	Rounds Played	Cuts Made	Wins	Top-5s	Top-10s	Top-25s	Scoring Average	Money
1996	14	35	4	0	0	0	0	72.51	$11,734

Best finish for 1996: T-43rd at the B.C. Open

Year	Starts	Rounds Played	Cuts Made	Wins	Top-5s	Top-10s	Top-25s	Scoring Average	Money
1997	5	10	0	0	0	0	0	75.70	
1998	5	14	2	0	0	0	0	71.71	$5,475

Best finish for 1998: T-62nd at the Deposit Guaranty Golf Classic

Year	Starts	Rounds Played	Cuts Made	Wins	Top-5s	Top-10s	Top-25s	Scoring Average	Money
1999	1	2	0	0	0	0	0	73.50	
2000	1	1	0	0	0	0	0	79.00	
Period Totals	**Starts**	**Rounds Played**	**Cuts Made**	**Wins**	**Top-5s**	**Top-10s**	**Top-25s**	**Scoring Average**	**Money**
	338	1010	172	1	10	22	49	72.03	$1,169,376

Larry Silveira

Year	Starts	Rounds Played	Cuts Made	Wins	Top-5s	Top-10s	Top-25s	Scoring Average	Money
1988	1	2	0	0	0	0	0	72.50	
1989	28	81	14	0	0	0	4	71.37	$60,712

Best finish for 1989: T-18th at the Canadian Open

Year	Starts	Rounds Played	Cuts Made	Wins	Top-5s	Top-10s	Top-25s	Scoring Average	Money
1990	29	83	14	0	0	1	3	71.73	$65,696

Best finish for 1990: T-10th at the Deposit Guaranty

Year	Starts	Rounds Played	Cuts Made	Wins	Top-5s	Top-10s	Top-25s	Scoring Average	Money
1991	29	79	10	1	1	1	3	72.08	$93,893

Best finish for 1991: Win at the Deposit Guaranty Classic

Year	Starts	Rounds Played	Cuts Made	Wins	Top-5s	Top-10s	Top-25s	Scoring Average	Money
1992	18	54	9	0	1	1	2	71.91	$66,697

Best finish for 1992: T-4th at the Buick Southern Open

Year	Starts	Rounds Played	Cuts Made	Wins	Top-5s	Top-10s	Top-25s	Scoring Average	Money
1993	1	2	0	0	0	0	0	71.50	
1994	28	77	12	0	0	1	3	71.94	$99,671

Best finish for 1994: T-8th at the Motorola Western Open

Year	Starts	Rounds Played	Cuts Made	Wins	Top-5s	Top-10s	Top-25s	Scoring Average	Money
1997	24	59	6	0	0	0	1	72.92	$37,356

Best finish for 1997: T-20th at the AT&T Pebble Beach Pro-Am

	Starts	Rounds Played	Cuts Made	Wins	Top-5s	Top-10s	Top-25s	Scoring Average	Money
Period Totals	158	437	65	1	2	4	16	71.95	$424,025

Michael Sim

Year	Starts	Rounds Played	Cuts Made	Wins	Top-5s	Top-10s	Top-25s	Scoring Average	Money
2005	1	2	0	0	0	0	0	74.50	
2006	1	2	0	0	0	0	0	71.00	
2007	17	52	9	0	0	1	4	70.94	$399,900

Best finish for 2007: T-9th at the Ginn sur Mer Classic at Tesoro

Year	Starts	Rounds Played	Cuts Made	Wins	Top-5s	Top-10s	Top-25s	Scoring Average	Money
2008	7	27	6	0	0	1	3	70.93	$269,864

Best finish for 2008: T-7th at the Frys.Com Open

Period Totals	Starts	Rounds Played	Cuts Made	Wins	Top-5s	Top-10s	Top-25s	Scoring Average	Money
	26	83	15	0	0	2	7	71.02	$669,764

Gaylon Simon

Year	Starts	Rounds Played	Cuts Made	Wins	Top-5s	Top-10s	Top-25s	Scoring Average	Money
1964	19	34	1	0	0	0	0	75.62	$177

Best finish for 1964: T-46th at the Buick Open

Year	Starts	Rounds Played	Cuts Made	Wins	Top-5s	Top-10s	Top-25s	Scoring Average	Money
1967	9	17	0	0	0	0	0	77.12	
1968	7	14	1	0	0	0	0	74.21	

Best finish for 1968: T-59th at the Robinson Open

Year	Starts	Rounds Played	Cuts Made	Wins	Top-5s	Top-10s	Top-25s	Scoring Average	Money
1969	4	10	2	0	0	0	0	75.00	$296

Best finish for 1969: T-62nd at the Heritage Golf Classic

Year	Starts	Rounds Played	Cuts Made	Wins	Top-5s	Top-10s	Top-25s	Scoring Average	Money
1970	3	5	0	0	0	0	0	79.80	$500
1974	1	2	0	0	0	0	0	75.50	
1975	1	2	0	0	0	0	0	75.00	
1978	1	2	0	0	0	0	0	80.50	
Period Totals	Starts	Rounds Played	Cuts Made	Wins	Top-5s	Top-10s	Top-25s	Scoring Average	Money
	45	86	4	0	0	0	0	75.95	$974

Jim Simons

Year	Starts	Rounds Played	Cuts Made	Wins	Top-5s	Top-10s	Top-25s	Scoring Average	Money
1967	1	2	0	0	0	0	0	82.00	
1968	1	4	1	0	0	0	0	77.50	

Best finish for 1968: 63rd at the U.S. Open

| 1970 | 1 | 2 | 0 | 0 | 0 | 0 | 0 | 73.50 | |
| 1971 | 4 | 12 | 2 | 0 | 1 | 1 | 1 | 74.25 | |

Best finish for 1971: T-5th at the U.S. Open

| 1972 | 6 | 24 | 6 | 0 | 0 | 0 | 1 | 73.25 | $1,511 |

Best finish for 1972: T-15th at the U.S. Open

| 1973 | 33 | 110 | 19 | 0 | 1 | 2 | 2 | 72.92 | $20,486 |

Best finish for 1973: 2nd at the Tallahassee Open

| 1974 | 25 | 83 | 16 | 0 | 1 | 2 | 7 | 72.33 | $28,238 |

Best finish for 1974: T-5th at the Tallahassee Open

| 1975 | 30 | 106 | 23 | 0 | 3 | 4 | 8 | 71.89 | $47,725 |

Best finish for 1975: T-3rd at the Pleasant Valley Classic

| 1976 | 34 | 114 | 23 | 0 | 2 | 4 | 8 | 72.13 | $45,717 |

Best finish for 1976: T-3rd at the Phoenix Open

| 1977 | 25 | 91 | 20 | 1 | 3 | 4 | 10 | 71.54 | $81,397 |

Best finish for 1977: Win at the First NBC New Orleans Open

| 1978 | 28 | 97 | 21 | 1 | 1 | 3 | 10 | 72.08 | $92,021 |

Best finish for 1978: Win at the Memorial Tournament

| 1979 | 34 | 118 | 24 | 0 | 2 | 3 | 8 | 72.49 | $76,350 |

Best finish for 1979: T-2nd at the Greater Milwaukee Open & Buick Goodwrench Open

| 1980 | 28 | 88 | 17 | 0 | 1 | 4 | 8 | 71.86 | $86,027 |

Best finish for 1980: 2nd at the Sammy Davis, Jr. - Greater Hartford Open

| 1981 | 31 | 108 | 25 | 0 | 2 | 4 | 13 | 71.18 | $109,760 |

Best finish for 1981: T-2nd at the Western Open

| 1982 | 28 | 93 | 19 | 1 | 2 | 3 | 8 | 71.48 | $117,367 |

Best finish for 1982: Win at the Bing Crosby Pro-Am

| 1983 | 27 | 87 | 16 | 0 | 0 | 2 | 5 | 71.68 | $59,277 |

Best finish for 1983: T-6th at the USF&G Classic

| 1984 | 22 | 74 | 16 | 0 | 1 | 2 | 6 | 71.38 | $87,458 |

Best finish for 1984: 2nd at the Bob Hope Chrysler Classic

| 1985 | 21 | 72 | 14 | 0 | 0 | 1 | 5 | 71.97 | $62,558 |

Best finish for 1985: T-6th at the Hawaiian Open

| 1986 | 25 | 77 | 15 | 0 | 0 | 0 | 5 | 72.55 | $56,397 |

Best finish for 1986: T-12th at the Byron Nelson Golf Classic

| 1987 | 23 | 55 | 6 | 0 | 0 | 0 | 0 | 72.82 | $9,880 |

Best finish for 1987: T-32nd at the Southwest Golf Classic

| 1988 | 16 | 38 | 2 | 0 | 0 | 0 | 0 | 74.29 | $2,142 |

Best finish for 1988: T-47th at the B.C. Open

Year	Starts	Rounds Played	Cuts Made	Wins	Top-5s	Top-10s	Top-25s	Scoring Average	Money
1989	3	6	0	0	0	0	0	75.83	
1990	1	2	0	0	0	0	0	83.00	
Period Totals	Starts	Rounds Played	Cuts Made	Wins	Top-5s	Top-10s	Top-25s	Scoring Average	Money
	447	1463	285	3	20	39	105	72.17	$984,309

Scott Simpson

Year	Starts	Rounds Played	Cuts Made	Wins	Top-5s	Top-10s	Top-25s	Scoring Average	Money
1975	1	2	0	0	0	0	0	78.00	
1976	1	4	1	0	0	0	0	74.50	

Best finish for 1976: 71st at the Glen Campbell Los Angeles Open

1977	1	2	0	0	0	0	0	72.50	
1978	1	4	1	0	0	0	1	71.50	$3,100

Best finish for 1978: T-14th at the Andy Williams-San Diego Open

1979	29	100	21	0	1	2	6	72.03	$51,414

Best finish for 1979: T-4th at the Manufactures Hanover Westchester Classic

1980	31	108	24	1	3	4	11	71.86	$144,403

Best finish for 1980: Win at the Western Open

1981	31	101	21	0	2	3	14	71.55	$110,843

Best finish for 1981: 2nd at the Pleasant Valley Jimmy Fund Classic

1982	26	94	21	0	2	4	12	70.90	$146,903

Best finish for 1982: T-2nd at the Hawaiian Open & Tournament Players Championship

1983	26	98	23	0	2	5	12	71.47	$144,092

Best finish for 1983: T-2nd at the Kemper Open

1984	27	98	23	1	4	8	14	71.12	$248,606

Best finish for 1984: Win at the Manufactures Hanover Westchester Classic

1985	26	95	23	0	2	5	14	71.09	$180,745

Best finish for 1985: T-3rd at the MONY Tournament Of Champions & Anheuser-Busch Golf Classic

1986	25	77	20	0	2	3	9	71.29	$207,298

Best finish for 1986: 2nd at the Seiko Tucson-Match Play Championship

1987	27	94	23	2	6	10	13	70.94	$624,191

Best finish for 1987: Win at the Greater Greensboro Open & U.S. Open

1988	23	71	13	0	0	1	6	71.62	$110,802

Best finish for 1988: T-6th at the U.S. Open

1989	24	76	16	1	1	3	7	71.67	$308,200

Best finish for 1989: Win at the BellSouth Atlanta Golf Classic

1990	21	67	13	0	2	3	6	72.12	$242,941

Best finish for 1990: T-2nd at the Bob Hope Chrysler Classic

1991	19	70	15	0	2	3	9	70.47	$329,900

Best finish for 1991: 2nd at the U.S. Open

1992	22	73	15	0	0	1	6	70.92	$155,549

Best finish for 1992: T-8th at the Nissan Los Angeles Open

1993	23	82	20	1	4	6	10	70.72	$746,436

Best finish for 1993: Win at the GTE Byron Nelson Classic

1994	22	72	15	0	2	2	6	71.17	$310,056

Best finish for 1994: 2nd at the Southwestern Bell Colonial

1995	25	88	19	0	5	6	12	70.16	$796,834

Best finish for 1995: T-2nd at the Northern Telecom Open, Motorola Western Open & Anheuser-Busch Golf Classic

1996	22	70	14	0	3	4	5	71.43	$310,948

Best finish for 1996: T-2nd at the Nissan Open

1997	25	80	16	0	0	0	3	71.46	$129,448

Best finish for 1997: T-13th at the United Airlines Hawaiian Open

1998	20	57	8	1	1	1	2	72.61	$456,277

Best finish for 1998: Win at the Buick Invitational

1999	20	57	8	0	0	1	3	72.98	$179,006

Best finish for 1999: T-7th at the Buick Invitational

2001	22	73	13	0	1	1	3	70.71	$512,530

Best finish for 2001: T-2nd at the Greater Greensboro Chrysler Classic

2002	25	61	6	0	0	0	2	72.25	$122,115

Best finish for 2002: T-17th at the Verizon Byron Nelson Classic

2003	18	46	5	0	0	0	0	72.17	$78,153

Best finish for 2003: T-27th at the MCI Heritage

2004	18	55	9	0	0	1	2	71.58	$190,986

Best finish for 2004: T-10th at the Valero Texas Open

2005	9	25	3	0	0	0	0	72.08	$35,556

Best finish for 2005: T-33rd at the Chrysler Classic of Tucson

2006	1	3	0	0	0	0	0	73.67	
2007	1	3	0	0	0	0	0	77.00	
Period Totals	Starts	Rounds Played	Cuts Made	Wins	Top-5s	Top-10s	Top-25s	Scoring Average	Money
	612	2006	409	7	45	77	188	71.43	$6,877,333

Tim Simpson

Year	Starts	Rounds Played	Cuts Made	Wins	Top-5s	Top-10s	Top-25s	Scoring Average	Money
1977	10	31	6	0	0	0	1	73.16	$2,512

Best finish for 1977: T-19th at the Ohio Kings Island Open

1978	28	93	18	0	2	4	7	71.95	$38,454

Best finish for 1978: T-4th at the Greater Milwaukee Open

1979	30	99	19	0	1	1	6	72.66	$36,823

Best finish for 1979: T-5th at the American Optical Classic

1980	28	83	16	0	0	2	2	72.35	$29,072

Best finish for 1980: T-7th at the Joe Garagiola Tucson Open

1981	32	110	22	0	2	3	7	71.78	$62,063

Best finish for 1981: T-5th at the Greater Milwaukee Open & Sammy Davis, Jr. - Greater Hartford Open

1982	33	114	24	0	1	3	8	71.86	$62,803

Best finish for 1982: 4th at the Tallahassee Open

1983	33	103	19	0	1	3	10	71.72	$97,605

Best finish for 1983: T-5th at the Phoenix Open

1984	30	101	20	0	3	6	11	71.43	$157,082

Best finish for 1984: T-2nd at the Danny Thomas Memphis Classic

1985	31	107	23	1	3	4	7	71.10	$165,702

Best finish for 1985: Win at the Southern Open

1986	31	98	22	0	4	7	11	71.38	$242,011

Best finish for 1986: T-2nd at the Southern Open

1987	31	110	26	0	2	3	11	70.94	$168,258

Best finish for 1987: 4th at the Provident Classic

1988	31	101	19	0	1	4	11	70.95	$204,248

Best finish for 1988: T-4th at the Federal Express St. Jude Classic

1989	31	109	25	2	5	8	20	70.40	$764,097

Best finish for 1989: Win at the USF&G Classic & Walt Disney World/Oldsmobile Classic

1990	28	98	22	1	6	12	20	70.28	$840,911

Best finish for 1990: Win at the Walt Disney World/Oldsmobile Classic

1991	26	87	17	0	2	3	4	71.16	$205,046

Best finish for 1991: 3rd at the Bob Hope Chrysler Classic

1992	24	69	11	0	0	0	3	71.39	$85,314

Best finish for 1992: T-11th at the Walt Disney World/Oldsmobile Classic

1993	27	86	18	0	0	1	5	71.35	$111,436

Best finish for 1993: T-8th at the Hardee's Golf Classic

1994	31	91	15	0	0	1	5	71.59	$127,861

Best finish for 1994: T-10th at the Kemper Open

1995	1	5	1	0	0	0	0	69.60	$2,688

Best finish for 1995: T-54th at the Bob Hope Chrysler Classic

1996	8	24	4	0	0	0	0	71.17	$13,953

Best finish for 1996: T-40th at the Greater Milwaukee Open

1997	25	63	7	0	0	0	1	72.37	$33,166

Best finish for 1997: T-23rd at the Honda Classic

1998	3	9	2	0	0	0	0	72.33	$7,423

Best finish for 1998: T-49th at the United Airlines Hawaiian Open

Period Totals	Starts	Rounds Played	Cuts Made	Wins	Top-5s	Top-10s	Top-25s	Scoring Average	Money
	552	1791	356	4	33	65	150	71.48	$3,458,527

Joey Sindelar

Year	Starts	Rounds Played	Cuts Made	Wins	Top-5s	Top-10s	Top-25s	Scoring Average	Money
1980	1	2	0	0	0	0	0	73.50	
1981	1	2	0	0	0	0	0	75.50	
1982	2	4	0	0	0	0	0	75.50	$600
1983	3	12	2	0	0	0	1	71.00	$4,696

Best finish for 1983: T-21st at the Bank of Boston Classic

1984	33	114	23	0	3	3	9	72.31	$116,528

Best finish for 1984: T-2nd at the Bank of Boston Classic

1985	33	120	28	2	3	7	15	71.38	$282,762

Best finish for 1985: Win at the Greater Greensboro Open & B.C. Open

1986	35	117	29	0	4	7	17	71.24	$343,331

Best finish for 1986: 2nd at the Federal Express St. Jude Classic & Pensacola Open

1987	33	113	25	1	2	4	10	71.52	$235,700

Best finish for 1987: Win at the B.C. Open

1988	31	111	27	2	7	10	16	70.65	$814,732

Best finish for 1988: Win at the Honda Classic & The International

1989	28	95	20	0	1	3	9	71.33	$198,592

Best finish for 1989: T-5th at the Canadian Open

1990	27	80	15	1	1	3	5	71.89	$307,207

Best finish for 1990: Win at the Hardee's Golf Classic

1991	28	94	19	0	0	2	6	71.40	$168,349

Best finish for 1991: T-6th at the NEC World Series of Golf

Year	Starts	Rounds Played	Cuts Made	Wins	Top-5s	Top-10s	Top-25s	Scoring Average	Money
1992	32	107	22	0	2	6	13	70.96	$395,354

Best finish for 1992: T-3rd at the Memorial Tournament

| 1993 | 22 | 70 | 14 | 0 | 3 | 5 | 8 | 71.49 | $392,649 |

Best finish for 1993: 2nd at the United Airlines Hawaiian Open

| 1994 | 22 | 65 | 12 | 0 | 1 | 1 | 3 | 71.35 | $114,563 |

Best finish for 1994: T-3rd at the Greater Milwaukee Open

| 1995 | 24 | 71 | 14 | 0 | 1 | 3 | 7 | 71.10 | $202,896 |

Best finish for 1995: T-4th at the Ideon Classic

| 1996 | 28 | 87 | 18 | 0 | 0 | 3 | 7 | 71.08 | $275,531 |

Best finish for 1996: T-6th at the B.C. Open

| 1997 | 31 | 102 | 19 | 0 | 0 | 1 | 3 | 71.55 | $200,069 |

Best finish for 1997: T-10th at the PGA Championship

| 1998 | 27 | 96 | 22 | 0 | 0 | 4 | 10 | 71.10 | $466,797 |

Best finish for 1998: T-6th at the MCI Classic & Buick Open

| 1999 | 24 | 72 | 13 | 0 | 0 | 4 | 8 | 71.58 | $414,993 |

Best finish for 1999: T-8th at the Greater Milwaukee Open

| 2000 | 30 | 84 | 14 | 0 | 2 | 2 | 4 | 71.48 | $388,341 |

Best finish for 2000: T-5th at the BellSouth Classic & Buick Classic

| 2001 | 25 | 66 | 12 | 0 | 1 | 2 | 5 | 70.94 | $654,864 |

Best finish for 2001: T-2nd at the Bell Canadian Open

| 2002 | 32 | 102 | 19 | 0 | 2 | 3 | 6 | 70.97 | $791,750 |

Best finish for 2002: T-2nd at the Honda Classic

| 2003 | 29 | 91 | 17 | 0 | 1 | 1 | 4 | 70.91 | $692,328 |

Best finish for 2003: 3rd at the Buick Classic

| 2004 | 31 | 98 | 18 | 1 | 2 | 2 | 3 | 71.11 | $1,539,881 |

Best finish for 2004: Win at the Wachovia Championship

| 2005 | 29 | 104 | 23 | 0 | 2 | 3 | 8 | 70.95 | $1,060,238 |

Best finish for 2005: T-4th at the Deutsche Bank Championship

| 2006 | 29 | 90 | 15 | 0 | 0 | 4 | 6 | 71.60 | $804,507 |

Best finish for 2006: T-6th at the Wachovia Championship & U.S. Bank Championship in Milwaukee

| 2007 | 25 | 75 | 12 | 0 | 0 | 0 | 2 | 71.80 | $312,717 |

Best finish for 2007: T-13th at the Wyndham Championship

| 2008 | 5 | 15 | 2 | 0 | 0 | 0 | 0 | 73.07 | $34,351 |

Best finish for 2008: T-28th at the Mayakoba Golf Classic

Period Totals	Starts	Rounds Played	Cuts Made	Wins	Top-5s	Top-10s	Top-25s	Scoring Average	Money
	700	2259	454	7	38	83	185	71.34	$11,214,327

Vijay Singh

Year	Starts	Rounds Played	Cuts Made	Wins	Top-5s	Top-10s	Top-25s	Scoring Average	Money
1989	1	4	1	0	0	0	1	71.00	$10,773

Best finish for 1989: T-23rd at the British Open

| 1990 | 1 | 4 | 1 | 0 | 0 | 0 | 1 | 70.00 | $29,639 |

Best finish for 1990: T-12th at the British Open

| 1991 | 1 | 4 | 1 | 0 | 0 | 0 | 1 | 70.00 | $28,728 |

Best finish for 1991: T-12th at the British Open

| 1992 | 5 | 20 | 5 | 0 | 0 | 1 | 3 | 70.55 | $78,830 |

Best finish for 1992: T-7th at the Memorial Tournament

| 1993 | 15 | 53 | 13 | 1 | 5 | 6 | 10 | 70.57 | $665,030 |

Best finish for 1993: Win at the Buick Classic

| 1994 | 21 | 71 | 16 | 0 | 3 | 3 | 8 | 71.31 | $347,409 |

Best finish for 1994: T-2nd at the Northern Telecom Open & Northern Telecom Open & The Nestle Invitational

| 1995 | 22 | 79 | 17 | 2 | 4 | 9 | 13 | 70.80 | $1,021,413 |

Best finish for 1995: Win at the Phoenix Open & Buick Classic

| 1996 | 24 | 90 | 24 | 0 | 3 | 9 | 16 | 70.52 | $855,140 |

Best finish for 1996: T-2nd at the Doral-Ryder Open

| 1997 | 21 | 83 | 21 | 2 | 2 | 4 | 9 | 71.16 | $1,059,236 |

Best finish for 1997: Win at the Memorial Tournament & Buick Open

| 1998 | 26 | 93 | 23 | 2 | 6 | 7 | 18 | 70.57 | $2,243,998 |

Best finish for 1998: Win at the PGA Championship & Sprint International

| 1999 | 29 | 101 | 26 | 1 | 8 | 11 | 21 | 70.66 | $2,284,483 |

Best finish for 1999: Win at the Honda Classic

| 2000 | 26 | 92 | 24 | 1 | 5 | 8 | 15 | 70.32 | $2,575,835 |

Best finish for 2000: Win at the Masters

| 2001 | 26 | 92 | 24 | 0 | 8 | 14 | 22 | 69.34 | $3,440,829 |

Best finish for 2001: 2nd at the AT&T Pebble Beach & The Players Championship

| 2002 | 28 | 96 | 24 | 2 | 6 | 11 | 17 | 69.76 | $3,760,513 |

Best finish for 2002: Win at the Shell Houston Open & The Tour Championship

| 2003 | 27 | 102 | 26 | 4 | 13 | 18 | 24 | 69.11 | $7,573,907 |

Best finish for 2003: Win at the Phoenix Open, EDS Byron Nelson Championship, John Deere Classic & FUNAI Classic at the Walt Disney World Resort

| 2004 | 29 | 110 | 28 | 9 | 14 | 18 | 24 | 69.19 | $10,905,166 |

Best finish for 2004: Win at the AT&T Pebble Beach National Pro-Am, Shell Houston Open, HP Classic of New Orleans, Buick Open, PGA Championship, Deutsche

Bank Championship, Bell Canadian Open, 84 Lumber Classic & Chrysler Championship

Year	Starts	Rounds Played	Cuts Made	Wins	Top-5s	Top-10s	Top-25s	Scoring Average	Money
2005	30	109	26	4	13	18	25	69.59	$8,017,336

Best finish for 2005: Win at the Sony Open in Hawaii, Shell Houston Open, Wachovia Championship & Buick Open

2006	27	100	25	1	5	13	17	70.21	$4,609,314

Best finish for 2006: Win at the Barclays Classic

2007	27	100	25	2	4	7	16	70.39	$4,730,876

Best finish for 2007: Win at the Mercedes Championships & Arnold Palmer Invitational

2008	23	78	18	3	8	8	14	70.27	$6,601,094

Best finish for 2008: Win at the WGC-Bridgestone Invitational, Barclays Classic & Deutsche Bank Championship

Period Totals	Starts	Rounds Played	Cuts Made	Wins	Top-5s	Top-10s	Top-25s	Scoring Average	Money
	409	1481	368	34	107	165	275	70.18	$60,839,548

Geoffrey Sisk

Year	Starts	Rounds Played	Cuts Made	Wins	Top-5s	Top-10s	Top-25s	Scoring Average	Money
1992	1	2	0	0	0	0	0	74.50	
1995	1	2	0	0	0	0	0	77.00	$1,000
1996	1	2	0	0	0	0	0	72.50	
1999	31	79	9	0	0	0	1	72.70	$91,260

Best finish for 1999: T-19th at the Doral-Ryder Open

2003	1	2	0	0	0	0	0	73.00	$1,000
2004	2	6	1	0	0	0	0	74.33	$30,672

Best finish for 2004: T-40th at the U.S. Open

2005	1	2	0	0	0	0	0	71.00	
2007	1	2	0	0	0	0	0	78.00	$2,000

Period Totals	Starts	Rounds Played	Cuts Made	Wins	Top-5s	Top-10s	Top-25s	Scoring Average	Money
	39	97	10	0	0	0	1	73.00	$125,932

Sonny Skinner

Year	Starts	Rounds Played	Cuts Made	Wins	Top-5s	Top-10s	Top-25s	Scoring Average	Money
1990	27	75	11	0	0	0	2	72.49	$29,565

Best finish for 1990: T-19th at the B.C. Open

1991	2	8	2	0	0	0	0	68.13	$4,013

Best finish for 1991: T-36th at the Chattanooga Classic

1992	28	73	9	0	0	0	1	71.99	$26,454

Best finish for 1992: T-23rd at the Canon Greater Hartford Open

1993	1	4	1	0	0	0	0	68.75	$1,557

Best finish for 1993: T-32nd at the Deposit Guaranty Classic

1997	25	71	9	0	0	0	1	71.93	$46,313

Best finish for 1997: T-13th at the Deposit Guaranty Golf Classic

1998	31	86	14	0	0	0	3	72.09	$109,418

Best finish for 1998: T-20th at the B.C. Open

2006	1	4	1	0	0	0	0	73.75	$9,646

Best finish for 2006: 79th at the BellSouth Classic

2007	1	2	0	0	0	0	0	75.00	
2008	1	2	0	0	0	0	0	76.50	

Period Totals	Starts	Rounds Played	Cuts Made	Wins	Top-5s	Top-10s	Top-25s	Scoring Average	Money
	117	325	47	0	0	0	7	72.05	$226,966

Heath Slocum

Year	Starts	Rounds Played	Cuts Made	Wins	Top-5s	Top-10s	Top-25s	Scoring Average	Money
2001	8	28	6	0	0	0	0	71.25	$45,670

Best finish for 2001: T-37th at the Southern Farm Bureau Classic

2002	32	92	15	0	1	2	6	71.51	$865,615

Best finish for 2002: 2nd at the WorldCom Classic

2003	32	98	18	0	2	2	5	71.22	$815,812

Best finish for 2003: T-2nd at the Greater Milwaukee Open

2004	31	90	14	1	1	3	6	71.04	$1,068,837

Best finish for 2004: Win at the Chrysler Classic of Tucson

2005	29	99	22	1	2	4	9	70.56	$1,606,185

Best finish for 2005: Win at the Southern Farm Bureau Classic

2006	30	93	18	0	2	3	8	71.04	$1,180,681

Best finish for 2006: T-3rd at the Chrysler Classic of Tucson & John Deere Classic

2007	28	101	22	0	3	6	16	70.13	$2,184,379

Best finish for 2007: T-2nd at the PODS Championship

2008	29	104	23	0	2	5	7	71.17	$1,491,916

Best finish for 2008: 4th at the Travelers Championship

Period Totals	Starts	Rounds Played	Cuts Made	Wins	Top-5s	Top-10s	Top-25s	Scoring Average	Money
	219	705	138	2	13	25	57	70.96	$9,259,094

Jeff Sluman

Year	Starts	Rounds Played	Cuts Made	Wins	Top-5s	Top-10s	Top-25s	Scoring Average	Money
1980	1	2	0	0	0	0	0	77.50	

Year	Starts	Rounds Played	Cuts Made	Wins	Top-5s	Top-10s	Top-25s	Scoring Average	Money
1981	1	0	0	0	0	0	0		
1983	19	59	11	0	0	0	2	72.34	$13,643

Best finish for 1983: T-25th at the Manufactures Hanover Westchester Classic & Texas Open

1984	1	4	1	0	0	0	0	74.50	$603

Best finish for 1984: T-69th at the B.C. Open

1985	26	88	18	0	2	4	10	71.82	$100,523

Best finish for 1985: T-5th at the Greater Greensboro Open & Southwest Golf Classic

1986	34	105	24	0	0	7	12	71.33	$154,159

Best finish for 1986: T-6th at the Pensacola Open

1987	33	108	22	0	2	6	11	70.97	$335,590

Best finish for 1987: T-2nd at the Tournament Players Championship & B.C. Open

1988	33	120	30	1	4	6	15	70.63	$504,321

Best finish for 1988: Win at the PGA Championship

1989	24	76	15	0	0	4	6	71.62	$156,307

Best finish for 1989: T-6th at the MONY Tournament Of Champions

1990	32	110	23	0	1	2	8	71.66	$275,566

Best finish for 1990: T-2nd at the Kmart Greater Greensboro Open

1991	31	113	25	0	4	7	14	70.38	$559,019

Best finish for 1991: 2nd at the Nissan Los Angeles Open & Kemper Open

1992	31	113	26	0	5	9	17	70.28	$730,227

Best finish for 1992: 2nd at the AT&T Pebble Beach Pro-Am & U.S. Open

1993	28	99	21	0	0	1	6	71.63	$188,765

Best finish for 1993: T-9th at the Kmart Greater Greensboro Open

1994	30	92	16	0	1	4	8	71.57	$301,178

Best finish for 1994: 2nd at the B.C. Open

1995	29	101	20	0	4	7	12	70.43	$563,681

Best finish for 1995: T-2nd at the Kmart Greater Greensboro Open

1996	30	105	23	0	2	7	14	70.24	$651,628

Best finish for 1996: 2nd at the MasterCard Colonial

1997	29	98	20	1	2	3	9	71.09	$635,503

Best finish for 1997: Win at the Tucson Chrysler Classic

1998	30	106	24	1	3	5	11	70.56	$1,148,975

Best finish for 1998: Win at the Greater Milwaukee Open

1999	31	111	26	1	4	6	13	70.81	$1,622,491

Best finish for 1999: Win at the Sony Open in Hawaii

2000	32	111	25	0	0	1	16	70.59	$878,390

Best finish for 2000: 7th at the National Car Rental Golf Classic/Disney

2001	30	104	23	1	4	7	15	69.67	$1,843,952

Best finish for 2001: Win at the B.C. Open

2002	32	117	27	1	4	6	15	70.44	$2,250,187

Best finish for 2002: Win at the Greater Milwaukee Open

2003	31	104	22	0	1	3	15	70.26	$1,616,722

Best finish for 2003: 3rd at the Bank of America Colonial

2004	28	97	22	0	0	3	8	70.63	$1,007,635

Best finish for 2004: T-6th at the Buick Open

2005	28	94	20	0	2	3	6	70.97	$1,089,506

Best finish for 2005: T-3rd at the Memorial Tournament

2006	29	101	21	0	2	4	6	70.93	$1,254,275

Best finish for 2006: 3rd at the U.S. Bank Championship in Milwaukee

2007	21	60	8	0	0	1	2	72.53	$277,692

Best finish for 2007: T-9th at the U.S. Bank Championship in Milwaukee

2008	2	6	0	0	0	0	0	71.50	
Period Totals	Starts	Rounds Played	Cuts Made	Wins	Top-5s	Top-10s	Top-25s	Scoring Average	Money
	706	2404	513	6	47	106	251	70.91	$18,160,538

Mike Small

Year	Starts	Rounds Played	Cuts Made	Wins	Top-5s	Top-10s	Top-25s	Scoring Average	Money
1990	1	2	0	0	0	0	0	72.00	
1991	2	4	0	0	0	0	0	74.00	
1993	1	2	0	0	0	0	0	78.50	
1994	4	8	0	0	0	0	0	75.25	$1,000
1995	2	5	1	0	0	0	1	70.20	$17,875

Best finish for 1995: T-12th at the Quad City Classic

1998	26	65	8	0	0	1	3	72.05	$113,336

Best finish for 1998: T-9th at the Bell Canadian Open

1999	1	2	0	0	0	0	0	71.50	
2001	1	2	0	0	0	0	0	75.50	
2003	1	4	1	0	0	0	0	71.25	$14,430

Best finish for 2003: T-43rd at the 100th Western Open

2004	2	6	1	0	0	0	0	72.50	$35,360

Best finish for 2004: T-27th at the Cialis Western Open

2005	2	8	2	0	0	0	0	74.38	$21,900

Best finish for 2005: 70th at the Cialis Western Open

Year	Starts	Rounds Played	Cuts Made	Wins	Top-5s	Top-10s	Top-25s	Scoring Average	Money
2006	9	27	4	0	0	0	0	71.41	$42,506

Best finish for 2006: T-38th at the U.S. Bank Championship in Milwaukee

Year	Starts	Rounds Played	Cuts Made	Wins	Top-5s	Top-10s	Top-25s	Scoring Average	Money
2007	2	6	1	0	0	0	0	76.50	$15,050

Best finish for 2007: T-69th at the PGA Championship

Period Totals	Starts	Rounds Played	Cuts Made	Wins	Top-5s	Top-10s	Top-25s	Scoring Average	Money
	54	141	18	0	0	1	4	72.55	$261,457

Terry Small

Year	Starts	Rounds Played	Cuts Made	Wins	Top-5s	Top-10s	Top-25s	Scoring Average	Money
1964	1	4	1	0	0	0	0	75.00	

Best finish for 1964: T-60th at the Almaden Open

Year	Starts	Rounds Played	Cuts Made	Wins	Top-5s	Top-10s	Top-25s	Scoring Average	Money
1969	1	2	0	0	0	0	0	77.50	
1971	1	2	0	0	0	0	0	73.00	
1972	1	2	0	0	0	0	0	81.00	$500
1973	20	56	9	0	0	0	1	73.32	$4,189

Best finish for 1973: T-15th at the Greater Milwaukee Open

Year	Starts	Rounds Played	Cuts Made	Wins	Top-5s	Top-10s	Top-25s	Scoring Average	Money
1974	16	45	6	0	0	0	2	73.16	$3,234

Best finish for 1974: T-20th at the Quad Cities Open

Year	Starts	Rounds Played	Cuts Made	Wins	Top-5s	Top-10s	Top-25s	Scoring Average	Money
1975	12	30	4	0	0	0	0	74.80	$1,560

Best finish for 1975: T-38th at the Greater Milwaukee Open

Year	Starts	Rounds Played	Cuts Made	Wins	Top-5s	Top-10s	Top-25s	Scoring Average	Money
1976	4	7	0	0	0	0	0	77.14	

Best finish for 1976: 100 at the Western Open

Year	Starts	Rounds Played	Cuts Made	Wins	Top-5s	Top-10s	Top-25s	Scoring Average	Money
1977	1	2	0	0	0	0	0	78.00	
1983	1	2	0	0	0	0	0	75.50	

Period Totals	Starts	Rounds Played	Cuts Made	Wins	Top-5s	Top-10s	Top-25s	Scoring Average	Money
	58	152	20	0	0	0	3	74.03	$9,483

Bob-E. Smith

Year	Starts	Rounds Played	Cuts Made	Wins	Top-5s	Top-10s	Top-25s	Scoring Average	Money
1967	3	10	2	0	0	1	1	72.90	$1,472

Best finish for 1967: T-8th at the Cajun Classic

Year	Starts	Rounds Played	Cuts Made	Wins	Top-5s	Top-10s	Top-25s	Scoring Average	Money
1968	32	118	27	0	2	6	13	71.35	$28,983

Best finish for 1968: T-5th at the Rebel Yell Open & Western Open

Year	Starts	Rounds Played	Cuts Made	Wins	Top-5s	Top-10s	Top-25s	Scoring Average	Money
1969	36	121	26	0	0	1	9	72.16	$19,646

Best finish for 1969: T-6th at the Minnesota Classic

Year	Starts	Rounds Played	Cuts Made	Wins	Top-5s	Top-10s	Top-25s	Scoring Average	Money
1970	34	115	25	0	1	3	11	71.96	$29,698

Best finish for 1970: T-5th at the Los Angeles Open

Year	Starts	Rounds Played	Cuts Made	Wins	Top-5s	Top-10s	Top-25s	Scoring Average	Money
1971	34	112	25	0	0	3	12	71.71	$36,211

Best finish for 1971: T-9th at the Tucson Open & Monsanto Open

Year	Starts	Rounds Played	Cuts Made	Wins	Top-5s	Top-10s	Top-25s	Scoring Average	Money
1972	33	117	25	0	1	3	10	71.95	$38,621

Best finish for 1972: T-4th at the Jackie Gleason's Inverrary Classic

Year	Starts	Rounds Played	Cuts Made	Wins	Top-5s	Top-10s	Top-25s	Scoring Average	Money
1973	36	118	21	0	2	3	10	72.29	$40,241

Best finish for 1973: T-3rd at the Liggett Meyers Open & B.C. Open

Year	Starts	Rounds Played	Cuts Made	Wins	Top-5s	Top-10s	Top-25s	Scoring Average	Money
1974	30	87	14	0	0	2	5	73.18	$16,772

Best finish for 1974: T-9th at the Bing Crosby Pro-Am & Greater Milwaukee Open

Year	Starts	Rounds Played	Cuts Made	Wins	Top-5s	Top-10s	Top-25s	Scoring Average	Money
1975	29	104	24	0	1	1	6	72.12	$44,720

Best finish for 1975: 2nd at the Byron Nelson Golf Classic

Year	Starts	Rounds Played	Cuts Made	Wins	Top-5s	Top-10s	Top-25s	Scoring Average	Money
1976	30	103	23	0	3	8	12	71.61	$55,547

Best finish for 1976: T-4th at the Southern Open

Year	Starts	Rounds Played	Cuts Made	Wins	Top-5s	Top-10s	Top-25s	Scoring Average	Money
1977	27	78	15	0	0	0	4	72.96	$20,009

Best finish for 1977: T-14th at the Colgate Hall Of Fame Golf Classic

Year	Starts	Rounds Played	Cuts Made	Wins	Top-5s	Top-10s	Top-25s	Scoring Average	Money
1978	25	73	11	0	0	0	1	73.34	$8,769

Best finish for 1978: T-23rd at the Ed McMahon Quad City Open

Year	Starts	Rounds Played	Cuts Made	Wins	Top-5s	Top-10s	Top-25s	Scoring Average	Money
1979	23	64	11	0	0	1	4	71.91	$16,919

Best finish for 1979: T-10th at the Tallahassee Open

Year	Starts	Rounds Played	Cuts Made	Wins	Top-5s	Top-10s	Top-25s	Scoring Average	Money
1980	20	56	9	0	0	0	0	73.54	$7,936

Best finish for 1980: T-28th at the Buick Goodwrench Open

Year	Starts	Rounds Played	Cuts Made	Wins	Top-5s	Top-10s	Top-25s	Scoring Average	Money
1981	9	22	2	0	0	0	0	73.32	$2,820

Best finish for 1981: T-33rd at the Manufactures Hanover Westchester Classic

Year	Starts	Rounds Played	Cuts Made	Wins	Top-5s	Top-10s	Top-25s	Scoring Average	Money
1982	1	2	0	0	0	0	0	83.50	$600
1983	4	13	1	0	0	0	0	73.38	$1,410

Best finish for 1983: T-37th at the B.C. Open

Year	Starts	Rounds Played	Cuts Made	Wins	Top-5s	Top-10s	Top-25s	Scoring Average	Money
1984	1	2	0	0	0	0	0	75.00	$600
1985	1	4	1	0	0	0	0	71.25	$606

Best finish for 1985: 69th at the Lite Quad Cities Open

Year	Starts	Rounds Played	Cuts Made	Wins	Top-5s	Top-10s	Top-25s	Scoring Average	Money
1986	3	10	2	0	0	0	0	72.10	$1,248

Best finish for 1986: 49th at the Provident Classic

Year	Starts	Rounds Played	Cuts Made	Wins	Top-5s	Top-10s	Top-25s	Scoring Average	Money
1989	1	2	0	0	0	0	0	73.50	$800

Period Totals	Starts	Rounds Played	Cuts Made	Wins	Top-5s	Top-10s	Top-25s	Scoring Average	Money
	412	1331	264	0	10	32	98	72.26	$373,628

Chris Smith

Year	Starts	Rounds Played	Cuts Made	Wins	Top-5s	Top-10s	Top-25s	Scoring Average	Money
1987	1	2	0	0	0	0	0	73.50	
1991	1	2	0	0	0	0	0	79.50	
1993	3	8	1	0	0	1	1	72.38	$24,000

Best finish for 1993: T-8th at the B.C. Open

1994	2	6	1	0	0	0	0	73.00	$3,075

Best finish for 1994: T-67th at the Kmart Greater Greensboro Open

1996	28	80	12	0	0	0	0	72.65	$41,112

Best finish for 1996: T-29th at the GTE Byron Nelson Classic

1997	6	24	6	0	1	1	3	69.83	$120,768

Best finish for 1997: 4th at the CVS Charity Classic

1998	31	92	16	0	0	2	2	71.64	$184,933

Best finish for 1998: T-7th at the Deposit Guaranty Golf Classic

1999	28	78	11	0	0	0	1	72.38	$116,794

Best finish for 1999: T-20th at the COMPAQ Classic of New Orleans

2001	30	98	20	0	2	5	8	70.44	$933,810

Best finish for 2001: T-3rd at the BellSouth Classic

2002	30	100	21	1	2	5	8	70.72	$1,361,963

Best finish for 2002: Win at the Buick Classic

2003	30	92	15	0	1	1	6	71.75	$480,523

Best finish for 2003: T-5th at the Greater Milwaukee Open

2004	33	105	19	0	1	1	4	71.30	$693,785

Best finish for 2004: 3rd at the Chrysler Classic of Greensboro

2005	32	93	14	0	1	1	4	71.33	$454,375

Best finish for 2005: T-5th at the U.S. Bank Championship in Milwaukee

2006	21	67	12	0	0	0	1	71.37	$183,410

Best finish for 2006: T-24th at the B.C. Open

2007	8	23	4	0	0	0	0	72.26	$50,381

Best finish for 2007: T-37th at the U.S. Bank Championship in Milwaukee

2008	5	13	1	0	0	0	0	73.08	$22,775

Best finish for 2008: T-28th at the Puerto Rico Open

Period Totals	Starts	Rounds Played	Cuts Made	Wins	Top-5s	Top-10s	Top-25s	Scoring Average	Money
	289	883	153	1	8	17	38	71.51	$4,671,704

Dick Smith

Year	Starts	Rounds Played	Cuts Made	Wins	Top-5s	Top-10s	Top-25s	Scoring Average	Money
1958	1	1	0	0	0	0	0	85.00	
1959	1	2	0	0	0	0	0	76.00	
1960	1	4	1	0	0	0	0	74.25	

Best finish for 1960: T-40th at the British Open

1966	3	6	0	0	0	0	0	77.17	
1968	1	2	0	0	0	0	0	74.50	
1969	1	2	0	0	0	0	0	74.00	
1970	1	4	1	0	0	0	0	75.50	$975

Best finish for 1970: T-44th at the U.S. Open

1971	3	10	2	0	0	0	1	72.10	$1,648

Best finish for 1971: T-18th at the IVB Philadelphia Golf Classic

1972	4	10	1	0	0	0	0	73.70	$200

Best finish for 1972: T-67th at the Greater New Orleans Open

1973	1	2	0	0	0	0	0	74.00	
1974	2	4	0	0	0	0	0	75.25	
1975	2	4	1	0	0	0	0	73.75	$199

Best finish for 1975: T-61st at the IVB Philadelphia Golf Classic

1978	2	6	1	0	0	0	1	73.17	$3,553

Best finish for 1978: T-17th at the IVB Philadelphia Golf Classic

1979	1	2	0	0	0	0	0	72.00	
1982	1	2	0	0	0	0	0	78.50	$650

Period Totals	Starts	Rounds Played	Cuts Made	Wins	Top-5s	Top-10s	Top-25s	Scoring Average	Money
	25	61	7	0	0	0	2	74.39	$7,225

Ivan Smith

Year	Starts	Rounds Played	Cuts Made	Wins	Top-5s	Top-10s	Top-25s	Scoring Average	Money
1983	22	55	4	0	0	1	1	73.40	$14,563

Best finish for 1983: T-6th at the Bank of Boston Classic

1985	21	55	7	0	0	0	1	73.49	$9,992

Best finish for 1985: T-16th at the Lite Quad Cities Open

1986	1	3	0	0	0	0	0	72.67	
1987	2	4	0	0	0	0	0	77.25	$600
1990	1	2	0	0	0	0	0	74.00	$1,000

Period Totals	Starts	Rounds Played	Cuts Made	Wins	Top-5s	Top-10s	Top-25s	Scoring Average	Money
	47	119	11	0	0	1	2	73.56	$26,156

Jerry Smith

Year	Starts	Rounds Played	Cuts Made	Wins	Top-5s	Top-10s	Top-25s	Scoring Average	Money
1988	2	6	1	0	0	0	0	71.83	$2,368

Best finish for 1988: T-55th at the Hardee's Golf Classic

1993	1	2	0	0	0	0	0	74.00	$1,000
1994	1	4	1	0	0	0	0	71.00	$1,990

Best finish for 1994: T-70th at the Hardee's Golf Classic

2000	32	101	20	0	0	1	4	71.04	$406,591

Best finish for 2000: 9th at the GTE Byron Nelson Classic

2001	31	95	16	0	1	3	6	70.78	$592,030

Best finish for 2001: T-3rd at the National Car Rental Golf Classic/Disney

2002	33	87	12	0	1	1	1	72.21	$269,953

Best finish for 2002: T-5th at the AT&T Pebble Beach

2003	1	2	0	0	0	0	0	71.50	
2004	1	2	0	0	0	0	0	72.50	
2005	1	2	0	0	0	0	0	74.50	$2,000
2006	29	92	17	0	1	1	3	70.90	$568,213

Best finish for 2006: 5th at the Shell Houston Open

2007	19	49	5	0	0	0	0	72.33	$63,334

Best finish for 2007: T-38th at the Zurich Classic of New Orleans

Period Totals	Starts	Rounds Played	Cuts Made	Wins	Top-5s	Top-10s	Top-25s	Scoring Average	Money
	151	442	72	0	3	6	14	71.38	$1,907,480

Mike Smith

Year	Starts	Rounds Played	Cuts Made	Wins	Top-5s	Top-10s	Top-25s	Scoring Average	Money
1980	6	14	1	0	0	0	0	73.07	$508

Best finish for 1980: T-64th at the Buick Goodwrench Open

1981	22	59	9	0	0	0	3	72.20	$11,582

Best finish for 1981: T-17th at the Quad Cities Open

1982	20	57	8	0	0	0	1	72.79	$11,348

Best finish for 1982: T-15th at the LaJet Classic

1984	21	69	13	0	0	2	2	72.14	$42,045

Best finish for 1984: T-6th at the Byron Nelson Golf Classic

1985	27	77	14	0	2	2	5	72.04	$159,518

Best finish for 1985: 2nd at the Panasonic Las Vegas Invitational

1986	28	72	10	0	0	0	1	73.01	$19,759

Best finish for 1986: T-12th at the Hardee's Golf Classic

1987	27	78	13	0	0	0	3	72.08	$33,634

Best finish for 1987: T-15th at the Deposit Guaranty Golf Classic

1988	5	18	4	0	0	0	0	71.78	$8,092

Best finish for 1988: T-30th at the Deposit Guaranty Golf Classic

1989	1	2	0	0	0	0	0	73.50	$800
1990	28	91	17	0	1	3	6	71.82	$170,034

Best finish for 1990: T-3rd at the Bank of Boston Classic

1991	31	102	19	0	1	1	4	70.92	$149,612

Best finish for 1991: T-4th at the AT&T Pebble Beach Pro-Am

1992	31	105	21	0	0	1	8	70.96	$179,082

Best finish for 1992: T-9th at the Buick Classic

1993	33	90	11	0	1	2	2	72.12	$107,375

Best finish for 1993: T-5th at the Buick Classic

1994	15	39	5	0	0	1	1	72.44	$57,848

Best finish for 1994: T-8th at the Kmart Greater Greensboro Open

1995	25	72	10	0	0	0	1	71.85	$48,076

Best finish for 1995: T-20th at the Buick Challenge

1996	6	16	2	0	0	0	0	70.94	$11,200

Best finish for 1996: T-26th at the Deposit Guaranty Golf Classic

1997	3	10	2	0	0	0	0	71.00	$7,059

Best finish for 1997: T-41st at the B.C. Open

1998	3	8	1	0	0	0	0	72.13	$2,806

Best finish for 1998: T-79th at the Quad City Classic

2000	1	2	0	0	0	0	0	74.50	

Period Totals	Starts	Rounds Played	Cuts Made	Wins	Top-5s	Top-10s	Top-25s	Scoring Average	Money
	333	981	160	0	5	12	37	71.92	$1,020,380

Taylor Smith

Year	Starts	Rounds Played	Cuts Made	Wins	Top-5s	Top-10s	Top-25s	Scoring Average	Money
1987	1	2	0	0	0	0	0	74.50	
1991	1	4	1	0	0	0	0	74.50	$1,980

Best finish for 1991: 71st at the BellSouth Atlanta Golf Classic

1992	1	4	1	0	0	0	0	72.25	$2,232

Best finish for 1992: T-76th at the United Airlines Hawaiian Open

Year	Starts	Rounds Played	Cuts Made	Wins	Top-5s	Top-10s	Top-25s	Scoring Average	Money
1996	27	76	15	0	2	2	4	71.59	$221,517

Best finish for 1996: T-2nd at the Greater Vancouver Open

Year	Starts	Rounds Played	Cuts Made	Wins	Top-5s	Top-10s	Top-25s	Scoring Average	Money
1997	28	81	13	0	0	1	2	72.35	$110,947

Best finish for 1997: T-9th at the United Airlines Hawaiian Open

Year	Starts	Rounds Played	Cuts Made	Wins	Top-5s	Top-10s	Top-25s	Scoring Average	Money
1998	2	8	2	0	0	0	0	71.00	$6,360

Best finish for 1998: T-57th at the United Airlines Hawaiian Open

Period Totals	Starts	Rounds Played	Cuts Made	Wins	Top-5s	Top-10s	Top-25s	Scoring Average	Money
	60	175	32	0	2	3	6	72.03	$343,036

Des Smyth

Year	Starts	Rounds Played	Cuts Made	Wins	Top-5s	Top-10s	Top-25s	Scoring Average	Money
1975	1	2	0	0	0	0	0	78.00	$220
1976	1	2	0	0	0	0	0	76.50	$180
1977	1	3	0	0	0	0	0	74.00	$340
1980	4	11	1	0	0	0	0	74.09	$1,461

Best finish for 1980: T-48th at the Doral-Eastern Open

Year	Starts	Rounds Played	Cuts Made	Wins	Top-5s	Top-10s	Top-25s	Scoring Average	Money
1981	1	4	1	0	0	0	0	72.75	$1,750

Best finish for 1981: T-31st at the British Open

Year	Starts	Rounds Played	Cuts Made	Wins	Top-5s	Top-10s	Top-25s	Scoring Average	Money
1982	1	4	1	0	1	1	1	71.50	$18,700

Best finish for 1982: T-4th at the British Open

Year	Starts	Rounds Played	Cuts Made	Wins	Top-5s	Top-10s	Top-25s	Scoring Average	Money
1983	1	2	0	0	0	0	0	74.50	$375
1984	1	2	0	0	0	0	0	75.00	$429
1985	1	3	0	0	0	0	0	75.00	$1,015
1986	1	2	0	0	0	0	0	76.50	$600
1987	1	2	0	0	0	0	0	73.50	$640
1988	1	2	0	0	0	0	0	73.50	
1989	1	2	0	0	0	0	0	73.50	$800
1990	1	2	0	0	0	0	0	73.50	$996
1991	1	4	1	0	0	0	0	71.25	$7,114

Best finish for 1991: T-44th at the British Open

Year	Starts	Rounds Played	Cuts Made	Wins	Top-5s	Top-10s	Top-25s	Scoring Average	Money
1992	1	2	0	0	0	0	0	73.50	$1,200
1993	1	4	1	0	0	0	0	70.25	$11,126

Best finish for 1993: T-27th at the British Open

Year	Starts	Rounds Played	Cuts Made	Wins	Top-5s	Top-10s	Top-25s	Scoring Average	Money
1994	1	2	0	0	0	0	0	74.50	$972
1996	1	1	0	0	0	0	0	72.00	$1,008
1998	1	4	1	0	0	0	1	72.25	$38,904

Best finish for 1998: T-15th at the British Open

Year	Starts	Rounds Played	Cuts Made	Wins	Top-5s	Top-10s	Top-25s	Scoring Average	Money
1999	1	2	0	0	0	0	0	78.50	$1,406
2001	1	4	1	0	0	0	1	70.00	$57,310

Best finish for 2001: T-13th at the British Open

Year	Starts	Rounds Played	Cuts Made	Wins	Top-5s	Top-10s	Top-25s	Scoring Average	Money
2002	1	4	1	0	0	0	0	71.00	$37,925

Best finish for 2002: T-28th at the British Open

Period Totals	Starts	Rounds Played	Cuts Made	Wins	Top-5s	Top-10s	Top-25s	Scoring Average	Money
	26	70	8	0	1	1	3	73.31	$184,471

J.C. Snead

Year	Starts	Rounds Played	Cuts Made	Wins	Top-5s	Top-10s	Top-25s	Scoring Average	Money
1968	15	39	5	0	0	0	1	73.23	$690

Best finish for 1968: T-21st at the Robinson Open

Year	Starts	Rounds Played	Cuts Made	Wins	Top-5s	Top-10s	Top-25s	Scoring Average	Money
1969	18	51	8	0	1	2	3	72.82	$10,140

Best finish for 1969: T-3rd at the Michigan Golf Classic

Year	Starts	Rounds Played	Cuts Made	Wins	Top-5s	Top-10s	Top-25s	Scoring Average	Money
1970	26	76	12	0	0	1	2	73.05	$9,852

Best finish for 1970: T-6th at the Robinson Open Golf Classic

Year	Starts	Rounds Played	Cuts Made	Wins	Top-5s	Top-10s	Top-25s	Scoring Average	Money
1971	35	115	26	2	3	5	12	71.88	$87,877

Best finish for 1971: Win at the Tucson Open & Doral-Eastern Open

Year	Starts	Rounds Played	Cuts Made	Wins	Top-5s	Top-10s	Top-25s	Scoring Average	Money
1972	32	114	25	1	2	7	13	71.99	$80,248

Best finish for 1972: Win at the IVB Philadelphia Golf Classic

Year	Starts	Rounds Played	Cuts Made	Wins	Top-5s	Top-10s	Top-25s	Scoring Average	Money
1973	30	110	24	0	7	8	16	71.65	$93,735

Best finish for 1973: 2nd at the Masters

Year	Starts	Rounds Played	Cuts Made	Wins	Top-5s	Top-10s	Top-25s	Scoring Average	Money
1974	29	110	26	0	7	12	20	70.85	$146,674

Best finish for 1974: T-2nd at the Western Open, Tournament Players Championship & Southern Open

Year	Starts	Rounds Played	Cuts Made	Wins	Top-5s	Top-10s	Top-25s	Scoring Average	Money
1975	28	101	22	1	2	7	12	71.83	$91,822

Best finish for 1975: Win at the Andy Williams-San Diego Open

Year	Starts	Rounds Played	Cuts Made	Wins	Top-5s	Top-10s	Top-25s	Scoring Average	Money
1976	29	107	25	2	6	9	15	71.20	$192,646

Best finish for 1976: Win at the Andy Williams-San Diego Open & Kaiser International Open

Year	Starts	Rounds Played	Cuts Made	Wins	Top-5s	Top-10s	Top-25s	Scoring Average	Money
1977	32	116	26	0	2	4	11	71.92	$68,970

Best finish for 1977: 3rd at the Pensacola Open

Year	Starts	Rounds Played	Cuts Made	Wins	Top-5s	Top-10s	Top-25s	Scoring Average	Money
1978	29	96	20	0	1	5	9	71.85	$63,561

Best finish for 1978: T-2nd at the U.S. Open

Year	Starts	Rounds Played	Cuts Made	Wins	Top-5s	Top-10s	Top-25s	Scoring Average	Money
1979	31	113	26	0	4	6	16	71.28	$130,535

Best finish for 1979: T-3rd at the Kemper Open & IVB Philadelphia Golf Classic

Year	Starts	Rounds Played	Cuts Made	Wins	Top-5s	Top-10s	Top-25s	Scoring Average	Money
1980	32	113	26	0	0	3	12	71.43	$76,791

Best finish for 1980: T-6th at the Anheuser-Busch Golf Classic

Year	Starts	Rounds Played	Cuts Made	Wins	Top-5s	Top-10s	Top-25s	Scoring Average	Money
1981	32	101	20	1	2	5	14	71.33	$127,675

Best finish for 1981: Win at the Southern Open

| 1982 | 33 | 113 | 25 | 0 | 0 | 3 | 13 | 71.40 | $98,906 |

Best finish for 1982: T-7th at the Danny Thomas Memphis Classic & Manufactures Hanover Westchester Classic

| 1983 | 30 | 108 | 23 | 0 | 1 | 4 | 11 | 71.65 | $111,995 |

Best finish for 1983: T-4th at the Panasonic Las Vegas Pro Celebrity

| 1984 | 30 | 94 | 17 | 0 | 1 | 1 | 4 | 73.00 | $68,724 |

Best finish for 1984: 3rd at the Honda Classic

| 1985 | 29 | 96 | 18 | 0 | 0 | 2 | 4 | 71.56 | $65,697 |

Best finish for 1985: T-7th at the Manufactures Hanover Westchester Classic

| 1986 | 31 | 95 | 20 | 0 | 2 | 3 | 3 | 72.01 | $147,882 |

Best finish for 1986: T-2nd at the Buick Open

| 1987 | 28 | 87 | 17 | 1 | 2 | 3 | 5 | 71.54 | $235,837 |

Best finish for 1987: Win at the Manufactures Hanover Westchester Classic

| 1988 | 29 | 82 | 15 | 0 | 1 | 2 | 5 | 71.93 | $99,262 |

Best finish for 1988: T-5th at the MONY Tournament Of Champions

| 1989 | 25 | 86 | 17 | 0 | 1 | 2 | 6 | 70.93 | $124,005 |

Best finish for 1989: T-5th at the Manufactures Hanover Westchester Classic

| 1990 | 22 | 73 | 14 | 0 | 0 | 0 | 1 | 71.92 | $53,291 |

Best finish for 1990: T-24th at the Hardee's Golf Classic

1991	2	4	0	0	0	0	0	75.75	
Period Totals	Starts	Rounds Played	Cuts Made	Wins	Top-5s	Top-10s	Top-25s	Scoring Average	Money
	657	2200	457	8	45	94	208	71.76	$2,186,814

Sam Snead

Year	Starts	Rounds Played	Cuts Made	Wins	Top-5s	Top-10s	Top-25s	Scoring Average	Money
1958	14	51	12	2	8	10	11	70.02	$21,805

Best finish for 1958: Win at the Greenbrier Invitational & Dallas Open

| 1959 | 8 | 32 | 8 | 1 | 3 | 5 | 7 | 70.47 | $10,522 |

Best finish for 1959: Win at the Sam Snead Festival

| 1960 | 12 | 48 | 10 | 2 | 6 | 7 | 12 | 70.21 | $19,956 |

Best finish for 1960: Win at the De Soto Open Invitational & Greater Greensboro Open Invitational

| 1961 | 12 | 48 | 9 | 1 | 5 | 7 | 11 | 70.82 | $23,907 |

Best finish for 1961: Win Tournament of Champions

| 1962 | 10 | 41 | 9 | 0 | 1 | 3 | 6 | 72.59 | $7,920 |

Best finish for 1962: T-3rd at the Greater Greensboro Open Invitational

| 1963 | 11 | 45 | 10 | 0 | 5 | 6 | 6 | 71.58 | $91,431 |

Best finish for 1963: T-2nd at the Doral Country Club Open Invitational

| 1964 | 8 | 28 | 6 | 0 | 2 | 2 | 4 | 71.96 | $8,384 |

Best finish for 1964: 3rd at the Greater Greensboro Open

| 1965 | 17 | 60 | 13 | 1 | 4 | 6 | 12 | 71.82 | $41,639 |

Best finish for 1965: Win at the Greater Greensboro Open

| 1966 | 7 | 28 | 7 | 0 | 0 | 2 | 4 | 72.18 | $12,110 |

Best finish for 1966: T-6th at the PGA Championship

| 1967 | 7 | 26 | 6 | 0 | 0 | 2 | 3 | 72.08 | $7,142 |

Best finish for 1967: T-10th at the Greater Greensboro Open & The Masters

| 1968 | 11 | 35 | 7 | 0 | 3 | 4 | 4 | 71.89 | $38,125 |

Best finish for 1968: 2nd at the Greater Milwaukee Open Invitational

| 1969 | 13 | 50 | 12 | 0 | 1 | 2 | 5 | 71.62 | $27,851 |

Best finish for 1969: 2nd at the Canadian Open

| 1970 | 14 | 42 | 9 | 0 | 1 | 1 | 6 | 72.38 | $23,949 |

Best finish for 1970: T-2nd at the National 4 Ball Championship PGA Players

| 1971 | 12 | 38 | 8 | 0 | 1 | 2 | 3 | 71.89 | $20,578 |

Best finish for 1971: T-4th at the Westchester Classic

| 1972 | 9 | 36 | 9 | 0 | 2 | 4 | 6 | 71.06 | $31,084 |

Best finish for 1972: T-4th at the Doral-Eastern Open & PGA Championship

| 1973 | 13 | 56 | 13 | 0 | 1 | 3 | 7 | 71.71 | $36,888 |

Best finish for 1973: T-4th at the Jackie Gleason's Inverrary Classic

| 1974 | 14 | 50 | 11 | 0 | 3 | 3 | 7 | 70.98 | $41,647 |

Best finish for 1974: T-2nd at the Glen Campbell Los Angeles Open

| 1975 | 12 | 33 | 5 | 0 | 0 | 1 | 2 | 72.64 | $10,036 |

Best finish for 1975: T-8th at the B.C. Open

| 1976 | 9 | 26 | 4 | 0 | 0 | 0 | 0 | 73.31 | $4,474 |

Best finish for 1976: T-30th at the Glen Campbell Los Angeles Open

| 1977 | 8 | 16 | 1 | 0 | 0 | 0 | 0 | 75.44 | $2,488 |

Best finish for 1977: T-54th at the PGA Championship

| 1978 | 4 | 9 | 1 | 0 | 0 | 0 | 0 | 75.00 | $1,885 |

Best finish for 1978: T-63rd at the Sea Pines Heritage Classic

| 1979 | 6 | 19 | 4 | 0 | 0 | 0 | 0 | 72.47 | $6,171 |

Best finish for 1979: T-28th at the Jackie Gleason's Inverrary Classic

| 1980 | 4 | 5 | 0 | 0 | 0 | 0 | 0 | 78.00 | $1,500 |

Year	Starts	Rounds Played	Cuts Made	Wins	Top-5s	Top-10s	Top-25s	Scoring Average	Money
1981	4	6	0	0	0	0	0	76.00	$1,500
1982	4	7	0	0	0	0	0	78.86	$1,500
1983	2	2	0	0	0	0	0	75.50	$1,500
Period Totals	Starts	Rounds Played	Cuts Made	Wins	Top-5s	Top-10s	Top-25s	Scoring Average	Money
	245	837	174	7	46	70	116	71.83	$495,991

PGA Tour career totals from 1935 to 1983

	Starts	Rounds Played	Cuts Made	Wins	Top-5s	Top-10s	Top-25s	Scoring Average	Money
	601	1746	530	82	N/A	345	454	N/A	$826,028

Brandt Snedeker

Year	Starts	Rounds Played	Cuts Made	Wins	Top-5s	Top-10s	Top-25s	Scoring Average	Money
2004	9	26	4	0	0	0	0	72.77	$54,215

Best finish for 2004: T-27th at the EDS Byron Nelson Championship

| 2005 | 2 | 6 | 1 | 0 | 0 | 0 | 0 | 74.33 | $14,731 |

Best finish for 2005: T-47th at the MCI Heritage

| 2007 | 29 | 105 | 23 | 1 | 3 | 6 | 13 | 70.50 | $2,836,643 |

Best finish for 2007: Win at the Wyndham Championship

| 2008 | 26 | 84 | 19 | 0 | 1 | 5 | 7 | 71.27 | $1,531,442 |

Best finish for 2008: T-3rd at the Masters

Period Totals	Starts	Rounds Played	Cuts Made	Wins	Top-5s	Top-10s	Top-25s	Scoring Average	Money
	66	221	47	1	4	11	20	71.16	$4,437,031

Ed Sneed

Year	Starts	Rounds Played	Cuts Made	Wins	Top-5s	Top-10s	Top-25s	Scoring Average	Money
1967	1	2	0	0	0	0	0	76.50	
1968	3	6	0	0	0	0	0	75.83	
1969	13	38	6	0	0	0	1	73.61	$3,835

Best finish for 1969: T-11th at the Kaiser International Open

| 1970 | 19 | 51 | 7 | 0 | 0 | 0 | 0 | 73.86 | $1,303 |

Best finish for 1970: T-61st at the Cleveland Open

| 1971 | 24 | 72 | 11 | 0 | 1 | 1 | 3 | 73.42 | $7,432 |

Best finish for 1971: T-4th at the Tallahassee Open

| 1972 | 26 | 79 | 13 | 0 | 0 | 1 | 3 | 73.30 | $10,958 |

Best finish for 1972: T-8th at the Walt Disney World Open

| 1973 | 38 | 133 | 28 | 1 | 1 | 4 | 10 | 72.08 | $65,366 |

Best finish for 1973: Win at the Kaiser International Open

| 1974 | 28 | 87 | 16 | 1 | 1 | 2 | 8 | 72.17 | $50,280 |

Best finish for 1974: Win at the Greater Milwaukee Open

| 1975 | 29 | 107 | 24 | 0 | 2 | 2 | 9 | 72.30 | $47,885 |

Best finish for 1975: 3rd at the Western Open

| 1976 | 29 | 98 | 22 | 0 | 5 | 8 | 12 | 71.61 | $90,005 |

Best finish for 1976: T-3rd at the Greater Milwaukee Open & B.C. Open

| 1977 | 26 | 87 | 17 | 1 | 1 | 3 | 9 | 72.46 | $50,638 |

Best finish for 1977: Win at the Tallahassee Open

| 1978 | 27 | 90 | 18 | 0 | 5 | 5 | 12 | 72.10 | $86,843 |

Best finish for 1978: 2nd at the Anheuser-Busch Golf Classic

| 1979 | 26 | 94 | 22 | 0 | 3 | 5 | 12 | 71.91 | $125,470 |

Best finish for 1979: T-2nd at the Sea Pines Heritage Classic & Masters

| 1980 | 26 | 86 | 18 | 0 | 3 | 5 | 8 | 72.28 | $84,798 |

Best finish for 1980: T-3rd at the Hawaiian Open & Sea Pines Heritage Classic

| 1981 | 30 | 88 | 16 | 0 | 1 | 1 | 8 | 72.31 | $48,678 |

Best finish for 1981: T-5th at the Hall of Fame Tournament

| 1982 | 27 | 100 | 23 | 1 | 2 | 5 | 12 | 71.34 | $148,553 |

Best finish for 1982: Win at the Michelob Houston Open

| 1983 | 25 | 77 | 12 | 0 | 1 | 2 | 3 | 73.10 | $39,413 |

Best finish for 1983: T-5th at the Phoenix Open

| 1984 | 19 | 50 | 4 | 0 | 0 | 0 | 0 | 74.68 | $4,443 |

Best finish for 1984: T-69th at the Doral-Eastern Open

| 1985 | 10 | 24 | 1 | 0 | 0 | 0 | 0 | 74.33 | $995 |

Best finish for 1985: T-70th at the Honda Classic

| 1986 | 7 | 16 | 1 | 0 | 0 | 0 | 0 | 74.00 | $1,030 |

Best finish for 1986: T-55th at the Sea Pines Heritage Classic

1987	1	2	0	0	0	0	0	75.50	
1988	1	2	0	0	0	0	0	78.00	$765
1991	3	9	0	0	0	0	0	73.56	
1992	2	6	0	0	0	0	0	74.67	
1993	3	10	2	0	0	0	0	74.10	$3,124

Best finish for 1993: T-72nd at the Shell Houston Open

| 1994 | 3 | 9 | 1 | 0 | 0 | 0 | 1 | 74.22 | $7,583 |

Best finish for 1994: T-20th at the Deposit Guaranty Golf Classic

Period Totals	Starts	Rounds Played	Cuts Made	Wins	Top-5s	Top-10s	Top-25s	Scoring Average	Money
	446	1423	262	4	26	44	111	72.59	$879,399

Terry Snodgrass

Year	Starts	Rounds Played	Cuts Made	Wins	Top-5s	Top-10s	Top-25s	Scoring Average	Money
1982	1	2	0	0	0	0	0	74.50	
1985	23	62	8	0	0	0	1	72.61	$14,201

Best finish for 1985: T-21st at the Buick Open

Year	Starts	Rounds Played	Cuts Made	Wins	Top-5s	Top-10s	Top-25s	Scoring Average	Money
1986	1	2	0	0	0	0	0	73.50	
1991	1	4	1	0	0	0	0	76.25	$4,958

Best finish for 1991: T-63rd at the U.S. Open

Period Totals	Starts	Rounds Played	Cuts Made	Wins	Top-5s	Top-10s	Top-25s	Scoring Average	Money
	26	70	9	0	0	0	1	72.90	$19,159

John Snyder

Year	Starts	Rounds Played	Cuts Made	Wins	Top-5s	Top-10s	Top-25s	Scoring Average	Money
1987	1	2	0	0	0	0	0	75.50	
1988	23	46	1	0	0	0	0	74.35	$1,338

Best finish for 1988: T-58th at the Hardee's Golf Classic

Year	Starts	Rounds Played	Cuts Made	Wins	Top-5s	Top-10s	Top-25s	Scoring Average	Money
1990	1	2	0	0	0	0	0	75.00	$1,000
1995	1	2	0	0	0	0	0	77.50	$1,000

Period Totals	Starts	Rounds Played	Cuts Made	Wins	Top-5s	Top-10s	Top-25s	Scoring Average	Money
	26	52	1	0	0	0	0	74.54	$3,338

Joey Snyder III

Year	Starts	Rounds Played	Cuts Made	Wins	Top-5s	Top-10s	Top-25s	Scoring Average	Money
2005	31	98	20	0	1	3	8	71.06	$1,042,696

Best finish for 2005: 4th at the Southern Farm Bureau Classic

Year	Starts	Rounds Played	Cuts Made	Wins	Top-5s	Top-10s	Top-25s	Scoring Average	Money
2006	6	14	1	0	0	0	0	73.29	$13,432

Best finish for 2006: T-48th at the Ford Championship at Doral

Period Totals	Starts	Rounds Played	Cuts Made	Wins	Top-5s	Top-10s	Top-25s	Scoring Average	Money
	37	112	21	0	1	3	8	71.34	$1,056,128

Mick Soli

Year	Starts	Rounds Played	Cuts Made	Wins	Top-5s	Top-10s	Top-25s	Scoring Average	Money
1979	8	22	3	0	0	0	0	74.45	$4,762

Best finish for 1979: T-30th at the American Optical Classic

| 1980 | 19 | 53 | 10 | 0 | 0 | 0 | 2 | 72.53 | $13,835 |

Best finish for 1980: T-14th at the San Antonio Texas Open

| 1981 | 22 | 59 | 9 | 0 | 1 | 1 | 2 | 73.36 | $19,259 |

Best finish for 1981: T-5th at the Bay Hill Classic

| 1982 | 24 | 70 | 11 | 0 | 0 | 0 | 1 | 73.10 | $15,318 |

Best finish for 1982: T-12th at the Bank of Boston Classic

| 1983 | 29 | 83 | 12 | 0 | 0 | 0 | 6 | 72.69 | $29,804 |

Best finish for 1983: T-16th at the Georgia-Pacific Atlanta Golf Classic

| 1984 | 22 | 62 | 9 | 0 | 0 | 0 | 0 | 73.18 | $13,164 |

Best finish for 1984: T-26th at the Walt Disney World Golf Classic

| 1985 | 23 | 69 | 10 | 0 | 0 | 0 | 0 | 73.52 | $10,476 |

Best finish for 1985: T-36th at the Manufactures Hanover Westchester Classic

1994	1	2	0	0	0	0	0	77.00	$1,000
1995	1	3	0	0	0	0	0	74.33	
1998	1	3	0	0	0	0	0	75.00	
1999	1	3	0	0	0	0	0	76.67	
2006	1	3	0	0	0	0	0	74.67	

Period Totals	Starts	Rounds Played	Cuts Made	Wins	Top-5s	Top-10s	Top-25s	Scoring Average	Money
	152	432	64	0	1	1	11	73.21	$107,619

Ramon Sota

Year	Starts	Rounds Played	Cuts Made	Wins	Top-5s	Top-10s	Top-25s	Scoring Average	Money
1958	1	2	0	0	0	0	0	75.50	
1959	1	2	0	0	0	0	0	76.00	
1960	1	4	1	0	0	0	1	71.75	$168

Best finish for 1960: 15th at the British Open

| 1961 | 1 | 4 | 1 | 0 | 0 | 0 | 1 | 73.75 | |

Best finish for 1961: T-12th at the British Open

| 1962 | 1 | 2 | 0 | 0 | 0 | 0 | 0 | 79.00 | |
| 1963 | 1 | 4 | 1 | 0 | 0 | 1 | 1 | 71.75 | $700 |

Best finish for 1963: T-7th at the British Open

| 1964 | 8 | 32 | 8 | 0 | 0 | 1 | 2 | 72.81 | $5,414 |

Best finish for 1964: 6th at the Greater Greensboro Open

| 1965 | 3 | 12 | 3 | 0 | 0 | 1 | 2 | 72.75 | $4,914 |

Best finish for 1965: T-6th at the Masters

| 1966 | 2 | 8 | 2 | 0 | 0 | 0 | 0 | 74.88 | $2,293 |

Best finish for 1966: T-27th at the Carling World Open

1967	2	8	2	0	0	0	0	73.88	$1,300

Best finish for 1967: T-31st at the Masters

1969	1	2	0	0	0	0	0	77.00	
1970	1	3	0	0	0	0	0	74.00	
1971	1	4	1	0	0	0	1	71.75	$2,760

Best finish for 1971: T-11th at the British Open

1972	2	4	0	0	0	0	0	77.50	$1,125
Period Totals	Starts	Rounds Played	Cuts Made	Wins	Top-5s	Top-10s	Top-25s	Scoring Average	Money
	26	91	19	0	0	3	8	73.58	$18,674

Mike Souchak

Year	Starts	Rounds Played	Cuts Made	Wins	Top-5s	Top-10s	Top-25s	Scoring Average	Money
1958	34	124	28	1	4	8	23	71.39	$18,840

Best finish for 1958: Win at the St. Paul Open

1959	24	4	19	3	11	13	20	70.47	$42,348

Best finish for 1959: Win at the Tournament of Champions, Western Open Championship & Motor City Open Invitational

1960	19	77	18	2	6	10	17	70.74	$29,353

Best finish for 1960: Win at the San Diego Open Invitational & Buick Open Invitational

1961	20	80	19	1	4	5	9	71.13	$17,797

Best finish for 1961: Win at the Greater Greensboro Open Invitational

1962	21	83	18	0	3	5	13	70.90	$18,912

Best finish for 1962: T-2nd at the Greater Greensboro Open Invitational

1963	24	96	24	0	1	3	8	71.84	$13,434

Best finish for 1963: T-2nd at the Hot Springs Open Invitational

1964	31	101	19	2	4	5	13	72.09	$39,440

Best finish for 1964: Win at the Houston Classic & Memphis Open

1965	31	109	23	0	1	2	9	72.86	$20,244

Best finish for 1965: T-5th at the Cleveland Open

1966	28	87	15	0	1	1	5	73.03	$13,327

Best finish for 1966: T-3rd at the Bob Hope Desert Classic

1967	14	50	10	0	0	2	4	72.38	$8,797

Best finish for 1967: T-8th at the Los Angeles Open

1968	11	33	4	0	0	0	0	73.45	$1,604

Best finish for 1968: T-29th at the Los Angeles Open Invitational

1969	9	22	2	0	0	0	0	74.45	$1,196

Best finish for 1969: T-42nd at the U.S. Open

1970	4	10	0	0	0	0	0	76.40	
1971	2	5	0	0	0	0	0	78.20	$500
1972	2	6	1	0	0	0	0	73.33	$1,497

Best finish for 1972: T-29th at the PGA Championship

1973	1	2	0	0	0	0	0	77.50	
1976	2	4	0	0	0	0	0	80.50	$680
1978	1	3	0	0	0	0	0	79.00	
1980	1	3	0	0	0	0	0	77.67	
Period Totals	Starts	Rounds Played	Cuts Made	Wins	Top-5s	Top-10s	Top-25s	Scoring Average	Money
	279	990	200	9	35	54	121	71.99	$227,968

PGA Tour career totals from 1953 to 1980

	Starts	Rounds Played	Cuts Made	Wins	Top-5s	Top-10s	Top-25s	Scoring Average	Money
	390	1425	310	15	57	98	194	N/A	$303,404

Bruce Soulsby

Year	Starts	Rounds Played	Cuts Made	Wins	Top-5s	Top-10s	Top-25s	Scoring Average	Money
1984	3	10	2	0	0	0	0	73.20	$1,396

Best finish for 1984: T-48th at the B.C. Open

1985	4	10	1	0	0	0	0	73.10	$1,230

Best finish for 1985: T-61st at the B.C. Open

1986	2	4	0	0	0	0	0	74.25	
1987	30	90	17	0	0	0	4	71.87	$54,563

Best finish for 1987: T-14th at the Manufactures Hanover Westchester Classic

1988	23	61	9	0	0	0	1	71.97	$24,570

Best finish for 1988: T-19th at the Federal Express St. Jude Classic

1989	2	0	1	0	0	0	0		$2,060

Best finish for 1989: T-65th at the International

1990	1	2	0	0	0	0	0	77.00	$1,000
Period Totals	Starts	Rounds Played	Cuts Made	Wins	Top-5s	Top-10s	Top-25s	Scoring Average	Money
	65	177	30	0	0	0	5	72.16	$84,820

Bob Sowards

Year	Starts	Rounds Played	Cuts Made	Wins	Top-5s	Top-10s	Top-25s	Scoring Average	Money
1997	1	2	0	0	0	0	0	75.50	$1,300
2001	1	2	0	0	0	0	0	75.00	$2,000

Year	Starts	Rounds Played	Cuts Made	Wins	Top-5s	Top-10s	Top-25s	Scoring Average	Money
2003	1	2	0	0	0	0	0	79.50	$2,000
2004	1	2	0	0	0	0	0	77.50	$2,000
2005	7	18	2	0	0	0	0	72.72	$19,162

Best finish for 2005: T-65th at the FUNAI Classic at the Walt Disney World Resort

2008	22	61	9	0	0	1	2	71.79	$263,327

Best finish for 2008: T-9th at the Wyndham Championship

Period Totals	Starts	Rounds Played	Cuts Made	Wins	Top-5s	Top-10s	Top-25s	Scoring Average	Money
	33	87	11	0	0	1	2	72.45	$289,789

Mike Spang

Year	Starts	Rounds Played	Cuts Made	Wins	Top-5s	Top-10s	Top-25s	Scoring Average	Money
1965	1	2	0	0	0	0	0	77.00	
1966	1	2	0	0	0	0	0	75.50	
1971	1	4	1	0	0	0	0	72.50	

Best finish for 1971: T-44th at the Bahamas National Open

1972	21	55	7	0	0	0	1	73.82	$3,429

Best finish for 1972: T-17th at the Cleveland Open

1973	8	18	1	0	0	0	0	75.72	

Best finish for 1973: T-71st at the Monsanto Open

Period Totals	Starts	Rounds Played	Cuts Made	Wins	Top-5s	Top-10s	Top-25s	Scoring Average	Money
	32	81	9	0	0	0	1	74.30	$3,429

Bob Spence

Year	Starts	Rounds Played	Cuts Made	Wins	Top-5s	Top-10s	Top-25s	Scoring Average	Money
1960	1	4	1	0	0	0	0	72.00	$025

Best finish for 1960: T-33rd at the Mobile Sertoma Open Invitational

1964	1	4	1	0	0	0	0	74.00	

Best finish for 1964: T-37th at the Azalea Open

1965	5	12	1	0	0	0	0	75.42	

Best finish for 1965: T-58th at the Azalea Open

1966	12	32	4	0	0	0	0	74.53	$250

Best finish for 1966: T-36th at the Portland Open Invitational

1972	3	6	0	0	0	0	0	75.17	
1976	3	8	1	0	0	0	0	75.00	

Best finish for 1976: T-74th at the World Open

1979	1	2	0	0	0	0	0	77.50	

Period Totals	Starts	Rounds Played	Cuts Made	Wins	Top-5s	Top-10s	Top-25s	Scoring Average	Money
	26	68	8	0	0	0	0	74.71	$275

Craig-A. Spence

Year	Starts	Rounds Played	Cuts Made	Wins	Top-5s	Top-10s	Top-25s	Scoring Average	Money
1999	8	20	3	0	1	1	1	73.55	$92,520

Best finish for 1999: T-4th at the B.C. Open

2000	31	85	12	0	1	1	3	72.11	$347,569

Best finish for 2000: 5th at the International presented by Quest

2001	19	42	2	0	0	0	1	73.19	$31,548

Best finish for 2001: T-25th at the Greater Milwaukee Open

Period Totals	Starts	Rounds Played	Cuts Made	Wins	Top-5s	Top-10s	Top-25s	Scoring Average	Money
	58	147	17	0	2	2	5	72.61	$471,636

Joel Spinola

Year	Starts	Rounds Played	Cuts Made	Wins	Top-5s	Top-10s	Top-25s	Scoring Average	Money
1964	26	53	5	0	0	0	0	75.23	$462

Best finish for 1964: T-29th at the Sahara Invitational

1965	1	3	0	0	0	0	0	77.33	

Period Totals	Starts	Rounds Played	Cuts Made	Wins	Top-5s	Top-10s	Top-25s	Scoring Average	Money
	27	56	5	0	0	0	0	75.34	$462

Mike Sposa

Year	Starts	Rounds Played	Cuts Made	Wins	Top-5s	Top-10s	Top-25s	Scoring Average	Money
1991	1	2	0	0	0	0	0	73.50	
1997	2	4	0	0	0	0	0	75.50	$1,000
1999	31	89	17	0	0	1	4	71.53	$255,408

Best finish for 1999: T-10th at the Kemper Open

2000	26	73	11	0	0	1	2	71.18	$201,360

Best finish for 2000: T-7th at the Shell Houston Open

2001	29	93	20	0	0	0	9	70.62	$578,312

Best finish for 2001: T-11th at the MasterCard Colonial

2002	34	109	21	0	1	1	4	71.07	$463,418

Best finish for 2002: T-4th at the COMPAQ Classic of New Orleans

2003	25	70	11	0	0	1	3	70.99	$276,447

Best finish for 2003: T-10th at the Chrysler Classic of Tucson

Year	Starts	Rounds Played	Cuts Made	Wins	Top-5s	Top-10s	Top-25s	Scoring Average	Money
2004	1	2	0	0	0	0	0	72.00	
2006	25	65	10	0	0	0	1	71.82	$132,131

Best finish for 2006: T-24th at the Chrysler Classic of Tucson

Period Totals	Starts	Rounds Played	Cuts Made	Wins	Top-5s	Top-10s	Top-25s	Scoring Average	Money
	174	507	90	0	1	4	23	71.22	$1,908,075

Jack Spradlin

Year	Starts	Rounds Played	Cuts Made	Wins	Top-5s	Top-10s	Top-25s	Scoring Average	Money
1975	12	33	4	0	0	0	0	73.79	$1,522

Best finish for 1975: T-28th at the Ed McMahon Quad City Open

1977	6	17	3	0	0	0	1	72.65	$2,088

Best finish for 1977: T-16th at the San Antonio Texas Open

1978	22	52	7	0	0	0	0	73.19	$4,909

Best finish for 1978: T-27th at the Glen Campbell Los Angeles Open

1979	20	57	8	0	0	0	0	72.93	$4,746

Best finish for 1979: T-43rd at the Andy Williams-San Diego Open

1980	5	7	1	0	0	0	1	74.71	$2,170

Best finish for 1980: T-23rd at the World Disney World National Team Championship

1981	2	3	0	0	0	0	0	75.67	
1983	1	2	0	0	0	0	0	74.00	
1984	24	52	2	0	0	0	0	74.38	$2,471

Best finish for 1984: T-41st at the Isuzu/Andy Williams San Diego Open

Period Totals	Starts	Rounds Played	Cuts Made	Wins	Top-5s	Top-10s	Top-25s	Scoring Average	Money
	92	223	25	0	0	0	2	73.54	$17,906

Steve Spray

Year	Starts	Rounds Played	Cuts Made	Wins	Top-5s	Top-10s	Top-25s	Scoring Average	Money
1961	1	2	0	0	0	0	0	79.50	
1964	2	6	1	0	0	0	0	72.83	$251

Best finish for 1964: T-39th at the Western Open

1965	15	42	6	0	0	0	0	74.36	$798

Best finish for 1965: T-33rd at the Buick Open

1966	29	93	18	0	0	3	7	72.46	$16,540

Best finish for 1966: T-6th at the Buick Open Invitational & Minnesota Golf Classic

1967	25	78	16	0	1	3	8	72.67	$27,701

Best finish for 1967: 2nd at the Sahara Open

1968	33	115	23	0	1	2	8	72.62	$18,245

Best finish for 1968: T-5th at the U.S. Open

1969	27	80	13	1	1	2	4	73.05	$28,510

Best finish for 1969: Win at the San Francisco Open

1970	35	115	23	0	2	3	8	72.35	$30,380

Best finish for 1970: 4th at the Greater Greensboro Open

1971	28	77	10	0	0	0	1	73.83	$4,197

Best finish for 1971: T-15th at the Tucson Open

1972	18	61	11	0	0	1	2	73.36	$6,512

Best finish for 1972: T-8th at the Robinson's Fall Golf Classic

1973	10	26	2	0	0	0	0	75.35	$959

Best finish for 1973: T-32nd at the Glen Campbell Los Angeles Open

1974	4	10	2	0	0	0	1	72.40	$1,416

Best finish for 1974: T-25th at the Greater Jacksonville Open

1975	7	16	1	0	0	0	0	76.81	

Best finish for 1975: T-76th at the Greater Jacksonville Open

1977	3	6	0	0	0	0	0	77.83	$500
1978	3	8	1	0	0	0	0	74.38	$688

Best finish for 1978: T-60th at the Andy Williams-San Diego Open

1979	7	17	1	0	0	0	0	75.65	$1,566

Best finish for 1979: T-48th at the Andy Williams-San Diego Open

1980	1	2	0	0	0	0	0	79.00	$500
1982	3	8	1	0	0	0	0	75.13	$1,161

Best finish for 1982: T-76th at the Phoenix Open

1989	1	2	0	0	0	0	0	74.00	$1,000

Period Totals	Starts	Rounds Played	Cuts Made	Wins	Top-5s	Top-10s	Top-25s	Scoring Average	Money
	252	764	129	1	5	14	39	73.26	$140,923

Mike Springer

Year	Starts	Rounds Played	Cuts Made	Wins	Top-5s	Top-10s	Top-25s	Scoring Average	Money
1987	1	4	1	0	0	1	1	68.50	

Best finish for 1987: 9th at the Seiko-Tucson Open

1988	2	6	1	0	0	0	0	72.00	

Best finish for 1988: T-30th at the Los Angeles Open

1991	28	90	16	0	2	3	6	70.71	$178,588

Best finish for 1991: T-3rd at the BellSouth Atlanta Golf Classic

1992	30	85	13	0	1	2	4	71.52	$144,316

Year	Starts	Rounds Played	Cuts Made	Wins	Top-5s	Top-10s	Top-25s	Scoring Average	Money
Best finish for 1992: T-2nd at the Kemper Open									
1993	25	79	14	0	2	4	5	71.47	$216,929
Best finish for 1993: T-3rd at the Phoenix Open									
1994	25	89	18	2	4	5	10	70.84	$783,633
Best finish for 1994: Win at the Kmart Greater Greensboro Open & Greater Milwaukee Open									
1995	27	67	6	0	0	0	1	73.52	$59,883
Best finish for 1995: T-20th at the NEC World Series of Golf									
1996	29	85	13	0	0	3	4	71.33	$164,666
Best finish for 1996: T-8th at the Walt Disney World/Oldsmobile Classic									
1997	22	66	11	0	2	3	3	71.83	$191,422
Best finish for 1997: T-3rd at the Kemper Open									
1998	34	105	19	0	0	0	7	71.38	$230,795
Best finish for 1998: T-11th at the Westin Texas Open									
1999	33	87	11	0	0	1	3	72.16	$165,675
Best finish for 1999: T-8th at the Canon Greater Hartford Open									
2000	31	81	13	0	0	0	4	71.46	$182,726
Best finish for 2000: T-22nd at the Greater Milwaukee Open									
2001	10	26	3	0	0	0	1	72.65	$81,141
Best finish for 2001: T-13th at the AT&T Pebble Beach									
2002	12	36	6	0	0	0	1	72.44	$59,193
Best finish for 2002: T-25th at the B.C. Open									
2003	9	25	4	0	0	0	0	72.00	$53,452
Best finish for 2003: T-31st at the B.C. Open									
2004	10	29	4	0	0	0	0	72.41	$44,616
Best finish for 2004: T-35th at the Chrysler Classic of Greensboro									
2005	5	14	2	0	0	0	1	71.00	$59,269
Best finish for 2005: T-13th at the B.C. Open									
2006	6	13	0	0	0	0	0	73.62	
Period Totals	Starts	Rounds Played	Cuts Made	Wins	Top-5s	Top-10s	Top-25s	Scoring Average	Money
	339	987	155	2	11	22	51	71.67	$2,616,304

Craig Stadler

Year	Starts	Rounds Played	Cuts Made	Wins	Top-5s	Top-10s	Top-25s	Scoring Average	Money
1973	2	4	0	0	0	0	0	77.50	
1974	3	8	1	0	0	1	1	73.88	$1,700
Best finish for 1974: T-6th at the Glen Campbell Los Angeles Open									
1975	2	6	1	0	0	0	1	74.33	$1,250
Best finish for 1975: T-25th at the Glen Campbell Los Angeles Open									
1976	8	26	5	0	0	0	0	72.31	$2,702
Best finish for 1976: T-35th at the Pensacola Open									
1977	30	96	18	0	2	4	9	72.52	$41,289
Best finish for 1977: 4th at the Glen Campbell Los Angeles Open									
1978	28	94	20	0	1	5	11	72.19	$56,486
Best finish for 1978: 4th at the Greater Greensboro Open									
1979	33	116	24	0	1	4	11	72.14	$74,342
Best finish for 1979: 4th at the Ed McMahon Quad City Open									
1980	26	95	23	2	3	9	13	71.54	$228,054
Best finish for 1980: Win at the Bob Hope Chrysler Classic & Greater Greensboro Open									
1981	30	101	21	1	6	8	12	71.34	$219,829
Best finish for 1981: Win at the Kemper Open									
1982	26	102	24	4	9	11	18	70.86	$447,879
Best finish for 1982: Win at the Joe Garagiola Tucson Open, Masters, Kemper Open & World Series Of Golf									
1983	28	101	21	0	5	11	15	71.35	$225,371
Best finish for 1983: T-2nd at the Greater Greensboro Open & Manufactures Hanover Westchester Classic									
1984	23	86	21	1	5	8	16	70.83	$328,702
Best finish for 1984: Win at the Byron Nelson Golf Classic									
1985	25	89	20	0	5	8	14	71.15	$299,541
Best finish for 1985: T-2nd at the Bob Hope Chrysler Classic, Hawaiian Open & Greater Greensboro Open									
1986	27	83	17	0	3	8	10	71.33	$172,176
Best finish for 1986: T-3rd at the Southwest Golf Classic									
1987	21	78	17	0	2	7	12	70.88	$259,914
Best finish for 1987: T-2nd at the Hawaiian Open									
1988	22	77	17	0	3	5	11	71.29	$282,605
Best finish for 1988: T-3rd at the Masters & Kemper Open									
1989	24	84	21	0	3	4	14	70.60	$431,719
Best finish for 1989: 2nd at the Independent Insurance Agent Open									
1990	20	68	16	0	2	5	9	71.75	$279,479
Best finish for 1990: T-3rd at the Hawaiian Open									
1991	22	74	17	1	5	7	12	70.51	$832,668
Best finish for 1991: Win at the Tour Championship									
1992	26	86	19	1	1	4	10	71.05	$493,911
Best finish for 1992: Win at the NEC World Series of Golf									

Year	Starts	Rounds Played	Cuts Made	Wins	Top-5s	Top-10s	Top-25s	Scoring Average	Money
1993	24	80	17	0	4	5	7	71.11	$554,823

Best finish for 1993: 2nd at the NEC World Series of Golf & Las Vegas Invitational

| 1994 | 23 | 73 | 16 | 1 | 3 | 4 | 8 | 70.51 | $490,246 |

Best finish for 1994: Win at the Buick Invitational of California

| 1995 | 21 | 69 | 15 | 0 | 3 | 4 | 9 | 70.45 | $404,853 |

Best finish for 1995: T-3rd at the B.C. Open

| 1996 | 18 | 56 | 12 | 1 | 1 | 1 | 4 | 71.16 | $338,120 |

Best finish for 1996: Win at the Nissan Open

| 1997 | 21 | 69 | 15 | 0 | 3 | 6 | 9 | 70.48 | $526,644 |

Best finish for 1997: 2nd at the Buick Invitational & Nissan Open

| 1998 | 18 | 61 | 15 | 0 | 0 | 2 | 7 | 70.87 | $350,091 |

Best finish for 1998: T-7th at the Honda Classic

| 1999 | 17 | 50 | 11 | 0 | 1 | 1 | 6 | 71.46 | $455,841 |

Best finish for 1999: 3rd at the AT&T Pebble Beach Pro-Am

| 2000 | 21 | 66 | 13 | 0 | 1 | 2 | 6 | 71.52 | $637,752 |

Best finish for 2000: 2nd at the Shell Houston Open

| 2001 | 19 | 39 | 6 | 0 | 1 | 1 | 1 | 72.64 | $201,073 |

Best finish for 2001: T-5th at the Accenture Match Play Championship

| 2002 | 22 | 68 | 13 | 0 | 0 | 1 | 6 | 71.09 | $505,778 |

Best finish for 2002: T-10th at the WorldCom Classic

| 2003 | 11 | 26 | 4 | 1 | 1 | 1 | 1 | 72.19 | $584,830 |

Best finish for 2003: Win at the B.C. Open

| 2004 | 6 | 20 | 4 | 0 | 0 | 0 | 1 | 71.95 | $142,475 |

Best finish for 2004: T-21st at the B.C. Open

| 2005 | 6 | 24 | 5 | 0 | 0 | 1 | 2 | 71.63 | $256,110 |

Best finish for 2005: T-9th at the Sony Open in Hawaii

| 2006 | 4 | 10 | 1 | 0 | 0 | 0 | 0 | 73.70 | $21,259 |

Best finish for 2006: T-42nd at the AT&T Pebble Beach National Pro-Am

| 2007 | 1 | 4 | 1 | 0 | 0 | 0 | 0 | 76.25 | $18,560 |

Best finish for 2007: T-49th at the Masters

2008	2	5	0	0	0	0	0	75.40	
Period Totals	Starts	Rounds Played	Cuts Made	Wins	Top-5s	Top-10s	Top-25s	Scoring Average	Money
	660	2194	471	13	74	138	266	71.36	$10,168,075

Kevin Stadler

Year	Starts	Rounds Played	Cuts Made	Wins	Top-5s	Top-10s	Top-25s	Scoring Average	Money
2002	1	2	0	0	0	0	0	74.00	
2003	2	2	0	0	0	0	0	71.00	
2004	5	16	4	0	0	0	0	72.88	$49,541

Best finish for 2004: T-40th at the B.C. Open

| 2005 | 33 | 92 | 14 | 0 | 0 | 2 | 3 | 71.46 | $367,775 |

Best finish for 2005: T-9th at the Chrysler Classic of Tucson

| 2006 | 6 | 22 | 5 | 0 | 0 | 0 | 2 | 72.64 | $172,972 |

Best finish for 2006: T-13th at the WGC-NEC Invitational

| 2007 | 31 | 95 | 16 | 0 | 1 | 2 | 5 | 72.13 | $810,876 |

Best finish for 2007: T-2nd at the Reno-Tahoe Open

| 2008 | 30 | 90 | 15 | 0 | 1 | 1 | 5 | 71.56 | $598,945 |

Best finish for 2008: T-4th at the Puerto Rico Open

Period Totals	Starts	Rounds Played	Cuts Made	Wins	Top-5s	Top-10s	Top-25s	Scoring Average	Money
	108	319	54	0	2	5	15	71.85	$2,000,110

Mike Standly

Year	Starts	Rounds Played	Cuts Made	Wins	Top-5s	Top-10s	Top-25s	Scoring Average	Money
1986	1	2	0	0	0	0	0	75.00	
1987	1	2	0	0	0	0	0	72.50	
1988	1	4	1	0	0	0	0	72.00	$800

Best finish for 1988: 70th at the Gatlin Brothers - Southwest Golf Classic

| 1991 | 31 | 88 | 14 | 0 | 0 | 0 | 2 | 71.95 | $55,846 |

Best finish for 1991: T-18th at the Phoenix Open

| 1992 | 29 | 99 | 22 | 0 | 1 | 2 | 5 | 71.06 | $213,712 |

Best finish for 1992: T-2nd at the Freeport-McMoRan Classic

| 1993 | 30 | 92 | 17 | 1 | 2 | 2 | 5 | 71.85 | $325,386 |

Best finish for 1993: Win at the Freeport-McMoRan Classic

| 1994 | 30 | 92 | 19 | 0 | 0 | 0 | 6 | 71.79 | $179,850 |

Best finish for 1994: T-12th at the AT&T Pebble Beach Pro-Am

| 1995 | 30 | 93 | 17 | 0 | 1 | 3 | 3 | 71.54 | $178,920 |

Best finish for 1995: T-5th at the Freeport-McMoRan Classic

| 1996 | 31 | 81 | 11 | 0 | 1 | 1 | 2 | 71.78 | $99,034 |

Best finish for 1996: T-4th at the CVS Charity Classic

| 1997 | 28 | 86 | 14 | 0 | 2 | 3 | 6 | 71.21 | $320,239 |

Best finish for 1997: 2nd at the Deposit Guaranty Golf Classic

| 1998 | 31 | 86 | 12 | 0 | 0 | 1 | 3 | 72.05 | $191,976 |

Best finish for 1998: T-7th at the Bell Canadian Open

Year	Starts	Rounds Played	Cuts Made	Wins	Top-5s	Top-10s	Top-25s	Scoring Average	Money
1999	15	42	6	0	0	0	1	72.29	$47,814

Best finish for 1999: T-21st at the John Deere Classic

| 2000 | 13 | 37 | 6 | 0 | 0 | 0 | 1 | 70.89 | $72,948 |

Best finish for 2000: T-24th at the COMPAQ Classic of New Orleans

| 2001 | 6 | 15 | 1 | 0 | 0 | 0 | 0 | 71.73 | $5,766 |

Best finish for 2001: T-75th at the Greater Milwaukee Open

| 2002 | 11 | 29 | 4 | 0 | 0 | 0 | 1 | 72.07 | $68,210 |

Best finish for 2002: T-18th at the Air Canada Championship

| 2003 | 9 | 27 | 4 | 0 | 0 | 0 | 0 | 71.56 | $62,991 |

Best finish for 2003: T-30th at the Bell Canadian Open

| 2004 | 9 | 20 | 1 | 0 | 0 | 0 | 0 | 72.95 | $6,000 |

Best finish for 2004: T-69th at the B.C. Open

| 2005 | 2 | 6 | 1 | 0 | 0 | 0 | 0 | 71.17 | $8,904 |

Best finish for 2005: T-48th at the Valero Texas Open

2006	1	2	0	0	0	0	0	71.50	
2007	1	2	0	0	0	0	0	75.00	
2008	1	2	0	0	0	0	0	73.50	
Period Totals	Starts	Rounds Played	Cuts Made	Wins	Top-5s	Top-10s	Top-25s	Scoring Average	Money
	311	907	150	1	7	12	35	71.70	$1,838,397

Paul Stankowski

Year	Starts	Rounds Played	Cuts Made	Wins	Top-5s	Top-10s	Top-25s	Scoring Average	Money
1994	29	77	10	0	1	3	4	71.66	$171,392

Best finish for 1994: T-5th at the Las Vegas Invitational

| 1995 | 31 | 91 | 14 | 0 | 1 | 1 | 3 | 71.93 | $145,758 |

Best finish for 1995: T-4th at the Shell Houston Open

| 1996 | 25 | 71 | 11 | 1 | 1 | 3 | 3 | 71.87 | $392,075 |

Best finish for 1996: Win at the BellSouth Classic

| 1997 | 29 | 101 | 22 | 1 | 5 | 5 | 15 | 71.12 | $930,495 |

Best finish for 1997: Win at the United Airlines Hawaiian Open

| 1998 | 26 | 77 | 14 | 0 | 0 | 2 | 6 | 70.92 | $324,536 |

Best finish for 1998: T-6th at the Las Vegas Invitational

| 1999 | 28 | 77 | 11 | 0 | 1 | 2 | 6 | 71.99 | $362,889 |

Best finish for 1999: T-3rd at the Southern Farm Bureau Classic

| 2000 | 22 | 73 | 16 | 0 | 0 | 3 | 9 | 70.47 | $669,709 |

Best finish for 2000: T-10th at the GTE Byron Nelson Classic & Bell Canadian Open

| 2001 | 27 | 88 | 19 | 0 | 1 | 2 | 5 | 71.02 | $744,603 |

Best finish for 2001: 2nd at the Bob Hope Chrysler Classic

| 2002 | 31 | 98 | 18 | 0 | 0 | 2 | 6 | 71.23 | $565,294 |

Best finish for 2002: T-9th at the Invensys Classic at Las Vegas

| 2003 | 21 | 67 | 13 | 0 | 2 | 4 | 6 | 70.54 | $719,436 |

Best finish for 2003: T-4th at the Southern Farm Bureau Classic

| 2004 | 14 | 43 | 7 | 0 | 0 | 1 | 4 | 71.02 | $442,872 |

Best finish for 2004: T-9th at the FedEx St. Jude Classic

| 2005 | 1 | 1 | 0 | 0 | 0 | 0 | 0 | 71.00 | |
| 2006 | 22 | 70 | 13 | 0 | 0 | 0 | 3 | 71.47 | $319,597 |

Best finish for 2006: T-12th at the B.C. Open

| 2007 | 18 | 52 | 7 | 0 | 0 | 0 | 4 | 71.69 | $282,388 |

Best finish for 2007: T-12th at the Reno-Tahoe Open

| 2008 | 13 | 38 | 5 | 0 | 0 | 0 | 3 | 71.50 | $156,077 |

Best finish for 2008: T-12th at the Mayakoba Golf Classic

Period Totals	Starts	Rounds Played	Cuts Made	Wins	Top-5s	Top-10s	Top-25s	Scoring Average	Money
	337	1024	180	2	12	28	77	71.32	$6,227,122

Bob Stanton

Year	Starts	Rounds Played	Cuts Made	Wins	Top-5s	Top-10s	Top-25s	Scoring Average	Money
1966	2	8	2	0	0	0	0	75.25	$1,099

Best finish for 1966: T-27th at the British Open

| 1967 | 17 | 55 | 11 | 0 | 0 | 1 | 4 | 73.64 | $9,918 |

Best finish for 1967: T-6th at the Buick Open

| 1968 | 17 | 57 | 12 | 0 | 2 | 3 | 5 | 71.58 | $19,888 |

Best finish for 1968: 3rd at the Western Open

| 1969 | 24 | 85 | 18 | 0 | 1 | 3 | 7 | 72.06 | $31,477 |

Best finish for 1969: 2nd at the AVCO Classic

| 1970 | 32 | 104 | 21 | 0 | 4 | 6 | 10 | 71.89 | $53,939 |

Best finish for 1970: T-2nd at the Florida Citrus Open Invitational

| 1971 | 20 | 55 | 8 | 0 | 0 | 0 | 0 | 73.25 | $2,507 |

Best finish for 1971: T-39th at the Doral-Eastern Open & Southern Open

| 1972 | 10 | 25 | 3 | 0 | 0 | 0 | 1 | 72.72 | $3,274 |

Best finish for 1972: T-22nd at the Monsanto Open

| 1973 | 7 | 20 | 3 | 0 | 0 | 0 | 2 | 73.15 | $2,775 |

Best finish for 1973: T-21st at the Ohio Kings Island Open & Kaiser International Open

Year	Starts	Rounds Played	Cuts Made	Wins	Top-5s	Top-10s	Top-25s	Scoring Average	Money
1974	30	105	22	0	1	5	9	71.50	$43,810

Best finish for 1974: 5th at the World Open

| 1975 | 30 | 97 | 18 | 0 | 0 | 1 | 8 | 72.29 | $29,737 |

Best finish for 1975: T-8th at the Kemper Open

| 1976 | 13 | 33 | 4 | 0 | 0 | 0 | 0 | 74.24 | $1,675 |

Best finish for 1976: T-49th at the Bing Crosby Pro-Am

Period Totals	Starts	Rounds Played	Cuts Made	Wins	Top-5s	Top-10s	Top-25s	Scoring Average	Money
	202	644	122	0	8	19	46	72.38	$200,100

Nate Starks

Year	Starts	Rounds Played	Cuts Made	Wins	Top-5s	Top-10s	Top-25s	Scoring Average	Money
1971	1	2	0	0	0	0	0	77.00	$500
1973	2	8	1	0	0	1	1	74.50	$3,900

Best finish for 1973: T-9th at the Walt Disney World Open

| 1974 | 24 | 75 | 13 | 0 | 0 | 0 | 3 | 72.80 | $13,040 |

Best finish for 1974: T-16th at the Greater New Orleans Open

| 1975 | 21 | 69 | 14 | 0 | 1 | 1 | 4 | 72.77 | $8,966 |

Best finish for 1975: T-20th at the Tallahassee Open

| 1976 | 19 | 60 | 12 | 0 | 0 | 0 | 2 | 72.82 | $7,709 |

Best finish for 1976: T-24th at the Pleasant Valley Classic

| 1977 | 15 | 40 | 5 | 0 | 0 | 0 | 0 | 73.25 | $1,760 |

Best finish for 1977: T-32nd at the Southern Open

| 1978 | 1 | 4 | 1 | 0 | 0 | 0 | 0 | 75.50 | $1,275 |

Best finish for 1978: T-53rd at the U.S. Open

Period Totals	Starts	Rounds Played	Cuts Made	Wins	Top-5s	Top-10s	Top-25s	Scoring Average	Money
	83	258	46	0	1	2	10	72.99	$37,150

B.J. Staten

Year	Starts	Rounds Played	Cuts Made	Wins	Top-5s	Top-10s	Top-25s	Scoring Average	Money
2006	18	46	7	0	1	1	1	71.87	$253,088

Best finish for 2006: T-5th at the John Deere Classic

| 2007 | 7 | 21 | 3 | 0 | 0 | 1 | 1 | 71.48 | $175,505 |

Best finish for 2007: T-9th at the Travelers Championship

Period Totals	Starts	Rounds Played	Cuts Made	Wins	Top-5s	Top-10s	Top-25s	Scoring Average	Money
	25	67	10	0	1	2	2	71.75	$428,593

Kenneth Staton

Year	Starts	Rounds Played	Cuts Made	Wins	Top-5s	Top-10s	Top-25s	Scoring Average	Money
1999	2	4	0	0	0	0	0	72.75	
2002	36	102	14	0	2	2	4	71.45	$453,816

Best finish for 2002: T-4th at the Touchstone Energy Tucson Open

| 2003 | 22 | 57 | 7 | 0 | 0 | 0 | 0 | 71.98 | $83,386 |

Best finish for 2003: T-31st at the Shell Houston Open

Period Totals	Starts	Rounds Played	Cuts Made	Wins	Top-5s	Top-10s	Top-25s	Scoring Average	Money
	60	163	21	0	2	2	4	71.67	$537,202

Iain Steel

Year	Starts	Rounds Played	Cuts Made	Wins	Top-5s	Top-10s	Top-25s	Scoring Average	Money
1996	1	2	0	0	0	0	0	74.50	$1,008
1998	24	62	7	0	0	0	0	73.19	$29,143

Best finish for 1998: T-40th at the United Airlines Hawaiian Open

| 2002 | 1 | 4 | 1 | 0 | 0 | 0 | 0 | 72.00 | $7,560 |

Best finish for 2002: T-73rd at the Bell Canadian Open

Period Totals	Starts	Rounds Played	Cuts Made	Wins	Top-5s	Top-10s	Top-25s	Scoring Average	Money
	26	68	8	0	0	0	0	73.16	$37,710

Jerry Steelsmith

Year	Starts	Rounds Played	Cuts Made	Wins	Top-5s	Top-10s	Top-25s	Scoring Average	Money
1958	1	4	1	0	0	0	1	71.50	$348

Best finish for 1958: T-21st at the Los Angeles Open

| 1961 | 17 | 68 | 16 | 0 | 1 | 4 | 12 | 71.10 | $9,530 |

Best finish for 1961: T-2nd at the Hot Springs Open Invitational

| 1962 | 22 | 87 | 21 | 0 | 3 | 6 | 9 | 71.22 | $14,960 |

Best finish for 1962: T-2nd at the Azalea Open Invitational

| 1963 | 22 | 88 | 20 | 0 | 1 | 3 | 11 | 71.47 | $15,710 |

Best finish for 1963: T-2nd at the Frank Sinatra Open Invitational

| 1964 | 28 | 107 | 24 | 0 | 1 | 7 | 12 | 71.83 | $19,957 |

Best finish for 1964: T-2nd at the Almaden Open

| 1965 | 29 | 96 | 16 | 0 | 0 | 2 | 6 | 72.49 | $10,096 |

Best finish for 1965: T-6th at the Portland Open

| 1966 | 16 | 49 | 9 | 0 | 0 | 0 | 0 | 71.69 | $2,483 |

Best finish for 1966: T-28th at the Greater Seattle-Everett Open Invitational

| 1967 | 27 | 94 | 19 | 0 | 1 | 1 | 7 | 72.64 | $17,651 |

Best finish for 1967: T-4th at the Carling World Open

| 1968 | 27 | 84 | 15 | 0 | 0 | 0 | 3 | 72.60 | $4,610 |

Best finish for 1968: T-14th at the AZALEA Open Invitational

| 1969 | 4 | 12 | 2 | 0 | 0 | 0 | 1 | 72.00 | $1,865 |

Best finish for 1969: T-25th at the Phoenix Open

| 1970 | 5 | 11 | 2 | 0 | 0 | 0 | 1 | 72.55 | $1,162 |

Best finish for 1970: T-24th at the Los Angeles Open

| 1971 | 3 | 8 | 1 | 0 | 0 | 0 | 0 | 73.25 | $526 |

Best finish for 1971: T-40th at the Bing Crosby Pro-Am

| 1972 | 2 | 6 | 1 | 0 | 0 | 0 | 0 | 75.33 | $333 |

Best finish for 1972: T-62nd at the PGA Championship

| 1973 | 1 | 4 | 1 | 0 | 0 | 0 | 0 | 74.50 | $360 |

Best finish for 1973: T-66th at the PGA Championship

| 1974 | 2 | 5 | 1 | 0 | 0 | 0 | 0 | 74.00 | |

Best finish for 1974: 76th at the B.C. Open

| 1975 | 1 | 2 | 0 | 0 | 0 | 0 | 0 | 74.00 | |
| 1976 | 1 | 2 | 0 | 0 | 0 | 0 | 0 | 72.00 | |

Best finish for 1976: T-100 at the B.C. Open

Period Totals	Starts	Rounds Played	Cuts Made	Wins	Top-5s	Top-10s	Top-25s	Scoring Average	Money
	208	727	149	0	7	23	63	72.01	$99,591

Jeff Steinberg

Year	Starts	Rounds Played	Cuts Made	Wins	Top-5s	Top-10s	Top-25s	Scoring Average	Money
1973	5	12	1	0	0	0	0	74.75	$205

Best finish for 1973: T-56th at the B.C. Open

| 1974 | 13 | 32 | 3 | 0 | 0 | 0 | 0 | 75.72 | $502 |

Best finish for 1974: T-63rd at the B.C. Open

| 1975 | 6 | 14 | 1 | 0 | 0 | 0 | 0 | 75.29 | $218 |

Best finish for 1975: T-63rd at the Greater Milwaukee Open

| 1976 | 3 | 8 | 1 | 0 | 0 | 0 | 1 | 73.63 | $925 |

Best finish for 1976: T-25th at the Southern Open

| 1977 | 1 | 2 | 0 | 0 | 0 | 0 | 0 | 76.00 | |
| 1980 | 6 | 14 | 1 | 0 | 0 | 0 | 0 | 73.43 | $444 |

Best finish for 1980: T-57th at the Quad Cities Open

Period Totals	Starts	Rounds Played	Cuts Made	Wins	Top-5s	Top-10s	Top-25s	Scoring Average	Money
	34	82	7	0	0	0	1	74.91	$2,294

Henrik Stenson

Year	Starts	Rounds Played	Cuts Made	Wins	Top-5s	Top-10s	Top-25s	Scoring Average	Money
2001	1	2	0	0	0	0	0	76.00	$1,287
2005	4	16	4	0	1	1	2	70.25	$501,986

Best finish for 2005: T-3rd at the WGC-American Express Championship

| 2006 | 10 | 32 | 8 | 0 | 1 | 1 | 4 | 71.88 | $826,678 |

Best finish for 2006: T-3rd at the Players Championship

| 2007 | 15 | 46 | 10 | 1 | 1 | 2 | 6 | 72.30 | $1,908,632 |

Best finish for 2007: Win at the WGC-Accenture Match Play Championship

| 2008 | 9 | 30 | 8 | 0 | 3 | 4 | 6 | 72.07 | $1,937,992 |

Best finish for 2008: T-3rd at the WGC-Accenture Match Play Championship & British Open

Period Totals	Starts	Rounds Played	Cuts Made	Wins	Top-5s	Top-10s	Top-25s	Scoring Average	Money
	39	126	30	1	6	8	18	71.94	$5,176,575

Scott Sterling

Year	Starts	Rounds Played	Cuts Made	Wins	Top-5s	Top-10s	Top-25s	Scoring Average	Money
2006	1	4	1	0	0	0	0	71.00	$20,280

Best finish for 2006: T-38th at the FedEx St. Jude Classic

| 2008 | 28 | 89 | 17 | 0 | 0 | 2 | 4 | 70.92 | $624,822 |

Best finish for 2008: T-6th at the Children's Miracle Network Classic

Period Totals	Starts	Rounds Played	Cuts Made	Wins	Top-5s	Top-10s	Top-25s	Scoring Average	Money
	29	93	18	0	0	2	4	70.92	$645,102

Earl Stewart

Year	Starts	Rounds Played	Cuts Made	Wins	Top-5s	Top-10s	Top-25s	Scoring Average	Money
1958	5	18	4	0	0	1	3	72.94	$1,642

Best finish for 1958: 7th at the Dallas Open

| 1959 | 2 | 8 | 2 | 0 | 1 | 1 | 1 | 72.25 | $1,967 |

Best finish for 1959: T-2nd at the Dallas Open Invitational

| 1960 | 6 | 25 | 5 | 0 | 1 | 1 | 2 | 71.96 | $2,586 |

Best finish for 1960: T-5th at the Dallas Open Invitational

Year	Starts	Rounds Played	Cuts Made	Wins	Top-5s	Top-10s	Top-25s	Scoring Average	Money
1961	2	8	2	1	1	1	1	71.50	$4,390

Best finish for 1961: Win at the Dallas Open Invitational

| 1962 | 7 | 28 | 7 | 0 | 0 | 1 | 5 | 72.07 | $4,247 |

Best finish for 1962: T-10th at the Houston Classic

| 1963 | 4 | 16 | 3 | 0 | 0 | 0 | 1 | 72.13 | $2,091 |

Best finish for 1963: T-16th at the Houston Classic

| 1964 | 2 | 7 | 1 | 0 | 0 | 0 | 0 | 74.29 | $262 |

Best finish for 1964: T-36th at the Colonial National Invitational

| 1965 | 1 | 4 | 1 | 0 | 0 | 0 | 0 | 76.00 | $150 |

Best finish for 1965: 59th at the Colonial National Invitational

| 1966 | 4 | 14 | 3 | 0 | 0 | 0 | 2 | 72.07 | $2,811 |

Best finish for 1966: T-13th at the Dallas Open Invitational

| 1967 | 5 | 16 | 4 | 0 | 0 | 0 | 3 | 72.00 | $5,102 |

Best finish for 1967: T-18th at the Greater New Orleans Open

| 1968 | 4 | 16 | 4 | 0 | 0 | 1 | 3 | 71.25 | $6,994 |

Best finish for 1968: T-6th at the Colonial National Invitational

| 1969 | 17 | 54 | 10 | 0 | 0 | 1 | 3 | 73.28 | $6,840 |

Best finish for 1969: T-6th at the Heritage Golf Classic

| 1971 | 1 | 2 | 0 | 0 | 0 | 0 | 0 | 74.50 | |
| 1972 | 1 | 2 | 0 | 0 | 0 | 0 | 0 | 80.50 | |

Period Totals	Starts	Rounds Played	Cuts Made	Wins	Top-5s	Top-10s	Top-25s	Scoring Average	Money
	61	218	46	1	3	7	24	72.60	$39,084

PGA Tour career totals from 1942 to 1972

	Starts	Rounds Played	Cuts Made	Wins	Top-5s	Top-10s	Top-25s	Scoring Average	Money
	183	700	168	3	N/A	35	101	N/A	$91,800

Payne Stewart

Year	Starts	Rounds Played	Cuts Made	Wins	Top-5s	Top-10s	Top-25s	Scoring Average	Money
1979	1	2	0	0	0	0	0	75.00	
1981	12	34	6	0	0	1	2	71.71	$14,500

Best finish for 1981: T-9th at the Southern Open

| 1982 | 23 | 71 | 13 | 1 | 2 | 3 | 6 | 72.18 | $85,836 |

Best finish for 1982: Win at the Miller High-Life Quad Cities Open

| 1983 | 32 | 111 | 23 | 1 | 3 | 7 | 12 | 71.43 | $178,909 |

Best finish for 1983: Win at the Walt Disney World Golf Classic

| 1984 | 32 | 112 | 25 | 0 | 4 | 6 | 18 | 71.19 | $291,188 |

Best finish for 1984: 2nd at the Colonial National Invitational & Buick Open

| 1985 | 28 | 100 | 25 | 0 | 6 | 7 | 16 | 70.82 | $288,079 |

Best finish for 1985: 2nd at the Byron Nelson Golf Classic & British Open

| 1986 | 29 | 97 | 23 | 0 | 8 | 16 | 17 | 70.44 | $540,141 |

Best finish for 1986: 2nd at the AT&T Pebble Beach Pro-Am, Colonial National Invitational & Vantage Championship

| 1987 | 29 | 101 | 23 | 1 | 6 | 8 | 18 | 70.50 | $561,226 |

Best finish for 1987: Win at the Hertz Bay Hill Classic

| 1988 | 29 | 107 | 26 | 0 | 5 | 13 | 22 | 69.99 | $589,270 |

Best finish for 1988: T-2nd at the Honda Classic & Provident Classic

| 1989 | 26 | 89 | 20 | 2 | 9 | 12 | 16 | 70.27 | $1,234,902 |

Best finish for 1989: Win at the MCI Heritage Classic & PGA Championship

| 1990 | 28 | 99 | 23 | 2 | 6 | 9 | 17 | 70.85 | $1,085,881 |

Best finish for 1990: Win at the MCI Heritage Classic & GTE Byron Nelson Classic

| 1991 | 21 | 76 | 17 | 1 | 2 | 2 | 12 | 70.64 | $487,935 |

Best finish for 1991: Win at the U.S. Open

| 1992 | 24 | 86 | 20 | 0 | 2 | 5 | 10 | 70.47 | $347,758 |

Best finish for 1992: T-3rd at the Memorial Tournament

| 1993 | 27 | 100 | 23 | 0 | 8 | 12 | 17 | 70.12 | $1,015,985 |

Best finish for 1993: T-2nd at the Nissan Los Angeles Open, Freeport-McMoRan Classic, U.S. Open & Hardee's Golf Classic

| 1994 | 24 | 78 | 15 | 0 | 1 | 2 | 5 | 71.60 | $149,159 |

Best finish for 1994: 5th at the Bob Hope Chrysler Classic

| 1995 | 27 | 97 | 22 | 1 | 4 | 6 | 15 | 70.69 | $866,219 |

Best finish for 1995: Win at the Shell Houston Open

| 1996 | 25 | 87 | 18 | 0 | 4 | 7 | 9 | 70.52 | $538,793 |

Best finish for 1996: 2nd at the Walt Disney World/Oldsmobile Classic

| 1997 | 23 | 87 | 20 | 0 | 2 | 7 | 8 | 70.66 | $538,289 |

Best finish for 1997: T-2nd at the Honda Classic

| 1998 | 21 | 76 | 18 | 0 | 5 | 6 | 13 | 70.63 | $1,191,496 |

Best finish for 1998: 2nd at the U.S. Open & Greater Vancouver Open

| 1999 | 20 | 68 | 16 | 2 | 5 | 5 | 11 | 71.21 | $2,077,950 |

Best finish for 1999: Win at the AT&T Pebble Beach Pro-Am & U.S. Open

Period Totals	Starts	Rounds Played	Cuts Made	Wins	Top-5s	Top-10s	Top-25s	Scoring Average	Money
	481	1678	376	11	82	134	244	70.79	$12,083,519

Ray Stewart

Year	Starts	Rounds Played	Cuts Made	Wins	Top-5s	Top-10s	Top-25s	Scoring Average	Money
1980	1	2	0	0	0	0	0	79.50	
1983	18	50	6	0	0	0	1	73.72	$7,576

Best finish for 1983: T-17th at the Sammy Davis, Jr. - Greater Hartford Open

1984	1	4	1	0	0	0	0	74.75	$892

Best finish for 1984: T-57th at the Canadian Open

1985	1	4	1	0	0	0	0	74.50	$1,002

Best finish for 1985: T-64th at the Canadian Open

1986	2	4	0	0	0	0	0	79.75	$600
1987	30	90	17	0	1	2	3	71.91	$72,136

Best finish for 1987: T-2nd at the Bank of Boston Classic

1988	31	93	16	0	0	1	1	71.92	$45,107

Best finish for 1988: 8th at the Pensacola Open

1989	22	65	12	0	1	3	4	71.75	$133,944

Best finish for 1989: 2nd at the Chattanooga Classic

1990	29	95	18	0	1	2	5	71.59	$139,536

Best finish for 1990: T-4th at the Greater Milwaukee Open

1991	31	93	16	0	0	1	3	71.74	$81,495

Best finish for 1991: T-10th at the Canadian Open

1992	10	27	4	0	0	0	0	72.19	$7,131

Best finish for 1992: T-46th at the Chattanooga Classic

1993	1	4	1	0	0	0	0	73.50	$2,670

Best finish for 1993: T-45th at the Canadian Open

1994	1	2	0	0	0	0	0	75.50	
1995	21	66	11	0	0	0	0	71.61	$48,965

Best finish for 1995: T-27th at the Greater Milwaukee Open

1996	1	2	0	0	0	0	0	73.50	
1997	1	4	1	0	0	0	0	69.50	$4,290

Best finish for 1997: T-45th at the Greater Vancouver Open

1998	1	4	1	0	0	0	0	72.25	$3,700

Best finish for 1998: T-77th at the Greater Vancouver Open

1999	2	6	1	0	0	0	0	72.67	$5,125

Best finish for 1999: T-65th at the Air Canada Championship

2000	1	2	0	0	0	0	0	71.50	
2001	1	2	0	0	0	0	0	71.50	
Period Totals	Starts	Rounds Played	Cuts Made	Wins	Top-5s	Top-10s	Top-25s	Scoring Average	Money
	206	619	106	0	3	9	17	72.08	$554,169

Darron Stiles

Year	Starts	Rounds Played	Cuts Made	Wins	Top-5s	Top-10s	Top-25s	Scoring Average	Money
1999	1	2	0	0	0	0	0	73.50	
2003	29	90	17	0	0	0	3	71.41	$346,694

Best finish for 2003: T-11th at the Greater Hartford Open

2005	26	76	14	0	0	2	4	70.67	$499,827

Best finish for 2005: T-9th at the Chrysler Classic of Tucson & Buick Championship

2006	15	42	7	0	0	0	1	70.93	$157,559

Best finish for 2006: T-22nd at the FedEx St. Jude Classic

2007	24	65	8	0	0	0	2	71.68	$217,379

Best finish for 2007: T-22nd at the John Deere Classic

Period Totals	Starts	Rounds Played	Cuts Made	Wins	Top-5s	Top-10s	Top-25s	Scoring Average	Money
	95	275	46	0	0	2	10	71.21	$1,221,458

Ken Still

Year	Starts	Rounds Played	Cuts Made	Wins	Top-5s	Top-10s	Top-25s	Scoring Average	Money
1958	2	4	0	0	0	0	0	79.00	
1959	1	2	0	0	0	0	0	80.00	
1961	16	64	15	0	1	2	10	71.17	$5,520

Best finish for 1961: T-2nd at the Cajun Classic Open Invitational

1962	11	43	11	0	0	0	5	71.51	$3,665

Best finish for 1962: T-13th at the Sahara Invitational

1963	11	44	9	0	0	0	5	72.39	$4,382

Best finish for 1963: T-18th at the "500" Festival Open Invitational

1964	22	67	10	0	0	1	4	73.30	$3,773

Best finish for 1964: T-6th at the Fresno Open

1965	30	102	21	0	1	3	9	72.21	$14,029

Best finish for 1965: T-3rd at the Almaden Open

1966	32	123	29	0	1	3	10	71.85	$24,024

Best finish for 1966: T-2nd at the Texas Open Invitational

1967	29	98	18	0	3	4	9	72.28	$33,245

Best finish for 1967: 2nd at the Phoenix Open

Year	Starts	Rounds Played	Cuts Made	Wins	Top-5s	Top-10s	Top-25s	Scoring Average	Money
1968	34	124	28	0	4	6	13	71.56	$47,105

Best finish for 1968: 2nd at the Minnesota Golf Classic

1969	32	116	26	2	2	4	9	71.84	$68,600

Best finish for 1969: Win at the Citrus Open & Greater Milwaukee Open

1970	26	80	17	1	3	5	6	72.46	$54,949

Best finish for 1970: Win at the Kaiser International Open

1971	32	106	23	0	1	3	8	72.36	$38,222

Best finish for 1971: 3rd at the U.S. Professional Match Play Championship

1972	32	124	30	0	0	3	11	71.84	$39,796

Best finish for 1972: T-7th at the Greater Hartford Open Invitational

1973	33	127	28	0	1	4	7	71.94	$50,279

Best finish for 1973: T-2nd at the Greater Greensboro Open

1974	26	88	18	0	0	1	8	71.92	$28,713

Best finish for 1974: T-9th at the Westchester Classic

1975	27	94	20	0	0	3	7	72.17	$31,514

Best finish for 1975: T-6th at the Greater Greensboro Open

1976	29	86	15	0	0	1	4	72.67	$17,596

Best finish for 1976: T-7th at the IVB - Bicentennial Golf Classic

1977	30	89	14	0	0	0	2	73.35	$11,213

Best finish for 1977: T-16th at the Florida Citrus Open Invitational

1978	24	62	7	0	0	0	1	73.77	$3,748

Best finish for 1978: T-22nd at the Doral-Eastern Open

1979	14	42	7	0	1	1	1	73.33	$17,089

Best finish for 1979: 3rd at the Ed McMahon Quad City Open

1980	5	10	0	0	0	0	0	73.90	
1981	5	12	1	0	0	0	0	72.58	$438

Best finish for 1981: T-57th at the Quad Cities Open

1982	5	10	0	0	0	0	0	75.10	
1983	2	4	0	0	0	0	0	81.50	$600
1984	1	2	0	0	0	0	0	77.50	
1985	1	2	0	0	0	0	0	75.00	
Period Totals	Starts	Rounds Played	Cuts Made	Wins	Top-5s	Top-10s	Top-25s	Scoring Average	Money
	512	1725	347	3	18	44	129	72.31	$498,500

Adrian Stills

Year	Starts	Rounds Played	Cuts Made	Wins	Top-5s	Top-10s	Top-25s	Scoring Average	Money
1986	22	63	11	0	0	0	0	73.14	$11,662

Best finish for 1986: 35th at the Deposit Guaranty Golf Classic

1987	1	2	0	0	0	0	0	73.50	
1989	1	2	0	0	0	0	0	77.00	
1998	1	2	0	0	0	0	0	83.00	$1,000
Period Totals	Starts	Rounds Played	Cuts Made	Wins	Top-5s	Top-10s	Top-25s	Scoring Average	Money
	25	69	11	0	0	0	0	73.55	$12,662

Dave Stockton

Year	Starts	Rounds Played	Cuts Made	Wins	Top-5s	Top-10s	Top-25s	Scoring Average	Money
1964	2	8	2	0	0	1	2	72.25	$1,203

Best finish for 1964: T-10th at the Almaden Open

1965	24	78	14	0	0	0	4	72.86	$5,410

Best finish for 1965: T-19th at the Canadian Open

1966	29	100	20	0	2	2	5	72.71	$11,159

Best finish for 1966: 4th at the Los Angeles Open Invitational

1967	32	116	26	1	2	6	13	71.63	$55,727

Best finish for 1967: Win at the Colonial National Invitational

1968	29	101	22	2	5	9	15	71.14	$98,004

Best finish for 1968: Win at the Cleveland Open Invitational & Greater Milwaukee Open Invitational

1969	32	116	27	0	5	8	17	71.55	$68,955

Best finish for 1969: T-2nd at the National Airlines Open

1970	32	110	25	1	4	11	18	71.42	$106,973

Best finish for 1970: Win at the PGA Championship

1971	27	98	24	1	3	6	13	71.31	$83,558

Best finish for 1971: Win at the Massachusetts Classic

1972	30	105	24	0	3	7	13	72.10	$61,948

Best finish for 1972: T-3rd at the Greater Greensboro Open & Colonial National Invitational

1973	31	119	28	1	3	6	15	71.45	$91,693

Best finish for 1973: Win at the Greater Milwaukee Open

1974	29	111	26	3	5	7	14	71.49	$153,187

Best finish for 1974: Win at the Glen Campbell Los Angeles Open, Quad Cities Open & Sammy Davis, Jr. - Greater Hartford Open

1975	29	106	24	0	1	5	12	71.56	$72,885

Best finish for 1975: 2nd at the Tournament Players Championship

1976	29	101	21	1	2	5	13	72.12	$94,974

Best finish for 1976: Win at the PGA Championship

Year	Starts	Rounds Played	Cuts Made	Wins	Top-5s	Top-10s	Top-25s	Scoring Average	Money
1977	26	90	18	0	1	3	9	72.43	$58,823

Best finish for 1977: 2nd at the Phoenix Open

1978	26	87	17	0	3	5	8	71.86	$66,516

Best finish for 1978: T-2nd at the U.S. Open

1979	26	87	17	0	0	1	5	72.34	$37,101

Best finish for 1979: T-9th at the Houston Open

1980	25	75	13	0	0	0	3	72.36	$24,152

Best finish for 1980: T-15th at the Kemper Open

1981	23	68	10	0	0	1	3	72.57	$26,347

Best finish for 1981: T-7th at the Greater Greensboro Open

1982	20	59	9	0	0	2	2	73.12	$21,326

Best finish for 1982: T-8th at the Bing Crosby Pro-Am

1983	17	58	11	0	0	0	0	72.76	$11,304

Best finish for 1983: T-28th at the Byron Nelson Golf Classic

1984	19	54	8	0	1	1	2	72.87	$33,613

Best finish for 1984: T-2nd at the Miller High-Life Quad Cities Open

1985	16	48	7	0	0	0	0	72.85	$8,294

Best finish for 1985: T-36th at the Phoenix Open

1986	17	51	7	0	0	0	0	72.61	$10,867

Best finish for 1986: T-32nd at the Hardee's Golf Classic

1987	18	56	11	0	0	0	0	72.36	$19,206

Best finish for 1987: T-38th at the Greater Greensboro Open

1988	13	40	6	0	0	0	0	72.63	$15,846

Best finish for 1988: T-31st at the Kemper Open

1989	10	31	4	0	0	1	1	72.26	$33,240

Best finish for 1989: T-10th at the AT&T Pebble Beach Pro-Am

1990	12	31	3	0	0	0	0	74.35	$6,691

Best finish for 1990: T-70th at the Greater Milwaukee Open

1991	14	30	0	0	0	0	0	72.47	$1,000
1994	2	7	1	0	0	0	0	72.14	$3,845

Best finish for 1994: T-47th at the Southwestern Bell Colonial

1995	1	4	1	0	0	0	0	72.00	$3,122

Best finish for 1995: T-57th at the AT&T Pebble Beach Pro-Am

1997	2	5	0	0	0	0	0	74.20	$1,000
1998	1	2	0	0	0	0	0	73.00	
1999	2	5	1	0	0	0	1	73.20	$20,920

Best finish for 1999: T-25th at the AT&T Pebble Beach Pro-Am

2001	1	2	0	0	0	0	0	74.50	
Period Totals Starts	Rounds Played	Cuts Made	Wins	Top-5s	Top-10s	Top-25s	Scoring Average	Money	
646	2159	427	10	40	87	188	72.09	$1,308,888	

Dave Stockton, Jr.

Year	Starts	Rounds Played	Cuts Made	Wins	Top-5s	Top-10s	Top-25s	Scoring Average	Money
1990	2	4	0	0	0	0	0	74.50	
1991	3	7	0	0	0	0	0	74.57	
1994	31	90	15	0	2	3	4	71.59	$185,209

Best finish for 1994: T-3rd at the Canon Greater Hartford Open & Canon Greater Hartford Open & Deposit Guaranty Golf Classic

1995	32	93	14	0	1	1	2	71.69	$149,579

Best finish for 1995: T-2nd at the Canon Greater Hartford Open

1996	34	92	14	0	2	2	3	71.66	$176,056

Best finish for 1996: T-3rd at the Buick Open

1997	32	99	17	0	0	1	3	71.63	$136,158

Best finish for 1997: T-8th at the B.C. Open

1998	22	65	12	0	0	3	4	70.89	$218,934

Best finish for 1998: T-6th at the Shell Houston Open

1999	32	89	13	0	0	1	2	72.09	$197,127

Best finish for 1999: T-6th at the Canon Greater Hartford Open

2000	31	87	12	0	1	2	3	71.52	$290,426

Best finish for 2000: T-5th at the B.C. Open

2001	21	61	8	0	0	0	1	72.39	$90,132

Best finish for 2001: T-19th at the Michelob Championship at Kingsmill

2002	4	11	0	0	0	0	0	71.82	
2003	31	77	7	0	0	0	3	72.30	$214,876

Best finish for 2003: T-12th at the Chrysler Classic of Greensboro

2004	1	3	0	0	0	0	0	76.00	
Period Totals Starts	Rounds Played	Cuts Made	Wins	Top-5s	Top-10s	Top-25s	Scoring Average	Money	
276	778	112	0	6	13	25	71.80	$1,658,498	

Waddy Stokes

Year	Starts	Rounds Played	Cuts Made	Wins	Top-5s	Top-10s	Top-25s	Scoring Average	Money
1978	2	6	1	0	0	0	0	76.00	

Best finish for 1978: 77th at the Colgate Hall Of Fame Classic

Year	Starts	Rounds Played	Cuts Made	Wins	Top-5s	Top-10s	Top-25s	Scoring Average	Money
1979	8	18	1	0	0	0	0	73.78	$915

Best finish for 1979: T-66th at the B.C. Open

| 1980 | 14 | 28 | 2 | 0 | 0 | 0 | 0 | 74.14 | $1,206 |

Best finish for 1980: T-68th at the Anheuser-Busch Golf Classic

| 1985 | 1 | 2 | 0 | 0 | 0 | 0 | 0 | 75.50 | |
| 1986 | 1 | 4 | 1 | 0 | 0 | 0 | 0 | 70.50 | $636 |

Best finish for 1986: T-63rd at the Provident Classic

Period Totals	Starts	Rounds Played	Cuts Made	Wins	Top-5s	Top-10s	Top-25s	Scoring Average	Money
	26	58	5	0	0	0	0	74.02	$2,757

Andre Stolz

Year	Starts	Rounds Played	Cuts Made	Wins	Top-5s	Top-10s	Top-25s	Scoring Average	Money
2003	1	2	0	0	0	0	0	79.00	$2,000
2004	20	53	7	1	1	1	1	72.21	$808,373

Best finish for 2004: Win at the Michelin Championship at Las Vegas

| 2005 | 12 | 28 | 3 | 0 | 0 | 0 | 1 | 73.75 | $104,775 |

Best finish for 2005: 22nd at the Mercedes Championships

Period Totals	Starts	Rounds Played	Cuts Made	Wins	Top-5s	Top-10s	Top-25s	Scoring Average	Money
	33	83	10	1	1	1	2	72.89	$915,148

Bob Stone

Year	Starts	Rounds Played	Cuts Made	Wins	Top-5s	Top-10s	Top-25s	Scoring Average	Money
1958	1	4	1	0	0	0	0	72.25	

Best finish for 1958: T-41st at the Kansas City Open

1961	1	2	0	0	0	0	0	75.00	
1962	1	4	0	0	0	0	1	67.25	$750
1963	2	6	1	0	0	0	1	74.83	$555

Best finish for 1963: T-24th at the Oklahoma City Open Invitational

| 1965 | 1 | 4 | 1 | 0 | 0 | 0 | 0 | 73.75 | |

Best finish for 1965: T-67th at the Cajun Classic

| 1967 | 4 | 12 | 2 | 0 | 0 | 0 | 1 | 73.00 | $1,151 |

Best finish for 1967: T-17th at the Cajun Classic

| 1968 | 24 | 73 | 11 | 0 | 0 | 1 | 3 | 72.85 | $6,210 |

Best finish for 1968: T-9th at the AZALEA Open Invitational

| 1969 | 22 | 65 | 10 | 0 | 1 | 1 | 3 | 73.38 | $8,782 |

Best finish for 1969: T-2nd at the Azalea Open

| 1970 | 34 | 127 | 29 | 0 | 1 | 3 | 9 | 72.16 | $30,253 |

Best finish for 1970: T-3rd at the Canadian Open

| 1971 | 34 | 117 | 23 | 0 | 1 | 1 | 7 | 72.57 | $23,043 |

Best finish for 1971: T-3rd at the Andy Williams-San Diego Open

| 1972 | 21 | 52 | 5 | 0 | 0 | 0 | 0 | 74.08 | $1,663 |

Best finish for 1972: T-34th at the American Golf Classic

| 1974 | 1 | 4 | 1 | 0 | 0 | 0 | 0 | 76.00 | $935 |

Best finish for 1974: T-45th at the U.S. Open

| 1975 | 4 | 10 | 1 | 0 | 0 | 0 | 0 | 74.90 | |

Best finish for 1975: T-75th at the Danny Thomas Memphis Classic

Period Totals	Starts	Rounds Played	Cuts Made	Wins	Top-5s	Top-10s	Top-25s	Scoring Average	Money
	150	480	85	0	3	6	25	72.87	$73,342

Tom Storey

Year	Starts	Rounds Played	Cuts Made	Wins	Top-5s	Top-10s	Top-25s	Scoring Average	Money
1965	1	2	0	0	0	0	0	78.50	
1966	2	4	0	0	0	0	0	76.00	
1973	1	2	0	0	0	0	0	77.50	
1974	1	2	0	0	0	0	0	82.00	$500
1976	13	34	4	0	1	1	1	73.21	$6,786

Best finish for 1976: T-3rd at the Tallahassee Open

| 1977 | 16 | 39 | 3 | 0 | 0 | 0 | 0 | 74.77 | $1,562 |

Best finish for 1977: T-32nd at the Atlanta Classic

| 1978 | 22 | 66 | 11 | 0 | 0 | 0 | 0 | 72.45 | $8,156 |

Best finish for 1978: T-29th at the Atlanta Classic

| 1979 | 27 | 76 | 11 | 0 | 0 | 1 | 1 | 73.03 | $14,222 |

Best finish for 1979: T-10th at the Hawaiian Open

| 1980 | 23 | 56 | 6 | 0 | 0 | 0 | 0 | 73.45 | $3,349 |

Best finish for 1980: T-57th at the Hawaiian Open

| 1981 | 25 | 69 | 10 | 0 | 0 | 0 | 2 | 72.62 | $9,491 |

Best finish for 1981: T-17th at the Tallahassee Open

| 1983 | 1 | 4 | 0 | 0 | 0 | 0 | 0 | 74.25 | |
| 1993 | 1 | 2 | 0 | 0 | 0 | 0 | 0 | 79.00 | |

Period Totals	Starts	Rounds Played	Cuts Made	Wins	Top-5s	Top-10s	Top-25s	Scoring Average	Money
	133	356	45	0	1	2	4	73.30	$44,067

Dick Stranahan

Year	Starts	Rounds Played	Cuts Made	Wins	Top-5s	Top-10s	Top-25s	Scoring Average	Money
1959	4	15	4	0	0	0	2	72.27	$935

Best finish for 1959: T-13th at the Orange County Open Invitational

1960	7	27	7	0	0	0	1	73.22	$6,316

Best finish for 1960: T-20th at the Hesperia Open Invitational

1961	4	16	4	0	0	0	3	71.44	$1,554

Best finish for 1961: T-20th at the Portland Open Invitational

1962	3	10	3	0	0	0	1	72.50	$446

Best finish for 1962: T-21st at the Baton Rouge Open Invitational

1963	2	8	2	0	0	0	2	73.25	$159

Best finish for 1963: T-25th at the Puerto Rico Open Invitational & Jamaica Open Invitational

1964	12	28	3	0	0	0	0	74.39	$562

Best finish for 1964: T-28th at the Greater Hartford Open

1965	6	16	1	0	0	0	0	74.31	$150

Best finish for 1965: T-54th at the Los Angeles Open

1967	3	7	0	0	0	0	0	76.71	
1968	1	2	0	0	0	0	0	76.00	
1969	1	4	1	0	0	0	0	71.25	$160

Best finish for 1969: T-61st at the Greater Hartford Open

1971	1	2	0	0	0	0	0	77.00	$500
1972	2	6	1	0	0	0	0	73.50	$273

Best finish for 1972: T-47th at the Greater Hartford Open Invitational

1973	2	4	0	0	0	0	0	71.00	$060
1974	1	3	0	0	0	0	0	78.00	
1977	1	2	0	0	0	0	0	73.50	
Period Totals	Starts	Rounds Played	Cuts Made	Wins	Top-5s	Top-10s	Top-25s	Scoring Average	Money
	50	150	26	0	0	0	9	73.47	$11,116

Frank Stranahan

Year	Starts	Rounds Played	Cuts Made	Wins	Top-5s	Top-10s	Top-25s	Scoring Average	Money
1958	32	121	29	1	3	7	18	71.42	$16,881

Best finish for 1958: Win at the Los Angeles Open

1959	20	78	17	0	0	1	10	71.94	$5,675

Best finish for 1959: T-9th at the Greater Greensboro Open Invitational

1960	15	61	14	0	2	3	8	72.02	$12,375

Best finish for 1960: T-2nd at the Texas Open Invitational

1961	8	28	7	0	1	1	2	72.68	$2,185

Best finish for 1961: T-4th at the San Diego Open

1962	5	20	5	0	0	1	5	71.70	$5,242

Best finish for 1962: T-7th at the American Golf Classic

1963	7	26	6	0	0	0	0	73.15	$1,433

Best finish for 1963: T-32nd at the Thunderbird Classic Invitational

1964	14	46	6	0	0	0	0	72.89	$2,505

Best finish for 1964: T-28th at the Los Angeles Open

Period Totals	Starts	Rounds Played	Cuts Made	Wins	Top-5s	Top-10s	Top-25s	Scoring Average	Money
	101	380	84	1	6	13	43	72.03	$46,296

PGA Tour career totals from 1942 to 1964

Starts	Rounds Played	Cuts Made	Wins	Top-5s	Top-10s	Top-25s	Scoring Average	Money
297	N/A	N/A	6	N/A	63	163	N/A	N/A

Curtis Strange

Year	Starts	Rounds Played	Cuts Made	Wins	Top-5s	Top-10s	Top-25s	Scoring Average	Money
1974	1	2	0	0	0	0	0	74.50	
1975	3	8	1	0	0	0	0	75.25	$1,250

Best finish for 1975: T-48th at the World Open

1976	5	14	2	0	0	0	1	74.57	$555

Best finish for 1976: T-15th at the Masters

1977	17	54	11	0	2	2	3	72.13	$32,928

Best finish for 1977: 2nd at the Pensacola Open

1978	28	86	16	0	0	3	7	72.33	$29,346

Best finish for 1978: T-7th at the Colgate Hall Of Fame Classic & Pensacola Open

1979	34	116	24	1	3	9	16	71.37	$138,718

Best finish for 1979: Win at the Pensacola Open

1980	31	114	28	2	7	10	22	70.90	$280,108

Best finish for 1980: Win at the Michelob Houston Open & Manufactures Hanover Westchester Classic

1981	29	102	24	0	4	12	20	70.60	$203,833

Best finish for 1981: 2nd at the Tournament Players Championship

1982	30	113	27	0	10	12	20	70.47	$270,008

Best finish for 1982: 2nd at the Byron Nelson Golf Classic & Texas Open

Year	Starts	Rounds Played	Cuts Made	Wins	Top-5s	Top-10s	Top-25s	Scoring Average	Money
1983	29	105	23	1	3	6	14	71.53	$204,064

Best finish for 1983: Win at the Sammy Davis, Jr. - Greater Hartford Open

1984	26	97	23	1	7	9	18	71.03	$277,773

Best finish for 1984: Win at the LaJet Golf Classic

1985	25	96	22	3	7	7	12	71.15	$543,321

Best finish for 1985: Win at the Honda Classic, Panasonic Las Vegas Invitational & Canadian Open

1986	26	92	20	1	2	6	13	71.49	$256,550

Best finish for 1986: Win at the Houston Open

1987	27	98	23	3	8	11	16	70.56	$925,941

Best finish for 1987: Win at the Canadian Open, Federal Express St. Jude Classic & NEC World Series of Golf

1988	26	94	22	4	4	6	13	70.81	$1,171,444

Best finish for 1988: Win at the Independent Insurance Agent Open, Memorial Tournament, U.S. Open & Nabisco Golf Championship

1989	23	83	20	1	6	9	16	70.61	$756,867

Best finish for 1989: Win at the U.S. Open

1990	21	74	17	0	2	6	10	71.30	$279,167

Best finish for 1990: T-4th at the Nestle Invitational

1991	21	70	14	0	2	3	5	71.30	$345,699

Best finish for 1991: T-2nd at the Phoenix Open & Doral-Ryder Open

1992	18	62	13	0	0	2	6	71.34	$153,039

Best finish for 1992: T-9th at the Honda Classic

1993	24	78	16	0	1	5	8	70.71	$265,396

Best finish for 1993: T-3rd at the Anheuser-Busch Golf Classic

1994	23	83	18	0	3	5	9	70.84	$390,881

Best finish for 1994: T-3rd at the Buick Open

1995	24	84	17	0	2	4	9	70.90	$359,212

Best finish for 1995: T-3rd at the Bob Hope Chrysler Classic

1996	24	79	15	0	0	1	4	71.22	$183,383

Best finish for 1996: T-9th at the Nortel Open

1997	20	63	12	0	1	1	3	71.40	$173,392

Best finish for 1997: T-2nd at the Buick Open

1998	16	50	8	0	0	0	1	72.02	$79,836

Best finish for 1998: T-19th at the British Open

1999	16	48	7	0	0	0	3	72.04	$119,138

Best finish for 1999: T-22nd at the Greater Milwaukee Open

2000	12	39	7	0	0	0	1	71.87	$91,387

Best finish for 2000: T-15th at the MCI Classic

2001	11	30	3	0	1	1	1	72.10	$150,632

Best finish for 2001: T-5th at the FedEx St. Jude Classic

2002	11	26	2	0	0	0	0	74.00	$18,207

Best finish for 2002: T-64th at the Bay Hill Invitational & Buick Challenge

Year	Starts	Rounds Played	Cuts Made	Wins	Top-5s	Top-10s	Top-25s	Scoring Average	Money
2003	8	15	0	0	0	0	0	73.93	
2004	4	7	0	0	0	0	0	76.57	
Period Totals	613	2082	435	17	75	130	251	71.29	$7,702,077

Ron Streck

Year	Starts	Rounds Played	Cuts Made	Wins	Top-5s	Top-10s	Top-25s	Scoring Average	Money
1977	16	50	10	0	0	0	2	72.40	$9,982

Best finish for 1977: T-16th at the Colgate Hall Of Fame Golf Classic

1978	21	57	7	1	1	1	3	72.98	$46,618

Best finish for 1978: Win at the San Antonio Texas Open

1979	35	97	14	0	1	1	3	73.47	$40,584

Best finish for 1979: 4th at the PGA Championship

1980	35	110	23	0	0	4	8	72.34	$55,398

Best finish for 1980: T-6th at the Byron Nelson Golf Classic

1981	31	102	22	1	2	4	11	71.69	$117,455

Best finish for 1981: Win at the Michelob Houston Open

1982	29	99	20	0	1	2	5	72.22	$67,962

Best finish for 1982: T-2nd at the MONY Tournament Of Champions

1983	26	91	18	0	0	4	9	71.76	$68,950

Best finish for 1983: T-7th at the Miller High-Life Quad Cities Open

1984	31	99	19	0	1	2	7	71.97	$73,235

Best finish for 1984: 5th at the Texas Open

1985	27	98	23	0	2	5	6	71.54	$143,448

Best finish for 1985: 2nd at the Isuzu/Andy Williams San Diego Open

1986	25	72	11	0	1	1	2	72.36	$21,605

Best finish for 1986: T-5th at the Deposit Guaranty Golf Classic

1987	31	98	21	0	0	0	4	71.27	$61,756

Best finish for 1987: T-17th at the Hardee's Golf Classic

1988	22	67	12	0	0	0	1	71.04	$31,094

Best finish for 1988: T-23rd at the B.C. Open

1989	11	35	7	0	0	1	4	70.63	$50,444

Best finish for 1989: T-9th at the Anheuser-Busch Golf Classic

Year	Starts	Rounds Played	Cuts Made	Wins	Top-5s	Top-10s	Top-25s	Scoring Average	Money
1990	7	20	3	0	0	0	1	70.70	$10,356

Best finish for 1990: T-21st at the Deposit Guaranty

| 1991 | 6 | 16 | 2 | 0 | 0 | 0 | 1 | 70.75 | $13,914 |

Best finish for 1991: T-15th at the Chattanooga Classic

| 1992 | 6 | 18 | 3 | 0 | 0 | 0 | 0 | 70.83 | $9,917 |

Best finish for 1992: T-27th at the Buick Open

| 1993 | 2 | 6 | 1 | 0 | 0 | 0 | 0 | 70.17 | $885 |

Best finish for 1993: T-44th at the Deposit Guaranty Classic

| 1994 | 4 | 9 | 1 | 0 | 0 | 0 | 0 | 72.78 | $2,189 |

Best finish for 1994: T-69th at the Anheuser-Busch Golf Classic

1995	1	2	0	0	0	0	0	78.50	
1996	1	2	0	0	0	0	0	83.50	
1997	1	2	0	0	0	0	0	76.50	
1999	3	6	0	0	0	0	0	76.33	
Period Totals	Starts	Rounds Played	Cuts Made	Wins	Top-5s	Top-10s	Top-25s	Scoring Average	Money
	371	1156	217	2	9	25	67	72.02	$825,793

Kevin Streelman

Year	Starts	Rounds Played	Cuts Made	Wins	Top-5s	Top-10s	Top-25s	Scoring Average	Money
2003	1	2	0	0	0	0	0	77.50	
2004	1	3	0	0	0	0	0	74.00	
2005	2	6	1	0	0	0	0	70.17	$21,695

Best finish for 2005: T-29th at the U.S. Bank Championship in Milwaukee

| 2008 | 32 | 114 | 24 | 0 | 1 | 4 | 8 | 70.63 | $1,352,705 |

Best finish for 2008: T-4th at the Barclays Classic

Period Totals	Starts	Rounds Played	Cuts Made	Wins	Top-5s	Top-10s	Top-25s	Scoring Average	Money
	36	125	25	0	1	4	8	70.80	$1,374,399

Steve Stricker

Year	Starts	Rounds Played	Cuts Made	Wins	Top-5s	Top-10s	Top-25s	Scoring Average	Money
1990	1	4	1	0	0	0	0	69.75	$3,974

Best finish for 1990: T-35th at the Greater Milwaukee Open

| 1991 | 1 | 2 | 0 | 0 | 0 | 0 | 0 | 71.50 | |
| 1992 | 2 | 6 | 1 | 0 | 0 | 0 | 0 | 71.83 | $5,550 |

Best finish for 1992: T-31st at the Greater Milwaukee Open

| 1993 | 6 | 17 | 2 | 0 | 1 | 1 | 1 | 72.47 | $46,171 |

Best finish for 1993: T-4th at the Canadian Open

| 1994 | 26 | 93 | 21 | 0 | 3 | 4 | 6 | 70.67 | $334,409 |

Best finish for 1994: T-2nd at the Northern Telecom Open

| 1995 | 23 | 83 | 20 | 0 | 1 | 4 | 13 | 70.57 | $438,931 |

Best finish for 1995: 4th at the Nestle Invitational

| 1996 | 22 | 82 | 19 | 2 | 7 | 7 | 10 | 70.76 | $1,385,239 |

Best finish for 1996: Win at the Kemper Open & Motorola Western Open

| 1997 | 20 | 59 | 13 | 0 | 0 | 1 | 3 | 71.76 | $173,952 |

Best finish for 1997: T-7th at the Quad City Classic

| 1998 | 21 | 82 | 20 | 0 | 6 | 10 | 12 | 70.38 | $1,313,948 |

Best finish for 1998: 2nd at the Greater Milwaukee Open

| 1999 | 21 | 69 | 15 | 0 | 1 | 4 | 9 | 71.35 | $665,617 |

Best finish for 1999: 5th at the U.S. Open

| 2000 | 21 | 61 | 11 | 0 | 1 | 1 | 5 | 71.93 | $422,452 |

Best finish for 2000: T-4th at the COMPAQ Classic of New Orleans

| 2001 | 20 | 65 | 15 | 1 | 1 | 4 | 7 | 70.54 | $1,677,229 |

Best finish for 2001: Win at the Accenture Match Play Championship

| 2002 | 22 | 63 | 13 | 0 | 0 | 1 | 9 | 71.13 | $796,713 |

Best finish for 2002: T-6th at the Verizon Byron Nelson Classic

| 2003 | 21 | 56 | 8 | 0 | 0 | 0 | 1 | 71.59 | $150,590 |

Best finish for 2003: T-18th at the Phoenix Open

| 2004 | 27 | 78 | 13 | 0 | 1 | 1 | 3 | 71.45 | $441,906 |

Best finish for 2004: T-4th at the John Deere Classic

| 2005 | 21 | 62 | 10 | 0 | 1 | 1 | 4 | 70.76 | $397,640 |

Best finish for 2005: 4th at the Chrysler Classic of Tucson

| 2006 | 17 | 62 | 15 | 0 | 2 | 7 | 10 | 69.55 | $1,811,811 |

Best finish for 2006: T-2nd at the Booz Allen Classic

| 2007 | 23 | 80 | 19 | 1 | 6 | 9 | 14 | 70.19 | $4,663,077 |

Best finish for 2007: Win at the Barclays Classic

| 2008 | 22 | 72 | 16 | 0 | 2 | 6 | 13 | 70.83 | $2,438,304 |

Best finish for 2008: 2nd at the Mercedes Championships

Period Totals	Starts	Rounds Played	Cuts Made	Wins	Top-5s	Top-10s	Top-25s	Scoring Average	Money
	337	1096	232	4	33	61	120	70.89	$17,167,512

Bobby Stroble

Year	Starts	Rounds Played	Cuts Made	Wins	Top-5s	Top-10s	Top-25s	Scoring Average	Money
1976	9	22	2	0	0	0	0	75.64	$1,435

Best finish for 1976: T-54th at the Western Open

| 1977 | 14 | 35 | 4 | 0 | 0 | 0 | 0 | 74.46 | $1,131 |

Best finish for 1977: T-57th at the Canadian Open

| 1978 | 13 | 34 | 5 | 0 | 0 | 0 | 0 | 74.35 | $995 |

Best finish for 1978: T-49th at the Buick Goodwrench Open

| 1979 | 2 | 3 | 0 | 0 | 0 | 0 | 0 | 74.33 | |
| 1984 | 5 | 12 | 1 | 0 | 0 | 0 | 0 | 73.42 | $998 |

Best finish for 1984: T-31st at the Miller High-Life Quad Cities Open

Period Totals	Starts	Rounds Played	Cuts Made	Wins	Top-5s	Top-10s	Top-25s	Scoring Average	Money
	43	106	12	0	0	0	0	74.55	$4,560

Chris Stroud

Year	Starts	Rounds Played	Cuts Made	Wins	Top-5s	Top-10s	Top-25s	Scoring Average	Money
2004	1	4	1	0	0	0	0	71.50	$10,350

Best finish for 2004: T-57th at the Chrysler Classic of Greensboro

| 2005 | 1 | 2 | 0 | 0 | 0 | 0 | 0 | 73.00 | |
| 2007 | 24 | 66 | 9 | 0 | 1 | 2 | 5 | 71.27 | $675,106 |

Best finish for 2007: T-5th at the Zurich Classic of New Orleans

| 2008 | 29 | 81 | 12 | 0 | 0 | 2 | 4 | 71.54 | $482,405 |

Best finish for 2008: T-6th at the Valero Texas Open

Period Totals	Starts	Rounds Played	Cuts Made	Wins	Top-5s	Top-10s	Top-25s	Scoring Average	Money
	55	153	22	0	1	4	9	71.44	$1,167,862

Glenn Stuart

Year	Starts	Rounds Played	Cuts Made	Wins	Top-5s	Top-10s	Top-25s	Scoring Average	Money
1964	11	28	3	0	1	1	1	73.54	$3,400

Best finish for 1964: T-2nd at the New Orleans Open

| 1965 | 15 | 47 | 8 | 0 | 0 | 1 | 1 | 73.43 | $2,808 |

Best finish for 1965: T-7th at the Greater Greensboro Open

| 1966 | 7 | 16 | 1 | 0 | 0 | 0 | 0 | 75.75 | $562 |

Best finish for 1966: T-29th at the Bing Crosby National Professional-Amateur

| 1967 | 3 | 6 | 0 | 0 | 0 | 0 | 0 | 77.67 | |
| 1968 | 2 | 6 | 1 | 0 | 0 | 0 | 0 | 74.83 | |

Best finish for 1968: T-72nd at the Buick Open Invitational

| 1969 | 4 | 8 | 0 | 0 | 0 | 0 | 0 | 76.13 | |
| 1974 | 1 | 2 | 0 | 0 | 0 | 0 | 0 | 80.00 | |

Period Totals	Starts	Rounds Played	Cuts Made	Wins	Top-5s	Top-10s	Top-25s	Scoring Average	Money
	43	113	13	0	1	2	2	74.39	$6,770

Larry Stubblefield

Year	Starts	Rounds Played	Cuts Made	Wins	Top-5s	Top-10s	Top-25s	Scoring Average	Money
1972	3	6	0	0	0	0	0	75.33	$500
1973	23	60	7	0	0	0	1	73.35	$3,280

Best finish for 1973: T-19th at the Southern Open

| 1974 | 9 | 20 | 1 | 0 | 0 | 0 | 1 | 73.05 | $1,400 |

Best finish for 1974: T-16th at the Southern Open

| 1975 | 4 | 10 | 1 | 0 | 0 | 0 | 0 | 73.10 | $210 |

Best finish for 1975: T-40th at the Tallahassee Open

Period Totals	Starts	Rounds Played	Cuts Made	Wins	Top-5s	Top-10s	Top-25s	Scoring Average	Money
	39	96	9	0	0	0	2	73.39	$5,390

Hideyo Sugimoto

Year	Starts	Rounds Played	Cuts Made	Wins	Top-5s	Top-10s	Top-25s	Scoring Average	Money
1965	4	12	2	0	0	0	1	74.08	$2,062

Best finish for 1965: T-13th at the Carling Open

| 1966 | 1 | 4 | 1 | 0 | 0 | 0 | 0 | 74.75 | $1,118 |

Best finish for 1966: T-27th at the Carling World Open

| 1967 | 2 | 2 | 0 | 0 | 0 | 0 | 0 | 76.00 | |
| 1968 | 17 | 52 | 9 | 0 | 0 | 0 | 0 | 73.21 | $3,379 |

Best finish for 1968: T-31st at the American Golf Classic

| 1969 | 1 | 4 | 1 | 0 | 0 | 0 | 0 | 72.75 | $167 |

Best finish for 1969: T-60th at the Hawaiian Open

Period Totals	Starts	Rounds Played	Cuts Made	Wins	Top-5s	Top-10s	Top-25s	Scoring Average	Money
	25	74	13	0	0	0	1	73.49	$6,726

Buddy Sullivan

Year	Starts	Rounds Played	Cuts Made	Wins	Top-5s	Top-10s	Top-25s	Scoring Average	Money
1958	9	33	7	0	0	0	3	71.76	$1,012

Best finish for 1958: T-18th at the St. Paul Open

Year	Starts	Rounds Played	Cuts Made	Wins	Top-5s	Top-10s	Top-25s	Scoring Average	Money
1959	4	11	2	0	0	0	0	76.09	$093

Best finish for 1959: T-59th at the Houston Classic

1960	6	24	6	0	0	1	3	71.54	$2,198

Best finish for 1960: T-9th at the Eastern Open Invitational

1961	10	40	9	0	1	2	8	70.35	$6,287

Best finish for 1961: T-3rd at the Home Of The Sun Open Invitational

1962	6	24	6	0	0	2	3	71.71	$3,777

Best finish for 1962: T-6th at the Tucson Open Invitational

1963	1	2	0	0	0	0	0	74.50	
1964	5	14	1	0	0	0	0	73.93	$375

Best finish for 1964: T-32nd at the Greater Hartford Open

1968	2	4	0	0	0	0	0	73.25	
1969	2	8	1	0	0	0	1	74.50	$750

Best finish for 1969: T-16th at the Alameda County Open

1970	2	5	0	0	0	0	0	77.20	
1971	2	5	0	0	0	0	0	76.00	
1972	2	5	0	0	0	0	0	78.20	
Period Totals	**Starts**	**Rounds Played**	**Cuts Made**	**Wins**	**Top-5s**	**Top-10s**	**Top-25s**	**Scoring Average**	**Money**
	51	175	32	0	1	5	18	72.50	$14,491

Chip Sullivan

Year	Starts	Rounds Played	Cuts Made	Wins	Top-5s	Top-10s	Top-25s	Scoring Average	Money
1988	1	2	0	0	0	0	0	73.00	
1991	1	2	0	0	0	0	0	76.00	
1997	27	77	11	0	0	0	0	72.29	$41,019

Best finish for 1997: T-36th at the CVS Charity Classic

1999	3	8	1	0	0	0	0	73.25	$5,225

Best finish for 1999: T-65th at the MCI Classic

2001	1	2	0	0	0	0	0	74.50	
2002	1	4	1	0	0	0	0	70.75	$12,966

Best finish for 2002: T-40th at the Michelob Championship at Kingsmill

2003	2	6	1	0	0	0	0	73.50	$11,675

Best finish for 2003: T-59th at the FBR Capital Open

2004	1	4	1	0	0	0	0	71.75	$34,250

Best finish for 2004: T-31st at the PGA Championship

2006	1	2	0	0	0	0	0	75.50	$2,250
2007	1	2	0	0	0	0	0	79.00	$2,500
2008	6	18	3	0	0	0	0	72.67	$45,559

Best finish for 2008: T-33rd at the Zurich Classic of New Orleans

Period Totals	**Starts**	**Rounds Played**	**Cuts Made**	**Wins**	**Top-5s**	**Top-10s**	**Top-25s**	**Scoring Average**	**Money**
	45	127	18	0	0	0	0	72.65	$155,445

Dennis Sullivan

Year	Starts	Rounds Played	Cuts Made	Wins	Top-5s	Top-10s	Top-25s	Scoring Average	Money
1971	1	2	0	0	0	0	0	83.00	
1978	1	2	0	0	0	0	0	76.50	$600
1979	23	68	11	0	0	0	2	73.09	$12,922

Best finish for 1979: T-15th at the Ed McMahon Quad City Open

1980	16	32	0	0	0	0	0	75.34	
Period Totals	**Starts**	**Rounds Played**	**Cuts Made**	**Wins**	**Top-5s**	**Top-10s**	**Top-25s**	**Scoring Average**	**Money**
	41	104	11	0	0	0	2	74.04	$13,522

Mike Sullivan

Year	Starts	Rounds Played	Cuts Made	Wins	Top-5s	Top-10s	Top-25s	Scoring Average	Money
1977	20	51	6	0	1	1	1	73.04	$10,936

Best finish for 1977: T-4th at the Doral-Eastern Open

1978	28	87	15	0	1	3	8	72.30	$40,995

Best finish for 1978: 2nd at the Buick Goodwrench Open

1979	31	96	16	0	0	2	7	72.57	$38,596

Best finish for 1979: T-9th at the Anheuser-Busch Golf Classic & San Antonio Texas Open

1980	29	95	19	1	4	8	11	71.49	$147,759

Best finish for 1980: Win at the Southern Open

1981	32	108	23	0	3	4	11	71.75	$95,444

Best finish for 1981: 2nd at the Southern Open

1982	29	97	19	0	1	1	6	72.07	$38,607

Best finish for 1982: T-4th at the Pensacola Open

1983	29	99	20	0	1	3	11	71.49	$101,097

Best finish for 1983: T-3rd at the Honda Inverrary Classic

1984	26	92	18	0	1	5	9	71.78	$111,844

Best finish for 1984: T-5th at the Georgia-Pacific Atlanta Golf Classic

1985	26	78	11	0	0	2	6	72.00	$45,032

Best finish for 1985: T-8th at the Greater Milwaukee Open

Year	Starts	Rounds Played	Cuts Made	Wins	Top-5s	Top-10s	Top-25s	Scoring Average	Money
1986	25	82	22	0	2	3	8	71.11	$150,407

Best finish for 1986: T-2nd at the Walt Disney World/Oldsmobile Classic

| 1987 | 27 | 85 | 16 | 0 | 0 | 1 | 6 | 71.89 | $79,455 |

Best finish for 1987: T-9th at the Doral-Ryder Open

| 1988 | 30 | 92 | 17 | 0 | 2 | 2 | 6 | 71.33 | $115,994 |

Best finish for 1988: T-4th at the Canadian Open

| 1989 | 25 | 79 | 17 | 1 | 2 | 2 | 5 | 71.66 | $273,962 |

Best finish for 1989: Win at the Independent Insurance Agent Open

| 1990 | 27 | 82 | 16 | 0 | 0 | 1 | 3 | 72.11 | $81,038 |

Best finish for 1990: T-9th at the B.C. Open

| 1991 | 29 | 88 | 16 | 0 | 0 | 0 | 5 | 71.39 | $106,048 |

Best finish for 1991: T-16th at the MCI Heritage Classic

| 1992 | 28 | 80 | 13 | 0 | 0 | 2 | 3 | 71.30 | $115,441 |

Best finish for 1992: T-8th at the United Airlines Hawaiian Open & Buick Open

| 1993 | 15 | 47 | 9 | 0 | 0 | 0 | 2 | 72.28 | $68,587 |

Best finish for 1993: T-12th at the Kmart Greater Greensboro Open

| 1994 | 26 | 71 | 11 | 1 | 2 | 2 | 3 | 71.55 | $299,586 |

Best finish for 1994: Win at the B.C. Open

| 1995 | 26 | 86 | 17 | 0 | 0 | 1 | 3 | 71.93 | $168,986 |

Best finish for 1995: 8th at the NEC World Series of Golf

| 1996 | 28 | 85 | 17 | 0 | 0 | 1 | 2 | 71.49 | $126,069 |

Best finish for 1996: T-8th at the Kemper Open

| 1997 | 14 | 38 | 5 | 0 | 0 | 0 | 2 | 71.79 | $43,122 |

Best finish for 1997: T-21st at the Buick Classic

| 1998 | 8 | 18 | 2 | 0 | 0 | 0 | 1 | 72.11 | $21,582 |

Best finish for 1998: T-22nd at the Shell Houston Open

| 1999 | 7 | 17 | 2 | 0 | 0 | 0 | 0 | 73.06 | $17,105 |

Best finish for 1999: T-31st at the Greater Milwaukee Open

| 2000 | 3 | 10 | 2 | 0 | 0 | 0 | 0 | 70.80 | $10,458 |

Best finish for 2000: T-47th at the Greater Milwaukee Open

2001	2	4	0	0	0	0	0	72.50	
2002	3	5	0	0	0	0	0	74.20	
2003	1	2	0	0	0	0	0	71.00	
2004	1	4	1	0	0	0	0	72.25	$5,520

Best finish for 2004: 78th at the B.C. Open

Period Totals	Starts	Rounds Played	Cuts Made	Wins	Top-5s	Top-10s	Top-25s	Scoring Average	Money
	575	1778	330	3	20	44	119	71.81	$2,313,670

Boyd Summerhays

Year	Starts	Rounds Played	Cuts Made	Wins	Top-5s	Top-10s	Top-25s	Scoring Average	Money
2004	8	17	1	0	0	0	1	72.47	$37,126

Best finish for 2004: T-25th at the AT&T Pebble Beach National Pro-Am

| 2005 | 8 | 16 | 0 | 0 | 0 | 0 | 0 | 73.31 | |
| 2006 | 13 | 29 | 2 | 0 | 0 | 0 | 0 | 72.83 | $20,794 |

Best finish for 2006: 67th at the Booz Allen Classic

Period Totals	Starts	Rounds Played	Cuts Made	Wins	Top-5s	Top-10s	Top-25s	Scoring Average	Money
	29	62	3	0	0	0	1	72.85	$57,920

David Sutherland

Year	Starts	Rounds Played	Cuts Made	Wins	Top-5s	Top-10s	Top-25s	Scoring Average	Money
1991	28	76	11	0	1	1	1	72.33	$71,629

Best finish for 1991: T-3rd at the Buick Southern Open

| 1992 | 10 | 30 | 5 | 0 | 0 | 0 | 1 | 72.00 | $11,297 |

Best finish for 1992: T-22nd at the Deposit Guaranty Classic

| 1995 | 1 | 3 | 0 | 0 | 0 | 0 | 0 | 72.67 | |
| 1997 | 28 | 82 | 14 | 0 | 1 | 2 | 6 | 71.09 | $288,663 |

Best finish for 1997: T-2nd at the Greater Milwaukee Open

| 1998 | 31 | 93 | 17 | 0 | 0 | 0 | 7 | 71.48 | $239,330 |

Best finish for 1998: T-16th at the Players Championship

| 1999 | 31 | 90 | 15 | 0 | 1 | 2 | 3 | 71.72 | $338,129 |

Best finish for 1999: T-3rd at the Bell Canadian Open

| 2000 | 32 | 106 | 22 | 0 | 0 | 2 | 6 | 71.29 | $500,421 |

Best finish for 2000: T-7th at the Shell Houston Open

| 2001 | 2 | 5 | 1 | 0 | 0 | 0 | 0 | 71.20 | $7,752 |

Best finish for 2001: T-54th at the Buick Challenge

| 2002 | 11 | 34 | 6 | 0 | 0 | 0 | 0 | 71.68 | $63,052 |

Best finish for 2002: T-37th at the Nissan Open

| 2003 | 25 | 73 | 13 | 0 | 0 | 1 | 6 | 71.23 | $451,442 |

Best finish for 2003: 9th at the Reno-Tahoe Open

| 2004 | 16 | 43 | 6 | 0 | 0 | 0 | 2 | 71.74 | $216,419 |

Best finish for 2004: T-11th at the Bell Canadian Open

Period Totals	Starts	Rounds Played	Cuts Made	Wins	Top-5s	Top-10s	Top-25s	Scoring Average	Money
	215	635	110	0	3	8	32	71.56	$2,188,134

Kevin Sutherland

Year	Starts	Rounds Played	Cuts Made	Wins	Top-5s	Top-10s	Top-25s	Scoring Average	Money
1991	1	4	1	0	0	0	0	73.75	$2,030

Best finish for 1991: T-68th at the USF&G Classic

| 1995 | 1 | 3 | 0 | 0 | 0 | 0 | 0 | 76.00 | |
| 1996 | 33 | 107 | 21 | 0 | 0 | 1 | 4 | 71.58 | $145,828 |

Best finish for 1996: T-9th at the Canon Greater Hartford Open

| 1997 | 27 | 85 | 17 | 0 | 2 | 4 | 6 | 70.91 | $455,860 |

Best finish for 1997: 2nd at the Shell Houston Open

| 1998 | 30 | 100 | 22 | 0 | 1 | 3 | 9 | 70.98 | $445,429 |

Best finish for 1998: T-3rd at the Buick Invitational

| 1999 | 29 | 96 | 21 | 0 | 1 | 4 | 8 | 70.80 | $665,641 |

Best finish for 1999: T-4th at the Buick Invitational

| 2000 | 27 | 94 | 21 | 0 | 1 | 4 | 12 | 70.32 | $730,635 |

Best finish for 2000: T-5th at the Buick Invitational

| 2001 | 30 | 98 | 21 | 0 | 3 | 7 | 13 | 70.10 | $1,525,572 |

Best finish for 2001: 2nd at the Touchstone Energy Tucson Open

| 2002 | 28 | 90 | 18 | 1 | 1 | 3 | 7 | 71.18 | $1,577,689 |

Best finish for 2002: Win at the WGC-Accenture Match Play Championship

| 2003 | 27 | 94 | 21 | 0 | 1 | 3 | 9 | 70.66 | $1,092,918 |

Best finish for 2003: T-5th at the John Deere Classic

| 2004 | 27 | 82 | 16 | 0 | 0 | 4 | 5 | 71.05 | $931,760 |

Best finish for 2004: T-6th at The Players Championship

| 2005 | 26 | 87 | 19 | 0 | 0 | 3 | 9 | 70.70 | $845,875 |

Best finish for 2005: T-6th at the Buick Invitational

| 2006 | 29 | 96 | 21 | 0 | 0 | 0 | 7 | 70.68 | $751,626 |

Best finish for 2006: T-11th at the Reno-Tahoe Open & Frys.Com Open-Vegas

| 2007 | 25 | 85 | 17 | 0 | 1 | 3 | 7 | 71.16 | $1,351,942 |

Best finish for 2007: 2nd at the AT&T Pebble Beach National Pro-Am

| 2008 | 26 | 98 | 22 | 0 | 3 | 6 | 12 | 70.22 | $2,581,311 |

Best finish for 2008: T-2nd at the Barclays Classic & Frys.Com Open

Period Totals	Starts	Rounds Played	Cuts Made	Wins	Top-5s	Top-10s	Top-25s	Scoring Average	Money
	366	1219	258	1	14	45	108	70.82	$13,104,117

Hal Sutton

Year	Starts	Rounds Played	Cuts Made	Wins	Top-5s	Top-10s	Top-25s	Scoring Average	Money
1980	3	10	2	0	0	0	0	74.40	

Best finish for 1980: 52nd at the Masters

| 1981 | 7 | 19 | 3 | 0 | 0 | 0 | 0 | 74.74 | $2,100 |

Best finish for 1981: T-47th at the British Open

| 1982 | 31 | 111 | 24 | 1 | 6 | 8 | 15 | 71.18 | $237,367 |

Best finish for 1982: Win at the Disney World

| 1983 | 31 | 117 | 26 | 2 | 6 | 12 | 16 | 70.95 | $428,865 |

Best finish for 1983: Win at the Tournament Players Championship & PGA Championship

| 1984 | 27 | 98 | 23 | 0 | 4 | 11 | 16 | 71.09 | $229,903 |

Best finish for 1984: T-2nd at the B.C. Open

| 1985 | 26 | 101 | 23 | 2 | 5 | 7 | 16 | 71.10 | $365,340 |

Best finish for 1985: Win at the St. Jude Memphis Classic & Southwest Golf Classic

| 1986 | 28 | 95 | 23 | 2 | 5 | 9 | 11 | 71.06 | $430,934 |

Best finish for 1986: Win at the Phoenix Open & Memorial Tournament

| 1987 | 27 | 94 | 21 | 0 | 5 | 6 | 17 | 70.61 | $501,096 |

Best finish for 1987: T-2nd at the Phoenix Open, Panasonic Las Vegas Invitational & Seiko-Tucson Open

| 1988 | 28 | 90 | 16 | 0 | 0 | 1 | 8 | 71.86 | $139,561 |

Best finish for 1988: 10th at the Los Angeles Open

| 1989 | 31 | 100 | 20 | 0 | 3 | 7 | 12 | 70.66 | $425,203 |

Best finish for 1989: T-2nd at the USF&G Classic & Anheuser-Busch Golf Classic

| 1990 | 28 | 90 | 18 | 0 | 1 | 4 | 8 | 71.49 | $209,584 |

Best finish for 1990: T-5th at the Nissan Los Angeles Open

| 1991 | 28 | 101 | 23 | 0 | 2 | 5 | 13 | 70.32 | $347,408 |

Best finish for 1991: T-3rd at the GTE Byron Nelson Classic

| 1992 | 29 | 76 | 8 | 0 | 0 | 0 | 1 | 72.64 | $41,934 |

Best finish for 1992: T-14th at the GTE Byron Nelson Classic

| 1993 | 29 | 85 | 13 | 0 | 0 | 1 | 2 | 72.42 | $74,144 |

Best finish for 1993: T-9th at the Buick Invitational of California

| 1994 | 29 | 97 | 23 | 0 | 3 | 4 | 15 | 70.64 | $540,162 |

Best finish for 1994: T-2nd at the Shell Houston Open & Federal Express St. Jude Classic

| 1995 | 31 | 94 | 17 | 1 | 4 | 4 | 8 | 70.86 | $557,433 |

Best finish for 1995: Win at the B.C. Open

| 1996 | 29 | 88 | 17 | 0 | 0 | 1 | 7 | 71.49 | $196,522 |

Best finish for 1996: T-10th at the GTE Byron Nelson Classic

| 1997 | 29 | 96 | 18 | 0 | 4 | 4 | 9 | 70.90 | $455,228 |

Best finish for 1997: T-3rd at the Buick Challenge

Year	Starts	Rounds Played	Cuts Made	Wins	Top-5s	Top-10s	Top-25s	Scoring Average	Money
1998	30	104	21	2	4	9	16	70.25	$1,834,740

Best finish for 1998: Win at the Westin Texas Open & The Tour Championship

Year	Starts	Rounds Played	Cuts Made	Wins	Top-5s	Top-10s	Top-25s	Scoring Average	Money
1999	25	90	22	1	5	13	17	70.58	$2,132,578

Best finish for 1999: Win at the Bell Canadian Open

Year	Starts	Rounds Played	Cuts Made	Wins	Top-5s	Top-10s	Top-25s	Scoring Average	Money
2000	25	89	20	2	7	11	14	70.24	$3,065,420

Best finish for 2000: Win at the Players Championship & Greater Greensboro Chrysler Classic

Year	Starts	Rounds Played	Cuts Made	Wins	Top-5s	Top-10s	Top-25s	Scoring Average	Money
2001	26	95	23	1	3	3	9	70.18	$1,723,946

Best finish for 2001: Win at the Shell Houston Open

Year	Starts	Rounds Played	Cuts Made	Wins	Top-5s	Top-10s	Top-25s	Scoring Average	Money
2002	26	73	11	0	0	0	3	72.16	$324,557

Best finish for 2002: T-12th at the MasterCard Colonial

Year	Starts	Rounds Played	Cuts Made	Wins	Top-5s	Top-10s	Top-25s	Scoring Average	Money
2003	24	81	16	0	2	4	6	70.56	$944,488

Best finish for 2003: T-3rd at the MCI Heritage

Year	Starts	Rounds Played	Cuts Made	Wins	Top-5s	Top-10s	Top-25s	Scoring Average	Money
2004	16	42	5	0	0	0	1	72.12	$105,698

Best finish for 2004: T-25th at the HP Classic of New Orleans

Year	Starts	Rounds Played	Cuts Made	Wins	Top-5s	Top-10s	Top-25s	Scoring Average	Money
2005	10	23	2	0	0	0	0	74.22	$18,320

Best finish for 2005: 74th at the Valero Texas Open

Year	Starts	Rounds Played	Cuts Made	Wins	Top-5s	Top-10s	Top-25s	Scoring Average	Money
2006	1	2	0	0	0	0	0	74.50	
Period Totals	**Starts**	**Rounds Played**	**Cuts Made**	**Wins**	**Top-5s**	**Top-10s**	**Top-25s**	**Scoring Average**	**Money**
	654	2161	438	14	69	124	240	71.13	$15,332,532

Mike Swartz

Year	Starts	Rounds Played	Cuts Made	Wins	Top-5s	Top-10s	Top-25s	Scoring Average	Money
1988	1	2	0	0	0	0	0	74.00	$1,000
1989	1	4	1	0	0	0	1	68.75	$10,500

Best finish for 1989: T-16th at the Phoenix Open

Year	Starts	Rounds Played	Cuts Made	Wins	Top-5s	Top-10s	Top-25s	Scoring Average	Money
1990	1	2	0	0	0	0	0	72.00	
1992	1	2	0	0	0	0	0	81.00	$1,000
1993	2	4	0	0	0	0	0	71.25	
1995	1	2	0	0	0	0	0	76.00	
1996	29	73	8	0	0	1	1	72.41	$77,616

Best finish for 1996: T-7th at the FedEx St. Jude Classic

Year	Starts	Rounds Played	Cuts Made	Wins	Top-5s	Top-10s	Top-25s	Scoring Average	Money
1997	1	2	0	0	0	0	0	74.50	$1,000
Period Totals	**Starts**	**Rounds Played**	**Cuts Made**	**Wins**	**Top-5s**	**Top-10s**	**Top-25s**	**Scoring Average**	**Money**
	37	91	9	0	0	1	2	72.54	$91,116

Roger Tambellini

Year	Starts	Rounds Played	Cuts Made	Wins	Top-5s	Top-10s	Top-25s	Scoring Average	Money
2004	28	78	12	0	0	0	2	72.09	$235,164

Best finish for 2004: T-14th at the BellSouth Classic

Year	Starts	Rounds Played	Cuts Made	Wins	Top-5s	Top-10s	Top-25s	Scoring Average	Money
2006	25	61	7	0	0	0	1	72.38	$116,685

Best finish for 2006: T-21st at the Shell Houston Open

Period Totals	Starts	Rounds Played	Cuts Made	Wins	Top-5s	Top-10s	Top-25s	Scoring Average	Money
	53	139	19	0	0	0	3	72.22	$351,849

Hidemichi Tanaka

Year	Starts	Rounds Played	Cuts Made	Wins	Top-5s	Top-10s	Top-25s	Scoring Average	Money
1996	4	16	4	0	0	0	1	72.38	$38,999

Best finish for 1996: T-23rd at the NEC World Series of Golf

Year	Starts	Rounds Played	Cuts Made	Wins	Top-5s	Top-10s	Top-25s	Scoring Average	Money
1997	2	4	0	0	0	0	0	74.25	
1998	1	2	0	0	0	0	0	72.00	
1999	5	12	1	0	0	0	0	75.08	$8,543

Best finish for 1999: T-70th at the Memorial Tournament

Year	Starts	Rounds Played	Cuts Made	Wins	Top-5s	Top-10s	Top-25s	Scoring Average	Money
2000	3	12	3	0	0	0	2	71.67	$124,917

Best finish for 2000: T-11th at the American Express Championship

Year	Starts	Rounds Played	Cuts Made	Wins	Top-5s	Top-10s	Top-25s	Scoring Average	Money
2001	7	14	2	0	0	0	1	73.50	$68,650

Best finish for 2001: T-17th at the Accenture Match Play Championship

Year	Starts	Rounds Played	Cuts Made	Wins	Top-5s	Top-10s	Top-25s	Scoring Average	Money
2002	31	102	20	0	1	2	10	70.72	$766,423

Best finish for 2002: T-4th at the Disney Golf Classic

Year	Starts	Rounds Played	Cuts Made	Wins	Top-5s	Top-10s	Top-25s	Scoring Average	Money
2003	30	112	25	0	3	4	9	70.51	$1,024,678

Best finish for 2003: T-4th at the Bell Canadian Open & Southern Farm Bureau Classic

Year	Starts	Rounds Played	Cuts Made	Wins	Top-5s	Top-10s	Top-25s	Scoring Average	Money
2004	27	89	18	0	2	2	7	71.26	$795,206

Best finish for 2004: T-3rd at the B.C. Open

Year	Starts	Rounds Played	Cuts Made	Wins	Top-5s	Top-10s	Top-25s	Scoring Average	Money
2005	34	102	19	0	1	2	5	70.89	$686,113

Best finish for 2005: T-3rd at the Chrysler Championship

Year	Starts	Rounds Played	Cuts Made	Wins	Top-5s	Top-10s	Top-25s	Scoring Average	Money
2006	31	73	7	0	0	0	0	73.27	$69,435

Best finish for 2006: T-56th at the Buick Invitational

Period Totals	Starts	Rounds Played	Cuts Made	Wins	Top-5s	Top-10s	Top-25s	Scoring Average	Money
	175	538	99	0	7	10	35	71.41	$3,582,965

Toru Taniguchi

Year	Starts	Rounds Played	Cuts Made	Wins	Top-5s	Top-10s	Top-25s	Scoring Average	Money
1998	1	2	0	0	0	0	0	74.00	$1,316
2001	9	22	4	0	2	2	2	72.23	$590,914

Best finish for 2001: 3rd at the Accenture Match Play Championship

2002	8	20	4	0	1	1	1	72.30	$205,273

Best finish for 2002: 5th at the Nissan Open

2003	4	8	0	0	0	0	0	78.38	$11,179
2005	7	16	1	0	0	0	1	73.31	$46,384

Best finish for 2005: T-24th at the Buick Invitational

2006	2	6	1	0	0	0	0	75.67	$37,500

Best finish for 2006: T-59th at the WGC-American Express Championship

2007	4	10	1	0	0	0	0	74.40	$26,094

Best finish for 2007: T-60th at the British Open

2008	7	16	3	0	0	0	0	72.75	$122,620

Best finish for 2008: T-26th at the WGC-CA Championship

Period Totals	Starts	Rounds Played	Cuts Made	Wins	Top-5s	Top-10s	Top-25s	Scoring Average	Money
	42	100	14	0	3	3	4	73.45	$1,041,281

Alan Tapie

Year	Starts	Rounds Played	Cuts Made	Wins	Top-5s	Top-10s	Top-25s	Scoring Average	Money
1974	2	8	2	0	0	0	1	75.38	$3,245

Best finish for 1974: T-13th at the British Open

1975	28	92	18	0	0	2	7	72.16	$23,416

Best finish for 1975: T-9th at the Houston Open

1976	25	87	18	0	0	0	7	72.21	$25,258

Best finish for 1976: T-12th at the Memorial Tournament

1977	26	82	14	0	0	1	4	72.83	$18,372

Best finish for 1977: T-8th at the Bob Hope Chrysler Classic

1978	26	94	21	0	2	7	10	71.68	$58,865

Best finish for 1978: T-5th at the Greater Greensboro Open & American Express Westchester Classic

1979	31	103	21	0	2	4	11	71.87	$86,763

Best finish for 1979: T-2nd at the Anheuser-Busch Golf Classic

1980	31	96	16	0	0	0	8	72.35	$39,328

Best finish for 1980: T-12th at the Western Open

1981	15	50	10	0	0	0	1	73.28	$13,954

Best finish for 1981: T-14th at the Atlanta Classic

1982	10	30	4	0	0	0	0	72.20	$5,350

Best finish for 1982: T-30th at the Joe Garagiola Tucson Open

1985	1	2	0	0	0	0	0	77.00	$544
1987	1	2	0	0	0	0	0	77.50	$600
1989	1	3	0	0	0	0	0	73.67	

Period Totals	Starts	Rounds Played	Cuts Made	Wins	Top-5s	Top-10s	Top-25s	Scoring Average	Money
	197	649	124	0	4	14	49	72.33	$275,694

Phil Tataurangi

Year	Starts	Rounds Played	Cuts Made	Wins	Top-5s	Top-10s	Top-25s	Scoring Average	Money
1994	24	66	9	0	0	0	2	71.89	$47,587

Best finish for 1994: T-16th at the Buick Classic

1996	1	4	1	0	0	0	0	71.00	$3,742

Best finish for 1996: T-49th at the Kemper Open

1997	27	76	12	0	1	2	6	71.37	$256,930

Best finish for 1997: 3rd at the Bell Canadian Open

1998	28	79	13	0	1	1	5	71.58	$336,820

Best finish for 1998: 2nd at the Michelob Championship at Kingsmill

1999	29	71	8	0	1	2	3	72.69	$232,078

Best finish for 1999: T-4th at the Air Canada Championship

2000	4	5	0	0	0	0	0	80.60	
2001	12	32	4	0	0	0	2	71.59	$141,581

Best finish for 2001: T-12th at the Greater Greensboro Chrysler Classic

2002	25	84	19	1	3	4	8	70.58	$1,644,686

Best finish for 2002: Win at the Invensys Classic at Las Vegas

2003	11	30	6	0	0	1	3	72.50	$354,083

Best finish for 2003: T-7th at the AT&T Pebble Beach National Pro-Am

2004	8	15	1	0	0	0	0	74.00	$6,540

Best finish for 2004: T-60th at the Reno-Tahoe Open

2006	20	46	4	0	0	0	0	73.54	$57,792

Best finish for 2006: T-34th at the EDS Byron Nelson Championship

2007	8	21	2	0	0	0	1	72.29	$77,102

Best finish for 2007: T-14th at the Frys.Com Open-Vegas

Year	Starts	Rounds Played	Cuts Made	Wins	Top-5s	Top-10s	Top-25s	Scoring Average	Money
2008	6	13	0	0	0	0	0	74.00	
Period Totals	Starts	Rounds Played	Cuts Made	Wins	Top-5s	Top-10s	Top-25s	Scoring Average	Money
	203	542	79	1	6	10	30	72.03	$3,158,942

Harry Taylor

Year	Starts	Rounds Played	Cuts Made	Wins	Top-5s	Top-10s	Top-25s	Scoring Average	Money
1965	1	4	1	0	0	0	0	72.25	

Best finish for 1965: T-50th at the Almaden Open

| 1980 | 16 | 45 | 7 | 0 | 0 | 0 | 1 | 72.71 | $6,283 |

Best finish for 1980: T-24th at the Southern Open

| 1986 | 22 | 62 | 10 | 0 | 0 | 0 | 3 | 72.60 | $23,985 |

Best finish for 1986: T-15th at the Anheuser-Busch Golf Classic

| 1987 | 30 | 81 | 17 | 0 | 0 | 0 | 4 | 71.89 | $53,485 |

Best finish for 1987: T-11th at the Manufactures Hanover Westchester Classic

| 1988 | 22 | 55 | 9 | 0 | 0 | 0 | 2 | 72.00 | $32,432 |

Best finish for 1988: T-12th at the Provident Classic

| 1989 | 4 | 15 | 4 | 0 | 0 | 0 | 0 | 69.60 | $6,081 |

Best finish for 1989: T-26th at the Deposit Guaranty Golf Classic

| 1990 | 19 | 58 | 11 | 0 | 1 | 1 | 1 | 71.67 | $45,647 |

Best finish for 1990: T-5th at the Chattanooga Classic

| 1991 | 3 | 8 | 1 | 0 | 0 | 0 | 0 | 69.63 | $4,355 |

Best finish for 1991: T-29th at the Chattanooga Classic

| 1992 | 3 | 6 | 0 | 0 | 0 | 0 | 0 | 73.33 | |
| 1993 | 29 | 88 | 17 | 0 | 0 | 0 | 4 | 71.39 | $105,846 |

Best finish for 1993: T-12th at the Greater Milwaukee Open

| 1994 | 11 | 27 | 4 | 0 | 0 | 0 | 1 | 71.63 | $16,482 |

Best finish for 1994: T-19th at the Buick Southern Open

| 1995 | 28 | 85 | 14 | 0 | 0 | 1 | 2 | 71.42 | $94,265 |

Best finish for 1995: T-7th at the Bob Hope Chrysler Classic

1996	2	4	0	0	0	0	0	72.25	
Period Totals	Starts	Rounds Played	Cuts Made	Wins	Top-5s	Top-10s	Top-25s	Scoring Average	Money
	190	538	95	0	1	2	18	71.78	$388,863

Joe Taylor

Year	Starts	Rounds Played	Cuts Made	Wins	Top-5s	Top-10s	Top-25s	Scoring Average	Money
1958	1	4	1	0	0	0	1	70.75	

Best finish for 1958: T-25th at the Greenbrier Invitational

| 1960 | 1 | 2 | 0 | 0 | 0 | 0 | 0 | 74.50 | |
| 1961 | 2 | 8 | 2 | 0 | 0 | 0 | 0 | 72.38 | $463 |

Best finish for 1961: T-31st at the Phoenix Open Invitational

| 1962 | 1 | 3 | 1 | 0 | 0 | 0 | 0 | 75.67 | |
| 1964 | 9 | 28 | 4 | 0 | 0 | 0 | 1 | 73.82 | $825 |

Best finish for 1964: T-13th at the Tucson Open

| 1965 | 6 | 21 | 3 | 0 | 0 | 0 | 0 | 73.76 | $094 |

Best finish for 1965: T-48th at the Bing Crosby Pro-Am & Bob Hope Classic

| 1966 | 4 | 17 | 4 | 0 | 0 | 0 | 1 | 72.47 | $1,344 |

Best finish for 1966: T-17th at the Phoenix Open Invitational

| 1967 | 4 | 14 | 2 | 0 | 0 | 0 | 0 | 73.93 | $279 |

Best finish for 1967: T-38th at the Tucson Open

1968	1	2	0	0	0	0	0	75.00	
Period Totals	Starts	Rounds Played	Cuts Made	Wins	Top-5s	Top-10s	Top-25s	Scoring Average	Money
	29	99	17	0	0	0	3	73.44	$3,005

Steve Taylor

Year	Starts	Rounds Played	Cuts Made	Wins	Top-5s	Top-10s	Top-25s	Scoring Average	Money
1974	1	2	0	0	0	0	0	75.50	
1975	6	12	0	0	0	0	0	74.58	
1976	12	36	6	0	0	0	2	73.75	$3,794

Best finish for 1976: T-20th at the San Antonio Texas Open

| 1977 | 18 | 56 | 10 | 0 | 1 | 1 | 3 | 72.89 | $17,498 |

Best finish for 1977: T-2nd at the Southern Open

| 1978 | 8 | 18 | 1 | 0 | 0 | 0 | 0 | 75.56 | $989 |

Best finish for 1978: T-34th at the Anheuser-Busch Golf Classic

1979	1	2	0	0	0	0	0	76.00	
Period Totals	Starts	Rounds Played	Cuts Made	Wins	Top-5s	Top-10s	Top-25s	Scoring Average	Money
	46	126	17	0	1	1	5	73.77	$22,281

Vaughn Taylor

Year	Starts	Rounds Played	Cuts Made	Wins	Top-5s	Top-10s	Top-25s	Scoring Average	Money
1998	1	2	0	0	0	0	0	76.00	
2000	1	2	0	0	0	0	0	76.00	

Year	Starts	Rounds Played	Cuts Made	Wins	Top-5s	Top-10s	Top-25s	Scoring Average	Money
2004	27	82	16	1	2	4	8	70.67	$1,176,434

Best finish for 2004: Win at the Reno-Tahoe Open

2005	32	99	19	1	3	4	8	70.76	$1,827,574

Best finish for 2005: Win at the Reno-Tahoe Open

2006	26	88	18	0	3	6	9	70.86	$1,791,195

Best finish for 2006: T-3rd at the Verizon Heritage

2007	28	91	18	0	2	3	5	71.20	$1,322,169

Best finish for 2007: 3rd at the Arnold Palmer Invitational

2008	32	103	21	0	1	2	7	70.84	$1,053,423

Best finish for 2008: T-2nd at the Ginn sur Mer Classic

Period Totals	Starts	Rounds Played	Cuts Made	Wins	Top-5s	Top-10s	Top-25s	Scoring Average	Money
	147	467	92	2	11	19	37	70.91	$7,170,794

Lance Ten Broeck

Year	Starts	Rounds Played	Cuts Made	Wins	Top-5s	Top-10s	Top-25s	Scoring Average	Money
1975	1	4	1	0	0	0	0	74.75	

Best finish for 1975: T-49th at the U.S. Open

1980	29	81	12	0	0	0	1	73.31	$10,230

Best finish for 1980: T-24th at the Southern Open

1981	19	44	4	0	0	0	1	73.70	$5,784

Best finish for 1981: T-21st at the B.C. Open

1982	25	77	14	0	0	0	4	72.38	$24,374

Best finish for 1982: T-12th at the Hall of Fame

1983	19	57	10	0	0	0	3	72.04	$20,050

Best finish for 1983: T-12th at the Miller High-Life Quad Cities Open

1984	17	52	9	0	0	2	5	72.27	$40,785

Best finish for 1984: T-9th at the Western Open & Sammy Davis, Jr. - Greater Hartford Open

1985	34	95	12	0	0	0	1	73.26	$24,191

Best finish for 1985: T-20th at the Canadian Open

1986	5	14	3	0	0	1	2	72.50	$18,165

Best finish for 1986: T-10th at the Honda Classic

1987	4	9	1	0	0	0	0	73.56	$1,920

Best finish for 1987: T-73rd at the Doral-Ryder Open

1988	27	81	13	0	0	3	6	71.20	$65,988

Best finish for 1988: T-7th at the Southern Open

1989	28	78	13	0	2	2	8	71.00	$108,838

Best finish for 1989: T-3rd at the Deposit Guaranty Golf Classic

1990	34	96	15	0	0	0	4	72.31	$72,900

Best finish for 1990: T-13th at the Phoenix Open

1991	14	51	11	0	1	2	3	71.00	$146,089

Best finish for 1991: 2nd at the Chattanooga Classic

1992	34	107	19	0	0	0	6	71.58	$114,617

Best finish for 1992: T-11th at the New England Classic

1993	32	97	16	0	0	0	3	71.69	$88,263

Best finish for 1993: T-17th at the Shell Houston Open

1994	11	30	5	0	0	0	0	73.13	$10,843

Best finish for 1994: T-50th at the Deposit Guaranty Golf Classic

1995	3	6	0	0	0	0	0	75.17	
1996	6	10	0	0	0	0	0	74.90	
1997	3	6	0	0	0	0	0	75.33	
1998	4	10	1	0	0	0	0	74.40	$3,030

Best finish for 1998: T-68th at the CVS Charity Classic

2008	1	2	0	0	0	0	0	83.50	

Period Totals	Starts	Rounds Played	Cuts Made	Wins	Top-5s	Top-10s	Top-25s	Scoring Average	Money
	350	1007	159	0	3	10	47	72.29	$756,066

Brian Tennyson

Year	Starts	Rounds Played	Cuts Made	Wins	Top-5s	Top-10s	Top-25s	Scoring Average	Money
1986	4	9	1	0	0	0	0	73.44	$5,209

Best finish for 1986: T-31st at the Vantage Championship

1987	5	14	2	0	0	0	0	71.50	$5,294

Best finish for 1987: T-35th at the Kemper Open

1988	32	99	19	0	1	1	5	71.51	$109,040

Best finish for 1988: T-4th at the Independent Insurance Agent Open

1989	31	102	22	0	1	2	8	71.13	$190,345

Best finish for 1989: T-2nd at the Hardee's Golf Classic

1990	30	96	19	0	5	8	11	71.03	$443,508

Best finish for 1990: T-2nd at the Bob Hope Chrysler Classic

1991	32	91	13	0	1	1	3	71.87	$112,302

Best finish for 1991: T-5th at the Northern Telecom Open

1992	17	49	7	0	0	0	2	72.31	$38,614

Best finish for 1992: T-13th at the Deposit Guaranty Classic

Year	Starts	Rounds Played	Cuts Made	Wins	Top-5s	Top-10s	Top-25s	Scoring Average	Money
1994	1	2	0	0	0	0	0	73.00	
1996	22	75	15	0	0	1	3	71.52	$96,329

Best finish for 1996: T-9th at the Quad City Classic

1997	2	4	0	0	0	0	0	77.00	$1,000
Period Totals	Starts	Rounds Played	Cuts Made	Wins	Top-5s	Top-10s	Top-25s	Scoring Average	Money
	176	541	98	0	8	13	32	71.56	$1,001,642

Peter Teravainen

Year	Starts	Rounds Played	Cuts Made	Wins	Top-5s	Top-10s	Top-25s	Scoring Average	Money
1980	16	31	1	0	0	0	0	74.55	$1,472

Best finish for 1980: T-36th at the Canadian Open

1981	2	6	1	0	0	0	0	75.17	$612

Best finish for 1981: T-68th at the Glen Campbell Los Angeles Open

1984	1	2	0	0	0	0	0	75.00	$429
1985	1	3	0	0	0	0	0	74.67	$1,015
1986	1	2	0	0	0	0	0	77.00	$600
1989	1	4	1	0	0	0	0	73.75	$3,840

Best finish for 1989: T-73rd at the British Open

1991	1	4	1	0	0	0	0	72.50	$5,040

Best finish for 1991: T-92nd at the British Open

1996	1	2	0	0	0	0	0	77.00	$1,000
1997	4	14	3	0	0	0	0	74.14	$32,289

Best finish for 1997: 45th at the NEC World Series of Golf

Period Totals	Starts	Rounds Played	Cuts Made	Wins	Top-5s	Top-10s	Top-25s	Scoring Average	Money
	28	68	7	0	0	0	0	74.51	$46,296

Ron Terry

Year	Starts	Rounds Played	Cuts Made	Wins	Top-5s	Top-10s	Top-25s	Scoring Average	Money
1972	1	2	0	0	0	0	0	84.00	$500
1976	6	14	1	0	0	0	0	73.79	$304

Best finish for 1976: T-59th at the Ohio Kings Island Open

1977	2	4	0	0	0	0	0	76.50	
1979	21	61	10	0	0	0	1	72.75	$11,359

Best finish for 1979: T-13th at the American Optical Classic

1980	21	56	7	0	0	0	1	73.18	$4,430

Best finish for 1980: T-25th at the Tallahassee Open

1983	2	5	1	0	0	0	0	75.20	$3,687

Best finish for 1983: T-34th at the U.S. Open

1984	1	2	0	0	0	0	0	77.00	$600
1989	1	2	0	0	0	0	0	73.00	
1992	1	2	0	0	0	0	0	74.50	
Period Totals	Starts	Rounds Played	Cuts Made	Wins	Top-5s	Top-10s	Top-25s	Scoring Average	Money
	56	148	19	0	0	0	2	73.43	$20,879

Doug Tewell

Year	Starts	Rounds Played	Cuts Made	Wins	Top-5s	Top-10s	Top-25s	Scoring Average	Money
1974	1	4	1	0	0	0	0	73.25	$075

Best finish for 1974: T-70th at the Phoenix Open

1975	11	26	2	0	0	0	0	73.92	$790

Best finish for 1975: T-46th at the Western Open

1976	14	31	3	0	0	0	0	73.42	$1,064

Best finish for 1976: T-55th at the NBC Tucson Open

1977	21	72	16	0	1	2	5	71.93	$32,952

Best finish for 1977: T-4th at the Kemper Open

1978	25	80	15	0	0	1	2	72.38	$23,289

Best finish for 1978: T-6th at the Andy Williams-San Diego Open

1979	26	88	17	0	2	5	10	71.33	$84,850

Best finish for 1979: T-2nd at the San Antonio Texas Open

1980	27	91	20	2	3	5	11	72.05	$163,854

Best finish for 1980: Win at the Sea Pines Heritage Classic & IVB Golf Classic

1981	28	87	17	0	0	1	7	72.06	$43,640

Best finish for 1981: T-6th at the MONY Tournament Of Champions

1982	25	90	20	0	1	4	8	71.74	$78,770

Best finish for 1982: T-4th at the Sea Pines Heritage Classic

1983	27	87	18	0	0	4	12	71.45	$112,287

Best finish for 1983: T-6th at the Bob Hope Chrysler Classic, USF&G Classic & Tournament Players Championship

1984	25	81	18	0	3	5	9	71.49	$118,588

Best finish for 1984: T-3rd at the USF&G Classic

1985	25	79	18	0	2	4	9	71.70	$137,426

Best finish for 1985: T-2nd at the Phoenix Open

1986	30	95	20	1	3	10	15	70.77	$311,785

Best finish for 1986: Win at the Los Angeles Open

| 1987 | 25 | 76 | 14 | 1 | 1 | 4 | 6 | 71.46 | $153,216 |

Best finish for 1987: Win at the Pensacola Open

| 1988 | 27 | 79 | 16 | 0 | 1 | 3 | 8 | 71.81 | $209,242 |

Best finish for 1988: 2nd at the Buick Open

| 1989 | 25 | 79 | 16 | 0 | 1 | 1 | 5 | 71.82 | $176,107 |

Best finish for 1989: T-2nd at the Buick Open

| 1990 | 25 | 78 | 14 | 0 | 1 | 2 | 6 | 71.46 | $137,795 |

Best finish for 1990: T-3rd at the B.C. Open

| 1991 | 22 | 68 | 13 | 0 | 0 | 2 | 6 | 71.25 | $137,360 |

Best finish for 1991: T-6th at the Federal Express St. Jude Classic

| 1992 | 23 | 76 | 16 | 0 | 0 | 0 | 7 | 70.41 | $159,856 |

Best finish for 1992: T-11th at the Doral-Ryder Open

| 1993 | 20 | 63 | 11 | 0 | 0 | 1 | 6 | 71.65 | $132,478 |

Best finish for 1993: T-7th at the Sprint Western Open

| 1994 | 27 | 84 | 18 | 0 | 0 | 3 | 7 | 71.35 | $177,388 |

Best finish for 1994: T-7th at the Walt Disney World/Oldsmobile Classic

| 1995 | 21 | 55 | 7 | 0 | 0 | 0 | 2 | 71.47 | $45,878 |

Best finish for 1995: T-11th at the Deposit Guaranty Golf Classic

| 1997 | 10 | 26 | 4 | 0 | 0 | 0 | 0 | 72.65 | $15,374 |

Best finish for 1997: T-38th at the LaCantera Texas Open

| 1998 | 15 | 46 | 9 | 0 | 1 | 2 | 3 | 70.61 | $200,466 |

Best finish for 1998: T-4th at the Canon Greater Hartford Open

| 1999 | 8 | 30 | 7 | 0 | 0 | 0 | 0 | 71.00 | $65,152 |

Best finish for 1999: T-26th at the Phoenix Open

| 2002 | 1 | 4 | 1 | 0 | 0 | 0 | 0 | 71.75 | $8,080 |

Best finish for 2002: T-68th at the WorldCom Classic

| 2005 | 1 | 4 | 1 | 0 | 0 | 0 | 0 | 75.25 | $10,088 |

Best finish for 2005: 73rd at the MCI Heritage

Period Totals	Starts	Rounds Played	Cuts Made	Wins	Top-5s	Top-10s	Top-25s	Scoring Average	Money
	535	1679	332	4	20	59	144	71.62	$2,737,850

Roland Thatcher

Year	Starts	Rounds Played	Cuts Made	Wins	Top-5s	Top-10s	Top-25s	Scoring Average	Money
2003	2	5	0	0	0	0	0	74.80	$1,000
2004	23	66	9	0	1	1	2	71.56	$247,986

Best finish for 2004: T-5th at the Reno-Tahoe Open

| 2005 | 26 | 73 | 12 | 0 | 0 | 1 | 3 | 71.44 | $326,299 |

Best finish for 2005: T-8th at the FedEx St. Jude Classic

| 2006 | 1 | 4 | 1 | 0 | 0 | 0 | 1 | 70.50 | $74,250 |

Best finish for 2006: T-19th at the Shell Houston Open

| 2008 | 15 | 41 | 7 | 0 | 0 | 2 | 4 | 71.68 | $445,212 |

Best finish for 2008: T-7th at the EDS Byron Nelson Championship

Period Totals	Starts	Rounds Played	Cuts Made	Wins	Top-5s	Top-10s	Top-25s	Scoring Average	Money
	67	189	29	0	1	4	10	71.60	$1,094,748

Tim Thelen

Year	Starts	Rounds Played	Cuts Made	Wins	Top-5s	Top-10s	Top-25s	Scoring Average	Money
1984	1	4	1	0	0	0	0	74.25	

Best finish for 1984: 71st at the Houston Coca-Cola Open

1985	1	2	0	0	0	0	0	78.00	
1993	1	2	0	0	0	0	0	71.00	
1997	1	2	0	0	0	0	0	75.00	
1998	1	2	0	0	0	0	0	76.50	
1999	1	2	0	0	0	0	0	77.50	$1,750
2000	2	6	1	0	0	0	0	75.33	$7,656

Best finish for 2000: T-67th at the Shell Houston Open

| 2001 | 7 | 17 | 2 | 0 | 0 | 0 | 1 | 71.35 | $53,780 |

Best finish for 2001: T-12th at the B.C. Open

2002	3	6	0	0	0	0	0	73.50	$2,000
2003	1	2	0	0	0	0	0	77.00	$2,000
2004	5	12	1	0	0	0	0	71.75	$21,306

Best finish for 2004: T-29th at the Valero Texas Open

2005	1	2	0	0	0	0	0	75.00	$2,000
2007	2	4	0	0	0	0	0	75.50	$2,500
2008	1	2	0	0	0	0	0	78.50	

Period Totals	Starts	Rounds Played	Cuts Made	Wins	Top-5s	Top-10s	Top-25s	Scoring Average	Money
	28	65	5	0	0	0	1	73.58	$92,992

Stan Thirsk

Year	Starts	Rounds Played	Cuts Made	Wins	Top-5s	Top-10s	Top-25s	Scoring Average	Money
1959	1	2	0	0	0	0	0	79.50	
1962	2	4	1	0	0	0	0	75.75	

Best finish for 1962: T-200 at the PGA Championship

Year	Starts	Rounds Played	Cuts Made	Wins	Top-5s	Top-10s	Top-25s	Scoring Average	Money
1963	4	17	4	0	0	0	2	73.53	$1,555

Best finish for 1963: T-17th at the Cajun Classic Open Invitational

Year	Starts	Rounds Played	Cuts Made	Wins	Top-5s	Top-10s	Top-25s	Scoring Average	Money
1964	6	20	3	0	0	0	0	73.85	$550

Best finish for 1964: T-26th at the Palm Springs Classic

Year	Starts	Rounds Played	Cuts Made	Wins	Top-5s	Top-10s	Top-25s	Scoring Average	Money
1965	4	13	1	0	0	1	1	73.00	$2,850

Best finish for 1965: T-7th at the Bob Hope Classic

Year	Starts	Rounds Played	Cuts Made	Wins	Top-5s	Top-10s	Top-25s	Scoring Average	Money
1966	6	20	3	0	0	0	0	74.95	$1,199

Best finish for 1966: T-37th at the PGA Championship

Year	Starts	Rounds Played	Cuts Made	Wins	Top-5s	Top-10s	Top-25s	Scoring Average	Money
1967	1	2	0	0	0	0	0	72.00	
1968	4	12	2	0	0	0	0	74.67	

Best finish for 1968: T-57th at the Bing Crosby National Professional-Amateur

Year	Starts	Rounds Played	Cuts Made	Wins	Top-5s	Top-10s	Top-25s	Scoring Average	Money
1969	2	8	2	0	0	0	0	75.38	$541

Best finish for 1969: T-33rd at the Alameda County Open

Year	Starts	Rounds Played	Cuts Made	Wins	Top-5s	Top-10s	Top-25s	Scoring Average	Money
1971	2	4	0	0	0	0	0	76.00	
1972	1	4	1	0	0	0	0	76.50	$333

Best finish for 1972: T-72nd at the PGA Championship

Year	Starts	Rounds Played	Cuts Made	Wins	Top-5s	Top-10s	Top-25s	Scoring Average	Money
1973	1	2	0	0	0	0	0	76.50	$500
1975	1	2	0	0	0	0	0	76.50	$500
1976	1	4	1	0	0	0	0	76.25	$450

Best finish for 1976: T-71st at the PGA Championship

Year	Starts	Rounds Played	Cuts Made	Wins	Top-5s	Top-10s	Top-25s	Scoring Average	Money
1978	1	2	0	0	0	0	0	81.50	$303
1979	1	2	0	0	0	0	0	84.00	$600
Period Totals	Starts	Rounds Played	Cuts Made	Wins	Top-5s	Top-10s	Top-25s	Scoring Average	Money
	38	118	18	0		1	3	74.85	$9,382

Dave Thomas

Year	Starts	Rounds Played	Cuts Made	Wins	Top-5s	Top-10s	Top-25s	Scoring Average	Money
1958	5	19	4	0	1	1	3	76.11	$2,127

Best finish for 1958: 2nd at the British Open

Year	Starts	Rounds Played	Cuts Made	Wins	Top-5s	Top-10s	Top-25s	Scoring Average	Money
1959	3	12	3	0	0	0	1	72.83	$802

Best finish for 1959: T-15th at the Greater Greensboro Open Invitational

Year	Starts	Rounds Played	Cuts Made	Wins	Top-5s	Top-10s	Top-25s	Scoring Average	Money
1961	1	4	1	0	0	0	1	75.00	

Best finish for 1961: T-23rd at the British Open

Year	Starts	Rounds Played	Cuts Made	Wins	Top-5s	Top-10s	Top-25s	Scoring Average	Money
1962	1	4	1	0	0	1	1	73.25	

Best finish for 1962: T-8th at the British Open

Year	Starts	Rounds Played	Cuts Made	Wins	Top-5s	Top-10s	Top-25s	Scoring Average	Money
1963	2	8	2	0	0	0	1	72.25	$1,168

Best finish for 1963: T-22nd at the Sahara Invitational

Year	Starts	Rounds Played	Cuts Made	Wins	Top-5s	Top-10s	Top-25s	Scoring Average	Money
1964	12	37	6	0	0	1	2	73.27	$1,366

Best finish for 1964: T-9th at the Azalea Open

Year	Starts	Rounds Played	Cuts Made	Wins	Top-5s	Top-10s	Top-25s	Scoring Average	Money
1965	2	8	2	0	0	0	0	74.75	$795

Best finish for 1965: 39th at the British Open

Year	Starts	Rounds Played	Cuts Made	Wins	Top-5s	Top-10s	Top-25s	Scoring Average	Money
1966	2	6	1	0	1	1	1	73.00	$4,780

Best finish for 1966: T-2nd at the British Open

Year	Starts	Rounds Played	Cuts Made	Wins	Top-5s	Top-10s	Top-25s	Scoring Average	Money
1967	7	18	3	0	0	0	0	73.61	$1,614

Best finish for 1967: T-40th at the Pensacola Open

Year	Starts	Rounds Played	Cuts Made	Wins	Top-5s	Top-10s	Top-25s	Scoring Average	Money
1968	1	4	1	0	0	0	0	75.50	$403

Best finish for 1968: T-27th at the British Open

Year	Starts	Rounds Played	Cuts Made	Wins	Top-5s	Top-10s	Top-25s	Scoring Average	Money
1969	1	3	0	0	0	0	0	76.00	
1970	1	4	1	0	0	0	0	74.25	$420

Best finish for 1970: T-32nd at the British Open

Year	Starts	Rounds Played	Cuts Made	Wins	Top-5s	Top-10s	Top-25s	Scoring Average	Money
1972	1	2	0	0	0	0	0	77.50	$125
Period Totals	Starts	Rounds Played	Cuts Made	Wins	Top-5s	Top-10s	Top-25s	Scoring Average	Money
	39	129	25	0	2	4	10	73.99	$13,600

Steve Thomas

Year	Starts	Rounds Played	Cuts Made	Wins	Top-5s	Top-10s	Top-25s	Scoring Average	Money
1982	1	3	1	0	0	0	0	71.67	$1,355

Best finish for 1982: T-36th at the USF&G Classic

Year	Starts	Rounds Played	Cuts Made	Wins	Top-5s	Top-10s	Top-25s	Scoring Average	Money
1984	5	12	1	0	0	0	0	74.67	$658

Best finish for 1984: 76th at the Anheuser-Busch Golf Classic

Year	Starts	Rounds Played	Cuts Made	Wins	Top-5s	Top-10s	Top-25s	Scoring Average	Money
1985	1	1	0	0	0	0	0	74.00	
1988	30	77	9	0	0	1	2	72.58	$22,669

Best finish for 1988: T-8th at the Deposit Guaranty Golf Classic

Year	Starts	Rounds Played	Cuts Made	Wins	Top-5s	Top-10s	Top-25s	Scoring Average	Money
1989	7	15	1	0	0	0	0	73.40	$502

Best finish for 1989: T-47th at the Deposit Guaranty Golf Classic

Year	Starts	Rounds Played	Cuts Made	Wins	Top-5s	Top-10s	Top-25s	Scoring Average	Money
1993	1	4	1	0	0	0	0	71.00	$597

Best finish for 1993: T-70th at the Deposit Guaranty Classic

Period Totals	Starts	Rounds Played	Cuts Made	Wins	Top-5s	Top-10s	Top-25s	Scoring Average	Money
	45	112	13	0	0	1	2	72.85	$25,781

Barney Thompson

Year	Starts	Rounds Played	Cuts Made	Wins	Top-5s	Top-10s	Top-25s	Scoring Average	Money
1972	2	4	0	0	0	0	0	77.75	$500
1973	2	8	1	0	0	0	0	75.25	$308

Best finish for 1973: T-57th at the Walt Disney World Open

1974	27	78	13	0	0	1	3	72.79	$11,405

Best finish for 1974: T-9th at the Bing Crosby Pro-Am

1975	20	56	8	0	0	0	2	73.14	$7,991

Best finish for 1975: T-17th at the Florida Citrus Open Invitational & Greater Jacksonville Open

1976	18	50	7	0	0	1	3	73.00	$6,339

Best finish for 1976: T-8th at the Ed McMahon Quad City Open

1977	16	49	10	0	1	1	5	71.92	$12,646

Best finish for 1977: T-5th at the Greater Milwaukee Open

1978	22	66	13	0	0	1	4	72.32	$13,231

Best finish for 1978: T-6th at the Buick Goodwrench Open

1979	17	51	9	0	0	1	4	72.06	$21,389

Best finish for 1979: 6th at the Southern Open

1980	19	54	10	0	0	1	4	72.20	$28,192

Best finish for 1980: T-8th at the Michelob Houston Open

1981	27	82	17	0	1	1	4	72.29	$38,707

Best finish for 1981: T-2nd at the Bing Crosby Pro-Am

1982	14	37	4	0	0	0	1	73.49	$6,313

Best finish for 1982: T-17th at the Doral-Eastern Open

1986	1	2	0	0	0	0	0	81.50	$600
1993	1	4	1	0	0	0	0	72.50	$5,122

Best finish for 1993: T-77th at the U.S. Open

Period Totals	Starts	Rounds Played	Cuts Made	Wins	Top-5s	Top-10s	Top-25s	Scoring Average	Money
	186	541	93	0	2	7	30	72.66	$152,742

Dicky Thompson

Year	Starts	Rounds Played	Cuts Made	Wins	Top-5s	Top-10s	Top-25s	Scoring Average	Money
1991	31	86	13	0	0	1	3	71.72	$87,480

Best finish for 1991: T-9th at the Las Vegas Invitational

1992	27	70	9	0	0	0	2	72.21	$47,770

Best finish for 1992: T-11th at the Buick Southern Open

1994	1	2	0	0	0	0	0	72.50	
1995	25	70	9	0	1	1	1	71.90	$53,380

Best finish for 1995: T-4th at the Deposit Guaranty Golf Classic

1996	2	6	1	0	0	0	0	73.00	$5,200

Best finish for 1996: T-39th at the BellSouth Classic

1997	1	2	0	0	0	0	0	75.00	
1998	1	2	0	0	0	0	0	73.50	

Period Totals	Starts	Rounds Played	Cuts Made	Wins	Top-5s	Top-10s	Top-25s	Scoring Average	Money
	88	238	32	0	1	2	6	72.00	$193,829

Kyle Thompson

Year	Starts	Rounds Played	Cuts Made	Wins	Top-5s	Top-10s	Top-25s	Scoring Average	Money
2003	1	2	0	0	0	0	0	73.00	
2006	1	3	0	0	0	0	0	71.67	
2007	1	4	1	0	0	0	1	70.50	$42,900

Best finish for 2007: T-25th at the AT&T Pebble Beach National Pro-Am

2008	26	70	9	0	0	0	1	72.40	$154,447

Best finish for 2008: T-15th at the Puerto Rico Open

Period Totals	Starts	Rounds Played	Cuts Made	Wins	Top-5s	Top-10s	Top-25s	Scoring Average	Money
	29	79	10	0	0	0	2	72.29	$197,347

Leonard Thompson

Year	Starts	Rounds Played	Cuts Made	Wins	Top-5s	Top-10s	Top-25s	Scoring Average	Money
1971	4	14	3	0	0	1	2	72.36	$5,817

Best finish for 1971: T-7th at the Walt Disney World Open

1972	29	85	15	0	3	4	7	72.45	$37,611

Best finish for 1972: 2nd at the Tallahassee Open

1973	37	139	31	0	3	7	15	71.52	$87,626

Best finish for 1973: T-3rd at the Kemper Open & World Open

1974	32	109	23	1	5	7	16	71.49	$120,110

Best finish for 1974: Win at the Jackie Gleason's Inverrary Classic

1975	30	105	23	0	0	4	12	71.81	$48,308

Best finish for 1975: T-6th at the Bing Crosby Pro-Am

1976	36	127	27	0	0	1	7	72.58	$26,566

Best finish for 1976: T-10th at the Ohio Kings Island Open

1977	32	114	25	1	3	7	9	71.60	$107,293

Best finish for 1977: Win at the Pensacola Open

Year	Starts	Rounds Played	Cuts Made	Wins	Top-5s	Top-10s	Top-25s	Scoring Average	Money
1978	32	119	27	0	1	4	10	71.77	$52,231

Best finish for 1978: T-4th at the MONY Tournament Of Champions

1979	31	104	22	0	1	5	13	71.69	$91,065

Best finish for 1979: T-4th at the Bing Crosby Pro-Am

1980	28	100	24	0	2	8	14	71.34	$144,689

Best finish for 1980: T-2nd at the Bay Hill Classic & Canadian Open

1981	31	102	22	0	1	5	12	71.77	$95,517

Best finish for 1981: T-5th at the Doral-Eastern Open

1982	35	112	22	0	1	2	10	71.68	$60,998

Best finish for 1982: T-5th at the Texas Open

1983	28	93	19	0	0	4	8	72.41	$76,926

Best finish for 1983: T-6th at the Bank of Boston Classic

1984	34	105	21	0	0	0	3	72.94	$36,920

Best finish for 1984: 11th at the Pensacola Open

1985	27	84	14	0	1	1	4	72.27	$48,395

Best finish for 1985: T-2nd at the Bank of Boston Classic

1986	32	93	15	0	3	3	4	72.00	$84,419

Best finish for 1986: T-3rd at the Greater Greensboro Open & Pensacola Open

1987	34	102	18	0	0	0	3	71.89	$52,325

Best finish for 1987: T-15th at the AT&T Pebble Beach Pro-Am & Provident Classic

1988	36	103	17	0	0	2	4	71.83	$84,659

Best finish for 1988: T-6th at the Provident Classic

1989	32	94	16	1	1	2	5	71.69	$262,397

Best finish for 1989: Win at the Buick Open

1990	31	92	15	0	0	1	2	72.40	$79,517

Best finish for 1990: T-7th at the Buick Open

1991	30	80	12	0	1	2	4	71.20	$114,275

Best finish for 1991: T-4th at the Hardee's Golf Classic

1992	27	69	9	0	0	0	0	72.45	$30,540

Best finish for 1992: T-29th at the Centel Western Open & Canadian Open

1993	12	33	5	0	0	0	0	73.00	$15,153

Best finish for 1993: T-30th at the New England Classic

1994	11	32	7	0	0	0	2	71.66	$32,992

Best finish for 1994: T-16th at the Deposit Guaranty Golf Classic

1995	5	9	0	0	0	0	0	73.89	
1996	11	28	3	0	0	0	1	72.11	$29,790

Best finish for 1996: T-14th at the Quad City Classic

Period Totals	Starts	Rounds Played	Cuts Made	Wins	Top-5s	Top-10s	Top-25s	Scoring Average	Money
	707	2247	435	3	26	70	167	71.95	$1,826,139

Nicholas Thompson

Year	Starts	Rounds Played	Cuts Made	Wins	Top-5s	Top-10s	Top-25s	Scoring Average	Money
2006	32	93	15	0	0	1	1	71.97	$266,717

Best finish for 2006: T-6th at the B.C. Open

2008	36	113	21	0	4	6	11	71.38	$1,869,329

Best finish for 2008: T-2nd at the Ginn sur Mer Classic

Period Totals	Starts	Rounds Played	Cuts Made	Wins	Top-5s	Top-10s	Top-25s	Scoring Average	Money
	68	206	36	0	4	7	12	71.65	$2,136,046

Robert Thompson

Year	Starts	Rounds Played	Cuts Made	Wins	Top-5s	Top-10s	Top-25s	Scoring Average	Money
1980	2	6	1	0	0	0	0	70.83	$925

Best finish for 1980: T-41st at the San Antonio Texas Open

1981	3	6	0	0	0	0	0	74.00	$600
1982	19	49	5	0	0	0	0	73.39	$3,438

Best finish for 1982: T-57th at the Phoenix Open

1984	1	2	0	0	0	0	0	76.50	$600
1986	2	4	0	0	0	0	0	73.50	
1987	26	77	13	0	1	2	3	71.84	$58,026

Best finish for 1987: T-5th at the Provident Classic

1988	33	96	17	0	1	1	2	71.85	$46,688

Best finish for 1988: T-4th at the Deposit Guaranty Golf Classic

1989	27	72	10	0	1	1	2	71.71	$36,113

Best finish for 1989: T-3rd at the Deposit Guaranty Golf Classic

1990	2	8	2	0	0	0	0	71.13	$8,360

Best finish for 1990: T-26th at the Deposit Guaranty

1991	25	61	4	0	0	1	1	72.90	$40,895

Best finish for 1991: T-6th at the Federal Express St. Jude Classic

1992	3	10	2	0	0	1	1	71.20	$10,864

Best finish for 1992: T-10th at the Deposit Guaranty Classic

1997	1	2	0	0	0	0	0	74.00	

Year	Starts	Rounds Played	Cuts Made	Wins	Top-5s	Top-10s	Top-25s	Scoring Average	Money
1998	3	8	1	0	0	0	0	72.38	$6,087

Best finish for 1998: T-53rd at the Shell Houston Open

2000	2	6	1	0	0	0	0	70.50	$8,320

Best finish for 2000: T-44th at the Westin Texas Open at LaCantera

2001	2	6	1	0	0	0	0	72.83	$6,936

Best finish for 2001: T-67th at the Shell Houston Open

2002	2	6	1	0	0	0	0	74.50	$10,120

Best finish for 2002: T-68th at the Shell Houston Open

2003	2	4	0	0	0	0	0	71.50	
2004	1	2	0	0	0	0	0	78.00	$2,000
Period Totals	Starts	Rounds Played	Cuts Made	Wins	Top-5s	Top-10s	Top-25s	Scoring Average	Money
	156	425	58	0	3	6	9	72.26	$239,972

Rocky Thompson

Year	Starts	Rounds Played	Cuts Made	Wins	Top-5s	Top-10s	Top-25s	Scoring Average	Money
1964	17	48	6	0	0	0	2	73.48	$1,152

Best finish for 1964: T-20th at the Portland Open & Sunset-Camellia Open

1965	25	78	13	0	1	2	5	72.67	$8,616

Best finish for 1965: T-5th at the Seattle Open

1966	30	105	22	0	0	2	6	72.65	$11,730

Best finish for 1966: T-8th at the Dallas Open Invitational & Texas Open Invitational

1967	29	100	21	0	1	2	6	72.85	$17,583

Best finish for 1967: 3rd at the Azalea Open

1968	31	90	15	0	3	3	8	72.61	$21,185

Best finish for 1968: T-3rd at the Atlanta Classic & Robinson Open

1969	30	86	14	0	1	1	4	73.22	$20,423

Best finish for 1969: 2nd at the Western Open

1970	26	80	15	0	0	0	5	72.60	$11,501

Best finish for 1970: T-13th at the Robinson Open Golf Classic

1971	17	48	7	0	0	0	2	73.29	$3,762

Best finish for 1971: T-24th at the Colonial National Invitational

1972	13	36	5	0	0	0	1	73.81	$2,370

Best finish for 1972: T-21st at the San Antonio Texas Open

1973	24	69	10	0	0	0	2	72.65	$7,166

Best finish for 1973: T-11th at the Shrine-Robinson Golf Classic

1974	18	45	4	0	0	0	0	74.09	$1,796

Best finish for 1974: T-29th at the Quad Cities Open

1975	16	41	4	0	0	0	1	74.32	$3,077

Best finish for 1975: T-15th at the IVB Philadelphia Golf Classic

1976	13	33	6	0	0	0	0	74.58	$789

Best finish for 1976: T-52nd at the Ed McMahon Quad City Open

1978	10	23	2	0	0	0	1	73.35	$3,642

Best finish for 1978: T-13th at the Southern Open

1979	23	56	6	0	0	0	0	73.82	$3,306

Best finish for 1979: T-53rd at the Southern Open

1980	9	19	1	0	0	0	0	74.00	$704

Best finish for 1980: T-52nd at the Phoenix Open

1982	9	20	1	0	0	0	1	75.20	$6,910

Best finish for 1982: T-11th at the Hawaiian Open

1983	2	8	1	0	0	0	0	76.88	$1,898

Best finish for 1983: T-68th at the U.S. Open

1984	2	4	0	0	0	0	0	80.00	$600
1985	4	8	0	0	0	0	0	76.25	
1986	2	4	0	0	0	0	0	74.25	
1987	5	10	1	0	0	0	0	72.10	$2,858

Best finish for 1987: T-30th at the Provident Classic

1988	6	11	0	0	0	0	0	73.18	
1989	9	25	4	0	0	0	0	73.20	$4,683

Best finish for 1989: T-58th at the Shearson Lehman Hutton Open

1990	1	3	1	0	0	0	0	71.33	$3,333

Best finish for 1990: T-40th at the GTE Byron Nelson Classic

1992	1	2	0	0	0	0	0	72.50	
Period Totals	Starts	Rounds Played	Cuts Made	Wins	Top-5s	Top-10s	Top-25s	Scoring Average	Money
	372	1052	159	0	6	10	44	73.26	$139,082

Jeff Thomsen

Year	Starts	Rounds Played	Cuts Made	Wins	Top-5s	Top-10s	Top-25s	Scoring Average	Money
1978	1	2	0	0	0	0	0	76.50	$332
1979	11	25	2	0	0	1	1	73.44	$5,656

Best finish for 1979: T-10th at the American Optical Classic

1980	19	53	7	0	0	0	0	73.32	$3,737

Best finish for 1980: T-41st at the B.C. Open

Year	Starts	Rounds Played	Cuts Made	Wins	Top-5s	Top-10s	Top-25s	Scoring Average	Money
1981	9	28	5	0	0	0	0	73.14	$3,690

Best finish for 1981: T-36th at the Hall of Fame Tournament

1982	17	39	3	0	0	0	0	73.15	$2,322

Best finish for 1982: T-42nd at the Greater Milwaukee Open

1983	1	2	0	0	0	0	0	77.00	$600
1984	2	8	2	0	0	0	0	72.00	$1,441

Best finish for 1984: T-51st at the Miller High-Life Quad Cities Open

1985	1	4	1	0	0	0	0	71.00	$990

Best finish for 1985: T-55th at the Phoenix Open

1988	1	2	0	0	0	0	0	73.00	
1990	1	2	0	0	0	0	0	76.50	$1,000
1998	1	2	0	0	0	0	0	77.00	$1,500
Period Totals	**Starts**	**Rounds Played**	**Cuts Made**	**Wins**	**Top-5s**	**Top-10s**	**Top-25s**	**Scoring Average**	**Money**
	64	167	20	0	0	1	1	73.31	$21,269

Peter Thomson

Year	Starts	Rounds Played	Cuts Made	Wins	Top-5s	Top-10s	Top-25s	Scoring Average	Money
1958	8	31	7	1	3	3	5	74.19	$6,039

Best finish for 1958: Win at the British Open

1959	5	19	3	0	0	2	4	72.05	$2,667

Best finish for 1959: T-6th at the Greater Greensboro Open Invitational

1960	3	12	3	0	0	1	1	73.00	$503

Best finish for 1960: T-9th at the British Open

1961	8	30	7	0	0	2	6	72.30	$5,735

Best finish for 1961: T-7th at the British Open

1962	1	4	1	0	0	1	1	73.00	

Best finish for 1962: T-6th at the British Open

1963	1	4	1	0	1	1	1	71.25	$1,400

Best finish for 1963: 5th at the British Open

1964	2	8	2	0	0	0	1	74.38	$836

Best finish for 1964: T-24th at the British Open

1965	4	14	3	1	1	1	2	73.50	$6,412

Best finish for 1965: Win at the British Open

1966	8	26	5	0	0	3	4	72.35	$9,428

Best finish for 1966: T-7th at the Colonial National Invitation

1967	4	16	4	0	0	1	2	72.63	$3,638

Best finish for 1967: T-8th at the British Open

1968	1	4	1	0	0	0	1	75.25	$468

Best finish for 1968: T-24th at the British Open

1969	2	6	1	0	1	1	1	72.67	$5,100

Best finish for 1969: T-3rd at the British Open

1970	1	4	1	0	0	1	1	72.25	$2,880

Best finish for 1970: T-9th at the British Open

1971	1	4	1	0	0	1	1	71.25	$3,720

Best finish for 1971: T-9th at the British Open

1972	1	4	1	0	0	0	0	73.50	$512

Best finish for 1972: T-31st at the British Open

1973	1	4	1	0	0	0	0	73.50	$552

Best finish for 1973: T-31st at the British Open

1974	1	2	0	0	0	0	0	80.00	$120
1975	1	3	0	0	0	0	0	76.33	$330
1976	1	2	0	0	0	0	0	77.00	$180
1977	2	6	1	0	0	0	1	71.83	$3,740

Best finish for 1977: T-13th at the British Open

1978	1	4	1	0	0	0	1	72.50	$1,302

Best finish for 1978: T-24th at the British Open

1979	1	4	1	0	0	0	0	74.25	$1,864

Best finish for 1979: T-26th at the British Open

1984	1	3	0	0	0	0	0	73.67	$793
Period Totals	**Starts**	**Rounds Played**	**Cuts Made**	**Wins**	**Top-5s**	**Top-10s**	**Top-25s**	**Scoring Average**	**Money**
	59	214	45	2	6	18	33	73.08	$58,218

PGA Tour career totals from 1950 to 1984

	Starts	Rounds Played	Cuts Made	Wins	Top-5s	Top-10s	Top-25s	Scoring Average	Money
	136	N/A	N/A	6	N/A	43	88	N/A	N/A

David Thore

Year	Starts	Rounds Played	Cuts Made	Wins	Top-5s	Top-10s	Top-25s	Scoring Average	Money
1977	8	18	1	0	0	0	0	73.06	$352

Best finish for 1977: T-64th at the Sammy Davis, Jr. - Greater Hartford Open

1978	8	20	3	0	0	0	0	74.25	$672

Best finish for 1978: T-47th at the Tallahassee Open

Year	Starts	Rounds Played	Cuts Made	Wins	Top-5s	Top-10s	Top-25s	Scoring Average	Money
1979	12	38	7	0	0	0	0	71.84	$6,180

Best finish for 1979: T-28th at the Southern Open

1980	22	59	8	0	0	0	1	72.88	$10,811

Best finish for 1980: T-12th at the B.C. Open

1981	19	48	7	0	0	2	2	72.85	$22,017

Best finish for 1981: T-6th at the Danny Thomas Memphis Classic

1982	16	39	4	0	0	0	0	74.54	$2,518

Best finish for 1982: T-45th at the Tallahassee Open

1985	26	74	11	0	0	0	3	72.70	$25,020

Best finish for 1985: T-20th at the Greater Milwaukee Open

1986	3	10	2	0	0	0	0	73.50	$4,438

Best finish for 1986: T-33rd at the Greater Greensboro Open

1987	2	4	0	0	0	0	0	77.25	
1988	5	10	0	0	0	0	0	75.50	$2,765
1992	1	2	0	0	0	0	0	77.00	
1995	1	2	0	0	0	0	0	73.00	
1996	1	2	0	0	0	0	0	74.50	
1999	1	2	0	0	0	0	0	77.50	
Period Totals	Starts	Rounds Played	Cuts Made	Wins	Top-5s	Top-10s	Top-25s	Scoring Average	Money
	125	328	43	0	0	2	6	73.22	$74,774

Chuck Thorpe

Year	Starts	Rounds Played	Cuts Made	Wins	Top-5s	Top-10s	Top-25s	Scoring Average	Money
1971	2	6	1	0	0	0	0	73.00	$171

Best finish for 1971: T-61st at the Walt Disney World Open

1972	33	112	23	0	1	4	5	72.49	$24,179

Best finish for 1972: T-5th at the Houston Open

1973	23	71	12	0	0	1	2	72.70	$11,972

Best finish for 1973: T-10th at the Houston Open

1974	9	25	4	0	0	0	1	72.68	$2,934

Best finish for 1974: T-23rd at the Doral-Eastern Open

1980	1	2	0	0	0	0	0	73.50	$600
1982	1	2	0	0	0	0	0	74.50	
1984	1	4	1	0	0	0	0	72.00	$896

Best finish for 1984: T-57th at the Georgia-Pacific Atlanta Golf Classic

Period Totals	Starts	Rounds Played	Cuts Made	Wins	Top-5s	Top-10s	Top-25s	Scoring Average	Money
	70	222	41	0	1	5	8	72.61	$40,752

Jim Thorpe

Year	Starts	Rounds Played	Cuts Made	Wins	Top-5s	Top-10s	Top-25s	Scoring Average	Money
1976	8	20	2	0	0	0	0	73.40	$1,140

Best finish for 1976: T-28th at the Ohio Kings Island Open

1979	27	86	18	0	1	2	6	72.15	$49,336

Best finish for 1979: T-2nd at the Joe Garagiola Tucson Open

1980	26	80	15	0	0	2	5	71.90	$33,671

Best finish for 1980: T-6th at the Pleasant Valley Jimmy Fund Classic

1981	30	92	16	0	0	1	6	72.21	$43,011

Best finish for 1981: T-10th at the Canadian Open

1982	28	97	21	0	2	3	7	72.15	$67,879

Best finish for 1982: T-4th at the Western Open & Miller High-Life Quad Cities Open

1983	31	106	21	0	3	3	9	71.97	$118,197

Best finish for 1983: T-2nd at the Houston Coca-Cola Open & Bank of Boston Classic

1984	30	97	20	0	3	5	11	71.64	$137,318

Best finish for 1984: T-3rd at the Kemper Open

1985	28	94	21	2	5	6	9	71.28	$379,091

Best finish for 1985: Win at the Greater Milwaukee Open & Seiko Tucson-Match Play Championship

1986	29	87	19	1	3	7	11	71.63	$326,272

Best finish for 1986: Win at the Seiko Tucson-Match Play Championship

1987	24	60	9	0	0	1	4	73.07	$58,638

Best finish for 1987: T-9th at the U.S. Open

1988	10	24	3	0	0	0	0	74.54	$6,534

Best finish for 1988: T-56th at the Provident Classic

1989	29	83	11	0	1	1	4	71.77	$104,704

Best finish for 1989: T-2nd at the Kemper Open

1990	28	87	16	0	1	1	8	71.86	$212,297

Best finish for 1990: 2nd at the Phoenix Open

1991	27	81	13	0	0	0	1	71.69	$46,039

Best finish for 1991: T-23rd at the Greater Milwaukee Open

1992	21	56	6	0	0	0	1	72.29	$28,235

Best finish for 1992: T-14th at the Buick Classic

1993	19	56	9	0	0	0	4	71.84	$71,376

Best finish for 1993: T-14th at the H-E-B Texas Open

Year	Starts	Rounds Played	Cuts Made	Wins	Top-5s	Top-10s	Top-25s	Scoring Average	Money
1994	26	76	14	0	1	3	6	71.49	$186,714

Best finish for 1994: T-4th at the Doral-Ryder Open

| 1995 | 15 | 34 | 3 | 0 | 0 | 0 | 0 | 73.21 | $12,945 |

Best finish for 1995: T-32nd at the Shell Houston Open

| 1996 | 22 | 55 | 8 | 0 | 0 | 0 | 0 | 73.09 | $25,130 |

Best finish for 1996: T-43rd at the Buick Classic

| 1997 | 12 | 33 | 5 | 0 | 0 | 0 | 1 | 71.55 | $32,680 |

Best finish for 1997: T-19th at the Greater Vancouver Open

| 1998 | 9 | 18 | 1 | 0 | 0 | 0 | 0 | 73.11 | $3,980 |

Best finish for 1998: T-70th at the Greater Vancouver Open

Period Totals	Starts	Rounds Played	Cuts Made	Wins	Top-5s	Top-10s	Top-25s	Scoring Average	Money
	479	1422	251	3	20	35	93	72.05	$1,945,187

Chris Tidland

Year	Starts	Rounds Played	Cuts Made	Wins	Top-5s	Top-10s	Top-25s	Scoring Average	Money
1998	1	2	0	0	0	0	0	78.00	$1,000
1999	1	4	1	0	0	0	0	74.75	$10,305

Best finish for 1999: T-51st at the U.S. Open

| 2000 | 3 | 8 | 1 | 0 | 0 | 0 | 0 | 72.25 | $15,438 |

Best finish for 2000: T-36th at the Touchstone Energy Tucson Open

| 2001 | 29 | 80 | 14 | 0 | 0 | 0 | 1 | 71.36 | $191,738 |

Best finish for 2001: T-23rd at the Southern Farm Bureau Classic

2002	1	2	0	0	0	0	0	73.50	
2005	1	2	0	0	0	0	0	72.00	
2007	21	59	8	0	0	1	2	71.81	$339,483

Best finish for 2007: T-6th at the AT&T Classic

Period Totals	Starts	Rounds Played	Cuts Made	Wins	Top-5s	Top-10s	Top-25s	Scoring Average	Money
	57	157	24	0	0	1	3	71.78	$557,963

Dennis Tiziani

Year	Starts	Rounds Played	Cuts Made	Wins	Top-5s	Top-10s	Top-25s	Scoring Average	Money
1966	1	2	0	0	0	0	0	78.00	
1969	3	8	1	0	0	0	0	77.50	$185

Best finish for 1969: 79th at the Canadian Open

| 1970 | 9 | 20 | 1 | 0 | 0 | 0 | 0 | 75.25 | $152 |

Best finish for 1970: T-54th at the Greater Milwaukee Open

| 1971 | 11 | 28 | 3 | 0 | 0 | 0 | 0 | 74.14 | $438 |

Best finish for 1971: T-32nd at the Canadian Open

1972	2	4	0	0	0	0	0	73.25	
1973	1	2	0	0	0	0	0	77.50	
1974	1	2	0	0	0	0	0	75.00	
1975	1	2	0	0	0	0	0	74.50	
1976	3	10	2	0	0	0	0	73.50	$1,287

Best finish for 1976: T-46th at the Greater Milwaukee Open

1977	3	6	0	0	0	0	0	76.17	$500
1978	1	2	0	0	0	0	0	74.00	
1979	1	2	0	0	0	0	0	75.00	
1980	1	2	0	0	0	0	0	74.50	
1983	1	4	1	0	0	0	0	71.75	$548

Best finish for 1983: T-58th at the Greater Milwaukee Open

1984	2	4	0	0	0	0	0	77.75	$600
1985	1	2	0	0	0	0	0	76.50	
1993	1	2	0	0	0	0	0	72.50	
1994	1	2	0	0	0	0	0	74.50	
1995	1	2	0	0	0	0	0	73.00	

Period Totals	Starts	Rounds Played	Cuts Made	Wins	Top-5s	Top-10s	Top-25s	Scoring Average	Money
	45	106	8	0	0	0	0	74.85	$3,709

Mario Tiziani

Year	Starts	Rounds Played	Cuts Made	Wins	Top-5s	Top-10s	Top-25s	Scoring Average	Money
1995	1	2	0	0	0	0	0	74.50	
1996	3	6	0	0	0	0	0	73.67	
1997	2	4	0	0	0	0	0	74.75	
1999	1	2	0	0	0	0	0	74.00	
2000	2	4	0	0	0	0	0	76.00	$1,000
2002	3	10	2	0	0	0	0	71.70	$23,603

Best finish for 2002: T-38th at the Bell Canadian Open

| 2003 | 1 | 4 | 1 | 0 | 0 | 0 | 0 | 69.50 | $17,780 |

Best finish for 2003: T-32nd at the Greater Milwaukee Open

| 2004 | 1 | 2 | 0 | 0 | 0 | 0 | 0 | 74.50 | |
| 2005 | 23 | 65 | 11 | 0 | 0 | 0 | 1 | 71.12 | $181,618 |

Best finish for 2005: T-12th at the Southern Farm Bureau Classic

2006	1	2	0	0	0	0	0	69.50	
Period Totals	Starts	Rounds Played	Cuts Made	Wins	Top-5s	Top-10s	Top-25s	Scoring Average	Money
	38	101	14	0	0	0	1	71.76	$224,001

Rick Todd

Year	Starts	Rounds Played	Cuts Made	Wins	Top-5s	Top-10s	Top-25s	Scoring Average	Money
1990	25	56	2	0	0	0	0	74.41	$2,367

Best finish for 1990: T-70th at the Phoenix Open

| 1991 | 1 | 4 | 1 | 0 | 0 | 0 | 0 | 73.75 | $1,850 |

Best finish for 1991: T-77th at the Canadian Open

| 1996 | 3 | 11 | 3 | 0 | 0 | 0 | 0 | 73.00 | $14,471 |

Best finish for 1996: T-56th at the Memorial Tournament

| 1997 | 2 | 8 | 2 | 0 | 0 | 0 | 1 | 70.75 | $30,628 |

Best finish for 1997: T-12th at the Greater Vancouver Open

1998	2	4	0	0	0	0	0	76.00	$1,000
1999	1	2	0	0	0	0	0	74.50	
Period Totals	Starts	Rounds Played	Cuts Made	Wins	Top-5s	Top-10s	Top-25s	Scoring Average	Money
	34	85	8	0	0	0	1	73.93	$50,316

John Toepel

Year	Starts	Rounds Played	Cuts Made	Wins	Top-5s	Top-10s	Top-25s	Scoring Average	Money
1972	12	32	4	0	0	0	0	73.56	$2,442

Best finish for 1972: T-26th at the American Golf Classic & Greater Hartford Open Invitational

| 1973 | 26 | 68 | 8 | 0 | 0 | 0 | 0 | 73.90 | $3,113 |

Best finish for 1973: T-39th at the Liggett Meyers Open

| 1974 | 21 | 51 | 5 | 0 | 0 | 0 | 1 | 73.84 | $4,137 |

Best finish for 1974: T-16th at the Westchester Classic

| 1975 | 16 | 47 | 7 | 0 | 0 | 1 | 1 | 73.40 | $4,903 |

Best finish for 1975: T-6th at the Tallahassee Open

| 1976 | 12 | 32 | 4 | 0 | 0 | 0 | 1 | 73.34 | $2,081 |

Best finish for 1976: T-22nd at the Houston Open

Period Totals	Starts	Rounds Played	Cuts Made	Wins	Top-5s	Top-10s	Top-25s	Scoring Average	Money
	87	230	28	0	0	1	3	73.66	$16,677

Esteban Toledo

Year	Starts	Rounds Played	Cuts Made	Wins	Top-5s	Top-10s	Top-25s	Scoring Average	Money
1986	2	4	0	0	0	0	0	76.25	
1989	1	3	0	0	0	0	0	77.33	
1992	1	3	0	0	0	0	0	73.67	
1994	28	78	12	0	0	0	3	71.60	$66,049

Best finish for 1994: T-16th at the Deposit Guaranty Golf Classic

| 1995 | 1 | 2 | 0 | 0 | 0 | 0 | 0 | 74.00 | |
| 1998 | 30 | 93 | 18 | 0 | 1 | 2 | 6 | 70.96 | $327,244 |

Best finish for 1998: T-3rd at the BellSouth Classic

| 1999 | 33 | 107 | 20 | 0 | 0 | 2 | 5 | 71.27 | $382,046 |

Best finish for 1999: 7th at the Buick Open

| 2000 | 35 | 111 | 20 | 0 | 1 | 2 | 8 | 70.85 | $673,387 |

Best finish for 2000: 2nd at the B.C. Open

| 2001 | 36 | 114 | 21 | 0 | 1 | 1 | 7 | 70.91 | $684,751 |

Best finish for 2001: T-3rd at the Michelob Championship at Kingsmill

| 2002 | 32 | 102 | 21 | 0 | 1 | 3 | 5 | 70.81 | $766,463 |

Best finish for 2002: T-2nd at the Buick Open

| 2003 | 35 | 109 | 19 | 0 | 0 | 1 | 4 | 71.12 | $487,495 |

Best finish for 2003: T-9th at the Bank of America Colonial

| 2004 | 36 | 90 | 8 | 0 | 0 | 0 | 1 | 72.12 | $115,184 |

Best finish for 2004: T-21st at the B.C. Open

| 2005 | 7 | 17 | 2 | 0 | 0 | 0 | 1 | 70.76 | $76,887 |

Best finish for 2005: T-13th at the John Deere Classic

| 2006 | 2 | 7 | 1 | 0 | 0 | 0 | 0 | 71.57 | $15,567 |

Best finish for 2006: T-32nd at the B.C. Open

| 2007 | 2 | 7 | 1 | 0 | 0 | 0 | 0 | 71.29 | $12,250 |

Best finish for 2007: T-41st at the Mayakoba Golf Classic

| 2008 | 3 | 12 | 3 | 0 | 0 | 0 | 1 | 70.58 | $111,305 |

Best finish for 2008: 11th at the Mayakoba Golf Classic

Period Totals	Starts	Rounds Played	Cuts Made	Wins	Top-5s	Top-10s	Top-25s	Scoring Average	Money
	284	859	146	0	4	11	41	71.22	$3,718,629

Tommy Tolles

Year	Starts	Rounds Played	Cuts Made	Wins	Top-5s	Top-10s	Top-25s	Scoring Average	Money
1988	1	2	0	0	0	0	0	78.00	
1991	2	4	0	0	0	0	0	74.25	$1,000
1995	27	79	13	0	1	2	5	71.14	$166,431

Best finish for 1995: T-3rd at the Bob Hope Chrysler Classic

Year	Starts	Rounds Played	Cuts Made	Wins	Top-5s	Top-10s	Top-25s	Scoring Average	Money
1996	25	95	21	0	5	6	10	70.39	$871,589

Best finish for 1996: T-2nd at the Players Championship

| 1997 | 25 | 89 | 22 | 0 | 4 | 9 | 12 | 70.79 | $825,778 |

Best finish for 1997: 3rd at the Masters

| 1998 | 28 | 81 | 13 | 0 | 1 | 2 | 6 | 72.25 | $261,553 |

Best finish for 1998: T-3rd at the Kemper Open

| 1999 | 27 | 77 | 12 | 0 | 1 | 4 | 4 | 72.34 | $458,066 |

Best finish for 1999: T-2nd at the Sony Open in Hawaii

| 2000 | 20 | 60 | 9 | 0 | 0 | 0 | 2 | 71.90 | $142,248 |

Best finish for 2000: T-14th at the Tampa Bay Classic

| 2001 | 31 | 86 | 12 | 0 | 1 | 1 | 2 | 71.69 | $304,644 |

Best finish for 2001: T-4th at the Texas Open at LaCantera

| 2002 | 20 | 64 | 12 | 0 | 0 | 0 | 3 | 71.39 | $213,740 |

Best finish for 2002: T-13th at the B.C. Open

| 2004 | 25 | 67 | 8 | 0 | 0 | 0 | 1 | 72.06 | $151,852 |

Best finish for 2004: T-13th at the B.C. Open

2005	1	2	0	0	0	0	0	77.00	
Period Totals	Starts	Rounds Played	Cuts Made	Wins	Top-5s	Top-10s	Top-25s	Scoring Average	Money
	232	706	122	0	13	24	45	71.55	$3,396,900

David Toms

Year	Starts	Rounds Played	Cuts Made	Wins	Top-5s	Top-10s	Top-25s	Scoring Average	Money
1989	5	12	1	0	0	0	0	72.58	$1,463

Best finish for 1989: T-65th at the Hardee's Golf Classic

| 1990 | 3 | 6 | 0 | 0 | 0 | 0 | 0 | 74.50 | |
| 1992 | 30 | 87 | 14 | 0 | 1 | 1 | 4 | 71.63 | $148,712 |

Best finish for 1992: 3rd at the Northern Telecom Open

| 1993 | 31 | 85 | 12 | 0 | 0 | 3 | 5 | 72.39 | $120,952 |

Best finish for 1993: T-8th at the Buick Southern Open

| 1994 | 32 | 92 | 16 | 0 | 0 | 0 | 4 | 71.93 | $87,607 |

Best finish for 1994: T-15th at the Buick Invitational of California

| 1996 | 29 | 89 | 16 | 0 | 0 | 2 | 8 | 71.13 | $206,188 |

Best finish for 1996: 6th at the Kemper Open

| 1997 | 27 | 88 | 17 | 1 | 2 | 2 | 7 | 71.02 | $462,655 |

Best finish for 1997: Win at the Quad City Classic

| 1998 | 26 | 85 | 18 | 0 | 2 | 3 | 11 | 70.88 | $636,573 |

Best finish for 1998: T-2nd at the Tucson Chrysler Classic

| 1999 | 32 | 103 | 21 | 2 | 5 | 7 | 17 | 70.83 | $1,967,422 |

Best finish for 1999: Win at the Sprint International & Buick Challenge

| 2000 | 31 | 109 | 26 | 1 | 4 | 6 | 19 | 70.38 | $2,002,068 |

Best finish for 2000: Win at the Michelob Championship at Kingsmill

| 2001 | 28 | 96 | 23 | 3 | 4 | 9 | 16 | 69.71 | $3,793,169 |

Best finish for 2001: Win at the COMPAQ Classic of New Orleans, PGA Championship & Michelob Championship at Kingsmill

| 2002 | 27 | 102 | 25 | 0 | 9 | 12 | 20 | 69.64 | $3,463,794 |

Best finish for 2002: T-2nd at the Mercedes Championships, MasterCard Colonial & Buick Challenge

| 2003 | 26 | 81 | 19 | 2 | 5 | 7 | 11 | 70.22 | $3,714,879 |

Best finish for 2003: Win at the Wachovia Championship & FedEx St. Jude Classic

| 2004 | 24 | 74 | 17 | 1 | 3 | 7 | 13 | 70.62 | $2,362,531 |

Best finish for 2004: Win at the FedEx St. Jude Classic

| 2005 | 25 | 77 | 19 | 1 | 6 | 11 | 14 | 70.05 | $3,970,518 |

Best finish for 2005: Win at the WGC-Accenture Match Play Championship

| 2006 | 22 | 69 | 17 | 1 | 3 | 6 | 13 | 70.57 | $2,918,187 |

Best finish for 2006: Win at the Sony Open in Hawaii

| 2007 | 22 | 77 | 19 | 0 | 2 | 7 | 11 | 70.88 | $2,101,284 |

Best finish for 2007: 3rd at the Stanford St. Jude Classic

| 2008 | 20 | 68 | 16 | 0 | 0 | 1 | 6 | 71.13 | $799,114 |

Best finish for 2008: T-8th at the Viking Classic

| Period Totals | Starts | Rounds Played | Cuts Made | Wins | Top-5s | Top-10s | Top-25s | Scoring Average | Money |
| | 440 | 1400 | 296 | 12 | 46 | 84 | 179 | 70.83 | $28,757,114 |

Sam Torrance

Year	Starts	Rounds Played	Cuts Made	Wins	Top-5s	Top-10s	Top-25s	Scoring Average	Money
1972	1	4	1	0	0	0	0	74.00	$358

Best finish for 1972: T-46th at the British Open

1973	1	3	0	0	0	0	0	75.33	$195
1974	1	2	0	0	0	0	0	81.50	$120
1975	1	4	1	0	0	0	1	72.25	$1,692

Best finish for 1975: T-19th at the British Open

1976	1	2	0	0	0	0	0	76.50	$180
1977	2	6	0	0	0	0	0	75.00	$340
1978	1	3	0	0	0	0	0	74.67	$428

Year	Starts	Rounds Played	Cuts Made	Wins	Top-5s	Top-10s	Top-25s	Scoring Average	Money
1979	1	2	0	0	0	0	0	76.50	$420
1980	2	4	1	0	0	0	0	72.75	$1,440

Best finish for 1980: T-38th at the British Open

| 1981 | 1 | 4 | 1 | 0 | 1 | 1 | 1 | 71.00 | $17,000 |

Best finish for 1981: 5th at the British Open

| 1982 | 2 | 8 | 2 | 0 | 0 | 0 | 2 | 73.63 | $15,260 |

Best finish for 1982: 12th at the British Open

| 1983 | 3 | 10 | 2 | 0 | 1 | 1 | 1 | 70.50 | $28,088 |

Best finish for 1983: 2nd at the Southern Open

| 1984 | 5 | 17 | 2 | 0 | 0 | 1 | 1 | 72.82 | $15,562 |

Best finish for 1984: T-9th at the British Open

| 1985 | 2 | 8 | 2 | 0 | 0 | 0 | 1 | 72.50 | $15,900 |

Best finish for 1985: T-16th at the British Open

| 1986 | 1 | 4 | 1 | 0 | 0 | 0 | 1 | 73.50 | $7,533 |

Best finish for 1986: T-21st at the British Open

| 1987 | 1 | 4 | 1 | 0 | 0 | 0 | 0 | 73.75 | $4,040 |

Best finish for 1987: T-50th at the British Open

| 1988 | 1 | 4 | 1 | 0 | 0 | 0 | 0 | 73.50 | $5,185 |

Best finish for 1988: T-48th at the British Open

| 1989 | 1 | 2 | 0 | 0 | 0 | 0 | 0 | 73.50 | $800 |
| 1990 | 1 | 4 | 1 | 0 | 0 | 0 | 0 | 71.25 | $7,632 |

Best finish for 1990: T-39th at the British Open

| 1991 | 3 | 8 | 1 | 0 | 0 | 0 | 0 | 72.63 | $8,114 |

Best finish for 1991: T-44th at the British Open

| 1992 | 1 | 2 | 0 | 0 | 0 | 0 | 0 | 72.50 | $1,200 |
| 1993 | 1 | 4 | 1 | 0 | 0 | 0 | 0 | 71.25 | $6,709 |

Best finish for 1993: T-51st at the British Open

| 1994 | 6 | 22 | 5 | 0 | 1 | 1 | 2 | 72.00 | $124,464 |

Best finish for 1994: 3rd at the Freeport-McMoRan Classic

| 1995 | 2 | 8 | 2 | 0 | 0 | 0 | 2 | 70.50 | $56,970 |

Best finish for 1995: T-11th at the British Open

| 1996 | 6 | 16 | 2 | 0 | 0 | 0 | 1 | 73.13 | $45,262 |

Best finish for 1996: T-16th at the U.S. Open

| 1997 | 5 | 13 | 2 | 0 | 0 | 0 | 0 | 74.69 | $20,158 |

Best finish for 1997: T-39th at the Masters

| 1998 | 1 | 4 | 1 | 0 | 0 | 0 | 1 | 72.75 | $20,530 |

Best finish for 1998: T-24th at the British Open

1999	1	2	0	0	0	0	0	74.50	$1,000
2000	2	4	0	0	0	0	0	76.75	$3,672
Period Totals	**Starts**	**Rounds Played**	**Cuts Made**	**Wins**	**Top-5s**	**Top-10s**	**Top-25s**	**Scoring Average**	**Money**
	57	178	30	0	3	4	14	73.05	$410,250

Harry Toscano

Year	Starts	Rounds Played	Cuts Made	Wins	Top-5s	Top-10s	Top-25s	Scoring Average	Money
1964	1	2	0	0	0	0	0	77.50	
1966	3	8	1	0	0	0	0	74.50	$888

Best finish for 1966: T-34th at the Western Open

| 1967 | 26 | 81 | 12 | 0 | 0 | 0 | 2 | 73.68 | $5,012 |

Best finish for 1967: T-13th at the "500" Festival Open

| 1968 | 16 | 44 | 6 | 0 | 0 | 0 | 2 | 73.34 | $2,227 |

Best finish for 1968: T-21st at the Rebel Yell Open

| 1969 | 19 | 57 | 10 | 0 | 0 | 0 | 1 | 73.23 | $2,723 |

Best finish for 1969: T-18th at the Minnesota Classic

| 1970 | 22 | 66 | 13 | 0 | 0 | 2 | 5 | 72.35 | $9,319 |

Best finish for 1970: T-10th at the Greater Milwaukee Open & Green Island Open Invitational

| 1971 | 22 | 65 | 10 | 0 | 0 | 0 | 2 | 72.82 | $5,354 |

Best finish for 1971: T-18th at the Southern Open

| 1972 | 23 | 68 | 12 | 0 | 0 | 0 | 1 | 73.21 | $5,853 |

Best finish for 1972: T-19th at the Greater St. Louis Classic

| 1973 | 19 | 54 | 6 | 0 | 0 | 0 | 0 | 74.11 | $1,794 |

Best finish for 1973: T-34th at the Greater Milwaukee Open

| 1974 | 2 | 6 | 1 | 0 | 0 | 0 | 0 | 72.83 | $511 |

Best finish for 1974: T-47th at the Pleasant Valley Classic

| 1975 | 2 | 6 | 1 | 0 | 0 | 0 | 0 | 73.50 | $482 |

Best finish for 1975: T-43rd at the Doral-Eastern Open

| 1976 | 8 | 20 | 2 | 0 | 0 | 0 | 0 | 74.30 | $875 |

Best finish for 1976: T-61st at the Pleasant Valley Classic

| 1977 | 6 | 16 | 2 | 0 | 0 | 0 | 0 | 74.56 | $819 |

Best finish for 1977: T-31st at the Tallahassee Open

| 1978 | 1 | 4 | 1 | 0 | 0 | 0 | 0 | 75.75 | $1,255 |

Best finish for 1978: T-55th at the U.S. Open

1984	1	2	0	0	0	0	0	77.50	$600
Period Totals	**Starts**	**Rounds Played**	**Cuts Made**	**Wins**	**Top-5s**	**Top-10s**	**Top-25s**	**Scoring Average**	**Money**
	171	499	77	0	0	2	13	73.39	$37,710

Bob Toski

Year	Starts	Rounds Played	Cuts Made	Wins	Top-5s	Top-10s	Top-25s	Scoring Average	Money
1958	12	42	10	0	1	1	4	72.69	$2,008

Best finish for 1958: T-2nd at the Jackson Open

Year	Starts	Rounds Played	Cuts Made	Wins	Top-5s	Top-10s	Top-25s	Scoring Average	Money
1959	9	34	8	0	1	1	2	72.21	$1,903

Best finish for 1959: T-5th at the Puerto Rico Open Invitational

| 1960 | 4 | 16 | 4 | 0 | 2 | 2 | 3 | 70.50 | $1,952 |

Best finish for 1960: T-3rd at the Jamaica Open Invitational

| 1961 | 1 | 2 | 1 | 0 | 0 | 0 | 0 | 75.00 | |

Best finish for 1961: T-200 at the PGA Championship

| 1964 | 2 | 4 | 0 | 0 | 0 | 0 | 0 | 75.25 | |
| 1965 | 2 | 6 | 1 | 0 | 0 | 0 | 0 | 72.83 | $220 |

Best finish for 1965: T-46th at the Greater Hartford Open

| 1966 | 3 | 7 | 0 | 0 | 0 | 0 | 0 | 75.14 | |
| 1967 | 1 | 4 | 1 | 0 | 0 | 0 | 0 | 74.25 | $430 |

Best finish for 1967: T-51st at the PGA Championship

| 1968 | 4 | 12 | 2 | 0 | 0 | 0 | 0 | 73.83 | $068 |

Best finish for 1968: T-49th at the Greater New Orleans Open Invitational

| 1969 | 2 | 4 | 0 | 0 | 0 | 0 | 0 | 73.25 | |
| 1970 | 2 | 6 | 1 | 0 | 0 | 0 | 0 | 73.50 | $217 |

Best finish for 1970: T-54th at the Bahama Islands Open

| 1972 | 2 | 6 | 2 | 0 | 0 | 0 | 0 | 72.67 | $1,112 |

Best finish for 1972: T-27th at the Sea Pines Heritage Classic

1974	1	2	0	0	0	0	0	75.00	
1975	1	2	0	0	0	0	0	75.00	
1976	1	2	0	0	0	0	0	71.50	
1980	1	2	0	0	0	0	0	74.50	
Period Totals	Starts	Rounds Played	Cuts Made	Wins	Top-5s	Top-10s	Top-25s	Scoring Average	Money
	48	151	30	0	4	4	9	72.81	$7,910

PGA Tour career totals from 1947 to 1980

	Starts	Rounds Played	Cuts Made	Wins	Top-5s	Top-10s	Top-25s	Scoring Average	Money
	235	N/A	N/A	5	N/A	39	112	N/A	N/A

Ken Towns

Year	Starts	Rounds Played	Cuts Made	Wins	Top-5s	Top-10s	Top-25s	Scoring Average	Money
1964	2	6	1	0	0	0	1	73.67	$650

Best finish for 1964: T-14th at the Almaden Open

| 1965 | 19 | 52 | 7 | 0 | 0 | 0 | 2 | 73.54 | $1,718 |

Best finish for 1965: T-23rd at the Oklahoma City Open

| 1966 | 29 | 94 | 17 | 0 | 0 | 0 | 4 | 72.97 | $8,410 |

Best finish for 1966: 12th at the Bing Crosby National Professional-Amateur

| 1967 | 3 | 9 | 1 | 0 | 0 | 0 | 0 | 74.33 | |

Best finish for 1967: T-61st at the Bob Hope Classic

| 1968 | 1 | 2 | 0 | 0 | 0 | 0 | 0 | 82.50 | $500 |
| 1969 | 4 | 15 | 3 | 0 | 0 | 0 | 1 | 72.87 | $889 |

Best finish for 1969: T-19th at the Alameda County Open

| 1970 | 3 | 7 | 0 | 0 | 0 | 0 | 0 | 75.71 | |
| 1971 | 3 | 9 | 1 | 0 | 0 | 0 | 0 | 76.00 | $258 |

Best finish for 1971: T-75th at the PGA Championship

1972	3	7	0	0	0	0	0	76.57	
1973	3	7	0	0	0	0	0	77.43	
1974	2	5	0	0	0	0	0	77.60	
1975	3	7	0	0	0	0	0	75.57	
1976	1	2	0	0	0	0	0	79.00	
1977	2	5	0	0	0	0	0	75.20	
1978	1	3	0	0	0	0	0	76.00	
1981	1	3	0	0	0	0	0	77.00	
Period Totals	Starts	Rounds Played	Cuts Made	Wins	Top-5s	Top-10s	Top-25s	Scoring Average	Money
	80	233	30	0	0	0	8	74.05	$12,424

Peter Townsend

Year	Starts	Rounds Played	Cuts Made	Wins	Top-5s	Top-10s	Top-25s	Scoring Average	Money
1966	1	4	1	0	0	0	1	73.75	

Best finish for 1966: T-23rd at the British Open

| 1967 | 2 | 4 | 0 | 0 | 0 | 0 | 0 | 77.25 | |
| 1968 | 13 | 37 | 5 | 0 | 0 | 0 | 1 | 73.32 | $1,095 |

Best finish for 1968: T-16th at the Magnolia State Classic

| 1969 | 26 | 87 | 18 | 0 | 1 | 4 | 7 | 72.38 | $20,876 |

Best finish for 1969: 4th at the Western Open

| 1970 | 19 | 51 | 6 | 0 | 0 | 0 | 2 | 73.63 | $3,410 |

Best finish for 1970: T-12th at the Tallahassee Open

Year	Starts	Rounds Played	Cuts Made	Wins	Top-5s	Top-10s	Top-25s	Scoring Average	Money
1971	5	13	1	0	0	0	0	74.38	$408

Best finish for 1971: T-40th at the British Open

| 1972 | 8 | 22 | 3 | 0 | 0 | 0 | 3 | 73.64 | $7,544 |

Best finish for 1972: T-13th at the British Open

| 1973 | 1 | 4 | 1 | 0 | 0 | 0 | 0 | 75.00 | $325 |

Best finish for 1973: 55th at the British Open

| 1974 | 1 | 4 | 1 | 0 | 0 | 0 | 1 | 74.00 | $2,400 |

Best finish for 1974: T-13th at the British Open

| 1975 | 1 | 4 | 1 | 0 | 0 | 0 | 0 | 74.50 | $385 |

Best finish for 1975: T-57th at the British Open

1976	1	2	0	0	0	0	0	79.50	$180
1978	1	2	0	0	0	0	0	74.50	$332
1980	1	2	0	0	0	0	0	75.00	$540
1981	1	4	1	0	0	0	1	72.25	$4,025

Best finish for 1981: T-19th at the British Open

| 1982 | 1 | 4 | 1 | 0 | 0 | 0 | 0 | 75.75 | $1,020 |

Best finish for 1982: T-54th at the British Open

Period Totals	Starts	Rounds Played	Cuts Made	Wins	Top-5s	Top-10s	Top-25s	Scoring Average	Money
	82	244	39	0	1	4	16	73.36	$42,542

D.J. Trahan

Year	Starts	Rounds Played	Cuts Made	Wins	Top-5s	Top-10s	Top-25s	Scoring Average	Money
2001	1	2	0	0	0	0	0	76.50	
2003	6	14	1	0	0	0	0	72.43	$7,880

Best finish for 2003: T-71st at the Greater Hartford Open

| 2004 | 1 | 2 | 0 | 0 | 0 | 0 | 0 | 75.00 | |
| 2005 | 28 | 77 | 14 | 0 | 0 | 3 | 7 | 70.94 | $806,304 |

Best finish for 2005: T-9th at the Zurich Classic of New Orleans & Wachovia Championship

| 2006 | 33 | 90 | 13 | 1 | 2 | 2 | 4 | 71.48 | $1,037,242 |

Best finish for 2006: Win at the Southern Farm Bureau Classic

| 2007 | 30 | 99 | 18 | 0 | 1 | 3 | 3 | 71.39 | $1,108,874 |

Best finish for 2007: 2nd at the Frys.Com Open-Vegas

| 2008 | 27 | 94 | 21 | 1 | 3 | 4 | 10 | 70.89 | $2,304,368 |

Best finish for 2008: Win at the Bob Hope Chrysler Classic

Period Totals	Starts	Rounds Played	Cuts Made	Wins	Top-5s	Top-10s	Top-25s	Scoring Average	Money
	126	378	67	2	6	12	24	71.28	$5,264,668

John Traub

Year	Starts	Rounds Played	Cuts Made	Wins	Top-5s	Top-10s	Top-25s	Scoring Average	Money
1979	1	4	1	0	0	0	0	73.25	$675

Best finish for 1979: T-43rd at the Buick Goodwrench Open

| 1981 | 21 | 46 | 2 | 0 | 0 | 0 | 1 | 75.72 | $6,131 |

Best finish for 1981: 24th at the World Series Of Golf

| 1982 | 6 | 14 | 1 | 0 | 0 | 0 | 0 | 75.07 | $1,429 |

Best finish for 1982: 73rd at the Canadian Open

1985	1	2	0	0	0	0	0	73.00	
1989	1	2	0	0	0	0	0	85.50	$1,000
1990	1	2	0	0	0	0	0	75.00	
1994	1	4	1	0	0	0	0	74.50	$2,310

Best finish for 1994: 65th at the Buick Open

| 2003 | 1 | 2 | 0 | 0 | 0 | 0 | 0 | 75.50 | |

Period Totals	Starts	Rounds Played	Cuts Made	Wins	Top-5s	Top-10s	Top-25s	Scoring Average	Money
	33	76	5	0	0	0	1	75.57	$11,545

Lee Trevino

Year	Starts	Rounds Played	Cuts Made	Wins	Top-5s	Top-10s	Top-25s	Scoring Average	Money
1966	1	4	1	0	0	0	0	75.75	$600

Best finish for 1966: T-54th at the U.S. Open

| 1967 | 14 | 50 | 11 | 0 | 1 | 4 | 8 | 71.88 | $26,473 |

Best finish for 1967: 5th at the U.S. Open

| 1968 | 31 | 112 | 25 | 2 | 6 | 12 | 21 | 70.71 | $129,276 |

Best finish for 1968: Win at the U.S. Open & Hawaiian Open

| 1969 | 33 | 121 | 29 | 1 | 8 | 12 | 21 | 71.36 | $108,763 |

Best finish for 1969: Win at the Tucson Open

| 1970 | 34 | 122 | 30 | 2 | 10 | 13 | 22 | 70.74 | $157,631 |

Best finish for 1970: Win at the Tucson Open & National Airlines Open

| 1971 | 31 | 113 | 25 | 6 | 13 | 15 | 21 | 69.79 | $240,332 |

Best finish for 1971: Win at the Tallahassee Open, Danny Thomas Memphis Classic, U.S. Open, Canadian Open, British Open & Sahara Invitational

| 1972 | 31 | 114 | 28 | 4 | 11 | 14 | 20 | 70.86 | $221,005 |

Best finish for 1972: Win at the Danny Thomas Memphis Classic, Greater Hartford Open Invitational, British Open & Greater St. Louis Classic

| 1973 | 27 | 99 | 24 | 2 | 9 | 11 | 20 | 70.88 | $208,615 |

Best finish for 1973: Win at the Jackie Gleason's Inverrary Classic & Doral-Eastern Open

Year	Starts	Rounds Played	Cuts Made	Wins	Top-5s	Top-10s	Top-25s	Scoring Average	Money
1974	26	100	24	2	10	14	19	70.72	$200,808

Best finish for 1974: Win at the Greater New Orleans Open & PGA Championship

| 1975 | 28 | 103 | 24 | 1 | 5 | 10 | 18 | 71.19 | $134,686 |

Best finish for 1975: Win at the Florida Citrus Open Invitational

| 1976 | 22 | 80 | 18 | 1 | 5 | 8 | 14 | 70.68 | $138,214 |

Best finish for 1976: Win at the Colonial National Invitational

| 1977 | 21 | 78 | 19 | 1 | 2 | 4 | 10 | 71.63 | $93,608 |

Best finish for 1977: Win at the Canadian Open

| 1978 | 26 | 103 | 25 | 1 | 9 | 12 | 19 | 70.42 | $229,724 |

Best finish for 1978: Win at the Colonial National Invitational

| 1979 | 25 | 93 | 20 | 1 | 8 | 10 | 16 | 71.04 | $243,982 |

Best finish for 1979: Win at the Canadian Open

| 1980 | 22 | 86 | 22 | 3 | 12 | 14 | 17 | 69.70 | $427,814 |

Best finish for 1980: Win at the Tournament Players Championship, Danny Thomas Memphis Classic & San Antonio Texas Open

| 1981 | 22 | 78 | 18 | 1 | 2 | 4 | 14 | 71.05 | $146,901 |

Best finish for 1981: Win at the MONY Tournament Of Champions

| 1982 | 19 | 53 | 8 | 0 | 0 | 1 | 5 | 72.55 | $36,953 |

Best finish for 1982: T-9th at the Colonial National Invitational

| 1983 | 17 | 64 | 15 | 0 | 3 | 4 | 9 | 71.20 | $131,500 |

Best finish for 1983: T-2nd at the Houston Coca-Cola Open & LaJet Coors Classic

| 1984 | 17 | 59 | 12 | 1 | 3 | 4 | 8 | 71.37 | $291,684 |

Best finish for 1984: Win at the PGA Championship

| 1985 | 13 | 46 | 10 | 0 | 2 | 4 | 7 | 71.87 | $149,110 |

Best finish for 1985: 2nd at the PGA Championship

| 1986 | 14 | 48 | 12 | 0 | 1 | 2 | 6 | 71.60 | $89,203 |

Best finish for 1986: T-4th at the U.S. Open

| 1987 | 13 | 36 | 6 | 0 | 1 | 2 | 3 | 72.19 | $65,232 |

Best finish for 1987: T-4th at the Canon Sammy Davis, Jr. - Greater Hartford Open

| 1988 | 11 | 34 | 6 | 0 | 0 | 0 | 2 | 72.26 | $29,550 |

Best finish for 1988: T-19th at the Canon Sammy Davis, Jr. - Greater Hartford Open

| 1989 | 15 | 46 | 10 | 0 | 2 | 2 | 4 | 71.46 | $126,588 |

Best finish for 1989: T-4th at the Canon Greater Hartford Open

| 1990 | 4 | 15 | 3 | 0 | 0 | 0 | 2 | 71.73 | $27,054 |

Best finish for 1990: T-24th at the Masters

| 1991 | 3 | 10 | 2 | 0 | 0 | 0 | 1 | 72.10 | $21,426 |

Best finish for 1991: T-17th at the British Open

| 1992 | 1 | 4 | 1 | 0 | 0 | 0 | 0 | 71.75 | $10,167 |

Best finish for 1992: T-39th at the British Open

1994	1	2	0	0	0	0	0	73.50	$972
1995	1	2	0	0	0	0	0	76.00	$1,037
2000	1	2	0	0	0	0	0	78.50	$1,064
Period Totals	Starts	Rounds Played	Cuts Made	Wins	Top-5s	Top-10s	Top-25s	Scoring Average	Money
	524	1877	428	29	123	176	307	71.04	$3,689,969

Kirk Triplett

Year	Starts	Rounds Played	Cuts Made	Wins	Top-5s	Top-10s	Top-25s	Scoring Average	Money
1986	1	2	0	0	0	0	0	78.00	$600
1987	1	2	0	0	0	0	0	74.50	$600
1990	26	77	13	0	2	2	5	71.95	$184,464

Best finish for 1990: 3rd at the Buick Classic

| 1991 | 28 | 92 | 18 | 0 | 0 | 0 | 6 | 70.98 | $138,302 |

Best finish for 1991: T-11th at the Shearson Lehman Brothers Open

| 1992 | 25 | 69 | 10 | 0 | 1 | 1 | 2 | 72.55 | $177,422 |

Best finish for 1992: 2nd at the Shell Houston Open

| 1993 | 27 | 92 | 19 | 0 | 1 | 2 | 6 | 71.26 | $189,417 |

Best finish for 1993: T-3rd at the Phoenix Open

| 1994 | 27 | 92 | 19 | 0 | 1 | 8 | 15 | 70.47 | $423,143 |

Best finish for 1994: T-2nd at the AT&T Pebble Beach National Pro-Am

| 1995 | 27 | 100 | 24 | 0 | 5 | 7 | 17 | 70.24 | $644,607 |

Best finish for 1995: T-2nd at the Buick Invitational of California & Canon Greater Hartford Open

| 1996 | 22 | 73 | 16 | 0 | 1 | 3 | 8 | 70.90 | $324,514 |

Best finish for 1996: 2nd at the Deposit Guaranty Golf Classic

| 1997 | 26 | 88 | 19 | 0 | 2 | 4 | 10 | 70.66 | $541,023 |

Best finish for 1997: 3rd at the Greater Greensboro Chrysler Classic

| 1998 | 25 | 82 | 18 | 0 | 0 | 4 | 10 | 70.83 | $474,645 |

Best finish for 1998: T-7th at the Deposit Guaranty Golf Classic & FedEx St. Jude Classic

| 1999 | 26 | 86 | 19 | 0 | 2 | 5 | 12 | 70.72 | $864,399 |

Best finish for 1999: T-3rd at the Touchstone Energy Tucson Open & John Deere Classic

| 2000 | 28 | 97 | 21 | 1 | 5 | 10 | 14 | 70.22 | $2,104,943 |

Best finish for 2000: Win at the Nissan Open

| 2001 | 26 | 83 | 19 | 0 | 1 | 5 | 12 | 70.00 | $1,388,202 |

Best finish for 2001: 2nd at the Michelob Championship at Kingsmill

Year	Starts	Rounds Played	Cuts Made	Wins	Top-5s	Top-10s	Top-25s	Scoring Average	Money
2002	25	79	18	0	1	3	8	70.46	$844,273

Best finish for 2002: 3rd at the John Deere Classic

2003	25	90	20	1	3	5	12	70.44	$2,006,561

Best finish for 2003: Win at the Reno-Tahoe Open

2004	24	84	19	0	1	6	13	70.24	$1,568,426

Best finish for 2004: 5th at the Chrysler Championship

2005	18	52	9	0	0	1	7	71.27	$598,145

Best finish for 2005: T-9th at the WGC-Accenture Match Play Championship

2006	18	56	11	1	1	1	2	71.55	$768,843

Best finish for 2006: Win at the Chrysler Classic of Tucson

2007	25	77	12	0	0	0	3	71.96	$318,034

Best finish for 2007: T-16th at the Mercedes Championships

2008	9	25	4	0	0	0	0	71.80	$32,794

Best finish for 2008: T-50th at the John Deere Classic

Period Totals	Starts	Rounds Played	Cuts Made	Wins	Top-5s	Top-10s	Top-25s	Scoring Average	Money
	459	1498	308	3	27	67	162	70.90	$13,593,357

Paul Trittler

Year	Starts	Rounds Played	Cuts Made	Wins	Top-5s	Top-10s	Top-25s	Scoring Average	Money
1988	28	67	5	0	0	0	0	73.79	$7,524

Best finish for 1988: T-32nd at the Gatlin Brothers - Southwest Golf Classic

1990	29	84	15	0	0	0	3	72.15	$67,149

Best finish for 1990: T-13th at the Canon Greater Hartford Open

1991	4	12	2	0	0	0	0	70.92	$8,768

Best finish for 1991: T-33rd at the Doral-Ryder Open

1992	2	6	1	0	0	0	0	71.67	$3,311

Best finish for 1992: T-45th at the Honda Classic

1993	2	6	1	0	0	0	0	73.83	$2,632

Best finish for 1993: 76th at the Doral-Ryder Open

1994	2	8	2	0	0	0	0	72.88	$6,580

Best finish for 1994: T-39th at the Honda Classic

1996	1	2	0	0	0	0	0	77.50	
1997	1	4	1	0	0	0	0	72.75	$3,390

Best finish for 1997: T-55th at the Honda Classic

2007	1	4	1	0	0	0	0	72.25	$7,640

Best finish for 2007: T-74th at the Frys.Com Open-Vegas

2008	1	2	0	0	0	0	0	73.00	

Period Totals	Starts	Rounds Played	Cuts Made	Wins	Top-5s	Top-10s	Top-25s	Scoring Average	Money
	71	195	28	0	0	0	3	72.78	$106,994

Gary Trivisonno

Year	Starts	Rounds Played	Cuts Made	Wins	Top-5s	Top-10s	Top-25s	Scoring Average	Money
1977	1	2	0	0	0	0	0	73.00	
1980	3	6	0	0	0	0	0	74.17	$600
1981	15	37	5	0	1	1	1	74.76	$16,562

Best finish for 1981: 4th at the Pleasant Valley Jimmy Fund Classic

1982	15	43	6	0	0	0	0	73.12	$5,270

Best finish for 1982: T-26th at the Joe Garagiola Tucson Open

1991	1	2	0	0	0	0	0	76.00	$1,000
1993	1	2	0	0	0	0	0	75.00	$1,200
1995	1	2	0	0	0	0	0	74.00	$1,200
1996	1	4	1	0	0	0	0	74.75	$5,075

Best finish for 1996: 103 at the U.S. Open

Period Totals	Starts	Rounds Played	Cuts Made	Wins	Top-5s	Top-10s	Top-25s	Scoring Average	Money
	38	98	12	0	1	1	1	73.98	$30,907

Dennis Trixler

Year	Starts	Rounds Played	Cuts Made	Wins	Top-5s	Top-10s	Top-25s	Scoring Average	Money
1980	8	16	1	0	0	0	0	72.81	$465

Best finish for 1980: T-53rd at the Southern Open

1981	5	15	2	0	0	0	0	73.80	$1,113

Best finish for 1981: T-69th at the Phoenix Open

1982	1	2	0	0	0	0	0	72.00	
1983	3	8	1	0	0	0	0	74.88	$1,370

Best finish for 1983: T-52nd at the Bing Crosby Pro-Am

1984	1	3	0	0	0	0	0	77.00	
1985	30	84	11	0	0	0	0	73.42	$12,807

Best finish for 1985: T-36th at the Manufactures Hanover Westchester Classic

1986	30	78	13	0	0	2	3	73.12	$42,015

Best finish for 1986: T-10th at the Los Angeles Open & Tallahassee Open

1987	15	40	6	0	0	0	0	71.98	$6,876

Best finish for 1987: T-41st at the Byron Nelson Golf Classic

Year	Starts	Rounds Played	Cuts Made	Wins	Top-5s	Top-10s	Top-25s	Scoring Average	Money
1988	3	9	1	0	0	0	0	73.22	$3,896

Best finish for 1988: T-54th at the U.S. Open

Year	Starts	Rounds Played	Cuts Made	Wins	Top-5s	Top-10s	Top-25s	Scoring Average	Money
1989	5	17	4	0	0	0	2	70.47	$26,767

Best finish for 1989: T-17th at the AT&T Pebble Beach Pro-Am

Year	Starts	Rounds Played	Cuts Made	Wins	Top-5s	Top-10s	Top-25s	Scoring Average	Money
1990	3	9	1	0	0	0	0	71.89	$684

Best finish for 1990: T-54th at the Deposit Guaranty

Year	Starts	Rounds Played	Cuts Made	Wins	Top-5s	Top-10s	Top-25s	Scoring Average	Money
1991	1	3	0	0	0	0	0	74.67	
1992	1	4	1	0	0	0	0	70.00	$576

Best finish for 1992: T-73rd at the Deposit Guaranty Classic

Year	Starts	Rounds Played	Cuts Made	Wins	Top-5s	Top-10s	Top-25s	Scoring Average	Money
1993	29	82	13	0	0	0	3	72.37	$75,032

Best finish for 1993: T-11th at the GTE Byron Nelson Classic

Year	Starts	Rounds Played	Cuts Made	Wins	Top-5s	Top-10s	Top-25s	Scoring Average	Money
1994	2	6	1	0	0	0	0	72.33	$7,609

Best finish for 1994: T-29th at the AT&T Pebble Beach Pro-Am

Year	Starts	Rounds Played	Cuts Made	Wins	Top-5s	Top-10s	Top-25s	Scoring Average	Money
1995	1	3	0	0	0	0	0	76.67	
1997	2	5	0	0	0	0	0	73.40	$1,000
1998	1	1	0	0	0	0	0	76.00	
Period Totals	Starts	Rounds Played	Cuts Made	Wins	Top-5s	Top-10s	Top-25s	Scoring Average	Money
	141	385	55	0	0	2	8	72.84	$180,211

Ted Tryba

Year	Starts	Rounds Played	Cuts Made	Wins	Top-5s	Top-10s	Top-25s	Scoring Average	Money
1987	1	2	0	0	0	0	0	73.50	
1989	1	2	0	0	0	0	0	72.00	
1990	18	48	6	0	0	0	0	72.77	$10,708

Best finish for 1990: T-40th at the Chattanooga Classic

1993	33	94	16	0	1	2	2	71.97	$136,670

Best finish for 1993: T-3rd at the Walt Disney World/Oldsmobile Classic

1994	34	108	22	0	0	2	10	71.28	$247,681

Best finish for 1994: T-6th at the United Airlines Hawaiian Open

1995	35	104	17	1	2	3	5	71.68	$453,183

Best finish for 1995: Win at the Anheuser-Busch Golf Classic

1996	36	103	16	0	1	1	2	71.86	$166,744

Best finish for 1996: T-3rd at the Michelob Championship at Kingsmill

1997	35	103	18	0	1	2	6	71.76	$304,399

Best finish for 1997: T-3rd at the Walt Disney World/Oldsmobile Classic

1998	32	105	21	0	1	2	8	71.35	$421,786

Best finish for 1998: T-4th at the B.C. Open

1999	32	110	22	1	5	5	9	71.30	$1,534,886

Best finish for 1999: Win at the FedEx St. Jude Classic

2000	37	111	19	0	0	0	2	72.15	$258,109

Best finish for 2000: T-21st at the Doral Ryder Open

2001	33	106	21	0	0	0	3	71.02	$308,049

Best finish for 2001: T-12th at the B.C. Open

2002	9	22	2	0	0	0	0	72.23	$17,706

Best finish for 2002: T-43rd at the FedEx St. Jude Classic

2004	9	18	0	0	0	0	0	74.00	
2005	2	6	1	0	0	0	0	71.67	$10,437

Best finish for 2005: T-62nd at the FedEx St. Jude Classic

2006	1	2	0	0	0	0	0	72.50	
2007	1	2	0	0	0	0	0	74.00	
Period Totals	Starts	Rounds Played	Cuts Made	Wins	Top-5s	Top-10s	Top-25s	Scoring Average	Money
	349	1046	181	2	11	17	47	71.71	$3,870,357

Ty Tryon

Year	Starts	Rounds Played	Cuts Made	Wins	Top-5s	Top-10s	Top-25s	Scoring Average	Money
2001	3	10	2	0	0	0	0	70.50	

Best finish for 2001: T-37th at the B.C. Open

2002	6	14	1	0	0	0	0	72.71	$8,620

Best finish for 2002: T-41st at the Tampa Bay Classic presented by Buick

2003	21	50	4	0	0	1	1	73.26	$125,875

Best finish for 2003: T-10th at the Bay Hill Invitational

Period Totals	Starts	Rounds Played	Cuts Made	Wins	Top-5s	Top-10s	Top-25s	Scoring Average	Money
	30	74	7	0	0	1	1	72.78	$134,495

Chris Tucker

Year	Starts	Rounds Played	Cuts Made	Wins	Top-5s	Top-10s	Top-25s	Scoring Average	Money
1990	1	2	0	0	0	0	0	79.00	$1,000
1991	2	6	1	0	0	0	0	73.17	$1,910

Best finish for 1991: T-74th at the MCI Heritage Classic

1992	34	83	9	0	1	1	3	72.52	$92,537

Best finish for 1992: T-3rd at the Buick Invitational of California

1993	14	35	4	0	0	0	1	73.00	$17,473

Best finish for 1993: T-20th at the Canon Greater Hartford Open

Year	Starts	Rounds Played	Cuts Made	Wins	Top-5s	Top-10s	Top-25s	Scoring Average	Money
1996	1	2	0	0	0	0	0	73.50	$1,300
1997	1	2	0	0	0	0	0	76.50	$1,300
1998	3	6	0	0	0	0	0	78.67	$1,500
1999	2	4	0	0	0	0	0	76.00	$1,750
2002	1	2	0	0	0	0	0	73.50	
Period Totals	Starts	Rounds Played	Cuts Made	Wins	Top-5s	Top-10s	Top-25s	Scoring Average	Money
	59	142	14	0	1	1	4	73.20	$118,770

Dick Turner

Year	Starts	Rounds Played	Cuts Made	Wins	Top-5s	Top-10s	Top-25s	Scoring Average	Money
1958	1	4	1	0	0	0	0	72.00	

Best finish for 1958: T-36th at the Texas Open

1960	1	4	1	0	0	0	1	72.00	$753

Best finish for 1960: T-11th at the Texas Open Invitational

1963	1	4	1	0	0	0	0	75.25	$200

Best finish for 1963: T-69th at the PGA Championship

1964	14	35	5	0	0	0	1	73.29	$612

Best finish for 1964: T-25th at the Greater Greensboro Open

1965	1	2	0	0	0	0	0	76.00	
1966	1	2	0	0	0	0	0	73.50	
1967	3	8	1	0	0	0	0	73.38	

Best finish for 1967: T-55th at the Phoenix Open

1968	3	8	1	0	0	0	0	74.63	

Best finish for 1968: T-76th at the Tucson Open Invitational

1969	3	10	2	0	0	0	0	72.70	$310

Best finish for 1969: T-52nd at the Tucson Open

1970	1	2	0	0	0	0	0	73.50	
1971	2	4	0	0	0	0	0	73.50	
1973	1	2	0	0	0	0	0	75.00	
Period Totals	Starts	Rounds Played	Cuts Made	Wins	Top-5s	Top-10s	Top-25s	Scoring Average	Money
	32	85	12	0	0	0	2	73.45	$1,875

Jim Turnesa

Year	Starts	Rounds Played	Cuts Made	Wins	Top-5s	Top-10s	Top-25s	Scoring Average	Money
1958	32	114	25	0	0	1	10	72.49	$4,464

Best finish for 1958: T-8th at the Miller Open

1959	10	37	7	0	0	0	2	72.14	$1,828

Best finish for 1959: T-15th at the Sam Snead Festival

1960	8	33	8	0	0	0	1	73.36	$1,702

Best finish for 1960: T-22nd at the Coral Gables Open Invitational

1961	5	14	3	0	0	0	0	72.57	$772

Best finish for 1961: T-26th at the Houston Classic

1962	3	8	1	0	0	0	0	75.63	$555

Best finish for 1962: T-65th at the Thunderbird Classic Invitational

1963	1	2	1	0	0	0	0	78.50	

Best finish for 1963: T-200 at the PGA Championship

1964	7	18	1	0	0	0	0	74.94	$220

Best finish for 1964: T-62nd at the PGA Championship

1965	2	4	0	0	0	0	0	77.50	
1966	2	4	0	0	0	0	0	75.75	
1967	4	8	0	0	0	0	0	75.00	
1968	8	16	0	0	0	0	0	75.31	
1969	8	19	2	0	0	0	0	74.63	$241

Best finish for 1969: T-67th at the Azalea Open

Period Totals	Starts	Rounds Played	Cuts Made	Wins	Top-5s	Top-10s	Top-25s	Scoring Average	Money
	90	277	48	0	0	1	13	73.35	$9,782

PGA Tour career totals from 1922 to 1969

	Starts	Rounds Played	Cuts Made	Wins	Top-5s	Top-10s	Top-25s	Scoring Average	Money
	344	N/A	N/A	2	N/A	70	167	N/A	N/A

Marc Turnesa

Year	Starts	Rounds Played	Cuts Made	Wins	Top-5s	Top-10s	Top-25s	Scoring Average	Money
2008	29	87	13	1	2	2	4	71.16	$1,329,920

Best finish for 2008: Win at the Justin Timberlake Shriners Hospitals for Children Open

Period Totals	Starts	Rounds Played	Cuts Made	Wins	Top-5s	Top-10s	Top-25s	Scoring Average	Money

Billy Tuten

Year	Starts	Rounds Played	Cuts Made	Wins	Top-5s	Top-10s	Top-25s	Scoring Average	Money
1983	1	2	0	0	0	0	0	74.50	
1984	5	12	1	0	0	0	0	74.50	$800

Best finish for 1984: 70th at the Western Open

Year	Starts	Rounds Played	Cuts Made	Wins	Top-5s	Top-10s	Top-25s	Scoring Average	Money
1985	1	2	0	0	0	0	0	77.50	
1989	25	72	11	0	0	0	1	72.03	$27,135

Best finish for 1989: T-12th at the Southern Open

1990	4	16	4	0	0	0	2	70.19	$25,870

Best finish for 1990: T-11th at the Chattanooga Classic

1991	5	14	2	0	0	0	0	70.57	$4,294

Best finish for 1991: T-30th at the Deposit Guaranty Classic

1993	1	2	0	0	0	0	0	76.00	$1,000
1994	1	2	1	0	0	0	0	69.50	$2,733

Best finish for 1994: T-50th at the GTE Byron Nelson Classic

2001	2	4	0	0	0	0	0	71.50	
Period Totals	Starts	Rounds Played	Cuts Made	Wins	Top-5s	Top-10s	Top-25s	Scoring Average	Money
	45	126	19	0	0	0	3	72.00	$61,832

Bob Tway

Year	Starts	Rounds Played	Cuts Made	Wins	Top-5s	Top-10s	Top-25s	Scoring Average	Money
1981	4	12	2	0	0	0	0	75.92	$2,082

Best finish for 1981: T-66th at the Memorial Tournament

1982	9	32	7	0	0	0	1	72.75	$9,039

Best finish for 1982: T-16th at the Greater Milwaukee Open

1983	8	28	6	0	0	0	2	71.86	$12,089

Best finish for 1983: T-14th at the Greater Milwaukee Open

1984	2	7	1	0	0	0	0	75.00	$1,719

Best finish for 1984: T-74th at the Panasonic Las Vegas Invitational

1985	25	76	14	0	4	4	9	71.55	$164,023

Best finish for 1985: 2nd at the Lite Quad Cities Open

1986	33	112	29	4	4	13	21	70.54	$656,493

Best finish for 1986: Win at the Shearson Lehman/Andy Williams San Diego, Manufactures Hanover Westchester Classic, Georgia-Pacific Atlanta Golf Classic & PGA Championship

1987	28	92	20	0	1	7	12	71.39	$219,459

Best finish for 1987: T-3rd at the Phoenix Open

1988	32	112	26	0	3	4	14	70.82	$393,866

Best finish for 1988: T-2nd at the AT&T Pebble Beach National Pro-Am & Southern Open

1989	30	98	20	1	4	4	9	71.43	$496,120

Best finish for 1989: Win at the Memorial Tournament

1990	31	99	20	1	2	5	8	71.30	$496,857

Best finish for 1990: Win at the Las Vegas Invitational

1991	25	80	16	0	2	6	8	71.03	$381,831

Best finish for 1991: T-2nd at the Northern Telecom Open

1992	22	67	12	0	0	0	0	72.27	$48,832

Best finish for 1992: T-29th at the Centel Western Open

1993	25	68	12	0	1	2	4	72.62	$150,320

Best finish for 1993: 4th at the Hardee's Golf Classic

1994	29	80	13	0	0	0	4	71.48	$116,376

Best finish for 1994: T-13th at the Bell Canadian Open

1995	27	94	22	1	3	8	15	70.30	$789,585

Best finish for 1995: Win at the MCI Classic

1996	25	80	17	0	3	5	11	70.78	$531,764

Best finish for 1996: 2nd at the Nortel Open

1997	26	93	21	0	2	5	14	70.59	$513,864

Best finish for 1997: T-5th at the GTE Byron Nelson Classic & U.S. Open

1998	28	100	24	0	3	9	18	70.31	$1,080,092

Best finish for 1998: 3rd at the U.S. Open

1999	29	92	20	0	2	5	11	71.23	$901,203

Best finish for 1999: T-2nd at the Buick Open

2000	30	89	16	0	0	1	8	71.01	$425,710

Best finish for 2000: T-10th at the Tampa Bay Classic

2001	29	106	25	0	3	5	11	70.08	$1,121,858

Best finish for 2001: T-2nd at the Nissan Open

2002	28	99	22	0	2	6	10	70.38	$1,162,399

Best finish for 2002: T-4th at the Memorial Tournament

2003	26	85	17	1	5	7	9	70.31	$2,604,600

Best finish for 2003: Win at the Bell Canadian Open

2004	26	85	20	0	0	3	6	71.27	$967,553

Best finish for 2004: T-6th at the WGC-NEC Invitational

2005	26	83	18	0	2	4	8	70.77	$1,074,387

Best finish for 2005: T-3rd at the EDS Byron Nelson Championship

2006	25	78	15	0	0	0	1	71.47	$299,726

Best finish for 2006: T-14th at the Chrysler Classic of Tucson

2007	32	103	19	0	0	0	2	71.25	$456,768

Best finish for 2007: T-13th at the EDS Byron Nelson Championship

Year	Starts	Rounds Played	Cuts Made	Wins	Top-5s	Top-10s	Top-25s	Scoring Average	Money
2008	20	70	14	0	1	1	7	69.94	$785,641

Best finish for 2008: T-4th at the Buick Open

Period Totals	Starts	Rounds Played	Cuts Made	Wins	Top-5s	Top-10s	Top-25s	Scoring Average	Money
	680	2220	468	8	47	104	223	71.04	$15,864,254

Greg Twiggs

Year	Starts	Rounds Played	Cuts Made	Wins	Top-5s	Top-10s	Top-25s	Scoring Average	Money
1984	1	2	0	0	0	0	0	73.00	
1985	30	82	10	0	1	1	2	73.79	$33,559

Best finish for 1985: T-3rd at the Greater Milwaukee Open

1986	21	68	13	0	0	0	4	71.37	$41,418

Best finish for 1986: T-12th at the Federal Express St. Jude Classic

1987	15	48	9	0	0	0	1	71.88	$21,443

Best finish for 1987: T-12th at the Georgia-Pacific Atlanta Golf Classic

1988	2	6	1	0	0	0	0	69.83	$2,999

Best finish for 1988: T-26th at the Provident Classic

1989	26	72	11	1	1	1	1	73.42	$154,302

Best finish for 1989: Win at the Shearson Lehman Hutton Open

1990	31	89	12	0	0	0	1	73.00	$49,696

Best finish for 1990: T-16th at the Federal Express St. Jude Classic

1991	30	82	10	0	0	1	3	71.83	$65,081

Best finish for 1991: T-9th at the B.C. Open

1992	16	52	10	0	1	1	4	71.54	$75,027

Best finish for 1992: T-2nd at the Deposit Guaranty Classic

1993	29	89	16	0	2	3	8	71.58	$231,823

Best finish for 1993: T-3rd at the AT&T Pebble Beach Pro-Am

1994	29	64	2	0	0	0	0	73.78	$13,676

Best finish for 1994: T-27th at the Freeport-McMoRan Classic

1995	9	29	6	0	0	0	2	71.00	$42,474

Best finish for 1995: T-18th at the Ideon Classic

1996	3	8	1	0	0	0	0	73.75	$2,688

Best finish for 1996: T-56th at the Buick Invitational

1997	4	12	2	0	0	0	0	71.42	$10,015

Best finish for 1997: T-38th at the Shell Houston Open

1998	5	13	2	0	0	0	0	72.31	$10,107

Best finish for 1998: T-40th at the B.C. Open

1999	2	4	0	0	0	0	0	72.75	
2000	2	6	1	0	0	0	0	72.00	$4,540

Best finish for 2000: T-54th at the B.C. Open

2001	1	4	1	0	0	0	0	72.50	$3,540

Best finish for 2001: T-81st at the B.C. Open

2002	1	4	1	0	0	0	0	70.00	$5,171

Best finish for 2002: T-48th at the B.C. Open

2003	1	2	0	0	0	0	0	72.00	

Period Totals	Starts	Rounds Played	Cuts Made	Wins	Top-5s	Top-10s	Top-25s	Scoring Average	Money
	258	736	108	1	5	7	26	72.40	$767,559

Howard Twitty

Year	Starts	Rounds Played	Cuts Made	Wins	Top-5s	Top-10s	Top-25s	Scoring Average	Money
1970	1	2	0	0	0	0	0	76.00	
1971	1	2	0	0	0	0	0	75.50	
1974	1	4	1	0	0	0	0	72.25	$322

Best finish for 1974: T-55th at the Phoenix Open

1975	9	28	5	0	1	2	2	71.75	$8,182

Best finish for 1975: T-5th at the Ed McMahon Quad City Open

1976	25	89	19	0	1	3	11	71.71	$45,268

Best finish for 1976: 2nd at the NBC Tucson Open

1977	33	110	21	0	1	2	13	71.93	$58,191

Best finish for 1977: 3rd at the Anheuser-Busch Golf Classic

1978	30	113	26	0	3	7	15	71.36	$92,409

Best finish for 1978: T-2nd at the Colgate Hall Of Fame Classic

1979	31	112	25	1	4	8	13	71.57	$179,620

Best finish for 1979: Win at the B.C. Open

1980	32	108	23	1	6	6	9	71.88	$166,790

Best finish for 1980: Win at the Sammy Davis, Jr. - Greater Hartford Open

1981	36	113	23	0	2	3	7	72.35	$59,503

Best finish for 1981: T-5th at the B.C. Open & Pensacola Open

1982	36	113	20	0	1	2	7	72.19	$58,005

Best finish for 1982: T-5th at the Disney World

1983	34	100	16	0	0	0	1	72.89	$20,600

Best finish for 1983: T-18th at the Greater Milwaukee Open

1984	31	101	19	0	0	1	5	72.12	$51,971

Best finish for 1984: 6th at the Texas Open

Year	Starts	Rounds Played	Cuts Made	Wins	Top-5s	Top-10s	Top-25s	Scoring Average	Money
1985	34	114	21	0	1	1	5	71.86	$93,558

Best finish for 1985: 3rd at the Southwest Golf Classic

1986	30	100	25	0	1	3	11	71.54	$157,149

Best finish for 1986: 3rd at the B.C. Open

1987	29	94	20	0	2	3	8	71.39	$170,442

Best finish for 1987: T-2nd at the Kemper Open

1988	33	105	20	0	0	2	6	71.48	$86,293

Best finish for 1988: T-10th at the Federal Express St. Jude Classic & Gatlin Brothers - Southwest Golf Classic

1989	25	82	17	0	0	0	4	71.41	$107,200

Best finish for 1989: T-11th at the Kemper Open

1990	33	95	17	0	0	1	7	71.81	$129,444

Best finish for 1990: T-8th at the BellSouth Atlanta Golf Classic

1991	30	102	22	0	0	2	11	70.89	$226,476

Best finish for 1991: T-6th at the Buick Open

1992	28	84	15	0	1	3	7	70.68	$265,242

Best finish for 1992: T-2nd at the Kemper Open

1993	30	96	21	1	1	2	9	71.09	$428,550

Best finish for 1993: Win at the United Airlines Hawaiian Open

1994	30	93	18	0	0	1	3	71.72	$141,237

Best finish for 1994: T-8th at the Mercedes Championship

1995	29	87	16	0	0	1	6	71.14	$140,695

Best finish for 1995: T-8th at the Ideon Classic

1996	8	22	3	0	0	0	0	73.55	$13,738

Best finish for 1996: T-26th at the Nissan Open

1997	17	48	8	0	0	0	0	72.46	$25,766

Best finish for 1997: T-39th at the FedEx St. Jude Classic

1998	14	30	1	0	0	0	0	73.27	$9,874

Best finish for 1998: T-35th at the United Airlines Hawaiian Open

1999	2	4	0	0	0	0	0	76.25	
2003	1	2	0	0	0	0	0	72.00	
Period Totals	Starts	Rounds Played	Cuts Made	Wins	Top-5s	Top-10s	Top-25s	Scoring Average	Money
	673	2153	422	3	25	53	160	71.75	$2,736,525

Tray Tyner

Year	Starts	Rounds Played	Cuts Made	Wins	Top-5s	Top-10s	Top-25s	Scoring Average	Money
1987	2	8	2	0	0	0	0	71.00	$957

Best finish for 1987: T-46th at the Colonial National Invitational

1988	1	2	0	0	0	0	0	73.50	
1991	1	4	1	0	0	0	0	70.00	$1,940

Best finish for 1991: T-72nd at the Hardee's Golf Classic

1992	27	63	5	0	0	0	1	72.87	$39,047

Best finish for 1992: T-17th at the U.S. Open

1994	1	4	1	0	0	0	0	71.25	$7,193

Best finish for 1994: T-32nd at the Shell Houston Open

1995	31	82	12	0	1	1	2	72.26	$126,339

Best finish for 1995: T-4th at the Shell Houston Open

1996	18	51	8	0	0	0	1	71.71	$50,426

Best finish for 1996: T-12th at the Canon Greater Hartford Open

1997	27	74	9	0	0	0	1	72.35	$57,355

Best finish for 1997: T-15th at the Buick Open

1998	1	4	1	0	0	0	0	71.50	$2,592

Best finish for 1998: T-62nd at the Deposit Guaranty Golf Classic

Period Totals	Starts	Rounds Played	Cuts Made	Wins	Top-5s	Top-10s	Top-25s	Scoring Average	Money
	109	292	39	0	1	1	5	72.24	$285,850

Tom Ulozas

Year	Starts	Rounds Played	Cuts Made	Wins	Top-5s	Top-10s	Top-25s	Scoring Average	Money
1970	1	4	1	0	0	0	0	72.25	$720

Best finish for 1970: T-46th at the Dow Jones Open Invitational

1971	15	40	5	0	0	0	0	73.68	$1,935

Best finish for 1971: T-36th at the Greater Jacksonville Open

1972	19	59	11	0	1	2	4	72.76	$24,243

Best finish for 1972: 2nd at the American Golf Classic

1973	20	47	5	0	0	0	1	74.30	$4,269

Best finish for 1973: T-16th at the USI Classic

1974	3	8	1	0	0	0	0	75.75	$935

Best finish for 1974: T-45th at the U.S. Open

1975	1	2	0	0	0	0	0	77.50	$500
1976	1	4	1	0	0	0	0	74.00	$450

Best finish for 1976: T-57th at the PGA Championship

1977	1	2	0	0	0	0	0	74.00	$500

Year	Starts	Rounds Played	Cuts Made	Wins	Top-5s	Top-10s	Top-25s	Scoring Average	Money
1978	1	4	1	0	0	0	0	75.00	$1,350

Best finish for 1978: T-46th at the U.S. Open

1981	1	2	0	0	0	0	0	77.50	$550
Period Totals	Starts	Rounds Played	Cuts Made	Wins	Top-5s	Top-10s	Top-25s	Scoring Average	Money
	63	172	25	0	1	2	5	73.73	$35,452

Hal Underwood

Year	Starts	Rounds Played	Cuts Made	Wins	Top-5s	Top-10s	Top-25s	Scoring Average	Money
1964	1	4	1	0	0	0	0	76.50	

Best finish for 1964: 67th at the Houston Classic

1965	1	4	1	0	0	0	0	75.25	

Best finish for 1965: 72nd at the Texas Open

1966	1	4	1	0	0	0	0	73.25	

Best finish for 1966: T-60th at the Houston Champions International

1967	1	4	1	0	0	0	0	72.50	

Best finish for 1967: T-31st at the Houston Championship International

1968	1	4	1	0	0	0	0	72.25	$430

Best finish for 1968: 44th at the Houston Champions International

1969	12	36	6	0	1	1	4	71.67	$12,395

Best finish for 1969: T-4th at the Danny Thomas-Diplomat Classic

1970	13	46	9	0	1	1	3	72.13	$8,890

Best finish for 1970: T-4th at the Robinson Open Golf Classic

1971	22	67	13	0	1	1	1	72.72	$19,370

Best finish for 1971: 2nd at the Greater Jacksonville Open

1972	1	4	1	0	0	1	1	69.25	$3,530

Best finish for 1972: T-8th at the Phoenix Open

1989	1	2	0	0	0	0	0	73.50	
1991	1	2	0	0	0	0	0	80.00	
1992	1	2	0	0	0	0	0	73.50	
1993	1	2	0	0	0	0	0	72.50	
Period Totals	Starts	Rounds Played	Cuts Made	Wins	Top-5s	Top-10s	Top-25s	Scoring Average	Money
	57	181	34	0	3	4	9	72.51	$44,615

Bob Unger

Year	Starts	Rounds Played	Cuts Made	Wins	Top-5s	Top-10s	Top-25s	Scoring Average	Money
1964	1	4	1	0	0	0	0	78.50	

Best finish for 1964: 73rd at the Los Angeles Open

1973	1	2	0	0	0	0	0	77.50	
1974	28	82	13	0	0	0	4	72.85	$12,306

Best finish for 1974: T-14th at the Florida Citrus Open Invitational & IVB Philadelphia Golf Classic

1975	19	51	7	0	0	0	1	73.41	$3,356

Best finish for 1975: T-20th at the Phoenix Open

1976	1	2	0	0	0	0	0	75.00	
Period Totals	Starts	Rounds Played	Cuts Made	Wins	Top-5s	Top-10s	Top-25s	Scoring Average	Money
	50	141	21	0	0	0	5	73.31	$15,662

Carl Unis

Year	Starts	Rounds Played	Cuts Made	Wins	Top-5s	Top-10s	Top-25s	Scoring Average	Money
1964	2	7	1	0	0	0	0	74.29	

Best finish for 1964: 66th at the Cleveland Open

1965	8	22	3	0	0	0	0	76.77	

Best finish for 1965: 69th at the Oklahoma City Open

1966	9	22	2	0	0	0	0	75.55	

Best finish for 1966: T-64th at the Texas Open Invitational

1969	1	4	1	0	0	0	0	74.00	$200

Best finish for 1969: T-59th at the Greater Milwaukee Open

1971	5	10	0	0	0	0	0	75.00	
1972	1	2	0	0	0	0	0	76.50	
1973	1	2	0	0	0	0	0	78.00	
1977	1	2	0	0	0	0	0	76.00	
1978	1	2	0	0	0	0	0	77.00	
1979	1	2	0	0	0	0	0	77.50	
1983	1	2	0	0	0	0	0	76.50	
1984	1	2	0	0	0	0	0	76.00	
Period Totals	Starts	Rounds Played	Cuts Made	Wins	Top-5s	Top-10s	Top-25s	Scoring Average	Money
	32	79	7	0	0	0	0	75.85	$200

Brett Upper

Year	Starts	Rounds Played	Cuts Made	Wins	Top-5s	Top-10s	Top-25s	Scoring Average	Money
1981	1	0	1	0	0	0	0		$1,680

Best finish for 1981: T-29th at the World Disney World National Team Championship

1984	31	96	15	0	0	3	3	72.91	$37,782

Best finish for 1984: T-7th at the LaJet Golf Classic

Year	Starts	Rounds Played	Cuts Made	Wins	Top-5s	Top-10s	Top-25s	Scoring Average	Money
1985	31	104	23	0	1	3	11	71.30	$136,187

Best finish for 1985: T-3rd at the Lite Quad Cities Open

| 1986 | 31 | 97 | 19 | 0 | 1 | 3 | 5 | 72.60 | $95,518 |

Best finish for 1986: T-4th at the Tournament Players Championship

| 1987 | 31 | 81 | 11 | 0 | 0 | 1 | 2 | 72.74 | $34,618 |

Best finish for 1987: T-7th at the USF&G Classic

| 1988 | 29 | 83 | 14 | 0 | 0 | 1 | 1 | 71.88 | $56,573 |

Best finish for 1988: T-6th at the Canon Sammy Davis, Jr. - Greater Hartford Open

| 1989 | 5 | 12 | 1 | 0 | 0 | 0 | 0 | 72.50 | $2,569 |

Best finish for 1989: T-47th at the Canon Greater Hartford Open

| 1990 | 1 | 3 | 0 | 0 | 0 | 0 | 0 | 71.67 | |
| 1991 | 6 | 18 | 3 | 0 | 0 | 0 | 0 | 71.94 | $19,881 |

Best finish for 1991: T-31st at the Buick Classic

1992	1	2	0	0	0	0	0	77.00	$1,000
1999	1	2	0	0	0	0	0	78.50	$1,750
2000	2	4	0	0	0	0	0	73.50	
2001	2	4	0	0	0	0	0	73.75	
2004	2	4	0	0	0	0	0	75.75	
Period Totals	Starts	Rounds Played	Cuts Made	Wins	Top-5s	Top-10s	Top-25s	Scoring Average	Money
	174	510	87	0	2	11	22	72.35	$387,558

Omar Uresti

Year	Starts	Rounds Played	Cuts Made	Wins	Top-5s	Top-10s	Top-25s	Scoring Average	Money
1991	1	2	0	0	0	0	0	73.50	
1995	31	96	16	0	0	0	4	71.67	$104,876

Best finish for 1995: T-12th at the Shell Houston Open

| 1996 | 32 | 94 | 14 | 0 | 0 | 2 | 7 | 71.73 | $171,797 |

Best finish for 1996: T-7th at the Nortel Open

| 1997 | 32 | 101 | 18 | 0 | 1 | 2 | 3 | 71.63 | $203,516 |

Best finish for 1997: T-3rd at the Bay Hill Invitational

| 1998 | 35 | 109 | 19 | 0 | 1 | 1 | 6 | 71.20 | $282,347 |

Best finish for 1998: T-5th at the Greater Vancouver Open

| 1999 | 31 | 103 | 20 | 0 | 1 | 2 | 8 | 71.55 | $406,201 |

Best finish for 1999: T-4th at the Buick Invitational

| 2000 | 34 | 94 | 13 | 0 | 0 | 1 | 3 | 71.74 | $213,433 |

Best finish for 2000: T-8th at the Greater Greensboro Chrysler Classic

| 2001 | 3 | 10 | 2 | 0 | 0 | 0 | 2 | 69.90 | $47,450 |

Best finish for 2001: T-23rd at the B.C. Open

| 2004 | 28 | 85 | 14 | 0 | 0 | 1 | 4 | 71.34 | $346,797 |

Best finish for 2004: T-10th at the Sony Open in Hawaii

| 2005 | 27 | 84 | 16 | 0 | 0 | 1 | 4 | 70.86 | $538,238 |

Best finish for 2005: T-6th at the EDS Byron Nelson Championship

| 2006 | 22 | 59 | 8 | 0 | 2 | 2 | 2 | 70.81 | $583,704 |

Best finish for 2006: T-3rd at the EDS Byron Nelson Championship

| 2007 | 4 | 10 | 1 | 0 | 0 | 0 | 1 | 71.40 | $64,350 |

Best finish for 2007: T-19th at the AT&T Pebble Beach National Pro-Am

| 2008 | 24 | 74 | 13 | 0 | 0 | 0 | 4 | 71.05 | $346,285 |

Best finish for 2008: T-11th at the U.S. Bank Championship in Milwaukee

| Period Totals | Starts | Rounds Played | Cuts Made | Wins | Top-5s | Top-10s | Top-25s | Scoring Average | Money |
| | 304 | 921 | 154 | 0 | 5 | 12 | 48 | 71.38 | $3,308,995 |

Stan Utley

Year	Starts	Rounds Played	Cuts Made	Wins	Top-5s	Top-10s	Top-25s	Scoring Average	Money
1986	1	2	0	0	0	0	0	83.00	$600
1987	1	2	0	0	0	0	0	75.00	
1988	3	10	2	0	0	0	0	71.70	$2,819

Best finish for 1988: T-43rd at the Provident Classic

| 1989 | 9 | 28 | 5 | 1 | 1 | 1 | 2 | 70.96 | $108,400 |

Best finish for 1989: Win at the Chattanooga Classic

| 1990 | 34 | 106 | 20 | 0 | 0 | 1 | 5 | 72.12 | $143,604 |

Best finish for 1990: T-6th at the International

| 1991 | 32 | 92 | 13 | 0 | 0 | 2 | 4 | 71.64 | $128,849 |

Best finish for 1991: T-7th at the Southwestern Bell Colonial

| 1992 | 30 | 73 | 6 | 0 | 0 | 0 | 0 | 73.08 | $14,944 |

Best finish for 1992: T-48th at the Kemper Open

| 1993 | 5 | 18 | 4 | 0 | 0 | 1 | 1 | 71.06 | $17,370 |

Best finish for 1993: T-10th at the Deposit Guaranty Classic

| 1994 | 29 | 73 | 9 | 0 | 0 | 1 | 2 | 72.21 | $63,345 |

Best finish for 1994: T-8th at the Deposit Guaranty Golf Classic

| 1995 | 1 | 2 | 0 | 0 | 0 | 0 | 0 | 75.50 | |
| 1996 | 9 | 21 | 2 | 0 | 0 | 0 | 0 | 73.29 | $4,438 |

Best finish for 1996: 70th at the B.C. Open

Year	Starts	Rounds Played	Cuts Made	Wins	Top-5s	Top-10s	Top-25s	Scoring Average	Money
1997	2	5	0	0	0	0	0	71.00	
1998	7	18	2	0	0	0	1	71.61	$20,802

Best finish for 1998: T-17th at the Quad City Classic

| 2000 | 4 | 12 | 2 | 0 | 0 | 0 | 0 | 71.17 | $15,336 |

Best finish for 2000: T-40th at the Westin Texas Open at LaCantera

| 2001 | 3 | 8 | 1 | 0 | 0 | 0 | 0 | 73.00 | $3,540 |

Best finish for 2001: T-81st at the B.C. Open

| 2002 | 7 | 22 | 4 | 0 | 0 | 0 | 0 | 71.41 | $28,423 |

Best finish for 2002: T-40th at the John Deere Classic

| 2003 | 11 | 35 | 6 | 0 | 0 | 0 | 0 | 71.20 | $78,946 |

Best finish for 2003: T-26th at the Greater Hartford Open

| 2004 | 8 | 23 | 3 | 0 | 0 | 0 | 0 | 71.04 | $45,610 |

Best finish for 2004: T-32nd at the John Deere Classic

2005	2	5	0	0	0	0	0	72.80	
2006	1	3	0	0	0	0	0	76.33	
2007	1	3	0	0	0	0	0	73.00	
Period Totals	Starts	Rounds Played	Cuts Made	Wins	Top-5s	Top-10s	Top-25s	Scoring Average	Money
	200	561	79	1	1	6	15	72.05	$677,026

Tommy Valentine

Year	Starts	Rounds Played	Cuts Made	Wins	Top-5s	Top-10s	Top-25s	Scoring Average	Money
1977	9	22	2	0	0	0	0	74.91	$787

Best finish for 1977: T-48th at the Western Open

| 1978 | 19 | 49 | 6 | 0 | 0 | 0 | 1 | 74.69 | $3,972 |

Best finish for 1978: T-25th at the B.C. Open

| 1979 | 24 | 66 | 9 | 0 | 0 | 0 | 5 | 72.64 | $16,815 |

Best finish for 1979: T-14th at the Buick Goodwrench Open

| 1980 | 26 | 74 | 14 | 0 | 0 | 2 | 10 | 72.30 | $40,369 |

Best finish for 1980: T-8th at the World Disney World National Team Championship

| 1981 | 33 | 102 | 20 | 0 | 2 | 4 | 11 | 71.83 | $97,323 |

Best finish for 1981: 2nd at the Atlanta Classic

| 1982 | 36 | 103 | 16 | 0 | 2 | 3 | 5 | 73.03 | $66,745 |

Best finish for 1982: T-3rd at the Canadian Open

| 1983 | 35 | 95 | 12 | 0 | 0 | 0 | 1 | 73.58 | $15,448 |

Best finish for 1983: T-21st at the Panasonic Las Vegas Pro Celebrity

| 1984 | 26 | 77 | 12 | 0 | 1 | 2 | 4 | 73.08 | $39,850 |

Best finish for 1984: T-5th at the Bank of Boston Classic

| 1985 | 33 | 83 | 8 | 0 | 1 | 1 | 3 | 73.10 | $36,228 |

Best finish for 1985: T-4th at the Canadian Open

| 1986 | 23 | 57 | 8 | 0 | 0 | 0 | 1 | 73.18 | $10,093 |

Best finish for 1986: T-21st at the Tallahassee Open

| 1987 | 5 | 12 | 1 | 0 | 0 | 0 | 0 | 74.33 | $1,095 |

Best finish for 1987: T-59th at the Centel Classic

1988	3	6	0	0	0	0	0	74.67	
Period Totals	Starts	Rounds Played	Cuts Made	Wins	Top-5s	Top-10s	Top-25s	Scoring Average	Money
	272	746	108	0	6	12	41	73.05	$328,725

Jean Van de Velde

Year	Starts	Rounds Played	Cuts Made	Wins	Top-5s	Top-10s	Top-25s	Scoring Average	Money
1989	1	2	0	0	0	0	0	71.00	
1991	2	5	0	0	0	0	0	74.80	$1,008
1993	1	4	1	0	0	0	0	70.50	$9,517

Best finish for 1993: T-34th at the British Open

| 1994 | 1 | 4 | 1 | 0 | 0 | 0 | 0 | 70.00 | $9,882 |

Best finish for 1994: T-38th at the British Open

| 1997 | 1 | 2 | 0 | 0 | 0 | 0 | 0 | 76.50 | $1,173 |
| 1999 | 4 | 16 | 4 | 0 | 1 | 1 | 1 | 72.44 | $382,276 |

Best finish for 1999: T-2nd at the British Open

| 2000 | 22 | 67 | 13 | 0 | 2 | 2 | 5 | 71.04 | $775,249 |

Best finish for 2000: 2nd at the Reno-Tahoe Open

| 2001 | 17 | 45 | 9 | 0 | 0 | 1 | 3 | 71.84 | $248,301 |

Best finish for 2001: T-9th at the Accenture Match Play Championship

| 2002 | 1 | 4 | 1 | 0 | 0 | 0 | 0 | 73.75 | $20,072 |

Best finish for 2002: T-45th at the U.S. Open

2005	1	2	0	0	0	0	0	75.00	$3,942
Period Totals	Starts	Rounds Played	Cuts Made	Wins	Top-5s	Top-10s	Top-25s	Scoring Average	Money
	51	151	29	0	3	4	9	71.71	$1,451,421

Tjaart van der Walt

Year	Starts	Rounds Played	Cuts Made	Wins	Top-5s	Top-10s	Top-25s	Scoring Average	Money
2005	1	2	0	0	0	0	0	73.50	

Year	Starts	Rounds Played	Cuts Made	Wins	Top-5s	Top-10s	Top-25s	Scoring Average	Money
2000	1	4	1	0	0	0	0	74.50	$27,750

Best finish for 2000: T-50th at the American Express Championship

2004	12	35	6	0	0	0	1	71.97	$138,785

Best finish for 2004: T-21st at the EDS Byron Nelson Championship

2005	18	54	9	0	1	1	1	71.39	$544,058

Best finish for 2005: 2nd at the Buick Championship

2006	21	57	10	0	0	1	1	71.40	$234,918

Best finish for 2006: T-10th at the FedEx St. Jude Classic

Period Totals	Starts	Rounds Played	Cuts Made	Wins	Top-5s	Top-10s	Top-25s	Scoring Average	Money
	53	152	26	0	1	2	3	71.64	$945,510

Bo Van Pelt

Year	Starts	Rounds Played	Cuts Made	Wins	Top-5s	Top-10s	Top-25s	Scoring Average	Money
1999	28	73	7	0	0	0	1	73.36	$70,080

Best finish for 1999: T-20th at the Bell Canadian Open

2002	28	78	10	0	0	0	1	72.08	$139,357

Best finish for 2002: T-25th at the BellSouth Classic

2004	30	104	23	0	3	5	13	70.38	$1,553,825

Best finish for 2004: T-4th at the Buick Invitational & Booz Allen Classic

2005	33	112	23	0	4	6	12	70.67	$1,611,082

Best finish for 2005: T-3rd at the Memorial Tournament & Chrysler Championship

2006	28	102	23	0	1	4	11	70.79	$1,394,574

Best finish for 2006: T-5th at the Southern Farm Bureau Classic

2007	30	104	22	0	1	4	13	70.27	$1,561,681

Best finish for 2007: T-5th at the Frys.Com Open-Vegas

2008	32	101	20	0	1	1	7	70.96	$903,967

Best finish for 2008: T-2nd at the Puerto Rico Open

Period Totals	Starts	Rounds Played	Cuts Made	Wins	Top-5s	Top-10s	Top-25s	Scoring Average	Money
	209	674	128	0	10	20	58	71.08	$7,234,565

Bruce Vaughan

Year	Starts	Rounds Played	Cuts Made	Wins	Top-5s	Top-10s	Top-25s	Scoring Average	Money
1990	1	2	0	0	0	0	0	75.00	$1,000
1993	2	4	0	0	0	0	0	73.25	$1,000
1994	1	2	0	0	0	0	0	73.50	$972
1995	30	93	15	0	0	0	4	71.72	$78,561

Best finish for 1995: T-22nd at the LaCantera Texas Open

2006	1	2	0	0	0	0	0	76.00	$3,718

Period Totals	Starts	Rounds Played	Cuts Made	Wins	Top-5s	Top-10s	Top-25s	Scoring Average	Money
	35	103	15	0	0	0	4	71.96	$85,251

Vance Veazey

Year	Starts	Rounds Played	Cuts Made	Wins	Top-5s	Top-10s	Top-25s	Scoring Average	Money
1998	29	67	6	0	0	0	0	72.57	$41,145

Best finish for 1998: T-33rd at the Michelob Championship at Kingsmill

2002	1	2	0	0	0	0	0	72.00	
2003	26	66	8	0	0	0	1	72.18	$111,157

Best finish for 2003: T-20th at the FedEx St. Jude Classic

2004	1	4	1	0	0	0	0	72.25	$9,776

Best finish for 2004: 66th at the FedEx St. Jude Classic

2005	1	2	0	0	0	0	0	72.50	
2006	20	59	10	0	0	0	3	72.02	$207,077

Best finish for 2006: T-23rd at the Honda Classic

2007	9	27	4	0	0	1	1	71.89	$185,208

Best finish for 2007: T-10th at the Stanford St. Jude Classic

2008	1	2	0	0	0	0	0	73.00	

Period Totals	Starts	Rounds Played	Cuts Made	Wins	Top-5s	Top-10s	Top-25s	Scoring Average	Money
	88	229	29	0	0	1	5	72.23	$554,363

Ken Venturi

Year	Starts	Rounds Played	Cuts Made	Wins	Top-5s	Top-10s	Top-25s	Scoring Average	Money
1958	27	108	27	4	13	17	24	70.23	$37,758

Best finish for 1958: Win at the Thunderbird Invitational, Phoenix Open, Baton Rouge Open & Gleneagles-Chicago Open

1959	23	90	20	2	5	8	14	70.82	$26,712

Best finish for 1959: Win at the Los Angeles Open Invitational & Gleneagles-Chicago Open Invitational

1960	24	97	21	2	13	18	21	69.31	$41,290

Best finish for 1960: Win at the Bing Crosby National & Milwaukee Open Invitational

1961	22	89	19	0	5	10	17	70.46	$24,811

Best finish for 1961: T-2nd at the Houston Classic & Eastern Open Invitational

1962	11	44	11	0	1	2	3	72.30	$6,046

Best finish for 1962: T-5th at the Bing Crosby National

1963	8	32	8	0	0	0	2	71.94	$3,858

Best finish for 1963: T-19th at the Insurance City Open Invitational

Year	Starts	Rounds Played	Cuts Made	Wins	Top-5s	Top-10s	Top-25s	Scoring Average	Money
1964	30	111	23	3	8	11	15	71.22	$62,847

Best finish for 1964: Win at the U.S. Open, Greater Hartford Open & American Classic

| 1965 | 10 | 25 | 2 | 0 | 0 | 0 | 0 | 75.12 | $295 |

Best finish for 1965: T-35th at the Almaden Open

| 1966 | 21 | 76 | 16 | 1 | 1 | 2 | 7 | 72.71 | $21,462 |

Best finish for 1966: Win at the Lucky International Open Invitational

| 1967 | 23 | 79 | 16 | 0 | 0 | 0 | 6 | 72.86 | $16,847 |

Best finish for 1967: T-11th at the PGA Championship

| 1968 | 20 | 61 | 11 | 0 | 0 | 0 | 0 | 73.74 | $2,993 |

Best finish for 1968: 41st at the Thunderbird Classic

| 1969 | 15 | 31 | 2 | 0 | 0 | 0 | 1 | 74.32 | $1,839 |

Best finish for 1969: T-18th at the American Classic

| 1970 | 11 | 23 | 1 | 0 | 0 | 0 | 0 | 75.17 | $262 |

Best finish for 1970: 64th at the Bing Crosby Pro-Am

| 1971 | 8 | 10 | 0 | 0 | 0 | 0 | 0 | 75.90 | |
| 1972 | 7 | 17 | 2 | 0 | 0 | 0 | 0 | 74.71 | $538 |

Best finish for 1972: T-50th at the American Golf Classic

| 1973 | 16 | 40 | 5 | 0 | 0 | 0 | 0 | 73.90 | $1,568 |

Best finish for 1973: T-55th at the Kemper Open & USI Classic

| 1974 | 11 | 25 | 2 | 0 | 0 | 0 | 1 | 74.40 | $1,780 |

Best finish for 1974: T-24th at the Bing Crosby Pro-Am

| 1975 | 15 | 35 | 2 | 0 | 0 | 0 | 0 | 75.09 | $407 |

Best finish for 1975: T-61st at the Andy Williams-San Diego Open

1976	6	13	3	0	0	0	0	75.92	
1977	1	3	0	0	0	0	0	74.33	
1980	1	0	0	0	0	0	0		
1981	1	0	0	0	0	0	0		
1983	1	2	0	0	0	0	0	76.00	
Period Totals	Starts	Rounds Played	Cuts Made	Wins	Top-5s	Top-10s	Top-25s	Scoring Average	Money
	312	1011	191	12	46	68	111	72.07	$251,314

PGA Tour career totals from 1954 to 1983

	Starts	Rounds Played	Cuts Made	Wins	Top-5s	Top-10s	Top-25s	Scoring Average	Money
	331	1087	210	14	50	79	128	N/A	$270,076

Maurie Ver Brugge

Year	Starts	Rounds Played	Cuts Made	Wins	Top-5s	Top-10s	Top-25s	Scoring Average	Money
1970	2	5	0	0	0	0	0	76.00	
1971	1	3	0	0	0	0	0	77.33	

Best finish for 1971: T-100 at the Bing Crosby Pro-Am

| 1972 | 1 | 4 | 1 | 0 | 0 | 0 | 0 | 74.50 | $280 |

Best finish for 1972: T-57th at the Bing Crosby Pro-Am

| 1973 | 2 | 6 | 1 | 0 | 0 | 0 | 1 | 73.50 | $2,430 |

Best finish for 1973: T-17th at the Bing Crosby Pro-Am

| 1974 | 1 | 3 | 1 | 0 | 0 | 0 | 0 | 74.33 | $227 |

Best finish for 1974: T-59th at the Bing Crosby Pro-Am

| 1975 | 2 | 7 | 1 | 0 | 0 | 0 | 0 | 76.00 | $429 |

Best finish for 1975: T-60th at the PGA Championship

1976	2	5	3	0	0	0	0	77.20	$250
1977	1	3	0	0	0	0	0	74.00	
1978	1	3	0	0	0	0	0	78.00	
1979	1	3	0	0	0	0	0	77.00	
1980	1	3	0	0	0	0	0	74.67	
1981	1	3	0	0	0	0	0	78.33	
1983	1	3	0	0	0	0	0	76.33	
1984	1	3	0	0	0	0	0	76.33	
1985	1	3	0	0	0	0	0	79.33	
1986	1	3	0	0	0	0	0	78.33	
1987	1	3	0	0	0	0	0	77.33	
1988	1	3	0	0	0	0	0	78.33	
1989	1	3	0	0	0	0	0	75.00	
1990	1	3	0	0	0	0	0	81.67	
1991	1	2	0	0	0	0	0	84.00	
1992	1	3	0	0	0	0	0	77.67	
1994	1	3	0	0	0	0	0	78.00	
Period Totals	Starts	Rounds Played	Cuts Made	Wins	Top-5s	Top-10s	Top-25s	Scoring Average	Money
	27	80	7	0	0	0	1	76.76	$3,616

Steve Veriato

Year	Starts	Rounds Played	Cuts Made	Wins	Top-5s	Top-10s	Top-25s	Scoring Average	Money
1976	24	70	14	0	0	1	2	73.57	$10,964

Best finish for 1976: T-9th at the Western Open

Year	Starts	Rounds Played	Cuts Made	Wins	Top-5s	Top-10s	Top-25s	Scoring Average	Money
1977	18	45	5	0	1	1	2	73.73	$25,641

Best finish for 1977: 2nd at the Atlanta Classic

| 1978 | 23 | 59 | 7 | 0 | 0 | 0 | 1 | 74.15 | $7,384 |

Best finish for 1978: T-13th at the Bob Hope Chrysler Classic

| 1979 | 20 | 53 | 6 | 0 | 0 | 0 | 1 | 73.55 | $6,838 |

Best finish for 1979: T-22nd at the IVB Philadelphia Golf Classic

| 1980 | 18 | 45 | 5 | 0 | 0 | 0 | 0 | 73.73 | $5,851 |

Best finish for 1980: T-32nd at the Jackie Gleason's Inverrary Classic & Kemper Open

| 1982 | 1 | 4 | 1 | 0 | 0 | 1 | 1 | 68.00 | $6,768 |

Best finish for 1982: T-7th at the Texas Open

| 1984 | 1 | 2 | 0 | 0 | 0 | 0 | 0 | 73.50 | |
| 1985 | 2 | 6 | 1 | 0 | 0 | 0 | 0 | 72.50 | $1,829 |

Best finish for 1985: T-51st at the Texas Open

| 1986 | 2 | 4 | 0 | 0 | 0 | 0 | 0 | 73.25 | $1,000 |
| 1987 | 4 | 10 | 1 | 0 | 0 | 0 | 0 | 74.30 | $1,687 |

Best finish for 1987: T-54th at the Pensacola Open

1988	3	6	0	0	0	0	0	73.50	$1,000
1991	1	2	0	0	0	0	0	81.00	$1,000
1992	1	4	1	0	0	0	0	75.00	$2,325

Best finish for 1992: T-76th at the PGA Championship

1994	1	2	0	0	0	0	0	75.00	
Period Totals	Starts	Rounds Played	Cuts Made	Wins	Top-5s	Top-10s	Top-25s	Scoring Average	Money
	119	312	41	0	1	3	7	73.72	$72,286

Scott Verplank

Year	Starts	Rounds Played	Cuts Made	Wins	Top-5s	Top-10s	Top-25s	Scoring Average	Money
1983	1	2	0	0	0	0	0	77.50	
1984	1	4	1	0	0	0	0	72.00	

Best finish for 1984: T-34th at the LaJet Golf Classic

| 1985 | 5 | 14 | 2 | 1 | 1 | 1 | 1 | 72.21 | |

Best finish for 1985: Win at the Western Open

| 1986 | 19 | 52 | 8 | 0 | 1 | 2 | 4 | 72.19 | $21,857 |

Best finish for 1986: T-4th at the MONY Tournament Of Champions

| 1987 | 31 | 85 | 12 | 0 | 0 | 0 | 2 | 72.38 | $36,236 |

Best finish for 1987: T-20th at the Greater Greensboro Open

| 1988 | 30 | 98 | 19 | 1 | 2 | 3 | 9 | 71.12 | $367,809 |

Best finish for 1988: Win at the Buick Open

| 1989 | 28 | 87 | 15 | 0 | 0 | 1 | 3 | 72.22 | $84,845 |

Best finish for 1989: T-6th at the Memorial Tournament

| 1990 | 27 | 88 | 18 | 0 | 2 | 4 | 7 | 71.89 | $303,588 |

Best finish for 1990: 2nd at the Bank of Boston Classic

| 1991 | 26 | 54 | 1 | 0 | 0 | 0 | 0 | 74.46 | $3,195 |

Best finish for 1991: T-63rd at the Las Vegas Invitational

| 1992 | 12 | 27 | 1 | 0 | 0 | 0 | 0 | 74.67 | $1,760 |

Best finish for 1992: T-58th at the B.C. Open

| 1994 | 19 | 64 | 14 | 0 | 1 | 1 | 8 | 70.95 | $183,015 |

Best finish for 1994: T-4th at the Anheuser-Busch Golf Classic

| 1995 | 25 | 85 | 20 | 0 | 2 | 4 | 10 | 70.41 | $334,086 |

Best finish for 1995: T-4th at the BellSouth Classic

| 1996 | 12 | 43 | 10 | 0 | 0 | 0 | 4 | 71.09 | $88,800 |

Best finish for 1996: T-15th at the Freeport-McDermott Classic

| 1997 | 21 | 62 | 10 | 0 | 0 | 1 | 4 | 71.60 | $113,254 |

Best finish for 1997: T-10th at the Quad City Classic

| 1998 | 27 | 96 | 22 | 0 | 5 | 9 | 13 | 70.39 | $1,223,436 |

Best finish for 1998: 2nd at the Greater Greensboro Chrysler Classic & Buick Open

| 1999 | 26 | 89 | 19 | 0 | 0 | 1 | 8 | 71.52 | $479,260 |

Best finish for 1999: T-8th at the John Deere Classic

| 2000 | 28 | 106 | 24 | 1 | 2 | 6 | 16 | 70.21 | $1,751,619 |

Best finish for 2000: Win at the Reno-Tahoe Open

| 2001 | 26 | 97 | 24 | 1 | 6 | 8 | 16 | 69.48 | $2,788,401 |

Best finish for 2001: Win at the Bell Canadian Open

| 2002 | 26 | 91 | 21 | 0 | 2 | 4 | 12 | 70.22 | $1,220,022 |

Best finish for 2002: 4th at the Canon Greater Hartford Open

| 2003 | 26 | 96 | 23 | 0 | 4 | 8 | 13 | 69.93 | $2,313,483 |

Best finish for 2003: T-2nd at the FUNAI Classic at the Walt Disney World Resort

| 2004 | 24 | 91 | 23 | 0 | 2 | 6 | 13 | 70.02 | $2,365,592 |

Best finish for 2004: 2nd at the Ford Championship at Doral

| 2005 | 25 | 86 | 21 | 0 | 3 | 5 | 13 | 70.23 | $2,582,213 |

Best finish for 2005: T-2nd at The Players Championship & U.S. Bank Championship in Milwaukee

| 2006 | 25 | 86 | 20 | 0 | 3 | 4 | 9 | 70.57 | $1,733,569 |

Best finish for 2006: T-2nd at the Bob Hope Chrysler Classic & FBR Open

Year	Starts	Rounds Played	Cuts Made	Wins	Top-5s	Top-10s	Top-25s	Scoring Average	Money
2007	23	81	19	1	4	10	11	70.56	$3,114,289

Best finish for 2007: Win at the EDS Byron Nelson Championship

2008	24	81	18	0	2	3	8	70.84	$1,359,620

Best finish for 2008: T-3rd at the Children's Miracle Network Classic

Period Totals	Starts	Rounds Played	Cuts Made	Wins	Top-5s	Top-10s	Top-25s	Scoring Average	Money
	537	1765	365	5	42	81	184	71.01	$22,469,952

Bob Verwey

Year	Starts	Rounds Played	Cuts Made	Wins	Top-5s	Top-10s	Top-25s	Scoring Average	Money
1960	4	16	4	0	0	1	2	72.56	$2,455

Best finish for 1960: T-7th at the Oklahoma City Open Invitational

1961	2	6	1	0	0	0	1	74.67	$285

Best finish for 1961: T-23rd at the Greater Greensboro Open Invitational

1962	4	13	2	0	0	1	1	73.85	$1,327

Best finish for 1962: T-10th at the Memphis Open Invitational

1964	25	78	13	0	1	2	6	72.28	$9,492

Best finish for 1964: 3rd at the Oklahoma City Open

1965	23	82	18	1	3	4	9	72.21	$22,176

Best finish for 1965: Win at the Almaden Open

1966	29	101	20	0	0	1	4	73.16	$11,800

Best finish for 1966: T-9th at the Memphis Open Invitational

1967	23	82	17	0	1	3	7	72.46	$12,891

Best finish for 1967: 2nd at the Minnesota Golf Classic

1968	25	73	12	0	0	0	4	72.97	$6,131

Best finish for 1968: T-15th at the Rebel Yell Open

1969	8	15	0	0	0	0	0	74.60	

Period Totals	Starts	Rounds Played	Cuts Made	Wins	Top-5s	Top-10s	Top-25s	Scoring Average	Money
	143	466	87	1	5	12	34	72.76	$66,557

Camilo Villegas

Year	Starts	Rounds Played	Cuts Made	Wins	Top-5s	Top-10s	Top-25s	Scoring Average	Money
2004	10	30	5	0	0	1	2	70.83	$238,984

Best finish for 2004: T-7th at the B.C. Open

2005	2	6	1	0	0	0	0	71.17	$16,300

Best finish for 2005: T-40th at the Cialis Western Open

2006	29	93	18	0	4	4	7	71.08	$1,744,362

Best finish for 2006: T-2nd at the FBR Open & Ford Championship at Doral

2007	24	82	17	0	2	6	9	70.93	$1,866,961

Best finish for 2007: T-2nd at the Honda Classic

2008	22	78	19	2	5	7	10	70.60	$4,422,641

Best finish for 2008: Win at the BMW Championship & The Tour Championship

Period Totals	Starts	Rounds Played	Cuts Made	Wins	Top-5s	Top-10s	Top-25s	Scoring Average	Money
	87	289	60	2	11	18	28	70.88	$8,289,247

Everett Vinzant

Year	Starts	Rounds Played	Cuts Made	Wins	Top-5s	Top-10s	Top-25s	Scoring Average	Money
1958	20	63	11	0	0	1	2	73.89	$998

Best finish for 1958: T-9th at the St. Petersburg Open

1959	2	7	2	0	0	0	1	71.57	$260

Best finish for 1959: T-23rd at the Tucson Open Invitational

1964	6	9	0	0	0	0	0	77.67	
1965	3	6	0	0	0	0	0	75.33	
1966	1	2	0	0	0	0	0	73.50	
1967	2	4	0	0	0	0	0	73.50	
1968	1	2	0	0	0	0	0	76.00	$500
1969	19	54	8	0	0	0	2	73.65	$2,168

Best finish for 1969: T-22nd at the Bob Hope Desert Classic

1970	1	2	0	0	0	0	0	81.00	$500
1972	1	2	0	0	0	0	0	81.00	$500
1973	1	2	0	0	0	0	0	78.50	
1974	1	2	0	0	0	0	0	80.50	

Period Totals	Starts	Rounds Played	Cuts Made	Wins	Top-5s	Top-10s	Top-25s	Scoring Average	Money
	58	155	21	0	0	1	5	74.32	$4,926

Wayne Vollmer

Year	Starts	Rounds Played	Cuts Made	Wins	Top-5s	Top-10s	Top-25s	Scoring Average	Money
1967	1	2	0	0	0	0	0	72.50	
1968	3	8	1	0	0	0	0	72.13	$740

Best finish for 1968: T-30th at the Canadian Open

1969	13	42	8	0	0	0	2	72.50	$5,751

Best finish for 1969: T-13th at the Doral Open

1970	21	65	11	0	0	0	2	73.37	$6,492

Best finish for 1970: T-15th at the Azalea Open Invitational

Year	Starts	Rounds Played	Cuts Made	Wins	Top-5s	Top-10s	Top-25s	Scoring Average	Money
1971	13	36	5	0	0	0	2	72.94	$4,216

Best finish for 1971: T-12th at the Greater New Orleans Open

Year	Starts	Rounds Played	Cuts Made	Wins	Top-5s	Top-10s	Top-25s	Scoring Average	Money
1972	9	21	1	0	0	0	0	75.86	$216

Best finish for 1972: T-74th at the Sahara Invitational

Period Totals	Starts	Rounds Played	Cuts Made	Wins	Top-5s	Top-10s	Top-25s	Scoring Average	Money
	60	174	26	0	0	0	6	73.30	$17,416

Ernie Vossler

Year	Starts	Rounds Played	Cuts Made	Wins	Top-5s	Top-10s	Top-25s	Scoring Average	Money
1958	28	104	24	1	4	9	16	71.16	$17,760

Best finish for 1958: Win at the Kansas City Open

Year	Starts	Rounds Played	Cuts Made	Wins	Top-5s	Top-10s	Top-25s	Scoring Average	Money
1959	24	96	20	1	4	7	17	71.18	$15,882

Best finish for 1959: Win at the Tijuana Open Invitational

| 1960 | 20 | 76 | 18 | 2 | 3 | 3 | 13 | 71.42 | $11,676 |

Best finish for 1960: Win at the Panama Open Invitational & Carling Open Invitational

| 1961 | 6 | 22 | 5 | 0 | 0 | 0 | 3 | 72.32 | $3,063 |

Best finish for 1961: T-15th at the PGA Championship & Houston Classic

| 1962 | 7 | 27 | 7 | 0 | 0 | 1 | 2 | 72.52 | $2,268 |

Best finish for 1962: T-7th at the Puerto Rico Open Invitational

| 1963 | 4 | 16 | 4 | 0 | 1 | 2 | 2 | 73.00 | $2,488 |

Best finish for 1963: T-5th at the Jamaica Open Invitational

| 1964 | 6 | 22 | 5 | 0 | 0 | 0 | 1 | 73.64 | $1,375 |

Best finish for 1964: T-14th at the Bing Crosby Pro-Am

| 1965 | 6 | 22 | 4 | 0 | 0 | 0 | 1 | 74.09 | $2,126 |

Best finish for 1965: T-12th at the Oklahoma City Open

| 1966 | 8 | 30 | 6 | 0 | 0 | 0 | 2 | 72.97 | $3,858 |

Best finish for 1966: T-18th at the PGA Championship

| 1967 | 8 | 30 | 6 | 0 | 0 | 0 | 1 | 72.97 | $3,446 |

Best finish for 1967: T-13th at the Byron Nelson Dallas Open

| 1968 | 2 | 8 | 1 | 0 | 0 | 0 | 0 | 75.75 | $167 |

Best finish for 1968: T-59th at the Colonial National Invitational

| 1969 | 5 | 17 | 3 | 0 | 0 | 0 | 0 | 74.06 | $545 |

Best finish for 1969: T-53rd at the Colonial National Invitational

| 1970 | 2 | 8 | 1 | 0 | 0 | 0 | 0 | 74.38 | $192 |

Best finish for 1970: T-67th at the Colonial National Invitational

1971	2	6	0	0	0	0	0	75.50	
1972	2	6	0	0	0	0	0	75.50	
1973	1	4	0	0	0	0	0	75.00	

Period Totals	Starts	Rounds Played	Cuts Made	Wins	Top-5s	Top-10s	Top-25s	Scoring Average	Money
	131	494	104	4	12	22	58	72.21	$64,847

PGA Tour career totals from 1954 to 1973

Starts	Rounds Played	Cuts Made	Wins	Top-5s	Top-10s	Top-25s	Scoring Average	Money
185	707	158	4	18	32	84	N/A	$82,193

Bobby Wadkins

Year	Starts	Rounds Played	Cuts Made	Wins	Top-5s	Top-10s	Top-25s	Scoring Average	Money
1974	1	2	0	0	0	0	0	77.00	
1975	27	91	18	0	0	1	6	72.42	$23,330

Best finish for 1975: T-8th at the Tournament Players Championship

| 1976 | 33 | 108 | 22 | 0 | 0 | 0 | 4 | 72.48 | $22,431 |

Best finish for 1976: T-12th at the Western Open

| 1977 | 33 | 97 | 17 | 0 | 0 | 0 | 3 | 72.74 | $20,601 |

Best finish for 1977: T-11th at the Memorial Tournament

| 1978 | 32 | 109 | 23 | 0 | 5 | 5 | 10 | 71.72 | $69,626 |

Best finish for 1978: 2nd at the Joe Garagiola Tucson Open

| 1979 | 32 | 104 | 21 | 0 | 4 | 6 | 12 | 71.81 | $121,043 |

Best finish for 1979: T-2nd at the IVB Philadelphia Golf Classic & Anheuser-Busch Golf Classic

| 1980 | 35 | 116 | 23 | 0 | 0 | 2 | 9 | 72.08 | $56,728 |

Best finish for 1980: T-9th at the Pleasant Valley Jimmy Fund Classic & Anheuser-Busch Golf Classic

| 1981 | 34 | 118 | 25 | 0 | 1 | 2 | 7 | 71.63 | $59,846 |

Best finish for 1981: T-5th at the Hall of Fame Tournament

| 1982 | 34 | 118 | 26 | 0 | 0 | 2 | 12 | 71.70 | $69,400 |

Best finish for 1982: T-9th at the Tallahassee Open

| 1983 | 33 | 112 | 22 | 0 | 1 | 1 | 6 | 72.38 | $56,363 |

Best finish for 1983: T-5th at the Colonial National Invitational

| 1984 | 31 | 110 | 22 | 0 | 2 | 3 | 9 | 71.95 | $109,335 |

Best finish for 1984: 3rd at the Houston Coca-Cola Open

| 1985 | 31 | 108 | 22 | 0 | 1 | 1 | 3 | 71.94 | $84,542 |

Best finish for 1985: 2nd at the Sea Pines Heritage Classic

| 1986 | 31 | 107 | 25 | 0 | 5 | 7 | 15 | 70.92 | $226,079 |

Best finish for 1986: 3rd at the Byron Nelson Golf Classic

Year	Starts	Rounds Played	Cuts Made	Wins	Top-5s	Top-10s	Top-25s	Scoring Average	Money
1987	31	102	22	0	4	7	17	70.60	$342,174

Best finish for 1987: T-2nd at the Shearson Lehman/Andy Williams San Diego

1988	31	113	25	0	2	3	13	70.88	$195,521

Best finish for 1988: T-4th at the Georgia-Pacific Atlanta Golf Classic

1989	31	105	22	0	1	1	7	71.32	$153,184

Best finish for 1989: T-3rd at the Chattanooga Classic

1990	28	103	23	0	1	2	7	71.64	$190,613

Best finish for 1990: T-5th at the Canadian Open

1991	31	103	20	0	0	2	7	71.08	$208,503

Best finish for 1991: T-7th at the H-E-B Texas Open

1992	15	43	6	0	0	0	1	71.98	$30,382

Best finish for 1992: T-20th at the United Airlines Hawaiian Open

1993	24	65	8	0	0	0	1	72.43	$39,153

Best finish for 1993: T-25th at the Memorial Tournament

1994	22	67	14	0	1	2	5	70.97	$208,358

Best finish for 1994: T-2nd at the Kemper Open

1995	30	96	16	0	1	1	4	71.71	$167,727

Best finish for 1995: 3rd at the Buick Classic

1996	32	92	17	0	0	1	3	71.36	$142,003

Best finish for 1996: T-10th at the Deposit Guaranty Golf Classic

1997	6	20	4	0	0	0	1	70.75	$29,789

Best finish for 1997: T-20th at the MCI Classic

1998	32	90	15	0	0	0	3	71.92	$171,854

Best finish for 1998: T-15th at the Nissan Open

1999	5	14	2	0	0	0	0	72.07	$26,672

Best finish for 1999: T-28th at the Touchstone Energy Tucson Open

2000	4	8	0	0	0	0	0	73.50	
2001	1	4	1	0	0	0	0	70.25	$4,887

Best finish for 2001: T-50th at the B.C. Open

2007	1	2	0	0	0	0	0	76.00	
Period Totals	Starts	Rounds Played	Cuts Made	Wins	Top-5s	Top-10s	Top-25s	Scoring Average	Money
	711	2327	461	0	29	49	165	71.72	$2,830,142

Lanny Wadkins

Year	Starts	Rounds Played	Cuts Made	Wins	Top-5s	Top-10s	Top-25s	Scoring Average	Money
1969	1	4	1	0	0	0	0	72.25	

Best finish for 1969: T-67th at the Greater Greensboro Open

1970	2	6	1	0	1	1	1	72.50	

Best finish for 1970: 2nd at the Heritage Classic

1971	10	34	7	0	1	2	5	72.56	$15,017

Best finish for 1971: T-3rd at the Walt Disney World Open

1972	32	112	26	1	6	7	17	71.77	$105,462

Best finish for 1972: Win at the Sahara Invitational

1973	27	105	24	2	9	14	18	71.08	$197,694

Best finish for 1973: Win at the Byron Nelson Golf Classic & USI Classic

1974	29	87	16	0	2	3	7	72.43	$47,730

Best finish for 1974: 2nd at the Phoenix Open

1975	27	78	13	0	1	1	3	72.97	$23,772

Best finish for 1975: 3rd at the First NBC New Orleans Open

1976	27	90	18	0	2	3	6	72.17	$43,099

Best finish for 1976: T-3rd at the Pleasant Valley Classic

1977	28	101	22	2	6	9	14	71.26	$244,882

Best finish for 1977: Win at the PGA Championship & World Series Of Golf

1978	23	76	14	0	2	5	9	71.95	$52,895

Best finish for 1978: 4th at the World Series Of Golf

1979	24	91	22	2	4	6	12	71.70	$195,710

Best finish for 1979: Win at the Glen Campbell Los Angeles Open & Tournament Players Championship

1980	27	90	18	0	2	6	8	71.87	$69,878

Best finish for 1980: T-4th at the Hall of Fame Tournament

1981	27	92	19	0	0	1	10	71.64	$51,704

Best finish for 1981: T-7th at the Memorial Tournament

1982	26	93	21	3	5	9	12	71.20	$306,827

Best finish for 1982: Win at the Phoenix Open, MONY Tournament Of Champions & Buick Open

1983	26	90	19	2	7	11	17	70.90	$321,568

Best finish for 1983: Win at the Greater Greensboro Open & MONY Tournament Of Champions

1984	24	84	20	0	4	8	11	71.43	$226,236

Best finish for 1984: T-2nd at the PGA Championship

1985	25	91	22	3	5	12	18	70.57	$447,908

Best finish for 1985: Win at the Bob Hope Chrysler Classic, Los Angeles Open & Walt Disney World/Oldsmobile Classic

1986	26	89	24	0	4	5	11	71.08	$264,931

Best finish for 1986: T-2nd at the U.S. Open & NEC World Series of Golf

1987	24	88	20	1	6	6	9	70.80	$508,448

Best finish for 1987: Win at the Doral-Ryder Open

Year	Starts	Rounds Played	Cuts Made	Wins	Top-5s	Top-10s	Top-25s	Scoring Average	Money
1988	26	98	24	2	4	6	15	70.52	$623,651

Best finish for 1988: Win at the Hawaiian Open & Colonial National Invitational

1989	26	86	17	0	2	6	10	71.23	$244,643

Best finish for 1989: T-4th at the Bob Hope Chrysler Classic

1990	25	84	18	1	4	6	10	71.48	$675,428

Best finish for 1990: Win at the Anheuser-Busch Golf Classic

1991	24	90	20	1	5	7	10	70.86	$656,535

Best finish for 1991: Win at the United Hawaiian Open

1992	25	91	19	1	1	2	9	70.96	$377,187

Best finish for 1992: Win at the Canon Greater Hartford Open

1993	23	72	12	0	2	2	7	71.17	$245,468

Best finish for 1993: T-3rd at the Masters & Anheuser-Busch Golf Classic

1994	25	67	8	0	0	0	2	72.66	$54,114

Best finish for 1994: T-18th at the Masters

1995	21	59	8	0	0	1	3	71.81	$98,985

Best finish for 1995: T-7th at the Nissan Open

1996	21	62	9	0	0	1	1	72.65	$66,294

Best finish for 1996: T-6th at the Nissan Open

1997	20	71	14	0	0	1	2	71.24	$155,962

Best finish for 1997: T-6th at the Shell Houston Open

1998	12	29	3	0	0	0	1	72.69	$32,436

Best finish for 1998: T-18th at the MasterCard Colonial

1999	20	57	7	0	0	0	1	72.79	$73,433

Best finish for 1999: T-17th at the Michelob Championship at Kingsmill

2000	2	6	0	0	0	0	0	73.83	$2,000
2001	1	2	0	0	0	0	0	85.50	$2,000
2005	1	4	0	0	0	0	0	74.50	
Period Totals	Starts	Rounds Played	Cuts Made	Wins	Top-5s	Top-10s	Top-25s	Scoring Average	Money
	707	2379	486	21	85	141	259	71.56	$6,431,897

Fred Wadsworth

Year	Starts	Rounds Played	Cuts Made	Wins	Top-5s	Top-10s	Top-25s	Scoring Average	Money
1984	1	2	0	0	0	0	0	74.50	
1985	1	2	0	0	0	0	0	75.00	$600
1986	6	18	4	1	1	2	3	70.33	$75,692

Best finish for 1986: Win at the Southern Open

1987	35	104	17	0	0	1	5	72.49	$83,084

Best finish for 1987: T-8th at the Hardee's Golf Classic

1988	30	73	7	0	0	0	1	73.52	$24,129

Best finish for 1988: T-20th at the MCI Heritage Classic

1989	10	24	3	0	0	0	0	72.75	$10,587

Best finish for 1989: T-30th at the NEC World Series of Golf

1990	4	10	1	0	0	0	0	71.80	$684

Best finish for 1990: T-54th at the Deposit Guaranty

1991	5	12	1	0	0	0	0	71.17	$1,292

Best finish for 1991: T-37th at the Deposit Guaranty Classic

1992	3	6	0	0	0	0	0	73.50	
1993	3	8	1	0	0	0	0	73.38	$609

Best finish for 1993: T-68th at the Deposit Guaranty Classic

1995	1	2	0	0	0	0	0	73.50	
1996	7	16	1	0	0	0	0	72.44	$2,368

Best finish for 1996: T-51st at the Greater Vancouver Open

1997	3	6	0	0	0	0	0	73.50	
1998	5	12	1	0	0	0	1	72.17	$23,250

Best finish for 1998: T-16th at the B.C. Open

1999	1	2	0	0	0	0	0	75.00	
2000	1	2	0	0	0	0	0	72.00	
2001	6	13	0	0	0	0	0	73.46	
2002	18	38	3	0	0	0	0	74.74	$16,854

Best finish for 2002: 72nd at the Michelob Championship at Kingsmill

2003	2	2	0	0	0	0	0	76.00	
Period Totals	Starts	Rounds Played	Cuts Made	Wins	Top-5s	Top-10s	Top-25s	Scoring Average	Money
	142	352	39	1	1	3	10	72.93	$239,149

Johnson Wagner

Year	Starts	Rounds Played	Cuts Made	Wins	Top-5s	Top-10s	Top-25s	Scoring Average	Money
2004	1	2	0	0	0	0	0	77.00	$1,000
2007	33	97	15	0	1	2	7	71.27	$1,015,024

Best finish for 2007: 2nd at the Viking Classic

2008	26	83	15	1	1	1	2	71.65	$1,431,001

Best finish for 2008: Win at the Shell Houston Open

Period Totals	Starts	Rounds Played	Cuts Made	Wins	Top-5s	Top-10s	Top-25s	Scoring Average	Money
	60	182	30	1	2	3	9	71.51	$2,447,026

Grant Waite

Year	Starts	Rounds Played	Cuts Made	Wins	Top-5s	Top-10s	Top-25s	Scoring Average	Money
1988	3	8	1	0	0	0	0	72.88	$1,494

Best finish for 1988: T-50th at the Bank of Boston Classic

1990	27	73	11	0	0	1	1	73.03	$50,076

Best finish for 1990: T-6th at the Hawaiian Open

1991	4	13	2	0	0	1	1	71.31	$9,307

Best finish for 1991: T-7th at the Deposit Guaranty Classic

1992	2	2	0	0	0	0	0	75.00	
1993	30	90	17	1	2	4	6	71.76	$412,605

Best finish for 1993: Win at the Kemper Open

1994	25	70	13	0	0	0	2	72.46	$73,195

Best finish for 1994: T-18th at the Phoenix Open

1995	26	84	16	0	1	2	5	71.01	$241,922

Best finish for 1995: T-2nd at the Canon Greater Hartford Open

1996	26	75	12	0	1	2	6	71.53	$304,588

Best finish for 1996: T-2nd at the Kemper Open

1997	31	102	22	0	1	4	6	71.16	$362,320

Best finish for 1997: T-2nd at the Michelob Championship at Kingsmill

1998	31	95	16	0	0	0	6	71.63	$248,136

Best finish for 1998: T-11th at the Deposit Guaranty Golf Classic

1999	31	97	18	0	0	1	5	71.30	$253,209

Best finish for 1999: T-10th at the BellSouth Classic

2000	26	85	18	0	2	4	10	70.26	$1,142,789

Best finish for 2000: 2nd at the Air Canada Championship & Bell Canadian Open

2001	28	76	13	0	1	2	4	71.13	$544,227

Best finish for 2001: 3rd at the Bay Hill Invitational

2002	31	96	17	0	0	1	2	71.05	$332,947

Best finish for 2002: T-6th at the Bell Canadian Open

2003	18	47	6	0	0	0	1	71.45	$151,969

Best finish for 2003: T-12th at the Greater Milwaukee Open

2004	29	77	10	0	0	0	2	72.14	$239,318

Best finish for 2004: T-11th at the BellSouth Classic

2005	6	19	3	0	0	0	0	71.16	$38,855

Best finish for 2005: T-31st at the B.C. Open

2006	8	21	2	0	0	0	1	71.90	$96,950

Best finish for 2006: T-13th at the Booz Allen Classic

2007	12	37	6	0	0	0	1	72.97	$75,347

Best finish for 2007: T-25th at the Reno-Tahoe Open

2008	8	17	1	0	0	0	0	73.00	$12,540

Best finish for 2008: T-61st at the AT&T Pebble Beach National Pro-Am

Period Totals	Starts	Rounds Played	Cuts Made	Wins	Top-5s	Top-10s	Top-25s	Scoring Average	Money
	402	1184	204	1	8	22	59	71.58	$4,591,793

Rocky Walcher

Year	Starts	Rounds Played	Cuts Made	Wins	Top-5s	Top-10s	Top-25s	Scoring Average	Money
1991	1	2	0	0	0	0	0	76.00	$1,000
1994	23	64	9	0	0	0	2	72.61	$41,759

Best finish for 1994: T-22nd at the Canon Greater Hartford Open

1995	4	10	1	0	0	1	1	71.10	$20,300

Best finish for 1995: T-8th at the Deposit Guaranty Golf Classic

1998	1	4	1	0	0	0	0	75.75	$7,696

Best finish for 1998: 59th at the U.S. Open

2001	26	59	3	0	0	0	0	73.25	$32,942

Best finish for 2001: T-32nd at the National Car Rental Golf Classic/Disney

Period Totals	Starts	Rounds Played	Cuts Made	Wins	Top-5s	Top-10s	Top-25s	Scoring Average	Money
	55	139	14	0	0	1	3	72.91	$103,697

Duffy Waldorf

Year	Starts	Rounds Played	Cuts Made	Wins	Top-5s	Top-10s	Top-25s	Scoring Average	Money
1985	2	6	1	0	0	0	0	74.67	

Best finish for 1985: 69th at the Los Angeles Open

1986	3	6	0	0	0	0	0	73.83	
1987	32	95	17	0	0	1	4	72.00	$52,175

Best finish for 1987: T-9th at the Deposit Guaranty Golf Classic

1988	30	92	16	0	0	1	3	71.65	$59,228

Best finish for 1988: T-9th at the Bank of Boston Classic

1989	28	85	16	0	1	3	9	71.08	$150,945

Best finish for 1989: T-3rd at the Texas Open

Year	Starts	Rounds Played	Cuts Made	Wins	Top-5s	Top-10s	Top-25s	Scoring Average	Money
1990	28	88	16	0	0	0	2	72.14	$71,664

Best finish for 1990: T-13th at the H-E-B Texas Open

| 1991 | 29 | 96 | 20 | 0 | 1 | 2 | 9 | 70.58 | $196,081 |

Best finish for 1991: T-5th at the Independent Insurance Agent Open

| 1992 | 26 | 90 | 20 | 0 | 5 | 8 | 13 | 70.36 | $597,520 |

Best finish for 1992: 2nd at the Phoenix Open & Buick Classic

| 1993 | 26 | 84 | 16 | 0 | 1 | 4 | 6 | 71.90 | $212,042 |

Best finish for 1993: T-4th at the Southwestern Bell Colonial

| 1994 | 26 | 80 | 14 | 0 | 1 | 4 | 8 | 71.50 | $274,971 |

Best finish for 1994: 3rd at the Sprint International

| 1995 | 26 | 90 | 21 | 1 | 3 | 4 | 9 | 70.47 | $525,622 |

Best finish for 1995: Win at the LaCantera Texas Open

| 1996 | 21 | 67 | 12 | 0 | 3 | 5 | 6 | 71.31 | $606,682 |

Best finish for 1996: T-2nd at the Greater Greensboro Chrysler Classic & NEC World Series of Golf

| 1997 | 26 | 89 | 20 | 0 | 4 | 4 | 4 | 71.31 | $459,344 |

Best finish for 1997: T-2nd at the Buick Invitational & Michelob Championship at Kingsmill

| 1998 | 26 | 82 | 15 | 0 | 1 | 2 | 6 | 71.06 | $290,092 |

Best finish for 1998: T-4th at the Canon Greater Hartford Open

| 1999 | 26 | 90 | 19 | 2 | 3 | 3 | 7 | 71.32 | $1,302,784 |

Best finish for 1999: Win at the Buick Classic & Westin Texas Open

| 2000 | 23 | 75 | 17 | 1 | 2 | 6 | 9 | 70.89 | $1,390,508 |

Best finish for 2000: Win at the National Car Rental Golf Classic/Disney

| 2001 | 27 | 72 | 15 | 0 | 1 | 1 | 4 | 71.53 | $429,461 |

Best finish for 2001: T-5th at the Reno-Tahoe Open

| 2002 | 27 | 87 | 19 | 0 | 1 | 4 | 10 | 70.43 | $911,003 |

Best finish for 2002: T-5th at the Advil Western Open

| 2003 | 25 | 86 | 19 | 0 | 2 | 3 | 9 | 70.51 | $1,206,005 |

Best finish for 2003: T-2nd at the FBR Capital Open

| 2004 | 26 | 73 | 16 | 0 | 4 | 5 | 11 | 70.49 | $1,488,912 |

Best finish for 2004: T-4th at the Buick Invitational, EDS Byron Nelson Championship & The International

| 2005 | 28 | 82 | 16 | 0 | 0 | 0 | 5 | 71.23 | $462,725 |

Best finish for 2005: T-13th at the Reno-Tahoe Open

| 2006 | 28 | 92 | 19 | 0 | 1 | 1 | 5 | 71.03 | $627,513 |

Best finish for 2006: T-3rd at the Chrysler Classic of Tucson

| 2007 | 23 | 69 | 11 | 0 | 0 | 0 | 3 | 71.55 | $363,335 |

Best finish for 2007: T-12th at the Stanford St. Jude Classic

| 2008 | 4 | 11 | 1 | 0 | 0 | 0 | 0 | 73.73 | $7,350 |

Best finish for 2008: T-61st at the Puerto Rico Open

Period Totals	Starts	Rounds Played	Cuts Made	Wins	Top-5s	Top-10s	Top-25s	Scoring Average	Money
	566	1787	356	4	34	61	142	71.19	$11,685,963

Jimmy Walker

Year	Starts	Rounds Played	Cuts Made	Wins	Top-5s	Top-10s	Top-25s	Scoring Average	Money
2001	3	8	1	0	0	0	0	72.50	$13,164

Best finish for 2001: T-52nd at the U.S. Open

2002	1	2	0	0	0	0	0	76.50	$1,000
2003	1	2	0	0	0	0	0	71.50	
2004	1	2	0	0	0	0	0	73.00	
2005	9	23	3	0	0	0	2	72.57	$155,850

Best finish for 2005: 17th at the MCI Heritage

| 2006 | 21 | 58 | 9 | 0 | 0 | 0 | 1 | 71.62 | $153,950 |

Best finish for 2006: T-24th at the U.S. Bank Championship in Milwaukee

| 2008 | 24 | 73 | 13 | 0 | 0 | 0 | 3 | 71.45 | $282,249 |

Best finish for 2008: T-19th at the U.S. Bank Championship in Milwaukee & Valero Texas Open

Period Totals	Starts	Rounds Played	Cuts Made	Wins	Top-5s	Top-10s	Top-25s	Scoring Average	Money
	60	168	26	0	0	0	6	71.79	$606,214

Art Wall

Year	Starts	Rounds Played	Cuts Made	Wins	Top-5s	Top-10s	Top-25s	Scoring Average	Money
1958	35	136	33	1	10	19	26	70.63	$30,616

Best finish for 1958: Win at the Eastern Open & Rubber City Open

| 1959 | 29 | 115 | 24 | 4 | 13 | 15 | 26 | 70.12 | $53,123 |

Best finish for 1959: Win at the Bing Crosby National, Azalea Open Invitational, Buick Open Invitational & Masters

| 1960 | 21 | 85 | 14 | 1 | 8 | 11 | 17 | 70.21 | $26,455 |

Best finish for 1960: Win at the Canadian Open Invitational

| 1961 | 20 | 81 | 20 | 0 | 5 | 8 | 13 | 69.53 | $18,278 |

Best finish for 1961: T-2nd at the Los Angeles Open & Denver Open Invitational

| 1962 | 19 | 75 | 16 | 0 | 2 | 5 | 16 | 71.08 | $18,212 |

Best finish for 1962: T-2nd at the Insurance City Open Invitational

| 1963 | 23 | 93 | 23 | 0 | 4 | 7 | 17 | 71.45 | $24,389 |

Best finish for 1963: T-4th at the Bing Crosby National

| 1964 | 15 | 56 | 12 | 1 | 3 | 6 | 10 | 71.59 | $19,344 |

Best finish for 1964: Win at the San Diego Open

Year	Starts	Rounds Played	Cuts Made	Wins	Top-5s	Top-10s	Top-25s	Scoring Average	Money
1965	14	51	10	0	0	0	6	72.06	$9,832

Best finish for 1965: T-13th at the Los Angeles Open & San Diego Open

| 1966 | 9 | 27 | 5 | 1 | 1 | 1 | 1 | 72.70 | $21,589 |

Best finish for 1966: Win at the Insurance City Open Invitational

| 1967 | 19 | 72 | 17 | 0 | 3 | 5 | 8 | 71.75 | $55,416 |

Best finish for 1967: T-2nd at the Doral Open, Canadian Open & Thunderbird Classic

| 1968 | 18 | 54 | 11 | 0 | 1 | 3 | 6 | 71.67 | $30,214 |

Best finish for 1968: T-2nd at the Kemper Open Invitational

| 1969 | 14 | 47 | 9 | 0 | 1 | 1 | 3 | 72.70 | $10,660 |

Best finish for 1969: 4th at the Bob Hope Desert Classic

| 1970 | 22 | 70 | 15 | 0 | 1 | 2 | 7 | 72.10 | $18,940 |

Best finish for 1970: 5th at the Houston Champions International

| 1971 | 24 | 76 | 17 | 0 | 2 | 4 | 9 | 71.70 | $51,782 |

Best finish for 1971: 2nd at the Canadian Open

| 1972 | 29 | 99 | 21 | 0 | 1 | 3 | 11 | 72.03 | $37,461 |

Best finish for 1972: T-3rd at the Tallahassee Open

| 1973 | 26 | 93 | 20 | 0 | 0 | 2 | 9 | 72.39 | $29,823 |

Best finish for 1973: T-6th at the Kemper Open

| 1974 | 22 | 73 | 15 | 0 | 0 | 0 | 5 | 72.41 | $14,552 |

Best finish for 1974: T-15th at the Kemper Open

| 1975 | 22 | 69 | 13 | 1 | 1 | 2 | 5 | 72.28 | $44,390 |

Best finish for 1975: Win at the Greater Milwaukee Open

| 1976 | 25 | 80 | 17 | 0 | 0 | 1 | 3 | 72.38 | $22,635 |

Best finish for 1976: 7th at the MONY Tournament Of Champions

| 1977 | 23 | 78 | 15 | 0 | 0 | 0 | 3 | 72.50 | $22,319 |

Best finish for 1977: T-12th at the Bing Crosby Pro-Am & Anheuser-Busch Golf Classic

| 1978 | 9 | 25 | 2 | 0 | 0 | 0 | 0 | 75.12 | $2,535 |

Best finish for 1978: T-62nd at the Pensacola Open

| 1979 | 10 | 31 | 6 | 0 | 0 | 0 | 0 | 73.00 | $6,181 |

Best finish for 1979: T-39th at the Bob Hope Chrysler Classic & Memorial Tournament

| 1980 | 5 | 12 | 1 | 0 | 0 | 0 | 0 | 75.58 | $1,500 |

Best finish for 1980: 51st at the Masters

1981	3	6	0	0	0	0	0	73.50	$1,500
1982	3	6	0	0	0	0	0	75.33	$1,500
1983	2	4	0	0	0	0	0	76.75	$1,500
1984	1	2	0	0	0	0	0	78.00	$1,500
1985	1	2	0	0	0	0	0	78.50	$1,500
1987	1	2	0	0	0	0	0	80.50	$1,500
1988	1	2	0	0	0	0	0	82.50	$1,500
Period Totals	Starts	Rounds Played	Cuts Made	Wins	Top-5s	Top-10s	Top-25s	Scoring Average	Money
	465	1622	336	10	56	95	201	71.71	$580,744

PGA Tour career totals from 1949 to 1988

	Starts	Rounds Played	Cuts Made	Wins	Top-5s	Top-10s	Top-25s	Scoring Average	Money
	583	2270	502	14	N/A	144	303	N/A	$647,585

Dave Walters

Year	Starts	Rounds Played	Cuts Made	Wins	Top-5s	Top-10s	Top-25s	Scoring Average	Money
1969	15	38	4	0	0	0	0	76.24	$594

Best finish for 1969: T-56th at the Alameda County Open

| 1970 | 8 | 18 | 1 | 0 | 0 | 0 | 0 | 73.61 | $342 |

Best finish for 1970: T-28th at the Azalea Open Invitational

| 1972 | 6 | 14 | 1 | 0 | 0 | 0 | 0 | 75.86 | $227 |

Best finish for 1972: T-56th at the Phoenix Open

1973	1	2	0	0	0	0	0	81.00	
Period Totals	Starts	Rounds Played	Cuts Made	Wins	Top-5s	Top-10s	Top-25s	Scoring Average	Money
	30	72	6	0	0	0	0	75.64	$1,164

Bobby Walzel

Year	Starts	Rounds Played	Cuts Made	Wins	Top-5s	Top-10s	Top-25s	Scoring Average	Money
1973	4	14	2	0	0	0	0	75.36	$390

Best finish for 1973: T-62nd at the Houston Open

| 1974 | 25 | 67 | 9 | 0 | 0 | 0 | 3 | 73.21 | $7,560 |

Best finish for 1974: T-16th at the Southern Open & Kaiser International Open

| 1975 | 23 | 69 | 11 | 0 | 0 | 0 | 4 | 72.72 | $9,320 |

Best finish for 1975: T-18th at the Kaiser International Open

| 1976 | 29 | 95 | 21 | 0 | 0 | 0 | 5 | 72.57 | $21,983 |

Best finish for 1976: T-12th at the Phoenix Open

| 1977 | 24 | 66 | 11 | 0 | 2 | 3 | 6 | 72.82 | $33,861 |

Best finish for 1977: 3rd at the Bob Hope Chrysler Classic & Tallahassee Open

| 1978 | 29 | 84 | 17 | 0 | 0 | 3 | 6 | 72.20 | $27,023 |

Best finish for 1978: T-6th at the Ed McMahon Quad City Open

Year	Starts	Rounds Played	Cuts Made	Wins	Top-5s	Top-10s	Top-25s	Scoring Average	Money
1979	25	76	15	0	1	3	6	72.03	$39,058

Best finish for 1979: T-5th at the Tallahassee Open

| 1980 | 28 | 83 | 15 | 0 | 0 | 3 | 5 | 72.41 | $38,306 |

Best finish for 1980: T-7th at the Andy Williams-San Diego Open

| 1981 | 23 | 63 | 9 | 0 | 0 | 1 | 3 | 72.56 | $22,777 |

Best finish for 1981: T-7th at the Greater Greensboro Open

| 1982 | 1 | 2 | 0 | 0 | 0 | 0 | 0 | 83.00 | |
| 1984 | 4 | 10 | 1 | 0 | 0 | 0 | 0 | 72.80 | $618 |

Best finish for 1984: T-66th at the Southern Open

1988	1	2	0	0	0	0	0	73.00	
Period Totals	Starts	Rounds Played	Cuts Made	Wins	Top-5s	Top-10s	Top-25s	Scoring Average	Money
	216	631	111	0	3	13	38	72.64	$200,896

Fred Wampler

Year	Starts	Rounds Played	Cuts Made	Wins	Top-5s	Top-10s	Top-25s	Scoring Average	Money
1958	7	22	4	0	0	0	0	73.27	$226

Best finish for 1958: T-28th at the Mayfair Inn Open

| 1959 | 4 | 15 | 4 | 0 | 0 | 0 | 1 | 73.80 | $590 |

Best finish for 1959: T-20th at the St. Petersburg Open Invitational

| 1960 | 2 | 6 | 1 | 0 | 0 | 0 | 0 | 74.83 | $200 |

Best finish for 1960: T-49th at the PGA Championship

| 1961 | 5 | 19 | 5 | 0 | 0 | 0 | 1 | 71.63 | $612 |

Best finish for 1961: T-25th at the Home Of The Sun Open Invitational

| 1962 | 1 | 4 | 1 | 0 | 0 | 0 | 0 | 72.25 | $110 |

Best finish for 1962: T-45th at the Lucky International Open

| 1963 | 3 | 10 | 2 | 0 | 0 | 1 | 1 | 73.20 | $1,414 |

Best finish for 1963: T-8th at the Phoenix Open Invitational

| 1964 | 5 | 10 | 1 | 0 | 0 | 0 | 0 | 73.80 | $402 |

Best finish for 1964: T-44th at the PGA Championship

| 1965 | 2 | 6 | 1 | 0 | 0 | 0 | 0 | 76.50 | $402 |

Best finish for 1965: T-54th at the PGA Championship

| 1967 | 2 | 6 | 1 | 0 | 0 | 0 | 0 | 74.00 | $632 |

Best finish for 1967: T-38th at the PGA Championship

1968	1	2	0	0	0	0	0	75.00	
1969	2	4	0	0	0	0	0	76.75	
1971	2	5	0	0	0	0	0	78.80	

Best finish for 1971: T-100 at the Bing Crosby Pro-Am

1972	1	2	0	0	0	0	0	76.00	
1973	1	2	0	0	0	0	0	78.00	
1974	2	4	0	0	0	0	0	76.25	
1975	3	8	1	0	0	0	0	76.13	$929

Best finish for 1975: T-54th at the PGA Championship

1976	2	4	0	0	0	0	0	77.50	$500
1978	1	2	0	0	0	0	0	79.00	$600
Period Totals	Starts	Rounds Played	Cuts Made	Wins	Top-5s	Top-10s	Top-25s	Scoring Average	Money
	46	131	21	0	0	1	3	74.29	$6,618

PGA Tour career totals from 1948 to 1978

	Starts	Rounds Played	Cuts Made	Wins	Top-5s	Top-10s	Top-25s	Scoring Average	Money
	162	N/A	N/A	1	3	14	54	N/A	N/A

Charles Warren

Year	Starts	Rounds Played	Cuts Made	Wins	Top-5s	Top-10s	Top-25s	Scoring Average	Money
1999	26	69	8	0	0	0	1	72.93	$67,784

Best finish for 1999: T-24th at the Reno-Tahoe Open

| 2000 | 1 | 4 | 1 | 0 | 0 | 0 | 0 | 74.50 | $22,056 |

Best finish for 2000: T-37th at the U.S. Open

| 2003 | 2 | 7 | 1 | 0 | 0 | 0 | 0 | 74.00 | $11,984 |

Best finish for 2003: T-62nd at the Wachovia Championship

| 2004 | 1 | 2 | 0 | 0 | 0 | 0 | 0 | 76.00 | |
| 2005 | 31 | 87 | 14 | 0 | 1 | 4 | 7 | 71.28 | $1,007,276 |

Best finish for 2005: T-3rd at the Chrysler Classic of Greensboro

| 2006 | 27 | 90 | 20 | 0 | 0 | 2 | 9 | 70.69 | $1,018,841 |

Best finish for 2006: T-6th at the 84 Lumber Classic

| 2007 | 29 | 101 | 21 | 0 | 1 | 3 | 6 | 70.89 | $1,068,440 |

Best finish for 2007: T-2nd at the Reno-Tahoe Open

| 2008 | 29 | 79 | 12 | 0 | 1 | 2 | 4 | 72.08 | $800,694 |

Best finish for 2008: 3rd at the FBR Open

| **Period Totals** | Starts | Rounds Played | Cuts Made | Wins | Top-5s | Top-10s | Top-25s | Scoring Average | Money |
| | 146 | 439 | 77 | 0 | 3 | 11 | 27 | 71.56 | $3,997,075 |

Randy Watkins

Year	Starts	Rounds Played	Cuts Made	Wins	Top-5s	Top-10s	Top-25s	Scoring Average	Money
1984	25	69	8	0	0	1	1	73.48	$14,593

Best finish for 1984: T-8th at the Miller High-Life Quad Cities Open

Year	Starts	Rounds Played	Cuts Made	Wins	Top-5s	Top-10s	Top-25s	Scoring Average	Money
1986	1	4	1	0	0	0	0	70.75	$434

Best finish for 1986: T-59th at the Deposit Guaranty Golf Classic

Year	Starts	Rounds Played	Cuts Made	Wins	Top-5s	Top-10s	Top-25s	Scoring Average	Money
1987	1	2	0	0	0	0	0	71.50	
1993	2	4	0	0	0	0	0	75.25	
1994	1	2	0	0	0	0	0	75.50	
1996	1	2	0	0	0	0	0	74.00	
1998	1	2	0	0	0	0	0	73.00	
Period Totals	Starts	Rounds Played	Cuts Made	Wins	Top-5s	Top-10s	Top-25s	Scoring Average	Money
	32	85	9	0	0	1	1	73.44	$15,027

Scott Watkins

Year	Starts	Rounds Played	Cuts Made	Wins	Top-5s	Top-10s	Top-25s	Scoring Average	Money
1980	26	75	14	0	0	0	0	72.97	$12,945

Best finish for 1980: T-27th at the Andy Williams-San Diego Open & World Disney World National Team Championship

Year	Starts	Rounds Played	Cuts Made	Wins	Top-5s	Top-10s	Top-25s	Scoring Average	Money
1981	22	61	8	0	0	0	0	72.13	$10,114

Best finish for 1981: T-27th at the B.C. Open

Year	Starts	Rounds Played	Cuts Made	Wins	Top-5s	Top-10s	Top-25s	Scoring Average	Money
1982	19	52	6	0	0	0	1	72.48	$9,998

Best finish for 1982: T-18th at the Bay Hill Classic

Year	Starts	Rounds Played	Cuts Made	Wins	Top-5s	Top-10s	Top-25s	Scoring Average	Money
1984	22	58	6	0	0	0	0	73.81	$7,400

Best finish for 1984: T-46th at the Honda Classic

Year	Starts	Rounds Played	Cuts Made	Wins	Top-5s	Top-10s	Top-25s	Scoring Average	Money
1987	3	7	0	0	0	0	0	72.71	
1988	2	5	0	0	0	0	0	74.40	
1989	1	2	0	0	0	0	0	76.50	
1992	2	7	1	0	0	0	0	71.00	$2,265

Best finish for 1992: T-52nd at the Phoenix Open

Year	Starts	Rounds Played	Cuts Made	Wins	Top-5s	Top-10s	Top-25s	Scoring Average	Money
1994	1	4	1	0	0	0	0	71.25	$2,508

Best finish for 1994: T-65th at the Phoenix Open

Year	Starts	Rounds Played	Cuts Made	Wins	Top-5s	Top-10s	Top-25s	Scoring Average	Money
1995	1	2	0	0	0	0	0	71.50	
1998	2	4	0	0	0	0	0	74.50	
1999	2	4	0	0	0	0	0	75.00	
2002	1	4	1	0	0	0	0	70.50	$6,300

Best finish for 2002: T-64th at the Touchstone Energy Tucson Open

Period Totals	Starts	Rounds Played	Cuts Made	Wins	Top-5s	Top-10s	Top-25s	Scoring Average	Money
	104	285	37	0	0	0	1	72.85	$51,531

Nick Watney

Year	Starts	Rounds Played	Cuts Made	Wins	Top-5s	Top-10s	Top-25s	Scoring Average	Money
2003	8	18	2	0	0	1	1	72.11	$73,255

Best finish for 2003: T-10th at the Reno-Tahoe Open

Year	Starts	Rounds Played	Cuts Made	Wins	Top-5s	Top-10s	Top-25s	Scoring Average	Money
2004	1	3	0	0	0	0	0	72.67	
2005	31	89	14	0	0	2	4	71.08	$605,369

Best finish for 2005: T-6th at the Michelin Championship at Las Vegas

Year	Starts	Rounds Played	Cuts Made	Wins	Top-5s	Top-10s	Top-25s	Scoring Average	Money
2006	29	95	19	0	2	6	11	70.82	$1,243,816

Best finish for 2006: T-5th at the Reno-Tahoe Open & FUNAI Classic at the Walt Disney World Resort

Year	Starts	Rounds Played	Cuts Made	Wins	Top-5s	Top-10s	Top-25s	Scoring Average	Money
2007	26	87	17	1	1	3	7	71.13	$1,843,129

Best finish for 2007: Win at the Zurich Classic of New Orleans

Year	Starts	Rounds Played	Cuts Made	Wins	Top-5s	Top-10s	Top-25s	Scoring Average	Money
2008	27	96	21	0	1	1	5	71.02	$878,173

Best finish for 2008: T-5th at the Mercedes Championships

Period Totals	Starts	Rounds Played	Cuts Made	Wins	Top-5s	Top-10s	Top-25s	Scoring Average	Money
	122	388	73	1	4	13	28	71.07	$4,643,743

Bob Watson

Year	Starts	Rounds Played	Cuts Made	Wins	Top-5s	Top-10s	Top-25s	Scoring Average	Money
1958	6	24	6	0	0	1	2	71.67	$1,345

Best finish for 1958: T-8th at the Carling Open

Year	Starts	Rounds Played	Cuts Made	Wins	Top-5s	Top-10s	Top-25s	Scoring Average	Money
1959	5	19	5	0	1	2	3	72.53	$2,138

Best finish for 1959: T-4th at the Puerto Rico Open Invitational

Year	Starts	Rounds Played	Cuts Made	Wins	Top-5s	Top-10s	Top-25s	Scoring Average	Money
1960	3	12	3	0	1	2	3	72.75	$1,400

Best finish for 1960: T-5th at the Jamaica Open Invitational

Year	Starts	Rounds Played	Cuts Made	Wins	Top-5s	Top-10s	Top-25s	Scoring Average	Money
1962	1	3	1	0	0	0	0	73.33	$080

Best finish for 1962: T-77th at the Thunderbird Classic Invitational

Year	Starts	Rounds Played	Cuts Made	Wins	Top-5s	Top-10s	Top-25s	Scoring Average	Money
1963	2	6	1	0	0	0	0	74.17	$330

Best finish for 1963: T-61st at the Thunderbird Classic Invitational

Year	Starts	Rounds Played	Cuts Made	Wins	Top-5s	Top-10s	Top-25s	Scoring Average	Money
1964	14	33	4	0	0	0	1	74.58	$507

Best finish for 1964: T-15th at the St. Petersburg Open

Year	Starts	Rounds Played	Cuts Made	Wins	Top-5s	Top-10s	Top-25s	Scoring Average	Money
1965	3	8	0	0	0	0	0	75.25	
1966	3	6	0	0	0	0	0	78.67	$300

Year	Starts	Rounds Played	Cuts Made	Wins	Top-5s	Top-10s	Top-25s	Scoring Average	Money
1967	1	2	0	0	0	0	0	78.00	
1968	2	4	0	0	0	0	0	75.25	
1969	1	3	0	0	0	0	0	77.67	
1970	1	2	0	0	0	0	0	76.50	
1972	1	2	0	0	0	0	0	76.00	
1975	1	2	0	0	0	0	0	78.50	
1976	1	2	0	0	0	0	0	77.00	
1977	1	2	0	0	0	0	0	80.00	
Period Totals	Starts	Rounds Played	Cuts Made	Wins	Top-5s	Top-10s	Top-25s	Scoring Average	Money
	46	130	20	0	2	5	9	74.13	$6,100

Bubba Watson

Year	Starts	Rounds Played	Cuts Made	Wins	Top-5s	Top-10s	Top-25s	Scoring Average	Money
2002	1	2	0	0	0	0	0	75.50	
2004	1	2	0	0	0	0	0	73.50	$1,000
2006	27	79	15	0	2	3	6	70.66	$1,019,264
Best finish for 2006: T-3rd at the Chrysler Classic of Tucson									
2007	26	80	13	0	4	5	9	71.24	$1,657,306
Best finish for 2007: T-2nd at the Shell Houston Open									
2008	29	97	19	0	1	3	7	71.07	$1,533,523
Best finish for 2008: T-2nd at the Buick Open									
Period Totals	Starts	Rounds Played	Cuts Made	Wins	Top-5s	Top-10s	Top-25s	Scoring Average	Money
	84	260	47	0	7	11	22	71.05	$4,211,093

Denis Watson

Year	Starts	Rounds Played	Cuts Made	Wins	Top-5s	Top-10s	Top-25s	Scoring Average	Money
1979	1	4	1	0	0	0	0	75.00	$1,003
Best finish for 1979: T-41st at the British Open									
1980	4	11	1	0	0	0	1	73.09	$6,590
Best finish for 1980: T-19th at the World Series Of Golf									
1981	12	42	9	0	1	4	7	71.17	$49,153
Best finish for 1981: T-4th at the Danny Thomas Memphis Classic									
1982	21	58	10	0	2	3	6	72.57	$73,870
Best finish for 1982: T-2nd at the Bay Hill Classic & Tallahassee Open									
1983	20	64	12	0	1	2	2	72.48	$59,659
Best finish for 1983: T-2nd at the Greater Greensboro Open									
1984	27	87	16	3	3	4	9	71.61	$408,562
Best finish for 1984: Win at the Buick Open, NEC World Series of Golf & Panasonic Las Vegas Invitational									
1985	20	70	15	0	2	2	5	72.53	$158,931
Best finish for 1985: T-2nd at the U.S. Open & NEC World Series of Golf									
1986	23	66	12	0	0	0	6	72.15	$61,553
Best finish for 1986: T-12th at the U.S. Open & Canon Sammy Davis, Jr. - Greater Hartford Open									
1987	29	94	21	0	3	5	8	71.29	$231,074
Best finish for 1987: T-2nd at the Federal Express St. Jude Classic									
1988	26	77	14	0	0	0	2	72.66	$52,238
Best finish for 1988: T-11th at the Kemper Open									
1989	9	16	1	0	0	0	0	75.38	$3,958
Best finish for 1989: T-43rd at the Doral-Ryder Open									
1990	13	33	3	0	1	1	1	72.88	$43,013
Best finish for 1990: T-5th at the Kemper Open									
1991	22	57	8	0	0	0	0	72.11	$17,749
Best finish for 1991: T-46th at the Northern Telecom Open									
1992	16	39	5	0	0	0	0	73.33	$17,105
Best finish for 1992: T-29th at the Canadian Open									
1993	24	61	9	0	1	1	1	73.02	$111,977
Best finish for 1993: 2nd at the B.C. Open									
1994	16	35	1	0	0	0	0	75.54	$4,250
Best finish for 1994: 85th at the Players Championship									
1996	11	27	3	0	0	0	0	72.22	$12,118
Best finish for 1996: T-28th at the Greater Vancouver Open									
1997	2	4	0	0	0	0	0	76.25	
1998	1	1	0	0	0	0	0	78.00	
1999	3	5	0	0	0	0	0	73.80	
2002	1	2	0	0	0	0	0	72.50	
2003	1	1	0	0	0	0	0	76.00	
2007	1	2	0	0	0	0	0	79.00	$2,500
Period Totals	Starts	Rounds Played	Cuts Made	Wins	Top-5s	Top-10s	Top-25s	Scoring Average	Money
	303	856	141	3	14	22	48	72.51	$1,315,304

Tom Watson

Year	Starts	Rounds Played	Cuts Made	Wins	Top-5s	Top-10s	Top-25s	Scoring Average	Money
1970	1	2	0	0	0	0	0	76.50	
1971	4	14	3	0	0	0	0	73.21	$1,461

Best finish for 1971: T-28th at the Kaiser International Open

Year	Starts	Rounds Played	Cuts Made	Wins	Top-5s	Top-10s	Top-25s	Scoring Average	Money
1972	31	103	20	0	1	1	7	72.64	$29,248

Best finish for 1972: 2nd at the Quad Cities Open

Year	Starts	Rounds Played	Cuts Made	Wins	Top-5s	Top-10s	Top-25s	Scoring Average	Money
1973	30	110	22	0	4	7	12	71.67	$71,710

Best finish for 1973: 3rd at the Hawaiian Open

Year	Starts	Rounds Played	Cuts Made	Wins	Top-5s	Top-10s	Top-25s	Scoring Average	Money
1974	29	111	27	1	6	10	20	70.96	$131,537

Best finish for 1974: Win at the Western Open

Year	Starts	Rounds Played	Cuts Made	Wins	Top-5s	Top-10s	Top-25s	Scoring Average	Money
1975	26	98	23	2	4	13	22	70.84	$170,296

Best finish for 1975: Win at the Byron Nelson Golf Classic & British Open

Year	Starts	Rounds Played	Cuts Made	Wins	Top-5s	Top-10s	Top-25s	Scoring Average	Money
1976	25	93	21	0	7	11	15	71.10	$137,213

Best finish for 1976: T-2nd at the Glen Campbell Los Angeles Open & American Express Westchester Classic

Year	Starts	Rounds Played	Cuts Made	Wins	Top-5s	Top-10s	Top-25s	Scoring Average	Money
1977	24	94	23	5	12	18	21	70.20	$327,653

Best finish for 1977: Win at the Bing Crosby Pro-Am, Andy Williams-San Diego Open, Masters, Western Open & British Open

Year	Starts	Rounds Played	Cuts Made	Wins	Top-5s	Top-10s	Top-25s	Scoring Average	Money
1978	25	97	23	5	11	15	22	70.21	$366,989

Best finish for 1978: Win at the Joe Garagiola Tucson Open, Bing Crosby Pro-Am, Byron Nelson Golf Classic, Colgate Hall Of Fame Classic & Anheuser-Busch Golf Classic

Year	Starts	Rounds Played	Cuts Made	Wins	Top-5s	Top-10s	Top-25s	Scoring Average	Money
1979	22	86	21	5	12	15	18	70.45	$465,100

Best finish for 1979: Win at the Sea Pines Heritage Classic, MONY Tournament Of Champions, Byron Nelson Golf Classic, Memorial Tournament & Colgate Hall Of Fame Classic

Year	Starts	Rounds Played	Cuts Made	Wins	Top-5s	Top-10s	Top-25s	Scoring Average	Money
1980	23	92	23	7	13	17	23	69.86	$590,808

Best finish for 1980: Win at the Andy Williams-San Diego Open, Glen Campbell Los Angeles Open, MONY Tournament Of Champions, Greater New Orleans Open, Byron Nelson Golf Classic, British Open & World Series Of Golf

Year	Starts	Rounds Played	Cuts Made	Wins	Top-5s	Top-10s	Top-25s	Scoring Average	Money
1981	22	81	20	3	7	10	17	70.83	$350,647

Best finish for 1981: Win at the Masters, USF&G New Orleans Open & Atlanta Classic

Year	Starts	Rounds Played	Cuts Made	Wins	Top-5s	Top-10s	Top-25s	Scoring Average	Money
1982	21	82	20	4	8	13	18	70.48	$370,883

Best finish for 1982: Win at the Glen Campbell Los Angeles Open, Sea Pines Heritage Classic, U.S. Open & British Open

Year	Starts	Rounds Played	Cuts Made	Wins	Top-5s	Top-10s	Top-25s	Scoring Average	Money
1983	18	70	17	1	7	11	15	70.77	$297,519

Best finish for 1983: Win at the British Open

Year	Starts	Rounds Played	Cuts Made	Wins	Top-5s	Top-10s	Top-25s	Scoring Average	Money
1984	21	75	18	3	8	10	16	70.89	$517,730

Best finish for 1984: Win at the Seiko Tucson-Match Play Championship, MONY Tournament Of Champions & Western Open

Year	Starts	Rounds Played	Cuts Made	Wins	Top-5s	Top-10s	Top-25s	Scoring Average	Money
1985	20	72	18	0	4	7	11	71.19	$245,264

Best finish for 1985: 2nd at the Hertz Bay Hill Classic

Year	Starts	Rounds Played	Cuts Made	Wins	Top-5s	Top-10s	Top-25s	Scoring Average	Money
1986	21	65	18	0	4	9	13	70.51	$283,090

Best finish for 1986: T-3rd at the AT&T Pebble Beach Pro-Am, Hawaiian Open, Houston Open & Colonial National Invitational

Year	Starts	Rounds Played	Cuts Made	Wins	Top-5s	Top-10s	Top-25s	Scoring Average	Money
1987	22	71	16	1	2	6	13	70.44	$653,151

Best finish for 1987: Win at the Nabisco Championship of Golf

Year	Starts	Rounds Played	Cuts Made	Wins	Top-5s	Top-10s	Top-25s	Scoring Average	Money
1988	20	69	16	0	1	6	11	70.74	$281,036

Best finish for 1988: 2nd at the NEC World Series of Golf

Year	Starts	Rounds Played	Cuts Made	Wins	Top-5s	Top-10s	Top-25s	Scoring Average	Money
1989	19	63	14	0	2	3	8	71.44	$249,398

Best finish for 1989: T-3rd at the Manufactures Hanover Westchester Classic

Year	Starts	Rounds Played	Cuts Made	Wins	Top-5s	Top-10s	Top-25s	Scoring Average	Money
1990	18	59	13	0	0	5	9	71.86	$215,984

Best finish for 1990: 7th at the Masters, GTE Byron Nelson Classic & Centel Western Open

Year	Starts	Rounds Played	Cuts Made	Wins	Top-5s	Top-10s	Top-25s	Scoring Average	Money
1991	17	55	13	0	3	6	10	70.64	$367,217

Best finish for 1991: T-2nd at the Phoenix Open

Year	Starts	Rounds Played	Cuts Made	Wins	Top-5s	Top-10s	Top-25s	Scoring Average	Money
1992	16	50	12	0	1	5	7	70.94	$302,018

Best finish for 1992: T-2nd at the Players Championship

Year	Starts	Rounds Played	Cuts Made	Wins	Top-5s	Top-10s	Top-25s	Scoring Average	Money
1993	17	58	14	0	2	4	8	70.88	$342,946

Best finish for 1993: T-5th at the U.S. Open & PGA Championship

Year	Starts	Rounds Played	Cuts Made	Wins	Top-5s	Top-10s	Top-25s	Scoring Average	Money
1994	16	58	15	0	1	5	10	70.69	$411,698

Best finish for 1994: T-2nd at the AT&T Pebble Beach Pro-Am

Year	Starts	Rounds Played	Cuts Made	Wins	Top-5s	Top-10s	Top-25s	Scoring Average	Money
1995	16	56	14	0	1	3	7	70.93	$320,785

Best finish for 1995: T-5th at the Memorial Tournament

Year	Starts	Rounds Played	Cuts Made	Wins	Top-5s	Top-10s	Top-25s	Scoring Average	Money
1996	15	54	14	1	3	4	7	70.37	$762,738

Best finish for 1996: Win at the Memorial Tournament

Year	Starts	Rounds Played	Cuts Made	Wins	Top-5s	Top-10s	Top-25s	Scoring Average	Money
1997	16	52	12	0	2	5	8	70.98	$480,446

Best finish for 1997: T-3rd at the GTE Byron Nelson Classic

Year	Starts	Rounds Played	Cuts Made	Wins	Top-5s	Top-10s	Top-25s	Scoring Average	Money
1998	15	49	10	1	3	4	5	70.61	$985,401

Best finish for 1998: Win at the MasterCard Colonial

Year	Starts	Rounds Played	Cuts Made	Wins	Top-5s	Top-10s	Top-25s	Scoring Average	Money
1999	13	35	7	0	0	0	1	73.40	$149,879

Best finish for 1999: T-16th at the Sony Open in Hawaii

Year	Starts	Rounds Played	Cuts Made	Wins	Top-5s	Top-10s	Top-25s	Scoring Average	Money
2000	4	14	3	0	0	1	1	72.50	$163,409

Best finish for 2000: T-9th at the PGA Championship

Year	Starts	Rounds Played	Cuts Made	Wins	Top-5s	Top-10s	Top-25s	Scoring Average	Money
2001	4	10	1	0	0	0	0	73.10	$16,237

Best finish for 2001: T-66th at the PGA Championship

Year	Starts	Rounds Played	Cuts Made	Wins	Top-5s	Top-10s	Top-25s	Scoring Average	Money
2002	4	14	3	0	0	1	1	73.00	$183,290

Best finish for 2002: 7th at the MasterCard Colonial

Year	Starts	Rounds Played	Cuts Made	Wins	Top-5s	Top-10s	Top-25s	Scoring Average	Money
2003	4	12	2	0	0	0	1	73.00	$115,017

Best finish for 2003: T-18th at the British Open

Year	Starts	Rounds Played	Cuts Made	Wins	Top-5s	Top-10s	Top-25s	Scoring Average	Money
2004	2	6	1	0	0	0	0	74.00	$15,350

Best finish for 2004: T-66th at the Bay Hill Invitational

Year	Starts	Rounds Played	Cuts Made	Wins	Top-5s	Top-10s	Top-25s	Scoring Average	Money
2005	2	6	1	0	0	0	0	73.33	$31,243

Best finish for 2005: T-41st at the British Open

| 2006 | 2 | 6 | 1 | 0 | 0 | 0 | 0 | 73.67 | $26,578 |

Best finish for 2006: T-48th at the British Open

| 2007 | 2 | 6 | 1 | 0 | 0 | 0 | 1 | 72.33 | $64,350 |

Best finish for 2007: T-19th at the AT&T Pebble Beach National Pro-Am

2008	2	4	0	0	0	0	0	75.00	
Period Totals	Starts	Rounds Played	Cuts Made	Wins	Top-5s	Top-10s	Top-25s	Scoring Average	Money
	609	2152	500	39	129	225	358	71.02	$10,495,320

Brian Watts

Year	Starts	Rounds Played	Cuts Made	Wins	Top-5s	Top-10s	Top-25s	Scoring Average	Money
1986	2	4	0	0	0	0	0	76.50	
1988	2	6	1	0	0	0	0	72.17	$816

Best finish for 1988: T-67th at the Gatlin Brothers - Southwest Golf Classic

| 1989 | 4 | 13 | 3 | 0 | 0 | 0 | 2 | 70.46 | $26,814 |

Best finish for 1989: T-17th at the Federal Express St. Jude Classic

| 1990 | 4 | 14 | 3 | 0 | 0 | 0 | 1 | 70.57 | $12,535 |

Best finish for 1990: T-21st at the Bank of Boston Classic

| 1991 | 29 | 79 | 11 | 0 | 0 | 1 | 1 | 71.90 | $40,197 |

Best finish for 1991: T-7th at the Deposit Guaranty Classic

| 1992 | 1 | 4 | 1 | 0 | 0 | 0 | 0 | 69.25 | $663 |

Best finish for 1992: T-57th at the Deposit Guaranty Classic

| 1993 | 4 | 8 | 2 | 0 | 0 | 0 | 0 | 74.00 | $24,159 |

Best finish for 1993: T-32nd at the NEC World Series of Golf

| 1994 | 1 | 4 | 1 | 0 | 0 | 0 | 0 | 70.75 | $7,614 |

Best finish for 1994: T-55th at the British Open

| 1995 | 3 | 10 | 2 | 0 | 0 | 0 | 1 | 72.30 | $34,925 |

Best finish for 1995: T-20th at the NEC World Series of Golf

| 1996 | 2 | 6 | 1 | 0 | 0 | 0 | 0 | 73.00 | $7,008 |

Best finish for 1996: T-47th at the PGA Championship

| 1997 | 3 | 8 | 1 | 0 | 0 | 0 | 0 | 74.25 | $18,040 |

Best finish for 1997: T-37th at the Players Championship

| 1998 | 4 | 14 | 3 | 0 | 1 | 1 | 1 | 71.36 | $335,735 |

Best finish for 1998: 2nd at the British Open

| 1999 | 24 | 84 | 20 | 0 | 1 | 4 | 11 | 71.27 | $767,409 |

Best finish for 1999: T-3rd at the GTE Byron Nelson Classic

| 2000 | 29 | 88 | 18 | 0 | 0 | 1 | 4 | 71.59 | $316,802 |

Best finish for 2000: T-9th at the Westin Texas Open at LaCantera

| 2001 | 16 | 56 | 12 | 0 | 0 | 2 | 5 | 70.21 | $457,293 |

Best finish for 2001: T-6th at the Verizon Byron Nelson Classic

| 2002 | 21 | 54 | 7 | 0 | 0 | 0 | 1 | 72.24 | $162,704 |

Best finish for 2002: 13th at the International presented by Quest

| 2003 | 13 | 34 | 5 | 0 | 0 | 0 | 2 | 71.79 | $134,905 |

Best finish for 2003: T-22nd at the AT&T Pebble Beach & Ford Championship at Doral

| 2004 | 9 | 23 | 3 | 0 | 0 | 0 | 0 | 72.43 | $23,770 |

Best finish for 2004: T-52nd at the Valero Texas Open

| 2005 | 7 | 14 | 2 | 0 | 0 | 0 | 0 | 72.64 | $18,520 |

Best finish for 2005: T-64th at the International

Period Totals	Starts	Rounds Played	Cuts Made	Wins	Top-5s	Top-10s	Top-25s	Scoring Average	Money
	178	523	96	0	2	9	29	71.65	$2,389,910

Bert Weaver

Year	Starts	Rounds Played	Cuts Made	Wins	Top-5s	Top-10s	Top-25s	Scoring Average	Money
1957	14	56	14	0	1	3	7	72.02	$3,959

Best finish for 1958: 3rd at the Azalea Open

| 1958 | 34 | 121 | 27 | 0 | 3 | 4 | 14 | 72.02 | $6,735 |

Best finish for 1958: T-4th at the Lafayette Open

| 1959 | 21 | 83 | 19 | 0 | 2 | 4 | 15 | 71.52 | $8,602 |

Best finish for 1959: T-4th at the Azalea Open Invitational & Orange County Open Invitational

| 1960 | 19 | 74 | 19 | 0 | 0 | 0 | 13 | 71.92 | $5,963 |

Best finish for 1960: T-12th at the Azalea Open Invitational

| 1961 | 19 | 76 | 18 | 0 | 2 | 4 | 10 | 71.28 | $8,600 |

Best finish for 1961: T-2nd at the Beaumont Open Invitational

| 1962 | 23 | 90 | 18 | 0 | 2 | 6 | 15 | 71.04 | $15,622 |

Best finish for 1962: T-2nd at the Carling Open Invitational

| 1963 | 10 | 40 | 10 | 0 | 0 | 0 | 4 | 72.23 | $3,321 |

Best finish for 1963: T-18th at the Hot Springs Open Invitational

| 1964 | 17 | 60 | 10 | 0 | 1 | 1 | 3 | 72.13 | $3,637 |

Best finish for 1964: T-4th at the Pensacola Open

Year	Starts	Rounds Played	Cuts Made	Wins	Top-5s	Top-10s	Top-25s	Scoring Average	Money
1965	21	78	18	1	3	6	12	71.79	$34,841

Best finish for 1965: Win at the Jacksonville Open

| 1966 | 16 | 52 | 9 | 0 | 0 | 1 | 3 | 72.65 | $7,914 |

Best finish for 1966: T-6th at the Jacksonville Open Invitational

| 1967 | 18 | 61 | 12 | 0 | 2 | 2 | 7 | 72.02 | $17,019 |

Best finish for 1967: T-5th at the Western Open & Thunderbird Classic

| 1968 | 16 | 49 | 9 | 0 | 0 | 1 | 1 | 71.94 | $7,113 |

Best finish for 1968: T-8th at the Western Open

| 1969 | 12 | 36 | 7 | 0 | 1 | 1 | 3 | 72.36 | $5,526 |

Best finish for 1969: T-3rd at the Indian Ridge Hospital Open

| 1970 | 9 | 30 | 7 | 0 | 0 | 2 | 2 | 71.47 | $6,227 |

Best finish for 1970: T-7th at the Green Island Open Invitational

| 1971 | 13 | 34 | 5 | 0 | 0 | 0 | 2 | 72.21 | $7,797 |

Best finish for 1971: T-11th at the Western Open

| 1972 | 3 | 8 | 1 | 0 | 1 | 1 | 1 | 74.38 | $10,825 |

Best finish for 1972: T-3rd at the Danny Thomas Memphis Classic

| 1973 | 2 | 6 | 1 | 0 | 0 | 0 | 0 | 73.83 | $842 |

Best finish for 1973: T-36th at the Danny Thomas Memphis Classic

| 1974 | 2 | 2 | 0 | 0 | 0 | 0 | 0 | 79.50 | |
| 1975 | 1 | 4 | 1 | 0 | 0 | 0 | 0 | 73.25 | $333 |

Best finish for 1975: T-60th at the Danny Thomas Memphis Classic

| 1976 | 2 | 6 | 1 | 0 | 0 | 0 | 0 | 74.33 | $450 |

Best finish for 1976: T-51st at the PGA Championship

1977	2	4	0	0	0	0	0	77.50	$250
1979	1	2	0	0	0	0	0	77.00	
Period Totals	**Starts**	**Rounds Played**	**Cuts Made**	**Wins**	**Top-5s**	**Top-10s**	**Top-25s**	**Scoring Average**	**Money**
	275	972	206	1	18	36	114	71.94	$155,575

Dewitt Weaver

Year	Starts	Rounds Played	Cuts Made	Wins	Top-5s	Top-10s	Top-25s	Scoring Average	Money
1964	10	27	3	0	0	0	0	74.00	

Best finish for 1964: T-44th at the Sunset-Camellia Open

| 1965 | 9 | 21 | 1 | 0 | 0 | 0 | 0 | 76.00 | |

Best finish for 1965: T-51st at the Houston Classic

| 1966 | 3 | 6 | 0 | 0 | 0 | 0 | 0 | 75.50 | $300 |
| 1967 | 17 | 48 | 7 | 0 | 0 | 1 | 1 | 73.81 | $4,674 |

Best finish for 1967: T-6th at the Atlanta Classic

| 1968 | 24 | 76 | 15 | 0 | 1 | 1 | 4 | 73.26 | $11,125 |

Best finish for 1968: T-2nd at the Jacksonville Open Invitational

| 1969 | 29 | 87 | 14 | 0 | 1 | 1 | 3 | 73.23 | $9,640 |

Best finish for 1969: T-3rd at the Greater Jacksonville Open

| 1970 | 22 | 70 | 13 | 0 | 0 | 1 | 4 | 73.20 | $13,183 |

Best finish for 1970: T-7th at the Sahara Invitational

| 1971 | 33 | 108 | 22 | 1 | 2 | 5 | 9 | 72.40 | $72,926 |

Best finish for 1971: Win at the U.S. Professional Match Play Championship

| 1972 | 31 | 98 | 20 | 1 | 2 | 3 | 8 | 73.52 | $48,311 |

Best finish for 1972: Win at the Southern Open

| 1973 | 29 | 92 | 19 | 0 | 2 | 4 | 10 | 72.43 | $52,811 |

Best finish for 1973: 2nd at the U.S. Professional Match Play Championship

| 1974 | 23 | 74 | 13 | 0 | 1 | 3 | 5 | 73.03 | $23,267 |

Best finish for 1974: T-4th at the Greater Jacksonville Open

| 1975 | 19 | 46 | 3 | 0 | 0 | 0 | 1 | 74.07 | $4,088 |

Best finish for 1975: T-25th at the Greater Jacksonville Open

| 1976 | 11 | 24 | 1 | 0 | 0 | 0 | 0 | 74.25 | $1,668 |

Best finish for 1976: T-26th at the Greater Greensboro Open

| 1977 | 3 | 12 | 3 | 0 | 0 | 0 | 0 | 72.00 | $981 |

Best finish for 1977: T-45th at the Southern Open

| 1978 | 5 | 14 | 2 | 0 | 0 | 0 | 0 | 73.36 | $1,548 |

Best finish for 1978: T-42nd at the PGA Championship

| 1979 | 6 | 22 | 5 | 0 | 0 | 0 | 1 | 72.95 | $5,464 |

Best finish for 1979: T-23rd at the Jackie Gleason's Inverrary Classic

| 1980 | 12 | 32 | 4 | 0 | 0 | 0 | 1 | 73.28 | $3,665 |

Best finish for 1980: T-25th at the Greater New Orleans Open

| 1981 | 10 | 24 | 3 | 0 | 0 | 0 | 1 | 73.33 | $3,936 |

Best finish for 1981: T-25th at the Atlanta Classic

| 1982 | 10 | 24 | 2 | 0 | 0 | 0 | 0 | 72.83 | $1,351 |

Best finish for 1982: T-45th at the Tallahassee Open

| 1983 | 12 | 38 | 6 | 0 | 0 | 0 | 1 | 72.79 | $7,643 |

Best finish for 1983: T-19th at the B.C. Open

| 1984 | 2 | 4 | 0 | 0 | 0 | 0 | 0 | 74.75 | |
| 1985 | 2 | 6 | 1 | 0 | 0 | 0 | 0 | 72.17 | $724 |

Best finish for 1985: T-67th at the Southern Open

Year	Starts	Rounds Played	Cuts Made	Wins	Top-5s	Top-10s	Top-25s	Scoring Average	Money
1986	2	6	1	0	0	0	0	71.33	$1,183

Best finish for 1986: T-32nd at the Deposit Guaranty Golf Classic

Year	Starts	Rounds Played	Cuts Made	Wins	Top-5s	Top-10s	Top-25s	Scoring Average	Money
1987	1	2	0	0	0	0	0	72.00	
1988	3	6	0	0	0	0	0	73.33	
1989	7	14	0	0	0	0	0	76.14	
1990	1	2	0	0	0	0	0	73.50	
1992	1	2	0	0	0	0	0	77.50	
1994	1	2	0	0	0	0	0	75.50	
Period Totals	Starts	Rounds Played	Cuts Made	Wins	Top-5s	Top-10s	Top-25s	Scoring Average	Money
	338	987	158	2	9	19	49	73.26	$268,488

Doug Weaver

Year	Starts	Rounds Played	Cuts Made	Wins	Top-5s	Top-10s	Top-25s	Scoring Average	Money
1988	1	2	0	0	0	0	0	75.50	
1989	25	69	9	0	0	0	0	72.59	$19,769

Best finish for 1989: T-26th at the B.C. Open

| 1990 | 5 | 12 | 1 | 0 | 0 | 0 | 0 | 72.58 | $1,020 |

Best finish for 1990: T-43rd at the Deposit Guaranty

| 1993 | 1 | 4 | 1 | 0 | 0 | 0 | 0 | 73.75 | $4,680 |

Best finish for 1993: T-85th at the U.S. Open

2000	1	2	0	0	0	0	0	76.50	
2002	1	1	0	0	0	0	0	78.00	
Period Totals	Starts	Rounds Played	Cuts Made	Wins	Top-5s	Top-10s	Top-25s	Scoring Average	Money
	34	90	11	0	0	0	0	72.86	$25,470

Larry Webb

Year	Starts	Rounds Played	Cuts Made	Wins	Top-5s	Top-10s	Top-25s	Scoring Average	Money
1974	1	2	0	0	0	0	0	78.50	$500
1977	6	11	0	0	0	0	0	75.00	
1979	17	50	9	0	0	0	0	73.12	$5,641

Best finish for 1979: T-30th at the Tallahassee Open

| 1984 | 4 | 12 | 1 | 0 | 0 | 0 | 0 | 74.42 | $6,900 |

Best finish for 1984: 40th at the NEC World Series of Golf

1986	1	2	0	0	0	0	0	75.00	$1,000
Period Totals	Starts	Rounds Played	Cuts Made	Wins	Top-5s	Top-10s	Top-25s	Scoring Average	Money
	29	77	10	0	0	0	0	73.78	$14,041

Ron Weber

Year	Starts	Rounds Played	Cuts Made	Wins	Top-5s	Top-10s	Top-25s	Scoring Average	Money
1960	1	2	0	0	0	0	0	77.50	
1962	3	10	2	0	0	1	2	71.20	$1,700

Best finish for 1962: T-6th at the Portland Open Invitational

| 1963 | 5 | 20 | 5 | 0 | 0 | 1 | 1 | 71.45 | $1,184 |

Best finish for 1963: T-7th at the Jamaica Open Invitational

| 1966 | 3 | 8 | 1 | 0 | 0 | 0 | 0 | 73.13 | $046 |

Best finish for 1966: T-49th at the Thunderbird Classic

| 1967 | 7 | 19 | 3 | 0 | 0 | 0 | 0 | 74.16 | |

Best finish for 1967: T-50th at the San Diego Open

1968	1	2	0	0	0	0	0	73.50	
1970	1	2	0	0	0	0	0	75.50	
1971	1	4	1	0	0	0	0	75.50	$217

Best finish for 1971: 71st at the Houston Champions International

| 1972 | 2 | 6 | 1 | 0 | 0 | 0 | 0 | 73.67 | $340 |

Best finish for 1972: T-44th at the San Antonio Texas Open

1975	1	2	0	0	0	0	0	79.00	
1976	1	2	0	0	0	0	0	76.00	
1977	1	2	0	0	0	0	0	76.00	
1978	1	2	0	0	0	0	0	75.00	
1979	1	2	0	0	0	0	0	82.50	
Period Totals	Starts	Rounds Played	Cuts Made	Wins	Top-5s	Top-10s	Top-25s	Scoring Average	Money
	29	83	13	0	0	2	3	73.60	$3,486

Boo Weekley

Year	Starts	Rounds Played	Cuts Made	Wins	Top-5s	Top-10s	Top-25s	Scoring Average	Money
2002	24	57	5	0	0	0	2	72.16	$95,206

Best finish for 2002: T-19th at the FedEx St. Jude Classic

| 2007 | 29 | 101 | 20 | 1 | 3 | 5 | 9 | 70.95 | $2,613,211 |

Best finish for 2007: Win at the Verizon Heritage

| 2008 | 23 | 79 | 18 | 1 | 2 | 5 | 11 | 71.16 | $2,388,182 |

Best finish for 2008: Win at the Verizon Heritage

Period Totals	Starts	Rounds Played	Cuts Made	Wins	Top-5s	Top-10s	Top-25s	Scoring Average	Money
	76	237	43	2	5	10	22	71.31	$5,096,599

D.A. Weibring

Year	Starts	Rounds Played	Cuts Made	Wins	Top-5s	Top-10s	Top-25s	Scoring Average	Money
1977	8	22	3	0	0	0	0	72.77	$1,681

Best finish for 1977: T-35th at the Colgate Hall Of Fame Golf Classic

1978	27	86	17	0	3	4	7	71.72	$40,192

Best finish for 1978: T-3rd at the Ed McMahon Quad City Open

1979	33	106	20	1	1	2	5	72.29	$71,720

Best finish for 1979: Win at the Ed McMahon Quad City Open

1980	29	93	21	0	2	4	6	71.89	$82,111

Best finish for 1980: 2nd at the Andy Williams-San Diego Open

1981	30	101	21	0	2	6	8	71.89	$92,365

Best finish for 1981: T-2nd at the Hall of Fame Tournament

1982	30	113	26	0	3	7	12	71.04	$118,591

Best finish for 1982: 3rd at the Sea Pines Heritage Classic

1983	23	77	14	0	2	3	7	71.61	$61,731

Best finish for 1983: T-3rd at the Bay Hill Classic

1984	28	96	21	0	1	4	11	72.00	$110,325

Best finish for 1984: 5th at the Western Open

1985	25	80	15	0	1	2	9	71.93	$176,250

Best finish for 1985: 2nd at the Tournament Players Championship

1986	25	85	20	0	2	3	11	71.01	$173,302

Best finish for 1986: T-3rd at the Southwest Golf Classic

1987	27	87	19	1	2	5	10	71.20	$391,962

Best finish for 1987: Win at the Beatrice Western Open

1988	26	81	17	0	2	5	9	71.21	$188,177

Best finish for 1988: T-3rd at the U.S. Open

1989	24	77	17	0	0	0	5	71.77	$98,686

Best finish for 1989: T-12th at the Independent Insurance Agent Open

1990	22	65	13	0	1	2	6	71.58	$156,235

Best finish for 1990: T-3rd at the Bank of Boston Classic

1991	24	85	20	1	4	5	8	70.68	$558,648

Best finish for 1991: Win at the Hardee's Golf Classic

1992	24	81	19	0	1	3	9	71.00	$255,218

Best finish for 1992: T-3rd at the International

1993	22	76	18	0	2	2	6	71.00	$299,293

Best finish for 1993: T-2nd at the GTE Byron Nelson Classic & Hardee's Golf Classic

1994	21	65	14	0	2	3	4	71.22	$256,729

Best finish for 1994: T-2nd at the Kemper Open

1995	24	83	18	1	3	4	8	70.67	$517,065

Best finish for 1995: Win at the Quad City Classic

1996	17	53	11	1	1	2	5	71.45	$437,775

Best finish for 1996: Win at the Canon Greater Hartford Open

1997	20	62	13	0	0	1	2	71.66	$124,044

Best finish for 1997: T-7th at the Kemper Open

1998	24	69	12	0	1	1	3	71.28	$174,504

Best finish for 1998: T-5th at the Quad City Classic

1999	17	53	9	0	0	1	3	72.11	$182,713

Best finish for 1999: T-10th at the John Deere Classic

2000	14	42	7	0	0	0	2	71.24	$87,620

Best finish for 2000: T-25th at the FedEx St. Jude Classic & Canon Greater Hartford Open

2001	10	34	7	0	0	0	1	70.56	$99,843

Best finish for 2001: T-17th at the B.C. Open

2002	10	25	3	0	0	0	1	72.00	$41,044

Best finish for 2002: T-25th at the Valero Texas Open

2003	2	8	2	0	0	0	0	71.25	$17,289

Best finish for 2003: T-53rd at the John Deere Classic

Period Totals	Starts	Rounds Played	Cuts Made	Wins	Top-5s	Top-10s	Top-25s	Scoring Average	Money
	586	1905	397	5	36	69	158	71.47	$4,815,113

Mike Weir

Year	Starts	Rounds Played	Cuts Made	Wins	Top-5s	Top-10s	Top-25s	Scoring Average	Money
1989	1	2	0	0	0	0	0	75.50	
1992	2	4	0	0	0	0	0	76.75	
1993	2	6	1	0	0	0	0	73.33	$1,940

Best finish for 1993: T-70th at the Buick Open

1994	1	2	0	0	0	0	0	74.00	
1995	1	2	0	0	0	0	0	74.50	
1996	5	14	2	0	1	1	1	71.43	$36,624

Best finish for 1996: T-5th at the Greater Vancouver Open

1997	4	8	1	0	0	0	0	72.50	$7,709

Best finish for 1997: T-31st at the B.C. Open

Year	Starts	Rounds Played	Cuts Made	Wins	Top-5s	Top-10s	Top-25s	Scoring Average	Money
1998	27	77	13	0	1	2	5	71.78	$218,967

Best finish for 1998: T-5th at the Greater Vancouver Open

| 1999 | 30 | 101 | 20 | 1 | 4 | 7 | 12 | 71.10 | $1,492,139 |

Best finish for 1999: Win at the Air Canada Championship

| 2000 | 28 | 96 | 23 | 1 | 4 | 8 | 16 | 70.42 | $2,547,828 |

Best finish for 2000: Win at the American Express Championship

| 2001 | 23 | 86 | 20 | 1 | 5 | 6 | 13 | 70.06 | $2,779,367 |

Best finish for 2001: Win at The Tour Championship

| 2002 | 25 | 92 | 22 | 0 | 0 | 0 | 11 | 70.79 | $845,154 |

Best finish for 2002: T-11th at the Honda Classic

| 2003 | 21 | 75 | 20 | 3 | 7 | 10 | 16 | 69.89 | $4,918,910 |

Best finish for 2003: Win at the Bob Hope Chrysler Classic, Nissan Open & Masters

| 2004 | 22 | 73 | 16 | 1 | 6 | 7 | 10 | 70.71 | $2,768,536 |

Best finish for 2004: Win at the Nissan Open

| 2005 | 23 | 66 | 14 | 0 | 2 | 2 | 6 | 71.80 | $1,367,409 |

Best finish for 2005: 2nd at the AT&T Pebble Beach National Pro-Am

| 2006 | 24 | 85 | 20 | 0 | 2 | 6 | 12 | 70.76 | $1,883,724 |

Best finish for 2006: T-3rd at the AT&T Pebble Beach National Pro-Am

| 2007 | 23 | 81 | 19 | 1 | 1 | 4 | 9 | 71.16 | $1,988,553 |

Best finish for 2007: Win at the Fry's Electronics Open

| 2008 | 26 | 87 | 20 | 0 | 5 | 8 | 13 | 70.68 | $3,020,135 |

Best finish for 2008: T-2nd at the Memorial Tournament & Deutsche Bank Championship

Period Totals	Starts	Rounds Played	Cuts Made	Wins	Top-5s	Top-10s	Top-25s	Scoring Average	Money
	288	957	211	8	38	61	124	70.90	$23,876,997

Tom Weiskopf

Year	Starts	Rounds Played	Cuts Made	Wins	Top-5s	Top-10s	Top-25s	Scoring Average	Money
1964	1	4	1	0	0	0	0	71.50	$488

Best finish for 1964: T-30th at the Western Open

| 1965 | 27 | 89 | 17 | 0 | 1 | 1 | 6 | 73.24 | $11,264 |

Best finish for 1965: T-5th at the Greater Hartford Open

| 1966 | 29 | 104 | 23 | 0 | 5 | 6 | 14 | 71.91 | $38,042 |

Best finish for 1966: T-2nd at the San Diego Open Invitational, Greater Greensboro Open Invitational & Oklahoma City Open Invitational

| 1967 | 34 | 123 | 27 | 0 | 1 | 5 | 17 | 71.98 | $40,331 |

Best finish for 1967: T-3rd at the Hawaiian Open

| 1968 | 30 | 115 | 27 | 2 | 9 | 11 | 21 | 71.07 | $142,577 |

Best finish for 1968: Win at the Andy Williams-San Diego Open Invitational & Buick Open Invitational

| 1969 | 27 | 102 | 24 | 0 | 6 | 8 | 19 | 71.47 | $80,618 |

Best finish for 1969: T-2nd at the Greater Greensboro Open & The Masters

| 1970 | 26 | 91 | 21 | 0 | 8 | 12 | 18 | 70.77 | $94,592 |

Best finish for 1970: T-2nd at the Kemper Open & AVCO Classic

| 1971 | 31 | 98 | 22 | 2 | 5 | 7 | 12 | 71.44 | $101,750 |

Best finish for 1971: Win at the Kemper Open & IVB Philadelphia Golf Classic

| 1972 | 26 | 90 | 22 | 1 | 3 | 11 | 17 | 71.52 | $128,500 |

Best finish for 1972: Win at the Jackie Gleason's Inverrary Classic

| 1973 | 22 | 78 | 19 | 5 | 13 | 15 | 16 | 70.27 | $271,206 |

Best finish for 1973: Win at the Colonial National Invitational, Kemper Open, IVB Philadelphia Golf Classic, British Open & Canadian Open

| 1974 | 24 | 82 | 18 | 0 | 6 | 10 | 14 | 71.38 | $127,502 |

Best finish for 1974: T-2nd at the Masters, Western Open & Pleasant Valley Classic

| 1975 | 24 | 85 | 19 | 2 | 9 | 10 | 14 | 71.14 | $222,331 |

Best finish for 1975: Win at the Greater Greensboro Open & Canadian Open

| 1976 | 27 | 88 | 19 | 0 | 5 | 11 | 18 | 71.15 | $133,065 |

Best finish for 1976: T-2nd at the Kemper Open & U.S. Open

| 1977 | 24 | 86 | 20 | 1 | 7 | 10 | 17 | 71.12 | $198,808 |

Best finish for 1977: Win at the Kemper Open

| 1978 | 21 | 72 | 15 | 1 | 3 | 6 | 13 | 71.81 | $113,371 |

Best finish for 1978: Win at the Doral-Eastern Open

| 1979 | 27 | 88 | 20 | 0 | 2 | 3 | 10 | 72.27 | $77,769 |

Best finish for 1979: 2nd at the Southern Open

| 1980 | 25 | 92 | 21 | 0 | 1 | 7 | 11 | 71.84 | $96,720 |

Best finish for 1980: T-4th at the Memorial Tournament

| 1981 | 20 | 72 | 16 | 1 | 3 | 4 | 10 | 71.32 | $177,396 |

Best finish for 1981: Win at the LaJet Classic

| 1982 | 20 | 69 | 14 | 1 | 3 | 4 | 9 | 72.07 | $153,219 |

Best finish for 1982: Win at the Western Open

| 1983 | 18 | 65 | 15 | 0 | 0 | 2 | 6 | 72.95 | $48,622 |

Best finish for 1983: T-8th at the Doral-Eastern Open & Anheuser-Busch Golf Classic

| 1984 | 9 | 28 | 5 | 0 | 0 | 0 | 0 | 73.43 | $9,657 |

Best finish for 1984: T-29th at the Western Open

| 1986 | 7 | 21 | 4 | 0 | 0 | 0 | 0 | 73.43 | $7,342 |

Best finish for 1986: T-29th at the Doral-Eastern Open

| 1987 | 1 | 2 | 0 | 0 | 0 | 0 | 0 | 75.00 | |

Year	Starts	Rounds Played	Cuts Made	Wins	Top-5s	Top-10s	Top-25s	Scoring Average	Money
1988	1	2	0	0	0	0	0	74.00	
1989	2	4	0	0	0	0	0	74.25	$800
1990	5	12	2	0	0	0	0	74.75	$5,321

Best finish for 1990: T-51st at the GTE Byron Nelson Classic

Year	Starts	Rounds Played	Cuts Made	Wins	Top-5s	Top-10s	Top-25s	Scoring Average	Money
1991	4	10	1	0	0	0	0	73.40	$5,040
1992	14	35	4	0	0	0	1	72.37	$16,496

Best finish for 1992: T-25th at the Buick Invitational of California

Year	Starts	Rounds Played	Cuts Made	Wins	Top-5s	Top-10s	Top-25s	Scoring Average	Money
1995	1	2	0	0	0	0	0	75.50	$1,037
1996	1	2	0	0	0	0	0	75.50	$1,000
2004	1	2	0	0	0	0	0	80.00	$3,745
Period Totals	Starts	Rounds Played	Cuts Made	Wins	Top-5s	Top-10s	Top-25s	Scoring Average	Money
	529	1813	396	16	90	143	263	71.73	$2,308,606

Kevin Wentworth

Year	Starts	Rounds Played	Cuts Made	Wins	Top-5s	Top-10s	Top-25s	Scoring Average	Money
1993	1	2	0	0	0	0	0	72.50	$1,000
1998	28	78	12	0	0	2	7	71.65	$246,174

Best finish for 1998: T-9th at the Greater Milwaukee Open

Year	Starts	Rounds Played	Cuts Made	Wins	Top-5s	Top-10s	Top-25s	Scoring Average	Money
1999	27	71	9	0	1	4	6	71.99	$413,601

Best finish for 1999: T-4th at the FedEx St. Jude Classic

Year	Starts	Rounds Played	Cuts Made	Wins	Top-5s	Top-10s	Top-25s	Scoring Average	Money
2000	31	80	9	0	1	1	1	72.05	$332,293

Best finish for 2000: T-2nd at the Honda Classic

Year	Starts	Rounds Played	Cuts Made	Wins	Top-5s	Top-10s	Top-25s	Scoring Average	Money
2001	14	32	2	0	0	0	0	73.41	$20,820

Best finish for 2001: T-43rd at the AT&T Pebble Beach

Year	Starts	Rounds Played	Cuts Made	Wins	Top-5s	Top-10s	Top-25s	Scoring Average	Money
2002	4	10	1	0	0	0	1	73.00	$32,400

Best finish for 2002: T-24th at the AT&T Pebble Beach

Period Totals	Starts	Rounds Played	Cuts Made	Wins	Top-5s	Top-10s	Top-25s	Scoring Average	Money
	105	273	33	0	2	7	15	72.12	$1,046,288

Mike West

Year	Starts	Rounds Played	Cuts Made	Wins	Top-5s	Top-10s	Top-25s	Scoring Average	Money
1986	29	77	10	0	0	0	2	73.00	$20,238

Best finish for 1986: T-14th at the Deposit Guaranty Golf Classic

Year	Starts	Rounds Played	Cuts Made	Wins	Top-5s	Top-10s	Top-25s	Scoring Average	Money
1987	3	8	1	0	0	0	1	69.88	$2,240

Best finish for 1987: T-21st at the Deposit Guaranty Golf Classic

Year	Starts	Rounds Played	Cuts Made	Wins	Top-5s	Top-10s	Top-25s	Scoring Average	Money
1988	1	4	1	0	0	0	1	69.25	$2,600

Best finish for 1988: T-19th at the Deposit Guaranty Golf Classic

Year	Starts	Rounds Played	Cuts Made	Wins	Top-5s	Top-10s	Top-25s	Scoring Average	Money
1991	1	2	0	0	0	0	0	72.00	
1992	1	2	0	0	0	0	0	75.50	$1,200
1993	1	2	0	0	0	0	0	73.50	
Period Totals	Starts	Rounds Played	Cuts Made	Wins	Top-5s	Top-10s	Top-25s	Scoring Average	Money
	36	95	12	0	0	0	4	72.62	$26,278

Lee Westwood

Year	Starts	Rounds Played	Cuts Made	Wins	Top-5s	Top-10s	Top-25s	Scoring Average	Money
1995	1	4	1	0	0	0	0	74.75	$6,380

Best finish for 1995: T-96th at the British Open

Year	Starts	Rounds Played	Cuts Made	Wins	Top-5s	Top-10s	Top-25s	Scoring Average	Money
1996	1	2	0	0	0	0	0	72.50	$1,008
1997	5	20	5	0	0	1	4	71.35	$155,645

Best finish for 1997: T-10th at the British Open

Year	Starts	Rounds Played	Cuts Made	Wins	Top-5s	Top-10s	Top-25s	Scoring Average	Money
1998	8	29	7	1	2	3	4	72.03	$601,086

Best finish for 1998: Win at the Freeport-McDermott Classic

Year	Starts	Rounds Played	Cuts Made	Wins	Top-5s	Top-10s	Top-25s	Scoring Average	Money
1999	11	33	9	0	1	3	5	72.27	$620,764

Best finish for 1999: T-4th at the American Express Championship

Year	Starts	Rounds Played	Cuts Made	Wins	Top-5s	Top-10s	Top-25s	Scoring Average	Money
2000	10	31	8	0	2	2	6	71.68	$916,636

Best finish for 2000: 2nd at the American Express Championship

Year	Starts	Rounds Played	Cuts Made	Wins	Top-5s	Top-10s	Top-25s	Scoring Average	Money
2001	6	18	3	0	0	0	1	72.17	$77,821

Best finish for 2001: T-17th at the Bay Hill Invitational

Year	Starts	Rounds Played	Cuts Made	Wins	Top-5s	Top-10s	Top-25s	Scoring Average	Money
2002	9	24	5	0	0	0	3	72.71	$217,326

Best finish for 2002: T-15th at the Nissan Open & WGC-NEC Invitational

Year	Starts	Rounds Played	Cuts Made	Wins	Top-5s	Top-10s	Top-25s	Scoring Average	Money
2003	8	24	5	0	0	0	0	72.54	$143,359

Best finish for 2003: T-29th at the Memorial Tournament

Year	Starts	Rounds Played	Cuts Made	Wins	Top-5s	Top-10s	Top-25s	Scoring Average	Money
2004	11	34	8	0	1	2	4	71.50	$769,899

Best finish for 2004: 4th at the British Open

Year	Starts	Rounds Played	Cuts Made	Wins	Top-5s	Top-10s	Top-25s	Scoring Average	Money
2005	15	48	12	0	0	0	5	71.83	$511,524

Best finish for 2005: T-17th at the WGC-Accenture Match Play Championship & PGA Championship

Year	Starts	Rounds Played	Cuts Made	Wins	Top-5s	Top-10s	Top-25s	Scoring Average	Money
2006	14	41	8	0	2	2	2	71.93	$635,566

Best finish for 2006: T-5th at the Nissan Open & Bay Hill Invitational

Year	Starts	Rounds Played	Cuts Made	Wins	Top-5s	Top-10s	Top-25s	Scoring Average	Money
2007	8	28	8	0	0	0	1	72.86	$288,280

Best finish for 2007: T-22nd at the WGC-Bridgestone Invitational

Year	Starts	Rounds Played	Cuts Made	Wins	Top-5s	Top-10s	Top-25s	Scoring Average	Money
2008	10	30	7	0	2	2	5	72.07	$1,550,880

Best finish for 2008: T-2nd at the WGC-Bridgestone Invitational

Period Totals	Starts	Rounds Played	Cuts Made	Wins	Top-5s	Top-10s	Top-25s	Scoring Average	Money
	117	366	86	1	10	15	40	72.08	$6,496,174

Brett Wetterich

Year	Starts	Rounds Played	Cuts Made	Wins	Top-5s	Top-10s	Top-25s	Scoring Average	Money
1998	1	2	0	0	0	0	0	79.00	$1,000
2000	9	21	1	0	0	0	0	73.43	$7,174
Best finish for 2000: T-63rd at the COMPAQ Classic of New Orleans									
2001	1	2	0	0	0	0	0	74.00	
2002	32	87	12	0	0	1	1	72.06	$203,034
Best finish for 2002: T-8th at the Honda Classic									
2003	1	2	0	0	0	0	0	73.50	
2005	28	74	10	0	0	2	5	71.01	$576,029
Best finish for 2005: T-6th at the Honda Classic									
2006	25	82	16	1	4	6	9	70.68	$3,030,082
Best finish for 2006: Win at the EDS Byron Nelson Championship									
2007	28	87	17	0	2	4	7	71.60	$2,215,164
Best finish for 2007: T-2nd at the WGC-CA Championship & Deutsche Bank Championship									
2008	11	36	7	0	0	0	0	73.03	$121,675
Best finish for 2008: T-37th at the Buick Invitational									
Period Totals	Starts	Rounds Played	Cuts Made	Wins	Top-5s	Top-10s	Top-25s	Scoring Average	Money
	136	393	63	1	6	13	22	71.69	$6,154,158

Frank Wharton

Year	Starts	Rounds Played	Cuts Made	Wins	Top-5s	Top-10s	Top-25s	Scoring Average	Money
1958	3	12	3	0	0	0	0	72.58	$145
Best finish for 1958: T-28th at the Dallas Open									
1959	7	26	4	0	0	1	3	72.35	$1,404
Best finish for 1959: T-7th at the Lafayette Open Invitational									
1960	6	23	5	0	0	0	2	71.74	$1,611
Best finish for 1960: T-20th at the West Palm Beach Open Invitational									
1961	6	24	6	0	0	0	5	70.46	$2,601
Best finish for 1961: T-13th at the Phoenix Open Invitational									
1962	7	28	6	0	0	1	3	70.79	$2,807
Best finish for 1962: T-7th at the St. Paul Open Invitational									
1963	6	24	6	0	0	0	2	71.67	$2,206
Best finish for 1963: T-11th at the Insurance City Open Invitational									
1964	32	79	8	0	0	0	1	73.89	$1,257
Best finish for 1964: T-22nd at the Seattle Open									
1965	25	88	17	0	0	0	2	72.75	$5,901
Best finish for 1965: T-12th at the Western Open									
1966	11	38	7	0	0	0	0	73.34	$1,012
Best finish for 1966: T-29th at the San Diego Open Invitational									
1967	9	28	4	0	0	0	1	73.46	$417
Best finish for 1967: T-22nd at the Cajun Classic									
1968	9	23	3	0	0	0	1	73.48	$1,368
Best finish for 1968: T-12th at the Cajun Classic									
1969	3	6	0	0	0	0	0	74.00	
1970	1	4	1	0	0	0	0	74.75	$273
Best finish for 1970: T-69th at the American Golf Classic									
1971	3	6	0	0	0	0	0	75.50	
1972	2	4	0	0	0	0	0	76.50	
1973	3	6	0	0	0	0	0	75.83	$500
1974	1	2	0	0	0	0	0	77.00	
1975	1	2	0	0	0	0	0	77.50	
1976	1	2	0	0	0	0	0	79.50	
Period Totals	Starts	Rounds Played	Cuts Made	Wins	Top-5s	Top-10s	Top-25s	Scoring Average	Money
	136	425	70	0	0	2	20	72.92	$21,502

Steve Wheatcroft

Year	Starts	Rounds Played	Cuts Made	Wins	Top-5s	Top-10s	Top-25s	Scoring Average	Money
2001	1	2	0	0	0	0	0	76.00	
2005	2	4	0	0	0	0	0	73.00	
2007	25	73	10	0	0	0	1	71.88	$153,246
Best finish for 2007: T-18th at the U.S. Bank Championship in Milwaukee									
Period Totals	Starts	Rounds Played	Cuts Made	Wins	Top-5s	Top-10s	Top-25s	Scoring Average	Money
	28	79	10	0	0	0	1	72.04	$153,246

Greg Whisman

Year	Starts	Rounds Played	Cuts Made	Wins	Top-5s	Top-10s	Top-25s	Scoring Average	Money
1991	29	84	13	0	0	0	3	71.56	$68,975
Best finish for 1991: T-14th at the Northern Telecom Open									
1992	29	78	11	0	0	0	3	71.88	$83,322
Best finish for 1992: 13th at the International									

1993	2	8	2	0	0	0	0	71.50	$3,392

Best finish for 1993: T-47th at the Buick Invitational of California

Period Totals	Starts	Rounds Played	Cuts Made	Wins	Top-5s	Top-10s	Top-25s	Scoring Average	Money
	60	170	26	0	0	0	6	71.71	$155,689

Carlton White

Year	Starts	Rounds Played	Cuts Made	Wins	Top-5s	Top-10s	Top-25s	Scoring Average	Money
1975	2	6	1	0	0	0	0	76.50	$800

Best finish for 1975: 66th at the U.S. Open

| 1976 | 16 | 46 | 7 | 0 | 0 | 0 | 1 | 73.57 | $8,445 |

Best finish for 1976: T-13th at the American Express Westchester Classic

| 1977 | 15 | 37 | 3 | 0 | 1 | 1 | 1 | 73.86 | $7,524 |

Best finish for 1977: T-4th at the San Antonio Texas Open

| 1978 | 21 | 61 | 9 | 0 | 0 | 0 | 3 | 72.80 | $9,163 |

Best finish for 1978: T-11th at the Buick Goodwrench Open

| 1979 | 27 | 71 | 8 | 0 | 0 | 0 | 1 | 73.65 | $5,045 |

Best finish for 1979: T-24th at the Tallahassee Open

| 1980 | 2 | 2 | 0 | 0 | 0 | 0 | 0 | 75.00 | |
| 1981 | 4 | 10 | 1 | 0 | 0 | 0 | 0 | 73.30 | $510 |

Best finish for 1981: 68th at the Greater Milwaukee Open

Period Totals	Starts	Rounds Played	Cuts Made	Wins	Top-5s	Top-10s	Top-25s	Scoring Average	Money
	87	233	29	0	1	1	6	73.52	$31,487

Jim White

Year	Starts	Rounds Played	Cuts Made	Wins	Top-5s	Top-10s	Top-25s	Scoring Average	Money
1977	8	16	0	0	0	0	0	74.75	
1978	11	32	4	0	0	0	0	74.03	$1,546

Best finish for 1978: T-36th at the Bob Hope Chrysler Classic

| 1979 | 14 | 34 | 2 | 0 | 0 | 0 | 0 | 74.41 | $1,548 |

Best finish for 1979: T-53rd at the Danny Thomas Memphis Classic

1981	3	7	0	0	0	0	0	74.14	
1982	1	3	0	0	0	0	0	76.67	
1983	1	2	0	0	0	0	0	76.00	$100
1985	1	2	0	0	0	0	0	74.50	$1,000
1986	1	2	0	0	0	0	0	75.00	$1,000
1987	1	2	0	0	0	0	0	74.00	$600
1991	1	2	0	0	0	0	0	81.50	$1,000
1994	1	2	0	0	0	0	0	74.50	$1,200
1997	1	2	0	0	0	0	0	78.50	$1,300
1999	1	2	0	0	0	0	0	79.50	$1,000

Period Totals	Starts	Rounds Played	Cuts Made	Wins	Top-5s	Top-10s	Top-25s	Scoring Average	Money
	45	108	6	0	0	0	0	74.73	$10,294

Larry White

Year	Starts	Rounds Played	Cuts Made	Wins	Top-5s	Top-10s	Top-25s	Scoring Average	Money
1971	16	44	7	0	0	0	0	74.16	$2,215

Best finish for 1971: T-29th at the Cleveland Open

| 1972 | 18 | 55 | 10 | 0 | 0 | 0 | 2 | 74.15 | $6,889 |

Best finish for 1972: T-11th at the Kaiser International Open

| 1973 | 19 | 57 | 9 | 0 | 0 | 0 | 0 | 73.16 | $2,985 |

Best finish for 1973: T-45th at the Quad Cities Open

| 1974 | 2 | 4 | 0 | 0 | 0 | 0 | 0 | 77.50 | |
| 1975 | 1 | 4 | 1 | 0 | 0 | 0 | 0 | 74.00 | $066 |

Best finish for 1975: T-70th at the Danny Thomas Memphis Classic

| 1977 | 1 | 2 | 0 | 0 | 0 | 0 | 0 | 75.50 | |

Period Totals	Starts	Rounds Played	Cuts Made	Wins	Top-5s	Top-10s	Top-25s	Scoring Average	Money
	57	166	27	0	0	0	2	73.90	$12,155

Don Whitt

Year	Starts	Rounds Played	Cuts Made	Wins	Top-5s	Top-10s	Top-25s	Scoring Average	Money
1958	33	109	22	0	1	2	13	71.87	$7,634

Best finish for 1958: T-5th at the Insurance City Open

| 1959 | 23 | 90 | 21 | 2 | 5 | 6 | 13 | 71.10 | $17,497 |

Best finish for 1959: Win at the Memphis Open Invitational & Kentucky Derby Open Invitational

| 1960 | 20 | 80 | 19 | 0 | 3 | 5 | 14 | 70.84 | $12,868 |

Best finish for 1960: T-3rd at the Azalea Open Invitational & Greater Greensboro Open Invitational

| 1961 | 14 | 57 | 13 | 0 | 2 | 3 | 9 | 71.04 | $11,912 |

Best finish for 1961: T-2nd at the Lucky International Open

| 1962 | 10 | 40 | 10 | 0 | 1 | 1 | 5 | 71.68 | $5,720 |

Best finish for 1962: T-5th at the Puerto Rico Open Invitational

| 1963 | 12 | 46 | 12 | 0 | 0 | 3 | 8 | 71.80 | $8,339 |

Best finish for 1963: T-6th at the Sahara Invitational

Year	Starts	Rounds Played	Cuts Made	Wins	Top-5s	Top-10s	Top-25s	Scoring Average	Money
1964	12	39	5	0	1	1	2	72.85	$3,876

Best finish for 1964: T-5th at the "500" Festival Open

1965	1	3	1	0	0	0	0	76.00	

Best finish for 1965: 101 at the Bob Hope Classic

1967	5	14	2	0	0	0	0	74.29	$952

Best finish for 1967: T-34th at the Atlanta Classic

1968	18	53	9	0	0	0	2	72.72	$3,711

Best finish for 1968: T-19th at the Minnesota Golf Classic

1969	13	32	3	0	1	1	2	73.88	$9,948

Best finish for 1969: 2nd at the Alameda County Open

Period Totals	Starts	Rounds Played	Cuts Made	Wins	Top-5s	Top-10s	Top-25s	Scoring Average	Money
	161	563	117	2	14	22	68	71.84	$82,457

PGA Tour career totals from 1955 to 1969

	Starts	Rounds Played	Cuts Made	Wins	Top-5s	Top-10s	Top-25s	Scoring Average	Money
	217	779	173	2	15	25	71	N/A	$94,343

Ron Whittaker

Year	Starts	Rounds Played	Cuts Made	Wins	Top-5s	Top-10s	Top-25s	Scoring Average	Money
1995	4	10	1	0	0	0	0	72.70	$14,650

Best finish for 1995: T-40th at the NEC World Series of Golf

1996	23	58	8	0	0	0	0	72.34	$29,656

Best finish for 1996: T-33rd at the Deposit Guaranty Golf Classic & Buick Open

2006	28	79	13	0	0	1	2	71.59	$300,033

Best finish for 2006: T-9th at the Frys.Com Open-Vegas

2008	22	54	5	0	0	0	0	71.70	$59,977

Best finish for 2008: T-36th at the Mayakoba Golf Classic

Period Totals	Starts	Rounds Played	Cuts Made	Wins	Top-5s	Top-10s	Top-25s	Scoring Average	Money
	77	201	27	0	0	1	2	71.90	$404,316

Charlie Wi

Year	Starts	Rounds Played	Cuts Made	Wins	Top-5s	Top-10s	Top-25s	Scoring Average	Money
2002	1	4	1	0	0	0	0	72.75	$28,625

Best finish for 2002: T-63rd at the WGC-NEC Invitational

2005	23	65	11	0	1	1	2	71.63	$250,081

Best finish for 2005: T-5th at the Southern Farm Bureau Classic

2006	1	2	0	0	0	0	0	72.50	
2007	27	90	18	0	2	3	8	70.86	$1,145,975

Best finish for 2007: T-2nd at the U.S. Bank Championship in Milwaukee

2008	27	97	21	0	2	4	11	70.41	$1,515,395

Best finish for 2008: T-2nd at the Valero Texas Open

Period Totals	Starts	Rounds Played	Cuts Made	Wins	Top-5s	Top-10s	Top-25s	Scoring Average	Money
	79	258	51	0	5	8	21	70.93	$2,940,076

Mark Wiebe

Year	Starts	Rounds Played	Cuts Made	Wins	Top-5s	Top-10s	Top-25s	Scoring Average	Money
1981	2	6	1	0	0	0	0	73.50	$2,538

Best finish for 1981: T-27th at the LaJet Classic

1982	1	2	0	0	0	0	0	74.50	
1983	2	9	2	0	0	0	1	70.22	$6,628

Best finish for 1983: T-21st at the Isuzu/Andy Williams San Diego Open

1984	19	57	8	0	0	1	1	73.05	$16,257

Best finish for 1984: T-8th at the B.C. Open

1985	29	87	15	1	4	5	5	71.93	$183,494

Best finish for 1985: Win at the Anheuser-Busch Golf Classic

1986	30	93	22	1	3	5	7	71.52	$260,180

Best finish for 1986: Win at the Hardee's Golf Classic

1987	33	115	26	0	1	2	5	71.89	$128,651

Best finish for 1987: T-3rd at the MCI Heritage Classic

1988	33	116	27	0	3	7	16	70.76	$390,166

Best finish for 1988: T-2nd at the Anheuser-Busch Golf Classic

1989	29	98	20	0	3	4	12	70.93	$297,770

Best finish for 1989: T-2nd at the Shearson Lehman Hutton Open

1990	31	100	21	0	2	2	7	71.83	$211,437

Best finish for 1990: 2nd at the B.C. Open

1991	31	91	14	0	0	0	4	71.59	$100,046

Best finish for 1991: T-12th at the Walt Disney World/Oldsmobile Classic

1992	26	83	17	0	1	2	6	70.98	$174,763

Best finish for 1992: T-4th at the AT&T Pebble Beach Pro-Am

1993	27	90	19	0	2	5	9	71.16	$360,212

Best finish for 1993: 2nd at the Buick Classic

1994	9	26	5	0	0	0	0	71.65	$16,032

Best finish for 1994: T-33rd at the Texas Open

Year	Starts	Rounds Played	Cuts Made	Wins	Top-5s	Top-10s	Top-25s	Scoring Average	Money
1995	23	64	11	0	1	3	3	72.14	$168,832

Best finish for 1995: T-3rd at the Sprint International

| 1996 | 25 | 74 | 13 | 0 | 1 | 2 | 5 | 71.50 | $201,058 |

Best finish for 1996: T-2nd at the Nissan Open

| 1997 | 25 | 77 | 14 | 0 | 1 | 1 | 5 | 71.82 | $287,814 |

Best finish for 1997: 2nd at the Kemper Open

| 1998 | 26 | 79 | 13 | 0 | 1 | 3 | 5 | 71.03 | $283,711 |

Best finish for 1998: T-3rd at the Freeport-McDermott Classic

| 1999 | 27 | 76 | 11 | 0 | 1 | 2 | 8 | 71.74 | $385,508 |

Best finish for 1999: 4th at the Shell Houston Open

| 2000 | 28 | 92 | 19 | 0 | 1 | 1 | 4 | 71.28 | $511,414 |

Best finish for 2000: 2nd at the Westin Texas Open at LaCantera

| 2001 | 24 | 62 | 8 | 0 | 1 | 2 | 3 | 71.63 | $310,365 |

Best finish for 2001: T-5th at the Touchstone Energy Tucson Open

2002	11	18	0	0	0	0	0	79.33	
2003	2	2	0	0	0	0	0	76.50	
2004	6	15	2	0	0	0	0	71.87	$25,435

Best finish for 2004: T-29th at the B.C. Open

2005	1	0	0	0	0	0	0		
Period Totals	Starts	Rounds Played	Cuts Made	Wins	Top-5s	Top-10s	Top-25s	Scoring Average	Money
	500	1532	288	2	26	47	106	71.63	$4,322,311

Jim Wiechers

Year	Starts	Rounds Played	Cuts Made	Wins	Top-5s	Top-10s	Top-25s	Scoring Average	Money
1965	1	4	1	0	0	1	1	69.25	

Best finish for 1965: T-8th at the Western Open

| 1967 | 23 | 71 | 12 | 0 | 0 | 0 | 2 | 73.56 | $3,728 |

Best finish for 1967: T-23rd at the Pensacola Open

| 1968 | 30 | 98 | 19 | 0 | 1 | 2 | 6 | 72.36 | $17,194 |

Best finish for 1968: T-3rd at the Robinson Open

| 1969 | 32 | 111 | 25 | 1 | 4 | 6 | 12 | 71.57 | $37,388 |

Best finish for 1969: Win at the West End Classic

| 1970 | 35 | 117 | 23 | 0 | 0 | 0 | 4 | 72.47 | $15,150 |

Best finish for 1970: T-16th at the Phoenix Open & Bing Crosby Pro-Am

| 1971 | 32 | 112 | 23 | 0 | 2 | 2 | 8 | 72.21 | $28,116 |

Best finish for 1971: 2nd at the Tallahassee Open

| 1972 | 32 | 118 | 27 | 0 | 3 | 5 | 9 | 71.88 | $47,511 |

Best finish for 1972: T-3rd at the Western Open

| 1973 | 30 | 107 | 22 | 0 | 5 | 8 | 15 | 71.37 | $74,807 |

Best finish for 1973: T-2nd at the Greater Jacksonville Open

| 1974 | 28 | 98 | 21 | 0 | 2 | 4 | 11 | 71.93 | $48,151 |

Best finish for 1974: T-4th at the Greater Jacksonville Open & Pleasant Valley Classic

| 1975 | 31 | 103 | 20 | 0 | 1 | 1 | 5 | 72.63 | $22,135 |

Best finish for 1975: T-5th at the B.C. Open

| 1976 | 20 | 53 | 10 | 0 | 0 | 0 | 0 | 73.32 | $7,199 |

Best finish for 1976: T-28th at the Western Open

| 1977 | 22 | 68 | 11 | 0 | 0 | 0 | 2 | 73.21 | $9,944 |

Best finish for 1977: T-20th at the American Express Westchester Classic

1978	10	21	0	0	0	0	0	75.14	
1979	1	2	0	0	0	0	0	75.00	
Period Totals	Starts	Rounds Played	Cuts Made	Wins	Top-5s	Top-10s	Top-25s	Scoring Average	Money
	327	1083	214	1	18	29	75	72.34	$311,321

Phil Wiechman

Year	Starts	Rounds Played	Cuts Made	Wins	Top-5s	Top-10s	Top-25s	Scoring Average	Money
1962	1	4	1	0	0	0	0	72.50	$052

Best finish for 1962: T-32nd at the Mobile Sertoma Open Invitational

| 1963 | 3 | 10 | 2 | 0 | 0 | 0 | 2 | 73.80 | $990 |

Best finish for 1963: T-20th at the Cajun Classic Open Invitational

| 1964 | 12 | 30 | 3 | 0 | 0 | 0 | 1 | 75.10 | $902 |

Best finish for 1964: T-20th at the Buick Open

| 1965 | 9 | 22 | 2 | 0 | 0 | 0 | 0 | 75.77 | |

Best finish for 1965: T-53rd at the Portland Open

1967	1	2	0	0	0	0	0	78.50	
1968	1	2	0	0	0	0	0	72.00	
1969	1	2	0	0	0	0	0	74.00	
1970	1	2	0	0	0	0	0	75.50	
Period Totals	Starts	Rounds Played	Cuts Made	Wins	Top-5s	Top-10s	Top-25s	Scoring Average	Money
	29	74	8	0	0	0	3	74.97	$1,945

Terry Wilcox

Year	Starts	Rounds Played	Cuts Made	Wins	Top-5s	Top-10s	Top-25s	Scoring Average	Money
1962	1	4	1	0	0	1	1	72.25	$1,100

Best finish for 1962: T-9th at the Oklahoma City Open Invitational

| 1963 | 2 | 8 | 2 | 0 | 0 | 0 | 0 | 73.13 | $753 |

Best finish for 1963: T-32nd at the Oklahoma City Open Invitational

| 1964 | 16 | 41 | 5 | 0 | 0 | 0 | 1 | 74.66 | $650 |

Best finish for 1964: T-14th at the Almaden Open

| 1965 | 8 | 26 | 5 | 0 | 0 | 1 | 1 | 72.73 | $2,580 |

Best finish for 1965: T-10th at the Bing Crosby Pro-Am

| 1966 | 12 | 39 | 7 | 0 | 0 | 0 | 2 | 72.69 | $2,719 |

Best finish for 1966: T-21st at the Lucky International Open Invitational

| 1967 | 17 | 59 | 11 | 0 | 0 | 0 | 3 | 83.51 | $6,882 |

Best finish for 1967: T-22nd at the Westchester Classic & Thunderbird Classic

| 1968 | 25 | 84 | 18 | 0 | 0 | 1 | 5 | 72.15 | $13,284 |

Best finish for 1968: T-10th at the Kemper Open Invitational

| 1969 | 29 | 86 | 15 | 0 | 2 | 5 | 7 | 72.24 | $24,415 |

Best finish for 1969: T-2nd at the Azalea Open

| 1970 | 29 | 94 | 18 | 0 | 1 | 2 | 7 | 72.69 | $34,468 |

Best finish for 1970: 2nd at the IVB Philadelphia Golf Classic

| 1971 | 19 | 61 | 10 | 0 | 0 | 1 | 1 | 73.10 | $10,655 |

Best finish for 1971: T-6th at the Canadian Open

| 1972 | 15 | 47 | 7 | 0 | 0 | 0 | 2 | 73.85 | $5,041 |

Best finish for 1972: T-12th at the Greater New Orleans Open

| 1973 | 14 | 43 | 6 | 0 | 0 | 0 | 1 | 73.74 | $2,227 |

Best finish for 1973: T-22nd at the Tallahassee Open

| 1974 | 13 | 36 | 4 | 0 | 0 | 0 | 0 | 73.44 | $1,924 |

Best finish for 1974: T-35th at the Dean Martin Tucson Open

| 1975 | 7 | 21 | 2 | 0 | 0 | 0 | 0 | 74.24 | $888 |

Best finish for 1975: T-48th at the Greater Greensboro Open

1976	6	14	0	0	0	0	0	75.50	$250
1977	4	9	0	0	0	0	0	76.22	
1978	2	6	0	0	0	0	0	74.67	
1979	3	8	0	0	0	0	0	74.25	
Period Totals	Starts	Rounds Played	Cuts Made	Wins	Top-5s	Top-10s	Top-25s	Scoring Average	Money
	222	686	111	0	3	11	31	74.03	$107,836

Tim Wilkinson

Year	Starts	Rounds Played	Cuts Made	Wins	Top-5s	Top-10s	Top-25s	Scoring Average	Money
2003	1	4	1	0	0	0	0	73.25	$9,900

Best finish for 2003: 71st at the Deutsche Bank Championship

| 2004 | 1 | 4 | 1 | 0 | 0 | 0 | 0 | 69.00 | $29,820 |

Best finish for 2004: T-27th at the Buick Championship

| 2008 | 29 | 95 | 17 | 0 | 2 | 3 | 5 | 71.02 | $1,167,607 |

Best finish for 2008: T-2nd at the Valero Texas Open

| Period Totals | Starts | Rounds Played | Cuts Made | Wins | Top-5s | Top-10s | Top-25s | Scoring Average | Money |
| | 31 | 103 | 19 | 0 | 2 | 3 | 5 | 71.03 | $1,207,327 |

Harold Williams

Year	Starts	Rounds Played	Cuts Made	Wins	Top-5s	Top-10s	Top-25s	Scoring Average	Money
1958	4	12	3	0	0	1	2	74.00	$315

Best finish for 1958: T-9th at the Jackson Open

| 1961 | 1 | 2 | 0 | 0 | 0 | 0 | 0 | 80.50 | |
| 1962 | 5 | 20 | 4 | 0 | 1 | 1 | 2 | 71.50 | $1,880 |

Best finish for 1962: T-5th at the Hot Springs Open Invitational

| 1963 | 1 | 4 | 1 | 0 | 0 | 1 | 1 | 71.00 | $925 |

Best finish for 1963: T-9th at the Hot Springs Open Invitational

1964	6	13	0	0	0	0	0	75.08	
1965	3	6	0	0	0	0	0	74.50	
1966	12	38	7	0	0	0	0	73.55	$663

Best finish for 1966: T-36th at the Pensacola Open Invitational

| 1967 | 6 | 14 | 1 | 0 | 0 | 0 | 0 | 74.29 | |

Best finish for 1967: T-52nd at the Memphis Open

| Period Totals | Starts | Rounds Played | Cuts Made | Wins | Top-5s | Top-10s | Top-25s | Scoring Average | Money |
| | 38 | 109 | 16 | 0 | 1 | 3 | 5 | 73.59 | $3,784 |

Jay Williamson

Year	Starts	Rounds Played	Cuts Made	Wins	Top-5s	Top-10s	Top-25s	Scoring Average	Money
1995	22	65	11	0	1	3	3	72.00	$120,180

Best finish for 1995: T-4th at the Ideon Classic

| 1996 | 27 | 77 | 13 | 0 | 0 | 1 | 2 | 72.12 | $82,773 |

Best finish for 1996: T-7th at the Buick Open

Year	Starts	Rounds Played	Cuts Made	Wins	Top-5s	Top-10s	Top-25s	Scoring Average	Money
1997	2	6	1	0	0	0	0	71.33	$3,409

Best finish for 1997: T-53rd at the Canon Greater Hartford Open

| 1999 | 31 | 82 | 12 | 0 | 1 | 1 | 4 | 71.83 | $264,618 |

Best finish for 1999: T-4th at the AT&T Pebble Beach National Pro-Am

| 2000 | 32 | 102 | 20 | 0 | 0 | 1 | 6 | 70.80 | $460,024 |

Best finish for 2000: T-7th at the Bay Hill Invitational

| 2001 | 35 | 90 | 13 | 0 | 0 | 3 | 4 | 71.20 | $477,031 |

Best finish for 2001: T-6th at the Marconi Pennsylvania Classic

| 2002 | 30 | 91 | 16 | 0 | 1 | 2 | 6 | 71.07 | $515,445 |

Best finish for 2002: T-5th at the Southern Farm Bureau Classic

| 2003 | 31 | 92 | 17 | 0 | 1 | 1 | 4 | 71.14 | $627,132 |

Best finish for 2003: T-3rd at the BellSouth Classic

| 2004 | 33 | 98 | 16 | 0 | 0 | 2 | 8 | 71.08 | $660,038 |

Best finish for 2004: T-7th at the Nissan Open

| 2005 | 16 | 53 | 10 | 0 | 0 | 1 | 3 | 71.45 | $382,653 |

Best finish for 2005: T-10th at the BellSouth Classic

| 2006 | 18 | 48 | 6 | 0 | 0 | 0 | 0 | 72.54 | $86,150 |

Best finish for 2006: T-34th at the EDS Byron Nelson Championship

| 2007 | 14 | 50 | 11 | 0 | 1 | 1 | 3 | 70.64 | $835,516 |

Best finish for 2007: 2nd at the Travelers Championship

| 2008 | 33 | 96 | 18 | 0 | 1 | 1 | 3 | 71.52 | $758,862 |

Best finish for 2008: T-2nd at the John Deere Classic

Period Totals	Starts	Rounds Played	Cuts Made	Wins	Top-5s	Top-10s	Top-25s	Scoring Average	Money
	324	950	164	0	6	17	46	71.40	$5,273,831

Garrett Willis

Year	Starts	Rounds Played	Cuts Made	Wins	Top-5s	Top-10s	Top-25s	Scoring Average	Money
1995	1	2	0	0	0	0	0	81.50	
1998	1	2	0	0	0	0	0	76.50	$1,000
1999	1	2	0	0	0	0	0	75.50	$1,000
2001	33	86	11	1	1	1	3	71.65	$686,038

Best finish for 2001: Win at the Touchstone Energy Tucson Open

| 2002 | 29 | 78 | 13 | 0 | 1 | 1 | 3 | 72.36 | $444,483 |

Best finish for 2002: T-2nd at the Valero Texas Open

| 2003 | 32 | 96 | 16 | 0 | 0 | 0 | 5 | 71.34 | $467,213 |

Best finish for 2003: T-11th at the Bell Canadian Open

| 2004 | 17 | 49 | 7 | 0 | 0 | 0 | 2 | 71.45 | $165,210 |

Best finish for 2004: T-12th at the Chrysler Classic of Tucson

| 2005 | 7 | 21 | 3 | 0 | 0 | 0 | 1 | 71.33 | $52,251 |

Best finish for 2005: T-20th at the John Deere Classic

| 2006 | 10 | 27 | 4 | 0 | 0 | 0 | 0 | 71.22 | $60,541 |

Best finish for 2006: T-27th at the John Deere Classic

| 2007 | 13 | 38 | 6 | 0 | 0 | 1 | 2 | 71.08 | $233,569 |

Best finish for 2007: T-7th at the Frys.Com Open-Vegas

| 2008 | 11 | 34 | 6 | 0 | 0 | 0 | 2 | 71.50 | $176,815 |

Best finish for 2008: T-15th at the Wyndham Championship

Period Totals	Starts	Rounds Played	Cuts Made	Wins	Top-5s	Top-10s	Top-25s	Scoring Average	Money
	155	435	66	1	2	3	18	71.67	$2,288,118

Brian Wilson

Year	Starts	Rounds Played	Cuts Made	Wins	Top-5s	Top-10s	Top-25s	Scoring Average	Money
1988	1	2	0	0	0	0	0	75.00	
2001	31	86	12	0	0	0	2	71.51	$169,440

Best finish for 2001: 20th at the Buick Open

| 2002 | 1 | 4 | 1 | 0 | 0 | 0 | 0 | 69.50 | $10,860 |

Best finish for 2002: T-33rd at the B.C. Open

| 2004 | 1 | 2 | 0 | 0 | 0 | 0 | 0 | 75.50 | |

Period Totals	Starts	Rounds Played	Cuts Made	Wins	Top-5s	Top-10s	Top-25s	Scoring Average	Money
	34	94	13	0	0	0	2	71.59	$180,300

Dean Wilson

Year	Starts	Rounds Played	Cuts Made	Wins	Top-5s	Top-10s	Top-25s	Scoring Average	Money
2001	2	6	1	0	0	0	0	73.00	$31,486

Best finish for 2001: T-30th at the U.S. Open

| 2002 | 4 | 12 | 2 | 0 | 0 | 0 | 1 | 71.50 | $46,900 |

Best finish for 2002: T-23rd at the Sony Open in Hawaii

| 2003 | 27 | 82 | 14 | 0 | 0 | 2 | 7 | 71.16 | $657,345 |

Best finish for 2003: T-6th at the Chrysler Classic of Tucson

| 2004 | 33 | 99 | 16 | 0 | 1 | 1 | 4 | 71.12 | $561,340 |

Best finish for 2004: T-3rd at the Valero Texas Open

| 2005 | 27 | 86 | 17 | 0 | 0 | 4 | 7 | 70.70 | $821,903 |

Best finish for 2005: 6th at the Barclays Classic

Year	Starts	Rounds Played	Cuts Made	Wins	Top-5s	Top-10s	Top-25s	Scoring Average	Money
2006	34	111	23	1	2	6	11	70.71	$2,511,857

Best finish for 2006: Win at The International

| 2007 | 28 | 92 | 18 | 0 | 1 | 4 | 9 | 71.28 | $1,261,007 |

Best finish for 2007: T-5th at the Stanford St. Jude Classic

| 2008 | 32 | 109 | 22 | 0 | 2 | 3 | 8 | 70.98 | $1,350,002 |

Best finish for 2008: T-3rd at the AT&T National & U.S. Bank Championship in Milwaukee

Period Totals	Starts	Rounds Played	Cuts Made	Wins	Top-5s	Top-10s	Top-25s	Scoring Average	Money
	187	597	113	1	6	20	47	71.02	$7,241,840

Jeff Wilson

Year	Starts	Rounds Played	Cuts Made	Wins	Top-5s	Top-10s	Top-25s	Scoring Average	Money
1982	1	2	0	0	0	0	0	76.50	
1990	28	75	11	0	0	1	3	72.12	$71,011

Best finish for 1990: T-7th at the Buick Southern Open

| 1991 | 3 | 8 | 1 | 0 | 0 | 0 | 0 | 71.38 | $2,864 |

Best finish for 1991: T-47th at the AT&T Pebble Beach Pro-Am

| 1992 | 1 | 3 | 0 | 0 | 0 | 0 | 0 | 72.33 | |
| 1993 | 3 | 8 | 1 | 0 | 0 | 0 | 0 | 74.88 | $5,508 |

Best finish for 1993: T-36th at the AT&T Pebble Beach Pro-Am

| 1995 | 1 | 3 | 0 | 0 | 0 | 0 | 0 | 73.00 | |
| 2000 | 1 | 4 | 1 | 0 | 0 | 0 | 0 | 76.00 | |

Best finish for 2000: 59th at the U.S. Open

2008	1	2	0	0	0	0	0	79.50	
Period Totals	Starts	Rounds Played	Cuts Made	Wins	Top-5s	Top-10s	Top-25s	Scoring Average	Money
	39	105	14	0	0	1	3	72.68	$79,382

Jim Wilson

Year	Starts	Rounds Played	Cuts Made	Wins	Top-5s	Top-10s	Top-25s	Scoring Average	Money
1986	1	3	0	0	0	0	0	78.00	
1987	27	62	4	0	0	0	0	73.90	$4,995

Best finish for 1987: T-41st at the Honda Classic

Period Totals	Starts	Rounds Played	Cuts Made	Wins	Top-5s	Top-10s	Top-25s	Scoring Average	Money
	28	65	4	0	0	0	0	74.09	$4,995

John Wilson

Year	Starts	Rounds Played	Cuts Made	Wins	Top-5s	Top-10s	Top-25s	Scoring Average	Money
1991	29	85	12	0	0	0	3	71.88	$44,041

Best finish for 1991: T-19th at the Deposit Guaranty Classic & Federal Express St. Jude Classic

| 1992 | 1 | 4 | 1 | 0 | 0 | 0 | 0 | 70.00 | $576 |

Best finish for 1992: T-73rd at the Deposit Guaranty Classic

| 1994 | 29 | 84 | 14 | 0 | 2 | 2 | 4 | 71.14 | $155,058 |

Best finish for 1994: T-4th at the Anheuser-Busch Golf Classic

| 1995 | 29 | 95 | 17 | 0 | 0 | 1 | 4 | 71.34 | $149,280 |

Best finish for 1995: T-8th at the Shell Houston Open

| 1996 | 26 | 81 | 13 | 0 | 1 | 2 | 5 | 71.49 | $183,421 |

Best finish for 1996: T-4th at the Phoenix Open

| 1997 | 30 | 92 | 14 | 0 | 0 | 0 | 2 | 72.07 | $112,836 |

Best finish for 1997: T-12th at the B.C. Open

Period Totals	Starts	Rounds Played	Cuts Made	Wins	Top-5s	Top-10s	Top-25s	Scoring Average	Money
	144	441	71	0	3	5	18	71.57	$645,213

Mark Wilson

Year	Starts	Rounds Played	Cuts Made	Wins	Top-5s	Top-10s	Top-25s	Scoring Average	Money
1996	1	2	0	0	0	0	0	83.50	
1998	2	4	0	0	0	0	0	74.00	$1,000
1999	1	4	1	0	0	0	0	69.00	$12,765

Best finish for 1999: T-31st at the Greater Milwaukee Open

| 2000 | 1 | 4 | 1 | 0 | 0 | 0 | 0 | 69.50 | $8,500 |

Best finish for 2000: T-43rd at the Greater Milwaukee Open

| 2001 | 2 | 8 | 2 | 0 | 0 | 0 | 0 | 71.13 | $13,727 |

Best finish for 2001: T-52nd at the Advil Western Open

| 2002 | 1 | 2 | 0 | 0 | 0 | 0 | 0 | 72.00 | |
| 2003 | 30 | 80 | 11 | 0 | 1 | 1 | 3 | 71.83 | $482,502 |

Best finish for 2003: 4th at the HP Classic of New Orleans

| 2004 | 19 | 62 | 12 | 0 | 1 | 1 | 2 | 70.97 | $300,317 |

Best finish for 2004: T-5th at the Reno-Tahoe Open

| 2005 | 25 | 70 | 12 | 0 | 1 | 3 | 3 | 70.99 | $573,218 |

Best finish for 2005: T-3rd at the Valero Texas Open

| 2006 | 24 | 76 | 16 | 0 | 0 | 1 | 4 | 70.80 | $444,318 |

Best finish for 2006: T-9th at the Chrysler Classic of Tucson

| 2007 | 25 | 87 | 18 | 1 | 1 | 3 | 6 | 71.07 | $1,639,612 |

Best finish for 2007: Win at the Honda Classic

	Starts	Rounds Played	Cuts Made	Wins	Top-5s	Top-10s	Top-25s	Scoring Average	Money
2008	29	107	25	0	1	5	12	70.44	$1,578,337

Best finish for 2008: T-2nd at the Valero Texas Open

Period Totals	Starts	Rounds Played	Cuts Made	Wins	Top-5s	Top-10s	Top-25s	Scoring Average	Money
	160	506	98	1	5	14	30	71.04	$5,054,297

Bo Wininger

Year	Starts	Rounds Played	Cuts Made	Wins	Top-5s	Top-10s	Top-25s	Scoring Average	Money
1958	32	125	30	0	5	9	21	71.31	$16,184

Best finish for 1958: T-2nd at the Tijuana Open

| 1959 | 19 | 76 | 18 | 0 | 5 | 8 | 15 | 70.67 | $17,552 |

Best finish for 1959: T-3rd at the San Diego Open Invitational, Canadian Open Championship & Miller Open Invitational

| 1960 | 10 | 38 | 8 | 0 | 1 | 1 | 3 | 72.16 | $5,085 |

Best finish for 1960: T-2nd at the Dallas Open Invitational

| 1961 | 5 | 21 | 5 | 0 | 0 | 1 | 3 | 71.81 | $2,318 |

Best finish for 1961: T-10th at the Bing Crosby National

| 1962 | 14 | 56 | 13 | 2 | 4 | 5 | 8 | 71.27 | $17,038 |

Best finish for 1962: Win at the Greater New Orleans Open Invitational & Carling Open Invitational

| 1963 | 20 | 80 | 20 | 1 | 1 | 6 | 10 | 71.44 | $21,040 |

Best finish for 1963: Win at the Greater New Orleans Open Invitational

| 1964 | 8 | 31 | 6 | 0 | 1 | 2 | 3 | 72.55 | $8,865 |

Best finish for 1964: T-2nd at the Bing Crosby Pro-Am

| 1965 | 9 | 36 | 8 | 0 | 1 | 1 | 4 | 72.58 | $13,076 |

Best finish for 1965: 4th at the PGA Championship

| 1966 | 8 | 27 | 4 | 0 | 0 | 1 | 2 | 74.44 | $5,084 |

Best finish for 1966: T-7th at the Colonial National Invitation

| 1967 | 5 | 19 | 3 | 0 | 0 | 0 | 0 | 75.47 | $150 |

Best finish for 1967: T-44th at the Oklahoma City Open

Period Totals	Starts	Rounds Played	Cuts Made	Wins	Top-5s	Top-10s	Top-25s	Scoring Average	Money
	130	509	115	3	18	34	69	71.80	$106,391

PGA Tour career totals from 1949 to 1958

	Starts	Rounds Played	Cuts Made	Wins	Top-5s	Top-10s	Top-25s	Scoring Average	Money
	255	705	990	6	N/A	77	152	N/A	$168,659

Terry Winter

Year	Starts	Rounds Played	Cuts Made	Wins	Top-5s	Top-10s	Top-25s	Scoring Average	Money
1967	1	4	1	0	0	0	0	74.00	

Best finish for 1967: T-45th at the "500" Festival Open

| 1968 | 16 | 39 | 4 | 0 | 0 | 0 | 0 | 74.85 | |

Best finish for 1968: T-56th at the Buick Open Invitational

| 1969 | 9 | 26 | 4 | 0 | 0 | 0 | 1 | 73.27 | $989 |

Best finish for 1969: T-25th at the Indian Ridge Hospital Open

Period Totals	Starts	Rounds Played	Cuts Made	Wins	Top-5s	Top-10s	Top-25s	Scoring Average	Money
	26	69	9	0	0	0	1	74.20	$989

Gary Wintz

Year	Starts	Rounds Played	Cuts Made	Wins	Top-5s	Top-10s	Top-25s	Scoring Average	Money
1975	21	57	8	0	0	1	3	73.05	$6,136

Best finish for 1975: T-10th at the Southern Open

| 1976 | 28 | 89 | 19 | 0 | 0 | 0 | 2 | 72.93 | $10,019 |

Best finish for 1976: T-17th at the Pensacola Open

| 1977 | 13 | 28 | 1 | 0 | 0 | 0 | 0 | 74.82 | $424 |

Best finish for 1977: T-51st at the First NBC New Orleans Open

| 1978 | 4 | 9 | 2 | 0 | 0 | 0 | 0 | 73.11 | $1,605 |

Best finish for 1978: T-32nd at the Florida Citrus Open Invitational

| 1979 | 5 | 12 | 1 | 0 | 0 | 0 | 0 | 73.50 | $455 |

Best finish for 1979: T-43rd at the Tallahassee Open

| 1980 | 3 | 4 | 0 | 0 | 0 | 0 | 0 | 76.50 | |
| 1981 | 17 | 35 | 2 | 0 | 0 | 0 | 0 | 74.43 | $1,525 |

Best finish for 1981: T-57th at the Quad Cities Open

Period Totals	Starts	Rounds Played	Cuts Made	Wins	Top-5s	Top-10s	Top-25s	Scoring Average	Money
	91	234	33	0	0	1	5	73.51	$20,164

Larry Wise

Year	Starts	Rounds Played	Cuts Made	Wins	Top-5s	Top-10s	Top-25s	Scoring Average	Money
1964	1	2	0	0	0	0	0	77.50	
1966	1	4	1	0	0	0	0	72.75	

Best finish for 1966: T-62nd at the Cajun Classic

| 1967 | 13 | 33 | 3 | 0 | 0 | 0 | 0 | 75.06 | $242 |

Best finish for 1967: T-37th at the Cajun Classic

Year	Starts	Rounds Played	Cuts Made	Wins	Top-5s	Top-10s	Top-25s	Scoring Average	Money
1968	8	23	3	0	0	0	0	73.39	$535

Best finish for 1968: T-45th at the PGA Championship

Year	Starts	Rounds Played	Cuts Made	Wins	Top-5s	Top-10s	Top-25s	Scoring Average	Money
1970	1	2	0	0	0	0	0	76.50	
1971	1	2	0	0	0	0	0	76.00	$500
1972	1	4	1	0	0	0	1	72.50	$2,385

Best finish for 1972: T-20th at the PGA Championship

Year	Starts	Rounds Played	Cuts Made	Wins	Top-5s	Top-10s	Top-25s	Scoring Average	Money
1973	18	60	10	0	1	2	4	72.45	$12,154

Best finish for 1973: T-5th at the Liggett Meyers Open

Year	Starts	Rounds Played	Cuts Made	Wins	Top-5s	Top-10s	Top-25s	Scoring Average	Money
1974	22	63	9	0	0	0	2	73.10	$8,429

Best finish for 1974: T-15th at the Kemper Open

Year	Starts	Rounds Played	Cuts Made	Wins	Top-5s	Top-10s	Top-25s	Scoring Average	Money
1975	14	41	6	0	0	0	1	73.20	$2,965

Best finish for 1975: T-20th at the Tallahassee Open

1986	1	0	0	0	0	0	0		
Period Totals	Starts	Rounds Played	Cuts Made	Wins	Top-5s	Top-10s	Top-25s	Scoring Average	Money
	81	234	33	0	1	2	8	73.33	$27,209

Casey Wittenberg

Year	Starts	Rounds Played	Cuts Made	Wins	Top-5s	Top-10s	Top-25s	Scoring Average	Money
2002	2	4	0	0	0	0	0	72.75	
2003	1	2	0	0	0	0	0	74.50	
2004	9	26	4	0	0	0	3	72.50	$85,670

Best finish for 2004: T-13th at the Masters

2005	9	26	4	0	0	0	0	72.58	$69,548

Best finish for 2005: T-33rd at the Masters

2006	1	4	1	0	0	0	0	72.75	$10,868

Best finish for 2006: T-65th at the FedEx St. Jude Classic

2008	4	12	2	0	1	1	1	71.58	$167,520

Best finish for 2008: T-4th at the Viking Classic

Period Totals	Starts	Rounds Played	Cuts Made	Wins	Top-5s	Top-10s	Top-25s	Scoring Average	Money
	26	74	11	0	1	1	4	72.46	$333,606

Jimmy Wittenberg

Year	Starts	Rounds Played	Cuts Made	Wins	Top-5s	Top-10s	Top-25s	Scoring Average	Money
1974	1	2	0	0	0	0	0	73.00	
1975	15	35	3	0	0	0	0	73.77	$1,226

Best finish for 1975: T-43rd at the Kaiser International Open

1977	17	44	6	0	0	0	1	72.89	$3,569

Best finish for 1977: T-25th at the Canadian Open

1978	3	7	0	0	0	0	0	76.29	$600
Period Totals	Starts	Rounds Played	Cuts Made	Wins	Top-5s	Top-10s	Top-25s	Scoring Average	Money
	36	88	9	0	0	0	1	73.51	$5,395

Bob Wolcott

Year	Starts	Rounds Played	Cuts Made	Wins	Top-5s	Top-10s	Top-25s	Scoring Average	Money
1986	3	6	0	0	0	0	0	73.67	
1987	2	6	1	0	0	0	1	69.67	$3,793

Best finish for 1987: T-23rd at the Provident Classic

1988	2	6	1	0	0	0	1	69.33	$9,112

Best finish for 1988: T-12th at the Provident Classic

1989	26	64	8	0	0	1	1	71.91	$20,688

Best finish for 1989: T-7th at the Deposit Guaranty Golf Classic

1990	29	86	15	0	1	1	5	71.59	$133,261

Best finish for 1990: T-3rd at the Anheuser-Busch Golf Classic

1991	36	119	23	0	1	1	3	71.78	$145,389

Best finish for 1991: T-3rd at the Kmart Greater Greensboro Open

1992	36	102	15	0	0	1	2	71.77	$68,358

Best finish for 1992: T-10th at the Deposit Guaranty Classic

1993	3	8	1	0	0	0	0	73.50	$702

Best finish for 1993: T-51st at the Deposit Guaranty Classic

1994	1	2	0	0	0	0	0	74.50	
1997	27	71	8	0	0	1	2	72.04	$62,652

Best finish for 1997: T-10th at the Quad City Classic

1998	1	2	0	0	0	0	0	72.50	
2003	1	2	0	0	0	0	0	75.00	
Period Totals	Starts	Rounds Played	Cuts Made	Wins	Top-5s	Top-10s	Top-25s	Scoring Average	Money
	167	474	72	0	2	5	15	71.82	$443,956

Randy Wolff

Year	Starts	Rounds Played	Cuts Made	Wins	Top-5s	Top-10s	Top-25s	Scoring Average	Money
1969	18	53	9	0	0	0	1	73.83	$3,105

Best finish for 1969: T-16th at the Tallahassee Open

1970	27	82	15	0	1	1	4	72.54	$12,032

Best finish for 1970: 5th at the Byron Nelson Golf Classic

Year	Starts	Rounds Played	Cuts Made	Wins	Top-5s	Top-10s	Top-25s	Scoring Average	Money
1971	27	91	18	0	1	1	6	72.30	$21,835

Best finish for 1971: T-2nd at the Danny Thomas Memphis Classic

| 1972 | 24 | 71 | 11 | 0 | 0 | 0 | 0 | 73.86 | $3,237 |

Best finish for 1972: T-35th at the Greater Hartford Open Invitational

| 1973 | 11 | 27 | 3 | 0 | 0 | 0 | 0 | 73.67 | $816 |

Best finish for 1973: T-30th at the Tallahassee Open

Period Totals	Starts	Rounds Played	Cuts Made	Wins	Top-5s	Top-10s	Top-25s	Scoring Average	Money
	107	324	56	0	2	2	11	73.06	$41,025

Larry Wood

Year	Starts	Rounds Played	Cuts Made	Wins	Top-5s	Top-10s	Top-25s	Scoring Average	Money
1964	2	4	0	0	0	0	0	74.00	
1965	13	34	4	0	0	0	1	74.24	$941

Best finish for 1965: T-19th at the Seattle Open

| 1966 | 19 | 50 | 6 | 0 | 0 | 0 | 1 | 74.40 | $1,098 |

Best finish for 1966: T-25th at the Azalea Open Invitational

| 1967 | 16 | 44 | 5 | 0 | 0 | 0 | 1 | 74.30 | $1,390 |

Best finish for 1967: T-24th at the "500" Festival Open

| 1968 | 15 | 46 | 8 | 0 | 0 | 1 | 1 | 73.17 | $1,550 |

Best finish for 1968: T-6th at the AZALEA Open Invitational

| 1969 | 3 | 8 | 1 | 0 | 0 | 0 | 0 | 73.63 | |

Best finish for 1969: T-37th at the Azalea Open

| 1970 | 19 | 62 | 12 | 0 | 0 | 0 | 2 | 73.11 | $5,910 |

Best finish for 1970: T-11th at the Byron Nelson Golf Classic

| 1971 | 31 | 106 | 21 | 0 | 1 | 2 | 3 | 72.97 | $24,395 |

Best finish for 1971: T-4th at the Monsanto Open

| 1972 | 35 | 109 | 19 | 0 | 1 | 1 | 5 | 72.56 | $27,561 |

Best finish for 1972: T-2nd at the Walt Disney World Open

| 1973 | 36 | 109 | 17 | 0 | 0 | 0 | 1 | 73.56 | $7,930 |

Best finish for 1973: T-11th at the San Antonio Texas Open

| 1974 | 23 | 62 | 7 | 0 | 0 | 0 | 0 | 74.10 | $2,163 |

Best finish for 1974: T-38th at the Greater New Orleans Open & Southern Open

| 1975 | 4 | 8 | 0 | 0 | 0 | 0 | 0 | 74.75 | |

Period Totals	Starts	Rounds Played	Cuts Made	Wins	Top-5s	Top-10s	Top-25s	Scoring Average	Money
	216	642	100	0	2	4	15	73.44	$72,939

Willie Wood

Year	Starts	Rounds Played	Cuts Made	Wins	Top-5s	Top-10s	Top-25s	Scoring Average	Money
1980	1	2	0	0	0	0	0	75.00	
1982	2	6	1	0	0	0	0	76.33	

Best finish for 1982: T-41st at the Masters

| 1983 | 2 | 8 | 2 | 0 | 0 | 1 | 1 | 73.25 | $8,400 |

Best finish for 1983: T-10th at the LaJet Coors Classic

| 1984 | 30 | 99 | 20 | 0 | 1 | 3 | 10 | 71.83 | $115,741 |

Best finish for 1984: 2nd at the Anheuser-Busch Golf Classic

| 1985 | 30 | 108 | 26 | 0 | 3 | 4 | 11 | 71.32 | $154,306 |

Best finish for 1985: 3rd at the Honda Classic

| 1986 | 31 | 96 | 23 | 0 | 3 | 3 | 7 | 71.53 | $173,629 |

Best finish for 1986: 2nd at the Manufactures Hanover Westchester Classic

| 1987 | 30 | 97 | 19 | 0 | 0 | 1 | 7 | 71.49 | $95,917 |

Best finish for 1987: T-8th at the Federal Express St. Jude Classic

| 1988 | 30 | 78 | 10 | 0 | 1 | 1 | 3 | 72.53 | $53,064 |

Best finish for 1988: T-5th at the Shearson Lehman/Andy Williams San Diego

| 1989 | 23 | 53 | 3 | 0 | 0 | 0 | 0 | 73.34 | $9,677 |

Best finish for 1989: T-46th at the Nissan Los Angeles Open

| 1990 | 25 | 70 | 10 | 0 | 1 | 2 | 5 | 72.17 | $179,972 |

Best finish for 1990: T-2nd at the Hardee's Golf Classic

| 1991 | 27 | 77 | 13 | 0 | 0 | 0 | 0 | 71.77 | $48,033 |

Best finish for 1991: T-30th at the GTE Byron Nelson Classic & The International

| 1992 | 8 | 26 | 5 | 0 | 0 | 1 | 2 | 71.12 | $57,748 |

Best finish for 1992: T-6th at the Hardee's Golf Classic

| 1993 | 25 | 78 | 16 | 0 | 0 | 3 | 5 | 71.32 | $147,206 |

Best finish for 1993: T-6th at the New England Classic

| 1994 | 26 | 77 | 15 | 0 | 0 | 0 | 2 | 71.62 | $87,102 |

Best finish for 1994: T-18th at the Hardee's Golf Classic

| 1995 | 11 | 37 | 8 | 0 | 0 | 0 | 3 | 71.38 | $64,697 |

Best finish for 1995: T-12th at the Shell Houston Open

| 1996 | 10 | 32 | 9 | 1 | 1 | 1 | 3 | 70.06 | $255,158 |

Best finish for 1996: Win at the Deposit Guaranty Golf Classic

| 1997 | 27 | 86 | 17 | 0 | 0 | 1 | 3 | 71.48 | $190,283 |

Best finish for 1997: T-9th at the MCI Classic

Year	Starts	Rounds Played	Cuts Made	Wins	Top-5s	Top-10s	Top-25s	Scoring Average	Money
1998	27	83	15	0	2	2	5	71.30	$398,110

Best finish for 1998: T-2nd at the Sprint International

1999	27	72	10	0	0	0	1	72.06	$120,884

Best finish for 1999: T-18th at the Phoenix Open

2000	14	38	6	0	0	0	0	72.21	$45,345

Best finish for 2000: T-41st at the SEI Pennsylvania Classic

2001	16	52	10	0	0	0	2	70.94	$197,113

Best finish for 2001: 12th at the Southern Farm Bureau Classic

2002	16	44	6	0	0	0	1	71.48	$85,871

Best finish for 2002: T-23rd at the Kemper Insurance Open

2003	11	34	6	0	0	0	1	71.56	$118,280

Best finish for 2003: T-18th at the Greater Hartford Open

2004	9	26	4	0	0	0	1	71.54	$78,936

Best finish for 2004: T-18th at the Reno-Tahoe Open

2005	4	9	0	0	0	0	0	73.11	
2006	11	26	3	0	0	0	0	72.42	$27,774

Best finish for 2006: T-60th at the FedEx St. Jude Classic

2007	6	14	1	0	0	0	0	72.07	$8,700

Best finish for 2007: 83rd at the Wyndham Championship

2008	5	11	0	0	0	0	0	74.64	
Period Totals	Starts	Rounds Played	Cuts Made	Wins	Top-5s	Top-10s	Top-25s	Scoring Average	Money
	484	1439	258	1	12	23	73	71.74	$2,721,946

Tom Woodard

Year	Starts	Rounds Played	Cuts Made	Wins	Top-5s	Top-10s	Top-25s	Scoring Average	Money
1981	7	15	2	0	0	0	0	74.07	$1,504

Best finish for 1981: T-42nd at the B.C. Open

1982	11	29	3	0	0	0	1	73.69	$2,771

Best finish for 1982: T-24th at the Miller High-Life Quad Cities Open

1985	10	22	1	0	0	0	0	74.91	$724

Best finish for 1985: T-79th at the Doral-Eastern Open

1988	1	2	0	0	0	0	0	79.50	$1,000
1991	1	2	0	0	0	0	0	80.00	$1,000
1993	1	2	0	0	0	0	0	74.00	$1,000
Period Totals	Starts	Rounds Played	Cuts Made	Wins	Top-5s	Top-10s	Top-25s	Scoring Average	Money
	31	72	6	0	0	0	1	74.49	$7,999

Jeff Woodland

Year	Starts	Rounds Played	Cuts Made	Wins	Top-5s	Top-10s	Top-25s	Scoring Average	Money
1989	1	4	1	0	0	0	0	71.75	$6,560

Best finish for 1989: T-39th at the British Open

1990	1	2	0	0	0	0	0	72.00	$996
1991	3	6	1	0	0	0	1	71.00	$20,500

Best finish for 1991: T-11th at the New England Classic

1992	1	2	0	0	0	0	0	71.00	
1993	27	79	14	0	0	1	3	72.04	$73,367

Best finish for 1993: T-10th at the Deposit Guaranty Classic

1994	30	83	13	0	0	1	6	71.78	$117,627

Best finish for 1994: T-8th at the GTE Byron Nelson Classic

1995	9	17	0	0	0	0	0	73.76	
Period Totals	Starts	Rounds Played	Cuts Made	Wins	Top-5s	Top-10s	Top-25s	Scoring Average	Money
	72	193	29	0	0	2	10	72.03	$219,050

Tiger Woods

Year	Starts	Rounds Played	Cuts Made	Wins	Top-5s	Top-10s	Top-25s	Scoring Average	Money
1992	1	2	0	0	0	0	0	73.50	
1993	3	6	0	0	0	0	0	75.17	
1994	3	6	0	0	0	0	0	75.17	
1995	4	13	3	0	0	0	0	73.31	

Best finish for 1995: T-41st at the Masters

1996	11	41	10	2	5	5	8	69.41	$790,594

Best finish for 1996: Win at the Las Vegas Invitational & Walt Disney World/Oldsmobile Classic

1997	21	81	20	4	7	9	14	69.75	$2,066,833

Best finish for 1997: Win at the Mercedes Championship, Masters, GTE Byron Nelson Classic & Motorola Western Open

1998	20	73	19	1	8	13	17	70.10	$1,841,117

Best finish for 1998: Win at the BellSouth Classic

1999	21	75	21	8	13	16	18	69.56	$6,616,585

Best finish for 1999: Win at the Buick Invitational, Memorial Tournament, Motorola Western Open, PGA Championship, WGC-NEC Invitational, National Car Rental Golf Classic/Disney, The Tour Championship & American Express Championship

2000	20	76	20	9	17	17	20	68.17	$9,188,321

Best finish for 2000: Win at the Mercedes Championships, AT&T Pebble Beach, Bay Hill Invitational, Memorial Tournament, U.S. Open, British Open, PGA Championship, WGC-NEC Invitational & Bell Canadian Open

Year	Starts	Rounds Played	Cuts Made	Wins	Top-5s	Top-10s	Top-25s	Scoring Average	Money
2001	19	76	19	5	8	9	18	68.87	$5,687,778

Best finish for 2001: Win at the Bay Hill Invitational, The Players Championship, Masters, Memorial Tournament & WGC-NEC Invitational

| 2002 | 18 | 68 | 18 | 5 | 11 | 13 | 16 | 69.00 | $6,912,625 |

Best finish for 2002: Win at the Bay Hill Invitational, Masters, U.S. Open, Buick Open & American Express Championship

| 2003 | 18 | 68 | 18 | 5 | 11 | 12 | 16 | 69.38 | $6,623,463 |

Best finish for 2003: Win at the Buick Invitational, WGC-Accenture Match Play Championship, Bay Hill Invitational, 100th Western Open & American Express Championship

| 2004 | 19 | 72 | 19 | 1 | 9 | 14 | 18 | 69.68 | $5,365,472 |

Best finish for 2004: Win at the WGC-Accenture Match Play Championship

| 2005 | 21 | 74 | 19 | 6 | 13 | 13 | 17 | 69.11 | $10,628,024 |

Best finish for 2005: Win at the Buick Invitational, Ford Championship at Doral, Masters, British Open, WGC-NEC Invitational & WGC-American Express Championship

| 2006 | 15 | 52 | 13 | 8 | 10 | 11 | 13 | 68.73 | $9,943,563 |

Best finish for 2006: Win at the Buick Invitational, Ford Championship at Doral, British Open, Buick Open, PGA Championship, WGC-NEC Invitational, Deutsche Bank Championship & WGC-American Express Championship

| 2007 | 16 | 60 | 16 | 7 | 10 | 12 | 15 | 69.10 | $10,867,052 |

Best finish for 2007: Win at the Buick Invitational, WGC-CA Championship, Wachovia Championship, WGC-Bridgestone Invitational, PGA Championship, BMW Championship & The Tour Championship

| 2008 | 6 | 20 | 6 | 4 | 6 | 6 | 6 | 68.90 | $5,775,000 |

Best finish for 2008: Win at the Buick Invitational & WGC-Accenture Match Play Championship, Arnold Palmer Invitational & U.S. Open

Period Totals	Starts	Rounds Played	Cuts Made	Wins	Top-5s	Top-10s	Top-25s	Scoring Average	Money
	236	863	221	65	128	150	196	69.39	$82,306,426

Jim Woodward

Year	Starts	Rounds Played	Cuts Made	Wins	Top-5s	Top-10s	Top-25s	Scoring Average	Money
1980	1	2	0	0	0	0	0	76.50	
1986	3	10	1	0	0	0	0	72.40	$927

Best finish for 1986: T-66th at the Los Angeles Open

| 1987 | 3 | 10 | 2 | 0 | 0 | 0 | 1 | 73.40 | $11,487 |

Best finish for 1987: T-17th at the U.S. Open

| 1990 | 28 | 73 | 8 | 0 | 1 | 1 | 2 | 72.34 | $118,462 |

Best finish for 1990: T-2nd at the Canadian Open

| 1991 | 29 | 81 | 11 | 0 | 0 | 0 | 1 | 72.11 | $28,307 |

Best finish for 1991: T-24th at the Nissan Los Angeles Open

| 1992 | 25 | 70 | 11 | 0 | 1 | 2 | 6 | 71.56 | $161,301 |

Best finish for 1992: T-5th at the GTE Byron Nelson Classic

| 1993 | 19 | 50 | 8 | 0 | 0 | 0 | 1 | 72.30 | $52,731 |

Best finish for 1993: T-11th at the Phoenix Open

| 1994 | 16 | 43 | 6 | 0 | 0 | 0 | 0 | 72.53 | $20,996 |

Best finish for 1994: T-27th at the Nissan Los Angeles Open

2000	1	2	0	0	0	0	0	77.50	$2,000
2001	1	2	0	0	0	0	0	75.00	$2,000
Period Totals	Starts	Rounds Played	Cuts Made	Wins	Top-5s	Top-10s	Top-25s	Scoring Average	Money
	126	343	47	0	2	3	11	72.25	$398,212

Len Woodward

Year	Starts	Rounds Played	Cuts Made	Wins	Top-5s	Top-10s	Top-25s	Scoring Average	Money
1960	8	30	6	0	0	2	4	70.57	$3,542

Best finish for 1960: T-6th at the Portland Open Invitational

| 1961 | 5 | 20 | 4 | 0 | 0 | 1 | 1 | 71.95 | $1,474 |

Best finish for 1961: T-9th at the Greater Greensboro Open Invitational

| 1963 | 4 | 16 | 4 | 0 | 0 | 0 | 1 | 70.94 | $1,380 |

Best finish for 1963: T-17th at the Portland Open Invitational

| 1964 | 20 | 43 | 1 | 0 | 0 | 0 | 0 | 74.56 | |

Best finish for 1964: T-32nd at the Azalea Open

Period Totals	Starts	Rounds Played	Cuts Made	Wins	Top-5s	Top-10s	Top-25s	Scoring Average	Money
	37	109	15	0	0	3	6	72.45	$6,397

Ian Woosnam

Year	Starts	Rounds Played	Cuts Made	Wins	Top-5s	Top-10s	Top-25s	Scoring Average	Money
1982	1	3	0	0	0	0	0	77.00	$638
1983	1	2	0	0	0	0	0	75.00	$375
1984	2	7	1	0	0	0	1	71.71	$14,513

Best finish for 1984: T-12th at the NEC World Series of Golf

| 1985 | 1 | 4 | 1 | 0 | 0 | 0 | 1 | 71.75 | $11,455 |

Best finish for 1985: T-16th at the British Open

| 1986 | 2 | 8 | 2 | 0 | 1 | 1 | 1 | 71.75 | $56,500 |

Best finish for 1986: T-3rd at the British Open

| 1987 | 3 | 10 | 2 | 0 | 0 | 1 | 1 | 73.10 | $34,846 |

Best finish for 1987: T-8th at the British Open

| 1988 | 7 | 18 | 2 | 0 | 0 | 0 | 2 | 74.11 | $19,314 |

Best finish for 1988: T-19th at the Hertz Bay Hill Classic

Year	Starts	Rounds Played	Cuts Made	Wins	Top-5s	Top-10s	Top-25s	Scoring Average	Money
1989	6	24	6	0	1	2	4	72.08	$151,763

Best finish for 1989: T-2nd at the U.S. Open

| 1990 | 6 | 23 | 6 | 0 | 2 | 2 | 3 | 71.39 | $144,538 |

Best finish for 1990: T-3rd at the Independent Insurance Agent Open

| 1991 | 7 | 27 | 7 | 2 | 2 | 3 | 5 | 70.96 | $501,916 |

Best finish for 1991: Win at the USF&G Classic & Masters

| 1992 | 7 | 22 | 4 | 0 | 1 | 2 | 3 | 72.41 | $113,389 |

Best finish for 1992: T-5th at the British Open

| 1993 | 7 | 24 | 5 | 0 | 0 | 0 | 2 | 72.00 | $62,134 |

Best finish for 1993: T-17th at the Masters

| 1994 | 7 | 22 | 4 | 0 | 0 | 1 | 1 | 73.36 | $53,867 |

Best finish for 1994: T-9th at the PGA Championship

| 1995 | 8 | 30 | 7 | 0 | 1 | 1 | 4 | 71.53 | $175,664 |

Best finish for 1995: 3rd at the Honda Classic

| 1996 | 6 | 20 | 4 | 0 | 0 | 0 | 1 | 72.60 | $42,704 |

Best finish for 1996: T-23rd at the BellSouth Classic

| 1997 | 7 | 21 | 4 | 0 | 0 | 0 | 1 | 72.81 | $43,038 |

Best finish for 1997: T-24th at the British Open

| 1998 | 7 | 22 | 4 | 0 | 0 | 1 | 2 | 72.64 | $124,005 |

Best finish for 1998: T-8th at the Freeport-McDermott Classic

| 1999 | 7 | 20 | 5 | 0 | 0 | 0 | 2 | 73.35 | $131,228 |

Best finish for 1999: T-14th at the Masters

| 2000 | 5 | 18 | 4 | 0 | 0 | 0 | 0 | 73.33 | $77,092 |

Best finish for 2000: T-33rd at the WGC-NEC Invitational

| 2001 | 5 | 15 | 3 | 0 | 1 | 1 | 1 | 72.07 | $230,878 |

Best finish for 2001: T-3rd at the British Open

| 2002 | 3 | 8 | 1 | 0 | 0 | 0 | 0 | 73.75 | $33,732 |

Best finish for 2002: T-37th at the British Open

| 2003 | 2 | 6 | 1 | 0 | 0 | 0 | 0 | 76.17 | $18,432 |

Best finish for 2003: 72nd at the British Open

2004	2	4	0	0	0	0	0	76.00	$7,000
2005	2	4	0	0	0	0	0	76.00	$9,380
2006	1	2	0	0	0	0	0	74.50	$5,000
2008	1	4	1	0	0	0	0	75.00	$26,250

Best finish for 2008: 44th at the Masters

Period Totals	Starts	Rounds Played	Cuts Made	Wins	Top-5s	Top-10s	Top-25s	Scoring Average	Money
	113	368	74	2	9	15	35	72.63	$2,089,650

Robert Wrenn

Year	Starts	Rounds Played	Cuts Made	Wins	Top-5s	Top-10s	Top-25s	Scoring Average	Money
1982	2	5	1	0	0	0	0	74.20	$582

Best finish for 1982: T-69th at the Bing Crosby Pro-Am

1983	1	3	0	0	0	0	0	74.33	
1984	2	5	0	0	0	0	0	76.80	
1985	27	84	13	0	0	1	3	72.70	$36,396

Best finish for 1985: T-9th at the Kemper Open

| 1986 | 33 | 95 | 15 | 0 | 0 | 0 | 1 | 72.16 | $22,869 |

Best finish for 1986: T-24th at the Shearson Lehman/Andy Williams San Diego

| 1987 | 27 | 80 | 15 | 1 | 2 | 3 | 5 | 71.60 | $204,157 |

Best finish for 1987: Win at the Buick Open

| 1988 | 30 | 103 | 23 | 0 | 1 | 3 | 11 | 71.06 | $209,404 |

Best finish for 1988: 2nd at the Texas Open

| 1989 | 27 | 87 | 18 | 0 | 1 | 1 | 5 | 71.17 | $244,638 |

Best finish for 1989: T-2nd at the Las Vegas Invitational

| 1990 | 29 | 96 | 20 | 0 | 0 | 3 | 7 | 71.27 | $174,398 |

Best finish for 1990: T-7th at the Buick Open

| 1991 | 29 | 89 | 17 | 0 | 1 | 1 | 5 | 70.79 | $141,255 |

Best finish for 1991: T-5th at the Shearson Lehman Brothers Open

| 1992 | 29 | 82 | 13 | 0 | 1 | 1 | 5 | 71.43 | $127,730 |

Best finish for 1992: T-3rd at the Buick Invitational of California

| 1993 | 28 | 81 | 13 | 0 | 1 | 1 | 1 | 72.32 | $103,929 |

Best finish for 1993: T-3rd at the Phoenix Open

| 1994 | 17 | 52 | 9 | 0 | 0 | 1 | 3 | 71.87 | $77,279 |

Best finish for 1994: T-6th at the Hardee's Golf Classic

| 1995 | 1 | 2 | 0 | 0 | 0 | 0 | 0 | 72.50 | |
| 1996 | 25 | 72 | 12 | 0 | 0 | 0 | 1 | 72.01 | $81,690 |

Best finish for 1996: T-12th at the Canon Greater Hartford Open

| 1998 | 1 | 2 | 0 | 0 | 0 | 0 | 0 | 72.50 | |

Period Totals	Starts	Rounds Played	Cuts Made	Wins	Top-5s	Top-10s	Top-25s	Scoring Average	Money
	308	938	169	1	7	15	47	71.69	$1,424,326

Jimmy Wright

Year	Starts	Rounds Played	Cuts Made	Wins	Top-5s	Top-10s	Top-25s	Scoring Average	Money
1962	4	14	3	0	0	1	2	72.71	$1,095

Best finish for 1962: T-9th at the Beaumont Open Invitational

| 1963 | 9 | 34 | 8 | 0 | 0 | 0 | 6 | 72.09 | $5,124 |

Best finish for 1963: T-13th at the Doral Country Club Open Invitational & Houston Classic

| 1964 | 2 | 8 | 2 | 0 | 0 | 0 | 0 | 72.00 | |

Best finish for 1964: T-60th at the Greater Hartford Open

| 1965 | 5 | 15 | 1 | 0 | 0 | 0 | 0 | 73.53 | |

Best finish for 1965: T-64th at the San Diego Open

| 1966 | 1 | 4 | 1 | 0 | 0 | 0 | 0 | 73.75 | |

Best finish for 1966: T-64th at the Thunderbird Classic

| 1967 | 3 | 8 | 1 | 0 | 0 | 0 | 0 | 74.13 | $430 |

Best finish for 1967: T-51st at the PGA Championship

| 1968 | 10 | 30 | 5 | 0 | 0 | 0 | 0 | 73.03 | $688 |

Best finish for 1968: T-29th at the Doral Open Invitational

| 1969 | 10 | 32 | 6 | 0 | 1 | 2 | 3 | 72.13 | $13,869 |

Best finish for 1969: 4th at the PGA Championship

| 1970 | 15 | 40 | 7 | 0 | 0 | 0 | 2 | 73.28 | $5,991 |

Best finish for 1970: T-11th at the Los Angeles Open

| 1971 | 3 | 7 | 0 | 0 | 0 | 0 | 0 | 77.71 | $500 |
| 1972 | 10 | 38 | 8 | 0 | 0 | 0 | 2 | 72.55 | $6,074 |

Best finish for 1972: T-20th at the Liggett Meyers Open

| 1973 | 4 | 13 | 1 | 0 | 0 | 1 | 1 | 72.85 | $3,765 |

Best finish for 1973: T-8th at the Dean Martin Tucson Open

| 1974 | 4 | 10 | 1 | 0 | 0 | 0 | 0 | 76.00 | $608 |

Best finish for 1974: T-66th at the World Open

| 1975 | 2 | 6 | 1 | 0 | 0 | 0 | 0 | 74.50 | $429 |

Best finish for 1975: T-54th at the PGA Championship

| 1976 | 3 | 12 | 3 | 0 | 0 | 0 | 1 | 72.08 | $3,166 |

Best finish for 1976: T-23rd at the American Express Westchester Classic

| 1977 | 3 | 6 | 0 | 0 | 0 | 0 | 0 | 76.00 | $750 |
| 1978 | 2 | 6 | 1 | 0 | 0 | 0 | 1 | 72.50 | $4,500 |

Best finish for 1978: T-16th at the American Express Westchester Classic

| 1979 | 1 | 4 | 1 | 0 | 0 | 0 | 0 | 72.00 | $1,050 |

Best finish for 1979: T-42nd at the PGA Championship

1981	1	2	0	0	0	0	0	78.50	$600
1982	3	6	0	0	0	0	0	80.83	$1,250
1984	1	2	0	0	0	0	0	78.00	$1,000
Period Totals	Starts	Rounds Played	Cuts Made	Wins	Top-5s	Top-10s	Top-25s	Scoring Average	Money
	96	297	50	0	1	4	18	73.28	$50,887

Mark Wurtz

Year	Starts	Rounds Played	Cuts Made	Wins	Top-5s	Top-10s	Top-25s	Scoring Average	Money
1994	29	81	13	0	0	1	4	71.75	$104,252

Best finish for 1994: T-8th at the Motorola Western Open

| 1995 | 28 | 84 | 13 | 0 | 0 | 0 | 1 | 72.07 | $59,949 |

Best finish for 1995: T-21st at the GTE Byron Nelson Classic

| 1996 | 1 | 4 | 1 | 0 | 0 | 0 | 1 | 69.50 | $13,040 |

Best finish for 1996: T-18th at the Greater Vancouver Open

| 1998 | 23 | 55 | 4 | 0 | 0 | 0 | 1 | 72.75 | $40,215 |

Best finish for 1998: T-17th at the Buick Classic

| 2001 | 2 | 6 | 1 | 0 | 0 | 0 | 0 | 71.83 | $7,388 |

Best finish for 2001: T-48th at the Touchstone Energy Tucson Open

| 2002 | 3 | 8 | 1 | 0 | 0 | 0 | 0 | 71.75 | $6,660 |

Best finish for 2002: T-58th at the Reno-Tahoe Open

2003	2	5	0	0	0	0	0	74.00	$1,000
Period Totals	Starts	Rounds Played	Cuts Made	Wins	Top-5s	Top-10s	Top-25s	Scoring Average	Money
	88	243	33	0	0	1	7	72.10	$232,504

Lee Wykle

Year	Starts	Rounds Played	Cuts Made	Wins	Top-5s	Top-10s	Top-25s	Scoring Average	Money
1972	14	38	5	0	0	0	2	73.11	$4,616

Best finish for 1972: T-19th at the Greater St. Louis Classic

| 1973 | 20 | 64 | 10 | 0 | 0 | 0 | 2 | 73.64 | $7,968 |

Best finish for 1973: T-11th at the Bob Hope Chrysler Classic

| 1974 | 17 | 47 | 6 | 0 | 0 | 0 | 0 | 73.53 | $3,202 |

Best finish for 1974: T-33rd at the B.C. Open

| 1976 | 3 | 10 | 2 | 0 | 0 | 0 | 1 | 72.00 | $1,528 |

Best finish for 1976: T-15th at the Tallahassee Open

| 1978 | 2 | 3 | 0 | 0 | 0 | 0 | 0 | 79.33 | |

1980	1	0	0	0	0	0	0		
Period Totals	Starts	Rounds Played	Cuts Made	Wins	Top-5s	Top-10s	Top-25s	Scoring Average	Money
	57	162	23	0	0	0	5	73.49	$17,314

Bob Wynn

Year	Starts	Rounds Played	Cuts Made	Wins	Top-5s	Top-10s	Top-25s	Scoring Average	Money
1967	1	2	0	0	0	0	0	77.50	
1970	11	25	3	0	0	0	1	73.00	$1,220

Best finish for 1970: T-23rd at the Robinson Open Golf Classic

| 1971 | 22 | 61 | 12 | 0 | 0 | 1 | 2 | 72.57 | $8,537 |

Best finish for 1971: T-10th at the Greater New Orleans Open

| 1972 | 27 | 68 | 11 | 0 | 2 | 2 | 4 | 73.51 | $15,236 |

Best finish for 1972: T-5th at the Greater St. Louis Classic & Quad Cities Open

| 1973 | 30 | 92 | 18 | 0 | 0 | 1 | 4 | 72.48 | $14,947 |

Best finish for 1973: T-6th at the Quad Cities Open

| 1974 | 28 | 83 | 18 | 0 | 2 | 3 | 4 | 71.70 | $36,620 |

Best finish for 1974: 3rd at the Sammy Davis, Jr. - Greater Hartford Open

| 1975 | 29 | 96 | 21 | 0 | 2 | 4 | 7 | 71.74 | $45,424 |

Best finish for 1975: 3rd at the IVB Philadelphia Golf Classic

| 1976 | 31 | 91 | 16 | 1 | 2 | 4 | 8 | 72.05 | $77,164 |

Best finish for 1976: Win at the B.C. Open

| 1977 | 31 | 87 | 14 | 0 | 0 | 0 | 7 | 73.00 | $21,835 |

Best finish for 1977: T-12th at the Atlanta Classic

| 1978 | 20 | 59 | 9 | 0 | 1 | 2 | 3 | 72.93 | $25,860 |

Best finish for 1978: T-3rd at the Hawaiian Open

| 1979 | 16 | 41 | 5 | 0 | 0 | 0 | 1 | 73.71 | $4,180 |

Best finish for 1979: T-21st at the Pensacola Open

| 1980 | 4 | 14 | 2 | 0 | 0 | 0 | 0 | 74.21 | $1,658 |

Best finish for 1980: T-34th at the Pensacola Open

1981	2	5	0	0	0	0	0	74.60	
1983	1	3	0	0	0	0	0	75.33	
1984	1	3	0	0	0	0	0	79.00	
1986	1	2	0	0	0	0	0	71.50	
1988	1	3	0	0	0	0	0	78.67	
1989	1	0	0	0	0	0	0		
1990	1	2	0	0	0	0	0	75.00	
Period Totals	Starts	Rounds Played	Cuts Made	Wins	Top-5s	Top-10s	Top-25s	Scoring Average	Money
	258	737	129	1	9	17	41	72.66	$252,683

Mike Wynn

Year	Starts	Rounds Played	Cuts Made	Wins	Top-5s	Top-10s	Top-25s	Scoring Average	Money
1971	1	2	0	0	0	0	0	74.50	$500
1972	13	44	9	0	0	1	2	72.91	$7,000

Best finish for 1972: T-7th at the Greater St. Louis Classic

| 1973 | 30 | 94 | 16 | 0 | 0 | 2 | 3 | 72.67 | $16,259 |

Best finish for 1973: T-6th at the St. Louis Children's Hospital Golf Classic

| 1974 | 21 | 55 | 8 | 0 | 0 | 1 | 3 | 73.04 | $8,885 |

Best finish for 1974: T-8th at the B.C. Open

| 1975 | 26 | 80 | 14 | 0 | 0 | 0 | 4 | 72.83 | $12,122 |

Best finish for 1975: T-12th at the Houston Open

| 1976 | 20 | 52 | 7 | 0 | 0 | 0 | 2 | 73.29 | $8,479 |

Best finish for 1976: T-13th at the American Express Westchester Classic

| 1977 | 15 | 36 | 4 | 0 | 0 | 0 | 0 | 73.81 | $2,880 |

Best finish for 1977: T-26th at the Doral-Eastern Open

1982	1	2	0	0	0	0	0	74.50	$650
1983	3	6	0	0	0	0	0	76.17	$100
Period Totals	Starts	Rounds Played	Cuts Made	Wins	Top-5s	Top-10s	Top-25s	Scoring Average	Money
	130	371	58	0	0	4	14	73.06	$56,875

Dudley Wysong

Year	Starts	Rounds Played	Cuts Made	Wins	Top-5s	Top-10s	Top-25s	Scoring Average	Money
1958	1	4	1	0	0	0	0	74.75	

Best finish for 1958: 66th at the Dallas Open

| 1960 | 1 | 2 | 0 | 0 | 0 | 0 | 0 | 78.00 | |
| 1962 | 2 | 6 | 1 | 0 | 0 | 0 | 0 | 74.67 | |

Best finish for 1962: T-33rd at the Dallas Open Invitational

| 1963 | 8 | 32 | 8 | 0 | 0 | 0 | 0 | 72.09 | $1,660 |

Best finish for 1963: T-29th at the Fig Garden Village Open Invitational & Almaden Open Invitational

| 1964 | 29 | 93 | 16 | 0 | 1 | 1 | 7 | 72.57 | $7,821 |

Best finish for 1964: T-4th at the Seattle Open

| 1965 | 28 | 94 | 19 | 0 | 1 | 3 | 9 | 72.17 | $15,953 |

Best finish for 1965: 2nd at the Cajun Classic

Year	Starts	Rounds Played	Cuts Made	Wins	Top-5s	Top-10s	Top-25s	Scoring Average	Money
1966	32	104	20	1	3	4	11	72.65	$41,037

Best finish for 1966: Win at the Phoenix Open Invitational

| 1967 | 30 | 111 | 25 | 1 | 1 | 3 | 8 | 72.63 | $36,411 |

Best finish for 1967: Win at the Hawaiian Open

| 1968 | 29 | 95 | 19 | 0 | 1 | 3 | 7 | 72.31 | $27,867 |

Best finish for 1968: 3rd at the Philadelphia Golf Classic

| 1969 | 27 | 86 | 15 | 0 | 0 | 0 | 3 | 72.70 | $9,826 |

Best finish for 1969: T-11th at the Minnesota Classic

| 1970 | 24 | 63 | 7 | 0 | 0 | 0 | 1 | 73.48 | $3,624 |

Best finish for 1970: T-25th at the Danny Thomas Memphis Classic

| 1971 | 3 | 8 | 1 | 0 | 0 | 0 | 0 | 74.63 | $172 |

Best finish for 1971: 78th at the Byron Nelson Golf Classic

1989	3	6	0	0	0	0	0	76.00	
1991	1	2	0	0	0	0	0	75.00	
Period Totals	Starts	Rounds Played	Cuts Made	Wins	Top-5s	Top-10s	Top-25s	Scoring Average	Money
	218	706	132	2	7	14	46	72.68	$144,371

Bert Yancey

Year	Starts	Rounds Played	Cuts Made	Wins	Top-5s	Top-10s	Top-25s	Scoring Average	Money
1964	28	86	15	0	0	2	6	72.57	$10,857

Best finish for 1964: T-6th at the Greater Hartford Open

| 1965 | 32 | 115 | 25 | 0 | 3 | 4 | 10 | 72.40 | $23,186 |

Best finish for 1965: 2nd at the Phoenix Open

| 1966 | 34 | 117 | 24 | 3 | 3 | 5 | 9 | 72.15 | $48,724 |

Best finish for 1966: Win at the Azalea Open Invitational, Memphis Open Invitational & Portland Open Invitational

| 1967 | 30 | 114 | 26 | 1 | 4 | 8 | 16 | 72.01 | $69,105 |

Best finish for 1967: Win at the Byron Nelson Dallas Open

| 1968 | 31 | 103 | 24 | 0 | 6 | 6 | 14 | 71.49 | $65,843 |

Best finish for 1968: 2nd at the Greater New Orleans Open Invitational

| 1969 | 36 | 132 | 31 | 1 | 4 | 9 | 19 | 71.56 | $77,961 |

Best finish for 1969: Win at the Atlanta Classic

| 1970 | 31 | 104 | 23 | 1 | 5 | 6 | 14 | 71.17 | $82,922 |

Best finish for 1970: Win at the Bing Crosby Pro-Am

| 1971 | 33 | 117 | 28 | 0 | 5 | 6 | 17 | 71.42 | $81,364 |

Best finish for 1971: 2nd at the Colonial National Invitational & Robinson Open Golf Classic

| 1972 | 34 | 119 | 25 | 1 | 3 | 5 | 14 | 71.90 | $73,375 |

Best finish for 1972: Win at the American Golf Classic

| 1973 | 30 | 120 | 28 | 0 | 3 | 6 | 16 | 71.75 | $66,394 |

Best finish for 1973: T-3rd at the St. Louis Children's Hospital Golf Classic

| 1974 | 30 | 100 | 21 | 0 | 4 | 5 | 12 | 71.52 | $68,871 |

Best finish for 1974: 2nd at the Bob Hope Chrysler Classic

| 1975 | 18 | 58 | 11 | 0 | 2 | 2 | 4 | 72.53 | $31,790 |

Best finish for 1975: T-2nd at the Doral-Eastern Open & Tallahassee Open

1976	12	26	0	0	0	0	0	79.77	
1981	2	2	0	0	0	0	0	77.50	
1982	5	11	0	0	0	0	0	76.82	
1983	1	2	0	0	0	0	0	81.50	
1984	1	2	0	0	0	0	0	79.00	
1986	1	4	1	0	0	0	0	72.50	$468

Best finish for 1986: T-52nd at the Tallahassee Open

| 1987 | 14 | 33 | 2 | 0 | 0 | 0 | 0 | 73.36 | $1,356 |

Best finish for 1987: T-52nd at the Deposit Guaranty Golf Classic

| 1988 | 9 | 21 | 1 | 0 | 0 | 0 | 0 | 76.62 | $388 |

Best finish for 1988: 73rd at the Deposit Guaranty Golf Classic

1992	1	2	0	0	0	0	0	71.00	
1993	1	2	0	0	0	0	0	77.50	
Period Totals	Starts	Rounds Played	Cuts Made	Wins	Top-5s	Top-10s	Top-25s	Scoring Average	Money
	414	1390	285	7	42	64	151	72.17	$702,605

Y.E. Yang

Year	Starts	Rounds Played	Cuts Made	Wins	Top-5s	Top-10s	Top-25s	Scoring Average	Money
2005	3	10	2	0	0	0	0	71.80	$27,236

Best finish for 2005: T-47th at the PGA Championship

| 2007 | 8 | 20 | 4 | 0 | 0 | 0 | 0 | 74.65 | $139,796 |

Best finish for 2007: T-30th at the Masters

| 2008 | 23 | 68 | 12 | 0 | 0 | 1 | 3 | 71.59 | $392,048 |

Best finish for 2008: T-9th at the AT&T Pebble Beach National Pro-Am

| Period Totals | Starts | Rounds Played | Cuts Made | Wins | Top-5s | Top-10s | Top-25s | Scoring Average | Money |
| | 34 | 98 | 18 | 0 | 0 | 1 | 3 | 72.23 | $559,081 |

Wayne Yates

Year	Starts	Rounds Played	Cuts Made	Wins	Top-5s	Top-10s	Top-25s	Scoring Average	Money
1966	21	66	13	0	0	0	2	73.15	$3,516

Best finish for 1966: T-13th at the Azalea Open Invitational

1967	25	83	15	0	0	2	4	72.98	$10,706

Best finish for 1967: T-6th at the Philadelphia Classic

1968	25	83	16	0	1	1	3	72.28	$6,952

Best finish for 1968: T-3rd at the Rebel Yell Open

1969	16	48	9	0	0	1	1	73.42	$5,009

Best finish for 1969: T-6th at the Minnesota Classic

1970	6	16	2	0	0	0	0	73.88	$1,652

Best finish for 1970: T-27th at the Atlanta Classic

1971	6	16	3	0	0	0	1	72.19	$1,867

Best finish for 1971: T-22nd at the Tallahassee Open

1972	6	17	3	0	0	0	1	73.59	$3,051

Best finish for 1972: T-22nd at the Westchester Classic

1973	8	23	4	0	0	0	1	73.39	$3,579

Best finish for 1973: T-21st at the Kemper Open

1974	4	8	1	0	0	0	0	73.75	$519

Best finish for 1974: T-56th at the Kemper Open

1975	11	27	3	0	0	0	0	73.85	$229

Best finish for 1975: T-46th at the Ed McMahon Quad City Open

1976	1	1	0	0	0	0	0	75.00	
1977	1	4	1	0	0	0	0	72.50	$475

Best finish for 1977: T-50th at the Atlanta Classic

1978	1	2	0	0	0	0	0	74.50	
Period Totals	Starts	Rounds Played	Cuts Made	Wins	Top-5s	Top-10s	Top-25s	Scoring Average	Money
	131	394	70	0	1	4	13	73.05	$37,557

Kaname Yokoo

Year	Starts	Rounds Played	Cuts Made	Wins	Top-5s	Top-10s	Top-25s	Scoring Average	Money
1996	1	2	0	0	0	0	0	76.00	
1999	7	24	5	0	0	1	1	71.79	$111,395

Best finish for 1999: T-7th at the Memorial Tournament

2000	5	16	3	0	0	0	0	70.94	$41,286

Best finish for 2000: T-26th at the Sony Open in Hawaii

2001	27	81	13	0	0	3	5	71.28	$477,989

Best finish for 2001: T-6th at the Texas Open at LaCantera

2002	28	72	8	0	1	1	3	71.69	$491,473

Best finish for 2002: T-2nd at the Phoenix Open

2003	22	54	5	0	0	0	0	72.65	$56,088

Best finish for 2003: T-58th at the WGC-NEC Invitational

2006	2	6	1	0	0	0	0	71.67	$9,180

Best finish for 2006: 80th at the Sony Open in Hawaii

2007	2	6	1	0	0	0	0	72.00	$18,640

Best finish for 2007: T-46th at the Sony Open in Hawaii

2008	1	2	0	0	0	0	0	73.00	
Period Totals	Starts	Rounds Played	Cuts Made	Wins	Top-5s	Top-10s	Top-25s	Scoring Average	Money
	95	263	36	0	1	5	9	71.78	$1,206,051

Kim Young

Year	Starts	Rounds Played	Cuts Made	Wins	Top-5s	Top-10s	Top-25s	Scoring Average	Money
1977	6	11	0	0	0	0	0	76.27	
1978	6	15	1	0	0	0	0	75.00	

Best finish for 1978: T-75th at the Phoenix Open

1984	1	2	0	0	0	0	0	76.00	$600
1988	26	73	10	0	1	1	3	72.29	$32,186

Best finish for 1988: T-4th at the Deposit Guaranty Golf Classic

1989	1	2	0	0	0	0	0	70.00	
1991	22	53	4	0	0	0	0	72.40	$9,022

Best finish for 1991: T-41st at the Independent Insurance Agent Open

1992	25	67	10	0	0	0	2	72.22	$55,048

Best finish for 1992: T-12th at the AT&T Pebble Beach Pro-Am

1993	17	33	1	0	0	0	0	73.55	$2,343

Best finish for 1993: T-60th at the Northern Telecom Open

1995	1	2	0	0	0	0	0	74.50	$1,000
Period Totals	Starts	Rounds Played	Cuts Made	Wins	Top-5s	Top-10s	Top-25s	Scoring Average	Money
	105	258	26	0	1	1	5	72.81	$100,199

Bruce Zabriski

Year	Starts	Rounds Played	Cuts Made	Wins	Top-5s	Top-10s	Top-25s	Scoring Average	Money
1984	3	6	0	0	0	0	0	74.33	
1985	1	2	0	0	0	0	0	80.00	
1986	3	6	0	0	0	0	0	75.50	$1,200
1988	29	83	11	0	0	0	1	72.75	$21,460

Best finish for 1988: T-12th at the Deposit Guaranty Golf Classic

Year	Starts	Rounds Played	Cuts Made	Wins	Top-5s	Top-10s	Top-25s	Scoring Average	Money
1989	1	2	0	0	0	0	0	73.00	
1991	1	2	0	0	0	0	0	77.00	$1,000
1992	30	82	12	0	0	0	5	71.70	$86,275

Best finish for 1992: T-12th at the United Airlines Hawaiian Open

Year	Starts	Rounds Played	Cuts Made	Wins	Top-5s	Top-10s	Top-25s	Scoring Average	Money
1993	8	25	4	0	0	0	0	72.56	$16,828

Best finish for 1993: T-30th at the Canon Greater Hartford Open

Year	Starts	Rounds Played	Cuts Made	Wins	Top-5s	Top-10s	Top-25s	Scoring Average	Money
1994	2	4	0	0	0	0	0	74.50	$1,200
1995	1	2	0	0	0	0	0	72.50	$1,200
1996	1	4	1	0	0	0	0	72.00	$3,506

Best finish for 1996: T-43rd at the Buick Classic

Year	Starts	Rounds Played	Cuts Made	Wins	Top-5s	Top-10s	Top-25s	Scoring Average	Money
1997	2	4	0	0	0	0	0	77.00	$1,300
1998	6	16	2	0	0	0	0	75.06	$38,372

Best finish for 1998: T-32nd at the U.S. Open

Year	Starts	Rounds Played	Cuts Made	Wins	Top-5s	Top-10s	Top-25s	Scoring Average	Money
1999	1	4	1	0	0	0	0	74.50	$6,675

Best finish for 1999: T-68th at the PGA Championship

Year	Starts	Rounds Played	Cuts Made	Wins	Top-5s	Top-10s	Top-25s	Scoring Average	Money
2001	1	2	0	0	0	0	0	72.50	$2,000
2002	1	2	0	0	0	0	0	76.00	$2,000
Period Totals	Starts	Rounds Played	Cuts Made	Wins	Top-5s	Top-10s	Top-25s	Scoring Average	Money
	91	246	31	0	0	0	6	72.87	$183,017

Joe Zakarian

Year	Starts	Rounds Played	Cuts Made	Wins	Top-5s	Top-10s	Top-25s	Scoring Average	Money
1958	17	55	9	0	0	0	1	73.76	$661

Best finish for 1958: T-15th at the Eastern Open

Year	Starts	Rounds Played	Cuts Made	Wins	Top-5s	Top-10s	Top-25s	Scoring Average	Money
1959	1	4	1	0	0	0	0	73.75	$100

Best finish for 1959: T-44th at the Bing Crosby National

Year	Starts	Rounds Played	Cuts Made	Wins	Top-5s	Top-10s	Top-25s	Scoring Average	Money
1960	2	8	1	0	0	0	1	73.00	$280

Best finish for 1960: T-24th at the Baton Rouge Open Invitational

Year	Starts	Rounds Played	Cuts Made	Wins	Top-5s	Top-10s	Top-25s	Scoring Average	Money
1961	1	2	0	0	0	0	0	79.50	
1962	2	4	1	0	0	0	0	76.75	

Best finish for 1962: T-200 at the PGA Championship

Year	Starts	Rounds Played	Cuts Made	Wins	Top-5s	Top-10s	Top-25s	Scoring Average	Money
1963	2	6	1	0	0	0	0	76.33	$485

Best finish for 1963: T-49th at the PGA Championship

Year	Starts	Rounds Played	Cuts Made	Wins	Top-5s	Top-10s	Top-25s	Scoring Average	Money
1964	4	10	0	0	0	0	0	75.30	
1965	1	2	0	0	0	0	0	75.50	
1966	2	6	1	0	0	0	0	78.50	$520

Best finish for 1966: 64th at the U.S. Open

Year	Starts	Rounds Played	Cuts Made	Wins	Top-5s	Top-10s	Top-25s	Scoring Average	Money
1968	1	1	0	0	0	0	0	75.00	
1969	1	2	0	0	0	0	0	78.50	
Period Totals	Starts	Rounds Played	Cuts Made	Wins	Top-5s	Top-10s	Top-25s	Scoring Average	Money
	34	100	14	0	0	0	2	74.67	$2,047

Kermit Zarley

Year	Starts	Rounds Played	Cuts Made	Wins	Top-5s	Top-10s	Top-25s	Scoring Average	Money
1963	3	12	3	0	0	0	2	71.33	$1,673

Best finish for 1963: T-18th at the Houston Classic

Year	Starts	Rounds Played	Cuts Made	Wins	Top-5s	Top-10s	Top-25s	Scoring Average	Money
1964	20	65	11	0	0	3	3	73.02	$6,082

Best finish for 1964: T-8th at the Greater Hartford Open

Year	Starts	Rounds Played	Cuts Made	Wins	Top-5s	Top-10s	Top-25s	Scoring Average	Money
1965	31	107	21	0	2	3	10	72.50	$14,686

Best finish for 1965: T-5th at the Pensacola Open & Cajun Classic

Year	Starts	Rounds Played	Cuts Made	Wins	Top-5s	Top-10s	Top-25s	Scoring Average	Money
1966	30	111	25	0	4	6	11	71.93	$44,992

Best finish for 1966: T-2nd at the Doral Open Invitational & Buick Open Invitational

Year	Starts	Rounds Played	Cuts Made	Wins	Top-5s	Top-10s	Top-25s	Scoring Average	Money
1967	29	103	21	0	5	6	9	72.14	$37,779

Best finish for 1967: T-2nd at the Byron Nelson Dallas Open

Year	Starts	Rounds Played	Cuts Made	Wins	Top-5s	Top-10s	Top-25s	Scoring Average	Money
1968	25	96	23	1	2	4	12	71.33	$62,815

Best finish for 1968: Win at the Kaiser International Open Invitational

Year	Starts	Rounds Played	Cuts Made	Wins	Top-5s	Top-10s	Top-25s	Scoring Average	Money
1969	32	108	24	0	0	3	11	72.13	$21,633

Best finish for 1969: T-8th at the Sahara Invitational

Year	Starts	Rounds Played	Cuts Made	Wins	Top-5s	Top-10s	Top-25s	Scoring Average	Money
1970	30	101	22	1	1	2	11	71.95	$50,826

Best finish for 1970: Win at the Canadian Open

Year	Starts	Rounds Played	Cuts Made	Wins	Top-5s	Top-10s	Top-25s	Scoring Average	Money
1971	31	104	23	0	2	4	12	71.92	$46,312

Best finish for 1971: 3rd at the Florida Citrus Open Invitational

Year	Starts	Rounds Played	Cuts Made	Wins	Top-5s	Top-10s	Top-25s	Scoring Average	Money
1972	28	101	22	0	0	3	9	72.35	$33,475

Best finish for 1972: 6th at the U.S. Open

| 1973 | 31 | 111 | 23 | 0 | 2 | 6 | 14 | 71.74 | $62,089 |

Best finish for 1973: T-2nd at the Quad Cities Open

| 1974 | 29 | 101 | 22 | 0 | 0 | 3 | 10 | 72.23 | $40,323 |

Best finish for 1974: T-6th at the Dean Martin Tucson Open & Byron Nelson Golf Classic

| 1975 | 29 | 95 | 18 | 0 | 0 | 1 | 8 | 72.37 | $25,898 |

Best finish for 1975: T-10th at the World Open

| 1976 | 29 | 101 | 24 | 0 | 1 | 4 | 7 | 72.24 | $32,032 |

Best finish for 1976: 2nd at the Florida Citrus Open Invitational

| 1977 | 33 | 112 | 24 | 0 | 0 | 5 | 10 | 72.06 | $50,891 |

Best finish for 1977: T-6th at the Byron Nelson Golf Classic

| 1978 | 32 | 105 | 21 | 0 | 0 | 2 | 6 | 72.33 | $35,253 |

Best finish for 1978: T-6th at the Houston Open

| 1979 | 31 | 111 | 24 | 0 | 2 | 3 | 9 | 72.04 | $63,414 |

Best finish for 1979: T-3rd at the Glen Campbell Los Angeles Open

| 1980 | 25 | 71 | 10 | 0 | 0 | 0 | 1 | 73.18 | $13,949 |

Best finish for 1980: T-18th at the Buick Goodwrench Open

| 1981 | 6 | 13 | 1 | 0 | 0 | 0 | 0 | 73.31 | $732 |

Best finish for 1981: T-64th at the USF&G New Orleans Open

| 1982 | 13 | 35 | 4 | 0 | 0 | 0 | 2 | 72.43 | $14,765 |

Best finish for 1982: T-15th at the Western Open

| 1983 | 4 | 16 | 4 | 0 | 0 | 0 | 0 | 71.44 | $3,979 |

Best finish for 1983: T-37th at the B.C. Open

| 1984 | 2 | 8 | 2 | 0 | 0 | 0 | 0 | 73.13 | $1,744 |

Best finish for 1984: T-58th at the Texas Open

| 1985 | 4 | 12 | 2 | 0 | 0 | 0 | 0 | 72.25 | $2,376 |

Best finish for 1985: T-44th at the St. Jude Memphis Classic

| 1986 | 7 | 20 | 3 | 0 | 0 | 0 | 0 | 71.70 | $2,753 |

Best finish for 1986: T-32nd at the Deposit Guaranty Golf Classic

| 1987 | 8 | 24 | 4 | 0 | 0 | 0 | 1 | 71.08 | $6,800 |

Best finish for 1987: T-24th at the Deposit Guaranty Golf Classic

Period Totals	Starts	Rounds Played	Cuts Made	Wins	Top-5s	Top-10s	Top-25s	Scoring Average	Money
	542	1843	381	2	21	58	158	72.15	$677,271

Bob Zender

Year	Starts	Rounds Played	Cuts Made	Wins	Top-5s	Top-10s	Top-25s	Scoring Average	Money
1970	1	2	0	0	0	0	0	77.50	
1971	5	12	1	0	0	0	0	73.25	$668

Best finish for 1971: T-37th at the Kaiser International Open

| 1972 | 24 | 73 | 12 | 0 | 0 | 0 | 2 | 73.59 | $6,287 |

Best finish for 1972: T-19th at the Greater St. Louis Classic

| 1973 | 27 | 79 | 11 | 0 | 0 | 0 | 1 | 73.08 | $8,628 |

Best finish for 1973: T-16th at the Doral-Eastern Open

| 1974 | 24 | 65 | 8 | 0 | 1 | 1 | 2 | 73.95 | $12,040 |

Best finish for 1974: T-3rd at the Greater Milwaukee Open

| 1975 | 29 | 86 | 15 | 0 | 0 | 1 | 3 | 72.59 | $14,813 |

Best finish for 1975: T-10th at the World Open

| 1976 | 25 | 62 | 8 | 0 | 0 | 1 | 1 | 73.39 | $7,366 |

Best finish for 1976: T-10th at the Ohio Kings Island Open

| 1977 | 25 | 77 | 14 | 0 | 2 | 2 | 5 | 72.97 | $21,920 |

Best finish for 1977: T-4th at the Ed McMahon Quad City Open

| 1978 | 31 | 108 | 22 | 0 | 1 | 4 | 7 | 72.05 | $39,063 |

Best finish for 1978: T-4th at the Anheuser-Busch Golf Classic

| 1979 | 23 | 64 | 11 | 0 | 0 | 1 | 5 | 72.88 | $23,268 |

Best finish for 1979: T-7th at the Colgate Hall Of Fame Classic

| 1980 | 17 | 38 | 3 | 0 | 0 | 0 | 1 | 73.50 | $4,028 |

Best finish for 1980: T-20th at the Quad Cities Open

Period Totals	Starts	Rounds Played	Cuts Made	Wins	Top-5s	Top-10s	Top-25s	Scoring Average	Money
	231	666	105	0	4	10	27	73.03	$138,081

Larry Ziegler

Year	Starts	Rounds Played	Cuts Made	Wins	Top-5s	Top-10s	Top-25s	Scoring Average	Money
1965	1	2	0	0	0	0	0	78.50	
1966	12	32	4	0	0	0	2	74.28	$1,559

Best finish for 1966: T-18th at the Tucson Open Invitational & Azalea Open Invitational

| 1967 | 21 | 71 | 14 | 0 | 0 | 0 | 2 | 73.41 | $3,348 |

Best finish for 1967: T-19th at the Hawaiian Open

| 1968 | 24 | 67 | 10 | 0 | 0 | 0 | 1 | 73.28 | $3,050 |

Best finish for 1968: T-24th at the U.S. Open

| 1969 | 36 | 123 | 26 | 1 | 2 | 7 | 13 | 71.89 | $58,234 |

Best finish for 1969: Win at the Michigan Golf Classic

| 1970 | 36 | 121 | 25 | 0 | 3 | 6 | 9 | 72.19 | $48,157 |

Best finish for 1970: 2nd at the Bob Hope Chrysler Classic

Year	Starts	Rounds Played	Cuts Made	Wins	Top-5s	Top-10s	Top-25s	Scoring Average	Money
1971	38	121	26	0	0	3	8	72.21	$30,864

Best finish for 1971: T-6th at the Danny Thomas Memphis Classic & Southern Open

1972	34	118	26	0	1	2	11	72.13	$33,624

Best finish for 1972: 2nd at the Liggett Meyers Open

1973	37	125	25	0	3	5	14	71.94	$48,751

Best finish for 1973: T-3rd at the B.C. Open

1974	32	110	25	0	2	4	18	71.33	$76,573

Best finish for 1974: T-2nd at the Canadian Open

1975	30	94	18	1	1	2	5	72.23	$54,765

Best finish for 1975: Win at the Greater Jacksonville Open

1976	29	87	18	1	4	4	9	71.85	$84,415

Best finish for 1976: Win at the First NBC New Orleans Open

1977	27	88	18	0	0	2	6	72.20	$30,223

Best finish for 1977: T-9th at the Andy Williams-San Diego Open

1978	25	75	15	0	0	0	1	72.32	$9,250

Best finish for 1978: T-25th at the Andy Williams-San Diego Open

1979	27	85	17	0	0	1	4	72.18	$37,336

Best finish for 1979: T-10th at the American Optical Classic

1980	28	84	14	0	0	0	2	72.87	$19,871

Best finish for 1980: T-17th at the San Antonio Texas Open

1981	20	57	9	0	1	2	5	71.96	$38,593

Best finish for 1981: T-4th at the American Motors Inverrary Classic

1982	16	53	10	0	2	3	5	71.83	$49,419

Best finish for 1982: 4th at the Texas Open

1983	21	57	6	0	0	0	0	73.26	$6,866

Best finish for 1983: T-26th at the Buick Open

1984	13	39	7	0	0	0	1	72.44	$9,663

Best finish for 1984: T-22nd at the Georgia-Pacific Atlanta Golf Classic

1985	14	37	4	0	0	0	0	72.70	$6,304

Best finish for 1985: T-34th at the Texas Open

1986	15	42	7	0	0	0	2	72.33	$17,235

Best finish for 1986: T-12th at the Bank of Boston Classic

1987	14	41	7	0	1	1	1	72.39	$31,759

Best finish for 1987: T-4th at the Greater Milwaukee Open

1988	15	41	5	0	0	0	0	71.85	$9,300

Best finish for 1988: T-26th at the Centel Classic

1989	10	24	2	0	0	0	1	72.00	$4,935

Best finish for 1989: T-16th at the Deposit Guaranty Golf Classic

Period Totals	Starts	Rounds Played	Cuts Made	Wins	Top-5s	Top-10s	Top-25s	Scoring Average	Money
	575	1794	338	3	20	42	120	72.28	$714,096

Bob Zimmerman

Year	Starts	Rounds Played	Cuts Made	Wins	Top-5s	Top-10s	Top-25s	Scoring Average	Money
1958	1	2	0	0	0	0	0	83.00	
1962	1	2	0	0	0	0	0	76.00	
1965	26	86	17	0	1	3	6	72.53	$11,837

Best finish for 1965: T-5th at the Azalea Open

1966	27	81	14	0	0	1	2	73.30	$6,311

Best finish for 1966: 6th at the San Diego Open Invitational

1967	12	31	5	0	0	0	0	74.32	$1,622

Best finish for 1967: T-38th at the PGA Championship

1968	2	5	1	0	0	0	0	75.00	

Best finish for 1968: 67th at the Phoenix Open Invitational

1973	1	2	0	0	0	0	0	79.50	

Period Totals	Starts	Rounds Played	Cuts Made	Wins	Top-5s	Top-10s	Top-25s	Scoring Average	Money
	70	209	37	0	1	4	8	73.35	$19,771

Billy Ziobro

Year	Starts	Rounds Played	Cuts Made	Wins	Top-5s	Top-10s	Top-25s	Scoring Average	Money
1970	1	2	0	0	0	0	0	78.00	
1971	1	2	0	0	0	0	0	77.00	
1972	24	69	10	0	1	1	3	73.58	$12,676

Best finish for 1972: T-4th at the Greater New Orleans Open

1973	31	96	16	0	0	3	4	72.99	$17,070

Best finish for 1973: T-6th at the Shrine-Robinson Golf Classic

1974	26	77	13	0	0	0	4	73.10	$12,447

Best finish for 1974: T-11th at the Greater New Orleans Open & Southern Open

1975	25	62	8	0	0	0	0	73.87	$3,869

Best finish for 1975: T-32nd at the Greater Greensboro Open& Houston Open

1976	4	8	0	0	0	0	0	75.25	$250
1977	1	2	0	0	0	0	0	74.00	$500
1983	1	2	0	0	0	0	0	78.50	

Period Totals	Starts	Rounds Played	Cuts Made	Wins	Top-5s	Top-10s	Top-25s	Scoring Average	Money
	114	320	47	0	1	4	11	73.47	$46,812

Fuzzy Zoeller

Year	Starts	Rounds Played	Cuts Made	Wins	Top-5s	Top-10s	Top-25s	Scoring Average	Money
1975	21	63	10	0	1	1	3	73.43	$7,195

Best finish for 1975: T-14th at the Hawaiian Open & San Antonio Texas Open

Year	Starts	Rounds Played	Cuts Made	Wins	Top-5s	Top-10s	Top-25s	Scoring Average	Money
1976	26	86	18	0	2	4	6	72.10	$52,557

Best finish for 1976: T-2nd at the Ed McMahon Quad City Open & American Express Westchester Classic

1977	31	111	23	0	4	7	12	71.77	$76,417

Best finish for 1977: T-3rd at the Glen Campbell Los Angeles Open & Jackie Gleason's Inverrary Classic

1978	29	103	23	0	4	5	15	71.15	$109,685

Best finish for 1978: T-2nd at the Greater Greensboro Open & First NBC New Orleans Open

1979	25	89	20	2	5	6	12	71.57	$198,181

Best finish for 1979: Win at the Andy Williams-San Diego Open & Masters

1980	24	82	20	0	3	8	13	71.67	$104,051

Best finish for 1980: T-3rd at the IVB Golf Classic & San Antonio Texas Open

1981	26	88	20	1	3	4	12	71.03	$155,091

Best finish for 1981: Win at the Colonial National Invitational

1982	26	96	21	0	2	7	11	71.29	$142,037

Best finish for 1982: 2nd at the Bank of Boston Classic

1983	29	110	24	2	8	12	19	70.87	$425,757

Best finish for 1983: Win at the Sea Pines Heritage Classic & Panasonic Las Vegas Pro Celebrity

1984	22	75	16	1	1	3	8	70.88	$166,237

Best finish for 1984: Win at the U.S. Open

1985	22	79	19	1	3	7	12	71.22	$262,033

Best finish for 1985: Win at the Hertz Bay Hill Classic

1986	21	74	17	3	3	5	11	71.23	$385,114

Best finish for 1986: Win at the AT&T Pebble Beach Pro-Am, Sea Pines Heritage Classic & Anheuser-Busch Golf Classic

1987	23	76	17	0	2	5	10	71.29	$230,041

Best finish for 1987: T-2nd at the Seiko-Tucson Open

1988	23	81	19	0	2	4	9	71.15	$215,324

Best finish for 1988: T-3rd at the Bank of Boston Classic & Walt Disney World/Oldsmobile Classic

1989	20	69	14	0	2	4	7	71.36	$220,542

Best finish for 1989: 2nd at the Memorial Tournament

1990	20	71	13	0	1	2	8	71.62	$199,629

Best finish for 1990: T-2nd at the Buick Open

1991	17	60	13	0	3	3	8	70.52	$391,177

Best finish for 1991: 2nd at the Players Championship

1992	18	62	11	0	1	1	4	71.13	$126,003

Best finish for 1992: T-4th at the MCI Heritage Classic

1993	19	75	18	0	3	4	9	70.33	$401,605

Best finish for 1993: 2nd at the Buick Open

1994	20	77	17	0	6	7	10	70.03	$1,136,684

Best finish for 1994: 2nd at the Bob Hope Chrysler Classic, The Nestle Invitational, The Players Championship, Walt Disney World/Oldsmobile Classic & The Tour Championship

1995	15	55	12	0	1	1	5	70.76	$172,206

Best finish for 1995: T-5th at the Canon Greater Hartford Open

1996	16	53	9	0	2	3	5	70.87	$350,137

Best finish for 1996: T-3rd at the Canon Greater Hartford Open

1997	16	52	9	0	0	0	2	71.42	$136,076

Best finish for 1997: T-14th at the Players Championship

1998	20	68	14	0	0	2	6	71.22	$306,041

Best finish for 1998: T-6th at the AT&T Pebble Beach Pro-Am

1999	19	54	6	0	0	0	1	72.74	$60,046

Best finish for 1999: T-23rd at the Bay Hill Invitational

2000	14	32	1	0	0	0	0	73.97	$9,550

Best finish for 2000: 79th at the Greater Milwaukee Open

2001	15	41	5	0	0	0	0	72.39	$43,530

Best finish for 2001: T-43rd at the AT&T Pebble Beach

2002	2	4	0	0	0	0	0	75.25	$7,000
2003	1	2	0	0	0	0	0	77.50	$5,000
2004	1	2	0	0	0	0	0	80.00	$5,000
2005	1	2	0	0	0	0	0	81.00	$5,000
2006	1	2	0	0	0	0	0	79.50	$5,000
2007	1	4	1	0	0	0	0	78.25	$15,950

Best finish for 2007: 60th at the Masters

2008	1	2	0	0	0	0	0	80.00	

Period Totals	Starts	Rounds Played	Cuts Made	Wins	Top-5s	Top-10s	Top-25s	Scoring Average	Money
	585	2000	410	10	62	105	218	71.42	$6,125,896

Richard Zokol

Year	Starts	Rounds Played	Cuts Made	Wins	Top-5s	Top-10s	Top-25s	Scoring Average	Money
1978	1	2	0	0	0	0	0	82.00	
1982	18	49	7	0	1	1	1	72.84	$14,766
Best finish for 1982: T-5th at the Greater Milwaukee Open									
1983	30	82	9	0	0	1	4	72.62	$38,107
Best finish for 1983: T-6th at the Greater Milwaukee Open									
1984	27	79	13	0	1	2	4	72.67	$56,605
Best finish for 1984: T-5th at the Canadian Open									
1985	27	88	17	0	1	1	7	72.01	$71,792
Best finish for 1985: 4th at the Southwest Golf Classic									
1986	31	87	14	0	0	1	3	72.22	$37,878
Best finish for 1986: T-9th at the Deposit Guaranty Golf Classic									
1987	21	64	13	0	1	3	9	70.70	$114,056
Best finish for 1987: T-3rd at the Deposit Guaranty Golf Classic									
1988	25	76	14	0	1	2	5	72.05	$142,251
Best finish for 1988: 2nd at the Hawaiian Open									
1989	27	77	11	0	1	1	1	72.03	$51,323
Best finish for 1989: T-5th at the Chattanooga Classic									
1990	20	63	13	0	1	3	5	71.11	$191,634
Best finish for 1990: 2nd at the Chattanooga Classic									
1991	25	69	10	0	0	0	5	71.75	$78,426
Best finish for 1991: T-12th at the GTE Byron Nelson Classic									
1992	23	67	12	2	2	2	6	71.15	$311,511
Best finish for 1992: Win at the Deposit Guaranty Classic & Greater Milwaukee Open									
1993	25	73	14	0	1	2	7	71.75	$215,919
Best finish for 1993: T-4th at the Greater Milwaukee Open									
1994	26	74	14	0	0	0	3	71.92	$78,074
Best finish for 1994: T-19th at the Anheuser-Busch Golf Classic & Buick Southern Open									
1995	10	26	4	0	0	0	1	72.00	$23,371
Best finish for 1995: T-17th at the Greater Milwaukee Open									
1996	7	21	4	0	0	0	2	71.14	$30,260
Best finish for 1996: T-18th at the Greater Vancouver Open									
1997	6	17	3	0	0	0	2	70.29	$53,705
Best finish for 1997: T-12th at the Greater Vancouver Open									
1998	7	22	4	0	0	0	0	70.64	$29,905
Best finish for 1998: T-28th at the Greater Vancouver Open									
1999	6	15	2	0	0	0	0	72.33	$28,022
Best finish for 1999: T-29th at the Bell Canadian Open									
2000	11	34	6	0	1	1	2	71.21	$169,492
Best finish for 2000: T-5th at the B.C. Open									
2001	3	11	2	0	0	0	1	72.09	$32,803
Best finish for 2001: T-23rd at the Southern Farm Bureau Classic									
2002	20	51	6	0	0	0	0	72.49	$53,437
Best finish for 2002: T-38th at the Bell Canadian Open									
2003	13	31	2	0	0	0	0	73.32	$19,155
Best finish for 2003: T-46th at the Reno-Tahoe Open									
2004	1	2	0	0	0	0	0	75.00	
2005	1	2	0	0	0	0	0	80.50	
Period Totals	Starts	Rounds Played	Cuts Made	Wins	Top-5s	Top-10s	Top-25s	Scoring Average	Money
	411	1182	194	2	11	20	68	71.95	$1,842,492

PART TWO:
TOURNAMENT RESULTS, 1958–2008

1958

It was a year of firsts: Arnold Palmer won his first major championship, holding off late charges by Doug Ford and Fred Hawkins to claim the Masters. Dow Finsterwald won the first PGA Championship contested at medal play, beating Billy Casper by two shots at Llanerch Country Club in Havertown, Pennsylvania. Gary Player won his first PGA Tour event, the Kentucky Derby Open in Louisville. Tommy Bolt notched his first major; he was the only player not to post 75 or higher during a brutally hot U.S. Open week at Southern Hills. Only the outcome of the British Open at Royal Lytham was familiar—Peter Thomson won it for the fourth time in five years. George Bayer won the Havana Open, the last professional golf tournament to be contested in Cuba before the European Challenge Tour held its 1999 season-ending Grand Finale on the island.

Los Angeles Open

Course: Rancho Municipal G.C., Los Angeles, Calif.
Par: 71 Yardage: 6,827
Last day of event: Monday, January 6, 1958

Player	Place	Score	Earnings
Frank Stranahan	Win	68-73-67-67=275	$7,000.00
Dutch Harrison	2	68-70-71-69=278	$3,750.00
Gay Brewer	3	71-69-67-72=279	$2,600.00
Billy Casper	4	74-68-68-70=280	$2,200.00
Bo Wininger	T-5	69-72-70-70=281	$1,675.00
Al Balding	T-5	71-72-68-70=281	$1,675.00
Art Wall	T-6	71-72-69-70=282	$1,183.34
Dave Ragan	T-6	70-72-70-70=282	$1,183.33
Tommy Jacobs	T-6	71-69-70-72=282	$1,183.33
Johnny Pott	T-9	74-67-74-68=283	$816.67
Paul O'Leary	T-9	73-71-70-69=283	$816.67
Ken Venturi	T-9	72-69-72-70=283	$816.66

Bing Crosby National Pro-Am

Courses: Pebble Beach G.L., Monterey Peninsula C.C., Cypress Point C.C., Pebble Beach, Calif.
Home Course / Pebble Beach G.L., Par: 72 Yardage: 6,747
Last day of event: Sunday, January 12, 1958

Player	Place	Score	Earnings
Billy Casper	Win	71-66-69-71=277	$4,000.00
Dave Marr	2	69-70-70-72=281	$2,400.00
Ken Venturi	T-3	68-74-70-72=284	$1,633.34
Jack Burke Jr.	T-3	72-68-71-73=284	$1,633.33
Dow Finsterwald	T-3	73-67-69-75=284	$1,633.33
Jay Hebert	6	69-72-71-73=285	$1,300.00
Bob Harris	T-7	71-69-71-75=286	$1,116.67
Tommy Bolt	T-7	67-71-74-74=286	$1,116.67
Cary Middlecoff	T-7	72-69-72-73=286	$1,116.66
Bob Rosburg	T-10	65-67-74-81=287	$975.00
Chick Harbert	T-10	71-68-74-74=287	$975.00

Tijuana Open

Course: Caliente C.C., Tijuana, Mexico
Par: N/A Yardage: N/A
Last day of event: Monday, January 20, 1958

Player	Place	Score	Earnings
Dutch Harrison	Win	71-71-69-69=280	$2,000.00
Bo Wininger	T-2	65-69-77-70=281	$1,150.00
Jerry Barber	T-2	68-69-73-71=281	$1,150.00
Arnold Palmer	T-2	70-70-71-70=281	$1,150.00
Fred Hawkins	T-2	68-73-68-72=281	$1,150.00
J.C. Goosie	T-6	72-69-67-74=282	$725.00
Lionel Hebert	T-6	69-70-72-71=282	$725.00
Dave Ragan	T-6	74-67-69-72=282	$725.00
Gene Littler	T-6	71-71-68-72=282	$725.00
Mike Souchak	T-10	73-71-69-70=283	$550.00
Stan Leonard	T-10	68-70-70-75=283	$550.00
Bill Johnston	T-10	71-69-70-73=283	$550.00

Thunderbird Invitational

Course: Thunderbird C.C., Palm Springs, Calif.
Par: N/A Yardage: N/A
Last day of event: Sunday, January 26, 1958

Player	Place	Score	Earnings
Ken Venturi	Win	70-63-66-70=269	$1,500.00
Jimmy Demaret	T-2	68-65-71-69=273	$875.00
Gene Littler	T-2	67-71-65-70=273	$875.00
Jack Burke Jr.	T-4	70-70-68-66=274	$566.66
Stan Leonard	T-4	74-68-66-66=274	$566.66
Don Fairfield	T-4	68-68-69-69=274	$566.66
Tommy Bolt	7	67-69-69-70=275	$450.00
Dick Mayer	T-8	69-69-68-70=276	$343.75
Dave Marr	T-8	65-70-73-68=276	$343.75
Frank Stranahan	T-8	68-72-68-68=276	$343.75
Billy Maxwell	T-8	69-69-68-70=276	$343.75

Phoenix Open

Course: Phoenix C.C., Phoenix, Ariz.
Par: 71 Yardage: 6,726
Last day of event: Sunday, February 2, 1958

Player	Place	Score	Earnings
Ken Venturi	Win	70-68-66-70=274	$2,000.00
Walter Burkemo	T-2	72-69-69-65=275	$1,350.00
Jay Hebert	T-2	69-67-69-70=275	$1,350.00
Bill Collins	T-4	70-70-72-67=279	$950.00
John Mcmullin	T-4	68-71-70-70=279	$950.00
Paul Harney	6	70-68-70-72=280	$800.00
Billy Casper	T-7	72-69-74-67=282	$575.00
Lionel Hebert	T-7	71-71-73-67=282	$575.00
Tommy Bolt	T-7	70-70-72-70=282	$575.00
Dow Finsterwald	T-7	66-73-72-71=282	$575.00
Fred Hawkins	T-7	74-70-69-69=282	$575.00
Jerry Barber	T-7	68-71-72-71=282	$575.00
Billy Maxwell	T-7	69-68-72-73=282	$575.00
Wes Ellis	T-7	68-71-68-75=282	$575.00

Tucson Open

Course: El Rio G&C.C., Tucson, Ariz.
Par: 70 Yardage: 6,418
Last day of event: Sunday, February 9, 1958

Player	Place	Score	Earnings
Lionel Hebert	Win	66-67-66-66=265	$2,000.00
Don January	2	67-67-64-69=267	$1,500.00
John Barnum	3	65-69-68-67=269	$1,200.00
Jay Hebert	T-4	67-68-72-65=272	$862.50
Dow Finsterwald	T-4	67-69-71-65=272	$862.50
Ken Venturi	T-4	69-70-67-66=272	$862.50
Stan Leonard	T-4	69-64-71-68=272	$862.50

Player	Place	Score	Earnings
Walter Burkemo	T-8	69-68-72-64=273	$675.00
Jim Riggins	T-8	65-67-69-72=273	$675.00
Bob Duden	10	69-67-66-72=274	$600.00

Texas Open

Course: Brackenridge Park G.C., San Antonio, Texas
Par: 71 Yardage: 6,185
Last day of event: Sunday, February 16, 1958

Player	Place	Score	Earnings
Bill Johnston	Win	69-71-66-68=274	$2,000.00
Bob Rosburg	2	74-69-69-65=277	$1,500.00
Bo Wininger	T-3	70-71-69-68=278	$975.00
Jimmy Demaret	T-3	70-72-68-68=278	$975.00
Dave Marr	T-3	63-71-71-73=278	$975.00
Billy Maxwell	T-3	70-71-69-68=278	$975.00
Bill Parker	T-7	71-74-69-66=280	$675.00
Jerry Magee	T-7	73-68-70-69=280	$675.00
Ed Griffiths	T-7	72-70-68-70=280	$675.00
Bob Goalby	T-7	73-71-66-70=280	$675.00

Houston Open

Course: Memorial Park G.C., Houston, Texas
Par: 70 Yardage: 7,212
Last day of event: Monday, February 24, 1958

Player	Place	Score	Earnings
Ed Oliver	Win	68-73-73-67=281	$4,300.00
Roberto De Vicenzo	T-2	70-70-71-71=282	$2,500.00
Jay Hebert	T-2	69-73-70-70=282	$2,500.00
Dave Ragan	T-4	72-69-73-69=283	$1,533.34
Marty Furgol	T-4	68-72-71-72=283	$1,533.33
Jimmy Demaret	T-4	70-70-69-74=283	$1,533.33
Johnny Pott	T-7	73-72-72-68=285	$1,200.00
Frank Stranahan	T-7	72-71-71-71=285	$1,200.00
Milon Marusic	T-7	68-73-73-71=285	$1,200.00
Ken Venturi	T-10	71-73-72-70=286	$950.00
Al Besselink	T-10	73-72-72-69=286	$950.00
Dow Finsterwald	T-10	74-70-68-74=286	$950.00

Baton Rouge Open

Course: Baton Rouge C.C., Baton Rouge, La.
Par: N/A Yardage: N/A
Last day of event: Sunday, March 2, 1958

Player	Place	Score	Earnings
Ken Venturi	Win	69-69-69-69=276	$2,000.00
Arnold Palmer	T-2	67-71-71-71=280	$1,350.00
Lionel Hebert	T-2	71-68-68-73=280	$1,350.00
Fred Haas	4	71-69-69-74=283	$1,000.00
Peter Thomson	5	68-71-76-69=284	$900.00
Otto Greiner	T-6	68-71-77-69=285	$775.00
Bob Hill	T-6	72-75-68-70=285	$775.00
Joe Conrad	T-8	76-74-67-70=287	$600.00
Doug Ford	T-8	72-72-72-71=287	$600.00
Dave Ragan	T-8	71-75-69-72=287	$600.00
Julius Boros	T-8	71-71-71-74=287	$600.00
Bill Ogden	T-8	70-71-72-74=287	$600.00

Greater New Orleans Open

Course: City Park G.C., New Orleans, La.
Par: 72 Yardage: 6,656
Last day of event: Tuesday, March 11, 1958

Player	Place	Score	Earnings
Billy Casper	Win	69-70-70-69=278	$2,800.00
Ken Venturi	T-2	68-71-73-66=278	$1,900.00
Walter Burkemo	T-3	71-68-71-71=281	$1,300.00
Arnold Palmer	T-3	73-67-71-70=281	$1,300.00
Doug Ford	T-5	69-72-69-72=282	$1,000.00
Julius Boros	T-5	73-68-71-70=282	$1,000.00
Mike Krak	T-5	72-68-69-73=282	$1,000.00
Bill Ezinicki	8	72-69-72-70=283	$850.00
Gardner Dickinson	T-9	73-68-73-70=284	$753.34
Howie Johnson	T-9	70-71-70-73=284	$753.33
Billy Maxwell	T-9	68-72-72-72=284	$753.33

Pensacola Open

Course: Pensacola C.C., Pensacola, Fla.
Par: 72 Yardage: 6,500
Last day of event: Sunday, March 16, 1958

Player	Place	Score	Earnings
Doug Ford	Win	70-65-70-73=278	$2,000.00
Art Wall	T-2	71-67-73-69=280	$1,350.00
Ken Venturi	T-2	70-66-72-72=280	$1,350.00
Wes Ellis	4	69-69-72-72=282	$1,000.00
Frank Stranahan	5	68-70-74-71=283	$900.00
Billy Casper	6	74-70-72-68=284	$800.00
Lionel Hebert	T-7	72-72-72-69=285	$650.00
Jay Hebert	T-7	73-70-71-71=285	$650.00
Walter Burkemo	T-7	70-71-72-72=285	$650.00
Al Balding	T-7	69-73-72-71=285	$650.00
Dave Ragan	T-7	69-74-70-72=285	$650.00

St. Petersburg Open Invitational

Course: Lakewood C.C., St. Petersburg, Fla.
Par: 72 Yardage: 6,519
Last day of event: Sunday, March 23, 1958

Player	Place	Score	Earnings
Arnold Palmer	Win	70-69-72-65=276	$2,000.00
Fred Hawkins	T-2	72-72-67-66=277	$1,350.00
Dow Finsterwald	T-2	70-70-67-70=277	$1,350.00
Leo Biagetti	4	74-70-66-69=279	$1,000.00
Billy Casper	5	73-73-67-67=280	$900.00
Bo Wininger	6	73-72-68-68=281	$800.00
Don Fairfield	T-7	74-70-69-69=282	$725.00
Mike Dietz	T-7	74-73-67-68=282	$725.00
Everett Vinzant	T-9	72-74-70-67=283	$625.00
Doug Ford	T-9	74-71-69-69=283	$625.00

Azalea Open

Course: Cape Fear C.C., Wilmington, N.C.
Par: 72 Yardage: 6,651
Last day of event: Sunday, March 30, 1958

Player	Place	Score	Earnings
Howie Johnson	Win	74-68-72-68=282	$2,000.00
Arnold Palmer	2	66-73-75-68=282	$1,500.00
Billy Casper	3	69-70-74-73=286	$1,200.00
George Bayer	T-4	69-73-69-76=287	$862.50
Roberto De Vicenzo	T-4	74-70-70-73=287	$862.50
Art Wall	T-4	70-71-71-75=287	$862.50

Dow Finsterwald	T-4	67-70-75-75=287	$862.50
Doug Ford	T-8	70-74-71-73=288	$675.00
Jay Hebert	T-8	71-69-75-73=288	$675.00
Bill Nary	T-10	70-77-70-73=290	$575.00
John Ruedi	T-10	72-74-72-72=290	$575.00

Masters

Course: Augusta National G.C., Augusta, Ga.
Par: 72 Yardage: 6,925
Last day of event: Sunday, April 6, 1958

Player	Place	Score	Earnings
Arnold Palmer	Win	70-73-68-73=284	$11,250.00
Fred Hawkins	T-2	71-75-68-71=285	$4,500.00
Doug Ford	T-2	74-71-70-70=285	$4,500.00
Ken Venturi	T-4	68-72-74-72=286	$1,968.75
Stan Leonard	T-4	72-70-73-71=286	$1,968.75
Cary Middlecoff	T-6	70-73-69-75=287	$1,518.75
Art Wall	T-6	71-72-70-74=287	$1,518.75
Billy-Joe Patton	8	72-69-73-74=288	
Billy Maxwell	T-9	71-70-72-76=289	$1,265.63
Al Mengert	T-9	73-71-69-76=289	$1,265.63
Jay Hebert	T-9	72-73-73-71=289	$1,265.63
Claude Harmon	T-9	71-76-72-70=289	$1,265.63

Greater Greensboro Open

Course: Starmount Forest C.C., Greensboro, N.C.
Par: 71 Yardage: 6,630
Last day of event: Sunday, April 13, 1958

Player	Place	Score	Earnings
Bob Goalby	Win	71-69-69-66=275	$2,000.00
Don January	T-2	73-69-71-64=277	$1,080.00
Dow Finsterwald	T-2	70-69-68-70=277	$1,080.00
Sam Snead	T-2	70-69-66-72=277	$1,080.00
Art Wall	T-2	70-69-71-67=277	$1,080.00
Tony Lema	T-2	69-69-70-69=277	$1,080.00
Gary Player	T-7	70-70-69-69=278	$700.00
Mike Souchak	T-7	78-66-68-66=278	$700.00
Al Balding	T-7	68-68-72-70=278	$700.00
Frank Phillips	T-10	72-69-71-67=279	$550.00
Doug Ford	T-10	70-71-70-68=279	$550.00
Billy Maxwell	T-10	72-67-71-69=279	$550.00

Kentucky Derby Open

Course: Seneca G.C., Louisville, Ky.
Par: N/A Yardage: 6,526
Last day of event: Sunday, April 20, 1958

Player	Place	Score	Earnings
Gary Player	Win	68-68-69-69=274	$2,800.00
Chick Harbert	T-2	66-69-74-68=277	$1,650.00
Ernie Vossler	T-2	71-70-67-69=277	$1,650.00
Peter Thomson	T-4	70-70-71-67=278	$1,150.00
Tom Nieporte	T-4	68-67-71-72=278	$1,150.00
Tony Lema	T-6	67-67-75-70=279	$950.00
Don Fairfield	T-6	70-67-68-74=279	$950.00
Al Besselink	T-8	69-72-70-69=280	$777.50
Paul Harney	T-8	68-66-69-77=280	$777.50
Tommy Bolt	T-8	67-73-72-68=280	$777.50
Bob Keller	T-8	70-70-72-68=280	$777.50

Lafayette Open

Course: Oakbourne C.C., Lafayette, Ky.
Par: 71 Yardage: 6,947
Last day of event: Sunday, April 27, 1958

Player	Place	Score	Earnings
Jay Hebert	Win	69-69-68-67=273	$2,000.00
Bob Rosburg	T-2	71-70-68-69=278	$1,350.00
Leo Biagetti	T-2	70-68-67-73=278	$1,350.00
Gay Brewer	T-4	71-70-70-68=279	$950.00
Bert Weaver	T-4	69-73-70-67=279	$950.00
Bill Collins	T-6	70-68-67-75=280	$750.00
Gary Player	T-6	69-69-70-72=280	$750.00
Ernie Vossler	T-6	73-68-68-71=280	$750.00
Bill Webb	9	73-71-71-67=282	$650.00
Paul O'Leary	10	71-72-69-71=283	$600.00

Tournament of Champions

Course: Desert Inn C.C., Las Vegas,, Nev.
Par: 72 Yardage: 7,209
Last day of event: Sunday, April 27, 1958

Player	Place	Score	Earnings
Stan Leonard	Win	69-69-69-68=275	$10,000.00
Billy Casper	2	65-70-71-70=276	$5,000.00
Frank Stranahan	3	66-71-72-71=280	$2,500.00
Tommy Bolt	T-4	69-67-71-74=281	$1,390.00
Gene Littler	T-4	68-74-71-68=281	$1,390.00
E. Harrison	T-6	70-70-72-70=282	$1,310.00
Arnold Palmer	T-6	72-68-72-70=282	$1,310.00
George Bayer	T-8	78-66-68-71=283	$1,260.00
Gardner Dickinson	T-8	73-70-68-72=283	$1,260.00
Ken Venturi	T-8	72-71-71-69=283	$1,260.00

Colonial National Invitational

Course: Colonial C.C., Fort Worth, Texas
Par: 70 Yardage: 7,021
Last day of event: Sunday, May 4, 1958

Player	Place	Score	Earnings
Tommy Bolt	Win	68-70-70-74=282	$5,000.00
Ken Venturi	2	72-73-69-69=283	$3,000.00
Gardner Dickinson	T-3	69-74-72-69=284	$1,900.00
Ted Kroll	T-3	74-72-68-70=284	$1,900.00
Don January	T-5	73-72-71-69=285	$1,416.67
Lloyd Mangrum	T-5	68-73-70-74=285	$1,416.67
Ben Hogan	T-5	73-69-70-73=285	$1,416.66
Dow Finsterwald	8	72-73-70-71=286	$1,100.00
Stan Leonard	T-9	68-72-72-75=287	$950.00
Ed Oliver	T-9	70-73-70-74=287	$950.00

Arlington Hotel Open

Course: Hot Springs Country Club, Hot Springs, Ark.
Par: 72 Yardage: 7,011
Last day of event: Sunday, May 11, 1958

Player	Place	Score	Earnings
Julius Boros	Win	70-64-68-71=273	$2,800.00
Cary Middlecoff	2	72-66-69-67=274	$1,900.00
Don January	T-3	72-69-67-67=275	$1,300.00
Bob Rosburg	T-3	67-69-70-69=275	$1,300.00
Ted Kroll	T-5	71-70-68-69=278	$1,000.00
Bo Wininger	T-5	70-69-70-69=278	$1,000.00
Gay Brewer	T-5	71-68-72-67=278	$1,000.00

Ernie Vossler	8	72-67-69-71=279	$850.00
Art Wall	T-9	72-69-71-68=280	$732.50
Gardner Dickinson	T-9	72-68-70-70=280	$732.50
Tommy Bolt	T-9	66-70-71-73=280	$732.50
Gene Littler	T-9	71-67-71-71=280	$732.50

Memphis Invitational Open

Course: Colonial C.C., Memphis, Tenn.
Par: 70 Yardage: 6,466
Last day of event: Sunday, May 18, 1958

Player	Place	Score	Earnings
Billy Maxwell	Win	69-65-68-65=267	$2,800.00
Cary Middlecoff	2	67-67-68-66=268	$1,900.00
Mason Rudolph	3	65-66-68-70=269	
Paul Harney	T-4	69-69-67-66=271	$1,300.00
Marty Furgol	T-4	66-67-69-69=271	$1,300.00
Jay Hebert	T-6	69-67-67-69=272	$1,050.00
Fred Haas	T-6	67-70-68-67=272	$1,050.00
Arnold Palmer	8	69-70-66-68=273	$850.00
Hillman Robbins	9	67-69-68-70=274	
Ted Kroll	10	69-67-68-71=275	$800.00

Greenbrier Invitational

Course: The Greenbrier, White Sulphur Springs, W.Va.
Par: N/A Yardage: N/A
Last day of event: Sunday, May 18, 1958

Player	Place	Score	Earnings
Sam Snead	Win	66-66-65-67=264	$2,300.00
Gary Player	2	66-65-67-66=264	$1,300.00
Ben Hogan	3	65-64-68-68=265	$700.00
Doug Sanders	4	70-72-63-68=273	$500.00
Clarence Doser	T-5	74-67-64-69=274	$400.00
Al Mengert	T-5	67-67-69-71=274	$400.00
Stan Mosel	T-5	65-73-65-71=274	$400.00
George Fazio	8	71-68-71-65=275	$300.00
Al Smith	T-9	72-69-65-70=276	$262.20
Ed Oliver	T-9	68-71-67-70=276	$262.20

Kansas City Open

Course: Hillcrest C.C., Kansas City, Mo.
Par: N/A Yardage: 6,668
Last day of event: Sunday, May 25, 1958

Player	Place	Score	Earnings
Ernie Vossler	Win	67-65-70-67=269	$2,800.00
Billy Maxwell	2	68-71-65-67=271	$1,900.00
Lionel Hebert	3	66-68-71-69=274	$1,400.00
Gary Player	4	67-67-71-70=275	$1,200.00
Tommy Jacobs	5	64-70-73-70=277	$1,100.00
Gene Littler	T-6	73-71-66-68=278	$916.67
Art Wall	T-6	71-68-70-69=278	$916.67
Marty Furgol	T-6	69-70-70-69=278	$916.66
Dick Mayer	T-9	73-71-70-65=279	$753.34
Wes Ellis	T-9	70-69-72-68=279	$753.33
Jim Ferree	T-9	74-68-66-71=279	$753.33

Western Open

Course: Red Run G.C., Royal Oak, Mich.
Par: 72 Yardage: 6,801
Last day of event: Sunday, June 1, 1958

Player	Place	Score	Earnings
Doug Sanders	Win	69-68-70-68=275	$5,000.00
Dow Finsterwald	2	69-68-68-71=276	$2,500.00
Julius Boros	T-3	70-73-70-66=279	$1,600.00
Bob Rosburg	T-3	67-70-71-71=279	$1,600.00
Mike Souchak	T-3	68-70-67-74=279	$1,600.00
Tommy Jacobs	6	64-71-72-73=280	$1,100.00
Sam Snead	T-7	70-68-73-70=281	$815.00
Arnold Palmer	T-7	66-73-72-70=281	$815.00
Frank Stranahan	T-7	67-71-70-73=281	$815.00
Ken Venturi	T-7	71-70-65-75=281	$815.00
Dave Ragan	T-7	69-71-65-76=281	$815.00

Dallas Open

Course: Oak Cliff C.C., Dallas, Texas
Par: 71 Yardage: 6,836
Last day of event: Sunday, June 8, 1958

Player	Place	Score	Earnings
Sam Snead	Win	67-67-69-69=272	$3,500.00
Julius Boros	T-2	67-66-70-69=272	$1,866.67
Gary Player	T-2	66-66-72-68=272	$1,866.67
John Mcmullin	T-2	64-65-69-74=272	$1,866.66
Bert Weaver	T-5	68-67-71-67=273	$1,250.00
Tommy Bolt	T-5	68-62-71-72=273	$1,250.00
Earl Stewart	7	68-66-69-71=274	$1,100.00
Bruce Crampton	T-8	69-65-72-69=275	$950.00
Bo Wininger	T-8	68-70-66-71=275	$950.00
Art Wall	T-8	69-65-69-72=275	$950.00

Insurance City Open

Course: Wethersfield C.C., Wethersfield, CT.
Par: 71 Yardage: 6,568
Last day of event: Friday, June 13, 1958

Player	Place	Score	Earnings
Jack Burke Jr.	Win	63-67-69-69=268	$3,500.00
Art Wall	T-2	67-70-65-69=271	$2,050.00
Dow Finsterwald	T-2	68-66-69-68=271	$2,050.00
Wes Ellis	4	68-72-63-69=272	$1,500.00
George Bayer	T-5	65-69-70-69=273	$1,200.00
Paul Harney	T-5	70-66-69-68=273	$1,200.00
Don Whitt	T-5	70-68-66-69=273	$1,200.00
Billy Casper	T-8	68-68-69-69=274	$900.00
Gene Littler	T-8	67-69-69-69=274	$900.00
Ted Kroll	T-8	67-72-66-69=274	$900.00
Gary Player	T-8	66-71-68-69=274	$900.00
Arnold Palmer	T-8	66-68-70-70=274	$900.00

U.S. Open

Course: Southern Hills, Tulsa, Okla.
Par: 70 Yardage: 6,907
Last day of event: Saturday, June 14, 1958

Player	Place	Score	Earnings
Tommy Bolt	Win	71-71-69-72=283	$8,000.00
Gary Player	2	75-68-73-71=287	$5,000.00
Julius Boros	3	71-75-72-71=289	$3,000.00
Gene Littler	4	74-73-67-76=290	$2,000.00

Walter Burkemo	T-5	75-74-70-72=291	$1,625.00
Bob Rosburg	T-5	75-74-72-70=291	$1,625.00
Don January	T-7	79-73-68-73=293	$1,016.67
Dick Metz	T-7	71-78-73-71=293	$1,016.67
Jay Hebert	T-7	77-76-71-69=293	$1,016.66
Frank Stranahan	T-10	72-72-75-75=294	$566.67
Tommy Jacobs	T-10	76-75-71-72=294	$566.67
Ben Hogan	T-10	75-73-75-71=294	$566.66

Buick Open

Course: Warwick Hills C.C., Grand Blanc, Mich.
Par: 72 Yardage: 7,014
Last day of event: Monday, June 23, 1958

Player	Place	Score	Earnings
Billy Casper	Win	70-73-71-71=285	$9,000.00
Arnold Palmer	T-2	76-71-70-69=286	$3,800.00
Ted Kroll	T-2	71-71-69-75=286	$3,800.00
Tommy Bolt	T-4	69-72-72-74=287	$2,450.00
Doug Ford	T-4	74-71-72-70=287	$2,450.00
Art Wall	T-6	72-72-73-72=289	$2,000.00
Julius Boros	T-6	73-72-69-75=289	$2,000.00
Billy Maxwell	T-8	76-71-71-72=290	$1,600.00
Max Evans	T-8	72-73-73-72=290	$1,600.00
Jack Fleck	T-8	73-71-69-77=290	$1,600.00

Pepsi Open

Course: Pine Hollow C.C., East Norwich, N.Y.
Par: 71 Yardage: 6,860
Last day of event: Sunday, June 29, 1958

Player	Place	Score	Earnings
Arnold Palmer	Win	66-69-67-71=273	$9,000.00
Jay Hebert	2	70-70-70-68=278	$4,600.00
Don Fairfield	3	73-66-70-70=279	$3,000.00
Sam Snead	T-4	69-73-68-70=280	$2,333.34
Ted Kroll	T-4	69-71-67-73=280	$2,333.33
Bob Rosburg	T-4	72-70-68-70=280	$2,333.33
Al Mengert	T-7	72-72-70-67=281	$1,675.00
Doug Ford	T-7	73-70-68-70=281	$1,675.00
Stan Leonard	T-7	73-72-67-69=281	$1,675.00
Henry Ransom	T-7	69-70-71-71=281	$1,675.00

British Open

Course: Royal Lytham & St. Annes G.C., Lytham, Lancashire, England
Par: 71 Yardage: 6,635
Last day of event: Friday, July 4, 1958

Player	Place	Score	Earnings
Peter Thomson	Win	66-72-67-73-139=278	$2,800.00
Dave Thomas	2	70-68-69-71-143=278	$1,400.00
Christy O'Connor	T-3	67-68-73-71=279	N/A
Eric Brown	T-3	73-70-65-71=279	N/A
Flory Van Donck	T-5	70-70-67-74=281	N/A
Leopoldo Ruiz	T-5	71-65-72-73=281	N/A
Gary Player	7	68-74-70-71=283	N/A
Eric Lester	T-8	73-66-71-74=284	N/A
Henry Cotton	T-8	68-75-69-72=284	N/A
Harry Weetman	T-8	73-67-73-71=284	N/A

Rubber City Open

Course: Firestone C.C., Akron, Ohio
Par: 70 Yardage: N/A
Last day of event: Sunday, July 6, 1958

Player	Place	Score	Earnings
Dow Finsterwald	Win	70-65-69-65=269	$1,900.00
Art Wall	T-2	65-67-68-69=269	$2,800.00
Bob Goalby	3	70-67-66-67=270	$1,400.00
Mike Souchak	T-4	67-67-69-69=272	$1,150.00
Jack Burke Jr.	T-4	70-68-68-66=272	$1,150.00
Jack Fleck	6	68-66-69-70=273	$1,000.00
Dick Mayer	T-7	67-69-72-66=274	$850.00
Bob Rosburg	T-7	68-67-71-68=274	$850.00
Tommy Bolt	T-7	68-65-71-70=274	$850.00
Charles Sifford	T-10	70-64-73-68=275	$730.00
Huston La Clair	T-10	71-69-67-68=275	$730.00

PGA Championship

Course: Llanerch C.C., Havertown, Pa.
Par: 70 Yardage: 6,710
Last day of event: Sunday, July 20, 1958

Player	Place	Score	Earnings
Dow Finsterwald	Win	67-72-70-67=276	$5,500.00
Billy Casper	2	73-67-68-70=278	$3,500.00
Sam Snead	3	73-67-67-73=280	$2,400.00
Jack Burke Jr.	4	70-72-69-70=281	$2,000.00
Jay Hebert	T-5	68-71-73-73=285	$1,600.00
Julius Boros	T-5	72-68-73-72=285	$1,600.00
Tommy Bolt	T-5	72-70-73-70=285	$1,600.00
Mike Souchak	T-8	75-69-69-74=287	$1,300.00
Buster Cupit	T-8	71-74-69-73=287	$1,300.00
Ed Oliver	T-8	74-73-71-69=287	$1,300.00

Eastern Open

Course: Mt. Pleasant Municipal Golf Club, Baltimore, Md.
Par: 72 Yardage: 6,895
Last day of event: Sunday, July 27, 1958

Player	Place	Score	Earnings
Art Wall	Win	69-69-71-67=276	$2,800.00
Bob Rosburg	T-2	68-70-71-67=276	$1,650.00
Jack Burke Jr.	T-2	71-69-69-67=276	$1,650.00
Gary Player	4	68-68-72-69=277	$1,200.00
Jim Ferree	T-5	71-72-73-67=283	$1,050.00
Mike Fetchick	T-5	68-73-71-71=283	$1,050.00
Don Fairfield	T-7	72-72-69-71=284	$875.00
Gene Littler	T-7	73-72-67-72=284	$875.00
Sam Snead	T-9	72-72-67-74=285	$691.66
Bob Goalby	T-9	72-68-73-72=285	$691.66
George Bayer	T-9	71-72-71-71=285	$691.67
Marty Furgol	T-9	70-75-70-70=285	$691.67
Jay Hebert	T-9	70-72-73-70=285	$691.67
Clarence Doser	T-9	73-71-71-70=285	$691.67

Gleneagles-Chicago Open

Course: Gleneagles C.C., Lemont, Ill.
Par: 70 Yardage: 6,350
Last day of event: Monday, August 4, 1958

Player	Place	Score	Earnings
Ken Venturi	Win	65-67-68-72=272	$9,000.00
Julius Boros	T-2	73-69-66-65=273	$3,800.00

Jack Burke Jr.	T-2	68-67-68-70=273	$3,800.00
Bob Rosburg	T-4	70-68-69-67=274	$2,333.34
J.C. Goosie	T-4	73-66-67-68=274	$2,333.33
Gary Player	T-4	69-68-67-70=274	$2,333.33
Billy Casper	7	80-64-64-67=275	$1,900.00
Marty Furgol	8	68-70-67-71=276	$1,700.00
Ted Kroll	9	69-66-74-68=277	$1,600.00
Doug Sanders	T-10	67-68-72-71=278	$1,212.50
Fred Haas	T-10	68-73-68-69=278	$1,212.50
Bob Harris	T-10	66-72-70-70=278	$1,212.50
Don Whitt	T-10	67-71-72-68=278	$1,212.50
Dave Ragan	T-10	72-73-65-68=278	$1,212.50
Art Wall	T-10	74-67-70-67=278	$1,212.50
Don Fairfield	T-10	68-71-69-70=278	$1,212.50
Ernie Vossler	T-10	75-65-65-73=278	$1,212.50

Miller Open

Course: Tripoli G.C., Milwaukee, Wis.
Par: 70 Yardage: 6,514
Last day of event: Monday, August 11, 1958

Player	Place	Score	Earnings
Cary Middlecoff	Win	67-64-66-67=264	$5,300.00
Bob Rosburg	2	67-69-66-64=266	$3,400.00
Billy Casper	3	70-64-66-67=267	$2,200.00
Bob Goalby	T-4	66-68-66-70=270	$1,800.00
Sam Snead	T-4	68-67-69-66=270	$1,800.00
Paul Harney	T-6	63-68-70-70=271	$1,450.00
Chick Harbert	T-6	66-68-69-68=271	$1,450.00
Ken Venturi	T-8	66-69-68-69=272	$1,100.00
Jack Burke Jr.	T-8	66-69-71-66=272	$1,100.00
Gary Player	T-8	67-65-72-68=272	$1,100.00
Jay Hebert	T-8	68-69-69-66=272	$1,100.00
Jim Turnesa	T-8	65-68-72-67=272	$1,100.00

St. Paul Open

Course: Keller G.C., St. Paul, Minn. .
Par: 72 Yardage: N/A
Last day of event: Sunday, August 17, 1958

Player	Place	Score	Earnings
Mike Souchak	Win	66-64-68-65=263	$3,500.00
Sam Snead	T-2	65-66-66-70=267	$2,050.00
Julius Boros	T-2	66-70-67-64=267	$2,050.00
Art Wall	4	66-68-69-66=269	$1,500.00
Ernie Vossler	T-5	67-64-69-70=270	$1,075.00
Lionel Hebert	T-5	64-68-69-69=270	$1,075.00
Frank Stranahan	T-5	65-69-69-67=270	$1,075.00
Cary Middlecoff	T-5	65-67-70-68=270	$1,075.00
Ken Venturi	T-5	66-66-68-70=270	$1,075.00
Dow Finsterwald	T-5	66-72-64-68=270	$1,075.00

Canadian Open

Course: Mayfair G&C.C., Edmonton, Alberta, Canada
Par: 70 Yardage: N/A
Last day of event: Saturday, August 23, 1958

Player	Place	Score	Earnings
Wes Ellis	Win	67-69-65-66=267	$3,500.00
Jay Hebert	2	66-68-65-69=268	$2,300.00
George Bayer	3	70-70-64-65=269	$1,800.00
Stan Leonard	T-4	67-66-69-68=270	$1,220.00
Mike Souchak	T-4	67-67-69-67=270	$1,220.00
Bob Goetz	T-4	67-65-69-69=270	$1,220.00
Don Fairfield	T-4	69-66-69-66=270	$1,220.00
Art Wall	T-4	70-66-69-65=270	$1,220.00
Al Balding	T-9	69-65-68-69=271	$900.00
Tommy Jacobs	T-9	66-67-68-70=271	$900.00
Lionel Hebert	T-9	66-67-73-65=271	$900.00

Vancouver Open

Course: Point Grey Course, Vancouver. B.C., Canada
Par: 72 Yardage: 6,505
Last day of event: Monday, September 1, 1958

Player	Place	Score	Earnings
Jim Ferree	Win	69-61-69-71=270	$6,400.00
Billy Casper	2	71-66-68-66=271	$3,600.00
Dow Finsterwald	T-3	69-65-71-68=273	$2,350.00
Ken Venturi	T-3	70-67-68-68=273	$2,350.00
Stan Leonard	5	70-68-71-65=274	$1,900.00
Fred Hawkins	6	68-70-65-72=275	$1,700.00
Ed Oliver	7	69-70-71-66=276	$1,600.00
Mike Souchak	8	69-65-73-70=277	$1,500.00
Don January	T-9	74-68-64-73=279	$1,250.00
Koichi Ono	T-9	68-70-71-70=279	$1,250.00
Art Wall	T-9	69-70-70-70=279	$1,250.00
Gene Littler	T-9	69-70-70-70=279	$1,250.00

Utah Open

Course: Salt Lake C.C., Salt Lake City, Utah
Par: 71 Yardage: 6,394
Last day of event: Monday, September 8, 1958

Player	Place	Score	Earnings
Dow Finsterwald	Win	69-65-67-66=267	$2,000.00
Fred Hawkins	T-2	70-67-62-69=268	$1,350.00
Arnold Palmer	T-2	65-69-68-66=268	$1,350.00
Bill Collins	4	67-67-69-68=271	$1,000.00
Art Wall	T-5	68-70-68-66=272	$816.67
Bob Rosburg	T-5	67-68-66-71=272	$816.67
Tom Nieporte	T-5	67-65-70-70=272	$816.66
John Mcmullin	8	70-67-69-68=274	$700.00
Bo Wininger	T-9	66-68-73-68=275	$625.00
Don Fairfield	T-9	70-68-67-70=275	$625.00

Denver Open

Course: Wellshire Golf Course, Denver, Colo.
Par: 70 Yardage: 6,642
Last day of event: Sunday, September 14, 1958

Player	Place	Score	Earnings
Tommy Jacobs	Win	65-67-67-67=266	$2,800.00
Ernie Vossler	2	68-70-65-64=267	$1,900.00
Howie Johnson	T-3	73-67-66-64=270	$1,300.00
Arnold Palmer	T-3	67-68-66-69=270	$1,300.00
Bill Bisdorf	T-5	70-69-70-65=274	$930.00
Bob Goalby	T-5	71-66-72-65=274	$930.00
Ed Oliver	T-5	69-70-68-67=274	$930.00
Tony Lema	T-5	72-69-66-67=274	$930.00
Bert Weaver	T-5	70-68-64-72=274	$930.00
Billy Maxwell	T-10	70-69-70-66=275	$670.00
Don January	T-10	73-73-64-65=275	$670.00
Tom Nieporte	T-10	76-67-64-68=275	$670.00
John Mcmullin	T-10	66-68-67-74=275	$670.00
Doug Sanders	T-10	67-74-63-71=275	$670.00

Hesperia Open

Course: Hesperia C.C., Hesperia, Calif.
Par: 72 Yardage: 7,054
Last day of event: Sunday, September 21, 1958

Player	Place	Score	Earnings
John Mcmullin	Win	69-68-67-67=271	$2,000.00
Gene Littler	2	67-62-72-71=272	$1,500.00
Dow Finsterwald	3	73-67-65-69=274	$1,200.00
Wes Ellis	T-4	67-68-73-67=275	$862.50
Fred Hawkins	T-4	70-67-66-72=275	$862.50
Ken Venturi	T-4	68-67-70-70=275	$862.50
Jerry Barber	T-4	63-68-72-72=275	$862.50
Bob Rosburg	T-8	67-68-71-71=277	$675.00
Bo Wininger	T-8	69-69-70-69=277	$675.00
Lloyd Mangrum	T-10	65-68-72-73=278	$575.00
Zell Eaton	T-10	69-68-71-70=278	$575.00

Carling Open

Course: Cherokee Town & C.C., Atlanta, Ga.
Par: 72 Yardage: 7,004
Last day of event: Sunday, November 9, 1958

Player	Place	Score	Earnings
Julius Boros	Win	74-66-70-74=284	$8,500.00
Billy Casper	2	72-69-71-74=286	$2,300.00
Bill Collins	3	68-70-75-74=287	$1,800.00
Pete Cooper	T-4	73-73-72-70=288	$1,400.00
Fred Hawkins	T-4	70-75-70-73=288	$1,400.00
Billy Maxwell	T-6	72-64-77-76=289	$1,150.00
Tommy Bolt	T-6	74-74-65-76=289	$1,150.00
Bob Watson	T-8	71-70-71-78=290	$975.00
Doug Sanders	T-8	72-70-75-73=290	$975.00
Ernie Vossler	T-10	70-72-70-79=291	$875.00
Bob Rosburg	T-10	75-70-77-69=291	$875.00

Havana Invitational

Course: Villa Real G.C., East Havana, Cuba
Par: 70 Yardage: 7,009
Last day of event: Sunday, November 16, 1958

Player	Place	Score	Earnings
George Bayer	Win	75-64-74-73=286	$6,500.00
Sam Snead	T-2	70-72-70-74=286	$3,600.00
Doug Ford	3	70-71-74-76=291	$2,500.00
Billy Casper	4	72-72-74-74=292	$2,200.00
Julius Boros	5	73-76-74-70=293	$2,000.00
Tony Lema	T-6	74-73-72-75=294	$1,600.00
Ernie Vossler	T-6	75-71-76-72=294	$1,600.00
Ed Oliver	T-6	73-77-72-72=294	$1,600.00
Ted Kroll	T-9	73-76-73-73=295	$1,350.00
Dow Finsterwald	T-9	72-72-79-72=295	$1,350.00

West Palm Beach Open

Course: West Palm Beach C.C., West Palm Beach, Fla.
Par: 72 Yardage: 6,745
Last day of event: Sunday, November 23, 1958

Player	Place	Score	Earnings
Pete Cooper	Win	68-63-68-70=269	$2,000.00
Wes Ellis	T-2	65-68-63-73=269	$1,500.00
Dow Finsterwald	T-3	66-70-68-69=273	$1,100.00
Billy Casper	T-3	67-70-68-68=273	$1,100.00

Tommy Jacobs	5	72-68-66-69=275	$900.00
Arnold Palmer	T-6	70-66-67-74=277	$725.00
Art Wall	T-6	71-66-68-72=277	$725.00
Julius Boros	T-6	70-70-71-66=277	$725.00
Jay Hebert	T-6	68-72-69-68=277	$725.00
Bert Weaver	T-10	65-70-72-71=278	$550.00
Don January	T-10	71-71-67-69=278	$550.00
Doug Sanders	T-10	71-67-68-72=278	$550.00

Mayfair Inn Open

Course: Mayfair C.C., Sanford, Fla.
Par: 71 Yardage: 6,600
Last day of event: Sunday, December 7, 1958

Player	Place	Score	Earnings
George Bayer	Win	68-67-69-68=272	$2,000.00
Chick Harbert	2	68-68-71-66=273	$1,500.00
Dow Finsterwald	3	71-66-70-67=274	$1,200.00
Julius Boros	T-4	69-70-70-66=275	$830.00
Tom Nieporte	T-4	71-73-66-65=275	$830.00
Art Wall	T-4	69-68-71-67=275	$830.00
Bo Wininger	T-4	68-70-69-68=275	$830.00
Jay Hebert	T-4	69-72-66-68=275	$830.00
Tommy Bolt	9	66-70-71-69=276	$650.00
Ed Oliver	T-10	70-71-68-68=277	$575.00
Wes Ellis	T-10	68-70-68-71=277	$575.00

1959

Art Wall, who claimed to have made 42 holes-in-one during his career, played the last four holes at Augusta National in 5 under par to win the Masters. Billy Casper one-putted 31 times en route to victory at the U.S. Open; he took 114 putts all week at Winged Foot. Gary Player won the first of his nine majors, against a British Open field at Muirfield that included no Americans of note. Bob Rosburg, who would gain fame as a TV commentator, made up a 6-shot deficit after 54 holes to win the PGA Championship at Minneapolis Golf Club. Arnold Palmer and Mark McCormack made a handshake agreement that the young lawyer from Cleveland would represent the business interests of the charismatic golfer from Latrobe, Pa. They never formalized the deal with a contract, even as McCormack's management company, IMG, evolved into one of the most influential entities in golf. The United States won the Ryder Cup, 8 to 3, beginning a streak of 13 consecutive victories in the biennial match between America and Great Britain (plus Ireland beginning in 1973 and Europe beginning in 1979).

Los Angeles Open

Course: Rancho Municipal G.C.
Los Angeles, Calif.
Par: 71 Yardage: 7,000
Last day of event: Monday, January 5, 1959

Player	Place	Score	Earnings
Ken Venturi	Win	72-71-72-63=278	$5,300.00
Art Wall	2	71-68-68-73=280	$3,400.00
Billy Maxwell	3	67-70-72-72=281	$2,200.00
Doug Sanders	4	66-69-73-74=282	$1,900.00
Paul Harney	T-5	71-69-74-69=283	$1,533.34
Mike Souchak	T-5	69-72-69-73=283	$1,533.33
Tommy Bolt	T-5	69-70-71-73=283	$1,533.33
Al Geiberger	T-5	70-70-74-69=283	
Julius Boros	9	68-74-71-71=284	$1,300.00
John Mcmullin	T-10	66-70-74-75=285	$1,062.50
Howie Johnson	T-10	69-71-71-74=285	$1,062.50
Jack Fleck	T-10	68-75-70-72=285	$1,062.50
Arnold Palmer	T-10	72-69-72-72=285	$1,062.50

Tijuana Open Invitational

Course: Tijuana C.C., Tijuana, Mexico
Par: 72 Yardage: 7,400
Last day of event: Monday, January 12, 1959

Player	Place	Score	Earnings
Ernie Vossler	Win	69-65-71-68=273	$2,800.00
John Mcmullin	2	66-69-71-69=275	$1,900.00
Jack Fleck	3	69-67-72-68=276	$1,400.00
Mike Fetchick	T-4	70-66-71-70=277	$1,150.00
Jay Hebert	T-4	69-67-70-71=277	$1,150.00
Mike Souchak	6	70-71-66-71=278	$1,000.00
Lionel Hebert	T-7	73-67-69-70=279	$802.00
Bill Collins	T-7	74-69-66-70=279	$802.00
Paul Runyan	T-7	70-70-69-70=279	$802.00
Jerry Barber	T-7	66-71-72-70=279	$802.00
Doug Ford	T-7	67-73-69-70=279	$802.00

Bing Crosby National Pro-Am

Courses: Pebble Beach G.L. - Home
Monterey Peninsula C.C., Cypress Point C.C., Pebble Beach, Calif.
Home Course Par: 72 Yardage: 6,747
Last day of event: Sunday, January 18, 1959

Player	Place	Score	Earnings
Art Wall	Win	69-65-70-75=279	$4,000.00
Gene Littler	T-2	73-67-70-71=281	$1,250.00
Jimmy Demaret	T-2	74-64-70-73=281	$1,250.00
John Mcmullin	T-4	68-73-71-71=283	$1,500.00
Bob Rosburg	T-4	71-70-70-72=283	$1,500.00
Don January	T-6	70-72-70-73=285	$1,250.00
Doug Ford	T-6	73-74-68-70=285	$1,250.00
Billy Maxwell	T-8	67-74-72-73=286	$1,025.00
Lloyd Mangrum	T-8	73-71-70-72=286	$1,025.00
Arnold Palmer	T-8	69-77-67-73=286	$1,025.00
Jack Fleck	T-8	75-69-73-69=286	$1,025.00

Thunderbird Invitational

Course: Thunderbird C.C., Palm Springs, Calif.
Par: 71 Yardage: 6,680
Last day of event: Sunday, January 25, 1959

Player	Place	Score	Earnings
Arnold Palmer	Win	67-70-67-62=266	$1,500.00
Jimmy Demaret	T-2	69-66-64-70=269	$875.00
Ken Venturi	T-2	68-67-68-66=269	$875.00
Lloyd Mangrum	4	68-68-68-66=270	$650.00
Wes Ellis	5	67-66-68-70=271	$550.00
Jack Burke Jr.	T-6	69-67-68-68=272	$475.00
Bo Wininger	T-6	69-64-70-69=272	$475.00
Tommy Jacobs	T-8	68-70-69-66=273	$358.34
Stan Leonard	T-8	70-68-68-67=273	$358.33
Julius Boros	T-8	69-71-67-66=273	$358.33

San Diego Open

Course: Mission Valley C.C., San Diego, Calif.
Home Course -Par: 72 Yardage: 6,700
Last day of event: Sunday, February 1, 1959

Player	Place	Score	Earnings
Marty Furgol	Win	70-71-64-69=274	$2,800.00
Mike Souchak	T-2	65-68-69-73=275	$1,320.00
Bo Wininger	T-2	66-68-71-70=275	$1,320.00
Joe Campbell	T-2	67-69-68-71=275	$1,320.00
Dave Ragan	T-2	69-68-66-72=275	$1,320.00
Billy Casper	T-2	67-69-69-70=275	$1,320.00
Bob Harris	7	71-69-67-69=276	$900.00
Bob Rosburg	T-8	68-66-69-74=277	$756.00
Jack Burke Jr.	T-8	68-71-67-71=277	$756.00
Bob Duden	T-8	65-71-70-71=277	$756.00
Doug Sanders	T-8	66-66-73-72=277	$756.00
Fred Hawkins	T-8	73-67-68-69=277	$756.00

Phoenix Open

Course: Arizona C.C., Phoenix, Ariz.
Par: 70 Yardage: 6,216
Last day of event: Sunday, February 8, 1959

Player	Place	Score	Earnings
Gene Littler	Win	67-63-67-71=268	$2,400.00
Art Wall	2	70-65-68-66=269	$1,700.00
Jimmy Clark	T-3	68-68-69-70=275	$1,133.34
Marty Furgol	T-3	67-67-70-71=275	$1,133.33
John Mcmullin	T-3	65-67-71-72=275	$1,133.33
Paul Harney	T-6	68-68-69-71=276	$806.25
Dick Mayer	T-6	72-67-70-67=276	$806.25
Lloyd Mangrum	T-6	72-67-69-68=276	$806.25
Tommy Jacobs	T-6	66-69-73-68=276	$806.25
Joe Campbell	10	64-68-73-72=277	$675.00

Tucson Open

Course: El Rio G&C.C., Tucson, Ariz.
Par: 70 Yardage: 6,434
Last day of event: Sunday, February 15, 1959

Player	Place	Score	Earnings
Gene Littler	Win	65-67-68-66=266	$2,000.00
Joe Campbell	T-2	65-64-65-73=267	$1,350.00
Art Wall	T-2	66-64-67-70=267	$1,350.00
Bill Johnston	T-4	67-68-66-67=268	$900.00
Arnold Palmer	T-4	70-68-64-66=268	$900.00
Doug Sanders	T-4	68-67-68-65=268	$900.00
Paul O'Leary	T-7	69-70-64-66=269	$675.00
Marty Furgol	T-7	62-68-72-67=269	$675.00
Walter Burkemo	T-7	67-66-67-69=269	$675.00
Lloyd Mangrum	T-7	66-65-71-67=269	$675.00

Texas Open

Course: Brackenridge Park G.C., San Antonio, Texas
Par: 71 Yardage: 6,490
Last day of event: Sunday, February 22, 1959

Player	Place	Score	Earnings
Wes Ellis	Win	66-71-72-67=276	$2,800.00
Bill Johnston	T-2	68-70-70-70=278	$1,650.00
Tom Nieporte	T-2	72-69-68-69=278	$1,650.00
Doug Ford	T-4	72-69-69-70=280	$1,150.00
Tommy Jacobs	T-4	71-71-65-73=280	$1,150.00
Mike Souchak	6	72-66-71-72=281	$1,000.00
Al Balding	T-7	70-71-68-73=282	$875.00
Fred Hawkins	T-7	71-69-72-70=282	$875.00
Chandler Harper	9	73-75-68-67=283	$800.00
Joe Jimenez	T-10	69-67-76-72=284	$690.00
Tony Lema	T-10	74-71-67-72=284	$690.00
Gene Littler	T-10	76-72-67-69=284	$690.00
Jim Turnesa	T-10	72-70-70-72=284	$690.00

Baton Rouge Open Invitational

Course: Baton Rouge C.C., Baton Rouge, La.
Par: 72 Yardage: 6,450
Last day of event: Sunday, March 1, 1959

Player	Place	Score	Earnings
Howie Johnson	Win	72-71-70-70=283	$2,000.00
Jay Hebert	2	70-71-68-75=284	$1,500.00
John Mcmullin	3	65-73-75-72=285	$1,200.00
Doug Ford	T-4	72-70-72-72=286	$950.00
Paul Harney	T-4	68-72-72-74=286	$950.00
Bert Weaver	T-6	69-73-75-70=287	$650.00
Lionel Hebert	T-6	72-70-69-76=287	$650.00
Billy Maxwell	T-6	67-75-74-71=287	$650.00
Bob Goalby	T-6	68-74-74-71=287	$650.00
Bill Ezinicki	T-6	71-74-68-74=287	$650.00
Mike Souchak	T-6	68-71-76-72=287	$650.00
Gene Littler	T-6	70-70-71-76=287	$650.00

Greater New Orleans Open

Course: City Park G.C., New Orleans, La.
Par: 72 Yardage: 6,656
Last day of event: Monday, March 9, 1959

Player	Place	Score	Earnings
Bill Collins	Win	68-72-70-70=280	$2,800.00
Tom Nieporte	T-2	70-70-75-68=283	$1,650.00
Jack Burke Jr.	T-2	75-70-71-67=283	$1,650.00
Huston La Clair	T-4	73-68-72-71=284	$1,100.00
Gene Littler	T-4	73-64-72-75=284	$1,100.00
Moe Norman	T-4	70-72-70-72=284	$1,100.00
Howie Johnson	T-7	73-71-71-70=285	$850.00
Dow Finsterwald	T-7	69-74-70-72=285	$850.00
Wes Ellis	T-7	70-71-72-72=285	$850.00
Bob Goalby	T-10	72-72-72-70=286	$710.00
Billy Maxwell	T-10	70-70-73-73=286	$710.00
Don January	T-10	74-73-68-71=286	$710.00

Pensacola Open

Course: Pensacola C.C., Pensacola, Fla.
Par: 72 Yardage: 6,500
Last day of event: Sunday, March 15, 1959

Player	Place	Score	Earnings
Paul Harney	Win	69-65-65-70=269	$2,000.00
Jay Hebert	2	68-72-65-67=272	$1,500.00
Bob Rosburg	T-3	75-67-62-72=276	$1,100.00
Chandler Harper	T-3	69-67-70-70=276	$1,100.00
Ken Venturi	T-5	72-72-67-66=277	$850.00
Fred Haas	T-5	68-72-66-71=277	$850.00
Art Wall	T-7	68-69-72-69=278	$725.00
Arnold Palmer	T-7	68-69-69-72=278	$725.00
Dave Ragan	T-9	69-72-69-70=280	$625.00
Billy Casper	T-9	75-66-70-69=280	$625.00

St. Petersburg Open Invitational

Course: Lakewood C.C., St. Petersburg, Fla.
Par: 72 Yardage: 6,519
Last day of event: Monday, March 23, 1959

Player	Place	Score	Earnings
Cary Middlecoff	Win	70-69-67-69=275	$2,000.00
Pete Cooper	2	68-70-69-71=278	$1,500.00
Bob Goalby	3	70-66-69-75=280	$1,200.00

Gene Littler	T-4	72-70-72-68=282	$900.00
George Bayer	T-4	66-69-77-70=282	$900.00
Wes Ellis	T-4	70-66-74-72=282	$900.00
Al Balding	T-7	68-74-73-68=283	$725.00
Chick Harbert	T-7	71-68-71-73=283	$725.00
Billy Casper	T-9	72-71-72-69=284	$625.00
Doug Ford	T-9	72-70-71-71=284	$625.00

Azalea Open

Course: Cape Fear C.C., Wilmington, N.C.
Par: 72 Yardage: 6,651
Last day of event: Monday, March 30, 1959

Player	Place	Score	Earnings
Art Wall	Win	72-66-71-73=282	$2,000.00
Mike Souchak	2	72-72-70-71=285	$1,500.00
Dow Finsterwald	3	73-71-75-68=287	$1,200.00
Bert Weaver	4	71-73-74-72=290	$1,000.00
Don Whitt	T-5	71-71-73-76=291	$850.00
Doug Ford	T-5	74-73-74-70=291	$850.00
Bob Goalby	7	70-72-76-74=292	$750.00
Bob Rosburg	8	76-73-75-70=294	$700.00
Billy Maxwell	T-9	73-72-74-76=295	$575.00
Al Besselink	T-9	72-74-75-74=295	$575.00
Tom Nieporte	T-9	74-74-71-76=295	$575.00

Masters

Course: Augusta National G.C., Augusta, Ga.
Par: 72 Yardage: 6,925
Last day of event: Sunday, April 5, 1959

Player	Place	Score	Earnings
Art Wall	Win	73-74-71-66=284	$15,000.00
Cary Middlecoff	2	74-71-68-72=285	$7,500.00
Arnold Palmer	3	71-70-71-74=286	$4,500.00
Stan Leonard	T-4	69-74-69-75=287	$2,625.00
Dick Mayer	T-4	73-75-71-68=287	$2,625.00
Charles Coe	6	74-74-67-73=288	
Fred Hawkins	7	77-71-68-73=289	$2,100.00
Billy Maxwell	T-8	73-71-72-74=290	$1,740.00
Billy-Joe Patton	T-8	75-70-71-74=290	
Jay Hebert	T-8	72-73-72-73=290	$1,740.00
Julius Boros	T-8	75-69-74-72=290	$1,740.00
Gene Littler	T-8	72-75-72-71=290	$1,740.00
Gary Player	T-8	73-75-71-71=290	$1,740.00

Greater Greensboro Open

Course: Starmount Forest C.C., Greensboro, N.C.
Par: 71 Yardage: 6,630
Last day of event: Sunday, April 12, 1959

Player	Place	Score	Earnings
Dow Finsterwald	Win	68-68-65-77=278	$2,000.00
Art Wall	2	69-67-70-74=280	$1,500.00
Sam Snead	T-3	73-69-69-70=281	$1,100.00
Billy Casper	T-3	73-68-68-72=281	$1,100.00
Tom Nieporte	T-5	70-70-70-73=283	$816.67
Peter Thomson	T-5	71-70-68-74=283	$816.67
Billy Maxwell	T-5	67-71-70-75=283	$816.66
Doug Ford	T-8	69-71-74-70=284	$650.00
Frank Stranahan	T-8	71-70-69-74=284	$650.00
Mike Fetchick	T-8	66-67-72-79=284	$650.00

Houston Classic

Course: Memorial Park G.C., Houston, Texas
Par: 72 Yardage: 7,133
Last day of event: Sunday, April 19, 1959

Player	Place	Score	Earnings
Jack Burke Jr.	Win	69-66-72-70=277	$4,300.00
Julius Boros	2	68-71-70-68=277	$3,000.00
Arnold Palmer	T-3	66-68-71-73=278	$1,850.00
Mike Souchak	T-3	70-71-70-67=278	$1,850.00
Chick Harbert	T-5	70-74-67-68=279	$1,400.00
Fred Haas	T-5	68-66-72-73=279	$1,400.00
Cary Middlecoff	T-5	67-70-71-71=279	$1,400.00
Jay Hebert	T-8	67-69-71-73=280	$1,150.00
Billy Maxwell	T-8	69-72-70-69=280	$1,150.00
Wes Ellis	T-10	70-68-73-71=282	$975.00
Paul Harney	T-10	70-68-73-71=282	$975.00

Tournament of Champions

Course: Desert Inn C.C., Las Vegas,, Nev.
Par: 72 Yardage: 7,073
Last day of event: Sunday, April 26, 1959

Player	Place	Score	Earnings
Mike Souchak	Win	66-70-68-77=281	$10,000.00
Art Wall	2	72-68-69-74=283	$5,000.00
Gene Littler	3	71-72-71-71=285	$3,000.00
Julius Boros	T-4	70-70-75-74=289	$1,606.67
Doug Sanders	T-4	71-73-72-73=289	$1,606.67
Stan Leonard	T-4	71-73-70-75=289	$1,606.66
Billy Maxwell	T-7	72-73-73-72=290	$1,360.00
Ken Venturi	T-7	71-75-72-72=290	$1,360.00
Ernie Vossler	T-7	69-71-74-76=290	$1,360.00
Billy Casper	T-10	72-75-73-72=292	$1,300.00
Pete Cooper	T-10	69-77-73-73=292	$1,300.00
John McMullen	T-10	68-72-76-76=292	$1,300.00

Colonial National Invitational

Course: Colonial C.C., Fort Worth, Texas
Par: 70 Yardage: 7,021
Last day of event: Friday, May 1, 1959

Player	Place	Score	Earnings
Ben Hogan	Win	69-67-77-72=285	$5,000.00
Fred Hawkins	2	72-69-73-71=285	$3,000.00
Billy Maxwell	T-3	74-71-72-69=286	$1,900.00
Tommy Jacobs	T-3	70-70-73-73=286	$1,900.00
Ted Kroll	T-5	68-71-71-77=287	$1,500.00
Lionel Hebert	T-5	67-67-78-75=287	$1,500.00
Dow Finsterwald	T-7	70-73-76-69=288	$1,116.67
Ernie Vossler	T-7	73-70-73-72=288	$1,116.67
Bo Wininger	T-7	73-69-73-73=288	$1,116.66
Peter Thomson	10	75-72-72-70=289	$900.00

Oklahoma City Open

Course: Twin Oaks G & C.C., Oklahoma City, Okla.
Par: 72 Yardage: 6,640
Last day of event: Monday, May 11, 1959

Player	Place	Score	Earnings
Arnold Palmer	Win	73-64-67-69=273	$3,500.00
Bob Goalby	2	69-68-71-67=275	$2,300.00
Tommy Jacobs	3	66-67-73-70=276	$1,800.00
Mike Souchak	T-4	71-70-70-68=279	$1,400.00
Ted Kroll	T-4	70-71-70-68=279	$1,400.00
Don Fairfield	6	71-67-70-72=280	$1,200.00
Glen Fowler	7	68-70-72-71=281	
Fred Hawkins	8	75-70-69-68=282	$1,100.00
Bob Rosburg	9	74-67-74-68=283	$1,000.00
Ernie Vossler	10	73-72-71-68=284	$950.00

Arlington Hotel Open Invitational

Course: Hot Springs Country Club, Hot Springs, Ark.
Par: 72 Yardage: 7,011
Last day of event: Sunday, May 17, 1959

Player	Place	Score	Earnings
Gene Littler	Win	67-69-64-70=270	$2,800.00
Jim Ferree	2	67-69-68-67=271	$1,900.00
Doug Ford	3	69-70-67-67=273	$1,400.00
Johnny Palmer	T-4	69-71-68-68=276	$1,150.00
Art Wall	T-4	63-73-71-69=276	$1,150.00
Wes Ellis	T-6	67-69-73-68=277	$950.00
Don January	T-6	69-70-70-68=277	$950.00
Jay Hebert	T-8	71-70-69-68=278	$777.50
Tommy Bolt	T-8	70-67-72-69=278	$777.50
Bob Goalby	T-8	68-68-70-72=278	$777.50
George Bayer	T-8	68-63-71-76=278	$777.50

Sam Snead Festival

Course: The Greenbrier, White Sulphur Springs, W.Va.
Par: 70 Yardage: N/A
Last day of event: Sunday, May 17, 1959

Player	Place	Score	Earnings
Sam Snead	Win	68-69-59-63=259	$2,300.00
Mike Souchak	2	68-71-66-65=270	$1,300.00
Dutch Harrison	3	68-68-68-69=273	$700.00
Al Besselink	4	70-70-71-64=275	$500.00
Dave Marr	T-5	73-68-67-68=276	$375.00
Dave Douglas	T-5	71-70-68-67=276	$375.00
Doug Sanders	T-5	67-71-69-69=276	$375.00
Bruce Crampton	T-5	67-73-70-66=276	$375.00
Mike Homa	9	71-71-79-65=286	$275.00
H. Williams, Jr.	10	69-72-69-68=278	$250.00

Memphis Invitational Open

Course: Colonial C.C., Memphis, Tenn.
Par: 70 Yardage: 6,501
Last day of event: Monday, May 25, 1959

Player	Place	Score	Earnings
Don Whitt	Win	67-70-64-71=272	$3,500.00
Gary Player	T-2	69-68-68-67=272	$2,050.00
Al Balding	T-2	68-69-68-67=272	$2,050.00
Art Wall	T-4	66-69-69-69=273	$1,400.00
Lionel Hebert	T-4	72-70-63-68=273	$1,400.00
Doug Ford	6	66-70-69-70=275	$1,200.00
Wes Ellis	T-7	69-70-69-69=277	$960.00
Pete Cooper	T-7	66-72-70-69=277	$960.00
Paul Harney	T-7	71-67-70-69=277	$960.00
Jay Hebert	T-7	65-68-69-75=277	$960.00
Al Besselink	T-7	65-69-70-73=277	$960.00

Kentucky Derby Open Invitational

Course: Seneca G.C., Louisville, Ky.
Par: 71 Yardage: 6,452
Last day of event: Sunday, May 31, 1959

Player	Place	Score	Earnings
Don Whitt	Win	70-64-73-67=274	$2,800.00
Jim Ferree	2	70-68-69-68=275	$1,900.00
Ernie Vossler	T-3	66-70-72-68=276	$1,175.00
Dick Knight	T-3	72-67-70-67=276	$1,175.00
Dave Ragan	T-3	72-73-64-67=276	$1,175.00
Doug Ford	T-3	69-70-67-70=276	$1,175.00
Billy Casper	T-7	73-73-64-67=277	$850.00
Tommy Jacobs	T-7	71-69-69-68=277	$850.00
J.C. Goosie	T-7	73-68-66-70=277	$850.00
Bo Wininger	T-10	74-72-66-66=278	$730.00
Bob Goalby	T-10	64-68-69-77=278	$730.00

Eastern Open Invitational

Course: Pine Ridge G.C., Baltimore, Md.
Par: 72 Yardage: N/A
Last day of event: Sunday, June 7, 1959

Player	Place	Score	Earnings
Dave Ragan	Win	69-68-66-70=273	$2,800.00
Gene Littler	2	65-67-71-71=274	$1,900.00
Henry Ransom	T-3	70-66-70-69=275	$1,300.00
Don Whitt	T-3	69-68-69-69=275	$1,300.00
Ed Oliver	5	66-67-73-70=276	$1,100.00
Billy Maxwell	T-6	68-69-70-70=277	$950.00
Ken Venturi	T-6	72-70-69-66=277	$950.00
Fred Hawkins	T-8	67-68-73-70=278	$25.00
Don January	T-8	67-71-73-67=278	$25.00
Bill Collins	T-10	70-69-69-72=280	$710.00
Ted Kroll	T-10	70-68-73-69=280	$710.00
Mike Souchak	T-10	74-67-69-70=280	$710.00

U.S. Open

Course: Winged Foot G.C. (West), Mamaroneck, N.Y.
Par: 70 Yardage: 6,873
Last day of event: Saturday, June 13, 1959

Player	Place	Score	Earnings
Billy Casper	Win	71-68-69-74=282	$12,000.00
Bob Rosburg	2	75-70-67-71=283	$6,600.00
Mike Souchak	T-3	71-70-72-71=284	$3,600.00
Claude Harmon	T-3	72-71-70-71=284	$3,600.00
Arnold Palmer	T-5	71-69-72-74=286	$2,100.00
Doug Ford	T-5	72-69-72-73=286	$2,100.00
Ernie Vossler	T-5	72-70-72-72=286	$2,100.00
Ben Hogan	T-8	69-71-71-76=287	$1,350.00
Sam Snead	T-8	73-72-67-75=287	$1,350.00
Dick Knight	10	69-75-73-73=290	$900.00

Canadian Open

Course: Islesmere G&C.C., Montreal, Quebec, Canada
Par: 72 Yardage: 6,695
Last day of event: Sunday, June 21, 1959

Player	Place	Score	Earnings
Doug Ford	Win	68-69-69-70=276	$3,500.00
Dow Finsterwald	T-2	67-69-69-73=278	$1,866.67
Bo Wininger	T-2	71-69-70-68=278	$1,866.67
Art Wall	T-2	67-69-70-72=278	$1,866.66

Bruce Crampton	T-5	68-67-70-75=280	$1,200.00
Bob Rosburg	T-5	67-69-72-72=280	$1,200.00
Don Fairfield	T-5	69-69-72-70=280	$1,200.00
Billy Maxwell	T-8	68-70-72-71=281	$950.00
Jay Hebert	T-8	69-68-70-74=281	$950.00
Paul Harney	T-8	73-69-69-70=281	$950.00

Gleneagles-Chicago Open Invitational

Course: Gleneagles C.C., Lemont, Ill.
Par: 70 Yardage: 6,350
Last day of event: Sunday, June 28, 1959

Player	Place	Score	Earnings
Ken Venturi	Win	64-75-68-66=273	$9,000.00
Johnny Pott	2	63-67-72-72=274	$4,600.00
Gene Littler	3	67-72-69-68=276	$3,000.00
Bo Wininger	4	66-66-73-72=277	$2,600.00
Sam Snead	T-5	70-69-70-70=279	$2,100.00
Don Whitt	T-5	67-72-70-70=279	$2,100.00
Jim Ferree	T-5	73-70-68-68=279	$2,100.00
Lionel Hebert	T-8	70-71-68-71=280	$1,600.00
Monte Bradley	T-8	71-70-71-68=280	$1,600.00
Paul Harney	T-8	71-68-72-69=280	$1,600.00

British Open

Course: Muirfield G.C., Muirfield, East Lothian, Scotland
Par: 71 Yardage: 6,806
Last day of event: Friday, July 3, 1959

Player	Place	Score	Earnings
Gary Player	Win	75-71-70-68=284	$2,800.00
Fred Bullock	T-2	68-70-74-74=286	
Flory Van Donck	T-2	70-70-73-73=286	
Syd Scott	4	73-70-73-71=287	
Sam King	T-5	70-74-68-76=288	
Reid Jack	T-5	71-75-68-74=288	
John Panton	T-5	72-72-71-73=288	
Christy O'Connor	T-5	73-74-72-69=288	
Leopoldo Ruiz	T-9	72-74-69-74=289	
Dai Rees	T-9	73-73-69-74=289	

Buick Open

Course: Warwick Hills C.C., Grand Blanc, Mich.
Par: 72 Yardage: 7,014
Last day of event: Sunday, July 5, 1959

Player	Place	Score	Earnings
Art Wall	Win	71-67-72-72=282	$9,000.00
Dow Finsterwald	2	71-68-71-72=282	$4,600.00
Cary Middlecoff	T-3	75-72-71-65=283	$2,800.00
Jerry Barber	T-3	74-70-72-67=283	$2,800.00
Pete Cooper	T-5	72-69-74-69=284	$2,200.00
Jay Hebert	T-5	68-73-74-69=284	$2,200.00
Ken Venturi	7	75-70-69-71=285	$1,900.00
Julius Boros	T-8	73-69-73-71=286	$1,650.00
Arnold Palmer	T-8	72-74-69-71=286	$1,650.00
Don Fairfield	T-10	73-76-70-68=287	$1,450.00
Mike Souchak	T-10	70-75-73-69=287	$1,450.00

Western Open

Course: Pittsburgh Field Club, Fox Chapel, Pa.
Par: 70 Yardage: 6,625
Last day of event: Sunday, July 12, 1959

Player	Place	Score	Earnings
Mike Souchak	Win	67-67-73-65=272	$5,000.00
Arnold Palmer	2	67-66-69-71=273	$2,500.00
George Bayer	3	69-67-72-66=274	$2,000.00
Ted Kroll	4	71-67-70-67=275	$1,500.00
Fred Hawkins	T-5	68-69-71-68=276	$1,200.00
Pete Cooper	T-5	71-66-72-67=276	$1,200.00
Dutch Harrison	T-7	72-71-63-71=277	$900.00
Jack Fleck	T-7	70-67-70-70=277	$900.00
Julius Boros	T-7	69-75-66-67=277	$900.00
Joe Campbell	10	65-71-66-76=278	$725.00

Insurance City Open

Course: Wethersfield C.C., Wethersfield, CT.
Par: 71 Yardage: 6,568
Last day of event: Sunday, July 19, 1959

Player	Place	Score	Earnings
Gene Littler	Win	64-66-72-70=272	$3,500.00
Tom Nieporte	2	68-69-67-69=273	$2,300.00
Doug Ford	3	70-69-69-66=274	$1,800.00
Fred Hawkins	T-4	67-69-71-69=276	$1,400.00
Jack Burke Jr.	T-4	69-71-68-68=276	$1,400.00
Bob Watson	T-6	72-67-70-69=278	$1,150.00
Ken Venturi	T-6	70-70-70-68=278	$1,150.00
Bob Goalby	T-9	68-67-71-73=279	$950.00
Arnold Palmer	T-9	68-71-68-72=279	$950.00
Dick Knight	T-9	70-74-66-69=279	$950.00

PGA Championship

Course: Minneapolis G.C., St. Louis Park, Minn. .
Par: 70 Yardage: 6,850
Last day of event: Sunday, August 2, 1959

Player	Place	Score	Earnings
Bob Rosburg	Win	71-72-68-66=277	$8,250.00
Jerry Barber	T-2	69-65-71-73=278	$3,562.50
Doug Sanders	T-2	72-66-68-72=278	$3,562.00
Dow Finsterwald	4	71-68-71-70=280	$2,500.00
Mike Souchak	T-5	69-67-71-74=281	$2,000.00
Ken Venturi	T-5	70-72-70-69=281	$2,000.00
Bob Goalby	T-5	72-69-72-68=281	$2,000.00
Cary Middlecoff	T-8	72-68-70-72=282	$1,600.00
Sam Snead	T-8	71-73-68-70=282	$1,600.00
Gene Littler	T-10	69-70-72-73=284	$1,450.00

Carling Open Invitational

Course: Seneca G.C., Cleveland, Ohio
Par: 71 Yardage: 6,955
Last day of event: Sunday, August 9, 1959

Player	Place	Score	Earnings
Dow Finsterwald	Win	74-68-66-68=276	$3,500.00
Mike Souchak	T-2	70-65-72-70=277	$2,050.00
Gene Littler	T-2	71-64-70-72=277	$2,050.00
Paul Harney	T-4	72-63-70-73=278	$1,333.34
Doug Sanders	T-4	70-66-71-71=278	$1,333.33
Dick Knight	T-4	70-70-67-71=278	$1,333.33
Bert Weaver	7	69-69-72-69=279	$1,100.00

Gardner Dickinson	T-8	70-69-70-71=280	$925.00
Pete Cooper	T-8	67-67-73-73=280	$925.00
Jack Fleck	T-8	70-70-73-67=280	$925.00
Art Wall	T-8	70-69-69-72=280	$925.00

Motor City Open Invitational

Course: Meadowbrook C.C., Detroit, Mich..
Par: 71 Yardage: 6,616
Last day of event: Sunday, August 16, 1959

Player	Place	Score	Earnings
Mike Souchak	Win	69-63-67-69=268	$3,500.00
Doug Ford	T-2	70-70-67-70=277	$2,050.00
Billy Casper	T-2	71-67-70-69=277	$2,050.00
Arnold Palmer	T-4	69-66-71-73=279	$1,333.34
Art Wall	T-4	70-68-69-72=279	$1,333.33
Dutch Harrison	T-4	69-71-70-69=279	$1,333.33
Paul Harney	7	69-71-72-69=281	$1,100.00
Dow Finsterwald	T-8	68-73-72-71=284	$900.00
Tom Nieporte	T-8	69-75-67-73=284	$900.00
Max Evans	T-8	72-66-72-74=284	$900.00
Mason Rudolph	T-8	67-75-72-70=284	$900.00
Bob Rosburg	T-8	69-73-72-70=284	$900.00

Rubber City Open Invitational

Course: Firestone G.C., Akron, Ohio
Par: 70 Yardage: 6,620
Last day of event: Sunday, August 23, 1959

Player	Place	Score	Earnings
Tom Nieporte	Win	67-69-65-66=267	$2,800.00
Bob Goalby	2	66-66-70-68=270	$1,900.00
Bill Collins	3	70-70-66-65=271	$1,400.00
Tommy Bolt	T-4	70-67-68-67=272	$1,100.00
Arnold Palmer	T-4	66-69-68-69=272	$1,100.00
Don January	T-4	70-69-65-68=272	$1,100.00
Billy Casper	T-7	67-69-67-70=273	$875.00
Ted Kroll	T-7	66-70-70-67=273	$875.00
Doug Ford	T-9	70-70-66-68=274	$775.00
Doug Sanders	T-9	67-67-71-69=274	$775.00

Miller Open Invitational

Course: Tripoli G.C., Milwaukee, Wis.
Par: 70 Yardage: 6,355
Last day of event: Sunday, August 30, 1959

Player	Place	Score	Earnings
Gene Littler	Win	68-66-64-67=265	$5,300.00
Bob Rosburg	T-2	69-67-64-66=266	$2,500.00
Bo Wininger	T-2	66-65-64-71=266	$2,500.00
Ted Kroll	T-4	67-67-66-68=268	$2,500.00
Art Wall	5	68-69-66-66=269	$1,700.00
Ed Oliver	T-6	68-67-69-66=270	$1,450.00
Bill Collins	T-6	70-67-65-68=270	$1,450.00
Don January	T-8	67-68-69-68=272	$1,150.00
Doug Sanders	T-8	65-67-72-68=272	$1,150.00
Doug Ford	T-8	66-66-70-70=272	$1,150.00
Paul Harney	T-8	68-65-69-70=272	$1,150.00

Kansas City Open Invitational
Course: Blue Hills C.C., Kansas City, Mo.
Par: 70 Yardage: 6,542
Last day of event: Monday, September 7, 1959

Player	Place	Score	Earnings
Dow Finsterwald	Win	68-69-69-69=275	$2,800.00
Don Fairfield	2	70-71-67-67=275	$1,900.00
Dutch Harrison	T-3	67-71-71-67=276	$1,175.00
Bob Goalby	T-3	69-66-71-70=276	$1,175.00
Pete Cooper	T-3	71-70-67-68=276	$1,175.00
Bruce Crampton	T-3	70-67-72-67=276	$1,175.00
Joe Campbell	T-7	71-70-68-68=277	$850.00
Ron Reif	T-7	69-71-71-66=277	$850.00
Doug Sanders	T-7	68-69-70-70=277	$850.00
Mason Rudolph	T-10	66-72-72-69=279	$710.00
Jim Ferree	T-10	69-70-68-72=279	$710.00
Don Whitt	T-10	70-67-71-71=279	$710.00

Dallas Open
Course: Oak Cliff C.C., Dallas, Texas
Par: 71 Yardage: 6,836
Last day of event: Monday, September 14, 1959

Player	Place	Score	Earnings
Julius Boros	Win	68-66-70-70=274	$3,500.00
Earl Stewart	T-2	72-64-75-64=275	$1,866.67
Dow Finsterwald	T-2	68-72-70-65=275	$1,866.67
Bo Wininger	T-2	67-69-71-68=275	$1,866.66
Jon Gustin	5	69-68-67-72=276	$1,300.00
Gardner Dickinson	T-6	72-71-67-67=277	$1,100.00
Gay Brewer	T-6	68-72-72-65=277	$1,100.00
Don January	T-6	72-69-67-69=277	$1,100.00
Paul Harney	T-7	74-71-68-65=278	$925.00
Doug Sanders	T-7	72-71-68-67=278	$925.00
Cary Middlecoff	T-9	71-72-68-68=279	$800.00
Huston La Clair	T-9	72-69-70-68=279	$800.00
Tommy Jacobs	T-9	71-72-70-66=279	$800.00

El Paso Open Invitational
Course: El Paso C.C., El Paso, Texas
Par: 72 Yardage: 6,700
Last day of event: Sunday, September 20, 1959

Player	Place	Score	Earnings
Marty Furgol	Win	73-69-66-65=273	$2,800.00
Ernie Vossler	T-2	69-70-68-70=277	$1,650.00
Jay Hebert	T-2	69-71-69-68=277	$1,650.00
Bob Goalby	4	71-70-70-67=278	$1,200.00
Doug Ford	T-5	65-71-71-73=280	$1,050.00
Art Wall	T-5	74-69-69-68=280	$1,050.00
Fred Hawkins	T-7	71-68-70-72=281	$825.00
Iverson Martin	T-7	68-67-75-71=281	$825.00
Billy Maxwell	T-7	72-67-72-70=281	$825.00
Monte Bradley	T-7	71-69-72-69=281	$825.00

Golden Gate Championship
Course: Harding Park G.C., San Francisco, Calif.
Par: 71 Yardage: 6,628
Last day of event: Sunday, September 27, 1959

Player	Place	Score	Earnings
Mason Rudolph	Win	67-72-67-69=275	$6,400.00
Dow Finsterwald	T-2	70-68-70-69=277	$3,050.00

Bob Goalby	T-2	69-68-73-67=277	$3,050.00
Jerry Barber	T-4	70-66-74-68=278	$2,050.00
Don Whitt	T-4	69-72-69-68=278	$2,050.00
Billy Casper	T-6	70-71-68-70=279	$1,650.00
Tommy Jacobs	T-6	72-72-63-72=279	$1,650.00
Jim Ferree	T-8	69-71-70-70=280	$1,450.00
Tommy Bolt	T-8	69-67-74-70=280	$1,450.00
Doug Sanders	T-10	73-69-69-70=281	$1,100.00
Eric Monti	T-10	73-70-69-69=281	$1,100.00
Mike Souchak	T-10	68-72-72-69=281	$1,100.00
Bob Rosburg	T-10	70-73-71-67=281	$1,100.00
Gene Littler	T-10	74-70-70-67=281	$1,100.00

Portland Centennial Open Invitational
Course: Portland G.C.
Portland, Ore.
Par: 72 Yardage: 6,604
Last day of event: Sunday, October 4, 1959

Player	Place	Score	Earnings
Billy Casper	Win	69-64-67-69=269	$2,800.00
Bob Duden	T-2	68-68-68-68=272	$1,650.00
Dave Ragan	T-2	71-67-67-67=272	$1,650.00
Mason Rudolph	4	72-67-69-66=274	$1,200.00
Billy Maxwell	T-5	68-69-69-69=275	$1,000.00
Tony Lema	T-5	65-68-69-73=275	$1,000.00
Bob Rosburg	T-5	70-64-68-73=275	$1,000.00
Charles Sifford	8	72-66-69-69=276	$850.00
Doug Sanders	T-9	70-71-66-70=277	$753.34
Don January	T-9	69-68-70-70=277	$753.33
Jim Ferree	T-9	67-69-70-71=277	$753.33

Hesperia Open Invitational
Course: Hesperia C.C., Hesperia, Calif.
Par: 72 Yardage: 7,127
Last day of event: Sunday, October 11, 1959

Player	Place	Score	Earnings
Eric Monti	Win	70-68-64-69=271	$2,000.00
Bob Duden	T-2	68-70-66-71=275	$1,233.34
Jack Fleck	T-2	66-71-67-71=275	$1,233.33
Jay Hebert	T-2	71-68-66-70=275	$1,233.33
Paul Harney	5	69-69-72-67=277	$900.00
Billy Casper	6	69-72-66-71=278	$800.00
Bob Goalby	7	68-71-70-70=279	$750.00
Don Fairfield	T-8	70-67-71-72=280	$75.00
Joe Kirkwood, Jr.	T-8	67-68-70-75=280	$75.00
Chuck Rotar	T-10	71-71-69-70=281	$550.00
Gene Littler	T-10	70-68-72-71=281	$550.00
Doug Sanders	T-10	68-66-69-78=281	$550.00

Orange County Open
Course: Mesa Verde C.C., Costa Mesa, Calif.
Par: 71 Yardage: 6,650
Last day of event: Sunday, October 18, 1959

Player	Place	Score	Earnings
Jay Hebert	Win	68-68-68-69=273	$2,000.00
Jerry Magee	T-2	69-70-65-71=275	$1,350.00
Jack Fleck	T-2	70-67-68-70=275	$1,350.00
Bert Weaver	T-4	68-70-69-69=276	$862.50
Jerry Barber	T-4	68-71-69-68=276	$862.50
Billy Maxwell	T-4	71-69-67-69=276	$862.50
George Bayer	T-7	70-70-68-70=278	$625.00

Miller Barber	T-7	69-71-69-69=278	$625.00
Don Fairfield	T-7	72-70-67-69=278	$625.00
Gene Littler	T-7	68-70-68-72=278	$625.00

Lafayette Open Invitational
Course: Oakbourne C.C., Lafayette, La.
Par: 71 Yardage: 6,700
Last day of event: Sunday, November 15, 1959

Player	Place	Score	Earnings
Billy Casper	Win	69-64-71-69=273	$2,000.00
George Bayer	2	70-67-72-68=277	$1,500.00
Jim Ferree	T-3	68-68-72-70=278	$1,100.00
Billy Maxwell	T-3	67-70-71-70=278	$1,100.00
Gay Brewer	5	69-69-73-70=281	$900.00
Bill Johnston	6	69-69-71-73=282	$800.00
Frank Wharton	T-7	69-69-75-70=283	$700.00
Arnold Palmer	T-7	74-69-73-67=283	$700.00
Bob Goalby	T-7	71-66-79-67=283	$700.00
Monte Bradley	T-10	72-70-70-72=284	$550.00
Jon Gustin	T-10	71-69-73-71=284	$550.00
Doug Ford	T-10	71-74-70-69=284	$550.00

Mobile Sertoma Open Invitational
Course: Mobile Municipal Golf Club, Mobile, Ala.
Par: 72 Yardage: 6,383
Last day of event: Sunday, November 22, 1959

Player	Place	Score	Earnings
Billy Casper	Win	71-68-68-73=280	$2,000.00
Wes Ellis	T-2	72-71-66-73=282	$1,350.00
Dave Ragan	T-2	72-70-70-70=282	$1,350.00
Jon Gustin	T-4	71-68-72-72=283	$900.00
Walter Burkemo	T-4	70-70-74-69=283	$900.00
Johnny Pott	T-4	73-71-70-69=283	$900.00
Joe Campbell	T-7	71-72-69-72=284	$725.00
John Barnum	T-7	69-72-75-68=284	$725.00
Howie Johnson	T-9	70-71-77-67=285	$575.00
Dick Knight	T-9	73-73-70-69=285	$575.00
Miller Barber	T-9	70-72-71-72=285	$575.00
Gay Brewer	T-9	73-67-74-71=285	$575.00

West Palm Beach Open Invitational
Course: West Palm Beach C.C., West Palm Beach, Fla.
Par: 72 Yardage: 6,745
Last day of event: Sunday, November 29, 1959

Player	Place	Score	Earnings
Arnold Palmer	Win	72-67-66-76=281	$2,000.00
Gay Brewer	T-2	72-66-68-75=281	$1,350.00
Pete Cooper	T-2	70-69-68-74=281	$1,350.00
Chick Harbert	T-4	71-73-69-70=283	$950.00
Billy Casper	T-4	72-70-68-73=283	$950.00
Dave Ragan	6	70-65-70-79=284	$800.00
Julius Boros	7	72-72-70-71=285	$750.00
Billy Maxwell	T-8	72-73-69-72=286	$625.00
Doug Sanders	T-8	69-73-71-73=286	$625.00
Bill Johnston	T-8	72-70-67-77=286	$625.00
Dick Knight	T-8	72-69-71-74=286	$625.00

Coral Gables Open Invitational
Course: Biltmore C.C., Coral Gables, Fla.
Par: 71 Yardage: 6,563
Last day of event: Sunday, December 6, 1959

Player	Place	Score	Earnings
Doug Sanders	Win	68-71-69-65=273	$2,800.00
Dow Finsterwald	2	68-70-69-69=276	$1,900.00
Julius Boros	T-3	67-73-72-67=279	$1,233.34
Johnny Pott	T-3	70-70-70-69=279	$1,233.33
Arnold Palmer	T-3	69-72-66-72=279	$1,233.33
Al Besselink	T-6	76-67-70-67=280	$950.00
Jay Hebert	T-6	70-69-72-69=280	$950.00
Jim Ferree	T-8	70-69-72-70=281	$825.00
Bill Collins	T-8	70-70-69-72=281	$825.00
Don Fairfield	10	71-73-69-69=282	$750.00

1960

Beginning his reign as "The King," Arnold Palmer birdied the final two holes to win the Masters by a shot over a shellshocked Ken Venturi, then roared back from a 7-shot deficit after 54 holes and won the U.S. Open by two strokes. The Open runner-up at Cherry Hills was a chubby amateur from Ohio State named Jack Nicklaus. Kel Nagle of Australia won the British Open at St. Andrews, but it was Palmer's closing 68 to take second place that revived Americans' interest in golf's oldest championship. Jay Hebert won the PGA Championship, matching his brother Lionel's feat of three years earlier. Palmer wound up with eight victories in '60.

Los Angeles Open
Course: Rancho Municipal G.C., Los Angeles, Calif.
Par: 71 Yardage: 7,171
Last day of event: Saturday, January 9, 1960

Player	Place	Score	Earnings
Dow Finsterwald	Win	70-68-71-71=280	$5,500.00
Dave Ragan	T-2	69-71-71-72=283	$2,633.34
Jay Herbert	T-2	72-70-70-71=283	$2,633.33
Bill Collins	T-2	70-70-71-72=283	$2,633.33
Don January	T-5	72-69-71-72=284	$1,650.00
Tommy Bolt	T-5	72-71-72-69=284	$1,650.00
Eric Monti	T-7	66-71-68-80=285	$1,400.00
Fred Hawkins	T-7	71-72-71-71=285	$1,400.00
Bill Blanton	T-7	72-70-73-70=285	$1,400.00
Gay Brewer	T-10	71-72-69-74=286	$920.00
Jimmy Clark	T-10	67-76-71-72=286	$920.00
Dick Knight	T-10	74-66-72-74=286	$920.00
Johnny Bulla	T-10	68-72-74-72=286	$920.00
Smiley Quick	T-10	70-72-73-71=286	$920.00
Jack Fleck	T-10	68-73-74-71=286	$920.00
Johnny Pott	T-10	70-75-71-70=286	$920.00
Doug Sanders	T-10	68-73-74-71=286	$920.00
Monte Bradley	T-10	68-73-74-71=286	$920.00

Yorba Linda Open Invitational
Course: Yorba Linda C.C., Yorba Linda, Calif.
Par: 72 Yardage: 7,203
Last day of event: Monday, January 18, 1960

Player	Place	Score	Earnings
Jerry Barber	Win	67-70-69-72=278	$2,800.00
Billy Maxwell	2	71-71-68-69=279	$1,900.00
Harry Weetman	T-3	68-71-70-72=281	$1,300.00
Tom Nieporte	T-3	71-73-69-68=281	$1,300.00
Bob Goalby	5	71-72-69-71=283	$1,100.00

Julius Boros	T-6	67-72-73-72=284	$860.00
Mike Souchak	T-6	72-71-72-69=284	$860.00
Lionel Hebert	T-6	68-72-74-70=284	$860.00
Doug Sanders	T-6	68-73-72-71=284	$860.00
Billy Casper	T-6	70-72-71-71=284	$860.00

Bing Crosby National Pro-Am
Courses: Pebble Beach G.L. - Home
Monterey Peninsula C.C., Cypress Point C.C., Pebble Beach, Calif.
Home Course Par: 72 Yardage: 6,747
Last day of event: Sunday, January 24, 1960

Player	Place	Score	Earnings
Ken Venturi	Win	70-71-68-77=286	$4,000.00
Tommy Jacobs	T-2	70-74-70-75=289	$2,150.00
Julius Boros	T-2	73-71-72-73=289	$2,150.00
Ed Oliver	T-4	73-68-73-76=290	$1,500.00
Don January	T-4	72-71-69-78=290	$1,500.00
Gene Littler	T-6	67-73-71-80=291	$1,250.00
Billy Maxwell	T-6	71-74-68-78=291	$1,250.00
Doug Ford	8	73-76-70-73=292	$1,100.00
Billy Casper	T-9	74-73-72-75=294	$1,025.00
Paul Harney	T-9	75-73-70-76=294	$1,025.00

San Diego Open
Course: Mission Valley C.C., San Diego, Calif.
Home Course -Par: 72 Yardage: 6,716
Last day of event: Sunday, January 31, 1960

Player	Place	Score	Earnings
Mike Souchak	Win	67-68-67-67=269	$2,800.00
Johnny Pott	T-2	69-66-66-69=270	$1,900.00
Art Wall	T-3	68-68-69-68=273	$1,400.00
Billy Casper	T-4	72-68-65-69=274	$1,100.00
Al Geiberger	T-4	64-72-69-69=274	$1,100.00
Dave Marr	T-4	66-71-70-67=274	$1,100.00
Arnold Palmer	T-7	71-69-65-70=275	$850.00
Bob Goalby	T-7	69-66-70-70=275	$850.00
Don January	T-7	67-72-70-66=275	$850.00
Al Besselink	T-10	73-67-68-68=276	$730.00
Howie Johnson	T-10	71-71-67-67=276	$730.00

Palm Springs Golf Classic
Course: Thunderbird C.C.—Home Course
Tamarisk C.C., Bermuda Dunes, Indian Wells, Palm Desert, Calif.
Par: 72 Yardage: 6,680
Last day of event: Sunday, February 7, 1960

Player	Place	Score	Earnings
Arnold Palmer	Win	67-73-67-66-65=338	$12,000.00
Fred Hawkins	2	69-69-71-67-65=341	$6,600.00
Johnny Palmer	T-3	67-70-69-66-70=342	$3,350.00
Bob Goalby	T-3	67-70-69-68-68=342	$3,350.00
Ken Venturi	T-5	70-71-67-69-67=344	$2,387.50
Jack Fleck	T-5	68-72-66-70-68=344	$2,387.50
Bill Johnston	T-5	69-67-71-67-70=344	$2,387.50
Jay Herbert	T-5	71-69-69-66-69=344	$2,387.50
Gene Littler	T-9	72-68-69-69-68=346	$1,716.67
Al Besselink	T-9	68-69-70-70-69=346	$1,716.67
Tommy Bolt	T-9	73-71-69-63-70=346	$1,716.66

Phoenix Open
Course: Phoenix C.C., Phoenix, Ariz.
Par: 71 Yardage: 6,585
Last day of event: Monday, February 15, 1960

Player	Place	Score	Earnings
Jack Fleck	Win	68-68-71-66=273	$3,150.00
Bill Collins	2	70-70-64-69=273	$2,100.00
Frank Stranahan	T-3	73-68-67-67=275	$1,475.00
Jerry Barber	T-3	67-71-71-66=275	$1,475.00
Ken Venturi	T-5	68-70-66-72=276	$1,100.00
Doug Ford	T-5	66-70-69-71=276	$1,100.00
Don Whitt	T-5	70-64-72-70=276	$1,100.00
Don January	T-8	72-69-69-67=277	$875.00
Wes Ellis	T-8	72-68-68-69=277	$875.00
Lloyd Mangrum	T-8	70-69-69-69=277	$875.00
Bill Johnston	T-8	72-70-64-71=277	$875.00

Tucson Open
Course: El Rio G&C.C., Tucson, Ariz.
Par: 70 Yardage: 6,413
Last day of event: Sunday, February 21, 1960

Player	Place	Score	Earnings
Don January	Win	67-67-68-69=271	$2,800.00
Bob Harris	2	69-69-68-68=274	$1,900.00
Dutch Harrison	T-3	69-69-65-72=275	$1,300.00
Jack Harden	T-3	69-71-69-66=275	$1,300.00
Al Besselink	T-5	70-71-71-64=276	$872.86
Joe Campbell	T-5	70-71-66-69=276	$872.86
Gay Brewer	T-5	68-69-69-70=276	$872.86
Pete Mazor	T-5	70-72-67-67=276	$872.86
Arnold Palmer	T-5	65-74-69-68=276	$872.86
Butch Baird	T-5	72-70-65-69=276	$872.85
Paul Harney	T-5	64-71-72-69=276	$872.85

Texas Open
Course: Fort Sam Houston G.C., San Antonio, Texas
Par: 72 Yardage: 6,566
Last day of event: Sunday, February 28, 1960

Player	Place	Score	Earnings
Arnold Palmer	Win	69-65-67-75=276	$2,800.00
Frank Stranahan	T-2	64-73-68-73=278	$1,650.00
Doug Ford	T-2	68-71-69-70=278	$1,650.00
Wes Ellis	4	69-69-71-75=284	$1,200.00
Mason Rudolph	5	70-71-71-73=285	$1,100.00
Rex Baxter	6	71-69-71-75=286	$1,000.00
Dave Marr	T-7	74-69-69-75=287	$875.00
Fred Hawkins	T-7	73-70-71-73=287	$875.00
George Bayer	T-9	71-72-73-72=288	$753.34
Hugh Royer	T-9	72-71-70-75=288	$753.33
Dick Turner	T-9	72-71-71-74=288	$753.33

Baton Rouge Open Invitational
Course: Baton Rouge C.C., Baton Rouge, La.
Par: 72 Yardage: 6,700
Last day of event: Sunday, March 6, 1960

Player	Place	Score	Earnings
Arnold Palmer	Win	71-71-69-68=279	$2,000.00
Ron Reif	T-2	74-74-72-66=286	$1,233.34
Jay Herbert	T-2	72-72-72-70=286	$1,233.33
Doug Sanders	T-2	77-69-69-71=286	$1,233.33

Bob Goalby	T-5	73-71-76-70=290	$760.00
Lionel Hebert	T-5	75-74-72-69=290	$760.00
Don Fairfield	T-5	73-74-74-69=290	$760.00
Jack McGowan	T-5	72-73-75-70=290	$760.00
Doug Ford	T-5	77-71-69-73=290	$760.00
Jimmy Clark	T-10	76-71-71-73=291	$575.00
Dave Ragan	T-10	72-74-71-74=291	$575.00

Pensacola Open

Course: Pensacola C.C., Pensacola, Fla.
Par: 72 Yardage: 6,500
Last day of event: Sunday, March 13, 1960

Player	Place	Score	Earnings
Arnold Palmer	Win	68-65-73-67=273	$2,000.00
Doug Sanders	2	70-72-67-65=274	$1,500.00
Fred Haas	3	69-69-0-68=206	$1,200.00
Al Geiberger	4	64-70-73-70=277	$1,000.00
Ken Venturi	5	68-0-69-72=209	$900.00
Joe Campbell	T-6	68-70-66-76=280	$700.00
George Bayer	T-6	68-68-71-73=280	$700.00
Billy Maxwell	T-6	69-69-74-68=280	$700.00
Bill Collins	T-6	70-69-73-68=280	$700.00
Julius Boros	T-6	68-68-72-72=280	$700.00

St. Petersburg Open Invitational

Course: Lakewood C.C., St. Petersburg, Fla.
Par: 72 Yardage: 6,329
Last day of event: Monday, March 21, 1960

Player	Place	Score	Earnings
George Bayer	Win	66-69-75-72=282	$2,000.00
Jack Fleck	2	69-72-72-69=282	$1,500.00
Fred Hawkins	T-3	70-75-69-69=283	$1,100.00
Ken Venturi	T-3	75-72-65-71=283	$1,100.00
Arnold Palmer	5	70-72-70-72=284	$900.00
Mason Rudolph	T-6	72-72-72-69=285	$5.00
Joe Campbell	T-6	67-76-71-71=285	$5.00
Chick Harbert	T-8	74-72-69-71=286	$25.00
Fred Haas	T-8	75-69-68-74=286	$25.00
Doug Ford	T-8	71-70-72-73=286	$25.00
Dave Marr	T-8	71-72-70-73=286	$25.00

De Soto Open Invitational

Course: De Soto Lakes G & C.C., Bradenton, Fla.
Par: 71 Yardage: 6,902
Last day of event: Sunday, March 27, 1960

Player	Place	Score	Earnings
Sam Snead	Win	69-72-67-68=276	$5,300.00
Jerry Barber	2	69-68-69-71=277	$3,400.00
Dow Finsterwald	3	73-67-69-69=278	$2,200.00
Billy Casper	4	71-70-68-74=283	$1,900.00
Billy Maxwell	T-5	75-69-71-69=284	$1,475.00
Arnold Palmer	T-5	71-71-70-72=284	$1,475.00
Bob Goalby	T-5	67-74-70-73=284	$1,475.00
Doug Sanders	T-5	69-70-69-76=284	$1,475.00
Mike Souchak	T-9	73-72-71-69=285	$1,062.50
Ken Venturi	T-9	72-73-69-71=285	$1,062.50
Dave Marr	T-9	72-70-71-72=285	$1,062.50
Ted Kroll	T-9	73-70-68-74=285	$1,062.50

Azalea Open

Course: Cape Fear C.C., Wilmington, N.C.
Par: 72 Yardage: 6,651
Last day of event: Sunday, April 3, 1960

Player	Place	Score	Earnings
Tom Nieporte	Win	64-68-72-73=277	$2,000.00
Gay Brewer	2	67-71-71-70=279	$1,500.00
Don Whitt	T-3	73-67-74-67=281	$1,100.00
Dow Finsterwald	T-3	71-66-70-74=281	$1,100.00
Jerry Barber	5	67-72-72-71=282	$900.00
Bill Collins	6	74-69-73-67=283	$800.00
Don January	7	74-71-69-71=285	$750.00
Fred Hawkins	T-8	71-73-71-71=286	$650.00
Jon Gustin	T-8	75-70-69-72=286	$650.00
Jerry Pittman	T-8	69-70-71-76=286	$650.00

Masters

Course: Augusta National G.C., Augusta, Ga.
Par: 72 Yardage: 6,925
Last day of event: Sunday, April 10, 1960

Player	Place	Score	Earnings
Arnold Palmer	Win	67-73-72-70=282	$17,500.00
Ken Venturi	2	73-69-71-70=283	$10,500.00
Dow Finsterwald	3	71-70-72-71=284	$7,000.00
Billy Casper	4	71-71-71-74=287	$5,250.00
Julius Boros	5	72-71-70-75=288	$4,200.00
Ben Hogan	T-6	73-68-72-76=289	$2,800.00
Gary Player	T-6	72-71-72-74=289	$2,800.00
Walter Burkemo	T-6	72-69-75-73=289	$2,800.00
Lionel Hebert	T-9	74-70-73-73=290	$1,575.00
Stan Leonard	T-9	72-72-72-74=290	$1,575.00

Greater Greensboro Open

Course: Starmount Forest C.C., Greensboro, N.C.
Par: 71 Yardage: 6,630
Last day of event: Sunday, April 17, 1960

Player	Place	Score	Earnings
Sam Snead	Win	68-66-67-69=270	$2,800.00
Dow Finsterwald	2	67-67-70-68=272	$1,900.00
Don Whitt	3	71-71-69-66=277	$1,400.00
Lee Woodward	4	67-70-70-71=278	$1,200.00
Gary Player	5	70-68-72-69=279	$1,100.00
Mike Souchak	T-6	73-70-68-69=280	$950.00
Billy Maxwell	T-6	72-69-71-68=280	$950.00
Mason Rudolph	8	71-70-70-70=281	$850.00
Bruce Crampton	T-9	74-68-73-67=282	$775.00
Doug Sanders	T-9	71-71-70-70=282	$775.00

Greater New Orleans Open

Course: City Park G.C., New Orleans, La.
Par: 72 Yardage: 6,589
Last day of event: Sunday, April 24, 1960

Player	Place	Score	Earnings
Dow Finsterwald	Win	69-66-66-69=270	$3,500.00
Al Besselink	2	68-67-71-70=276	$2,300.00
Doug Sanders	T-3	70-70-65-72=277	$1,450.00
Huston La Clair	T-3	67-69-72-69=277	$1,450.00
Johnny Pott	T-3	71-72-63-71=277	$1,450.00
Bob Rosburg	T-3	71-66-70-70=277	$1,450.00
Jon Gustin	7	70-69-70-69=278	$1,100.00

Dick Knight	8	70-71-73-65=279	$1,000.00
Gary Player	T-9	72-72-67-69=280	$925.00
Pete Cooper	T-9	71-70-71-68=280	$925.00

Houston Classic

Course: Memorial Park G.C., Houston, Texas
Par: 72 Yardage: 7,122
Last day of event: Monday, May 2, 1960

Player	Place	Score	Earnings
Bill Collins	Win	66-71-68-75=280	$5,300.00
Arnold Palmer	2	66-71-70-73=280	$3,400.00
Jack Fleck	3	68-69-72-72=281	$2,200.00
Doug Sanders	T-4	75-72-69-68=284	$1,800.00
Gary Player	T-4	73-71-71-69=284	$1,800.00
Richard Crawford	T-4	69-75-67-73=284	
Fred Haas	T-7	70-70-75-70=285	$1,450.00
Billy Maxwell	T-7	67-72-74-72=285	$1,450.00
Fred Hawkins	T-9	73-73-73-67=286	$1,150.00
Ed Oliver	T-9	75-72-71-68=286	$1,150.00
Dave Hill	T-9	68-73-75-70=286	$1,150.00
Dave Ragan	T-9	67-75-73-71=286	$1,150.00

Tournament of Champions

Course: Desert Inn C.C., Las Vegas,, Nev.
Par: 72 Yardage: 7,000
Last day of event: Sunday, May 8, 1960

Player	Place	Score	Earnings
Jerry Barber	Win	69-66-66-67=268	$10,000.00
Jay Hebert	2	68-68-68-68=272	$5,000.00
Julius Boros	3	70-67-66-71=274	$4,000.00
Don Whitt	4	67-72-68-68=275	$3,000.00
Billy Casper	T-5	73-67-66-70=276	$1,650.00
Arnold Palmer	T-5	72-65-70-69=276	$1,650.00
Doug Sanders	7	74-67-69-68=278	$1,280.00
Doug Ford	T-8	70-73-69-67=279	$1,250.00
Art Wall	T-8	69-70-73-67=279	$1,250.00
Tom Nieporte	10	73-65-73-69=280	$1,220.00

Colonial National Invitational

Course: Colonial C.C., Fort Worth, Texas
Par: 70 Yardage: 7,041
Last day of event: Sunday, May 15, 1960

Player	Place	Score	Earnings
Julius Boros	Win	70-71-69-70=280	$5,000.00
Gene Littler	T-2	69-70-70-72=281	$2,500.00
Kel Nagle	T-2	69-68-72-72=281	$2,500.00
Ted Kroll	4	75-69-69-69=282	$1,700.00
Mike Souchak	T-5	74-69-71-70=284	$1,400.00
Ken Venturi	T-5	69-74-72-69=284	$1,400.00
Jerry Barber	T-5	68-72-73-71=284	$1,400.00
Ben Hogan	8	69-72-75-69=285	$1,200.00
Tommy Bolt	T-9	71-77-71-67=286	$1,050.00
Jay Herbert	T-9	72-75-70-69=286	$1,050.00

Hot Springs Open Invitational

Course: Hot Springs C.C.
Hot Springs, Ark., Par: 72 Yardage: 7,011
Last day of event: Sunday, May 22, 1960

Player	Place	Score	Earnings
Bill Collins	Win	68-70-68-69=275	$2,800.00
Pete Cooper	2	72-70-69-67=278	$1,900.00
Fred Hawkins	T-3	70-73-70-66=279	$1,223.34
Paul Harney	T-3	71-71-68-69=279	$1,223.33
Al Balding	T-3	70-70-71-68=279	$1,223.33
Al Geiberger	6	67-73-70-70=280	$1,000.00
Stan Leonard	T-7	68-74-70-69=281	$802.00
Art Wall	T-7	72-68-67-74=281	$802.00
Jack Fleck	T-7	69-71-68-73=281	$802.00
Dave Hill	T-7	70-70-70-71=281	$802.00
Doug Ford	T-7	70-69-71-71=281	$802.00

Sam Snead Festival

Course: The Greenbrier, White Sulphur Springs, W.Va.
Par: 70 Yardage: N/A
Last day of event: Sunday, May 22, 1960

Player	Place	Score	Earnings
Dave Marr	Win	67-67-67-64=265	$2,000.00
Babe Lichardus	2	70-66-67-69=272	$1,300.00
Gardner Dickinson	3	65-72-65-71=273	$700.00
Sam Snead	4	70-69-67-68=274	$550.00
Mike Souchak	T-5	74-67-66-68=275	$450.00
Clarence Doser	T-5	72-72-66-65=275	$450.00
Gary Player	7	72-69-65-70=276	$350.00
Al Besselink	T-8	71-66-71-69=277	$287.50
Errie Ball	T-8	70-69-69-69=277	$287.50
Frank Boynton	T-10	70-72-65-71=278	$237.50
D-Lee Raymond	T-10	75-64-70-69=278	$237.50

"500" Festival Open

Course: Speedway G.C., Indianapolis, Ind.
Par: 71 Yardage: 6,605
Last day of event: Sunday, May 29, 1960

Player	Place	Score	Earnings
Doug Ford	Win	66-68-68-68=270	$9,000.00
Jerry Barber	2	63-69-67-73=272	$4,600.00
Dow Finsterwald	T-3	67-69-71-66=273	$2,800.00
Doug Sanders	T-3	68-65-69-71=273	$2,800.00
Ken Venturi	5	67-70-69-68=274	$2,300.00
Don Whitt	T-6	67-71-71-66=275	$1,760.00
Johnny Pott	T-6	66-68-73-68=275	$1,760.00
Bob Goalby	T-6	66-73-67-69=275	$1,760.00
Gene Littler	T-9	67-70-68-700=905	$1,760.00
Jerry Pittman	T-10	67-69-68-71=275	$1,760.00

Memphis Invitational Open

Course: Colonial C.C., Memphis, Tenn.
Par: 70 Yardage: 6,500
Last day of event: Sunday, June 5, 1960

Player	Place	Score	Earnings
Tommy Bolt	Win	72-69-65-67=273	$4,300.00
Ben Hogan	T-2	66-66-73-68=273	$2,500.00
Gene Littler	T-2	74-70-65-64=273	$2,500.00
Bill Collins	T-4	66-69-68-71=274	$1,533.34
J.C. Goosie	T-4	67-65-71-71=274	$1,533.33

Bob Rosburg	T-4	65-67-73-69=274	$1,533.33
Don January	7	67-69-74-65=275	$1,300.00
Don Fairfield	T-8	71-73-69-63=276	$1,030.00
Dave Marr	T-8	68-72-69-67=276	$1,030.00
Joe Campbell	T-8	70-72-67-67=276	$1,030.00
Julius Boros	T-8	72-66-69-69=276	$1,030.00
Cary Middlecoff	T-8	70-69-66-71=276	$1,030.00

Oklahoma City Open

Course: Twin Oaks G & C.C., Oklahoma City, Okla.
Par: 71 Yardage: 6,640
Last day of event: Sunday, June 12, 1960

Player	Place	Score	Earnings
Gene Littler	Win	71-64-70-68=273	$4,300.00
Art Wall	2	70-70-67-67=274	$3,000.00
Arnold Palmer	3	68-66-75-67=276	$2,000.00
Johnny Pott	4	67-71-71-69=278	$1,700.00
Mike Souchak	5	70-69-71-69=279	$1,500.00
Denis Hutchinson	T-6	70-70-72-68=280	$1,300.00
Bob Verwey	T-6	74-66-73-67=280	$1,300.00
Bob Goetz	T-6	66-70-73-71=280	$1,300.00
Doug Sanders	T-9	69-74-75-63=281	$1,050.00
Jimmy Clark	T-9	74-69-71-67=281	$1,050.00

U.S. Open

Course: Cherry Hills C.C., Englewood, Colo.
Par: 71 Yardage: 7,089
Last day of event: Saturday, June 18, 1960

Player	Place	Score	Earnings
Arnold Palmer	Win	72-71-72-65=280	$14,400.00
Jack Nicklaus	2	71-71-69-71=282	
Dow Finsterwald	T-3	71-69-70-73=283	$3,950.00
Dutch Harrison	T-3	74-70-70-69=283	$3,950.00
Jack Fleck	T-3	70-70-72-71=283	$3,950.00
Julius Boros	T-3	73-69-68-73=283	$3,950.00
Mike Souchak	T-3	68-67-73-75=283	$3,950.00
Ted Kroll	T-3	72-69-75-67=283	$3,950.00
Ben Hogan	T-9	75-67-69-73=284	$1,950.00
Don Cherry	T-9	70-71-71-72=284	
Jerry Barber	T-9	69-71-70-74=284	$1,950.00

Buick Open

Course: Warwick Hills C.C., Grand Blanc, Mich.
Par: 72 Yardage: 7,014
Last day of event: Monday, July 4, 1960

Player	Place	Score	Earnings
Mike Souchak	Win	71-68-74-69=282	$9,000.00
Art Wall	T-2	74-68-72-69=283	$3,800.00
Gay Brewer	T-2	75-68-69-71=283	$3,800.00
Dave Hill	T-4	68-73-74-71=286	$2,333.34
Don January	T-4	71-69-72-74=286	$2,333.33
Gene Littler	T-4	69-70-73-74=286	$2,333.33
Johnny Pott	T-7	70-72-73-72=287	$1,800.00
Al Geiberger	T-7	73-72-69-73=287	$1,800.00
Sam Snead	T-9	74-71-69-74=288	$1,550.00
Mason Rudolph	T-9	71-70-71-76=288	$1,550.00

British Open

Course: Old Course at St. Andrews, St. Andrews, Fife, Scotland
Par: 72 Yardage: 6,936
Last day of event: Friday, July 8, 1960

Player	Place	Score	Earnings
Kel Nagle	Win	69-67-71-71=278	$3,500.00
Arnold Palmer	2	70-71-70-68=279	$2,520.00
Bernard Hunt	T-3	72-73-71-66=282	$1,493.34
Harold Henning	T-3	72-72-69-69=282	$1,493.34
Roberto De Vicenzo	T-3	67-67-75-73=282	$1,493.34
Guy Wolstenholme	6	74-70-71-68=283	
Gary Player	7	72-71-72-69=284	$700.00
Joe Carr	8	72-73-67-73=285	
Dai Rees	T-9	73-71-73-69=286	$242.70
David Blair	T-9	70-73-71-72=286	
Eric Brown	T-9	75-68-72-71=286	$242.70
Harry Weetman	T-9	74-70-71-71=286	$242.70
Peter Thomson	T-9	72-69-75-70=286	$242.70
Syd Scott	T-9	73-71-67-75=286	$242.70

Canadian Open

Course: St. George's G&C.C., Toronto, Ontario, Canada
Par: 72 Yardage: N/A
Last day of event: Saturday, July 9, 1960

Player	Place	Score	Earnings
Art Wall	Win	66-67-67-69=269	$3,500.00
Jay Herbert	T-2	69-67-72-67=275	$2,050.00
Bob Goalby	T-2	68-68-67-72=275	$2,050.00
Bob Shave, Jr.	4	67-74-67-69=277	$1,500.00
Ken Venturi	T-5	69-71-69-69=278	$1,250.00
Tommy Bolt	T-5	69-66-70-73=278	$1,250.00
Johnny Pott	7	71-70-69-69=279	$1,100.00
Ted Kroll	8	67-73-71-69=280	$1,000.00
Don January	T-9	65-77-73-66=281	$875.00
Doug Ford	T-9	68-70-71-72=281	$875.00
Sam Snead	T-9	67-69-68-77=281	$875.00
Gene Littler	T-9	68-68-68-77=281	$875.00

Western Open

Course: Western G&C.C., Detroit, Mich.
Par: 72 Yardage: 6,808
Last day of event: Sunday, July 17, 1960

Player	Place	Score	Earnings
Stan Leonard	Win	71-68-71-68=278	$5,000.00
Art Wall	2	71-66-67-74=278	$2,500.00
Doug Sanders	T-3	71-69-70-69=279	$1,750.00
Gene Littler	T-3	73-69-68-69=279	$1,750.00
Jerry Barber	T-5	71-70-70-69=280	$1,133.34
Dave Ragan	T-5	70-70-70-70=280	$1,133.33
Mike Souchak	T-5	74-67-68-71=280	$1,133.33
Ken Venturi	T-8	71-69-71-70=281	$730.00
Bob Rosburg	T-8	69-72-72-68=281	$730.00
Julius Boros	T-8	71-69-70-71=281	$730.00
Doug Ford	T-8	72-69-68-72=281	$730.00
Jim Ferree	T-8	71-68-70-72=281	$730.00

PGA Championship

Course: Firestone C.C. (South), Akron, Ohio
Par: 70 Yardage: 7,165
Last day of event: Sunday, July 24, 1960

Player	Place	Score	Earnings
Jay Hebert	Win	72-67-72-70=281	$11,000.00
Jim Ferrier	2	71-74-66-71=282	$5,500.00
Doug Sanders	T-3	70-71-69-73=283	$3,350.00
Sam Snead	T-3	68-73-70-72=283	$3,350.00
Don January	5	70-70-72-72=284	$2,800.00
Wes Ellis	6	72-72-72-69=285	$2,500.00
Arnold Palmer	T-7	67-74-75-70=286	$2,125.00
Doug Ford	T-7	75-70-69-72=286	$2,125.00
Ken Venturi	9	70-72-73-72=287	$1,900.00
Dave Marr	T-10	75-71-69-73=288	$1,750.00
Fred Hawkins	T-10	73-69-72-74=288	$1,750.00

Eastern Open Invitational

Course: Pine Ridge G.C., Baltimore, Md.
Par: 72 Yardage: N/A
Last day of event: Sunday, July 31, 1960

Player	Place	Score	Earnings
Gene Littler	Win	65-68-73-67=273	$3,500.00
Gary Player	2	72-68-68-67=275	$2,300.00
Al Besselink	3	70-66-71-69=276	$1,800.00
Chi Chi Rodriguez	T-4	67-67-76-67=277	$1,400.00
Bobby Nichols	T-4	71-68-71-67=277	$1,400.00
Doug Ford	T-6	68-66-75-70=279	$1,150.00
Charles Sifford	T-6	72-66-71-70=279	$1,150.00
Tom Nieporte	T-8	72-72-70-66=280	$950.00
Buddy Sullivan	T-8	69-69-71-71=280	$950.00
Jack Burke Jr.	T-8	67-69-71-73=280	$950.00

Insurance City Open

Course: Wethersfield C.C., Wethersfield, CT.
Par: 71 Yardage: 6,568
Last day of event: Sunday, August 7, 1960

Player	Place	Score	Earnings
Arnold Palmer	Win	70-68-66-66=270	$3,500.00
Bill Collins	T-2	70-65-66-69=270	$2,050.00
Jack Fleck	T-2	69-65-65-71=270	$2,050.00
Ken Venturi	4	69-66-68-70=273	$1,500.00
Lionel Hebert	T-5	69-66-70-69=274	$1,250.00
Fred Hawkins	T-5	69-70-63-72=274	$1,250.00
Chick Harbert	T-7	71-69-70-67=277	$987.50
Doug Ford	T-7	67-69-72-69=277	$987.50
Dow Finsterwald	T-7	67-67-70-73=277	$987.50
Wes Ellis	T-7	70-70-63-74=277	$987.50

St. Paul Open

Course: Keller G.C., St. Paul, Minn. .
Par: 72 Yardage: 6,557
Last day of event: Sunday, August 21, 1960

Player	Place	Score	Earnings
Don Fairfield	Win	66-68-65-67=266	$4,300.00
Lionel Hebert	T-2	64-69-6-69=208	$2,500.00
Billy Casper	T-3	66-67-71-64=268	$2,500.00
Sam Snead	T-4	68-68-70-64=270	$1,533.34
Don Whitt	T-4	68-67-70-65=270	$1,533.33
Al Geiberger	T-4	67-68-68-67=270	$1,533.33

Gordon Jones	7	68-67-68-68=271	$1,300.00
Jerry Barber	8	67-70-68-67=272	$1,200.00
Art Wall	9	70-68-67-68=273	$1,100.00
Jerry Pittman	T-10	72-68-69-65=274	$900.00
Tommy Jacobs	T-10	68-69-71-66=274	$900.00
Mason Rudolph	T-10	68-69-69-68=274	$900.00
Tommy Bolt	T-10	67-70-67-70=274	$900.00
George Bayer	T-10	71-68-65-70=274	$900.00

Milwaukee Open Invitational

Course: North Hills C.C., Milwaukee, Wis.
Par: 70 Yardage: 6,410
Last day of event: Sunday, August 28, 1960

Player	Place	Score	Earnings
Ken Venturi	Win	65-69-68-69=271	$4,300.00
Billy Casper	2	71-68-66-68=273	$3,000.00
Bob Goalby	T-3	66-69-70-69=274	$1,850.00
Arnold Palmer	T-3	69-65-70-70=274	$1,850.00
Fred Hawkins	T-5	69-65-70-71=275	$1,450.00
Mason Rudolph	T-5	67-69-68-71=275	$1,450.00
Johnny Pott	T-7	65-72-72-67=276	$1,450.00
John Mcmullin	T-7	69-70-65-72=276	$1,450.00
Ted Kroll	T-7	68-70-67-71=276	$1,450.00
Art Wall	10	70-71-67-69=277	$1,000.00

Dallas Open

Course: Oak Cliff C.C., Dallas, Texas
Par: 71 Yardage: 6,826
Last day of event: Monday, September 5, 1960

Player	Place	Score	Earnings
Johnny Pott	Win	70-66-71-68=275	$3,500.00
Bo Wininger	T-2	70-70-68-67=275	$2,050.00
Ted Kroll	T-2	72-69-68-66=275	$2,050.00
Art Wall	4	69-70-68-70=277	$1,500.00
Earl Stewart	5	67-68-73-70=278	$1,300.00
Gardner Dickinson	T-6	70-71-71-67=279	$1,000.00
Doug Ford	T-6	71-71-69-68=279	$1,000.00
Len Woodward	T-6	68-68-73-70=279	$1,000.00
Bob Goalby	T-6	74-68-68-69=279	$1,000.00
Tommy Bolt	T-6	67-71-70-71=279	$1,000.00
Doug Sanders	T-6	70-68-70-71=279	$1,000.00

Utah Open Invitational

Course: Salt Lake C.C., Salt Lake City, Utah
Par: 71 Yardage: 6,310
Last day of event: Monday, September 12, 1960

Player	Place	Score	Earnings
Bill Johnston	Win	66-67-66-63=262	$2,800.00
Art Wall	2	67-66-65-66=264	$1,900.00
Bill Collins	T-3	64-66-67-68=265	$1,300.00
Ken Venturi	T-3	69-65-65-66=265	$1,300.00
Doug Sanders	5	64-67-64-71=266	$1,100.00
Don Fairfield	T-6	67-67-68-65=267	$950.00
Dow Finsterwald	T-6	65-64-69-69=267	$950.00
Fred Hawkins	8	66-66-67-69=268	$850.00
Huston La Clair	T-9	65-70-68-66=269	$775.00
Julius Boros	T-9	67-65-68-69=269	$775.00

Carling Open Invitational

Course: Fircrest C.C., Tacoma, Wash.
Par: 71 Yardage: N/A
Last day of event: Sunday, September 18, 1960

Player	Place	Score	Earnings
Ernie Vossler	Win	69-69-66-68=272	$3,500.00
Paul Harney	2	71-66-66-70=273	$2,300.00
Ken Venturi	T-3	69-67-72-67=275	$1,650.00
Lionel Hebert	T-3	67-69-69-70=275	$1,650.00
Fred Hawkins	T-5	70-67-69-70=276	$1,200.00
Billy Casper	T-5	67-70-69-70=276	$1,200.00
Bob Duden	T-5	68-69-68-71=276	$1,200.00
Don January	T-8	63-75-70-69=277	$900.00
Don Fairfield	T-8	70-72-66-69=277	$900.00
Dow Finsterwald	T-8	72-69-66-70=277	$900.00
George Bayer	T-8	70-70-65-72=277	$900.00

Portland Open Invitational

Course: Portland G.C., Portland, Ore.
Par: 72 Yardage: 6,586
Last day of event: Sunday, September 25, 1960

Player	Place	Score	Earnings
Billy Casper	Win	68-67-66-65=266	$2,800.00
Paul Harney	2	66-69-68-65=268	$1,900.00
Don January	3	67-65-70-67=269	$1,400.00
Bob Rosburg	4	68-65-69-68=270	$1,150.00
Arnold Palmer	T-4	66-70-67-67=270	$1,150.00
Len Woodward	6	68-67-69-69=273	$1,000.00
Mason Rudolph	T-7	65-69-71-69=274	$850.00
Charles Sifford	T-7	67-71-68-68=274	$850.00
Lionel Hebert	T-7	72-68-67-67=274	$850.00
Ken Venturi	T-10	70-65-72-68=275	$730.00
Bill Collins	T-10	68-68-71-68=275	$730.00

Hesperia Open Invitational

Course: Hesperia C.C., Hesperia, Calif.
Par: 72 Yardage: 7,127
Last day of event: Monday, October 3, 1960

Player	Place	Score	Earnings
Billy Casper	Win	70-68-67-70=275	$2,000.00
Bob Rosburg	2	70-69-68-73=280	$1,500.00
Tom Nieporte	3	70-66-73-72=281	$1,200.00
Jay Herbert	4	75-67-69-71=282	$1,000.00
Ken Venturi	T-5	70-74-71-68=283	$876.67
Eric Monti	T-5	72-68-70-73=283	$876.66
Miller Barber	T-5	72-67-71-73=283	$876.66
Paul Harney	8	72-74-70-68=284	$700.00
Don January	9	71-67-72-75=285	$650.00
Butch Baird	T-10	74-70-73-69=286	$550.00
Tommy Jacobs	T-10	70-73-74-69=286	$550.00
Bill Johnston	T-10	69-72-74-71=286	$550.00

Orange County Open

Course: Mesa Verde C.C., Costa Mesa, Calif.
Par: 71 Yardage: 6,650
Last day of event: Sunday, October 16, 1960

Player	Place	Score	Earnings
Billy Casper	Win	70-68-69-69=276	$2,000.00
Charles Sifford	2	70-68-69-70=277	$1,500.00
Jay Herbert	3	71-73-64-70=278	$1,200.00

Tom Nieporte	4	67-71-71-70=279	$1,000.00
Tommy Bolt	T-5	69-65-74-72=280	$850.00
Al Geiberger	T-5	69-68-70-73=280	$850.00
Paul Harney	T-7	69-74-68-70=281	$675.00
John Mcmullin	T-7	69-73-70-69=281	$675.00
Bill Eggers	T-7	75-67-68-71=281	$675.00
Jack Fleck	T-7	73-70-65-73=281	$675.00

Cajun Classic Open Invitational

Course: Oakbourne C.C., Lafayette, La.
Par: 71 Yardage: 6,530
Last day of event: Sunday, November 20, 1960

Player	Place	Score	Earnings
Lionel Hebert	Win	68-69-66-69=272	$2,000.00
Johnny Pott	T-2	70-66-69-69=274	$1,350.00
Jon Gustin	T-2	67-69-71-67=274	$1,350.00
Billy Casper	T-4	70-69-1-66=206	$950.00
Jay Herbert	T-5	67-71-71-67=276	$950.00
Wes Ellis	6	69-72-69-67=277	$800.00
Gay Brewer	T-7	69-71-70-68=278	$575.00
Howie Johnson	T-7	70-69-71-68=278	$575.00
Bob Goetz	T-7	71-72-68-67=278	$575.00
Al Balding	T-7	70-67-72-69=278	$575.00
Jerry Pittman	T-7	65-76-69-68=278	$575.00
Frank Boynton	T-7	67-71-69-71=278	$575.00
Fred Haas	T-7	70-72-67-69=278	$575.00
Don Fairfield	T-7	71-72-65-70=278	$575.00

Mobile Sertoma Open Invitational

Course: Mobile Municipal Golf Club, Mobile, Ala.
Par: 72 Yardage: 6,383
Last day of event: Sunday, November 27, 1960

Player	Place	Score	Earnings
Arnold Palmer	Win	68-67-74-65=274	$2,000.00
Johnny Pott	2	68-66-71-71=276	$1,500.00
Dave Hill	3	68-70-69-70=277	$1,200.00
Fred Haas	4	66-68-71-73=278	$1,000.00
Billy Casper	T-5	74-70-70-66=280	$760.00
Fred Hawkins	T-5	72-70-71-67=280	$760.00
Mason Rudolph	T-5	73-65-74-68=280	$760.00
Jon Gustin	T-5	66-69-72-73=280	$760.00
George Bayer	T-5	71-70-68-71=280	$760.00
Frank Stranahan	T-10	73-70-69-69=281	$575.00
Gay Brewer	T-10	68-71-72-70=281	$575.00

West Palm Beach Open Invitational

Course: West Palm Beach C.C., West Palm Beach, Fla.
Par: 72 Yardage: 6,745
Last day of event: Sunday, December 4, 1960

Player	Place	Score	Earnings
Johnny Pott	Win	72-71-67-68=278	$2,000.00
Sam Snead	2	68-70-69-74=281	$1,500.00
Art Wall	3	69-73-70-70=282	$1,200.00
Bobby Nichols	4	72-71-69-75=287	$1,000.00
Ted Kroll	T-5	69-76-71-72=288	$816.67
Wes Ellis	T-5	74-73-70-71=288	$816.66
Arnold Palmer	T-5	71-72-69-76=288	$816.66
Fred Hawkins	T-8	75-71-75-68=289	$625.00
Tom Nieporte	T-8	73-77-70-69=289	$625.00
John Barnum	T-8	72-68-73-76=289	$625.00
Bob Goetz	T-8	74-72-70-73=289	$625.00

Coral Gables Open Invitational

Course: Biltmore C.C., Coral Gables, Fla.
Par: 71 Yardage: 6,563
Last day of event: Sunday, December 11, 1960

Player	Place	Score	Earnings
Bob Goalby	Win	67-67-71-67=272	$2,800.00
Dow Finsterwald	2	69-68-67-69=273	$1,900.00
Ted Kroll	3	68-68-66-72=274	$1,400.00
Don Fairfield	4	70-68-71-70=279	$1,200.00
Dave Hill	T-5	71-68-73-68=280	$930.00
Marty Furgol	T-5	66-71-72-71=280	$930.00
H. Williams, Jr.	T-5	69-66-73-72=280	$930.00
Wes Ellis	T-5	68-67-72-73=280	$930.00
John Barnum	T-5	65-74-69-72=280	$930.00
Bill Collins	T-10	68-71-74-68=281	$730.00
Arnold Palmer	T-10	68-72-68-73=281	$730.00

1961

Bob Goalby scored a record eight consecutive birdies (since tied by five players) in the final round of the St. Petersburg Open. Gary Player endured a one-day weather delay and won the Masters by a shot over Arnold Palmer and lanky amateur Charlie Coe. Trailing Doug Sanders by three shots after 54 holes, Gene Littler shot a closing 68 to win the U.S. Open at Oakland Hills. In winning his first British Open, by a shot over Dai Rees, Palmer became immortalized in that championship's lore when he slashed an approach shot from the side of a dune at Royal Birkdale's 15th hole and made par during Round 4. Holing putts of 20, 40 and 60 feet, Jerry Barber came back from four shots down with three holes to play to catch Don January, then won the PGA Championship in a playoff. Of more social significance, the PGA of America struck the "Caucasian only" membership clause from its bylaws.

Los Angeles Open

Course: Rancho Municipal G.C., Los Angeles, Calif.
Par: 71 Yardage: 6,827
Last day of event: Monday, January 9, 1961

Player	Place	Score	Earnings
Bob Goalby	Win	67-70-71-67=275	$7,500.00
Eric Brown	T-2	71-69-72-66=278	$3,225.00
Art Wall	T-2	70-72-69-67=278	$3,225.00
Ken Venturi	T-4	69-68-74-68=279	$2,133.34
Billy Casper	T-4	71-69-69-70=279	$2,133.33
Paul Harney	T-4	68-68-71-72=279	$2,133.33
Gardner Dickinson	T-7	69-71-72-68=280	$1,500.00
Bill Collins	T-7	67-71-73-69=280	$1,500.00
Gary Player	T-7	70-71-69-70=280	$1,500.00
Tommy Aaron	T-7	74-66-70-70=280	$1,500.00
Lionel Hebert	T-7	68-70-70-72=280	$1,500.00

San Diego Open

Course: Mission Valley C.C., San Diego, Calif.
Home Course -Par: 72 Yardage: 6,619
Last day of event: Sunday, January 15, 1961

Player	Place	Score	Earnings
Arnold Palmer	Win	69-68-69-65=271	$2,800.00
Al Balding	2	69-66-70-66=271	$1,900.00
Gary Player	3	67-69-71-68=275	$1,400.00
Frank Stranahan	T-4	69-68-71-68=276	$1,100.00
Don January	T-4	68-72-68-68=276	$1,100.00
Dow Finsterwald	T-4	72-66-68-70=276	$1,100.00
Johnny Pott	T-7	71-69-70-67=277	$850.00
Mason Rudolph	T-7	72-68-69-68=277	$850.00

Bobby Nichols	T-7	71-67-69-70=277	$850.00
Tommy Bolt	T-10	71-70-71-66=278	$710.00
Bill Collins	T-10	69-70-70-69=278	$710.00
Stan Leonard	T-10	70-65-70-73=278	$710.00

Bing Crosby National Pro-Am

Courses: Pebble Beach G.L., Monterey Peninsula C.C., Cypress Point C.C., Pebble Beach, Calif.
Home Course / Pebble Beach G.L, Par: 72 Yardage: 6,747
Last day of event: Sunday, January 22, 1961

Player	Place	Score	Earnings
Bob Rosburg	Win	69-67-74-72=282	$5,300.00
Dave Ragan	T-2	68-71-70-74=283	$2,800.00
Roberto De Vicenzo	T-2	72-66-70-75=283	$2,800.00
Gardner Dickinson	T-4	70-71-72-71=284	$1,625.00
Arnold Palmer	T-4	70-68-71-75=284	$1,625.00
Ted Kroll	T-4	69-66-68-81=284	$1,625.00
Bill Collins	T-4	67-68-74-75=284	$1,625.00
Johnny Pott	8	73-72-69-71=285	$1,300.00
Jack Burke Jr.	T-9	68-69-75-74=286	$1,030.00
Bo Wininger	T-9	70-72-70-74=286	$1,030.00
Ken Venturi	T-9	67-71-74-74=286	$1,030.00
Dow Finsterwald	T-9	69-70-72-75=286	$1,030.00
Marty Furgol	T-9	70-72-67-77=286	$1,030.00

Lucky International Open

Course: Harding Park G.C., San Francisco, Calif.
Par: 71 Yardage: 6,772
Last day of event: Sunday, January 29, 1961

Player	Place	Score	Earnings
Gary Player	Win	70-69-68-65=272	$9,000.00
Don Whitt	T-2	70-70-66-68=274	$3,800.00
George Bayer	T-2	65-66-72-71=274	$3,800.00
Don January	T-4	68-67-72-68=275	$2,450.00
Al Geiberger	T-4	70-66-69-70=275	$2,450.00
Jay Hebert	T-6	70-69-68-69=276	$2,000.00
Ted Kroll	T-6	66-69-68-73=276	$2,000.00
Stan Leonard	T-8	66-69-74-68=277	$1,500.00
Jack Burke Jr.	T-8	72-67-69-69=277	$1,500.00
Ken Venturi	T-8	70-68-69-70=277	$1,500.00
Arnold Palmer	T-8	66-69-72-70=277	$1,500.00
Billy Casper	T-8	66-69-71-71=277	$1,500.00

Palm Springs Golf Classic

Course: Tamarisk C.C.—Home Course
Thunderbird C.C., Bermuda Dunes C.C., Indian Wells C.C.
Eldorado, C.C., Palm Desert, Calif.
Par: 72 Yardage: 6,837
Last day of event: Sunday, February 5, 1961

Player	Place	Score	Earnings
Billy Maxwell	Win	68-70-68-68-71=345	$5,300.00
Doug Sanders	2	68-73-71-66-69=347	$3,400.00
Arnold Palmer	3	69-68-70-72-69=348	$2,200.00
Billy Casper	4	68-69-69-68-75=349	$1,900.00
Ken Venturi	T-5	65-71-67-71-76=350	$1,600.00
Bob Rosburg	T-5	65-69-68-73-75=350	$1,600.00
Don Whitt	7	66-70-73-72-70=351	$1,400.00
Jack Fleck	T-8	70-71-73-67-71=352	$1,200.00
Stan Leonard	T-8	71-69-71-69-72=352	$1,200.00
Al Mengert	T-8	68-65-68-76-75=352	$1,200.00

Phoenix Open

Course: Arizona C.C., Phoenix, Ariz.
Par: 71 Yardage: 6,216
Last day of event: Sunday, February 12, 1961

Player	Place	Score	Earnings
Arnold Palmer	Win	69-65-66-70=270	$4,300.00
Doug Sanders	2	71-67-70-62=270	$3,000.00
Jack Fleck	3	68-67-67-69=271	$2,000.00
Don January	4	67-67-69-69=272	$1,700.00
Johnny Pott	T-5	70-65-70-69=274	$1,450.00
Dave Marr	T-5	66-67-72-69=274	$1,450.00
Bill Collins	T-7	66-69-68-72=275	$1,250.00
Jacky Cupit	T-7	69-68-69-69=275	$1,250.00
Al Balding	T-9	68-69-71-68=276	$1,016.67
Jim Ferrier	T-9	69-66-71-70=276	$1,016.67
Wes Ellis	T-9	70-69-67-70=276	$1,016.66

Tucson Open

Course: El Rio G&C.C., Tucson, Ariz.
Par: 70 Yardage: 6,418
Last day of event: Sunday, February 19, 1961

Player	Place	Score	Earnings
Dave Hill	Win	69-66-69-65=269	$2,800.00
Tommy Bolt	T-2	69-64-69-67=269	$1,650.00
Buddy Sullivan	T-2	66-65-68-70=269	$1,650.00
Art Wall	T-4	69-67-9-66=211	$1,150.00
Charles Sifford	T-5	69-66-65-71=271	$1,150.00
Dave Marr	T-6	66-72-70-64=272	$835.00
Mason Rudolph	T-6	70-69-66-67=272	$835.00
Marty Furgol	T-6	67-66-70-69=272	$835.00
Jay Hebert	T-6	65-66-72-69=272	$835.00
Jacky Cupit	T-6	71-65-67-69=272	$835.00
Gary Player	T-6	68-68-67-69=272	$835.00

Baton Rouge Open Invitational

Course: Baton Rouge C.C., Baton Rouge, La.
Par: 72 Yardage: 6,700
Last day of event: Sunday, February 26, 1961

Player	Place	Score	Earnings
Arnold Palmer	Win	65-67-68-66=266	$2,800.00
Wes Ellis	2	68-68-68-69=273	$1,900.00
Johnny Pott	T-3	68-71-66-69=274	$1,233.34
Buster Cupit	T-3	67-71-66-70=274	$1,233.33
Gary Player	T-3	71-67-69-67=274	$1,233.33
Jack Burke Jr.	6	65-68-69-74=276	$1,000.00
Bobby Nichols	7	69-66-71-71=277	$900.00
George Knudson	T-8	66-72-71-70=279	$825.00
Jacky Cupit	T-8	69-76-66-68=279	$825.00
Butch Baird	T-10	70-71-70-69=280	$710.00
Paul Harney	T-10	70-72-69-69=280	$710.00
Frank Boynton	T-10	66-71-70-73=280	$710.00

Greater New Orleans Open

Course: City Park G.C., New Orleans, La.
Par: 72 Yardage: 6,656
Last day of event: Sunday, March 5, 1961

Player	Place	Score	Earnings
Doug Sanders	Win	68-65-69-70=272	$4,300.00
Gay Brewer	T-2	72-65-66-74=277	$2,500.00
Mac Main	T-2	72-70-68-67=277	$2,500.00

Gary Player	T-4	73-68-69-70=280	$1,600.00
Johnny Pott	T-4	68-68-68-76=280	$1,600.00
Arnold Palmer	T-6	70-71-72-70=283	$1,300.00
Mason Rudolph	T-6	73-72-66-72=283	$1,300.00
Lionel Hebert	T-6	72-69-70-72=283	$1,300.00
Jacky Cupit	T-9	72-69-72-71=284	$907.15
Jerry Pittman	T-9	70-74-68-72=284	$907.15
Al Geiberger	T-9	73-69-70-72=284	$907.14
Bob Brue	T-9	74-70-69-71=284	$907.14
Tommy Jacobs	T-9	70-73-69-72=284	$907.14
Howie Johnson	T-9	70-71-68-75=284	$907.14
Paul Harney	T-9	70-72-68-74=284	$907.14

Pensacola Open

Course: Pensacola C.C., Pensacola, Fla.
Par: 72 Yardage: 6,500
Last day of event: Sunday, March 12, 1961

Player	Place	Score	Earnings
Tommy Bolt	Win	72-68-68-67=275	$2,800.00
Gary Player	2	75-64-73-65=277	$1,900.00
Dow Finsterwald	3	72-70-67-70=279	$1,400.00
Dave Ragan	T-4	70-69-72-69=280	$1,100.00
Marty Furgol	T-4	71-70-68-71=280	$1,100.00
Gay Brewer	T-4	73-68-69-70=280	$1,100.00
Arnold Palmer	7	73-65-72-71=281	$900.00
Johnny Pott	T-8	75-72-67-68=282	$800.00
Tommy Jacobs	T-8	72-70-68-72=282	$800.00
George Bayer	T-8	70-70-70-72=282	$800.00

St. Petersburg Open Invitational

Course: Lakewood C.C., St. Petersburg, Fla.
Par: 72 Yardage: 6,329
Last day of event: Sunday, March 19, 1961

Player	Place	Score	Earnings
Bob Goalby	Win	67-62-67-65=261	$2,800.00
Ted Kroll	2	67-64-66-67=264	$1,900.00
Gary Player	3	66-68-64-68=266	$1,400.00
Bob Goetz	T-4	67-68-68-65=268	$1,010.00
Mason Rudolph	T-4	65-67-68-68=268	$1,010.00
Julius Boros	T-4	69-68-66-65=268	$1,010.00
Doug Ford	T-4	67-66-67-68=268	$1,010.00
Don Fairfield	T-4	66-67-67-68=268	$1,010.00
Joe Campbell	T-9	67-71-66-65=269	$775.00
Bob Brue	T-9	67-65-68-69=269	$775.00

Sunshine Open Invitational

Course: Bayshore C.C., Miami Beach, Fla.
Par: N/A Yardage: N/A
Last day of event: Sunday, March 26, 1961

Player	Place	Score	Earnings
Gary Player	Win	69-68-67-69=273	$3,500.00
Arnold Palmer	2	68-70-70-66=274	$2,300.00
Mike Souchak	3	70-70-68-67=275	$1,800.00
Dave Ragan	T-4	70-72-69-65=276	$1,333.34
Gay Brewer	T-4	70-65-69-72=276	$1,333.33
Julius Boros	T-4	68-67-69-72=276	$1,333.33
Billy Casper	7	70-69-71-67=277	$1,100.00
Sam Snead	T-8	70-69-70-69=278	$950.00
Bobby Nichols	T-8	71-68-70-69=278	$950.00
Jay Hebert	T-8	66-68-75-69=278	$950.00

Masters

Course: Augusta National G.C., Augusta, Ga.
Par: 72 Yardage: 6,925
Last day of event: Monday, April 10, 1961

Player	Place	Score	Earnings
Gary Player	Win	69-68-69-74=280	$20,000.00
Arnold Palmer	T-2	68-69-73-71=281	$12,000.00
Charles Coe	T-2	72-71-69-69=281	
Don January	T-4	74-68-72-71=285	$7,000.00
Tommy Bolt	T-4	72-71-74-68=285	$7,000.00
Paul Harney	6	71-73-68-74=286	$4,800.00
Bill Collins	T-7	74-72-67-74=287	$3,200.00
Billy Casper	T-7	72-77-69-69=287	$3,200.00
Jack Burke Jr.	T-7	76-70-68-73=287	$3,200.00
Jack Nicklaus	T-7	70-75-70-72=287	

Greater Greensboro Open

Course: Sedgefield C.C., Greensboro, N.C.
Par: 70 Yardage: 6,680
Last day of event: Sunday, April 16, 1961

Player	Place	Score	Earnings
Mike Souchak	Win	70-68-69-69=276	$3,200.00
Sam Snead	2	71-72-69-71=283	$2,100.00
Billy Maxwell	3	69-69-71-75=284	$1,650.00
Stan Leonard	T-4	74-69-69-73=285	$1,300.00
Charles Sifford	T-4	68-72-70-75=285	$1,300.00
Al Johnston	6	73-71-72-70=286	$110.00
Tommy Jacobs	T-7	73-71-72-71=287	$975.00
Peter Thomson	T-7	74-71-70-72=287	$975.00
Len Woodward	9	77-72-69-70=288	$900.00
Bert Weaver	T-10	73-71-73-72=289	$800.00
Gene Littler	T-10	71-71-74-73=289	$800.00
Doug Sanders	T-10	74-70-69-76=289	$800.00

Houston Classic

Course: Memorial Park G.C., Houston, Texas
Par: 70 Yardage: 7,212
Last day of event: Sunday, April 23, 1961

Player	Place	Score	Earnings
Jay Hebert	Win	69-71-69-67=276	$7,000.00
Ken Venturi	2	70-70-68-68=276	$3,600.00
Tommy Bolt	3	69-69-70-70=278	$2,500.00
Lionel Hebert	4	69-68-73-69=279	$2,200.00
Julius Boros	5	67-73-69-71=280	$1,900.00
Henry Ransom	T-6	75-68-71-67=281	$1,650.00
Fred Haas	T-6	68-71-71-71=281	$1,650.00
Jack Burke Jr.	8	67-73-75-67=282	$1,500.00
Billy Casper	T-9	71-70-72-70=283	$1,200.00
Paul Harney	T-9	71-71-71-70=283	$1,200.00
Gary Player	T-9	72-69-70-72=283	$1,200.00
Arnold Palmer	T-9	68-69-73-73=283	$1,200.00
Peter Thomson	T-9	65-71-72-75=283	$1,200.00

Texas Open

Course: Fort Sam Houston G.C., San Antonio, Texas
Par: 70 Yardage: 6,566
Last day of event: Sunday, April 30, 1961

Player	Place	Score	Earnings
Arnold Palmer	Win	67-63-72-68=270	$4,300.00
Al Balding	2	64-70-68-69=271	$3,000.00

Player	Place	Score	Earnings
Paul Harney	3	66-70-65-71=272	$2,000.00
Al Geiberger	T-4	68-65-68-72=273	$1,600.00
Doug Sanders	T-4	66-70-66-71=273	$1,600.00
Jay Hebert	T-6	69-68-69-68=274	$1,350.00
Rex Baxter	T-6	69-67-66-72=274	$1,350.00
Billy Casper	T-8	70-70-70-65=275	$1,062.50
Jacky Cupit	T-8	69-70-68-68=275	$1,062.50
Dave Hill	T-8	67-72-67-69=275	$1,062.50
Gay Brewer	T-8	70-65-70-70=275	$1,062.50

Waco Turner Open Invitational

Course: Turner Lodge & C.C., Burneyville, Okla.
Par: 72 Yardage: N/A
Last day of event: Sunday, May 7, 1961

Player	Place	Score	Earnings
Butch Baird	Win	73-72-68-68=281	$2,800.00
Rex Baxter	2	68-72-69-73=282	$1,900.00
Buster Cupit	3	70-72-72-70=284	$1,400.00
Paul Harney	4	72-69-75-70=286	$1,200.00
Jacky Cupit	T-5	72-73-73-69=287	$1,050.00
Hal Mccommas	T-5	71-68-72-76=287	$1,050.00
Jimmy Clark	T-7	71-74-69-74=288	$802.00
Bob Pratt	T-7	72-72-73-71=288	$802.00
Tony Lema	T-7	70-73-71-74=288	$802.00
Tom Nieporte	T-7	73-70-75-70=288	$802.00
Peter Thomson	T-7	71-71-74-72=288	$802.00

Tournament of Champions

Course: Desert Inn C.C., Las Vegas,, Nev.
Par: 72 Yardage: 7,209
Last day of event: Sunday, May 7, 1961

Player	Place	Score	Earnings
Sam Snead	Win	68-67-69-69=273	$10,000.00
Tommy Bolt	2	67-69-73-71=280	$5,000.00
Bill Collins	3	71-68-73-69=281	$3,000.00
Bob Rosburg	4	73-70-71-68=282	$2,500.00
Doug Ford	5	67-69-74-73=283	$2,100.00
Jay Hebert	T-6	66-67-78-73=284	$1,760.00
Stan Leonard	T-6	69-67-74-74=284	$1,760.00
Gary Player	T-6	70-70-69-75=284	$1,760.00
Julius Boros	T-9	67-71-75-74=287	$1,640.00
Billy Casper	T-9	68-70-73-76=287	$1,640.00
Doug Sanders	T-9	70-74-71-72=287	$1,640.00

Colonial National Invitational

Course: Colonial C.C., Fort Worth, Texas
Par: 70 Yardage: 7,021
Last day of event: Sunday, May 14, 1961

Player	Place	Score	Earnings
Doug Sanders	Win	69-75-67-70=281	$7,000.00
Kel Nagle	2	65-76-74-67=282	$3,500.00
Billy Casper	3	69-72-69-73=283	$2,500.00
Don Whitt	T-4	71-74-69-70=284	$1,900.00
Gene Littler	T-4	72-70-67-75=284	$1,900.00
Arnold Palmer	6	68-73-69-76=286	$1,700.00
Doug Ford	T-7	71-71-75-70=287	$1,550.00
Stan Leonard	T-7	72-72-68-75=287	$1,550.00
Gary Player	T-9	74-75-71-68=288	$1,158.34
Gardner Dickinson	T-9	71-73-68-76=288	$1,158.34
Ted Kroll	T-9	74-75-70-69=288	$1,158.33
Jack Burke Jr.	T-9	71-73-73-71=288	$1,158.33

Paul Harney	T-9	73-73-71-71=288	$1,158.33
Jay Hebert	T-9	71-76-69-72=288	$1,158.33

Hot Springs Open Invitational

Course: Hot Springs C.C., Hot Springs, Ark.
Par: 72 Yardage: 7,011
Last day of event: Sunday, May 21, 1961

Player	Place	Score	Earnings
Doug Sanders	Win	68-68-69-68=273	$2,800.00
Jerry Steelsmith	T-2	67-70-70-67=274	$1,650.00
Dave Ragan	T-2	68-70-70-66=274	$1,650.00
Al Geiberger	4	68-70-70-67=275	$1,200.00
Bobby Nichols	T-5	72-70-68-68=278	$962.50
Buster Cupit	T-5	65-72-72-69=278	$962.50
Art Wall	T-5	65-73-71-69=278	$962.50
Tommy Aaron	T-5	73-68-66-71=278	$962.50
Bill Collins	T-9	72-73-71-64=280	$732.50
Ken Still	T-9	69-70-72-69=280	$732.50
Mason Rudolph	T-9	68-68-72-72=280	$732.50
Johnny Pott	T-9	69-72-67-72=280	$732.50

"500" Festival Open

Course: Speedway G.C., Indianapolis, Ind.
Par: 71 Yardage: 6,605
Last day of event: Sunday, May 28, 1961

Player	Place	Score	Earnings
Doug Ford	Win	69-69-67-68=273	$9,000.00
Arnold Palmer	2	67-70-70-66=273	$4,600.00
Gary Player	3	70-70-67-67=274	$3,000.00
Billy Casper	T-4	69-74-70-66=279	$2,450.00
Mason Rudolph	T-4	70-69-73-67=279	$2,450.00
Jim Ferree	T-6	67-76-70-67=280	$1,900.00
Billy Maxwell	T-6	68-73-70-69=280	$1,900.00
Art Wall	T-6	68-72-69-71=280	$1,900.00
Dave Ragan	T-9	69-75-69-69=282	$1,400.00
Johnny Pott	T-9	67-72-73-70=282	$1,400.00
Bob Shave, Jr.	T-9	68-74-69-71=282	$1,400.00
Peter Thomson	T-9	68-71-70-73=282	$1,400.00
Paul Harney	T-9	69-71-72-70=282	$1,400.00

Memphis Invitational Open

Course: Colonial C.C., Memphis, Tenn.
Par: 70 Yardage: 6,466
Last day of event: Sunday, June 4, 1961

Player	Place	Score	Earnings
Cary Middlecoff	Win	67-68-64-67=266	$4,300.00
Mike Souchak	T-2	68-68-68-67=271	$2,500.00
Gardner Dickinson	T-2	63-65-70-73=271	$2,500.00
Bob Shave, Jr.	4	67-69-73-63=272	$1,700.00
Gene Littler	T-5	66-69-69-69=273	$1,400.00
Buddy Sullivan	T-5	68-70-66-69=273	$1,400.00
Lionel Hebert	T-5	69-69-69-66=273	$1,400.00
Tommy Bolt	T-8	66-69-69-70=274	$1,150.00
Ken Venturi	T-8	68-67-71-68=274	$1,150.00
Don Fairfield	10	68-72-65-70=275	$1,000.00

U.S. Open

Course: Oakland Hills C.C., Birmingham, Mich.
Par: 70 Yardage: 6,927
Last day of event: Saturday, June 17, 1961

Player	Place	Score	Earnings
Gene Littler	Win	73-68-72-68=281	$14,000.00
Bob Goalby	T-2	70-72-69-71=282	$6,000.00
Doug Sanders	T-2	72-67-71-72=282	$6,000.00
Jack Nicklaus	T-4	75-69-70-70=284	
Mike Souchak	T-4	73-70-68-73=284	$4,000.00
Doug Ford	T-6	72-69-71-74=286	$2,616.67
Dow Finsterwald	T-6	72-71-71-72=286	$2,616.66
Eric Monti	T-6	74-67-72-73=286	$2,616.67
Gardner Dickinson	T-9	72-69-71-75=287	$1,750.00
Gary Player	T-9	75-72-69-71=287	$1,750.00
Jacky Cupit	T-9	72-72-67-76=287	$1,750.00

Western Open

Course: Blythefield C.C., Grand Rapids, Mich.
Par: 71 Yardage: 6,730
Last day of event: Sunday, June 25, 1961

Player	Place	Score	Earnings
Arnold Palmer	Win	65-70-67-69=271	$5,000.00
Sam Snead	2	66-74-67-66=273	$2,800.00
Johnny Pott	3	67-71-69-67=274	$1,800.00
Billy Casper	4	69-69-71-66=275	$1,550.00
Doug Sanders	5	66-71-67-72=276	$1,350.00
Mac Main	6	70-70-69-68=277	$1,250.00
Bob Goetz	T-7	70-74-71-63=278	$1,056.67
Dave Hill	T-7	66-71-73-68=278	$1,056.67
Gene Littler	T-7	69-74-68-67=278	$1,056.66
Bob Duden	T-10	69-71-72-67=279	$870.00
Don Fairfield	T-10	70-70-71-68=279	$870.00
Stan Leonard	T-10	71-70-69-69=279	$870.00
Ted Kroll	T-10	66-71-70-72=279	$870.00

Buick Open

Course: Warwick Hills C.C., Grand Blanc, Mich.
Par: 72 Yardage: 7,014
Last day of event: Sunday, July 2, 1961

Player	Place	Score	Earnings
Jack Burke Jr.	Win	71-71-72-70=284	$9,000.00
Billy Casper	2	72-68-71-73=284	$3,800.00
Johnny Pott	2	72-68-71-73=284	$3,800.00
Dave Ragan	4	71-69-71-74=285	$2,600.00
Mason Rudolph	T-5	72-74-74-67=287	$2,000.00
Al Balding	T-5	71-70-74-72=287	$2,000.00
Ted Kroll	T-5	73-74-70-70=287	$2,000.00
Bob Rosburg	T-5	74-70-72-71=287	$2,000.00
Gardner Dickinson	T-9	71-72-75-70=288	$1,550.00
Stan Leonard	T-9	73-72-72-71=288	$1,550.00

St. Paul Open

Course: Keller G.C., St. Paul, Minn. .
Par: 72 Yardage: N/A
Last day of event: Sunday, July 9, 1961

Player	Place	Score	Earnings
Don January	Win	66-71-68-64=269	$4,300.00
Buster Cupit	2	66-67-68-69=270	$3,000.00
Dave Hill	3	70-65-68-69=272	$2,000.00

Johnny Pott	T-4	66-68-70-69=273	$1,475.00
Dave Ragan	T-4	72-69-66-66=273	$1,475.00
Mac Main	T-4	71-71-64-67=273	$1,475.00
Tommy Aaron	T-4	67-69-68-69=273	$1,475.00
Paul Harney	8	72-70-67-65=274	$1,200.00
Jim Ferrier	T-9	70-69-70-66=275	$1,016.67
Billy Casper	T-9	71-69-67-68=275	$1,016.67
Jacky Cupit	T-9	70-67-70-68=275	$1,016.66

British Open

Course: Royal Birkdale G.C., Southport, Lancashire, England
Par: 73 Yardage: 6,844
Last day of event: Friday, July 14, 1961

Player	Place	Score	Earnings
Arnold Palmer	Win	70-73-69-72=284	$3,920.00
Dai Rees	T-2	68-74-71-72=285	$2,800.00
Neil Coles	T-3	70-77-69-72=288	$1,988.00
Christy O'Connor	T-3	71-77-67-73=288	$1,988.00
Eric Brown	T-5	73-76-70-70=289	$1,120.00
Kel Nagle	T-5	68-75-75-71=289	$1,120.00
Peter Thomson	T-7	75-72-70-73=290	$770.00
Ken Bousfield	T-8	71-77-75-68=291	N/A
Peter Alliss	T-8	73-75-72-71=291	N/A
Syd Scott	T-10	76-75-71-71=293	N/A
Harold Henning	T-10	68-74-75-76=293	N/A

Canadian Open

Course: Niakwa C.C., Winnipeg, Manitoba, Canada
Par: N/A Yardage: N/A
Last day of event: Saturday, July 15, 1961

Player	Place	Score	Earnings
Jacky Cupit	Win	66-69-64-71=270	$4,300.00
Dow Finsterwald	T-2	72-68-68-67=275	$2,333.34
Buster Cupit	T-2	70-67-63-75=275	$2,333.33
Bobby Nichols	T-2	69-70-67-69=275	$2,333.33
Mac Main	T-5	68-69-69-70=276	$1,450.00
Johnny Pott	T-5	69-70-69-68=276	$1,450.00
Dave Hill	T-7	67-69-70-71=277	$1,250.00
Tony Lema	T-7	65-70-72-70=277	$1,250.00
Al Balding	T-9	70-75-67-66=278	$1,016.67
Stan Leonard	T-9	72-70-68-68=278	$1,016.67
Billy Casper	T-9	71-73-64-70=278	$1,016.66

Milwaukee Open Invitational

Course: North Hills C.C., Milwaukee, Wis.
Par: 70 Yardage: 6,410
Last day of event: Sunday, July 23, 1961

Player	Place	Score	Earnings
Bruce Crampton	Win	70-64-67-71=272	$4,300.00
Gay Brewer	T-2	68-70-68-67=273	$2,500.00
Bob Goalby	T-2	69-68-67-69=273	$2,500.00
Billy Casper	T-4	69-67-70-68=274	$1,600.00
Don Massengale	T-4	65-70-69-70=274	$1,600.00
Tony Lema	T-6	69-68-72-66=275	$1,300.00
Tom Nieporte	T-6	68-69-72-66=275	$1,300.00
Jack Nicklaus	T-6	67-72-67-69=275	
Gary Player	T-6	68-68-69-70=275	$1,300.00
Paul Harney	T-10	67-72-67-70=276	$1,050.00
Tommy Bolt	T-10	67-68-71-70=276	$1,050.00

PGA Championship

Course: Olympia Fields C.C., Olympia Fields, Il.
Par: 70 Yardage: 6,722
Last day of event: Monday, July 31, 1961

Player	Place	Score	Earnings
Jerry Barber	Win	69-67-71-70=277	$11,000.00
Playoff: Beat Don January in18-hole playoff (Barber 67, January 68)			
Don January	2	72-66-67-72=277	$5,500.00
Doug Sanders	3	70-68-74-68=280	$3,600.00
Ted Kroll	4	72-68-70-71=281	$3,100.00
Arnold Palmer	T-5	73-72-69-68=282	$2,208.34
Art Wall	T-5	67-72-73-70=282	$2,208.33
Doug Ford	T-5	69-73-74-66=282	$2,208.33
Gene Littler	T-5	71-70-72-69=282	$2,208.33
Johnny Pott	T-5	71-73-67-71=282	$2,208.33
Wes Ellis	T-5	71-71-68-72=282	$2,208.34

Eastern Open Invitational

Course: Pine Ridge G.C., Baltimore, Md.
Par: 72 Yardage: N/A
Last day of event: Sunday, August 6, 1961

Player	Place	Score	Earnings
Doug Sanders	Win	72-66-68-69=275	$5,300.00
Ken Venturi	2	68-69-69-70=276	$3,400.00
Harold Kneece	T-3	71-69-71-67=278	$2,050.00
Joe Campbell	T-3	71-69-68-70=278	$2,050.00
Mason Rudolph	5	70-74-65-70=279	$1,700.00
Billy Maxwell	T-6	72-67-72-69=280	$1,207.15
Joe Moore Jr.	T-6	71-70-68-71=280	$1,207.15
Bob Shave, Jr.	T-6	71-69-69-71=280	$1,207.14
Bobby Nichols	T-6	71-69-70-70=280	$1,207.14
Charles Bassler	T-6	70-72-68-70=280	$1,207.14
Bob McCallister	T-6	73-67-68-72=280	$1,207.14
Gay Brewer	T-6	72-66-68-74=280	$1,207.14

Insurance City Open

Course: Wethersfield C.C., Wethersfield, CT.
Par: 71 Yardage: 6,568
Last day of event: Sunday, August 13, 1961

Player	Place	Score	Earnings
Billy Maxwell	Win	69-68-68-66=271	$4,300.00
Ted Kroll	2	67-62-70-72=271	$3,000.00
Joe Campbell	3	66-67-66-73=272	$2,000.00
Doug Sanders	T-4	67-69-70-68=274	$1,533.34
Frank Boynton	T-4	66-67-71-70=274	$1,533.33
Phil Rodgers	T-4	67-66-68-73=274	$1,533.33
Gene Littler	T-7	70-68-67-70=275	$1,250.00
John Frillman	T-7	68-71-66-70=275	$1,250.00
Jim Ferree	T-9	69-66-71-70=276	$1,016.67
Ken Venturi	T-9	69-68-68-71=276	$1,016.67
Julius Boros	T-9	67-68-68-73=276	$1,016.66

Carling Open Invitational

Course: Indian Springs C.C., Silver Springs, Md.
Par: N/A Yardage: N/A
Last day of event: Sunday, August 20, 1961

Player	Place	Score	Earnings
Gay Brewer	Win	72-72-66-67=277	$5,300.00
Billy Maxwell	2	69-69-71-69=278	$3,400.00
Paul Harney	T-3	73-69-66-71=279	$2,050.00

Player	Place	Score	Earnings
Billy Casper	T-3	66-71-69-73=279	$2,050.00
Doug Ford	T-5	72-73-71-65=281	$1,420.00
Dan Sikes	T-5	72-69-70-70=281	$1,420.00
Lionel Hebert	T-5	73-71-66-71=281	$1,420.00
Ted Kroll	T-5	72-74-64-71=281	$1,420.00
Al Geiberger	T-5	69-71-70-71=281	$1,420.00
Dow Finsterwald	10	74-67-69-72=282	$1,100.00

American Golf Classic

Course: Firestone C.C. (South), Akron, Ohio
Par: 70 Yardage: 7,180
Last day of event: Sunday, August 27, 1961

Player	Place	Score	Earnings
Jay Hebert	Win	70-67-68-73=278	$9,000.00
Gary Player	2	71-67-68-72=278	$4,600.00
Don Fairfield	3	73-68-65-74=280	$3,000.00
Arnold Palmer	T-4	70-70-69-72=281	$2,600.00
Sam Snead	T-5	71-71-72-69=283	$2,200.00
Doug Ford	T-5	71-70-72-70=283	$2,200.00
Ken Venturi	T-7	69-73-72-70=284	$1,733.34
Bob Goalby	T-7	68-69-75-72=284	$1,733.33
Art Wall	T-7	67-73-70-74=284	$1,733.33
Dutch Harrison	T-10	72-76-69-68=285	$1,450.00
Billy Maxwell	T-10	68-73-72-72=285	$1,450.00

Dallas Open

Course: Oak Cliff C.C., Dallas, Texas
Par: 71 Yardage: 6,836
Last day of event: Monday, September 4, 1961

Player	Place	Score	Earnings
Earl Stewart	Win	67-72-68-71=278	$4,300.00
Gay Brewer	T-2	71-71-70-67=279	$2,233.34
Doug Sanders	T-2	70-73-70-66=279	$2,233.33
Arnold Palmer	T-2	67-69-72-71=279	$2,233.33
Art Wall	T-5	72-70-70-70=282	$1,450.00
Johnny Pott	T-5	67-72-71-72=282	$1,450.00
Billy Maxwell	T-7	71-69-73-70=283	$1,250.00
George Bayer	T-7	71-73-68-71=283	$1,250.00
Bert Weaver	T-9	71-71-73-69=284	$1,050.00
Jacky Cupit	T-9	73-69-72-70=284	$1,050.00

Denver Open Invitational

Course: Meadow Hill C.C., Denver, Colo.
Par: 70 Yardage: N/A
Last day of event: Sunday, September 10, 1961

Player	Place	Score	Earnings
Dave Hill	Win	63-64-67-69=263	$3,500.00
Art Wall	T-2	72-61-69-67=269	$2,050.00
Bob Goalby	T-2	69-65-67-68=269	$2,050.00
Doug Sanders	T-4	67-67-65-71=270	$1,400.00
Bob Rosburg	T-4	65-67-67-71=270	$1,400.00
Dave Ragan	T-6	68-69-68-66=271	$1,150.00
Bill Collins	T-6	66-72-67-66=271	$1,150.00
Don Fairfield	T-8	66-70-66-70=272	$975.00
Mason Rudolph	T-8	69-65-71-67=272	$975.00
Frank Boynton	T-10	67-69-66-71=273	$850.00
George Bayer	T-10	67-68-70-68=273	$850.00
Tony Lema	T-10	70-68-65-70=273	$850.00

Greater Seattle Open Invitational

Course: Broadmoor C.C., Seattle, Wash.
Par: 70 Yardage: N/A
Last day of event: Sunday, September 17, 1961

Player	Place	Score	Earnings
Dave Marr	Win	67-69-66-63=265	$3,500.00
Bob Rosburg	T-2	68-65-68-64=265	$2,050.00
Jacky Cupit	T-2	66-69-64-66=265	$2,050.00
Gary Player	4	69-64-66-67=266	$1,500.00
Gay Brewer	5	69-65-64-69=267	$1,300.00
Doug Sanders	6	67-69-65-67=268	$1,200.00
Phil Rodgers	T-7	68-67-65-69=269	$1,050.00
Jay Hebert	T-7	68-65-71-65=269	$1,050.00
Bill Collins	T-9	64-69-68-69=270	$925.00
Ken Venturi	T-9	70-65-65-70=270	$925.00

Portland Open Invitational

Course: Portland G.C., Portland, Ore.
Par: 72 Yardage: 6,586
Last day of event: Sunday, September 24, 1961

Player	Place	Score	Earnings
Billy Casper	Win	68-71-67-67=273	$3,500.00
Dave Hill	2	66-68-69-71=274	$2,300.00
Al Balding	T-3	70-67-72-68=277	$1,380.00
Bob Harrison	T-3	69-68-71-69=277	$1,380.00
Lionel Hebert	T-3	72-67-68-70=277	$1,380.00
Jerry Steelsmith	T-3	65-69-71-72=277	$1,380.00
Bruce Crampton	T-3	69-68-68-72=277	$1,380.00
Mike Souchak	T-8	75-68-70-65=278	$875.00
Butch Baird	T-8	71-69-69-69=278	$875.00
Gary Player	T-8	69-72-67-70=278	$875.00
Tommy Aaron	T-8	66-70-72-70=278	$875.00
Al Geiberger	T-8	71-67-70-70=278	$875.00
Gordon Jones	T-8	69-69-67-73=278	$875.00

Bakersfield Open

Course: Bakersfield C.C., Bakersfield, Calif.
Par: N/A Yardage: N/A
Last day of event: Sunday, October 1, 1961

Player	Place	Score	Earnings
Jack Fleck	Win	71-71-69-65=276	$3,500.00
Bob Rosburg	2	69-66-71-70=276	$2,300.00
Jim Ferree	3	71-70-69-67=277	$1,800.00
Gay Brewer	4	70-72-71-65=278	$1,500.00
Eric Monti	T-5	71-73-67-68=279	$1,200.00
George Bayer	T-5	70-66-74-69=279	$1,200.00
Jon Gustin	T-5	67-71-67-74=279	$1,200.00
Bob Harrison	8	71-73-67-69=280	$1,000.00
Marty Furgol	T-9	69-72-70-70=281	$925.00
Jerry Barber	T-9	70-70-71-70=281	$925.00

Ontario Open

Course: Whispering Lake G.C., Ontario, Calif.
Par: N/A Yardage: N/A
Last day of event: Sunday, October 15, 1961

Player	Place	Score	Earnings
Eric Monti	Win	68-71-68-70=277	$2,800.00
George Bayer	T-2	64-71-72-70=277	$1,650.00
Bobby Nichols	T-2	66-71-72-68=277	$1,650.00
Jon Gustin	4	65-74-71-68=278	$1,200.00

Gary Player	T-5	70-72-70-68=280	$1,050.00
Billy Maxwell	T-5	69-69-73-69=280	$1,050.00
Dave Hill	7	69-69-72-72=282	$900.00
Jack Ellis	T-8	72-73-69-69=283	$825.00
Don Collett	T-8	67-76-70-70=283	$825.00
Bob Duden	T-10	69-72-76-67=284	$710.00
Jim Ferrier	T-10	68-73-74-69=284	$710.00
Lloyd Mangrum	T-10	74-69-69-72=284	$710.00

Orange County Open

Course: Mesa Verde C.C., Costa Mesa, Calif.
Par: 71 Yardage: 6,650
Last day of event: Sunday, October 22, 1961

Player	Place	Score	Earnings
Bob McCallister	Win	69-70-73-66=278	$2,400.00
Phil Rodgers	T-2	67-72-72-69=280	$1,200.00
Al Geiberger	T-2	68-71-71-70=280	$1,200.00
Jacky Cupit	T-2	72-66-72-70=280	$1,200.00
Marty Furgol	T-2	71-69-68-72=280	$1,200.00
Don Fairfield	T-2	69-70-68-73=280	$1,200.00
Bob Shave, Jr.	T-7	72-68-69-72=281	$783.34
Jack Fleck	T-7	71-70-68-72=281	$783.33
Billy Casper	T-7	72-68-69-72=281	$783.33
Bobby Nichols	T-10	71-69-72-70=282	$655.00
Jon Gustin	T-10	68-73-71-70=282	$655.00

Almaden Open

Course: Almaden C.C., Almaden, Calif.
Par: 72 Yardage: 7,035
Last day of event: Sunday, November 5, 1961

Player	Place	Score	Earnings
Jim Ferrier	Win	69-72-66-72=279	$1,200.00
Bob Rosburg	2	72-69-67-72=280	$1,000.00
Charles Sifford	T-3	69-70-71-71=281	$900.00
John Lotz	T-3	67-68-77-69=281	
Ken Venturi	5	73-70-67-72=282	$800.00
Jerry Magee	T-6	74-71-71-68=284	$650.00
Al Geiberger	T-6	73-70-69-72=284	$650.00
Marty Furgol	T-6	70-73-70-71=284	$650.00
Bob McCallister	T-9	69-73-71-72=285	$550.00
Jack O'Keefe	T-9	69-73-71-72=285	$550.00

Beaumont Open Invitational

Course: Tyrrell Park Course, Beaumont, Texas
Par: N/A Yardage: N/A
Last day of event: Sunday, November 12, 1961

Player	Place	Score	Earnings
Joe Campbell	Win	72-71-68-66=277	$2,800.00
Bert Weaver	2	71-69-72-66=278	$1,900.00
Gordon Jones	3	70-71-71-67=279	$1,400.00
Eddie Merrins	T-4	69-71-71-69=280	$1,100.00
Jay Hebert	T-4	68-70-68-74=280	$1,100.00
Jacky Cupit	T-4	73-71-67-69=280	$1,100.00
Henry Ransom	T-7	71-69-72-69=281	$825.00
Jerry Steelsmith	T-7	71-71-69-70=281	$825.00
Don Massengale	T-7	70-74-68-69=281	$825.00
Don Fairfield	T-7	66-70-72-73=281	$825.00

Cajun Classic Open Invitational

Course: Oakbourne C.C., Lafayette, La.
Par: 71 Yardage: 6,530
Last day of event: Sunday, November 19, 1961

Player	Place	Score	Earnings
Doug Sanders	Win	67-67-67-69=270	$2,000.00
Ken Still	2	67-69-68-72=276	$1,500.00
Bob Rosburg	3	72-63-68-74=277	$1,200.00
Don Massengale	T-4	71-71-69-67=278	$900.00
Gay Brewer	T-4	73-69-69-67=278	$900.00
Julius Boros	T-4	71-70-68-69=278	$900.00
Johnny Pott	T-7	70-70-72-67=279	$700.00
Dave Ragan	T-7	71-70-69-69=279	$700.00
Don Fairfield	T-7	73-69-66-71=279	$700.00
Jim Ferree	T-10	70-70-71-69=280	$500.00
Jay Hebert	T-10	70-73-68-69=280	$500.00
Al Balding	T-10	74-69-68-69=280	$500.00
Butch Baird	T-10	74-69-67-70=280	$500.00
Tommy Aaron	T-10	72-67-65-76=280	$500.00

Mobile Sertoma Open Invitational

Course: Mobile Municipal Golf Club, Mobile, Ala.
Par: 72 Yardage: 6,383
Last day of event: Sunday, November 26, 1961

Player	Place	Score	Earnings
Gay Brewer	Win	69-66-74-66=275	$2,000.00
Johnny Pott	2	70-69-71-66=276	$1,500.00
Doug Sanders	T-3	74-71-71-65=281	$1,100.00
Arnold Palmer	T-3	72-70-70-69=281	$1,100.00
George Knudson	5	70-70-72-71=283	$900.00
Jerry Steelsmith	6	74-72-70-68=284	$800.00
Dan Sikes	7	71-71-70-73=285	$750.00
Fred Haas	T-8	75-68-73-70=286	$675.00
Pete Cooper	T-8	71-73-71-71=286	$675.00
Mason Rudolph	T-10	72-76-69-70=287	$525.00
Leo Biagetti	T-10	69-70-76-72=287	$525.00
John Barnum	T-10	71-72-72-72=287	$525.00
Frank Boynton	T-10	75-68-72-72=287	$525.00

West Palm Beach Open Invitational

Course: West Palm Beach C.C., West Palm Beach, Fla.
Par: 72 Yardage: 6,745
Last day of event: Sunday, December 3, 1961

Player	Place	Score	Earnings
Gay Brewer	Win	69-64-70-71=274	$2,800.00
Arnold Palmer	2	73-67-70-68=278	$1,900.00
Johnny Pott	T-3	72-68-71-68=279	$1,300.00
Bert Weaver	T-3	69-72-67-71=279	$1,300.00
John Barnum	5	73-71-68-68=280	$1,100.00
Bobby Nichols	T-6	71-68-71-71=281	$916.67
Sam Snead	T-6	70-72-67-72=281	$916.67
Don Massengale	T-6	67-69-74-71=281	$916.66
Ted Kroll	T-9	71-74-68-69=282	$775.00
Frank Boynton	T-9	70-69-72-71=282	$775.00

Coral Gables Open Invitational

Course: Biltmore C.C., Coral Gables, Fla.
Par: 71 Yardage: 6,563
Last day of event: Sunday, December 10, 1961

Player	Place	Score	Earnings
George Knudson	Win	65-71-71-66=273	$2,800.00

Gay Brewer	2	69-69-71-65=274	$1,900.00
Dan Sikes	T-3	66-71-68-72=277	$1,300.00
Chico Miartuz	T-3	65-74-69-69=277	$1,300.00
Sam Snead	5	70-71-68-69=278	$1,100.00
Marty Furgol	T-6	72-70-70-67=279	$887.50
Ed Furgol	T-6	68-70-71-70=279	$887.50
Dave Ragan	T-6	69-68-72-70=279	$887.50
Tommy Aaron	T-6	70-71-67-71=279	$887.50
Phil Rodgers	T-10	70-71-71-68=280	$670.00
Dave Marr	T-10	67-70-72-71=280	$670.00
Don Fairfield	T-10	71-70-68-71=280	$670.00
Chick Harbert	T-10	71-72-66-71=280	$670.00
Bill Collins	T-10	70-66-72-72=280	$670.00

1962

Arnold Palmer shot 31 on Augusta National's back nine for a 68 that bested Gary Player (71) and Dow Finsterwald (77) in a playoff for the Masters green jacket. At the U.S. Open, however, rookie Jack Nicklaus—who had won the U.S. Amateur nine months earlier—beat Palmer 71-74 in a playoff on Arnold's home turf at Oakmont. Palmer came back to win the British Open by six shots at Royal Troon. Player won the PGA Championship by a shot over Bob Goalby (who closed with 67), earning his third different major title in four years.

Los Angeles Open

Course: Rancho Municipal G.C., Los Angeles, Calif.
Par: 71 Yardage: 6,827
Last day of event: Monday, January 8, 1962

Player	Place	Score	Earnings
Phil Rodgers	Win	67-71-68-62=268	$7,500.00
Bob Goalby	T-2	64-71-73-69=277	$3,325.00
Fred Hawkins	T-2	68-70-68-71=277	$3,325.00
Jack Burke Jr.	4	72-68-70-68=278	$2,400.00
George Bayer	T-5	73-70-68-68=279	$1,900.00
Bobby Nichols	T-5	72-68-70-69=279	$1,900.00
Tony Lema	T-5	70-66-73-70=279	$1,900.00
Dave Ragan	T-8	73-71-69-67=280	$1,450.00
Don January	T-8	70-70-72-68=280	$1,450.00
Bob Rosburg	T-8	69-70-72-69=280	$1,450.00
Julius Boros	T-8	69-71-70-70=280	$1,450.00

San Diego Open

Course: Stardust C.C., San Diego, Calif.
Home Course -Par: 71 Yardage: 6,725
Last day of event: Sunday, January 14, 1962

Player	Place	Score	Earnings
Tommy Jacobs	Win	72-70-70-65=277	$3,500.00
Johnny Pott	2	71-67-70-69=277	$2,300.00
George Bayer	T-3	68-71-75-64=278	$1,650.00
Art Wall	T-3	69-70-69-70=278	$1,650.00
Bob Goalby	T-5	65-70-73-71=279	$1,200.00
Jay Hebert	T-5	69-69-70-71=279	$1,200.00
Mike Souchak	T-5	67-72-68-72=279	$1,200.00
Joe Campbell	T-8	71-68-71-70=280	$900.00
Gardner Dickinson	T-8	68-71-73-68=280	$900.00
Al Feldman	T-8	68-71-71-70=280	$900.00
Eric Monti	T-8	71-69-71-69=280	$900.00
Gary Player	T-8	69-68-71-72=280	$900.00

Bing Crosby National Pro-Am

Courses: Pebble Beach G.L. - Home
Monterey Peninsula C.C., Cypress Point C.C., Pebble Beach, Calif.
Home Course Par: 72 Yardage: 6,747
Last day of event: Saturday, January 20, 1962

Player	Place	Score	Earnings
Doug Ford	Win	70-73-69-74=286	$5,300.00
Joe Campbell	2	67-71-72-76=286	$3,400.00
Phil Rodgers	3	67-75-72-74=288	$2,200.00
Dave Ragan	T-4	70-74-73-73=290	$1,800.00
Ken Venturi	T-4	72-69-73-76=290	$1,800.00
Johnny Pott	T-6	69-75-73-74=291	$1,400.00
Mason Rudolph	T-6	68-77-71-75=291	$1,400.00
Tommy Jacobs	T-6	71-75-70-75=291	$1,400.00
Don Massengale	T-9	72-76-73-71=292	$1,000.00
Paul Harney	T-9	70-76-73-73=292	$1,000.00
Butch Baird	T-9	74-73-73-72=292	$1,000.00
Bernard Hunt	T-9	70-76-70-76=292	$1,000.00
Stan Leonard	T-9	74-74-71-73=292	$1,000.00
Ted Kroll	T-9	74-75-68-75=292	$1,000.00

Lucky International Open

Course: Harding Park G.C., San Francisco, Calif.
Par: 71 Yardage: 6,772
Last day of event: Sunday, January 28, 1962

Player	Place	Score	Earnings
Gene Littler	Win	65-68-68-73=274	$9,000.00
George Knudson	2	71-69-67-69=276	$4,600.00
Bob Rosburg	T-3	70-69-68-70=277	$2,800.00
Billy Casper	T-3	69-70-68-70=277	$2,800.00
Dow Finsterwald	T-5	69-71-71-68=279	$2,200.00
Bruce Crampton	T-5	69-72-69-69=279	$2,200.00
Al Geiberger	7	71-71-69-69=280	$1,900.00
Harold Kneece	T-8	68-73-71-69=281	$1,550.00
Lionel Hebert	T-8	73-72-66-70=281	$1,550.00
Don January	T-8	72-69-70-70=281	$1,550.00
Tommy Jacobs	T-8	70-68-72-71=281	$1,550.00

Palm Springs Golf Classic

Course: Bermuda Dunes C.C. -Home Course
Eldorado C.C., Indian Wells C.C., La Quinta C.C., La Quinta, Calif.
Par: 72 Yardage: N/A
Last day of event: Sunday, February 4, 1962

Player	Place	Score	Earnings
Arnold Palmer	Win	69-67-66-71-69=342	$5,300.00
Gene Littler	T-2	67-71-64-68-75=345	$2,800.00
Jay Herbert	T-2	69-70-66-69-71=345	$2,800.00
Tommy Aaron	T-4	69-69-68-70-70=346	$1,700.00
Gardner Dickinson	T-4	68-66-66-72-74=346	$1,700.00
Al Geiberger	T-4	71-71-67-67-70=346	$1,700.00
Don January	T-7	74-75-66-67-65=347	$1,350.00
Neil Coles	T-7	68-67-71-74-67=347	$1,350.00
Art Wall	9	72-72-69-67-68=348	$1,200.00
Dick Mayer	T-10	71-68-68-70-72=349	$1,050.00
Jim Ferree	T-10	68-69-73-68-71=349	$1,050.00

Phoenix Open

Course: Phoenix C.C., Phoenix, Ariz.
Par: 71 Yardage: 6,765
Last day of event: Sunday, February 11, 1962

Player	Place	Score	Earnings
Arnold Palmer	Win	64-68-71-66=269	$5,300.00
Bob McCallister	T-2	70-69-71-71=281	$2,300.00
Billy Casper	T-2	72-68-68-73=281	$2,300.00
Don Fairfield	T-2	70-70-70-71=281	$2,300.00
Jack Nicklaus	T-2	69-73-68-71=281	$2,300.00
Dave Hill	T-6	70-71-75-66=282	$1,350.00
Dave Marr	T-6	73-73-68-68=282	$1,350.00
Fred Hawkins	T-6	69-74-69-70=282	$1,350.00
Bill Collins	T-6	70-71-69-72=282	$1,350.00
Bruce Crampton	T-10	69-75-71-68=283	$933.34
Paul Harney	T-10	73-72-70-68=283	$933.34
Don January	T-10	70-73-70-70=283	$933.33
Jack Fleck	T-10	71-71-69-72=283	$933.33
Gay Brewer	T-10	74-67-70-72=283	$933.33
Bo Wininger	T-10	72-68-70-73=283	$933.33

Tucson Open

Course: El Rio G&C.C., Tucson, Ariz.
Par: 70 Yardage: 6,484
Last day of event: Sunday, February 18, 1962

Player	Place	Score	Earnings
Phil Rodgers	Win	76-68-65-66=275	$2,800.00
Jim Ferrier	2	66-72-66-62=266	$1,900.00
Gene Littler	T-3	67-67-67-66=267	$1,175.00
Charles Sifford	T-3	68-68-65-66=267	$1,175.00
Paul Harney	T-3	68-65-67-67=267	$1,175.00
Buddy Sullivan	T-3	61-69-69-68=267	$1,175.00
Ed Updegraff	T-7	63-68-69-68=268	
Bob Duden	T-7	65-66-69-68=268	$850.00
Fred Hawkins	T-7	69-66-63-70=268	$850.00
Art Wall	T-7	66-65-68-69=268	$850.00

Greater New Orleans Open

Course: City Park G.C., New Orleans, La.
Par: 72 Yardage: 6,656
Last day of event: Sunday, February 25, 1962

Player	Place	Score	Earnings
Bo Wininger	Win	69-71-73-68=281	$4,300.00
Bob Rosburg	2	70-73-71-69=283	$3,000.00
Doug Sanders	3	68-74-72-71=285	$2,000.00
Bert Weaver	4	71-77-69-70=287	$1,700.00
Lionel Hebert	T-5	74-73-71-70=288	$1,400.00
Jerry Steelsmith	T-5	74-69-73-72=288	$1,400.00
Phil Rodgers	T-5	69-69-76-74=288	$1,400.00
Paul Harney	T-8	75-72-71-71=289	$1,150.00
Dan Sikes	T-8	74-71-70-74=289	$1,150.00
Dow Finsterwald	T-10	69-74-76-72=291	$851.43
Bob Goalby	T-10	73-77-70-71=291	$851.43
Gay Brewer	T-10	71-74-74-72=291	$851.43
Jack McGowan	T-10	74-77-69-71=291	$851.43
Johnny Pott	T-10	74-73-72-72=291	$851.43
Ed Oldfield	T-10	68-76-73-74=291	$851.43
Wes Ellis	T-10	68-72-77-74=291	$851.42

Baton Rouge Open Invitational

Course: Baton Rouge C.C., Baton Rouge, La.
Par: 72 Yardage: 6,700
Last day of event: Sunday, March 4, 1962

Player	Place	Score	Earnings
Joe Campbell	Win	68-70-67-69=274	$2,800.00
Bob Rosburg	2	70-71-67-68=276	$1,900.00
Mason Rudolph	T-3	69-69-69-70=277	$1,300.00
Doug Sanders	T-3	69-69-68-71=277	$1,300.00
Wes Ellis	5	70-69-71-68=278	$1,100.00
Gay Brewer	T-6	72-69-70-68=279	$916.67
Howie Johnson	T-6	71-68-72-68=279	$916.67
Dave Hill	T-6	68-70-68-73=279	$916.66
Bob Goalby	T-9	74-69-68-69=280	$753.34
Jack Nicklaus	T-9	72-68-69-71=280	$753.33
Arnold Palmer	T-9	70-70-71-69=280	$753.33

Pensacola Open

Course: Pensacola C.C., Pensacola, Fla.
Par: 72 Yardage: 6,700
Last day of event: Sunday, March 11, 1962

Player	Place	Score	Earnings
Doug Sanders	Win	67-67-67-69=270	$2,800.00
Don Fairfield	2	67-70-67-67=271	$1,900.00
Billy Maxwell	T-3	69-70-65-69=273	$1,300.00
Paul Harney	T-3	70-67-67-69=273	$1,300.00
Arnold Palmer	T-5	66-71-68-69=274	$1,000.00
Johnny Pott	T-5	70-68-69-67=274	$1,000.00
Mike Souchak	T-5	70-71-67-66=274	$1,000.00
Dan Sikes	8	70-68-71-67=276	$850.00
Tommy Aaron	T-9	70-73-66-68=277	$775.00
Dow Finsterwald	T-9	71-69-67-70=277	$775.00

St Petersburg Open Invitational

Course: Lakewood C.C., St. Petersburg, Fla.
Par: 72 Yardage: 6,215
Last day of event: Sunday, March 18, 1962

Player	Place	Score	Earnings
Bobby Nichols	Win	71-67-70-64=272	$2,800.00
Frank Boynton	2	65-69-73-67=274	$1,900.00
Bob Goalby	3	70-72-68-66=276	$1,400.00
Mike Souchak	4	73-68-70-66=277	$1,200.00
Dave Ragan	T-5	70-70-72-66=278	$1,050.00
John Barnum	T-5	69-73-68-68=278	$1,050.00
Jerry Steelsmith	T-7	73-71-72-64=280	$850.00
Doug Sanders	T-7	69-69-73-69=280	$850.00
Don Fairfield	T-7	69-72-66-73=280	$850.00
Tommy Aaron	T-10	69-71-72-69=281	$730.00
Dave Marr	T-10	70-71-68-72=281	$730.00

Doral Open

Course: Doral C.C. (Blue), Miami, Fla.
Par: 72 Yardage: 7,028
Last day of event: Sunday, March 25, 1962

Player	Place	Score	Earnings
Billy Casper	Win	70-67-75-71=283	$9,000.00
Paul Bondeson	2	71-73-67-73=284	$4,600.00
Jack Nicklaus	3	69-74-69-73=285	$3,000.00
Ben Hogan	T-4	74-72-71-69=286	$2,450.00
Ted Kroll	T-4	72-72-70-72=286	$2,450.00

Bob Goalby	6	70-69-72-76=287	$2,100.00
Bobby Nichols	7	69-77-72-71=289	$1,900.00
Dave Ragan	8	74-71-69-76=290	$1,700.00
Buddy Sullivan	T-9	72-73-77-69=291	$1,550.00
Jon Gustin	T-9	74-71-76-70=291	$1,550.00

Azalea Open

Course: Cape Fear C.C., Wilmington, N.C.
Par: 72 Yardage: 6,700
Last day of event: Sunday, April 1, 1962

Player	Place	Score	Earnings
Dave Marr	Win	73-66-71-71=281	$2,800.00
Jerry Steelsmith	2	73-70-70-68=281	$1,900.00
Mason Rudolph	3	69-71-69-73=282	$1,400.00
Tommy Bolt	T-4	75-68-72-68=283	$1,100.00
Billy Casper	T-4	70-71-73-69=283	$1,100.00
Howie Johnson	T-4	72-69-71-71=283	$1,100.00
Jerry Magee	7	71-72-69-72=284	$900.00
Tom Nieporte	T-8	68-76-73-68=285	$777.50
Jack McGowan	T-8	70-72-71-72=285	$777.50
Billy Maxwell	T-8	73-67-69-76=285	$777.50
Tommy Jacobs	T-8	74-68-69-74=285	$777.50

Masters

Course: Augusta National G.C., Augusta, Ga.
Par: 72 Yardage: 6,925
Last day of event: Monday, April 9, 1962

Player	Place	Score	Earnings
Arnold Palmer	Win	70-66-69-75-68=280	$20,000.00

Playoff: Beat Gary Player and Dow Finsterwald in18 hole playoff (Palmer 68, Player 71, Finsterwald 77)

Gary Player	2	67-71-71-71-71=280	$12,000.00
Dow Finsterwald	2	74-68-65-73-77=280	$8,000.00
Gene Littler	4	71-68-71-72=282	$6,000.00
Billy Maxwell	T-5	71-73-72-71=287	$3,600.00
Jerry Barber	T-5	72-72-69-74=287	$3,600.00
Jimmy Demaret	T-5	73-73-71-70=287	$3,600.00
Mike Souchak	T-5	70-72-74-71=287	$3,600.00
Charles Coe	T-9	72-74-71-71=288	
Ken Venturi	T-9	75-70-71-72=288	$2,000.00

Greater Greensboro Open

Course: Sedgefield C.C., Greensboro, N.C.
Par: 70 Yardage: 6,680
Last day of event: Sunday, April 15, 1962

Player	Place	Score	Earnings
Billy Casper	Win	69-70-68-68=275	$5,300.00
Mike Souchak	2	68-69-70-69=276	$3,400.00
Sam Snead	3	70-72-67-69=278	$2,200.00
Billy Maxwell	4	70-67-73-72=282	$1,900.00
Arnold Palmer	T-5	71-76-68-69=284	$1,600.00
Mason Rudolph	T-5	69-70-72-73=284	$1,600.00
Dave Marr	T-7	70-70-75-71=286	$1,300.00
Jack Nicklaus	T-7	70-72-74-70=286	$1,300.00
Jim Ferrier	T-7	69-71-72-74=286	$1,300.00
George Bayer	T-10	69-73-71-74=287	$1,016.67
Julius Boros	T-10	67-76-69-75=287	$1,016.67
Jerry Steelsmith	T-10	70-69-70-78=287	$1,016.66

Houston Classic

Course: Memorial Park G.C., Houston, Texas
Par: 70 Yardage: 7,212
Last day of event: Sunday, April 22, 1962

Player	Place	Score	Earnings
Bobby Nichols	Win	68-69-71-70=278	$9,000.00
Dan Sikes	T-2	71-68-71-68=278	$3,800.00
Jack Nicklaus	T-2	68-70-68-72=278	$3,800.00
Billy Casper	4	70-69-71-69=279	$2,600.00
Billy Maxwell	T-5	69-76-69-67=281	$2,100.00
Dave Marr	T-5	69-70-73-69=281	$2,100.00
Doug Sanders	T-5	70-70-68-73=281	$2,100.00
Al Geiberger	8	73-70-70-69=282	$1,700.00
Jack Burke Jr.	9	71-73-70-69=283	$1,600.00
Earl Stewart	T-10	71-70-74-69=284	$1,310.00
Lionel Hebert	T-10	68-73-73-70=284	$1,310.00
Rex Baxter	T-10	71-68-72-73=284	$1,310.00
Jacky Cupit	T-10	67-75-69-73=284	$1,310.00
Jay Herbert	T-10	67-71-71-75=284	$1,310.00

Waco Turner Open Invitational

Course: Turner Lodge & C.C., Burneyville, Okla.
Par: 72 Yardage: N/A
Last day of event: Sunday, May 6, 1962

Player	Place	Score	Earnings
Johnny Pott	Win	68-71-69-68=276	$2,800.00
Mason Rudolph	2	69-72-72-69=282	$1,900.00
Buster Cupit	T-3	71-77-72-65=285	$1,233.34
Tommy Aaron	T-3	70-70-75-70=285	$1,233.33
Jack Nicklaus	T-3	71-73-70-71=285	$1,233.33
Jon Gustin	T-6	72-75-72-68=287	$916.67
Bob Shave, Jr.	T-6	70-73-74-70=287	$916.67
Marty Furgol	T-6	72-73-71-71=287	$916.66
Don Massengale	T-9	75-72-73-68=288	$775.00
Rex Baxter	T-9	71-70-77-70=288	$775.00

Tournament of Champions

Course: Desert Inn C.C., Las Vegas,, Nev.
Par: 72 Yardage: 7,209
Last day of event: Sunday, May 6, 1962

Player	Place	Score	Earnings
Arnold Palmer	Win	69-70-69-68=276	$11,000.00
Billy Casper	2	73-67-69-68=277	$5,800.00
Earl Stewart	3	72-68-69-70=279	$3,800.00
Doug Sanders	4	69-72-69-70=280	$3,300.00
Jay Hebert	5	71-76-68-68=283	$2,900.00
Eric Monti	6	74-70-70-70=284	$2,500.00
Gay Brewer	T-7	70-74-69-72=285	$2,125.00
Phil Rodgers	T-7	71-71-70-73=285	$2,125.00
Gene Littler	9	72-71-71-73=287	$1,850.00
Doug Ford	T-10	70-69-74-75=288	$1,650.00
Don January	T-10	75-72-70-71=288	$1,650.00

Colonial National Invitational

Course: Colonial C.C., Fort Worth, Texas
Par: 70 Yardage: 7,021
Last day of event: Sunday, May 13, 1962

Player	Place	Score	Earnings
Arnold Palmer	Win	67-72-66-76=281	$7,000.00
Johnny Pott	2	69-70-73-69=281	$3,500.00

Bruce Crampton	3	71-70-67-74=282	$2,500.00
Jack Nicklaus	4	69-71-74-69=283	$2,000.00
Jim Ferree	T-5	71-73-71-69=284	$1,750.00
Gay Brewer	T-5	70-75-67-72=284	$1,750.00
Bo Wininger	T-7	68-73-73-71=285	$1,550.00
Doug Ford	T-7	68-72-69-76=285	$1,550.00
Doug Sanders	T-9	71-71-72-72=286	$1,350.00
Gary Player	T-9	68-70-70-78=286	$1,350.00

Hot Springs Open Invitational
Course: Hot Springs C.C., Hot Springs, Ark.
Par: 72 Yardage: 7,011
Last day of event: Sunday, May 20, 1962

Player	Place	Score	Earnings
Al Johnston	Win	69-70-8-66=213	$2,800.00
Bill Collins	2	65-68-72-68=273	$1,900.00
Buster Cupit	3	67-68-70-70=275	$1,700.00
Al Geiberger	4	67-71-67-72=277	$1,200.00
Harold Williams	5	69-70-69-70=278	$1,100.00
Butch Baird	T-6	69-70-69-71=279	$950.00
Bobby Nichols	T-6	72-64-70-73=279	$950.00
Dave Hill	T-8	70-73-71-66=280	$800.00
Jack McGowan	T-8	68-75-68-69=280	$800.00
Julius Boros	T-8	69-70-69-72=280	$800.00

"500" Festival Open
Course: Speedway G.C., Indianapolis, Ind.
Par: 71 Yardage: 6,605
Last day of event: Sunday, May 27, 1962

Player	Place	Score	Earnings
Billy Casper	Win	66-67-67-64=264	$9,000.00
George Bayer	T-2	66-67-69-63=265	$3,800.00
Jerry Steelsmith	T-2	67-68-66-64=265	$3,800.00
Bruce Crampton	T-4	70-67-67-64=268	$2,450.00
Bill Collins	T-4	69-65-67-67=268	$2,450.00
Dave Ragan	6	66-65-72-66=269	$2,100.00
Gary Player	T-7	72-68-64-66=270	$1,733.34
Don Fairfield	T-7	69-66-67-68=270	$1,733.33
Joe Campbell	T-7	63-68-69-70=270	$1,733.33
Mike Souchak	T-10	69-68-68-66=271	$1,400.00
Bob Goetz	T-10	68-69-65-69=271	$1,400.00
Dave Hill	T-10	66-68-66-71=271	$1,400.00

Memphis Invitational Open
Course: Colonial C.C.
Memphis, Tenn.
Par: 70 Yardage: 6,466
Last day of event: Sunday, June 3, 1962

Player	Place	Score	Earnings
Lionel Hebert	Win	67-69-64-67=267	$6,400.00
Gary Player	T-2	65-66-68-68=267	$3,050.00
Gene Littler	T-2	66-67-68-66=267	$3,050.00
Bruce Crampton	T-4	70-63-68-67=268	$2,050.00
Jay Herbert	T-4	68-65-65-70=268	$2,050.00
Don January	T-6	65-67-73-67=272	$650.00
Tommy Jacobs	T-6	68-65-68-71=272	$650.00
Billy Maxwell	T-8	65-70-70-68=273	$1,450.00
Bert Weaver	T-8	69-68-67-69=273	$1,450.00
Bob Verwey	T-10	69-68-69-68=274	$1,200.00
Gay Brewer	T-10	64-71-68-71=274	$1,200.00
Julius Boros	T-10	67-70-66-71=274	$1,200.00

Thunderbird Classic Invitational
Course: Upper Montclair C.C., Clifton, N.J.
Par: 71 Yardage: 7,055
Last day of event: Sunday, June 10, 1962

Player	Place	Score	Earnings
Gene Littler	Win	67-71-70-67=275	$25,000.00
Jack Nicklaus	2	69-73-65-70=277	$10,000.00
Dow Finsterwald	T-3	72-68-67-73=280	$5,000.00
Wes Ellis	T-3	73-67-69-71=280	$5,000.00
Butch Baird	5	73-68-68-72=281	$3,500.00
Bob Goalby	T-6	70-71-71-70=282	$2,900.00
Paul Harney	T-6	71-68-70-73=282	$2,900.00
Bruce Crampton	T-8	73-70-75-65=283	$2,300.00
Fred Hawkins	T-8	68-73-69-73=283	$2,300.00
Sam Snead	T-10	70-66-78-70=284	$1,900.00
Jim Ferrier	T-10	74-70-69-71=284	$1,900.00
Jack Burke Jr.	T-10	69-72-70-73=284	$1,900.00

U.S. Open
Course: Oakmont C.C., Oakmont, Pa.
Par: 71 Yardage: 6,893
Last day of event: Sunday, June 17, 1962

Player	Place	Score	Earnings
Jack Nicklaus	Win	72-70-72-69-71=283	$17,500.00
Playoff: Beat Arnold Palmer in 18 hole playoff (Nicklaus 71, Palmer 74)			
Arnold Palmer	2	71-68-73-71-74=283	$10,500.00
Bobby Nichols	T-3	70-72-70-73=285	$5,500.00
Phil Rodgers	T-3	74-70-69-72=285	$5,500.00
Gay Brewer	5	73-72-73-69=287	$4,000.00
Gary Player	T-6	71-71-72-74=288	$2,750.00
Tommy Jacobs	T-6	74-71-73-70=288	$2,750.00
Billy Maxwell	T-8	71-70-75-74=290	$1,766.67
Doug Ford	T-8	74-75-71-70=290	$1,766.67
Gene Littler	T-8	69-74-72-75=290	$1,766.66

Eastern Open Invitational
Course: Mount Pleasant C.C., Baltimore, Md.
Par: 72 Yardage: N/A
Last day of event: Sunday, June 24, 1962

Player	Place	Score	Earnings
Doug Ford	Win	69-65-73-72=279	$5,300.00
Bob Goalby	2	71-73-67-69=280	$3,400.00
Tony Lema	3	75-67-70-69=281	$2,200.00
Ted Kroll	4	72-74-67-69=282	$1,900.00
Bobby Nichols	5	70-70-73-70=283	$1,700.00
Charles Bassler	T-6	70-72-68-75=285	$1,450.00
Chi Chi Rodriguez	T-6	73-70-69-73=285	$1,450.00
Stan Leonard	T-8	72-70-75-69=286	$1,250.00
Howie Johnson	T-8	73-67-74-72=286	$1,250.00
Jim Ferrier	T-10	73-70-74-70=287	$933.34
Doug Sanders	T-10	74-72-70-71=287	$933.34
Julius Boros	T-10	70-70-76-71=287	$933.33
Al Geiberger	T-10	73-72-72-70=287	$933.33
Bob Shave, Jr.	T-10	71-70-74-72=287	$933.33
Charles Sifford	T-10	70-72-70-75=287	$933.33

Texas Open

Course: Oak Hills C.C., San Antonio, Texas
Par: 70 Yardage: 6,576
Last day of event: Friday, June 29, 1962

Player	Place	Score	Earnings
Arnold Palmer	Win	67-69-70-67=273	$4,300.00
Mason Rudolph	T-2	70-67-70-67=274	$2,050.00
Doug Sanders	T-2	70-69-66-69=274	$2,050.00
Joe Campbell	T-2	67-68-69-70=274	$2,050.00
Gene Littler	T-2	68-69-68-69=274	$2,050.00
Dave Marr	6	69-67-70-70=276	$1,400.00
Dave Hill	T-7	71-71-69-66=277	$1,250.00
Jack Burke Jr.	T-7	72-69-69-67=277	$1,250.00
Bob Goalby	T-9	68-72-72-66=278	$933.34
Tommy Aaron	T-9	72-72-67-67=278	$933.34
Mike Souchak	T-9	70-70-67-71=278	$933.33
Phil Rodgers	T-9	72-70-65-71=278	$933.33
Jon Gustin	T-9	69-70-68-71=278	$933.33
Dan Sikes	T-9	73-65-70-70=278	$933.33

Western Open

Course: Medinah C.C. (No 3), Medinah, Ill.
Par: 71 Yardage: 7,014
Last day of event: Sunday, July 1, 1962

Player	Place	Score	Earnings
Jacky Cupit	Win	69-70-71-71=281	$11,000.00
Billy Casper	2	72-73-71-67=283	$5,500.00
Fred Hawkins	T-3	68-72-76-70=286	$3,075.00
Gary Player	T-3	72-69-69-76=286	$3,075.00
Al Geiberger	T-5	71-75-72-69=287	$2,200.00
Julius Boros	T-5	73-72-70-72=287	$2,200.00
Arnold Palmer	7	73-74-72-69=288	$1,900.00
Harold Kneece	T-8	72-72-74-73=291	$1,500.00
Dow Finsterwald	T-8	71-75-72-73=291	$1,500.00
Jack Nicklaus	T-8	70-73-73-75=291	$1,500.00
Stan Leonard	T-8	76-69-72-74=291	$1,500.00
Jim Ferree	T-8	75-70-70-76=291	$1,500.00

Buick Open

Course: Warwick Hills C.C., Grand Blanc, Mich.
Par: 72 Yardage: 7,014
Last day of event: Sunday, July 8, 1962

Player	Place	Score	Earnings
Bill Collins	Win	70-71-71-72=284	$9,000.00
Dave Ragan	2	71-75-67-72=285	$4,600.00
Billy Casper	T-3	74-70-72-70=286	$2,800.00
Doug Sanders	T-3	73-69-72-72=286	$2,800.00
Joe Campbell	5	74-71-69-73=287	$2,300.00
Johnny Pott	T-6	70-73-73-72=288	$1,825.00
Jerry Barber	T-6	71-71-72-74=288	$1,825.00
Bob Goalby	T-6	71-73-71-73=288	$1,825.00
Tony Lema	T-6	71-69-72-76=288	$1,825.00
Rex Baxter	T-10	72-74-73-70=289	$1,350.00
Bob Shave, Jr.	T-10	72-72-73-72=289	$1,350.00
Al Geiberger	T-10	72-71-73-73=289	$1,350.00
Pete Cooper	T-10	71-69-72-77=289	$1,350.00

British Open

Course: Royal Troon G.C., Troon, Ayrshire, Scotland
Par: 72 Yardage: 7,045
Last day of event: Friday, July 13, 1962

Player	Place	Score	Earnings
Arnold Palmer	Win	71-69-67-69=276	$3,920.00
Kel Nagle	2	71-71-70-70=282	$2,800.00
Brian Huggett	T-3	75-71-74-69=289	$1,988.00
Phil Rodgers	T-3	75-70-72-72=289	$1,988.00
Bob Charles	5	75-70-70-75=290	$1,330.00
Peter Thomson	T-6	70-77-75-70=292	$840.00
Sam Snead	T-6	76-73-72-71=292	$840.00
Dave Thomas	T-8	77-70-71-75=293	$532.00
Peter Alliss	T-8	77-69-74-73=293	$532.00
Syd Scott	10	77-74-75-68=294	$406.00

Motor City Open Invitational

Course: Knollwood C.C., Detroit, Mich..
Par: 71 Yardage: N/A
Last day of event: Sunday, July 15, 1962

Player	Place	Score	Earnings
Bruce Crampton	Win	66-65-70-66=267	$5,300.00
Dave Hill	T-2	71-66-69-64=270	$2,800.00
Don Massengale	T-2	67-66-68-69=270	$2,800.00
Dave Ragan	4	66-66-69-70=271	$1,900.00
Billy Casper	5	66-67-71-68=272	$1,700.00
Doug Ford	6	70-67-68-69=274	$1,500.00
Butch Baird	T-7	73-67-67-68=275	$1,350.00
Julius Boros	T-7	71-68-68-70=275	$1,350.00
Mason Rudolph	T-9	70-70-66-70=276	$1,062.50
Pete Cooper	T-9	65-72-68-71=276	$1,062.50
Tommy Jacobs	T-9	69-68-69-70=276	$1,062.50
Bob Goalby	T-9	70-67-67-72=276	$1,062.50

PGA Championship

Course: Aronimink G.C., Newton Square, Pa.
Par: 70 Yardage: 7,045
Last day of event: Sunday, July 22, 1962

Player	Place	Score	Earnings
Gary Player	Win	72-67-69-70=278	$13,000.00
Bob Goalby	2	69-72-71-67=279	$6,700.00
George Bayer	T-3	69-70-71-71=281	$3,450.00
Jack Nicklaus	T-3	71-74-69-67=281	$3,450.00
Doug Ford	5	69-69-73-71=282	$2,900.00
Bobby Nichols	6	72-70-71-70=283	$2,500.00
Dave Ragan	T-7	72-74-70-68=284	$2,066.67
Jack Fleck	T-7	74-69-70-71=284	$2,066.66
Paul Harney	T-7	70-73-72-69=284	$2,066.67
Jay Hebert	10	73-72-70-70=285	$1,750.00

Canadian Open

Course: Laval sur le lac, Laval sur le lac, Quebec, Canada
Par: N/A Yardage: N/A
Last day of event: Sunday, July 29, 1962

Player	Place	Score	Earnings
Ted Kroll	Win	71-68-69-70=278	$4,300.00
Charles Sifford	2	71-67-70-72=280	$3,000.00
Art Wall	3	72-73-70-66=281	$2,000.00
Bruce Crampton	4	71-68-76-67=282	$1,700.00
Jack Nicklaus	T-5	70-75-68-71=284	$1,450.00

Bob Shave, Jr.	T-5	70-71-73-70=284	$1,450.00
Don Fairfield	T-7	69-71-75-70=285	$1,250.00
Wilf Homenuik	T-7	70-69-75-71=285	$1,250.00
George Bayer	T-9	69-72-75-70=286	$987.50
Jim Ferrier	T-9	73-74-71-68=286	$987.50
Al Geiberger	T-9	72-73-68-73=286	$987.50
Bob Rosburg	T-9	71-71-72-72=286	$987.50

Insurance City Open

Course: Wethersfield C.C., Wethersfield, CT.
Par: 71 Yardage: 6,568
Last day of event: Sunday, August 5, 1962

Player	Place	Score	Earnings
Bob Goalby	Win	69-69-66-67=271	$5,300.00
Art Wall	2	65-70-66-70=271	$3,400.00
Julius Boros	T-3	69-65-72-66=272	$2,050.00
Jerry Steelsmith	T-3	67-67-69-69=272	$2,050.00
Gene Littler	T-5	68-66-71-68=273	$1,600.00
Paul Harney	T-5	66-66-71-70=273	$1,600.00
Bruce Crampton	7	70-67-68-69=274	$1,400.00
Al Geiberger	8	69-68-69-69=275	$1,300.00
Howie Johnson	T-9	73-64-68-71=276	$1,150.00
Jack Burke Jr.	T-9	70-64-70-72=276	$1,150.00

American Golf Classic

Course: Firestone C.C. (South), Akron, Ohio
Par: 70 Yardage: 7,180
Last day of event: Sunday, August 12, 1962

Player	Place	Score	Earnings
Arnold Palmer	Win	67-69-70-70=276	$9,000.00
Mason Rudolph	2	73-73-69-66=281	$4,600.00
Jack Nicklaus	T-3	72-70-71-71=284	$2,500.00
Al Geiberger	T-3	73-73-66-72=284	$2,500.00
Billy Maxwell	T-3	74-69-70-71=284	$2,500.00
Don January	T-3	71-70-72-71=284	$2,500.00
Frank Stranahan	T-7	73-71-75-68=287	$1,800.00
Gene Littler	T-7	72-71-73-71=287	$1,800.00
Fred Hawkins	T-9	74-71-72-71=288	$1,550.00
Bob Goalby	T-9	73-69-70-76=288	$1,550.00

St. Paul Open

Course: Keller G.C., St. Paul, Minn. .
Par: 72 Yardage: N/A
Last day of event: Sunday, August 19, 1962

Player	Place	Score	Earnings
Doug Sanders	Win	66-69-69-65=269	$4,300.00
Dave Hill	2	67-70-68-67=272	$3,000.00
Gary Player	T-3	70-67-69-67=273	$1,850.00
Dave Ragan	T-3	66-68-71-68=273	$1,850.00
Phil Rodgers	T-5	72-68-68-67=275	$1,450.00
Johnny Pott	T-5	67-67-70-71=275	$1,450.00
Frank Wharton	7	66-71-67-72=276	$1,300.00
Jimmy Powell	T-8	71-69-70-67=277	$1,100.00
Dow Finsterwald	T-8	68-69-73-67=277	$1,100.00
Tommy Bolt	T-8	68-69-71-69=277	$1,100.00
George Boutell	T-8	70-70-68-69=277	

Oklahoma City Open

Course: Quail Creek C.C., Oklahoma City, Okla.
Par: 72 Yardage: 7,173
Last day of event: Sunday, August 26, 1962

Player	Place	Score	Earnings
Doug Sanders	Win	70-69-74-67=280	$5,300.00
Johnny Pott	2	68-73-71-70=282	$3,400.00
Don Massengale	3	69-68-70-77=284	$2,200.00
Terry Dill	T-4	68-72-76-69=285	$1,800.00
Tony Lema	T-4	77-68-70-70=285	$1,800.00
Dave Hill	T-6	72-68-76-70=286	$1,400.00
Tommy Jacobs	T-6	71-71-73-71=286	$1,400.00
Frank Boynton	T-6	74-68-72-72=286	$1,400.00
Terry Wilcox	T-9	75-69-74-71=289	$1,100.00
Gene Littler	T-9	69-72-74-74=289	$1,100.00
Bob Goalby	T-9	74-69-73-73=289	$1,100.00

Dallas Open

Course: Oak Cliff C.C., Dallas, Texas
Par: 71 Yardage: 6,836
Last day of event: Monday, September 3, 1962

Player	Place	Score	Earnings
Billy Maxwell	Win	68-70-68-71=277	$5,300.00
Johnny Pott	2	69-71-70-71=281	$3,400.00
Charles Sifford	T-3	69-71-75-67=282	$2,050.00
Chi Chi Rodriguez	T-3	67-75-69-71=282	$2,050.00
Doug Sanders	T-5	70-72-72-69=283	$1,420.00
Gene Littler	T-5	72-69-74-68=283	$1,420.00
Jay Herbert	T-5	73-72-70-68=283	$1,420.00
Bruce Crampton	T-5	69-71-72-71=283	$1,420.00
Jack Nicklaus	T-5	72-71-68-72=283	$1,420.00
Mason Rudolph	10	73-69-71-71=284	$1,100.00

Denver Open Invitational

Course: Denver C.C., Denver, Colo.
Par: N/A Yardage: N/A
Last day of event: Sunday, September 9, 1962

Player	Place	Score	Earnings
Bob Goalby	Win	72-69-67-69=277	$4,300.00
Jack Fleck	T-2	69-68-74-67=278	$1,816.67
Billy Maxwell	T-2	71-70-70-67=278	$1,816.67
Bob Duden	T-2	70-72-68-68=278	$1,816.67
Bill Johnston	T-2	67-71-69-71=278	$1,816.67
George Bayer	T-2	68-69-71-70=278	$1,816.66
Art Wall	T-2	68-69-72-69=278	$1,816.66
Dow Finsterwald	T-8	67-74-74-64=279	$1,062.50
Julius Boros	T-8	74-71-67-67=279	$1,062.50
Don Massengale	T-8	68-72-72-67=279	$1,062.50
Dave Marr	T-8	70-67-73-69=279	$1,062.50

Seattle World's Fair Open Invitational

Course: Broadmoor C.C., Seattle, Wash.
Par: 70 Yardage: N/A
Last day of event: Sunday, September 16, 1962

Player	Place	Score	Earnings
Jack Nicklaus	Win	67-65-65-68=265	$4,300.00
Tony Lema	2	72-66-66-63=267	$3,000.00
Art Wall	3	69-66-67-66=268	$2,000.00
Bob Harrison	4	67-67-68-67=269	$1,700.00
Gary Player	5	68-67-64-71=270	$1,500.00

Julius Boros	T-6	68-66-69-68=271	$1,250.00
Don January	T-6	68-68-67-68=271	$1,250.00
Arnold Palmer	T-6	70-65-68-68=271	$1,250.00
Al Johnston	T-6	71-67-64-69=271	$1,250.00
Tommy Jacobs	T-10	69-72-69-62=272	$828.75
George Bayer	T-10	71-68-68-65=272	$828.75
Larry Mowry	T-10	65-71-69-67=272	$828.75
Billy Maxwell	T-10	67-65-72-68=272	$828.75
Jack Fleck	T-10	68-68-67-69=272	$828.75
Fred Hawkins	T-10	67-67-69-69=272	$828.75
Billy Casper	T-10	67-63-71-71=272	$828.75
Bob Rosburg	T-10	69-67-65-71=272	$828.75

Portland Open Invitational

Course: Portland G.C., Portland, Ore.
Par: 72 Yardage: 6,586
Last day of event: Sunday, September 23, 1962

Player	Place	Score	Earnings
Jack Nicklaus	Win	64-69-67-69=269	$3,500.00
George Bayer	2	67-69-69-65=270	$2,300.00
Billy Casper	3	66-68-67-71=272	$1,800.00
Doug Sanders	T-4	69-68-68-69=274	$1,275.00
Don January	T-4	70-70-66-68=274	$1,275.00
Ron Weber	T-4	67-70-67-70=274	$1,275.00
Butch Baird	T-4	68-67-68-71=274	$1,275.00
Phil Rodgers	T-8	70-71-70-64=275	$950.00
Gay Brewer	T-8	72-68-67-68=275	$950.00
Dutch Harrison	T-8	69-69-68-69=275	$950.00

Sahara Invitational

Course: Paradise Valley C.C., Las Vegas, Nev.
Par: 71 Yardage: 7,069
Last day of event: Sunday, September 30, 1962

Player	Place	Score	Earnings
Tony Lema	Win	69-67-66-68=270	$2,800.00
Don January	2	69-67-67-70=273	$1,900.00
Billy Casper	3	68-67-72-69=276	$1,400.00
Dave Hill	4	69-69-67-72=277	$1,200.00
Jacky Cupit	T-5	71-68-69-70=278	$962.50
Charles Sifford	T-5	70-69-69-70=278	$962.50
Jay Herbert	T-5	70-67-72-69=278	$962.50
Julius Boros	T-5	71-66-70-71=278	$962.50
Bob Brue	9	71-69-69-71=280	$800.00
Don Massengale	T-10	71-71-67-72=281	$650.00
Rex Baxter	T-10	71-69-68-73=281	$650.00
George Bayer	T-10	69-71-68-73=281	$650.00
Ken Still	T-10	71-68-69-73=281	$650.00
Frank Wharton	T-10	67-71-73-70=281	$650.00
Jon Gustin	T-10	72-63-76-70=281	$650.00

Beaumont Open Invitational

Course: Tyrrell Park Course, Beaumont, Texas
Par: N/A Yardage: N/A
Last day of event: Sunday, November 4, 1962

Player	Place	Score	Earnings
Dave Ragan	Win	70-72-71-70=283	$2,800.00
Don Massengale	T-2	70-72-77-67=286	$1,500.00
Dow Finsterwald	T-2	73-70-70-73=286	$1,500.00
Lionel Hebert	T-2	71-69-70-76=286	$1,500.00
Bo Wininger	T-5	67-75-77-68=287	$1,000.00
Rex Baxter	T-5	71-70-75-71=287	$1,000.00

Jerry Steelsmith	T-5	70-74-72-71=287	$1,000.00
Doug Sanders	T-8	73-71-75-69=288	$800.00
Jimmy Wright	T-8	70-72-73-73=288	$800.00
Bert Weaver	T-8	73-67-73-75=288	$800.00

Cajun Classic Open Invitational

Course: Oakbourne C.C., Lafayette, La.
Par: 71 Yardage: 6,750
Last day of event: Sunday, November 11, 1962

Player	Place	Score	Earnings
John Barnum	Win	68-70-63-69=270	$2,400.00
Gay Brewer	2	66-71-69-70=276	$1,700.00
Bo Wininger	3	73-68-66-68=275	$1,300.00
Dave Hill	T-4	69-74-71-66=280	$1,050.00
Dave Ragan	T-4	71-70-68-71=280	$1,050.00
Lionel Hebert	6	70-69-70-73=282	$900.00
Bob Goetz	T-7	69-74-71-69=283	$775.00
Jerry Pittman	T-7	69-71-72-71=283	$775.00
Bob Brue	T-7	69-74-67-73=283	$775.00
Cashere Jawor	T-10	73-67-74-70=284	$607.50
Jack McGowan	T-10	70-72-70-72=284	$607.50
Don Fairfield	T-10	68-72-70-74=284	$607.50
John Langford	T-10	72-70-69-73=284	$607.50

Mobile Sertoma Open Invitational

Course: Mobile Municipal Golf Club, Mobile, Al.
Par: 72 Yardage: 6,383
Last day of event: Sunday, November 18, 1962

Player	Place	Score	Earnings
Tony Lema	Win	67-68-68-70=273	$2,000.00
Doug Sanders	2	71-71-71-67=280	$1,500.00
Dave Ragan	T-3	71-70-70-70=281	$1,033.34
George Knudson	T-3	68-69-73-71=281	$1,033.33
Jim Ferree	T-3	69-75-66-71=281	$1,033.33
Jerry Pittman	6	74-68-71-69=282	$800.00
Don Fairfield	T-7	70-72-68-73=283	$725.00
Harold Kneece	T-7	70-72-68-73=283	$725.00
Gay Brewer	T-9	69-68-74-73=284	$625.00
Bert Weaver	T-9	70-71-69-74=284	$625.00

Carling Open Invitational

Course: Rio Pinar C.C., Orlando, Fla.
Par: 71 Yardage: 6,873
Last day of event: Sunday, November 25, 1962

Player	Place	Score	Earnings
Bo Wininger	Win	71-71-65-67=274	$5,300.00
Bert Weaver	2	65-73-68-69=275	$3,400.00
Dow Finsterwald	3	69-69-71-68=277	$2,200.00
Miller Barber	T-4	71-71-72-65=279	$1,800.00
Ted Kroll	T-4	69-68-71-71=279	$1,800.00
Dan Sikes	T-6	70-71-71-69=281	$1,400.00
Johnny Pott	T-6	73-71-68-69=281	$1,400.00
Paul Bondeson	T-6	71-68-70-72=281	$1,400.00
J.C. Goosie	T-9	74-72-69-67=282	$1,030.00
Bob Cajda	T-9	69-71-73-69=282	$1,030.00
George Bayer	T-9	71-68-74-69=282	$1,030.00
Joe Lopez, Jr.	T-9	69-72-71-70=282	$1,030.00
Jay Herbert	T-9	70-70-70-72=282	$1,030.00

West Palm Beach Open Invitational

Course: West Palm Beach C.C., West Palm Beach, Fla.
Par: 72 Yardage: 6,745
Last day of event: Sunday, December 2, 1962

Player	Place	Score	Earnings
Dave Ragan	Win	70-72-67-68=277	$2,800.00
Doug Sanders	2	70-67-70-70=277	$1,900.00
Dow Finsterwald	3	70-72-66-70=278	$1,400.00
Jon Gustin	T-4	72-67-73-67=279	$1,100.00
Jerry Pittman	T-4	72-69-69-69=279	$1,100.00
J.C. Goosie	T-4	72-69-68-70=279	$1,100.00
Joe Campbell	T-7	69-69-72-70=280	$875.00
George Knudson	T-7	75-66-70-69=280	$875.00
Mason Rudolph	9	71-73-70-67=281	$800.00
Paul Harney	T-10	73-72-71-66=282	$730.00
Bobby Nichols	T-10	69-70-69-74=282	$730.00

Coral Gables Open Invitational

Course: Biltmore C.C., Coral Gables, Fla.
Par: 71 Yardage: 6,563
Last day of event: Sunday, December 9, 1962

Player	Place	Score	Earnings
Gardner Dickinson	Win	70-66-67-71=274	$2,800.00
Bill Collins	T-2	67-66-69-73=275	$1,650.00
Don Fairfield	T-2	73-66-68-68=275	$1,650.00
Dow Finsterwald	4	70-70-69-67=276	$1,200.00
Rex Baxter	5	67-70-69-71=277	$1,100.00
Dave Ragan	6	66-71-70-71=278	$1,000.00
Bert Weaver	T-7	74-69-68-68=279	$802.00
Doug Sanders	T-7	71-69-69-70=279	$802.00
Jerry Pittman	T-7	69-70-70-70=279	$802.00
George Bayer	T-7	72-71-66-70=279	$802.00
Mason Rudolph	T-7	69-70-67-73=279	$802.00

1963

Jack Nicklaus won five times in 1963, including the Masters and the PGA Championship, and he was third at the British Open. Nicklaus fended off Tony Lema by a shot at Augusta and beat Dave Ragan by two strokes in the PGA at Dallas Athletic Club. Smooth-swinging Julius Boros shot 70 to win a U.S. Open playoff against Jackie Cupit (73) and Arnold Palmer (76). Cupit had dropped three shots over the final two holes of regulation; Palmer missed a 2-foot putt at the 71st hole. Bob Charles became the first left-hander to win a major, beating Phil Rodgers by eight strokes in a 36-hole British Open playoff at Royal Lytham.

Los Angeles Open

Course: Rancho Municipal G.C., Los Angeles, Calif.
Par: 71 Yardage: 6,827
Last day of event: Monday, January 7, 1963

Player	Place	Score	Earnings
Arnold Palmer	Win	69-69-70-66=274	$9,000.00
Al Balding	T-2	68-69-73-67=277	$3,800.00
Gary Player	T-2	71-69-68-69=277	$3,800.00
Tommy Jacobs	T-4	73-68-71-66=278	$2,120.00
Bob Rosburg	T-4	66-70-75-67=278	$2,120.00
Gene Littler	T-4	65-72-71-70=278	$2,120.00
Phil Rodgers	T-4	71-69-69-69=278	$2,120.00
Don Fairfield	T-4	71-70-67-70=278	$2,120.00
Mike Souchak	T-9	68-71-71-69=279	$1,358.34
Al Geiberger	T-9	72-73-65-69=279	$1,358.34
Fred Hawkins	T-9	72-72-66-69=279	$1,358.33
Dutch Harrison	T-9	69-67-73-70=279	$1,358.33
Billy Casper	T-9	71-68-69-71=279	$1,358.33
Art Wall	T-9	68-70-67-74=279	$1,358.33

San Diego Open

Course: Stardust C.C., San Diego, Calif.
Home Course -Par: 71 Yardage: 6,725
Last day of event: Sunday, January 13, 1963

Player	Place	Score	Earnings
Gary Player	Win	65-65-70-70=270	$3,500.00
Tony Lema	2	65-68-71-67=271	$2,300.00
Charles Sifford	T-3	67-69-67-69=272	$1,650.00
Billy Casper	T-3	64-68-69-71=272	$1,650.00
Julius Boros	5	66-70-68-69=273	$1,300.00
Miller Barber	6	68-67-66-73=274	$1,200.00
Art Wall	T-7	68-69-68-70=275	$1,050.00
Jacky Cupit	T-7	66-65-73-71=275	$1,050.00
Bob McCallister	T-9	69-68-74-65=276	$925.00
Dan Sikes	T-9	69-69-72-66=276	$925.00

Bing Crosby National Pro-Am

Courses: Pebble Beach G.L. - Home
Monterey Peninsula C.C., Cypress Point C.C., Pebble Beach, Calif.
Home Course Par: 72 Yardage: 6,747
Last day of event: Sunday, January 20, 1963

Player	Place	Score	Earnings
Billy Casper	Win	73-65-73-74=285	$5,300.00
Bob Rosburg	T-2	71-74-70-71=286	$2,140.00
Dave Hill	T-2	68-69-76-73=286	$2,140.00
Art Wall	T-2	71-71-72-72=286	$2,140.00
Gary Player	T-2	73-69-70-74=286	$2,140.00
Jack Nicklaus	T-2	71-69-76-70=286	$2,140.00
Bob Duden	7	70-73-67-77=287	$1,400.00
Julius Boros	T-8	66-75-70-77=288	$1,200.00
George Bayer	T-8	68-73-71-76=288	$1,200.00
Doug Sanders	T-8	74-74-69-71=288	$1,200.00

Lucky International Open

Course: Harding Park G.C., San Francisco, Calif.
Par: 71 Yardage: 6,772
Last day of event: Sunday, January 27, 1963

Player	Place	Score	Earnings
Jack Burke Jr.	Win	70-69-70-67=276	$9,000.00
Don January	2	70-70-68-71=279	$4,600.00
Paul Harney	T-3	72-71-69-68=280	$2,633.34
George Knudson	T-3	69-71-69-71=280	$2,633.33
Charles Sifford	T-3	68-71-70-71=280	$2,633.33
Dave Marr	T-6	74-70-72-65=281	$2,000.00
Miller Barber	T-6	69-70-73-69=281	$2,000.00
Gardner Dickinson	T-8	69-71-71-71=282	$1,600.00
Jack Fleck	T-8	70-71-70-71=282	$1,600.00
Tony Lema	T-8	73-67-70-72=282	$1,600.00

Palm Springs Golf Classic

Course: Indian Wells C.C.—Home Course

Tamarisk C.C., Eldorado C.C., Bermuda Dunes C.C., Indian Wells, Calif.

Par: 72 Yardage: N/A

Last day of event: Sunday, February 3, 1963

Player	Place	Score	Earnings
Jack Nicklaus	Win	69-66-67-71-72=345	$9,000.00
Gary Player	T-2	67-69-73-69-67=345	$4,600.00
Tommy Bolt	3	69-70-71-70-66=346	$3,000.00
Gene Littler	T-4	70-73-72-68-64=347	$2,450.00
Gardner Dickinson	T-4	66-73-70-70-68=347	$2,450.00
Arnold Palmer	T-6	71-72-71-68-67=349	$2,000.00
Jack Fleck	T-6	72-69-73-66-69=349	$2,000.00
Tony Lema	T-8	72-70-74-67-68=351	$1,450.00
Mason Rudolph	T-8	71-71-71-69-69=351	$1,450.00
Dan Sikes	T-8	74-68-69-70-70=351	$1,450.00
George Bayer	T-8	69-70-73-69-70=351	$1,450.00
Bob Shave, Jr.	T-8	67-69-72-72-71=351	$1,450.00
Wes Ellis	T-8	73-72-69-65-72=351	$1,450.00

Phoenix Open

Course: Arizona C.C., Phoenix, Ariz.

Par: 71 Yardage: 6,216

Last day of event: Tuesday, February 12, 1963

Player	Place	Score	Earnings
Arnold Palmer	Win	68-67-68-70=273	$5,300.00
Gary Player	2	67-69-68-70=274	$3,400.00
Jack Nicklaus	3	67-70-67-71=275	$2,200.00
Gardner Dickinson	4	69-68-68-71=276	$1,900.00
Tony Lema	T-5	72-71-65-69=277	$1,600.00
Jay Herbert	T-5	67-67-72-71=277	$1,600.00
Dan Sikes	T-7	69-71-72-67=279	$1,250.00
Fred Wampler	T-7	69-72-69-69=279	$1,250.00
Don January	T-7	71-67-67-74=279	$1,250.00
Johnny Pott	T-7	70-67-69-73=279	$1,250.00

Tucson Open

Course: 49er C.C., Tucson, Ariz.

Par: 72 Yardage: 6,722

Last day of event: Sunday, February 17, 1963

Player	Place	Score	Earnings
Don January	Win	65-67-69-65=266	$3,500.00
Phil Rodgers	T-2	71-69-71-66=277	$2,050.00
Gene Littler	T-2	69-70-69-69=277	$2,050.00
Tom Nieporte	T-4	69-73-68-68=278	$1,275.00
Al Balding	T-4	71-73-66-68=278	$1,275.00
Rex Baxter	T-4	68-72-69-69=278	$1,275.00
Frank Boynton	T-4	69-68-71-70=278	$1,275.00
Ed Updegraff	8	69-70-73-67=279	
Tony Lema	T-9	73-71-69-67=280	$975.00
Bob Harris	T-9	69-74-67-70=280	$975.00

Greater New Orleans Open

Course: Lakewood C.C., New Orleans, La.

Par: 72 Yardage: 7,080

Last day of event: Monday, March 4, 1963

Player	Place	Score	Earnings
Bo Wininger	Win	68-70-72-69=279	$6,400.00
Bob Rosburg	T-2	67-74-67-74=282	$3,050.00
Tony Lema	T-2	72-69-68-73=282	$3,050.00

Player	Place	Score	Earnings
Jacky Cupit	T-4	74-69-71-69=283	$2,050.00
Doug Sanders	T-4	75-69-68-71=283	$2,050.00
Gary Player	6	70-72-70-72=284	$1,700.00
Al Geiberger	7	72-74-71-69=286	$1,600.00
Jack Nicklaus	T-8	74-73-69-72=288	$1,450.00
Jerry Edwards	T-8	70-73-70-75=288	$1,450.00
Bob Charles	T-10	70-76-74-69=289	$1,150.00
Billy Casper	T-10	70-70-78-71=289	$1,150.00
Dave Ragan	T-10	72-71-72-74=289	$1,150.00
Dow Finsterwald	T-10	75-71-67-74=289	$1,150.00

Pensacola Open

Course: Pensacola C.C., Pensacola, Fla.

Par: 72 Yardage: 6,700

Last day of event: Sunday, March 10, 1963

Player	Place	Score	Earnings
Arnold Palmer	Win	69-68-69-67=273	$3,500.00
Harold Kneece	T-2	69-70-63-73=275	$2,050.00
Gary Player	T-2	67-72-67-69=275	$2,050.00
Tommy Bolt	4	69-71-68-68=276	$1,500.00
Mason Rudolph	T-5	71-67-71-68=277	$1,150.00
Bo Wininger	T-5	69-70-70-68=277	$1,150.00
Johnny Pott	T-5	68-68-71-70=277	$1,150.00
Bob Charles	T-5	70-70-66-71=277	$1,150.00
Dave Ragan	T-9	71-70-70-67=278	$875.00
Doug Sanders	T-9	67-73-70-68=278	$875.00
Julius Boros	T-9	67-70-71-70=278	$875.00
Bob Duden	T-9	70-69-68-71=278	$875.00

St. Petersburg Open Invitational

Course: Lakewood C.C., St. Petersburg, Fla.

Par: 72 Yardage: 6,329

Last day of event: Sunday, March 17, 1963

Player	Place	Score	Earnings
Ray Floyd	Win	67-71-69-67=274	$3,500.00
Dave Marr	2	67-69-66-73=275	$2,300.00
Mason Rudolph	T-3	72-66-70-68=276	$1,650.00
Tommy Bolt	T-3	65-72-69-70=276	$1,650.00
Billy Maxwell	T-5	66-72-69-71=278	$1,150.00
Doug Ford	T-5	73-69-65-71=278	$1,150.00
Bob Goalby	T-5	69-74-68-67=278	$1,150.00
Julius Boros	T-5	67-73-68-70=278	$1,150.00
Doug Sanders	T-9	68-67-76-68=279	$925.00
Dow Finsterwald	T-9	73-70-67-69=279	$925.00

Doral Open

Course: Doral C.C. (Blue), Miami, Fla.

Par: 72 Yardage: 6,939

Last day of event: Sunday, March 24, 1963

Player	Place	Score	Earnings
Dan Sikes	Win	76-70-67-70=283	$9,000.00
Sam Snead	2	71-69-73-71=284	$4,600.00
Tony Lema	3	75-72-70-69=286	$3,000.00
Dave Ragan	T-4	75-72-70-70=287	$2,333.34
Al Balding	T-4	74-72-70-71=287	$2,333.33
Paul Harney	T-4	68-72-73-74=287	$2,333.33
Billy Casper	T-7	73-71-76-70=290	$1,800.00
Arnold Palmer	T-7	71-71-75-73=290	$1,800.00
Gene Littler	T-9	70-71-73-77=291	$1,400.00
Jacky Cupit	T-9	74-72-71-74=291	$1,400.00
Art Wall	T-9	73-74-70-74=291	$1,400.00

Player	Place	Score	Earnings
Jack Nicklaus	T-9	73-73-72-73=291	$1,400.00
Jimmy Wright	T-9	77-72-71-71=291	$1,400.00

Azalea Open
Course: Cape Fear C.C., Wilmington, N.C.
Par: 72 Yardage: 6,700
Last day of event: Sunday, March 31, 1963

Player	Place	Score	Earnings
Jerry Barber	Win	69-68-70-67=274	$2,800.00
Jack Rule	T-2	70-74-66-69=279	$1,320.00
Larry Beck	T-2	70-68-71-70=279	$1,320.00
Bruce Crampton	T-2	72-71-65-71=279	$1,320.00
Doug Ford	T-2	74-64-71-70=279	$1,320.00
Billy Maxwell	T-2	70-71-67-71=279	$1,320.00
Jerry Steelsmith	T-7	74-67-70-69=280	$875.00
Gene Littler	T-7	67-70-72-71=280	$875.00
Dave Marr	T-9	73-70-69-69=281	$753.34
Billy Dunk	T-9	71-70-71-69=281	$753.33
Lionel Herbert	T-9	70-71-70-70=281	$753.33

Masters
Course: Augusta National G.C., Augusta, Ga.
Par: 72 Yardage: 6,925
Last day of event: Sunday, April 7, 1963

Player	Place	Score	Earnings
Jack Nicklaus	Win	74-66-74-72=286	$20,000.00
Tony Lema	2	74-69-74-70=287	$12,000.00
Julius Boros	T-3	76-69-71-72=288	$70,000.00
Sam Snead	T-3	70-73-74-71=288	$70,000.00
Dow Finsterwald	T-5	74-73-73-69=289	$4,000.00
Ed Furgol	T-5	70-71-74-74=289	$4,000.00
Gary Player	T-5	71-74-74-70=289	$4,000.00
Bo Wininger	8	69-72-77-72=290	$2,400.00
Arnold Palmer	T-9	74-73-73-71=291	$1,800.00
Don January	T-9	73-75-72-71=291	$1,800.00

Greater Greensboro Open
Course: Sedgefield C.C., Greensboro, N.C.
Par: 70 Yardage: 6,680
Last day of event: Sunday, April 14, 1963

Player	Place	Score	Earnings
Doug Sanders	Win	68-65-68-69=270	$5,500.00
Jimmy Clark	2	68-70-68-68=274	$3,500.00
Kel Nagle	3	69-68-69-69=275	$2,400.00
Bob Charles	T-4	68-71-71-67=277	$1,766.67
Art Wall	T-4	70-71-68-68=277	$1,766.67
Harold Kneece	T-4	69-70-70-68=277	$1,766.66
Jack McGowan	T-7	72-70-68-68=278	$1,400.00
Gary Player	T-7	66-74-69-69=278	$1,400.00
Sam Snead	T-7	69-69-69-71=278	$1,400.00
Tommy Aaron	T-10	68-69-75-67=279	$1,100.00
Bob Goetz	T-10	71-68-70-70=279	$1,100.00
Dave Marr	T-10	69-67-72-71=279	$1,100.00

Houston Classic
Course: Memorial Park G.C., Houston, Texas
Par: 70 Yardage: 7,212
Last day of event: Sunday, April 21, 1963

Player	Place	Score	Earnings
Bob Charles	Win	67-66-66-69=268	$9,000.00
Fred Hawkins	2	71-65-67-66=269	$4,600.00

Player	Place	Score	Earnings
Homero Blancas	3	68-68-70-64=270	
Jack Nicklaus	4	65-69-68-71=273	$3,000.00
Miller Barber	T-5	68-69-69-69=275	$2,450.00
Dow Finsterwald	T-5	72-67-67-69=275	$2,450.00
Jay Herbert	T-7	70-71-67-69=277	$1,825.00
Gay Brewer	T-7	73-68-67-69=277	$1,825.00
Charles Sifford	T-7	67-69-70-71=277	$1,825.00
Tommy Aaron	T-7	64-73-69-71=277	$1,825.00

Texas Open
Course: Oak Hills C.C., San Antonio, Texas
Par: 70 Yardage: 6,576
Last day of event: Sunday, April 28, 1963

Player	Place	Score	Earnings
Phil Rodgers	Win	66-71-66-65=268	$4,300.00
Johnny Pott	2	66-71-66-67=270	$3,000.00
Jack Fleck	3	69-67-70-66=272	$2,000.00
Bruce Crampton	T-4	64-72-69-69=274	$1,600.00
Bobby Nichols	T-4	69-71-65-69=274	$1,600.00
Bob Duden	T-6	72-68-67-68=275	$1,300.00
Jerry Steelsmith	T-6	68-70-68-69=275	$1,300.00
Gene Bone	T-6	70-68-69-68=275	$1,300.00
Arnold Palmer	T-9	71-68-70-67=276	$1,050.00
Doug Sanders	T-9	68-72-66-70=276	$1,050.00

Waco Turner Open Invitational
Course: Turner Lodge & C.C., Burneyville, Okla.
Par: 72 Yardage: N/A
Last day of event: Sunday, May 5, 1963

Player	Place	Score	Earnings
Gay Brewer	Win	72-70-71-67=280	$2,800.00
Ted Ball	2	69-71-72-69=281	$1,900.00
Billy Dunk	3	73-68-71-70=282	$1,400.00
Jack Rule	4	74-71-70-69=284	$1,200.00
Frank Beard	T-5	70-73-73-69=285	$1,000.00
Tommy Aaron	T-5	70-71-75-69=285	$1,000.00
Bob Goetz	T-5	69-73-72-71=285	$1,000.00
Moon Mullins	T-8	76-70-71-69=286	$825.00
Bruce Devlin	T-8	72-68-72-74=286	$825.00
Ron Thomas	T-10	72-73-72-70=287	$690.00
Bob Pratt	T-10	69-73-74-71=287	$690.00
Chi Chi Rodriguez	T-10	72-70-73-72=287	$690.00
Charles Coe	T-10	70-73-73-71=287	
Jimmy Wright	T-10	73-71-70-73=287	$690.00

Tournament of Champions
Course: Desert Inn C.C., Las Vegas,, Nev.
Par: 72 Yardage: 7,209
Last day of event: Sunday, May 5, 1963

Player	Place	Score	Earnings
Jack Nicklaus	Win	64-68-72-69=273	$13,000.00
Tony Lema	T-2	72-69-71-66=278	$5,300.00
Arnold Palmer	T-2	66-71-73-68=278	$5,300.00
Gardner Dickinson	T-4	71-71-70-69=281	$2,900.00
Bob Goalby	T-4	73-68-68-72=281	$2,900.00
Ted Kroll	T-4	72-71-69-69=281	$2,900.00
Doug Sanders	7	70-72-72-69=283	$2,250.00
Jerry Barber	T-8	71-69-74-70=284	$1,850.00
Jacky Cupit	T-8	71-70-72-71=284	$1,850.00
Gene Littler	T-8	73-74-68-69=284	$1,850.00

Colonial National Invitational

Course: Colonial C.C., Fort Worth, Texas
Par: 70 Yardage: 7,021
Last day of event: Sunday, May 12, 1963

Player	Place	Score	Earnings
Julius Boros	Win	71-66-71-71=279	$12,000.00
Gary Player	2	73-71-72-67=283	$6,000.00
Jack Nicklaus	3	71-69-74-70=284	$3,500.00
Doug Sanders	T-4	67-72-72-75=286	$2,800.00
Tony Lema	T-4	71-69-73-73=286	$2,800.00
Jerry Edwards	T-6	72-70-75-70=287	$2,200.00
Gene Littler	T-6	74-71-69-73=287	$2,200.00
Gardner Dickinson	T-8	71-75-76-66=288	$1,850.00
Jack Burke Jr.	T-8	74-67-78-69=288	$1,850.00
Phil Rodgers	T-10	71-71-74-73=289	$1,550.00
Bruce Crampton	T-10	71-69-74-75=289	$1,550.00
Bobby Nichols	T-10	73-67-74-75=289	$1,550.00

Oklahoma City Open

Course: Quail Creek C.C., Oklahoma City, Okla.
Par: 72 Yardage: 7,173
Last day of event: Sunday, May 19, 1963

Player	Place	Score	Earnings
Don Fairfield	Win	72-71-68-69=280	$5,300.00
Julius Boros	2	70-72-71-68=281	$3,400.00
Dow Finsterwald	3	71-70-71-70=282	$2,200.00
Miller Barber	T-4	70-72-71-70=283	$1,800.00
Frank Beard	T-4	70-73-69-71=283	$1,800.00
Fred Hawkins	T-6	70-72-72-70=284	$1,350.00
Bruce Crampton	T-6	75-73-67-69=284	$1,350.00
Bob Goalby	T-6	71-71-72-70=284	$1,350.00
Ernie Vossler	T-6	69-74-69-72=284	$1,350.00
Bobby Nichols	10	70-72-71-72=285	$1,100.00

Memphis Invitational Open

Course: Colonial C.C., Memphis, Tenn.
Par: 70 Yardage: 6,466
Last day of event: Monday, May 27, 1963

Player	Place	Score	Earnings
Tony Lema	Win	67-67-68-68=270	$9,000.00
Tommy Aaron	2	69-67-66-68=270	$4,600.00
Bruce Crampton	T-3	70-67-69-68=274	$2,800.00
Harold Kneece	T-3	71-65-65-73=274	$2,800.00
Gary Player	5	70-69-69-67=275	$2,300.00
Gene Littler	T-6	76-67-63-70=276	$1,900.00
George Bayer	T-6	72-68-67-69=276	$1,900.00
Dow Finsterwald	T-6	70-69-68-69=276	$1,900.00
Jay Herbert	T-9	69-71-70-67=277	$1,550.00
Dave Marr	T-9	72-68-67-70=277	$1,550.00

"500" Festival Open

Course: Speedway G.C., Indianapolis, Ind.
Par: 71 Yardage: 6,605
Last day of event: Monday, June 3, 1963

Player	Place	Score	Earnings
Dow Finsterwald	Win	68-68-64-68=268	$10,000.00
Bobby Nichols	T-2	69-69-68-64=270	$3,400.00
Tony Lema	T-2	70-64-69-67=270	$3,400.00
Julius Boros	T-2	68-67-65-70=270	$3,400.00
Tommy Aaron	T-2	71-64-66-69=270	$3,400.00
Chi Chi Rodriguez	T-6	67-68-69-67=271	$2,100.00

Bob Duden	T-6	69-68-66-68=271	$2,100.00
Fred Hawkins	T-6	64-69-69-69=271	$2,100.00
Jim Ferrier	9	70-70-61-71=272	$1,700.00
Sam Carmichael	T-10	66-70-70-68=274	$1,450.00
Miller Barber	T-10	67-68-70-69=274	$1,450.00
Bill Collins	T-10	67-67-71-69=274	$1,450.00
Claude King	T-10	67-65-72-70=274	$1,450.00

Buick Open

Course: Warwick Hills C.C., Grand Blanc, Mich.
Par: 72 Yardage: 7,014
Last day of event: Sunday, June 9, 1963

Player	Place	Score	Earnings
Julius Boros	Win	66-71-68-69=274	$9,000.00
Dow Finsterwald	2	70-72-70-67=279	$4,600.00
George Bayer	3	71-70-71-68=280	$3,000.00
George Knudson	4	71-70-71-69=281	$2,600.00
Art Wall	T-5	71-71-69-72=283	$2,100.00
Mason Rudolph	T-5	71-72-72-68=283	$2,100.00
Gene Littler	T-5	69-73-69-72=283	$2,100.00
Bob Rosburg	8	72-75-72-66=285	$1,700.00
Jerry Pittman	9	68-76-72-71=287	$1,600.00
Tommy Jacobs	T-10	72-74-70-72=288	$1,310.00
Tony Lema	T-10	71-74-73-70=288	$1,310.00
Bob Goalby	T-10	73-76-71-68=288	$1,310.00
Gardner Dickinson	T-10	73-71-74-70=288	$1,310.00
Jay Herbert	T-10	74-74-68-72=288	$1,310.00

Thunderbird Classic Invitational

Course: Westchester C.C., Harrison, N.Y.
Par: 72 Yardage: 6,573
Last day of event: Sunday, June 16, 1963

Player	Place	Score	Earnings
Arnold Palmer	Win	67-70-68-72=277	$25,000.00
Paul Harney	2	69-73-66-69=277	$10,000.00
Gene Littler	3	71-71-69-67=278	$5,700.00
Dow Finsterwald	T-4	70-69-71-69=279	$4,200.00
Bill Collins	T-4	72-70-68-69=279	$4,200.00
Gary Player	T-6	69-70-74-67=280	$3,000.00
Tom Nieporte	T-6	76-67-69-68=280	$3,000.00
Jay Herbert	T-8	71-68-72-70=281	$2,250.00
Bobby Nichols	T-8	71-66-70-74=281	$2,250.00
Joe Campbell	T-8	72-67-70-72=281	$2,250.00

U.S. Open

Course: The Country Club, Brookline, Mass.
Par: 71 Yardage: 6,870
Last day of event: Sunday, June 23, 1963

Player	Place	Score	Earnings
Julius Boros	Win	71-74-76-72-70=293	$17,500.00

Playoff: Beat Jacky Cupit and Arnold Palmer in 18 hole playoff (Boros 70, Cupit 73, Palmer 76)

Player	Place	Score	Earnings
Arnold Palmer	T-2	73-69-77-74-76=293	$8,500.00
Jacky Cupit	T-2	70-72-76-75-73=293	$8,500.00
Paul Harney	4	78-70-73-73=294	$5,000.00
Billy Maxwell	T-5	73-73-75-74=295	$3,166.66
Bruce Crampton	T-5	74-72-75-74=295	$3,166.67
Tony Lema	T-5	71-74-74-76=295	$3,166.67
Gary Player	T-8	74-75-75-72=296	$1,875.00
Walter Burkemo	T-8	72-71-76-77=296	$1,875.00
Dan Sikes	10	77-73-73-74=297	$1,550.00

Cleveland Open Invitational

Course: Beechmont C.C., Cleveland, Ohio
Par: 71 Yardage: 6,643
Last day of event: Monday, July 1, 1963

Player	Place	Score	Earnings
Arnold Palmer	Win	71-68-66-68=273	$22,000.00
Tommy Aaron	T-2	69-66-72-66=273	$8,550.00
Tony Lema	T-2	68-68-69-68=273	$8,550.00
Julius Boros	T-4	69-69-71-65=274	$4,316.67
Sam Snead	T-4	68-69-70-67=274	$4,316.67
Jack Burke Jr.	T-4	69-70-68-67=274	$4,316.66
Jack Nicklaus	7	68-68-69-70=275	$3,450.00
Art Wall	T-8	69-70-70-67=276	$2,725.00
Jay Herbert	T-8	70-69-70-67=276	$2,725.00
Don January	T-8	70-67-70-69=276	$2,725.00
Gary Player	T-8	66-69-71-70=276	$2,725.00

Canadian Open

Course: Scarboro G&C.C., Toronto, Ontario, Canada
Par: N/A Yardage: N/A
Last day of event: Saturday, July 6, 1963

Player	Place	Score	Earnings
Doug Ford	Win	69-67-74-70=280	$9,000.00
Al Geiberger	2	74-71-71-65=281	$4,600.00
George Bayer	T-3	70-70-75-67=282	$2,633.34
Fred Hawkins	T-3	69-74-72-67=282	$2,633.33
Bruce Crampton	T-3	73-72-71-66=282	$2,633.33
Bob Rosburg	6	70-72-74-67=283	$2,100.00
George Knudson	T-7	72-68-74-70=284	$1,733.34
Dan Keefe	T-7	71-73-69-71=284	$1,733.33
Herman Keiser	T-7	70-68-74-72=284	$1,733.33
Al Johnston	T-10	75-69-75-66=285	$1,400.00
Charles Sifford	T-10	75-68-71-71=285	$1,400.00
Tommy Aaron	T-10	69-74-75-70=285	$1,400.00

British Open

Course: Royal Lytham & St. Annes G.C., Lytham, Lancashire, England
Par: 71 Yardage: 6,836
Last day of event: Saturday July 13, 1963

Player	Place	Score	Earnings
Bob Charles	Win	68-72-66-71=277	$4,200.00

Playoff: Beat Phil Rodgers in 36 hole playoff (Charles 69-71=140, Rodgers 72-76=148)

Player	Place	Score	Earnings
Phil Rodgers	2	67-68-73-69=277	$2,800.00
Jack Nicklaus	3	71-67-70-70=278	$2,240.00
Kel Nagle	4	69-70-73-71=283	$1,820.00
Peter Thomson	5	67-69-71-78=285	$1,400.00
Christy O'Connor	6	74-68-76-68=286	$980.00
Gary Player	T-7	75-70-72-70=287	$700.00
Ramon Sota	T-7	69-73-73-72=287	$700.00
Jean Garaialde	T-9	72-69-72-75=288	$455.00
Sebastian Miguel	T-9	73-69-73-73=288	$455.00

Hot Springs Open Invitational

Course: Hot Springs C.C., Hot Springs, Ark.
Par: 72 Yardage: 7,011
Last day of event: Sunday, July 14, 1963

Player	Place	Score	Earnings
Dave Hill	Win	69-70-70-68=277	$3,500.00
Mike Souchak	2	69-67-72-69=277	$2,300.00
Rex Baxter	T-3	71-66-71-73=281	$1,650.00
Al Johnston	T-3	72-67-69-73=281	$1,650.00
Bob Goalby	5	69-70-70-73=282	$1,300.00
Harold Kneece	T-6	68-72-70-73=283	$1,100.00
Bo Wininger	T-6	72-70-67-74=283	$1,100.00
Dutch Harrison	T-6	68-71-70-74=283	$1,100.00
Harold Williams	T-9	73-68-69-74=284	$925.00
Paul Bondeson	T-9	69-71-70-74=284	$925.00

PGA Championship

Course: Dallas Athletic Club, Dallas, Texas
Par: 71 Yardage: 7,046
Last day of event: Sunday, July 21, 1963

Player	Place	Score	Earnings
Jack Nicklaus	Win	69-73-69-68=279	$13,000.00
Dave Ragan	2	75-70-67-69=281	$7,000.00
Bruce Crampton	T-3	70-73-65-74=282	$3,750.00
Dow Finsterwald	T-3	72-72-66-72=282	$3,750.00
Al Geiberger	T-5	72-73-69-70=284	$3,125.00
Billy Maxwell	T-5	73-71-69-71=284	$3,125.00
Jim Ferrier	7	73-73-70-69=285	$2,750.00
Art Wall	T-8	73-76-66-71=286	$2,090.00
Bill Johnston	T-8	71-72-72-71=286	$2,090.00
Gardner Dickinson	T-8	72-74-74-66=286	$2,090.00
Gary Player	T-8	74-75-67-70=286	$2,090.00
Tommy Jacobs	T-8	74-72-70-70=286	$2,090.00

Western Open

Course: Beverly C.C., Chicago, Ill.
Par: 71 Yardage: 6,923
Last day of event: Monday, July 29, 1963

Player	Place	Score	Earnings
Arnold Palmer	Win	73-67-67-73=280	$1,000.00
Julius Boros	2	72-67-74-67=280	$4,450.00
Jack Nicklaus	T-2	69-74-71-66=280	$4,450.00
Charles Sifford	T-4	72-69-72-69=282	$2,525.00
Sam Snead	T-4	71-68-68-75=282	$2,525.00
Tommy Jacobs	T-6	72-72-71-68=283	$1,900.00
Harold Kneece	T-6	74-67-72-70=283	$1,900.00
Fred Hawkins	T-6	67-68-76-72=283	$1,900.00
Lionel Herbert	9	71-69-72-72=284	$1,600.00
Jerry Pittman	10	69-76-71-69=285	$1,500.00

St. Paul Open

Course: Keller G.C., St. Paul, Minn. .
Par: N/A Yardage: N/A
Last day of event: Sunday, August 4, 1963

Player	Place	Score	Earnings
Jack Rule	Win	67-61-65-73=266	$5,300.00
Fred Hawkins	2	70-65-65-71=271	$3,400.00
Dave Hill	T-3	71-66-70-66=273	$2,050.00
Bruce Crampton	T-3	68-69-68-68=273	$2,050.00
George Bayer	5	71-67-72-64=274	$1,700.00
Charles Sifford	T-6	71-65-71-68=275	$1,450.00
Bruce Devlin	T-6	71-68-66-70=275	$1,450.00
Gene Littler	T-8	71-68-69-68=276	$1,150.00
Don Fairfield	T-8	65-69-73-69=276	$1,150.00
Harold Kneece	T-8	73-66-68-69=276	$1,150.00
Claude King	T-8	72-67-67-70=276	$1,150.00

Insurance City Open

Course: Wethersfield C.C., Wethersfield, CT.
Par: 71 Yardage: 6,568
Last day of event: Sunday, August 18, 1963

Player	Place	Score	Earnings
Billy Casper	Win	67-68-71-65=271	$6,400.00
George Bayer	2	69-65-67-71=272	$3,600.00
Wes Ellis	3	66-67-71-71=275	$2,500.00
Doug Ford	4	69-71-71-66=277	$2,200.00
Art Wall	T-5	69-66-73-70=278	$1,675.00
Dave Marr	T-5	69-69-70-70=278	$1,675.00
Jack Nicklaus	T-5	73-67-67-71=278	$1,675.00
Bo Wininger	T-5	72-65-69-72=278	$1,675.00
Lionel Herbert	9	69-66-68-76=279	$1,400.00
Jay Herbert	T-10	69-70-73-68=280	$1,250.00
Frank Wharton	T-10	70-68-73-69=280	$1,250.00

American Golf Classic

Course: Firestone C.C. (South), Akron, Ohio
Par: 70 Yardage: 7,180
Last day of event: Sunday, August 25, 1963

Player	Place	Score	Earnings
Johnny Pott	Win	67-68-71-70=276	$9,000.00
Arnold Palmer	2	70-71-66-73=280	$4,600.00
Julius Boros	3	67-73-70-71=281	$3,000.00
Dave Hill	4	69-70-74-69=282	$2,600.00
Jack Nicklaus	T-5	70-70-71-72=283	$2,200.00
Bob Charles	T-5	72-72-68-71=283	$2,200.00
Paul Bondeson	7	73-71-72-68=284	$1,900.00
Bobby Nichols	8	71-67-70-77=285	$1,700.00
Gary Player	T-9	71-71-74-70=286	$1,400.00
Jay Herbert	T-9	69-73-74-70=286	$1,400.00
Bruce Crampton	T-9	69-70-72-75=286	$1,400.00
Tony Lema	T-9	71-71-70-74=286	$1,400.00
Harold Kneece	T-9	73-70-68-75=286	$1,400.00

Denver Open Invitational

Course: Denver C.C., Denver, Colo.
Par: N/A Yardage: N/A
Last day of event: Sunday, September 1, 1963

Player	Place	Score	Earnings
Chi Chi Rodriguez	Win	68-74-65-69=276	$5,300.00
Bill Eggers	2	67-70-71-70=278	$3,400.00
Al Geiberger	T-3	72-64-71-72=279	$1,933.34
Jay Herbert	T-3	72-64-71-72=279	$1,933.33
Dave Hill	T-3	68-67-69-75=279	$1,933.33
Rex Baxter	6	67-71-71-71=280	$1,500.00
Jim Ferree	T-7	71-68-71-71=281	$1,350.00
Bob Rosburg	T-7	70-70-69-72=281	$1,350.00
Bo Wininger	T-9	73-72-70-67=282	$1,062.50
Bill Johnston	T-9	66-75-71-70=282	$1,062.50
Bob McCallister	T-9	70-71-70-71=282	$1,062.50
Jacky Cupit	T-9	68-70-68-76=282	$1,062.50

Utah Open Invitational

Course: Salt Lake C.C., Salt Lake City, Utah
Par: 71 Yardage: 6,310
Last day of event: Sunday, September 8, 1963

Player	Place	Score	Earnings
Tommy Jacobs	Win	68-72-62-70=272	$6,500.00

Player	Place	Score	Earnings
Don January	2	66-67-72-68=273	$3,600.00
Gary Player	3	66-69-70-70=275	$2,500.00
Jack Rule	T-4	71-72-66-69=278	$2,050.00
Billy Casper	T-4	75-65-69-69=278	$2,050.00
Paul Bondeson	T-6	69-73-67-70=279	$1,650.00
Bob Goalby	T-6	70-68-70-71=279	$1,650.00
Doug Sanders	T-8	71-74-67-68=280	$1,350.00
Mason Rudolph	T-8	68-71-71-70=280	$1,350.00
Bill Eggers	T-8	72-68-68-72=280	$1,350.00
Billy Maxwell	T-8	66-68-74-72=280	$1,350.00

Seattle Open Invitational

Course: Inglewood C.C., Seattle, Wash.
Par: 72 Yardage: N/A
Last day of event: Sunday, September 15, 1963

Player	Place	Score	Earnings
Bobby Nichols	Win	66-68-68-70=272	$5,300.00
Stan Leonard	T-2	66-67-72-69=274	$2,800.00
Ray Floyd	T-2	66-69-66-73=274	$2,800.00
Dow Finsterwald	4	70-68-66-74=278	$1,900.00
Larry Mowry	5	69-69-69-72=279	$1,700.00
Al Balding	T-6	70-72-70-69=281	$1,400.00
Doug Sanders	T-6	67-72-70-72=281	$1,400.00
Gardner Dickinson	T-6	71-70-67-73=281	$1,400.00
Billy Casper	9	70-67-70-75=282	$1,200.00
Bob McCallister	T-10	67-75-74-67=283	$933.34
Rod Funseth	T-10	72-72-69-70=283	$933.34
Lionel Herbert	T-10	70-71-70-72=283	$933.33
Pete Fleming	T-10	73-70-68-72=283	$933.33
Jerry Steelsmith	T-10	72-68-70-73=283	$933.33
Don January	T-10	71-71-69-72=283	$933.33

Portland Open Invitational

Course: Portland G.C., Portland, Ore.
Par: 72 Yardage: 6,586
Last day of event: Sunday, September 22, 1963

Player	Place	Score	Earnings
George Knudson	Win	69-67-68-67=271	$4,300.00
Mason Rudolph	2	69-64-67-71=271	$3,000.00
Dave Hill	3	70-66-69-68=273	$2,000.00
Dave Marr	T-4	73-67-68-66=274	$1,533.34
Gardner Dickinson	T-4	69-69-67-69=274	$1,533.33
Mike Souchak	T-4	69-69-67-69=274	$1,533.33
Billy Casper	T-7	72-70-66-68=276	$1,200.00
Tommy Jacobs	T-7	69-67-71-69=276	$1,200.00
Buster Cupit	T-7	68-69-67-72=276	$1,200.00
Bob Duden	T-10	70-72-67-68=277	$925.00
Jack Nicklaus	T-10	72-67-68-70=277	$925.00
Jack Rule	T-10	71-66-69-71=277	$925.00
Frank Beard	T-10	67-71-68-71=277	$925.00

Whitemarsh Open Invitational

Course: Whitemarsh Valley C.C., Chestnut Hill, Pa.
Par: 72 Yardage: 6,708
Last day of event: Sunday, October 6, 1963

Player	Place	Score	Earnings
Arnold Palmer	Win	70-71-66-74=281	$26,000.00
Lionel Herbert	2	72-74-65-71=282	$13,000.00
Sam Snead	T-3	72-71-74-66=283	$6,750.00
Al Balding	T-3	70-68-73-72=283	$6,750.00
Don January	T-5	70-73-70-71=284	$4,700.00

Player	Place	Score	Earnings
Mason Rudolph	T-5	67-72-71-74=284	$4,700.00
Julius Boros	T-7	73-75-70-67=285	$3,400.00
Gene Littler	T-7	69-72-72-72=285	$3,400.00
Tommy Jacobs	T-7	72-67-74-72=285	$3,400.00
Gary Player	10	71-72-70-73=286	$2,800.00

Sahara Invitational
Course: Paradise Valley C.C., Las Vegas, Nev.
Par: 71 Yardage: 7,069
Last day of event: Sunday, October 20, 1963

Player	Place	Score	Earnings
Jack Nicklaus	Win	75-66-66-69=276	$13,000.00
Gay Brewer	T-2	68-69-70-70=277	$5,250.00
Al Geiberger	T-2	67-71-69-70=277	$5,250.00
Bobby Nichols	T-4	69-71-69-69=278	$3,233.34
Tommy Aaron	T-4	69-73-68-68=278	$3,233.33
Don Whitt	T-4	73-68-67-70=278	$3,233.33
Rex Baxter	T-7	71-71-70-68=280	$2,500.00
Don January	T-7	69-71-70-70=280	$2,500.00
Frank Beard	T-9	70-74-67-70=281	$2,033.34
Miller Barber	T-9	73-70-68-70=281	$2,033.33
Claude King	T-9	71-68-69-73=281	$2,033.33

Fig Garden Village Open Invitational
Course: San Joaquin C.C., Fresno, Calif.
Par: N/A Yardage: N/A
Last day of event: Sunday, October 27, 1963

Player	Place	Score	Earnings
Mason Rudolph	Win	66-67-71-71=275	$3,500.00
Tommy Aaron	T-2	68-70-69-71=278	$2,050.00
Al Geiberger	T-2	72-71-68-67=278	$2,050.00
Randy Glover	T-4	77-71-67-68=283	$1,333.34
Buster Cupit	T-4	71-68-71-73=283	$1,333.33
George Knudson	T-4	71-69-70-73=283	$1,333.33
Don Whitt	T-7	72-71-72-69=284	$1,050.00
Gardner Dickinson	T-7	72-72-69-71=284	$1,050.00
Bob Goalby	T-9	75-71-71-68=285	$900.00
Billy Maxwell	T-9	78-70-67-70=285	$900.00
Dutch Harrison	T-9	75-69-71-70=285	$900.00

Almaden Open
Course: Almaden C.C., Almaden, Calif.
Par: 72 Yardage: 7,035
Last day of event: Sunday, November 3, 1963

Player	Place	Score	Earnings
Al Geiberger	Win	69-67-67-74=277	$3,500.00
Dick Lotz	T-2	72-68-69-69=278	
Dutch Harrison	T-2	66-73-70-69=278	$2,300.00
Jay Herbert	4	68-70-69-72=279	$1,800.00
George Bayer	T-5	72-71-68-69=280	$1,333.34
Bob Rosburg	T-5	69-68-72-71=280	$1,333.33
Alex Sutton	T-5	68-71-68-73=280	$1,333.33
Jim Ferree	T-8	68-69-74-70=281	$1,050.00
Lionel Herbert	T-8	69-72-69-71=281	$1,050.00
Mason Rudolph	T-10	71-71-70-70=282	$825.00
Dale Douglass	T-10	74-70-68-70=282	$825.00
Jerry Pittman	T-10	74-68-69-71=282	$825.00
Bob Goetz	T-10	70-69-70-73=282	$825.00
Ray Floyd	T-10	70-70-70-72=282	$825.00
Charles Sifford	T-10	77-65-68-72=282	$825.00

Frank Sinatra Open Invitational
Course: Canyon C.C., Palm Springs, Calif.
Par: N/A Yardage: N/A
Last day of event: Sunday, November 10, 1963

Player	Place	Score	Earnings
Frank Beard	Win	68-72-69-69=278	$9,000.00
Jerry Steelsmith	2	71-70-69-69=279	$4,600.00
Dow Finsterwald	T-3	69-69-73-69=280	$2,800.00
Mason Rudolph	T-3	71-72-67-70=280	$2,800.00
Al Geiberger	5	71-70-72-69=282	$2,300.00
Bob Goalby	T-6	73-69-72-69=283	$1,760.00
Dan Sikes	T-6	73-67-71-72=283	$1,760.00
Billy Casper	T-6	69-70-73-71=283	$1,760.00
Gardner Dickinson	T-6	73-68-71-71=283	$1,760.00
Tommy Bolt	T-6	69-73-67-74=283	$1,760.00

Cajun Classic Open Invitational
Course: Oakbourne C.C., Lafayette, La.
Par: 71 Yardage: 6,750
Last day of event: Sunday, November 24, 1963

Player	Place	Score	Earnings
Rex Baxter	Win	68-71-68-68=275	$2,800.00
Bob Shave, Jr.	2	70-71-67-69=277	$1,900.00
Tommy Aaron	T-3	70-70-69-69=278	$1,300.00
Jack Rule	T-3	69-67-68-74=278	$1,300.00
Jack Nicklaus	T-5	69-72-69-69=279	$1,050.00
Bob Goetz	T-5	68-67-74-70=279	$1,050.00
Bob Duden	T-7	72-71-72-65=280	$875.00
Dave Marr	T-7	67-69-73-71=280	$875.00
Al Balding	T-9	71-72-71-67=281	$775.00
John Barnum	T-9	72-71-66-72=281	$775.00

1964

Arnold Palmer would win 19 more tournaments in his illustrious career, but his six-shot victory over Jack Nicklaus and Dave Marr at the Masters was his last major title. Ken Venturi famously beat the heat and slogged through the national championship's last 36-hole Saturday to win the U.S. Open by four shots at Congressional. The ebullient "Champagne" Tony Lema scored a five-shot victory over Nicklaus in the British Open at St. Andrews. Bobby Nichols led wire-to-wire at the PGA Championship, beating Palmer—who became the first player to post four rounds in the 60s at a major championship—and Nicklaus by two shots.

Los Angeles Open
Course: Rancho Municipal G.C., Los Angeles, Calif.
Par: 71 Yardage: 6,827
Last day of event: Monday, January 6, 1964

Player	Place	Score	Earnings
Paul Harney	Win	71-72-66-71=280	$7,500.00
Bobby Nichols	2	69-68-73-71=281	$4,000.00
Bob Goalby	T-3	69-74-72-67=282	$2,775.00
Dow Finsterwald	T-3	69-73-72-68=282	$2,775.00
Arnold Palmer	T-3	70-70-72-70=282	$2,775.00
Al Geiberger	T-3	70-69-73-70=282	$2,775.00
Dave Marr	T-7	72-71-72-68=283	$1,950.00
Tommy Jacobs	T-7	69-68-76-70=283	$1,950.00
Julius Boros	T-9	76-70-71-68=285	$1,550.00
James Black	T-9	67-74-73-71=285	$1,550.00

San Diego Open
Course: Rancho Bernardo C.C., San Diego, Calif.
Home Course -Par: 72 Yardage: 6,455
Last day of event: Sunday, January 12, 1964

Player	Place	Score	Earnings
Art Wall	Win	71-65-68-70=274	$4,000.00
Tony Lema	T-2	67-70-72-67=276	$2,300.00
Bob Rosburg	T-2	66-69-71-70=276	$2,300.00
Bob Charles	T-4	69-69-73-66=277	$1,550.00
George Archer	T-4	71-66-73-67=277	$1,550.00
Rex Baxter	T-4	70-70-69-68=277	$1,550.00
Harold Kneece	T-4	70-71-68-68=277	$1,550.00
Ray Floyd	8	73-65-74-66=278	$1,300.00
Jerry Barber	T-9	69-72-68-70=279	$1,150.00
Al Geiberger	T-9	69-67-72-71=279	$1,150.00

Bing Crosby National Pro-Am
Courses: Pebble Beach G.L. - Home
Monterey Peninsula C.C., Cypress Point C.C., Pebble Beach, Calif.
Home Course Par: 72 Yardage: 6,747
Last day of event: Sunday, January 19, 1964

Player	Place	Score	Earnings
Tony Lema	Win	70-68-70-76=284	$5,800.00
Gay Brewer	T-2	76-68-70-73=287	$3,100.00
Bo Wininger	T-2	69-73-70-75=287	$3,100.00
Al Geiberger	T-4	80-67-68-73=288	$2,150.00
Tommy Aaron	T-4	70-68-73-77=288	$2,150.00
George Knudson	T-6	72-76-68-73=289	$1,650.00
Gardner Dickinson	T-6	71-73-70-75=289	$1,650.00
Bruce Devlin	T-6	69-67-74-79=289	$1,650.00
Dave Marr	T-6	72-69-72-76=289	$1,650.00
Bob Charles	T-10	68-71-76-75=290	$1,250.00
Dow Finsterwald	T-10	70-73-69-78=290	$1,250.00
Billy Casper	T-10	71-68-75-76=290	$1,250.00
Paul Harney	T-10	76-71-66-77=290	$1,250.00
Glen Fowler	0	76=76	

Lucky International Open
Course: Harding Park G.C., San Francisco, Calif.
Par: 71 Yardage: 6,772
Last day of event: Sunday, January 26, 1964

Player	Place	Score	Earnings
Chi Chi Rodriguez	Win	72-69-65-66=272	$7,500.00
Don January	2	66-68-70-68=272	$4,000.00
Arnold Palmer	T-3	67-66-72-70=275	$3,100.00
Ray Floyd	T-3	69-67-69-70=275	$3,100.00
Mason Rudolph	T-5	68-67-71-71=277	$2,450.00
Gene Littler	T-5	70-69-67-71=277	$2,450.00
Billy Casper	T-7	70-70-70-68=278	$1,950.00
Tommy Jacobs	T-7	69-69-70-70=278	$1,950.00
Jon Gustin	T-9	73-72-68-66=279	$1,500.00
Art Wall	T-9	73-69-70-67=279	$1,500.00
Dave Ragan	T-9	69-67-70-73=279	$1,500.00

Palm Springs Golf Classic
Course: Eldorado C.C.—Home Course
La Quinta C.C., Indian Wells, Bermuda Dunes C.C., Palm Desert, Calif.
Par: 72 Yardage: N/A
Last day of event: Sunday, February 2, 1964

Player	Place	Score	Earnings
Tommy Jacobs	Win	66-74-74-69-70=353	$7,500.00
Jimmy Demaret	2	75-68-67-72-71=353	$4,000.00
Don January	T-3	69-71-74-69-71=354	$3,100.00
Bob Charles	T-3	67-72-69-73-73=354	$3,100.00
Bob Goalby	T-5	67-72-72-73-71=355	$2,450.00
Chuck Courtney	T-5	71-72-69-67-76=355	$2,450.00
Bruce Devlin	T-7	70-74-68-70-74=356	$1,680.00
Dave Marr	T-7	71-70-75-67-73=356	$1,680.00
George Knudson	T-7	71-70-75-67-73=356	$1,680.00
Billy Casper	T-7	70-72-67-70-77=356	$1,680.00
Charles Sifford	T-7	66-71-71-73-75=356	$1,680.00

Phoenix Open
Course: Phoenix C.C., Phoenix, Ariz.
Par: 71 Yardage: 6,726
Last day of event: Sunday, February 9, 1964

Player	Place	Score	Earnings
Jack Nicklaus	Win	71-66-68-66=271	$7,500.00
Bob Brue	2	70-67-67-70=274	$4,000.00
Gene Littler	T-3	71-68-69-67=275	$3,100.00
Gary Player	T-3	72-65-66-72=275	$3,100.00
George Bayer	5	69-68-65-74=276	$2,600.00
Tony Lema	T-6	68-68-71-70=277	$2,066.67
Julius Boros	T-6	69-68-70-70=277	$2,066.67
Dave Marr	T-6	69-69-69-70=277	$2,066.66
Arnold Palmer	T-9	70-72-69-67=278	$1,450.00
Jack Rule	T-9	71-74-65-68=278	$1,450.00
Gay Brewer	T-9	70-69-71-68=278	$1,450.00
Bob Rosburg	T-9	70-68-69-71=278	$1,450.00

Tucson Open
Course: 49er C.C., Tucson, Ariz.
Par: 72 Yardage: 6,722
Last day of event: Sunday, February 16, 1964

Player	Place	Score	Earnings
Jacky Cupit	Win	69-68-66-71=274	$4,000.00
Rex Baxter	2	66-70-71-69=276	$2,700.00
Bruce Crampton	3	70-68-71-69=278	$1,900.00
Dave Hill	T-4	72-69-71-67=279	$1,600.00
Tommy Aaron	T-4	68-71-67-73=279	$1,600.00
Chuck Courtney	T-4	67-71-69-72=279	$1,600.00
Don Massengale	T-7	67-72-69-72=280	$1,350.00
Al Johnston	T-7	73-73-64-70=280	$1,350.00
Gay Brewer	T-9	73-72-67-69=281	$1,100.00
Phil Rodgers	T-9	71-68-70-72=281	$1,100.00
Bruce Devlin	T-9	69-67-71-74=281	$1,100.00

Greater New Orleans Open
Course: Lakewood C.C., New Orleans, La.
Par: 72 Yardage: 7,080
Last day of event: Monday, March 2, 1964

Player	Place	Score	Earnings
Mason Rudolph	Win	68-70-70-75=283	$7,500.00
Chi Chi Rodriguez	T-2	72-76-69-67=284	$3,400.00

Jack Nicklaus	T-2	70-70-72-72=284	$3,400.00
Glenn Stuart	T-2	75-70-70-69=284	$3,400.00
Bob Charles	5	76-68-71-70=285	$2,600.00
Paul Bondeson	6	79-71-68-68=286	$2,300.00
Wes Ellis	7	73-73-67-74=287	$2,100.00
Bruce Crampton	T-8	72-73-73-70=288	$1,700.00
Al Balding	T-8	75-70-71-72=288	$1,700.00
Arnold Palmer	10	76-71-72-70=289	$1,500.00

Pensacola Open

Course: Pensacola C.C., Pensacola, Fla.
Par: 72 Yardage: 6,700
Last day of event: Sunday, March 8, 1964

Player	Place	Score	Earnings
Gary Player	Win	71-68-66-69=274	$4,000.00
Arnold Palmer	T-2	69-68-68-69=274	$2,300.00
Miller Barber	T-2	69-68-68-69=274	$2,300.00
Doug Sanders	T-4	69-69-72-69=279	$1,500.00
Johnny Pott	T-4	69-72-68-68=277	$1,500.00
Bert Weaver	T-4	71-69-68-69=277	$1,500.00
Jack Rule	T-4	70-69-70-68=277	$1,500.00
Jay Hebert	T-4	69-71-67-70=277	$1,500.00
George Bayer	T-9	69-69-71-69=278	$1,100.00
Ken Venturi	T-9	71-65-74-68=278	$1,100.00
Gardner Dickinson	T-9	68-71-68-71=278	$1,100.00

St. Petersburg Open Invitational

Course: Lakewood C.C., St. Petersburg, Fla.
Par: 72 Yardage: 6,329
Last day of event: Sunday, March 15, 1964

Player	Place	Score	Earnings
Bruce Devlin	Win	69-64-69-70=272	$3,300.00
Dan Sikes	2	70-70-68-68=276	$2,100.00
Jacky Cupit	3	70-70-69-68=277	$1,700.00
Dave Ragan	T-4	70-68-72-68=278	$1,400.00
Joe Campbell	T-4	69-69-71-69=278	$1,400.00
Jack Nicklaus	T-4	71-69-68-70=278	$1,400.00
Dow Finsterwald	7	69-73-69-68=279	$1,200.00
Dick Howell	T-8	73-69-70-68=280	$1,016.67
Mason Rudolph	T-8	72-67-71-70=280	$1,016.67
Don Fairfield	T-8	70-68-70-72=280	$1,016.66

Doral Open

Course: Doral C.C. (Blue), Miami, Fla.
Par: 72 Yardage: 6,939
Last day of event: Sunday, March 22, 1964

Player	Place	Score	Earnings
Billy Casper	Win	70-70-67-70=277	$7,500.00
Jack Nicklaus	2	70-66-73-69=278	$4,000.00
Rex Baxter	3	70-66-72-71=279	$3,300.00
Sam Snead	T-4	68-69-73-71=281	$2,750.00
Jack Rule	T-4	71-70-68-72=281	$2,750.00
Jay Hebert	T-6	70-69-75-68=282	$2,200.00
Bob Shave, Jr.	T-6	69-67-73-73=282	$2,200.00
Chick Harbert	8	72-73-69-69=283	$1,800.00
Dave Marr	T-9	70-70-74-70=284	$1,500.00
Frank Beard	T-9	75-69-67-73=284	$1,500.00
Mason Rudolph	T-9	72-70-70-72=284	$1,500.00

Azalea Open

Course: Cape Fear C.C., Wilmington, N.C.
Par: 72 Yardage: 6,700
Last day of event: Monday, March 30, 1964

Player	Place	Score	Earnings
Al Besselink	Win	70-65-72-75=282	$2,700.00
Lionel Hebert	2	70-70-70-73=283	$1,800.00
Tommy Jacobs	3	69-70-71-74=284	$1,500.00
Billy Casper	T-4	72-70-71-72=285	$1,250.00
Larry Mowry	T-4	71-68-71-75=285	$1,250.00
Doug Ford	T-6	73-69-71-73=286	$1,000.00
Bob Gajda	T-6	68-68-75-75=286	$1,000.00
Joe Campbell	T-6	67-73-69-77=286	$1,000.00
Dave Thomas	T-9	72-72-70-74=288	$775.00
Jack McGowan	T-9	69-72-70-77=288	$775.00

Greater Greensboro Open

Course: Sedgefield C.C., Greensboro, N.C.
Par: 70 Yardage: 6,680
Last day of event: Sunday, April 5, 1964

Player	Place	Score	Earnings
Julius Boros	Win	68-70-73-66=277	$6,600.00
Doug Sanders	2	73-70-66-68=277	$3,800.00
Sam Snead	3	64-71-74-69=278	$3,000.00
Jack Nicklaus	4	70-69-67-73=279	$2,550.00
Al Geiberger	5	71-69-70-70=280	$2,250.00
Ramon Sota	6	72-70-73-67=282	$2,000.00
Mason Rudolph	7	72-71-69-71=283	$1,800.00
Tommy Jacobs	T-8	73-70-69-72=284	$1,500.00
Gordon Jones	T-8	70-72-71-71=284	$1,500.00
Billy Dunk	T-8	67-71-71-75=284	$1,500.00

Masters

Course: Augusta National G.C., Augusta, Ga.
Par: 72 Yardage: 6,925
Last day of event: Sunday, April 12, 1964

Player	Place	Score	Earnings
Arnold Palmer	Win	69-68-69-70=276	$20,000.00
Dave Marr	T-2	70-73-69-70=282	$10,100.00
Jack Nicklaus	T-2	71-73-71-67=282	$10,100.00
Bruce Devlin	4	72-72-67-73=284	$6,100.00
Billy Casper	T-5	76-76-68-66=286	$3,700.00
Jim Ferrier	T-5	71-73-69-73=286	$3,700.00
Paul Harney	T-5	73-72-71-70=286	$3,700.00
Gary Player	T-5	69-72-72-73=286	$3,700.00
Ben Hogan	T-9	73-75-67-72=287	$1,700.00
Mike Souchak	T-9	73-74-70-70=287	$1,700.00
Tony Lema	T-9	75-68-74-70=287	$1,700.00
Dow Finsterwald	T-9	71-72-75-69=287	$1,700.00

Houston Classic

Course: Sharpstown C.C., Houston, Texas
Par: 71 Yardage: 7,021
Last day of event: Sunday, April 19, 1964

Player	Place	Score	Earnings
Mike Souchak	Win	71-69-68-70=278	$7,500.00
Jack Nicklaus	2	76-66-66-71=279	$4,000.00
Chi Chi Rodriguez	3	72-70-70-68=280	$3,300.00
Rex Baxter	T-4	69-73-72-67=281	$2,600.00
Butch Baird	T-4	70-70-70-71=281	$2,600.00

Al Geiberger	T-4	74-70-65-72=281	$2,600.00
Johnny Pott	T-7	74-73-69-66=282	$1,950.00
Buster Cupit	T-7	71-68-73-70=282	$1,950.00
Bobby Nichols	T-9	70-75-68-70=283	$1,450.00
Tommy Aaron	T-9	71-71-71-70=283	$1,450.00
Lionel Hebert	T-9	69-72-70-72=283	$1,450.00
Don Fairfield	T-9	74-72-66-71=283	$1,450.00

Texas Open

Course: Oak Hills C.C., San Antonio, Texas
Par: 70 Yardage: 6,576
Last day of event: Sunday, April 26, 1964

Player	Place	Score	Earnings
Bruce Crampton	Win	71-69-68-65=273	$5,800.00
Bob Charles	T-2	67-69-69-69=274	$3,100.00
Chi Chi Rodriguez	T-2	72-68-65-69=274	$3,100.00
Miller Barber	T-4	69-68-69-69=275	$1,950.00
Gene Littler	T-4	67-67-71-70=275	$1,950.00
Mason Rudolph	T-4	68-71-67-69=275	$1,950.00
Don January	T-4	67-71-67-70=275	$1,950.00
Terry Dill	T-8	67-67-72-70=276	$1,450.00
Jerry Steelsmith	T-8	67-70-69-70=276	$1,450.00
Dan Sikes	T-8	69-66-69-72=276	$1,450.00
Dutch Harrison	T-8	67-69-66-74=276	$1,450.00

Tournament of Champions

Course: Desert Inn C.C., Las Vegas,, Nev.
Par: 72 Yardage: 7,209
Last day of event: Sunday, May 3, 1964

Player	Place	Score	Earnings
Jack Nicklaus	Win	68-73-65-73=279	$12,000.00
Al Geiberger	T-2	70-75-67-69=281	$6,000.00
Doug Sanders	T-2	71-73-71-66=281	$6,000.00
Julius Boros	T-4	72-76-66-68=282	$3,020.00
Don Fairfield	T-4	72-72-67-71=282	$3,020.00
Paul Harney	T-4	72-71-70-69=282	$3,020.00
Tommy Jacobs	T-4	70-75-68-69=282	$3,020.00
Chi Chi Rodriguez	T-4	69-70-70-73=282	$3,020.00
Arnold Palmer	9	72-72-70-70=284	$1,850.00
Gary Player	T-10	71-71-70-73=285	$1,650.00
Art Wall	T-10	72-73-70-70=285	$1,650.00

Colonial National Invitational

Course: Colonial C.C., Fort Worth, Texas
Par: 70 Yardage: 7,021
Last day of event: Sunday, May 10, 1964

Player	Place	Score	Earnings
Billy Casper	Win	72-67-70-70=279	$14,000.00
Tommy Jacobs	2	69-69-71-74=283	$7,000.00
Gene Littler	3	71-71-68-75=285	$4,000.00
Gay Brewer	T-4	70-73-72-72=287	$3,160.00
Dow Finsterwald	T-4	74-69-74-70=287	$3,160.00
Ben Hogan	T-4	72-72-72-71=287	$3,160.00
Arnold Palmer	T-4	75-71-69-72=287	$3,160.00
Gary Player	T-4	68-71-74-74=287	$3,160.00
Kel Nagle	9	71-76-68-73=288	$2,500.00
Dave Marr	T-10	76-71-72-70=289	$2,175.00
Mason Rudolph	T-10	72-72-71-74=289	$2,175.00

Oklahoma City Open

Course: Quail Creek C.C., Oklahoma City, Okla.
Par: 72 Yardage: 7,173
Last day of event: Monday, May 18, 1964

Player	Place	Score	Earnings
Arnold Palmer	Win	72-69-69-67=277	$5,800.00
Lionel Hebert	2	70-68-69-72=279	$3,500.00
Bob Verwey	3	69-71-71-70=281	$2,700.00
Mike Souchak	T-4	68-71-71-72=282	$2,150.00
Jack McGowan	T-4	69-71-69-73=282	$2,150.00
Dave Marr	6	72-71-72-68=283	$1,800.00
Bob Rosburg	7	70-71-73-70=284	$1,700.00
Bruce Devlin	T-8	73-71-69-72=285	$1,400.00
Miller Barber	T-8	73-74-69-69=285	$1,400.00
Jerry Steelsmith	T-8	72-75-72-66=285	$1,400.00
Tony Lema	T-8	70-72-77-66=285	$1,400.00
Johnny Pott	T-8	69-70-74-72=285	$1,400.00

Memphis Invitational Open

Course: Colonial C.C., Memphis, Tenn.
Par: 70 Yardage: 6,466
Last day of event: Sunday, May 24, 1964

Player	Place	Score	Earnings
Mike Souchak	Win	69-65-67-69=270	$7,500.00
Tommy Jacobs	T-2	69-68-66-68=271	$3,650.00
Billy Casper	T-2	69-63-69-70=271	$3,650.00
Bob Rosburg	T-4	69-67-69-67=272	$2,216.67
Art Wall	T-4	68-68-68-68=272	$2,216.67
Gay Brewer	T-4	66-71-68-67=272	$2,216.67
Doug Sanders	T-4	67-68-66-71=272	$2,216.67
Gene Littler	T-4	66-69-66-71=272	$2,216.66
Mason Rudolph	T-4	67-69-66-70=272	$2,216.66
Jerry Steelsmith	T-10	70-69-67-67=273	$1,450.00
Johnny Pott	T-10	71-66-67-69=273	$1,450.00

"500" Festival Open

Course: Speedway G.C., Indianapolis, Ind.
Par: 71 Yardage: 6,605
Last day of event: Sunday, May 31, 1964

Player	Place	Score	Earnings
Gary Player	Win	70-66-70-67=273	$12,000.00
Doug Sanders	T-2	68-71-73-64=276	$5,250.00
Art Wall	T-2	70-67-70-67=274	$5,250.00
George Bayer	4	66-67-72-70=275	$3,700.00
Cliff Brown	T-5	72-68-69-67=276	$2,933.34
Don Whitt	T-5	68-72-68-68=276	$2,933.33
Billy Casper	T-5	68-70-69-69=276	$2,933.33
Gay Brewer	T-8	68-69-72-68=277	$2,300.00
Kel Nagle	T-8	66-69-73-69=277	$2,300.00
Dow Finsterwald	T-10	70-71-69-68=278	$1,850.00
Jerry Steelsmith	T-10	71-71-67-69=278	$1,850.00
Harold Kneece	T-10	65-72-70-71=278	$1,850.00
Gene Littler	T-10	71-69-68-70=278	$1,850.00

Thunderbird Classic

Course: Westchester C.C., Harrison, N.Y.
Par: 72 Yardage: 6,573
Last day of event: Sunday, June 7, 1964

Player	Place	Score	Earnings
Tony Lema	Win	68-67-70-71=276	$20,000.00

Mike Souchak	2	69-68-71-69=277	$12,000.00
Billy Casper	T-3	71-67-73-68=279	$6,250.00
Ken Venturi	T-3	67-70-72-70=279	$6,250.00
Chi Chi Rodriguez	T-5	71-70-70-69=280	$4,050.00
Phil Rodgers	T-5	67-71-72-70=280	$4,050.00
Kel Nagle	T-7	68-70-73-70=281	$2,975.00
Dan Sikes	T-7	71-69-72-69=281	$2,975.00
Charles Sifford	T-7	75-67-71-68=281	$2,975.00
Mason Rudolph	T-7	72-74-68-67=281	$2,975.00

Buick Open

Course: Warwick Hills C.C., Grand Blanc, Mich.
Par: 72 Yardage: 7,014
Last day of event: Sunday, June 14, 1964

Player	Place	Score	Earnings
Tony Lema	Win	69-66-72-70=277	$8,177.42
Dow Finsterwald	2	70-70-67-71=278	$4,477.42
Bob Charles	3	71-73-72-67=283	$3,677.42
Mason Rudolph	4	68-70-73-73=284	$3,177.42
Charles Sifford	5	75-71-68-71=285	$2,877.42
Tommy Bolt	T-6	72-75-71-68=286	$2,344.09
Lionel Hebert	T-6	73-75-69-69=286	$2,344.09
Ken Venturi	T-6	72-74-69-71=286	$2,344.09
Bill Collins	T-9	71-71-76-69=287	$1,827.42
Kel Nagle	T-9	73-70-75-69=287	$1,827.42
Art Wall	T-9	75-71-70-71=287	$1,827.42
Don January	T-9	70-74-70-73=287	$1,827.42

U.S. Open

Course: Congressional C.C., Bethesda, Md.
Par: 70 Yardage: 7,053
Last day of event: Saturday, June 20, 1964

Player	Place	Score	Earnings
Ken Venturi	Win	72-70-66-70=278	$17,500.00
Tommy Jacobs	2	72-64-70-76=282	$8,500.00
Bob Charles	3	72-72-71-68=283	$6,000.00
Billy Casper	4	71-74-69-71=285	$5,000.00
Arnold Palmer	T-5	68-69-75-74=286	$3,750.00
Gay Brewer	T-5	76-69-73-68=286	$3,750.00
Bill Collins	7	70-71-74-72=287	$3,000.00
Dow Finsterwald	8	73-72-71-72=288	$2,500.00
Johnny Pott	T-9	71-73-73-72=289	$1,950.00
Bob Rosburg	T-9	73-73-70-73=289	$1,950.00

Cleveland Open

Course: Highland Park G.C., Cleveland, Ohio
Par: N/A Yardage: N/A
Last day of event: Sunday, June 28, 1964

Player	Place	Score	Earnings
Tony Lema	Win	65-70-70-65=270	$20,000.00
Arnold Palmer	2	67-64-71-68=270	$12,000.00
Terry Dill	T-3	69-66-71-66=272	$6,250.00
Jack Nicklaus	T-3	68-65-69-70=272	$6,250.00
Ed Griffiths	T-5	69-68-71-66=274	$3,650.00
Bruce Devlin	T-5	71-70-67-66=274	$3,650.00
Don January	T-5	69-68-69-68=274	$3,650.00
Billy Casper	T-5	66-71-68-69=274	$3,650.00
R.H. Sikes	T-9	68-64-73-70=275	$2,700.00
Don Fairfield	T-9	68-68-69-70=275	$2,700.00

Whitemarsh Open

Course: Whitemarsh Valley C.C., Chestnut Hill, Pa.
Par: 72 Yardage: 6,708
Last day of event: Sunday, July 5, 1964

Player	Place	Score	Earnings
Jack Nicklaus	Win	69-70-70-67=276	$24,042.12
Gary Player	2	69-70-69-69=277	$16,042,12
Arnold Palmer	3	68-70-67-73=278	$10,042.12
Dave Marr	T-4	67-68-69-75=279	$7,042.12
Chi Chi Rodriguez	T-4	66-68-69-76=279	$7,042.12
Tom Shaw	T-6	66-72-72-70=280	$3,917.12
Billy Casper	T-6	70-69-71-70=280	$3,917.12
Tony Lema	T-6	66-72-67-75=280	$3,917.11
George Knudson	T-6	67-71-68-74=280	$3,917.11
Doug Sanders	T-10	73-72-68-68=281	$1,892.11
Dan Sikes	T-10	70-66-74-71=281	$1,892.11
Tommy Bolt	T-10	73-70-67-71=281	$1,892.11
Jerry Steelsmith	T-10	72-67-70-72=281	$1,892.11
Don Fairfield	T-10	69-67-71-74=281	$1,892.11
Billy Maxwell	T-10	71-70-65-75=281	$1,892.11

British Open

Course: Old Course at St. Andrews, St. Andrews, Fife, Scotland
Par: 72 Yardage: 6,926
Last day of event: Friday, July 10, 1964

Player	Place	Score	Earnings
Tony Lema	Win	73-68-68-70=279	$4,200.00
Jack Nicklaus	2	76-74-66-68=284	$2,800.00
Roberto De Vicenzo	3	76-72-70-67=285	$2,240.00
Bernard Hunt	4	73-74-70-70=287	$1,820.00
Bruce Devlin	5	72-72-73-73=290	$1,400.00
Christy O'Connor	T-6	71-73-74-73=291	$875.00
Harry Weetman	T-6	72-71-75-73=291	$875.00
Angel Miguel	T-8	73-76-72-71=292	$520.00
Gary Player	T-8	78-71-73-70=292	$520.00
Harold Henning	T-8	78-73-71-70=292	$520.00

PGA Championship

Course: Columbus C.C., Columbus, Ohio
Par: 70 Yardage: 6,851
Last day of event: Sunday, July 19, 1964

Player	Place	Score	Earnings
Bobby Nichols	Win	64-71-69-67=271	$18,000.00
Jack Nicklaus	T-2	67-73-70-64=274	$9,000.00
Arnold Palmer	T-2	68-68-69-69=274	$9,000.00
Mason Rudolph	4	73-66-68-69=276	$5,000.00
Tom Nieporte	T-5	68-71-68-72=279	$3,850.00
Ken Venturi	T-5	72-65-73-69=279	$3,850.00
Bo Wininger	7	69-68-73-70=280	$3,200.00
Gay Brewer	8	72-71-71-67=281	$2,900.00
Billy Casper	T-9	68-72-70-72=282	$2,300.00
Jon Gustin	T-9	69-76-71-66=282	$2,300.00
Ben Hogan	T-9	70-72-68-72=282	$2,300.00
Tony Lema	T-9	71-68-72-71=282	$2,300.00

Insurance City Open

Course: Wethersfield C.C., Wethersfield, CT.
Par: 71 Yardage: 6,568
Last day of event: Sunday July 26, 1964

Player	Place	Score	Earnings
Ken Venturi	Win	70-63-69-71=273	$7,500.00
Al Besselink	T-2	66-67-69-72=274	$3,400.00
Paul Bondeson	T-2	72-68-69-65=274	$3,400.00
Sam Carmichael	T-2	67-68-68-71=274	$3,400.00
Jim Grant	T-2	70-67-70-67=274	
Bill Collins	T-6	69-69-67-70=275	$2,450.00
Bert Yancey	T-6	66-67-71-71=275	$2,450.00
Billy Casper	T-8	69-69-71-67=276	$1,750.00
Richard Crawford	T-8	69-67-72-68=276	$1,750.00
Jerry Edwards	T-8	71-66-71-68=276	$1,750.00
Kermit Zarley	T-8	71-72-68-65=276	$1,750.00

Canadian Open

Course: Pinegrove C.C., St. Luc, Quebec, Canada
Par: 71 Yardage: N/A
Last day of event: Sunday, August 2, 1964

Player	Place	Score	Earnings
Kel Nagle	Win	73-71-66-67=277	$7,500.00
Arnold Palmer	2	71-67-71-70=279	$4,000.00
Ray Floyd	3	73-68-68-71=280	$3,300.00
Dan Sikes	4	73-70-68-70=281	$2,900.00
Billy Casper	T-5	73-66-72-71=282	$2,080.00
Bill Collins	T-5	70-68-71-73=282	$2,080.00
Jay Hebert	T-5	71-74-69-68=282	$2,080.00
Jack Nicklaus	T-5	70-72-71-69=282	$2,080.00
Gary Player	T-5	72-69-70-71=282	$2,080.00
Bob Verwey	10	70-71-71-73=285	$1,500.00

Western Open

Course: Tam O'Shanter C.C., Niles, Ill.
Par: 71 Yardage: 6,686
Last day of event: Sunday, August 9, 1964

Player	Place	Score	Earnings
Chi Chi Rodriguez	Win	64-69-68-67=268	$11,000.00
Arnold Palmer	2	68-66-67-68=269	$5,750.00
Jack Nicklaus	T-3	72-71-65-67=275	$3,300.00
Don Massengale	T-3	71-65-69-70=275	$3,300.00
Ken Venturi	5	68-71-68-70=277	$2,500.00
Stan Leonard	T-6	74-69-69-66=278	$1,960.00
Tony Lema	T-6	70-69-70-69=278	$1,960.00
Jim Ferrier	T-6	67-69-73-69=278	$1,960.00
Tom Veech	T-6	68-71-69-70=278	$1,960.00
Billy Casper	T-6	64-71-71-72=278	$1,960.00

St. Paul Open

Course: Keller G.C., St. Paul, Minn. .
Par: 71 Yardage: N/A
Last day of event: Sunday, August 16, 1964

Player	Place	Score	Earnings
Chuck Courtney	Win	68-72-66-66=272	$11,500.00
Charles Sifford	T-2	70-70-68-67=275	$4,433.34
Rod Funseth	T-2	68-71-69-67=275	$4,433.33
Jack McGowan	T-2	68-71-68-68=275	$4,433.33
Julius Boros	T-5	68-71-71-66=276	$2,560.00
Bobby Nichols	T-5	67-72-70-67=276	$2,560.00
Labron Harris, Jr.	T-5	68-69-70-69=276	$2,560.00
Bruce Devlin	T-5	72-69-66-69=276	$2,560.00
Howie Johnson	T-5	69-69-68-70=276	$2,560.00
Bob Bruno	T-10	71-72-68-66=277	$1,675.00
Don Massengale	T-10	70-70-70-67=277	$1,675.00
John-H. Cook	T-10	66-70-73-68=277	$1,675.00
Lionel Hebert	T-10	71-71-67-68=277	$1,675.00

American Golf Classic

Course: Firestone C.C. (South), Akron, Ohio
Par: 70 Yardage: 7,165
Last day of event: Sunday, August 23, 1964

Player	Place	Score	Earnings
Ken Venturi	Win	71-66-69-69=275	$7,500.00
Mason Rudolph	2	70-68-70-72=280	$4,000.00
Arnold Palmer	3	68-73-71-68=280	$3,300.00
Jack Nicklaus	4	73-69-70-73=285	$2,900.00
Tommy Aaron	T-5	74-70-73-69=286	$2,200.00
George Knudson	T-5	72-72-71-71=286	$2,200.00
Tony Lema	T-5	69-71-70-76=286	$2,200.00
R.H. Sikes	T-5	74-73-71-68=286	$2,200.00
Bob McCallister	9	72-69-72-74=287	$1,600.00
Frank Beard	T-10	73-68-74-73=288	$1,450.00
Dave Marr	T-10	76-73-69-70=288	$1,450.00

Carling World Open Championship

Course: Oakland Hills C.C., Birmingham, Mich.
Par: 71 Yardage: N/A
Last day of event: Sunday, August 30, 1964

Player	Place	Score	Earnings
Bobby Nichols	Win	72-68-66-72=278	$35,000.00
Arnold Palmer	2	70-71-67-71=279	$17,000.00
Gary Player	3	72-72-67-70=281	$8,500.00
Ben Hogan	T-4	72-70-72-68=282	$6,850.00
Pete Brown	T-4	71-73-69-69=282	$6,850.00
Bruce Devlin	T-6	68-74-72-69=283	$5,500.00
Terry Dill	T-6	74-71-68-70=283	$5,500.00
Jay Hebert	T-8	73-69-73-70=285	$4,033.34
Gene Littler	T-8	73-71-70-71=285	$4,033.33
Billy Casper	T-8	70-72-71-72=285	$4,033.33

Dallas Open

Course: Oak Cliff C.C., Dallas, Texas
Par: 71 Yardage: 6,836
Last day of event: Monday, September 7, 1964

Player	Place	Score	Earnings
Charles Coody	Win	67-67-68-69=271	$5,800.00
Jerry Edwards	2	71-66-68-67=272	$3,500.00
Fred Haas	T-3	66-72-67-68=273	$2,500.00
Billy Casper	T-3	69-67-67-70=273	$2,500.00
Ray Floyd	5	69-70-67-68=274	$2,000.00
Frank Beard	T-6	66-71-71-67=275	$1,750.00
Johnny Pott	T-6	72-68-69-66=275	$1,750.00
Gay Brewer	8	69-67-67-73=276	$1,600.00
Kermit Zarley	T-9	69-73-68-67=277	$1,300.00
Don Massengale	T-9	70-71-68-68=277	$1,300.00
Don January	T-9	67-71-69-70=277	$1,300.00
Tommy Bolt	T-9	69-66-72-70=277	$1,300.00
Don Cherry	T-9	67-68-71-71=277	$1,300.00

Portland Open

Course: Portland G.C., Portland, Ore.
Par: 72 Yardage: 6,586
Last day of event: Sunday, September 20, 1964

Player	Place	Score	Earnings
Jack Nicklaus	Win	68-72-68-67=275	$5,800.00
Ken Venturi	2	69-69-69-71=278	$3,500.00
Mason Rudolph	3	72-66-71-70=279	$2,700.00
Jim Ferree	T-4	73-68-72-68=281	$2,150.00
Paul Bondeson	T-4	73-71-65-72=281	$2,150.00
Billy Casper	6	72-71-70-69=282	$1,800.00
Don Massengale	T-7	72-73-70-68=283	$1,450.00
Jerry Steelsmith	T-7	73-72-69-69=283	$1,450.00
George Knudson	T-7	73-71-70-69=283	$1,450.00
Gardner Dickinson	T-7	74-72-66-71=283	$1,450.00
Bob Batdorff	T-7	73-70-68-74=285	$1,450.00
Al Geiberger	T-7	70-69-70-74=283	$1,450.00

Seattle Open

Course: Broadmoor C.C., Seattle, Wash.
Par: 70 Yardage: N/A
Last day of event: Sunday, September 27, 1964

Player	Place	Score	Earnings
Billy Casper	Win	68-67-66-64=265	$5,800.00
Mason Rudolph	2	67-70-66-64=267	$3,500.00
Al Geiberger	3	65-68-66-69=268	$2,700.00
Chuck Congdon	T-4	71-68-62-68=269	$2,150.00
Dudley Wysong	T-4	66-69-65-69=269	$2,150.00
Doug Sanders	T-6	69-66-70-65=270	$1,750.00
Tommy Aaron	T-6	69-65-67-69=270	$1,750.00
Bobby Nichols	T-8	68-66-67-70=271	$1,450.00
Labron Harris, Jr.	T-8	69-66-68-68=271	$1,450.00
Fred Marti	T-8	67-66-66-72=271	$1,450.00
Lionel Hebert	T-8	69-65-67-70=271	$1,450.00

Fresno Open

Course: San Joaquin C.C., Fresno, Calif.
Par: N/A Yardage: N/A
Last day of event: Sunday, October 4, 1964

Player	Place	Score	Earnings
George Knudson	Win	73-69-71-67=280	$5,000.00
Al Balding	2	67-75-66-72=280	$3,200.00
Jay Hebert	T-3	72-69-68-74=283	$2,033.34
Frank Beard	T-3	73-69-68-73=283	$2,033.33
Bob McCallister	T-3	69-68-72-74=283	$2,033.33
Ken Still	T-6	73-72-69-70=284	$1,500.00
Jerry Edwards	T-6	75-72-67-70=284	$1,500.00
Gardner Dickinson	T-6	70-70-74-70=284	$1,500.00
Jack McGowan	9	67-74-75-69=285	$1,300.00
Tommy Jacobs	10	72-73-70-72=287	$1,200.00

Sunset-Camellia Open

Course: Sunset Oaks C.C., Sunset City, Calif.
Par: N/A Yardage: N/A
Last day of event: Sunday, October 11, 1964

Player	Place	Score	Earnings
Bob McCallister	Win	69-71-71-70=281	$3,300.00
Stan Leonard	T-2	70-72-72-68=282	$1,900.00
Pete Brown	T-2	72-70-71-69=282	$1,900.00
George Bayer	4	73-69-74-67=283	$1,500.00

Claude King	T-5	70-72-73-69=284	$1,300.00
Al Geiberger	T-5	71-68-71-74=284	$1,300.00
Bob Batdorff	T-5	73-70-69-72=284	$1,300.00
Butch Baird	T-8	75-68-71-71=285	$1,050.00
Jack Rule	T-8	71-70-71-73=285	$1,050.00
Frank Beard	T-9	76-72-73-65=286	$900.00
Randy Glover	T-9	70-72-74-70=286	$900.00
Dick Sikes	T-9	71-73-70-72=286	$900.00

Sahara Invitational

Course: Paradise Valley C.C., Las Vegas, Nev.
Par: 71 Yardage: 7,069
Last day of event: Sunday, October 18, 1964

Player	Place	Score	Earnings
R.H. Sikes	Win	62-71-70-72=275	$12,000.00
Billy Casper	2	70-70-69-67=276	$6,500.00
Jack Nicklaus	T-3	70-71-69-67=277	$3,666.67
Phil Rodgers	T-3	69-70-67-71=277	$3,666.67
Jack McGowan	T-3	71-67-68-71=277	$3,666.66
Frank Beard	6	70-71-66-71=278	$2,900.00
Ken Venturi	T-7	71-67-69-72=279	$2,500.00
Al Geiberger	T-7	68-68-69-74=279	$2,500.00
Tommy Bolt	T-9	70-69-72-69=280	$2,033.34
Bill Johnston	T-9	70-69-68-73=280	$2,033.33
Bert Yancey	T-9	69-71-64-76=280	$2,033.33

Mountain View Open

Course: Mountain View C.C., Corona, Calif.
Par: N/A Yardage: N/A
Last day of event: Sunday, October 25, 1964

Player	Place	Score	Earnings
Jack McGowan	Win	66-68-65-74=273	$5,800.00
R.H. Sikes	2	69-69-69-70=277	$3,500.00
Jack Rule	3	68-69-70-71=278	$2,700.00
Charles Coody	4	69-71-68-71=279	$2,300.00
Billy Casper	T-5	72-72-71-65=280	$1,833.34
George Archer	T-5	73-73-68-66=280	$1,833.33
Howie Johnson	T-5	66-72-71-71=280	$1,833.33
Bud Holscher	T-8	74-65-71-71=281	$1,550.00
Jacky Cupit	T-8	68-68-71-74=281	$1,550.00
Dave Hill	10	69-74-70-69=282	$1,400.00

Almaden Open

Course: Almaden C.C., Almaden, Calif.
Par: 72 Yardage: 7,035
Last day of event: Sunday, November 1, 1964

Player	Place	Score	Earnings
Billy Casper	Win	68-70-73-68=279	$3,300.00
Pete Brown	T-2	72-71-67-69=279	$1,900.00
Jerry Steelsmith	T-2	67-70-72-70=279	$1,900.00
Ken Venturi	4	72-71-67-70=280	$1,500.00
Chuck Courtney	5	70-68-70-73=281	$1,400.00
Charles Sifford	T-6	74-69-66-73=282	$1,250.00
Sam Carmichael	T-6	69-70-71-72=282	$1,250.00
Jim Ferree	8	75-69-71-68=283	$1,100.00
Jacky Cupit	9	72-70-73-70=285	$1,000.00
James Black	T-10	76-69-72-69=286	$875.00
Dave Stockton	T-10	74-72-68-72=286	$875.00
Dick Lotz	T-10	74-70-70-72=286	$875.00
Tony Lema	T-10	70-71-73-72=286	$875.00

Cajun Classic

Course: Oakbourne C.C., Lafayette, La.
Par: 71 Yardage: 6,750
Last day of event: Sunday, November 22, 1964

Player	Place	Score	Earnings
Miller Barber	Win	72-70-68-67=277	$3,300.00
Jack Nicklaus	T-2	68-71-72-71=282	$1,900.00
Gay Brewer	T-2	70-69-74-69=282	$1,900.00
Arnold Palmer	4	68-74-71-71=284	$1,500.00
Gordon Jones	5	72-74-71-68=285	$1,400.00
Frank Beard	T-6	67-79-71-69=286	$1,200.00
Don Massengale	T-6	70-73-69-74=286	$1,200.00
Dick Lotz	T-6	70-71-77-68=286	$1,200.00
Lionel Hebert	T-9	72-74-71-71=288	$900.00
Dave Ragan	T-9	72-74-74-68=288	$900.00
Jack Burke Jr.	T-9	74-74-68-72=288	$900.00
Tommy Aaron	T-9	69-73-74-72=288	$900.00
Kermit Zarley	T-9	69-71-75-73=288	$900.00

1965

Sam Snead won the Greensboro Open for the eighth time, becoming the oldest winner (50 years, 10 months, 21 days) of a PGA Tour event. Jack Nicklaus posted a tournament record 271 to win the Masters by nine shots over Gary Player and Arnold Palmer. Player completed his career Grand Slam with a victory at the U.S. Open, which was scheduled to finish on a Sunday for the first time but was extended to Monday for a playoff between Player (71) and Kel Nagle (74). Peter Thomson of Australia won his fifth British Open, beating Brian Huggen and Christy O'Connor Sr. by two shots at Royal Birkdale. Dave Marr, who would become a popular TV commentator, won the PGA Championship by two shots over Billy Casper and Jack Nicklaus at Laurel Valley.

Los Angeles Open

Course: Rancho Municipal G.C., Los Angeles, Calif.
Par: 71 Yardage: 6,827
Last day of event: Monday, January 11, 1965

Player	Place	Score	Earnings
Paul Harney	Win	68-71-68-69=276	$12,000.00
Dan Sikes	2	71-67-71-70=279	$6,500.00
Billy Casper	2	66-72-72-71=281	$4,000.00
Tony Lema	T-4	70-71-72-69=282	$3,300.00
George Knudson	T-4	76-68-68-70=282	$3,300.00
Bobby Nichols	T-4	70-72-69-71=282	$3,300.00
Charles Coody	T-7	72-72-69-70=283	$2,500.00
Howie Johnson	T-7	69-72-69-73=283	$2,500.00
Gene Littler	T-9	73-69-73-69=284	$1,975.00
Arnold Palmer	T-9	72-73-70-69=284	$1,975.00
Jim Ferree	T-9	74-71-69-70=284	$1,975.00
Charles Sifford	T-9	74-71-68-71=284	$1,975.00

San Diego Open

Course: Stardust C.C., San Diego, Calif.
Home Course -Par: 71 Yardage: 6,725
Last day of event: Sunday, January 17, 1965

Player	Place	Score	Earnings
Wes Ellis	Win	66-65-71-65=267	$4,850.00
Billy Casper	2	70-68-65-64=267	$3,100.00
Johnny Pott	3	66-69-68-65=268	$2,200.00
George Knudson	4	69-68-68-64=269	$2,000.00
Jay Dolan	T-5	66-68-70-68=272	$1,700.00
Bud Holscher	T-5	64-70-70-68=272	$1,700.00
Frank Beard	T-7	69-70-70-64=273	$1,450.00
Bruce Devlin	T-7	70-66-67-70=273	$1,450.00

Jacky Cupit	T-9	71-72-66-65=274	$1,200.00
Charles Sifford	T-9	68-66-69-71=274	$1,200.00
Gene Littler	T-9	62-70-71-71=274	$1,200.00

Bing Crosby National Pro-Am

Courses: Pebble Beach G.L. - Home
Monterey Peninsula C.C., Cypress Point C.C., Pebble Beach, Calif.
Home Course Par: 72 Yardage: 6,747
Last day of event: Sunday, January 24, 1965

Player	Place	Score	Earnings
Bruce Crampton	Win	75-67-73-69=284	$7,500.00
Tony Lema	2	71-65-79-72=287	$4,000.00
Jack Nicklaus	T-3	72-68-77-71=288	$3,100.00
Billy Casper	T-3	70-70-76-72=288	$3,100.00
Al Mengert	T-5	78-67-74-70=289	$2,450.00
Harold Kneece	T-5	69-76-69-75=289	$2,450.00
Ken Still	T-7	76-69-75-70=290	$1,833.34
Jacky Cupit	T-7	77-69-69-75=290	$1,833.33
Rocky Thompson	T-7	74-70-68-78=290	$1,833.33
Terry Wilcox	T-10	72-74-71-74=291	$1,400.00
Jon Gustin	T-10	70-72-76-73=291	$1,400.00
Mike Fetchick	T-10	74-69-78-70=291	$1,400.00

Lucky International Open

Course: Harding Park G.C., San Francisco, Calif.
Par: 71 Yardage: 6,772
Last day of event: Sunday, January 31, 1965

Player	Place	Score	Earnings
George Archer	Win	68-73-69-68=278	$8,500.00
Bob Charles	2	71-67-71-69=278	$4,600.00
George Knudson	T-3	71-69-73-68=281	$3,450.00
Gardner Dickinson	T-3	68-71-71-71=281	$3,450.00
Bud Holscher	T-5	70-73-65-74=282	$2,625.00
Billy Maxwell	T-5	70-70-72-70=282	$2,625.00
John Lotz	T-7	74-71-69-69=283	$1,910.00
Miller Barber	T-7	70-71-72-70=283	$1,910.00
Mike Souchak	T-7	72-70-68-73=283	$1,910.00
Bill Martindale	T-7	69-69-74-71=283	$1,910.00
Jack McGowan	T-7	68-71-68-76=283	$1,910.00

Bob Hope Classic

Course: Bermuda Dunes C.C.—Home Course
Eldorado C.C., Indian Wells C.C., La Quinta C.C.
Home Course Par: 72 Yardage: N/A
Last day of event: Sunday, February 7, 1965

Player	Place	Score	Earnings
Billy Casper	Win	70-70-69-67-72=348	$15,000.00
Arnold Palmer	T-2	70-70-72-67-70=349	$6,600.00
Tommy Aaron	T-2	69-69-69-72-70=349	$6,600.00
Jack Nicklaus	T-4	71-71-69-72-69=352	$3,666.67
Frank Beard	T-4	66-71-73-68-74=352	$3,666.67
Dave Marr	T-4	71-71-68-69-73=352	$3,666.66
Stan Thirsk	T-7	67-67-75-73-71=353	$2,850.00
Don January	T-7	68-67-73-72-73=353	$2,850.00
Al Geiberger	T-9	71-70-68-74-71=354	$2,400.00
Butch Baird	T-9	71-69-68-74-72=354	$2,400.00

Phoenix Open
Course: Arizona C.C., Phoenix, Ariz.
Par: 71 Yardage: 6,216
Last day of event: Sunday, February 14, 1965

Player	Place	Score	Earnings
Rod Funseth	Win	71-68-68-67=274	$10,500.00
Bert Yancey	2	67-70-69-71=277	$6,250.00
Doug Sanders	T-3	73-68-71-66=278	$4,025.00
Don January	T-3	72-68-69-69=278	$4,025.00
Billy Maxwell	T-5	75-70-70-64=279	$2,916.67
Al Geiberger	T-5	68-69-70-72=279	$2,916.67
Frank Beard	T-5	68-69-72-70=279	$2,916.66
Dick Sikes	T-8	72-72-69-67=280	$2,075.00
Randy Glover	T-8	73-68-72-67=280	$2,075.00
Jack Nicklaus	T-8	70-69-70-71=280	$2,075.00
George Knudson	T-8	73-69-69-69=280	$2,075.00

Tucson Open
Course: Tucson National G.C.
Starr Pass G.C., Tucson, Ariz.
Par: 72 Yardage: 7,305
Last day of event: Sunday, February 21, 1965

Player	Place	Score	Earnings
Bob Charles	Win	65-69-67-70=271	$6,800.00
Al Geiberger	T-2	70-70-66-69=275	$3,850.00
Don January	T-2	74-70-69-63=276	$3,850.00
Billy Casper	4	68-72-70-67=277	$2,600.00
Dick Sikes	5	71-69-69-69=278	$2,300.00
Bob Johnson	T-6	69-70-74-66=279	$2,000.00
Tommy Jacobs	T-6	72-69-66-72=279	$2,000.00
Bert Weaver	8	72-68-68-72=280	$1,640.00
Rex Baxter	T-9	74-72-68-67=281	$1,470.00
Jay Hebert	T-9	72-70-71-68=281	$1,470.00

Pensacola Open
Course: Pensacola C.C. Pensacola, Fla.
Par: 72 Yardage: 6,700
Last day of event: Sunday, February 28, 1965

Player	Place	Score	Earnings
Doug Sanders	Win	68-71-65-73=277	$10,000.00
Jack Nicklaus	2	68-71-67-71=277	$6,000.00
Billy Casper	T-3	69-73-67-71=280	$3,850.00
Bill Martindale	T-3	69-68-72-71=280	$3,850.00
Kermit Zarley	5	70-77-65-70=282	$3,100.00
Doug Ford	T-6	71-69-72-71=283	$2,320.00
Jack Rule	T-6	73-72-68-70=283	$2,320.00
Gary Player	T-6	72-70-70-71=283	$2,320.00
Joe Campbell	T-6	73-70-68-72=283	$2,320.00
Arnold Palmer	T-10	71-73-73-67=284	$1,600.00
Bruce Crampton	T-10	72-72-72-68=284	$1,600.00
Dave Marr	T-10	68-72-72-72=284	$1,600.00
Kel Nagle	T-10	68-74-69-73=284	$1,600.00
Don January	T-10	72-72-66-74=284	$1,600.00

Doral Open
Course: Doral C.C. (Blue), Miami, Fla.
Par: 72 Yardage: 6,939
Last day of event: Sunday, March 7, 1965

Player	Place	Score	Earnings
Doug Sanders	Win	65-71-71-67=274	$11,000.00

Bruce Devlin	2	68-67-70-70=275	$6,200.00
Randy Glover	3	70-71-69-68=278	$4,300.00
Terry Dill	4	71-67-71-70=279	$3,700.00
Sam Snead	T-5	73-68-71-70=282	$2,750.00
Fred Marti	T-5	71-73-68-70=282	$2,750.00
Jack Nicklaus	T-5	70-73-69-70=282	$2,750.00
Dave Marr	T-5	68-71-71-72=282	$2,750.00
Lionel Hebert	9	70-73-68-72=283	$2,200.00
Miller Barber	T-10	69-77-68-70=284	$1,750.00
Gardner Dickinson	T-10	70-72-72-70=284	$1,750.00
Dave Hill	T-10	71-69-73-71=284	$1,750.00
Bert Yancey	T-10	71-70-71-72=284	$1,750.00
Jay Hebert	T-10	70-69-72-73=284	$1,750.00
Jack McGowan	T-10	67-74-68-75=284	$1,750.00

Jacksonville Open
Course: Selva Marina C.C., Atlantic Beach, Fla.
Par: 72 Yardage: 6,906
Last day of event: Sunday, March 14, 1965

Player	Place	Score	Earnings
Bert Weaver	Win	70-70-73-72=285	$8,500.00
Bob Charles	T-2	69-70-75-72=286	$3,575.00
Jack Nicklaus	T-2	72-69-73-72=286	$3,575.00
Bruce Devlin	T-2	69-70-73-74=286	$3,575.00
Dave Marr	T-2	71-69-73-73=286	$3,575.00
Sam Snead	T-6	73-73-70-71=287	$2,350.00
Dan Sikes	T-6	74-68-69-76=287	$2,350.00
Gordon Jones	T-8	75-70-72-71=288	$1,825.00
Doug Sanders	T-8	72-71-73-72=288	$1,825.00
Ray Floyd	T-8	77-68-71-72=288	$1,825.00
Phil Rodgers	T-8	72-65-75-76=288	$1,825.00

Azalea Open
Course: Cape Fear C.C., Wilmington, N.C.
Par: 72 Yardage: 6,700
Last day of event: Sunday, March 21, 1965

Player	Place	Score	Earnings
Dick Hart	Win	70-65-72-69=276	$3,850.00
Phil Rodgers	2	68-70-68-70=276	$2,600.00
Joe Campbell	3	69-70-69-70=278	$1,875.00
Jacky Cupit	4	68-73-70-70=281	$1,650.00
Bill Martindale	T-5	68-69-76-69=282	$1,450.00
Butch Baird	T-5	73-69-70-70=282	$1,450.00
Bob Zimmerman	T-5	71-69-71-71=282	$1,450.00
Bob Batdorff	8	69-76-68-70=283	$1,250.00
George Bayer	T-9	71-71-71-71=284	$1,061.67
Harold Kneece	T-9	71-72-69-72=284	$1,061.67
Claude King	T-9	65-72-75-72=284	$1,061.66

Greater Greensboro Open
Course: Sedgefield C.C., Greensboro, N.C.
Par: 70 Yardage: 6,680
Last day of event: Sunday, March 28, 1965

Player	Place	Score	Earnings
Sam Snead	Win	68-69-68-68=273	$11,000.00
Jack McGowan	T-2	71-71-69-67=278	$4,733.34
Billy Casper	T-2	70-67-72-69=278	$4,733.33
Phil Rodgers	T-2	69-71-69-69=278	$4,733.33
Labron Harris, Jr.	5	70-70-67-72=279	$3,200.00
Tony Lema	6	71-74-68-67=280	$2,900.00
Miller Barber	T-7	71-71-69-70=281	$2,275.00

Dan Sikes	T-7	71-70-71-69=281	$2,275.00
Glenn Stuart	T-7	71-73-70-67=281	$2,275.00
Bert Weaver	T-7	70-71-73-67=281	$2,275.00

Masters
Course: Augusta National G.C., Augusta, Ga.
Par: 72 Yardage: 6,925
Last day of event: Sunday, April 4, 1965

Player	Place	Score	Earnings
Jack Nicklaus	Win	67-71-64-69=271	$20,000.00
Gary Player	T-2	65-73-69-73=280	$10,200.00
Arnold Palmer	T-2	70-68-72-70=280	$10,200.00
Mason Rudolph	4	70-75-66-72=283	$6,200.00
Dan Sikes	5	67-72-71-75=285	$5,000.00
Gene Littler	T-6	71-74-67-74=286	$3,800.00
Ramon Sota	T-6	71-73-70-72=286	$3,800.00
Tommy Bolt	T-8	69-78-69-71=287	$2,400.00
Frank Beard	T-8	68-77-72-70=287	$2,400.00
George Knudson	10	72-73-69-74=288	$1,800.00

Houston Classic
Course: Sharpstown C.C., Houston, Texas
Par: 71 Yardage: 7,021
Last day of event: Sunday, April 11, 1965

Player	Place	Score	Earnings
Bobby Nichols	Win	67-69-67-70=273	$12,000.00
Bruce Devlin	T-2	68-69-69-68=274	$5,600.00
Chi Chi Rodriguez	T-2	73-69-68-64=274	$5,600.00
Don January	T-4	71-66-68-72=277	$3,800.00
Bert Yancey	T-4	65-70-68-74=277	$3,800.00
Lou Graham	6	70-70-68-70=278	$3,100.00
Miller Barber	T-7	68-71-70-70=279	$2,425.00
Homero Blancas	T-7	66-72-69-72=279	$2,425.00
Claude King	T-7	70-69-68-72=279	$2,425.00
Dave Marr	T-7	68-72-70-69=279	$2,425.00

Texas Open
Course: Oak Hills C.C., San Antonio, Texas
Par: 70 Yardage: 6,576
Last day of event: Sunday, April 18, 1965

Player	Place	Score	Earnings
Frank Beard	Win	70-67-65-68=270	$7,500.00
Gardner Dickinson	2	65-72-68-68=273	$4,000.00
Tommy Aaron	T-3	66-66-72-70=274	$2,933.34
Bob Verwey	T-3	72-67-66-69=274	$2,933.33
Steve Oppermann	T-3	68-71-65-70=274	$2,933.33
Larry Mowry	T-6	70-68-69-68=275	$2,066.67
Jacky Cupit	T-6	66-70-64-75=275	$2,066.67
Jack Rule	T-6	67-69-67-72=275	$2,066.66
Gay Brewer	T-9	70-70-71-65=276	$1,300.00
Joe Conrad	T-9	73-70-67-66=276	$1,300.00
Bill Martindale	T-9	69-68-72-67=276	$1,300.00
Charles Coody	T-9	71-68-69-68=276	$1,300.00
Pete Brown	T-9	72-67-66-71=276	$1,300.00
Bert Weaver	T-9	66-68-69-73=276	$1,300.00
Johnny Pott	T-9	70-67-66-73=276	$1,300.00

Tournament of Champions
Course: Desert Inn C.C., Las Vegas,, Nev.
Par: 72 Yardage: 7,209
Last day of event: Sunday, April 25, 1965

Player	Place	Score	Earnings
Arnold Palmer	Win	66-69-71-71=277	$14,000.00
Chi Chi Rodriguez	T-2	70-67-72-70=279	$8,000.00
Doug Sanders	T-3	69-68-72-72=281	$6,000.00
Sam Snead	T-4	68-71-74-70=283	$4,750.00
Kel Nagle	T-5	71-73-69-70=283	$4,750.00
Miller Barber	T-6	73-70-72-71=286	$3,750.00
Billy Casper	T-7	68-71-72-75=286	$3,750.00
Bruce Crampton	T-8	69-70-76-72=287	$2,900.00
Dan Sikes	T-9	68-74-68-77=287	$2,900.00
George Knudson	T-10	69-74-72-74=289	$2,400.00

Colonial National Invitational
Course: Colonial C.C., Fort Worth, Texas
Par: 70 Yardage: 7,021
Last day of event: Tuesday, May 11, 1965

Player	Place	Score	Earnings
Bruce Crampton	Win	71-68-71-66=276	$20,000.00
George Knudson	2	68-71-70-70=279	$11,500.00
Gardner Dickinson	T-3	72-69-71-68=280	$5,100.00
Don January	T-3	72-72-68-68=280	$5,100.00
Tony Lema	T-3	71-69-70-70=280	$5,100.00
Chi Chi Rodriguez	T-3	70-73-69-68=280	$5,100.00
Julius Boros	7	72-68-72-69=281	$3,400.00
Gene Littler	T-8	69-71-73-69=282	$2,850.00
Doug Sanders	T-8	70-72-70-70=282	$2,850.00
Ben Hogan	T-10	69-71-75-69=284	$2,233.34
Bill Martindale	T-10	72-72-70-70=284	$2,233.33
Bobby Nichols	T-10	73-71-71-69=284	$2,233.33

Greater New Orleans Open
Course: Lakewood C.C., New Orleans, La.
Par: 72 Yardage: 7,080
Last day of event: Sunday, May 16, 1965

Player	Place	Score	Earnings
Dick Mayer	Win	72-67-66-68=273	$20,000.00
Bill Martindale	T-2	65-71-68-70=274	$9,400.00
Bruce Devlin	T-2	70-67-67-70=274	$9,400.00
George Knudson	T-4	69-68-70-68=275	$4,500.00
Jacky Cupit	T-4	68-69-70-68=275	$4,500.00
Jack Nicklaus	T-4	65-69-72-69=275	$4,500.00
Homero Blancas	T-7	66-70-73-68=277	$3,200.00
Bobby Nichols	T-7	67-71-69-70=277	$3,200.00
Gene Littler	T-7	65-73-69-70=277	$3,200.00
Howie Johnson	T-10	70-70-74-64=278	$2,150.00
Johnny Pott	T-10	70-69-70-69=278	$2,150.00
Bob McCallister	T-10	70-67-72-69=278	$2,150.00
Kermit Zarley	T-10	68-70-70-70=278	$2,150.00
Lionel Hebert	T-10	70-70-69-69=278	$2,150.00
Miller Barber	T-10	67-70-70-71=278	$2,150.00

Memphis Invitational Open

Course: Colonial C.C., Memphis, Tenn.
Par: 70 Yardage: 6,466
Last day of event: Sunday, May 23, 1965

Player	Place	Score	Earnings
Jack Nicklaus	Win	67-68-71-65=271	$9,000.00
Johnny Pott	2	69-67-67-68=271	$5,000.00
Lou Graham	T-3	71-66-71-65=273	$3,175.00
Bob McCallister	T-3	65-71-66-71=273	$3,175.00
Julius Boros	T-3	66-64-71-72=273	$3,175.00
Bert Yancey	T-3	68-68-68-69=273	$3,175.00
Bruce Crampton	T-7	70-65-69-70=274	$2,225.00
Bob Verwey	T-7	68-69-68-69=274	$2,225.00
Jack McGowan	9	67-70-68-71=276	$2,000.00
Deane Beman	T-10	71-71-69-66=277	
Randy Glover	T-10	69-69-69-70=277	$1,800.00

"500" Festival Open

Course: Speedway G.C., Indianapolis, Ind.
Par: 71 Yardage: 6,605
Last day of event: Sunday, May 30, 1965

Player	Place	Score	Earnings
Bruce Crampton	Win	71-70-67-71=279	$15,200.00
Lionel Hebert	T-2	72-68-70-70=280	$6,625.00
Jacky Cupit	T-2	73-71-67-69=280	$6,625.00
Chi Chi Rodriguez	T-4	71-69-71-70=281	$4,200.00
Dan Sikes	T-4	70-70-70-71=281	$4,200.00
Johnny Pott	T-6	70-71-71-70=282	$3,320.00
Miller Barber	T-6	70-70-70-72=282	$3,320.00
Don Massengale	8	73-70-69-71=283	$2,870.00
Don January	T-9	75-72-72-65=284	$2,456.67
Dale Douglass	T-9	73-75-68-68=284	$2,456.67
Mason Rudolph	T-9	71-72-70-71=284	$2,456.66

Buick Open

Course: Warwick Hills C.C., Grand Blanc, Mich.
Par: 72 Yardage: 7,014
Last day of event: Sunday, June 6, 1965

Player	Place	Score	Earnings
Tony Lema	Win	71-70-69-70=280	$20,000.00
Johnny Pott	2	70-71-70-71=282	$12,000.00
Julius Boros	3	69-70-72-72=283	$6,800.00
Jack Nicklaus	4	70-71-70-73=284	$5,000.00
Bert Weaver	5	70-71-71-74=286	$4,500.00
Doug Sanders	6	70-71-74-72=287	$4,000.00
Bob Zimmerman	7	73-70-71-74=288	$3,500.00
Miller Barber	T-8	73-70-76-70=289	$2,550.00
Bruce Devlin	T-8	72-73-72-72=289	$2,550.00
Jacky Cupit	T-8	75-68-73-73=289	$2,550.00
Howie Johnson	T-8	75-69-71-74=289	$2,550.00
George Archer	T-8	75-68-71-75=289	$2,550.00
Gary Player	T-8	73-68-74-74=289	$2,550.00

Cleveland Open

Course: Highland Park G.C., Cleveland, Ohio
Par: N/A Yardage: N/A
Last day of event: Sunday, June 13, 1965

Player	Place	Score	Earnings
Dan Sikes	Win	68-70-68-66=272	$25,000.00
Tony Lema	2	67-70-68-70=275	$13,000.00
Bruce Devlin	3	70-71-68-65=274	$9,000.00
Bert Weaver	4	71-67-70-71=279	$7,000.00
Mike Souchak	T-5	74-70-70-66=280	$4,650.00
Julius Boros	T-5	71-69-70-70=280	$4,650.00
R.H. Sikes	T-5	72-69-69-70=280	$4,650.00
Tommy Aaron	T-5	68-67-71-74=280	$4,650.00
Bob Rosburg	9	71-71-68-71=281	$3,100.00
Arnold Palmer	T-10	71-70-70-71=282	$2,505.00
Randy Glover	T-10	69-70-70-73=282	$2,505.00
Billy Maxwell	T-10	72-69-69-73=283	$2,505.00
Gordon Jones	T-10	71-66-68-77=282	$2,505.00

U.S. Open

Course: Bellerive C.C., St. Louis, Mo.
Par: 70 Yardage: 7,191
Last day of event: Sunday, June 20, 1965

Player	Place	Score	Earnings
Gary Player	Win	70-70-71-71=282	$26,000.00
Playoff: Beat Kel Nagle in18 hole playoff (Player 71, Nagle 74)			
Kel Nagle	T-2	68-73-72-69=282	$13,500.00
Frank Beard	3	74-69-70-71=284	$9,000.00
Al Geiberger	T-4	70-76-70-71=287	$6,500.00
Julius Boros	T-4	72-75-70-70=287	$6,500.00
Ray Floyd	T-6	72-72-76-68=288	$4,500.00
Bruce Devlin	T-6	72-73-72-71=288	$4,500.00
Gene Littler	T-8	73-71-73-72=289	$2,500.00
Tony Lema	T-8	72-74-73-70=289	$2,500.00
Dudley Wysong	T-8	72-75-70-72=289	$2,500.00

St. Paul Open

Course: Keller G.C., St. Paul, Minn.
Par: 71 Yardage: 6,700
Last day of event: Sunday, June 27, 1965

Player	Place	Score	Earnings
Ray Floyd	Win	66-70-65-69=270	$20,000.00
Tommy Aaron	T-2	67-66-69-72=274	$9,400.00
Gene Littler	T-2	67-70-67-70=274	$9,400.00
Dean Refram	4	66-69-73-67=275	$5,000.00
Jack Nicklaus	T-5	70-69-69-68=276	$4,250.00
Bruce Devlin	T-5	70-67-67-72=276	$4,250.00
Gardner Dickinson	T-7	72-68-73-64=277	$3,050.00
Joe Campbell	T-7	65-70-71-71=277	$3,050.00
Dick Sikes	T-7	69-69-68-71=277	$3,050.00
Arnold Palmer	T-7	66-69-70-72=277	$3,050.00

Western Open

Course: Tam O'Shanter C.C., Niles, Ill.
Par: 71 Yardage: 6,686
Last day of event: Sunday, July 4, 1965

Player	Place	Score	Earnings
Billy Casper	Win	70-66-70-74=280	$11,000.00
Chi Chi Rodriguez	T-2	67-71-68-66=272	$4,950.00
Jack McGowan	T-2	71-68-65-68=272	$4,950.00
Gene Littler	T-4	69-69-73-64=275	$3,066.67
Tony Lema	T-4	69-69-68-69=275	$3,066.67
Joe Campbell	T-4	68-70-69-68=275	$3,066.66
Rod Funseth	7	70-70-66-70=276	$2,400.00
Tommy Aaron	T-8	68-73-69-67=277	$2,050.00

Jerry Steelsmith	T-8	69-72-68-68=277	$2,050.00
Al Geiberger	T-8	70-65-69-73=277	$2,050.00
Jim Wiechers	T-8	70-69-67-71=277	

British Open

Course: Royal Birkdale G.C., Southport, Lancashire, England
Par: 72 Yardage: 7,037
Last day of event: Friday, July 9, 1965

Player	Place	Score	Earnings
Peter Thomson	Win	74-68-72-71=285	$4,900.00
Brian Huggett	T-2	73-68-76-70=287	$3,150.00
Christy O'Connor	T-2	69-73-74-71=287	$3,150.00
Roberto De Vicenzo	4	74-69-73-72=288	$2,100.00
Bernard Hunt	T-5	74-74-70-71=289	$1,330.00
Kel Nagle	T-5	74-70-73-72=289	$1,330.00
Tony Lema	T-5	68-72-75-74=289	$1,330.00
Bruce Devlin	T-8	71-69-75-75=290	$770.00
Sebastian Miguel	T-8	72-73-72-73=290	$770.00
John Panton	T-10	74-74-75-70=293	$518.00
Max Faulkner	T-10	74-72-74-73=293	$518.00

Canadian Open

Course: Mississaugua G. & C.C., Mississaugua, Ontario, Canada
Par: 70 Yardage: 6,828
Last day of event: Saturday, July 17, 1965

Player	Place	Score	Earnings
Gene Littler	Win	70-68-69-66=273	$20,000.00
Jack Nicklaus	2	69-66-72-67=274	$12,000.00
Homero Blancas	T-3	75-67-70-68=280	$4,760.00
Joe Campbell	T-3	66-70-73-69=278	$4,760.00
Rod Funseth	T-3	70-71-68-69=278	$4,760.00
Randy Glover	T-3	70-69-69-70=278	$4,760.00
Mason Rudolph	T-3	67-71-69-71=278	$4,760.00
Charles Sifford	T-8	68-71-70-70=279	$3,050.00
Bruce Devlin	T-8	68-68-71-74=281	$3,050.00
Billy Casper	T-10	69-70-71-70=280	$2,500.00
Rex Baxter	T-10	73-67-69-71=280	$2,500.00

Insurance City Open

Course: Wethersfield C.C., Wethersfield, CT.
Par: 71 Yardage: 6,568
Last day of event: Sunday, July 25, 1965

Player	Place	Score	Earnings
Billy Casper	Win	70-72-66-66=274	$11,000.00
Johnny Pott	T-2	71-68-66-69=274	$6,200.00
Bob Goalby	T-3	64-71-70-70=275	$4,000.00
Dave Marr	T-3	67-67-70-71=275	$4,000.00
Al Geiberger	T-5	69-67-70-70=276	$2,883.34
Bob Crowley	T-5	70-67-69-70=276	$2,883.33
Tom Weiskopf	T-5	69-69-67-71=276	$2,883.33
Tommy Aaron	T-8	67-70-72-68=277	$2,050.00
John Berry	T-8	67-72-73-65=277	$2,050.00
Homero Blancas	T-8	70-67-72-68=277	$2,050.00
Dave Hill	T-8	67-66-73-71=277	$2,050.00
Phil Rodgers	T-8	68-71-69-69=277	$2,050.00

Thunderbird Classic

Course: Westchester C.C., Harrison, N.Y.
Par: 72 Yardage: 6,573
Last day of event: Sunday, August 1, 1965

Player	Place	Score	Earnings
Jack Nicklaus	Win	67-66-69-68=270	$20,000.00
Gary Player	2	69-67-65-71=272	$12,000.00
Gardner Dickinson	3	70-71-69-69=279	$6,800.00
Bobby Nichols	4	68-73-67-68=276	$5,000.00
Billy Casper	5	67-67-69-74=277	$4,500.00
Jim Ferree	T-6	71-70-67-70=278	$3,566.67
R.H. Sikes	T-6	69-72-69-68=278	$3,566.67
Mason Rudolph	T-6	70-68-69-71=278	$3,566.66
Pete Brown	T-9	67-73-72-67=279	$2,750.00
Miller Barber	T-9	71-67-70-71=279	$2,750.00

Philadelphia Classic

Course: Whitemarsh Valley C.C., Chestnut Hill, Pa.
Par: 72 Yardage: 6,708
Last day of event: Sunday, August 8, 1965

Player	Place	Score	Earnings
Jack Nicklaus	Win	71-65-73-68=277	$24,300.00
Doug Sanders	T-2	73-68-67-70=278	$13,200.00
Joe Campbell	T-2	72-66-72-68=278	$13,200.00
Randy Glover	4	72-71-67-70=280	$8,100.00
Gary Player	T-5	72-70-70-69=281	$5,600.00
Tony Lema	T-5	71-69-67-74=281	$5,600.00
Gardner Dickinson	T-7	75-72-66-69=282	$3,600.00
Tommy Jacobs	T-7	74-70-69-69=282	$3,600.00
R.H. Sikes	T-7	64-71-73-74=282	$3,600.00
Billy Casper	10	71-72-71-69=283	$2,600.00

PGA Championship

Course: Laurel Valley G.C., Ligonier, Pa.
Par: 71 Yardage: 7,090
Last day of event: Sunday, August 15, 1965

Player	Place	Score	Earnings
Dave Marr	Win	70-69-70-71=280	$25,000.00
Billy Casper	T-2	70-70-71-71=282	$12,500.00
Jack Nicklaus	T-2	69-70-72-71=282	$12,500.00
Bo Wininger	4	73-72-72-66=283	$8,000.00
Gardner Dickinson	5	67-74-69-74=284	$7,000.00
Bruce Devlin	T-6	68-75-72-70=285	$5,750.00
Sam Snead	T-6	68-75-70-72=285	$5,750.00
Tommy Aaron	T-8	66-71-72-78=287	$4,040.00
Jack Burke Jr.	T-8	75-71-72-69=287	$4,040.00
Jacky Cupit	T-8	72-76-70-69=287	$4,040.00
Rod Funseth	T-8	75-72-69-71=287	$4,040.00
Bob McCallister	T-8	76-68-70-73=287	$4,040.00

Carling Open

Course: Pleasant Valley C.C., Sutton, Mass.
Par: 71 Yardage: 6,713
Last day of event: Monday, August 23, 1965

Player	Place	Score	Earnings
Tony Lema	Win	71-71-67-70=279	$35,000.00

Arnold Palmer	2	69-73-70-69=281	$17,000.00
Joe Campbell	3	69-70-73-70=282	$8,500.00
Sam Snead	T-4	72-68-73-70=283	$6,850.00
Gary Player	T-4	71-69-72-71=283	$6,850.00
Dave Marr	T-6	73-69-71-71=284	$5,500.00
Homero Blancas	T-6	71-67-71-75=284	$5,500.00
Claude King	8	70-70-73-72=285	$4,600.00
Christy O'Connor	T-9	74-72-72-68=286	$3,350.00
Jack Rule	T-9	72-70-75-69=286	$3,350.00
Jacky Cupit	T-9	72-70-72-72=286	$3,350.00
Charles Sifford	T-9	73-70-70-73=286	$3,350.00

American Golf Classic

Course: Firestone C.C. (South)
Akron, Ohio
Par: 70 Yardage: 7,165
Last day of event: Sunday, August 29, 1965

Player	Place	Score	Earnings
Al Geiberger	Win	70-69-69-72=280	$20,000.00
Arnold Palmer	2	70-70-74-70=284	$12,000.00
Jacky Cupit	3	72-71-73-69=285	$6,800.00
Bob Charles	4	71-69-76-70=286	$5,000.00
Jack Rule	T-5	73-68-78-70=289	$3,800.00
Bobby Nichols	T-5	69-70-74-76=289	$3,800.00
Johnny Pott	T-5	68-78-69-74=289	$3,800.00
Tony Lema	T-5	71-73-72-73=289	$3,800.00
Doug Sanders	T-9	70-74-75-71=290	$2,525.00
Jack McGowan	T-9	73-72-73-72=290	$2,525.00
Bruce Devlin	T-9	75-71-72-72=290	$2,525.00
George Knudson	T-9	72-70-73-75=290	$2,525.00

Oklahoma City Open

Course: Quail Creek C.C., Oklahoma City, Okla.
Par: 72 Yardage: 7,173
Last day of event: Sunday, September 5, 1965

Player	Place	Score	Earnings
Jack Rule	Win	72-71-70-70=283	$10,000.00
Bobby Nichols	2	71-74-71-68=284	$6,000.00
Phil Rodgers	T-3	72-71-69-73=285	$3,850.00
Randy Glover	T-3	73-69-71-72=285	$3,850.00
Johnny Pott	5	72-71-71-72=286	$3,100.00
Tommy Aaron	6	71-72-72-72=287	$2,800.00
Chuck Rotar	T-7	71-76-72-69=288	$2,200.00
Dave Hill	T-7	74-69-72-73=288	$2,200.00
Tommy Jacobs	T-7	76-70-70-72=288	$2,200.00
Dave Marr	T-7	71-69-74-74=288	$2,200.00

Portland Open

Course: Portland G.C., Portland, Ore.
Par: 72 Yardage: 6,586
Last day of event: Sunday, September 19, 1965

Player	Place	Score	Earnings
Jack Nicklaus	Win	69-68-68-68=273	$6,600.00
Dave Marr	2	69-64-74-69=276	$6,800.00
Billy Maxwell	3	68-69-71-70=278	$3,000.00
Bob Verwey	4	73-71-68-67=279	$2,550.00
Billy Casper	5	70-68-71-71=280	$2,250.00
Al Geiberger	T-6	71-72-72-67=282	$1,800.00

Dudley Wysong	T-6	70-73-70-69=282	$1,800.00
Jerry Steelsmith	T-6	74-70-69-69=282	$1,800.00
Miller Barber	T-9	72-71-72-68=283	$1,450.00
Don Massengale	T-9	73-72-68-70=283	$1,450.00

Seattle Open

Course: Inglewood C.C., Seattle, Wash.
Par: 72 Yardage: 6,707
Last day of event: Sunday, September 26, 1965

Player	Place	Score	Earnings
Gay Brewer	Win	69-72-66-72=279	$6,600.00
Doug Sanders	2	72-71-67-69=279	$3,800.00
Don Massengale	T-3	69-73-72-68=282	$2,775.00
Charles Coody	T-3	68-72-68-74=282	$2,775.00
Phil Rodgers	T-5	72-73-70-68=283	$2,016.67
Rocky Thompson	T-5	71-74-65-73=283	$2,016.67
Howie Johnson	T-5	75-69-68-71=283	$2,016.66
Bob Zimmerman	8	70-74-69-71=284	$1,600.00
Don Bies	T-9	69-74-74-68=285	$1,207.15
Charles Sifford	T-9	72-72-72-69=285	$1,207.15
Jack Nicklaus	T-9	69-74-72-70=285	$1,207.14
Ken Still	T-9	73-73-69-70=285	$1,207.14
Randy Glover	T-9	70-77-68-70=285	$1,207.14
Al Geiberger	T-9	69-70-73-73=285	$1,207.14
Bob McCallister	T-9	68-73-67-77=285	$1,207.14

Sahara Invitational

Course: Paradise Valley C.C.
Las Vegas, Nev.
Par: 71 Yardage: 7,069
Last day of event: Saturday, October 23, 1965

Player	Place	Score	Earnings
Billy Casper	Win	66-66-68-69=269	$20,000.00
Bill Martindale	2	71-70-68-63=272	$12,000.00
Bobby Nichols	3	68-71-68-66=273	$7,500.00
Doug Sanders	T-4	70-69-70-65=274	$4,650.00
Randy Glover	T-4	70-65-68-71=274	$4,650.00
Jack Nicklaus	T-6	71-67-70-68=276	$3,600.00
Tommy Aaron	T-6	70-73-65-68=276	$3,600.00
Bruce Crampton	8	70-70-66-71=277	$3,100.00
George Knudson	9	73-67-70-69=279	$2,800.00
Frank Beard	T-10	72-70-74-65=281	$2,300.00
Al Geiberger	T-10	73-67-72-69=281	$2,300.00
Tommy Bolt	T-10	75-68-69-69=281	$2,300.00
Billy Maxwell	T-10	71-68-69-73=281	$2,300.00

Almaden Open

Course: Almaden C.C., Almaden, Calif.
Par: 72 Yardage: 7,035
Last day of event: Sunday, October 31, 1965

Player	Place	Score	Earnings
Bob Verwey	Win	69-66-67-71=273	$6,800.00
Bill Martindale	2	70-67-69-69=275	$3,850.00
Ken Still	T-3	67-70-65-74=276	$2,825.00
Jim Ferree	T-3	66-67-69-74=276	$2,825.00
George Archer	T-5	71-68-70-68=277	$2,100.00
Gardner Dickinson	T-5	69-69-70-69=277	$2,100.00
Dean Refram	T-5	70-68-70-69=277	$2,100.00

Steve Reid	T-8	69-71-68-70=278	$1,475.00
Al Geiberger	T-8	65-73-69-71=278	$1,475.00
Bob Duden	T-8	71-68-66-73=278	$1,475.00
Mason Rudolph	T-8	69-69-68-72=278	$1,475.00

Hawaiian Open

Course: Waialae C.C., Honolulu, Hi.
Par: 71 Yardage: 7,234
Last day of event: Sunday, November 7, 1965

Player	Place	Score	Earnings
Gay Brewer	Win	74-72-67-68=281	$9,000.00
Bob Goalby	2	73-69-70-69=281	$5,000.00
Frank Beard	T-3	69-71-75-67=282	$3,400.00
George Archer	T-3	70-68-72-72=282	$3,400.00
Al Besselink	T-3	70-71-70-71=282	$3,400.00
Al Geiberger	6	68-71-72-72=283	$2,500.00
Billy Casper	T-7	76-73-68-67=284	$2,225.00
Dick Hart	T-7	73-71-69-71=284	$2,225.00
Paul Bondeson	T-9	73-68-73-71=285	$1,833.34
Charles Coody	T-9	74-75-68-70=285	$1,833.33
Pete Brown	T-9	72-71-70-72=285	$1,833.33

Cajun Classic

Course: Oakbourne C.C., Lafayette, La.
Par: 72 Yardage: 6,550
Last day of event: Sunday, November 28, 1965

Player	Place	Score	Earnings
Babe Hiskey	Win	68-69-71-67=275	$4,250.00
Dudley Wysong	2	72-67-70-66=275	$2,900.00
Rex Baxter	T-3	72-66-70-68=276	$1,900.00
Jack Nicklaus	T-3	69-67-71-69=276	$1,900.00
Jack McGowan	T-5	69-72-69-67=277	$1,650.00
Kermit Zarley	T-5	71-68-69-69=277	$1,650.00
Harold Kneece	7	68-72-69-69=278	$1,500.00
Dave Ragan	8	72-71-67-69=279	$1,400.00
Fred Haas	T-9	69-69-70-72=280	$1,183.34
Claude King	T-9	70-70-68-72=280	$1,183.33
Tom Nieporte	T-9	69-69-70-72=280	$1,183.33

1966

It ranks among the most storied collapses in golf history: Arnold Palmer blew a 7-shot lead after 63 holes in the U.S. Open at the Olympic Club, falling into a playoff with Billy Casper, who beat Palmer 69 to 73 over the extra 18. Years later, Palmer would write that he violated every rule his father had ever taught him about tournament golf: "Never quit, never look up, and most of all, never lose focus until you've completely taken care of business." Jack Nicklaus won the Masters in a playoff with Gay Brewer and Tommy Jacobs, then completed his career Grand Slam by winning the British Open at Muirfield (the first Open Championship contested over four days). Al Geiberger notched a four-shot victory over Dudley Wysong at the PGA Championship. Later that afternoon, popular "Champagne" Tony Lema, who had recorded eight top 10s in his most recent 15 majors—including a victory at the 1964 British Open—was killed in a plane crash. He was 32.

Los Angeles Open

Course: Rancho Municipal G.C., Los Angeles, Calif.
Par: 71 Yardage: 6,890
Last day of event: Sunday, January 9, 1966

Player	Place	Score	Earnings
Arnold Palmer	Win	72-66-62-73=273	$11,000.00

Miller Barber	T-2	71-69-69-67=276	$5,250.00
Paul Harney	T-2	71-71-67-67=276	$5,250.00
Dave Stockton	4	71-69-69-68=277	$3,700.00
Dave Ragan	T-5	67-70-72-69=278	$3,050.00
Billy Casper	T-5	70-71-66-71=278	$3,050.00
Don January	7	72-71-66-70=279	$2,550.00
Al Besselink	T-8	73-68-71-68=280	$2,050.00
Dave Hill	T-8	73-71-68-68=280	$2,050.00
Howie Johnson	T-8	73-69-68-70=280	$2,050.00
Charles Sifford	T-8	71-69-69-71=280	$2,050.00
Dave Marr	T-8	69-71-69-71=280	$2,050.00

San Diego Open

Course: Stardust C.C., San Diego, Calif.
Home Course -Par: 71 Yardage: 6,738
Last day of event: Sunday, January 16, 1966

Player	Place	Score	Earnings
Billy Casper	Win	70-66-68-64=268	$5,800.00
Tom Weiskopf	T-2	68-68-68-68=272	$3,100.00
Tommy Aaron	T-2	65-71-64-72=272	$3,100.00
Don January	T-4	68-68-66-73=273	$2,150.00
Paul Bondeson	T-4	67-65-71-70=273	$2,150.00
Bob Zimmerman	6	67-71-64-72=274	$1,800.00
Dave Hill	T-7	70-68-69-69=276	$1,600.00
Ronnie Rief	T-7	70-68-68-70=276	$1,600.00
Charles Coody	T-7	70-65-70-71=276	$1,600.00
Chris Blocker	10	65-68-74-70=277	$1,400.00

Bing Crosby National Pro-Am

Courses: Pebble Beach G.L. - Home
Monterey Peninsula C.C., Cypress Point C.C., Pebble Beach, Calif.
Home Course Par: 72 Yardage: 6,747
Last day of event: Sunday, January 23, 1966

Player	Place	Score	Earnings
Don Massengale	Win	70-67-76-70=283	$11,000.00
Arnold Palmer	2	70-70-73-71=284	$6,200.00
Bill Martindale	T-3	72-71-69-73=285	$4,000.00
Al Geiberger	T-3	68-74-67-76=285	$4,000.00
Doug Sanders	T-5	75-70-71-71=287	$3,050.00
Randy Glover	T-5	73-72-72-70=287	$3,050.00
R.H. Sikes	T-7	74-74-70-71=289	$2,366.67
Jack Rule	T-7	75-70-70-74=289	$2,366.67
Joe Campbell	T-7	71-75-73-70=289	$2,366.66
Mason Rudolph	T-10	74-74-70-72=290	$1,950.00
Bob Goalby	T-10	74-74-67-75=290	$1,950.00

Lucky International Open

Course: Harding Park G.C., San Francisco, Calif.
Par: 71 Yardage: 6,692
Last day of event: Monday, January 31, 1966

Player	Place	Score	Earnings
Ken Venturi	Win	68-68-71-66=273	$8,500.00
Frank Beard	2	66-67-70-71=274	$4,600.00
George Archer	T-3	73-69-68-65=275	$3,037.50
Tom Weiskopf	T-3	68-69-70-68=275	$3,037.50
Arnold Palmer	T-3	73-66-68-68=275	$3,037.50
Ray Floyd	T-3	69-67-69-70=275	$3,037.50
Joe Campbell	7	68-70-69-69=276	$2,250.00
Charles Sifford	T-8	72-70-69-66=277	$1,833.34
Terry Dill	T-8	69-69-70-69=277	$1,833.33
Dave Ragan	T-8	69-67-71-70=277	$1,833.33

Bob Hope Desert Classic
Course: Indian Wells C.C.
La Quinta C.C., Eldorado C.C., Bermuda Dune C.C., Indian Wells, Calif.
Par: 72 Yardage: 6,651
Last day of event: Sunday, February 6, 1966

Player	Place	Score	Earnings
Doug Sanders	Win	70-72-68-73-66=349	$15,000.00
Playoff: Beat Arnold Palmer with birdie on first extra hole			
Arnold Palmer	2	71-70-71-67-70=349	$8,000.00
Phil Rodgers	T-3	72-71-68-72-67=350	$4,050.00
Dave Marr	T-3	68-73-72-70-67=350	$4,050.00
Mike Souchak	T-3	71-74-67-69-69=350	$4,050.00
Harold Kneece	T-3	68-68-69-72-73=350	$4,050.00
Al Geiberger	T-7	69-73-71-71-67=351	$2,625.00
Julius Boros	T-7	74-71-69-69-68=351	$2,625.00
Billy Casper	T-7	69-73-65-74-70=351	$2,625.00
Al Besselink	T-7	67-75-69-68-72=351	$2,625.00

Phoenix Open
Course: Phoenix C.C., Phoenix, Ariz.
Par: 71 Yardage: 6,765
Last day of event: Monday, February 14, 1966

Player	Place	Score	Earnings
Dudley Wysong	Win	73-69-70-66=278	$9,000.00
Gardner Dickinson	2	66-69-70-73=278	$5,000.00
Gene Littler	3	70-71-69-70=280	$4,000.00
Johnny Pott	T-4	72-73-70-67=282	$4,000.00
Mason Rudolph	T-4	68-71-73-70=282	$4,000.00
George Archer	6	73-68-73-69=283	$25,000.00
Dave Marr	T-7	73-69-73-69=284	$2,225.00
R.H. Sikes	T-7	74-70-70-70=284	$2,225.00
Bill Ezinicki	T-9	71-73-71-70=285	$1,720.00
Richard Crawford	T-9	69-72-72-72=285	$1,720.00
Bob Rosburg	T-9	69-71-69-76=285	$1,720.00
Charles Coody	T-9	69-74-69-73=285	$1,720.00
Doug Sanders	T-9	70-71-69-75=285	$1,720.00

Tucson Open
Course: Tucson National G.C., Starr Pass G.C., Tucson, Ariz.
Par: 72 Yardage: 7,200
Last day of event: Sunday, February 20, 1966

Player	Place	Score	Earnings
Joe Campbell	Win	69-70-69-70=278	$9,000.00
Playoff: Beat Gene Litter with birdie on first extra hole			
Gene Littler	2	71-71-68-68=278	$5,000.00
R.H. Sikes	T-3	72-69-70-69=280	$3,400.00
Jay Hebert	T-3	75-67-65-73=280	$3,400.00
Lionel Hebert	T-3	74-67-70-69=280	$3,400.00
Tommy Aaron	T-6	73-72-68-68=281	$2,316.67
Doug Sanders	T-6	69-70-72-70=281	$2,316.67
George Archer	T-6	69-73-68-71=281	$2,316.66
George Knudson	T-9	75-71-68-68=282	$1,833.34
Frank Beard	T-9	74-69-70-69=282	$1,833.33
Johnny Pott	T-9	70-66-75-71=282	$1,833.33

Pensacola Open
Course: Pensacola C.C., Pensacola, Fla.
Par: 72 Yardage: 6,380
Last day of event: Monday, March 7, 1966

Player	Place	Score	Earnings
Gay Brewer	Win	65-69-67-71=272	$10,000.00
Bruce Devlin	2	66-72-70-67=275	$6,000.00
Jacky Cupit	3	70-68-70-68=276	$4,200.00
Mason Rudolph	4	71-67-69-70=277	$3,500.00
Gordon Jones	T-5	71-71-68-68=278	$2,950.00
Randy Glover	T-5	69-72-66-71=278	$2,950.00
Ray Floyd	7	70-68-71-70=279	$2,500.00
Don Massengale	T-8	70-72-70-68=280	$1,960.00
Dan Sikes	T-8	70-72-71-67=280	$1,960.00
R.H. Sikes	T-8	70-72-71-67=280	$1,960.00
Dick Hart	T-8	69-68-70-73=280	$1,960.00
Julius Boros	T-8	68-70-69-73=280	$1,960.00

Doral Open
Course: Doral C.C. (Blue), Miami, Fla.
Par: 72 Yardage: 7,028
Last day of event: Sunday, March 13, 1966

Player	Place	Score	Earnings
Phil Rodgers	Win	69-69-70-70=278	$20,000.00
Jay Dolan	T-2	66-72-69-72=279	$9,750.00
Kermit Zarley	T-2	65-72-71-71=279	$9,750.00
Frank Beard	T-4	71-67-74-69=281	$3,920.00
Ray Floyd	T-4	75-68-71-67=281	$3,920.00
Jack McGowan	T-4	68-72-73-68=281	$3,920.00
Arnold Palmer	T-4	69-70-71-71=281	$3,920.00
Johnny Pott	T-4	68-70-74-69=281	$3,920.00
Julius Boros	T-9	71-72-67-72=282	$2,400.00
Gay Brewer	T-9	75-73-67-67=282	$2,400.00
Jacky Cupit	T-9	74-66-70-72=282	$2,400.00
Bruce Devlin	T-9	73-68-69-72=282	$2,400.00
Sam Snead	T-9	71-69-72-70=282	$2,400.00

Florida Citrus Open
Course: Rio Pinar C.C., Orlando, Fla.
Par: 71 Yardage: 6,873
Last day of event: Sunday, March 20, 1966

Player	Place	Score	Earnings
Lionel Hebert	Win	71-70-69-69=279	$21,000.00
Charles Coody	T-2	72-74-67-68=281	$8,833.34
Jack Nicklaus	T-2	70-73-68-70=281	$8,833.33
Dick Lytle	T-2	73-67-70-71=281	$8,833.33
Randy Glover	T-5	74-68-73-67=282	$4,150.00
Billy Maxwell	T-5	69-70-74-69=282	$4,150.00
Bob Shave, Jr.	T-5	70-72-72-68=282	$4,150.00
Mason Rudolph	T-5	70-73-68-71=282	$4,150.00
John Lotz	T-9	68-74-69-72=283	$2,800.00
Gay Brewer	T-9	71-69-70-73=283	$2,800.00
Al Besselink	T-9	74-71-66-72=283	$2,800.00
Gardner Dickinson	T-9	69-68-71-75=283	$2,800.00

Jacksonville Open Invitational

Course: Selva Marina C.C., Atlantic Beach, Fla.
Par: 72 Yardage: 6,906
Last day of event: Sunday, March 27, 1966

Player	Place	Score	Earnings
Doug Sanders	Win	71-65-66-71=273	$13,500.00
Gay Brewer	2	67-66-71-70=274	$7,200.00
Gary Player	3	72-67-68-70=277	$5,200.00
Frank Beard	T-4	74-70-66-68=278	$4,100.00
Tommy Bolt	T-4	66-70-68-74=278	$4,100.00
Tony Lema	T-6	74-68-68-69=279	$3,250.00
Bert Weaver	T-6	71-71-66-71=279	$3,250.00
Jack Nicklaus	T-8	70-72-71-67=280	$2,420.00
Tommy Aaron	T-8	71-72-69-68=280	$2,420.00
Ken Still	T-8	74-69-69-68=280	$2,420.00
Ray Floyd	T-8	69-72-70-69=280	$2,420.00
Bruce Devlin	T-8	71-69-69-71=280	$2,420.00

Greater Greensboro Open

Course: Sedgefield C.C., Greensboro, N.C.
Par: 71 Yardage: 7,017
Last day of event: Sunday, April 3, 1966

Player	Place	Score	Earnings
Doug Sanders	Win	65-70-71-70=276	$20,000.00
Playoff: Beat Tom Weiskopf on second extra hole			
Tom Weiskopf	2	68-67-71-70=276	$12,000.00
Miller Barber	T-3	71-73-68-65=277	$6,250.00
Dave Ragan	T-3	69-68-70-70=277	$6,250.00
Dave Marr	5	74-68-68-68=278	$4,300.00
Al Geiberger	T-6	66-70-73-70=279	$3,433.34
Arnold Palmer	T-6	71-71-68-69=279	$3,433.33
R.H. Sikes	T-6	68-69-68-74=279	$3,433.33
Bobby Nichols	T-9	68-74-69-69=280	$2,700.00
Howie Johnson	T-9	67-71-68-74=280	$2,700.00

Masters

Course: Augusta National G.C., Augusta, Ga.
Par: 72 Yardage: 6,980
Last day of event: Monday, April 11, 1966

Player	Place	Score	Earnings
Jack Nicklaus	Win	68-76-72-72=288	$20,000.00
Playoff: Beat Tommy Jacobs and Gay Brewer in 18-hole playoff. (Nicklaus 70, Jacobs 72, Brewer 78)			
Tommy Jacobs	2	75-71-70-72=288	$12,300.00
Gay Brewer	2	74-72-72-70=288	$8,300.00
Arnold Palmer	T-4	74-70-74-72=290	$5,700.00
Doug Sanders	T-4	74-70-75-71=290	$5,700.00
George Knudson	T-6	73-76-72-71=292	$3,900.00
Don January	T-6	71-73-73-75=292	$3,900.00
Ray Floyd	T-8	72-73-74-74=293	$2,500.00
Paul Harney	T-8	75-68-76-74=293	$2,500.00
Jay Hebert	T-10	72-74-73-75=294	$1,770.00
Bob Rosburg	T-10	73-71-76-74=294	$1,770.00
Billy Casper	T-10	71-75-76-72=294	$1,770.00

Azalea Open

Course: Cape Fear C.C., Wilmington, N.C.
Par: 72 Yardage: 6,744
Last day of event: Sunday, April 17, 1966

Player	Place	Score	Earnings
Bert Yancey	Win	74-69-67-68=278	$3,200.00
Bob Johnson	2	72-71-69-67=279	$2,100.00
Dave Marad	3	72-72-68-69=281	$1,650.00
Tom Weiskopf	4	68-73-69-72=282	$1,400.00
Dick Lytle	T-5	74-71-68-70=283	$1,116.67
Al Besselink	T-5	71-69-72-71=283	$1,116.67
Larry Beck	T-5	71-67-72-73=283	$1,116.66
Marvin Fitts	T-8	71-72-70-71=284	$900.00
Kel Nagle	T-8	70-74-70-70=284	$900.00
Roger Ginsberg	T-8	75-72-67-70=284	$900.00
Jerry Barber	T-8	70-70-72-72=284	$900.00
Roberto De Vicenzo	T-8	72-70-69-73=284	$900.00

Tournament of Champions

Course: Desert Inn C.C., Las Vegas,, Nev.
Par: 72 Yardage: 7,209
Last day of event: Monday, April 18, 1966

Player	Place	Score	Earnings
Arnold Palmer	Win	74-70-70-69=283	$20,000.00
Playoff: Beat Gay Brewer in 18 hole playoff (Palmer 69, Brewer 73)			
Gay Brewer	2	70-69-70-74=283	$12,000.00
Billy Casper	3	70-71-74-70=285	$8,000.00
Don Massengale	4	74-72-69-72=287	$5,600.00
Bruce Crampton	T-5	72-71-71-74=288	$4,250.00
Jack Nicklaus	T-5	76-71-69-72=288	$4,250.00
Frank Beard	T-7	75-68-76-70=289	$3,233.34
Dave Marr	T-7	71-72-71-75=289	$3,233.33
Bobby Nichols	T-7	73-72-70-74=289	$3,233.33
Phil Rodgers	T-10	74-74-69-73=290	$2,800.00
Dudley Wysong	T-10	71-70-80-69=290	$2,800.00

Dallas Open

Course: Oak Cliff C.C., Dallas, Texas
Par: 71 Yardage: 6,836
Last day of event: Tuesday, April 26, 1966

Player	Place	Score	Earnings
Roberto De Vicenzo	Win	71-69-69-67=276	$15,000.00
Ray Floyd	T-2	72-67-71-67=277	$5,800.00
Joe Campbell	T-2	70-69-69-69=277	$5,800.00
Harold Henning	T-2	72-68-65-72=277	$5,800.00
Kel Nagle	T-5	72-70-69-67=278	$3,433.34
Tommy Jacobs	T-5	72-66-71-69=278	$3,433.33
John Lotz	T-5	71-71-63-73=278	$3,433.33
Mason Rudolph	T-8	73-70-67-69=279	$2,410.00
Dow Finsterwald	T-8	70-70-70-69=279	$2,410.00
Rocky Thompson	T-8	72-68-68-71=279	$2,410.00
Paul Bondeson	T-8	75-69-65-70=279	$2,410.00
Doug Sanders	T-8	67-70-70-72=279	$2,410.00

Texas Open

Course: Oak Hills C.C., San Antonio, Texas
Par: 70 Yardage: 6,715
Last day of event: Sunday, May 1, 1966

Player	Place	Score	Earnings
Harold Henning	Win	72-67-65-68=272	$13,000.00

Wes Ellis	T-2	68-71-68-68=275	$5,433.34
Ken Still	T-2	70-69-66-70=275	$5,433.33
Gene Littler	T-2	65-70-67-73=275	$5,433.33
Jay Hebert	T-5	67-72-68-69=276	$3,333.34
Terry Dill	T-5	69-67-69-71=276	$3,333.33
Dave Marr	T-5	70-67-67-72=276	$3,333.33
Doug Ford	T-8	70-68-70-69=277	$2,185.72
Rocky Thompson	T-8	69-70-69-69=277	$2,185.72
Al Geiberger	T-8	67-70-70-70=277	$2,185.72
Bob Rosburg	T-8	68-67-70-72=277	$2,185.71
Phil Rodgers	T-8	68-65-72-72=277	$2,185.71
Joe Campbell	T-8	68-70-66-73=277	$2,185.71
Tommy Aaron	T-8	66-68-70-73=277	$2,185.71

Greater New Orleans Open

Course: Lakewood C.C., New Orleans, La.
Par: 72 Yardage: 7,020
Last day of event: Monday, May 16, 1966

Player	Place	Score	Earnings
Frank Beard	Win	68-71-70-67=276	$20,000.00
Gardner Dickinson	2	72-72-66-68=278	$12,000.00
Miller Barber	T-3	72-72-69-66=279	$5,150.00
Tony Lema	T-3	68-71-69-71=279	$5,150.00
Bob Goalby	T-3	68-69-72-70=279	$5,150.00
Jack Nicklaus	T-3	68-70-70-71=279	$5,150.00
Johnny Pott	T-7	72-72-67-69=280	$3,250.00
Billy Casper	T-7	70-70-70-70=280	$3,250.00
Harold Kneece	9	70-73-68-70=281	$2,800.00
Doug Sanders	10	71-70-71-70=282	$2,600.00

Colonial National Invitational

Course: Colonial C.C., Fort Worth, Texas
Par: 70 Yardage: 7,100
Last day of event: Sunday, May 22, 1966

Player	Place	Score	Earnings
Bruce Devlin	Win	67-68-70-75=280	$22,000.00
R.H. Sikes	2	76-67-67-71=281	$12,540.00
Al Geiberger	T-3	70-69-72-71=282	$6,765.00
Tony Lema	T-3	71-71-69-71=282	$6,765.00
Ben Hogan	T-5	72-72-71-69=284	$4,455.00
Jack McGowan	T-5	73-69-68-74=284	$4,455.00
Gardner Dickinson	T-7	74-72-70-69=285	$2,887.50
Bo Wininger	T-7	72-72-71-70=285	$2,887.50
Peter Thomson	T-7	68-72-71-74=285	$2,887.50
Johnny Pott	T-7	70-72-71-72=285	$2,887.50
Don January	T-7	69-73-70-73=285	$2,887.50
Gene Littler	T-7	69-69-70-77=285	$2,887.50

Oklahoma City Open

Course: Quail Creek C.C., Oklahoma City, Okla.
Par: 72 Yardage: 7,173
Last day of event: Sunday, May 29, 1966

Player	Place	Score	Earnings
Tony Lema	Win	69-68-69-65=271	$8,500.00
Tom Weiskopf	2	68-69-68-72=277	$4,600.00
Jack Nicklaus	3	73-70-65-71=279	$3,700.00
Kermit Zarley	4	72-71-67-70=280	$3,200.00
Bruce Devlin	5	68-72-71-70=281	$2,800.00
Frank Beard	T-6	73-72-68-69=282	$2,216.67
Gary Player	T-6	76-70-66-70=282	$2,216.67
Johnny Pott	T-6	64-69-74-75=282	$2,216.67

| Dave Hill | T-9 | 71-70-72-70=283 | $1,775.00 |
| George Archer | T-9 | 70-72-71-70=283 | $1,775.00 |

Memphis Invitational Open

Course: Colonial C.C., Memphis, Tenn.
Par: 70 Yardage: 6,466
Last day of event: Sunday, June 5, 1966

Player	Place	Score	Earnings
Bert Yancey	Win	63-69-67-66=265	$20,000.00
Gene Littler	2	66-66-66-72=270	$12,000.00
Johnny Pott	3	72-64-68-67=271	$7,500.00
Jack Nicklaus	T-4	72-64-68-68=272	$4,650.00
Bruce Devlin	T-4	67-69-66-70=272	$4,650.00
Dale Douglass	T-6	66-71-66-70=273	$3,600.00
Wright Garrett	T-6	66-70-66-71=273	$3,600.00
Gay Brewer	8	70-68-68-70=276	$3,100.00
Jay Dolan	T-9	69-71-72-65=277	$2,175.00
Roger Ginsberg	T-9	67-70-72-68=277	$2,175.00
Dave Hill	T-9	70-67-72-68=277	$2,175.00
Tony Lema	T-9	69-70-69-69=277	$2,175.00
Julius Boros	T-9	72-67-67-71=277	$2,175.00
Jack Rule	T-9	67-68-71-71=277	$2,175.00
Ben Hogan	T-9	71-69-67-70=277	$2,175.00
Bob Verwey	T-9	69-71-65-72=277	$2,175.00

Buick Open

Course: Warwick Hills C.C., Grand Blanc, Mich.
Par: 72 Yardage: 7,280
Last day of event: Sunday, June 12, 1966

Player	Place	Score	Earnings
Phil Rodgers	Win	70-73-71-70=284	$20,000.00
Johnny Pott	T-2	74-71-68-73=286	$9,750.00
Kermit Zarley	T-2	71-74-71-70=286	$9,750.00
Tony Lema	T-4	78-66-70-73=287	$4,650.00
Fred Marti	T-4	70-69-75-73=287	$4,650.00
Steve Spray	T-6	75-73-71-69=288	$3,600.00
Jay Hebert	T-6	73-74-71-70=288	$3,600.00
Arnold Palmer	T-8	73-74-72-70=289	$2,950.00
Doug Sanders	T-8	73-71-71-74=289	$2,950.00
Al Geiberger	T-10	71-76-69-74=290	$2,500.00
Tom Weiskopf	T-10	72-71-72-75=290	$2,500.00

U.S. Open

Course: Olympic Golf Club, San Francisco, Calif.
Par: 70 Yardage: 6,727
Last day of event: Monday, June 20, 1966

Player	Place	Score	Earnings
Billy Casper	Win	69-68-73-68-69=278	$26,500.00

Playoff: Beat Arnold Palmer in a 18 hole playoff (Casper 69, Palmer 73)

Arnold Palmer	2	71-66-70-71-73=278	$14,000.00
Jack Nicklaus	3	71-71-69-74=285	$9,000.00
Tony Lema	T-4	71-74-70-71=286	$6,500.00
Dave Marr	T-4	71-74-68-73=286	$6,500.00
Phil Rodgers	6	70-70-73-74=287	$5,000.00
Bobby Nichols	7	74-72-71-72=289	$4,000.00
Johnny Miller	T-8	70-72-74-74=290	
Doug Sanders	T-8	70-75-74-71=290	$2,800.00
Wes Ellis	T-8	71-75-74-70=290	$2,800.00
Mason Rudolph	T-8	74-72-71-73=290	$2,800.00

Western Open

Course: Medinah C.C. (No 3), Medinah, Ill.
Par: 71 Yardage: 7,014
Last day of event: Sunday, June 26, **1966**

Player	Place	Score	Earnings
Billy Casper	Win	69-72-72-70=283	$20,000.00
Gay Brewer	2	75-71-69-71=286	$12,000.00
Tommy Aaron	T-3	75-68-69-75=287	$6,250.00
Kermit Zarley	T-3	71-69-73-74=287	$6,250.00
Bruce Crampton	T-5	73-73-72-70=288	$3,650.00
Tony Lema	T-5	71-71-75-71=288	$3,650.00
Homero Blancas	T-5	71-69-74-74=288	$3,650.00
Jack McGowan	T-5	71-71-72-74=288	$3,650.00
Billy Maxwell	T-9	72-75-74-68=289	$2,400.00
Charles Coody	T-9	74-71-73-71=289	$2,400.00
Arnold Palmer	T-9	72-70-75-72=289	$2,400.00
George Archer	T-9	73-76-67-73=289	$2,400.00
Ken Venturi	T-9	72-70-71-76=289	$2,400.00

British Open

Course: Muirfield G.C., Muirfield, East Lothian, Scotland
Par: 71 Yardage: 6,887
Last day of event: Saturday, July 9, **1966**

Player	Place	Score	Earnings
Jack Nicklaus	Win	70-67-75-70=282	$5,880.00
Dave Thomas	T-2	72-73-69-69=283	$3,780.00
Doug Sanders	T-2	71-70-72-70=283	$3,780.00
Bruce Devlin	T-4	73-69-74-70=286	$1,974.00
Gary Player	T-4	72-74-71-69=286	$1,974.00
Kel Nagle	T-4	72-68-76-70=286	$1,974.00
Phil Rodgers	T-4	74-66-70-76=286	$1,974.00
Arnold Palmer	T-8	73-72-69-74=288	$924.00
Dave Marr	T-8	73-76-69-70=288	$924.00
Peter Thomson	T-8	73-75-69-71=288	$924.00
Sebastian Miguel	T-8	74-72-70-72=288	$924.00

Minnesota Golf Classic

Course: Keller G.C., St. Paul, Minn. .
Par: 71 Yardage: 6,702
Last day of event: Sunday, July 17, **1966**

Player	Place	Score	Earnings
Bobby Nichols	Win	67-67-66-70=270	$20,000.00
John Schlee	2	66-72-67-66=271	$12,000.00
Terry Dill	T-3	74-65-66-67=272	$6,250.00
Jacky Cupit	T-3	65-66-71-70=272	$6,250.00
Doug Sanders	5	68-69-68-68=273	$4,300.00
Billy Casper	T-6	69-65-73-67=274	$3,433.34
Steve Spray	T-6	66-70-68-70=274	$3,433.33
Dan Sikes	T-6	68-69-66-71=274	$3,433.33
Babe Hiskey	T-9	68-73-67-67=275	$2,700.00
Homero Blancas	T-9	68-70-68-69=275	$2,700.00

PGA Championship

Course: Firestone C.C. (South), Akron, Ohio
Par: 70 Yardage: 7,180
Last day of event: Sunday, July 24, **1966**

Player	Place	Score	Earnings
Al Geiberger	Win	68-72-68-72=280	$25,000.00
Dudley Wysong	T-2	74-72-66-72=284	$15,000.00
Billy Casper	T-3	73-73-70-70=286	$8,333.34
Gene Littler	T-3	75-71-71-69=286	$8,333.33
Gary Player	T-3	73-70-70-73=286	$8,333.33
Julius Boros	T-6	69-72-75-71=287	$5,000.00
Jacky Cupit	T-6	70-73-73-71=287	$5,000.00
Arnold Palmer	T-6	75-73-71-68=287	$5,000.00
Doug Sanders	T-6	69-74-73-71=287	$5,000.00
Sam Snead	T-6	68-71-75-73=287	$5,000.00

"500" Festival Open

Course: Speedway G.C., Indianapolis, Ind.
Par: 72 Yardage: 7,179
Last day of event: Sunday, July 31, **1966**

Player	Place	Score	Earnings
Billy Casper	Win	69-70-68-70=277	$16,400.00
R.H. Sikes	2	69-70-68-73=280	$8,500.00
Jacky Cupit	3	73-68-71-70=282	$5,600.00
Gene Littler	4	71-69-73-70=283	$4,800.00
Chi Chi Rodriguez	5	72-66-73-73=284	$4,100.00
Dale Douglass	6	68-75-73-69=285	$3,700.00
Bobby Nichols	T-7	77-73-68-69=287	$2,820.00
Miller Barber	T-7	71-71-74-71=287	$2,820.00
Don January	T-7	69-74-72-72=287	$2,820.00
Julius Boros	T-7	71-72-70-74=287	$2,820.00
Lionel Hebert	T-7	70-69-73-75=287	$2,820.00

Cleveland Open Invitational

Course: Lakewood C.C., Westlake, Ohio
Par: 71 Yardage: 6,695
Last day of event: Sunday, August 7, **1966**

Player	Place	Score	Earnings
R.H. Sikes	Win	69-68-63-68=268	$20,000.00
Bob Goalby	2	68-67-64-72=271	$12,000.00
Don January	3	71-66-71-66=274	$7,500.00
Bobby Nichols	T-4	67-70-68-70=275	$4,650.00
Julius Boros	T-4	72-64-68-71=275	$4,650.00
Kermit Zarley	T-6	72-69-68-67=276	$3,600.00
Tommy Bolt	T-6	67-71-68-70=276	$3,600.00
Gene Littler	T-8	68-69-72-68=277	$2,620.00
Labron Harris, Jr.	T-8	65-72-70-70=277	$2,620.00
Al Geiberger	T-8	68-73-66-70=277	$2,620.00
Charles Coody	T-8	71-71-65-70=277	$2,620.00
Johnny Pott	T-8	66-70-66-75=277	$2,620.00

Thunderbird Classic

Course: Upper Montclair C.C., Clifton, N.J.
Par: 72 Yardage: 7,055
Last day of event: Sunday, August 14, **1966**

Player	Place	Score	Earnings
Mason Rudolph	Win	69-70-70-69=278	$20,000.00
Jack Nicklaus	2	71-72-66-70=279	$12,000.00
Bill Martindale	3	72-69-66-74=281	$7,500.00
Tommy Aaron	4	74-68-67-73=282	$5,000.00
Dudley Wysong	T-5	69-75-69-71=284	$4,050.00
Jacky Cupit	T-5	72-71-68-73=284	$4,050.00
George Knudson	T-7	69-71-73-72=285	$2,975.00
Jack McGowan	T-7	71-72-70-72=285	$2,975.00
Julius Boros	T-7	71-73-68-73=285	$2,975.00
Gary Player	T-7	69-72-71-73=285	$2,975.00

Insurance City Open

Course: Wethersfield C.C., Wethersfield, CT.
Par: 71 Yardage: 6,568
Last day of event: Sunday, August 21, **1966**

Player	Place	Score	Earnings
Art Wall	Win	65-64-69-68=266	$20,000.00
Wes Ellis	2	65-65-68-70=268	$12,000.00
Billy Casper	T-3	69-69-64-67=269	$6,250.00
George Archer	T-3	71-67-64-67=269	$6,250.00
Julius Boros	5	67-65-70-68=270	$4,300.00
Jim Grant	T-6	68-69-70-64=271	
Paul Bondeson	T-6	69-68-68-66=271	$3,800.00
Homero Blancas	8	65-71-69-67=272	$3,400.00
Kel Nagle	T-9	66-72-70-65=273	$2,620.00
Paul Harney	T-9	68-67-71-67=273	$2,620.00
Kermit Zarley	T-9	69-70-66-68=273	$2,620.00
Al Geiberger	T-9	67-70-68-68=273	$2,620.00
Bob Rosburg	T-9	70-68-67-68=273	$2,620.00

Philadelphia Golf Classic

Course: Whitemarsh Valley C.C., Chestnut Hill, Pa.
Par: 72 Yardage: 6,708
Last day of event: Sunday, August 28, **1966**

Player	Place	Score	Earnings
Don January	Win	69-69-69-71=278	$21,000.00
Jack Nicklaus	2	72-70-70-67=279	$13,000.00
Bob Goalby	T-3	68-72-71-70=281	$6,100.00
Gene Littler	T-3	71-68-71-71=281	$6,100.00
Arnold Palmer	T-3	71-71-65-74=281	$6,100.00
Chuck Courtney	T-6	71-70-72-69=282	$4,100.00
George Knudson	T-6	71-68-69-74=282	$4,100.00
Bill Martindale	T-8	70-68-76-69=283	$3,350.00
Bob Charles	T-8	70-69-74-70=283	$3,350.00
Dan Sikes	T-10	68-76-72-68=284	$2,700.00
Roberto De Vicenzo	T-10	72-67-75-70=284	$2,700.00
Bruce Crampton	T-10	72-69-70-73=284	$2,700.00

Carling World Open

Course: Royal Birkdale G.C., Southport, Lancashire, England
Par: 73 Yardage: 7,037
Last day of event: Saturday, September 3, **1966**

Player	Place	Score	Earnings
Bruce Devlin	Win	73-70-74-69=286	$35,000.00
Billy Casper	2	73-74-69-71=287	$17,000.00
Neil Coles	3	71-72-75-70=288	$8,500.00
Harold Henning	T-4	71-74-75-71=291	$6,500.00
Kel Nagle	T-4	68-74-73-76=291	$6,500.00
Roberto De Vicenzo	T-4	74-73-71-73=291	$6,500.00
Bert Yancey	7	73-68-76-75=292	$5,200.00
Sewsunker Sewgolum	T-8	71-75-75-72=293	$3,416.75
George Archer	T-8	75-71-75-72=293	$3,416.75
Barry Coxon	T-8	75-70-74-74=293	$3,416.75
Peter Thomson	T-8	70-75-73-75=293	$3,416.75
Terry Dill	T-8	71-73-74-75=293	$3,416.75
Bob Charles	T-8	70-74-75-74=293	$3,416.75

Portland Open Invitational

Course: Columbia-Edgewater C.C., Portland, Ore.
Par: 72 Yardage: 6,390
Last day of event: Sunday, September 18, **1966**

Player	Place	Score	Earnings
Bert Yancey	Win	68-68-68-67=271	$6,800.00
Billy Casper	2	67-71-67-69=274	$3,900.00
Pete Brown	3	67-68-69-72=276	$3,100.00
Bruce Crampton	T-4	70-70-68-69=277	$2,450.00
Wright Garrett	T-4	72-69-65-71=277	$2,450.00
Jack Nicklaus	T-6	72-72-65-70=279	$1,616.67
Laurie Hammer	T-6	68-70-69-72=279	$1,616.67
George Knudson	T-6	72-70-66-71=279	$1,616.67
Gay Brewer	T-6	69-67-72-71=279	$1,616.67
Paul Bondeson	T-6	72-69-66-72=279	$1,616.66
Bob Goalby	T-6	67-67-71-74=279	$1,616.66

Greater Seattle-Everett Open Invitational

Course: Everett C.C., Everett, Wash.
Par: 71 Yardage: 6,123
Last day of event: Sunday, September 25, **1966**

Player	Place	Score	Earnings
Homero Blancas	Win	66-65-65-70=266	$6,600.00
Jacky Cupit	2	69-65-67-66=267	$3,800.00
Paul Bondeson	T-3	69-67-67-68=271	$2,775.00
Don Bies	T-3	69-66-67-69=271	$2,775.00
Dave Hill	5	68-70-68-68=274	$2,250.00
Chi Chi Rodriguez	T-6	70-68-70-68=276	$1,900.00
Bob Goalby	T-6	65-73-67-71=276	$1,900.00
Bob Rosburg	8	69-69-68-71=277	$1,600.00
Dan Sikes	T-9	72-67-70-69=278	$1,450.00
Lou Graham	T-9	72-69-70-67=278	$1,450.00

Canadian Open

Course: Shaughnessy Golf & Country Club, Vancouver. B.C., Canada
Par: 71 Yardage: 6,907
Last day of event: Sunday, October 2, **1966**

Player	Place	Score	Earnings
Don Massengale	Win	70-70-70-70=280	$20,000.00
Chi Chi Rodriguez	2	73-68-67-75=283	$12,000.00
R.H. Sikes	T-3	72-76-69-67=284	$4,516.67
Tommy Aaron	T-3	70-76-71-67=284	$4,516.67
Randy Glover	T-3	70-70-69-75=284	$4,516.67
Rod Funseth	T-3	72-69-73-70=284	$4,516.67
Lou Graham	T-3	73-71-66-74=284	$4,516.66
Homero Blancas	T-3	70-73-70-71=284	$4,516.66
Steve Spray	T-9	73-73-71-68=285	$2,700.00
Bob Goalby	T-9	74-71-70-70=285	$2,700.00

Sahara Invitational

Course: Paradise Valley C.C., Las Vegas, Nev.
Par: 71 Yardage: 7,069
Last day of event: Saturday, October 15, **1966**

Player	Place	Score	Earnings
Jack Nicklaus	Win	71-77-68-66=282	$20,000.00
Miller Barber	T-2	72-79-64-70=285	$9,750.00
Arnold Palmer	T-2	71-80-67-67=285	$9,750.00
Gardner Dickinson	T-4	72-76-71-68=287	$4,650.00
George Archer	T-4	69-79-70-69=287	$4,650.00
Chi Chi Rodriguez	6	71-77-71-70=289	$3,800.00

Billy Casper	T-7	73-78-65-74=290	$3,250.00
Bob McCallister	T-7	71-74-71-74=290	$3,250.00
Rex Baxter	9	73-79-72-67=291	$2,800.00
Dale Douglass	10	74-76-70-72=292	$2,600.00

Hawaiian Open

Course: Waialae C.C., Honolulu, Hi.
Par: 72 Yardage: 7,020
Last day of event: Sunday, October 30, **1966**

Player	Place	Score	Earnings
Ted Makalena	Win	66-71-66-68=271	$8,500.00
Billy Casper	T-2	72-66-67-69=274	$4,125.00
Gay Brewer	T-2	70-67-69-68=274	$4,125.00
Gene Littler	4	72-69-70-65=276	$3,150.00
Doug Sanders	5	66-67-73-72=278	$2,750.00
Ken Still	T-6	67-69-72-71=279	$2,200.00
Al Geiberger	T-6	70-71-67-71=279	$2,200.00
Jack McGowan	T-6	70-68-69-72=279	$2,200.00

Houston Champions International

Course: Champions G.C., Houston, Texas
Par: 71 Yardage: 7,118
Last day of event: Sunday, November 20, **1966**

Player	Place	Score	Earnings
Arnold Palmer	Win	70-68-68-69=275	$21,000.00
Gardner Dickinson	2	69-67-69-71=276	$13,000.00
George Archer	3	68-71-70-68=277	$8,000.00
Lionel Hebert	T-4	70-70-72-66=278	$5,150.00
Julius Boros	T-4	66-72-71-69=278	$5,150.00
Doug Sanders	6	70-67-72-70=279	$4,300.00
Bert Yancey	T-7	71-70-72-67=280	$3,375.00
Jacky Cupit	T-7	68-74-71-67=280	$3,375.00
Al Geiberger	T-7	70-68-69-73=280	$3,375.00
Tommy Bolt	T-7	74-66-68-72=280	$3,375.00

Cajun Classic

Course: Oakbourne C.C., Lafayette, La.
Par: 72 Yardage: 6,550
Last day of event: Sunday, November 27, **1966**

Player	Place	Score	Earnings
Jacky Cupit	Win	68-66-65-72=271	$4,850.00
Playoff: Beat Chi Chi Rodriguez on second extra hole			
Chi Chi Rodriguez	2	67-68-67-69=271	$3,100.00
Dan Sikes	3	70-67-69-67=273	$2,200.00
Dave Hill	4	69-68-67-70=274	$2,000.00
Wright Garrett	T-5	66-68-72-69=275	$1,700.00
Dave Stockton	T-5	72-66-69-68=275	$1,700.00
Gardner Dickinson	7	69-68-70-69=276	$1,500.00
Doug Sanders	T-8	70-70-69-68=277	$1,300.00
John Josephson	T-8	68-68-72-69=277	$1,300.00
Jack McGowan	T-8	69-71-67-70=277	$1,300.00

1967

Gay Brewer, who had lost in a playoff the year before, won the Masters with a closing 67. Jack Nicklaus won the U.S. Open by four shots over Arnold Palmer. Lee Trevino, a 27-year-old Mexican American, arrived on the scene that week with a fifth-place finish at Baltusrol, where Ben Hogan tied for 34th in his last U.S. Open. The British Open went to Roberto de Vicenzo of Argentina, who bested Nicklaus by two shots at Hoylake. Don January won the PGA Championship in a playoff against Don Massingale. At age 47, Julius Boros won three times in 1967.

San Diego Open

Course: Stardust C.C., San Diego, Calif.
Home Course -Par: 72 Yardage: 6,738
Last day of event: Sunday, January 15, 1967

Player	Place	Score	Earnings
Bob Goalby	Win	68-64-68-69=269	$13,200.00
Gay Brewer	2	66-72-68-64=270	$7,920.00
Bob Charles	3	69-70-68-66=273	$4,950.00
Dave Hill	T-4	69-68-69-68=274	$3,069.00
Al Geiberger	T-4	69-69-67-69=274	$3,069.00
Billy Casper	T-6	71-70-68-66=275	$2,161.50
Ronnie Reif	T-6	68-68-71-68=275	$2,161.50
Pete Brown	T-6	71-69-67-68=275	$2,161.50
Randy Glover	T-6	65-67-74-69=275	$2,161.50
Richard Crawford	T-10	71-70-71-64=276	$1,336.50
George Archer	T-10	68-71-71-66=276	$1,336.50
Bill Ezinicki	T-10	70-68-71-67=276	$1,336.50
Tommy Aaron	T-10	68-75-66-67=276	$1,336.50
Hugh Royer	T-10	70-72-66-68=276	$1,336.50
Chris Blocker	T-10	68-67-72-69=276	$1,336.50
Art Wall	T-10	71-65-70-70=276	$1,336.50
Doug Sanders	T-10	69-69-67-71=276	$1,336.50

Bing Crosby National Pro-Am

Courses: Pebble Beach G.L., Spyglass Hill G.C., Cypress Point C.C., Pebble Beach, Calif.
Home Course / Pebble Beach G.L., Par: 72 Yardage: 6,747
Last day of event: Sunday, January 22, 1967

Player	Place	Score	Earnings
Jack Nicklaus	Win	69-73-74-68=284	$16,000.00
Billy Casper	2	72-74-69-74=289	$9,600.00
Arnold Palmer	3	74-75-67-75=291	$6,000.00
Bob Rosburg	T-4	72-75-72-74=293	$3,493.34
Jack Burke Jr.	T-4	70-75-74-74=293	$3,493.33
Bill Parker	T-4	75-72-70-76=293	$3,493.33
Doug Sanders	T-7	73-78-72-71=294	$2,040.00
Dave Hill	T-7	73-80-70-71=294	$2,040.00
Frank Beard	T-7	72-75-75-72=294	$2,040.00
Gardner Dickinson	T-7	75-74-73-72=294	$2,040.00
Howie Johnson	T-7	73-76-72-73=294	$2,040.00
Bob McCallister	T-7	73-71-75-75=294	$2,040.00
Wes Ellis	T-7	73-75-71-75=294	$2,040.00
Al Geiberger	T-7	70-77-71-76=294	$2,040.00

Los Angles Open

Course: Rancho Municipal G.C., Los Angeles, Calif.
Par: 71 Yardage: 6,821
Last day of event: Sunday, January 29, 1967

Player	Place	Score	Earnings
Arnold Palmer	Win	70-64-67-68=269	$20,000.00
Gay Brewer	2	67-70-68-69=274	$12,000.00
Julius Boros	T-3	67-72-69-67=275	$5,600.00
Don Massengale	T-3	67-65-74-69=275	$5,600.00
Lou Graham	T-3	67-72-67-69=275	$5,600.00
Bruce Crampton	T-6	70-71-67-69=277	$3,600.00
Billy Casper	T-6	72-70-66-69=277	$3,600.00
Jacky Cupit	T-8	66-71-74-67=278	$2,833.34
Bob Goalby	T-8	70-68-72-68=278	$2,833.34
Mike Souchak	T-8	71-68-71-68=278	$2,833.33

Bob Hope Classic

Course: La Quinta C.C., Indian Wells C.C., Eldorado C.C., Bermuda Dunes C.C.
Home Course / La Quinta, Par: 72 Yardage: 6,904
Last day of event: Sunday, February 5, 1967

Player	Place	Score	Earnings
Tom Nieporte	Win	76-68-68-68-69=349	$17,600.00
Doug Sanders	2	70-73-69-67-71=350	$10,560.00
Chi Chi Rodriguez	3	70-71-70-73-70=354	$6,600.00
Paul Harney	T-4	73-68-72-72-70=355	$3,630.00
Jack Nicklaus	T-4	75-70-67-71-72=355	$3,630.00
Bert Yancey	T-4	72-72-71-69-71=355	$3,630.00
George Archer	T-4	73-70-72-66-74=355	$3,630.00
Billy Casper	T-8	69-75-68-73-71=356	$2,493.34
Dale Douglass	T-8	70-70-75-71-70=356	$2,493.33
Bob Charles	T-8	71-71-72-69-73=356	$2,493.33

Phoenix Open

Course: Arizona C.C., Phoenix, Ariz.
Par: 71 Yardage: 6,489
Last day of event: Sunday, February 12, 1967

Player	Place	Score	Earnings
Julius Boros	Win	69-67-69-67=272	$14,000.00
Ken Still	2	66-74-70-63=273	$8,400.00
Gardner Dickinson	T-3	71-67-67-69=274	$4,375.00
Rod Funseth	T-3	68-64-70-72=274	$4,375.00
Tommy Aaron	T-5	69-73-68-65=275	$2,835.00
Dean Refram	T-5	66-72-65-72=275	$2,835.00
George Knudson	7	69-68-72-67=276	$2,380.00
Doug Sanders	T-8	69-68-73-67=277	$1,907.50
Roger Ginsberg	T-8	69-69-69-70=277	$1,907.50
Jack Rule	T-8	66-70-70-71=277	$1,907.50
Jerry Mowlds	T-8	72-67-66-72=277	$1,907.50

Tucson Open

Course: Tucson National G.C., Starr Pass G.C., Tucson, Ariz.
Par: 72 Yardage: 7,200
Last day of event: Sunday, February 19, 1967

Player	Place	Score	Earnings
Arnold Palmer	Win	66-67-67-73=273	$12,000.00
Chuck Courtney	2	67-69-68-70=274	$7,200.00
Bruce Crampton	3	67-71-66-71=275	$4,500.00
John Schlee	4	71-66-69-71=277	$3,000.00
Paul Bondeson	T-5	72-66-71-69=278	$2,430.00
Rod Funseth	T-5	71-68-66-73=278	$2,430.00
Dick Hart	7	73-68-68-70=279	$2,040.00
Tommy Jacobs	T-8	69-73-69-69=280	$1,635.00
Bob Harris	T-8	71-71-70-68=280	$1,635.00
Charles Sifford	T-8	69-70-69-72=280	$1,635.00
Randy Glover	T-8	68-72-67-73=280	$1,635.00

Doral Open

Course: Doral C.C. (Blue), Miami, Fla.
Par: 72 Yardage: 7,002
Last day of event: Sunday, March 5, 1967

Player	Place	Score	Earnings
Doug Sanders	Win	68-71-66-70=275	$20,000.00
Art Wall	T-2	71-67-69-69=276	$9,750.00
Harold Henning	T-2	68-69-67-72=276	$9,750.00
Jack Nicklaus	4	68-71-66-72=277	$5,880.00
George Archer	T-5	68-71-71-68=278	$3,480.00

Lionel Hebert	T-5	72-68-69-69=278	$3,480.00
Bobby Nichols	T-5	70-70-67-71=278	$3,480.00
Miller Barber	T-5	69-70-67-72=278	$3,480.00
Tommy Aaron	T-5	66-70-67-75=278	$3,480.00
John Schlee	T-10	73-70-69-67=279	$2,085.72
Don January	T-10	71-70-70-68=279	$2,085.72
Kermit Zarley	T-10	71-66-71-71=279	$2,085.72
Arnold Palmer	T-10	67-72-69-71=279	$2,085.71
Billy Maxwell	T-10	70-69-68-72=279	$2,085.71
Dan Sikes	T-10	73-68-67-71=279	$2,085.71
Dave Stockton	T-10	73-67-68-71=279	$2,085.71

Florida Citrus Open

Course: Rio Pinar C.C., Orlando, Fla.
Par: 71 Yardage: 7,012
Last day of event: Sunday, March 12, 1967

Player	Place	Score	Earnings
Julius Boros	Win	70-67-67-70=274	$23,000.00
Arnold Palmer	T-2	67-69-71-68=275	$11,212.50
George Knudson	T-2	70-70-69-66=275	$11,212.50
Dean Refram	4	66-68-70-72=276	$5,750.00
Mason Rudolph	T-5	74-69-70-64=277	$4,657.50
Kermit Zarley	T-5	69-69-66-73=277	$4,657.50
Bobby Nichols	T-7	71-67-71-69=278	$3,565.00
Jack Nicklaus	T-7	71-69-69-69=278	$3,565.00
Bert Yancey	T-7	69-70-68-71=278	$3,565.00
Ken Still	T-10	72-69-72-66=279	$3,565.00
Bruce Devlin	T-10	69-68-72-70=279	$3,565.00
Gardner Dickinson	T-10	69-73-68-69=279	$3,565.00
Johnny Pott	T-10	71-67-70-71=279	$3,565.00
Jack McGowan	T-10	70-71-68-70=279	$3,565.00
Doug Sanders	T-10	66-66-73-74=279	$3,565.00

Jacksonville Open

Course: Deerwood Club, Jacksonville, Fla.
Par: 72 Yardage: 7,075
Last day of event: Sunday, March 19, 1967

Player	Place	Score	Earnings
Dan Sikes	Win	67-69-70-73=279	$20,000.00
Bill Collins	2	71-69-73-67=280	$12,000.00
Gay Brewer	T-3	68-70-71-72=281	$6,250.00
Jim Colbert	T-3	68-72-72-69=281	$6,250.00
Bob Goalby	T-5	70-69-71-72=282	$4,050.00
Chuck Courtney	T-5	70-71-69-72=282	$4,050.00
Julius Boros	7	71-69-73-70=283	$3,400.00
Don January	8	70-70-74-70=284	$3,100.00
Gary Player	T-9	72-72-73-68=285	$2,500.00
Billy Maxwell	T-9	73-70-72-70=285	$2,500.00
Jacky Cupit	T-9	71-69-74-71=285	$2,500.00
Mason Rudolph	T-9	69-73-69-74=285	$2,500.00

Pensacola Open

Course: Pensacola C.C., Pensacola, Fla.
Par: 72 Yardage: 6,380
Last day of event: Sunday, March 26, 1967

Player	Place	Score	Earnings
Gay Brewer	Win	66-64-61-71=262	$15,000.00
Bob Keller	2	65-72-66-65=268	$9,000.00
Doug Sanders	3	69-71-65-64=269	$5,625.00
Ken Still	4	67-66-67-71=271	$3,750.00
Jim Colbert	T-5	66-71-68-67=272	$2,610.00

Dan Sikes	T-5	70-66-68-68=272	$2,610.00
Bobby Nichols	T-5	68-65-71-68=272	$2,610.00
George Archer	T-5	68-70-65-69=272	$2,610.00
Tommy Jacobs	T-5	73-65-65-69=272	$2,610.00
Frank Beard	T-10	71-70-68-64=273	$1,612.50
Miller Barber	T-10	72-67-69-65=273	$1,612.50
Deane Beman	T-10	68-71-68-66=273	
Mike Souchak	T-10	68-68-67-70=273	$1,612.50
Chuck Courtney	T-10	67-70-64-72=273	$1,612.50
Phil Rodgers	T-10	67-66-67-73=273	$1,612.50
Homero Blancas	T-10	65-67-69-72=273	$1,612.50

Greater Greensboro Open

Course: Sedgefield C.C., Greensboro, N.C.
Par: 71 Yardage: 7,017
Last day of event: Sunday, April 2, 1967

Player	Place	Score	Earnings
George Archer	Win	67-64-68-68=267	$25,000.00
Doug Sanders	2	67-68-70-64=269	$15,000.00
Arnold Palmer	3	69-68-68-66=271	$9,375.00
Dave Stockton	4	67-67-65-74=273	$6,250.00
Charles Sifford	5	69-70-67-68=274	$5,375.00
Gene Littler	6	70-70-68-67=275	$4,750.00
Rex Baxter	7	73-68-66-69=276	$4,250.00
Paul Harney	T-8	72-67-70-68=277	$3,687.50
John Schlee	T-8	71-71-72-63=277	$3,687.50
Al Geiberger	T-10	71-70-71-66=278	$3,125.00
Sam Snead	T-10	70-68-72-68=278	$3,125.00

Masters

Course: Augusta National G.C., Augusta, Ga.
Par: 72 Yardage: 6,980
Last day of event: Sunday, April 9, 1967

Player	Place	Score	Earnings
Gay Brewer	Win	73-68-72-67=280	$20,000.00
Bobby Nichols	2	72-69-70-70=281	$14,000.00
Bert Yancey	3	67-73-71-73=284	$9,000.00
Arnold Palmer	4	73-73-70-69=285	$6,600.00
Julius Boros	5	71-70-70-75=286	$5,500.00
Gary Player	T-6	75-69-72-71=287	$4,150.00
Paul Harney	T-6	73-71-74-69=287	$4,150.00
Lionel Hebert	T-8	77-71-67-73=288	$3,350.00
Tommy Aaron	T-8	75-68-74-71=288	$3,350.00
Ben Hogan	T-10	74-73-66-77=290	$2,720.00
Sam Snead	T-10	72-76-71-71=290	$2,720.00
Mason Rudolph	T-10	72-76-72-70=290	$2,720.00
Roberto De Vicenzo	T-10	73-72-74-71=290	$2,720.00
Bruce Devlin	T-10	74-70-75-71=290	$2,720.00

Azalea Open

Course: Cape Fear C.C., Wilmington, N.C.
Par: 72 Yardage: 6,744
Last day of event: Sunday, April 16, 1967

Player	Place	Score	Earnings
Randy Glover	Win	68-69-67-74=278	$5,000.00
Playoff: Beat Joe Campbell with birdie on second extra hole			
Joe Campbell	2	68-71-73-66=278	$6,600.00
Rocky Thompson	3	70-71-70-68=279	$2,500.00
Howell Fraser	T-4	70-68-70-72=280	$1,975.00
John-H. Cook	T-4	74-69-69-68=280	$1,975.00
Bob Verwey	T-6	72-66-69-74=281	$1,550.00

Jack McGowan	T-6	68-73-68-72=281	$1,550.00
Kel Nagle	T-8	70-69-69-74=282	$1,250.00
Bill Ezinicki	T-8	70-75-68-69=282	$1,250.00
Larry Mowry	T-8	65-67-76-74=282	$1,250.00
Monty Kaser	9	74-70-69-70=283	$1,000.00
Art Proctor	T-10	71-73-72-68=284	$875.00
Dave Marad	T-10	73-71-72-68=284	$875.00
Wright Garrett	T-10	72-71-72-69=284	$875.00
Dale Douglass	T-10	70-71-71-72=284	$875.00

Tournament of Champions

Course: Stardust C.C., Las Vegas, Nev.
Home course / Par: 71 Yardage: 6,625
Last day of event: Sunday, April 16, 1967

Player	Place	Score	Earnings
Frank Beard	Win	65-68-74-71=278	$20,000.00
Arnold Palmer	2	68-73-74-64=279	$12,000.00
George Archer	3	68-74-72-68=282	$8,000.00
Bobby Nichols	T-4	68-71-75-70=284	$4,700.00
Jack Nicklaus	T-4	68-68-75-73=284	$4,700.00
Doug Sanders	T-4	67-69-77-71=284	$4,700.00
Roberto De Vicenzo	T-7	70-74-68-73=285	$3,233.33
Dan Sikes	T-7	68-68-73-76=285	$3,233.33
R.H. Sikes	T-7	69-70-75-71=285	$3,233.34
Bert Yancey	10	70-75-71-70=286	$2,850.00

Byron Nelson Dallas Open

Course: Oak Cliff C.C., Dallas, Texas
Par: 71 Yardage: 6,777
Last day of event: Sunday, April 23, 1967

Player	Place	Score	Earnings
Bert Yancey	Win	68-69-66-71=274	$20,000.00
Roberto De Vicenzo	T-2	70-64-73-68=275	$9,750.00
Kermit Zarley	T-2	66-70-68-71=275	$9,750.00
Bob Goalby	T-4	69-66-70-71=276	$4,650.00
Doug Sanders	T-4	70-69-67-70=276	$4,650.00
Charles Sifford	6	68-67-70-72=277	$3,800.00
Bob Charles	T-7	73-68-65-73=279	$3,100.00
Bruce Crampton	T-7	69-69-70-71=279	$3,100.00
Johnny Pott	T-7	70-71-67-71=279	$3,100.00
Rex Baxter	T-10	72-65-72-71=280	$2,400.00
Billy Casper	T-10	67-70-71-72=280	$2,400.00
Dale Douglass	T-10	70-73-70-67=280	$2,400.00

Texas Open

Course: Pecan Valley, San Antonio, Texas
Par: 71 Yardage: 7,138
Last day of event: Sunday, April 30, 1967

Player	Place	Score	Earnings
Chi Chi Rodriguez	Win	68-73-70-66=277	$20,000.00
Bob Goalby	T-2	72-66-72-68=278	$9,750.00
Bob Charles	T-2	71-67-73-67=278	$9,750.00
Billy Casper	T-4	71-70-69-72=282	$4,650.00
Miller Barber	T-4	72-71-67-72=282	$4,650.00
Rex Baxter	T-6	72-70-73-68=283	$3,275.00
Tom Weiskopf	T-6	70-70-74-69=283	$3,275.00
Harold Henning	T-6	72-69-72-70=283	$3,275.00
R.H. Sikes	T-6	74-70-68-71=283	$3,275.00
Roberto De Vicenzo	10	70-70-73-71=284	$2,600.00

Houston Championship International

Course: Champions G.C., Houston, Texas
Par: 71 Yardage: 7,118
Last day of event: Sunday, May 7, 1967

Player	Place	Score	Earnings
Frank Beard	Win	67-70-70-67=274	$23,000.00
Arnold Palmer	2	68-66-70-71=275	$13,800.00
Charles Coody	T-3	70-72-69-67=278	$7,187.50
Ben Hogan	T-3	69-69-72-68=278	$7,187.50
Julius Boros	T-5	70-73-71-65=279	$4,657.50
Harold Henning	T-5	68-71-70-70=279	$4,657.50
Tom Weiskopf	7	72-68-70-70=280	$3,910.00
Billy Casper	T-8	73-68-65-75=281	$3,392.50
Dave Hill	T-8	71-67-72-71=281	$3,392.50
Dan Sikes	10	67-72-70-73=282	$2,990.00

Greater New Orleans Open

Course: Lakewood C.C., New Orleans, La.
Par: 72 Yardage: 7,020
Last day of event: Sunday, May 14, 1967

Player	Place	Score	Earnings
George Knudson	Win	71-66-70-70=277	$20,000.00
Jack Nicklaus	2	70-68-69-71=278	$12,000.00
Frank Beard	3	68-71-70-70=279	$7,500.00
Billy Casper	T-4	73-71-69-67=280	$3,920.00
Cobie Legrange	T-4	73-71-69-67=280	$3,920.00
Gardner Dickinson	T-4	68-74-69-69=280	$3,920.00
Bob Charles	T-4	70-68-70-72=280	$3,920.00
Tommy Bolt	T-4	73-69-68-70=280	$3,920.00
Phil Rodgers	T-9	74-72-66-69=281	$2,700.00
George Archer	T-9	71-70-71-69=281	$2,700.00

Colonial National Invitational

Course: Colonial C.C., Fort Worth, Texas
Par: 70 Yardage: 7,100
Last day of event: Sunday, May 21, 1967

Player	Place	Score	Earnings
Dave Stockton	Win	65-66-74-73=278	$23,000.00
Charles Coody	2	74-67-70-69=280	$13,800.00
George Archer	T-3	72-68-69-72=281	$7,187.50
Ben Hogan	T-3	67-72-69-73=281	$7,187.50
Gene Littler	5	71-73-68-71=283	$4,945.00
Gardner Dickinson	T-6	72-67-72-73=284	$4,140.00
Arnold Palmer	T-6	73-73-67-71=284	$4,140.00
Jack Nicklaus	T-8	72-71-72-70=285	$3,258.34
Frank Beard	T-8	72-71-68-74=285	$3,258.33
Dan Sikes	T-8	70-72-71-72=285	$3,258.33

Oklahoma City Open

Course: Quail Creek C.C., Oklahoma City, Okla.
Par: 72 Yardage: 7,173
Last day of event: Sunday, May 28, 1967

Player	Place	Score	Earnings
Miller Barber	Win	70-72-68-68=278	$13,200.00
Playoff: Beat Gary Player with birdie on the third extra hole			
Gary Player	2	70-73-67-68=278	$7,920.00
George Archer	3	73-70-68-69=280	$4,950.00
Billy Casper	T-4	74-69-70-69=282	$3,069.00
Kermit Zarley	T-4	69-75-69-69=282	$3,069.00
Bob Charles	T-6	71-75-70-67=283	$2,376.00

Dave Stockton	T-6	71-71-68-73=283	$2,376.00
Jim Colbert	8	71-72-72-71=286	$2,046.00
Babe Hiskey	T-9	71-75-70-71=287	$1,716.00
Harold Henning	T-9	72-73-71-71=287	$1,716.00
Chuck Courtney	T-9	73-75-68-71=287	$1,716.00

Memphis Open

Course: Colonial C.C., Memphis, Tenn.
Par: 70 Yardage: 6,466
Last day of event: Sunday, June 4, 1967

Player	Place	Score	Earnings
Dave Hill	Win	65-66-68-73=272	$20,000.00
Johnny Pott	2	72-71-65-66=274	$12,000.00
Harold Henning	3	67-69-71-68=275	$12,000.00
Randy Glover	T-4	69-73-67-67=276	$4,650.00
Dan Sikes	T-4	71-68-66-71=276	$4,650.00
Chuck Courtney	T-6	70-65-73-69=277	$3,140.00
Jerry McGee	T-6	72-68-68-69=277	$3,140.00
Gary Player	T-6	67-68-69-73=277	$3,140.00
Labron Harris, Jr.	T-6	71-68-67-71=277	$3,140.00
Don January	T-6	72-70-65-70=277	$3,140.00

Buick Open

Course: Warwick Hills C.C., Grand Blanc, Mich.
Par: 72 Yardage: 7,126
Last day of event: Sunday, June 11, 1967

Player	Place	Score	Earnings
Julius Boros	Win	72-72-70-69=283	$20,000.00
Bert Yancey	T-2	73-71-74-68=286	$8,166.67
R.H. Sikes	T-2	75-71-69-71=286	$8,166.67
Bob Goalby	T-2	69-73-74-70=286	$8,166.66
Kermit Zarley	5	71-72-71-73=287	$4,300.00
Bob Stanton	T-6	71-75-75-68=289	$3,433.34
Tom Weiskopf	T-6	74-70-74-71=289	$3,433.33
Bruce Crampton	T-6	77-67-71-74=289	$3,433.33
Sam Carmichael	T-9	73-76-72-69=290	$2,500.00
Al Geiberger	T-9	72-72-73-73=290	$2,500.00
Tommy Aaron	T-9	72-70-75-73=290	$2,500.00
Bob Verwey	T-9	74-74-69-73=290	$2,500.00

U.S. Open

Course: Baltusrol G.C. (Lower Course), Springfield, N.J.
Par: 70 Yardage: 7,065
Last day of event: Sunday, June 18, 1967

Player	Place	Score	Earnings
Jack Nicklaus	Win	71-67-72-65=275	$30,000.00
Arnold Palmer	2	69-68-73-69=279	$15,000.00
Don January	3	69-72-70-70=281	$10,000.00
Billy Casper	4	69-70-71-72=282	$7,500.00
Lee Trevino	5	72-70-71-70=283	$6,000.00
Deane Beman	T-6	69-71-71-73=284	$4,166.67
Gardner Dickinson	T-6	70-73-68-73=284	$4,166.66
Bob Goalby	T-6	72-71-70-71=284	$4,166.67
Kel Nagle	T-9	70-72-72-71=285	$2,566.67
Art Wall	T-9	69-73-72-71=285	$2,566.67
Dave Marr	T-9	70-74-70-71=285	$2,566.66

Cleveland Open

Course: Aurora C.C., Aurora, Ohio
Par: 70 Yardage: 6,611
Last day of event: Sunday, June 25, 1967

Player	Place	Score	Earnings
Gardner Dickinson	Win	68-66-67-70=271	$20,700.00
Miller Barber	T-2	69-69-68-69=275	$10,091.25
Homero Blancas	T-2	71-65-67-72=275	$10,091.25
Tommy Aaron	T-4	69-73-69-66=277	$4,057.20
Jerry Edwards	T-4	72-67-70-68=277	$4,057.20
Allan Henning	T-4	70-66-72-69=277	$4,057.20
Lou Graham	T-4	69-71-65-72=277	$4,057.20
Phil Rodgers	T-4	71-69-66-71=277	$4,057.20
Cobie Legrange	T-9	71-69-71-67=278	$2,691.00
Wayne Yates	T-9	66-66-72-74=278	$2,691.00
Arnold Palmer	T-9	67-68-70-73=278	$2,691.00

Canadian Open

Course: Montreal Municipal G.C., Montreal, Quebec, Canada
Par: 71 Yardage: 6,600
Last day of event: Monday, July 3, 1967

Player	Place	Score	Earnings
Billy Casper	Win	69-70-71-69=279	$30,000.00
Playoff: Beat Art Wall in 18-hole playoff (Casper 65, Wall 69)			
Art Wall	2	67-70-70-72=279	$18,500.00
Julius Boros	T-3	72-71-69-68=280	$10,816.67
Jack Nicklaus	T-3	69-72-70-69=280	$10,816.67
Steve Reid	T-3	67-73-69-71=280	$10,816.66
Al Geiberger	6	70-72-68-71=281	$7,500.00
Arnold Palmer	T-7	72-70-70-70=282	$6,500.00
Tommy Aaron	T-7	72-71-69-70=282	$6,500.00
Gene Littler	T-7	75-70-66-71=282	$6,500.00
Charles Coody	T-10	72-71-70-70=283	$5,250.00
Charles Sifford	T-10	73-70-67-73=283	$5,250.00

"500" Festival Open

Course: Speedway G.C., Indianapolis, Ind.
Par: 72 Yardage: 7,179
Last day of event: Sunday, July 9, 1967

Player	Place	Score	Earnings
Frank Beard	Win	70-71-69-69=279	$20,000.00
Rod Funseth	T-2	67-70-71-74=282	$9,750.00
Rives McBee	T-2	73-69-71-69=282	$9,750.00
Joe Campbell	4	73-70-70-70=283	$5,000.00
Gene Littler	5	71-68-73-72=284	$4,300.00
Bob Goalby	6	73-72-69-71=285	$3,800.00
Billy Casper	T-7	72-73-70-71=286	$3,100.00
Steve Spray	T-7	70-73-71-72=286	$3,100.00
R.H. Sikes	T-7	67-72-72-75=286	$3,100.00
Roger Ginsberg	10	74-69-73-71=287	$2,600.00

British Open

Course: Royal Liverpool G.C., Hoylake, Cheshire, England
Par: 72 Yardage: 6,955
Last day of event: Saturday, July 15, 1967

Player	Place	Score	Earnings
Roberto De Vicenzo	Win	70-71-67-70=278	$5,880.00
Jack Nicklaus	2	71-69-71-69=280	$4,200.00
Clive Clark	T-3	70-73-69-72=284	$3,150.00
Gary Player	T-3	72-71-67-74=284	$3,150.00
Tony Jacklin	5	73-69-73-70=285	$2,170.00
Harold Henning	T-6	74-70-71-71=286	$1,610.00
Sebastian Miguel	T-6	72-74-68-72=286	$1,610.00
Al Balding	T-8	74-71-69-73=287	$926.80
Bruce Devlin	T-8	70-70-72-75=287	$926.80
Hugh Boyle	T-8	74-74-71-68=287	$926.80
Peter Thomson	T-8	71-74-70-72=287	$926.80
Tommy Horton	T-8	74-74-69-70=287	$926.80

PGA Championship

Course: Columbine C.C., Denver, Colo.
Par: 72 Yardage: 7,436
Last day of event: Monday, July 24, 1967

Player	Place	Score	Earnings
Don January	Win	71-72-70-68=281	$25,000.00
Playoff: Beat Don Massengale in 18-hole playoff (January 69, Massengale 71)			
Don Massengale	T-2	70-75-70-66=281	$15,000.00
Jack Nicklaus	T-3	67-75-69-71=282	$9,000.00
Dan Sikes	T-3	69-70-70-73=282	$9,000.00
Julius Boros	T-5	69-76-70-68=283	$6,500.00
Al Geiberger	T-5	73-71-69-70=283	$6,500.00
Frank Beard	T-7	71-74-70-70=285	$4,750.00
Don Bies	T-7	69-70-76-70=285	$4,750.00
Bob Goalby	T-7	70-74-68-73=285	$4,750.00
Gene Littler	T-7	73-72-71-69=285	$4,750.00

Minnesota Golf Classic

Course: Hazeltine National G.C., Chaska, Minn.
Par: 72 Yardage: 7,285
Last day of event: Sunday, July 30, 1967

Player	Place	Score	Earnings
Lou Graham	Win	76-68-70-72=286	$20,000.00
Bob Verwey	2	72-73-75-67=287	$1,200.00
Julius Boros	3	70-72-76-71=289	$7,500.00
Ken Still	T-4	74-72-74-70=290	$4,366.67
Doug Ford	T-4	74-71-74-71=290	$4,366.67
Al Geiberger	T-4	74-73-71-72=290	$4,366.66
Ray Floyd	T-7	70-74-72-75=291	$2,860.00
David Jimenez	T-7	75-72-72-72=291	$2,860.00
Dudley Wysong	T-7	72-71-71-77=291	$2,860.00
Dave Stockton	T-7	74-73-70-74=291	$2,860.00
Harold Henning	T-7	71-74-73-73=291	$2,860.00

Western Open

Course: Beverly C.C., Chicago, Ill.
Par: 71 Yardage: 6,857
Last day of event: Sunday, August 6, 1967

Player	Place	Score	Earnings
Jack Nicklaus	Win	72-68-65-69=274	$20,000.00
Doug Sanders	2	69-68-67-72=276	$12,000.00
Steve Oppermann	T-3	67-71-69-71=278	$6,250.00
Miller Barber	T-3	69-73-67-69=278	$6,250.00
Phil Rodgers	T-5	72-69-70-68=279	$3,480.00
George Knudson	T-5	70-71-67-71=279	$3,480.00
Bert Weaver	T-5	72-69-68-70=279	$3,480.00
George Archer	T-5	69-71-67-72=279	$3,480.00
Tom Veech	T-5	72-68-65-74=279	$3,480.00
Bob Shave, Jr.	T-10	70-72-69-69=280	$2,400.00
Dave Stockton	T-10	72-68-69-71=280	$2,400.00
Julius Boros	T-10	68-68-73-71=280	$2,400.00

American Golf Classic

Course: Firestone C.C. (South), Akron, Ohio
Par: 70 Yardage: 7,180
Last day of event: Sunday, August 13, 1967

Player	Place	Score	Earnings
Arnold Palmer	Win	70-67-72-67=276	$20,000.00
Doug Sanders	2	70-71-69-69=279	$12,000.00
Jack McGowan	T-3	69-67-72-72=280	$5,600.00
Kermit Zarley	T-3	69-71-68-72=280	$5,600.00
Jack Nicklaus	T-3	70-69-70-71=280	$5,600.00
Gardner Dickinson	T-6	70-70-74-67=281	$3,433.34
Bert Yancey	T-6	71-69-73-68=281	$3,433.33
Bobby Nichols	T-6	70-69-73-69=281	$3,433.33
Al Balding	T-9	72-71-70-69=282	$2,500.00
Kel Nagle	T-9	71-73-67-71=282	$2,500.00
Tom Weiskopf	T-9	74-68-69-71=282	$2,500.00
Allan Henning	T-9	73-66-69-74=282	$2,500.00

Insurance City Open

Course: Wethersfield C.C., Wethersfield, Conn.
Par: 71 Yardage: 6,568
Last day of event: Sunday, August 20, 1967

Player	Place	Score	Earnings
Charles Sifford	Win	69-70-69-64=272	$20,000.00
Steve Oppermann	2	70-67-69-67=273	$12,000.00
Ray Floyd	T-3	68-70-68-68=274	$5,150.00
Doug Ford	T-3	68-67-69-70=274	$5,150.00
Gary Player	T-3	65-69-71-69=274	$5,150.00
Dan Sikes	T-3	72-65-67-70=274	$5,150.00
Frank Beard	T-7	68-69-69-69=275	$3,100.00
Terry Dill	T-7	66-68-69-72=275	$3,100.00
Kel Nagle	T-7	69-68-70-68=275	$3,100.00
Al Balding	T-10	71-69-69-67=276	$2,150.00
Bobby Cole	T-10	70-68-70-68=276	$2,150.00
Al Geiberger	T-10	71-70-68-67=276	$2,150.00
Dave Hill	T-10	72-61-71-72=276	$2,150.00
Dave Marr	T-10	69-68-67-72=276	$2,150.00
Lee Trevino	T-10	67-69-72-68=276	$2,150.00

Westchester Classic

Course: Westchester C.C., Harrison, N.Y.
Par: 72 Yardage: 6,573
Last day of event: Wednesday, August 30, 1967

Player	Place	Score	Earnings
Jack Nicklaus	Win	67-69-65-71=272	$50,000.00
Dan Sikes	2	72-62-70-69=273	$30,000.00
Roberto De Vicenzo	3	69-67-68-70=274	$18,750.00
Gary Player	4	66-70-68-71=275	$12,500.00
Arnold Palmer	5	69-69-67-71=276	$10,750.00
Doug Sanders	6	69-68-69-71=277	$9,500.00
Chi Chi Rodriguez	T-7	70-69-69-70=278	$8,125.00
Lee Trevino	T-7	68-68-73-69=278	$8,125.00
Frank Beard	T-9	68-67-70-74=279	$6,500.00
Bob Charles	T-9	67-67-71-74=279	$6,500.00
Charles Coody	T-9	71-69-73-66=279	$6,500.00

Carling World Open

Course: Board of Trade C.C., Toronto, Ontario, Canada
Par: 71 Yardage: 7,024
Last day of event: Monday, September 4, 1967

Player	Place	Score	Earnings
Billy Casper	Win	74-68-70-69=281	$35,000.00
Playoff: Beat Al Geiberger with par on first extra hole			
Al Geiberger	2	72-67-70-72=281	$17,000.00
Gary Player	3	69-68-75-71=283	$8,500.00
Randy Glover	T-4	70-72-69-73=284	$6,500.00
Doug Ford	T-4	71-69-70-74=284	$6,500.00
Jerry Steelsmith	T-4	73-69-69-73=284	$6,500.00
Julius Boros	T-7	73-72-70-70=285	$4,325.00
Tony Jacklin	T-7	70-72-72-71=285	$4,325.00
Lee Trevino	T-7	70-69-73-73=285	$4,325.00
R.H. Sikes	T-7	68-74-70-73=285	$4,325.00

Philadelphia Classic

Course: Whitemarsh Valley C.C., Chestnut Hill, Pa.
Par: 72 Yardage: 6,708
Last day of event: Sunday, September 17, 1967

Player	Place	Score	Earnings
Dan Sikes	Win	71-68-69-68=276	$22,000.00
George Archer	2	68-66-70-74=278	$13,200.00
Billy Casper	T-3	69-68-73-70=280	$6,160.00
Mason Rudolph	T-3	68-74-67-71=280	$6,160.00
Bob Charles	T-3	68-71-71-70=280	$6,160.00
Miller Barber	T-6	68-73-73-68=282	$3,454.00
Arnold Palmer	T-6	70-72-72-68=282	$3,454.00
Wayne Yates	T-6	70-72-72-68=282	$3,454.00
Bobby Nichols	T-6	72-70-69-71=282	$3,454.00
Jim Colbert	T-6	70-71-71-70=282	$3,454.00

Thunderbird Classic

Course: Upper Montclair C.C., Clifton, N.J.
Par: 72 Yardage: 7,055
Last day of event: Sunday, September 24, 1967

Player	Place	Score	Earnings
Arnold Palmer	Win	71-71-72-69=283	$30,000.00
Charles Coody	T-2	71-72-69-72=284	$12,250.00
Art Wall	T-2	70-72-70-72=284	$12,250.00
Jack Nicklaus	T-2	73-70-69-72=284	$12,250.00
Harold Henning	T-5	72-69-74-70=285	$5,475.00
Julius Boros	T-5	71-72-70-72=285	$5,475.00
Bert Weaver	T-5	71-71-71-72=285	$5,475.00
Billy Casper	T-5	69-72-71-73=285	$5,475.00
Bob Goalby	9	73-72-68-73=286	$4,200.00
Pat Schwab	T-10	69-72-75-71=287	$3,750.00
Gary Player	T-10	71-71-69-76=287	$3,750.00

Atlanta Classic

Course: Atlanta C.C., Atlanta, Ga.
Par: 72 Yardage: 7,049
Last day of event: Sunday, October 1, 1967

Player	Place	Score	Earnings
Bob Charles	Win	72-71-69-70=282	$22,000.00
Tommy Bolt	T-2	73-72-67-72=284	$8,983.33
Richard Crawford	T-2	73-73-70-68=284	$8,983.33
Gardner Dickinson	T-2	75-74-68-67=284	$8,983.34
Bruce Crampton	5	75-71-72-67=285	$4,730.00

Dave Marr	T-6	71-70-72-73=286	$3,602.50
Billy Maxwell	T-6	71-73-71-71=286	$3,602.50
Steve Spray	T-6	75-70-72-69=286	$3,602.50
Dewitt Weaver	T-6	71-73-73-69=286	$3,602.50
Dave Hill	10	74-73-72-68=287	$2,860.00

Sahara Open
Course: Paradise Valley C.C., Las Vegas, Nev.
Par: 71 Yardage: 7,069
Last day of event: Sunday, October 29, 1967

Player	Place	Score	Earnings
Jack Nicklaus	Win	68-69-62-71=270	$20,000.00
Steve Spray	2	69-64-67-71=271	$12,000.00
Hugh Royer	3	69-72-67-68=276	$7,500.00
Frank Beard	T-4	67-70-72-68=277	$4,366.67
Rives McBee	T-4	70-70-68-69=277	$4,366.67
Terry Dill	T-4	67-68-70-72=277	$4,366.66
Jack McGowan	T-7	69-69-73-67=278	$2,975.00
Dudley Wysong	T-7	74-67-68-69=278	$2,975.00
Deane Beman	T-7	72-69-69-68=278	$2,975.00
Julius Boros	T-7	67-73-68-70=278	$2,975.00

Hawaiian Open
Course: Waialae C.C., Honolulu, Ha.
Par: 72 Yardage: 7,020
Last day of event: Saturday, November 4, 1967

Player	Place	Score	Earnings
Dudley Wysong	Win	72-69-70-73=284	$20,000.00
Playoff: Beat Billy Casper with par on first extra hole			
Billy Casper	2	71-71-70-72=284	$20,000.00
Tom Weiskopf	T-3	68-77-70-72=287	$5,150.00
Babe Hiskey	T-3	78-70-68-71=287	$5,150.00
Deane Beman	T-3	72-71-72-72=287	$5,150.00
Doug Sanders	T-3	73-72-71-71=287	$5,150.00
Ted Makalena	T-7	78-70-71-69=288	$2,975.00
Ray Floyd	T-7	72-70-71-75=288	$2,975.00
Bert Yancey	T-7	71-73-73-71=288	$2,975.00
R.H. Sikes	T-7	74-68-70-76=288	$2,975.00

Cajun Classic
Course: Oakbourne C.C., Lafayette, La.
Par: 72 Yardage: 6,550
Last day of event: Sunday, December 3, 1967

Player	Place	Score	Earnings
Marty Fleckman	Win	67-68-71-69=275	$5,000.00
Playoff: Beat Jack Montgomery with birdie on first extra hole			
Jack Montgomery	2	64-72-71-68=275	$3,300.00
Jim Grant	T-3	70-67-71-68=276	$2,300.00
Laurie Hammer	T-3	67-68-73-68=276	$2,300.00
Richard Crawford	5	70-66-69-73=278	$1,850.00
Lou Graham	T-6	68-69-67-75=279	$1,550.00
Jimmy Picard	T-6	73-68-71-67=279	$1,550.00
Rocky Thompson	T-8	68-73-72-67=280	$1,300.00
Bob-E. Smith	T-8	71-65-74-70=280	$1,300.00
Miller Barber	T-8	71-65-74-70=280	$1,300.00

1968

Roberto de Vicenzo was penalized one stroke for signing an incorrect score card (giving himself a 4 at the 17th hole instead of a 3), a gaffe that handed a Masters victory to Bob Goalby. Both players had shot a final-round 66. The Argentine's lament—"What a stupid I am."—became etched in golf lore. Lee Trevino became the first to break 70 in all four rounds of a U.S. Open, beating Jack Nicklaus by four shots at Oak Hill. Gary Player beat Nicklaus and Bob Charles to win the British Open by two shots at Carnoustie. Billy Casper led the Tour with six victories. Former U.S Open, British Open and PGA Championship winner Tommy Armour died in September at age 73. Julius Boros held off Charles and Arnold Palmer to win the PGA Championship by one stroke. Of more significance to future generations of pro golfers, Boros ignited a marketing revolution when he appeared at the PGA wearing a bucket hat that was embroidered with the name of appliance maker Amana. Boros was paid $50 a week for the endorsement.

Bing Crosby National Pro-Am
Courses: Pebble Beach G.L., Spyglass Hill G.C., Cypress Point C.C., Pebble Beach, Calif.
Home Course / Pebble Beach G.L., Par: 72 Yardage: 6,745
Last day of event: Sunday, January 14, 1968

Player	Place	Score	Earnings
Johnny Pott	Win	70-71-71-73=285	$16,000.00
Playoff: Beat Billy Casper and Bruce Devlin with birdie on first extra hole			
Billy Casper	T-2	73-69-73-70=285	$7,800.00
Bruce Devlin	T-2	73-69-73-70=285	$7,800.00
Deane Beman	4	74-71-72-70=287	$4,000.00
Ray Floyd	T-5	79-68-71-70=288	$3,066.67
George Knudson	T-5	73-71-74-70=288	$3,066.67
Bobby Nichols	T-5	76-68-72-72=288	$3,066.66
Jack Nicklaus	8	71-75-70-73=289	$2,480.00
Jack Rule	9	73-76-69-72=290	$2,240.00
Dale Douglass	T-10	75-73-73-70=291	$1,840.00
Miller Barber	T-10	74-75-71-71=291	$1,840.00
Dave Hill	T-10	69-77-73-72=291	$1,840.00
Tony Jacklin	T-10	72-75-71-73=291	$1,840.00

Kaiser International Open Invitational
Course: Silverado C.C. (North Course, South Course), Napa, Calif.
Home Course -Par: 72 Yardage: 6,849
Last day of event: Sunday, January 21, 1968

Player	Place	Score	Earnings
Kermit Zarley	Win	71-67-70-65=273	$25,000.00
Dave Marr	2	68-69-67-70=274	$15,000.00
George Archer	T-3	70-68-68-70=276	$7,812.50
Gene Littler	T-3	71-70-66-69=276	$7,812.50
Bert Greene	5	69-71-71-68=279	$5,375.00
Lou Graham	T-6	74-69-71-68=282	$4,291.67
Bruce Crampton	T-6	71-70-72-69=282	$4,291.67
Richard Crawford	T-6	71-71-70-70=282	$4,291.66
Dave Hill	T-9	73-72-70-68=283	$3,000.00
Billy Farrell	T-9	74-71-69-69=283	$3,000.00
Eldridge Miles	T-9	76-68-70-69=283	$3,000.00
Al Geiberger	T-9	72-69-72-70=283	$3,000.00
Miller Barber	T-9	73-72-68-70=283	$3,000.00

Los Angeles Open Invitational
Course: Brookside Park G.C., Pasadena, Calif.
Par: 71 Yardage: 7,021
Last day of event: Sunday, January 28, 1968

Player	Place	Score	Earnings
Billy Casper	Win	70-67-68-69=274	$20,000.00
Arnold Palmer	2	69-71-69-68=277	$12,000.00
Al Geiberger	3	67-70-69-72=278	$7,500.00
George Archer	T-4	68-69-75-68=280	$4,366.67
Dave Marr	T-4	68-69-74-69=280	$4,366.67
John Schlee	T-4	71-70-65-74=280	$4,366.66
Dave Hill	7	70-70-71-70=281	$3,400.00
Ray Floyd	T-8	68-71-75-68=282	$2,950.00
Lee Trevino	T-8	70-68-73-71=282	$2,950.00
Gardner Dickinson	T-10	70-70-73-70=283	$2,400.00
George Knudson	T-10	68-73-72-70=283	$2,400.00
Miller Barber	T-10	74-71-65-73=283	$2,400.00

Bob Hope Desert Classic
Course: Bermuda Dunes C.C, La Quinta C.C., Indian Wells C.C., Eldorado C.C.
Home Course / Bermuda Dunes, Par: 72 Yardage: N/A
Last day of event: Sunday, February 4, 1968

Player	Place	Score	Earnings
Arnold Palmer	Win	72-70-67-71-68=348	$20,000.00

Playoff: Beat Deane Beman with par on second extra hole

Player	Place	Score	Earnings
Deane Beman	2	72-74-70-67-65=348	$12,000.00
Harold Henning	3	76-69-67-69-68=349	$7,500.00
Tom Weiskopf	T-4	72-69-68-72-69=350	$4,650.00
Billy Casper	T-4	70-72-69-68-71=350	$4,650.00
Lee Trevino	T-6	68-73-70-71-69=351	$3,600.00
Charles Coody	T-6	69-72-69-72-69=351	$3,600.00
Ted Makalena	T-8	69-72-74-68-69=352	$2,833.34
Bruce Devlin	T-8	71-67-72-72-70=352	$2,833.33
George Knudson	T-8	70-73-68-70-71=352	$2,833.33

Andy Williams-San Diego Open Invitational
Course: Torrey Pines (South), San Diego, Calif.
Home Course -Par: 72 Yardage: 6,808
Last day of event: Sunday, February 11, 1968

Player	Place	Score	Earnings
Tom Weiskopf	Win	66-68-71-68=273	$30,000.00
Al Geiberger	2	68-69-68-69=274	$18,000.00
Ray Floyd	3	66-73-69-67=275	$11,250.00
Bob Lunn	4	69-71-66-70=276	$7,500.00
Jack Nicklaus	5	67-69-69-72=277	$6,450.00
Jimmy Powell	6	64-76-69-69=278	$5,700.00
Harold Henning	T-7	71-71-68-69=279	$4,875.00
Paul Harney	T-7	72-70-68-69=279	$4,875.00
Bobby Nichols	T-9	69-72-68-71=280	$3,900.00
Marty Fleckman	T-9	67-72-69-72=280	$3,900.00
Dave Hill	T-9	67-68-72-73=280	$3,900.00

Phoenix Open Invitational
Course: Phoenix C.C., Phoenix, Ariz.
Par: 71 Yardage: 6,765
Last day of event: Sunday, February 18, 1968

Player	Place	Score	Earnings
George Knudson	Win	67-64-70-71=272	$20,000.00
Julius Boros	T-2	70-69-69-67=275	$8,166.67
Jack Montgomery	T-2	67-68-72-68=275	$8,166.67
Sam Carmichael	T-2	70-66-68-71=275	$8,166.66
Frank Beard	T-5	72-68-68-68=276	$4,050.00
Bert Yancey	T-5	70-70-65-71=276	$4,050.00
Frank Boynton	T-7	66-72-70-69=277	$3,100.00
Gene Littler	T-7	71-68-68-70=277	$3,100.00
Tom Shaw	T-7	67-66-69-75=277	$3,100.00
Bob-E. Smith	T-10	70-69-73-66=278	$2,300.00
Gardner Dickinson	T-10	73-67-69-69=278	$2,300.00
Tommy Aaron	T-10	68-67-73-70=278	$2,300.00
Terry Dill	T-10	70-67-68-73=278	$2,300.00

Tucson Open Invitational
Course: Tucson National G.C., Starr Pass G.C., Tucson, Ariz.
Par: 72 Yardage: 7,200
Last day of event: Sunday, February 25, 1968

Player	Place	Score	Earnings
George Knudson	Win	70-67-71-65=273	$20,000.00
Frank Boynton	T-2	71-69-67-67=274	$9,750.00
Frank Beard	T-2	71-69-65-69=274	$9,750.00
Bill Ogden	T-4	69-66-70-70=275	$4,366.67
Dale Douglass	T-4	72-63-70-70=275	$4,366.67
Harold Henning	T-4	70-66-68-71=275	$4,366.66
Al Geiberger	7	71-68-67-70=276	$3,400.00
Tony Jacklin	T-8	72-68-70-68=278	$2,950.00
Jack Montgomery	T-8	69-67-70-72=278	$2,950.00
Bruce Crampton	10	68-71-66-74=279	$2,600.00

Doral Open Invitational
Course: Doral C.C. (Blue), Miami, Fla.
Par: 72 Yardage: 7,002
Last day of event: Sunday, March 10, 1968

Player	Place	Score	Earnings
Gardner Dickinson	Win	65-71-67-72=275	$20,000.00
Tom Weiskopf	2	70-67-66-73=276	$12,000.00
Bert Yancey	3	69-70-69-69=277	$7,500.00
Charles Coody	T-4	69-69-72-69=279	$4,650.00
Miller Barber	T-4	71-70-68-70=279	$4,650.00
Dan Sikes	6	70-70-69-71=280	$3,800.00
George Archer	T-7	70-72-71-68=281	$3,250.00
Fred Marti	T-7	70-70-68-73=281	$3,250.00
Frank Beard	T-9	70-71-71-70=282	$2,700.00
Howie Johnson	T-9	67-71-68-76=282	$2,700.00

Florida Citrus Open
Course: Rio Pinar C.C., Orlando, Fla.
Par: 72 Yardage: 6,839
Last day of event: Sunday, March 17, 1968

Player	Place	Score	Earnings
Dan Sikes	Win	71-67-70-66=274	$23,000.00
Tom Weiskopf	2	68-72-69-66=275	$13,800.00
Jack Nicklaus	3	67-68-73-68=276	$8,625.00
Miller Barber	T-4	67-71-70-69=277	$5,347.50
Tony Jacklin	T-4	70-72-67-68=277	$5,347.50
Bob Charles	T-6	68-69-71-70=278	$3,948.34
Bruce Crampton	T-6	72-67-72-67=278	$3,948.34
Rod Funseth	T-6	70-71-68-69=278	$3,948.33
Tom Nieporte	T-9	70-70-69-70=279	$2,990.00
Lee Trevino	T-9	69-72-68-70=279	$2,990.00
Art Wall	T-9	73-68-69-69=279	$2,990.00

Pensacola Open Invitational

Course: Pensacola C.C., Pensacola, Fla.
Par: 72 Yardage: 6,380
Last day of event: Monday, March 25, 1968

Player	Place	Score	Earnings
George Archer	Win	66-68-69-65=268	$16,000.00
Tony Jacklin	T-2	66-69-68-66=269	$7,800.00
Dave Marr	T-2	66-70-68-65=269	$7,800.00
Gary Player	4	67-72-69-63=271	$4,000.00
Ray Floyd	5	68-70-64-70=272	$3,440.00
Tom Shaw	6	63-67-74-69=273	$3,040.00
Richard Martinez	7	69-70-70-65=274	$2,720.00
Rafe Botts	T-8	66-72-72-65=275	$2,360.00
Steve Oppermann	T-8	68-70-70-67=275	$2,360.00
Lee Trevino	10	70-73-69-64=276	$2,080.00

Jacksonville Open Invitational

Course: Deerwood Club, Jacksonville, Fla.
Par: 72 Yardage: 7,221
Last day of event: Sunday, March 31, 1968

Player	Place	Score	Earnings
Tony Jacklin	Win	68-65-69-71=273	$20,000.00
Gardner Dickinson	T-2	66-69-70-70=275	$6,520.00
Don January	T-2	67-69-68-71=275	$6,520.00
Chi Chi Rodriguez	T-2	67-68-70-70=275	$6,520.00
Doug Sanders	T-2	65-68-69-73=275	$6,520.00
Dewitt Weaver	T-2	66-69-70-70=275	$6,520.00
Bob Charles	T-7	70-69-67-70=276	$3,100.00
Arnold Palmer	T-7	70-65-68-73=276	$3,100.00
Gary Player	T-7	69-68-70-69=276	$3,100.00
Rex Baxter	T-10	69-69-69-70=277	$2,400.00
Julius Boros	T-10	66-70-68-73=277	$2,400.00
Hugh Royer	T-10	68-66-69-74=277	$2,400.00

Greater Greensboro Open Invitational

Course: Sedgefield C.C., Greensboro, N.C.
Par: 71 Yardage: 7,034
Last day of event: Monday, April 8, 1968

Player	Place	Score	Earnings
Billy Casper	Win	65-67-69-66=267	$27,500.00
George Archer	T-2	68-71-67-65=271	$11,229.17
Gene Littler	T-2	69-66-69-67=271	$11,229.17
Bobby Nichols	T-2	69-65-72-65=271	$11,229.16
Al Geiberger	T-5	66-71-67-69=273	$5,270.84
Arnold Palmer	T-5	69-71-66-67=273	$5,270.83
Doug Sanders	T-5	71-69-70-73=273	$5,270.84
Miller Barber	T-8	70-67-66-71=274	$3,895.84
Don January	T-8	68-67-66-73=274	$3,895.84
Gary Player	T-8	69-67-69-69=274	$3,895.83

Masters

Course: Augusta National G.C., Augusta, Ga.
Par: 72 Yardage: 6,980
Last day of event: Sunday, April 14, 1968

Player	Place	Score	Earnings
Bob Goalby	Win	70-70-71-66=277	$20,000.00
Roberto De Vicenzo	2	69-73-70-66=278	$15,000.00
Bert Yancey	3	71-71-72-65=279	$10,000.00
Bruce Devlin	4	69-73-69-69=280	$7,500.00
Frank Beard	T-5	75-65-71-70=281	$5,500.00
Jack Nicklaus	T-5	69-71-74-67=281	$5,500.00
Ray Floyd	T-7	71-71-69-71=282	$3,460.00
Jerry Pittman	T-7	70-73-70-69=282	$3,460.00
Gary Player	T-7	72-67-71-72=282	$3,460.00
Lionel Hebert	T-7	72-71-71-68=282	$3,460.00
Tommy Aaron	T-7	69-72-72-69=282	$3,460.00

Rebel Yell Open

Course: Holston Hills C.C., Knoxville, Tenn.
Par: 72 Yardage: 7,009
Last day of event: Sunday, April 14, 1968

Player	Place	Score	Earnings
Larry Mowry	Win	71-69-68-71=279	$2,800.00
Playoff: Beat Chris Blocker with par on first extra hole			
Chris Blocker	2	73-67-70-69=279	$1,900.00
Wayne Yates	T-3	71-70-69-70=280	$1,300.00
Bob Lunn	T-3	70-71-68-71=280	$1,300.00
John Lotz	T-5	73-69-71-68=281	$1,050.00
Bob-E. Smith	T-5	73-68-70-69=281	$1,050.00
Dick Lotz	T-7	75-67-70-70=282	$825.00
Hugh Royer	T-7	72-71-68-71=282	$825.00
Herb Hooper	T-7	73-66-71-72=282	$825.00
Dave Eichelberger	T-7	69-74-69-70=282	$825.00

Tournament of Champions

Course: Stardust C.C., Las Vegas, Nev.
Home course / Par: 71 Yardage: 6,708
Last day of event: Sunday, April 21, 1968

Player	Place	Score	Earnings
Don January	Win	70-68-69-69=276	$30,000.00
Julius Boros	2	70-70-71-66=277	$18,000.00
Randy Glover	3	70-71-70-68=279	$12,000.00
Gardner Dickinson	T-4	68-71-73-69=281	$9,175.00
Bob Goalby	T-4	70-70-66-75=281	$9,175.00
George Archer	6	71-69-71-71=282	$7,250.00
Bob Charles	T-7	73-68-74-68=283	$5,750.00
Tony Jacklin	T-7	74-70-69-70=283	$5,750.00
Billy Casper	T-9	70-74-70-70=284	$4,350.00
Dave Stockton	T-9	72-69-75-68=284	$4,350.00

Azalea Open Invitational

Course: Cape Fear C.C., Wilmington, N.C.
Par: 71 Yardage: 6,575
Last day of event: Sunday, April 21, 1968

Player	Place	Score	Earnings
Steve Reid	Win	65-71-66-69=271	$5,000.00
Playoff: Beat Gary Player with birdie on second extra hole			
Gary Player	2	68-68-69-66=271	$3,300.00
Bruce Devlin	3	70-68-66-68=272	$2,500.00
Sam Carmichael	T-4	67-73-67-66=273	$1,975.00
Bob Lunn	T-4	63-66-71-73=273	$1,975.00
Claude King	T-6	70-68-67-70=275	$1,500.00
Larry Wood	T-6	68-71-67-69=275	$1,500.00
Dick Rhyan	T-6	66-67-69-73=275	$1,500.00
R.H. Sikes	T-9	68-73-67-68=276	$1,110.00
Dave Gumlia	T-9	70-73-65-68=276	$1,110.00
Jerry McGee	T-9	68-71-67-70=276	$1,110.00
Bob Stone	T-9	68-69-69-70=276	$1,110.00
Wilf Homenuik	T-9	69-69-66-72=276	$1,110.00

Byron Nelson Golf Classic

Course: Preston Trail G.C., Dallas, Texas
Par: 70 Yardage: 7,086
Last day of event: Sunday, April 28, 1968

Player	Place	Score	Earnings
Miller Barber	Win	67-68-65-70=270	$20,000.00
Kermit Zarley	2	71-68-68-64=271	$12,000.00
Harold Henning	3	67-69-69-68=273	$7,500.00
Gary Player	T-4	66-71-70-70=277	$4,650.00
Jack Montgomery	T-4	67-70-71-69=277	$4,650.00
Dave Stockton	T-6	70-73-68-67=278	$3,275.00
Tom Weiskopf	T-6	72-71-67-68=278	$3,275.00
Jack McGowan	T-6	71-65-74-68=278	$3,275.00
Arnold Palmer	T-6	71-68-69-70=278	$3,275.00
Jack Nicklaus	10	73-67-70-69=279	$2,600.00

Houston Champions International

Course: Champions G.C., Houston, Texas
Par: 71 Yardage: 7,118
Last day of event: Sunday, May 5, 1968

Player	Place	Score	Earnings
Roberto De Vicenzo	Win	67-68-71-68=274	$20,000.00
Lee Trevino	2	69-69-66-71=275	$12,000.00
Dan Sikes	3	66-68-69-73=276	$7,500.00
Jack Nicklaus	4	65-69-72-72=278	$5,000.00
Tommy Aaron	T-5	73-67-70-69=279	$4,050.00
Miller Barber	T-5	67-68-69-75=279	$4,050.00
Frank Beard	T-7	69-70-73-68=280	$3,100.00
Dale Douglass	T-7	69-71-71-69=280	$3,100.00
Al Geiberger	T-7	68-71-69-72=280	$3,100.00
Steve Spray	10	69-69-71-72=281	$2,600.00

Greater New Orleans Open Invitational

Course: Lakewood C.C., New Orleans, La.
Par: 72 Yardage: 6,960
Last day of event: Sunday, May 12, 1968

Player	Place	Score	Earnings
George Archer	Win	69-65-70-67=271	$20,000.00
Bert Yancey	2	69-69-69-66=273	$12,000.00
Miller Barber	T-3	69-66-68-73=276	$5,600.00
Bobby Cole	T-3	69-72-65-70=276	$5,600.00
Tom Weiskopf	T-3	66-70-67-73=276	$5,600.00
John Lotz	6	70-71-67-70=278	$3,800.00
Tommy Aaron	T-7	68-69-71-71=279	$3,250.00
Frank Beard	T-7	71-71-68-69=279	$3,250.00
Chris Blocker	T-9	68-70-68-74=280	$2,500.00
Bob Charles	T-9	69-72-69-70=280	$2,500.00
Dave Marr	T-9	67-70-70-73=280	$2,500.00
Gary Player	T-9	66-70-73-71=280	$2,500.00

Colonial National Invitational

Course: Colonial C.C., Fort Worth, Texas
Par: 70 Yardage: 7,100
Last day of event: Sunday, May 19, 1968

Player	Place	Score	Earnings
Billy Casper	Win	68-71-68-68=275	$25,000.00
Gene Littler	2	71-72-69-68=280	$15,000.00
Tommy Aaron	3	69-74-68-70=281	$9,375.00
Gary Player	T-4	70-68-69-76=283	$5,812.50
Lee Trevino	T-4	71-71-70-71=283	$5,812.50

Julius Boros	T-6	73-71-70-71=285	$4,291.66
Harold Henning	T-6	71-73-70-71=285	$4,291.67
Earl Stewart	T-6	69-73-69-74=285	$4,291.67
Tommy Bolt	T-9	70-72-73-71=286	$3,375.00
Dudley Wysong	T-9	72-73-70-71=286	$3,375.00

Magnolia State Classic

Course: Hattiesburg C.C., Hattiesburg, Miss.
Par: 72 Yardage: 6,800
Last day of event: Sunday, May 19, 1968

Player	Place	Score	Earnings
Mac McLendon	Win	65-69-69-66=269	$2,800.00
Playoff: Beat Pete Fleming with birdie on ninth extra hole			
Pete Fleming	2	65-70-66-68=269	$1,900.00
Ron Cerrudo	3	69-67-69-66=272	$1,400.00
Dick Lotz	4	64-70-67-71=272	$1,200.00
Bobby Mitchell	T-5	70-67-68-68=273	$1,050.00
Mya Aye	T-5	66-68-70-69=273	$1,050.00
Allan Henning	7	67-72-66-69=274	$900.00
Fred Marti	8	69-69-69-68=275	$850.00
Bert Greene	T-9	67-73-65-71=276	$753.34
Richard Martinez	T-9	71-71-67-67=276	$753.33
Bob Murphy	T-9	69-68-69-70=276	$753.33

Memphis Open Invitational

Course: Colonial C.C., Memphis, Tenn.
Par: 70 Yardage: 6,466
Last day of event: Saturday, May 25, 1968

Player	Place	Score	Earnings
Bob Lunn	Win	65-68-68-67=268	$20,000.00
Monty Kaser	2	70-68-65-66=269	$12,000.00
Mac McLendon	T-3	65-67-69-69=270	$6,250.00
Lou Graham	T-3	67-66-66-71=270	$6,250.00
Miller Barber	T-5	68-71-65-67=271	$3,833.34
Gay Brewer	T-5	67-67-68-69=271	$3,833.33
Bob McCallister	T-5	68-70-65-68=271	$3,833.33
Billy Maxwell	T-8	69-68-68-67=272	$2,620.00
Dave Marr	T-8	69-67-68-68=272	$2,620.00
Gene Littler	T-8	73-67-65-67=272	$2,620.00
Jack McGowan	T-8	66-68-69-69=272	$2,620.00
Arnold Palmer	T-8	69-65-68-70=272	$2,620.00

Atlanta Classic

Course: Atlanta C.C., Atlanta, Ga.
Par: 72 Yardage: 6,893
Last day of event: Sunday, June 2, 1968

Player	Place	Score	Earnings
Bob Lunn	Win	70-71-70-69=280	$23,000.00
Lee Trevino	2	70-74-70-69=283	$13,800.00
Paul Bondeson	T-3	72-72-68-73=285	$5,922.50
Frank Boynton	T-3	72-74-69-70=285	$5,922.50
Lou Graham	T-3	71-76-66-72=285	$5,922.50
Rocky Thompson	T-3	74-70-71-70=285	$5,922.50
Tommy Aaron	T-7	69-70-75-72=286	$3,289.00
George Archer	T-7	70-75-69-72=286	$3,289.00
Bruce Devlin	T-7	72-73-68-73=286	$3,289.00
Gary Player	T-7	73-70-70-73=286	$3,289.00
Dave Stockton	T-7	76-73-69-68=286	$3,289.00

"500" Festival Open Invitational
Course: Speedway G.C., Indianapolis, Ind.
Par: 72 Yardage: 7,179
Last day of event: Sunday, June 9, 1968

Player	Place	Score	Earnings
Billy Casper	Win	70-71-69-70=280	$20,000.00
Frank Beard	T-2	70-71-72-68=281	$9,750.00
Mike Hill	T-2	71-69-66-75=281	$9,750.00
Lou Graham	T-4	74-66-72-70=282	$3,920.00
Sam Snead	T-4	71-69-69-73=282	$3,920.00
Fred Marti	T-4	72-71-68-71=282	$3,920.00
R.H. Sikes	T-4	71-73-67-71=282	$3,920.00
Dutch Harrison	T-4	71-70-69-72=282	$3,920.00
Ken Still	9	71-71-70-71=283	$2,800.00
Mac McLendon	10	75-71-70-69=285	$2,800.00

U.S. Open
Course: Oak Hill C.C., Rochester, N.Y.
Par: 70 Yardage: 6,962
Last day of event: Sunday, June 16, 1968

Player	Place	Score	Earnings
Lee Trevino	Win	69-68-69-69=275	$30,000.00
Jack Nicklaus	2	72-70-70-67=279	$15,000.00
Bert Yancey	3	67-68-70-76=281	$10,000.00
Bobby Nichols	4	74-71-68-69=282	$7,500.00
Don Bies	T-5	70-70-75-69=284	$5,500.00
Steve Spray	T-5	73-75-71-65=284	$5,500.00
Jerry Pittman	T-7	73-67-74-71=285	$3,750.00
Bob Charles	T-7	73-69-72-71=285	$3,750.00
Bruce Devlin	T-9	71-69-75-71=286	$2,516.67
Gay Brewer	T-9	71-71-75-69=286	$2,516.67
Billy Casper	T-9	75-68-71-72=286	$2,516.67
Sam Snead	T-9	73-71-74-68=286	$2,516.66
Dave Stockton	T-9	72-73-69-72=286	$2,516.66
Al Geiberger	T-9	72-74-68-72=286	$2,516.67

Canadian Open
Course: Royal St. George, Toronto, Ontario, Canada
Par: 70 Yardage: 6,756
Last day of event: Sunday, June 23, 1968

Player	Place	Score	Earnings
Bob Charles	Win	70-68-70-66=274	$23,225.00
Jack Nicklaus	2	73-68-68-67=276	$13,935.00
Bruce Crampton	3	71-68-72-66=277	$8,709.38
Tommy Aaron	T-4	70-72-67-70=279	$4,790.16
R.H. Sikes	T-4	69-71-69-70=279	$4,790.16
Sam Snead	T-4	71-72-68-68=279	$4,790.16
Tom Weiskopf	T-4	69-71-69-70=279	$4,790.16
Billy Casper	T-8	69-71-69-71=280	$3,425.69
Jack Montgomery	T-8	75-71-69-65=280	$3,425.69
Al Balding	T-10	71-70-72-68=281	$3,425.69
Bruce Devlin	T-10	67-68-75-71=281	$3,425.69
George Knudson	T-10	75-69-64-73=281	$3,425.69
Gary Player	T-10	74-68-72-67=281	$3,425.69
Bob-E. Smith	T-10	71-69-72-69=281	$3,425.69
Ken Still	T-10	67-71-72-71=281	$3,425.69

Cleveland Open Invitational
Course: Lakewood C.C., Lakewood, Ohio
Par: 71 Yardage: 6,742
Last day of event: Sunday, June 30, 1968

Player	Place	Score	Earnings
Dave Stockton	Win	69-68-67-72=276	$22,000.00
Bob Dickson	2	72-66-70-70=278	$13,200.00
Julius Boros	T-3	70-71-68-70=279	$6,160.00
Roberto De Vicenzo	T-3	69-68-69-73=279	$6,160.00
Don January	T-3	71-67-69-72=279	$6,160.00
Bobby Cole	T-6	71-68-67-74=280	$3,776.66
Tony Jacklin	T-6	66-75-68-71=280	$3,776.67
Lee Trevino	T-6	72-71-70-67=280	$3,776.67
Tommy Aaron	T-9	70-66-72-73=281	$2,548.33
Frank Beard	T-9	71-69-73-68=281	$2,548.34
Bob Murphy	T-9	74-68-70-69=281	$2,548.33
Kel Nagle	T-9	75-67-68-71=281	$2,548.33
Gary Player	T-9	73-70-70-68=281	$2,548.34
R.H. Sikes	T-9	72-70-69-70=281	$2,548.33

Buick Open Invitational
Course: Warwick Hills C.C., Grand Blanc, Mich.
Par: 72 Yardage: 7,001
Last day of event: Sunday, July 7, 1968

Player	Place	Score	Earnings
Tom Weiskopf	Win	73-67-71-69=280	$25,000.00
Mike Hill	2	75-67-67-72=281	$15,000.00
Rod Horn	3	69-72-67-74=282	$9,375.00
Bob Lunn	T-4	72-71-72-68=283	$5,812.50
Rocky Thompson	T-4	71-71-71-70=283	$5,812.50
Julius Boros	T-6	70-69-75-70=284	$4,291.67
Johnny Pott	T-6	73-68-70-73=284	$4,291.66
Lee Trevino	T-6	70-68-70-76=284	$4,291.67
Frank Beard	T-9	70-74-70-71=285	$3,375.00
Fred Marti	T-9	70-70-72-73=285	$3,375.00

British Open
Course: Carnoustie G.C., Carnoustie, Angus, Scotland
Par: 72 Yardage: 7,252
Last day of event: Saturday, July 13, 1968

Player	Place	Score	Earnings
Gary Player	Win	74-71-71-73=289	$7,200.00
Bob Charles	T-2	72-72-71-76=291	$4,171.20
Jack Nicklaus	T-2	76-69-73-73=291	$4,171.20
Billy Casper	4	72-68-74-78=292	$2,940.00
Maurice Bembridge	5	71-75-73-74=293	$2,400.00
Brian Barnes	T-6	70-74-80-71=295	$1,579.20
Gay Brewer	T-6	74-73-72-76=295	$1,579.20
Neil Coles	T-6	75-76-71-73=295	$1,579.20
Al Balding	9	74-76-74-72=296	$1,140.00
Arnold Palmer	T-10	77-71-72-77=297	$964.80
Bruce Devlin	T-10	77-73-72-75=297	$964.80
Roberto De Vicenzo	T-10	77-72-74-74=297	$964.80

Greater Milwaukee Open Invitational
Course: Northshore C.C., Mequon, Wis.
Par: 72 Yardage: 7,155
Last day of event: Sunday, July 14, 1968

Player	Place	Score	Earnings
Dave Stockton	Win	68-67-71-69=275	$40,000.00

Sam Snead	2	72-65-75-67=279	$24,000.00
Tom Weiskopf	T-3	72-72-68-69=281	$12,500.00
Dave Marr	T-3	72-68-69-72=281	$12,500.00
Charles Coody	T-5	74-66-73-69=282	$7,300.00
Ron Cerrudo	T-5	71-68-72-71=282	$7,300.00
Bruce Crampton	T-5	72-68-71-71=282	$7,300.00
Mac McLendon	T-5	66-71-73-72=282	$7,300.00
Frank Beard	T-9	74-68-73-68=283	$4,633.34
Bob McCallister	T-9	72-72-69-70=283	$4,633.34

PGA Championship
Course: Pecan Valley, San Antonio, Texas
Par: 70 Yardage: 7,096
Last day of event: Sunday, July 21, 1968

Player	Place	Score	Earnings
Julius Boros	Win	71-71-70-69=281	$25,000.00
Bob Charles	T-2	72-70-70-70=282	$12,500.00
Arnold Palmer	T-2	71-69-72-70=282	$12,500.00
George Archer	T-4	71-69-74-69=283	$7,500.00
Marty Fleckman	T-4	66-72-72-73=283	$7,500.00
Frank Beard	T-6	68-70-72-74=284	$5,750.00
Billy Casper	T-6	74-70-70-70=284	$5,750.00
Miller Barber	T-8	70-70-72-73=285	$3,405.55
Frank Boynton	T-8	70-73-72-70=285	$3,405.56
Charles Coody	T-8	70-77-70-68=285	$3,405.56
Al Geiberger	T-8	70-73-71-71=285	$3,405.56
Bob Goalby	T-8	73-72-70-70=285	$3,405.56
Lou Graham	T-8	73-70-70-72=285	$3,405.55
Doug Sanders	T-8	72-67-73-73=285	$3,405.55
Dan Sikes	T-8	70-72-73-70=285	$3,405.56
Kermit Zarley	T-8	72-75-68-70=285	$3,405.55

Minnesota Golf Classic
Course: Keller G.C., St. Paul, Minn. .
Par: 71 Yardage: 6,702
Last day of event: Sunday, July 28, 1968

Player	Place	Score	Earnings
Dan Sikes	Win	71-66-71-64=272	$25,000.00
Ken Still	2	69-67-69-68=273	$12,000.00
Tom Weiskopf	3	67-69-74-64=274	$7,500.00
Pete Brown	T-4	66-67-71-71=275	$4,366.67
Bob Dickson	T-4	68-70-69-68=275	$4,366.67
Lou Graham	T-4	69-68-67-71=275	$4,366.66
Tommy Aaron	T-7	69-66-70-71=276	$2,750.00
Dale Douglass	T-7	70-67-72-67=276	$2,750.00
Billy Maxwell	T-7	69-69-72-66=276	$2,750.00
Steve Oppermann	T-7	69-70-67-70=276	$2,750.00
Phil Rodgers	T-7	69-72-70-65=276	$2,750.00
Bob Stanton	T-7	66-71-71-68=276	$2,750.00

Western Open
Course: Olympia Fields (North Course), Olympia Fields, Ill.
Par: 71 Yardage: 6,749
Last day of event: Sunday, August 4, 1968

Player	Place	Score	Earnings
Jack Nicklaus	Win	65-72-65-71=273	$26,000.00
Miller Barber	2	67-70-73-66=276	$15,600.00
Bob Stanton	3	70-67-69-71=277	$9,750.00
Julius Boros	4	70-71-67-70=278	$6,500.00
Bob-E. Smith	T-5	72-72-69-66=279	$4,983.34
George Archer	T-5	72-72-69-66=279	$4,983.33

Homero Blancas	T-5	69-68-72-70=279	$4,983.33
Bert Weaver	T-8	71-71-70-68=280	$3,835.00
Bobby Nichols	T-8	70-66-75-69=280	$3,835.00
Tom Weiskopf	T-10	70-73-72-66=281	$2,990.00
Gay Brewer	T-10	74-71-70-66=281	$2,990.00
Billy Maxwell	T-10	69-68-75-69=281	$2,990.00
Tommy Aaron	T-10	71-72-67-71=281	$2,990.00

American Golf Classic
Course: Firestone C.C. (South), Akron, Ohio
Par: 70 Yardage: 7,180
Last day of event: Sunday, August 11, 1968

Player	Place	Score	Earnings
Jack Nicklaus	Win	70-69-72-69=280	$25,000.00
Playoff: Beat Lee Elder with birdie on fifth extra hole (Frank Beard eliminated with par on first hole)			
Lee Elder	T-2	68-70-72-70=280	$12,187.50
Frank Beard	T-2	70-71-69-70=280	$12,187.50
Julius Boros	T-4	73-69-69-70=281	$5,156.25
Bert Yancey	T-4	73-68-69-71=281	$5,156.25
Don Bies	T-4	69-73-64-75=281	$5,156.25
Bob Stanton	T-4	73-71-68-69=281	$5,156.25
Bob Lunn	T-8	67-72-72-71=282	$3,541.67
Art Wall	T-8	68-72-70-72=282	$3,541.66
George Knudson	T-8	70-68-72-72=282	$3,541.67

Westchester Classic
Course: Westchester C.C., Harrison, N.Y.
Par: 72 Yardage: 6,573
Last day of event: Sunday, August 18, 1968

Player	Place	Score	Earnings
Julius Boros	Win	70-65-69-68=272	$50,000.00
Bob Murphy	T-2	64-69-68-72=273	$20,416.66
Jack Nicklaus	T-3	67-68-72-66=273	$20,416.67
Dan Sikes	T-3	65-70-70-68=273	$20,416.67
Billy Casper	5	70-71-67-67=275	$10,750.00
Rives McBee	T-6	69-66-70-71=276	$9,000.00
Dudley Wysong	T-6	68-69-72-67=276	$9,000.00
Frank Beard	T-8	71-67-69-70=277	$7,083.33
Bruce Crampton	T-8	68-68-73-68=277	$7,083.34
Dale Douglass	T-8	70-65-73-69=277	$7,083.33

Philadelphia Golf Classic
Course: Whitemarsh Valley C.C., Chestnut Hill, Pa.
Par: 72 Yardage: 6,708
Last day of event: Sunday, August 25, 1968

Player	Place	Score	Earnings
Bob Murphy	Win	69-71-66-70=276	$20,000.00
Playoff: Beat Labron Harris, Jr. with birdie on the third extra hole			
Labron Harris, Jr.	2	71-67-70-68=276	$12,000.00
Dudley Wysong	3	65-74-68-70=277	$7,500.00
Frank Beard	T-4	73-72-68-65=278	$4,366.67
Charles Coody	T-4	70-73-67-68=278	$4,366.67
Jack Nicklaus	T-4	73-69-66-70=278	$4,366.66
Dean Refram	7	71-68-69-71=279	$3,400.00
Gardner Dickinson	T-8	70-70-72-68=280	$2,725.00
George Knudson	T-8	70-69-72-69=280	$2,725.00
Chi Chi Rodriguez	T-8	72-69-70-69=280	$2,725.00
Lee Elder	T-8	71-71-66-72=280	$2,725.00

Thunderbird Classic

Course: Upper Montclair C.C., Clifton, N.J.

Par: 72 Yardage: 7,055

Last day of event: Monday, September 2, 1968

Player	Place	Score	Earnings
Bob Murphy	Win	68-70-71-68=277	$30,000.00
Bruce Crampton	T-2	70-68-73-69=280	$14,625.00
Bob Lunn	T-2	71-72-68-69=280	$14,625.00
Homero Blancas	4	70-71-69-72=282	$7,500.00
Jack Nicklaus	T-5	73-69-70-71=283	$5,750.00
Gary Player	T-5	70-67-70-76=283	$5,750.00
Dan Sikes	T-5	72-72-69-70=283	$5,750.00
Larry Mowry	T-8	74-70-71-69=284	$4,425.00
Mason Rudolph	T-8	70-69-76-69=284	$4,425.00
Tommy Aaron	T-10	73-68-73-72=286	$3,450.00
Charles Coody	T-10	71-74-70-71=286	$3,450.00
Arnold Palmer	T-10	71-70-74-71=286	$3,450.00
Chi Chi Rodriguez	T-10	70-71-73-72=286	$3,450.00

Greater Hartford Open Invitational

Course: Wethersfield C.C., Wethersfield, Conn.

Par: 71 Yardage: 6,568

Last day of event: Sunday, September 8, 1968

Player	Place	Score	Earnings
Billy Casper	Win	68-65-67-66=266	$20,000.00
Bruce Crampton	2	65-67-70-67=269	$12,000.00
Ray Floyd	3	69-67-68-67=271	$7,500.00
Dave Stockton	4	68-68-67-71=274	$5,000.00
Mason Rudolph	T-5	67-70-70-68=275	$4,050.00
Ken Still	T-5	67-71-67-70=275	$4,050.00
Howie Johnson	T-7	68-69-70-69=276	$2,975.00
Dave Marr	T-7	68-71-67-70=276	$2,975.00
Jack Montgomery	T-7	72-67-69-68=276	$2,975.00
Bob-E. Smith	T-7	69-71-70-66=276	$2,975.00

Kemper Open Invitational

Course: Pleasant Valley, Sutton, Mass.

Par: 72 Yardage: 7,250

Last day of event: Sunday, September 15, 1968

Player	Place	Score	Earnings
Arnold Palmer	Win	69-70-70-67=276	$30,000.00
Bruce Crampton	T-2	69-71-67-73=280	$14,625.00
Art Wall	T-2	69-68-73-70=280	$14,625.00
John Lively	T-4	71-72-70-68=281	$6,975.00
Orville Moody	T-4	71-68-67-75=281	$6,975.00
Dow Finsterwald	T-6	72-70-71-69=282	$4,912.50
Al Geiberger	T-6	70-70-74-68=282	$4,912.50
Phil Rodgers	T-6	69-73-71-69=282	$4,912.50
Doug Sanders	T-6	71-68-70-73=282	$4,912.50
Harold Henning	T-10	72-72-69-70=283	$3,600.00
Steve Reid	T-10	75-71-69-68=283	$3,600.00
Terry Wilcox	T-10	71-72-70-70=283	$3,600.00

Robinson Open

Course: Crawford C.C., Robinson, Ill.

Par: 72 Yardage: 6,460

Last day of event: Sunday, September 29, 1968

Player	Place	Score	Earnings
Dean Refram	Win	68-67-70-65=270	$5,000.00
Mike Hill	2	65-72-69-69=275	$3,000.00

Jim Grant	T-3	70-69-68-72=279	$1,400.00
Rocky Thompson	T-3	66-69-72-72=279	$1,400.00
Jim Wiechers	T-3	68-68-73-70=279	$1,400.00
J.C. Goosie	T-6	72-70-68-70=280	$900.00
Orville Moody	T-6	72-68-67-73=280	$900.00
Deane Beman	T-8	73-68-73-67=281	$655.00
Bobby Mitchell	T-8	73-67-67-74=281	$655.00
John Schlee	T-8	72-72-68-69=281	$655.00
Chick Evans	T-8	70-70-70-71=281	$655.00
Mac McLendon	T-8	68-71-69-73=281	$655.00

Sahara Invitational

Course: Paradise Valley C.C., Las Vegas, Nev.

Home course / Par: 71 Yardage: 7,091

Last day of event: Sunday, October 20, 1968

Player	Place	Score	Earnings
Chi Chi Rodriguez	Win	70-71-69-64=274	$20,000.00
Playoff: Beat Dale Douglass with par on first extra hole			
Dale Douglass	2	67-68-69-70=274	$12,000.00
Ron Cerrudo	T-3	70-67-69-69=275	$5,150.00
George Archer	T-3	69-71-71-64=275	$5,150.00
Lee Trevino	T-3	70-68-70-67=275	$5,150.00
Billy Casper	T-3	71-67-67-70=275	$5,150.00
Howie Johnson	T-7	70-68-71-67=276	$3,100.00
Kermit Zarley	T-7	68-69-69-70=276	$3,100.00
Julius Boros	T-7	68-70-69-69=276	$3,100.00
Frank Beard	T-10	73-68-70-67=278	$2,500.00
Dave Marr	T-10	70-71-69-68=278	$2,500.00

Haig Open Invitational

Course: Mesa Verde C.C., Costa Mesa, Calif.

Par: 71 Yardage: 6,650

Last day of event: Sunday, October 27, 1968

Player	Place	Score	Earnings
Bob Dickson	Win	68-65-69-69=271	$22,000.00
Chi Chi Rodriguez	2	67-69-66-71=273	$13,200.00
Bill Collins	3	69-66-70-69=274	$8,250.00
Bobby Mitchell	4	68-69-72-66=275	$5,500.00
Jack Montgomery	T-5	69-67-71-69=276	$3,828.00
Billy Casper	T-5	68-68-69-71=276	$3,828.00
Ken Still	T-5	71-65-69-71=276	$3,828.00
Don Massengale	T-5	67-70-68-71=276	$3,828.00
Bob-E. Smith	T-9	69-72-69-67=277	$2,442.00
Dow Finsterwald	T-9	69-70-69-69=277	$2,442.00
Al Geiberger	T-9	65-72-70-70=277	$2,442.00
Mac McLendon	T-9	70-70-68-69=277	$2,442.00

Lucky International Open Invitational

Course: Harding Park G.C., San Francisco, Calif.

Par: 71 Yardage: 6,692

Last day of event: Monday, November 4, 1968

Player	Place	Score	Earnings
Billy Casper	Win	68-65-70-66=269	$20,000.00
Ray Floyd	T-2	70-69-66-68=273	$9,750.00
Don Massengale	T-2	68-67-69-69=273	$9,750.00
Miller Barber	T-4	66-69-68-71=274	$4,125.00
Bob Murphy	T-4	72-68-65-69=274	$4,125.00
Ken Still	T-4	70-66-69-69=274	$4,125.00
Dave Stockton	T-4	67-66-69-72=274	$4,125.00
Tommy Aaron	8	69-71-63-72=275	$3,100.00
George Archer	T-9	66-73-67-70=276	$2,400.00

Charles Coody	T-9	71-65-71-69=276	$2,400.00
Gene Littler	T-9	72-69-67-68=276	$2,400.00
Bob Lunn	T-9	70-68-70-68=276	$2,400.00
Mac McLendon	T-9	69-68-70-69=276	$2,400.00

Hawaiian Open Invitational
Course: Waialae C.C., Honolulu, Ha.
Par: 72 Yardage: 7,020
Last day of event: Sunday, November 10, 1968

Player	Place	Score	Earnings
Lee Trevino	Win	68-71-65-68=272	$25,000.00
George Archer	2	64-70-69-71=274	$15,000.00
Dale Douglass	3	69-68-69-70=276	$9,375.00
Mac McLendon	4	66-70-69-72=277	$6,250.00
Frank Beard	T-5	69-69-72-68=278	$5,062.00
Dick Lotz	T-5	65-69-69-75=278	$5,062.00
Jim Wiechers	7	73-67-71-69=280	$4,250.00
Charles Coody	T-8	69-71-72-69=281	$3,541.67
Bruce Crampton	T-8	68-71-71-71=281	$3,541.67
Gene Littler	T-8	65-66-70-70=281	$3,541.66

Cajun Classic
Course: Oakbourne C.C., Lafayette, La.
Par: 72 Yardage: 6,550
Last day of event: Sunday, November 24, 1968

Player	Place	Score	Earnings
Ron Cerrudo	Win	69-67-66-68=270	$5,000.00
Charles Sifford	T-2	70-67-70-67=274	$2,900.00
Bobby Mitchell	T-2	68-71-67-68=274	$2,900.00
Dave Stockton	T-4	66-70-71-68=275	$1,975.00
Miller Barber	T-4	65-72-69-69=275	$1,975.00
Homero Blancas	T-6	72-66-67-71=276	$1,550.00
Dan Sikes	T-6	66-71-70-69=276	$1,550.00
Deane Beman	T-8	69-71-71-66=277	$1,250.00
Howie Johnson	T-8	70-73-68-66=277	$1,250.00
Mac McLendon	T-8	69-71-70-67=277	$1,250.00
Jerry McGee	T-8	71-69-68-69=277	$1,250.00

1969

Lanky George Archer won the Masters by a shot over Billy Casper, George Knudson and Tom Weiskopf. Orville Moody, who had honed his game in the Army, took the U.S. Open, besting Deane Beman, Al Geiberger and Bob Rosburg by a stroke. Englishman Tony Jacklin energized golf in his home country by winning the British Open, beating Bob Charles by two shots at Royal Lytham. Raymond Floyd scored a one-shot victory at the PGA Championship over South Africa's Gary Player, who was dogged throughout the competition at NCR Country Club by anti-apartheid protestors. Joseph C. Dey Jr. became director of the Tournament Players Division of the PGA of America, an entity formed as a compromise between jealous club professionals and rebellious touring pros. Eleven-time major winner Walter Hagen, who elevated the status of pro golfers in the 1920s, died in October at age 76.

Alameda County Open
Course: Sunol Valley G.C. (Palm Course), Sunol, Calif.
Par: 72 Yardage: 7,015
Last day of event: Sunday, January 12, 1969

Player	Place	Score	Earnings
Dick Lotz	Win	72-71-74-73=290	$10,000.00
Don Whitt	2	72-77-69-73=291	$5,700.00
Bob Erickson	3	77-71-68-76=292	$3,550.00
Dave Ragan	4	75-70-71-78=294	$2,350.00

Bill Ogden	T-5	70-72-75-78=295	$1,925.00
Tommy Jacobs	T-5	75-76-70-74=295	$1,925.00
Bob Lunn	T-7	75-69-73-79=296	$1,419.00
John Lotz	T-7	74-75-70-77=296	$1,419.00
John Jacobs	T-7	74-74-76-72=296	$1,419.00
Bob Brue	T-7	73-75-72-76=296	$1,419.00

Los Angeles Open
Course: Rancho Municipal G.C., Los Angeles, Calif.
Par: 71 Yardage: 6,827
Last day of event: Sunday, January 12, 1969

Player	Place	Score	Earnings
Charles Sifford	Win	63-71-71-71=276	$20,000.00
Playoff: Beat Harold Henning with birdie on first extra hole			
Harold Henning	2	74-68-66-68=276	$11,400.00
Billy Casper	T-3	69-69-72-67=277	$5,900.00
Bruce Devlin	T-3	69-72-69-67=277	$5,900.00
Dave Hill	5	66-73-69-70=278	$4,100.00
Bert Yancey	6	75-67-71-67=280	$3,600.00
Howell Fraser	7	72-73-70-66=281	$3,200.00
Mac McLendon	T-8	69-68-77-68=282	$2,716.67
Roy Pace	T-8	71-69-72-70=282	$2,716.67
Tom Shaw	T-8	69-68-73-72=282	$2,716.66

Kaiser International Open
Course: Silverado C.C. (North Course), Silverado C.C. (South Course), Napa, Calif.
Home Course -Par: 72 Yardage: 6,849
Last day of event: Friday, January 17, 1969

Player	Place	Score	Earnings
Miller Barber	Win	68-67=135 $13,500.00	
Bruce Devlin	2	69-67=136 $7,700.00	
Arnold Palmer	3	69-68=137 $4,785.00	
Charles Coody	T-4	70-68=138 $2,917.25	
Bob Lunn	T-4	65-73=138 $2,917.25	
Bob Brue	T-6	71-68=139 $1,792.82	
Jim Colbert	T-6	71-68=139 $1,792.82	
Jacky Cupit	T-6	66-73=139 $1,792.82	
Gene Littler	T-6	69-70=139 $1,792.82	
John Lotz	T-6	72-67=139 $1,792.82	
Bob McCallister	T-6	69-70=139 $1,792.82	
Orville Moody	T-6	69-70=139 $1,792.82	
Lee Trevino	T-6	68-71=139 $1,792.82	

Bing Crosby National Pro-Am
Courses: Pebble Beach G.L., Spyglass Hill G.C., Cypress Point C.C., Pebble Beach, Calif.
Home Course / Pebble Beach G.L., Par: 72 Yardage: 6,747
Last day of event: Monday, January 27, 1969

Player	Place	Score	Earnings
George Archer	Win	72-68-72-71=283	$25,000.00
Bob Dickson	T-2	73-69-74-68=284	$9,666.67
Dale Douglass	T-2	71-69-70-74=284	$9,666.67
Howie Johnson	T-2	71-69-71-73=284	$9,666.66
John Lotz	5	71-75-67-72=285	$5,125.00
Jack Nicklaus	6	71-73-73-70=287	$4,500.00
Lee Elder	7	71-75-73-69=288	$4,000.00
Ron Cerrudo	T-8	75-72-71-71=289	$2,901.43
Bill Collins	T-8	71-73-76-69=289	$2,901.43
Bruce Devlin	T-8	69-75-78-67=289	$2,901.43
Rod Funseth	T-8	72-71-73-73=289	$2,901.42

Gene Littler	T-8	73-74-70-72=289	$2,901.43
Don Massengale	T-8	72-75-70-72=289	$2,901.43
Jimmy Powell	T-8	73-76-68-72=289	$2,901.43

Andy Williams-San Diego Open
Course: Torrey Pines (South), San Diego, Calif.
Home Course -Par: 72 Yardage: 6,792
Last day of event: Sunday, February 2, 1969

Player	Place	Score	Earnings
Jack Nicklaus	Win	68-72-71-73=284	$30,000.00
Gene Littler	2	70-72-67-76=285	$17,100.00
Dave Stockton	T-3	74-72-70-70=286	$8,850.00
Tommy Aaron	T-3	74-72-70-70=286	$8,850.00
Dow Finsterwald	5	69-75-72-71=287	$6,150.00
Lee Trevino	T-6	75-69-74-70=288	$4,875.00
Larry Ziegler	T-6	70-69-76-73=288	$4,875.00
Phil Rodgers	T-6	75-72-68-73=288	$4,875.00
Frank Beard	T-9	74-72-75-68=289	$3,325.00
Ray Floyd	T-9	73-75-69-72=289	$3,325.00
Bruce Devlin	T-9	72-72-72-73=289	$3,325.00
Don January	T-9	74-73-70-72=289	$3,325.00
Bob Charles	T-9	74-69-72-74=289	$3,325.00
Dick Lotz	T-9	72-71-71-75=289	$3,325.00

Bob Hope Desert Classic
Course: Indian Wells C.C., Tamarisk C.C., Bermuda Dunes C.C., La Quinta, Calif.
Home course / Indian Wells, Par: 72 Yardage: 6,711
Last day of event: Sunday, February 9, 1969

Player	Place	Score	Earnings
Billy Casper	Win	71-68-71-69-66=345	$20,000.00
Dave Hill	2	69-72-70-71-66=348	$11,400.00
Jack Montgomery	3	70-68-74-67-70=349	$7,100.00
Art Wall	4	69-69-71-70-71=350	$4,700.00
Deane Beman	T-5	72-77-72-68-62=351	$3,175.00
Bob Charles	T-5	74-67-69-72-69=351	$3,175.00
Gene Littler	T-5	67-74-68-73-69=351	$3,175.00
Orville Moody	T-5	72-69-68-72-70=351	$3,175.00
Frank Beard	T-5	70-68-71-68-74=351	$3,175.00
George Knudson	T-5	72-71-68-69-71=351	$3,175.00

Phoenix Open
Course: Arizona C.C., Phoenix, Ariz.
Par: 71 Yardage: 6,389
Last day of event: Sunday, February 16, 1969

Player	Place	Score	Earnings
Gene Littler	Win	69-66-62-66=263	$20,000.00
Don January	T-2	67-65-67-66=265	$7,733.34
Billy Maxwell	T-2	65-66-68-66=265	$7,733.33
Miller Barber	T-2	65-70-66-64=265	$7,733.33
Terry Wilcox	T-5	65-69-66-67=267	$3,633.34
Jack Ewing	T-5	67-66-66-68=267	$3,633.33
Ray Floyd	T-5	69-65-68-65=267	$3,633.33
Dave Hill	T-8	68-71-63-67=269	$2,825.00
Larry Ziegler	T-8	65-70-70-64=269	$2,825.00
Jerry Abbott	T-8	67-69-63-70=269	$2,200.00

Tucson Open
Course: Tucson National G.C., Starr Pass G.C., Tucson, Ariz.
Par: 72 Yardage: 7,200
Last day of event: Sunday, February 23, 1969

Player	Place	Score	Earnings
Lee Trevino	Win	67-70-68-66=271	$20,000.00
Miller Barber	2	65-72-73-68=278	$11,400.00
Bert Yancey	3	70-70-70-69=279	$7,100.00
Gene Littler	T-4	74-70-68-68=280	$4,400.00
Don Bies	T-4	72-67-72-69=280	$4,400.00
Phil Rodgers	6	69-71-74-67=281	$3,600.00
Dale Douglass	T-7	67-69-78-68=282	$2,837.50
Ron Cerrudo	T-7	68-73-73-68=282	$2,837.50
Jimmy Wright	T-7	69-69-73-71=282	$2,837.50
Johnny Pott	T-7	70-65-75-72=282	$2,837.50

Doral Open
Course: Doral C.C. (Blue), Miami, Fla.
Par: 72 Yardage: 7,002
Last day of event: Sunday, March 2, 1969

Player	Place	Score	Earnings
Tom Shaw	Win	65-70-71-70=276	$30,000.00
Tommy Aaron	2	67-68-71-71=277	$17,100.00
Dan Sikes	3	65-70-72-71=278	$10,650.00
Homero Blancas	T-4	71-68-70-70=279	$6,600.00
Jack Nicklaus	T-4	72-71-64-72=279	$6,600.00
Tommy Bolt	6	69-69-69-73=280	$5,400.00
Gay Brewer	7	73-68-72-68=281	$4,800.00
Tony Jacklin	T-8	70-68-72-72=282	$4,237.50
Hugh Royer	T-8	73-72-69-68=282	$4,237.50
Richard Crawford	T-10	72-70-73-68=283	$3,450.00
Bobby Nichols	T-10	77-67-72-67=283	$3,450.00
Arnold Palmer	T-10	68-69-73-73=283	$3,450.00

Florida Citrus Open
Course: Rio Pinar C.C., Orlando, Fla.
Par: 72 Yardage: 6,849
Last day of event: Sunday, March 9, 1969

Player	Place	Score	Earnings
Ken Still	Win	74-67-67-70=278	$23,000.00
Miller Barber	2	69-68-72-70=279	$13,100.00
Orville Moody	T-3	70-70-72-68=280	$6,790.00
Johnny Pott	T-3	70-66-70-74=280	$6,790.00
Gay Brewer	5	70-72-67-72=281	$4,720.00
Lee Elder	T-6	70-71-67-74=282	$3,577.50
Dave Stockton	T-6	72-67-69-74=282	$3,577.50
Lee Trevino	T-6	74-70-68-70=282	$3,577.50
Tom Weiskopf	T-6	68-71-71-72=282	$3,577.50
Dale Douglass	T-10	72-67-68-76=283	$2,438.00
Jack Nicklaus	T-10	70-71-71-71=283	$2,438.00
Dean Refram	T-10	71-68-69-75=283	$2,438.00
Dan Sikes	T-10	69-70-70-74=283	$2,438.00
Bert Yancey	T-10	70-66-70-77=283	$2,438.00

Monsanto Open
Course: Pensacola C.C., Pensacola, Fla.
Par: 71 Yardage: 6,575
Last day of event: Tuesday, March 18, 1969

Player	Place	Score	Earnings
Jim Colbert	Win	69-67-64-67=267	$20,000.00

Deane Beman	2	70-68-63-68=269	$11,400.00
Lee Trevino	3	67-69-66-68=270	$7,100.00
Ray Floyd	4	70-66-67-68=271	$4,700.00
Larry Hinson	T-5	67-71-69-68=275	$3,633.34
Tommy Aaron	T-5	67-70-67-71=275	$3,633.33
Gary Player	T-5	70-68-65-72=275	$3,633.33
Steve Reid	T-8	71-72-67-67=277	$2,612.50
Doug Sanders	T-8	69-69-70-69=277	$2,612.50
Bruce Crampton	T-8	67-71-70-69=277	$2,612.50
Richard Crawford	T-8	68-67-69-73=277	$2,612.50

Greater Jacksonville Open

Course: Deerwood C.C., Jacksonville, Fla.
Par: 72 Yardage: 7,221
Last day of event: Sunday, March 23, 1969

Player	Place	Score	Earnings
Ray Floyd	Win	68-71-68-71=278	$20,000.00
Playoff: Beat Gardner Dickinson with birdie on first extra hole			
Gardner Dickinson	2	68-70-70-70=278	$11,400.00
Lee Trevino	T-3	69-69-72-70=280	$5,300.00
Dewitt Weaver	T-3	68-74-66-72=280	$5,300.00
Bobby Cole	T-5	69-69-78-65=281	$3,400.00
Arnold Palmer	T-5	70-68-72-71=281	$3,400.00
Jim Colbert	T-7	72-71-71-68=282	$2,612.50
Bob Charles	T-7	71-72-70-69=282	$2,612.50
Billy Casper	T-7	71-70-72-69=282	$2,612.50
Bob Murphy	T-7	71-74-67-70=282	$2,612.50

National Airlines Open

Course: C.C. of Miami, Miami, Fla.
Par: 72 Yardage: 6,927
Last day of event: Sunday, March 30, 1969

Player	Place	Score	Earnings
Bunky Henry	Win	69-73-66-70=278	$40,000.00
Bruce Crampton	T-2	68-70-75-66=279	$13,650.00
Dan Sikes	T-2	70-70-71-68=279	$13,650.00
Bob Murphy	T-2	69-66-68-76=279	$13,650.00
Dave Stockton	T-2	68-72-67-72=279	$13,650.00
Butch Baird	6	68-69-70-73=280	$7,200.00
Dale Douglass	T-7	68-68-73-72=281	$6,150.00
Lionel Hebert	T-7	68-69-69-75=281	$6,150.00
Terry Dill	T-9	71-67-72-72=282	$6,150.00
Terry Wilcox	T-9	69-69-71-73=282	$6,150.00
Deane Beman	T-9	69-72-69-72=282	$6,150.00

Greater Greensboro Open

Course: Sedgefield C.C., Greensboro, N.C.
Par: 71 Yardage: 7,034
Last day of event: Sunday, April 6, 1969

Player	Place	Score	Earnings
Gene Littler	Win	66-70-69-69=274	$32,000.00
Playoff: Beat Julius Boros and Orville Moody with birdie on the fifth extra hole			
(Tom Weiskopf eliminated with bogey on first extra hole)			
Orville Moody	T-2	69-70-68-67=274	$12,373.34
Julius Boros	T-2	67-71-67-69=274	$12,373.33
Tom Weiskopf	T-2	67-72-67-68=274	$12,373.33
Gary Player	T-5	69-68-68-70=275	$6,560.00
Bobby Cole	T-6	70-69-69-68=276	$5,440.00
Chi Chi Rodriguez	T-6	69-68-69-70=276	$5,440.00
Deane Beman	T-8	68-69-67-73=277	$4,520.00
Ken Still	T-8	69-72-68-68=277	$4,520.00
Bruce Crampton	T-10	68-69-70-71=278	$4,000.00

Masters

Course: Augusta National G.C., Augusta, Ga.
Par: 72 Yardage: 6,980
Last day of event: Sunday, April 13, 1969

Player	Place	Score	Earnings
George Archer	Win	67-73-69-72=281	$20,000.00
Tom Weiskopf	T-2	71-71-69-71=282	$12,333.34
George Knudson	T-2	70-73-69-70=282	$12,333.33
Billy Casper	T-2	66-71-71-74=282	$12,333.33
Charles Coody	T-5	74-68-69-72=283	$6,750.00
Don January	T-5	74-73-70-66=283	$6,750.00
Miller Barber	7	71-71-68-74=284	$5,000.00
Lionel Hebert	T-8	69-73-70-73=285	$3,600.00
Gene Littler	T-8	69-75-70-71=285	$3,600.00
Tommy Aaron	T-8	71-71-73-70=285	$3,600.00

Tallahassee Open

Course: Killearn C.C., Tallahassee, Fla.
Par: 72 Yardage: 7,008
Last day of event: Sunday, April 20, 1969

Player	Place	Score	Earnings
Chuck Courtney	Win	72-69-71-70=282	$5,000.00
Jacky Cupit	T-2	71-72-73-67=283	$2,633.34
Bob Shaw	T-2	68-74-68-73=283	$2,633.33
Bert Greene	T-2	70-72-71-70=283	$2,633.33
John Jacobs	T-5	74-70-69-71=284	$1,650.00
Jim Wiechers	T-5	76-68-69-71=284	$1,650.00
Jack Ewing	T-5	71-72-72-69=284	$1,650.00
Larry Hinson	8	70-64-77-74=285	$1,400.00
Jerry Abbott	9	73-72-75-66=286	$1,300.00
Grier Jones	T-10	74-69-73-71=287	$1,062.50
Tommy Aaron	T-10	72-71-69-75=287	$1,062.50
Richard Crawford	T-10	71-73-71-72=287	$1,062.50
Bob Boldt	T-10	77-70-69-71=287	$1,062.50

Azalea Open

Course: Cape Fear C.C., Wilmington, N.C.
Par: 71 Yardage: 6,575
Last day of event: Sunday, April 20, 1969

Player	Place	Score	Earnings
Dale Douglass	Win	70-70-66-69=275	$5,000.00
Jim Langley	T-2	67-70-70-71=278	$2,437.50
Larry Mowry	T-2	68-67-73-70=278	$2,437.50
Bob Stone	T-2	66-70-73-69=278	$2,437.50
Terry Wilcox	T-2	69-66-72-71=278	$2,437.50
Joe Campbell	T-6	66-71-70-72=279	$1,550.00
Randy Petri	T-6	68-68-68-75=279	$1,550.00
Tommy Bolt	8	67-71-71-71=280	$1,400.00
Bobby Mitchell	T-9	69-71-70-71=281	$1,200.00
Mac McLendon	T-9	69-71-70-71=281	$1,200.00
Bob Duden	T-9	70-67-72-72=281	$1,200.00

Tournament of Champions

Course: La Costa C.C., Carlsbad, Calif.
Par: 72 Yardage: 7,114
Last day of event: Sunday, April 20, 1969

Player	Place	Score	Earnings
Gary Player	Win	69-74-69-72=284	$30,000.00
Lee Trevino	2	74-68-70-74=286	$17,000.00
Arnold Palmer	T-3	69-74-75-71=289	$10,000.00
Dave Stockton	T-3	69-75-75-70=289	$10,000.00

Gene Littler	5	75-68-75-72=290	$8,000.00
George Archer	6	71-71-74-75=291	$7,000.00
Bob Charles	T-7	73-73-74-72=292	$5,500.00
Dick Lotz	T-7	67-78-70-77=292	$5,500.00
Billy Casper	T-9	71-76-71-75=293	$4,116.66
Ron Cerrudo	T-9	74-73-75-71=293	$4,116.67
Dan Sikes	T-9	73-73-77-70=293	$4,116.67

Byron Nelson Golf Classic
Course: Preston Trail G.C., Dallas, Texas
Par: 70 Yardage: 7,086
Last day of event: Sunday, April 27, 1969

Player	Place	Score	Earnings
Bruce Devlin	Win	71-66-70-70=277	$20,000.00
Frank Beard	T-2	70-67-70-71=278	$9,250.00
Bruce Crampton	T-2	69-70-70-69=278	$9,250.00
Bob Charles	4	69-70-67-73=279	$4,700.00
Don January	T-5	72-72-71-65=280	$3,633.34
Bert Greene	T-5	66-71-73-70=280	$3,633.33
Lee Trevino	T-5	69-70-67-74=280	$3,633.33
Bob Lunn	T-8	69-74-68-71=282	$2,825.00
Arnold Palmer	T-8	69-75-69-69=282	$2,825.00
Pete Brown	T-10	73-75-69-66=283	$2,400.00
Orville Moody	T-10	69-71-71-72=283	$2,400.00

Greater New Orleans Open
Course: Lakewood C.C., New Orleans, La.
Par: 72 Yardage: 6,960
Last day of event: Sunday, May 4, 1969

Player	Place	Score	Earnings
Larry Hinson	Win	69-68-71-67=275	$20,000.00
Playoff: Beat Frank Beard with par on first extra hole			
Frank Beard	2	67-67-69-72=275	$1,140.00
Joel Goldstrand	T-3	70-67-69-70=276	$5,300.00
Dave Hill	T-3	67-68-68-73=276	$5,300.00
Bobby Mitchell	T-3	70-70-69-67=276	$5,300.00
Johnny Pott	6	68-68-71-70=277	$3,600.00
Lee Elder	T-7	66-73-68-71=278	$2,950.00
Lionel Hebert	T-7	68-70-69-71=278	$2,950.00
Herb Hooper	T-7	67-70-72-69=278	$2,950.00
Deane Beman	T-10	71-70-69-69=279	$1,810.00
Bob Charles	T-10	73-64-70-72=279	$1,810.00
Bruce Devlin	T-10	71-70-69-69=279	$1,810.00
Gardner Dickinson	T-10	72-67-71-69=279	$1,810.00
Rod Funseth	T-10	69-69-70-71=279	$1,810.00
Labron Harris, Jr.	T-10	72-70-71-66=279	$1,810.00
John Jacobs	T-10	68-68-71-72=279	$1,810.00
Grier Jones	T-10	68-72-67-72=279	$1,810.00
Dan Sikes	T-10	67-72-71-69=279	$1,810.00
Bob Stanton	T-10	68-70-72-69=279	$1,810.00

Texas Open
Course: Pecan Valley C.C., San Antonio, Texas
Par: 71 Yardage: 7,138
Last day of event: Monday, May 12, 1969

Player	Place	Score	Earnings
Deane Beman	Win	70-69-70-65=274	$20,000.00
Playoff: Beat Jack McGowan with birdie on first extra hole			
Jack McGowan	2	70-68-67-69=274	$20,000.00
Tommy Aaron	T-3	71-70-68-68=277	$5,300.00
Lee Trevino	T-3	74-68-67-68=277	$5,300.00

Dave Hill	T-3	70-68-73-66=277	$5,300.00
Bob Charles	T-6	70-68-69-71=278	$6,400.00
Steve Reid	T-6	67-71-70-70=278	$6,400.00
Doug Sanders	8	69-68-71-71=279	$2,950.00
Bert Yancey	T-9	69-68-71-72=280	$2,600.00
Jacky Cupit	T-9	70-67-71-72=280	$2,600.00

Colonial National Invitational
Course: Colonial C.C., Fort Worth, Texas
Par: 70 Yardage: 7,142
Last day of event: Sunday, May 18, 1969

Player	Place	Score	Earnings
Gardner Dickinson	Win	71-68-73-66=278	$25,000.00
Gary Player	2	70-68-72-69=279	$14,300.00
Don January	3	71-70-70-69=280	$8,850.00
Bob Charles	T-4	69-72-73-68=282	$5,487.50
Jack Nicklaus	T-4	68-70-73-71=282	$5,487.50
Bruce Crampton	T-6	70-69-69-75=283	$3,890.00
Dave Hill	T-6	74-69-72-68=283	$3,890.00
George Knudson	T-6	74-72-71-66=283	$3,890.00
Bob Lunn	T-6	72-71-73-67=283	$3,890.00
Frank Beard	10	73-68-76-67=284	$3,125.00

Atlanta Classic
Course: Atlanta C.C., Atlanta, Ga.
Par: 72 Yardage: 7,053
Last day of event: Sunday, May 25, 1969

Player	Place	Score	Earnings
Bert Yancey	Win	71-68-69-69=277	$23,000.00
Playoff: Beat Bruce Devlin with birdie on second extra hole			
Bruce Devlin	2	71-69-68-69=277	$13,100.00
Gary Player	3	72-70-66-70=278	$8,170.00
Bruce Crampton	4	69-69-68-73=279	$5,410.00
Pete Brown	T-5	69-66-74-71=280	$4,180.00
Grier Jones	T-5	71-67-74-68=280	$4,180.00
George Knudson	T-5	67-71-71-71=280	$4,180.00
Bob Charles	8	69-70-71-71=281	$3,390.00
Bob Erickson	T-9	69-69-71-73=282	$2,987.50
Dan Sikes	T-9	74-69-72-67=282	$2,987.50

Memphis Open
Course: Colonial C.C., Memphis, Tenn.
Par: 70 Yardage: 6,486
Last day of event: Sunday, June 1, 1969

Player	Place	Score	Earnings
Dave Hill	Win	67-67-66-65=265	$30,000.00
Lee Elder	2	64-67-66-70=267	$17,100.00
Tommy Aaron	T-3	66-69-68-65=268	$8,850.00
Charles Coody	T-3	66-68-67-67=268	$8,850.00
Steve Reid	5	69-70-61-69=269	$6,150.00
Don January	6	69-70-64-67=270	$5,400.00
Lee Trevino	T-7	65-69-69-68=271	$4,425.00
Lou Graham	T-7	65-69-66-71=271	$4,425.00
Dale Douglass	T-7	66-66-70-69=271	$4,425.00
Hale Irwin	T-10	67-65-72-68=272	$3,600.00
Dan Sikes	T-10	66-66-68-72=272	$3,600.00

Western Open

Course: Midlothian C.C., Midlothian, Ill.
Par: 71 Yardage: 6,654
Last day of event: Sunday, June 8, 1969

Player	Place	Score	Earnings
Billy Casper	Win	72-69-68-67=276	$26,000.00
Rocky Thompson	2	67-70-74-69=280	$14,800.00
Frank Beard	3	66-71-70-74=281	$9,240.00
Peter Townsend	4	71-72-68-72=283	$6,120.00
Gary Player	T-5	68-72-72-72=284	$4,302.00
Dick Rhyan	T-5	67-70-75-72=284	$4,302.00
Homero Blancas	T-5	70-73-67-74=284	$4,302.00
Tom Weiskopf	T-5	73-70-67-74=284	$4,302.00
Tony Jacklin	T-5	75-68-72-69=284	$4,302.00
Julius Boros	T-10	72-72-69-72=285	$2,990.00
Gay Brewer	T-10	69-67-74-75=285	$2,990.00
Ken Still	T-10	72-66-72-75=285	$2,990.00

U.S. Open

Course: Champions G.C., Houston, Texas
Par: 70 Yardage: 6,967
Last day of event: Sunday, June 15, 1969

Player	Place	Score	Earnings
Orville Moody	Win	71-70-68-72=281	$30,000.00
Deane Beman	T-2	68-69-73-72=282	$11,000.00
Bob Rosburg	T-2	70-69-72-71=282	$11,000.00
Al Geiberger	T-2	68-72-72-70=282	$11,000.00
Bob Murphy	5	66-72-74-71=283	$7,000.00
Miller Barber	T-6	67-71-68-78=284	$5,000.00
Arnold Palmer	T-6	70-73-69-72=284	$5,000.00
Bruce Crampton	T-6	73-72-68-71=284	$5,000.00
Bunky Henry	9	70-72-68-75=285	$3,500.00
George Archer	T-10	69-74-73-70=286	$2,800.00
Dave Marr	T-10	75-69-71-71=286	$2,800.00
Bruce Devlin	T-10	73-74-70-69=286	$2,800.00

Kemper Insurance Open

Course: Quail Hollow C.C., Charlotte, N.C.
Par: 72 Yardage: 7,205
Last day of event: Sunday, June 22, 1969

Player	Place	Score	Earnings
Dale Douglass	Win	69-70-68-67=274	$30,000.00
Charles Coody	2	73-69-71-65=278	$17,100.00
Bruce Crampton	T-3	72-68-69-70=279	$8,850.00
Gary Player	T-3	70-73-67-69=279	$8,850.00
George Archer	T-5	67-73-68-72=280	$5,193.75
Joel Goldstrand	T-5	71-72-68-69=280	$5,193.75
Tony Jacklin	T-5	70-69-70-71=280	$5,193.75
Arnold Palmer	T-5	73-71-70-66=280	$5,193.75
Bob Charles	T-9	68-70-70-73=281	$3,750.00
George Knudson	T-9	71-69-70-71=281	$3,750.00
Larry Ziegler	T-9	70-73-70-68=281	$3,750.00

Cleveland Open

Course: Aurora C.C., Aurora, Ohio
Par: 70 Yardage: 6,661
Last day of event: Sunday, June 29, 1969

Player	Place	Score	Earnings
Charles Coody	Win	67-64-71-69=271	$22,000.00
Bruce Crampton	2	69-66-69-69=273	$12,500.00

Bob Murphy	3	70-71-69-65=275	$7,850.00
Bert Yancey	T-4	69-70-72-65=276	$4,840.00
Frank Beard	T-4	69-70-71-68=276	$4,840.00
John Schlee	6	69-66-71-71=277	$3,960.00
John Levinson	T-7	73-72-65-68=278	$3,382.50
Bob Charles	T-7	73-67-68-70=278	$3,382.50
Harold Henning	T-9	69-70-72-68=279	$2,438.34
Gordon Jones	T-9	72-71-67-69=279	$2,438.34
Terry Dill	T-9	69-73-68-69=279	$2,438.34
Arnold Palmer	T-9	74-69-66-70=279	$2,438.33
J.C. Goosie	T-9	70-70-68-71=279	$2,438.33
Gardner Dickinson	T-9	69-70-68-72=279	$2,438.33

Buick Open

Course: Warwick Hills C.C., Grand Blanc, Mich.
Par: 72 Yardage: 7,001
Last day of event: Sunday, July 6, 1969

Player	Place	Score	Earnings
Dave Hill	Win	68-68-71-70=277	$25,000.00
Frank Beard	2	70-68-70-71=279	$14,300.00
Homero Blancas	3	65-73-70-72=280	$8,850.00
Dan Sikes	4	72-69-69-71=281	$5,850.00
Terry Dill	5	67-71-73-71=282	$5,125.00
Herb Hooper	T-6	69-71-72-72=284	$4,061.67
Bobby Nichols	T-6	71-69-72-72=284	$4,061.67
Julius Boros	T-6	69-69-70-76=284	$4,061.66
Don Bies	T-9	67-71-76-71=285	$3,125.00
R.H. Sikes	T-9	65-76-73-71=285	$3,125.00
Jim Wiechers	T-9	71-69-77-68=285	$3,125.00

British Open

Course: Royal Lytham & St. Annes G.C., Lytham, Lancashire, England
Par: 71 Yardage: 6,848
Last day of event: Saturday, July 12, 1969

Player	Place	Score	Earnings
Tony Jacklin	Win	68-70-70-72=280	$10,200.00
Bob Charles	2	66-69-75-72=282	$7,200.00
Peter Thomson	T-3	71-70-70-72=283	$5,100.00
Roberto De Vicenzo	T-3	72-73-66-72=283	$5,100.00
Christy O'Connor	5	71-65-74-74=284	$4,200.00
Davis Love Jr.	T-6	70-73-71-71=285	$3,300.00
Jack Nicklaus	T-6	75-70-68-72=285	$3,300.00
Peter Alliss	8	73-74-73-66=286	$2,640.00
Kel Nagle	9	74-71-72-70=287	$2,400.00
Miller Barber	10	69-75-75-69=288	$2,160.00

Minnesota Classic

Course: Braemar G.C., Edina, Minn. .
Par: 71 Yardage: 6,919
Last day of event: Sunday, July 13, 1969

Player	Place	Score	Earnings
Frank Beard	Win	69-67-67-66=269	$20,000.00
Tommy Aaron	T-2	70-69-69-68=276	$9,250.00
Hugh Inggs	T-2	72-65-69-70=276	$9,250.00
Labron Harris, Jr.	T-4	70-70-67-70=277	$4,400.00
Dave Stockton	T-4	68-67-69-73=277	$4,400.00
Terry Dill	T-6	69-71-67-71=278	$2,990.00
Howie Johnson	T-6	69-71-69-69=278	$2,990.00
R.H. Sikes	T-6	70-68-71-69=278	$2,990.00
Bob-E. Smith	T-6	69-71-71-67=278	$2,990.00
Wayne Yates	T-6	70-68-70-70=278	$2,990.00

Philadelphia Classic

Course: Whitemarsh Valley C.C., Chestnut Hill, Pa.
Par: 72 Yardage: 6,708
Last day of event: Sunday, July 20, 1969

Player	Place	Score	Earnings
Dave Hill	Win	71-71-68-69=279	$30,000.00
Playoff: Beat Gay Brewer, Tommy Jacobs and R.H. Sikes with birdie on first extra hole			
Gay Brewer	T-2	71-72-70-66=279	$11,600.00
Tommy Jacobs	T-2	69-70-68-72=279	$11,600.00
R.H. Sikes	T-2	73-71-68-67=279	$11,600.00
Frank Beard	5	72-72-70-66=280	$6,150.00
Deane Beman	T-6	69-74-68-70=281	$4,485.00
Bruce Devlin	T-6	72-71-73-65=281	$4,485.00
Lou Graham	T-6	68-73-70-70=281	$4,485.00
Grier Jones	T-6	72-69-66-74=281	$4,485.00
Mac McLendon	T-6	68-74-71-68=281	$4,485.00

American Golf Classic

Course: Firestone C.C. (South), Akron, Ohio
Par: 70 Yardage: 7,180
Last day of event: Sunday, July 27, 1969

Player	Place	Score	Earnings
Ray Floyd	Win	67-68-68-65=268	$25,000.00
Bobby Nichols	2	68-70-67-67=272	$14,300.00
Tom Weiskopf	3	68-73-67-66=274	$8,850.00
Gene Littler	T-4	68-69-71-68=276	$5,487.50
Bobby Mitchell	T-4	65-68-70-73=276	$5,487.50
Jack Nicklaus	T-6	66-66-71-75=278	$4,250.00
Al Geiberger	T-6	68-73-68-69=278	$4,250.00
R.H. Sikes	T-8	71-68-74-66=279	$3,530.00
Frank Beard	T-8	68-67-72-72=279	$3,530.00
Jim Colbert	T-10	70-70-71-69=280	$2,875.00
Don Bies	T-10	71-69-68-72=280	$2,875.00
Peter Townsend	T-10	68-72-68-72=280	$2,875.00

Canadian Open

Course: Pinegrove C.C., St. Luc, Quebec, Canada
Par: 72 Yardage: 7,076
Last day of event: Sunday, July 27, 1969

Player	Place	Score	Earnings
Tommy Aaron	Win	71-70-70-64=275	$25,000.00
Playoff: Beat Sam Snead in 18-hole playoff (Aaron 70, Snead 72)			
Sam Snead	2	67-68-70-70=275	$14,300.00
Billy Casper	3	72-71-70-67=280	$8,850.00
Takaaki Kono	4	72-68-70-71=281	$5,850.00
Bob Charles	T-5	71-73-68-70=282	$4,812.50
Al Balding	T-5	70-70-74-68=282	$4,812.50
John Jacobs	T-7	74-72-68-69=283	$3,546.25
Jack Ewing	T-7	73-69-72-70=283	$3,546.25
George Knudson	T-7	71-72-72-68=283	$3,546.25
Bob Rosburg	T-7	71-74-72-66=283	$3,546.25
Doug Sanders	T-7	71-70-75-70=286	$3,546.25
Jimmy Day	T-7	72-70-71-73=286	$3,546.25
Johnny Stevens	T-7	71-70-73-72=286	$3,546.25
Roberto De Vicenzo	T-7	69-67-78-72=286	$3,546.25

Westchester Classic

Course: Westchester C.C., Harrison, N.Y.
Par: 72 Yardage: 6,677
Last day of event: Sunday, August 3, 1969

Player	Place	Score	Earnings
Frank Beard	Win	69-72-67-67=275	$50,000.00
Bert Greene	2	67-69-68-72=276	$28,500.00
Dan Sikes	3	71-67-70-69=277	$17,750.00
Harold Henning	4	68-72-68-70=278	$11,750.00
Tommy Aaron	T-5	70-67-72-70=279	$9,625.00
Lee Trevino	T-5	71-70-67-71=279	$9,625.00
Bruce Crampton	7	68-73-68-71=280	$8,000.00
Dick Lotz	T-8	71-71-69-70=281	$7,062.50
Jerry Pittman	T-8	71-71-69-70=281	$7,062.50
Roberto De Vicenzo	T-10	73-70-71-68=282	$5,500.00
Bob Goalby	T-10	71-69-71-71=282	$5,500.00
Howie Johnson	T-10	75-69-71-67=282	$5,500.00
Al Mengert	T-10	70-71-68-73=282	$5,500.00

Greater Milwaukee Open

Course: Northshore C.C., Mequon, Wis.
Par: 72 Yardage: 7,075
Last day of event: Sunday, August 10, 1969

Player	Place	Score	Earnings
Ken Still	Win	74-71-67-65=277	$20,000.00
Gary Player	2	73-70-71-65=279	$11,400.00
Lee Elder	3	73-73-68-66=280	$7,100.00
Jim Wiechers	4	70-73-69-69=281	$4,700.00
Bob Lunn	5	70-73-68-71=282	$4,100.00
Chuck Courtney	T-6	72-72-68-71=283	$3,112.50
Terry Dill	T-6	74-71-66-72=283	$3,112.50
Peter Townsend	T-6	67-75-69-72=283	$3,112.50
Larry Ziegler	T-6	70-74-70-69=283	$3,112.50
Jerry Abbott	T-10	71-72-70-71=284	$2,120.00
Ron Cerrudo	T-10	76-73-69-66=284	$2,120.00
Fred Marti	T-10	71-70-71-72=284	$2,120.00
Phil Rodgers	T-10	72-71-69-72=284	$2,120.00
Kermit Zarley	T-10	71-73-72-68=284	$2,120.00

PGA Championship

Course: NCR C.C. (South Course), Dayton, Ohio
Par: 71 Yardage: 6,915
Last day of event: Sunday, August 17, 1969

Player	Place	Score	Earnings
Ray Floyd	Win	69-66-67-74=276	$35,000.00
Gary Player	2	71-65-71-70=277	$20,000.00
Bert Greene	3	71-68-68-71=278	$12,400.00
Jimmy Wright	4	71-68-69-71=279	$8,300.00
Miller Barber	T-5	73-75-64-68=280	$6,725.00
Larry Ziegler	T-5	69-71-70-70=280	$6,725.00
Charles Coody	T-7	69-71-72-69=281	$5,143.33
Orville Moody	T-7	70-68-71-72=281	$5,143.33
Terry Wilcox	T-7	72-71-72-66=281	$5,143.34
Frank Beard	10	70-75-68-69=282	$4,375.00

Indian Ridge Hospital Open
Course: Indian Ridge C.C., Andover, Mass.
Par: 71 Yardage: 6,805
Last day of event: Sunday, August 17, 1969

Player	Place	Score	Earnings
Monty Kaser	Win	72-64-69-69=274	$8,020.00
Steve Oppermann	2	69-68-69-69=275	$4,772.00
Bert Weaver	T-3	69-70-69-68=276	$2,386.00
Mike Hill	T-3	69-69-68-70=276	$2,386.00
Joel Goldstrand	T-5	71-67-70-69=277	$1,424.00
Jack Montgomery	T-5	69-71-67-70=277	$1,424.00
Laurie Hammer	7	72-68-71-67=278	$1,193.00
Ross Coon	8	68-74-69-68=279	$1,143.00
Peter Townsend	T-9	67-70-73-70=280	$1,052.50
Rod Funseth	T-9	67-72-70-71=280	$1,052.50

AVCO Classic
Course: Pleasant Valley C.C., Sutton, Mass.
Par: 72 Yardage: 7,212
Last day of event: Sunday, August 24, 1969

Player	Place	Score	Earnings
Tom Shaw	Win	68-68-67-77=280	$30,000.00
Bob Stanton	2	73-71-66-71=281	$17,100.00
Tom Weiskopf	3	73-75-69-66=283	$10,650.00
Julius Boros	T-4	71-74-71-68=284	$5,850.00
George Knudson	T-4	69-72-73-70=284	$5,850.00
Fred Marti	T-4	75-74-69-66=284	$5,850.00
Bobby Mitchell	T-4	72-71-70-71=284	$5,850.00
Larry Ziegler	8	73-74-71-67=285	$4,425.00
Bruce Crampton	T-9	72-71-70-73=286	$3,325.00
Lee Elder	T-9	74-74-69-69=286	$3,325.00
Dick Lotz	T-9	74-71-71-70=286	$3,325.00
Bob Lunn	T-9	75-69-67-75=286	$3,325.00
Mac McLendon	T-9	72-70-74-70=286	$3,325.00
Roy Pace	T-9	72-73-73-68=286	$3,325.00

Greater Hartford Open
Course: Wethersfield C.C., Wethersfield, Conn.
Par: 71 Yardage: 6,568
Last day of event: Monday, September 1, 1969

Player	Place	Score	Earnings
Bob Lunn	Win	67-68-66-67=268	$20,000.00
Playoff: Beat Dave Hill with birdie on fourth extra hole			
Dave Hill	2	68-68-66-66=268	$11,400.00
Dave Stockton	3	69-67-67-66=269	$7,100.00
Gay Brewer	T-4	68-66-69-68=271	$4,400.00
Bert Greene	T-4	69-67-70-65=271	$4,400.00
Howie Johnson	6	72-67-63-70=272	$3,600.00
Jack Nicklaus	7	68-68-69-68=273	$3,200.00
J.C. Snead	T-8	66-74-66-68=274	$2,510.00
Deane Beman	T-8	70-69-65-70=274	$2,510.00
R.H. Sikes	T-8	67-70-67-70=274	$2,510.00
Lou Graham	T-8	72-67-68-67=274	$2,510.00
Larry Hinson	T-8	69-69-68-68=274	$2,510.00

Michigan Golf Classic
Course: Shenandoah G. & C.C., Walled Lake, Mich.
Par: 71 Yardage: 6,708
Last day of event: Sunday, September 7, 1969

Player	Place	Score	Earnings
Larry Ziegler	Win	72-70-66-64=272	$20,000.00
Playoff: Beat Homero Blancas with birdie on second extra hole			
Homero Blancas	2	71-71-65-65=272	$11,400.00
Phil Rodgers	T-3	69-70-67-67=273	$5,900.00
J.C. Snead	T-3	71-70-65-67=273	$5,900.00
Grier Jones	T-5	65-73-70-66=274	$3,462.50
Cashere Jawor	T-5	69-70-69-66=274	$3,462.50
Mike Hill	T-5	68-71-68-67=274	$3,462.50
Larry Hinson	T-5	69-68-68-69=274	$3,462.50
Joel Goldstrand	T-9	69-69-69-68=275	$2,500.00
Jerry McGee	T-9	68-69-70-68=275	$2,500.00
Kermit Zarley	T-9	68-68-69-70=275	$2,500.00

Robinson Open
Course: Crawford C.C., Robinson, Ill.
Par: 72 Yardage: 6,460
Last day of event: Sunday, September 28, 1969

Player	Place	Score	Earnings
Bob Goalby	Win	62-71-73-67=273	$15,000.00
Playoff: Beat Jim Wiechers with birdie on first extra hole			
Jim Wiechers	2	70-68-66-69=273	$9,000.00
Howie Johnson	3	71-68-70-65=274	$5,625.00
Howell Fraser	T-4	68-70-69-68=275	$3,275.00
Bob Payne	T-4	72-69-66-68=275	$3,275.00
Billy Maxwell	T-4	66-69-67-73=275	$3,275.00
Terry Wilcox	T-7	70-66-73-67=276	$2,231.25
Bob Stanton	T-7	71-64-70-71=276	$2,231.25
Bill Garrett	T-7	68-68-70-70=276	$2,231.25
Richard Martinez	T-7	65-69-70-72=276	$2,231.25

Robinson Open
Course: Portland G.C., Portland, Ore.
Par: 72 Yardage: 6,541
Last day of event: Sunday, September 28, 1969

Player	Place	Score	Earnings
Billy Casper	Win	70-68-70-66=274	$55,000.00
Lee Trevino	2	70-67-69-69=275	$15,000.00
Frank Beard	3	71-70-69-68=278	$7,000.00
Dan Sikes	4	69-72-68-70=279	$5,800.00
Lou Graham	5	69-72-70-69=280	$4,500.00
Gay Brewer	T-6	71-68-71-71=281	$4,100.00
Jean Garaialde	T-6	71-69-73-68=281	$4,100.00
Hubert Green	T-8	70-68-72-72=282	$3,600.00
Dave Hill	T-8	74-72-66-70=282	$3,600.00
Gene Littler	T-8	72-68-73-69=282	$3,600.00

Sahara Invitational
Course: Sahara Nevada C.C., Las Vegas, Nev.
Home course / Par: 71 Yardage: 6,751
Last day of event: Sunday, October 19, 1969

Player	Place	Score	Earnings
Jack Nicklaus	Win	69-68-70-65=272	$20,000.00
Frank Beard	2	69-72-65-70=276	$11,400.00
Dale Douglass	T-3	72-68-71-66=277	$5,900.00
Dave Hill	T-3	71-67-70-69=277	$5,900.00

Tony Jacklin	T-5	70-69-70-69=278	$3,850.00
Grier Jones	T-5	69-72-69-68=278	$3,850.00
Richard Crawford	7	70-72-68-69=279	$3,200.00
Steve Spray	T-8	67-70-75-68=280	$2,172.23
Dave Stockton	T-8	71-73-68-68=280	$2,172.23
Homero Blancas	T-8	72-70-69-69=280	$2,172.22
Terry Dill	T-8	71-66-74-69=280	$2,172.22
Rod Funseth	T-8	70-71-69-70=280	$2,172.22
Steve Reid	T-8	70-68-71-71=280	$2,172.22
Chi Chi Rodriguez	T-8	69-68-73-70=280	$2,172.22
Hugh Royer	T-8	71-71-68-70=280	$2,172.22
Kermit Zarley	T-8	68-70-72-70=280	$2,172.22

San Francisco Open

Course: Harding Park G.C., San Francisco, Calif.
Par: 71 Yardage: 6,677
Last day of event: Sunday, October 26, 1969

Player	Place	Score	Earnings
Steve Spray	Win	70-63-66-70=269	$20,000.00
Chi Chi Rodriguez	2	69-68-67-66=270	$11,400.00
Bob Lunn	3	65-68-69-69=271	$7,100.00
Bob Charles	T-4	68-69-67-68=272	$4,400.00
Dave Hill	T-4	67-69-67-69=272	$4,400.00
Homero Blancas	T-6	68-71-67-67=273	$3,112.50
Billy Casper	T-6	70-68-66-69=273	$3,112.50
Jerry Heard	T-6	65-69-70-69=273	$3,112.50
R.H. Sikes	T-6	68-69-66-70=273	$3,112.50
Deane Beman	T-10	69-69-65-71=274	$2,200.00
Lee Elder	T-10	66-68-70-70=274	$2,200.00
Jim Wiechers	T-10	70-68-67-69=274	$2,200.00
Bert Yancey	T-10	73-67-69-65=274	$2,200.00

Kaiser International Open

Course: Silverado C.C. (North Course), Silverado C.C. (South Course), Napa, Calif.
Home Course -Par: 72 Yardage: 6,849
Last day of event: Sunday, November 2, 1969

Player	Place	Score	Earnings
Jack Nicklaus	Win	66-67-69-71=273	$28,000.00

Playoff: Beat George Archer and Billy Casper with birdie on second extra hole (Don January eliminated with par on first hole)

George Archer	T-2	69-69-66-69=273	$10,826.67
Billy Casper	T-2	68-69-69-67=273	$10,826.67
Don January	T-2	67-71-69-66=273	$10,826.66
Lou Graham	5	66-69-70-69=274	$4,760.00
Chi Chi Rodriguez	T-6	68-68-69-70=275	$4,760.00
Dan Sikes	T-6	72-65-71-67=275	$4,760.00
Arnold Palmer	T-8	71-69-68-69=277	$3,803.33
R.H. Sikes	T-8	69-72-68-68=277	$3,803.34
Dave Stockton	T-8	71-67-66-73=277	$3,803.33

Hawaiian Open

Course: Waialae C.C., Honolulu, Ha.
Par: 72 Yardage: 7,020
Last day of event: Sunday, November 9, 1969

Player	Place	Score	Earnings
Bruce Crampton	Win	71-71-65-67=274	$25,000.00
Jack Nicklaus	2	63-71-74-70=278	$14,300.00
John Schroeder	T-3	68-72-74-66=280	$6,350.00
Chi Chi Rodriguez	T-3	71-71-71-67=280	$6,350.00
Jack McGowan	T-5	68-72-71-70=281	$4,812.50

Tom Weiskopf	T-5	70-68-71-72=281	$4,812.50
George Archer	T-7	71-71-72-68=282	$3,546.25
Gay Brewer	T-7	72-72-69-69=282	$3,546.25
Billy Casper	T-7	73-68-71-70=282	$3,546.25
Don Bies	T-7	71-73-66-72=282	$3,546.25

Heritage Golf Classic

Course: Harbour Town G.L., Hilton Head, S.C.
Par: 71 Yardage: 6,655
Last day of event: Sunday, November 30, 1969

Player	Place	Score	Earnings
Arnold Palmer	Win	68-71-70-74=283	$20,000.00
Richard Crawford	T-2	71-69-72-74=286	$9,250.00
Bert Yancey	T-2	76-68-70-72=286	$9,250.00
Doug Ford	4	74-68-75-70=287	$4,700.00
Homero Blancas	5	74-69-69-76=288	$4,100.00
Jack Ewing	T-6	75-74-70-70=289	$3,250.00
Jack Nicklaus	T-6	71-72-71-75=289	$3,250.00
Earl Stewart	T-6	72-73-70-74=289	$3,250.00
Richard Hart	T-9	72-74-71-73=290	$2,400.00
Bob Murphy	T-9	73-70-75-72=290	$2,400.00
Doug Sanders	T-9	74-70-75-71=290	$2,400.00
Tom Weiskopf	T-9	74-65-74-77=290	$2,400.00

Danny Thomas-Diplomat Classic

Course: Diplomat C.C., Hollywood, Fla.
Par: 72 Yardage: 6,964
Last day of event: Sunday, December 7, 1969

Player	Place	Score	Earnings
Arnold Palmer	Win	68-67-70-65=270	$25,000.00
Gay Brewer	2	65-66-68-73=272	$14,300.00
Lee Trevino	3	70-69-69-66=274	$8,850.00
Larry Hinson	T-4	69-69-68-69=275	$5,487.50
Hal Underwood	T-4	68-67-71-69=275	$5,487.50
George Archer	6	70-75-67-64=276	$4,500.00
Fred Marti	7	69-70-69-69=277	$4,000.00
Jim Jamieson	T-8	67-73-66-72=278	$3,530.00
Sam Snead	T-8	70-67-71-70=278	$3,530.00
Bert Yancey	T-10	68-70-69-72=279	$2,875.00
Homero Blancas	T-10	68-73-71-67=279	$2,875.00
Gardner Dickinson	T-10	70-69-69-71=279	$2,875.00

West End Classic

Course: Grand Bahama Hotel & C.C., West End, Bahama Islands
Par: 72 Yardage: 6,836
Last day of event: Sunday, December 7, 1969

Player	Place	Score	Earnings
Jim Wiechers	Win	70-68-69-70=277	$5,000.00
Johnny Pott	T-2	64-70-71-74=279	$2,437.50
Al Besselink	T-2	75-66-67-71=279	$2,437.50
Mike Reasor	4	68-69-74-72=283	$1,250.00
Art Silvestrone	5	70-72-69-73=284	$1,075.00
Bobby Greenwood	6	70-70-74-71=285	$950.00
Malcolm Gregson	7	72-72-70-72=286	$850.00
Carl Lohren	T-8	74-74-67-72=287	$681.25
Steve Reid	T-8	70-71-73-73=287	$681.25
Jerry Abbott	T-8	70-74-70-73=287	$681.25
Gene Borek	T-8	73-69-70-75=287	$681.25

1970

Billy Casper posted four victories in 1970, including the Masters, where he bested Gene Littler 69 to 74 in a playoff. Tony Jacklin scored a seven-shot victory in the U.S. Open at Hazeltine National, which was famously referred to as a "cow pasture" by Dave Hill, who was fined $150 by the USGA. Jacklin, who had won the 1969 British Open, became the first Englishman since Harry Vardon in 1900 to hold both Open titles simultaneously. (No European has won the U.S. Open since Jacklin did it.) Jack Nicklaus won the British Open in a playoff against Doug Sanders, who had missed a 3-foot putt on the 72nd hole at St. Andrews. Dave Stockton notched a 2-shot victory at the PGA Championship at Southern Hills. Arnold Palmer's tie (with Bob Murphy) for second place marked the last time he was a contender in the PGA, the only major title that eluded him.

Los Angles Open

Course: Rancho Municipal G.C., Los Angeles, Calif.
Par: 71 Yardage: 6,827
Last day of event: Sunday, January 11, 1970

Player	Place	Score	Earnings
Billy Casper	Win	68-68-68-72=276	$20,000.00
Playoff: Beat Hale Irwin with birdie on first extra hole			
Hale Irwin	2	70-66-67-73=276	$11,400.00
Dave Hill	T-3	66-71-70-70=277	$5,900.00
Bob Lunn	T-3	66-72-68-71=277	$5,900.00
Terry Dill	T-5	69-69-70-70=278	$3,850.00
Bob-E. Smith	T-5	71-67-74-66=278	$3,850.00
Don Massengale	T-7	67-69-72-71=279	$2,837.50
Ken Still	T-7	68-68-71-72=279	$2,837.50
Grier Jones	T-7	69-72-67-71=279	$2,837.50
Dave Stockton	T-7	68-69-69-74=279	$2,837.50

Phoenix Open

Course: Phoenix C.C., Phoenix, Ariz.
Par: 71 Yardage: 6,765
Last day of event: Sunday, January 18, 1970

Player	Place	Score	Earnings
Dale Douglass	Win	71-66-68-66=271	$20,000.00
Howie Johnson	T-2	67-68-69-68=272	$9,250.00
Gene Littler	T-2	67-68-67-70=272	$9,250.00
Dave Hill	T-4	69-70-67-67=273	$3,710.00
Bob Lunn	T-4	71-69-65-68=273	$3,710.00
Orville Moody	T-4	71-69-66-67=273	$3,710.00
Dave Marr	T-4	72-69-65-67=273	$3,710.00
Tom Weiskopf	T-4	73-67-63-70=273	$3,710.00
Homero Blancas	9	67-69-67-71=274	$2,700.00
Bruce Crampton	T-10	67-71-67-70=275	$2,120.00
Bert Greene	T-10	64-72-69-70=275	$2,120.00
Chi Chi Rodriguez	T-10	67-72-67-69=275	$2,120.00
Frank Beard	T-10	69-72-67-67=275	$2,120.00
Johnny Miller	T-10	72-71-61-71=275	$2,120.00

Bing Crosby National Pro-Am

Courses: Pebble Beach G.L., Spyglass Hill G.C., Cypress Point C.C., Pebble Beach, Calif.
Home Course / Pebble Beach G.L., Par: 72 Yardage: 6,815
Last day of event: Sunday, January 25, 1970

Player	Place	Score	Earnings
Bert Yancey	Win	67-70-72-69=278	$25,000.00
Jack Nicklaus	2	70-72-72-65=279	$14,300.00
Bobby Nichols	T-3	71-73-69-70=283	$7,350.00
Howie Johnson	T-3	68-74-71-70=283	$7,350.00

Player	Place	Score	Earnings
Paul Harney	T-5	69-72-72-71=284	$4,327.50
George Archer	T-5	68-73-71-72=284	$4,327.50
Don Massengale	T-5	70-70-70-74=284	$4,327.50
John Jacobs	T-5	74-72-69-69=284	$4,327.50
Bob Stone	T-9	72-74-68-71=285	$3,000.00
Rod Funseth	T-9	74-68-68-75=285	$3,000.00
Tom Weiskopf	T-9	71-76-68-70=285	$3,000.00

Andy Williams-San Diego Open

Course: Torrey Pines (South), Torrey Pines (North)), San Diego, Calif.
Home Course -Par: 72 Yardage: 7,021
Last day of event: Sunday, February 1, 1970

Player	Place	Score	Earnings
Pete Brown	Win	76-67-67-65=275	$30,000.00
Playoff: Beat Tony Jacklin with par on first extra hole			
Tony Jacklin	2	66-67-71-71=275	$17,100.00
Jack Nicklaus	3	65-68-70-73=276	$10,650.00
Tom Weiskopf	4	72-67-70-69=278	$7,050.00
Grier Jones	T-5	72-68-73-66=279	$5,775.00
Terry Dill	T-5	68-67-70-74=279	$5,775.00
George Knudson	T-7	70-68-71-71=280	$4,095.00
Tommy Aaron	T-7	71-71-70-68=280	$4,095.00
Frank Beard	T-7	71-71-71-67=280	$4,095.00
Don January	T-7	72-68-70-70=280	$4,095.00
Dave Hill	T-7	73-72-68-67=280	$4,095.00

Bob Hope Chrysler Classic

Course: La Quinta C.C., Indian Wells C.C., Eldorado C.C., Bermuda Dunes C.C.
Home Course / La Quinta, Par: 72 Yardage: 6,911
Last day of event: Sunday, February 8, 1970

Player	Place	Score	Earnings
Bruce Devlin	Win	67-68-68-70-66=339	$25,000.00
Larry Ziegler	2	67-65-68-71-72=343	$14,300.00
Larry Hinson	3	69-72-66-67-73=347	$8,850.00
Arnold Palmer	4	68-71-70-69-70=348	$5,850.00
Bob Murphy	T-5	69-70-69-71-70=349	$4,812.50
Gene Littler	T-5	72-69-72-70-66=349	$4,812.50
Don Bies	T-7	69-70-72-69-70=350	$3,842.50
Tommy Aaron	T-7	76-69-69-69-67=350	$3,842.50
Terry Wilcox	T-9	70-71-72-70-68=351	$3,125.00
Gardner Dickinson	T-9	72-69-69-70-71=351	$3,125.00
Billy Casper	T-9	71-69-67-74-70=351	$3,125.00

Tucson Open

Course: Tucson National G.C., Starr Pass G.C., Tucson, Ariz.
Par: 72 Yardage: 7,305
Last day of event: Sunday, February 15, 1970

Player	Place	Score	Earnings
Lee Trevino	Win	66-68-72-69=275	$20,000.00
Playoff: Beat Bob Murphy with birdie on first extra hole			
Bob Murphy	2	66-68-72-69=275	$11,400.00
Charles Coody	3	70-70-69-68=277	$7,100.00
Bob Lunn	4	72-66-70-70=278	$4,700.00
John Lotz	5	69-64-74-72=279	$4,100.00
Frank Beard	T-6	69-72-70-69=280	$3,400.00
Fred Marti	T-6	68-70-73-69=280	$3,400.00
Don Bies	T-8	71-69-70-71=281	$2,716.67
Tom Shaw	T-8	68-74-68-71=281	$2,716.66
Steve Reid	T-8	69-67-75-70=281	$2,716.67

San Antonio Texas Open

Course: Pecan Valley C.C., San Antonio, Texas
Par: 70 Yardage: 7,183
Last day of event: Sunday, February 22, 1970

Player	Place	Score	Earnings
Ron Cerrudo	Win	71-65-69-68=273	$20,000.00
Dick Lotz	2	77-68-65-68=278	$11,400.00
Rod Funseth	T-3	67-70-72-70=279	$5,900.00
Miller Barber	T-3	73-71-67-68=279	$5,900.00
John Schlee	T-5	70-70-71-71=282	$3,850.00
Al Geiberger	T-5	75-67-70-70=282	$3,850.00
Chris Blocker	T-7	72-71-69-71=283	$2,837.50
Dave Stockton	T-7	72-70-72-69=283	$2,837.50
Kermit Zarley	T-7	71-69-73-70=283	$2,837.50
Orville Moody	T-7	76-71-68-68=283	$2,837.50

Doral-Eastern Open

Course: Doral C.C. (Blue), Miami, Fla.
Par: 72 Yardage: 6,939
Last day of event: Sunday, March 1, 1970

Player	Place	Score	Earnings
Mike Hill	Win	70-69-69-71=279	$30,000.00
Jim Colbert	2	69-70-72-72=283	$17,100.00
Larry Hinson	T-3	69-71-72-74=286	$7,950.00
Brian Barnes	T-3	69-74-74-69=286	$7,950.00
Bruce Devlin	T-3	75-70-69-72=286	$7,950.00
Jack McGowan	6	67-75-69-76=287	$5,400.00
Gibby Gilbert	7	70-68-76-74=288	$4,800.00
Larry Ziegler	T-8	72-71-73-73=289	$3,612.50
Tony Jacklin	T-8	70-72-73-74=289	$3,612.50
George Knudson	T-8	73-74-72-70=289	$3,612.50
Bob Stanton	T-8	74-71-74-70=289	$3,612.50
Deane Beman	T-8	74-69-75-71=289	$3,612.50
Don Bies	T-8	76-71-70-72=289	$3,612.50

Florida Citrus Open Invitational

Course: Rio Pinar C.C., Orlando, Fla.
Par: 72 Yardage: 7,012
Last day of event: Sunday, March 8, 1970

Player	Place	Score	Earnings
Bob Lunn	Win	66-68-67-70=271	$30,000.00
Bob Stanton	T-2	71-68-65-68=272	$13,875.00
Arnold Palmer	T-2	64-72-64-72=272	$13,875.00
Dick Lotz	4	69-69-69-68=275	$7,050.00
Tom Shaw	T-5	69-68-69-70=276	$5,450.00
Tom Weiskopf	T-5	68-71-69-68=276	$5,450.00
Richard Crawford	T-5	65-72-70-69=276	$5,450.00
Bruce Crampton	T-8	67-71-68-71=277	$4,075.00
Howie Johnson	T-8	66-69-70-72=277	$4,075.00
Bruce Devlin	T-8	67-67-69-74=277	$4,075.00

Monsanto Open

Course: Pensacola C.C., Pensacola, Fla.
Par: 71 Yardage: 6,679
Last day of event: Sunday, March 15, 1970

Player	Place	Score	Earnings
Dick Lotz	Win	68-70-69-68=275	$30,000.00
Dave Stockton	2	68-70-73-67=278	$17,100.00
Ray Floyd	3	68-72-68-72=280	$10,650.00
Tony Jacklin	T-4	74-70-66-71=281	$6,600.00

Homero Blancas	T-4	75-71-71-64=281	$6,600.00
Bob Charles	T-6	71-72-70-69=282	$5,100.00
Johnny Miller	T-6	72-73-67-70=282	$5,100.00
Paul Harney	T-8	70-70-73-70=283	$4,075.00
Bob Stanton	T-8	70-73-73-67=283	$4,075.00
Gary Player	T-8	71-71-68-73=283	$4,075.00

Greater Jacksonville Open

Course: Hidden Hills C.C., Jacksonville, Fla.
Par: 72 Yardage: 6,943
Last day of event: Monday, March 23, 1970

Player	Place	Score	Earnings
Don January	Win	68-75-70-66=279	$20,000.00
Playoff: Beat Dale Douglass in 18-hole playoff (January 69, Douglass 72)			
Dale Douglass	2	69-69-72-69=279	$11,400.00
Tony Jacklin	3	70-72-72-67=281	$7,100.00
Dave Stockton	4	72-71-70-69=282	$4,700.00
Jack Nicklaus	T-5	70-71-72-70=283	$3,850.00
Dan Sikes, Jr.	T-5	71-69-72-71=283	$3,850.00
Lee Trevino	7	70-67-76-71=284	$3,200.00
Don Bies	T-8	69-71-72-73=285	$2,825.00
Hale Irwin	T-8	73-72-71-69=285	$2,825.00
Bob Charles	T-10	71-73-72-70=286	$1,985.72
Billy Maxwell	T-10	73-70-73-70=286	$1,985.72
Ron Cerrudo	T-10	68-73-74-71=286	$1,985.72
Lionel Hebert	T-10	70-71-71-74=286	$1,985.71
Dick Rhyan	T-10	72-69-71-74=286	$1,985.71
Bob Lunn	T-10	75-71-68-72=286	$1,985.71
Bobby Mitchell	T-10	69-68-76-73=286	$1,985.71

National Airlines Open

Course: C.C. of Miami, Miami, Fla.
Par: 72 Yardage: 6,970
Last day of event: Sunday, March 29, 1970

Player	Place	Score	Earnings
Lee Trevino	Win	69-66-68-71=274	$40,000.00
Playoff: Beat Bob Menne with par on second extra hole			
Bob Menne	2	64-69-70-71=274	$22,800.00
Bob Stanton	3	68-73-67-67=275	$14,200.00
Dick Lotz	4	71-66-68-72=277	$9,400.00
Marty Fleckman	T-5	70-70-71-67=278	$6,925.00
Chi Chi Rodriguez	T-5	68-67-71-72=278	$6,925.00
Frank Beard	T-5	69-69-72-68=278	$6,925.00
Bruce Devlin	T-5	72-66-70-70=278	$6,925.00
R.H. Sikes	T-9	66-70-72-71=279	$4,800.00
Orville Moody	T-9	70-70-67-72=279	$4,800.00
Homero Blancas	T-9	71-71-72-65=279	$4,800.00
Bob-E. Smith	T-9	72-69-71-67=279	$4,800.00

Greater Greensboro Open

Course: Sedgefield C.C., Greensboro, N.C.
Par: 71 Yardage: 7,034
Last day of event: Sunday, April 5, 1970

Player	Place	Score	Earnings
Gary Player	Win	70-63-73-65=271	$36,000.00
Miller Barber	2	69-64-72-68=273	$20,500.00
R.H. Sikes	3	65-67-73-69=274	$12,800.00
Steve Spray	4	70-67-71-67=275	$8,460.00
Lee Trevino	T-5	71-66-71-68=276	$6,540.00
Tommy Aaron	T-5	64-69-72-71=276	$6,540.00
Arnold Palmer	T-5	64-67-74-71=276	$6,540.00

Larry Hinson	T-8	68-69-71-69=277	$5,085.00
Chi Chi Rodriguez	T-8	69-69-72-67=277	$5,085.00
Billy Maxwell	10	69-68-73-68=278	$4,500.00

Masters
Course: Augusta National G.C., Augusta, Ga.
Par: 72 Yardage: 6,925
Last day of event: Monday, April 11, 1970

Player	Place	Score	Earnings
Billy Casper	Win	72-68-68-71-69=279	$25,000.00
Playoff: Beat Gene Littler in 18-hole playoff (Casper 69, Littler 74)			
Gene Littler	2	69-70-70-70-74=279	$17,500.00
Gary Player	3	74-68-68-70=280	$14,000.00
Bert Yancey	4	69-70-72-70=281	$10,000.00
Dave Stockton	T-5	72-72-69-70=283	$6,667.00
Dave Hill	T-5	73-70-70-70=283	$6,667.00
Tommy Aaron	T-5	68-74-69-72=283	$6,667.00
Jack Nicklaus	8	71-75-69-69=284	$4,500.00
Frank Beard	9	71-76-68-70=285	$4,000.00
Bob Lunn	T-10	70-70-75-72=287	$3,500.00
Chi Chi Rodriguez	T-10	70-76-73-68=287	$3,500.00

Greater New Orleans Open
Course: Lakewood C.C., New Orleans, La.
Par: 72 Yardage: 7,080
Last day of event: Sunday, April 19, 1970

Player	Place	Score	Earnings
Miller Barber	Win	68-71-69-70=278	$25,000.00
Playoff: Beat Bob Charles and Howie Johnson with birdie on second extra hole			
Bob Charles	2	71-70-70-67=278	$11,575.00
Howie Johnson	2	69-66-72-71=278	$11,575.00
Lou Graham	4	68-68-72-71=279	$5,850.00
George Archer	5	66-67-72-76=281	$5,125.00
Dave Stockton	T-6	68-69-73-72=282	$3,737.00
Gary Player	T-6	66-74-70-72=282	$3,737.00
Jim Colbert	T-6	67-74-71-70=282	$3,737.00
Billy Casper	T-6	71-67-74-70=282	$3,737.00
Rod Curl	T-6	72-70-65-75=282	$3,737.00

Tournament of Champions
Course: La Costa C.C., Carlsbad, Calif.
Par: 72 Yardage: 6,911
Last day of event: Sunday, April 26, 1970

Player	Place	Score	Earnings
Frank Beard	Win	70-64-68-71=273	$30,000.00
Gary Player	T-2	68-72-69-71=280	$11,633.33
Billy Casper	T-2	71-69-68-72=280	$11,633.33
Tony Jacklin	T-2	69-68-67-76=280	$11,633.34
Arnold Palmer	5	70-72-69-70=281	$7,400.00
Orville Moody	6	72-71-71-70=284	$6,400.00
Dale Douglass	T-7	70-71-71-74=286	$4,766.66
Jack Nicklaus	T-7	71-69-72-74=286	$4,766.67
Bruce Crampton	T-7	69-69-72-76=286	$4,766.67
Larry Ziegler	T-10	72-71-73-71=287	$3,675.00
Ken Still	T-10	78-72-69-68=287	$3,675.00

Tallahassee Open
Course: Killearn C.C., Tallahassee, Fla.
Par: 72 Yardage: 7,124
Last day of event: Sunday, April 26, 1970

Player	Place	Score	Earnings
Harold Henning	Win	67-76-64-70=277	$10,000.00
Rives McBee	2	71-72-68-67=278	$6,000.00
Fred Marti	T-3	70-69-69-73=281	$2,800.00
Joe Porter	T-3	70-73-67-71=281	$2,800.00
Homero Blancas	T-3	74-69-70-68=281	$2,800.00
Johnny Miller	T-6	69-70-71-72=282	$1,637.50
Bert Greene	T-6	69-70-72-71=282	$1,637.50
Larry Mowry	T-6	70-70-70-72=282	$1,637.50
Sam Carmichael	T-6	73-70-67-72=282	$1,637.50
Bobby Greenwood	T-10	70-68-73-72=283	$1,250.00
Bobby Mitchell	T-10	72-73-71-67=283	$1,250.00

Byron Nelson Golf Classic
Course: Preston Trail G.C., Dallas, Texas
Par: 70 Yardage: 6,993
Last day of event: Sunday, May 3, 1970

Player	Place	Score	Earnings
Jack Nicklaus	Win	67-68-68-71=274	$20,000.00
Playoff: Beat Arnold Palmer with birdie on first extra hole			
Arnold Palmer	2	66-71-68-69=274	$11,400.00
John Schroeder	T-3	73-66-69-67=275	$5,900.00
Lee Trevino	T-3	74-68-67-66=275	$5,900.00
Randy Wolff	5	71-71-66-68=276	$4,100.00
Pete Brown	T-6	69-70-67-70=278	$3,400.00
Dan Sikes, Jr.	T-6	70-67-71-70=278	$3,400.00
Jerry Abbott	8	69-71-72-67=279	$2,950.00
Harold Henning	T-9	70-73-71-67=281	$2,600.00
Dave Stockton	T-9	73-71-70-67=281	$2,600.00

Houston Champions International
Course: Champions G.C., Houston, Texas
Par: 71 Yardage: 7,166
Last day of event: Sunday, May 10, 1970

Player	Place	Score	Earnings
Gibby Gilbert	Win	69-72-71-70=282	$23,000.00
Playoff: Beat Bruce Crampton with par on third extra hole			
Bruce Crampton	2	69-68-72-73=282	$13,100.00
Bert Greene	3	69-74-68-72=283	$8,220.00
Gary Player	4	72-72-72-68=284	$5,460.00
Art Wall, Jr.	5	71-72-70-72=285	$4,770.00
Jim Colbert	T-6	72-71-71-72=286	$3,786.66
Dale Douglass	T-6	70-72-71-73=286	$3,786.67
Julius Boros	T-6	71-72-73-70=286	$3,786.67
Bob Murphy	T-9	72-72-71-72=287	$2,600.00
Dave Hill	T-9	70-73-70-74=287	$2,600.00
Lee Trevino	T-9	70-75-72-70=287	$2,600.00
Ben Hogan	T-9	71-75-71-70=287	$2,600.00
Dick Lotz	T-9	76-72-69-70=287	$2,600.00
Johnny Miller	T-9	76-74-70-67=287	$2,600.00

Colonial National Invitational

Course: Colonial C.C., Fort Worth, Texas
Par: 70 Yardage: 7,142
Last day of event: Sunday, May 17, 1970

Player	Place	Score	Earnings
Homero Blancas	Win	69-68-69-67=273	$25,000.00
Lee Trevino	T-2	66-70-69-69=274	$11,575.00
Gene Littler	T-2	69-72-66-67=274	$11,575.00
Kel Nagle	4	70-71-69-68=278	$5,850.00
Bob Charles	T-5	69-70-72-68=279	$4,812.50
Hale Irwin	T-5	73-68-69-69=279	$4,812.50
Dick Lotz	T-7	69-72-71-68=280	$3,842.50
Tom Shaw	T-7	68-73-69-70=280	$3,842.50
Lionel Hebert	T-9	70-70-71-70=281	$3,125.00
Bob-E. Smith	T-9	67-69-73-72=281	$3,125.00
Howie Johnson	T-9	76-71-66-68=281	$3,125.00

Atlanta Classic

Course: Atlanta C.C., Atlanta, Ga.
Par: 72 Yardage: 7,007
Last day of event: Sunday, May 24, 1970

Player	Place	Score	Earnings
Tommy Aaron	Win	68-68-70-69=275	$25,000.00
Dan Sikes, Jr.	2	71-65-71-69=276	$14,300.00
Bert Yancey	T-3	67-70-70-70=277	$6,081.25
Arnold Palmer	T-3	69-70-70-68=277	$6,081.25
Gary Player	T-3	68-68-69-72=277	$6,081.25
Tom Weiskopf	T-3	65-68-71-73=277	$6,081.25
George Knudson	T-7	70-69-68-71=278	$3,412.00
Jack Nicklaus	T-7	69-69-68-72=278	$3,412.00
Bob Lunn	T-7	69-68-72-69=278	$3,412.00
Chuck Courtney	T-7	67-67-71-73=278	$3,412.00
Homero Blancas	T-7	65-74-70-69=278	$3,412.00

Danny Thomas Memphis Classic,

Course: Colonial C.C., Memphis, Tenn.
Par: 70 Yardage: 6,466
Last day of event: Sunday, May 31, 1970

Player	Place	Score	Earnings
Dave Hill	Win	63-69-67-68=267	$30,000.00
Homero Blancas	T-2	66-65-67-70=268	$11,600.00
Frank Beard	T-2	70-65-66-67=268	$11,600.00
Bob Charles	T-2	71-65-69-63=268	$11,600.00
George Archer	T-5	67-67-68-68=270	$4,965.00
Dan Sikes, Jr.	T-5	68-68-67-67=270	$4,965.00
Billy Maxwell	T-5	66-68-69-67=270	$4,965.00
Steve Spray	T-5	69-66-65-70=270	$4,965.00
Joe Campbell	T-5	70-64-68-68=270	$4,965.00
Joe Carr	T-10	68-70-67-66=271	$3,600.00
Bob Murphy	T-10	68-70-68-65=271	$3,600.00

Kemper Open

Course: Quail Hollow C.C., Charlotte, N.C.
Par: 72 Yardage: 7,205
Last day of event: Sunday, June 7, 1970

Player	Place	Score	Earnings
Dick Lotz	Win	72-66-69-71=278	$30,000.00
Grier Jones	T-2	69-69-70-72=280	$10,237.50
Larry Hinson	T-2	73-65-70-72=280	$10,237.50
Lou Graham	T-2	67-68-71-74=280	$10,237.50
Tom Weiskopf	T-2	68-74-72-66=280	$10,237.50
Dan Sikes, Jr.	T-6	71-69-71-70=281	$4,668.75
Bob Lunn	T-6	68-73-69-71=281	$4,668.75
Steve Reid	T-6	69-71-68-73=281	$4,668.75
Lionel Hebert	T-6	66-71-70-74=281	$4,668.75
Rod Funseth	10	70-69-73-70=282	$3,750.00

Western Open

Course: Beverly C.C., Chicago, Ill.
Par: 71 Yardage: 6,923
Last day of event: Sunday, June 14, 1970

Player	Place	Score	Earnings
Hugh Royer, Jr.	Win	67-65-72-69=273	$26,000.00
Dale Douglass	2	68-70-67-69=274	$14,800.00
Tom Weiskopf	T-3	69-68-70-71=278	$5,906.00
Jim Jamieson	T-3	71-67-69-71=278	$5,906.00
Bert Yancey	T-3	72-68-68-70=278	$5,906.00
Jack Nicklaus	T-3	72-70-67-69=278	$5,906.00
Bobby Nichols	T-3	67-69-67-75=278	$5,906.00
Arnold Palmer	8	67-69-71-72=279	$3,830.00
Julius Boros	T-9	69-71-69-71=280	$3,250.00
Bob Brue	T-9	71-69-67-73=280	$3,250.00
Rives McBee	T-9	73-69-66-72=280	$3,250.00

U.S. Open

Course: Hazeltine National G.C., Chaska, Minn. .
Par: 72 Yardage: 7,151
Last day of event: Sunday, June 21, 1970

Player	Place	Score	Earnings
Tony Jacklin	Win	71-70-70-70=281	$30,000.00
Dave Hill	2	75-69-71-73=288	$15,000.00
Bob Charles	T-3	76-71-75-67=289	$9,000.00
Bob Lunn	T-3	77-72-70-70=289	$9,000.00
Ken Still	5	78-71-71-71=291	$7,000.00
Miller Barber	6	75-75-72-70=292	$6,000.00
Gay Brewer	7	75-71-71-76=293	$5,000.00
Larry Ziegler	T-8	75-73-73-73=294	$3,325.00
Billy Casper	T-8	75-75-71-73=294	$3,325.00
Bruce Devlin	T-8	75-75-71-73=294	$3,325.00
Lee Trevino	T-8	77-73-74-70=294	$3,325.00

Cleveland Open

Course: Aurora C>C, Aurora, Ohio
Par: 70 Yardage: 6,661
Last day of event: Sunday, June 28, 1970

Player	Place	Score	Earnings
Bruce Devlin	Win	69-69-66-64=268	$30,000.00
Steve Eichstaedt	2	70-65-69-68=272	$17,100.00
Bob Murphy	T-3	68-69-68-68=273	$8,850.00
Larry Hinson	T-3	65-71-71-66=273	$8,850.00
Lou Graham	T-5	68-70-70-66=274	$5,450.00
Dave Hill	T-5	66-71-68-69=274	$5,450.00
Lee Trevino	T-5	66-71-70-67=274	$5,450.00
Tom Weiskopf	8	68-67-67-73=275	$4,425.00
Bob Goalby	T-9	69-68-70-69=276	$3,900.00
Homero Blancas	T-9	73-68-66-69=276	$3,900.00

Canadian Open

Course: London Hunt & C.C., London, Ontario, Canada
Par: 72 Yardage: 7,168
Last day of event: Sunday, July 5, 1970

Player	Place	Score	Earnings
Kermit Zarley	Win	69-73-70-67=279	$25,000.00
Gibby Gilbert	2	65-77-69-71=282	$14,300.00
Bob Stone	T-3	68-68-73-74=283	$7,350.00
Chi Chi Rodriguez	T-3	72-67-69-75=283	$7,350.00
Labron Harris, Jr.	5	71-70-67-76=284	$5,125.00
Phil Rodgers	6	69-70-73-73=285	$4,500.00
Steve Spray	T-7	72-72-71-71=286	$3,412.00
Bob Murphy	T-7	70-73-74-69=286	$3,412.00
Art Wall, Jr.	T-7	66-71-75-74=286	$3,412.00
Johnny Miller	T-7	75-71-70-70=286	$3,412.00
George Archer	T-7	66-72-71-77=286	$3,412.00

Greater Milwaukee Open

Course: Northshore C.C., Mequon, Wis.
Par: 72 Yardage: 7,075
Last day of event: Sunday, July 12, 1970

Player	Place	Score	Earnings
Deane Beman	Win	68-71-68-69=276	$22,000.00
Don Massengale	T-2	69-68-70-72=279	$8,510.00
Richard Crawford	T-2	68-73-69-69=279	$8,510.00
Ted Hayes, Jr.	T-2	68-70-73-68=279	$8,510.00
Jack Lewis, Jr.	T-5	69-69-72-70=280	$4,230.00
Chi Chi Rodriguez	T-5	72-67-72-69=280	$4,230.00
Terry Dill	T-7	68-72-69-72=281	$3,245.00
Chuck Courtney	T-7	70-72-71-68=281	$3,245.00
Bruce Crampton	T-7	71-70-72-68=281	$3,245.00
Harry Toscano	T-10	68-71-73-70=282	$2,640.00
Dave Eichelberger	T-10	76-67-73-66=282	$2,640.00

British Open

Course: Old Course at St. Andrews, St. Andrews, Fife, Scotland
Par: 72 Yardage: 6,951
Last day of event: Sunday, July 12, 1970

Player	Place	Score	Earnings
Jack Nicklaus	Win	68-69-73-73-72=283	$12,600.00

Playoff: Beat Doug Sanders in 18-hole playoff (Nicklaus 72, Sanders 73)

Player	Place	Score	Earnings
Doug Sanders	2	68-71-71-73-73=283	$9,000.00
Harold Henning	T-3	67-72-73-73=285	$6,600.00
Lee Trevino	T-3	68-68-72-77=285	$6,600.00
Tony Jacklin	5	67-70-73-76=286	$5,280.00
Neil Coles	T-6	65-74-72-76=287	$4,200.00
Peter Oosterhuis	T-6	73-69-69-76=287	$4,200.00
Hugh Jackson	8	69-72-73-74=288	$3,360.00
John Panton	T-9	72-73-73-71=289	$2,880.00
Peter Thomson	T-9	68-74-73-74=289	$2,880.00
Tommy Horton	T-9	66-73-75-75=289	$2,880.00

IVB Philadelphia Golf Classic

Course: Whitemarsh Valley C.C., Chestnut Hill, Pa.
Par: 72 Yardage: 6,708
Last day of event: Sunday, July 19, 1970

Player	Place	Score	Earnings
Billy Casper	Win	68-67-71-68=274	$30,000.00
Terry Wilcox	2	71-69-68-69=277	$17,100.00
Richard Crawford	T-3	70-71-67-71=279	$7,950.00
Frank Beard	T-3	71-69-70-69=279	$7,950.00
Bunky Henry	T-3	69-69-72-69=279	$7,950.00
Bob Murphy	6	67-70-75-68=280	$5,400.00
Deane Beman	T-7	70-72-69-70=281	$4,256.25
Bruce Devlin	T-7	69-73-73-66=281	$4,256.25
Charles Coody	T-7	68-68-74-71=281	$4,256.25
Jerry Heard	T-7	77-68-68-68=281	$4,256.25

National 4 Ball Championship PGA Players

Course: Laurel Valley G.C., Ligonier, Pa.
Par: 71 Yardage: 7,045
Last day of event: Sunday, July 26, 1970

Player	Place	Score	Earnings
Jack Nicklaus	Win	61-67-64-67=259	$20,000.00
Partner: Arnold Palmer			
Arnold Palmer	Win	61-67-64-67=259	$20,000.00
Partner: Jack Nicklaus			
Bruce Crampton	T-2	67-63-64-68=262	$8,166.66
Partner: Orville Moody			
Orville Moody	T-2	67-63-64-68=262	$8,166.66
Partner: Bruce Crampton			
Gardner Dickinson	T-2	67-61-68-66=262	$8,166.67
Partner: Sam Snead			
Sam Snead	T-2	67-61-68-66=262	$8,166.67
Partner: Gardner Dickinson			
George Archer	T-2	67-64-68-63=262	$8,166.67
Partner: Bobby Nichols			
Bobby Nichols	T-2	67-64-68-63=262	$8,166.67
Partner: George Archer			
Miller Barber	T-5	66-64-66-67=263	$3,650.00
Partner: Don January			
Don January	T-5	66-64-66-67=263	$3,650.00
Partner: Miller Barber			
Gene Littler	T-5	69-65-65-64=263	$3,650.00
Partner: Ken Still			
Ken Still	T-5	69-65-65-64=263	$3,650.00
Partner: Gene Littler			
Dave Hill	T-5	69-65-65-64=263	$3,650.00
Partner: Mike Hill			
Mike Hill	T-5	69-65-65-64=263	$3,650.00
Partner: Dave Hill			
Bob Charles	T-5	65-66-70-62=263	$3,650.00
Partner: Bruce Devlin			
Bruce Devlin	T-5	65-66-70-62=263	$3,650.00
Partner: Bob Charles			
Dave Eichelberger	T-9	64-65-63-72=264	$2,725.00
Partner: J.C. Goosie			
J.C. Goosie	T-9	64-65-63-72=264	$2,725.00
Partner: Dave Eichelberger			
Jim Colbert	T-9	64-65-68-67=264	$2,725.00
Partner: Dean Refram			
Dean Refram	T-9	64-65-68-67=264	$2,725.00
Partner: Jim Colbert			

Westchester Classic

Course: Westchester C.C., Harrison, N.Y.
Par: 72 Yardage: 6,700
Last day of event: Sunday, August 2, 1970

Player	Place	Score	Earnings
Bruce Crampton	Win	67-71-68-67=273	$50,000.00
Larry Hinson	T-2	67-70-69-68=274	$23,125.00
Jack Nicklaus	T-2	72-67-67-68=274	$23,125.00
Ray Floyd	T-4	68-73-68-68=277	$11,000.00

Jerry Heard	T-4	73-68-69-67=277	$11,000.00
Tommy Aaron	T-6	70-69-69-70=278	$6,910.71
Frank Beard	T-6	68-71-70-69=278	$6,910.71
John Schroeder	T-6	69-68-71-70=278	$6,910.71
Phil Rodgers	T-6	69-70-72-67=278	$6,910.72
Dave Hill	T-6	72-72-63-71=278	$6,910.71
Arnold Palmer	T-6	72-69-69-68=278	$6,910.72
Tom Weiskopf	T-6	72-71-70-65=278	$6,910.72

American Golf Classic

Course: Firestone C.C. (South), Akron, Ohio
Par: 70 Yardage: 7,180
Last day of event: Sunday, August 9, 1970

Player	Place	Score	Earnings
Frank Beard	Win	73-65-67-71=276	$30,000.00
Bruce Crampton	T-2	69-68-70-71=278	$11,600.00
Tommy Aaron	T-2	69-69-68-72=278	$11,600.00
Jack Nicklaus	T-2	73-67-69-69=278	$11,600.00
George Archer	5	67-69-70-73=279	$6,150.00
Dale Douglass	T-6	72-69-71-68=280	$5,100.00
Tom Shaw	T-6	70-66-69-75=280	$5,100.00
Gary Player	T-8	72-68-72-69=281	$4,237.50
Bob Murphy	T-8	71-75-67-68=281	$4,237.50
Dave Stockton	T-10	71-69-71-71=282	$3,180.00
George Knudson	T-10	74-71-70-67=282	$3,180.00
Bob Goalby	T-10	69-75-68-70=282	$3,180.00
Bob Stone	T-10	71-71-65-75=282	$3,180.00
Bert Yancey	T-10	76-67-69-70=282	$3,180.00

PGA Championship

Course: Southern Hills C.C., Tulsa, Okla.
Par: 70 Yardage: 6,962
Last day of event: Sunday, August 16, 1970

Player	Place	Score	Earnings
Dave Stockton	Win	70-70-66-73=279	$40,000.00
Arnold Palmer	T-2	70-72-69-70=281	$18,500.00
Bob Murphy	T-2	71-73-71-66=281	$18,500.00
Gene Littler	T-4	72-71-69-70=282	$8,800.00
Larry Hinson	T-4	69-71-74-68=282	$8,800.00
Bruce Crampton	T-6	73-75-68-67=283	$6,800.00
Jack Nicklaus	T-6	68-76-73-66=283	$6,800.00
Ray Floyd	T-8	71-73-65-75=284	$5,650.00
Dick Lotz	T-8	72-70-75-67=284	$5,650.00
Mason Rudolph	T-10	71-70-73-71=285	$4,800.00
Billy Maxwell	T-10	72-71-73-69=285	$4,800.00

AVCO Classic

Course: Pleasant Valley C.C., Sutton, Mass.
Par: 72 Yardage: 7,110
Last day of event: Monday, August 24, 1970

Player	Place	Score	Earnings
Billy Casper	Win	68-67-73-69=277	$32,000.00
Tom Weiskopf	T-2	70-69-70-71=280	$14,800.00
Rod Funseth	T-2	72-70-72-66=280	$14,800.00
Lou Graham	T-4	70-69-71-71=281	$5,936.00
Larry Hinson	T-4	71-70-72-68=281	$5,936.00
Larry Ziegler	T-4	72-68-70-71=281	$5,936.00
Mac McLendon	T-4	72-73-69-67=281	$5,936.00
Charles Coody	T-4	73-72-69-67=281	$5,936.00
John Schroeder	T-9	71-73-71-67=282	$3,840.00
Dave Hill	T-9	72-70-67-73=282	$3,840.00

| Dan Sikes, Jr. | T-9 | 66-74-69-73=282 | $3,840.00 |
| Paul Harney | T-9 | 72-74-67-69=282 | $3,840.00 |

Dow Jones Open Invitational

Course: Upper Montclair C.C., Clifton, N.J.
Par: 72 Yardage: 7,085
Last day of event: Sunday, August 30, 1970

Player	Place	Score	Earnings
Bobby Nichols	Win	68-70-69-69=276	$60,000.00
Labron Harris, Jr.	2	69-68-70-70=277	$34,200.00
Dan Sikes, Jr.	3	71-73-67-68=279	$21,300.00
Larry Hinson	4	70-69-70-71=280	$14,100.00
Charles Coody	5	71-71-69-70=281	$12,300.00
Homero Blancas	T-6	71-69-70-72=282	$9,337.50
Bruce Devlin	T-6	71-72-70-69=282	$9,337.50
Johnny Miller	T-6	69-71-69-73=282	$9,337.50
Orville Moody	T-6	72-64-75-71=282	$9,337.50
Bruce Crampton	T-10	68-68-74-73=283	$7,200.00
Tom Weiskopf	T-10	71-69-74-69=283	$7,200.00

Greater Hartford Open Invitational

Course: Wethersfield C.C.
Wethersfield, Conn., Par: 71 Yardage: 6,568
Last day of event: Monday, September 7, 1970

Player	Place	Score	Earnings
Bob Murphy	Win	66-66-66-69=267	$20,000.00
Paul Harney	2	70-65-69-67=271	$11,400.00
Tom Weiskopf	3	69-66-70-67=272	$7,100.00
Steve Oppermann	T-4	67-68-67-71=273	$4,400.00
Jim Grant	T-4	69-64-71-69=273	$4,400.00
Doug Sanders	T-6	67-70-69-68=274	$3,400.00
Dave Stockton	T-6	72-67-69-66=274	$3,400.00
Pete Brown	T-8	66-70-69-70=275	$2,510.00
Homero Blancas	T-8	70-67-69-69=275	$2,510.00
Billy Maxwell	T-8	67-68-71-69=275	$2,510.00
Deane Beman	T-8	71-67-67-70=275	$2,510.00
Grier Jones	T-8	68-68-73-66=275	$2,510.00
Charles Coody	T-8	75-63-70-68=275	$2,510.00

Robinson Open Golf Classic

Course: Crawford C.C., Robinson, Ill.
Par: 71 Yardage: 6,625
Last day of event: Sunday, September 20, 1970

Player	Place	Score	Earnings
George Knudson	Win	67-69-69-63=268	$20,000.00
Playoff: Beat George Archer with par on fourth extra hole			
George Archer	2	67-67-68-66=268	$11,400.00
Larry Ziegler	3	69-67-68-67=271	$7,100.00
Grier Jones	T-4	67-69-70-68=274	$4,400.00
Hal Underwood	T-4	68-71-66-69=274	$4,400.00
Mason Rudolph	T-6	69-67-69-70=275	$3,250.00
Charles Sifford	T-6	67-71-68-69=275	$3,250.00
J.C. Snead	T-6	68-72-68-67=275	$3,250.00
Hale Irwin	T-9	67-69-68-72=276	$2,400.00
Dave Eichelberger	T-9	68-72-69-67=276	$2,400.00
Bert Weaver	T-9	68-72-71-65=276	$2,400.00
Deane Beman	T-9	69-65-72-70=276	$2,400.00

Green Island Open Invitational
Course: Green Island C.C., Columbus, Ga.
Par: 70 Yardage: 6,791
Last day of event: Sunday, September 27, 1970

Player	Place	Score	Earnings
Mason Rudolph	Win	75-68-67-64=274	$12,000.00
Chris Blocker	2	68-69-69-70=276	$6,840.00
Jim Jamieson	3	70-70-70-68=278	$4,285.00
Herb Hooper	T-4	69-71-70-69=279	$2,580.00
Bob Stanton	T-4	66-70-74-69=279	$2,580.00
Bunky Henry	6	67-71-75-67=280	$1,850.00
Tom Shaw	T-7	69-69-72-71=281	$1,600.00
Bert Greene	T-7	75-67-71-68=281	$1,600.00
Bert Weaver	T-7	75-67-71-68=281	$1,600.00
Davis Love, Jr.	T-10	70-69-72-71=282	$1,281.00
John Schlee	T-10	72-70-68-72=282	$1,281.00
Homero Blancas	T-10	73-66-71-72=282	$1,281.00
Harry Toscano	T-10	66-70-72-74=282	$1,281.00
Bobby Cole	T-10	74-70-73-65=282	$1,281.00

Azalea Open Invitational
Course: Cape Fear C.C., Wilmington, N.C.
Par: 71 Yardage: 6,567
Last day of event: Sunday, October 4, 1970

Player	Place	Score	Earnings
Cesar Sanudo	Win	66-68-68-67=269	$12,000.00
Bobby Mitchell	2	66-64-68-72=270	$6,840.00
John Schlee	3	67-67-75-62=271	$4,285.00
Hugh Royer, Jr.	T-4	68-66-70-68=272	$2,580.00
Bob Stanton	T-4	71-67-69-65=272	$2,580.00
Mason Rudolph	T-6	69-67-67-70=273	$1,775.00
Rolf Deming	T-6	70-69-65-69=273	$1,775.00
Howell Fraser	T-8	68-67-68-71=274	$1,550.00
Al Balding	T-8	66-68-74-66=274	$1,550.00
Joe Campbell	T-10	66-70-70-69=275	$1,281.00
Labron Harris, Jr.	T-10	70-67-69-69=275	$1,281.00
Ted Hayes, Jr.	T-10	70-70-70-65=275	$1,281.00
Wilf Homeniuik	T-10	65-70-71-69=275	$1,281.00
Dale Douglass	T-10	69-63-72-71=275	$1,281.00

Kaiser International Open
Course: Silverado C.C., Napa, Calif.
Home Course -Par: 72 Yardage: 6,849
Last day of event: Sunday, October 25, 1970

Player	Place	Score	Earnings
Ken Still	Win	68-69-71-72=280	$30,000.00
Playoff: Beat Lee Trevino and Bert Yancey with birdie on first extra hole			
Bert Yancey	T-2	68-71-69-70=278	$13,875.00
Lee Trevino	T-2	69-68-70-71=278	$13,875.00
Jack Montgomery	T-4	65-72-71-71=279	$6,200.00
Dave Hill	T-4	68-69-72-70=279	$6,200.00
Jerry Heard	T-4	69-73-70-67=279	$6,200.00
Tommy Aaron	T-7	70-72-70-68=280	$4,425.00
Gene Littler	T-7	70-72-71-67=280	$4,425.00
Phil Rodgers	T-7	72-69-67-72=280	$4,425.00
Bruce Crampton	T-10	71-70-72-69=282	$3,450.00
Don January	T-10	72-70-68-72=282	$3,450.00
Steve Reid	T-10	74-70-66-72=282	$3,450.00

Sahara Invitational
Course: Paradise Valley C.C., Las Vegas, Nev.
Home course / Par: 72 Yardage: 7,143
Last day of event: Sunday, November 1, 1970

Player	Place	Score	Earnings
Babe Hiskey	Win	70-70-65-71=276	$20,000.00
Terry Dill	T-2	68-71-73-65=277	$7,733.34
Miller Barber	T-2	73-68-68-68=277	$7,733.33
Bob Goalby	T-2	71-74-66-66=277	$7,733.33
Larry Hinson	T-5	67-71-71-69=278	$3,850.00
Tommy Aaron	T-5	64-71-72-71=278	$3,850.00
Johnny Miller	T-7	68-71-70-70=279	$2,730.00
Dave Stockton	T-7	70-67-71-71=279	$2,730.00
Billy Casper	T-7	70-72-69-68=279	$2,730.00
Dewitt Weaver	T-7	71-72-66-70=279	$2,730.00
Chi Chi Rodriguez	T-7	68-72-74-65=279	$2,730.00

Heritage Classic
Course: Harbour Town G.L., Hilton Head, S.C.
Par: 71 Yardage: 6,657
Last day of event: Sunday, November 29, 1970

Player	Place	Score	Earnings
Bob Goalby	Win	74-70-70-66=280	$20,000.00
Lanny Wadkins	2	73-74-69-68=284	
Billy Maxwell	T-3	72-73-70-71=286	$7,733.33
Arnold Palmer	T-3	73-70-72-71=286	$7,733.34
Bob Murphy	T-3	75-71-70-70=286	$7,733.33
Jack Lewis, Jr.	T-6	75-74-65-73=287	$3,850.00
Phil Rodgers	T-6	75-73-67-72=287	$3,850.00
John Schlee	8	75-73-68-72=288	$3,200.00
Mason Rudolph	T-9	72-72-73-72=289	$2,825.00
Richard Crawford	T-9	76-72-69-72=289	$2,825.00

Coral Springs Open Invitational
Course: Coral Springs C.C., Coral Springs, Fla.
Par: 71 Yardage: 6,843
Last day of event: Sunday, December 6, 1970

Player	Place	Score	Earnings
Bill Garrett	Win	71-64-68-69=272	$25,000.00
Bob Murphy	2	69-71-68-65=273	$14,300.00
Vic Loustalot	T-3	69-70-69-66=274	$7,350.00
Lee Trevino	T-3	68-67-68-71=274	$7,350.00
Julius Boros	5	73-67-65-70=275	$5,125.00
Fred Marti	T-6	69-70-67-70=276	$3,890.00
Gardner Dickinson	T-6	68-67-70-71=276	$3,890.00
Herb Hooper	T-6	68-70-67-71=276	$3,890.00
Arnold Palmer	T-6	72-70-68-66=276	$3,890.00
Homero Blancas	10	68-69-68-72=277	$3,125.00

Bahama Islands Open
Course: Kings Inn & G.C. (Emerald Course), Freeport, Bahama
Par: 72 Yardage: 7,005
Last day of event: Sunday, December 13, 1970

Player	Place	Score	Earnings
Doug Sanders	Win	66-70-68-68=272	$26,000.00
Playoff: Beat Chris Blocker with par on second extra hole			
Chris Blocker	2	69-66-71-66=272	$14,800.00
Lee Trevino	3	73-70-67-65=275	$9,240.00
Richard Crawford	4	76-68-67-65=276	$6,120.00
Tommy Aaron	5	70-70-72-65=277	$5,330.00

Gay Brewer	6	70-69-70-69=278	$4,680.00
Dave Hill	7	71-70-72-66=279	$4,160.00
Arnold Palmer	8	68-69-75-69=281	$3,830.00
Bruce Crampton	9	71-72-70-70=283	$3,510.00
Bob Payne	T-10	71-70-72-71=284	$2,665.00
Jim Jamieson	T-10	72-69-71-72=284	$2,665.00
Jerry McGee	T-10	73-69-73-69=284	$2,665.00
Gardner Dickinson	T-10	69-74-71-70=284	$2,665.00
Lee Elder	T-10	74-71-72-67=284	$2,665.00
Jerry Heard	T-10	71-75-71-67=284	$2,665.00

1971

For the only time in the history of the modern major championships, the PGA Championship was contested before the other three. Jack Nicklaus won that February tournament at PGA National, becoming the first player to win all four modern majors twice. Nicklaus led the Masters through 54 holes, but it was Charles Coody who earned a green jacket thanks to a pair of 70s over the weekend. Nicklaus also was runner-up at the U.S. Open, losing in a playoff with Lee Trevino at Merion—where Trevino famously tossed a rubber snake at Nicklaus on the first tee before the extra session began. Trevino won the British Open, edging Liang-Huan Lu of Taiwan by a stroke at Royal Birkdale. Johnny Miller scored his first PGA Tour win, the Southern Open Invitational. Bobby Jones, winner of 13 majors including the original Grand Slam in 1930, died in December at age 69.

Glen Campbell Los Angeles Open

Course: Rancho Municipal G.C., Los Angeles, Calif.
Par: 71 Yardage: 6,827
Last day of event: Sunday, January 10, 1971

Player	Place	Score	Earnings
Bob Lunn	Win	68-69-70-67=274	$22,000.00
Playoff: Beat Billy Casper with birdie on fourth extra hole			
Billy Casper	2	66-72-69-67=274	$12,500.00
Art Wall, Jr.	3	70-67-70-68=275	$7,850.00
Gibby Gilbert	T-4	69-70-68-70=277	$4,290.00
Don January	T-4	69-68-71-69=277	$4,290.00
Phil Rodgers	T-4	70-67-72-68=277	$4,290.00
Bobby Greenwood	T-4	69-69-66-73=277	$4,290.00
Bob Goalby	T-8	70-71-68-69=278	$3,107.00
Lee Trevino	T-8	71-69-67-71=278	$3,107.00
Monte Sanders	T-10	71-70-68-70=279	$2,640.00
Bill Garrett	T-10	69-69-72-69=279	$2,640.00

Bing Crosby Pro-Am

Courses: Pebble Beach G.L., Spyglass Hill G.C.,fCypress Point C.C., Pebble Beach, Calif.
Home Course / Pebble Beach G.L.,Par: 72 Yardage: 6,815
Last day of event: Sunday, January 17, 1971

Player	Place	Score	Earnings
Tom Shaw	Win	68-71-69-70=278	$27,000.00
Arnold Palmer	2	72-68-69-71=280	$15,400.00
Bob Murphy	3	71-69-73-69=282	$9,570.00
Tom Weiskopf	T-4	71-73-68-72=284	$5,581.00
Howie Johnson	T-4	69-70-71-74=284	$5,581.00
Jerry Heard	T-4	72-74-71-67=284	$5,581.00
Bobby Nichols	7	68-72-71-74=285	$4,320.00
Dave Eichelberger	T-8	72-71-71-72=286	$3,666.00
Johnny Miller	T-8	73-74-72-67=286	$3,666.00
Miller Barber	T-8	74-69-71-72=286	$3,666.00

Phoenix Open

Course: Arizona C.C., Phoenix, Ariz.
Par: 71 Yardage: 6,216
Last day of event: Sunday, January 24, 1971

Player	Place	Score	Earnings
Miller Barber	Win	65-64-67-65=261	$25,000.00
Dan Sikes, Jr.	T-2	66-67-66-64=263	$11,575.00
Billy Casper	T-2	67-68-66-62=263	$11,575.00
Dave Hill	T-4	65-66-66-67=264	$5,158.00
Rod Curl	T-4	67-67-67-65=264	$5,158.00
Homero Blancas	T-4	65-69-63-67=264	$5,158.00
George Archer	T-7	65-67-66-67=265	$3,280.00
Don Massengale	T-7	64-67-68-66=265	$3,280.00
Hale Irwin	T-7	66-65-68-66=265	$3,280.00
Howard Johnston	T-7	65-66-69-65=265	$3,280.00
Kermit Zarley	T-7	69-66-64-66=265	$3,280.00
Paul Harney	T-7	65-64-65-71=265	$3,280.00

Andy Williams-San Diego Open

Course: Torrey Pines (South), Torrey Pines (North), San Diego, Calif.
Home Course -Par: 72 Yardage: 7,021
Last day of event: Sunday, January 31, 1971

Player	Place	Score	Earnings
George Archer	Win	67-72-68-65=272	$30,000.00
Dave Eichelberger	2	66-70-71-68=275	$17,100.00
Paul Harney	T-3	67-70-69-69=277	$7,312.00
Miller Barber	T-3	68-69-70-70=277	$7,312.00
Bob Stone	T-3	69-71-67-70=277	$7,312.00
Jack Nicklaus	T-3	69-71-71-66=277	$7,312.00
Dick Lotz	T-7	71-68-70-69=278	$4,612.00
John Schlee	T-7	71-70-70-67=278	$4,612.00
Dow Finsterwald	T-9	68-69-71-71=279	$3,600.00
Lee Elder	T-9	72-66-69-72=279	$3,600.00
Art Wall, Jr.	T-9	72-67-70-70=279	$3,600.00
Frank Beard	T-9	69-74-68-68=279	$3,600.00

Hawaiian Open

Course: Waialae C.C., Honolulu, Ha.
Par: 72 Yardage: 7,234
Last day of event: Sunday, February 7, 1971

Player	Place	Score	Earnings
Tom Shaw	Win	68-67-69-69=273	$40,000.00
Miller Barber	2	72-67-67-68=274	$22,800.00
Dewitt Weaver	3	68-68-68-71=275	$14,200.00
Arnold Palmer	T-4	67-69-68-73=277	$8,266.00
Lee Trevino	T-4	68-73-66-70=277	$8,266.00
Hubert Green	T-4	73-67-69-68=277	$8,266.00
Bruce Crampton	7	69-69-68-72=278	$6,400.00
Bob Charles	T-8	72-68-69-70=279	$5,433.00
Bob Murphy	T-8	73-68-69-69=279	$5,433.00
John Schlee	T-8	66-74-70-69=279	$5,433.00

Bob Hope Chrysler Classic

Course: Bermuda Dunes C.C., La Quinta C.C., Indian Wells C.C., Tamarisk C.C.
Home Course / Bermuda Dunes, Par: 72 Yardage: 6,837
Last day of event: Sunday, February 14, 1971

Player	Place	Score	Earnings
Arnold Palmer	Win	67-71-66-68-70=342	$28,000.00
Playoff: Beat Ray Floyd with birdie on second extra hole			
Ray Floyd	2	68-71-70-66-67=342	$16,000.00

Bert Yancey	3	69-69-71-66-71=346	$9,900.00
Billy Casper	4	71-68-68-71-70=348	$6,580.00
Bob Rosburg	T-5	69-70-71-67-72=349	$5,390.00
Jim Wiechers	T-5	70-70-64-73-72=349	$5,390.00
Charles Coody	T-7	70-71-69-69-71=350	$4,305.00
Johnny Miller	T-7	71-71-71-66-71=350	$4,305.00
Marty Fleckman	9	66-77-69-70-67=351	$3,780.00
Al Mengert	T-10	71-72-70-68-71=352	$2,968.00
Tom Shaw	T-10	72-71-70-68-71=352	$2,968.00
Bob Murphy	T-10	70-68-73-69-72=352	$2,968.00
Bobby Nichols	T-10	71-73-72-70-66=352	$2,968.00
George Hixon	T-10	68-70-74-69-71=352	$2,968.00

Tucson Open

Course: Tucson National G.C., Starr Pass G.C., Tucson, Ariz.
Par: 72 Yardage: 7,305
Last day of event: Sunday, February 21, 1971

Player	Place	Score	Earnings
J.C. Snead	Win	66-71-70-66=273	$22,000.00
Dale Douglass	2	69-68-70-67=274	$12,500.00
Al Mengert	T-3	72-71-68-68=279	$5,843.00
George Archer	T-3	68-73-68-70=279	$5,843.00
Hale Irwin	T-3	72-74-66-67=279	$5,843.00
Dewitt Weaver	T-6	66-72-71-71=280	$3,575.00
Frank Beard	T-6	72-68-68-72=280	$3,575.00
Jacky Cupit	T-6	71-73-70-66=280	$3,575.00
Bob-E. Smith	T-9	72-71-68-70=281	$2,750.00
Orville Moody	T-9	70-73-70-68=281	$2,750.00
Bob Charles	T-9	73-70-70-68=281	$2,750.00

PGA Championship

Course: PGA National G.C. (JDM C.C.), Palm Beach Gardens, Fla.
Par: 72 Yardage: 7,096
Last day of event: Sunday, February 28, 1971

Player	Place	Score	Earnings
Jack Nicklaus	Win	69-69-70-73=281	$40,000.00
Billy Casper	2	71-73-71-68=283	$22,800.00
Tommy Bolt	3	72-74-69-69=284	$14,200.00
Gary Player	T-4	71-73-68-73=285	$8,800.00
Miller Barber	T-4	72-68-75-70=285	$8,800.00
Jim Jamieson	T-6	72-72-72-70=286	$6,500.00
Gibby Gilbert	T-6	74-67-72-73=286	$6,500.00
Dave Hill	T-6	74-71-71-70=286	$6,500.00
Bob Lunn	T-9	72-70-73-72=287	$4,800.00
Jerry Heard	T-9	73-71-72-71=287	$4,800.00
Fred Marti	T-9	72-71-74-70=287	$4,800.00
Bob Rosburg	T-9	74-72-70-71=287	$4,800.00

Doral-Eastern Open

Course: Doral C.C. (Blue), Miami, Fla.
Par: 72 Yardage: 6,939
Last day of event: Sunday, March 7, 1971

Player	Place	Score	Earnings
J.C. Snead	Win	70-70-66-69=275	$30,000.00
Gardner Dickinson	2	68-70-69-69=276	$17,100.00
Miller Barber	3	76-65-69-68=278	$10,650.00
Gibby Gilbert	4	69-70-69-71=279	$7,050.00
Terry Dill	T-5	72-71-66-71=280	$5,450.00
Bruce Fleisher	T-5	72-67-72-69=280	$5,450.00
Bruce Devlin	T-5	72-69-70-69=280	$5,450.00
Mike Hill	8	74-70-69-68=281	$4,425.00

| Homero Blancas | T-9 | 69-73-70-70=282 | $3,900.00 |
| Jack Nicklaus | T-9 | 74-68-67-73=282 | $3,900.00 |

Florida Citrus Open Invitational

Course: Rio Pinar C.C., Orlando, Fla.
Par: 72 Yardage: 7,012
Last day of event: Sunday, March 14, 1971

Player	Place	Score	Earnings
Arnold Palmer	Win	66-68-68-68=270	$30,000.00
Julius Boros	2	67-68-67-69=271	$17,100.00
Kermit Zarley	3	68-64-72-69=273	$10,650.00
Jerry Heard	T-4	66-70-69-69=274	$6,600.00
Tom Weiskopf	T-4	71-69-66-68=274	$6,600.00
Lionel Hebert	T-6	69-69-68-69=275	$4,668.00
Dave Stockton	T-6	69-67-69-70=275	$4,668.00
Frank Beard	T-6	69-70-67-69=275	$4,668.00
Gibby Gilbert	T-6	70-69-66-70=275	$4,668.00
Orville Moody	10	68-65-70-73=276	$3,750.00

Greater Jacksonville Open

Course: Hidden Hills C.C., Jacksonville, Fla.
Par: 72 Yardage: 6,943
Last day of event: Sunday, March 21, 1971

Player	Place	Score	Earnings
Gary Player	Win	70-70-72-69=281	$25,000.00
Playoff: Beat Hal Underwood with par on second extra hole			
Hal Underwood	2	67-70-71-71=281	$14,300.00
Johnny Miller	T-3	73-68-69-72=282	$7,350.00
Lee Trevino	T-3	66-74-71-71=282	$7,350.00
Don January	T-5	70-67-76-71=284	$5,125.00
Steve Melnyk	T-5	66-71-77-70=284	
Bob Erickson	7	70-72-74-69=285	$4,500.00
John Schlee	8	68-75-70-73=286	$4,000.00
Dave Eichelberger	T-9	69-71-73-74=287	$2,295.00
Bob Charles	T-9	73-73-74-67=287	$2,295.00
Jack Nicklaus	T-9	71-75-72-69=287	$2,295.00

National Airlines Open

Course: C.C. of Miami, Miami, Fla.
Par: 72 Yardage: 6,970
Last day of event: Sunday, March 28, 1971

Player	Place	Score	Earnings
Gary Player	Win	69-67-70-68=274	$40,000.00
Lee Trevino	2	67-69-71-69=276	$22,800.00
Jerry McGee	3	72-67-72-66=277	$14,200.00
Bruce Crampton	T-4	68-68-70-72=278	$8,800.00
Charles Coody	T-4	70-66-72-70=278	$8,800.00
Arnold Palmer	T-6	70-69-71-69=279	$6,225.00
Johnny Pott	T-6	71-69-70-69=279	$6,225.00
Cesar Sanudo	T-6	72-71-69-67=279	$6,225.00
Jerry Heard	T-6	66-70-74-69=279	$6,225.00
Bob-E. Smith	T-10	71-69-71-69=280	$4,240.00
John Schroeder	T-10	72-71-68-69=280	$4,240.00
Bruce Devlin	T-10	68-69-70-73=280	$4,240.00
Dan Sikes, Jr.	T-10	69-68-73-70=280	$4,240.00
Deane Beman	T-10	73-68-71-68=280	$4,240.00

Greater Greensboro Open

Course: Sedgefield C.C., Greensboro, N.C.
Par: 71 Yardage: 7,034
Last day of event: Sunday, April 4, 1971

Player	Place	Score	Earnings
Bud Allin	Win	75-64-67-69=275	$38,000.00
Playoff: Beat Dave Eichelberger and Rod Funseth with birdie on first extra hole			
Dave Eichelberger	2	66-71-67-69=275	$17,575.00
Rod Funseth	2	73-66-65-71=275	$17,575.00
Pete Brown	4	68-69-70-69=276	$8,930.00
Terry Dill	T-5	70-68-71-68=277	$7,315.00
Miller Barber	T-6	67-70-69-71=277	$7,315.00
Bob Charles	T-7	67-72-68-71=278	$5,605.00
Tony Jacklin	T-7	70-69-72-67=278	$5,605.00
Al Geiberger	T-7	72-70-69-67=278	$5,605.00
Jerry Heard	T-10	71-67-71-70=279	$4,180.00
Lee Trevino	T-10	67-72-71-69=279	$4,180.00
Tommy Aaron	T-10	72-71-67-69=279	$4,180.00
Don January	T-10	73-70-67-69=279	$4,180.00

Masters

Course: Augusta National G.C., Augusta, Ga.
Par: 72 Yardage: 6,925
Last day of event: Sunday, April 11, 1971

Player	Place	Score	Earnings
Charles Coody	Win	66-73-70-70=279	$25,000.00
Jack Nicklaus	T-2	70-71-68-72=281	$17,500.00
Johnny Miller	T-2	72-73-68-68=281	$17,500.00
Don January	T-4	69-69-73-72=283	$9,050.00
Gene Littler	T-4	72-69-73-69=283	$9,050.00
Tom Weiskopf	T-6	71-69-72-72=284	$5,600.00
Ken Still	T-6	72-71-72-69=284	$5,600.00
Gary Player	T-6	72-72-71-69=284	$5,600.00
Dave Stockton	T-9	72-73-69-72=286	$3,767.00
Frank Beard	T-9	74-73-69-70=286	$3,767.00
Roberto De Vicenzo	T-9	76-69-72-69=286	$3,767.00

Monsanto Open

Course: Pensacola C.C., Pensacola, Fla.
Par: 71 Yardage: 6,679
Last day of event: Sunday, April 18, 1971

Player	Place	Score	Earnings
Gene Littler	Win	71-67-71-67=276	$30,000.00
George Archer	T-2	71-70-68-70=279	$13,875.00
Pete Brown	T-2	72-69-71-67=279	$13,875.00
Bob Murphy	T-4	70-70-70-70=280	$6,600.00
Larry Wood	T-4	66-70-73-71=280	$6,600.00
Mason Rudolph	T-6	69-70-69-73=281	$4,875.00
Ron Cerrudo	T-6	74-70-68-69=281	$4,875.00
Johnny Pott	T-6	74-71-68-68=281	$4,875.00
Billy Maxwell	T-9	68-72-69-73=282	$3,600.00
Bob-E. Smith	T-9	69-71-73-69=282	$3,600.00
Al Geiberger	T-9	68-73-67-74=282	$3,600.00
John Lotz	T-9	75-70-70-67=282	$3,600.00

Tournament of Champions

Course: La Costa C.C., Carlsbad, Calif.
Par: 72 Yardage: 6,911
Last day of event: Sunday, April 25, 1971

Player	Place	Score	Earnings
Jack Nicklaus	Win	69-71-69-70=279	$33,000.00
Dave Stockton	T-2	71-72-72-72=287	$12,760.00
Bruce Devlin	T-2	72-70-72-73=287	$12,760.00
Gary Player	T-2	70-71-74-72=287	$12,760.00
Gene Littler	5	72-71-74-71=288	$6,770.00
Bobby Nichols	6	71-75-72-71=289	$5,940.00
Frank Beard	T-7	70-73-73-74=290	$4,930.00
Charles Coody	T-7	74-68-73-75=290	$4,930.00
Gibby Gilbert	9	73-71-73-74=291	$4,350.00
Dave Hill	10	72-76-71-73=292	$4,050.00

Tallahassee Open

Course: Killearn C.C., Tallahassee, Fla.
Par: 72 Yardage: 7,124
Last day of event: Sunday, April 25, 1971

Player	Place	Score	Earnings
Lee Trevino	Win	69-67-69-68=273	$12,000.00
Jim Wiechers	2	64-72-72-68=276	$7,200.00
Hubert Green	3	68-68-66-75=277	$4,500.00
Ed Sneed	T-4	70-70-70-68=278	$2,620.00
Jack Ewing	T-4	69-71-67-71=278	$2,620.00
Rod Funseth	T-4	68-74-67-69=278	$2,620.00
Roy Pace	7	71-69-71-68=279	$2,040.00
Ted Hayes, Jr.	T-8	68-68-73-71=280	$1,770.00
Johnny Pott	T-8	70-73-69-68=280	$1,770.00
Jim Jamieson	T-10	68-71-72-70=281	$1,332.00
Charles Sifford	T-10	69-70-70-72=281	$1,332.00
Mike Hill	T-10	69-72-72-68=281	$1,332.00
Steve Reid	T-10	69-68-73-71=281	$1,332.00
Wilf Homeniuik	T-10	69-73-68-71=281	$1,332.00

Greater New Orleans Open

Course: Lakewood C.C., New Orleans, La.
Par: 72 Yardage: 7,080
Last day of event: Sunday, May 2, 1971

Player	Place	Score	Earnings
Frank Beard	Win	70-71-67-68=276	$25,000.00
Hubert Green	2	68-69-69-71=277	$14,300.00
George Johnson	T-3	68-71-71-68=278	$7,350.00
Lee Elder	T-3	67-73-67-71=278	$7,350.00
Charles Coody	5	70-73-67-70=280	$5,125.00
Miller Barber	T-6	70-67-72-72=281	$3,890.00
John Lotz	T-6	70-69-70-72=281	$3,890.00
Dave Hill	T-6	67-73-70-71=281	$3,890.00
Jack Ewing	T-6	73-71-67-70=281	$3,890.00
Bob Wynn	T-10	69-72-70-71=282	$3,000.00
Bob Murphy	T-10	69-73-68-72=282	$3,000.00

Byron Nelson Golf Classic

Course: Preston Trail G.C., Dallas, Texas
Par: 70 Yardage: 6,993
Last day of event: Sunday, May 9, 1971

Player	Place	Score	Earnings
Jack Nicklaus	Win	69-71-68-66=274	$25,000.00
Frank Beard	T-2	69-70-70-67=276	$11,575.00

Player	Place	Score	Earnings
Jerry McGee	T-2	66-71-74-65=276	$11,575.00
Charles Coody	4	69-66-72-71=278	$5,850.00
Lee Trevino	T-5	68-70-70-71=279	$4,541.00
Bert Yancey	T-5	71-72-69-67=279	$4,541.00
Bobby Nichols	T-5	73-68-69-69=279	$4,541.00
Hugh Royer, Jr.	T-8	69-70-71-70=280	$3,530.00
Dan Sikes, Jr.	T-8	72-69-68-70=280	$3,530.00
Ted Hayes, Jr.	T-10	68-72-69-72=281	$2,482.00
Gay Brewer	T-10	68-72-70-71=281	$2,482.00
Arnold Palmer	T-10	70-71-68-72=281	$2,482.00
Larry Hinson	T-10	72-70-69-70=281	$2,482.00
Homero Blancas	T-10	69-70-69-73=281	$2,482.00
Chi Chi Rodriguez	T-10	69-68-73-71=281	$2,482.00
Jim Colbert	T-10	79-66-69-67=281	$2,482.00

Houston Champions International

Course: Champions G.C., Houston, Texas
Par: 71 Yardage: 7,166
Last day of event: Sunday, May 16, 1971

Player	Place	Score	Earnings
Hubert Green	Win	68-69-72-71=280	$25,000.00
Playoff: Beat Don January with birdie on second extra hole			
Don January	2	71-73-68-68=280	$14,300.00
Bob Murphy	T-3	69-73-68-71=281	$7,350.00
Lee Trevino	T-3	76-72-66-67=281	$7,350.00
Lou Graham	T-5	72-69-69-72=282	$4,812.00
Dan Sikes, Jr.	T-5	70-75-71-66=282	$4,812.00
Homero Blancas	T-7	70-68-73-72=283	$3,842.00
Ben Crenshaw	T-7	70-69-73-71=283	
Dewitt Weaver	T-7	70-69-69-75=283	$3,842.00
Johnny Miller	T-10	73-67-72-72=284	$3,250.00
Charles Coody	T-10	72-70-67-75=284	$3,250.00

Colonial National Invitational

Course: Colonial C.C., Fort Worth, Texas
Par: 70 Yardage: 7,142
Last day of event: Sunday, May 23, 1971

Player	Place	Score	Earnings
Gene Littler	Win	72-68-74-69=283	$25,000.00
Bert Yancey	2	69-73-72-70=284	$14,300.00
Orville Moody	T-3	71-73-72-69=285	$6,081.00
Fred Marti	T-3	68-72-71-74=285	$6,081.00
George Knudson	T-3	67-69-76-73=285	$6,081.00
Julius Boros	T-3	71-71-67-76=285	$6,081.00
Bert Greene	T-7	68-74-72-72=286	$3,412.00
Gary Player	T-7	73-70-74-69=286	$3,412.00
Homero Blancas	T-7	67-73-71-75=286	$3,412.00
Jerry McGee	T-7	71-68-75-72=286	$3,412.00
Bob Rosburg	T-7	75-66-73-72=286	$3,412.00

Danny Thomas Memphis Classic

Course: Colonial C.C., Memphis, Tenn.
Par: 70 Yardage: 6,466
Last day of event: Sunday, May 30, 1971

Player	Place	Score	Earnings
Lee Trevino	Win	66-66-69-67=268	$35,000.00
Hale Irwin	T-2	69-69-66-68=272	$12,706.00
Lee Elder	T-2	71-68-67-66=272	$12,706.00
Randy Wolff	T-2	65-68-72-64=272	$12,706.00
Jerry Heard	T-2	67-74-67-64=272	$12,706.00
Don January	T-6	68-70-68-67=273	$6,787.00

Player	Place	Score	Earnings
Larry Ziegler	T-6	62-71-71-69=273	$6,787.00
Chuck Courtney	T-8	70-67-70-67=274	$4,312.00
Chi Chi Rodriguez	T-8	66-68-71-69=274	$4,312.00
Labron Harris, Jr.	T-8	68-70-71-65=274	$4,312.00
Ken Still	T-8	73-69-69-63=274	$4,312.00

Atlanta Classic

Course: Atlanta C.C., Atlanta, Ga.
Par: 72 Yardage: 7,007
Last day of event: Sunday, June 6, 1971

Player	Place	Score	Earnings
Gardner Dickinson	Win	68-68-69-70=275	$25,000.00
Playoff: Beat Jack Nicklaus with par on first extra hole			
Jack Nicklaus	2	67-68-70-70=275	$14,300.00
Lee Trevino	T-3	68-70-68-70=276	$7,350.00
Gary Player	T-3	69-68-67-72=276	$7,350.00
Steve Reid	T-5	71-70-69-68=278	$4,321.00
Johnny Miller	T-5	65-70-71-72=278	$4,321.00
Ray Floyd	T-5	67-70-69-72=278	$4,321.00
Tommy Aaron	T-5	71-72-68-67=278	$4,321.00
Dale Douglass	T-9	69-70-70-70=279	$3,250.00
Bob Lunn	T-9	68-71-69-71=279	$3,250.00

Kemper Open

Course: Quail Hollow C.C., Charlotte, N.C.
Par: 72 Yardage: 7,205
Last day of event: Sunday, June 13, 1971

Player	Place	Score	Earnings
Tom Weiskopf	Win	66-72-70-69=277	$30,000.00
Playoff: Beat Dale Douglass, Gary Player and Lee Trevino with birdie on first extra hole			
Dale Douglass	2	71-65-71-70=277	$11,600.00
Gary Player	2	72-67-69-69=277	$11,600.00
Lee Trevino	2	69-73-66-69=277	$11,600.00
Rod Funseth	T-5	69-70-71-69=279	$5,450.00
George Johnson	T-5	72-70-67-70=279	$5,450.00
Bob Lunn	T-5	69-66-71-73=279	$5,450.00
Babe Hiskey	T-8	71-71-70-68=280	$3,918.00
Larry Hinson	T-8	69-70-72-69=280	$3,918.00
Kermit Zarley	T-8	72-71-70-67=280	$3,918.00
Bob Charles	T-8	69-73-69-69=280	$3,918.00

U.S. Open

Course: Merion G.C., Ardmore, Pa.
Par: 70 Yardage: 6,544
Last day of event: Monday, June 21, 1971

Player	Place	Score	Earnings
Lee Trevino	Win	70-72-69-69-68=280	$30,000.00
Playoff: Beat Jack Nicklaus in18-hole playoff (Trevino 68, Nicklaus 71)			
Jack Nicklaus	2	69-72-68-71-71=280	$15,000.00
Bob Rosburg	T-3	71-72-70-69=282	$9,000.00
Jim Colbert	T-3	69-69-73-71=282	$9,000.00
George Archer	T-5	71-70-70-72=283	$6,500.00
Johnny Miller	T-5	70-73-70-70=283	$6,500.00
Jim Simons	T-5	71-71-65-76=283	
Ray Floyd	8	71-75-67-71=284	$5,000.00
Gay Brewer	T-9	70-70-73-72=285	$3,325.00
Larry Hinson	T-9	71-71-70-73=285	$3,325.00
Bobby Nichols	T-9	69-72-69-75=285	$3,325.00
Bert Yancey	T-9	75-69-69-72=285	$3,325.00

Cleveland Open

Course: Beechmont C.C., Cleveland, Ohio
Par: 71 Yardage: 6,643
Last day of event: Sunday, June 27, 1971

Player	Place	Score	Earnings
Bobby Mitchell	Win	66-64-67-65=262	$30,000.00
Charles Coody	2	67-72-62-68=269	$17,100.00
Bruce Crampton	3	68-66-67-69=270	$10,650.00
Jerry McGee	T-4	67-69-67-68=271	$6,200.00
Phil Rodgers	T-4	69-67-67-68=271	$6,200.00
Gene Littler	6	66-68-70-68=272	$4,800.00
Billy Casper	T-7	67-69-68-69=273	$4,237.00
Dan Sikes, Jr.	T-7	64-67-71-71=273	$4,237.00
Bobby Cole	T-9	69-65-70-70=274	$3,600.00
Deane Beman	T-9	69-68-67-70=274	$3,600.00

Canadian Open

Course: Richelieu Valley G. & C.C., Ste. Julie De Vercheres, Quebec, Canada
Par: 72 Yardage: 6,920
Last day of event: Sunday, July 4, 1971

Player	Place	Score	Earnings
Lee Trevino	Win	73-68-67-67=275	$30,000.00
Playoff: Beat Art Wall, Jr. with birdie on second extra hole			
Art Wall, Jr.	2	70-67-69-69=275	$17,000.00
Phil Rodgers	3	67-72-73-69=281	$10,650.00
R.H. Sikes	4	71-71-73-68=283	$7,050.00
Bob Rosburg	5	71-72-67-74=284	$6,150.00
Terry Wilcox	T-6	72-72-68-73=285	$4,875.00
George Archer	T-6	72-74-70-69=285	$4,875.00
Lou Graham	T-6	67-71-72-75=285	$4,875.00
Rod Funseth	T-9	67-73-71-75=286	$3,900.00
Dewitt Weaver	T-9	69-75-70-72=286	$3,900.00

British Open

Course: Royal Birkdale G.C., Southport, Lancashire, England
Par: 73 Yardage: 7,080
Last day of event: Saturday, July 10, 1971

Player	Place	Score	Earnings
Lee Trevino	Win	69-70-69-70=278	$13,200.00
Lu Liang-Huan	2	70-70-69-70=279	$9,600.00
Tony Jacklin	3	69-70-70-71=280	$7,800.00
Craig Defoy	4	72-72-68-69=281	$6,600.00
Jack Nicklaus	T-5	71-71-72-69=283	$5,520.00
Charles Coody	T-5	74-71-70-68=283	$5,520.00
Gary Player	7	71-70-71-72=284	$4,260.00
Billy Casper	T-7	70-72-75-67=284	$4,260.00
Peter Thomson	T-9	70-73-73-69=285	$3,720.00
Doug Sanders	T-9	73-71-74-67=285	$3,720.00

Greater Milwaukee Open

Course: Tripoli G.C., Milwaukee, Wis.
Par: 71 Yardage: 6,514
Last day of event: Sunday, July 11, 1971

Player	Place	Score	Earnings
Dave Eichelberger	Win	64-70-68-68=270	$25,000.00
Bob Shaw	T-2	67-69-69-66=271	$11,575.00
Ralph Johnston	T-2	69-66-69-67=271	$11,575.00
Bruce Crampton	4	68-67-72-65=272	$5,850.00
Rod Funseth	5	68-67-66-72=273	$5,125.00
Roy Pace	T-6	67-69-69-69=274	$3,737.00

Player	Place	Score	Earnings
Lionel Hebert	T-6	69-67-69-69=274	$3,737.00
Lou Graham	T-6	67-68-69-70=274	$3,737.00
Paul Moran	T-6	70-68-69-67=274	$3,737.00
Dean Refram	T-6	68-66-68-72=274	$3,737.00

Western Open

Course: Olympia Fields (North), Olympia Fields, Ill.
Par: 71 Yardage: 6,749
Last day of event: Sunday, July 18, 1971

Player	Place	Score	Earnings
Bruce Crampton	Win	66-73-69-71=279	$30,000.00
Bobby Nichols	2	71-67-70-73=281	$17,100.00
Jerry Heard	T-3	71-68-72-71=282	$8,850.00
Tommy Aaron	T-3	67-74-70-71=282	$8,850.00
Dick Lotz	5	69-69-71-74=283	$6,250.00
Bert Greene	6	72-69-70-74=285	$5,400.00
Gardner Dickinson	T-7	73-70-72-71=286	$4,256.00
Dale Douglass	T-7	68-72-74-72=286	$4,256.00
Larry Mowry	T-7	71-75-71-69=286	$4,256.00
Babe Hiskey	T-7	71-69-76-70=286	$4,256.00

Westchester Classic

Course: Westchester C.C., Harrison, N.Y.
Par: 72 Yardage: 6,700
Last day of event: Sunday, July 25, 1971

Player	Place	Score	Earnings
Arnold Palmer	Win	64-70-68-68=270	$50,000.00
Gibby Gilbert	T-2	67-70-68-70=275	$23,125.00
Hale Irwin	T-2	70-70-67-68=275	$23,125.00
Frank Beard	T-4	69-69-71-68=277	$11,000.00
Sam Snead	T-4	71-70-68-68=277	$11,000.00
Bobby Nichols	T-6	70-69-70-70=279	$8,125.00
Larry Wood	T-6	65-72-71-71=279	$8,125.00
Mason Rudolph	T-6	71-73-70-65=279	$8,125.00
George Boutell	T-9	68-70-72-70=280	$6,500.00
Jack Nicklaus	T-9	72-69-72-67=280	$6,500.00

American Golf Classic

Course: Firestone C.C. (South), Akron, Ohio
Par: 70 Yardage: 7,180
Last day of event: Sunday, August 8, 1971

Player	Place	Score	Earnings
Jerry Heard	Win	67-66-68-74=275	$30,000.00
Dale Douglass	2	69-68-69-72=278	$17,100.00
Bob Murphy	3	74-67-71-67=279	$10,650.00
Jack Nicklaus	4	73-68-69-70=280	$7,050.00
Steve Reid	5	71-70-69-71=281	$6,150.00
Chi Chi Rodriguez	T-6	70-71-73-68=282	$4,875.00
Arnold Palmer	T-6	70-73-72-67=282	$4,875.00
Mike Hill	T-6	67-71-76-68=282	$4,875.00
Johnny Miller	T-9	69-72-72-70=283	$3,325.00
Bert Greene	T-9	70-69-72-72=283	$3,325.00
Phil Rodgers	T-9	72-70-71-70=283	$3,325.00
Johnny Pott	T-9	70-73-70-70=283	$3,325.00
Dick Lotz	T-9	72-73-70-68=283	$3,325.00
Gay Brewer	T-9	68-71-67-77=283	$3,325.00

Massachusetts Classic

Course: Pleasant Valley C.C., Sutton, Mass.
Par: 72 Yardage: 7,241
Last day of event: Sunday, August 15, 1971

Player	Place	Score	Earnings
Dave Stockton	Win	71-69-69-66=275	$33,000.00
Ray Floyd	2	69-70-69-68=276	$18,810.00
Rod Funseth	3	69-72-68-69=278	$11,715.00
Bruce Crampton	4	72-71-65-71=279	$7,755.00
Mike Hill	T-5	70-69-71-71=281	$5,467.00
Mike Reasor	T-5	71-67-72-71=281	$5,467.00
Charles Coody	T-5	71-72-71-67=281	$5,467.00
Homero Blancas	T-5	73-68-68-72=281	$5,467.00
Lionel Hebert	T-5	71-75-67-68=281	$5,467.00
Bob Rosburg	T-10	71-71-71-69=282	$3,498.00
Jerry Heard	T-10	70-70-72-70=282	$3,498.00
J.C. Snead	T-10	72-72-68-70=282	$3,498.00
Bob Charles	T-10	73-69-70-70=282	$3,498.00
Lou Graham	T-10	69-70-68-75=282	$3,498.00

IVB Philadelphia Golf Classic

Course: Whitemarsh Valley C.C., Chestnut Hill, Pa.
Par: 72 Yardage: 6,708
Last day of event: Sunday, August 22, 1971

Player	Place	Score	Earnings
Tom Weiskopf	Win	67-71-66-70=274	$30,000.00
Dave Hill	2	68-68-71-68=275	$17,100.00
Jack Nicklaus	3	66-73-70-67=276	$10,650.00
George Knudson	4	71-68-69-69=277	$7,050.00
Lou Graham	T-5	70-71-68-71=280	$5,450.00
Dale Douglass	T-5	70-70-68-72=280	$5,450.00
Bob Murphy	T-5	67-70-73-70=280	$5,450.00
Lee Elder	T-8	72-72-69-68=281	$4,237.00
Phil Rodgers	T-8	68-75-69-69=281	$4,237.00
Homero Blancas	10	69-73-70-70=282	$3,750.00

U.S. Professional Match Play Championship

Course: C.C. Of North Carolina, Pinehurst, N.C.
Par: 72 Yardage: 6,988
Last day of event: Sunday, August 29, 1971

Player	Place	Score	Earnings
Dewitt Weaver	Win		$35,000.00

Round One - Beat George Archer 72-74
Round Two - Beat Doug Sanders 72-76
Round Three - Beat Julius Boros 71-74
Quarterfinals - Beat Lou Graham 71-72
Semifinals - Beat Bruce Crampton 77-78
Finals - Beat Phil Rodgers 71-77

| Phil Rodgers | 2 | | $17,500.00 |

Round One - Beat Bob Goalby 72-77
Round Two - Beat Mason Rudolph 71-72
Round Three - Beat Gene Littler on the first hole of playoff after both shot 76
Quarterfinals - Beat George Knudson 70-73
Semifinals - Beat Ken Still 69-76
Finals - Lost to DeWitt Weaver 71-77

| Ken Still | 3 | | $10,000.00 |

Round One - Beat Rod Funseth 71-73
Round Two - Beat Lee Elder on third hole of playoff after both shot 72
Round Three - Beat Dave Stockton 70-74
Quarterfinals - Beat Tom Weiskopf on the first hole of a playoff after both shot 71
Semifinals - Lost to Phil Rodgers 69-76
Consolation - Beat Bruce Crampton 74-76

| Bruce Crampton | 4 | | $75,000.00 |

Round One - Beat Bob Rosburg on first hole of playoff after both shot 75
Round Two - Beat Fred Marti 72-78
Round Three - Beat Gardner Dickinson 71-75
Quarterfinals - Beat Arnold Palmer 69-72
Semifinals - Lost to DeWitt Weaver 77-78
Consolation - Lost to Ken Still 74-76

| Tom Weiskopf | T-5 | | $5,000.00 |

Round One - Beat Bert Yancey 73-74
Round Two - Beat Johnny Miller 69-70
Round Three - Beat Ray Floyd 71-73
Quarterfinals - Lost to Ken Still on the first hole of a playoff after both shot 71

| George Knudson | T-5 | | $5,000.00 |

Round One - Beat Don January 72-75
Round Two - Beat Charles Coody 68-69
Round Three - Beat Pete Brown 66-75
Quarterfinals - Lost to Phil Rodgers 70-73

| Lou Graham | T-5 | | $5,000.00 |

Round One - Beat Frank Beard 73-76
Round Two - Beat Bobby Mitchell 69-75
Round Three - Beat Art Wall, Jr. 70-73
Quarterfinals - Lost to DeWitt Weaver 71-72

| Arnold Palmer | T-5 | | $5,000.00 |

Round One - Beat Bruce Devlin 68 to 71
Round Two - Beat Mike Hill 68-71
Round Three - Beat Dave Eichelberger 69-72
Quarterfinals - Lost to Bruce Crampton 69-72

| Ray Floyd | T-9 | | $3,750.00 |

Round One - Beat Jack Nicklaus 67-69
Round Two - Beat Bob E. Smith 73-74
Round Three - Lost to Tom Weiskopf 71-73

| Dave Stockton | T-9 | | $3,750.00 |

Round One - Beat John Schlee 72-74
Round Two - Beat Bud Allin 70-72
Round Three - Lost to Ken Still 70-74

| Pete Brown | T-9 | | $3,750.00 |

Round One - Beat Bobby Nickols 70-72
Round Two - Beat Homero Blancas 72-73
Round Three - Lost to George Knudson 66-75

| Gene Littler | T-9 | | $3,750.00 |

Round One - Beat Dan Sikes 73-75
Round Two - Beat Dave Hill on the first hole of a playoff after both shot 71
Round Three - Lost to Phil Rodgers on the first hole of a playoff after both shot 76

| Gardner Dickinson | T-9 | | $3,750.00 |

Round One - Beat Bill Garrett 72-75
Round Two - Beat Fred Hinson on first hole of playoff after both shot 73
Round Three - Lost to Bruce Crampton 71-75

| Julius Boros | T-9 | | $3,750.00 |

Round One - Beat Miller Barber 71-75
Round Two - Beat Terry Dill 73-76
Round Three - Lost to DeWitt Weaver 71-74

| Art Wall, Jr. | T-9 | | $3,750.00 |

Round One - Beat Cesar Sanudo on the third hole of playoff after both shot 73
Round Two - Beat Hubert Green 71-73
Round Three - Lost to Lou Graham 70-73

| Dave Eichelberger | T-9 | | $3,750.00 |

Round One - Beat Tommy Aaron on first hole of playoff after both shot 68
Round Two - Beat Lionel Hebert 72-76
Round Three - Lost to Arnold Palmer 69-72

Greater Hartford Open Invitational

Course: Wethersfield C.C., Wethersfield, Conn.
Par: 71 Yardage: 6,568
Last day of event: Monday, September 6, 1971

Player	Place	Score	Earnings
George Archer	Win	68-66-68-66=268	$22,000.00
Playoff: Beat Lou Graham and J.C. Snead with birdie on first extra hole			
Lou Graham	2	68-67-67-66=268	$10,175.00
J.C. Snead	2	65-69-67-67=268	$10,175.00
Dave Stockton	T-4	65-69-68-68=270	$4,290.00
Deane Beman	T-4	66-69-67-68=270	$4,290.00
Jack Ewing	T-4	65-67-70-68=270	$4,290.00
Hubert Green	T-4	66-68-70-66=270	$4,290.00
Tom Weiskopf	T-8	69-68-69-65=271	$2,988.00
R.H. Sikes	T-8	68-70-66-67=271	$2,988.00
Gay Brewer	T-8	71-67-65-68=271	$2,988.00

Southern Open

Course: Green Island C.C., Columbus, Ga.
Par: 70 Yardage: 6,791
Last day of event: Sunday, September 12, 1971

Player	Place	Score	Earnings
Johnny Miller	Win	65-67-68-67=267	$20,000.00
Deane Beman	2	73-67-66-66=272	$11,400.00
Bobby Mitchell	3	71-69-62-71=273	$7,100.00
Tommy Aaron	4	72-68-67-67=274	$4,700.00
Frank Beard	5	68-71-69-67=275	$4,100.00
Jim Colbert	T-6	71-66-71-68=276	$3,250.00
Larry Ziegler	T-6	73-64-68-71=276	$3,250.00
Gay Brewer	T-6	68-64-69-75=276	$3,250.00
Pete Brown	T-9	68-72-71-66=277	$2,500.00
John Schroeder	T-9	73-68-68-68=277	$2,500.00
Jack Ewing	T-9	68-74-65-70=277	$2,500.00

Robinson Open Golf Classic

Course: Crawford C.C., Robinson, Ill.
Par: 71 Yardage: 6,685
Last day of event: Sunday, September 26, 1971

Player	Place	Score	Earnings
Labron Harris, Jr.	Win	68-70-69-67=274	$20,000.00
Playoff: Beat Bert Yancey with birdie on third extra hole			
Bert Yancey	2	70-70-67-67=274	$11,400.00
Gay Brewer	T-3	70-69-68-69=276	$5,300.00
Larry Hinson	T-3	68-71-70-67=276	$5,300.00
Jim Colbert	T-3	69-66-73-68=276	$5,300.00
Jim Jamieson	T-6	71-70-64-72=277	$3,250.00
Chuck Courtney	T-6	72-71-69-65=277	$3,250.00
J.C. Snead	T-6	73-69-68-67=277	$3,250.00
Lou Graham	T-9	71-70-69-68=278	$2,500.00
Jacky Cupit	T-9	69-72-68-69=278	$2,500.00
Gardner Dickinson	T-9	72-69-71-66=278	$2,500.00

Kaiser International Open

Course: Silverado C.C., Napa, Calif.
Home Course -Par: 72 Yardage: 6,849
Last day of event: Sunday, October 24, 1971

Player	Place	Score	Earnings
Billy Casper	Win	67-65-69-68=269	$30,000.00
Fred Marti	2	68-70-68-67=273	$17,100.00
Tommy Aaron	3	66-69-68-71=274	$10,650.00

George Johnson	4	69-68-67-72=276	$7,050.00
Miller Barber	T-5	69-70-70-70=279	$5,775.00
Mike Hill	T-5	67-70-68-74=279	$5,775.00
Hale Irwin	T-7	69-70-71-70=280	$4,256.00
Dave Eichelberger	T-7	69-71-70-70=280	$4,256.00
Lou Graham	T-7	68-72-70-70=280	$4,256.00
John Schlee	T-7	69-72-70-69=280	$4,256.00

Sahara Invitational

Course: Paradise Valley C.C., Las Vegas, Nev.
Home course / Par: 72 Yardage: 7,143
Last day of event: Sunday, October 31, 1971

Player	Place	Score	Earnings
Lee Trevino	Win	69-72-73-66=280	$27,000.00
George Archer	2	72-72-71-66=281	$15,400.00
Bob Dickson	3	68-74-68-72=282	$9,570.00
Kermit Zarley	4	73-70-70-71=284	$5,535.00
Ron Cerrudo	5	73-75-69-68=285	$4,860.00
Gay Brewer	T-6	74-71-70-71=286	$4,150.00
Fred Marti	T-6	71-79-67-69=286	$4,150.00
Jim Jamieson	T-8	71-73-73-70=287	$3,378.00
Lanny Wadkins	T-8	73-76-67-71=287	$3,378.00
Dave Eichelberger	T-8	72-77-68-70=287	$3,378.00

Sea Pines Heritage Classic

Course: Harbour Town G.L., Hilton Head, S.C.
Par: 71 Yardage: 6,657
Last day of event: Sunday, November 28, 1971

Player	Place	Score	Earnings
Hale Irwin	Win	68-73-68-70=279	$22,000.00
Bob Lunn	2	71-68-71-70=280	$12,500.00
Jack Nicklaus	T-3	71-69-71-70=281	$6,515.00
Frank Beard	T-3	75-68-71-67=281	$6,515.00
Arnold Palmer	5	69-74-69-74=284	$4,500.00
Deane Beman	6	71-72-72-70=285	$3,575.00
George Knudson	T-7	74-66-76-71=287	$3,575.00
Mac McLendon	T-7	71-67-72-77=287	$3,575.00
Dave Marr	9	76-70-72-70=288	$2,970.00
Homero Blancas	T-10	72-73-74-70=289	$2,640.00
Larry Ziegler	T-10	76-68-74-71=289	$2,640.00

Walt Disney World Open

Course: Walt Disney (Magnolia), Lake Buena Vista, Fla.
Par: 72 Yardage: 7,190
Last day of event: Monday, December 6, 1971

Player	Place	Score	Earnings
Jack Nicklaus	Win	67-68-70-68=273	$30,000.00
Deane Beman	2	70-71-66-69=276	$17,100.00
Lanny Wadkins	T-3	70-68-69-71=278	$8,850.00
Arnold Palmer	T-3	71-66-71-70=278	$8,850.00
Frank Beard	T-5	69-68-71-71=279	$5,775.00
Hale Irwin	T-5	69-72-70-68=279	$5,775.00
Sam Snead	T-7	69-70-70-71=280	$4,095.00
Lou Graham	T-7	69-71-68-72=280	$4,095.00
Jim Colbert	T-7	70-72-72-66=280	$4,095.00
John Schlee	T-7	70-69-73-68=280	$4,095.00
Leonard Thompson	T-7	75-69-67-69=280	$4,095.00

Bahamas National Open

Course: Lucayan C.C., Freeport, Bahama Islands
Par: 71 Yardage: 6,805
Last day of event: Sunday, December 12, 1971

Player	Place	Score	Earnings
Bob Goalby	Win	69-70-66-70=275	$26,000.00
George Archer	2	66-67-71-72=276	$14,800.00
Bert Yancey	T-3	67-69-70-71=277	$7,680.00
Tommy Aaron	T-3	70-68-73-66=277	$7,680.00
Ralph Johnston	5	70-69-70-69=278	$5,330.00
Julius Boros	T-6	67-72-69-72=280	$4,420.00
Grier Jones	T-6	65-70-70-75=280	$4,420.00
Jerry Heard	T-8	71-71-70-69=281	$3,670.00
Bobby Mitchell	T-8	73-71-70-67=281	$3,670.00
George Johnson	T-10	68-71-72-71=282	$3,120.00
Tom Shaw	T-10	73-67-73-69=282	$3,120.00

1972

Jack Nicklaus won the Masters and the U.S. Open, both by three shots over Bruce Crampton (and Bobby Mitchell and Tom Weiskopf at the Masters). Nicklaus' Grand Slam bid was halted by Lee Trevino, who made a remarkable number of chip-ins and long putts at Muirfield and beat Nicklaus by a shot. Gary Player won the PGA Championship by two shots at Oakland Hills, a victory he secured by making birdie from trouble on the 70th hole. David Graham, who had moved to the United States after going bankrupt as a club pro in Tasmania, won his first PGA Tour event, the Cleveland Open.

Glen Campbell Los Angeles Open

Course: Rancho Municipal G.C., Los Angeles, Calif.
Par: 71 Yardage: 6,827
Last day of event: Sunday, January 9, 1972

Player	Place	Score	Earnings
George Archer	Win	66-69-69-66=270	$25,000.00

Playoff: Beat Tommy Aaron and Dave Hill in 18-hole playoff (Archer 66, Aaron 68, Hill 68)

Player	Place	Score	Earnings
Tommy Aaron	2	69-65-67-69=270	$11,575.00
Dave Hill	2	70-67-67-66=270	$11,575.00
Chris Blocker	4	69-71-65-70=275	$5,850.00
Bob Rosburg	T-5	71-68-71-66=276	$4,812.50
Hale Irwin	T-5	66-74-68-68=276	$4,812.50
Tom Weiskopf	7	68-68-71-70=277	$4,000.00
Johnny Miller	T-8	69-68-70-71=278	$3,265.00
Forrest Fezler	T-8	69-72-72-65=278	$3,265.00
Curtis Sifford	T-8	66-68-71-73=278	$3,265.00
Bob-E. Smith	T-8	66-73-67-72=278	$3,265.00

Bing Crosby Pro-Am

Courses: Pebble Beach G.L., Spyglass Hill G.C., Cypress Point C.C., Pebble Beach, Calif.
Home Course / Pebble Beach G.L., Par: 72 Yardage: 6,815
Last day of event: Sunday, January 16, 1972

Player	Place	Score	Earnings
Jack Nicklaus	Win	66-74-71-73=284	$28,000.00

Playoff: Beat Johnny Miller with birdie on first extra hole

Player	Place	Score	Earnings
Johnny Miller	2	75-68-67-74=284	$16,000.00
Lee Trevino	3	69-74-70-73=286	$9,900.00
Fred Marti	T-4	72-73-71-71=287	$6,160.00
Bruce Crampton	T-4	73-72-69-73=287	$6,160.00
Dan Sikes, Jr.	T-6	76-72-66-74=288	$4,357.50
George Archer	T-6	76-73-69-70=288	$4,357.50
Bob Murphy	T-6	76-74-69-69=288	$4,357.50
Tony Jacklin	T-6	70-70-71-77=288	$4,357.50
Kermit Zarley	T-10	72-73-74-70=289	$3,080.00
Tom Weiskopf	T-10	70-73-75-71=289	$3,080.00
Gay Brewer	T-10	75-72-68-74=289	$3,080.00
Mac Hunter, Jr.	T-10	76-73-68-72=289	$3,080.00

Tucson Open

Course: Tucson National G.C., Starr Pass G.C., Tucson, Ariz.
Par: 72 Yardage: 7,305
Last day of event: Sunday, January 23, 1972

Player	Place	Score	Earnings
Miller Barber	Win	68-73-67-65=273	$30,000.00

Playoff: Beat George Archer with birdie on third extra hole after both shot 72 in playoff

Player	Place	Score	Earnings
George Archer	2	65-71-69-68=273	$17,100.00
Bobby Nichols	3	67-70-67-71=275	$10,650.00
Bob Murphy	T-4	67-70-69-70=276	$6,600.00
Dale Douglass	T-4	68-70-68-70=276	$6,600.00
Marty Fleckman	T-6	70-69-70-69=278	$4,875.00
Dave Hill	T-6	68-69-70-71=278	$4,875.00
Don Bies	T-6	73-66-70-69=278	$4,875.00
Jim Jamieson	T-9	67-71-70-71=279	$3,325.00
Al Mengert	T-9	70-71-67-71=279	$3,325.00
Grier Jones	T-9	71-72-67-69=279	$3,325.00
J.C. Snead	T-9	66-73-68-72=279	$3,325.00
Jack Montgomery	T-9	67-70-73-69=279	$3,325.00
Don Massengale	T-9	70-69-67-73=279	$3,325.00

Andy Williams-San Diego Open

Course: Torrey Pines (South), Torrey Pines (North), San Diego, Calif.
Home Course -Par: 72 Yardage: 7,021
Last day of event: Sunday, January 30, 1972

Player	Place	Score	Earnings
Paul Harney	Win	68-71-66-70=275	$30,000.00
Hale Irwin	2	69-68-67-72=276	$17,100.00
Gardner Dickinson	3	70-70-69-68=277	$10,650.00
Bruce Crampton	4	71-66-69-72=278	$7,050.00
Bert Yancey	T-5	73-68-68-70=279	$5,193.75
George Knudson	T-5	70-74-67-68=279	$5,193.75
Dave Eichelberger	T-5	74-69-67-69=279	$5,193.75
Miller Barber	T-5	74-69-69-67=279	$5,193.75
Labron Harris, Jr.	T-9	71-68-70-71=280	$3,325.00
Phil Rodgers	T-9	69-71-68-72=280	$3,325.00
Homero Blancas	T-9	69-69-72-70=280	$3,325.00
Bobby Mitchell	T-9	71-70-67-72=280	$3,325.00
Bob Murphy	T-9	72-68-68-72=280	$3,325.00
John Lotz	T-9	73-70-68-69=280	$3,325.00

Hawaiian Open

Course: Waialae C.C., Honolulu, Ha.
Par: 72 Yardage: 7,234
Last day of event: Sunday, February 6, 1972

Player	Place	Score	Earnings
Grier Jones	Win	65-73-72-64=274	$40,000.00

Playoff: Beat Bob Murphy with par on first extra hole

Player	Place	Score	Earnings
Bob Murphy	2	65-70-70-69=274	$22,800.00
Charles Coody	3	66-72-69-68=275	$14,200.00
Marty Fleckman	4	66-71-71-68=276	$9,400.00
Don Bies	5	67-71-74-65=277	$8,200.00
Jim Jamieson	T-6	68-70-70-70=278	$5,980.00
John Schlee	T-6	68-71-71-68=278	$5,980.00

Bunky Henry	T-6	71-69-70-68=278	$5,980.00
Curtis Sifford	T-6	66-72-69-71=278	$5,980.00
Bob Rosburg	T-6	73-70-70-65=278	$5,980.00

Bob Hope Chrysler Classic
Course: Indian Wells C.C., Tamarisk C.C., Bermuda Dunes C.C., La Quinta C.C.
Home Course / Indian Wells, Par: 72 Yardage: 6,478
Last day of event: Sunday, February 13, 1972

Player	Place	Score	Earnings
Bob Rosburg	Win	66-69-72-70-67=344	$29,000.00
Lanny Wadkins	2	70-69-70-69-67=345	$16,530.00
Jerry Heard	T-3	66-70-69-70-71=346	$8,555.00
Johnny Miller	T-3	71-67-70-71-67=346	$8,555.00
Bob Murphy	5	70-71-71-69-66=347	$5,945.00
Arnold Palmer	6	69-68-76-66-69=348	$5,220.00
Billy Casper	T-7	71-68-70-73-67=349	$4,278.33
Grier Jones	T-7	74-70-70-69-66=349	$4,278.33
Deane Beman	T-7	72-65-72-75-65=349	$4,278.34
Larry Hinson	T-10	70-72-68-71-70=351	$3,190.00
Jack Nicklaus	T-10	68-72-74-69-68=351	$3,190.00
Kermit Zarley	T-10	71-72-74-69-65=351	$3,190.00
Bobby Nichols	T-10	73-74-70-68-66=351	$3,190.00

Phoenix Open
Course: Phoenix C.C., Phoenix, Ariz.
Par: 71 Yardage: 6,726
Last day of event: Sunday, February 20, 1972

Player	Place	Score	Earnings
Homero Blancas	Win	70-61-73-69=273	$25,000.00
Playoff: Beat Lanny Wadkins with birdie on first extra hole			
Lanny Wadkins	2	70-70-67-66=273	$14,300.00
Marty Fleckman	3	69-68-69-68=274	$8,850.00
Jim Wiechers	T-4	68-70-70-68=276	$4,868.75
Gene Littler	T-4	67-68-70-71=276	$4,868.75
Tony Jacklin	T-4	70-68-66-72=276	$4,868.75
Paul Moran	T-4	66-74-66-70=276	$4,868.75
Hal Underwood	T-8	71-69-69-68=277	$3,530.00
Hubert Green	T-8	69-70-72-66=277	$3,530.00
Babe Hiskey	T-10	68-72-69-69=278	$2,875.00
Steve Melnyk	T-10	71-72-67-68=278	$2,875.00
Dan Sikes, Jr.	T-10	72-70-67-69=278	$2,875.00

Jackie Gleason's Inverrary Classic
Course: Inverrary G. & C.C. (East), Lauderhill, Fla.
Par: 72 Yardage: 7,128
Last day of event: Sunday, February 27, 1972

Player	Place	Score	Earnings
Tom Weiskopf	Win	69-72-69-68=278	$52,000.00
Jack Nicklaus	2	73-68-71-67=279	$29,640.00
Mac McLendon	3	68-72-70-70=280	$18,460.00
Tony Jacklin	T-4	69-71-72-70=282	$10,140.00
Bob-E. Smith	T-4	68-73-72-69=282	$10,140.00
Chi Chi Rodriguez	T-4	74-72-69-67=282	$10,140.00
Bud Allin	T-4	72-66-75-69=282	$10,140.00
Bruce Devlin	8	75-69-71-68=283	$7,670.00
Lanny Wadkins	T-9	69-72-72-71=284	$5,763.34
John Schlee	T-9	69-69-73-73=284	$5,763.33
Art Wall, Jr.	T-9	70-70-73-71=284	$5,763.34
Phil Rodgers	T-9	71-70-70-73=284	$5,763.33
Dick Lotz	T-9	70-68-74-72=284	$5,763.33
Gary Player	T-9	72-69-69-74=284	$5,763.33

Doral-Eastern Open
Course: Doral C.C. (Blue), Miami, Fla.
Par: 72 Yardage: 6,939
Last day of event: Sunday, March 5, 1972

Player	Place	Score	Earnings
Jack Nicklaus	Win	71-71-64-70=276	$30,000.00
Bob Rosburg	T-2	69-71-70-68=278	$13,875.00
Lee Trevino	T-2	69-69-68-72=278	$13,875.00
Sam Snead	4	71-68-68-72=279	$7,050.00
Julius Boros	T-5	71-70-70-69=280	$5,450.00
George Shortridge	T-5	71-71-70-68=280	$5,450.00
Bruce Crampton	T-5	72-70-69-69=280	$5,450.00
Johnny Miller	T-8	73-70-66-73=281	$4,075.00
Paul Harney	T-8	70-69-68-74=281	$4,075.00
Bert Yancey	T-8	71-74-70-66=281	$4,075.00

Florida Citrus Open Invitational
Course: Rio Pinar C.C., Orlando, Fla.
Par: 72 Yardage: 7,012
Last day of event: Sunday, March 12, 1972

Player	Place	Score	Earnings
Jerry Heard	Win	70-67-70-69=276	$30,000.00
Bobby Mitchell	2	66-78-68-66=278	$17,100.00
Leonard Thompson	T-3	70-73-67-69=279	$8,850.00
Jim Jamieson	T-3	73-73-63-70=279	$8,850.00
George Archer	T-5	70-70-71-69=280	$4,965.00
Bruce Crampton	T-5	72-70-69-69=280	$4,965.00
Chris Blocker	T-5	67-66-74-73=280	$4,965.00
Rod Funseth	T-5	69-74-69-68=280	$4,965.00
Bob Murphy	T-5	76-66-69-69=280	$4,965.00
Jack Nicklaus	T-10	70-72-70-69=281	$3,600.00
Gary Player	T-10	69-75-71-66=281	$3,600.00

Greater Jacksonville Open
Course: Hidden Hills C.C., Jacksonville, Fla.
Par: 72 Yardage: 6,943
Last day of event: Sunday, March 19, 1972

Player	Place	Score	Earnings
Tony Jacklin	Win	70-71-74-68=283	$25,000.00
Playoff: Beat John Jacobs with par on first extra hole			
John Jacobs	2	72-70-71-70=283	$14,300.00
Bruce Crampton	T-3	73-72-69-70=284	$7,350.00
Rod Funseth	T-3	74-70-69-71=284	$7,350.00
Bob Murphy	5	70-70-73-72=285	$5,125.00
John Schlee	6	72-78-67-69=286	$4,500.00
Jerry Heard	T-7	73-73-74-67=287	$3,842.50
Arnold Palmer	T-7	71-72-75-69=287	$3,842.50
Grier Jones	T-9	70-72-73-73=288	$3,000.00
Lee Trevino	T-9	73-73-70-72=288	$3,000.00
Bobby Nichols	T-9	72-74-72-70=288	$3,000.00
Mike Hill	T-9	73-76-67-72=288	$3,000.00

Greater New Orleans Open
Course: Lakewood C.C., New Orleans, La.
Par: 72 Yardage: 7,080
Last day of event: Sunday, March 26, 1972

Player	Place	Score	Earnings
Gary Player	Win	73-69-68-69=279	$58,000.00
Dave Eichelberger	T-2	67-70-72-71=280	$11,575.00
Jack Nicklaus	T-2	66-70-71-73=280	$11,575.00

John Lister	T-4	71-71-68-71=281	$5,498.50
Billy Ziobro	T-4	67-73-71-70=281	$5,498.50
Mike Reasor	T-6	68-74-71-69=282	$4,250.00
Ron Cerrudo	T-6	70-74-70-68=282	$4,250.00
Mike Hill	T-8	71-69-71-72=283	$3,265.00
George Knudson	T-8	71-71-72-69=283	$3,265.00
Ralph Johnston	T-8	67-70-74-72=283	$3,265.00
Billy Casper	T-8	66-68-73-76=283	$3,265.00

Greater Greensboro Open

Course: Sedgefield C.C., Greensboro, N.C.
Par: 71 Yardage: 7,034
Last day of event: Sunday, April 2, 1972

Player	Place	Score	Earnings
George Archer	Win	70-68-66-68=272	$40,000.00
Playoff: Beat Tommy Aaron with par on second extra hole			
Tommy Aaron	2	71-67-67-67=272	$22,800.00
Chi Chi Rodriguez	T-3	68-69-69-67=273	$9,750.00
Dave Stockton	T-3	69-69-68-67=273	$9,750.00
J.C. Snead	T-3	66-69-70-68=273	$9,750.00
Arnold Palmer	T-3	69-66-68-70=273	$9,750.00
Tony Jacklin	T-7	69-68-69-69=275	$5,900.00
Julius Boros	T-7	66-69-68-72=275	$5,900.00
Bruce Crampton	T-7	67-65-70-73=275	$5,900.00
Lou Graham	T-10	68-69-70-69=276	$4,400.00
Hale Irwin	T-10	69-68-69-70=276	$4,400.00
Jerry McGee	T-10	70-67-69-70=276	$4,400.00
Bob Charles	T-10	70-68-68-70=276	$4,400.00

Masters

Course: Augusta National G.C., Augusta, Ga.
Par: 72 Yardage: 6,925
Last day of event: Sunday, April 9, 1972

Player	Place	Score	Earnings
Jack Nicklaus	Win	68-71-73-74=286	$25,000.00
Bobby Mitchell	T-2	73-72-71-73=289	$15,833.00
Tom Weiskopf	T-2	74-71-70-74=289	$15,833.00
Bruce Crampton	T-2	72-75-69-73=289	$15,833.00
Jerry Heard	T-5	73-71-72-74=290	$6,200.00
Jerry McGee	T-5	73-74-71-72=290	$6,200.00
Bruce Devlin	T-5	74-75-70-71=290	$6,200.00
Homero Blancas	T-5	76-71-69-74=290	$6,200.00
Jim Jamieson	T-5	72-70-71-77=290	$6,200.00
Gary Player	T-10	73-75-72-71=291	$3,600.00
Dave Stockton	T-10	76-70-74-71=291	$3,600.00

Monsanto Open

Course: Pensacola C.C., Pensacola, Fla.
Par: 71 Yardage: 6,679
Last day of event: Sunday, April 16, 1972

Player	Place	Score	Earnings
Dave Hill	Win	64-68-68-71=271	$30,000.00
Jerry Heard	2	72-66-69-65=272	$17,100.00
Chris Blocker	3	67-71-67-69=274	$10,650.00
Bob Goalby	4	68-74-68-65=275	$7,050.00
Ray Floyd	5	68-71-68-69=276	$6,150.00
Lee Elder	T-6	70-70-69-70=279	$4,668.75
Jim Colbert	T-6	67-70-71-71=279	$4,668.75
Dan Sikes, Jr.	T-6	72-68-68-71=279	$4,668.75
Bob-E. Smith	T-6	65-71-70-73=279	$4,668.75
Bruce Crampton	T-10	71-71-72-66=280	$3,450.00

| Dave Marr | T-10 | 72-72-66-70=280 | $3,450.00 |
| Lloyd Monroe | T-10 | 73-68-70-69=280 | $3,450.00 |

Tournament of Champions

Course: La Costa C.C., Carlsbad, Calif.
Par: 72 Yardage: 6,911
Last day of event: Sunday, April 23, 1972

Player	Place	Score	Earnings
Bobby Mitchell	Win	71-65-74-70=280	$33,000.00
Playoff: Beat Jack Nicklaus with birdie on first extra hole			
Jack Nicklaus	2	70-71-67-72=280	$19,000.00
Lee Trevino	3	75-67-68-72=282	$12,000.00
Jerry Heard	T-4	70-70-72-72=284	$7,150.00
Bruce Crampton	T-4	70-72-71-71=284	$7,150.00
Dave Hill	T-4	71-71-70-72=284	$7,150.00
Homero Blancas	T-4	75-65-77-67=284	$7,150.00
Tom Weiskopf	8	74-70-71-71=286	$5,700.00
Arnold Palmer	T-9	74-74-70-71=289	$5,033.34
Bob Rosburg	T-9	73-76-68-72=289	$5,033.33
Dave Stockton	T-9	76-74-68-71=289	$5,033.33

Tallahassee Open

Course: Killearn C.C., Tallahassee, Fla.
Par: 72 Yardage: 7,124
Last day of event: Sunday, April 23, 1972

Player	Place	Score	Earnings
Bob Shaw	Win	70-67-68-68=273	$15,000.00
Leonard Thompson	2	66-71-70-68=275	$8,550.00
Rod Funseth	T-3	70-70-68-69=277	$3,975.00
Art Wall, Jr.	T-3	71-68-68-70=277	$3,975.00
Steve Melnyk	T-3	69-72-68-68=277	$3,975.00
Fred Marti	T-6	67-70-71-70=278	$2,550.00
Bert Yancey	T-6	71-71-70-66=278	$2,550.00
Bert Greene	T-8	72-70-69-68=279	$2,120.00
Larry Hinson	T-8	67-68-73-71=279	$2,120.00
John Mahaffey	T-10	66-71-71-72=280	$1,650.00
Monty Kaser	T-10	70-72-69-69=280	$1,650.00
Ken Still	T-10	71-69-68-72=280	$1,650.00
Chuck Thorpe	T-10	73-72-70-65=280	$1,650.00

Byron Nelson Golf Classic

Course: Preston Trail G.C., Dallas, Texas
Par: 70 Yardage: 6,993
Last day of event: Sunday, April 30, 1972

Player	Place	Score	Earnings
Chi Chi Rodriguez	Win	66-68-69-70=273	$25,000.00
Playoff: Beat Billy Casper with birdie on first extra hole			
Billy Casper	2	68-65-69-71=273	$14,300.00
Bruce Crampton	T-3	67-70-69-69=275	$6,608.34
Wilf Homeniuik	T-3	67-67-71-70=275	$6,608.33
Charles Coody	T-3	68-68-71-68=275	$6,608.33
Arnold Palmer	6	70-71-67-68=276	$4,500.00
Chuck Thorpe	7	72-72-65-68=277	$4,000.00
Dave Stockton	T-8	69-70-69-70=278	$3,137.00
Miller Barber	T-8	68-68-71-71=278	$3,137.00
Tom Weiskopf	T-8	68-68-70-72=278	$3,137.00
Lee Trevino	T-8	66-68-73-71=278	$3,137.00
John Schlee	T-8	68-67-69-74=278	$3,137.00

Houston Open

Course: Westwood C.C., Houston, Texas
Par: 72 Yardage: 6,998
Last day of event: Sunday, May 7, 1972

Player	Place	Score	Earnings
Bruce Devlin	Win	69-70-67-72=278	$25,000.00
Doug Sanders	T-2	68-71-70-71=280	$9,666.66
Lou Graham	T-2	72-70-71-67=280	$9,666.67
Tommy Aaron	T-2	73-69-69-69=280	$9,666.67
Chuck Thorpe	T-5	66-71-72-72=281	$4,541.67
Jack Ewing	T-5	68-72-69-72=281	$4,541.66
Chuck Courtney	T-5	70-72-70-69=281	$4,541.67
Hale Irwin	8	67-67-74-74=282	$3,685.00
Bert Greene	T-9	71-72-69-71=283	$3,000.00
Larry Hinson	T-9	72-71-69-71=283	$3,000.00
Grier Jones	T-9	73-73-68-69=283	$3,000.00
Don Bies	T-9	67-73-76-67=283	$3,000.00

Colonial National Invitational

Course: Colonial C.C., Fort Worth, Texas
Par: 70 Yardage: 7,142
Last day of event: Sunday, May 14, 1972

Player	Place	Score	Earnings
Jerry Heard	Win	69-66-67-73=275	$25,100.00
Fred Marti	2	66-70-69-72=277	$14,357.00
Dave Stockton	3	67-68-71-72=278	$8,885.50
Phil Rodgers	4	68-69-68-74=279	$5,873.50
Bob Murphy	5	74-67-70-69=280	$5,145.50
Bert Greene	6	67-73-69-72=281	$4,518.00
George Johnson	T-7	73-71-68-70=282	$3,701.42
Bruce Crampton	T-7	66-74-71-71=282	$3,701.42
Bobby Nichols	T-7	71-69-68-74=282	$3,701.41
Mason Rudolph	T-10	72-71-68-72=283	$2,660.60
Bruce Devlin	T-10	72-68-72-71=283	$2,660.60
Ray Floyd	T-10	71-72-67-73=283	$2,660.60
Lee Elder	T-10	69-67-72-75=283	$2,660.60
Don Bies	T-10	76-68-68-71=283	$2,660.60

Danny Thomas Memphis Classic

Course: Colonial C.C. (South), Cordova, Tenn.
Par: 70 Yardage: 6,883
Last day of event: Sunday, May 21, 1972

Player	Place	Score	Earnings
Lee Trevino	Win	70-72-72-67=281	$35,000.00
John Mahaffey	2	74-71-71-69=285	$19,950.00
George Hixon	T-3	72-71-73-70=286	$10,325.00
Bert Weaver	T-3	71-69-72-74=286	$10,325.00
Doug Sanders	5	71-71-72-73=287	$7,175.00
Dave Stockton	T-6	71-73-72-72=288	$5,446.25
Gibby Gilbert	T-6	69-74-73-72=288	$5,446.25
J.C. Snead	T-6	71-70-72-75=288	$5,446.25
Bob Dickson	T-6	76-71-71-70=288	$5,446.25
Chuck Courtney	T-10	71-72-72-74=289	$4,025.00
Arnold Palmer	T-10	71-71-74-73=289	$4,025.00
Mason Rudolph	T-10	73-69-76-71=289	$4,025.00

Atlanta Classic

Course: Atlanta C.C., Atlanta, Ga.
Par: 72 Yardage: 7,007
Last day of event: Sunday, May 28, 1972

Player	Place	Score	Earnings
Bob Lunn	Win	67-68-71-69=275	$26,000.00
Gary Player	2	71-65-70-71=277	$14,800.00
Lou Graham	3	68-69-71-70=278	$9,240.00
Dave Hill	T-4	67-72-69-71=279	$5,725.00
Homero Blancas	T-4	69-68-73-69=279	$5,725.00
Gay Brewer	6	75-68-68-69=280	$4,680.00
Bob Murphy	T-7	71-70-71-69=281	$3,687.50
Labron Harris, Jr.	T-7	72-68-71-70=281	$3,687.50
Doug Sanders	T-7	69-72-73-67=281	$3,687.50
Tom Weiskopf	T-7	72-67-69-73=281	$3,687.50

Kemper Open

Course: Quail Hollow C.C., Charlotte, N.C.
Par: 72 Yardage: 7,205
Last day of event: Sunday, June 4, 1972

Player	Place	Score	Earnings
Doug Sanders	Win	71-68-68-68=275	$35,000.00
Lee Trevino	2	69-69-69-69=276	$19,950.00
Labron Harris, Jr.	3	69-69-71-68=277	$7,233.34
Cesar Sanudo	T-4	65-71-71-71=278	$7,233.33
Gary Player	T-4	71-68-70-69=278	$7,233.33
Bruce Devlin	T-4	73-70-66-69=278	$7,233.33
Dave Hill	T-7	70-66-72-71=279	$5,161.66
Tom Shaw	T-7	73-68-68-70=279	$5,161.67
Ray Floyd	T-7	73-70-70-66=279	$5,161.67
Bob Lunn	10	74-69-68-69=280	$4,375.00

IVB Philadelphia Golf Classic

Course: Whitemarsh Valley C.C., Chestnut Hill, Pa.
Par: 72 Yardage: 6,708
Last day of event: Sunday, June 11, 1972

Player	Place	Score	Earnings
J.C. Snead	Win	70-71-69-72=282	$30,000.00
Chi Chi Rodriguez	2	71-68-70-74=283	$17,100.00
Dick Rhyan	T-3	73-69-73-70=285	$8,850.00
Jim Jamieson	T-3	67-69-76-73=285	$8,850.00
Dave Hill	5	70-71-75-70=286	$6,150.00
Hubert Green	T-6	68-74-74-71=287	$4,875.00
Homero Blancas	T-6	74-68-72-73=287	$4,875.00
Bob Murphy	T-6	68-69-75-75=287	$4,875.00
Art Wall, Jr.	T-9	72-71-75-70=288	$3,900.00
Gay Brewer	T-9	67-73-71-77=288	$3,900.00

U.S. Open

Courses: Pebble Beach G.L. , Pebble Beach, Calif.
Par: 72 Yardage: 6,815
Last day of event: Sunday, June 18, 1972

Player	Place	Score	Earnings
Jack Nicklaus	Win	71-73-72-74=290	$30,000.00
Bruce Crampton	2	74-70-73-76=293	$15,000.00
Arnold Palmer	3	77-68-73-76=294	$10,000.00
Homero Blancas	T-4	74-70-76-75=295	$7,500.00
Lee Trevino	T-4	74-72-71-78=295	$7,500.00
Kermit Zarley	6	71-73-73-79=296	$6,000.00
Johnny Miller	7	74-73-71-79=297	$5,000.00

Tom Weiskopf	8	73-74-73-78=298	$4,000.00
Chi Chi Rodriguez	T-9	71-75-78-75=299	$3,250.00
Cesar Sanudo	T-9	72-72-78-77=299	$3,250.00

Western Open

Course: Sunset Ridge, Winnetka, Ill.
Par: 71 Yardage: 6,716
Last day of event: Sunday, June 25, 1972

Player	Place	Score	Earnings
Jim Jamieson	Win	68-67-67-69=271	$30,000.00
Labron Harris, Jr.	2	73-70-69-65=277	$17,100.00
Hale Irwin	T-3	69-72-71-68=280	$7,950.00
Jim Wiechers	T-3	70-74-68-68=280	$7,950.00
Bob Lunn	T-3	75-68-68-69=280	$7,950.00
David Graham	T-6	70-72-72-67=281	$4,485.00
Bobby Nichols	T-6	72-70-69-70=281	$4,485.00
Tom Weiskopf	T-6	69-73-71-68=281	$4,485.00
J.C. Snead	T-6	71-67-73-70=281	$4,485.00
Tommy Aaron	T-6	78-65-67-71=281	$4,485.00

Cleveland Open

Course: Tanglewood C.C., Chagrin Falls, Ohio
Par: 71 Yardage: 6,907
Last day of event: Monday, July 3, 1972

Player	Place	Score	Earnings
David Graham	Win	68-73-68-69=278	$30,000.00

Playoff: Beat Bruce Devlin with birdie on second extra hole

Bruce Devlin	2	73-69-66-70=278	$17,100.00
Larry Hinson	3	65-72-69-73=279	$10,650.00
Lanny Wadkins	T-4	68-71-67-74=280	$6,600.00
Miller Barber	T-4	68-69-74-69=280	$6,600.00
George Knudson	6	67-74-69-71=281	$5,400.00
Bud Allin	T-7	68-72-69-73=282	$4,095.00
Grier Jones	T-7	68-70-73-71=282	$4,095.00
George Archer	T-7	69-70-73-70=282	$4,095.00
Bobby Mitchell	T-7	71-74-69-68=282	$4,095.00
Cesar Sanudo	T-7	73-67-67-75=282	$4,095.00

Canadian Open

Course: Cherry Hill Club, Ridgeway, Ontario, Canada
Par: 71 Yardage: 6,751
Last day of event: Sunday, July 9, 1972

Player	Place	Score	Earnings
Gay Brewer	Win	67-70-68-70=275	$30,000.00
Sam Adams	T-2	67-72-71-66=276	$13,875.00
Dave Hill	T-2	70-66-73-67=276	$13,875.00
Phil Rodgers	4	72-68-68-69=277	$7,050.00
Lou Graham	5	67-69-72-70=278	$6,150.00
Chi Chi Rodriguez	T-6	70-69-73-67=279	$5,100.00
George Knudson	T-6	73-70-69-67=279	$5,100.00
Grier Jones	T-8	70-72-70-69=281	$4,237.50
Bunky Henry	T-8	65-74-71-71=281	$4,237.50
Deane Beman	T-10	69-70-73-70=282	$3,075.00
Lee Trevino	T-10	69-73-70-70=282	$3,075.00
Bud Allin	T-10	70-73-67-72=282	$3,075.00
Gary Player	T-10	71-69-73-69=282	$3,075.00
Sam Snead	T-10	67-74-72-69=282	$3,075.00
Bruce Crampton	T-10	68-70-70-74=282	$3,075.00

British Open

Course: Muirfield G.C., Muirfield, East Lothian, Scotland
Par: 71 Yardage: 6,892
Last day of event: Saturday, July 15, 1972

Player	Place	Score	Earnings
Lee Trevino	Win	71-70-66-71=278	$13,750.00
Jack Nicklaus	2	70-72-71-66=279	$10,000.00
Tony Jacklin	3	69-72-67-72=280	$8,125.00
Doug Sanders	4	71-71-69-70=281	$6,875.00
Brian Barnes	5	71-72-69-71=283	$6,125.00
Gary Player	6	71-71-76-67=285	$5,375.00
Arnold Palmer	T-6	73-73-69-71=286	$4,157.50
Tom Weiskopf	T-6	73-74-70-69=286	$4,157.50
David Vaughan	T-6	74-73-70-69=286	$4,157.50
Guy Hunt	T-6	75-72-67-72=286	$4,157.50

Greater Milwaukee Open

Course: Tripoli G.C., Milwaukee, Wis.
Par: 71 Yardage: 6,514
Last day of event: Sunday, July 16, 1972

Player	Place	Score	Earnings
Jim Colbert	Win	66-67-69-69=271	$25,000.00
Grier Jones	T-2	68-69-68-67=272	$8,531.25
Bud Allin	T-2	69-66-69-68=272	$8,531.25
George Johnson	T-2	65-68-69-70=272	$8,531.25
Chuck Courtney	T-2	69-65-74-64=272	$8,531.25
Jim Wiechers	T-6	67-70-68-68=273	$4,061.67
Bert Greene	T-6	71-67-67-68=273	$4,061.66
Rod Funseth	T-6	67-67-73-66=273	$4,061.67
Mike Hill	T-9	67-69-69-69=274	$3,000.00
Bob Dickson	T-9	66-70-71-67=274	$3,000.00
Roy Pace	T-9	67-71-68-68=274	$3,000.00
Tom Ulozas	T-9	65-69-72-68=274	$3,000.00

American Golf Classic

Course: Firestone C.C. (South), Akron, Ohio
Par: 70 Yardage: 7,180
Last day of event: Sunday, July 23, 1972

Player	Place	Score	Earnings
Bert Yancey	Win	69-68-67-72=276	$30,000.00

Playoff: Beat Tom Ulozas with par on first extra hole

Tom Ulozas	2	70-69-69-68=276	$17,100.00
Hale Irwin	3	70-69-70-68=277	$10,650.00
George Knudson	4	72-70-66-70=278	$7,050.00
Jim Wiechers	5	70-68-75-66=279	$6,150.00
Chuck Thorpe	T-6	71-72-68-69=280	$5,100.00
Cesar Sanudo	T-6	74-69-70-67=280	$5,100.00
Steve Melnyk	T-8	69-68-73-71=281	$4,237.50
Bobby Cole	T-8	71-75-67-68=281	$4,237.50
Arnold Palmer	T-10	68-70-70-74=282	$3,600.00
Jerry Heard	T-10	74-67-68-73=282	$3,600.00

PGA Championship

Course: Oakland Hills C.C., Birmingham, Mich.
Par: 70 Yardage: 6,815
Last day of event: Sunday, August 6, 1972

Player	Place	Score	Earnings
Gary Player	Win	71-71-67-72=281	$45,000.00
Tommy Aaron	T-2	71-71-70-71=283	$20,850.00
Jim Jamieson	T-2	69-72-72-70=283	$20,850.00

Player	Place	Score	Earnings
Ray Floyd	T-4	69-71-74-70=284	$9,275.00
Sam Snead	T-4	70-74-71-69=284	$9,275.00
Billy Casper	T-4	73-70-67-74=284	$9,275.00
Doug Sanders	T-7	72-72-68-73=285	$6,383.00
Jerry Heard	T-7	69-70-72-74=285	$6,383.00
Gay Brewer	T-7	71-70-70-74=285	$6,383.00
Phil Rodgers	T-7	71-72-68-74=285	$6,383.00

Westchester Classic
Course: Westchester C.C., Harrison, N.Y.
Par: 72 Yardage: 6,700
Last day of event: Sunday, August 13, 1972

Player	Place	Score	Earnings
Jack Nicklaus	Win	65-67-70-68=270	$50,000.00
Jim Colbert	2	70-68-70-65=273	$28,500.00
Dwight Nevil	3	66-65-73-71=275	$17,750.00
Homero Blancas	4	71-68-72-65=276	$11,750.00
George Archer	T-5	69-70-70-68=277	$9,625.00
Dewitt Weaver	T-5	64-73-72-68=277	$9,625.00
Charles Sifford	T-7	68-70-70-70=278	$7,687.50
Gay Brewer	T-7	69-69-68-72=278	$7,687.50
Bob Rosburg	T-9	69-71-71-68=279	$6,250.00
Tommy Aaron	T-9	71-68-71-69=279	$6,250.00
Chi Chi Rodriguez	T-9	71-68-71-69=279	$6,250.00

USI Classic
Course: Pleasant Valley C.C., Sutton, Mass.
Par: 72 Yardage: 7,241
Last day of event: Sunday, August 20, 1972

Player	Place	Score	Earnings
Bruce Devlin	Win	69-68-69-69=275	$40,000.00
Lee Elder	2	70-67-71-70=278	$22,800.00
John Mahaffey	T-3	71-67-70-71=279	$11,800.00
Tommy Aaron	T-3	67-69-74-69=279	$11,800.00
John Schlee	5	67-72-72-69=280	$8,200.00
Rik Massengale	6	68-71-73-69=281	$7,200.00
Hubert Green	7	69-76-70-67=282	$6,400.00
Bobby Greenwood	8	72-72-69-70=283	$5,900.00
Frank Beard	T-9	71-68-74-71=284	$5,200.00
Hale Irwin	T-9	69-67-76-72=284	$5,200.00

Liggett Meyers Open
Course: C.C. Of North Carolina, Pinehurst, N.C.
Par: 72 Yardage: 6,988
Last day of event: Sunday, August 27, 1972

Player	Place	Score	Earnings
Lou Graham	Win	71-74-70-70=285	$20,000.00

Playoff: Beat Hale Irwin with a birdie on third extra hole (David Graham and Larry Ziegler were eliminated on first hole)

Player	Place	Score	Earnings
Hale Irwin	2	70-72-71-72=285	$7,733.34
Larry Ziegler	2	70-72-70-73=285	$7,733.33
David Graham	2	72-72-68-73=285	$7,733.33
Mason Rudolph	T-5	71-73-69-73=286	$3,633.33
Doug Sanders	T-5	73-71-73-69=286	$3,633.34
Charles Coody	T-5	69-74-73-70=286	$3,633.33
John Schlee	T-8	71-72-72-72=287	$2,510.00
J.C. Snead	T-8	70-73-70-74=287	$2,510.00
Ken Still	T-8	71-70-72-74=287	$2,510.00
John Schroeder	T-8	69-72-75-71=287	$2,510.00
Bobby Greenwood	T-8	69-76-71-71=287	$2,510.00

U.S. Professional Match Play Championship
Course: C.C. Of North Carolina, Pinehurst, N.C.
Par: 72 Yardage: 6,988
Last day of event: Sunday, August 27, 1972

Player	Place	Score	Earnings
Jack Nicklaus	Win		$40,000.00

Round One - Beat Deane Beman 1 up
Round Two - Beat Lanny Wadkins 2 & 1
Semifinals - Beat Don Bies 2 & 1
Finals - Beat Frank Beard 2 & 1

| Frank Beard | 2 | | $22,000.00 |

Round One - Beat Paul Moran 1 up
Round Two - Beat Lee Trevino 2 & 1
Semifinals - Beat Babe Hiskey 1 up
Finals - Lost to Jack Nicklaus 2 & 1

| Don Bies | T-3 | | $10,000.00 |

Round One - Beat Arnold Palmer 5 & 4
Round Two - Beat Leonard Thompson 2 & 1
Semifinals - Lost to Jack Nicklaus 2 & 1

| Babe Hiskey | T-3 | | $10,000.00 |

Round One - Beat George Archer 1 up
Round Two - Beat Dave Stockton 3 & 1
Semifinals - Lost to Frank Beard 1 up

| Lanny Wadkins | T-5 | | $7,000.00 |

Round One - Beat Miller Barber 2 & 1
Round Two - Lost to Jack Nicklaus 5 & 3

| Leonard Thompson | T-5 | | $7,000.00 |

Round One - Beat Jerry Heard 1 up
Round Two - Lost to Don Bies 2 & 1

| Lee Trevino | T-5 | | $7,000.00 |

Round One - Beat DeWitt Weaver 2 & 1
Round Two - Lost to Frank Beard 2 & 1

| Dave Stockton | T-5 | | $7,000.00 |

Round One - Beat Bob Barbarossa 1 up
Round Two - Lost to Babe Hiskey 3 & 1

| Deane Beman | T-9 | | $5,000.00 |

Round One - Lost to Jack Nicklaus 1 up

| Miller Barber | T-9 | | $5,000.00 |

Round One - Lost to Lanny Wadkins 2 & 1

| Arnold Palmer | T-9 | $5,000.00 | |

Round One - Lost to Don Bies 5 & 4

| Jerry Heard | T-9 | | $5,000.00 |

Round One - Lost to Leonard Thompson 1 up

| Dewitt Weaver | T-9 | | $5,000.00 |

Round One - Lost to Lee Trevino 2 & 1

| Paul Moran | T-9 | | $5,000.00 |

Round One - Lost to Frank Beard 1 up

| George Archer | T-9 | | $5,000.00 |

Round One - Lost to Babe Hiskey 1 up

| Bob Barbarossa | T-9 | | $5,000.00 |

Round One - Lost to Dave Stockton 1 up

Greater Hartford Open Invitational
Course: Wethersfield C.C., Wethersfield, Conn.
Par: 71 Yardage: 6,568
Last day of event: Monday, September 4, 1972

Player	Place	Score	Earnings
Lee Trevino	Win	64-68-72-65=269	$25,000.00

Playoff: Beat Lee Elder with birdie on first extra hole

Player	Place	Score	Earnings
Lee Elder	2	64-69-69-67=269	$14,300.00
Ralph Johnston	T-3	67-67-67-69=270	$7,350.00
Deane Beman	T-3	66-66-70-68=270	$7,350.00
Homero Blancas	T-5	71-69-69-64=273	$4,812.50

Player	Place	Score	Earnings
Curtis Sifford	T-5	65-69-67-72=273	$4,812.50
Chi Chi Rodriguez	T-7	69-68-70-67=274	$3,686.67
Ken Still	T-7	68-70-65-71=274	$3,686.66
Tom Shaw	T-7	67-66-72-69=274	$3,686.67
Lou Graham	10	70-67-69-69=275	$3,125.00

Southern Open

Course: Green Island C.C., Columbus, Ga.
Par: 70 Yardage: 6,791
Last day of event: Sunday, September 10, 1972

Player	Place	Score	Earnings
Dewitt Weaver	Win	65-67-72-72=276	$20,000.00

Playoff: Beat Chuck Courtney with par on first extra hole

Player	Place	Score	Earnings
Chuck Courtney	2	69-68-69-70=276	$11,400.00
Chi Chi Rodriguez	3	66-72-68-71=277	$7,100.00
Deane Beman	T-4	71-68-68-71=278	$4,400.00
Dick Rhyan	T-4	72-69-67-70=278	$4,400.00
George Archer	T-6	72-67-71-69=279	$3,250.00
Jim Colbert	T-6	68-74-67-70=279	$3,250.00
Dwight Nevil	T-6	75-70-63-71=279	$3,250.00
Jack Ewing	T-9	70-71-70-69=280	$2,400.00
John Schroeder	T-9	72-69-70-69=280	$2,400.00
George Johnson	T-9	67-70-67-76=280	$2,400.00
Frank Beard	T-9	72-63-69-76=280	$2,400.00

Greater St. Louis Classic

Course: Norwood Hills C.C., Normandy, Mo.
Par: 70 Yardage: 6,544
Last day of event: Sunday, September 17, 1972

Player	Place	Score	Earnings
Lee Trevino	Win	65-68-66-70=269	$30,000.00
Deane Beman	2	64-67-67-72=270	$17,100.00
Don Bies	T-3	68-66-72-68=274	$8,850.00
Bob Goalby	T-3	67-68-66-73=274	$8,850.00
Bob Wynn	5	68-71-68-68=275	$6,150.00
John Schroeder	6	70-66-72-68=276	$5,400.00
Jerry McGee	T-7	68-72-68-69=277	$4,256.25
Mike Wynn	T-7	72-68-70-67=277	$4,256.25
Chris Blocker	T-7	68-69-73-67=277	$4,256.25
Mike Hill	T-7	73-70-69-65=277	$4,256.25

Robinson's Fall Golf Classic

Course: Crawford C.C., Robinson, Ill.
Par: 71 Yardage: 6,556
Last day of event: Sunday, September 24, 1972

Player	Place	Score	Earnings
Grier Jones	Win	66-72-67-68=273	$20,000.00

Playoff: Beat Dave Marad with par on second extra hole

Player	Place	Score	Earnings
Dave Marad	2	71-67-66-69=273	$11,400.00
Jim Colbert	3	69-68-71-67=275	$7,100.00
Labron Harris, Jr.	T-4	68-71-67-70=276	$4,400.00
Mac McLendon	T-4	71-69-68-68=276	$4,400.00
John Schlee	T-6	69-71-70-67=277	$3,400.00
Larry Hinson	T-6	71-68-68-70=277	$3,400.00
Don Bies	T-8	69-71-67-71=278	$2,408.33
Orville Moody	T-8	70-68-71-69=278	$2,408.33
Steve Spray	T-8	71-69-68-70=278	$2,408.33
Chuck Courtney	T-8	71-69-70-68=278	$2,408.34
Bill Johnston	T-8	71-69-70-68=278	$2,408.34
Bob Menne	T-8	70-66-68-74=278	$2,408.33

Quad Cities Open

Course: Crow Valley C.C., Bettendorf, Iowa
Par: 71 Yardage: 6,501
Last day of event: Sunday, October 1, 1972

Player	Place	Score	Earnings
Deane Beman	Win	72-69-71-67=279	$20,000.00
Tom Watson	2	73-72-69-66=280	$11,400.00
Don Iverson	3	67-71-70-73=281	$7,100.00
Lanny Wadkins	4	71-69-70-72=282	$4,700.00
Grier Jones	T-5	72-71-69-71=283	$3,462.50
Gibby Gilbert	T-5	68-72-73-70=283	$3,462.50
Bob Wynn	T-5	71-69-70-73=283	$3,462.50
Doug Olson	T-5	69-71-75-68=283	$3,462.50
Rod Curl	T-9	71-72-76-65=284	$2,600.00
Jacky Cupit	T-9	72-76-67-69=284	$2,600.00

Kaiser International Open

Course: Silverado C.C., Napa, Calif.
Home Course -Par: 72 Yardage: 6,849
Last day of event: Sunday, October 22, 1972

Player	Place	Score	Earnings
George Knudson	Win	66-69-66-70=271	$30,000.00
Bobby Nichols	T-2	70-70-70-64=274	$13,875.00
Hale Irwin	T-2	74-69-65-66=274	$13,875.00
Grier Jones	4	67-70-70-69=276	$7,050.00
Bobby Mitchell	5	68-69-70-70=277	$6,150.00
Don Iverson	6	69-73-70-67=279	$5,400.00
Jim Wiechers	T-7	68-71-72-69=280	$4,612.50
Bud Allin	T-7	68-68-71-73=280	$4,612.50
Jack Nicklaus	T-9	69-71-69-72=281	$3,900.00
J.C. Snead	T-9	72-67-71-71=281	$3,900.00

Sahara Invitational

Course: Paradise Valley C.C., Las Vegas, Nev.
Home course / Par: 72 Yardage: 7,143
Last day of event: Sunday, October 29, 1972

Player	Place	Score	Earnings
Lanny Wadkins	Win	65-69-70-69=273	$27,000.00
Arnold Palmer	2	65-69-71-69=274	$15,400.00
Hale Irwin	T-3	70-69-67-69=275	$7,960.00
Gay Brewer	T-3	71-69-67-68=275	$7,960.00
Bob Eastwood	T-5	69-68-71-68=276	$5,197.50
Jack Nicklaus	T-5	66-69-73-68=276	$5,197.50
Lionel Hebert	T-7	72-69-67-69=277	$3,981.67
John Mahaffey	T-7	68-66-73-70=277	$3,981.67
George Knudson	T-7	65-70-66-76=277	$3,981.66
Cesar Sanudo	T-10	70-71-71-66=278	$2,970.00
Jerry Heard	T-10	71-66-71-70=278	$2,970.00
Doug Sanders	T-10	65-72-73-68=278	$2,970.00
Jim Ferriell	T-10	69-73-70-66=278	$2,970.00

San Antonio Texas Open

Course: Woodlake G.C., San Antonio, Texas
Par: 72 Yardage: 7,143
Last day of event: Sunday, November 5, 1972

Player	Place	Score	Earnings
Mike Hill	Win	67-68-69-69=273	$25,000.00
Lee Trevino	2	71-69-68-67=275	$14,300.00
Phil Rodgers	3	71-69-70-67=277	$8,850.00
Brad Anderson	T-4	70-70-70-68=278	$4,632.00

Player	Place	Score	Earnings
Chi Chi Rodriguez	T-4	70-70-70-68=278	$4,632.00
Bobby Nichols	T-4	70-71-69-68=278	$4,632.00
Charles Coody	T-4	71-67-69-71=278	$4,632.00
Ben Kern	T-4	69-70-72-67=278	$4,632.00
Forrest Fezler	9	68-69-71-71=279	$3,375.00
Grier Jones	T-10	71-70-69-70=280	$3,000.00
Dan Sikes, Jr.	T-10	66-72-70-72=280	$3,000.00

Sea Pines Heritage Classic

Course: Harbour Town G.L., Ocean Course, Hilton Head, S.C.
Par: 71 Yardage: 6,657
Last day of event: Sunday, November 26, 1972

Player	Place	Score	Earnings
Johnny Miller	Win	71-65-75-70=281	$25,000.00
Tom Weiskopf	2	71-73-72-66=282	$14,300.00
Lon Hinkle	T-3	68-72-72-71=283	$7,350.00
Ben Crenshaw	T-3	73-72-71-67=283	
Bobby Nichols	T-3	70-69-77-67=283	$7,350.00
Steve Melnyk	T-6	71-73-71-69=284	$4,541.67
Allen Miller	T-6	68-71-75-70=284	$4,541.66
Lou Graham	T-6	71-68-75-70=284	$4,541.67
Larry Ziegler	T-9	70-73-71-71=285	$2,901.43
Jim Jamieson	T-9	72-73-70-70=285	$2,901.43
Mason Rudolph	T-9	73-69-72-71=285	$2,901.43
Gardner Dickinson	T-9	71-72-74-68=285	$2,901.43
Dan Sikes, Jr.	T-9	74-71-71-69=285	$2,901.43
Pat Fitzsimons	T-9	74-71-74-66=285	$2,901.43
Forrest Fezler	T-9	70-66-76-73=285	$2,901.42

Walt Disney World Open

Course: Walt Disney (Magnolia, Palm), Lake Buena Vista, Fla.
Home course / Magnolia, Par: 72 Yardage: 7,190
Last day of event: Sunday, December 3, 1972

Player	Place	Score	Earnings
Jack Nicklaus	Win	68-68-67-64=267	$30,000.00
Jim Dent	T-2	71-69-65-71=276	$11,600.00
Bobby Mitchell	T-2	73-69-68-66=276	$11,600.00
Larry Wood	T-2	69-74-66-67=276	$11,600.00
Frank Beard	T-5	68-70-70-69=277	$5,450.00
Bob Goalby	T-5	71-71-65-70=277	$5,450.00
Bert Yancey	T-5	70-74-64-69=277	$5,450.00
Leonard Thompson	T-8	71-68-69-70=278	$3,765.00
Dave Marr	T-8	70-72-65-71=278	$3,765.00
Sam Snead	T-8	72-71-70-65=278	$3,765.00
Tommy Aaron	T-8	69-69-73-67=278	$3,765.00
Ed Sneed	T-8	66-73-75-64=278	$3,765.00

1973

This year is remembered for Johnny Miller's historic victory at the U.S. Open, where he shot a final-round 63 at Oakmont that erased a 6-shot deficit after 54 holes. Runner-up John Schlee finished one back. Tommy Aaron won the Masters by a shot over J.C. Snead (Sam's nephew). In the British Open at Troon, Tom Weiskopf notched the only major victory of his career, a perplexing underachievement given his immense talent. Weiskopf won five times in 1973. Jack Nicklaus' victory in the PGA Championship set a career record for modern majors (12), eclipsing Walter Hagen's 11. (Thanks to a pair of U.S. Amateur victories, Nicklaus also displaced Bobby Jones as the pre-modern major king, 14 to 13.) Arnold Palmer won the Bob Hope Desert Classic, the last of his 60 victories on the PGA Tour. Ben Crenshaw won his first PGA Tour start, the San Antonio Texas Open.

Glen Campbell Los Angeles Open

Course: Riviera C.C., Pacific Palisades, Calif.
Par: 71 Yardage: 7,029
Last day of event: Sunday, January 7, 1973

Player	Place	Score	Earnings
Rod Funseth	Win	73-69-65-69=276	$27,000.00
Tom Weiskopf	T-2	70-70-70-69=279	$9,213.75
David Graham	T-2	69-69-70-71=279	$9,213.75
Don Bies	T-2	69-69-72-69=279	$9,213.75
Dave Hill	T-2	73-68-69-69=279	$9,213.75
Jack Nicklaus	6	69-70-71-70=280	$4,860.00
John Mahaffey	T-7	71-71-71-68=281	$3,982.67
Sam Snead	T-7	70-70-68-73=281	$3,982.67
Gay Brewer	T-7	75-70-65-71=281	$3,982.66
Larry Ziegler	T-10	70-71-71-70=282	$2,970.00
Julius Boros	T-10	67-70-73-72=282	$2,970.00
Ken Still	T-10	70-70-73-69=282	$2,970.00
Bud Allin	T-10	71-67-74-70=282	$2,970.00

Phoenix Open

Course: Arizona C.C., Phoenix, Ariz.
Par: 70 Yardage: 6,216
Last day of event: Sunday, January 14, 1973

Player	Place	Score	Earnings
Bruce Crampton	Win	68-67-68-65=268	$30,000.00
Steve Melnyk	T-2	69-66-69-65=269	$13,875.00
Lanny Wadkins	T-2	69-65-70-65=269	$13,875.00
Paul Harney	T-4	69-69-65-67=270	$5,850.00
J.C. Snead	T-4	62-67-71-70=270	$5,850.00
Grier Jones	T-4	64-68-66-72=270	$5,850.00
Tommy Aaron	T-4	66-73-67-64=270	$5,850.00
Leonard Thompson	T-8	68-69-67-67=271	$3,612.50
Gene Littler	T-8	69-69-64-69=271	$3,612.50
Bob Dickson	T-8	64-70-70-67=271	$3,612.50
Dave Hill	T-8	65-68-68-70=271	$3,612.50
Rod Funseth	T-8	67-70-70-64=271	$3,612.50
Ray Floyd	T-8	68-70-66-67=271	$3,612.50

Dean Martin Tucson Open

Course: Tucson National G.C., Starr Pass G.C., Tucson, Ariz.
Par: 72 Yardage: 7,305
Last day of event: Sunday, January 21, 1973

Player	Place	Score	Earnings
Bruce Crampton	Win	70-70-66-71=277	$30,000.00
Labron Harris, Jr.	T-2	71-71-70-70=282	$11,600.00
George Archer	T-2	70-68-72-72=282	$11,600.00
Gay Brewer	T-2	71-72-69-70=282	$11,600.00
Bobby Nichols	T-5	69-69-73-72=283	$5,450.00
Richie Karl	T-5	72-71-67-73=283	$5,450.00
Rod Funseth	T-5	69-70-70-74=283	$5,450.00
Frank Beard	T-8	69-72-71-72=284	$3,765.00
Jerry Heard	T-8	71-73-68-72=284	$3,765.00
Jerry McGee	T-8	73-71-71-69=284	$3,765.00
Dave Hill	T-8	70-74-72-68=284	$3,765.00
Jimmy Wright	T-8	75-71-70-68=284	$3,765.00

Bing Crosby Pro-Am

Courses: Pebble Beach G.L., Spyglass Hill G.C., Cypress Point C.C., Pebble Beach, Calif.

Home Course / Pebble Beach G.L., Par: 72 Yardage: 6,815

Last day of event: Sunday, January 28, 1973

Player	Place	Score	Earnings
Jack Nicklaus	Win	71-69-71-71=282	$36,000.00
Playoff: Beat Ray Floyd and Orville Moody with birdie on first extra hole			
Ray Floyd	2	71-70-70-71=282	$16,500.00
Orville Moody	2	71-66-69-76=282	$16,500.00
Dave Marr	4	71-71-70-73=285	$8,460.00
Rod Funseth	T-5	72-74-71-69=286	$6,930.00
Lee Elder	T-5	76-68-69-73=286	$6,930.00
Don Iverson	T-7	72-68-70-77=287	$5,535.00
Billy Casper	T-7	66-67-78-76=287	$5,535.00
Howie Johnson	T-9	73-71-73-71=288	$4,320.00
Gibby Gilbert	T-9	74-67-73-74=288	$4,320.00
Lee Trevino	T-9	74-70-73-71=288	$4,320.00
Butch Baird	T-9	72-72-75-69=288	$4,320.00

Hawaiian Open

Course: Waialae C.C., Honolulu, Ha.

Par: 72 Yardage: 7,234

Last day of event: Sunday, February 4, 1973

Player	Place	Score	Earnings
John Schlee	Win	70-68-67-68=273	$40,000.00
Orville Moody	2	72-66-68-69=275	$22,800.00
Tom Watson	3	68-65-68-75=276	$14,200.00
Gay Brewer	4	68-72-68-69=277	$9,400.00
J.C. Snead	5	70-71-68-69=278	$8,200.00
Hale Irwin	T-6	71-71-71-66=279	$6,800.00
Johnny Miller	T-6	73-72-65-69=279	$6,800.00
Lanny Wadkins	8	69-73-72-66=280	$5,900.00
George Archer	T-9	68-71-71-71=281	$4,433.33
Chi Chi Rodriguez	T-9	71-72-71-67=281	$4,433.34
Bud Allin	T-9	72-70-68-71=281	$4,433.33
Larry Ziegler	T-9	72-71-69-69=281	$4,433.34
Billy Casper	T-9	73-68-70-70=281	$4,433.33
Dewitt Weaver	T-9	74-72-66-69=281	$4,433.33

Bob Hope Chrysler Classic

Course: Bermuda Dunes C.C., La Quinta C.C., Indian Wells C.C., Eldorado C.C.

Home Course / Bermuda Dunes, Par: 72 Yardage: 6,837

Last day of event: Sunday, February 11, 1973

Player	Place	Score	Earnings
Arnold Palmer	Win	71-66-69-68-69=343	$32,000.00
Jack Nicklaus	T-2	64-70-71-68-72=345	$14,800.00
Johnny Miller	T-2	70-70-70-63-72=345	$14,800.00
Gay Brewer	T-4	66-70-70-68-72=346	$7,040.00
Jim Wiechers	T-4	70-69-73-66-68=346	$7,040.00
John Schlee	6	70-68-69-70-71=348	$5,760.00
Lanny Wadkins	7	71-70-70-69-69=349	$4,520.00
Kermit Zarley	T-8	68-72-70-71-69=350	$4,520.00
John Mahaffey	T-8	68-73-69-68-72=350	$4,520.00
Charles Coody	10	67-75-68-69-72=351	$4,000.00

Andy Williams-San Diego Open

Course: Torrey Pines (South), Torrey Pines (North), San Diego, Calif.

Home Course -Par: 72 Yardage: 7,021

Last day of event: Sunday, February 18, 1973

Player	Place	Score	Earnings
Bob Dickson	Win	69-68-69-72=278	$34,000.00
Billy Casper	T-2	69-69-72-71=281	$11,602.50
Phil Rodgers	T-2	71-73-71-66=281	$11,602.50
Grier Jones	T-2	69-66-71-75=281	$11,602.50
Bruce Crampton	T-2	67-70-68-76=281	$11,602.50
Dave Eichelberger	T-6	71-68-70-73=282	$5,291.25
Tommy Jacobs	T-6	74-71-72-65=282	$5,291.25
Miller Barber	T-6	70-71-75-66=282	$5,291.25
Chuck Courtney	T-9	70-73-68-72=283	$4,080.00
Doug Sanders	T-9	68-74-71-70=283	$4,080.00

Jackie Gleason's Inverrary Classic

Course: Inverrary G. & C.C. (East), Lauderhill, Fla.

Par: 72 Yardage: 7,128

Last day of event: Sunday, February 25, 1973

Player	Place	Score	Earnings
Lee Trevino	Win	69-69-69-72=279	$52,000.00
Forrest Fezler	2	67-69-68-76=280	$29,640.00
Bob Murphy	3	73-71-66-71=281	$18,460.00
Bruce Devlin	T-4	72-69-69-72=282	$11,440.00
Sam Snead	T-4	74-69-68-71=282	$11,440.00
Johnny Miller	T-6	71-71-70-71=283	$8,092.50
Jack Nicklaus	T-6	73-69-70-71=283	$8,092.50
Gibby Gilbert	T-6	69-70-70-74=283	$8,092.50
Jerry Heard	T-6	74-69-68-72=283	$8,092.50
Ed Sneed	10	72-71-70-71=284	$6,500.00

Florida Citrus Open Invitational

Course: Rio Pinar C.C., Orlando, Fla.

Par: 72 Yardage: 7,012

Last day of event: Sunday, March 4, 1973

Player	Place	Score	Earnings
Bud Allin	Win	66-65-67-67=265	$30,000.00
Charles Coody	2	70-70-67-66=273	$17,100.00
Homero Blancas	T-3	68-69-68-69=274	$7,312.50
Grier Jones	T-3	71-68-68-67=274	$7,312.50
Chi Chi Rodriguez	T-3	64-70-68-72=274	$7,312.50
Kermit Zarley	T-3	73-70-67-64=274	$7,312.50
Gibby Gilbert	7	64-68-71-72=275	$4,800.00
Dave Hill	T-8	67-69-70-70=276	$4,075.00
Bob Dickson	T-8	70-68-69-69=276	$4,075.00
Johnny Miller	T-8	71-66-74-65=276	$4,075.00

Doral-Eastern Open

Course: Doral C.C. (Blue), Miami, Fla.

Par: 72 Yardage: 6,939

Last day of event: Sunday, March 11, 1973

Player	Place	Score	Earnings
Lee Trevino	Win	64-70-71-71=276	$30,000.00
Tom Weiskopf	T-2	72-68-70-67=277	$13,875.00
Bruce Crampton	T-2	73-70-69-65=277	$13,875.00
Rod Curl	T-4	70-68-72-70=280	$6,600.00
Ralph Johnston	T-4	71-72-69-68=280	$6,600.00
Dave Hill	T-6	70-69-70-72=281	$5,100.00
Jerry Heard	T-6	72-70-69-70=281	$5,100.00

Player	Place	Score	Earnings
Bud Allin	T-8	70-70-70-72=282	$4,075.00
John Mahaffey	T-8	72-72-71-67=282	$4,075.00
Homero Blancas	T-8	74-66-71-71=282	$4,075.00

Greater Jacksonville Open
Course: Deerwood C.C., Jacksonville, Fla.
Par: 72 Yardage: 7,088
Last day of event: Sunday, March 18, 1973

Player	Place	Score	Earnings
Jim Colbert	Win	70-65-71-73=279	$26,000.00
Johnny Miller	T-2	66-72-71-71=280	$8,872.50
Dan Sikes, Jr.	T-2	68-70-70-72=280	$8,872.50
Jim Wiechers	T-2	70-68-70-72=280	$8,872.50
Lou Graham	T-2	68-67-73-72=280	$8,872.50
Don Massengale	6	68-71-72-71=282	$4,680.00
Steve Melnyk	T-7	67-72-72-72=283	$3,549.00
Bruce Crampton	T-7	69-72-70-72=283	$3,549.00
John Mahaffey	T-7	71-73-71-68=283	$3,549.00
Homero Blancas	T-7	67-69-74-73=283	$3,549.00
Forrest Fezler	T-7	68-72-74-69=283	$3,549.00

Greater New Orleans Open
Course: Lakewood C.C., New Orleans, La.
Par: 72 Yardage: 7,080
Last day of event: Sunday, March 25, 1973

Player	Place	Score	Earnings
Jack Nicklaus	Win	68-72-71-69=280	$25,000.00
Playoff: Beat Miller Barber with birdie on second extra hole			
Miller Barber	2	70-69-71-70=280	$14,250.00
Lou Graham	3	69-71-68-73=281	$8,875.00
Billy Casper	T-4	70-73-73-67=283	$5,500.00
Tom Watson	T-4	67-74-73-69=283	$5,500.00
Larry Hinson	T-6	72-70-71-71=284	$4,062.33
Leonard Thompson	T-6	74-72-70-68=284	$4,062.34
Lee Elder	T-6	65-74-75-70=284	$4,062.33
Lanny Wadkins	9	71-73-71-70=285	$3,375.00
Gene Littler	T-10	71-71-72-72=286	$2,650.00
John Mahaffey	T-10	71-73-72-70=286	$2,650.00
Ed Sneed	T-10	72-72-73-69=286	$2,650.00
Deane Beman	T-10	73-69-72-72=286	$2,650.00
Labron Harris, Jr.	T-10	74-70-72-70=286	$2,650.00

Greater Greensboro Open
Course: Sedgefield C.C., Greensboro, N.C.
Par: 71 Yardage: 7,012
Last day of event: Monday, April 2, 1973

Player	Place	Score	Earnings
Chi Chi Rodriguez	Win	68-66-67-66=267	$42,000.00
Lou Graham	T-2	68-64-67-69=268	$19,425.00
Ken Still	T-2	69-65-70-64=268	$19,425.00
Gay Brewer	T-4	68-68-70-64=270	$19,425.00
Billy Casper	T-4	67-64-68-71=270	$19,425.00
Bobby Nichols	6	66-71-67-67=271	$7,560.00
Doug Sanders	T-7	65-68-69-70=272	$6,195.00
Rod Funseth	T-7	65-69-68-70=272	$6,195.00
Lee Elder	T-7	64-72-68-68=272	$6,195.00
Bud Allin	T-10	68-67-71-67=273	$5,040.00
Jim Wiechers	T-10	71-67-66-69=273	$5,040.00

Masters
Course: Augusta National G.C., Augusta, Ga.
Par: 72 Yardage: 6,925
Last day of event: Sunday, April 8, 1973

Player	Place	Score	Earnings
Tommy Aaron	Win	68-73-74-68=283	$30,000.00
J.C. Snead	2	70-71-73-70=284	$22,500.00
Jim Jamieson	T-3	73-71-70-71=285	$12,500.00
Peter Oosterhuis	T-3	73-70-68-74=285	$12,500.00
Jack Nicklaus	T-3	69-77-73-66=285	$12,500.00
Bob Goalby	T-6	73-70-71-74=288	$6,250.00
Johnny Miller	T-6	75-69-71-73=288	$6,250.00
Bruce Devlin	T-8	73-72-72-72=289	$4,250.00
Jumbo Ozaki	T-8	69-74-73-73=289	$4,250.00
Gardner Dickinson	T-10	74-70-72-75=291	$3,425.00
Don January	T-10	75-71-75-70=291	$3,425.00
Chi Chi Rodriguez	T-10	72-70-73-76=291	$3,425.00
Gay Brewer	T-10	75-66-74-76=291	$3,425.00

Monsanto Open
Course: Pensacola C.C., Pensacola, Fla.
Par: 72 Yardage: 6,679
Last day of event: Sunday, April 15, 1973

Player	Place	Score	Earnings
Homero Blancas	Win	67-69-66-75=277	$30,000.00
Frank Beard	2	72-66-68-72=278	$17,100.00
Andy North	3	72-68-67-72=279	$10,650.00
Dave Hill	T-4	75-69-68-69=281	$6,200.00
Miller Barber	T-5	73-67-70-71=281	$6,200.00
Bob Charles	T-5	69-71-66-75=281	$6,200.00
Chuck Courtney	T-7	69-72-72-70=283	$4,425.00
Lou Graham	T-7	71-70-70-72=283	$4,425.00
Doug Sanders	T-7	68-71-71-73=283	$4,425.00
Tom Watson	T-10	71-72-72-69=284	$3,075.00
Mike Kallam	T-10	70-72-73-69=284	$3,075.00
Fred Marti	T-10	71-70-70-73=284	$3,075.00
Jim Wiechers	T-10	72-69-73-70=284	$3,075.00
Hale Irwin	T-10	72-71-73-68=284	$3,075.00
Lee Elder	T-10	73-70-71-70=284	$3,075.00

Tournament of Champions
Course: La Costa C.C., Carlsbad, Calif.
Par: 72 Yardage: 6,911
Last day of event: Sunday, April 22, 1973

Player	Place	Score	Earnings
Jack Nicklaus	Win	70-70-68-68=276	$40,000.00
Lee Trevino	2	68-71-71-67=277	$23,404.00
Jim Colbert	3	66-76-70-69=281	$14,628.00
Chi Chi Rodriguez	4	71-72-70-69=282	$9,384.00
Dewitt Weaver	T-5	71-73-70-71=285	$6,921.40
J.C. Snead	T-5	72-68-72-73=285	$6,921.40
Bruce Crampton	T-5	73-68-70-74=285	$6,921.40
Lanny Wadkins	T-5	70-75-70-70=285	$6,921.40
Jim Jamieson	T-5	68-76-70-71=285	$6,921.40
Bob Dickson	T-10	70-73-72-73=288	$5,516.00
Grier Jones	T-10	69-75-73-71=288	$5,516.00

Tallahassee Open

Course: Killearn C.C., Tallahassee, Fla.
Par: 72 Yardage: 7,124
Last day of event: Sunday, April 22, 1973

Player	Place	Score	Earnings
Hubert Green	Win	69-67-70-71=277	$15,000.00
Jim Simons	2	69-71-68-70=278	$8,550.00
Dave Hill	T-3	70-70-71-68=279	$4,425.00
Bob Murphy	T-3	70-67-70-72=279	$4,425.00
Wilf Homeniuik	T-5	69-71-71-69=280	$2,381.33
Allen Miller	T-5	71-71-68-70=280	$2,381.33
Charles Sifford	T-5	69-70-69-72=280	$2,381.33
Tom Watson	T-5	71-69-72-68=280	$2,381.34
Frank Beard	T-5	72-69-67-72=280	$2,381.33
Richard Crawford	T-5	68-71-73-68=280	$2,381.34

Byron Nelson Golf Classic

Course: Preston Trail G.C., Dallas, Texas
Par: 70 Yardage: 6,993
Last day of event: Sunday, April 29, 1973

Player	Place	Score	Earnings
Lanny Wadkins	Win	71-68-71-67=277	$30,000.00
Playoff: Beat Dan Sikes, Jr. with par on first extra hole			
Dan Sikes, Jr.	2	70-68-68-71=277	$17,100.00
Bob Dickson	3	69-66-71-73=279	$10,650.00
Bruce Crampton	4	71-70-69-70=280	$7,050.00
Bert Greene	5	70-70-70-71=281	$6,150.00
Chuck Courtney	T-6	71-71-72-68=282	$5,100.00
Bert Yancey	T-6	69-69-71-73=282	$5,100.00
Tom Weiskopf	T-8	69-70-71-73=283	$3,765.00
Leonard Thompson	T-8	72-68-70-73=283	$3,765.00
Ron Cerrudo	T-8	73-70-71-69=283	$3,765.00
Dave Stockton	T-8	72-68-74-69=283	$3,765.00
Julius Boros	T-8	70-68-76-69=283	$3,765.00

Houston Open

Course: Quail Valley G.C., Houston, Texas
Par: 72 Yardage: 6,905
Last day of event: Sunday, May 6, 1973

Player	Place	Score	Earnings
Bruce Crampton	Win	72-66-67-72=277	$41,000.00
Dave Stockton	2	70-71-70-67=278	$23,370.00
Lanny Wadkins	3	71-69-69-72=281	$14,555.00
Leonard Thompson	T-4	72-71-69-70=282	$9,020.00
Charles Coody	T-4	72-69-72-69=282	$9,020.00
Rod Funseth	T-6	71-71-71-70=283	$7,380.00
Ben Crenshaw	T-6	69-71-72-71=283	
David Graham	T-8	72-72-71-69=284	$6,304.00
David Glenz	T-8	74-70-71-69=284	$6,304.00
Ed Sneed	T-10	72-70-71-72=285	$5,330.00
Chuck Thorpe	T-10	72-70-72-71=285	$5,330.00

Colonial National Invitational

Course: Colonial C.C., Fort Worth, Texas
Par: 70 Yardage: 7,142
Last day of event: Sunday, May 13, 1973

Player	Place	Score	Earnings
Tom Weiskopf	Win	69-68-70-69=276	$30,000.00
Jerry Heard	T-2	69-69-71-68=277	$13,875.00
Bruce Crampton	T-2	66-69-69-73=277	$13,875.00

Lee Elder	4	70-68-69-71=278	$7,050.00
Julius Boros	5	69-72-70-69=280	$6,150.00
Kermit Zarley	T-6	71-70-71-69=281	$5,100.00
Hale Irwin	T-6	70-69-72-70=281	$5,100.00
Mason Rudolph	T-8	73-69-67-73=282	$4,075.00
John Mahaffey	T-8	73-70-69-70=282	$4,075.00
Leonard Thompson	T-8	74-67-71-70=282	$4,075.00

Danny Thomas Memphis Classic

Course: Colonial C.C. (South), Cordova, Tenn.
Par: 72 Yardage: 7,282
Last day of event: Sunday, May 20, 1973

Player	Place	Score	Earnings
Dave Hill	Win	68-69-74-72=283	$35,000.00
Lee Trevino	T-2	71-72-71-70=284	$16,187.50
Allen Miller	T-2	70-73-72-69=284	$16,187.50
Gene Littler	T-4	71-73-70-71=285	$6,492.60
David Glenz	T-4	72-71-73-69=285	$6,492.60
Charles Sifford	T-4	72-73-73-67=285	$6,492.60
Hale Irwin	T-4	76-73-66-70=285	$6,492.60
Larry Ziegler	T-4	74-68-74-79=285	$6,492.60
Hubert Green	T-9	72-71-72-71=286	$4,550.00
Bert Greene	T-9	71-74-69-72=286	$4,550.00

Atlanta Classic

Course: Atlanta C.C., Atlanta, Ga.
Par: 72 Yardage: 7,007
Last day of event: Sunday, May 27, 1973

Player	Place	Score	Earnings
Jack Nicklaus	Win	67-66-66-73=272	$30,000.00
Tom Weiskopf	2	70-67-68-69=274	$17,100.00
Al Geiberger	3	70-69-68-72=279	$11,650.00
Hubert Green	T-4	68-71-69-73=281	$5,775.00
Doug Sanders	T-4	72-73-68-68=281	$5,775.00
Johnny Miller	T-6	70-71-70-71=282	$4,425.00
Lee Elder	T-6	70-73-70-69=282	$4,425.00
Gay Brewer	T-6	70-73-65-74=282	$4,425.00
Pat Fitzsimons	T-9	70-71-72-70=283	$3,600.00
Lou Graham	T-9	73-66-73-71=283	$3,600.00

Kemper Open

Course: Quail Hollow C.C., Charlotte, N.C.
Par: 72 Yardage: 7,205
Last day of event: Sunday, June 3, 1973

Player	Place	Score	Earnings
Tom Weiskopf	Win	65-70-68-68=271	$40,000.00
Lanny Wadkins	2	66-68-71-69=274	$22,800.00
Dave Hill	T-3	71-68-67-71=277	$10,600.00
Lou Graham	T-3	72-66-72-67=277	$10,600.00
Leonard Thompson	T-3	67-65-74-71=277	$10,600.00
Art Wall, Jr.	T-6	70-68-70-70=278	$5,750.00
John Lister	T-6	71-70-70-67=278	$5,750.00
Mac McLendon	T-6	67-72-72-67=278	$5,750.00
Dan Sikes, Jr.	T-6	70-69-72-67=278	$5,750.00
Cesar Sanudo	T-6	71-69-66-72=278	$5,750.00
Ken Still	T-6	67-67-71-73=278	$5,750.00

IVB Philadelphia Golf Classic

Course: Whitemarsh Valley C.C., Chestnut Hill, Pa.
Par: 72 Yardage: 6,708
Last day of event: Sunday, June 10, 1973

Player	Place	Score	Earnings
Tom Weiskopf	Win	67-71-65-71=274	$30,045.00
Jim Barber	2	65-67-76-70=278	$17,125.65
Forrest Fezler	T-3	68-67-72-72=279	$8,863.28
Johnny Miller	T-3	74-65-69-71=279	$8,863.28
Gay Brewer	T-5	70-70-71-69=280	$5,201.54
Dave Eichelberger	T-5	72-71-70-67=280	$5,201.54
John Schlee	T-5	70-66-73-71=280	$5,201.54
Jack Nicklaus	T-5	73-70-70-67=280	$5,201.55
Miller Barber	T-9	68-71-71-71=281	$3,605.40
Dave Barber	T-9	69-67-73-72=281	$3,605.40
Bruce Crampton	T-9	71-73-67-70=281	$3,605.40
Ken Still	T-9	74-70-68-69=281	$3,605.40

U.S. Open

Course: Oakmont C.C., Oakmont, Pa.
Par: 71 Yardage: 6,921
Last day of event: Sunday, June 17, 1973

Player	Place	Score	Earnings
Johnny Miller	Win	71-69-76-63=279	$35,000.00
John Schlee	2	73-70-67-70=280	$18,000.00
Tom Weiskopf	3	73-69-69-70=281	$13,000.00
Lee Trevino	T-4	70-72-70-70=282	$9,000.00
Arnold Palmer	T-4	71-71-68-72=282	$9,000.00
Jack Nicklaus	T-4	71-69-74-68=282	$9,000.00
Julius Boros	T-7	73-69-68-73=283	$6,000.00
Jerry Heard	T-7	74-70-66-73=283	$6,000.00
Lanny Wadkins	T-7	74-69-75-65=283	$6,000.00
Jim Colbert	10	70-68-74-72=284	$4,000.00

American Golf Classic

Course: Firestone C.C. (South), Akron, Ohio
Par: 70 Yardage: 7,180
Last day of event: Sunday, June 24, 1973

Player	Place	Score	Earnings
Bruce Crampton	Win	70-67-68-68=273	$32,000.00
Lanny Wadkins	T-2	71-67-70-68=276	$12,373.33
Gay Brewer	T-2	72-69-64-71=276	$12,373.33
Bob Murphy	T-2	72-68-69-67=276	$12,373.34
Tom Weiskopf	T-5	74-66-64-73=277	$6,160.00
Forrest Fezler	T-5	67-65-70-75=277	$6,160.00
Gene Littler	7	72-69-66-71=278	$5,120.00
Julius Boros	8	71-70-68-70=279	$4,720.00
Arnold Palmer	T-9	68-71-71-70=280	$3,680.00
Frank Beard	T-9	70-72-71-67=280	$3,680.00
Jack Nicklaus	T-9	69-70-73-68=280	$3,680.00
Bert Yancey	T-9	71-65-73-71=280	$3,680.00
John Mahaffey	T-9	71-67-75-67=280	$3,680.00

Western Open

Course: Midlothian C.C., Midlothian, Ill.
Par: 71 Yardage: 6,654, Last day of event: Sunday, July 1, 1973

Player	Place	Score	Earnings
Billy Casper	Win	67-69-67-69=272	$35,000.00
Larry Hinson	T-2	68-70-68-67=273	$16,187.50
Hale Irwin	T-2	67-66-71-69=273	$16,187.50

Hubert Green	T-4	68-71-70-65=274	$7,233.34
J.C. Snead	T-4	67-72-69-66=274	$7,233.33
Bruce Crampton	T-4	66-69-66-73=274	$7,233.33
Arnold Palmer	T-7	66-71-68-71=276	$5,381.50
Art Wall, Jr.	T-7	72-70-67-67=276	$5,381.50
John Mahaffey	9	68-71-68-70=277	$4,725.00
George Archer	T-10	69-72-70-67=278	$4,025.00
Bob Murphy	T-10	73-67-72-66=278	$4,025.00
Bruce Devlin	T-10	68-69-74-67=278	$4,025.00

Greater Milwaukee Open

Course: Tuckaway C.C., Franklin, Wis.
Par: 72 Yardage: 7,030
Last day of event: Sunday, July 8, 1973

Player	Place	Score	Earnings
Dave Stockton	Win	69-63-71-73=276	$26,000.00
Homero Blancas	T-2	67-71-71-68=277	$12,025.00
Hubert Green	T-2	68-70-71-68=277	$12,025.00
George Knudson	4	71-71-69-67=278	$6,110.00
Bob Goalby	5	65-71-69-74=279	$5,330.00
Bud Allin	T-6	66-73-71-70=280	$4,420.00
Charles Sifford	T-6	71-69-74-66=280	$4,420.00
Roy Pace	T-8	68-71-70-72=281	$3,672.50
Jerry Heard	T-8	69-71-72-69=281	$3,672.50
Jim Ferriell	T-10	70-73-69-70=282	$3,120.00
Billy Ziobro	T-10	70-75-70-67=282	$3,120.00

British Open

Course: Royal Troon G.C., Troon, Ayrshire, Scotland
Par: 72 Yardage: 7,064
Last day of event: Saturday, July 14, 1973

Player	Place	Score	Earnings
Tom Weiskopf	Win	68-67-71-70=276	$14,300.00
Johnny Miller	T-2	70-68-69-72=279	$9,425.00
Neil Coles	T-2	71-72-70-66=279	$9,425.00
Jack Nicklaus	4	69-70-76-65=280	$7,150.00
Bert Yancey	5	69-69-73-70=281	$6,370.00
Peter Butler	6	71-72-74-69=286	$5,590.00
Bob Charles	T-7	73-71-73-71=288	$4,463.34
Lanny Wadkins	T-7	71-73-70-74=288	$4,463.34
Christy O'Connor	T-7	73-68-74-73=288	$4,463.34
Harold Henning	T-10	73-73-73-70=289	$3,510.00
Lee Trevino	T-10	75-73-73-68=289	$3,510.00
Brian Barnes	T-10	76-67-70-76=289	$3,510.00
Gay Brewer	T-10	76-71-72-70=289	$3,510.00

Shrine-Robinson Golf Classic

Course: Crawford C.C., Robinson, Ill.
Par: 71 Yardage: 6,556
Last day of event: Sunday, July 15, 1973

Player	Place	Score	Earnings
Deane Beman	Win	69-68-67-67=271	$25,000.00
Bunky Henry	T-2	69-69-68-66=272	$11,562.50
Bob Dickson	T-2	70-68-68-66=272	$11,562.50
Chuck Courtney	4	68-70-66-69=273	$5,875.00
Larry Hinson	5	71-72-64-67=274	$5,125.00
George Archer	T-6	68-70-69-68=275	$4,250.00
Andy North	T-6	73-65-67-70=275	$4,250.00
Bob Lewis, Jr.	T-6	71-67-68-70=276	$3,395.66
Billy Ziobro	T-6	71-68-69-68=276	$3,395.67
Labron Harris, Jr.	T-6	66-72-69-69=276	$3,395.67

St. Louis Children's Hospital Golf Classic
Course: Norwood Hills C.C., Normandy, Mo.
Par: 70 Yardage: 6,544
Last day of event: Sunday, July 22, 1973

Player	Place	Score	Earnings
Gene Littler	Win	66-66-68-68=268	$42,000.00
Bruce Crampton	2	71-66-65-67=269	$23,940.00
Bert Yancey	T-3	68-69-68-66=271	$11,130.00
Bob Goalby	T-3	65-68-67-71=271	$11,130.00
Lee Trevino	T-3	69-64-66-72=271	$11,130.00
Jim Ferriell	T-6	67-67-70-68=272	$6,279.00
Mike Wynn	T-6	67-67-70-68=272	$6,279.00
Hubert Green	T-6	70-68-67-67=272	$6,279.00
Tom Watson	T-6	72-67-66-67=272	$6,279.00
Tom Shaw	T-6	73-63-69-67=272	$6,279.00

Canadian Open
Course: Richelieu Valley G. & C.C., Ste. Julie De Vercheres, Quebec, Canada
Par: 72 Yardage: 6,905
Last day of event: Sunday, July 29, 1973

Player	Place	Score	Earnings
Tom Weiskopf	Win	67-73-68-70=278	$35,000.00
Forrest Fezler	2	67-71-71-71=280	$19,950.00
Bobby Cole	3	68-74-73-66=281	$12,425.00
Hale Irwin	4	65-75-74-68=282	$8,225.00
Chuck Courtney	5	71-70-70-72=283	$7,175.00
Bruce Crampton	T-6	72-69-72-71=284	$5,447.00
Jim Ferriell	T-6	71-70-70-73=284	$5,447.00
Bobby Mitchell	T-6	69-70-71-74=284	$5,447.00
Jim Colbert	T-6	71-75-69-69=284	$5,447.00
Tommy Aaron	T-10	74-71-72-68=285	$4,025.00
Arnold Palmer	T-10	70-75-70-70=285	$4,025.00
Hubert Green	T-10	67-71-77-70=285	$4,025.00

Westchester Classic
Course: Westchester C.C., Harrison, N.Y.
Par: 72 Yardage: 6,614
Last day of event: Sunday, August 5, 1973

Player	Place	Score	Earnings
Bobby Nichols	Win	70-67-70-65=272	$50,000.00
Playoff: Beat Bob Murphy with birdie on second extra hole			
Bob Murphy	2	67-70-68-67=272	$28,500.00
Tom Weiskopf	T-3	64-69-69-71=273	$28,500.00
Dan Sikes, Jr.	T-3	70-65-67-71=273	$28,500.00
Frank Beard	T-5	68-67-68-71=274	$9,083.33
Gene Littler	T-5	68-69-71-66=274	$9,083.33
Gibby Gilbert	T-5	67-72-68-67=274	$9,083.34
David Glenz	8	69-70-66-70=275	$7,375.00
Jack Nicklaus	T-9	70-68-69-69=276	$6,250.00
Bob-E. Smith	T-9	69-70-71-66=276	$6,250.00
Bobby Cole	T-9	70-68-65-73=276	$6,250.00

PGA Championship
Course: Canterbury G.C., Cleveland, Ohio
Par: 71 Yardage: 6,852
Last day of event: Sunday, August 12, 1973

Player	Place	Score	Earnings
Jack Nicklaus	Win	72-68-68-69=277	$45,000.00
Bruce Crampton	2	71-73-67-70=281	$25,700.00
Mason Rudolph	T-3	69-70-70-73=282	$11,908.33
Lanny Wadkins	T-3	73-69-71-69=282	$11,908.33
J.C. Snead	T-3	71-74-68-69=282	$11,908.34
Tom Weiskopf	T-6	70-71-71-71=283	$7,311.67
Dan Sikes, Jr.	T-6	72-68-72-71=283	$7,311.67
Don Iverson	T-6	67-72-70-74=283	$7,311.66
Sam Snead	T-9	71-71-71-71=284	$5,625.00
Kermit Zarley	T-9	76-71-68-69=284	$5,625.00
Hale Irwin	T-9	76-72-68-68=284	$5,625.00

USI Classic
Course: Pleasant Valley C.C., Sutton, Mass.
Par: 72 Yardage: 7,241
Last day of event: Sunday, August 19, 1973

Player	Place	Score	Earnings
Lanny Wadkins	Win	71-69-70-69=279	$40,000.00
Tom Jenkins	T-2	69-71-70-71=281	$15,466.66
Lee Elder	T-2	72-70-70-69=281	$15,466.67
Rik Massengale	T-2	68-70-69-74=281	$15,466.67
Bobby Mitchell	T-5	70-67-73-72=282	$7,700.00
Jim Wiechers	T-5	71-67-71-73=282	$7,700.00
Roy Pace	T-7	69-73-73-68=283	$5,900.00
Miller Barber	T-7	71-70-73-69=283	$5,900.00
Bert Yancey	T-7	68-75-72-68=283	$5,900.00
Tom Shaw	T-10	73-66-73-72=284	$4,400.00
Gene Littler	T-10	73-70-71-70=284	$4,400.00
Larry Hinson	T-10	73-72-71-68=284	$4,400.00
Frank Beard	T-10	74-69-70-71=284	$4,400.00

U.S. Professional Match Play Championship
Course: MacGregor Downs C.C., Gary, N.C.
Par: 71 Yardage: 6,786
Last day of event: Sunday, August 26, 1973

Player	Place	Score	Earnings
John Schroeder	Win		$40,000.00
Round One - Beat Grier Jones 1 up			
Round Two - Beat Bud Allin 5 & 4			
Semifinals - Beat Lee Trevino 1 up			
Finals - Beat DeWitt Weaver 2 up			
Dewitt Weaver	2		$22,000.00
Round One - Beat George Archer 1 up			
Round Two - Beat Artie McNickle 2 & 1			
Semifinals - Beat Tom Weiskopf 4 & 3			
Finals - Lost to John Schroeder 2 up			
Lee Trevino	T-3	$10,000.00	
Round One - Beat Dan Sikes 1 up			
Round Two - Beat Jack Nicklaus 4 & 3			
Semifinals - Lost to John Schroeder 1 up			
Tom Weiskopf	T-3	$10,000.00	
Round One - Beat Allen Miller 3 & 2			
Round Two - Beat J.C. Snead 4 & 3			
Semifinals - Lost to DeWitt Weaver 1 up			
Jack Nicklaus	T-5	$7,000.00	
Round One - Beat Joe Porter 2 up			
Round Two - Lost to Lee Trevino 4 & 3			
Bud Allin	T-5	$7,000.00	
Round One - Beat Tommy Aaron 2 up			
Round Two - Lost to John Schroeder 5 & 4			
Artie McNickle	T-5	$7,000.00	
Round One - Beat Johnny Miller 2 & 1			
Round Two - Lost to DeWitt Weaver 2 & 1			
J.C. Snead	T-5	$7,000.00	
Round One - Beat Jerry Heard 1 up			
Round Two - Lost to Tom Weiskopf 4 & 3			

Joe Porter	T-9		$5,000.00
Round One - Lost to Jack Nicklaus 2 up			
Dan Sikes, Jr.	T-9		$5,000.00
Round One - Lost to Lee Trevino 1 up			
Tommy Aaron	T-9		$5,000.00
Round One - Lost to Bud Allin 2 up			
Grier Jones	T-9		$5,000.00
Round One - Lost to John Schroeder 1 up			
Johnny Miller	T-9		$5,000.00
Round One - Lost to Artie McNickle 2 & 1			
George Archer	T-9		$5,000.00
Round One - Lost to DeWitt Weaver 1 up			
Allen Miller	T-9		$5,000.00
Round One - Lost to Tom Weiskopf 3 & 2			
Jerry Heard	T-9		$5,000.00
Round One - Lost to J.C. Snead 1 up			

Liggett Meyers Open

Course: MacGregor Downs C.C., Gary, N.C.
Par: 71 Yardage: 6,786
Last day of event: Sunday, August 26, 1973

Player	Place	Score	Earnings
Bert Greene	Win	68-73-67-70=278	$20,000.00
Playoff: Beat Miller Barber with birdie on fifth extra hole			
Miller Barber	2	73-70-68-67=278	$11,400.00
Lanny Wadkins	T-3	71-69-70-69=279	$5,967.50
Bob-E. Smith	T-3	72-68-69-70=279	$5,967.50
Larry Wise	T-5	70-71-71-68=280	$3,961.00
Rod Curl	T-5	72-70-74-64=280	$3,961.00
Lionel Hebert	7	74-70-68-69=281	$3,292.00
Rik Massengale	T-8	71-69-71-71=282	$2,906.50
Tom Jenkins	T-8	71-71-72-68=282	$2,906.50
Julius Boros	T-10	71-71-69-72=283	$2,469.00
Dave Stockton	T-10	67-73-70-73=283	$2,469.00

Sammy Davis, Jr. - Greater Hartford Open

Course: Wethersfield C.C., Wethersfield, Conn.
Par: 71 Yardage: 6,568
Last day of event: Monday, September 3, 1973

Player	Place	Score	Earnings
Billy Casper	Win	67-65-68-64=264	$40,000.00
Bruce Devlin	2	65-67-67-66=265	$22,800.00
Lee Elder	T-3	67-68-67-64=266	$9,750.00
Arnold Palmer	T-3	68-65-67-66=266	$9,750.00
Jim Wiechers	T-3	65-66-69-66=266	$9,750.00
Lee Trevino	T-3	67-65-69-65=266	$9,750.00
Gary Player	T-7	66-67-67-67=267	$5,460.00
Don Bies	T-7	66-67-70-64=267	$5,460.00
Bob Payne	T-7	70-66-64-67=267	$5,460.00
Tom Kite	T-7	68-71-63-65=267	$5,460.00
Hubert Green	T-7	63-73-63-68=267	$5,460.00

Southern Open

Course: Green Island C.C., Columbus, Ga.
Par: 70 Yardage: 6,791
Last day of event: Sunday, September 9, 1973

Player	Place	Score	Earnings
Gary Player	Win	69-65-67-69=270	$20,030.00
Forrest Fezler	2	69-68-66-68=271	$11,417.10
Jerry McGee	3	69-69-67-69=274	$7,110.75
Curtis Sifford	T-4	68-69-69-70=276	$4,406.60

Sam Adams	T-4	72-69-66-69=276	$4,406.60
Dewitt Weaver	T-6	70-68-67-72=277	$3,254.88
Grier Jones	T-6	67-67-73-70=277	$3,254.88
Dick Rhyan	T-6	75-69-63-70=277	$3,254.89
Roy Pace	T-9	70-71-70-67=278	$2,403.60
Bob Menne	T-9	71-67-72-68=278	$2,403.60
John Schroeder	T-9	67-65-73-73=278	$2,403.60
Butch Baird	T-9	70-73-69-66=278	$2,403.60

Sea Pines Heritage Classic

Course: Harbour Town G.L., Hilton Head, S.C.
Par: 71 Yardage: 6,657
Last day of event: Sunday, September 16, 1973

Player	Place	Score	Earnings
Hale Irwin	Win	69-66-65-72=272	$30,000.00
Jerry Heard	T-2	69-71-67-70=277	$13,875.00
Grier Jones	T-2	70-68-71-68=277	$13,875.00
Jim Wiechers	4	67-73-72-68=280	$7,050.00
Gary Player	5	69-72-68-72=281	$6,150.00
Andy North	T-6	71-71-70-70=282	$5,100.00
Jerry McGee	T-6	74-66-72-70=282	$5,100.00
Dave Eichelberger	T-8	73-68-70-72=283	$4,237.50
Ben Crenshaw	T-8	69-75-69-70=283	$4,237.50
Arnold Palmer	T-10	70-73-71-70=284	$3,300.00
Bert Greene	T-10	71-71-69-73=284	$3,300.00
Jim Jamieson	T-10	73-71-72-68=284	$3,300.00
Forrest Fezler	T-10	70-71-68-75=284	$3,300.00

B.C. Open

Course: En-Joie G.C., Endicott, N.Y.
Par: 71 Yardage: 6,966
Last day of event: Sunday, September 23, 1973

Player	Place	Score	Earnings
Hubert Green	Win	69-65-65-67=266	$20,000.00
Dwight Nevil	2	68-66-72-66=272	$11,400.00
Bob-E. Smith	T-3	65-69-72-70=276	$5,900.00
Larry Ziegler	T-3	70-72-67-67=276	$5,900.00
John Lister	T-5	70-70-70-67=277	$3,850.00
Bert Greene	T-5	68-68-68-73=277	$3,850.00
Mike Wynn	T-7	68-72-68-70=278	$2,837.50
Tommy McGinnis	T-7	68-71-72-67=278	$2,837.50
Bob Allard	T-7	69-72-70-67=278	$2,837.50
Jim Simons	T-7	72-67-71-68=278	$2,837.50

Quad Cities Open

Course: Crow Valley C.C., Bettendorf, Iowa
Par: 71 Yardage: 6,501
Last day of event: Sunday, September 30, 1973

Player	Place	Score	Earnings
Sam Adams	Win	72-64-64-68=268	$20,000.00
Dwight Nevil	T-2	64-71-67-69=271	$9,250.00
Kermit Zarley	T-2	66-66-72-67=271	$9,250.00
Dave Stockton	T-4	64-69-70-69=272	$4,400.00
Bob Goalby	T-4	65-69-71-67=272	$4,400.00
Hale Irwin	T-6	68-66-70-70=274	$3,250.00
Deane Beman	T-6	68-69-67-70=274	$3,250.00
Bob Wynn	T-6	70-65-68-71=274	$3,250.00
Bob Payne	T-9	69-68-69-69=275	$2,142.86
Jim Ahern	T-9	68-69-70-68=275	$2,142.86
Rod Curl	T-9	69-70-69-67=275	$2,142.86
David Glenz	T-9	68-71-68-68=275	$2,142.86

Player	Place	Score	Earnings
Frank Beard	T-9	68-73-64-70=275	$2,142.85
Larry Wise	T-9	74-69-72-70=275	$2,142.85

Ohio Kings Island Open
Course: Jack Nicklaus Golf Center, Mason, Ohio
Par: 71 Yardage: 6,915
Last day of event: Sunday, October 7, 1973

Player	Place	Score	Earnings
Jack Nicklaus	Win	68-69-62-72=271	$25,000.00
Lee Trevino	2	72-68-69-68=277	$14,250.00
Tom Weiskopf	T-3	70-70-70-71=281	$7,375.00
Andy North	T-3	74-68-70-69=281	$7,375.00
Tom Kite	5	70-72-72-68=282	$5,125.00
John Lister	6	72-69-67-75=283	$4,500.00
Tom Watson	T-7	71-71-70-72=284	$3,687.33
Rod Curl	T-7	69-71-70-74=284	$3,687.33
Billy Ziobro	T-7	70-75-70-69=284	$3,687.34
J.C. Snead	T-10	71-70-70-74=285	$2,650.00
John Schroeder	T-10	69-75-73-68=285	$2,650.00
Mac McLendon	T-10	72-75-69-69=285	$2,650.00
Curtis Sifford	T-10	75-72-70-68=285	$2,650.00
Bobby Nichols	T-10	75-71-72-67=285	$2,650.00

Kaiser International Open
Course: Silverado C.C., Napa, Calif.
Home Course -Par: 72 Yardage: 6,849
Last day of event: Sunday, October 21, 1973

Player	Place	Score	Earnings
Ed Sneed	Win	68-66-69-72=275	$30,091.60

Playoff: Beat John Schlee with par on first extra hole

Player	Place	Score	Earnings
John Schlee	2	66-67-70-72=275	$17,152.15
Hale Irwin	3	69-66-69-73=277	$10,682.55
John Mahaffey	4	68-70-72-69=279	$7,071.55
Lou Graham	T-5	71-69-69-71=280	$4,980.19
George Archer	T-5	67-72-71-70=280	$4,980.19
Dan Sikes, Jr.	T-5	72-67-70-71=280	$4,980.19
Jim Ferriell	T-5	72-68-72-68=280	$4,980.19
Bert Yancey	T-5	74-69-67-70=280	$4,980.19
Dave Stockton	T-10	70-70-71-70=281	$3,460.57
Dave Eichelberger	T-10	69-69-72-71=281	$3,460.57
Kermit Zarley	T-10	70-69-69-73=281	$3,460.56

Sahara Invitational
Course: Sahara Nevada C.C., Las Vegas, Nev.
Home course / Par: 71 Yardage: 6,880
Last day of event: Sunday, October 28, 1973

Player	Place	Score	Earnings
John Mahaffey	Win	68-66-69-68=271	$27,000.00
Dave Eichelberger	2	70-69-71-64=274	$15,390.00
Allen Miller	T-3	65-72-70-68=275	$7,965.00
Jim Ferriell	T-3	68-67-73-67=275	$7,965.00
Mike Hill	T-5	71-70-71-64=276	$4,905.00
Larry Ziegler	T-5	72-67-65-72=276	$4,905.00
Lou Graham	T-5	67-67-69-73=276	$4,905.00
Hubert Green	8	70-71-70-66=277	$3,983.00
John Schroeder	9	69-72-69-68=278	$3,645.00
Ben Kern	T-10	67-71-70-71=279	$3,240.00
Jim Wiechers	T-10	71-70-68-70=279	$3,240.00

San Antonio Texas Open
Course: Woodlake G.C., San Antonio, Texas
Par: 71 Yardage: 6,990
Last day of event: Sunday, November 4, 1973

Player	Place	Score	Earnings
Ben Crenshaw	Win	65-72-66-67=270	$25,000.00
Orville Moody	2	68-70-67-67=272	$14,250.00
George Archer	3	68-69-67-69=273	$8,875.00
Rod Funseth	4	69-70-68-69=276	$5,875.00
Dave Eichelberger	T-5	70-70-69-68=277	$4,812.50
Jack Ewing	T-5	73-70-68-66=277	$4,812.50
Steve Melnyk	T-7	69-70-69-70=278	$3,546.75
Tom Jenkins	T-7	71-71-69-67=278	$3,546.75
John Mahaffey	T-7	69-70-72-67=278	$3,546.75
Homero Blancas	T-7	72-68-71-67=278	$3,546.75

World Open
Course: Pinehurst C.C. (No 2 & No 4), Pinehurst, N.C.
Par: 71 Yardage: 7,007
Last day of event: Saturday, November 17, 1973

Player	Place	Score	Earnings
Miller Barber	Win	68-74-73-74-67-73-72-69=570	$100,000.00
Ben Crenshaw	2	75-71-73-75-71-64-73-71=573	$44,175.00
Leonard Thompson	3	73-71-74-72-69-72-73-71=575	$27,513.00
Al Geiberger	T-4	72-72-73-68-74-73-74-70=576	$17,050.00
Tom Watson	T-4	74-74-69-68-62-76-76-77=576	$17,050.00
Jim Jamieson	6	74-72-73-72-73-70-71-72=577	$13,950.00
Hale Irwin	T-7	74-74-75-74-71-73-69-68=578	$11,915.00
Bobby Mitchell	T-7	72-73-70-72-69-75-70-77=578	$11,915.00
Mike McCullough	T-9	69-77-72-71-74-71-71-74=579	$10,075.00
Jerry Heard	T-9	72-70-71-74-70-72-77-73=579	$10,075.00

Walt Disney World Open
Course: Walt Disney (Magnolia, Palm), Lake Buena Vista, Fla.
Home course / Magnolia, Par: 72 Yardage: 7,190
Last day of event: Saturday, December 1, 1973

Player	Place	Score	Earnings
Jack Nicklaus	Win	70-71-67-67=275	$30,000.00
Mason Rudolph	2	71-70-67-68=276	$17,100.00
John Mahaffey	3	69-68-69-71=277	$10,650.00
Lou Graham	T-4	69-70-70-69=278	$6,200.00
John Schlee	T-4	70-71-67-70=278	$6,200.00
Hubert Green	T-4	72-74-63-69=278	$6,200.00
Miller Barber	7	74-68-67-70=279	$4,800.00
Rod Curl	8	69-71-69-71=280	$4,425.00
Nate Starks	T-9	69-70-69-73=281	$3,900.00
Homero Blancas	T-9	73-73-67-68=281	$3,900.00

1974

Johnny Miller posted eight victories in 1974, but his best finish in a major was 10th at the British Open. Gary Player won his second Masters, the victory coming 13 years after Player had donned his first green jacket. Hale Irwin shot 7-over-par 287 to win the U.S. Open, later dubbed the "Massacre at Winged Foot." Player scored a 4-shot victory in the British Open, which featured a now-familiar international flavor with five Americans, two South Africans, an Englishman, a Taiwanese and a Belgian in the top 10. Lee Trevino notched a one-shot victory over Jack Nicklaus at the PGA Championship, where Sam Snead, at age 62, tied for third. Tom Watson won the Western Open, the first of his 39 PGA Tour career victories. Deane Beman began his 21-year reign as commissioner of the PGA Tour.

Bing Crosby Pro-Am

Courses: Pebble Beach G.L., Spyglass Hill G.C., Cypress Point C.C., Pebble Beach, Calif.
Home Course / Pebble Beach, G.L., Par: 72 Yardage: 6,815
Last day of event: Sunday, January 6, 1974

Player	Place	Score	Earnings
Johnny Miller	Win	68-70-70=208	$27,750.00
Grier Jones	2	71-69-72=212	$15,817.50
Rod Funseth	T-3	72-70-72=214	$6,764.06
John Jacobs	T-3	74-68-72=214	$6,764.06
Bruce Summerhays	T-3	74-71-69=214	$6,764.07
David Glenz	T-7	70-72-73=215	$4,266.38
Dave Eichelberger	T-7	69-74-72=215	$4,266.37
Dave Stockton	T-9	73-70-73=216	$3,075.62
Bruce Crampton	T-9	73-72-71=216	$3,075.63
Bob Eastwood	T-9	71-71-74=216	$3,075.63
Barney Thompson	T-9	67-75-74=216	$3,075.62
Bob-E. Smith	T-9	74-75-67=216	$3,075.63
Mike Morley	T-9	76-69-71=216	$3,075.62

Phoenix Open

Course: Phoenix C.C., Phoenix, Ariz.
Par: 71 Yardage: 6,726
Last day of event: Sunday, January 13, 1974

Player	Place	Score	Earnings
Johnny Miller	Win	69-69-66-67=271	$30,000.00
Lanny Wadkins	2	69-69-69-65=272	$17,100.00
Miller Barber	T-3	68-68-68-70=274	$7,950.00
Hubert Green	T-3	69-70-69-66=274	$7,950.00
John Schroeder	T-3	69-70-69-66=274	$7,950.00
Dave Stockton	T-6	72-68-68-67=275	$5,100.00
Gene Littler	T-6	74-68-65-68=275	$5,100.00
John Mahaffey	8	69-70-66-72=277	$4,425.00
Mark Hayes	T-9	67-72-70-69=278	$3,750.00
Mike McCullough	T-9	69-69-72-68=278	$3,750.00
Dewitt Weaver	T-9	72-70-67-69=278	$3,750.00

Dean Martin Tucson Open

Course: Tucson National G.C., Starr Pass G.C., Tucson, Ariz.
Par: 72 Yardage: 7,305
Last day of event: Sunday, January 20, 1974

Player	Place	Score	Earnings
Johnny Miller	Win	62-71-71-68=272	$30,000.00
Ben Crenshaw	2	70-69-67-69=275	$17,100.00
J.C. Snead	T-3	70-71-65-70=276	$8,850.00
Jerry Heard	T-3	66-73-68-69=276	$8,850.00
Rod Curl	5	69-70-71-67=277	$6,150.00
Kermit Zarley	T-6	68-71-68-71=278	$4,875.00
Bobby Mitchell	T-6	69-73-69-67=278	$4,875.00
Al Geiberger	T-6	69-74-69-66=278	$4,875.00
Jim Colbert	T-9	71-67-70-71=279	$3,750.00
Grier Jones	T-9	72-71-69-67=279	$3,750.00
Gene Littler	T-9	69-75-67-68=279	$3,750.00

Andy Williams-San Diego Open

Course: Torrey Pines (South), Torrey Pines (North), San Diego, Calif.
Home Course -Par: 72 Yardage: 7,021
Last day of event: Sunday, January 27, 1974

Player	Place	Score	Earnings
Bobby Nichols	Win	69-69-68-69=275	$34,000.00
Gene Littler	T-2	68-71-71-66=276	$15,725.00
Rod Curl	T-2	71-68-67-70=276	$15,725.00
Tom Watson	T-4	70-72-66-70=278	$7,480.00
Miller Barber	T-4	74-66-69-69=278	$7,480.00
Ben Crenshaw	6	65-72-71-71=279	$6,120.00
Billy Casper	7	72-68-68-72=280	$5,440.00
J.C. Snead	T-8	71-69-71-70=281	$4,618.34
Bobby Mitchell	T-8	68-71-70-72=281	$4,618.33
Mike Morley	T-8	74-65-71-71=281	$4,618.33

Hawaiian Open

Course: Waialae C.C., Honolulu, Ha.
Par: 72 Yardage: 7,234
Last day of event: Sunday, February 3, 1974

Player	Place	Score	Earnings
Jack Nicklaus	Win	65-67-69-70=271	$44,000.00
Eddie Pearce	2	70-67-71-66=274	$25,080.00
J.C. Snead	3	72-68-67-68=275	$15,620.00
Hale Irwin	T-4	71-70-69-66=276	$9,680.00
Dwight Nevil	T-4	65-72-71-68=276	$9,680.00
Bobby Nichols	T-6	70-69-70-68=277	$7,480.00
Gibby Gilbert	T-6	67-69-71-70=277	$7,480.00
Andy North	8	69-74-67-68=278	$6,490.00
Dewitt Weaver	T-9	69-69-71-70=279	$5,720.00
Tom Watson	T-9	72-67-69-71=279	$5,720.00

Bob Hope Chrysler Classic

Course: Indian Wells C.C., Eldorado C.C., Bermuda Dunes C.C., La Quinta C.C.
Home course / Indian Wells, Par: 72 Yardage: 6,478
Last day of event: Sunday, February 10, 1974

Player	Place	Score	Earnings
Hubert Green	Win	72-69-66-69-65=341	$32,048.00
Bert Yancey	2	71-72-61-69-70=343	$18,276.40
John Mahaffey	3	71-70-71-68-69=347	$11,377.15
Johnny Miller	T-4	72-69-69-69-70=349	$6,249.39
Mike McCullough	T-4	69-73-70-70-67=349	$6,249.40
Mark Hayes	T-4	68-74-67-72-68=349	$6,249.39
Bob Murphy	T-4	74-69-70-70-66=349	$6,249.40
George Knudson	T-9	72-71-70-70-67=350	$4,526.78
Dwight Nevil	T-9	74-69-71-69-67=350	$4,526.78
Labron Harris, Jr.	T-10	70-70-71-71-69=351	$3,685.52
David Graham	T-10	74-72-65-70-70=351	$3,685.52
Bud Allin	T-10	80-67-71-66-69=351	$3,685.52

Glen Campbell Los Angeles Open

Course: Riviera C.C., Pacific Palisades, Calif.
Par: 71 Yardage: 7,029
Last day of event: Sunday, February 17, 1974

Player	Place	Score	Earnings
Dave Stockton	Win	68-68-71-69=276	$30,000.00
John Mahaffey	T-2	70-69-68-71=278	$13,875.00
Sam Snead	T-2	73-68-66-71=278	$13,875.00
Tom Watson	4	68-72-68-72=280	$7,050.00
Johnny Miller	5	71-66-71-73=281	$6,150.00
Tom Kite	T-6	69-71-72-70=282	$5,400.00
Craig Stadler	T-6	71-69-73-69=282	
Tom Weiskopf	8	71-71-65-76=283	$4,800.00
Dave Hill	T-9	72-66-73-73=284	$4,237.50
Forrest Fezler	T-9	73-67-70-74=284	$4,237.50

Jackie Gleason's Inverrary Classic

Course: Inverrary G. & C.C. (East), Lauderhill, Fla.
Par: 72 Yardage: 7,128
Last day of event: Sunday, February 24, 1974

Player	Place	Score	Earnings
Leonard Thompson	Win	72-69-69-68=278	$52,000.00
Hale Irwin	2	73-69-69-68=279	$29,640.00
Julius Boros	3	73-71-69-67=280	$18,460.00
Lee Trevino	T-4	70-70-72-69=281	$10,140.00
Lanny Wadkins	T-4	71-72-73-65=281	$10,140.00
Andy North	T-4	73-70-70-68=281	$10,140.00
Jack Nicklaus	T-4	74-73-69-65=281	$10,140.00
Roy Pace	T-8	72-71-67-72=282	$7,345.00
Gene Littler	T-8	67-75-74-66=282	$7,345.00
Tom Kite	T-10	72-69-73-69=283	$5,980.00
Chi Chi Rodriguez	T-10	73-68-70-72=283	$5,980.00
Jim Dent	T-10	71-70-76-66=283	$5,980.00

Florida Citrus Open Invitational

Course: Rio Pinar C.C., Orlando, Fla.
Par: 72 Yardage: 7,012
Last day of event: Sunday, March 3, 1974

Player	Place	Score	Earnings
Jerry Heard	Win	67-68-69-69=273	$30,000.00
Homero Blancas	T-2	71-69-66-70=276	$13,875.00
Jim Jamieson	T-2	70-72-67-67=276	$13,875.00
Bobby Cole	T-4	70-71-67-69=277	$6,600.00
Bob Murphy	T-4	71-67-68-71=277	$6,600.00
Lee Elder	T-6	71-70-68-69=278	$4,668.75
Leonard Thompson	T-6	68-69-69-72=278	$4,668.75
Lanny Wadkins	8	70-67-71-73=281	$2,100.00
Jim Dent	T-9	71-69-71-71=282	$1,335.00
Mike Hill	T-9	70-72-72-68=282	$1,335.00
Dave Eichelberger	T-9	72-69-71-70=282	$1,335.00
Roy Pace	T-9	71-70-68-73=282	$1,335.00
Grier Jones	T-9	70-69-74-69=282	$1,335.00

Doral-Eastern Open

Course: Doral C.C. (Blue), Miami, Fla.
Par: 72 Yardage: 6,939
Last day of event: Sunday, March 10, 1974

Player	Place	Score	Earnings
Bud Allin	Win	66-71-68-67=272	$30,000.00
Jerry Heard	2	65-68-72-68=273	$17,100.00

Player	Place	Score	Earnings
Bruce Devlin	T-3	67-69-67-71=274	$8,850.00
Bruce Crampton	T-3	67-72-67-68=274	$8,850.00
Tom Weiskopf	T-5	69-65-69-72=275	$5,775.00
Bert Yancey	T-5	69-69-72-65=275	$5,775.00
Bobby Nichols	T-7	68-69-69-70=276	$4,612.50
Tom Kite	T-7	70-73-68-65=276	$4,612.50
Lee Trevino	T-9	67-69-72-69=277	$3,750.00
Gibby Gilbert	T-9	68-69-72-68=277	$3,750.00
Tom Watson	T-9	72-68-68-69=277	$3,750.00

Greater Jacksonville Open

Course: Deerwood C.C., Jacksonville, Fla.
Par: 72 Yardage: 7,088
Last day of event: Sunday, March 17, 1974

Player	Place	Score	Earnings
Hubert Green	Win	70-67-68-71=276	$30,000.00
John Mahaffey	2	68-70-69-72=279	$17,100.00
Jerry Heard	3	72-71-69-68=280	$10,650.00
Leonard Thompson	T-4	69-70-72-70=281	$6,200.00
Dewitt Weaver	T-4	70-72-68-71=281	$6,200.00
Jim Wiechers	T-4	72-67-66-76=281	$6,200.00
Hale Irwin	7	71-70-70-71=282	$4,800.00
Tom Weiskopf	T-8	72-68-70-74=284	$3,482.14
Larry Nelson	T-8	74-68-68-74=284	$3,482.15
Chi Chi Rodriguez	T-8	74-67-73-70=284	$3,482.15
Labron Harris, Jr.	T-8	68-72-69-75=284	$3,482.14
Homero Blancas	T-8	71-67-71-75=284	$3,482.14
Bob Charles	T-8	73-68-68-75=284	$3,482.14
Larry Ziegler	T-8	76-67-68-73=284	$3,482.14

Sea Pines Heritage Classic

Course: Harbour Town G.L., Hilton Head, S.C.
Par: 71 Yardage: 6,657
Last day of event: Sunday, March 24, 1974

Player	Place	Score	Earnings
Johnny Miller	Win	67-67-72-70=276	$40,000.00
Gibby Gilbert	2	71-71-68-69=279	$22,800.00
Richard Crawford	3	74-70-66-70=280	$14,200.00
Tom Kite	4	73-68-71-69=281	$9,400.00
Leonard Thompson	5	71-74-67-70=282	$8,200.00
Tom Weiskopf	T-6	72-71-67-73=283	$6,500.00
Homero Blancas	T-6	75-72-69-67=283	$6,500.00
Ray Floyd	T-6	77-71-70-65=283	$6,500.00
Don Bies	T-9	72-69-73-71=285	$5,200.00
Rod Curl	T-9	72-79-69-65=285	$5,200.00

Greater New Orleans Open

Course: Lakewood C.C., New Orleans, La.
Par: 72 Yardage: 7,080
Last day of event: Sunday, March 31, 1974

Player	Place	Score	Earnings
Lee Trevino	Win	67-68-67-65=267	$30,000.00
Ben Crenshaw	T-2	71-70-64-70=275	$13,875.00
Bobby Cole	T-2	68-66-68-73=275	$13,875.00
Rod Curl	T-4	67-71-69-69=276	$6,600.00
Larry Hinson	T-4	67-68-69-72=276	$6,600.00
Jack Nicklaus	T-7	66-71-70-70=277	$4,875.00
Jerry McGee	T-7	68-72-68-69=277	$4,875.00
David Graham	T-7	70-69-65-73=277	$4,875.00
Gay Brewer	T-9	69-69-69-71=278	$3,900.00
Tom Watson	T-9	67-69-72-70=278	$3,900.00

Greater Greensboro Open

Course: Sedgefield C.C., Greensboro, N.C.
Par: 71 Yardage: 7,012
Last day of event: Sunday, April 7, 1974

Player	Place	Score	Earnings
Bob Charles	Win	65-70-67-68=270	$44,066.00
Ray Floyd	T-2	66-68-70-67=271	$20,380.50
Lee Trevino	T-2	66-69-70-66=271	$20,380.50
Bruce Fleisher	T-4	69-68-68-67=272	$9,694.50
John Mahaffey	T-4	67-66-70-69=272	$9,694.50
Jim Jamieson	6	66-67-70-70=273	$7,931.90
Forrest Fezler	T-7	70-67-69-68=274	$6,499.76
Wilf Homeniuik	T-7	68-67-72-67=274	$6,499.77
J.C. Snead	T-7	73-68-67-66=274	$6,499.77
Jim Wiechers	T-10	67-68-71-69=275	$5,067.60
Al Geiberger	T-10	70-68-71-66=275	$5,067.60
Mike Hill	T-10	69-66-73-67=275	$5,067.60

Masters

Course: Augusta National G.C., Augusta, Ga.
Par: 72 Yardage: 6,925
Last day of event: Sunday, April 14, 1974

Player	Place	Score	Earnings
Gary Player	Win	71-71-66-70=278	$35,000.00
Tom Weiskopf	T-2	71-69-70-70=280	$21,250.00
Dave Stockton	T-2	71-66-70-73=280	$21,250.00
Hale Irwin	T-4	68-70-72-71=281	$10,833.00
Jack Nicklaus	T-4	69-71-72-69=281	$10,833.00
Jim Colbert	T-4	67-72-69-73=281	$10,833.00
Phil Rodgers	T-7	72-69-68-73=282	$4,750.00
Bobby Nichols	T-7	73-68-68-73=282	$4,750.00
Hubert Green	T-9	68-70-74-71=283	$3,900.00
Maurice Bembridge	T-9	73-74-72-64=283	$3,900.00

Monsanto Open

Course: Pensacola C.C., Pensacola, Fla.
Par: 71 Yardage: 6,679
Last day of event: Sunday, April 21, 1974

Player	Place	Score	Earnings
Lee Elder	Win	67-69-71-67=274	$30,045.00
Playoff: Beat Peter Oosterhuis with birdie on fourth extra hole			
Peter Oosterhuis	2	70-63-72-69=274	$17,125.65
Al Geiberger	3	68-72-66-70=276	$10,666.00
Ray Floyd	T-4	69-71-70-68=278	$6,609.92
Miller Barber	T-4	69-73-68-68=278	$6,609.93
Gibby Gilbert	6	73-70-68-69=280	$5,408.10
Marion Heck	7	71-70-69-71=281	$4,807.20
Jack Ewing	8	74-66-69-73=282	$4,431.65
Bob Stanton	T-9	71-71-72-69=283	$3,905.88
Frank Beard	T-9	68-70-71-74=283	$3,905.87

Tournament of Champions

Course: La Costa C.C., Carlsbad, Calif.
Par: 72 Yardage: 6,911
Last day of event: Sunday, April 28, 1974

Player	Place	Score	Earnings
Johnny Miller	Win	75-69-67-69=280	$40,000.00
John Mahaffey	T-2	70-70-71-70=281	$19,500.00
Bud Allin	T-2	66-69-75-71=281	$19,500.00
Billy Casper	4	75-69-68-71=283	$10,000.00

Jerry Heard	T-5	71-71-72-71=285	$8,133.33
Hubert Green	T-5	73-72-66-74=285	$8,133.33
Gene Littler	T-5	70-69-75-71=285	$8,133.34
Bob Charles	8	70-72-67-77=286	$7,200.00
Leonard Thompson	T-9	72-72-72-71=287	$6,200.00
Dave Hill	T-9	70-72-73-72=287	$6,200.00
Jack Nicklaus	T-9	72-71-69-75=287	$6,200.00
Bruce Crampton	T-9	73-70-69-75=287	$6,200.00

Tallahassee Open

Course: Killearn C.C., Tallahassee, Fla.
Par: 72 Yardage: 7,124
Last day of event: Sunday, April 28, 1974

Player	Place	Score	Earnings
Allen Miller	Win	65-69-67-73=274	$18,000.00
Eddie Pearce	T-2	68-68-70-69=275	$6,960.00
Dan Sikes, Jr.	T-2	67-69-67-72=275	$6,960.00
Joe Inman	T-2	73-68-63-71=275	$6,960.00
Gil Morgan	T-5	69-70-67-70=276	$2,979.00
Jack Ewing	T-5	70-69-70-67=276	$2,979.00
Jim Dent	T-5	70-68-67-71=276	$2,979.00
Jim Simons	T-5	73-66-66-71=276	$2,979.00
George Johnson	T-5	73-69-67-67=276	$2,979.00
Larry Hinson	10	68-69-71-69=277	$2,250.00

Byron Nelson Golf Classic

Course: Preston Trail G.C., Dallas, Texas
Par: 71 Yardage: 6,993
Last day of event: Sunday, May 5, 1974

Player	Place	Score	Earnings
Bud Allin	Win	69-69-63-68=269	$30,045.00
Lee Trevino	T-2	69-69-66-69=273	$10,252.87
Tom Watson	T-2	70-66-67-70=273	$10,252.87
Charles Coody	T-2	70-69-68-66=273	$10,252.88
Homero Blancas	T-2	65-70-67-71=273	$10,252.88
Kermit Zarley	6	72-65-71-66=274	$5,408.10
Jim Simons	T-7	68-65-72-70=275	$4,619.42
Bob Charles	T-7	67-73-66-69=275	$4,619.43
Bob Wynn	T-9	71-69-68-68=276	$3,755.65
Butch Baird	T-9	71-70-70-65=276	$3,755.65
Bruce Crampton	T-9	67-69-68-72=276	$3,755.65

Houston Open

Course: Quail Valley G.C., Houston, Texas
Par: 72 Yardage: 6,905
Last day of event: Sunday, May 12, 1974

Player	Place	Score	Earnings
Dave Hill	Win	70-67-74-65=276	$30,000.00
Rod Curl	T-2	69-71-68-69=277	$11,600.00
Steve Melnyk	T-2	72-65-70-70=277	$11,600.00
Andy North	T-2	73-68-67-69=277	$11,600.00
Joe Inman	T-5	71-69-67-71=278	$5,775.00
Dave Stockton	T-5	73-69-71-65=278	$5,775.00
Bob Rosburg	T-7	70-73-67-69=279	$4,612.50
Hubert Green	T-7	73-69-71-66=279	$4,612.50
Gibby Gilbert	T-9	72-68-72-69=281	$3,450.00
Allen Miller	T-9	72-69-72-68=281	$3,450.00
Bob Stanton	T-9	70-68-69-74=281	$3,450.00
Dick Lotz	T-9	71-69-67-74=281	$3,450.00
Mark Hayes	T-9	74-70-68-69=281	$3,450.00

Colonial National Invitational

Course: Colonial C.C., Fort Worth, Texas
Par: 70 Yardage: 7,142
Last day of event: Sunday, May 19, 1974

Player	Place	Score	Earnings
Rod Curl	Win	70-67-71-68=276	$50,000.00
Jack Nicklaus	2	71-69-69-68=277	$28,500.00
Chuck Courtney	3	70-66-70-72=278	$17,750.00
Julius Boros	4	69-70-72-68=279	$11,750.00
Lee Trevino	5	72-69-71-68=280	$10,250.00
Gary Player	6	74-68-70-70=282	$9,000.00
Steve Melnyk	T-7	72-69-72-70=283	$7,093.75
Charles Coody	T-7	68-72-74-69=283	$7,093.75
Gary McCord	T-7	72-74-66-71=283	$7,093.75
Lou Graham	T-7	74-72-71-66=283	$7,093.75

Danny Thomas Memphis Classic

Course: Colonial C.C. (South), Cordova, Tenn.
Par: 72 Yardage: 7,282
Last day of event: Sunday, May 26, 1974

Player	Place	Score	Earnings
Gary Player	Win	65-72-69-67=273	$35,000.00
Lou Graham	T-2	67-71-67-70=275	$16,187.50
Hubert Green	T-2	66-66-70-73=275	$16,187.50
Bob Wynn	T-4	66-70-69-71=276	$7,233.33
Don Bies	T-4	68-72-66-70=276	$7,233.33
Tom Watson	T-4	68-66-74-68=276	$7,233.34
Bobby Mitchell	T-7	71-66-70-71=278	$5,381.50
Larry Ziegler	T-7	66-72-69-71=278	$5,381.50
Ray Floyd	9	72-68-69-70=279	$4,725.00
Chuck Courtney	T-10	70-71-69-71=281	$4,025.00
Gary Groh	T-10	70-71-72-68=281	$4,025.00
Forrest Fezler	T-10	71-66-74-70=281	$4,025.00

Kemper Open

Course: Quail Hollow C.C., Charlotte, N.C.
Par: 72 Yardage: 7,205
Last day of event: Sunday, June 2, 1974

Player	Place	Score	Earnings
Bob Menne	Win	67-69-67-67=270	$50,000.00

Playoff: Beat Jerry Heard with birdie on first extra hole

Player	Place	Score	Earnings
Jerry Heard	2	69-66-65-70=270	$28,500.00
Dave Hill	3	70-70-66-65=271	$17,750.00
Lee Trevino	4	70-64-69-69=272	$11,750.00
J.C. Snead	T-5	69-66-69-69=273	$9,625.00
Billy Casper	T-5	69-68-67-69=273	$9,625.00
Kermit Zarley	7	68-68-70-69=275	$8,000.00
Chi Chi Rodriguez	T-8	70-65-71-70=276	$6,791.67
Bruce Crampton	T-8	66-72-69-69=276	$6,791.67
Hubert Green	T-8	68-68-68-72=276	$6,791.66

IVB Philadelphia Golf Classic

Course: Whitemarsh Valley C.C., Chestnut Hill, Pa.
Par: 72 Yardage: 6,708
Last day of event: Sunday, June 9, 1974

Player	Place	Score	Earnings
Hubert Green	Win	70-67-66-68=271	$30,000.00
Hale Irwin	2	69-72-68-66=275	$17,100.00
Tom Jenkins	T-3	67-71-68-71=277	$8,850.00
Johnny Miller	T-3	72-67-66-72=277	$8,850.00
Tom Weiskopf	5	71-71-68-69=279	$6,150.00

Mike Hill	6	69-70-70-71=280	$5,400.00
Joe Inman	7	69-72-71-69=281	$4,800.00
Tom Kite	T-8	68-72-69-73=282	$4,075.00
Jim Dent	T-8	74-71-67-70=282	$4,075.00
John Schlee	T-8	66-72-69-75=282	$4,075.00

U.S. Open

Course: Winged Foot G.C. (West), Mamaroneck, N.Y.
Par: 70 Yardage: 6,961
Last day of event: Sunday, June 16, 1974

Player	Place	Score	Earnings
Hale Irwin	Win	73-70-71-73=287	$35,000.00
Forrest Fezler	2	75-70-74-70=289	$18,000.00
Lou Graham	T-3	71-75-74-70=290	$11,500.00
Bert Yancey	T-3	76-69-73-72=290	$11,500.00
Arnold Palmer	T-5	73-70-73-76=292	$8,000.00
Jim Colbert	T-5	72-77-69-74=292	$8,000.00
Tom Watson	T-5	73-71-69-79=292	$8,000.00
Gary Player	T-8	70-73-77-73=293	$5,500.00
Tom Kite	T-8	74-70-77-72=293	$5,500.00
Jack Nicklaus	T-10	75-74-76-69=294	$3,750.00
Bud Allin	T-10	76-71-74-73=294	$3,750.00

American Golf Classic

Course: Firestone C.C. (South), Akron, Ohio
Par: 70 Yardage: 7,180
Last day of event: Sunday, June 23, 1974

Player	Place	Score	Earnings
Jim Colbert	Win	70-67-74-70=281	$34,000.00

Playoff: Beat Ray Floyd with par on second extra hole (Gay Brewer, Forrest Fezler eliminated on first hole)

Player	Place	Score	Earnings
Gay Brewer	T-2	69-70-71-71=281	$13,146.66
Forrest Fezler	T-2	69-71-68-73=281	$13,146.66
Ray Floyd	T-2	65-71-75-70=281	$13,146.67
J.C. Snead	T-5	71-69-71-71=282	$5,886.25
Dwight Nevil	T-5	70-68-72-72=282	$5,886.25
Bert Yancey	T-5	71-68-71-72=282	$5,886.25
Jim Jamieson	T-5	70-70-69-73=282	$5,886.25
Tom Kite	9	71-68-70-74=283	$4,590.00
Mason Rudolph	T-10	70-73-71-70=284	$3,910.00
Bruce Crampton	T-10	72-69-70-73=284	$3,910.00
Jerry McGee	T-10	67-69-74-74=284	$3,910.00

Western Open

Course: Butler National G.C., Oak Brook, Ill.
Par: 71 Yardage: 7,002
Last day of event: Sunday, June 30, 1974

Player	Place	Score	Earnings
Tom Watson	Win	72-71-75-69=287	$40,000.00
J.C. Snead	T-2	75-71-71-72=289	$18,500.00
Tom Weiskopf	T-2	71-70-71-77=289	$18,500.00
Hale Irwin	4	71-75-75-72=293	$9,400.00
Arnold Palmer	T-5	74-72-74-74=294	$6,925.00
Butch Baird	T-5	76-70-73-75=294	$6,925.00
Gene Littler	T-5	73-71-79-71=294	$6,925.00
Larry Nelson	T-5	79-70-74-71=294	$6,925.00
Jim Wiechers	9	73-77-73-72=295	$5,400.00
Gary McCord	T-10	70-74-76-76=296	$4,400.00
Charles Sifford	T-10	74-76-72-74=296	$4,400.00
Roy Pace	T-10	75-73-76-72=296	$4,400.00
Al Geiberger	T-10	71-71-80-74=296	$4,400.00

Greater Milwaukee Open

Course: Tuckaway C.C., Franklin, Wis.
Par: 72 Yardage: 7,030
Last day of event: Saturday, July 6, 1974

Player	Place	Score	Earnings
Ed Sneed	Win	66-67-71-72=276	$26,000.00
Grier Jones	2	72-71-66-71=280	$14,820.00
Chuck Courtney	T-3	71-69-72-69=281	$6,890.00
Bob Zender	T-3	69-70-69-73=281	$6,890.00
Dave Hill	T-3	73-67-68-73=281	$6,890.00
Lee Trevino	T-6	71-69-71-71=282	$4,225.00
Larry Hinson	T-6	70-72-69-71=282	$4,225.00
Tommy Aaron	T-6	68-68-75-71=282	$4,225.00
Bob-E. Smith	T-9	73-68-70-72=283	$3,380.00
Lou Graham	T-9	73-72-68-70=283	$3,380.00

British Open

Course: Royal Lytham & St. Annes G.C., Lytham, Lancashire, Scotland
Par: 71 Yardage: 6,822
Last day of event: Saturday, July 13, 1974

Player	Place	Score	Earnings
Gary Player	Win	69-68-75-70=282	$13,200.00
Peter Oosterhuis	2	71-71-73-71=286	$9,600.00
Jack Nicklaus	3	74-72-70-71=287	$7,800.00
Hubert Green	4	71-74-72-71=288	$6,600.00
Lu Liang-Huan	T-5	72-72-75-73=292	$5,520.00
Danny Edwards	T-5	70-73-76-73=292	$5,520.00
Tom Weiskopf	T-7	72-72-74-75=293	$4,120.80
Bobby Cole	T-7	70-72-76-75=293	$4,120.80
Donald Swaelens	T-7	77-73-74-69=293	$4,120.80
Johnny Miller	10	72-75-73-74=294	$3,600.00

Quad Cities Open

Course: Crow Valley C.C., Bettendorf, Iowa
Par: 71 Yardage: 6,501
Last day of event: Sunday, July 14, 1974

Player	Place	Score	Earnings
Dave Stockton	Win	68-68-71-64=271	$20,000.00
Bruce Fleisher	2	70-63-71-68=272	$11,400.00
George Johnson	3	72-67-70-64=273	$7,100.00
Sam Snead	4	69-65-69-72=275	$4,700.00
Rafe Botts	5	69-69-69-69=276	$4,100.00
Joe Inman	T-6	70-68-69-70=277	$2,990.00
Gary McCord	T-6	72-70-65-70=277	$2,990.00
Ed Sneed	T-6	67-65-73-72=277	$2,990.00
Mike Morley	T-6	69-64-71-73=277	$2,990.00
Gary Sanders	T-6	73-66-68-70=277	$2,990.00

B.C. Open

Course: En-Joie G.C., Endicott, N.Y.
Par: 71 Yardage: 6,966
Last day of event: Sunday, July 21, 1974

Player	Place	Score	Earnings
Richie Karl	Win	70-67-68-68=273	$30,000.00
Playoff: Beat Bruce Crampton with birdie on first extra hole			
Bruce Crampton	2	71-66-70-66=273	$17,100.00
Ray Floyd	3	69-72-68-68=277	$10,650.00
Rod Curl	4	70-68-73-65=276	$7,050.00
Curtis Sifford	T-5	68-67-70-72=277	$5,775.00
John Schlee	T-5	68-74-65-70=277	$5,775.00
Dan Sikes, Jr.	7	71-68-72-67=278	$4,800.00

Player	Place	Score	Earnings
Sam Adams	T-8	69-71-69-70=279	$3,612.50
Mark Hayes	T-8	66-70-72-71=279	$3,612.50
Tim Collins	T-8	68-67-72-71=279	$3,612.50
Mike Wynn	T-8	68-69-72-70=279	$3,612.50
Mike Hill	T-8	69-69-72-69=279	$3,612.50
Dale Douglass	T-8	71-67-72-69=279	$3,612.50

Canadian Open

Course: Mississaugua G. & C.C., Mississaugua, Ontario, Canada
Par: 70 Yardage: 6,788
Last day of event: Sunday, July 28, 1974

Player	Place	Score	Earnings
Bobby Nichols	Win	67-67-68-68=270	$40,000.00
John Schlee	T-2	69-66-69-70=274	$18,500.00
Larry Ziegler	T-2	69-63-73-69=274	$18,500.00
Lou Graham	T-4	70-71-67-67=275	$7,420.00
Dale Douglass	T-4	71-65-71-68=275	$7,420.00
Ray Floyd	T-4	71-67-69-68=275	$7,420.00
Lee Trevino	T-4	66-69-68-72=275	$7,420.00
Chi Chi Rodriguez	T-4	68-63-74-70=275	$7,420.00
Ben Crenshaw	T-9	67-68-71-70=276	$4,800.00
Lionel Hebert	T-9	69-66-70-71=276	$4,800.00
Gary Sanders	T-9	68-67-72-69=276	$4,800.00
Steve Melnyk	T-9	69-72-67-68=276	$4,800.00

Pleasant Valley Classic

Course: Pleasant Valley C.C., Sutton, Mass.
Par: 71 Yardage: 7,110
Last day of event: Sunday, August 4, 1974

Player	Place	Score	Earnings
Victor Regalado	Win	68-72-69-69=278	$40,000.00
Tom Weiskopf	2	71-65-71-72=279	$22,800.00
Dave Hill	3	69-65-71-75=280	$14,200.00
Lee Elder	T-4	70-70-71-72=283	$7,800.00
Dale Douglass	T-4	71-69-72-71=283	$7,800.00
Bobby Nichols	T-4	74-70-70-69=283	$7,800.00
Jim Wiechers	T-4	72-67-68-76=283	$7,800.00
Jerry Heard	8	68-70-72-74=284	$5,900.00
Larry Hinson	T-9	70-72-71-73=286	$4,285.71
Dan Sikes, Jr.	T-9	73-70-72-71=286	$4,285.72
Dwight Nevil	T-9	73-71-71-71=286	$4,285.71
J.C. Snead	T-9	68-71-74-73=286	$4,285.71
Bobby Cole	T-9	74-69-70-73=286	$4,285.71
Ben Crenshaw	T-9	74-68-74-70=286	$4,285.72
Bruce Crampton	T-9	74-70-74-68=286	$4,285.72

PGA Championship

Course: Tanglewood G.C., Clemmons, N.C.
Par: 70 Yardage: 7,050
Last day of event: Sunday, August 11, 1974

Player	Place	Score	Earnings
Lee Trevino	Win	73-66-68-69=276	$45,000.00
Jack Nicklaus	2	69-69-70-69=277	$25,700.00
Bobby Cole	T-3	69-68-71-71=279	$10,956.25
Sam Snead	T-3	69-71-71-68=279	$10,956.25
Hubert Green	T-3	68-68-73-70=279	$10,956.25
Dave Hill	T-3	74-69-67-69=279	$10,956.25
Gary Player	7	73-64-73-70=280	$7,200.00
Al Geiberger	8	70-70-75-66=281	$6,635.00
John Mahaffey	T-9	72-72-71-67=282	$5,850.00
Don Bies	T-9	73-71-68-70=282	$5,850.00

Sammy Davis, Jr. - Greater Hartford Open

Course: Wethersfield C.C., Wethersfield, Conn.

Par: 70 Yardage: 6,568

Last day of event: Sunday, August 18, 1974

Player	Place	Score	Earnings
Dave Stockton	Win	65-65-69-69=268	$40,000.00
Ray Floyd	2	69-68-69-66=272	$22,800.00
Bob Wynn	3	68-64-71-70=273	$14,200.00
Lee Trevino	4	68-65-69-72=274	$9,400.00
Bruce Crampton	T-5	70-65-70-70=275	$6,350.00
Jim Colbert	T-5	70-67-70-68=275	$6,350.00
Jerry McGee	T-5	67-69-71-68=275	$6,350.00
Bobby Cole	T-5	70-66-68-71=275	$6,350.00
Mike Hill	T-5	71-67-69-68=275	$6,350.00
Billy Casper	T-5	71-68-68-68=275	$6,350.00

Westchester Classic

Course: Westchester C.C., Harrison, N.Y.

Par: 72 Yardage: 6,614

Last day of event: Sunday, August 25, 1974

Player	Place	Score	Earnings
Johnny Miller	Win	69-68-65-67=269	$50,000.00
Don Bies	2	70-65-70-66=271	$28,500.00
Tom Weiskopf	3	70-66-68-68=272	$17,750.00
Jerry McGee	4	68-68-70-68=274	$11,750.00
Jack Nicklaus	T-5	68-69-68-70=275	$9,625.00
Larry Ziegler	T-5	67-67-72-69=275	$9,625.00
Dale Douglass	T-7	67-66-72-71=276	$7,687.50
Bruce Crampton	T-7	68-68-72-68=276	$7,687.50
David Graham	T-9	70-69-68-70=277	$5,750.00
Ken Still	T-9	70-69-68-70=277	$5,750.00
Jim Colbert	T-9	70-69-70-68=277	$5,750.00
Miller Barber	T-9	67-71-69-70=277	$5,750.00
Tom Watson	T-9	68-74-68-67=277	$5,750.00

Tournament Players Championship

Course: Atlanta C.C., Atlanta, Ga.

Par: 72 Yardage: 6,883

Last day of event: Monday, September 2, 1974

Player	Place	Score	Earnings
Jack Nicklaus	Win	66-71-68-67=272	$50,000.00
J.C. Snead	2	64-71-67-72=274	$28,500.00
Bruce Crampton	3	69-68-72-67=276	$17,750.00
Gene Littler	4	72-69-69-67=277	$11,750.00
Lou Graham	5	67-67-73-71=278	$10,250.00
Bob Murphy	T-6	71-71-68-69=279	$8,500.00
Hubert Green	T-6	70-67-72-70=279	$8,500.00
Dave Hill	8	70-66-72-72=280	$7,375.00
Charles Coody	T-9	67-71-71-72=281	$6,250.00
Bud Allin	T-9	71-67-71-72=281	$6,250.00
Eddie Pearce	T-9	73-67-69-72=281	$6,250.00

Southern Open

Course: Green Island C.C., Columbus, Ga.

Par: 70 Yardage: 6,791

Last day of event: Sunday, September 8, 1974

Player	Place	Score	Earnings
Forrest Fezler	Win	70-68-68-65=271	$20,000.00
Bruce Crampton	T-2	70-69-68-65=272	$9,250.00
J.C. Snead	T-2	68-71-66-67=272	$9,250.00

Mike Hill	4	71-69-68-67=275	$4,750.00
Phil Rodgers	T-5	69-70-68-70=277	$3,633.34
Jim Ferriell	T-5	67-71-70-69=277	$3,633.33
Ben Crenshaw	T-5	71-65-69-72=277	$3,633.33
Dwight Nevil	T-8	71-68-69-70=278	$2,321.67
Bob Dickson	T-8	69-72-68-69=278	$2,321.67
Tommy Aaron	T-8	70-70-65-73=278	$2,321.66

World Open

Course: Pinehurst C.C. (No 2 & No 4), Pinehurst, N.C.

Par: 71 Yardage: 7,007

Last day of event: Sunday, September 15, 1974

Player	Place	Score	Earnings
Johnny Miller	Win	73-63-73-72=281	$60,000.00
Playoff: Beat Jack Nicklaus, Frank Beard and Bob Murphy with birdie on second extra hole			
Jack Nicklaus	2	68-71-70-72=281	$23,200.00
Bob Murphy	2	65-74-73-69=281	$23,200.00
Frank Beard	2	67-70-75-69=281	$23,200.00
Bob Stanton	5	72-69-74-67=282	$12,300.00
Charles Coody	T-6	68-72-71-72=283	$9,750.00
Gene Littler	T-6	69-70-73-71=283	$9,750.00
Jim Dent	T-6	71-70-76-66=283	$9,750.00
Bruce Devlin	T-9	72-68-71-73=284	$7,800.00
David Graham	T-9	70-68-74-72=284	$7,800.00

Ohio Kings Island Open

Course: Jack Nicklaus Golf Center, Mason, Ohio

Par: 71 Yardage: 6,915

Last day of event: Sunday, September 22, 1974

Player	Place	Score	Earnings
Miller Barber	Win	68-68-69-72=277	$30,000.00
George Johnson	2	73-70-68-69=280	$17,100.00
Victor Regalado	T-3	69-70-69-73=281	$8,850.00
Leonard Thompson	T-3	72-73-69-67=281	$8,850.00
Graham Marsh	T-5	69-71-70-73=283	$5,775.00
Jerry McGee	T-5	73-70-73-67=283	$5,775.00
Bob Panasiuk	T-7	71-72-71-70=284	$4,256.25
David Graham	T-7	72-71-70-71=284	$4,256.25
Gil Morgan	T-7	69-72-73-70=284	$4,256.25
Jack Nicklaus	T-7	71-71-69-73=284	$4,256.25

Kaiser International Open

Course: Silverado C.C., Napa, Calif.

Home Course -Par: 72 Yardage: 6,849

Last day of event: Sunday, September 29, 1974

Player	Place	Score	Earnings
Johnny Miller	Win	69-69-67-66=271	$30,000.00
Billy Casper	T-2	65-70-72-72=279	$13,875.00
Lee Trevino	T-2	70-73-69-67=279	$13,875.00
Leonard Thompson	4	70-71-70-69=280	$7,050.00
Tim Collins	T-5	71-70-69-71=281	$5,775.00
Mike Reasor	T-5	74-68-69-70=281	$5,775.00
Gene Littler	T-7	69-71-72-70=282	$4,612.50
Charles Coody	T-7	72-72-70-68=282	$4,612.50
Al Geiberger	T-9	70-69-73-71=283	$3,900.00
Bud Allin	T-9	75-69-71-68=283	$3,900.00

Sahara Invitational

Course: Sahara Nevada C.C., Las Vegas, Nev.
Home course / Par: 71 Yardage: 6,880
Last day of event: Sunday, October 6, 1974

Player	Place	Score	Earnings
Al Geiberger	Win	70-68-66-69=273	$27,000.00
Mike Hill	T-2	68-71-69-68=276	$9,213.75
Jerry Heard	T-2	69-70-66-71=276	$9,213.75
Dave Hill	T-2	73-66-65-72=276	$9,213.75
Wally Armstrong	T-2	74-69-65-68=276	$9,213.75
Chi Chi Rodriguez	T-6	68-68-69-72=277	$4,387.67
Johnny Miller	T-6	71-69-72-65=277	$4,387.67
David Graham	T-6	73-70-67-67=277	$4,387.66
Charles Sifford	T-9	70-68-70-70=278	$3,240.00
Bob Stanton	T-9	70-72-64-72=278	$3,240.00
J.C. Snead	T-9	67-71-67-73=278	$3,240.00
Dave Eichelberger	T-9	67-68-73-70=278	$3,240.00

San Antonio Texas Open

Course: Woodlake G.C., San Antonio, Texas
Par: 72 Yardage: 7,143
Last day of event: Sunday, October 20, 1974

Player	Place	Score	Earnings
Terry Diehl	Win	68-65-65-71=269	$25,000.00
Mike Hill	2	67-67-68-68=270	$14,250.00
Andy North	T-3	69-69-67-66=271	$7,375.00
Wally Armstrong	T-3	69-69-69-64=271	$7,375.00
Gil Morgan	T-5	68-68-66-70=272	$4,812.50
Al Geiberger	T-5	70-65-69-68=272	$4,812.50
Bob Stanton	T-7	67-68-69-69=273	$3,687.33
Bobby Mitchell	T-7	69-69-69-66=273	$3,687.34
Bobby Greenwood	T-7	67-68-70-68=273	$3,687.33
Eddie Pearce	T-10	68-69-68-69=274	$2,875.00
Jim Jamieson	T-10	69-67-69-69=274	$2,875.00
Lee Trevino	T-10	68-70-69-67=274	$2,875.00

1975

Jack Nicklaus eked out a victory at the Masters by one shot over Tom Weiskopf and Johnny Miller, both of whom missed birdie putts at the 72nd hole. It was Weiskopf's fourth runner-up finish at Augusta; Miller closed with 65-66. Lee Elder, thanks to winning the Monsanto Open the previous year, gained a spot in the Masters field, making him the first African American to participate in the tournament. Lou Graham won the U.S. Open at Medinah, besting John Mahaffey 71 to 73 in a playoff. Tom Watson won his first major—and the first of his five British Opens—beating Jack Newton 71 to 72 in a playoff at Carnoustie. Nicklaus won the PGA Championship at Firestone by two shots over Bruce Crampton, marking the fourth time Crampton was runner-up to Jack at a major. Billy Casper won the New Orleans Open, the last of his 51 career victories.

Phoenix Open

Course: Phoenix C.C., Phoenix, Ariz.
Par: 71 Yardage: 6,726
Last day of event: Sunday, January 12, 1975

Player	Place	Score	Earnings
Johnny Miller	Win	67-61-68-64=260	$30,000.00
Jerry Heard	2	74-68-67-65=274	$17,100.00
Tommy Aaron	3	68-72-69-67=276	$10,650.00
Mike Hill	4	71-63-69-74=277	$7,050.00
Roy Pace	5	68-69-69-72=278	$6,150.00
J.C. Snead	6	68-72-67-72=279	$5,400.00
John Mahaffey	T-7	67-71-72-70=280	$4,095.00
Dick Lotz	T-7	69-68-72-71=280	$4,095.00

Player	Place	Score	Earnings
Gene Littler	T-7	71-67-70-72=280	$4,095.00
Tom Watson	T-7	73-71-68-68=280	$4,095.00
Butch Baird	T-7	71-74-67-68=280	$4,095.00

Dean Martin Tucson Open

Course: Tucson National G.C., Starr Pass G.C., Tucson, Ariz.
Par: 72 Yardage: 7,305
Last day of event: Sunday, January 19, 1975

Player	Place	Score	Earnings
Johnny Miller	Win	66-69-67-61=263	$40,000.00
John Mahaffey	2	67-69-69-67=272	$22,800.00
Tom Watson	3	72-67-67-67=273	$14,200.00
Mike Hill	T-4	68-72-67-69=276	$8,800.00
Don Iverson	T-4	67-74-66-69=276	$8,800.00
Al Geiberger	6	71-69-69-69=278	$7,200.00
Leonard Thompson	T-7	68-70-69-72=279	$5,900.00
Tommy Aaron	T-7	71-66-70-72=279	$5,900.00
Bruce Crampton	T-7	71-72-70-66=279	$5,900.00
Arnold Palmer	10	72-71-67-70=280	$5,000.00

Bing Crosby Pro-Am

Courses: Pebble Beach G.L. - Home
Spyglass Hill G.C., Cypress Point C.C., Pebble Beach, Calif.
Home Course Par: 72 Yardage: 6,815
Last day of event: Sunday, January 26, 1975

Player	Place	Score	Earnings
Gene Littler	Win	68-71-68-73=280	$37,000.00
Hubert Green	2	66-75-74-69=284	$21,090.00
Tom Kite	3	70-76-69-70=285	$13,135.00
Lou Graham	4	72-70-70-75=287	$8,695.00
Forrest Fezler	5	71-73-72-72=288	$7,585.00
Johnny Miller	T-6	71-74-70-74=289	$5,318.66
Jack Nicklaus	T-6	71-74-72-72=289	$5,318.67
Rik Massengale	T-6	72-71-74-72=289	$5,318.67
Leonard Thompson	T-6	74-71-71-73=289	$5,318.67
Bruce Devlin	T-6	73-71-69-76=289	$5,318.66
Dave Hill	T-6	76-72-69-72=289	$5,318.67

Hawaiian Open

Course: Waialae C.C., Honolulu, Ha.
Par: 72 Yardage: 7,234
Last day of event: Sunday, February 2, 1975

Player	Place	Score	Earnings
Gary Groh	Win	68-68-70-68=274	$44,000.00
Al Geiberger	2	66-69-71-69=275	$25,080.00
Arnold Palmer	3	69-67-69-71=276	$15,620.00
Bruce Crampton	T-4	69-70-70-68=277	$9,680.00
Lou Graham	T-4	69-71-65-72=277	$9,680.00
Forrest Fezler	6	69-67-68-74=278	$7,920.00
Bill Rogers	T-7	69-71-71-68=279	$6,765.00
Richard Crawford	T-7	72-70-66-71=279	$6,765.00
Eddie Pearce	T-9	67-69-72-72=280	$5,060.00
Allen Miller	T-9	67-72-69-72=280	$5,060.00
John Mahaffey	T-9	69-72-68-71=280	$5,060.00
Tom Kite	T-9	69-74-69-68=280	$5,060.00
Dale Douglass	T-9	69-74-69-78=280	$5,060.00

Bob Hope Chrysler Classic
Course: Bermuda Dunes C.C., La Quinta C.C., Indian Wells C.C., Tamarisk C.C.
Home course Par: 72 Yardage: 6,837
Last day of event: Sunday, February 9, 1975

Player	Place	Score	Earnings
Johnny Miller	Win	64-69-72-66-68=339	$32,000.00
Bob Murphy	2	74-67-67-68-66=342	$18,240.00
Jerry Heard	3	68-70-68-68-69=343	$11,360.00
Tom Shaw	4	70-66-69-71-69=345	$7,520.00
John Mahaffey	T-5	70-67-69-69-71=346	$6,160.00
Pat Fitzsimons	T-5	73-73-67-67-66=346	$6,160.00
Mac McLendon	T-7	68-68-71-74-66=347	$4,921.00
Billy Casper	T-7	75-68-66-68-70=347	$4,921.00
Miller Barber	T-9	68-69-69-70-72=348	$4,160.00
Don Bies	T-9	71-67-66-72-72=348	$4,160.00

Andy Williams-San Diego Open
Course: Torrey Pines (South), Torrey Pines (North), San Diego, Calif.
Home Course -Par: 72 Yardage: 7,021
Last day of event: Sunday, February 16, 1975

Player	Place	Score	Earnings
J.C. Snead	Win	69-71-71-68=279	$34,000.00

Playoff: Beat Ray Floyd and Bobby Nichols with birdie on fourth extra hole

Player	Place	Score	Earnings
Bobby Nichols	T-2	71-69-68-71=279	$15,725.00
Ray Floyd	T-2	68-71-68-72=279	$15,725.00
Rod Funseth	4	70-67-69-74=280	$7,990.00
Tom Kite	5	72-68-70-71=281	$6,970.00
John Mahaffey	T-6	69-71-71-71=282	$5,525.00
Billy Casper	T-6	69-68-72-73=282	$5,525.00
Hale Irwin	T-6	70-71-73-68=282	$5,525.00
Dale Douglass	T-9	71-71-72-70=284	$4,250.00
Pat Fitzsimons	T-9	71-74-71-68=284	$4,250.00
Leonard Thompson	T-9	72-69-68-75=284	$4,250.00

Glen Campbell Los Angeles Open
Course: Riviera C.C., Pacific Palisades, Calif.
Par: 71 Yardage: 7,029
Last day of event: Sunday, February 23, 1975

Player	Place	Score	Earnings
Pat Fitzsimons	Win	70-71-64-70=275	$30,000.00
Tom Kite	2	71-69-71-68=279	$17,100.00
Jack Nicklaus	3	69-75-71-65=280	$10,650.00
Hale Irwin	T-4	72-72-71-67=282	$6,600.00
Tom Weiskopf	T-4	67-75-72-68=282	$6,600.00
Tom Watson	T-6	67-73-72-71=283	$4,668.75
Jim Dent	T-6	69-73-71-70=283	$4,668.75
Jerry McGee	T-6	70-73-70-70=283	$4,668.75
Billy Casper	T-6	69-74-71-69=283	$4,668.75
Dale Douglass	T-10	68-69-74-73=284	$3,600.00
Dave Stockton	T-10	68-75-69-72=284	$3,600.00

Jackie Gleason's Inverrary Classic
Course: Inverrary G. & C.C. (East), Lauderhill, Fla.
Par: 72 Yardage: 7,128
Last day of event: Sunday, March 2, 1975

Player	Place	Score	Earnings
Bob Murphy	Win	68-71-66-68=273	$52,000.00
Eddie Pearce	2	67-64-72-71=274	$29,640.00
Jack Nicklaus	3	67-69-68-73=275	$18,460.00
Miller Barber	4	67-70-71-68=276	$12,220.00

Lee Trevino	T-5	70-70-71-66=277	$10,010.00
Hale Irwin	T-5	69-66-72-70=277	$10,010.00
Tom Weiskopf	T-7	72-68-66-73=279	$7,995.00
Arnold Palmer	T-7	68-66-71-74=279	$7,995.00
Charles Coody	T-9	68-69-71-72=280	$6,240.00
Gene Littler	T-9	70-66-72-72=280	$6,240.00
Rik Massengale	T-9	68-74-65-73=280	$6,240.00
Tom Kite	T-9	68-67-70-75=280	$6,240.00

Florida Citrus Open Invitational
Course: Rio Pinar C.C., Orlando, Fla.
Par: 72 Yardage: 7,012
Last day of event: Sunday, March 9, 1975

Player	Place	Score	Earnings
Lee Trevino	Win	69-66-70-71=276	$40,000.00
Hale Irwin	2	68-67-74-68=277	$22,800.00
Ben Crenshaw	3	72-68-67-71=278	$14,200.00
Charles Coody	4	71-66-71-71=279	$9,400.00
Rik Massengale	T-5	68-71-72-70=281	$7,266.67
Bruce Devlin	T-5	72-71-66-72=281	$7,266.66
Forrest Fezler	T-5	71-74-69-67=281	$7,266.67
Larry Ziegler	T-8	71-70-72-69=282	$5,225.00
John Schlee	T-8	72-72-69-69=282	$5,225.00
Tom Watson	T-8	70-69-73-70=282	$5,225.00
Larry Hinson	T-8	68-68-74-72=282	$5,225.00

Doral-Eastern Open
Course: Doral C.C. (Blue), Miami, Fla.
Par: 72 Yardage: 6,939
Last day of event: Sunday, March 16, 1975

Player	Place	Score	Earnings
Jack Nicklaus	Win	69-70-69-68=276	$30,000.00
Forrest Fezler	T-2	71-70-67-71=279	$13,875.00
Bert Yancey	T-2	71-72-69-67=279	$13,875.00
Johnny Miller	4	72-69-72-67=280	$7,050.00
Bruce Crampton	T-5	73-69-68-71=281	$5,775.00
Bud Allin	T-5	73-72-70-69=281	$5,775.00
Mike Hill	T-7	69-71-72-70=282	$4,612.50
Steve Melnyk	T-7	72-71-70-69=282	$4,612.50
Lee Trevino	T-9	70-71-71-71=283	$3,325.00
Rod Curl	T-9	70-72-70-71=283	$3,325.00
Joe Porter	T-9	72-70-69-72=283	$3,325.00
John Lister	T-9	72-71-69-71=283	$3,325.00
Tom Jenkins	T-9	73-69-70-71=283	$3,325.00
Wally Armstrong	T-9	68-70-77-68=283	$3,325.00

Greater Jacksonville Open
Course: Deerwood C.C., Jacksonville, Fla.
Par: 72 Yardage: 7,143
Last day of event: Sunday, March 23, 1975

Player	Place	Score	Earnings
Larry Ziegler	Win	73-69-69-65=276	$30,000.00
Mac McLendon	T-2	67-72-71-68=278	$13,875.00
Mike Morley	T-2	72-71-65-70=278	$13,875.00
Lou Graham	4	74-69-71-65=279	$7,050.00
Andy North	T-5	71-71-70-68=280	$5,450.00
Tom Shaw	T-5	70-67-72-71=280	$5,450.00
Wally Armstrong	T-5	71-73-66-70=280	$5,450.00
Bob Dickson	T-8	68-71-71-71=281	$3,765.00
Jerry McGee	T-8	70-68-71-72=281	$3,765.00
Ben Crenshaw	T-8	68-73-69-71=281	$3,765.00

Joe Inman	T-8	70-68-73-70=281	$3,765.00
Bobby Cole	T-8	69-69-74-69=281	$3,765.00

Sea Pines Heritage Classic

Course: Harbour Town G.L., Hilton Head, S.C.
Par: 71 Yardage: 6,657
Last day of event: Sunday, March 30, 1975

Player	Place	Score	Earnings
Jack Nicklaus	Win	66-63-74-68=271	$40,000.00
Tom Weiskopf	2	70-65-68-71=274	$22,800.00
Charles Coody	3	71-69-74-65=279	$14,200.00
John Mahaffey	4	70-70-70-70=280	$9,400.00
Bruce Crampton	T-5	69-70-71-71=281	$7,700.00
Tom Kite	T-5	69-68-69-75=281	$7,700.00
Mac McLendon	7	73-68-72-69=282	$6,400.00
John Schlee	8	73-70-68-72=283	$5,900.00
Miller Barber	T-9	72-66-74-72=284	$4,800.00
Hale Irwin	T-9	69-68-72-75=284	$4,800.00
Don January	T-9	69-70-69-76=284	$4,800.00
George Archer	T-9	71-68-76-69=284	$4,800.00

Greater Greensboro Open

Course: Sedgefield C.C., Greensboro, N.C.
Par: 71 Yardage: 6,643
Last day of event: Sunday, April 6, 1975

Player	Place	Score	Earnings
Tom Weiskopf	Win	64-71-72-68=275	$45,000.00
Al Geiberger	2	71-75-66-66=278	$25,650.00
Jerry McGee	3	77-67-68-68=280	$15,975.00
Lee Trevino	4	71-70-72-68=281	$10,575.00
Dave Hill	5	67-73-72-70=282	$9,225.00
Johnny Miller	T-6	72-70-70-71=283	$7,650.00
Ken Still	T-6	74-68-69-72=283	$7,650.00
Maurice Bembridge	8	72-73-70-69=284	$6,650.00
Graham Marsh	T-9	73-70-72-70=285	$5,625.00
Mason Rudolph	T-9	73-72-70-70=285	$5,625.00
Steve Melnyk	T-9	77-70-70-68=285	$5,625.00

Masters

Course: Augusta National G.C., Augusta, Ga.
Par: 72 Yardage: 6,925
Last day of event: Sunday, April 13, 1975

Player	Place	Score	Earnings
Jack Nicklaus	Win	68-67-73-68=276	$40,000.00
Tom Weiskopf	T-2	69-72-66-70=277	$21,250.00
Johnny Miller	T-2	75-71-65-66=277	$21,250.00
Bobby Nichols	T-4	67-74-72-69=282	$12,500.00
Hale Irwin	T-4	73-74-71-64=282	$12,500.00
Billy Casper	6	70-70-73-70=283	$7,500.00
Dave Hill	7	75-71-70-68=284	$6,000.00
Tom Watson	T-8	70-70-72-73=285	$4,500.00
Hubert Green	T-8	74-71-70-70=285	$4,500.00
Lee Trevino	T-10	71-70-74-71=286	$3,600.00
Tom Kite	T-10	72-74-71-69=286	$3,600.00
J.C. Snead	T-10	69-72-75-70=286	$3,600.00

Pensacola Open

Course: Pensacola C.C., Pensacola, Fla.
Par: 71 Yardage: 6,679
Last day of event: Sunday, April 20, 1975

Player	Place	Score	Earnings
Jerry McGee	Win	69-66-66-70=271	$25,000.00
Wally Armstrong	2	70-66-66-71=273	$14,250.00
Miller Barber	T-3	67-69-70-68=274	$6,625.00
Dwight Nevil	T-3	71-69-69-65=274	$6,625.00
Bruce Crampton	T-3	65-72-68-69=274	$6,625.00
Jerry Pate	6	69-71-69-66=275	
Dan Sikes, Jr.	T-7	72-69-66-69=276	$4,062.33
Bob Murphy	T-7	69-73-67-67=276	$4,062.33
Bobby Mitchell	T-7	73-70-67-66=276	$4,062.34
Lou Graham	T-10	68-70-70-69=277	$2,770.83
Roger Maltbie	T-10	69-67-69-72=277	$2,770.83
Andy North	T-10	64-73-70-70=277	$2,770.83
Charles Coody	T-10	65-71-73-68=277	$2,770.84
Doug Sanders	T-10	73-64-71-69=277	$2,770.84
Lee Elder	T-10	73-68-69-70=277	$2,770.83

MONY Tournament of Champions

Course: La Costa C.C., Carlsbad, Calif.
Par: 72 Yardage: 6,911
Last day of event: Sunday, April 27, 1975

Player	Place	Score	Earnings
Al Geiberger	Win	67-67-70-73=277	$40,000.00
Playoff: Beat Gary Player with birdie on first extra hole			
Gary Player	2	72-70-68-67=277	$23,700.00
Lee Trevino	3	72-65-70-71=278	$14,812.00
Jim Colbert	4	65-73-70-71=279	$9,503.00
Hale Irwin	T-5	70-73-71-70=284	$7,792.50
Bud Allin	T-5	73-69-70-72=284	$7,792.50
Gene Littler	T-7	69-72-74-70=285	$6,667.50
Tom Watson	T-7	69-75-71-70=285	$6,667.50
Dave Stockton	T-9	72-71-71-73=287	$5,945.00
Jack Nicklaus	T-9	70-72-71-74=287	$5,945.00

Tallahassee Open

Course: Killearn C.C., Tallahassee, Fla.
Par: 72 Yardage: 7,124
Last day of event: Sunday, April 27, 1975

Player	Place	Score	Earnings
Rik Massengale	Win	67-67-68-72=274	$12,000.00
Bert Yancey	T-2	69-70-68-69=276	$5,550.00
Spike Kelley	T-2	69-70-69-68=276	$5,550.00
Ralph Johnston	4	67-70-69-72=278	$2,820.00
Bob Charles	5	71-69-70-69=279	$2,460.00
Sam Adams	T-6	73-70-70-67=280	$2,040.00
John Toepel	T-6	67-69-75-69=280	$2,040.00
Terry Dill	T-8	70-71-69-71=281	$1,567.50
Bobby Mitchell	T-8	67-70-72-72=281	$1,567.50
Pete Brown	T-8	71-69-69-72=281	$1,567.50
Bob Panasiuk	T-8	73-69-69-70=281	$1,567.50

Houston Open
Course: Woodlands C.C., The Woodlands, Texas
Par: 72 Yardage: 6,929
Last day of event: Sunday, May 4, 1975

Player	Place	Score	Earnings
Bruce Crampton	Win	68-70-66-69=273	$30,000.00
Gil Morgan	2	70-68-67-70=275	$17,100.00
Joe Inman	3	68-70-71-67=276	$10,650.00
John Schroeder	4	68-72-67-71=278	$7,050.00
Eddie Pearce	T-5	67-70-71-71=279	$5,193.75
Larry Nelson	T-5	68-71-70-70=279	$5,193.75
Lionel Hebert	T-5	69-71-70-69=279	$5,193.75
Tom Kite	T-5	70-71-70-68=279	$5,193.75
Roger Maltbie	T-9	69-70-70-71=280	$3,900.00
Alan Tapie	T-9	67-71-73-69=280	$3,900.00

Byron Nelson Golf Classic
Course: Preston Trail G.C., Dallas, Texas
Par: 72 Yardage: 6,993
Last day of event: Monday, May 12, 1975

Player	Place	Score	Earnings
Tom Watson	Win	72-63-69-65=269	$35,000.00
Bob-E. Smith	2	67-68-69-67=271	$19,950.00
Jack Ewing	3	74-63-68-67=272	$12,425.00
Rod Funseth	T-4	69-68-66-70=273	$7,700.00
Larry Nelson	T-4	69-65-71-68=273	$7,700.00
Bruce Crampton	T-6	66-70-67-71=274	$5,950.00
Dwight Nevil	T-6	68-68-71-67=274	$5,950.00
George Knudson	T-8	68-69-68-70=275	$4,392.60
Miller Barber	T-8	68-69-67-71=275	$4,392.60
Lon Hinkle	T-8	69-71-68-67=275	$4,392.60
Mike Morley	T-8	71-71-65-68=275	$4,392.60
Bob Eastwood	T-8	73-65-65-72=275	$4,392.60

First NBC New Orleans Open
Course: Lakewood C.C., New Orleans, La.
Par: 72 Yardage: 7,080
Last day of event: Sunday, May 18, 1975

Player	Place	Score	Earnings
Billy Casper	Win	67-68-66-70=271	$30,000.00
Peter Oosterhuis	2	68-68-69-68=273	$17,100.00
Lanny Wadkins	3	69-68-70-69=276	$10,650.00
Bob Wynn	4	71-66-70-70=277	$7,050.00
Steve Melnyk	T-5	69-69-68-72=278	$5,450.00
Don January	T-5	69-72-71-66=278	$5,450.00
Larry Hinson	T-5	73-70-67-68=278	$5,450.00
Tom Shaw	T-8	69-67-73-70=279	$4,075.00
David Graham	T-8	70-69-73-67=279	$4,075.00
Joe Porter	T-8	74-66-71-68=279	$4,075.00

Danny Thomas Memphis Classic
Course: Colonial C.C. (South), Cordova, Tenn.
Par: 72 Yardage: 7,282
Last day of event: Sunday, May 25, 1975

Player	Place	Score	Earnings
Gene Littler	Win	67-68-69-66=270	$35,000.00
John Mahaffey	2	65-68-71-71=275	$19,500.00
Tom Weiskopf	T-3	65-71-73-68=277	$10,325.00
Jack Nicklaus	T-3	66-70-73-68=277	$10,325.00
Jim Simons	T-5	69-70-72-70=281	$6,737.50

Player	Place	Score	Earnings
Tom Kite	T-5	67-73-70-71=281	$6,737.50
Tom Watson	7	69-72-73-68=282	$5,600.00
Jim Dent	8	72-70-74-67=283	$5,163.00
Joe Inman	T-9	71-72-71-70=284	$3,750.00
Gibby Gilbert	T-9	72-71-71-70=284	$3,750.00
John Lister	T-9	68-71-73-72=284	$3,750.00
Don January	T-9	73-71-69-71=284	$3,750.00
Ray Floyd	T-9	69-74-69-72=284	$3,750.00
Roy Pace	T-9	74-70-69-71=284	$3,750.00
Lee Trevino	T-9	74-67-73-70=284	$3,750.00

Atlanta Classic
Course: Atlanta C.C., Atlanta, Ga.
Par: 72 Yardage: 7,007
Last day of event: Sunday, June 1, 1975

Player	Place	Score	Earnings
Hale Irwin	Win	66-69-68-68=271	$45,000.00
Tom Watson	2	71-71-65-68=275	$25,650.00
Charles Coody	3	71-68-67-70=276	$15,975.00
Johnny Miller	T-4	68-71-68-70=277	$9,300.00
Jack Nicklaus	T-4	68-73-67-69=277	$9,300.00
Miller Barber	T-4	71-64-73-69=277	$9,300.00
Jim Dent	T-4	70-68-69-72=279	$6,925.00
Jim Colbert	T-4	70-74-68-67=279	$6,925.00
Billy Casper	T-9	66-73-70-71=280	$5,625.00
John Schlee	T-9	71-74-68-67=280	$5,625.00
Gibby Gilbert	T-9	75-65-70-70=280	$5,625.00

Kemper Open
Course: Quail Hollow C.C., Charlotte, N.C.
Par: 72 Yardage: 7,205
Last day of event: Sunday, June 8, 1975

Player	Place	Score	Earnings
Ray Floyd	Win	65-71-73-69=278	$50,000.00
John Mahaffey	T-2	71-69-71-70=281	$23,125.00
Gary Player	T-2	69-70-69-73=281	$23,125.00
Jerry Heard	4	71-70-69-72=282	$11,750.00
Bob Murphy	T-5	68-72-72-71=283	$9,083.33
Peter Oosterhuis	T-5	70-73-69-71=283	$9,083.34
Jim Masserio	T-5	71-70-69-73=283	$9,083.33
David Graham	T-8	73-68-71-72=284	$6,531.25
Steve Melnyk	T-8	71-68-74-71=284	$6,531.25
Bob Stanton	T-8	70-75-69-70=284	$6,531.25
Bobby Nichols	T-8	71-69-69-75=284	$6,531.25

IVB Philadelphia Golf Classic
Course: Whitemarsh Valley C.C., Chestnut Hill, Pa.
Par: 71 Yardage: 6,687
Last day of event: Sunday, June 15, 1975

Player	Place	Score	Earnings
Tom Jenkins	Win	69-65-69-72=275	$30,000.00
Johnny Miller	2	71-69-68-68=276	$17,100.00
Bob Wynn	3	73-70-65-69=277	$10,650.00
Jim Simons	4	69-71-68-71=279	$7,050.00
Bud Allin	5	71-70-69-70=280	$6,150.00
Tom Shaw	T-6	70-71-70-70=281	$4,485.00
Don Bies	T-6	71-71-71-68=281	$4,485.00
Jerry McGee	T-6	69-72-68-72=281	$4,485.00
J.C. Snead	T-6	69-72-69-71=281	$4,485.00
Gary Groh	T-6	73-71-71-66=281	$4,485.00

U.S. Open

Course: Medinah C.C. (No 3), Medinah, Ill.
Par: 71 Yardage: 7,032
Last day of event: Monday, June 23, 1975

Player	Place	Score	Earnings
Lou Graham	Win	74-72-68-73-71=287	$40,000.00
Playoff: Beat John Mahaffey in 18-hole playoff (Graham 71, Mahaffey 73)			
John Mahaffey	2	73-71-72-71-73=287	$20,000.00
Hale Irwin	T-3	74-71-73-70=288	$10,875.00
Bob Murphy	T-3	74-73-72-69=288	$10,875.00
Ben Crenshaw	T-3	70-68-76-74=288	$10,875.00
Frank Beard	T-3	74-69-67-78=288	$10,875.00
Peter Oosterhuis	T-7	69-73-72-75=289	$7,500.00
Jack Nicklaus	T-7	72-70-75-72=289	$7,500.00
Arnold Palmer	T-9	69-75-73-73=290	$5,000.00
Pat Fitzsimons	T-9	67-73-73-77=290	$5,000.00
Tom Watson	T-9	67-68-78-77=290	$5,000.00

Western Open

Course: Butler National G.C., Oak Brook, Ill.
Par: 71 Yardage: 7,002
Last day of event: Sunday, June 29, 1975

Player	Place	Score	Earnings
Hale Irwin	Win	71-68-71-73=283	$40,000.00
Bobby Cole	2	74-71-70-69=284	$22,800.00
Ed Sneed	3	71-74-69-73=287	$14,200.00
Gibby Gilbert	T-4	71-71-73-73=288	$8,266.66
Jerry Heard	T-4	69-74-72-73=288	$8,266.67
John Lister	T-4	76-75-65-72=288	$8,266.67
Florentino Molina	T-7	70-73-71-75=289	$5,460.00
Jim Simons	T-7	71-73-70-75=289	$5,460.00
Gay Brewer	T-7	75-70-69-75=289	$5,460.00
Al Geiberger	T-7	71-73-76-69=289	$5,460.00
George Johnson	T-7	72-66-72-79=289	$5,460.00

Greater Milwaukee Open

Course: Tuckaway C.C., Franklin, Wis.
Par: 72 Yardage: 7,030
Last day of event: Saturday, July 5, 1975

Player	Place	Score	Earnings
Art Wall, Jr.	Win	67-67-67-70=271	$26,000.00
Gary McCord	2	69-71-65-67=272	$14,820.00
Rod Curl	3	69-70-66-68=273	$9,230.00
Dave Hill	T-4	68-68-69-69=274	$5,720.00
Gibby Gilbert	T-4	69-66-69-70=274	$5,720.00
Dave Stockton	6	68-71-68-68=275	$4,680.00
Ken Still	7	68-67-70-71=276	$4,160.00
Lee Elder	T-8	69-69-70-69=277	$3,672.50
Mark Hayes	T-8	71-68-66-72=277	$3,672.50
Lionel Hebert	T-10	69-71-68-70=278	$3,120.00
Roger Maltbie	T-10	72-67-68-71=278	$3,120.00

British Open

Course: Carnoustie G.C., Carnoustie, Angus, Scotland
Par: 72 Yardage: 7,065
Last day of event: Sunday, July 13, 1975

Player	Place	Score	Earnings
Tom Watson	Win	71-67-69-72=279	$16,500.00
Playoff: Beat Jack Newton in 18-hole playoff (Watson 71, Newton 72)			
Jack Newton	2	69-71-65-74=279	$13,200.00
Jack Nicklaus	T-3	69-71-68-72=280	$8,507.40
Johnny Miller	T-3	71-69-66-74=280	$8,507.40
Bobby Cole	T-3	72-66-66-76=280	$8,507.40
Graham Marsh	6	72-67-71-71=281	$6,600.00
Peter Oosterhuis	T-7	68-70-71-73=282	$5,940.00
Neil Coles	7	72-69-67-74=282	$5,940.00
Hale Irwin	9	69-70-69-75=283	$5,280.00
George Burns	T-10	71-73-69-71=284	$4,675.00
John Mahaffey	T-10	71-68-69-76=284	$4,675.00

Ed McMahon Quad City Open

Course: Oakwood C.C., Coal Valley, Ill.
Par: 71 Yardage: 6,305
Last day of event: Sunday, July 13, 1975

Player	Place	Score	Earnings
Roger Maltbie	Win	74-65-72-64=275	$15,000.00
Dave Eichelberger	2	67-65-72-72=276	$8,550.00
Mark Hayes	3	70-68-70-69=277	$5,325.00
Gary McCord	4	72-66-70-70=278	$3,525.00
Terry Dill	T-5	67-71-69-72=279	$2,725.00
Howard Twitty	T-5	66-73-68-72=279	$2,725.00
Homero Blancas	T-5	70-67-73-69=279	$2,725.00
Antonio Cerda	8	73-73-68-66=280	$2,213.00
Mike Reasor	T-9	71-70-70-70=281	$1,725.00
Dave Stockton	T-9	69-70-70-72=281	$1,725.00
Ralph Johnston	T-9	71-69-72-69=281	$1,725.00
Frank Beard	T-9	68-70-69-74=281	$1,725.00
Bruce Lietzke	T-9	69-70-74-68=281	$1,725.00

Pleasant Valley Classic

Course: Pleasant Valley C.C., Sutton, Mass.
Par: 71 Yardage: 7,110
Last day of event: Sunday, July 20, 1975

Player	Place	Score	Earnings
Roger Maltbie	Win	72-71-67-66=276	$40,000.00
Mac McLendon	2	70-68-70-69=277	$22,800.00
Ben Crenshaw	T-3	69-68-71-70=278	$9,750.00
Bud Allin	T-3	70-67-72-69=278	$9,750.00
Miller Barber	T-3	67-74-69-68=278	$9,750.00
Jim Simons	T-3	69-70-74-65=278	$9,750.00
George Knudson	T-7	69-69-72-70=280	$6,150.00
Lee Trevino	T-7	70-66-74-70=280	$6,150.00
Al Geiberger	T-9	70-71-70-70=281	$4,600.00
George Johnson	T-9	69-68-72-72=281	$4,600.00
Rod Curl	T-9	66-71-71-73=281	$4,600.00
Lee Elder	T-9	68-67-73-73=281	$4,600.00
Hale Irwin	T-9	70-68-73-70=281	$4,600.00

Canadian Open

Course: Royal Montreal G.C., Ile-Bizard, Quebec, Canada
Par: 70 Yardage: 6,628
Last day of event: Sunday, July 27, 1975

Player	Place	Score	Earnings
Tom Weiskopf	Win	65-74-68-67=274	$40,000.00
Playoff: Beat Jack Nicklaus with birdie on first extra hole			
Jack Nicklaus	2	65-71-70-68=274	$22,800.00
Gay Brewer	3	68-68-70-69=275	$14,200.00
Arnold Palmer	4	68-73-69-67=277	$9,400.00
Bruce Crampton	5	74-68-67-69=278	$8,200.00
J.C. Snead	6	73-68-72-66=279	$7,200.00
Lee Trevino	T-7	71-72-68-69=280	$5,675.00

Gary Player	T-7	67-73-73-67=280	$5,675.00
Bob Wynn	T-7	69-74-69-68=280	$5,675.00
Ken Still	T-7	70-67-74-69=280	$5,675.00

Westchester Classic
Course: Westchester C.C., Harrison, N.Y.
Par: 72 Yardage: 6,614
Last day of event: Sunday, August 3, 1975

Player	Place	Score	Earnings
Gene Littler	Win	68-68-69-66=271	$50,000.00

Playoff: Beat Julius Boros with par on first extra hole

Julius Boros	2	70-66-70-65=271	$28,500.00
Tom Weiskopf	3	66-63-72-71=272	$17,750.00
Bruce Lietzke	4	70-71-66-67=274	$11,750.00
Pat Fitzsimons	5	67-70-66-73=276	$10,250.00
Hale Irwin	T-6	72-65-71-69=277	$8,125.00
Tom Shaw	T-6	72-71-67-67=277	$8,125.00
Jerry Heard	T-6	73-70-67-67=277	$8,125.00
George Cadle	T-9	71-69-69-69=278	$6,000.00
Art Wall, Jr.	T-9	72-68-69-69=278	$6,000.00
Dan Sikes, Jr.	T-9	72-71-69-66=278	$6,000.00
Rik Massengale	T-9	65-74-72-67=278	$6,000.00

PGA Championship
Course: Firestone C.C. (South), Akron, Ohio
Par: 70 Yardage: 7,180
Last day of event: Sunday, August 10, 1975

Player	Place	Score	Earnings
Jack Nicklaus	Win	70-68-67-71=276	$45,000.00
Bruce Crampton	2	71-63-75-69=278	$25,700.00
Tom Weiskopf	3	70-71-70-68=279	$16,000.00
Andy North	4	72-74-70-65=281	$10,500.00
Billy Casper	T-5	69-72-72-70=283	$8,662.50
Hale Irwin	T-5	72-65-73-73=283	$8,662.50
Dave Hill	T-7	71-71-74-68=284	$6,917.50
Gene Littler	T-7	76-71-66-71=284	$6,917.50
Tom Watson	9	70-71-71-73=285	$6,075.00
Ray Floyd	T-10	70-73-72-71=286	$4,467.86
Don January	T-10	72-70-71-73=286	$4,467.85
Bud Allin	T-10	73-72-70-71=286	$4,467.86
Ben Crenshaw	T-10	73-72-71-70=286	$4,467.86
David Graham	T-10	72-70-70-74=286	$4,467.85
Leonard Thompson	T-10	74-69-72-71=286	$4,467.86
John Schlee	T-10	71-68-75-72=286	$4,467.86

Sammy Davis, Jr. - Greater Hartford Open
Course: Wethersfield C.C., Wethersfield, Conn.
Par: 71 Yardage: 6,568
Last day of event: Sunday, August 17, 1975

Player	Place	Score	Earnings
Don Bies	Win	65-66-67-69=267	$40,000.00

Playoff: Beat Hubert Green with birdie on second extra hole

Hubert Green	2	66-65-68-68=267	$22,800.00
J.C. Snead	3	66-68-67-67=268	$14,200.00
Larry Nelson	T-4	68-66-67-68=269	$8,800.00
Victor Regalado	T-4	69-68-65-67=269	$8,800.00
Homero Blancas	6	67-69-68-66=270	$7,200.00
Andy North	T-7	66-69-67-69=271	$6,150.00
Johnny Miller	T-7	69-67-68-67=271	$6,150.00
Gary Player	T-9	69-68-69-66=272	$5,200.00
Ray Floyd	T-9	67-69-71-65=272	$5,200.00

Tournament Players Championship
Course: Colonial C.C., Fort Worth, Texas
Par: 70 Yardage: 7,160
Last day of event: Sunday, August 24, 1975

Player	Place	Score	Earnings
Al Geiberger	Win	66-68-67-69=270	$50,000.00
Dave Stockton	2	72-64-68-69=273	$28,500.00
Hubert Green	3	71-65-70-69=275	$17,730.00
Mason Rudolph	T-4	69-70-72-70=281	$10,333.34
Bob Dickson	T-4	67-69-72-73=281	$10,333.34
Bob Murphy	T-4	73-69-71-68=281	$10,333.34
Hale Irwin	7	67-72-72-72=283	$8,000.00
Joe Porter	T-8	72-72-68-72=284	$6,791.67
Tom Watson	T-8	73-69-75-67=284	$6,791.67
Bobby Wadkins	T-8	76-69-68-71=284	$6,791.66

B.C. Open
Course: En-Joie G.C., Endicott, N.Y.
Par: 71 Yardage: 6,966
Last day of event: Monday, September 1, 1975

Player	Place	Score	Earnings
Don Iverson	Win	66-69-71-68=274	$35,000.00
Jim Colbert	T-2	69-69-69-68=275	$16,187.50
David Graham	T-2	68-68-71-68=275	$16,187.50
Terry Diehl	4	69-69-71-66=276	$8,225.00
Hubert Green	T-5	70-69-71-67=277	$6,358.33
Jerry McGee	T-5	69-72-70-66=277	$6,358.34
Jim Wiechers	T-5	72-67-71-67=277	$6,358.33
Sam Snead	T-8	69-73-69-67=278	$4,944.00
Butch Baird	T-8	66-67-71-74=278	$4,944.00
Gary McCord	T-10	70-70-71-68=279	$4,025.00
Mark Hayes	T-10	71-69-68-71=279	$4,025.00

Southern Open
Course: Green Island C.C., Columbus, Ga.
Par: 70 Yardage: 6,791
Last day of event: Sunday, September 7, 1975

Player	Place	Score	Earnings
Hubert Green	Win	68-66-66-64=264	$20,000.00
John Schroeder	2	65-66-68-68=267	$11,400.00
Terry Dill	3	66-69-69-68=272	$7,100.00
Bill Rogers	4	70-69-63-71=273	$4,700.00
Gibby Gilbert	5	69-68-69-68=274	$4,100.00
Ben Crenshaw	6	68-69-70-68=275	$3,600.00
George Burns	T-7	70-65-71-70=276	$2,950.00
Larry Nelson	T-7	70-71-70-65=276	$2,950.00
J.C. Snead	T-7	68-68-72-68=276	$2,950.00
Allen Miller	T-10	70-69-68-70=277	$2,120.00
Mac McLendon	T-10	65-69-71-72=277	$2,120.00
Gary Wintz	T-10	70-72-68-67=277	$2,120.00
Alan Tapie	T-10	67-66-70-74=277	$2,120.00
Mark Hayes	T-10	70-65-74-68=277	$2,120.00

World Open
Course: Pinehurst C.C. (No 2), Pinehurst, N.C.
Par: 71 Yardage: 7,007
Last day of event: Sunday, September 14, 1975

Player	Place	Score	Earnings
Jack Nicklaus	Win	70-71-70-69=280	$40,000.00

Playoff: Beat Billy Casper with par on first extra hole

Billy Casper	2	70-72-68-70=280	$22,800.00
Tom Weiskopf	3	67-71-68-75=281	$14,200.00
Pat Fitzsimons	4	67-69-71-75=282	$9,400.00
Ed Sneed	5	68-70-70-75=283	$8,200.00
John Schlee	T-6	68-72-73-71=284	$6,225.00
John Mahaffey	T-6	70-71-70-73=284	$6,225.00
Rod Funseth	T-6	67-70-74-73=284	$6,225.00
Larry Nelson	T-6	70-71-69-74=284	$6,225.00
Bob Zender	T-10	72-71-71-71=285	$4,240.00
Bruce Lietzke	T-10	72-72-71-70=285	$4,240.00
Wally Armstrong	T-10	69-72-71-73=285	$4,240.00
Kermit Zarley	T-10	71-69-74-71=285	$4,240.00
Howard Twitty	T-10	69-68-73-75=285	$4,240.00

Sahara Invitational

Course: Sahara Nevada C.C., Las Vegas, Nev.
Home course / Par: 71 Yardage: 6,880
Last day of event: Sunday, September 28, 1975

Player	Place	Score	Earnings
Dave Hill	Win	68-66-67-69=270	$27,000.00
Playoff: Beat Rik Massengale with par on first extra hole			
Rik Massengale	2	70-64-67-69=270	$15,390.00
Joe Inman	T-3	67-70-67-67=271	$7,965.00
Bobby Mitchell	T-3	70-64-67-70=271	$7,965.00
George Cadle	T-5	69-66-67-70=272	$4,674.50
Charles Coody	T-5	70-69-65-68=272	$4,674.50
Don January	T-5	70-66-70-66=272	$4,674.50
Bruce Crampton	T-5	72-65-65-70=272	$4,674.50
Chuck Courtney	T-9	68-68-68-69=273	$3,375.00
Bob Wynn	T-9	64-70-68-71=273	$3,375.00
Gary McCord	T-9	67-70-71-65=273	$3,375.00

Kaiser International Open

Course: Silverado C.C., Napa, Calif.
Home Course -Par: 72 Yardage: 6,849
Last day of event: Sunday, October 5, 1975

Player	Place	Score	Earnings
Johnny Miller	Win	68-67-68-69=272	$35,000.00
Rod Curl	2	73-67-64-71=275	$19,950.00
Marty Fleckman	T-3	68-67-71-70=276	$9,275.00
Gene Littler	T-3	65-70-69-72=276	$9,275.00
Lee Trevino	T-3	70-65-72-69=276	$9,275.00
Jack Nicklaus	6	72-67-69-69=277	$6,300.00
Bruce Lietzke	T-7	70-70-68-70=278	$5,381.50
Antonio Cerda	T-7	69-70-73-66=278	$5,381.50
Gibby Gilbert	T-9	68-71-68-72=279	$4,200.00
Lou Graham	T-9	69-70-72-68=279	$4,200.00
Jerry Heard	T-9	73-67-72-67=279	$4,200.00
Don January	T-9	70-64-75-70=279	$4,200.00

San Antonio Texas Open

Course: Woodlake G.C., San Antonio, Texas
Par: 72 Yardage: 7,143
Last day of event: Sunday, October 19, 1975

Player	Place	Score	Earnings
Don January	Win	71-67-71-66=275	$25,000.00
Playoff: Beat Larry Hinson with birdie on second extra hole			
Larry Hinson	2	70-73-64-68=275	$14,250.00
Gil Morgan	3	66-68-75-68=277	$8,875.00
Miller Barber	T-4	66-71-70-71=278	$5,166.66
Bruce Lietzke	T-4	70-71-70-67=278	$5,166.67

Ralph Johnston	T-4	67-68-73-70=278	$5,166.67
Mike McCullough	7	73-67-70-69=279	$4,000.00
Bob Shaw	T-8	71-72-68-69=280	$3,137.40
Charles Coody	T-8	68-69-70-73=280	$3,137.40
Richard Crawford	T-8	68-69-70-73=280	$3,137.40
Rod Funseth	T-8	73-69-66-72=280	$3,137.40
Bobby Cole	T-8	74-66-71-69=280	$3,137.40

1976

Raymond Floyd won the Masters by a shot over Ben Crenshaw, setting 36-hole (65-66-131) and 54-hole (70-201) scoring records in the process. Jerry Pate, at age 22, won the U.S. Open at the Atlanta Athletic Club, which had become the Open venue thanks to a request to the USGA by Bobby Jones shortly before his death in 1971. Frequently relying on his 1-iron off the tee, Johnny Miller scored a 6-shot victory in the British Open at Royal Birkdale. But it was19-year-old Seve Ballesteros, the 54-hole leader and eventual co-runnerup with Jack Nicklaus, who stole the show with his flamboyant play amid the dunes at Birkdale. Dave Stockton won his second PGA Championship, this one by a shot over Floyd and Don January. Roger Maltbie, who would gain greater fame as a TV commentator, won the first Memorial Tournament at Nicklaus' Muirfield Village.

NBC Tucson Open

Course: Tucson National G.C., Starr Pass G.C., Tucson, Ariz.
Par: 72 Yardage: 7,305
Last day of event: Sunday, January 11, 1976

Player	Place	Score	Earnings
Johnny Miller	Win	70-69-67-68=274	$40,000.00
Howard Twitty	2	71-70-68-68=277	$14,200.00
Tom Weiskopf	3	67-71-67-73=278	$14,200.00
Dave Hill	T-4	68-69-71-71=279	$7,083.33
Bruce Lietzke	T-4	72-67-70-70=279	$7,083.33
Jerry McGee	T-4	72-69-71-67=279	$7,083.34
Tom Watson	T-4	70-68-68-73=279	$7,083.33
Dave Stockton	T-4	73-66-69-71=279	$7,083.33
Pat Fitzsimons	T-4	72-65-74-68=279	$7,083.34
Jerry Heard	T-10	69-71-71-69=280	$4,600.00
Don January	T-10	71-70-68-71=280	$4,600.00
Billy Casper	T-10	72-70-68-70=280	$4,600.00

Phoenix Open

Course: Phoenix C.C., Phoenix, Ariz.
Par: 71 Yardage: 6,726
Last day of event: Sunday, January 18, 1976

Player	Place	Score	Earnings
Bob Gilder	Win	68-67-66-67=268	$40,000.00
Roger Maltbie	2	65-65-70-70=270	$22,800.00
Rod Curl	T-3	70-70-68-65=273	$9,750.00
Lee Trevino	T-3	66-68-68-71=273	$9,750.00
Jim Simons	T-3	71-67-66-69=273	$9,750.00
Bruce Lietzke	T-3	67-74-65-67=273	$9,750.00
Hale Irwin	T-7	69-65-71-69=274	$6,150.00
Johnny Miller	T-7	69-67-72-66=274	$6,150.00
Gary McCord	T-9	68-69-69-69=275	$5,000.00
Ben Crenshaw	T-9	67-70-70-68=275	$5,000.00
Jim Colbert	T-9	68-65-70-72=275	$5,000.00

Bing Crosby Pro-Am

Courses: Pebble Beach G.L. - Home
Spyglass Hill G.C., Cypress Point C.C., Pebble Beach, Calif.
Home Course Par: 72 Yardage: 6,815
Last day of event: Sunday, January 25, 1976

Player	Place	Score	Earnings
Ben Crenshaw	Win	75-67-70-69=281	$37,000.00
Mike Morley	2	67-72-71-73=283	$21,090.00
George Burns	T-3	74-72-69-69=284	$10,915.00
Dave Hill	T-3	71-65-76-72=284	$10,915.00
Tom Watson	T-5	73-72-70-71=286	$7,122.50
David Graham	T-5	69-69-73-75=286	$7,122.50
Bud Allin	T-7	74-68-71-74=287	$5,688.50
Bruce Crampton	T-7	72-76-72-67=287	$5,688.50
Charles Coody	T-9	72-71-72-73=288	$4,810.00
Tom Weiskopf	T-9	76-70-70-72=288	$4,810.00

Hawaiian Open

Course: Waialae C.C., Honolulu, Ha.
Par: 72 Yardage: 7,234
Last day of event: Sunday, February 1, 1976

Player	Place	Score	Earnings
Ben Crenshaw	Win	70-69-65-66=270	$46,000.00
Larry Nelson	T-2	69-69-67-69=274	$21,275.00
Hale Irwin	T-2	66-69-66-73=274	$21,275.00
Charles Coody	T-4	68-70-68-69=275	$8,970.00
Al Geiberger	T-4	66-70-68-71=275	$8,970.00
Lou Graham	T-4	67-69-71-68=275	$8,970.00
Mike Morley	T-4	74-67-68-66=275	$8,970.00
Lee Trevino	T-8	69-69-69-69=276	$5,539.17
Mac McLendon	T-8	69-69-71-67=276	$5,539.17
Wally Armstrong	T-8	71-70-65-70=276	$5,539.16
Gene Littler	T-8	71-70-69-66=276	$5,539.17
Bob Murphy	T-8	66-69-67-74=276	$5,539.16
Ed Sneed	T-8	66-74-67-69=276	$5,539.17

Bob Hope Chrysler Classic

Course: Indian Wells C.C., Eldorado C.C., Bermuda Dunes C.C., La Quinta C.C.
Home course Par: 72 Yardage: 6,478
Last day of event: Sunday, February 8, 1976

Player	Place	Score	Earnings
Johnny Miller	Win	71-69-73-68-63=344	$36,000.00
Rik Massengale	2	69-72-71-68-67=347	$20,520.00
Bud Allin	3	67-68-75-71-67=348	$12,780.00
Jerry Heard	T-4	73-72-70-69-67=351	$7,740.00
Dave Newquist	T-4	74-70-67-71-69=351	$7,740.00
Jim Colbert	T-4	67-73-77-70-64=351	$7,740.00
Jack Nicklaus	T-7	69-70-72-69-72=352	$5,535.00
Lee Elder	T-7	71-70-73-69-69=352	$5,535.00
Billy Casper	9	72-65-74-68-74=353	$4,860.00
Bill Rogers	T-10	69-71-74-70-70=354	$4,320.00
Bob Murphy	T-10	70-68-76-74-66=354	$4,320.00

Andy Williams-San Diego Open

Course: Torrey Pines (South), Torrey Pines (North), San Diego, Calif.
Home Course -Par: 72 Yardage: 7,021
Last day of event: Sunday, February 15, 1976

Player	Place	Score	Earnings
J.C. Snead	Win	65-68-67-72=272	$36,000.00
Don Bies	2	66-68-71-68=273	$20,520.00

Player	Place	Score	Earnings
Don January	T-3	71-65-69-70=275	$9,540.00
Bruce Crampton	T-3	66-68-73-68=275	$9,540.00
Mike Morley	T-3	67-66-73-69=275	$9,540.00
Bud Allin	6	68-70-70-68=276	$6,480.00
Jerry Pate	T-7	66-71-70-70=277	$4,914.00
Bob Dickson	T-7	67-72-68-70=277	$4,914.00
Tom Kite	T-7	67-72-70-68=277	$4,914.00
Jim Colbert	T-7	72-70-67-68=277	$4,914.00
Rod Funseth	T-7	68-73-69-67=277	$4,914.00

Glen Campbell Los Angeles Open

Course: Riviera C.C., Pacific Palisades, Calif.
Par: 71 Yardage: 7,029
Last day of event: Sunday, February 22, 1976

Player	Place	Score	Earnings
Hale Irwin	Win	69-69-66-68=272	$37,000.00
Tom Watson	2	67-66-68-73=274	$21,090.00
Gary Player	3	72-71-67-67=277	$13,135.00
Tom Shaw	T-4	71-70-68-69=278	$8,140.00
Lanny Wadkins	T-4	68-71-73-66=278	$8,140.00
Gil Morgan	6	74-68-70-68=280	$6,660.00
Tom Jenkins	T-7	66-72-72-71=281	$5,457.33
Gene Littler	T-7	72-70-71-68=281	$5,457.34
Don January	T-7	68-67-73-73=281	$5,457.33
Tom Kite	10	71-73-69-69=282	$4,625.00

Tournament Players Championship

Course: Inverrary G. & C.C. (East), Lauderhill, Fla.
Par: 72 Yardage: 7,127
Last day of event: Monday, March 1, 1976

Player	Place	Score	Earnings
Jack Nicklaus	Win	66-70-68-65=269	$60,000.00
J.C. Snead	2	67-69-68-68=272	$34,200.00
Roger Maltbie	T-3	70-70-65-71=276	$17,700.00
Jim Masserio	T-3	69-68-72-67=276	$17,700.00
Mark Hayes	5	71-67-67-72=277	$12,300.00
Lee Elder	6	69-72-70-67=278	$10,800.00
Butch Baird	T-7	71-67-72-70=280	$9,225.00
Don January	T-7	67-68-73-72=280	$9,225.00
David Graham	T-9	70-71-71-69=281	$7,500.00
Gary Player	T-9	73-70-71-67=281	$7,500.00
Tom Watson	T-9	67-70-70-74=281	$7,500.00

Florida Citrus Open Invitational

Course: Rio Pinar C.C., Orlando, Fla.
Par: 72 Yardage: 7,012
Last day of event: Sunday, March 7, 1976

Player	Place	Score	Earnings
Hale Irwin	Win	74-66-64-66=270	$40,000.00
Playoff: Beat Kermit Zarley with par on sixth extra hole			
Kermit Zarley	2	67-66-68-69=270	$2,280.00
J.C. Snead	3	70-68-69-66=273	$14,200.00
John Mahaffey	4	69-67-69-69=274	$9,400.00
Larry Ziegler	T-5	72-66-68-69=275	$7,700.00
Mike Hill	T-5	65-73-67-70=275	$7,700.00
Bob Murphy	7	69-68-69-70=276	$6,400.00
Victor Regalado	T-8	70-69-70-68=277	$5,433.34
Mark Hayes	T-8	65-70-71-71=277	$5,433.33
Al Geiberger	T-8	73-67-67-70=277	$5,433.33

Doral-Eastern Open
Course: Doral C.C. (Blue), Miami, Fla.
Par: 72 Yardage: 6,939
Last day of event: Sunday, March 14, 1976

Player	Place	Score	Earnings
Hubert Green	Win	66-70-65-69=270	$40,000.00
Mark Hayes	T-2	67-68-70-71=276	$18,500.00
Jack Nicklaus	T-2	69-71-68-68=276	$18,500.00
Ben Crenshaw	4	66-71-69-71=277	$9,400.00
Bobby Mitchell	T-5	68-69-68-73=278	$7,700.00
David Graham	T-5	69-73-64-72=278	$7,700.00
Rod Curl	7	71-69-71-68=279	$6,400.00
Tom Weiskopf	8	70-71-69-71=281	$5,900.00
Tom Kite	T-9	70-70-72-70=282	$5,000.00
Gene Littler	T-9	70-71-72-69=282	$5,000.00
Gary Player	T-9	69-71-69-73=282	$5,000.00

Greater Jacksonville Open
Course: Deerwood C.C., Jacksonville, Fla.
Par: 72 Yardage: 7,143
Last day of event: Sunday, March 21, 1976

Player	Place	Score	Earnings
Hubert Green	Win	72-67-67-70=276	$35,000.00
Miller Barber	2	72-67-68-71=278	$19,950.00
Mike Hill	T-3	69-68-71-71=279	$10,325.00
Ed Dougherty	T-3	73-72-67-67=279	$10,325.00
Lou Graham	5	71-73-65-71=280	$7,175.00
Gary Player	6	73-69-69-70=281	$6,300.00
Ben Crenshaw	7	70-71-71-70=282	$5,600.00
Lee Elder	8	70-73-69-71=283	$5,163.00
Rik Massengale	T-9	70-72-70-72=284	$3,879.16
Mike McCullough	T-9	70-72-72-70=284	$3,879.17
Peter Oosterhuis	T-9	69-73-73-69=284	$3,879.17
Dave Stockton	T-9	73-70-72-69=284	$3,879.17
Ray Floyd	T-9	68-71-74-71=284	$3,879.16
Dale Douglass	T-9	71-69-74-70=284	$3,879.17

Sea Pines Heritage Classic
Course: Harbour Town G.L., Hilton Head, S.C.
Par: 71 Yardage: 6,657
Last day of event: Sunday, March 28, 1976

Player	Place	Score	Earnings
Hubert Green	Win	68-67-66-73=274	$43,000.00
Jerry McGee	2	71-69-71-68=279	$24,510.00
Gibby Gilbert	T-3	68-70-69-73=280	$11,395.00
Don January	T-3	67-72-74-67=280	$11,395.00
Hale Irwin	T-3	69-67-77-67=280	$11,395.00
Kermit Zarley	T-6	70-71-71-69=281	$6,428.00
Andy North	T-6	69-70-72-70=281	$6,428.00
Lanny Wadkins	T-6	69-73-69-70=281	$6,428.00
Graham Marsh	T-6	69-69-69-74=281	$6,428.00
Bob Murphy	T-6	66-71-68-76=281	$6,428.00

Greater Greensboro Open
Course: Sedgefield C.C., Greensboro, N.C.
Par: 71 Yardage: 6,643
Last day of event: Sunday, April 4, 1976

Player	Place	Score	Earnings
Al Geiberger	Win	70-65-65-68=268	$46,000.00
Lee Trevino	2	68-71-66-65=270	$26,220.00

Player	Place	Score	Earnings
Miller Barber	3	68-67-69-67=271	$16,330.00
Lou Graham	T-4	67-69-70-67=273	$10,120.00
George Burns	T-4	69-68-70-66=273	$10,120.00
Bob Menne	T-6	69-67-69-69=274	$7,475.00
Tom Weiskopf	T-6	69-68-68-69=274	$7,475.00
Eddie Pearce	T-6	71-68-70-65=274	$7,475.00
Dave Stockton	9	67-74-66-68=275	$6,210.00
Ron Cerrudo	T-10	69-67-70-70=276	$4,715.00
Mark Hayes	T-10	70-67-68-71=276	$4,715.00
Mike Hill	T-10	70-65-69-72=276	$4,715.00
Stan Lee	T-10	72-69-65-70=276	$4,715.00
Victor Regalado	T-10	72-68-69-67=276	$4,715.00
Gene Littler	T-10	73-68-67-68=276	$4,715.00

Masters
Course: Augusta National G.C., Augusta, Ga.
Par: 72 Yardage: 6,925
Last day of event: Sunday, April 11, 1976

Player	Place	Score	Earnings
Ray Floyd	Win	65-66-70-70=271	$40,000.00
Ben Crenshaw	2	70-70-72-67=279	$25,000.00
Larry Ziegler	T-3	67-71-72-72=282	$16,250.00
Jack Nicklaus	T-3	67-69-73-73=282	$16,250.00
Tom Kite	T-5	73-67-72-73=285	$11,167.00
Charles Coody	T-5	72-69-70-74=285	$11,167.00
Hale Irwin	T-5	71-77-67-70=285	$11,167.00
Billy Casper	8	71-76-71-69=287	$8,000.00
Tom Weiskopf	T-9	73-71-70-74=288	$6,000.00
Roger Maltbie	T-9	72-75-70-71=288	$6,000.00
Graham Marsh	T-9	73-68-75-72=288	$6,000.00

MONY Tournament of Champions
Course: La Costa C.C., Carlsbad, Calif.
Par: 72 Yardage: 6,911
Last day of event: Sunday, April 18, 1976

Player	Place	Score	Earnings
Don January	Win	71-68-69-69=277	$45,000.00
Hubert Green	2	69-71-73-69=282	$27,000.00
Bruce Crampton	T-3	71-70-72-70=283	$14,625.00
Al Geiberger	T-3	71-74-69-69=283	$14,625.00
Ben Crenshaw	5	72-72-72-68=284	$10,230.00
Tom Watson	6	72-74-71-69=286	$9,753.00
Art Wall, Jr.	7	74-71-72-70=287	$9,298.00
Ray Floyd	8	78-70-70-72=290	$8,848.00
Dave Hill	9	73-75-75-68=291	$8,398.00
J.C. Snead	T-10	72-70-76-74=292	$7,273.00
Lou Graham	T-10	73-69-76-74=292	$7,273.00
Don Bies	T-10	76-73-73-70=292	$7,273.00
Johnny Miller	T-10	77-72-73-70=292	$7,273.00

Tallahassee Open
Course: Killearn C.C., Tallahassee, Fla.
Par: 72 Yardage: 7,124
Last day of event: Sunday, April 18, 1976

Player	Place	Score	Earnings
Gary Koch	Win	71-69-67-70=277	$16,000.00
John Mahaffey	2	69-71-66-72=278	$9,120.00
Tom Storey	T-3	69-72-70-69=280	$4,720.00
Victor Regalado	T-3	69-73-70-68=280	$4,720.00
Wally Armstrong	T-5	70-72-72-68=282	$4,720.00
Ron Cerrudo	T-5	72-70-69-71=282	$4,720.00

Joe Porter	T-5	73-69-70-70=282	$4,720.00
Bob Eastwood	T-5	66-69-70-77=282	$4,720.00
Dave Newquist	T-9	70-71-72-70=283	$1,773.33
Mac McLendon	T-9	72-70-69-72=283	$1,773.33
Lyn Lott	T-9	67-69-73-74=283	$1,773.33
Marty Fleckman	T-9	69-74-73-67=283	$1,773.34
Fuzzy Zoeller	T-9	73-66-74-70=283	$1,773.33
George Cadle	T-9	74-67-73-69=283	$1,773.34

First NBC New Orleans Open
Course: Lakewood C.C., New Orleans, La.
Par: 72 Yardage: 7,080
Last day of event: Sunday, April 25, 1976

Player	Place	Score	Earnings
Larry Ziegler	Win	69-68-67-70=274	$35,000.00
Victor Regalado	2	68-69-69-69=275	$19,950.00
Tom Watson	3	68-72-72-64=276	$12,425.00
Billy Casper	T-4	67-71-70-70=278	$5,937.57
John Mahaffey	T-4	68-71-68-71=278	$5,937.57
Lee Elder	T-4	68-69-71-70=278	$5,937.57
Jim Colbert	T-4	71-66-71-70=278	$5,937.57
Gene Littler	T-4	69-69-72-68=278	$5,937.57
Gibby Gilbert	T-4	72-70-68-68=278	$5,937.58
Jack Nicklaus	T-4	68-67-74-69=278	$5,937.57

Houston Open
Course: Woodlands C.C., The Woodlands, Texas
Par: 72 Yardage: 6,997
Last day of event: Sunday, May 2, 1976

Player	Place	Score	Earnings
Lee Elder	Win	70-72-67-69=278	$40,000.00
Forrest Fezler	2	67-71-74-67=279	$22,800.00
Wally Armstrong	T-3	67-69-72-72=280	$11,800.00
George Burns	T-3	68-70-70-72=280	$11,800.00
Lee Trevino	T-5	70-70-70-71=281	$7,700.00
Miller Barber	T-5	72-69-69-71=281	$7,700.00
Barry Jaeckel	T-7	69-69-72-72=282	$5,900.00
Ed Sneed	T-7	69-70-70-73=282	$5,900.00
Mark Hayes	T-7	67-74-70-71=282	$5,900.00
Gil Morgan	T-10	71-70-71-71=283	$4,600.00
Bruce Devlin	T-10	69-70-72-72=283	$4,600.00
Charles Coody	T-10	70-72-67-74=283	$4,600.00

Byron Nelson Golf Classic
Course: Preston Trail G.C., Dallas, Texas
Par: 71 Yardage: 6,993
Last day of event: Sunday, May 9, 1976

Player	Place	Score	Earnings
Mark Hayes	Win	66-67-71-69=273	$40,000.00
Don Bies	2	67-70-70-68=275	$2,280.00
Ray Floyd	3	70-67-71-69=277	$14,200.00
Hale Irwin	4	70-68-72-68=278	$9,400.00
Ben Crenshaw	5	70-71-69-69=279	$8,200.00
Dave Stockton	T-6	69-71-70-70=280	$6,800.00
Larry Nelson	T-6	70-71-68-71=280	$6,800.00
Jack Nicklaus	T-8	71-68-71-71=281	$4,487.50
Monty Kaser	T-8	71-70-70-70=281	$4,487.50
Bill Rogers	T-8	69-68-72-72=281	$4,487.50
David Graham	T-8	70-70-72-69=281	$4,487.50
Mac McLendon	T-8	71-73-67-70=281	$4,487.50
Jerry McGee	T-8	73-72-67-69=281	$4,487.50

Bob-E. Smith	T-8	68-67-74-72=281	$4,487.50
Homero Blancas	T-8	74-69-70-68=281	$4,487.50

Colonial National Invitational
Course: Colonial C.C., Fort Worth, Texas
Par: 70 Yardage: 7,142
Last day of event: Sunday, May 16, 1976

Player	Place	Score	Earnings
Lee Trevino	Win	68-64-68-73=273	$40,000.00
Mike Morley	2	70-68-67-69=274	$22,800.00
Tom Weiskopf	T-3	68-71-67-71=277	$11,800.00
Don January	T-3	68-68-69-72=277	$11,800.00
Tom Kite	T-5	69-68-72-69=278	$7,266.67
John Mahaffey	T-5	69-72-68-69=278	$7,266.66
Bob Gilder	T-5	69-73-66-70=278	$7,266.67
Hubert Green	T-8	67-72-70-70=279	$5,225.00
Bob-E. Smith	T-8	70-72-68-69=279	$5,225.00
Grier Jones	T-8	72-69-71-67=279	$5,225.00
Miller Barber	T-8	68-65-70-76=279	$5,225.00

Danny Thomas Memphis Classic
Course: Colonial C.C. (South), Cordova, Tenn.
Par: 72 Yardage: 7,282
Last day of event: Sunday, May 23, 1976

Player	Place	Score	Earnings
Gibby Gilbert	Win	68-67-66-72=273	$40,000.00
John Lister	T-2	69-71-69-68=277	$15,466.67
Forrest Fezler	T-2	70-69-67-71=277	$15,466.66
Gil Morgan	T-2	70-69-65-73=277	$15,466.67
George Cadle	5	71-69-69-69=278	$8,200.00
Tom Kite	T-6	72-67-71-69=279	$6,800.00
Fred Marti	T-6	65-68-74-72=279	$6,800.00
Gene Littler	T-8	71-71-69-69=280	$5,225.00
Grier Jones	T-8	68-69-72-71=280	$5,225.00
Howard Twitty	T-8	68-72-70-70=280	$5,225.00
Al Geiberger	T-8	74-70-64-72=280	$5,225.00

Memorial Tournament
Course: Muirfield Village G.C., Dubin, Ohio
Par: 72 Yardage: 7,027
Last day of event: Sunday, May 30, 1976

Player	Place	Score	Earnings
Roger Maltbie	Win	71-71-70-76=288	$40,000.00
Playoff: Beat Hale Irwin with birdie on fourth extra hole			
Hale Irwin	2	71-74-74-69=288	$22,800.00
Don Bies	3	68-75-71-75=289	$14,200.00
Jerry McGee	T-4	71-73-72-74=290	$8,800.00
Jerry Pate	T-4	74-73-70-73=290	$8,800.00
Lou Graham	T-6	72-74-73-72=291	$6,800.00
Tom Kite	T-6	74-74-70-73=291	$6,800.00
Jack Nicklaus	T-8	71-72-73-73=292	$6,560.00
Rod Funseth	T-8	76-67-72-77=292	$6,560.00
Ed Sneed	T-10	73-71-73-76=293	$4,800.00
Tom Weiskopf	T-10	77-74-70-72=293	$4,800.00

IVB - Bicentennial Golf Classic

Course: Whitemarsh Valley C.C., Chestnut Hill, Pa.
Par: 71　Yardage: 6,687
Last day of event: Sunday, June 6, 1976

Player	Place	Score	Earnings
Tom Kite	Win	71-70-70-66=277	$40,000.00
Playoff: Beat Terry Diehl with par on fifth extra hole			
Terry Diehl	2	69-70-70-68=277	$22,800.00
Jerry Pate	3	70-67-71-70=278	$14,200.00
Ray Floyd	T-4	67-71-71-70=279	$8,266.67
Jerry McGee	T-4	70-67-71-71=279	$8,266.66
Larry Nelson	T-4	71-71-66-71=279	$8,266.67
Ken Still	T-7	70-72-66-72=280	$6,150.00
Grier Jones	T-7	73-72-65-70=280	$6,150.00
Bob Gilder	9	73-73-69-66=281	$5,400.00
Calvin Peete	T-10	71-70-74-67=282	$4,800.00
Fuzzy Zoeller	T-10	73-67-75-67=282	$4,800.00

Kemper Open

Course: Quail Hollow C.C., Charlotte, N.C.
Par: 72　Yardage: 7,205
Last day of event: Sunday, June 13, 1976

Player	Place	Score	Earnings
Joe Inman	Win	70-69-67-71=277	$50,000.00
Tom Weiskopf	T-2	71-70-67-70=278	$23,125.00
Grier Jones	T-2	71-69-65-73=278	$23,125.00
Charles Coody	T-4	68-70-71-71=280	$9,750.00
Lou Graham	T-4	70-71-68-71=280	$9,750.00
Roger Maltbie	T-4	70-69-71-70=280	$9,750.00
J.C. Snead	T-4	67-73-69-71=280	$9,750.00
Bob Wynn	T-8	71-70-70-70=281	$6,531.25
Terry Diehl	T-8	71-72-68-70=281	$6,531.25
Mark Hayes	T-8	69-69-69-74=281	$6,531.25
Bob Murphy	T-8	74-67-68-72=281	$6,531.25

U.S. Open

Course: Atlanta Athletic Club, Duluth, Ga.
Par: 70　Yardage: 7,015
Last day of event: Sunday, June 20, 1976

Player	Place	Score	Earnings
Jerry Pate	Win	71-69-69-68=277	$42,000.00
Al Geiberger	T-2	70-69-71-69=279	$18,000.00
Tom Weiskopf	T-2	73-70-68-68=279	$18,000.00
Butch Baird	T-4	71-71-71-67=280	$11,250.00
John Mahaffey	T-4	70-68-69-73=280	$11,250.00
Hubert Green	6	72-70-71-69=282	$9,500.00
Tom Watson	7	74-72-68-70=284	$8,500.00
Lyn Lott	T-8	71-71-70-73=285	$7,000.00
Ben Crenshaw	T-8	72-68-72-73=285	$7,000.00
Johnny Miller	10	74-72-69-71=286	$5,500.00

Western Open

Course: Butler National G.C., Oak Brook, Ill.
Par: 71　Yardage: 7,002
Last day of event: Sunday, June 27, 1976

Player	Place	Score	Earnings
Al Geiberger	Win	71-71-73-73=288	$40,000.00
Joe Porter	2	71-74-71-73=289	$22,800.00
Hale Irwin	T-3	71-74-72-73=290	$10,600.00
Charles Coody	T-3	70-72-73-75=290	$10,600.00
Bob Dickson	T-3	67-69-74-80=290	$10,600.00
Bill Mallon	6	74-72-71-74=291	$7,200.00
Andy North	T-7	74-75-73-70=292	$6,150.00
George Burns	T-7	70-73-76-73=292	$6,150.00
Steve Veriato	T-9	73-71-74-75=293	$5,000.00
Peter Oosterhuis	T-9	73-73-72-75=293	$5,000.00
Gil Morgan	T-9	71-72-73-77=293	$5,000.00

Greater Milwaukee Open

Course: Tuckaway C.C., Franklin, Wis.
Par: 72　Yardage: 7,030
Last day of event: Sunday, July 4, 1976

Player	Place	Score	Earnings
Dave Hill	Win	66-67-68-69=270	$26,000.00
John Jacobs	2	67-69-70-67=273	$14,820.00
Ed Sneed	T-3	71-66-69-70=276	$26,000.00
Dave Eichelberger	T-3	70-71-72-63=276	$7,670.00
Bob-E. Smith	T-5	71-68-71-68=278	$5,005.00
Homero Blancas	T-5	67-70-68-73=278	$5,005.00
Andy North	T-7	68-71-71-69=279	$3,549.00
Bill Kratzert	T-7	71-70-68-70=279	$3,549.00
Gibby Gilbert	T-7	72-70-68-69=279	$3,549.00
Joe Porter	T-7	74-67-68-70=279	$3,549.00
Howard Twitty	T-7	70-75-69-65=279	$3,549.00

British Open

Course: Royal Birkdale G.C., Southport, Lancashire, England
Par: 72　Yardage: 7,001
Last day of event: Saturday, July 10, 1976

Player	Place	Score	Earnings
Johnny Miller	Win	72-68-73-66=279	$13,500.00
Seve Ballesteros	T-2	69-69-73-74=285	$9,450.00
Jack Nicklaus	T-2	74-70-72-69=285	$9,450.00
Ray Floyd	4	76-67-73-70=286	$6,840.00
Tom Kite	T-5	70-74-73-71=288	$5,076.00
Tommy Horton	T-5	74-69-72-73=288	$5,076.00
Christy O'Connor, Jr.	T-5	69-73-75-71=288	$5,076.00
Mark James	T-5	76-72-74-66=288	$5,076.00
Hubert Green	T-5	72-70-78-68=288	$5,076.00
Peter Butler	T-10	74-72-73-70=289	$3,555.00
Norio Suzuki	T-10	69-75-75-70=289	$3,555.00
George Burns	T-10	75-69-75-70=289	$3,555.00
Vicente Fernandez	T-10	79-71-69-70=289	$3,555.00

Ed McMahon Quad City Open

Course: Oakwood C.C., Coal Valley, Ill.
Par: 71　Yardage: 6,305
Last day of event: Sunday, July 11, 1976

Player	Place	Score	Earnings
John Lister	Win	68-68-65-67=268	$20,000.00
Fuzzy Zoeller	2	63-71-68-68=270	$11,400.00
Rex Caldwell	3	66-68-69-69=272	$7,100.00
George Archer	4	74-62-69-70=275	$4,700.00
Tommy McGinnis	5	67-73-65-71=276	$4,100.00
Bud Allin	T-6	72-68-67-70=277	$3,400.00
Barry Jaeckel	T-6	67-74-70-66=277	$3,400.00
Terry Dill	T-8	70-71-68-69=278	$2,612.50
Stanton Altgelt	T-8	71-68-70-69=278	$2,612.50
Barney Thompson	T-8	71-70-68-69=278	$2,612.50
Joe Porter	T-8	66-71-72-69=278	$2,612.50

American Express Westchester Classic

Course: Westchester C.C., Harrison, N.Y.
Par: 71 Yardage: 6,603
Last day of event: Sunday, July 18, 1976

Player	Place	Score	Earnings
David Graham	Win	63-68-70-71=272	$60,000.00
Ben Crenshaw	T-2	69-68-69-69=275	$23,200.00
Fuzzy Zoeller	T-2	66-72-69-68=275	$23,200.00
Tom Watson	T-2	64-72-73-66=275	$23,200.00
Miller Barber	T-5	69-68-70-70=277	$8,793.75
Dan Sikes, Jr.	T-5	70-69-70-68=277	$8,793.75
Larry Ziegler	T-5	68-67-71-71=277	$8,793.75
Rik Massengale	T-5	70-71-68-68=277	$8,793.75
Ed Sneed	T-5	71-67-71-68=277	$8,793.75
John Mahaffey	T-5	71-70-69-67=277	$8,793.75
Mike Hill	T-5	65-72-71-69=277	$8,793.75
Bud Allin	T-5	70-68-72-67=277	$8,793.75

Canadian Open

Course: Essex G. & C.C., Windsor, Ontario, Canada
Par: 70 Yardage: 6,696
Last day of event: Sunday, July 25, 1976

Player	Place	Score	Earnings
Jerry Pate	Win	69-67-68-63=267	$40,000.00
Jack Nicklaus	2	67-67-72-65=271	$22,800.00
Lyn Lott	3	68-70-67-69=274	$14,200.00
Ed Sneed	4	68-71-69-67=275	$9,400.00
Bob Eastwood	T-5	69-69-71-68=277	$7,700.00
Bob Wynn	T-5	68-68-66-75=277	$7,700.00
Ben Crenshaw	T-7	68-70-68-72=278	$5,250.00
Johnny Miller	T-7	69-72-70-67=278	$5,250.00
Andy North	T-7	72-70-69-67=278	$5,250.00
Tony Jacklin	T-7	73-66-71-68=278	$5,250.00
Richard Crawford	T-7	67-74-67-70=278	$5,250.00
J.C. Snead	T-7	70-66-74-68=278	$5,250.00

Pleasant Valley Classic

Course: Pleasant Valley C.C., Sutton, Mass.
Par: 71 Yardage: 7,110
Last day of event: Sunday, August 1, 1976

Player	Place	Score	Earnings
Bud Allin	Win	72-67-68-70=277	$40,000.00
Ben Crenshaw	2	70-67-71-70=278	$22,800.00
Bob Menne	T-3	71-71-65-72=279	$10,600.00
Lee Elder	T-3	67-72-66-74=279	$10,600.00
Lanny Wadkins	T-3	65-76-69-69=279	$10,600.00
Rex Caldwell	T-6	67-70-71-72=280	$5,528.57
Bruce Lietzke	T-6	68-72-68-72=280	$5,528.57
Tom Jenkins	T-6	69-70-69-72=280	$5,528.57
Mark Hayes	T-6	69-69-72-70=280	$5,528.57
John Lister	T-6	68-73-72-67=280	$5,528.58
George Burns	T-6	73-69-67-71=280	$5,528.57
Bob Wynn	T-6	69-74-67-70=280	$5,528.57

B.C. Open

Course: En-Joie G.C., Endicott, N.Y.
Par: 71 Yardage: 6,966
Last day of event: Sunday, August 8, 1976

Player	Place	Score	Earnings
Bob Wynn	Win	65-71-66-69=271	$40,000.00
Bob Gilder	2	69-65-69-69=272	$22,800.00
Jerry McGee	T-3	65-70-70-69=274	$9,750.00
George Knudson	T-3	67-70-67-70=274	$9,750.00
Terry Diehl	T-3	68-70-69-67=274	$9,750.00
Ed Sneed	T-3	68-66-69-71=274	$9,750.00
Larry Nelson	7	69-70-68-68=275	$6,400.00
Dave Hill	T-8	67-70-72-67=276	$5,650.00
Wally Armstrong	T-8	73-67-69-67=276	$5,650.00
Kermit Zarley	T-10	68-69-69-71=277	$4,600.00
Dan Sikes, Jr.	T-10	71-66-69-71=277	$4,600.00
Bud Allin	T-10	63-67-74-73=277	$4,600.00

PGA Championship

Course: Congressional C.C., Bethesda, Md.
Par: 70 Yardage: 7,054
Last day of event: Sunday, August 15, 1976

Player	Place	Score	Earnings
Dave Stockton	Win	70-72-69-70=281	$45,000.00
Don January	T-2	70-69-71-72=282	$20,000.00
Ray Floyd	T-2	72-68-71-71=282	$20,000.00
David Graham	T-4	70-71-70-72=283	$9,750.00
John Schlee	T-4	72-71-70-70=283	$9,750.00
Jerry Pate	T-4	69-73-72-69=283	$9,750.00
Jack Nicklaus	T-4	71-69-69-74=283	$9,750.00
Jerry McGee	T-8	68-72-72-72=284	$6,000.00
Tom Weiskopf	T-8	65-74-73-72=284	$6,000.00
Ben Crenshaw	T-8	71-69-74-70=284	$6,000.00
Gil Morgan	T-8	66-68-75-75=284	$6,000.00
Charles Coody	T-8	68-72-67-77=284	$6,000.00

Sammy Davis, Jr. - Greater Hartford Open

Course: Wethersfield C.C., Wethersfield, Conn.
Par: 71 Yardage: 6,568
Last day of event: Sunday, August 22, 1976

Player	Place	Score	Earnings
Rik Massengale	Win	65-65-70-66=266	$42,000.00
J.C. Snead	T-2	67-64-69-68=268	$19,425.00
Al Geiberger	T-2	70-66-68-64=268	$19,425.00
Lee Trevino	4	68-70-66-67=271	$9,870.00
Chi Chi Rodriguez	T-5	67-69-68-68=272	$7,271.25
Barry Jaeckel	T-5	71-68-66-67=272	$7,271.25
Wally Armstrong	T-5	71-69-66-66=272	$7,271.25
Ray Floyd	T-5	73-67-67-65=272	$7,271.25
Mac McLendon	T-9	68-67-69-69=273	$5,250.00
Hubert Green	T-9	70-68-67-68=273	$5,250.00
Billy Casper	T-9	67-68-71-67=273	$5,250.00

American Golf Classic

Course: Firestone C.C. (North), Akron, Ohio
Par: 72 Yardage: 7,085
Last day of event: Sunday, August 29, 1976

Player	Place	Score	Earnings
David Graham	Win	69-67-69-69=274	$40,000.00
Lou Graham	2	72-73-65-68=278	$22,800.00
Tom Jenkins	3	71-67-71-70=279	$14,200.00
Bob Gilder	T-4	72-67-71-70=280	$8,266.67
Ed Sneed	T-4	67-72-68-73=280	$8,266.67
Jim Simons	T-4	71-68-67-74=280	$8,266.66
Rik Massengale	T-7	72-69-67-73=281	$5,900.00
Wally Armstrong	T-7	71-68-68-74=281	$5,900.00
Ray Floyd	T-7	69-68-68-76=281	$5,900.00

Jerry Pate	T-10	70-72-70-71=283	$4,240.00
Tom Watson	T-10	70-72-68-73=283	$4,240.00
Miller Barber	T-10	74-69-69-71=283	$4,240.00
Jerry McGee	T-10	68-72-67-76=283	$4,240.00
Bob-E. Smith	T-10	71-69-67-76=283	$4,240.00

World Series of Golf

Course: Firestone C.C. (South), Akron, Ohio
Par: 70 Yardage: 7,149
Last day of event: Sunday, September 5, 1976

Player	Place	Score	Earnings
Jack Nicklaus	Win	68-70-69-68=275	$100,000.00
Hale Irwin	2	71-70-71-67=279	$50,000.00
Dave Hill	3	67-70-73-70=280	$20,000.00
David Graham	4	70-71-71-69=281	$15,000.00
Hubert Green	5	71-65-73-73=282	$13,000.00
Lee Trevino	T-6	71-70-72-70=283	$10,250.00
Tom Watson	T-6	70-73-70-70=283	$10,250.00
Al Geiberger	8	73-67-72-73=285	$8,000.00
Jerry Pate	T-9	71-72-72-71=286	$7,100.00
J.C. Snead	T-9	70-71-71-74=286	$7,100.00
Takashi Murakami	T-9	67-72-70-77=286	$7,100.00

World Open

Course: Pinehurst C.C. (No 2), Pinehurst, N.C.
Par: 71 Yardage: 7,007
Last day of event: Sunday, September 12, 1976

Player	Place	Score	Earnings
Ray Floyd	Win	69-67-67-71=274	$40,000.00
Playoff: Beat Jerry McGee with birdie on first extra hole			
Jerry McGee	2	67-70-71-66=274	$22,800.00
George Burns	3	65-68-69-73=275	$14,200.00
Tom Watson	4	65-71-69-71=276	$9,400.00
Bob-E. Smith	T-5	65-71-70-72=278	$7,266.67
Hale Irwin	T-5	68-67-71-72=278	$7,266.66
Rik Massengale	T-5	69-70-72-67=278	$7,266.67
Bill Mallon	8	70-70-72-67=279	$5,900.00
David Graham	T-9	67-70-72-71=280	$5,200.00
Jim Simons	T-9	69-72-71-68=280	$5,200.00

Ohio Kings Island Open

Course: Jack Nicklaus Golf Center, Mason, Ohio
Par: 70 Yardage: 6,837
Last day of event: Sunday, September 19, 1976

Player	Place	Score	Earnings
Ben Crenshaw	Win	69-69-67-66=271	$30,000.00
Andy North	2	68-69-66-69=272	$17,100.00
Tom Weiskopf	3	69-68-68-69=274	$10,650.00
Danny Edwards	T-4	66-71-70-68=275	$6,600.00
Ed Sabo	T-4	69-71-69-66=275	$6,600.00
Bob-E. Smith	T-6	67-70-71-68=276	$4,668.75
Kermit Zarley	T-6	70-68-71-67=276	$4,668.75
Jack Nicklaus	T-6	71-69-69-67=276	$4,668.75
Bruce Lietzke	T-6	69-68-72-67=276	$4,668.75
Bill Kratzert	T-10	67-72-72-66=277	$3,450.00
Bob Zender	T-10	68-69-72-68=277	$3,450.00
Leonard Thompson	T-10	67-74-68-68=277	$3,450.00

Kaiser International Open

Course: Silverado C.C., Napa, Calif.
Home Course -Par: 72 Yardage: 6,849
Last day of event: Sunday, September 26, 1976

Player	Place	Score	Earnings
J.C. Snead	Win	66-70-70-68=274	$35,000.00
Johnny Miller	T-2	63-72-72-69=276	$16,187.50
Gibby Gilbert	T-2	66-74-65-71=276	$16,187.50
Miller Barber	4	69-70-67-71=277	$8,225.00
Lyn Lott	T-5	70-67-70-72=279	$6,358.33
Jack Ewing	T-5	71-72-68-68=279	$6,358.33
Don Massengale	T-5	72-70-70-67=279	$6,358.34
Andy North	8	69-72-70-69=280	$5,163.00
Hale Irwin	T-9	71-71-69-70=281	$4,025.00
Don January	T-9	65-71-73-72=281	$4,025.00
Billy Casper	T-9	69-69-73-70=281	$4,025.00
Lee Trevino	T-9	72-67-69-73=281	$4,025.00
Charles Coody	T-9	73-70-70-68=281	$4,025.00

The **Sahara Invitational**

Course: Sahara Nevada C.C., Las Vegas, Nev.
Home course / Par: 71 Yardage: 6,880
Last day of event: Sunday, October 3, 1976

Player	Place	Score	Earnings
George Archer	Win	67-66-69-69=271	$27,000.00
Dave Hill	T-2	70-65-71-67=273	$12,487.50
Don January	T-2	66-68-67-72=273	$12,487.50
Gil Morgan	T-4	68-68-71-67=274	$5,940.00
Mike McCullough	T-4	68-66-72-68=274	$5,940.00
Gene Littler	T-6	71-70-67-68=276	$4,036.60
Rik Massengale	T-6	71-67-71-67=276	$4,036.60
Wally Armstrong	T-6	64-73-70-69=276	$4,036.60
George Burns	T-6	67-65-73-71=276	$4,036.60
Bruce Lietzke	T-6	66-67-76-67=276	$4,036.60

San Antonio Texas Open

Course: Woodlake G.C., San Antonio, Texas
Par: 72 Yardage: 7,143
Last day of event: Sunday, October 17, 1976

Player	Place	Score	Earnings
Butch Baird	Win	68-70-70-65=273	$25,000.00
Playoff: Beat Miller Barber with birdie on first extra hole			
Miller Barber	2	68-70-65-70=273	$14,500.00
Bruce Lietzke	3	70-68-70-67=275	$8,875.00
Al Geiberger	T-4	69-69-69-71=278	$4,637.40
Dave Hill	T-4	70-70-71-67=278	$4,637.40
Sandy Galbraith	T-4	71-68-68-71=278	$4,637.40
George Cadle	T-4	71-66-71-70=278	$4,637.40
Gary Koch	T-4	73-68-67-70=278	$4,637.40
Tom Jenkins	T-9	68-69-71-71=279	$2,593.75
Jim Simons	T-9	70-69-71-69=279	$2,593.75
Dave Eichelberger	T-9	72-68-71-68=279	$2,593.75
Fred Marti	T-9	68-71-67-73=279	$2,593.75
Bill Kratzert	T-9	71-70-65-73=279	$2,593.75
Mason Rudolph	T-9	71-66-73-69=279	$2,593.75
Frank Conner	T-9	67-74-69-69=279	$2,593.75
Richard Crawford	T-9	68-74-69-68=279	$2,593.75

Southern Open

Course: Green Island C.C., Columbus, Ga.
Par: 70 Yardage: 6,791
Last day of event: Sunday, October 24, 1976

Player	Place	Score	Earnings
Mac McLendon	Win	68-69-69-68=274	$25,000.00
Hubert Green	2	68-68-72-68=276	$14,500.00
Jerry McGee	3	70-68-69-70=277	$8,875.00
Jim Colbert	T-4	67-71-72-69=279	$4,637.40
Bob-E. Smith	T-4	71-73-67-68=279	$4,637.40
Peter Oosterhuis	T-4	71-73-71-64=279	$4,637.40
Richard Crawford	T-4	73-70-66-70=279	$4,637.40
Tommy Aaron	T-4	73-70-68-68=279	$4,637.40
Grier Jones	T-9	72-68-70-70=280	$3,125.00
Chi Chi Rodriguez	T-9	73-68-72-67=280	$3,125.00
Terry Diehl	T-9	75-67-74-64=280	$3,125.00

Pensacola Open

Course: Pensacola C.C., Pensacola, Fla.
Par: 71 Yardage: 6,549
Last day of event: Monday, November 1, 1976

Player	Place	Score	Earnings
Mark Hayes	Win	68-72-69-66=275	$25,000.00
Lee Elder	2	68-71-70-68=277	$14,250.00
Frank Beard	T-3	69-70-69-70=278	$7,375.00
Tom Purtzer	T-3	72-69-68-69=278	$7,375.00
Phil Rodgers	T-5	71-69-70-69=279	$4,328.00
George Archer	T-5	71-70-69-69=279	$4,328.00
Jerry McGee	T-5	67-70-72-70=279	$4,328.00
Chi Chi Rodriguez	T-5	72-71-68-68=279	$4,328.00
Bob-E. Smith	T-9	68-73-70-69=280	$3,250.00
Bob Murphy	T-9	67-76-67-70=280	$3,250.00

1977

Tom Watson vs. Jack Nicklaus in the British Open at Turnberry ranks as the most memorable duel in major championship history. Both players posted 68-70-65 for 54 holes before Watson birdied the 72nd hole and his closing 65 was good enough to pip Nicklaus by a shot. Watson's 268 broke the Open Championship scoring record by eight strokes. At 269, Nicklaus finished 10 shots ahead of third-place Hubert Green. Three months earlier, Watson had beaten Nicklaus by two shots at the Masters, and a month earlier Green, ignoring a death threat, had won the U.S. Open at Southern Hills. At the PGA Championship, Lanny Wadkins won the first sudden-death playoff at a major, beating Gene Littler (who had bogeyed five holes in the final nine of regulation) on the third extra hole at Pebble Beach. Al Geiberger became the first to shoot 59 in a PGA Tour event, setting the record in the second round en route to victory at the Danny Thomas Memphis Classic. Augusta National Golf Club and Masters co-founder Clifford Roberts committed suicide in September at age 83.

Phoenix Open

Course: Phoenix C.C., Phoenix, Ariz.
Par: 71 Yardage: 6,726
Last day of event: Sunday, January 9, 1977

Player	Place	Score	Earnings
Jerry Pate	Win	67-67-70-73=277	$40,000.00
Playoff: Beat Dave Stockton with birdie on first extra hole			
Dave Stockton	2	69-72-64-72=277	$22,800.00
Larry Nelson	3	68-68-71-71=278	$14,200.00
Bruce Lietzke	T-4	71-70-69-69=279	$8,800.00
George Burns	T-4	67-69-73-70=279	$8,800.00
Fuzzy Zoeller	T-6	70-70-70-70=280	$6,225.00
George Cadle	T-6	71-68-69-72=280	$6,225.00
Bill Garrett	T-6	72-70-67-71=280	$6,225.00
Gary McCord	T-6	69-73-65-73=280	$6,225.00
Dave Hill	T-10	71-68-71-71=281	$4,600.00
Lon Hinkle	T-10	69-72-71-69=281	$4,600.00
Miller Barber	T-10	72-69-67-73=281	$4,600.00

Joe Garagiola Tucson Open

Course: Tucson National G.C., Starr Pass G.C., Tucson, Ariz.
Par: 72 Yardage: 7,305
Last day of event: Sunday, January 16, 1977

Player	Place	Score	Earnings
Bruce Lietzke	Win	70-66-70-69=275	$40,000.00
Playoff: Beat Gene Littler with birdie on fourth extra hole			
Gene Littler	2	71-67-70-67=275	$22,800.00
Andy North	3	67-72-71-66=276	$14,200.00
Tom Watson	4	67-71-73-68=279	$9,400.00
Bill Mallon	T-5	71-70-70-69=280	$7,266.67
Gil Morgan	T-5	67-70-71-72=280	$7,266.66
Gary McCord	T-5	67-73-71-69=280	$7,266.67
Don Bies	T-8	71-72-68-70=281	$5,650.00
Larry Nelson	T-8	72-72-66-71=281	$5,650.00
Jim Dent	T-10	69-71-71-71=282	$3,850.00
Tom Purtzer	T-10	71-70-71-70=282	$3,850.00
Phil Rodgers	T-10	71-72-70-69=282	$3,850.00
Rik Massengale	T-10	69-71-69-73=282	$3,850.00
Tommy Aaron	T-10	69-73-67-73=282	$3,850.00
Charles Coody	T-10	70-68-71-73=282	$3,850.00
Billy Casper	T-10	72-67-69-74=282	$3,850.00
Andy Bean	T-10	74-64-72-72=282	$3,850.00

Bing Crosby Pro-Am

Courses: Pebble Beach G.L. - Home
Monterey Peninsula C.C., Cypress Point C.C., Pebble Beach, Calif.
Home Course Par: 72 Yardage: 6,815
Last day of event: Sunday, January 23, 1977

Player	Place	Score	Earnings
Tom Watson	Win	66-69-67-71=273	$40,000.00
Tony Jacklin	2	69-66-68-71=274	$22,800.00
Lee Elder	3	69-66-69-71=275	$14,200.00
Bill Rogers	4	68-68-70-71=277	$9,400.00
Bruce Devlin	T-5	69-68-71-70=278	$6,620.00
Craig Stadler	T-5	72-68-71-67=278	$6,620.00
Victor Regalado	T-5	67-67-71-73=278	$6,620.00
Leonard Thompson	T-5	69-69-73-67=278	$6,620.00
Hubert Green	T-5	65-76-68-69=278	$6,620.00
Don Bies	10	68-72-67-72=279	$5,000.00

Andy Williams-San Diego Open

Course: Torrey Pines (South), Torrey Pines (North), San Diego, Calif.
Home Course -Par: 72 Yardage: 7,021
Last day of event: Sunday, January 30, 1977

Player	Place	Score	Earnings
Tom Watson	Win	66-67-67-69=269	$36,000.00
Larry Nelson	T-2	68-69-68-69=274	$16,650.00
John Schroeder	T-2	68-69-70-67=274	$16,650.00
Jerry McGee	T-4	70-71-66-68=275	$7,920.00
Bob Shearer	T-4	67-66-69-73=275	$7,920.00
Jay Haas	6	67-73-68-68=276	$6,480.00
Andy Bean	T-7	68-69-72-68=277	$5,535.00
Lon Hinkle	T-7	66-67-73-71=277	$5,535.00
Miller Barber	T-9	68-68-71-71=278	$3,990.00
Larry Ziegler	T-9	68-68-71-71=278	$3,990.00

George Archer	T-9	69-69-71-69=278	$3,990.00
Bob Murphy	T-9	71-68-72-67=278	$3,990.00
George Burns	T-9	68-71-73-66=278	$3,990.00
Rod Funseth	T-9	68-68-74-68=278	$3,990.00

Hawaiian Open

Course: Waialae C.C., Honolulu, Ha.
Par: 72 Yardage: 7,234
Last day of event: Sunday, February 6, 1977

Player	Place	Score	Earnings
Bruce Lietzke	Win	67-70-67-69=273	$48,000.00
Don January	T-2	71-64-69-72=276	$22,200.00
Takashi Murakami	T-2	73-63-71-69=276	$22,200.00
Andy Bean	4	72-67-69-69=277	$11,280.00
Bill Kratzert	T-5	71-69-71-67=278	$8,310.00
Steve Melnyk	T-5	68-73-68-69=278	$8,310.00
Tom Watson	T-5	68-74-66-70=278	$8,310.00
Lance Suzuki	T-5	75-65-72-66=278	$8,310.00
Roger Maltbie	T-9	73-71-68-67=279	$6,240.00
Bill Rogers	T-9	75-67-68-69=279	$6,240.00

Bob Hope Chrysler Classic

Course: La Quinta C.C., Indian Wells C.C., Tamarisk C.C., Bermuda Dunes C.C.
Home course / La Quinta, Calif.
Par: 72 Yardage: 6,911
Last day of event: Sunday, February 13, 1977

Player	Place	Score	Earnings
Rik Massengale	Win	64-66-70-70-67=337	$40,000.00
Bruce Lietzke	2	67-67-70-72-67=343	$22,800.00
Bobby Walzel	3	72-74-67-70-64=347	$14,200.00
Mike Morley	T-4	70-72-68-71-67=348	$8,800.00
Bob Shearer	T-4	69-73-67-67-72=348	$8,800.00
Roger Maltbie	6	70-72-67-70-70=349	$7,200.00
Gary Player	7	70-71-68-70-71=350	$6,400.00
Alan Tapie	T-8	67-70-72-70-72=351	$5,225.00
Hubert Green	T-8	69-68-69-72-73=351	$5,225.00
Charles Coody	T-8	70-70-71-67-73=351	$5,225.00

Glen Campbell Los Angeles Open

Course: Riviera C.C., Pacific Palisades, Calif.
Par: 71 Yardage: 7,029
Last day of event: Sunday, February 20, 1977

Player	Place	Score	Earnings
Tom Purtzer	Win	68-67-66-72=273	$40,000.00
Lanny Wadkins	2	66-69-69-70=274	$22,800.00
Fuzzy Zoeller	3	72-71-68-65=276	$14,200.00
Craig Stadler	4	69-68-70-70=277	$9,400.00
Bob Gilder	T-5	67-71-68-72=278	$7,700.00
Graham Marsh	T-5	73-67-70-68=278	$7,700.00
Jerry McGee	T-7	70-72-71-67=280	$6,150.00
Don January	T-7	68-73-72-67=280	$6,150.00
Jim Masserio	T-9	70-70-68-73=281	$5,200.00
Gil Morgan	T-9	77-69-67-68=281	$5,200.00

Jackie Gleason's Inverrary Classic

Course: Inverrary G. & C.C. (East), Lauderhill, Fla.
Par: 72 Yardage: 7,128
Last day of event: Sunday, February 27, 1977

Player	Place	Score	Earnings
Jack Nicklaus	Win	70-66-69-70=275	$50,000.00
Gary Player	2	68-73-66-73=280	$28,500.00
Jim Simons	T-3	70-71-71-70=282	$13,250.00
Fuzzy Zoeller	T-3	70-71-68-73=282	$13,250.00
Gil Morgan	T-3	74-67-65-76=282	$13,250.00
Hubert Green	6	72-70-70-71=283	$9,000.00
Andy North	T-7	71-71-71-71=284	$7,375.00
Hale Irwin	T-7	71-71-70-72=284	$7,375.00
Jerry McGee	T-7	74-66-75-69=284	$7,375.00
Tom Kite	T-10	72-73-69-72=286	$6,000.00
Tom Weiskopf	T-10	74-68-69-75=286	$6,000.00

Florida Citrus Open Invitational

Course: Rio Pinar C.C., Orlando, Fla.
Par: 72 Yardage: 7,012
Last day of event: Monday, March 7, 1977

Player	Place	Score	Earnings
Gary Koch	Win	70-69-65-70=274	$40,000.00
Joe Inman	T-2	68-69-71-68=276	$18,500.00
Dale Hayes	T-2	71-69-68-68=276	$18,500.00
Steve Melnyk	4	72-68-69-68=277	$9,400.00
Bob Zender	T-5	69-67-71-71=278	$7,266.67
Graham Marsh	T-5	70-69-68-71=278	$7,266.66
Victor Regalado	T-5	67-74-72-65=278	$7,266.67
Bill Rogers	8	66-71-69-73=279	$5,900.00
Dale Douglass	T-9	69-71-71-69=280	$4,285.72
Miller Barber	T-9	71-69-71-69=280	$4,285.72
Ray Floyd	T-9	71-70-70-69=280	$4,285.71
Bill Kratzert	T-9	70-73-68-69=280	$4,285.71
Mike Reid	T-9	71-68-68-73=280	$4,285.71
Grier Jones	T-9	71-73-67-69=280	$4,285.71
Fuzzy Zoeller	T-9	73-67-71-69=280	$4,285.72

Doral-Eastern Open

Course: Doral C.C. (Blue), Miami, Fla.
Par: 72 Yardage: 6,939
Last day of event: Sunday, March 13, 1977

Player	Place	Score	Earnings
Andy Bean	Win	67-67-71-72=277	$40,000.00
David Graham	2	71-67-71-69=278	$22,800.00
Tom Weiskopf	3	73-69-69-68=279	$14,200.00
Mike Sullivan	T-4	70-71-68-72=281	$8,800.00
Lanny Wadkins	T-4	70-73-66-72=281	$8,800.00
Miller Barber	T-6	68-71-73-70=282	$5,980.00
Leonard Thompson	T-6	68-70-70-74=282	$5,980.00
Graham Marsh	T-6	72-70-74-66=282	$5,980.00
Chi Chi Rodriguez	T-6	73-69-66-74=282	$5,980.00
Bill Kratzert	T-6	74-70-67-71=282	$5,980.00

Tournament Players Championship

Course: Sawgrass C.C., Ponte Vedra Beach, Fla.
Par: 72 Yardage: 7,174
Last day of event: Sunday, March 20, 1977

Player	Place	Score	Earnings
Mark Hayes	Win	72-74-71-72=289	$60,000.00

Player	Place	Score	Earnings
Mike McCullough	2	66-74-76-75=291	$34,200.00
Hale Irwin	T-3	72-77-69-74=292	$17,700.00
Bruce Devlin	T-3	69-79-72-72=292	$17,700.00
Jack Nicklaus	T-5	73-74-72-74=293	$10,900.00
Tom Watson	T-5	68-74-74-77=293	$10,900.00
Graham Marsh	T-5	73-77-72-71=293	$10,900.00
Larry Nelson	T-8	74-74-73-73=294	$8,150.00
Steve Melnyk	T-8	73-76-73-72=294	$8,150.00
Bill Rogers	T-8	75-72-76-71=294	$8,150.00

Sea Pines Heritage Classic
Course: Harbour Town G.L., Hilton Head, S.C.
Par: 71 Yardage: 6,657
Last day of event: Sunday, March 27, 1977

Player	Place	Score	Earnings
Graham Marsh	Win	65-72-67-69=273	$45,000.00
Ben Crenshaw	2	66-74-68-68=276	$15,975.00
Tom Watson	2	67-67-68-74=276	$25,650.00
Ray Floyd	T-4	67-72-66-72=277	$9,900.00
Gene Littler	T-4	72-70-70-65=277	$9,900.00
George Cadle	6	70-69-68-72=279	$8,100.00
Gary Player	T-7	71-70-68-71=280	$6,641.67
Jack Nicklaus	T-7	68-72-70-70=280	$6,641.67
Ed Sneed	T-9	71-68-69-72=280	$6,641.66
Bill Kratzert	10	71-68-71-71=281	$5,625.00

Greater Greensboro Open
Course: Forest Oaks C.C., Greensboro, N.C.
Par: 71 Yardage: 7,075
Last day of event: Sunday, April 3, 1977

Player	Place	Score	Earnings
Danny Edwards	Win	68-68-68-72=276	$47,000.00
George Burns	T-2	68-72-68-72=280	$21,737.50
Larry Nelson	T-2	70-66-72-72=280	$21,737.50
Grier Jones	4	72-70-70-69=281	$11,045.00
Gil Morgan	5	71-70-71-70=282	$9,635.00
Rik Massengale	T-6	71-67-74-71=283	$7,990.00
Howard Twitty	T-6	74-73-69-67=283	$7,990.00
Al Geiberger	T-8	71-72-70-71=284	$5,659.66
Andy North	T-8	72-69-72-71=284	$5,659.67
George Cadle	T-8	74-69-71-70=284	$5,659.67
Jim Colbert	T-8	74-73-70-67=284	$5,659.67
Hale Irwin	T-8	70-66-73-75=284	$5,659.66
Ed Dougherty	T-8	75-69-71-69=284	$5,659.67

Masters
Course: Augusta National G.C., Augusta, Ga.
Par: 72 Yardage: 6,925
Last day of event: Sunday, April 10, 1977

Player	Place	Score	Earnings
Tom Watson	Win	70-69-70-67=276	$40,000.00
Jack Nicklaus	2	72-70-70-66=278	$30,000.00
Rik Massengale	T-3	70-73-67-70=280	$17,500.00
Tom Kite	T-3	70-73-70-67=280	$17,500.00
Hale Irwin	5	70-74-70-68=282	$12,500.00
David Graham	T-6	75-67-73-69=284	$10,500.00
Lou Graham	T-6	75-71-69-69=284	$10,500.00
Ray Floyd	T-8	71-72-71-71=285	$5,667.00
Gene Littler	T-8	71-72-73-69=285	$5,667.00
Hubert Green	T-8	67-74-72-72=285	$5,667.00
John Schlee	T-8	75-73-69-68=285	$5,667.00
Don January	T-8	69-76-69-71=285	$5,667.00
Ben Crenshaw	T-8	71-69-69-76=285	$5,667.00

MONY Tournament of Champions
Course: La Costa C.C., Carlsbad, Calif.
Par: 72 Yardage: 6,911
Last day of event: Sunday, April 17, 1977

Player	Place	Score	Earnings
Jack Nicklaus	Win	71-69-70-71=281	$45,000.00
Playoff: Beat Bruce Lietzke with birdie on third extra hole			
Bruce Lietzke	2	71-70-74-66=281	$26,000.00
Graham Marsh	T-3	73-72-72-66=283	$11,949.67
Johnny Miller	T-3	67-74-73-69=283	$11,949.67
Tom Purtzer	T-3	74-68-68-73=283	$11,949.67
Rik Massengale	6	72-72-71-69=284	$7,925.00
David Graham	7	71-72-70-72=285	$7,514.99
Joe Inman	T-8	69-73-71-73=286	$6,917.50
Gary Koch	T-8	69-72-73-72=286	$6,917.50
Danny Edwards	T-10	73-73-70-71=287	$5,929.67
George Archer	T-10	71-74-70-72=287	$5,929.67
Mark Hayes	T-10	70-72-69-76=287	$5,929.66

Tallahassee Open
Course: Killearn C.C., Tallahassee, Fla.
Par: 72 Yardage: 7,124
Last day of event: Sunday, April 17, 1977

Player	Place	Score	Earnings
Ed Sneed	Win	68-70-68-70=276	$16,000.00
Playoff: Beat Lon Hinkle with birdie on first extra hole			
Lon Hinkle	2	70-69-69-68=276	$91,200.00
Bobby Walzel	3	69-68-70-71=278	$5,680.00
Jack Ewing	T-4	68-68-71-72=279	$3,520.00
Jim Simons	T-4	69-73-71-66=279	$3,520.00
Ed Dougherty	T-6	68-72-69-71=280	$2,490.00
Dale Hayes	T-6	68-72-70-70=280	$2,490.00
Bill Rogers	T-6	72-72-68-68=280	$2,490.00
Bobby Cole	T-6	73-67-69-71=280	$2,490.00
Lyn Lott	T-10	70-71-70-70=281	$1,920.00
Jim Dent	T-10	71-72-69-69=281	$1,920.00

First NBC New Orleans Open
Course: Lakewood C.C., New Orleans, La.
Par: 72 Yardage: 7,080
Last day of event: Sunday, April 24, 1977

Player	Place	Score	Earnings
Jim Simons	Win	70-69-67-67=273	$35,000.00
Stan Lee	2	69-68-70-69=276	$19,950.00
Tom Watson	3	68-68-71-70=277	$12,425.00
Ben Crenshaw	T-4	69-69-71-69=278	$7,700.00
Lou Graham	T-4	71-69-69-69=278	$7,700.00
Doug Tewell	6	70-69-71-69=279	$6,300.00
Don January	T-7	68-70-71-72=281	$5,381.50
Leonard Thompson	T-7	72-71-70-68=281	$5,381.50
Lyn Lott	T-9	72-72-66-72=282	$4,375.00
Miller Barber	T-9	66-74-69-73=282	$4,375.00
Chi Chi Rodriguez	T-9	68-74-70-70=282	$4,375.00

Houston Open

Course: Woodlands C.C., The Woodlands, Texas
Par: 72 Yardage: 6,997
Last day of event: Sunday, May 1, 1977

Player	Place	Score	Earnings
Gene Littler	Win	70-65-67-74=276	$40,000.00
Lanny Wadkins	2	71-68-70-70=279	$22,800.00
Chi Chi Rodriguez	3	72-66-71-71=280	$14,220.00
Andy North	T-4	71-70-69-71=281	$8,800.00
Bill Kratzert	T-4	71-72-66-72=281	$8,800.00
Dave Eichelberger	T-6	72-67-70-73=282	$5,980.00
Lon Hinkle	T-6	73-69-70-70=282	$5,980.00
Leonard Thompson	T-6	70-68-70-74=282	$5,980.00
Jack Nicklaus	T-6	69-75-67-71=282	$5,980.00
George Knudson	T-6	69-68-76-69=282	$5,980.00

Byron Nelson Golf Classic

Course: Preston Trail G.C., Dallas, Texas
Par: 71 Yardage: 6,993
Last day of event: Sunday, May 8, 1977

Player	Place	Score	Earnings
Ray Floyd	Win	69-70-68-69=276	$40,000.00
Ben Crenshaw	2	69-70-68-71=278	$22,800.00
Andy Bean	T-3	79-68-65-67=279	$11,800.00
Lyn Lott	T-3	79-68-65-67=279	$11,800.00
Don January	5	72-70-70-68=280	$8,200.00
Kermit Zarley	T-6	72-75-69-75=291	$6,500.00
Jerry McGee	T-7	70-71-71-69=281	$6,500.00
David Graham	T-7	74-71-68-68=281	$6,500.00
Jim Dent	T-9	71-72-70-69=282	$5,200.00
Bill Kratzert	T-9	74-69-68-71=282	$5,200.00

Colonial National Invitational

Course: Colonial C.C., Fort Worth, Texas
Par: 70 Yardage: 7,142
Last day of event: Sunday, May 15, 1977

Player	Place	Score	Earnings
Ben Crenshaw	Win	65-70-68-69=272	$40,000.00
John Schroeder	2	66-65-71-71=273	$22,800.00
Tom Watson	3	67-72-68-67=274	$14,200.00
Lyn Lott	T-4	72-72-67-66=277	$8,800.00
Al Geiberger	T-4	65-71-73-68=277	$8,800.00
Ed Sneed	T-6	67-70-71-71=279	$6,500.00
Butch Baird	T-6	68-73-68-70=279	$6,500.00
Miller Barber	T-6	69-73-69-68=279	$6,500.00
Hubert Green	T-9	69-73-70-68=280	$5,200.00
Wally Armstrong	T-9	70-73-69-68=280	$5,200.00

Memorial Tournament

Course: Muirfield Village G.C., Dubin, Ohio
Par: 72 Yardage: 7,101
Last day of event: Sunday, May 22, 1977

Player	Place	Score	Earnings
Jack Nicklaus	Win	72-68-70-71=281	$45,000.00
Hubert Green	2	71-71-72-69=283	$25,650.00
Tom Watson	3	71-70-73-71=285	$15,975.00
Lou Graham	4	77-70-70-70=287	$10,575.00
Chi Chi Rodriguez	T-5	70-76-73-69=288	$8,662.50
Fuzzy Zoeller	T-5	72-67-78-71=288	$8,662.50
Bob Murphy	T-7	72-72-73-72=289	$6,375.00
Joe Inman	T-7	71-73-71-74=289	$6,375.00
Lee Trevino	T-7	72-74-72-71=289	$6,375.00
Gary Player	T-7	70-68-76-75=289	$6,375.00

Atlanta Classic

Course: Atlanta C.C., Atlanta, Ga.
Par: 72 Yardage: 7,007
Last day of event: Sunday, May 29, 1977

Player	Place	Score	Earnings
Hale Irwin	Win	70-70-66-67=273	$40,000.00
Steve Veriato	2	70-70-66-68=274	$22,800.00
Lou Graham	3	69-71-71-68=279	$14,200.00
Lanny Wadkins	4	72-68-65-72=277	$9,400.00
Jack Nicklaus	5	70-73-67-68=278	$8,200.00
Dave Stockton	6	68-69-71-71=279	$7,200.00
Mac McLendon	T-7	68-69-73-70=280	$5,675.00
Jim Dent	T-7	68-70-73-69=280	$5,675.00
Charles Coody	T-7	73-68-68-71=280	$5,675.00
Roger Maltbie	T-7	73-67-70-70=280	$5,675.00

Kemper Open

Course: Quail Hollow C.C., Charlotte, N.C.
Par: 72 Yardage: 7,205
Last day of event: Sunday, June 5, 1977

Player	Place	Score	Earnings
Tom Weiskopf	Win	67-71-69-70=277	$50,000.00
George Burns	T-2	70-71-66-72=279	$23,125.00
Bill Rogers	T-2	72-67-68-72=279	$23,125.00
Doug Tewell	T-4	71-69-68-72=280	$11,000.00
Lou Graham	T-4	72-67-69-72=280	$11,000.00
Hubert Green	T-6	70-72-69-70=281	$7,187.50
J.C. Snead	T-6	71-69-72-69=281	$7,187.50
Craig Stadler	T-6	72-71-67-71=281	$7,187.50
Lanny Wadkins	T-6	69-74-69-69=281	$7,187.50
Allen Miller	T-6	70-74-67-70=281	$7,187.50
Bill Calfee	T-6	71-74-68-68=281	$7,187.50

Danny Thomas Memphis Classic

Course: Colonial C.C. (South), Cordova, Tenn.
Par: 72 Yardage: 7,282
Last day of event: Sunday, June 12, 1977

Player	Place	Score	Earnings
Al Geiberger	Win	72-59-72-70=273	$40,000.00
Jerry McGee	T-2	70-70-69-67=276	$18,500.00
Gary Player	T-2	67-71-69-69=276	$18,500.00
Mike Morley	T-4	69-70-71-69=279	$8,800.00
Tom Weiskopf	T-5	71-68-69-69=277	$8,800.00
Rod Curl	T-6	72-68-72-67=279	$6,800.00
Dave Eichelberger	T-6	74-67-70-68=279	$6,800.00
Kermit Zarley	8	75-67-70-68=280	$5,900.00
Johnny Miller	T-9	71-72-67-71=281	$4,600.00
Gene Littler	T-9	71-72-71-67=281	$4,600.00
Lee Trevino	T-9	72-68-70-71=281	$4,600.00
Lon Hinkle	T-9	72-69-72-68=281	$4,600.00
Grier Jones	T-9	74-69-69-69=281	$4,600.00

U.S. Open

Course: Southern Hills C.C., Tulsa, Okla.
Par: 70 Yardage: 6,873
Last day of event: Sunday, June 19, 1977

Player	Place	Score	Earnings
Hubert Green	Win	69-67-72-70=278	$45,000.00
Lou Graham	2	72-71-68-68=279	$23,500.00
Tom Weiskopf	3	71-71-68-71=281	$16,000.00
Tom Purtzer	4	69-69-72-72=282	$13,000.00
Jay Haas	T-5	72-68-71-72=283	$10,875.00
Gary Jacobsen	T-5	73-70-67-73=283	$10,875.00
Lyn Lott	T-7	73-73-68-70=284	$8,000.00
Terry Diehl	T-7	69-68-73-74=284	$8,000.00
Tom Watson	T-7	74-72-71-67=284	$8,000.00
Mike McCullough	T-10	73-73-69-70=285	$4,100.00
Rod Funseth	T-10	69-70-72-74=285	$4,100.00
Peter Oosterhuis	T-10	71-70-74-70=285	$4,100.00
Jack Nicklaus	T-10	74-68-71-72=285	$4,100.00
Al Geiberger	T-10	70-71-75-69=285	$4,100.00
Gary Player	T-10	72-67-71-75=285	$4,100.00

Western Open

Course: Butler National G.C., Oak Brook, Ill.
Par: 72 Yardage: 7,097
Last day of event: Sunday, June 26, 1977

Player	Place	Score	Earnings
Tom Watson	Win	70-69-75-69=283	$40,000.00
Wally Armstrong	T-2	72-73-69-70=284	$18,500.00
Johnny Miller	T-2	72-74-69-69=284	$18,500.00
Tom Weiskopf	4	75-69-70-71=285	$9,400.00
Bill Kratzert	5	72-71-72-71=286	$8,200.00
Tom Kite	T-6	73-73-72-69=287	$6,800.00
Rik Massengale	T-6	71-74-71-71=287	$6,800.00
Hubert Green	8	77-72-74-66=289	$5,900.00
J.C. Snead	T-9	70-74-72-74=290	$5,000.00
Gary McCord	T-9	67-73-75-75=290	$5,000.00
Phil Hancock	T-9	71-70-75-74=290	$5,000.00

Greater Milwaukee Open

Course: Tuckaway C.C., Franklin, Wis.
Par: 72 Yardage: 7,030
Last day of event: Sunday, July 3, 1977

Player	Place	Score	Earnings
Dave Eichelberger	Win	71-68-69-70=278	$26,000.00
Mike Morley	T-2	69-70-70-71=280	$10,053.33
Gary McCord	T-2	69-70-73-68=280	$10,053.33
Morris Hatalsky	T-2	75-66-69-70=280	$10,053.34
Frank Beard	T-5	71-68-71-71=281	$4,501.25
Barney Thompson	T-5	70-69-69-73=281	$4,501.25
Keith Fergus	T-5	69-67-74-71=281	$4,501.25
Miller Barber	T-5	74-69-68-70=281	$4,501.25
Lanny Wadkins	T-9	73-74-70-65=282	$3,380.00
Bill Rogers	T-9	74-70-68-70=282	$3,380.00

British Open

Course: Turnberry (Ailsa Course), Turnberry, Ayrshire, Scotland
Par: 70 Yardage: 6,875
Last day of event: Saturday, July 9, 1977

Player	Place	Score	Earnings
Tom Watson	Win	68-70-65-65=268	$17,000.00
Jack Nicklaus	2	68-70-65-66=269	$13,600.00
Hubert Green	3	72-66-74-67=279	$10,200.00
Lee Trevino	4	68-70-72-70=280	$8,500.00
George Burns	T-5	70-70-72-69=281	$7,225.00
Ben Crenshaw	T-5	71-69-66-75=281	$7,225.00
Arnold Palmer	7	73-73-67-69=282	$6,375.00
Ray Floyd	8	70-73-68-72=283	$5,950.00
John Schroeder	T-9	66-74-73-71=284	$4,887.50
Johnny Miller	T-9	69-74-67-74=284	$4,887.50
Tommy Horton	T-9	70-74-65-75=284	$4,887.50
Mark Hayes	T-9	76-63-72-73=284	$4,887.50

Ed McMahon Quad City Open

Course: Oakwood C.C., Coal Valley, Ill.
Par: 71 Yardage: 6,602
Last day of event: Sunday, July 10, 1977

Player	Place	Score	Earnings
Mike Morley	Win	68-69-64-66=267	$25,000.00
Victor Regalado	T-2	67-66-67-69=269	$11,562.50
Bob Murphy	T-2	69-66-68-66=269	$11,562.50
Bob Zender	T-4	67-67-67-69=270	$5,500.00
Don Pooley	T-4	70-64-66-70=270	$5,500.00
Rod Curl	T-6	67-68-68-68=271	$4,250.00
Jack Renner	T-6	71-65-69-66=271	$4,250.00
Bill Rogers	T-8	72-67-68-65=272	$3,265.50
Keith Fergus	T-9	67-67-69-69=272	$3,265.50
Craig Stadler	T-9	67-67-68-70=272	$3,265.50
Fuzzy Zoeller	T-9	67-66-73-66=272	$3,265.50

Pleasant Valley Classic

Course: Pleasant Valley C.C., Sutton, Mass.
Par: 71 Yardage: 7,110
Last day of event: Sunday, July 17, 1977

Player	Place	Score	Earnings
Ray Floyd	Win	67-68-67-69=271	$50,000.00
Jack Nicklaus	2	68-67-70-67=272	$28,500.00
Miller Barber	3	73-68-68-65=274	$17,500.00
Rik Massengale	4	69-74-63-69=275	$11,500.00
Gary Player	T-5	70-67-69-70=276	$9,625.00
Bruce Lietzke	T-5	70-69-68-69=276	$9,625.00
Kermit Zarley	T-7	70-70-69-68=277	$7,093.75
Dave Eichelberger	T-7	69-70-71-67=277	$7,093.75
Victor Regalado	T-7	68-72-68-69=277	$7,093.75
Roger Maltbie	T-7	72-71-67-67=277	$7,093.75

Canadian Open

Course: Glen Abbey G.C., Oakville, Ontario, Canada
Par: 72 Yardage: 7,096
Last day of event: Sunday, July 24, 1977

Player	Place	Score	Earnings
Lee Trevino	Win	67-68-71-74=280	$45,000.00
Peter Oosterhuis	2	73-69-72-70=284	$25,650.00
Tom Kite	3	68-70-74-73=285	$15,975.00
Bill Kratzert	T-4	72-72-71-71=286	$7,970.83
Charles Coody	T-4	71-71-73-71=286	$7,970.84
Mike McCullough	T-4	71-73-72-70=286	$7,970.84
Jack Nicklaus	T-4	68-70-74-74=286	$7,970.83
Ray Floyd	T-4	72-67-73-74=286	$7,970.83
Mike Morley	T-4	68-77-69-72=286	$7,970.83
Tom Shaw	10	72-74-71-70=287	$5,625.00

IVB Philadelphia Golf Classic
Course: Whitemarsh Valley C.C., Chestnut Hill, Pa.
Par: 71 Yardage: 6,687
Last day of event: Sunday, July 31, 1977

Player	Place	Score	Earnings
Jerry McGee	Win	70-68-65-69=272	$40,000.00
Bob Shearer	T-2	70-71-68-67=276	$18,500.00
John Lister	T-2	70-65-69-72=276	$18,500.00
Bob Gilder	4	68-70-65-74=277	$9,400.00
Grier Jones	T-5	69-69-69-71=278	$6,925.00
Bob Murphy	T-5	72-66-69-71=278	$6,925.00
Rod Curl	T-5	68-73-65-72=278	$6,925.00
Lyn Lott	T-8	69-71-70-69=279	$4,800.00
Ray Floyd	T-8	68-71-72-68=279	$4,800.00
Victor Regalado	T-8	69-69-72-69=279	$4,800.00
Mac McLendon	T-8	72-70-71-66=279	$4,800.00

Sammy Davis, Jr. - Greater Hartford Open
Course: Wethersfield C.C., Wethersfield, Conn.
Par: 71 Yardage: 6,568
Last day of event: Sunday, August 7, 1977

Player	Place	Score	Earnings
Bill Kratzert	Win	66-66-64-69=265	$42,000.00
Larry Nelson	T-2	68-66-69-65=268	$19,425.00
Grier Jones	T-2	69-69-65-65=268	$19,425.00
Victor Regalado	4	67-63-72-69=271	$9,240.00
Curtis Strange	5	65-66-68-70=269	$9,240.00
Rod Curl	T-6	67-69-65-69=270	$6,825.00
Calvin Peete	T-6	67-67-69-67=270	$6,825.00
Lee Elder	T-6	64-67-67-72=270	$6,825.00
Terry Diehl	T-9	65-69-68-69=271	$5,460.00
Kermit Zarley	T-9	65-68-73-65=271	$5,460.00

PGA Championship
Courses: Pebble Beach G.L., Pebble Beach, Calif.
Home Course Par: 72 Yardage: 6,804
Last day of event: Sunday, August 14, 1977

Player	Place	Score	Earnings
Lanny Wadkins	Win	69-71-72-70=282	$45,000.00

Playoff: Beat Gene Littler with par on third extra hole

Player	Place	Score	Earnings
Gene Littler	T-2	67-69-70-76=282	$25,000.00
Jack Nicklaus	3	69-71-70-73=283	$15,000.00
Charles Coody	4	70-71-70-73=284	$12,000.00
Jerry Pate	5	73-70-69-73=285	$10,000.00
Al Geiberger	T-6	71-70-73-72=286	$7,300.00
Lou Graham	T-6	71-73-71-71=286	$7,300.00
Tom Watson	T-6	68-73-71-74=286	$7,300.00
Don January	T-6	75-69-70-72=286	$7,300.00
Jerry McGee	T-6	68-70-77-71=286	$7,300.00

American Express Westchester Classic
Course: Westchester C.C., Harrison, N.Y.
Par: 72 Yardage: 6,603
Last day of event: Sunday, August 21, 1977

Player	Place	Score	Earnings
Andy North	Win	66-70-65-71=272	$60,000.00
George Archer	2	70-69-68-67=274	$34,200.00
Tom Weiskopf	3	71-64-69-72=276	$21,300.00
Andy Bean	T-4	71-66-71-69=277	$13,200.00
George Burns	T-4	69-67-75-66=277	$13,200.00
Tom Watson	T-6	71-68-68-71=278	$10,200.00
Leonard Thompson	T-6	69-66-70-73=278	$10,200.00
Charles Coody	T-8	67-68-72-72=279	$7,530.00
Mac McLendon	T-8	71-66-70-72=279	$7,530.00
Rod Curl	T-8	68-67-74-70=279	$7,530.00
Jack Nicklaus	T-8	71-74-68-66=279	$7,530.00
Don Pooley	T-8	74-66-72-67=279	$7,530.00

Colgate Hall Of Fame Golf Classic
Course: Pinehurst C.C. (No 2), Pinehurst, N.C.
Par: 71 Yardage: 7,007
Last day of event: Sunday, August 28, 1977

Player	Place	Score	Earnings
Hale Irwin	Win	65-62-69-68=264	$50,000.00
Leonard Thompson	2	64-69-70-66=269	$28,500.00
Jeff Mitchell	3	72-68-65-67=272	$17,750.00
Lou Graham	T-4	68-70-66-70=274	$11,000.00
J.C. Snead	T-4	63-72-71-68=274	$11,000.00
Charles Coody	T-6	67-68-70-70=275	$8,125.00
Jerry Pate	T-6	68-71-67-69=275	$8,125.00
Tom Weiskopf	T-6	70-68-71-66=275	$8,125.00
Tom Watson	9	70-72-65-69=276	$6,750.00
Bobby Cole	T-10	70-68-68-71=277	$5,500.00
Miller Barber	T-10	67-67-72-71=277	$5,500.00
Jack Newton	T-10	73-66-68-70=277	$5,500.00
Lon Hinkle	T-10	65-67-69-76=277	$5,500.00

World Series of Golf
Course: Firestone C.C. (South), Akron, Ohio
Par: 70 Yardage: 7,149
Last day of event: Monday, September 5, 1977

Player	Place	Score	Earnings
Lanny Wadkins	Win	69-66-67-65=267	$100,000.00
Hale Irwin	T-2	67-71-65-69=272	$35,000.00
Tom Weiskopf	T-2	67-68-72-65=272	$35,000.00
Mark Hayes	4	68-69-70-69=276	$15,000.00
Gary Player	T-5	69-70-70-69=278	$11,166.67
Ray Floyd	T-5	67-71-71-69=278	$11,166.67
Jack Nicklaus	T-5	69-73-68-68=278	$11,166.66
Graham Marsh	8	69-70-71-70=280	$8,000.00
Seve Ballesteros	9	69-73-70-69=281	$7,500.00
Tom Watson	10	72-72-69-69=282	$7,000.00

B.C. Open
Course: En-Joie G.C., Endicott, N.Y.
Par: 71 Yardage: 6,966
Last day of event: Sunday, September 11, 1977

Player	Place	Score	Earnings
Gil Morgan	Win	67-65-69-69=270	$40,000.00
Lee Elder	2	65-70-70-70=275	$22,800.00
Mac McLendon	3	66-74-68-68=276	$14,200.00
Florentino Molina	4	73-65-70-69=277	$9,400.00
Tom Kite	5	69-75-68-66=278	$8,200.00
Bob Payne	6	67-70-72-70=279	$7,200.00
Bob Menne	T-7	70-71-70-69=280	$5,900.00
Dave Stockton	T-7	71-69-70-70=280	$5,900.00
Miller Barber	T-7	67-71-75-67=280	$5,900.00
Joe Inman	T-10	69-72-71-69=281	$4,240.00
Jerry Pate	T-10	72-67-70-72=281	$4,240.00
Ray Arinno	T-10	72-72-66-71=281	$4,240.00
George Archer	T-10	72-72-70-67=281	$4,240.00
Kermit Zarley	T-10	67-73-71-70=281	$4,240.00

Ohio Kings Island Open

Course: Jack Nicklaus Golf Center, Mason, Ohio
Par: 70 Yardage: 6,837
Last day of event: Sunday, September 25, 1977

Player	Place	Score	Earnings
Mike Hill	Win	68-65-72-64=269	$30,000.00
Tom Kite	2	66-69-73-62=270	$17,100.00
Ben Crenshaw	T-3	67-67-71-70=275	$8,850.00
Jim Dent	T-3	69-69-71-66=275	$8,850.00
Fred Marti	5	70-67-73-67=277	$6,150.00
Lanny Wadkins	T-6	71-69-70-68=278	$4,875.00
Antonio Cerda	T-6	68-68-72-70=278	$4,875.00
Barry Jaeckel	T-6	72-69-71-66=278	$4,875.00
Don Pooley	T-9	68-72-70-69=279	$3,600.00
Miller Barber	T-9	72-69-68-70=279	$3,600.00
Gary Groh	T-9	69-67-73-70=279	$3,600.00
Jerry Pate	T-9	70-67-73-69=279	$3,600.00

Anheuser-Busch Golf Classic

Course: Silverado C.C., Napa, Calif.
Home Course -Par: 72 Yardage: 6,849
Last day of event: Sunday, October 2, 1977

Player	Place	Score	Earnings
Miller Barber	Win	71-66-70-65=272	$40,000.00
George Archer	2	69-69-63-73=274	$22,800.00
Howard Twitty	3	73-71-69-62=275	$14,200.00
John Schroeder	4	73-70-68-66=277	$9,400.00
Grier Jones	T-5	68-68-71-71=278	$7,700.00
Mac McLendon	T-5	67-69-69-73=278	$7,700.00
Bruce Lietzke	7	70-68-69-72=279	$6,400.00
Roger Maltbie	T-8	69-70-69-72=280	$5,225.00
Tom Watson	T-8	72-68-69-71=280	$5,225.00
Pat Fitzsimons	T-8	68-69-74-69=280	$5,225.00
Jim Dent	T-8	72-68-66-74=280	$5,225.00

San Antonio Texas Open

Course: Oak Hill C.C., San Antonio, Texas
Par: 70 Yardage: 6,576
Last day of event: Sunday, October 16, 1977

Player	Place	Score	Earnings
Hale Irwin	Win	68-67-64-67=266	$30,000.00
Miller Barber	2	68-64-70-66=268	$17,000.00
Tom Kite	3	68-66-65-71=270	$10,650.00
George Archer	T-4	64-67-72-69=272	$6,600.00
Carlton White	T-4	67-66-67-72=272	$6,600.00
Lou Graham	6	70-67-68-70=275	$5,400.00
Pat Fitzsimons	T-7	69-69-70-68=276	$4,425.00
Grier Jones	T-7	71-68-68-69=276	$4,425.00
Bob Murphy	T-7	72-70-66-68=276	$4,425.00
Bill Kratzert	T-10	69-71-70-67=277	$3,450.00
Homero Blancas	T-10	70-69-65-73=277	$3,450.00
Bill Garrett	T-10	70-69-65-73=277	$3,450.00

Southern Open

Course: Green Island C.C., Columbus, Ga.
Par: 70 Yardage: 6,791
Last day of event: Sunday, October 23, 1977

Player	Place	Score	Earnings
Jerry Pate	Win	64-67-69-66=266	$25,000.00
Phil Hancock	T-2	69-69-68-67=273	$8,531.25

Johnny Miller	T-2	67-68-68-70=273	$8,531.25
Mac McLendon	T-2	69-66-70-68=273	$8,531.25
Steve Taylor	T-2	73-68-63-67=273	$8,531.25
Wally Armstrong	T-6	68-68-69-69=274	$4,250.00
Miller Barber	T-6	70-68-68-68=274	$4,250.00
Bill Kratzert	8	72-71-65-67=275	$3,687.00
Forrest Fezler	9	71-69-69-67=276	$3,375.00
Larry Ziegler	T-10	69-71-66-71=277	$3,000.00
Andy Bean	T-10	72-69-64-72=277	$3,000.00

Pensacola Open

Course: Pensacola C.C., Pensacola, Fla.
Par: 71 Yardage: 6,549
Last day of event: Sunday, October 30, 1977

Player	Place	Score	Earnings
Leonard Thompson	Win	70-65-65-68=268	$25,000.00
Curtis Strange	2	70-68-64-68=270	$14,250.00
J.C. Snead	3	73-67-65-67=272	$8,875.00
Fuzzy Zoeller	T-4	69-68-67-69=273	$5,166.66
Butch Baird	T-4	70-68-68-67=273	$5,166.67
Bill Kratzert	T-4	71-69-68-65=273	$5,166.67
Andy Bean	T-7	69-71-66-68=274	$3,412.40
Steve Melnyk	T-7	71-66-67-70=274	$3,412.40
Jim Simons	T-7	68-67-67-72=274	$3,412.40
Bobby Walzel	T-7	68-72-65-69=274	$3,412.40
Mac McLendon	T-7	66-71-73-64=274	$3,412.40

1978

Gary Player made seven birdies over the last 10 holes to win the Masters, the last major victory of his illustrious career. Taking only 114 putts for the week, Andy North nevertheless carded a 1-over-par 285 to win the U.S. Open at Cherry Hills. Jack Nicklaus notched a two-shot victory in the British Open at St. Andrews, becoming the first player to win all four majors at least three times. John Mahaffey roared back from a seven-shot deficit after 54 holes and won the PGA Championship in a playoff with Jerry Pate and Tom Watson at Oakmont. Nicklaus missed the cut at the PGA, ending a streak of 33 consecutive majors, beginning with his British Open victory in 1970, during which he won eight times and finished no worst than 13th. Seve Ballesteros, age 21, won his first PGA Tour event, the Greater Greensboro Open.

Joe Garagiola Tucson Open

Course: Tucson National G.C., Starr Pass G.C., Tucson, Ariz.
Par: 72 Yardage: 7,305
Last day of event: Sunday, January 8, 1978

Player	Place	Score	Earnings
Tom Watson	Win	63-68-73-72=274	$40,000.00
Bobby Wadkins	2	69-66-71-72=277	$22,000.00
Howard Twitty	3	70-69-71-68=278	$14,200.00
Keith Fergus	T-4	68-71-70-70=279	$8,266.67
Lee Trevino	T-4	70-67-71-71=279	$8,266.66
Charles Coody	T-4	66-74-69-70=279	$8,266.67
Lou Graham	T-7	71-71-71-67=280	$5,460.00
Bill Rogers	T-7	67-69-72-72=280	$5,460.00
John Schroeder	T-7	71-72-68-69=280	$5,460.00
Lon Hinkle	T-7	72-71-68-69=280	$5,460.00
J.C. Snead	T-7	68-67-74-71=280	$5,460.00

Phoenix Open

Course: Phoenix C.C., Phoenix, Ariz.
Par: 71 Yardage: 6,726
Last day of event: Sunday, January 15, 1978

Player	Place	Score	Earnings
Miller Barber	Win	68-69-70-65=272	$40,000.00
Lee Trevino	T-2	69-68-67-69=273	$18,500.00
Jerry Pate	T-2	69-65-70-69=273	$18,500.00
Rod Funseth	4	67-65-73-69=274	$9,400.00
Arnold Palmer	5	69-68-71-67=275	$8,200.00
John Schroeder	T-6	69-69-69-69=276	$5,750.00
Andy Bean	T-6	68-70-69-69=276	$5,750.00
Jack Renner	T-6	70-68-71-67=276	$5,750.00
Jim Simons	T-6	68-66-70-72=276	$5,750.00
Joe Inman	T-6	72-69-66-69=276	$5,750.00
George Knudson	T-6	65-72-66-73=276	$5,750.00

Bing Crosby Pro-Am

Courses: Pebble Beach G.L., Spyglass Hill G.C., Cypress Point C.C., Pebble Beach, Calif.
Home Course Par: 72 Yardage: 6,815
Last day of event: Monday, January 23, 1978

Player	Place	Score	Earnings
Tom Watson	Win	66-74-71-69=280	$45,000.00
Playoff: Beat Ben Crenshaw with par on second extra hole			
Ben Crenshaw	2	69-71-73-67=280	$25,650.00
Hale Irwin	3	69-70-74-68=281	$15,975.00
Don Bies	T-4	70-70-73-70=283	$9,300.00
Mike Morley	T-4	71-73-68-71=283	$9,300.00
Hubert Green	T-4	69-71-74-69=283	$9,300.00
Andy North	7	74-70-69-71=284	$7,200.00
Tom Weiskopf	T-8	70-71-71-73=285	$6,116.66
Tony Jacklin	T-8	74-70-73-68=285	$6,116.67
Don Pooley	T-8	70-70-75-70=285	$6,116.67

Andy Williams-San Diego Open

Course: Torrey Pines (South), Torrey Pines (North), San Diego, Calif.
Home Course -Par: 72 Yardage: 7,021
Last day of event: Sunday, January 29, 1978

Player	Place	Score	Earnings
Jay Haas	Win	72-64-72-70=278	$40,000.00
Andy Bean	T-2	71-71-70-69=281	$15,466.00
John Schroeder	T-2	69-72-71-69=281	$15,466.00
Gene Littler	T-2	73-68-68-72=281	$15,466.00
Fuzzy Zoeller	5	70-70-71-71=282	$8,200.00
Doug Tewell	T-6	69-71-70-73=283	$6,225.00
Grier Jones	T-6	73-68-70-72=283	$6,225.00
Mark Pfeil	T-6	66-74-70-73=283	$6,225.00
Bill Rogers	T-6	76-68-71-68=283	$6,225.00
Alan Tapie	10	70-71-73-70=284	$5,000.00

Hawaiian Open

Course: Waialae C.C., Honolulu, Ha.
Par: 72 Yardage: 7,234
Last day of event: Sunday, February 5, 1978

Player	Place	Score	Earnings
Hubert Green	Win	69-66-68-71=274	$50,000.00
Playoff: Beat Bill Kratzert with par on second extra hole			
Bill Kratzert	2	70-67-69-68=274	$28,500.00
Hale Irwin	T-3	69-70-67-69=275	$13,250.00
Bob Wynn	T-3	67-69-71-68=275	$13,250.00
Mike Morley	T-3	68-73-68-66=275	$13,250.00
Gene Littler	6	65-73-68-70=276	$9,000.00
Chi Chi Rodriguez	T-7	71-69-67-70=277	$7,687.50
Bill Calfee	T-7	72-70-65-70=277	$7,687.50
Jim Chancey	T-9	72-68-68-70=278	$5,750.00
Gil Morgan	T-9	71-73-68-66=278	$5,750.00
Bob Gilder	T-9	71-73-69-65=278	$5,750.00
Dave Stockton	T-9	67-75-68-68=278	$5,750.00
Mark Hayes	T-9	67-75-69-67=278	$5,750.00

Bob Hope Chrysler Classic

Course: Bermuda Dunes C.C.,La Quinta C.C., Indian Wells C.C., Eldorado C.C.
Home course / Bermuda Dunes, Par: 72 Yardage: 6,837
Last day of event: Saturday, February 11, 1978

Player	Place	Score	Earnings
Bill Rogers	Win	69-67-67-67-69=339	$45,000.00
Jerry McGee	2	71-68-65-70-67=341	$25,650.00
Peter Oosterhuis	3	67-71-68-66-71=343	$15,975.00
Rex Caldwell	4	71-68-71-69-66=345	$10,575.00
Tom Watson	5	69-68-66-72-71=346	$9,225.00
Lon Hinkle	T-6	71-67-70-71-68=347	$7,316.66
Keith Fergus	T-6	68-72-70-69-68=347	$7,316.67
J.C. Snead	T-6	70-70-69-72-66=347	$7,316.67
Tim Simpson	T-9	72-69-68-68-71=348	$5,850.00
Lee Trevino	T-9	72-67-72-69-68=348	$5,850.00

Glen Campbell Los Angeles Open

Course: Riviera C.C., Pacific Palisades, Calif.
Par: 71 Yardage: 7,029
Last day of event: Sunday, February 19, 1978

Player	Place	Score	Earnings
Gil Morgan	Win	66-69-73-70=278	$40,000.00
Jack Nicklaus	2	72-66-70-72=280	$22,800.00
Forrest Fezler	3	68-76-71-68=283	$14,200.00
Lyn Lott	T-4	72-72-71-70=285	$7,800.00
Bill Rogers	T-4	72-72-71-70=285	$7,800.00
Barry Jaeckel	T-4	69-70-75-71=285	$7,800.00
Charles Coody	T-4	77-72-71-65=285	$7,800.00
Gary Koch	T-8	70-72-72-72=286	$5,225.00
Mike McCullough	T-8	74-68-72-72=286	$5,225.00
Tom Purtzer	T-8	72-69-75-70=286	$5,225.00
Lanny Wadkins	T-8	69-76-68-73=286	$5,225.00

Jackie Gleason's Inverrary Classic

Course: Inverrary G. & C.C. (East), Lauderhill, Fla.
Par: 72 Yardage: 7,128
Last day of event: Sunday, February 26, 1978

Player	Place	Score	Earnings
Jack Nicklaus	Win	70-75-66-65=276	$50,000.00
Grier Jones	2	67-72-71-67=277	$28,500.00
Hale Irwin	3	69-71-69-69=278	$17,750.00
Jerry Pate	T-4	70-71-71-67=279	$11,000.00
Andy Bean	T-4	69-69-72-69=279	$11,000.00
Bob Gilder	6	70-73-68-69=280	$9,000.00
Lou Graham	T-7	72-72-70-70=284	$7,375.00
Howard Twitty	T-7	71-69-70-74=284	$7,375.00
Lyn Lott	T-7	70-75-69-70=284	$7,375.00
J.C. Snead	T-10	72-71-71-71=285	$5,750.00
Pat McGowan	T-10	70-70-72-73=285	$5,750.00
Danny Edwards	T-10	69-69-75-72=285	$5,750.00

Florida Citrus Open Invitational
Course: Rio Pinar C.C., Orlando, Fla.
Par: 72 Yardage: 7,012
Last day of event: Monday, March 6, 1978

Player	Place	Score	Earnings
Mac McLendon	Win	69-65-69-68=271	$40,000.00
David Graham	2	66-68-73-66=273	$22,800.00
Ben Crenshaw	T-3	68-69-69-68=274	$11,800.00
Tom Kite	T-3	65-70-69-70=274	$11,800.00
Hale Irwin	5	67-71-69-68=275	$8,200.00
George Burns	T-6	71-68-69-69=277	$6,500.00
Bruce Lietzke	T-6	71-71-68-67=277	$6,500.00
Howard Twitty	T-6	68-72-69-68=277	$6,500.00
Sammy Rachels	T-9	70-69-68-71=278	$5,000.00
Leonard Thompson	T-9	70-69-74-65=278	$5,000.00
Wally Armstrong	T-9	70-67-75-66=278	$5,000.00

Doral-Eastern Open
Course: Doral C.C. (Blue), Miami, Fla.
Par: 72 Yardage: 6,939
Last day of event: Sunday, March 12, 1978

Player	Place	Score	Earnings
Tom Weiskopf	Win	67-70-67-68=272	$40,000.00
Jack Nicklaus	2	67-69-72-65=273	$22,800.00
John Mahaffey	3	67-69-70-72=278	$14,200.00
Eddie Pearce	T-4	70-69-70-70=279	$8,226.67
Ed Fiori	T-4	65-72-72-70=279	$8,226.66
Bob Gilder	T-4	72-69-65-73=279	$8,226.67
Steve Melnyk	7	70-71-70-69=280	$6,400.00
Bruce Lietzke	T-8	70-71-71-69=281	$5,225.00
Lon Hinkle	T-8	72-68-69-72=281	$5,225.00
Alan Tapie	T-8	71-74-69-67=281	$5,225.00
Gibby Gilbert	T-8	67-70-69-75=281	$5,225.00

Tournament Players Championship
Course: Sawgrass C.C., Ponte Vedra Beach, Fla.
Par: 72 Yardage: 7,174
Last day of event: Sunday, March 19, 1978

Player	Place	Score	Earnings
Jack Nicklaus	Win	70-71-73-75=289	$60,000.00
Lou Graham	2	71-70-74-75=290	$34,200.00
Lou Hinkle	3	75-72-74-70=291	$21,300.00
Andy North	T-4	74-71-74-73=292	$11,700.00
Larry Nelson	T-4	71-72-75-74=292	$11,700.00
John Schroeder	T-4	70-75-76-71=292	$11,700.00
Ben Crenshaw	T-4	70-71-77-74=292	$11,700.00
Jim Colbert	8	74-74-74-72=294	$8,850.00
Peter Oosterhuis	T-9	73-73-75-74=295	$7,500.00
Hubert Green	T-9	76-77-71-71=295	$7,500.00
Victor Regalado	T-9	70-79-76-70=295	$7,500.00

Sea Pines Heritage Classic
Course: Harbour Town G.L., Hilton Head, S.C.
Par: 71 Yardage: 6,657
Last day of event: Sunday, March 26, 1978

Player	Place	Score	Earnings
Hubert Green	Win	70-70-70-67=277	$45,000.00
Hale Irwin	2	69-68-73-70=280	$25,650.00
Mac McLendon	T-3	72-73-68-68=281	$7,793.75
Orville Moody	T-3	73-70-67-71=281	$13,275.00
Larry Nelson	T-3	69-68-68-76=281	$13,275.00

Alan Tapie	T-6	71-69-72-70=282	$7,793.75
Craig Stadler	T-6	70-70-67-75=282	$7,793.75
Graham Marsh	T-6	72-71-69-78=282	$7,793.75
Gibby Gilbert	T-9	69-71-72-72=283	$4,987.50
Andy North	T-9	71-72-69-71=283	$4,987.50
Bob Gilder	T-9	72-69-70-72=283	$4,987.50
Lou Graham	T-9	67-71-71-74=283	$3,600.00
Howard Twitty	T-9	67-74-70-72=283	$4,987.50
George Burns	T-9	72-65-74-72=283	$4,987.50
Bob Wynn	T-9	73-67-74-69=283	$4,987.50

Greater Greensboro Open
Course: Forest Oaks C.C., Greensboro, N.C.
Par: 72 Yardage: 6,958
Last day of event: Sunday, April 2, 1978

Player	Place	Score	Earnings
Seve Ballesteros	Win	72-75-69-66=282	$48,000.00
Fuzzy Zoeller	T-2	72-71-71-69=283	$22,200.00
Jack Renner	T-2	71-67-73-72=283	$22,200.00
Craig Stadler	4	71-70-73-70=284	$11,280.00
Lee Elder	T-5	70-71-73-71=285	$6,760.00
Tim Simpson	T-5	71-72-73-69=285	$6,760.00
Alan Tapie	T-5	72-68-72-73=285	$6,760.00
Wally Armstrong	T-5	67-70-74-74=285	$6,760.00
Dave Eichelberger	T-5	69-71-71-74=285	$6,760.00
Bobby Wadkins	T-5	72-71-74-68=285	$6,760.00
Lanny Wadkins	T-5	72-71-74-68=285	$6,760.00
Florentino Molina	T-5	66-71-77-71=285	$6,760.00
Bob Shearer	T-5	69-71-77-68=285	$6,760.00

Masters
Course: Augusta National G.C., Augusta, Ga.
Par: 72 Yardage: 6,925
Last day of event: Sunday, April 9, 1978

Player	Place	Score	Earnings
Gary Player	Win	72-72-69-64=277	$45,000.00
Hubert Green	T-2	72-69-65-72=278	$21,667.00
Rod Funseth	T-2	73-66-70-69=278	$21,667.00
Tom Watson	T-2	73-68-68-69=278	$21,667.00
Wally Armstrong	T-5	72-70-70-68=280	$11,750.00
Bill Kratzert	T-5	70-74-67-69=280	$11,750.00
Jack Nicklaus	7	72-73-69-67=281	$10,000.00
Hale Irwin	8	73-67-71-71=282	$8,500.00
Joe Inman	T-9	69-73-72-69=283	$6,750.00
David Graham	T-9	75-69-67-72=283	$6,750.00

MONY Tournament of Champions
Course: La Costa C.C., Carlsbad, Calif.
Par: 72 Yardage: 6,911
Last day of event: Sunday, April 16, 1978

Player	Place	Score	Earnings
Gary Player	Win	70-68-76-67=281	$45,000.00
Lee Trevino	T-2	73-69-70-71=283	$21,937.50
Andy North	T-2	76-70-68-69=283	$21,937.50
Leonard Thompson	T-4	72-70-71-71=284	$9,527.00
Mac McLendon	T-4	70-70-71-73=284	$9,527.00
Bill Kratzert	T-4	70-67-75-72=284	$9,527.00
Jerry Pate	T-7	71-73-69-73=286	$7,389.00
Ray Floyd	T-7	73-70-74-69=286	$7,389.00
Seve Ballesteros	T-7	69-65-73-79=286	$7,389.00
Gil Morgan	10	74-72-72-69=287	$6,569.00

Tallahassee Open

Course: Killearn C.C., Tallahassee, Fla.
Par: 72 Yardage: 7,124
Last day of event: Sunday, April 16, 1978

Player	Place	Score	Earnings
Barry Jaeckel	Win	70-67-71-65=273	$16,000.00

Playoff: Beat Bruce Lietzke with par on first extra hole

Player	Place	Score	Earnings
Bruce Lietzke	2	69-66-68-70=273	$9,120.00
Bobby Wadkins	T-3	71-68-65-70=274	$4,720.00
Jim Nelford	T-3	66-67-72-69=274	$4,720.00
Ed Dougherty	5	69-68-74-65=276	$3,280.00
Rex Caldwell	6	69-69-69-70=277	$2,880.00
Mike McCullough	7	73-67-68-70=278	$2,560.00
Bob Murphy	T-8	72-66-69-72=279	$2,090.00
Mike Walters	T-8	72-67-71-69=279	$2,090.00
Gary Koch	T-8	72-69-69-69=279	$2,090.00
Allen Miller	T-8	69-66-73-71=279	$2,090.00

Houston Open

Course: Woodlands C.C., The Woodlands, Texas
Par: 72 Yardage: 6,997
Last day of event: Sunday, April 23, 1978

Player	Place	Score	Earnings
Gary Player	Win	64-67-70-69=270	$40,000.00
Andy Bean	2	67-65-66-73=271	$22,800.00
Bob Murphy	T-3	66-66-70-70=272	$11,800.00
Bill Kratzert	T-3	70-67-69-66=272	$11,800.00
Mike Reid	5	68-72-67-67=274	$8,200.00
Jack Renner	T-6	71-65-68-71=275	$6,500.00
Kermit Zarley	T-6	69-68-72-66=275	$6,500.00
Tom Kite	T-6	72-69-64-70=275	$6,500.00
Mike Sullivan	T-9	70-69-68-69=276	$5,200.00
Gary Koch	T-9	68-71-66-71=276	$5,200.00

First NBC New Orleans Open

Course: Lakewood C.C., New Orleans, La.
Par: 72 Yardage: 7,080
Last day of event: Sunday, April 30, 1978

Player	Place	Score	Earnings
Lon Hinkle	Win	74-67-64-66=271	$40,000.00
Fuzzy Zoeller	T-2	70-65-70-67=272	$18,500.00
Gibby Gilbert	T-2	70-68-67-67=272	$18,500.00
Grier Jones	4	69-69-69-67=274	$9,400.00
Calvin Peete	T-5	71-69-69-68=277	$6,925.00
Bob Murphy	T-5	71-68-71-67=277	$6,925.00
Gary Player	T-5	69-67-69-72=277	$6,925.00
D.A. Weibring	T-5	69-64-73-71=277	$6,925.00
Lou Graham	T-9	69-70-70-69=278	$4,600.00
Mike Sullivan	T-9	69-71-68-70=278	$4,600.00
Fred Marti	T-9	71-67-69-71=278	$4,600.00
Jack Renner	T-9	71-67-70-70=278	$4,600.00
Gary Koch	T-9	72-68-67-71=278	$4,600.00

Byron Nelson Golf Classic

Course: Preston Trail G.C., Dallas, Texas
Par: 70 Yardage: 6,993
Last day of event: Sunday, May 7, 1978

Player	Place	Score	Earnings
Tom Watson	Win	69-67-70-66=272	$40,000.00
Lee Trevino	2	70-69-68-66=273	$22,800.00

Player	Place	Score	Earnings
Ed Sneed	T-3	70-67-71-68=276	$9,750.00
Joe Inman	T-3	72-70-65-69=276	$9,750.00
Don January	T-3	69-73-67-67=276	$9,750.00
Dave Stockton	T-3	75-69-65-67=276	$9,750.00
Ray Floyd	7	68-75-67-67=277	$6,400.00
Jim Dent	T-8	65-71-71-71=278	$5,650.00
Andy Bean	T-8	70-72-66-70=278	$5,650.00
Alan Tapie	T-10	71-72-68-68=279	$4,100.00
Jerry McGee	T-10	72-71-70-66=279	$4,100.00
David Graham	T-10	71-69-73-66=279	$4,100.00
Bill Kratzert	T-10	71-73-69-66=279	$4,100.00
Barry Jaeckel	T-10	67-74-70-68=279	$4,100.00
Calvin Peete	T-10	74-71-67-67=279	$4,100.00

Colonial National Invitational

Course: Colonial C.C., Fort Worth, Texas
Par: 70 Yardage: 7,142
Last day of event: Sunday, May 14, 1978

Player	Place	Score	Earnings
Lee Trevino	Win	66-68-68-66=268	$40,000.00
Jerry Heard	T-2	67-66-71-68=272	$18,500.00
Jerry Pate	T-2	69-67-71-65=272	$18,500.00
Tom Watson	T-4	69-68-68-68=273	$8,800.00
Steve Melnyk	T-4	65-68-70-70=273	$8,800.00
Tom Weiskopf	6	72-68-71-65=276	$7,200.00
Gary Koch	7	70-69-69-69=277	$6,400.00
Jim Simons	T-8	70-67-71-71=279	$5,020.00
Tom Kite	T-8	68-69-70-72=279	$5,020.00
John Mahaffey	T-8	71-69-72-67=279	$5,020.00
Andy Bean	T-8	67-70-73-69=279	$5,020.00
Tom Purtzer	T-8	70-68-68-73=279	$5,020.00

Memorial Tournament

Course: Muirfield Village G.C., Dubin, Ohio
Par: 72 Yardage: 7,101
Last day of event: Sunday, May 21, 1978

Player	Place	Score	Earnings
Jim Simons	Win	68-69-73-74=284	$50,000.00
Bill Kratzert	2	72-70-69-74=285	$28,500.00
Fuzzy Zoeller	3	71-73-73-70=287	$17,750.00
Gary Player	T-4	67-72-75-74=288	$10,333.33
Jack Nicklaus	T-4	67-76-71-74=288	$10,333.33
Ed Sneed	T-4	69-70-78-71=288	$10,333.34
Bob Shearer	T-7	72-72-70-75=289	$7,687.50
Morris Hatalsky	T-7	74-68-75-72=289	$7,687.50
Gil Morgan	9	74-67-76-74=291	$6,750.00
Tom Watson	T-10	73-72-72-75=292	$5,300.00
Jay Haas	T-10	71-76-73-72=292	$5,300.00
Jerry Pate	T-10	76-73-74-69=292	$5,300.00
Curtis Strange	T-10	69-76-77-70=292	$5,300.00
David Graham	T-10	78-69-72-73=292	$5,300.00

Atlanta Classic

Course: Atlanta C.C., Atlanta, Ga.
Par: 72 Yardage: 7,007
Last day of event: Sunday, May 28, 1978

Player	Place	Score	Earnings
Jerry Heard	Win	67-67-68-67=269	$40,000.00
Tom Watson	T-2	68-66-69-68=271	$15,466.67
Bob Murphy	T-2	64-70-67-70=271	$15,466.66
Lou Graham	T-2	71-67-67-66=271	$15,466.67

Gibby Gilbert	5	70-67-66-70=273	$8,200.00
Lanny Wadkins	6	70-67-68-69=274	$7,200.00
Jim Colbert	7	70-66-69-70=275	$6,400.00
Dave Stockton	T-8	66-73-72-65=276	$5,433.34
Tom Weiskopf	T-8	70-67-73-66=276	$5,433.33
Rod Curl	T-8	73-69-65-69=276	$5,433.33

Kemper Open

Course: Quail Hollow C.C., Charlotte, N.C.
Par: 72 Yardage: 7,205
Last day of event: Sunday, June 4, 1978

Player	Place	Score	Earnings
Andy Bean	Win	72-67-68-66=273	$60,000.00
Mark Hayes	T-2	69-71-68-70=278	$27,750.00
Andy North	T-2	72-69-68-69=278	$27,750.00
Steve Melnyk	4	73-67-69-70=279	$14,100.00
Hale Irwin	T-5	71-68-71-70=280	$9,525.00
Ed Sneed	T-5	70-69-72-69=280	$9,525.00
Charles Coody	T-5	70-69-68-73=280	$9,525.00
Wally Armstrong	T-5	70-70-67-73=280	$9,525.00
Dave Eichelberger	T-5	72-69-73-66=280	$9,525.00
Alan Pate	T-5	70-71-65-74=280	$9,525.00

Danny Thomas Memphis Classic

Course: Colonial C.C. (South), Cordova, Tenn.
Par: 72 Yardage: 7,282
Last day of event: Sunday, June 11, 1978

Player	Place	Score	Earnings
Andy Bean	Win	70-68-69-70=277	$50,000.00
Playoff: Beat Lee Trevino with birdie on first extra hole			
Lee Trevino	2	68-71-73-65=277	$28,500.00
Tom Kite	3	74-70-68-66=278	$17,750.00
Tom Purtzer	T-4	69-70-69-71=279	$10,333.33
John Lister	T-4	69-70-71-69=279	$10,333.34
Gary Koch	T-4	69-72-70-68=279	$10,333.33
Bob Gilder	T-7	68-70-71-71=280	$6,825.00
Kermit Zarley	T-7	70-67-72-71=280	$6,825.00
Gil Morgan	T-7	70-72-67-71=280	$6,825.00
J.C. Snead	T-7	72-70-68-70=280	$6,825.00
Barry Jaeckel	T-7	67-73-68-72=280	$6,825.00

U.S. Open

Course: Cherry Hills C.C., Englewood, Colo.
Par: 71 Yardage: 7,083
Last day of event: Sunday, June 18, 1978

Player	Place	Score	Earnings
Andy North	Win	70-70-71-74=285	$45,000.00
J.C. Snead	T-2	70-72-72-72=286	$19,750.00
Dave Stockton	T-2	71-73-70-72=286	$19,750.00
Hale Irwin	T-4	69-74-75-70=288	$13,000.00
Tom Weiskopf	T-4	77-73-70-68=288	$13,000.00
Andy Bean	T-6	72-72-71-74=289	$7,548.34
Bill Kratzert	T-6	72-74-70-73=289	$7,548.33
Jack Nicklaus	T-6	73-69-74-73=289	$7,548.33
Tom Watson	T-6	74-75-70-70=289	$7,548.34
Gary Player	T-6	71-71-70-77=289	$7,548.33
Johnny Miller	T-6	78-69-68-74=289	$7,548.33

Buick Goodwrench Open

Course: Warwick Hills C.C., Grand Blanc, Mich.
Par: 72 Yardage: 7,014
Last day of event: Sunday, June 18, 1978

Player	Place	Score	Earnings
Jack Newton	Win	72-67-70-71=280	$20,000.00
Playoff: Beat Mike Sullivan with birdie on first extra hole			
Mike Sullivan	2	73-69-69-69=280	$11,400.00
Greg Powers	T-3	69-70-71-71=281	$5,300.00
Rex Caldwell	T-3	69-72-69-71=281	$5,300.00
Bobby Cole	T-3	72-70-68-71=281	$5,300.00
Barney Thompson	T-6	68-73-70-71=282	$3,400.00
Jim Nelford	T-6	69-75-70-68=282	$3,400.00
Craig Stadler	8	70-69-70-74=283	$2,950.00
Bob Zender	T-9	73-72-70-69=284	$2,600.00
Alan Tapie	T-9	75-68-70-71=284	$2,600.00

Canadian Open

Course: Glen Abbey G.C., Oakville, Ontario, Canada
Par: 71 Yardage: 7,050
Last day of event: Sunday, June 25, 1978

Player	Place	Score	Earnings
Bruce Lietzke	Win	76-67-67-73=283	$50,000.00
Pat McGowan	2	72-68-72-72=284	$28,500.00
Ben Crenshaw	T-3	70-74-69-72=285	$14,750.00
Lee Trevino	T-3	74-71-69-71=285	$14,750.00
Mike McCullough	T-5	73-70-72-71=286	$9,083.33
George Burns	T-5	73-70-73-70=286	$9,083.33
Ray Floyd	T-5	74-74-69-69=286	$9,083.34
Jim Colbert	T-8	71-70-73-73=287	$5,803.57
Jeff Hawkes	T-8	67-73-72-75=287	$5,803.57
John Schroeder	T-8	74-67-71-75=287	$5,803.57
Arnold Palmer	T-8	70-76-73-68=287	$5,803.58
Bill Kratzert	T-8	76-70-69-72=287	$5,803.57
Tom Purtzer	T-8	76-69-72-70=287	$5,803.57
Bunky Henry	T-8	77-70-71-69=287	$5,803.57

Western Open

Course: Butler National G.C., Oak Brook, Ill.
Par: 72 Yardage: 7,097
Last day of event: Sunday, July 2, 1978

Player	Place	Score	Earnings
Andy Bean	Win	70-71-75-66=282	$45,000.00
Playoff: Beat Bill Rogers with par on first extra hole			
Bill Rogers	2	70-71-69-72=282	$25,650.00
Tom Kite	3	72-72-71-68=283	$15,975.00
Hale Irwin	T-4	71-70-71-72=284	$9,900.00
Phil Hancock	T-4	70-74-70-70=284	$9,900.00
Tom Watson	T-6	71-69-74-71=285	$7,650.00
Cesar Sanudo	T-6	67-76-74-68=285	$7,650.00
Rex Caldwell	T-8	72-73-70-71=286	$6,116.66
Terry Diehl	T-8	72-71-73-70=286	$6,116.67
Marty Fleckman	T-8	70-72-78-66=286	$6,116.67

Greater Milwaukee Open

Course: Tuckaway C.C., Franklin, Wis.
Par: 72 Yardage: 7,030
Last day of event: Sunday, July 9, 1978

Player	Place	Score	Earnings
Lee Elder	Win	66-70-70-69=275	$30,000.00

Playoff: Beat Lee Trevino with par on eighth extra hole

Player	Place	Score	Earnings
Lee Trevino	2	69-70-68-68=275	$17,100.00
Miller Barber	3	74-69-67-68=278	$17,100.00
Dave Barr	T-4	68-70-70-71=279	$6,200.00
Lou Graham	T-4	68-71-69-71=279	$6,200.00
Tim Simpson	T-4	69-71-68-71=279	$6,200.00
Jay Haas	T-7	70-70-70-70=280	$3,782.14
Bob Zender	T-7	69-69-71-71=280	$3,782.14
Homero Blancas	T-7	69-71-68-72=280	$3,782.14
Gibby Gilbert	T-7	72-68-69-71=280	$3,782.14
Dave Eichelberger	T-7	72-70-70-68=280	$3,782.15
Grier Jones	T-7	72-73-66-69=280	$3,782.15
Mac McLendon	T-7	73-69-68-70=280	$3,782.14

British Open

Course: Old Course at St. Andrews, St. Andrews, Fife, Scotland
Par: 72 Yardage: 6,933
Last day of event: Saturday, July 15, 1978

Player	Place	Score	Earnings
Jack Nicklaus	Win	71-72-69-69=281	$23,750.00
Tom Kite	T-2	72-69-72-70=283	$13,893.75
Ben Crenshaw	T-2	70-69-73-71=283	$13,893.75
Ray Floyd	T-2	69-75-71-68=283	$13,893.75
Simon Owen	T-2	70-75-67-71=283	$13,893.75
Peter Oosterhuis	6	72-70-69-73=284	$9,500.00
Nick Faldo	T-7	71-72-70-72=285	$7,481.25
Isao Aoki	T-7	68-71-73-73=285	$7,481.25
Bob Shearer	T-7	71-69-74-71=285	$7,481.25
John Schroeder	T-7	74-69-70-72=285	$7,481.25

Ed McMahon Quad City Open

Course: Oakwood C.C., Coal Valley, Ill.
Par: 71 Yardage: 6,561
Last day of event: Sunday, July 16, 1978

Player	Place	Score	Earnings
Victor Regalado	Win	67-64-68-70=269	$30,000.00
Fred Marti	2	66-67-67-70=270	$17,100.00
D.A. Weibring	T-3	67-69-67-69=272	$7,950.00
Jack Renner	T-3	67-66-70-69=272	$7,950.00
Don Iverson	T-3	67-69-72-64=272	$7,950.00
Terry Diehl	T-6	68-69-70-67=274	$4,875.00
Bobby Walzel	T-6	70-68-66-70=274	$4,875.00
Dave Eichelberger	T-6	70-70-66-68=274	$4,875.00
Bob Murphy	T-9	70-67-69-69=275	$3,600.00
John Lister	T-9	71-69-65-70=275	$3,600.00
Bob Zender	T-9	70-72-67-66=275	$3,600.00
Bob Eastwood	T-9	74-65-69-67=275	$3,600.00

IVB Philadelphia Golf Classic

Course: Whitemarsh Valley C.C., Chestnut Hill, Pa.
Par: 71 Yardage: 6,687
Last day of event: Sunday, July 23, 1978

Player	Place	Score	Earnings
Jack Nicklaus	Win	66-64-72-68=270	$50,000.00
Gil Morgan	2	68-72-64-67=271	$28,500.00
Hale Irwin	T-3	67-71-68-67=273	$14,750.00
Jerry Pate	T-3	71-69-67-66=273	$14,750.00
Hubert Green	5	65-73-66-70=274	$10,250.00
Lee Elder	T-6	68-67-70-70=275	$7,781.25
Miller Barber	T-6	69-65-71-70=275	$7,781.25
Mark Hayes	T-6	70-72-67-66=275	$7,781.25

Player	Place	Score	Earnings
Bruce Lietzke	T-6	67-68-66-74=275	$7,781.25
John Lister	T-10	68-67-71-70=276	$5,500.00
Andy Bean	T-10	68-69-71-68=276	$5,500.00
Lee Trevino	T-10	69-67-72-68=276	$5,500.00
Bill Kratzert	T-10	73-67-69-67=276	$5,500.00

Sammy Davis, Jr. - Greater Hartford Open

Course: Wethersfield C.C., Wethersfield, Conn.
Par: 71 Yardage: 6,568
Last day of event: Sunday, July 30, 1978

Player	Place	Score	Earnings
Rod Funseth	Win	65-67-68-64=264	$42,000.00
Lee Elder	T-2	67-68-66-67=268	$16,240.00
Bill Kratzert	T-2	66-67-69-66=268	$16,240.00
Dale Douglass	T-2	66-69-67-66=268	$16,240.00
Rex Caldwell	T-5	66-66-70-68=270	$8,085.00
Howard Twitty	T-5	70-63-66-71=270	$8,085.00
Gil Morgan	T-7	66-67-69-69=271	$6,457.50
Joe Inman	T-7	69-62-73-67=271	$6,457.50
Bob Eastwood	T-9	68-67-69-68=272	$4,357.50
Rod Curl	T-9	69-70-65-68=272	$4,357.50
Laurie Hammer	T-9	70-67-66-69=272	$4,357.50
Grier Jones	T-9	70-66-68-68=272	$4,357.50
Larry Nelson	T-9	64-67-70-71=272	$4,357.50
Stan Lee	T-9	68-67-66-71=272	$4,357.50
Bobby Walzel	T-9	73-63-65-71=272	$4,357.50
Victor Regalado	T-9	73-67-64-68=272	$4,357.50

PGA Championship

Course: Oakmont C.C., Oakmont, Pa.
Par: 71 Yardage: 6,989
Last day of event: Sunday, August 6, 1978

Player	Place	Score	Earnings
John Mahaffey	Win	75-67-68-66=276	$50,000.00

Playoff: Beat Jerry Pate and Tom Watson with birdie on second extra hole

Player	Place	Score	Earnings
Jerry Pate	T-2	72-70-66-68=276	$25,000.00
Tom Watson	T-2	67-69-67-73=276	$25,000.00
Tom Weiskopf	T-4	73-67-69-71=280	$14,500.00
Gil Morgan	T-4	76-71-66-67=280	$14,500.00
Craig Stadler	6	70-74-67-71=282	$10,000.00
Andy Bean	T-7	72-72-70-70=284	$8,000.00
Lee Trevino	T-7	69-73-70-72=284	$8,000.00
Graham Marsh	T-7	72-74-68-70=284	$8,000.00
Fuzzy Zoeller	10	75-69-73-68=285	$6,500.00

American Optical Classic

Course: Pleasant Valley C.C., Sutton, Mass.
Par: 71 Yardage: 7,110
Last day of event: Sunday, August 13, 1978

Player	Place	Score	Earnings
John Mahaffey	Win	71-65-67-67=270	$45,000.00
Ray Floyd	T-2	67-68-70-67=272	$20,812.50
Gil Morgan	T-2	70-67-66-69=272	$20,812.50
Miller Barber	T-4	66-71-70-69=276	$8,775.00
Bob Shearer	T-4	68-71-69-68=276	$8,775.00
Bruce Lietzke	T-4	68-71-70-67=276	$8,775.00
Mark Hayes	T-4	67-66-69-74=276	$8,775.00
Mike McCullough	8	70-67-72-68=277	$6,650.00
Lanny Wadkins	T-9	71-70-70-67=278	$5,625.00
Craig Stadler	T-9	69-67-72-70=278	$5,625.00
Bob Gilder	T-9	70-65-75-68=278	$5,625.00

American Express Westchester Classic

Course: Westchester C.C., Harrison, N.Y.
Par: 71 Yardage: 6,603
Last day of event: Sunday, August 20, 1978

Player	Place	Score	Earnings
Lee Elder	Win	71-68-68-67=274	$60,000.00
Mark Hayes	2	70-67-72-66=275	$34,200.00
Hubert Green	3	70-68-68-70=276	$21,300.00
Bill Kratzert	4	71-72-67-67=277	$14,100.00
Dave Eichelberger	T-5	70-71-66-71=278	$9,930.00
Bob Murphy	T-5	71-72-66-69=278	$9,930.00
Gibby Gilbert	T-5	69-68-68-73=278	$9,930.00
Alan Tapie	T-5	70-68-67-73=278	$9,930.00
Dave Stockton	T-5	74-69-69-66=278	$9,930.00
Tom Watson	T-10	70-68-70-71=279	$6,150.00
Rod Curl	T-10	71-70-67-71=279	$6,150.00
Jack Nicklaus	T-10	67-69-71-72=279	$6,150.00
Grier Jones	T-10	69-72-66-72=279	$6,150.00
Larry Nelson	T-10	69-69-73-68=279	$6,150.00
David Graham	T-10	69-68-76-66=279	$6,150.00

Colgate Hall of Fame Classic

Course: Pinehurst C.C. (No 2), Pinehurst, N.C.
Par: 71 Yardage: 7,050
Last day of event: Sunday, August 27, 1978

Player	Place	Score	Earnings
Tom Watson	Win	72-67-67-71=277	$50,000.00
Tom Kite	T-2	69-68-70-71=278	$19,333.33
Howard Twitty	T-2	69-69-73-67=278	$19,333.33
Hale Irwin	T-2	73-63-69-73=278	$19,333.34
Danny Edwards	5	70-72-72-65=279	$10,250.00
Jerry Pate	6	67-73-72-70=282	$9,000.00
Bob Gilder	T-7	72-71-71-69=283	$7,687.50
Curtis Strange	T-7	71-70-69-73=283	$7,687.50
Phil Hancock	T-9	71-74-68-71=284	$6,250.00
Mike McCullough	T-9	73-66-74-71=284	$6,250.00
Peter Jacobsen	T-9	75-70-70-69=284	$6,250.00

B.C. Open

Course: En-Joie G.C., Endicott, N.Y.
Par: 71 Yardage: 6,966
Last day of event: Monday, September 4, 1978

Player	Place	Score	Earnings
Tom Kite	Win	66-65-68-68=267	$45,000.00
Mark Hayes	2	70-69-65-68=272	$25,650.00
Peter Jacobsen	3	70-69-67-69=275	$15,975.00
Gil Morgan	T-4	69-69-68-70=276	$9,300.00
John Mahaffey	T-4	68-71-67-70=276	$9,300.00
Ed Sneed	T-4	69-71-68-68=276	$9,300.00
Rex Caldwell	T-7	68-68-70-71=277	$6,641.67
Artie McNickle	T-7	68-68-71-70=277	$6,641.66
Bobby Walzel	T-7	69-69-71-68=277	$6,641.67
Bob Byman	T-10	70-68-69-71=278	$4,950.00
Miller Barber	T-10	71-66-70-71=278	$4,950.00
Tom Purtzer	T-10	66-73-72-67=278	$4,950.00
Rod Curl	T-10	70-64-71-73=278	$4,950.00

Southern Open

Course: Green Island C.C., Columbus, Ga.
Par: 70 Yardage: 6,791
Last day of event: Sunday, September 10, 1978

Player	Place	Score	Earnings
Jerry Pate	Win	67-67-66-69=269	$35,000.00
Phil Hancock	2	66-72-68-64=270	$19,950.00
Don January	T-3	69-66-70-68=273	$10,325.00
Jim Nelford	T-3	68-66-75-64=273	$10,325.00
George Cadle	T-5	68-70-67-69=274	$6,358.33
Bobby Wadkins	T-5	68-66-69-71=274	$6,358.33
Chi Chi Rodriguez	T-5	68-68-71-67=274	$6,358.34
Keith Fergus	T-8	70-66-70-69=275	$4,392.60
Rex Caldwell	T-8	66-67-72-70=275	$4,392.60
Greg Powers	T-8	68-65-70-72=275	$4,392.60
Mark Hayes	T-8	72-66-70-67=275	$4,392.60
Tim Simpson	T-8	74-67-66-68=275	$4,392.60

San Antonio Texas Open

Course: Oak Hill C.C., San Antonio, Texas
Par: 70 Yardage: 6,576
Last day of event: Sunday, September 17, 1978

Player	Place	Score	Earnings
Ron Streck	Win	73-67-63-62=265	$40,000.00
Lon Hinkle	T-2	68-67-67-64=266	$18,500.00
Hubert Green	T-2	62-70-68-66=266	$18,500.00
Ben Crenshaw	4	65-63-70-69=267	$9,400.00
George Burns	T-5	69-66-65-69=269	$7,266.67
Lee Trevino	T-5	69-66-65-69=269	$7,266.67
Lou Graham	T-5	63-67-70-69=269	$7,266.66
Tom Purtzer	T-8	66-67-70-67=270	$5,225.00
Hale Irwin	T-8	67-67-71-65=270	$5,225.00
Leonard Thompson	T-8	69-65-65-71=270	$5,225.00
Peter Oosterhuis	T-8	69-63-72-66=270	$5,225.00

Anheuser-Busch Golf Classic

Course: Silverado C.C., Napa, Calif.
Home Course -Par: 72 Yardage: 6,849
Last day of event: Sunday, September 24, 1978

Player	Place	Score	Earnings
Tom Watson	Win	68-69-66-67=270	$40,000.00
Ed Sneed	2	66-68-69-70=273	$22,800.00
Barry Jaeckel	3	69-67-67-72=275	$14,200.00
Orville Moody	T-4	70-69-70-67=276	$7,800.00
D.A. Weibring	T-4	71-67-69-69=276	$7,800.00
Bob Gilder	T-4	71-68-68-69=276	$7,800.00
Bob Zender	T-4	67-72-66-71=276	$7,800.00
Danny Edwards	T-8	70-68-69-70=277	$5,225.00
Lou Graham	T-8	72-65-71-69=277	$5,225.00
Bruce Lietzke	T-8	68-69-66-74=277	$5,225.00
Jay Haas	T-8	66-70-66-75=277	$5,225.00

World Series of Golf

Course: Firestone C.C. (South), Akron, Ohio
Par: 70 Yardage: 7,149
Last day of event: Sunday, October 1, 1978

Player	Place	Score	Earnings
Gil Morgan	Win	71-72-67-68=278	$100,000.00
Playoff: Beat Hubert Green with par on first extra hole			
Hubert Green	2	70-67-71-70=278	$45,000.00
Tom Watson	3	74-70-69-67=280	$19,000.00
Lanny Wadkins	4	70-73-73-66=282	$12,500.00
Tom Kite	5	71-69-72-71=283	$10,000.00
Hale Irwin	6	71-71-70-72=284	$8,400.00
Jack Nicklaus	7	72-76-70-67=285	$6,900.00

Gary Player	8	76-72-69-69=286	$6,600.00
Bill Kratzert	T-9	72-71-73-71=287	$6,450.00
Seve Ballesteros	T-9	69-70-76-72=287	$6,450.00

Pensacola Open

Course: Perdido Bay C.C., Pensacola, Fla.
Par: 72 Yardage: 7,133
Last day of event: Sunday, October 29, 1978

Player	Place	Score	Earnings
Mac McLendon	Win	65-67-67-73=272	$25,000.00
Playoff: Beat Mike Reid with par on first extra hole			
Mike Reid	2	68-70-68-66=272	$14,250.00
Wayne Levi	3	68-70-64-71=273	$8,875.00
Allen Miller	T-4	69-70-66-69=274	$5,500.00
Bobby Wadkins	T-4	70-69-66-69=274	$5,500.00
Keith Fergus	6	71-66-71-68=276	$4,500.00
Leonard Thompson	T-7	70-69-70-68=277	$3,151.72
Curtis Strange	T-7	69-70-67-71=277	$3,151.71
Howard Twitty	T-7	69-71-69-68=277	$3,151.72
Andy Bean	T-7	70-71-68-68=277	$3,151.72
D.A. Weibring	T-7	68-69-67-73=277	$3,151.71
Mark McCumber	T-7	70-70-64-73=277	$3,151.71
Lon Hinkle	T-7	71-73-66-67=277	$3,151.71

1979

This was the year charismatic Seve Ballesteros began his reign atop European golf, winning the British Open at Royal Lytham, where he made birdie at the 70th hole after hitting his approach shot from a parking lot. Frank Urban "Fuzzy" Zoeller won the Masters' first sudden-death playoff, bouncing Tom Watson and Ed Sneed on the second hole. (Sneed bogeyed the last three holes in regulation.) Thanks to a 6-shot cushion after 63 holes, Hale Irwin won the U.S. Open by two strokes despite shooting 40 over his final nine holes at Inverness. David Graham shot a closing 65, which included double-bogey at the 72nd hole, then beat Ben Crenshaw on the third hole of sudden death to win the PGA Championship at Oakland Hills.

Bob Hope Chrysler Classic

Course: Indian Wells C.C., Tamarisk C.C., Bermuda Dunes C.C.
Home course /Indian Wells, La Quinta, Calif.
Par: 72 Yardage: 6,478
Last day of event: Sunday, January 14, 1979

Player	Place	Score	Earnings
John Mahaffey	Win	66-66-71-71-69=343	$50,000.00
Lee Trevino	2	71-68-66-70-69=344	$29,700.00
Mark Hayes	3	70-72-68-69-66=345	$18,700.00
Grier Jones	4	70-68-71-69-68=346	$13,200.00
Lanny Wadkins	5	71-66-74-69-68=348	$10,450.00
Keith Fergus	T-6	69-70-72-71-67=349	$10,450.00
Bobby Wadkins	T-6	69-70-72-71-67=349	$8,275.00
Tom Purtzer	T-6	69-68-70-74-68=349	$8,275.00
Leonard Thompson	T-6	69-66-69-75-70=349	$8,275.00
Jack Nicklaus	T-10	71-69-69-72-69=350	$6,325.00
Jerry Pate	T-10	71-72-70-69-68=350	$6,325.00
Alan Tapie	T-10	71-72-70-69-68=350	$6,325.00
Lon Hinkle	T-10	72-67-73-69-69=350	$6,325.00

Phoenix Open

Course: Phoenix C.C., Phoenix, Ariz.
Par: 71 Yardage: 6,726
Last day of event: Monday, January 22, 1979

Player	Place	Score	Earnings
Ben Crenshaw	Win	67-61-71=199	$33,750.00
Jay Haas	2	65-67-68=200	$20,250.00
Tom Kite	3	73-66-63=202	$12,750.00
Lon Hinkle	T-4	66-69-68=203	$7,382.81
Andy Bean	T-4	66-66-71=203	$7,382.81
Jerry Pate	T-4	66-66-71=203	$7,382.81
Pat McGowan	T-4	71-66-66=203	$7,382.82
Phil Hancock	T-8	68-68-69=205	$5,250.00
Joe Inman	T-8	69-68-68=205	$5,250.00
Rod Funseth	T-8	70-66-69=205	$5,250.00
Wayne Levi	T-8	71-68-66=205	$5,250.00

Andy Williams-San Diego Open

Course: Torrey Pines (South), Torrey Pines (North), San Diego, Calif.
Home Course -Par: 72 Yardage: 7,021
Last day of event: Sunday, January 28, 1979

Player	Place	Score	Earnings
Fuzzy Zoeller	Win	76-67-67-72=282	$45,000.00
Artie McNickle	T-2	73-71-71-72=287	$16,500.00
Bill Kratzert	T-2	73-68-72-74=287	$16,500.00
Tom Watson	T-2	74-70-72-71=287	$16,500.00
Wayne Levi	T-2	79-68-72-68=287	$16,500.00
Victor Regalado	T-6	71-73-70-74=288	$8,093.75
Jerry Pate	T-6	72-70-72-74=288	$8,093.75
Lee Trevino	T-6	75-69-70-74=288	$8,093.75
Jerry McGee	T-6	71-67-74-76=288	$8,093.75
Scott Simpson	T-10	73-73-71-72=289	$6,000.00
Howard Twitty	T-10	73-73-71-72=289	$6,000.00
Keith Fergus	T-10	74-73-72-70=289	$6,000.00
Larry Nelson	T-10	77-68-70-74=289	$6,000.00

Bing Crosby Pro-Am

Courses: Pebble Beach G.L., Spyglass Hill G.C., Cypress Point C.C., Pebble Beach, Calif.
Home Course/ Pebble Beach, Par: 72 Yardage: 6,815
Last day of event: Sunday, February 4, 1979

Player	Place	Score	Earnings
Lon Hinkle	Win	70-68-69-77=284	$54,000.00
Playoff: Beat Andy Bean and Mark Hayes with birdie on third extra hole			
Andy Bean	T-2	72-73-70-69=284	$26,400.00
Mark Hayes	T-2	73-73-66-72=284	$26,400.00
Brad Bryant	T-4	71-70-73-72=286	$13,200.00
Leonard Thompson	T-4	71-69-76-70=286	$13,200.00
Jim Nelford	T-6	72-74-70-71=287	$10,425.00
Jay Haas	T-6	68-77-74-68=287	$10,425.00
Gibby Gilbert	T-8	72-73-70-73=288	$8,700.00
Curtis Strange	T-8	70-70-74-74=288	$8,700.00
J.C. Snead	T-8	74-72-69-73=288	$8,700.00

Hawaiian Open

Course: Waialae C.C., Honolulu, Ha.
Par: 72 Yardage: 7,234
Last day of event: Sunday, February 11, 1979

Player	Place	Score	Earnings
Hubert Green	Win	68-67-63-69=267	$54,000.00

Fuzzy Zoeller	2	66-68-71-65=270	$32,400.00
Larry Nelson	3	66-69-70-67=272	$20,400.00
Miller Barber	T-4	65-70-68-70=273	$12,400.00
Charles Coody	T-4	66-72-66-69=273	$12,400.00
Don January	T-6	68-70-66-70=274	$9,675.00
Dan Halldorson	T-6	68-66-69-71=274	$9,675.00
Hale Irwin	T-8	67-70-67-71=275	$8,400.00
George Burns	T-8	71-63-68-73=275	$8,400.00
Tom Storey	T-10	68-70-66-72=276	$7,200.00
John Schroeder	T-10	68-73-70-65=276	$7,200.00

Joe Garagiola Tucson Open

Course: Randolph Park Municipal, Tucson, Ariz.
Par: 70 Yardage: 6,860
Last day of event: Sunday, February 18, 1979

Player	Place	Score	Earnings
Bruce Lietzke	Win	63-66-68-68=265	$45,000.00
Jim Thorpe	T-2	67-65-67-68=267	$18,666.67
Tom Watson	T-2	67-66-66-68=267	$18,666.67
Buddy Gardner	T-2	69-66-67-65=267	$18,666.66
Victor Regalado	T-5	66-68-67-67=268	$8,781.25
Marty Fleckman	T-5	66-67-66-69=268	$8,781.25
Howard Twitty	T-5	69-68-66-65=268	$8,781.25
Curtis Strange	T-5	64-71-67-66=268	$8,781.25
Lee Trevino	T-9	67-68-66-68=269	$7,000.00
Dave Barr	T-9	69-67-66-67=269	$7,000.00

Glen Campbell Los Angeles Open

Course: Riviera C.C., Pacific Palisades, Calif.
Par: 71 Yardage: 7,029
Last day of event: Sunday, February 25, 1979

Player	Place	Score	Earnings
Lanny Wadkins	Win	66-72-69-69=276	$45,000.00
Lon Hinkle	2	67-69-71-70=277	$27,000.00
Kermit Zarley	T-3	68-71-68-71=278	$14,500.00
Andy Bean	T-3	71-69-68-70=278	$14,500.00
Ed Sneed	T-5	69-72-69-69=279	$9,500.00
Fuzzy Zoeller	T-5	70-67-72-70=279	$9,500.00
Jim Colbert	T-7	73-67-71-69=280	$7,791.66
Tommy Aaron	T-7	73-70-68-69=280	$7,791.67
Rod Curl	T-7	73-73-68-66=280	$7,791.67
Artie McNickle	10	71-69-72-69=281	$6,750.00

Bay Hill Citrus Classic

Course: Bay Hill Club, Orlando, Fla.
Par: 71 Yardage: 7,103
Last day of event: Sunday, March 4, 1979

Player	Place	Score	Earnings
Bob Byman	Win	67-70-70-71=278	$45,000.00
Playoff: Beat John Schroeder with par on second extra hole			
John Schroeder	2	68-68-72-70=278	$27,000.00
Hale Irwin	T-3	69-70-72-68=279	$13,000.00
Bill Rogers	T-3	67-69-74-69=279	$13,000.00
Andy Bean	T-3	64-69-76-70=279	$13,000.00
Alan Tapie	T-6	70-71-72-70=283	$7,562.50
Tom Watson	T-6	72-68-71-72=283	$7,562.50
Grier Jones	T-6	69-69-73-72=283	$7,562.50
David Edwards	T-6	68-70-71-74=283	$7,562.50
Jay Haas	T-6	69-70-74-70=283	$7,562.50
Jerry Pate	T-6	68-68-77-70=283	$7,562.50

Jackie Gleason's Inverrary Classic

Course: Inverrary G. & C.C. (East), Lauderhill, Fla.
Par: 72 Yardage: 7,128
Last day of event: Sunday, March 11, 1979

Player	Place	Score	Earnings
Larry Nelson	Win	67-69-67-71=274	$54,000.00
Grier Jones	2	71-67-69-70=277	$32,400.00
Hale Irwin	3	73-62-72-73=280	$20,400.00
Lee Elder	T-4	72-71-68-70=281	$13,200.00
Tommy Aaron	T-4	66-69-74-72=281	$13,200.00
Ray Floyd	6	69-72-67-74=282	$10,800.00
Andy North	7	69-71-71-72=283	$10,050.00
Charles Coody	T-8	68-69-74-73=284	$8,700.00
Pat McGowan	T-8	72-74-67-71=284	$8,700.00
Bob Gilder	T-8	76-69-68-71=284	$8,700.00

Doral-Eastern Open

Course: Doral C.C. (Blue), Miami, Fla.
Par: 72 Yardage: 6,939
Last day of event: Sunday, March 18, 1979

Player	Place	Score	Earnings
Mark McCumber	Win	67-71-69-72=279	$45,000.00
Bill Rogers	2	70-68-70-72=280	$27,000.00
Rod Curl	3	67-76-70-68=281	$17,000.00
Kermit Zarley	T-4	73-72-66-71=282	$9,843.75
Mike McCullough	T-4	70-71-74-67=282	$9,843.75
Alan Tapie	T-4	66-71-69-76=282	$9,843.75
Gibby Gilbert	T-4	67-77-70-68=282	$9,843.75
Bill Kratzert	T-8	67-69-75-72=283	$7,750.00
David Graham	T-9	69-72-73-70=284	$6,750.00
Bobby Wadkins	T-9	73-70-71-70=284	$6,750.00
Tom Kite	T-9	73-72-70-69=284	$6,750.00

Tournament Players Championship

Course: Sawgrass C.C., Ponte Vedra Beach, Fla.
Par: 72 Yardage: 7,174
Last day of event: Sunday, March 25, 1979

Player	Place	Score	Earnings
Lanny Wadkins	Win	67-68-76-72=283	$72,000.00
Tom Watson	2	70-72-75-71=288	$43,200.00
Jack Renner	3	73-70-71-75=289	$27,200.00
Phil Hancock	4	69-73-75-74=291	$19,200.00
Wayne Levi	T-5	69-72-77-75=293	$14,600.00
Bill Kratzert	T-5	69-70-75-79=293	$14,600.00
Lee Trevino	T-5	70-69-75-79=293	$14,600.00
Andy Bean	8	72-73-74-75=294	$12,400.00
Tom Kite	T-9	72-73-75-75=295	$10,800.00
Jay Haas	T-9	71-74-74-76=295	$10,800.00
Jack Newton	T-9	69-74-77-75=295	$10,800.00

Sea Pines Heritage Classic

Course: Harbour Town G.L., Hilton Head, S.C.
Par: 71 Yardage: 6,657
Last day of event: Sunday, April 1, 1979

Player	Place	Score	Earnings
Tom Watson	Win	65-65-69-71=270	$54,000.00
Ed Sneed	2	69-69-71-66=275	$32,400.00
Tom Kite	T-3	69-68-71-71=279	$17,400.00
Mike Morley	T-3	69-68-72-70=279	$17,400.00
Bill Rogers	T-5	69-68-72-71=280	$11,400.00

Ray Floyd	T-5	72-68-69-71=280	$11,400.00
George Burns	T-7	67-72-72-70=281	$9,675.00
Bob Murphy	T-7	71-67-74-69=281	$9,675.00
Don January	T-9	72-70-69-71=282	$8,400.00
Lanny Wadkins	T-9	66-67-74-75=282	$8,400.00

Greater Greensboro Open

Course: Forest Oaks C.C., Greensboro, N.C.
Par: 72 Yardage: 6,958
Last day of event: Sunday, April 8, 1979

Player	Place	Score	Earnings
Ray Floyd	Win	73-71-71-67=282	$45,000.00
Gary Player	T-2	70-71-71-71=283	$22,000.00
George Burns	T-2	73-71-69-70=283	$22,000.00
Bobby Wadkins	4	70-73-67-74=284	$12,000.00
Rex Caldwell	5	70-74-71-72=287	$10,000.00
Lee Elder	T-6	73-73-69-73=288	$8,375.00
Doug Tewell	T-6	72-74-71-71=288	$8,375.00
Tom Purtzer	T-6	70-71-72-75=288	$8,375.00
Bobby Walzel	T-9	68-75-74-72=289	$6,750.00
Curtis Strange	T-9	71-75-71-72=289	$6,750.00
Jack Renner	T-9	68-71-70-80=289	$6,750.00

Masters

Course: Augusta National G.C., Augusta, Ga.
Par: 72 Yardage: 6,925
Last day of event: Sunday, April 15, 1979

Player	Place	Score	Earnings
Fuzzy Zoeller	Win	70-71-69-70=280	$50,000.00

Playoff: Beat Ed Sneed and Tom Watson with birdie on second extra hole

Tom Watson	T-2	68-71-70-71=280	$30,000.00
Ed Sneed	T-2	68-67-69-76=280	$30,000.00
Jack Nicklaus	4	69-71-72-69=281	$15,000.00
Tom Kite	5	71-72-68-72=283	$13,000.00
Bruce Lietzke	6	67-75-68-74=284	$11,500.00
Lanny Wadkins	T-7	73-69-70-73=285	$9,000.00
Leonard Thompson	T-7	68-70-73-74=285	$9,000.00
Craig Stadler	T-7	69-66-74-76=285	$9,000.00
Gene Littler	T-10	74-71-69-72=286	$6,500.00
Hubert Green	T-10	74-69-72-71=286	$6,500.00

MONY Tournament of Champions

Course: La Costa C.C., Carlsbad, Calif.
Par: 72 Yardage: 6,911
Last day of event: Sunday, April 22, 1979

Player	Place	Score	Earnings
Tom Watson	Win	69-66-70-70=275	$54,000.00
Bruce Lietzke	T-2	72-66-70-73=281	$29,500.00
Jerry Pate	T-2	72-71-65-73=281	$29,500.00
Gary Player	4	71-69-74-68=282	$18,000.00
Lee Trevino	T-5	72-68-72-72=284	$15,000.00
Larry Nelson	T-5	74-69-69-72=284	$15,000.00
Tom Kite	7	76-69-68-72=285	$12,000.00
Lee Elder	T-8	72-73-68-75=288	$10,625.00
Ben Crenshaw	T-8	75-71-75-67=288	$10,625.00
Hubert Green	T-10	73-71-73-74=291	$8,750.00
Lon Hinkle	T-10	75-70-73-73=291	$8,750.00
Andy Bean	T-10	75-72-71-73=291	$8,750.00

Tallahassee Open

Course: Killearn C.C., Tallahassee, Fla.
Par: 72 Yardage: 7,124
Last day of event: Sunday, April 22, 1979

Player	Place	Score	Earnings
Chi Chi Rodriguez	Win	66-69-67-67=269	$18,000.00
Lindy Miller	2	65-72-67-68=272	$10,000.00
Bobby Wadkins	3	68-69-65-72=274	$6,800.00
Rex Caldwell	4	69-67-68-71=275	$4,950.00
Bob Eastwood	T-5	68-69-70-69=276	$3,660.00
Bobby Walzel	T-5	70-68-68-70=276	$3,660.00
Bob Mann	T-5	64-71-70-71=276	$3,660.00
Gary Koch	T-5	68-68-71-69=276	$3,660.00
Billy Casper	T-5	68-71-70-67=276	$3,660.00
Jim Thorpe	T-10	68-69-69-71=277	$2,600.00
Bob-E. Smith	T-10	71-70-68-68=277	$2,600.00
Wayne Levi	T-10	67-69-68-73=277	$2,600.00

First NBC New Orleans Open

Course: Lakewood C.C., New Orleans, La.
Par: 72 Yardage: 7,080
Last day of event: Sunday, April 29, 1979

Player	Place	Score	Earnings
Hubert Green	Win	69-67-69-68=273	$45,000.00
Lee Trevino	T-2	68-67-69-70=274	$16,500.00
Steve Melnyk	T-2	68-68-70-68=274	$16,500.00
Bruce Lietzke	T-2	68-70-69-67=274	$16,500.00
Frank Conner	T-2	65-71-68-70=274	$16,500.00
Calvin Peete	T-6	70-67-69-69=275	$8,375.00
Curtis Strange	T-6	66-70-67-72=275	$8,375.00
Bob Gilder	T-6	71-73-62-69=275	$8,375.00
Jim Colbert	9	66-71-71-68=276	$7,250.00
Doug Tewell	T-10	66-72-68-71=277	$6,500.00
Leonard Thompson	T-10	72-68-69-68=277	$6,500.00

Houston Open

Course: Woodlands C.C., The Woodlands, Texas
Par: 71 Yardage: 6,918
Last day of event: Sunday, May 6, 1979

Player	Place	Score	Earnings
Wayne Levi	Win	69-65-63-71=268	$54,000.00
Michael Brannan	2	68-66-66-70=270	$32,400.00
Bob Gilder	T-3	70-64-70-68=272	$14,400.00
Sammy Rachels	T-3	68-65-68-71=272	$14,400.00
Hale Irwin	T-3	69-64-71-68=272	$14,400.00
Orville Moody	T-3	72-64-67-69=272	$14,400.00
Bill Rogers	T-7	67-69-69-68=273	$9,675.00
Calvin Peete	T-7	70-70-68-65=273	$9,675.00
John Schroeder	T-9	68-66-70-70=274	$8,400.00
Dave Stockton	T-9	72-66-67-69=274	$8,400.00

Byron Nelson Golf Classic

Course: Preston Trail G.C., Dallas, Texas
Par: 70 Yardage: 6,993
Last day of event: Sunday, May 13, 1979

Player	Place	Score	Earnings
Tom Watson	Win	64-72-69-70=275	$54,000.00

Playoff: Beat Bill Rogers with birdie on first extra hole

Bill Rogers	2	68-73-68-66=275	$32,400.00
Larry Nelson	3	65-68-74-69=276	$20,400.00

Jerry Pate	4	69-70-67-72=278	$14,400.00
Morris Hatalsky	T-5	67-71-72-69=279	$10,537.50
Jerry McGee	T-5	71-72-69-67=279	$10,537.50
Calvin Peete	T-5	68-70-73-68=279	$10,537.50
Michael Brannan	T-5	69-73-69-68=279	$10,537.50
Gene Littler	T-9	69-72-71-68=280	$8,400.00
Brad Bryant	T-9	67-73-73-67=280	$8,400.00

Colonial National Invitational

Course: Colonial C.C., Fort Worth, Texas
Par: 70 Yardage: 7,096
Last day of event: Sunday, May 20, 1979

Player	Place	Score	Earnings
Al Geiberger	Win	68-69-64-73=274	$54,000.00
Gene Littler	T-2	70-70-67-68=275	$26,400.00
Don January	T-2	72-70-68-65=275	$26,400.00
Jim Colbert	T-4	70-73-64-69=276	$13,200.00
Tom Watson	T-4	71-73-65-67=276	$13,200.00
Fuzzy Zoeller	T-6	70-68-70-70=278	$10,425.00
Leonard Thompson	T-6	65-68-73-72=278	$10,425.00
Wayne Levi	T-8	68-71-71-69=279	$8,100.00
Bruce Lietzke	T-8	66-73-74-66=279	$8,100.00
Lindy Miller	T-8	68-74-70-67=279	$8,100.00
Ed Sneed	T-8	69-74-69-67=279	$8,100.00
Jack Renner	T-8	70-74-66-69=279	$8,100.00

Memorial Tournament

Course: Muirfield Village G.C., Dubin, Ohio
Par: 72 Yardage: 7,101
Last day of event: Sunday, May 27, 1979

Player	Place	Score	Earnings
Tom Watson	Win	73-69-72-71=285	$54,000.00
Miller Barber	2	74-73-71-70=288	$32,400.00
Bob Gilder	3	74-80-68-69=291	$20,400.00
Tom Kite	T-4	74-72-74-72=292	$13,200.00
Lanny Wadkins	T-4	69-79-73-71=292	$13,200.00
Ed Sneed	6	71-78-75-69=293	$10,800.00
Howard Twitty	T-7	75-76-74-69=294	$9,350.00
Bill Rogers	T-7	77-75-71-71=294	$9,350.00
Jim Colbert	T-7	73-78-73-70=294	$9,350.00
Jay Haas	T-10	73-78-73-71=295	$7,800.00
George Burns	T-10	76-78-73-68=295	$7,800.00

Kemper Open

Course: Quail Hollow C.C., Charlotte, N.C.
Par: 72 Yardage: 7,205
Last day of event: Sunday, June 3, 1979

Player	Place	Score	Earnings
Jerry McGee	Win	61-74-69-68=272	$63,000.00
Jerry Pate	2	71-70-64-68=273	$37,800.00
J.C. Snead	T-3	71-65-71-70=277	$20,300.00
Andy Bean	T-3	69-68-72-68=277	$20,300.00
Ray Floyd	5	70-68-68-72=278	$14,000.00
Mark Hayes	6	69-71-68-71=279	$12,600.00
Bill Rogers	T-7	69-71-70-70=280	$10,185.00
Bobby Walzel	T-7	68-71-69-72=280	$10,185.00
Victor Regalado	T-7	71-66-72-71=280	$10,185.00
Homero Blancas	T-7	71-68-72-69=280	$10,185.00
Craig Stadler	T-7	62-69-73-76=280	$10,185.00

Atlanta Classic

Course: Atlanta C.C., Atlanta, Ga.
Par:72 Yardage: 7,007
Last day of event: Sunday, June 10, 1979

Player	Place	Score	Earnings
Andy Bean	Win	70-67-61-67=265	$54,000.00
Joe Inman	2	71-64-68-70=273	$32,400.00
Grier Jones	T-3	68-68-70-70=276	$17,400.00
David Graham	T-3	71-70-67-68=276	$17,400.00
Fuzzy Zoeller	5	68-71-64-74=277	$12,000.00
Wally Armstrong	6	71-71-70-67=279	$10,800.00
Jack Renner	T-7	68-71-70-71=280	$9,350.00
Hubert Green	T-7	69-71-70-70=280	$9,350.00
Doug Tewell	T-7	72-70-69-69=280	$9,350.00
Curtis Strange	T-10	70-71-70-70=281	$7,200.00
Ed Dougherty	T-10	71-73-65-72=281	$7,200.00
Barry Jaeckel	T-10	67-72-68-74=281	$7,200.00
Bob Murphy	T-10	68-71-74-68=281	$7,200.00

U.S. Open

Course: Inverness Club, Toledo, Ohio
Par: 71 Yardage: 6,982
Last day of event: Sunday, June 17, 1979

Player	Place	Score	Earnings
Hale Irwin	Win	74-68-67-75=284	$50,000.00
Gary Player	T-2	73-73-72-68=286	$22,250.00
Jerry Pate	T-2	71-74-69-72=286	$22,250.00
Bill Rogers	T-4	71-72-73-72=288	$13,733.33
Tom Weiskopf	T-4	71-74-67-76=288	$13,733.33
Larry Nelson	T-4	71-68-76-73=288	$13,733.33
David Graham	7	73-73-70-73=289	$10,000.00
Tom Purtzer	8	70-69-75-76=290	$9,000.00
Keith Fergus	T-9	70-77-72-72=291	$7,500.00
Jack Nicklaus	T-9	74-77-72-68=291	$7,500.00

Canadian Open

Course: Glen Abbey G.C., Oakville, Ontario, Canada
Par: 71 Yardage: 7,059
Last day of event: Sunday, June 24, 1979

Player	Place	Score	Earnings
Lee Trevino	Win	67-71-72-71=281	$63,000.00
Ben Crenshaw	2	70-70-73-71=284	$37,800.00
Tom Watson	3	66-69-72-78=285	$23,800.00
Bob Gilder	4	70-70-76-70=286	$16,800.00
Bruce Lietzke	T-5	71-74-72-70=287	$12,775.00
David Graham	T-5	72-70-74-71=287	$12,775.00
Howard Twitty	T-5	69-76-73-69=287	$12,775.00
Jim Nelford	8	71-72-73-72=288	$10,850.00
Eddie Pearce	T-9	74-72-72-71=289	$9,100.00
Johnny Miller	T-9	67-73-75-74=289	$9,100.00
Keith Fergus	T-9	70-75-71-73=289	$9,100.00
D.A. Weibring	T-9	68-70-75-76=289	$9,100.00

Danny Thomas Memphis Classic

Course: Colonial C.C. (South), Cordova, Tenn.
Par: 72 Yardage: 7,282
Last day of event: Sunday, July 1, 1979

Player	Place	Score	Earnings
Gil Morgan	Win	72-71-69-66=278	$54,000.00

Playoff: Beat Larry Nelson with birdie on second extra hole

Larry Nelson	2	72-71-70-65=278	$32,400.00
Tom Kite	3	71-70-69-70=280	$20,400.00
Graham Marsh	T-4	72-70-70-70=282	$11,812.50
Bruce Lietzke	T-4	71-73-72-66=282	$11,812.50
Mark Hayes	T-4	71-70-74-67=282	$11,812.50
J.C. Snead	T-4	69-70-76-67=282	$11,812.50
Peter Jacobsen	T-8	71-71-69-72=283	$8,100.00
Cesar Sanudo	T-8	72-68-71-72=283	$8,100.00
Andy Bean	T-8	71-74-68-70=283	$8,100.00
Tom Purtzer	T-8	74-72-70-67=283	$8,100.00
Bob Byman	T-8	71-69-75-68=283	$8,100.00

Western Open

Course: Butler National G.C., Oak Brook, Ill.
Par: 72 Yardage: 7,097
Last day of event: Sunday, July 8, 1979

Player	Place	Score	Earnings
Larry Nelson	Win	71-69-70-76=286	$54,000.00
Playoff: Beat Ben Crenshaw with birdie on first extra hole			
Ben Crenshaw	2	75-69-71-71=286	$32,400.00
Dan Pohl	T-3	71-72-71-73=287	$17,400.00
Bruce Douglass	T-3	69-71-76-71=287	$17,400.00
Bruce Lietzke	5	73-73-73-69=288	$12,000.00
Mark Hayes	T-6	75-71-72-71=289	$9,712.50
John Schroeder	T-6	75-73-74-67=289	$9,712.50
Jim Simons	T-6	69-76-72-72=289	$9,712.50
Tom Watson	T-6	70-73-68-78=289	$9,712.50
Calvin Peete	T-10	70-75-74-71=290	$7,500.00
Graham Marsh	T-10	72-74-75-69=290	$7,500.00
Bobby Wadkins	T-10	75-72-70-73=290	$7,500.00

Greater Milwaukee Open

Course: Tuckaway C.C., Franklin, Wis.
Par: 72 Yardage: 7,030
Last day of event: Sunday, July 15, 1979

Player	Place	Score	Earnings
Calvin Peete	Win	69-67-68-65=269	$36,000.00
Lee Trevino	T-2	70-68-66-70=274	$14,933.33
Victor Regalado	T-2	66-68-69-71=274	$14,933.34
Jim Simons	T-2	68-68-71-67=274	$14,933.34
John Lister	T-5	67-69-71-68=275	$7,600.00
Ed Dougherty	T-5	67-66-70-72=275	$7,600.00
Brad Bryant	T-7	69-70-70-67=276	$6,450.00
David Graham	T-7	68-67-71-70=276	$6,450.00
Jim Dent	T-9	70-67-70-70=277	$5,400.00
Grier Jones	T-9	69-67-71-70=277	$5,400.00
Rex Caldwell	T-9	71-71-69-66=277	$5,400.00

British Open

Course: Royal Lytham & St. Annes G.C., Lytham, Lancashire, England
Par: 71 Yardage: 6,822
Last day of event: Saturday, July 21, 1979

Player	Place	Score	Earnings
Seve Ballesteros	Win	73-65-75-70=283	$31,500.00
Ben Crenshaw	T-2	72-71-72-71=286	$23,625.00
Jack Nicklaus	T-2	72-69-73-72=286	$23,625.00
Mark James	4	76-69-69-73=287	$15,750.00
Rodger Davis	5	75-70-70-73=288	$13,650.00
Hale Irwin	6	68-68-75-78=289	$12,600.00
Isao Aoki	T-7	70-74-72-75=291	$10,500.00
Graham Marsh	T-7	74-68-75-74=291	$10,500.00

Bob Byman	T-7	73-70-72-76=291	$10,500.00
Jumbo Ozaki	T-10	75-69-75-73=292	$8,400.00
Greg Norman	T-10	73-71-72-76=292	$8,400.00
Bob Charles	T-10	78-72-70-72=292	$8,400.00

Ed McMahon Quad City Open

Course: Oakwood C.C., Coal Valley, Ill.
Par: 70 Yardage: 6,514
Last day of event: Sunday, July 22, 1979

Player	Place	Score	Earnings
D.A. Weibring	Win	67-65-69-65=266	$36,000.00
Calvin Peete	2	68-70-67-63=268	$21,600.00
Ken Still	3	67-68-67-68=270	$13,600.00
Craig Stadler	4	70-66-66-69=271	$9,600.00
Lonnie Nielsen	T-5	66-69-68-69=272	$7,300.00
Ed Sabo	T-5	71-66-69-66=272	$7,300.00
Victor Regalado	T-5	64-70-72-66=272	$7,300.00
Dan Pohl	T-8	68-70-70-65=273	$5,000.00
Curtis Strange	T-8	69-70-66-68=273	$5,000.00
Mike Morley	T-8	70-68-69-66=273	$5,000.00
Brad Bryant	T-8	70-70-69-64=273	$5,000.00
Morris Hatalsky	T-8	66-71-67-69=273	$5,000.00
Rod Curl	T-8	67-65-70-71=273	$5,000.00
Dan Halldorson	T-8	65-68-67-73=273	$5,000.00

IVB Philadelphia Golf Classic

Course: Whitemarsh Valley C.C., Chestnut Hill, Pa.
Par: 71 Yardage: 6,687
Last day of event: Sunday, July 22, 1979

Player	Place	Score	Earnings
Lou Graham	Win	68-70-71-64=273	$45,000.00
Playoff: Beat Bobby Wadkins with birdie on first extra hole			
Bobby Wadkins	2	67-69-67-70=273	$27,000.00
Mark Hayes	T-3	68-70-67-69=274	$13,000.00
Jack Nicklaus	T-3	72-70-67-65=274	$13,000.00
J.C. Snead	T-3	68-64-73-69=274	$13,000.00
David Graham	T-6	65-69-70-71=275	$8,687.50
Bill Kratzert	T-6	69-72-68-66=275	$8,687.50
Jerry Pate	T-8	69-71-70-66=276	$7,250.00
Ray Floyd	T-8	71-68-70-67=276	$7,250.00
Ben Crenshaw	T-8	69-66-72-69=276	$7,250.00

PGA Championship

Course: Oakland Hills C.C., Birmingham, Mich.
Par: 70 Yardage: 7,014
Last day of event: Sunday, August 5, 1979

Player	Place	Score	Earnings
David Graham	Win	69-68-70-65=272	$60,000.00
Playoff: Beat Ben Crenshaw with birdie on third extra hole			
Ben Crenshaw	T-2	69-67-69-67=272	$40,000.00
Rex Caldwell	3	67-70-66-71=274	$25,000.00
Ron Streck	4	68-71-69-68=276	$20,000.00
Jerry Pate	T-5	69-69-69-71=278	$14,500.00
Gibby Gilbert	T-5	69-72-68-69=278	$14,500.00
Don January	T-7	69-70-71-69=279	$9,200.00
Jay Haas	T-7	68-69-73-69=279	$9,200.00
Howard Twitty	T-7	70-73-69-67=279	$9,200.00
Gary Koch	T-10	71-71-71-67=280	$6,750.00
Lou Graham	T-10	69-74-68-69=280	$6,750.00

Sammy Davis, Jr. - Greater Hartford Open

Course: Wethersfield C.C., Wethersfield, Conn.
Par: 71 Yardage: 6,568
Last day of event: Sunday, August 12, 1979

Player	Place	Score	Earnings
Jerry McGee	Win	68-67-67-65=267	$54,000.00
Jack Renner	2	68-67-66-67=268	$32,400.00
Curtis Strange	T-3	70-66-69-65=270	$17,400.00
George Cadle	T-3	62-73-66-69=270	$17,400.00
Lou Graham	T-5	69-69-67-66=271	$10,950.00
J.C. Snead	T-5	65-66-71-69=271	$10,950.00
Mark Hayes	T-5	66-66-73-66=271	$10,950.00
Michael Brannan	T-8	67-67-70-68=272	$9,000.00
Hubert Green	T-8	67-71-68-66=272	$9,000.00
Peter Oosterhuis	T-10	67-68-69-69=273	$7,200.00
Victor Regalado	T-10	69-70-67-67=273	$7,200.00
Ray Floyd	T-10	70-69-67-67=273	$7,200.00
Dave Eichelberger	T-10	69-71-67-66=273	$7,200.00

Manufacturers Hanover Westchester Classic

Course: Westchester C.C., Harrison, N.Y.
Par: 71 Yardage: 6,603
Last day of event: Sunday, August 19, 1979

Player	Place	Score	Earnings
Jack Renner	Win	69-71-70-67=277	$72,000.00
Howard Twitty	T-2	70-70-71-67=278	$35,200.00
David Graham	T-2	65-73-69-71=278	$35,200.00
Scott Simpson	T-4	70-68-70-71=279	$17,600.00
Peter Oosterhuis	T-4	70-75-71-63=279	$17,600.00
Tom Kite	6	69-67-74-70=280	$14,400.00
George Burns	T-7	69-70-72-70=281	$12,466.67
Bob Murphy	T-7	73-68-69-71=281	$12,466.66
J.C. Snead	T-7	73-68-71-69=281	$12,466.67
Lon Hinkle	T-10	70-69-72-71=282	$10,000.00
Tom Watson	T-10	69-75-70-68=282	$10,000.00
Gil Morgan	T-10	71-68-76-67=282	$10,000.00

Colgate Hall of Fame Classic

Course: Pinehurst C.C. (No 2), Pinehurst, N.C.
Par: 71 Yardage: 7,020
Last day of event: Sunday, August 26, 1979

Player	Place	Score	Earnings
Tom Watson	Win	70-68-65-69=272	$45,000.00
Playoff: Beat Johnny Miller with par on second extra hole			
Johnny Miller	2	69-63-70-70=272	$27,000.00
Keith Fergus	3	68-68-67-71=274	$17,000.00
Danny Edwards	4	67-68-69-71=275	$12,000.00
Andy North	5	69-70-67-70=276	$10,000.00
Bill Rogers	6	74-66-69-69=278	$9,000.00
Bob Zender	T-7	73-71-69-66=279	$8,062.50
Michael Brannan	T-7	67-68-74-70=279	$8,062.50
Kermit Zarley	T-9	68-70-70-72=280	$3,750.00
Lyn Lott	T-9	72-70-72-66=280	$3,750.00
Bruce Devlin	T-9	70-67-70-73=280	$3,750.00

B.C. Open

Course: En-Joie G.C., Endicott, N.Y.
Par: 71 Yardage: 6,966
Last day of event: Sunday, September 2, 1979

Player	Place	Score	Earnings
Howard Twitty	Win	69-70-64-67=270	$49,500.00

Player	Place	Score	Earnings
Tom Purtzer	2	70-67-68-66=271	$29,700.00
Doug Tewell	3	67-69-66-70=272	$18,700.00
Rod Curl	T-4	70-66-70-68=274	$12,100.00
Tom Kite	T-4	72-68-67-67=274	$12,100.00
Brad Bryant	6	67-67-68-73=275	$9,900.00
Jay Haas	T-7	71-66-68-71=276	$8,850.00
Curtis Strange	T-7	64-73-68-71=276	$8,850.00
Craig Stadler	T-9	69-70-69-69=277	$6,600.00
Chi Chi Rodriguez	T-9	70-69-70-68=277	$6,600.00
Grier Jones	T-9	71-68-70-68=277	$6,600.00
Parker Moore	T-9	69-72-66-70=277	$6,600.00
Jerry Pate	T-9	72-66-69-70=277	$6,600.00
Peter Jacobsen	T-9	68-69-75-65=277	$6,600.00

American Optical Classic

Course: Pleasant Valley C.C., Sutton, Mass.
Par: 71 Yardage: 7,110
Last day of event: Sunday, September 9, 1979

Player	Place	Score	Earnings
Lou Graham	Win	68-67-71-69=275	$45,000.00
Ben Crenshaw	2	67-71-68-70=276	$27,000.00
Terry Diehl	3	66-71-69-72=278	$17,000.00
Jeff Mitchell	4	70-70-67-72=279	$12,000.00
Rex Caldwell	T-5	69-71-72-69=281	$8,475.00
Bruce Devlin	T-5	70-70-69-72=281	$8,475.00
Tim Simpson	T-5	70-70-69-72=281	$8,475.00
David Eger	T-5	69-69-70-73=281	$8,475.00
Rod Curl	T-5	74-68-69-70=281	$8,475.00
Jeff Thomsen	T-10	70-71-71-70=282	$5,250.00
Larry Ziegler	T-10	71-73-71-67=282	$5,250.00
David Edwards	T-10	72-67-66-77=282	$5,250.00

Buick Goodwrench Open

Course: Warwick Hills C.C., Grand Blanc, Mich.
Par: 72 Yardage: 7,014
Last day of event: Sunday, September 16, 1979

Player	Place	Score	Earnings
John Fought	Win	71-72-68-69=280	$27,000.00
Playoff: Beat Jim Simons with par on second extra hole			
Jim Simons	2	72-71-70-67=280	$16,200.00
Dave Eichelberger	3	68-70-72-71=281	$10,200.00
Jim Colbert	4	69-72-72-69=282	$7,425.00
Bill Kratzert	T-5	71-72-70-70=283	$6,000.00
Lon Hinkle	T-5	73-69-73-68=283	$6,000.00
Bob Eastwood	T-5	68-75-74-66=283	$6,000.00
George Burns	T-8	68-72-72-72=284	$4,075.00
David Edwards	T-8	72-70-71-71=284	$4,075.00
Dana Quigley	T-8	70-71-70-73=284	$4,075.00
David Graham	T-8	68-74-70-72=284	$4,075.00
Tom Weiskopf	T-8	69-74-70-71=284	$4,075.00
Lindy Miller	T-8	71-71-75-67=284	$4,075.00

Anheuser-Busch Golf Classic

Course: Silverado C.C., Napa, Calif.
Home Course -Par: 72 Yardage: 6,849
Last day of event: Sunday, September 23, 1979

Player	Place	Score	Earnings
John Fought	Win	69-68-71-69=277	$54,000.00
Bobby Wadkins	T-2	66-72-71-69=278	$22,400.00
Buddy Gardner	T-2	68-72-68-70=278	$22,400.00
Alan Tapie	T-2	68-75-69-66=278	$22,400.00
Bill Rogers	5	68-71-72-68=279	$12,000.00

Andy North	T-6	71-69-71-69=280	$10,050.00
Mark Lye	T-6	66-72-67-75=280	$10,050.00
Lon Hinkle	T-6	69-66-70-75=280	$10,050.00
Mike Sullivan	T-9	70-70-70-71=281	$7,800.00
Bruce Lietzke	T-9	71-68-71-71=281	$7,800.00
Rod Curl	T-9	73-69-73-66=281	$7,800.00
Bob Gilder	T-9	69-68-70-74=281	$7,800.00

World Series of Golf

Course: Firestone C.C. (South), Akron, Ohio
Par: 70 Yardage: 7,149
Last day of event: Sunday, September 30, 1979

Player	Place	Score	Earnings
Lon Hinkle	Win	67-67-71-67=272	$100,000.00
Bill Rogers	T-2	69-67-68-69=273	$37,266.67
Larry Nelson	T-2	68-67-68-70=273	$37,266.67
Lee Trevino	T-2	67-68-72-66=273	$37,266.66
Hale Irwin	T-5	69-70-70-65=274	$15,000.00
Tom Watson	T-5	68-65-72-69=274	$15,000.00
Tom Kite	7	67-68-70-70=275	$12,800.00
Howard Twitty	8	69-67-71-69=276	$11,600.00
Bob Gilder	9	74-67-67-70=278	$10,400.00
Bruce Lietzke	T-10	71-68-71-69=279	$9,400.00
Andy Bean	T-10	64-75-70-70=279	$9,400.00

San Antonio Texas Open

Course: Oak Hill C.C., San Antonio, Texas
Par: 70 Yardage: 6,576
Last day of event: Sunday, October 7, 1979

Player	Place	Score	Earnings
Lou Graham	Win	69-64-69-66=268	$45,000.00
Eddie Pearce	T-2	69-65-65-70=269	$18,666.67
Doug Tewell	T-2	66-68-63-72=269	$18,666.67
Bill Rogers	T-2	72-68-62-67=269	$18,666.66
Lee Trevino	T-5	68-65-69-69=271	$8,781.25
Keith Fergus	T-5	69-65-69-68=271	$8,781.25
Ben Crenshaw	T-5	70-65-68-68=271	$8,781.25
Gary McCord	T-5	70-69-67-65=271	$8,781.25
Mike Sullivan	T-9	68-69-68-67=272	$7,000.00
Bob Gilder	T-9	72-68-67-65=272	$7,000.00

Southern Open

Course: Green Island C.C., Columbus, Ga.
Par: 70 Yardage: 6,791
Last day of event: Sunday, October 14, 1979

Player	Place	Score	Earnings
Ed Fiori	Win	69-72-65-68=274	$36,000.00
Playoff: Beat Tom Weiskopf with birdie on second extra hole			
Tom Weiskopf	2	69-67-68-70=274	$21,600.00
Artie McNickle	T-3	70-68-68-69=275	$10,400.00
Mike Reid	T-3	67-69-68-71=275	$10,400.00
Calvin Peete	T-3	69-67-67-72=275	$10,400.00
Barney Thompson	6	69-70-68-69=276	$7,200.00
Gibby Gilbert	T-7	69-66-71-71=277	$6,450.00
David Edwards	T-7	72-69-67-69=277	$6,450.00
Michael Brannan	T-9	68-69-72-69=278	$5,600.00
Jerry Pate	T-9	66-69-69-74=278	$5,600.00

Pensacola Open

Course: Perdido Bay C.C., Pensacola, Fla.
Par: 72 Yardage: 7,133
Last day of event: Sunday, October 21, 1979

Player	Place	Score	Earnings
Curtis Strange	Win	69-71-62-69=271	$36,000.00
Bill Kratzert	2	64-70-70-68=272	$21,600.00
John Mahaffey	T-3	67-67-70-70=274	$11,600.00
Morris Hatalsky	T-3	64-69-72-69=274	$11,600.00
Keith Fergus	T-5	69-69-68-69=275	$7,025.00
Don January	T-5	70-67-68-70=275	$7,025.00
Terry Diehl	T-5	67-71-69-68=275	$7,025.00
Orville Moody	T-5	68-67-68-72=275	$7,025.00
Bob Murphy	T-9	70-69-69-68=276	$5,600.00
Dan Pohl	T-9	68-69-67-72=276	$5,600.00

1980

Tom Watson won seven times on the PGA Tour, including the British Open at Muirfield, where he finished four shots ahead of runner-up Lee Trevino. Jack Nicklaus had his last monster year in the majors, winning the U.S. Open by two shots over Asao Aoki at Baltusrol and cruising to a seven-shot victory over Andy Bean in the PGA Championship at Oak Hill. Seve Ballesteros won the Masters in typical Seve fashion, taking a 10-shot lead into the back nine but dropping four shots to par over the next four holes before righting the ship and winning by four. (This was the Masters where Tom Weiskopf famously made a 13 at the par-3 12th hole after hitting five balls into Rae's Creek during Round 1.) The movie Caddyshack was released in 1980.

Bob Hope Chrysler Classic

Course: La Quinta C.C.—Home course
Indian Wells C.C., Eldorado C.C., Bermuda Dunes C.C, La Quinta, Calif.
Par: 72 Yardage: 6,911
Last day of event: Sunday, January 13, 1980

Player	Place	Score	Earnings
Craig Stadler	Win	69-68-70-69-67=343	$50,000.00
Tom Purtzer	T-2	70-70-68-69-68=345	$24,200.00
Mike Sullivan	T-2	71-70-65-71-68=345	$24,200.00
Larry Nelson	4	70-65-70-71-70=346	$13,200.00
Mark Hayes	5	69-69-70-71-68=347	$11,000.00
Bob Murphy	T-6	70-69-69-71-69=348	$8,312.50
Tom Kite	T-6	70-71-70-69-68=348	$8,312.50
D.A. Weibring	T-6	71-69-72-69-67=348	$8,312.50
George Cadle	T-6	73-71-65-69-70=348	$8,312.50
Lanny Wadkins	T-6	74-66-68-71-69=348	$8,312.50
Dave Hill	T-6	74-70-69-67-68=348	$8,312.50

Phoenix Open

Course: Phoenix C.C., Phoenix, Ariz.
Par: 71 Yardage: 6,726
Last day of event: Sunday, January 20, 1980

Player	Place	Score	Earnings
Jeff Mitchell	Win	69-67-69-67=272	$54,000.00
Rik Massengale	2	73-71-67-65=276	$32,400.00
Mike Sullivan	3	65-71-72-69=277	$20,400.00
Charles Coody	T-4	69-68-71-70=278	$11,310.00
Rod Curl	T-4	69-68-71-70=278	$11,310.00
Bill Rogers	T-4	68-69-73-68=278	$11,310.00
Jack Renner	T-4	69-66-73-70=278	$11,310.00
Tom Kite	T-4	69-73-70-66=278	$11,310.00
Ben Crenshaw	T-9	71-71-69-68=279	$7,800.00
Jerry Pate	T-9	66-73-72-68=279	$7,800.00

Hubert Green	T-9	67-71-68-73=279	$7,800.00
Dan Pohl	T-9	67-73-70-69=279	$7,800.00

Andy Williams-San Diego Open

Course: Torrey Pines (South), Torrey Pines (North), San Diego, Calif.
Home Course -Par: 72 Yardage: 7,021
Last day of event: Sunday, January 27, 1980

Player	Place	Score	Earnings
Tom Watson	Win	68-69-68-70=275	$45,000.00

Playoff: Beat D.A. Weibring with par on first extra hole

D.A. Weibring	2	66-71-73-65=275	$27,000.00
Lon Hinkle	3	73-67-67-71=278	$17,000.00
Keith Fergus	T-4	67-71-71-71=280	$11,000.00
Andy North	T-4	70-71-70-69=280	$11,000.00
Ray Floyd	6	70-67-70-74=281	$9,000.00
J.C. Snead	T-7	70-69-72-71=282	$7,020.84
Leonard Thompson	T-7	70-71-72-69=282	$7,020.84
Jay Haas	T-7	71-72-69-70=282	$7,020.83
Bobby Walzel	T-7	66-71-74-71=282	$7,020.83
Forrest Fezler	T-7	70-69-69-74=282	$7,020.83
Tom Purtzer	T-7	71-71-66-74=282	$7,020.83

Bing Crosby Pro-Am

Courses: Pebble Beach G.L.—Home Course
Spyglass Hill G.C., Cypress Point C.C., Pebble Beach, Calif.
Home Course Par: 72 Yardage: 6,815
Last day of event: Saturday, February 2, 1980

Player	Place	Score	Earnings
George Burns	Win	71-69-71-69=280	$54,000.00
Dan Pohl	2	72-70-72-67=281	$32,400.00
Keith Fergus	T-3	70-71-71-70=282	$14,400.00
Larry Nelson	T-3	70-70-70-72=282	$14,400.00
John Mahaffey	T-3	68-74-72-68=282	$14,400.00
Bill Kratzert	T-3	70-74-68-70=282	$14,400.00
Mike Reid	T-7	69-72-71-71=283	$9,037.50
Gil Morgan	T-7	70-69-71-73=283	$9,037.50
David Edwards	T-7	67-69-72-75=283	$9,037.50
Tom Weiskopf	T-7	70-77-67-69=283	$9,037.50

Hawaiian Open

Course: Waialae C.C., Honolulu, Ha.
Par: 72 Yardage: 7,234
Last day of event: Sunday, February 10, 1980

Player	Place	Score	Earnings
Andy Bean	Win	71-63-66-66=266	$58,500.00
Lee Trevino	2	69-69-65-66=269	$35,100.00
Ed Sneed	3	67-69-66-68=270	$22,100.00
Mark Lye	T-4	69-69-66-67=271	$14,300.00
George Burns	T-4	65-69-66-71=271	$14,300.00
Larry Nelson	6	68-69-68-67=272	$11,700.00
Tom Watson	T-7	67-72-66-68=273	$10,900.00
John Schroeder	T-8	67-70-70-67=274	$9,750.00
Frank Conner	T-8	68-67-67-72=274	$9,750.00
Don January	T-10	69-68-70-68=275	$7,800.00
Artie McNickle	T-10	70-67-69-69=275	$7,800.00
Chi Chi Rodriguez	T-10	67-70-71-67=275	$7,800.00
Bill Kratzert	T-10	68-71-67-69=275	$7,800.00

Joe Garagiola Tucson Open

Course: Tucson National G.C., Starr Pass G.C., Tucson, Ariz.
Par: 73 Yardage: 7,305
Last day of event: Sunday, February 17, 1980

Player	Place	Score	Earnings
Jim Colbert	Win	66-68-66-70=270	$54,000.00
Dan Halldorson	2	67-71-69-67=274	$32,400.00
Allen Miller	3	69-72-67-67=275	$20,400.00
Tom Purtzer	4	68-67-72-69=276	$14,400.00
Andy Bean	T-5	70-71-67-70=278	$11,400.00
Bruce Lietzke	T-5	72-69-66-71=278	$11,400.00
Tim Simpson	T-7	69-70-71-69=279	$9,350.00
Bud Allin	T-7	68-69-72-70=279	$9,350.00
Keith Fergus	T-7	67-71-73-68=279	$9,350.00
George Archer	T-10	71-71-70-68=280	$7,200.00
Rex Caldwell	T-10	65-73-72-70=280	$7,200.00
Dave Barr	T-10	67-71-69-73=280	$7,200.00
Peter Jacobsen	T-10	68-75-70-67=280	$7,200.00

Glen Campbell Los Angeles Open

Course: Riviera C.C., Pacific Palisades, Calif.
Par: 71 Yardage: 7,029
Last day of event: Sunday, February 24, 1980

Player	Place	Score	Earnings
Tom Watson	Win	69-66-70-71=276	$45,000.00
Don January	T-2	69-67-70-71=277	$22,000.00
Bob Gilder	T-2	70-66-68-73=277	$22,000.00
Don Pooley	4	70-69-72-69=280	$12,000.00
Mike Reid	T-5	70-72-72-67=281	$9,500.00
Scott Simpson	T-5	72-67-71-71=281	$9,500.00
Johnny Miller	T-7	69-71-71-71=282	$6,291.67
Gil Morgan	T-7	70-70-71-71=282	$6,291.67
Tom Weiskopf	T-7	67-71-72-72=282	$6,291.67
Jay Haas	T-7	70-68-72-72=282	$6,291.67
John Fought	T-7	70-70-70-72=282	$6,291.66
Fuzzy Zoeller	T-7	72-69-71-70=282	$6,291.67
Hale Irwin	T-7	73-68-68-73=282	$6,291.66
George Archer	T-7	74-68-68-72=282	$6,291.66
Lanny Wadkins	T-7	70-75-68-69=282	$6,291.67

Bay Hill Classic

Course: Bay Hill Club, Orlando, Fla.
Par: 71 Yardage: 7,103
Last day of event: Sunday, March 2, 1980

Player	Place	Score	Earnings
Dave Eichelberger	Win	69-66-70-74=279	$54,000.00
Leonard Thompson	2	66-72-70-74=282	$32,400.00
Jim Colbert	T-3	67-71-73-77=288	$17,400.00
Dan Pohl	T-3	64-72-74-78=288	$17,400.00
David Graham	T-5	74-68-72-75=289	$10,950.00
Lanny Wadkins	T-5	70-72-71-76=289	$10,950.00
Bill Calfee	T-5	73-72-65-79=289	$10,950.00
Craig Stadler	T-8	74-71-72-73=290	$8,700.00
Fuzzy Zoeller	T-8	68-69-76-77=290	$8,700.00
Ray Floyd	T-8	69-77-72-72=290	$8,700.00

Jackie Gleason's Inverrary Classic

Course: Inverrary G. & C.C. (East), Lauderhill, Fla.
Par: 72 Yardage: 7,128
Last day of event: Sunday, March 9, 1980

Player	Place	Score	Earnings
Johnny Miller	Win	70-68-66-70=274	$54,000.00
Charles Coody	T-2	69-71-69-67=276	$26,400.00
Bruce Lietzke	T-2	69-74-68-65=276	$26,400.00
Larry Nelson	T-4	68-72-68-69=277	$13,200.00
Bill Rogers	T-4	69-73-66-69=277	$13,200.00
Doug Tewell	T-6	71-68-69-70=278	$9,712.50
Dave Eichelberger	T-6	71-68-70-69=278	$9,712.50
Jim Simons	T-6	68-70-72-68=278	$9,712.50
Mike Hill	T-6	69-67-70-72=278	$9,712.50
Morris Hatalsky	T-10	70-69-70-70=279	$7,500.00
Bruce Fleisher	T-10	71-69-71-68=279	$7,500.00
Chi Chi Rodriguez	T-10	67-73-71-68=279	$7,500.00

Doral-Eastern Open

Course: Doral C.C. (Blue), Miami, Fla.
Par: 72 Yardage: 6,939
Last day of event: Sunday, March 16, 1980

Player	Place	Score	Earnings
Ray Floyd	Win	74-69-70-66=279	$45,000.00

Playoff: Beat Jack Nicklaus with birdie on second extra hole

Player	Place	Score	Earnings
Jack Nicklaus	2	72-67-71-69=279	$27,000.00
Keith Fergus	3	68-73-69-70=280	$17,000.00
Wayne Levi	4	69-71-71-72=283	$12,000.00
Ed Fiori	T-5	72-70-72-70=284	$9,500.00
Ben Crenshaw	T-5	71-68-74-71=284	$9,500.00
Grier Jones	T-7	73-68-73-71=285	$7,275.00
Terry Diehl	T-7	73-69-73-70=285	$7,275.00
Leonard Thompson	T-7	69-68-74-74=285	$7,275.00
Bruce Lietzke	T-7	70-68-72-75=285	$7,275.00
Andy Bean	T-7	75-69-70-71=285	$7,275.00

Tournament Players Championship

Course: Sawgrass C.C., Ponte Vedra Beach, Fla.
Par: 72 Yardage: 7,174
Last day of event: Sunday, March 23, 1980

Player	Place	Score	Earnings
Lee Trevino	Win	68-72-68-70=278	$72,000.00
Ben Crenshaw	2	71-73-69-66=279	$43,200.00
Tom Watson	T-3	69-71-72-68=280	$23,200.00
Seve Ballesteros	T-3	69-73-69-69=280	$23,200.00
John Mahaffey	T-5	70-71-72-69=282	$14,600.00
Mike Reid	T-5	70-72-72-68=282	$14,600.00
Peter Jacobsen	T-5	68-74-69-71=282	$14,600.00
Gary Player	T-8	70-71-69-73=283	$10,400.00
Jay Haas	T-8	72-73-67-71=283	$10,400.00
Dan Pohl	T-8	73-72-69-69=283	$10,400.00
Danny Edwards	T-8	68-74-72-69=283	$10,400.00
Hubert Green	T-8	72-71-66-74=283	$10,400.00
Grier Jones	T-8	74-69-72-68=283	$10,400.00

Sea Pines Heritage Classic

Course: Harbour Town G.L., Hilton Head, S.C.
Par: 71 Yardage: 6,657
Last day of event: Sunday, March 30, 1980

Player	Place	Score	Earnings
Doug Tewell	Win	69-66-72-73=280	$54,000.00

Playoff: Beat Jerry Pate with par on first extra hole

Player	Place	Score	Earnings
Jerry Pate	2	66-69-73-72=280	$32,400.00
Gary Player	T-3	70-71-69-72=282	$14,400.00
Lon Hinkle	T-3	73-69-70-70=282	$14,400.00
Ed Sneed	T-3	70-74-70-68=282	$14,400.00
John Mahaffey	T-3	68-69-70-75=282	$14,400.00
George Burns	T-7	69-70-72-72=283	$9,350.00
Bob Murphy	T-7	72-68-70-73=283	$9,350.00
Fuzzy Zoeller	T-7	73-65-73-72=283	$9,350.00
Gary Koch	T-10	71-69-72-72=284	$6,650.00
Tom Watson	T-10	70-71-73-70=284	$6,650.00
Gil Morgan	T-10	71-69-73-71=284	$6,650.00
Tom Kite	T-10	72-69-70-73=284	$6,650.00
Ray Floyd	T-10	70-70-75-69=284	$6,650.00
George Archer	T-10	75-66-72-71=284	$6,650.00

Greater Greensboro Open

Course: Forest Oaks C.C., Greensboro, N.C.
Par: 72 Yardage: 6,958
Last day of event: Sunday, April 6, 1980

Player	Place	Score	Earnings
Craig Stadler	Win	67-69-71-68=275	$45,000.00
Bill Kratzert	T-2	70-69-72-70=281	$16,500.00
Jack Newton	T-2	69-71-73-68=281	$16,500.00
George Burns	T-2	68-74-70-69=281	$16,500.00
Jerry Pate	T-2	70-74-70-67=281	$16,500.00
Jeff Mitchell	6	72-68-72-71=283	$9,000.00
Ray Floyd	T-7	70-69-72-73=284	$7,531.25
Mike Reid	T-7	70-71-70-73=284	$7,531.25
Fuzzy Zoeller	T-7	73-67-71-73=284	$7,531.25
Morris Hatalsky	T-7	69-74-72-69=284	$7,531.25

Masters

Course: Augusta National G.C., Augusta, Ga.
Par: 72 Yardage: 6,925
Last day of event: Sunday, April 13, 1980

Player	Place	Score	Earnings
Seve Ballesteros	Win	66-69-68-72=275	$55,000.00
Jack Newton	T-2	68-74-69-68=279	$30,500.00
Gibby Gilbert	T-2	70-74-68-67=279	$30,500.00
Hubert Green	4	68-74-71-67=280	$15,750.00
David Graham	5	66-73-72-70=281	$13,200.00
Gary Player	T-6	71-71-71-70=283	$9,958.00
Larry Nelson	T-6	69-72-73-69=283	$9,958.00
Ed Fiori	T-6	71-70-69-73=283	$9,958.00
Tom Kite	T-6	69-71-74-69=283	$9,958.00
Jerry Pate	T-6	72-68-76-67=283	$9,958.00
Ben Crenshaw	T-6	76-70-68-69=283	$9,958.00

MONY Tournament of Champions

Course: La Costa C.C., Carlsbad, Calif.
Par: 72 Yardage: 6,911
Last day of event: Sunday, April 20, 1980

Player	Place	Score	Earnings
Tom Watson	Win	65-66-72-73=276	$54,000.00
Jim Colbert	2	67-71-71-70=279	$34,000.00
Curtis Strange	T-3	72-70-72-67=281	$20,000.00
George Burns	T-3	70-73-72-66=281	$20,000.00
Lou Graham	5	66-67-77-72=282	$15,000.00
Ray Floyd	T-6	66-73-72-72=283	$12,500.00
Craig Stadler	T-6	69-69-74-71=283	$12,500.00
Gil Morgan	T-8	71-71-69-73=284	$10,625.00

Jack Renner	T-8	71-71-73-69=284	$10,625.00
Johnny Miller	10	73-68-73-71=285	$9,500.00

Tallahassee Open

Course: Killearn C.C., Tallahassee, Fla.
Par: 72 Yardage: 7,124
Last day of event: Sunday, April 20, 1980

Player	Place	Score	Earnings
Mark Pfeil	Win	69-66-71-71=277	$18,000.00
Mark Lye	T-2	68-72-68-70=278	$8,800.00
Bill Rogers	T-2	68-67-69-74=278	$8,800.00
Bobby Cole	T-4	72-67-69-71=279	$4,675.00
Bob Murphy	T-4	65-71-70-73=279	$4,675.00
Steve Melnyk	T-6	68-70-72-70=280	$3,475.00
Terry Mauney	T-6	70-72-68-70=280	$3,475.00
Mike Sullivan	T-6	74-68-69-69=280	$3,475.00
Rex Caldwell	T-6	67-68-75-70=280	$3,475.00
Ron Streck	T-10	70-72-71-68=281	$2,600.00
David Edwards	T-10	73-67-70-71=281	$2,600.00
Bobby Walzel	T-10	74-70-68-69=281	$2,600.00

Greater New Orleans Open

Course: Lakewood C.C., New Orleans, La.
Par: 72 Yardage: 7,080
Last day of event: Monday, April 28, 1980

Player	Place	Score	Earnings
Tom Watson	Win	66-68-66-73=273	$45,000.00
Lee Trevino	2	67-71-68-69=275	$27,000.00
Mike Reid	3	67-71-67-71=276	$17,000.00
Larry Nelson	T-4	71-66-68-72=277	$11,000.00
Hubert Green	T-4	66-68-69-74=277	$11,000.00
Calvin Peete	6	72-67-68-71=278	$9,000.00
Leonard Thompson	7	71-69-68-71=279	$8,375.00
Lou Graham	T-8	69-70-72-69=280	$7,500.00
Mark Hayes	T-8	70-72-67-71=280	$7,500.00
Dana Quigley	T-10	68-71-71-71=281	$5,541.67
Mike Peck	T-10	69-71-72-69=281	$5,541.67
Peter Oosterhuis	T-10	71-70-68-72=281	$5,541.66
Gene Littler	T-10	68-72-68-73=281	$5,541.66
Bud Allin	T-10	68-73-67-73=281	$5,541.67
Bob Murphy	T-10	68-74-69-70=281	$5,541.67

Michelob Houston Open

Course: Woodlands C.C., The Woodlands, Texas
Par: 71 Yardage: 6,918
Last day of event: Sunday, May 4, 1980

Player	Place	Score	Earnings
Curtis Strange	Win	66-63-66-71=266	$63,000.00
Playoff: Beat Lee Trevino with birdie on first extra hole			
Lee Trevino	2	67-66-68-65=266	$37,800.00
Mike Reid	T-3	69-64-69-66=268	$20,300.00
Bob Gilder	T-3	70-65-69-64=268	$20,300.00
D.A. Weibring	T-5	68-68-66-68=270	$13,300.00
Tom Kite	T-5	70-69-65-66=270	$13,300.00
Bill Rogers	7	67-68-68-69=272	$11,725.00
Ron Streck	T-8	68-68-68-69=273	$9,800.00
George Burns	T-8	68-67-70-68=273	$9,800.00
Barney Thompson	T-8	69-67-70-67=273	$9,800.00
Jerry Pate	T-8	72-66-66-69=273	$9,800.00

Byron Nelson Golf Classic

Course: Preston Trail G.C., Dallas, Texas
Par: 70 Yardage: 6,993
Last day of event: Sunday, May 11, 1980

Player	Place	Score	Earnings
Tom Watson	Win	64-70-69-71=274	$54,000.00
Bill Rogers	2	69-69-70-67=275	$32,400.00
Bill Kratzert	3	71-67-68-71=277	$20,400.00
George Cadle	4	66-73-67-72=278	$14,400.00
Curtis Strange	5	66-69-70-74=279	$12,000.00
Wayne Levi	T-6	71-70-71-68=280	$10,050.00
Ron Streck	T-6	67-72-69-72=280	$10,050.00
George Burns	T-6	67-70-73-70=280	$10,050.00
Andy Bean	T-9	71-68-71-71=281	$8,100.00
Michael Brannan	T-9	67-71-72-71=281	$8,100.00
Hale Irwin	T-9	69-72-71-69=281	$8,100.00

Colonial National Invitational

Course: Colonial C.C., Fort Worth, Texas
Par: 70 Yardage: 7,096
Last day of event: Sunday, May 18, 1980

Player	Place	Score	Earnings
Bruce Lietzke	Win	63-68-71-69=271	$54,000.00
Ben Crenshaw	2	67-66-70-69=272	$32,400.00
Jeff Mitchell	3	65-73-70-65=273	$20,400.00
Tom Watson	T-4	66-68-71-69=274	$13,200.00
Doug Tewell	T-4	71-65-69-69=274	$13,200.00
Andy Bean	6	70-67-71-67=275	$10,800.00
Bob Murphy	T-7	70-69-67-70=276	$9,675.00
Lon Hinkle	T-7	71-64-72-69=276	$9,675.00
Ed Fiori	T-9	70-69-68-70=277	$7,800.00
Ed Sneed	T-9	68-71-71-67=277	$7,800.00
Lee Trevino	T-9	66-72-69-70=277	$7,800.00
Tom Kite	T-9	67-71-67-72=277	$7,800.00

Memorial Tournament

Course: Muirfield Village G.C., Dubin, Ohio
Par: 72 Yardage: 7,116
Last day of event: Sunday, May 25, 1980

Player	Place	Score	Earnings
David Graham	Win	73-67-70-70=280	$54,000.00
Tom Watson	2	74-67-69-71=281	$32,400.00
Mike Reid	3	69-73-70-70=282	$20,400.00
Tom Weiskopf	T-4	69-71-71-72=283	$13,200.00
Miller Barber	T-4	72-66-72-73=283	$13,200.00
Hale Irwin	T-6	72-71-71-70=284	$10,425.00
Dan Halldorson	T-6	73-71-68-72=284	$10,425.00
Lanny Wadkins	T-8	71-72-71-71=285	$7,800.00
Scott Simpson	T-8	72-72-69-72=285	$7,800.00
Ray Floyd	T-8	68-73-71-73=285	$7,800.00
John Mahaffey	T-8	72-67-72-74=285	$7,800.00
Bob Murphy	T-8	70-71-75-69=285	$7,800.00
Jay Haas	T-8	75-68-71-71=285	$7,800.00

Kemper Open

Course: Congressional C.C., Bethesda, Md.
Par: 72 Yardage: 7,173
Last day of event: Sunday, June 1, 1980

Player	Place	Score	Earnings
John Mahaffey	Win	68-72-67-68=275	$72,000.00

Craig Stadler	2	73-69-69-67=278	$43,200.00
Gil Morgan	3	71-68-70-70=279	$27,200.00
Lee Trevino	T-4	69-70-69-72=280	$17,600.00
Jack Newton	T-4	72-68-69-71=280	$17,600.00
Bob Gilder	T-6	70-71-71-69=281	$13,400.00
Tom Watson	T-6	71-69-73-68=281	$13,400.00
Hale Irwin	T-6	74-66-70-71=281	$13,400.00
Jay Haas	9	68-73-70-71=282	$11,600.00
Mark Hayes	T-10	71-72-70-70=283	$9,200.00
Larry Nelson	T-10	71-71-72-69=283	$9,200.00
Jeff Mitchell	T-10	71-70-69-73=283	$9,200.00
Artie McNickle	T-10	73-70-70-70=283	$9,200.00
Andy Bean	T-10	76-68-70-69=283	$9,200.00

Atlanta Classic

Course: Atlanta C.C., Atlanta, Ga.
Par: 72 Yardage: 7,007
Last day of event: Sunday, June 8, 1980

Player	Place	Score	Earnings
Larry Nelson	Win	66-69-68-67=270	$54,000.00
Andy Bean	T-2	67-69-69-72=277	$26,400.00
Don Pooley	T-2	68-74-70-65=277	$26,400.00
Calvin Peete	4	68-70-70-70=278	$14,400.00
Bob Shearer	T-5	63-71-72-73=279	$11,400.00
Mike Reid	T-5	73-70-66-70=279	$11,400.00
Ed Fiori	7	72-69-69-70=280	$10,050.00
Mike Nicolette	8	66-70-71-74=281	$9,300.00
Curtis Strange	T-9	70-70-71-71=282	$6,500.00
Tom Shaw	T-9	68-72-71-71=282	$6,500.00
Brad Bryant	T-9	69-72-70-71=282	$6,500.00
Gibby Gilbert	T-9	71-70-69-72=282	$6,500.00
Lyn Lott	T-9	66-73-73-70=282	$6,500.00
J.C. Snead	T-9	68-70-71-73=282	$6,500.00
David Edwards	T-9	73-70-68-71=282	$6,500.00
Doug Tewell	T-9	67-74-71-70=282	$6,500.00
Sammy Rachels	T-9	70-67-71-74=282	$6,500.00

U.S. Open

Course: Baltusrol G.C., Springfield, N.J.
Par: 70 Yardage: 7,076
Last day of event: Sunday, June 15, 1980

Player	Place	Score	Earnings
Jack Nicklaus	Win	63-71-70-68=272	$55,000.00
Isao Aoki	2	68-68-68-70=274	$29,500.00
Keith Fergus	T-3	66-70-70-70=276	$17,400.00
Lon Hinkle	T-3	66-70-69-71=276	$17,400.00
Tom Watson	T-3	71-68-67-70=276	$17,400.00
Mark Hayes	T-6	66-71-69-74=280	$11,950.00
Mike Reid	T-6	69-67-75-69=280	$11,950.00
Ed Sneed	T-8	72-70-70-70=282	$8,050.00
Hale Irwin	T-8	70-70-73-69=282	$8,050.00
Mike Morley	T-8	73-68-69-72=282	$8,050.00
Andy North	T-8	68-75-72-67=282	$8,050.00

Canadian Open

Course: Royal Montreal G.C., Ile-Bizard, Quebec, Canada
Par: 70 Yardage: 6,628
Last day of event: Sunday, June 22, 1980

Player	Place	Score	Earnings
Bob Gilder	Win	67-67-70-70=274	$63,000.00
Jerry Pate	T-2	72-69-65-70=276	$30,800.00

Leonard Thompson	T-2	68-73-68-67=276	$30,800.00
Ben Crenshaw	4	69-70-68-70=277	$16,800.00
Lee Trevino	T-5	71-67-70-70=278	$12,775.00
George Burns	T-5	66-71-72-69=278	$12,775.00
Danny Edwards	T-5	70-72-67-69=278	$12,775.00
Johnny Miller	8	67-72-69-71=279	$10,850.00
Tom Weiskopf	T-9	71-71-69-69=280	$9,450.00
Don Pooley	T-9	69-72-67-72=280	$9,450.00
Bill Kratzert	T-9	69-70-72-69=280	$9,450.00

Danny Thomas Memphis Classic

Course: Colonial C.C. (South), Cordova, Tenn.
Par: 72 Yardage: 7,282
Last day of event: Sunday, June 29, 1980

Player	Place	Score	Earnings
Lee Trevino	Win	67-68-68-69=272	$54,000.00
Tom Purtzer	2	67-68-71-67=273	$32,400.00
Miller Barber	T-3	70-65-68-72=275	$17,400.00
Jerry Pate	T-3	66-67-74-68=275	$17,400.00
Danny Edwards	5	69-71-67-70=277	$12,000.00
Morris Hatalsky	6	68-68-73-69=278	$10,800.00
Bruce Lietzke	7	73-65-71-70=279	$10,050.00
Lonnie Nielsen	T-8	70-71-68-71=280	$8,700.00
Leonard Thompson	T-8	68-70-73-69=280	$8,700.00
Terry Mauney	T-8	69-68-73-70=280	$8,700.00

Western Open

Course: Butler National G.C., Oak Brook, Ill.
Par: 72 Yardage: 7,097
Last day of event: Sunday, July 6, 1980

Player	Place	Score	Earnings
Scott Simpson	Win	70-69-70-72=281	$54,000.00
Andy Bean	2	71-69-75-71=286	$32,400.00
Hale Irwin	T-3	69-71-74-73=287	$17,400.00
Don Pooley	T-3	74-69-75-69=287	$17,400.00
Calvin Peete	5	76-68-74-70=288	$12,000.00
David Graham	T-6	72-71-75-71=289	$10,050.00
Rex Caldwell	T-6	70-71-76-72=289	$10,050.00
Tom Kite	T-6	69-72-78-70=289	$10,050.00
Jim Simons	T-9	73-69-74-74=290	$8,100.00
Bill Kratzert	T-9	73-72-76-69=290	$8,100.00
Bruce Lietzke	T-9	73-76-72-69=290	$8,100.00

Greater Milwaukee Open

Course: Tuckaway C.C., Franklin, Wis.
Par: 72 Yardage: 7,030
Last day of event: Sunday, July 13, 1980

Player	Place	Score	Earnings
Bill Kratzert	Win	67-66-67-66=266	$36,000.00
Howard Twitty	2	67-68-66-69=270	$21,600.00
Mark Lye	T-3	67-70-66-68=271	$10,400.00
Curtis Strange	T-3	71-67-69-64=271	$10,400.00
George Cadle	T-3	66-73-66-66=271	$10,400.00
Dana Quigley	6	70-68-65-70=273	$7,200.00
Calvin Peete	T-7	66-72-70-66=274	$6,233.33
Dan Pohl	T-7	67-67-72-68=274	$6,233.33
Hale Irwin	T-7	69-67-72-66=274	$6,233.34
Joe Hager	T-10	68-69-69-69=275	$5,000.00
Chi Chi Rodriguez	T-10	68-68-68-71=275	$5,000.00
Gibby Gilbert	T-10	69-68-72-66=275	$5,000.00

Quad Cities Open

Course: Oakwood C.C., Coal Valley, Ill.
Par: 70 Yardage: 6,514
Last day of event: Sunday, July 20, 1980

Player	Place	Score	Earnings
Scott Hoch	Win	63-66-68-69=266	$36,000.00
Curtis Strange	2	69-68-66-66=269	$21,600.00
Pat McGowan	T-3	67-68-70-65=270	$11,600.00
Gary Hallberg	T-3	72-66-64-68=270	$11,600.00
Howard Twitty	5	66-67-66-72=271	$8,000.00
Mike Sullivan	6	66-67-72-67=272	$7,200.00
Rod Curl	T-7	68-68-68-69=273	$6,450.00
Wayne Levi	T-7	68-69-69-67=273	$6,450.00
Brad Bryant	T-9	68-66-69-71=274	$4,628.57
Skip Dunaway	T-9	68-71-67-68=274	$4,628.57
Don Pooley	T-9	70-68-65-71=274	$4,628.57
Gary Koch	T-9	66-72-68-68=274	$4,628.57
Bill Britton	T-9	72-65-69-68=274	$4,628.57
Tommy Valentine	T-9	66-68-67-73=274	$4,628.57
Calvin Peete	T-9	66-73-69-66=274	$4,628.58

British Open

Course: Muirfield G.C., Muirfield, East Lothian, Scotland
Par: 71 Yardage: 6,926
Last day of event: Sunday, July 20, 1980

Player	Place	Score	Earnings
Tom Watson	Win	68-70-64-69=271	$60,000.00
Lee Trevino	2	68-67-71-69=275	$42,000.00
Ben Crenshaw	3	70-70-68-69=277	$32,400.00
Carl Mason	T-4	72-69-70-69=280	$22,200.00
Jack Nicklaus	T-4	73-67-71-69=280	$22,200.00
Andy Bean	T-6	71-69-70-72=282	$17,400.00
Craig Stadler	T-6	72-70-69-71=282	$17,400.00
Ken Brown	T-6	70-68-68-76=282	$17,400.00
Hubert Green	T-6	77-69-64-72=282	$17,400.00
Gil Morgan	T-10	70-70-71-72=283	$13,800.00
Jack Newton	T-10	69-71-73-70=283	$13,800.00

Sammy Davis, Jr. - Greater Hartford Open

Course: Wethersfield C.C., Wethersfield, Conn.
Par: 71 Yardage: 6,568
Last day of event: Sunday, July 27, 1980

Player	Place	Score	Earnings
Howard Twitty	Win	68-66-63-69=266	$54,000.00
Playoff: Beat Jim Simons with birdie on sixth extra hole			
Jim Simons	2	62-70-67-67=266	$32,400.00
Jay Haas	3	68-70-66-65=269	$20,400.00
Lindy Miller	4	67-67-66-70=270	$14,400.00
Butch Baird	T-5	69-68-67-67=271	$10,170.00
Jaime Gonzalez	T-5	64-70-67-70=271	$10,170.00
Lee Trevino	T-5	65-68-68-70=271	$10,170.00
John Fought	T-5	67-66-68-70=271	$10,170.00
Gary Hallberg	T-5	68-70-63-70=271	$10,170.00
Leonard Thompson	T-10	68-68-69-67=272	$7,200.00
Tony Hollifield	T-10	69-67-70-66=272	$7,200.00
Curtis Strange	T-10	70-66-67-69=272	$7,200.00
Jim Thorpe	T-10	65-72-67-68=272	$7,200.00

IVB Golf Classic

Course: Whitemarsh Valley C.C., Chestnut Hill, Pa.
Par: 71 Yardage: 6,687
Last day of event: Sunday, August 3, 1980

Player	Place	Score	Earnings
Doug Tewell	Win	67-73-65-67=272	$45,000.00
Tom Kite	2	67-71-65-70=273	$27,000.00
Ben Crenshaw	T-3	64-71-69-70=274	$11,275.00
Lou Graham	T-3	65-69-69-71=274	$11,275.00
Jack Renner	T-3	65-68-71-70=274	$11,275.00
Fuzzy Zoeller	T-3	67-66-72-69=274	$11,275.00
Calvin Peete	T-3	69-72-65-68=274	$11,275.00
Jerry Pate	T-8	68-70-68-70=276	$6,750.00
Ron Streck	T-8	68-70-68-70=276	$6,750.00
Roger Maltbie	T-8	69-69-70-68=276	$6,750.00
D.A. Weibring	T-8	70-70-69-67=276	$6,750.00
John Cook	T-8	67-70-66-73=276	$6,750.00

PGA Championship

Course: Oak Hill C.C., Rochester, N.Y.
Par: 70 Yardage: 6,964
Last day of event: Sunday, August 10, 1980

Player	Place	Score	Earnings
Jack Nicklaus	Win	70-69-66-69=274	$60,000.00
Andy Bean	2	72-71-68-70=281	$40,000.00
Gil Morgan	T-3	68-70-73-72=283	$22,500.00
Lon Hinkle	T-3	70-69-69-75=283	$22,500.00
Curtis Strange	T-5	68-72-72-72=284	$14,500.00
Howard Twitty	T-5	68-74-71-71=284	$14,500.00
Lee Trevino	7	74-71-71-69=285	$11,000.00
Bill Rogers	T-8	71-71-72-72=286	$8,500.00
Bobby Walzel	T-8	68-76-71-71=286	$8,500.00
Tom Weiskopf	T-10	71-73-72-72=288	$6,000.00
Jerry Pate	T-10	72-73-70-73=288	$6,000.00
Peter Jacobsen	T-10	71-73-74-70=288	$6,000.00
Tom Watson	T-10	75-74-72-67=288	$6,000.00
Terry Diehl	T-10	72-72-68-76=288	$6,000.00

Manufacturers Hanover Westchester Classic

Course: Westchester C.C., Harrison, N.Y.
Par: 71 Yardage: 6,603
Last day of event: Sunday, August 17, 1980

Player	Place	Score	Earnings
Curtis Strange	Win	69-65-70-69=273	$72,000.00
Gibby Gilbert	2	69-69-70-67=275	$43,200.00
Phil Hancock	3	67-70-70-69=276	$27,200.00
Mike Reid	T-4	66-70-72-69=277	$16,533.34
Tom Watson	T-4	68-66-70-73=277	$16,533.33
George Cadle	T-4	68-65-70-74=277	$16,533.33
Roger Maltbie	T-7	69-68-70-71=278	$11,640.00
George Burns	T-7	65-72-69-72=278	$11,640.00
Mike Sullivan	T-7	69-67-72-70=278	$11,640.00
Mark Lye	T-7	72-66-72-68=278	$11,640.00
David Graham	T-7	65-67-77-69=278	$11,640.00

World Series of Golf

Course: Firestone C.C. (South), Akron, Ohio
Par: 70 Yardage: 7,149
Last day of event: Sunday, August 24, 1980

Player	Place	Score	Earnings
Tom Watson	Win	65-75-65-65=270	$100,000.00
Ray Floyd	2	69-68-70-65=272	$55,000.00
Jerry Pate	3	72-64-70-67=273	$34,500.00
Lee Trevino	T-4	69-69-67-69=274	$19,600.00
Hale Irwin	T-4	68-74-66-66=274	$19,600.00

Player	Place	Score	Earnings
Lon Hinkle	T-6	68-69-69-69=275	$15,000.00
Ben Crenshaw	T-6	67-69-70-69=275	$15,000.00
Mike Reid	T-6	68-70-69-68=275	$15,000.00
Craig Stadler	9	67-68-70-73=278	$13,000.00
Bob Gilder	10	69-70-68-72=279	$12,000.00

Buick Goodwrench Open

Course: Warwick Hills C.C., Grand Blanc, Mich.
Par: 72 Yardage: 7,014
Last day of event: Sunday, August 24, 1980

Player	Place	Score	Earnings
Peter Jacobsen	Win	70-70-69-67=276	$45,000.00
Mark Lye	T-2	70-68-72-67=277	$22,000.00
Bill Kratzert	T-2	72-69-70-66=277	$22,000.00
Victor Regalado	T-4	73-70-66-69=278	$10,333.34
Tom Purtzer	T-4	74-65-69-70=278	$10,333.33
Rex Caldwell	T-4	66-66-71-75=278	$10,333.33
Phil Hancock	7	69-71-70-69=279	$8,375.00
Tom Weiskopf	T-8	68-69-72-71=280	$7,250.00
Bobby Clampett	T-8	71-72-70-67=280	$7,250.00
John Fought	T-8	72-72-72-64=280	$7,250.00

B.C. Open

Course: En-Joie G.C., Endicott, N.Y.
Par: 71 Yardage: 6,966
Last day of event: Sunday, August 31, 1980

Player	Place	Score	Earnings
Don Pooley	Win	68-69-66-68=271	$49,500.00
Peter Jacobsen	2	70-66-69-67=272	$29,700.00
Howard Twitty	T-3	67-69-69-68=273	$14,300.00
Bob Murphy	T-3	69-68-70-66=273	$14,300.00
Lee Trevino	T-3	72-64-67-70=273	$14,300.00
Terry Diehl	6	70-68-69-67=274	$9,900.00
Doug Johnson	7	68-69-67-71=275	$9,175.00
Brad Bryant	8	70-69-65-72=276	$8,525.00
Gary Hallberg	T-9	70-67-70-70=277	$7,425.00
Tom Jenkins	T-9	69-72-67-69=277	$7,425.00
Mike Sullivan	T-9	71-72-66-68=277	$7,425.00

Pleasant Valley Jimmy Fund Classic

Course: Pleasant Valley C.C., Sutton, Mass.
Par: 71 Yardage: 7,110
Last day of event: Sunday, September 7, 1980

Player	Place	Score	Earnings
Wayne Levi	Win	71-71-65-66=273	$54,000.00
Playoff: Beat Gil Morgan with par on fourth extra hole			
Gil Morgan	2	67-69-67-70=273	$32,400.00
Mike Reid	3	68-69-69-68=274	$20,400.00
Jack Renner	T-4	69-68-68-71=276	$13,200.00
John Cook	T-4	66-67-72-71=276	$13,200.00
Ray Floyd	T-6	70-72-67-68=277	$10,050.00
Jim Thorpe	T-6	72-68-70-67=277	$10,050.00
Jim Simons	T-6	73-69-70-65=277	$10,050.00
Bobby Wadkins	T-9	69-70-71-68=278	$8,400.00
George Burns	T-9	68-72-69-69=278	$8,400.00

Hall of Fame Tournament

Course: Pinehurst C.C. (No 2), Pinehurst, N.C.
Par: 71 Yardage: 7,020
Last day of event: Sunday, September 14, 1980

Player	Place	Score	Earnings
Phil Hancock	Win	71-67-67-70=275	$45,000.00
Scott Simpson	2	69-73-70-64=276	$27,000.00
Howard Twitty	3	68-70-69-70=277	$17,000.00
Lanny Wadkins	T-4	70-68-71-69=278	$10,333.34
Tom Kite	T-4	72-67-67-72=278	$10,333.33
Bill Rogers	T-4	72-67-67-72=278	$10,333.33
Larry Nelson	T-7	71-68-71-69=279	$7,275.00
Jerry Pate	T-7	72-68-67-72=279	$7,275.00
Jay Haas	T-7	71-73-67-68=279	$7,275.00
Ben Crenshaw	T-7	69-66-74-70=279	$7,275.00
Fuzzy Zoeller	T-7	72-68-75-64=279	$7,275.00

San Antonio Texas Open

Course: Oak Hill C.C., San Antonio, Texas
Par: 70 Yardage: 6,576
Last day of event: Sunday, September 21, 1980

Player	Place	Score	Earnings
Lee Trevino	Win	66-67-67-65=265	$45,000.00
Terry Diehl	2	65-67-67-67=266	$27,000.00
Fuzzy Zoeller	3	64-68-66-69=267	$17,000.00
Ed Sneed	T-4	67-68-67-66=268	$11,000.00
Lon Hinkle	T-4	67-70-65-66=268	$11,000.00
John Adams	6	71-67-66-65=269	$9,000.00
Bob Murphy	7	68-65-67-70=270	$8,375.00
Bill Rogers	8	64-67-71-69=271	$7,750.00
Bruce Devlin	T-9	68-68-67-69=272	$6,500.00
Forrest Fezler	T-9	65-70-69-68=272	$6,500.00
Mark McCumber	T-9	69-63-68-72=272	$6,500.00
George Burns	T-9	72-68-62-70=272	$6,500.00

Anheuser-Busch Golf Classic

Course: Silverado C.C., Napa, Calif.
Home Course -Par: 72 Yardage: 6,849
Last day of event: Sunday, September 28, 1980

Player	Place	Score	Earnings
Ben Crenshaw	Win	66-67-68-71=272	$54,000.00
Jack Renner	2	67-72-67-70=276	$32,400.00
Gary Hallberg	T-3	67-71-72-68=278	$17,400.00
Tom Watson	T-3	68-72-70-68=278	$17,400.00
Lon Hinkle	5	68-74-68-69=279	$12,000.00
Tom Weiskopf	T-6	68-70-72-70=280	$10,050.00
J.C. Snead	T-6	68-72-67-73=280	$10,050.00
Mike Reid	T-6	68-70-74-68=280	$10,050.00
Bobby Wadkins	9	73-69-68-71=281	$8,700.00
John Schroeder	T-10	68-72-72-70=282	$6,900.00
Dave Eichelberger	T-10	71-72-67-72=282	$6,900.00
Johnny Miller	T-10	68-69-72-73=282	$6,900.00
Bill Rogers	T-10	68-73-72-69=282	$6,900.00
Craig Stadler	T-10	74-71-71-66=282	$6,900.00

Southern Open

Course: Green Island C.C., Columbus, Ga.
Par: 71 Yardage: 6,791
Last day of event: Sunday, October 5, 1980

Player	Place	Score	Earnings
Mike Sullivan	Win	68-63-69-69=269	$36,000.00

Johnny Miller	T-2	69-71-65-69=274	$17,600.00
Dave Eichelberger	T-2	69-72-66-67=274	$17,600.00
Hale Irwin	T-4	68-70-68-69=275	$8,800.00
George Burns	T-4	67-66-74-68=275	$8,800.00
Wayne Levi	T-6	69-69-72-67=277	$6,950.00
Bill Kratzert	T-6	72-67-69-69=277	$6,950.00
Rik Massengale	8	69-69-69-71=278	$6,200.00
Joe Inman	T-9	70-71-71-67=279	$5,200.00
George Cadle	T-9	68-72-70-69=279	$5,200.00
Jerry Pate	T-9	67-71-67-74=279	$5,200.00
Gary Hallberg	T-9	68-69-74-68=279	$5,200.00

Pensacola Open
Course: Perdido Bay C.C., Pensacola, Fla.
Par: 72 Yardage: 7,133
Last day of event: Sunday, October 12, 1980

Player	Place	Score	Earnings
Dan Halldorson	Win	68-67-70-70=275	$36,000.00
Gary Hallberg	T-2	68-67-71-71=277	$17,600.00
Mike Sullivan	T-2	69-72-66-70=277	$17,600.00
Lyn Lott	T-4	69-68-71-70=278	$7,875.00
Mike Gove	T-4	70-67-68-73=278	$7,875.00
Tom Kite	T-4	65-70-69-74=278	$7,875.00
Dave Eichelberger	T-4	74-66-68-70=278	$7,875.00
Miller Barber	T-8	69-71-71-68=279	$6,000.00
Don Pooley	T-8	71-71-68-69=279	$6,000.00
Gibby Gilbert	T-10	69-71-70-70=280	$4,150.00
Chip Beck	T-10	66-72-72-70=280	$4,150.00
Lanny Wadkins	T-10	72-65-72-71=280	$4,150.00
Mark Hayes	T-10	72-68-69-71=280	$4,150.00
Mark McCumber	T-10	66-71-70-73=280	$4,150.00
Tim Simpson	T-10	67-70-74-69=280	$4,150.00
Jon Chaffee	T-10	74-70-67-69=280	$4,150.00
Bob Mann	T-10	68-71-63-78=280	$4,150.00

World Disney World National Team Championship
Course: Walt Disney (Magnolia, Palm), Lake Buena Vista C.C., Lake Buena Vista, Fla.
Home course / Magnolia, Par: 72 Yardage: 7,170
Last day of event: Sunday, October 19, 1980

Player	Place	Score	Earnings
Danny Edwards	Win	60-63-65-65=253	$31,500.00
Partner: David Edwards			
David Edwards	Win	60-63-65-65=253	$31,500.00
Partner: Danny Edwards			
Mike Harmon	T-2	63-64-66-62=255	$14,700.00
Partner: Barry Harwell			
Barry Harwell	T-2	63-64-66-62=255	$14,700.00
Partner: Mike Harmon			
Gibby Gilbert	T-2	65-67-62-61=255	$14,700.00
Partner: Grier Jones			
Grier Jones	T-2	65-67-62-61=255	$14,700.00
Partner: Gibby Gilbert			
Dan Halldorson	T-2	66-61-66-62=255	$14,700.00
Partner: Dana Quigley			
Dana Quigley	T-2	66-61-66-62=255	$14,700.00
Partner: Dan Halldorson			
Hubert Green	5	69-65-61-61=256	$7,980.00
Partner: Fuzzy Zoeller			
Fuzzy Zoeller	5	69-65-61-61=256	$7,980.00
Partner: Hubert Green			
Doug Campbell	T-6	64-61-64-68=257	$6,720.00
Partner: Mike Gove			
Mike Gove	T-6	64-61-64-68=257	$6,720.00
Partner: Doug Campbell			
Gary Koch	T-6	65-66-60-66=257	$6,720.00
Partner: Curtis Strange			
Curtis Strange	T-6	65-66-60-66=257	$6,720.00
Partner: Gary Koch			
Dave Barr	T-8	62-67-64-65=258	$4,363.33
Partner: Ed Fiori			
Ed Fiori	T-8	62-67-64-65=258	$4,363.33
Partner: Dave Barr			
Ed Dougherty	T-8	63-67-65-63=258	$4,363.34
Partner: Tommy Valentine			
Tommy Valentine	T-8	63-67-65-63=258	$4,363.34
Partner: Ed Dougherty			
George Burns	T-8	64-65-64-65=258	$4,363.33
Partner: Ben Crenshaw			
Ben Crenshaw	T-8	64-65-64-65=258	$4,363.33
Partner: George Burns			
Jim Dent	T-8	64-65-63-66=258	$4,363.33
Partner: Artie McNickle			
Artie McNickle	T-8	64-65-63-66=258	$4,363.33
Partner: Jim Dent			
Buddy Gardner	T-8	64-64-66-64=258	$4,363.33
Partner: Roger Maltbie			
Roger Maltbie	T-8	64-64-66-64=258	$4,363.33
Partner: Buddy Gardner			
R.W. Eaks	T-8	66-63-67-62=258	$4,363.34
Partner: Mark Rohde			
Mark Rohde	T-8	66-63-67-62=258	$4,363.34
Partner: R.W. Eaks			
Mac McLendon	T-8	66-62-65-65=258	$4,363.33
Partner: Leonard Thompson			
Leonard Thompson	T-8	66-62-65-65=258	$4,363.33
Partner: Mac McLendon			
Morris Hatalsky	T-8	66-64-64-64=258	$4,363.33
Partner: Don Pooley			
Don Pooley	T-8	66-64-64-64=258	$4,363.33
Partner: Morris Hatalsky			
Lon Hinkle	T-8	67-63-63-65=258	$4,363.33
Partner: Craig Stadler			
Craig Stadler	T-8	67-63-63-65=258	$4,363.33
Partner: Lon Hinkle			

1981

Tom Watson scored a two-shot victory over Johnny Miller and Jack Nicklaus at the Masters. Trailing by three shots after 54 holes, David Graham fired a closing 67 to win the U.S. Open at Merion, a classic Philadelphia course that fell out of USGA favor because of its lack of length but was awarded an Open reprieve in 2013. Bill Rogers won the British Open by four shots at Sandwich. Larry Nelson, who took up the game after serving in Vietnam, won the PGA Championship by four shots over Fuzzy Zoeller at the Atlanta Athletic Club.

Joe Garagiola Tucson Open
Course: Randolph Park Municipal, Tucson, Ariz.
Par: 70 Yardage: 6,860
Last day of event: Sunday, January 11, 1981

Player	Place	Score	Earnings
Johnny Miller	Win	66-64-70-65=265	$54,000.00
Lon Hinkle	2	65-69-67-66=267	$32,400.00
Dan Halldorson	3	63-69-66-71=269	$20,400.00
John Mahaffey	T-4	66-69-68-68=271	$13,200.00
Dan Pohl	T-4	67-65-68-71=271	$13,200.00
Michael Brannan	6	67-67-70-68=272	$10,800.00
Mike Donald	T-7	68-66-69-70=273	$9,675.00
Bill Rogers	T-7	69-65-69-70=273	$9,675.00

Player	Place	Score	Earnings
Scott Simpson	9	67-70-68-69=274	$8,700.00
Ed Fiori	T-10	68-70-68-69=275	$7,500.00
Lee Trevino	T-10	68-70-69-68=275	$7,500.00
David Edwards	T-10	73-63-71-68=275	$7,500.00

Bob Hope Chrysler Classic

Course: Bermuda Dunes C.C., La Quinta C.C., Indian Wells C.C.,Tamarisk C.C.

Home course / Bermuda Dunes, Par: 72 Yardage: 6,837

Last day of event: Sunday, January 18, 1981

Player	Place	Score	Earnings
Bruce Lietzke	Win	65-66-65-70-69=335	$50,000.00
Jerry Pate	2	66-67-68-67-69=337	$29,700.00
David Edwards	3	67-68-68-67-71=341	$18,700.00
D.A. Weibring	T-4	70-68-67-69-68=342	$11,366.67
Bill Rogers	T-4	70-65-66-69-72=342	$11,366.66
J.C. Snead	T-4	66-70-66-74-66=342	$11,366.67
Ben Crenshaw	7	68-68-68-69-70=343	$9,175.00
Ray Floyd	T-8	66-70-70-70-68=344	$7,975.00
Jack Renner	T-8	71-67-72-67-67=344	$7,975.00
Tom Kite	T-8	71-73-67-64-69=344	$7,975.00

Phoenix Open

Course: Phoenix C.C., Phoenix, Ariz.

Par: 71 Yardage: 6,726

Last day of event: Saturday, January 24, 1981

Player	Place	Score	Earnings
David Graham	Win	65-68-69-66=268	$54,000.00
Lon Hinkle	2	73-66-67-63=269	$32,400.00
Mike Reid	T-3	70-66-67-68=271	$17,400.00
Calvin Peete	T-3	72-67-65-67=271	$17,400.00
Jerry Pate	T-5	68-68-68-68=272	$10,950.00
Mike Sullivan	T-5	71-66-70-65=272	$10,950.00
Mark Lye	T-5	67-65-72-68=272	$10,950.00
John Schroeder	8	66-72-68-67=273	$9,300.00
Mark O'Meara	T-9	71-68-67-68=274	$8,400.00
D.A. Weibring	T-9	68-72-65-69=274	$8,400.00

Bing Crosby Pro-Am

Courses: Pebble Beach G.L., Spyglass Hill G.C., Cypress Point C.C., Pebble Beach, Calif.

Home Course / Pebble Beach, Par: 72 Yardage: 6,815

Last day of event: Sunday, February 1, 1981

Player	Place	Score	Earnings
John Cook	Win	66-71-72=209	$40,500.00
Hale Irwin	T-2	70-69-70=209	$14,850.00
Bobby Clampett	T-2	67-71-71=209	$14,850.00
Barney Thompson	T-2	71-71-67=209	$14,850.00
Ben Crenshaw	T-2	67-70-72=209	$14,850.00
Andy Bean	T-6	70-69-71=210	$7,042.50
Mike Reid	T-6	70-72-68=210	$7,042.50
Jerry Pate	T-6	69-68-73=210	$7,042.50
Tom Watson	T-6	67-69-74=210	$7,042.50
Brad Bryant	T-6	69-67-74=210	$7,042.50

Wickes/Andy Williams San Diego Open

Course: Torrey Pines (South), Torrey Pines (North), San Diego, Calif.

Home Course -Par: 72 Yardage: 7,021

Last day of event: Sunday, February 8, 1981

Player	Place	Score	Earnings
Bruce Lietzke	Win	68-72-70-68=278	$45,000.00

Playoff: Beat Ray Floyd and Tom Jenkins with birdie on second extra hole

Player	Place	Score	Earnings
Ray Floyd	T-2	70-66-71-71=278	$22,000.00
Tom Jenkins	T-2	65-72-71-70=278	$22,000.00
George Burns	T-4	69-70-69-71=279	$10,333.33
Gary Hallberg	T-4	67-72-73-67=279	$10,333.34
Jeff Mitchell	T-4	73-67-68-71=279	$10,333.33
Jim Simons	T-7	69-68-72-71=280	$7,791.67
Craig Stadler	T-7	73-67-67-73=280	$7,791.66
Jack Renner	T-7	74-69-67-70=280	$7,791.67
Tom Kite	T-10	71-70-70-70=281	$6,000.00
Ron Streck	T-10	65-72-71-73=281	$6,000.00
Johnny Miller	T-10	67-70-73-71=281	$6,000.00
Keith Fergus	T-10	66-72-74-69=281	$6,000.00

Hawaiian Open

Course: Waialae C.C., Honolulu, Ha.

Par: 72 Yardage: 7,234

Last day of event: Saturday, February 14, 1981

Player	Place	Score	Earnings
Hale Irwin	Win	68-66-62-69=265	$58,500.00
Don January	2	67-68-68-68=271	$35,100.00
Isao Aoki	T-3	69-68-66-69=272	$16,900.00
Terry Diehl	T-3	67-69-66-70=272	$16,900.00
Ben Crenshaw	T-3	68-70-67-67=272	$16,900.00
John Mahaffey	T-6	68-68-70-67=273	$10,175.00
Tom Watson	T-6	66-68-71-68=273	$10,175.00
Andy Bean	T-6	69-65-72-67=273	$10,175.00
John Schroeder	T-6	70-65-66-72=273	$10,175.00
George Archer	T-6	73-67-66-67=273	$10,175.00

Glen Campbell Los Angeles Open

Course: Riviera C.C., Pacific Palisades, Calif.

Par: 71 Yardage: 7,029

Last day of event: Sunday, February 22, 1981

Player	Place	Score	Earnings
Johnny Miller	Win	66-69-67-68=270	$54,000.00
Tom Weiskopf	2	71-65-68-68=272	$32,400.00
Gil Morgan	T-3	65-69-69-70=273	$17,400.00
Miller Barber	T-3	66-67-71-69=273	$17,400.00
Bruce Lietzke	T-5	66-70-69-69=274	$11,400.00
George Archer	T-5	70-68-70-66=274	$11,400.00
Craig Stadler	T-7	69-70-66-70=275	$9,675.00
Ben Crenshaw	T-7	70-67-66-72=275	$9,675.00
George Cadle	T-9	68-70-69-69=276	$7,800.00
Nick Faldo	T-9	69-70-67-70=276	$7,800.00
Bob Gilder	T-9	70-67-69-70=276	$7,800.00
Larry Ziegler	T-9	70-69-69-68=276	$7,800.00

Bay Hill Classic

Course: Bay Hill Club, Orlando, Fla.

Par: 71 Yardage: 7,103

Last day of event: Sunday, March 1, 1981

Player	Place	Score	Earnings
Andy Bean	Win	68-62-67-69=266	$54,000.00
Tom Watson	2	64-66-70-73=273	$32,400.00
Curtis Strange	3	68-68-72-67=275	$20,400.00
Mark O'Meara	4	67-68-69-72=276	$14,400.00
Mick Soli	T-5	69-70-67-71=277	$10,950.00
Mike Donald	T-5	72-68-66-71=277	$10,950.00
Brad Bryant	T-5	70-73-67-67=277	$10,950.00
Tom Purtzer	8	68-69-72-69=278	$9,300.00

Player	Place	Score	Earnings
Don Pooley	T-9	72-63-72-72=279	$8,100.00
Phil Hancock	T-9	71-69-73-66=279	$8,100.00
Ray Floyd	T-9	73-68-68-70=279	$8,100.00

American Motors Inverrary Classic
Course: Inverrary G. & C.C. (East), Lauderhill, Fla.
Par: 72 Yardage: 7,128
Last day of event: Sunday, March 8, 1981

Player	Place	Score	Earnings
Tom Kite	Win	69-68-68-69=274	$54,000.00
Jack Nicklaus	2	65-73-69-68=275	$32,400.00
Curtis Strange	3	68-67-66-75=276	$20,400.00
Andy Bean	T-4	69-71-69-68=277	$13,200.00
Larry Ziegler	T-4	65-68-72-72=277	$13,200.00
Charles Coody	T-6	67-72-70-69=278	$10,425.00
Johnny Miller	T-6	70-70-66-72=278	$10,425.00
Hale Irwin	T-8	76-69-67-67=279	$9,300.00
Mark O'Meara	T-9	71-74-66-69=280	$8,100.00
Vance Heafner	T-9	74-69-68-69=280	$8,100.00
Jerry Pate	T-9	76-65-71-68=280	$8,100.00

Doral-Eastern Open
Course: Doral C.C. (Blue), Miami, Fla.
Par: 72 Yardage: 6,939
Last day of event: Sunday, March 15, 1981

Player	Place	Score	Earnings
Ray Floyd	Win	66-68-71-68=273	$45,000.00
Keith Fergus	T-2	67-71-69-67=274	$22,000.00
David Graham	T-2	66-73-68-67=274	$22,000.00
Tom Kite	4	69-69-70-67=275	$12,000.00
Gil Morgan	T-5	66-69-71-70=276	$9,500.00
Leonard Thompson	T-5	68-68-71-69=276	$9,500.00
Bruce Lietzke	7	73-66-69-69=277	$8,375.00
Bob Murphy	T-8	68-71-69-70=278	$7,500.00
Bud Allin	T-8	72-67-70-69=278	$7,500.00
Mike Sullivan	T-10	70-69-70-70=279	$6,500.00
Mike Reid	T-10	70-70-68-71=279	$6,500.00

Tournament Players Championship
Course: Sawgrass C.C., Ponte Vedra Beach, Fla.
Par: 72 Yardage: 7,174
Last day of event: Sunday, March 22, 1981

Player	Place	Score	Earnings
Ray Floyd	Win	72-74-71-68=285	$72,000.00
Playoff: Beat Barry Jaeckel and Curtis Strange with par on first extra hole			
Curtis Strange	2	72-72-71-70=285	$35,200.00
Barry Jaeckel	2	69-70-72-74=285	$35,200.00
Jim Simons	T-4	73-68-73-73=287	$15,750.00
Bruce Lietzke	T-4	73-75-68-71=287	$15,750.00
Miller Barber	T-4	72-78-69-68=287	$15,750.00
Jim Colbert	T-4	78-69-69-71=287	$15,750.00
Gary Hallberg	T-8	71-73-72-72=288	$11,200.00
Dan Halldorson	T-8	70-70-74-74=288	$11,200.00
Frank Conner	T-8	74-72-70-72=288	$11,200.00
Leonard Thompson	T-8	71-76-72-69=288	$11,200.00

Sea Pines Heritage Classic
Course: Harbour Town G.L., Hilton Head, S.C.
Par: 71 Yardage: 6,657
Last day of event: Sunday, March 29, 1981

Player	Place	Score	Earnings
Bill Rogers	Win	71-69-68-70=278	$54,000.00
Bruce Devlin	T-2	70-71-71-67=279	$19,800.00
Craig Stadler	T-2	71-70-71-67=279	$19,800.00
Gil Morgan	T-2	67-72-72-68=279	$19,800.00
Hale Irwin	T-2	68-70-73-68=279	$19,800.00
Tom Weiskopf	6	71-69-72-70=282	$10,800.00
Andy Bean	T-7	71-72-71-69=283	$9,037.50
Greg Norman	T-7	71-72-72-68=283	$9,037.50
Roger Maltbie	T-7	71-68-73-71=283	$9,037.50
Terry Diehl	T-7	73-69-70-71=283	$9,037.50

Greater Greensboro Open
Course: Forest Oaks C.C., Greensboro, N.C.
Par: 72 Yardage: 6,984
Last day of event: Sunday, April 5, 1981

Player	Place	Score	Earnings
Larry Nelson	Win	69-68-69-75=281	$54,000.00
Playoff: Beat Mark Hayes with birdie on second extra hole			
Mark Hayes	2	70-69-68-74=281	$32,400.00
Nick Faldo	3	72-73-68-69=282	$20,400.00
Lee Trevino	4	69-72-70-72=283	$14,400.00
Ben Crenshaw	T-5	73-72-70-71=286	$11,400.00
George Burns	T-5	69-76-72-69=286	$11,400.00
Bob Shearer	T-7	73-72-70-72=287	$8,121.43
Bobby Walzel	T-7	70-74-70-73=287	$8,121.43
Dan Pohl	T-7	71-72-70-74=287	$8,121.43
Dave Stockton	T-7	74-72-69-72=287	$8,121.43
Ed Fiori	T-7	70-75-68-74=287	$8,121.42
Bill Rogers	T-7	75-71-70-71=287	$8,121.43
Jay Haas	T-7	68-72-76-71=287	$8,121.43

Masters
Course: Augusta National G.C., Augusta, Ga.
Par: 72 Yardage: 6,925
Last day of event: Sunday, April 12, 1981

Player	Place	Score	Earnings
Tom Watson	Win	71-68-70-71=280	$60,000.00
Johnny Miller	T-2	69-72-73-68=282	$30,500.00
Jack Nicklaus	T-2	70-65-75-72=282	$30,500.00
Greg Norman	4	69-70-72-72=283	$16,000.00
Jerry Pate	T-5	71-72-71-70=284	$12,667.00
Tom Kite	T-5	74-72-70-68=284	$12,667.00
David Graham	7	70-70-74-71=285	$11,167.00
Ben Crenshaw	T-8	71-72-70-73=286	$9,667.00
John Mahaffey	T-8	72-71-69-74=286	$9,667.00
Ray Floyd	T-8	75-71-71-69=286	$9,667.00

MONY Tournament of Champions
Course: La Costa C.C., Carlsbad, Calif.
Par: 72 Yardage: 6,911
Last day of event: Sunday, April 19, 1981

Player	Place	Score	Earnings
Lee Trevino	Win	67-67-70-69=273	$54,000.00
Ray Floyd	2	69-67-69-70=275	$35,000.00
Bruce Lietzke	3	68-71-69-70=278	$23,500.00
Bill Rogers	4	68-72-69-71=280	$17,100.00
Larry Nelson	5	71-67-72-71=281	$15,000.00
Curtis Strange	T-6	66-73-71-73=283	$12,000.00
Tom Kite	T-6	69-73-73-68=283	$12,000.00
Doug Tewell	T-6	71-73-70-69=283	$12,000.00
Tom Watson	9	74-72-68-70=284	$10,250.00
David Graham	10	73-69-71-72=285	$9,500.00

Tallahassee Open,

Course: Killearn C.C., Tallahassee, Fla.
Par: 72 Yardage: 7,124
Last day of event: Sunday, April 19, 1981

Player	Place	Score	Earnings
Dave Eichelberger	Win	66-66-69-70=271	$18,000.00

Playoff: Beat Bob Murphy and Mark O'Meara with birdie on first extra hole

Player	Place	Score	Earnings
Bob Murphy	T-2	67-67-68-69=271	$8,800.00
Mark O'Meara	T-2	65-74-65-67=271	$8,800.00
Greg Powers	4	68-68-64-72=272	$4,950.00
Chi Chi Rodriguez	5	72-66-67-69=274	$4,400.00
Brad Bryant	6	73-67-68-67=275	$4,000.00
Mike Donald	T-7	67-70-69-70=276	$3,300.00
Lou Graham	T-7	70-71-68-67=276	$3,300.00
Terry Mauney	T-7	71-65-71-69=276	$3,300.00
Tommy Valentine	T-10	70-69-68-70=277	$2,400.00
Dana Quigley	T-10	71-71-69-66=277	$2,400.00
Sammy Rachels	T-10	69-69-72-67=277	$2,400.00
Gary McCord	T-10	71-68-66-72=277	$2,400.00
Jerry Heard	T-10	67-70-67-73=277	$2,400.00

USF&G New Orleans Open

Course: Lakewood C.C., New Orleans, La.
Par: 72 Yardage: 7,080
Last day of event: Sunday, April 26, 1981

Player	Place	Score	Earnings
Tom Watson	Win	69-69-64-68=270	$63,000.00
Bruce Fleisher	2	71-67-68-66=272	$37,800.00
Gil Morgan	3	68-66-68-71=273	$23,800.00
Barry Jaeckel	4	69-67-70-69=275	$16,800.00
Ron Streck	T-5	69-68-70-69=276	$12,293.75
Jay Haas	T-5	70-66-69-71=276	$12,293.75
Fred Couples	T-5	71-66-69-70=276	$12,293.75
Lon Hinkle	T-5	68-70-72-66=276	$12,293.75
Rod Curl	T-9	70-67-69-71=277	$9,800.00
David Edwards	T-9	71-65-69-72=277	$9,800.00

Michelob Houston Open

Course: Woodlands C.C., The Woodlands, Texas
Par: 71 Yardage: 7,031
Last day of event: Saturday, May 2, 1981

Player	Place	Score	Earnings
Ron Streck	Win	68-68-62=198	$47,250.00
Jerry Pate	T-2	67-68-66=201	$23,100.00
Hale Irwin	T-2	65-69-67=201	$23,100.00
Jay Haas	T-4	67-67-68=202	$11,550.00
Ben Crenshaw	T-4	65-70-67=202	$11,550.00
Tom Kite	T-6	65-68-70=203	$8,793.75
Bruce Lietzke	T-6	66-70-67=203	$8,793.75
Bob Gilder	T-6	68-64-71=203	$8,793.75
Mike Morley	T-9	70-66-68=204	$7,350.00
Mike Holland	T-9	66-67-71=204	$7,350.00

Byron Nelson Golf Classic

Course: Preston Trail G.C., Dallas, Texas
Par: 70 Yardage: 6,993
Last day of event: Sunday, May 10, 1981

Player	Place	Score	Earnings
Bruce Lietzke	Win	68-74-69-70=281	$54,000.00

Playoff: Beat Tom Watson with par on first extra hole

Player	Place	Score	Earnings
Tom Watson	2	66-70-72-73=281	$32,400.00

Player	Place	Score	Earnings
Tom Purtzer	T-3	72-68-72-71=283	$17,400.00
Bobby Clampett	T-3	69-73-67-74=283	$17,400.00
Ben Crenshaw	5	75-68-72-69=284	$12,000.00
Curtis Strange	T-6	69-74-70-72=285	$10,050.00
Cesar Sanudo	T-6	70-70-75-70=285	$10,050.00
Ray Floyd	T-6	68-69-77-71=285	$10,050.00
Bruce Devlin	T-9	72-71-72-71=286	$8,400.00
Fred Couples	T-9	70-76-69-71=286	$8,400.00

Colonial National Invitational

Course: Colonial C.C., Fort Worth, Texas
Par: 70 Yardage: 7,096
Last day of event: Sunday, May 17, 1981

Player	Place	Score	Earnings
Fuzzy Zoeller	Win	67-69-68-70=274	$54,000.00
Hale Irwin	2	69-68-71-70=278	$32,400.00
Scott Simpson	T-3	69-70-70-70=279	$15,600.00
Tom Kite	T-3	67-71-71-70=279	$15,600.00
Curtis Strange	T-3	69-71-67-72=279	$15,600.00
Frank Conner	6	70-72-68-70=280	$10,800.00
Don January	T-7	70-69-70-72=281	$9,675.00
Ray Floyd	T-7	66-74-71-70=281	$9,675.00
Rod Curl	T-9	67-73-74-68=282	$8,400.00
Jerry Heard	T-9	74-65-72-71=282	$8,400.00

Memorial Tournament

Course: Muirfield Village G.C., Dubin, Ohio
Par: 72 Yardage: 7,116
Last day of event: Sunday, May 24, 1981

Player	Place	Score	Earnings
Keith Fergus	Win	71-68-74-71=284	$63,000.00
Jack Renner	2	75-70-69-71=285	$37,800.00
Tom Purtzer	T-3	68-74-72-73=287	$16,800.00
Tom Watson	T-3	72-72-69-74=287	$16,800.00
Craig Stadler	T-3	70-71-71-75=287	$16,800.00
George Archer	T-3	74-69-69-75=287	$16,800.00
Fuzzy Zoeller	T-7	73-72-72-71=288	$10,185.00
Dan Halldorson	T-7	70-70-74-74=288	$10,185.00
Mark Hayes	T-7	67-75-74-72=288	$10,185.00
Lanny Wadkins	T-7	68-72-75-73=288	$10,185.00
Tom Kite	T-7	71-72-69-76=288	$10,185.00

Kemper Open

Course: Congressional C.C., Bethesda, Md.
Par: 72 Yardage: 7,173
Last day of event: Sunday, May 31, 1981

Player	Place	Score	Earnings
Craig Stadler	Win	67-69-66-68=270	$72,000.00
Tom Watson	T-2	71-69-69-67=276	$35,200.00
Tom Weiskopf	T-2	68-68-68-72=276	$35,200.00
John Cook	4	65-72-67-73=277	$19,200.00
David Edwards	5	71-68-68-71=278	$16,000.00
Tom Kite	T-6	70-70-68-71=279	$13,400.00
Danny Edwards	T-6	67-67-73-72=279	$13,400.00
D.A. Weibring	T-6	68-74-67-70=279	$13,400.00
Beau Baugh	T-9	69-70-69-72=280	$10,400.00
Dan Pohl	T-9	69-68-72-71=280	$10,400.00
Andy North	T-9	70-68-72-70=280	$10,400.00
Jack Renner	T-9	74-68-67-71=280	$10,400.00

Atlanta Classic

Course: Atlanta C.C., Atlanta, Ga.
Par: 72 Yardage: 7,007
Last day of event: Sunday, June 7, 1981

Player	Place	Score	Earnings
Tom Watson	Win	68-70-68-71=277	$54,000.00

Playoff: Beat Tommy Valentine with par on third extra hole

Player	Place	Score	Earnings
Tommy Valentine	2	68-65-72-72=277	$32,400.00
Mike Morley	T-3	70-66-72-71=279	$15,600.00
Calvin Peete	T-3	68-68-69-74=279	$15,600.00
Lee Elder	T-3	71-65-74-69=279	$15,600.00
Bill Britton	T-6	69-73-71-67=280	$10,050.00
Ray Floyd	T-6	69-66-74-71=280	$10,050.00
Frank Conner	T-6	70-67-69-74=280	$10,050.00
Jack Nicklaus	T-9	68-72-69-72=281	$8,100.00
Jerry Pate	T-9	71-72-68-70=281	$8,100.00
Pat Lindsey	T-9	70-73-70-68=281	$8,100.00

Manufacturers Hanover Westchester Classic

Course: Westchester C.C., Harrison, N.Y.
Par: 71 Yardage: 6,603
Last day of event: Sunday, June 14, 1981

Player	Place	Score	Earnings
Ray Floyd	Win	70-68-68-69=275	$72,000.00
Gibby Gilbert	T-2	68-68-71-70=277	$29,866.67
Craig Stadler	T-2	69-68-68-72=277	$29,866.66
Bobby Clampett	T-2	72-69-68-68=277	$29,866.67
George Burns	5	71-74-69-65=279	$16,000.00
Lee Elder	T-6	68-70-72-70=280	$12,520.00
Leonard Thompson	T-6	71-65-73-71=280	$12,520.00
Ron Streck	T-6	72-69-66-73=280	$12,520.00
Tom Kite	T-6	73-65-68-74=280	$12,520.00
J.C. Snead	T-6	74-65-67-74=280	$12,520.00

U.S. Open

Course: Merion G.C., Ardmore, Pa.
Par: 70 Yardage: 6,544
Last day of event: Sunday, June 21, 1981

Player	Place	Score	Earnings
David Graham	Win	68-68-70-67=273	$55,000.00
Bill Rogers	T-2	70-68-69-69=276	$24,650.00
George Burns	T-2	69-66-68-73=276	$24,650.00
John Cook	T-4	68-70-71-70=279	$16,200.00
John Schroeder	T-4	71-68-69-71=279	$16,200.00
Lon Hinkle	T-6	69-71-70-70=280	$9,920.00
Sammy Rachels	T-6	70-71-69-70=280	$9,920.00
Jack Nicklaus	T-6	69-68-71-72=280	$9,920.00
Frank Conner	T-6	71-72-69-68=280	$9,920.00
Chi Chi Rodriguez	T-6	68-73-67-72=280	$9,920.00

Danny Thomas Memphis Classic

Course: Colonial C.C. (South), Cordova, Tenn.
Par: 72 Yardage: 7,282
Last day of event: Sunday, June 28, 1981

Player	Place	Score	Earnings
Jerry Pate	Win	69-70-66-69=274	$54,000.00
Bruce Lietzke	T-2	71-71-67-67=276	$26,400.00
Tom Kite	T-2	67-73-68-68=276	$26,400.00
Denis Watson	T-4	72-72-69-68=281	$13,200.00
Peter Jacobsen	T-4	73-69-64-75=281	$13,200.00

Player	Place	Score	Earnings
Lee Trevino	T-6	70-71-72-69=282	$10,425.00
David Thore	T-6	72-68-71-71=282	$10,425.00
Jim Simons	8	73-72-69-69=283	$9,300.00
Bill Kratzert	T-9	71-71-71-71=284	$7,800.00
Curtis Strange	T-9	69-70-73-72=284	$7,800.00
Leonard Thompson	T-9	70-73-70-71=284	$7,800.00
Tim Norris	T-9	73-74-68-69=284	$7,800.00

Western Open

Course: Butler National G.C., Oak Brook, Ill.
Par: 72 Yardage: 7,097
Last day of event: Sunday, July 5, 1981

Player	Place	Score	Earnings
Ed Fiori	Win	74-67-69-67=277	$54,000.00
Jim Simons	T-2	69-71-71-70=281	$22,400.00
Jim Colbert	T-2	71-70-70-70=281	$22,400.00
Greg Powers	T-2	69-67-75-70=281	$22,400.00
Bill Rogers	5	69-73-66-74=282	$12,000.00
J.C. Snead	6	71-74-69-70=284	$10,800.00
Tom Kite	T-7	72-68-72-74=286	$9,037.50
Curtis Strange	T-7	73-70-69-74=286	$9,037.50
Don Pooley	T-7	68-70-73-75=286	$9,037.50
Jack Nicklaus	T-7	75-72-70-69=286	$9,037.50

Greater Milwaukee Open

Course: Tuckaway C.C., Franklin, Wis.
Par: 72 Yardage: 7,030
Last day of event: Sunday, July 12, 1981

Player	Place	Score	Earnings
Jay Haas	Win	68-66-67-73=274	$45,000.00
Chi Chi Rodriguez	2	68-69-71-69=277	$27,000.00
Lyn Lott	T-3	68-71-68-71=278	$14,500.00
Danny Edwards	T-3	72-69-69-68=278	$14,500.00
Tim Simpson	T-5	68-70-71-70=279	$8,475.00
Bill Kratzert	T-5	72-69-69-69=279	$8,475.00
Jeff Mitchell	T-5	72-69-69-69=279	$8,475.00
Jim Colbert	T-5	69-73-67-70=279	$8,475.00
Rex Caldwell	T-5	74-65-67-73=279	$8,475.00
Bobby Cole	T-10	69-71-69-71=280	$6,250.00
John Adams	T-10	71-71-71-67=280	$6,250.00
George Archer	T-10	68-72-71-69=280	$6,250.00

Quad Cities Open

Course: Oakwood C.C., Coal Valley, Ill.
Par: 70 Yardage: 6,602
Last day of event: Sunday, July 19, 1981

Player	Place	Score	Earnings
Dave Barr	Win	69-64-71-66=270	$36,000.00

Playoff: Beat Woody Blackburn, Frank Conner, Dan Halldorson and Victor
Regalado with par on eighth extra hole

Player	Place	Score	Earnings
Frank Conner	T-2	67-67-67-69=270	$13,200.00
Dan Halldorson	T-2	70-65-66-69=270	$13,200.00
Woody Blackburn	T-2	70-66-67-67=270	$13,200.00
Victor Regalado	T-2	69-64-66-71=270	$13,200.00
Dan Pohl	T-6	69-69-64-69=271	$6,475.00
Jack Renner	T-6	66-69-70-66=271	$6,475.00
Mark McCumber	T-6	70-64-67-70=271	$6,475.00
Calvin Peete	T-6	70-65-69-67=271	$6,475.00
Curtis Strange	10	69-65-69-69=272	$5,400.00

British Open

Course: Royal St. George's G.C., Sandwich, Kent, England
Par: 70 Yardage: 6,829
Last day of event: Sunday, July 19, 1981

Player	Place	Score	Earnings
Bill Rogers	Win	72-66-67-71=276	$50,000.00
Bernhard Langer	2	73-67-70-70=280	$35,000.00
Mark James	T-3	72-70-68-73=283	$23,500.00
Ray Floyd	T-3	74-70-69-70=283	$23,500.00
Sam Torrance	5	72-69-73-70=284	$17,000.00
Manuel Pinero	T-6	73-74-68-70=285	$15,500.00
Bruce Lietzke	T-6	76-69-71-69=285	$15,500.00
Ben Crenshaw	T-8	72-67-76-71=286	$13,000.00
Howard Clark	T-8	72-76-70-68=286	$13,000.00
Brian Jones	T-8	73-76-66-71=286	$13,000.00

Anheuser-Busch Golf Classic

Course: Kingsmill G.C., Williamsburg, Va.
Par: 71 Yardage: 6,776
Last day of event: Sunday, July 26, 1981

Player	Place	Score	Earnings
John Mahaffey	Win	72-67-70-67=276	$54,000.00
Andy North	2	73-70-67-68=278	$32,400.00
Mike Sullivan	T-3	71-70-69-71=281	$15,600.00
Tom Purtzer	T-3	72-70-71-68=281	$15,600.00
Greg Powers	T-3	78-67-69-67=281	$15,600.00
Jack Renner	T-6	70-72-70-70=282	$10,050.00
Curtis Strange	T-6	75-70-64-73=282	$10,050.00
Mark McCumber	T-6	75-68-69-70=282	$10,050.00
D.A. Weibring	T-9	69-73-71-70=283	$6,712.50
Bobby Clampett	T-9	73-72-68-70=283	$6,712.50
Danny Edwards	T-9	73-71-71-68=283	$6,712.50
Wayne Levi	T-9	70-67-74-72=283	$6,712.50
Lyn Lott	T-9	74-70-67-72=283	$6,712.50
Mark Lye	T-9	74-69-70-70=283	$6,712.50
Bruce Fleisher	T-9	75-71-68-69=283	$6,712.50
Denis Watson	T-9	75-71-71-66=283	$6,712.50

Canadian Open

Course: Glen Abbey G.C., Oakville, Ontario, Canada
Par: 71 Yardage: 7,060
Last day of event: Sunday, August 2, 1981

Player	Place	Score	Earnings
Peter Oosterhuis	Win	69-69-72-70=280	$76,500.00
Jack Nicklaus	T-2	70-70-70-71=281	$31,733.33
Bruce Lietzke	T-2	71-70-70-70=281	$31,733.34
Andy North	T-2	73-68-69-71=281	$31,733.33
David Graham	T-5	70-72-70-70=282	$16,150.00
Mark Hayes	T-5	72-67-69-74=282	$16,150.00
Tom Kite	T-7	69-72-68-74=283	$13,246.67
Bob Eastwood	T-7	69-71-76-67=283	$13,246.67
Leonard Thompson	T-7	72-62-73-76=283	$13,246.66
Jim Thorpe	T-10	69-72-71-72=284	$10,200.00
Scott Hoch	T-10	73-69-71-71=284	$10,200.00
Jerry Pate	T-10	70-74-72-68=284	$10,200.00
Tom Purtzer	T-10	71-70-69-74=284	$10,200.00

PGA Championship

Course: Atlanta Athletic Club, Duluth, Ga.
Par: 70 Yardage: 7,070
Last day of event: Sunday, August 9, 1981

Player	Place	Score	Earnings
Larry Nelson	Win	70-66-66-71=273	$60,000.00
Fuzzy Zoeller	2	70-68-68-71=277	$40,000.00
Dan Pohl	3	69-67-73-69=278	$25,000.00
Bruce Lietzke	T-4	70-70-71-68=279	$13,146.43
Jack Nicklaus	T-4	71-68-71-69=279	$13,146.43
Keith Fergus	T-4	71-71-69-68=279	$13,146.43
Tom Kite	T-4	71-67-69-72=279	$13,146.42
Greg Norman	T-4	73-67-68-71=279	$13,146.43
Bob Gilder	T-4	74-69-70-66=279	$13,146.43
Isao Aoki	T-4	75-68-66-70=279	$13,146.43

Sammy Davis, Jr. - Greater Hartford Open

Course: Wethersfield C.C., Wethersfield, Conn.
Par: 71 Yardage: 6,568
Last day of event: Sunday, August 16, 1981

Player	Place	Score	Earnings
Hubert Green	Win	68-65-67-64=264	$54,000.00
Roger Maltbie	T-2	65-68-64-68=265	$22,400.00
Fred Couples	T-2	67-69-63-66=265	$22,400.00
Bobby Clampett	T-2	67-65-69-64=265	$22,400.00
Tim Simpson	5	66-68-67-65=266	$12,000.00
Curtis Strange	T-6	68-66-65-68=267	$10,425.00
Jack Renner	T-6	68-65-67-67=267	$10,425.00
Jay Haas	T-8	65-68-68-67=268	$8,400.00
Greg Powers	T-8	69-69-64-66=268	$8,400.00
John Mazza	T-8	66-67-70-65=268	$8,400.00
George Archer	T-8	72-67-65-64=268	$8,400.00

Buick Open

Course: Warwick Hills C.C., Grand Blanc, Mich.
Par: 72 Yardage: 7,014
Last day of event: Sunday, August 23, 1981

Player	Place	Score	Earnings
Hale Irwin	Win	65-73-67-72=277	$63,000.00

Playoff: Beat Bobby Clampett, Peter Jacobsen and Gil Morgan with birdie on second extra hole

Player	Place	Score	Earnings
Bobby Clampett	T-2	69-69-69-70=277	$26,133.33
Peter Jacobsen	T-2	68-69-71-69=277	$26,133.34
Gil Morgan	T-2	71-69-69-68=277	$26,133.33
Hubert Green	T-5	70-70-70-68=278	$12,775.00
Roger Maltbie	T-5	68-68-71-71=278	$12,775.00
Dan Halldorson	T-5	66-68-75-69=278	$12,775.00
Don Pooley	T-8	69-72-70-68=279	$10,150.00
Steve Melnyk	T-8	70-67-70-72=279	$10,150.00
Tom Kite	T-8	73-68-70-68=279	$10,150.00

World Series of Golf

Course: Firestone C.C. (South), Akron, Ohio
Par: 70 Yardage: 7,149
Last day of event: Sunday, August 30, 1981

Player	Place	Score	Earnings
Bill Rogers	Win	68-69-71-67=275	$100,000.00
Tom Kite	2	72-71-66-67=276	$55,000.00
Hale Irwin	T-3	68-68-70-72=278	$27,850.00
Isao Aoki	T-3	74-65-72-67=278	$27,850.00
Ray Floyd	5	71-73-69-67=280	$18,000.00
Bernhard Langer	T-6	68-69-72-72=281	$14,500.00
David Graham	T-6	72-69-69-71=281	$14,500.00
Larry Nelson	T-6	71-66-71-73=281	$14,500.00
Bruce Lietzke	T-6	74-67-72-68=281	$14,500.00

Player	Place	Score	Earnings
Curtis Strange	T-10	69-71-71-72=283	$11,500.00
Jack Nicklaus	T-10	71-67-71-74=283	$11,500.00

B.C. Open
Course: En-Joie G.C., Endicott, N.Y.
Par: 71 Yardage: 6,966
Last day of event: Sunday, September 6, 1981

Player	Place	Score	Earnings
Jay Haas	Win	67-65-69-69=270	$49,500.00
Tom Kite	2	67-68-69-69=273	$29,700.00
Bobby Clampett	T-3	70-65-70-70=275	$15,950.00
Barry Jaeckel	T-3	68-71-68-68=275	$15,950.00
Howard Twitty	5	70-70-69-67=276	$11,000.00
Calvin Peete	T-6	64-70-73-70=277	$9,200.00
Dan Pohl	T-6	67-68-74-68=277	$9,200.00
Chip Beck	T-6	74-69-67-67=277	$9,200.00
Denis Watson	9	67-68-70-73=278	$7,975.00
Don Pooley	T-10	69-71-68-71=279	$7,150.00
D.A. Weibring	T-10	71-70-68-70=279	$7,150.00

Pleasant Valley Jimmy Fund Classic
Course: Pleasant Valley C.C., Sutton, Mass.
Par: 71 Yardage: 7,110
Last day of event: Sunday, September 13, 1981

Player	Place	Score	Earnings
Jack Renner	Win	68-68-68-69=273	$54,000.00
Scott Simpson	2	68-69-70-68=275	$32,400.00
Tom Kite	3	68-70-68-70=276	$20,400.00
Gary Trivisonno	4	69-71-68-69=277	$14,400.00
Gibby Gilbert	T-5	69-69-70-70=278	$10,950.00
Don Pooley	T-5	71-69-71-67=278	$10,950.00
Mark Lye	T-5	74-66-69-69=278	$10,950.00
George Burns	T-8	70-71-67-71=279	$7,500.00
Jeff Mitchell	T-8	68-69-70-72=279	$7,500.00
Denis Watson	T-8	69-67-71-72=279	$7,500.00
Bill Calfee	T-8	70-72-67-70=279	$7,500.00
Ed Dougherty	T-8	72-68-68-71=279	$7,500.00
Mike Reid	T-8	72-71-68-68=279	$7,500.00
Tommy Valentine	T-8	70-67-67-75=279	$7,500.00

LaJet Classic
Course: Fairway Oaks C.C., Abilene, Texas
Par: 72 Yardage: 7,166
Last day of event: Sunday, September 20, 1981

Player	Place	Score	Earnings
Tom Weiskopf	Win	73-67-70-68=278	$63,000.00
Gil Morgan	2	71-66-74-69=280	$37,800.00
Craig Stadler	T-3	69-68-74-70=281	$18,200.00
Fuzzy Zoeller	T-3	70-67-74-70=281	$18,200.00
Tommy Valentine	T-3	66-70-75-70=281	$18,200.00
Joe Inman	T-6	70-72-70-71=283	$11,331.25
J.C. Snead	T-6	69-74-69-71=283	$11,331.25
Jack Renner	T-6	70-74-69-70=283	$11,331.25
Bob Eastwood	T-6	70-71-74-68=283	$11,331.25
Bill Britton	T-10	70-70-73-73=286	$9,100.00
John Mahaffey	T-10	75-68-71-72=286	$9,100.00

Hall of Fame Tournament
Course: Pinehurst C.C. (No 2), Pinehurst, N.C.
Par: 71 Yardage: 7,005
Last day of event: Sunday, September 27, 1981

Player	Place	Score	Earnings
Morris Hatalsky	Win	65-71-68-71=275	$45,000.00
Jerry Pate	T-2	66-68-71-72=277	$22,000.00
D.A. Weibring	T-2	72-69-66-70=277	$22,000.00
Keith Fergus	4	71-66-73-68=278	$12,000.00
Mike Reid	T-5	71-70-69-69=279	$9,125.00
Ed Sneed	T-5	71-73-68-67=279	$9,125.00
Bobby Wadkins	T-5	74-69-69-67=279	$9,125.00
Ray Floyd	T-8	70-70-70-70=280	$7,250.00
David Thore	T-8	70-69-71-70=280	$7,250.00
Terry Diehl	T-8	70-70-71-69=280	$7,250.00

Texas Open
Course: Oak Hill C.C., San Antonio, Texas
Par: 70 Yardage: 6,576
Last day of event: Sunday, October 4, 1981

Player	Place	Score	Earnings
Bill Rogers	Win	67-66-70-63=266	$45,000.00
Playoff: Beat Ben Crenshaw with birdie on first extra hole			
Ben Crenshaw	2	65-67-70-64=266	$27,000.00
Bob Murphy	T-3	67-69-69-64=269	$13,000.00
Craig Stadler	T-3	63-67-69-70=269	$13,000.00
Jim Colbert	T-3	66-64-69-70=269	$13,000.00
Don Levin	T-6	67-67-67-69=270	$8,375.00
Tom Kite	T-6	68-68-65-69=270	$8,375.00
Bobby Wadkins	T-6	68-69-67-66=270	$8,375.00
Tom Purtzer	9	68-69-65-69=271	$7,250.00
Wayne Levi	T-10	66-67-70-69=272	$6,250.00
Bobby Clampett	T-10	66-67-68-71=272	$6,250.00
Tim Simpson	T-10	69-65-67-71=272	$6,250.00

Southern Open
Course: Green Island C.C., Columbus, Ga.
Par: 70 Yardage: 6,791
Last day of event: Sunday, October 11, 1981

Player	Place	Score	Earnings
J.C. Snead	Win	67-68-70-66=271	$36,000.00
Playoff: Beat Mike Sullivan with par on second extra hole			
Mike Sullivan	2	66-71-70-64=271	$21,600.00
Jeff Mitchell	3	69-68-65-70=272	$13,600.00
Peter Jacobsen	T-4	67-70-67-69=273	$8,800.00
Jim Booros	T-4	71-68-66-68=273	$8,800.00
Vance Heafner	T-6	68-69-68-69=274	$6,700.00
George Burns	T-6	66-69-69-70=274	$6,700.00
Greg Powers	T-6	69-67-72-66=274	$6,700.00
Dave Eichelberger	T-9	70-68-68-69=275	$5,200.00
Scott Hoch	T-9	71-70-66-68=275	$5,200.00
Calvin Peete	T-9	68-67-68-72=275	$5,200.00
Payne Stewart	T-9	67-65-70-73=275	$5,200.00

Pensacola Open

Course: Perdido Bay C.C., Pensacola, Fla.
Par: 72 Yardage: 7,133
Last day of event: Sunday, October 18, 1981

Player	Place	Score	Earnings
Jerry Pate	Win	66-69-65-71=271	$36,000.00
Steve Melnyk	2	67-69-68-70=274	$21,600.00
Fred Couples	T-3	68-65-71-71=275	$11,600.00
Tom Kite	T-3	72-70-64-69=275	$11,600.00
Bruce Lietzke	T-5	67-68-71-70=276	$7,300.00
George Cadle	T-5	70-66-69-71=276	$7,300.00
Howard Twitty	T-5	67-67-72-70=276	$7,300.00
Gary Hallberg	T-8	70-69-68-70=277	$6,000.00
Gibby Gilbert	T-8	65-72-68-72=277	$6,000.00
Vance Heafner	T-10	69-68-70-71=278	$4,433.34
Mike Holland	T-10	70-70-67-71=278	$4,433.33
Ed Fiori	T-10	68-66-72-72=278	$4,433.33
Mike Donald	T-10	70-66-72-70=278	$4,433.34
George Archer	T-10	72-66-69-71=278	$4,433.33
Ray Floyd	T-10	70-68-67-73=278	$4,433.33

World Disney World National Team Championship

Course: Walt Disney (Magnolia, Palm), Lake Buena Vista C.C., Lake Buena Vista, Fla.
Home course / Magnolia, Par: 72 Yardage: 7,170
Last day of event: Sunday, October 25, 1981

Player	Place	Score	Earnings
Vance Heafner	Win	60-62-61-63=246	$36,000.00
Partner: Mike Holland			
Mike Holland	Win	60-62-61-63=246	$36,000.00
Partner: Vance Heafner			
Chip Beck	2	66-61-58-66=251	$23,200.00
Partner: Rex Caldwell			
Rex Caldwell	2	66-61-58-66=251	$23,200.00
Partner: Chip Beck			
Danny Edwards	3	62-64-64-62=252	$16,000.00
Partner: David Edwards			
David Edwards	3	62-64-64-62=252	$16,000.00
Partner: Danny Edwards			
Scott Hoch	4	64-63-63-63=253	$11,200.00
Partner: Calvin Peete			
Calvin Peete	4	64-63-63-63=253	$11,200.00
Partner: Scott Hoch			
Jim Dent	5	65-61-63-65=254	$9,120.00
Partner: Clarence Rose			
Clarence Rose	5	65-61-63-65=254	$9,120.00
Partner: Jim Dent			
Jim Booros	6	63-62-65-65=255	$8,000.00
Partner: Tim Norris			
Tim Norris	6	63-62-65-65=255	$8,000.00
Partner: Jim Booros			
Tom Purtzer	T-7	63-64-64-65=256	$6,720.00
Partner: Howard Twitty			
Howard Twitty	T-7	63-64-64-65=256	$6,720.00
Partner: Tom Purtzer			
Brad Bryant	T-7	63-63-68-62=256	$6,720.00
Partner: Joe Hager			
Joe Hager	T-7	63-63-68-62=256	$6,720.00
Partner: Brad Bryant			
Bruce Douglass	T-7	63-63-64-66=256	$6,720.00
Partner: Mike McCullough			
Mike McCullough	T-7	63-63-64-66=256	$6,720.00
Partner: Bruce Douglass			
Forrest Fezler	T-10	62-65-67-63=257	$4,577.14
Partner: Greg Powers			
Greg Powers	T-10	62-65-67-63=257	$4,577.14
Partner: Forrest Fezler			
Mark Lye	T-10	63-64-63-67=257	$4,577.14
Partner: Dan Pohl			
Dan Pohl	T-10	63-64-63-67=257	$4,577.14
Partner: Mark Lye			
David Canipe	T-10	64-63-65-65=257	$4,577.14
Partner: Tom McGinnis			
Tom McGinnis	T-10	64-63-65-65=257	$4,577.14
Partner: David Canipe			
Bruce Fleisher	T-10	64-65-62-66=257	$4,577.14
Partner: Tom Jenkins			
Tom Jenkins	T-10	64-65-62-66=257	$4,577.14
Partner: Bruce Fleisher			
Keith Fergus	T-10	65-66-63-63=257	$4,577.14
Partner: Phil Hancock			
Phil Hancock	T-10	65-66-63-63=257	$4,577.14
Partner: Keith Fergus			
Pat McGowan	T-10	66-61-65-65=257	$4,577.15
Partner: Jim Nelford			
Jim Nelford	T-10	66-61-65-65=257	$4,577.15
Partner: Pat McGowan			
Arthur Perry	T-10	67-64-61-65=257	$4,577.15
Partner: Doug Black			
Doug Black	T-10	67-64-61-65=257	$4,577.15
Partner: Arthur Perry			

1982

It was a big year for Tom Watson. He made the sports highlight reels when he chipped in at No. 17, then birdied the 72nd hole to beat Jack Nicklaus by two shots in the U.S. Open at Pebble Beach. Trailing Nick Price by four shots after 54 holes at Royal Troon, Watson shot a closing 70 to beat Price and Peter Oosterhuis by one stroke at the British Open. Craig Stadler won the Masters, surviving a sudden death playoff against Dan Pohl, who had caught Stadler with a closing 67. The PGA Championship went to Raymond Floyd, who opened with a 63 and went on to beat Lanny Wadkins by three shots at Southern Hills. Wayne Levi won the Hawaiian Open using an orange-colored golf ball. "I think you'll be seeing more and more of them used in the future," Levi predicted. Straight-hitting Calvin Peete, one of the few African-Americans to play on the PGA Tour, won four times in 1982. Jerry Pate won the first Players Championship played at TPC Sawgrass, then shoved commissioner Deane Beman and course architect Pete Dye into the lake beside the 18th green.

Joe Garagiola Tucson Open

Course: Randolph Park Municipal, Tucson, Ariz.
Par: 70 Yardage: 6,860
Last day of event: Sunday, January 10, 1982

Player	Place	Score	Earnings
Craig Stadler	Win	65-64-66-71=266	$54,000.00
Vance Heafner	T-2	68-68-69-64=269	$26,400.00
John Mahaffey	T-2	71-66-67-65=269	$26,400.00
Bob Gilder	4	68-70-67-65=270	$14,400.00
Jay Haas	5	67-68-67-69=271	$12,000.00
Leonard Thompson	T-6	67-69-69-67=272	$8,764.29
Greg Powers	T-6	69-69-65-69=272	$8,764.28
Peter Jacobsen	T-6	68-70-67-67=272	$8,764.29
Andy Bean	T-6	70-65-70-67=272	$8,764.29
John Jackson	T-6	71-68-66-67=272	$8,764.28
Keith Fergus	T-6	71-69-65-67=272	$8,764.28
Joe Hager	T-6	69-72-66-65=272	$8,764.29

Bob Hope Chrysler Classic

Course: Indian Wells C.C.,Eldorado C.C., Bermuda Dunes C.C., La Quinta CC

Home course / Indian Wells, Par: 72 Yardage: 6,478

Last day of event: Sunday, January 17, 1982

Player	Place	Score	Earnings
Ed Fiori	Win	70-65-66-67-67=335	$50,000.00
Tom Kite	2	68-66-66-69-66=335	$29,700.00
Rex Caldwell	3	64-69-70-66-68=337	$18,700.00
Scott Hoch	4	68-69-69-67-65=338	$13,200.00
Curtis Strange	5	67-70-69-68-65=339	$11,000.00
Mark O'Meara	T-6	71-70-65-64-70=340	$9,537.50
Wayne Levi	T-6	68-68-73-67-64=340	$9,537.50
Mike Reid	8	70-71-68-65-67=341	$8,525.00
Calvin Peete	9	69-65-71-68-69=342	$7,975.00
Forrest Fezler	10	66-70-67-67-73=343	$7,425.00

Phoenix Open

Course: Phoenix C.C., Phoenix, Ariz.

Par: 71 Yardage: 6,726

Last day of event: Monday, January 25, 1982

Player	Place	Score	Earnings
Lanny Wadkins	Win	65-70-63-65=263	$54,000.00
Jerry Pate	2	71-69-64-65=269	$32,400.00
Mike Reid	3	70-68-66-66=270	$20,400.00
Morris Hatalsky	T-4	67-67-68-69=271	$12,400.00
Andy Bean	T-4	70-67-69-65=271	$12,400.00
Larry Nelson	T-4	63-70-71-67=271	$12,400.00
D.A. Weibring	T-7	71-69-65-67=272	$9,675.00
Fuzzy Zoeller	T-7	76-65-65-66=272	$9,675.00
Tom Purtzer	T-9	66-69-70-68=273	$7,800.00
John Cook	T-9	70-66-67-70=273	$7,800.00
Jim Simons	T-9	67-71-69-66=273	$7,800.00
Scott Simpson	T-9	75-66-63-69=273	$7,800.00

Wickes/Andy Williams San Diego Open

Course: Torrey Pines (South), Torrey Pines (North), San Diego, Calif.

Home Course -Par: 72 Yardage: 7,021

Last day of event: Sunday, January 31, 1982

Player	Place	Score	Earnings
Johnny Miller	Win	65-67-68-70=270	$54,000.00
Jack Nicklaus	2	69-68-70-64=271	$32,400.00
Tom Weiskopf	T-3	69-67-68-69=273	$17,400.00
Tom Kite	T-3	72-65-66-70=273	$17,400.00
Curtis Strange	5	68-67-71-68=274	$12,000.00
Andy Bean	6	70-66-71-68=275	$10,800.00
Fuzzy Zoeller	T-7	65-70-70-71=276	$8,730.00
Gil Morgan	T-7	66-71-69-70=276	$8,730.00
Tom Watson	T-7	67-69-69-71=276	$8,730.00
Gary Hallberg	T-7	70-67-71-68=276	$8,730.00
Hale Irwin	T-7	70-67-74-65=276	$8,730.00

Bing Crosby Pro-Am

Courses: Pebble Beach G.L., Spyglass Hill G.C., Cypress Point C.C., Pebble Beach, Calif.

Home Course / Pebble Beach, Par: 72 Yardage: 6,815

Last day of event: Sunday, February 7, 1982

Player	Place	Score	Earnings
Jim Simons	Win	71-66-71-66=274	$54,000.00
Craig Stadler	2	71-71-64-70=276	$32,400.00
Jack Nicklaus	T-3	69-70-71-70=280	$13,530.00

Johnny Miller	T-3	71-71-71-67=280	$13,530.00
Joe Inman	T-3	73-69-69-69=280	$13,530.00
Rex Caldwell	T-3	73-67-73-67=280	$13,530.00
Mike Morley	T-3	72-76-65-67=280	$13,530.00
Gene Littler	T-8	70-71-71-69=281	$8,400.00
Dave Stockton	T-8	71-70-70-70=281	$8,400.00
Tommy Valentine	T-8	70-71-73-67=281	$8,400.00
George Burns	T-8	67-69-77-68=281	$8,400.00

Hawaiian Open

Course: Waialae C.C., Honolulu, Ha.

Par: 72 Yardage: 7,234

Last day of event: Sunday, February 14, 1982

Player	Place	Score	Earnings
Wayne Levi	Win	72-68-67-70=277	$58,500.00
Scott Simpson	2	70-69-70-69=278	$35,100.00
Chip Beck	3	72-68-71-68=279	$22,100.00
Bobby Clampett	T-4	67-72-70-71=280	$13,433.33
Ben Crenshaw	T-4	70-72-68-70=280	$13,433.34
Andy North	T-4	69-69-69-73=280	$13,433.33
Jim Booros	T-7	72-72-70-67=281	$10,133.34
Nick Faldo	T-7	73-67-73-68=281	$10,133.33
Bruce Lietzke	T-7	77-68-68-68=281	$10,133.33
Dan Halldorson	10	75-66-71-70=282	$8,775.00

Glen Campbell Los Angeles Open

Course: Riviera C.C., Pacific Palisades, Calif.

Par: 71 Yardage: 7,029

Last day of event: Sunday, February 21, 1982

Player	Place	Score	Earnings
Tom Watson	Win	69-67-68-67=271	$54,000.00
Johnny Miller	2	68-68-66-69=271	$32,400.00
Tom Weiskopf	3	67-67-68-73=275	$20,400.00
Bill Rogers	T-4	70-68-68-70=276	$13,200.00
Lennie Clements	T-4	74-68-68-66=276	$13,200.00
Tim Simpson	6	73-66-70-68=277	$10,800.00
Jim Nelford	T-7	70-70-70-68=278	$9,350.00
Vance Heafner	T-7	68-68-71-71=278	$9,350.00
Jay Haas	T-7	69-69-69-71=278	$9,350.00
Tom Kite	T-10	71-70-66-72=279	$7,500.00
Mike Morley	T-10	67-69-70-73=279	$7,500.00
Jack Ferenz	T-10	74-69-69-67=279	$7,500.00

Doral-Eastern Open

Course: Doral C.C. (Blue), Miami, Fla.

Par: 72 Yardage: 6,939

Last day of event: Sunday, February 28, 1982

Player	Place	Score	Earnings
Andy Bean	Win	68-69-72-69=278	$54,000.00
Jerry Pate	T-2	70-70-69-70=279	$22,400.00
Mike Nicolette	T-2	68-70-71-70=279	$22,400.00
Scott Hoch	T-2	69-70-71-69=279	$22,400.00
Calvin Peete	T-5	68-72-70-71=281	$10,950.00
Craig Stadler	T-5	66-69-73-73=281	$10,950.00
Curtis Strange	T-5	70-76-68-67=281	$10,950.00
Eric Batten	T-8	67-72-72-71=282	$9,000.00
Jim Dent	T-8	71-72-72-67=282	$9,000.00
Seve Ballesteros	10	69-71-75-68=283	$8,100.00

Bay Hill Classic
Course: Bay Hill Club, Orlando, Fla.
Par: 71 Yardage: 7,103
Last day of event: Sunday, March 7, 1982

Player	Place	Score	Earnings
Tom Kite	Win	69-70-70-69=278	$54,000.00
Denis Watson	T-2	69-68-69-72=278	$26,400.00
Jack Nicklaus	T-2	69-67-67-75=278	$26,400.00
Lanny Wadkins	T-4	69-69-70-71=279	$13,200.00
Craig Stadler	T-4	66-70-73-70=279	$13,200.00
Fuzzy Zoeller	T-6	67-74-72-67=280	$10,425.00
Ray Floyd	T-6	68-70-66-76=280	$10,425.00
Scott Hoch	T-8	65-71-73-72=281	$8,700.00
Tom Jenkins	T-8	69-73-70-69=281	$8,700.00
Gil Morgan	T-8	67-74-72-68=281	$8,700.00

Honda Inverarry Classic
Course: Inverrary G. & C.C. (East), Lauderhill, Fla.
Par: 72 Yardage: 7,128
Last day of event: Sunday, March 14, 1982

Player	Place	Score	Earnings
Hale Irwin	Win	65-71-67-66=269	$72,000.00
George Burns	T-2	66-67-67-70=270	$35,200.00
Tom Kite	T-2	65-67-71-67=270	$35,200.00
Bobby Clampett	4	68-70-67-66=271	$19,200.00
Calvin Peete	5	70-66-67-69=272	$16,000.00
Ray Floyd	6	68-69-69-68=274	$14,400.00
Ed Sneed	7	68-71-69-67=275	$13,400.00
Peter Oosterhuis	8	70-67-68-71=276	$12,400.00
Andy Bean	T-9	68-68-73-68=277	$11,200.00
David Graham	T-9	67-74-69-67=277	$11,200.00

Tournament Players Championship
Course: TPC at Sawgrass, Ponte Vedra Beach, Fla.
Par: 72 Yardage: 6,857
Last day of event: Sunday, March 21, 1982

Player	Place	Score	Earnings
Jerry Pate	Win	70-73-70-67=280	$90,000.00
Brad Bryant	T-2	70-69-71-72=282	$44,000.00
Scott Simpson	T-2	68-70-73-71=282	$44,000.00
Bruce Lietzke	4	69-72-69-73=283	$24,000.00
Roger Maltbie	5	69-72-73-70=284	$20,000.00
Seve Ballesteros	T-6	73-72-69-72=286	$16,187.50
Craig Stadler	T-6	71-68-75-72=286	$16,187.50
Hubert Green	T-6	73-75-70-68=286	$16,187.50
Tom Watson	T-6	70-76-68-72=286	$16,187.50
Jim Booros	T-10	73-72-71-71=287	$12,500.00
Ed Sneed	T-10	68-71-74-74=287	$12,500.00
Larry Nelson	T-10	67-72-77-71=287	$12,500.00

Sea Pines Heritage Classic
Course: Harbour Town G.L., Hilton Head, S.C.
Par: 71 Yardage: 6,657
Last day of event: Sunday, March 28, 1982

Player	Place	Score	Earnings
Tom Watson	Win	69-68-72-71=280	$54,000.00
Playoff: Beat Frank Conner with par on third extra hole			
Frank Conner	2	71-66-70-73=280	$32,400.00
D.A. Weibring	3	69-73-70-70=282	$20,400.00
Bob Shearer	T-4	69-71-71-72=283	$12,400.00
Bobby Clampett	T-4	70-71-72-70=283	$12,400.00
Doug Tewell	T-4	68-71-71-73=283	$12,400.00
Craig Stadler	T-7	69-70-71-74=284	$9,350.00
Ed Sneed	T-7	74-69-68-73=284	$9,350.00
Fred Couples	T-7	69-68-71-76=284	$9,350.00
Gil Morgan	10	72-71-72-70=285	$8,100.00

Greater Greensboro Open
Course: Forest Oaks C.C., Greensboro, N.C.
Par: 72 Yardage: 6,984
Last day of event: Monday, April 5, 1982

Player	Place	Score	Earnings
Danny Edwards	Win	66-72-72-75=285	$54,000.00
Bobby Clampett	2	69-72-72-73=286	$32,400.00
Jack Renner	3	73-72-72-70=287	$20,400.00
Woody Blackburn	4	70-70-75-73=288	$14,400.00
Bill Rogers	T-5	69-74-74-72=289	$11,400.00
Ben Crenshaw	T-5	69-73-78-69=289	$11,400.00
Doug Black	T-7	69-70-75-76=290	$9,037.50
D.A. Weibring	T-7	71-68-75-76=290	$9,037.50
Lanny Wadkins	T-7	69-71-73-77=290	$9,037.50
Denis Watson	T-7	72-65-76-77=290	$9,037.50

Masters
Course: Augusta National G.C., Augusta, Ga.
Par: 72 Yardage: 6,925
Last day of event: Sunday, April 11, 1982

Player	Place	Score	Earnings
Craig Stadler	Win	75-69-67-73=284	$64,000.00
Playoff: Beat Dan Pohl with par on first extra hole			
Dan Pohl	2	75-75-67-67=284	$39,000.00
Seve Ballesteros	T-3	73-73-68-71=285	$21,000.00
Jerry Pate	T-3	74-73-67-71=285	$21,000.00
Tom Kite	T-5	76-69-73-69=287	$13,500.00
Tom Watson	T-5	77-69-70-71=287	$13,500.00
Ray Floyd	T-7	74-72-69-74=289	$11,067.00
Curtis Strange	T-7	74-70-73-72=289	$11,067.00
Larry Nelson	T-7	79-71-70-69=289	$11,067.00
Mark Hayes	T-10	74-73-73-70=290	$8,550.00
Tom Weiskopf	T-10	75-72-68-75=290	$8,550.00
Andy Bean	T-10	75-72-73-70=290	$8,550.00
Fuzzy Zoeller	T-10	72-76-70-72=290	$8,550.00

MONY Tournament of Champions
Course: La Costa C.C., Carlsbad, Calif.
Par: 72 Yardage: 6,911
Last day of event: Sunday, April 18, 1982

Player	Place	Score	Earnings
Lanny Wadkins	Win	67-72-68-73=280	$63,000.00
David Graham	T-2	70-72-70-71=283	$26,162.50
Andy Bean	T-2	70-72-71-70=283	$26,162.50
Ron Streck	T-2	72-70-68-73=283	$26,162.50
Craig Stadler	T-2	74-72-73-64=283	$26,162.50
Wayne Levi	T-6	71-72-71-70=284	$12,840.00
Danny Edwards	T-6	73-72-71-68=284	$12,840.00
Tom Kite	T-6	72-74-65-73=284	$12,840.00
Johnny Miller	T-6	74-70-73-67=284	$12,840.00
Tom Watson	T-6	69-68-72-75=284	$12,840.00

Tallahassee Open
Course: Killearn C.C., Tallahassee, Fla.
Par: 72 Yardage: 7,124
Last day of event: Sunday, April 18, 1982

Player	Place	Score	Earnings
Bob Shearer	Win	69-69-68-66=272	$18,000.00
Denis Watson	T-2	69-68-69-67=273	$8,800.00
Hal Sutton	T-2	66-69-72-66=273	$8,800.00
Tim Simpson	4	69-68-69-68=274	$4,950.00
John Adams	T-5	68-70-70-67=275	$3,825.00
Bob Murphy	T-5	70-67-68-70=275	$3,825.00
Rik Massengale	T-5	71-67-71-66=275	$3,825.00
Mark Lye	T-5	72-69-67-67=275	$3,825.00
Bobby Wadkins	T-9	68-71-67-70=276	$2,900.00
Bob Byman	T-9	67-69-66-74=276	$2,900.00

USF&G Classic
Course: Lakewood C.C., New Orleans, La.
Par: 72 Yardage: 7,080
Last day of event: Sunday, April 25, 1982

Player	Place	Score	Earnings
Scott Hoch	Win	67-69-70=206	$54,000.00
Bob Shearer	T-2	66-71-71=208	$26,400.00
Tom Watson	T-2	71-70-67=208	$26,400.00
Steve Melnyk	4	69-72-68=209	$14,400.00
Lon Hinkle	T-5	70-69-71=210	$10,537.50
Don Pooley	T-5	72-68-70=210	$10,537.50
Vance Heafner	T-5	72-70-68=210	$10,537.50
Jodie Mudd	T-5	72-71-67=210	$10,537.50
Bob Eastwood	T-9	71-69-71=211	$7,200.00
Bruce Fleisher	T-9	71-69-71=211	$7,200.00
Gil Morgan	T-9	71-69-71=211	$7,200.00
Chip Beck	T-9	71-70-70=211	$7,200.00
Larry Ziegler	T-9	68-71-72=211	$7,200.00
Jay Haas	T-9	69-73-69=211	$7,200.00

Byron Nelson Golf Classic
Course: Preston Trail G.C., Dallas, Texas
Par: 70 Yardage: 6,993
Last day of event: Sunday, May 2, 1982

Player	Place	Score	Earnings
Bob Gilder	Win	67-65-67-67=266	$63,000.00
Curtis Strange	2	65-72-65-69=271	$37,800.00
Dan Halldorson	T-3	68-68-69-68=273	$18,200.00
David Graham	T-3	68-69-66-70=273	$18,200.00
Tom Watson	T-3	71-68-67-67=273	$18,200.00
Bruce Lietzke	T-6	69-69-70-66=274	$11,331.25
Phil Hancock	T-6	70-68-66-70=274	$11,331.25
George Archer	T-6	65-68-71-70=274	$11,331.25
Bob Shearer	T-6	68-68-71-67=274	$11,331.25
Bobby Wadkins	T-10	68-69-70-69=276	$7,758.33
Jack Newton	T-10	71-69-67-69=276	$7,758.33
Jim Colbert	T-10	68-72-66-70=276	$7,758.33
Lon Hinkle	T-10	69-68-72-67=276	$7,758.34
Pat Lindsey	T-10	70-72-69-65=276	$7,758.34
Scott Hoch	T-10	72-68-68-68=276	$7,758.33

Michelob Houston Open
Course: Woodlands C.C., The Woodlands, Texas
Par: 71 Yardage: 7,031
Last day of event: Sunday, May 9, 1982

Player	Place	Score	Earnings
Ed Sneed	Win	64-70-71-70=275	$63,000.00
Bob Shearer	2	69-67-64-75=275	$37,800.00
Danny Edwards	3	71-68-69-68=276	$23,800.00
George Burns	4	73-68-69-67=277	$16,800.00
Tommy Valentine	T-5	68-71-72-67=278	$13,300.00
Tom Kite	T-5	70-69-73-66=278	$13,300.00
Peter Oosterhuis	T-7	68-68-72-71=279	$11,287.50
Scott Hoch	T-7	65-73-69-72=279	$11,287.50
Jay Haas	T-9	72-69-69-70=280	$9,450.00
Jim Dent	T-9	73-67-71-69=280	$9,450.00
Ron Streck	T-9	70-69-67-74=280	$9,450.00

Colonial National Invitational
Course: Colonial C.C., Fort Worth, Texas
Par: 70 Yardage: 7,096
Last day of event: Sunday, May 16, 1982

Player	Place	Score	Earnings
Jack Nicklaus	Win	66-70-70-67=273	$63,000.00
Andy North	2	68-69-67-72=276	$37,800.00
Jerry Pate	3	69-68-69-71=277	$23,800.00
Tom Kite	4	68-68-74-68=278	$16,800.00
Joe Inman	T-5	68-73-70-69=280	$12,293.75
Tom Purtzer	T-5	69-74-67-70=280	$12,293.75
Bob Eastwood	T-5	74-71-70-65=280	$12,293.75
Lennie Clements	T-5	66-69-75-70=280	$12,293.75
Lee Trevino	T-9	72-74-67-68=281	$9,800.00
Danny Edwards	T-9	72-68-66-75=281	$9,800.00

Georgia-Pacific Atlanta Golf Classic
Course: Atlanta C.C., Atlanta, Ga.
Par: 72 Yardage: 7,007
Last day of event: Sunday, May 23, 1982

Player	Place	Score	Earnings
Keith Fergus	Win	66-72-66-69=273	$54,000.00
Playoff: Beat Ray Floyd with birdie on first extra hole			
Ray Floyd	2	72-69-64-68=273	$32,400.00
Wayne Levi	3	69-68-69-68=274	$20,400.00
Larry Nelson	4	66-67-68-74=275	$14,400.00
Gibby Gilbert	T-5	69-69-69-69=276	$10,170.00
Peter Jacobsen	T-5	68-69-67-72=276	$10,170.00
David Edwards	T-5	72-69-68-67=276	$10,170.00
Steve Melnyk	T-5	70-73-66-67=276	$10,170.00
Scott Hoch	T-5	67-67-74-68=276	$10,170.00
Joe Inman	10	67-72-71-67=277	$8,100.00

Memorial Tournament
Course: Muirfield Village G.C., Dubin, Ohio
Par: 72 Yardage: 7,116
Last day of event: Sunday, May 30, 1982

Player	Place	Score	Earnings
Ray Floyd	Win	74-69-67-71=281	$63,000.00
Gil Morgan	T-2	72-70-67-74=283	$23,100.00
Peter Jacobsen	T-2	74-69-68-72=283	$23,100.00
Wayne Levi	T-2	74-70-69-70=283	$23,100.00
Roger Maltbie	T-2	68-66-75-74=283	$23,100.00
Dan Pohl	T-6	70-72-70-72=284	$12,162.50
Bruce Lietzke	T-6	73-70-71-70=284	$12,162.50
Jay Haas	T-8	70-72-70-73=285	$10,150.00
Scott Simpson	T-8	71-69-71-74=285	$10,150.00
Tom Purtzer	T-8	74-69-68-74=285	$10,150.00

Kemper Open

Course: Congressional C.C., Bethesda, Md.
Par: 72 Yardage: 7,173
Last day of event: Sunday, June 6, 1982

Player	Place	Score	Earnings
Craig Stadler	Win	72-67-67-69=275	$72,000.00
Seve Ballesteros	2	72-69-72-69=282	$43,200.00
Gil Morgan	T-3	68-72-70-73=283	$23,200.00
Jack Nicklaus	T-3	72-65-72-74=283	$23,200.00
George Burns	5	75-66-73-70=284	$16,000.00
Steve Melnyk	6	72-71-71-72=286	$14,400.00
Bob Eastwood	T-7	71-72-72-72=287	$12,050.00
Calvin Peete	T-7	69-74-73-71=287	$12,050.00
Dan Halldorson	T-7	74-69-69-75=287	$12,050.00
Jim Nelford	T-7	77-69-73-68=287	$12,050.00

Danny Thomas Memphis Classic

Course: Colonial C.C. (South), Cordova, Tenn.
Par: 72 Yardage: 7,282
Last day of event: Sunday, June 13, 1982

Player	Place	Score	Earnings
Ray Floyd	Win	67-68-67-69=271	$72,000.00
Mike Holland	2	72-67-68-70=277	$43,200.00
Curtis Strange	3	72-70-67-69=278	$27,200.00
Mark McNulty	4	74-67-67-71=279	$19,200.00
Mark Lye	5	67-71-71-71=280	$16,000.00
Scott Hoch	6	73-71-68-69=281	$14,400.00
J.C. Snead	T-7	70-72-68-72=282	$12,900.00
Tom Purtzer	T-7	72-67-69-74=282	$12,900.00
Larry Nelson	T-9	72-69-72-70=283	$10,400.00
Bob Murphy	T-9	70-74-69-70=283	$10,400.00
Hal Sutton	T-9	72-67-70-74=283	$10,400.00
Payne Stewart	T-9	75-72-67-69=283	$10,400.00

U.S. Open

Courses: Pebble Beach G.L. , Pebble Beach, Calif.
Par: 72 Yardage: 6,815
Last day of event: Sunday, June 20, 1982

Player	Place	Score	Earnings
Tom Watson	Win	72-72-68-70=282	$60,000.00
Jack Nicklaus	2	74-70-71-69=284	$34,506.00
Bobby Clampett	T-3	71-73-72-70=286	$14,967.00
Bill Rogers	T-3	70-73-69-74=286	$14,967.00
Dan Pohl	T-3	72-74-70-70=286	$14,967.00
David Graham	T-6	73-72-69-73=287	$8,011.00
Jay Haas	T-6	75-74-70-68=287	$8,011.00
Lanny Wadkins	T-6	73-76-67-71=287	$8,011.00
Gary Koch	T-6	78-73-69-67=287	$8,011.00
Calvin Peete	T-10	71-72-72-73=288	$6,332.00
Bruce Devlin	T-10	70-69-75-74=288	$6,332.00

Manufacturers Hanover Westchester Classic

Course: Westchester C.C., Harrison, N.Y.
Par: 70 Yardage: 6,329
Last day of event: Sunday, June 27, 1982

Player	Place	Score	Earnings
Bob Gilder	Win	64-63-65-69=261	$72,000.00
Tom Kite	T-2	66-64-68-68=266	$35,200.00
Peter Jacobsen	T-2	68-62-70-66=266	$35,200.00
Don Pooley	T-4	69-66-68-67=270	$17,600.00
Wayne Levi	T-4	70-65-67-68=270	$17,600.00
Jerry Pate	6	72-68-68-64=272	$14,400.00
J.C. Snead	T-7	67-70-69-67=273	$12,900.00
Jim Colbert	T-7	69-65-68-71=273	$12,900.00
Bill Rogers	T-9	69-69-67-69=274	$11,200.00
D.A. Weibring	T-9	67-68-71-68=274	$11,200.00

Western Open

Course: Butler National G.C., Oak Brook, Ill.
Par: 72 Yardage: 7,097
Last day of event: Sunday, July 4, 1982

Player	Place	Score	Earnings
Tom Weiskopf	Win	69-67-70-70=276	$63,000.00
Larry Nelson	2	66-72-68-71=277	$37,800.00
Bob Gilder	3	64-71-74-69=278	$23,800.00
Bill Rogers	T-4	69-72-69-70=280	$15,400.00
Jim Thorpe	T-4	67-75-68-70=280	$15,400.00
Curtis Strange	6	69-72-72-69=282	$12,600.00
Mark Pfeil	7	70-72-69-72=283	$11,725.00
Tom Jenkins	T-8	69-72-73-70=284	$9,800.00
George Burns	T-8	68-74-71-71=284	$9,800.00
Doug Tewell	T-8	70-76-68-70=284	$9,800.00
Lanny Wadkins	T-8	76-72-68-68=284	$9,800.00

Greater Milwaukee Open

Course: Tuckaway C.C., Franklin, Wis.
Par: 72 Yardage: 7,030
Last day of event: Sunday, July 11, 1982

Player	Place	Score	Earnings
Calvin Peete	Win	70-66-69-69=274	$45,000.00
Victor Regalado	2	71-66-68-71=276	$27,000.00
Terry Diehl	3	65-69-72-71=277	$17,000.00
Jim Colbert	4	67-69-70-72=278	$12,000.00
Morris Hatalsky	T-5	68-70-70-71=279	$9,125.00
Larry Ziegler	T-5	72-69-68-70=279	$9,125.00
Richard Zokol	T-5	65-69-70-75=279	$9,125.00
David Edwards	T-8	65-72-71-72=280	$7,500.00
Wayne Levi	T-8	68-68-68-76=280	$7,500.00
Dan Pohl	T-10	70-71-71-69=281	$6,000.00
Howard Twitty	T-10	71-71-68-71=281	$6,000.00
Dave Stockton	T-10	70-68-70-73=281	$6,000.00
Andy Bean	T-10	68-70-69-74=281	$6,000.00

Miller High-Life **Quad Cities Open**

Course: Oakwood C.C., Coal Valley, Ill.
Par: 70 Yardage: 6,602
Last day of event: Sunday, July 18, 1982

Player	Place	Score	Earnings
Payne Stewart	Win	66-71-68-63=268	$36,000.00
Brad Bryant	T-2	69-67-68-66=270	$17,600.00
Pat McGowan	T-2	71-67-65-67=270	$17,600.00
Jim Thorpe	4	72-67-66-66=271	$9,600.00
Allen Miller	T-5	68-70-71-64=273	$7,300.00
Jeff Mitchell	T-5	69-63-71-70=273	$7,300.00
Barry Jaeckel	T-5	72-63-71-67=273	$7,300.00
Dave Eichelberger	T-8	68-69-68-69=274	$4,825.00
Rod Curl	T-8	69-69-68-68=274	$4,825.00
Vance Heafner	T-8	69-66-70-69=274	$4,825.00
Gary McCord	T-8	70-67-70-67=274	$4,825.00
Lyn Lott	T-8	68-66-71-69=274	$4,825.00
Don Pooley	T-8	72-67-67-68=274	$4,825.00

Bob Eastwood	T-8	72-68-66-68=274	$4,825.00
Jim Dent	T-8	74-66-67-67=274	$4,825.00

British Open

Course: Royal Troon G.C., Troon, Ayrshire, Scotland
Par: 72 Yardage: 7,067
Last day of event: Sunday, July 18, 1982

Player	Place	Score	Earnings
Tom Watson	Win	69-71-74-70=284	$54,400.00
Nick Price	T-2	69-69-74-73=285	$32,810.00
Peter Oosterhuis	T-2	74-67-74-70=285	$32,810.00
Massy Kuramoto	T-4	71-73-71-71=286	$18,700.00
Nick Faldo	T-4	73-73-71-69=286	$18,700.00
Des Smyth	T-4	70-69-74-73=286	$18,700.00
Tom Purtzer	T-4	76-66-75-69=286	$18,700.00
Fuzzy Zoeller	T-8	73-71-73-70=287	$14,875.00
Sandy Lyle	T-8	74-66-73-74=287	$14,875.00
Jack Nicklaus	T-10	77-70-72-69=288	$12,495.00
Bobby Clampett	T-10	67-66-78-77=288	$12,495.00

Anheuser-Busch Golf Classic

Course: Kingsmill G.C., Williamsburg, Va.
Par: 71 Yardage: 6,776
Last day of event: Sunday, July 25, 1982

Player	Place	Score	Earnings
Calvin Peete	Win	66-68-69=203	$63,000.00
Bruce Lietzke	2	65-74-66=205	$37,800.00
Hal Sutton	T-3	68-69-69=206	$20,300.00
Rik Massengale	T-3	68-68-70=206	$20,300.00
Bill Rogers	5	66-70-71=207	$14,000.00
David Edwards	T-6	68-70-70=208	$11,331.25
Victor Regalado	T-6	70-71-67=208	$11,331.00
Peter Oosterhuis	T-6	71-69-68=208	$11,331.00
Doug Tewell	T-6	72-69-67=208	$11,331.00
Pat McGowan	T-10	69-71-69=209	$9,100.00
Ed Dougherty	T-10	72-68-69=209	$9,100.00

Canadian Open

Course: Glen Abbey G.C., Oakville, Ontario, Canada
Par: 71 Yardage: 7,060
Last day of event: Sunday, August 1, 1982

Player	Place	Score	Earnings
Bruce Lietzke	Win	68-68-68-73=277	$76,500.00
Hal Sutton	2	68-68-72-71=279	$45,900.00
Charles Coody	T-3	71-70-72-67=280	$24,650.00
Tommy Valentine	T-3	70-68-68-74=280	$24,650.00
Andy Bean	T-5	70-71-69-71=281	$13,919.16
Johnny Miller	T-5	71-71-70-69=281	$13,919.17
Vance Heafner	T-5	71-72-67-71=281	$13,919.16
Nick Faldo	T-5	68-70-73-70=281	$13,919.17
Larry Nelson	T-5	73-71-67-70=281	$13,919.17
Lou Graham	T-5	68-70-75-68=281	$13,919.17

PGA Championship

Course: Southern Hills C.C., Tulsa, Okla.
Par: 70 Yardage: 6,862
Last day of event: Sunday, August 8, 1982

Player	Place	Score	Earnings
Ray Floyd	Win	63-69-68-72=272	$65,000.00

Lanny Wadkins	2	71-68-69-67=275	$45,000.00
Calvin Peete	T-3	69-70-68-69=276	$27,500.00
Fred Couples	T-3	67-71-72-66=276	$27,500.00
Greg Norman	T-5	66-69-70-72=277	$16,000.00
Jay Haas	T-5	71-66-68-72=277	$16,000.00
Jim Simons	T-5	68-67-73-69=277	$16,000.00
Bob Gilder	8	66-68-72-72=278	$11,000.00
Lon Hinkle	T-9	70-68-71-71=280	$7,918.75
Jerry Pate	T-9	72-69-70-69=280	$7,918.75
Tom Watson	T-9	72-69-71-68=280	$7,918.75
Tom Kite	T-9	73-70-70-67=280	$7,918.75

Sammy Davis, Jr. - Greater Hartford Open

Course: Wethersfield C.C., Wethersfield, Conn.
Par: 71 Yardage: 6,568
Last day of event: Sunday, August 15, 1982

Player	Place	Score	Earnings
Tim Norris	Win	63-64-66-66=259	$54,000.00
Hubert Green	T-2	66-66-66-67=265	$26,400.00
Ray Floyd	T-2	65-65-67-68=265	$26,400.00
Peter Jacobsen	T-4	65-67-67-67=266	$11,310.00
Mark McNulty	T-4	66-65-68-67=266	$11,310.00
D.A. Weibring	T-4	66-65-68-67=266	$11,310.00
Gavin Levenson	T-4	66-64-69-67=266	$11,310.00
Curtis Strange	T-4	68-66-69-63=266	$11,310.00
David Edwards	T-9	68-64-67-68=267	$8,400.00
Dana Quigley	T-9	70-69-61-67=267	$8,400.00

Buick Open

Course: Warwick Hills C.C., Grand Blanc, Mich.
Par: 72 Yardage: 7,014
Last day of event: Sunday, August 22, 1982

Player	Place	Score	Earnings
Lanny Wadkins	Win	66-71-71-65=273	$63,000.00
Tom Kite	2	71-67-69-67=274	$37,800.00
Curtis Strange	T-3	66-69-69-72=276	$18,200.00
Payne Stewart	T-3	68-69-67-72=276	$18,200.00
George Archer	T-3	74-67-69-66=276	$18,200.00
Hale Irwin	T-6	70-68-69-71=278	$12,162.50
Jack Renner	T-6	73-68-69-68=278	$12,162.50
John Cook	T-8	65-72-71-71=279	$10,150.00
Bob Eastwood	T-8	67-71-69-72=279	$10,150.00
Peter Jacobsen	T-8	72-67-68-72=279	$10,150.00

World Series of Golf

Course: Firestone C.C. (South), Akron, Ohio
Par: 70 Yardage: 7,149
Last day of event: Sunday, August 29, 1982

Player	Place	Score	Earnings
Craig Stadler	Win	70-68-75-65=278	$100,000.00
Playoff: Beat Ray Floyd with par on fourth extra hole			
Ray Floyd	2	69-71-68-70=278	$55,000.00
Isao Aoki	3	77-66-70-67=280	$34,500.00
Curtis Strange	T-4	71-71-72-68=282	$19,600.00
Bob Shearer	T-4	69-69-73-71=282	$19,600.00
Lanny Wadkins	T-6	70-72-72-71=285	$15,000.00
Tom Kite	T-6	73-68-73-71=285	$15,000.00
Jack Nicklaus	T-6	71-75-72-67=285	$15,000.00
Bill Rogers	9	76-72-71-67=286	$13,000.00
Tom Watson	T-10	75-74-69-69=287	$11,500.00
Jerry Pate	T-10	76-72-70-69=287	$11,500.00

B.C. Open

Course: En-Joie G.C., Endicott, N.Y.
Par: 71 Yardage: 6,966
Last day of event: Sunday, September 5, 1982

Player	Place	Score	Earnings
Calvin Peete	Win	69-63-64-69=265	$49,500.00
Jerry Pate	2	67-66-66-73=272	$29,700.00
Fuzzy Zoeller	3	68-62-67-76=273	$18,700.00
Craig Stadler	4	71-68-69-66=274	$13,200.00
Michael Brannan	T-5	68-70-70-67=275	$10,450.00
Tom Kite	T-5	67-67-68-73=275	$10,450.00
Antonio Cerda	T-7	70-72-67-67=276	$8,850.00
Doug Tewell	T-7	69-67-67-73=276	$8,850.00
Gary McCord	T-9	70-70-70-67=277	$7,700.00
Don Pooley	T-9	68-71-69-69=277	$7,700.00

Bank of Boston Classic

Course: Pleasant Valley C.C., Sutton, Mass.
Par: 71 Yardage: 7,110
Last day of event: Sunday, September 12, 1982

Player	Place	Score	Earnings
Bob Gilder	Win	67-67-70-67=271	$54,000.00
Fuzzy Zoeller	2	69-69-68-67=273	$32,400.00
Mike McCullough	T-3	72-64-66-72=274	$17,400.00
Gil Morgan	T-3	72-66-68-68=274	$17,400.00
David Graham	T-5	69-69-68-69=275	$10,170.00
Ed Sneed	T-5	66-72-68-69=275	$10,170.00
Brad Bryant	T-5	68-72-64-71=275	$10,170.00
Peter Jacobsen	T-5	70-67-66-72=275	$10,170.00
John Cook	T-5	73-67-66-69=275	$10,170.00
Tom Jenkins	T-10	69-70-68-69=276	$7,800.00
George Archer	T-10	66-68-69-73=276	$7,800.00

Hall of Fame

Course: Pinehurst C.C. (No 2), Pinehurst, N.C.
Par: 71 Yardage: 7,020
Last day of event: Sunday, September 19, 1982

Player	Place	Score	Earnings
Jay Haas	Win	70-70-70-66=276	$45,000.00
Playoff: Beat John Adams with par on second extra hole			
John Adams	2	67-69-71-69=276	$27,000.00
Curtis Strange	3	69-70-69-69=277	$17,000.00
Bobby Clampett	T-4	69-71-70-69=279	$10,333.33
Allen Miller	T-4	69-72-71-67=279	$10,333.33
Morris Hatalsky	T-4	70-68-73-68=279	$10,333.34
Mike Reid	T-7	70-69-70-71=280	$8,062.50
D.A. Weibring	T-7	73-71-66-70=280	$8,062.50
Roger Maltbie	T-9	71-72-71-67=281	$7,000.00
Jack Renner	T-9	72-64-71-74=281	$7,000.00

Southern Open

Course: Green Island C.C., Columbus, Ga.
Par: 70 Yardage: 6,791
Last day of event: Sunday, September 26, 1982

Player	Place	Score	Earnings
Bobby Clampett	Win	65-69-68-64=266	$45,000.00
Hale Irwin	2	67-72-68-61=268	$27,000.00
George Burns	3	67-68-66-68=269	$17,000.00
Hal Sutton	4	69-68-67-66=270	$12,000.00
Andy Bean	5	69-67-69-66=271	$10,000.00

Gary Hallberg	T-6	69-68-68-67=272	$8,687.50
Jim Thorpe	T-6	70-67-69-66=272	$8,687.50
Vance Heafner	T-8	69-70-66-68=273	$7,500.00
Larry Rinker	T-8	67-72-66-68=273	$7,500.00
John Fought	T-10	67-66-70-71=274	$6,500.00
John Mahaffey	T-10	71-71-66-66=274	$6,500.00

Texas Open

Course: Oak Hill C.C., San Antonio, Texas
Par: 70 Yardage: 6,576
Last day of event: Sunday, October 3, 1982

Player	Place	Score	Earnings
Jay Haas	Win	63-67-67-65=262	$45,000.00
Curtis Strange	2	65-66-66-68=265	$27,000.00
Keith Fergus	3	65-66-69-67=267	$17,000.00
Larry Ziegler	4	66-68-67-68=269	$12,000.00
D.A. Weibring	T-5	67-64-69-70=270	$9,500.00
Leonard Thompson	T-5	68-67-64-71=270	$9,500.00
Peter Oosterhuis	T-7	68-69-67-68=272	$6,767.86
Bill Calfee	T-7	67-68-67-70=272	$6,767.85
Steve Veriato	T-7	68-70-70-64=272	$6,767.86
Gary McCord	T-7	70-65-71-66=272	$6,767.86
David Graham	T-7	71-68-65-68=272	$6,767.85
Tim Simpson	T-7	71-69-69-63=272	$6,767.86
Tom Kite	T-7	74-65-68-65=272	$6,767.86

LaJet Classic

Course: Fairway Oaks C.C., Abilene, Texas
Par: 72 Yardage: 7,166
Last day of event: Sunday, October 10, 1982

Player	Place	Score	Earnings
Wayne Levi	Win	64-71-68-68=271	$63,000.00
Thomas Gray	2	73-71-66-67=277	$37,800.00
Bobby Cole	T-3	67-71-69-71=278	$20,300.00
Johnny Miller	T-3	68-74-69-67=278	$20,300.00
Gary Koch	5	67-71-70-71=279	$14,000.00
Bruce Devlin	6	67-70-72-71=280	$12,600.00
Steven Liebler	T-7	68-71-72-70=281	$11,287.50
Hal Sutton	T-7	71-72-71-67=281	$11,287.50
Ed Fiori	T-9	68-73-69-72=282	$9,800.00
Gil Morgan	T-9	71-73-67-71=282	$9,800.00

Pensacola Open

Course: Perdido Bay C.C., Pensacola, Fla.
Par: 71 Yardage: 7,093
Last day of event: Sunday, October 24, 1982

Player	Place	Score	Earnings
Calvin Peete	Win	65-66-72-65=268	$36,000.00
Dan Halldorson	T-2	69-73-66-67=275	$17,600.00
Hal Sutton	T-2	66-67-68-74=275	$17,600.00
Tom Watson	T-4	69-67-70-70=276	$7,540.00
George Burns	T-4	66-68-70-72=276	$7,540.00
Brad Bryant	T-4	64-73-71-68=276	$7,540.00
Mike Sullivan	T-4	68-69-66-73=276	$7,540.00
John Fought	T-4	68-67-75-66=276	$7,540.00
Pat Lindsey	T-9	69-69-70-69=277	$4,800.00
Mark McCumber	T-9	71-69-69-68=277	$4,800.00
Larry Mize	T-9	66-68-71-72=277	$4,800.00
J.C. Snead	T-9	68-68-72-69=277	$4,800.00
Jerry Pate	T-9	71-68-66-72=277	$4,800.00
Steven Liebler	T-9	64-66-74-73=277	$4,800.00

Walt Disney World Golf Classic

Course: Walt Disney (Magnolia, Palm), Lake Buena Vista C.C., Lake Buena Vista, Fla.

Home course / Magnolia, Par: 72 Yardage: 7,190

Last day of event: Sunday, October 31, 1982

Player	Place	Score	Earnings
Hal Sutton	Win	71-63-68-67=269	$72,000.00
Bill Britton	2	69-67-69-64=269	$43,200.00
Jay Haas	3	66-66-65-73=270	$27,200.00
Don Pooley	4	71-66-68-66=271	$19,200.00
Howard Twitty	T-5	67-66-70-70=273	$15,200.00
Larry Nelson	T-5	71-64-67-71=273	$15,200.00
Wayne Levi	T-7	70-67-70-67=274	$12,050.00
Pat Lindsey	T-7	70-67-70-67=274	$12,050.00
Mark Lye	T-7	72-67-65-70=274	$12,050.00
Bob Gilder	T-7	73-69-64-68=274	$12,050.00

1983

Seve Ballesteros scored a four-shot victory at the Masters. Larry Nelson shot 65-67 over the weekend to surge from 25th place after 36 holes of the U.S. Open at Oakmont and beat Tom Watson by a stroke. Watson bounced back at the British Open, winning it for the fifth time. Watson's one-shot victory over Andy Bean and Hale Irwin at Royal Birkdale was his last victory in a major. Hal Sutton collected the first six-figure paycheck awarded at a major, earning $100,000 for his one-shot victory over Jack Nicklaus in the PGA Championship at Riviera. An Australian named Greg Norman joined the PGA Tour, which had put its all-exempt qualifying system into place in 1983. On July 24, Jack Newton, the 1979 Australian Open winner and runner-up in the 1975 British Open and 1980 Masters, lost his right arm and right eye after walking into a spinning airplane propeller at an airport in New South Wales.

Joe Garagiola Tucson Open

Course: Randolph Park Municipal, Tucson, Ariz.

Par: 70 Yardage: 6,860

Last day of event: Sunday, January 9, 1983

Player	Place	Score	Earnings
Gil Morgan	Win	65-71-68-67=271	$54,000.00
Playoff: Beat Curtis Strange and Lanny Wadkins with birdie on second extra hole			
Lanny Wadkins	T-2	68-67-68-68=271	$26,400.00
Curtis Strange	T-2	72-67-67-65=271	$26,400.00
Andy Bean	T-4	69-69-68-66=272	$11,812.50
Calvin Peete	T-4	68-67-66-71=272	$11,812.50
Fuzzy Zoeller	T-4	71-65-68-68=272	$11,812.50
Fred Couples	T-4	66-73-67-66=272	$11,812.50
Scott Hoch	8	67-63-72-71=273	$9,300.00
Payne Stewart	T-9	69-68-69-68=274	$8,100.00
Keith Fergus	T-9	68-67-70-69=274	$8,100.00
Johnny Miller	T-9	66-69-67-72=274	$8,100.00

Glen Campbell Los Angeles Open

Course: Rancho Municipal G.C., Los Angeles, Calif.

Par: 71 Yardage: 6,827

Last day of event: Sunday, January 16, 1983

Player	Place	Score	Earnings
Gil Morgan	Win	71-68-63-68=270	$54,000.00
Lanny Wadkins	T-2	68-67-67-70=272	$22,400.00
Mark McCumber	T-2	69-68-65-70=272	$22,400.00
Gibby Gilbert	T-2	65-66-72-69=272	$22,400.00
George Archer	5	72-70-61-70=273	$12,000.00
Tom Watson	T-6	67-68-69-70=274	$9,712.50
Andy North	T-6	70-67-68-69=274	$9,712.50
Fuzzy Zoeller	T-6	64-70-69-71=274	$9,712.50
Joe Inman	T-6	71-69-67-67=274	$9,712.50

Player	Place	Score	Earnings
J.C. Snead	T-10	68-71-66-70=275	$7,800.00
Arnold Palmer	T-10	66-69-68-72=275	$7,800.00

Bob Hope Chrysler Classic

Course: La Quinta C.C.—Home course

Indian Wells C.C., Tamarisk C.C., Bermuda Dunes C.C., La Quinta, Calif.

Par: 72 Yardage: 6,911

Last day of event: Sunday, January 23, 1983

Player	Place	Score	Earnings
Keith Fergus	Win	71-69-65-65-65=335	$67,500.00
Playoff: Beat Rex Caldwell with par on first extra hole			
Rex Caldwell	2	67-69-69-65-65=335	$40,500.00
Craig Stadler	3	63-66-72-69-69=339	$25,500.00
Chip Beck	T-4	70-66-67-69-68=340	$16,500.00
John Fought	T-4	69-68-62-70-71=340	$16,500.00
Doug Tewell	6	68-71-69-66-68=342	$13,500.00
T.C. Chen	T-7	70-69-69-71-64=343	$11,687.50
Ray Floyd	T-7	68-67-67-68-73=343	$11,687.50
Bob Gilder	T-7	74-67-65-68-69=343	$11,687.50
Hal Sutton	T-10	66-69-69-71-69=344	$9,750.00
Mark Lye	T-10	67-69-72-68-68=344	$9,750.00

Phoenix Open

Course: Phoenix C.C., Phoenix, Ariz.

Par: 71 Yardage: 6,726

Last day of event: Sunday, January 30, 1983

Player	Place	Score	Earnings
Bob Gilder	Win	68-68-66-69=271	$63,000.00
Playoff: Beat Rex Caldwell, Johnny Miller and Mark O'Meara with par on eighth extra hole			
Rex Caldwell	T-2	69-65-67-70=271	$26,133.33
Johnny Miller	T-2	67-65-71-68=271	$26,133.34
Mark O'Meara	T-2	71-66-68-66=271	$26,133.33
Calvin Peete	T-5	67-69-69-67=272	$11,865.00
Scott Hoch	T-5	67-70-67-68=272	$11,865.00
Ed Sneed	T-5	65-71-70-66=272	$11,865.00
Tim Simpson	T-5	68-66-71-67=272	$11,865.00
Hal Sutton	T-5	65-68-72-67=272	$11,865.00
Lanny Wadkins	T-10	68-68-67-70=273	$8,400.00
Fuzzy Zoeller	T-10	71-69-69-64=273	$8,400.00
Dan Pohl	T-10	68-67-72-66=273	$8,400.00
Jack Renner	T-10	65-66-74-68=273	$8,400.00

Bing Crosby Pro-Am

Courses: Pebble Beach G.L., Spyglass Hill G.C., Cypress Point C.C., Pebble Beach, Calif.

Home Course / Pebble Beach, Par: 72 Yardage: 6,815

Last day of event: Sunday, February 6, 1983

Player	Place	Score	Earnings
Tom Kite	Win	69-72-62-73=276	$58,500.00
Calvin Peete	T-2	68-70-70-70=278	$28,600.00
Rex Caldwell	T-2	69-70-66-73=278	$28,600.00
Danny Edwards	T-4	70-69-69-71=279	$14,300.00
Bob Gilder	T-4	72-69-66-72=279	$14,300.00
Jack Nicklaus	6	71-71-66-72=280	$11,700.00
Tom Watson	T-7	67-73-72-69=281	$10,487.50
Ken Green	T-7	66-68-71-76=281	$10,487.50
Mike McCullough	T-9	69-72-70-71=282	$8,450.00
Ben Crenshaw	T-9	70-72-68-72=282	$8,450.00
David Graham	T-9	72-70-70-70=282	$8,450.00
Gil Morgan	T-9	67-73-71-71=282	$8,450.00

Hawaiian Open

Course: Waialae C.C., Honolulu, Ha.
Par: 72 Yardage: 7,234
Last day of event: Sunday, February 13, 1983

Player	Place	Score	Earnings
Isao Aoki	Win	66-70-65-67=268	$58,500.00
Jack Renner	2	69-68-66-66=269	$35,100.00
Ben Crenshaw	3	68-68-69-66=271	$22,100.00
Peter Jacobsen	T-4	69-66-67-70=272	$12,800.00
Ed Fiori	T-4	68-67-66-71=272	$12,800.00
Andy Bean	T-4	70-64-71-67=272	$12,800.00
Hale Irwin	T-4	73-67-67-65=272	$12,800.00
Dave Eichelberger	T-8	69-69-69-66=273	$9,750.00
Don Pooley	T-8	72-68-65-68=273	$9,750.00
Dan Pohl	T-10	66-70-69-69=274	$8,125.00
Leonard Thompson	T-10	67-68-70-69=274	$8,125.00
J.C. Snead	T-10	74-67-68-65=274	$8,125.00

Isuzu/Andy Williams San Diego Open

Course: Torrey Pines (South), Torrey Pines (North), San Diego, Calif.
Home Course -Par: 72 Yardage: 7,021
Last day of event: Sunday, February 20, 1983

Player	Place	Score	Earnings
Gary Hallberg	Win	69-67-69-66=271	$54,000.00
Tom Kite	2	68-65-68-71=272	$32,400.00
Ben Crenshaw	T-3	66-70-70-68=274	$17,400.00
John Cook	T-3	71-65-71-67=274	$17,400.00
Ray Floyd	T-5	71-70-70-64=275	$11,400.00
Tom Watson	T-5	72-66-69-68=275	$11,400.00
Scott Simpson	7	66-73-70-67=276	$10,050.00
Jim Booros	T-8	71-67-70-69=277	$9,000.00
Ron Streck	T-8	70-68-73-66=277	$9,000.00
Craig Stadler	T-10	70-71-70-67=278	$6,650.00
Mark Lye	T-10	71-70-67-70=278	$6,650.00
Barry Jaeckel	T-10	67-71-72-68=278	$6,650.00
Lon Hinkle	T-10	68-69-69-72=278	$6,650.00
Don Pooley	T-10	72-65-70-71=278	$6,650.00
Gil Morgan	T-10	71-66-68-73=278	$6,650.00

Doral-Eastern Open

Course: Doral C.C. (Blue), Miami, Fla.
Par: 72 Yardage: 6,939
Last day of event: Sunday, February 27, 1983

Player	Place	Score	Earnings
Gary Koch	Win	69-67-65-70=271	$54,000.00
Ed Fiori	2	65-73-67-71=276	$32,400.00
George Burns	3	69-67-70-71=277	$20,400.00
Ray Floyd	T-4	71-68-69-70=278	$13,200.00
Tom Kite	T-4	68-68-72-70=278	$13,200.00
Tom Purtzer	T-6	69-68-70-72=279	$10,425.00
Massy Kuramoto	T-6	71-68-72-68=279	$10,425.00
Jack Nicklaus	T-8	70-70-69-71=280	$9,000.00
Tom Weiskopf	T-8	71-67-70-72=280	$9,000.00
Ed Sneed	10	70-68-72-71=281	$8,100.00

Honda Inverarry Classic

Course: Inverrary G. & C.C. (East), Lauderhill, Fla.
Par: 72 Yardage: 7,128
Last day of event: Sunday, March 6, 1983

Player	Place	Score	Earnings
Johnny Miller	Win	68-73-68-69=278	$72,000.00

Jack Nicklaus	2	72-72-70-66=280	$43,200.00
Fred Couples	T-3	70-70-70-71=281	$20,800.00
Mike Sullivan	T-3	68-72-71-70=281	$20,800.00
Mike Donald	T-3	70-68-72-71=281	$20,800.00
Hal Sutton	T-6	72-71-69-70=282	$12,950.00
Tom Kite	T-6	71-73-69-69=282	$12,950.00
Wayne Levi	T-6	71-67-70-74=282	$12,950.00
Ray Floyd	T-6	67-67-78-70=282	$12,950.00
Payne Stewart	T-10	65-72-73-73=283	$8,044.45
David Edwards	T-10	69-69-72-73=283	$8,044.44
Mark Hayes	T-10	69-70-73-71=283	$8,044.44
Jay Haas	T-10	69-71-73-70=283	$8,044.45
John Adams	T-10	72-71-73-67=283	$8,044.44
Dan Forsman	T-10	69-71-69-74=283	$8,044.45
Mike McCullough	T-10	69-70-74-70=283	$8,044.45
Allen Miller	T-10	69-73-74-67=283	$8,044.44
Gary Koch	T-10	68-71-68-76=283	$8,044.44

Bay Hill Classic

Course: Bay Hill Club, Orlando, Fla.
Par: 71 Yardage: 7,103
Last day of event: Sunday, March 13, 1983

Player	Place	Score	Earnings
Mike Nicolette	Win	66-72-71-74=283	$63,000.00
Playoff: Beat Greg Norman with par on first extra hole			
Greg Norman	2	72-71-72-68=283	$37,800.00
Bill Rogers	T-3	71-74-72-69=286	$20,300.00
D.A. Weibring	T-3	71-75-70-70=286	$20,300.00
Jack Nicklaus	T-5	72-72-73-70=287	$12,293.75
Seve Ballesteros	T-5	70-74-71-72=287	$12,293.75
Gil Morgan	T-5	72-74-72-69=287	$12,293.75
Hale Irwin	T-5	76-73-70-68=287	$12,293.75
Fuzzy Zoeller	T-9	72-74-74-68=288	$9,800.00
Tom Watson	T-9	73-71-74-70=288	$9,800.00

USF&G Classic

Course: Lakewood C.C., New Orleans, La.
Par: 72 Yardage: 7,080
Last day of event: Sunday, March 20, 1983

Player	Place	Score	Earnings
Bill Rogers	Win	69-67-69-69=274	$72,000.00
Jay Haas	T-2	68-70-71-68=277	$29,866.67
David Edwards	T-2	71-67-69-70=277	$29,866.67
Vance Heafner	T-2	71-70-67-69=277	$29,866.66
Greg Norman	5	73-67-68-70=278	$16,000.00
Doug Tewell	T-6	69-70-68-72=279	$13,900.00
Jim Simons	T-6	69-72-68-70=279	$13,900.00
John Cook	T-8	70-70-70-70=280	$12,000.00
Lon Hinkle	T-8	72-69-68-71=280	$12,000.00
Pat McGowan	T-10	70-70-71-70=281	$9,600.00
Bob Shearer	T-10	70-71-71-69=281	$9,600.00
Jim Colbert	T-10	71-72-68-70=281	$9,600.00
Curtis Strange	T-10	71-69-72-69=281	$9,600.00

Tournament Players Championship

Course: TPC at Sawgrass, Ponte Vedra Beach, Fla.
Par: 72 Yardage: 6,857
Last day of event: Monday, March 28, 1983

Player	Place	Score	Earnings
Hal Sutton	Win	73-71-70-69=283	$126,000.00
Bob Eastwood	2	69-75-71-69=284	$75,600.00
John Mahaffey	T-3	72-74-72-67=285	$36,400.00

Bruce Lietzke	T-3	68-75-71-71=285	$36,400.00
John Cook	T-3	69-70-71-75=285	$36,400.00
Vance Heafner	T-6	72-71-69-74=286	$24,325.00
Doug Tewell	T-6	72-74-70-70=286	$24,325.00
Ed Fiori	T-8	72-73-71-71=287	$21,000.00
Curtis Strange	T-8	72-75-70-70=287	$21,000.00
Ben Crenshaw	T-10	70-74-69-75=288	$17,500.00
Don Pooley	T-10	71-70-72-75=288	$17,500.00
Bobby Clampett	T-10	69-72-70-77=288	$17,500.00

Greater Greensboro Open

Course: Forest Oaks C.C., Greensboro, N.C.
Par: 72 Yardage: 6,984
Last day of event: Sunday, April 3, 1983

Player	Place	Score	Earnings
Lanny Wadkins	Win	72-69-67-67=275	$72,000.00
Denis Watson	T-2	69-72-67-72=280	$35,200.00
Craig Stadler	T-2	71-70-67-72=280	$35,200.00
Tommy Nakajima	4	74-70-66-71=281	$19,200.00
Bobby Clampett	5	72-69-69-72=282	$16,000.00
Nick Faldo	6	71-71-71-70=283	$14,400.00
Bob Eastwood	T-7	70-69-73-72=284	$12,466.66
Phil Hancock	T-7	73-68-70-73=284	$12,466.67
Peter Oosterhuis	T-7	73-73-66-72=284	$12,466.67
Ron Streck	T-10	72-69-70-74=285	$10,400.00
Miller Barber	T-10	73-69-74-69=285	$10,400.00

Masters

Course: Augusta National G.C., Augusta, Ga.
Par: 72 Yardage: 6,925
Last day of event: Monday, April 11, 1983

Player	Place	Score	Earnings
Seve Ballesteros	Win	68-70-73-69=280	$90,000.00
Tom Kite	T-2	70-72-73-69=284	$44,000.00
Ben Crenshaw	T-2	76-70-70-68=284	$44,000.00
Tom Watson	T-4	70-71-71-73=285	$22,000.00
Ray Floyd	T-4	67-72-71-75=285	$22,000.00
Hale Irwin	T-6	72-73-72-69=286	$17,400.00
Craig Stadler	T-6	69-72-69-76=286	$17,400.00
Lanny Wadkins	T-8	73-70-73-71=287	$14,500.00
Dan Pohl	T-8	74-72-70-71=287	$14,500.00
Gil Morgan	T-8	67-70-76-74=287	$14,500.00

Sea Pines Heritage Classic

Course: Harbour Town G.L., Hilton Head, S.C.
Par: 71 Yardage: 6,657
Last day of event: Monday, April 18, 1983

Player	Place	Score	Earnings
Fuzzy Zoeller	Win	67-72-65-71=275	$63,000.00
Jim Nelford	2	68-68-70-71=277	$37,800.00
Mac O'Grady	T-3	68-65-73-73=279	$20,300.00
Bob Eastwood	T-3	67-67-71-74=279	$20,300.00
David Graham	T-5	70-69-69-72=280	$11,462.50
Craig Stadler	T-5	70-71-67-72=280	$11,462.50
Calvin Peete	T-5	72-68-70-70=280	$11,462.50
Hale Irwin	T-5	70-66-71-73=280	$11,462.50
Mark McCumber	T-5	70-69-68-73=280	$11,462.50
Tom Kite	T-5	75-68-67-70=280	$11,462.50

MONY Tournament of Champions

Course: La Costa C.C., Carlsbad, Calif.
Par: 72 Yardage: 6,911
Last day of event: Sunday, April 24, 1983

Player	Place	Score	Earnings
Lanny Wadkins	Win	67-70-71-72=280	$72,000.00
Ray Floyd	2	68-72-72-69=281	$48,000.00
Jay Haas	3	70-70-69-73=282	$32,000.00
Hal Sutton	4	67-70-72-74=283	$24,000.00
Bobby Clampett	T-5	72-71-70-71=284	$18,333.33
Isao Aoki	T-5	73-69-72-70=284	$18,333.34
Fuzzy Zoeller	T-5	74-72-68-70=284	$18,333.33
Wayne Levi	8	72-69-74-70=285	$15,000.00
Craig Stadler	9	69-73-73-71=286	$14,000.00
Calvin Peete	T-10	71-71-74-71=287	$12,500.00
Jack Nicklaus	T-10	65-72-77-73=287	$12,500.00

Byron Nelson Golf Classic

Course: Las Colinas Sports Club, Irving, Texas
Par: 70 Yardage: 6,982
Last day of event: Sunday, May 1, 1983

Player	Place	Score	Earnings
Ben Crenshaw	Win	71-69-67-66=273	$72,000.00
Brad Bryant	T-2	69-68-69-68=274	$35,200.00
Hal Sutton	T-2	72-66-67-69=274	$35,200.00
Mark Hayes	T-4	70-67-71-69=277	$13,971.43
Gary McCord	T-4	71-68-70-68=277	$13,971.43
Tom Purtzer	T-4	71-64-70-72=277	$13,971.43
Mike Donald	T-4	71-64-72-70=277	$13,971.43
Bruce Lietzke	T-4	72-67-69-69=277	$13,971.43
Lanny Wadkins	T-4	67-69-68-73=277	$13,971.42
Tom Watson	T-4	75-67-69-66=277	$13,971.43

Houston Coca-Cola Open

Course: Woodlands C.C., The Woodlands, Texas
Par: 71 Yardage: 7,031
Last day of event: Sunday, May 8, 1983

Player	Place	Score	Earnings
David Graham	Win	66-72-73-64=275	$72,000.00
Jim Thorpe	T-2	71-68-71-70=280	$29,866.66
Lee Trevino	T-2	68-68-71-73=280	$29,866.67
Lee Elder	T-2	69-73-69-69=280	$29,866.67
David Edwards	5	72-71-69-69=281	$16,000.00
Ed Fiori	T-6	71-70-71-70=282	$11,685.72
Fred Couples	T-6	71-67-72-72=282	$11,685.71
Jim Nelford	T-6	66-72-71-73=282	$11,685.72
Bob Boyd	T-6	68-73-71-70=282	$11,685.71
Tom Purtzer	T-6	73-73-70-66=282	$11,685.72
John Cook	T-6	67-73-68-74=282	$11,685.71
Larry Mize	T-6	71-71-74-66=282	$11,685.71

Colonial National Invitational

Course: Colonial C.C., Fort Worth, Texas
Par: 70 Yardage: 7,096
Last day of event: Sunday, May 15, 1983

Player	Place	Score	Earnings
Jim Colbert	Win	69-67-70-72=278	$72,000.00

Playoff: Beat Fuzzy Zoeller with par on sixth extra hole

Fuzzy Zoeller	2	68-70-68-72=278	$43,200.00
Bruce Lietzke	T-3	69-67-72-71=279	$23,200.00

Lon Hinkle	T-3	70-72-67-70=279	$23,200.00
Gary Koch	T-5	69-69-72-70=280	$12,657.15
Mark McNulty	T-5	70-67-72-71=280	$12,657.14
Mike Reid	T-5	67-69-70-74=280	$12,657.14
Bobby Wadkins	T-5	68-64-74-74=280	$12,657.14
Peter Jacobsen	T-5	70-69-67-74=280	$12,657.14
Gary Hallberg	T-5	66-67-75-72=280	$12,657.14
Bob Murphy	T-5	70-66-75-69=280	$12,657.15

Georgia-Pacific Atlanta Golf Classic
Course: Atlanta C.C., Atlanta, Ga.
Par: 72 Yardage: 7,007
Last day of event: Sunday, May 22, 1983

Player	Place	Score	Earnings
Calvin Peete	Win	68-75-63=206	$72,000.00
Jim Colbert	T-2	69-67-72=208	$29,866.66
Don Pooley	T-2	70-66-72=208	$29,866.67
Chip Beck	T-2	65-73-70=208	$29,866.67
Greg Powers	5	69-71-69=209	$16,000.00
Larry Nelson	6	71-70-69=210	$14,400.00
Scott Simpson	T-7	71-69-71=211	$12,050.00
Mike Sullivan	T-7	71-69-71=211	$12,050.00
Gary Koch	T-7	70-72-69=211	$12,050.00
David Edwards	T-7	72-68-71=211	$12,050.00

Memorial Tournament
Course: Muirfield Village G.C., Dubin, Ohio
Par: 72 Yardage: 7,116
Last day of event: Sunday, May 29, 1983

Player	Place	Score	Earnings
Hale Irwin	Win	71-71-70-69=281	$72,000.00
Ben Crenshaw	T-2	67-71-73-71=282	$35,200.00
David Graham	T-2	72-67-69-74=282	$35,200.00
Jim Thorpe	4	74-69-70-70=283	$19,200.00
Andy Bean	T-5	69-67-74-74=284	$15,200.00
Scott Hoch	T-5	72-68-70-74=284	$15,200.00
Calvin Peete	T-7	72-71-69-73=285	$12,900.00
Jay Haas	T-7	72-68-73-72=285	$12,900.00
Jim Nelford	T-9	69-72-73-72=286	$10,000.00
Jack Renner	T-9	73-68-71-74=286	$10,000.00
Bill Rogers	T-9	74-71-69-72=286	$10,000.00
Lanny Wadkins	T-9	67-72-75-72=286	$10,000.00
Bob Murphy	T-9	78-71-69-68=286	$10,000.00

Kemper Open
Course: Congressional C.C., Bethesda, Md.
Par: 72 Yardage: 7,173
Last day of event: Sunday, June 5, 1983

Player	Place	Score	Earnings
Fred Couples	Win	71-71-68-77=287	$72,000.00

Playoff: Beat Gil Morgan, Barry Jaeckel, T.C. Chen and Scott Simpson with birdie on second extra hole

Barry Jaeckel	T-2	71-75-71-70=287	$26,400.00
Gil Morgan	T-2	75-70-72-70=287	$26,400.00
T.C. Chen	T-2	69-73-69-76=287	$26,400.00
Scott Simpson	T-2	68-68-74-77=287	$26,400.00
Roger Maltbie	T-6	73-72-72-71=288	$13,400.00
Andy Bean	T-6	69-75-72-72=288	$13,400.00
Hal Sutton	T-6	73-77-68-70=288	$13,400.00
Chip Beck	T-9	74-73-70-72=289	$10,400.00
Tom Kite	T-9	68-70-76-75=289	$10,400.00

Buddy Gardner	T-9	71-72-76-70=289	$10,400.00
Nick Price	T-9	76-70-70-73=289	$10,400.00

Manufacturers Hanover Westchester Classic
Course: Westchester C.C., Harrison, N.Y.
Par: 71 Yardage: 6,687
Last day of event: Sunday, June 12, 1983

Player	Place	Score	Earnings
Seve Ballesteros	Win	69-67-70-70=276	$81,000.00
Craig Stadler	T-2	71-66-73-68=278	$39,600.00
Andy Bean	T-2	73-68-70-67=278	$39,600.00
Mike Reid	T-4	71-71-67-70=279	$18,600.00
Mark McCumber	T-4	71-69-71-68=279	$18,600.00
Fuzzy Zoeller	T-4	68-68-71-72=279	$18,600.00
Roger Maltbie	7	72-66-70-72=280	$15,075.00
Fred Couples	T-8	71-69-71-71=282	$13,500.00
Jerry Pate	T-8	73-69-70-70=282	$13,500.00
Dan Halldorson	T-10	72-72-68-71=283	$9,975.00
Tom Kite	T-10	72-71-73-67=283	$9,975.00
Ron Streck	T-10	73-72-72-66=283	$9,975.00
Wayne Levi	T-10	72-75-71-65=283	$9,975.00
Lee Elder	T-10	74-69-65-75=283	$9,975.00
Gary Koch	T-10	75-69-70-69=283	$9,975.00

U.S. Open
Course: Oakmont C.C., Oakmont, Pa.
Par: 71 Yardage: 6,972
Last day of event: Sunday, June 19, 1983

Player	Place	Score	Earnings
Larry Nelson	Win	75-73-65-67=280	$72,000.00
Tom Watson	2	72-70-70-69=281	$44,000.00
Gil Morgan	3	73-72-70-68=283	$29,000.00
Seve Ballesteros	T-4	69-74-69-74=286	$17,968.50
Calvin Peete	T-4	75-68-70-73=286	$17,968.50
Hal Sutton	6	73-70-73-71=287	$13,254.00
Lanny Wadkins	7	72-73-74-69=288	$12,088.00
David Graham	T-8	74-75-73-69=291	$10,711.00
Ralph Landrum	T-8	75-73-69-74=291	$10,711.00
Chip Beck	T-10	73-74-74-71=292	$8,976.34
Andy North	T-10	73-71-72-76=292	$8,976.33
Craig Stadler	T-10	76-74-73-69=292	$8,976.33

Danny Thomas Memphis Classic
Course: Colonial C.C. (South), Cordova, Tenn.
Par: 72 Yardage: 7,282
Last day of event: Sunday, June 26, 1983

Player	Place	Score	Earnings
Larry Mize	Win	70-65-69-70=274	$72,000.00
Sammy Rachels	T-2	69-69-69-68=275	$29,866.67
Chip Beck	T-2	65-68-71-71=275	$29,866.66
Fuzzy Zoeller	T-2	68-68-67-72=275	$29,866.67
John Fought	T-5	68-68-70-71=277	$14,600.00
Mark O'Meara	T-5	71-66-71-69=277	$14,600.00
John Mahaffey	T-5	71-67-70-69=277	$14,600.00
Mark McCumber	T-8	68-71-71-68=278	$11,600.00
Tim Simpson	T-8	70-69-68-71=278	$11,600.00
Mike Sullivan	T-8	70-68-67-73=278	$11,600.00

Western Open

Course: Butler National G.C., Oak Brook, Ill.
Par: 72 Yardage: 7,097
Last day of event: Sunday, July 3, 1983

Player	Place	Score	Earnings
Mark McCumber	Win	74-71-68-71=284	$72,000.00
Tom Watson	2	67-71-75-72=285	$43,200.00
Mike Nicolette	T-3	71-73-73-71=288	$20,800.00
Mark Lye	T-3	71-74-71-72=288	$20,800.00
Curtis Strange	T-3	75-70-70-73=288	$20,800.00
Clarence Rose	T-6	72-73-73-71=289	$13,900.00
Payne Stewart	T-6	73-70-72-74=289	$13,900.00
Mike Gove	T-8	74-70-73-73=290	$10,800.00
Phil Hancock	T-8	74-70-73-73=290	$10,800.00
Pat Lindsey	T-8	74-71-74-71=290	$10,800.00
David Edwards	T-8	70-72-73-75=290	$10,800.00
Bob Gilder	T-8	75-72-72-71=290	$10,800.00

Greater Milwaukee Open

Course: Tuckaway C.C., Franklin, Wis.
Par: 72 Yardage: 7,030
Last day of event: Sunday, July 10, 1983

Player	Place	Score	Earnings
Morris Hatalsky	Win	70-68-71-66=275	$45,000.00
George Cadle	2	71-70-70-64=275	$27,000.00
Payne Stewart	T-3	70-69-70-67=276	$13,000.00
Larry Mize	T-3	72-70-66-68=276	$13,000.00
Skeeter Heath	T-3	74-67-69-66=276	$13,000.00
Dan Pohl	T-6	70-70-67-70=277	$8,375.00
Mark Calcavecchia	T-6	69-72-66-70=277	$8,375.00
Richard Zokol	T-6	70-72-66-69=277	$8,375.00
Jim Colbert	T-9	69-71-71-67=278	$6,250.00
Jay Haas	T-9	72-70-69-67=278	$6,250.00
D.A. Weibring	T-9	72-70-71-65=278	$6,250.00
Don Pooley	T-9	69-68-68-73=278	$6,250.00
T.C. Chen	T-9	73-68-68-69=278	$6,250.00

Miller High-Life Quad Cities Open

Course: Oakwood C.C., Coal Valley, Ill.
Par: 70 Yardage: 6,602
Last day of event: Sunday, July 17, 1983

Player	Place	Score	Earnings
Danny Edwards	Win	66-64-69-67=266	$36,000.00
Morris Hatalsky	2	68-64-67-67=266	$21,600.00
Lennie Clements	T-3	67-68-65-67=267	$11,600.00
Scott Hoch	T-3	69-65-67-66=267	$11,600.00
D.A. Weibring	T-5	65-66-69-68=268	$7,600.00
David Peoples	T-5	69-65-67-67=268	$7,600.00
Ron Streck	T-7	66-68-67-68=269	$6,450.00
Payne Stewart	T-7	65-68-66-70=269	$6,450.00
Lon Hinkle	9	69-66-66-69=270	$5,800.00
Jim Dent	T-10	69-69-67-66=271	$5,200.00
Sammy Rachels	T-10	67-64-69-71=271	$5,200.00

British Open

Course: Royal Birkdale G.C., Southport, Lancashire, England
Par: 71 Yardage: 6,968
Last day of event: Sunday, July 17, 1983

Player	Place	Score	Earnings
Tom Watson	Win	67-68-70-70=275	$60,000.00
Andy Bean	T-2	70-69-70-67=276	$34,500.00
Hale Irwin	T-2	69-68-72-67=276	$34,500.00
Graham Marsh	4	69-70-74-64=277	$22,500.00
Lee Trevino	5	69-66-73-70=278	$20,400.00
Harold Henning	T-6	71-69-70-69=279	$18,375.00
Seve Ballesteros	T-6	71-71-69-68=279	$18,375.00
Christy O'Connor, Jr.	T-8	72-69-71-68=280	$14,437.50
Bill Rogers	T-8	67-71-73-69=280	$14,437.50
Nick Faldo	T-8	68-68-71-73=280	$14,437.50
Denis Durnian	T-8	73-66-74-67=280	$14,437.50

Anheuser-Busch Golf Classic

Course: Kingsmill G.C., Williamsburg, Va.
Par: 71 Yardage: 6,776
Last day of event: Sunday, July 24, 1983

Player	Place	Score	Earnings
Calvin Peete	Win	66-75-66-69=276	$63,000.00
Tim Norris	2	67-74-68-68=277	$37,800.00
Lanny Wadkins	T-3	71-76-63-68=278	$20,300.00
Hal Sutton	T-3	67-65-69-77=278	$20,300.00
Ralph Landrum	T-5	72-70-70-67=279	$13,300.00
Scott Simpson	T-5	64-74-70-71=279	$13,300.00
Bruce Lietzke	7	68-72-70-70=280	$11,725.00
Jon Chaffee	T-8	71-70-70-70=281	$8,443.75
Ray Floyd	T-8	68-71-72-70=281	$8,443.75
Leonard Thompson	T-8	69-72-68-72=281	$8,443.75
Morris Hatalsky	T-8	69-72-71-69=281	$8,443.75
Curtis Strange	T-8	72-69-71-69=281	$8,443.75
John Fought	T-8	72-71-69-69=281	$8,443.75
Bob Eastwood	T-8	69-74-70-68=281	$8,443.75
Tom Weiskopf	T-8	66-73-75-67=281	$8,443.75

Canadian Open

Course: Glen Abbey G.C., Oakville, Ontario, Canada
Par: 71 Yardage: 7,055
Last day of event: Sunday, July 31, 1983

Player	Place	Score	Earnings
John Cook	Win	68-71-70-68=277	$63,000.00
Johnny Miller	2	75-68-67-67=277	$37,800.00
Jack Nicklaus	3	73-68-70-67=278	$23,800.00
David Graham	T-4	68-71-71-69=279	$14,466.67
Ralph Landrum	T-4	65-75-67-72=279	$14,466.67
Andy Bean	T-4	70-70-77-62=279	$14,466.66
Bruce Lietzke	T-7	72-67-70-72=281	$11,287.50
Peter Oosterhuis	T-7	70-69-74-68=281	$11,287.50
Frank Conner	T-9	72-71-67-72=282	$9,100.00
Mark Pfeil	T-9	69-71-73-69=282	$9,100.00
Tony Sills	T-9	72-73-66-71=282	$9,100.00
Tom Purtzer	T-9	72-66-70-74=282	$9,100.00

PGA Championship

Course: Riviera C.C., Pacific Palisades, Calif.
Par: 71 Yardage: 6,946
Last day of event: Sunday, August 7, 1983

Player	Place	Score	Earnings
Hal Sutton	Win	65-66-72-71=274	$100,000.00
Jack Nicklaus	2	73-65-71-66=275	$60,000.00
Peter Jacobsen	3	73-70-68-65=276	$40,000.00
Pat McGowan	4	68-67-73-69=277	$30,000.00
John Fought	5	67-69-71-71=278	$25,000.00
Bruce Lietzke	T-6	67-71-70-71=279	$19,000.00

Fuzzy Zoeller	T-6	72-71-67-69=279	$19,000.00
Dan Pohl	8	72-70-69-69=280	$16,000.00
Mike Reid	T-9	69-71-72-70=282	$10,800.00
Scott Simpson	T-9	66-73-70-73=282	$10,800.00
Jay Haas	T-9	68-72-69-73=282	$10,800.00
Doug Tewell	T-9	74-72-69-67=282	$10,800.00
Ben Crenshaw	T-9	68-66-71-77=282	$10,800.00

Buick Open

Course: Warwick Hills C.C., Grand Blanc, Mich.
Par: 72 Yardage: 7,014
Last day of event: Sunday, August 14, 1983

Player	Place	Score	Earnings
Wayne Levi	Win	72-64-71-65=272	$63,000.00
Calvin Peete	T-2	66-70-70-67=273	$30,800.00
Isao Aoki	T-2	68-66-70-69=273	$30,800.00
John Cook	4	67-69-70-68=274	$16,800.00
Lanny Wadkins	T-5	70-67-68-70=275	$13,300.00
Frank Conner	T-5	73-67-65-70=275	$13,300.00
David Graham	T-7	70-67-69-70=276	$9,829.17
Fred Couples	T-7	67-71-70-68=276	$9,829.16
Brad Faxon	T-7	69-71-67-69=276	$9,829.17
Peter Jacobsen	T-7	70-68-67-71=276	$9,829.17
Craig Stadler	T-7	70-68-71-67=276	$9,829.16
Forrest Fezler	T-7	72-67-67-70=276	$9,829.17

Sammy Davis, Jr. - Greater Hartford Open

Course: Wethersfield C.C., Wethersfield, Conn.
Par: 71 Yardage: 6,568
Last day of event: Sunday, August 21, 1983

Player	Place	Score	Earnings
Curtis Strange	Win	69-62-69-68=268	$54,000.00
Jay Haas	T-2	69-66-69-65=269	$26,400.00
Jack Renner	T-2	66-68-64-71=269	$26,400.00
Don Pooley	4	70-67-64-69=270	$14,400.00
Hale Irwin	T-5	65-68-68-70=271	$10,950.00
Tom Jenkins	T-5	67-71-67-66=271	$10,950.00
John Adams	T-5	72-66-65-68=271	$10,950.00
Isao Aoki	8	66-67-71-68=272	$9,300.00
Rex Caldwell	T-9	66-68-70-69=273	$7,800.00
Danny Edwards	T-9	68-70-68-67=273	$7,800.00
Terry Diehl	T-9	69-69-70-65=273	$7,800.00
Bob Murphy	T-9	67-68-64-74=273	$7,800.00

World Series of Golf

Course: Firestone C.C. (South), Akron, Ohio
Par: 70 Yardage: 7,149
Last day of event: Sunday, August 28, 1983

Player	Place	Score	Earnings
Nick Price	Win	66-68-69-67=270	$100,000.00
Jack Nicklaus	2	67-73-69-65=274	$60,000.00
Johnny Miller	3	71-69-68-67=275	$40,000.00
Ray Floyd	T-4	69-68-70-69=276	$19,125.00
Hale Irwin	T-4	68-70-67-71=276	$19,125.00
Tom Watson	T-4	70-70-71-65=276	$19,125.00
Mark McCumber	T-4	71-68-68-69=276	$19,125.00
Isao Aoki	8	76-64-67-70=277	$12,000.00
Hal Sutton	9	70-71-70-67=278	$11,000.00
David Graham	10	70-69-71-69=279	$10,000.00

B.C. Open

Course: En-Joie G.C., Endicott, N.Y.
Par: 71 Yardage: 6,966
Last day of event: Sunday, September 4, 1983

Player	Place	Score	Earnings
Pat Lindsey	Win	71-64-65-68=268	$54,000.00
Gil Morgan	2	70-67-68-67=272	$32,400.00
John Adams	T-3	68-67-70-68=273	$17,400.00
Wayne Levi	T-3	69-70-70-64=273	$17,400.00
Mike Reid	T-5	71-67-67-69=274	$11,400.00
Don Pooley	T-5	67-66-72-69=274	$11,400.00
Pat McGowan	7	73-70-65-67=275	$10,050.00
Steven Liebler	T-8	70-69-68-69=276	$8,400.00
Victor Regalado	T-8	67-68-69-72=276	$8,400.00
Sammy Rachels	T-8	69-72-67-68=276	$8,400.00
Craig Stadler	T-8	72-68-71-65=276	$8,400.00

Bank of Boston Classic

Course: Pleasant Valley C.C., Sutton, Mass.
Par: 71 Yardage: 7,110
Last day of event: Sunday, September 11, 1983

Player	Place	Score	Earnings
Mark Lye	Win	69-69-71-64=273	$63,000.00
Sammy Rachels	T-2	68-68-69-69=274	$26,133.33
Jim Thorpe	T-2	72-67-67-68=274	$26,133.33
John Mahaffey	T-2	65-69-67-73=274	$26,133.34
Fuzzy Zoeller	5	67-68-69-71=275	$14,000.00
Ivan Smith	T-6	70-69-69-68=276	$12,162.50
Leonard Thompson	T-6	70-65-72-69=276	$12,162.50
Dale Douglass	T-8	70-69-69-69=277	$9,800.00
Wayne Levi	T-8	66-70-70-71=277	$9,800.00
George Burns	T-8	72-69-67-69=277	$9,800.00
Joe Inman	T-8	69-69-66-73=277	$9,800.00

LaJet Coors Classic

Course: Fairway Oaks C.C.
Abilene, Texas
Par: 72 Yardage: 7,166
Last day of event: Sunday, September 25, 1983

Player	Place	Score	Earnings
Rex Caldwell	Win	68-72-76-66=282	$63,000.00
Lee Trevino	2	70-72-68-73=283	$37,800.00
Andy Bean	T-3	67-74-71-73=285	$20,300.00
David Graham	T-3	75-73-67-70=285	$20,300.00
Lyn Lott	5	74-65-77-70=286	$14,000.00
Hal Sutton	T-6	73-73-73-68=287	$11,725.00
Ben Crenshaw	T-6	74-69-70-74=287	$11,725.00
John Cook	T-6	71-70-75-71=287	$11,725.00
Hale Irwin	9	74-68-75-71=288	$10,150.00
Keith Fergus	T-10	70-73-74-72=289	$8,400.00
J.C. Snead	T-10	72-70-73-74=289	$8,400.00
Willie Wood	T-10	72-74-70-73=289	$8,400.00
Frank Conner	T-10	78-70-70-71=289	$8,400.00

Panasonic Las Vegas Pro Celebrity

Course: Las Vegas C.C., Dunes C.C., Desert Inn C.C., Showboat C.C., Las Vegas, Nev.
Home course / Las Vegas C.C., Par: 71 Yardage: 7,164
Last day of event: Wednesday, September 28, 1983

Player	Place	Score	Earnings
Fuzzy Zoeller	Win	63-70-70-64-73=340	$135,000.00

Player	Place	Score	Earnings
Rex Caldwell	2	71-66-66-70-71=344	$81,000.00
Ed Fiori	3	67-67-72-69-70=345	$51,000.00
Scott Hoch	T-4	69-71-69-68-70=347	$33,000.00
J.C. Snead	T-4	67-67-69-72-72=347	$33,000.00
Tim Simpson	T-6	69-67-69-72-71=348	$22,687.50
Peter Jacobsen	T-6	69-72-69-68-70=348	$22,687.50
Tom Watson	T-6	72-71-68-70-67=348	$22,687.50
Gil Morgan	T-6	69-66-70-73-70=348	$22,687.50
David Graham	T-6	66-72-68-68-74=348	$22,687.50
Hale Irwin	T-6	66-72-69-66-75=348	$22,687.50

Texas Open

Course: Oak Hill C.C., San Antonio, Texas
Par: 70 Yardage: 6,576
Last day of event: Sunday, October 2, 1983

Player	Place	Score	Earnings
Jim Colbert	Win	66-62-66-67=261	$54,000.00
Mark Pfeil	2	70-63-63-70=266	$32,400.00
Tony Sills	3	67-64-69-67=267	$20,400.00
Curt Byrum	4	71-66-65-66=268	$14,400.00
Gary Koch	T-5	68-68-67-67=270	$10,537.50
George Cadle	T-5	66-64-70-70=270	$10,537.50
Jay Haas	T-5	69-64-67-70=270	$10,537.50
Brad Bryant	T-5	70-66-67-67=270	$10,537.50
Lee Trevino	T-9	69-68-66-68=271	$7,800.00
Fred Couples	T-9	64-70-70-67=271	$7,800.00
Jeff Sanders	T-9	67-70-66-68=271	$7,800.00
Lee Elder	T-9	67-65-72-67=271	$7,800.00

Southern Open

Course: Green Island C.C., Columbus, Ga.
Par: 70 Yardage: 6,791
Last day of event: Sunday, October 9, 1983

Player	Place	Score	Earnings
Ronnie Black	Win	68-69-65-69=271	$45,000.00
Playoff: Beat Sam Torrance with birdie on fourth extra hole			
Sam Torrance	2	66-67-66-72=271	$27,000.00
Wally Armstrong	3	68-68-70-68=274	$17,000.00
Payne Stewart	T-4	65-72-68-70=275	$11,000.00
Joe Inman	T-4	70-65-73-67=275	$11,000.00
Mark Lye	T-6	71-70-70-65=276	$8,687.50
Scott Hoch	T-6	70-66-73-67=276	$8,687.50
Mike Nicolette	T-8	69-70-70-68=277	$7,000.00
Dave Eichelberger	T-8	68-71-67-71=277	$7,000.00
Rod Curl	T-8	71-67-68-71=277	$7,000.00
John Mahaffey	T-8	71-66-72-68=277	$7,000.00

Walt Disney World Golf Classic

Course: Walt Disney (Magnolia, Palm), Lake Buena Vista C.C., Lake Buena Vista, Fla.
Home course / Magnolia, Par: 72 Yardage: 7,190
Last day of event: Sunday, October 23, 1983

Player	Place	Score	Earnings
Payne Stewart	Win	69-64-69-67=269	$72,000.00
Mark McCumber	T-2	64-69-71-67=271	$35,200.00
Nick Faldo	T-2	72-65-68-66=271	$35,200.00
Scott Hoch	4	68-68-66-70=272	$19,200.00
Craig Stadler	T-5	68-69-69-67=273	$14,050.00
Gary Koch	T-5	69-68-69-67=273	$14,050.00
Morris Hatalsky	T-5	66-70-68-69=273	$14,050.00
Larry Nelson	T-5	67-67-71-68=273	$14,050.00

Dave Barr	T-9	66-70-68-70=274	$10,800.00
Leonard Thompson	T-9	69-67-70-68=274	$10,800.00
Denis Watson	T-9	67-71-71-65=274	$10,800.00

Pensacola Open

Course: Perdido Bay C.C., Pensacola, Fla.
Par: 71 Yardage: 7,093
Last day of event: Sunday, October 30, 1983

Player	Place	Score	Earnings
Mark McCumber	Win	68-68-65-65=266	$45,000.00
Lon Hinkle	T-2	67-68-67-68=270	$22,000.00
Mark Lye	T-2	63-70-72-65=270	$22,000.00
Calvin Peete	4	68-68-68-67=271	$12,000.00
Mark Hayes	T-5	70-66-67-69=272	$9,500.00
Lyn Lott	T-5	70-65-65-72=272	$9,500.00
Jim Simons	T-7	70-69-66-68=273	$7,531.25
Gary Hallberg	T-7	70-70-70-63=273	$7,531.25
Dan Pohl	T-7	66-71-66-70=273	$7,531.25
Jon Chaffee	T-7	70-66-66-71=273	$7,531.25

1984

In his second full season on the PGA Tour, Greg Norman served notice of things to come with a 1-2-10-1-2 stretch, winning the Kemper Open and Canadian Open, en route to seven top 10 finishes. Norman famously waved a flag of surrender at the conclusion of a 67-75 playoff loss to Fuzzy Zoeller at the U.S. Open at Winged Foot. Ben Crenshaw won his first major, beating Tom Watson by two shots at the Masters. Nick Faldo posted his first victory in the United States, the Sea Pines Heritage Classic. Seve Ballesteros won his second British Open, besting Bernhard Langer and Tom Watson by two shots at St. Andrews. Watson's last serious bid to tie Harry Vardon's record of six Open Championships was foiled when he overshot the Road Hole green in Round 4, leading to bogey as Ballesteros was making birdie at the 18th. Lee Trevino won his second PGA Championship, besting Gary Player and Lanny Wadkins by four shots at Shoal Creek.

Seiko Tucson-Match Play Championship

Course: Randolph Park Municipal, Tucson, Ariz.
Par: 70 Yardage: 6,860
Last day of event: Sunday, January 8, 1984

Player	Place	Score	Earnings
Tom Watson	Win		$100,000.00
Was given a bye to fifth round			
Round Five - Beat Jim Dent 3 & 2			
Quarterfinals - Beat Lon Hinkle 2 & 1			
Semifinals - Beat Scott Hoch 2 & 1			
Finals - Beat Gil Morgan 2 & 1			
Gil Morgan	2		$60,000.00
Was given a bye to fifth round			
Round Five - Beat Keith Fergus 1 up			
Quarterfinals - Beat Mark Hayes 5 & 4			
Semifinals - Beat Lanny Wadkins 1 up			
Finals - Tom Watson beats him 2 & 1			
Scott Hoch	3		$35,000.00
Round One - Beat George Archer 2 & 1			
Round Two - Beat Ron Streck 20 holes			
Round Three - Beat Lee Elder 1 up			
Round Four - Beat Doug Tewell 4 & 3			
Round Five - Beat Hal Sutton 3 & 2			
Quarterfinals - Beat Tom Kite 5 & 4			
Semifinals - Tom Watson beats him 2 & 1			
Consolation - Beat Lanny Wadkins 2 & 1			
Lanny Wadkins	4		$25,000.00
Was given a bye to fifth round			

Round Five - Beat T.C. Chen 6 & 4
Quarterfinals - Beat Ben Crenshaw 19 holes
Semifinals - Gil Morgan beats him 1 up
Consolation - Scott Hoch beats him 2 & 1

Mark Hayes	T-5	$20,000.00

Round One - Beat Willie Wood 4 & 2
Round Two - Beat John Fought 2 & 1
Round Three - Beat Jim Nelford 3 & 2
Round Four - Beat D.A. Weibring 2 up
Round Five - Beat Fuzzy Zoeller 1 up
Quarterfinals - Gil Morgan beats him 5 & 4

Lon Hinkle	T-5	$20,000.00

Round One - Beat Tom Jenkins 2 & 1
Round Two - Beat Joey Rassett 2 & 1
Round Three - Beat Fred Couples 3 & 2
Round Four - Beat Brad Bryant 2 & 1
Round Five - Beat Calvin Peete 6 & 5
Quarterfinals - Tom Watson beats him 2 & 1

Ben Crenshaw	T-5	$20,000.00

Was given a bye to fifth round
Round Five - Beat Richard Zokol 20 holes
Quarterfinals - Lanny Wadkins beats him 20 holes

Tom Kite	T-5	$20,000.00

Was given a bye to fifth round
Round Five - Beat Victor Regalado 1 up
Quarterfinals - Scott Hoch beats him 5 & 4

Keith Fergus	T-9	$15,000.00

Round One - Beat Lyn Lott 1 up
Round Two - Beat Dave Barr 2 up
Round Three - Beat Mark McCumber 2 & 1
Round Four - Beat Dave Stockton 1 up
Round Five - Gil Morgan beats him 1 up

T.C. Chen	T-9	$15,000.00

Round One - Beat Mark Calcavecchia 21st hole
Round Two - Beat Scott Simpson 3 & 2
Round Three - Beat Vance Heafner 2 & 1
Round Four - Beat Tom Purtzer 20 holes
Round Five - Lanny Wadkins beats him 6 & 4

Richard Zokol	T-9	$15,000.00

Round One - Beat Mike Reid 3 & 2
Round Two - Beat Bill Kratzert 3 & 2
Round Three - Beat Curtis Strange 19 holes
Round Four - Beat Allen Miller 4 & 2
Round Five - Ben Crenshaw beats him 20 holes

Jim Dent	T-9	$15,000.00

Round One - Beat Peter Jacobsen 4 & 3
Round Two - Beat Mark Pfeil 21 holes
Round Three - Beat Gary McCord 2 up
Round Four - Beat Payne Stewart 3 & 2
Round Five - Tom Watson beats him 3 & 2

Victor Regalado	T-9	$15,000.00

Round One - Beat Tim Simpson 2 & 1
Round Two - Beat Pat Lindsey 2 up
Round Three - Beat Jim Colbert 2 & 1
Round Four - Beat Morris Hatalsky 4 & 2
Round Five - Tom Kite beats him 1 up

Calvin Peete	T-9	$15,000.00

Was given a bye to fifth round
Round Five - Lon Hinkle beats him 6 & 5

Hal Sutton	T-9	$15,000.00

Was given a bye to fifth round
Round Five - Scott Hoch beats him 3 & 2

Fuzzy Zoeller	T-9	$15,000.00

Was given a bye to fifth round
Round Five - Mark Hayes beats him 1 up

Bob Hope Chrysler Classic

Course: Bermuda Dunes C.C., La Quinta C.C., Indian Wells C.C., Tamarisk C.C.
Home course / Bermuda Dunes, Par: 72　Yardage: 6,837
Last day of event: Sunday, January 15, 1984

Player	Place	Score	Earnings
John Mahaffey	Win	66-70-70-68-66=340	$72,000.00

Playoff: Beat Jim Simons with par on second extra hole

Player	Place	Score	Earnings
Jim Simons	2	69-63-70-69-69=340	$43,200.00
Johnny Miller	3	67-69-65-69-72=342	$27,200.00
Curtis Strange	T-4	70-70-67-68-68=343	$17,600.00
Peter Jacobsen	T-4	70-67-69-72-65=343	$17,600.00
Jack Renner	T-6	69-67-68-68-72=344	$13,400.00
Gary Koch	T-6	72-71-67-67-67=344	$13,400.00
Tim Norris	T-6	68-68-74-66-68=344	$13,400.00
Sammy Rachels	T-9	68-69-72-68-69=346	$10,000.00
Lee Elder	T-9	69-68-67-70-72=346	$10,000.00
Doug Tewell	T-9	69-72-67-67-71=346	$10,000.00
Ronnie Black	T-9	67-68-70-73-68=346	$10,000.00
Mike Reid	T-9	73-68-67-68-70=346	$10,000.00

Phoenix Open

Course: Phoenix C.C., Phoenix, Ariz.
Par: 71　Yardage: 6,726
Last day of event: Sunday, January 22, 1984

Player	Place	Score	Earnings
Tom Purtzer	Win	68-67-68-65=268	$72,000.00
Corey Pavin	2	66-67-68-68=269	$43,200.00
Larry Mize	T-3	67-68-67-68=270	$23,200.00
Curtis Strange	T-3	68-66-69-67=270	$23,200.00
Bill Sander	T-5	70-66-69-67=272	$14,600.00
George Burns	T-5	70-70-65-67=272	$14,600.00
Doug Tewell	T-5	72-68-66-66=272	$14,600.00
Tim Norris	T-8	69-69-68-67=273	$10,000.00
Tommy Nakajima	T-8	69-69-69-66=273	$10,000.00
Fuzzy Zoeller	T-8	69-70-68-66=273	$10,000.00
Lon Hinkle	T-8	68-71-65-69=273	$10,000.00
Jim Simons	T-8	68-69-72-64=273	$10,000.00
Hale Irwin	T-8	72-68-64-69=273	$10,000.00
Tim Simpson	T-8	73-68-69-63=273	$10,000.00

Isuzu/Andy Williams San Diego Open

Course: Torrey Pines (South), Torrey Pines (North), San Diego, Calif.
Home Course -Par: 72　Yardage: 7,021
Last day of event: Sunday, January 29, 1984

Player	Place	Score	Earnings
Gary Koch	Win	68-70-69-65=272	$72,000.00

Playoff: Beat Gary Hallberg with birdie on second extra hole

Player	Place	Score	Earnings
Gary Hallberg	2	72-66-66-68=272	$43,200.00
Dan Pohl	T-3	68-68-69-68=273	$19,200.00
Chip Beck	T-3	66-68-69-70=273	$19,200.00
Don Pooley	T-3	66-68-71-68=273	$19,200.00
Craig Stadler	T-3	68-72-66-67=273	$19,200.00
Larry Mize	T-7	70-70-67-67=274	$12,050.00
Doug Tewell	T-7	70-71-67-66=274	$12,050.00
Andy Bean	T-7	67-68-67-72=274	$12,050.00
Peter Oosterhuis	T-7	72-69-67-66=274	$12,050.00

Bing Crosby Pro-Am

Courses: Pebble Beach G.L., Spyglass Hill G.C., Cypress Point C.C., Pebble Beach, Calif.

Home Course / Pebble Beach, Par: 72 Yardage: 6,815

Last day of event: Sunday, February 5, 1984

Player	Place	Score	Earnings
Hale Irwin	Win	69-69-68-72=278	$72,000.00
Playoff: Beat Jim Nelford with birdie on second extra hole			
Jim Nelford	2	67-73-70-68=278	$43,200.00
Mark O'Meara	T-3	68-74-68-70=280	$23,200.00
Fred Couples	T-3	74-67-69-70=280	$23,200.00
Nick Faldo	5	70-72-71-68=281	$16,000.00
Hal Sutton	T-6	69-70-71-72=282	$13,900.00
Craig Stadler	T-6	72-66-74-70=282	$13,900.00
John Fought	T-8	72-72-70-69=283	$11,600.00
Lon Hinkle	T-8	72-71-72-68=283	$11,600.00
David Edwards	T-8	69-70-69-75=283	$11,600.00

Hawaiian Open

Course: Waialae C.C., Honolulu, Ha.

Par: 72 Yardage: 7,234

Last day of event: Sunday, February 12, 1984

Player	Place	Score	Earnings
Jack Renner	Win	70-66-68-67=271	$90,000.00
Playoff: Beat Wayne Levi with par on second extra hole			
Wayne Levi	2	70-66-65-70=271	$54,000.00
Gil Morgan	T-3	66-70-68-69=273	$29,000.00
Chip Beck	T-3	74-65-70-64=273	$29,000.00
David Edwards	T-5	70-68-68-69=275	$18,250.00
Calvin Peete	T-5	65-69-70-71=275	$18,250.00
Bernhard Langer	T-5	69-66-72-68=275	$18,250.00
Hale Irwin	T-8	69-69-70-68=276	$15,000.00
Mike Sullivan	T-8	66-70-68-72=276	$15,000.00

Los Angeles Open

Course: Riviera C.C., Pacific Palisades, Calif.

Par: 71 Yardage: 7,029

Last day of event: Sunday, February 19, 1984

Player	Place	Score	Earnings
David Edwards	Win	70-73-72-64=279	$72,000.00
Jack Renner	2	71-75-67-69=282	$43,200.00
Jack Nicklaus	3	73-71-70-69=283	$27,200.00
Mark McCumber	T-4	71-72-71-70=284	$17,600.00
Dan Pohl	T-4	74-70-74-66=284	$17,600.00
Johnny Miller	T-6	71-72-72-70=285	$13,900.00
Jim Colbert	T-6	71-75-69-70=285	$13,900.00
Craig Stadler	8	72-73-73-68=286	$12,400.00
Allen Miller	T-9	72-71-73-72=288	$10,000.00
Gary Koch	T-9	73-70-72-73=288	$10,000.00
T.C. Chen	T-9	72-73-69-74=288	$10,000.00
Fred Couples	T-9	71-71-71-75=288	$10,000.00
Rex Caldwell	T-9	72-69-76-72=289	$10,000.00

Honda Classic

Course: TPC at Eagle Trace, Coral Springs, Fla.

Par: 72 Yardage: 7,030

Last day of event: Sunday, March 4, 1984

Player	Place	Score	Earnings
Bruce Lietzke	Win	72-70-70-68=280	$90,000.00
Playoff: Beat Andy Bean with par on first extra hole			

Player	Place	Score	Earnings
Andy Bean	2	69-71-68-72=280	$54,000.00
J.C. Snead	3	68-71-72-70=281	$34,000.00
Mark McCumber	4	77-67-66-72=282	$24,000.00
Joey Sindelar	5	70-73-70-70=283	$20,000.00
Hubert Green	T-6	72-72-72-68=284	$16,187.50
Tommy Nakajima	T-6	70-71-70-73=284	$16,187.50
Jim Colbert	T-6	73-68-71-72=284	$16,187.50
Gary Koch	T-6	74-74-66-70=284	$16,187.50
Phil Hancock	T-10	71-71-73-70=285	$13,000.00
Fred Couples	T-10	75-71-70-69=285	$13,000.00

Doral-Eastern Open

Course: Doral C.C. (Blue), Miami, Fla.

Par: 72 Yardage: 6,939

Last day of event: Sunday, March 11, 1984

Player	Place	Score	Earnings
Tom Kite	Win	68-69-70-65=272	$72,000.00
Jack Nicklaus	2	67-69-70-68=274	$43,200.00
George Archer	T-3	71-65-69-70=275	$23,200.00
Bruce Lietzke	T-3	71-67-67-70=275	$23,200.00
Gary Hallberg	5	67-70-69-70=276	$16,000.00
Johnny Miller	T-6	68-70-68-71=277	$12,950.00
Ben Crenshaw	T-6	69-71-71-66=277	$12,950.00
Andy Bean	T-6	72-69-69-67=277	$12,950.00
Bob Shearer	T-6	70-66-73-68=277	$12,950.00
Gibby Gilbert	T-10	70-70-69-69=278	$10,000.00
Tony Sills	T-10	69-71-69-69=278	$10,000.00
Wayne Levi	T-10	70-68-69-71=278	$10,000.00

Bay Hill Classic

Course: Bay Hill Club, Orlando, Fla.

Par: 71 Yardage: 7,103

Last day of event: Sunday, March 18, 1984

Player	Place	Score	Earnings
Gary Koch	Win	69-68-72-63=272	$72,000.00
Playoff: Beat George Burns with birdie on second extra hole			
George Burns	2	67-69-69-67=272	$43,200.00
Bernhard Langer	3	70-68-69-66=273	$27,200.00
Hal Sutton	4	67-69-67-72=275	$19,200.00
Sammy Rachels	5	69-69-68-70=276	$16,000.00
Ray Floyd	T-6	67-69-70-71=277	$13,900.00
Greg Norman	T-6	71-62-71-73=277	$13,900.00
Roger Maltbie	8	73-68-70-68=279	$12,400.00
Tom Watson	T-9	70-70-70-70=280	$9,600.00
Bruce Lietzke	T-9	70-71-68-71=280	$9,600.00
Craig Stadler	T-9	71-71-71-67=280	$9,600.00
Nick Faldo	T-9	72-68-68-72=280	$9,600.00
Jack Nicklaus	T-9	69-72-73-66=280	$9,600.00
Dan Pohl	T-9	73-71-67-69=280	$9,600.00

USF&G Classic

Course: Lakewood C.C., New Orleans, La.

Par: 72 Yardage: 7,080

Last day of event: Sunday, March 25, 1984

Player	Place	Score	Earnings
Bob Eastwood	Win	66-68-68-70=272	$72,000.00
Larry Rinker	2	71-66-70-68=275	$43,200.00
John Mahaffey	T-3	68-70-68-71=277	$20,800.00
John Adams	T-3	69-70-71-67=277	$20,800.00
Doug Tewell	T-3	70-69-66-72=277	$20,800.00
Bernhard Langer	6	67-69-72-70=278	$14,400.00

Don Pooley	T-7	71-70-68-70=279	$12,900.00
Larry Mize	T-7	66-71-74-68=279	$12,900.00
Ben Crenshaw	T-9	69-70-72-69=280	$10,000.00
Wayne Levi	T-9	69-70-72-69=280	$10,000.00
Calvin Peete	T-9	71-70-72-67=280	$10,000.00
Denis Watson	T-9	72-68-70-70=280	$10,000.00
Mike Nicolette	T-9	74-66-72-68=280	$10,000.00

Tournament Players Championship

Course: TPC at Sawgrass, Ponte Vedra Beach, Fla.
Par: 72 Yardage: 6,857
Last day of event: Sunday, April 1, 1984

Player	Place	Score	Earnings
Fred Couples	Win	71-64-71-71=277	$144,000.00
Lee Trevino	2	76-66-68-68=278	$86,400.00
Seve Ballesteros	T-3	70-68-70-74=282	$46,400.00
Craig Stadler	T-3	74-70-66-72=282	$46,400.00
Mark O'Meara	T-5	72-69-69-73=283	$30,400.00
Lanny Wadkins	T-5	72-66-78-67=283	$30,400.00
Nick Price	7	70-72-74-68=284	$26,800.00
Dan Pohl	T-8	74-69-71-71=285	$24,000.00
Tom Watson	T-8	75-67-67-76=285	$24,000.00
John Mahaffey	T-10	69-74-69-74=286	$20,800.00
Jim Thorpe	T-10	68-69-78-71=286	$20,800.00

Greater Greensboro Open

Course: Forest Oaks C.C., Greensboro, N.C.
Par: 72 Yardage: 6,984
Last day of event: Sunday, April 8, 1984

Player	Place	Score	Earnings
Andy Bean	Win	71-67-72-70=280	$72,000.00
George Archer	2	72-73-68-69=282	$43,200.00
Scott Simpson	T-3	72-71-70-72=285	$18,040.00
Fred Couples	T-3	72-71-71-71=285	$18,040.00
Buddy Gardner	T-3	69-73-70-73=285	$18,040.00
Ben Crenshaw	T-3	73-72-73-67=285	$18,040.00
Jack Renner	T-3	72-67-74-72=285	$18,040.00
Clarence Rose	T-8	71-72-70-73=286	$10,800.00
Nick Faldo	T-8	71-70-73-72=286	$10,800.00
Steven Liebler	T-8	73-71-71-71=286	$10,800.00
David Peoples	T-8	70-71-71-74=286	$10,800.00
Tom Purtzer	T-8	71-72-74-69=286	$10,800.00

Masters

Course: Augusta National G.C., Augusta, Ga.
Par: 72 Yardage: 6,925
Last day of event: Sunday, April 15, 1984

Player	Place	Score	Earnings
Ben Crenshaw	Win	67-72-70-68=277	$108,000.00
Tom Watson	2	74-67-69-69=279	$64,800.00
David Edwards	T-3	71-70-72-67=280	$34,800.00
Gil Morgan	T-3	73-71-69-67=280	$34,800.00
Larry Nelson	5	76-69-66-70=281	$24,000.00
David Graham	T-6	69-70-70-73=282	$19,425.00
Mark Lye	T-6	69-66-73-74=282	$19,425.00
Ronnie Black	T-6	71-74-69-68=282	$19,425.00
Tom Kite	T-6	70-68-69-75=282	$19,425.00
Fred Couples	10	71-73-67-72=283	$16,200.00

Sea Pines Heritage Classic

Course: Harbour Town G.L., Hilton Head, S.C.
Par: 71 Yardage: 6,657
Last day of event: Sunday, April 22, 1984

Player	Place	Score	Earnings
Nick Faldo	Win	66-67-68-69=270	$72,000.00
Tom Kite	2	68-67-70-66=271	$43,200.00
Ronnie Black	T-3	69-67-71-67=274	$23,200.00
Gil Morgan	T-3	64-73-71-66=274	$23,200.00
Dan Pohl	5	69-67-69-71=276	$16,000.00
Hal Sutton	T-6	69-70-69-70=278	$13,400.00
Chip Beck	T-6	72-68-68-70=278	$13,400.00
Andy Bean	T-6	70-74-67-67=278	$13,400.00
Jim Thorpe	T-9	69-71-70-69=279	$11,200.00
Hubert Green	T-9	69-70-68-72=279	$11,200.00

Houston Coca-Cola Open

Course: Woodlands C.C., The Woodlands, Texas
Par: 71 Yardage: 7,031
Last day of event: Sunday, April 29, 1984

Player	Place	Score	Earnings
Corey Pavin	Win	70-68-68-68=274	$90,000.00
Buddy Gardner	2	70-67-69-69=275	$54,000.00
Bobby Wadkins	3	66-67-73-70=276	$34,000.00
Nick Price	4	67-72-69-69=277	$24,000.00
Doug Tewell	5	68-70-68-72=278	$20,000.00
Bruce Lietzke	T-6	70-69-69-71=279	$15,650.00
Ron Streck	T-6	66-71-70-72=279	$15,650.00
Gary McCord	T-6	65-71-73-70=279	$15,650.00
Mark O'Meara	T-6	69-68-69-73=279	$15,650.00
John Mahaffey	T-6	68-68-68-75=279	$15,650.00

MONY Tournament of Champions

Course: La Costa C.C., Carlsbad, Calif.
Par: 72 Yardage: 7,022
Last day of event: Sunday, May 6, 1984

Player	Place	Score	Earnings
Tom Watson	Win	69-71-67-67=274	$72,000.00
Bruce Lietzke	2	72-68-71-68=279	$43,200.00
Seve Ballesteros	3	71-70-71-70=282	$27,200.00
David Graham	4	64-77-68-74=283	$20,300.00
Hal Sutton	5	69-67-77-71=284	$18,500.00
Lanny Wadkins	T-6	70-71-71-73=285	$15,666.66
Tom Kite	T-6	71-67-74-73=285	$15,666.67
Calvin Peete	T-6	74-73-67-71=285	$15,666.67
John Mahaffey	T-9	71-71-71-73=286	$11,500.00
Larry Nelson	T-9	71-73-69-73=286	$11,500.00
Andy Bean	T-9	72-73-70-71=286	$11,500.00
Wayne Levi	T-9	74-68-72-72=286	$11,500.00
Hale Irwin	T-9	72-67-75-72=286	$11,500.00

Byron Nelson Golf Classic

Course: Las Colinas Sports Club, Irving, Texas
Par: 71 Yardage: 6,982
Last day of event: Sunday, May 13, 1984

Player	Place	Score	Earnings
Craig Stadler	Win	70-71-64-71=276	$90,000.00
David Edwards	2	68-75-69-65=277	$54,000.00
Tom Watson	3	73-72-66-68=279	$34,000.00
Dave Barr	T-4	67-73-73-67=280	$22,000.00

Andy Bean	T-4	74-69-69-68=280	$22,000.00
Dan Pohl	T-6	73-71-71-66=281	$16,750.00
Ben Crenshaw	T-6	73-72-70-66=281	$16,750.00
Mike Smith	T-6	74-67-68-72=281	$16,750.00
Tom Kite	T-9	72-73-68-69=282	$12,500.00
Mark O'Meara	T-9	74-71-66-71=282	$12,500.00
Wayne Levi	T-9	74-73-69-66=282	$12,500.00
Payne Stewart	T-9	75-70-68-69=282	$12,500.00
Hal Sutton	T-9	75-68-71-68=282	$12,500.00

Colonial National Invitational

Course: Colonial C.C., Fort Worth, Texas
Par: 70 Yardage: 7,096
Last day of event: Sunday, May 20, 1984

Player	Place	Score	Earnings
Peter Jacobsen	Win	64-71-65-70=270	$90,000.00

Playoff: Beat Payne Stewart with birdie on first extra hole

Payne Stewart	2	68-66-64-72=270	$54,000.00
Gil Morgan	3	66-67-70-72=275	$34,000.00
Tony Sills	T-4	67-71-69-70=277	$18,850.00
Ben Crenshaw	T-4	69-71-68-69=277	$18,850.00
Tom Kite	T-4	70-69-67-71=277	$18,850.00
Tom Watson	T-4	66-72-69-70=277	$18,850.00
Mark Pfeil	T-4	72-67-69-69=277	$18,850.00
Mike Sullivan	T-9	68-71-70-69=278	$14,000.00
Ray Floyd	T-9	72-68-69-69=278	$14,000.00

Memorial Tournament

Course: Muirfield Village G.C., Dubin, Ohio
Par: 72 Yardage: 7,116
Last day of event: Sunday, May 27, 1984

Player	Place	Score	Earnings
Jack Nicklaus	Win	69-70-71-70=280	$90,000.00

Playoff: Beat Andy Bean with par on third extra hole

Andy Bean	2	71-75-67-67=280	$54,000.00
Roger Maltbie	T-3	70-73-73-67=283	$26,000.00
Chip Beck	T-3	69-72-68-74=283	$26,000.00
Payne Stewart	T-3	67-75-72-69=283	$26,000.00
Hal Sutton	T-6	71-73-73-68=285	$17,375.00
Gil Morgan	T-6	67-73-74-71=285	$17,375.00
Larry Mize	T-8	72-73-71-70=286	$15,000.00
Larry Nelson	T-8	68-73-75-70=286	$15,000.00
Gary Koch	T-10	69-71-73-74=287	$12,500.00
Mark McCumber	T-10	73-75-75-64=287	$12,500.00
Bob Murphy	T-10	67-73-76-71=287	$12,500.00

Kemper Open

Course: Congressional C.C., Bethesda, Md.
Par: 72 Yardage: 7,173
Last day of event: Sunday, June 3, 1984

Player	Place	Score	Earnings
Greg Norman	Win	68-68-71-73=280	$72,000.00
Mark O'Meara	2	73-71-72-69=285	$43,200.00
Gil Morgan	T-3	72-70-73-72=287	$17,100.00
Mike Donald	T-3	72-73-72-70=287	$17,100.00
Scott Hoch	T-3	73-72-70-72=287	$17,100.00
Jim Thorpe	T-3	70-72-74-71=287	$17,100.00
Mike Reid	T-3	72-71-74-70=287	$17,100.00
Hal Sutton	T-3	73-76-69-69=287	$17,100.00
Scott Simpson	T-9	70-72-73-73=288	$9,600.00
Ralph Landrum	T-9	70-73-73-72=288	$9,600.00

Peter Jacobsen	T-9	71-72-73-72=288	$9,600.00
Hale Irwin	T-9	72-73-73-70=288	$9,600.00
John Mahaffey	T-9	73-71-70-74=288	$9,600.00
Curtis Strange	T-9	75-74-71-68=288	$9,600.00

Manufacturers Hanover Westchester Classic

Course: Westchester C.C., Harrison, N.Y.
Par: 71 Yardage: 6,687
Last day of event: Sunday, June 10, 1984

Player	Place	Score	Earnings
Scott Simpson	Win	66-68-70-65=269	$90,000.00
Mark O'Meara	T-2	69-68-70-67=274	$37,333.33
Jay Haas	T-2	67-68-68-71=274	$37,333.33
David Graham	T-2	68-71-69-66=274	$37,333.34
Chip Beck	5	63-69-70-73=275	$20,000.00
Gary McCord	T-6	68-72-67-69=276	$17,375.00
Tom Kite	T-6	70-66-68-72=276	$17,375.00
Mike Sullivan	T-8	69-70-70-68=277	$15,000.00
Fred Couples	T-8	67-69-73-68=277	$15,000.00
Allen Miller	T-10	70-70-68-70=278	$11,500.00
D.A. Weibring	T-10	67-71-71-69=278	$11,500.00
Loren Roberts	T-10	68-69-70-71=278	$11,500.00
Gil Morgan	T-10	71-66-71-70=278	$11,500.00
Calvin Peete	T-10	71-68-69-70=278	$11,500.00

U.S. Open

Course: Winged Foot G.C. (West), Mamaroneck, N.Y.
Par: 70 Yardage: 6,930
Last day of event: Sunday, June 17, 1984

Player	Place	Score	Earnings
Fuzzy Zoeller	Win	71-66-69-70-67=276	$94,000.00

Playoff: Beat Greg Norman in18-hole playoff (Zoeller 67, Norman 75)

Greg Norman	2	70-68-69-69-75=276	$47,000.00
Curtis Strange	3	69-70-74-68=281	$36,000.00
Jim Thorpe	T-4	68-71-70-73=282	$22,335.00
Johnny Miller	T-4	74-68-70-70=282	$22,335.00
Hale Irwin	6	68-68-69-79=284	$16,238.00
Peter Jacobsen	T-7	72-73-73-67=285	$14,237.00
Mark O'Meara	T-7	71-74-71-69=285	$14,237.00
Fred Couples	T-9	69-71-74-72=286	$12,122.00
Lee Trevino	T-9	71-72-69-74=286	$12,122.00

Georgia-Pacific Atlanta Golf Classic

Course: Atlanta C.C., Atlanta, Ga.
Par: 72 Yardage: 7,007
Last day of event: Sunday, June 24, 1984

Player	Place	Score	Earnings
Tom Kite	Win	69-67-66-67=269	$72,000.00
Don Pooley	2	68-68-67-71=274	$43,200.00
Tim Simpson	T-3	70-70-68-67=275	$23,200.00
Mike Donald	T-3	64-73-69-69=275	$23,200.00
Mike Sullivan	T-5	67-71-70-69=277	$13,560.00
Jay Haas	T-5	71-72-67-67=277	$13,560.00
Jim Colbert	T-5	72-69-67-69=277	$13,560.00
Scott Simpson	T-5	70-73-63-71=277	$13,560.00
Bobby Wadkins	T-5	70-66-74-67=277	$13,560.00
Joe Inman	T-10	69-68-71-70=278	$10,000.00
Greg Norman	T-10	72-70-68-68=278	$10,000.00
Tommy Valentine	T-10	70-63-72-73=278	$10,000.00

Canadian Open

Course: Glen Abbey G.C., Oakville, Ontario, Canada
Par: 72 Yardage: 7,102
Last day of event: Sunday, July 1, 1984

Player	Place	Score	Earnings
Greg Norman	Win	73-68-70-67=278	$72,000.00
Jack Nicklaus	2	73-69-69-69=280	$43,200.00
Mark Pfeil	T-3	74-72-66-71=283	$23,200.00
Nick Price	T-3	67-67-73-76=283	$23,200.00
Clarence Rose	T-5	71-70-72-71=284	$14,050.00
John Cook	T-5	71-69-71-73=284	$14,050.00
Richard Zokol	T-5	69-74-71-70=284	$14,050.00
Corey Pavin	T-5	73-67-74-70=284	$14,050.00
Mark Lye	T-9	75-73-69-68=285	$11,200.00
Hal Sutton	T-9	76-70-69-70=285	$11,200.00

Western Open

Course: Butler National G.C., Oak Brook, Ill.
Par: 72 Yardage: 7,097
Last day of event: Sunday, July 8, 1984

Player	Place	Score	Earnings
Tom Watson	Win	71-69-70-70=280	$72,000.00
Playoff: Beat Greg Norman with birdie on third extra hole			
Greg Norman	2	68-70-71-71=280	$43,200.00
Mark O'Meara	3	71-71-71-70=283	$27,200.00
Scott Hoch	4	69-70-73-72=284	$19,200.00
D.A. Weibring	5	68-69-76-72=285	$16,000.00
T.C. Chen	6	70-67-74-76=287	$14,400.00
Joe Inman	T-7	70-74-69-75=288	$12,900.00
George Burns	T-7	71-68-72-77=288	$12,900.00
Russ Cochran	T-9	70-73-72-74=289	$10,400.00
Corey Pavin	T-9	71-72-72-74=289	$10,400.00
Lance Ten Broeck	T-9	68-73-75-73=289	$10,400.00
Ben Crenshaw	T-9	75-70-74-70=289	$10,400.00

Anheuser-Busch Golf Classic

Course: Kingsmill G.C., Williamsburg, Va.
Par: 71 Yardage: 6,776
Last day of event: Sunday, July 15, 1984

Player	Place	Score	Earnings
Ronnie Black	Win	69-69-66-63=267	$63,000.00
Willie Wood	2	63-68-66-71=268	$37,800.00
Curtis Strange	3	65-68-69-67=269	$23,800.00
Wayne Levi	4	70-63-68-69=270	$16,800.00
Vance Heafner	5	67-72-68-69=276	$14,000.00
Scott Hoch	6	77-67-69-65=278	$12,600.00
Tim Norris	T-7	70-71-71-67=279	$8,808.33
Ken Green	T-7	71-69-69-70=279	$8,808.34
Tim Simpson	T-7	67-70-70-72=279	$8,808.33
Bill Kratzert	T-7	68-67-72-72=279	$8,808.33
Scott Simpson	T-7	68-71-72-68=279	$8,808.34
Larry Rinker	T-7	69-68-70-72=279	$8,808.33
Joe Inman	T-7	69-70-72-68=279	$8,808.33
John Adams	T-7	72-69-69-69=279	$8,808.34
Lanny Wadkins	T-7	67-71-67-74=279	$8,808.33

Miller High-Life Quad Cities Open

Course: Oakwood C.C., Coal Valley, Ill.
Par: 70 Yardage: 6,602
Last day of event: Sunday, July 22, 1984

Player	Place	Score	Earnings
Scott Hoch	Win	67-67-66-66=266	$36,000.00
Vance Heafner	T-2	64-67-69-71=271	$14,933.33
Dave Stockton	T-2	64-66-71-70=271	$14,933.33
George Archer	T-2	72-69-66-64=271	$14,933.34
Curt Byrum	T-5	70-66-67-69=272	$7,600.00
Gary Hallberg	T-5	71-67-69-65=272	$7,600.00
T.C. Chen	7	72-66-65-70=273	$6,700.00
Lindy Miller	T-8	68-70-67-69=274	$5,200.00
Brett Upper	T-8	67-69-67-71=274	$5,200.00
Jim Gallagher, Jr.	T-8	67-71-67-69=274	$5,200.00
Bill Calfee	T-8	68-68-67-71=274	$5,200.00
Woody Blackburn	T-8	68-69-65-72=274	$5,200.00
Randy Watkins	T-8	71-65-66-72=274	$5,200.00

British Open

Course: Old Course at St. Andrews, St. Andrews, Fife, Scotland
Par: 72 Yardage: 6,933
Last day of event: Sunday, July 22, 1984

Player	Place	Score	Earnings
Seve Ballesteros	Win	69-68-70-69=276	$71,500.00
Bernhard Langer	T-2	71-68-68-71=278	$41,470.00
Tom Watson	T-2	71-68-66-73=278	$41,470.00
Lanny Wadkins	T-4	70-69-73-69=281	$25,740.00
Fred Couples	T-4	70-69-74-68=281	$25,740.00
Greg Norman	T-6	67-74-74-67=282	$21,307.00
Nick Faldo	T-6	69-68-76-69=282	$21,307.00
Mark McCumber	8	74-67-72-70=283	$18,590.00
Hugh Baiocchi	T-9	72-70-70-72=284	$14,643.20
Graham Marsh	T-9	70-74-73-67=284	$14,643.20
Ronan Rafferty	T-9	74-72-67-71=284	$14,643.20
Sam Torrance	T-9	74-74-66-70=284	$14,643.20
Ian Baker-Finch	T-9	68-66-71-79=284	$14,643.20

Sammy Davis, Jr. - Greater Hartford Open

Course: TPC of Connecticut, Cromwell, Conn.
Par: 71 Yardage: 6,786
Last day of event: Sunday, July 29, 1984

Player	Place	Score	Earnings
Peter Jacobsen	Win	67-69-63-70=269	$72,000.00
Mark O'Meara	2	70-67-63-71=271	$43,200.00
Bill Kratzert	T-3	70-68-64-71=273	$23,200.00
Gary Hallberg	T-3	70-72-67-64=273	$23,200.00
Curtis Strange	T-5	69-72-69-66=276	$15,200.00
George Burns	T-5	65-73-68-70=276	$15,200.00
Mike Reid	T-7	69-69-70-69=277	$12,900.00
Mark Lye	T-7	70-69-68-70=277	$12,900.00
Chi Chi Rodriguez	T-9	70-69-69-70=278	$11,200.00
Lance Ten Broeck	T-9	67-70-72-69=278	$11,200.00

Danny Thomas Memphis Classic

Course: Colonial C.C. (South), Cordova, Tenn.
Par: 72 Yardage: 7,282
Last day of event: Sunday, August 5, 1984

Player	Place	Score	Earnings
Bob Eastwood	Win	71-69-68-72=280	$90,000.00
Ralph Landrum	T-2	71-74-70-67=282	$37,333.34
Tim Simpson	T-2	74-68-70-70=282	$37,333.33
Mark O'Meara	T-2	75-69-69-69=282	$37,333.33
Mark Lye	T-5	70-72-70-71=283	$19,000.00
Loren Roberts	T-5	67-70-70-76=283	$19,000.00

Roger Maltbie	T-7	72-70-71-71=284	$15,583.33
Bill Kratzert	T-7	70-69-74-71=284	$15,583.33
Willie Wood	T-7	67-71-75-71=284	$15,583.34
Mark Brooks	T-10	72-71-72-70=285	$13,000.00
Curtis Strange	T-10	70-71-71-73=285	$13,000.00

Buick Open

Course: Warwick Hills C.C., Grand Blanc, Mich.
Par: 72 Yardage: 7,014
Last day of event: Sunday, August 12, 1984

Player	Place	Score	Earnings
Denis Watson	Win	70-70-63-68=271	$72,000.00
Payne Stewart	2	69-65-69-69=272	$43,200.00
Scott Hoch	3	70-65-69-69=273	$27,200.00
Isao Aoki	T-4	68-68-67-71=274	$15,750.00
Lee Trevino	T-4	70-64-69-71=274	$15,750.00
Dave Barr	T-4	71-70-66-67=274	$15,750.00
Rex Caldwell	T-4	71-71-66-66=274	$15,750.00
Lanny Wadkins	T-8	69-67-71-68=275	$12,000.00
Mark O'Meara	T-8	69-69-64-73=275	$12,000.00
Chip Beck	T-10	69-69-68-70=276	$10,000.00
D.A. Weibring	T-10	68-71-67-70=276	$10,000.00
Jack Renner	T-10	68-71-69-68=276	$10,000.00

PGA Championship

Course: Shoal Creek C.C., Birmingham, Al.
Par: 72 Yardage: 7,145
Last day of event: Sunday, August 19, 1984

Player	Place	Score	Earnings
Lee Trevino	Win	69-68-67-69=273	$125,000.00
Lanny Wadkins	T-2	68-69-68-72=277	$62,500.00
Gary Player	T-2	74-63-69-71=277	$62,500.00
Calvin Peete	4	71-70-69-68=278	$35,000.00
Seve Ballesteros	5	70-69-70-70=279	$25,000.00
Gary Hallberg	T-6	69-71-68-72=280	$17,150.00
Scott Simpson	T-6	69-69-72-70=280	$17,150.00
Larry Mize	T-6	71-69-67-73=280	$17,150.00
Hal Sutton	T-6	74-73-64-69=280	$17,150.00
Victor Regalado	T-10	69-69-73-70=281	$12,083.33
Russ Cochran	T-10	73-68-73-67=281	$12,083.34
Tommy Nakajima	T-10	72-68-67-74=281	$12,083.33

NEC World Series of Golf

Course: Firestone C.C. (South), Akron, Ohio
Par: 70 Yardage: 7,149
Last day of event: Sunday, August 26, 1984

Player	Place	Score	Earnings
Denis Watson	Win	69-62-70-70=271	$126,000.00
Bruce Lietzke	2	66-68-69-70=273	$75,600.00
Peter Jacobsen	T-3	70-67-69-69=275	$40,600.00
Bob Eastwood	T-3	70-70-66-69=275	$40,600.00
Craig Stadler	T-5	69-70-68-70=277	$26,600.00
Scott Simpson	T-5	71-69-70-67=277	$26,600.00
Pat Lindsey	7	70-70-72-66=278	$23,400.00
Greg Norman	T-8	70-73-70-66=279	$21,000.00
Tom Kite	T-8	73-69-65-72=279	$21,000.00
Jack Nicklaus	10	72-73-69-66=280	$18,900.00

B.C. Open

Course: En-Joie G.C., Endicott, N.Y.
Par: 71 Yardage: 6,966
Last day of event: Sunday, September 2, 1984

Player	Place	Score	Earnings
Wayne Levi	Win	67-71-71-66=275	$54,000.00
Hal Sutton	T-2	69-69-68-70=276	$26,400.00
Russ Cochran	T-2	69-71-69-67=276	$26,400.00
Larry Mize	T-4	70-68-71-69=278	$13,200.00
Mike Donald	T-4	66-74-69-69=278	$13,200.00
Dan Halldorson	T-6	67-72-70-70=279	$10,425.00
Loren Roberts	T-6	71-73-69-66=279	$10,425.00
Mark Wiebe	T-8	71-69-72-68=280	$8,700.00
Brett Upper	T-8	72-71-67-70=280	$8,700.00
George Burns	T-8	73-68-71-68=280	$8,700.00

Bank of Boston Classic

Course: Pleasant Valley C.C., Sutton, Mass.
Par: 71 Yardage: 7,110
Last day of event: Sunday, September 9, 1984

Player	Place	Score	Earnings
George Archer	Win	69-66-70-65=270	$63,000.00
Joey Sindelar	T-2	71-64-69-72=276	$30,800.00
Frank Conner	T-2	72-68-71-65=276	$30,800.00
Jerry Pate	4	71-72-67-68=278	$16,800.00
Jim Thorpe	T-5	69-71-70-69=279	$12,775.00
Curtis Strange	T-5	68-69-73-69=279	$12,775.00
Tommy Valentine	T-5	72-67-67-73=279	$12,775.00
Lou Graham	T-8	69-69-71-71=280	$8,750.00
Tom Jenkins	T-8	70-72-67-71=280	$8,750.00
Tim Simpson	T-8	72-67-70-71=280	$8,750.00
John Mahaffey	T-8	70-69-68-73=280	$8,750.00
Mike Smith	T-8	74-70-66-70=280	$8,750.00
Calvin Peete	T-8	66-71-68-75=280	$8,750.00
George Burns	T-8	75-67-67-71=280	$8,750.00

Greater Milwaukee Open

Course: Tuckaway C.C., Franklin, Wis.
Par: 72 Yardage: 7,030
Last day of event: Sunday, September 16, 1984

Player	Place	Score	Earnings
Mark O'Meara	Win	67-68-69-68=272	$54,000.00
Tom Watson	2	68-69-70-70=277	$32,400.00
Keith Fergus	3	68-72-68-70=278	$20,400.00
Dan Pohl	T-4	65-71-71-72=279	$13,200.00
Mark Calcavecchia	T-4	70-72-71-66=279	$13,200.00
Jim Nelford	T-6	68-70-70-72=280	$9,712.50
Brad Faxon	T-6	68-70-72-70=280	$9,712.50
Bill Sander	T-6	68-70-73-69=280	$9,712.50
Calvin Peete	T-6	73-71-70-66=280	$9,712.50
Mark McCumber	T-10	69-71-69-72=281	$7,500.00
Gary Pinns	T-10	69-72-68-72=281	$7,500.00
Nick Price	T-10	73-70-73-65=281	$7,500.00

Panasonic Las Vegas Invitational

Course: Las Vegas C.C.,Tropicana C.C., Desert Inn C.C., Showboat C.C., Las Vegas, Nev.
Home course / Las Vegas C.C., Par: 71 Yardage: 7,164
Last day of event: Sunday, September 23, 1984

Player	Place	Score	Earnings
Denis Watson	Win	69-66-68-70-68=341	$162,000.00

Andy Bean	2	69-65-69-71-68=342	$97,200.00
Craig Stadler	T-3	67-68-68-67-73=343	$52,200.00
Payne Stewart	T-3	67-73-67-64-72=343	$52,200.00
Johnny Miller	5	70-69-64-67-75=345	$36,000.00
Mark Pfeil	T-6	70-68-71-71-66=346	$29,137.50
Dave Barr	T-6	65-71-68-70-72=346	$29,137.50
Mike Donald	T-6	66-68-70-70-72=346	$29,137.50
Mark O'Meara	T-6	68-75-67-67-69=346	$29,137.50
Bruce Fleisher	T-10	67-70-68-71-71=347	$20,700.00
Jack Renner	T-10	70-71-67-69-70=347	$20,700.00
Gibby Gilbert	T-10	71-70-66-71-69=347	$20,700.00
Lon Hinkle	T-10	62-68-73-72-72=347	$20,700.00
Russ Cochran	T-10	69-70-68-74-66=347	$20,700.00

LaJet Golf Classic

Course: Fairway Oaks C.C., Abilene, Texas
Par: 72 Yardage: 7,166
Last day of event: Sunday, September 30, 1984

Player	Place	Score	Earnings
Curtis Strange	Win	68-67-67-71=273	$63,000.00
Mark O'Meara	2	68-70-71-66=275	$37,800.00
Vance Heafner	T-3	67-72-69-70=278	$20,300.00
Dan Halldorson	T-3	67-68-73-70=278	$20,300.00
Hubert Green	T-5	68-72-69-70=279	$13,300.00
Tim Simpson	T-5	69-72-69-69=279	$13,300.00
Brett Upper	T-7	66-72-71-71=280	$10,908.33
Tony Sills	T-7	68-72-71-69=280	$10,908.34
Dan Forsman	T-7	67-73-71-69=280	$10,908.33
Scott Simpson	10	68-72-70-71=281	$9,450.00

Texas Open

Course: Oak Hill C.C., San Antonio, Texas
Par: 70 Yardage: 6,576
Last day of event: Sunday, October 7, 1984

Player	Place	Score	Earnings
Calvin Peete	Win	67-67-66-66=266	$63,000.00
Bruce Lietzke	2	67-71-66-65=269	$37,800.00
Mike Reid	T-3	69-69-65-67=270	$20,300.00
Mark O'Meara	T-3	67-66-72-65=270	$20,300.00
Ron Streck	5	65-68-69-69=271	$14,000.00
Howard Twitty	6	67-70-71-64=272	$12,600.00
Dan Forsman	T-7	69-70-66-68=273	$10,543.75
Mike Nicolette	T-7	70-68-67-68=273	$10,543.75
Lanny Wadkins	T-7	66-71-69-67=273	$10,543.75
Keith Fergus	T-7	75-64-65-69=273	$10,543.75

Southern Open

Course: Green Island C.C., Columbus, Ga.
Par: 70 Yardage: 6,791
Last day of event: Sunday, October 14, 1984

Player	Place	Score	Earnings
Hubert Green	Win	65-66-67-67=265	$54,000.00
Rex Caldwell	T-2	68-68-69-66=271	$22,400.00
Corey Pavin	T-2	69-66-68-68=271	$22,400.00
Scott Hoch	T-2	68-65-68-70=271	$22,400.00
Andy Bean	T-5	71-68-65-68=272	$11,400.00
Gary Hallberg	T-5	65-67-72-68=272	$11,400.00
Willie Wood	T-7	64-70-69-70=273	$9,037.50
Peter Oosterhuis	T-7	67-70-68-68=273	$9,037.50
Mike Sullivan	T-7	66-67-72-68=273	$9,037.50
Gibby Gilbert	T-7	69-66-72-66=273	$9,037.50

Walt Disney World Golf Classic

Course: Walt Disney (Magnolia, Palm), Lake Buena Vista C.C., Lake Buena Vista, Fla.
Home course / Magnolia, Par: 72 Yardage: 7,190
Last day of event: Sunday, October 21, 1984

Player	Place	Score	Earnings
Larry Nelson	Win	66-66-64-70=266	$72,000.00
Hubert Green	2	67-65-67-68=267	$43,200.00
Brad Faxon	T-3	67-65-69-69=270	$20,800.00
Jay Haas	T-3	66-66-70-68=270	$20,800.00
Chip Beck	T-3	64-66-68-72=270	$20,800.00
Payne Stewart	T-6	70-64-68-69=271	$13,400.00
Larry Rinker	T-6	69-71-64-67=271	$13,400.00
Mark Lye	T-6	68-73-61-69=271	$13,400.00
Bobby Wadkins	T-9	67-68-69-68=272	$10,800.00
Dave Barr	T-9	68-67-70-67=272	$10,800.00
D.A. Weibring	T-9	70-67-70-65=272	$10,800.00

Pensacola Open

Course: Perdido Bay C.C., Pensacola, Fla.
Par: 71 Yardage: 7,093
Last day of event: Sunday, October 28, 1984

Player	Place	Score	Earnings
Bill Kratzert	Win	67-66-71-66=270	$54,000.00
Ken Brown	T-2	66-68-69-69=272	$26,400.00
John Mahaffey	T-2	67-67-70-68=272	$26,400.00
Ralph Landrum	4	63-69-73-69=274	$14,400.00
Gene Sauers	T-5	70-69-68-69=276	$9,825.00
Danny Edwards	T-5	66-68-71-71=276	$9,825.00
Tim Norris	T-5	67-68-71-70=276	$9,825.00
Joey Sindelar	T-5	70-68-66-72=276	$9,825.00
Gibby Gilbert	T-5	70-67-72-67=276	$9,825.00
Mark McCumber	T-5	70-67-73-66=276	$9,825.00

1985

Bernhard Langer became the first man from Germany to win a major championship, claiming the Masters by two shots over Seve Ballesteros, Raymond Floyd and Curtis Strange. Andy North won his second U.S. Open, this time by one shot at Oakland Hills, where co-runnerup T.C. Chen of Taiwan became etched in golf lore. Leading by four shots after four holes in Round 4, Chen double-hit a wedge shot en route to a quadruple-bogey 8 at No. 5—prompting golfers forever after to refer to a double-hit as a "T.C. Chen." Sandy Lyle beat Payne Stewart by a shot at Sandwich, becoming the first resident Scotsman to win the British Open since George Duncan in 1920. Hubert Green won his second major, scoring a one-shot victory over Lee Trevino in the PGA Championship at Cherry Hills. Amateur Scott Verplank won the Western Open. The United States lost the Ryder Cup for the first time in 28 years, ushering in an era of intense competition between America and Europe.

Bob Hope Chrysler Classic

Course: Indian Wells C.C., Tamarisk C.C., Bermuda Dunes C.C., La Quinta C.C.
Home course / Indian Wells, Par: 72 Yardage: 6,478
Last day of event: Sunday, January 13, 1985

Player	Place	Score	Earnings
Lanny Wadkins	Win	67-67-68-66-65=333	$90,000.00
Playoff: Beat Craig Stadler with birdie on fifth extra hole			
Craig Stadler	2	66-68-64-69-66=333	$54,000.00
Hubert Green	3	68-68-69-70-65=340	$34,000.00
Ron Streck	4	68-67-66-70-70=341	$24,000.00
Ray Floyd	T-5	70-69-66-70-67=342	$18,250.00
Larry Mize	T-5	68-68-67-68-71=342	$18,250.00

Buddy Gardner	T-5	74-64-67-71-66=342	$18,250.00
Jack Renner	T-8	70-70-67-68-68=343	$14,500.00
Ed Fiori	T-8	71-67-67-69-69=343	$14,500.00
John Mahaffey	T-8	66-69-72-72-64=343	$14,500.00

Phoenix Open

Course: Phoenix C.C., Phoenix, Ariz.
Par: 71 Yardage: 6,726
Last day of event: Sunday, January 20, 1985

Player	Place	Score	Earnings
Calvin Peete	Win	65-65-72-68=270	$81,000.00
Morris Hatalsky	T-2	66-70-66-70=272	$39,600.00
Doug Tewell	T-2	67-68-65-72=272	$39,600.00
Corey Pavin	T-4	70-69-67-69=275	$16,312.50
Don Pooley	T-4	70-67-70-68=275	$16,312.50
Dan Forsman	T-4	70-69-70-66=275	$16,312.50
John Mahaffey	T-4	68-72-72-63=275	$16,312.50
Loren Roberts	T-4	69-72-66-68=275	$16,312.50
Nick Faldo	T-4	67-73-69-66=275	$16,312.50
Ed Fiori	10	69-71-65-71=276	$12,150.00

Los Angeles Open

Course: Riviera C.C., Pacific Palisades, Calif.
Par: 71 Yardage: 7,029
Last day of event: Sunday, January 27, 1985

Player	Place	Score	Earnings
Lanny Wadkins	Win	63-70-67-64=264	$72,000.00
Hal Sutton	2	66-66-70-69=271	$43,200.00
Corey Pavin	3	68-70-64-70=272	$27,200.00
Craig Stadler	T-4	68-69-70-66=273	$16,533.33
Gary Koch	T-4	66-66-70-71=273	$16,533.33
Chip Beck	T-4	71-66-66-70=273	$16,533.34
Don Pooley	T-7	69-66-70-70=275	$12,050.00
Larry Rinker	T-7	71-70-65-69=275	$12,050.00
Scott Simpson	T-7	66-71-66-72=275	$12,050.00
Larry Mize	T-7	70-62-71-72=275	$12,050.00

Bing Crosby Pro-Am

Courses: Pebble Beach G.L., Spyglass Hill G.C., Cypress Point C.C., Pebble Beach, Calif.
Home Course / Pebble Beach, G.L., Par: 72 Yardage: 6,815
Last day of event: Sunday, February 3, 1985

Player	Place	Score	Earnings
Mark O'Meara	Win	70-72-68-73=283	$90,000.00
Kikuo Aoki	T-2	73-69-71-71=284	$37,333.33
Larry Rinker	T-2	73-72-70-69=284	$37,333.34
Curtis Strange	T-2	75-69-68-72=284	$37,333.33
Payne Stewart	T-5	72-73-74-66=285	$19,000.00
Rex Caldwell	T-5	75-72-72-66=285	$19,000.00
Bernhard Langer	T-7	73-71-71-71=286	$15,583.33
Greg Norman	T-7	74-68-73-71=286	$15,583.34
Tom Watson	T-7	75-71-71-69=286	$15,583.33
Doug Tewell	T-10	72-70-72-73=287	$11,500.00
Lanny Wadkins	T-10	73-74-68-72=287	$11,500.00
Corey Pavin	T-10	74-72-73-68=287	$11,500.00
George Archer	T-10	69-70-76-72=287	$11,500.00
Johnny Miller	T-10	68-71-77-71=287	$11,500.00

Hawaiian Open

Course: Waialae C.C., Honolulu, Ha.
Par: 72 Yardage: 6,975
Last day of event: Sunday, February 10, 1985

Player	Place	Score	Earnings
Mark O'Meara	Win	67-66-65-69=267	$90,000.00
Craig Stadler	2	68-70-66-64=268	$54,000.00
Larry Mize	T-3	67-67-69-69=272	$29,000.00
Ed Fiori	T-3	68-68-67-69=272	$29,000.00
Buddy Gardner	5	69-70-65-69=273	$20,000.00
Dan Pohl	T-6	67-68-72-67=274	$16,750.00
Jim Simons	T-6	68-66-68-72=274	$16,750.00
Andy North	T-6	66-67-73-68=274	$16,750.00
Scott Simpson	T-9	66-68-70-71=275	$13,000.00
Fred Couples	T-9	67-71-69-68=275	$13,000.00
Jay Delsing	T-9	69-69-71-66=275	$13,000.00
Larry Nelson	T-9	70-64-68-73=275	$13,000.00

Isuzu/Andy Williams San Diego Open

Course: Torrey Pines (South), Torrey Pines (North), San Diego, Calif.
Home Course -Par: 72 Yardage: 7,021
Last day of event: Sunday, February 17, 1985

Player	Place	Score	Earnings
Woody Blackburn	Win	66-66-66-71=269	$72,000.00
Playoff: Beat Ron Streck with par on fourth extra hole			
Ron Streck	2	67-66-66-70=269	$43,200.00
Loren Roberts	3	65-68-69-68=270	$27,200.00
Dan Pohl	T-4	67-65-70-69=271	$17,600.00
Rex Caldwell	T-4	71-66-69-65=271	$17,600.00
Mark Pfeil	T-6	68-69-67-69=273	$13,900.00
Fred Couples	T-6	67-69-65-72=273	$13,900.00
Ed Fiori	T-8	66-68-70-70=274	$11,200.00
Don Pooley	T-8	64-69-70-71=274	$11,200.00
Bill Glasson	T-8	68-68-67-71=274	$11,200.00
Vance Heafner	T-8	65-70-66-73=274	$11,200.00

Doral-Eastern Open

Course: Doral C.C. (Blue), Miami, Fla.
Par: 72 Yardage: 6,939
Last day of event: Sunday, February 24, 1985

Player	Place	Score	Earnings
Mark McCumber	Win	70-71-72-71=284	$72,000.00
Tom Kite	2	71-70-71-73=285	$43,200.00
Roger Maltbie	T-3	71-74-72-70=287	$23,200.00
Jack Nicklaus	T-3	76-68-69-74=287	$23,200.00
Andy Bean	T-5	70-74-72-72=288	$13,560.00
Calvin Peete	T-5	73-71-70-74=288	$13,560.00
Mark Pfeil	T-5	74-73-69-72=288	$13,560.00
Loren Roberts	T-5	75-69-72-72=288	$13,560.00
Bill Kratzert	T-5	70-73-69-76=288	$13,560.00
Andrew Magee	T-10	71-73-72-73=289	$8,571.43
Morris Hatalsky	T-10	73-69-73-74=289	$8,571.43
Lee Trevino	T-10	69-75-71-74=289	$8,571.42
George Archer	T-10	75-70-71-73=289	$8,571.43
Scott Hoch	T-10	75-71-70-73=289	$8,571.43
Fred Couples	T-10	69-76-74-70=289	$8,571.43
Peter Oosterhuis	T-10	70-72-71-76=289	$8,571.43

Honda Classic

Course: TPC at Eagle Trace, Coral Springs, Fla.
Par: 72 Yardage: 7,030
Last day of event: Sunday, March 3, 1985

Player	Place	Score	Earnings
Curtis Strange	Win	67-64-70-74=275	$90,000.00
Playoff: Beat Peter Jacobsen with par on first extra hole			
Peter Jacobsen	2	66-71-70-68=275	$54,000.00
Willie Wood	3	65-72-70-71=278	$34,000.00
Ray Floyd	T-4	69-72-68-70=279	$22,000.00
Fred Couples	T-4	63-68-70-78=279	$22,000.00
Gary Koch	T-6	68-68-72-72=280	$17,375.00
Tom Kite	T-6	69-69-75-67=280	$17,375.00
Dan Forsman	T-8	72-71-70-68=281	$14,500.00
Andy Bean	T-8	70-69-69-73=281	$14,500.00
Dave Barr	T-8	67-69-70-75=281	$14,500.00

Hertz Bay Hill Classic

Course: Bay Hill Club, Orlando, Fla.
Par: 71 Yardage: 7,103
Last day of event: Sunday, March 10, 1985

Player	Place	Score	Earnings
Fuzzy Zoeller	Win	70-72-66-67=275	$90,000.00
Tom Watson	2	73-67-70-67=277	$54,000.00
Mark Lye	3	71-72-68-67=278	$34,000.00
Curtis Strange	4	73-67-68-72=280	$24,000.00
Larry Nelson	T-5	72-68-70-71=281	$18,250.00
Paul Azinger	T-5	72-65-74-70=281	$18,250.00
Bill Glasson	T-5	70-75-68-68=281	$18,250.00
Corey Pavin	T-8	72-67-72-71=282	$14,000.00
Andy Bean	T-8	73-68-69-72=282	$14,000.00
Bill Kratzert	T-8	72-66-75-69=282	$14,000.00
Andy North	T-8	75-70-69-68=282	$14,000.00

USF&G Classic

Course: Lakewood C.C., New Orleans, La.
Par: 72 Yardage: 7,080
Last day of event: Sunday, March 17, 1985

Player	Place	Score	Earnings
Seve Ballesteros	Win	68-69-68=205	$72,000.00
Peter Jacobsen	T-2	65-72-70=207	$35,200.00
John Mahaffey	T-2	63-73-71=207	$35,200.00
Mark Lye	T-4	67-72-69=208	$17,600.00
Tony Sills	T-4	66-69-73=208	$17,600.00
Kikuo Arai	T-6	69-70-70=209	$12,520.00
Joe Inman	T-6	68-70-71=209	$12,520.00
Hal Sutton	T-6	70-71-68=209	$12,520.00
Clarence Rose	T-6	71-68-70=209	$12,520.00
Lanny Wadkins	T-6	67-72-70=209	$12,520.00

Panasonic Las Vegas Invitational

Course: Las Vegas C.C., Tropicana C.C., Desert Inn C.C., Las Vegas, Nev.
Home course / Las Vegas C.C., Par: 71 Yardage: 7,164
Last day of event: Sunday, March 24, 1985

Player	Place	Score	Earnings
Curtis Strange	Win	69-73-64-66-66=338	$171,000.00
Mike Smith	2	67-69-66-71-66=339	$102,600.00
Mac O'Grady	3	67-71-70-65-67=340	$64,600.00
Tom Watson	T-4	66-65-68-71-71=341	$41,800.00
Fred Couples	T-4	67-69-71-69-65=341	$41,800.00

Greg Norman	6	68-70-71-67-66=342	$34,200.00
Jay Haas	T-7	68-70-67-67-71=343	$30,637.50
Fuzzy Zoeller	T-7	73-69-67-71-63=343	$30,637.50
Mike Reid	T-9	69-71-68-66-70=344	$25,650.00
Barry Jaeckel	T-9	69-70-71-68-66=344	$25,650.00
Johnny Miller	T-9	67-73-66-68-70=344	$25,650.00

Tournament Players Championship

Course: TPC at Sawgrass, Ponte Vedra Beach, Fla.
Par: 72 Yardage: 6,857
Last day of event: Sunday, March 31, 1985

Player	Place	Score	Earnings
Calvin Peete	Win	70-69-69-66=274	$162,000.00
D.A. Weibring	2	68-68-72-69=277	$97,200.00
Larry Rinker	3	68-72-71-70=281	$61,200.00
Gary Hallberg	4	72-71-67-72=282	$43,200.00
Dan Halldorson	T-5	70-68-72-73=283	$34,200.00
Hale Irwin	T-5	67-72-69-75=283	$34,200.00
Bruce Lietzke	T-7	71-72-70-71=284	$27,112.50
Lon Hinkle	T-7	71-72-71-70=284	$27,112.50
Bernhard Langer	T-7	68-70-75-71=284	$27,112.50
Isao Aoki	T-7	70-75-74-65=284	$27,112.50

Greater Greensboro Open

Course: Forest Oaks C.C., Greensboro, N.C.
Par: 72 Yardage: 6,984
Last day of event: Sunday, April 7, 1985

Player	Place	Score	Earnings
Joey Sindelar	Win	68-76-72-69=285	$72,000.00
Craig Stadler	T-2	70-74-71-71=286	$35,200.00
Isao Aoki	T-2	71-69-74-72=286	$35,200.00
Corey Pavin	4	75-70-71-71=287	$19,200.00
Doug Tewell	T-5	71-72-71-74=288	$13,560.00
Bill Kratzert	T-5	71-74-69-74=288	$13,560.00
Ed Fiori	T-5	74-73-71-70=288	$13,560.00
Dan Pohl	T-5	68-74-71-75=288	$13,560.00
Jeff Sluman	T-5	66-71-77-74=288	$13,560.00
Nick Faldo	T-10	73-73-70-73=289	$9,200.00
Lanny Wadkins	T-10	69-74-72-74=289	$9,200.00
Fuzzy Zoeller	T-10	72-72-74-71=289	$9,200.00
Jodie Mudd	T-10	70-75-74-70=289	$9,200.00
Brad Faxon	T-10	71-71-77-70=289	$9,200.00

Masters

Course: Augusta National G.C., Augusta, Ga.
Par: 72 Yardage: 6,925
Last day of event: Sunday, April 14, 1985

Player	Place	Score	Earnings
Bernhard Langer	Win	72-74-68-68=282	$126,000.00
Seve Ballesteros	T-2	72-71-71-70=284	$52,267.00
Ray Floyd	T-2	70-73-69-72=284	$52,267.00
Curtis Strange	T-2	80-65-68-71=284	$52,267.00
Jay Haas	5	73-73-72-67=285	$28,000.00
Bruce Lietzke	T-6	72-71-73-70=286	$22,663.00
Jack Nicklaus	T-6	71-74-72-69=286	$22,663.00
Gary Hallberg	T-6	68-73-75-70=286	$22,663.00
Craig Stadler	T-6	73-67-76-70=286	$22,663.00
Lee Trevino	T-10	70-73-72-72=287	$16,800.00
David Graham	T-10	74-71-71-71=287	$16,800.00
Tom Watson	T-10	69-71-75-72=287	$16,800.00
Fred Couples	T-10	75-73-69-70=287	$16,800.00

Sea Pines Heritage Classic

Course: Harbour Town G.L., Hilton Head, S.C.
Par: 71 Yardage: 6,657
Last day of event: Sunday, April 21, 1985

Player	Place	Score	Earnings
Bernhard Langer	Win	68-66-69-70=273	$72,000.00

Playoff: Beat Bobby Wadkins with par on first extra hole

Player	Place	Score	Earnings
Bobby Wadkins	2	65-68-72-68=273	$43,200.00
Tim Norris	T-3	70-71-66-67=274	$23,200.00
Hal Sutton	T-3	72-67-68-67=274	$23,200.00
Mike Smith	5	73-67-68-67=275	$16,000.00
Larry Nelson	6	67-69-70-70=276	$14,400.00
Jim Thorpe	T-7	67-68-72-70=277	$12,050.00
Larry Mize	T-7	68-70-67-72=277	$12,050.00
Dan Pohl	T-7	68-67-72-70=277	$12,050.00
Danny Edwards	T-7	71-65-68-73=277	$12,050.00

Houston Open

Course: TPC at The Woodlands, The Woodlands, Texas
Par: 72 Yardage: 7,042
Last day of event: Sunday, April 28, 1985

Player	Place	Score	Earnings
Ray Floyd	Win	69-70-69-69=277	$90,000.00
David Frost	T-2	67-71-71-69=278	$44,000.00
Bob Lohr	T-2	73-68-70-67=278	$44,000.00
Payne Stewart	T-4	66-72-70-71=279	$19,687.50
Keith Fergus	T-4	67-72-69-71=279	$19,687.50
Russ Cochran	T-4	72-68-69-70=279	$19,687.50
Bob Murphy	T-4	71-68-73-67=279	$19,687.50
Calvin Peete	T-8	67-72-71-70=280	$15,000.00
Phil Blackmar	T-8	69-72-68-71=280	$15,000.00
John Mahaffey	T-10	70-70-70-71=281	$13,000.00
Donnie Hammond	T-10	70-70-71-70=281	$13,000.00

MONY Tournament of Champions

Course: La Costa C.C., Carlsbad, Calif.
Par: 72 Yardage: 7,022
Last day of event: Sunday, May 5, 1985

Player	Place	Score	Earnings
Tom Kite	Win	64-72-70-69=275	$72,000.00
Mark McCumber	2	69-71-71-70=281	$49,000.00
Scott Simpson	3	72-70-67-73=282	$32,500.00
Fuzzy Zoeller	T-4	68-72-70-73=283	$22,875.00
Mark O'Meara	T-4	73-73-70-67=283	$22,875.00
Larry Nelson	6	70-69-72-73=284	$18,250.00
Craig Stadler	T-7	73-71-71-70=285	$15,133.33
Lanny Wadkins	T-7	69-68-73-75=285	$15,133.33
Ray Floyd	T-7	70-75-72-68=285	$15,133.34
Joey Sindelar	10	70-74-72-70=286	$13,100.00

Byron Nelson Golf Classic

Course: Las Colinas Sports Club, Irving, Texas
Par: 70 Yardage: 6,982
Last day of event: Sunday, May 12, 1985

Player	Place	Score	Earnings
Bob Eastwood	Win	69-66-70-67=272	$90,000.00

Playoff: Beat Payne Stewart with bogey on first extra hole

Player	Place	Score	Earnings
Payne Stewart	2	67-71-66-68=272	$54,000.00
Tom Watson	T-3	67-69-73-66=275	$29,000.00
Mac O'Grady	T-3	63-69-69-74=275	$29,000.00

Craig Stadler	T-5	67-70-69-71=277	$18,250.00
Lee Trevino	T-5	70-71-69-67=277	$18,250.00
Chi Chi Rodriguez	T-5	72-70-69-66=277	$18,250.00
Russ Cochran	T-8	71-67-71-69=278	$14,000.00
Ron Streck	T-8	71-67-71-69=278	$14,000.00
Phil Blackmar	T-8	69-73-70-66=278	$14,000.00
Bob Lohr	T-8	73-69-66-70=278	$14,000.00

Colonial National Invitational

Course: Colonial C.C., Fort Worth, Texas
Par: 70 Yardage: 7,096
Last day of event: Sunday, May 19, 1985

Player	Place	Score	Earnings
Corey Pavin	Win	66-64-68-68=266	$90,000.00
Bob Murphy	2	68-70-65-67=270	$54,000.00
Scott Hoch	3	69-68-66-69=272	$34,000.00
Nick Price	T-4	69-70-70-64=273	$22,000.00
Mark O'Meara	T-4	66-68-71-68=273	$22,000.00
Larry Mize	6	71-70-65-68=274	$18,000.00
Buddy Gardner	T-7	68-70-68-69=275	$15,062.50
John Mahaffey	T-7	70-66-71-68=275	$15,062.50
Willie Wood	T-7	66-69-72-68=275	$15,062.50
Joey Sindelar	T-7	71-72-62-70=275	$15,062.50

Memorial Tournament

Course: Muirfield Village G.C., Dubin, Ohio
Par: 72 Yardage: 7,106
Last day of event: Sunday, May 26, 1985

Player	Place	Score	Earnings
Hale Irwin	Win	68-68-73-72=281	$100,000.00
Lanny Wadkins	2	69-72-67-74=282	$60,000.00
Bill Kratzert	3	69-71-71-73=284	$37,780.00
Keith Fergus	T-4	73-72-69-72=286	$22,963.33
Corey Pavin	T-4	72-74-70-70=286	$22,963.33
George Burns	T-4	72-74-71-69=286	$22,963.34
Bill Rogers	7	73-70-70-74=287	$18,610.00
Gil Morgan	T-8	70-72-75-71=288	$16,665.00
Jack Renner	T-8	76-73-70-69=288	$16,665.00
Doug Tewell	T-10	71-71-74-73=289	$12,856.00
Paul Azinger	T-10	74-74-74-67=289	$12,856.00
Mark O'Meara	T-10	70-74-70-75=289	$12,856.00
Roger Maltbie	T-10	72-70-72-75=289	$12,856.00
Lon Hinkle	T-10	67-75-71-76=289	$12,856.00

Kemper Open

Course: Congressional C.C., Bethesda, Md.
Par: 72 Yardage: 7,173
Last day of event: Sunday, June 2, 1985

Player	Place	Score	Earnings
Bill Glasson	Win	72-70-70-66=278	$90,000.00
Corey Pavin	T-2	72-70-68-69=279	$44,000.00
Larry Mize	T-2	70-68-68-73=279	$44,000.00
Willie Wood	T-4	69-71-74-67=281	$22,000.00
Curtis Strange	T-4	70-72-74-65=281	$22,000.00
Greg Norman	6	73-70-73-66=282	$18,000.00
Jeff Sluman	T-7	71-70-72-70=283	$16,125.00
Lanny Wadkins	T-7	71-73-73-66=283	$16,125.00
Dave Barr	T-9	71-72-73-68=284	$13,500.00
Robert Wrenn	T-9	70-74-72-68=284	$13,500.00
George Archer	T-9	68-69-75-72=284	$13,500.00

Manufacturers Hanover Westchester Classic

Course: Westchester C.C., Harrison, N.Y.
Par: 71 Yardage: 6,722
Last day of event: Sunday, June 9, 1985

Player	Place	Score	Earnings
Roger Maltbie	Win	70-63-72-70=275	$90,000.00
Playoff: Beat George Burns and Ray Floyd with birdie on first extra hole			
Ray Floyd	T-2	69-72-69-65=275	$44,000.00
George Burns	T-2	66-66-73-70=275	$44,000.00
Mark Wiebe	4	68-72-70-67=277	$24,000.00
Willie Wood	5	72-66-71-70=279	$20,000.00
Peter Jacobsen	6	74-68-69-69=280	$18,000.00
J.C. Snead	T-7	70-68-72-71=281	$15,583.34
Barry Jaeckel	T-7	72-69-69-71=281	$15,583.33
Wayne Levi	T-7	72-71-65-73=281	$15,583.33
Tony Sills	T-10	70-71-71-70=282	$13,000.00
Don Pooley	T-10	68-74-70-70=282	$13,000.00

U.S. Open

Course: Oakland Hills C.C., Birmingham, Mich.
Par: 70 Yardage: 6,996
Last day of event: Sunday, June 16, 1985

Player	Place	Score	Earnings
Andy North	Win	70-65-70-74=279	$103,000.00
Dave Barr	T-2	70-68-70-72=280	$39,185.00
Denis Watson	T-2	72-65-73-70=280	$39,185.00
T.C. Chen	T-2	65-69-69-77=280	$39,185.00
Payne Stewart	T-5	70-70-71-70=281	$18,458.67
Seve Ballesteros	T-5	71-70-69-71=281	$18,458.67
Lanny Wadkins	T-5	70-72-69-70=281	$18,458.67
Johnny Miller	8	74-71-68-69=282	$14,921.00
Fuzzy Zoeller	T-9	71-69-72-71=283	$12,439.75
Jack Renner	T-9	72-69-72-70=283	$12,439.75
Corey Pavin	T-9	72-68-73-70=283	$12,439.75
Rick Fehr	T-9	69-67-73-74=283	$12,439.75

Georgia-Pacific Atlanta Golf Classic

Course: Atlanta C.C., Atlanta, Ga.
Par: 72 Yardage: 7,007
Last day of event: Sunday, June 23, 1985

Player	Place	Score	Earnings
Wayne Levi	Win	71-68-67-67=273	$90,000.00
Playoff: Beat Steve Pate with birdie on second extra hole			
Steve Pate	2	67-66-71-69=273	$54,000.00
Ray Floyd	3	68-68-68-70=274	$34,000.00
Mac O'Grady	T-4	67-70-70-69=276	$22,000.00
David Frost	T-4	69-69-64-74=276	$22,000.00
Scott Simpson	T-6	68-69-69-71=277	$17,375.00
Danny Edwards	T-6	69-65-68-75=277	$17,375.00
Tony Sills	T-8	65-72-72-69=278	$14,000.00
Tim Simpson	T-8	67-73-69-69=278	$14,000.00
Jim Colbert	T-8	70-68-73-67=278	$14,000.00
Larry Mize	T-8	73-67-69-69=278	$14,000.00

St. Jude Memphis Classic

Course: Colonial C.C. (South), Cordova, Tenn.
Par: 72 Yardage: 7,282
Last day of event: Sunday, June 30, 1985

Player	Place	Score	Earnings
Hal Sutton	Win	65-76-73-65=279	$90,000.00

Playoff: Beat David Ogrin with birdie on first extra hole

Player	Place	Score	Earnings
David Ogrin	2	66-70-72-71=279	$54,000.00
Russ Cochran	T-3	70-68-71-71=280	$29,000.00
Gil Morgan	T-3	69-72-72-67=280	$29,000.00
Tony Sills	T-5	68-72-70-71=281	$19,000.00
Bob Tway	T-5	69-69-73-70=281	$19,000.00
Wayne Grady	T-7	70-72-71-69=282	$13,535.71
Johnny Miller	T-7	71-68-72-71=282	$13,535.72
Bill Kratzert	T-7	72-68-71-71=282	$13,535.72
Bill Sander	T-7	65-71-73-73=282	$13,535.71
Scott Hoch	T-7	73-70-69-70=282	$13,535.72
Andy Bean	T-7	69-70-69-74=282	$13,535.71
George Burns	T-7	67-69-70-76=282	$13,535.71

Canadian Open

Course: Glen Abbey G.C., Oakville, Ontario, Canada
Par: 72 Yardage: 7,102
Last day of event: Sunday, July 7, 1985

Player	Place	Score	Earnings
Curtis Strange	Win	69-69-68-73=279	$86,506.52
Greg Norman	T-2	67-68-73-73=281	$42,144.20
Jack Nicklaus	T-2	70-73-66-72=281	$42,144.21
Peter Jacobsen	T-4	70-72-70-70=282	$18,262.48
Fuzzy Zoeller	T-4	73-66-71-72=282	$18,262.49
Tommy Valentine	T-4	73-69-70-70=282	$18,262.49
Johnny Miller	T-4	68-75-72-67=282	$18,262.49
Bill Sander	T-4	75-68-69-70=282	$18,262.49
Bruce Lietzke	T-9	69-73-68-74=284	$12,476.90
Jim Colbert	T-9	70-74-67-73=284	$12,476.91
Larry Mize	T-9	72-66-72-74=284	$12,476.91
Corey Pavin	T-9	76-70-68-70=284	$12,476.90

Anheuser-Busch Golf Classic

Course: Kingsmill G.C., Williamsburg, Va.
Par: 71 Yardage: 6,776
Last day of event: Sunday, July 14, 1985

Player	Place	Score	Earnings
Mark Wiebe	Win	70-69-64-70=273	$90,000.00
Playoff: Beat John Mahaffey with birdie on first extra hole			
John Mahaffey	2	69-68-67-69=273	$54,000.00
Joey Sindelar	T-3	71-66-69-68=274	$26,000.00
Danny Edwards	T-3	70-64-68-72=274	$26,000.00
Scott Simpson	T-3	68-67-73-66=274	$26,000.00
Keith Fergus	6	69-64-71-71=275	$18,000.00
Donnie Hammond	T-7	68-70-70-68=276	$14,041.67
Jay Haas	T-7	66-71-71-68=276	$14,041.66
Frank Conner	T-7	67-68-70-71=276	$14,041.67
Roger Maltbie	T-7	68-66-70-72=276	$14,041.66
Wayne Grady	T-7	67-67-73-69=276	$14,041.67
Hal Sutton	T-7	68-69-73-66=276	$14,041.67

Lite Quad Cities Open

Course: Oakwood C.C., Coal Valley, Ill.
Par: 70 Yardage: 6,602
Last day of event: Sunday, July 21, 1985

Player	Place	Score	Earnings
Dan Forsman	Win	68-69-63-67=267	$54,000.00
Bob Tway	2	64-67-70-67=268	$32,400.00
Brett Upper	T-3	68-64-69-68=269	$17,400.00
Brad Fabel	T-3	69-67-68-65=269	$17,400.00
Dan Halldorson	T-5	68-68-67-67=270	$10,950.00

Jim Thorpe	T-5	68-68-69-65=270	$10,950.00
Mark Wiebe	T-5	72-64-66-68=270	$10,950.00
Roger Maltbie	T-8	68-68-67-68=271	$8,700.00
Bill Calfee	T-8	70-68-67-66=271	$8,700.00
Scott Hoch	T-8	67-65-71-68=271	$8,700.00

British Open

Course: Royal St. George's G.C., Sandwich, Kent, England
Par: 70 Yardage: 6,857
Last day of event: Sunday, July 21, 1985

Player	Place	Score	Earnings
Sandy Lyle	Win	68-71-73-70=282	$94,250.00
Payne Stewart	2	70-75-70-68=283	$62,350.00
Mark O'Meara	T-3	70-72-70-72=284	$34,220.00
Jose Rivero	T-3	74-72-70-68=284	$34,220.00
David Graham	T-3	68-71-70-75=284	$34,220.00
Bernhard Langer	T-3	72-69-68-75=284	$34,220.00
Christy O'Connor, Jr.	T-3	64-76-72-72=284	$34,220.00
Tom Kite	T-8	73-73-67-72=285	$22,570.70
D.A. Weibring	T-8	69-71-74-71=285	$22,570.70
Anders Forsbrand	T-8	70-76-69-70=285	$22,570.70

Canon Sammy Davis, Jr. - Greater Hartford Open

Course: TPC of Connecticut, Cromwell, Conn.
Par: 71 Yardage: 6,786
Last day of event: Sunday, July 28, 1985

Player	Place	Score	Earnings
Phil Blackmar	Win	72-67-64-68=271	$108,000.00
Playoff: Beat Jodie Mudd and Dan Pohl with birdie on first extra hole			
Dan Pohl	T-2	68-69-68-66=271	$52,800.00
Jodie Mudd	T-2	68-67-70-66=271	$52,800.00
Ray Floyd	T-4	64-68-68-72=272	$26,400.00
Wayne Grady	T-4	70-65-65-72=272	$26,400.00
Lon Hinkle	T-6	70-66-69-68=273	$19,425.00
Brett Upper	T-6	71-68-66-68=273	$19,425.00
Peter Jacobsen	T-6	71-69-67-66=273	$19,425.00
Andrew Magee	T-6	72-68-65-68=273	$19,425.00
Mark Wiebe	T-10	68-71-68-67=274	$14,400.00
Larry Rinker	T-10	69-68-66-71=274	$14,400.00
Scott Hoch	T-10	69-71-66-68=274	$14,400.00
John Cook	T-10	66-69-72-67=274	$14,400.00

Western Open

Course: Butler National G.C., Oak Brook, Ill.
Par: 72 Yardage: 7,097
Last day of event: Sunday, August 4, 1985

Player	Place	Score	Earnings
Scott Verplank	Win	68-68-69-74=279	
Playoff: Beat Jim Thorpe with par on second extra hole			
(Verplank an amateur so first place check went to Thorpe)			
Jim Thorpe	2	75-66-66-72=279	$90,000.00
Seve Ballesteros	3	75-68-72-68=283	$54,000.00
Bobby Clampett	T-4	73-73-71-69=286	$22,550.00
Dan Halldorson	T-4	73-73-71-69=286	$22,550.00
Andy North	T-4	71-74-71-70=286	$22,550.00
Bruce Lietzke	T-4	74-70-68-74=286	$22,550.00
Corey Pavin	T-4	75-67-70-74=286	$22,550.00
Steve Pate	T-9	73-73-71-70=287	$14,500.00
Danny Edwards	T-9	69-74-72-72=287	$14,500.00
Ron Streck	T-9	72-73-74-68=287	$14,500.00

PGA Championship

Course: Cherry Hills C.C., Englewood, Colo.
Par: 71 Yardage: 7,089
Last day of event: Sunday, August 11, 1985

Player	Place	Score	Earnings
Hubert Green	Win	67-69-70-72=278	$125,000.00
Lee Trevino	2	66-68-75-71=280	$75,000.00
Andy Bean	T-3	71-70-72-68=281	$42,500.00
T.M. Chen	T-3	69-76-71-65=281	$42,500.00
Nick Price	5	73-73-65-71=282	$25,000.00
Buddy Gardner	T-6	73-73-70-67=283	$17,125.00
Tom Watson	T-6	67-70-74-72=283	$17,125.00
Corey Pavin	T-6	66-75-73-69=283	$17,125.00
Fred Couples	T-6	70-65-76-72=283	$17,125.00
Lanny Wadkins	T-10	70-69-73-72=284	$12,625.00
Peter Jacobsen	T-10	66-71-75-72=284	$12,625.00

Buick Open

Course: Warwick Hills C.C., Grand Blanc, Mich.
Par: 72 Yardage: 7,014
Last day of event: Sunday, August 18, 1985

Player	Place	Score	Earnings
Ken Green	Win	69-65-67-67=268	$81,000.00
Wayne Grady	2	69-64-69-70=272	$48,600.00
Mac O'Grady	3	70-69-67-68=274	$30,600.00
George Burns	T-4	68-70-68-69=275	$18,600.00
Gary Hallberg	T-4	68-72-67-68=275	$18,600.00
Gene Sauers	T-4	72-64-66-73=275	$18,600.00
Roger Maltbie	T-7	69-68-68-71=276	$14,512.50
Brett Upper	T-7	71-69-66-70=276	$14,512.50
Calvin Peete	T-9	68-70-69-70=277	$11,250.00
Andy Bean	T-9	70-70-71-66=277	$11,250.00
Jack Renner	T-9	68-72-69-68=277	$11,250.00
David Graham	T-9	69-72-67-69=277	$11,250.00
Donnie Hammond	T-9	69-67-67-74=277	$11,250.00

NEC World Series of Golf

Course: Firestone C.C. (South), Akron, Ohio
Par: 70 Yardage: 7,149
Last day of event: Sunday, August 25, 1985

Player	Place	Score	Earnings
Roger Maltbie	Win	65-69-68-66=268	$126,000.00
Denis Watson	2	65-71-66-70=272	$75,600.00
Tom Kite	T-3	67-68-70-68=273	$40,600.00
Calvin Peete	T-3	66-69-71-67=273	$40,600.00
Hal Sutton	5	68-68-70-68=274	$28,000.00
Ray Floyd	6	70-71-70-64=275	$25,200.00
Larry Nelson	T-7	69-68-70-69=276	$20,400.00
Woody Blackburn	T-7	67-71-67-71=276	$20,400.00
Greg Norman	T-7	71-68-70-67=276	$20,400.00
Gordon J. Brand	T-7	67-67-70-72=276	$20,400.00
Andy North	T-7	69-69-73-65=276	$20,400.00

B.C. Open

Course: En-Joie G.C., Endicott, N.Y.
Par: 71 Yardage: 6,966
Last day of event: Sunday, September 1, 1985

Player	Place	Score	Earnings
Joey Sindelar	Win	66-71-69-68=274	$54,000.00
Mike Reid	2	67-71-69-68=275	$32,400.00

Bill Glasson	3	68-72-69-67=276	$20,400.00
David Lundstrom	T-4	70-68-69-70=277	$13,200.00
Bruce Lietzke	T-4	66-72-68-71=277	$13,200.00
Pat Lindsey	6	70-68-69-71=278	$10,800.00
Ken Green	T-7	70-70-69-70=279	$9,675.00
Jay Delsing	T-7	73-62-72-72=279	$9,675.00
Andrew Magee	T-9	67-72-70-71=280	$8,400.00
Mac O'Grady	T-9	72-70-69-69=280	$8,400.00

Bank of Boston Classic
Course: Pleasant Valley C.C., Sutton, Mass.
Par: 71 Yardage: 7,110
Last day of event: Sunday, September 8, 1985

Player	Place	Score	Earnings
George Burns	Win	67-66-68-66=267	$72,000.00
Greg Norman	T-2	67-68-68-70=273	$26,400.00
Jodie Mudd	T-2	69-67-70-67=273	$26,400.00
Leonard Thompson	T-2	66-71-69-67=273	$26,400.00
John Mahaffey	T-2	65-70-66-72=273	$26,400.00
Calvin Peete	6	71-69-68-66=274	$14,400.00
Joey Sindelar	T-7	70-68-67-70=275	$12,466.67
Brad Fabel	T-7	65-72-68-70=275	$12,466.66
Lennie Clements	T-7	74-63-68-70=275	$12,466.67
Steve Pate	T-10	68-70-68-70=276	$9,200.00
Chris Perry	T-10	68-68-71-69=276	$9,200.00
Fuzzy Zoeller	T-10	71-68-69-68=276	$9,200.00
Wayne Levi	T-10	68-68-72-68=276	$9,200.00
Frank Conner	T-10	69-67-72-68=276	$9,200.00

Greater Milwaukee Open
Course: Tuckaway C.C., Franklin, Wis.
Par: 72 Yardage: 7,030
Last day of event: Sunday, September 15, 1985

Player	Place	Score	Earnings
Jim Thorpe	Win	73-69-62-70=274	$54,000.00
Jack Nicklaus	2	70-69-67-71=277	$32,400.00
Tim Simpson	T-3	70-71-66-72=279	$13,530.00
Greg Twiggs	T-3	68-68-70-73=279	$13,530.00
Larry Rinker	T-3	68-70-68-73=279	$13,530.00
Brad Fabel	T-3	68-73-69-69=279	$13,530.00
Pat McGowan	T-3	72-73-69-65=279	$13,530.00
David Frost	T-8	70-68-70-72=280	$8,700.00
Jodie Mudd	T-8	72-70-66-72=280	$8,700.00
Mike Sullivan	T-8	68-74-71-67=280	$8,700.00

Southwest Golf Classic
Course: Fairway Oaks C.C., Abilene, Texas
Par: 72 Yardage: 7,166
Last day of event: Sunday, September 22, 1985

Player	Place	Score	Earnings
Hal Sutton	Win	68-67-67-71=273	$72,000.00
Playoff: Beat Mike Reid with birdie on first extra hole			
Mike Reid	2	68-66-67-72=273	$43,200.00
Howard Twitty	3	69-68-68-69=274	$27,200.00
Richard Zokol	4	69-72-64-70=275	$19,200.00
Jack Renner	T-5	72-68-67-70=277	$14,600.00
Jeff Sluman	T-5	72-68-69-68=277	$14,600.00
Andy Bean	T-5	66-67-68-76=277	$14,600.00
Wayne Levi	8	70-71-68-69=278	$12,400.00
Dan Pohl	9	68-69-68-74=279	$11,600.00
Charles Bolling	T-10	71-69-69-71=280	$10,400.00
Pat Lindsey	T-10	70-72-69-69=280	$10,400.00

Texas Open
Course: Oak Hill C.C., San Antonio, Texas
Par: 70 Yardage: 6,576
Last day of event: Sunday, September 29, 1985

Player	Place	Score	Earnings
John Mahaffey	Win	68-68-65-67=268	$63,000.00
Playoff: Beat Jodie Mudd with par on second extra hole			
Jodie Mudd	2	64-65-68-71=268	$37,800.00
Mark Hayes	T-3	66-67-69-69=271	$20,300.00
Mark O'Meara	T-3	69-68-67-67=271	$20,300.00
Jim Colbert	5	72-66-66-68=272	$14,000.00
Steve Jones	T-6	66-68-71-68=273	$12,162.50
Andrew Magee	T-6	71-71-67-64=273	$12,162.50
Lanny Wadkins	T-8	68-70-69-69=276	$9,800.00
Gary Koch	T-8	70-69-68-69=276	$9,800.00
J.C. Snead	T-8	71-70-67-68=276	$9,800.00
Tom Kite	T-8	69-68-67-72=276	$9,800.00

Southern Open
Course: Green Island C.C., Columbus, Ga.
Par: 70 Yardage: 6,791
Last day of event: Sunday, October 6, 1985

Player	Place	Score	Earnings
Tim Simpson	Win	64-64-69-67=264	$63,000.00
Clarence Rose	2	64-66-69-67=266	$37,800.00
Bob Tway	3	68-66-65-68=267	$23,800.00
Jim Thorpe	T-4	66-69-69-67=271	$15,400.00
Tony Sills	T-4	68-67-69-67=271	$15,400.00
Payne Stewart	T-6	68-68-69-67=272	$11,725.00
Jack Renner	T-6	66-68-71-67=272	$11,725.00
Bobby Clampett	T-6	71-65-67-69=272	$11,725.00
Joey Sindelar	9	63-68-72-70=273	$10,150.00
Corey Pavin	T-10	67-70-69-68=274	$8,400.00
Paul Azinger	T-10	68-70-70-66=274	$8,400.00
Jeff Sluman	T-10	67-66-70-71=274	$8,400.00
Mike Sullivan	T-10	69-65-68-72=274	$8,400.00

Walt Disney World/Oldsmobile Classic
Course: Walt Disney (Magnolia, Palm), Lake Buena Vista C.C., Lake Buena Vista, Fla.
Home course / Magnolia, Par: 72 Yardage: 7,190
Last day of event: Sunday, October 13, 1985

Player	Place	Score	Earnings
Lanny Wadkins	Win	68-67-69-63=267	$72,000.00
Mike Donald	T-2	66-69-66-67=268	$35,200.00
Scott Hoch	T-2	69-63-67-69=268	$35,200.00
Payne Stewart	T-4	69-69-65-66=269	$17,600.00
Gary Koch	T-4	66-68-72-63=269	$17,600.00
Gary McCord	6	67-68-70-66=271	$14,400.00
Andy Bean	7	70-68-66-68=272	$13,400.00
Craig Stadler	T-8	65-70-69-69=273	$11,600.00
Don Pooley	T-8	70-66-69-68=273	$11,600.00
Donnie Hammond	T-8	70-68-68-67=273	$11,600.00

Pensacola Open
Course: Perdido Bay C.C., Pensacola, Fla.
Par: 71 Yardage: 7,093
Last day of event: Sunday, October 20, 1985

Player	Place	Score	Earnings
Danny Edwards	Win	67-68-67-67=269	$54,000.00

Gil Morgan	T-2	65-68-70-67=270	$26,400.00
John Mahaffey	T-2	70-69-65-66=270	$26,400.00
Mark McCumber	4	69-66-68-68=271	$14,400.00
Calvin Peete	T-5	68-68-67-69=272	$10,950.00
Tony Sills	T-5	70-68-70-64=272	$10,950.00
Tim Simpson	T-5	65-69-71-67=272	$10,950.00
Dan Pohl	T-8	70-68-68-67=273	$8,400.00
Bill Kratzert	T-8	66-68-71-68=273	$8,400.00
Steve Bowman	T-8	71-66-66-70=273	$8,400.00
Kenny Knox	T-8	73-68-66-66=273	$8,400.00

Seiko Tucson-Match Play Championship
Course: Randolph Park Municipal, Tucson, Ariz.
Par: 70 Yardage: 6,860
Last day of event: Sunday, October 27, 1985

Player	Place	Score	Earnings
Jim Thorpe	Win		$150,000.00

Round One - Beat Tony Sills 1 up
Round Two - Beat Dan Pohl 1 up
Round Three - Beat Jodie Mudd 2 & 1
Quarterfinals - Beat Mark Wiebe 6 & 5
Semifinals - Beat Mac O'Grady 1 up
Finals - Beat Jack Renner 4 & 3

Jack Renner	2		$90,000.00

Round One - Beat Mark O'Meara 2 & 1
Round Two - Beat Scott Hoch 2 & 1
Round Three - Beat Clarence Rose 2 & 1
Quarterfinals - Beat Phil Blackmar 4 & 3
Semifinals - Beat Bob Tway 22nd hole
Finals - Jim Thorpe beats him 4 & 3

Bob Tway	3		$60,000.00

Round One - Beat Lanny Wadkins 2 up
Round Two - Beat Wayne Grady 3 & 2
Round Three - Beat Ron Steck 3 & 2
Quarterfinals - Beat Danny Edwards 6 & 5
Semifinals - Jack Renner beats him 22nd hole
Consolation - Beat Mac O'Grady 1 up

Mac O'Grady	4		$40,000.00

Round One - Beat Bob Eastwood 1 up
Round Two - Beat Jay Haas 1 up
Round Three - Beat Larry Rinker 3 & 2
Quarterfinals - Beat Tom Watson 1 up
Semifinals - Jim Thorpe beats him 1 up
Consolation - Bob Tway beats him 1 up

Tom Watson	T-5		$25,000.00

Round One - Beat Lon Hinkle 5 & 3
Round Two - Beat Mike Reid 4 & 2
Round Three - Beat Wayne Levi 1 up
Quarterfinals - Mac O'Grady beats him 1 up

Mark Wiebe	T-5		$25,000.00

Round One - Beat Bill Kratzert 4 & 2
Round Two - Beat Roger Maltbie 19th hole
Round Three - Beat Dan Forsman 1 up
Quarterfinals - Jim Thorpe beats him 6 & 5

Danny Edwards	T-5		$25,000.00

Round One - Beat Willie Wood 19th hole
Round Two - Beat John Mahaffey 3 & 1
Round Three - Beat Tom Kite 19th hole
Quarterfinals - Bob Tway beats him 6 & 5

Phil Blackmar	T-5		$25,000.00

Round One - Beat Tim Simpson 22nd hole
Round Two - Beat Calvin Peete 20th hole
Round Three - Beat Peter Jacobsen 2 & 1
Quarterfinals - Jack Renner beats him 4 & 3

Wayne Levi	T-9		$12,500.00

Round One - Beat Gil Morgan 3 & 2
Round Two - Beat Brett Upper 2 up
Round Three - Tom Watson beats him 1 up

Larry Rinker	T-9		$12,500.00

Round One - Beat D.A. Weibring 1 up
Round Two - Beat David Frost 1 up
Round Three - Mac O'Grady beats him 3 & 2

Jodie Mudd	T-9		$12,500.00

Round One - Beat Don Pooley 1 up
Round Two - Beat Corey Pavin 20th hole
Round Three - Jim Thorpe beats him 2 & 1

Dan Forsman	T-9		$12,500.00

Round One - Beat Bill Glasson 2 up
Round Two - Beat Dave Barr 2 & 1
Round Three - Mark Wiebe beats him 1 up

Ron Streck	T-9		$12,500.00

Round One - Beat Payne Stewart 1 up
Round Two - Beat Andy North 3 & 2
Round Three - Bob Tway beats him 3 & 2

Tom Kite	T-9		$12,500.00

Round One - Beat Buddy Gardner 5 & 4
Round Two - Beat Mark McCumber 1 up
Round Three - Danny Edwards beats him 19th hole

Peter Jacobsen	T-9		$12,500.00

Round One - Beat Doug Tewell 19th hole
Round Two - Beat Larry Mize 4 & 2
Round Three - Phil Blackmar beats him 2 & 1

Clarence Rose	T-9		$12,500.00

Round One - Beat Fuzzy Zoeller 2 up
Round Two - Beat Larry Nelson 3 & 2
Round Three - Jack Renner beats him 2 & 1

1986

Greg Norman was the 54-hole leader at all four majors in 1986, but managed to win only one. With son Jackie caddying for him, 46-year-old Jack Nicklaus scored an emotional victory at the Masters, making birdie at No. 9 in the final round then closing with scores of 3-3-4-4-4-3-2-3-4 (six under par). In winning the last of his 18 professional majors, Nicklaus edged Tom Kite and Norman by a shot. Raymond Floyd, 43, who like Nicklaus was suspected to be past his prime, needed only 111 putts during a two-shot victory over Chip Beck and Lanny Wadkins at the U.S. Open, which returned to storied Shinnecock Hills for the first time in 90 years. (Norman shot 75 in Round 4.) Norman prevailed over the wind-swept links at Turnberry, riding a second-round 63 to a five-shot victory over Gordon Brand in the British Open. Bob Tway holed a bunker shot for birdie at the 72nd hole of the PGA Championship for a two-shot victory over Norman, who had started Round 4 with a four-shot lead. Norman was part of another history footnote in 1986: The Panasonic Las Vegas Open offered the first $1 million purse in PGA Tour history, and it was Norman who took home the winner's share of $207,000.

MONY Tournament of Champions
Course: La Costa C.C., Carlsbad, Calif.
Par: 72 Yardage: 7,022
Last day of event: Saturday, January 11, 1986

Player	Place	Score	Earnings
Calvin Peete	Win	68-67-64-68=267	$90,000.00
Mark O'Meara	2	70-65-67-71=273	$57,000.00
Phil Blackmar	3	74-68-66-69=277	$37,000.00
Bernhard Langer	T-4	69-69-71-70=279	$25,000.00
Danny Edwards	T-4	70-69-69-71=279	$25,000.00
Scott Verplank	T-4	72-67-68-72=279	
Jim Thorpe	T-7	70-68-71-72=281	$19,166.67
Tim Simpson	T-7	72-73-66-70=281	$19,166.66
Hal Sutton	T-7	71-77-66-67=281	$19,166.67
Tom Kite	10	69-66-73-75=283	$16,500.00

Bob Hope Chrysler Classic

Course: Bermuda Dunes C.C., La Quinta C.C., Indian Wells C.C., Eldorado C.C.
Home course / Bermuda Dunes, Par: 72 Yardage: 6,837
Last day of event: Sunday, January 19, 1986

Player	Place	Score	Earnings
Donnie Hammond	Win	69-64-68-68-66=335	$108,000.00
Playoff: Beat John Cook with birdie on first extra hole			
John Cook	T-2	68-67-65-69-66=335	$64,800.00
Jodie Mudd	3	72-65-63-68-69=337	$40,800.00
Hal Sutton	4	65-70-69-65-69=338	$28,800.00
Gary Koch	T-5	67-68-68-68-68=339	$21,900.00
Craig Stadler	T-5	67-65-69-70-68=339	$21,900.00
Payne Stewart	T-5	72-67-71-64-65=339	$21,900.00
David Graham	8	69-73-63-67-68=340	$18,600.00
Lennie Clements	T-9	71-68-72-64-66=341	$16,800.00
Ray Floyd	T-9	68-70-65-73-65=341	$16,800.00

Phoenix Open

Course: Phoenix C.C., Phoenix, Ariz.
Par: 72 Yardage: 6,726
Last day of event: Sunday, January 26, 1986

Player	Place	Score	Earnings
Hal Sutton	Win	64-64-68-71=267	$90,000.00
Tony Sills	T-2	68-68-65-68=269	$44,000.00
Calvin Peete	T-2	64-69-68-68=269	$44,000.00
Dan Forsman	4	70-68-66-66=270	$24,000.00
Greg Norman	T-5	64-71-66-70=271	$19,000.00
Don Pooley	T-5	74-61-67-69=271	$19,000.00
Bernhard Langer	T-7	69-68-67-69=273	$14,041.66
Andy Bean	T-7	66-69-68-70=273	$14,041.67
Larry Mize	T-7	64-71-68-70=273	$14,041.67
John Mahaffey	T-7	67-65-70-71=273	$14,041.67
Joey Sindelar	T-7	69-64-69-71=273	$14,041.67
Ronnie Black	T-7	66-66-69-72=273	$14,041.66

AT&T Pebble Beach Pro-Am

Courses: Pebble Beach G.L., Spyglass Hill G.C., Cypress Point C.C., Pebble Beach, Calif.
Home Course / Pebble Beach GL., Par: 72 Yardage: 6,815
Last day of event: Sunday, February 2, 1986

Player	Place	Score	Earnings
Fuzzy Zoeller	Win	69-66-70=205	$108,000.00
Payne Stewart	2	71-69-70=210	$64,800.00
Mark Wiebe	T-3	70-69-72=211	$31,200.00
Tony Sills	T-3	72-68-71=211	$31,200.00
Tom Watson	T-3	71-67-73=211	$31,200.00
Dan Pohl	T-6	71-70-72=213	$19,425.00
Bob Eastwood	T-6	70-70-73=213	$19,425.00
Mark Pfeil	T-6	73-67-73=213	$19,425.00
Ken Brown	T-6	74-73-66=213	$19,425.00
Chi Chi Rodriguez	T-10	72-72-70=214	$15,000.00
Jim Thorpe	T-10	72-68-74=214	$15,000.00
Andy Bean	T-10	75-71-68=214	$15,000.00

Shearson Lehman/Andy Williams San Diego

Course: Torrey Pines (South), Torrey Pines (North), San Diego, Calif.
Home Course -Par: 72 Yardage: 7,021
Last day of event: Sunday, February 9, 1986

Player	Place	Score	Earnings
Bob Tway	Win	67-68-69=204	$81,000.00

Playoff: Beat Bernhard Langer with par on second extra hole

Player	Place	Score	Earnings
Bernhard Langer	T-2	70-66-68=204	$48,600.00
Paul Azinger	T-3	67-69-69=205	$23,400.00
Mike Hulbert	T-3	69-69-67=205	$23,400.00
Mark Lye	T-3	70-66-69=205	$23,400.00
Gary Hallberg	T-6	70-69-67=206	$15,075.00
Gary Koch	T-6	70-69-67=206	$15,075.00
Larry Rinker	T-6	66-72-68=206	$15,075.00
Don Pooley	T-9	68-70-69=207	$12,600.00
Danny Edwards	T-9	66-69-72=207	$12,600.00

Hawaiian Open

Course: Waialae C.C., Honolulu, Ha.
Par: 72 Yardage: 6,975
Last day of event: Sunday, February 16, 1986

Player	Place	Score	Earnings
Corey Pavin	Win	67-67-72-66=272	$90,000.00
Paul Azinger	2	70-65-69-70=274	$54,000.00
Tom Watson	T-3	68-69-66-73=276	$29,000.00
Bernhard Langer	T-3	67-74-67-68=276	$29,000.00
Andy Dillard	T-5	69-71-69-68=277	$18,250.00
Hubert Green	T-5	71-68-68-70=277	$11,571.43
David Ogrin	T-5	66-70-74-67=277	$15,500.00
Jodie Mudd	8	71-69-66-72=278	$11,571.43
Bobby Wadkins	T-9	68-70-71-70=279	$11,571.43
Wayne Levi	T-9	67-70-70-72=279	$11,571.42
Dave Rummells	T-9	68-68-72-71=279	$11,571.43
Jay Haas	T-9	68-72-72-67=279	$11,571.43
Isao Aoki	T-9	72-69-70-68=279	$11,571.43
Craig Stadler	T-9	67-72-67-73=279	$11,571.43
Bob Tway	T-9	70-68-68-73=279	$11,571.43

Los Angeles Open

Course: Riviera C.C., Pacific Palisades, Calif.
Par: 71 Yardage: 7,029
Last day of event: Sunday, February 23, 1986

Player	Place	Score	Earnings
Doug Tewell	Win	69-72-66-63=270	$81,000.00
Clarence Rose	2	73-70-66-68=277	$48,600.00
Willie Wood	3	72-69-67-70=278	$30,600.00
Jim Gallagher, Jr.	T-4	71-71-68-69=279	$19,800.00
Jay Delsing	T-4	66-74-71-68=279	$19,800.00
Lanny Wadkins	T-6	71-70-67-72=280	$14,568.75
Barry Jaeckel	T-6	73-70-67-70=280	$14,568.75
Antonio Cerda	T-6	74-67-69-70=280	$14,568.75
Corey Pavin	T-6	74-68-69-69=280	$14,568.75
Lennie Clements	T-10	69-70-71-71=281	$10,800.00
Massy Kuramoto	T-10	72-69-70-70=281	$10,800.00
Dennis Trixler	T-10	66-71-71-73=281	$10,800.00
Mark Lye	T-10	72-66-73-70=281	$10,800.00

Honda Classic

Course: TPC at Eagle Trace, Coral Springs, Fla.
Par: 72 Yardage: 7,030
Last day of event: Sunday, March 2, 1986

Player	Place	Score	Earnings
Kenny Knox	Win	66-71-80-70=287	$90,000.00
Clarence Rose	T-2	70-73-72-73=288	$33,000.00
Jodie Mudd	T-2	70-72-75-71=288	$33,000.00
John Mahaffey	T-2	74-70-76-68=288	$33,000.00
Andy Bean	T-2	69-69-77-73=288	$33,000.00

Barry Jaeckel	6	76-70-74-69=289	$18,000.00
Tom Purtzer	7	71-71-80-68=290	$16,750.00
Payne Stewart	T-8	69-74-73-75=291	$15,000.00
Mike Reid	T-8	69-78-72-72=291	$15,000.00
Bruce Lietzke	T-10	72-70-77-73=292	$13,000.00
Lance Ten Broeck	T-10	74-69-78-71=292	$13,000.00

Doral-Eastern Open
Course: Doral C.C. (Blue), Miami, Fla.
Par: 72 Yardage: 6,939
Last day of event: Sunday, March 9, 1986

Player	Place	Score	Earnings
Andy Bean	Win	71-68-68-69=276	$90,000.00
Playoff: Beat Hubert Green with birdie on fourth extra hole			
Hubert Green	T-2	70-70-64-72=276	$54,000.00
Tom Kite	T-3	66-67-73-71=277	$29,000.00
Mark O'Meara	T-3	70-67-74-66=277	$29,000.00
Mike Sullivan	T-5	71-69-69-70=279	$19,000.00
Mac O'Grady	T-5	73-67-69-70=279	$19,000.00
Tom Purtzer	7	66-71-73-70=280	$16,750.00
Mark Calcavecchia	T-8	65-72-72-72=281	$13,500.00
Bobby Wadkins	T-8	72-69-69-71=281	$13,500.00
Bill Kratzert	T-8	72-70-69-70=281	$13,500.00
David Frost	T-8	69-70-73-69=281	$13,500.00
Ed Fiori	T-8	68-68-74-71=281	$13,500.00

Hertz Bay Hill Classic
Course: Bay Hill Club, Orlando, Fla.
Par: 71 Yardage: 7,103
Last day of event: Sunday, March 16, 1986

Player	Place	Score	Earnings
Dan Forsman	Win	68-67-67=202	$90,000.00
Ray Floyd	T-2	68-69-66=203	$44,000.00
Mike Hulbert	T-2	70-69-64=203	$44,000.00
Wayne Levi	4	70-67-67=204	$24,000.00
Dan Pohl	T-5	68-70-67=205	$19,000.00
Curtis Strange	T-5	70-70-65=205	$19,000.00
Corey Pavin	T-7	69-70-67=206	$15,583.33
Mark Wiebe	T-7	70-70-66=206	$15,583.33
Bernhard Langer	T-7	72-66-68=206	$15,583.34
Bob Tway	10	66-72-69=207	$13,500.00

USF&G Classic
Course: Lakewood C.C., New Orleans, La.
Par: 72 Yardage: 7,080
Last day of event: Sunday, March 23, 1986

Player	Place	Score	Earnings
Calvin Peete	Win	68-67-66-68=269	$90,000.00
Pat McGowan	2	69-69-68-68=274	$54,000.00
Doug Tewell	T-3	71-69-69-68=277	$24,000.00
Nick Faldo	T-3	68-72-68-69=277	$24,000.00
Tom Sieckmann	T-3	73-70-67-67=277	$24,000.00
Greg Ladehoff	T-3	75-68-64-70=277	$24,000.00
Don Pooley	T-7	71-71-70-69=281	$14,550.00
Dave Barr	T-7	73-72-67-69=281	$14,550.00
Tom Watson	T-7	71-74-66-70=281	$14,550.00
Dick Mast	T-7	72-64-71-74=281	$14,550.00
Bill Israelson	T-7	73-65-74-69=281	$14,550.00

Tournament Players Championship
Course: TPC at Sawgrass, Ponte Vedra Beach, Fla.
Par: 72 Yardage: 6,857
Last day of event: Sunday, March 30, 1986

Player	Place	Score	Earnings
John Mahaffey	Win	69-70-65-71=275	$162,000.00
Larry Mize	2	66-68-66-76=276	$97,200.00
Tim Simpson	3	72-70-66-72=280	$61,200.00
Tom Kite	T-4	69-69-71-72=281	$37,200.00
Brett Upper	T-4	71-65-73-72=281	$37,200.00
Jim Thorpe	T-4	69-68-74-70=281	$37,200.00
Hal Sutton	T-7	71-72-68-71=282	$28,050.00
John Cook	T-7	71-73-70-68=282	$28,050.00
Jay Haas	T-7	73-68-73-68=282	$28,050.00
Bob Tway	T-10	66-73-72-72=283	$21,600.00
Doug Tewell	T-10	68-68-74-73=283	$21,600.00
Payne Stewart	T-10	71-67-75-70=283	$21,600.00
Dave Rummells	T-10	70-65-79-69=283	$21,600.00

Greater Greensboro Open
Course: Forest Oaks C.C., Greensboro, N.C.
Par: 72 Yardage: 6,984
Last day of event: Sunday, April 6, 1986

Player	Place	Score	Earnings
Sandy Lyle	Win	68-64-73-70=275	$90,000.00
Andy Bean	2	68-70-72-67=277	$54,000.00
Leonard Thompson	T-3	66-72-72-69=279	$29,000.00
Isao Aoki	T-3	73-71-69-66=279	$29,000.00
Lanny Wadkins	5	75-68-68-69=280	$20,000.00
Craig Stadler	T-6	69-69-71-72=281	$15,125.00
David Frost	T-6	69-72-68-72=281	$15,125.00
Chip Beck	T-6	72-69-71-69=281	$15,125.00
Tom Purtzer	T-6	68-72-68-73=281	$15,125.00
David Edwards	T-6	67-72-74-68=281	$15,125.00
Payne Stewart	T-6	70-70-74-67=281	$15,125.00

Masters
Course: Augusta National G.C., Augusta, Ga.
Par: 72 Yardage: 6,925
Last day of event: Sunday, April 13, 1986

Player	Place	Score	Earnings
Jack Nicklaus	Win	74-71-69-65=279	$144,000.00
Greg Norman	T-2	70-72-68-70=280	$70,400.00
Tom Kite	T-2	70-74-68-68=280	$70,400.00
Seve Ballesteros	4	71-68-72-70=281	$38,400.00
Nick Price	5	79-69-63-71=282	$32,000.00
Tom Watson	T-6	70-74-68-71=283	$27,800.00
Jay Haas	T-6	76-69-71-67=283	$27,800.00
Tommy Nakajima	T-8	70-71-71-72=284	$23,200.00
Bob Tway	T-8	70-73-71-70=284	$23,200.00
Payne Stewart	T-8	75-71-69-69=284	$23,200.00

Deposit Guaranty Golf Classic
Course: Hattiesburg C.C., Hattiesburg, Miss.
Par: 70 Yardage: 6,594
Last day of event: Sunday, April 13, 1986

Player	Place	Score	Earnings
Dan Halldorson	Win	64-67-66-66=263	$36,000.00
Paul Azinger	2	64-69-66-66=265	$21,600.00
Scott Hoch	3	67-69-65-67=268	$13,600.00

John Adams	4	66-69-71-64=270	$9,600.00
Ron Streck	T-5	66-69-67-69=271	$7,025.00
Eduardo Romero	T-5	66-70-68-67=271	$7,025.00
Vance Heafner	T-5	67-69-70-65=271	$7,025.00
Tom Byrum	T-5	68-65-70-68=271	$7,025.00
Antonio Cerda	T-9	67-67-69-69=272	$5,000.00
Richard Zokol	T-9	64-71-71-66=272	$5,000.00
Rocco Mediate	T-9	65-66-70-71=272	$5,000.00
Gibby Gilbert	T-9	68-68-72-64=272	$5,000.00
Gary Martin	T-9	67-74-66-65=272	$5,000.00

Sea Pines Heritage Classic

Course: Harbour Town G.L., Hilton Head, S.C.
Par: 71 Yardage: 6,657
Last day of event: Sunday, April 20, 1986

Player	Place	Score	Earnings
Fuzzy Zoeller	Win	68-68-69-71=276	$81,000.00
Chip Beck	T-2	70-67-70-70=277	$33,600.00
Greg Norman	T-2	70-68-69-70=277	$33,600.00
Roger Maltbie	T-2	67-72-69-69=277	$33,600.00
Jay Haas	5	71-70-66-71=278	$18,000.00
Ken Green	T-6	71-70-71-67=279	$15,075.00
Ray Floyd	T-6	69-72-72-66=279	$15,075.00
Tom Kite	T-6	70-72-70-67=279	$15,075.00
Hal Sutton	T-9	71-71-69-70=281	$12,150.00
Danny Edwards	T-9	74-70-70-67=281	$12,150.00
Don Pooley	T-9	69-66-75-71=281	$12,150.00

Houston Open

Course: TPC at The Woodlands, The Woodlands, Texas
Par: 72 Yardage: 7,045
Last day of event: Sunday, April 27, 1986

Player	Place	Score	Earnings
Curtis Strange	Win	72-68-68-66=274	$90,000.00
Playoff: Beat Calvin Peete with birdie on third extra hole			
Calvin Peete	T-2	65-70-70-69=274	$54,000.00
Tom Watson	3	69-68-68-71=276	$34,000.00
Bruce Lietzke	T-4	68-72-71-68=279	$20,666.67
David Edwards	T-4	73-71-66-69=279	$20,666.67
Jay Haas	T-4	68-70-67-74=279	$20,666.66
Doug Tewell	T-7	71-70-71-68=280	$16,125.00
Payne Stewart	T-7	69-73-71-67=280	$16,125.00
Craig Stadler	T-9	69-70-71-72=282	$12,500.00
Lennie Clements	T-9	72-69-72-69=282	$12,500.00
Bill Glasson	T-9	72-71-70-69=282	$12,500.00
Charles Bolling	T-9	73-67-72-70=282	$12,500.00
Brian Claar	T-9	74-71-67-70=282	$12,500.00

Panasonic Las Vegas Invitational

Course: Las Vegas C.C., Spanish Trail G. & C.C., Desert Inn C.C., Las Vegas, Nev.
Home course / Las Vegas C.C., Par: 72 Yardage: 7,164
Last day of event: Sunday, May 4, 1986

Player	Place	Score	Earnings
Greg Norman	Win	73-63-68-64-65=333	$207,000.00
Dan Pohl	2	68-70-67-66-69=340	$124,200.00
Larry Nelson	T-3	67-69-67-69-69=341	$66,700.00
Steve Pate	T-3	67-73-69-65-67=341	$66,700.00
Andy Bean	T-5	70-69-66-69-68=342	$43,700.00
Don Pooley	T-5	70-70-67-68-67=342	$43,700.00
John Cook	T-7	66-68-70-71-68=343	$35,843.33
Gil Morgan	T-7	67-67-70-71-68=343	$35,843.33

Bob Tway	T-7	70-71-63-68-71=343	$35,843.34
Wayne Levi	T-10	69-69-68-68-70=344	$25,491.67
Jim Colbert	T-10	69-71-64-69-71=344	$25,491.66
John Mahaffey	T-10	69-70-65-71-69=344	$25,491.67
Bob Lohr	T-10	67-65-70-72-70=344	$25,491.66
Hal Sutton	T-10	67-69-69-73-66=344	$25,491.67
Tom Watson	T-10	73-68-66-69-68=344	$25,491.67

Byron Nelson Golf Classic

Course: TPC at Las Colinas, Irving, Texas
Par: 70 Yardage: 6,767
Last day of event: Sunday, May 11, 1986

Player	Place	Score	Earnings
Andy Bean	Win	66-68-67-68=269	$108,000.00
Mark Wiebe	2	69-66-68-67=270	$64,800.00
Bobby Wadkins	3	68-69-66-70=273	$40,800.00
Craig Stadler	T-4	69-69-65-71=274	$23,625.00
Payne Stewart	T-4	70-66-67-71=274	$23,625.00
Gene Sauers	T-4	71-68-66-69=274	$23,625.00
Mark Hayes	T-4	64-72-68-70=274	$23,625.00
Bob Lohr	T-8	70-70-67-68=275	$16,800.00
D.A. Weibring	T-8	71-68-68-68=275	$16,800.00
Dan Halldorson	T-8	72-69-64-70=275	$16,800.00
Nick Price	T-8	73-66-69-67=275	$16,800.00

Colonial National Invitational

Course: Colonial C.C., Fort Worth, Texas
Par: 70 Yardage: 7,096
Last day of event: Sunday, May 18, 1986

Player	Place	Score	Earnings
Dan Pohl	Win	68-69-68=205	$108,000.00
Playoff: Beat Payne Stewart with birdie on first extra hole			
Payne Stewart	T-2	72-67-66=205	$64,800.00
Bernhard Langer	T-3	70-70-67=207	$31,200.00
Bill Rogers	T-3	67-71-69=207	$31,200.00
Tom Watson	T-3	75-68-64=207	$31,200.00
Mike Sullivan	T-6	70-69-69=208	$20,100.00
David Frost	T-6	70-71-67=208	$20,100.00
Gene Sauers	T-6	66-72-70=208	$20,100.00
Ronnie Black	T-9	71-68-70=209	$15,600.00
Bob Tway	T-9	69-68-72=209	$15,600.00
David Edwards	T-9	69-67-73=209	$15,600.00
Paul Azinger	T-9	75-67-67=209	$15,600.00

Memorial Tournament

Course: Muirfield Village G.C., Dubin, Ohio
Par: 72 Yardage: 7,106
Last day of event: Sunday, May 25, 1986

Player	Place	Score	Earnings
Hal Sutton	Win	68-69-66-68=271	$100,000.00
Don Pooley	2	69-67-70-69=275	$60,000.00
Johnny Miller	T-3	70-69-69-68=276	$32,225.00
Mark O'Meara	T-3	68-75-67-66=276	$32,225.00
John Mahaffey	T-5	68-71-69-69=277	$21,110.00
Jack Nicklaus	T-5	66-70-72-69=277	$21,110.00
Chip Beck	T-7	71-66-70-71=278	$17,313.33
Scott Simpson	T-7	70-72-68-68=278	$17,313.34
Payne Stewart	T-7	72-69-69-68=278	$17,313.33
Craig Stadler	T-10	72-69-71-67=279	$13,335.00
Doug Tewell	T-10	66-70-70-73=279	$13,335.00
Tom Purtzer	T-10	68-69-73-69=279	$13,335.00
Greg Norman	T-10	73-67-71-68=279	$13,335.00

Kemper Open

Course: Congressional C.C., Bethesda, Md.
Par: 72 Yardage: 7,173
Last day of event: Sunday, June 1, 1986

Player	Place	Score	Earnings
Greg Norman	Win	72-69-70-66=277	$90,000.00
Playoff: Beat Larry Mize with par on six extra hole			
Larry Mize	T-2	67-71-70-69=277	$54,000.00
Mike Reid	T-3	68-70-71-70=279	$29,000.00
John Cook	T-3	72-69-71-67=279	$29,000.00
Bobby Wadkins	5	70-71-73-66=280	$20,000.00
Curtis Strange	6	73-67-71-71=282	$18,000.00
Buddy Gardner	T-7	72-70-71-70=283	$15,583.33
Bob Gilder	T-7	73-71-73-66=283	$15,583.34
Chip Beck	T-7	74-70-68-71=283	$15,583.33
Roger Maltbie	T-10	71-70-73-70=284	$11,500.00
Craig Stadler	T-10	73-68-73-70=284	$11,500.00
David Ogrin	T-10	68-74-70-72=284	$11,500.00
Donnie Hammond	T-10	71-68-75-70=284	$11,500.00
Gil Morgan	T-10	75-71-66-72=284	$11,500.00

Manufacturers Hanover Westchester Classic

Course: Westchester C.C., Harrison, N.Y.
Par: 71 Yardage: 6,723
Last day of event: Sunday, June 8, 1986

Player	Place	Score	Earnings
Bob Tway	Win	73-63-69-67=272	$108,000.00
Willie Wood	2	71-63-73-66=273	$64,800.00
Gil Morgan	T-3	69-69-70-67=275	$34,800.00
Scott Simpson	T-3	71-67-70-67=275	$34,800.00
Mike Reid	5	68-69-68-72=277	$24,000.00
Andrew Magee	T-6	72-67-71-70=280	$20,850.00
Mark Wiebe	T-6	68-71-73-68=280	$20,850.00
Tom Watson	T-8	72-70-70-69=281	$16,800.00
Jay Haas	T-8	65-73-73-70=281	$16,800.00
Brett Upper	T-8	68-66-74-73=281	$16,800.00
Doug Tewell	T-8	70-66-74-71=281	$16,800.00

U.S. Open

Course: Shinnecock Hills G.C., Southampton, N.Y.
Par: 70 Yardage: 6,912
Last day of event: Sunday, June 15, 1986

Player	Place	Score	Earnings
Ray Floyd	Win	75-68-70-66=279	$115,000.00
Lanny Wadkins	T-2	74-70-72-65=281	$47,646.00
Chip Beck	T-2	75-73-68-65=281	$47,646.00
Lee Trevino	T-4	74-68-69-71=282	$26,269.00
Hal Sutton	T-4	75-70-66-71=282	$26,269.00
Payne Stewart	T-6	76-68-69-70=283	$19,009.00
Ben Crenshaw	T-6	76-69-69-69=283	$19,009.00
Bob Tway	T-8	70-73-69-72=284	$14,500.75
Mark McCumber	T-8	74-71-68-71=284	$14,500.75
Bernhard Langer	T-8	74-70-70-70=284	$14,500.00
Jack Nicklaus	T-8	77-72-67-68=284	$14,500.75

Provident Classic

Course: ValleyBrook C.C., Hixson, Tenn.
Par: 70 Yardage: 6,641
Last day of event: Sunday, June 15, 1986

Player	Place	Score	Earnings
Brad Faxon	Win	67-62-69-63=261	$54,000.00

Scott Hoch	2	67-63-66-66=262	$32,400.00
Clarence Rose	3	65-66-65-69=265	$20,400.00
Bill Bergin	T-4	67-69-65-66=267	$12,400.00
Loren Roberts	T-4	67-68-69-63=267	$12,400.00
Gary McCord	T-4	69-67-63-68=267	$12,400.00
J.C. Snead	T-7	69-68-67-64=268	$9,675.00
Tommy Armour III	T-7	71-62-67-68=268	$9,675.00
Jim Gallagher, Jr.	T-9	64-68-69-68=269	$7,800.00
Brian Claar	T-9	67-69-65-68=269	$7,800.00
Steve Jones	T-9	70-67-64-68=269	$7,800.00
Ken Brown	T-9	71-66-65-67=269	$7,800.00

Georgia-Pacific Atlanta Golf Classic

Course: Atlanta C.C., Atlanta, Ga.
Par: 72 Yardage: 7,007
Last day of event: Sunday, June 22, 1986

Player	Place	Score	Earnings
Bob Tway	Win	68-66-71-64=269	$90,000.00
Hal Sutton	2	66-68-67-70=271	$54,000.00
Scott Hoch	T-3	67-66-70-70=273	$24,000.00
Mark O'Meara	T-3	67-67-70-69=273	$24,000.00
Willie Wood	T-3	67-68-70-68=273	$24,000.00
Greg Norman	T-3	71-72-66-64=273	$24,000.00
Gary Koch	7	72-63-72-67=274	$16,750.00
Tom Purtzer	8	69-69-66-71=275	$15,500.00
David Graham	T-9	71-71-67-67=276	$13,500.00
Rex Caldwell	T-9	71-72-65-68=276	$13,500.00
Doug Tewell	T-9	68-64-71-73=276	$13,500.00

Canadian Open

Course: Glen Abbey G.C., Oakville, Ontario, Canada
Par: 72 Yardage: 7,102
Last day of event: Sunday, June 29, 1986

Player	Place	Score	Earnings
Bob Murphy	Win	71-70-68-71=280	$108,000.00
Greg Norman	2	72-76-62-73=283	$64,800.00
Mike Donald	T-3	69-73-69-73=284	$31,200.00
Andy Bean	T-3	69-69-74-72=284	$31,200.00
Davis Love III	T-3	72-68-70-74=284	$31,200.00
Brian Claar	T-6	73-73-69-70=285	$20,100.00
Mac O'Grady	T-6	73-68-69-75=285	$20,100.00
Clarence Rose	T-6	69-76-70-70=285	$20,100.00
Bob Tway	T-9	70-71-72-73=286	$13,885.71
Nick Price	T-9	71-71-71-73=286	$13,885.72
Jeff Sluman	T-9	72-73-70-71=286	$13,885.71
Curtis Strange	T-9	73-70-70-73=286	$13,885.72
David Ogrin	T-9	73-71-72-70=286	$13,885.72
Bobby Cole	T-9	71-72-69-74=286	$13,885.71
Jay Delsing	T-9	75-69-71-71=286	$13,885.71

Canon Sammy Davis, Jr. - Greater Hartford Open

Course: TPC of Connecticut, Cromwell, Conn.
Par: 71 Yardage: 6,786
Last day of event: Sunday, July 6, 1986

Player	Place	Score	Earnings
Mac O'Grady	Win	71-69-67-62=269	$126,000.00
Playoff: Beat Roger Maltbie with par on first extra hole			
Roger Maltbie	T-2	66-67-70-66=269	$75,600.00
Paul Azinger	T-3	67-70-66-69=272	$36,400.00
Scott Hoch	T-3	71-66-68-67=272	$36,400.00
Mark O'Meara	T-3	69-72-64-67=272	$36,400.00
Tom Watson	T-6	65-67-70-71=273	$23,450.00

Curtis Strange	T-6	71-69-65-68=273	$23,450.00
Tim Simpson	T-6	64-66-74-69=273	$23,450.00
John Cook	T-9	68-69-69-68=274	$18,900.00
Mike Donald	T-9	69-68-68-69=274	$18,900.00
Chip Beck	T-9	66-73-65-70=274	$18,900.00

Anheuser-Busch Golf Classic
Course: Kingsmill G.C., Williamsburg, Va.
Par: 71 Yardage: 6,776
Last day of event: Sunday, July 13, 1986

Player	Place	Score	Earnings
Fuzzy Zoeller	Win	70-68-72-64=274	$90,000.00
Jodie Mudd	2	65-70-72-69=276	$54,000.00
Joey Sindelar	3	70-68-72-67=277	$34,000.00
Mac O'Grady	T-4	69-72-70-67=278	$22,000.00
Scott Hoch	T-4	68-69-74-67=278	$22,000.00
Clarence Rose	T-6	69-71-70-69=279	$16,187.50
T.C. Chen	T-6	71-70-70-68=279	$16,187.50
David Frost	T-6	68-71-72-68=279	$16,187.50
Rick Fehr	T-6	71-67-72-69=279	$16,187.50
Hale Irwin	T-10	70-69-71-70=280	$11,500.00
Don Pooley	T-10	67-72-72-69=280	$11,500.00
Corey Pavin	T-10	70-72-69-69=280	$11,500.00
Jeff Sluman	T-10	66-73-74-67=280	$11,500.00
Tony Sills	T-10	70-65-75-70=280	$11,500.00

Hardee's Golf Classic
Course: Oakwood C.C., Coal Valley, Ill.
Par: 70 Yardage: 6,602
Last day of event: Sunday, July 20, 1986

Player	Place	Score	Earnings
Mark Wiebe	Win	69-65-66-68=268	$72,000.00
Curt Byrum	2	64-70-64-71=269	$43,200.00
Pat Lindsey	3	73-66-66-66=271	$27,200.00
Bill Glasson	4	72-68-66-66=272	$19,200.00
Bob Lohr	T-5	63-71-69-70=273	$14,600.00
Calvin Peete	T-5	68-67-72-66=273	$14,600.00
Morris Hatalsky	T-5	72-68-65-68=273	$14,600.00
George Archer	T-8	69-67-68-70=274	$11,200.00
Russ Cochran	T-8	66-67-70-71=274	$11,200.00
Mark Brooks	T-8	67-70-66-71=274	$11,200.00
Brett Upper	T-8	71-70-65-68=274	$11,200.00

British Open
Course: Turnberry (Ailsa Course), Turnberry, Ayrshire, Scotland
Par: 70 Yardage: 6,957
Last day of event: Sunday, July 20, 1986

Player	Place	Score	Earnings
Greg Norman	Win	74-63-74-69=280	$105,000.00
Gordon J. Brand	2	71-68-75-71=285	$75,000.00
Ian Woosnam	T-3	70-74-70-72=286	$52,500.00
Bernhard Langer	T-3	72-70-76-68=286	$52,500.00
Nick Faldo	5	71-70-76-70=287	$37,500.00
Gary Koch	T-6	73-72-72-71=288	$33,000.00
Seve Ballesteros	T-6	76-75-73-64=288	$33,000.00
Fuzzy Zoeller	T-8	75-73-72-69=289	$25,999.50
Tommy Nakajima	T-8	74-67-71-77=289	$25,999.50
Brian Marchbank	T-8	78-70-72-69=289	$25,999.50

Buick Open
Course: Warwick Hills C.C., Grand Blanc, Mich.
Par: 72 Yardage: 7,014
Last day of event: Sunday, July 27, 1986

Player	Place	Score	Earnings
Ben Crenshaw	Win	69-67-66-68=270	$90,000.00
J.C. Snead	T-2	67-70-68-66=271	$44,000.00
Doug Tewell	T-2	70-68-67-66=271	$44,000.00
Ed Fiori	4	66-69-70-67=272	$24,000.00
Bobby Wadkins	T-5	69-66-70-68=273	$19,000.00
Davis Love III	T-5	65-67-70-71=273	$19,000.00
Gene Sauers	T-7	69-67-67-71=274	$16,125.00
Steve Pate	T-7	70-67-65-72=274	$16,125.00
Jeff Sluman	T-9	69-67-69-70=275	$11,571.42
Lee Trevino	T-9	69-68-70-68=275	$11,571.43
Scott Hoch	T-9	70-69-66-70=275	$11,571.43
Kenny Knox	T-9	68-68-68-71=275	$11,571.43
Brian Claar	T-9	68-68-71-68=275	$11,571.43
Wayne Levi	T-9	71-67-68-69=275	$11,571.43
Tom Purtzer	T-9	68-68-66-73=275	$11,571.43

Western Open
Course: Butler National G.C., Oak Brook, Ill.
Par: 72 Yardage: 7,097
Last day of event: Sunday, August 3, 1986

Player	Place	Score	Earnings
Tom Kite	Win	70-75-73-68=286	$90,000.00

Playoff: Beat Fred Couples, David Frost and Nick Price with birdie on first extra hole

Nick Price	T-2	71-71-73-71=286	$37,333.34
Fred Couples	T-2	70-68-73-75=286	$37,333.33
David Frost	T-2	74-66-71-75=286	$37,333.33
Dick Mast	T-5	69-73-72-73=287	$16,950.00
Leonard Thompson	T-5	71-73-69-74=287	$16,950.00
Greg Norman	T-5	71-74-72-70=287	$16,950.00
Bruce Lietzke	T-5	74-70-73-70=287	$16,950.00
Bobby Wadkins	T-5	69-69-74-75=287	$16,950.00
Mark Pfeil	T-10	72-71-73-73=289	$12,000.00
Danny Edwards	T-10	75-72-73-69=289	$12,000.00
Tom Byrum	T-10	70-70-72-77=289	$12,000.00
George Burns	T-10	71-70-71-77=289	$12,000.00

PGA Championship
Course: Inverness Club, Toledo, Ohio
Par: 71 Yardage: 6,982
Last day of event: Monday, August 11, 1986

Player	Place	Score	Earnings
Bob Tway	Win	72-70-64-70=276	$140,000.00
Greg Norman	2	65-68-69-76=278	$80,000.00
Peter Jacobsen	3	68-70-70-71=279	$60,000.00
D.A. Weibring	4	71-72-68-69=280	$42,865.00
Bruce Lietzke	T-5	69-71-70-71=281	$32,500.00
Payne Stewart	T-5	70-67-72-72=281	$32,500.00
Jim Thorpe	T-7	71-67-73-71=282	$20,833.33
Mike Hulbert	T-7	69-68-74-71=282	$20,833.34
David Graham	T-7	75-69-71-67=282	$20,833.33
Doug Tewell	T-10	73-71-68-71=283	$15,000.00

The International

Course: Castle Pine G.C., Castle Rock, Colo.

Par: 72 Yardage: 7,559

Last day of event: Monday, August 18, 1986

Player	Place	Score	Earnings
Ken Green	Win	8-4-7-12=31	$180,000.00
Bernhard Langer	2	-1-9-10-9=27	$113,000.00
J.C. Snead	T-3	3-5-7-8=23	$63,000.00
Joey Sindelar	T-3	7-12-8-8=35	$63,000.00
Nick Price	5	4-3-9-6=22	$45,000.00
Howard Twitty	6	3-7-11-5=26	$41,000.00
Kenny Knox	T-7	9-3-5-4=21	$37,250.00
Bruce Lietzke	T-7	11-9-5-4=29	$37,250.00
Andy Dillard	9	5-5-6-1=17	$34,000.00
Tom Kite	T-10	5-6-7-0=18	$31,000.00
Donnie Hammond	T-10	10-4-6-0=20	$31,000.00

NEC World Series of Golf

Course: Firestone C.C. (South), Akron, Ohio

Par: 70 Yardage: 7,149

Last day of event: Sunday, August 24, 1986

Player	Place	Score	Earnings
Dan Pohl	Win	69-66-71-71=277	$126,000.00
Lanny Wadkins	2	68-68-70-72=278	$75,600.00
Bobby Cole	3	74-67-68-70=279	$47,600.00
John Mahaffey	4	71-66-72-71=280	$33,600.00
Rodger Davis	T-5	72-69-69-71=281	$24,550.00
Tim Simpson	T-5	71-73-72-65=281	$24,550.00
Donnie Hammond	T-5	66-68-73-74=281	$24,550.00
Andy Bean	T-5	72-74-69-66=281	$24,550.00
Tom Kite	T-9	71-69-71-71=282	$16,800.00
Jim Thorpe	T-9	70-72-68-72=282	$16,800.00
Calvin Peete	T-9	72-70-71-69=282	$16,800.00
David Ishii	T-9	67-71-73-71=282	$16,800.00
Jack Nicklaus	T-9	71-69-69-73=282	$16,800.00
Bob Tway	T-9	74-72-66-70=282	$16,800.00

Federal Express St. Jude Classic

Course: Colonial C.C. (South), Cordova, Tenn.

Par: 72 Yardage: 7,282

Last day of event: Sunday, August 31, 1986

Player	Place	Score	Earnings
Mike Hulbert	Win	71-72-68-69=280	$109,064.00
Joey Sindelar	2	71-71-71-68=281	$65,438.00
Payne Stewart	3	71-70-71-70=282	$41,202.00
Larry Nelson	4	76-70-67-70=283	$29,084.00
Gary Koch	T-5	73-69-69-73=284	$23,024.50
Larry Mize	T-5	73-70-68-73=284	$23,024.50
Fuzzy Zoeller	T-7	70-74-71-70=285	$17,632.00
Howard Twitty	T-7	71-67-73-74=285	$17,632.00
Tony Sills	T-7	74-70-69-72=285	$17,632.00
Jeff Sluman	T-7	74-70-70-71=285	$17,632.00
Eugene Elliott	T-7	76-72-68-69=285	$17,632.00

B.C. Open

Course: En-Joie G.C., Endicott, N.Y.

Par: 71 Yardage: 6,966

Last day of event: Sunday, September 7, 1986

Player	Place	Score	Earnings
Rick Fehr	Win	65-66-67-69=267	$72,000.00

Larry Mize	2	64-67-70-68=269	$43,200.00
Howard Twitty	3	69-68-68-66=271	$27,200.00
Bobby Wadkins	4	66-68-73-65=272	$19,200.00
Bill Glasson	T-5	66-70-71-67=274	$15,200.00
Calvin Peete	T-5	71-67-70-66=274	$15,200.00
Jay Haas	T-7	70-69-69-67=275	$12,900.00
Jack Renner	T-7	72-68-67-68=275	$12,900.00
Tom Purtzer	9	69-68-70-69=276	$11,600.00
Jeff Sluman	T-10	69-68-71-69=277	$10,000.00
Tony Sills	T-10	71-67-70-69=277	$10,000.00
Dick Mast	T-10	68-69-68-72=277	$10,000.00

Bank of Boston Classic

Course: Pleasant Valley C.C., Sutton, Mass.

Par: 71 Yardage: 7,110

Last day of event: Sunday, September 14, 1986

Player	Place	Score	Earnings
Gene Sauers	Win	70-71-64-69=274	$81,000.00
Playoff: Beat Blaine McCallister with birdie on third extra hole			
Blaine McCallister	T-2	72-68-67-67=274	$48,600.00
Curt Byrum	3	71-68-69-68=276	$30,600.00
Wayne Levi	T-4	68-71-70-68=277	$19,800.00
Jack Renner	T-4	73-70-68-66=277	$19,800.00
Paul Azinger	6	71-71-69-67=278	$16,200.00
Mark Calcavecchia	T-7	70-69-68-72=279	$14,512.50
Curtis Strange	T-7	73-65-68-73=279	$14,512.50
Larry Rinker	9	68-74-66-73=281	$13,050.00
Wayne Grady	T-10	66-73-71-72=282	$11,700.00
Ernie Gonzalez	T-10	71-71-66-74=282	$11,700.00

Greater Milwaukee Open

Course: Tuckaway C.C., Franklin, Wis.

Par: 72 Yardage: 7,030

Last day of event: Sunday, September 21, 1986

Player	Place	Score	Earnings
Corey Pavin	Win	66-72-67-67=272	$72,000.00
Playoff: Beat Dave Barr with birdie on fourth extra hole			
Dave Barr	T-2	69-64-69-70=272	$43,200.00
David Frost	3	69-66-68-70=273	$27,200.00
Buddy Gardner	T-4	69-68-67-70=274	$16,533.33
Tom Purtzer	T-4	66-71-68-69=274	$16,533.34
Roger Maltbie	T-4	72-68-67-67=274	$16,533.33
Ronnie Black	T-7	68-69-68-70=275	$12,900.00
Joey Sindelar	T-7	70-67-67-71=275	$12,900.00
Rick Fehr	T-9	68-70-68-70=276	$10,800.00
Morris Hatalsky	T-9	68-67-70-71=276	$10,800.00
Mark Calcavecchia	T-9	73-70-63-70=276	$10,800.00

Southwest Golf Classic

Course: Fairway Oaks C.C., Abilene, Texas

Par: 72 Yardage: 7,189

Last day of event: Sunday, September 28, 1986

Player	Place	Score	Earnings
Mark Calcavecchia	Win	68-70-66-71=275	$72,000.00
Tom Byrum	2	68-74-67-69=278	$43,200.00
Craig Stadler	T-3	72-72-72-63=279	$20,800.00
Morris Hatalsky	T-3	66-74-71-68=279	$20,800.00
D.A. Weibring	T-3	66-76-68-69=279	$20,800.00
Ronnie Black	6	69-74-69-69=281	$14,400.00
Jeff Maggert	7	68-73-70-71=282	$13,400.00
Ben Crenshaw	T-8	73-72-71-67=283	$11,600.00

Doug Tewell	T-8	69-74-69-71=283	$11,600.00
Corey Pavin	T-8	70-74-69-70=283	$11,600.00

Southern Open

Course: Green Island C.C., Columbus, Ga.
Par: 70 Yardage: 6,791
Last day of event: Sunday, October 5, 1986

Player	Place	Score	Earnings
Fred Wadsworth	Win	67-67-68-67=269	$63,000.00
George Archer	T-2	69-66-67-69=271	$23,100.00
Tim Simpson	T-2	68-67-70-66=271	$23,100.00
Jim Thorpe	T-2	65-71-64-71=271	$23,100.00
John Cook	T-2	70-71-65-65=271	$23,100.00
Jack Renner	T-6	70-69-65-68=272	$11,725.00
Joey Sindelar	T-6	70-70-67-65=272	$11,725.00
Payne Stewart	T-6	66-67-68-71=272	$11,725.00
Brad Fabel	9	70-65-69-69=273	$10,150.00
Kenny Knox	T-10	67-69-68-70=274	$8,050.00
Mike McCullough	T-10	69-65-70-70=274	$8,050.00
Larry Nelson	T-10	69-67-68-70=274	$8,050.00
Joe Inman	T-10	71-70-65-68=274	$8,050.00
Bob Gilder	T-10	72-65-70-67=274	$8,050.00

Pensacola Open

Course: Perdido Bay C.C., Pensacola, Fla.
Par: 71 Yardage: 7,093
Last day of event: Sunday, October 12, 1986

Player	Place	Score	Earnings
Ernie Gonzalez	Win	65-63=128	$40,500.00
Joey Sindelar	2	67-62=129	$24,300.00
Leonard Thompson	3	66-65=131	$15,300.00
Kenny Knox	T-4	66-67=133	$9,900.00
Mike Hulbert	T-4	68-65=133	$9,900.00
Paul Azinger	T-6	67-67=134	$6,342.18
Tom Byrum	T-6	66-68=134	$6,342.19
Bob Murphy	T-6	66-68=134	$6,342.18
Rick Fehr	T-6	68-66=134	$6,342.19
Bob Gilder	T-6	68-66=134	$6,342.19
Tim Simpson	T-6	68-66=134	$6,342.19
Jeff Sluman	T-6	65-69=134	$6,342.19
Fred Wadsworth	T-6	69-65=134	$6,342.19

Walt Disney World/Oldsmobile Classic

Course: Walt Disney (Magnolia, Palm), Lake Buena Vista C.C., Lake Buena Vista, Fla.
Home course / Magnolia, Par: 72 Yardage: 7,190
Last day of event: Sunday, October 19, 1986

Player	Place	Score	Earnings
Ray Floyd	Win	68-66-70-71=275	$90,000.00
Playoff: Beat Mike Sullivan and Lon Hinkle with par on first extra hole			
Mike Sullivan	T-2	65-69-70-71=275	$44,000.00
Lon Hinkle	T-2	67-69-68-71=275	$44,000.00
Pat McGowan	T-4	69-70-69-68=276	$20,666.67
Gary Koch	T-4	66-73-68-69=276	$20,666.66
Payne Stewart	T-4	65-66-71-74=276	$20,666.67
Andy North	T-7	71-69-69-69=278	$16,125.00
Phil Blackmar	T-7	67-73-68-70=278	$16,125.00
Bob Murphy	9	68-72-69-70=279	$14,500.00
Chris Perry	T-10	72-70-68-70=280	$13,000.00
Tom Purtzer	T-10	69-71-67-73=280	$13,000.00

Vantage Championship

Course: Oak Hill C.C., San Antonio, Texas
Par: 70 Yardage: 6,576
Last day of event: Sunday, October 26, 1986

Player	Place	Score	Earnings
Ben Crenshaw	Win	65-67-64=196	$180,000.00
Payne Stewart	2	67-65-65=197	$108,000.00
Phil Blackmar	T-3	66-67-68=201	$48,000.00
Bobby Clampett	T-3	67-68-66=201	$48,000.00
Ronnie Black	T-3	68-66-67=201	$48,000.00
Ernie Gonzalez	T-3	68-67-66=201	$48,000.00
Jeff Sluman	T-7	67-67-68=202	$27,071.43
Nick Price	T-7	67-68-67=202	$27,071.42
Tom Kite	T-7	68-67-67=202	$27,071.43
Kenny Knox	T-7	66-67-69=202	$27,071.43
Larry Mize	T-7	67-66-69=202	$27,071.43
Mac O'Grady	T-7	70-64-68=202	$27,071.43
Don Pooley	T-7	70-65-67=202	$27,071.43

Tallahassee Open

Course: Killearn C.C., Tallahassee, Fla.
Par: 72 Yardage: 7,124
Last day of event: Sunday, November 2, 1986

Player	Place	Score	Earnings
Mark Hayes	Win	68-67-68-70=273	$36,000.00
Russ Cochran	2	66-72-66-70=274	$21,600.00
Danny Briggs	T-3	67-69-70-69=275	$10,400.00
Tom Sieckmann	T-3	68-70-71-66=275	$10,400.00
Jim Gallagher, Jr.	T-3	73-69-68-65=275	$10,400.00
Scott Verplank	T-6	68-70-68-70=276	$6,950.00
Steve Jones	T-6	68-70-69-69=276	$6,950.00
Kenny Knox	8	71-68-68-70=277	$6,200.00
John Adams	9	70-70-68-71=279	$5,800.00
Jeff Grygiel	T-10	70-68-72-70=280	$4,800.00
Loren Roberts	T-10	72-67-70-71=280	$4,800.00
Charles Bolling	T-10	74-67-71-68=280	$4,800.00
Dennis Trixler	T-10	68-66-70-76=280	$4,800.00

Seiko Tucson-Match Play Championship

Course: Randolph Park Municipal, Tucson, Ariz.
Par: 70 Yardage: 6,860
Last day of event: Sunday, November 2, 1986

Player	Place	Score	Earnings
Jim Thorpe	Win		$150,000.00

Round One - Beat Brad Faxon 68-70
Round Two - Beat Dan Forsman with a par on second extra hole after both shot 70
Round Three - Beat Ben Crenshaw 65-67
Quarterfinals - Beat Tim Simpson 69-71
Semifinals - Beat Phil Blackmar 68-71
Finals - Beat Scott Simpson 67-71

Scott Simpson	2		$90,000.00

Round One - Beat Dan Pohl with a birdie on the first extra hole after both shot 72
Round Two - Beat Danny Edwards 70-74
Round Three - Beat Gary Koch 66-73
Quarterfinals - Beat Lanny Wadkins 65-68
Semifinals - Beat Ken Green 69-70
Finals - Jim Thorpe beats him 67-71

Ken Green	3		$60,000.00

Round One - Beat Bill Glasson 69-71
Round Two - Beat Brian Claar 71-73
Round Three - Beat Steve Pate 69-70
Quarterfinals - Beat David Edwards 70-71

Semifinals -Scott Simpson beats him 69-70
Consolation - Beat Phil Blackmar 67-74

| Phil Blackmar | 4 | | $40,000.00 |

Round One - Beat Willie Wood 68-69
Round Two - Beat Bob Gilder with a birdie on the fourth extra hole after both shot 69
Round Three - Beat Dave Barr 65-69
Quarterfinals - Beat Don Pooley 71-75
Semifinals - Jim Thorpe beats him 68-71
Consolation - Ken Green beats him 67-74

| Tim Simpson | T-5 | | $25,000.00 |

Round One - Beat J.C. Snead with a birdie on the fourth extra hole after both shot 67
Round Two - Beat Morris Hatalsky 71-72
Round Three - Beat Lennie Clements 66-67
Quarterfinals - Jim Thorpe beats him 69-71

| Don Pooley | T-5 | | $25,000.00 |

Round One - Beat Mike Reid 65-71
Round Two - Beat Davis Love III 67-70
Round Three - Beat Tom Purtzer 69-70
Quarterfinals - Phil Blackmar beats him 71-75

| David Edwards | T-5 | | $25,000.00 |

Round One - Beat Tom Watson 66-72
Round Two - Beat Gene Sauers 70-72
Round Three - Beat Mark Calcavecchia 67-69
Quarterfinals - Ken Green beats him 70-71

| Lanny Wadkins | T-5 | | $25,000.00 |

Round One - Beat Pat McGowan 67-72
Round Two - Beat Mark McCumber 69-74
Round Three - Beat Jim Colbert 70-71
Quarterfinals - Scott Simpson beats him 65-68

| Ben Crenshaw | T-9 | | $12,500.00 |

Round One - Beat Fred Couples 66-73
Round Two - Beat Hubert Green 72-75
Round Three - Jim Thorpe beats him 65-67

| Lennie Clements | T-9 | | $12,500.00 |

Round One - Beat John Mahaffey 65-70
Round Two - Beat Roger Maltbie 70-73
Round Three - Tim Simpson beats him 66-67

| Dave Barr | T-9 | | $12,500.00 |

Round One - Beat David Frost with a birdie on first extra hole after both shot 67
Round Two - Beat Mac O'Grady 71-73
Round Three - Phil Blackmar beats him 65-69

| Tom Purtzer | T-9 | | $12,500.00 |

Round One - Beat Bobby Clampett 66-72
Round Two - Beat Howard Twitty with par on second extra hole after both shot 70
Round Three - Don Pooley beats him 69-70

| Steve Pate | T-9 | | $12,500.00 |

Round One - Beat Craig Stadler 65-68
Round Two - Beat Bob Tway 69-73
Round Three - Ken Green beats him 69-70

| Mark Calcavecchia | T-9 | | $12,500.00 |

Round One - Beat Nick Price 67-69
Round Two - Beat Mike Donald with a birdie at the second extra hole after both shot 73
Round Three - David Edwards beats him 67-69

| Gary Koch | T-9 | | $12,500.00 |

Round One - Beat Jeff Sluman 66-71
Round Two - Beat Lon Hinkle 71-72
Round Three - Scott Simpson beats him 66-73

| Jim Colbert | T-9 | | $12,500.00 |

Round One - Beat Paul Azinger with a birdie on the third extra hole after both shot 69
Round Two - Beat Wayne Levi with a par on fourth extra hole after both shot 72
Round Three - Lanny Wadkins beats him 70-71

1987

In what was becoming an all too familiar scene, Greg Norman watched in disbelief as Larry Mize chipped in for birdie on the second hole (No. 11) of sudden death to win the Masters. (Largely forgotten is that Seve Ballesteros also made the playoff, but was eliminated on the first extra hole.) Scott Simpson won the U.S. Open by one shot over Tom Watson, who bogeyed three of the first five holes in Round 4 at the Olympic Club. Playing the kind of textbook golf that would become his trademark, Nick Faldo made 18 pars in the final round of the British Open to beat Paul Azinger and Rodger Davis by a shot at Muirfield. Larry Nelson claimed his second PGA Championship when Lanny Wadkins bogeyed the first hole of a sudden-death playoff at PGA National. Europe retained the Ryder Cup with a 15 to 13 victory at Muirfield Village, its first win on American soil.

MONY Tournament of Champions
Course: La Costa C.C., Carlsbad, Calif.
Par: 72 Yardage: 7,022
Last day of event: Saturday, January 10, 1987

Player	Place	Score	Earnings
Mac O'Grady	Win	65-72-70-71=278	$90,000.00
Rick Fehr	2	68-67-73-71=279	$55,000.00
Greg Norman	T-3	69-70-70-71=280	$29,800.00
Mark Calcavecchia	T-3	65-75-70-70=280	$29,800.00
Hal Sutton	T-5	72-69-69-71=281	$20,000.00
Ben Crenshaw	T-5	72-70-71-68=281	$20,000.00
Ray Floyd	7	70-68-74-70=282	$17,500.00
Donnie Hammond	T-8	70-71-71-71=283	$15,566.67
Doug Tewell	T-8	70-70-72-71=283	$15,566.66
Sandy Lyle	T-8	72-72-71-68=283	$15,566.67

Bob Hope Chrysler Classic
Course: PGA West/Staduim, Bermuda Dunes C.C., Indian Wells C.C., Tamarisk C.C.
Home course / PGA West, Par: 72 Yardage: 7,114
Last day of event: Sunday, January 18, 1987

Player	Place	Score	Earnings
Corey Pavin	Win	72-71-65-66-67=341	$162,000.00
Bernhard Langer	2	68-66-68-70-70=342	$97,200.00
Mark Calcavecchia	3	69-67-71-66-72=345	$61,200.00
David Frost	T-4	68-71-72-69-68=348	$39,600.00
Andy Bean	T-4	63-68-75-72-70=348	$39,600.00
Blaine McCallister	T-6	70-69-71-69-71=350	$29,137.50
Ed Fiori	T-6	67-68-72-72-71=350	$29,137.50
T.C. Chen	T-6	70-73-67-72-68=350	$29,137.50
Jeff Sluman	T-6	68-71-68-67-76=350	$29,137.50
Larry Rinker	T-10	68-70-72-70-71=351	$22,500.00
Charles Bolling	T-10	70-67-70-71-73=351	$22,500.00
Bob Tway	T-10	67-69-70-74-71=351	$22,500.00

Phoenix Open
Course: TPC of Scottsdale, Scottsdale, Ariz.
Par: 71 Yardage: 6,992
Last day of event: Sunday, January 25, 1987

Player	Place	Score	Earnings
Paul Azinger	Win	67-69-65-67=268	$108,000.00
Hal Sutton	2	67-71-67-64=269	$64,800.00
Fuzzy Zoeller	T-3	67-69-66-70=272	$31,200.00
Mark Calcavecchia	T-3	68-66-70-68=272	$31,200.00
Bob Tway	T-3	71-69-63-69=272	$31,200.00
Mark O'Meara	T-6	63-71-70-69=273	$20,100.00
Corey Pavin	T-6	65-69-66-73=273	$20,100.00

Bobby Clampett	T-6	65-73-69-66=273	$20,100.00
Calvin Peete	T-9	69-69-69-67=274	$15,000.00
Don Pooley	T-9	70-68-67-69=274	$15,000.00
Andy North	T-9	70-70-65-69=274	$15,000.00
Gene Sauers	T-9	68-67-71-68=274	$15,000.00
Payne Stewart	T-9	69-71-70-64=274	$15,000.00

AT&T Pebble Beach Pro-Am

Courses: Pebble Beach G.L., Spyglass Hill G.C., Cypress Point C.C., Pebble Beach, Calif.
Home Course / Pebble Beach G.L., Par: 72 Yardage: 6,815
Last day of event: Sunday, February 1, 1987

Player	Place	Score	Earnings
Johnny Miller	Win	72-72-68-66=278	$108,000.00
Payne Stewart	2	69-69-69-72=279	$64,800.00
Lanny Wadkins	T-3	68-69-72-71=280	$34,800.00
Bernhard Langer	T-3	72-69-68-71=280	$34,800.00
Fred Couples	5	70-70-72-69=281	$24,000.00
Larry Mize	T-6	71-71-71-69=282	$19,425.00
Danny Edwards	T-6	70-69-72-71=282	$19,425.00
Bob Tway	T-6	72-71-72-67=282	$19,425.00
Dan Pohl	T-6	69-75-71-67=282	$19,425.00
Mark Wiebe	T-10	71-72-73-67=283	$15,000.00
Ken Brown	T-10	73-70-71-69=283	$15,000.00
Rick Fehr	T-10	71-74-73-65=283	$15,000.00

Hawaiian Open

Course: Waialae C.C., Honolulu, Ha.
Par: 72 Yardage: 6,975
Last day of event: Sunday, February 8, 1987

Player	Place	Score	Earnings
Corey Pavin	Win	65-75-66-64=270	$108,000.00
Playoff: Beat Craig Stadler with birdie on second extra hole			
Craig Stadler	T-2	70-68-62-70=270	$64,800.00
Paul Azinger	3	70-66-65-70=271	$40,800.00
Lanny Wadkins	T-4	69-68-67-68=272	$26,400.00
Larry Mize	T-4	69-66-70-67=272	$26,400.00
Curt Byrum	T-6	69-68-69-67=273	$17,528.57
Steve Jones	T-6	70-67-68-68=273	$17,528.57
Fred Couples	T-6	69-65-68-71=273	$17,528.57
John Cook	T-6	69-71-64-69=273	$17,528.57
Curtis Strange	T-6	69-71-64-69=273	$17,528.57
Jodie Mudd	T-6	69-72-67-65=273	$17,528.58
Ben Crenshaw	T-6	75-66-66-66=273	$17,528.57

Shearson Lehman/Andy Williams San Diego

Course: Torrey Pines (South), Torrey Pines (North), San Diego, Calif.
Home Course -Par: 72 Yardage: 7,021
Last day of event: Sunday, February 15, 1987

Player	Place	Score	Earnings
George Burns	Win	63-68-70-65=266	$90,000.00
Bobby Wadkins	T-2	68-66-67-69=270	$44,000.00
J.C. Snead	T-2	64-69-66-71=270	$44,000.00
Pat McGowan	T-4	66-69-69-68=272	$22,000.00
Buddy Gardner	T-4	69-68-65-70=272	$22,000.00
Peter Jacobsen	T-6	67-70-67-69=273	$14,607.15
Curt Byrum	T-6	69-65-70-69=273	$14,607.14
Bill Sander	T-6	70-68-69-66=273	$14,607.14
David Frost	T-6	67-71-65-70=273	$14,607.14
Scott Simpson	T-6	69-66-71-67=273	$14,607.14
David Edwards	T-6	70-66-65-72=273	$14,607.14
Ray Floyd	T-6	65-68-66-74=273	$14,607.15

Los Angeles Open

Course: Riviera C.C., Pacific Palisades, Calif.
Par: 71 Yardage: 7,029
Last day of event: Sunday, February 22, 1987

Player	Place	Score	Earnings
T.C. Chen	Win	70-67-67-71=275	$108,000.00
Playoff: Beat Ben Crenshaw with par on first extra hole			
Ben Crenshaw	T-2	71-69-66-69=275	$64,800.00
Danny Edwards	3	73-64-68-71=276	$40,800.00
Don Pooley	T-4	70-69-69-69=277	$23,626.00
Steve Pate	T-4	71-71-68-67=277	$23,626.00
Bobby Wadkins	T-4	66-72-68-71=277	$23,626.00
Lanny Wadkins	T-4	73-65-73-66=277	$23,626.00
Donnie Hammond	8	70-72-67-69=278	$18,600.00
Seve Ballesteros	9	69-70-69-71=279	$17,400.00
Scott Hoch	T-10	69-69-72-70=280	$12,857.14
Rick Dalpos	T-10	70-72-67-71=280	$12,857.14
Pat McGowan	T-10	71-72-65-72=280	$12,857.15
Mark O'Meara	T-10	73-71-66-70=280	$12,857.14
Nick Price	T-10	72-67-75-66=280	$12,857.14
Bob Tway	T-10	75-70-66-69=280	$12,857.15
Bill Sander	T-10	70-66-79-65=280	$12,857.14

Doral-Ryder Open

Course: Doral C.C. (Blue), Miami, Fla.
Par: 72 Yardage: 6,939
Last day of event: Sunday, March 1, 1987

Player	Place	Score	Earnings
Lanny Wadkins	Win	75-66-66-70=277	$180,000.00
Don Pooley	T-2	70-69-71-70=280	$74,666.67
Seve Ballesteros	T-2	71-66-74-69=280	$74,666.66
Tom Kite	T-2	67-76-69-68=280	$74,666.67
David Edwards	5	73-70-71-67=281	$40,000.00
Bruce Lietzke	T-6	70-71-72-69=282	$33,500.00
J.C. Snead	T-6	71-73-68-70=282	$33,500.00
Fred Couples	T-6	73-64-74-71=282	$33,500.00
Scott Simpson	T-9	71-69-72-71=283	$24,000.00
Ed Fiori	T-9	72-71-71-69=283	$24,000.00
Ken Brown	T-9	68-72-69-74=283	$24,000.00
Lennie Clements	T-9	69-68-74-72=283	$24,000.00
Dave Rummells	T-9	74-71-70-68=283	$24,000.00
Mike Sullivan	T-9	73-68-76-66=283	$24,000.00

Honda Classic

Course: TPC at Eagle Trace, Coral Springs, Fla.
Par: 72 Yardage: 7,030
Last day of event: Sunday, March 8, 1987

Player	Place	Score	Earnings
Mark Calcavecchia	Win	69-72-68-70=279	$108,000.00
Bernhard Langer	T-2	70-67-70-75=282	$52,800.00
Payne Stewart	T-2	75-68-68-71=282	$52,800.00
Bruce Lietzke	4	69-70-70-75=284	$28,800.00
Isao Aoki	T-5	74-76-67-68=285	$21,900.00
Greg Norman	T-5	77-72-67-69=285	$21,900.00
Clarence Rose	T-5	72-79-65-69=285	$21,900.00
Steve Elkington	T-8	73-73-68-72=286	$17,400.00
Brad Fabel	T-8	74-75-68-69=286	$17,400.00
John Mahaffey	T-8	78-70-71-67=286	$17,400.00

Hertz Bay Hill Classic

Course: Bay Hill Club, Orlando, Fla.
Par: 71 Yardage: 7,103
Last day of event: Sunday, March 15, 1987

Player	Place	Score	Earnings
Payne Stewart	Win	69-67-63-65=264	$108,000.00
David Frost	2	67-68-65-67=267	$64,800.00
Dan Pohl	3	70-70-65-70=275	$40,800.00
Larry Mize	4	69-69-72-66=276	$28,800.00
Ben Crenshaw	5	75-67-71-64=277	$24,000.00
Bernhard Langer	T-6	69-70-69-70=278	$20,850.00
Tommy Nakajima	T-6	70-70-68-70=278	$20,850.00
Scott Simpson	T-8	71-69-70-69=279	$18,000.00
Chip Beck	T-8	72-66-72-69=279	$18,000.00
Tom Kite	T-10	68-72-71-69=280	$14,400.00
Curt Byrum	T-10	70-71-72-67=280	$14,400.00
Davis Love III	T-10	74-73-66-67=280	$14,400.00
Curtis Strange	T-10	71-66-68-75=280	$14,400.00

USF&G Classic

Course: Lakewood C.C., New Orleans, La.
Par: 72 Yardage: 7,080
Last day of event: Sunday, March 22, 1987

Player	Place	Score	Earnings
Ben Crenshaw	Win	66-68-67-67=268	$90,000.00
Curtis Strange	2	67-71-66-67=271	$54,000.00
Ronnie Black	3	67-67-69-70=273	$34,000.00
Sam Randolph	T-4	67-71-70-67=275	$20,666.66
Keith Clearwater	T-4	69-70-65-71=275	$20,666.67
Dick Mast	T-4	64-68-73-70=275	$20,666.67
Brett Upper	T-7	67-69-69-71=276	$14,041.66
John Mahaffey	T-7	71-68-68-69=276	$14,041.67
Ken Brown	T-7	71-70-68-67=276	$14,041.67
Jay Haas	T-7	67-71-66-72=276	$14,041.66
Tom Watson	T-7	69-69-66-72=276	$14,041.67
Jay Delsing	T-7	69-72-65-70=276	$14,041.67

Tournament Players Championship

Course: TPC at Sawgrass, Ponte Vedra Beach, Fla.
Par: 72 Yardage: 6,857
Last day of event: Sunday, March 29, 1987

Player	Place	Score	Earnings
Sandy Lyle	Win	67-71-66-70=274	$180,000.00

Playoff: Beat Jeff Sluman with par on third extra hole

Player	Place	Score	Earnings
Jeff Sluman	T-2	70-66-69-69=274	$108,000.00
Mark O'Meara	3	68-65-69-73=275	$68,000.00
Greg Norman	T-4	67-68-71-70=276	$44,000.00
Scott Simpson	T-4	69-65-68-74=276	$44,000.00
Paul Azinger	6	68-70-68-71=277	$36,000.00
Bill Glasson	T-7	69-69-68-72=278	$32,250.00
Dan Pohl	T-7	68-66-75-69=278	$32,500.00
Tom Purtzer	T-9	69-67-72-71=279	$27,000.00
Tom Kite	T-9	72-70-67-70=279	$27,000.00
Ben Crenshaw	T-9	70-68-66-75=279	$27,000.00

Greater Greensboro Open

Course: Forest Oaks C.C., Greensboro, N.C.
Par: 72 Yardage: 6,984
Last day of event: Sunday, April 5, 1987

Player	Place	Score	Earnings
Scott Simpson	Win	70-73-69-70=282	$108,000.00

Player	Place	Score	Earnings
Clarence Rose	2	72-68-75-69=284	$64,800.00
Tom Byrum	T-3	71-70-72-72=285	$31,200.00
Payne Stewart	T-3	74-71-70-70=285	$31,200.00
Kenny Knox	T-3	75-72-71-67=285	$31,200.00
John Cook	6	72-73-72-69=286	$21,600.00
Chip Beck	T-7	73-71-73-70=287	$18,075.00
Mark O'Meara	T-7	74-69-74-70=287	$18,075.00
Bill Sander	T-7	70-72-75-70=287	$18,075.00
Howard Twitty	T-7	73-68-75-71=287	$18,075.00

Deposit Guaranty Golf Classic

Course: Hattiesburg C.C., Hattiesburg, Miss.
Par: 70 Yardage: 6,594
Last day of event: Sunday, April 12, 1987

Player	Place	Score	Earnings
David Ogrin	Win	66-68-69-64=267	$36,000.00
Nick Faldo	2	67-67-67-67=268	$21,600.00
Bill Glasson	T-3	65-69-67-68=269	$10,400.00
Jeff Grygiel	T-3	67-69-64-69=269	$10,400.00
Richard Zokol	T-3	69-67-65-68=269	$10,400.00
Tom Pernice, Jr.	T-6	66-68-67-69=270	$6,700.00
Ed Dougherty	T-6	66-68-66-70=270	$6,700.00
John Inman	T-6	64-71-70-65=270	$6,700.00
Duffy Waldorf	T-9	66-67-69-69=271	$4,800.00
John McComish	T-9	68-66-68-69=271	$4,800.00
Rex Caldwell	T-9	69-68-70-64=271	$4,800.00
Aki Ohmachi	T-9	68-71-66-66=271	$4,800.00
Robert Wrenn	T-9	69-62-68-72=271	$4,800.00
Steve Elkington	T-9	72-63-67-69=271	$4,800.00

Masters

Course: Augusta National G.C., Augusta, Ga.
Par: 72 Yardage: 6,925
Last day of event: Sunday, April 12, 1987

Player	Place	Score	Earnings
Larry Mize	Win	70-72-72-71=285	$162,000.00

Playoff: Beat Greg Norman with birdie on second extra hole (Seve Ballesteros eliminated on first hole)

Player	Place	Score	Earnings
Seve Ballesteros	T-2	73-71-70-71=285	$79,200.00
Greg Norman	T-2	73-74-66-72=285	$79,200.00
Jodie Mudd	T-4	74-72-71-69=286	$37,200.00
Ben Crenshaw	T-4	75-70-67-74=286	$37,200.00
Roger Maltbie	T-4	76-66-70-74=286	$37,200.00
Jay Haas	T-7	72-72-72-73=289	$26,200.00
Tom Watson	T-7	71-72-74-72=289	$26,200.00
Jack Nicklaus	T-7	74-72-73-70=289	$26,200.00
D.A. Weibring	T-7	72-75-71-71=289	$26,200.00
Bernhard Langer	T-7	71-72-70-76=289	$26,200.00

MCI Heritage Classic

Course: Harbour Town G.L., Hilton Head, S.C.
Par: 71 Yardage: 6,657
Last day of event: Sunday, April 19, 1987

Player	Place	Score	Earnings
Davis Love III	Win	70-67-67-67=271	$117,000.00
Steve Jones	2	67-66-67-72=272	$70,200.00
Mark Wiebe	T-3	69-67-70-67=273	$37,700.00
Gene Sauers	T-3	69-67-64-73=273	$37,700.00
Bob Murphy	T-5	69-70-66-69=274	$23,725.00
Howard Twitty	T-5	66-69-72-67=274	$23,725.00
Mark Calcavecchia	T-5	66-73-67-68=274	$23,725.00
Larry Nelson	T-8	69-70-66-70=275	$17,550.00

Player	Place	Score	Earnings
David Frost	T-8	67-71-71-66=275	$17,550.00
Jay Haas	T-8	71-70-65-69=275	$17,550.00
Tom Kite	T-8	71-72-67-65=275	$17,550.00
Mark Hayes	T-8	64-68-70-73=275	$17,550.00

Big I Houston Open

Course: TPC at The Woodlands, The Woodlands, Texas
Par: 72 Yardage: 7,042
Last day of event: Sunday, April 26, 1987

Player	Place	Score	Earnings
Jay Haas	Win	69-69-71-67=276	$108,000.00
Playoff: Beat Buddy Gardner with par on first extra hole			
Buddy Gardner	T-2	69-70-67-70=276	$64,800.00
Payne Stewart	3	70-68-72-67=277	$40,800.00
Wayne Levi	T-4	70-67-71-71=279	$26,400.00
Nick Price	T-4	71-69-68-71=279	$26,400.00
Aki Ohmachi	T-6	69-69-71-71=280	$20,100.00
Gary Hallberg	T-6	70-72-69-69=280	$20,100.00
George Burns	T-6	73-70-68-69=280	$20,100.00
Ken Brown	T-9	71-71-69-70=281	$15,600.00
Andrew Magee	T-9	70-72-70-69=281	$15,600.00
Russ Cochran	T-9	69-70-74-68=281	$15,600.00
Steve Pate	T-9	74-69-68-70=281	$15,600.00

Panasonic Las Vegas Invitational

Course: Las Vegas C.C., Spanish Trail G. & C.C., Desert Inn C.C., Las Vegas, Nev.
Home course / Las Vegas C.C., Par: 72 Yardage: 7,164
Last day of event: Sunday, May 3, 1987

Player	Place	Score	Earnings
Paul Azinger	Win	68-72-67-64=271	$225,000.00
Hal Sutton	2	67-66-72-67=272	$135,000.00
Curtis Strange	3	70-69-67-67=273	$85,000.00
Kenny Perry	T-4	68-67-70-69=274	$55,000.00
Ken Brown	T-4	64-71-70-69=274	$55,000.00
David Frost	T-6	70-69-67-69=275	$43,437.50
Payne Stewart	T-6	67-71-69-68=275	$43,437.50
Donnie Hammond	T-8	69-70-70-67=276	$36,250.00
Denis Watson	T-8	65-72-71-68=276	$36,250.00
Fred Couples	T-8	66-73-68-69=276	$36,250.00

Byron Nelson Golf Classic

Course: TPC at Las Colinas, Irving, Texas
Par: 70 Yardage: 6,767
Last day of event: Sunday, May 10, 1987

Player	Place	Score	Earnings
Fred Couples	Win	65-67-64-70=266	$108,000.00
Playoff: Beat Mark Calcavecchia with par on third extra hole			
Mark Calcavecchia	T-2	73-66-63-64=266	$64,800.00
Bob Lohr	3	69-62-67-69=267	$40,800.00
Donnie Hammond	T-4	68-63-68-69=268	$26,400.00
Craig Stadler	T-4	69-67-67-65=268	$26,400.00
Tom Byrum	T-6	66-65-69-69=269	$19,425.00
Greg Norman	T-6	64-68-67-70=269	$19,425.00
Tom Kite	T-6	70-65-68-66=269	$19,425.00
Ben Crenshaw	T-6	66-65-67-71=269	$19,425.00
Ray Barr, Jr.	T-10	69-66-67-68=270	$15,600.00
David Frost	T-10	67-70-66-67=270	$15,600.00

Colonial National Invitational

Course: Colonial C.C., Fort Worth, Texas
Par: 70 Yardage: 7,096
Last day of event: Sunday, May 17, 1987

Player	Place	Score	Earnings
Keith Clearwater	Win	67-71-64-64=266	$108,000.00
Davis Love III	2	69-69-65-66=269	$64,800.00
Dan Pohl	3	69-67-66-68=270	$40,800.00
Scott Simpson	T-4	67-66-70-69=272	$26,400.00
Curtis Strange	T-4	68-66-70-68=272	$26,400.00
Jeff Sluman	T-6	68-69-68-68=273	$20,100.00
Larry Mize	T-6	68-69-69-67=273	$20,100.00
Ben Crenshaw	T-6	67-69-65-72=273	$20,100.00
Tom Byrum	T-9	67-69-67-71=274	$16,200.00
Scott Hoch	T-9	68-68-71-67=274	$16,200.00
Doug Tewell	T-9	68-66-68-72=274	$16,200.00

Georgia-Pacific Atlanta Golf Classic

Course: Atlanta C.C., Atlanta, Ga.
Par: 72 Yardage: 7,007
Last day of event: Sunday, May 24, 1987

Player	Place	Score	Earnings
Dave Barr	Win	66-68-66-65=265	$108,000.00
Larry Mize	2	71-64-69-65=269	$64,800.00
Chip Beck	T-3	67-68-68-67=270	$34,800.00
Lanny Wadkins	T-3	66-68-70-66=270	$34,800.00
Gary Hallberg	T-5	70-69-66-66=271	$22,800.00
Steve Pate	T-5	67-66-67-71=271	$22,800.00
Bobby Wadkins	7	66-68-65-73=272	$20,100.00
Bob Tway	8	71-69-67-66=273	$18,600.00
Bill Sander	T-9	69-69-68-68=274	$16,200.00
Dan Pohl	T-9	68-67-70-69=274	$16,200.00
Don Pooley	T-9	70-68-69-67=274	$16,200.00

Memorial Tournament

Course: Muirfield Village G.C., Dubin, Ohio
Par: 72 Yardage: 7,104
Last day of event: Sunday, May 31, 1987

Player	Place	Score	Earnings
Don Pooley	Win	70-67-65-70=272	$140,000.00
Curt Byrum	2	64-71-69-71=275	$84,000.00
Chip Beck	T-3	70-69-69-68=276	$40,443.00
Denis Watson	T-3	75-66-65-70=276	$40,443.00
Scott Hoch	T-3	67-64-67-78=276	$40,443.00
David Frost	T-6	68-70-70-69=277	$26,038.00
Larry Nelson	T-6	69-69-70-69=277	$26,038.00
Sandy Lyle	T-6	69-70-69-69=277	$26,038.00
Craig Stadler	T-9	71-67-71-69=278	$19,480.00
Scott Simpson	T-9	68-68-72-70=278	$19,480.00
John Cook	T-9	69-69-72-68=278	$19,480.00
John Mahaffey	T-9	69-69-65-73=278	$19,480.00
Hal Sutton	T-9	74-64-68-72=278	$19,480.00

Kemper Open

Course: TPC at Avenel, Potomac, Md.
Par: 71 Yardage: 6,864
Last day of event: Sunday, June 7, 1987

Player	Place	Score	Earnings
Tom Kite	Win	64-69-68-69=270	$126,000.00
Howard Twitty	T-2	66-67-73-71=277	$61,600.00

Chris Perry	T-2	66-66-70-75=277	$61,600.00
Mike Reid	T-4	69-69-69-71=278	$28,933.00
Scott Simpson	T-4	70-67-70-71=278	$28,933.00
Greg Norman	T-4	64-73-68-73=278	$28,933.00
Ken Green	T-7	72-71-68-68=279	$22,575.00
Roger Maltbie	T-7	74-67-69-69=279	$22,575.00
Larry Mize	T-9	67-67-72-74=280	$18,900.00
Scott Hoch	T-9	65-68-72-75=280	$18,900.00
George Burns	T-9	69-67-68-76=280	$18,900.00

Manufacturers Hanover Westchester Classic
Course: Westchester C.C., Harrison, N.Y.
Par: 71 Yardage: 6,769
Last day of event: Sunday, June 14, 1987

Player	Place	Score	Earnings
J.C. Snead	Win	71-70-65-70=276	$108,000.00
Playoff: Beat Seve Ballesteros with par on first extra hole			
Seve Ballesteros	T-2	66-67-71-72=276	$64,800.00
Roger Maltbie	3	71-67-68-71=277	$40,800.00
Mike Donald	T-4	69-70-72-67=278	$24,800.00
Morris Hatalsky	T-4	71-68-72-67=278	$24,800.00
Mike Reid	T-4	68-66-69-75=278	$24,800.00
Sandy Lyle	T-7	65-72-71-71=279	$19,350.00
Fred Couples	T-7	70-69-73-67=279	$19,350.00
Aki Ohmachi	T-9	72-72-68-68=280	$16,800.00
Chris Perry	T-9	69-69-67-75=280	$16,800.00

U.S. Open
Course: The Olympic Club (Lake Course), San Francisco, Calif.
Par: 70 Yardage: 6,714
Last day of event: Sunday, June 21, 1987

Player	Place	Score	Earnings
Scott Simpson	Win	71-68-70-68=277	$150,000.00
Tom Watson	2	72-65-71-70=278	$75,000.00
Seve Ballesteros	3	68-75-68-71=282	$46,240.00
Bobby Wadkins	T-4	71-71-70-71=283	$24,542.80
Ben Crenshaw	T-4	67-72-72-72=283	$24,542.80
Larry Mize	T-4	71-68-72-72=283	$24,542.80
Curtis Strange	T-4	71-72-69-71=283	$24,542.80
Bernhard Langer	T-4	69-69-73-72=283	$24,542.80
Mac O'Grady	T-9	71-69-72-72=284	$15,004.20
Jim Thorpe	T-9	70-68-73-73=284	$15,004.20
Tommy Nakajima	T-9	68-70-74-72=284	$15,004.20
Lennie Clements	T-9	70-70-70-74=284	$15,004.20
Dan Pohl	T-9	75-71-69-69=284	$15,004.20

Canon Sammy Davis, Jr. - Greater Hartford Open
Course: TPC of Connecticut, Cromwell, Conn.
Par: 71 Yardage: 6,786
Last day of event: Sunday, June 28, 1987

Player	Place	Score	Earnings
Paul Azinger	Win	69-65-63-72=269	$126,000.00
Dan Forsman	T-2	65-69-69-67=270	$61,600.00
Wayne Levi	T-2	64-68-68-70=270	$61,600.00
Gene Sauers	T-4	66-68-68-70=272	$30,800.00
Lee Trevino	T-4	67-69-70-66=272	$30,800.00
Doug Tewell	T-6	68-68-68-69=273	$24,325.00
John Inman	T-6	70-66-67-70=273	$24,325.00
Bob Lohr	T-8	68-68-67-71=274	$20,300.00
Bernhard Langer	T-8	65-65-72-72=274	$20,300.00
Denis Watson	T-8	65-72-69-68=274	$20,300.00

Canadian Open
Course: Glen Abbey G.C., Oakville, Ontario, Canada
Par: 72 Yardage: 7,102
Last day of event: Sunday, July 5, 1987

Player	Place	Score	Earnings
Curtis Strange	Win	71-70-66-69=276	$108,000.00
David Frost	T-2	71-67-72-69=279	$44,800.00
Nick Price	T-2	72-67-70-70=279	$44,800.00
Jodie Mudd	T-2	73-69-69-68=279	$44,800.00
Mark McCumber	T-5	72-70-72-67=281	$22,800.00
Mike McCullough	T-5	72-67-68-74=281	$22,800.00
Pat McGowan	T-7	71-69-72-70=282	$16,500.00
Brad Faxon	T-7	72-69-72-69=282	$16,500.00
Joey Sindelar	T-7	68-74-69-71=282	$16,500.00
Richard Zokol	T-7	70-68-69-75=282	$16,500.00
Craig Stadler	T-7	75-67-68-72=282	$16,500.00
John Cook	T-7	75-71-66-70=282	$16,500.00

Anheuser-Busch Golf Classic
Course: Kingsmill G.C., Williamsburg, Va.
Par: 71 Yardage: 6,776
Last day of event: Sunday, July 12, 1987

Player	Place	Score	Earnings
Mark McCumber	Win	65-69-67-66=267	$110,160.00
Bobby Clampett	2	69-66-65-68=268	$66,096.00
Scott Hoch	3	67-66-68-69=270	$41,616.00
John Cook	4	66-67-66-72=271	$29,376.00
Denis Watson	T-5	68-69-69-66=272	$23,256.00
Chris Perry	T-5	69-69-68-66=272	$23,256.00
D.A. Weibring	T-7	68-71-66-69=274	$19,737.00
Tim Simpson	T-7	67-65-69-73=274	$19,737.00
Tom Sieckmann	T-9	65-68-69-73=275	$17,136.00
Vance Heafner	T-9	71-65-66-73=275	$17,136.00

Hardee's Golf Classic
Course: Oakwood C.C., Coal Valley, Ill.
Par: 70 Yardage: 6,606
Last day of event: Sunday, July 19, 1987

Player	Place	Score	Earnings
Kenny Knox	Win	67-66-66-66=265	$90,000.00
Gil Morgan	2	66-69-63-68=266	$54,000.00
Mark McCumber	3	64-67-69-67=267	$34,000.00
Scott Hoch	4	68-68-65-67=268	$24,000.00
Brad Fabel	5	64-65-71-69=269	$20,000.00
Perry Arthur	T-6	67-67-69-67=270	$17,375.00
Jack Renner	T-6	69-69-69-63=270	$17,375.00
Tom Shaw	T-8	68-67-68-68=271	$13,000.00
Fred Wadsworth	T-8	65-67-68-71=271	$13,000.00
Jim Gallagher, Jr.	T-8	69-63-71-68=271	$13,000.00
Bob Eastwood	T-8	71-66-66-68=271	$13,000.00
Chris Perry	T-8	71-66-69-65=271	$13,000.00
Jeff Sluman	T-8	65-72-67-67=271	$13,000.00

British Open
Course: Muirfield G.C., Muirfield, East Lothian, Scotland
Par: 71 Yardage: 6,963
Last day of event: Sunday, July 19, 1987

Player	Place	Score	Earnings
Nick Faldo	Win	68-69-71-71=279	$120,000.00
Paul Azinger	T-2	68-68-71-73=280	$79,200.00

Rodger Davis	T-2	64-73-74-69=280	$79,200.00
Payne Stewart	T-4	71-66-72-72=281	$49,600.00
Ben Crenshaw	T-4	73-68-72-68=281	$49,600.00
David Frost	6	70-68-70-74=282	$41,600.00
Tom Watson	7	69-69-71-74=283	$36,800.00
Ian Woosnam	T-8	71-69-72-72=284	$29,865.60
Nick Price	T-8	68-71-72-73=284	$29,865.60
Craig Stadler	T-8	69-69-71-75=284	$29,865.60

Buick Open

Course: Warwick Hills C.C., Grand Blanc, Mich.
Par: 72 Yardage: 7,014
Last day of event: Sunday, July 26, 1987

Player	Place	Score	Earnings
Robert Wrenn	Win	65-63-67-67=262	$108,000.00
Dan Pohl	2	69-68-67-65=269	$64,800.00
Scott Hoch	3	67-68-69-66=270	$40,800.00
Ken Green	4	66-66-69-70=271	$28,800.00
Jodie Mudd	T-5	67-67-69-69=272	$21,900.00
Gil Morgan	T-5	67-69-68-68=272	$21,900.00
Don Pooley	T-5	68-66-69-69=272	$21,900.00
Brad Faxon	T-8	70-68-67-68=273	$17,400.00
Trevor Dodds	T-8	70-69-63-71=273	$17,400.00
Tom Kite	T-8	72-67-69-65=273	$17,400.00

Federal Express St. Jude Classic

Course: Colonial C.C. (South), Cordova, Tenn.
Par: 72 Yardage: 7,282
Last day of event: Sunday, August 2, 1987

Player	Place	Score	Earnings
Curtis Strange	Win	70-68-68-69=275	$130,328.00
Mike Donald	T-2	72-67-68-69=276	$47,787.00
Tom Kite	T-2	72-70-67-67=276	$47,787.00
Russ Cochran	T-2	66-73-68-69=276	$47,787.00
Denis Watson	T-2	74-65-71-66=276	$47,787.00
Fuzzy Zoeller	6	71-66-70-70=277	$26,066.00
Bob Tway	7	70-70-69-69=278	$24,255.00
Ronnie Black	T-8	68-72-72-67=279	$20,273.00
Willie Wood	T-8	71-72-70-66=279	$20,273.00
Curt Byrum	T-8	72-70-70-67=279	$20,273.00
Gil Morgan	T-8	69-70-74-66=279	$20,273.00

PGA Championship

Course: PGA National G.C. (Champion), Palm Beach Gardens, Fla.
Par: 72 Yardage: 7,002
Last day of event: Sunday, August 9, 1987

Player	Place	Score	Earnings
Larry Nelson	Win	70-72-73-72=287	$150,000.00
Playoff: Beat Lanny Wadkins with par on first extra hole			
Lanny Wadkins	T-2	70-70-74-73=287	$90,000.00
Scott Hoch	T-3	74-74-71-69=288	$58,750.00
D.A. Weibring	T-3	73-72-67-76=288	$58,750.00
Don Pooley	T-5	73-71-73-72=289	$37,500.00
Mark McCumber	T-5	74-69-69-77=289	$37,500.00
Ben Crenshaw	T-7	72-70-74-74=290	$27,500.00
Bobby Wadkins	T-7	68-74-71-77=290	$27,500.00
Curtis Strange	9	70-76-71-74=291	$22,500.00
David Frost	T-10	75-70-71-76=292	$17,000.00
Nick Price	T-10	76-71-70-75=292	$17,000.00
Tom Kite	T-10	72-77-71-72=292	$17,000.00
Seve Ballesteros	T-10	72-70-72-78=292	$17,000.00

The International

Course: Castle Pine G.C., Castle Rock, Colo.
Par: 72 Yardage: 7,559
Last day of event: Sunday, August 16, 1987

Player	Place	Score	Earnings
John Cook	Win	1-0-4-11=16	$180,000.00
Ken Green	2	5-4-10-9=28	$108,000.00
Ben Crenshaw	T-3	4-2-6-6=18	$48,000.00
Scott Simpson	T-3	7-1-4-6=18	$48,000.00
Mike Hulbert	T-3	7-2-4-6=19	$48,000.00
Chip Beck	T-3	13--1-13-6=31	$48,000.00
D.A. Weibring	T-7	3-0-7-5=15	$32,250.00
Fuzzy Zoeller	T-7	7-4-4-5=20	$32,250.00
Corey Pavin	T-9	3-4-6-4=17	$28,000.00
Tom Watson	T-9	7-0-6-4=17	$28,000.00

Beatrice Western Open

Course: Butler National G.C., Oak Brook, Ill.
Par: 72 Yardage: 6,752
Last day of event: Sunday, August 23, 1987

Player	Place	Score	Earnings
D.A. Weibring	Win	70-69-68=207	$144,000.00
Greg Norman	T-2	69-70-69=208	$70,400.00
Larry Nelson	T-2	72-67-69=208	$70,400.00
Lennie Clements	T-4	70-69-70=209	$31,500.00
David Frost	T-4	70-71-68=209	$31,500.00
Mike Reid	T-4	71-69-69=209	$31,500.00
Greg Powers	T-4	71-70-68=209	$31,500.00
Davis Love III	T-8	70-70-70=210	$21,600.00
Bob Tway	T-8	69-71-70=210	$21,600.00
Bobby Wadkins	T-8	69-72-69=210	$21,600.00
Brian Fogt	T-8	71-67-72=210	$21,600.00
Mark Hayes	T-8	72-68-70=210	$21,600.00

NEC World Series of Golf

Course: Firestone C.C. (South), Akron, Ohio
Par: 70 Yardage: 7,149
Last day of event: Sunday, August 30, 1987

Player	Place	Score	Earnings
Curtis Strange	Win	70-66-68-71=275	$144,000.00
Fulton Allem	2	71-70-67-70=278	$86,400.00
Mac O'Grady	3	69-72-69-69=279	$54,400.00
Fred Couples	T-4	70-71-69-70=280	$33,066.67
Larry Nelson	T-4	69-73-70-68=280	$33,066.66
Bobby Wadkins	T-4	64-74-70-72=280	$33,066.67
Mike Hulbert	T-7	68-74-68-71=281	$25,800.00
Paul Azinger	T-7	69-69-74-69=281	$25,800.00
Tom Kite	9	70-73-65-74=282	$23,200.00
Greg Norman	T-10	70-69-71-73=283	$20,033.33
Rick Fehr	T-10	72-69-69-73=283	$20,033.34
Ben Crenshaw	T-10	73-72-71-67=283	$20,033.33

Provident Classic

Course: ValleyBrook C.C., Hixson, Tenn.
Par: 70 Yardage: 6,641
Last day of event: Sunday, August 30, 1987

Player	Place	Score	Earnings
John Inman	Win	65-67-67-66=265	$81,000.00
Bill Glasson	T-2	65-69-66-66=266	$39,600.00
Rocco Mediate	T-2	66-63-69-68=266	$39,600.00

Player	Place	Score	Earnings
Tim Simpson	4	64-71-66-66=267	$21,600.00
Blaine McCallister	T-5	67-67-65-69=268	$17,100.00
Robert Thompson	T-5	67-69-62-70=268	$17,100.00
Richard Zokol	T-7	69-67-66-67=269	$14,025.00
Joey Sindelar	T-7	62-68-70-69=269	$14,025.00
Morris Hatalsky	T-7	64-67-74-64=269	$14,025.00
Greg Powers	T-10	66-66-69-69=270	$10,350.00
Ray Stewart	T-10	67-66-69-68=270	$10,350.00
Jim Carter	T-10	68-65-68-69=270	$10,350.00
Jay Don Blake	T-10	69-68-66-67=270	$10,350.00
Andrew Magee	T-10	65-67-72-66=270	$10,350.00

B.C. Open

Course: En-Joie G.C., Endicott, N.Y.
Par: 71 Yardage: 6,966
Last day of event: Sunday, September 6, 1987

Player	Place	Score	Earnings
Joey Sindelar	Win	65-63-69-69=266	$72,000.00
Jeff Sluman	2	69-68-68-65=270	$43,200.00
Tony Sills	T-3	69-68-69-69=275	$23,200.00
Mike McCullough	T-3	69-71-69-66=275	$23,200.00
Tim Simpson	T-5	69-70-67-70=276	$14,050.00
Wayne Levi	T-5	71-67-69-69=276	$14,050.00
Ken Green	T-5	69-72-66-69=276	$14,050.00
Mike Nicolette	T-5	72-69-67-68=276	$14,050.00
Paul Azinger	T-9	69-70-69-69=277	$11,200.00
Craig Stadler	T-9	68-69-72-68=277	$11,200.00

Bank of Boston Classic

Course: Pleasant Valley C.C., Sutton, Mass.
Par: 71 Yardage: 7,110
Last day of event: Sunday, September 13, 1987

Player	Place	Score	Earnings
Sam Randolph	Win	67-68-64=199	$90,000.00
Wayne Grady	T-2	67-68-68=203	$37,333.34
Gene Sauers	T-2	68-67-68=203	$37,333.33
Ray Stewart	T-2	65-73-65=203	$37,333.33
Clarence Rose	T-5	68-67-69=204	$17,562.50
Steve Pate	T-5	69-66-69=204	$17,562.50
Curtis Strange	T-5	65-69-70=204	$17,562.50
John Mahaffey	T-5	65-71-68=204	$17,562.50
Tom Byrum	T-9	68-69-68=205	$13,000.00
Larry Rinker	T-9	69-66-70=205	$13,000.00
Gary Hallberg	T-9	71-68-66=205	$13,000.00
Lee Trevino	T-9	66-67-72=205	$13,000.00

Greater Milwaukee Open

Course: Tuckaway C.C., Franklin, Wis.
Par: 72 Yardage: 7,030
Last day of event: Monday, September 21, 1987

Player	Place	Score	Earnings
Gary Hallberg	Win	70-66-67-66=269	$108,000.00
Wayne Levi	T-2	68-68-68-67=271	$52,800.00
Robert Wrenn	T-2	65-68-70-68=271	$52,800.00
Larry Ziegler	T-4	64-68-72-68=272	$26,400.00
Dan Pohl	T-4	67-67-72-66=272	$26,400.00
Bill Kratzert	T-6	68-71-67-68=274	$20,100.00
Tom Byrum	T-6	72-67-68-67=274	$20,100.00
Nick Price	T-6	67-65-74-68=274	$20,100.00
Fred Couples	9	71-69-65-70=275	$17,400.00
Mark Calcavecchia	T-10	68-68-70-71=277	$14,400.00

Player	Place	Score	Earnings
Corey Pavin	T-10	69-67-71-70=277	$14,400.00
Wayne Grady	T-10	71-70-66-70=277	$14,400.00
Gene Sauers	T-10	71-70-67-69=277	$14,400.00

Southwest Golf Classic

Course: Fairway Oaks C.C., Abilene, Texas
Par: 72 Yardage: 7,166
Last day of event: Sunday, September 27, 1987

Player	Place	Score	Earnings
Steve Pate	Win	67-71-68-67=273	$72,000.00
Mark O'Meara	T-2	68-70-67-69=274	$26,400.00
Bob Eastwood	T-2	65-69-69-71=274	$26,400.00
Dan Halldorson	T-2	66-66-72-70=274	$26,400.00
David Edwards	T-2	70-67-65-72=274	$26,400.00
Tony Sills	T-6	71-67-71-68=277	$13,900.00
Paul Azinger	T-6	69-67-72-69=277	$13,900.00
Ronnie Black	T-8	67-71-69-71=278	$12,000.00
Vance Heafner	T-8	69-68-70-71=278	$12,000.00
Russ Cochran	T-10	70-70-69-70=279	$10,000.00
Mike Hulbert	T-10	73-67-72-67=279	$10,000.00
Hale Irwin	T-10	70-68-65-76=279	$10,000.00

Southern Open

Course: Green Island C.C., Columbus, Ga.
Par: 70 Yardage: 6,791
Last day of event: Sunday, October 4, 1987

Player	Place	Score	Earnings
Ken Brown	Win	65-64-69-68=266	$72,000.00
Larry Mize	T-2	70-65-70-68=273	$29,866.66
Mike Hulbert	T-2	65-66-72-70=273	$29,866.67
David Frost	T-2	63-71-73-66=273	$29,866.67
Rex Caldwell	5	69-67-70-68=274	$16,000.00
Mark Lye	6	70-68-68-69=275	$14,400.00
Hale Irwin	7	66-68-69-73=276	$13,400.00
Wayne Levi	T-8	70-69-69-69=277	$12,000.00
Larry Nelson	T-8	71-66-72-68=277	$12,000.00
Vance Heafner	10	65-69-77-67=278	$10,800.00

Pensacola Open

Course: Perdido Bay C.C., Pensacola, Fla.
Par: 71 Yardage: 7,093
Last day of event: Sunday, October 11, 1987

Player	Place	Score	Earnings
Doug Tewell	Win	69-66-66-68=269	$54,000.00
Danny Edwards	T-2	67-67-68-70=272	$26,400.00
Phil Blackmar	T-2	67-69-66-70=272	$26,400.00
Mark McCumber	T-4	72-68-68-67=275	$13,200.00
David Ogrin	T-4	72-71-66-66=275	$13,200.00
Jeff Sluman	T-6	67-71-69-69=276	$10,425.00
Clarence Rose	T-6	71-70-70-65=276	$10,425.00
John Mahaffey	T-8	66-69-73-69=277	$9,000.00
David Canipe	T-8	75-67-69-66=277	$9,000.00
Mike Reid	T-10	69-69-69-71=278	$7,800.00
Mike Hulbert	T-10	70-70-66-72=278	$7,800.00

Walt Disney World/Oldsmobile Classic

Course: Walt Disney (Magnolia, Palm), Lake Buena Vista C.C., Lake Buena Vista, Fla.
Home course / Magnolia, Par: 72 Yardage: 7,190
Last day of event: Sunday, October 18, 1987

Player	Place	Score	Earnings
Larry Nelson	Win	68-69-68-63=268	$108,000.00
Morris Hatalsky	T-2	68-67-67-67=269	$52,800.00
Mark O'Meara	T-2	63-68-69-69=269	$52,800.00
Steve Pate	4	66-68-65-71=270	$28,800.00
Mac O'Grady	T-5	68-68-67-68=271	$21,900.00
David Frost	T-5	69-65-68-69=271	$21,900.00
Mike Reid	T-5	69-67-68-67=271	$21,900.00
Nick Price	8	68-68-68-68=272	$18,600.00
Don Shirey Jr.	T-9	70-70-70-63=273	$15,600.00
Tom Kite	T-9	69-65-71-68=273	$15,600.00
Fuzzy Zoeller	T-9	69-69-71-64=273	$15,600.00
Donnie Hammond	T-9	71-65-71-66=273	$15,600.00

Seiko-Tucson Open

Course: TPC At StarPass, Tucson, Ariz.
Par: 72 Yardage: 7,010
Last day of event: Sunday, October 25, 1987

Player	Place	Score	Earnings
Mike Reid	Win	64-69-68-67=268	$108,000.00
Mark Calcavecchia	T-2	67-71-65-69=272	$39,600.00
Chip Beck	T-2	69-65-67-71=272	$39,600.00
Hal Sutton	T-2	69-62-68-73=272	$39,600.00
Fuzzy Zoeller	T-2	67-66-64-75=272	$39,600.00
Dan Pohl	T-6	71-64-70-68=273	$20,100.00
Jay Haas	T-6	68-68-65-72=273	$20,100.00
Corey Pavin	T-6	70-66-73-64=273	$20,100.00
Mike Springer	9	70-67-69-68=274	
Fred Couples	T-10	68-66-71-70=275	$16,200.00
Robert Thompson	T-10	71-66-70-68=275	$16,200.00
Craig Stadler	T-10	69-67-67-72=275	$16,200.00

Centel Classic

Course: Killearn C.C., Tallahassee, Fla.
Par: 72 Yardage: 7,124
Last day of event: Sunday, November 1, 1987

Player	Place	Score	Earnings
Keith Clearwater	Win	71-68-68-71=278	$90,000.00
Bill Glasson	T-2	70-71-69-69=279	$33,000.00
Bill Kratzert	T-2	69-67-72-71=279	$33,000.00
Bob Lohr	T-2	70-72-67-70=279	$33,000.00
Joey Sindelar	T-2	71-69-67-72=279	$33,000.00
Bob Gilder	T-6	71-70-71-68=280	$15,125.00
Hubert Green	T-6	69-71-68-72=280	$15,125.00
Buddy Gardner	T-6	69-68-72-71=280	$15,125.00
Mike Hulbert	T-6	69-72-70-69=280	$15,125.00
Greg Powers	T-6	69-72-71-68=280	$15,125.00
John Mahaffey	T-6	71-71-72-66=280	$15,125.00

Nabisco Championship of Golf

Course: Oak Hills C.C., San Antonio, Texas
Par: 70 Yardage: 6,576
Last day of event: Sunday, November 1, 1987

Player	Place	Score	Earnings
Tom Watson	Win	65-66-69-68=268	$360,000.00
Chip Beck	2	71-67-68-64=270	$216,000.00
Greg Norman	3	67-70-68-66=271	$138,000.00

Player	Place	Score	Earnings
Paul Azinger	4	73-66-67-67=273	$96,000.00
Mark Calcavecchia	T-5	67-68-69-70=274	$68,800.00
Nick Price	T-5	67-71-69-67=274	$68,800.00
Hal Sutton	T-5	71-69-67-67=274	$68,800.00
Corey Pavin	T-5	73-65-68-68=274	$68,800.00
Ben Crenshaw	T-5	68-67-75-64=274	$68,800.00
Mark O'Meara	T-10	69-69-66-71=275	$55,400.00
Don Pooley	T-10	71-68-68-68=275	$55,400.00

Nabisco year-end Bonus

Player	Place	Earnings
Curtis Strange	Win	$175,000.00
Ben Crenshaw	2	$106,000.00
Paul Azinger	3	$68,000.00
Larry Mize	4	$47,000.00
Scott Simpson	5	$40,000.00
David Frost	6	$36,000.00
Greg Norman	7	$34,000.00
Dan Pohl	8	$32,000.00
Tom Kite	9	$30,000.00
Mark Calcavecchia	10	$28,000.00

1988

Sandy Lyle hit a memorable 7-iron from the fairway bunker on Augusta National's 18th hole, setting up a birdie that secured a one-shot Masters victory. Shooting 71 to Nick Faldo's 75 in an 18-hole playoff at The Country Club, Curtis Strange won the first of his back-to-back U.S. Opens. (Strange would go on to become the first player to win $1 million in a season.) Seve Ballesteros scored a closing 65 and won the British Open by two shots over Nick Price at Royal Lytham. Thanks to a final-round 65, Jeff Sluman won the PGA Championship by three shots over Paul Azinger.

MONY Tournament of Champions

Course: La Costa C.C., Carlsbad, Calif.
Par: 72 Yardage: 7,022
Last day of event: Sunday, January 17, 1988

Player	Place	Score	Earnings
Steve Pate	Win	66-66-70=202	$90,000.00
Larry Nelson	2	68-67-68=203	$54,000.00
Nick Faldo	T-3	70-65-71=206	$29,000.00
Dave Barr	T-3	67-66-73=206	$29,000.00
J.C. Snead	T-5	69-69-71=209	$19,000.00
Keith Clearwater	T-5	69-67-73=209	$19,000.00
Payne Stewart	T-7	68-71-71=210	$15,062.50
Doug Tewell	T-7	69-71-70=210	$15,062.50
Mark McCumber	T-7	72-68-70=210	$15,062.50
Paul Azinger	T-7	68-73-69=210	$15,162.50

Bob Hope Chrysler Classic

Course: Indian Wells C.C., PGA West/Palmer, Bermuda Dunes C.C., La Quinta C.C.
Home course / Indian Wells, Par: 72 Yardage: 6,478
Last day of event: Sunday, January 24, 1988

Player	Place	Score	Earnings
Jay Haas	Win	63-68-69-68-70=338	$180,000.00
David Edwards	2	66-71-71-65-67=340	$108,000.00
Bob Tway	3	69-66-67-67-72=341	$68,000.00
Mark O'Meara	T-4	71-66-68-68-69=342	$44,000.00
Payne Stewart	T-4	72-71-67-67-65=342	$44,000.00
Scott Hoch	6	69-66-72-68-68=343	$36,000.00
Gil Morgan	T-7	71-67-71-67-68=344	$31,166.67
Chip Beck	T-7	72-67-69-66-70=344	$31,166.67
Leonard Thompson	T-7	68-66-76-70-64=344	$31,166.66
Gene Sauers	T-10	69-67-69-70-70=345	$26,000.00
Paul Azinger	T-10	67-68-65-70-75=345	$26,000.00

Phoenix Open

Course: TPC of Scottsdale, Scottsdale, Ariz.
Par: 71 Yardage: 6,992
Last day of event: Sunday, January 31, 1988

Player	Place	Score	Earnings
Sandy Lyle	Win	68-68-68-65=269	$117,000.00

Playoff: Beat Fred Couples with bogey on third extra hole

Player	Place	Score	Earnings
Fred Couples	2	67-65-67-70=269	$70,200.00
David Frost	3	67-66-70-68=271	$44,200.00
Davis Love III	4	63-68-66-76=273	$31,200.00
Bob Lohr	T-5	68-70-70-66=274	$22,831.25
Ken Green	T-5	70-68-67-69=274	$22,831.25
Ken Brown	T-5	66-71-70-67=274	$22,831.25
Gil Morgan	T-5	68-66-71-69=274	$22,831.25
T.C. Chen	T-9	68-68-70-69=275	$17,550.00
Jim Carter	T-9	71-68-66-70=275	$17,550.00
Chip Beck	T-9	66-63-75-71=275	$17,550.00

AT&T Pebble Beach Pro-Am

Courses: Pebble Beach G.L., Spyglass Hill G.C., Cypress Point C.C., Pebble Beach, Calif.
Home Course / Pebble Beach G.L., Par: 72 Yardage: 6,815
Last day of event: Sunday, February 7, 1988

Player	Place	Score	Earnings
Steve Jones	Win	72-64-70-74=280	$126,000.00

Playoff: Beat Bob Tway with birdie on second extra hole

Player	Place	Score	Earnings
Bob Tway	T-2	72-73-67-68=280	$75,600.00
Greg Norman	3	68-75-72-66=281	$47,600.00
Jim Carter	T-4	70-71-70-71=282	$27,562.50
Craig Stadler	T-4	68-70-71-73=282	$27,562.50
Bernhard Langer	T-4	72-67-70-73=282	$27,562.50
Tom Sieckmann	T-4	69-68-75-70=282	$27,562.50
Mark Calcavecchia	8	67-69-75-72=283	$21,700.00
Tom Watson	T-9	68-72-72-72=284	$18,900.00
Mark O'Meara	T-9	69-73-71-71=284	$18,900.00
David Canipe	T-9	70-76-68-70=284	$18,900.00

Hawaiian Open

Course: Waialae C.C., Honolulu, Ha.
Par: 72 Yardage: 6,975
Last day of event: Sunday, February 14, 1988

Player	Place	Score	Earnings
Lanny Wadkins	Win	68-71-66-66=271	$108,000.00
Richard Zokol	2	66-71-65-70=272	$64,800.00
John Huston	3	72-67-69-66=274	$40,800.00
Gene Sauers	4	71-68-67-69=275	$28,800.00
Fulton Allem	5	69-69-68-70=276	$24,000.00
Jim Carter	T-6	69-68-71-69=277	$19,425.00
Tom Watson	T-6	69-70-66-72=277	$19,425.00
Loren Roberts	T-6	68-66-70-73=277	$19,425.00
Bob Eastwood	T-6	69-69-73-66=277	$19,425.00
David Ishii	T-10	70-68-69-71=278	$15,000.00
J.C. Snead	T-10	70-67-73-68=278	$15,000.00
Dave Eichelberger	T-10	75-66-69-68=278	$15,000.00

Shearson Lehman/Andy Williams San Diego

Course: Torrey Pines (South), Torrey Pines (North), San Diego, Calif.
Home Course -Par: 72 Yardage: 7,021
Last day of event: Sunday, February 21, 1988

Player	Place	Score	Earnings
Steve Pate	Win	68-66-67-68=269	$117,000.00

Player	Place	Score	Earnings
Jay Haas	2	69-67-68-66=270	$70,200.00
Joey Sindelar	T-3	68-67-68-68=271	$37,700.00
Gil Morgan	T-3	74-62-67-68=271	$37,700.00
Roger Maltbie	T-5	67-68-68-69=272	$22,035.00
Willie Wood	T-5	66-68-68-70=272	$22,035.00
Mark Calcavecchia	T-5	66-68-70-68=272	$22,035.00
Tom Kite	T-5	68-65-69-70=272	$22,035.00
Brad Faxon	T-5	69-65-66-72=272	$22,035.00
Gary Koch	T-10	66-68-69-70=273	$15,600.00
Fred Couples	T-10	63-71-68-71=273	$15,600.00
Don Pooley	T-10	67-65-71-70=273	$15,600.00
Jay Don Blake	T-10	69-71-67-66=273	$15,600.00

Los Angeles Open

Course: Riviera C.C., Pacific Palisades, Calif.
Par: 71 Yardage: 7,029
Last day of event: Sunday, February 28, 1988

Player	Place	Score	Earnings
Chip Beck	Win	65-69-65-68=267	$135,000.00
Mac O'Grady	T-2	69-68-66-68=271	$66,000.00
Bill Sander	T-2	79-69-66-66=280	$66,000.00
Mike Reid	T-4	67-69-67-69=272	$33,000.00
Ed Fiori	T-4	66-68-68-70=272	$33,000.00
Tom Purtzer	T-6	69-68-67-69=273	$26,062.50
Jay Haas	T-6	65-68-69-71=273	$26,062.50
Steve Elkington	T-8	69-67-66-72=274	$22,500.00
Donnie Hammond	T-8	66-68-73-67=274	$22,500.00
Hal Sutton	10	70-68-68-69=275	$20,250.00

Doral-Ryder Open

Course: Doral C.C. (Blue), Miami, Fla.
Par: 72 Yardage: 6,939
Last day of event: Sunday, March 6, 1988

Player	Place	Score	Earnings
Ben Crenshaw	Win	70-69-69-66=274	$180,000.00
Chip Beck	T-2	68-68-70-69=275	$88,000.00
Mark McCumber	T-2	71-68-68-68=275	$88,000.00
Ray Floyd	4	69-71-68-68=276	$48,000.00
Larry Nelson	T-5	68-71-70-68=277	$36,500.00
Joey Sindelar	T-5	71-69-69-68=277	$36,500.00
John Mahaffey	T-5	69-72-69-67=277	$36,500.00
Bruce Lietzke	T-8	69-71-68-70=278	$29,000.00
Scott Hoch	T-8	72-70-68-68=278	$29,000.00
Gil Morgan	T-8	69-69-73-67=278	$29,000.00

Honda Classic

Course: TPC at Eagle Trace
Coral Springs, Fla.
Par: 72 Yardage: 7,030
Last day of event: Sunday, March 13, 1988

Player	Place	Score	Earnings
Joey Sindelar	Win	68-70-68-70=276	$126,000.00
Ed Fiori	T-2	70-67-71-70=278	$52,266.67
Payne Stewart	T-2	73-71-67-67=278	$52,266.67
Sandy Lyle	T-2	74-64-70-70=278	$52,266.66
Tom Byrum	T-5	70-68-71-70=279	$24,587.50
Jodie Mudd	T-5	70-67-72-70=279	$24,587.50
Wayne Grady	T-5	72-69-70-68=279	$24,587.50
Bob Lohr	T-5	73-73-66-67=279	$24,587.50
Ray Floyd	T-9	71-69-68-72=280	$18,900.00
Ken Green	T-9	70-70-73-67=280	$18,900.00
Fred Couples	T-9	73-70-69-68=280	$18,900.00

Hertz Bay Hill Classic
Course: Bay Hill Club, Orlando, Fla.
Par: 71 Yardage: 7,103
Last day of event: Sunday, March 20, 1988

Player	Place	Score	Earnings
Paul Azinger	Win	66-66-73-66=271	$135,000.00
Tom Kite	2	69-68-69-70=276	$81,000.00
Andrew Magee	T-3	66-70-73-71=280	$43,500.00
David Frost	T-3	70-66-75-69=280	$43,500.00
Don Pooley	T-5	68-74-73-66=281	$30,000.00
Payne Stewart	T-6	68-72-70-72=282	$23,475.00
Bruce Lietzke	T-6	69-72-71-70=282	$23,475.00
Joey Sindelar	T-6	68-73-73-68=282	$23,475.00
Craig Stadler	T-6	73-68-70-71=282	$23,475.00
Dave Eichelberger	T-6	72-65-71-74=282	$23,475.00

The Players Championship
Course: TPC at Sawgrass, Ponte Vedra Beach, Fla.
Par: 72 Yardage: 6,857
Last day of event: Sunday, March 27, 1988

Player	Place	Score	Earnings
Mark McCumber	Win	65-72-67-69=273	$225,000.00
Mike Reid	2	68-69-73-67=277	$135,000.00
David Frost	T-3	67-71-68-72=278	$65,000.00
Curt Byrum	T-3	66-73-69-70=278	$65,000.00
Fulton Allem	T-3	73-72-65-68=278	$65,000.00
Gil Morgan	T-6	69-70-71-69=279	$43,437.50
Lanny Wadkins	T-6	70-72-67-70=279	$43,437.50
Wayne Levi	T-8	70-71-71-68=280	$36,250.00
Dan Pohl	T-8	69-69-70-72=280	$36,250.00
Payne Stewart	T-8	71-65-71-73=280	$36,250.00

Kmart Greater Greensboro Open
Course: Forest Oaks C.C., Greensboro, N.C.
Par: 72 Yardage: 6,984
Last day of event: Sunday, April 3, 1988

Player	Place	Score	Earnings
Sandy Lyle	Win	68-63-68-72=271	$180,000.00
Playoff: Beat Ken Green with birdie on first extra hole			
Ken Green	T-2	68-67-69-67=271	$108,000.00
Jeff Sluman	3	64-65-73-71=273	$68,000.00
Scott Hoch	4	67-67-72-72=278	$48,000.00
Gil Morgan	5	68-68-71-72=279	$40,000.00
Kenny Perry	T-6	71-70-70-70=281	$32,375.00
Chip Beck	T-6	70-70-72-69=281	$32,375.00
Donnie Hammond	T-6	67-67-73-74=281	$32,375.00
Tom Purtzer	T-6	74-66-72-69=281	$32,375.00
Joey Sindelar	T-10	70-72-72-68=282	$23,000.00
Mark Wiebe	T-10	69-71-69-73=282	$23,000.00
Keith Clearwater	T-10	69-73-71-69=282	$23,000.00
Bobby Clampett	T-10	74-70-67-71=282	$23,000.00
T.C. Chen	T-10	66-71-75-70=282	$23,000.00

Masters
Course: Augusta National G.C., Augusta, Ga.
Par: 72 Yardage: 6,925
Last day of event: Sunday, April 10, 1988

Player	Place	Score	Earnings
Sandy Lyle	Win	71-67-72-71=281	$183,800.00
Mark Calcavecchia	2	71-69-72-70=282	$110,200.00
Craig Stadler	3	76-69-70-68=283	$69,400.00
Ben Crenshaw	4	72-73-67-72=284	$48,900.00
Don Pooley	T-5	71-72-72-70=285	$36,500.00
Fred Couples	T-5	75-68-71-71=285	$36,500.00
Greg Norman	T-5	77-73-71-64=285	$36,500.00
David Frost	8	73-74-71-68=286	$31,000.00
Bernhard Langer	T-9	71-72-71-73=287	$28,000.00
Tom Watson	T-9	72-71-73-71=287	$28,000.00

Deposit Guaranty Golf Classic
Course: Hattiesburg C.C., Hattiesburg, Miss.
Par: 70 Yardage: 6,594
Last day of event: Sunday, April 10, 1988

Player	Place	Score	Earnings
Frank Conner	Win	65-70-69-63=267	$36,000.00
Brian Mogg	2	68-67-70-67=272	$21,600.00
David Ogrin	3	68-69-68-68=273	$13,600.00
Kim Young	T-4	68-70-66-70=274	$7,875.00
Jeff Hart	T-4	70-68-70-66=274	$7,875.00
John Adams	T-4	69-71-66-68=274	$7,875.00
Robert Thompson	T-4	72-64-69-69=274	$7,875.00
Rick Pearson	T-8	71-70-64-70=275	$5,600.00
Rocco Mediate	T-8	72-67-66-70=275	$5,600.00
Lance Ten Broeck	T-8	72-64-66-73=275	$5,600.00
Steve Thomas	T-8	73-69-66-67=275	$5,600.00

MCI Heritage Classic
Course: Harbour Town G.L., Hilton Head, S.C.
Par: 71 Yardage: 6,657
Last day of event: Sunday, April 17, 1988

Player	Place	Score	Earnings
Greg Norman	Win	65-69-71-66=271	$126,000.00
David Frost	T-2	69-64-69-70=272	$61,600.00
Gil Morgan	T-2	71-64-69-68=272	$61,600.00
Fred Couples	4	68-65-68-73=274	$33,600.00
David Ogrin	T-5	67-69-71-69=276	$26,600.00
Paul Azinger	T-5	65-70-73-68=276	$26,600.00
D.A. Weibring	T-7	68-71-68-70=277	$21,816.66
Curtis Strange	T-7	70-70-71-66=277	$21,816.67
Doug Tewell	T-7	72-69-69-67=277	$21,816.67
Steve Pate	T-10	71-69-70-68=278	$17,500.00
Mark McCumber	T-10	72-67-69-70=278	$17,500.00
Russ Cochran	T-10	73-68-69-68=278	$17,500.00

USF&G Classic
Course: Lakewood C.C., New Orleans, La.
Par: 72 Yardage: 7,080
Last day of event: Sunday, April 24, 1988

Player	Place	Score	Earnings
Chip Beck	Win	69-64-65-64=262	$135,000.00
Lanny Wadkins	2	67-65-69-68=269	$81,000.00
Dan Forsman	3	68-68-70-65=271	$51,000.00
Calvin Peete	4	69-70-67-66=272	$36,000.00
Larry Mize	5	68-68-70-67=273	$30,000.00
Greg Ladehoff	6	68-68-68-70=274	$27,000.00
Brad Fabel	T-7	70-67-68-70=275	$24,187.50
John Cook	T-7	70-70-67-68=275	$24,187.50
Robert Wrenn	T-9	68-71-68-69=276	$18,000.00
Tom Watson	T-9	68-69-71-68=276	$18,000.00
Donnie Hammond	T-9	68-71-70-67=276	$18,000.00
Lennie Clements	T-9	69-68-68-71=276	$18,000.00

Player	Place	Score	Earnings
Russ Cochran	T-9	71-69-66-70=276	$18,000.00
Mark Lye	T-9	71-70-68-67=276	$18,000.00

Independent Insurance Agent Open
Course: TPC at The Woodlands, The Woodlands, Texas
Par: 72 Yardage: 7,045
Last day of event: Sunday, May 1, 1988

Player	Place	Score	Earnings
Curtis Strange	Win	69-68-66-67=270	$126,000.00
Playoff: Beat Greg Norman with birdie on third extra hole			
Greg Norman	T-2	65-70-68-67=270	$75,600.00
Tom Kite	3	69-69-66-68=272	$47,600.00
Brian Tennyson	T-4	68-68-70-69=275	$30,800.00
Jim Carter	T-4	71-69-68-67=275	$30,800.00
Tim Simpson	6	68-70-69-69=276	$25,200.00
Mike Donald	T-7	67-69-72-70=278	$22,575.00
Bruce Lietzke	T-7	73-68-69-68=278	$22,575.00
Jack Renner	T-9	70-70-68-71=279	$18,900.00
Dave Rummells	T-9	72-68-70-69=279	$18,900.00
Bobby Clampett	T-9	73-68-70-68=279	$18,900.00

Panasonic Las Vegas Invitational
Course: Las Vegas C.C.—Home course
Spanish Trail G. & C.C., Desert Inn C.C., Las Vegas, Nev.
Home course / Par: 72 Yardage: 7,164
Last day of event: Sunday, May 8, 1988

Player	Place	Score	Earnings
Gary Koch	Win	68-73-66-67=274	$250,000.00
Peter Jacobsen	T-2	71-66-68-70=275	$122,222.00
Mark O'Meara	T-2	65-75-69-66=275	$122,222.00
Gene Sauers	T-4	69-71-68-68=276	$52,361.40
David Canipe	T-4	71-69-68-68=276	$52,361.40
Curt Byrum	T-4	65-72-67-72=276	$52,361.40
Joey Sindelar	T-4	70-72-68-66=276	$52,361.40
Rick Fehr	T-4	67-74-67-68=276	$52,361.40
Payne Stewart	T-9	70-72-66-69=277	$38,889.00
Donnie Hammond	T-9	68-75-66-68=277	$38,889.00

GTE Byron Nelson Classic
Course: TPC at Las Colinas , Irving, Texas
Par: 70 Yardage: 6,767
Last day of event: Sunday, May 15, 1988

Player	Place	Score	Earnings
Bruce Lietzke	Win	66-69-66-70=271	$135,000.00
Playoff: Beat Clarence Rose with birdie on first extra hole			
Clarence Rose	T-2	66-69-67-69=271	$81,000.00
David Graham	T-3	68-69-67-68=272	$43,500.00
Ben Crenshaw	T-3	66-65-70-71=272	$43,500.00
John Cook	T-5	70-64-69-70=273	$27,375.00
Mark Calcavecchia	T-5	70-66-68-69=273	$27,375.00
Paul Azinger	T-5	73-68-63-69=273	$27,375.00
Nick Price	T-8	71-68-66-69=274	$22,500.00
Craig Stadler	T-8	68-66-68-72=274	$22,500.00
David Frost	T-10	66-70-70-69=275	$18,750.00
Fred Couples	T-10	70-71-65-69=275	$18,750.00
Tom Watson	T-10	67-73-71-64=275	$18,750.00

Colonial National Invitational
Course: Colonial C.C., Fort Worth, Texas
Par: 70 Yardage: 7,096

Last day of event: Sunday, May 22, 1988

Player	Place	Score	Earnings
Lanny Wadkins	Win	67-68-70-65=270	$135,000.00
Mark Calcavecchia	T-2	68-69-68-66=271	$56,000.00
Ben Crenshaw	T-2	69-67-68-67=271	$56,000.00
Joey Sindelar	T-2	71-65-67-68=271	$56,000.00
Clarence Rose	5	67-68-65-74=274	$30,000.00
Scott Hoch	T-6	67-68-71-69=275	$23,125.00
David Graham	T-6	71-66-70-68=275	$23,125.00
Mark Wiebe	T-6	72-67-69-67=275	$23,125.00
Chip Beck	T-9	71-70-69-67=277	$21,000.00
David Frost	T-9	74-66-69-68=277	$21,000.00

Memorial Tournament
Course: Muirfield Village G.C., Dubin, Ohio
Par: 72 Yardage: 7,104
Last day of event: Sunday, May 29, 1988

Player	Place	Score	Earnings
Curtis Strange	Win	73-70-64-67=274	$160,000.00
David Frost	T-2	69-70-68-69=276	$78,200.00
Hale Irwin	T-2	70-68-68-70=276	$78,200.00
John Huston	T-4	69-70-72-71=282	$39,115.00
Andrew Magee	T-4	70-70-68-74=282	$39,115.00
Peter Jacobsen	T-6	68-74-72-69=283	$26,881.00
Greg Norman	T-6	71-74-67-71=283	$26,881.00
Scott Hoch	T-6	74-73-64-72=283	$26,881.00
Payne Stewart	T-6	72-69-67-75=283	$26,881.00
Jay Haas	T-6	72-75-69-67=283	$26,881.00
Lanny Wadkins	T-6	79-66-71-67=283	$26,881.00

Kemper Open
Course: TPC at Avenel, Potomac, Md.
Par: 71 Yardage: 6,867
Last day of event: Sunday, June 5, 1988

Player	Place	Score	Earnings
Morris Hatalsky	Win	68-66-68-72=274	$144,000.00
Playoff: Beat Tom Kite with par on second extra hole			
Tom Kite	T-2	67-67-71-69=274	$86,400.00
Mike Reid	T-3	69-68-67-72=276	$46,400.00
Craig Stadler	T-3	70-70-64-72=276	$46,400.00
Jim Hallet	T-5	68-65-72-72=277	$30,400.00
Bob Gilder	T-5	72-65-71-69=277	$30,400.00
Calvin Peete	T-7	68-70-70-70=278	$24,100.00
Larry Mize	T-7	69-70-69-70=278	$24,100.00
Dick Mast	T-7	72-68-68-70=278	$24,100.00
John Mahaffey	T-7	68-68-68-74=278	$24,100.00

Manufacturers Hanover Westchester Classic
Course: Westchester C.C., Harrison, N.Y.
Par: 71 Yardage: 6,779
Last day of event: Sunday, June 12, 1988

Player	Place	Score	Earnings
Seve Ballesteros	Win	72-68-69-67=276	$126,000.00
Playoff: Beat David Frost, Greg Norman and Ken Green with birdie on first extra hole			
Ken Green	T-2	71-68-67-70=276	$52,267.00
David Frost	T-2	71-68-69-68=276	$52,267.00
Greg Norman	T-2	73-69-70-64=276	$52,267.00
Steve Elkington	5	68-70-69-71=278	$28,000.00
Bob Eastwood	T-6	69-72-72-67=280	$22,662.00

Loren Roberts	T-6	66-71-73-70=280	$22,662.00
Brandel Chamblee	T-6	70-68-73-69=280	$22,662.00
Dick Mast	T-6	71-68-68-73=280	$22,662.00
Tommy Armour III	T-10	73-69-71-68=281	$18,200.00
Jeff Sluman	T-10	74-70-68-69=281	$18,200.00

U.S. Open

Course: The Country Club, Brookline, Mass.
Par: 71 Yardage: 7,010
Last day of event: Monday, June 20, 1988

Player	Place	Score	Earnings
Curtis Strange	Win	70-67-69-72-71=278	$180,000.00

Playoff: Beat Nick Faldo in 18-hole playoff (Strange 71, Faldo 75)

Nick Faldo	2	72-67-68-71-75=278	$90,000.00
D.A. Weibring	T-3	71-69-68-72=280	$41,370.00
Mark O'Meara	T-3	71-72-66-71=280	$41,370.00
Steve Pate	T-3	72-69-72-67=280	$41,370.00
Scott Simpson	T-6	69-66-72-74=281	$25,414.50
Paul Azinger	T-6	69-70-76-66=281	$25,414.50
Fuzzy Zoeller	T-8	73-72-71-66=282	$20,903.50
Bob Gilder	T-8	68-69-70-75=282	$20,903.50
Fred Couples	T-10	72-67-71-73=283	$17,870.50
Payne Stewart	T-10	73-73-70-67=283	$17,870.50

Georgia-Pacific Atlanta Golf Classic

Course: Atlanta C.C., Atlanta, Ga.
Par: 72 Yardage: 7,007
Last day of event: Sunday, June 26, 1988

Player	Place	Score	Earnings
Larry Nelson	Win	63-66-66-73=268	$126,000.00
Chip Beck	2	67-66-70-66=269	$75,600.00
Paul Azinger	3	66-67-66-71=270	$47,600.00
Dave Rummells	T-4	67-69-67-69=272	$28,933.33
Lanny Wadkins	T-4	69-68-70-65=272	$28,933.34
Bobby Wadkins	T-4	64-69-68-71=272	$28,933.33
Clarence Rose	T-7	68-71-66-68=273	$22,575.00
Nick Price	T-7	68-71-68-66=273	$22,575.00
Scott Hoch	T-9	70-65-68-71=274	$20,300.00
Wayne Levi	T-10	68-69-68-70=275	$18,200.00
Mark Calcavecchia	T-10	67-71-67-70=275	$18,200.00

Beatrice Western Open

Course: Butler National G.C., Oak Brook, Ill.
Par: 72 Yardage: 7,097
Last day of event: Sunday, July 3, 1988

Player	Place	Score	Earnings
Jim Benepe	Win	71-68-69-70=278	$162,000.00
Peter Jacobsen	2	70-65-69-75=279	$97,200.00
Brad Faxon	T-3	71-69-71-69=280	$52,200.00
Isao Aoki	T-3	71-73-67-69=280	$52,200.00
D.A. Weibring	T-5	70-71-69-71=281	$34,200.00
Dan Forsman	T-5	68-69-71-73=281	$34,200.00
Bill Glasson	T-7	69-73-71-69=282	$27,112.50
Mark Calcavecchia	T-7	71-71-67-73=282	$27,112.50
Hale Irwin	T-7	73-69-69-71=282	$27,112.50
Morris Hatalsky	T-7	66-79-68-69=282	$27,112.50

Anheuser-Busch Golf Classic

Course: Kingsmill G.C., Williamsburg, Va.
Par: 71 Yardage: 6,776

Last day of event: Sunday, July 10, 1988

Player	Place	Score	Earnings
Tom Sieckmann	Win	69-66-66-69=270	$117,000.00
Mark Wiebe	T-2	68-70-64-68=270	$70,200.00
Kenny Knox	T-3	67-69-65-71=272	$37,700.00
Gene Sauers	T-3	68-71-67-66=272	$37,700.00
Mark McCumber	T-5	68-69-69-67=273	$24,700.00
Jeff Sluman	T-5	70-67-72-64=273	$24,700.00
Fuzzy Zoeller	T-7	67-68-69-70=274	$19,581.25
Tim Simpson	T-7	69-71-69-65=274	$19,581.25
Peter Jacobsen	T-7	67-65-69-73=274	$19,581.25
Jeff Coston	T-7	75-67-65-67=274	$19,581.25

Hardee's Golf Classic

Course: Oakwood C.C., Coal Valley, Ill.
Par: 70 Yardage: 6,606
Last day of event: Sunday, July 17, 1988

Player	Place	Score	Earnings
Blaine McCallister	Win	68-62-63-68=261	$108,000.00
Dan Forsman	2	64-66-67-67=264	$64,800.00
Sam Randolph	3	64-67-69-66=266	$40,800.00
Brad Fabel	T-4	67-66-67-67=267	$24,800.00
Steve Jones	T-4	67-69-67-64=267	$24,800.00
Scott Hoch	T-4	69-65-67-66=267	$24,800.00
Bob Lohr	T-7	68-68-66-66=268	$19,350.00
Russ Cochran	T-7	66-64-69-69=268	$19,350.00
Jim Dent	T-9	66-68-68-67=269	$15,600.00
Tom Sieckmann	T-9	67-67-69-66=269	$15,600.00
Dave Barr	T-9	69-67-67-66=269	$15,600.00
Ray Barr, Jr.	T-9	66-67-70-66=269	$15,600.00

British Open

Course: Royal Lytham & St. Annes G.C., Lytham, Lancashire, England
Par: 71 Yardage: 6,857
Last day of event: Monday, July 18, 1988

Player	Place	Score	Earnings
Seve Ballesteros	Win	67-71-70-65=273	$136,000.00
Nick Price	2	70-67-69-69=275	$102,000.00
Nick Faldo	3	71-69-68-71=279	$79,900.00
Gary Koch	T-4	71-72-70-68=281	$56,950.00
Fred Couples	T-4	73-69-71-68=281	$56,950.00
Peter Senior	6	70-73-70-69=282	$45,900.00
Isao Aoki	T-7	72-71-73-67=283	$35,700.00
Sandy Lyle	T-7	73-69-67-74=283	$35,700.00
David Frost	T-7	71-75-69-68=283	$35,700.00
Payne Stewart	T-7	73-75-68-67=283	$35,700.00

Canon Sammy Davis, Jr. - Greater Hartford Open

Course: TPC of Connecticut, Cromwell, Conn.
Par: 71 Yardage: 6,786
Last day of event: Sunday, July 24, 1988

Player	Place	Score	Earnings
Mark Brooks	Win	66-65-69-69=269	$126,000.00

Playoff: Beat Dave Barr and Joey Sindelar with birdie on second extra hole

Dave Barr	T-2	69-67-70-63=269	$61,600.00
Joey Sindelar	T-2	65-72-67-65=269	$61,600.00
Ronnie Black	T-4	66-69-65-70=270	$30,800.00
Mark Calcavecchia	T-4	67-66-67-70=270	$30,800.00
Brett Upper	T-6	67-66-69-69=271	$24,325.00
Roger Maltbie	T-6	64-68-72-67=271	$24,325.00

Brad Faxon	T-8	65-69-69-69=272	$19,600.00
Blaine McCallister	T-8	68-66-69-69=272	$19,600.00
Lennie Clements	T-8	68-70-68-66=272	$19,600.00
George Archer	T-8	70-66-67-69=272	$19,600.00

Buick Open

Course: Warwick Hills C.C., Grand Blanc, Mich.
Par: 72 Yardage: 7,014
Last day of event: Sunday, July 31, 1988

Player	Place	Score	Earnings
Scott Verplank	Win	66-66-70-66=268	$126,000.00
Doug Tewell	2	68-70-68-64=270	$75,600.00
Fred Couples	3	66-69-71-65=271	$47,600.00
Tim Norris	4	69-66-71-66=272	$33,600.00
Jim Hallet	T-5	67-69-69-69=274	$26,600.00
Ben Crenshaw	T-5	70-71-66-67=274	$26,600.00
Kenny Knox	T-7	69-68-69-69=275	$20,370.00
Dave Rummells	T-7	68-71-66-70=275	$20,370.00
Gene Sauers	T-7	68-71-68-68=275	$20,370.00
Scott Hoch	T-7	66-72-68-69=275	$20,370.00
Jack Renner	T-7	68-72-68-67=275	$20,370.00

Federal Express St. Jude Classic

Course: Colonial C.C. (South), Cordova, Tenn.
Par: 72 Yardage: 7,282
Last day of event: Sunday, August 7, 1988

Player	Place	Score	Earnings
Jodie Mudd	Win	68-68-67-70=273	$171,692.00
Peter Jacobsen	T-2	68-68-72-66=274	$83,938.00
Nick Price	T-2	73-64-71-66=274	$83,938.00
Larry Mize	T-4	70-68-70-68=276	$39,425.33
Dave Rummells	T-4	70-69-66-71=276	$39,425.34
Tim Simpson	T-4	68-68-68-72=276	$39,425.33
Curtis Strange	T-7	69-71-67-70=277	$30,761.50
Tom Kite	T-7	71-69-67-70=277	$30,761.50
Fulton Allem	9	69-69-71-69=278	$27,661.00
Howard Twitty	T-10	70-69-69-71=279	$21,143.16
Scott Hoch	T-10	71-68-69-71=279	$21,143.17
Loren Roberts	T-10	70-72-72-65=279	$21,143.17
Richard Zokol	T-10	71-70-73-65=279	$21,143.17
Larry Nelson	T-10	73-70-66-70=279	$21,143.17
Tommy Armour III	T-10	69-69-74-67=279	$21,143.16

PGA Championship

Course: Oak Tree G.C., Edmond, Okla.
Par: 71 Yardage: 7,015
Last day of event: Sunday, August 14, 1988

Player	Place	Score	Earnings
Jeff Sluman	Win	69-70-68-65=272	$160,000.00
Paul Azinger	2	67-66-71-71=275	$100,000.00
Tommy Nakajima	3	69-68-74-67=278	$70,000.00
Nick Faldo	T-4	67-71-70-71=279	$45,800.00
Tom Kite	T-4	72-69-71-67=279	$45,800.00
Bob Gilder	T-6	66-75-71-68=280	$32,500.00
Dave Rummells	T-6	73-64-68-75=280	$32,500.00
Dan Pohl	8	69-71-70-71=281	$28,000.00
Mark O'Meara	T-9	70-71-70-71=282	$21,500.00
Greg Norman	T-9	68-71-72-71=282	$21,500.00
Steve Jones	T-9	69-68-72-73=282	$21,500.00
Payne Stewart	T-9	70-69-70-73=282	$21,500.00
Kenny Knox	T-9	72-69-68-73=282	$21,500.00
Ray Floyd	T-9	68-68-74-72=282	$21,500.00

The International

Course: Castle Pine G.C., Castle Rock, Colo. (Stableford format)
Par: 72 Yardage: 7,559
Last day of event: Sunday, August 21, 1988

Player	Place	Score	Earnings
Joey Sindelar	Win	3-11-7-17=38	$180,000.00
Dan Pohl	T-2	6-6-8-13=33	$88,000.00
Steve Pate	T-2	6-9-7-13=35	$88,000.00
Mark Wiebe	4	2-8-10-12=32	$48,000.00
Chip Beck	5	4-7-11-11=33	$40,000.00
Davis Love III	6	3-7-8-9=27	$36,000.00
Ben Crenshaw	7	10-4-13-8=35	$33,500.00
Bruce Lietzke	8	1-9-14-6=30	$31,000.00
Bill Glasson	9	1-6-6-5=18	$29,000.00
Tom Kite	10	2-2-11-3=18	$27,000.00

NEC World Series of Golf

Course: Firestone C.C. (South), Akron, Ohio
Par: 70 Yardage: 7,149
Last day of event: Sunday, August 28, 1988

Player	Place	Score	Earnings
Mike Reid	Win	70-65-71-69=275	$162,000.00
Playoff: Beat Tom Watson with par on first extra hole			
Tom Watson	2	74-69-64-68=275	$97,200.00
Ian Baker-Finch	T-3	68-67-71-71=277	$52,200.00
Larry Nelson	T-3	70-70-66-71=277	$52,200.00
Sandy Lyle	5	69-67-71-71=278	$36,000.00
Chip Beck	T-6	71-69-69-70=279	$31,350.00
Steve Pate	T-6	74-67-74-64=279	$31,350.00
Ben Crenshaw	8	73-67-68-72=280	$28,100.00
Bruce Lietzke	T-9	70-69-72-70=281	$25,300.00
Jay Haas	T-9	69-73-69-70=281	$25,300.00

Provident Classic

Course: ValleyBrook C.C., Hixson, Tenn.,
Par: 70 Yardage: 6,641
Last day of event: Sunday, August 28, 1988

Player	Place	Score	Earnings
Phil Blackmar	Win	66-64-69-65=264	$81,000.00
Playoff: Beat Payne Stewart with birdie on first extra hole			
Payne Stewart	2	65-67-67-65=264	$48,600.00
Billy Ray Brown	T-3	69-69-65-66=269	$23,400.00
Jim Dent	T-3	66-66-67-70=269	$23,400.00
Mark Hayes	T-3	70-69-63-67=269	$23,400.00
Leonard Thompson	T-6	66-67-69-68=270	$13,612.50
Russ Cochran	T-6	66-69-67-68=270	$13,612.50
Jim Hallet	T-6	67-65-69-69=270	$13,612.50
Bill Glasson	T-6	68-69-68-65=270	$13,612.50
Bill Bergin	T-6	69-67-65-69=270	$13,612.50
Bill Britton	T-6	63-70-66-71=270	$13,612.50

Canadian Open

Course: Glen Abbey G.C., Oakville, Ontario, Canada
Par: 72 Yardage: 7,102
Last day of event: Sunday, September 4, 1988

Player	Place	Score	Earnings
Ken Green	Win	70-65-68-72=275	$135,000.00
Scott Verplank	T-2	69-70-67-70=276	$66,000.00
Bill Glasson	T-2	70-71-68-67=276	$66,000.00

Mike Sullivan	T-4	71-70-69-67=277	$33,000.00
Dave Barr	T-4	72-68-71-66=277	$33,000.00
Mark Wiebe	6	72-69-70-67=278	$27,000.00
Gordon Smith	T-7	71-71-70-67=279	$22,593.75
Wayne Grady	T-7	69-72-68-70=279	$22,593.75
Jay Delsing	T-7	70-67-68-74=279	$22,593.75
Larry Rinker	T-7	77-65-65-72=279	$22,593.75

Greater Milwaukee Open

Course: Tuckaway C.C., Franklin, Wis.
Par: 72 Yardage: 7,030
Last day of event: Sunday, September 11, 1988

Player	Place	Score	Earnings
Ken Green	Win	70-69-61-68=268	$126,000.00
Donnie Hammond	T-2	68-69-68-69=274	$46,200.00
Mark Calcavecchia	T-2	71-68-69-66=274	$46,200.00
Jim Gallagher, Jr.	T-2	67-67-72-68=274	$46,200.00
Dan Pohl	T-2	70-72-66-66=274	$46,200.00
Nick Price	6	70-71-67-67=275	$25,200.00
David Ogrin	T-7	70-66-70-70=276	$21,816.66
Tim Simpson	T-7	70-70-70-66=276	$21,816.67
Corey Pavin	T-7	66-72-70-68=276	$21,816.67
Dave Barr	10	66-68-68-75=277	$18,900.00

Bank of Boston Classic

Course: Pleasant Valley C.C., Sutton, Mass.
Par: 71 Yardage: 7,110
Last day of event: Sunday, September 18, 1988

Player	Place	Score	Earnings
Mark Calcavecchia	Win	71-67-70-66=274	$108,000.00
Don Pooley	2	75-68-69-63=275	$64,800.00
Fuzzy Zoeller	T-3	68-69-69-70=276	$31,200.00
John Mahaffey	T-3	70-69-70-67=276	$31,200.00
Dave Rummells	T-3	70-69-70-67=276	$31,200.00
Wayne Levi	T-6	71-67-69-70=277	$20,100.00
Wayne Grady	T-6	71-68-69-69=277	$20,100.00
Steve Pate	T-6	68-68-69-72=277	$20,100.00
Roger Maltbie	T-9	71-71-66-70=278	$14,400.00
Duffy Waldorf	T-9	71-70-69-68=278	$14,400.00
Clarence Rose	T-9	71-70-71-66=278	$14,400.00
Donnie Hammond	T-9	67-73-71-67=278	$14,400.00
D.A. Weibring	T-9	68-68-69-73=278	$14,400.00
Blaine McCallister	T-9	73-69-70-66=278	$14,400.00

B.C. Open

Course: En-Joie G.C., Endicott, N.Y.
Par: 71 Yardage: 6,966
Last day of event: Sunday, September 25, 1988

Player	Place	Score	Earnings
Bill Glasson	Win	66-68-65-69=268	$90,000.00
Wayne Levi	T-2	66-71-66-67=270	$44,000.00
Bruce Lietzke	T-2	68-71-67-64=270	$44,000.00
Don Pooley	T-4	67-66-70-68=271	$22,000.00
Jeff Sluman	T-4	68-70-68-65=271	$22,000.00
Brad Bryant	T-6	68-68-67-70=273	$16,750.00
Fred Couples	T-6	70-67-69-67=273	$16,750.00
Ken Green	T-6	66-70-72-65=273	$16,750.00
Kenny Knox	T-9	68-70-68-68=274	$12,500.00
Ian Baker-Finch	T-9	69-68-67-70=274	$12,500.00
Kenny Perry	T-9	69-70-66-69=274	$12,500.00
Lance Ten Broeck	T-9	66-69-68-71=274	$12,500.00
Joey Sindelar	T-9	67-65-70-72=274	$12,500.00

Southern Open

Course: Green Island C.C., Columbus, Ga.
Par: 70 Yardage: 6,791
Last day of event: Sunday, October 2, 1988

Player	Place	Score	Earnings
David Frost	Win	70-68-65-67=270	$72,000.00
Playoff: Beat Bob Tway with birdie on first extra hole			
Bob Tway	2	71-66-66-67=270	$43,200.00
Dan Forsman	T-3	67-66-69-69=271	$20,800.00
George Archer	T-3	70-66-70-65=271	$20,800.00
Dave Barr	T-3	72-68-61-70=271	$20,800.00
Mike Hulbert	6	67-66-69-70=272	$14,400.00
Corey Pavin	T-7	69-70-66-68=273	$12,050.00
Mike Donald	T-7	67-70-71-65=273	$12,050.00
Lance Ten Broeck	T-7	68-65-69-71=273	$12,050.00
Jeff Sluman	T-7	63-67-74-69=273	$12,050.00

Gatlin Brothers - Southwest Golf Classic

Course: Fairway Oaks C.C., Abilene, Texas
Par: 72 Yardage: 7,166
Last day of event: Sunday, October 9, 1988

Player	Place	Score	Earnings
Tom Purtzer	Win	64-72-69-64=269	$72,000.00
Playoff: Beat Mark Brooks with par on first extra hole			
Mark Brooks	2	64-68-70-67=269	$43,200.00
Buddy Gardner	3	69-68-69-65=271	$27,200.00
Brad Bryant	T-4	66-68-68-70=272	$17,600.00
Dan Pohl	T-4	70-69-66-67=272	$17,600.00
Dave Barr	T-6	69-67-68-69=273	$12,950.00
Paul Azinger	T-6	66-70-69-68=273	$12,950.00
Tommy Armour III	T-6	71-70-64-68=273	$12,950.00
Mark O'Meara	T-6	71-70-68-64=273	$12,950.00
Howard Twitty	T-10	68-68-70-68=274	$10,400.00
Davis Love III	T-10	73-65-70-66=274	$10,400.00

Texas Open

Course: Oak Hill C.C., San Antonio, Texas
Par: 70 Yardage: 6,576
Last day of event: Sunday, October 16, 1988

Player	Place	Score	Earnings
Corey Pavin	Win	64-63-66-66=259	$108,000.00
Robert Wrenn	2	69-68-68-62=267	$64,800.00
Pat McGowan	3	68-68-67-65=268	$40,800.00
Tom Kite	4	67-64-69-69=269	$28,800.00
Roger Maltbie	T-5	68-67-68-67=270	$20,340.00
Payne Stewart	T-5	69-65-68-68=270	$20,340.00
Bobby Wadkins	T-5	64-71-69-66=270	$20,340.00
Tom Pernice, Jr.	T-5	65-66-67-72=270	$20,340.00
Mike Sullivan	T-5	63-67-77-63=270	$20,340.00
Don Pooley	T-10	67-69-69-66=271	$14,400.00
Ben Crenshaw	T-10	67-65-69-70=271	$14,400.00
Jodie Mudd	T-10	68-66-70-67=271	$14,400.00
Jay Haas	T-10	66-65-73-67=271	$14,400.00

Pensacola Open

Course: Tiger Point G. & C.C., Gulf Breeze, Fla.
Par: 72 Yardage: 7,033
Last day of event: Sunday, October 23, 1988

Player	Place	Score	Earnings
Andrew Magee	Win	70-68-67-66=271	$72,000.00

Ken Green	T-2	68-68-69-67=272	$29,866.67
Bruce Lietzke	T-2	71-67-67-67=272	$29,866.66
Tom Byrum	T-2	72-64-65-71=272	$29,866.67
Dan Pohl	5	66-71-70-67=274	$16,000.00
Bobby Wadkins	T-6	70-68-68-69=275	$13,900.00
Jim Hallet	T-6	72-70-68-65=275	$13,900.00
Ray Stewart	8	71-66-68-71=276	$12,400.00
Dave Rummells	T-9	70-70-69-68=277	$9,600.00
Lennie Clements	T-9	69-71-69-68=277	$9,600.00
Mike McCullough	T-9	68-72-70-67=277	$9,600.00
Jay Don Blake	T-9	72-68-69-68=277	$9,600.00
Billy Andrade	T-9	66-73-69-69=277	$9,600.00
Scott Hoch	T-9	68-67-74-68=277	$9,600.00

Walt Disney World/Oldsmobile Classic

Course: Walt Disney (Magnolia, Palm), Lake Buena Vista C.C., Lake Buena Vista, Fla.

Home course / Magnolia, Par: 72 Yardage: 7,190

Last day of event: Saturday, October 29, 1988

Player	Place	Score	Earnings
Bob Lohr	Win	62-67-66-68=263	$126,000.00
Playoff: Beat Chip Beck with par on fifth extra hole			
Chip Beck	2	66-63-66-66=263	$75,600.00
Bruce Lietzke	T-3	69-67-65-68=269	$40,600.00
Fuzzy Zoeller	T-3	64-69-66-70=269	$40,600.00
Dan Pohl	T-5	68-68-68-66=270	$25,550.00
Mike Donald	T-5	68-67-70-65=270	$25,550.00
Paul Azinger	T-5	67-68-62-73=270	$25,550.00
Gene Sauers	T-8	69-67-67-68=271	$19,600.00
Mark Wiebe	T-8	69-67-68-67=271	$19,600.00
Robert Wrenn	T-8	66-66-71-68=271	$19,600.00
Larry Nelson	T-8	72-63-67-69=271	$19,600.00

Northern Telecom Tucson Open

Course: TPC At StarPass, Tucson, Ariz.

Par: 72 Yardage: 7,010

Last day of event: Sunday, November 6, 1988

Player	Place	Score	Earnings
David Frost	Win	66-66-67-67=266	$108,000.00
Mark O'Meara	T-2	67-69-65-70=271	$52,800.00
Mark Calcavecchia	T-2	66-73-63-69=271	$52,800.00
Ken Green	T-4	71-66-67-68=272	$26,400.00
Mark Wiebe	T-4	73-65-61-73=272	$26,400.00
Andrew Magee	6	68-73-67-65=273	$21,600.00
D.A. Weibring	T-7	68-69-67-70=274	$17,460.00
Don Pooley	T-7	70-65-68-71=274	$17,460.00
Jim Carter	T-7	71-68-64-71=274	$17,460.00
Curt Byrum	T-7	68-68-65-73=274	$17,460.00
Tom Kite	T-7	68-73-67-66=274	$17,460.00

Centel Classic

Course: Killearn C.C., Tallahassee, Fla.

Par: 72 Yardage: 7,124

Last day of event: Sunday, November 13, 1988

Player	Place	Score	Earnings
Bill Glasson	Win	67-69-68-68=272	$90,000.00
Tommy Armour III	2	70-71-65-68=274	$54,000.00
Chris Perry	T-3	67-71-66-71=275	$29,000.00
Bob Lohr	T-3	69-67-68-71=275	$29,000.00
Buddy Gardner	T-5	68-69-70-69=276	$18,250.00
Mike Donald	T-5	70-66-70-70=276	$18,250.00

Kenny Perry	T-5	69-66-69-72=276	$18,250.00
George Archer	T-8	68-69-70-70=277	$14,500.00
Bernhard Langer	T-8	66-70-71-70=277	$14,500.00
Jay Overton	T-8	68-70-73-66=277	$14,500.00

Nabisco Golf Championship

Course: Pebble Beach G.C., Pebble Beach, Calif.

Par: 72 Yardage: 6,815

Last day of event: Sunday, November 13, 1988

Player	Place	Score	Earnings
Curtis Strange	Win	64-71-70-74=279	$360,000.00
Playoff: Beat Tom Kite with birdie on second extra hole			
Tom Kite	2	72-65-70-72=279	$216,000.00
Payne Stewart	T-3	73-70-64-73=280	$104,666.67
Ken Green	T-3	67-70-69-74=280	$104,666.66
Mark Calcavecchia	T-3	70-71-65-74=280	$104,666.67
Peter Jacobsen	6	71-70-67-73=281	$72,000.00
Fred Couples	7	75-67-67-73=282	$68,000.00
Mike Reid	T-8	72-72-68-73=285	$55,800.00
Scott Verplank	T-8	69-70-72-74=285	$55,800.00
Gary Koch	T-8	71-72-68-74=285	$55,800.00
Bob Tway	T-8	69-70-71-75=285	$55,800.00
Jodie Mudd	T-8	70-71-68-76=285	$55,800.00
Bruce Lietzke	T-8	69-68-70-78=285	$55,800.00

Nabisco year-end bonus

Player	Place	Earnings
Curtis Strange	Win	$175,000.00
Chip Beck	2	$106,000.00
Joey Sindelar	3	$68,000.00
Ken Green	4	$47,000.00
Tom Kite	5	$40,000.00
Mark Calcavecchia	6	$36,000.00
Sandy Lyle	7	$34,000.00
Ben Crenshaw	8	$32,000.00
David Frost	9	$30,000.00
Lanny Wadkins	10	$28,000.00

1989

Bouncing back from a third-round 77, Nick Faldo closed with 65 to tie Scott Hoch for first place after 72 holes at the Masters. The ensuing sudden-death playoff would be remembered for the phrase "Hoch, as in choke," referring to the 2-foot par putt Hoch missed on the first extra hole, sending it to No. 11 where Faldo made a 25-foot birdie putt for the victory. Curtis Strange shot 2-under 278 to successfully defend his U.S. Open title at Oak Hill, where four players made holes in one on the same hole using the same choice of club during Round 1. Accomplishing the feat—at No. 6, using 7-irons on the 167-yard hole—were Doug Weaver, Jerry Pate, Nick Price and Mark Weibe. In the first four-hole aggregate playoff to settle a major, Mark Calcaveccia shot 4-3-3-3 to best Greg Norman (who had closed with 64) and Wayne Grady in the British Open at Royal Troon. Finally gaining more attention for his play than his attire, Payne Stewart summoned four birdies over the final five holes to edge Mike Reid, Andy Bean and Curtis Strange by a shot at the PGA Championship at Kemper Lakes. Europe kept the Ryder Cup with a 14-14 deadlock at The Belfry.

MONY Tournament of Champions

Course: La Costa C.C., Carlsbad, Calif.

Par: 72 Yardage: 7,022

Last day of event: Sunday, January 8, 1989

Player	Place	Score	Earnings
Steve Jones	Win	69-69-72-69=279	$135,000.00
David Frost	T-2	72-70-72-68=282	$67,000.00
Jay Haas	T-2	75-67-72-68=282	$67,000.00
Greg Norman	4	71-72-72-68=283	$37,000.00

Chip Beck	5	69-70-74-71=284	$31,000.00
Jeff Sluman	T-6	70-71-73-71=285	$26,500.00
Lanny Wadkins	T-6	71-70-71-73=285	$26,500.00
Morris Hatalsky	T-6	74-74-70-67=285	$26,500.00
Bill Glasson	9	75-73-67-71=286	$23,000.00
Bob Lohr	T-10	70-74-70-73=287	$20,000.00
Sandy Lyle	T-10	71-71-71-74=287	$20,000.00
Ben Crenshaw	T-10	70-72-70-75=287	$20,000.00
Curtis Strange	T-10	77-70-69-71=287	$20,000.00

Bob Hope Chrysler Classic

Course: Bermuda Dunes C.C., PGA West/Palmer, Indian Wells C.C., Eldorado C.C.

Home course / Bermuda Dunes, Par: 72 Yardage: 6,837

Last day of event: Sunday, January 15, 1989

Player	Place	Score	Earnings
Steve Jones	Win	76-68-67-63-69=343	$180,000.00

Playoff: Beat Paul Azinger and Sandy Lyle with birdie on first extra hole

Paul Azinger	T-2	69-68-70-67-69=343	$88,000.00
Sandy Lyle	T-2	70-68-68-68-69=343	$88,000.00
Lanny Wadkins	T-4	68-70-68-70-68=344	$39,375.00
Fred Couples	T-4	65-71-71-68-69=344	$39,375.00
Kenny Knox	T-4	68-71-69-67-69=344	$39,375.00
Mark Calcavecchia	T-4	71-67-67-67-72=344	$39,375.00
Bernhard Langer	T-8	70-68-68-69-70=345	$29,000.00
Tom Kite	T-8	68-69-68-69-71=345	$29,000.00
Hubert Green	T-8	73-70-65-68-69=345	$29,000.00

Phoenix Open

Course: TPC of Scottsdale, Scottsdale, Ariz.

Par: 71 Yardage: 6,992

Last day of event: Sunday, January 22, 1989

Player	Place	Score	Earnings
Mark Calcavecchia	Win	66-68-65-64=263	$126,000.00
Chip Beck	2	67-70-66-67=270	$75,600.00
Paul Azinger	T-3	68-68-68-67=271	$36,400.00
Scott Hoch	T-3	64-70-69-68=271	$36,400.00
Bill Glasson	T-3	65-68-73-65=271	$36,400.00
Mark McCumber	6	64-69-69-70=272	$25,200.00
Jim Carter	T-7	68-68-70-67=273	$21,087.50
Larry Mize	T-7	70-69-67-67=273	$21,087.50
Ted Schulz	T-7	64-70-71-68=273	$21,087.50
Steve Elkington	T-7	66-73-64-70=273	$21,087.50

AT&T Pebble Beach Pro-Am

Courses: Pebble Beach G.L., Spyglass Hill G.C., Cypress Point C.C., Pebble Beach, Calif.

Home Course / Pebble Beach G.L., Par: 72 Yardage: 6,815

Last day of event: Sunday, January 29, 1989

Player	Place	Score	Earnings
Mark O'Meara	Win	66-68-73-70=277	$180,000.00
Tom Kite	2	67-70-72-69=278	$108,000.00
Sandy Lyle	T-3	68-72-72-68=280	$52,000.00
Jim Carter	T-3	70-72-69-69=280	$52,000.00
Nick Price	T-3	66-74-67-73=280	$52,000.00
Steve Jones	T-6	71-69-71-70=281	$32,375.00
Steve Pate	T-6	72-72-66-71=281	$32,375.00
Hal Sutton	T-6	70-73-70-68=281	$32,375.00
Lanny Wadkins	T-6	73-69-72-67=281	$32,375.00
Loren Roberts	T-10	67-72-76-67=282	$26,000.00
Dave Stockton	T-10	65-70-78-69=282	$26,000.00

Nissan Los Angeles Open

Course: Riviera C.C., Pacific Palisades, Calif.

Par: 71 Yardage: 7,029

Last day of event: Sunday, February 5, 1989

Player	Place	Score	Earnings
Mark Calcavecchia	Win	68-66-70-68=272	$180,000.00
Sandy Lyle	2	68-66-68-71=273	$108,000.00
Hale Irwin	3	70-67-69-68=274	$68,000.00
Steve Pate	T-4	67-71-68-70=276	$41,333.33
Gene Sauers	T-4	67-70-72-67=276	$41,333.34
Phil Blackmar	T-4	68-72-67-69=276	$41,333.33
Fred Couples	T-7	69-68-69-71=277	$33,500.00
Tom Kite	T-8	73-70-66-69=278	$31,000.00
Ben Crenshaw	T-9	70-71-70-69=280	$25,000.00
Johnny Miller	T-9	71-70-70-69=280	$25,000.00
Donnie Hammond	T-9	68-73-68-71=280	$25,000.00
Mike Reid	T-9	68-69-73-70=280	$25,000.00
Tom Purtzer	T-9	71-66-73-70=280	$25,000.00

Hawaiian Open

Course: Waialae C.C., Honolulu, Ha.

Par: 72 Yardage: 6,975

Last day of event: Sunday, February 12, 1989

Player	Place	Score	Earnings
Gene Sauers	Win	65-67-65=197	$135,000.00
David Ogrin	2	65-67-66=198	$81,000.00
Dave Rummells	3	70-65-64=199	$51,000.00
Jim Carter	4	64-66-70=200	$36,000.00
Chip Beck	T-5	69-64-69=202	$28,500.00
Don Reese	T-5	69-69-64=202	$28,500.00
Rex Caldwell	7	69-67-67=203	$25,125.00
Lon Hinkle	T-8	66-70-68=204	$21,000.00
Bill Glasson	T-8	67-67-70=204	$21,000.00
Paul Azinger	T-8	68-70-66=204	$21,000.00
Kazunari Takahashi	T-8	70-67-67=204	$21,000.00

Shearson Lehman Hutton Open

Course: Torrey Pines (South), Torrey Pines (North), San Diego, Calif.

Home Course -Par: 72 Yardage: 7,021

Last day of event: Sunday, February 19, 1989

Player	Place	Score	Earnings
Greg Twiggs	Win	68-70-64-69=271	$126,000.00
Brad Faxon	T-2	67-69-69-68=273	$46,200.00
Mark Wiebe	T-2	68-65-70-70=273	$46,200.00
Mark O'Meara	T-2	68-67-72-66=273	$46,200.00
Steve Elkington	T-2	70-63-67-73=273	$46,200.00
John McComish	T-6	68-69-67-70=274	$23,450.00
Sam Randolph	T-6	71-69-66-68=274	$23,450.00
Dan Forsman	T-6	73-64-70-67=274	$23,450.00
Duffy Waldorf	T-9	68-69-69-69=275	$18,900.00
Phil Blackmar	T-9	69-68-70-68=275	$18,900.00
John Cook	T-9	70-68-69-68=275	$18,900.00

Doral-Ryder Open

Course: Doral C.C. (Blue), Miami, Fla.

Par: 72 Yardage: 6,939

Last day of event: Sunday, February 26, 1989

Player	Place	Score	Earnings
Bill Glasson	Win	71-65-67-72=275	$234,000.00
Fred Couples	2	69-69-70-68=276	$140,400.00

Bruce Lietzke	T-3	68-71-68-71=278	$67,600.00
Curtis Strange	T-3	73-67-69-69=278	$67,600.00
Mark Calcavecchia	T-3	65-73-66-74=278	$67,600.00
John Huston	T-6	69-69-70-71=279	$43,550.00
Wayne Levi	T-6	68-69-73-69=279	$43,550.00
Dan Pohl	T-6	69-71-73-66=279	$43,550.00
Ben Crenshaw	T-9	67-72-72-70=281	$35,100.00
Paul Azinger	T-9	73-71-66-71=281	$35,100.00
Buddy Gardner	T-9	70-68-69-74=281	$35,100.00

Honda Classic
Course: TPC at Eagle Trace, Coral Springs, Fla.
Par: 72 Yardage: 7,030
Last day of event: Sunday, March 5, 1989

Player	Place	Score	Earnings
Blaine McCallister	Win	70-67-65-64=266	$144,000.00
Payne Stewart	2	68-65-70-67=270	$86,400.00
Steve Pate	T-3	70-67-64-70=271	$46,400.00
Curtis Strange	T-3	68-71-67-65=271	$46,400.00
Dan Pohl	5	66-62-75-69=272	$32,000.00
Tom Byrum	T-6	65-69-70-69=273	$27,800.00
Paul Azinger	T-6	67-66-72-68=273	$27,800.00
Fuzzy Zoeller	8	70-66-70-68=274	$24,800.00
Gary Koch	T-9	69-68-68-70=275	$20,800.00
Davis Love III	T-9	70-67-68-70=275	$20,800.00
Nick Price	T-9	69-66-69-71=275	$20,800.00
Mike Hulbert	T-9	71-67-67-70=275	$20,800.00
Bruce Lietzke	T-10	68-69-69-70=276	$14,133.33
J.C. Snead	T-10	68-69-71-68=276	$14,133.34
Gene Sauers	T-10	68-72-66-70=276	$14,133.33
Mark McCumber	T-10	68-67-72-69=276	$14,133.34
John Huston	T-10	68-66-73-69=276	$14,133.33
Larry Rinker	T-10	67-68-67-74=276	$14,133.33

The Nestle Invitational
Course: Bay Hill Club, Orlando, Fla.
Par: 71 Yardage: 7,103
Last day of event: Sunday, March 12, 1989

Player	Place	Score	Earnings
Tom Kite	Win	68-72-67-71=278	$144,000.00
Playoff: Beat Davis Love III with par on second extra hole			
Davis Love III	2	72-67-66-73=278	$86,400.00
Curtis Strange	3	73-72-69-65=279	$54,400.00
Loren Roberts	T-4	66-73-69-72=280	$33,066.66
Don Pooley	T-4	69-73-68-70=280	$33,066.67
Payne Stewart	T-4	76-69-65-70=280	$33,066.67
Dan Pohl	7	70-70-71-70=281	$26,800.00
Larry Rinker	T-8	72-68-68-74=282	$24,000.00
Nick Price	T-8	67-77-71-67=282	$24,000.00
Larry Mize	T-10	70-71-69-73=283	$20,000.00
Blaine McCallister	T-10	71-73-74-65=283	$20,000.00
Tommy Armour III	T-10	75-69-69-70=283	$20,000.00

The Players Championship
Course: TPC at Sawgrass, Ponte Vedra Beach, Fla.
Par: 72 Yardage: 6,857
Last day of event: Sunday, March 19, 1989

Player	Place	Score	Earnings
Tom Kite	Win	69-70-69-71=279	$243,000.00
Chip Beck	2	71-68-68-73=280	$145,800.00
Bruce Lietzke	3	66-69-74-72=281	$91,800.00

Fred Couples	T-4	68-70-71-73=282	$59,400.00
Greg Norman	T-4	74-67-69-72=282	$59,400.00
Gil Morgan	T-6	71-69-70-73=283	$46,912.50
Mark McCumber	T-6	69-70-70-74=283	$46,912.50
David Frost	T-8	66-71-75-72=284	$39,150.00
Gary Koch	T-8	70-69-70-75=284	$39,150.00
Andy Bean	T-8	68-76-69-71=284	$39,150.00

USF&G Classic
Course: English Turn G. & C.C., New Orleans, La.
Par: 72 Yardage: 7,106
Last day of event: Sunday, March 26, 1989

Player	Place	Score	Earnings
Tim Simpson	Win	68-67-70-69=274	$135,000.00
Hal Sutton	T-2	71-68-67-70=276	$66,000.00
Greg Norman	T-2	68-68-68-72=276	$66,000.00
Mark Hayes	4	72-71-67-68=278	$36,000.00
Bill Sander	T-5	68-71-70-70=279	$26,343.75
Payne Stewart	T-5	70-69-69-71=279	$26,343.75
P.H. Horgan III	T-5	70-70-67-72=279	$26,343.75
Mark O'Meara	T-5	72-67-72-68=279	$26,343.75
Pat McGowan	T-9	68-70-71-71=280	$18,750.00
Lanny Wadkins	T-9	72-70-67-71=280	$18,750.00
David Edwards	T-9	72-68-72-68=280	$18,570.00
Dan Forsman	T-9	66-69-71-74=280	$18,750.00
Chip Beck	T-9	74-67-68-71=280	$18,750.00

Independent Insurance Agent Open
Course: TPC at The Woodlands, The Woodlands, Texas
Par: 72 Yardage: 7,042
Last day of event: Sunday, April 2, 1989

Player	Place	Score	Earnings
Mike Sullivan	Win	76-71-68-65=280	$144,000.00
Craig Stadler	2	72-71-68-70=281	$86,400.00
Seve Ballesteros	T-3	69-69-72-72=282	$41,600.00
Mike Reid	T-3	72-69-71-70=282	$41,600.00
Mike Donald	T-3	67-67-74-74=282	$41,600.00
Curtis Strange	T-6	69-70-72-72=283	$26,800.00
David Frost	T-6	70-74-70-69=283	$26,800.00
Hal Sutton	T-6	74-69-68-72=283	$26,800.00
Bob Gilder	T-9	70-71-71-72=284	$21,600.00
Mike Hulbert	T-9	68-76-71-69=284	$21,600.00
Gil Morgan	T-9	70-77-69-68=284	$21,600.00

Masters
Course: Augusta National G.C., Augusta, Ga.
Par: 72 Yardage: 6,925
Last day of event: Sunday, April 9, 1989

Player	Place	Score	Earnings
Nick Faldo	Win	68-73-77-65=283	$200,000.00
Playoff: Beat Scott Hoch with birdie on second extra hole			
Scott Hoch	T-2	69-74-71-69=283	$120,000.00
Ben Crenshaw	T-3	71-72-70-71=284	$64,450.00
Greg Norman	T-3	74-75-68-67=284	$64,450.00
Seve Ballesteros	5	71-72-73-69=285	$44,400.00
Mike Reid	6	72-71-71-72=286	$40,000.00
Jodie Mudd	7	73-76-72-66=287	$37,200.00
Jeff Sluman	T-8	74-72-74-68=288	$32,200.00
Chip Beck	T-8	74-76-70-68=288	$32,200.00
Jose Maria Olazabal	T-8	77-73-70-68=288	$32,200.00

Deposit Guaranty Golf Classic

Course: Hattiesburg C.C., Hattiesburg, Miss.

Par: 70 Yardage: 6,594

Last day of event: Sunday, April 9, 1989

Player	Place	Score	Earnings
Jim Booros	Win	64-69-66=199	$36,000.00
Mike Donald	2	68-65-66=199	$21,600.00
David Peoples	T-3	68-68-65=201	$9,600.00
Lance Ten Broeck	T-3	69-65-67=201	$9,600.00
Robert Thompson	T-3	65-71-65=201	$9,600.00
Fred Funk	T-3	71-65-65=201	$9,600.00
Steve Lowery	T-7	68-69-65=202	$6,233.33
P.H. Horgan III	T-7	69-69-64=202	$6,233.34
Bob Wolcott	T-7	70-66-66=202	$6,233.34
Perry Arthur	10	69-68-67=204	$5,400.00

MCI Heritage Classic

Course: Harbour Town G.L., Hilton Head, S.C.

Par: 71 Yardage: 6,657

Last day of event: Sunday, April 16, 1989

Player	Place	Score	Earnings
Payne Stewart	Win	65-67-67-69=268	$144,000.00
Kenny Perry	2	65-67-70-71=273	$86,400.00
Bernhard Langer	T-3	69-70-67-71=277	$46,400.00
Fred Couples	T-3	71-72-69-65=277	$46,400.00
Craig Stadler	T-5	70-70-70-68=278	$29,200.00
Kenny Knox	T-5	69-70-67-72=278	$29,200.00
Lanny Wadkins	T-5	72-69-70-67=278	$29,200.00
Tom Kite	T-8	72-67-70-70=279	$23,200.00
Mark McCumber	T-8	71-64-69-75=279	$23,200.00
Tim Simpson	T-8	75-68-68-68=279	$23,200.00

Kmart Greater Greensboro Open

Course: Forest Oaks C.C., Greensboro, N.C.

Par: 72 Yardage: 6,984

Last day of event: Sunday, April 23, 1989

Player	Place	Score	Earnings
Ken Green	Win	73-66-66-72=277	$180,000.00
John Huston	2	71-69-67-72=279	$108,000.00
Ed Fiori	3	70-71-73-67=281	$68,000.00
Dave Eichelberger	4	72-67-72-71=282	$48,000.00
Jim Booros	T-5	69-70-72-72=283	$36,500.00
Greg Norman	T-5	73-72-70-68=283	$36,500.00
Mike Sullivan	T-5	70-74-70-69=283	$36,500.00
Kenny Perry	T-8	70-70-72-72=284	$30,000.00
Mark Wiebe	T-8	72-69-71-72=284	$30,000.00
Dave Barr	10	71-69-73-73=286	$27,000.00

Las Vegas Invitational

Course: Las Vegas C.C., Spanish Trail G. & C.C., Desert Inn C.C., Las Vegas, Nev.

Home course / Las Vegas C.C., Par: 72 Yardage: 7,164

Last day of event: Sunday, April 30, 1989

Player	Place	Score	Earnings
Scott Hoch	Win	69-64-68-65-70=336	$225,000.00
Robert Wrenn	T-2	69-66-66-69-66=336	$135,000.00
Craig Stadler	T-3	69-67-65-69-67=337	$72,500.00
Gil Morgan	T-3	70-63-73-64-67=337	$72,500.00
Brad Bryant	T-5	67-68-69-70-64=338	$43,906.25
Russ Cochran	T-5	70-70-66-64-68=338	$43,906.25
Dan Pohl	T-5	69-66-64-68-71=338	$43,906.25

Mark Wiebe	T-5	71-67-66-68-66=338	$43,906.25
Tony Sills	T-9	67-69-69-68-67=340	$33,750.00
Jim Carter	T-9	70-67-65-67-71=340	$33,750.00
Gene Sauers	T-9	65-69-72-66-68=340	$33,750.00

GTE Byron Nelson Classic

Course: TPC at Las Colinas, Irving, Texas

Par: 70 Yardage: 6,767

Last day of event: Sunday, May 7, 1989

Player	Place	Score	Earnings
Jodie Mudd	Win	68-66-66-65=265	$180,000.00
Playoff: Beat Larry Nelson with birdie on first extra hole			
Larry Nelson	T-2	63-68-67-67=265	$108,000.00
Mark O'Meara	3	67-68-65-66=266	$68,000.00
Loren Roberts	4	65-68-66-68=267	$48,000.00
Chris Perry	T-5	65-65-70-68=268	$36,500.00
Wayne Levi	T-5	62-67-68-71=268	$36,500.00
Larry Mize	T-5	67-67-63-71=268	$36,500.00
Ted Schulz	T-8	69-66-66-68=269	$29,000.00
Dave Rummells	T-8	64-68-67-70=269	$29,000.00
Payne Stewart	T-8	64-70-68-67=269	$29,000.00

Memorial Tournament

Course: Muirfield Village G.C., Dubin, Ohio

Par: 72 Yardage: 7,104

Last day of event: Sunday, May 14, 1989

Player	Place	Score	Earnings
Bob Tway	Win	71-69-68-69=277	$160,000.00
Fuzzy Zoeller	2	69-66-72-72=279	$96,000.00
Payne Stewart	3	70-73-73-65=281	$60,440.00
Mark Calcavecchia	T-4	72-68-73-70=283	$40,835.00
Bruce Lietzke	T-4	73-70-69-71=283	$40,835.00
Scott Verplank	T-6	72-73-69-70=284	$32,610.00
Mark O'Meara	T-6	75-68-72-69=284	$32,610.00
Larry Nelson	T-8	72-72-72-69=285	$26,610.00
Ray Floyd	T-8	73-67-73-72=285	$26,610.00
David Frost	T-8	75-71-72-67=285	$26,610.00
Scott Hoch	T-8	72-76-69-68=285	$26,610.00

Southwestern Bell Colonial

Course: Colonial C.C., Fort Worth, Texas

Par: 70 Yardage: 7,096

Last day of event: Sunday, May 21, 1989

Player	Place	Score	Earnings
Ian Baker-Finch	Win	65-70-65-70=270	$180,000.00
David Edwards	2	72-69-68-65=274	$108,000.00
David Frost	T-3	70-66-71-69=276	$58,000.00
Tim Simpson	T-3	71-71-66-68=276	$58,000.00
Nick Price	T-5	70-66-68-73=277	$36,500.00
Lon Hinkle	T-5	74-69-66-68=277	$36,500.00
Curtis Strange	T-5	74-71-66-66=277	$36,500.00
Payne Stewart	T-8	70-70-70-68=278	$28,000.00
Scott Simpson	T-8	71-67-70-70=278	$28,000.00
Isao Aoki	T-8	66-74-66-72=278	$28,000.00
Paul Azinger	T-8	70-74-69-65=278	$28,000.00

BellSouth Atlanta Golf Classic

Course: Atlanta C.C., Atlanta, Ga.

Par: 72 Yardage: 7,007

Last day of event: Sunday, May 28, 1989

Player	Place	Score	Earnings
Scott Simpson	Win	72-68-71-67=278	$162,000.00
Playoff: Beat Bob Tway with par on first extra hole			
Bob Tway	T-2	70-70-71-67=278	$97,200.00
Davis Love III	T-3	71-69-69-70=279	$52,200.00
Jay Don Blake	T-3	66-71-70-72=279	$52,200.00
David Peoples	T-5	70-71-70-69=280	$34,200.00
David Canipe	T-5	71-70-70-69=280	$34,200.00
Wayne Levi	T-7	72-70-72-67=281	$28,050.00
Ray Stewart	T-7	69-68-75-69=281	$28,050.00
Wayne Grady	T-7	70-66-75-70=281	$28,050.00
Ronnie Black	T-10	71-68-72-71=282	$19,950.00
Gene Sauers	T-10	72-70-71-69=282	$19,950.00
Larry Mize	T-10	71-69-69-73=282	$19,950.00
Mike Miles	T-10	71-73-66-72=282	$19,950.00
Don Pooley	T-10	68-72-74-68=282	$19,950.00
Tim Simpson	T-10	75-68-71-68=282	$19,950.00

Kemper Open
Course: TPC at Avenel, Potomac, Md.
Par: 71 Yardage: 6,917
Last day of event: Sunday, June 4, 1989

Player	Place	Score	Earnings
Tom Byrum	Win	66-69-65-68=268	$162,000.00
Billy Ray Brown	T-2	69-67-70-67=273	$67,200.00
Jim Thorpe	T-2	70-69-67-67=273	$67,200.00
Tommy Armour III	T-2	68-70-64-71=273	$67,200.00
Gil Morgan	5	70-71-68-66=275	$36,000.00
Mark McCumber	T-6	69-69-66-72=276	$31,275.00
Andrew Magee	T-6	73-69-65-69=276	$31,275.00
Lon Hinkle	T-8	68-70-68-71=277	$26,100.00
Mike Hulbert	T-8	68-72-67-70=277	$26,100.00
Jay Don Blake	T-8	68-64-75-70=277	$26,100.00

Manufacturers Hanover Westchester Classic
Course: Westchester C.C., Harrison, N.Y.
Par: 71 Yardage: 6,779
Last day of event: Sunday, June 11, 1989

Player	Place	Score	Earnings
Wayne Grady	Win	69-65-71-72=277	$180,000.00
Playoff: Beat Ronnie Black with birdie on first extra hole			
Ronnie Black	T-2	69-71-69-68=277	$108,000.00
Tom Watson	T-3	71-69-70-68=278	$58,000.00
Clarence Rose	T-3	72-69-67-70=278	$58,000.00
Billy Andrade	T-5	69-69-70-71=279	$35,125.00
Fred Couples	T-5	66-72-70-71=279	$35,125.00
Tom Kite	T-5	70-67-72-70=279	$35,125.00
J.C. Snead	T-5	67-68-70-74=279	$35,125.00
Mike Reid	T-9	69-72-68-71=280	$27,000.00
Mark Lye	T-9	66-70-71-73=280	$27,000.00
Nick Price	T-9	74-67-69-70=280	$27,000.00

U.S. Open
Course: Oak Hill C.C., Rochester, N.Y.
Par: 70 Yardage: 6,902
Last day of event: Sunday, June 18, 1989

Player	Place	Score	Earnings
Curtis Strange	Win	71-64-73-70=278	$200,000.00
Chip Beck	T-2	71-69-71-68=279	$67,823.00
Mark McCumber	T-2	70-68-72-69=279	$67,823.00
Ian Woosnam	T-2	70-68-73-68=279	$67,823.00
Brian Claar	5	71-72-68-69=280	$34,345.00
Jumbo Ozaki	T-6	70-71-68-72=281	$28,220.50
Scott Simpson	T-6	67-69-70-75=281	$28,220.50
Peter Jacobsen	8	71-70-71-70=282	$24,307.00
Jose Maria Olazabal	T-9	69-72-70-72=283	$19,968.50
Paul Azinger	T-9	71-72-70-70=283	$19,968.50
Hubert Green	T-9	69-72-74-68=283	$19,968.50
Tom Kite	T-9	67-69-69-78=283	$19,968.50

Canadian Open
Course: Glen Abbey G.C., Oakville, Ontario, Canada
Par: 72 Yardage: 7,102
Last day of event: Sunday, June 25, 1989

Player	Place	Score	Earnings
Steve Jones	Win	67-64-70-70=271	$162,000.00
Mark Calcavecchia	T-2	67-69-68-69=273	$67,200.00
Mike Hulbert	T-2	71-66-72-64=273	$67,200.00
Clark Burroughs	T-2	69-66-64-74=273	$67,200.00
Mark McCumber	T-5	69-69-69-67=274	$32,850.00
Joey Sindelar	T-5	69-72-65-68=274	$32,850.00
Mark Brooks	T-5	67-73-68-66=274	$32,850.00
Dave Barr	T-8	69-69-69-68=275	$27,000.00
Jim Gallagher, Jr.	T-8	64-68-71-72=275	$27,000.00
Bill Sander	T-10	67-69-70-70=276	$18,675.00
Jack Nicklaus	T-10	68-69-69-70=276	$18,675.00
John Adams	T-10	70-70-69-67=276	$18,675.00
Corey Pavin	T-10	70-70-69-67=276	$18,675.00
David Ogrin	T-10	68-69-68-71=276	$18,675.00
Dan Halldorson	T-10	68-70-67-71=276	$18,675.00
Lon Hinkle	T-10	69-68-66-73=276	$18,675.00
Fred Couples	T-10	73-67-69-67=276	$18,675.00

Beatrice Western Open
Course: Butler National G.C., Oak Brook, Ill.
Par: 72 Yardage: 7,097
Last day of event: Monday, July 3, 1989

Player	Place	Score	Earnings
Mark McCumber	Win	68-67-71-69=275	$180,000.00
Playoff: Beat Peter Jacobsen with par on first extra hole			
Peter Jacobsen	2	69-69-69-68=275	$108,000.00
Paul Azinger	3	67-68-72-69=276	$68,000.00
Jim Gallagher, Jr.	4	71-72-70-66=279	$48,000.00
L.T. Broeck	T-5	68-71-72-69=280	$38,000.00
Lee Trevino	T-5	73-71-67-69=280	$38,000.00
Joey Sindelar	T-7	71-71-70-69=281	$30,125.00
Jodie Mudd	T-7	69-73-72-67=281	$30,125.00
Chip Beck	T-7	65-71-75-70=281	$30,125.00
Larry Mize	T-7	69-70-67-75=281	$30,125.00

Canon Greater Hartford Open
Course: TPC of Connecticut, Cromwell, Conn.
Par: 71 Yardage: 6,786
Last day of event: Sunday, July 9, 1989

Player	Place	Score	Earnings
Paul Azinger	Win	65-70-67-65=267	$180,000.00
Wayne Levi	2	69-68-64-67=268	$108,000.00
Dave Rummells	3	70-67-67-66=270	$68,000.00
Mark Calcavecchia	T-4	67-68-67-69=271	$41,333.33
Lee Trevino	T-4	70-64-70-67=271	$41,333.33
Jim Carter	T-4	66-68-71-66=271	$41,333.34
Roger Maltbie	T-7	66-69-69-68=272	$29,100.00

Blaine McCallister	T-7	69-69-67-67=272	$29,100.00
Clark Burroughs	T-7	66-67-70-69=272	$29,100.00
Don Shirey Jr.	T-7	70-67-68-67=272	$29,100.00
Hal Sutton	T-7	67-71-68-66=272	$29,100.00

Anheuser-Busch Golf Classic

Course: Kingsmill G.C., Williamsburg, Va.
Par: 71 Yardage: 6,776
Last day of event: Sunday, July 16, 1989

Player	Place	Score	Earnings
Mike Donald	Win	67-66-70-65=268	$153,000.00

Playoff: Beat Tim Simpson with birdie on fourth extra hole (Hal Sutton eliminated on third hole)

Tim Simpson	T-2	64-70-67-67=268	$74,800.00
Hal Sutton	T-2	64-71-65-68=268	$74,800.00
Mike Hulbert	4	65-66-68-70=269	$40,800.00
Tom Byrum	5	70-70-64-66=270	$34,000.00
Blaine McCallister	T-6	67-70-66-68=271	$28,475.00
Brian Tennyson	T-6	67-71-67-66=271	$28,475.00
Roger Maltbie	T-6	72-63-67-69=271	$28,475.00
Ron Streck	T-9	68-67-69-68=272	$22,950.00
John Mahaffey	T-9	69-67-69-67=272	$22,950.00
Chris Perry	T-9	65-73-65-69=272	$22,950.00

Hardee's Golf Classic

Course: Oakwood C.C., Coal Valley, Ill.
Par: 70 Yardage: 6,606
Last day of event: Sunday, July 23, 1989

Player	Place	Score	Earnings
Curt Byrum	Win	66-67-69-66=268	$126,000.00
Brian Tennyson	T-2	69-69-67-64=269	$61,600.00
Bill Britton	T-2	70-65-69-65=269	$61,600.00
Jim Gallagher, Jr.	T-4	69-68-69-65=271	$30,800.00
Barry Jaeckel	T-4	70-71-67-63=271	$30,800.00
John Adams	T-6	67-68-67-70=272	$24,325.00
Dan Forsman	T-6	74-65-68-65=272	$24,325.00
Tom Sieckmann	T-8	69-68-69-67=273	$19,600.00
Greg Ladehoff	T-8	69-65-69-70=273	$19,600.00
Andrew Magee	T-8	71-69-67-66=273	$19,600.00
Jay Haas	T-8	72-68-67-66=273	$19,600.00

British Open

Course: Royal Troon G.C.,Troon, Ayrshire, Scotland
Par: 72 Yardage: 7,067
Last day of event: Sunday, July 23, 1989

Player	Place	Score	Earnings
Mark Calcavecchia	Win	71-68-68-68=275	$128,000.00

Playoff: Won four-hole aggregate playoff (4-3-3-3=13) with Wayne Grady (4-4-4-4=16) and Greg Norman (3-3-4-x)

Wayne Grady	T-2	68-67-69-71=275	$88,000.00
Greg Norman	T-2	69-70-72-64=275	$88,000.00
Tom Watson	4	69-68-68-72=277	$64,000.00
Jodie Mudd	5	73-67-68-70=278	$48,000.00
Fred Couples	T-6	68-71-68-72=279	$41,600.00
David Feherty	T-6	71-67-69-72=279	$41,600.00
Paul Azinger	T-8	68-73-67-72=280	$33,600.00
Payne Stewart	T-8	72-65-69-74=280	$33,600.00
Eduardo Romero	T-8	68-70-75-67=280	$33,600.00

Buick Open

Course: Warwick Hills C.C., Grand Blanc, Mich.
Par: 72 Yardage: 7,014
Last day of event: Sunday, July 30, 1989

Player	Place	Score	Earnings
Leonard Thompson	Win	65-71-69-68=273	$180,000.00
Doug Tewell	T-2	69-66-70-69=274	$74,667.00
Billy Andrade	T-2	67-71-69-67=274	$74,667.00
Payne Stewart	T-2	71-67-64-72=274	$74,667.00
Mark O'Meara	T-5	66-70-71-68=275	$36,500.00
Hal Sutton	T-5	67-68-68-72=275	$36,500.00
Bob Eastwood	T-5	73-66-66-70=275	$36,500.00
Tom Kite	T-8	69-70-71-66=276	$29,000.00
Gil Morgan	T-8	71-70-67-68=276	$29,000.00
Wayne Grady	T-8	67-69-72-68=276	$29,000.00

Federal Express St. Jude Classic

Course: TPC at Southwind, Germantown, Tenn.
Par: 71 Yardage: 7,006
Last day of event: Sunday, August 6, 1989

Player	Place	Score	Earnings
John Mahaffey	Win	70-71-66-65=272	$180,000.00
Bob Tway	2	66-72-68-69=275	$66,000.00
Bernhard Langer	T-3	67-69-68-71=275	$66,000.00
Bob Gilder	T-3	68-66-70-71=275	$66,000.00
Hubert Green	T-3	70-69-73-63=275	$66,000.00
Jay Haas	T-6	70-70-68-69=277	$32,375.00
Mike Donald	T-6	70-67-69-71=277	$32,375.00
Jim Hallet	T-6	70-70-71-66=277	$32,375.00
Rick Fehr	T-6	71-71-69-66=277	$32,375.00
Bob Lohr	10	69-73-72-64=278	$27,000.00

PGA Championship

Course: Kemper Lakes G.C., Hawthorn Woods, Ill.
Par: 72 Yardage: 7,217
Last day of event: Sunday, August 13, 1989

Player	Place	Score	Earnings
Payne Stewart	Win	74-66-69-67=276	$200,000.00
Curtis Strange	T-2	70-68-70-69=277	$83,333.33
Mike Reid	T-2	66-67-70-74=277	$83,333.33
Andy Bean	T-2	70-67-74-66=277	$83,333.34
Dave Rummells	5	68-69-69-72=278	$45,000.00
Ian Woosnam	6	68-70-70-71=279	$40,000.00
Scott Hoch	T-7	69-69-69-73=280	$36,250.00
Craig Stadler	T-7	71-64-72-73=280	$36,250.00
Nick Faldo	T-9	70-73-69-69=281	$30,000.00
Tom Watson	T-9	67-69-74-71=281	$30,000.00
Ed Fiori	T-9	70-67-75-69=281	$30,000.00

The International

Course: Castle Pine G.C., Castle Rock, Colo. (Stableford format)
Par: 72 Yardage: 7,559
Last day of event: Sunday, August 20, 1989

Player	Place	Score	Earnings
Greg Norman	Win	5-4-11-13=20	$180,000.00
Clarence Rose	2	-2-8-6-11=23	$108,000.00
Chip Beck	3	8-3-11-9=31	$68,000.00
Mark Lye	T-4	5-2-9-8=24	$44,000.00
Billy Andrade	T-4	7-3-13-8=31	$44,000.00
David Frost	6	7-4-7-7=25	$36,000.00

Jim Carter	T-7	7-4-10-6=27	$32,250.00
Dan Forsman	T-7	9-2-12-6=29	$32,250.00
Jack Nicklaus	9	8-5-7-5=25 $29,000.00	
Ray Stewart	T-10	3-7-9-4=23 $26,000.00	
Mac O'Grady	T-10	8-5-7-4=24 $26,000.00	

NEC World Series of Golf
Course: Firestone C.C. (South), Akron, Ohio
Par: 70 Yardage: 7,149
Last day of event: Sunday, August 27, 1989

Player	Place	Score	Earnings
David Frost	Win	70-68-69-69=276	$180,000.00
Ben Crenshaw	2	64-72-72-68=276	$108,000.00
Payne Stewart	3	72-67-68-71=278	$68,000.00
Greg Norman	4	73-65-70-71=279	$48,000.00
Mike Reid	T-5	68-71-70-71=280	$38,000.00
Larry Mize	T-5	73-66-70-71=280	$38,000.00
Paul Azinger	7	72-68-67-74=281	$33,500.00
Bill Glasson	T-8	69-74-73-66=282	$29,166.67
Mark Calcavecchia	T-8	71-67-74-70=282	$29,166.67
Steve Jones	T-8	76-63-69-74=282	$29,166.66

Chattanooga Classic
Course: ValleyBrook C.C., Hixson, Tenn.
Par: 70 Yardage: 6,641
Last day of event: Sunday, August 27, 1989

Player	Place	Score	Earnings
Stan Utley	Win	69-66-64-64=263	$90,000.00
Ray Stewart	2	71-63-67-63=264	$54,000.00
Bobby Wadkins	T-3	67-67-65-66=265	$29,000.00
Don Shirey Jr.	T-3	65-65-68-67=265	$29,000.00
Russ Cochran	T-5	66-67-67-66=266	$17,562.50
John Inman	T-5	66-68-67-65=266	$17,562.50
Richard Zokol	T-5	68-67-65-66=266	$17,562.50
Bob Estes	T-5	69-65-66-66=266	$17,562.50
Fred Funk	T-9	68-64-67-68=267	$12,500.00
Steve Lowery	T-9	66-69-67-65=267	$12,500.00
Ted Schulz	T-9	66-63-70-68=267	$12,500.00
Lennie Clements	T-9	70-65-67-65=267	$12,500.00
Kenny Perry	T-9	70-67-66-64=267	$12,500.00

Greater Milwaukee Open
Course: Tuckaway C.C., Franklin, Wis.
Par: 72 Yardage: 7,030
Last day of event: Sunday, September 3, 1989

Player	Place	Score	Earnings
Greg Norman	Win	64-69-66-70=269	$144,000.00
Andy Bean	2	70-69-67-66=272	$86,400.00
Ted Schulz	T-3	68-69-68-68=273	$46,400.00
Mark Lye	T-3	67-66-72-68=273	$46,400.00
Wayne Levi	T-5	69-66-68-71=274	$30,400.00
Tom Purtzer	T-5	72-67-66-69=274	$30,400.00
Larry Mize	T-7	68-67-70-70=275	$21,657.14
Joey Sindelar	T-7	70-69-67-69=275	$21,657.14
Steve Pate	T-7	65-71-70-69=275	$21,657.15
David Frost	T-7	67-67-70-71=275	$21,657.14
Duffy Waldorf	T-7	68-67-69-71=275	$21,657.14
Loren Roberts	T-7	69-67-68-71=275	$21,657.14
Jeff Sluman	T-7	70-71-66-68=275	$21,657.15

B.C. Open
Course: En-Joie G.C., Endicott, N.Y.
Par: 71 Yardage: 6,966
Last day of event: Sunday, September 10, 1989

Player	Place	Score	Earnings
Mike Hulbert	Win	69-66-68-65=268	$90,000.00
Playoff: Beat Bob Estes with par on first extra hole			
Bob Estes	2	66-68-66-68=268	$54,000.00
Steve Elkington	3	68-72-67-62=269	$34,000.00
Fuzzy Zoeller	T-4	69-67-66-69=271	$22,000.00
Dave Eichelberger	T-4	67-67-67-70=271	$22,000.00
Wayne Levi	6	69-73-64-66=272	$18,000.00
Gil Morgan	7	67-67-71-68=273	$36,750.00
Nolan Henke	8	69-67-73-65=274	$15,500.00
Jeff Sluman	T-9	69-68-69-69=275	$11,571.43
Steve Lowery	T-9	69-69-70-67=275	$11,571.43
Barry Jaeckel	T-9	70-67-68-70=275	$11,571.43
Tom Pernice, Jr.	T-9	71-68-67-69=275	$11,571.43
Mark Hayes	T-9	71-68-68-68=275	$11,571.43
Mark Lye	T-9	69-69-72-65=275	$11,571.43
Jim Booros	T-9	70-65-68-72=275	$11,571.42

Bank of Boston Classic
Course: Pleasant Valley C.C., Sutton, Mass.
Par: 71 Yardage: 7,110
Last day of event: Sunday, September 17, 1989

Player	Place	Score	Earnings
Blaine McCallister	Win	67-67-71-66=271	$126,000.00
Brad Faxon	2	66-67-70-69=272	$75,600.00
Mark Calcavecchia	T-3	67-68-69-69=273	$36,400.00
Chris Perry	T-3	68-69-70-66=273	$36,400.00
Don Pooley	T-3	66-65-72-70=273	$36,400.00
Fuzzy Zoeller	T-6	68-67-70-69=274	$22,662.50
Mark Lye	T-6	68-71-66-69=274	$22,662.50
Steve Jones	T-6	68-70-71-65=274	$22,662.50
Nick Price	T-6	70-68-74-62=274	$22,662.50
Webb Heintzelman	T-10	68-69-69-69=275	$18,200.00
Wayne Grady	T-10	69-70-71-65=275	$18,200.00

Southern Open
Course: Green Island C.C., Columbus, Ga.
Par: 70 Yardage: 6,791
Last day of event: Sunday, September 24, 1989

Player	Place	Score	Earnings
Ted Schulz	Win	66-66-68-66=266	$72,000.00
Jay Haas	T-2	68-67-64-68=267	$35,200.00
Tim Simpson	T-2	66-73-65-63=267	$35,200.00
Bob Tway	T-4	69-69-65-67=270	$16,533.34
Lance Ten Broeck	T-4	70-66-65-69=270	$16,533.33
Larry Rinker	T-4	70-68-64-68=270	$16,533.33
Steve Pate	T-7	64-68-70-69=271	$12,466.67
Andrew Magee	T-7	66-70-66-69=271	$12,466.67
Kenny Knox	T-7	65-68-67-71=271	$12,466.66
Mike Donald	T-10	68-70-66-68=272	$10,400.00
Dave Rummells	T-10	68-64-67-73=272	$10,400.00

Centel Classic

Course: Killearn C.C. & Inn, Tallahassee, Fla.
Par: 72 Yardage: 7,098
Last day of event: Sunday, October 1, 1989

Player	Place	Score	Earnings
Bill Britton	Win	71-66-63=200	$135,000.00
Ronnie Black	2	67-67-70=204	$81,000.00
Gary Hallberg	3	68-71-66=205	$51,000.00
Mike Reid	T-4	69-68-69=206	$31,000.00
Bill Buttner	T-4	69-66-71=206	$31,000.00
Tom Pernice, Jr.	T-4	68-65-73=206	$31,000.00
Peter Jacobsen	T-7	69-69-69=207	$20,303.57
Kenny Knox	T-7	69-69-69=207	$20,303.57
Tom Byrum	T-7	68-69-70=207	$20,303.57
Tim Simpson	T-7	68-69-70=207	$20,303.57
Tim Norris	T-7	70-68-69=207	$20,303.57
Leonard Thompson	T-7	72-70-65=207	$20,303.58
Hale Irwin	T-7	67-73-67=207	$20,303.57

Texas Open

Course: Oak Hill C.C., San Antonio, Texas
Par: 70 Yardage: 6,576
Last day of event: Sunday, October 8, 1989

Player	Place	Score	Earnings
Donnie Hammond	Win	65-64-65-64=258	$108,000.00
Paul Azinger	2	64-62-70-69=265	$64,800.00
Mark Wiebe	T-3	62-68-70-67=267	$31,200.00
Bob Lohr	T-3	66-64-66-71=267	$31,200.00
Duffy Waldorf	T-3	67-63-66-71=267	$31,200.00
Jay Don Blake	T-6	67-65-68-68=268	$20,100.00
Bill Britton	T-6	67-65-67-69=268	$20,100.00
Lanny Wadkins	T-6	62-68-68-70=268	$20,100.00
Hal Sutton	T-9	66-66-69-68=269	$15,000.00
Davis Love III	T-9	67-68-65-69=269	$15,000.00
Bob Eastwood	T-9	66-68-65-70=269	$15,000.00
Don Pooley	T-9	64-66-67-72=269	$15,000.00
Loren Roberts	T-9	66-64-72-67=269	$15,000.00

Walt Disney World/Oldsmobile Classic

Course: Walt Disney (Magnolia, Palm), Lake Buena Vista C.C., Lake Buena Vista, Fla.
Home course / Magnolia, Par: 72 Yardage: 7,190
Last day of event: Saturday, October 21, 1989

Player	Place	Score	Earnings
Tim Simpson	Win	65-67-70-70=272	$144,000.00
Donnie Hammond	2	72-65-65-71=273	$86,400.00
Fred Couples	T-3	70-65-69-70=274	$41,600.00
Paul Azinger	T-3	65-70-71-68=274	$41,600.00
Kenny Knox	T-3	70-65-71-68=274	$41,600.00
Jay Haas	T-6	71-66-70-68=275	$27,800.00
Ted Schulz	T-6	65-69-72-69=275	$27,800.00
Bob Gilder	T-8	70-65-69-72=276	$24,000.00
Curtis Strange	T-8	72-66-72-66=276	$24,000.00
Mike Hulbert	T-10	68-69-69-71=277	$19,200.00
Nick Price	T-10	72-69-67-69=277	$19,200.00
Jim Hallet	T-10	72-69-69-67=277	$19,200.00
Roger Maltbie	T-10	71-63-74-69=277	$19,200.00

Nabisco Championships

Course: Harbour Town G.L., Hilton Head, S.C.
Par: 71 Yardage: 6,657
Last day of event: Sunday, October 29, 1989

Player	Place	Score	Earnings
Tom Kite	Win	69-65-74-68=276	$450,000.00

Playoff: Beat Payne Stewart with par on second extra hole

Player	Place	Score	Earnings
Payne Stewart	2	69-70-71-66=276	$270,000.00
Wayne Levi	T-3	71-72-63-72=278	$146,250.00
Paul Azinger	T-3	71-73-67-67=278	$146,250.00
Donnie Hammond	5	65-73-69-72=279	$100,000.00
Mark O'Meara	6	67-71-71-71=280	$90,000.00
Scott Hoch	T-7	71-71-68-71=281	$82,500.00
Fred Couples	T-7	68-74-67-72=281	$82,500.00
Chip Beck	T-9	71-68-73-71=283	$73,000.00
Mark Calcavecchia	T-9	70-75-68-70=283	$73,000.00

Nabisco year-end bonus

Player	Place	Earnings
Tom Kite	Win	$175,000.00
Payne Stewart	2	$106,000.00
Paul Azinger	3	$68,000.00
Greg Norman	4	$47,000.00
Mark Calcavecchia	5	$40,000.00
Tim Simpson	6	$36,000.00
Curtis Strange	7	$34,000.00
Steve Jones	8	$32,000.00
Chip Beck	9	$30,000.00
Scott Hoch	10	$28,000.00

1990

This year will be remembered for Shoal Creek, the PGA Championship venue in Birmingham, Ala., that drew outrage for its exclusionary membership policies—an episode that prompted the PGA Tour to require tournament venues be free of discriminatory membership rules. (Addressing criticism of Shoal Creek's all-white membership, club founder Hall Thompson noted that Shoal Creek had Jewish and women members, adding: "I think we've said we don't discriminate in any other area except blacks." Thompson said members were welcome to bring black guests to the club, but when asked if that had ever happened, he responded: "No. That's just not done in Birmingham.") Pressure mounted with the defection of several corporate sponsors, and the controversy was diffused when Thompson apologized and offered an honorary membership to Louis Willie, a local black businessman. Wayne Grady won the tournament by three shots over Fred Couples, who bogeyed four of the last six holes. With a par on the second hole of sudden death against Raymond Floyd, Nick Faldo successfully defended his 1989 title at the Masters. Trailing Mike Donald by four shots after 54 holes at the U.S. Open, Hale Irwin, age 45, posted a final-round 67—punctuated by a 45-foot birdie on the 72nd hole—to catch Donald and force a playoff at Medinah. Both players shot 74 on Monday, and Irwin claimed his third national championship with a birdie on the first hole of sudden death. Nick Faldo dismantled the Old Course at St. Andrews, shooting 18-under-par 288 and winning the British Open by five shots over Payne Stewart and Mark McNulty.

Infiniti Tournament of Champions

Course: La Costa C.C., Carlsbad, Calif.
Par: 72 Yardage: 7,022
Last day of event: Sunday, January 7, 1990

Player	Place	Score	Earnings
Paul Azinger	Win	66-68-69-69=272	$135,000.00
Ian Baker-Finch	2	66-67-72-68=273	$82,000.00
Mark O'Meara	3	69-73-65-69=276	$52,000.00
Wayne Grady	4	69-68-72-69=278	$36,800.00
Scott Hoch	T-5	69-68-71-71=279	$29,750.00
Greg Norman	T-5	66-72-71-70=279	$29,750.00
Curtis Strange	T-7	71-73-70-67=281	$24,666.67

Mike Hulbert	T-7	72-68-73-68=281	$24,666.67
Mark Calcavecchia	T-7	70-68-68-75=281	$24,666.66
Mark McCumber	T-10	69-73-69-73=284	$19,625.00
Tim Simpson	T-10	69-73-71-71=284	$19,625.00
Bob Tway	T-10	71-73-68-72=284	$19,625.00
Payne Stewart	T-10	67-75-69-73=284	$19,625.00

Northern Telecom Tucson Open

Course: TPC At StarPass, Randolph Park Municipal, Tucson, Ariz.
Par: 72 Yardage: 7,010
Last day of event: Sunday, January 14, 1990

Player	Place	Score	Earnings
Robert Gamez	Win	65-66-69-70=270	$162,000.00
Mark Calcavecchia	T-2	68-67-70-69=274	$79,200.00
Jay Haas	T-2	66-64-72-72=274	$79,200.00
Corey Pavin	T-4	67-70-69-69=275	$35,437.50
Dan Forsman	T-4	70-67-69-69=275	$35,437.50
Davis Love III	T-4	68-65-73-69=275	$35,437.50
Bill Sander	T-4	68-69-73-65=275	$35,437.50
Joel Edwards	T-8	67-71-71-67=276	$27,000.00
David Frost	T-8	70-60-71-75=276	$27,000.00
Mike Reid	10	67-71-68-71=277	$24,300.00

Bob Hope Chrysler Classic

Course: PGA West/Palmer, Bermuda Dunes C.C., Indian Wells C.C., Tamarisk C.C.
Home course / PGA West, Par: 72 Yardage: 6,924
Last day of event: Sunday, January 21, 1990

Player	Place	Score	Earnings
Peter Jacobsen	Win	67-66-69-66-71=339	$180,000.00
Scott Simpson	T-2	68-69-67-68-68=340	$88,000.00
Brian Tennyson	T-2	73-68-66-67-66=340	$88,000.00
Tom Kite	T-4	70-69-64-69-69=341	$41,333.33
Ted Schulz	T-4	70-66-69-67-69=341	$41,333.33
Tim Simpson	T-4	70-70-67-68-66=341	$41,333.34
Bob Tway	T-7	67-68-69-69-69=342	$32,250.00
Davis Love III	T-7	67-72-67-69-67=342	$32,250.00
Andrew Magee	T-9	68-69-68-69-69=343	$26,000.00
Scott Hoch	T-9	68-69-69-68-69=343	$26,000.00
Bill Glasson	T-9	67-71-71-65-69=343	$26,000.00
Bobby Wadkins	T-9	71-70-65-71-66=343	$26,000.00

Phoenix Open

Course: TPC of Scottsdale, Scottsdale, Ariz.
Par: 71 Yardage: 6,992
Last day of event: Sunday, January 28, 1990

Player	Place	Score	Earnings
Tommy Armour III	Win	65-67-67-68=267	$162,000.00
Jim Thorpe	2	69-69-66-68=272	$97,200.00
Billy Ray Brown	T-3	69-66-70-69=274	$52,200.00
Fred Couples	T-3	75-66-66-67=274	$52,200.00
Bob Tway	T-5	71-67-71-66=275	$32,850.00
Brian Tennyson	T-5	70-67-65-73=275	$32,850.00
Billy Mayfair	T-5	73-66-70-66=275	$32,850.00
Paul Azinger	T-8	69-67-71-70=277	$27,000.00
Jay Delsing	T-8	69-67-68-73=277	$27,000.00
Sandy Lyle	T-10	67-71-67-73=278	$22,500.00
Clark Burroughs	T-10	68-67-70-73=278	$22,500.00
Dave Barr	T-10	67-68-68-75=278	$22,500.00

A

T&T Pebble Beach Pro-Am

Courses: Pebble Beach G.L., Spyglass Hill G.C., Cypress Point C.C., Pebble Beach, Calif.
Home Course / Pebble Beach G.L., Par: 72 Yardage: 6,815
Last day of event: Sunday, February 4, 1990

Player	Place	Score	Earnings
Mark O'Meara	Win	67-73-69-72=281	$180,000.00
Kenny Perry	2	73-71-69-70=283	$108,000.00
Payne Stewart	T-3	66-71-74-73=284	$58,000.00
Tom Kite	T-3	69-69-75-71=284	$58,000.00
David Frost	5	74-71-73-67=285	$40,000.00
Mark Calcavecchia	T-6	69-71-74-72=286	$34,750.00
Richard Zokol	T-6	75-71-71-69=286	$34,750.00
Rick Fehr	T-8	70-72-73-72=287	$29,000.00
Brad Faxon	T-8	75-69-74-69=287	$29,000.00
Rocco Mediate	T-8	69-68-73-77=287	$29,000.00

Hawaiian Open

Course: Waialae C.C., Honolulu, Ha.
Par: 72 Yardage: 6,975
Last day of event: Sunday, February 11, 1990

Player	Place	Score	Earnings
David Ishii	Win	72-67-68-72=279	$180,000.00
Paul Azinger	2	68-71-71-70=280	$108,000.00
Craig Stadler	T-3	71-67-72-71=281	$52,000.00
Jodie Mudd	T-3	72-72-68-69=281	$52,000.00
Clark Dennis	T-3	70-73-68-70=281	$52,000.00
Grant Waite	T-6	72-67-72-71=282	$30,250.00
Tim Simpson	T-6	72-69-71-70=282	$30,250.00
Billy Ray Brown	T-6	72-71-69-70=282	$30,250.00
Jim Hallet	T-6	69-73-70-70=282	$30,250.00
Peter Persons	T-6	72-68-73-69=282	$30,250.00
Billy Mayfair	T-6	74-71-67-70=282	$30,250.00

Shearson Lehman Hutton Open

Course: Torrey Pines (South), Torrey Pines (North), San Diego, Calif.
Home Course -Par: 72 Yardage: 7,021
Last day of event: Sunday, February 18, 1990

Player	Place	Score	Earnings
Dan Forsman	Win	68-63-72-72=275	$162,000.00
Tommy Armour III	2	66-66-73-72=277	$97,200.00
Tom Byrum	3	70-71-69-68=278	$61,200.00
Craig Stadler	T-4	67-70-70-72=279	$32,625.00
Kirk Triplett	T-4	71-66-72-70=279	$32,625.00
Steve Elkington	T-4	72-69-70-68=279	$32,625.00
Mark O'Meara	T-4	66-74-67-72=279	$32,625.00
Fred Couples	T-4	68-68-74-69=279	$32,625.00
Tom Sieckmann	T-4	69-64-76-70=279	$32,625.00
Bob Estes	10	67-71-74-68=280	$24,300.00

Nissan Los Angeles Open

Course: Riviera C.C., Pacific Palisades, Calif.
Par: 71 Yardage: 7,029
Last day of event: Sunday, February 25, 1990

Player	Place	Score	Earnings
Fred Couples	Win	68-67-62-69=266	$180,000.00
Gil Morgan	2	67-67-65-70=269	$108,000.00
Peter Jacobsen	T-3	65-69-70-66=270	$58,000.00
Rocco Mediate	T-3	65-67-67-71=270	$58,000.00
Hal Sutton	T-5	68-67-67-69=271	$38,000.00
Tom Kite	T-5	67-70-69-65=271	$38,000.00
Tony Sills	T-7	70-64-70-68=272	$33,500.00

Mark Calcavecchia	T-7	70-68-69-65=272	$28,000.00
John Mahaffey	T-9	69-69-67-68=273	$28,000.00
Tom Sieckmann	T-10	68-68-68-69=273	$28,000.00
Craig Stadler	T-10	68-66-72-67=273	$28,000.00

Doral-Ryder Open

Course: Doral C.C. (Blue), Miami, Fla.
Par: 72 Yardage: 6,939
Last day of event: Sunday, March 4, 1990

Player	Place	Score	Earnings
Greg Norman	Win	68-73-70-62=273	$252,000.00

Playoff: Beat Paul Azinger, Mark Calcavecchia and Tim Simpson with eagle on first extra hole

Paul Azinger	T-2	68-66-70-69=273	$104,533.33
Tim Simpson	T-2	70-71-66-66=273	$104,533.33
Mark Calcavecchia	T-2	68-67-73-65=273	$104,533.34
Tom Purtzer	T-5	67-70-70-68=275	$53,200.00
Mike Reid	T-5	67-72-66-70=275	$53,200.00
Fred Couples	7	67-67-70-72=276	$46,900.00
Ken Green	T-8	68-71-70-68=277	$39,200.00
Wayne Grady	T-8	69-71-71-66=277	$39,200.00
Peter Jacobsen	T-8	68-72-72-65=277	$39,200.00
David Edwards	T-8	69-75-68-65=277	$39,200.00

Honda Classic

Course: TPC at Eagle Trace, Coral Springs, Fla.
Par: 72 Yardage: 7,030
Last day of event: Sunday, March 11, 1990

Player	Place	Score	Earnings
John Huston	Win	68-73-70-71=282	$180,000.00
Mark Calcavecchia	2	70-76-69-69=284	$108,000.00
Mark Brooks	T-3	71-71-70-73=285	$48,000.00
Ray Floyd	T-3	73-72-70-70=285	$48,000.00
Bruce Lietzke	T-3	75-69-73-68=285	$48,000.00
Billy Ray Brown	T-3	72-76-68-69=285	$48,000.00
Dave Rummells	7	75-73-69-70=287	$33,500.00
Tom Watson	T-8	73-69-73-73=288	$27,000.00
Ken Green	T-8	75-71-70-72=288	$27,000.00
George Burns	T-8	75-71-71-71=288	$27,000.00
Bob Eastwood	T-8	76-67-73-72=288	$27,000.00
Brad Bryant	T-8	73-71-77-67=288	$27,000.00

The Players Championship

Course: TPC at Sawgrass, Ponte Vedra Beach, Fla.
Par: 72 Yardage: 6,857
Last day of event: Sunday, March 18, 1990

Player	Place	Score	Earnings
Jodie Mudd	Win	67-72-70-69=278	$270,000.00
Mark Calcavecchia	2	67-75-68-69=279	$162,000.00
Tom Purtzer	T-3	71-73-69-71=284	$87,000.00
Steve Jones	T-3	75-71-69-69=284	$87,000.00
Tom Kite	T-5	72-70-70-73=285	$52,687.50
Billy Ray Brown	T-5	73-72-69-71=285	$52,687.50
Hale Irwin	T-5	70-68-74-73=285	$52,687.50
Ken Green	T-5	71-69-70-75=285	$52,687.50
Andy Bean	T-9	73-68-72-73=286	$42,000.00
Mark McCumber	T-9	73-72-73-68=286	$42,000.00

The Nestle Invitational

Course: Bay Hill Club, Orlando, Fla.
Par: 72 Yardage: 7,114
Last day of event: Sunday, March 25, 1990

Player	Place	Score	Earnings
Robert Gamez	Win	71-69-68-66=274	$162,000.00
Greg Norman	2	74-68-65-68=275	$97,200.00
Larry Mize	3	71-70-67-68=276	$61,200.00
Scott Hoch	T-4	69-68-70-70=277	$37,200.00
Curtis Strange	T-4	69-70-68-70=277	$37,200.00
Fulton Allem	T-4	74-69-65-69=277	$37,200.00
Paul Azinger	7	70-70-70-68=278	$30,150.00
Corey Pavin	T-8	69-69-72-70=280	$27,000.00
Nick Price	T-8	72-68-72-68=280	$27,000.00
Tom Watson	T-10	71-68-72-70=281	$22,500.00
Jose Maria Olazabal	T-10	68-73-71-69=281	$22,500.00
Mark O'Meara	T-10	70-73-74-64=281	$22,500.00

Independent Insurance Agent Open

Course: TPC at The Woodlands, The Woodlands, Texas
Par: 72 Yardage: 7,042
Last day of event: Sunday, April 1, 1990

Player	Place	Score	Earnings
Tony Sills	Win	67-72-65=204	$180,000.00

Playoff: Beat Gil Morgan with par on first extra hole

Gil Morgan	T-2	67-70-67=204	$108,000.00
Fred Couples	T-3	67-69-69=205	$39,062.50
Scott Simpson	T-3	68-68-69=205	$39,062.50
Larry Mize	T-3	68-69-68=205	$39,062.50
Seve Ballesteros	T-3	69-68-68=205	$39,062.50
Ian Woosnam	T-3	69-69-67=205	$39,062.50
Bruce Lietzke	T-3	67-70-68=205	$39,062.50
David Peoples	T-3	67-66-72=205	$39,062.50
Brad Bryant	T-3	68-73-64=205	$39,062.50

Masters

Course: Augusta National G.C., Augusta, Ga.
Par: 72 Yardage: 6,925
Last day of event: Sunday, April 8, 1990

Player	Place	Score	Earnings
Nick Faldo	Win	71-72-66-69=278	$225,000.00

Playoff: Beat Ray Floyd with par on second extra hole

Ray Floyd	T-2	70-68-68-72=278	$135,000.00
Lanny Wadkins	T-3	72-73-70-68=283	$72,500.00
John Huston	T-3	66-74-68-75=283	$72,500.00
Fred Couples	5	74-69-72-69=284	$50,000.00
Jack Nicklaus	6	72-70-69-74=285	$45,000.00
Curtis Strange	T-7	70-73-71-72=286	$35,150.00
Bill Britton	T-7	68-74-71-73=286	$35,150.00
Bernhard Langer	T-7	70-73-69-74=286	$35,150.00
Scott Simpson	T-7	74-71-68-73=286	$35,150.00
Seve Ballesteros	T-7	74-73-68-71=286	$35,150.00
Tom Watson	T-7	77-71-67-71=286	$35,150.00

Deposit Guaranty Classic

Course: Hattiesburg C.C., Hattiesburg, Miss.
Par: 70 Yardage: 6,594
Last day of event: Sunday, April 8, 1990

Player	Place	Score	Earnings
Gene Sauers	Win	67-65-68-68=268	$54,000.00
Jack Ferenz	T-2	71-64-68-67=270	$32,400.00

David Ogrin	T-3	67-70-69-65=271	$17,400.00
Mike McCullough	T-3	68-67-70-66=271	$17,400.00
Lee Janzen	5	69-64-71-68=272	$12,000.00
Nolan Henke	T-6	68-69-68-68=273	$9,712.50
Ray Stewart	T-6	67-70-68-68=273	$9,712.50
Jim Booros	T-6	69-68-66-70=273	$9,712.50
Tommy Moore	T-6	66-67-71-69=273	$9,712.50
Larry Silveira	T-10	68-69-69-68=274	$7,500.00
Mike Smith	T-10	67-70-68-69=274	$7,500.00
Neal Lancaster	T-10	72-68-68-66=274	$7,500.00

MCI Heritage Classic
Course: Harbour Town G.L., Hilton Head, S.C.
Par: 71 Yardage: 6,657
Last day of event: Sunday, April 15, 1990

Player	Place	Score	Earnings
Payne Stewart	Win	70-69-66-71=276	$180,000.00
Playoff: Beat Steve Jones and Larry Mize with birdie on second extra hole			
Larry Mize	T-2	71-69-70-66=276	$88,000.00
Steve Jones	T-2	68-73-66-69=276	$88,000.00
Greg Norman	T-4	70-70-67-70=277	$44,000.00
Steve Pate	T-4	67-69-73-68=277	$44,000.00
Andy Bean	6	74-68-69-67=278	$36,000.00
Loren Roberts	T-7	71-70-67-71=279	$32,250.00
Gene Sauers	T-7	66-72-72-69=279	$32,250.00
Bob Estes	T-9	71-70-70-69=280	$23,142.86
Tom Kite	T-9	68-70-72-70=280	$23,142.85
Calvin Peete	T-9	70-66-72-72=280	$23,142.85
Lanny Wadkins	T-9	70-71-73-66=280	$23,142.86
David Edwards	T-9	71-73-71-65=280	$23,142.86
Hal Sutton	T-9	72-67-73-68=280	$23,142.86
Chip Beck	T-9	74-70-68-68=280	$23,142.86

Kmart Greater Greensboro Open
Course: Forest Oaks C.C., Greensboro, N.C.
Par: 72 Yardage: 6,984
Last day of event: Sunday, April 22, 1990

Player	Place	Score	Earnings
Steve Elkington	Win	74-71-71-66=282	$225,000.00
Jeff Sluman	T-2	71-74-68-71=284	$110,000.00
Mike Reid	T-2	72-70-67-75=284	$110,000.00
Fred Couples	T-4	71-70-71-73=285	$51,666.66
Paul Azinger	T-4	72-73-73-67=285	$51,666.67
Mike Hulbert	T-4	73-70-73-69=285	$51,666.67
Chip Beck	T-7	72-72-70-72=286	$38,958.33
John Huston	T-7	74-69-71-72=286	$38,958.33
Joey Sindelar	T-7	70-73-75-68=286	$38,958.34
Bill Glasson	T-10	72-71-72-72=287	$25,138.89
Lanny Wadkins	T-10	71-73-73-70=287	$25,138.89
Jim Gallagher, Jr.	T-10	70-70-74-73=287	$25,138.89
Phil Blackmar	T-10	70-71-74-72=287	$25,138.89
Nick Price	T-10	71-71-71-74=287	$25,138.88
Jay Delsing	T-10	74-73-71-69=287	$25,138.89
Lennie Clements	T-10	69-74-75-69=287	$25,138.89
David Edwards	T-10	70-75-72-70=287	$25,138.89
Donnie Hammond	T-10	71-71-76-69=287	$25,138.89

USF&G Classic
Course: English Turn G. & C.C., New Orleans, La.
Par: 72 Yardage: 7,106
Last day of event: Sunday, April 29, 1990

Player	Place	Score	Earnings
David Frost	Win	71-70-66-69=276	$180,000.00

Greg Norman	2	73-68-71-65=277	$108,000.00
Russ Cochran	3	72-69-71-67=279	$68,000.00
Brian Tennyson	4	69-70-69-75=283	$48,000.00
Jay Delsing	5	73-69-73-69=284	$40,000.00
Tim Simpson	6	73-69-71-72=285	$36,000.00
David Edwards	T-7	71-71-72-72=286	$29,100.00
Brad Bryant	T-7	70-73-73-70=286	$29,100.00
Tommy Moore	T-7	73-71-69-73=286	$29,100.00
Mike Smith	T-7	73-72-69-72=286	$29,100.00
Hal Sutton	T-7	74-69-74-69=286	$29,100.00

GTE Byron Nelson Classic
Course: TPC at Las Colinas, Irving, Texas
Par: 70 Yardage: 6,767
Last day of event: Sunday, May 6, 1990

Player	Place	Score	Earnings
Payne Stewart	Win	67-68-67=202	$180,000.00
Lanny Wadkins	2	72-67-65=204	$108,000.00
Mark Calcavecchia	T-3	69-69-69=207	$58,000.00
Bruce Lietzke	T-3	71-68-68=207	$58,000.00
Andrew Magee	T-5	69-68-71=208	$38,000.00
Tim Simpson	T-5	72-66-70=208	$38,000.00
Tom Watson	T-7	71-69-69=209	$30,125.00
Fred Funk	T-7	71-71-67=209	$30,125.00
Tom Purtzer	T-7	70-67-72=209	$30,125.00
Greg Norman	T-7	73-67-69=209	$30,125.00

Memorial Tournament
Course: Muirfield Village G.C., Dubin, Ohio
Par: 72 Yardage: 7,104
Last day of event: Sunday, May 13, 1990

Player	Place	Score	Earnings
Greg Norman	Win	73-74-69=216	$180,000.00
Payne Stewart	2	74-74-69=217	$108,000.00
Don Pooley	T-3	73-71-74=218	$48,000.00
Fred Couples	T-3	69-74-75=218	$48,000.00
Mark Brooks	T-3	76-70-72=218	$48,000.00
Brad Faxon	T-3	77-69-72=218	$48,000.00
Bill Sander	T-7	75-72-72=219	$32,250.00
Peter Jacobsen	T-7	76-72-71=219	$32,250.00
Paul Azinger	T-9	74-73-73=220	$26,000.00
Steve Pate	T-9	75-75-70=220	$26,000.00
Bill Glasson	T-9	78-71-71=220	$26,000.00
Gil Morgan	T-9	79-72-69=220	$26,000.00

Southwestern Bell Colonial
Course: Colonial C.C., Fort Worth, Texas
Par: 70 Yardage: 7,096
Last day of event: Sunday, May 20, 1990

Player	Place	Score	Earnings
Ben Crenshaw	Win	69-65-72-66=272	$180,000.00
Corey Pavin	T-2	66-71-70-68=275	$74,666.67
John Mahaffey	T-2	67-72-70-66=275	$74,666.67
Nick Price	T-2	72-68-67-68=275	$74,666.66
Curtis Strange	T-5	68-69-69-70=276	$38,000.00
Mike Hulbert	T-5	71-70-72-63=276	$38,000.00
Andrew Magee	T-7	71-71-69-66=277	$30,125.00
Payne Stewart	T-7	70-72-68-67=277	$30,125.00
Brian Tennyson	T-7	73-68-70-66=277	$30,125.00
Gene Sauers	T-7	72-74-69-62=277	$30,125.00

BellSouth Atlanta Golf Classic

Course: Atlanta C.C., Atlanta, Ga.
Par: 72 Yardage: 7,007
Last day of event: Sunday, May 27, 1990

Player	Place	Score	Earnings
Wayne Levi	Win	72-66-68-69=275	$180,000.00
Nick Price	T-2	68-69-69-70=276	$74,666.66
Larry Mize	T-2	66-69-71-70=276	$74,666.67
Keith Clearwater	T-2	70-68-66-72=276	$74,666.67
Kenny Perry	T-5	69-70-70-69=278	$38,000.00
Mike Donald	T-5	68-72-68-70=278	$38,000.00
Brian Claar	7	69-71-69-70=279	$33,500.00
Scott Verplank	T-8	70-71-71-68=280	$28,000.00
Howard Twitty	T-8	68-68-72-72=280	$28,000.00
Tom Kite	T-8	72-69-68-71=280	$28,000.00
Don Pooley	T-8	72-68-70-70=280	$28,000.00

Kemper Open

Course: TPC at Avenel, Potomac, Md.
Par: 71 Yardage: 6,917
Last day of event: Sunday, June 3, 1990

Player	Place	Score	Earnings
Gil Morgan	Win	68-67-70-69=274	$180,000.00
Ian Baker-Finch	2	67-72-70-66=275	$108,000.00
Scott Hoch	T-3	68-68-69-71=276	$58,000.00
Hale Irwin	T-3	69-73-65-69=276	$58,000.00
Tom Kite	T-5	70-70-67-70=277	$38,000.00
Denis Watson	T-5	67-72-70-68=277	$38,000.00
Billy Ray Brown	T-7	68-70-72-70=280	$28,083.34
Mark Hayes	T-7	72-70-70-68=280	$28,083.34
Pat McGowan	T-7	65-72-70-73=280	$28,083.33
Clark Burroughs	T-7	69-70-66-75=280	$28,083.33
Joel Edwards	T-7	70-71-64-75=280	$28,083.33
Steve Jones	T-7	69-68-65-78=280	$28,083.33

Centel Western Open

Course: Butler National G.C., Oak Brook, Ill.
Par: 72 Yardage: 7,097
Last day of event: Sunday, June 10, 1990

Player	Place	Score	Earnings
Wayne Levi	Win	70-66-70-69=275	$180,000.00
Payne Stewart	2	68-67-72-72=279	$108,000.00
Peter Jacobsen	T-3	72-70-70-68=280	$58,000.00
Loren Roberts	T-3	65-75-69-71=280	$58,000.00
Greg Norman	T-5	71-69-71-70=281	$38,000.00
Mark Brooks	T-5	71-65-73-72=281	$38,000.00
Tom Watson	7	69-71-69-73=282	$33,500.00
Jose Maria Olazabal	T-8	71-68-72-72=283	$30,000.00
Curtis Strange	T-8	73-71-69-70=283	$30,000.00
Wayne Grady	T-10	70-71-73-70=284	$26,000.00
Steve Pate	T-10	71-68-73-72=284	$26,000.00

U.S. Open

Course: Medinah C.C. (No 3), Medinah, Ill.
Par: 72 Yardage: 6,996
Last day of event: Monday, June 18, 1990

Player	Place	Score	Earnings
Hale Irwin	Win	69-70-74-67=280	$220,000.00

Playoff: Beat Mike Donald with a birdie on the 19th hole (tied 18-hole playoff at 74)

Mike Donald	T-2	67-70-72-71=280	$110,000.00
Billy Ray Brown	T-3	69-71-69-72=281	$56,878.50
Nick Faldo	T-3	72-72-68-69=281	$56,878.50
Mark Brooks	T-5	68-70-72-73=283	$33,271.33
Greg Norman	T-5	72-73-69-69=283	$33,271.33
Tim Simpson	T-5	66-69-75-73=283	$33,271.34
Craig Stadler	T-8	71-70-72-71=284	$22,236.67
Scott Hoch	T-8	70-73-69-72=284	$22,236.67
Jose Maria Olazabal	T-8	73-69-69-73=284	$22,236.66
Fuzzy Zoeller	T-8	73-70-68-73=284	$22,236.67
Tom Sieckmann	T-8	70-74-68-72=284	$22,236.67
Steve Jones	T-8	67-76-74-67=284	$22,236.66

Buick Classic

Course: Westchester C.C., Harrison, N.Y.
Par: 71 Yardage: 6,779
Last day of event: Sunday, June 24, 1990

Player	Place	Score	Earnings
Hale Irwin	Win	66-69-68-66=269	$180,000.00
Paul Azinger	2	67-70-69-65=271	$108,000.00
Kirk Triplett	3	65-74-67-66=272	$68,000.00
Ken Green	4	70-67-69-67=273	$48,000.00
Jim Gallagher, Jr.	T-5	69-68-70-67=274	$38,000.00
Blaine McCallister	T-5	66-67-70-71=274	$38,000.00
Lee Janzen	T-7	69-70-69-68=276	$30,125.00
Craig Stadler	T-7	67-71-68-70=276	$30,125.00
Loren Roberts	T-7	71-67-69-69=276	$30,125.00
Ray Floyd	T-7	70-73-65-68=276	$30,125.00

Canon Greater Hartford Open

Course: TPC of Connecticut, Cromwell, Conn.
Par: 70 Yardage: 6,531
Last day of event: Sunday, July 1, 1990

Player	Place	Score	Earnings
Wayne Levi	Win	67-66-67-67=267	$180,000.00
Mark Calcavecchia	T-2	67-67-68-67=269	$66,000.00
Chris Perry	T-2	63-69-68-69=269	$66,000.00
Rocco Mediate	T-2	65-69-70-65=269	$66,000.00
Brad Fabel	T-2	67-65-67-70=269	$66,000.00
Loren Roberts	T-6	67-66-68-69=270	$32,375.00
Brian Tennyson	T-6	69-69-65-67=270	$32,375.00
Bob Lohr	T-6	70-68-68-64=270	$32,375.00
Nolan Henke	T-6	65-67-67-71=270	$32,375.00
Robert Wrenn	T-10	70-66-70-65=271	$25,000.00
John Cook	T-10	70-63-67-71=271	$25,000.00
David Canipe	T-10	67-68-72-64=271	$25,000.00

Anheuser-Busch Golf Classic

Course: Kingsmill G.C., Williamsburg, Va.
Par: 71 Yardage: 6,776
Last day of event: Sunday, July 8, 1990

Player	Place	Score	Earnings
Lanny Wadkins	Win	65-66-67-68=266	$180,000.00
Larry Mize	2	66-69-68-68=271	$108,000.00
Scott Verplank	T-3	69-64-69-70=272	$58,000.00
Bob Wolcott	T-3	69-65-68-70=272	$58,000.00
Russ Cochran	T-5	66-71-69-67=273	$36,500.00
Chris Perry	T-5	67-67-68-71=273	$36,500.00
Ian Baker-Finch	T-5	69-71-66-67=273	$36,500.00
D.A. Weibring	T-8	67-70-69-68=274	$30,000.00
Curtis Strange	T-8	67-66-68-73=274	$30,000.00

| Tim Simpson | T-10 | 71-65-69-70=275 | $26,000.00 |
| Jerry Haas | T-10 | 68-68-66-73=275 | $26,000.00 |

Bank of Boston Classic
Course: Pleasant Valley C.C., Sutton, Mass.
Par: 71 Yardage: 7,110
Last day of event: Sunday, July 15, 1990

Player	Place	Score	Earnings
Morris Hatalsky	Win	70-68-69-68=275	$162,000.00
Scott Verplank	2	67-68-68-73=276	$97,200.00
Rick Fehr	T-3	68-71-68-70=277	$46,800.00
Mike Smith	T-3	65-72-69-71=277	$46,800.00
D.A. Weibring	T-3	68-69-72-68=277	$46,800.00
Brad Bryant	T-6	69-69-70-70=278	$27,225.00
Bill Glasson	T-6	67-70-70-71=278	$27,225.00
Willie Wood	T-6	69-71-66-72=278	$27,225.00
Billy Mayfair	T-6	70-68-72-68=278	$27,225.00
Steve Pate	T-6	72-65-70-71=278	$27,225.00
Brian Tennyson	T-6	71-68-65-74=278	$27,225.00

British Open
Course: Old Course at St. Andrews, St. Andrews, Fife, Scotland
Par: 72 Yardage: 6,933
Last day of event: Sunday, July 22, 1990

Player	Place	Score	Earnings
Nick Faldo	Win	67-65-67-71=270	$153,850.00
Payne Stewart	T-2	68-68-68-71=275	$108,600.00
Mark McNulty	T-2	74-68-68-65=275	$108,600.00
Ian Woosnam	T-4	68-69-70-69=276	$72,400.00
Jodie Mudd	T-4	72-66-72-66=276	$72,400.00
Ian Baker-Finch	T-6	68-72-64-73=277	$51,585.00
Greg Norman	T-6	66-66-76-69=277	$51,585.00
Donnie Hammond	T-8	70-71-68-70=279	$39,820.00
Corey Pavin	T-8	71-69-68-71=279	$39,820.00
Steve Pate	T-8	70-68-72-69=279	$39,820.00
David Graham	T-8	72-71-70-66=279	$39,820.00

Buick Open
Course: Warwick Hills C.C., Grand Blanc, Mich.
Par: 72 Yardage: 7,014
Last day of event: Sunday, July 29, 1990

Player	Place	Score	Earnings
Chip Beck	Win	66-70-71-65=272	$180,000.00
Mike Donald	T-2	65-69-69-70=273	$74,666.67
Fuzzy Zoeller	T-2	66-69-66-72=273	$74,666.67
Hale Irwin	T-2	69-63-67-74=273	$74,666.66
Fred Funk	5	69-71-69-65=274	$40,000.00
Ken Green	6	71-63-71-70=275	$36,000.00
Leonard Thompson	T-7	66-72-67-71=276	$30,125.00
Robert Wrenn	T-7	67-69-68-72=276	$30,125.00
Dave Barr	T-7	69-66-68-73=276	$30,125.00
Doug Tewell	T-7	71-65-66-74=276	$30,125.00

Federal Express St. Jude Classic
Course: TPC at Southwind, Germantown, Tenn.
Par: 71 Yardage: 7,006
Last day of event: Sunday, August 5, 1990

Player	Place	Score	Earnings
Tom Kite	Win	72-68-62-67=269	$180,000.00

Playoff: Beat John Cook with birdie on first extra hole

John Cook	T-2	69-67-66-67=269	$108,000.00
David Canipe	3	66-73-64-69=272	$68,000.00
Bob Estes	T-4	67-69-69-69=274	$41,333.33
Tim Simpson	T-4	69-68-67-70=274	$41,333.33
David Frost	T-4	69-70-68-67=274	$41,333.34
Billy Andrade	T-7	68-70-70-67=275	$31,166.67
Billy Mayfair	T-7	71-65-69-70=275	$31,166.66
Loren Roberts	T-7	66-68-73-68=275	$31,166.67
Neal Lancaster	T-10	71-65-70-70=276	$26,000.00
Brian Claar	T-10	72-65-68-71=276	$26,000.00

PGA Championship
Course: Shoal Creek C.C., Birmingham, Al.
Par: 72 Yardage: 7,145
Last day of event: Sunday, August 12, 1990

Player	Place	Score	Earnings
Wayne Grady	Win	72-67-72-71=282	$225,000.00
Fred Couples	2	69-71-73-72=285	$135,000.00
Gil Morgan	3	77-72-65-72=286	$90,000.00
Bill Britton	4	72-74-72-71=289	$73,500.00
Billy Mayfair	T-5	70-71-75-74=290	$51,666.67
Loren Roberts	T-5	73-71-70-76=290	$51,666.66
Chip Beck	T-5	71-70-78-71=290	$51,666.67
Tim Simpson	T-8	71-73-75-73=292	$34,375.00
Mark McNulty	T-8	74-72-75-71=292	$34,375.00
Don Pooley	T-8	75-74-71-72=292	$34,375.00
Payne Stewart	T-8	71-72-70-79=292	$34,375.00

The International
Course: Castle Pine G.C., Castle Rock, Colo. (Stableford format)
Par: 72 Yardage: 7,559
Last day of event: Sunday, August 19, 1990

Player	Place	Score	Earnings
Davis Love III	Win	8-0-15-14=37	$180,000.00
Steve Pate	T-2	4-6-7-11=28	$74,666.00
Peter Senior	T-2	4-6-8-11=29	$74,666.00
Eduardo Romero	T-2	9-11-6-11=37	$74,666.00
Ben Crenshaw	5	6-0-10-9=25	$40,000.00
Jim Gallagher, Jr.	T-6	2-4-10-8=24	$33,500.00
John Adams	T-6	4-4-8-8=24	$33,500.00
Stan Utley	T-6	3-14-2-8=27	$33,500.00
Dillard Pruitt	T-9	5-6-7-7=25	$27,000.00
Mark McCumber	T-9	5-12-3-7=27	$27,000.00
Bob Lohr	T-9	7-9-5-7=28	$27,000.00

NEC World Series of Golf
Course: Firestone C.C. (South), Akron, Ohio
Par: 70 Yardage: 7,149
Last day of event: Sunday, August 26, 1990

Player	Place	Score	Earnings
Jose Maria Olazabal	Win	61-67-67-67=262	$198,000.00
Lanny Wadkins	2	70-68-70-66=274	$118,600.00
Hale Irwin	3	70-67-66-74=277	$74,600.00
Donnie Hammond	4	73-65-70-71=279	$52,600.00
Larry Mize	5	66-71-73-70=280	$44,000.00
Chip Beck	T-6	71-69-69-72=281	$38,025.00
Greg Norman	T-6	71-73-69-68=281	$38,025.00
Paul Azinger	T-8	69-71-72-70=282	$31,833.33
Tom Kite	T-8	70-71-72-69=282	$31,833.34
Trevor Dodds	T-8	72-71-68-71=282	$31,833.33

Chattanooga Classic

Course: ValleyBrook C.C., Hixson, Tenn.
Par: 70 Yardage: 6,641
Last day of event: Sunday, August 26, 1990

Player	Place	Score	Earnings
Peter Persons	Win	64-64-65-67=260	$108,000.00
Richard Zokol	2	65-66-65-66=262	$64,800.00
Fred Funk	T-3	65-67-66-66=264	$34,800.00
Kenny Knox	T-3	68-70-61-65=264	$34,800.00
Harry Taylor	T-5	66-66-67-67=266	$21,900.00
David Peoples	T-5	67-66-67-66=266	$21,900.00
Ray Pearce	T-5	70-66-64-66=266	$21,900.00
John Adams	T-8	65-68-67-67=267	$17,400.00
Dave Eichelberger	T-8	65-69-64-69=267	$17,400.00
Steve Lowery	T-8	62-68-71-66=267	$17,400.00

Greater Milwaukee Open

Course: Tuckaway C.C., Franklin, Wis.
Par: 72 Yardage: 7,030
Last day of event: Saturday, September 1, 1990

Player	Place	Score	Earnings
Jim Gallagher, Jr.	Win	69-70-66-66=271	$162,000.00
Playoff: Beat Billy Mayfair and Ed Dougherty with par on first extra hole			
Billy Mayfair	T-2	66-69-68-68=271	$79,200.00
Ed Dougherty	T-2	69-69-67-66=271	$79,200.00
Scott Hoch	T-4	70-66-69-67=272	$37,200.00
Steve Lowery	T-4	69-67-71-65=272	$37,200.00
Ray Stewart	T-4	63-70-67-72=272	$37,200.00
Hal Sutton	T-7	70-68-66-69=273	$29,025.00
Chris Perry	T-7	67-71-68-67=273	$29,025.00
Corey Pavin	T-9	68-70-66-70=274	$24,300.00
Gene Sauers	T-9	67-73-70-64=274	$24,300.00
Scott Verplank	T-9	74-62-67-71=274	$24,300.00

Hardee's Golf Classic

Course: Oakwood C.C., Coal Valley, Ill.
Par: 70 Yardage: 6,606
Last day of event: Sunday, September 9, 1990

Player	Place	Score	Earnings
Joey Sindelar	Win	70-65-67-66=268	$180,000.00
Playoff: Beat Willie Wood with par on first extra hole			
Willie Wood	T-2	68-63-68-69=268	$108,000.00
Jim Gallagher, Jr.	T-3	68-66-67-68=269	$45,100.00
Ian Baker-Finch	T-3	67-69-69-64=269	$45,100.00
Bill Britton	T-3	69-67-68-65=269	$45,100.00
Jay Delsing	T-3	66-65-70-68=269	$45,100.00
Dave Barr	T-3	67-70-65-67=269	$45,100.00
Emlyn Aubrey	T-8	66-68-69-67=270	$28,000.00
Bob Tway	T-8	68-64-67-71=270	$28,000.00
Mark Lye	T-8	71-66-67-66=270	$28,000.00
Jeff Sluman	T-8	64-72-65-69=270	$28,000.00

Canadian Open

Course: Glen Abbey G.C., Oakville, Ontario, Canada
Par: 72 Yardage: 7,102
Last day of event: Sunday, September 16, 1990

Player	Place	Score	Earnings
Wayne Levi	Win	68-68-72-70=278	$180,000.00
Ian Baker-Finch	T-2	68-70-73-68=279	$88,000.00
Jim Woodward	T-2	68-71-74-66=279	$88,000.00

Andy North	4	71-71-70-69=281	$48,000.00
Paul Azinger	T-5	70-71-71-70=282	$32,750.00
Bobby Wadkins	T-5	68-72-69-73=282	$32,750.00
Mark Wiebe	T-5	69-73-68-72=282	$32,750.00
Brian Tennyson	T-5	70-67-73-72=282	$32,750.00
Brad Faxon	T-5	65-74-71-72=282	$32,750.00
Buddy Gardner	T-5	72-68-67-75=282	$32,750.00

B.C. Open

Course: En-Joie G.C., Endicott, N.Y.
Par: 71 Yardage: 6,966
Last day of event: Sunday, September 23, 1990

Player	Place	Score	Earnings
Nolan Henke	Win	66-64-70-68=268	$126,000.00
Mark Wiebe	2	70-69-68-64=271	$75,600.00
Jim Benepe	T-3	68-69-67-68=272	$33,600.00
Barry Jaeckel	T-3	70-68-65-69=272	$33,600.00
Brian Tennyson	T-3	70-70-66-66=272	$33,600.00
Doug Tewell	T-3	71-64-70-67=272	$33,600.00
Blaine McCallister	7	71-66-69-68=274	$23,450.00
Brad Bryant	8	74-65-68-68=275	$21,700.00
Mike Sullivan	T-9	69-68-69-70=276	$18,200.00
Trevor Dodds	T-9	69-69-67-71=276	$18,200.00
Jim Hallet	T-9	66-66-72-72=276	$18,200.00
Robert Wrenn	T-9	68-68-72-68=276	$18,200.00

Buick Southern Open

Course: Green Island C.C., Columbus, Ga.
Par: 70 Yardage: 6,791
Last day of event: Sunday, September 30, 1990

Player	Place	Score	Earnings
Kenny Knox	Win	69-62-68-66=265	$108,000.00
Playoff: Beat Jim Hallet with birdie on second extra hole			
Jim Hallet	T-2	68-66-65-66=265	$64,800.00
Jim Booros	T-3	67-67-68-66=268	$40,800.00
Larry Nelson	T-4	70-67-68-64=269	$23,625.00
Tommy Moore	T-5	69-68-65-67=269	$23,625.00
David Peoples	T-6	67-62-70-70=269	$23,625.00
Jeff Wilson	T-7	67-64-69-69=269	$23,625.00
John Cook	T-8	70-69-67-64=270	$18,000.00
Bob Estes	T-9	67-68-66-69=270	$18,000.00
Tom Eubank	T-10	66-70-70-65=271	$12,450.00

H-E-B Texas Open

Course: Oak Hill C.C., San Antonio, Texas
Par: 70 Yardage: 6,576
Last day of event: Sunday, October 7, 1990

Player	Place	Score	Earnings
Mark O'Meara	Win	64-68-66-63=261	$144,000.00
Gary Hallberg	T-2	63-69-64-66=262	$86,400.00
Nick Price	T-3	65-66-63-69=263	$54,400.00
Loren Roberts	T-4	70-65-64-65=264	$38,400.00
Corey Pavin	T-5	67-68-62-68=265	$32,000.00
Mark Brooks	T-6	69-64-65-68=266	$28,800.00
Emlyn Aubrey	T-7	63-69-70-65=267	$25,800.00
Steve Jones	T-8	65-63-70-69=267	$25,800.00
Larry Mize	T-9	70-65-66-67=268	$20,000.00
Scott Hoch	T-10	68-67-66-67=268	$20,000.00

Tim Simpson	8		$32,000.00
Fred Couples	9		$30,000.00
Mark O'Meara	10		$28,000.00

Las Vegas Invitational

Course: Las Vegas C.C., Spanish Trail G. & C.C., Desert Inn C.C., Las Vegas, Nev.
Home course / Las Vegas C.C., Par: 72 Yardage: 7,164
Last day of event: Sunday, October 14, 1990

Player	Place	Score	Earnings
Bob Tway	Win	67-67-65-65-70=334	$234,000.00
Playoff: Beat John Cook with par on first extra hole			
John Cook	T-2	64-70-66-67-67=334	$140,400.00
Phil Blackmar	T-3	67-69-68-66-67=337	$75,400.00
Corey Pavin	T-3	72-68-66-68-63=337	$75,400.00
Nolan Henke	T-5	69-69-70-66-64=338	$49,400.00
Mark O'Meara	T-5	67-64-67-69-71=338	$49,400.00
Paul Azinger	7	69-67-71-68-64=339	$43,550.00
Richard Zokol	T-8	69-68-66-67-70=340	$37,700.00
Steve Elkington	T-8	69-71-71-62-67=340	$37,700.00
Joey Sindelar	T-8	72-68-70-66-64=340	$37,700.00

Walt Disney World/Oldsmobile Classic

Course: Walt Disney (Magnolia, Palm), Lake Buena Vista C.C., Lake Buena Vista, Fla.
Home course / Magnolia, Par: 72 Yardage: 7,190
Last day of event: Saturday, October 20, 1990

Player	Place	Score	Earnings
Tim Simpson	Win	64-64-65-71=264	$180,000.00
John Mahaffey	2	67-66-68-64=265	$108,000.00
Davis Love III	3	68-65-66-67=266	$68,000.00
Gene Sauers	4	68-65-67-67=267	$48,000.00
Paul Azinger	5	67-65-68-68=268	$40,000.00
David Peoples	6	68-69-65-67=269	$36,000.00
Bob Gilder	7	68-65-68-69=270	$33,500.00
Bruce Lietzke	T-8	68-68-68-67=271	$28,000.00
Chip Beck	T-8	70-67-65-69=271	$28,000.00
Dan Forsman	T-8	70-68-65-68=271	$28,000.00
Larry Nelson	T-8	72-66-66-67=271	$28,000.00

Nabisco Championships

Course: Champions G.C., Houston, Texas
Par: 71 Yardage: 7,187
Last day of event: Sunday, October 28, 1990

Player	Place	Score	Earnings
Jodie Mudd	Win	68-69-68-68=273	$450,000.00
Playoff: Beat Billy Mayfair with birdie on first extra hole			
Billy Mayfair	T-2	69-66-70-68=273	$270,000.00
Ian Baker-Finch	T-3	71-70-67-68=276	$146,250.00
Wayne Levi	T-3	75-71-67-63=276	$146,250.00
Nick Price	5	68-68-71-70=277	$100,000.00
Chip Beck	6	69-68-71-70=278	$90,000.00
Greg Norman	T-7	66-71-71-71=279	$82,500.00
Tim Simpson	T-7	66-73-70-70=279	$82,500.00
Wayne Grady	9	72-67-73-69=281	$75,000.00
Steve Elkington	10	72-72-66-72=282	$71,000.00

Nabisco year-end bonus

Player	Place	Earnings
Greg Norman	Win	$175,000.00
Wayne Levi	2	$106,000.00
Payne Stewart	3	$68,000.00
Paul Azinger	4	$47,000.00
Jodie Mudd	5	$40,000.00
Mark Calcavecchia	6	$37,750.00
Hale Irwin	7	$36,000.00

1991

Long-hitting John Daly, who entered the tournament as ninth alternate and played no practice rounds, became an instant cult hero ("Grip it and rip it.") with his 3-shot victory over Bruce Lietzke in the PGA Championship at Crooked Stick. Daly used a driver with a head made of Kevlar, a compound used in bullet-proof vests, because the force of impact generated by his swing speed caused the face of conventional metal drivers to cave in. Ian Woosnam, a 5-foot-4 former boxer from Wales, won the Masters by a shot over Jose-Maria Olazabal. Payne Stewart notched his second major title, beating Scott Simpson 75 to 77 in an 18-hole U.S. Open playoff at Hazeltine. Ian Baker-Finch followed his third-round 64 with five birdies over the first seven holes in Round 4, cruising to a two-shot victory over Mike Harwood in the British Open at Royal Birkdale. In Round 3 of the Las Vegas Invitational, Chip Beck became the second man in PGA Tour history to shoot 59. A 20-year-old amateur named Phil Mickelson won the Northern Telecom Open. The United States wrested the Ryder Cup away from Europe with a contentious 14 ½ to 13 ½ victory in the "War by the Shore" at Kiawah Island.

Infiniti Tournament of Champions

Course: La Costa C.C., Carlsbad, Calif.
Par: 72 Yardage: 7,022
Last day of event: Sunday, January 6, 1991

Player	Place	Score	Earnings
Tom Kite	Win	68-67-68-69=272	$144,000.00
Lanny Wadkins	2	65-67-73-68=273	$86,400.00
Chip Beck	T-3	68-69-70-69=276	$41,600.00
Fred Couples	T-3	70-68-67-71=276	$41,600.00
Wayne Levi	T-3	70-71-69-66=276	$41,600.00
Tommy Armour III	T-6	72-71-72-66=281	$26,800.00
Greg Norman	T-6	70-71-73-67=281	$26,800.00
Bob Tway	T-6	73-67-70-71=281	$26,800.00
Wayne Grady	T-9	69-72-72-69=282	$21,275.00
Mark O'Meara	T-9	72-69-70-71=282	$21,275.00
Nolan Henke	T-9	72-72-70-68=282	$21,275.00
Ben Crenshaw	T-9	74-70-67-71=282	$21,275.00

Northern Telecom Open

Course: TPC At StarPass, Tucson National G.C., Tucson, Ariz.
Par: 72 Yardage: 7,010
Last day of event: Sunday, January 13, 1991

Player	Place	Score	Earnings
Phil Mickelson	Win	65-71-65-71=272	
Tom Purtzer	T-2	70-70-66-67=273	$144,000.00
Bob Tway	T-2	64-70-71-68=273	$144,000.00
Craig Stadler	4	69-64-72-70=275	$68,000.00
Jeff Maggert	T-5	68-69-70-69=276	$39,375.00
Brian Tennyson	T-5	69-65-73-69=276	$39,375.00
David Peoples	T-5	70-67-66-73=276	$39,375.00
John Cook	T-5	66-69-75-66=276	$39,375.00
Rocco Mediate	T-9	67-69-70-71=277	$27,000.00
Dave Rummells	T-9	71-71-67-68=277	$27,000.00
Neal Lancaster	T-9	70-68-72-67=277	$27,000.00
Scott Hoch	T-9	68-66-70-73=277	$27,000.00
Corey Pavin	T-9	67-67-69-74=277	$27,000.00

United Hawaiian Open

Course: Waialae C.C., Honolulu, Ha.
Par: 72 Yardage: 6,975
Last day of event: Sunday, January 20, 1991

Player	Place	Score	Earnings
Lanny Wadkins	Win	69-67-69-65=270	$198,000.00
John Cook	2	64-66-69-75=274	$118,800.00
Ed Dougherty	3	70-68-66-71=275	$74,800.00
Phil Blackmar	T-4	66-70-71-69=276	$41,470.00
Mark Calcavecchia	T-4	68-67-72-69=276	$41,470.00
Hale Irwin	T-4	66-69-68-73=276	$41,470.00
Chip Beck	T-4	66-66-70-74=276	$41,470.00
Gil Morgan	T-4	66-66-69-75=276	$41,470.00
Mark Lye	T-9	66-70-71-70=277	$25,457.15
Bart Bryant	T-9	70-66-70-71=277	$25,457.14
Buddy Gardner	T-9	68-65-72-72=277	$25,457.14
Larry Mize	T-9	64-70-70-73=277	$25,457.14
Craig Stadler	T-9	67-73-66-71=277	$25,457.15
Fred Funk	T-9	69-64-71-73=277	$25,457.14
Dave Rummells	T-9	67-70-65-75=277	$25,457.14

Phoenix Open

Course: TPC of Scottsdale, Scottsdale, Ariz.
Par: 71 Yardage: 6,992
Last day of event: Sunday, January 27, 1991

Player	Place	Score	Earnings
Nolan Henke	Win	65-66-66-71=268	$180,000.00
Tom Watson	T-2	68-68-68-65=269	$74,666.67
Gil Morgan	T-2	66-67-70-66=269	$74,666.67
Curtis Strange	T-2	64-67-71-67=269	$74,666.66
Bruce Lietzke	T-5	67-68-68-67=270	$35,125.00
Jay Don Blake	T-5	68-66-70-66=270	$35,125.00
Mike Hulbert	T-5	68-72-65-65=270	$35,125.00
Andrew Magee	T-5	72-65-67-66=270	$35,125.00
Gene Sauers	T-9	65-69-68-69=271	$27,000.00
Bob Tway	T-9	65-69-68-69=271	$27,000.00
Rocco Mediate	T-9	70-68-68-65=271	$27,000.00

AT&T Pebble Beach Pro-Am

Courses: Pebble Beach G.L., Spyglass Hill G.C., Poppy Hills G.C., Pebble Beach, Calif.
Home Course / Pebble Beach G.L., Par: 72 Yardage: 6,815
Last day of event: Sunday, February 3, 1991

Player	Place	Score	Earnings
Paul Azinger	Win	67-67-73-67=274	$198,000.00
Corey Pavin	T-2	71-71-69-67=278	$96,800.00
Brian Claar	T-2	66-73-71-68=278	$96,800.00
Davis Love III	T-4	67-70-69-73=279	$45,466.66
Mike Smith	T-4	70-73-71-65=279	$45,466.67
Rocco Mediate	T-4	69-67-69-74=279	$45,466.67
John Cook	T-7	66-72-69-73=280	$34,283.33
Larry Mize	T-7	71-66-73-70=280	$34,283.33
Jay Haas	T-7	68-70-74-68=280	$34,283.34
Mark Calcavecchia	10	71-72-71-67=281	$29,700.00

Bob Hope Chrysler Classic

Course: Indian Wells C.C., PGA West/Palmer, Bermuda Dunes C.C., La Quinta C.C.
Home course / Indian Wells, Par: 72 Yardage: 6,478
Last day of event: Sunday, February 10, 1991

Player	Place	Score	Earnings
Corey Pavin	Win	65-69-66-66-65=331	$198,000.00

Playoff: Beat Mark O'Meara with birdie on first extra hole

Player	Place	Score	Earnings
Mark O'Meara	2	66-65-67-67-67=331	$118,800.00
Tim Simpson	3	67-64-66-68-67=332	$74,800.00
Ray Floyd	4	71-68-66-64-64=333	$54,800.00
Fred Couples	5	67-69-64-67-67=334	$44,000.00
Blaine McCallister	6	66-70-63-68-68=335	$39,600.00
Bob Tway	T-7	66-68-71-68-64=337	$34,283.34
Jeff Sluman	T-7	71-65-69-67-65=337	$34,283.33
Scott Hoch	T-7	72-64-69-63-69=337	$34,283.33
Jim McGovern	T-10	66-67-69-69-67=338	$27,500.00
Bob Lohr	T-10	69-68-68-69-64=338	$27,500.00
Jim Hallet	T-10	67-70-70-67-64=338	$27,500.00

Shearson Lehman Brothers Open

Course: Torrey Pines (South), Torrey Pines (North), San Diego, Calif.
Home Course -Par: 72 Yardage: 7,021
Last day of event: Sunday, February 17, 1991

Player	Place	Score	Earnings
Jay Don Blake	Win	69-65-67-67=268	$180,000.00
Bill Sander	2	68-65-71-66=270	$108,000.00
Dan Forsman	3	68-64-71-68=271	$68,000.00
Ben Crenshaw	4	65-68-70-69=272	$48,000.00
Jim Hallet	T-5	68-69-66-70=273	$36,500.00
Robert Wrenn	T-5	68-66-68-71=273	$36,500.00
Steve Pate	T-5	67-65-67-74=273	$36,500.00
Ed Humenik	T-8	69-70-68-67=274	$29,000.00
Dudley Hart	T-8	68-70-71-65=274	$29,000.00
Brad Faxon	T-8	69-64-67-74=274	$29,000.00

Nissan Los Angeles Open

Course: Riviera C.C., Pacific Palisades, Calif.
Par: 71 Yardage: 7,029
Last day of event: Sunday, February 24, 1991

Player	Place	Score	Earnings
Ted Schulz	Win	69-66-69-68=272	$180,000.00
Jeff Sluman	2	66-69-68-70=273	$108,000.00
Davis Love III	T-3	70-65-69-70=274	$52,000.00
Craig Stadler	T-3	66-71-71-66=274	$52,000.00
Bruce Lietzke	T-3	70-63-70-71=274	$52,000.00
Rocco Mediate	T-6	70-69-66-70=275	$33,500.00
Scott Simpson	T-6	71-68-67-69=275	$33,500.00
Sam Randolph	T-6	72-65-69-69=275	$33,500.00
Andrew Magee	T-9	66-69-70-71=276	$27,000.00
Rick Fehr	T-9	68-69-71-68=276	$27,000.00
Duffy Waldorf	T-9	66-72-72-66=276	$27,000.00

Doral-Ryder Open

Course: Doral C.C. (Blue)
Par: 72 Yardage: 6,939
Last day of event: Monday, March 4, 1991

Player	Place	Score	Earnings
Rocco Mediate	Win	66-70-68-72=276	$252,000.00

Playoff: Beat Curtis Strange with birdie on first extra hole

Player	Place	Score	Earnings
Curtis Strange	2	69-68-72-67=276	$151,200.00
Russ Cochran	T-3	69-67-68-73=277	$81,200.00
Andy Bean	T-3	68-68-67-74=277	$81,200.00
Davis Love III	T-5	71-68-68-72=279	$53,200.00
Jack Nicklaus	T-5	71-63-75-70=279	$53,200.00
Mark Calcavecchia	7	68-70-69-73=280	$46,900.00

Player	Place	Score	Earnings
Lanny Wadkins	8	71-67-70-73=281	$43,400.00
Wayne Levi	9	67-70-71-74=282	$40,600.00
Tom Sieckmann	10	68-72-71-72=283	$37,800.00

Honda Classic
Course: TPC at Eagle Trace, Coral Springs, Fla.
Par: 72 Yardage: 7,030
Last day of event: Sunday, March 10, 1991

Player	Place	Score	Earnings
Steve Pate	Win	69-65-70-75=279	$180,000.00
Paul Azinger	T-2	68-67-75-72=282	$88,000.00
Dan Halldorson	T-3	67-67-78-70=282	$88,000.00
Bruce Lietzke	T-4	72-67-70-74=283	$41,333.33
Billy Andrade	T-4	68-72-75-68=283	$41,333.34
John Daly	T-4	68-68-76-71=283	$41,333.33
Bart Bryant	7	69-71-72-72=284	$33,500.00
Dave Barr	8	70-66-74-75=285	$31,000.00
Andy Bean	T-9	70-71-73-72=286	$26,000.00
Blaine McCallister	T-9	69-70-73-74=286	$26,000.00
Andrew Magee	T-9	70-71-71-74=286	$26,000.00
Davis Love III	T-9	74-70-68-74=286	$26,000.00

The Nestle Invitational
Course: Bay Hill Club, Orlando, Fla.
Par: 72 Yardage: 7,114
Last day of event: Sunday, March 17, 1991

Player	Place	Score	Earnings
Andrew Magee	Win	68-69-66=203	$180,000.00
Tom Sieckmann	2	70-65-70=205	$108,000.00
Mark Calcavecchia	T-3	66-69-71=206	$58,000.00
Steve Pate	T-3	72-66-68=206	$58,000.00
Mark O'Meara	5	68-69-70=207	$40,000.00
Jay Don Blake	6	69-69-70=208	$36,000.00
Bernhard Langer	T-7	70-69-70=209	$28,083.33
Ian Woosnam	T-7	70-70-69=209	$28,083.34
Nick Faldo	T-7	67-71-71=209	$28,083.33
Bob Tway	T-7	70-71-68=209	$28,083.34
Rocco Mediate	T-7	68-69-72=209	$28,083.33
Scott Hoch	T-7	70-66-73=209	$28,083.33

USF&G Classic
Course: English Turn G. & C.C., New Orleans, La.
Par: 72 Yardage: 7,106
Last day of event: Sunday, March 24, 1991

Player	Place	Score	Earnings
Ian Woosnam	Win	73-67-68-67=275	$180,000.00
Playoff: Beat Jim Hallet with par on second extra hole			
Jim Hallet	2	69-71-65-70=275	$108,000.00
Tom Sieckmann	3	71-68-70-68=277	$68,000.00
John Huston	4	72-70-68-68=278	$48,000.00
Tim Simpson	T-5	71-72-71-65=279	$36,500.00
Joel Edwards	T-5	73-71-64-71=279	$36,500.00
Ronnie Black	T-5	68-74-66-71=279	$36,500.00
Curt Byrum	T-8	72-72-68-68=280	$29,000.00
Tom Watson	T-8	67-72-73-68=280	$29,000.00
Kenny Knox	T-8	68-75-66-71=280	$29,000.00

The Players Championship
Course: TPC at Sawgrass, Ponte Vedra Beach, Fla.
Par: 72 Yardage: 6,857
Last day of event: Sunday, March 31, 1991

Player	Place	Score	Earnings
Steve Elkington	Win	66-70-72-68=276	$288,000.00
Fuzzy Zoeller	2	68-68-69-72=277	$172,800.00
Phil Blackmar	T-3	67-72-69-70=278	$83,200.00
John Cook	T-3	71-73-69-65=278	$83,200.00
Paul Azinger	T-3	67-68-69-74=278	$83,200.00
Bernhard Langer	T-6	70-70-71-69=280	$53,600.00
Curtis Strange	T-6	71-68-70-71=280	$53,600.00
Bruce Lietzke	T-6	71-72-68-69=280	$53,600.00
Bob Lohr	T-9	68-71-68-74=281	$41,600.00
Gene Sauers	T-9	68-74-68-71=281	$41,600.00
Bobby Wadkins	T-9	68-74-69-70=281	$41,600.00
Nick Price	T-9	68-75-67-71=281	$41,600.00

Deposit Guaranty Classic
Course: Hattiesburg C.C., Hattiesburg, Miss.
Par: 70 Yardage: 6,594
Last day of event: Sunday, April 14, 1991

Player	Place	Score	Earnings
Larry Silveira	Win	66-66-71-63=266	$54,000.00
Mike Nicolette	T-2	65-65-68-68=266	$26,400.00
Russ Cochran	T-2	69-65-69-63=266	$26,400.00
Fred Funk	4	66-67-68-66=267	$14,400.00
Jerry Haas	T-5	66-69-66-67=268	$11,400.00
Brandel Chamblee	T-5	71-67-64-66=268	$11,400.00
Chris Perry	T-7	68-67-67-67=269	$7,819.00
Dan Halldorson	T-7	68-68-66-67=269	$7,819.00
Brian Watts	T-7	65-68-69-67=269	$7,819.00
Frank Conner	T-7	65-66-68-70=269	$7,819.00
Mike Springer	T-7	66-70-66-67=269	$7,819.00
Greg Ladehoff	T-7	70-64-67-68=269	$7,819.00
Brad Fabel	T-7	70-65-67-67=269	$7,819.00
Grant Waite	T-7	63-73-66-67=269	$7,819.00

Masters
Course: Augusta National G.C., Augusta, Ga.
Par: 72 Yardage: 6,925
Last day of event: Sunday, April 14, 1991

Player	Place	Score	Earnings
Ian Woosnam	Win	72-66-67-72=277	$243,000.00
Jose Maria Olazabal	2	68-71-69-70=278	$145,800.00
Lanny Wadkins	T-3	67-71-70-71=279	$64,800.00
Tom Watson	T-3	68-68-70-73=279	$64,800.00
Ben Crenshaw	T-3	70-73-68-68=279	$64,800.00
Steve Pate	T-3	72-73-69-65=279	$64,800.00
Jodie Mudd	T-7	70-70-71-69=280	$42,100.00
Ian Baker-Finch	T-7	71-70-69-70=280	$42,100.00
Andrew Magee	T-7	70-72-68-70=280	$42,100.00
Tommy Nakajima	T-10	74-71-67-69=281	$35,150.00
Hale Irwin	T-10	70-70-75-66=281	$35,150.00

MCI Heritage Classic
Course: Harbour Town G.L., Hilton Head, S.C.
Par: 71 Yardage: 6,657
Last day of event: Sunday, April 21, 1991

Player	Place	Score	Earnings
Davis Love III	Win	65-68-68-70=271	$180,000.00
Ian Baker-Finch	2	75-64-65-69=273	$108,000.00
Lanny Wadkins	3	68-68-70-68=274	$68,000.00
Mark O'Meara	T-4	68-69-68-70=275	$41,333.33
Payne Stewart	T-4	68-68-70-69=275	$41,333.34
Hale Irwin	T-4	70-70-66-69=275	$41,333.33

Player	Place	Score	Earnings
Fred Funk	T-7	69-69-68-71=277	$31,166.67
Billy Mayfair	T-7	68-72-66-71=277	$31,166.67
Chip Beck	T-7	68-64-73-72=277	$31,166.66
Bobby Clampett	10	72-66-67-73=278	$27,000.00

Kmart Greater Greensboro Open
Course: Forest Oaks C.C., Greensboro, N.C.
Par: 72 Yardage: 6,984
Last day of event: Sunday, April 28, 1991

Player	Place	Score	Earnings
Mark Brooks	Win	71-70-70-64=275	$225,000.00
Playoff: Beat Gene Sauers with par on third extra hole			
Gene Sauers	2	70-64-72-69=275	$135,000.00
Bob Wolcott	T-3	67-69-68-72=276	$72,500.00
John Huston	T-3	74-68-69-65=276	$72,500.00
Bill Britton	T-5	70-70-69-68=277	$43,906.25
Mike Hulbert	T-5	70-70-69-68=277	$43,906.25
Jeff Sluman	T-5	69-67-70-71=277	$43,906.25
Lanny Wadkins	T-5	69-65-72-71=277	$43,906.25
Loren Roberts	T-9	71-71-68-68=278	$33,750.00
Marco Dawson	T-9	71-71-69-67=278	$33,750.00
Davis Love III	T-9	75-67-67-69=278	$33,750.00

GTE Byron Nelson Classic
Course: TPC at Las Colinas, Irving, Texas
Par: 70 Yardage: 6,767
Last day of event: Sunday, May 5, 1991

Player	Place	Score	Earnings
Nick Price	Win	68-64-70-68=270	$198,000.00
Craig Stadler	2	68-66-70-67=271	$118,800.00
Scott Simpson	T-3	68-68-68-68=272	$52,800.00
Ray Floyd	T-3	67-69-67-69=272	$52,800.00
Corey Pavin	T-3	68-66-69-69=272	$52,800.00
Hal Sutton	T-3	68-68-67-69=272	$52,800.00
Lanny Wadkins	7	66-71-68-68=273	$36,850.00
Tom Watson	T-8	65-69-70-71=275	$30,800.00
Loren Roberts	T-8	71-68-66-70=275	$30,800.00
Phil Blackmar	T-8	70-66-66-73=275	$30,800.00
Tom Kite	T-8	68-66-66-75=275	$30,800.00

BellSouth Atlanta Golf Classic
Course: Atlanta C.C., Atlanta, Ga.
Par: 72 Yardage: 7,007
Last day of event: Sunday, May 12, 1991

Player	Place	Score	Earnings
Corey Pavin	Win	68-67-67-70=272	$180,000.00
Playoff: Beat Steve Pate with par on second extra hole			
Steve Pate	2	68-70-68-66=272	$108,000.00
Hale Irwin	T-3	71-69-67-66=273	$52,000.00
Mike Springer	T-3	68-63-69-73=273	$52,000.00
Tom Kite	T-3	64-68-67-74=273	$52,000.00
David Edwards	T-6	70-68-68-68=274	$34,750.00
Fred Funk	T-6	62-77-67-68=274	$34,750.00
Jodie Mudd	T-8	69-69-68-69=275	$29,000.00
Leonard Thompson	T-8	70-69-67-69=275	$29,000.00
Jay Don Blake	T-8	68-73-68-66=275	$29,000.00

Memorial Tournament
Course: Muirfield Village G.C., Dubin, Ohio
Par: 72 Yardage: 7,104
Last day of event: Sunday, May 19, 1991

Player	Place	Score	Earnings
Kenny Perry	Win	70-63-69-71=273	$216,000.00
Hale Irwin	2	73-69-65-66=273	$129,600.00
Corey Pavin	3	66-71-67-71=275	$81,600.00
Craig Stadler	T-4	71-70-70-68=279	$52,800.00
Mike Hulbert	T-4	73-67-72-67=279	$52,800.00
Ian Baker-Finch	T-6	69-73-69-69=280	$41,700.00
Chip Beck	T-6	70-66-74-70=280	$41,700.00
Andy Bean	T-8	69-69-72-71=281	$30,000.00
Doug Tewell	T-8	69-69-72-71=281	$30,000.00
Jay Don Blake	T-8	69-71-72-69=281	$30,000.00
John Cook	T-8	72-72-69-68=281	$30,000.00
David Frost	T-8	69-71-73-68=281	$30,000.00
Larry Mize	T-8	72-69-73-67=281	$30,000.00
Ted Schulz	T-8	69-71-67-74=281	$30,000.00

Southwestern Bell Colonial
Course: Colonial C.C., Fort Worth, Texas
Par: 70 Yardage: 7,096
Last day of event: Sunday, May 26, 1991

Player	Place	Score	Earnings
Tom Purtzer	Win	70-66-67-64=267	$216,000.00
David Edwards	T-2	66-68-68-68=270	$89,600.00
Scott Hoch	T-2	67-67-70-66=270	$89,600.00
Bob Lohr	T-2	68-68-63-71=270	$89,600.00
Mark Calcavecchia	T-5	65-68-68-70=271	$45,600.00
Fred Funk	T-5	65-68-68-70=271	$45,600.00
Tom Watson	T-7	68-66-69-69=272	$36,150.00
Wayne Grady	T-7	68-67-67-70=272	$36,150.00
Stan Utley	T-7	68-64-69-71=272	$36,150.00
Ian Baker-Finch	T-7	70-65-71-66=272	$36,150.00

Kemper Open
Course: TPC at Avenel, Potomac, Md.
Par: 71 Yardage: 6,904
Last day of event: Sunday, June 2, 1991

Player	Place	Score	Earnings
Billy Andrade	Win	68-64-64-67=263	$180,000.00
Playoff: Beat Jeff Sluman with birdie on first extra hole			
Jeff Sluman	2	70-64-64-65=263	$108,000.00
Bill Britton	3	67-67-66-66=266	$68,000.00
Mark Brooks	T-4	67-67-68-65=267	$41,333.34
Greg Norman	T-4	67-65-64-71=267	$41,333.33
Hal Sutton	T-4	66-65-64-72=267	$41,333.33
Scott Hoch	7	69-69-65-65=268	$33,500.00
Stan Utley	T-8	68-70-64-67=269	$30,000.00
Steve Jones	T-9	71-65-65-68=269	$30,000.00
David Edwards	10	68-69-66-67=270	$27,000.00

Buick Classic
Course: Westchester C.C., Harrison, N.Y.
Par: 71 Yardage: 6,779
Last day of event: Sunday, June 9, 1991

Player	Place	Score	Earnings
Billy Andrade	Win	68-68-69-68=273	$180,000.00
Brad Bryant	2	66-70-68-71=275	$108,000.00
Nolan Henke	T-3	69-70-67-70=276	$58,000.00
Hale Irwin	T-3	67-69-67-73=276	$58,000.00
Seve Ballesteros	T-5	70-67-69-71=277	$36,500.00
Wayne Levi	T-5	71-72-67-67=277	$36,500.00
Larry Rinker	T-5	68-73-65-71=277	$36,500.00
Ray Floyd	T-8	69-68-69-72=278	$30,000.00

Player	Place	Score	Earnings
Fulton Allem	T-8	66-69-70-73=278	$30,000.00
Howard Twitty	T-10	70-70-70-69=279	$24,000.00
Greg Norman	T-10	70-68-70-71=279	$24,000.00
Fred Couples	T-10	70-65-72-72=279	$24,000.00
Loren Roberts	T-10	68-73-67-71=279	$24,000.00

U.S. Open

Course: Hazeltine National G.C., Chaska, Minn. .
Par: 72 Yardage: 7,149
Last day of event: Sunday, June 16, 1991

Player	Place	Score	Earnings
Payne Stewart	Win	67-70-73-72=282	$235,000.00

Playoff: Beat Scott Simpson in18-hole playoff (Stewart 75, Simpson 77)

Player	Place	Score	Earnings
Scott Simpson	2	70-68-72-72=282	$117,500.00
Larry Nelson	T-3	73-72-72-68=285	$62,574.00
Fred Couples	T-3	70-70-75-70=285	$62,574.00
Fuzzy Zoeller	5	72-73-74-67=286	$41,542.00
Scott Hoch	6	69-71-74-73=287	$36,090.00
Nolan Henke	7	67-71-77-73=288	$32,176.00
Jose Maria Olazabal	T-8	73-71-75-70=289	$26,958.33
Ray Floyd	T-8	73-72-76-68=289	$26,958.34
Corey Pavin	T-8	71-67-79-72=289	$26,958.33

Anheuser-Busch Golf Classic

Course: Kingsmill G.C., Williamsburg, Va.
Par: 71 Yardage: 6,776
Last day of event: Sunday, June 23, 1991

Player	Place	Score	Earnings
Mike Hulbert	Win	66-67-65-68=266	$180,000.00

Playoff: Beat Kenny Knox with par on first extra hole

Player	Place	Score	Earnings
Kenny Knox	2	67-69-62-68=266	$108,000.00
Ian Baker-Finch	T-3	62-68-68-69=267	$58,000.00
Fuzzy Zoeller	T-3	67-69-66-65=267	$58,000.00
Bob Gilder	T-5	63-68-70-68=269	$38,000.00
Brian Claar	T-5	68-68-62-71=269	$38,000.00
Brad Fabel	7	66-67-68-70=271	$33,500.00
Nick Price	T-8	67-69-69-68=273	$25,000.00
Keith Clearwater	T-8	69-66-69-69=273	$25,000.00
Bill Britton	T-8	69-69-68-67=273	$25,000.00
Kenny Perry	T-8	67-68-68-70=273	$25,000.00
Jay Don Blake	T-8	67-68-70-68=273	$25,000.00
Mike Donald	T-8	66-64-68-75=273	$25,000.00
Dan Pohl	T-8	64-67-65-77=273	$25,000.00

Federal Express St. Jude Classic

Course: TPC at Southwind, Germantown, Tenn.
Par: 71 Yardage: 7,006
Last day of event: Sunday, June 30, 1991

Player	Place	Score	Earnings
Fred Couples	Win	68-67-66-68=269	$180,000.00
Rick Fehr	2	64-70-71-67=272	$108,000.00
David Canipe	T-3	69-69-70-65=273	$58,000.00
Jay Haas	T-3	70-65-73-65=273	$58,000.00
Russ Cochran	5	66-67-73-68=274	$40,000.00
Doug Tewell	T-6	68-71-66-70=275	$32,375.00
Nick Price	T-6	71-65-69-70=275	$32,375.00
Robert Thompson	T-6	67-72-69-67=275	$32,375.00
Mark Brooks	T-6	68-66-69-72=275	$32,375.00
Greg Ladehoff	T-10	70-71-67-68=276	$25,000.00
Peter Persons	T-10	67-70-65-74=276	$25,000.00
Bob Gilder	T-10	68-74-67-67=276	$25,000.00

Centel Western Open

Course: Cog Hill G. & C.C. (Dubsdread), Lemont, Ill.
Par: 72 Yardage: 7,040
Last day of event: Sunday, July 7, 1991

Player	Place	Score	Earnings
Russ Cochran	Win	66-72-68-69=275	$180,000.00
Greg Norman	2	69-66-71-71=277	$108,000.00
Fred Couples	3	70-68-68-72=278	$68,000.00
Bob Gilder	4	70-71-70-70=281	$48,000.00
Nick Price	T-5	71-71-70-70=282	$32,750.00
John Huston	T-5	72-70-71-69=282	$32,750.00
D.A. Weibring	T-5	71-72-73-66=282	$32,750.00
Kenny Knox	T-5	73-69-70-70=282	$32,750.00
Gary Hallberg	T-5	67-71-70-74=282	$32,750.00
Dave Barr	T-5	70-74-68-70=282	$32,750.00

New England Classic

Course: Pleasant Valley C.C., Sutton, Mass.
Par: 71 Yardage: 7,110
Last day of event: Sunday, July 14, 1991

Player	Place	Score	Earnings
Bruce Fleisher	Win	64-67-73-64=268	$180,000.00

Playoff: Beat Ian Baker-Finch with birdie on seventh extra hole

Player	Place	Score	Earnings
Ian Baker-Finch	2	66-68-66-68=268	$108,000.00
Gene Sauers	3	67-67-66-69=269	$68,000.00
Ted Schulz	4	65-69-71-67=272	$48,000.00
Ed Dougherty	T-5	69-67-70-67=273	$35,125.00
Barry Jaeckel	T-5	70-65-68-70=273	$35,125.00
Brad Faxon	T-5	70-68-65-70=273	$35,125.00
Charles Bowles	T-5	68-68-71-66=273	$35,125.00
John Adams	T-9	69-68-67-70=274	$28,000.00
Lance Ten Broeck	T-9	70-66-72-66=274	$28,000.00

Chattanooga Classic

Course: ValleyBrook C.C., Hixson, Tenn.
Par: 70 Yardage: 6,641
Last day of event: Sunday, July 21, 1991

Player	Place	Score	Earnings
Dillard Pruitt	Win	66-65-65-64=260	$126,000.00
Lance Ten Broeck	2	64-65-66-67=262	$75,600.00
John Daly	T-3	65-66-67-66=264	$33,600.00
Jim Gallagher, Jr.	T-3	64-68-65-67=264	$33,600.00
Steve Lowery	T-3	63-65-69-67=264	$33,600.00
Dave Rummells	T-3	69-66-68-61=264	$33,600.00
Perry Arthur	T-7	67-64-67-67=265	$21,087.50
Brad Fabel	T-7	67-65-66-67=265	$21,087.50
Russ Cochran	T-7	68-66-67-64=265	$21,087.50
Kenny Knox	T-7	70-63-67-65=265	$21,087.50

British Open

Course: Royal Birkdale G.C., Southport, Lancashire, England
Par: 70 Yardage: 6,940
Last day of event: Sunday, July 21, 1991

Player	Place	Score	Earnings
Ian Baker-Finch	Win	71-71-64-66=272	$151,200.00
Mike Harwood	2	68-70-69-67=274	$117,600.00
Mark O'Meara	T-3	71-68-67-69=275	$92,400.00
Fred Couples	T-3	72-69-70-64=275	$92,400.00
Jodie Mudd	T-5	72-70-72-63=277	$57,400.01
Eamonn Darcy	T-5	73-68-66-70=277	$57,400.01

Player	Place	Score	Earnings
Bob Tway	T-5	75-66-70-66=277	$57,400.01
Craig Parry	8	71-70-69-68=278	$46,200.00
Bernhard Langer	T-9	71-71-70-67=279	$38,359.99
Seve Ballesteros	T-9	66-73-69-71=279	$38,359.99
Greg Norman	T-9	74-68-71-66=279	$38,359.99

Canon Greater Hartford Open
Course: TPC at River Highlands, Cromwell, Conn.
Par: 70 Yardage: 6,820
Last day of event: Sunday, July 28, 1991

Player	Place	Score	Earnings
Billy Ray Brown	Win	67-72-65-67=271	$180,000.00
Playoff: Beat Corey Pavin and Rick Fehr with birdie on first extra hole
Corey Pavin	T-2	65-67-70-69=271	$88,000.00
Rick Fehr	T-2	68-67-66-70=271	$88,000.00
Loren Roberts	T-4	68-69-68-67=272	$41,333.34
Jim Gallagher, Jr.	T-4	68-65-70-69=272	$41,333.33
Billy Andrade	T-4	72-66-66-68=272	$41,333.33
Dan Pohl	T-7	70-69-67-67=273	$31,166.67
Larry Rinker	T-7	71-66-66-70=273	$31,166.66
Mike Reid	T-7	71-69-68-65=273	$31,166.67
Kenny Perry	T-10	67-67-70-70=274	$24,000.00
Dan Forsman	T-10	67-67-71-69=274	$24,000.00
Dave Barr	T-10	67-69-71-67=274	$24,000.00
Ken Green	T-10	67-69-71-67=274	$24,000.00

Buick Open
Course: Warwick Hills C.C., Grand Blanc, Mich.
Par: 72 Yardage: 7,014
Last day of event: Sunday, August 4, 1991

Player	Place	Score	Earnings
Brad Faxon	Win	66-68-71-66=271	$180,000.00
Playoff: Beat Chip Beck with par on first extra hole
Chip Beck	2	67-67-68-69=271	$108,000.00
Steve Pate	T-3	68-69-69-66=272	$52,000.00
Scott Hoch	T-3	63-70-72-67=272	$52,000.00
John Cook	T-3	68-73-66-65=272	$52,000.00
Gene Sauers	T-6	67-68-69-69=273	$32,375.00
Hal Sutton	T-6	69-69-66-69=273	$32,375.00
Nick Faldo	T-6	68-69-65-71=273	$32,375.00
Howard Twitty	T-6	71-66-66-70=273	$32,375.00
Greg Norman	T-10	67-65-71-71=274	$23,000.00
Wayne Grady	T-10	68-66-71-69=274	$23,000.00
Bill Britton	T-10	69-69-65-71=274	$23,000.00
Tim Simpson	T-10	72-68-64-70=274	$23,000.00
Marco Dawson	T-10	66-70-64-74=274	$23,000.00

PGA Championship
Course: Crooked Stick G.C., Carmel, Ind.
Par: 72 Yardage: 7,295
Last day of event: Sunday, August 11, 1991

Player	Place	Score	Earnings
John Daly	Win	69-67-69-71=276	$230,000.00
Bruce Lietzke	2	68-69-72-70=279	$140,000.00
Jim Gallagher, Jr.	3	70-72-72-67=281	$95,000.00
Kenny Knox	4	67-71-70-74=282	$75,000.00
Steven Richardson	T-5	70-72-72-69=283	$60,000.00
Bob Gilder	T-5	73-70-67-73=283	$60,000.00
John Huston	T-7	70-72-70-72=284	$38,000.00
Ray Floyd	T-7	69-74-72-69=284	$38,000.00
David Feherty	T-7	71-74-71-68=284	$38,000.00
Hal Sutton	T-7	74-67-72-71=284	$38,000.00
Steve Pate	T-7	70-75-70-69=284	$38,000.00
Craig Stadler	T-7	68-71-69-76=284	$38,000.00

The International
Course: Castle Pine G.C., Castle Rock, Colo. (Stableford format)
Par: 72 Yardage: 7,559
Last day of event: Sunday, August 18, 1991

Player	Place	Score	Earnings
Jose Maria Olazabal	Win	5-6-8-19-10=10	$198,000.00
Scott Gump	T-2	9-5-3-17-7=7	$82,133.33
Bob Lohr	T-2	2-11-5-18-7=7	$82,133.34
Ian Baker-Finch	T-2	12-9-5-26-7=7	$82,133.33
Ted Schulz	T-5	4-4-8-16-6=6	$38,637.50
Tom Watson	T-5	6-0-14-20-6=6	$38,637.50
Larry Mize	T-5	11-2-8-21-6=6	$38,637.50
Bobby Clampett	T-5	12-6-11-29-6=6	$38,637.50
Rocco Mediate	T-9	2-7-15-24-5=5	$30,800.00
Keith Clearwater	T-9	18-4-6-28-5=5	$30,800.00

NEC World Series of Golf
Course: Firestone C.C. (South), Akron, Ohio
Par: 70 Yardage: 7,149
Last day of event: Sunday, August 25, 1991

Player	Place	Score	Earnings
Tom Purtzer	Win	72-69-67-71=279	$216,000.00
Playoff: Beat Davis Love III and Jim Gallagher, Jr. with par on second extra hole
Davis Love III	T-2	72-66-72-69=279	$105,600.00
Jim Gallagher, Jr.	T-2	72-68-70-69=279	$105,600.00
Mark Brooks	T-4	72-64-74-70=280	$52,800.00
Fred Couples	T-4	74-70-69-67=280	$52,800.00
Joe Ozaki	T-6	72-70-68-72=282	$38,850.00
Nick Price	T-6	72-70-71-69=282	$38,850.00
Joey Sindelar	T-6	70-68-73-71=282	$38,850.00
Dillard Pruitt	T-6	71-66-68-77=282	$38,850.00
Steve Elkington	T-10	71-70-71-71=283	$30,000.00
Andrew Magee	T-10	73-68-70-72=283	$30,000.00
Corey Pavin	T-10	72-68-74-69=283	$30,000.00

Greater Milwaukee Open
Course: Tuckaway C.C., Franklin, Wis.
Par: 72 Yardage: 7,030
Last day of event: Sunday, September 1, 1991

Player	Place	Score	Earnings
Mark Brooks	Win	63-67-70-70=270	$180,000.00
Robert Gamez	2	61-66-74-70=271	$108,000.00
Steve Jones	3	71-66-69-67=273	$68,000.00
Jeff Maggert	4	65-65-71-73=274	$48,000.00
John Adams	T-5	68-68-72-68=276	$38,000.00
Neal Lancaster	T-5	67-66-73-70=276	$38,000.00
D.A. Weibring	T-7	67-67-72-71=277	$31,166.67
Nick Price	T-7	72-67-72-66=277	$31,166.67
Hal Sutton	T-7	65-66-74-72=277	$31,166.66
Ken Green	T-10	70-69-70-69=278	$23,000.00
Jay Haas	T-10	67-70-70-71=278	$23,000.00
Joey Sindelar	T-10	66-70-72-70=278	$23,000.00
Chris Perry	T-10	68-68-72-70=278	$23,000.00
Jodie Mudd	T-10	72-68-70-68=278	$23,000.00

Canadian Open

Course: Glen Abbey G.C., Oakville, Ontario, Canada
Par: 72 Yardage: 7,102
Last day of event: Sunday, September 8, 1991

Player	Place	Score	Earnings
Nick Price	Win	71-69-67-66=273	$180,000.00
David Edwards	2	69-69-68-68=274	$108,000.00
Fred Couples	T-3	69-69-68-69=275	$58,000.00
Ken Green	T-3	68-69-68-70=275	$58,000.00
Jeff Sluman	T-5	69-72-72-64=277	$38,000.00
D.A. Weibring	T-5	69-64-69-75=277	$38,000.00
Jim Benepe	7	64-67-75-72=278	$33,500.00
Neal Lancaster	T-8	70-70-70-69=279	$30,000.00
Brian Kamm	T-8	65-67-74-73=279	$30,000.00
Bob Lohr	T-10	69-69-71-71=280	$24,000.00
Ian Baker-Finch	T-10	68-72-71-69=280	$24,000.00
Paul Azinger	T-10	70-68-70-72=280	$24,000.00
Ray Stewart	T-10	68-69-70-73=280	$24,000.00

Hardee's Golf Classic

Course: Oakwood C.C., Coal Valley, Ill.
Par: 70 Yardage: 6,796
Last day of event: Sunday, September 15, 1991

Player	Place	Score	Earnings
D.A. Weibring	Win	68-67-68-64=267	$180,000.00
Paul Azinger	T-2	65-65-70-68=268	$88,000.00
Peter Jacobsen	T-2	65-66-72-65=268	$88,000.00
Scott Hoch	T-4	69-65-69-66=269	$41,333.34
Greg Norman	T-4	64-67-70-68=269	$41,333.33
Leonard Thompson	T-4	67-62-73-67=269	$41,333.33
Steve Jones	T-7	68-69-64-69=270	$31,166.67
Brad Fabel	T-7	68-69-67-66=270	$31,166.67
Steve Lowery	T-7	65-66-70-69=270	$31,166.66
Tom Purtzer	T-10	68-69-68-66=271	$24,000.00
David Frost	T-10	66-71-66-68=271	$24,000.00
John Huston	T-10	67-71-66-67=271	$24,000.00
David Edwards	T-10	66-69-64-72=271	$24,000.00

B.C. Open

Course: En-Joie G.C., Endicott, N.Y.
Par: 71 Yardage: 6,966
Last day of event: Sunday, September 22, 1991

Player	Place	Score	Earnings
Fred Couples	Win	66-67-68-68=269	$144,000.00
Peter Jacobsen	2	68-68-68-68=272	$86,400.00
Blaine McCallister	T-3	64-68-72-69=273	$46,400.00
Brad Faxon	T-3	65-64-71-73=273	$46,400.00
David Peoples	5	69-70-66-69=274	$32,000.00
Lee Janzen	6	73-68-65-69=275	$28,800.00
Steve Pate	T-7	68-70-68-70=276	$25,800.00
Mark Lye	T-7	70-70-70-66=276	$25,800.00
Jerry Haas	T-9	70-70-70-67=277	$20,800.00
Paul Broadhurst	T-9	66-69-71-71=277	$20,800.00
Mike McCullough	T-9	70-70-66-71=277	$20,800.00
Greg Twiggs	T-9	71-68-69-69=277	$20,800.00

Buick Southern Open

Course: Callaway Gardens Resort, Pine Mountain, Ga.
Par: 72 Yardage: 7,057
Last day of event: Sunday, September 29, 1991

Player	Place	Score	Earnings
David Peoples	Win	67-71-72-66=276	$126,000.00
Robert Gamez	2	71-70-66-70=277	$75,600.00
David Sutherland	T-3	67-71-70-71=279	$40,600.00
Larry Nelson	T-3	69-68-70-72=279	$40,600.00
Morris Hatalsky	T-5	71-70-69-72=282	$25,550.00
Dudley Hart	T-5	71-72-69-70=282	$25,550.00
Buddy Gardner	T-5	73-69-71-69=282	$25,550.00
Bob Lohr	T-8	71-70-71-71=283	$20,300.00
Scott Hoch	T-8	70-72-73-68=283	$20,300.00
David Canipe	T-8	73-72-71-67=283	$20,300.00

H-E-B Texas Open

Course: Oak Hill C.C., San Antonio, Texas
Par: 70 Yardage: 6,576
Last day of event: Sunday, October 6, 1991

Player	Place	Score	Earnings
Blaine McCallister	Win	66-64-69-70=269	$162,000.00
Playoff: Beat Gary Hallberg with birdie on second extra hole			
Gary Hallberg	2	70-65-65-69=269	$97,200.00
Bob Lohr	T-3	68-67-69-69=273	$43,200.00
Ben Crenshaw	T-3	67-68-68-70=273	$43,200.00
Bill Britton	T-3	66-68-68-71=273	$43,200.00
Brian Claar	T-3	68-66-72-67=273	$43,200.00
Bob Estes	T-7	69-68-67-70=274	$25,275.00
Jeff Sluman	T-7	70-67-68-69=274	$25,275.00
Mark Calcavecchia	T-7	65-71-68-70=274	$25,275.00
Bobby Wadkins	T-7	71-64-70-69=274	$25,275.00
Lee Janzen	T-7	71-68-69-66=274	$25,275.00
John Cook	T-7	67-67-66-74=274	$25,275.00

Las Vegas Invitational

Course: Las Vegas C.C., Sunrise C.C., Desert Inn C.C., Las Vegas, Nev.
Home course / Las Vegas C.C., Par: 72 Yardage: 7,164
Last day of event: Sunday, October 13, 1991

Player	Place	Score	Earnings
Andrew Magee	Win	69-65-67-62-66=329	$270,000.00
Playoff: Beat D.A. Weibring with par on second extra hole			
D.A. Weibring	2	70-64-65-64-66=329	$162,000.00
Ted Schulz	T-3	65-68-67-66-65=331	$78,000.00
Jim Gallagher, Jr.	T-3	69-65-69-61-67=331	$78,000.00
Chip Beck	T-3	65-72-59-68-67=331	$78,000.00
Bruce Lietzke	6	68-63-65-67-69=332	$54,000.00
Ed Humenik	T-7	66-69-68-64-66=333	$48,375.00
Mark McCumber	T-7	69-64-67-66-67=333	$48,375.00
Dicky Thompson	T-9	70-68-68-61-67=334	$42,000.00
Ken Green	T-9	70-65-67-67-65=334	$42,000.00

Walt Disney World/Oldsmobile Classic

Course: Walt Disney (Magnolia, Palm), Lake Buena Vista C.C., Lake Buena Vista, Fla.
Home course / Magnolia, Par: 72 Yardage: 7,190
Last day of event: Saturday, October 19, 1991

Player	Place	Score	Earnings
Mark O'Meara	Win	66-66-71-64=267	$180,000.00
David Peoples	2	68-67-68-65=268	$108,000.00
Paul Azinger	3	72-65-65-67=269	$68,000.00
Steve Elkington	4	65-71-67-67=270	$48,000.00
John Cook	T-5	69-69-68-65=271	$36,500.00
Davis Love III	T-5	71-66-66-68=271	$36,500.00
Scott Gump	T-5	71-67-66-67=271	$36,500.00

Player	Place	Score	Earnings
Ken Green	T-8	69-68-67-68=272	$28,000.00
Larry Nelson	T-8	65-70-70-67=272	$28,000.00
Nolan Henke	T-8	67-70-69-66=272	$28,000.00
Robert Gamez	T-8	68-71-68-65=272	$28,000.00

Independent Insurance Agent Open
Course: TPC at The Woodlands, The Woodlands, Texas
Par: 72 Yardage: 7,042
Last day of event: Saturday, October 26, 1991

Player	Place	Score	Earnings
Fulton Allem	Win	71-69-67-66=273	$144,000.00
Billy Ray Brown	T-2	67-67-69-71=274	$59,733.34
Mike Hulbert	T-2	68-69-66-71=274	$59,733.33
Tom Kite	T-2	69-73-64-68=274	$59,733.33
Mike Springer	T-5	71-70-69-65=275	$30,400.00
Duffy Waldorf	T-5	67-67-72-69=275	$30,400.00
Gary Hallberg	T-7	68-69-70-69=276	$23,280.00
Bryan Norton	T-7	70-70-69-67=276	$23,280.00
Mike Reid	T-7	67-68-68-73=276	$23,280.00
Donnie Hammond	T-7	69-68-66-73=276	$23,280.00
Steve Jones	T-7	65-74-70-67=276	$23,280.00

The Tour Championship
Course: Pinehurst C.C. (No 2), Pinehurst, N.C.
Par: 71 Yardage: 7,005
Last day of event: Sunday, November 3, 1991

Player	Place	Score	Earnings
Craig Stadler	Win	66-68-72-71=277	$360,000.00

Playoff: Beat Russ Cochran with birdie on second extra hole

Russ Cochran	2	68-69-71-71=279	$216,000.00
John Daly	3	68-76-68-70=282	$138,000.00
Bruce Lietzke	4	71-69-72-71=283	$96,000.00
Chip Beck	T-5	72-70-72-71=285	$71,000.00
Nolan Henke	T-5	69-70-74-72=285	$71,000.00
Jim Gallagher, Jr.	T-5	71-74-69-71=285	$71,000.00
Nick Price	T-5	70-67-75-73=285	$71,000.00
Steve Elkington	9	69-75-71-71=286	$60,000.00
Jeff Sluman	T-10	74-71-69-73=287	$54,000.00
Corey Pavin	T-10	74-69-72-72=287	$54,000.00
Ian Baker-Finch	T-10	68-76-71-72=287	$54,000.00

1992

This was a breakthrough year for Fred Couples, Tom Kite and Nick Price, each of whom won his first major. Couples scored a two-shot victory over Raymond Floyd at the Masters. Kite, who at 42 may have held the "best player never to have won a major" title longer than any other, beat Jeff Sluman by two shots in a windy, rainy U.S. Open at Pebble Beach. At the PGA Championship, Price was the only player to post four rounds under par and won by three shots at Bellerive. The parade of first-time major winners was interrupted at the British Open by Nick Faldo, who birdied two of Muirfield's last four holes and notched a one-shot victory over John Cook.

Infiniti Tournament of Champions
Course: La Costa C.C., Carlsbad, Calif.
Par: 72 Yardage: 7,022
Last day of event: Sunday, January 12, 1992

Player	Place	Score	Earnings
Steve Elkington	Win	69-71-67-72=279	$144,000.00

Playoff: Beat Brad Faxon with birdie on first extra hole

Brad Faxon	2	68-70-71-70=279	$86,400.00
Billy Andrade	T-3	71-68-70-71=280	$41,600.00

Fred Couples	T-3	72-70-68-70=280	$41,600.00
Rocco Mediate	T-3	73-68-68-71=280	$41,600.00
Paul Azinger	6	67-76-69-70=282	$28,800.00
Davis Love III	T-7	69-71-73-70=283	$25,800.00
Jay Don Blake	T-7	73-66-74-70=283	$25,800.00
Mark O'Meara	9	70-71-71-72=284	$23,200.00
Blaine McCallister	10	65-75-74-71=285	$21,700.00

Bob Hope Chrysler Classic
Course: Bermuda Dunes C.C., PGA West/Palmer, Indian Wells C.C., La Quinta C.C.
Home course / Bermuda Dunes, Par: 72 Yardage: 6,927
Last day of event: Sunday, January 19, 1992

Player	Place	Score	Earnings
John Cook	Win	65-73-63-69-66=336	$198,000.00

Playoff: Beat Gene Sauers with eagle on fourth extra hole. Mark O'Meara and Tom Kite eliminated with pars on first hole; Fehr (bogey) eliminated on second hole.

Mark O'Meara	T-2	66-69-65-67-69=336	$72,600.00
Gene Sauers	T-2	69-65-64-70-68=336	$72,600.00
Rick Fehr	T-2	64-72-66-71-63=336	$72,600.00
Tom Kite	T-2	65-73-68-67-63=336	$72,600.00
Fred Couples	T-6	68-67-69-64-69=337	$38,225.00
David Peoples	T-6	64-71-68-66-68=337	$38,225.00
Davis Love III	T-8	67-68-68-67-68=338	$30,800.00
Kenny Perry	T-8	69-65-66-68-70=338	$30,800.00
Tom Lehman	T-8	70-65-70-67-66=338	$30,800.00
Brian Claar	T-8	71-63-67-68-69=338	$30,800.00

Phoenix Open
Course: TPC of Scottsdale, Scottsdale, Ariz.
Par: 71 Yardage: 6,992
Last day of event: Sunday, January 26, 1992

Player	Place	Score	Earnings
Mark Calcavecchia	Win	69-65-67-63=264	$180,000.00
Duffy Waldorf	2	68-67-67-67=269	$108,000.00
Rocco Mediate	3	69-66-69-67=271	$68,000.00
John Huston	T-4	69-64-69-70=272	$41,333.34
Mark O'Meara	T-4	70-68-65-69=272	$41,333.33
Jay Delsing	T-4	66-65-69-72=272	$41,333.33
Bob Lohr	T-7	68-68-67-70=273	$29,100.00
Gary Hallberg	T-7	69-70-68-66=273	$29,100.00
Nick Price	T-7	66-68-71-68=273	$29,100.00
Ed Fiori	T-7	72-63-70-68=273	$29,100.00
Bruce Lietzke	T-7	73-67-67-66=273	$29,100.00

AT&T Pebble Beach Pro-Am
Courses: Pebble Beach G.L., Spyglass Hill G.C., Poppy Hills G.C., Pebble Beach, Calif.
Home Course / Pebble Beach G.L., Par: 72 Yardage: 6,815
Last day of event: Sunday, February 2, 1992

Player	Place	Score	Earnings
Mark O'Meara	Win	69-68-68-70=275	$198,000.00

Playoff: Beat Jeff Sluman with par on first extra hole

Jeff Sluman	2	64-73-70-68=275	$118,800.00
Paul Azinger	3	74-70-64-68=276	$74,800.00
Steve Elkington	T-4	70-70-69-68=277	$45,466.67
Tom Lehman	T-4	70-71-67-69=277	$45,466.66
Mark Wiebe	T-4	64-74-70-69=277	$45,466.67
Gil Morgan	T-7	71-69-69-70=279	$35,475.00
Larry Rinker	T-7	72-66-72-69=279	$35,475.00
Tom Watson	T-9	70-69-71-70=280	$29,700.00

Player	Place	Score	Earnings
Ben Crenshaw	T-9	71-71-71-67=280	$29,700.00
Chip Beck	T-9	67-71-73-69=280	$29,700.00

United Airlines Hawaiian Open
Course: Waialae C.C., Honolulu, Ha.
Par: 72 Yardage: 6,975
Last day of event: Sunday, February 9, 1992

Player	Place	Score	Earnings
John Cook	Win	67-68-65-65=265	$216,000.00
Paul Azinger	2	65-67-68-67=267	$129,600.00
Jeff Maggert	3	68-68-67-68=271	$81,600.00
Wayne Levi	4	69-63-72-68=272	$57,600.00
Tom Lehman	T-5	68-69-66-70=273	$45,600.00
Keith Clearwater	T-5	68-70-66-69=273	$45,600.00
Jim Woodward	7	67-71-70-66=274	$40,200.00
Mike Sullivan	T-8	69-67-69-70=275	$33,600.00
Jim Gallagher, Jr.	T-8	69-70-66-70=275	$33,600.00
Larry Mize	T-8	70-70-70-65=275	$33,600.00
Mark Brooks	T-8	69-71-65-70=275	$33,600.00

Northern Telecom Open
Course: Tucson National G.C., Tucson, Ariz.
Par: 72 Yardage: 7,010
Last day of event: Sunday, February 16, 1992

Player	Place	Score	Earnings
Lee Janzen	Win	71-67-67-65=270	$198,000.00
Bill Britton	2	67-70-68-66=271	$118,800.00
David Toms	3	71-68-70-63=272	$74,800.00
Jay Don Blake	T-4	68-70-67-69=274	$39,875.00
Buddy Gardner	T-4	68-70-70-66=274	$39,875.00
Olin Browne	T-4	70-68-70-66=274	$39,875.00
Dudley Hart	T-4	69-69-65-71=274	$39,875.00
Ken Green	T-4	71-65-68-70=274	$39,875.00
Jim Gallagher, Jr.	T-4	72-65-68-69=274	$39,875.00
Bruce Fleisher	T-10	66-68-70-71=275	$28,600.00
Gary McCord	T-10	73-69-68-65=275	$28,600.00

Buick Invitational of California
Course: Torrey Pines (South), Torrey Pines (North), San Diego, Calif.
Home Course -Par: 72 Yardage: 7,021
Last day of event: Sunday, February 23, 1992

Player	Place	Score	Earnings
Steve Pate	Win	64-69-67=200	$180,000.00
Chip Beck	2	70-65-66=201	$108,000.00
Steve Elkington	T-3	65-68-69=202	$52,000.00
Robert Wrenn	T-3	63-69-70=202	$52,000.00
Chris Tucker	T-3	67-65-70=202	$52,000.00
D.A. Weibring	T-6	68-67-68=203	$30,250.00
Jodie Mudd	T-6	68-69-66=203	$30,250.00
Tom Lehman	T-6	71-67-65=203	$30,250.00
Tom Watson	T-6	63-68-72=203	$30,250.00
Mike Springer	T-6	66-65-72=203	$30,250.00
Bob Lohr	T-6	72-65-66=203	$30,250.00

Nissan Los Angeles Open
Course: Riviera C.C., Pacific Palisades, Calif.
Par: 71 Yardage: 7,029
Last day of event: Sunday, March 1, 1992

Player	Place	Score	Earnings
Fred Couples	Win	68-67-64-70=269	$180,000.00

Playoff: Beat Davis Love III with birdie on second extra hole

Player	Place	Score	Earnings
Davis Love III	2	67-63-70-69=269	$108,000.00
Jay Haas	T-3	67-69-69-65=270	$58,000.00
Yoshinori Kaneko	T-3	69-69-67-65=270	$58,000.00
Rocco Mediate	5	67-68-66-70=271	$40,000.00
Sandy Lyle	6	67-67-66-72=272	$36,000.00
Doug Martin	7	68-68-69-68=273	$33,500.00
Mark McCumber	T-8	68-70-69-67=274	$28,000.00
John Daly	T-8	68-70-70-66=274	$28,000.00
Scott Simpson	T-8	70-67-70-67=274	$28,000.00
Steve Elkington	T-8	70-70-68-66=274	$28,000.00

Doral-Ryder Open
Course: Doral C.C. (Blue), Miami, Fla.
Par: 72 Yardage: 6,939
Last day of event: Sunday, March 8, 1992

Player	Place	Score	Earnings
Ray Floyd	Win	67-67-67-70=271	$252,000.00
Fred Couples	T-2	66-69-69-69=273	$123,200.00
Keith Clearwater	T-2	68-67-70-68=273	$123,200.00
Ken Green	T-4	69-70-68-67=274	$61,600.00
Davis Love III	T-4	71-68-68-67=274	$61,600.00
Howard Twitty	6	68-69-68-70=275	$50,400.00
Hale Irwin	T-7	70-66-70-70=276	$42,175.00
Mark O'Meara	T-7	70-71-65-70=276	$42,175.00
Larry Nelson	T-7	68-71-65-72=276	$42,175.00
Tom Kite	T-7	73-68-66-69=276	$42,175.00

Honda Classic
Course: Weston Hills G. & C.C., Ft. Lauderdale, Fla.
Par: 72 Yardage: 7,069
Last day of event: Sunday, March 15, 1992

Player	Place	Score	Earnings
Corey Pavin	Win	68-67-70-68=273	$198,000.00

Playoff: Beat Fred Couples with birdie on second extra hole

Player	Place	Score	Earnings
Fred Couples	2	69-68-65-71=273	$118,800.00
Keith Clearwater	T-3	66-70-70-68=274	$49,610.00
Blaine McCallister	T-3	68-68-68-70=274	$49,610.00
Ray Floyd	T-3	66-68-71-69=274	$49,610.00
Mark Brooks	T-3	69-70-64-71=274	$49,610.00
Billy Ray Brown	T-3	71-70-68-65=274	$49,610.00
Bruce Lietzke	8	70-66-71-68=275	$34,100.00
Andrew Magee	T-9	71-70-68-67=276	$30,800.00
Curtis Strange	T-9	72-70-68-66=276	$30,800.00

The Nestle Invitational
Course: Bay Hill Club, Orlando, Fla.
Par: 72 Yardage: 7,114
Last day of event: Sunday, March 22, 1992

Player	Place	Score	Earnings
Fred Couples	Win	67-69-63-70=269	$180,000.00
Gene Sauers	2	70-70-65-73=278	$108,000.00
John Huston	T-3	68-71-73-69=281	$45,100.00
Dan Pohl	T-3	71-73-67-70=281	$45,100.00
Jeff Sluman	T-3	73-71-68-69=281	$45,100.00
Duffy Waldorf	T-3	74-69-70-68=281	$45,100.00
Mark Brooks	T-3	68-75-69-69=281	$45,100.00
Brad Faxon	T-8	71-73-68-70=282	$29,000.00
Davis Love III	T-8	74-70-67-71=282	$29,000.00
Tom Kite	T-8	76-69-67-70=282	$29,000.00

The Players Championship

Course: TPC at Sawgrass, Ponte Vedra Beach, Fla.
Par: 72 Yardage: 6,857
Last day of event: Sunday, March 29, 1992

Player	Place	Score	Earnings
Davis Love III	Win	67-68-71-67=273	$324,000.00
Tom Watson	T-2	68-70-70-69=277	$118,800.00
Ian Baker-Finch	T-2	70-67-68-72=277	$118,800.00
Phil Blackmar	T-2	67-69-68-73=277	$118,800.00
Nick Faldo	T-2	68-68-67-74=277	$118,800.00
Tom Sieckmann	T-6	71-72-67-68=278	$62,550.00
Craig Parry	T-6	67-68-73-70=278	$62,550.00
Nick Price	8	71-67-69-72=279	$55,800.00
John Mahaffey	T-9	71-71-69-69=280	$46,800.00
Mark Brooks	T-9	67-70-70-73=280	$46,800.00
Mark O'Meara	T-9	69-69-74-68=280	$46,800.00
Jose Maria Olazabal	T-9	69-65-75-71=280	$46,800.00

Freeport-McMoRan Classic

Course: English Turn G. & C.C., New Orleans, La.
Par: 72 Yardage: 7,106
Last day of event: Sunday, April 5, 1992

Player	Place	Score	Earnings
Chip Beck	Win	67-65-74-70=276	$180,000.00
Greg Norman	T-2	70-68-70-69=277	$88,000.00
Mike Standly	T-2	69-73-66-69=277	$88,000.00
Brad Bryant	T-4	67-69-71-72=279	$44,000.00
Jeff Maggert	T-4	68-69-67-75=279	$44,000.00
Neal Lancaster	T-6	69-71-71-70=281	$30,250.00
Duffy Waldorf	T-6	68-71-70-72=281	$30,250.00
Craig Parry	T-6	72-68-71-70=281	$30,250.00
Larry Rinker	T-6	70-69-69-73=281	$30,250.00
John Inman	T-6	73-67-69-72=281	$30,250.00
Nick Faldo	T-6	74-69-69-69=281	$30,250.00

Masters

Course: Augusta National G.C., Augusta, Ga.
Par: 72 Yardage: 6,925
Last day of event: Sunday, April 12, 1992

Player	Place	Score	Earnings
Fred Couples	Win	69-67-69-70=275	$270,000.00
Ray Floyd	2	69-68-69-71=277	$162,000.00
Corey Pavin	3	72-71-68-67=278	$102,000.00
Jeff Sluman	T-4	65-74-70-71=280	$66,000.00
Mark O'Meara	T-4	74-67-69-70=280	$66,000.00
Nolan Henke	T-6	70-71-70-70=281	$43,829.00
Ted Schulz	T-6	68-69-72-72=281	$43,829.00
Nick Price	T-6	70-71-67-73=281	$43,829.00
Greg Norman	T-6	70-70-73-68=281	$43,829.00
Larry Mize	T-6	73-69-71-68=281	$43,829.00
Steve Pate	T-6	73-71-70-67=281	$43,829.00
Ian Baker-Finch	T-6	70-69-68-74=281	$43,829.00

Deposit Guaranty Classic

Course: Hattiesburg C.C., Hattiesburg, Miss.
Par: 70 Yardage: 6,594
Last day of event: Sunday, April 12, 1992

Player	Place	Score	Earnings
Richard Zokol	Win	67-67-66-67=267	$54,000.00
Greg Twiggs	T-2	65-69-65-69=268	$19,800.00

Bob Eastwood	T-2	67-65-69-67=268	$19,800.00
Mike Donald	T-2	68-62-67-71=268	$19,800.00
Mike Nicolette	T-2	71-64-64-69=268	$19,800.00
Jack Renner	T-6	68-69-69-63=269	$9,713.00
Frank Conner	T-6	69-66-66-68=269	$9,713.00
Marco Dawson	T-6	67-68-70-64=269	$9,713.00
Mike Tschetter	T-6	70-64-71-64=269	$9,713.00
Bob Wolcott	T-10	69-68-66-67=270	$7,500.00
Robert Thompson	T-10	69-69-67-65=270	$7,500.00
Michael Cunning	T-10	66-70-66-68=270	$7,500.00

MCI Heritage Classic

Course: Harbour Town G.L., Hilton Head, S.C.
Par: 71 Yardage: 6,657
Last day of event: Sunday, April 19, 1992

Player	Place	Score	Earnings
Davis Love III	Win	67-67-67-68=269	$180,000.00
Chip Beck	2	69-65-71-68=273	$108,000.00
Nick Price	3	71-71-66-66=274	$68,000.00
Russ Cochran	T-4	70-69-70-66=275	$44,000.00
Fuzzy Zoeller	T-4	73-67-67-68=275	$44,000.00
Wayne Levi	T-6	69-68-69-70=276	$30,250.00
Wayne Grady	T-6	69-70-70-67=276	$30,250.00
Craig Stadler	T-6	71-68-70-67=276	$30,250.00
Mark O'Meara	T-6	69-65-70-72=276	$30,250.00
Kenny Perry	T-6	72-70-66-68=276	$30,250.00
Brad Faxon	T-6	68-73-67-68=276	$30,250.00

Kmart Greater Greensboro Open

Course: Forest Oaks C.C., Greensboro, N.C.
Par: 72 Yardage: 6,984
Last day of event: Sunday, April 26, 1992

Player	Place	Score	Earnings
Davis Love III	Win	71-68-71-62=272	$225,000.00
John Cook	2	73-71-66-68=278	$135,000.00
Tom Kite	T-3	70-70-70-69=279	$53,437.50
Tom Byrum	T-3	71-67-70-71=279	$53,437.50
Paul Azinger	T-3	68-69-72-70=279	$53,437.50
Mike Reid	T-3	68-67-73-71=279	$53,437.50
Craig Parry	T-3	73-69-68-69=279	$53,437.50
Chip Beck	T-3	69-67-75-68=279	$53,437.50
Rocco Mediate	9	72-66-69-73=280	$36,250.00
Mark Brooks	T-10	68-71-71-71=281	$33,750.00
Mike Hulbert	T-10	70-70-71-71=282	$23,333.33
Jay Delsing	T-10	69-71-72-70=282	$23,333.33
Dillard Pruitt	T-10	71-71-68-72=282	$23,333.33
Ken Green	T-10	71-70-72-69=282	$23,333.34
Bill Britton	T-10	67-73-71-71=282	$23,333.33
Brad Faxon	T-10	70-68-70-74=282	$23,333.33
Jeff Sluman	T-10	70-69-74-69=282	$23,333.34
Wayne Levi	T-10	72-68-74-68=282	$23,333.34
Phil Blackmar	T-10	67-66-78-71=282	$23,333.33

Shell Houston Open

Course: TPC at The Woodlands, The Woodlands, Texas
Par: 72 Yardage: 7,042
Last day of event: Sunday, May 3, 1992

Player	Place	Score	Earnings
Fred Funk	Win	68-72-62-70=272	$216,000.00
Kirk Triplett	2	68-70-69-67=274	$129,600.00
Billy Ray Brown	3	72-71-68-64=275	$81,600.00

Player	Place	Score	Earnings
Fulton Allem	4	67-70-66-73=276	$57,600.00
Blaine McCallister	T-5	69-69-69-70=277	$45,600.00
Mark Brooks	T-5	71-67-67-72=277	$45,600.00
Rick Fehr	T-7	70-69-68-71=278	$36,150.00
Nick Price	T-7	72-67-69-70=278	$36,150.00
Dan Forsman	T-7	69-69-73-67=278	$36,150.00
Robert Gamez	T-7	70-67-77-64=278	$36,150.00

BellSouth Classic

Course: Atlanta C.C., Atlanta, Ga.
Par: 72 Yardage: 7,007
Last day of event: Sunday, May 10, 1992

Player	Place	Score	Earnings
Tom Kite	Win	70-65-72-65=272	$180,000.00
Jay Don Blake	2	69-68-70-68=275	$108,000.00
Larry Mize	T-3	70-69-71-69=279	$58,000.00
Russ Cochran	T-3	73-66-71-69=279	$58,000.00
David Peoples	5	73-67-72-68=280	$40,000.00
Patrick Burke	T-6	72-69-68-72=281	$34,750.00
Kenny Perry	T-6	72-71-68-70=281	$34,750.00
Lanny Wadkins	8	72-74-69-67=282	$31,000.00
Dave Barr	T-9	71-70-71-71=283	$26,000.00
Steve Pate	T-9	71-70-72-70=283	$26,000.00
Brad Bryant	T-9	70-69-71-73=283	$26,000.00
Paul Azinger	T-9	74-71-65-73=283	$26,000.00

GTE Byron Nelson Classic

Course: TPC at Las Colinas, Irving, Texas
Par: 70 Yardage: 6,850
Last day of event: Sunday, May 17, 1992

Player	Place	Score	Earnings
Billy Ray Brown	Win	69-64-66=199	$198,000.00
Playoff: Beat Ray Floyd, Ben Crenshaw and Bruce Lietzke with birdie on first extra hole			
Bruce Lietzke	T-2	65-67-67=199	$82,133.33
Ben Crenshaw	T-2	65-68-66=199	$82,133.33
Ray Floyd	T-2	66-68-65=199	$82,133.34
Jay Haas	T-5	65-66-69=200	$40,150.00
Jim Woodward	T-5	69-68-63=200	$40,150.00
Marco Dawson	T-5	70-63-67=200	$40,150.00
Dudley Hart	T-8	67-68-66=201	$31,900.00
Bill Glasson	T-8	68-66-67=201	$31,900.00
Jeff Sluman	T-8	73-66-62=201	$31,900.00

Southwestern Bell Colonial

Course: Colonial C.C., Fort Worth, Texas
Par: 70 Yardage: 7,096
Last day of event: Sunday, May 24, 1992

Player	Place	Score	Earnings
Bruce Lietzke	Win	69-68-64-66=267	$234,000.00
Playoff: Beat Corey Pavin with birdie on first extra hole			
Corey Pavin	2	68-64-70-65=267	$140,400.00
Jim Gallagher, Jr.	3	70-68-63-68=269	$88,400.00
Mark Brooks	T-4	69-66-68-67=270	$57,200.00
Rick Fehr	T-4	69-68-69-64=270	$57,200.00
Keith Clearwater	T-6	66-69-69-68=272	$42,087.50
Dillard Pruitt	T-6	67-68-69-68=272	$42,087.50
Greg Norman	T-6	70-68-69-65=272	$42,087.50
John Cook	T-6	69-71-67-65=272	$42,087.50
Bruce Fleisher	T-10	68-69-70-66=273	$28,816.67
Mark Calcavecchia	T-10	69-66-68-70=273	$28,816.66
Ben Crenshaw	T-10	70-67-70-66=273	$28,816.67
Craig Stadler	T-10	66-67-71-69=273	$28,816.66
Fulton Allem	T-10	69-65-71-68=273	$28,816.67
Jeff Sluman	T-10	72-65-68-68=273	$28,816.67

Kemper Open

Course: TPC at Avenel, Potomac, Md.
Par: 71 Yardage: 7,005
Last day of event: Sunday, May 31, 1992

Player	Place	Score	Earnings
Bill Glasson	Win	69-68-71-68=276	$198,000.00
John Daly	T-2	68-69-70-70=277	$72,600.00
Ken Green	T-2	68-70-71-68=277	$72,600.00
Mike Springer	T-2	70-68-71-68=277	$72,600.00
Howard Twitty	T-2	71-70-69-67=277	$72,600.00
Payne Stewart	T-6	70-68-70-70=278	$34,430.00
Mark Calcavecchia	T-6	67-69-71-71=278	$34,430.00
Mark Brooks	T-6	71-70-70-67=278	$34,430.00
Greg Kraft	T-6	67-68-73-70=278	$34,430.00
Wayne Riley	T-6	71-67-73-67=278	$34,430.00

Memorial Tournament

Course: Muirfield Village G.C., Dubin, Ohio
Par: 72 Yardage: 7,104
Last day of event: Sunday, June 7, 1992

Player	Place	Score	Earnings
David Edwards	Win	71-65-70-67=273	$234,000.00
Playoff: Beat Rick Fehr with par on second extra hole			
Rick Fehr	2	69-70-67-67=273	$140,400.00
Payne Stewart	T-3	72-70-66-66=274	$75,400.00
Joey Sindelar	T-3	69-65-67-73=274	$75,400.00
Nolan Henke	T-5	65-69-71-70=275	$49,400.00
Mark Brooks	T-5	67-68-69-71=275	$49,400.00
Bob Gilder	T-7	71-67-68-70=276	$37,830.00
David Frost	T-7	72-70-69-65=276	$37,830.00
Vijay Singh	T-7	73-68-66-69=276	$37,830.00
Larry Mize	T-7	73-66-69-68=276	$37,830.00
Tom Kite	T-7	74-67-67-68=276	$37,830.00

Federal Express St. Jude Classic

Course: TPC at Southwind, Germantown, Tenn.
Par: 71 Yardage: 7,006
Last day of event: Sunday, June 14, 1992

Player	Place	Score	Earnings
Jay Haas	Win	68-67-64-64=263	$198,000.00
Dan Forsman	T-2	64-66-68-68=266	$96,800.00
Robert Gamez	T-2	68-69-66-63=266	$96,800.00
Jim McGovern	4	70-62-67-68=267	$52,800.00
Jim Gallagher, Jr.	5	69-65-66-68=268	$44,000.00
Peter Persons	T-6	63-70-69-67=269	$35,612.50
Joe Ozaki	T-6	65-68-70-66=269	$35,612.50
Scott Gump	T-6	68-70-64-67=269	$35,612.50
Howard Twitty	T-6	68-70-66-65=269	$35,612.50
Dan Halldorson	T-10	66-67-68-69=270	$27,500.00
Russ Cochran	T-10	67-65-69-69=270	$27,500.00
Paul Azinger	T-10	67-69-68-66=270	$27,500.00

U.S. Open

Courses: Pebble Beach G.L. , Pebble Beach, Calif.
Par: 72 Yardage: 6,809
Last day of event: Sunday, June 21, 1992

Player	Place	Score	Earnings
Tom Kite	Win	71-72-70-72=285	$275,000.00
Jeff Sluman	2	73-74-69-71=287	$137,500.00
Colin Montgomerie	3	70-71-77-70=288	$84,245.00
Nick Faldo	T-4	70-76-68-77=291	$54,924.00
Nick Price	T-4	71-72-77-71=291	$54,924.00
Billy Andrade	T-6	72-74-72-74=292	$32,316.00
Jay Don Blake	T-6	70-74-75-73=292	$32,316.00
Bob Gilder	T-6	73-70-75-74=292	$32,316.00
Mike Hulbert	T-6	74-73-70-75=292	$32,316.00
Tom Lehman	T-6	69-74-72-77=292	$32,316.00
Joey Sindelar	T-6	74-72-68-78=292	$32,316.00
Ian Woosnam	T-6	72-72-69-79=292	$32,316.00

Buick Classic

Course: Westchester C.C., Harrison, N.Y.
Par: 71 Yardage: 6,779
Last day of event: Sunday, June 28, 1992

Player	Place	Score	Earnings
David Frost	Win	67-68-67-66=268	$180,000.00
Duffy Waldorf	2	69-67-69-71=276	$108,000.00
Fred Funk	T-3	69-67-71-70=277	$52,000.00
Lee Janzen	T-3	70-71-67-69=277	$52,000.00
Paul Azinger	T-3	75-67-69-66=277	$52,000.00
Tom Kite	T-6	70-70-67-71=278	$33,500.00
Craig Parry	T-6	68-72-72-66=278	$33,500.00
Greg Norman	T-6	71-73-65-69=278	$33,500.00
Steve Elkington	T-9	67-71-70-71=279	$25,000.00
Bill Britton	T-9	71-67-69-72=279	$25,000.00
Fred Couples	T-9	71-67-72-69=279	$25,000.00
Craig Stadler	T-9	72-67-71-69=279	$25,000.00
Mike Smith	T-9	73-69-67-70=279	$25,000.00

Centel Western Open

Course: Cog Hill G. & C.C. (Dubsdread), Lemont, Ill.
Par: 72 Yardage: 7,040
Last day of event: Sunday, July 5, 1992

Player	Place	Score	Earnings
Ben Crenshaw	Win	70-72-65-69=276	$198,000.00
Greg Norman	2	68-69-68-72=277	$118,800.00
Fred Couples	T-3	70-69-69-70=278	$52,800.00
Chip Beck	T-3	70-71-70-67=278	$52,800.00
Duffy Waldorf	T-3	68-68-70-72=278	$52,800.00
Blaine McCallister	T-3	64-73-71-70=278	$52,800.00
Jeff Sluman	T-7	72-72-63-72=279	$35,475.00
Tom Purtzer	T-7	73-69-68-69=279	$35,475.00
Brian Claar	T-9	68-71-71-70=280	$25,457.14
Tom Watson	T-9	70-69-70-71=280	$25,457.14
Bruce Fleisher	T-9	71-71-68-70=280	$25,457.15
Tom Lehman	T-9	67-72-70-71=280	$25,457.14
Nick Price	T-9	69-69-72-70=280	$25,457.14
Russ Cochran	T-9	71-72-69-68=280	$25,457.15
Ian Baker-Finch	T-9	65-72-74-69=280	$25,457.14

Anheuser-Busch Golf Classic

Course: Kingsmill G.C., Williamsburg, Va.
Par: 71 Yardage: 6,776
Last day of event: Sunday, July 12, 1992

Player	Place	Score	Earnings
David Peoples	Win	66-69-67-69=271	$198,000.00
Jim Gallagher, Jr.	T-2	69-67-68-68=272	$82,133.33
Ed Dougherty	T-3	66-69-66-71=272	$82,133.33
Bill Britton	T-3	68-71-64-69=272	$82,133.34
Tom Lehman	5	67-68-71-67=273	$44,000.00
J.P. Hayes	T-6	70-70-67-68=275	$35,612.50
Peter Parsons	T-6	66-68-71-70=275	$35,612.50
P.H. Horgan III	T-6	71-68-66-70=275	$35,612.50
Bruce Lietzke	T-6	72-63-68-72=275	$35,612.50
Curtis Strange	10	75-63-67-71=276	$29,700.00

Chattanooga Classic

Course: Council Fire G. & C.C., Chattanooga, Tenn.
Par: 72 Yardage: 6,999
Last day of event: Sunday, July 19, 1992

Player	Place	Score	Earnings
Mark Carnevale	Win	68-71-66-64=269	$144,000.00
Dan Forsman	T-2	67-68-69-67=271	$70,400.00
Ed Dougherty	T-2	69-69-62-71=271	$70,400.00
Brad Fabel	T-4	69-66-70-68=273	$33,066.67
David Edwards	T-4	66-71-67-69=273	$33,066.66
Steve Lamontagne	T-4	66-72-69-66=273	$33,066.67
John Inman	T-7	66-70-68-70=274	$23,280.00
John Mahaffey	T-7	67-69-67-71=274	$23,280.00
Andy Bean	T-7	68-71-64-71=274	$23,280.00
Dick Mast	T-7	69-71-66-68=274	$23,280.00
Kelly Gibson	T-7	71-70-70-63=274	$23,280.00

British Open

Course: Muirfield G.C., Muirfield, East Lothian, Scotland
Par: 71 Yardage: 6,970
Last day of event: Sunday, July 19, 1992

Player	Place	Score	Earnings
Nick Faldo	Win	66-64-69-73=272	$190,000.00
John Cook	2	66-67-70-70=273	$150,000.00
Jose Maria Olazabal	3	70-67-69-68=274	$128,000.00
Steve Pate	4	64-70-69-73=276	$106,000.00
Robert Karlsson	T-5	70-68-70-71=279	$60,142.86
Malcolm Mackenzie	T-5	71-67-70-71=279	$60,142.86
Andrew Magee	T-5	67-72-70-70=279	$60,142.86
Ian Woosnam	T-5	65-73-70-71=279	$60,142.86
Gordon Brand Jr.	T-5	65-68-72-74=279	$60,142.86
Ernie Els	T-5	66-69-70-74=279	$60,142.86
Donnie Hammond	T-5	70-65-70-74=279	$60,142.86

New England Classic

Course: Pleasant Valley C.C., Sutton, Mass.
Par: 71 Yardage: 7,110
Last day of event: Sunday, July 26, 1992

Player	Place	Score	Earnings
Brad Faxon	Win	66-67-67-68=268	$180,000.00
Phil Mickelson	2	66-69-69-66=270	$108,000.00
Steve Elkington	T-3	66-68-69-68=271	$48,000.00
John Cook	T-3	68-66-68-69=271	$48,000.00
Gene Sauers	T-3	69-70-66-66=271	$48,000.00
David Peoples	T-3	70-66-67-68=271	$48,000.00
Wayne Levi	T-7	66-68-68-70=272	$30,125.00
Kelly Gibson	T-7	66-67-70-69=272	$30,125.00

Player	Place	Score	Earnings
Lon Hinkle	T-7	69-67-66-70=272	$30,125.00
Roger Maltbie	T-7	65-66-69-72=272	$30,125.00

Canon Greater Hartford Open
Course: TPC at River Highlands, Cromwell, Conn.
Par: 70 Yardage: 6,820
Last day of event: Sunday, August 2, 1992

Player	Place	Score	Earnings
Lanny Wadkins	Win	68-70-71-65=274	$180,000.00
Dan Forsman	T-2	69-69-68-70=276	$74,666.67
Donnie Hammond	T-2	66-70-68-72=276	$74,666.66
Nick Price	T-2	68-67-72-69=276	$74,666.67
Jeff Sluman	T-5	67-70-70-70=277	$36,500.00
Gil Morgan	T-5	66-68-71-72=277	$36,500.00
Bob Estes	T-5	68-69-68-72=277	$36,500.00
Ken Green	T-8	68-72-70-68=278	$29,000.00
Billy Mayfair	T-8	69-66-71-72=278	$29,000.00
Phil Blackmar	T-8	69-72-70-67=278	$29,000.00

Buick Open
Course: Warwick Hills C.C., Grand Blanc, Mich.
Par: 72 Yardage: 7,014
Last day of event: Sunday, August 9, 1992

Player	Place	Score	Earnings
Dan Forsman	Win	72-67-70-67=276	$180,000.00

Playoff: Beat Steve Elkington with par on second extra hole (Brad Faxon eliminated on first hole)

Player	Place	Score	Earnings
Brad Faxon	T-2	69-69-70-68=276	$88,000.00
Steve Elkington	T-2	70-69-67-70=276	$88,000.00
John Huston	T-4	69-68-71-69=277	$44,000.00
Robin Freeman	T-4	74-69-66-68=277	$44,000.00
Greg Lesher	T-6	68-71-71-68=278	$34,750.00
Tom Kite	T-6	72-69-72-65=278	$34,750.00
Dave Rummells	T-8	71-68-70-70=279	$30,000.00
Mike Sullivan	T-8	69-69-68-73=279	$30,000.00
Keith Clearwater	T-10	70-68-70-72=280	$25,000.00
Mark Hayes	T-10	73-69-70-68=280	$25,000.00
Fred Funk	T-10	69-71-78-62=280	$25,000.00

PGA Championship
Course: Bellerive C.C., St Louis, Mo.
Par: 71 Yardage: 7,024
Last day of event: Sunday, August 16, 1992

Player	Place	Score	Earnings
Nick Price	Win	70-70-68-70=278	$280,000.00
John Cook	T-2	71-72-67-71=281	$101,250.00
Jim Gallagher, Jr.	T-2	72-66-72-71=281	$101,250.00
Gene Sauers	T-2	67-69-70-75=281	$101,250.00
Nick Faldo	T-2	68-70-76-67=281	$101,250.00
Jeff Maggert	6	71-72-65-74=282	$60,000.00
Dan Forsman	T-7	70-73-70-70=283	$52,500.00
Russ Cochran	T-7	69-69-76-69=283	$52,500.00
Brian Claar	T-9	68-73-73-70=284	$40,000.00
Anders Forsbrand	T-9	73-71-70-70=284	$40,000.00
Duffy Waldorf	T-9	74-73-68-69=284	$40,000.00

The International
Course: Castle Pine G.C., Castle Rock, Colo. (Stableford format)
Par: 72 Yardage: 7,559
Last day of event: Sunday, August 23, 1992

Player	Place	Score	Earnings
Brad Faxon	Win	4-7-7-18-14=14	$216,000.00
Lee Janzen	2	5-7-7-19-12=12	$129,600.00
Steve Elkington	T-3	8-3-8-19-10=10	$69,600.00
D.A. Weibring	T-3	0-12-7-19-10=10	$69,600.00
John Daly	5	8-8-15-31-9=9	$48,000.00
Bruce Lietzke	T-6	7-10-3-20-8=8	$40,200.00
Greg Norman	T-6	9-10-5-24-8=8	$40,200.00
Steve Pate	T-6	8-10-8-26-8=8	$40,200.00
Keith Clearwater	9	-4-9-12-17-7=7	$34,800.00
Tom Watson	10	3-7-6-16-6=6	$32,400.00

NEC World Series of Golf
Course: Firestone C.C. (South), Akron, Ohio
Par: 70 Yardage: 7,149
Last day of event: Sunday, August 30, 1992

Player	Place	Score	Earnings
Craig Stadler	Win	69-65-69-70=273	$252,000.00
Corey Pavin	2	69-71-69-65=274	$151,200.00
Fred Couples	3	67-70-70-68=275	$95,200.00
John Cook	4	70-74-66-68=278	$67,200.00
Nick Price	T-5	72-68-68-72=280	$53,200.00
David Peoples	T-5	68-70-68-74=280	$53,200.00
Andrew Magee	T-7	69-70-71-71=281	$45,150.00
Mark Calcavecchia	T-7	73-71-63-74=281	$45,150.00
D.A. Weibring	T-9	68-71-73-70=282	$39,200.00
Chip Beck	T-9	65-70-77-70=282	$39,200.00

Greater Milwaukee Open
Course: Tuckaway C.C., Franklin, Wis.
Par: 72 Yardage: 7,030
Last day of event: Sunday, September 6, 1992

Player	Place	Score	Earnings
Richard Zokol	Win	67-71-64-67=269	$180,000.00
Dick Mast	2	67-69-71-64=271	$108,000.00
Dudley Hart	T-3	69-67-69-68=273	$52,000.00
Tom Lehman	T-3	68-67-72-66=273	$52,000.00
Mark Brooks	T-3	70-66-65-72=273	$52,000.00
Larry Mize	T-6	70-67-69-68=274	$33,500.00
Nick Price	T-6	69-71-65-69=274	$33,500.00
Payne Stewart	T-6	68-72-67-67=274	$33,500.00
Joel Edwards	T-9	70-69-70-66=275	$27,000.00
Jay Haas	T-9	69-71-64-71=275	$27,000.00
Joey Sindelar	T-9	71-67-71-66=275	$27,000.00

Canadian Open
Course: Glen Abbey G.C., Oakville, Ontario, Canada
Par: 72 Yardage: 7,102
Last day of event: Sunday, September 13, 1992

Player	Place	Score	Earnings
Greg Norman	Win	73-66-71-70=280	$180,000.00

Playoff: Beat Bruce Lietzke with birdie on second extra hole

Player	Place	Score	Earnings
Bruce Lietzke	2	71-64-73-72=280	$108,000.00
Nick Price	3	69-70-73-69=281	$68,000.00
Jay Delsing	T-4	71-71-71-69=282	$41,333.33
Corey Pavin	T-4	67-74-71-70=282	$41,333.33
Joey Sindelar	T-4	70-74-71-67=282	$41,333.34
Keith Clearwater	7	73-71-71-68=283	$33,500.00
Don Pooley	T-8	67-73-73-71=284	$28,000.00
Fred Couples	T-8	71-69-71-73=284	$28,000.00
David Frost	T-8	71-70-73-70=284	$28,000.00
Mark Wiebe	T-8	76-66-71-71=284	$28,000.00

Hardee's Golf Classic

Course: Oakwood C.C., Coal Valley, Ill.
Par: 70 Yardage: 6,796
Last day of event: Sunday, September 20, 1992

Player	Place	Score	Earnings
David Frost	Win	62-68-64-72=266	$180,000.00
Tom Lehman	T-2	64-69-66-70=269	$88,000.00
Loren Roberts	T-2	67-66-66-70=269	$88,000.00
Jay Delsing	4	66-71-65-69=271	$48,000.00
Gil Morgan	5	68-67-68-69=272	$40,000.00
Joey Sindelar	T-6	69-68-67-69=273	$32,375.00
Bill Britton	T-6	69-70-65-69=273	$32,375.00
P.H. Horgan III	T-6	67-68-67-71=273	$32,375.00
Willie Wood	T-6	64-72-71-66=273	$32,375.00
Jerry Haas	T-10	66-70-68-70=274	$19,500.00
Dan Halldorson	T-10	67-68-70-69=274	$19,500.00
Brad Fabel	T-10	69-70-65-70=274	$19,500.00
Bart Bryant	T-10	64-71-71-68=274	$19,500.00
Bruce Fleisher	T-10	66-69-71-68=274	$19,500.00
Mike Hulbert	T-10	66-70-71-67=274	$19,500.00
Andrew Magee	T-10	67-71-67-69=274	$19,500.00
Dan Forsman	T-10	68-69-66-71=274	$19,500.00
Ed Fiori	T-10	69-68-66-71=274	$19,500.00
Paul Azinger	T-10	65-68-68-73=274	$19,500.00

B.C. Open

Course: En-Joie G.C., Endicott, N.Y.
Par: 70 Yardage: 6,966
Last day of event: Sunday, September 27, 1992

Player	Place	Score	Earnings
John Daly	Win	67-66-67-66=266	$144,000.00
Ken Green	T-2	65-69-69-69=272	$52,800.00
Joel Edwards	T-2	69-66-69-68=272	$52,800.00
Jay Haas	T-2	69-68-67-68=272	$52,800.00
Nolan Henke	T-2	67-67-68-70=272	$52,800.00
Keith Clearwater	6	67-69-70-68=274	$28,800.00
Jay Delsing	T-7	71-69-67-68=275	$25,800.00
Rocco Mediate	T-7	73-65-71-66=275	$25,800.00
Joey Sindelar	T-9	71-69-70-66=276	$22,400.00
Mike Hulbert	T-9	70-72-70-64=276	$22,400.00

Buick Southern Open

Course: Callaway Gardens Resort, Pine Mountain, Ga.
Par: 72 Yardage: 7,057
Last day of event: Sunday, October 4, 1992

Player	Place	Score	Earnings
Gary Hallberg	Win	68-69-69=206	$126,000.00
Jim Gallagher, Jr.	2	69-68-70=207	$75,600.00
Loren Roberts	3	71-70-68=209	$47,600.00
Larry Silveira	T-4	71-70-69=210	$27,562.50
Gene Sauers	T-4	71-71-68=210	$27,562.50
Ed Humenik	T-4	67-71-72=210	$27,562.50
Kelly Gibson	T-4	67-72-71=210	$27,562.50
Steve Pate	T-8	71-71-69=211	$20,300.00
John Daly	T-8	67-71-73=211	$20,300.00
Phil Mickelson	T-8	68-75-68=211	$20,300.00

Las Vegas Invitational

Course: TPC at Summerlin, Desert Inn C.C., Las Vegas C.C., Las Vegas, Nev.
Home course / TPC at Summerlin, Par: 72 Yardage: 7,243
Last day of event: Sunday, October 11, 1992

Player	Place	Score	Earnings
John Cook	Win	68-66-62-70-68=334	$234,000.00
David Frost	2	71-67-67-68-63=336	$140,400.00
John Adams	T-3	66-67-68-68-69=338	$62,400.00
Bob Estes	T-3	68-70-65-68-67=338	$62,400.00
Nolan Henke	T-3	68-68-71-63-68=338	$62,400.00
Davis Love III	T-3	70-66-71-64-67=338	$62,400.00
Robert Gamez	7	68-64-70-68-69=339	$43,550.00
Paul Azinger	T-8	66-69-68-68-69=340	$37,700.00
Keith Clearwater	T-8	70-66-66-68-70=340	$37,700.00
Mike Standly	T-8	66-71-65-72-66=340	$37,700.00

Walt Disney World/Oldsmobile Classic

Course: Walt Disney (Magnolia, Palm), Lake Buena Vista C.C., Lake Buena Vista, Fla.
Home course / Magnolia, Par: 72 Yardage: 7,190
Last day of event: Sunday, October 18, 1992

Player	Place	Score	Earnings
John Huston	Win	66-68-66-62=262	$180,000.00
Mark O'Meara	2	64-68-64-69=265	$108,000.00
Ted Schulz	3	66-66-64-71=267	$68,000.00
Payne Stewart	4	64-67-67-70=268	$48,000.00
Duffy Waldorf	5	65-68-67-69=269	$40,000.00
Lee Janzen	T-6	62-70-68-70=270	$34,750.00
Bill Britton	T-6	67-65-68-70=270	$34,750.00
Loren Roberts	T-8	69-65-69-68=271	$29,000.00
Rocco Mediate	T-8	69-65-67-70=271	$29,000.00
David Edwards	T-8	72-64-68-67=271	$29,000.00

H-E-B Texas Open

Course: Oak Hill C.C., San Antonio, Texas
Par: 72 Yardage: 6,650
Last day of event: Sunday, October 25, 1992

Player	Place	Score	Earnings
Nick Price	Win	67-62-68-66=263	$162,000.00

Playoff: Beat Steve Elkington with par on second extra hole

Player	Place	Score	Earnings
Steve Elkington	2	68-65-65-65=263	$97,200.00
David Edwards	T-3	66-68-68-65=267	$46,800.00
Jeff Maggert	T-3	67-65-67-68=267	$46,800.00
Corey Pavin	T-3	63-69-67-68=267	$46,800.00
Donnie Hammond	6	69-63-67-69=268	$32,400.00
Mark Brooks	T-7	66-67-68-68=269	$24,364.28
Lee Janzen	T-7	68-65-69-67=269	$24,364.29
Larry Rinker	T-7	69-67-65-68=269	$24,364.28
Brad Fabel	T-7	66-66-67-70=269	$24,364.28
Brad Bryant	T-7	67-65-71-66=269	$24,364.29
Morris Hatalsky	T-7	71-66-66-66=269	$24,364.29
Payne Stewart	T-7	68-66-72-63=269	$24,364.29

The Tour Championship

Course: Pinehurst C.C. (No 2), Pinehurst, N.C.
Par: 71 Yardage: 7,005
Last day of event: Sunday, November 1, 1992

Player	Place	Score	Earnings
Paul Azinger	Win	70-66-69-71=276	$360,000.00
Lee Janzen	T-2	70-69-72-68=279	$177,000.00
Corey Pavin	T-2	74-68-69-68=279	$177,000.00
Keith Clearwater	4	68-75-72-67=282	$96,000.00
Ray Floyd	T-5	72-71-71-69=283	$76,000.00
Fred Couples	T-5	73-78-66-66=283	$76,000.00
Brad Faxon	T-7	70-71-72-71=284	$59,000.00

Greg Norman	T-7	70-70-73-71=284	$59,000.00
Duffy Waldorf	T-7	70-73-70-71=284	$59,000.00
Jay Haas	T-7	72-66-73-73=284	$59,000.00
David Frost	T-7	69-68-74-73=284	$59,000.00
Dan Forsman	T-7	71-67-72-74=284	$59,000.00

1993

Bernhard Langer systematically won the Masters, scoring a four-shot victory over Chip Beck, who was harshly criticized for laying up at the par-5 15th hole in the final round, when he trailed Langer by three shots. Lee Janzen opened with two 67s and never gave up the lead en route to a two-shot U.S. Open victory over Payne Stewart at Baltusrol, where never-in-contention John Daly nevertheless dazzled spectators at the 630-yard 17th hole by hitting the green with driver/1-iron. It took an extraordinary week of scoring for Greg Norman to win the British Open by two shots over Nick Faldo at Sandwich, where Ernie Els posted four rounds in the 60s and tied for sixth. A month later at Inverness, Paul Azinger added to Norman's history of near misses by beating him in a playoff at the PGA Championship when Norman lipped out a 4-foot par putt on the second extra hole. Vijay Singh appeared on golf radar screens in the United States for the first time, thanks to a second-round 63 at the PGA. The Ryder Cup returned to America after the U.S. won 15 to 13 at The Belfry.

Infiniti Tournament of Champions

Course: La Costa C.C., Carlsbad, Calif.
Par: 72 Yardage: 7,022
Last day of event: Sunday, January 10, 1993

Player	Place	Score	Earnings
Davis Love III	Win	67-67-69-69=272	$144,000.00
Tom Kite	2	69-71-69-64=273	$86,400.00
Mark O'Meara	T-3	70-70-68-67=275	$46,400.00
Paul Azinger	T-3	65-69-70-71=275	$46,400.00
Brad Faxon	T-5	71-69-67-71=278	$31,000.00
John Cook	T-5	73-68-68-69=278	$31,000.00
Dan Forsman	T-7	68-71-69-71=279	$27,225.00
Steve Pate	T-7	73-66-71-69=279	$27,225.00
John Huston	9	70-73-68-70=281	$24,825.00
Mark Calcavecchia	T-10	68-72-70-72=282	$23,025.00
Fred Couples	T-10	70-70-72-70=282	$23,025.00

United Airlines Hawaiian Open

Course: Waialae C.C., Honolulu, Ha.
Par: 72 Yardage: 6,975
Last day of event: Sunday, January 17, 1993

Player	Place	Score	Earnings
Howard Twitty	Win	63-68-70-68=269	$216,000.00
Joey Sindelar	2	71-68-66-68=273	$129,600.00
Paul Azinger	3	67-68-69-70=274	$81,600.00
Brett Ogle	T-4	67-70-70-70=277	$49,600.00
Jeff Maggert	T-4	68-71-68-70=277	$49,600.00
Keith Clearwater	T-4	72-66-68-71=277	$49,600.00
Davis Love III	T-7	69-68-71-70=278	$38,700.00
Nolan Henke	T-7	69-71-71-67=278	$38,700.00
Duffy Waldorf	T-9	69-69-71-71=280	$31,200.00
Bill Glasson	T-9	65-71-73-71=280	$31,200.00
Mark O'Meara	T-9	66-73-71-70=280	$31,200.00
Wayne Levi	T-9	72-65-69-74=280	$31,200.00

Northern Telecom Open

Course: Tucson National G.C., Starr Pass G.C., Tucson, Ariz.
Par: 72 Yardage: 7,148
Last day of event: Sunday, January 24, 1993

Player	Place	Score	Earnings
Larry Mize	Win	68-66-70-67=271	$198,000.00
Jeff Maggert	2	70-66-70-67=273	$118,800.00
Michael Allen	T-3	68-70-68-68=274	$52,800.00
Robin Freeman	T-3	71-68-69-66=274	$52,800.00
Dudley Hart	T-3	66-66-69-73=274	$52,800.00
Jim Gallagher, Jr.	T-3	75-66-67-66=274	$52,800.00
Billy Andrade	7	63-73-69-70=275	$36,850.00
Lennie Clements	T-8	69-67-70-70=276	$29,700.00
Roger Maltbie	T-8	70-68-70-68=276	$29,700.00
Craig Parry	T-8	67-72-72-65=276	$29,700.00
Robert Gamez	T-8	69-67-72-68=276	$29,700.00
Phil Mickelson	T-8	67-65-69-75=276	$29,700.00

Phoenix Open

Course: TPC of Scottsdale, Scottsdale, Ariz.
Par: 71 Yardage: 6,992
Last day of event: Sunday, January 31, 1993

Player	Place	Score	Earnings
Lee Janzen	Win	67-65-73-68=273	$180,000.00
Andrew Magee	2	69-70-64-72=275	$108,000.00
Michael Allen	T-3	66-70-70-70=276	$48,000.00
Mike Springer	T-3	70-69-68-69=276	$48,000.00
Kirk Triplett	T-3	69-67-69-71=276	$48,000.00
Robert Wrenn	T-3	66-68-68-74=276	$48,000.00
Mark Wiebe	T-7	67-70-70-70=277	$32,250.00
Keith Clearwater	T-7	68-72-71-66=277	$32,250.00
Tom Lehman	T-9	69-66-73-70=278	$28,000.00
Gil Morgan	T-9	71-65-74-68=278	$28,000.00

AT&T Pebble Beach Pro-Am

Courses: Pebble Beach G.L., Spyglass Hill G.C., Poppy Hills G.C., Pebble Beach, Calif.
Home Course / Pebble Beach G.L., Par: 72 Yardage: 6,815
Last day of event: Sunday, February 7, 1993

Player	Place	Score	Earnings
Brett Ogle	Win	68-68-69-71=276	$225,000.00
Billy Ray Brown	2	70-68-69-72=279	$135,000.00
Joey Sindelar	T-3	69-72-70-69=280	$65,000.00
Greg Twiggs	T-3	69-72-70-69=280	$65,000.00
Trevor Dodds	T-3	70-68-70-72=280	$65,000.00
Lee Janzen	6	71-67-72-71=281	$45,000.00
Grant Waite	T-7	71-70-72-69=282	$40,312.50
Chip Beck	T-7	72-71-69-70=282	$40,312.50
Payne Stewart	T-9	72-70-71-70=283	$27,968.75
Brandel Chamblee	T-9	72-73-68-70=283	$27,968.75
Bobby Clampett	T-9	73-72-68-70=283	$27,968.75
Steve Elkington	T-9	68-71-74-70=283	$27,968.75
John Flannery	T-9	70-69-70-74=283	$27,968.75
Billy Andrade	T-9	70-74-68-71=283	$27,968.75
Gil Morgan	T-9	69-70-69-75=283	$27,968.75
Dan Forsman	T-9	73-71-64-75=283	$27,968.75

Bob Hope Chrysler Classic

Course: PGA West/Palmer, Bermuda Dunes C.C., Indian Wells C.C., Tamarisk C.C.
Home course / PGA West, Par: 72 Yardage: 6,924
Last day of event: Sunday, February 14, 1993

Player	Place	Score	Earnings
Tom Kite	Win	67-67-64-65-62=325	$198,000.00
Rick Fehr	2	66-66-70-62-67=331	$118,800.00

Scott Simpson	3	71-69-66-63-66=335	$74,800.00
Jim Gallagher, Jr.	T-4	69-68-67-69-63=336	$43,312.50
Bob Lohr	T-4	68-66-66-66-70=336	$43,312.50
Keith Clearwater	T-4	68-66-68-70-64=336	$43,312.50
Jay Haas	T-4	66-66-71-65-68=336	$43,312.50
Bill Glasson	8	70-64-66-67-70=337	$34,100.00
Wayne Levi	T-9	68-66-66-69-69=338	$29,700.00
Fred Couples	T-9	68-64-68-66-72=338	$29,700.00
Steve Elkington	T-9	69-63-66-68-72=338	$29,700.00

Buick Invitational of California

Course: Torrey Pines (South), Torrey Pines (North), San Diego, Calif.
Home Course -Par: 72 Yardage: 7,021
Last day of event: Sunday, February 21, 1993

Player	Place	Score	Earnings
Phil Mickelson	Win	75-69-69-65=278	$180,000.00
Dave Rummells	2	77-64-71-70=282	$108,000.00
Payne Stewart	3	72-66-75-70=283	$68,000.00
Jay Haas	T-4	70-72-71-72=285	$41,333.33
Greg Twiggs	T-4	73-73-69-70=285	$41,333.33
Jay Don Blake	T-4	73-75-70-67=285	$41,333.34
Keith Clearwater	T-7	75-72-70-69=286	$32,250.00
Joey Sindelar	T-7	77-68-70-71=286	$32,250.00
Hal Sutton	T-9	73-71-74-69=287	$24,000.00
Patrick Burke	T-9	74-74-68-71=287	$24,000.00
Craig Stadler	T-9	75-68-71-73=287	$24,000.00
Len Mattiace	T-9	76-68-71-72=287	$24,000.00
Mark Wiebe	T-9	76-73-71-67=287	$24,000.00
David Peoples	T-9	77-71-69-70=287	$24,000.00

Nissan Los Angeles Open

Course: Riviera C.C., Pacific Palisades, Calif.
Par: 71 Yardage: 7,029
Last day of event: Sunday, February 28, 1993

Player	Place	Score	Earnings
Tom Kite	Win	73-66-67=206	$180,000.00
Donnie Hammond	T-2	69-69-71=209	$66,000.00
Fred Couples	T-2	71-67-71=209	$66,000.00
Dave Barr	T-2	71-72-66=209	$66,000.00
Payne Stewart	T-2	72-66-71=209	$66,000.00
Jodie Mudd	T-6	71-68-71=210	$28,187.50
Jay Don Blake	T-6	67-72-71=210	$28,187.50
Howard Twitty	T-6	70-72-68=210	$28,187.50
Rick Fehr	T-6	72-67-71=210	$28,187.50
Greg Twiggs	T-6	72-67-71=210	$28,187.50
Paul Azinger	T-6	72-68-70=210	$28,187.50
Jeff Maggert	T-6	71-73-66=210	$28,187.50
Peter Jacobsen	T-6	73-68-69=210	$28,187.50

Doral-Ryder Open

Course: Doral C.C. (Blue), Miami, Fla.
Par: 72 Yardage: 6,939
Last day of event: Sunday, March 7, 1993

Player	Place	Score	Earnings
Greg Norman	Win	65-68-62-70=265	$252,000.00
Paul Azinger	T-2	67-66-68-68=269	$123,200.00
Mark McCumber	T-2	69-67-66-67=269	$123,200.00
David Frost	4	70-64-68-68=270	$67,200.00
Sandy Lyle	5	69-67-68-68=272	$56,000.00
Fred Couples	T-6	68-67-71-67=273	$48,650.00
Nick Faldo	T-6	72-65-70-66=273	$48,650.00

Tom Kite	8	66-73-69-67=275	$43,400.00
Scott Hoch	9	71-67-69-69=276	$40,600.00
Ed Humenik	T-10	67-71-69-70=277	$31,033.33
Lee Janzen	T-10	71-71-70-65=277	$31,033.34
Steve Elkington	T-10	68-72-67-70=277	$31,033.33
Chip Beck	T-10	70-72-72-63=277	$31,033.34
John Adams	T-10	72-67-70-68=277	$31,033.33
Jack Nicklaus	T-10	69-68-67-73=277	$31,033.33

Honda Classic

Course: Weston Hills G. & C.C., Ft. Lauderdale, Fla.
Par: 72 Yardage: 7,069
Last day of event: Sunday, March 14, 1993

Player	Place	Score	Earnings
Fred Couples	Win	64-73-70=207	$198,000.00
Playoff: Beat Robert Gamez with par on second extra hole			
Robert Gamez	2	68-71-68=207	$118,800.00
Larry Mize	3	69-67-72=208	$74,800.00
Dick Mast	4	68-69-72=209	$52,800.00
Craig Parry	5	67-71-72=210	$44,000.00
Jim McGovern	T-6	71-69-71=211	$32,135.71
Rocco Mediate	T-6	71-69-71=211	$32,135.71
Steve Pate	T-6	68-71-72=211	$32,135.71
Mike Smith	T-6	69-72-70=211	$32,135.72
David Frost	T-6	68-69-74=211	$32,135.71
Ed Dougherty	T-6	70-74-67=211	$32,135.72
Fuzzy Zoeller	T-6	66-75-70=211	$32,135.72

The Nestle Invitational

Course: Bay Hill Club, Orlando, Fla.
Par: 72 Yardage: 7,114
Last day of event: Sunday, March 21, 1993

Player	Place	Score	Earnings
Ben Crenshaw	Win	71-70-69-70=280	$180,000.00
Davis Love III	T-2	71-69-71-71=282	$74,666.66
Vijay Singh	T-2	70-72-71-69=282	$74,666.67
Rocco Mediate	T-2	72-72-70-68=282	$74,666.67
Ed Humenik	5	73-69-72-70=284	$40,000.00
Mark O'Meara	T-6	71-72-72-70=285	$33,500.00
Mark McCumber	T-6	72-71-71-71=285	$33,500.00
Bernhard Langer	T-6	71-70-71-73=285	$33,500.00
Joey Sindelar	9	72-70-73-71=286	$29,000.00
Jay Haas	T-10	71-73-71-72=287	$21,428.57
Greg Norman	T-10	72-73-69-73=287	$21,428.57
Billy Andrade	T-10	72-74-70-71=287	$21,428.58
Larry Mize	T-10	74-72-70-71=287	$21,428.57
Dan Pohl	T-10	70-72-70-75=287	$21,428.57
Bill Kratzert	T-10	72-70-70-75=287	$21,428.57
Nick Price	T-10	73-75-67-72=287	$21,428.57

The Players Championship

Course: TPC at Sawgrass, Ponte Vedra Beach, Fla.
Par: 72 Yardage: 6,857
Last day of event: Sunday, March 28, 1993

Player	Place	Score	Earnings
Nick Price	Win	64-68-71-67=270	$450,000.00
Bernhard Langer	2	65-69-70-71=275	$270,000.00
Greg Norman	T-3	66-70-68-72=276	$145,000.00
Gil Morgan	T-3	68-71-72-65=276	$145,000.00
Mark O'Meara	5	67-71-66-73=277	$100,000.00
Rocco Mediate	T-6	68-71-68-71=278	$80,937.50

Player	Place	Score	Earnings
Ken Green	T-6	70-67-69-72=278	$80,937.50
Joe Ozaki	T-6	72-68-68-70=278	$80,937.50
Paul Azinger	T-6	68-69-68-73=278	$80,937.50
Tom Watson	10	70-72-69-68=279	$67,500.00

Freeport-McMoRan Classic

Course: English Turn G. & C.C., New Orleans, La.
Par: 72 Yardage: 7,106
Last day of event: Sunday, April 4, 1993

Player	Place	Score	Earnings
Mike Standly	Win	71-71-72-67=281	$180,000.00
Payne Stewart	T-2	70-70-73-69=282	$88,000.00
Russ Cochran	T-2	75-68-70-69=282	$88,000.00
Greg Norman	4	77-69-70-68=284	$48,000.00
Vijay Singh	5	72-73-72-68=285	$40,000.00
Neal Lancaster	T-6	72-73-71-71=287	$32,375.00
Scott Hoch	T-6	72-74-72-69=287	$32,375.00
Greg Kraft	T-6	72-71-69-75=287	$32,375.00
Dick Mast	T-6	76-72-70-69=287	$32,375.00
Duffy Waldorf	T-10	71-73-72-72=288	$24,000.00
Mark Brooks	T-10	73-72-71-72=288	$24,000.00
Ed Fiori	T-10	71-75-71-71=288	$24,000.00
Jaime Gomez	T-10	75-70-72-71=288	$24,000.00

Masters

Course: Augusta National G.C., Augusta, Ga.
Par: 72 Yardage: 6,925
Last day of event: Sunday, April 11, 1993

Player	Place	Score	Earnings
Bernhard Langer	Win	69-70-69-70=278	$306,000.00
Chip Beck	2	72-67-72-70=281	$183,600.00
Steve Elkington	T-3	71-70-71-71=283	$81,600.00
Lanny Wadkins	T-3	69-72-71-71=283	$81,600.00
John Daly	T-3	70-71-73-69=283	$81,600.00
Tom Lehman	T-3	67-75-73-68=283	$81,600.00
Dan Forsman	T-7	69-69-73-73=284	$54,850.00
Jose Maria Olazabal	T-7	70-72-74-68=284	$54,850.00
Brad Faxon	T-9	71-70-72-72=285	$47,600.00
Payne Stewart	T-9	74-70-72-69=285	$47,600.00

Deposit Guaranty Classic

Course: Hattiesburg C.C., Hattiesburg, Miss.
Par: 70 Yardage: 6,594
Last day of event: Sunday, April 11, 1993

Player	Place	Score	Earnings
Greg Kraft	Win	65-70-64-68=267	$54,000.00
Morris Hatalsky	T-2	69-65-68-66=268	$26,400.00
Tad Rhyan	T-2	66-70-64-68=268	$26,400.00
Massy Kuramoto	T-4	69-68-66-66=269	$11,310.00
Len Mattiace	T-4	65-70-67-67=269	$11,310.00
Barry Jaeckel	T-4	68-65-66-70=269	$11,310.00
Doug Martin	T-4	70-66-68-65=269	$11,310.00
Grant Waite	T-4	72-65-69-63=269	$11,310.00
Jeff Barlow	9	69-69-65-67=270	$8,700.00
J.P. Hayes	T-10	68-66-68-69=271	$6,650.00
Stan Utley	T-10	68-66-69-68=271	$6,650.00
Mike Donald	T-10	65-70-69-67=271	$6,650.00
Bill Buttner	T-10	68-70-67-66=271	$6,650.00
Pat McGowan	T-10	70-69-66-66=271	$6,650.00
Jeff Woodland	T-10	64-68-71-68=271	$6,650.00

MCI Heritage Classic

Course: Harbour Town G.L., Hilton Head, S.C.
Par: 71 Yardage: 6,657
Last day of event: Sunday, April 18, 1993

Player	Place	Score	Earnings
David Edwards	Win	68-66-70-69=273	$202,500.00
David Frost	2	67-67-70-71=275	$121,500.00
Don Pooley	T-3	67-70-70-70=277	$50,737.60
Ian Baker-Finch	T-3	68-70-69-70=277	$50,737.60
Fuzzy Zoeller	T-3	70-69-68-70=277	$50,737.60
Mark McCumber	T-3	68-68-70-71=277	$50,737.60
Paul Azinger	T-3	70-68-66-73=277	$50,737.60
Tom Lehman	T-8	70-70-70-68=278	$31,500.00
Steve Pate	T-8	71-67-68-72=278	$31,500.00
Gil Morgan	T-8	71-72-69-66=278	$31,500.00
John Cook	T-8	69-67-69-73=278	$31,500.00

Kmart Greater Greensboro Open

Course: Forest Oaks C.C., Greensboro, N.C.
Par: 72 Yardage: 6,984
Last day of event: Sunday, April 25, 1993

Player	Place	Score	Earnings
Rocco Mediate	Win	74-67-71-69=281	$270,000.00
Playoff: Beat Steve Elkington with birdie on fourth extra hole			
Steve Elkington	2	71-68-69-73=281	$162,000.00
Gil Morgan	T-3	71-69-69-73=282	$78,000.00
Paul Azinger	T-3	73-67-70-72=282	$78,000.00
Dudley Hart	T-3	72-65-74-71=282	$78,000.00
Lee Janzen	T-6	71-71-70-71=283	$50,250.00
David Edwards	T-6	70-71-70-72=283	$50,250.00
Mark Wiebe	T-6	72-73-68-70=283	$50,250.00
Vijay Singh	T-9	72-67-72-73=284	$40,500.00
Billy Andrade	T-9	74-72-68-70=284	$40,500.00
Jeff Sluman	T-9	78-65-71-70=284	$40,500.00

Shell Houston Open

Course: TPC at The Woodlands, The Woodlands, Texas
Par: 72 Yardage: 7,042
Last day of event: Sunday, May 2, 1993

Player	Place	Score	Earnings
Jim McGovern	Win	67-64-68=199	$234,000.00
Playoff: Beat John Huston with birdie on second extra hole			
John Huston	2	65-66-68=199	$140,400.00
Payne Stewart	T-3	66-68-66=200	$67,600.00
Donnie Hammond	T-3	67-65-68=200	$67,600.00
Blaine McCallister	T-3	64-65-71=200	$67,600.00
Larry Mize	6	68-64-69=201	$46,800.00
Loren Roberts	T-7	67-67-69=203	$39,162.50
Fulton Allem	T-7	66-70-67=203	$39,162.50
Steve Elkington	T-7	70-65-68=203	$39,162.50
Mike Springer	T-7	70-69-64=203	$39,162.50

BellSouth Classic

Course: Atlanta C.C., Atlanta, Ga.
Par: 72 Yardage: 7,007
Last day of event: Sunday, May 9, 1993

Player	Place	Score	Earnings
Nolan Henke	Win	67-69-68-67=271	$216,000.00
Tom Sieckmann	T-2	70-64-70-69=273	$89,600.00
Mark Calcavecchia	T-2	67-67-67-72=273	$89,600.00

Nick Price	T-2	69-67-64-73=273	$89,600.00
Fulton Allem	5	73-68-67-66=274	$48,000.00
Mike Springer	6	69-66-68-72=275	$43,200.00
Larry Mize	T-7	69-69-68-70=276	$33,700.00
Brian Claar	T-7	70-68-67-71=276	$33,700.00
Billy Andrade	T-7	67-66-73-70=276	$33,700.00
Kirk Triplett	T-7	73-69-70-64=276	$33,700.00
Dillard Pruitt	T-7	66-68-68-74=276	$33,700.00
Jimmy Johnston	T-7	71-67-64-74=276	$33,700.00

GTE Byron Nelson Classic

Course: TPC at Las Colinas, Irving, Texas
Par: 70 Yardage: 6,850
Last day of event: Sunday, May 16, 1993

Player	Place	Score	Earnings
Scott Simpson	Win	65-66-68-71=270	$216,000.00
D.A. Weibring	T-2	68-65-69-69=271	$89,600.00
Corey Pavin	T-2	69-68-67-67=271	$89,600.00
Billy Mayfair	T-2	71-61-69-70=271	$89,600.00
David Frost	T-5	68-66-69-69=272	$43,800.00
Payne Stewart	T-5	70-66-68-68=272	$43,800.00
Fred Couples	T-5	71-63-70-68=272	$43,800.00
Larry Rinker	T-8	68-69-67-69=273	$34,800.00
Ray Floyd	T-8	66-69-70-68=273	$34,800.00
Mark Calcavecchia	T-8	67-65-74-67=273	$34,800.00

Kemper Open

Course: TPC at Avenel, Potomac, Md.
Par: 71 Yardage: 7,005
Last day of event: Sunday, May 23, 1993

Player	Place	Score	Earnings
Grant Waite	Win	66-67-72-70=275	$234,000.00
Tom Kite	2	70-65-69-72=276	$140,400.00
Scott Hoch	T-3	70-69-70-68=277	$75,400.00
Michael Bradley	T-3	69-71-69-68=277	$75,400.00
Bob Estes	5	68-70-74-66=278	$52,000.00
JC Anderson	6	68-73-68-70=279	$46,800.00
Craig Parry	T-7	71-69-71-69=280	$40,516.67
Billy Mayfair	T-7	70-69-72-69=280	$40,516.67
Lee Janzen	T-7	71-67-70-72=280	$40,516.66
Tommy Armour III	T-10	68-71-70-72=281	$31,200.00
Ed Fiori	T-10	67-73-70-71=281	$31,200.00
John Inman	T-10	71-68-69-73=281	$31,200.00
Morris Hatalsky	T-10	72-66-75-68=281	$31,200.00

Southwestern Bell Colonial

Course: Colonial C.C., Fort Worth, Texas
Par: 70 Yardage: 7,096
Last day of event: Sunday, May 30, 1993

Player	Place	Score	Earnings
Fulton Allem	Win	66-63-68-67=264	$234,000.00
Greg Norman	2	69-64-64-68=265	$140,400.00
Jeff Maggert	3	65-68-68-66=267	$88,400.00
Duffy Waldorf	T-4	65-69-69-65=268	$57,200.00
Loren Roberts	T-4	66-70-66-66=268	$57,200.00
John Huston	T-6	66-70-66-67=269	$43,550.00
David Edwards	T-6	69-67-63-70=269	$43,550.00
Tom Watson	T-6	69-64-71-65=269	$43,550.00
Corey Pavin	T-9	70-65-67-68=270	$36,400.00
Keith Clearwater	T-9	71-61-69-69=270	$36,400.00

Memorial Tournament

Course: Muirfield Village G.C., Dubin, Ohio
Par: 72 Yardage: 7,104
Last day of event: Sunday, June 6, 1993

Player	Place	Score	Earnings
Paul Azinger	Win	68-69-68-69=274	$252,000.00
Corey Pavin	2	69-70-69-67=275	$151,200.00
Payne Stewart	3	69-66-67-74=276	$95,200.00
Brad Faxon	T-4	69-69-70-69=277	$50,750.00
Jim McGovern	T-4	67-71-69-70=277	$50,750.00
Jay Haas	T-4	67-70-72-68=277	$50,750.00
Fred Couples	T-4	67-68-73-69=277	$50,750.00
Jumbo Ozaki	T-4	67-70-73-67=277	$50,750.00
Greg Norman	T-4	68-68-74-67=277	$50,750.00
Davis Love III	T-10	66-72-69-71=278	$36,400.00
Bill Glasson	T-10	69-69-68-72=278	$36,400.00

Buick Classic

Course: Westchester C.C., Harrison, N.Y.
Par: 71 Yardage: 6,779
Last day of event: Sunday, June 13, 1993

Player	Place	Score	Earnings
Vijay Singh	Win	72-68-74-66=280	$180,000.00
Playoff: Beat Mark Wiebe with birdie on third extra hole			
Mark Wiebe	2	72-75-67-66=280	$108,000.00
Lee Janzen	T-3	69-72-68-72=281	$58,000.00
David Frost	T-3	70-72-73-66=281	$58,000.00
Mike Smith	T-5	72-73-69-68=282	$38,000.00
Tom Lehman	T-5	74-69-70-69=282	$38,000.00
Bob Gilder	T-7	72-72-69-70=283	$31,166.66
Chip Beck	T-7	71-72-74-66=283	$31,166.67
Payne Stewart	T-7	74-72-68-69=283	$31,166.67
Tom Kite	T-10	68-71-75-70=284	$25,000.00
Duffy Waldorf	T-10	69-70-70-75=284	$25,000.00
Fred Funk	T-10	69-75-71-69=284	$25,000.00

U.S. Open

Course: Baltusrol G.C., Springfield, N.J.
Par: 70 Yardage: 7,152
Last day of event: Sunday, June 20, 1993

Player	Place	Score	Earnings
Lee Janzen	Win	67-67-69-69=272	$290,000.00
Payne Stewart	2	70-66-68-70=274	$145,000.00
Paul Azinger	T-3	71-68-69-69=277	$78,556.50
Craig Parry	T-3	66-74-69-68=277	$78,556.50
Scott Hoch	T-5	66-72-72-68=278	$48,730.00
Tom Watson	T-5	70-66-73-69=278	$48,730.00
Fred Funk	T-7	70-72-67-70=279	$35,481.25
Nolan Henke	T-7	72-71-67-69=279	$35,481.25
Ray Floyd	T-7	68-73-70-68=279	$35,481.25
Ernie Els	T-7	71-73-68-67=279	$35,481.25

Canon Greater Hartford Open

Course: TPC at River Highlands, Cromwell, Conn.
Par: 70 Yardage: 6,820
Last day of event: Sunday, June 27, 1993

Player	Place	Score	Earnings
Nick Price	Win	67-70-69-65=271	$180,000.00
Roger Maltbie	T-2	65-71-71-65=272	$88,000.00
Dan Forsman	T-2	66-69-72-65=272	$88,000.00

Corey Pavin	T-4	67-65-73-69=274	$48,000.00
Kenny Perry	T-5	68-69-70-68=275	$38,000.00
Mike Springer	T-5	69-65-73-68=275	$38,000.00
Don Pooley	T-7	70-70-66-71=277	$30,125.00
Rocco Mediate	T-7	68-70-72-67=277	$30,125.00
John Cook	T-7	73-68-71-65=277	$30,125.00
Brian Kamm	T-7	69-75-69-64=277	$30,125.00

Sprint Western Open

Course: Cog Hill G. & C.C. (Dubsdread)
Lemont, Ill.
Par: 72 Yardage: 7,040
Last day of event: Sunday, July 4, 1993

Player	Place	Score	Earnings
Nick Price	Win	64-71-67-67=269	$216,000.00
Greg Norman	2	69-68-67-70=274	$129,600.00
Bob Lohr	3	72-69-67-69=277	$81,600.00
John Adams	T-4	72-71-63-72=278	$49,600.00
Mark Wiebe	T-4	65-73-71-69=278	$49,600.00
Brian Henninger	T-4	71-73-66-68=278	$49,600.00
Michael Allen	T-7	71-68-70-70=279	$33,700.00
Rick Fehr	T-7	71-68-71-69=279	$33,700.00
Doug Tewell	T-7	70-69-68-72=279	$33,700.00
Dan Forsman	T-7	67-73-69-70=279	$33,700.00
Curtis Strange	T-7	69-68-69-73=279	$33,700.00
P.H. Horgan III	T-7	69-74-68-68=279	$33,700.00

Anheuser-Busch Golf Classic

Course: Kingsmill G.C., Williamsburg, Va.
Par: 71 Yardage: 6,776
Last day of event: Sunday, July 11, 1993

Player	Place	Score	Earnings
Jim Gallagher, Jr.	Win	66-68-70-65=269	$198,000.00
Chip Beck	2	68-68-67-68=271	$118,800.00
Curtis Strange	T-3	67-69-68-68=272	$57,200.00
Lanny Wadkins	T-3	67-71-64-70=272	$57,200.00
Dave Rummells	T-3	67-71-66-68=272	$57,200.00
Loren Roberts	T-6	70-68-69-66=273	$38,225.00
Jim Hallet	T-6	70-70-68-65=273	$38,225.00
Lennie Clements	T-8	70-66-69-69=274	$28,600.00
Fred Funk	T-8	70-66-67-71=274	$28,600.00
Bob Gilder	T-8	71-69-66-68=274	$28,600.00
Ted Tryba	T-8	68-65-72-69=274	$28,600.00
Tom Byrum	T-8	72-62-69-71=274	$28,600.00
Dillard Pruitt	T-8	70-68-62-74=274	$28,600.00

British Open

Course: Royal St. George's G.C., Sandwich, Kent, England
Par: 70 Yardage: 6,860
Last day of event: Sunday, July 18, 1993

Player	Place	Score	Earnings
Greg Norman	Win	66-68-69-64=267	$154,000.00
Nick Faldo	2	69-63-70-67=269	$123,200.00
Bernhard Langer	3	67-66-70-67=270	$103,180.00
Peter Senior	T-4	66-69-70-67=272	$77,770.00
Corey Pavin	T-4	68-66-68-70=272	$77,770.00
Ernie Els	T-6	68-69-69-68=274	$51,076.67
Nick Price	T-6	68-70-67-69=274	$51,076.67
Paul Lawrie	T-6	72-68-69-65=274	$51,076.67
Scott Simpson	T-9	68-70-71-66=275	$39,270.00
Fred Couples	T-9	68-66-72-69=275	$39,270.00
Wayne Grady	T-9	74-68-64-69=275	$39,270.00

New England Classic

Course: Pleasant Valley C.C., Sutton, Mass.
Par: 71 Yardage: 7,110
Last day of event: Sunday, July 25, 1993

Player	Place	Score	Earnings
Paul Azinger	Win	67-69-64-68=268	$180,000.00
Bruce Fleisher	T-2	70-67-66-69=272	$88,000.00
Jay Delsing	T-2	73-67-65-67=272	$88,000.00
Joey Sindelar	T-4	68-67-70-69=274	$44,000.00
Bobby Clampett	T-4	63-71-67-73=274	$44,000.00
Brad Bryant	T-6	70-65-70-70=275	$32,375.00
Curtis Strange	T-6	70-70-65-70=275	$32,375.00
Peter Jacobsen	T-6	68-71-68-68=275	$32,375.00
Willie Wood	T-6	68-65-70-72=275	$32,375.00
Barry Cheesman	T-10	69-71-67-69=276	$25,000.00
Steve Lowery	T-10	66-69-69-72=276	$25,000.00
David Peoples	T-10	72-69-62-73=276	$25,000.00

Federal Express St. Jude Classic

Course: TPC at Southwind, Germantown, Tenn.
Par: 71 Yardage: 7,006
Last day of event: Sunday, August 1, 1993

Player	Place	Score	Earnings
Nick Price	Win	69-65-66-66=266	$198,000.00
Rick Fehr	T-2	68-66-68-67=269	$96,800.00
Jeff Maggert	T-2	67-65-71-66=269	$96,800.00
Fuzzy Zoeller	4	67-68-65-70=270	$52,800.00
Gil Morgan	5	69-69-64-69=271	$44,000.00
Fred Funk	T-6	68-69-65-70=272	$38,225.00
Tom Kite	T-6	70-67-69-66=272	$38,225.00
Curtis Strange	T-8	71-66-69-67=273	$33,000.00
Jay Delsing	T-8	72-69-71-61=273	$33,000.00
Mark Brooks	T-10	70-69-64-71=274	$28,600.00
Dan Pohl	T-10	72-68-69-65=274	$28,600.00

Buick Open

Course: Warwick Hills C.C., Grand Blanc, Mich.
Par: 72 Yardage: 7,014
Last day of event: Sunday, August 8, 1993

Player	Place	Score	Earnings
Larry Mize	Win	64-69-71-68=272	$180,000.00
Fuzzy Zoeller	2	69-65-66-73=273	$108,000.00
Greg Norman	3	68-73-68-65=274	$68,000.00
Jay Don Blake	T-4	69-71-67-69=276	$44,000.00
Corey Pavin	T-4	71-65-71-69=276	$44,000.00
Steve Lamontagne	T-6	67-70-70-70=277	$33,500.00
Fred Funk	T-6	68-71-67-71=277	$33,500.00
Steve Elkington	T-6	67-72-70-68=277	$33,500.00
Payne Stewart	T-9	66-71-71-70=278	$27,000.00
Neal Lancaster	T-9	69-71-71-67=278	$27,000.00
David Toms	T-9	73-67-68-70=278	$27,000.00

PGA Championship

Course: Inverness Club, Toledo, Ohio
Par: 71 Yardage: 7,024
Last day of event: Sunday, August 15, 1993

Player	Place	Score	Earnings
Paul Azinger	Win	69-66-69-68=272	$300,000.00
Playoff: Beat Greg Norman with par on second extra hole			
Greg Norman	2	68-68-67-69=272	$155,000.00
Nick Faldo	3	68-68-69-68=273	$105,000.00

Player	Place	Score	Earnings
Vijay Singh	4	68-63-73-70=274	$90,000.00
Tom Watson	5	69-65-70-72=276	$75,000.00
Phil Mickelson	T-6	67-71-69-70=277	$47,812.50
Scott Simpson	T-6	64-70-71-72=277	$47,812.50
Dudley Hart	T-6	66-68-71-72=277	$47,812.50
John Cook	T-6	72-66-68-71=277	$47,812.50
Nolan Henke	T-6	72-70-67-68=277	$47,812.50
Hale Irwin	T-6	68-69-67-73=277	$47,812.50
Bob Estes	T-6	69-66-69-73=277	$47,812.50
Scott Hoch	T-6	74-68-68-67=277	$47,812.50

The International

Course: Castle Pine G.C., Castle Rock, Colo. (Stableford format)
Par: 72   Yardage: 7,559
Last day of event: Sunday, August 22, 1993

Player	Place	Score	Earnings
Phil Mickelson	Win	11-7-11-16=45	$234,000.00
Mark Calcavecchia	2	0-4-14-19=37	$140,400.00
Phil Blackmar	3	6-15-5-7=33	$88,400.00
Greg Norman	T-4	11-6-5-9=31	$57,200.00
Scott Simpson	T-5	2-13-8-8=31	$57,200.00
Steve Pate	T-6	14-1-5-8=28	$45,175.00
Brad Faxon	T-7	13-7-2-6=28	$45,175.00
Skip Kendall	8	12-9-1-4=26	$40,300.00
Rocco Mediate	9	8-1-5-11=25	$37,700.00
Craig Parry	10	4-3-12-4=23	$35,100.00

NEC World Series of Golf

Course: Firestone C.C. (South), Akron, Ohio
Par: 70   Yardage: 7,149
Last day of event: Sunday, August 29, 1993

Player	Place	Score	Earnings
Fulton Allem	Win	68-68-72-62=270	$360,000.00
Nick Price	T-2	69-67-71-68=275	$149,333.33
Craig Stadler	T-2	71-69-68-67=275	$149,333.34
Jim Gallagher, Jr.	T-2	66-75-66-68=275	$149,333.33
Vijay Singh	5	73-70-68-66=277	$80,000.00
David Edwards	6	66-69-72-72=279	$72,000.00
David Frost	T-7	68-69-71-72=280	$62,366.67
Steve Elkington	T-7	69-67-72-72=280	$62,366.67
Greg Norman	T-7	69-69-69-73=280	$62,366.66
Grant Waite	10	72-70-75-65=282	$54,100.00

Greater Milwaukee Open

Course: Tuckaway C.C., Franklin, Wis.
Par: 72   Yardage: 7,030
Last day of event: Sunday, September 5, 1993

Player	Place	Score	Earnings
Billy Mayfair	Win	67-66-69-68=270	$180,000.00

Playoff: Beat Mark Calcavecchia with birdie on fourth extra hole (Ted Schulz also in playoff)

Player	Place	Score	Earnings
Ted Schulz	T-2	69-67-68-66=270	$88,000.00
Mark Calcavecchia	T-2	72-64-67-67=270	$88,000.00
Richard Zokol	T-4	67-68-68-68=271	$44,000.00
Bruce Lietzke	T-4	69-66-69-67=271	$44,000.00
Ken Green	6	69-66-69-68=272	$36,000.00
Donnie Hammond	7	69-65-70-69=273	$33,500.00
Brian Kamm	T-8	69-69-69-67=274	$28,000.00
Gil Morgan	T-8	69-65-70-70=274	$28,000.00
Craig Parry	T-8	70-66-69-69=274	$28,000.00
Hale Irwin	T-8	70-66-70-68=274	$28,000.00

Canadian Open

Course: Glen Abbey G.C., Oakville, Ontario, Canada
Par: 72   Yardage: 7,102
Last day of event: Sunday, September 12, 1993

Player	Place	Score	Earnings
David Frost	Win	72-70-69-68=279	$180,000.00
Fred Couples	2	70-71-70-69=280	$108,000.00
Brad Bryant	3	68-70-70-74=282	$68,000.00
Bruce Lietzke	T-4	71-72-71-70=284	$41,333.33
Craig Stadler	T-4	71-73-71-69=284	$41,333.34
Steve Stricker	T-4	66-69-74-75=284	$41,333.33
Bill Glasson	7	70-73-71-71=285	$33,500.00
Phil Blackmar	T-8	69-71-72-74=286	$30,000.00
Dudley Hart	T-8	69-71-74-72=286	$30,000.00
P.H. Horgan III	T-10	72-73-72-70=287	$22,166.67
Nick Price	T-10	68-74-71-74=287	$22,166.67
Jim Gallagher, Jr.	T-10	73-74-68-72=287	$22,166.67
Kenny Perry	T-10	70-71-70-76=287	$22,166.66
Brandel Chamblee	T-10	70-70-76-71=287	$22,166.67
Ed Dougherty	T-10	71-70-70-76=287	$22,166.66

Hardee's Golf Classic

Course: Oakwood C.C., Coal Valley, Ill.
Par: 70   Yardage: 6,796
Last day of event: Sunday, September 19, 1993

Player	Place	Score	Earnings
David Frost	Win	68-63-64-64=259	$180,000.00
Payne Stewart	T-2	66-68-67-65=266	$88,000.00
D.A. Weibring	T-2	66-65-66-69=266	$88,000.00
Bob Tway	4	69-67-67-65=268	$48,000.00
Mike Schuchart	T-5	69-65-69-66=269	$36,500.00
David Ogrin	T-5	66-70-68-65=269	$36,500.00
John Huston	T-5	70-68-66-65=269	$36,500.00
P.H. Horgan III	T-8	68-68-66-68=270	$26,000.00
Willie Wood	T-8	66-69-67-68=270	$26,000.00
Andrew Magee	T-8	68-66-67-69=270	$26,000.00
Larry Rinker	T-8	69-67-65-69=270	$26,000.00
Tim Simpson	T-8	70-66-68-66=270	$26,000.00
Kenny Perry	T-8	65-70-64-71=270	$26,000.00

B.C. Open

Course: En-Joie G.C., Endicott, N.Y.
Par: 71   Yardage: 6,966
Last day of event: Sunday, September 26, 1993

Player	Place	Score	Earnings
Blaine McCallister	Win	68-71-65-67=271	$144,000.00
Denis Watson	2	69-70-68-65=272	$86,400.00
Bill Glasson	3	66-72-68-67=273	$54,400.00
Greg Kraft	T-4	70-70-68-67=275	$33,066.67
Mark Lye	T-4	67-71-69-68=275	$33,066.67
David Ogrin	T-4	71-71-64-69=275	$33,066.66
Dick Mast	7	68-72-71-65=276	$23,800.00
Chris Smith	T-8	70-71-66-70=277	$24,000.00
Rick Fehr	T-8	70-71-67-69=277	$24,000.00
Bobby Clampett	T-10	70-70-69-69=278	$17,733.33
Peter Jacobsen	T-10	69-68-70-71=278	$17,733.33
Billy Mayfair	T-10	70-71-69-68=278	$17,733.34
Ed Dougherty	T-10	71-69-70-68=278	$17,733.33
David Toms	T-10	71-70-71-66=278	$17,733.34
Ed Humenik	T-10	66-75-67-70=278	$17,733.33

Buick Southern Open

Course: Callaway Gardens Resort, Pine Mountain, Ga.
Par: 72 Yardage: 7,057
Last day of event: Friday, October 1, 1993

Player	Place	Score	Earnings
John Inman	Win	71-73-64-70=278	$126,000.00

Playoff: Beat Bob Estes, Billy Andrade, Brad Bryant and Mark Brooks with birdie on second extra hole

Player	Place	Score	Earnings
Brad Bryant	T-2	69-72-70-67=278	$46,200.00
Bob Estes	T-2	70-69-67-72=278	$46,200.00
Mark Brooks	T-2	72-70-72-64=278	$46,200.00
Billy Andrade	T-2	68-70-73-67=278	$46,200.00
Russ Cochran	T-6	74-71-65-69=279	$24,325.00
Tom Lehman	T-6	70-65-76-68=279	$24,325.00
Willie Wood	T-8	69-70-71-70=280	$20,300.00
Bill Glasson	T-8	71-73-69-67=280	$20,300.00
David Toms	T-8	72-69-74-65=280	$20,300.00

Walt Disney World/Oldsmobile Classic

Course: Walt Disney (Magnolia, Palm), Lake Buena Vista C.C., Lake Buena Vista, Fla.
Home course / Magnolia, Par: 72 Yardage: 7,190
Last day of event: Sunday, October 10, 1993

Player	Place	Score	Earnings
Jeff Maggert	Win	66-65-66-68=265	$198,000.00
Greg Kraft	2	69-69-64-66=268	$118,800.00
Craig Stadler	T-3	68-67-68-67=270	$52,800.00
Loren Roberts	T-3	66-68-67-69=270	$52,800.00
Ken Green	T-3	70-68-63-69=270	$52,800.00
Ted Tryba	T-3	64-68-67-71=270	$52,800.00
John Cook	7	70-67-65-69=271	$36,850.00
Tom Purtzer	T-8	64-68-71-69=272	$33,000.00
Billy Mayfair	T-8	68-68-71-65=272	$33,000.00
Tom Sieckmann	T-10	69-66-69-69=273	$23,571.00
Curtis Strange	T-10	65-70-69-69=273	$23,571.00
Scott Hoch	T-10	66-69-68-70=273	$23,571.00
Larry Mize	T-10	66-70-66-71=273	$23,571.00
Jay Delsing	T-10	69-67-71-66=273	$23,571.43
Keith Clearwater	T-10	64-67-68-74=273	$23,571.43
David Ogrin	T-10	74-69-65-65=273	$23,571.00

H-E-B Texas Open

Course: Oak Hill C.C., San Antonio, Texas
Par: 71 Yardage: 6,650
Last day of event: Sunday, October 17, 1993

Player	Place	Score	Earnings
Jay Haas	Win	68-65-66-64=263	$180,000.00

Playoff: Beat Bob Lohr with birdie on second extra hole

Player	Place	Score	Earnings
Bob Lohr	2	68-64-67-64=263	$108,000.00
Billy Andrade	3	66-66-69-66=267	$68,000.00
Bob Estes	4	66-71-64-67=268	$48,000.00
David Edwards	T-5	68-66-66-69=269	$32,750.00
Marco Dawson	T-5	69-67-65-68=269	$32,750.00
Dan Forsman	T-5	64-68-67-70=269	$32,750.00
Gil Morgan	T-5	66-66-70-67=269	$32,750.00
Mike Standly	T-5	66-71-65-67=269	$32,750.00
Tom Lehman	T-5	71-63-65-70=269	$32,750.00

Las Vegas Invitational

Course: TPC at Summerlin, Desert Inn C.C., Las Vegas C.C., Las Vegas, Nev.
Home course / TPC at Summerlin, Par: 72 Yardage: 7,243
Last day of event: Sunday, October 24, 1993

Player	Place	Score	Earnings
Davis Love III	Win	67-66-67-65-66=331	$252,000.00
Craig Stadler	2	67-66-69-72-65=339	$151,200.00
Bob Estes	T-3	68-68-68-67-69=340	$72,800.00
Paul Azinger	T-3	66-67-72-68-67=340	$72,800.00
David Edwards	T-3	72-66-68-67-67=340	$72,800.00
Richard Zokol	T-6	68-67-68-69-70=342	$46,900.00
John Huston	T-6	69-66-69-71-67=342	$46,900.00
Bob Tway	T-6	71-68-68-67-68=342	$46,900.00
Gil Morgan	T-9	64-68-72-70-69=343	$40,600.00
Brian Kamm	T-10	68-70-69-69-68=344	$35,000.00
Robert Gamez	T-10	66-70-68-69-71=344	$35,000.00
Dick Mast	T-10	72-68-66-68-70=344	$35,000.00

The Tour Championship

Course: The Olympic Club (Lake Course), San Francisco, Calif.
Par: 71 Yardage: 6,812
Last day of event: Sunday, October 31, 1993

Player	Place	Score	Earnings
Jim Gallagher, Jr.	Win	63-73-72-69=277	$540,000.00
Scott Simpson	T-2	68-70-70-70=278	$198,750.00
Greg Norman	T-2	72-67-68-71=278	$198,750.00
John Huston	T-2	72-68-68-70=278	$198,750.00
David Frost	T-2	68-68-69-73=278	$198,750.00
Rick Fehr	6	69-69-70-71=279	$108,000.00
Tom Kite	T-7	69-68-72-71=280	$96,000.00
Corey Pavin	T-7	68-73-72-67=280	$96,000.00
Mark Calcavecchia	T-7	69-69-75-67=280	$96,000.00
Jay Haas	T-10	70-69-72-70=281	$83,100.00
Fred Couples	T-10	74-72-70-65=281	$83,100.00

1994

Nick Price had his best season on the PGA Tour, with five victories that included the British Open and the PGA Championship. At Turnberry, Price eagled the 71st hole and beat Jesper Parnevik by one shot. At Southern Hills, Price shot 11-under-par 280, leaving his closest pursuer, Corey Pavin, six shots back. Displaying uncanny deftness around Augusta National's greens—30 one-putts, two chip-ins and 6-for-6 in sand saves—Jose-Maria Olazabal won the Masters by two shots over Tom Lehman. Ernie Els captured a marathon U.S. Open at Oakmont, surviving a Monday playoff against Colin Montgomerie, who was eliminated after 18 holes (74 to 78), and Loren Roberts, who made bogey on the 20th hole. The United States defeated the International side 20 to 12 in the inaugural Presidents Cup competition. Tim Finchem succeeded Deane Beman as commissioner of the PGA Tour in June. Five months later, Finchem didn't blink when challenged by a Greg Norman-led, proposed World Tour. He blunted the crisis by warning players they would jeopardize their PGA Tour status if they competed on the renegade circuit.

Mercedes Championships

Course: La Costa C.C., Carlsbad, Calif.
Par: 72 Yardage: 7,022
Last day of event: Sunday, January 9, 1994

Player	Place	Score	Earnings
Phil Mickelson	Win	70-68-70-68=276	$180,000.00

Playoff: Beat Fred Couples with par on second extra hole

Player	Place	Score	Earnings
Fred Couples	2	69-70-69-68=276	$120,000.00
Tom Kite	3	73-68-69-68=278	$80,000.00
Jay Haas	T-4	71-71-69-69=280	$46,625.00
Scott Simpson	T-4	70-72-70-68=280	$46,625.00
Davis Love III	T-4	71-69-72-68=280	$46,625.00
Jeff Maggert	T-4	72-74-65-69=280	$46,625.00
Howard Twitty	T-8	72-73-67-69=281	$34,000.00
David Edwards	T-8	75-68-66-72=281	$34,000.00
Greg Norman	10	70-73-69-70=282	$31,000.00

United Airlines Hawaiian Open
Course: Waialae C.C., Honolulu, Ha.
Par: 72 Yardage: 6,975
Last day of event: Sunday, January 16, 1994

Player	Place	Score	Earnings
Brett Ogle	Win	66-66-69-68=269	$216,000.00
Davis Love III	2	68-60-71-71=270	$129,600.00
John Huston	3	70-68-67-67=272	$81,600.00
Corey Pavin	4	68-70-70-65=273	$57,600.00
Jesper Parnevik	5	71-66-74-63=274	$48,000.00
Ted Tryba	T-6	69-71-68-67=275	$41,700.00
Craig Parry	T-6	66-70-72-67=275	$41,700.00
David Ishii	T-8	70-67-69-70=276	$31,200.00
Lennie Clements	T-8	69-66-70-71=276	$31,200.00
Jeff Maggert	T-8	69-67-68-72=276	$31,200.00
Seiki Okuda	T-8	71-69-72-64=276	$31,200.00
David Ogrin	T-8	72-69-68-67=276	$31,200.00
Paul Goydos	T-8	67-73-69-67=276	$31,200.00

Northern Telecom Open
Course: Tucson National G.C., Starr Pass G.C., Tucson, Ariz.
Par: 72 Yardage: 7,148
Last day of event: Sunday, January 23, 1994

Player	Place	Score	Earnings
Andrew Magee	Win	69-67-67-67=270	$198,000.00
Jay Don Blake	T-2	68-69-67-68=272	$72,600.00
Steve Stricker	T-2	68-69-68-67=272	$72,600.00
Vijay Singh	T-2	67-68-72-65=272	$72,600.00
Loren Roberts	T-2	68-68-72-64=272	$72,600.00
Olin Browne	6	70-70-66-67=273	$39,600.00
Robert Gamez	T-7	66-71-71-66=274	$35,475.00
Jim Furyk	T-7	68-68-67-71=274	$35,475.00
Kirk Triplett	T-9	69-69-70-68=276	$22,400.00
Phil Mickelson	T-9	69-70-70-67=276	$22,400.00
Jim Thorpe	T-9	69-70-70-67=276	$22,400.00
David Feherty	T-9	70-69-67-70=276	$22,400.00
John Huston	T-9	68-71-70-67=276	$22,400.00
Billy Mayfair	T-9	69-71-68-68=276	$22,400.00
Rocco Mediate	T-9	70-70-71-65=276	$22,400.00
Bob Burns	T-9	70-72-69-65=276	$22,400.00
Dillard Pruitt	T-9	64-71-68-73=276	$22,400.00
Mike Springer	T-9	70-65-73-68=276	$22,400.00
Rick Fehr	T-9	73-68-69-66=276	$22,400.00

Phoenix Open
Course: TPC of Scottsdale, Scottsdale, Ariz.
Par: 71 Yardage: 6,992
Last day of event: Sunday, January 30, 1994

Player	Place	Score	Earnings
Bill Glasson	Win	68-68-68-64=268	$216,000.00
Bob Estes	2	66-68-69-68=271	$129,600.00
Blaine McCallister	T-3	67-69-69-67=272	$62,400.00
Jeff Maggert	T-3	70-68-69-65=272	$62,400.00
Mike Springer	T-3	68-68-71-65=272	$62,400.00
Rick Fehr	T-6	66-67-69-71=273	$41,700.00
Tom Lehman	T-6	67-68-73-65=273	$41,700.00
Steve Pate	T-8	68-69-69-68=274	$32,400.00
Fred Funk	T-8	69-69-70-66=274	$32,400.00
Phil Mickelson	T-8	67-70-71-66=274	$32,400.00
Curtis Strange	T-8	71-70-69-64=274	$32,400.00
Scott Hoch	T-8	72-66-67-69=274	$32,400.00

AT&T Pebble Beach Pro-Am
Courses: Pebble Beach G.L., Spyglass Hill G.C., Poppy Hills G.C., Pebble Beach, Calif.
Home Course / Pebble Beach G.L., Par: 72 Yardage: 6,815
Last day of event: Sunday, February 6, 1994

Player	Place	Score	Earnings
Johnny Miller	Win	68-72-67-74=281	$225,000.00
Corey Pavin	T-2	69-71-71-71=282	$82,500.00
Jeff Maggert	T-2	68-72-72-70=282	$82,500.00
Tom Watson	T-2	69-67-72-74=282	$82,500.00
Kirk Triplett	T-2	69-74-67-72=282	$82,500.00
Tom Lehman	6	69-68-73-73=283	$45,000.00
Blaine McCallister	T-7	68-71-72-73=284	$36,375.00
Keith Clearwater	T-7	70-70-71-73=284	$36,375.00
Ted Tryba	T-7	70-70-70-74=284	$36,375.00
Jay Delsing	T-7	66-75-70-73=284	$36,375.00
Dudley Hart	T-7	65-71-70-78=284	$36,375.00

Nissan Los Angeles Open
Course: Riviera C.C., Pacific Palisades, Calif.
Par: 71 Yardage: 6,946
Last day of event: Sunday, February 13, 1994

Player	Place	Score	Earnings
Corey Pavin	Win	67-64-72-68=271	$180,000.00
Fred Couples	2	67-67-68-71=273	$108,000.00
Chip Beck	3	66-71-72-68=277	$68,000.00
Brad Faxon	4	70-71-68-69=278	$48,000.00
David Frost	5	67-74-71-67=279	$40,000.00
Tom Watson	T-6	69-71-71-69=280	$34,750.00
Peter Jacobsen	T-6	69-71-68-72=280	$34,750.00
Jay Delsing	T-8	67-72-69-73=281	$28,000.00
Craig Stadler	T-8	68-69-71-73=281	$28,000.00
Lennie Clements	T-8	68-74-68-71=281	$28,000.00
Kirk Triplett	T-8	68-76-69-68=281	$28,000.00

Bob Hope Chrysler Classic
Course: Indian Wells C.C., PGA West/Palmer, Bermuda Dunes C.C., La Quinta C.C.
Home course / Indian Wells C.C., Par: 72 Yardage: 6,478
Last day of event: Sunday, February 20, 1994

Player	Place	Score	Earnings
Scott Hoch	Win	66-62-70-66-70=334	$198,000.00
Fuzzy Zoeller	T-2	70-67-66-68-66=337	$82,133.34
Lennie Clements	T-2	67-69-61-72-68=337	$82,133.33
Jim Gallagher, Jr.	T-2	66-67-74-62-68=337	$82,133.33
Payne Stewart	5	67-69-71-68-63=338	$44,000.00
Guy Boros	T-6	66-67-68-69-69=339	$36,850.00
Paul Stankowski	T-6	67-66-69-68-69=339	$36,850.00
Keith Clearwater	T-6	67-64-70-68-70=339	$36,850.00
Bob Estes	T-9	66-69-70-67-68=340	$30,800.00
John Huston	T-9	66-68-66-68-72=340	$30,800.00

Buick Invitational of California
Course: Torrey Pines (South), Torrey Pines (North), San Diego, Calif.
Home Course -Par: 72 Yardage: 7,000
Last day of event: Sunday, February 27, 1994

Player	Place	Score	Earnings
Craig Stadler	Win	67-67-68-66=268	$198,000.00
Steve Lowery	2	67-68-66-68=269	$118,800.00
Phil Mickelson	3	68-69-69-64=270	$74,800.00

Hal Sutton	4	68-68-67-69=272	$52,800.00
Mark Carnevale	5	67-69-70-67=273	$44,000.00
Bob Estes	T-6	70-67-67-70=274	$36,850.00
Robin Freeman	T-6	68-67-71-68=274	$36,850.00
Kirk Triplett	T-6	71-63-68-72=274	$36,850.00
Paul Goydos	T-9	68-70-70-67=275	$28,600.00
Lennie Clements	T-9	66-69-68-72=275	$28,600.00
Mark Calcavecchia	T-9	69-72-69-65=275	$28,600.00
Doug Martin	T-9	65-73-68-69=275	$28,600.00

Doral-Ryder Open

Course: Doral C.C. (Blue), Miami, Fla.
Par: 72 Yardage: 6,939
Last day of event: Sunday, March 6, 1994

Player	Place	Score	Earnings
John Huston	Win	70-68-70-66=274	$252,000.00
Brad Bryant	T-2	70-69-69-69=277	$123,200.00
Billy Andrade	T-2	70-68-66-73=277	$123,200.00
Jim Thorpe	T-4	68-72-68-71=279	$57,866.67
Lennie Clements	T-4	72-70-66-71=279	$57,866.66
D.A. Weibring	T-4	74-69-65-71=279	$57,866.67
Loren Roberts	T-7	73-70-69-69=281	$43,633.33
Greg Norman	T-7	71-74-69-67=281	$43,633.33
Bruce Lietzke	T-7	74-69-71-67=281	$43,633.34
Mike Hulbert	T-10	72-74-70-66=282	$35,000.00
Larry Nelson	T-10	73-64-69-76=282	$35,000.00
Mark McCumber	T-10	76-69-68-69=282	$35,000.00

Honda Classic

Course: Weston Hills G. & C.C., Ft. Lauderdale, Fla.
Par: 71 Yardage: 6,964
Last day of event: Sunday, March 13, 1994

Player	Place	Score	Earnings
Nick Price	Win	70-67-73-66=276	$198,000.00
Craig Parry	2	68-73-69-67=277	$118,800.00
Brandel Chamblee	3	67-68-72-71=278	$74,800.00
Davis Love III	T-4	68-71-70-71=280	$43,312.50
Curtis Strange	T-4	71-67-72-70=280	$43,312.50
Bernhard Langer	T-4	67-72-73-68=280	$43,312.50
John Daly	T-4	69-70-73-68=280	$43,312.50
David Edwards	8	70-72-69-71=282	$34,100.00
Hal Sutton	T-9	71-72-70-70=283	$27,500.00
Tom Kite	T-9	71-72-71-69=283	$27,500.00
Bruce Fleisher	T-9	68-73-70-72=283	$27,500.00
Jim Gallagher, Jr.	T-9	68-71-74-70=283	$27,500.00
Sandy Lyle	T-9	71-74-72-66=283	$27,500.00

The Nestle Invitational

Course: Bay Hill Club, Orlando, Fla.
Par: 72 Yardage: 7,114
Last day of event: Sunday, March 20, 1994

Player	Place	Score	Earnings
Loren Roberts	Win	70-70-68-67=275	$216,000.00
Vijay Singh	T-2	68-69-68-71=276	$89,600.00
Nick Price	T-2	66-72-68-70=276	$89,600.00
Fuzzy Zoeller	T-2	72-68-67-69=276	$89,600.00
Larry Mize	5	68-69-71-69=277	$48,000.00
Greg Norman	T-6	68-72-71-67=278	$41,700.00
Tom Lehman	T-6	72-67-68-71=278	$41,700.00
Tom Watson	8	69-70-67-73=279	$37,200.00
Andrew Magee	9	70-67-69-74=280	$34,800.00

Glen Day	T-10	70-68-72-71=281	$30,000.00
Bill Glasson	T-10	70-72-71-68=281	$30,000.00
D.A. Weibring	T-10	71-73-70-67=281	$30,000.00

The Players Championship

Course: TPC at Sawgrass, Ponte Vedra Beach, Fla.
Par: 72 Yardage: 6,857
Last day of event: Sunday, March 27, 1994

Player	Place	Score	Earnings
Greg Norman	Win	63-67-67-67=264	$450,000.00
Fuzzy Zoeller	2	66-67-68-67=268	$270,000.00
Jeff Maggert	3	65-69-69-68=271	$170,000.00
Hale Irwin	4	67-70-70-69=276	$120,000.00
Nick Faldo	5	67-69-68-73=277	$100,000.00
Brad Faxon	T-6	68-68-70-72=278	$83,750.00
Davis Love III	T-6	68-66-70-74=278	$83,750.00
Steve Lowery	T-6	68-74-69-67=278	$83,750.00
Tom Kite	T-9	65-71-70-73=279	$65,000.00
Colin Montgomerie	T-9	65-73-71-70=279	$65,000.00
Gary Hallberg	T-9	68-69-69-73=279	$65,000.00
Nolan Henke	T-9	73-69-69-68=279	$65,000.00

Freeport-McMoRan Classic

Course: English Turn G. & C.C., New Orleans, La.
Par: 72 Yardage: 7,106
Last day of event: Sunday, April 3, 1994

Player	Place	Score	Earnings
Ben Crenshaw	Win	69-68-68-68=273	$216,000.00
Jose Maria Olazabal	2	63-74-70-69=276	$129,600.00
Sam Torrance	3	67-71-67-73=278	$81,600.00
Kenny Perry	T-4	69-72-68-70=279	$49,600.00
Mike Springer	T-4	73-69-69-68=279	$49,600.00
Dennis Paulson	T-4	74-62-75-68=279	$49,600.00
Bobby Clampett	T-7	70-68-72-71=281	$36,150.00
Steve Brodie	T-7	71-67-72-71=281	$36,150.00
Dick Mast	T-7	71-69-74-67=281	$36,150.00
Chris DiMarco	T-7	76-70-66-69=281	$36,150.00

Masters

Course: Augusta National G.C., Augusta, Ga.
Par: 72 Yardage: 6,925
Last day of event: Sunday, April 10, 1994

Player	Place	Score	Earnings
Jose Maria Olazabal	Win	74-67-69-69=279	$360,000.00
Tom Lehman	2	70-70-69-72=281	$216,000.00
Larry Mize	3	68-71-72-71=282	$136,000.00
Tom Kite	4	69-72-71-71=283	$96,000.00
Jim McGovern	T-5	72-70-71-72=285	$73,000.00
Jay Haas	T-5	72-72-72-69=285	$73,000.00
Loren Roberts	T-5	75-68-72-70=285	$73,000.00
Corey Pavin	T-8	71-72-73-70=286	$60,000.00
Ernie Els	T-8	74-67-74-71=286	$60,000.00
Ray Floyd	T-10	70-74-71-72=287	$50,000.00
Ian Baker-Finch	T-10	71-71-71-74=287	$50,000.00
John Huston	T-10	72-72-74-69=287	$50,000.00

MCI Heritage Classic

Course: Harbour Town G.L., Hilton Head, S.C.
Par: 71 Yardage: 6,657
Last day of event: Sunday, April 17, 1994

Player	Place	Score	Earnings
Hale Irwin	Win	68-65-65-68=266	$225,000.00
Greg Norman	2	67-66-67-68=268	$135,000.00
Loren Roberts	3	69-70-68-62=269	$85,000.00
Nolan Henke	T-4	69-69-66-66=270	$51,666.66
David Edwards	T-4	70-71-65-64=270	$51,666.67
David Frost	T-4	70-61-72-67=270	$51,666.67
Bob Estes	T-7	65-70-68-68=271	$40,312.50
Russ Cochran	T-7	67-67-66-71=271	$40,312.50
Jesper Parnevik	T-9	68-68-69-67=272	$35,000.00
Larry Mize	T-9	67-65-75-65=272	$35,000.00

Kmart Greater Greensboro Open

Course: Forest Oaks C.C., Greensboro, N.C.
Par: 72 Yardage: 6,984
Last day of event: Sunday, April 24, 1994

Player	Place	Score	Earnings
Mike Springer	Win	64-69-70-72=275	$270,000.00
Brad Bryant	T-2	68-71-68-71=278	$112,000.00
Hale Irwin	T-2	65-73-71-69=278	$112,000.00
Ed Humenik	T-2	72-65-73-68=278	$112,000.00
Bob Lohr	5	69-71-69-70=279	$60,000.00
Donnie Hammond	T-6	70-71-69-70=280	$52,125.00
John Morse	T-6	72-68-67-73=280	$52,125.00
Joel Edwards	T-8	69-69-73-70=281	$42,000.00
Mike Smith	T-8	69-73-69-70=281	$42,000.00
David Edwards	T-8	71-74-68-68=281	$42,000.00
Dudley Hart	T-8	75-69-67-70=281	$42,000.00

Shell Houston Open

Course: TPC at The Woodlands, The Woodlands, Texas
Par: 72 Yardage: 7,042
Last day of event: Sunday, May 1, 1994

Player	Place	Score	Earnings
Mike Heinen	Win	67-68-69-68=272	$234,000.00
Hal Sutton	T-2	68-70-68-69=275	$97,066.67
Tom Kite	T-2	68-65-71-71=275	$97,066.66
Jeff Maggert	T-2	70-66-68-71=275	$97,066.67
Vijay Singh	T-5	72-67-69-70=278	$49,400.00
Bob Gilder	T-5	66-76-69-67=278	$49,400.00
Gil Morgan	T-7	70-71-72-66=279	$40,516.67
Peter Jacobsen	T-7	68-73-69-69=279	$40,516.66
John Daly	T-7	68-74-70-67=279	$40,516.67
Fred Funk	T-10	71-67-71-71=280	$32,500.00
Dave Barr	T-10	66-72-71-71=280	$32,500.00
Curtis Strange	T-10	71-72-66-71=280	$32,500.00

BellSouth Classic

Course: Atlanta C.C., Atlanta, Ga.
Par: 72 Yardage: 7,007
Last day of event: Sunday, May 8, 1994

Player	Place	Score	Earnings
John Daly	Win	69-64-69-72=274	$216,000.00
Nolan Henke	T-2	70-67-69-69=275	$105,600.00
Brian Henninger	T-2	68-67-69-71=275	$105,600.00
Bob Estes	T-4	71-69-68-68=276	$52,800.00
David Peoples	T-4	73-65-68-70=276	$52,800.00
Russ Cochran	T-6	69-69-69-70=277	$38,850.00
Blaine McCallister	T-6	69-68-69-71=277	$38,850.00
Tom Kite	T-6	66-72-68-71=277	$38,850.00
Lennie Clements	T-6	68-69-72-68=277	$38,850.00
Clark Dennis	10	71-66-72-69=278	$32,400.00

GTE Byron Nelson Classic

Course: TPC at Las Colinas, Cottonwood Valley Course, Irving, Texas
Par: 70 Yardage: 6,850
Last day of event: Sunday, May 15, 1994

Player	Place	Score	Earnings
Neal Lancaster	Win	67-65=132	$216,000.00

Playoff: Beat Tom Byrum, Mark Carnevale, David Edwards, Yoshi Mizumaki and David Ogrin with birdie on first extra hole

Player	Place	Score	Earnings
Yoshinori Mizumaki	T-2	66-66=132	$72,000.00
Mark Carnevale	T-2	65-67=132	$72,000.00
David Edwards	T-2	67-65=132	$72,000.00
David Ogrin	T-2	64-68=132	$72,000.00
Tom Byrum	T-2	68-64=132	$72,000.00
Brad Bryant	7	66-67=133	$40,200.00
Mark Brooks	T-8	67-67=134	$31,200.00
Bob Gilder	T-8	67-67=134	$31,200.00
Ben Crenshaw	T-8	66-68=134	$31,200.00
Greg Norman	T-8	66-68=134	$31,200.00
Jeff Woodland	T-8	69-65=134	$31,200.00
Ronnie Black	T-8	70-64=134	$31,200.00

Memorial Tournament

Course: Muirfield Village G.C., Dubin, Ohio
Par: 72 Yardage: 7,104
Last day of event: Sunday, May 22, 1994

Player	Place	Score	Earnings
Tom Lehman	Win	67-67-67-67=268	$270,000.00
Greg Norman	2	70-69-70-64=273	$162,000.00
John Cook	3	67-69-69-71=276	$102,000.00
Donnie Hammond	4	69-69-70-69=277	$72,000.00
David Edwards	5	69-67-72-70=278	$60,000.00
Robert Gamez	6	77-69-66-67=279	$54,000.00
Ben Crenshaw	T-7	72-66-74-68=280	$48,375.00
Mark Brooks	T-7	64-75-70-71=280	$48,375.00
Brad Faxon	T-9	72-68-72-69=281	$42,000.00
Jeff Maggert	T-9	71-74-66-70=281	$42,000.00

Southwestern Bell Colonial

Course: Colonial C.C., Fort Worth, Texas
Par: 70 Yardage: 7,096
Last day of event: Monday, May 30, 1994

Player	Place	Score	Earnings
Nick Price	Win	65-70-67-64=266	$252,000.00

Playoff: Beat Scott Simpson with birdie on first extra hole

Player	Place	Score	Earnings
Scott Simpson	2	66-65-64-71=266	$151,200.00
Hale Irwin	3	64-70-68-65=267	$95,200.00
Pete Jordan	4	68-70-66-66=270	$67,200.00
Tom Lehman	T-5	66-66-69-70=271	$51,100.00
Brad Faxon	T-5	70-66-67-68=271	$51,100.00
Gary Hallberg	T-5	67-67-65-72=271	$51,100.00
Phil Mickelson	8	68-68-71-65=272	$43,400.00
Corey Pavin	T-9	68-67-69-70=274	$37,800.00
Mark McCumber	T-9	68-69-67-70=274	$37,800.00
John Cook	T-9	66-71-67-70=274	$37,800.00

Kemper Open

Course: TPC at Avenel, Potomac, Md.
Par: 71 Yardage: 7,005
Last day of event: Sunday, June 5, 1994

Player	Place	Score	Earnings
Mark Brooks	Win	65-68-69-69=271	$234,000.00
D.A. Weibring	T-2	70-68-68-68=274	$114,400.00
Bobby Wadkins	T-2	68-67-65-74=274	$114,400.00
Phil Mickelson	T-4	70-69-67-69=275	$57,200.00
Lee Janzen	T-4	70-71-68-66=275	$57,200.00
Joel Edwards	6	71-70-68-69=278	$46,800.00
Mark Lye	T-7	70-70-69-70=279	$40,516.66
Craig Parry	T-7	69-71-69-70=279	$40,516.67
Kenny Perry	T-7	72-72-68-67=279	$40,516.67
Wayne Levi	T-10	68-70-72-71=281	$26,975.00
Tim Simpson	T-10	71-72-70-68=281	$26,975.00
Brian Kamm	T-10	69-71-68-73=281	$26,975.00
Scott Hoch	T-10	69-72-67-73=281	$26,975.00
Michael Bradley	T-10	70-71-67-73=281	$26,975.00
Kirk Triplett	T-10	72-73-67-69=281	$26,975.00
Robert Gamez	T-10	72-66-69-74=281	$26,975.00
Kelly Gibson	T-10	75-64-71-71=281	$26,975.00

Buick Classic

Course: Westchester C.C., Harrison, N.Y.
Par: 71 Yardage: 6,779
Last day of event: Sunday, June 12, 1994

Player	Place	Score	Earnings
Lee Janzen	Win	69-69-64-66=268	$216,000.00
Ernie Els	2	68-66-69-68=271	$129,600.00
Jay Haas	T-3	68-70-69-67=274	$69,600.00
Brad Faxon	T-3	70-68-70-66=274	$69,600.00
Billy Andrade	T-5	70-71-66-69=276	$43,800.00
Bob Burns	T-5	71-67-70-68=276	$43,800.00
Steve Pate	T-5	66-72-69-69=276	$43,800.00
Robin Freeman	T-8	69-69-69-70=277	$32,400.00
Mark Brooks	T-8	71-70-66-70=277	$32,400.00
Joe Ozaki	T-8	69-67-69-72=277	$32,400.00
Hale Irwin	T-8	70-72-65-70=277	$32,400.00
Jeff Maggert	T-8	72-72-64-69=277	$32,400.00

U.S. Open

Course: Oakmont C.C., Oakmont, Pa.
Par: 71 Yardage: 6,946
Last day of event: Monday, June 20, 1994

Player	Place	Score	Earnings
Ernie Els	Win	69-71-66-73-74=279	$320,000.00

Playoff: Shot 74-4-4 to beat Loren Roberts (74-4-5) and Colin Montgomerie (78) in 18-hole playoff followed by sudden death

Player	Place	Score	Earnings
Colin Montgomerie	T-2	71-65-73-70-74=279	$141,827.50
Loren Roberts	T-2	76-69-64-70-77=279	$141,827.50
Curtis Strange	4	70-70-70-70=280	$75,728.00
John Cook	5	73-65-73-71=282	$61,318.00
Clark Dennis	T-6	71-71-70-71=283	$49,485.34
Greg Norman	T-6	71-71-69-72=283	$49,485.33
Tom Watson	T-6	68-73-68-74=283	$49,485.33
Jeff Sluman	T-9	72-69-72-71=284	$37,179.75
Duffy Waldorf	T-9	74-68-73-69=284	$37,179.75
Jeff Maggert	T-9	71-68-75-70=284	$37,179.75
Frank Nobilo	T-9	69-71-68-76=284	$37,179.75

Canon Greater Hartford Open

Course: TPC at River Highlands, Cromwell, Conn.
Par: 70 Yardage: 6,820
Last day of event: Sunday, June 26, 1994

Player	Place	Score	Earnings
David Frost	Win	65-68-66-69=268	$216,000.00
Greg Norman	2	69-65-66-69=269	$129,600.00
Dave Barr	T-3	68-70-68-65=271	$57,600.00
Steve Stricker	T-3	70-67-67-67=271	$57,600.00
Dave Stockton, Jr.	T-3	66-66-67-72=271	$57,600.00
Corey Pavin	T-3	65-73-66-67=271	$57,600.00
Wayne Levi	T-7	68-66-71-68=273	$38,700.00
Kirk Triplett	T-7	71-66-69-67=273	$38,700.00
Peter Jacobsen	T-9	68-68-70-69=275	$28,800.00
Ken Green	T-9	69-70-68-68=275	$28,800.00
Clark Dennis	T-9	65-72-66-72=275	$28,800.00
Mike Reid	T-9	66-68-69-72=275	$28,800.00
Glen Day	T-9	72-65-70-68=275	$28,800.00
John Cook	T-9	71-67-64-73=275	$28,800.00

Motorola Western Open

Course: Cog Hill G. & C.C. (Dubsdread), Lemont, Ill.
Par: 72 Yardage: 7,040
Last day of event: Sunday, July 3, 1994

Player	Place	Score	Earnings
Nick Price	Win	67-67-72-71=277	$216,000.00
Greg Kraft	2	67-70-68-73=278	$129,600.00
Bill Glasson	T-3	66-70-72-71=279	$62,400.00
Mark Calcavecchia	T-3	67-70-72-70=279	$62,400.00
Scott Hoch	T-3	67-69-73-70=279	$62,400.00
Kelly Gibson	T-6	69-72-72-67=280	$41,700.00
Jeff Sluman	T-6	68-69-69-74=280	$41,700.00
Mark Wurtz	T-8	70-70-70-71=281	$28,000.00
Andrew Magee	T-8	70-71-69-71=281	$28,000.00
Doug Tewell	T-8	69-72-71-69=281	$28,000.00
Jim Thorpe	T-8	71-72-71-67=281	$28,000.00
Tom Purtzer	T-8	68-72-73-68=281	$28,000.00
Jim Gallagher, Jr.	T-8	72-68-68-73=281	$28,000.00
Larry Silveira	T-8	73-71-68-69=281	$28,000.00
David Duval	T-8	73-70-70-68=281	$28,000.00
David Frost	T-8	71-68-74-68=281	$28,000.00

Anheuser-Busch Golf Classic

Course: Kingsmill G.C., Williamsburg, Va.
Par: 71 Yardage: 6,776
Last day of event: Sunday, July 10, 1994

Player	Place	Score	Earnings
Mark McCumber	Win	67-69-65-66=267	$198,000.00
Glen Day	2	64-68-72-66=270	$118,800.00
Justin Leonard	3	67-69-69-72=272	$74,800.00
Michael Bradley	T-4	68-69-69-67=273	$45,466.67
Scott Verplank	T-4	71-69-66-67=273	$45,466.66
John Wilson	T-4	64-70-72-67=273	$45,466.67
Tommy Armour III	T-7	69-71-67-67=274	$34,283.33
Bob Lohr	T-7	61-68-73-72=274	$34,283.33
Jay Haas	T-7	69-73-65-67=274	$34,283.34
Yoshinori Mizumaki	T-10	68-70-70-67=275	$28,600.00
Jim Furyk	T-10	70-70-66-69=275	$28,600.00

Deposit Guaranty Golf Classic

Course: Annandale G.C., Madison, Miss.
Par: 72 Yardage: 7,157
Last day of event: Sunday, July 17, 1994

Player	Place	Score	Earnings
Brian Henninger	Win	67-68=135	$126,000.00

Playoff: Beat Mike Sullivan with birdie on first extra hole

Player	Place	Score	Earnings
Mike Sullivan	T-2	66-69=135	$75,600.00
Guy Boros	T-3	69-67=136	$31,570.00
Scott Hoch	T-3	69-67=136	$31,570.00
Dave Stockton, Jr.	T-3	69-67=136	$31,570.00
Chris DiMarco	T-3	70-66=136	$31,570.00
Tommy Armour III	T-3	71-65=136	$31,570.00
Bobby Clampett	T-8	68-69=137	$20,300.00
Stan Utley	T-8	67-70=137	$20,300.00
Dicky Pride	T-8	73-64=137	$20,300.00

British Open

Course: Turnberry (Ailsa Course), Turnberry, Ayrshire, Scotland
Par: 70 Yardage: 6,957
Last day of event: Sunday, July 17, 1994

Player	Place	Score	Earnings
Nick Price	Win	69-66-67-66=268	$178,200.00
Jesper Parnevik	2	68-66-68-67=269	$142,560.00
Fuzzy Zoeller	3	71-66-64-70=271	$119,880.00
David Feherty	T-4	68-69-66-70=273	$82,080.01
Mark James	T-4	72-67-66-68=273	$82,080.01
Anders Forsbrand	T-4	72-71-66-64=273	$82,080.01
Brad Faxon	7	69-65-67-73=274	$58,320.00
Tom Kite	T-8	71-69-66-69=275	$48,600.00
Colin Montgomerie	T-8	72-69-65-69=275	$48,600.00
Nick Faldo	T-8	75-66-70-64=275	$48,600.00

New England Classic

Course: Pleasant Valley C.C., Sutton, Mass.
Par: 71 Yardage: 7,110
Last day of event: Sunday, July 24, 1994

Player	Place	Score	Earnings
Kenny Perry	Win	67-66-70-65=268	$180,000.00
David Feherty	2	65-69-68-67=269	$108,000.00
Ed Fiori	3	66-66-70-70=272	$68,000.00
Chris DiMarco	4	67-68-70-68=273	$48,000.00
Steve Gotsche	5	68-70-69-67=274	$40,000.00
Justin Leonard	T-6	69-68-70-68=275	$33,500.00
Billy Downes	T-6	71-68-69-67=275	$33,500.00
Fred Funk	T-6	68-66-75-66=275	$33,500.00
Wayne Levi	T-9	66-71-68-71=276	$23,142.85
Bill Glasson	T-9	68-68-71-69=276	$23,142.86
Jeff Maggert	T-9	68-69-71-68=276	$23,142.86
Guy Boros	T-9	65-69-70-72=276	$23,142.85
Fran Quinn	T-9	67-72-66-71=276	$23,142.86
Ken Green	T-9	68-72-68-68=276	$23,142.86
Blaine McCallister	T-9	68-73-69-66=276	$23,142.86

Federal Express St. Jude Classic

Course: TPC at Southwind, Germantown, Tenn.
Par: 71 Yardage: 7,006
Last day of event: Sunday, July 31, 1994

Player	Place	Score	Earnings
Dicky Pride	Win	66-67-67-67=267	$225,000.00

Playoff: Beat Gene Sauers and Hal Sutton with birdie on first extra hole

Player	Place	Score	Earnings
Gene Sauers	T-2	67-66-68-66=267	$110,000.00
Hal Sutton	T-2	67-68-68-64=267	$110,000.00
Nick Price	4	72-66-66-64=268	$60,000.00
Dave Barr	T-5	66-69-67-67=269	$45,625.00
Russ Cochran	T-5	67-68-65-69=269	$45,625.00
Wayne Grady	T-5	70-66-67-66=269	$45,625.00
Paul Stankowski	T-8	68-67-69-66=270	$37,500.00
Fuzzy Zoeller	T-8	66-65-70-69=270	$37,500.00
Brian Claar	T-10	69-67-68-67=271	$28,750.00
John Cook	T-10	67-70-65-69=271	$28,750.00
Duffy Waldorf	T-10	67-70-67-67=271	$28,750.00
Gil Morgan	T-10	70-67-63-71=271	$28,750.00
Jim Gallagher, Jr.	T-10	71-68-65-67=271	$28,750.00

Buick Open

Course: Warwick Hills C.C., Grand Blanc, Mich.
Par: 72 Yardage: 7,014
Last day of event: Sunday, August 7, 1994

Player	Place	Score	Earnings
Fred Couples	Win	72-65-65-68=270	$198,000.00
Corey Pavin	2	66-65-70-71=272	$118,800.00
Steve Pate	T-3	71-67-69-69=276	$57,200.00
Curtis Strange	T-3	71-70-67-68=276	$57,200.00
Greg Kraft	T-3	71-72-67-66=276	$57,200.00
Keith Clearwater	T-6	71-67-69-70=277	$38,225.00
Ben Crenshaw	T-6	72-68-69-68=277	$38,225.00
Tom Lehman	T-8	71-67-70-70=278	$31,900.00
Fred Funk	T-8	65-70-71-72=278	$31,900.00
Duffy Waldorf	T-8	69-67-74-68=278	$31,900.00

PGA Championship

Course: Southern Hills C.C., Tulsa, Okla.
Par: 70 Yardage: 6,824
Last day of event: Sunday, August 14, 1994

Player	Place	Score	Earnings
Nick Price	Win	67-65-70-67=269	$310,000.00
Corey Pavin	2	70-67-69-69=275	$160,000.00
Phil Mickelson	3	68-71-67-70=276	$110,000.00
John Cook	T-4	71-67-69-70=277	$76,666.66
Greg Norman	T-4	71-69-67-70=277	$76,666.67
Nick Faldo	T-4	73-67-71-66=277	$76,666.67
Jose Maria Olazabal	T-7	72-66-70-70=278	$57,500.00
Steve Elkington	T-7	73-70-66-69=278	$57,500.00
Loren Roberts	T-9	69-72-67-71=279	$41,000.00
Tom Watson	T-9	69-72-67-71=279	$41,000.00
Ben Crenshaw	T-9	70-67-70-72=279	$41,000.00
Tom Kite	T-9	72-68-69-70=279	$41,000.00
Ian Woosnam	T-9	68-72-73-66=279	$41,000.00

Sprint International

Course: Castle Pine G.C., Castle Rock, Colo. (Stableford format)
Par: 72 Yardage: 7,559
Last day of event: Sunday, August 21, 1994

Player	Place	Score	Earnings
Steve Lowery	Win	7-14-5-9=35	$252,000.00

Playoff: Beat Rick Fehr with par on first extra hole

Player	Place	Score	Earnings
Rick Fehr	2	10-5-9-11=35	$151,200.00
Duffy Waldorf	3	7-6-8-13=34	$95,200.00
Ernie Els	4	5-7-17-4=33	$67,200.00
Tom Kite	5	4-12-10-6=32	$56,000.00

John Adams	T-6	4-2-14-11=31	$48,650.00
Chris DiMarco	T-6	6-6-9-10=31	$48,650.00
Mark Calcavecchia	T-8	0-8-11-11=30	$42,000.00
Dave Stockton, Jr.	T-8	6-14-5-5=30	$42,000.00
Phil Mickelson	T-10	0-11-9-9=29	$36,400.00
Mike Reid	T-10	14-6-5-4=29	$36,400.00

NEC World Series of Golf

Course: Firestone C.C. (North), Akron, Ohio
Par: 71 Yardage: 6,918
Last day of event: Sunday, August 28, 1994

Player	Place	Score	Earnings
Jose Maria Olazabal	Win	66-67-69-67=269	$360,000.00
Scott Hoch	2	71-64-65-70=270	$216,000.00
Brad Faxon	T-3	69-68-65-69=271	$116,000.00
Steve Lowery	T-3	67-66-66-72=271	$116,000.00
Mark McNulty	T-5	69-68-65-70=272	$76,000.00
John Huston	T-5	73-64-64-71=272	$76,000.00
Mike Heinen	7	71-67-65-70=273	$67,000.00
Fred Couples	T-8	69-70-65-70=274	$60,000.00
Greg Norman	T-8	67-67-68-72=274	$60,000.00
Hale Irwin	T-10	70-65-71-70=276	$52,000.00
Nick Price	T-10	68-66-69-73=276	$52,000.00

Greater Milwaukee Open

Course: Brown Deer Park G.C., Milwaukee, Wis.
Par: 71 Yardage: 6,716
Last day of event: Sunday, September 4, 1994

Player	Place	Score	Earnings
Mike Springer	Win	69-67-65-67=268	$180,000.00
Loren Roberts	2	70-63-68-68=269	$108,000.00
Joey Sindelar	T-3	67-68-66-69=270	$48,000.00
Tom Purtzer	T-3	70-69-67-64=270	$48,000.00
Mark Calcavecchia	T-3	67-68-64-71=270	$48,000.00
Bob Estes	T-3	67-66-65-72=270	$48,000.00
Marco Dawson	T-7	68-66-69-68=271	$32,250.00
Dave Barr	T-7	69-64-70-68=271	$32,250.00
Mark O'Meara	T-9	68-69-67-68=272	$28,000.00
Steve Pate	T-9	68-70-65-69=272	$28,000.00

Bell Canadian Open

Course: Glen Abbey G.C., Oakville, Ontario, Canada
Par: 72 Yardage: 7,102
Last day of event: Sunday, September 11, 1994

Player	Place	Score	Earnings
Nick Price	Win	67-72-68-68=275	$234,000.00
Mark Calcavecchia	2	67-71-71-67=276	$140,400.00
Tom Lehman	3	69-69-70-69=277	$88,400.00
Mark McCumber	T-4	74-65-67-72=278	$57,200.00
Jay Don Blake	T-4	74-63-73-68=278	$57,200.00
Steve Stricker	T-6	69-70-69-71=279	$43,550.00
Fulton Allem	T-6	69-69-71-70=279	$43,550.00
Brian Kamm	T-6	71-71-69-68=279	$43,550.00
Mark O'Meara	9	66-72-72-70=280	$37,700.00
Payne Stewart	T-10	68-72-72-69=281	$32,500.00
Greg Kraft	T-10	72-70-70-69=281	$32,500.00
Bob Estes	T-10	72-73-68-68=281	$32,500.00

B.C. Open

Course: En-Joie G.C., Endicott, N.Y.
Par: 71 Yardage: 6,966
Last day of event: Sunday, September 18, 1994

Player	Place	Score	Earnings
Mike Sullivan	Win	65-67-68-66=266	$162,000.00
Jeff Sluman	2	63-68-67-72=270	$97,200.00
Mike Hulbert	T-3	67-67-68-70=272	$52,200.00
Brian Claar	T-3	68-68-65-71=272	$52,200.00
Russell Beiersdorf	T-5	69-66-68-70=273	$34,200.00
Curt Byrum	T-5	67-69-66-71=273	$34,200.00
Paul Goydos	T-7	68-68-67-71=274	$28,050.00
Bill Glasson	T-7	70-65-68-71=274	$28,050.00
Blaine McCallister	T-7	67-70-65-72=274	$28,050.00
P.H. Horgan III	T-10	68-67-69-71=275	$22,500.00
Mike Heinen	T-10	65-70-68-72=275	$22,500.00
Robin Freeman	T-10	68-65-69-73=275	$22,500.00

Hardee's Golf Classic

Course: Oakwood C.C., Coal Valley, Ill.
Par: 70 Yardage: 6,796
Last day of event: Sunday, September 25, 1994

Player	Place	Score	Earnings
Mark McCumber	Win	66-67-65-67=265	$180,000.00
Kenny Perry	2	67-66-65-68=266	$108,000.00
David Frost	T-3	68-67-67-65=267	$58,000.00
Mike Donald	T-3	70-66-64-67=267	$58,000.00
Russ Cochran	5	67-66-70-65=268	$40,000.00
Robert Wrenn	T-6	63-70-67-69=269	$32,375.00
Curt Byrum	T-6	69-65-65-70=269	$32,375.00
Tom Lehman	T-6	71-67-65-66=269	$32,375.00
John Huston	T-6	71-66-67-65=269	$32,375.00
Doug Tewell	T-10	65-69-69-67=270	$23,000.00
Mark Calcavecchia	T-10	66-69-69-66=270	$23,000.00
Kirk Triplett	T-10	67-65-70-68=270	$23,000.00
Wayne Levi	T-10	67-70-65-68=270	$23,000.00
Michael Bradley	T-10	72-67-62-69=270	$23,000.00

Buick Southern Open

Course: Callaway Gardens Resort, Pine Mountain, Ga.
Par: 72 Yardage: 7,057
Last day of event: Sunday, October 2, 1994

Player	Place	Score	Earnings
Steve Elkington	Win	66-66-68=200	$144,000.00
Steve Rintoul	2	70-65-70=205	$86,400.00
Brad Bryant	3	70-68-69=207	$54,400.00
Steve Pate	T-4	69-71-68=208	$33,066.67
Buddy Gardner	T-4	71-69-68=208	$33,066.67
Gene Sauers	T-4	72-67-69=208	$33,066.66
Jeff Sluman	T-7	69-70-70=209	$24,100.00
Blaine McCallister	T-7	69-71-69=209	$24,100.00
Bobby Wadkins	T-7	69-72-68=209	$24,100.00
Larry Mize	T-7	69-73-67=209	$24,100.00

Walt Disney World/Oldsmobile Classic

Course: Walt Disney (Magnolia, Palm, Eagle Pines), Lake Buena Vista, Fla.
Home course / Magnolia, Par: 72 Yardage: 7,190
Last day of event: Sunday, October 9, 1994

Player	Place	Score	Earnings
Rick Fehr	Win	63-70-68-68=269	$198,000.00

Player	Place	Score	Earnings
Fuzzy Zoeller	T-2	66-70-69-66=271	$96,800.00
Craig Stadler	T-2	68-66-67-70=271	$96,800.00
Trevor Dodds	T-4	68-66-70-68=272	$48,400.00
Steve Stricker	T-4	72-67-66-67=272	$48,400.00
Robert Gamez	6	68-69-68-68=273	$39,600.00
Brian Kamm	T-7	69-69-68-68=274	$33,137.50
Doug Tewell	T-7	69-66-71-68=274	$33,137.50
Glen Day	T-7	65-68-72-69=274	$33,137.50
Donnie Hammond	T-7	68-72-67-67=274	$33,137.50

Texas Open

Course: Oak Hill C.C., San Antonio, Texas
Par: 71 Yardage: 6,650
Last day of event: Sunday, October 16, 1994

Player	Place	Score	Earnings
Bob Estes	Win	62-65-68-70=265	$180,000.00
Gil Morgan	2	66-68-65-67=266	$108,000.00
Don Pooley	3	69-65-65-68=267	$68,000.00
Bruce Lietzke	4	68-69-64-69=270	$48,000.00
Craig Stadler	T-5	68-66-69-68=271	$36,500.00
John Wilson	T-5	66-68-67-70=271	$36,500.00
Mark McNulty	T-5	70-65-67-69=271	$36,500.00
Bob Burns	T-8	65-69-68-70=272	$25,000.00
Brad Bryant	T-8	66-67-70-69=272	$25,000.00
Dillard Pruitt	T-8	70-68-67-67=272	$25,000.00
Mark O'Meara	T-8	70-69-67-66=272	$25,000.00
Ben Crenshaw	T-8	70-69-68-65=272	$25,000.00
JC Anderson	T-8	67-64-70-71=272	$25,000.00
Blaine McCallister	T-8	70-65-72-65=272	$25,000.00

Las Vegas Invitational

Course: TPC at Summerlin, Las Vegas C.C., Las Vegas Hilton C.C., Las Vegas, Nev.
Home course / TPC at Summerlin, Par: 72 Yardage: 7,243
Last day of event: Sunday, October 23, 1994

Player	Place	Score	Earnings
Bruce Lietzke	Win	66-67-68-66-65=332	$270,000.00
Robert Gamez	2	66-70-64-69-64=333	$162,000.00
Billy Andrade	T-3	66-68-67-67-67=335	$87,000.00
Phil Mickelson	T-3	70-66-66-70-63=335	$87,000.00
Jim Furyk	T-5	67-64-69-66-70=336	$54,750.00
Bill Glasson	T-5	67-68-70-65-66=336	$54,750.00
Paul Stankowski	T-5	70-66-66-69-65=336	$54,750.00
Sean Murphy	T-8	64-69-67-69-68=337	$42,000.00
Scott Hoch	T-8	66-63-70-70-68=337	$42,000.00
Kirk Triplett	T-8	69-65-65-68-70=337	$42,000.00
Guy Boros	T-8	70-63-67-68-69=337	$42,000.00

The Tour Championship

Course: The Olympic Club (Lake Course), San Francisco, Calif.
Par: 71 Yardage: 6,812
Last day of event: Sunday, October 30, 1994

Player	Place	Score	Earnings
Mark McCumber	Win	66-71-69-68=274	$540,000.00
Playoff: Beat Fuzzy Zoeller with birdie on first extra hole			
Fuzzy Zoeller	2	71-69-66-68=274	$324,000.00
Brad Bryant	3	72-68-67-68=275	$207,000.00
Bill Glasson	T-4	66-68-71-71=276	$132,000.00
David Frost	T-4	66-69-75-66=276	$132,000.00
Jay Haas	6	69-71-71-66=277	$108,000.00
Jeff Maggert	7	72-66-70-70=278	$102,000.00

Player	Place	Score	Earnings
Loren Roberts	T-8	71-70-68-70=279	$93,000.00
Steve Lowery	T-8	66-69-72-72=279	$93,000.00
Bruce Lietzke	T-10	69-71-71-69=280	$81,000.00
Corey Pavin	T-10	69-69-70-72=280	$81,000.00
John Huston	T-10	74-68-66-72=280	$81,000.00

1995

Only a week after the death of his mentor Harvey Penick, Ben Crenshaw was the inspired winner of the Masters, holding off Davis Love III (final-round 66) to win by a shot. The U.S. Open also produced an unlikely winner, the diminutive but tenacious Corey Pavin, who beat Greg Norman by two shots at Shinnecock Hills. And who could have predicted John Daly's victory in the British Open at St. Andrews? After completing his final-round 71, Daly watched as the only man with a chance to beat him, Costantino Rocca, flubbed a chip shot at the 18th, then holed a monster putt from the Valley of Sin to force a playoff. Daly won the four-hole aggregate playoff 15 to 19. The PGA Championship featured extraordinary scoring at Riviera, with the top 22 players posting 67 rounds in the 60s and only five rounds over par. Steve Elkington and Colin Montgomerie both shot 17-under-par 267, with Elkington making a 25-foot birdie putt to win on the first hole of sudden death. Europe scored a 14 ½ to 13 ½ victory in the Ryder Cup at Oak Hill.

Mercedes Championshipss

Course: La Costa C.C., Carlsbad, Calif.
Par: 72 Yardage: 7,022
Last day of event: Sunday, January 8, 1995

Player	Place	Score	Earnings
Steve Elkington	Win	69-71-71-67=278	$180,000.00
Playoff: Beat Bruce Lietzke with birdie on second extra hole			
Bruce Lietzke	2	71-69-71-67=278	$108,000.00
Bill Glasson	3	70-69-73-67=279	$68,000.00
Craig Stadler	4	71-65-73-71=280	$48,000.00
Fred Couples	T-5	73-68-68-72=281	$35,250.00
Rick Fehr	T-5	71-74-70-66=281	$35,250.00
Ben Crenshaw	T-5	71-67-75-68=281	$35,250.00
Tom Lehman	T-5	75-68-72-66=281	$35,250.00
Lee Janzen	T-9	72-63-76-71=282	$28,750.00
John Huston	T-9	67-66-72-77=282	$28,750.00

United Airlines Hawaiian Open

Course: Waialae C.C., Honolulu, Ha.
Par: 72 Yardage: 6,975
Last day of event: Sunday, January 15, 1995

Player	Place	Score	Earnings
John Morse	Win	71-65-65-68=269	$216,000.00
Tom Lehman	T-2	68-70-67-67=272	$105,600.00
Duffy Waldorf	T-2	68-65-71-68=272	$105,600.00
Dan Pohl	T-4	69-67-69-69=274	$49,600.00
Bill Glasson	T-4	70-70-68-66=274	$49,600.00
Paul Azinger	T-4	72-67-69-66=274	$49,600.00
Mark Brooks	T-7	68-69-68-70=275	$38,700.00
John Huston	T-7	72-68-69-66=275	$38,700.00
Chip Beck	9	71-66-66-73=276	$34,800.00
Grant Waite	T-10	71-69-66-71=277	$31,200.00
David Ishii	T-10	71-69-68-69=277	$31,200.00

Northern Telecom Open

Course: Tucson National G.C., Starr Pass G.C., Tucson, Ariz.
Par: 72 Yardage: 7,148
Last day of event: Sunday, January 22, 1995

Player	Place	Score	Earnings
Phil Mickelson	Win	65-66-70-68=269	$225,000.00

Jim Gallagher, Jr.	T-2	68-64-69-69=270	$110,000.00
Scott Simpson	T-2	69-65-68-68=270	$110,000.00
Brett Ogle	4	68-65-68-70=271	$60,000.00
Jim Furyk	5	69-69-67-67=272	$50,000.00
David Duval	T-6	67-70-67-70=274	$37,812.50
Joe Ozaki	T-6	68-67-70-69=274	$37,812.50
Woody Austin	T-6	68-69-70-67=274	$37,812.50
Bob Tway	T-6	70-65-69-70=274	$37,812.50
Tom Kite	T-6	71-66-67-70=274	$37,812.50
Don Pooley	T-6	71-66-65-72=274	$37,812.50

Phoenix Open

Course: TPC of Scottsdale, Scottsdale, Ariz.
Par: 71 Yardage: 6,992
Last day of event: Sunday, January 29, 1995

Player	Place	Score	Earnings
Vijay Singh	Win	70-67-66-66=269	$234,000.00

Playoff: Beat Billy Mayfair with par on first extra hole

Billy Mayfair	2	69-67-67-66=269	$140,400.00
Ben Crenshaw	3	68-64-70-69=271	$88,400.00
Steve Jones	T-4	68-69-68-67=272	$53,733.33
Payne Stewart	T-4	71-68-67-66=272	$53,733.33
Bruce Lietzke	T-4	72-65-69-66=272	$53,733.34
Steve Lowery	T-7	70-68-65-70=273	$37,830.00
Joe Ozaki	T-7	68-71-67-67=273	$37,830.00
John Adams	T-7	71-66-66-70=273	$37,830.00
Hale Irwin	T-7	66-66-72-69=273	$37,830.00
Mark Calcavecchia	T-7	72-67-66-68=273	$37,830.00

AT&T Pebble Beach Pro-Am

Courses: Pebble Beach G.L., Spyglass Hill G.C., Poppy Hills G.C., Pebble Beach, Calif.
Home Course / Pebble Beach G.L., Par: 72 Yardage: 6,799
Last day of event: Sunday, February 5, 1995

Player	Place	Score	Earnings
Peter Jacobsen	Win	67-73-66-65=271	$252,000.00
David Duval	2	72-67-67-67=273	$151,200.00
Davis Love III	T-3	65-71-71-68=275	$81,200.00
Kenny Perry	T-3	68-68-67-72=275	$81,200.00
Payne Stewart	5	71-67-69-70=277	$56,000.00
Jack Nicklaus	T-6	71-70-67-70=278	$46,900.00
Guy Boros	T-6	69-66-71-72=278	$46,900.00
Brad Faxon	T-6	70-64-72-72=278	$46,900.00
Nick Faldo	T-9	66-72-69-72=279	$36,400.00
Emlyn Aubrey	T-9	70-69-68-72=279	$36,400.00
John Adams	T-9	72-66-71-70=279	$36,400.00
Mark O'Meara	T-9	73-68-70-68=279	$36,400.00

Buick Invitational of California

Course: Torrey Pines (South), Torrey Pines (North), San Diego, Calif.
Home Course -Par: 72 Yardage: 7,000
Last day of event: Sunday, February 12, 1995

Player	Place	Score	Earnings
Peter Jacobsen	Win	68-65-68-68=269	$216,000.00
Hal Sutton	T-2	67-69-68-69=273	$79,200.00
Kirk Triplett	T-2	69-69-66-69=273	$79,200.00
Mike Hulbert	T-2	70-65-70-68=273	$79,200.00
Mark Calcavecchia	T-2	71-67-67-68=273	$79,200.00
Dillard Pruitt	T-6	69-70-68-68=275	$41,700.00
Dan Pohl	T-6	65-74-66-70=275	$41,700.00
John Huston	T-8	69-71-67-69=276	$33,600.00

Nolan Henke	T-8	68-66-73-69=276	$33,600.00
Brandel Chamblee	T-8	66-66-74-70=276	$33,600.00
David Ogrin	T-8	66-69-74-67=276	$33,600.00

Bob Hope Chrysler Classic

Course: Bermuda Dunes C.C., Indian Ridge, Indian Wells C.C., La Quinta C.C.
Home course / Bermuda Dunes, Par: 72 Yardage: 6,927
Last day of event: Sunday, February 19, 1995

Player	Place	Score	Earnings
Kenny Perry	Win	63-71-64-67-70=335	$216,000.00
David Duval	2	67-68-65-67-69=336	$129,600.00
Dillard Pruitt	T-3	65-70-69-68-65=337	$62,400.00
Tommy Tolles	T-3	66-69-68-64-70=337	$62,400.00
Curtis Strange	T-3	64-73-67-63-70=337	$62,400.00
Robert Gamez	6	70-68-66-68-66=338	$43,200.00
Tommy Armour III	T-7	66-67-69-68-69=339	$34,920.00
Donnie Hammond	T-7	67-69-66-69-68=339	$34,920.00
Mark Brooks	T-7	67-68-69-65-70=339	$34,920.00
Kelly Gibson	T-7	65-71-67-67-69=339	$34,920.00
Harry Taylor	T-7	66-64-66-71-72=339	$34,920.00

Nissan Open

Course: Riviera C.C., Pacific Palisades, Calif.
Par: 71 Yardage: 6,946
Last day of event: Sunday, February 26, 1995

Player	Place	Score	Earnings
Corey Pavin	Win	67-66-68-67=268	$216,000.00
Jay Don Blake	T-2	69-67-66-69=271	$105,600.00
Kenny Perry	T-2	70-62-68-71=271	$105,600.00
Craig Stadler	T-4	67-68-67-70=272	$52,800.00
Scott Simpson	T-4	70-66-68-68=272	$52,800.00
Jodie Mudd	6	66-71-69-67=273	$43,200.00
Jay Haas	T-7	69-70-68-67=274	$38,700.00
Lanny Wadkins	T-7	67-72-66-69=274	$38,700.00
Mike Reid	T-9	69-69-69-69=276	$30,000.00
Mike Hulbert	T-9	71-66-68-71=276	$30,000.00
Ronnie Black	T-9	72-68-66-70=276	$30,000.00
Jim Furyk	T-9	67-74-65-70=276	$30,000.00
Brian Kamm	T-9	67-74-67-68=276	$30,000.00

Doral-Ryder Open

Course: Doral C.C. (Blue), Miami, Fla.
Par: 72 Yardage: 6,939
Last day of event: Sunday, March 5, 1995

Player	Place	Score	Earnings
Nick Faldo	Win	67-71-66-69=273	$270,000.00
Greg Norman	T-2	68-68-65-73=274	$132,000.00
Peter Jacobsen	T-2	68-69-64-73=274	$132,000.00
Davis Love III	T-4	65-69-70-71=275	$62,000.00
Justin Leonard	T-4	68-68-71-68=275	$62,000.00
Steve Elkington	T-4	67-72-67-69=275	$62,000.00
Hale Irwin	T-7	70-70-67-69=276	$48,375.00
Woody Austin	T-7	66-71-68-71=276	$48,375.00
Steve Stricker	9	70-68-71-68=277	$43,500.00
Mark O'Meara	T-10	69-72-66-71=278	$39,000.00
Steve Lowery	T-10	65-72-73-68=278	$39,000.00

Honda Classic

Course: Weston Hills G. & C.C., Ft. Lauderdale, Fla.
Par: 71 Yardage: 6,964
Last day of event: Sunday, March 12, 1995

Player	Place	Score	Earnings
Mark O'Meara	Win	68-65-71-71=275	$216,000.00
Nick Faldo	2	67-71-69-69=276	$129,600.00
Ian Woosnam	3	68-72-69-68=277	$81,600.00
Andrew Magee	4	69-67-76-67=279	$57,600.00
Blaine McCallister	5	70-66-73-71=280	$48,000.00
Bill Britton	6	71-69-72-69=281	$43,200.00
Mike Standly	7	71-66-75-70=282	$40,200.00
Brian Claar	T-8	69-70-72-72=283	$32,400.00
Keith Fergus	T-8	69-72-71-71=283	$32,400.00
Michael Bradley	T-8	73-69-73-68=283	$32,400.00
Scott Verplank	T-8	74-67-73-69=283	$32,400.00
Seve Ballesteros	T-8	70-68-76-69=283	$32,400.00

The Nestle Invitational

Course: Bay Hill Club, Orlando, Fla.
Par: 72 Yardage: 7,114
Last day of event: Sunday, March 19, 1995

Player	Place	Score	Earnings
Loren Roberts	Win	68-65-68-71=272	$216,000.00
Brad Faxon	2	69-70-64-71=274	$129,600.00
Peter Jacobsen	3	70-68-68-69=275	$81,600.00
Steve Stricker	4	67-72-69-69=277	$57,600.00
Mark McCumber	T-5	69-70-69-70=278	$39,300.00
Jesper Parnevik	T-5	67-72-67-72=278	$39,300.00
Bob Lohr	T-5	69-70-67-72=278	$39,300.00
Duffy Waldorf	T-5	71-72-70-65=278	$39,300.00
Jay Haas	T-5	72-69-69-68=278	$39,300.00
Nick Faldo	T-5	71-73-66-68=278	$39,300.00

The Players Championship

Course: TPC at Sawgrass, Ponte Vedra Beach, Fla.
Par: 72 Yardage: 6,857
Last day of event: Sunday, March 26, 1995

Player	Place	Score	Earnings
Lee Janzen	Win	69-74-69-71=283	$540,000.00
Bernhard Langer	2	69-71-71-73=284	$324,000.00
Payne Stewart	T-3	69-73-71-72=285	$156,000.00
Corey Pavin	T-3	66-73-72-74=285	$156,000.00
Gene Sauers	T-3	67-72-78-68=285	$156,000.00
Brad Bryant	T-6	72-71-72-71=286	$104,250.00
Davis Love III	T-6	73-67-74-72=286	$104,250.00
Billy Andrade	T-8	74-69-73-71=287	$87,000.00
Joe Ozaki	T-8	74-70-72-71=287	$87,000.00
Larry Mize	T-8	69-77-72-69=287	$87,000.00

Freeport-McMoRan Classic

Course: English Turn G. & C.C., New Orleans, La.
Par: 72 Yardage: 7,106
Last day of event: Sunday, April 2, 1995

Player	Place	Score	Earnings
Davis Love III	Win	68-69-66-71=274	$216,000.00

Playoff: Beat Mike Heinen with birdie on second extra hole

Player	Place	Score	Earnings
Mike Heinen	2	66-71-71-66=274	$129,600.00
David Duval	3	67-68-71-69=275	$81,600.00
Craig Parry	4	71-69-66-70=276	$57,600.00

Player	Place	Score	Earnings
David Peoples	T-5	70-69-66-72=277	$43,800.00
Jeff Maggert	T-5	72-66-70-69=277	$43,800.00
Mike Standly	T-5	70-65-69-73=277	$43,800.00
Scott Simpson	T-8	68-70-71-69=278	$36,000.00
Brad Bryant	T-8	65-74-69-70=278	$36,000.00
Brian Claar	T-10	68-70-71-70=279	$27,600.00
Lennie Clements	T-10	69-68-70-72=279	$27,600.00
Kirk Triplett	T-10	66-73-71-69=279	$27,600.00
Danny Briggs	T-10	69-71-73-66=279	$27,600.00
Mark Wiebe	T-10	70-68-68-73=279	$27,600.00

Masters

Course: Augusta National G.C., Augusta, Ga.
Par: 72 Yardage: 6,925
Last day of event: Sunday, April 9, 1995

Player	Place	Score	Earnings
Ben Crenshaw	Win	70-67-69-68=274	$396,000.00
Davis Love III	2	69-69-71-66=275	$237,600.00
Jay Haas	T-3	71-64-72-70=277	$127,600.00
Greg Norman	T-3	73-68-68-68=277	$127,600.00
David Frost	T-5	66-71-71-71=279	$83,600.00
Steve Elkington	T-5	73-67-67-72=279	$83,600.00
Phil Mickelson	T-7	66-71-70-73=280	$70,950.00
Scott Hoch	T-7	69-67-71-73=280	$70,950.00
Curtis Strange	9	72-71-65-73=281	$63,800.00
Fred Couples	T-10	71-69-67-75=282	$57,200.00
Brian Henninger	T-10	70-68-68-76=282	$57,200.00

MCI Classic

Course: Harbour Town G.L., Hilton Head, S.C.
Par: 71 Yardage: 6,657
Last day of event: Sunday, April 16, 1995

Player	Place	Score	Earnings
Bob Tway	Win	67-69-72-67=275	$234,000.00

Playoff: Beat Nolan Henke and David Frost with par on second extra hole

Player	Place	Score	Earnings
David Frost	T-2	71-68-66-70=275	$114,400.00
Nolan Henke	T-2	66-72-70-67=275	$114,400.00
Mark McCumber	T-4	70-71-64-71=276	$53,733.33
Woody Austin	T-4	71-72-69-64=276	$53,733.34
Nick Faldo	T-4	74-64-70-68=276	$53,733.33
Tom Watson	T-7	70-68-68-71=277	$36,508.33
Nick Price	T-7	69-72-71-65=277	$36,508.34
David Edwards	T-7	70-69-66-72=277	$36,508.33
Steve Lowery	T-7	68-73-66-70=277	$36,508.33
Gil Morgan	T-7	73-71-62-71=277	$36,508.33
Ernie Els	T-7	73-70-64-70=277	$36,508.34

Kmart Greater Greensboro Open

Course: Forest Oaks C.C., Greensboro, N.C.
Par: 72 Yardage: 6,984
Last day of event: Sunday, April 23, 1995

Player	Place	Score	Earnings
Jim Gallagher, Jr.	Win	69-70-69-66=274	$270,000.00
Peter Jacobsen	T-2	69-65-69-72=275	$132,000.00
Jeff Sluman	T-2	70-65-66-74=275	$132,000.00
John Adams	4	70-66-70-70=276	$72,000.00
Mark Calcavecchia	5	68-73-67-69=277	$60,000.00
Jesper Parnevik	6	70-68-68-72=278	$54,000.00
Ted Tryba	T-7	69-70-69-71=279	$43,650.00
Brad Faxon	T-7	65-71-71-72=279	$43,650.00
Vijay Singh	T-7	65-72-69-73=279	$43,650.00

Player	Place	Score	Earnings
Steve Stricker	T-7	68-73-66-72=279	$43,650.00
Guy Boros	T-7	73-67-70-69=279	$43,650.00

Shell Houston Open
Course: TPC at The Woodlands, The Woodlands, Texas
Par: 72 Yardage: 7,042
Last day of event: Sunday, April 30, 1995

Player	Place	Score	Earnings
Payne Stewart	Win	73-65-70-68=276	$252,000.00
Playoff: Beat Scott Hoch with birdie on first extra hole			
Scott Hoch	2	68-64-69-75=276	$151,200.00
Charlie Rymer	3	69-69-68-71=277	$95,200.00
Tray Tyner	T-4	70-69-68-71=278	$61,600.00
Paul Stankowski	T-4	71-68-71-68=278	$61,600.00
Brett Ogle	T-6	68-69-71-71=279	$48,650.00
Brian Claar	T-6	73-68-67-71=279	$48,650.00
Vijay Singh	T-8	70-70-70-70=280	$40,600.00
John Wilson	T-8	71-69-68-72=280	$40,600.00
Steve Rintoul	T-8	66-70-71-73=280	$40,600.00

BellSouth Classic
Course: Atlanta C.C., Atlanta, Ga.
Par: 72 Yardage: 7,007
Last day of event: Sunday, May 7, 1995

Player	Place	Score	Earnings
Mark Calcavecchia	Win	67-69-69-66=271	$234,000.00
Jim Gallagher, Jr.	2	65-70-68-70=273	$140,400.00
Stephen Keppler	3	67-69-67-71=274	$88,400.00
Curtis Strange	T-4	70-71-69-65=275	$53,733.34
Guy Boros	T-4	71-67-67-70=275	$53,733.33
Scott Verplank	T-4	72-67-67-69=275	$53,733.33
Brandel Chamblee	T-7	68-70-69-69=276	$37,830.00
Tommy Tolles	T-7	70-69-68-69=276	$37,830.00
Scott Hoch	T-7	69-71-71-65=276	$37,830.00
Lennie Clements	T-7	70-66-72-68=276	$37,830.00
Billy Andrade	T-7	72-68-69-67=276	$37,830.00

GTE Byron Nelson Classic
Course: TPC at Las Colinas, Cottonwood Valley, Irving, Texas
Home course / TPC at Los Colinas, Par: 70 Yardage: 6,850
Last day of event: Sunday, May 14, 1995

Player	Place	Score	Earnings
Ernie Els	Win	69-61-65-68=263	$234,000.00
Mike Heinen	T-2	67-66-67-66=266	$97,066.67
Robin Freeman	T-2	65-65-68-68=266	$97,066.66
D.A. Weibring	T-2	65-69-67-65=266	$97,066.67
Gil Morgan	T-5	68-66-68-66=268	$45,662.50
Jay Don Blake	T-5	64-69-69-66=268	$45,662.50
Scott Verplank	T-5	67-69-67-65=268	$45,662.50
Kenny Perry	T-5	65-66-70-67=268	$45,662.50
Bob Tway	T-9	68-66-69-66=269	$36,400.00
Loren Roberts	T-9	68-67-69-65=269	$36,400.00

Buick Classic
Course: Westchester C.C., Harrison, N.Y.
Par: 71 Yardage: 6,779
Last day of event: Sunday, May 21, 1995

Player	Place	Score	Earnings
Vijay Singh	Win	70-69-67-72=278	$216,000.00

Player	Place	Score	Earnings
Playoff: Beat Doug Martin with birdie on fifth extra hole			
Doug Martin	2	67-70-72-69=278	$129,600.00
Bobby Wadkins	3	72-66-69-72=279	$81,600.00
Fred Funk	T-4	71-68-71-70=280	$47,250.00
Nick Faldo	T-4	70-70-68-72=280	$47,250.00
Dillard Pruitt	T-4	72-69-70-69=280	$47,250.00
Ernie Els	T-4	68-69-75-68=280	$47,250.00
Blaine McCallister	T-8	69-71-69-72=281	$33,600.00
Bruce Fleisher	T-8	68-71-69-73=281	$33,600.00
Bob Gilder	T-8	73-70-68-70=281	$33,600.00
David Duval	T-8	69-75-67-70=281	$33,600.00

Colonial National Invitational
Course: Colonial C.C., Fort Worth, Texas
Par: 70 Yardage: 7,096
Last day of event: Sunday, May 28, 1995

Player	Place	Score	Earnings
Tom Lehman	Win	67-68-68-68=271	$252,000.00
Craig Parry	2	66-65-70-71=272	$151,200.00
D.A. Weibring	3	66-72-69-67=274	$95,200.00
Woody Austin	4	67-69-66-73=275	$67,200.00
Justin Leonard	T-5	68-72-68-68=276	$51,100.00
Mark McCumber	T-5	67-73-68-68=276	$51,100.00
Brad Faxon	T-5	67-70-75-64=276	$51,100.00
Rocco Mediate	T-8	69-68-70-70=277	$39,200.00
Billy Mayfair	T-8	68-71-67-71=277	$39,200.00
Mark Calcavecchia	T-8	70-67-68-72=277	$39,200.00
Jeff Maggert	T-8	66-68-74-69=277	$39,200.00

Memorial Tournament
Course: Muirfield Village G.C., Dubin, Ohio
Par: 72 Yardage: 7,104
Last day of event: Sunday, June 4, 1995

Player	Place	Score	Earnings
Greg Norman	Win	66-70-67-66=269	$306,000.00
Steve Elkington	T-2	69-68-69-67=273	$126,933.33
Mark Calcavecchia	T-2	69-71-66-67=273	$126,933.33
David Duval	T-2	70-71-64-68=273	$126,933.34
Ben Crenshaw	T-5	67-68-71-69=275	$57,630.00
Tom Watson	T-5	67-71-68-69=275	$57,630.00
Robert Gamez	T-5	68-67-69-71=275	$57,630.00
David Frost	T-5	68-72-65-70=275	$57,630.00
Jay Haas	T-5	72-72-66-65=275	$57,630.00
Nick Price	10	71-71-69-65=276	$45,900.00

Kemper Open
Course: TPC at Avenel, Potomac, Md.
Par: 71 Yardage: 7,005
Last day of event: Sunday, June 11, 1995

Player	Place	Score	Earnings
Lee Janzen	Win	68-69-68-67=272	$252,000.00
Playoff: Beat Corey Pavin with birdie on first extra hole			
Corey Pavin	2	73-68-63-68=272	$151,200.00
Robin Freeman	3	70-69-66-68=273	$95,200.00
Mark O'Meara	T-4	66-70-69-70=275	$52,780.00
Vijay Singh	T-4	65-71-71-68=275	$52,780.00
Justin Leonard	T-4	71-67-70-67=275	$52,780.00
Greg Norman	T-4	72-66-69-68=275	$52,780.00
Davis Love III	T-4	68-63-71-73=275	$52,780.00
Larry Mize	T-9	67-70-70-69=276	$35,000.00
Nick Price	T-9	70-68-70-68=276	$35,000.00

Player	Place	Score	Earnings
John Mahaffey	T-9	72-69-65-70=276	$35,000.00
Kenny Perry	T-9	72-68-69-67=276	$35,000.00
Payne Stewart	T-9	69-69-65-73=276	$35,000.00

U.S. Open
Course: Shinnecock Hills G.C., Southampton, N.Y.
Par: 70 Yardage: 6,944
Last day of event: Sunday, June 18, 1995

Player	Place	Score	Earnings
Corey Pavin	Win	72-69-71-68=280	$350,000.00
Greg Norman	2	68-67-74-73=282	$207,000.00
Tom Lehman	3	70-72-67-74=283	$131,974.00
Jay Haas	T-4	70-73-72-69=284	$66,633.66
Davis Love III	T-4	72-68-73-71=284	$66,633.66
Phil Mickelson	T-4	68-70-72-74=284	$66,633.67
Bill Glasson	T-4	69-70-76-69=284	$66,633.67
Jeff Maggert	T-4	69-72-77-66=284	$66,633.67
Neal Lancaster	T-4	70-72-77-65=284	$66,633.67
Vijay Singh	T-10	70-71-72-72=285	$44,184.33
Frank Nobilo	T-10	72-72-70-71=285	$44,184.33
Bob Tway	T-10	69-69-72-75=285	$44,184.34

Canon Greater Hartford Open
Course: TPC at River Highlands, Cromwell, Conn.
Par: 70 Yardage: 6,820
Last day of event: Sunday, June 25, 1995

Player	Place	Score	Earnings
Greg Norman	Win	67-64-65-71=267	$216,000.00
Dave Stockton, Jr.	T-2	65-68-68-68=269	$89,600.00
Kirk Triplett	T-2	64-67-69-69=269	$89,600.00
Grant Waite	T-2	66-67-67-69=269	$89,600.00
Fuzzy Zoeller	T-5	70-63-66-71=270	$43,800.00
Brian Henninger	T-5	66-67-72-65=270	$43,800.00
Don Pooley	T-5	67-72-66-65=270	$43,800.00
Michael Bradley	T-8	67-66-69-69=271	$34,800.00
Bob Estes	T-8	64-72-68-67=271	$34,800.00
Billy Andrade	T-8	74-65-62-70=271	$34,800.00

FedEx St. Jude Classic
Course: TPC at Southwind, Germantown, Tenn.
Par: 71 Yardage: 7,006
Last day of event: Sunday, July 2, 1995

Player	Place	Score	Earnings
Jim Gallagher, Jr.	Win	65-62-68-72=267	$225,000.00
Ken Green	T-2	68-67-65-68=268	$110,000.00
Jay Delsing	T-2	69-63-69-67=268	$110,000.00
Gene Sauers	4	68-65-63-73=269	$60,000.00
Steve Jones	T-5	68-69-65-68=270	$40,937.50
Larry Mize	T-5	69-66-67-68=270	$40,937.50
John Cook	T-5	65-70-67-68=270	$40,937.50
Brandel Chamblee	T-5	69-70-65-66=270	$40,937.50
Bob Tway	T-5	65-64-70-71=270	$40,937.50
Rocco Mediate	T-5	65-71-67-67=270	$40,937.50

Motorola Western Open
Course: Cog Hill G. & C.C. (Dubsdread), Lemont, Ill.
Par: 72 Yardage: 7,040
Last day of event: Sunday, July 9, 1995

Player	Place	Score	Earnings
Billy Mayfair	Win	73-70-69-67=279	$360,000.00

Player	Place	Score	Earnings
Justin Leonard	T-2	70-71-72-67=280	$132,000.00
Scott Simpson	T-2	71-72-69-68=280	$132,000.00
Jay Haas	T-2	69-68-73-70=280	$132,000.00
Jeff Maggert	T-2	74-73-69-64=280	$132,000.00
Steve Lowery	T-6	69-70-70-72=281	$64,750.00
Bob Estes	T-6	72-73-66-70=281	$64,750.00
John Huston	T-6	73-68-72-68=281	$64,750.00
Bob Tway	T-6	76-69-68-68=281	$64,750.00
Scott Hoch	T-10	73-69-70-70=282	$50,000.00
Woody Austin	T-10	74-70-69-69=282	$50,000.00
Scott Gump	T-10	74-70-72-66=282	$50,000.00

Anheuser-Busch Golf Classic
Course: Kingsmill G.C., Williamsburg, Va.
Par: 71 Yardage: 6,776
Last day of event: Sunday, July 16, 1995

Player	Place	Score	Earnings
Ted Tryba	Win	69-67-68-68=272	$198,000.00
Scott Simpson	2	69-69-68-67=273	$118,800.00
Lennie Clements	T-3	68-69-69-68=274	$57,200.00
Jim Carter	T-3	66-69-68-71=274	$57,200.00
Scott Hoch	T-3	67-69-71-67=274	$57,200.00
Curtis Strange	T-6	72-70-65-68=275	$38,225.00
Marco Dawson	T-6	68-71-73-63=275	$38,225.00
Fred Funk	T-8	68-68-70-71=277	$31,900.00
David Ogrin	T-8	71-71-66-69=277	$31,900.00
Jeff Sluman	T-8	72-69-67-69=277	$31,900.00

Deposit Guaranty Golf Classic
Course: Annandale G.C., Madison, Miss.
Par: 72 Yardage: 7,157
Last day of event: Sunday, July 23, 1995

Player	Place	Score	Earnings
Ed Dougherty	Win	68-68-70-66=272	$126,000.00
Gil Morgan	2	69-69-67-69=274	$75,600.00
Pete Jordan	3	71-67-69-68=275	$47,600.00
Tom Byrum	T-4	69-69-68-70=276	$27,562.50
Kirk Triplett	T-4	66-70-69-71=276	$27,562.50
Dicky Thompson	T-4	67-68-68-73=276	$27,562.50
Steve Rintoul	T-4	73-68-67-68=276	$27,562.50
Dicky Pride	T-8	66-68-70-73=277	$20,300.00
Bob Gilder	T-8	69-66-69-73=277	$20,300.00
Rocky Walcher	T-8	70-68-73-66=277	$20,300.00

British Open
Course: Old Course at St. Andrews, St. Andrews, Fife, Scotland
Par: 72 Yardage: 6,933
Last day of event: Sunday, July 23, 1995

Player	Place	Score	Earnings
John Daly	Win	67-71-73-71=282	$199,375.00
Playoff: Won four-hole aggregate playoff (4-3-4-4=15) with Costantino Rocca (5-4-7-3=19)			
Costantino Rocca	2	69-70-70-73=282	$159,500.00
Steven Bottomley	T-3	70-72-72-69=283	$104,738.33
Mark Brooks	T-3	70-69-73-71=283	$104,738.33
Michael Campbell	T-3	71-71-65-76=283	$104,738.33
Vijay Singh	T-6	68-72-73-71=284	$64,597.50
Steve Elkington	T-6	72-69-69-74=284	$64,597.50
Bob Estes	T-8	72-70-71-72=285	$53,166.66
Corey Pavin	T-8	69-70-72-74=285	$53,166.66
Mark James	T-8	72-75-68-70=285	$53,166.66

Ideon Classic

Course: Pleasant Valley C.C., Sutton, Mass.
Par: 71 Yardage: 7,110
Last day of event: Sunday, July 30, 1995

Player	Place	Score	Earnings
Fred Funk	Win	66-63-66-73=268	$180,000.00
Jim McGovern	2	66-66-67-70=269	$108,000.00
Don Pooley	3	70-64-68-68=270	$68,000.00
Jay Williamson	T-4	67-67-68-69=271	$39,375.00
Lennie Clements	T-4	67-68-69-67=271	$39,375.00
Roger Maltbie	T-4	68-67-69-67=271	$39,375.00
Joey Sindelar	T-4	69-66-70-66=271	$39,375.00
Howard Twitty	T-8	67-67-68-70=272	$29,000.00
Greg Kraft	T-8	70-67-66-69=272	$29,000.00
Dan Forsman	T-8	69-65-67-71=272	$29,000.00

Buick Open

Course: Warwick Hills C.C., Grand Blanc, Mich.
Par: 72 Yardage: 7,014
Last day of event: Sunday, August 6, 1995

Player	Place	Score	Earnings
Woody Austin	Win	63-68-72-67=270	$216,000.00
Playoff: Beat Mike Brisky with par on second extra hole			
Mike Brisky	2	67-68-67-68=270	$129,600.00
Ernie Els	T-3	69-68-66-68=271	$62,400.00
Tom Byrum	T-3	69-67-65-70=271	$62,400.00
Jeff Sluman	T-3	66-67-67-71=271	$62,400.00
Fred Couples	6	68-67-67-70=272	$43,200.00
Joel Edwards	7	69-65-68-71=273	$40,200.00
Payne Stewart	8	65-65-73-71=274	$37,200.00
Jonathan Kaye	T-9	69-67-69-70=275	$33,600.00
Tom Lehman	T-9	71-66-70-68=275	$33,600.00

PGA Championship

Course: Riviera C.C., Pacific Palisades, Calif.
Par: 71 Yardage: 6,956
Last day of event: Sunday, August 13, 1995

Player	Place	Score	Earnings
Steve Elkington	Win	68-67-68-64=267	$360,000.00
Playoff: Beat Colin Montgomerie with birdie on first extra hole			
Colin Montgomerie	2	68-67-67-65=267	$216,000.00
Jeff Maggert	T-3	66-69-65-69=269	$116,000.00
Ernie Els	T-3	66-65-66-72=269	$116,000.00
Brad Faxon	5	70-67-71-63=271	$80,000.00
Bob Estes	T-6	69-68-68-68=273	$68,500.00
Mark O'Meara	T-6	64-67-69-73=273	$68,500.00
Steve Lowery	T-8	69-68-68-69=274	$50,000.00
Justin Leonard	T-8	68-66-70-70=274	$50,000.00
Jeff Sluman	T-8	69-67-68-70=274	$50,000.00
Jay Haas	T-8	69-71-64-70=274	$50,000.00
Craig Stadler	T-8	71-66-66-71=274	$50,000.00

Sprint International

Course: Castle Pine G.C. Castle Rock, Colo. (Stableford format)
Par: 72 Yardage: 7,559
Last day of event: Sunday, August 20, 1995

Player	Place	Score	Earnings
Lee Janzen	Win	10-9-6-9=34	$270,000.00
Ernie Els	2	17-0-7-9=33	$162,000.00
Mark Wiebe	T-3	8-15--1-6=28	$87,000.00
Jay Haas	T-3	3-12-13-0=28	$87,000.00
David Duval	5	0-9-6-2=17	$60,000.00
Jose Maria Olazabal	T-6	7-5-6-8=26	$52,125.00
Tom Watson	T-6	7-8-9-2=26	$52,125.00
Greg Norman	T-8	14-3--2-9=24	$43,500.00
Dan Forsman	T-8	3-10-7-4=24	$43,500.00
Davis Love III	T-8	11-6-6-1=24	$43,500.00

NEC World Series of Golf

Course: Firestone C.C. (South), Akron, Ohio
Par: 70 Yardage: 7,149
Last day of event: Sunday, August 27, 1995

Player	Place	Score	Earnings
Greg Norman	Win	73-68-70-67=278	$360,000.00
Playoff: Beat Nick Price and Billy Mayfair with birdie on first extra hole			
Billy Mayfair	T-2	70-68-70-70=278	$176,000.00
Nick Price	T-2	72-69-69-68=278	$176,000.00
Phil Mickelson	T-4	69-74-70-66=279	$88,000.00
Vijay Singh	T-4	71-69-65-74=279	$88,000.00
Jim Gallagher, Jr.	T-6	66-71-70-73=280	$69,500.00
Fred Couples	T-6	68-76-68-68=280	$69,500.00
Mike Sullivan	8	71-67-74-69=281	$62,000.00
Loren Roberts	T-9	72-74-70-66=282	$56,000.00
Jose Maria Olazabal	T-9	68-70-69-75=282	$56,000.00

Greater Milwaukee Open

Course: Brown Deer Park G.C., Milwaukee, Wis.
Par: 71 Yardage: 6,716
Last day of event: Sunday, September 3, 1995

Player	Place	Score	Earnings
Scott Hoch	Win	68-71-65-65=269	$180,000.00
Marco Dawson	2	70-65-70-67=272	$108,000.00
Joe Acosta, Jr.	T-3	68-69-69-68=274	$52,000.00
Jim Gallagher, Jr.	T-3	68-71-68-67=274	$52,000.00
Jeff Sluman	T-3	72-71-65-66=274	$52,000.00
Lee Rinker	T-6	70-68-67-70=275	$32,375.00
Steve Lowery	T-6	70-69-71-65=275	$32,375.00
Duffy Waldorf	T-6	69-73-65-68=275	$32,375.00
Joey Sindelar	T-6	74-68-68-65=275	$32,375.00
Robert Gamez	T-10	67-69-70-70=276	$22,166.66
Mark O'Meara	T-10	69-71-68-68=276	$22,166.67
D.A. Weibring	T-10	70-69-71-66=276	$22,166.66
Bob Estes	T-10	71-70-71-64=276	$22,166.67
Andrew Magee	T-10	69-72-69-66=276	$22,166.67
Jay Haas	T-10	74-68-67-67=276	$22,166.67

Bell Canadian Open

Course: Glen Abbey G.C., Oakville, Ontario, Canada
Par: 72 Yardage: 7,102
Last day of event: Sunday, September 10, 1995

Player	Place	Score	Earnings
Mark O'Meara	Win	72-67-68-67=274	$234,000.00
Playoff: Beat Bob Lohr with par on first extra hole			
Bob Lohr	2	68-67-69-70=274	$140,400.00
Nick Price	3	72-69-68-68=277	$88,400.00
Hal Sutton	4	69-72-68-69=278	$62,400.00
Andrew Magee	T-5	68-68-73-71=280	$49,400.00
Bill Glasson	T-5	68-74-68-70=280	$49,400.00
Tony Sills	7	72-68-73-69=282	$43,550.00
Scott Dunlap	8	71-67-73-72=283	$40,300.00
Brian Kamm	T-9	74-71-70-69=284	$36,400.00
Bob Tway	T-9	69-72-68-75=284	$36,400.00

B.C. Open

Course: En-Joie G.C., Endicott, N.Y.
Par: 71 Yardage: 6,966
Last day of event: Sunday, September 17, 1995

Player	Place	Score	Earnings
Hal Sutton	Win	71-69-68-61=269	$180,000.00
Jim McGovern	2	71-67-69-63=270	$108,000.00
Craig Stadler	T-3	67-69-68-67=271	$58,000.00
Kirk Triplett	T-3	69-67-69-66=271	$58,000.00
Jay Haas	T-5	68-69-71-64=272	$38,000.00
Stewart Cink	T-5	71-70-66-65=272	$38,000.00
Jay Williamson	T-7	67-68-69-69=273	$29,100.00
Jeff Sluman	T-7	67-69-68-69=273	$29,100.00
Skip Kendall	T-7	66-69-68-70=273	$29,100.00
Joey Sindelar	T-7	68-68-70-67=273	$29,100.00
Jeff Leonard	T-7	69-66-71-67=273	$29,100.00

Quad City Classic

Course: Oakwood C.C., Coal Valley, Ill.
Par: 70 Yardage: 6,796
Last day of event: Sunday, September 24, 1995

Player	Place	Score	Earnings
D.A. Weibring	Win	64-65-68=197	$180,000.00
Jonathan Kaye	2	67-66-65=198	$108,000.00
Jay Delsing	3	69-64-67=200	$68,000.00
Jim McGovern	4	64-71-66=201	$48,000.00
Michael Allen	T-5	66-70-66=202	$36,500.00
Scott Hoch	T-5	71-65-66=202	$36,500.00
Dennis Paulson	T-5	71-66-65=202	$36,500.00
Curt Byrum	T-8	66-68-69=203	$30,000.00
Bob Gilder	T-8	68-69-66=203	$30,000.00
Bruce Fleisher	T-10	72-66-66=204	$26,000.00
Scott Verplank	T-10	65-73-66=204	$26,000.00

Buick Challenge

Course: Callaway Gardens Resort, Pine Mountain, Ga.
Par: 72 Yardage: 7,057
Last day of event: Sunday, October 1, 1995

Player	Place	Score	Earnings
Fred Funk	Win	69-67-69-67=272	$180,000.00
Loren Roberts	T-2	70-69-67-67=273	$88,000.00
John Morse	T-2	71-68-67-67=273	$88,000.00
Jeff Sluman	T-4	67-69-70-68=274	$41,333.33
Kirk Triplett	T-4	71-66-69-68=274	$41,333.34
Guy Boros	T-4	68-69-72-65=274	$41,333.33
David Ogrin	7	70-68-70-67=275	$33,500.00
Scott Hoch	T-8	70-70-69-67=276	$28,000.00
John Huston	T-8	67-71-70-68=276	$28,000.00
Larry Nelson	T-8	71-65-70-70=276	$28,000.00
Steve Stricker	T-8	66-67-72-71=276	$28,000.00

Walt Disney World/Oldsmobile Classic

Course: Walt Disney (Magnolia, Palm), Lake Buena Vista C.C., Lake Buena Vista, Fla.
Home course / Magnolia, Par: 72 Yardage: 7,190
Last day of event: Sunday, October 8, 1995

Player	Place	Score	Earnings
Brad Bryant	Win	67-63-68=198	$216,000.00
Hal Sutton	T-2	67-66-66=199	$105,600.00
Ted Tryba	T-2	69-65-65=199	$105,600.00

Mike Reid	T-4	68-66-67=201	$49,600.00
Joe Acosta, Jr.	T-4	68-67-66=201	$49,600.00
Bob Tway	T-4	65-70-66=201	$49,600.00
Mike Hulbert	T-7	68-66-68=202	$31,275.00
Lee Rinker	T-7	68-67-67=202	$31,275.00
Charlie Rymer	T-7	68-68-66=202	$31,275.00
Mike Heinen	T-7	65-68-69=202	$31,275.00
Russ Cochran	T-7	66-67-69=202	$31,275.00
Jay Williamson	T-7	69-65-68=202	$31,275.00
Patrick Burke	T-7	66-65-71=202	$31,275.00
Carl Paulson	T-7	62-68-72=202	$31,275.00

Las Vegas Invitational

Course: TPC at Summerlin, Las Vegas C.C., Las Vegas Hilton C.C., Las Vegas, Nev.
Home course / TPC at Summerlin, Par: 72 Yardage: 7,243
Last day of event: Sunday, October 15, 1995

Player	Place	Score	Earnings
Jim Furyk	Win	67-65-65-67-67=331	$270,000.00
Billy Mayfair	2	66-65-67-66-68=332	$162,000.00
Scott McCarron	3	71-65-69-64-65=334	$102,000.00
Brad Bryant	T-4	65-68-67-69-66=335	$62,000.00
Mark O'Meara	T-4	67-67-66-65-70=335	$62,000.00
Phil Blackmar	T-4	69-66-71-64-65=335	$62,000.00
Davis Love III	T-7	67-67-68-67-67=336	$46,750.00
David Edwards	T-7	67-66-64-69-70=336	$46,750.00
Glen Day	T-7	70-67-65-68-66=336	$46,750.00
Kirk Triplett	T-10	66-67-69-68-67=337	$36,000.00
Joe Ozaki	T-10	63-69-71-66-68=337	$36,000.00
Rick Fehr	T-10	64-68-71-67-67=337	$36,000.00
Bill Glasson	T-10	68-68-71-65-65=337	$36,000.00

LaCantera Texas Open

Course: LaCantera G.C., San Antonio, Texas
Par: 72 Yardage: 6,899
Last day of event: Sunday, October 22, 1995

Player	Place	Score	Earnings
Duffy Waldorf	Win	66-66-71-65=268	$198,000.00
Justin Leonard	2	67-70-69-68=274	$118,800.00
John Mahaffey	T-3	67-71-71-71=280	$57,200.00
John Morse	T-3	70-69-71-70=280	$57,200.00
Loren Roberts	T-3	64-72-73-71=280	$57,200.00
Mike Standly	T-6	68-71-74-68=281	$38,225.00
Jay Don Blake	T-6	67-67-70-77=281	$38,225.00
Jay Haas	8	68-68-74-72=282	$34,100.00
Mark Wiebe	T-9	74-69-70-70=283	$30,800.00
Lee Rinker	T-9	70-66-72-75=283	$30,800.00

The Tour Championship

Course: Southern Hills C.C., Tulsa, Okla.
Par: 70 Yardage: 6,834
Last day of event: Sunday, October 29, 1995

Player	Place	Score	Earnings
Billy Mayfair	Win	68-70-69-73=280	$540,000.00
Steve Elkington	T-2	71-72-67-73=283	$265,500.00
Corey Pavin	T-2	72-70-68-73=283	$265,500.00
Woody Austin	T-4	71-68-73-72=284	$132,000.00
Scott Simpson	T-4	71-70-74-69=284	$132,000.00
Vijay Singh	6	69-71-72-73=285	$108,000.00
Justin Leonard	T-7	70-70-72-74=286	$99,000.00
Brad Bryant	T-7	69-68-73-76=286	$99,000.00

Greg Norman	T-9	72-70-74-71=287	$87,600.00
David Duval	T-9	74-69-71-73=287	$87,600.00

1996

Tiger Woods, fresh off his third consecutive U.S. Amateur victory, turned pro in August and tied for 60th in his professional debut at the Greater Milwaukee Open. Woods won his fourth start, the Las Vegas Invitational, thereby earning a two-year PGA Tour exemption and invitation to compete in the 1997 Masters. If anyone still doubted the 20-year-old Woods might be someone special, those doubts were erased when Tiger won the Disney Classic and ended up banking $790,594 in eight starts, leaving him 24th on the PGA Tour money list. In yet another colossal setback at a major, Greg Norman forged a 6-shot lead after 54 holes at the Masters, then shot a final-round 78 that was painful to watch. Nick Faldo tried not to, posting a flawless 67 and winning by five shots. In the U.S. Open at Oakland Hills, Steve Jones scored a one-shot victory over Davis Love III, who bogeyed the last two holes, and Tom Lehman, whose drive at the 72nd hole came to rest in a bad lie in a fairway bunker, leading to bogey. Lehman bounced back at the British Open, firing a third-round 64 at Royal Lytham and coasting to a two-shot victory over Ernie Els and Mark McCumber. Mark Brooks birdied the 72nd hole to force a PGA Championship playoff against Kenny Perry, who had bogeyed the final hole and opted to join commentators in the TV broadcast booth at Valhalla rather than head to the range and stay focused for potential sudden death. Brooks won with a birdie on the first extra hole.

Mercedes Championships
Course: La Costa C.C., Carlsbad, Calif.
Par: 72 Yardage: 7,022
Last day of event: Sunday, January 7, 1996

Player	Place	Score	Earnings
Mark O'Meara	Win	68-69-66-68=271	$180,000.00
Scott Hoch	T-2	69-69-70-66=274	$88,000.00
Nick Faldo	T-2	70-69-68-67=274	$88,000.00
Bob Tway	4	71-69-70-66=276	$48,000.00
Brad Bryant	5	70-70-69-68=277	$40,000.00
Davis Love III	6	72-71-67-68=278	$36,000.00
Corey Pavin	T-7	67-71-70-71=279	$30,625.00
Jim Gallagher, Jr.	T-7	71-67-70-71=279	$30,625.00
Duffy Waldorf	T-7	71-70-69-69=279	$30,625.00
Lee Janzen	T-7	71-65-72-71=279	$30,625.00

Nortel Open
Course: Tucson National G.C.—Home course, Starr Pass G.C., Tucson, Ariz.
Home course / Par: 72 Yardage: 7,148
Last day of event: Sunday, January 14, 1996

Player	Place	Score	Earnings
Phil Mickelson	Win	69-66-71-67=273	$225,000.00
Bob Tway	2	69-71-68-67=275	$135,000.00
Fred Funk	T-3	70-69-68-69=276	$60,000.00
Bob Estes	T-3	69-67-71-69=276	$60,000.00
Lee Janzen	T-3	69-72-66-69=276	$60,000.00
Mike Hulbert	T-3	69-68-72-67=276	$60,000.00
Omar Uresti	T-7	68-70-72-67=277	$40,312.50
John Wilson	T-7	70-72-67-68=277	$40,312.50
Bruce Lietzke	T-9	71-68-68-71=278	$32,500.00
Ronnie Black	T-9	68-71-66-73=278	$32,500.00
Curtis Strange	T-9	68-73-67-70=278	$32,500.00
David Toms	T-9	69-66-69-74=278	$32,500.00

Bob Hope Chrysler Classic
Course: Indian Ridge C.C., Bermuda Dunes C.C., Indian Wells C.C., Tamarisk C.C., La Quinta C.C.
Home course / Indian Ridge C.C., Par: 72 Yardage: 7,037
Last day of event: Sunday, January 21, 1996

Player	Place	Score	Earnings
Mark Brooks	Win	66-68-69-67-67=337	$234,000.00
John Huston	2	69-71-65-65-68=338	$140,400.00
Scott Hoch	3	70-69-67-68-65=339	$88,400.00
Nolan Henke	T-4	69-69-64-69-69=340	$53,733.33
Payne Stewart	T-4	71-65-71-63-70=340	$53,733.33
Brad Bryant	T-4	71-65-65-71-68=340	$53,733.34
Paul Goydos	T-7	69-64-70-69-69=341	$39,162.50
Jeff Maggert	T-7	69-68-69-64-71=341	$39,162.50
Fred Couples	T-7	72-67-67-65-70=341	$39,162.50
Kenny Perry	T-7	75-69-67-65-65=341	$39,162.50

Phoenix Open
Course: TPC of Scottsdale, Scottsdale, Ariz.
Par: 71 Yardage: 6,992
Last day of event: Saturday, January 27, 1996

Player	Place	Score	Earnings
Phil Mickelson	Win	69-67-66-67=269	$234,000.00
Playoff: Beat Justin Leonard with birdie on third extra hole			
Justin Leonard	2	67-67-66-69=269	$140,400.00
Tom Scherrer	3	67-70-65-68=270	$88,400.00
John Wilson	T-4	67-71-67-66=271	$57,200.00
Mark Calcavecchia	T-4	72-69-68-62=271	$57,200.00
Rocco Mediate	T-6	70-67-68-67=272	$42,087.50
Scott Simpson	T-6	67-71-68-66=272	$42,087.50
Woody Austin	T-6	65-67-72-68=272	$42,087.50
Curt Byrum	T-6	69-69-72-62=272	$42,087.50
Kenny Perry	T-10	69-69-66-69=273	$31,200.00
Blaine McCallister	T-10	69-69-67-68=273	$31,200.00
Steve Jones	T-10	67-67-72-67=273	$31,200.00
Sandy Lyle	T-10	68-72-67-66=273	$31,200.00

Buick Invitational
Course: Torrey Pines (South), Torrey Pines (North), San Diego, Calif.
Home Course -Par: 72 Yardage: 7,022
Last day of event: Sunday, February 11, 1996

Player	Place	Score	Earnings
Davis Love III	Win	66-70-69-64=269	$216,000.00
Phil Mickelson	2	68-70-66-67=271	$129,600.00
Scott Simpson	T-3	66-69-69-68=272	$54,120.00
Tom Lehman	T-3	63-70-70-69=272	$54,120.00
Marco Dawson	T-3	66-70-70-66=272	$54,120.00
Lennie Clements	T-3	64-65-72-71=272	$54,120.00
Mark O'Meara	T-3	65-72-66-69=272	$54,120.00
Mark Calcavecchia	T-8	68-66-70-69=273	$36,000.00
Nick Faldo	T-8	69-70-70-64=273	$36,000.00
Joey Sindelar	T-10	69-66-70-69=274	$31,200.00
Jesper Parnevik	T-10	68-67-68-71=274	$31,200.00

United Airlines Hawaiian Open
Course: Waialae C.C., Honolulu, Ha.
Par: 72 Yardage: 6,975
Last day of event: Sunday, February 18, 1996

Player	Place	Score	Earnings
Jim Furyk	Win	68-71-69-69=277	$216,000.00

Playoff: Beat Brad Faxon with birdie on third extra hole

Player	Place	Score	Earnings
Brad Faxon	2	74-67-66-70=277	$129,600.00
Steve Stricker	3	69-70-68-71=278	$81,600.00
Larry Mize	T-4	71-71-67-70=279	$47,250.00
Tom Lehman	T-4	74-68-67-70=279	$47,250.00
David Ogrin	T-4	74-69-67-69=279	$47,250.00
Scott Simpson	T-4	68-76-67-68=279	$47,250.00
Vijay Singh	T-8	72-70-71-67=280	$34,800.00
Jeff Sluman	T-8	74-69-67-70=280	$34,800.00
John Morse	T-8	74-73-64-69=280	$34,800.00

Nissan Open

Course: Riviera C.C., Pacific Palisades, Calif.
Par: 71 Yardage: 6,946
Last day of event: Sunday, February 25, 1996

Player	Place	Score	Earnings
Craig Stadler	Win	67-70-73-68=278	$216,000.00
Scott Simpson	T-2	68-70-70-71=279	$79,200.00
Fred Couples	T-2	69-70-71-69=279	$79,200.00
Mark Wiebe	T-2	70-70-68-71=279	$79,200.00
Mark Brooks	T-2	74-69-72-64=279	$79,200.00
Kelly Gibson	T-6	70-69-71-70=280	$38,850.00
Lanny Wadkins	T-6	69-70-69-72=280	$38,850.00
Tom Lehman	T-6	70-70-68-72=280	$38,850.00
Hugh Royer III	T-6	71-70-73-66=280	$38,850.00
Peter Jacobsen	T-10	71-72-66-72=281	$28,800.00
Omar Uresti	T-10	71-72-69-69=281	$28,800.00
Steve Elkington	T-10	67-70-73-71=281	$28,800.00
Bob Tway	T-10	71-68-69-73=281	$28,800.00

Doral-Ryder Open

Course: Doral C.C. (Blue), Miami, Fla.
Par: 72 Yardage: 6,939
Last day of event: Sunday, March 3, 1996

Player	Place	Score	Earnings
Greg Norman	Win	67-69-67-66=269	$324,000.00
Vijay Singh	T-2	70-66-67-68=271	$158,400.00
Michael Bradley	T-2	64-71-70-66=271	$158,400.00
Jerry Kelly	T-4	67-71-69-67=274	$79,200.00
Fulton Allem	T-4	67-71-70-66=274	$79,200.00
Joe Ozaki	T-6	69-65-71-70=275	$62,550.00
Jay Haas	T-6	72-68-68-67=275	$62,550.00
Jesper Parnevik	T-8	68-71-69-69=277	$46,800.00
Ray Floyd	T-8	68-70-71-68=277	$46,800.00
Lennie Clements	T-8	71-67-68-71=277	$46,800.00
Jeff Sluman	T-8	66-71-72-68=277	$46,800.00
Larry Nelson	T-8	66-73-71-67=277	$46,800.00
Patrick Burke	T-8	67-73-68-69=277	$46,800.00

Honda Classic

Course: TPC at Eagle Trace, Coral Springs, Fla.
Par: 72 Yardage: 7,037
Last day of event: Sunday, March 10, 1996

Player	Place	Score	Earnings
Tim Herron	Win	62-68-72-69=271	$234,000.00
Mark McCumber	2	69-68-69-69=275	$140,400.00
Payne Stewart	T-3	70-70-68-68=276	$67,600.00
Nick Price	T-3	66-72-70-68=276	$67,600.00
Lee Rinker	T-3	64-75-68-69=276	$67,600.00
Mark O'Meara	6	70-71-65-71=277	$46,800.00
David Frost	T-7	70-69-70-70=279	$41,925.00

Player	Place	Score	Earnings
Michael Campbell	T-7	68-69-68-74=279	$41,925.00
Phil Blackmar	T-9	69-70-69-73=281	$35,100.00
Vijay Singh	T-9	73-70-71-67=281	$35,100.00
Nick Faldo	T-9	77-68-68-68=281	$35,100.00

Bay Hill Invitational

Course: Bay Hill Club, Orlando, Fla.
Par: 72 Yardage: 7,196
Last day of event: Sunday, March 17, 1996

Player	Place	Score	Earnings
Paul Goydos	Win	67-74-67-67=275	$216,000.00
Jeff Maggert	2	72-65-70-69=276	$129,600.00
Tom Purtzer	3	69-70-69-69=277	$81,600.00
Bill Glasson	T-4	71-70-68-70=279	$45,240.00
Mark O'Meara	T-4	67-72-69-71=279	$45,240.00
Corey Pavin	T-4	69-70-72-68=279	$45,240.00
Mark Calcavecchia	T-4	70-74-66-69=279	$45,240.00
Robert Gamez	T-4	74-67-69-69=279	$45,240.00
Steve Jones	T-9	69-70-70-71=280	$31,200.00
Glen Day	T-9	67-71-72-70=280	$31,200.00
Larry Nelson	T-9	71-70-67-72=280	$31,200.00
Tom Lehman	T-9	69-75-68-68=280	$31,200.00

Freeport-McDermott Classic

Course: English Turn G. & C.C., New Orleans, La.
Par: 72 Yardage: 7,116
Last day of event: Sunday, March 24, 1996

Player	Place	Score	Earnings
Scott McCarron	Win	68-67-69-71=275	$216,000.00
Tom Watson	2	68-66-72-74=280	$129,600.00
Tommy Tolles	3	70-69-66-76=281	$81,600.00
Joel Edwards	T-4	72-69-70-72=283	$43,500.00
Steve Lowery	T-4	71-71-68-73=283	$43,500.00
Payne Stewart	T-4	74-71-67-71=283	$43,500.00
Davis Love III	T-4	68-68-72-75=283	$43,500.00
Blaine McCallister	T-4	73-64-75-71=283	$43,500.00
Lennie Clements	T-4	67-66-74-76=283	$43,500.00
John Huston	T-10	69-73-71-71=284	$27,600.00
Brad Fabel	T-10	73-69-73-69=284	$27,600.00
Tom Lehman	T-10	69-71-70-74=284	$27,600.00
Jeff Gallagher	T-10	70-68-72-74=284	$27,600.00
Stuart Appleby	T-10	74-69-66-75=284	$27,600.00

The Players Championship

Course: TPC at SawgrassPonte Vedra Beach, Fla.
Par: 72 Yardage: 6,896
Last day of event: Sunday, March 31, 1996

Player	Place	Score	Earnings
Fred Couples	Win	66-72-68-64=270	$630,000.00
Colin Montgomerie	T-2	71-69-66-68=274	$308,000.00
Tommy Tolles	T-2	69-64-69-72=274	$308,000.00
Kenny Perry	T-4	65-71-70-69=275	$137,812.50
David Duval	T-4	70-66-68-71=275	$137,812.50
Fuzzy Zoeller	T-4	66-70-72-67=275	$137,812.50
Rocco Mediate	T-4	74-69-66-66=275	$137,812.50
Vijay Singh	T-8	70-68-68-70=276	$94,500.00
Jay Haas	T-8	68-68-69-71=276	$94,500.00
Ernie Els	T-8	71-70-65-70=276	$94,500.00
Grant Waite	T-8	68-72-68-68=276	$94,500.00
Tom Lehman	T-8	70-72-67-67=276	$94,500.00

BellSouth Classic

Course: Atlanta C.C., Atlanta, Ga.
Par: 72 Yardage: 7,007
Last day of event: Sunday, April 7, 1996

Player	Place	Score	Earnings
Paul Stankowski	Win	68-71-70-71=280	$234,000.00
Playoff: Beat Brandel Chamblee with birdie on first extra hole			
Brandel Chamblee	2	72-70-71-67=280	$140,400.00
Nick Price	T-3	68-70-73-71=282	$75,400.00
David Duval	T-3	68-70-68-76=282	$75,400.00
Fred Couples	T-5	71-73-66-73=283	$49,400.00
Tommy Tolles	T-5	69-70-69-75=283	$49,400.00
Neal Lancaster	T-7	67-70-75-72=284	$40,516.66
Corey Pavin	T-7	66-73-76-69=284	$40,516.67
Frank Lickliter II	T-7	69-72-76-67=284	$40,516.67
Lennie Clements	T-10	69-71-72-73=285	$33,800.00
Jerry Kelly	T-10	73-71-69-72=285	$33,800.00

Masters

Course: Augusta National G.C., Augusta, Ga.
Par: 72 Yardage: 6,925
Last day of event: Sunday, April 14, 1996

Player	Place	Score	Earnings
Nick Faldo	Win	69-67-73-67=276	$450,000.00
Greg Norman	2	63-69-71-78=281	$270,000.00
Phil Mickelson	3	65-73-72-72=282	$170,000.00
Frank Nobilo	4	71-71-72-69=283	$120,000.00
Duffy Waldorf	T-5	72-71-69-72=284	$95,000.00
Scott Hoch	T-5	67-73-73-71=284	$95,000.00
Jeff Maggert	T-7	71-73-72-69=285	$77,933.00
Davis Love III	T-7	72-71-74-68=285	$77,933.00
Corey Pavin	T-7	75-66-73-71=285	$77,933.00
David Frost	T-10	70-68-74-74=286	$65,000.00
Scott McCarron	T-10	70-70-72-74=286	$65,000.00

MCI Classic

Course: Harbour Town G.L., Hilton Head, S.C.
Par: 71 Yardage: 6,912
Last day of event: Sunday, April 21, 1996

Player	Place	Score	Earnings
Loren Roberts	Win	66-69-63-67=265	$252,000.00
Mark O'Meara	2	68-69-65-66=268	$151,200.00
Scott Hoch	3	71-68-65-66=270	$95,200.00
Davis Love III	4	68-68-68-67=271	$67,200.00
Vijay Singh	T-5	70-67-69-67=273	$51,100.00
Tom Watson	T-5	67-67-72-67=273	$51,100.00
Nick Price	T-5	72-67-69-65=273	$51,100.00
Larry Nelson	T-8	67-68-69-70=274	$37,800.00
Jeff Maggert	T-8	69-66-70-69=274	$37,800.00
Colin Montgomerie	T-8	69-66-70-69=274	$37,800.00
Rocco Mediate	T-8	68-68-71-67=274	$37,800.00
Gene Sauers	T-8	69-72-68-65=274	$37,800.00

Greater Greensboro Chrysler Classic, Course: Forest Oaks C.C.

Greensboro, N.C.
Par: 72 Yardage: 7,062
Last day of event: Sunday, April 28, 1996

Player	Place	Score	Earnings
Mark O'Meara	Win	75-68-62-69=274	$324,000.00
Duffy Waldorf	2	73-65-67-71=276	$194,400.00

Steve Stricker	3	72-69-70-67=278	$122,400.00
Emlyn Aubrey	4	72-67-68-72=279	$86,400.00
John Huston	T-5	71-71-73-65=280	$68,400.00
Billy Andrade	T-5	68-74-67-71=280	$68,400.00
Fuzzy Zoeller	T-7	72-70-70-69=281	$56,100.00
Jim Furyk	T-7	73-68-67-73=281	$56,100.00
Wayne Levi	T-7	74-67-71-69=281	$56,100.00
Woody Austin	10	71-68-72-71=282	$48,600.00

Shell Houston Open

Course: TPC at The Woodlands, The Woodlands, Texas
Par: 72 Yardage: 7,042
Last day of event: Sunday, May 5, 1996

Player	Place	Score	Earnings
Mark Brooks	Win	66-68-70-70=274	$270,000.00
Playoff: Beat Jeff Maggert with birdie on first extra hole			
Jeff Maggert	2	67-69-66-72=274	$162,000.00
David Duval	3	66-70-67-72=275	$102,000.00
Woody Austin	4	69-71-65-73=278	$72,000.00
Tommy Tolles	T-5	65-70-72-72=279	$54,750.00
Doug Martin	T-5	67-68-72-72=279	$54,750.00
Greg Kraft	T-5	67-70-74-68=279	$54,750.00
Andy Bean	8	69-74-69-68=280	$46,500.00
Payne Stewart	T-9	72-70-69-70=281	$37,500.00
Clarence Rose	T-9	68-72-68-73=281	$37,500.00
Bradley Hughes	T-9	73-68-71-69=281	$37,500.00
Mike Springer	T-9	65-70-74-72=281	$37,500.00
John Cook	T-9	72-66-69-74=281	$37,500.00

GTE Byron Nelson Classic

Course: TPC at Las Colinas, Cottonwood Valley Course, Irving, Texas
Home course / TPC at Los Colinas, Par: 70 Yardage: 6,899
Last day of event: Sunday, May 12, 1996

Player	Place	Score	Earnings
Phil Mickelson	Win	67-65-67-66=265	$270,000.00
Craig Parry	2	70-67-65-65=267	$162,000.00
David Duval	3	71-64-68-65=268	$102,000.00
Nick Price	T-4	67-66-69-67=269	$66,000.00
Jeff Sluman	T-4	69-68-65-67=269	$66,000.00
Mark Brooks	T-6	64-70-70-66=270	$48,562.50
Corey Pavin	T-6	67-66-67-70=270	$48,562.50
Mark Wiebe	T-6	68-69-63-70=270	$48,562.50
Gil Morgan	T-6	72-64-69-65=270	$48,562.50
Steve Elkington	T-10	67-69-66-69=271	$31,125.00
Allen Doyle	T-10	68-69-66-68=271	$31,125.00
Hal Sutton	T-10	69-69-66-67=271	$31,125.00
Brett Ogle	T-10	70-68-64-69=271	$31,125.00
Greg Kraft	T-10	70-69-67-65=271	$31,125.00
Jeff Maggert	T-10	67-71-66-67=271	$31,125.00
Kirk Triplett	T-10	71-68-68-64=271	$31,125.00
Brandel Chamblee	T-10	73-62-70-66=271	$31,125.00

Mastercard Colonial

Course: Colonial C.C., Fort Worth, Texas
Par: 70 Yardage: 7,010
Last day of event: Sunday, May 19, 1996

Player	Place	Score	Earnings
Corey Pavin	Win	69-67-67-69=272	$270,000.00
Jeff Sluman	2	69-67-70-68=274	$162,000.00
Rocco Mediate	3	68-66-68-73=275	$102,000.00
Fred Couples	4	70-67-68-71=276	$72,000.00

Davis Love III	5	72-70-68-67=277	$60,000.00
Ben Crenshaw	T-6	71-71-70-66=278	$48,562.50
Payne Stewart	T-6	69-69-72-68=278	$48,562.50
Tommy Tolles	T-6	72-64-75-67=278	$48,562.50
Steve Jones	T-6	67-76-68-67=278	$48,562.50
Jeff Gallagher	T-10	66-70-71-72=279	$39,000.00
Justin Leonard	T-10	73-69-66-71=279	$39,000.00

Kemper Open
Course: TPC at Avenel, Potomac, Md.
Par: 71 Yardage: 7,005
Last day of event: Sunday, May 26, 1996

Player	Place	Score	Earnings
Steve Stricker	Win	69-68-65-68=270	$270,000.00
Scott Hoch	T-2	69-68-68-68=273	$99,000.00
Mark O'Meara	T-2	67-69-70-67=273	$99,000.00
Brad Faxon	T-2	67-71-68-67=273	$99,000.00
Grant Waite	T-2	72-66-69-66=273	$99,000.00
David Toms	6	71-65-66-72=274	$54,000.00
Brad Fabel	7	67-70-66-72=275	$50,250.00
Mike Sullivan	T-8	67-69-71-69=276	$45,000.00
Larry Mize	T-8	68-67-70-71=276	$45,000.00
Payne Stewart	T-10	70-67-68-72=277	$37,500.00
Corey Pavin	T-10	70-72-72-63=277	$37,500.00
John Daly	T-10	69-67-68-73=277	$37,500.00

Memorial Tournament
Course: Muirfield Village G.C., Dubin, Ohio
Par: 72 Yardage: 7,104
Last day of event: Sunday, June 2, 1996

Player	Place	Score	Earnings
Tom Watson	Win	70-68-66-70=274	$324,000.00
David Duval	2	72-70-67-67=276	$194,400.00
Mark O'Meara	T-3	71-72-68-67=278	$104,400.00
David Frost	T-3	73-68-70-67=278	$104,400.00
John Huston	5	74-61-71-73=279	$72,000.00
Paul Stankowski	T-6	73-66-67-74=280	$56,340.00
Mike Hulbert	T-6	74-68-69-69=280	$56,340.00
Brad Faxon	T-6	74-72-68-66=280	$56,340.00
Ernie Els	T-6	70-67-68-75=280	$56,340.00
Davis Love III	T-6	76-68-65-71=280	$56,340.00

Buick Classic
Course: Westchester C.C., Harrison, N.Y.
Par: 71 Yardage: 6,779
Last day of event: Sunday, June 9, 1996

Player	Place	Score	Earnings
Ernie Els	Win	65-66-69-71=271	$216,000.00
Tom Lehman	T-2	71-71-67-70=279	$79,200.00
Steve Elkington	T-2	66-72-70-71=279	$79,200.00
Craig Parry	T-2	70-66-72-71=279	$79,200.00
Jeff Maggert	T-2	74-68-68-69=279	$79,200.00
Brad Faxon	T-6	70-72-67-71=280	$40,200.00
Fred Funk	T-6	72-70-67-71=280	$40,200.00
David Frost	T-6	67-69-74-70=280	$40,200.00
Corey Pavin	T-9	72-71-68-70=281	$33,600.00
Tim Herron	T-9	68-70-68-75=281	$33,600.00

U.S. Open
Course: Oakland Hills C.C., Birmingham, Mich.
Par: 70 Yardage: 6,974
Last day of event: Sunday, June 16, 1996

Player	Place	Score	Earnings
Steve Jones	Win	74-66-69-69=278	$425,000.00
Davis Love III	T-2	71-69-70-69=279	$204,801.00
Tom Lehman	T-2	71-72-65-71=279	$204,801.00
John Morse	4	68-74-68-70=280	$111,235.00
Ernie Els	T-5	72-67-72-70=281	$84,964.50
Jim Furyk	T-5	72-69-70-70=281	$84,964.50
Vijay Singh	T-7	71-72-70-69=282	$66,294.67
Ken Green	T-7	73-67-72-70=282	$66,294.67
Scott Hoch	T-7	73-71-71-67=282	$66,294.66
Colin Montgomerie	T-10	70-72-69-72=283	$52,591.00
Greg Norman	T-10	73-66-74-70=283	$52,591.00
Lee Janzen	T-10	68-75-71-69=283	$52,591.00

FedEx St. Jude Classic
Course: TPC at Southwind, Germantown, Tenn.
Par: 71 Yardage: 7,006
Last day of event: Sunday, June 23, 1996

Player	Place	Score	Earnings
John Cook	Win	64-62-63-69=258	$243,000.00
John Adams	2	65-64-66-70=265	$145,800.00
Kenny Perry	3	67-64-67-68=266	$91,800.00
Justin Leonard	T-4	70-64-66-67=267	$59,400.00
Gil Morgan	T-4	70-65-68-64=267	$59,400.00
Paul Stankowski	6	69-64-66-69=268	$48,600.00
Michael Bradley	T-7	69-67-67-66=269	$43,537.50
Mike Swartz	T-7	64-71-67-67=269	$43,537.50
John Huston	T-9	67-68-66-69=270	$36,450.00
Tom Purtzer	T-9	67-69-69-65=270	$36,450.00
Kirk Triplett	T-9	68-68-64-70=270	$36,450.00

Canon Greater Hartford Open
Course: TPC at River Highlands, Cromwell, Conn.
Par: 70 Yardage: 6,820
Last day of event: Sunday, June 30, 1996

Player	Place	Score	Earnings
D.A. Weibring	Win	68-65-70-67=270	$270,000.00
Tom Kite	2	72-68-66-68=274	$162,000.00
Dicky Pride	T-3	70-70-68-67=275	$78,000.00
Mark Calcavecchia	T-3	71-67-68-69=275	$78,000.00
Fuzzy Zoeller	T-3	75-66-66-68=275	$78,000.00
Joel Edwards	T-6	70-70-68-68=276	$52,125.00
Mike Brisky	T-6	71-72-63-70=276	$52,125.00
Brad Faxon	8	68-70-71-68=277	$46,500.00
Roger Maltbie	T-9	67-71-72-68=278	$40,500.00
Steve Jones	T-9	72-68-71-67=278	$40,500.00
Kevin Sutherland	T-9	67-65-72-74=278	$40,500.00

Motorola Western Open
Course: Cog Hill G. & C.C. (Dubsdread), Lemont, Ill.
Par: 72 Yardage: 7,073
Last day of event: Sunday, July 7, 1996

Player	Place	Score	Earnings
Steve Stricker	Win	65-69-67-69=270	$360,000.00
Billy Andrade	T-2	69-71-69-69=278	$176,000.00
Jay Don Blake	T-2	67-67-73-71=278	$176,000.00

Craig Parry	T-4	69-69-70-71=279	$78,750.00
Glen Day	T-4	70-71-69-69=279	$78,750.00
Mike Brisky	T-4	74-67-68-70=279	$78,750.00
Jim Gallagher, Jr.	T-4	74-68-70-67=279	$78,750.00
Vijay Singh	T-8	71-70-69-70=280	$54,000.00
Mark Brooks	T-8	68-70-70-72=280	$54,000.00
Justin Leonard	T-8	69-67-72-72=280	$54,000.00
Steve Elkington	T-8	70-72-67-71=280	$54,000.00
Lee Janzen	T-8	67-68-71-74=280	$54,000.00

Michelob Championship at Kingsmill
Course: Kingsmill G.C., Williamsburg, Va.
Par: 71 Yardage: 6,776
Last day of event: Sunday, July 14, 1996

Player	Place	Score	Earnings
Scott Hoch	Win	64-68-66-67=265	$225,000.00
Tom Purtzer	2	66-68-69-66=269	$135,000.00
Fred Funk	T-3	65-69-69-69=272	$65,000.00
Michael Bradley	T-3	69-67-70-66=272	$65,000.00
Ted Tryba	T-3	70-70-65-67=272	$65,000.00
Dicky Pride	6	67-68-67-71=273	$45,000.00
David Edwards	T-7	67-70-67-70=274	$40,312.50
Tommy Armour III	T-7	67-67-71-69=274	$40,312.50
Mark McCumber	T-9	68-67-70-70=275	$33,750.00
Donnie Hammond	T-9	69-68-70-68=275	$33,750.00
Olin Browne	T-9	69-69-70-67=275	$33,750.00

British Open
Course: Royal Lytham & St. Annes G.C., Lytham, Lancashire, England
Par: 71 Yardage: 6,892
Last day of event: Sunday, July 21, 1996

Player	Place	Score	Earnings
Tom Lehman	Win	67-67-64-73=271	$310,000.00
Mark McCumber	T-2	67-69-71-66=273	$193,750.00
Ernie Els	T-2	68-67-71-67=273	$193,750.00
Nick Faldo	4	68-68-68-70=274	$116,250.00
Mark Brooks	T-5	67-70-68-71=276	$77,500.00
Jeff Maggert	T-5	69-70-72-65=276	$77,500.00
Fred Couples	T-7	67-70-69-71=277	$54,250.00
Greg Norman	T-7	71-68-71-67=277	$54,250.00
Greg Turner	T-7	72-69-68-68=277	$54,250.00
Peter Hedblom	T-7	70-65-75-67=277	$54,250.00

Deposit Guaranty Golf Classic
Course: Annandale G.C., Madison, Miss.
Par: 72 Yardage: 7,157
Last day of event: Sunday, July 21, 1996

Player	Place	Score	Earnings
Willie Wood	Win	68-67-66-67=268	$180,000.00
Kirk Triplett	2	66-68-67-68=269	$108,000.00
Scott Hoch	T-3	69-69-68-65=271	$58,000.00
Greg Kraft	T-3	68-66-66-71=271	$58,000.00
David Ogrin	T-5	69-68-69-66=272	$35,125.00
Neal Lancaster	T-5	70-67-66-69=272	$35,125.00
Phil Blackmar	T-5	70-68-66-68=272	$35,125.00
David Edwards	T-5	68-67-66-71=272	$35,125.00
Robin Freeman	9	72-65-68-68=273	$29,000.00
Steve Jurgensen	T-10	68-68-69-69=274	$26,000.00
Bobby Wadkins	T-10	68-65-68-73=274	$26,000.00

CVS Charity Classic
Course: Pleasant Valley C.C., Sutton, Mass.
Par: 71 Yardage: 7,110
Last day of event: Sunday, July 28, 1996

Player	Place	Score	Earnings
John Cook	Win	65-67-67-69=268	$216,000.00
Russ Cochran	2	68-64-71-68=271	$129,600.00
Bruce Fleisher	3	65-67-70-72=274	$81,600.00
Mike Reid	T-4	67-70-70-68=275	$45,240.00
Marco Dawson	T-4	68-69-68-70=275	$45,240.00
Kenny Perry	T-4	66-71-69-69=275	$45,240.00
Mike Standly	T-4	68-67-71-69=275	$45,240.00
Charlie Rymer	T-4	72-66-66-71=275	$45,240.00
Brian Henninger	T-9	68-67-70-71=276	$32,400.00
Dudley Hart	T-9	70-71-69-66=276	$32,400.00
Brad Faxon	T-9	70-67-67-72=276	$32,400.00

Buick Open
Course: Warwick Hills C.C., Grand Blanc, Mich.
Par: 72 Yardage: 7,105
Last day of event: Sunday, August 4, 1996

Player	Place	Score	Earnings
Justin Leonard	Win	65-64-69-68=266	$216,000.00
Chip Beck	2	69-65-70-67=271	$129,600.00
Rick Fehr	T-3	64-67-70-72=273	$57,600.00
Jim Carter	T-3	65-67-72-69=273	$57,600.00
Dave Stockton, Jr.	T-3	69-66-66-72=273	$57,600.00
Woody Austin	T-3	72-65-68-68=273	$57,600.00
Olin Browne	T-7	70-69-67-68=274	$33,700.00
Wayne Levi	T-7	68-65-71-70=274	$33,700.00
Jay Williamson	T-7	67-69-66-72=274	$33,700.00
Fred Funk	T-7	68-72-66-68=274	$33,700.00
Mark McCumber	T-7	72-67-67-68=274	$33,700.00
Bob Tway	T-7	68-66-65-75=274	$33,700.00

PGA Championship
Course: Valhalla G.C., Louisville, Ky.
Par: 72 Yardage: 7,144
Last day of event: Sunday, August 11, 1996

Player	Place	Score	Earnings
Mark Brooks	Win	68-70-69-70=277	$430,000.00
Playoff: Beat Kenny Perry with birdie on first extra hole			
Kenny Perry	2	66-72-71-68=277	$260,000.00
Tommy Tolles	T-3	69-71-71-67=278	$140,000.00
Steve Elkington	T-3	67-74-67-70=278	$140,000.00
Vijay Singh	T-5	69-69-69-72=279	$86,666.66
Justin Leonard	T-5	71-66-72-70=279	$86,666.67
Jesper Parnevik	T-5	73-67-69-70=279	$86,666.67
Lee Janzen	T-8	68-71-71-70=280	$57,500.00
Larry Mize	T-8	71-70-69-70=280	$57,500.00
Nick Price	T-8	68-71-69-72=280	$57,500.00
Frank Nobilo	T-8	69-72-71-68=280	$57,500.00
Per-Ulrik Johansson	T-8	73-72-66-69=280	$57,500.00
Phil Mickelson	T-8	67-67-74-72=280	$57,500.00

Sprint International
Course: Castle Pine G.C., Castle Rock, Colo. (Stableford format)
Par: 72 Yardage: 7,559
Last day of event: Sunday, August 18, 1996

Player	Place	Score	Earnings
Clarence Rose	Win	6-3-12-10=31	$288,000.00

Playoff: Beat Brad Faxon with eagle on third extra hole

Player	Place	Score	Earnings
Brad Faxon	2	6-6-12-7=31	$172,800.00
Bob Tway	T-3	7-2-11-10=30	$92,800.00
Michael Bradley	T-3	9-3-11-7=30	$92,800.00
Justin Leonard	T-5	6-8-4-9=27	$60,800.00
Tom Lehman	T-5	7-4-8-8=27	$60,800.00
D.A. Weibring	7	4-2-12-7=25	$53,600.00
Kenny Perry	8	11-0-7-6=24	$49,600.00
Nick Faldo	T-9	6-4-8-5=23	$40,000.00
Woody Austin	T-9	10-3-5-5=23	$40,000.00
Billy Andrade	T-9	7-9-3-4=23	$40,000.00
Paul Goydos	T-9	2-10-9-2=23	$40,000.00
John Cook	T-9	10-8-3-2=23	$40,000.00

NEC World Series of Golf

Course: Firestone C.C. (South), Akron, Ohio
Par: 70 Yardage: 7,149
Last day of event: Sunday, August 25, 1996

Player	Place	Score	Earnings
Phil Mickelson	Win	70-66-68-70=274	$378,000.00
Billy Mayfair	T-2	66-71-70-70=277	$156,800.00
Duffy Waldorf	T-2	70-70-71-66=277	$156,800.00
Steve Stricker	T-2	68-72-69-68=277	$156,800.00
Greg Norman	5	70-68-69-71=278	$84,000.00
Alex Cejka	T-6	72-71-71-66=280	$72,975.00
Davis Love III	T-6	70-74-67-69=280	$72,975.00
John Cook	8	70-69-71-71=281	$65,100.00
Corey Pavin	9	73-70-70-69=282	$60,900.00
Fred Funk	T-10	72-70-73-68=283	$50,400.00
Mark Brooks	T-10	69-69-74-71=283	$50,400.00
Nick Faldo	T-10	70-71-68-74=283	$50,400.00
Tom Lehman	T-10	72-69-74-68=283	$50,400.00

Greater Vancouver Open

Course: Northview G. & C.C. (Ridge Course), Surrey, British Columbia, Canada
Par: 71 Yardage: 6,817
Last day of event: Sunday, August 25, 1996

Player	Place	Score	Earnings
Guy Boros	Win	71-65-65-71=272	$180,000.00
Emlyn Aubrey	T-2	68-68-70-67=273	$74,666.67
Lee Janzen	T-2	71-65-66-71=273	$74,666.67
Taylor Smith	T-2	71-65-65-72=273	$74,666.66
Kenny Perry	T-5	70-70-68-67=275	$33,900.00
Shane Bertsch	T-5	70-71-68-66=275	$33,900.00
Joey Gullion	T-5	71-69-67-68=275	$33,900.00
Mike Weir	T-5	72-68-65-70=275	$33,900.00
Russ Cochran	T-5	72-67-67-69=275	$33,900.00
Mike Brisky	T-10	67-71-68-70=276	$24,000.00
Andrew Magee	T-10	71-67-67-71=276	$24,000.00
Chris Perry	T-10	71-72-67-66=276	$24,000.00
Tom Byrum	T-10	72-71-69-64=276	$24,000.00

Greater Milwaukee Open

Course: Brown Deer Park G.C., Milwaukee, Wis.
Par: 71 Yardage: 6,739
Last day of event: Sunday, September 1, 1996

Player	Place	Score	Earnings
Loren Roberts	Win	66-65-66-68=265	$216,000.00
Playoff: Beat Jerry Kelly with birdie on first extra hole			
Jerry Kelly	2	67-66-68-64=265	$129,600.00
Steve Stricker	T-3	66-67-66-67=266	$57,600.00
Andrew Magee	T-3	68-70-65-63=266	$57,600.00
Nolan Henke	T-3	62-66-67-71=266	$57,600.00
Jesper Parnevik	T-3	65-66-63-72=266	$57,600.00
David Ogrin	T-7	68-66-66-67=267	$38,700.00
Olin Browne	T-7	67-67-69-64=267	$38,700.00
Fred Funk	T-9	69-66-67-66=268	$32,400.00
Duffy Waldorf	T-9	65-65-70-68=268	$32,400.00
Steve Lowery	T-9	70-64-67-67=268	$32,400.00

Bell Canadian Open

Course: Glen Abbey G.C., Oakville, Ontario, Canada
Par: 72 Yardage: 7,112
Last day of event: Sunday, September 8, 1996

Player	Place	Score	Earnings
Dudley Hart	Win	68-64-70=202	$270,000.00
David Duval	2	69-65-69=203	$162,000.00
Tom Byrum	T-3	70-66-69=205	$78,000.00
Taylor Smith	T-3	68-66-71=205	$78,000.00
Scott Dunlap	T-3	64-65-76=205	$78,000.00
Michael Bradley	6	70-64-72=206	$54,000.00
Tom Lehman	T-7	69-70-68=207	$45,187.50
Joey Sindelar	T-7	70-68-69=207	$45,187.50
Jesper Parnevik	T-7	66-71-70=207	$45,187.50
Mark Calcavecchia	T-7	71-68-68=207	$45,187.50

Quad City Classic

Course: Oakwood C.C., Coal Valley, Ill.
Par: 70 Yardage: 6,762
Last day of event: Sunday, September 15, 1996

Player	Place	Score	Earnings
Ed Fiori	Win	66-68-67-67=268	$216,000.00
Andrew Magee	2	69-70-69-62=270	$129,600.00
Steve Jones	T-3	68-68-67-68=271	$69,600.00
Chris Perry	T-3	68-70-67-66=271	$69,600.00
Phil Blackmar	T-5	69-71-65-67=272	$42,150.00
Hugh Royer III	T-5	71-68-65-68=272	$42,150.00
Tiger Woods	T-5	69-64-67-72=272	$42,150.00
Jeff Maggert	T-5	67-68-73-64=272	$42,150.00
Jeff Sluman	T-9	69-69-69-67=274	$30,000.00
Greg Kraft	T-9	68-70-67-69=274	$30,000.00
Loren Roberts	T-9	69-70-69-66=274	$30,000.00
Mike Springer	T-9	69-72-65-68=274	$30,000.00
Brian Tennyson	T-9	72-67-67-68=274	$30,000.00

B.C. Open

Course: En-Joie G.C., Endicott, N.Y.
Par: 71 Yardage: 6,920
Last day of event: Sunday, September 22, 1996

Player	Place	Score	Earnings
Fred Funk	Win	68-66-63=197	$180,000.00
Playoff: Beat Pete Jordan with birdie on first extra hole			
Pete Jordan	2	67-64-66=197	$108,000.00
Tiger Woods	T-3	68-66-66=200	$58,000.00
Patrick Burke	T-3	68-67-65=200	$58,000.00
Brian Claar	5	66-68-68=202	$40,000.00
Joey Sindelar	T-6	69-68-66=203	$33,500.00
Hugh Royer III	T-6	70-66-67=203	$33,500.00
Joe Daley	T-6	68-73-62=203	$33,500.00
Jeff Sluman	T-9	69-67-68=204	$27,000.00
David Ogrin	T-9	70-67-67=204	$27,000.00
Bradley Hughes	T-9	71-68-65=204	$27,000.00

Buick Challenge

Course: Callaway Gardens Resort, Pine Mountain, Ga.
Par: 72 Yardage: 7,057
Last day of event: Sunday, September 29, 1996

Player	Place	Score	Earnings
Michael Bradley	Win	66-68=134	$180,000.00

Playoff: Beat Fred Funk, Davis Love III, John Maginnes and Len Mattiace with birdie on first extra hole

Player	Place	Score	Earnings
Davis Love III	T-2	66-68=134	$66,000.00
Len Mattiace	T-2	66-68=134	$66,000.00
John Maginnes	T-2	68-66=134	$66,000.00
Fred Funk	T-2	69-65=134	$66,000.00
Fred Couples	T-6	68-67=135	$33,500.00
Brad Faxon	T-6	69-66=135	$33,500.00
Marco Dawson	T-6	70-65=135	$33,500.00
Brad Bryant	T-9	68-68=136	$28,000.00
Stewart Cink	T-9	66-70=136	$28,000.00

Las Vegas Invitational

Course: TPC at Summerlin, Desert Inn C.C., Las Vegas Hilton C.C., Las Vegas, Nev.
Home course / TPC at Summerlin, Par: 72 Yardage: 7,243
Last day of event: Sunday, October 6, 1996

Player	Place	Score	Earnings
Tiger Woods	Win	70-63-68-67-64=332	$297,000.00

Playoff: Beat Davis Love III with par on first extra hole

Player	Place	Score	Earnings
Davis Love III	2	66-67-64-68-67=332	$178,200.00
Kelly Gibson	T-3	69-69-65-65-65=333	$95,700.00
Mark Calcavecchia	T-3	72-67-65-64-65=333	$95,700.00
Dave Stockton, Jr.	T-5	67-68-67-64-69=335	$60,225.00
Ronnie Black	T-5	64-65-69-66-71=335	$60,225.00
Rick Fehr	T-5	64-62-69-73-67=335	$60,225.00
Phil Mickelson	T-8	68-67-68-67-66=336	$46,200.00
Fred Couples	T-8	66-67-66-67-70=336	$46,200.00
Paul Azinger	T-8	67-64-70-70-65=336	$46,200.00
Paul Goydos	T-8	67-71-66-65-67=336	$46,200.00

LaCantera Texas Open

Course: LaCantera G.C., San Antonio, Texas
Par: 72 Yardage: 7,001
Last day of event: Sunday, October 13, 1996

Player	Place	Score	Earnings
David Ogrin	Win	70-65-68-72=275	$216,000.00
Jay Haas	2	70-66-70-70=276	$129,600.00
Tiger Woods	3	69-68-73-67=277	$81,600.00
Greg Kraft	T-4	71-72-70-65=278	$52,800.00
Len Mattiace	T-4	73-71-65-69=278	$52,800.00
Keith Fergus	T-6	70-71-68-70=279	$40,200.00
Tim Herron	T-6	70-70-71-68=279	$40,200.00
John Huston	T-6	66-71-74-68=279	$40,200.00
Scott Dunlap	T-9	70-70-71-69=280	$33,600.00
Lee Janzen	T-9	73-67-70-70=280	$33,600.00

Walt Disney World/Oldsmobile Classic

Course: Walt Disney (Magnolia, Palm), Lake Buena Vista C.C., Lake Buena Vista, Fla.
Home course / Magnolia, Par: 72 Yardage: 7,190
Last day of event: Sunday, October 20, 1996

Player	Place	Score	Earnings
Tiger Woods	Win	69-63-69-66=267	$216,000.00
Payne Stewart	2	68-63-70-67=268	$129,600.00
Robert Gamez	3	66-66-70-67=269	$81,600.00
Nolan Henke	4	71-64-71-64=270	$57,600.00
Rick Fehr	T-5	65-65-70-71=271	$43,800.00
Jay Haas	T-5	65-67-68-71=271	$43,800.00
Lennie Clements	T-5	67-67-66-71=271	$43,800.00
Dudley Hart	T-8	68-66-69-69=272	$32,400.00
Jerry Kelly	T-8	69-64-69-70=272	$32,400.00
Mike Springer	T-8	69-67-70-66=272	$32,400.00
Ronnie Black	T-8	66-66-69-71=272	$32,400.00
Jim Carter	T-8	66-65-71-70=272	$32,400.00

The Tour Championship

Course: Southern Hills C.C., Tulsa, Okla.
Par: 70 Yardage: 6,834
Last day of event: Monday, October 28, 1996

Player	Place	Score	Earnings
Tom Lehman	Win	66-67-64-71=268	$540,000.00
Brad Faxon	2	68-72-66-68=274	$324,000.00
Steve Stricker	3	70-68-72-65=275	$207,000.00
Kenny Perry	4	73-68-70-66=277	$144,000.00
Fred Couples	5	68-73-68-69=278	$120,000.00
Tom Watson	T-6	70-70-69-70=279	$102,000.00
Justin Leonard	T-6	73-68-68-70=279	$102,000.00
Ernie Els	T-6	76-70-65-68=279	$102,000.00
Vijay Singh	T-9	66-71-69-74=280	$87,600.00
Jeff Sluman	T-9	71-74-67-68=280	$87,600.00

1997

Tiger Woods won four times in 1997, but it was his 12-shot victory at the Masters (Trivia answer: Tom Kite was runner-up.) that signaled a vibrant new era in golf. Pundits forecast an influx of minorities to the game. Augusta National would undergo a series of "Tiger-proofing" renovations. The PGA Tour was able to extract a $400 million deal from eager TV partners—double their previous arrangement—which set the table for a quantum leap in purses, from $75 million in 1997 to $131.7 in 1999 (the first year of the new contract). Ernie Els won his second U.S. Open, besting an agitated Colin Montgomerie again, this time by one shot at Congressional. Thanks to a closing 65 at Royal Troon, Justin Leonard won the British Open by three shots over Jesper Parnevik, who bogeyed the final three holes, and Darren Clarke. Davis Love III shed the "best player never to have won a major" label, posting a pair of 66s over the weekend at Winged Foot and beating runner-up Leonard by five shots. Ben Hogan, the steely winner of 68 tournaments including nine majors (and a career Grand Slam), died in July at age 84. With Seve Ballesteros at the helm as captain, Europe retained the Ryder Cup with a 14 ½ to 13 ½ victory at Valderrama.

Mercedes Championships

Course: La Costa C.C., Carlsbad, Calif.
Par: 72 Yardage: 7,022
Last day of event: Sunday, January 12, 1997

Player	Place	Score	Earnings
Tiger Woods	Win	70-67-65=202	$216,000.00

Playoff: Beat Tom Lehman with birdie on first extra hole

Player	Place	Score	Earnings
Tom Lehman	2	66-67-69=202	$129,600.00
Guy Boros	3	69-68-70=207	$81,600.00
Fred Couples	T-4	69-69-70=208	$52,800.00
Paul Goydos	T-4	67-71-70=208	$52,800.00
Steve Jones	T-6	70-71-68=209	$41,700.00
Davis Love III	T-6	70-67-72=209	$41,700.00
John Cook	T-8	70-71-69=210	$35,600.00
Corey Pavin	T-8	70-68-72=210	$35,600.00
Jim Furyk	T-8	67-68-75=210	$35,600.00

Bob Hope Chrysler Classic

Course: Indian Wells C.C., Indian Ridge C.C., Bermuda Dunes C.C., Tamarisk C.C., Indian Wells, Calif.

Home course / Indian Wells C.C., Par: 72 Yardage: 6,478

Last day of event: Sunday, January 19, 1997

Player	Place	Score	Earnings
John Cook	Win	66-69-67-62-63=327	$270,000.00
Mark Calcavecchia	2	64-67-66-64-67=328	$162,000.00
Jesper Parnevik	3	66-70-68-66-62=332	$102,000.00
Mark O'Meara	4	68-66-68-66-65=333	$72,000.00
Don Pooley	T-5	70-69-63-65-69=336	$57,000.00
Tommy Tolles	T-5	65-69-73-65-64=336	$57,000.00
John Daly	7	65-73-64-66-69=337	$50,250.00
Grant Waite	8	68-70-64-68-68=338	$46,500.00
Stewart Cink	T-9	68-68-69-68-66=339	$34,714.29
Craig Stadler	T-9	68-69-70-67-65=339	$34,714.28
Scott Hoch	T-9	71-66-67-67-68=339	$34,714.28
Fred Couples	T-9	71-71-64-68-65=339	$34,714.29
Larry Rinker	T-9	63-68-72-70-66=339	$34,714.29
Steve Jones	T-9	64-72-67-68-68=339	$34,714.28
Jay Don Blake	T-9	65-67-66-72-69=339	$34,714.29

Phoenix Open

Course: TPC of Scottsdale, Scottsdale, Ariz.

Par: 71 Yardage: 6,992

Last day of event: Sunday, January 26, 1997

Player	Place	Score	Earnings
Steve Jones	Win	62-64-65-67=258	$270,000.00
Jesper Parnevik	2	66-66-70-67=269	$162,000.00
Nick Price	3	64-72-65-69=270	$102,000.00
Mark Calcavecchia	T-4	68-66-67-71=272	$62,000.00
Rick Fehr	T-4	66-68-66-72=272	$62,000.00
Kenny Perry	T-4	74-67-66-65=272	$62,000.00
Tom Lehman	T-7	68-69-68-68=273	$40,607.14
Mike Hulbert	T-7	69-69-66-69=273	$40,607.14
Phil Mickelson	T-7	70-71-66-66=273	$40,607.15
Scott McCarron	T-7	71-68-64-70=273	$40,607.15
Dan Forsman	T-7	69-67-65-72=273	$40,607.14
Tommy Tolles	T-7	66-65-69-73=273	$40,607.14
Fulton Allem	T-7	67-67-66-73=273	$40,607.14

AT&T Pebble Beach Pro-Am

Courses: Pebble Beach G.L., Spyglass Hill G.C., Poppy Hills G.C., Pebble Beach, Calif.

Home Course / Pebble Beach G.L., Par: 72 Yardage: 6,799

Last day of event: Sunday, February 2, 1997

Player	Place	Score	Earnings
Mark O'Meara	Win	67-67-67-67=268	$342,000.00
David Duval	T-2	65-71-62-71=269	$167,200.00
Tiger Woods	T-2	70-72-63-64=269	$167,200.00
Jim Furyk	4	67-65-69-72=273	$91,200.00
Craig Stadler	T-5	70-69-66-69=274	$72,200.00
Jesper Parnevik	T-5	65-70-67-72=274	$72,200.00
Paul Azinger	T-7	69-70-67-69=275	$61,275.00
Billy Andrade	T-7	66-75-66-68=275	$61,275.00
Glen Day	T-9	70-69-67-70=276	$53,200.00
Mike Brisky	T-9	69-68-68-71=276	$53,200.00

Buick Invitational

Course: Torrey Pines (South), Torrey Pines (North), San Diego, Calif.

Home Course -Par: 72 Yardage: 7,022

Last day of event: Sunday, February 9, 1997

Player	Place	Score	Earnings
Mark O'Meara	Win	67-66-71-71=275	$270,000.00
David Ogrin	T-2	67-71-70-69=277	$78,107.15
Lee Janzen	T-2	71-65-71-70=277	$78,107.14
Craig Stadler	T-2	67-68-70-72=277	$78,107.14
Jesper Parnevik	T-2	70-66-69-72=277	$78,107.14
Duffy Waldorf	T-2	70-66-72-69=277	$78,107.14
Mike Hulbert	T-2	68-69-67-73=277	$78,107.14
Donnie Hammond	T-2	73-67-68-69=277	$78,107.15
Skip Kendall	T-9	67-71-71-69=278	$42,000.00
Steve Lowery	T-9	67-66-75-70=278	$42,000.00

United Airlines Hawaiian Open

Course: Waialae C.C., Honolulu, Ha.

Par: 72 Yardage: 7,012

Last day of event: Sunday, February 16, 1997

Player	Place	Score	Earnings
Paul Stankowski	Win	71-66-64-70=271	$216,000.00

Playoff: Beat Mike Reid and Jim Furyk with birdie on fourth extra hole

Player	Place	Score	Earnings
Jim Furyk	T-2	70-67-66-68=271	$105,600.00
Mike Reid	T-2	62-72-66-71=271	$105,600.00
Jay Don Blake	T-4	68-70-65-70=273	$52,800.00
Donnie Hammond	T-4	70-68-66-69=273	$52,800.00
Tom Lehman	6	65-69-69-71=274	$43,200.00
Paul Goydos	T-7	70-66-71-68=275	$38,700.00
Lee Porter	T-7	70-66-67-72=275	$38,700.00
Joe Durant	T-9	69-69-69-70=277	$31,200.00
Stuart Appleby	T-9	67-70-69-71=277	$31,200.00
Paul Azinger	T-9	67-70-69-71=277	$31,200.00
Taylor Smith	T-9	72-66-68-71=277	$31,200.00

Tucson Chrysler Classic

Course: Omni Tucson National Resort, Tucson, Ariz.

Par: 72 Yardage: 7,148

Last day of event: Sunday, February 23, 1997

Player	Place	Score	Earnings
Jeff Sluman	Win	75-68-65-67=275	$234,000.00
Steve Jones	2	66-68-72-70=276	$140,400.00
Paul Stankowski	T-3	72-65-69-71=277	$75,400.00
Brad Bryant	T-3	68-69-67-73=277	$75,400.00
Tom Kite	T-5	69-70-71-68=278	$44,070.00
Jeff Maggert	T-5	66-72-70-70=278	$44,070.00
Clarence Rose	T-5	67-72-68-71=278	$44,070.00
Lee Janzen	T-5	72-71-66-69=278	$44,070.00
Don Pooley	T-5	67-73-70-68=278	$44,070.00
Mike Reid	T-10	70-69-69-71=279	$32,500.00
Andrew Magee	T-10	70-72-67-70=279	$32,500.00
Jerry Kelly	T-10	72-68-69-70=279	$32,500.00

Nissan Open

Course: Riviera C.C., Pacific Palisades, Calif.

Par: 71 Yardage: 6,946

Last day of event: Sunday, March 2, 1997

Player	Place	Score	Earnings
Nick Faldo	Win	66-70-68-68=272	$252,000.00
Craig Stadler	2	71-66-68-70=275	$151,200.00
Scott Hoch	3	65-71-71-69=276	$95,200.00
Tom Purtzer	T-4	67-71-69-70=277	$61,600.00
Fred Funk	T-4	67-71-71-68=277	$61,600.00
Robin Freeman	T-6	69-71-68-70=278	$46,900.00
Omar Uresti	T-6	70-71-69-68=278	$46,900.00

Scott McCarron	T-6	68-73-64-73=278	$46,900.00
Fred Couples	T-9	68-70-70-71=279	$31,325.00
Payne Stewart	T-9	65-72-72-70=279	$31,325.00
Mark O'Meara	T-9	67-69-72-71=279	$31,325.00
David Ogrin	T-9	68-71-72-68=279	$31,325.00
Joe Ozaki	T-9	73-69-68-69=279	$31,325.00
Paul Goydos	T-9	66-74-70-69=279	$31,325.00
Ted Tryba	T-9	70-66-74-69=279	$31,325.00
Peter Jacobsen	T-9	68-75-68-68=279	$31,325.00

Doral-Ryder Open

Course: Doral C.C. (Blue), Miami, Fla.
Par: 72 Yardage: 6,939
Last day of event: Sunday, March 9, 1997

Player	Place	Score	Earnings
Steve Elkington	Win	70-66-70-69=275	$324,000.00
Nick Price	T-2	68-67-70-72=277	$158,400.00
Larry Nelson	T-2	72-66-69-70=277	$158,400.00
David Duval	4	68-66-70-74=278	$86,400.00
Fulton Allem	T-5	70-70-70-70=280	$65,700.00
Ronnie Black	T-5	67-71-70-72=280	$65,700.00
Robert Damron	T-5	72-66-71-71=280	$65,700.00
Brad Bryant	8	69-70-74-68=281	$55,800.00
Wayne Levi	T-9	70-72-68-72=282	$46,800.00
Craig Stadler	T-9	71-72-67-72=282	$46,800.00
Greg Norman	T-9	66-68-74-74=282	$46,800.00
Bob Tway	T-9	66-71-70-75=282	$46,800.00

Honda Classic

Course: TPC at Heron Bay, Coral Springs, Fla.
Par: 72 Yardage: 7,268
Last day of event: Sunday, March 16, 1997

Player	Place	Score	Earnings
Stuart Appleby	Win	68-68-67-71=274	$270,000.00
Payne Stewart	T-2	68-68-68-71=275	$132,000.00
Michael Bradley	T-2	69-65-73-68=275	$132,000.00
Colin Montgomerie	4	68-68-70-71=277	$72,000.00
Ronnie Black	T-5	69-71-68-70=278	$44,250.00
Joe Durant	T-5	69-71-68-70=278	$44,250.00
Mike Brisky	T-5	71-66-70-71=278	$44,250.00
Jesper Parnevik	T-5	71-69-68-70=278	$44,250.00
Doug Martin	T-5	69-66-72-71=278	$44,250.00
Robert Gamez	T-5	70-66-70-72=278	$44,250.00
Andrew Magee	T-5	70-68-68-72=278	$44,250.00
Paul Stankowski	T-5	67-66-72-73=278	$44,250.00
Craig Parry	T-5	74-64-70-70=278	$44,250.00

Bay Hill Invitational

Course: Bay Hill Club, Orlando, Fla.
Par: 72 Yardage: 7,207
Last day of event: Sunday, March 23, 1997

Player	Place	Score	Earnings
Phil Mickelson	Win	72-65-70-65=272	$270,000.00
Stuart Appleby	2	73-63-70-69=275	$162,000.00
Payne Stewart	T-3	69-70-70-67=276	$78,000.00
Omar Uresti	T-3	69-67-69-71=276	$78,000.00
Mark O'Meara	T-3	72-66-68-70=276	$78,000.00
Loren Roberts	T-6	70-67-70-70=277	$50,250.00
Tim Herron	T-6	70-70-66-71=277	$50,250.00
Michael Bradley	T-6	71-69-69-68=277	$50,250.00
Tiger Woods	T-9	68-71-71-68=278	$42,000.00
Davis Love III	T-9	73-68-67-70=278	$42,000.00

The Players Championship

Course: TPC at Sawgrass, Ponte Vedra Beach, Fla.
Par: 72 Yardage: 6,896
Last day of event: Sunday, March 30, 1997

Player	Place	Score	Earnings
Steve Elkington	Win	66-69-68-69=272	$630,000.00
Scott Hoch	2	69-71-65-74=279	$378,000.00
Loren Roberts	3	70-74-67-69=280	$238,000.00
Brad Faxon	4	70-69-72-70=281	$168,000.00
Billy Andrade	5	68-72-68-74=282	$140,000.00
Tom Lehman	6	67-71-73-72=283	$126,000.00
Colin Montgomerie	T-7	70-70-71-73=284	$109,083.33
Tommy Tolles	T-7	70-67-73-74=284	$109,083.33
Mark Brooks	T-7	72-68-70-74=284	$109,083.34
Russ Cochran	T-10	67-74-72-72=285	$84,000.00
Ernie Els	T-10	68-71-72-74=285	$84,000.00
Fred Couples	T-10	71-74-71-69=285	$84,000.00
Kirk Triplett	T-10	71-68-70-76=285	$84,000.00

Freeport-McDermott Classic

Course: English Turn G. & C.C., New Orleans, La.
Par: 72 Yardage: 7,116
Last day of event: Sunday, April 6, 1997

Player	Place	Score	Earnings
Brad Faxon	Win	68-69-66-69=272	$270,000.00
Bill Glasson	T-2	71-72-66-66=275	$132,000.00
Jesper Parnevik	T-2	72-69-68-66=275	$132,000.00
Scott McCarron	T-4	65-69-71-71=276	$66,000.00
Kirk Triplett	T-4	72-68-64-72=276	$66,000.00
Russ Cochran	6	70-71-67-69=277	$54,000.00
Jose Maria Olazabal	T-7	72-67-67-72=278	$45,187.50
Steve Lowery	T-7	72-71-66-69=278	$45,187.50
Yoshinori Kaneko	T-7	69-74-69-66=278	$45,187.50
Tommy Tolles	T-7	74-71-66-67=278	$45,187.50

Masters

Course: Augusta National G.C., Augusta, Ga.
Par: 72 Yardage: 6,925
Last day of event: Sunday, April 13, 1997

Player	Place	Score	Earnings
Tiger Woods	Win	70-66-65-69=270	$486,000.00
Tom Kite	2	77-69-66-70=282	$291,600.00
Tommy Tolles	3	72-72-72-67=283	$183,600.00
Tom Watson	4	75-68-69-72=284	$129,600.00
Paul Stankowski	T-5	68-74-69-74=285	$102,600.00
Costantino Rocca	T-5	71-69-70-75=285	$102,600.00
Davis Love III	T-7	72-71-72-71=286	$78,570.00
Fred Couples	T-7	72-69-73-72=286	$78,570.00
Bernhard Langer	T-7	72-72-74-68=286	$78,570.00
Jeff Sluman	T-7	74-67-72-73=286	$78,570.00
Justin Leonard	T-7	76-69-71-70=286	$78,570.00

MCI Classic

Course: Harbour Town G.L., Hilton Head, S.C.
Par: 71 Yardage: 6,915
Last day of event: Sunday, April 20, 1997

Player	Place	Score	Earnings
Nick Price	Win	65-69-69-66=269	$270,000.00
Brad Faxon	T-2	66-69-70-70=275	$132,000.00
Jesper Parnevik	T-2	72-71-66-66=275	$132,000.00
Tom Lehman	T-4	66-73-67-72=278	$62,000.00

Lennie Clements	T-4	67-68-73-70=278	$62,000.00
Hal Sutton	T-4	67-74-71-66=278	$62,000.00
Tom Watson	T-7	68-70-70-71=279	$48,375.00
John Cook	T-7	72-74-66-67=279	$48,375.00
Doug Martin	T-9	71-71-68-71=281	$37,500.00
Willie Wood	T-9	73-69-68-71=281	$37,500.00
Craig Stadler	T-9	68-71-74-68=281	$37,500.00
Scott Hoch	T-9	70-72-74-65=281	$37,500.00
Davis Love III	T-9	70-73-74-64=281	$37,500.00

Greater Greensboro Chrysler Classic

Course: Forest Oaks C.C., Greensboro, N.C.
Par: 72 Yardage: 7,062
Last day of event: Sunday, April 27, 1997

Player	Place	Score	Earnings
Frank Nobilo	Win	69-69-69-67=274	$342,000.00
Playoff: Beat Brad Faxon with par on first extra hole			
Brad Faxon	2	67-70-65-72=274	$205,200.00
Kirk Triplett	3	67-69-69-70=275	$129,200.00
Robert Damron	T-4	66-72-67-71=276	$83,600.00
Billy Andrade	T-4	72-68-67-69=276	$83,600.00
Davis Love III	6	72-69-69-67=277	$68,400.00
Mike Standly	T-7	68-68-71-71=278	$61,275.00
Tom Kite	T-7	67-68-67-76=278	$61,275.00
Phil Mickelson	T-9	71-68-70-70=279	$49,400.00
Rocco Mediate	T-9	72-66-69-72=279	$49,400.00
Mark O'Meara	T-9	72-67-73-67=279	$49,400.00
Ernie Els	T-9	69-69-67-74=279	$49,400.00

Shell Houston Open

Course: TPC at The Woodlands, The Woodlands, Texas
Par: 72 Yardage: 7,042
Last day of event: Sunday, May 4, 1997

Player	Place	Score	Earnings
Phil Blackmar	Win	68-71-67-70=276	$288,000.00
Playoff: Beat Kevin Sutherland with birdie on first extra hole			
Kevin Sutherland	2	68-72-66-70=276	$172,800.00
Steve Elkington	3	69-74-70-65=278	$108,800.00
Hal Sutton	T-4	68-72-71-68=279	$70,400.00
Scott Hoch	T-4	73-68-68-70=279	$70,400.00
Lanny Wadkins	T-6	73-70-71-67=281	$55,600.00
Jerry Kelly	T-6	70-68-69-74=281	$55,600.00
Larry Rinker	T-8	72-69-71-70=282	$43,200.00
J.P. Hayes	T-8	73-72-64-73=282	$43,200.00
Nolan Henke	T-8	73-71-68-70=282	$43,200.00
John Morse	T-8	68-74-69-71=282	$43,200.00
David Ogrin	T-8	69-68-74-71=282	$43,200.00

BellSouth Classic

Course: TPC at Sugarloaf, Duluth, Ga.
Par: 72 Yardage: 7,259
Last day of event: Sunday, May 11, 1997

Player	Place	Score	Earnings
Scott McCarron	Win	70-69-66-69=274	$270,000.00
Lee Janzen	T-2	69-70-70-68=277	$112,000.00
Brian Henninger	T-2	70-71-68-68=277	$112,000.00
David Duval	T-2	66-66-73-72=277	$112,000.00
David Toms	T-5	69-68-70-71=278	$52,687.50
Greg Norman	T-5	70-67-73-68=278	$52,687.50
Hal Sutton	T-5	69-74-68-67=278	$52,687.50
Nick Price	T-5	66-67-75-70=278	$52,687.50

Jay Haas	T-9	68-71-71-70=280	$37,500.00
Andrew Magee	T-9	70-71-68-71=280	$37,500.00
Kevin Sutherland	T-9	71-71-70-68=280	$37,500.00
Bruce Fleisher	T-9	70-72-70-68=280	$37,500.00
Don Pooley	T-9	64-70-77-69=280	$37,500.00

GTE Byron Nelson Classic

Course: TPC at Las Colinas, Cottonwood Valley Course, Irving, Texas
Home course / TPC at Las Colinas, Par: 70 Yardage: 6,899
Last day of event: Sunday, May 18, 1997

Player	Place	Score	Earnings
Tiger Woods	Win	64-64-67-68=263	$324,000.00
Lee Rinker	2	65-63-69-68=265	$194,400.00
Tom Watson	T-3	65-66-69-67=267	$104,400.00
Dan Forsman	T-3	67-64-66-70=267	$104,400.00
Andrew Magee	T-5	66-65-69-68=268	$56,957.15
Bob Tway	T-5	69-65-68-66=268	$56,957.15
Paul Stankowski	T-5	64-66-68-70=268	$56,957.14
Brad Bryant	T-5	65-67-66-70=268	$56,957.14
Chris Perry	T-5	65-67-66-70=268	$56,957.14
Jim Furyk	T-5	63-67-67-71=268	$56,957.14
Mike Standly	T-5	66-63-68-71=268	$56,957.14

Mastercard Colonial

Course: Colonial C.C., Fort Worth, Texas
Par: 70 Yardage: 7,010
Last day of event: Sunday, May 25, 1997

Player	Place	Score	Earnings
David Frost	Win	66-63-69-67=265	$288,000.00
Brad Faxon	T-2	63-66-70-68=267	$140,800.00
David Ogrin	T-2	66-67-62-72=267	$140,800.00
Paul Goydos	T-4	64-65-68-71=268	$70,400.00
Tiger Woods	T-4	67-65-64-72=268	$70,400.00
Dudley Hart	T-6	68-66-68-67=269	$55,600.00
Bob Tway	T-6	65-66-69-69=269	$55,600.00
Jim Furyk	8	64-67-67-72=270	$49,600.00
John Huston	9	67-67-67-70=271	$46,400.00
Glen Day	T-10	69-70-65-68=272	$40,000.00
Loren Roberts	T-10	67-68-66-71=272	$40,000.00
Steve Pate	T-10	69-66-64-73=272	$40,000.00

Memorial Tournament

Course: Muirfield Village G.C., Dubin, Ohio
Par: 72 Yardage: 7,118
Last day of event: Monday, June 2, 1997

Player	Place	Score	Earnings
Vijay Singh	Win	70-65-67=202	$342,000.00
Jim Furyk	T-2	71-66-67=204	$167,200.00
Greg Norman	T-2	71-69-64=204	$167,200.00
Lee Janzen	T-4	70-67-68=205	$78,533.00
Tommy Tolles	T-4	70-64-71=205	$78,533.00
Scott Hoch	T-4	67-65-73=205	$78,533.00
Frank Nobilo	7	71-67-68=206	$63,650.00
Jack Nicklaus	T-8	69-70-69=208	$57,000.00
Tim Herron	T-8	66-72-70=208	$57,000.00
Davis Love III	T-10	70-71-68=209	$45,600.00
Billy Andrade	T-10	66-72-71=209	$45,600.00
Glen Day	T-10	66-74-69=209	$45,600.00
Bob Tway	T-10	74-66-69=209	$45,600.00

Kemper Open

Course: TPC at Avenel, Potomac, Md.
Par: 71 Yardage: 7,005
Last day of event: Sunday, June 8, 1997

Player	Place	Score	Earnings
Justin Leonard	Win	69-69-69-67=274	$270,000.00
Mark Wiebe	2	69-67-66-73=275	$162,000.00
Nick Price	T-3	66-72-72-67=277	$72,000.00
Mike Springer	T-3	68-70-67-72=277	$72,000.00
Greg Norman	T-3	66-71-73-67=277	$72,000.00
Nick Faldo	T-3	73-65-68-71=277	$72,000.00
Loren Roberts	T-7	70-69-69-70=278	$45,187.50
Tim Herron	T-7	69-70-72-67=278	$45,187.50
Jim McGovern	T-7	72-69-68-69=278	$45,187.50
D.A. Weibring	T-7	69-67-75-67=278	$45,187.50

U.S. Open

Course: Congressional C.C., Bethesda, Md.
Par: 70 Yardage: 7,213
Last day of event: Sunday, June 15, 1997

Player	Place	Score	Earnings
Ernie Els	Win	71-67-69-69=276	$465,000.00
Colin Montgomerie	2	65-76-67-69=277	$275,000.00
Tom Lehman	3	67-70-68-73=278	$172,828.00
Jeff Maggert	4	73-66-68-74=281	$120,454.00
Olin Browne	T-5	71-71-69-71=282	$79,875.40
Bob Tway	T-5	71-71-70-70=282	$79,875.40
Jay Haas	T-5	73-69-68-72=282	$79,875.40
Tommy Tolles	T-5	74-67-69-72=282	$79,875.40
Jim Furyk	T-5	74-68-69-71=282	$79,875.40
Scott Hoch	T-10	71-68-72-72=283	$56,949.33
David Ogrin	T-10	70-69-71-73=283	$56,949.34
Scott McCarron	T-10	73-71-69-70=283	$56,949.33

Buick Classic

Course: Westchester C.C., Harrison, N.Y.
Par: 71 Yardage: 6,722
Last day of event: Sunday, June 22, 1997

Player	Place	Score	Earnings
Ernie Els	Win	64-68-67-69=268	$270,000.00
Jeff Maggert	2	67-69-66-68=270	$162,000.00
Jim Furyk	T-3	67-68-69-70=274	$87,000.00
Robert Damron	T-3	71-66-68-69=274	$87,000.00
Jim Carter	5	69-70-71-65=275	$60,000.00
Clarence Rose	T-6	69-69-70-69=277	$50,250.00
Bob Estes	T-6	71-67-71-68=277	$50,250.00
Stewart Cink	T-6	73-68-66-70=277	$50,250.00
Pete Jordan	T-9	69-68-69-72=278	$42,000.00
Brad Fabel	T-9	69-67-74-68=278	$42,000.00

FedEx St. Jude Classic

Course: TPC at Southwind, Germantown, Tenn.
Par: 71 Yardage: 7,006
Last day of event: Sunday, June 29, 1997

Player	Place	Score	Earnings
Greg Norman	Win	68-65-69-66=268	$270,000.00
Dudley Hart	2	69-68-66-66=269	$162,000.00
Craig Parry	T-3	69-69-66-66=270	$87,000.00
Robert Damron	T-3	65-66-69-70=270	$87,000.00
Nick Price	T-5	66-68-68-69=271	$52,687.50

Michael Bradley	T-5	68-67-66-70=271	$52,687.50
Jay Don Blake	T-5	70-64-68-69=271	$52,687.50
Justin Leonard	T-5	66-71-65-69=271	$52,687.50
Tom Byrum	T-9	69-69-67-67=272	$40,500.00
Gene Sauers	T-9	65-67-70-70=272	$40,500.00
Mike Hulbert	T-9	67-67-67-71=272	$40,500.00

Motorola Western Open

Course: Cog Hill G. & C.C. (Dubsdread), Lemont, Ill.
Par: 72 Yardage: 7,073
Last day of event: Sunday, July 6, 1997

Player	Place	Score	Earnings
Tiger Woods	Win	67-72-68-68=275	$360,000.00
Frank Nobilo	2	71-70-67-70=278	$216,000.00
Steve Lowery	T-3	70-72-66-71=279	$104,000.00
Justin Leonard	T-3	71-64-72-72=279	$104,000.00
Jeff Sluman	T-3	69-69-74-67=279	$104,000.00
Jim Furyk	6	67-74-67-72=280	$72,000.00
Jay Delsing	T-7	71-67-71-72=281	$56,166.67
Stuart Appleby	T-7	71-72-70-68=281	$56,166.66
Davis Love III	T-7	72-68-69-72=281	$56,166.67
Tom Watson	T-7	72-72-68-69=281	$56,166.67
Loren Roberts	T-7	70-71-66-74=281	$56,166.66
Steve Pate	T-7	75-67-67-72=281	$56,166.67

Quad City Classic

Course: Oakwood C.C., Coal Valley, Ill.
Par: 70 Yardage: 6,762
Last day of event: Sunday, July 13, 1997

Player	Place	Score	Earnings
David Toms	Win	67-66-67-65=265	$243,000.00
Robert Gamez	T-2	67-65-69-67=268	$100,800.00
Jimmy Johnston	T-2	70-67-69-62=268	$100,800.00
Brandel Chamblee	T-2	71-65-65-67=268	$100,800.00
Brad Fabel	T-5	68-67-65-69=269	$51,300.00
Frank Lickliter II	T-5	71-67-63-68=269	$51,300.00
Russ Cochran	T-7	66-67-68-69=270	$42,075.00
Steve Stricker	T-7	69-68-67-66=270	$42,075.00
Dave Rummells	T-7	68-70-65-67=270	$42,075.00
Kenny Perry	T-10	67-68-68-68=271	$28,012.50
Wayne Levi	T-10	68-67-68-68=271	$28,012.50
Scott Verplank	T-10	67-68-67-69=271	$28,012.50
John Adams	T-10	69-66-68-68=271	$28,012.50
Bob Wolcott	T-10	70-66-68-67=271	$28,012.50
Anthony Painter	T-10	70-69-65-67=271	$28,012.50
Ed Dougherty	T-10	67-65-71-68=271	$28,012.50
John Maginnes	T-10	71-66-67-67=271	$28,012.50

British Open

Course: Royal Troon G.C., Troon, Ayrshire, Scotland
Par: 71 Yardage: 7,079
Last day of event: Sunday, July 20, 1997

Player	Place	Score	Earnings
Justin Leonard	Win	69-66-72-65=272	$418,875.00
Darren Clarke	T-2	67-66-71-71=275	$251,325.00
Jesper Parnevik	T-2	70-66-66-73=275	$251,325.00
Jim Furyk	4	67-72-70-70=279	$150,795.00
Stephen Ames	T-5	74-69-66-71=280	$104,718.75
Padraig Harrington	T-5	75-69-69-67=280	$104,718.75
Peter O'Malley	T-7	73-70-70-68=281	$68,137.00
Fred Couples	T-7	69-68-70-74=281	$68,137.00

Eduardo Romero	T-7	74-68-67-72=281	$68,137.00
Tom Watson	T-10	71-70-70-71=282	$40,714.65
Lee Westwood	T-10	73-70-67-72=282	$40,714.65
Davis Love III	T-10	70-71-74-67=282	$40,714.65
Tom Kite	T-10	72-67-74-69=282	$40,714.65
Mark Calcavecchia	T-10	74-67-72-69=282	$40,714.65
Shigeki Maruyama	T-10	74-69-70-69=282	$40,714.65
Frank Nobilo	T-10	74-72-68-68=282	$40,714.65
Ernie Els	T-10	75-69-69-69=282	$40,714.65
Retief Goosen	T-10	75-69-70-68=282	$40,714.65
Robert Allenby	T-10	76-68-66-72=282	$40,714.65

Deposit Guaranty Golf Classic

Course: Annandale G.C., Madison, Miss.
Par: 72 Yardage: 7,157
Last day of event: Sunday, July 20, 1997

Player	Place	Score	Earnings
Billy Ray Brown	Win	69-66-69-67=271	$180,000.00
Mike Standly	2	69-67-70-66=272	$108,000.00
Mike Brisky	3	64-74-67-68=273	$68,000.00
Mike Springer	T-4	69-69-67-69=274	$36,250.00
Brian Rowell	T-4	69-68-69-68=274	$36,250.00
Brian Claar	T-4	67-69-68-70=274	$36,250.00
Steve Lowery	T-4	69-65-70-70=274	$36,250.00
Blaine McCallister	T-4	70-67-70-67=274	$36,250.00
Steve Jurgensen	T-4	66-67-69-72=274	$36,250.00
Brian Henninger	T-10	68-68-70-69=275	$25,000.00
Don Pooley	T-10	65-68-71-71=275	$25,000.00
Woody Austin	T-10	66-69-71-69=275	$25,000.00

Canon Greater Hartford Open

Course: TPC at River Highlands, Cromwell, Conn.
Par: 70 Yardage: 6,820
Last day of event: Sunday, July 27, 1997

Player	Place	Score	Earnings
Stewart Cink	Win	69-67-65-66=267	$270,000.00
Tom Byrum	T-2	66-68-65-69=268	$112,000.00
Brandel Chamblee	T-2	68-65-69-66=268	$112,000.00
Jeff Maggert	T-2	67-66-64-71=268	$112,000.00
Mark Calcavecchia	5	69-69-67-66=271	$60,000.00
P.H. Horgan III	T-6	67-71-68-66=272	$50,250.00
Wayne Levi	T-6	64-65-70-73=272	$50,250.00
Kelly Gibson	T-6	67-74-65-66=272	$50,250.00
Phil Tataurangi	T-9	69-69-68-67=273	$39,000.00
Steve Pate	T-9	65-68-70-70=273	$39,000.00
Mike Brisky	T-9	69-69-65-70=273	$39,000.00
Doug Barron	T-9	66-68-66-73=273	$39,000.00

Sprint International

Course: Castle Pine G.C., Castle Rock, Colo.(Stableford format)
Par: 72 Yardage: 7,559
Last day of event: Sunday, August 3, 1997

Player	Place	Score	Earnings
Phil Mickelson	Win	14-13-12-9=48	$306,000.00
Stuart Appleby	2	9-10-13-9=41	$183,600.00
Skip Kendall	3	10-12-12-4=38	$115,600.00
Dudley Hart	4	10-10-8-6=34	$81,600.00
Kevin Sutherland	T-5	3-14-8-8=33	$64,600.00
Jay Haas	T-5	15-4-10-4=33	$64,600.00
Jim Furyk	T-7	3-8-12-9=32	$52,983.34
Ernie Els	T-7	5-6-14-7=32	$52,983.33
Larry Mize	T-7	15-8-3-6=32	$52,983.33
Nick Price	10	6-14-7-4=31	$45,900.00

Buick Open

Course: Warwick Hills C.C., Grand Blanc, Mich.
Par: 72 Yardage: 7,105
Last day of event: Sunday, August 10, 1997

Player	Place	Score	Earnings
Vijay Singh	Win	67-73-67-66=273	$270,000.00
Joe Ozaki	T-2	67-71-70-69=277	$83,375.00
Brad Fabel	T-2	69-67-70-71=277	$83,375.00
Curtis Strange	T-2	72-66-68-71=277	$83,375.00
Tom Byrum	T-2	72-68-70-67=277	$83,375.00
Russ Cochran	T-2	68-69-73-67=277	$83,375.00
Ernie Els	T-2	68-63-72-74=277	$83,375.00
Rocco Mediate	T-8	70-71-67-70=278	$43,500.00
Tiger Woods	T-8	72-68-70-68=278	$43,500.00
Dan Forsman	T-8	68-67-73-70=278	$43,500.00

PGA Championship

Course: Winged Foot G.C. (West), Mamaroneck, N.Y.
Par: 70 Yardage: 6,987
Last day of event: Sunday, August 17, 1997

Player	Place	Score	Earnings
Davis Love III	Win	66-71-66-66=269	$470,000.00
Justin Leonard	2	68-70-65-71=274	$280,000.00
Jeff Maggert	3	69-69-73-65=276	$175,000.00
Lee Janzen	4	69-67-74-69=279	$125,000.00
Tom Kite	5	68-71-71-70=280	$105,000.00
Jim Furyk	T-6	69-72-72-68=281	$85,000.00
Scott Hoch	T-6	71-72-68-70=281	$85,000.00
Phil Blackmar	T-6	70-68-74-69=281	$85,000.00
Tom Byrum	9	69-73-70-70=282	$70,000.00
Tom Lehman	T-10	69-72-72-70=283	$60,000.00
Joey Sindelar	T-10	72-71-71-69=283	$60,000.00
Scott McCarron	T-10	74-71-67-71=283	$60,000.00

NEC World Series of Golf

Course: Firestone C.C. (South), Akron, Ohio
Par: 70 Yardage: 7,149
Last day of event: Sunday, August 24, 1997

Player	Place	Score	Earnings
Greg Norman	Win	68-68-70-67=273	$396,000.00
Phil Mickelson	2	67-72-66-72=277	$237,600.00
Fred Funk	T-3	70-69-71-68=278	$114,400.00
Tiger Woods	T-3	67-72-69-70=278	$114,400.00
John Cook	T-3	68-69-67-74=278	$114,400.00
Vijay Singh	6	71-71-71-66=279	$79,200.00
Tom Lehman	T-7	74-66-69-71=280	$70,950.00
Carlos Franco	T-7	75-67-68-70=280	$70,950.00
Davis Love III	T-9	68-71-70-72=281	$59,400.00
David Ogrin	T-9	71-70-67-73=281	$59,400.00
Nick Price	T-9	68-71-68-74=281	$59,400.00

Greater Vancouver Open

Course: Northview G. & C.C. (Ridge Course), Surrey, British Columbia, Canada
Par: 71 Yardage: 6,789
Last day of event: Sunday, August 24, 1997

Player	Place	Score	Earnings
Mark Calcavecchia	Win	68-66-65-66=265	$270,000.00
Andrew Magee	2	65-71-65-65=266	$162,000.00
Bob Estes	3	66-67-69-65=267	$102,000.00
Russ Cochran	4	69-68-66-66=269	$72,000.00

Player	Place	Score	Earnings
P.H. Horgan III	5	71-63-72-64=270	$60,000.00
David Sutherland	T-6	66-68-68-69=271	$45,375.00
Tim Herron	T-6	66-69-67-69=271	$45,375.00
Bill Glasson	T-6	67-68-67-69=271	$45,375.00
John Adams	T-6	66-68-67-70=271	$45,375.00
Payne Stewart	T-6	64-68-68-71=271	$45,375.00
Michael Christie	T-6	71-67-68-65=271	$45,375.00

Greater Milwaukee Open

Course: Brown Deer Park G.C., Milwaukee, Wis.
Par: 71 Yardage: 6,739
Last day of event: Sunday, August 31, 1997

Player	Place	Score	Earnings
Scott Hoch	Win	70-66-66-66=268	$234,000.00
Loren Roberts	T-2	67-69-67-66=269	$114,400.00
David Sutherland	T-2	70-65-65-69=269	$114,400.00
Tom Pernice, Jr.	4	68-69-64-69=270	$62,400.00
Lee Rinker	T-5	68-69-66-68=271	$47,450.00
Fulton Allem	T-5	67-69-64-71=271	$47,450.00
Clarence Rose	T-5	67-66-71-67=271	$47,450.00
Ronnie Black	T-8	70-68-70-64=272	$36,400.00
Bill Glasson	T-8	66-71-68-67=272	$36,400.00
Frank Lickliter II	T-8	67-71-68-66=272	$36,400.00
Jerry Kelly	T-8	71-66-66-69=272	$36,400.00

Bell Canadian Open

Course: Royal Montreal G.C., Ile-Bizard, Quebec, Canada
Par: 70 Yardage: 6,810
Last day of event: Sunday, September 7, 1997

Player	Place	Score	Earnings
Steve Jones	Win	71-68-67-69=275	$270,000.00
Greg Norman	2	66-72-69-69=276	$162,000.00
Phil Tataurangi	3	69-67-72-69=277	$102,000.00
Frank Lickliter II	T-4	68-72-68-70=278	$66,000.00
David Ogrin	T-4	69-70-72-67=278	$66,000.00
Justin Leonard	T-6	70-70-69-70=279	$52,125.00
Davis Love III	T-6	70-67-77-65=279	$52,125.00
David Frost	T-8	71-69-71-69=280	$43,500.00
Payne Stewart	T-8	66-72-72-70=280	$43,500.00
Fulton Allem	T-8	69-69-73-69=280	$43,500.00

CVS Charity Classic

Course: Pleasant Valley C.C., Sutton, Mass.
Par: 71 Yardage: 7,110
Last day of event: Sunday, September 14, 1997

Player	Place	Score	Earnings
Loren Roberts	Win	67-67-68-64=266	$216,000.00
Bill Glasson	2	66-67-67-67=267	$129,600.00
Peter Jacobsen	3	68-65-70-65=268	$81,600.00
Chris Smith	4	68-68-66-67=269	$57,600.00
Brian Henninger	5	72-67-63-68=270	$48,000.00
Kevin Burton	T-6	66-68-69-68=271	$40,200.00
Craig Parry	T-6	69-66-67-69=271	$40,200.00
Bob Estes	T-6	71-69-66-65=271	$40,200.00
Paul Azinger	T-9	69-69-69-65=272	$32,400.00
John Adams	T-9	66-68-67-71=272	$32,400.00
Tim Herron	T-9	71-68-68-65=272	$32,400.00

LaCantera Texas Open

Course: LaCantera G.C., San Antonio, Texas
Par: 72 Yardage: 7,001
Last day of event: Sunday, September 21, 1997

Player	Place	Score	Earnings
Tim Herron	Win	71-67-64-69=271	$252,000.00
Rick Fehr	T-2	70-67-66-70=273	$123,200.00
Brent Geiberger	T-2	67-72-69-65=273	$123,200.00
Duffy Waldorf	4	66-68-70-70=274	$67,200.00
Craig Parry	5	68-68-70-69=275	$56,000.00
Doug Barron	T-6	69-68-70-70=277	$45,325.00
Scott McCarron	T-6	68-71-71-67=277	$45,325.00
Mike Springer	T-6	69-69-67-72=277	$45,325.00
Gene Sauers	T-6	64-73-70-70=277	$45,325.00
Tom Byrum	T-10	70-70-69-70=279	$33,600.00
Steve Jones	T-10	67-71-72-69=279	$33,600.00
Mike Brisky	T-10	65-71-73-70=279	$33,600.00
P.H. Horgan III	T-10	68-70-66-75=279	$33,600.00

B.C. Open

Course: En-Joie G.C., Endicott, N.Y.
Par: 72 Yardage: 6,994
Last day of event: Sunday, September 28, 1997

Player	Place	Score	Earnings
Gabriel Hjertstedt	Win	70-69-66-70=275	$234,000.00
Chris Perry	T-2	69-69-69-69=276	$97,066.67
Andrew Magee	T-2	67-70-69-70=276	$97,066.66
Lee Rinker	T-2	70-68-72-66=276	$97,066.67
Bruce Fleisher	T-5	70-66-71-70=277	$47,450.00
Richard Green	T-5	71-68-69-69=277	$47,450.00
Robert Gamez	T-5	70-67-68-72=277	$47,450.00
Bradley Hughes	T-8	70-71-69-68=278	$36,400.00
Dick Mast	T-8	70-71-70-67=278	$36,400.00
Dave Stockton, Jr.	T-8	68-72-69-69=278	$36,400.00
Grant Waite	T-8	69-67-72-70=278	$36,400.00

Buick Challenge

Course: Callaway Gardens Resort, Pine Mountain, Ga.
Par: 72 Yardage: 7,057
Last day of event: Sunday, October 5, 1997

Player	Place	Score	Earnings
Davis Love III	Win	67-65-67-68=267	$216,000.00
Stewart Cink	2	70-64-67-70=271	$129,600.00
Steve Lowery	T-3	69-71-72-60=272	$69,600.00
Hal Sutton	T-3	67-65-74-66=272	$69,600.00
Jay Haas	5	70-69-68-67=274	$48,000.00
Brandel Chamblee	T-6	67-71-71-66=275	$40,200.00
Doug Martin	T-6	71-65-70-69=275	$40,200.00
Mike Hulbert	T-6	71-69-70-65=275	$40,200.00
David Berganio, Jr.	T-9	69-68-69-70=276	$26,850.00
Tommy Tolles	T-9	70-70-70-66=276	$26,850.00
Mike Brisky	T-9	66-71-69-70=276	$26,850.00
Michael Christie	T-9	69-71-69-67=276	$26,850.00
Grant Waite	T-9	71-70-65-70=276	$26,850.00
Jim Carter	T-9	71-69-68-68=276	$26,850.00
David Duval	T-9	72-69-69-66=276	$26,850.00
Steve Pate	T-9	68-65-75-68=276	$26,850.00

Michelob Championship at Kingsmill

Course: Kingsmill G.C., Williamsburg, Va.
Par: 71　Yardage: 6,797
Last day of event: Sunday, October 12, 1997

Player	Place	Score	Earnings
David Duval	Win	67-66-71-67=271	$279,000.00
Playoff: Beat Grant Waite and Duffy Waldorf with birdie on first extra hole			
Grant Waite	T-2	69-67-68-67=271	$136,400.00
Duffy Waldorf	T-2	63-69-69-70=271	$136,400.00
Fred Funk	4	69-65-70-69=273	$74,400.00
Scott Hoch	5	70-66-69-69=274	$62,000.00
Kirk Triplett	6	66-68-70-71=275	$55,800.00
John Cook	T-7	69-68-68-71=276	$49,987.50
Jim Gallagher, Jr.	T-7	69-68-71-68=276	$49,987.50
Payne Stewart	T-9	68-70-70-69=277	$43,400.00
Loren Roberts	T-9	70-67-71-69=277	$43,400.00

Walt Disney World/Oldsmobile Classic

Course: Walt Disney (Magnolia, Palm), Lake Buena Vista C.C., Lake Buena Vista, Fla.
Home course / Magnolia, Par: 72　Yardage: 7,190
Last day of event: Sunday, October 19, 1997

Player	Place	Score	Earnings
David Duval	Win	65-70-65-70=270	$270,000.00
Playoff: Beat Dan Forsman with par on first extra hole			
Dan Forsman	2	67-69-65-69=270	$162,000.00
Ted Tryba	T-3	67-68-68-69=272	$87,000.00
Len Mattiace	T-3	67-66-65-74=272	$87,000.00
Paul Goydos	5	69-70-68-66=273	$60,000.00
Olin Browne	6	74-64-66-70=274	$54,000.00
Joe Durant	T-7	68-66-71-70=275	$46,750.00
Lee Janzen	T-7	70-67-66-72=275	$46,750.00
Phil Blackmar	T-7	68-66-68-73=275	$46,750.00
Jeff Maggert	T-10	67-69-70-70=276	$32,142.86
Glen Day	T-10	69-70-69-68=276	$32,142.86
Andrew Magee	T-10	66-67-72-71=276	$32,142.86
John Cook	T-10	68-66-70-72=276	$32,142.85
Tommy Tolles	T-10	69-67-68-72=276	$32,142.86
Tom Lehman	T-10	73-65-67-71=276	$32,142.86
Payne Stewart	T-10	64-67-70-75=276	$32,142.85

Las Vegas Invitational

Course: TPC at Summerlin, Desert Inn C.C., Las Vegas Hilton C.C., Las Vegas, Nev.
Home course / TPC at Summerlin, Par: 72　Yardage: 7,243
Last day of event: Sunday, October 26, 1997

Player	Place	Score	Earnings
Bill Glasson	Win	63-65-75-71-66=340	$324,000.00
David Edwards	T-2	68-66-69-72-66=341	$158,400.00
Billy Mayfair	T-2	65-63-73-73-67=341	$158,400.00
Mark Calcavecchia	T-4	66-66-72-71-68=343	$79,200.00
Duffy Waldorf	T-4	65-63-69-75-71=343	$79,200.00
Mike Reid	T-6	67-67-70-70-71=345	$60,300.00
Lee Janzen	T-6	66-72-71-70-66=345	$60,300.00
Kevin Sutherland	T-6	69-63-70-73-70=345	$60,300.00
Brad Fabel	T-9	64-66-77-71-69=347	$50,400.00
Fred Couples	T-9	66-67-69-77-68=347	$50,400.00

The Tour Championship

Course: Champions G.C., Houston, Texas
Par: 71　Yardage: 7,200
Last day of event: Sunday, November 2, 1997

Player	Place	Score	Earnings
David Duval	Win	66-69-70-68=273	$720,000.00
Jim Furyk	2	66-68-73-67=274	$432,000.00
Davis Love III	3	68-68-69-70=275	$276,000.00
Bill Glasson	T-4	68-69-68-72=277	$176,000.00
Mark Calcavecchia	T-4	69-66-72-70=277	$176,000.00
Jesper Parnevik	T-6	66-73-69-70=278	$140,000.00
Brad Faxon	T-6	67-69-69-73=278	$140,000.00
Justin Leonard	T-8	70-69-72-68=279	$124,000.00
Loren Roberts	T-8	72-68-69-70=279	$124,000.00
Vijay Singh	T-10	70-70-70-70=280	$110,800.00
Scott Hoch	T-10	68-65-74-73=280	$110,800.00

1998

It was a huge year for Mark O'Meara, who at age 41 won the Masters and the British Open. At Augusta National, O'Meara birdied the last two holes and beat Fred Couples and David Duval by a shot. At Royal Birkdale, he beat Brian Watts in a four-hole aggregate playoff, 17 to 19. Lee Janzen won his second U.S. Open, closing with a 68 at the Olympic Club and edging Payne Stewart, who had led after each of the first three rounds, by a shot. Vijay Singh won his first major, beating Steve Stricker by two shots in the PGA Championship at Sahalee. Tiger Woods, meanwhile, spent the year rebuilding his swing under the direction of coach Butch Harmon.

Mercedes Championships

Course: La Costa C.C., Carlsbad, Calif.
Par: 72　Yardage: 7,022
Last day of event: Sunday, January 11, 1998

Player	Place	Score	Earnings
Phil Mickelson	Win	68-67-68-68=271	$306,000.00
Mark O'Meara	T-2	71-70-67-64=272	$149,600.00
Tiger Woods	T-2	72-67-69-64=272	$149,600.00
John Cook	T-4	65-70-70-70=275	$74,800.00
Nick Price	T-4	66-70-69-70=275	$74,800.00
Gabriel Hjertstedt	T-6	69-68-69-71=277	$55,462.50
Stewart Cink	T-6	71-67-71-68=277	$55,462.50
David Duval	T-6	68-70-66-73=277	$55,462.50
Mark Calcavecchia	T-6	70-74-66-67=277	$55,462.50
Ernie Els	T-10	67-71-71-69=278	$46,537.50
Frank Nobilo	T-10	67-69-70-72=278	$46,537.50

Bob Hope Chrysler Classic

Course: Bermuda Dunes C.C., PGA West/Palmer, Indian Wells C.C., La Quinta C.C.
Home course / Bermuda Dunes C.C., Par: 72　Yardage: 6,927
Last day of event: Sunday, January 18, 1998

Player	Place	Score	Earnings
Fred Couples	Win	64-70-66-66-66=332	$414,000.00
Playoff: Beat Bruce Lietzke with birdie on first extra hole			
Bruce Lietzke	2	65-71-62-69=332	$248,400.00
Andrew Magee	3	63-68-64-68-70=333	$156,400.00
David Duval	T-4	65-67-68-67-68=335	$101,200.00
Steve Jones	T-4	66-70-65-65-69=335	$101,200.00
Stewart Cink	T-6	65-67-67-68-69=336	$79,925.00
Mark O'Meara	T-6	67-67-65-68-69=336	$79,925.00
Skip Kendall	T-8	69-66-69-68-67=339	$69,000.00
Fuzzy Zoeller	T-8	66-69-68-66-70=339	$69,000.00
John Huston	T-10	67-70-67-68-68=340	$50,983.33
Paul Stankowski	T-10	69-69-65-70-67=340	$50,983.34
Brad Fabel	T-10	64-70-66-69-71=340	$50,983.33
Bob Tway	T-10	65-68-67-69-71=340	$50,983.33
Kirk Triplett	T-10	71-67-69-66-67=340	$50,983.34
Mark Wiebe	T-10	73-65-66-66-70=340	$50,983.33

Phoenix Open

Course: TPC of Scottsdale, Scottsdale, Ariz.
Par: 71 Yardage: 7,059
Last day of event: Sunday, January 25, 1998

Player	Place	Score	Earnings
Jesper Parnevik	Win	68-68-66-67=269	$450,000.00
Tom Watson	T-2	68-70-68-66=272	$165,000.00
Tommy Armour III	T-2	68-70-70-64=272	$165,000.00
Steve Pate	T-2	69-69-70-64=272	$165,000.00
Brent Geiberger	T-2	64-70-72-66=272	$165,000.00
Glen Day	T-6	68-70-69-67=274	$86,875.00
Billy Andrade	T-6	69-67-71-67=274	$86,875.00
Scott McCarron	T-8	67-70-70-68=275	$70,000.00
Dudley Hart	T-8	70-68-69-68=275	$70,000.00
Frank Lickliter II	T-8	72-67-66-70=275	$70,000.00
John Huston	T-8	73-67-68-67=275	$70,000.00

Buick Invitational

Course: Torrey Pines (South), Torrey Pines (North), San Diego, Calif.
Home Course -Par: 72 Yardage: 7,000
Last day of event: Sunday, February 8, 1998

Player	Place	Score	Earnings
Scott Simpson	Win	69-71-64=204	$378,000.00
Playoff: Beat Skip Kendall with birdie on first extra hole			
Skip Kendall	2	71-63-70=204	$226,800.00
Kevin Sutherland	T-3	68-67-70=205	$109,200.00
Tiger Woods	T-3	71-66-68=205	$109,200.00
Davis Love III	T-3	62-73-70=205	$109,200.00
Russ Cochran	T-6	67-70-69=206	$61,350.00
Spike McRoy	T-6	70-66-70=206	$61,350.00
J.L. Lewis	T-6	70-67-69=206	$61,350.00
Brent Geiberger	T-6	67-72-67=206	$61,350.00
Steve Jurgensen	T-6	63-73-70=206	$61,350.00
Tommy Armour III	T-6	67-73-66=206	$61,350.00
Steve Pate	T-6	67-65-74=206	$61,350.00

United Airlines Hawaiian Open

Course: Waialae C.C., Honolulu, Ha.
Par: 72 Yardage: 7,012
Last day of event: Sunday, February 15, 1998

Player	Place	Score	Earnings
John Huston	Win	63-65-66-66=260	$324,000.00
Tom Watson	2	67-64-70-66=267	$194,400.00
Trevor Dodds	3	65-70-65-68=268	$122,400.00
Brett Quigley	T-4	68-68-67-66=269	$74,400.00
Mike Reid	T-4	65-68-69-67=269	$74,400.00
Greg Kraft	T-4	69-67-63-70=269	$74,400.00
Steve Stricker	T-7	66-67-68-69=270	$54,225.00
Olin Browne	T-7	67-66-66-71=270	$54,225.00
Frank Lickliter II	T-7	68-64-66-72=270	$54,225.00
R.W. Eaks	T-7	72-63-70-65=270	$54,225.00

Tucson Chrysler Classic

Course: Omni Tucson National Resort, Tucson, Ariz.
Par: 72 Yardage: 7,148
Last day of event: Sunday, February 22, 1998

Player	Place	Score	Earnings
David Duval	Win	66-62-68-73=269	$360,000.00
Justin Leonard	T-2	65-70-68-70=273	$176,000.00
David Toms	T-2	70-67-68-68=273	$176,000.00

Steve Lowery	T-4	68-70-68-69=275	$88,000.00
Tim Herron	T-4	69-70-67-69=275	$88,000.00
Tom Lehman	T-6	66-71-69-70=276	$67,000.00
Bob Tway	T-6	70-68-71-67=276	$67,000.00
Andrew Magee	T-6	69-68-72-67=276	$67,000.00
Jim Furyk	T-9	69-70-68-70=277	$50,000.00
Tommy Tolles	T-9	69-70-68-70=277	$50,000.00
Scott Hoch	T-9	69-66-71-71=277	$50,000.00
Steve Pate	T-9	70-66-72-69=277	$50,000.00
Joey Sindelar	T-9	72-70-66-69=277	$50,000.00

Nissan Open

Course: Valencia C.C., Valencia, Calif.
Par: 71 Yardage: 6,987
Last day of event: Sunday, March 1, 1998

Player	Place	Score	Earnings
Billy Mayfair	Win	65-71-69-67=272	$378,000.00
Playoff: Beat Tiger Woods with birdie on first extra hole			
Tiger Woods	2	68-73-65-66=272	$226,800.00
Stephen Ames	3	66-71-70-68=275	$142,800.00
Payne Stewart	T-4	70-67-69-70=276	$92,400.00
John Daly	T-4	73-71-66-66=276	$92,400.00
Scott Hoch	T-6	67-71-68-71=277	$67,987.50
Bob Estes	T-6	69-70-67-71=277	$67,987.50
Jeff Gallagher	T-6	69-71-68-69=277	$67,987.50
Tommy Armour III	T-6	69-68-67-73=277	$67,987.50
Scott Verplank	T-10	68-72-70-68=278	$52,500.00
Barry Cheesman	T-10	72-73-67-66=278	$52,500.00
Jay Haas	T-10	73-70-67-68=278	$52,500.00

Doral-Ryder Open

Course: Doral C.C. (Blue), Miami, Fla.
Par: 72 Yardage: 7,125
Last day of event: Sunday, March 8, 1998

Player	Place	Score	Earnings
Michael Bradley	Win	71-66-70-71=278	$360,000.00
Billy Mayfair	T-2	72-70-68-69=279	$176,000.00
John Huston	T-2	70-69-73-67=279	$176,000.00
Mike Brisky	T-4	68-71-71-71=281	$82,666.67
Stewart Cink	T-4	70-68-71-72=281	$82,666.66
Vijay Singh	T-4	71-68-72-70=281	$82,666.67
Davis Love III	T-7	73-72-70-67=282	$64,500.00
Scott Hoch	T-7	72-66-74-70=282	$64,500.00
Bob Tway	T-9	68-71-72-72=283	$48,000.00
Tiger Woods	T-9	70-69-71-73=283	$48,000.00
Len Mattiace	T-9	73-67-72-71=283	$48,000.00
John Cook	T-9	71-66-74-72=283	$48,000.00
Tim Herron	T-9	70-67-76-70=283	$48,000.00
Jim Furyk	T-9	77-62-73-71=283	$48,000.00

Honda Classic

Course: TPC at Heron Bay, Coral Springs, Fla.
Par: 72 Yardage: 7,268
Last day of event: Sunday, March 15, 1998

Player	Place	Score	Earnings
Mark Calcavecchia	Win	70-67-68-65=270	$324,000.00
Vijay Singh	2	70-68-68-67=273	$194,400.00
Colin Montgomerie	3	69-69-71-66=275	$122,400.00
Stuart Appleby	T-4	70-67-72-67=276	$74,400.00
Jeff Maggert	T-4	67-68-76-65=276	$74,400.00
John Daly	T-4	68-76-68-64=276	$74,400.00

Player	Place	Score	Earnings
Kevin Sutherland	T-7	70-68-70-70=278	$52,380.00
Bob Estes	T-7	70-69-70-69=278	$52,380.00
Bob Friend	T-7	70-70-70-68=278	$52,380.00
Brent Geiberger	T-7	70-68-71-69=278	$52,380.00
Craig Stadler	T-7	73-66-71-68=278	$52,380.00

Bay Hill Invitational

Course: Bay Hill Club, Orlando, Fla.
Par: 72 Yardage: 7,207
Last day of event: Sunday, March 22, 1998

Player	Place	Score	Earnings
Ernie Els	Win	67-69-65-73=274	$360,000.00
Bob Estes	T-2	69-71-67-71=278	$176,000.00
Jeff Maggert	T-2	70-71-69-68=278	$176,000.00
Mark Calcavecchia	T-4	70-69-69-71=279	$88,000.00
Bernhard Langer	T-4	68-73-69-69=279	$88,000.00
Craig Parry	T-6	70-71-70-69=280	$69,500.00
Steve Stricker	T-6	67-72-68-73=280	$69,500.00
Jim Furyk	T-8	70-72-69-70=281	$60,000.00
Colin Montgomerie	T-8	71-68-73-69=281	$60,000.00
Craig Stadler	T-10	70-73-70-70=283	$50,000.00
Andrew Magee	T-10	69-74-70-70=283	$50,000.00
Stephen Ames	T-10	69-74-73-67=283	$50,000.00

The Players Championship

Course: TPC at Sawgrass, Ponte Vedra Beach, Fla.
Par: 72 Yardage: 6,950
Last day of event: Sunday, March 29, 1998

Player	Place	Score	Earnings
Justin Leonard	Win	72-69-70-67=278	$720,000.00
Tom Lehman	T-2	72-70-70-68=280	$352,000.00
Glen Day	T-2	66-73-70-71=280	$352,000.00
Mark Calcavecchia	4	69-75-68-69=281	$192,000.00
Len Mattiace	T-5	69-71-72-70=282	$146,000.00
Scott Hoch	T-5	73-69-70-70=282	$146,000.00
Lee Westwood	T-5	74-71-68-69=282	$146,000.00
Nick Price	T-8	71-72-70-70=283	$116,000.00
Phil Mickelson	T-8	69-73-70-71=283	$116,000.00
Payne Stewart	T-8	72-71-75-65=283	$116,000.00

Freeport-McDermott Classic

Course: English Turn G. & C.C., New Orleans, La.
Par: 72 Yardage: 7,116
Last day of event: Sunday, April 5, 1998

Player	Place	Score	Earnings
Lee Westwood	Win	69-68-67-69=273	$306,000.00
Steve Flesch	2	66-68-71-71=276	$183,600.00
Jim Carter	T-3	68-69-71-71=279	$81,600.00
Mark Wiebe	T-3	69-68-71-71=279	$81,600.00
Steve Lowery	T-3	72-66-70-71=279	$81,600.00
Glen Day	T-3	64-75-69-71=279	$81,600.00
Duffy Waldorf	7	67-69-70-74=280	$56,950.00
Ian Woosnam	T-8	70-70-71-71=282	$47,600.00
Trevor Dodds	T-8	67-72-71-72=282	$47,600.00
Bob Estes	T-8	70-71-72-69=282	$47,600.00
Lee Rinker	T-8	71-70-73-68=282	$47,600.00

Masters

Course: Augusta National G.C., Augusta, Ga.
Par: 72 Yardage: 6,925
Last day of event: Sunday, April 12, 1998

Player	Place	Score	Earnings
Mark O'Meara	Win	74-70-68-67=279	$576,000.00
Fred Couples	T-2	69-70-71-70=280	$281,600.00
David Duval	T-2	71-68-74-67=280	$281,600.00
Jim Furyk	4	76-70-67-68=281	$153,600.00
Paul Azinger	5	71-72-69-70=282	$128,000.00
Jack Nicklaus	T-6	73-72-70-68=283	$111,200.00
David Toms	T-6	75-72-72-64=283	$111,200.00
Tiger Woods	T-8	71-72-72-70=285	$89,600.00
Justin Leonard	T-8	74-73-69-69=285	$89,600.00
Colin Montgomerie	T-8	71-75-69-70=285	$89,600.00
Darren Clarke	T-8	76-73-67-69=285	$89,600.00

MCI Classic

Course: Harbour Town G.L., Hilton Head, S.C.
Par: 71 Yardage: 6,916
Last day of event: Sunday, April 19, 1998

Player	Place	Score	Earnings
Davis Love III	Win	67-68-66-65=266	$342,000.00
Glen Day	2	67-67-72-67=273	$205,200.00
Payne Stewart	T-3	69-71-64-72=276	$110,200.00
Phil Mickelson	T-3	67-71-65-73=276	$110,200.00
Fulton Allem	5	68-71-68-70=277	$76,000.00
Nick Price	T-6	67-69-70-72=278	$61,512.50
Joey Sindelar	T-6	69-67-70-72=278	$61,512.50
Doug Tewell	T-6	66-73-67-72=278	$61,512.50
Frank Lickliter II	T-6	67-66-75-70=278	$61,512.50
Larry Mize	T-10	69-70-70-70=279	$45,600.00
John Huston	T-10	66-73-67-73=279	$45,600.00
Ernie Els	T-10	73-68-70-68=279	$45,600.00
Kenny Perry	T-10	74-68-66-71=279	$45,600.00

Greater Greensboro Chrysler Classic

Course: Forest Oaks C.C., Greensboro, N.C.
Par: 72 Yardage: 7,062
Last day of event: Sunday, April 26, 1998

Player	Place	Score	Earnings
Trevor Dodds	Win	68-69-70-69=276	$396,000.00
Playoff: Beat Scott Verplank with par on first extra hole			
Scott Verplank	2	67-71-66-72=276	$237,600.00
Bob Estes	3	67-65-72-73=277	$149,600.00
Neal Lancaster	4	70-67-70-71=278	$105,600.00
Frank Nobilo	5	71-65-71-72=279	$88,000.00
Fred Funk	T-6	72-69-67-72=280	$76,450.00
Phil Mickelson	T-6	74-65-71-70=280	$76,450.00
Michael Bradley	T-8	69-71-72-69=281	$63,800.00
Lennie Clements	T-8	68-68-72-73=281	$63,800.00
Hal Sutton	T-8	65-67-74-75=281	$63,800.00

Shell Houston Open

Course: TPC at The Woodlands, The Woodlands, Texas
Par: 72 Yardage: 7,018
Last day of event: Sunday, May 3, 1998

Player	Place	Score	Earnings
David Duval	Win	69-70-73-64=276	$360,000.00
Jeff Maggert	2	71-71-64-71=277	$216,000.00

Player	Place	Score	Earnings
Fred Couples	3	72-68-70-68=278	$136,000.00
Lee Janzen	T-4	69-69-71-70=279	$88,000.00
Dudley Hart	T-4	70-72-70-67=279	$88,000.00
Jerry Kelly	T-6	71-71-70-68=280	$64,750.00
Hal Sutton	T-6	70-73-69-68=280	$64,750.00
Dan Forsman	T-6	68-70-68-74=280	$64,750.00
Dave Stockton, Jr.	T-6	74-71-67-68=280	$64,750.00
Stephen Ames	10	72-68-71-70=281	$54,000.00

BellSouth Classic

Course: TPC at Sugarloaf, Duluth, Ga.
Par: 72 Yardage: 7,259
Last day of event: Sunday, May 10, 1998

Player	Place	Score	Earnings
Tiger Woods	Win	69-67-63-72=271	$324,000.00
Jay Don Blake	2	67-68-67-70=272	$194,400.00
Steve Flesch	T-3	66-71-68-69=274	$104,400.00
Esteban Toledo	T-3	66-75-66-67=274	$104,400.00
John Huston	T-5	68-68-71-68=275	$61,020.00
Stewart Cink	T-5	67-71-65-72=275	$61,020.00
Bill Glasson	T-5	68-73-68-66=275	$61,020.00
Bob Tway	T-5	73-69-66-67=275	$61,020.00
Scott Verplank	T-5	67-74-69-65=275	$61,020.00
Trevor Dodds	T-10	71-67-72-66=276	$46,800.00
Clark Dennis	T-10	72-65-71-68=276	$46,800.00

GTE Byron Nelson Classic

Course: TPC at Las Colinas– Home course
Cottonwood Valley Course
Irving, Texas
Home course / Par: 70 Yardage: 6,924
Last day of event: Sunday, May 17, 1998

Player	Place	Score	Earnings
John Cook	Win	66-68-66-65=265	$450,000.00
Hal Sutton	T-2	66-65-68-69=268	$186,666.67
Harrison Frazar	T-2	64-68-66-70=268	$186,666.66
Fred Couples	T-2	66-67-63-72=268	$186,666.67
Steve Stricker	5	67-72-65-65=269	$100,000.00
Phil Mickelson	T-6	66-68-69-67=270	$83,750.00
Bob Friend	T-6	63-70-68-69=270	$83,750.00
Scott McCarron	T-6	66-72-68-64=270	$83,750.00
Jim Carter	T-9	68-68-66-69=271	$67,500.00
Tim Herron	T-9	69-69-67-66=271	$67,500.00
Clark Dennis	T-9	67-72-63-69=271	$67,500.00

Mastercard Colonial

Course: Colonial C.C., Fort Worth, Texas
Par: 70 Yardage: 7,010
Last day of event: Sunday, May 24, 1998

Player	Place	Score	Earnings
Tom Watson	Win	68-66-65-66=265	$414,000.00
Jim Furyk	2	66-67-66-68=267	$248,400.00
Jeff Sluman	3	67-67-66-69=269	$156,400.00
Harrison Frazar	4	64-67-68-71=270	$110,400.00
John Cook	5	68-66-69-68=271	$92,000.00
Jim Gallagher, Jr.	T-6	69-69-68-66=272	$79,925.00
Kenny Perry	T-6	68-65-69-70=272	$79,925.00
Brian Henninger	T-8	70-66-68-69=273	$69,000.00
Justin Leonard	T-8	70-70-67-66=273	$69,000.00
Stuart Appleby	T-10	68-69-69-68=274	$55,200.00
Craig Parry	T-10	68-69-69-68=274	$55,200.00

Player	Place	Score	Earnings
Dan Forsman	T-10	69-67-71-67=274	$55,200.00
Steve Flesch	T-10	68-66-72-68=274	$55,200.00

Memorial Tournament

Course: Muirfield Village G.C., Dubin, Ohio
Par: 72 Yardage: 7,163
Last day of event: Sunday, May 31, 1998

Player	Place	Score	Earnings
Fred Couples	Win	68-67-67-69=271	$396,000.00
Andrew Magee	2	67-71-68-69=275	$237,600.00
David Duval	3	74-66-67-69=276	$149,600.00
Jim Furyk	4	74-68-67-68=277	$105,600.00
Brandel Chamblee	T-5	71-72-66-69=278	$83,600.00
Davis Love III	T-5	66-73-66-73=278	$83,600.00
Mark Calcavecchia	T-7	68-69-72-70=279	$66,275.00
Tim Herron	T-7	72-72-67-68=279	$66,275.00
Ted Tryba	T-7	67-71-68-73=279	$66,275.00
Ernie Els	T-7	67-72-67-73=279	$66,275.00

Kemper Open

Course: TPC at Avenel, Potomac, Md.
Par: 71 Yardage: 7,005
Last day of event: Sunday, June 7, 1998

Player	Place	Score	Earnings
Stuart Appleby	Win	70-63-69-72=274	$360,000.00
Scott Hoch	2	69-68-68-70=275	$216,000.00
Mark O'Meara	T-3	68-70-71-69=278	$90,200.00
Brad Fabel	T-3	69-66-70-73=278	$90,200.00
Clark Dennis	T-3	70-65-70-73=278	$90,200.00
Tommy Tolles	T-3	70-68-66-74=278	$90,200.00
Fred Funk	T-3	64-66-71-77=278	$90,200.00
Steve Stricker	T-8	70-69-71-69=279	$58,000.00
Hal Sutton	T-8	69-69-69-72=279	$58,000.00
Craig Parry	T-8	67-66-76-70=279	$58,000.00

Buick Classic

Course: Westchester C.C., Harrison, N.Y.
Par: 71 Yardage: 6,722
Last day of event: Sunday, June 14, 1998

Player	Place	Score	Earnings
J.P. Hayes	Win	66-67-68=201	$324,000.00
Playoff: Beat Jim Furyk with birdie on first extra hole			
Jim Furyk	2	70-63-68=201	$194,400.00
Tom Lehman	3	67-72-65=204	$122,400.00
Bruce Fleisher	4	68-68-69=205	$86,400.00
Jeff Maggert	T-5	68-71-67=206	$68,400.00
Tom Byrum	T-5	69-71-66=206	$68,400.00
Bob Tway	T-7	66-70-71=207	$58,050.00
Kevin Sutherland	T-7	64-70-73=207	$58,050.00
Steve Lowery	9	66-72-70=208	$52,200.00
Chris Perry	T-10	72-69-68=209	$46,800.00
Jesper Parnevik	T-10	69-67-73=209	$46,800.00

U.S. Open

Course: The Olympic Club (Lake Course), San Francisco, Calif.
Par: 70 Yardage: 6,797
Last day of event: Sunday, June 21, 1998

Player	Place	Score	Earnings
Lee Janzen	Win	73-66-73-68=280	$535,000.00

Payne Stewart	2	66-71-70-74=281	$315,000.00
Bob Tway	3	68-70-73-73=284	$201,730.00
Nick Price	4	73-68-71-73=285	$140,597.00
Steve Stricker	T-5	73-71-69-73=286	$107,392.00
Tom Lehman	T-5	68-75-68-75=286	$107,392.00
Lee Westwood	T-7	72-74-70-71=287	$83,794.00
Jeff Maggert	T-7	69-69-75-74=287	$83,794.00
David Duval	T-7	75-68-75-69=287	$83,794.00
Phil Mickelson	T-10	71-73-74-70=288	$64,490.00
Jeff Sluman	T-10	72-74-74-68=288	$64,490.00
Stewart Cink	T-10	73-68-73-74=288	$64,490.00
Stuart Appleby	T-10	73-74-70-71=288	$64,490.00

Motorola Western Open

Course: Cog Hill G. & C.C. (Dubsdread), Lemont, Ill.
Par: 72 Yardage: 7,073
Last day of event: Sunday, June 28, 1998

Player	Place	Score	Earnings
Joe Durant	Win	68-67-70-66=271	$396,000.00
Vijay Singh	2	68-68-65-72=273	$237,600.00
Lee Janzen	T-3	68-69-69-71=277	$127,600.00
Dudley Hart	T-3	74-70-70-63=277	$127,600.00
Steve Stricker	T-5	71-69-67-71=278	$83,600.00
Greg Kraft	T-5	67-70-66-75=278	$83,600.00
Scott Hoch	T-7	71-67-70-71=279	$70,950.00
Jim Furyk	T-7	72-71-68-68=279	$70,950.00
Justin Leonard	T-9	72-72-69-68=281	$49,225.00
Joe Ozaki	T-9	71-69-68-73=281	$49,225.00
Clark Dennis	T-9	71-69-73-68=281	$49,225.00
Stuart Appleby	T-9	73-71-68-69=281	$49,225.00
Harrison Frazar	T-9	74-70-69-68=281	$49,225.00
Dan Forsman	T-9	74-71-68-68=281	$49,225.00
Scott Verplank	T-9	75-71-68-67=281	$49,225.00
Tiger Woods	T-9	76-67-69-69=281	$49,225.00

Canon Greater Hartford Open

Course: TPC at River Highlands, Cromwell, Conn.
Par: 70 Yardage: 6,820
Last day of event: Sunday, July 5, 1998

Player	Place	Score	Earnings
Olin Browne	Win	67-66-66-67=266	$360,000.00
Playoff: Beat Stewart Cink and Larry Mize with birdie on first extra hole			
Stewart Cink	T-2	67-65-67-67=266	$176,000.00
Larry Mize	T-2	68-63-66-69=266	$176,000.00
Doug Tewell	T-4	66-66-68-67=267	$82,666.66
Fred Funk	T-4	70-66-65-66=267	$82,666.67
Duffy Waldorf	T-4	70-67-64-66=267	$82,666.67
David Duval	T-7	68-65-66-69=268	$64,500.00
Scott Hoch	T-7	65-68-64-71=268	$64,500.00
Kenny Perry	T-9	65-69-67-68=269	$54,000.00
Len Mattiace	T-9	67-69-66-67=269	$54,000.00
Joey Sindelar	T-9	69-66-69-65=269	$54,000.00

Quad City Classic

Course: Oakwood C.C., Coal Valley, Ill.
Par: 70 Yardage: 6,762
Last day of event: Sunday, July 12, 1998

Player	Place	Score	Earnings
Steve Jones	Win	64-65-68-66=263	$279,000.00
Scott Gump	2	65-67-64-68=264	$167,400.00
Kenny Perry	3	65-65-67-68=265	$105,400.00

David Toms	4	65-65-65-71=266	$74,400.00
Scott McCarron	T-5	67-66-66-68=267	$54,443.75
Brad Fabel	T-5	68-66-65-68=267	$54,443.75
D.A. Weibring	T-5	64-68-65-70=267	$54,443.75
Fred Funk	T-5	66-70-65-66=267	$54,443.75
Russ Cochran	T-9	65-66-70-67=268	$40,300.00
Hal Sutton	T-9	64-68-71-65=268	$40,300.00
Dave Stockton, Jr.	T-9	64-71-68-65=268	$40,300.00
Scott Verplank	T-9	67-66-71-64=268	$40,300.00

British Open

Course: Royal Birkdale G.C., Southport, Lancashire, England
Par: 70 Yardage: 7,018
Last day of event: Sunday, July 19, 1998

Player	Place	Score	Earnings
Mark O'Meara	Win	72-68-72-68=280	$493,500.00
Playoff: Won four-hole aggregate playoff (4-4-5-4=17) with Brian Watts (5-4-5-5=19)			
Brian Watts	2	68-69-73-70=280	$309,260.00
Tiger Woods	3	65-73-77-66=281	$222,075.00
Jesper Parnevik	T-4	68-72-72-70=282	$126,116.67
Jim Furyk	T-4	70-70-72-70=282	$126,116.67
Raymond Russell	T-4	68-73-75-66=282	$126,116.67
Justin Rose	T-4	72-66-75-69=282	
Davis Love III	8	67-73-77-68=285	$81,427.50
Costantino Rocca	T-9	72-74-70-70=286	$67,198.25
Thomas Bjorn	T-9	68-71-76-71=286	$67,198.25

Deposit Guaranty Golf Classic

Course: Annandale G.C., Madison, Miss.
Par: 72 Yardage: 7,157
Last day of event: Sunday, July 19, 1998

Player	Place	Score	Earnings
Fred Funk	Win	69-64-69-68=270	$216,000.00
Tim Loustalot	T-2	69-69-68-66=272	$89,600.00
Franklin Langham	T-2	67-67-70-68=272	$89,600.00
Paul Goydos	T-2	66-66-72-68=272	$89,600.00
John Maginnes	T-5	70-71-66-66=273	$45,600.00
P.H. Horgan III	T-5	76-66-66-65=273	$45,600.00
Allen Doyle	T-7	67-69-69-69=274	$36,150.00
Jerry Kelly	T-7	70-66-70-68=274	$36,150.00
Chris Smith	T-7	66-68-71-69=274	$36,150.00
Kirk Triplett	T-7	68-72-68-66=274	$36,150.00

CVS Charity Classic

Course: Pleasant Valley C.C., Sutton, Mass.
Par: 71 Yardage: 7,110
Last day of event: Sunday, July 26, 1998

Player	Place	Score	Earnings
Steve Pate	Win	70-65-67-67=269	$270,000.00
Bradley Hughes	T-2	68-69-67-66=270	$132,000.00
Scott Hoch	T-2	68-68-69-65=270	$132,000.00
Willie Wood	T-4	64-69-68-70=271	$62,000.00
Nolan Henke	T-4	69-65-70-67=271	$62,000.00
Mike Heinen	T-4	74-65-65-67=271	$62,000.00
Mark Wiebe	T-7	69-67-68-68=272	$43,650.00
Bill Glasson	T-7	69-68-67-68=272	$43,650.00
Dave Stockton, Jr.	T-7	67-68-66-71=272	$43,650.00
Esteban Toledo	T-7	69-71-68-64=272	$43,650.00
Loren Roberts	T-7	71-70-65-66=272	$43,650.00

FedEx St. Jude Classic

Course: TPC at Southwind, Germantown, Tenn.
Par: 71 Yardage: 7,006
Last day of event: Sunday, August 2, 1998

Player	Place	Score	Earnings
Nick Price	Win	65-67-70-66=268	$324,000.00

Playoff: Beat Jeff Sluman with birdie on second extra hole

Player	Place	Score	Earnings
Jeff Sluman	2	70-67-66-65=268	$194,400.00
Glen Day	3	69-64-72-65=270	$122,400.00
Bob Estes	4	68-67-67-69=271	$86,400.00
Tim Conley	5	68-68-67-69=272	$72,000.00
Paul Goydos	6	72-66-69-67=274	$64,800.00
Kirk Triplett	T-7	68-70-69-68=275	$54,225.00
Jay Haas	T-7	70-67-70-68=275	$54,225.00
Paul Azinger	T-7	65-69-69-72=275	$54,225.00
Robert Damron	T-7	68-74-66-67=275	$54,225.00

Buick Open

Course: Warwick Hills C.C., Grand Blanc, Mich.
Par: 72 Yardage: 7,105
Last day of event: Sunday, August 9, 1998

Player	Place	Score	Earnings
Billy Mayfair	Win	70-69-65-67=271	$324,000.00
Scott Verplank	2	71-67-71-64=273	$194,400.00
Andrew Magee	3	69-71-70-64=274	$122,400.00
Tiger Woods	T-4	71-67-69-68=275	$79,200.00
Eric Booker	T-4	71-68-70-66=275	$79,200.00
Steve Stricker	T-6	69-67-68-72=276	$62,550.00
Joey Sindelar	T-6	69-71-72-64=276	$62,550.00
Jeff Gallagher	T-8	70-70-71-66=277	$50,400.00
Brandel Chamblee	T-8	65-68-72-72=277	$50,400.00
Vijay Singh	T-8	66-70-69-72=277	$50,400.00
Phil Blackmar	T-8	67-68-70-72=277	$50,400.00

PGA Championship

Course: Sahalee C.C., Redmond, Wash.
Par: 70 Yardage: 6,906
Last day of event: Sunday, August 16, 1998

Player	Place	Score	Earnings
Vijay Singh	Win	70-66-67-68=271	$540,000.00
Steve Stricker	2	69-68-66-70=273	$324,000.00
Steve Elkington	3	69-69-69-67=274	$204,000.00
Mark O'Meara	T-4	69-70-69-68=276	$118,000.00
Frank Lickliter II	T-4	68-71-69-68=276	$118,000.00
Nick Price	T-4	70-73-68-65=276	$118,000.00
Davis Love III	T-7	70-68-69-70=277	$89,500.00
Billy Mayfair	T-7	73-67-67-70=277	$89,500.00
John Cook	9	71-68-70-69=278	$80,000.00
Tiger Woods	T-10	66-72-70-71=279	$69,000.00
Kenny Perry	T-10	69-72-70-68=279	$69,000.00
Skip Kendall	T-10	72-68-68-71=279	$69,000.00

AT&T Pebble Beach Pro-Am

Courses: Pebble Beach G.L., Spyglass Hill G.C., Poppy Hills G.C., Pebble Beach, Calif.
Home Course / Pebble Beach G.L., Par: 72 Yardage: 6,799
Last day of event: Monday, August 17, 1998
(First two days played in February, but because of poor weather final round was postponed six months)

Player	Place	Score	Earnings
Phil Mickelson	Win	65-70-67=202	$450,000.00

Player	Place	Score	Earnings
Tom Pernice, Jr.	2	67-69-67=203	$270,000.00
Paul Azinger	T-3	67-69-68=204	$130,000.00
Jim Furyk	T-3	69-67-68=204	$130,000.00
J.P. Hayes	T-3	70-67-67=204	$130,000.00
Jay Haas	T-6	68-67-70=205	$83,750.00
Steve Elkington	T-6	70-68-67=205	$83,750.00
Fuzzy Zoeller	T-6	70-70-65=205	$83,750.00
Bob Gilder	T-9	68-70-68=206	$65,000.00
Chris Smith	T-9	69-67-70=206	$65,000.00
Tom Lehman	T-9	64-71-71=206	$65,000.00
Tom Watson	T-9	67-67-72=206	$65,000.00

Sprint International

Course: Castle Pine G.C., Castle Rock, Colo.(Stableford format)
Par: 72 Yardage: 7,559
Last day of event: Sunday, August 23, 1998

Player	Place	Score	Earnings
Vijay Singh	Win	15-12-6-14=47	$360,000.00
Phil Mickelson	T-2	8-5-16-12=41	$176,000.00
Willie Wood	T-2	9-8-15-9=41	$176,000.00
Tiger Woods	4	14-3-14-7=38	$96,000.00
Rocco Mediate	5	7-9-14-7=37	$80,000.00
Bob Tway	T-6	4-9-7-16=36	$64,750.00
Brad Faxon	T-6	3-9-11-13=36	$64,750.00
Brandt Jobe	T-6	13-9-5-9=36	$64,750.00
Steve Flesch	T-6	12-11-5-8=36	$64,750.00
Steve Elkington	10	9-8-8-10=35	$54,000.00

NEC World Series of Golf

Course: Firestone C.C. (South), Akron, Ohio
Par: 70 Yardage: 7,149
Last day of event: Sunday, August 30, 1998

Player	Place	Score	Earnings
David Duval	Win	69-66-66-68=269	$405,000.00
Phil Mickelson	2	66-71-66-68=271	$243,000.00
Davis Love III	3	71-69-67-65=272	$153,000.00
John Cook	4	71-69-62-71=273	$108,000.00
Tiger Woods	T-5	67-68-70-70=275	$85,500.00
Loren Roberts	T-5	72-67-69-67=275	$85,500.00
Mark O'Meara	T-7	72-67-65-72=276	$72,562.50
Joe Durant	T-7	73-67-70-66=276	$72,562.50
Scott Hoch	T-9	70-69-71-69=279	$63,000.00
Craig Parry	T-9	67-68-72-72=279	$63,000.00

Greater Vancouver Open

Course: Northview G. & C.C. (Ridge Course)
Surrey, British Columbia, Canada
Par: 71 Yardage: 6,789
Last day of event: Sunday, August 30, 1998

Player	Place	Score	Earnings
Brandel Chamblee	Win	67-64-68-66=265	$360,000.00
Payne Stewart	2	64-69-65-70=268	$216,000.00
Lee Porter	3	67-67-71-66=271	$136,000.00
Brian Claar	4	68-68-69-67=272	$96,000.00
Bob Estes	T-5	67-70-67-69=273	$65,500.00
Hugh Royer III	T-5	67-68-70-68=273	$65,500.00
Jeff Maggert	T-5	68-67-70-68=273	$65,500.00
Mike Weir	T-5	70-66-68-69=273	$65,500.00
Russ Cochran	T-5	71-67-66-69=273	$65,500.00
Omar Uresti	T-5	71-68-68-66=273	$65,500.00

Greater Milwaukee Open

Course: Brown Deer Park G.C., Milwaukee, Wis.
Par: 71 Yardage: 6,739
Last day of event: Sunday, September 6, 1998

Player	Place	Score	Earnings
Jeff Sluman	Win	68-66-63-68=265	$324,000.00
Steve Stricker	2	68-63-67-68=266	$194,400.00
Mark Calcavecchia	T-3	66-64-69-69=268	$93,600.00
Nolan Henke	T-3	70-62-67-69=268	$93,600.00
Chris Perry	T-3	68-62-67-71=268	$93,600.00
Doug Barron	6	67-67-68-67=269	$64,800.00
Mark Carnevale	T-7	66-66-69-69=270	$58,050.00
Fred Funk	T-7	68-70-65-67=270	$58,050.00
Gabriel Hjertstedt	T-9	66-67-69-69=271	$46,800.00
Tom Byrum	T-9	67-68-69-67=271	$46,800.00
Kevin Wentworth	T-9	68-65-68-70=271	$46,800.00
Billy Andrade	T-9	74-64-65-68=271	$46,800.00

Bell Canadian Open

Course: Glen Abbey G.C., Oakville, Ontario, Canada
Par: 72 Yardage: 7,112
Last day of event: Sunday, September 13, 1998

Player	Place	Score	Earnings
Billy Andrade	Win	68-69-69-69=275	$396,000.00
Playoff: Beat Bob Friend with par on first extra hole			
Bob Friend	2	69-67-68-71=275	$237,600.00
Mike Hulbert	3	72-70-66-68=276	$149,600.00
Hal Sutton	T-4	71-69-67-73=280	$90,933.33
Bradley Hughes	T-4	73-72-69-66=280	$90,933.34
Glen Day	T-4	74-71-64-71=280	$90,933.33
Mike Standly	T-7	72-71-71-67=281	$70,950.00
Sandy Lyle	T-7	75-70-66-70=281	$70,950.00
Mike Small	T-9	68-71-71-72=282	$57,200.00
Scott Verplank	T-9	68-71-71-72=282	$57,200.00
Chris DiMarco	T-9	73-65-71-73=282	$57,200.00
Jay Delsing	T-9	76-68-68-70=282	$57,200.00

B.C. Open

Course: En-Joie G.C., Endicott, N.Y.
Par: 72 Yardage: 6,994
Last day of event: Sunday, September 20, 1998

Player	Place	Score	Earnings
Chris Perry	Win	67-70-69-67=273	$270,000.00
Peter Jacobsen	2	68-70-71-67=276	$162,000.00
Nolan Henke	3	69-69-67-72=277	$102,000.00
Robert Allenby	T-4	69-70-71-68=278	$62,000.00
Ted Tryba	T-4	72-69-67-70=278	$62,000.00
Curt Byrum	T-4	71-73-69-65=278	$62,000.00
Doug Barron	T-7	67-71-70-71=279	$48,375.00
Mike Weir	T-7	71-68-69-71=279	$48,375.00
Skip Kendall	T-9	71-69-70-70=280	$34,714.29
Chris DiMarco	T-9	66-70-72-72=280	$34,714.29
Brian Henninger	T-9	69-69-70-72=280	$34,714.29
Brett Quigley	T-9	72-71-69-68=280	$34,714.29
Richard Coughlan	T-9	69-71-67-73=280	$34,714.28
R.W. Eaks	T-9	73-65-69-73=280	$34,714.28
Bruce Fleisher	T-9	69-72-63-76=280	$34,714.28

Westin Texas Open

Course: LaCantera G.C., San Antonio, Texas
Par: 72 Yardage: 7,001
Last day of event: Sunday, September 27, 1998

Player	Place	Score	Earnings
Hal Sutton	Win	67-68-67-68=270	$306,000.00
Justin Leonard	T-2	67-67-69-68=271	$149,600.00
Jay Haas	T-2	70-69-64-68=271	$149,600.00
Steve Lowery	T-4	70-70-69-64=273	$66,937.50
Loren Roberts	T-4	67-68-71-67=273	$66,937.50
Andrew Magee	T-4	68-72-67-66=273	$66,937.50
Mike Reid	T-4	70-69-72-62=273	$66,937.50
Scott Gump	T-8	68-70-65-71=274	$51,000.00
Jeff Maggert	T-8	71-68-69-66=274	$51,000.00
Corey Pavin	10	71-68-67-69=275	$45,900.00

Buick Challenge

Course: Callaway Gardens Resort, Pine Mountain, Ga.
Par: 72 Yardage: 7,057
Last day of event: Sunday, October 4, 1998

Player	Place	Score	Earnings
Steve Elkington	Win	66-70-66-65=267	$270,000.00
Playoff: Beat Fred Funk with par on first extra hole			
Fred Funk	2	63-67-68-69=267	$162,000.00
Bill Glasson	3	69-65-65-69=268	$102,000.00
J.L. Lewis	4	66-69-66-68=269	$72,000.00
Skip Kendall	5	71-70-67-63=271	$60,000.00
David Duval	T-6	66-68-70-69=273	$52,125.00
Steve Flesch	T-6	67-66-69-71=273	$52,125.00
Jeff Maggert	T-8	69-69-69-67=274	$39,000.00
Chris Perry	T-8	70-68-69-67=274	$39,000.00
Jim Carter	T-8	63-71-69-71=274	$39,000.00
Neal Lancaster	T-8	70-67-66-71=274	$39,000.00
Ben Bates	T-8	71-69-67-67=274	$39,000.00
Hal Sutton	T-8	72-66-67-69=274	$39,000.00

Michelob Championship at Kingsmill

Course: Kingsmill G.C., Williamsburg, Va.
Par: 71 Yardage: 6,797
Last day of event: Sunday, October 11, 1998

Player	Place	Score	Earnings
David Duval	Win	65-67-68-68=268	$342,000.00
Phil Tataurangi	2	65-68-69-69=271	$205,200.00
Barry Cheesman	3	69-68-69-66=272	$129,200.00
Bradley Hughes	T-4	68-67-69-69=273	$83,600.00
Payne Stewart	T-4	70-67-67-69=273	$83,600.00
Billy Mayfair	T-6	67-70-70-68=275	$61,512.50
John Huston	T-6	69-70-68-68=275	$61,512.50
Frank Lickliter II	T-6	66-67-70-72=275	$61,512.50
Gary Hallberg	T-6	68-67-66-74=275	$61,512.50
Corey Pavin	T-10	67-70-70-70=277	$47,500.00
Tommy Armour III	T-10	70-71-70-66=277	$47,500.00
Jeff Sluman	T-10	68-72-71-66=277	$47,500.00

Las Vegas Invitational

Course: TPC at Summerlin, Desert Inn C.C., Las Vegas Hilton C.C., Las Vegas, Nev.
Home course / TPC at Summerlin, Par: 72 Yardage: 7,243
Last day of event: Sunday, October 18, 1998

Player	Place	Score	Earnings
Jim Furyk	Win	67-68-69-63-68=335	$360,000.00
Mark Calcavecchia	2	65-71-69-65-66=336	$216,000.00
Scott Verplank	3	67-68-69-67-67=338	$136,000.00
Bob Tway	4	68-65-69-72-65=339	$96,000.00
Davis Love III	5	70-66-68-70-66=340	$80,000.00
Paul Stankowski	T-6	67-71-68-70-65=341	$69,500.00

Player	Place	Score	Earnings
Justin Leonard	T-6	70-66-71-66-68=341	$69,500.00
Rick Fehr	T-8	69-65-71-69-68=342	$60,000.00
Kirk Triplett	T-8	70-65-72-66-69=342	$60,000.00
Brandel Chamblee	T-10	69-68-70-68-68=343	$52,000.00
Kevin Wentworth	T-10	71-70-68-67-67=343	$52,000.00

Walt Disney World/Oldsmobile Classic

Course: Walt Disney (Magnolia, Palm), Lake Buena Vista, Fla.
Home course / Magnolia, Par: 72 Yardage: 7,190
Last day of event: Sunday, October 25, 1998

Player	Place	Score	Earnings
John Huston	Win	67-70-69-66=272	$360,000.00
Davis Love III	2	73-64-65-71=273	$216,000.00
Brent Geiberger	3	72-70-68-65=275	$136,000.00
Rocco Mediate	T-4	67-70-71-68=276	$82,666.67
Jesper Parnevik	T-4	66-72-69-69=276	$82,666.66
Tom Purtzer	T-4	69-68-72-67=276	$82,666.67
Doug Martin	T-7	69-68-68-72=277	$60,250.00
Nolan Henke	T-7	69-70-72-66=277	$60,250.00
Fred Funk	T-7	72-67-68-70=277	$60,250.00
Tiger Woods	T-7	66-73-68-70=277	$60,250.00

The Tour Championship

Course: East Lake G.C., Atlanta, Ga.
Par: 70 Yardage: 7,108
Last day of event: Sunday, November 1, 1998

Player	Place	Score	Earnings
Hal Sutton	Win	69-67-68-70=274	$720,000.00
Playoff: Beat Vijay Singh with birdie on first extra hole			
Vijay Singh	2	63-70-70-71=274	$432,000.00
Jesper Parnevik	T-3	70-70-67-68=275	$234,000.00
Jim Furyk	T-3	67-68-69-71=275	$234,000.00
Steve Stricker	T-5	69-71-71-69=280	$146,666.67
Scott Verplank	T-5	70-70-71-69=280	$146,666.67
Justin Leonard	T-5	68-72-68-72=280	$146,666.66
Davis Love III	T-8	70-71-70-70=281	$120,533.33
Bob Tway	T-8	71-70-70-70=281	$120,533.33
David Duval	T-8	75-69-69-68=281	$120,533.34

1999

David Duval started the season with a bang by winning the Mercedes Championships, then shooting the third 59 in PGA Tour history en route to victory at the Bob Hope Chrysler Classic. In April, Duval ascended to No. 1 in the Official World Golf Ranking, a position he held for 15 weeks. Armed with a retooled swing, Tiger Woods displaced Duval thanks to 11 victories worldwide in 1999, including the PGA Championship and seven other wins on the PGA Tour. Fully recovered from a mysterious foot injury that sidelined him for most of the previous two seasons, Jose Maria Olazabal won the Masters by two shots over Davis Love III. Paul Lawrie won a British Open that is better remembered for Jean Van de Velde's strategic blunders at the 72nd hole at Carnoustie, which cost him his 3-shot lead and the Claret Jug. Lawrie rarely gets credit for a closing 67—on a punishing Carnoustie setup that had made 19-year-old Sergio Garcia cry—which thrust him into the four-hole aggregate playoff with Van de Velde and Justin Leonard. The talented Garcia dried his eyes in time to dazzle PGA Championship spectators at Medinah, where he finished runner-up to Woods by one stroke. Garcia's defining moment came when he slashed a shot from the base of a tree on the 70th hole, hit the green and made an improbable par that kept him within striking distance. Payne Stewart notched his second U.S. Open title, making birdie at the 71st hole and a testy par putt at the last to beat Phil Mickelson by a shot at Pinehurst. On Oct. 25, Stewart was aboard a private jet that lost air pressure in the cabin, killing all five occupants. After flying aimlessly for several hours, the plane ran out of fuel and crashed in South Dakota. Golf also lost career Grand Slam winner (and inventor of the sand wedge) Gene Sarazen, who died in May at age 97. Europe suffered through a hostile Ryder Cup environment at The Country Club, where the United States won 14 ½ to 13 ½.

Mercedes Championshipss

Course: Kapalua Resort Plantation Course, Kapalua, Maui, Ha.
Par: 73 Yardage: 7,263
Last day of event: Sunday, January 10, 1999

Player	Place	Score	Earnings
David Duval	Win	67-63-68-68=266	$468,000.00
Mark O'Meara	T-2	70-68-69-68=275	$228,800.00
Billy Mayfair	T-2	66-69-69-71=275	$228,800.00
Vijay Singh	4	70-65-70-71=276	$124,800.00
Justin Leonard	T-5	68-72-68-69=277	$94,900.00
Tiger Woods	T-5	69-69-67-72=277	$94,900.00
Fred Funk	T-5	66-69-68-74=277	$94,900.00
Davis Love III	8	69-68-71-70=278	$81,900.00
Jim Furyk	9	68-69-68-75=280	$76,700.00
Fred Couples	10	69-68-73-71=281	$72,800.00

Sony Open in Hawaii

Course: Waialae C.C., Honolulu, Ha.
Par: 70 Yardage: 7,012
Last day of event: Sunday, January 17, 1999

Player	Place	Score	Earnings
Jeff Sluman	Win	69-70-66-66=271	$468,000.00
Chris Perry	T-2	69-69-69-66=273	$156,000.00
Jeff Maggert	T-2	69-70-66-68=273	$156,000.00
Len Mattiace	T-2	70-66-69-68=273	$156,000.00
Davis Love III	T-2	71-69-63-70=273	$156,000.00
Tommy Tolles	T-2	63-72-67-71=273	$156,000.00
Loren Roberts	T-7	69-69-69-67=274	$75,660.00
Chris Couch	T-7	69-70-68-67=274	$75,660.00
Jimmy Green	T-7	70-70-68-66=274	$75,660.00
Chris Riley	T-7	67-71-68-68=274	$75,660.00
Paul Goydos	T-7	72-68-67-67=274	$75,660.00

Bob Hope Chrysler Classic

Course: PGA West/Palmer, Bermuda Dunes C.C., Indian Wells C.C., Tamarisk C.C.
Home course / PGA West, Par: 72 Yardage: 6,950
Last day of event: Sunday, January 24, 1999

Player	Place	Score	Earnings
David Duval	Win	70-71-64-70-59=334	$540,000.00
Steve Pate	2	66-70-64-69-66=335	$324,000.00
John Huston	3	63-73-71-63-66=336	$204,000.00
Fred Funk	T-4	65-68-66-69-71=339	$132,000.00
Bob Estes	T-4	68-71-65-67-68=339	$132,000.00
Skip Kendall	6	67-73-66-64-70=340	$108,000.00
Jeff Maggert	7	69-72-66-68-66=341	$100,500.00
Jeff Sluman	T-8	68-68-70-68-68=342	$87,000.00
Paul Goydos	T-8	67-72-69-70-64=342	$87,000.00
Kevin Sutherland	T-8	69-72-66-67-68=342	$87,000.00

Phoenix Open

Course: TPC of Scottsdale, Scottsdale, Ariz.
Par: 71 Yardage: 7,083
Last day of event: Sunday, January 31, 1999

Player	Place	Score	Earnings
Rocco Mediate	Win	69-67-66-71=273	$540,000.00

Justin Leonard	2	67-75-67-66=275	$324,000.00
Tiger Woods	3	71-67-70-68=276	$204,000.00
Hal Sutton	4	69-70-71-69=279	$144,000.00
Bill Glasson	5	69-71-70-70=280	$120,000.00
Kenny Perry	T-6	72-70-68-72=282	$97,125.00
Jim Furyk	T-6	72-69-70-71=282	$97,125.00
Kevin Wentworth	T-6	72-72-71-67=282	$97,125.00
Harrison Frazar	T-6	74-69-66-73=282	$97,125.00
J.P. Hayes	T-10	70-71-69-73=283	$72,000.00
Lee Janzen	T-10	69-71-69-74=283	$72,000.00
Stewart Cink	T-10	74-69-71-69=283	$72,000.00
Dudley Hart	T-10	75-70-70-68=283	$72,000.00

AT&T Pebble Beach Pro-Am

Courses: Pebble Beach G.L., Spyglass Hill C.C., Poppy Hills G.C., Pebble Beach, Calif.
Home Course / Pebble Beach G.L., Par: 72 Yardage: 6,799
Last day of event: Sunday, February 7, 1999

Player	Place	Score	Earnings
Payne Stewart	Win	69-64-73=206	$504,000.00
Frank Lickliter II	2	68-68-71=207	$302,400.00
Craig Stadler	3	70-67-72=209	$190,400.00
Jay Williamson	T-4	69-70-71=210	$110,250.00
Ronnie Black	T-4	71-69-70=210	$110,250.00
Justin Leonard	T-4	70-72-68=210	$110,250.00
Fred Couples	T-4	72-65-73=210	$110,250.00
Tommy Tolles	T-8	71-70-70=211	$84,000.00
Neal Lancaster	T-8	73-70-68=211	$84,000.00
Paul Azinger	T-10	69-71-72=212	$64,400.00
Tim Herron	T-10	72-68-72=212	$64,400.00
Brett Quigley	T-10	66-73-73=212	$64,400.00
Davis Love III	T-10	73-65-74=212	$64,400.00
Vijay Singh	T-10	69-67-76=212	$64,400.00

Buick Invitational

Course: Torrey Pines (South), Torrey Pines (North), San Diego, Calif.
Home Course -Par: 72 Yardage: 7,000
Last day of event: Sunday, February 14, 1999

Player	Place	Score	Earnings
Tiger Woods	Win	68-71-62-65=266	$486,000.00
Billy Ray Brown	2	69-65-68-66=268	$291,600.00
Bill Glasson	3	68-67-68-67=270	$183,600.00
Kevin Sutherland	T-4	68-68-67-70=273	$111,600.00
Omar Uresti	T-4	71-66-69-67=273	$111,600.00
Chris Perry	T-4	66-69-72-66=273	$111,600.00
Loren Roberts	T-7	70-70-68-67=275	$81,337.50
Scott Simpson	T-7	71-68-66-70=275	$81,337.50
Chris Riley	T-7	72-65-68-70=275	$81,337.50
Dennis Paulson	T-7	67-64-74-70=275	$81,337.50

Nissan Open

Course: Riviera C.C., Pacific Palisades, Calif.
Par: 71 Yardage: 6,946
Last day of event: Sunday, February 21, 1999

Player	Place	Score	Earnings
Ernie Els	Win	68-66-68-68=270	$504,000.00
Davis Love III	T-2	69-65-68-70=272	$209,066.66
Tiger Woods	T-2	69-68-65-70=272	$209,066.67
Ted Tryba	T-2	70-69-61-72=272	$209,066.67
David Duval	T-5	66-71-67-69=273	$106,400.00
Nick Price	T-5	67-71-67-68=273	$106,400.00

Scott Hoch	T-7	71-69-68-66=274	$90,300.00
Bob Estes	T-7	66-67-72-69=274	$90,300.00
Jerry Kelly	T-9	68-69-67-71=275	$72,800.00
Mark Brooks	T-9	68-71-70-66=275	$72,800.00
Frank Lickliter II	T-9	71-68-66-70=275	$72,800.00
Robert Karlsson	T-9	71-66-70-68=275	$72,800.00

WGC-Andersen Consulting Match Play Championship

Course: La Costa Resort & Spa, Carlsbad, Calif.
Par: 72 Yardage: 7,022
Last day of event: Sunday, February 28, 1999

Player	Place	Earnings
Jeff Maggert	Win	$1,000,000.00

Round One - Beat Fred Funk 2 up
Round Two - Beat Nick Price 1 up
Round Three - Beat Bernhard Langer 1 up
Quarterfinals - Beat Tiger Woods 2 & 1
Semifinals - Beat Steve Pate 1 up
Finals - Beat Andrew Magee 38 holes

Andrew Magee	2	$500,000.00

Round One - Beat Darren Clarke 1 up
Round Two - Beat Thomas Bjorn 2 & 1
Round Three - Beat Bill Glasson 1 up
Quarterfinals - Beat Shigeki Maruyama
Semifinals - Beat John Huston 2 & 1
Finals - Jeff Maggert beat him 38 holes

John Huston	3	$400,000.00

Round One - Beat Bob Estes 3 & 2
Round Two - Beat Craig Stadler 2 & 1
Round Three - Beat Patrik Sjoland 1 up
Quarterfinals - Beat Jose Maria Olazabal 2 & 1
Semifinals - Andrew Magee beat him 3 & 1
Consolation - Beat Steve Pate 5 & 4

Steve Pate	4	$300,000.00

Round One - Beat Davis Love III 1 up
Round Two - Beat Brandt Jobe 1 up
Round Three - Beat Fred Couples 1 up
Quarterfinals - Beat Eduardo Romero 3 & 2
Semifinals - Jeff Maggert beat him 1 up
Consolation - John Huston beat him 5 & 4

Shigeki Maruyama	T-5	$150,000.00

Round One - Beat Steve Stricker 3 & 2
Round Two - Beat Justin Leonard 4 & 2
Round Three - Beat Loren Roberts 2 & 1
Quarterfinals - Andrew Magee beat him 1 up

Jose Maria Olazabal	T-5	$150,000.00

Round One - Beat Billy Mayfair 5 & 3
Round Two - Beat Michael Bradley 2 & 1
Round Three - Beat Steve Jones 5 & 4
Quarterfinals - John Huston beat him 2 & 1

Eduardo Romero	T-5	$150,000.00

Round One - Beat Lee Westwood 3 & 2
Round Two - Beat Greg Norman 21 holes
Round Three - Beat Phil Mickelson 2 & 1
Quarterfinals - Steve Pate beat him 1 up

Tiger Woods	T-5	$150,000.00

Round One - Beat Nick Faldo 4 & 3
Round Two - Beat Bob Tway 6 & 4
Round Three - Beat Stewart Cink 2 & 1
Quarterfinals - Jeff Maggert beat him 2 & 1

Stewart Cink	T-9	$75,000.00

Round One - Beat Payne Stewart 3 & 2
Round Two - Beat Craig Parry 3 & 2
Round Three - Tiger Woods beat him 2 & 1

Fred Couples	T-9	$75,000.00

Round One - Beat Dudley Hart 2 up
Round Two - Beat Scott Hoch 1 up
Round Three - Steve Pate beat him 1 up

Bill Glasson	T-9		$75,000.00

Round One - Beat Stuart Appleby 2 & 1
Round Two - Beat David Duval 2 & 1
Round Three - Andrew Magee beat him 1 up

Steve Jones	T-9		$75,000.00

Round One - Beat Steve Elkington 2 & 1
Round Two - Beat Scott Verplank 5 & 4
Round Three - Jose Maria Olazabal beat him 1 up

Bernhard Langer	T-9		$75,000.00

Round One - Beat Brad Faxon 4 & 2
Round Two - Beat Vijay Singh 2 & 1
Round Three - Jeff Maggert beat him 1 up

Phil Mickelson	T-9		$75,000.00

Round One - Beat Joe Ozaki 3 & 2
Round Two - Beat Lee Janzen 2 & 1
Round Three - Eduardo Romero beat him 2 & 1

Loren Roberts	T-9		$75,000.00

Round One - Beat Hal Sutton 5 & 4
Round Two - Beat Paul Azinger 2 & 1
Round Three - Shigeki Maruyama beat him 2 & 1

Patrik Sjoland	T-9		$75,000.00

Round One - Beat Jim Furyk 5 & 3
Round Two - Beat Carlos Franco 1 up
Round Three - John Huston beat him 1 up

Touchstone Energy Tucson Open
Course: Omni Tucson National Resort, Tucson, Ariz.
Par: 72 Yardage: 7,148
Last day of event: Sunday, February 28, 1999

Player	Place	Score	Earnings
Gabriel Hjertstedt	Win	67-68-73-68=276	$495,000.00

Playoff: Beat Tommy Armour III with birdie on first extra hole

Tommy Armour III	2	70-69-67-70=276	$297,000.00
Kirk Triplett	T-3	69-69-70-69=277	$159,500.00
Mike Reid	T-3	71-67-71-68=277	$159,500.00
Barry Cheesman	T-5	71-66-69-72=278	$104,500.00
Brent Geiberger	T-5	72-68-68-70=278	$104,500.00
Eric Rustand	T-7	70-69-70-70=279	$77,229.16
David Toms	T-7	68-69-71-71=279	$77,229.16
Franklin Langham	T-7	70-68-71-70=279	$77,229.17
Corey Pavin	T-7	71-68-71-69=279	$77,229.17
Nolan Henke	T-7	71-70-71-67=279	$77,229.17
Scott Gump	T-7	68-67-74-70=279	$77,229.17

Doral-Ryder Open
Course: Doral C.C. (Blue), Miami, Fla.
Par: 72 Yardage: 7,125
Last day of event: Sunday, March 7, 1999

Player	Place	Score	Earnings
Steve Elkington	Win	72-70-69-64=275	$540,000.00
Greg Kraft	2	68-67-70-71=276	$324,000.00
Jay Haas	T-3	70-69-70-68=277	$135,300.00
Tommy Armour III	T-3	67-71-71-68=277	$135,300.00
Ernie Els	T-3	71-66-70-70=277	$135,300.00
Scott Dunlap	T-3	67-72-69-69=277	$135,300.00
David Toms	T-3	70-73-67-67=277	$135,300.00
P.H. Horgan III	T-8	69-70-71-68=278	$90,000.00
Danny Briggs	T-8	71-72-68-67=278	$90,000.00
Guy Hill	T-10	71-69-70-69=279	$69,000.00
Glen Day	T-10	69-71-67-72=279	$69,000.00
Gabriel Hjertstedt	T-10	69-72-71-67=279	$69,000.00
Greg Chalmers	T-10	71-66-72-70=279	$69,000.00
Nick Price	T-10	72-69-70-68=279	$69,000.00

Honda Classic
Course: TPC at Heron Bay, Coral Springs, Fla.
Par: 72 Yardage: 7,268
Last day of event: Sunday, March 14, 1999

Player	Place	Score	Earnings
Vijay Singh	Win	71-69-68-69=277	$468,000.00
Payne Stewart	2	70-67-72-70=279	$280,800.00
Carlos Franco	T-3	72-68-71-69=280	$124,800.00
Mark O'Meara	T-3	68-70-69-73=280	$124,800.00
Doug Dunakey	T-3	70-65-75-70=280	$124,800.00
Eric Booker	T-3	65-66-72-77=280	$124,800.00
Hal Sutton	T-7	64-73-76-69=282	$83,850.00
Tommy Tolles	T-7	70-66-69-77=282	$83,850.00
Chris Riley	T-9	69-71-72-71=283	$70,200.00
Dudley Hart	T-9	70-72-72-69=283	$70,200.00
Stuart Appleby	T-9	69-70-69-75=283	$70,200.00

Bay Hill Invitational
Course: Bay Hill Club, Orlando, Fla.
Par: 72 Yardage: 7,196
Last day of event: Sunday, March 21, 1999

Player	Place	Score	Earnings
Tim Herron	Win	66-69-67-72=274	$450,000.00

Playoff: Beat Tom Lehman with birdie on second extra hole

Tom Lehman	2	69-68-66-71=274	$270,000.00
Davis Love III	3	69-66-67-73=275	$170,000.00
Robert Damron	4	70-71-68-67=276	$120,000.00
Dicky Pride	T-5	68-71-70-71=280	$81,875.00
Scott Hoch	T-5	71-70-70-69=280	$81,875.00
Bob Estes	T-5	70-70-68-72=280	$81,875.00
Craig Parry	T-5	72-67-72-69=280	$81,875.00
Brandel Chamblee	T-5	70-69-67-74=280	$81,875.00
Phil Mickelson	T-5	74-67-68-71=280	$81,875.00

The Players Championship
Course: TPC at Sawgrass, Ponte Vedra Beach, Fla.
Par: 72 Yardage: 6,950
Last day of event: Sunday, March 28, 1999

Player	Place	Score	Earnings
David Duval	Win	69-69-74-73=285	$900,000.00
Scott Gump	2	72-74-70-71=287	$540,000.00
Nick Price	3	74-67-74-73=288	$340,000.00
Hal Sutton	T-4	69-74-73-73=289	$220,000.00
Fred Couples	T-4	77-71-73-68=289	$220,000.00
Mark O'Meara	T-6	72-73-71-74=290	$161,875.00
Steve Stricker	T-6	73-73-70-74=290	$161,875.00
Scott Hoch	T-6	72-70-73-75=290	$161,875.00
Lee Westwood	T-6	73-69-75-73=290	$161,875.00
Joey Sindelar	T-10	72-71-74-74=291	$107,142.86
Tiger Woods	T-10	70-71-75-75=291	$107,142.85
Mark Calcavecchia	T-10	76-70-72-73=291	$107,142.86
Mark Brooks	T-10	71-77-71-72=291	$107,142.86
Skip Kendall	T-10	70-73-70-78=291	$107,142.85
Davis Love III	T-10	70-70-78-73=291	$107,142.86
Joe Ozaki	T-10	69-68-81-73=291	$107,142.86

BellSouth Classic

Course: TPC at Sugarloaf, Duluth, Ga.
Par: 72 Yardage: 7,259
Last day of event: Sunday, April 4, 1999

Player	Place	Score	Earnings
David Duval	Win	66-69-68-67=270	$450,000.00
Stewart Cink	2	71-65-66-70=272	$270,000.00
John Huston	T-3	71-65-67-70=273	$145,000.00
Rory Sabbatini	T-3	65-65-73-70=273	$145,000.00
Franklin Langham	T-5	69-67-68-70=274	$95,000.00
Mike Weir	T-5	69-65-68-72=274	$95,000.00
Davis Love III	T-7	69-69-69-68=275	$77,916.67
Phil Mickelson	T-7	69-71-64-71=275	$77,916.66
Glen Day	T-7	68-67-72-68=275	$77,916.67
Brent Geiberger	T-10	70-71-68-68=277	$55,416.67
Chris DiMarco	T-10	71-69-68-69=277	$55,416.67
David Toms	T-10	71-70-68-68=277	$55,416.67
Shigeki Maruyama	T-10	66-72-68-71=277	$55,416.66
Grant Waite	T-10	64-72-73-68=277	$55,416.67
Stuart Appleby	T-10	74-66-66-71=277	$55,416.66

Masters

Course: Augusta National G.C., Augusta, Ga.
Par: 72 Yardage: 6,985
Last day of event: Sunday, April 11, 1999

Player	Place	Score	Earnings
Jose Maria Olazabal	Win	70-66-73-71=280	$720,000.00
Davis Love III	2	69-72-70-71=282	$432,000.00
Greg Norman	3	71-68-71-73=283	$272,000.00
Bob Estes	T-4	71-72-69-72=284	$176,000.00
Steve Pate	T-4	71-75-65-73=284	$176,000.00
Nick Price	T-6	69-72-72-72=285	$125,200.00
Carlos Franco	T-6	72-72-68-73=285	$125,200.00
David Duval	T-6	71-74-70-70=285	$125,200.00
Phil Mickelson	T-6	74-69-71-71=285	$125,200.00
Lee Westwood	T-6	75-71-68-71=285	$125,200.00

MCI Classic

Course: Harbour Town G.L., Hilton Head, S.C.
Par: 71 Yardage: 6,916
Last day of event: Sunday, April 18, 1999

Player	Place	Score	Earnings
Glen Day	Win	70-68-70-66=274	$450,000.00

Playoff: Beat Payne Stewart and Jeff Sluman with birdie on first extra hole

Player	Place	Score	Earnings
Payne Stewart	T-2	68-64-72-70=274	$220,000.00
Jeff Sluman	T-2	72-67-68-67=274	$220,000.00
Chris Perry	4	69-66-68-72=275	$120,000.00
Corey Pavin	T-5	70-69-68-69=276	$91,250.00
Nolan Henke	T-5	71-70-65-70=276	$91,250.00
John Huston	T-5	68-67-69-72=276	$91,250.00
Lee Janzen	T-8	67-70-68-72=277	$75,000.00
Bob Tway	T-8	69-73-68-67=277	$75,000.00
Mike Weir	T-10	71-69-70-68=278	$65,000.00
Scott Gump	T-10	72-69-65-72=278	$65,000.00

Greater Greensboro Chrysler Classic

Course: Forest Oaks C.C., Greensboro, N.C.
Par: 72 Yardage: 7,062
Last day of event: Sunday, April 25, 1999

Player	Place	Score	Earnings
Jesper Parnevik	Win	65-63-67-70=265	$468,000.00

Player	Place	Score	Earnings
Jim Furyk	2	67-63-68-69=267	$280,800.00
Jeff Maggert	3	68-62-75-68=273	$176,800.00
Dudley Hart	4	66-65-71-72=274	$124,800.00
Tom Lehman	5	69-68-69-69=275	$104,000.00
Kirk Triplett	T-6	69-68-71-68=276	$90,350.00
Paul Stankowski	T-6	70-69-71-66=276	$90,350.00
Trevor Dodds	8	71-65-72-69=277	$80,600.00
Vijay Singh	T-9	70-70-70-68=278	$70,200.00
Phil Blackmar	T-9	71-69-70-68=278	$70,200.00
J.L. Lewis	T-9	70-65-74-69=278	$70,200.00

Shell Houston Open

Course: TPC at The Woodlands, The Woodlands, Texas
Par: 72 Yardage: 7,042
Last day of event: Sunday, May 2, 1999

Player	Place	Score	Earnings
Stuart Appleby	Win	70-68-70-71=279	$450,000.00
John Cook	T-2	68-74-68-70=280	$220,000.00
Hal Sutton	T-2	68-68-69-75=280	$220,000.00
Mark Wiebe	4	69-69-71-73=282	$120,000.00
Clark Dennis	T-5	72-69-71-71=283	$84,750.00
Vijay Singh	T-5	71-69-70-73=283	$84,750.00
J.P. Hayes	T-5	72-69-69-73=283	$84,750.00
Jonathan Kaye	T-5	74-70-67-72=283	$84,750.00
Loren Roberts	T-5	72-69-67-75=283	$84,750.00
Bradley Hughes	T-10	72-72-71-69=284	$53,571.43
Esteban Toledo	T-10	69-71-73-71=284	$53,571.43
Larry Mize	T-10	70-70-71-73=284	$53,571.43
Scott Hoch	T-10	73-70-67-74=284	$53,571.43
Brian Watts	T-10	70-70-69-75=284	$53,571.43
Frank Lickliter II	T-10	71-68-69-76=284	$53,571.43
Joey Sindelar	T-10	68-68-71-77=284	$53,571.42

COMPAQ Classic of New Orleans

Course: English Turn G. & C.C., New Orleans, La.
Par: 72 Yardage: 7,116
Last day of event: Sunday, May 9, 1999

Player	Place	Score	Earnings
Carlos Franco	Win	66-69-68-66=269	$468,000.00
Steve Flesch	T-2	66-67-68-70=271	$228,800.00
Harrison Frazar	T-2	68-70-65-68=271	$228,800.00
Dennis Paulson	T-4	69-69-68-67=273	$107,466.67
Craig Barlow	T-4	66-70-70-67=273	$107,466.67
Eric Booker	T-4	68-63-71-71=273	$107,466.66
Glen Day	T-7	67-69-71-67=274	$81,033.33
Hal Sutton	T-7	68-71-69-66=274	$81,033.34
Craig Parry	T-7	69-66-72-67=274	$81,033.33
Dudley Hart	T-10	68-70-65-72=275	$67,600.00
Jay Don Blake	T-10	72-69-65-69=275	$67,600.00

GTE Byron Nelson Classic

Course: TPC at Las Colinas, Cottonwood Valley Course, Irving, Texas
Home course / TPC at Las Colinas, Par: 70 Yardage: 6,899
Last day of event: Sunday, May 16, 1999

Player	Place	Score	Earnings
Loren Roberts	Win	66-66-62-68=262	$540,000.00

Playoff: Beat Steve Pate with par on first extra hole

Player	Place	Score	Earnings
Steve Pate	2	63-65-68-66=262	$324,000.00
Chris DiMarco	T-3	64-69-68-68=269	$144,000.00
Lee Janzen	T-3	68-64-68-69=269	$144,000.00
Sergio Garcia	T-3	62-67-71-69=269	$144,000.00
Brian Watts	T-3	65-71-65-68=269	$144,000.00

Player	Place	Score	Earnings
Emlyn Aubrey	T-7	64-69-69-69=271	$96,750.00
Tiger Woods	T-7	61-67-74-69=271	$96,750.00
Barry Cheesman	T-9	63-70-69-70=272	$81,000.00
Chris Perry	T-9	67-68-71-66=272	$81,000.00
Paul Goydos	T-9	62-76-66-68=272	$81,000.00

Mastercard Colonial

Course: Colonial C.C., Fort Worth, Texas
Par: 70 Yardage: 7,010
Last day of event: Sunday, May 23, 1999

Player	Place	Score	Earnings
Olin Browne	Win	73-67-66-66=272	$504,000.00
Fred Funk	T-2	68-68-69-68=273	$168,000.00
Tim Herron	T-2	68-69-69-67=273	$168,000.00
Paul Goydos	T-2	70-68-69-66=273	$168,000.00
Jeff Sluman	T-2	67-71-69-66=273	$168,000.00
Greg Kraft	T-2	75-67-61-70=273	$168,000.00
Bob Estes	T-7	70-68-68-68=274	$84,350.00
Billy Mayfair	T-7	68-67-68-71=274	$84,350.00
John Huston	T-7	72-65-71-66=274	$84,350.00
Craig Parry	T-7	72-68-68-66=274	$84,350.00

Kemper Open

Course: TPC at Avenel, Potomac, Md.
Par: 71 Yardage: 7,005
Last day of event: Sunday, May 30, 1999

Player	Place	Score	Earnings
Rich Beem	Win	66-67-71-70=274	$450,000.00
Bill Glasson	T-2	67-70-69-69=275	$220,000.00
Bradley Hughes	T-2	68-68-72-67=275	$220,000.00
David Toms	T-4	72-68-70-66=276	$110,000.00
Hal Sutton	T-4	73-72-66-65=276	$110,000.00
Tommy Armour III	T-6	68-68-68-73=277	$86,875.00
Stuart Appleby	T-6	74-66-69-68=277	$86,875.00
Emlyn Aubrey	T-8	71-70-66-71=278	$75,000.00
Dennis Paulson	T-8	72-67-71-68=278	$75,000.00
Tommy Tolles	T-10	68-70-70-71=279	$60,000.00
Dan Forsman	T-10	71-67-73-68=279	$60,000.00
Steve Stricker	T-10	71-67-73-68=279	$60,000.00
Mike Sposa	T-10	73-66-71-69=279	$60,000.00

Memorial Tournament

Course: Muirfield Village G.C., Dubin, Ohio
Par: 72 Yardage: 7,163
Last day of event: Sunday, June 6, 1999

Player	Place	Score	Earnings
Tiger Woods	Win	68-66-70-69=273	$459,000.00
Vijay Singh	2	68-67-71-69=275	$275,400.00
David Duval	T-3	72-68-69-70=279	$132,600.00
Olin Browne	T-3	72-70-72-65=279	$132,600.00
Carlos Franco	T-3	74-67-70-68=279	$132,600.00
Dennis Paulson	6	68-71-69-72=280	$91,800.00
Ernie Els	T-7	69-72-70-70=281	$76,818.75
Bill Glasson	T-7	70-68-71-72=281	$76,818.75
Kaname Yokoo	T-7	73-70-67-71=281	$76,818.75
Justin Leonard	T-7	68-69-74-70=281	$76,818.75

FedEx St. Jude Classic

Course: TPC at Southwind, Germantown, Tenn.
Par: 71 Yardage: 7,006
Last day of event: Monday, June 14, 1999

Player	Place	Score	Earnings
Ted Tryba	Win	68-64-67-66=265	$450,000.00
Tom Lehman	T-2	63-68-68-68=267	$220,000.00
Tim Herron	T-2	67-66-66-68=267	$220,000.00
Kevin Wentworth	T-4	69-69-63-67=268	$110,000.00
Jose Maria Olazabal	T-4	68-68-70-62=268	$110,000.00
Rick Fehr	T-6	66-69-66-69=270	$80,937.50
Paul Azinger	T-6	66-70-69-65=270	$80,937.50
Kevin Sutherland	T-6	69-65-66-70=270	$80,937.50
Hal Sutton	T-6	63-67-69-71=270	$80,937.50
Davis Love III	T-10	67-68-68-68=271	$57,500.00
Brett Quigley	T-10	70-65-66-70=271	$57,500.00
Omar Uresti	T-10	65-67-68-71=271	$57,500.00
Frank Lickliter II	T-10	65-71-66-69=271	$57,500.00
Miguel-A. Jimenez	T-10	68-67-71-65=271	$57,500.00

U.S. Open

Course: Pinehurst C.C. (No 2), Pinehurst, N.C.
Par: 70 Yardage: 7,175
Last day of event: Sunday, June 20, 1999

Player	Place	Score	Earnings
Payne Stewart	Win	68-69-72-70=279	$625,000.00
Phil Mickelson	2	67-70-73-70=280	$370,000.00
Tiger Woods	T-3	68-71-72-70=281	$196,791.50
Vijay Singh	T-3	69-70-73-69=281	$196,791.50
Steve Stricker	5	70-73-69-73=285	$130,655.00
Tim Herron	6	69-72-70-75=286	$116,935.00
Jeff Maggert	T-7	71-69-74-73=287	$96,260.33
David Duval	T-7	67-70-75-75=287	$96,260.33
Hal Sutton	T-7	69-70-76-72=287	$96,260.34
Darren Clarke	T-10	73-70-74-71=288	$78,862.50
Billy Mayfair	T-10	67-72-74-75=288	$78,862.50

Buick Classic

Course: Westchester C.C., Harrison, N.Y.
Par: 71 Yardage: 6,779
Last day of event: Sunday, June 27, 1999

Player	Place	Score	Earnings
Duffy Waldorf	Win	70-67-68-71=276	$450,000.00
Playoff: Beat Dennis Paulson with birdie on first extra hole			
Dennis Paulson	2	71-70-68-67=276	$270,000.00
Chris Perry	3	70-66-71-70=277	$170,000.00
Scott Hoch	4	73-70-66-69=278	$120,000.00
Gabriel Hjertstedt	T-5	69-70-69-71=279	$84,750.00
Loren Roberts	T-5	71-71-68-69=279	$84,750.00
Jim Carter	T-5	67-72-66-74=279	$84,750.00
Doug Barron	T-5	74-68-69-68=279	$84,750.00
Vijay Singh	T-5	75-69-67-68=279	$84,750.00
Bob Estes	T-10	70-71-69-70=280	$51,875.00
Tom Byrum	T-10	68-70-70-72=280	$51,875.00
Fred Couples	T-10	69-69-72-70=280	$51,875.00
Lee Janzen	T-10	71-67-69-73=280	$51,875.00
Steve Flesch	T-10	72-69-66-73=280	$51,875.00
David Sutherland	T-10	73-66-68-73=280	$51,875.00
David Duval	T-10	70-75-68-67=280	$51,875.00
Bob Tway	T-10	73-68-75-64=280	$51,875.00

Motorola Western Open

Course: Cog Hill G. & C.C. (Dubsdread), Lemont, Ill.
Par: 72 Yardage: 7,073
Last day of event: Sunday, July 4, 1999

Player	Place	Score	Earnings
Tiger Woods	Win	68-66-68-71=273	$450,000.00
Mike Weir	2	72-67-67-70=276	$270,000.00
Brent Geiberger	3	70-68-70-69=277	$170,000.00
Vijay Singh	4	67-70-71-70=278	$120,000.00
Dicky Pride	5	71-68-70-70=279	$100,000.00
John Maginnes	6	69-70-71-70=280	$90,000.00
Chris Perry	T-7	71-70-69-71=281	$80,625.00
Mike Reid	T-7	70-70-73-68=281	$80,625.00
Hal Sutton	T-9	67-70-73-72=282	$65,000.00
Glen Day	T-9	69-73-68-72=282	$65,000.00
Brian Henninger	T-9	74-67-67-74=282	$65,000.00
Joe Ogilvie	T-9	74-66-72-70=282	$65,000.00

Greater Milwaukee Open

Course: Brown Deer Park G.C., Milwaukee, Wis.
Par: 71 Yardage: 6,739
Last day of event: Sunday, July 11, 1999

Player	Place	Score	Earnings
Carlos Franco	Win	65-66-67-66=264	$414,000.00
Tom Lehman	2	68-67-65-66=266	$248,400.00
Jerry Kelly	3	66-65-66-71=268	$156,400.00
Dan Forsman	T-4	67-68-66-68=269	$101,200.00
Steve Lowery	T-4	70-70-68-61=269	$101,200.00
Chris Perry	T-6	65-68-67-70=270	$79,925.00
Skip Kendall	T-6	67-70-68-65=270	$79,925.00
Mark Calcavecchia	T-8	64-70-69-68=271	$69,000.00
Joey Sindelar	T-8	65-68-68-70=271	$69,000.00
Mark Wiebe	T-10	68-68-68-68=272	$49,285.71
Jay Haas	T-10	69-68-66-69=272	$49,285.71
Steve Stricker	T-10	69-67-69-67=272	$49,285.72
Jay Delsing	T-10	68-70-66-68=272	$49,285.71
Michael Bradley	T-10	70-67-69-66=272	$49,285.72
Ben Bates	T-10	62-73-70-67=272	$49,285.72
John Maginnes	T-10	66-64-74-68=272	$49,285.71

British Open

Course: Carnoustie G.C., Carnoustie, Angus, Scotland
Par: 71 Yardage: 7,361
Last day of event: Sunday, July 18, 1999

Player	Place	Score	Earnings
Paul Lawrie	Win	73-74-76-67=290	$546,805.00

Playoff: Won four-hole aggregate playoff (5-4-3-3=15) with Justin Leonard (5-4-4-5=18) and Jean Van de Velde (6-4-3-5=18)

Player	Place	Score	Earnings
Justin Leonard	T-2	73-74-71-72=290	$289,025.50
Jean Van de Velde	T-2	75-68-70-77=290	$289,025.50
Craig Parry	T-4	76-75-67-73=291	$156,230.00
Angel Cabrera	T-4	75-69-77-70=291	$156,230.00
Greg Norman	6	76-70-75-72=293	$109,361.00
Tiger Woods	T-7	74-72-74-74=294	$78,115.00
Davis Love III	T-7	74-74-77-69=294	$78,115.00
David Frost	T-7	80-69-71-74=294	$78,115.00
Retief Goosen	T-10	76-75-73-71=295	$54,368.04
Scott Dunlap	T-10	72-77-76-70=295	$54,368.04
Hal Sutton	T-10	73-78-72-72=295	$54,368.04
Jesper Parnevik	T-10	74-71-78-72=295	$54,268.04
Jim Furyk	T-10	78-71-76-70=295	$54,368.04

John Deere Classic

Course: Oakwood C.C., Coal Valley, Ill.
Par: 70 Yardage: 6,762
Last day of event: Sunday, July 25, 1999

Player	Place	Score	Earnings
J.L. Lewis	Win	66-65-65-65=261	$360,000.00

Playoff: Beat Mike Brisky with birdie on fifth extra hole

Player	Place	Score	Earnings
Mike Brisky	2	66-62-68-65=261	$216,000.00
Kirk Triplett	T-3	68-68-64-64=264	$116,000.00
Brian Henninger	T-3	66-63-64-71=264	$116,000.00
Pete Jordan	T-5	68-67-64-66=265	$73,000.00
Steve Jones	T-5	68-66-68-63=265	$73,000.00
Chris Perry	T-5	71-67-63-64=265	$73,000.00
Scott Verplank	T-8	66-67-66-67=266	$60,000.00
Dick Mast	T-8	69-67-64-66=266	$60,000.00
D.A. Weibring	T-10	67-67-65-68=267	$52,000.00
Robert Damron	T-10	64-67-65-71=267	$52,000.00

Canon Greater Hartford Open

Course: TPC at River Highlands, Cromwell, Conn.
Par: 70 Yardage: 6,820
Last day of event: Sunday, August 1, 1999

Player	Place	Score	Earnings
Brent Geiberger	Win	66-63-66-67=262	$450,000.00
Skip Kendall	2	63-68-68-66=265	$270,000.00
Justin Leonard	T-3	64-67-68-67=266	$130,000.00
Mark Calcavecchia	T-3	67-67-68-64=266	$130,000.00
Ted Tryba	T-3	72-64-62-68=266	$130,000.00
Dave Stockton, Jr.	T-6	68-68-64-67=267	$86,875.00
Pete Jordan	T-6	64-65-71-67=267	$86,875.00
Stewart Cink	T-8	64-68-68-68=268	$72,500.00
Mike Springer	T-8	63-73-65-67=268	$72,500.00
Tim Herron	T-8	66-73-67-62=268	$72,500.00

Buick Open

Course: Warwick Hills C.C., Grand Blanc, Mich.
Par: 72 Yardage: 7,101
Last day of event: Sunday, August 8, 1999

Player	Place	Score	Earnings
Tom Pernice, Jr.	Win	67-66-72-65=270	$432,000.00
Ted Tryba	T-2	66-70-69-66=271	$179,200.00
Bob Tway	T-2	67-69-70-65=271	$179,200.00
Tom Lehman	T-2	67-69-64-71=271	$179,200.00
Bob Estes	5	70-65-73-64=272	$96,000.00
Ernie Els	6	68-65-71-69=273	$86,400.00
Esteban Toledo	7	66-72-67-69=274	$80,400.00
Hal Sutton	8	69-70-70-66=275	$74,400.00
Tommy Armour III	T-9	70-67-69-70=276	$57,600.00
Brian Watts	T-9	70-70-67-69=276	$57,600.00
Loren Roberts	T-9	68-71-66-71=276	$57,600.00
Jim Furyk	T-9	70-67-71-68=276	$57,600.00
Rocco Mediate	T-9	69-64-72-71=276	$57,600.00
Joey Sindelar	T-9	70-72-64-70=276	$57,600.00

PGA Championship

Course: Medinah C.C. (No 3), Medinah, Ill.
Par: 72 Yardage: 7,401
Last day of event: Sunday, August 15, 1999

Player	Place	Score	Earnings
Tiger Woods	Win	70-67-68-72=277	$630,000.00

Sergio Garcia	2	66-73-68-71=278	$378,000.00
Stewart Cink	T-3	69-70-68-73=280	$203,000.00
Jay Haas	T-3	68-67-75-70=280	$203,000.00
Nick Price	5	70-71-69-71=281	$129,000.00
Bob Estes	T-6	71-70-72-69=282	$112,000.00
Colin Montgomerie	T-6	72-70-70-70=282	$112,000.00
Steve Pate	T-8	72-70-73-69=284	$96,500.00
Jim Furyk	T-8	71-70-69-74=284	$96,500.00
David Duval	T-10	70-71-72-72=285	$72,166.66
Chris Perry	T-10	70-73-71-71=285	$72,166.67
Jesper Parnevik	T-10	72-70-73-70=285	$72,166.67
Corey Pavin	T-10	69-74-71-71=285	$72,166.67
Miguel-A. Jimenez	T-10	70-70-75-70=285	$72,166.67
Mike Weir	T-10	68-68-69-80=285	$72,166.66

Sprint International

Course: Castle Pine G.C., Castle Rock, Colo. (Stableford format)
Par: 72 Yardage: 7,559
Last day of event: Sunday, August 22, 1999

Player	Place	Score	Earnings
David Toms	Win	16-13-10-8=47	$468,000.00
David Duval	2	10-15-11-8=44	$280,800.00
Stephen Ames	3	11-12-13-7=43	$176,800.00
Chris Perry	4	10-15-3-9=37	$124,800.00
Billy Mayfair	T-5	10-13-7-5=35	$98,800.00
Ernie Els	T-5	10-14-8-3=35	$98,800.00
Steve Elkington	7	13-10-4-7=34	$87,100.00
Jay Haas	T-8	10-5-5-12=32	$78,000.00
Olin Browne	T-8	7-14-7-4=32	$78,000.00
Kirk Triplett	T-10	7-8-5-11=31	$65,000.00
Eduardo Romero	T-10	5-8-11-7=31	$65,000.00
Steve Flesch	T-10	8-16-4-3=31	$65,000.00

WGC-NEC Invitational

Course: Firestone C.C. (South)
Akron, Ohio
Par: 70 Yardage: 7,139
Last day of event: Sunday, August 29, 1999

Player	Place	Score	Earnings
Tiger Woods	Win	66-71-62-71=270	$1,000,000.00
Phil Mickelson	2	69-67-70-65=271	$510,000.00
Nick Price	T-3	67-69-68-71=275	$327,500.00
Craig Parry	T-3	71-66-69-69=275	$327,500.00
Ernie Els	5	71-69-67-69=276	$234,000.00
Shigeki Maruyama	6	72-67-70-68=277	$179,000.00
Jeff Maggert	T-7	71-67-69-71=278	$154,000.00
Sergio Garcia	T-7	67-70-69-72=278	$154,000.00
Carlos Franco	T-7	68-67-70-73=278	$154,000.00
Jim Furyk	T-10	67-72-69-71=279	$129,000.00
Davis Love III	T-10	68-69-70-72=279	$129,000.00

Reno-Tahoe Open

Course: Montreux G. & C.C., Reno, Nev.
Par: 72 Yardage: 7,552
Last day of event: Sunday, August 29, 1999

Player	Place	Score	Earnings
Notah Begay III	Win	70-69-63-72=274	$495,000.00
David Toms	T-2	68-70-70-69=277	$242,000.00
Chris Perry	T-2	68-71-70-68=277	$242,000.00
John Cook	T-4	68-70-73-69=280	$113,666.67
Brandt Jobe	T-4	69-69-69-73=280	$113,666.66

Fred Funk	T-4	69-71-73-67=280	$113,666.67
Dennis Paulson	T-7	71-72-67-71=281	$88,687.50
Bob Tway	T-7	69-69-70-73=281	$88,687.50
Steve Jones	T-9	70-72-69-71=282	$61,531.25
Woody Austin	T-9	68-70-73-71=282	$61,531.25
Stewart Cink	T-9	68-70-73-71=282	$61,531.25
Emlyn Aubrey	T-9	69-71-73-69=282	$61,531.25
Mark Brooks	T-9	71-73-70-68=282	$61,531.25
Russ Cochran	T-9	72-70-73-67=282	$61,531.25
Jonathan Kaye	T-9	71-66-71-74=282	$61,531.25
Tom Scherrer	T-9	67-70-69-76=282	$61,531.25

Air Canada Championship

Course: Northview G. & C.C. (Ridge Course), Surrey, British Columbia, Canada
Par: 71 Yardage: 7,049
Last day of event: Sunday, September 5, 1999

Player	Place	Score	Earnings
Mike Weir	Win	68-70-64-64=266	$450,000.00
Fred Funk	2	71-64-65-68=268	$270,000.00
Carlos Franco	3	67-67-67-69=270	$170,000.00
Payne Stewart	T-4	68-67-69-68=272	$103,333.33
Phil Tataurangi	T-4	66-70-65-71=272	$103,333.33
Scott McCarron	T-4	72-67-72-61=272	$103,333.34
Charles Raulerson	7	65-68-69-71=273	$83,750.00
Kevin Wentworth	T-8	69-70-68-67=274	$75,000.00
Jay Delsing	T-8	70-68-72-64=274	$75,000.00
Steve Lowery	T-10	68-69-69-69=275	$62,500.00
Brad Fabel	T-10	71-66-68-70=275	$62,500.00
Bob Estes	T-10	73-67-67-68=275	$62,500.00

Bell Canadian Open

Course: Glen Abbey G.C., Oakville, Ontario, Canada
Par: 72 Yardage: 7,112
Last day of event: Sunday, September 12, 1999

Player	Place	Score	Earnings
Hal Sutton	Win	69-67-70-69=275	$450,000.00
Dennis Paulson	2	70-68-71-69=278	$270,000.00
Justin Leonard	T-3	72-67-72-70=281	$120,000.00
Dudley Hart	T-3	72-69-70-70=281	$120,000.00
David Sutherland	T-3	73-65-72-71=281	$120,000.00
Lee Janzen	T-3	66-71-68-76=281	$120,000.00
Scott Dunlap	7	72-74-66-70=282	$83,750.00
Nick Faldo	8	73-72-67-71=283	$77,500.00
Jesper Parnevik	T-9	68-73-73-70=284	$65,000.00
Charles Raulerson	T-9	67-74-70-73=284	$65,000.00
Phil Tataurangi	T-9	74-72-69-69=284	$65,000.00
Paul Azinger	T-9	71-66-70-77=284	$65,000.00

B.C. Open

Course: En-Joie G.C., Endicott, N.Y.
Par: 72 Yardage: 6,974
Last day of event: Sunday, September 19, 1999

Player	Place	Score	Earnings
Brad Faxon	Win	69-67-70-67=273	$288,000.00
Playoff: Beat Fred Funk with par on second extra hole			
Fred Funk	2	70-61-70-72=273	$172,800.00
Rory Sabbatini	3	69-67-68-70=274	$108,800.00
Mark Carnevale	T-4	69-70-70-67=276	$60,320.00
Stephen Ames	T-4	68-71-67-70=276	$60,320.00
Ronnie Black	T-4	71-67-68-70=276	$60,320.00
Jonathan Kaye	T-4	72-71-67-66=276	$60,320.00

Craig-A. Spence	T-4	74-69-68-65=276	$60,320.00
Peter Jacobsen	9	67-71-71-68=277	$46,400.00
Mike Weir	T-10	69-68-69-72=278	$41,600.00
Trevor Dodds	T-10	71-66-72-69=278	$41,600.00

Westin Texas Open

Course: LaCantera G.C., San Antonio, Texas

Par: 72 Yardage: 7,001

Last day of event: Sunday, September 26, 1999

Player	Place	Score	Earnings
Duffy Waldorf	Win	68-69-65-68=270	$360,000.00
Playoff: Beat Ted Tryba with birdie on first extra hole			
Ted Tryba	2	69-67-66-68=270	$216,000.00
Brent Geiberger	3	66-70-68-67=271	$136,000.00
Rich Beem	4	65-70-68-69=272	$96,000.00
Mike Reid	T-5	69-67-69-68=273	$73,000.00
Brian Henninger	T-5	68-66-70-69=273	$73,000.00
Jay Haas	T-5	69-70-69-65=273	$73,000.00
Jeff Brehaut	T-8	67-67-71-70=275	$60,000.00
Stephen Ames	T-8	64-69-67-75=275	$60,000.00
Steve Elkington	T-10	68-71-70-67=276	$52,000.00
Larry Mize	T-10	71-70-68-67=276	$52,000.00

Buick Challenge

Course: Callaway Gardens Resort, Pine Mountain, Ga.

Par: 72 Yardage: 7,057

Last day of event: Sunday, October 3, 1999

Player	Place	Score	Earnings
David Toms	Win	68-66-66-71=271	$324,000.00
Stuart Appleby	2	70-64-69-71=274	$194,400.00
Davis Love III	T-3	70-68-68-70=276	$93,600.00
Jay Delsing	T-3	70-68-71-67=276	$93,600.00
Craig Barlow	T-3	71-65-70-70=276	$93,600.00
Rocco Mediate	T-6	70-70-68-69=277	$52,585.71
Paul Azinger	T-6	70-70-70-67=277	$52,585.72
Scott Gump	T-6	67-71-70-69=277	$52,585.72
Dan Forsman	T-6	69-68-69-71=277	$52,585.71
Greg Kraft	T-6	71-66-69-71=277	$52,585.71
John Maginnes	T-6	70-71-64-72=277	$52,585.71
Stewart Cink	T-6	73-68-69-67=277	$52,585.72

Michelob Championship at Kingsmill

Course: Kingsmill G.C., Williamsburg, Va.

Par: 71 Yardage: 6,853

Last day of event: Sunday, October 10, 1999

Player	Place	Score	Earnings
Notah Begay III	Win	67-70-69-68=274	$450,000.00
Playoff: Beat Tom Byrum with par on second extra hole			
Tom Byrum	2	69-67-70-68=274	$270,000.00
Mike Weir	3	74-63-68-70=275	$170,000.00
Barry Cheesman	4	73-68-68-67=276	$120,000.00
Nick Faldo	T-5	70-70-70-67=277	$91,250.00
Tom Scherrer	T-5	72-70-66-69=277	$91,250.00
Jay Don Blake	T-5	73-68-70-66=277	$91,250.00
David Duval	T-8	70-70-69-69=278	$67,500.00
John Maginnes	T-8	70-70-71-67=278	$67,500.00
Ronnie Black	T-8	72-70-68-68=278	$67,500.00
Jay Delsing	T-8	73-70-65-70=278	$67,500.00
Brian Watts	T-8	75-68-67-68=278	$67,500.00

Las Vegas Invitational

Course: TPC at Summerlin, Desert Inn C.C., Las Vegas C.C., Las Vegas, Nev.

Home course / TPC at Summerlin, Par: 72 Yardage: 7,243

Last day of event: Sunday, October 17, 1999

Player	Place	Score	Earnings
Jim Furyk	Win	67-64-63-71-66=331	$450,000.00
Jonathan Kaye	2	63-66-66-73-64=332	$270,000.00
Dudley Hart	3	65-68-67-74-64=338	$170,000.00
Chris Perry	4	67-63-67-74-68=339	$120,000.00
Andrew Magee	5	63-67-70-72-68=340	$100,000.00
Brandel Chamblee	T-6	66-68-67-73-67=341	$83,750.00
Kevin Sutherland	T-6	67-69-63-73-69=341	$83,750.00
Robert Damron	T-6	65-67-67-75-67=341	$83,750.00
Stephen Ames	9	69-66-67-73-67=342	$72,500.00
Tommy Armour III	T-10	70-60-67-77-69=343	$62,500.00
Fred Couples	T-10	63-65-70-79-66=343	$62,500.00
Joe Ogilvie	T-10	63-70-66-79-65=343	$62,500.00

National Car Rental Golf Classic/Disney

Course: Walt Disney (Magnolia, Palm), Lake Buena Vista, Fla.

Home course / Magnolia, Par: 72 Yardage: 7,190

Last day of event: Sunday, October 24, 1999

Player	Place	Score	Earnings
Tiger Woods	Win	66-66-66-73=271	$450,000.00
Ernie Els	2	68-65-68-71=272	$270,000.00
Franklin Langham	T-3	67-67-68-72=274	$145,000.00
Bob Tway	T-3	67-65-66-76=274	$145,000.00
Vijay Singh	T-5	66-71-69-69=275	$95,000.00
John Huston	T-5	67-69-72-67=275	$95,000.00
Russ Cochran	T-7	68-69-68-72=277	$75,312.50
Jeff Sluman	T-7	70-65-70-72=277	$75,312.50
Glen Day	T-7	71-68-72-66=277	$75,312.50
Dudley Hart	T-7	70-67-67-73=277	$75,312.50

The Tour Championship

Course: Champions G.C., Houston, Texas

Par: 71 Yardage: 7,220

Last day of event: Sunday, October 31, 1999

Player	Place	Score	Earnings
Tiger Woods	Win	67-66-67-69=269	$900,000.00
Davis Love III	2	64-69-73-67=273	$540,000.00
Brent Geiberger	3	68-69-68-69=274	$345,000.00
Chris Perry	4	70-64-69-72=275	$240,000.00
Jeff Sluman	T-5	69-70-69-68=276	$177,500.00
Fred Funk	T-5	66-70-71-69=276	$177,500.00
John Huston	T-5	68-71-69-68=276	$177,500.00
Duffy Waldorf	T-5	66-74-66-70=276	$177,500.00
Tim Herron	T-9	66-72-71-68=277	$142,333.33
Hal Sutton	T-9	72-70-64-71=277	$142,333.33
Vijay Singh	T-9	74-68-70-65=277	$142,333.34

Southern Farm Bureau Classic

Course: Annandale G.C., Madison, Miss.

Par: 72 Yardage: 7,199

Last day of event: Monday, November 1, 1999

Player	Place	Score	Earnings
Brian Henninger	Win	67-66-69=202	$360,000.00
Chris DiMarco	2	65-68-72=205	$216,000.00
Perry Moss	T-3	67-69-70=206	$104,000.00
Paul Stankowski	T-3	70-69-67=206	$104,000.00

Glen Day	T-3	69-71-66=206	$104,000.00
Jonathan Kaye	6	71-68-68=207	$72,000.00
Kirk Triplett	T-7	69-70-69=208	$64,500.00
Rick Fehr	T-7	72-70-66=208	$64,500.00
Kevin Wentworth	T-9	69-71-69=209	$44,750.00
Mike Hulbert	T-9	70-68-71=209	$44,750.00
Jeff Gallagher	T-9	69-72-68=209	$44,750.00
Len Mattiace	T-9	69-72-68=209	$44,750.00
Blaine McCallister	T-9	72-67-70=209	$44,750.00
Mark Calcavecchia	T-9	72-69-68=209	$44,750.00
Russ Cochran	T-9	64-72-73=209	$44,750.00
Nolan Henke	T-9	66-73-70=209	$44,750.00

WGC-American Express Championship

Course: Valderrama G.C., Sotogrande, Andalucia, Spain
Par: 71 Yardage: 6,830
Last day of event: Sunday, November 7, 1999

Player	Place	Score	Earnings
Tiger Woods	Win	71-69-70-68=278	$1,000,000.00
Playoff: Beat Miguel Angel Jimenez with birdie on first extra hole			
Miguel-A. Jimenez	2	72-68-69-69=278	$400,000.00
Dudley Hart	3	75-68-70-70=283	$300,000.00
Lee Westwood	T-4	73-67-71-73=284	$176,666.67
Nick Price	T-4	69-71-70-74=284	$176,666.67
Stewart Cink	T-4	75-65-71-73=284	$176,666.66
Scott Hoch	T-7	69-70-72-74=285	$135,000.00
Fred Funk	T-7	71-68-74-72=285	$135,000.00
Sergio Garcia	T-7	74-69-69-73=285	$135,000.00
Chris Perry	T-7	70-67-72-76=285	$135,000.00

2000

Tiger Woods thoroughly dominated the first season of the new millennium. He won 10 times in 25 worldwide starts, including the U.S. Open, the British Open and the PGA Championship. His victory at Pebble Beach was by a U.S. Open record 15 shots over Ernie Els and Miguel Angel Jimenez. A 19-under-par total at St. Andrews was good for an 8-shot victory over Els and Thomas Bjorn; it also was the all-time best score in relation to par at any major. In the PGA at Valhalla, Woods birdied the final two holes of regulation to catch Bob May, then went birdie-par-par to beat May by a shot in the championship's first 3-hole aggregate playoff. Woods' scoring average of 68.11 for the season broke a 55-year-old record (68.33) held by Byron Nelson. Els also was the bridesmaid at the Masters, which Vijay Singh won by three shots.

Mercedes Championshipss

Course: Kapalua Resort Plantation Course, Kapalua, Maui, Ha.
Par: 73 Yardage: 7,263
Last day of event: Sunday, January 9, 2000

Player	Place	Score	Earnings
Tiger Woods	Win	71-66-71-68=276	$522,000.00
Playoff: Beat Ernie Els with birdie on second extra hole			
Ernie Els	2	71-70-67-68=276	$313,000.00
David Duval	3	72-73-67-68=280	$197,000.00
Jim Furyk	T-4	72-73-71-69=285	$127,500.00
Mike Weir	T-4	76-73-69-67=285	$127,500.00
Jesper Parnevik	T-6	69-74-73-71=287	$100,500.00
Carlos Franco	T-6	78-73-70-66=287	$100,500.00
Glen Day	T-8	74-75-69-71=289	$79,000.00
Brad Faxon	T-8	72-76-68-73=289	$79,000.00
Brent Geiberger	T-8	73-73-67-76=289	$79,000.00
Tom Pernice, Jr.	T-8	75-76-65-73=289	$79,000.00
Paul Lawrie	T-8	76-73-68-72=289	$79,000.00
Vijay Singh	T-8	73-77-67-72=289	$79,000.00

Sony Open in Hawaii

Course: Waialae C.C., Honolulu, Ha.
Par: 70 Yardage: 7,012
Last day of event: Sunday, January 16, 2000

Player	Place	Score	Earnings
Paul Azinger	Win	63-65-68-65=261	$522,000.00
Stuart Appleby	2	66-67-68-67=268	$313,200.00
John Huston	T-3	66-67-70-67=270	$168,200.00
Jesper Parnevik	T-3	70-65-66-69=270	$168,200.00
Ernie Els	5	67-68-69-67=271	$116,000.00
Scott Dunlap	T-6	68-67-67-70=272	$97,150.00
Tom Lehman	T-6	68-69-65-70=272	$97,150.00
Sean Murphy	T-6	68-67-70-67=272	$97,150.00
Shigeki Maruyama	T-9	67-69-70-69=275	$72,500.00
Bob Burns	T-9	70-69-67-69=275	$72,500.00
Jeff Maggert	T-9	69-67-68-71=275	$72,500.00
Jerry Kelly	T-9	67-67-69-72=275	$72,500.00
Carlos Franco	T-9	68-68-72-67=275	$72,500.00

Bob Hope Chrysler Classic

Course: Bermuda Dunes C.C., PGA West/Palmer, Indian Wells C.C., La Quinta C.C.
Home course / Bermuda Dunes, Par: 71 Yardage: 6,829
Last day of event: Sunday, January 23, 2000

Player	Place	Score	Earnings
Jesper Parnevik	Win	69-67-66-64-65=331	$540,000.00
Rory Sabbatini	2	67-67-66-64-68=332	$324,000.00
David Toms	T-3	63-68-66-70-66=333	$174,000.00
J.L. Lewis	T-3	65-66-70-66-66=333	$174,000.00
David Duval	T-5	68-67-63-68-69=335	$114,000.00
Hal Sutton	T-5	68-66-66-69-66=335	$114,000.00
John Huston	T-7	69-65-68-67-67=336	$93,500.00
Matt Gogel	T-7	66-67-64-68-71=336	$93,500.00
Fred Funk	T-7	68-68-74-63-63=336	$93,500.00
Andrew Magee	T-10	66-65-69-68-69=337	$78,000.00
Kirk Triplett	T-10	69-64-69-65-70=337	$78,000.00

Phoenix Open

Course: TPC of Scottsdale, Scottsdale, Ariz.
Par: 71 Yardage: 7,083
Last day of event: Sunday, January 30, 2000

Player	Place	Score	Earnings
Tom Lehman	Win	63-67-73-67=270	$576,000.00
Robert Allenby	T-2	67-67-68-69=271	$281,600.00
Rocco Mediate	T-2	67-70-67-67=271	$281,600.00
Hal Sutton	T-4	67-67-69-69=272	$132,266.66
Kirk Triplett	T-4	70-69-66-67=272	$132,266.67
Brandt Jobe	T-4	67-68-72-65=272	$132,266.67
Steve Flesch	T-7	70-65-68-70=273	$99,733.33
Mark Calcavecchia	T-7	71-68-66-68=273	$99,733.33
Edward Fryatt	T-7	73-67-68-65=273	$99,733.34
Kevin Sutherland	T-10	67-69-70-68=274	$66,400.00
Paul Stankowski	T-10	67-69-67-71=274	$66,400.00
Billy Mayfair	T-10	67-71-67-69=274	$66,400.00
Mike Weir	T-10	71-66-68-69=274	$66,400.00
Duffy Waldorf	T-10	71-68-69-66=274	$66,400.00
Stewart Cink	T-10	67-68-72-67=274	$66,400.00
Phil Mickelson	T-10	63-73-65-73=274	$66,400.00
Frank Lickliter II	T-10	67-64-69-74=274	$66,400.00

AT&T Pebble Beach National Pro-Am

Courses: Pebble Beach G.L., Spyglass Hill G.C., Poppy Hills G.C., Pebble Beach, Calif.

Home Course / Pebble Beach G.L., Par: 72 Yardage: 6,816

Last day of event: Monday, February 7, 2000

Player	Place	Score	Earnings
Tiger Woods	Win	68-73-68-64=273	$720,000.00
Matt Gogel	T-2	69-68-67-71=275	$352,000.00
Vijay Singh	T-2	66-67-72-70=275	$352,000.00
Jerry Kelly	T-4	71-70-68-67=276	$165,333.34
Notah Begay III	T-4	66-68-72-70=276	$165,333.33
Jimmy Green	T-4	72-68-68-68=276	$165,333.33
Tom Lehman	T-7	69-70-72-67=278	$120,500.00
Mike Weir	T-7	72-71-69-66=278	$120,500.00
Mark Brooks	T-7	71-67-66-74=278	$120,500.00
Andrew Magee	T-7	69-75-67-67=278	$120,500.00

Buick Invitational

Course: Torrey Pines (South), Torrey Pines (North), San Diego, Calif.

Home Course -Par: 72 Yardage: 7,000

Last day of event: Sunday, February 13, 2000

Player	Place	Score	Earnings
Phil Mickelson	Win	66-67-67-70=270	$540,000.00
Tiger Woods	T-2	71-68-67-68=274	$264,000.00
Shigeki Maruyama	T-2	69-64-69-72=274	$264,000.00
Davis Love III	4	65-71-69-70=275	$144,000.00
Fred Couples	T-5	68-71-67-70=276	$109,500.00
Kirk Triplett	T-5	69-64-73-70=276	$109,500.00
Kevin Sutherland	T-5	73-66-69-68=276	$109,500.00
Stephen Sear	T-8	72-67-69-69=277	$90,000.00
Bradley Hughes	T-8	68-67-73-69=277	$90,000.00
J.P. Hayes	T-10	67-71-72-69=279	$72,000.00
Brent Geiberger	T-10	69-72-70-68=279	$72,000.00
Steve Flesch	T-10	69-68-69-73=279	$72,000.00
Sandy Lyle	T-10	68-66-74-71=279	$72,000.00

Nissan Open

Course: Riviera C.C., Pacific Palisades, Calif.

Par: 71 Yardage: 7,056

Last day of event: Sunday, February 20, 2000

Player	Place	Score	Earnings
Kirk Triplett	Win	67-70-68-67=272	$558,000.00
Jesper Parnevik	2	71-67-67-68=273	$334,800.00
Robin Freeman	3	65-72-69-68=274	$210,800.00
Russ Cochran	4	69-71-66-69=275	$148,800.00
Stewart Cink	T-5	67-70-70-69=276	$105,090.00
Steve Flesch	T-5	69-69-70-68=276	$105,090.00
Tommy Armour III	T-5	68-68-69-71=276	$105,090.00
Bradley Hughes	T-5	69-66-71-70=276	$105,090.00
Fred Couples	T-5	72-66-68-70=276	$105,090.00
J.P. Hayes	T-10	64-70-72-71=277	$80,600.00
Brandel Chamblee	T-10	71-65-69-72=277	$80,600.00

WGC-Andersen Consulting Match Play Championship

Course: La Costa Resort & Spa, Carlsbad, Calif.

Par: 72 Yardage: 7,022

Last day of event: Sunday, February 27, 2000

Player	Place	Earnings
Darren Clarke	Win	$1,000,000.00

Round One - Beat Paul Azinger 2 & 1

Round Two - Beat Mark O'Meara 5 & 4

Round Three - Beat Thomas Bjorn 1 up

Quarterfinals - Beat Hal Sutton 1 up

Semifinals - Beat David Duval 4 & 2

Finals - Beat Tiger Woods 4 & 3

Tiger Woods	2	$500,000.00

Round One - Beat Michael Campbell 5 & 4

Round Two - Beat Retief Goosen 1 up

Round Three - Beat Shigeki Maruyama 4 & 3

Quarterfinals - Beat Paul Lawrie 1 up

Semifinals - Beat Davis Love III 5 & 4

Finals - Darren Clarke beat him 4 & 3

David Duval	3	$400,000.00

Round One - Beat Angel Cabrera 4 & 3

Round Two - Beat Tim Herron 2 & 1

Round Three - Beat Sergio Garcia 2 & 1

Quarterfinals - Beat Scott Hoch 5 & 4

Semifinals - Darren Clarke beat him 4 & 2

Consolation - Beat Davis Love III 5 & 4

Davis Love III	4	$300,000.00

Round One - Beat Olin Browne 2 & 1

Round Two - Beat Jeff Sluman 3 & 2

Round Three - Beat Jim Furyk 3 & 2

Quarterfinals - Beat Miguel Angel Jimenez 3 & 2

Semifinals - Tiger Woods beat him 5 & 4

Consolation - David Duval beat him 5 & 4

Paul Lawrie	T-5	$150,000.00

Round One - Beat Chris Perry 1 up

Round Two - Beat Billy Mayfair 3 & 2

Round Three - Beat Mark Calcavecchia 21 holes

Quarterfinals - Tiger Woods beat him 1 up

Hal Sutton	T-5	$150,000.00

Round One - Beat Ted Tryba 4 & 3

Round Two - Beat David Toms 1 up

Round Three - Beat Duffy Waldorf 2 & 1

Quarterfinals - Darren Clarke beat him 1 up

Miguel-A. Jimenez	T-5	$150,000.00

Round One - Beat Brent Geiberger holes

Round Two - Beat Tom Lehman 4 & 3

Round Three - Beat Bob Estes 2 & 1

Quarterfinals - Davis Love III beat him 3 & 2

Scott Hoch	T-5	$150,000.00

Round One - Beat Stuart Appleby 1 up

Round Two - Beat Lee Westwood 1 up

Round Three - Jesper Parnevik beat him 2 & 1

Quarterfinals - David Duval beat him 5 & 4

Shigeki Maruyama	T-9	$75,000.00

Round One - Beat John Huston 1 up

Round Two - Beat Justin Leonard 1 up

Round Three - Tiger Woods beat him 4 & 3

Mark Calcavecchia	T-9	$75,000.00

Round One - Beat Nick Price 2 & 1

Round Two - Beat Jose Maria Olazabal 4 & 3

Round Three - Paul Lawrie beat him 21 holes

Jim Furyk	T-9	$75,000.00

Round One - Beat Rocco Mediate 2 & 1

Round Two - Beat Bob Tway 2 & 1

Round Three - Davis Love III beat him 3 & 2

Bob Estes	T-9	$75,000.00

Round One - Beat Steve Pate 20 holes

Round Two - Beat Ernie Els 1 up

Round Three - Miguel Angel Jimenez beat him 2 & 1

Sergio Garcia	T-9	$75,000.00

Round One - Beat Loren Roberts 20 holes

Round Two - Beat Mike Weir 7 & 6

Round Three - David Duval beat him 2 & 1

Jesper Parnevik	T-9	$75,000.00

Round One - Beat Padraig Harrington 1 up
Round Two - Beat Joe Ozaki 19 holes
Round Three - Scott Hoch beat him 2 & 1

| Thomas Bjorn | T-9 | | $75,000.00 |

Round One - Beat Glen Day 1 up
Round Two - Beat Colin Montgomerie 23 holes
Round Three - Darren Clarke beat him 1 up

| Duffy Waldorf | T-9 | | $75,000.00 |

Round One - Beat Vijay Singh 2 & 1
Round Two - Beat Steve Stricker 2 & 1
Round Three - Hal Sutton beat him 2 & 1

Touchstone Energy Tucson Open

Course: Omni Tucson National Resort, Tucson, Ariz.
Par: 72 Yardage: 7,109
Last day of event: Sunday, February 27, 2000

Player	Place	Score	Earnings
Jim Carter	Win	66-68-69-66=269	$540,000.00
Jean Van de Velde	T-2	68-69-65-69=271	$224,000.00
Chris DiMarco	T-2	68-69-68-66=271	$224,000.00
Tom Scherrer	T-2	65-66-68-72=271	$224,000.00
Steve Jones	T-5	66-70-67-69=272	$114,000.00
Rick Fehr	T-5	69-71-66-66=272	$114,000.00
Steve Flesch	T-7	66-69-68-70=273	$90,375.00
Kirk Triplett	T-7	67-70-69-67=273	$90,375.00
Woody Austin	T-7	70-68-67-68=273	$90,375.00
Steve Lowery	T-7	64-72-71-66=273	$90,375.00

Doral-Ryder Open

Course: Doral C.C. (Blue), Miami, Fla.
Par: 72 Yardage: 7,125
Last day of event: Sunday, March 5, 2000

Player	Place	Score	Earnings
Jim Furyk	Win	65-67-68-65=265	$540,000.00
Franklin Langham	2	66-63-68-70=267	$324,000.00
Nick Price	3	66-71-66-67=270	$204,000.00
Shigeki Maruyama	T-4	67-65-70-69=271	$132,000.00
David Duval	T-4	71-64-70-66=271	$132,000.00
Scott Verplank	T-6	67-69-68-68=272	$104,250.00
Russ Cochran	T-6	69-67-69-67=272	$104,250.00
Stephen Ames	8	71-61-69-72=273	$93,000.00
Bruce Lietzke	T-9	65-70-69-70=274	$81,000.00
Jay Don Blake	T-9	69-70-71-64=274	$81,000.00
Edward Fryatt	T-9	75-62-71-66=274	$81,000.00

Honda Classic

Course: TPC at Heron Bay, Coral Springs, Fla.
Par: 72 Yardage: 7,268
Last day of event: Sunday, March 12, 2000

Player	Place	Score	Earnings
Dudley Hart	Win	65-69-70-65=269	$522,000.00
J.P. Hayes	T-2	65-67-68-70=270	$255,200.00
Kevin Wentworth	T-2	67-67-71-65=270	$255,200.00
Brian Gay	T-4	65-70-67-69=271	$127,600.00
Jim Furyk	T-4	68-71-65-67=271	$127,600.00
Jonathan Kaye	6	69-66-67-70=272	$104,400.00
Robert Damron	T-7	70-68-69-66=273	$84,390.00
Carlos Franco	T-7	65-69-71-68=273	$84,390.00
Rick Fehr	T-7	66-68-71-68=273	$84,390.00
Mark Calcavecchia	T-7	66-71-69-67=273	$84,390.00
Hal Sutton	T-7	67-66-72-68=273	$84,390.00

Bay Hill Invitational

Course: Bay Hill Club, Orlando, Fla.
Par: 72 Yardage: 7,239
Last day of event: Sunday, March 19, 2000

Player	Place	Score	Earnings
Tiger Woods	Win	69-64-67-70=270	$540,000.00
Davis Love III	2	72-67-63-72=274	$324,000.00
Skip Kendall	3	70-67-71-67=275	$204,000.00
Neal Lancaster	T-4	70-68-69-70=277	$132,000.00
Loren Roberts	T-4	71-69-70-67=277	$132,000.00
Stewart Cink	6	71-67-70-70=278	$108,000.00
Jay Williamson	T-7	72-70-69-68=279	$96,750.00
Mike Weir	T-7	70-64-72-73=279	$96,750.00
Woody Austin	9	71-67-71-71=280	$87,000.00
Paul Goydos	T-10	69-69-72-71=281	$72,000.00
Billy Mayfair	T-10	71-69-69-72=281	$72,000.00
Tim Herron	T-10	72-71-67-71=281	$72,000.00
Brandel Chamblee	T-10	76-68-68-69=281	$72,000.00

The Players Championship

Course: TPC at Sawgrass, Ponte Vedra Beach, Fla.
Par: 72 Yardage: 7,093
Last day of event: Monday, March 27, 2000

Player	Place	Score	Earnings
Hal Sutton	Win	69-69-69-71=278	$1,080,000.00
Tiger Woods	2	71-71-66-71=279	$648,000.00
Scott Dunlap	T-3	73-70-71-70=284	$270,600.00
Nick Price	T-3	73-71-73-67=284	$270,600.00
Colin Montgomerie	T-3	75-69-70-70=284	$270,600.00
Jeff Maggert	T-3	77-68-71-68=284	$270,600.00
Robert Damron	T-3	78-70-66-70=284	$270,600.00
Tom Lehman	8	71-68-72-74=285	$186,000.00
Lee Janzen	T-9	70-73-70-73=286	$156,000.00
Len Mattiace	T-9	70-72-73-71=286	$156,000.00
Greg Chalmers	T-9	71-75-69-71=286	$156,000.00
Mark O'Meara	T-9	75-74-70-67=286	$156,000.00

BellSouth Classic

Course: TPC at Sugarloaf, Duluth, Ga.
Par: 72 Yardage: 7,259
Last day of event: Sunday, April 2, 2000

Player	Place	Score	Earnings
Phil Mickelson	Win	67-69-69=205	$504,000.00
Playoff: Beat Gary Nicklaus with birdie on first extra hole			
Gary Nicklaus	2	68-69-68=205	$302,400.00
Kenny Perry	T-3	67-70-70=207	$162,400.00
Harrison Frazar	T-3	69-68-70=207	$162,400.00
Steve Jones	T-5	67-71-70=208	$94,920.00
Jay Don Blake	T-5	67-72-69=208	$94,920.00
John Huston	T-5	68-67-73=208	$94,920.00
Tom Pernice, Jr.	T-5	73-66-69=208	$94,920.00
Joey Sindelar	T-5	68-66-74=208	$94,920.00
Chris Perry	T-10	71-69-69=209	$64,400.00
Stewart Cink	T-10	71-71-67=209	$64,400.00
Blaine McCallister	T-10	67-70-72=209	$64,400.00
Steve Flesch	T-10	73-67-69=209	$64,400.00
Dicky Pride	T-10	73-68-68=209	$64,400.00

Masters

Course: Augusta National G.C., Augusta, Ga.
Par: 72 Yardage: 6,985
Last day of event: Sunday, April 9, 2000

Player	Place	Score	Earnings
Vijay Singh	Win	72-67-70-69=278	$828,000.00
Ernie Els	2	72-67-74-68=281	$496,800.00
Loren Roberts	T-3	73-69-71-69=282	$266,800.00
David Duval	T-3	73-65-74-70=282	$266,800.00
Tiger Woods	5	75-72-68-69=284	$184,000.00
Tom Lehman	6	69-72-75-69=285	$165,600.00
Davis Love III	T-7	75-72-68-71=286	$143,367.00
Phil Mickelson	T-7	71-68-76-71=286	$143,367.00
Carlos Franco	T-7	79-68-70-69=286	$143,367.00
Hal Sutton	10	72-75-71-69=287	$124,200.00

MCI Classic

Course: Harbour Town G.L., Hilton Head, S.C.
Par: 71 Yardage: 6,916
Last day of event: Sunday, April 16, 2000

Player	Place	Score	Earnings
Stewart Cink	Win	71-68-66-65=270	$540,000.00
Tom Lehman	2	70-70-67-65=272	$324,000.00
Dan Forsman	T-3	66-71-68-70=275	$128,250.00
Davis Love III	T-3	68-66-70-71=275	$128,250.00
Vijay Singh	T-3	70-70-71-64=275	$128,250.00
Larry Mize	T-3	73-67-65-70=275	$128,250.00
Edward Fryatt	T-3	67-74-65-69=275	$128,250.00
Ernie Els	T-3	68-67-66-74=275	$128,250.00
Jesper Parnevik	T-9	70-69-67-70=276	$84,000.00
John Huston	T-9	71-68-69-68=276	$84,000.00

Greater Greensboro Chrysler Classic

Course: Forest Oaks C.C., Greensboro, N.C.
Par: 72 Yardage: 7,062
Last day of event: Sunday, April 23, 2000

Player	Place	Score	Earnings
Hal Sutton	Win	67-64-72-71=274	$540,000.00
Andrew Magee	2	70-68-68-71=277	$324,000.00
Dudley Hart	T-3	72-67-69-70=278	$174,000.00
Mark Calcavecchia	T-3	72-70-71-65=278	$174,000.00
Chris Perry	T-5	71-71-69-70=281	$109,500.00
Doug Dunakey	T-5	67-71-72-71=281	$109,500.00
Jonathan Kaye	T-5	71-67-71-72=281	$109,500.00
Shigeki Maruyama	T-8	71-69-70-72=282	$81,000.00
Kenny Perry	T-8	73-70-69-70=282	$81,000.00
Scott Verplank	T-8	66-74-70-72=282	$81,000.00
Omar Uresti	T-8	67-72-69-74=282	$81,000.00
Jesper Parnevik	T-8	69-69-74-70=282	$81,000.00

Shell Houston Open

Course: TPC at The Woodlands, The Woodlands, Texas
Par: 72 Yardage: 7,018
Last day of event: Sunday, April 30, 2000

Player	Place	Score	Earnings
Robert Allenby	Win	68-67-68-72=275	$504,000.00
Playoff: Beat Craig Stadler with par on fourth extra hole			
Craig Stadler	2	66-69-69-71=275	$302,400.00
Joel Edwards	T-3	68-71-67-70=276	$162,400.00
Loren Roberts	T-3	68-67-72-69=276	$162,400.00

Player	Place	Score	Earnings
Brad Fabel	T-5	70-67-69-71=277	$106,400.00
Mark Brooks	T-5	69-67-72-69=277	$106,400.00
Mike Sposa	T-7	69-68-71-70=278	$84,350.00
David Sutherland	T-7	72-70-67-69=278	$84,350.00
Scott Hoch	T-7	71-65-69-73=278	$84,350.00
Steve Lowery	T-7	73-67-70-68=278	$84,350.00

COMPAQ Classic of New Orleans

Course: English Turn G. & C.C., New Orleans, La.
Par: 72 Yardage: 7,116
Last day of event: Sunday, May 7, 2000

Player	Place	Score	Earnings
Carlos Franco	Win	67-67-68-68=270	$612,000.00
Playoff: Beat Blaine McCallister with par on second extra hole			
Blaine McCallister	2	69-65-68-68=270	$367,200.00
Harrison Frazar	3	71-68-64-68=271	$231,200.00
Stephen Ames	T-4	69-67-68-68=272	$149,600.00
Steve Stricker	T-4	70-71-67-64=272	$149,600.00
Steve Flesch	T-6	69-68-67-69=273	$113,900.00
Kirk Triplett	T-6	72-69-67-65=273	$113,900.00
Bob Burns	T-6	67-73-64-69=273	$113,900.00
Joe Durant	T-9	71-68-68-67=274	$95,200.00
Scott Hoch	T-9	71-68-69-66=274	$95,200.00

GTE Byron Nelson Classic

Course: TPC at Las Colinas, Cottonwood Valley Course, Irving, Texas
Home Course / TPC at Las Colinas, Par: 70 Yardage: 6,994
Last day of event: Sunday, May 14, 2000

Player	Place	Score	Earnings
Jesper Parnevik	Win	70-65-68-66=269	$720,000.00
Playoff: Beat Davis Love III with par on third extra hole. Phil Mickelson (par) eliminated on second hole.			
Davis Love III	T-2	66-63-71-69=269	$352,000.00
Phil Mickelson	T-2	73-63-68-65=269	$352,000.00
John Huston	T-4	68-65-67-70=270	$176,000.00
Tiger Woods	T-4	73-67-67-63=270	$176,000.00
Bob Estes	6	69-68-68-66=271	$144,000.00
Mark Brooks	T-7	69-66-70-67=272	$129,000.00
Brandel Chamblee	T-7	72-65-71-64=272	$129,000.00
Jerry Smith	9	68-68-70-67=273	$116,000.00
Tommy Armour III	T-10	70-66-72-66=274	$100,000.00
Paul Stankowski	T-10	72-67-66-69=274	$100,000.00
Scott Dunlap	T-10	73-65-70-66=274	$100,000.00

Mastercard Colonial

Course: Colonial C.C., Fort Worth, Texas
Par: 70 Yardage: 7,080
Last day of event: Sunday, May 21, 2000

Player	Place	Score	Earnings
Phil Mickelson	Win	67-68-70-63=268	$594,000.00
Davis Love III	T-2	67-66-69-68=270	$290,400.00
Stewart Cink	T-2	70-64-65-71=270	$290,400.00
Rocco Mediate	T-4	68-67-69-68=272	$145,200.00
David Toms	T-4	67-66-72-67=272	$145,200.00
Greg Kraft	T-6	67-68-71-67=273	$114,675.00
Bob Estes	T-6	69-72-66-66=273	$114,675.00
John Cook	T-8	66-70-70-68=274	$89,100.00
Mike Weir	T-8	67-68-69-70=274	$89,100.00
Len Mattiace	T-8	67-72-67-68=274	$89,100.00
Jim Furyk	T-8	69-66-72-67=274	$89,100.00
Mark Calcavecchia	T-8	72-67-67-68=274	$89,100.00

Memorial Tournament

Course: Muirfield Village G.C., Dubin, Ohio
Par: 72 Yardage: 7,193
Last day of event: Monday, May 29, 2000

Player	Place	Score	Earnings
Tiger Woods	Win	71-63-65-70=269	$558,000.00
Justin Leonard	T-2	70-70-66-68=274	$272,800.00
Ernie Els	T-2	73-64-72-65=274	$272,800.00
Mike Weir	4	74-65-68-69=276	$148,800.00
Paul Azinger	T-5	72-71-69-66=278	$113,150.00
Steve Lowery	T-5	73-66-66-73=278	$113,150.00
Steve Flesch	T-5	76-68-64-70=278	$113,150.00
Hal Sutton	T-8	71-71-67-70=279	$93,000.00
Fred Couples	T-8	74-69-69-67=279	$93,000.00
Shigeki Maruyama	T-10	73-69-68-70=280	$80,600.00
J.P. Hayes	T-10	74-66-71-69=280	$80,600.00

Kemper Insurance Open

Course: TPC at Avenel, Potomac, Md.
Par: 71 Yardage: 7,005
Last day of event: Sunday, June 4, 2000

Player	Place	Score	Earnings
Tom Scherrer	Win	67-68-69-67=271	$540,000.00
Franklin Langham	T-2	70-67-66-70=273	$180,000.00
Steve Lowery	T-2	64-68-70-71=273	$180,000.00
Justin Leonard	T-2	65-68-71-69=273	$180,000.00
Greg Chalmers	T-2	65-71-69-68=273	$180,000.00
Kazuhiko Hosokawa	T-2	73-68-66-66=273	$180,000.00
Tim Herron	T-7	66-69-71-69=275	$93,500.00
David Peoples	T-7	71-68-67-69=275	$93,500.00
Stuart Appleby	T-7	70-73-64-68=275	$93,500.00
Bill Glasson	T-10	68-68-70-70=276	$75,000.00
Kirk Triplett	T-10	68-70-68-70=276	$75,000.00
Donnie Hammond	T-10	67-66-74-69=276	$75,000.00

Buick Classic

Course: Westchester C.C., Harrison, N.Y.
Par: 71 Yardage: 6,722
Last day of event: Sunday, June 11, 2000

Player	Place	Score	Earnings
Dennis Paulson	Win	65-68-75-68=276	$540,000.00
Playoff: Beat David Duval with par on fourth extra hole			
David Duval	2	70-67-70-69=276	$324,000.00
Sergio Garcia	3	74-70-65-68=277	$204,000.00
Greg Norman	4	71-72-68-67=278	$144,000.00
Jesper Parnevik	T-5	71-70-70-68=279	$101,700.00
Joey Sindelar	T-5	68-68-71-72=279	$101,700.00
John Cook	T-5	68-71-68-72=279	$101,700.00
Chris Perry	T-5	69-70-68-72=279	$101,700.00
Ernie Els	T-5	70-69-68-72=279	$101,700.00
Steve Lowery	10	70-69-69-72=280	$81,000.00

U.S. Open

Courses: Pebble Beach G.L., Pebble Beach, Calif.
Par: 71 Yardage: 6,846
Last day of event: Sunday, June 18, 2000

Player	Place	Score	Earnings
Tiger Woods	Win	65-69-71-67=272	$800,000.00
Ernie Els	T-2	74-73-68-72=287	$390,150.00
Miguel-A. Jimenez	T-2	66-74-76-71=287	$390,150.00
John Huston	4	67-75-76-70=288	$212,779.00

Padraig Harrington	T-5	73-71-72-73=289	$162,526.00
Lee Westwood	T-5	71-71-76-71=289	$162,526.00
Nick Faldo	7	69-74-76-71=290	$137,203.00
David Duval	T-8	75-71-74-71=291	$112,766.00
Stewart Cink	T-8	77-72-72-70=291	$112,766.00
Loren Roberts	T-8	68-78-73-72=291	$112,766.00
Vijay Singh	T-8	70-73-80-68=291	$112,766.00

FedEx St. Jude Classic

Course: TPC at Southwind, Germantown, Tenn.
Par: 71 Yardage: 7,006
Last day of event: Sunday, June 25, 2000

Player	Place	Score	Earnings
Notah Begay III	Win	66-69-67-69=271	$540,000.00
Chris DiMarco	T-2	66-68-69-69=272	$264,000.00
Bob May	T-2	66-66-69-71=272	$264,000.00
Joe Ogilvie	T-4	65-68-70-70=273	$124,000.00
Russ Cochran	T-4	67-66-71-69=273	$124,000.00
Pete Jordan	T-4	71-67-69-66=273	$124,000.00
Loren Roberts	T-7	67-70-69-68=274	$90,375.00
Craig Parry	T-7	70-65-69-70=274	$90,375.00
Tom Scherrer	T-7	69-71-68-66=274	$90,375.00
Robert Damron	T-7	71-64-71-68=274	$90,375.00

Canon Greater Hartford Open

Course: TPC at River Highlands, Cromwell, Conn.
Par: 70 Yardage: 6,820
Last day of event: Sunday, July 2, 2000

Player	Place	Score	Earnings
Notah Begay III	Win	64-65-67-64=260	$504,000.00
Mark Calcavecchia	2	65-64-64-68=261	$302,400.00
Kirk Triplett	3	64-72-61-67=264	$190,400.00
Jim Furyk	4	66-66-67-67=266	$134,400.00
Steve Flesch	T-5	67-67-67-67=268	$98,350.00
Doug Barron	T-5	65-69-67-67=268	$98,350.00
Chris DiMarco	T-5	69-66-67-66=268	$98,350.00
Edward Fryatt	T-5	67-64-66-71=268	$98,350.00
Scott Dunlap	T-9	68-68-66-67=269	$75,600.00
John Huston	T-9	67-70-66-66=269	$75,600.00
Kevin Sutherland	T-9	68-70-66-65=269	$75,600.00

Advil Western Open

Course: Cog Hill G. & C.C. (Dubsdread), Lemont, Ill.
Par: 72 Yardage: 7,073
Last day of event: Sunday, July 9, 2000

Player	Place	Score	Earnings
Robert Allenby	Win	69-69-68-68=274	$540,000.00
Playoff: Beat Nick Price with par on first extra hole			
Nick Price	2	63-72-70-69=274	$324,000.00
Greg Kraft	T-3	69-69-70-68=276	$156,000.00
Jim Furyk	T-3	66-70-69-71=276	$156,000.00
Shigeki Maruyama	T-3	72-68-66-70=276	$156,000.00
Jeff Maggert	T-6	70-71-68-68=277	$100,500.00
Franklin Langham	T-6	69-65-74-69=277	$100,500.00
Brian Henninger	T-6	70-63-70-74=277	$100,500.00
Carl Paulson	T-9	67-70-70-71=278	$72,000.00
David Toms	T-9	72-67-68-71=278	$72,000.00
Scott Hoch	T-9	72-68-69-69=278	$72,000.00
Fred Couples	T-9	67-68-73-70=278	$72,000.00
Frank Lickliter II	T-9	74-67-70-67=278	$72,000.00
Steve Flesch	T-9	69-66-68-75=278	$72,000.00

Greater Milwaukee Open

Course: Brown Deer Park G.C., Milwaukee, Wis.
Par: 71 Yardage: 6,759
Last day of event: Sunday, July 16, 2000

Player	Place	Score	Earnings
Loren Roberts	Win	65-66-63-66=260	$450,000.00
Franklin Langham	2	66-66-64-72=268	$270,000.00
Mathew Goggin	T-3	68-68-65-68=269	$120,000.00
J.P. Hayes	T-3	66-66-68-69=269	$120,000.00
Kenny Perry	T-3	64-70-67-68=269	$120,000.00
Steve Pate	T-3	70-64-70-65=269	$120,000.00
Joe Durant	T-7	66-70-69-65=270	$80,625.00
Russ Cochran	T-7	70-65-70-65=270	$80,625.00
Skip Kendall	T-9	69-68-66-68=271	$62,500.00
Chris Perry	T-9	66-67-68-70=271	$62,500.00
Olin Browne	T-9	68-69-70-64=271	$62,500.00
John Rollins	T-9	68-68-72-63=271	$62,500.00
Frank Lickliter II	T-9	65-66-67-73=271	$62,500.00

British Open

Course: Old Course at St. Andrews, St. Andrews, Fife, Scotland
Par: 72 Yardage: 7,115
Last day of event: Sunday, July 23, 2000

Player	Place	Score	Earnings
Tiger Woods	Win	67-66-67-69=269	$759,150.00
Thomas Bjorn	T-2	69-69-68-71=277	$371,983.50
Ernie Els	T-2	66-72-70-69=277	$371,983.50
Tom Lehman	T-4	68-70-70-70=278	$197,379.00
David Toms	T-4	69-67-71-71=278	$197,379.00
Fred Couples	6	70-68-72-69=279	$151,830.00
Pierre Fulke	T-7	69-72-70-69=280	$100,587.37
Paul Azinger	T-7	69-72-72-67=280	$100,587.37
Loren Roberts	T-7	69-68-70-73=280	$100,587.37
Darren Clarke	T-7	70-69-68-73=280	$100,587.37

B.C. Open

Course: En-Joie G.C., Endicott, N.Y.
Par: 72 Yardage: 6,974
Last day of event: Sunday, July 23, 2000

Player	Place	Score	Earnings
Brad Faxon	Win	68-66-68-68=270	$360,000.00
Esteban Toledo	2	64-67-71-69=271	$216,000.00
Bill Glasson	T-3	68-69-70-67=274	$116,000.00
Glen Hnatiuk	T-3	67-67-71-69=274	$116,000.00
Brett Quigley	T-5	69-69-69-68=275	$70,250.00
Richard Zokol	T-5	70-67-70-68=275	$70,250.00
Jerry Kelly	T-5	74-63-67-71=275	$70,250.00
Dave Stockton, Jr.	T-5	75-67-65-68=275	$70,250.00
Mathew Goggin	9	71-68-71-66=276	$58,000.00
Grant Waite	T-10	69-67-70-71=277	$46,000.00
Joe Ogilvie	T-10	69-70-67-71=277	$46,000.00
Andy Bean	T-10	69-69-72-67=277	$46,000.00
Paul Goydos	T-10	72-68-69-68=277	$46,000.00
Bob Heintz	T-10	71-65-73-68=277	$46,000.00

John Deere Classic

Course: TPC at Deere Run, Silvis, Ill.
Par: 71 Yardage: 7,183
Last day of event: Monday, July 31, 2000

Player	Place	Score	Earnings
Michael Clark II	Win	70-65-63-67=265	$468,000.00

Playoff: Beat Kirk Triplett with birdie on fourth extra hole

Player	Place	Score	Earnings
Kirk Triplett	2	67-66-62-70=265	$280,800.00
Charles Howell III	3	69-64-67-66=266	$176,800.00
Chris Riley	4	68-67-65-67=267	$124,800.00
Shaun Micheel	T-5	68-66-69-65=268	$98,800.00
Steve Lowery	T-5	67-70-68-63=268	$98,800.00
Tim Herron	7	65-65-70-69=269	$87,100.00
Neal Lancaster	T-8	69-68-67-66=270	$78,000.00
David Frost	T-8	65-62-70-73=270	$78,000.00
Jim McGovern	T-10	69-68-66-68=271	$67,600.00
Len Mattiace	T-10	70-68-65-68=271	$67,600.00

The International presented by Qwest

Course: Castle Pine G.C., Castle Rock, Colo. (Stableford format)
Par: 72 Yardage: 7,559
Last day of event: Sunday, August 6, 2000

Player	Place	Score	Earnings
Ernie Els	Win	15-19-6-8=48	$630,000.00
Phil Mickelson	2	10-8-14-12=44	$378,000.00
Stuart Appleby	3	14-14-2-11=41	$238,000.00
Greg Norman	4	12-14-6-6=38	$168,000.00
Craig-A. Spence	5	6-10-6-10=32	$140,000.00
Glen Hnatiuk	T-6	6-14-4-7=31	$121,625.00
Joe Ogilvie	T-6	2-8-11-10=31	$121,625.00
Stephen Ames	8	15-2-7-6=30	$108,500.00
Edward Fryatt	T-9	2-12-14-1=29	$98,000.00
Vijay Singh	T-9	3-8-9-9=29	$98,000.00

Buick Open

Course: Warwick Hills C.C., Grand Blanc, Mich.
Par: 72 Yardage: 7,101
Last day of event: Sunday, August 13, 2000

Player	Place	Score	Earnings
Rocco Mediate	Win	68-64-70-66=268	$486,000.00
Chris Perry	2	67-69-65-68=269	$291,600.00
Hal Sutton	3	67-67-69-68=271	$183,600.00
Phil Mickelson	T-4	69-71-65-68=273	$118,800.00
Woody Austin	T-4	63-67-73-70=273	$118,800.00
Joe Ozaki	T-6	66-69-69-70=274	$84,510.00
Jeff Maggert	T-6	69-70-67-68=274	$84,510.00
Dudley Hart	T-6	70-65-70-69=274	$84,510.00
Brad Faxon	T-6	70-69-66-69=274	$84,510.00
Carl Paulson	T-6	70-70-68-66=274	$84,510.00

PGA Championship

Course: Valhalla G.C., Louisville, Ky.
Par: 72 Yardage: 7,167
Last day of event: Sunday, August 20, 2000

Player	Place	Score	Earnings
Tiger Woods	Win	66-67-70-67=270	$900,000.00

Playoff: Won three-hole aggregate playoff (3-4-5=12) with Bob May (4-4-5=13)

Player	Place	Score	Earnings
Bob May	2	72-66-66-66=270	$540,000.00
Thomas Bjorn	3	72-68-67-68=275	$340,000.00
Stuart Appleby	T-4	70-69-68-69=276	$198,666.67
Greg Chalmers	T-4	71-69-66-70=276	$198,666.67
Jose Maria Olazabal	T-4	76-68-63-69=276	$198,666.66
Franklin Langham	7	72-71-65-69=277	$157,000.00
Notah Begay III	8	72-66-70-70=278	$145,000.00
Phil Mickelson	T-9	70-70-69-70=279	$112,500.00
Davis Love III	T-9	68-69-72-70=279	$112,500.00
Darren Clarke	T-9	68-72-72-67=279	$112,500.00
Fred Funk	T-9	69-68-74-68=279	$112,500.00

Scott Dunlap	T-9	66-68-70-75=279	$112,500.00
Tom Watson	T-9	76-70-65-68=279	$112,500.00

WGC-NEC Invitational
Course: Firestone C.C. (South), Akron, Ohio
Par: 70 Yardage: 7,139
Last day of event: Sunday, August 27, 2000

Player	Place	Score	Earnings
Tiger Woods	Win	64-61-67-67=259	$1,000,000.00
Phillip Price	T-2	66-69-66-69=270	$437,500.00
Justin Leonard	T-2	66-67-71-66=270	$437,500.00
Jim Furyk	T-4	65-69-69-68=271	$243,333.34
Phil Mickelson	T-4	66-66-69-70=271	$243,333.33
Hal Sutton	T-4	68-68-65-70=271	$243,333.33
Stewart Cink	7	72-69-68-63=272	$170,000.00
Paul Azinger	T-8	68-70-70-65=273	$147,500.00
Colin Montgomerie	T-8	71-69-66-67=273	$147,500.00
Thomas Bjorn	T-10	69-69-70-66=274	$125,000.00
Jose Maria Olazabal	T-10	67-73-69-65=274	$125,000.00

Reno-Tahoe Open
Course: Montreux G. & C.C., Reno, Nev.
Par: 72 Yardage: 7,552
Last day of event: Sunday, August 27, 2000

Player	Place	Score	Earnings
Scott Verplank	Win	69-68-71-67=275	$540,000.00

Playoff: Beat Jean Van De Velde with birdie on fourth extra hole

Jean Van de Velde	2	67-71-65-72=275	$324,000.00
Bob May	3	69-67-70-70=276	$204,000.00
Scott McCarron	T-4	66-70-71-71=278	$124,000.00
Brian Henninger	T-4	71-63-71-73=278	$124,000.00
Doug Dunakey	T-4	74-68-64-72=278	$124,000.00
Tom Byrum	T-7	69-72-68-70=279	$87,300.00
Duffy Waldorf	T-7	72-67-69-71=279	$87,300.00
Steve Flesch	T-7	67-68-73-71=279	$87,300.00
David Toms	T-7	72-65-69-73=279	$87,300.00
Franklin Langham	T-7	74-68-71-66=279	$87,300.00

Air Canada Championship
Course: Northview G. & C.C. (Ridge Course), Surrey, British Columbia, Canada
Par: 71 Yardage: 7,065
Last day of event: Sunday, September 3, 2000

Player	Place	Score	Earnings
Rory Sabbatini	Win	68-68-67-65=268	$540,000.00
Grant Waite	2	65-67-68-69=269	$324,000.00
Mark Calcavecchia	3	68-70-65-67=270	$204,000.00
Sergio Garcia	T-4	68-67-69-67=271	$118,125.00
Doug Barron	T-4	65-69-70-67=271	$118,125.00
Michael Clark II	T-4	68-70-70-63=271	$118,125.00
Chris Riley	T-4	71-64-68-68=271	$118,125.00
K.J. Choi	T-8	68-68-68-68=272	$87,000.00
Brent Geiberger	T-8	71-65-69-67=272	$87,000.00
Dave Stockton, Jr.	T-8	65-72-67-68=272	$87,000.00

Bell Canadian Open
Course: Glen Abbey G.C., Oakville, Ontario, Canada
Par: 72 Yardage: 7,112
Last day of event: Sunday, September 10, 2000

Player	Place	Score	Earnings
Tiger Woods	Win	72-65-64-65=266	$594,000.00

Grant Waite	2	69-64-68-66=267	$356,400.00
Sergio Garcia	3	67-69-70-67=273	$224,400.00
Greg Chalmers	T-4	69-65-71-69=274	$145,200.00
Craig Perks	T-4	72-69-67-66=274	$145,200.00
Rory Sabbatini	T-6	70-71-67-68=276	$106,837.50
Steve Flesch	T-6	71-68-68-69=276	$106,837.50
Scott Verplank	T-6	72-67-68-69=276	$106,837.50
Franklin Langham	T-6	73-67-68-68=276	$106,837.50
Keiichiro Fukabori	T-10	70-66-70-71=277	$64,350.00
Brandt Jobe	T-10	70-68-68-71=277	$64,350.00
Craig Stadler	T-10	71-70-69-67=277	$64,350.00
Kevin Sutherland	T-10	65-72-70-70=277	$64,350.00
Shaun Micheel	T-10	69-67-72-69=277	$64,350.00
Paul Stankowski	T-10	72-67-67-71=277	$64,350.00
Hal Sutton	T-10	72-72-65-68=277	$64,350.00
Paul Azinger	T-10	73-65-68-71=277	$64,350.00
J.L. Lewis	T-10	67-70-65-75=277	$64,350.00
Jim McGovern	T-10	76-67-66-68=277	$64,350.00

SEI Pennsylvania Classic
Course: Waynesborough C. C., Paoli, Pa.
Par: 71 Yardage: 6,939
Last day of event: Sunday, September 17, 2000

Player	Place	Score	Earnings
Chris DiMarco	Win	68-67-66-69=270	$576,000.00
Brad Elder	T-2	69-69-68-70=276	$192,000.00
Jonathan Kaye	T-2	68-69-68-71=276	$192,000.00
Mark Calcavecchia	T-2	68-66-70-72=276	$192,000.00
Chris Perry	T-2	72-68-66-70=276	$192,000.00
Scott Hoch	T-2	69-69-73-65=276	$192,000.00
Sandy Lyle	7	69-69-72-67=277	$107,200.00
Jeff Maggert	T-8	69-69-72-68=278	$92,800.00
Scott Verplank	T-8	72-68-70-68=278	$92,800.00
Loren Roberts	T-8	67-71-66-74=278	$92,800.00

Westin Texas Open at LaCantera
Course: LaCantera G.C., San Antonio, Texas
Par: 70 Yardage: 6,905
Last day of event: Sunday, September 24, 2000

Player	Place	Score	Earnings
Justin Leonard	Win	64-68-65-64=261	$468,000.00
Mark Wiebe	2	64-70-65-67=266	$280,800.00
Blaine McCallister	T-3	65-68-67-69=269	$150,800.00
Jim Gallagher, Jr.	T-3	67-70-64-68=269	$150,800.00
Frank Lickliter II	5	68-65-70-67=270	$104,000.00
Esteban Toledo	T-6	68-67-69-67=271	$87,100.00
Duffy Waldorf	T-6	69-67-69-66=271	$87,100.00
Len Mattiace	T-6	65-67-73-66=271	$87,100.00
Dan Forsman	T-9	69-66-68-69=272	$65,000.00
Ben Bates	T-9	67-70-67-68=272	$65,000.00
Brian Watts	T-9	65-69-71-67=272	$65,000.00
Loren Roberts	T-9	64-67-72-69=272	$65,000.00
Corey Pavin	T-9	66-72-66-68=272	$65,000.00

Buick Challenge
Course: Callaway Gardens Resort, Pine Mountain, Ga.
Par: 72 Yardage: 7,057
Last day of event: Sunday, October 1, 2000

Player	Place	Score	Earnings
David Duval	Win	68-69-67-65=269	$414,000.00
Jeff Maggert	T-2	63-69-69-70=271	$202,400.00
Nick Price	T-2	70-68-65-68=271	$202,400.00

Carl Paulson	4	70-67-69-67=273	$110,400.00
Scott Hoch	T-5	67-71-68-69=275	$83,950.00
Brent Geiberger	T-5	71-69-69-66=275	$83,950.00
Joel Edwards	T-5	72-69-68-66=275	$83,950.00
Greg Chalmers	T-8	69-70-68-69=276	$69,000.00
Paul Azinger	T-8	66-71-72-67=276	$69,000.00
Paul Goydos	T-10	69-70-68-70=277	$55,200.00
Billy Andrade	T-10	71-72-68-66=277	$55,200.00
Jay Don Blake	T-10	72-68-67-70=277	$55,200.00
Steve Elkington	T-10	70-73-66-68=277	$55,200.00

Michelob Championship at Kingsmill

Course: Kingsmill G.C., Williamsburg, Va.
Par: 71 Yardage: 6,776
Last day of event: Sunday, October 8, 2000

Player	Place	Score	Earnings
David Toms	Win	68-70-67-66=271	$540,000.00
Playoff: Beat Mike Weir with par on first extra hole			
Mike Weir	2	70-66-71-64=271	$324,000.00
Frank Lickliter II	3	67-69-68-69=273	$204,000.00
Tom Scherrer	4	71-64-72-67=274	$144,000.00
Stephen Ames	T-5	69-69-70-67=275	$105,375.00
Sean Murphy	T-5	66-72-69-68=275	$105,375.00
Bradley Hughes	T-5	68-63-72-72=275	$105,375.00
Mike Reid	T-5	73-68-65-69=275	$105,375.00
Scott Hoch	T-9	70-70-70-66=276	$81,000.00
Michael Bradley	T-9	68-67-71-70=276	$81,000.00
Chris Riley	T-9	69-67-68-72=276	$81,000.00

Invensys Classic at Las Vegas

Course: TPC at Summerlin, Desert Inn C.C., Southern Highlands G.C., Las Vegas, Nev.
Home course / TPC at Summerlin, Par: 72 Yardage: 7,243
Last day of event: Sunday, October 15, 2000

Player	Place	Score	Earnings
Billy Andrade	Win	67-67-63-67-68=332	$765,000.00
Phil Mickelson	2	69-65-67-66-66=333	$459,000.00
Stewart Cink	T-3	68-68-67-65-66=334	$246,500.00
Jonathan Kaye	T-3	68-70-67-67-62=334	$246,500.00
Shaun Micheel	T-5	68-69-66-63-69=335	$149,281.25
John Cook	T-5	65-70-65-68-67=335	$149,281.25
Chris DiMarco	T-5	66-69-70-67-63=335	$149,281.25
Scott McCarron	T-5	67-66-66-66-70=335	$149,281.25
Joe Durant	T-9	66-71-66-67-66=336	$114,750.00
Steve Flesch	T-9	66-71-66-67-66=336	$114,750.00
Tom Byrum	T-9	65-65-65-69-72=336	$114,750.00

Tampa Bay Classic

Course: Westin Innisbrook Resort (Copperhead Course), Palm Harbor, Fla.
Par: 71 Yardage: 7,295
Last day of event: Sunday, October 22, 2000

Player	Place	Score	Earnings
John Huston	Win	66-73-67-65=271	$432,000.00
Carl Paulson	2	66-66-70-72=274	$259,200.00
Frank Lickliter II	T-3	67-68-71-69=275	$139,200.00
Len Mattiace	T-3	68-66-70-71=275	$139,200.00
Joe Durant	5	68-69-73-66=276	$96,000.00
Lee Janzen	T-6	67-71-71-68=277	$80,400.00
Brad Faxon	T-6	70-71-71-65=277	$80,400.00
Steve Lowery	T-6	67-69-69-72=277	$80,400.00
Tim Herron	9	67-71-71-69=278	$69,600.00

Doug Barron	T-10	69-71-70-69=279	$57,600.00
Craig Barlow	T-10	70-70-71-68=279	$57,600.00
Bob Tway	T-10	71-68-71-69=279	$57,600.00
Andrew Magee	T-10	73-68-66-72=279	$57,600.00

National Car Rental Golf Classic/Disney

Course: Walt Disney (Magnolia, Palm), Lake Buena Vista, Fla.
Home course / Magnolia, Par: 72 Yardage: 7,243
Last day of event: Sunday, October 29, 2000

Player	Place	Score	Earnings
Duffy Waldorf	Win	65-66-69-62=262	$540,000.00
Steve Flesch	2	63-65-66-69=263	$324,000.00
Tiger Woods	3	63-67-66-69=265	$204,000.00
Fred Funk	T-4	66-69-66-65=266	$132,000.00
Scott Verplank	T-4	69-67-65-65=266	$132,000.00
Glen Day	6	66-68-66-67=267	$108,000.00
Jeff Sluman	7	68-64-67-70=269	$100,500.00
Steve Lowery	T-8	67-71-66-66=270	$90,000.00
David Sutherland	T-8	68-71-65-66=270	$90,000.00
Paul Azinger	T-10	67-69-67-68=271	$75,000.00
David Morland IV	T-10	66-69-70-66=271	$75,000.00
Carlos Franco	T-10	65-66-71-69=271	$75,000.00

Southern Farm Bureau Classic

Course: Annandale G.C., Madison, Miss.
Par: 72 Yardage: 7,199
Last day of event: Sunday, November 5, 2000

Player	Place	Score	Earnings
Steve Lowery	Win	64-67-65-70=266	$396,000.00
Playoff: Beat Skip Kendall with birdie on first extra hole			
Skip Kendall	2	67-68-65-66=266	$237,600.00
Kenny Perry	3	69-65-65-68=267	$149,600.00
Pete Jordan	T-4	69-64-72-64=269	$96,800.00
Brad Faxon	T-4	72-65-67-65=269	$96,800.00
Tom Byrum	T-6	69-67-66-68=270	$68,860.00
Chris Riley	T-6	69-67-67-67=270	$68,860.00
Grant Waite	T-6	66-67-67-70=270	$68,860.00
Brad Elder	T-6	70-64-69-67=270	$68,860.00
Fred Funk	T-6	70-65-64-71=270	$68,860.00

The Tour Championship

Course: East Lake G.C., Atlanta, Ga.
Par: 70 Yardage: 6,980
Last day of event: Sunday, November 5, 2000

Player	Place	Score	Earnings
Phil Mickelson	Win	67-69-65-66=267	$900,000.00
Tiger Woods	2	68-66-66-69=269	$540,000.00
Nick Price	T-3	70-68-68-67=273	$261,666.67
Ernie Els	T-3	64-72-68-69=273	$261,666.67
Vijay Singh	T-3	69-66-65-73=273	$261,666.66
David Duval	6	65-68-74-67=274	$180,000.00
Stuart Appleby	7	73-65-68-69=275	$170,000.00
Kirk Triplett	T-8	69-69-70-68=276	$150,666.67
Davis Love III	T-8	66-71-71-68=276	$150,666.66
Chris Perry	T-8	69-65-74-68=276	$150,666.67

WGC-American Express Championship

Course: Valderrama G.C., Sotogrande, Andalucia, Spain
Par: 72 Yardage: 6,974
Last day of event: Sunday, November 12, 2000

Player	Place	Score	Earnings
Mike Weir	Win	68-75-65-69=277	$1,000,000.00
Lee Westwood	2	72-72-68-67=279	$500,000.00
Vijay Singh	T-3	71-70-71-68=280	$287,000.00
Duffy Waldorf	T-3	70-69-72-69=280	$287,000.00
Tiger Woods	T-5	71-69-69-72=281	$157,500.00
Padraig Harrington	T-5	66-72-73-70=281	$157,500.00
Nick Price	T-5	63-72-74-72=281	$157,500.00
Sergio Garcia	T-5	69-74-74-64=281	$157,500.00
Michael Campbell	9	72-71-69-70=282	$115,000.00
Mark Calcavecchia	10	72-67-69-75=283	$105,000.00

2001

Tiger Woods completed the "Tiger Slam" by winning the Masters, his fourth consecutive victory in a major. Woods' two-shot victory over David Duval was one of his seven wins in 2001. Retief Goosen won the U.S. Open, shooting even-par 70 in a Monday playoff at Southern Hills, two strokes better than Mark Brooks. Goosen had missed a 2-foot par putt at the 72nd hole, just moments after watching Stewart Cink miss from even closer. David Duval finally cracked the major code, winning the British Open at Royal Lytham by two shots over Niclas Fasth. Thanks to a pair of 65s in the middle two rounds, including a hole-in-one Saturday, David Toms won the PGA Championship at Atlanta Athletic Club by one shot over Phil Mickelson. Mark Calcavecchia broke Mike Souchak's PGA Tour 72-hole scoring record (257, set in 1955), posting rounds of 65-60-64-67 for a 28-under-par 256 at the Phoenix Open. (Calcaveccia's record was broken two years later by Tommy Armour III.) The PGA Tour signed a $900 million TV deal that would extend its halcyon days through 2006. The Ryder Cup was postponed a year because of the 9/11 attacks.

WGC-Accenture Match Play Championship

Course: The Metropolitan G.C., Melbourne, South Oakleigh, Victoria, Australia
Par: 72 Yardage: 7,066
Last day of event: Sunday, January 7, 2001

Player	Place		Earnings
Steve Stricker	Win		$1,000,000.00

Round One - Beat Padraig Harrington 2 & 1
Round Two - Beat Scott Verplank 3 & 2
Round Three - Beat Justin Leonard 6 & 5
Quarterfinals - Beat Nick O'Hern 20 holes
Semifinals - Beat Toru Taniguchi 2 & 1
Finals - Beat Pierre Fulke 2 & 1

Pierre Fulke	2		$500,000.00

Round One - Beat Fred Funk 5 & 4
Round Two - Beat Glen Day 20 holes
Round Three - Beat Michael Campbell 1 up
Quarterfinals - Beat Brad Faxon 19 holes
Semifinals - Beat Ernie Els 2 & 1
Finals - Steve Stricker beat him 2 & 1

Toru Taniguchi	3		$400,000.00

Round One - Beat Bob Estes 3 & 2
Round Two - Beat Vijay Singh 1 up
Round Three - Beat Stuart Appleby 2 & 1
Quarterfinals - Beat Shigeki Maruyama 2 & 1
Semifinals - Steve Stricker beat him 2 & 1
Consolation - Beat Ernie Els 4 & 3

Ernie Els	4		$300,000.00

Round One - Beat Greg Kraft 3 & 2
Round Two - Beat Hidemichi Tanaka 1 up
Round Three - Beat Jean Van de Velde 19 holes
Quarterfinals - Beat Craig Stadler 1 up
Semifinals - Pierre Fulke beat him 2 & 1
Consolation - Toru Taniguchi beat him 4 & 3

Brad Faxon	T-5		$150,000.00

Round One - Beat Jose Coceres 3 & 2
Round Two - Beat Chris Perry 1 up
Round Three - Beat Tom Lehman 1 up
Quarterfinals - Pierre Fulke beat him 19 holes

Nick O'Hern	T-5		$150,000.00

Round One - Beat Hal Sutton 21 holes
Round Two - Beat Tim Herron 2 & 1
Round Three - Beat Dudley Hart 5 & 4
Quarterfinals - Steve Stricker beat him 20 holes

Shigeki Maruyama	T-5		$150,000.00

Round One - Beat Scott Dunlap 2 & 1
Round Two - Beat Bob May 22 holes
Round Three - Beat Mark McNulty 4 & 3
Quarterfinals - Toru Taniguchi beat him 2 & 1

Craig Stadler	T-5		$150,000.00

Round One - Beat John Huston 4 & 2
Round Two - Beat Craig Parry 7 & 6
Round Three - Beat Andrew Coltart 19 holes
Quarterfinals - Ernie Els beat him 1 up

Jean Van de Velde	T-9		$75,000.00

Round One - Beat Duffy Waldorf 19 holes
Round Two - Beat Retief Goosen 4 & 3
Round Three - Ernie Els beat him 19 holes

Andrew Coltart	T-9		$75,000.00

Round One - Beat Phillip Price 3 & 2
Round Two - Beat David Toms 3 & 2
Round Three - Craig Stadler beat him 19 holes

Tom Lehman	T-9		$75,000.00

Round One - Beat Greg Chalmers 2 & 1
Round Two - Beat Jeff Sluman 3 & 2
Round Three - Brad Faxon beat him 1 up

Michael Campbell	T-9		$75,000.00

Round One - Beat Mathias Gronberg 4 & 3
Round Two - Beat Toshi Izawa 5 & 4
Round Three - Pierre Fulke beat him 1 up

Dudley Hart	T-9		$75,000.00

Round One - Beat Skip Kendall 6 & 5
Round Two - Beat Robert Allenby 5 & 4
Round Three - Nick O'Hern beat him 5 & 4

Stuart Appleby	T-9		$75,000.00

Round One - Beat Kenny Perry 1 up
Round Two - Beat Per-Ulrik Johansson 4 & 3
Round Three - Toru Taniguchi beat him 2 & 1

Mark McNulty	T-9		$75,000.00

Round One - Beat Stewart Cink 1 up
Round Two - Beat Paul Lawrie 5 & 4
Round Three - Shigeki Maruyama beat him 4 & 3

Justin Leonard	T-9		$75,000.00

Round One - Beat Patrik Sjoland 6 & 5
Round Two - Beat Gary Orr 20 holes
Round Three - Steve Stricker beat him 6 & 5

Mercedes Championshipss

Course: Kapalua Resort Plantation Course, Kapalua, Maui, Ha.
Par: 73 Yardage: 7,263
Last day of event: Sunday, January 14, 2001

Player	Place	Score	Earnings
Jim Furyk	Win	69-69-69-67=274	$630,000.00
Rory Sabbatini	2	69-69-65-72=275	$380,000.00
Vijay Singh	T-3	71-67-67-71=276	$203,000.00
Ernie Els	T-3	68-66-73-69=276	$203,000.00
John Huston	5	74-67-69-67=277	$140,000.00
Rocco Mediate	6	70-69-70-69=278	$126,000.00
David Duval	7	73-71-65-70=279	$118,000.00
Michael Clark II	T-8	69-70-72-69=280	$99,000.00
David Toms	T-8	70-71-67-72=280	$99,000.00
Justin Leonard	T-8	67-73-69-71=280	$99,000.00
Tiger Woods	T-8	70-73-68-69=280	$99,000.00

Touchstone Energy Tucson Open

Course: Omni Tucson National Resort, The Gallery G.C., Tucson, Ariz.
Par: 72 Yardage: 7,109
Last day of event: Monday, January 15, 2001

Player	Place	Score	Earnings
Garrett Willis	Win	71-69-64-69=273	$540,000.00
Kevin Sutherland	2	67-72-67-68=274	$324,000.00
Geoff Ogilvy	T-3	67-72-68-68=275	$174,000.00
Bob Tway	T-3	73-69-67-66=275	$174,000.00
K.J. Choi	T-5	70-70-70-66=276	$105,375.00
Cliff Kresge	T-5	72-67-71-66=276	$105,375.00
Mark Wiebe	T-5	69-67-66-74=276	$105,375.00
Greg Kraft	T-5	74-65-69-68=276	$105,375.00
Bernhard Langer	T-9	68-69-70-70=277	$72,000.00
Jeff Maggert	T-9	70-68-70-69=277	$72,000.00
Mark Hensby	T-9	69-68-69-71=277	$72,000.00
Rich Beem	T-9	70-69-71-67=277	$72,000.00
Steve Flesch	T-9	72-69-66-70=277	$72,000.00
Harrison Frazar	T-9	68-73-66-70=277	$72,000.00

Sony Open in Hawaii

Course: Waialae C.C., Honolulu, Ha.
Par: 70 Yardage: 7,060
Last day of event: Sunday, January 21, 2001

Player	Place	Score	Earnings
Brad Faxon	Win	64-64-67-65=260	$720,000.00
Tom Lehman	2	66-67-65-66=264	$432,000.00
Ernie Els	3	68-65-65-69=267	$272,000.00
Billy Andrade	4	69-69-66-65=269	$192,000.00
Fred Funk	T-5	66-69-69-67=271	$135,600.00
Loren Roberts	T-5	67-67-69-68=271	$135,600.00
Greg Chalmers	T-5	69-69-66-67=271	$135,600.00
Joe Ozaki	T-5	66-70-68-67=271	$135,600.00
Briny Baird	T-5	68-70-68-65=271	$135,600.00
Tom Byrum	T-10	68-70-67-67=272	$96,000.00
Davis Love III	T-10	70-68-65-69=272	$96,000.00
Brian Gay	T-10	71-65-70-66=272	$96,000.00
Jeff Sluman	T-10	66-73-66-67=272	$96,000.00

Phoenix Open

Course: TPC of Scottsdale, Scottsdale, Ariz.
Par: 71 Yardage: 7,089
Last day of event: Sunday, January 28, 2001

Player	Place	Score	Earnings
Mark Calcavecchia	Win	65-60-64-67=256	$720,000.00
Rocco Mediate	2	68-63-64-69=264	$432,000.00
Steve Lowery	3	69-67-64-68=268	$272,000.00
Scott Verplank	4	64-66-70-70=270	$192,000.00
Chris DiMarco	T-5	68-67-65-71=271	$152,000.00
Tiger Woods	T-5	65-73-68-65=271	$152,000.00
Tom Lehman	T-7	64-70-69-69=272	$129,000.00
Steve Stricker	T-7	71-62-72-67=272	$129,000.00
David Toms	T-9	69-69-68-67=273	$104,000.00
John Daly	T-9	67-70-70-66=273	$104,000.00
Fred Funk	T-9	68-69-70-66=273	$104,000.00
Stewart Cink	T-9	65-66-71-71=273	$104,000.00

AT&T Pebble Beach National Pro-Am

Courses: Pebble Beach G.L., Spyglass Hill G.C., Poppy Hills G.C., Pebble Beach, Calif.
Home Course / Pebble Beach G.L., Par: 72 Yardage: 6,846
Last day of event: Sunday, February 4, 2001

Player	Place	Score	Earnings
Davis Love III	Win	71-69-69-63=272	$720,000.00
Vijay Singh	2	66-68-70-69=273	$432,000.00
Olin Browne	T-3	68-69-65-73=275	$232,000.00
Phil Mickelson	T-3	70-66-66-73=275	$232,000.00
Ronnie Black	5	67-68-70-71=276	$160,000.00
Craig Barlow	T-6	67-71-67-72=277	$139,000.00
Glen Day	T-6	68-75-69-65=277	$139,000.00
Franklin Langham	T-8	70-70-70-68=278	$112,000.00
Frank Nobilo	T-8	70-70-67-71=278	$112,000.00
Jerry Kelly	T-8	69-68-68-73=278	$112,000.00
Mike Weir	T-8	70-70-65-73=278	$112,000.00

Buick Invitational

Course: Torrey Pines (South), Torrey Pines (North), San Diego, Calif.
Home Course -Par: 72 Yardage: 7,055
Last day of event: Sunday, February 11, 2001

Player	Place	Score	Earnings
Phil Mickelson	Win	68-64-71-66=269	$630,000.00

Playoff: Beat Frank Lickliter II with double-bogey on third extra hole (Davis Love III eliminated with bogey on second hole)

Player	Place	Score	Earnings
Frank Lickliter II	T-2	68-67-68-66=269	$308,000.00
Davis Love III	T-2	65-67-70-67=269	$308,000.00
Tiger Woods	4	70-67-67-67=271	$168,000.00
Mike Weir	T-5	68-67-68-69=272	$133,000.00
Brent Geiberger	T-5	64-69-70-69=272	$133,000.00
Jay Don Blake	T-7	68-68-68-69=273	$109,083.33
Greg Kraft	T-7	69-68-66-70=273	$109,083.33
Jay Williamson	T-7	68-69-71-65=273	$109,083.34
Harrison Frazar	T-10	68-68-70-68=274	$87,500.00
Cameron Beckman	T-10	70-68-68-68=274	$87,500.00
Chris Smith	T-10	66-70-71-67=274	$87,500.00

Bob Hope Chrysler Classic

Course: PGA West/Palmer, Bermuda Dunes C.C., Indian Wells C.C., La Quinta C.C.
Home course / PGA West, Par: 72 Yardage: 6,950
Last day of event: Sunday, February 18, 2001

Player	Place	Score	Earnings
Joe Durant	Win	65-61-67-66-65=324	$630,000.00
Paul Stankowski	2	67-64-65-69-63=328	$378,000.00
Mark Calcavecchia	3	64-66-69-65-66=330	$238,000.00
Bob Tway	T-4	68-62-68-68-67=333	$144,666.66
Scott Verplank	T-4	66-68-70-62-67=333	$144,666.67
Brad Faxon	T-4	66-67-70-65-65=333	$144,666.67
Tom Pernice, Jr.	T-7	64-68-66-70-66=334	$112,875.00
Frank Lickliter II	T-7	70-66-64-68-66=334	$112,875.00
Kevin Sutherland	T-9	64-67-66-67-71=335	$98,000.00
Billy Mayfair	T-9	71-62-67-69-66=335	$98,000.00

Nissan Open

Course: Riviera C.C., Pacific Palisades, Calif.
Par: 71 Yardage: 7,078
Last day of event: Sunday, February 25, 2001

Player	Place	Score	Earnings
Robert Allenby	Win	73-64-69-70=276	$612,000.00

Playoff: Beat Brandel Chamblee, Toshi Izawa, Dennis Paulson, Jeff Sluman and Bob Tway with birdie on first extra hole

Player	Place	Score	Earnings
Jeff Sluman	T-2	68-69-70-69=276	$204,000.00
Dennis Paulson	T-2	70-68-68-70=276	$204,000.00
Bob Tway	T-2	67-71-70-68=276	$204,000.00
Brandel Chamblee	T-2	68-68-73-67=276	$204,000.00

Toshi Izawa	T-2	73-68-69-66=276	$204,000.00
Emanuele Canonica	7	68-70-71-68=277	$113,900.00
Neal Lancaster	T-8	69-68-71-70=278	$91,800.00
David Berganio, Jr.	T-8	71-67-70-70=278	$91,800.00
Chris Perry	T-8	68-68-72-70=278	$91,800.00
Jerry Kelly	T-8	72-69-70-67=278	$91,800.00
Davis Love III	T-8	68-67-68-75=278	$91,800.00

Genuity Championship

Course: Doral C.C. (Blue), Miami, Fla.
Par: 72 Yardage: 7,125
Last day of event: Sunday, March 4, 2001

Player	Place	Score	Earnings
Joe Durant	Win	68-70-67-65=270	$810,000.00
Mike Weir	2	62-70-69-71=272	$486,000.00
Jeff Sluman	T-3	69-66-69-70=274	$234,000.00
Vijay Singh	T-3	70-71-66-67=274	$234,000.00
Hal Sutton	T-3	66-66-70-72=274	$234,000.00
Davis Love III	6	65-70-69-71=275	$162,000.00
Nick Price	7	71-68-71-67=277	$150,750.00
Bob Estes	T-8	68-69-71-70=278	$126,000.00
Lee Porter	T-8	69-69-69-71=278	$126,000.00
Billy Andrade	T-8	67-67-74-70=278	$126,000.00
Chris Smith	T-8	69-66-76-67=278	$126,000.00

Honda Classic

Course: TPC at Heron Bay, Coral Springs, Fla.
Par: 72 Yardage: 7,268
Last day of event: Sunday, March 11, 2001

Player	Place	Score	Earnings
Jesper Parnevik	Win	65-67-66-72=270	$576,000.00
Mark Calcavecchia	T-2	67-68-66-70=271	$238,933.33
Craig Perks	T-2	67-70-68-66=271	$238,933.34
Geoff Ogilvy	T-2	65-72-65-69=271	$238,933.33
Joel Edwards	T-5	69-67-68-69=273	$121,600.00
Joe Durant	T-5	67-71-66-69=273	$121,600.00
Stuart Appleby	T-7	68-70-67-69=274	$96,400.00
Steve Flesch	T-7	69-70-67-68=274	$96,400.00
Kaname Yokoo	T-7	71-69-69-65=274	$96,400.00
Jim Furyk	T-7	70-72-67-65=274	$96,400.00

Bay Hill Invitational

Course: Bay Hill Club, Orlando, Fla.
Par: 72 Yardage: 7,239
Last day of event: Sunday, March 18, 2001

Player	Place	Score	Earnings
Tiger Woods	Win	71-67-66-69=273	$630,000.00
Phil Mickelson	2	66-72-70-66=274	$378,000.00
Grant Waite	3	66-71-72-69=278	$238,000.00
Steve Lowery	T-4	68-70-70-71=279	$137,812.50
Greg Norman	T-4	69-71-68-71=279	$137,812.50
Vijay Singh	T-4	71-70-66-72=279	$137,812.50
Sergio Garcia	T-4	71-66-68-74=279	$137,812.50
Lee Janzen	T-8	67-72-69-72=280	$91,000.00
Scott Hoch	T-8	68-72-69-71=280	$91,000.00
Paul Goydos	T-8	68-68-73-71=280	$91,000.00
Jeff Sluman	T-8	67-74-68-71=280	$91,000.00
Chris Perry	T-8	71-66-69-74=280	$91,000.00
Dennis Paulson	T-8	66-75-69-70=280	$91,000.00

The Players Championship

Course: TPC at Sawgrass, Ponte Vedra Beach, Fla.
Par: 72 Yardage: 7,093
Last day of event: Monday, March 26, 2001

Player	Place	Score	Earnings
Tiger Woods	Win	72-69-66-67=274	$1,080,000.00
Vijay Singh	2	67-70-70-68=275	$648,000.00
Bernhard Langer	3	73-68-68-67=276	$408,000.00
Jerry Kelly	4	69-66-70-73=278	$288,000.00
Billy Mayfair	T-5	68-72-70-71=281	$228,000.00
Hal Sutton	T-5	72-71-68-70=281	$228,000.00
Frank Lickliter II	T-7	72-72-70-68=282	$187,000.00
Paul Azinger	T-7	66-70-74-72=282	$187,000.00
Scott Hoch	T-7	67-70-71-74=282	$187,000.00
Joe Durant	T-10	73-73-67-70=283	$156,000.00
Nick Price	T-10	70-74-71-68=283	$156,000.00

BellSouth Classic

Course: TPC at Sugarloaf, Duluth, Ga.
Par: 72 Yardage: 7,279
Last day of event: Sunday, April 1, 2001

Player	Place	Score	Earnings
Scott McCarron	Win	68-67-72-73=280	$594,000.00
Mike Weir	2	76-67-73-67=283	$356,400.00
Chris Smith	T-3	73-70-72-69=284	$171,600.00
Phil Mickelson	T-3	70-66-73-75=284	$171,600.00
Dennis Paulson	T-3	72-65-72-75=284	$171,600.00
Stewart Cink	T-6	70-71-71-73=285	$103,290.00
Joey Sindelar	T-6	73-70-72-70=285	$103,290.00
Mathew Goggin	T-6	69-73-69-74=285	$103,290.00
Charles Howell III	T-6	70-68-74-73=285	$103,290.00
Chris DiMarco	T-6	68-67-73-77=285	$103,290.00

Masters

Course: Augusta National G.C., Augusta, Ga.
Par: 72 Yardage: 6,925
Last day of event: Sunday, April 8, 2001

Player	Place	Score	Earnings
Tiger Woods	Win	70-66-68-68=272	$1,008,000.00
David Duval	2	71-66-70-67=274	$604,800.00
Phil Mickelson	3	67-69-69-70=275	$380,800.00
Mark Calcavecchia	T-4	72-66-68-72=278	$246,400.00
Toshi Izawa	T-4	71-66-74-67=278	$246,400.00
Kirk Triplett	T-6	68-70-70-71=279	$181,300.00
Jim Furyk	T-6	69-71-70-69=279	$181,300.00
Ernie Els	T-6	71-68-68-72=279	$181,300.00
Bernhard Langer	T-6	73-69-68-69=279	$181,300.00
Steve Stricker	T-10	66-71-72-71=280	$128,800.00
Miguel-A. Jimenez	T-10	68-72-71-69=280	$128,800.00
Angel Cabrera	T-10	66-71-70-73=280	$128,800.00
Brad Faxon	T-10	73-68-68-71=280	$128,800.00
Chris DiMarco	T-10	65-69-72-74=280	$128,800.00

WorldCom Classic

Course: Harbour Town G.L., Hilton Head, S.C.
Par: 71 Yardage: 6,973
Last day of event: Monday, April 16, 2001

Player	Place	Score	Earnings
Jose Coceres	Win	68-70-64-71=273	$630,000.00

Playoff: Beat Billy Mayfair with par on fifth extra hole

Player	Place	Score	Earnings
Billy Mayfair	2	65-68-69-71=273	$378,000.00
Bernhard Langer	T-3	69-69-67-69=274	$168,000.00
Scott Verplank	T-3	68-67-69-70=274	$168,000.00
Carl Paulson	T-3	71-63-71-69=274	$168,000.00
Vijay Singh	T-3	65-68-67-74=274	$168,000.00
Mark Brooks	T-7	66-69-71-69=275	$109,083.33
Davis Love III	T-7	68-67-71-69=275	$109,083.33
Steve Flesch	T-7	71-69-72-63=275	$109,083.34
Stewart Cink	T-10	69-71-70-66=276	$91,000.00
Billy Andrade	T-10	66-67-73-70=276	$91,000.00

Shell Houston Open
Course: TPC at The Woodlands, The Woodlands, Texas
Par: 72 Yardage: 7,018
Last day of event: Sunday, April 22, 2001

Player	Place	Score	Earnings
Hal Sutton	Win	70-68-71-69=278	$612,000.00
Lee Janzen	T-2	67-68-73-73=281	$299,200.00
Joe Durant	T-2	67-69-71-74=281	$299,200.00
John Cook	T-4	69-72-72-69=282	$149,600.00
Justin Leonard	T-4	71-70-72-69=282	$149,600.00
Billy Mayfair	T-6	70-72-71-70=283	$113,900.00
Len Mattiace	T-6	72-69-73-69=283	$113,900.00
Vijay Singh	T-6	73-70-69-71=283	$113,900.00
Ben Ferguson	T-9	72-71-68-73=284	$88,400.00
David Toms	T-9	73-68-73-70=284	$88,400.00
Kevin Sutherland	T-9	69-69-72-74=284	$88,400.00
Chris DiMarco	T-9	69-70-71-74=284	$88,400.00

Greater Greensboro Chrysler Classic
Course: Forest Oaks C.C., Greensboro, N.C.
Par: 72 Yardage: 7,062
Last day of event: Sunday, April 29, 2001

Player	Place	Score	Earnings
Scott Hoch	Win	68-68-67-69=272	$630,000.00
Scott Simpson	T-2	66-69-70-68=273	$308,000.00
Brett Quigley	T-2	68-71-67-67=273	$308,000.00
Jeff Maggert	T-4	69-67-70-69=275	$131,950.00
Gabriel Hjertstedt	T-4	70-69-67-69=275	$131,950.00
Jerry Kelly	T-4	67-70-67-71=275	$131,950.00
David Berganio, Jr.	T-4	70-66-68-71=275	$131,950.00
K.J. Choi	T-4	72-66-70-67=275	$131,950.00
Kaname Yokoo	T-9	71-69-65-71=276	$94,500.00
Olin Browne	T-9	71-67-69-69=276	$94,500.00
Jim Furyk	T-9	69-72-66-69=276	$94,500.00

COMPAQ Classic of New Orleans
Course: English Turn G. & C.C., New Orleans, La.
Par: 72 Yardage: 7,116
Last day of event: Sunday, May 6, 2001

Player	Place	Score	Earnings
David Toms	Win	66-73-63-64=266	$720,000.00
Phil Mickelson	2	66-66-64-72=268	$432,000.00
Ernie Els	3	67-69-65-68=269	$272,000.00
Harrison Frazar	4	68-65-66-71=270	$192,000.00
Brian Gay	T-5	66-66-70-69=271	$152,000.00
Chris Smith	T-5	73-66-66-66=271	$152,000.00
Charles Howell III	7	69-71-63-69=272	$134,000.00
Stephen Ames	T-8	69-70-65-69=273	$116,000.00
Frank Lickliter II	T-8	67-71-67-68=273	$116,000.00
Steve Lowery	T-8	71-67-66-69=273	$116,000.00

Verizon Byron Nelson Classic
Course: TPC at Las Colinas Cottonwood Valley Course, Irving, Texas
Home Course / TPC at Las Colinas, Par: 70 Yardage: 7,017
Last day of event: Sunday, May 13, 2001

Player	Place	Score	Earnings
Robert Damron	Win	66-64-67-66=263	$810,000.00
Playoff: Beat Scott Verplank with birdie on fourth extra hole			
Scott Verplank	2	62-67-68-66=263	$486,000.00
Tiger Woods	T-3	66-68-69-63=266	$234,000.00
Nick Price	T-3	69-65-65-67=266	$234,000.00
David Duval	T-3	64-65-70-67=266	$234,000.00
Brian Watts	T-6	68-68-63-68=267	$156,375.00
Justin Leonard	T-6	68-69-61-69=267	$156,375.00
Kenny Perry	T-8	68-65-67-68=268	$130,500.00
David Peoples	T-8	66-69-67-66=268	$130,500.00
Sergio Garcia	T-8	71-68-64-65=268	$130,500.00

Mastercard Colonial
Course: Colonial C.C., Fort Worth, Texas
Par: 70 Yardage: 7,080
Last day of event: Sunday, May 20, 2001

Player	Place	Score	Earnings
Sergio Garcia	Win	69-69-66-63=267	$720,000.00
Brian Gay	T-2	66-69-69-65=269	$352,000.00
Phil Mickelson	T-2	65-68-66-70=269	$352,000.00
Glen Day	4	68-72-64-66=270	$192,000.00
Justin Leonard	T-5	69-67-70-66=272	$146,000.00
Shigeki Maruyama	T-5	72-65-65-70=272	$146,000.00
Brett Quigley	T-5	69-64-66-73=272	$146,000.00
David Toms	T-8	67-70-66-70=273	$116,000.00
Rocco Mediate	T-8	72-62-69-70=273	$116,000.00
Corey Pavin	T-8	68-64-73-68=273	$116,000.00

Kemper Insurance Open
Course: TPC at Avenel, Potomac, Md.
Par: 71 Yardage: 7,005
Last day of event: Monday, May 28, 2001

Player	Place	Score	Earnings
Frank Lickliter II	Win	69-65-66-68=268	$630,000.00
J.J. Henry	2	65-71-67-66=269	$378,000.00
Spike McRoy	T-3	71-66-67-68=272	$182,000.00
Phil Mickelson	T-3	68-67-72-65=272	$182,000.00
Bradley Hughes	T-3	70-63-72-67=272	$182,000.00
Tim Herron	T-6	69-68-68-69=274	$117,250.00
Scott Hoch	T-6	68-70-66-70=274	$117,250.00
Per-Ulrik Johansson	T-6	68-69-66-71=274	$117,250.00
Brent Schwarzrock	T-9	68-67-71-69=275	$94,500.00
Chris DiMarco	T-9	65-70-68-72=275	$94,500.00
Dan Forsman	T-9	68-67-67-73=275	$94,500.00

Memorial Tournament
Course: Muirfield Village G.C., Dubin, Ohio
Par: 72 Yardage: 7,221
Last day of event: Sunday, June 3, 2001

Player	Place	Score	Earnings
Tiger Woods	Win	68-69-68-66=271	$738,000.00
Sergio Garcia	T-2	68-69-70-71=278	$360,800.00
Paul Azinger	T-2	68-67-69-74=278	$360,800.00
Stewart Cink	4	72-69-67-71=279	$196,800.00
Vijay Singh	T-5	70-66-73-71=280	$155,800.00

Toru Taniguchi	T-5	68-74-69-69=280	$155,800.00
Kenny Perry	T-7	72-69-71-69=281	$127,783.34
Robert Allenby	T-7	69-69-70-73=281	$127,783.33
Stuart Appleby	T-7	67-71-69-74=281	$127,783.33
Scott Hoch	10	70-69-69-74=282	$110,700.00

FedEx St. Jude Classic
Course: TPC at Southwind, Germantown, Tenn.
Par: 71 Yardage: 7,030
Last day of event: Sunday, June 10, 2001

Player	Place	Score	Earnings
Bob Estes	Win	61-66-69-71=267	$630,000.00
Bernhard Langer	2	69-65-68-66=268	$378,000.00
Tom Lehman	T-3	69-68-66-66=269	$203,000.00
Scott McCarron	T-3	66-65-66-72=269	$203,000.00
Curtis Strange	T-5	65-67-69-69=270	$127,750.00
Paul Goydos	T-5	66-67-69-68=270	$127,750.00
John Daly	T-5	69-65-63-73=270	$127,750.00
Nick Price	T-8	68-67-69-67=271	$105,000.00
Jesper Parnevik	T-8	67-64-71-69=271	$105,000.00
Scott Hoch	T-10	68-68-67-69=272	$91,000.00
Nick Faldo	T-10	66-70-67-69=272	$91,000.00

U.S. Open
Course: Southern Hills C.C., Tulsa, Ok.
Par: 70 Yardage: 6,973
Last day of event: Monday, June 18, 2001

Player	Place	Score	Earnings
Retief Goosen	Win	66-70-69-71=276	$900,000.00
Playoff: Beat Mark Brooks in18-hole playoff (Goosen 70, Brooks 72)			
Mark Brooks	2	72-64-70-70=276	$530,000.00
Stewart Cink	3	69-69-67-72=277	$325,310.00
Rocco Mediate	4	71-68-67-72=278	$226,777.00
Tom Kite	T-5	73-72-72-64=281	$172,912.00
Paul Azinger	T-5	74-67-69-71=281	$172,912.00
Angel Cabrera	T-7	70-71-72-69=282	$125,172.00
Davis Love III	T-7	72-69-71-70=282	$125,172.00
Kirk Triplett	T-7	72-69-71-70=282	$125,172.00
Vijay Singh	T-7	74-70-74-64=282	$125,172.00
Phil Mickelson	T-7	70-69-68-75=282	$125,172.00

Buick Classic
Course: Westchester C.C., Harrison, N.Y.
Par: 71 Yardage: 6,722
Last day of event: Monday, June 25, 2001

Player	Place	Score	Earnings
Sergio Garcia	Win	68-67-66-67=268	$630,000.00
Scott Hoch	2	67-68-68-68=271	$378,000.00
J.P. Hayes	T-3	68-69-67-69=273	$182,000.00
Billy Andrade	T-3	70-69-68-66=273	$182,000.00
Stewart Cink	T-3	65-72-69-67=273	$182,000.00
Vijay Singh	T-6	67-70-70-67=274	$121,625.00
Brad Faxon	T-6	69-72-66-67=274	$121,625.00
Russ Cochran	T-8	71-68-67-69=275	$105,000.00
Robert Allenby	T-8	69-68-74-64=275	$105,000.00
Jay Williamson	10	70-72-65-69=276	$94,500.00

Canon Greater Hartford Open
Course: TPC at River Highlands, Cromwell, Conn.
Par: 70 Yardage: 6,820
Last day of event: Sunday, July 1, 2001

Player	Place	Score	Earnings
Phil Mickelson	Win	67-68-61-68=264	$558,000.00
Billy Andrade	2	68-65-66-66=265	$334,800.00
Chris DiMarco	T-3	65-67-66-68=266	$161,200.00
David Berganio, Jr.	T-3	67-66-64-69=266	$161,200.00
Dudley Hart	T-3	70-63-70-63=266	$161,200.00
Tom Pernice, Jr.	6	68-68-66-65=267	$111,600.00
Frank Lickliter II	T-7	65-69-68-67=269	$83,921.43
Jerry Kelly	T-7	67-65-69-68=269	$83,921.42
Kenny Perry	T-7	68-68-70-63=269	$83,921.43
Tripp Isenhour	T-7	69-70-67-63=269	$83,921.43
Kirk Triplett	T-7	68-71-65-65=269	$83,921.43
Olin Browne	T-7	68-71-67-63=269	$83,921.43
Shigeki Maruyama	T-7	63-69-73-64=269	$83,921.43

Advil Western Open
Course: Cog Hill G. & C.C. (Dubsdread)
Lemont, Ill.
Par: 72 Yardage: 7,073
Last day of event: Sunday, July 8, 2001

Player	Place	Score	Earnings
Scott Hoch	Win	69-68-66-64=267	$648,000.00
Davis Love III	2	66-67-69-66=268	$388,800.00
Brandel Chamblee	T-3	69-67-70-69=275	$208,800.00
Mike Weir	T-3	71-70-67-67=275	$208,800.00
Rory Sabbatini	T-5	71-68-70-67=276	$136,800.00
Jerry Kelly	T-5	67-73-69-67=276	$136,800.00
Dudley Hart	T-7	70-70-69-68=277	$112,200.00
Kevin Sutherland	T-7	70-70-69-68=277	$112,200.00
Steve Flesch	T-7	71-70-67-69=277	$112,200.00
Vijay Singh	T-10	69-70-70-69=278	$82,800.00
Frank Lickliter II	T-10	70-71-70-67=278	$82,800.00
Steve Stricker	T-10	72-70-68-68=278	$82,800.00
Mark Wiebe	T-10	65-74-67-72=278	$82,800.00
Matt Gogel	T-10	69-74-66-69=278	$82,800.00

Greater Milwaukee Open
Course: Brown Deer Park G.C., Milwaukee, Wis.
Par: 71 Yardage: 6,759
Last day of event: Sunday, July 15, 2001

Player	Place	Score	Earnings
Shigeki Maruyama	Win	68-65-67-66=266	$558,000.00
Playoff: Beat Charles Howell with birdie on first extra hole			
Charles Howell III	2	66-69-67-64=266	$334,800.00
Tim Herron	T-3	69-69-64-67=269	$179,800.00
J.P. Hayes	T-3	69-66-71-63=269	$179,800.00
Brent Geiberger	T-5	65-68-70-67=270	$105,090.00
Blaine McCallister	T-5	69-65-70-66=270	$105,090.00
Harrison Frazar	T-5	70-68-62-70=270	$105,090.00
K.J. Choi	T-5	70-68-66-66=270	$105,090.00
Kenny Perry	T-5	66-63-71-70=270	$105,090.00
Scott Hoch	T-10	67-68-68-68=271	$71,300.00
Jay Haas	T-10	64-71-69-67=271	$71,300.00
Jeff Sluman	T-10	67-68-64-72=271	$71,300.00
Bob Tway	T-10	69-72-66-64=271	$71,300.00
Steve Lowery	T-10	72-69-66-64=271	$71,300.00

British Open

Course: Royal Lytham & St. Annes G.C., Lytham, Lancashire, England
Par: 71 Yardage: 6,905
Last day of event: Sunday, July 22, 2001

Player	Place	Score	Earnings
David Duval	Win	69-73-65-67=274	$858,300.00
Niclas Fasth	2	69-69-72-67=277	$514,980.00
Darren Clarke	T-3	70-69-69-70=278	$202,654.64
Bernhard Langer	T-3	71-69-67-71=278	$202,654.64
Ernie Els	T-3	71-71-67-69=278	$202,654.64
Billy Mayfair	T-3	69-72-67-70=278	$202,654.64
Miguel-A. Jimenez	T-3	69-72-67-70=278	$202,654.64
Ian Woosnam	T-3	72-68-67-71=278	$202,654.64
Jesper Parnevik	T-9	69-68-71-71=279	$91,194.38
Sergio Garcia	T-9	70-72-67-70=279	$91,194.38
Mikko Ilonen	T-9	68-75-70-66=279	$91,194.38
Kevin Sutherland	T-9	75-69-68-67=279	$91,194.38

B.C. Open

Course: En-Joie G.C., Endicott, N.Y.
Par: 72 Yardage: 6,974
Last day of event: Sunday, July 22, 2001

Player	Place	Score	Earnings
Jeff Sluman	Win	67-68-65-66=266	$360,000.00

Playoff: Beat Paul Gow with birdie on second extra hole

Player	Place	Score	Earnings
Paul Gow	2	69-65-66-66=266	$216,000.00
Jonathan Kaye	3	67-65-70-67=269	$136,000.00
Jay Haas	4	68-68-66-68=270	$96,000.00
Steve Pate	5	69-69-67-66=271	$80,000.00
Stephen Ames	T-6	70-70-69-63=272	$69,500.00
Jim McGovern	T-6	67-66-68-71=272	$69,500.00
Brian Watts	T-8	66-72-67-68=273	$60,000.00
Brett Quigley	T-8	67-62-72-72=273	$60,000.00
Brad Fabel	T-10	66-71-69-68=274	$52,000.00
Trevor Dodds	T-10	74-67-69-64=274	$52,000.00

John Deere Classic

Course: TPC at Deere Run, Silvis, Ill.
Par: 71 Yardage: 7,183
Last day of event: Sunday, July 29, 2001

Player	Place	Score	Earnings
David Gossett	Win	67-64-68-66=265	$504,000.00
Briny Baird	2	69-65-66-66=266	$302,400.00
Pete Jordan	3	69-68-65-65=267	$190,400.00
Jeff Sluman	4	70-65-68-65=268	$134,400.00
Ian Leggatt	T-5	67-68-68-66=269	$106,400.00
Matt Gogel	T-5	68-66-67-68=269	$106,400.00
Paul Stankowski	7	67-67-66-70=270	$93,800.00
Woody Austin	T-8	69-66-69-67=271	$84,000.00
Brian Claar	T-8	66-69-66-70=271	$84,000.00
Paul Gow	T-10	65-69-69-69=272	$67,200.00
Jerry Smith	T-10	65-69-67-71=272	$67,200.00
Barry Cheesman	T-10	71-67-66-68=272	$67,200.00
Bradley Hughes	T-10	69-65-66-72=272	$67,200.00

The International presented by Qwest

Course: Castle Pine G.C., Castle Rock, Colo.(Stableford format)
Par: 72 Yardage: 7,559
Last day of event: Sunday, August 5, 2001

Player	Place	Score	Earnings
Tom Pernice, Jr.	Win	12-12-9-1=34	$720,000.00
Chris Riley	2	16-5-8-4=33	$432,000.00
Ernie Els	T-3	9-7-10-6=32	$208,000.00
Chris DiMarco	T-3	7-13-8-4=32	$208,000.00
Vijay Singh	T-3	9-9-12-2=32	$208,000.00
Brett Quigley	T-6	9-6-2-13=30	$139,000.00
Brad Faxon	T-6	8-10-4-8=30	$139,000.00
Woody Austin	8	11-8-8-1=28	$124,000.00
Mark O'Meara	T-9	12-3-4-8=27	$112,000.00
Edward Fryatt	T-9	9-11-2-5=27	$112,000.00

Buick Open

Course: Warwick Hills C.C., Grand Blanc, Mich.
Par: 72 Yardage: 7,127
Last day of event: Sunday, August 12, 2001

Player	Place	Score	Earnings
Kenny Perry	Win	66-64-64-69=263	$558,000.00
Chris DiMarco	T-2	68-67-65-65=265	$272,800.00
Jim Furyk	T-2	64-69-66-66=265	$272,800.00
Tom Pernice, Jr.	T-4	68-67-66-66=267	$136,400.00
Dudley Hart	T-4	68-70-65-64=267	$136,400.00
Padraig Harrington	T-6	67-67-65-69=268	$107,725.00
Brian Gay	T-6	70-67-66-65=268	$107,725.00
Ian Leggatt	T-8	66-68-69-66=269	$93,000.00
Jeff Maggert	T-8	69-66-68-66=269	$93,000.00
Bob Tway	T-10	68-65-67-70=270	$74,400.00
Frank Lickliter II	T-10	68-70-69-63=270	$74,400.00
Justin Leonard	T-10	69-68-63-70=270	$74,400.00
Phil Mickelson	T-10	65-70-71-64=270	$74,400.00

PGA Championship

Course: Atlanta Athletic Club, Duluth, Ga.
Par: 70 Yardage: 7,213
Last day of event: Sunday, August 19, 2001

Player	Place	Score	Earnings
David Toms	Win	66-65-65-69=265	$936,000.00
Phil Mickelson	2	66-66-66-68=266	$562,000.00
Steve Lowery	3	67-67-66-68=268	$354,000.00
Shingo Katayama	T-4	67-64-69-70=270	$222,500.00
Mark Calcavecchia	T-4	71-68-66-65=270	$222,500.00
Billy Andrade	6	68-70-68-66=272	$175,000.00
Scott Hoch	T-7	68-70-69-67=274	$152,333.34
Scott Verplank	T-7	69-68-70-67=274	$152,333.33
Jim Furyk	T-7	70-64-71-69=274	$152,333.33
Justin Leonard	T-10	70-69-67-69=275	$122,000.00
Kirk Triplett	T-10	68-70-71-66=275	$122,000.00
David Duval	T-10	66-68-67-74=275	$122,000.00

WGC-NEC Invitational

Course: Firestone C.C. (South), Akron, Ohio
Par: 70 Yardage: 7,139
Last day of event: Sunday, August 26, 2001

Player	Place	Score	Earnings
Tiger Woods	Win	66-67-66-69=268	$1,000,000.00

Playoff: Beat Jim Furyk with birdie on seventh extra hole

Player	Place	Score	Earnings
Jim Furyk	2	65-66-66-71=268	$500,000.00
Darren Clarke	3	66-68-68-69=271	$375,000.00
Colin Montgomerie	4	66-71-66-70=273	$300,000.00
Davis Love III	T-5	68-68-70-68=274	$201,666.67
Stuart Appleby	T-5	70-64-70-70=274	$201,666.67
Paul Azinger	T-5	67-70-65-72=274	$201,666.66
Phil Mickelson	T-8	67-66-70-72=275	$147,500.00
Ernie Els	T-8	67-70-66-72=275	$147,500.00
Retief Goosen	10	72-69-64-71=276	$131,000.00

Reno-Tahoe Open

Course: Montreux G. & C.C., Reno, Nev.
Par: 72 Yardage: 7,552
Last day of event: Sunday, August 26, 2001

Player	Place	Score	Earnings
John Cook	Win	69-64-74-64=271	$540,000.00
Jerry Kelly	2	66-68-67-71=272	$324,000.00
Bryce Molder	3	70-65-67-71=273	$204,000.00
Charles Howell III	4	68-66-69-71=274	$144,000.00
Duffy Waldorf	T-5	71-67-69-68=275	$114,000.00
Justin Leonard	T-5	71-69-69-66=275	$114,000.00
Tim Herron	T-7	66-70-71-69=276	$93,500.00
J.P. Hayes	T-7	68-68-71-69=276	$93,500.00
Dan Forsman	T-7	71-68-68-69=276	$93,500.00
Brian Gay	T-10	69-69-69-70=277	$78,000.00
Steve Flesch	T-10	67-74-67-69=277	$78,000.00

Air Canada Championship

Course: Northview G. & C.C. (Ridge Course), Surrey, British Columbia, Canada
Par: 71 Yardage: 7,072
Last day of event: Sunday, September 2, 2001

Player	Place	Score	Earnings
Joel Edwards	Win	65-67-68-65=265	$612,000.00
Steve Lowery	2	73-65-68-66=272	$367,200.00
Fred Funk	T-3	70-67-67-69=273	$197,200.00
Matt Kuchar	T-3	68-66-72-67=273	$197,200.00
Brent Geiberger	T-5	66-70-70-68=274	$124,100.00
David Gossett	T-5	67-68-69-70=274	$124,100.00
Kevin Sutherland	T-5	70-69-68-67=274	$124,100.00
Bob Estes	T-8	69-69-69-68=275	$82,025.00
Brent Schwarzrock	T-8	68-68-69-70=275	$82,025.00
Brett Quigley	T-8	68-70-67-70=275	$82,025.00
Chris Riley	T-8	66-71-71-67=275	$82,025.00
Jerry Smith	T-8	71-70-67-67=275	$82,025.00
J.J. Henry	T-8	67-72-66-70=275	$82,025.00
Grant Waite	T-8	70-68-65-72=275	$82,025.00
Edward Fryatt	T-8	72-67-66-70=275	$82,025.00

Bell Canadian Open

Course: Royal Montreal G.C., Ile-Bizard, Quebec, Canada
Par: 70 Yardage: 6,859
Last day of event: Sunday, September 9, 2001

Player	Place	Score	Earnings
Scott Verplank	Win	70-63-66-67=266	$684,000.00
Joey Sindelar	T-2	66-69-69-65=269	$334,400.00
Bob Estes	T-2	69-65-67-68=269	$334,400.00
John Daly	4	66-74-64-66=270	$182,400.00
Sergio Garcia	T-5	69-68-65-69=271	$138,700.00
Paul Gow	T-5	67-67-66-71=271	$138,700.00
David Morland IV	T-5	69-63-73-66=271	$138,700.00
K.J. Choi	T-8	67-68-69-68=272	$98,800.00
David Berganio, Jr.	T-8	69-68-69-66=272	$98,800.00
Michael Muehr	T-8	65-70-68-69=272	$98,800.00
Robert Allenby	T-8	70-68-69-65=272	$98,800.00
Matt Gogel	T-8	65-67-71-69=272	$98,800.00
Dudley Hart	T-8	69-68-71-64=272	$98,800.00

Marconi Pennsylvania Classic

Course: Laurel Valley G. C., Ligonier, Pa.
Par: 72 Yardage: 7,261
Last day of event: Sunday, September 23, 2001

Player	Place	Score	Earnings
Robert Allenby	Win	70-65-66-68=269	$594,000.00
Rocco Mediate	T-2	69-68-67-68=272	$290,400.00
Larry Mize	T-2	73-67-67-65=272	$290,400.00
Kevin Sutherland	4	76-65-64-68=273	$158,400.00
Nick Price	5	66-71-68-69=274	$132,000.00
Steve Elkington	T-6	70-68-69-70=277	$110,550.00
Matt Gogel	T-6	70-73-66-68=277	$110,550.00
Jay Williamson	T-6	74-68-67-68=277	$110,550.00
Glen Hnatiuk	9	70-73-66-69=278	$95,700.00
Cameron Beckman	10	70-71-65-73=279	$89,100.00

Texas Open at LaCantera

Course: LaCantera G.C., San Antonio, Texas
Par: 71 Yardage: 6,928
Last day of event: Sunday, September 30, 2001

Player	Place	Score	Earnings
Justin Leonard	Win	65-64-68-69=266	$540,000.00
Matt Kuchar	T-2	67-68-64-69=268	$264,000.00
J.J. Henry	T-2	70-64-68-66=268	$264,000.00
Bob Estes	T-4	67-68-69-67=271	$132,000.00
Tommy Tolles	T-4	68-69-66-68=271	$132,000.00
Kaname Yokoo	T-6	67-69-68-68=272	$104,250.00
Steve Elkington	T-6	67-70-68-67=272	$104,250.00
David Frost	T-8	70-65-70-68=273	$87,000.00
J.L. Lewis	T-8	71-68-69-65=273	$87,000.00
Bob Burns	T-8	66-72-67-68=273	$87,000.00

Michelob Championship at Kingsmill

Course: Kingsmill G.C., Williamsburg, Va.
Par: 71 Yardage: 6,853
Last day of event: Sunday, October 7, 2001

Player	Place	Score	Earnings
David Toms	Win	64-70-67-68=269	$630,000.00
Kirk Triplett	2	67-68-69-66=270	$378,000.00
Esteban Toledo	T-3	68-67-68-70=273	$203,000.00
Charles Howell III	T-3	70-65-71-67=273	$203,000.00
Len Mattiace	5	67-66-74-67=274	$140,000.00
J.J. Henry	6	65-71-72-67=275	$126,000.00
Michael Muehr	T-7	65-70-70-71=276	$101,850.00
Jim McGovern	T-7	71-68-68-69=276	$101,850.00
Neal Lancaster	T-7	65-69-70-72=276	$101,850.00
Rich Beem	T-7	66-70-72-68=276	$101,850.00
Jimmy Green	T-7	65-70-73-68=276	$101,850.00

Invensys Classic at Las Vegas

Course: TPC at Summerlin, TPC At The Canyons, Southern Highlands G.C., Las Vegas, Nev.
Home course / TPC at Summerlin, Par: 72 Yardage: 7,243
Last day of event: Sunday, October 14, 2001

Player	Place	Score	Earnings
Bob Estes	Win	65-66-67-68-63=329	$810,000.00
Tom Lehman	T-2	63-62-72-67-66=330	$396,000.00
Rory Sabbatini	T-2	64-67-72-63-64=330	$396,000.00
Davis Love III	T-4	69-65-68-69-61=332	$198,000.00
Scott McCarron	T-4	68-65-65-63-71=332	$198,000.00
Cameron Beckman	6	67-67-69-66-64=333	$162,000.00
Chris Riley	T-7	69-65-68-67=337	$135,562.50
Craig Parry	T-7	64-66-66-70-71=337	$135,562.50
Scott Verplank	T-7	67-67-71-65-67=337	$135,562.50
John Daly	T-7	67-62-72-69-67=337	$135,562.50

National Car Rental Golf Classic/Disney
Course: Walt Disney (Magnolia, Palm), Lake Buena Vista, Fla.
Home course / Magnolia, Par: 72 Yardage: 7,243
Last day of event: Sunday, October 21, 2001

Player	Place	Score	Earnings
Jose Coceres	Win	68-65-64-68=265	$612,000.00
Davis Love III	2	67-66-67-66=266	$367,200.00
David Peoples	T-3	69-65-68-66=268	$197,200.00
Jerry Smith	T-3	66-66-73-63=268	$197,200.00
Steve Flesch	5	73-65-66-65=269	$136,000.00
Vijay Singh	T-6	66-68-67-69=270	$99,328.57
David Toms	T-6	66-68-69-67=270	$99,328.57
Danny Ellis	T-6	67-68-70-65=270	$99,328.57
Skip Kendall	T-6	68-70-64-68=270	$99,328.57
Craig Perks	T-6	70-69-67-64=270	$99,328.58
Scott McCarron	T-6	65-71-65-69=270	$99,328.57
Jesper Parnevik	T-6	71-65-67-67=270	$99,328.57

Buick Challenge
Course: Callaway Gardens Resort, Pine Mountain, Ga.
Par: 72 Yardage: 7,057
Last day of event: Sunday, October 28, 2001

Player	Place	Score	Earnings
Chris DiMarco	Win	67-64-71-65=267	$612,000.00

Playoff: Beat David Duval with par on first extra hole

Player	Place	Score	Earnings
David Duval	2	67-69-68-63=267	$367,200.00
Neal Lancaster	T-3	65-67-68-69=269	$197,200.00
Bob Estes	T-3	71-63-69-66=269	$197,200.00
Davis Love III	5	68-62-69-71=270	$136,000.00
Jeff Maggert	6	67-66-72-66=271	$122,400.00
Per-Ulrik Johansson	T-7	65-70-68-69=272	$109,650.00
Joel Edwards	T-7	65-68-65-74=272	$109,650.00
Nick Price	9	70-68-69-67=274	$98,600.00
Chris Riley	T-10	68-69-69-69=275	$88,400.00
Vijay Singh	T-10	64-67-75-69=275	$88,400.00

Southern Farm Bureau Classic
Course: Annandale G.C., Madison, Miss.
Par: 72 Yardage: 7,199
Last day of event: Sunday, November 4, 2001

Player	Place	Score	Earnings
Cameron Beckman	Win	66-69-67-67=269	$432,000.00
Chad Campbell	2	70-64-65-71=270	$259,200.00
Fred Funk	3	65-69-69-68=271	$163,200.00
Dan Forsman	4	68-70-65-69=272	$115,200.00
Brett Quigley	5	68-69-69-67=273	$96,000.00
K.J. Choi	T-6	67-69-68-70=274	$72,600.00
J.J. Henry	T-6	69-67-68-70=274	$72,600.00
Chris Smith	T-6	70-68-69-67=274	$72,600.00
Carl Paulson	T-6	67-66-70-71=274	$72,600.00
Loren Roberts	T-6	70-71-67-66=274	$72,600.00
Dicky Pride	T-6	66-68-67-73=274	$72,600.00

The Tour Championship
Course: Champions G.C., Houston, Texas
Par: 71 Yardage: 7,220
Last day of event: Sunday, November 4, 2001

Player	Place	Score	Earnings
Mike Weir	Win	68-66-68-68=270	$900,000.00

Playoff: Beat Ernie Els, David Toms and Sergio Garcia with birdie on first extra hole

Player	Place	Score	Earnings
Sergio Garcia	T-2	69-67-66-68=270	$385,000.00
Ernie Els	T-2	69-68-65-68=270	$385,000.00
David Toms	T-2	73-66-64-67=270	$385,000.00
Kenny Perry	T-5	70-67-65-69=271	$202,500.00
Scott Verplank	T-5	67-65-68-71=271	$202,500.00
David Duval	T-7	69-69-63-71=272	$166,666.66
Jim Furyk	T-7	70-71-62-69=272	$166,666.67
Bob Estes	T-7	71-66-65-70=272	$166,666.67
Chris DiMarco	T-10	69-68-69-69=275	$136,666.67
Bernhard Langer	T-10	65-68-69-73=275	$136,666.66
Joe Durant	T-10	73-65-67-70=275	$136,666.67

2002

Tiger Woods won the Masters by three shots over Retief Goosen, but the pre-tournament headlines belonged to activist Martha Burk, who campaigned—unsuccessfully—for Augusta National to amend its all-male membership policy. Also among Woods' six victories in 2002 was the U.S. Open at Bethpage, where he beat Phil Mickelson by three shots. Ernie Els was the last man standing in a wild British Open week at Muirfield, where Woods shot 81 in a third-round gale. Steve Elkington, Stuart Appleby, Thomas Levet and Els finished regulation tied at 6-under-par 278. The two Australians, Elkington and Appleby, were eliminated in a four-hole aggregate playoff, then Els beat the pesky Frenchman Levet with a sand-save par on the first hole of sudden death. Despite Woods nipping at his heels, unheralded Rich Beem posted a closing 68 at Hazeltine to edge Woods by one shot in the PGA Championship. Sam Snead, the PGA Tour's all-time winner with 82 victories, died in May at age 89. Europe won the Ryder Cup 15 ½ to 12 ½ in a less combative resumption of the competition after a year's postponement due to 9/11.

Mercedes Championshipss
Course: Kapalua Resort Plantation Course, Kapalua, Maui, Ha.
Par: 73 Yardage: 7,263
Last day of event: Sunday, January 6, 2002

Player	Place	Score	Earnings
Sergio Garcia	Win	73-69-68-64=274	$720,000.00

Playoff: Beat David Toms with birdie on first extra hole

Player	Place	Score	Earnings
David Toms	2	69-66-72-67=274	$432,000.00
Kenny Perry	3	68-67-71-69=275	$275,000.00
Jim Furyk	4	67-72-73-65=277	$196,000.00
Chris DiMarco	T-5	67-72-68-71=278	$150,000.00
Scott McCarron	T-5	71-72-69-66=278	$150,000.00
Mark Calcavecchia	T-5	72-66-71-69=278	$150,000.00
Scott Verplank	8	67-69-70-73=279	$130,000.00
Brad Faxon	9	71-71-69-69=280	$120,000.00
Bob Estes	T-10	70-70-71-70=281	$105,000.00
Tiger Woods	T-10	68-74-74-65=281	$105,000.00

Sony Open in Hawaii
Course: Waialae C.C., Honolulu, Ha.
Par: 70 Yardage: 7,060
Last day of event: Monday, January 14, 2002

Player	Place	Score	Earnings
Jerry Kelly	Win	66-65-65-70=266	$720,000.00
John Cook	2	66-62-70-69=267	$432,000.00
Jay Don Blake	3	69-67-68-65=269	$272,000.00
Matt Kuchar	T-4	68-69-66-67=270	$165,333.34
David Toms	T-4	68-67-63-72=270	$165,333.33
Charles Howell III	T-4	72-62-66-70=270	$165,333.33
K.J. Choi	T-7	68-65-69-69=271	$112,333.33
Tommy Armour III	T-7	68-70-68-65=271	$112,333.34
Joel Edwards	T-7	70-66-68-67=271	$112,333.33
Stephen Ames	T-7	67-67-66-71=271	$112,333.33
Jim Furyk	T-7	69-66-64-72=271	$112,333.33
David Peoples	T-7	72-68-66-65=271	$112,333.34

Bob Hope Chrysler Classic

Course: PGA West/Palmer, Bermuda Dunes C.C., Indian Wells C.C., Tamarisk C.C., La Quinta, Calif.
Home course / PGA West, Par: 72 Yardage: 6,950
Last day of event: Sunday, January 20, 2002

Player	Place	Score	Earnings
Phil Mickelson	Win	64-67-70-65-64=330	$720,000.00
Playoff: Beat David Berganio, Jr. with birdie on first extra hole			
David Berganio, Jr.	2	69-66-65-64-66=330	$432,000.00
Briny Baird	T-3	67-67-68-66-64=332	$232,000.00
Cameron Beckman	T-3	67-67-64-65-69=332	$232,000.00
Jerry Kelly	5	64-69-65-68-67=333	$160,000.00
Chris DiMarco	T-6	67-69-64-67-67=334	$116,857.15
Brandel Chamblee	T-6	63-67-68-66-70=334	$116,857.14
Kirk Triplett	T-6	64-69-64-67-70=334	$116,857.14
Deane Pappas	T-6	66-68-63-67-70=334	$116,857.14
Justin Leonard	T-6	70-66-64-67-67=334	$116,857.14
Charles Howell III	T-6	65-67-71-66-65=334	$116,857.15
Kenny Perry	T-6	69-64-68-62-71=334	$116,857.14

Phoenix Open

Course: TPC of Scottsdale, Scottsdale, Ariz.
Par: 71 Yardage: 7,089
Last day of event: Sunday, January 27, 2002

Player	Place	Score	Earnings
Chris DiMarco	Win	68-64-66-69=267	$720,000.00
Kenny Perry	T-2	69-65-64-70=268	$352,000.00
Kaname Yokoo	T-2	70-66-68-64=268	$352,000.00
John Daly	T-4	68-65-66-70=269	$176,000.00
Lee Janzen	T-4	74-67-64-64=269	$176,000.00
Duffy Waldorf	6	65-65-67-73=270	$144,000.00
Per-Ulrik Johansson	7	67-68-65-71=271	$134,000.00
Kevin Sutherland	T-8	66-68-70-68=272	$100,000.00
Brent Geiberger	T-8	68-67-67-70=272	$100,000.00
Jeff Maggert	T-8	70-66-66-70=272	$100,000.00
John Huston	T-8	70-70-66-66=272	$100,000.00
Rory Sabbatini	T-8	67-64-70-71=272	$100,000.00
Rod Pampling	T-8	68-68-71-65=272	$100,000.00
Vijay Singh	T-8	66-65-72-69=272	$100,000.00

AT&T Pebble Beach National Pro-Am

Courses: Pebble Beach G.L., Spyglass Hill G.C., Poppy Hills G.C., Pebble Beach, Calif.
Home Course / Pebble Beach G.L., Par: 72 Yardage: 6,798
Last day of event: Sunday, February 3, 2002

Player	Place	Score	Earnings
Matt Gogel	Win	66-72-67-69=274	$720,000.00
Pat Perez	2	66-65-70-76=277	$432,000.00
Andrew Magee	T-3	69-70-67-72=278	$232,000.00
Lee Janzen	T-3	68-67-70-73=278	$232,000.00
Jose Maria Olazabal	T-5	70-71-71-68=280	$146,000.00
Jerry Smith	T-5	67-69-72-72=280	$146,000.00
Phil Tataurangi	T-5	67-72-70-71=280	$146,000.00
Vijay Singh	T-8	69-71-70-71=281	$112,000.00
Kent Jones	T-8	70-71-70-70=281	$112,000.00
Mathew Goggin	T-8	69-72-68-72=281	$112,000.00
Paul Goydos	T-8	72-70-67-72=281	$112,000.00

Buick Invitational

Course: Torrey Pines (South), Torrey Pines (North), San Diego, Calif.
Home Course -Par: 72 Yardage: 7,568
Last day of event: Sunday, February 10, 2002

Player	Place	Score	Earnings
Jose Maria Olazabal	Win	71-72-67-65=275	$648,000.00
Mark O'Meara	T-2	67-69-70-70=276	$316,800.00
J.L. Lewis	T-2	68-67-71-70=276	$316,800.00
John Daly	4	69-70-68-70=277	$172,800.00
Rory Sabbatini	T-5	70-66-71-71=278	$131,400.00
Bob Estes	T-5	75-66-71-66=278	$131,400.00
Tiger Woods	T-5	66-77-69-66=278	$131,400.00
John Rollins	T-8	70-67-71-71=279	$104,400.00
Chris Riley	T-8	66-73-71-69=279	$104,400.00
Jerry Kelly	T-8	73-67-66-73=279	$104,400.00

Nissan Open

Course: Riviera C.C., Pacific Palisades, Calif.
Par: 71 Yardage: 7,174
Last day of event: Sunday, February 17, 2002

Player	Place	Score	Earnings
Len Mattiace	Win	69-65-67-68=269	$666,000.00
Brad Faxon	T-2	67-67-68-68=270	$276,266.67
Rory Sabbatini	T-2	69-68-65-68=270	$276,266.67
Scott McCarron	T-2	69-65-65-71=270	$276,266.66
Toru Taniguchi	5	66-67-67-71=271	$148,000.00
Chris DiMarco	T-6	68-70-66-68=272	$123,950.00
Per-Ulrik Johansson	T-6	70-68-68-66=272	$123,950.00
Charles Howell III	T-6	68-71-64-69=272	$123,950.00
Fred Funk	T-9	69-68-69-68=274	$96,200.00
Jose Maria Olazabal	T-9	66-71-70-67=274	$96,200.00
Brian Gay	T-9	71-67-68-68=274	$96,200.00
Fred Couples	T-9	72-68-68-66=274	$96,200.00

WGC-Accenture Match Play Championship

Course: La Costa Resort & Spa, Carlsbad, Calif.
Par: 72 Yardage: 7,022
Last day of event: Sunday, February 24, 2002

Player	Place	Earnings
Kevin Sutherland	Win	$1,000,000.00
Round One - Beat David Duval 20 holes		
Round Two - Beat Paul McGinley 2 & 1		
Round Three - Beat Jim Furyk 4 & 3		
Quarterfinals - Beat David Toms 3 & 2		
Semifinals - Beat Brad Faxon 1 up		
Finals - Beat Scott McCarron 1 up		
Scott McCarron	2	$550,000.00
Round One - Beat Colin Montgomerie 2 & 1		
Round Two - Beat Mike Weir 1 up		
Round Three - Beat Sergio Garcia 1 up		
Quarterfinals - Beat Tom Lehman 2 & 1		
Semifinals - Beat Paul Azinger 1 up		
Finals - Kevin Sutherland beat him 1 up		
Brad Faxon	3	$450,000.00
Round One - Beat Kenny Perry 7 & 6		
Round Two - Beat Adam Scott 3 & 2		
Round Three - Beat John Cook 3 & 2		
Quarterfinals - Beat Jose Maria Olazabal 20 holes		
Semifinals - Kevin Sutherland beat him 1 up		
Consolation - Beat Paul Azinger 19th hole		
Paul Azinger	4	$360,000.00
Round One - Beat Jesper Parnevik 1 up		
Round Two - Beat Davis Love III 1 up		
Round Three - Beat Niclas Fasth 20 holes		
Quarter-finals - Beat Bob Estes 2 & 1		
Semifinals - Scott McCarron beat him 1 up		
Consolation - Brad Faxon beat him 19th hole		

Bob Estes	T-5		$175,000.00

Round One - Beat Stuart Appleby 1 up
Round Two - Beat Scott Verplank 19 holes
Round Three - Beat Nick Price 1 up
Quarterfinals - Paul Azinger beat him 2 & 1

Tom Lehman	T-5		$175,000.00

Round One - Beat Hal Sutton 2 & 1
Round Two - Beat Ernie Els 19 holes
Round Three - Beat Matt Gogel 4 & 3
Quarterfinals - Scott McCarron beat him 4 & 3

Jose Maria Olazabal	T-5		$175,000.00

Round One - Beat Justin Leonard 1 up
Round Two - Beat Retief Goosen 1 up
Round Three - Beat Mark Calcavecchia 2 up
Quarterfinals - Brad Faxon beat him 20 holes

David Toms	T-5		$175,000.00

Round One - Beat Rory Sabbatini 1 up
Round Two - Beat Rocco Mediate 1 up
Round Three - Beat Steve Flesch 1 up
Quarterfinals - Kevin Sutherland beat him 3 & 2

Nick Price	T-9		$85,000.00

Round One - Beat Angel Cabrera 2 & 1
Round Two - Beat Peter O'Malley 2 & 1
Round Three - Bob Estes beat him 1 up

Niclas Fasth	T-9		$85,000.00

Round One - Beat Michael Campbell 2 & 1
Round Two - Beat Vijay Singh 3 & 2
Round Three - Paul Azinger beat him 20 holes

Sergio Garcia	T-9		$85,000.00

Round One - Beat Lee Janzen 3 & 2
Round Two - Beat Charles Howell III 1 up
Round Three - Scott McCarron beat him 1 up

Matt Gogel	T-9		$85,000.00

Round One - Beat Darren Clarke 2 & 1
Round Two - Beat Steve Lowery 20 holes
Round Three - Tom Lehman beat him 4 & 3

John Cook	T-9		$85,000.00

Round One - Beat Phil Mickelson 3 & 2
Round Two - Beat Lee Westwood 1 up
Round Three - Brad Faxon beat him 3 & 2

Mark Calcavecchia	T-9		$85,000.00

Round One - Beat Jerry Kelly 3 & 2
Round Two - Beat Chris DiMarco 2 & 1
Round Three - Jose Maria Olazabal beat him 2 up

Jim Furyk	T-9		$85,000.00

Round One - Beat Billy Andrade 20 holes
Round Two - Beat Toshi Izawa 2 & 1
Round Three - Kevin Sutherland beat him 4 & 3

Steve Flesch	T-9		$85,000.00

Round One - Beat Padraig Harrington 3 & 2
Round Two - Beat Kirk Tripplett 3 & 2
Round Three - David Toms beat him 1 up

Touchstone Energy Tucson Open

Course: Omni Tucson National Resort, Tucson, Ariz.
Par: 72 Yardage: 7,109
Last day of event: Sunday, February 24, 2002

Player	Place	Score	Earnings
Ian Leggatt	Win	68-71-65-64=268	$540,000.00
David Peoples	T-2	67-68-68-67=270	$264,000.00
Loren Roberts	T-2	65-70-69-66=270	$264,000.00
Kenneth Staton	T-4	69-69-69-64=271	$132,000.00
Fred Funk	T-4	65-71-67-68=271	$132,000.00
Bob Tway	T-6	67-67-69-69=272	$84,562.50
Russ Cochran	T-6	67-69-68-68=272	$84,562.50

Greg Kraft	T-6	69-68-66-69=272	$84,562.50
Chris Smith	T-6	70-65-69-68=272	$84,562.50
Shigeki Maruyama	T-6	70-66-68-68=272	$84,562.50
Cameron Beckman	T-6	70-67-68-67=272	$84,562.50
Spike McRoy	T-6	67-71-70-64=272	$84,562.50
Heath Slocum	T-6	69-67-64-72=272	$84,562.50

Genuity Championship

Course: Doral C.C. (Blue), Miami, Fla.
Par: 72 Yardage: 7,125
Last day of event: Sunday, March 3, 2002

Player	Place	Score	Earnings
Ernie Els	Win	66-67-66-72=271	$846,000.00
Tiger Woods	2	67-70-70-66=273	$507,600.00
Peter Lonard	3	70-67-70-70=277	$319,600.00
Rich Beem	4	69-68-72-70=279	$225,600.00
Craig Perks	T-5	71-68-70-71=280	$159,330.00
Angel Cabrera	T-5	72-70-71-67=280	$159,330.00
Vijay Singh	T-5	66-73-70-71=280	$159,330.00
Steve Elkington	T-5	67-71-74-68=280	$159,330.00
Nick Price	T-5	69-69-75-67=280	$159,330.00
Jesper Parnevik	10	71-67-72-71=281	$126,900.00

Honda Classic

Course: TPC at Heron Bay, Coral Springs, Fla.
Par: 72 Yardage: 7,268
Last day of event: Sunday, March 10, 2002

Player	Place	Score	Earnings
Matt Kuchar	Win	68-69-66-66=269	$630,000.00
Brad Faxon	T-2	65-70-69-67=271	$308,000.00
Joey Sindelar	T-2	68-67-66-70=271	$308,000.00
J.L. Lewis	T-4	68-68-68-68=272	$144,666.67
Billy Andrade	T-4	68-70-67-67=272	$144,666.67
Brett Quigley	T-4	70-66-67-69=272	$144,666.66
Rod Pampling	7	67-67-71-68=273	$117,250.00
Peter Jacobsen	T-8	71-67-68-68=274	$101,500.00
John Riegger	T-8	63-69-72-70=274	$101,500.00
Brett Wetterich	T-8	68-66-68-72=274	$101,500.00

Bay Hill Invitational

Course: Bay Hill Club, Orlando, Fla.
Par: 72 Yardage: 7,239
Last day of event: Sunday, March 17, 2002

Player	Place	Score	Earnings
Tiger Woods	Win	67-65-74-69=275	$720,000.00
Michael Campbell	2	72-68-68-71=279	$432,000.00
Phil Mickelson	T-3	69-71-69-71=280	$192,000.00
Rocco Mediate	T-3	69-70-71-70=280	$192,000.00
John Huston	T-3	67-71-70-72=280	$192,000.00
Len Mattiace	T-3	73-66-68-73=280	$192,000.00
Harrison Frazar	T-7	69-70-71-71=281	$129,000.00
Jose Maria Olazabal	T-7	71-68-70-72=281	$129,000.00
Angel Cabrera	T-9	67-70-72-73=282	$100,000.00
Sergio Garcia	T-9	68-71-70-73=282	$100,000.00
Ernie Els	T-9	70-67-72-73=282	$100,000.00
Scott Hoch	T-9	71-68-70-73=282	$100,000.00
Pat Perez	T-9	70-69-69-74=282	$100,000.00

The Players Championship

Course: TPC at Sawgrass, Ponte Vedra Beach, Fla.
Par: 72 Yardage: 7,093
Last day of event: Sunday, March 24, 2002

Player	Place	Score	Earnings
Craig Perks	Win	71-68-69-72=280	$1,080,000.00
Stephen Ames	2	74-69-72-67=282	$648,000.00
Rocco Mediate	3	71-70-69-73=283	$408,000.00
Sergio Garcia	T-4	70-72-71-71=284	$226,200.00
Billy Andrade	T-4	73-69-70-72=284	$226,200.00
Jeff Sluman	T-4	69-69-72-74=284	$226,200.00
Scott Hoch	T-4	67-77-68-72=284	$226,200.00
Carl Paulson	T-4	69-69-69-77=284	$226,200.00
John Huston	T-9	73-69-73-70=285	$168,000.00
Nick Price	T-9	74-71-71-69=285	$168,000.00

Shell Houston Open

Course: TPC at The Woodlands, The Woodlands, Texas
Par: 72 Yardage: 7,018
Last day of event: Sunday, March 31, 2002

Player	Place	Score	Earnings
Vijay Singh	Win	67-65-66-68=266	$720,000.00
Darren Clarke	2	69-65-67-71=272	$432,000.00
Jose Maria Olazabal	3	71-68-64-70=273	$272,000.00
Jay Haas	T-4	67-70-69-69=275	$176,000.00
Shigeki Maruyama	T-4	68-71-66-70=275	$176,000.00
Justin Leonard	T-6	70-68-69-70=277	$129,500.00
Tom Pernice, Jr.	T-6	71-70-67-69=277	$129,500.00
Brandt Jobe	T-6	70-66-69-72=277	$129,500.00
Adam Scott	T-6	72-67-67-71=277	$129,500.00
J.P. Hayes	T-10	67-68-71-72=278	$104,000.00
Jim Carter	T-10	65-73-68-72=278	$104,000.00

BellSouth Classic

Course: TPC at Sugarloaf, Duluth, Ga.
Par: 72 Yardage: 7,293
Last day of event: Sunday, April 7, 2002

Player	Place	Score	Earnings
Retief Goosen	Win	68-66-68-70=272	$684,000.00
Jesper Parnevik	2	66-69-76-65=276	$410,400.00
Phil Mickelson	3	65-68-71-73=277	$258,400.00
Scott McCarron	4	67-72-71-68=278	$182,400.00
John Rollins	T-5	66-70-72-71=279	$144,400.00
Bob Tway	T-5	67-71-69-72=279	$144,400.00
Dudley Hart	7	66-72-70-72=280	$127,300.00
Steve Flesch	T-8	68-68-72-73=281	$106,400.00
K.J. Choi	T-8	70-68-70-73=281	$106,400.00
Padraig Harrington	T-8	69-65-73-74=281	$106,400.00
Phil Tataurangi	T-8	71-64-76-70=281	$106,400.00

Masters

Course: Augusta National G.C., Augusta, Ga.
Par: 72 Yardage: 7,270
Last day of event: Sunday, April 14, 2002

Player	Place	Score	Earnings
Tiger Woods	Win	70-69-66-71=276	$1,008,000.00
Retief Goosen	2	69-67-69-74=279	$604,800.00
Phil Mickelson	3	69-72-68-71=280	$380,800.00
Jose Maria Olazabal	4	70-69-71-71=281	$268,800.00
Padraig Harrington	T-5	69-70-72-71=282	$212,800.00
Ernie Els	T-5	70-67-72-73=282	$212,800.00
Vijay Singh	7	70-65-72-76=283	$187,600.00
Sergio Garcia	8	68-71-70-75=284	$173,600.00
Adam Scott	T-9	71-72-72-70=285	$151,200.00
Angel Cabrera	T-9	68-71-73-73=285	$151,200.00
Miguel-A. Jimenez	T-9	70-71-74-70=285	$151,200.00

WorldCom Classic

Course: Harbour Town G.L., Hilton Head, S.C.
Par: 71 Yardage: 6,973
Last day of event: Sunday, April 21, 2002

Player	Place	Score	Earnings
Justin Leonard	Win	67-64-66-73=270	$720,000.00
Heath Slocum	2	67-68-66-70=271	$432,000.00
Phil Mickelson	3	65-64-72-71=272	$272,000.00
Bernhard Langer	4	71-65-68-69=273	$192,000.00
Davis Love III	T-5	62-69-72-71=274	$146,000.00
Billy Mayfair	T-5	65-68-72-69=274	$146,000.00
Scott Verplank	T-5	67-68-72-67=274	$146,000.00
Glen Hnatiuk	T-8	68-71-66-70=275	$120,000.00
Angel Cabrera	T-8	66-67-70-72=275	$120,000.00
Craig Stadler	T-10	69-68-69-70=276	$92,000.00
Len Mattiace	T-10	70-68-66-72=276	$92,000.00
Frank Nobilo	T-10	72-69-69-66=276	$92,000.00
Mark Calcavecchia	T-10	68-70-73-65=276	$92,000.00
Jeff Sluman	T-10	73-66-65-72=276	$92,000.00

Greater Greensboro Chrysler Classic

Course: Forest Oaks C.C., Greensboro, N.C.
Par: 72 Yardage: 7,062
Last day of event: Sunday, April 28, 2002

Player	Place	Score	Earnings
Rocco Mediate	Win	68-67-66-71=272	$684,000.00
Mark Calcavecchia	2	65-69-69-72=275	$410,400.00
Jonathan Byrd	T-3	72-71-69-66=278	$220,400.00
Chad Campbell	T-3	67-72-66-73=278	$220,400.00
Jim Gallagher, Jr.	T-5	67-73-70-69=279	$144,400.00
Carl Paulson	T-5	68-70-73-68=279	$144,400.00
K.J. Choi	T-7	71-69-69-71=280	$118,433.33
Stephen Ames	T-7	71-69-72-68=280	$118,433.34
Robert Gamez	T-7	67-67-73-73=280	$118,433.33
Pat Bates	T-10	71-67-73-70=281	$91,200.00
Paul Stankowski	T-10	66-74-71-70=281	$91,200.00
Jonathan Kaye	T-10	69-72-66-74=281	$91,200.00
Kevin Sutherland	T-10	71-68-75-67=281	$91,200.00

COMPAQ Classic of New Orleans

Course: English Turn G. & C.C., New Orleans, La.
Par: 72 Yardage: 7,116
Last day of event: Sunday, May 5, 2002

Player	Place	Score	Earnings
K.J. Choi	Win	68-65-71-67=271	$810,000.00
Dudley Hart	T-2	68-71-69-67=275	$396,000.00
Geoff Ogilvy	T-2	70-67-71-67=275	$396,000.00
Dan Forsman	T-4	65-69-72-70=276	$177,187.50
Chris DiMarco	T-4	72-66-70-68=276	$177,187.50
Mike Sposa	T-4	72-68-68-68=276	$177,187.50
John Cook	T-4	74-67-69-66=276	$177,187.50
Nick Price	8	74-67-70-66=277	$139,500.00
David Toms	T-9	69-69-71-69=278	$112,500.00
Bryce Molder	T-9	69-67-69-73=278	$112,500.00

Scott Verplank	T-9	69-69-73-67=278	$112,500.00
Phil Mickelson	T-9	73-66-71-68=278	$112,500.00
Tim Clark	T-9	68-67-75-68=278	$112,500.00

Verizon Byron Nelson Classic
Course: TPC at Las Colinas, Cottonwood Valley Course, Irving, Texas
Home course / TPC at Las Colinas, Par: 70 Yardage: 7,017
Last day of event: Sunday, May 12, 2002

Player	Place	Score	Earnings
Shigeki Maruyama	Win	67-63-68-68=266	$864,000.00
Ben Crane	2	68-67-68-65=268	$518,400.00
Tiger Woods	3	71-65-69-65=270	$326,400.00
David Toms	T-4	68-68-70-66=272	$211,200.00
Ernie Els	T-4	69-70-64-69=272	$211,200.00
Steve Stricker	T-6	69-66-70-68=273	$166,800.00
Jim Carter	T-6	65-67-71-70=273	$166,800.00
Robert Allenby	T-8	69-69-67-69=274	$120,000.00
Frank Lickliter II	T-8	64-70-70-70=274	$120,000.00
Nick Price	T-8	64-71-69-70=274	$120,000.00
Loren Roberts	T-8	67-68-68-71=274	$120,000.00
Duffy Waldorf	T-8	71-67-66-70=274	$120,000.00
David Frost	T-8	66-72-68-68=274	$120,000.00
Cameron Beckman	T-8	70-65-66-73=274	$120,000.00

Mastercard Colonial
Course: Colonial C.C., Fort Worth, Texas
Par: 70 Yardage: 7,080
Last day of event: Sunday, May 19, 2002

Player	Place	Score	Earnings
Nick Price	Win	69-65-66-67=267	$774,000.00
Kenny Perry	T-2	70-66-69-67=272	$378,400.00
David Toms	T-2	71-71-64-66=272	$378,400.00
Dudley Hart	4	73-65-70-65=273	$206,400.00
Phil Tataurangi	T-5	70-69-66-69=274	$163,400.00
Davis Love III	T-5	70-70-67-67=274	$163,400.00
Tom Watson	7	68-72-66-69=275	$144,050.00
Steve Flesch	T-8	68-67-70-71=276	$120,400.00
Stuart Appleby	T-8	70-71-71-64=276	$120,400.00
Esteban Toledo	T-8	67-67-72-70=276	$120,400.00
Jonathan Byrd	T-8	73-67-68-68=276	$120,400.00

Memorial Tournament
Course: Muirfield Village G.C., Dubin, Ohio
Par: 72 Yardage: 7,224
Last day of event: Sunday, May 26, 2002

Player	Place	Score	Earnings
Jim Furyk	Win	71-70-68-65=274	$810,000.00
John Cook	T-2	73-69-65-69=276	$396,000.00
David Peoples	T-2	69-74-65-68=276	$396,000.00
Vijay Singh	T-4	69-67-72-69=277	$169,650.00
Bob Tway	T-4	65-71-68-73=277	$169,650.00
Shigeki Maruyama	T-4	74-66-67-70=277	$169,650.00
Harrison Frazar	T-4	70-65-75-67=277	$169,650.00
David Duval	T-4	75-69-67-66=277	$169,650.00
Jerry Kelly	T-9	71-71-68-68=278	$117,000.00
Billy Andrade	T-9	72-72-67-67=278	$117,000.00
Stewart Cink	T-9	66-70-69-73=278	$117,000.00
Phil Mickelson	T-9	73-66-70-69=278	$117,000.00

Kemper Insurance Open
Course: TPC at Avenel, Potomac, Md.
Par: 71 Yardage: 6,987
Last day of event: Sunday, June 2, 2002

Player	Place	Score	Earnings
Bob Estes	Win	65-69-69-70=273	$648,000.00
Rich Beem	2	68-68-69-69=274	$388,800.00
Steve Elkington	T-3	70-67-69-69=275	$208,800.00
Bob Burns	T-3	68-66-69-72=275	$208,800.00
Jonathan Kaye	T-5	69-69-69-69=276	$136,800.00
Justin Leonard	T-5	72-67-67-70=276	$136,800.00
Harrison Frazar	T-7	69-66-72-70=277	$116,100.00
Chris Smith	T-7	70-72-68-67=277	$116,100.00
Olin Browne	T-9	70-70-69-69=278	$93,600.00
Bart Bryant	T-9	72-70-66-70=278	$93,600.00
Duffy Waldorf	T-9	67-68-70-73=278	$93,600.00
Jay Williamson	T-9	66-71-67-74=278	$93,600.00

Buick Classic
Course: Westchester C.C., Harrison, N.Y.
Par: 71 Yardage: 6,722
Last day of event: Sunday, June 9, 2002

Player	Place	Score	Earnings
Chris Smith	Win	66-69-67-70=272	$630,000.00
Pat Perez	T-2	67-70-67-70=274	$261,333.33
Loren Roberts	T-2	64-68-71-71=274	$261,333.33
David Gossett	T-2	66-67-70-71=274	$261,333.34
Stewart Cink	T-5	67-69-71-68=275	$133,000.00
Ian Leggatt	T-5	69-68-67-71=275	$133,000.00
Jerry Kelly	T-7	65-70-70-71=276	$112,875.00
Tom Lehman	T-7	68-72-68-68=276	$112,875.00
Stephen Ames	T-9	70-71-66-71=278	$94,500.00
Peter Lonard	T-9	71-68-69-70=278	$94,500.00
Jim Furyk	T-9	68-69-74-67=278	$94,500.00

U.S. Open
Course: Bethpage State Park (Black Course), Farmingdale, N.Y.
Par: 70 Yardage: 7,214
Last day of event: Sunday, June 16, 2002

Player	Place	Score	Earnings
Tiger Woods	Win	67-68-70-72=277	$1,000,000.00
Phil Mickelson	2	70-73-67-70=280	$585,000.00
Jeff Maggert	3	69-73-68-72=282	$362,356.00
Sergio Garcia	4	68-74-67-74=283	$252,546.00
Billy Mayfair	T-5	69-74-68-74=285	$182,882.00
Scott Hoch	T-5	71-75-70-69=285	$182,882.00
Nick Faldo	T-5	70-76-66-73=285	$182,882.00
Tom Byrum	T-8	72-72-70-72=286	$138,669.00
Padraig Harrington	T-8	70-68-73-75=286	$138,669.00
Nick Price	T-8	72-75-69-70=286	$138,669.00

Canon Greater Hartford Open
Course: TPC at River Highlands, Cromwell, Conn.
Par: 70 Yardage: 6,820
Last day of event: Sunday, June 23, 2002

Player	Place	Score	Earnings
Phil Mickelson	Win	69-67-66-64=266	$720,000.00
Davis Love III	T-2	68-64-68-67=267	$352,000.00
Jonathan Kaye	T-2	65-67-65-70=267	$352,000.00
Scott Verplank	4	65-70-63-71=269	$192,000.00

Jim Carter	T-5	67-69-66-68=270	$152,000.00
Joel Edwards	T-5	68-71-68-63=270	$152,000.00
Dan Forsman	T-7	68-70-69-64=271	$124,666.67
Skip Kendall	T-7	65-72-67-67=271	$124,666.67
Scott Hoch	T-7	67-66-66-72=271	$124,666.66
Ernie Els	T-10	69-70-69-64=272	$100,000.00
David Frost	T-10	72-68-67-65=272	$100,000.00
Jeff Gove	T-10	73-64-68-67=272	$100,000.00

FedEx St. Jude Classic
Course: TPC at Southwind, Germantown, Tenn.
Par: 71 Yardage: 7,030
Last day of event: Sunday, June 30, 2002

Player	Place	Score	Earnings
Len Mattiace	Win	69-68-65-64=266	$684,000.00
Tim Petrovic	2	65-68-66-68=267	$410,400.00
Notah Begay III	3	66-65-68-69=268	$258,400.00
David Toms	4	68-68-65-68=269	$182,400.00
Jim Carter	T-5	68-67-67-68=270	$133,475.00
David Howser	T-5	66-70-70-64=270	$133,475.00
Matt Kuchar	T-5	66-66-67-71=270	$133,475.00
Tripp Isenhour	T-5	72-65-64-69=270	$133,475.00
Neal Lancaster	T-9	70-67-64-70=271	$95,000.00
Robert Gamez	T-9	70-64-69-68=271	$95,000.00
Justin Leonard	T-9	66-66-71-68=271	$95,000.00
Pat Bates	T-9	68-63-69-71=271	$95,000.00
Robert Allenby	T-9	72-67-66-66=271	$95,000.00

Advil Western Open
Course: Cog Hill G. & C.C. (Dubsdread), Lemont, Ill.
Par: 72 Yardage: 7,224
Last day of event: Sunday, July 7, 2002

Player	Place	Score	Earnings
Jerry Kelly	Win	67-69-68-65=269	$720,000.00
Davis Love III	2	67-70-68-66=271	$432,000.00
Brandt Jobe	3	69-69-69-66=273	$272,000.00
John Cook	4	67-66-72-69=274	$192,000.00
Chris Riley	T-5	70-70-66-69=275	$135,600.00
Duffy Waldorf	T-5	70-70-66-69=275	$135,600.00
Stuart Appleby	T-5	70-65-71-69=275	$135,600.00
Peter Lonard	T-5	71-71-68-65=275	$135,600.00
Neal Lancaster	T-5	68-68-67-72=275	$135,600.00
Bob Estes	T-10	66-70-68-72=276	$100,000.00
Nick Price	T-10	73-68-66-69=276	$100,000.00
Robert Allenby	T-10	69-67-65-75=276	$100,000.00

Greater Milwaukee Open
Course: Brown Deer Park G.C., Milwaukee, Wis.
Par: 71 Yardage: 6,759
Last day of event: Sunday, July 14, 2002

Player	Place	Score	Earnings
Jeff Sluman	Win	64-66-63-68=261	$558,000.00
Tim Herron	T-2	68-66-65-66=265	$272,800.00
Steve Lowery	T-2	66-65-64-70=265	$272,800.00
Kenny Perry	4	64-70-67-65=266	$148,800.00
Greg Chalmers	T-5	67-66-65-69=267	$113,150.00
J.P. Hayes	T-5	68-69-63-67=267	$113,150.00
Joey Sindelar	T-5	69-68-65-65=267	$113,150.00
Tommy Armour III	T-8	63-67-71-67=268	$93,000.00
Kirk Triplett	T-8	66-64-67-71=268	$93,000.00
Skip Kendall	T-10	68-67-69-65=269	$80,600.00
Chris Smith	T-10	67-70-64-68=269	$80,600.00

British Open
Course: Muirfield G.C., Muirfield, East Lothian, Scotland
Par: 71 Yardage: 7,034
Last day of event: Sunday, July 21, 2002

Player	Place	Score	Earnings
Ernie Els	Win	70-66-72-70=278	$1,106,140.00

Playoff: Beat Thomas Levet with par on first extra hole after four-hole aggregate playoff (Els 4-3-5-4=16) with Levet (4-3-5-4=16), Stewart Appleby (4-3-5-5=17) and Steve Elkington (5-3-4-5=17)

Steve Elkington	T-2	71-73-68-66=278	$452,990.66
Stuart Appleby	T-2	73-70-70-65=278	$452,990.66
Thomas Levet	T-2	72-66-74-66=278	$452,990.66
Gary Evans	T-5	72-68-74-65=279	$221,228.00
Shigeki Maruyama	T-5	68-68-75-68=279	$221,228.00
Padraig Harrington	T-5	69-67-76-67=279	$221,228.00
Sergio Garcia	T-8	71-69-71-69=280	$122,465.50
Soren Hansen	T-8	68-69-73-70=280	$122,465.50
Thomas Bjorn	T-8	68-70-73-69=280	$122,465.50
Retief Goosen	T-8	71-68-74-67=280	$122,465.50
Scott Hoch	T-8	74-69-71-66=280	$122,465.50
Peter O'Malley	T-8	72-68-75-65=280	$122,465.50

B.C. Open
Course: En-Joie G.C., Endicott, N.Y.
Par: 72 Yardage: 6,974
Last day of event: Sunday, July 21, 2002

Player	Place	Score	Earnings
Spike McRoy	Win	70-65-69-65=269	$378,000.00
Fred Funk	2	71-66-66-67=270	$226,800.00
Glen Day	T-3	67-69-67-68=271	$94,710.00
Robert Gamez	T-3	68-68-69-66=271	$94,710.00
Brian Henninger	T-3	67-69-70-65=271	$94,710.00
Cliff Kresge	T-3	72-67-70-62=271	$94,710.00
Shaun Micheel	T-3	65-65-67-74=271	$94,710.00
Eduardo Herrera	8	69-68-67-68=272	$65,100.00
John Rollins	T-9	71-69-65-68=273	$58,800.00
Paul Gow	T-9	67-66-67-73=273	$58,800.00

John Deere Classic
Course: TPC at Deere Run, Silvis, Ill.
Par: 71 Yardage: 7,183
Last day of event: Sunday, July 28, 2002

Player	Place	Score	Earnings
J.P. Hayes	Win	67-61-67-67=262	$540,000.00
Robert Gamez	2	65-64-66-71=266	$324,000.00
Kirk Triplett	3	68-67-66-66=267	$204,000.00
Pat Perez	4	68-65-69-66=268	$144,000.00
Briny Baird	T-5	67-64-68-70=269	$109,500.00
Chris Riley	T-5	69-64-66-70=269	$109,500.00
Mike Heinen	T-5	63-69-66-71=269	$109,500.00
Peter Jacobsen	T-8	66-67-69-68=270	$90,000.00
J.L. Lewis	T-8	67-69-66-68=270	$90,000.00
Paul Goydos	T-10	69-67-69-66=271	$69,000.00
David Gossett	T-10	65-69-67-70=271	$69,000.00
John Rollins	T-10	69-66-70-66=271	$69,000.00
Andrew Magee	T-10	70-67-70-64=271	$69,000.00
Notah Begay III	T-10	69-65-72-65=271	$69,000.00

The International presented by Qwest

Course: Castle Pine G.C., Castle Rock, Colo.(Stableford format)

Par: 72 Yardage: 7,559

Last day of event: Sunday, August 4, 2002

Player	Place	Score	Earnings
Rich Beem	Win	10-0-15-19=44	$810,000.00
Steve Lowery	2	8-13-6-16=43	$486,000.00
Mark Brooks	3	1-14-11-7=33	$306,000.00
Greg Norman	T-4	4-0-16-7=27	$198,000.00
Ernie Els	T-4	8-6-6-7=27	$198,000.00
Lee Janzen	6	6-4-6-10=26	$162,000.00
Frank Lickliter II	T-7	2--1-14-10=25	$145,125.00
Craig Barlow	T-7	7-10-11--3=25	$145,125.00
Tom Lehman	T-9	3--2-11-11=23	$126,000.00
Craig Perks	T-9	3-6-6-8=23	$126,000.00

Buick Open

Course: Warwick Hills C.C., Grand Blanc, Mich.

Par: 72 Yardage: 7,105

Last day of event: Sunday, August 11, 2002

Player	Place	Score	Earnings
Tiger Woods	Win	67-63-71-70=271	$594,000.00
Mark O'Meara	T-2	68-69-70-68=275	$217,800.00
Brian Gay	T-2	69-71-67-68=275	$217,800.00
Fred Funk	T-2	71-66-67-71=275	$217,800.00
Esteban Toledo	T-2	68-67-67-73=275	$217,800.00
Paul Azinger	T-6	69-70-69-68=276	$106,837.50
Tom Byrum	T-6	70-68-68-70=276	$106,837.50
Bob Tway	T-6	71-65-68-72=276	$106,837.50
Pat Bates	T-6	68-67-73-68=276	$106,837.50
David Toms	T-10	68-68-70-71=277	$79,200.00
Jim Furyk	T-10	69-67-70-71=277	$79,200.00
Steve Flesch	T-10	72-68-66-71=277	$79,200.00
J.J. Henry	T-10	67-67-76-67=277	$79,200.00

PGA Championship

Course: Hazeltine National G.C., Chaska, Minn. .

Par: 72 Yardage: 7,360

Last day of event: Sunday, August 18, 2002

Player	Place	Score	Earnings
Rich Beem	Win	72-66-72-68=278	$990,000.00
Tiger Woods	2	71-69-72-67=279	$594,000.00
Chris Riley	3	71-70-72-70=283	$374,000.00
Fred Funk	T-4	68-70-73-73=284	$235,000.00
Justin Leonard	T-4	72-66-69-77=284	$235,000.00
Rocco Mediate	6	72-73-70-70=285	$185,000.00
Mark Calcavecchia	7	70-68-74-74=286	$172,000.00
Vijay Singh	8	71-74-74-68=287	$159,000.00
Jim Furyk	9	68-73-76-71=288	$149,000.00
Steve Lowery	T-10	71-71-73-74=289	$110,714.28
Jose Coceres	T-10	72-71-72-74=289	$110,714.28
Ricardo Gonzalez	T-10	74-73-71-71=289	$110,714.28
Stewart Cink	T-10	74-74-72-69=289	$110,714.29
Sergio Garcia	T-10	75-73-73-68=289	$110,714.29
Robert Allenby	T-10	76-66-77-70=289	$110,714.29
Pierre Fulke	T-10	72-68-78-71=289	$110,714.29

WGC-NEC Invitational

Course: Sahalee C.C., Redmond, Wash.

Par: 71 Yardage: 6,949

Last day of event: Sunday, August 25, 2002

Player	Place	Score	Earnings
Craig Parry	Win	72-65-66-65=268	$1,000,000.00
Fred Funk	T-2	68-68-68-68=272	$410,000.00
Robert Allenby	T-2	69-63-71-69=272	$410,000.00
Tiger Woods	4	68-70-67-68=273	$215,000.00
Justin Rose	5	67-67-72-68=274	$187,500.00
Jim Furyk	T-6	70-67-68-70=275	$150,000.00
Rich Beem	T-6	74-67-67-67=275	$150,000.00
Steve Lowery	8	67-65-73-71=276	$120,000.00
Phil Mickelson	T-9	66-69-71-71=277	$105,000.00
Matt Gogel	T-9	68-69-68-72=277	$105,000.00

Reno-Tahoe Open

Course: Montreux G. & C.C., Reno, Nev.

Par: 72 Yardage: 7,472

Last day of event: Sunday, August 25, 2002

Player	Place	Score	Earnings
Chris Riley	Win	71-66-67-67=271	$540,000.00
Playoff: Beat Jonathan Kaye with par on first extra hole			
Jonathan Kaye	2	67-68-69-67=271	$324,000.00
J.J. Henry	T-3	68-69-70-68=275	$174,000.00
Charles Howell III	T-3	65-73-73-64=275	$174,000.00
Brian Gay	5	71-70-68-67=276	$120,000.00
Bob Tway	T-6	68-68-70-71=277	$97,125.00
Tom Pernice, Jr.	T-6	66-68-73-70=277	$97,125.00
Ben Crane	T-6	67-67-73-70=277	$97,125.00
Steve Flesch	T-6	70-64-70-73=277	$97,125.00
Woody Austin	T-10	68-71-69-70=278	$78,000.00
David Peoples	T-10	69-68-72-69=278	$78,000.00

Air Canada Championship

Course: Northview G. & C.C. (Ridge Course), Surrey, British Columbia, Canada

Par: 71 Yardage: 7,072

Last day of event: Sunday, September 1, 2002

Player	Place	Score	Earnings
Gene Sauers	Win	69-65-66-69=269	$630,000.00
Steve Lowery	2	67-67-68-68=270	$378,000.00
Vijay Singh	T-3	70-69-67-65=271	$182,000.00
Craig Barlow	T-3	67-65-71-68=271	$182,000.00
Robert Allenby	T-3	71-62-68-70=271	$182,000.00
Tom Scherrer	6	68-69-70-65=272	$126,000.00
Peter Lonard	T-7	66-67-68-72=273	$112,875.00
David Gossett	T-7	67-66-72-68=273	$112,875.00
John Senden	T-9	68-70-70-66=274	$94,500.00
Harrison Frazar	T-9	68-68-72-66=274	$94,500.00
Darren Clarke	T-9	72-67-66-69=274	$94,500.00

Bell Canadian Open

Course: Angus Glen C.C., Markham, Ontario, Canada

Par: 72 Yardage: 7,372

Last day of event: Sunday, September 8, 2002

Player	Place	Score	Earnings
John Rollins	Win	70-71-66-65=272	$720,000.00
Playoff: Beat Neal Lancaster and Justin Leonard with birdie on first extra hole			
Justin Leonard	T-2	69-68-66-69=272	$352,000.00
Neal Lancaster	T-2	66-67-67-72=272	$352,000.00
Greg Chalmers	T-4	66-71-65-71=273	$176,000.00
Steve Flesch	T-4	71-67-65-70=273	$176,000.00
Grant Waite	T-6	64-70-69-71=274	$134,000.00
Vijay Singh	T-6	67-70-66-71=274	$134,000.00
Geoff Ogilvy	T-6	68-74-64-68=274	$134,000.00

Player	Place	Score	Earnings
Bob Estes	T-9	68-71-68-68=275	$108,000.00
Jeff Sluman	T-9	71-68-66-70=275	$108,000.00
Lee Janzen	T-9	72-68-69-66=275	$108,000.00

SEI Pennsylvania Classic
Course: Waynesborough C. C., Paoli, Pa.
Par: 71 Yardage: 6,939
Last day of event: Sunday, September 15, 2002

Player	Place	Score	Earnings
Dan Forsman	Win	73-68-64-65=270	$594,000.00
Billy Andrade	T-2	66-68-68-69=271	$290,400.00
Robert Allenby	T-2	71-68-67-65=271	$290,400.00
John Huston	4	72-68-65-67=272	$158,400.00
Jeff Sluman	T-5	73-67-65-68=273	$125,400.00
Olin Browne	T-5	73-69-65-66=273	$125,400.00
Brent Geiberger	T-7	69-68-69-68=274	$99,412.50
Ian Leggatt	T-7	70-65-69-70=274	$99,412.50
Jeff Brehaut	T-7	69-68-66-71=274	$99,412.50
Hidemichi Tanaka	T-7	73-66-70-65=274	$99,412.50

WGC-American Express Championship
Course: Mount Juliet C.C., Thomastown, Kilkenny, Ireland
Par: 72 Yardage: 7,246
Last day of event: Sunday, September 22, 2002

Player	Place	Score	Earnings
Tiger Woods	Win	65-65-67-66=263	$1,000,000.00
Retief Goosen	2	67-67-68-62=264	$540,000.00
Vijay Singh	3	67-69-66-65=267	$367,500.00
David Toms	T-4	66-67-69-66=268	$235,000.00
Jerry Kelly	T-4	67-65-70-66=268	$235,000.00
Scott McCarron	6	71-67-64-67=269	$180,000.00
Sergio Garcia	7	69-69-70-62=270	$155,000.00
Davis Love III	8	69-67-68-67=271	$130,000.00
Bob Estes	T-9	68-68-69-67=272	$111,000.00
Michael Campbell	T-9	71-66-71-64=272	$111,000.00

Tampa Bay Classic presented by Buick
Course: Westin Innisbrook Resort (Copperhead Course), Palm Harbor, Fla.
Par: 71 Yardage: 7,295
Last day of event: Sunday, September 22, 2002

Player	Place	Score	Earnings
K.J. Choi	Win	63-68-68-68=267	$468,000.00
Glen Day	2	68-67-70-69=274	$280,800.00
Mark Brooks	3	73-65-70-67=275	$176,800.00
Rod Pampling	T-4	65-68-73-70=276	$114,400.00
John Morse	T-4	74-68-67-67=276	$114,400.00
Paul Gow	6	68-72-69-68=277	$93,600.00
Craig Barlow	T-7	68-73-68-69=278	$83,850.00
Pat Perez	T-7	67-67-70-74=278	$83,850.00
Matt Kuchar	T-9	70-69-70-70=279	$67,600.00
Tommy Armour III	T-9	71-69-70-69=279	$67,600.00
Peter Jacobsen	T-9	68-74-67-70=279	$67,600.00
Donnie Hammond	T-9	70-66-69-74=279	$67,600.00

Valero Texas Open
Course: LaCantera G.C., San Antonio, Texas
Par: 70 Yardage: 6,881
Last day of event: Sunday, September 29, 2002

Player	Place	Score	Earnings
Loren Roberts	Win	67-63-67-64=261	$630,000.00

Player	Place	Score	Earnings
Fred Couples	T-2	68-67-65-64=264	$261,333.34
Fred Funk	T-2	68-68-64-64=264	$261,333.33
Garrett Willis	T-2	71-61-66-66=264	$261,333.33
Joel Edwards	T-5	66-68-67-65=266	$118,650.00
Pat Perez	T-5	68-62-69-67=266	$118,650.00
Shaun Micheel	T-5	68-64-70-64=266	$118,650.00
J.L. Lewis	T-5	70-67-65-64=266	$118,650.00
Kenneth Staton	T-5	70-67-65-64=266	$118,650.00
Bob Estes	T-10	68-67-66-66=267	$84,000.00
Bob Tway	T-10	67-64-67-69=267	$84,000.00
Brian Gay	T-10	67-64-69-67=267	$84,000.00
Matt Peterson	T-10	69-62-67-69=267	$84,000.00

Michelob Championship at Kingsmill
Course: Kingsmill G.C., Williamsburg, Va.
Par: 71 Yardage: 6,853
Last day of event: Sunday, October 6, 2002

Player	Place	Score	Earnings
Charles Howell III	Win	70-65-68-67=270	$666,000.00
Scott Hoch	T-2	66-70-67-69=272	$325,600.00
Brandt Jobe	T-2	67-68-65-72=272	$325,600.00
Geoff Ogilvy	4	70-67-66-70=273	$177,600.00
Billy Mayfair	5	70-63-68-73=274	$148,000.00
Tim Clark	T-6	70-68-71-67=276	$119,787.50
Steve Flesch	T-6	72-67-66-71=276	$119,787.50
Corey Pavin	T-6	66-69-68-73=276	$119,787.50
Loren Roberts	T-6	66-69-73-68=276	$119,787.50
David Morland IV	T-10	68-69-69-71=277	$88,800.00
Scott Dunlap	T-10	69-70-67-71=277	$88,800.00
Harrison Frazar	T-10	70-67-71-69=277	$88,800.00
Tom Byrum	T-10	72-69-68-68=277	$88,800.00

Invensys Classic at Las Vegas
Course: TPC at Summerlin, TPC At The Canyons, Southern Highlands G.C., Las Vegas, Nev.
Home course / TPC at Summerlin, Par: 72 Yardage: 7,243
Last day of event: Sunday, October 13, 2002

Player	Place	Score	Earnings
Phil Tataurangi	Win	67-66-67-68-62=330	$900,000.00
Jeff Sluman	T-2	66-66-64-68-67=331	$440,000.00
Stuart Appleby	T-2	66-68-64-67-66=331	$440,000.00
Jim Furyk	4	66-65-64-69-68=332	$240,000.00
Rory Sabbatini	5	69-65-70-64-65=333	$200,000.00
Charles Howell III	T-6	67-65-66-69-67=334	$167,500.00
Dan Forsman	T-6	65-71-66-66-66=334	$167,500.00
David Duval	T-6	67-66-67-63-71=334	$167,500.00
John Cook	T-9	69-67-64-67-68=335	$130,000.00
Paul Stankowski	T-9	65-70-65-67-68=335	$130,000.00
Notah Begay III	T-9	65-70-70-65-65=335	$130,000.00
Joel Edwards	T-9	72-67-62-66-68=335	$130,000.00

Disney Golf Classic
Course: Walt Disney (Magnolia, Palm), Lake Buena Vista, Fla.
Home course / Magnolia, Par: 72 Yardage: 7,200
Last day of event: Sunday, October 20, 2002

Player	Place	Score	Earnings
Bob Burns	Win	63-68-67-65=263	$666,000.00
Chris DiMarco	2	64-63-69-68=264	$399,600.00
Tiger Woods	3	66-69-67-63=265	$251,600.00
Tim Herron	T-4	67-66-67-66=266	$162,800.00
Hidemichi Tanaka	T-4	63-67-70-66=266	$162,800.00
Tim Clark	T-6	65-68-68-66=267	$119,787.50

Player	Place	Score	Earnings
K.J. Choi	T-6	66-68-69-64=267	$119,787.50
David Toms	T-6	69-68-65-65=267	$119,787.50
John Rollins	T-6	66-71-64-66=267	$119,787.50
Carlos Franco	T-10	66-68-68-67=269	$88,800.00
Robert Damron	T-10	68-66-67-68=269	$88,800.00
Esteban Toledo	T-10	66-69-67-67=269	$88,800.00
Scott Hoch	T-10	64-65-69-71=269	$88,800.00

Buick Challenge

Course: Callaway Gardens Resort, Pine Mountain, Ga.
Par: 72 Yardage: 7,057
Last day of event: Sunday, October 27, 2002

Player	Place	Score	Earnings
Jonathan Byrd	Win	67-66-65-63=261	$666,000.00
David Toms	2	66-68-63-65=262	$399,600.00
Phil Mickelson	3	65-67-70-63=265	$251,600.00
Craig Parry	T-4	67-64-66-69=266	$152,933.33
John Huston	T-4	68-67-61-70=266	$152,933.33
Robert Allenby	T-4	67-71-63-65=266	$152,933.34
Kenny Perry	T-7	68-68-66-65=267	$115,316.67
Stewart Cink	T-7	69-66-65-67=267	$115,316.66
Joey Sindelar	T-7	69-68-65-65=267	$115,316.67
Billy Andrade	T-10	67-69-66-66=268	$92,500.00
Carlos Franco	T-10	66-71-67-64=268	$92,500.00
Tim Herron	T-10	63-68-65-72=268	$92,500.00

The Tour Championship

Course: East Lake G.C., Atlanta, Ga.
Par: 70 Yardage: 7,029
Last day of event: Sunday, November 3, 2002

Player	Place	Score	Earnings
Vijay Singh	Win	65-71-65-67=268	$900,000.00
Charles Howell III	2	66-69-69-66=270	$540,000.00
David Toms	3	70-66-70-67=273	$345,000.00
Jerry Kelly	4	71-69-67-67=274	$240,000.00
Phil Mickelson	T-5	70-69-67-69=275	$190,000.00
Davis Love III	T-5	72-70-68-65=275	$190,000.00
Chris DiMarco	T-7	70-68-69-69=276	$165,000.00
Tiger Woods	T-7	71-68-67-70=276	$165,000.00
K.J. Choi	T-9	71-68-70-68=277	$146,000.00
Retief Goosen	T-9	69-69-72-67=277	$146,000.00

Southern Farm Bureau Classic

Course: Annandale G.C., Madison, Miss.
Par: 72 Yardage: 7,199
Last day of event: Monday, November 4, 2002

Player	Place	Score	Earnings
Luke Donald	Win	66-68-67=201	$468,000.00
Deane Pappas	2	66-68-68=202	$280,800.00
Brad Elder	3	65-67-71=203	$176,800.00
Chad Campbell	4	69-66-69=204	$124,800.00
Chris Smith	T-5	67-69-69=205	$85,150.00
Spike McRoy	T-5	69-67-69=205	$85,150.00
Jonathan Byrd	T-5	66-68-71=205	$85,150.00
Brad Faxon	T-5	67-67-71=205	$85,150.00
Jay Williamson	T-5	71-68-66=205	$85,150.00
Robin Freeman	T-5	71-69-65=205	$85,150.00

2003

Tiger Woods won five times on the PGA Tour, but failed to bring home a major trophy. Instead, four players made career breakthroughs by winning their first major championships: Mike Weir at the Masters, Jim Furyk at the U.S. Open, Ben Curtis at the British Open, and Shaun Micheel at the PGA Championship. Weir prevailed on the first hole of a playoff against Len Mattiace, who shot a final-round 65. Furyk scored a three-shot victory over Stephen Leaney at Olympica Fields. Curtis edged Thomas Bjorn, who played the last four holes in 4 over par, and Vijay Singh by a shot at Sandwich. Micheel bested Chad Campbell by two strokes at Oak Hill. Annika Sorenstam, the world's top-ranked woman golfer, entered the Bank of America Colonial. She shot 71-74 and missed the cut by four shots. Tommy Armour III set a PGA Tour 72-hole scoring record, posting 64-62-63-65 for a 26-under par 254 at the Valero Texas Open. Mark McCormack, founder of powerhouse management company IMG, died at age 72.

Mercedes Championshipss

Course: Kapalua Resort Plantation Course, Kapalua, Maui, Ha.
Par: 73 Yardage: 7,263
Last day of event: Sunday, January 12, 2003

Player	Place	Score	Earnings
Ernie Els	Win	64-65-65-67=261	$1,000,000.00
Rocco Mediate	T-2	72-69-65-63=269	$450,000.00
K.J. Choi	T-2	67-67-62-73=269	$450,000.00
Vijay Singh	T-4	68-70-67-65=270	$224,000.00
Retief Goosen	T-4	70-65-66-69=270	$224,000.00
Chris Riley	T-6	65-70-67-69=271	$155,000.00
Bob Estes	T-6	66-66-70-69=271	$155,000.00
Jonathan Byrd	T-6	68-69-71-63=271	$155,000.00
Jim Furyk	T-6	64-72-67-68=271	$155,000.00
Jerry Kelly	T-10	65-70-67-70=272	$125,000.00
Gene Sauers	T-10	65-72-69-66=272	$125,000.00

Sony Open in Hawaii

Course: Waialae C.C., Honolulu, Ha.
Par: 70 Yardage: 7,060
Last day of event: Sunday, January 19, 2003

Player	Place	Score	Earnings
Ernie Els	Win	66-65-66-67=264	$810,000.00
Playoff: Beat Aaron Baddeley with birdie on second extra hole			
Aaron Baddeley	2	66-64-65-69=264	$486,000.00
Chris DiMarco	3	65-66-69-66=266	$306,000.00
Jerry Kelly	T-4	68-68-67-65=268	$198,000.00
Robert Allenby	T-4	68-69-65-66=268	$198,000.00
Stuart Appleby	6	68-71-67-63=269	$162,000.00
Chris Riley	T-7	65-69-69-67=270	$130,950.00
Shigeki Maruyama	T-7	66-66-69-69=270	$130,950.00
Fred Funk	T-7	66-68-69-67=270	$130,950.00
Joe Durant	T-7	67-69-67-67=270	$130,950.00
Briny Baird	T-7	68-65-67-70=270	$130,950.00

Phoenix Open

Course: TPC of Scottsdale, Scottsdale, Ariz.
Par: 71 Yardage: 7,089
Last day of event: Sunday, January 26, 2003

Player	Place	Score	Earnings
Vijay Singh	Win	67-66-65-63=261	$720,000.00
John Huston	2	64-67-66-67=264	$432,000.00
Retief Goosen	T-3	65-68-65-67=265	$192,000.00
Tim Petrovic	T-3	66-63-68-68=265	$192,000.00
Harrison Frazar	T-3	62-67-67-69=265	$192,000.00

Robert Gamez	T-3	70-65-64-66=265	$192,000.00
Joe Durant	T-7	69-65-66-66=266	$129,000.00
Alex Cejka	T-7	67-65-70-64=266	$129,000.00
Phil Mickelson	T-9	69-67-67-64=267	$112,000.00
Mike Weir	T-9	70-66-65-66=267	$112,000.00

Bob Hope Chrysler Classic

Course: PGA West/Palmer, Bermuda Dunes C.C., La Quinta C.C., Indian Wells C.C., La Quinta, Calif.
Home course / PGA West, Par: 72 Yardage: 6,930
Last day of event: Sunday, February 2, 2003

Player	Place	Score	Earnings
Mike Weir	Win	67-64-65-67-67=330	$810,000.00
Jay Haas	2	67-61-67-68-69=332	$486,000.00
Chris DiMarco	T-3	64-68-66-66-70=334	$261,000.00
Tim Herron	T-3	69-64-61-65-75=334	$261,000.00
David Gossett	5	69-67-62-66-72=336	$180,000.00
Phil Mickelson	T-6	70-68-63-69-67=337	$156,375.00
Pat Perez	T-6	69-61-70-66-71=337	$156,375.00
Justin Leonard	T-8	66-67-69-66-70=338	$126,000.00
Jonathan Kaye	T-8	66-71-64-70-67=338	$126,000.00
Harrison Frazar	T-8	67-62-72-66-71=338	$126,000.00
Stephen Ames	T-8	63-67-64-71-73=338	$126,000.00

AT&T Pebble Beach National Pro-Am

Courses: Pebble Beach G.L., Spyglass Hill G.C., Poppy Hills G.C., Pebble Beach, Calif.
Home Course / Pebble Beach G.L., Par: 72 Yardage: 6,798
Last day of event: Sunday, February 9, 2003

Player	Place	Score	Earnings
Davis Love III	Win	72-67-67-68=274	$900,000.00
Tom Lehman	2	68-70-70-67=275	$540,000.00
Tim Herron	T-3	69-69-72-66=276	$290,000.00
Mike Weir	T-3	67-74-67-68=276	$290,000.00
Rocco Mediate	T-5	70-71-68-70=279	$190,000.00
Jim Furyk	T-5	71-66-73-69=279	$190,000.00
Brad Faxon	T-7	70-70-70-70=280	$155,833.33
Phil Tataurangi	T-7	68-73-70-69=280	$155,833.34
Paul Stankowski	T-7	71-67-73-69=280	$155,833.33
Rory Sabbatini	T-10	71-69-70-71=281	$125,000.00
Rod Pampling	T-10	70-68-70-73=281	$125,000.00
Tim Clark	T-10	74-66-70-71=281	$125,000.00

Buick Invitational

Course: Torrey Pines (South), Torrey Pines (North), San Diego, Calif.
Home Course -Par: 72 Yardage: 7,568
Last day of event: Sunday, February 16, 2003

Player	Place	Score	Earnings
Tiger Woods	Win	70-66-68-68=272	$810,000.00
Carl Pettersson	2	69-68-70-69=276	$486,000.00
Brad Faxon	3	70-64-71-72=277	$306,000.00
Arron Oberholser	T-4	65-70-72-71=278	$186,000.00
Phil Mickelson	T-4	69-68-69-72=278	$186,000.00
Briny Baird	T-4	70-65-72-71=278	$186,000.00
Luke Donald	T-7	69-70-71-69=279	$130,950.00
Mark Calcavecchia	T-7	71-68-71-69=279	$130,950.00
Jonathan Kaye	T-7	68-67-72-72=279	$130,950.00
Charles Howell III	T-7	74-68-68-69=279	$130,950.00
Marco Dawson	T-7	68-66-76-69=279	$130,950.00

Nissan Open

Course: Riviera C.C., Pacific Palisades, Calif.
Par: 71 Yardage: 7,222
Last day of event: Sunday, February 23, 2003

Player	Place	Score	Earnings
Mike Weir	Win	72-68-69-66=275	$810,000.00
Playoff: Beat Charles Howell III with birdie on second extra hole			
Charles Howell III	2	69-65-68-73=275	$486,000.00
Nick Price	T-3	68-67-70-72=277	$261,000.00
Fred Funk	T-3	65-74-70-68=277	$261,000.00
K.J. Choi	T-5	70-69-67-72=278	$171,000.00
Tiger Woods	T-5	72-68-73-65=278	$171,000.00
Fred Couples	7	74-68-69-68=279	$150,750.00
Len Mattiace	T-8	69-67-71-73=280	$135,000.00
Chad Campbell	T-8	73-70-66-71=280	$135,000.00
Duffy Waldorf	T-10	70-69-70-72=281	$96,428.57
Bob Estes	T-10	69-71-68-73=281	$96,428.57
Marco Dawson	T-10	72-73-66-70=281	$96,428.57
Darren Clarke	T-10	71-74-68-68=281	$96,428.57
Rich Beem	T-10	73-65-69-74=281	$96,428.57
Shaun Micheel	T-10	74-69-72-66=281	$96,428.58
Dan Forsman	T-10	76-66-70-69=281	$96,428.57

WGC-Accenture Match Play Championship

Course: La Costa Resort & Spa, Carlsbad, Calif.
Par: 72 Yardage: 7,247
Last day of event: Sunday, March 2, 2003

Player	Place	Earnings
Tiger Woods	Win	$1,000,050.00
Round One - Beat Carl Pettersson 2 & 1		
Round Two - Beat K.J. Choi 5 & 3		
Round Three - Beat Stephen Leaney 7 & 6		
Quarterfinals - Beat Scott Hoch 5 & 4		
Semifinals - Beat Adam Scott 19 holes		
Finals - Beat David Toms 2 & 1		
David Toms	2	$600,000.00
Round One - Beat Anders Hansen 3 & 1		
Round Two - Beat Chris Riley 1 up		
Round Three - Beat Alex Cejka 1 up		
Quarterfinals - Beat Jerry Kelly 4 & 3		
Semifinals - Beat Peter Lonard 1 up		
Finals - Tiger Woods beat him 2 & 1		
Adam Scott	3	$480,000.00
Round One - Beat Bernhard Langer 3 & 2		
Round Two - Beat Rocco Mediate 1 up		
Round Three - Beat Kevin Sutherland 2 & 1		
Quarterfinals - Beat Jay Haas 2 & 1		
Semifinals - Tiger Woods beat him 19 holes		
Consolation - Beat Peter Lonard 1 up		
Peter Lonard	4	$390,000.00
Round One - Beat Kenny Perry 2 & 1		
Round Two - Beat Phil Tataurangi 5 & 4		
Round Three - Beat Robert Allenby 1 up		
Quarterfinals - Beat Darren Clarke 2 up		
Semifinals - David Toms beat him 1 up		
Consolation - Adam Scott beat him 1 up		
Scott Hoch	T-5	$200,000.00
Round One - Beat Tom Lehman 3 & 1		
Round Two - Beat Padraig Harrington 3 & 2		
Round Three - Beat Toshi Izawa 4 & 3		
Quarterfinals - Tiger Woods beat him 5 & 4		
Jay Haas	T-5	$200,000.00
Round One - Beat Retief Goosen 5 & 3		
Round Two - Beat Shigeki Maruyama 1 up		

Round Three - Beat Nick Price 2 & 1
Quarterfinals - Adam Scott beat him 2 & 1

Darren Clarke	T-5	$200,000.00

Round One - Beat Tim Clark 4 & 3
Round Two - Beat Davis Love III 7 & 6
Round Three - Beat Jim Furyk 2 up
Quarterfinals - Peter Lonard beat him 2 up

Jerry Kelly	T-5	$200,000.00

Round One - Beat Thomas Bjorn 5 & 4
Round Two - Beat Mike Weir 2 & 1
Round Three - Beat Phil Mickelson 3 & 2
Quarterfinals -David Toms beat him 4 & 3

Stephen Leaney	T-9	$95,000.00

Round One - Beat Bob Estes 2 & 1
Round Two - Beat Justin Leonard 6 & 5
Round Three - Tiger Woods beat him 7 & 6

Toshi Izawa	T-9	$95,000.00

Round One - Beat Chris DiMarco 2 & 1
Round Two - Beat Eduardo Romero 3 & 1
Round Three - Scott Hoch beat him 4 & 3

Nick Price	T-9	$95,000.00

Round One - Beat Paul Lawrie 4 & 3
Round Two - Beat Niclas Fasth 2 & 1
Round Three - Jay Haas beat him 20 holes

Kevin Sutherland	T-9	$95,000.00

Round One - Beat Sergio Garcia 2 & 1
Round Two - Beat Justin Rose 1 up
Round Three - Adam Scott beat him 2 & 1

Robert Allenby	T-9	$95,000.00

Round One - Beat Trevor Immelman 4 & 2
Round Two - Beat Jeff Sluman 1 up
Round Three - Peter Lonard beat him 1 up

Jim Furyk	T-9	$95,000.00

Round One - Beat Len Mattiace 2 & 1
Round Two - Beat Steve Lowery 6 & 5
Round Three - Darren Clarke beat him 2 up

Phil Mickelson	T-9	$95,000.00

Round One - Beat Robert Karlsson 1 up
Round Two - Beat Brad Faxon 3 & 2
Round Three - Jerry Kelly beat him 3 & 2

Alex Cejka	T-9	$95,000.00

Round One - Beat Colin Montgomerie 4 & 2
Round Two - Beat Angel Cabrera 4 & 2
Round Three - David Toms beat him 1 up

Chrysler Classic of Tucson

Course: Omni Tucson National Resort, Tucson, Ariz.
Par: 72 Yardage: 7,109
Last day of event: Sunday, March 2, 2003

Player	Place	Score	Earnings
Frank Lickliter II	Win	67-63-70-69=269	$540,000.00
Chad Campbell	2	70-71-63-67=271	$324,000.00
Brenden Pappas	3	71-66-67-68=272	$204,000.00
Bob Tway	T-4	71-67-68-67=273	$132,000.00
Aaron Barber	T-4	71-71-66-65=273	$132,000.00
Arron Oberholser	T-6	69-67-70-68=274	$97,125.00
Dean Wilson	T-6	68-69-71-66=274	$97,125.00
Stewart Cink	T-6	72-69-67-66=274	$97,125.00
Andrew Magee	T-6	68-74-64-68=274	$97,125.00
Steve Flesch	T-10	70-70-64-71=275	$75,000.00
Carlos Franco	T-10	72-66-68-69=275	$75,000.00
Mike Sposa	T-10	73-70-66-66=275	$75,000.00

Ford Championship at Doral

Course: Doral C.C. (Blue), Miami, Fla.
Par: 72 Yardage: 7,125
Last day of event: Sunday, March 9, 2003

Player	Place	Score	Earnings
Scott Hoch	Win	66-70-66-69=271	$900,000.00

Playoff: Beat Jim Furyk with birdie on third extra hole

Jim Furyk	2	68-66-69-68=271	$540,000.00
Bob Tway	3	65-68-69-71=273	$340,000.00
Tim Petrovic	4	70-72-65-67=274	$240,000.00
Heath Slocum	T-5	68-71-69-67=275	$182,500.00
Kenny Perry	T-5	69-71-71-64=275	$182,500.00
Jonathan Byrd	T-5	75-68-66-66=275	$182,500.00
Rod Pampling	T-8	64-71-70-71=276	$140,000.00
Cliff Kresge	T-8	71-66-68-71=276	$140,000.00
Shaun Micheel	T-8	67-72-70-67=276	$140,000.00
Skip Kendall	T-8	68-74-65-69=276	$140,000.00

Honda Classic

Course: C.C. at Mirasol (Sunset Course), Palm Beach Gardens, Fla.
Par: 72 Yardage: 7,157
Last day of event: Sunday, March 16, 2003

Player	Place	Score	Earnings
Justin Leonard	Win	63-70-64-67=264	$900,000.00
Davis Love III	T-2	66-65-65-69=265	$440,000.00
Chad Campbell	T-2	69-65-66-65=265	$440,000.00
Tim Herron	4	69-63-70-64=266	$240,000.00
Notah Begay III	T-5	63-67-69-68=267	$182,500.00
Jim Furyk	T-5	64-69-69-65=267	$182,500.00
Billy Mayfair	T-5	70-65-64-68=267	$182,500.00
Brian Gay	T-8	67-67-67-67=268	$130,000.00
Brett Quigley	T-8	68-66-66-68=268	$130,000.00
Chris DiMarco	T-8	69-68-65-66=268	$130,000.00
Woody Austin	T-8	66-70-63-69=268	$130,000.00
Jerry Kelly	T-8	70-62-67-69=268	$130,000.00
John Rollins	T-8	71-65-65-67=268	$130,000.00

Bay Hill Invitational

Course: Bay Hill Club, Orlando, Fla.
Par: 72 Yardage: 7,239
Last day of event: Sunday, March 23, 2003

Player	Place	Score	Earnings
Tiger Woods	Win	70-65-66-68=269	$810,000.00
Stewart Cink	T-2	69-69-70-72=280	$297,000.00
Kenny Perry	T-2	72-68-69-71=280	$297,000.00
Kirk Triplett	T-2	73-69-68-70=280	$297,000.00
Brad Faxon	T-2	70-71-65-74=280	$297,000.00
Aaron Baddeley	6	69-70-70-72=281	$162,000.00
J.L. Lewis	T-7	69-73-73-67=282	$140,250.00
Jeff Sluman	T-7	75-69-68-70=282	$140,250.00
Jerry Kelly	T-7	76-66-70-70=282	$140,250.00
Billy Andrade	T-10	72-71-69-71=283	$93,375.00
Steve Flesch	T-10	72-72-68-71=283	$93,375.00
Jonathan Kaye	T-10	69-70-73-71=283	$93,375.00
Ben Crane	T-10	70-73-68-72=283	$93,375.00
Stephen Ames	T-10	73-70-66-74=283	$93,375.00
Ty Tryon	T-10	73-67-74-69=283	$93,375.00
Pat Perez	T-10	74-69-69-71=283	$93,375.00
Jeff Brehaut	T-10	75-70-69-69=283	$93,375.00

The Players Championship
Course: TPC at Sawgrass, Ponte Vedra Beach, Fla.
Par: 72 Yardage: 7,093
Last day of event: Sunday, March 30, 2003

Player	Place	Score	Earnings
Davis Love III	Win	70-67-70-64=271	$1,170,000.00
Padraig Harrington	T-2	67-68-70-72=277	$572,000.00
Jay Haas	T-2	68-70-67-72=277	$572,000.00
Robert Allenby	T-4	70-71-72-65=278	$286,000.00
Jim Furyk	T-4	73-68-68-69=278	$286,000.00
Darren Clarke	T-6	71-70-67-71=279	$225,875.00
Chad Campbell	T-6	72-66-71-70=279	$225,875.00
Scott Verplank	T-8	71-72-68-69=280	$195,000.00
Kirk Triplett	T-8	72-70-71-67=280	$195,000.00
Fred Couples	10	67-71-69-74=281	$175,500.00

Player	Place	Score	Earnings
Woody Austin	2	68-70-65-68=271	$486,000.00
Geoff Ogilvy	T-3	68-67-70-67=272	$216,000.00
Chris Riley	T-3	69-70-66-67=272	$216,000.00
Hal Sutton	T-3	67-66-71-68=272	$216,000.00
David Gossett	T-3	71-67-68-66=272	$216,000.00
Steve Flesch	T-7	68-69-67-69=273	$140,250.00
Matt Gogel	T-7	69-67-69-68=273	$140,250.00
Tom Pernice, Jr.	T-7	67-70-68-68=273	$140,250.00
Peter Jacobsen	T-10	69-69-67-69=274	$93,375.00
Glen Hnatiuk	T-10	69-68-69-68=274	$93,375.00
Ernie Els	T-10	69-66-70-69=274	$93,375.00
Jim Furyk	T-10	70-66-69-69=274	$93,375.00
Rod Pampling	T-10	67-72-67-68=274	$93,375.00
Jeff Sluman	T-10	68-70-64-72=274	$93,375.00
Bob Estes	T-10	69-72-66-67=274	$93,375.00
Stewart Cink	T-10	67-65-69-73=274	$93,375.00

BellSouth Classic
Course: TPC at Sugarloaf, Duluth, Ga.
Par: 72 Yardage: 7,293
Last day of event: Sunday, April 6, 2003

Player	Place	Score	Earnings
Ben Crane	Win	73-72-64-63=272	$720,000.00
Bob Tway	2	70-66-69-71=276	$432,000.00
Hank Kuehne	T-3	71-69-67-70=277	$208,000.00
Jay Williamson	T-3	68-72-70-67=277	$208,000.00
Retief Goosen	T-3	68-70-74-65=277	$208,000.00
Tom Pernice, Jr.	T-6	70-70-66-72=278	$134,000.00
John Rollins	T-6	72-69-68-69=278	$134,000.00
Stewart Cink	T-6	72-70-67-69=278	$134,000.00
J.J. Henry	T-9	70-71-67-71=279	$104,000.00
Brenden Pappas	T-9	71-69-69-70=279	$104,000.00
Chris DiMarco	T-9	67-72-72-68=279	$104,000.00
Paul Lawrie	T-9	72-68-71-68=279	$104,000.00

Shell Houston Open
Course: Redstone G.C. (Fall Creek), Humble, Texas
Par: 72 Yardage: 7,508
Last day of event: Sunday, April 27, 2003

Player	Place	Score	Earnings
Fred Couples	Win	65-68-67-67=267	$810,000.00
Stuart Appleby	T-2	66-70-66-69=271	$336,000.00
Mark Calcavecchia	T-2	68-65-68-70=271	$336,000.00
Hank Kuehne	T-2	69-64-72-66=271	$336,000.00
Jay Haas	5	67-67-70-68=272	$180,000.00
Jeff Maggert	6	71-66-72-64=273	$162,000.00
John Daly	T-7	69-69-67-70=275	$145,125.00
Geoff Ogilvy	T-7	70-69-68-68=275	$145,125.00
Kevin Sutherland	T-9	69-70-67-70=276	$117,000.00
Vijay Singh	T-9	67-68-70-71=276	$117,000.00
Peter Jacobsen	T-9	67-71-69-69=276	$117,000.00
Steve Flesch	T-9	72-66-67-71=276	$117,000.00

Masters
Course: Augusta National G.C., Augusta, Ga.
Par: 72 Yardage: 7,290
Last day of event: Sunday, April 13, 2003

Player	Place	Score	Earnings
Mike Weir	Win	70-68-75-68=281	$1,080,000.00

Playoff: Beat Len Mattiace with bogey on first extra hole

Player	Place	Score	Earnings
Len Mattiace	2	73-74-69-65=281	$648,000.00
Phil Mickelson	3	73-70-72-68=283	$408,000.00
Jim Furyk	4	73-72-71-68=284	$288,000.00
Jeff Maggert	5	72-73-66-75=286	$240,000.00
Vijay Singh	T-6	73-71-70-73=287	$208,500.00
Ernie Els	T-6	79-66-72-70=287	$208,500.00
Jose Maria Olazabal	T-8	73-71-71-73=288	$162,000.00
David Toms	T-8	71-73-70-74=288	$162,000.00
Jonathan Byrd	T-8	74-71-71-72=288	$162,000.00
Mark O'Meara	T-8	76-71-70-71=288	$162,000.00
Scott Verplank	T-8	76-73-70-69=288	$162,000.00

HP Classic of New Orleans
Course: English Turn G. & C.C., New Orleans, La.
Par: 72 Yardage: 7,116
Last day of event: Sunday, May 4, 2003

Player	Place	Score	Earnings
Steve Flesch	Win	67-70-65-65=267	$900,000.00

Playoff: Beat Bob Estes with birdie on first extra hole

Player	Place	Score	Earnings
Bob Estes	2	66-66-66-69=267	$540,000.00
Scott Verplank	3	65-63-67-74=269	$340,000.00
Mark Wilson	4	65-67-69-69=270	$240,000.00
Jerry Kelly	T-5	67-69-65-70=271	$190,000.00
J.L. Lewis	T-5	68-68-65-70=271	$190,000.00
Woody Austin	7	66-72-65-69=272	$167,500.00
Briny Baird	T-8	68-71-66-68=273	$145,000.00
Chris DiMarco	T-8	69-68-65-71=273	$145,000.00
David Frost	T-8	70-65-71-67=273	$145,000.00

MCI Heritage
Course: Harbour Town G.L., Hilton Head, S.C.
Par: 71 Yardage: 6,973
Last day of event: Sunday, April 20, 2003

Player	Place	Score	Earnings
Davis Love III	Win	66-69-69-67=271	$810,000.00

Playoff: Beat Woody Austin with birdie on fourth extra hole

Wachovia Championship
Course: Quail Hollow Club, Charlotte, N.C.
Par: 72 Yardage: 7,396
Last day of event: Sunday, May 11, 2003

Player	Place	Score	Earnings
David Toms	Win	70-69-66-73=278	$1,008,000.00
Brent Geiberger	T-2	71-69-71-69=280	$418,133.33
Robert Gamez	T-2	72-67-71-70=280	$418,133.33
Vijay Singh	T-2	73-72-67-68=280	$418,133.34

Nick Price	T-5	66-71-74-70=281	$212,800.00
Kirk Triplett	T-5	69-74-67-71=281	$212,800.00
Greg Chalmers	T-7	71-71-71-69=282	$168,700.00
Charles Howell III	T-7	70-69-72-71=282	$168,700.00
Dean Wilson	T-7	70-72-70-70=282	$168,700.00
Tom Pernice, Jr.	T-7	73-67-74-68=282	$168,700.00

EDS Byron Nelson Championship

Course: TPC at Las Colinas, Cottonwood Valley Course, Irving, Texas
Home course / TPC at Los Colinas, Par: 70 Yardage: 7,017
Last day of event: Sunday, May 18, 2003

Player	Place	Score	Earnings
Vijay Singh	Win	65-65-69-66=265	$1,008,000.00
Nick Price	2	66-70-66-65=267	$604,800.00
Robert Allenby	3	67-67-69-65=268	$380,800.00
Scott Verplank	4	69-63-72-65=269	$268,800.00
Jim Furyk	5	64-70-70-66=270	$224,000.00
Per-Ulrik Johansson	T-6	66-69-67-69=271	$187,600.00
Hal Sutton	T-6	68-69-66-68=271	$187,600.00
David Toms	T-6	68-70-65-68=271	$187,600.00
Briny Baird	T-9	65-69-69-69=272	$140,000.00
Peter Lonard	T-9	68-67-68-69=272	$140,000.00
Andrew Magee	T-9	68-68-67-69=272	$140,000.00
Jerry Kelly	T-9	65-69-70-68=272	$140,000.00
Justin Leonard	T-9	67-70-69-66=272	$140,000.00

Bank of America Colonial

Course: Colonial C.C., Fort Worth, Texas
Par: 70 Yardage: 7,080
Last day of event: Sunday, May 25, 2003

Player	Place	Score	Earnings
Kenny Perry	Win	68-64-61-68=261	$900,000.00
Justin Leonard	2	68-72-66-61=267	$540,000.00
Jeff Sluman	3	68-68-67-65=268	$340,000.00
Brandt Jobe	4	67-70-68-64=269	$240,000.00
Jim Furyk	T-5	68-65-69-68=270	$175,625.00
Pat Bates	T-5	69-66-69-66=270	$175,625.00
Rory Sabbatini	T-5	64-70-67-69=270	$175,625.00
Hal Sutton	T-5	71-67-65-67=270	$175,625.00
Esteban Toledo	T-9	68-68-69-67=272	$130,000.00
Harrison Frazar	T-9	69-69-66-68=272	$130,000.00
Fred Funk	T-9	70-67-69-66=272	$130,000.00
Dan Forsman	T-9	66-66-73-67=272	$130,000.00

Memorial Tournament

Course: Muirfield Village G.C., Dubin, Ohio
Par: 72 Yardage: 7,265
Last day of event: Sunday, June 1, 2003

Player	Place	Score	Earnings
Kenny Perry	Win	65-68-70-72=275	$900,000.00
Lee Janzen	2	67-67-71-72=277	$540,000.00
Mike Weir	3	72-70-71-65=278	$340,000.00
Vijay Singh	T-4	67-69-72-71=279	$220,000.00
Tiger Woods	T-4	67-71-76-65=279	$220,000.00
Stewart Cink	6	70-69-72-69=280	$180,000.00
Retief Goosen	T-7	67-67-74-73=281	$161,250.00
Chad Campbell	T-7	67-70-74-70=281	$161,250.00
Mark Calcavecchia	9	69-70-70-73=282	$145,000.00
Jose Maria Olazabal	10	73-69-66-75=283	$135,000.00

FBR Capital Open

Course: TPC at Avenel, Potomac, Md.
Par: 71 Yardage: 6,987
Last day of event: Monday, June 9, 2003

Player	Place	Score	Earnings
Rory Sabbatini	Win	68-66-68-68=270	$810,000.00
Duffy Waldorf	T-2	71-68-66-69=274	$336,000.00
Fred Funk	T-2	70-70-66-68=274	$336,000.00
Joe Durant	T-2	69-70-69-66=274	$336,000.00
J.L. Lewis	T-5	71-67-68-69=275	$171,000.00
Bernhard Langer	T-5	70-68-69-68=275	$171,000.00
Niclas Fasth	T-7	68-68-67-73=276	$140,250.00
Tom Gillis	T-7	68-68-70-70=276	$140,250.00
Davis Love III	T-7	70-71-68-67=276	$140,250.00
Chris DiMarco	T-10	71-68-67-71=277	$112,500.00
Scott Laycock	T-10	71-67-70-69=277	$112,500.00
Todd Fischer	T-10	73-68-67-69=277	$112,500.00

U.S. Open

Course: Olympia Fields C.C. (North Course), Olympia Fields, Ill.
Par: 70 Yardage: 7,190
Last day of event: Sunday, June 15, 2003

Player	Place	Score	Earnings
Jim Furyk	Win	67-66-67-72=272	$1,080,000.00
Stephen Leaney	2	67-68-68-72=275	$650,000.00
Mike Weir	T-3	73-67-68-71=279	$341,367.00
Kenny Perry	T-3	72-71-69-67=279	$341,367.00
Nick Price	T-5	71-65-69-75=280	$185,934.00
Ernie Els	T-5	69-70-69-72=280	$185,934.00
Fredrik Jacobson	T-5	69-67-73-71=280	$185,934.00
David Toms	T-5	72-67-70-71=280	$185,934.00
Justin Rose	T-5	70-71-70-69=280	$185,934.00
Billy Mayfair	T-10	69-71-67-74=281	$124,936.00
Cliff Kresge	T-10	69-70-72-70=281	$124,936.00
Scott Verplank	T-10	76-67-68-70=281	$124,936.00
Jonathan Kaye	T-10	70-70-72-69=281	$124,936.00
Padraig Harrington	T-10	69-72-72-68=281	$124,936.00

Buick Classic

Course: Westchester C.C., Harrison, N.Y.
Par: 71 Yardage: 6,722
Last day of event: Sunday, June 22, 2003

Player	Place	Score	Earnings
Jonathan Kaye	Win	70-66-68-67=271	$900,000.00
Playoff: Beat John Rollins with eagle on first extra hole			
John Rollins	2	70-67-67-67=271	$540,000.00
Joey Sindelar	3	66-69-70-68=273	$340,000.00
Skip Kendall	T-4	68-66-70-70=274	$196,875.00
Sergio Garcia	T-4	70-69-66-69=274	$196,875.00
Fred Funk	T-4	71-70-64-69=274	$196,875.00
Jay Haas	T-4	74-68-67-65=274	$196,875.00
J.L. Lewis	T-8	68-68-70-69=275	$145,000.00
Tom Lehman	T-8	71-70-68-66=275	$145,000.00
Brad Faxon	T-8	69-67-74-65=275	$145,000.00

FedEx St. Jude Classic

Course: TPC at Southwind, Germantown, Tenn.
Par: 71 Yardage: 7,069
Last day of event: Sunday, June 29, 2003

Player	Place	Score	Earnings
David Toms	Win	68-67-65-64=264	$810,000.00

Nick Price	2	73-67-65-62=267	$486,000.00
Richard S. Johnson	T-3	64-66-69-69=268	$234,000.00
Fredrik Jacobson	T-3	66-67-68-67=268	$234,000.00
Bob Estes	T-3	67-70-66-65=268	$234,000.00
Lee Janzen	T-6	68-66-67-68=269	$156,375.00
Ben Crane	T-6	70-68-64-67=269	$156,375.00
David Peoples	8	65-66-70-69=270	$139,500.00
Jay Haas	T-9	64-70-69-68=271	$112,500.00
Kirk Triplett	T-9	67-67-69-68=271	$112,500.00
Chris DiMarco	T-9	68-70-65-68=271	$112,500.00
Hank Kuehne	T-9	68-68-69-66=271	$112,500.00
Fred Funk	T-9	71-69-65-66=271	$112,500.00

100th Western Open

Course: Cog Hill G. & C.C. (Dubsdread), Lemont, Ill.
Par: 72 Yardage: 7,320
Last day of event: Sunday, July 6, 2003

Player	Place	Score	Earnings
Tiger Woods	Win	63-70-65-69=267	$810,000.00
Rich Beem	2	69-71-65-67=272	$486,000.00
Mike Weir	T-3	67-70-69-68=274	$234,000.00
Jerry Kelly	T-3	66-72-68-68=274	$234,000.00
Jim Furyk	T-3	71-66-72-65=274	$234,000.00
Cliff Kresge	T-6	67-68-69-71=275	$156,375.00
Robert Allenby	T-6	69-67-68-71=275	$156,375.00
Dudley Hart	T-8	73-65-70-68=276	$130,500.00
Chad Campbell	T-8	67-73-69-67=276	$130,500.00
Fredrik Jacobson	T-8	69-74-67-66=276	$130,500.00

Greater Milwaukee Open

Course: Brown Deer Park G.C., Milwaukee, Wis.
Par: 70 Yardage: 6,759
Last day of event: Sunday, July 13, 2003

Player	Place	Score	Earnings
Kenny Perry	Win	69-67-66-66=268	$630,000.00
Steve Allan	T-2	69-66-68-66=269	$308,000.00
Heath Slocum	T-2	72-63-68-66=269	$308,000.00
Brett Quigley	4	66-67-72-65=270	$168,000.00
Brenden Pappas	T-5	72-68-63-69=272	$118,650.00
Dennis Paulson	T-5	68-69-69-66=272	$118,650.00
Billy Mayfair	T-5	67-72-67-66=272	$118,650.00
Jeff Gallagher	T-5	73-66-67-66=272	$118,650.00
Chris Smith	T-5	72-69-67-64=272	$118,650.00
Hal Sutton	T-10	69-70-67-67=273	$91,000.00
Spike McRoy	T-10	69-70-69-65=273	$91,000.00

British Open

Course: Royal St. George's G.C., Sandwich, Kent, England
Par: 71 Yardage: 7,106
Last day of event: Sunday, July 20, 2003

Player	Place	Score	Earnings
Ben Curtis	Win	72-72-70-69=283	$1,112,720.00
Thomas Bjorn	T-2	73-70-69-72=284	$548,412.00
Vijay Singh	T-2	75-70-69-70=284	$548,412.00
Davis Love III	T-4	69-72-72-72=285	$294,076.00
Tiger Woods	T-4	73-72-69-71=285	$294,076.00
Fredrik Jacobson	T-6	70-76-70-70=286	$213,801.20
Brian Davis	T-6	77-73-68-68=286	$213,801.20
Kenny Perry	T-8	74-70-70-73=287	$155,383.40
Nick Faldo	T-8	76-74-67-70=287	$155,383.40
Sergio Garcia	T-10	73-71-70-74=288	$108,092.80
Phillip Price	T-10	74-72-69-73=288	$108,092.80

Gary Evans	T-10	71-75-70-72=288	$108,092.80
Hennie Otto	T-10	68-76-75-69=288	$108,092.80
Retief Goosen	T-10	73-75-71-69=288	$108,092.80

B.C. Open

Course: En-Joie G.C., Endicott, N.Y.
Par: 72 Yardage: 6,974
Last day of event: Sunday, July 20, 2003

Player	Place	Score	Earnings
Craig Stadler	Win	67-69-68-63=267	$540,000.00
Steve Lowery	T-2	64-64-68-72=268	$264,000.00
Alex Cejka	T-2	66-66-69-67=268	$264,000.00
Rod Pampling	4	67-70-66-66=269	$144,000.00
John E. Morgan	T-5	68-65-68-70=271	$98,250.00
John Maginnes	T-5	66-69-67-69=271	$98,250.00
Steve Allan	T-5	68-65-71-67=271	$98,250.00
Glen Day	T-5	68-68-69-66=271	$98,250.00
Hank Kuehne	T-5	70-68-67-66=271	$98,250.00
Mike Grob	T-5	68-69-70-64=271	$98,250.00

Greater Hartford Open

Course: TPC at River Highlands, Cromwell, Conn.
Par: 70 Yardage: 6,820
Last day of event: Sunday, July 27, 2003

Player	Place	Score	Earnings
Peter Jacobsen	Win	63-67-69-67=266	$720,000.00
Chris Riley	2	72-65-63-68=268	$432,000.00
Todd Fischer	3	66-69-69-65=269	$272,000.00
Craig Barlow	T-4	65-68-68-69=270	$165,333.33
Kenny Perry	T-4	66-68-67-69=270	$165,333.33
Steve Pate	T-4	67-68-68-67=270	$165,333.34
Robert Damron	T-7	69-64-69-69=271	$124,666.66
Joe Durant	T-7	68-69-66-68=271	$124,666.67
Briny Baird	T-7	72-65-68-66=271	$124,666.67
Shaun Micheel	10	71-68-68-65=272	$108,000.00

Buick Open

Course: Warwick Hills C.C., Grand Blanc, Mich.
Par: 72 Yardage: 7,127
Last day of event: Sunday, August 3, 2003

Player	Place	Score	Earnings
Jim Furyk	Win	68-66-65-68=267	$720,000.00
Chris DiMarco	T-2	67-64-71-67=269	$264,000.00
Tiger Woods	T-2	69-65-69-66=269	$264,000.00
Briny Baird	T-2	70-68-65-66=269	$264,000.00
Geoff Ogilvy	T-2	70-65-69-65=269	$264,000.00
Neal Lancaster	T-6	67-68-66-69=270	$139,000.00
Paul Goydos	T-6	68-68-66-68=270	$139,000.00
Paul Gow	T-8	66-67-69-70=272	$112,000.00
Kenny Perry	T-8	69-67-66-70=272	$112,000.00
Andrew Magee	T-8	71-64-71-66=272	$112,000.00
Vijay Singh	T-8	69-67-70-66=272	$112,000.00

The International

Course: Castle Pine G.C., Castle Rock, Colo.(Stableford format)
Par: 72 Yardage: 7,559
Last day of event: Sunday, August 10, 2003

Player	Place	Score	Earnings
Davis Love III	Win	19-17-5-5=46	$900,000.00
Retief Goosen	T-2	2-15-9-8=34	$440,000.00

Vijay Singh	T-2	4-15-9-6=34	$440,000.00
Chris DiMarco	4	8-7-11-7=33	$240,000.00
John Rollins	5	11-15-5-0=31	$200,000.00
Ernie Els	T-6	4-5-4-13=26	$173,750.00
Phil Mickelson	T-6	8-14-1-3=26	$173,750.00
Geoff Ogilvy	8	9-3-8-5=25	$155,000.00
Charles Howell III	9	14-4-3-3=24	$145,000.00
Robert Allenby	T-10	7-3-5-8=23	$125,000.00
Paul Casey	T-10	7-9--2-9=23	$125,000.00
Bob Tway	T-10	12-6-0-5=23	$125,000.00

PGA Championship

Course: Oak Hill C.C., Rochester, N.Y.
Par: 70 Yardage: 7,134
Last day of event: Sunday, August 17, 2003

Player	Place	Score	Earnings
Shaun Micheel	Win	69-68-69-70=276	$1,080,000.00
Chad Campbell	2	69-72-65-72=278	$648,000.00
Tim Clark	3	72-70-68-69=279	$408,000.00
Alex Cejka	4	74-69-68-69=280	$288,000.00
Ernie Els	T-5	71-70-70-71=282	$214,000.00
Jay Haas	T-5	70-74-69-69=282	$214,000.00
Mike Weir	T-7	68-71-70-75=284	$175,666.67
Fred Funk	T-7	69-73-70-72=284	$175,666.67
Loren Roberts	T-7	70-73-70-71=284	$175,666.67
Billy Andrade	T-10	67-72-72-74=285	$135,500.00
Charles Howell III	T-10	70-72-70-73=285	$135,500.00
Niclas Fasth	T-10	76-70-71-68=285	$135,500.00
Kenny Perry	T-10	75-72-70-68=285	$135,500.00

WGC-NEC Invitational

Course: Firestone C.C. (South), Akron, Ohio
Par: 70 Yardage: 7,283
Last day of event: Sunday, August 24, 2003

Player	Place	Score	Earnings
Darren Clarke	Win	65-70-66-67=268	$1,050,000.00
Jonathan Kaye	2	68-69-65-70=272	$550,000.00
Davis Love III	3	66-70-68-69=273	$360,000.00
Chris Riley	T-4	66-67-70-71=274	$235,000.00
Tiger Woods	T-4	65-72-67-70=274	$235,000.00
Vijay Singh	T-6	69-65-72-69=275	$163,333.34
Jim Furyk	T-6	69-69-68-69=275	$163,333.33
Robert Allenby	T-6	69-69-68-69=275	$163,333.33
Brad Faxon	T-9	68-67-70-71=276	$116,750.00
Trevor Immelman	T-9	70-68-70-68=276	$116,750.00

Reno-Tahoe Open

Course: Montreux G. & C.C., Reno, Nev.
Par: 72 Yardage: 7,472
Last day of event: Sunday, August 24, 2003

Player	Place	Score	Earnings
Kirk Triplett	Win	67-68-73-63=271	$540,000.00
Tim Herron	2	69-65-69-71=274	$324,000.00
Dennis Paulson	T-3	68-66-73-68=275	$174,000.00
Rod Pampling	T-3	67-73-67-68=275	$174,000.00
Harrison Frazar	5	69-72-70-66=277	$120,000.00
Craig Barlow	T-6	70-65-68-75=278	$104,250.00
Hidemichi Tanaka	T-6	71-71-67-69=278	$104,250.00
J.P. Hayes	8	68-68-71-72=279	$93,000.00
David Sutherland	9	70-67-72-71=280	$87,000.00
Guy Boros	T-10	71-66-70-74=281	$66,500.00

Nick Watney	T-10	72-66-70-73=281	$66,500.00
Paul Stankowski	T-10	67-72-69-73=281	$66,500.00
Dicky Pride	T-10	71-68-72-70=281	$66,500.00
Mike Grob	T-10	69-74-68-70=281	$66,500.00
Scott McCarron	T-10	71-72-70-68=281	$66,500.00

Deutsche Bank Championship

Course: TPC of Boston, Norton, Mass.
Par: 71 Yardage: 7,415
Last day of event: Monday, September 1, 2003

Player	Place	Score	Earnings
Adam Scott	Win	69-62-67-66=264	$900,000.00
Rocco Mediate	2	67-70-66-65=268	$540,000.00
Justin Rose	3	63-71-68-67=269	$340,000.00
Vijay Singh	4	65-68-71-66=270	$240,000.00
Geoff Ogilvy	T-5	68-66-68-69=271	$190,000.00
Tim Herron	T-5	67-68-68-68=271	$190,000.00
Steve Flesch	T-7	66-69-69-69=273	$161,250.00
Tiger Woods	T-7	70-69-67-67=273	$161,250.00
Jonathan Kaye	T-9	71-67-63-74=275	$140,000.00
Darren Clarke	T-9	67-68-67-73=275	$140,000.00

Bell Canadian Open

Course: Hamilton Golf & C.C., Hamilton, Ontario, Canada
Par: 70 Yardage: 6,930
Last day of event: Sunday, September 7, 2003

Player	Place	Score	Earnings
Bob Tway	Win	70-70-66-66=272	$756,000.00
Playoff: Beat Brad Faxon with a bogey on third extra hole			
Brad Faxon	2	67-72-66-67=272	$453,600.00
Tom Pernice, Jr.	3	68-72-65-68=273	$285,600.00
Hidemichi Tanaka	T-4	66-70-67-71=274	$184,800.00
K.J. Choi	T-4	71-70-67-66=274	$184,800.00
Fred Funk	T-6	69-68-68-70=275	$145,950.00
Vijay Singh	T-6	75-67-65-68=275	$145,950.00
Loren Roberts	T-8	70-67-71-68=276	$126,000.00
Matt Gogel	T-8	69-70-70-67=276	$126,000.00
Mike Weir	10	69-69-70-69=277	$113,400.00

John Deere Classic

Course: TPC at Deere Run, Silvis, Ill.
Par: 71 Yardage: 7,183
Last day of event: Monday, September 15, 2003

Player	Place	Score	Earnings
Vijay Singh	Win	66-68-69-65=268	$630,000.00
J.L. Lewis	T-2	65-65-71-71=272	$261,333.33
Chris Riley	T-2	66-69-66-71=272	$261,333.34
Jonathan Byrd	T-2	65-67-72-68=272	$261,333.33
Paul Stankowski	T-5	70-65-68-70=273	$127,750.00
Hidemichi Tanaka	T-5	70-67-67-69=273	$127,750.00
Kevin Sutherland	T-5	69-67-71-66=273	$127,750.00
Notah Begay III	T-8	67-71-65-71=274	$105,000.00
Jerry Kelly	T-8	71-70-68-65=274	$105,000.00
Bernhard Langer	T-10	71-65-70-69=275	$91,000.00
Glen Day	T-10	72-65-70-68=275	$91,000.00

84 Lumber Classic of Pennsylvania

Course: Nemocolin Woodlands Resort (Mystic Rock Course), Farmington, Pa.
Par: 72 Yardage: 7,276
Last day of event: Sunday, September 21, 2003

Player	Place	Score	Earnings
J.L. Lewis	Win	69-67-68-62=266	$720,000.00
Tim Petrovic	T-2	67-69-65-67=268	$298,666.66
Stuart Appleby	T-2	69-68-64-67=268	$298,666.67
Frank Lickliter II	T-2	70-67-65-66=268	$298,666.67
Cameron Beckman	T-5	67-66-64-74=271	$146,000.00
Jesper Parnevik	T-5	68-66-70-67=271	$146,000.00
Rocco Mediate	T-5	68-70-67-66=271	$146,000.00
Robert Damron	T-8	67-66-66-73=272	$120,000.00
Craig Barlow	T-8	67-68-68-69=272	$120,000.00
Chris DiMarco	T-10	70-65-67-71=273	$100,000.00
Rory Sabbatini	T-10	68-70-64-71=273	$100,000.00
Shigeki Maruyama	T-10	68-70-67-68=273	$100,000.00

Valero Texas Open

Course: LaCantera G.C., San Antonio, Texas
Par: 70 Yardage: 6,881
Last day of event: Sunday, September 28, 2003

Player	Place	Score	Earnings
Tommy Armour III	Win	64-62-63-65=254	$630,000.00
Bob Tway	T-2	61-69-67-64=261	$308,000.00
Loren Roberts	T-2	64-66-69-62=261	$308,000.00
Duffy Waldorf	4	64-69-62-67=262	$168,000.00
Aaron Baddeley	5	62-70-69-62=263	$140,000.00
Dan Forsman	6	64-63-70-67=264	$126,000.00
Paul Goydos	T-7	65-64-68-68=265	$98,291.66
Glen Hnatiuk	T-7	65-68-64-68=265	$98,291.66
K.J. Choi	T-7	67-62-69-67=265	$98,291.67
Richard S. Johnson	T-7	66-67-66-66=265	$98,291.67
Steve Flesch	T-7	67-66-68-64=265	$98,291.67
Frank Lickliter II	T-7	68-69-64-64=265	$98,291.67

WGC-American Express Championship

Course: Capital City Club, Crabapple Course, Woodstock,, Ga.
Par: 70 Yardage: 7,189
Last day of event: Sunday, October 5, 2003

Player	Place	Score	Earnings
Tiger Woods	Win	67-66-69-72=274	$1,050,000.00
Vijay Singh	T-2	70-70-64-72=276	$405,000.00
Tim Herron	T-2	66-72-67-71=276	$405,000.00
Stuart Appleby	T-2	71-68-69-68=276	$405,000.00
David Toms	5	73-72-67-65=277	$235,000.00
K.J. Choi	T-6	67-71-68-73=279	$182,500.00
Padraig Harrington	T-6	71-73-69-66=279	$182,500.00
Retief Goosen	T-8	73-69-67-72=281	$137,500.00
Paul Casey	T-8	73-71-66-71=281	$137,500.00
Ignacio Garrido	T-10	68-71-69-74=282	$111,250.00
Fred Couples	T-10	71-73-70-68=282	$111,250.00

Southern Farm Bureau Classic

Course: Annandale G.C., Madison, Miss.
Par: 72 Yardage: 7,199
Last day of event: Sunday, October 5, 2003

Player	Place	Score	Earnings
John Huston	Win	66-66-68-68=268	$540,000.00
Brenden Pappas	2	72-69-66-62=269	$324,000.00
Shigeki Maruyama	3	68-68-68-66=270	$204,000.00
Hidemichi Tanaka	T-4	66-68-68-70=272	$124,000.00
Chris M. Anderson	T-4	69-66-67-70=272	$124,000.00
Paul Stankowski	T-4	68-68-66-70=272	$124,000.00
Tim Clark	T-7	69-66-69-69=273	$93,500.00
Glen Day	T-7	72-69-66-66=273	$93,500.00
Jose Coceres	T-7	71-67-70-65=273	$93,500.00
Luke Donald	T-10	69-67-67-71=274	$75,000.00
John E. Morgan	T-10	73-65-68-68=274	$75,000.00
Russ Cochran	T-10	71-69-68-66=274	$75,000.00

Las Vegas Invitational

Course: TPC at Summerlin, TPC At The Canyons, Southern Highlands G.C., Las Vegas, Nev.
Home course / TPC at Summerlin, Par: 72 Yardage: 7,243
Last day of event: Sunday, October 12, 2003

Player	Place	Score	Earnings
Stuart Appleby	Win	62-68-63-66-69=328	$720,000.00
Playoff: Beat Scott McCarron with birdie on first extra hole			
Scott McCarron	2	69-62-64-67-66=328	$432,000.00
Steve Lowery	T-3	65-64-70-65-67=331	$272,000.00
Scott Verplank	T-4	64-62-66-73-67=332	$192,000.00
David Frost	T-5	67-65-71-65-65=333	$160,000.00
Woody Austin	T-6	65-65-65-72-67=334	$139,000.00
Steve Flesch	T-6	62-64-66-68-74=334	$139,000.00
Billy Andrade	T-8	66-71-65-66-67=335	$124,000.00
Robert Allenby	T-9	66-65-66-73=336	$104,000.00
Jerry Kelly	T-9	65-67-65-73-66=336	$104,000.00
Phil Mickelson	T-9	67-64-69-68-68=336	$104,000.00
Rory Sabbatini	T-9	66-64-71-68-67=336	$104,000.00

Chrysler Classic of Greensboro

Course: Forest Oaks C.C., Greensboro, N.C.
Par: 72 Yardage: 7,311
Last day of event: Sunday, October 19, 2003

Player	Place	Score	Earnings
Shigeki Maruyama	Win	65-64-70-67=266	$810,000.00
Brad Faxon	2	67-67-68-69=271	$486,000.00
Matt Gogel	3	70-67-68-68=273	$306,000.00
Robert Allenby	4	70-70-66-68=274	$216,000.00
K.J. Choi	T-5	68-69-68-70=275	$142,392.85
Stephen Ames	T-5	64-71-71-69=275	$142,392.85
Jonathan Byrd	T-5	66-70-71-68=275	$142,392.86
Jay Haas	T-5	69-68-70-68=275	$142,392.86
Jeff Brehaut	T-5	69-70-68-68=275	$142,392.86
John E. Morgan	T-5	66-72-70-67=275	$142,392.86
Brenden Pappas	T-5	71-68-70-66=275	$142,392.86

FUNAI Classic at the Walt Disney World Resort

Course: Walt Disney (Magnolia, Palm), Lake Buena Vista, Fla.
Home course / Magnolia, Par: 72 Yardage: 7,200
Last day of event: Sunday, October 26, 2003

Player	Place	Score	Earnings
Vijay Singh	Win	64-65-69-67=265	$720,000.00
Scott Verplank	T-2	66-66-66-71=269	$298,666.67
Stewart Cink	T-2	67-65-66-71=269	$298,666.66
Tiger Woods	T-2	66-67-71-65=269	$298,666.67
John Rollins	T-5	66-65-67-72=270	$152,000.00
Davis Love III	T-5	67-65-69-69=270	$152,000.00
Bob Estes	T-7	67-63-72-69=271	$129,000.00
Michael Clark II	T-7	72-66-68-65=271	$129,000.00
Rocco Mediate	T-9	65-67-69-71=272	$108,000.00
Geoff Ogilvy	T-9	66-70-66-70=272	$108,000.00
Bob Tway	T-9	67-65-71-69=272	$108,000.00

Chrysler Championship

Course: Westin Innisbrook Resort (Copperhead Course), Palm Harbor, Fla.
Par: 71 Yardage: 7,315
Last day of event: Sunday, November 2, 2003

Player	Place	Score	Earnings
Retief Goosen	Win	69-66-67-70=272	$864,000.00
Vijay Singh	2	70-70-65-70=275	$518,400.00
Briny Baird	3	72-66-66-72=276	$326,400.00
Tim Petrovic	T-4	71-69-66-72=278	$211,200.00
Chad Campbell	T-4	68-69-72-69=278	$211,200.00
Thomas Levet	T-6	71-67-71-70=279	$160,800.00
Dan Forsman	T-6	67-75-69-68=279	$160,800.00
Davis Love III	T-6	69-72-72-66=279	$160,800.00
Geoff Ogilvy	T-9	71-71-68-70=280	$124,800.00
Brad Faxon	T-9	72-71-68-69=280	$124,800.00
Peter Lonard	T-9	71-71-70-68=280	$124,800.00
Stephen Ames	T-9	74-67-72-67=280	$124,800.00

The Tour Championship

Course: Champions G.C., Houston, Texas
Par: 71 Yardage: 7,301
Last day of event: Sunday, November 9, 2003

Player	Place	Score	Earnings
Chad Campbell	Win	70-69-61-68=268	$1,080,000.00
Charles Howell III	2	67-67-67-70=271	$648,000.00
Retief Goosen	3	69-67-67-69=272	$414,000.00
Chris Riley	4	69-68-66-70=273	$288,000.00
Davis Love III	T-5	73-67-67-69=276	$228,000.00
Vijay Singh	T-5	73-68-67-68=276	$228,000.00
Jonathan Kaye	7	69-70-68-70=277	$204,000.00
Jim Furyk	8	71-71-67-69=278	$192,000.00
Fred Funk	T-9	68-67-71-73=279	$163,650.00
Steve Flesch	T-9	71-68-67-73=279	$163,650.00
Kenny Perry	T-9	67-73-70-69=279	$163,650.00
Scott Verplank	T-9	71-71-69-68=279	$163,650.00

2004

Vijay Singh won nine times—including the PGA Championship in a playoff against Justin Leonard and Chris DiMarco—and displaced Tiger Woods atop the Official World Golf Ranking. Phil Mickelson birdied five of the final seven holes to beat Ernie Els by a stroke at the Masters—finally winning a major on his 47th attempt. Arnold Palmer played in his 50th consecutive, and final, Masters. Retief Goosen proved to be the most resilient at dealing with an out-of-control setup at Shinnecock Hills and won the U.S. Open by two shots over Mickelson. Unheralded Todd Hamilton won the British Open at Royal Troon, besting Els in a four-hole aggregate playoff, 15 to 16. Meanwhile, Tiger Woods parted with coach Butch Harmon and began to reconstruct his swing (for the second time since turning pro) under the direction of Hank Haney. Woods posted only one victory in 2004, at the WGC Accenture Match Play. Michelle Wie, 14, was given a sponsor's exemption into the Sony Open; she shot 72-68 and missed the cut by a shot. The U.S. was thrashed in the Ryder Cup, 18 to 9, at Oakland Hills.

Mercedes Champion111s

Course: Kapalua Resort Plantation Course, Kapalua, Maui, Ha.
Par: 73 Yardage: 7,263
Last day of event: Sunday, January 11, 2004

Player	Place	Score	Earnings
Stuart Appleby	Win	66-67-66-71=270	$1,060,000.00
Vijay Singh	2	68-64-69-70=271	$600,000.00
Darren Clarke	3	67-69-69-70=275	$400,000.00
Retief Goosen	T-4	70-70-64-73=277	$275,000.00
Tiger Woods	T-4	71-70-65-71=277	$275,000.00

Kirk Triplett	6	68-69-71-70=278	$204,000.00
Adam Scott	7	69-74-68-68=279	$180,000.00
Scott Hoch	8	68-71-69-72=280	$170,000.00
Davis Love III	T-9	69-71-69-72=281	$155,000.00
Ben Crane	T-9	71-74-66-70=281	$155,000.00

Sony Open in Hawaii

Course: Waialae C.C., Honolulu, Ha.
Par: 70 Yardage: 7,060
Last day of event: Sunday, January 18, 2004

Player	Place	Score	Earnings
Ernie Els	Win	67-64-66-65=262	$864,000.00
Playoff: Beat Harrison Frazar with birdie on third extra hole			
Harrison Frazar	2	67-63-66-66=262	$518,400.00
Davis Love III	3	70-65-63-67=265	$326,400.00
Frank Lickliter II	4	71-62-65-68=266	$230,400.00
Briny Baird	T-5	68-66-66-67=267	$182,400.00
Jerry Kelly	T-5	68-65-69-65=267	$182,400.00
John Riegger	7	68-66-67-67=268	$160,800.00
Craig Barlow	T-8	66-69-66-68=269	$144,000.00
Stephen Ames	T-8	66-70-65-68=269	$144,000.00
Paul Azinger	T-10	67-66-66-71=270	$110,400.00
Retief Goosen	T-10	67-69-65-69=270	$110,400.00
John Huston	T-10	67-67-69-67=270	$110,400.00
Vijay Singh	T-10	69-68-67-66=270	$110,400.00
Omar Uresti	T-10	72-66-67-65=270	$110,400.00

Bob Hope Chrysler Classic

Course: PGA West/Palmer, Bermuda Dunes C.C., La Quinta C.C., Indian Wells C.C., La Quinta, Calif.
Home course / PGA West, Par: 72 Yardage: 6,930
Last day of event: Sunday, January 25, 2004

Player	Place	Score	Earnings
Phil Mickelson	Win	68-63-64-67-68=330	$810,000.00
Playoff: Beat Skip Kendall with birdie on first extra hole			
Skip Kendall	2	63-68-68-66-65=330	$486,000.00
Jay Haas	3	65-68-64-67-67=331	$306,000.00
Jonathan Kaye	4	67-70-66-65-64=332	$216,000.00
Kenny Perry	T-5	64-66-69-64-71=334	$164,250.00
Ben Crane	T-5	68-64-65-69-68=334	$164,250.00
Jesper Parnevik	T-5	67-68-66-65-68=334	$164,250.00
Bernhard Langer	8	67-67-69-68-64=335	$139,500.00
Kirk Triplett	T-9	66-65-68-63-74=336	$104,142.85
Paul Azinger	T-9	67-65-66-69-69=336	$104,142.85
J.L. Lewis	T-9	68-68-69-64-67=336	$104,142.86
Harrison Frazar	T-9	73-67-66-63-67=336	$104,142.86
Kent Jones	T-9	69-65-68-68-66=336	$104,142.86
Rod Pampling	T-9	70-67-67-66-66=336	$104,142.86
Chris Riley	T-9	68-64-69-70-65=336	$104,142.86

FBR Open

Course: TPC of Scottsdale, Scottsdale, Ariz.
Par: 71 Yardage: 7,216
Last day of event: Sunday, February 1, 2004

Player	Place	Score	Earnings
Jonathan Kaye	Win	65-68-66-67=266	$936,000.00
Chris DiMarco	2	68-67-64-69=268	$561,600.00
Steve Flesch	T-3	66-69-68-66=269	$301,600.00
Vijay Singh	T-3	71-69-63-66=269	$301,600.00
Mike Weir	T-5	65-69-68-69=271	$197,600.00
Duffy Waldorf	T-5	70-68-68-65=271	$197,600.00

Phil Mickelson	T-7	64-68-68-72=272	$167,700.00
Scott Verplank	T-7	63-70-70-69=272	$167,700.00
Justin Leonard	T-9	69-67-66-71=273	$130,000.00
Fredrik Jacobson	T-9	68-68-67-70=273	$130,000.00
Sergio Garcia	T-9	71-67-65-70=273	$130,000.00
Kevin Sutherland	T-9	72-65-68-68=273	$130,000.00
Retief Goosen	T-9	70-68-68-67=273	$130,000.00

J.J. Henry	T-7	71-69-65-69=274	$149,600.00
Jay Williamson	T-7	69-69-72-64=274	$149,600.00
Tiger Woods	T-7	72-66-72-64=274	$149,600.00
Jeff Maggert	T-10	67-66-69-73=275	$110,400.00
Briny Baird	T-10	69-62-73-71=275	$110,400.00
Loren Roberts	T-10	70-65-69-71=275	$110,400.00
Tim Clark	T-10	72-69-64-70=275	$110,400.00
Bob Tway	T-10	68-67-71-69=275	$110,400.00

AT&T Pebble Beach National Pro-Am

Courses: Pebble Beach G.L., Spyglass Hill G.C., Poppy Hills G.C., Pebble Beach, Calif.
Home Course/ Pebble Beach G.L., Par: 72 Yardage: 6,816
Last day of event: Sunday, February 8, 2004

Player	Place	Score	Earnings
Vijay Singh	Win	67-68-68-69=272	$954,000.00
Jeff Maggert	2	71-68-67-69=275	$572,400.00
Phil Mickelson	3	68-68-71-69=276	$360,400.00
Arron Oberholser	T-4	69-67-67-76=279	$219,066.66
K.J. Choi	T-4	67-70-71-71=279	$219,066.67
Mike Weir	T-4	73-70-66-70=279	$219,066.67
Tom Pernice, Jr.	T-7	67-68-73-72=280	$165,183.33
Jesper Parnevik	T-7	70-67-73-70=280	$165,183.34
Mark Hensby	T-7	70-67-73-70=280	$165,183.33
Scott McCarron	T-10	69-68-71-73=281	$127,200.00
Bill Glasson	T-10	73-69-66-73=281	$127,200.00
Corey Pavin	T-10	69-68-73-71=281	$127,200.00
Kent Jones	T-10	67-71-74-69=281	$127,200.00

Buick Invitational

Course: Torrey Pines (South), Torrey Pines (North), San Diego, Calif.
Home Course -Par: 72 Yardage: 7,568
Last day of event: Sunday, February 15, 2004

Player	Place	Score	Earnings
John Daly	Win	69-66-68-75=278	$864,000.00

Playoff: Beat Chris Riley and Luke Donald with birdie on first extra hole

Chris Riley	T-2	67-71-71-69=278	$422,400.00
Luke Donald	T-2	69-69-71-69=278	$422,400.00
Jesper Parnevik	T-4	65-73-70-71=279	$174,000.00
Bo Van Pelt	T-4	68-68-73-70=279	$174,000.00
Duffy Waldorf	T-4	68-70-71-70=279	$174,000.00
Shigeki Maruyama	T-4	72-67-71-69=279	$174,000.00
Thomas Bjorn	T-4	70-69-72-68=279	$174,000.00
Phil Mickelson	T-4	74-69-69-67=279	$174,000.00
Stewart Cink	T-10	70-63-71-76=280	$106,400.00
Brandt Jobe	T-10	69-69-70-72=280	$106,400.00
Tom Pernice, Jr.	T-10	71-68-69-72=280	$106,400.00
Billy Mayfair	T-10	72-65-72-71=280	$106,400.00
Jay Haas	T-10	70-69-70-71=280	$106,400.00
Tiger Woods	T-10	71-68-72-69=280	$106,400.00

Nissan Open

Course: Riviera C.C., Pacific Palisades, Calif.
Par: 71 Yardage: 7,260
Last day of event: Sunday, February 22, 2004

Player	Place	Score	Earnings
Mike Weir	Win	66-64-66-71=267	$864,000.00
Shigeki Maruyama	2	64-66-71-67=268	$518,400.00
Stuart Appleby	3	70-64-70-66=270	$326,400.00
John Daly	4	68-64-72-67=271	$230,400.00
Hank Kuehne	5	65-72-68-67=272	$192,000.00
Kirk Triplett	6	66-67-72-68=273	$172,800.00

WGC-Accenture Match Play Championship

Course: La Costa Resort & Spa, Carlsbad, Calif.
Par: 72 Yardage: 7,247
Last day of event: Sunday, February 29, 2004

Player	Place	Earnings
Tiger Woods	Win	$1,200,000.00

Round One - Beat John Rollins 1 up
Round Two - Beat Trevor Immelman 5 & 4
Round Three - Beat Fredrik Jacobson 5 & 4
Quarterfinals - Beat Padraig Harrington 2 & 1
Semifinals - Beat Stephen Leaney 2 & 1
Finals - Beat Davis Love III 3 & 2

| Davis Love III | 2 | $700,000.00 |

Round One - Beat Briny Baird 2 up
Round Two - Beat Fred Couples 3 & 2
Round Three - Beat Scott Adams 4 & 3
Quarterfinals - Beat Phil Mickelson 1 up
Semifinals - Beat Darren Clarke 21 holes
Finals - Tiger Woods beat him 3 & 2

| Darren Clarke | 3 | $530,000.00 |

Round One - Beat Eduardo Romero 25 holes
Round Two - Beat Alex Cejka 6 & 5
Round Three - Beat Kenny Perry 3 & 2
Quarterfinals - Beat Jerry Kelly 5 & 3
Semifinals - Davis Love III beat him 21 holes
Consolation - Beat Stephen Leaney 2 up

| Stephen Leaney | 4 | $430,000.00 |

Round One - Beat Fred Funk 1 up
Round Two - Beat Mike Weir 3 & 2
Round Three - Beat Colin Montgomerie 1 up
Quarterfinals - Beat Ian Pouter 1 up
Semifinals - Tiger Woods beat him 2 & 1
Consolation - Darren Clarke beat him 2 up

| Padraig Harrington | T-5 | $225,000.00 |

Round One - Beat Toshi Izawa 1 & 1
Round Two - Beat Bob Estes 3 & 2
Round Three - Beat David Toms 1 up
Quarterfinals - Tiger Woods beat him 2 & 1

| Ian Poulter | T-5 | $225,000.00 |

Round One - Beat Chris Riley 1 up
Round Two - Beat Duffy Waldorf 7 & 5
Round Three - Beat John Huston 2 & 1
Quarterfinals - Stephen Leaney beat him 1 up

| Jerry Kelly | T-5 | $225,000.00 |

Round One - Beat Sergio Garcia 1 up
Round Two - Beat Vijay Singh 3 & 2
Round Three - Beat Chad Campbell 1 up
Quarterfinals - Darren Clarke beat him 5 & 3

| Phil Mickelson | T-5 | $225,000.00 |

Round One - Beat Lee Westwood 3 & 1
Round Two - Beat Ben Curtis 7 & 6
Round Three - Beat Chris DiMarco 3 & 2
Quarterfinals - Davis Love III beat him 1 up

| Fredrik Jacobson | T-9 | $115,000.00 |

Round One - Beat Phillip Price 5 & 4
Round Two - Beat Thomas Bjorn 5 & 4

Round Three - Tiger Woods beat him 5 & 4

Player	Place	Score	Earnings
David Toms	T-9		$115,000.00

Round One - Beat Niclas Fasth 19 holes
Round Two - Beat Shaun Micheel 4 & 3
Round Three - Padraig Harrington beat him 1 up

| Colin Montgomerie | T-9 | | $115,000.00 |

Round One - Beat Nick Price 20 holes
Round Two - Beat Stewart Cink 5 & 4
Round Three - Stephen Leaney beat him 1 up

| John Huston | T-9 | | $115,000.00 |

Round One - Beat Retief Goosen 2 & 1
Round Two - Beat Peter Lonard 1 up
Round Three - Ian Poulter beat 2 & 1

| Chad Campbell | T-9 | | $115,000.00 |

Round One - Beat Tim Herron 3 & 2
Round Two - Beat Loren Roberts 3 & 1
Round Three - Jerry Kelly beat him 1 up

| Kenny Perry | T-9 | | $115,000.00 |

Round One - Beat Jeff Sluman 6 & 4
Round Two - Beat Steve Flesch 1 up
Round Three - Darren Clarke beat 3 & 2

| Adam Scott | T-9 | | $115,000.00 |

Round One - Beat Miguel Angel Jimenez 2 & 1
Round Two - Beat Robert Allenby 23 holes
Round Three - Davis Love III beat him 4 & 3

| Chris DiMarco | T-9 | | $115,000.00 |

Round One - Beat Michael Campbell 2 up
Round Two - Beat Stuart Appleby 19 holes
Round Three - Phil Mickelson beat 3 & 2

Chrysler Classic of Tucson

Course: Tucson National Resort, Tucson, Ariz.
Par: 72 Yardage: 7,109
Last day of event: Sunday, February 29, 2004

Player	Place	Score	Earnings
Heath Slocum	Win	67-64-70-65=266	$540,000.00
Aaron Baddeley	2	68-69-64-66=267	$324,000.00
Mark Hensby	T-3	65-68-69-68=270	$156,000.00
Harrison Frazar	T-3	66-67-71-66=270	$156,000.00
Rory Sabbatini	T-3	69-68-69-64=270	$156,000.00
Bill Glasson	T-6	66-66-71-68=271	$104,250.00
Per-Ulrik Johansson	T-6	65-69-69-68=271	$104,250.00
Carlos Franco	T-8	65-69-68-70=272	$84,000.00
Mike Heinen	T-8	66-71-65-70=272	$84,000.00
Todd Fischer	T-8	68-68-69-67=272	$84,000.00
Tim Clark	T-8	66-68-72-66=272	$84,000.00

Ford Championship at Doral

Course: Doral C.C. (Blue), Miami, Fla.
Par: 72 Yardage: 7,266
Last day of event: Sunday, March 7, 2004

Player	Place	Score	Earnings
Craig Parry	Win	71-65-67-68=271	$900,000.00

Playoff: Beat Scott Verplank with eagle (holed out from fairway) on first extra hole

Scott Verplank	2	67-72-65-67=271	$540,000.00
Retief Goosen	3	67-68-71-66=272	$340,000.00
Joe Durant	4	66-72-67-68=273	$240,000.00
Gene Sauers	T-5	70-70-64-70=274	$175,625.00
K.J. Choi	T-5	70-69-66-69=274	$175,625.00
David Toms	T-5	72-68-65-69=274	$175,625.00
Bernhard Langer	T-5	75-68-66-65=274	$175,625.00
Danny Ellis	T-9	69-69-67-70=275	$140,000.00
Mark Calcavecchia	T-9	68-69-70-68=275	$140,000.00

Honda Classic

Course: C.C. at Mirasol (Sunrise Course), Palm Beach Gardens, Fla.
Par: 72 Yardage: 7,468
Last day of event: Sunday, March 14, 2004

Player	Place	Score	Earnings
Todd Hamilton	Win	68-66-68-74=276	$900,000.00
Davis Love III	2	69-69-70-69=277	$540,000.00
Brian Bateman	3	71-69-70-68=278	$340,000.00
Fredrik Jacobson	T-4	67-69-70-73=279	$196,875.00
Woody Austin	T-4	71-69-69-70=279	$196,875.00
Robert Allenby	T-4	68-74-67-70=279	$196,875.00
Kevin Na	T-4	67-72-71-69=279	$196,875.00
Brad Faxon	8	68-66-76-70=280	$155,000.00
Rory Sabbatini	T-9	66-72-71-72=281	$130,000.00
Lee Janzen	T-9	74-66-70-71=281	$130,000.00
Tommy Armour III	T-9	69-69-73-70=281	$130,000.00
Chad Campbell	T-9	71-70-71-69=281	$130,000.00

Bay Hill Invitational

Course: Bay Hill Club, Orlando, Fla.
Par: 72 Yardage: 7,267
Last day of event: Sunday, March 21, 2004

Player	Place	Score	Earnings
Chad Campbell	Win	66-68-70-66=270	$900,000.00
Stuart Appleby	2	67-67-66-76=276	$540,000.00
Adam Scott	T-3	68-70-68-71=277	$290,000.00
Scott Verplank	T-3	68-68-73-68=277	$290,000.00
Jerry Kelly	5	67-69-73-69=278	$200,000.00
Shigeki Maruyama	T-6	66-66-75-73=280	$161,875.00
Darren Clarke	T-6	66-68-74-72=280	$161,875.00
Zach Johnson	T-6	67-68-75-70=280	$161,875.00
Stephen Ames	T-6	72-65-73-70=280	$161,875.00
John Daly	T-10	68-70-70-73=281	$130,000.00
Dennis Paulson	T-10	72-67-72-70=281	$130,000.00

The Players Championship

Course: TPC at Sawgrass, Ponte Vedra Beach, Fla.
Par: 72 Yardage: 7,093
Last day of event: Sunday, March 28, 2004

Player	Place	Score	Earnings
Adam Scott	Win	65-72-69-70=276	$1,440,000.00
Padraig Harrington	2	68-70-73-66=277	$864,000.00
Frank Lickliter II	T-3	69-71-68-72=280	$416,000.00
Phil Mickelson	T-3	70-69-70-71=280	$416,000.00
Kenny Perry	T-3	69-71-69-71=280	$416,000.00
Kevin Sutherland	T-6	66-69-73-73=281	$268,000.00
Jerry Kelly	T-6	69-66-74-72=281	$268,000.00
Jay Haas	T-6	72-73-70-66=281	$268,000.00
Shaun Micheel	9	70-76-69-67=282	$232,000.00
Bob Burns	T-10	67-72-72-72=283	$200,000.00
Paul Casey	T-10	72-70-69-72=283	$200,000.00
Fred Funk	T-10	73-71-68-71=283	$200,000.00

BellSouth Classic

Course: TPC at Sugarloaf, Duluth, Ga.
Par: 72 Yardage: 7,293
Last day of event: Sunday, April 4, 2004

Player	Place	Score	Earnings
Zach Johnson	Win	69-66-68-72=275	$810,000.00
Mark Hensby	2	73-70-66-67=276	$486,000.00

Player	Place	Score	Earnings
Scott Hend	3	72-66-68-71=277	$306,000.00
Padraig Harrington	4	70-69-67-72=278	$216,000.00
Peter Lonard	5	73-67-69-71=280	$180,000.00
Ben Crane	T-6	68-69-71-73=281	$156,375.00
Lee Janzen	T-6	75-67-68-71=281	$156,375.00
Stewart Cink	T-8	75-67-69-71=282	$135,000.00
Luke Donald	T-8	72-70-71-69=282	$135,000.00
Phil Mickelson	10	69-72-71-71=283	$121,500.00

Masters

Course: Augusta National G.C., Augusta, Ga.
Par: 72 Yardage: 7,290
Last day of event: Sunday, April 11, 2004

Player	Place	Score	Earnings
Phil Mickelson	Win	72-69-69-69=279	$1,170,000.00
Ernie Els	2	70-72-71-67=280	$702,000.00
K.J. Choi	3	71-70-72-69=282	$442,000.00
Bernhard Langer	T-4	71-73-69-72=285	$286,000.00
Sergio Garcia	T-4	72-72-75-66=285	$286,000.00
Chris DiMarco	T-6	69-73-68-76=286	$189,893.00
Paul Casey	T-6	75-69-68-74=286	$189,893.00
Kirk Triplett	T-6	71-74-69-72=286	$189,893.00
Fred Couples	T-6	73-69-74-70=286	$189,893.00
Davis Love III	T-6	75-67-74-70=286	$189,893.00
Nick Price	T-6	72-73-71-70=286	$189,893.00
Vijay Singh	T-6	75-73-69-69=286	$189,893.00

MCI Heritage

Course: Harbour Town G.L., Hilton Head, S.C.
Par: 71 Yardage: 6,973
Last day of event: Sunday, April 18, 2004

Player	Place	Score	Earnings
Stewart Cink	Win	72-69-69-64=274	$864,000.00
Playoff: Beat Ted Purdy with birdie on fifth extra hole			
Ted Purdy	2	69-67-65-73=274	$518,400.00
Patrick Sheehan	T-3	71-66-69-70=276	$249,600.00
Ernie Els	T-3	69-70-68-69=276	$249,600.00
Carl Pettersson	T-3	72-71-66-67=276	$249,600.00
Fred Funk	6	69-69-69-70=277	$172,800.00
Stephen Ames	T-7	70-68-68-72=278	$144,600.00
Jay Haas	T-7	68-69-70-71=278	$144,600.00
Justin Rose	T-7	73-69-66-70=278	$144,600.00
Scott Hoch	T-7	70-68-71-69=278	$144,600.00

Shell Houston Open

Course: Redstone G.C. (Fall Creek), Humble, Texas
Par: 72 Yardage: 7,508
Last day of event: Monday, April 26, 2004

Player	Place	Score	Earnings
Vijay Singh	Win	74-66-69-68=277	$900,000.00
Scott Hoch	2	73-68-71-67=279	$540,000.00
John Huston	3	71-71-67-71=280	$340,000.00
Dudley Hart	T-4	69-72-71-70=282	$220,000.00
Stephen Ames	T-4	68-76-69-69=282	$220,000.00
Jose Coceres	T-6	73-69-68-73=283	$161,875.00
Paul Azinger	T-6	73-67-72-71=283	$161,875.00
John Daly	T-6	76-69-67-71=283	$161,875.00
Rory Sabbatini	T-6	74-70-69-70=283	$161,875.00
Geoff Ogilvy	10	71-70-71-72=284	$135,000.00

HP Classic of New Orleans

Course: English Turn G. & C.C., New Orleans, La.
Par: 72 Yardage: 7,078
Last day of event: Monday, May 3, 2004

Player	Place	Score	Earnings
Vijay Singh	Win	70-65-68-63=266	$918,000.00
Joe Ogilvie	T-2	66-67-66-68=267	$448,800.00
Phil Mickelson	T-2	67-65-69-66=267	$448,800.00
Hidemichi Tanaka	4	69-64-69-67=269	$244,800.00
Charles Howell III	T-5	66-64-71-70=271	$193,800.00
Justin Rose	T-5	67-70-65-69=271	$193,800.00
Brian Bateman	T-7	67-67-69-69=272	$158,950.00
K.J. Choi	T-7	67-68-68-69=272	$158,950.00
Stephen Ames	T-7	67-69-71-65=272	$158,950.00
Matt Kuchar	T-10	69-63-71-70=273	$132,600.00
Joe Durant	T-10	67-70-67-69=273	$132,600.00

Wachovia Championship

Course: Quail Hollow Club, Charlotte, N.C.
Par: 72 Yardage: 7,442
Last day of event: Sunday, May 9, 2004

Player	Place	Score	Earnings
Joey Sindelar	Win	69-69-70-69=277	$1,008,000.00
Playoff: Beat Arron Oberholser with par on second extra hole			
Arron Oberholser	2	69-68-68-72=277	$604,800.00
Carlos Franco	T-3	68-71-69-70=278	$324,800.00
Tiger Woods	T-3	69-66-75-68=278	$324,800.00
Notah Begay III	T-5	67-70-69-73=279	$196,700.00
Jeff Maggert	T-5	71-69-67-72=279	$196,700.00
Steve Flesch	T-5	72-72-66-69=279	$196,700.00
Phil Mickelson	T-5	70-70-72-67=279	$196,700.00
Mathias Gronberg	9	69-71-71-69=280	$162,400.00
Geoff Ogilvy	T-10	69-71-66-75=281	$128,800.00
Vijay Singh	T-10	68-70-71-72=281	$128,800.00
Heath Slocum	T-10	67-75-67-72=281	$128,800.00
Kevin Sutherland	T-10	71-68-71-71=281	$128,800.00
Lucas Glover	T-10	74-70-68-69=281	$128,800.00

EDS Byron Nelson Championship

Course: TPC at Las Colinas, Cottonwood Valley Course, Irving, Texas
Home course / TPC at Las Colinas, Par: 70 Yardage: 7,016
Last day of event: Sunday, May 16, 2004

Player	Place	Score	Earnings
Sergio Garcia	Win	66-68-65-71=270	$1,044,000.00
Playoff: Beat Dudley Hart and Robert Damron with par on first extra hole			
Dudley Hart	T-2	65-71-67-67=270	$510,400.00
Robert Damron	T-2	67-69-68-66=270	$510,400.00
Tiger Woods	T-4	65-67-70-69=271	$239,733.33
Duffy Waldorf	T-4	67-70-66-68=271	$239,733.33
Tim Herron	T-4	69-70-68-64=271	$239,733.34
Stephen Leaney	T-7	66-69-69-68=272	$174,725.00
Ernie Els	T-7	69-70-66-67=272	$174,725.00
Nick Price	T-7	66-71-69-66=272	$174,725.00
Shigeki Maruyama	T-7	70-70-66-66=272	$174,725.00

Bank of America Colonial

Course: Colonial C.C., Fort Worth, Texas
Par: 70 Yardage: 7,054
Last day of event: Sunday, May 23, 2004

Player	Place	Score	Earnings
Steve Flesch	Win	66-69-67-67=269	$954,000.00

Chad Campbell	2	70-71-61-68=270	$572,400.00
Stephen Ames	3	70-69-68-64=271	$360,400.00
Craig Perks	4	64-71-70-68=273	$254,400.00
Robert Gamez	T-5	71-64-71-68=274	$186,162.50
Tim Petrovic	T-5	66-71-69-68=274	$186,162.50
Skip Kendall	T-5	68-71-68-67=274	$186,162.50
Bo Van Pelt	T-5	68-69-72-65=274	$186,162.50
Mark Brooks	T-9	71-68-67-69=275	$143,100.00
Jeff Maggert	T-9	66-69-73-67=275	$143,100.00
John Senden	T-9	66-74-70-65=275	$143,100.00

FedEx St. Jude Classic

Course: TPC at Southwind, Germantown, Tenn.
Par: 71 Yardage: 7,069
Last day of event: Sunday, May 30, 2004

Player	Place	Score	Earnings
David Toms	Win	67-63-65-73=268	$846,000.00
Bob Estes	2	74-64-67-69=274	$507,600.00
Tim Herron	T-3	72-64-69-70=275	$272,600.00
Steve Lowery	T-3	74-64-70-67=275	$272,600.00
Vaughn Taylor	T-5	66-65-71-74=276	$165,087.50
Brian Gay	T-5	71-66-66-73=276	$165,087.50
Stewart Cink	T-5	68-70-69-69=276	$165,087.50
Fredrik Jacobson	T-5	75-68-64-69=276	$165,087.50
Hirofumi Miyase	T-9	68-69-67-73=277	$122,200.00
Craig Bowden	T-9	72-68-66-71=277	$122,200.00
Paul Stankowski	T-9	67-69-71-70=277	$122,200.00
Charles Howell III	T-9	70-70-68-69=277	$122,200.00

Memorial Tournament

Course: Muirfield Village G.C., Dubin, Ohio
Par: 72 Yardage: 7,265
Last day of event: Sunday, June 6, 2004

Player	Place	Score	Earnings
Ernie Els	Win	68-70-66-66=270	$945,000.00
Fred Couples	2	69-69-68-68=274	$567,000.00
Tiger Woods	3	72-68-67-69=276	$357,000.00
Justin Rose	4	70-67-69-71=277	$252,000.00
K.J. Choi	5	71-67-68-72=278	$210,000.00
Stephen Ames	T-6	69-68-70-72=279	$182,437.50
Kenny Perry	T-6	72-72-66-69=279	$182,437.50
Ben Curtis	T-8	68-69-73-72=282	$152,250.00
Jay Haas	T-8	70-72-69-71=282	$152,250.00
Retief Goosen	T-8	70-72-69-71=282	$152,250.00

Buick Classic

Course: Westchester C.C., Harrison, N.Y.
Par: 71 Yardage: 6,751
Last day of event: Sunday, June 13, 2004

Player	Place	Score	Earnings
Sergio Garcia	Win	70-67-68-67=272	$945,000.00

Playoff: Beat Rory Sabbatini with birdie on third extra hole (Padraig Harrington eliminated with bogey on second hole)

Rory Sabbatini	T-2	69-68-65-70=272	$462,000.00
Padraig Harrington	T-2	68-68-68-68=272	$462,000.00
Tom Byrum	T-4	71-64-68-71=274	$217,000.00
Vijay Singh	T-4	63-70-71-70=274	$217,000.00
Fred Couples	T-4	67-65-74-68=274	$217,000.00
Luke Donald	7	67-66-70-72=275	$175,875.00
Fredrik Jacobson	8	64-69-74-69=276	$162,750.00
Cameron Beckman	T-9	68-68-66-75=277	$131,250.00

Chris DiMarco	T-9	69-69-69-70=277	$131,250.00
Bo Van Pelt	T-9	68-71-68-70=277	$131,250.00
Tim Clark	T-9	68-72-68-69=277	$131,250.00
Kenny Perry	T-9	69-71-71-66=277	$131,250.00

U.S. Open

Course: Shinnecock Hills G.C., Southampton, N.Y.
Par: 70 Yardage: 6,996
Last day of event: Sunday, June 20, 2004

Player	Place	Score	Earnings
Retief Goosen	Win	70-66-69-71=276	$1,125,000.00
Phil Mickelson	2	68-66-73-71=278	$675,000.00
Jeff Maggert	3	68-67-74-72=281	$424,604.00
Shigeki Maruyama	T-4	66-68-74-76=284	$267,756.00
Mike Weir	T-4	69-70-71-74=284	$267,756.00
Fred Funk	6	70-66-72-77=285	$212,444.00
Steve Flesch	T-7	68-74-70-74=286	$183,828.00
Robert Allenby	T-7	70-72-74-70=286	$183,828.00
Ernie Els	T-9	70-67-70-80=287	$145,282.00
Chris DiMarco	T-9	71-71-70-75=287	$145,282.00
Stephen Ames	T-9	74-66-73-74=287	$145,282.00
Jay Haas	T-9	66-74-76-71=287	$145,282.00

Booz Allen Classic

Course: TPC at Avenel, Potomac, Md.
Par: 71 Yardage: 6,987
Last day of event: Sunday, June 27, 2004

Player	Place	Score	Earnings
Adam Scott	Win	66-62-67-68=263	$864,000.00
Charles Howell III	2	61-69-72-65=267	$518,400.00
Rory Sabbatini	3	67-67-69-66=269	$326,400.00
Arron Oberholser	T-4	69-65-68-70=272	$198,400.00
Tim Herron	T-4	69-68-68-67=272	$198,400.00
Bo Van Pelt	T-4	69-68-68-67=272	$198,400.00
Olin Browne	T-7	64-66-71-72=273	$154,800.00
Alex Cejka	T-7	74-63-67-69=273	$154,800.00
Aaron Barber	T-9	70-68-68-68=274	$134,400.00
Frank Lickliter II	T-9	67-69-72-66=274	$134,400.00

Cialis Western Open

Course: Cog Hill G. & C.C. (Dubsdread), Lemont, Ill.
Par: 71 Yardage: 7,326
Last day of event: Sunday, July 4, 2004

Player	Place	Score	Earnings
Stephen Ames	Win	67-73-64-70=274	$864,000.00
Steve Lowery	2	68-68-70-70=276	$518,400.00
Mark Hensby	T-3	67-70-67-73=277	$278,400.00
Luke Donald	T-3	72-68-70-67=277	$278,400.00
Geoff Ogilvy	T-5	68-69-68-73=278	$182,400.00
Stuart Appleby	T-5	71-68-67-72=278	$182,400.00
Jim Furyk	T-7	69-71-68-71=279	$144,600.00
Tiger Woods	T-7	70-73-65-71=279	$144,600.00
Carl Pettersson	T-7	71-70-69-69=279	$144,600.00
Davis Love III	T-7	70-74-67-68=279	$144,600.00

John Deere Classic
Course: TPC at Deere Run, Silvis, Ill.
Par: 71 Yardage: 7,193
Last day of event: Sunday, July 11, 2004

Player	Place	Score	Earnings
Mark Hensby	Win	68-65-69-66=268	$684,000.00

Playoff: Beat John E. Morgan with par on second extra hole

Player	Place	Score	Earnings
John E. Morgan	2	66-69-68-65=268	$410,400.00
Jose Coceres	3	62-68-68-71=269	$258,400.00
Greg Chalmers	T-4	64-67-69-70=270	$149,625.00
Steve Stricker	T-4	71-67-64-68=270	$149,625.00
Vijay Singh	T-4	69-67-67-67=270	$149,625.00
Joel Kribel	T-4	70-65-70-65=270	$149,625.00
Stewart Cink	T-8	70-65-67-69=271	$110,200.00
Jeff Sluman	T-8	69-68-66-68=271	$110,200.00
John Rollins	T-8	66-69-69-67=271	$110,200.00

British Open
Course: Royal Troon G.C., Troon, Ayrshire, Scotland
Par: 71 Yardage: 7,175
Last day of event: Sunday, July 18, 2004

Player	Place	Score	Earnings
Todd Hamilton	Win	71-67-67-69=274	$1,348,272.00

Playoff: Won four-hole aggregate playoff (4-4-3-4=15) with Ernie Els (4-4-4-4=16)

Player	Place	Score	Earnings
Ernie Els	2	69-69-68-68=274	$805,218.00
Phil Mickelson	3	73-66-68-68=275	$514,965.00
Lee Westwood	4	72-71-68-67=278	$393,246.00
Thomas Levet	T-5	66-70-71-72=279	$298,679.70
Davis Love III	T-5	72-69-71-67=279	$298,679.70
Retief Goosen	T-7	69-70-68-73=280	$220,030.50
Scott Verplank	T-7	69-70-70-71=280	$220,030.50
Tiger Woods	T-9	70-71-68-72=281	$167,597.70
Mike Weir	T-9	71-68-71-71=281	$167,597.70

B.C. Open
Course: En-Joie G.C., Endicott, N.Y.
Par: 72 Yardage: 6,974
Last day of event: Sunday, July 18, 2004

Player	Place	Score	Earnings
Jonathan Byrd	Win	67-65-68-68=268	$540,000.00
Ted Purdy	2	69-67-65-68=269	$324,000.00
Notah Begay III	T-3	73-62-66-69=270	$144,000.00
Hidemichi Tanaka	T-3	68-68-68-66=270	$144,000.00
Robin Freeman	T-3	70-67-67-66=270	$144,000.00
Todd Fischer	T-3	65-69-71-65=270	$144,000.00
Camilo Villegas	T-7	65-70-67-69=271	$93,500.00
Neal Lancaster	T-7	67-67-69-68=271	$93,500.00
Vaughn Taylor	T-7	71-66-68-66=271	$93,500.00
Robert Gamez	T-10	75-61-65-71=272	$75,000.00
John Senden	T-10	71-66-67-68=272	$75,000.00
Jim Gallagher, Jr.	T-10	70-68-66-68=272	$75,000.00

U.S. Bank Championship in Milwaukee
Course: Brown Deer Park G.C., Milwaukee, Wis.
Par: 70 Yardage: 6,759
Last day of event: Sunday, July 25, 2004

Player	Place	Score	Earnings
Carlos Franco	Win	68-63-69-67=267	$630,000.00
Brett Quigley	T-2	65-71-64-69=269	$308,000.00
Fred Funk	T-2	68-68-67-66=269	$308,000.00
Patrick Sheehan	T-4	65-68-67-70=270	$144,666.66
Olin Browne	T-4	65-70-68-67=270	$144,666.67
Billy Andrade	T-4	72-64-67-67=270	$144,666.67
Kenny Perry	T-7	69-67-65-70=271	$109,083.33
Danny Briggs	T-7	65-70-68-68=271	$109,083.33
Bo Van Pelt	T-7	65-68-71-67=271	$109,083.34
Scott Hoch	10	68-65-70-69=272	$94,500.00

Buick Open
Course: Warwick Hills C.C., Grand Blanc, Mich.
Par: 72 Yardage: 7,127
Last day of event: Sunday, August 1, 2004

Player	Place	Score	Earnings
Vijay Singh	Win	63-70-65-67=265	$810,000.00
John Daly	2	70-64-66-66=266	$486,000.00
Carlos Franco	T-3	67-67-67-66=267	$261,000.00
Tiger Woods	T-3	67-68-66-66=267	$261,000.00
Stewart Cink	5	69-65-70-66=270	$180,000.00
Jim Furyk	T-6	66-67-70-68=271	$156,375.00
Jeff Sluman	T-6	70-67-68-66=271	$156,375.00
Daniel Chopra	T-8	68-68-66-70=272	$135,000.00
Jerry Kelly	T-8	71-66-69-66=272	$135,000.00
Mark O'Meara	T-10	67-70-70-66=273	$117,000.00
Scott Verplank	T-10	70-67-70-66=273	$117,000.00

The International
Course: Castle Pine G.C., Castle Rock, Colo. (Stableford format)
Par: 72 Yardage: 7,619
Last day of event: Sunday, August 8, 2004

Player	Place	Score	Earnings
Rod Pampling	Win	15-7-7-2=31	$900,000.00
Alex Cejka	2	8-9-11-1=29	$540,000.00
Tom Pernice, Jr.	3	5-10-11-1=27	$340,000.00
Duffy Waldorf	4	8-3-7-8=26	$240,000.00
Jay Haas	5	10-3-8-4=25	$200,000.00
Chris DiMarco	T-6	14-17--2--5=24	$167,500.00
Tim Petrovic	T-6	9-5-8-2=24	$167,500.00
Stewart Cink	T-6	6-5-11-2=24	$167,500.00
Bob Tway	T-9	9-9-8--3=23	$135,000.00
Bernhard Langer	T-9	7-7-5-4=23	$135,000.00
Mathias Gronberg	T-9	2-6-9-6=23	$135,000.00

PGA Championship
Course: Whistling Straits Golf Club, Haven, Wis.
Par: 72 Yardage: 7,514
Last day of event: Sunday, August 15, 2004

Player	Place	Score	Earnings
Vijay Singh	Win	67-68-69-76=280	$1,125,000.00

Playoff: Won three-hole aggregate playoff (3-3-4=10) with Justin Leonard (4-3-4=11) and Chris DiMarco (4-3-4=11

Player	Place	Score	Earnings
Justin Leonard	T-2	66-69-70-75=280	$550,000.00
Chris DiMarco	T-2	68-70-71-71=280	$550,000.00
Ernie Els	T-4	66-70-72-73=281	$267,500.00
Chris Riley	T-4	69-70-69-73=281	$267,500.00
Phil Mickelson	T-6	69-72-67-74=282	$196,000.00
K.J. Choi	T-6	68-71-73-70=282	$196,000.00
Paul McGinley	T-6	69-74-70-69=282	$196,000.00
Stephen Ames	T-9	68-71-69-75=283	$152,000.00
Adam Scott	T-9	71-71-69-72=283	$152,000.00
Robert Allenby	T-9	71-70-72-70=283	$152,000.00
Ben Crane	T-9	70-74-69-70=283	$152,000.00

WGC-NEC Invitational

Course: Firestone C.C. (South), Akron, Ohio
Par: 70 Yardage: 7,360
Last day of event: Sunday, August 22, 2004

Player	Place	Score	Earnings
Stewart Cink	Win	63-68-68-70=269	$1,200,000.00
Tiger Woods	T-2	68-66-70-69=273	$552,500.00
Rory Sabbatini	T-2	68-66-71-68=273	$552,500.00
Angel Cabrera	T-4	69-70-67-68=274	$282,500.00
Davis Love III	T-4	68-68-72-66=274	$282,500.00
David Toms	T-6	69-66-69-71=275	$178,333.33
Chris DiMarco	T-6	68-69-67-71=275	$178,333.33
Bob Tway	T-6	67-73-67-68=275	$178,333.34
Charles Howell III	T-9	71-67-68-70=276	$116,000.00
Lee Westwood	T-9	69-69-69-69=276	$116,000.00
Robert Allenby	T-9	71-67-69-69=276	$116,000.00
Stuart Appleby	T-9	69-70-69-68=276	$116,000.00
Alex Cejka	T-9	72-67-71-66=276	$116,000.00

Reno-Tahoe Open

Course: Montreux G. & C.C., Reno, Nev.
Par: 72 Yardage: 7,472
Last day of event: Sunday, August 22, 2004

Player	Place	Score	Earnings
Vaughn Taylor	Win	67-67-69-75=278	$540,000.00

Playoff: Beat Steve Allan, Hunter Mahan and Scott McCarron with birdie on first extra hole

Player	Place	Score	Earnings
Steve Allan	T-2	68-68-68-74=278	$224,000.00
Hunter Mahan	T-2	69-67-68-74=278	$224,000.00
Scott McCarron	T-2	69-67-71-71=278	$224,000.00
Roland Thatcher	T-5	66-68-68-77=279	$109,500.00
Mark Wilson	T-5	67-71-69-72=279	$109,500.00
Carl Pettersson	T-5	69-67-74-69=279	$109,500.00
Woody Austin	8	71-67-70-72=280	$93,000.00
Joe Ogilvie	T-9	72-64-72-75=283	$75,000.00
Daniel Chopra	T-9	67-70-73-73=283	$75,000.00
Ken Duke	T-9	71-67-73-72=283	$75,000.00
Michael Allen	T-9	71-66-75-71=283	$75,000.00
Dennis Paulson	T-9	68-75-69-71=283	$75,000.00

Buick Championship

Course: TPC at River Highlands, Cromwell, Conn.
Par: 70 Yardage: 6,820
Last day of event: Sunday, August 29, 2004

Player	Place	Score	Earnings
Woody Austin	Win	68-70-66-66=270	$756,000.00

Playoff: Beat Tim Herron with birdie on first extra hole

Player	Place	Score	Earnings
Tim Herron	2	70-69-65-66=270	$453,600.00
Fred Funk	T-3	66-66-69-70=271	$218,400.00
Tom Pernice, Jr.	T-3	70-66-68-67=271	$218,400.00
Zach Johnson	T-3	67-65-73-66=271	$218,400.00
Corey Pavin	T-6	62-72-68-70=272	$140,700.00
Matt Gogel	T-6	67-69-69-67=272	$140,700.00
Jason Bohn	T-6	71-67-69-65=272	$140,700.00
Tom Byrum	T-9	69-66-67-71=273	$109,200.00
Kevin Sutherland	T-9	70-70-67-66=273	$109,200.00
Todd Fischer	T-9	71-69-67-66=273	$109,200.00
Jeff Sluman	T-9	72-69-70-62=273	$109,200.00

Deutsche Bank Championship

Course: TPC of Boston, Norton, Mass.
Par: 71 Yardage: 7,415
Last day of event: Monday, September 6, 2004

Player	Place	Score	Earnings
Vijay Singh	Win	68-63-68-69=268	$900,000.00
Tiger Woods	T-2	65-68-69-69=271	$440,000.00
Adam Scott	T-2	69-67-70-65=271	$440,000.00
Daniel Chopra	T-4	68-69-70-67=274	$220,000.00
John Rollins	T-4	67-66-75-66=274	$220,000.00
Shigeki Maruyama	T-6	68-66-71-70=275	$173,750.00
Hank Kuehne	T-6	68-68-71-68=275	$173,750.00
Jay Williamson	8	68-68-70-70=276	$155,000.00
Bill Haas	T-9	69-64-71-73=277	$135,000.00
Brad Faxon	T-9	72-69-68-68=277	$135,000.00
Charles Howell III	T-9	67-68-76-66=277	$135,000.00

Bell Canadian Open

Course: Glen Abbey G.C., Oakville, Ontario, Canada
Par: 71 Yardage: 7,222
Last day of event: Sunday, September 12, 2004

Player	Place	Score	Earnings
Vijay Singh	Win	68-66-72-69=275	$810,000.00

Playoff: Beat Mike Weir with par on third extra hole

Player	Place	Score	Earnings
Mike Weir	2	68-65-70-72=275	$486,000.00
Joe Ogilvie	3	70-69-69-69=277	$306,000.00
Stewart Cink	T-4	72-68-69-69=278	$177,187.50
Hunter Mahan	T-4	72-69-69-68=278	$177,187.50
Tom Lehman	T-4	74-70-70-64=278	$177,187.50
Justin Rose	T-4	70-70-75-63=278	$177,187.50
Robert Damron	8	72-71-70-66=279	$139,500.00
Jesper Parnevik	T-9	69-66-71-74=280	$126,000.00
Mark Hensby	T-9	70-69-70-71=280	$126,000.00

Valero Texas Open

Course: LaCantera G.C., San Antonio, Texas
Par: 70 Yardage: 6,881
Last day of event: Sunday, September 19, 2004

Player	Place	Score	Earnings
Bart Bryant	Win	67-67-60-67=261	$630,000.00
Patrick Sheehan	2	65-68-65-66=264	$378,000.00
Todd Fischer	T-3	68-67-63-67=265	$203,000.00
Dean Wilson	T-3	64-65-70-66=265	$203,000.00
Hunter Mahan	T-5	68-67-62-69=266	$118,650.00
J.J. Henry	T-5	64-67-67-68=266	$118,650.00
Tim Clark	T-5	64-70-64-68=266	$118,650.00
Ted Purdy	T-5	61-69-71-65=266	$118,650.00
Jerry Kelly	T-5	66-67-68-65=266	$118,650.00
Scott Simpson	T-10	65-67-66-69=267	$84,000.00
Heath Slocum	T-10	66-69-64-68=267	$84,000.00
Justin Leonard	T-10	65-68-68-66=267	$84,000.00
J.L. Lewis	T-10	69-67-68-63=267	$84,000.00

84 Lumber Classic

Course: Nemocolin Woodlands Resort (Mystic Rock Course), Farmington, Pa.
Par: 72 Yardage: 7,471
Last day of event: Sunday, September 26, 2004

Player	Place	Score	Earnings
Vijay Singh	Win	64-68-72-69=273	$756,000.00
Stewart Cink	2	71-71-67-65=274	$453,600.00

Player	Place	Score	Earnings
Chris DiMarco	T-3	70-65-71-70=276	$201,600.00
Jonathan Byrd	T-3	68-72-67-69=276	$201,600.00
Zach Johnson	T-3	69-69-70-68=276	$201,600.00
Pat Perez	T-3	67-73-69-67=276	$201,600.00
Duffy Waldorf	T-7	70-69-70-68=277	$135,450.00
K.J. Choi	T-7	71-68-73-65=277	$135,450.00
Frank Lickliter II	T-9	71-72-67-68=278	$117,600.00
Jose Maria Olazabal	T-9	73-70-70-65=278	$117,600.00

WGC-American Express Championship

Course: Mount Juliet C.C., Thomastown, Kilkenny, Ireland
Par: 72 Yardage: 7,256
Last day of event: Sunday, October 3, 2004

Player	Place	Score	Earnings
Ernie Els	Win	69-64-68-69=270	$1,200,000.00
Thomas Bjorn	2	68-69-66-68=271	$675,000.00
David Howell	3	69-69-66-71=275	$450,000.00
Sergio Garcia	T-4	67-72-67-70=276	$308,000.00
Darren Clarke	T-4	71-72-65-68=276	$308,000.00
Todd Hamilton	T-6	66-69-69-73=277	$200,000.00
Padraig Harrington	T-6	69-69-66-73=277	$200,000.00
Retief Goosen	T-6	68-69-68-72=277	$200,000.00
Tiger Woods	9	68-70-70-70=278	$155,000.00
Zach Johnson	10	68-71-69-71=279	$135,000.00

Southern Farm Bureau Classic

Course: Annandale G.C., Madison, Miss.
Par: 72 Yardage: 7,199
Last day of event: Sunday, October 3, 2004

Player	Place	Score	Earnings
Fred Funk	Win	69-67-64-66=266	$540,000.00
Ryan Palmer	2	69-68-66-64=267	$324,000.00
Kevin Na	T-3	71-65-66-66=268	$144,000.00
Loren Roberts	T-3	66-69-68-65=268	$144,000.00
J.J. Henry	T-3	70-67-66-65=268	$144,000.00
Glen Day	T-3	65-70-70-63=268	$144,000.00
Kirk Triplett	7	69-69-65-66=269	$100,500.00
Tim Clark	T-8	68-69-67-66=270	$90,000.00
Jonathan Byrd	T-8	70-69-66-65=270	$90,000.00
Chris Couch	T-10	70-63-68-70=271	$72,000.00
Greg Chalmers	T-10	68-67-67-69=271	$72,000.00
Pat Bates	T-10	69-66-68-68=271	$72,000.00
Carl Pettersson	T-10	67-69-67-68=271	$72,000.00

Michelin Championship at Las Vegas

Course: TPC at Summerlin, TPC At The Canyons, Bear's Best., Las Vegas, Nev.
Home course / TPC at Summerlin, Par: 72 Yardage: 7,243
Last day of event: Sunday, October 10, 2004

Player	Place	Score	Earnings
Andre Stolz	Win	67-67-65-67=266	$720,000.00
Tag Ridings	T-2	67-66-73-61=267	$298,666.67
Tom Lehman	T-2	64-68-66-69=267	$298,666.66
Harrison Frazar	T-2	64-68-68-67=267	$298,666.67
Dicky Pride	T-5	66-67-66-69=268	$152,000.00
Carl Pettersson	T-5	68-68-65-67=268	$152,000.00
Tim Petrovic	T-7	66-66-68-69=269	$120,500.00
Lee Janzen	T-7	68-66-70-65=269	$120,500.00
Danny Ellis	T-7	63-70-73-63=269	$120,500.00
David Frost	T-7	69-71-67-62=269	$120,500.00

Chrysler Classic of Greensboro

Course: Forest Oaks C.C., Greensboro, N.C.
Par: 72 Yardage: 7,311
Last day of event: Sunday, October 17, 2004

Player	Place	Score	Earnings
Brent Geiberger	Win	66-67-71-66=270	$828,000.00
Michael Allen	2	70-67-68-67=272	$496,800.00
Chris Smith	3	70-69-67-67=273	$312,800.00
Tom Lehman	T-4	69-66-69-70=274	$202,400.00
David Toms	T-4	69-65-71-69=274	$202,400.00
Arjun Atwal	6	71-70-68-66=275	$165,600.00
Tom Pernice, Jr.	7	66-68-73-69=276	$154,100.00
Joe Ogilvie	T-8	68-67-70-72=277	$110,975.00
Matt Gogel	T-8	70-69-66-72=277	$110,975.00
Jeff Brehaut	T-8	68-66-73-70=277	$110,975.00
Jerry Kelly	T-8	70-65-72-70=277	$110,975.00
Ben Crane	T-8	68-69-70-70=277	$110,975.00
Richard S. Johnson	T-8	67-71-69-70=277	$110,975.00
Jason Dufner	T-8	65-70-73-69=277	$110,975.00
Ted Purdy	T-8	71-68-74-64=277	$110,975.00

FUNAI Classic at the Walt Disney World Resort

Course: Walt Disney (Magnolia, Palm), Lake Buena Vista, Fla.
Home course / Magnolia, Par: 72 Yardage: 7,190
Last day of event: Sunday, October 24, 2004

Player	Place	Score	Earnings
Ryan Palmer	Win	68-68-68-62=266	$756,000.00
Briny Baird	T-2	65-66-68-70=269	$369,600.00
Vijay Singh	T-2	66-71-65-67=269	$369,600.00
Cameron Beckman	T-4	68-65-68-69=270	$184,800.00
Joey Sindelar	T-4	66-70-67-67=270	$184,800.00
Tom Lehman	T-6	66-66-67-72=271	$135,975.00
Mark Calcavecchia	T-6	71-66-65-69=271	$135,975.00
Tim Clark	T-6	69-69-64-69=271	$135,975.00
Mark Hensby	T-6	64-71-68-68=271	$135,975.00
Geoff Ogilvy	T-10	68-67-67-70=272	$93,100.00
John Huston	T-10	64-71-69-68=272	$93,100.00
Lucas Glover	T-10	68-68-68-68=272	$93,100.00
Neal Lancaster	T-10	69-69-67-67=272	$93,100.00
Vaughn Taylor	T-10	68-66-72-66=272	$93,100.00
Carl Pettersson	T-10	70-70-68-64=272	$93,100.00

Chrysler Championship

Course: Westin Innisbrook Resort (Copperhead Course), Palm Harbor, Fla.
Par: 71 Yardage: 7,340
Last day of event: Sunday, October 31, 2004

Player	Place	Score	Earnings
Vijay Singh	Win	65-69-67-65=266	$900,000.00
Tommy Armour III	T-2	70-64-68-69=271	$440,000.00
Jesper Parnevik	T-2	68-67-68-68=271	$440,000.00
Joe Durant	4	68-71-70-63=272	$240,000.00
Kirk Triplett	5	64-71-68-70=273	$200,000.00
Robert Allenby	T-6	70-67-69-68=274	$173,750.00
David Toms	T-6	70-69-67-68=274	$173,750.00
Carl Pettersson	T-8	68-68-70-69=275	$145,000.00
Spike McRoy	T-8	69-72-66-68=275	$145,000.00
Kenny Perry	T-8	70-68-70-67=275	$145,000.00

The Tour Championship

Course: East Lake G.C., Atlanta, Ga.

Par: 70 Yardage: 7,029

Last day of event: Sunday, November 7, 2004

Player	Place	Score	Earnings
Retief Goosen	Win	70-66-69-64=269	$1,080,000.00
Tiger Woods	2	72-64-65-72=273	$648,000.00
Jerry Kelly	3	67-71-71-65=274	$414,000.00
Stephen Ames	T-4	69-66-70-70=275	$248,000.00
Mike Weir	T-4	69-69-67-70=275	$248,000.00
Mark Hensby	T-4	69-70-69-67=275	$248,000.00
Jay Haas	T-7	67-66-68-75=276	$198,000.00
Scott Verplank	T-7	74-67-68-67=276	$198,000.00
Vijay Singh	9	69-73-70-65=277	$180,000.00
Rory Sabbatini	T-10	71-68-71-68=278	$158,200.00
David Toms	T-10	68-73-70-67=278	$158,200.00
Ernie Els	T-10	72-71-68-67=278	$158,200.00

2005

Tiger Woods silenced those who questioned his decision to revamp his swing under Hank Haney. Woods posted six victories on the PGA Tour, including the Masters and British Open, and regained the top spot in the Official World Golf Ranking. At Augusta, Woods beat Chris DiMarco with a birdie on their first playoff hole. He topped Colin Montgomerie by five strokes at St. Andrews, where Jack Nicklaus bid an emotional farewell to competitive golf. Phil Mickelson was a four-time winner, including the PGA Championship by a shot over Steve Elkington and Thomas Bjorn at Baltusrol, and was runner-up to Woods in a rousing duel at the Ford Championship at Doral. Vijay Singh was a four-time winner as well and posted top 10s in all four majors. The U.S. Open at Pinehurst was surprisingly won by Michael Campbell of New Zealand, who had struggled with injuries and confidence issues since leading the British Open through 59 holes in 1995. Campbell notched a two-shot victory over Woods, who rallied from an 8-shot deficit after 56 holes. At the EDS Byron Nelson Classic, Woods missed the cut for the first time in 143 starts; the 142-tournament streak is a PGA Tour record (by 39 over Byron Nelson). David Frost set a PGA Tour record for fewest putts in 72 holes, needing only 92 en route to a tie for 38th place at the MCI Heritage.

Mercedes Championshipss

Course: Kapalua Resort Plantation Course, Kapalua, Maui, Ha.

Par: 73 Yardage: 7,263

Last day of event: Sunday, January 9, 2005

Player	Place	Score	Earnings
Stuart Appleby	Win	74-64-66-67=271	$1,060,000.00
Jonathan Kaye	2	68-67-66-71=272	$600,000.00
Ernie Els	T-3	69-65-68-71=273	$350,000.00
Tiger Woods	T-3	68-68-69-68=273	$350,000.00
Vijay Singh	T-5	66-65-69-74=274	$211,333.33
Stewart Cink	T-5	68-68-67-71=274	$211,333.33
Adam Scott	T-5	69-72-68-65=274	$211,333.34
Vaughn Taylor	T-8	69-69-68-70=276	$165,000.00
David Toms	T-8	71-67-70-68=276	$165,000.00
Craig Parry	T-10	67-72-68-71=278	$145,000.00
Sergio Garcia	T-10	68-67-73-70=278	$145,000.00

Sony Open in Hawaii

Course: Waialae C.C., Honolulu, Ha.

Par: 70 Yardage: 7,060

Last day of event: Sunday, January 16, 2005

Player	Place	Score	Earnings
Vijay Singh	Win	69-68-67-65=269	$864,000.00
Ernie Els	2	71-67-70-62=270	$518,400.00
Shigeki Maruyama	T-3	67-65-68-71=271	$278,400.00
Charles Howell III	T-3	70-70-64-67=271	$278,400.00
Brett Quigley	T-5	66-67-68-71=272	$182,400.00
Stewart Cink	T-5	66-69-72-65=272	$182,400.00
Andrew Magee	T-7	67-68-71-67=273	$154,800.00
Tommy Armour III	T-7	69-71-67-66=273	$154,800.00
Robert Gamez	T-9	69-66-68-71=274	$124,800.00
Tom Lehman	T-9	67-68-70-69=274	$124,800.00
Bart Bryant	T-9	70-69-66-69=274	$124,800.00
Craig Stadler	T-9	71-69-67-67=274	$124,800.00

Buick Invitational

Course: Torrey Pines (South), Torrey Pines (North), San Diego, Calif.

Home Course -Par: 72 Yardage: 7,568

Last day of event: Sunday, January 23, 2005

Player	Place	Score	Earnings
Tiger Woods	Win	69-63-72-68=272	$864,000.00
Tom Lehman	T-2	62-67-73-73=275	$358,400.00
Luke Donald	T-2	68-67-67-73=275	$358,400.00
Charles Howell III	T-2	72-67-64-72=275	$358,400.00
Bernhard Langer	5	69-69-67-72=277	$192,000.00
Kevin Sutherland	T-6	68-66-72-72=278	$150,240.00
Pat Perez	T-6	66-69-72-71=278	$150,240.00
Ernie Els	T-6	65-71-71-71=278	$150,240.00
Arron Oberholser	T-6	64-72-72-70=278	$150,240.00
Scott McCarron	T-6	72-65-72-69=278	$150,240.00

Bob Hope Chrysler Classic

Course: PGA West/Palmer, Bermuda Dunes C.C., La Quinta C.C., Tamarisk C.C.

Home course / PGA West, Par: 72 Yardage: 6,930

Last day of event: Sunday, January 30, 2005

Player	Place	Score	Earnings
Justin Leonard	Win	66-67-68-64-67=332	$846,000.00
Joe Ogilvie	T-2	64-63-66-69-73=335	$413,600.00
Tim Clark	T-2	70-66-64-66-69=335	$413,600.00
Peter Lonard	T-4	67-64-64-69-72=336	$206,800.00
Loren Roberts	T-4	68-67-67-65-69=336	$206,800.00
John Senden	T-6	69-67-64-68-69=337	$163,325.00
Tim Herron	T-6	68-64-71-68-66=337	$163,325.00
Jim Furyk	T-8	67-70-65-65-71=338	$131,600.00
Ian Poulter	T-8	70-70-64-63-71=338	$131,600.00
Jerry Kelly	T-8	68-67-64-69-70=338	$131,600.00
Andrew Magee	T-8	68-69-65-69-67=338	$131,600.00

FBR Open

Course: TPC of Scottsdale, Scottsdale, Ariz.

Par: 71 Yardage: 7,216

Last day of event: Sunday, February 6, 2005

Player	Place	Score	Earnings
Phil Mickelson	Win	73-60-66-68=267	$936,000.00
Kevin Na	T-2	68-65-70-69=272	$457,600.00
Scott McCarron	T-2	72-70-65-65=272	$457,600.00
Steve Flesch	T-4	70-67-67-69=273	$214,933.33
David Toms	T-4	71-66-68-68=273	$214,933.34
Tim Herron	T-4	73-66-67-67=273	$214,933.33
Kenny Perry	7	70-67-67-70=274	$174,200.00
Charles Warren	8	69-68-69-69=275	$161,200.00
Mark Calcavecchia	T-9	74-66-65-71=276	$145,600.00
Hunter Mahan	T-9	68-69-72-67=276	$145,600.00

AT&T Pebble Beach National Pro-Am

Courses: Pebble Beach G.L, Spyglass Hill G.C., Poppy Hills G.C., Pebble Beach, Calif.

Home Course / Pebble Beach G.L., Par: 72 Yardage: 6,737

Last day of event: Sunday, February 13, 2005

Player	Place	Score	Earnings
Phil Mickelson	Win	62-67-67-73=269	$954,000.00
Mike Weir	2	66-67-73-67=273	$572,400.00
Greg Owen	3	67-69-67-72=275	$360,400.00
Paul Goydos	T-4	67-68-70-71=276	$233,200.00
Tim Clark	T-4	67-71-67-71=276	$233,200.00
Darren Clarke	T-6	70-66-70-71=277	$184,175.00
Arron Oberholser	T-6	71-66-69-71=277	$184,175.00
Graeme McDowell	8	68-69-70-71=278	$164,300.00
Jeff Sluman	T-9	71-66-69-73=279	$148,400.00
Davis Love III	T-9	65-72-71-71=279	$148,400.00

Nissan Open

Course: Riviera C.C., Pacific Palisades, Calif.

Par: 71 Yardage: 7,260

Last day of event: Monday, February 21, 2005

Player	Place	Score	Earnings
Adam Scott	Win	67-66=133	$864,000.00

Playoff: Beat Chad Campbell with par on first extra hole; victory unofficial (only 36 holes)

Player	Place	Score	Earnings
Chad Campbell	2	68-65=133	$518,400.00
Brian Davis	T-3	65-69=134	$278,400.00
Darren Clarke	T-3	66-68=134	$278,400.00
J.L. Lewis	T-5	70-65=135	$182,400.00
Colin Montgomerie	T-5	71-64=135	$182,400.00
Kevin Sutherland	T-7	67-69=136	$134,800.00
Bob Tway	T-7	68-68=136	$134,800.00
Fred Funk	T-7	69-67=136	$134,800.00
Robert Allenby	T-7	69-67=136	$134,800.00
Aaron Baddeley	T-7	69-67=136	$134,800.00
Billy Mayfair	T-7	70-66=136	$134,800.00

WGC-Accenture Match Play Championship

Course: La Costa Resort & Spa, Carlsbad, Calif.

Par: 72 Yardage: 7,277

Last day of event: Sunday, February 27, 2005

Player	Place	Earnings
David Toms	Win	$1,300,000.00

Round One - Beat Richard Green 1 up
Round Two - Beat Mark Hensby 2 up
Round Three - Beat Phil Mickelson 4 & 2
Quarterfinals - Beat Adam Scott 2 & 1
Semifinals - Beat Ian Poulter 3 & 2
Finals - Beat Chris DiMarco 6 & 5

Chris DiMarco	2	$750,000.00

Round One - Beat Tim Herron 1 up
Round Two - Beat John Daly 4 & 3
Round Three - Beat Jay Haas 2 & 1
Quarterfinals - Beat Stewart Cink 2 & 1
Semifinals - Beat Retief Goosen 2 & 1
Finals - David Toms beat him 6 & 5

Retief Goosen	3	$560,000.00

Round One - Beat Stephen Leaney 1 up
Round Two - Beat Fred Couples 1 up
Round Three - Beat Chad Campbell 19 holes
Quarterfinals - Beat Robert Allenby 4 & 3
Semifinals - Chris DiMarco beat him 2 & 1
Consolation - Beat Ian Poulter 20 holes

Ian Poulter	4	$450,000.00

Round One - Beat Jim Furyk 3 & 1
Round Two - Beat Stuart Appleby 6 & 5
Round Three - Beat Rory Sabbatini 1 up
Quarterfinals - Beat Nick O'Hern 3 & 1
Semifinals - David Toms beat him 2 & 2
Consolation - Retief Goosen beat him 20 holes

Stewart Cink	T-5	$240,000.00

Round One - Beat Fred Funk 2 up
Round Two - Beat Tom Lehman 2 & 1
Round Three - Beat Davis Love III 20 holes
Quarterfinals - Chris DiMarco beat him 2 & 1

Robert Allenby	T-5	$240,000.00

Round One - Beat Todd Hamilton 6 & 5
Round Two - Beat Graeme McDowell 1 up
Round Three - Beat Kirk Triplett 2 & 1
Quarterfinals - Retief Goosen beat him 4 &3

Nick O'Hern	T-5	$240,000.00

Round One - Beat Charles Howell III 19 holes
Round Two - Beat Tiger Woods 3 & 1
Round Three - Beat Luke Donald 5 & 4
Quarterfinals - Ian Poulter beat him 3 & 1

Adam Scott	T-5	$240,000.00

Round One - Beat Trevor Immelman 2 up
Round Two - Beat David Howell 2 & 1
Round Three - Beat Sergio Garcia 4 & 3
Quarterfinals - David Toms beat him 2 & 1

Phil Mickelson	T-9	$125,000.00

Round One - Beat Loren Roberts 3 & 1
Round Two - Beat Angel Cabrera 4 & 3
Round Three - David Toms beat him 4 & 2

Sergio Garcia	T-9	$125,000.00

Round One - Beat Alex Cejka 4 & 2
Round Two - Beat Jerry Kelly 19 holes
Round Three - Adam Scott beat him 4 & 3

Jay Haas	T-9	$125,000.00

Round One - Beat Jonathan Kaye 4 & 2
Round Two - Beat Vijay Singh 3 & 2
Round Three - Chris DiMarco beat him 2 & 1

Davis Love III	T-9	$125,000.00

Round One - Beat Chris Riley 1 up
Round Two - Beat Lee Westwood 7 & 6
Round Three - Stewart Cink beat him 20 holes

Chad Campbell	T-9	$125,000.00

Round One - Beat Fredrik Jacobson 2 up
Round Two - Beat Miguel Angel Jimenez 24 holes
Round Three - Retief Goosen beat him 19 holes

Kirk Triplett	T-9	$125,000.00

Round One - Beat Mike Weir 1 up
Round Two - Beat Craig Parry 5 & 4
Round Three - Robert Allenby beat him 2 & 1

Luke Donald	T-9	$125,000.00

Round One - Beat Zach Johnson 4 & 3
Round Two - Beat Kenny Perry 1 up
Round Three - Nick O'Hern beat him 5 & 4

Rory Sabbatini	T-9	$125,000.00

Round One - Beat Thomas Bjorn 6 & 5
Round Two - Beat Padraig Harrington 3 & 1
Round Three - Ian Poulter beat him 1 up

Chrysler Classic of Tucson

Course: Tucson National Resort, Tucson, Ariz.
Par: 72 Yardage: 7,109
Last day of event: Sunday, February 27, 2005

Player	Place	Score	Earnings
Geoff Ogilvy	Win	64-65-71-69=269	$540,000.00

Playoff: Beat Kevin Na with birdie on second extra hole (Mark Calcavecchia eliminated on first hole tih double bogey)

Player	Place	Score	Earnings
Kevin Na	T-2	67-66-65-71=269	$264,000.00
Mark Calcavecchia	T-2	64-65-71-69=269	$264,000.00
Steve Stricker	4	64-68-70-68=270	$144,000.00
Doug Barron	5	66-66-67-72=271	$120,000.00
Brent Geiberger	T-6	67-66-68-71=272	$100,500.00
Billy Mayfair	T-6	63-67-72-70=272	$100,500.00
Aaron Baddeley	T-6	73-64-67-68=272	$100,500.00
Lucas Glover	T-9	64-67-69-73=273	$67,125.00
Joe Ogilvie	T-9	66-66-69-72=273	$67,125.00
Darron Stiles	T-9	64-70-67-72=273	$67,125.00
Danny Briggs	T-9	69-64-69-71=273	$67,125.00
Todd Fischer	T-9	68-67-67-71=273	$67,125.00
Kevin Stadler	T-9	67-68-69-69=273	$67,125.00
Jose Maria Olazabal	T-9	68-69-68-68=273	$67,125.00
Kevin Sutherland	T-9	69-63-74-67=273	$67,125.00

Bay Hill Invitational

Course: Bay Hill Club, Orlando, Fla.
Par: 72 Yardage: 7,267
Last day of event: Sunday, March 20, 2005

Player	Place	Score	Earnings
Kenny Perry	Win	70-68-68-70=276	$900,000.00
Vijay Singh	T-2	72-68-69-69=278	$440,000.00
Graeme McDowell	T-2	69-73-70-66=278	$440,000.00
Retief Goosen	4	78-67-68-70=283	$240,000.00
Aaron Baddeley	T-5	70-74-68-72=284	$182,500.00
Corey Pavin	T-5	72-70-71-71=284	$182,500.00
Patrick Sheehan	T-5	71-71-75-67=284	$182,500.00
K.J. Choi	T-8	70-70-70-75=285	$109,545.45
Briny Baird	T-8	69-73-70-73=285	$109,545.45
Sergio Garcia	T-8	70-70-73-72=285	$109,545.45
Fred Couples	T-8	71-72-70-72=285	$109,545.45
Charles Howell III	T-8	71-68-75-71=285	$109,545.46
Joe Ogilvie	T-8	68-74-72-71=285	$109,545.45
Stewart Cink	T-8	74-70-70-71=285	$109,545.46
Zach Johnson	T-8	73-69-73-70=285	$109,545.46
Bart Bryant	T-8	72-73-71-69=285	$109,545.46
Chad Campbell	T-8	76-69-72-68=285	$109,545.46
Darren Clarke	T-8	76-71-70-68=285	$109,545.45

Ford Championship at Doral

Course: Doral C.C. (Blue), Miami, Fla.
Par: 72 Yardage: 7,266
Last day of event: Sunday, March 6, 2005

Player	Place	Score	Earnings
Tiger Woods	Win	65-70-63-66=264	$990,000.00
Phil Mickelson	2	64-66-66-69=265	$594,000.00
Zach Johnson	T-3	68-70-64-67=269	$319,000.00
Vijay Singh	T-3	68-67-68-66=269	$319,000.00
David Toms	5	69-66-69-67=271	$220,000.00
Craig Parry	T-6	69-66-67-70=272	$191,125.00
Jose Maria Olazabal	T-6	64-69-70-69=272	$191,125.00
Jim Furyk	T-8	70-66-67-70=273	$165,000.00
Retief Goosen	T-8	67-69-73-64=273	$165,000.00
Dudley Hart	T-10	70-67-68-69=274	$143,000.00
Angel Cabrera	T-10	68-69-70-67=274	$143,000.00

The Players Championship

Course: TPC at Sawgrass, Ponte Vedra Beach, Fla.
Par: 72 Yardage: 7,093
Last day of event: Monday, March 28, 2005

Player	Place	Score	Earnings
Fred Funk	Win	65-72-71-71=279	$1,440,000.00
Luke Donald	T-2	66-68-70-76=280	$597,333.33
Scott Verplank	T-2	71-67-72-70=280	$597,333.33
Tom Lehman	T-2	71-69-72-68=280	$597,333.34
Joe Durant	5	69-65-71-76=281	$320,000.00
Tim Herron	T-6	68-66-72-76=282	$278,000.00
Steve Elkington	T-6	72-66-71-73=282	$278,000.00
Zach Johnson	T-8	65-70-72-76=283	$224,000.00
Adam Scott	T-8	69-68-73-73=283	$224,000.00
Davis Love III	T-8	72-66-74-71=283	$224,000.00
J.L. Lewis	T-8	66-77-70-70=283	$224,000.00

Honda Classic

Course: C.C. at Mirasol (Sunrise Course), Palm Beach Gardens, Fla.
Par: 72 Yardage: 7,384
Last day of event: Sunday, March 13, 2005

Player	Place	Score	Earnings
Padraig Harrington	Win	73-69-69-63=274	$990,000.00

Playoff: Beat Vijay Singh with par on second extra hole (Joe Ogilvie eliminated on first hole with bogey)

Player	Place	Score	Earnings
Joe Ogilvie	T-2	73-66-67-68=274	$484,000.00
Vijay Singh	T-2	71-69-70-64=274	$484,000.00
Pat Perez	4	69-69-67-70=275	$264,000.00
David Toms	5	71-71-67-67=276	$220,000.00
Brett Wetterich	T-6	66-66-72-73=277	$184,250.00
Geoff Ogilvy	T-6	73-67-64-73=277	$184,250.00
Brad Faxon	T-6	69-71-72-65=277	$184,250.00
Jim Furyk	T-9	71-69-70-68=278	$154,000.00
Lucas Glover	T-9	70-71-74-63=278	$154,000.00

BellSouth Classic

Course: TPC at Sugarloaf, Duluth, Ga.
Par: 72 Yardage: 7,293
Last day of event: Monday, April 4, 2005

Player	Place	Score	Earnings
Phil Mickelson	Win	74-66-68=208	$900,000.00

Playoff: Beat Rich Beem with birdie on fourth extra hole (Jose Maria Olazabal eliminated on third hole; Brandt Jobe and Arjun Atwal eliminated on first hole)

Player	Place	Score	Earnings
Jose Maria Olazabal	T-2	70-69-69=208	$330,000.00
Rich Beem	T-2	70-70-68=208	$330,000.00
Brandt Jobe	T-2	72-69-67=208	$330,000.00
Arjun Atwal	T-2	77-67-64=208	$330,000.00
Scott Dunlap	T-6	72-68-69=209	$161,875.00
Arron Oberholser	T-6	72-68-69=209	$161,875.00
Tag Ridings	T-6	72-68-69=209	$161,875.00
Frank Lickliter II	T-6	71-70-68=209	$161,875.00
Lucas Glover	T-10	74-67-69=210	$115,000.00
Jay Williamson	T-10	72-71-67=210	$115,000.00
Dennis Paulson	T-10	75-68-67=210	$115,000.00
Hunter Haas	T-10	75-68-67=210	$115,000.00
Charles Warren	T-10	75-69-66=210	$115,000.00

Masters

Course: Augusta National G.C., Augusta, Ga.
Par: 72 Yardage: 7,290
Last day of event: Sunday, April 10, 2005

Player	Place	Score	Earnings
Tiger Woods	Win	74-66-65-71=276	$1,260,000.00

Playoff: Beat Chris DiMarco with birdie on first extra hole

Player	Place	Score	Earnings
Chris DiMarco	2	67-67-74-68=276	$756,000.00
Luke Donald	T-3	68-77-69-69=283	$406,000.00
Retief Goosen	T-3	71-75-70-67=283	$406,000.00
Trevor Immelman	T-5	73-73-65-73=284	$237,300.00
Vijay Singh	T-5	68-73-71-72=284	$237,300.00
Mark Hensby	T-5	69-73-70-72=284	$237,300.00
Mike Weir	T-5	74-71-68-71=284	$237,300.00
Rod Pampling	T-5	73-71-70-70=284	$237,300.00
Phil Mickelson	10	70-72-69-74=285	$189,000.00

MCI Heritage

Course: Harbour Town G.L., Hilton Head, S.C.
Par: 71 Yardage: 6,973
Last day of event: Sunday, April 17, 2005

Player	Place	Score	Earnings
Peter Lonard	Win	62-74-66-75=277	$936,000.00
Darren Clarke	T-2	65-65-73-76=279	$343,200.00
Davis Love III	T-2	69-70-69-71=279	$343,200.00
Jim Furyk	T-2	71-68-71-69=279	$343,200.00
Billy Andrade	T-2	72-69-70-68=279	$343,200.00
Rod Pampling	T-6	70-69-68-73=280	$174,200.00
Stephen Ames	T-6	71-69-69-71=280	$174,200.00
Thomas Levet	T-6	64-74-73-69=280	$174,200.00
Nick O'Hern	9	68-71-73-69=281	$150,800.00
Matt Kuchar	T-10	72-68-71-71=282	$130,000.00
Michael Allen	T-10	71-70-71-70=282	$130,000.00
Scott Verplank	T-10	73-70-70-69=282	$130,000.00

Shell Houston Open

Course: Redstone G.C. (Fall Creek), Humble, Texas
Par: 72 Yardage: 7,508
Last day of event: Sunday, April 24, 2005

Player	Place	Score	Earnings
Vijay Singh	Win	64-71-70-70=275	$900,000.00

Playoff: Beat John Daly with par on first extra hole

Player	Place	Score	Earnings
John Daly	2	68-67-73-67=275	$540,000.00
Jose Maria Olazabal	3	70-67-70-70=277	$340,000.00
Greg Owen	T-4	67-69-70-72=278	$220,000.00
Darren Clarke	T-4	71-69-71-67=278	$220,000.00
Joe Ogilvie	6	68-67-73-71=279	$180,000.00
Gavin Coles	T-7	65-69-71-75=280	$140,416.66
Jeff Maggert	T-7	67-68-74-71=280	$140,416.67
Kent Jones	T-7	70-71-68-71=280	$140,416.66
Bo Van Pelt	T-7	69-68-73-70=280	$140,416.67
Brian Davis	T-7	71-69-70-70=280	$140,416.67
Lucas Glover	T-7	70-71-72-67=280	$140,416.67

Zurich Classic of New Orleans

Course: TPC of Louisiana, Avondale, La.
Par: 72 Yardage: 7,520
Last day of event: Sunday, May 1, 2005

Player	Place	Score	Earnings
Tim Petrovic	Win	72-69-66-68=275	$990,000.00

Playoff: Beat James Driscoll with par on first extra hole

Player	Place	Score	Earnings
James Driscoll	2	68-71-66-70=275	$594,000.00
Chris DiMarco	T-3	65-71-68-72=276	$319,000.00
Lucas Glover	T-3	69-68-70-69=276	$319,000.00
Arjun Atwal	T-5	65-68-73-73=279	$193,187.50
J.J. Henry	T-5	67-67-74-71=279	$193,187.50
Bo Van Pelt	T-5	73-70-66-70=279	$193,187.50
Woody Austin	T-5	71-70-71-67=279	$193,187.50
Padraig Harrington	T-9	68-71-70-71=280	$137,500.00
Chris M. Anderson	T-9	70-70-69-71=280	$137,500.00
Daniel Chopra	T-9	71-70-68-71=280	$137,500.00
Richard S. Johnson	T-9	70-68-72-70=280	$137,500.00
D.J. Trahan	T-9	72-72-67-69=280	$137,500.00

Wachovia Championship

Course: Quail Hollow Club, Charlotte, N.C.
Par: 72 Yardage: 7,442
Last day of event: Sunday, May 8, 2005

Player	Place	Score	Earnings
Vijay Singh	Win	70-69-71-66=276	$1,080,000.00

Playoff: Beat Jim Furyk with par on fourth extra hole (Sergio Garcia eliminated on first hole with bogey)

Player	Place	Score	Earnings
Sergio Garcia	T-2	66-71-67-72=276	$528,000.00
Jim Furyk	T-2	69-72-69-66=276	$528,000.00
Chris DiMarco	4	74-67-73-66=280	$288,000.00
Vaughn Taylor	T-5	74-70-71-67=282	$228,000.00
Carlos Franco	T-5	72-74-70-66=282	$228,000.00
Greg Owen	T-7	74-67-71-71=283	$193,500.00
Phil Mickelson	T-7	71-73-73-66=283	$193,500.00
D.J. Trahan	9	72-67-71-74=284	$174,000.00
Billy Mayfair	10	76-72-70-67=285	$162,000.00

EDS Byron Nelson Championship

Course: TPC at Las Colinas, Cottonwood Valley Course, Irving, Texas
Home course / TPC at Las Colinas, Par: 70 Yardage: 7,022
Last day of event: Sunday, May 15, 2005

Player	Place	Score	Earnings
Ted Purdy	Win	65-67-68-65=265	$1,116,000.00
Sean O'Hair	2	66-65-67-68=266	$669,600.00
Doug Barron	T-3	69-66-65-69=269	$322,400.00
Bob Tway	T-3	68-68-66-67=269	$322,400.00
Vijay Singh	T-3	68-67-69-65=269	$322,400.00
Scott Verplank	T-6	68-67-65-70=270	$200,725.00
Shigeki Maruyama	T-6	67-67-68-68=270	$200,725.00
Nick Price	T-6	66-69-68-67=270	$200,725.00
Omar Uresti	T-6	65-70-69-66=270	$200,725.00
Jaxon Brigman	T-10	72-66-64-69=271	$148,800.00
J.J. Henry	T-10	67-69-67-68=271	$148,800.00
Ernie Els	T-10	64-72-69-66=271	$148,800.00
Mark Brooks	T-10	71-69-65-66=271	$148,800.00

Bank of America Colonial

Course: Colonial C.C., Fort Worth, Texas
Par: 70 Yardage: 7,054
Last day of event: Sunday, May 22, 2005

Player	Place	Score	Earnings
Kenny Perry	Win	65-63-64-69=261	$1,008,000.00
Billy Mayfair	2	67-66-66-69=268	$604,800.00
Peter Lonard	T-3	69-66-65-69=269	$291,200.00
Joe Durant	T-3	71-63-69-66=269	$291,200.00
David Toms	T-3	69-66-68-66=269	$291,200.00

Rod Pampling	T-6	66-67-68-69=270	$163,600.00
Brandt Jobe	T-6	65-69-67-69=270	$163,600.00
Aaron Baddeley	T-6	69-66-67-68=270	$163,600.00
Scott Hend	T-6	68-67-68-67=270	$163,600.00
Bernhard Langer	T-6	68-69-66-67=270	$163,600.00
Rory Sabbatini	T-6	67-69-68-66=270	$163,600.00
Tim Petrovic	T-6	71-69-66-64=270	$163,600.00

FedEx St. Jude Classic
Course: TPC at Southwind, Germantown, Tenn.
Par: 70 Yardage: 7,244
Last day of event: Sunday, May 29, 2005

Player	Place	Score	Earnings
Justin Leonard	Win	62-65-66-73=266	$882,000.00
David Toms	2	68-71-65-63=267	$529,200.00
Fred Funk	3	69-68-66-68=271	$333,200.00
Heath Slocum	T-4	68-66-67-71=272	$215,600.00
Davis Love III	T-4	65-70-68-69=272	$215,600.00
Fredrik Jacobson	T-6	68-64-72-69=273	$170,275.00
Richard S. Johnson	T-6	69-66-69-69=273	$170,275.00
Bob Estes	T-8	67-70-67-70=274	$142,100.00
Roland Thatcher	T-8	67-67-71-69=274	$142,100.00
Neal Lancaster	T-8	71-68-68-67=274	$142,100.00

Memorial Tournament
Course: Muirfield Village G.C., Dubin, Ohio
Par: 72 Yardage: 7,300
Last day of event: Sunday, June 5, 2005

Player	Place	Score	Earnings
Bart Bryant	Win	69-69-66-68=272	$990,000.00
Fred Couples	2	71-67-66-69=273	$594,000.00
Jeff Sluman	T-3	65-71-68-72=276	$286,000.00
Tiger Woods	T-3	69-68-71-68=276	$286,000.00
Bo Van Pelt	T-3	67-72-69-68=276	$286,000.00
Jonathan Kaye	T-6	67-70-68-72=277	$191,125.00
Nick O'Hern	T-6	67-70-70-70=277	$191,125.00
David Toms	T-8	70-70-64-74=278	$148,500.00
Richard Green	T-8	67-72-69-70=278	$148,500.00
Lucas Glover	T-8	67-70-73-68=278	$148,500.00
K.J. Choi	T-8	69-72-69-68=278	$148,500.00
Jim Furyk	T-8	73-73-64-68=278	$148,500.00

Booz Allen Classic
Course: Congressional C.C. (Blue Course), Bethesda, Md.
Par: 71 Yardage: 7,254
Last day of event: Sunday, June 12, 2005

Player	Place	Score	Earnings
Sergio Garcia	Win	71-68-66-65=270	$900,000.00
Adam Scott	T-2	68-67-69-68=272	$373,333.33
Ben Crane	T-2	67-70-68-67=272	$373,333.33
Davis Love III	T-2	69-68-69-66=272	$373,333.34
Ryuji Imada	5	70-71-66-67=274	$200,000.00
Rory Sabbatini	6	69-68-68-70=275	$180,000.00
Ernie Els	T-7	69-67-68-72=276	$140,416.66
Stuart Appleby	T-7	70-69-65-72=276	$140,416.66
Matt Gogel	T-7	63-72-70-71=276	$140,416.67
Joe Durant	T-7	70-67-70-69=276	$140,416.67
Rod Pampling	T-7	70-71-66-69=276	$140,416.67
Joey Snyder III	T-7	69-72-67-68=276	$140,416.67

U.S. Open
Course: Pinehurst C.C. (No 2), Pinehurst, N.C.
Par: 70 Yardage: 7,214
Last day of event: Sunday, June 19, 2005

Player	Place	Score	Earnings
Michael Campbell	Win	71-69-71-69=280	$1,170,000.00
Tiger Woods	2	70-71-72-69=282	$700,000.00
Mark Hensby	T-3	71-68-72-74=285	$320,039.00
Sergio Garcia	T-3	71-69-75-70=285	$320,039.00
Tim Clark	T-3	76-69-70-70=285	$320,039.00
Vijay Singh	T-6	70-70-74-72=286	$187,813.00
Rocco Mediate	T-6	67-74-74-71=286	$187,813.00
Davis Love III	T-6	77-70-70-69=286	$187,813.00
Arron Oberholser	T-9	76-67-71-73=287	$150,834.00
Nick Price	T-9	72-71-72-72=287	$150,834.00

Barclays Classic
Course: Westchester C.C., Harrison, N.Y.
Par: 71 Yardage: 6,839
Last day of event: Sunday, June 26, 2005

Player	Place	Score	Earnings
Padraig Harrington	Win	71-65-68-70=274	$1,035,000.00
Jim Furyk	2	65-69-70-71=275	$621,000.00
Brian Gay	T-3	69-66-71-73=279	$299,000.00
Brad Faxon	T-3	72-68-66-73=279	$299,000.00
Kenny Perry	T-3	68-68-72-71=279	$299,000.00
Dean Wilson	6	72-71-66-71=280	$207,000.00
John Senden	T-7	69-67-72-73=281	$173,218.75
Vijay Singh	T-7	68-71-69-73=281	$173,218.75
Justin Leonard	T-7	72-71-67-71=281	$173,218.75
Billy Mayfair	T-7	72-68-75-66=281	$173,218.75

Cialis Western Open
Course: Cog Hill G. & C.C. (Dubsdread), Lemont, Ill.
Par: 71 Yardage: 7,326
Last day of event: Sunday, July 3, 2005

Player	Place	Score	Earnings
Jim Furyk	Win	64-70-67-69=270	$900,000.00
Tiger Woods	2	73-66-67-66=272	$540,000.00
Ben Curtis	3	64-71-66-74=275	$340,000.00
Billy Mayfair	4	72-69-67-68=276	$240,000.00
Brett Quigley	T-5	69-69-69-70=277	$190,000.00
Pat Perez	T-5	74-66-67-70=277	$190,000.00
Shaun Micheel	T-7	71-67-68-72=278	$155,833.33
Heath Slocum	T-7	72-70-67-69=278	$155,833.33
Charles Warren	T-7	71-69-70-68=278	$155,833.34
Tim Herron	T-10	68-66-70-75=279	$125,000.00
Bob Tway	T-10	74-68-68-69=279	$125,000.00
Fredrik Jacobson	T-10	73-68-70-68=279	$125,000.00

John Deere Classic
Course: TPC at Deere Run, Silvis, Ill.
Par: 71 Yardage: 7,183
Last day of event: Sunday, July 10, 2005

Player	Place	Score	Earnings
Sean O'Hair	Win	66-69-68-65=268	$720,000.00
Hank Kuehne	T-2	68-66-67-68=269	$352,000.00
Robert Damron	T-2	65-68-69-67=269	$352,000.00
J.L. Lewis	T-4	64-65-69-72=270	$165,333.33
Wes Short, Jr.	T-4	66-67-71-66=270	$165,333.33

Player	Place	Score	Earnings
Mark Hensby	T-4	70-66-70-64=270	$165,333.34
Richard S. Johnson	T-7	65-68-68-70=271	$124,666.66
Shigeki Maruyama	T-7	68-63-72-68=271	$124,666.67
Hunter Mahan	T-7	63-68-74-66=271	$124,666.67
Jeff Brehaut	T-10	66-70-66-70=272	$100,000.00
Kevin Stadler	T-10	72-63-69-68=272	$100,000.00
D.J. Trahan	T-10	68-69-67-68=272	$100,000.00

British Open

Course: Old Course at St. Andrews, St. Andrews, Fife, Scotland
Par: 72 Yardage: 7,279
Last day of event: Sunday, July 17, 2005

Player	Place	Score	Earnings
Tiger Woods	Win	66-67-71-70=274	$1,261,584.00
Colin Montgomerie	2	71-66-70-72=279	$753,446.00
Jose Maria Olazabal	T-3	68-70-68-74=280	$424,908.50
Fred Couples	T-3	68-71-73-68=280	$424,908.50
Retief Goosen	T-5	68-73-66-74=281	$214,060.44
Sergio Garcia	T-5	70-69-69-73=281	$214,060.44
Vijay Singh	T-5	69-69-71-72=281	$214,060.44
Michael Campbell	T-5	69-72-68-72=281	$214,060.44
Bernhard Langer	T-5	71-69-70-71=281	$214,060.44
Geoff Ogilvy	T-5	71-74-67-69=281	$214,060.44

B.C. Open

Course: En-Joie G.C., Endicott, N.Y.
Par: 72 Yardage: 6,974
Last day of event: Sunday, July 17, 2005

Player	Place	Score	Earnings
Jason Bohn	Win	64-68-66-66=264	$540,000.00
Brendan Jones	T-2	67-64-66-68=265	$198,000.00
Ryan Palmer	T-2	67-64-67-67=265	$198,000.00
J.P. Hayes	T-2	67-68-64-66=265	$198,000.00
John Rollins	T-2	67-68-64-66=265	$198,000.00
Mathias Gronberg	T-6	65-67-68-66=266	$100,500.00
Ben Crane	T-6	64-69-69-64=266	$100,500.00
Michael Allen	T-6	72-67-63-64=266	$100,500.00
Arjun Atwal	T-9	65-68-65-70=268	$78,000.00
Jay Delsing	T-9	70-64-68-66=268	$78,000.00
Joey Sindelar	T-9	69-67-66-66=268	$78,000.00
Harrison Frazar	T-9	66-73-67-62=268	$78,000.00

U.S. Bank Championship in Milwaukee

Course: Brown Deer Park G.C., Milwaukee, Wis.
Par: 70 Yardage: 6,759
Last day of event: Sunday, July 24, 2005

Player	Place	Score	Earnings
Ben Crane	Win	62-65-64-69=260	$684,000.00
Scott Verplank	2	64-65-64-71=264	$410,400.00
Chad Campbell	3	66-68-66-65=265	$258,400.00
Jeff Sluman	4	64-64-70-68=266	$182,400.00
Chris Smith	T-5	64-67-65-71=267	$144,400.00
Steve Elkington	T-5	65-70-64-68=267	$144,400.00
Mark Calcavecchia	T-7	69-65-65-69=268	$122,550.00
Lee Janzen	T-7	69-66-68-65=268	$122,550.00
Kenny Perry	T-9	63-69-64-73=269	$95,000.00
John Huston	T-9	68-67-65-69=269	$95,000.00
Brad Faxon	T-9	67-64-70-68=269	$95,000.00
Dean Wilson	T-9	66-69-66-68=269	$95,000.00
Glen Day	T-9	67-70-66-66=269	$95,000.00

Buick Open

Course: Warwick Hills C.C., Grand Blanc, Mich.
Par: 72 Yardage: 7,127
Last day of event: Sunday, July 31, 2005

Player	Place	Score	Earnings
Vijay Singh	Win	65-66-63-70=264	$828,000.00
Zach Johnson	T-2	68-66-65-69=268	$404,800.00
Tiger Woods	T-2	71-61-70-66=268	$404,800.00
Robert Allenby	4	70-65-70-65=270	$220,800.00
Dudley Hart	5	68-66-71-66=271	$184,000.00
Jeff Brehaut	T-6	68-67-69-68=272	$159,850.00
Jim Furyk	T-6	66-71-67-68=272	$159,850.00
Sean O'Hair	T-8	70-66-66-71=273	$128,800.00
Craig Barlow	T-8	66-67-71-69=273	$128,800.00
Richard S. Johnson	T-8	69-69-67-68=273	$128,800.00
Heath Slocum	T-8	70-68-68-67=273	$128,800.00

The International

Course: Castle Pine G.C., Castle Rock, Colo.(Stableford format)
Par: 72 Yardage: 7,619
Last day of event: Sunday, August 7, 2005

Player	Place	Score	Earnings
Retief Goosen	Win	7-10-8-7=32	$900,000.00
Brandt Jobe	2	13-9-12--3=31	$540,000.00
Jeff Brehaut	3	7-6-6-10=29	$340,000.00
Hank Kuehne	4	3-8-6-10=27	$240,000.00
Charles Howell III	5	12-10--4-8=26	$200,000.00
Tim Petrovic	T-6	11-4-8-1=24	$161,875.00
Joey Snyder III	T-6	-1-13-8-4=24	$161,875.00
Rod Pampling	T-6	5-7-3-9=24	$161,875.00
Tim Clark	T-6	4-6-6-8=24	$161,875.00
Phil Mickelson	T-10	3-14--3-9=23	$130,000.00
Scott McCarron	T-10	5-5-13-0=23	$130,000.00

PGA Championship

Course: Baltusrol Golf Club, Springfield, N.J.
Par: 70 Yardage: 7,392
Last day of event: Monday, August 15, 2005

Player	Place	Score	Earnings
Phil Mickelson	Win	67-65-72-72=276	$1,170,000.00
Thomas Bjorn	T-2	71-71-63-72=277	$572,000.00
Steve Elkington	T-2	68-70-68-71=277	$572,000.00
Davis Love III	T-4	68-68-68-74=278	$286,000.00
Tiger Woods	T-4	75-69-66-68=278	$286,000.00
Pat Perez	T-6	68-71-67-73=279	$201,500.00
Retief Goosen	T-6	68-70-69-72=279	$201,500.00
Geoff Ogilvy	T-6	69-69-72-69=279	$201,500.00
Michael Campbell	T-6	73-68-69-69=279	$201,500.00
Vijay Singh	T-10	70-67-69-74=280	$131,800.00
Dudley Hart	T-10	70-73-66-71=280	$131,800.00
Steve Flesch	T-10	70-71-69-70=280	$131,800.00
David Toms	T-10	71-72-69-68=280	$131,800.00
Ted Purdy	T-10	69-75-70-66=280	$131,800.00

WGC-NEC Invitational

Course: Firestone C.C. (South), Akron, Ohio
Par: 70 Yardage: 7,360
Last day of event: Sunday, August 21, 2005

Player	Place	Score	Earnings
Tiger Woods	Win	66-70-67-71=274	$1,300,000.00

Chris DiMarco	2	67-70-70-68=275	$750,000.00
Paul McGinley	T-3	71-66-67-72=276	$353,666.66
Ryan Palmer	T-3	72-68-67-69=276	$353,666.66
Vijay Singh	T-3	66-71-72-67=276	$353,666.67
Kenny Perry	T-6	70-69-64-74=277	$200,000.00
David Howell	T-6	70-68-70-69=277	$200,000.00
Luke Donald	T-6	69-67-74-67=277	$200,000.00
Jose Maria Olazabal	T-9	72-68-66-72=278	$135,000.00
David Toms	T-9	71-67-69-71=278	$135,000.00
Zach Johnson	T-9	70-70-69-69=278	$135,000.00
Colin Montgomerie	T-9	70-72-68-68=278	$135,000.00

Reno-Tahoe Open

Course: Montreux G. & C.C., Reno, Nev.
Par: 72 Yardage: 7,472
Last day of event: Sunday, August 21, 2005

Player	Place	Score	Earnings
Vaughn Taylor	Win	64-67-64-72=267	$540,000.00
Jonathan Kaye	2	69-66-68-67=270	$324,000.00
Todd Fischer	3	65-67-69-70=271	$204,000.00
Aaron Baddeley	T-4	67-70-66-70=273	$124,000.00
J.P. Hayes	T-4	71-66-67-69=273	$124,000.00
J.J. Henry	T-4	70-67-70-66=273	$124,000.00
Tag Ridings	7	69-69-69-67=274	$100,500.00
Fredrik Jacobson	8	65-70-68-72=275	$93,000.00
Jesper Parnevik	T-9	67-68-67-74=276	$78,000.00
Dean Wilson	T-9	71-69-66-70=276	$78,000.00
Steve Allan	T-9	70-67-70-69=276	$78,000.00
Spike McRoy	T-9	69-69-70-68=276	$78,000.00

Buick Championship

Course: TPC at River Highlands, Cromwell, Conn.
Par: 70 Yardage: 6,820
Last day of event: Sunday, August 28, 2005

Player	Place	Score	Earnings
Brad Faxon	Win	69-71-65-61=266	$774,000.00

Playoff: Beat Tjaart van der Walt with birdie on first extra hole

Tjaart van der Walt	2	68-66-68-64=266	$464,400.00
Justin Rose	3	65-63-70-69=267	$292,400.00
Ben Curtis	T-4	64-68-67-69=268	$177,733.33
Jerry Kelly	T-4	68-67-67-66=268	$177,733.33
Michael Putnam	T-4	65-69-71-63=268	$177,733.34
Kenny Perry	7	70-69-67-63=269	$144,050.00
Corey Pavin	8	66-69-67-68=270	$133,300.00
Woody Austin	T-9	69-68-65-69=271	$116,100.00
Darron Stiles	T-9	71-69-63-68=271	$116,100.00
Nick Watney	T-9	69-66-70-66=271	$116,100.00

Deutsche Bank Championship

Course: TPC of Boston, Norton, Mass.
Par: 71 Yardage: 7,415
Last day of event: Monday, September 5, 2005

Player	Place	Score	Earnings
Olin Browne	Win	68-65-70-67=270	$990,000.00
Jason Bohn	2	68-68-67-68=271	$594,000.00
Vaughn Taylor	3	72-67-67-68=274	$374,000.00
Carl Pettersson	T-4	68-67-68-72=275	$216,562.50
Joey Sindelar	T-4	67-68-69-71=275	$216,562.50
Jeff Brehaut	T-4	67-66-72-70=275	$216,562.50
Charles Howell III	T-4	72-67-69-67=275	$216,562.50
Fred Couples	T-8	70-67-70-69=276	$165,000.00

Brandt Jobe	T-8	71-67-69-69=276	$165,000.00
Kent Jones	T-10	70-71-63-73=277	$126,500.00
Brett Wetterich	T-10	68-68-69-72=277	$126,500.00
Bo Van Pelt	T-10	71-69-65-72=277	$126,500.00
Marco Dawson	T-10	69-66-71-71=277	$126,500.00
Mark Wilson	T-10	67-70-71-69=277	$126,500.00

Bell Canadian Open

Course: Shaughnessy Golf & Country Club, Vancouver. B.C., Canada
Par: 70 Yardage: 7,010
Last day of event: Sunday, September 11, 2005

Player	Place	Score	Earnings
Mark Calcavecchia	Win	65-67-72-71=275	$900,000.00
Ryan Moore	T-2	69-70-67-70=276	$440,000.00
Ben Crane	T-2	74-66-70-66=276	$440,000.00
Jesper Parnevik	4	66-72-67-72=277	$240,000.00
Jerry Kelly	T-5	72-66-69-71=278	$190,000.00
Joey Sindelar	T-5	70-71-69-68=278	$190,000.00
Vijay Singh	T-7	73-66-68-72=279	$155,833.33
Stephen Ames	T-7	73-70-64-72=279	$155,833.33
Trevor Immelman	T-7	71-68-70-70=279	$155,833.34
Arjun Atwal	10	72-67-73-68=280	$135,000.00

84 Lumber Classic

Course: Nemocolin Woodlands Resort (Mystic Rock Course), Farmington, Pa.
Par: 72 Yardage: 7,516
Last day of event: Sunday, September 18, 2005

Player	Place	Score	Earnings
Jason Gore	Win	65-72-67-70=274	$792,000.00
Carlos Franco	2	69-69-68-69=275	$475,200.00
Ben Crane	3	67-70-73-67=277	$299,200.00
Tim Herron	4	70-68-70-70=278	$211,200.00
Cameron Beckman	T-5	69-65-73-72=279	$154,550.00
Chris DiMarco	T-5	70-70-67-72=279	$154,550.00
Jonathan Byrd	T-5	69-68-72-70=279	$154,550.00
John Huston	T-5	70-73-67-69=279	$154,550.00
Rod Pampling	T-9	70-67-69-74=280	$114,400.00
Tag Ridings	T-9	68-71-67-74=280	$114,400.00
Justin Leonard	T-9	73-64-70-73=280	$114,400.00
Stuart Appleby	T-9	67-66-75-72=280	$114,400.00

Valero Texas Open

Course: LaCantera G.C., San Antonio, Texas
Par: 70 Yardage: 6,881
Last day of event: Sunday, September 25, 2005

Player	Place	Score	Earnings
Robert Gamez	Win	62-68-68-64=262	$630,000.00
Olin Browne	2	65-65-71-64=265	$378,000.00
Woody Austin	T-3	63-67-67-69=266	$203,000.00
Mark Wilson	T-3	65-67-66-68=266	$203,000.00
Bob Heintz	T-5	65-65-69-68=267	$133,000.00
J.J. Henry	T-5	66-67-66-68=267	$133,000.00
Dean Wilson	7	66-62-70-70=268	$117,250.00
Jeff Maggert	T-8	63-66-70-70=269	$94,500.00
John Senden	T-8	63-66-70-70=269	$94,500.00
Steve Lowery	T-8	69-66-66-68=269	$94,500.00
Harrison Frazar	T-8	65-69-69-66=269	$94,500.00
Jay Delsing	T-8	67-71-68-63=269	$94,500.00

Chrysler Classic of Greensboro

Course: Forest Oaks C.C., Greensboro, N.C.
Par: 72 Yardage: 7,333
Last day of event: Sunday, October 2, 2005

Player	Place	Score	Earnings
K.J. Choi	Win	64-69-67-66=266	$900,000.00
Shigeki Maruyama	2	70-65-66-67=268	$540,000.00
Jason Bohn	T-3	71-65-65-70=271	$260,000.00
Brandt Jobe	T-3	72-65-67-67=271	$260,000.00
Charles Warren	T-3	62-74-70-65=271	$260,000.00
Justin Rose	T-6	69-65-68-71=273	$156,500.00
Tim Herron	T-6	70-66-67-70=273	$156,500.00
Tim Clark	T-6	66-69-70-68=273	$156,500.00
Jerry Kelly	T-6	70-68-67-68=273	$156,500.00
J.L. Lewis	T-6	72-68-67-66=273	$156,500.00

WGC-American Express Championship

Course: Harding Park Golf Course, San Francisco, Calif.
Par: 70 Yardage: 7,086
Last day of event: Sunday, October 9, 2005

Player	Place	Score	Earnings
Tiger Woods	Win	67-68-68-67=270	$1,300,000.00
Playoff: Beat John Daly with par on second extra hole			
John Daly	2	67-67-67-69=270	$750,000.00
Colin Montgomerie	T-3	64-69-69-70=272	$353,666.66
Sergio Garcia	T-3	67-69-67-69=272	$353,666.66
Henrik Stenson	T-3	70-67-67-68=272	$353,666.67
David Toms	T-6	68-68-70-69=275	$187,500.00
Vijay Singh	T-6	67-70-69-69=275	$187,500.00
Graeme McDowell	T-6	69-70-68-68=275	$187,500.00
David Howell	T-6	67-67-74-67=275	$187,500.00
Stephen Ames	10	72-64-71-69=276	$140,000.00

Michelin Championship at Las Vegas

Course: TPC at Summerlin, TPC At The Canyons, Las Vegas, Nev.
Home course / TPC at Summerlin, Par: 72 Yardage: 7,243
Last day of event: Sunday, October 16, 2005

Player	Place	Score	Earnings
Wes Short, Jr.	Win	67-67-66-66=266	$720,000.00
Playoff: Beat Jim Furyk with par on second extra hole			
Jim Furyk	2	66-66-69-65=266	$432,000.00
Ted Purdy	T-3	67-65-65-71=268	$232,000.00
Harrison Frazar	T-3	68-63-68-69=268	$232,000.00
Charles Howell III	5	63-69-67-70=269	$160,000.00
Shigeki Maruyama	T-6	65-65-72-68=270	$139,000.00
Nick Watney	T-6	67-67-70-66=270	$139,000.00
Briny Baird	T-8	62-66-78-65=271	$112,000.00
Will MacKenzie	T-8	65-69-70-67=271	$112,000.00
Hidemichi Tanaka	T-8	66-68-68-69=271	$112,000.00
Steve Lowery	T-8	67-68-64-72=271	$112,000.00

FUNAI Classic at the Walt Disney World Resort

Course: Walt Disney (Magnolia, Palm), Lake Buena Vista, Fla.
Home course / Magnolia, Par: 72 Yardage: 7,516
Last day of event: Sunday, October 23, 2005

Player	Place	Score	Earnings
Lucas Glover	Win	68-66-66-65=265	$792,000.00
Tom Pernice, Jr.	2	67-62-68-69=266	$475,200.00
Rich Beem	T-3	65-69-63-70=267	$198,440.00
Geoff Ogilvy	T-3	64-66-68-69=267	$198,440.00
Harrison Frazar	T-3	67-66-66-68=267	$198,440.00
Justin Rose	T-3	67-68-64-68=267	$198,440.00
Ryan Palmer	T-3	67-70-66-64=267	$198,440.00
Mark Calcavecchia	T-8	64-69-65-70=268	$132,000.00
Brandt Jobe	T-8	69-62-70-67=268	$132,000.00
Tim Clark	T-10	66-65-66-72=269	$110,000.00
Mark Wilson	T-10	67-68-63-71=269	$110,000.00
Tom Lehman	T-10	65-70-69-65=269	$110,000.00

Chrysler Championship

Course: Westin Innisbrook Resort (Copperhead Course)
Palm Harbor, Fla.
Par: 71 Yardage: 7,340
Last day of event: Monday, October 31, 2005

Player	Place	Score	Earnings
Carl Pettersson	Win	69-68-67-71=275	$954,000.00
Chad Campbell	2	70-70-69-67=276	$572,400.00
Steve Lowery	T-3	68-66-70-75=279	$216,164.28
Tom Pernice, Jr.	T-3	71-66-70-72=279	$216,164.28
Bo Van Pelt	T-3	71-65-73-70=279	$216,164.28
Tim Herron	T-3	71-67-71-70=279	$216,164.29
Hidemichi Tanaka	T-3	73-67-72-67=279	$216,164.29
Stewart Cink	T-3	71-70-71-67=279	$216,164.29
Tag Ridings	T-3	70-72-70-67=279	$216,164.29
Daniel Chopra	T-10	71-68-68-73=280	$132,500.00
Jeff Brehaut	T-10	65-74-69-72=280	$132,500.00
Sean O'Hair	T-10	73-69-69-69=280	$132,500.00

The Tour Championship

Course: East Lake G.C., Atlanta, Ga.
Par: 70 Yardage: 7,154
Last day of event: Sunday, November 6, 2005

Player	Place	Score	Earnings
Bart Bryant	Win	62-68-66-67=263	$1,170,000.00
Tiger Woods	2	66-67-67-69=269	$715,000.00
Scott Verplank	3	67-66-69-69=271	$461,500.00
Retief Goosen	T-4	64-66-69-74=273	$283,833.33
Davis Love III	T-4	68-71-65-69=273	$283,833.33
Vijay Singh	T-4	69-69-68-67=273	$283,833.34
Ben Crane	T-7	68-65-72-69=274	$209,625.00
Padraig Harrington	T-7	71-66-68-69=274	$209,625.00
Stuart Appleby	T-7	70-65-71-68=274	$209,625.00
Adam Scott	T-7	73-69-65-67=274	$209,625.00

Southern Farm Bureau Classic

Course: Annandale G.C., Madison, Miss.
Par: 72 Yardage: 7,199
Last day of event: Sunday, November 6, 2005

Player	Place	Score	Earnings
Heath Slocum	Win	69-68-64-66=267	$540,000.00
Loren Roberts	T-2	68-67-66-68=269	$264,000.00
Carl Pettersson	T-2	68-69-65-67=269	$264,000.00
Joey Snyder III	4	67-68-65-70=270	$144,000.00
Tag Ridings	T-5	68-66-68-69=271	$94,928.57
Bob Tway	T-5	64-70-71-66=271	$94,928.57
John Cook	T-5	69-65-71-66=271	$94,928.57
Charlie Wi	T-5	68-68-69-66=271	$94,928.57
Shaun Micheel	T-5	68-69-68-66=271	$94,928.57
Woody Austin	T-5	69-69-67-66=271	$94,928.57
Bo Van Pelt	T-5	66-69-71-65=271	$94,928.58

2006

Phil Mickelson won his second Masters, beating Tim Clark by two shots, but gained more notoriety with his 72nd-hole meltdown at the U.S. Open. Mickelson needed par to win but bounced his tee shot at Winged Foot's 18th off a corporate hospitality tent, then failed to execute a heroic recovery attempt and made double bogey. "I am such an idiot," Mickelson said. The victory went to Geoff Ogilvy, who had finished at 5-over-par 285 before the Mickelson debacle. Ogilvy also was the beneficiary of Colin Montgomerie's botched 72nd hole, where he was indecisive about club selection and missed the green from the center of the fairway, resulting in a double-bogey that left him a stroke behind Ogilvy. Tiger Woods scored an emotional 2-shot British Open victory over Chris DiMarco at Hoylake—Woods' first major win following the death of his father, Earl, in May—then won the PGA Championship by five shots over Shaun Micheel at Medinah. Woods won eight times, including his last six starts on Tour. There was much talk about him matching Byron Nelson's record of 11 consecutive victories, even though Woods' PGA Tour streak was interrupted by a T-9 at the HSBC World Match Play in England. Nelson, winner of 52 tournaments including five majors, died in September at age 93. The United States suffered another humiliation in the Ryder Cup, losing 14 to 9 in Ireland. Using a proposed "playoff" scheme as incentive, the PGA Tour finalized new six-year TV deals with CBS and NBC, and an eye-opening 15-year arrangement with the Golf Channel.

Mercedes Championipss

Course: Kapalua Resort Plantation Course, Kapalua, Maui, Ha.
Par: 73 Yardage: 7,411
Last day of event: Sunday, January 8, 2006

Player	Place	Score	Earnings
Stuart Appleby	Win	71-72-70-71=284	$1,080,000.00
Playoff: Beat Vijay Singh with birdie on first extra hole			
Vijay Singh	2	70-74-74-66=284	$630,000.00
Jim Furyk	3	72-72-72-72=288	$420,000.00
Michael Campbell	T-4	72-72-71-75=290	$287,500.00
Vaughn Taylor	T-4	74-73-72-71=290	$287,500.00
Lucas Glover	6	74-73-70-74=291	$217,000.00
Sergio Garcia	7	71-74-73-75=293	$195,000.00
Justin Leonard	8	72-78-72-72=294	$185,000.00
Bart Bryant	9	74-72-76-73=295	$175,000.00
Peter Lonard	10	74-74-73-75=296	$165,000.00

Sony Open in Hawaii

Course: Waialae C.C., Honolulu, Ha.
Par: 70 Yardage: 7,060
Last day of event: Sunday, January 15, 2006

Player	Place	Score	Earnings
David Toms	Win	66-69-61-65=261	$918,000.00
Chad Campbell	T-2	67-67-62-70=266	$448,800.00
Rory Sabbatini	T-2	65-72-67-62=266	$448,800.00
Bubba Watson	4	67-70-66-65=268	$244,800.00
Nathan Green	5	70-70-65-64=269	$204,000.00
Vijay Singh	6	71-69-65-66=271	$183,600.00
Jim Furyk	T-7	67-67-70-68=272	$158,950.00
Charles Warren	T-7	66-74-64-68=272	$158,950.00
Stuart Appleby	T-7	70-66-69-67=272	$158,950.00
J.B. Holmes	T-10	70-66-69-68=273	$127,500.00
Stewart Cink	T-10	71-69-66-67=273	$127,500.00
Carl Pettersson	T-10	71-68-68-66=273	$127,500.00

Bob Hope Chrysler Classic

Course: Classic Club, PGA West/Palmer, Bermuda Dunes C.C., La Quinta C.C.
Home Course / Classic Club, Par: 72 Yardage: 7,305
Last day of event: Sunday, January 22, 2006

Player	Place	Score	Earnings
Chad Campbell	Win	63-66-68-67-71=335	$900,000.00
Scott Verplank	T-2	68-68-65-64-73=338	$440,000.00
Jesper Parnevik	T-2	69-69-71-62-67=338	$440,000.00
John Huston	4	65-71-68-67-68=339	$240,000.00
John Senden	T-5	70-63-68-67-73=341	$182,500.00
Phil Mickelson	T-5	66-69-68-67-71=341	$182,500.00
Mike Weir	T-5	67-69-69-66-70=341	$182,500.00
Olin Browne	T-8	65-69-71-66-72=343	$150,000.00
Jeff Maggert	T-8	67-71-69-64-72=343	$150,000.00
Justin Rose	T-10	70-70-64-66-74=344	$110,833.33
Billy Mayfair	T-10	68-70-68-66-72=344	$110,833.33
Ryan Palmer	T-10	70-69-67-66-72=344	$110,833.34
Rory Sabbatini	T-10	71-68-68-64-73=344	$110,833.33
Bernhard Langer	T-10	70-70-67-65-72=344	$110,833.33
Lucas Glover	T-10	66-75-70-67-66=344	$110,833.34

Buick Invitational

Course: Torrey Pines (South), Torrey Pines (North)
San Diego, Calif. , Home Course -Par: 72 Yardage: 7,568
Last day of event: Sunday, January 29, 2006

Player	Place	Score	Earnings
Tiger Woods	Win	71-68-67-72=278	$918,000.00
Playoff: Beat Jose Maria Olazabal with par on second extra hole (Nathan Green eliminated on first hole with bogey)			
Nathan Green	T-2	67-70-69-72=278	$448,800.00
Jose Maria Olazabal	T-2	74-64-71-69=278	$448,800.00
Arjun Atwal	T-4	70-67-71-71=279	$200,812.50
Lucas Glover	T-4	71-67-70-71=279	$200,812.50
John Rollins	T-4	69-70-71-69=279	$200,812.50
Jonathan Kaye	T-4	67-73-71-68=279	$200,812.50
Sergio Garcia	T-8	69-68-68-75=280	$153,000.00
Phil Mickelson	T-8	71-67-69-73=280	$153,000.00
Rod Pampling	T-10	70-67-68-76=281	$117,300.00
Brandt Jobe	T-10	65-67-75-74=281	$117,300.00
Jesper Parnevik	T-10	67-67-73-74=281	$117,300.00
Tim Clark	T-10	68-66-74-73=281	$117,300.00
Henrik Bjornstad	T-10	68-72-70-71=281	$117,300.00

FBR Open

Course: TPC of Scottsdale, Scottsdale, Ariz.
Par: 71 Yardage: 7,216
Last day of event: Sunday, February 5, 2006

Player	Place	Score	Earnings
J.B. Holmes	Win	68-64-65-66=263	$936,000.00
J.J. Henry	T-2	67-61-70-72=270	$312,000.00
Ryan Palmer	T-2	68-66-64-72=270	$312,000.00
Camilo Villegas	T-2	68-67-66-69=270	$312,000.00
Scott Verplank	T-2	69-66-67-68=270	$312,000.00
Steve Lowery	T-2	65-68-70-67=270	$312,000.00
Justin Leonard	T-7	69-66-65-71=271	$162,066.66
Jonathan Byrd	T-7	70-65-68-68=271	$162,066.67
Phil Mickelson	T-7	69-66-70-66=271	$162,066.67
Dean Wilson	T-10	69-66-66-71=272	$135,200.00
Arron Oberholser	T-10	67-69-69-67=272	$135,200.00

AT&T Pebble Beach National Pro-Am

Courses: Pebble Beach G.L., Spyglass Hill G.C., Poppy Hills G.C., Pebble Beach, Calif.

Home Course / Pebble Beach G.L., Par: 72 Yardage: 6,816

Last day of event: Sunday, February 12, 2006

Player	Place	Score	Earnings
Arron Oberholser	Win	65-68-66-72=271	$972,000.00
Rory Sabbatini	2	69-69-68-70=276	$583,200.00
Mike Weir	T-3	63-67-69-78=277	$313,200.00
Jonathan Byrd	T-3	69-65-74-69=277	$313,200.00
Daniel Chopra	T-5	71-67-69-71=278	$205,200.00
Craig Barlow	T-5	69-68-72-69=278	$205,200.00
Luke Donald	T-7	62-72-71-74=279	$157,140.00
Nick Watney	T-7	65-71-70-73=279	$157,140.00
Brian Davis	T-7	66-72-68-73=279	$157,140.00
Tom Lehman	T-7	72-65-72-70=279	$157,140.00
Vijay Singh	T-7	68-71-72-68=279	$157,140.00

Nissan Open

Course: Riviera C.C., Pacific Palisades, Calif.

Par: 71 Yardage: 7,279

Last day of event: Sunday, February 19, 2006

Player	Place	Score	Earnings
Rory Sabbatini	Win	67-65-67-72=271	$918,000.00
Adam Scott	2	68-71-69-64=272	$550,800.00
Craig Barlow	3	67-69-67-70=273	$346,800.00
Fred Couples	4	66-72-65-71=274	$244,800.00
John Rollins	T-5	70-71-64-70=275	$193,800.00
Lee Westwood	T-5	71-66-70-68=275	$193,800.00
Trevor Immelman	T-7	67-70-67-72=276	$153,637.50
Dean Wilson	T-7	64-73-69-70=276	$153,637.50
Tom Lehman	T-7	67-70-70-69=276	$153,637.50
Carl Pettersson	T-7	70-70-68-68=276	$153,637.50

WGC-Accenture Match Play Championship

Course: La Costa Resort & Spa, Carlsbad, Calif.

Par: 72 Yardage: 7,277

Last day of event: Sunday, February 26, 2006

Player	Place	Earnings
Geoff Ogilvy	Win	$1,300,000.00

Round One - Beat Michael Campbell 19 holes
Round Two - Beat Nick O'Hern 21 holes
Round Three - Beat Mike Weir 21 holes
Quarterfinals - Beat David Howell 19 holes
Semifinals - Beat Tom Lehman 4 & 3
Finals - Beat Davis Love III 3 & 2

Davis Love III	T-2	$750,000.00

Round One - Beat Mark Hensby 2 & 1
Round Two - Beat Carl Pettersson 1 up
Round Three - Beat Chris DiMarco 3 & 1
Quarterfinals - Beat Padraig Harrington 1 up
Semifinals - Beat Zach Johnson 4 & 2
Finals - Geoff Ogilvy beat him 3 & 2

Zach Johnson	T-3	$560,000.00

Round One - Beat Jim Furyk 1 up
Round Two - Beat Sean O'Hair 1 up
Round Three - Beat Shingo Katayama 4 & 3
Quarterfinals - Beat Retief Goosen 3 & 2
Semifinals - Davis Love III beat him 4 & 2
Consolation - Beat Tom Lehman 1 up

Tom Lehman	T-4	$450,000.00

Round One - Beat Stuart Appleby 3 & 2

Round Two - Beat Adam Scott 1 up
Round Three - Beat David Lehman 4 & 3
Quarterfinals - Beat Chad Campbell 21 holes
Semifinals - Geoff Ogilvy beat him 4 & 3
Consolation - Zach Johnson beat him 1 up

Chad Campbell	T-5	$240,000.00

Round One - Beat Tim Herron 4 & 2
Round Two - Beat Henrik Stenson 1 up
Round Three - Beat Tiger Woods 1 up
Quarterfinals - Tom Lehman beat him 21 holes

Padraig Harrington	T-5	$240,000.00

Round One - Beat Rod Pampling 4 & 2
Round Two - Beat Angel Cabrera 19 holes
Round Three - Beat Vijay Singh 19 holes
Quarterfinals - Davis Love III beat him 1 up

Retief Goosen	T-5	$240,000.00

Round One - Beat Paul Broadhurst 5 & 4
Round Two - Beat Ben Crane 2 & 1
Round Three - Beat Luke Donald 1 up
Quarterfinals - Zach Johnson beat him 3 & 2

David Howell	T-5	$240,000.00

Round One - Beat Steve Elkington 22 holes
Round Two - Beat Scott Verplank 3 & 2
Round Three - Beat Phil Mickelson 3 & 1
Quarterfinals - Geoff Ogilvy beat him 19 holes

Tiger Woods	T-9	$125,000.00

Round One - Beat Stephen Ames 9 & 8
Round Two - Beat Robert Allenby 1 up
Round Three - Chad Campbell beat him 1 up

David Toms	T-9	$125,000.00

Round One - Beat Ian Poulter 19 holes
Round Two - Beat Jose Maria Olazabal 2 & 1
Round Three - Tom Lehman beat him 4 & 3

Vijay Singh	T-9	$125,000.00

Round One - Beat Graeme McDowell 5 & 4
Round Two - Beat Miguel Angel Jimenez 2 & 1
Round Three - Padraig Harrington beat him 19 holes

Chris DiMarco	T-9	$125,000.00

Round One - Beat Mark Calcavecchia 2 & 1
Round Two - Beat Arron Oberholser 6 & 5
Round Three - Davis Love III beat him 3 & 2

Luke Donald	T-9	$125,000.00

Round One - Beat Richard Green 2 & 1
Round Two - Beat Shigeki Maruyama 4 & 3
Round Three - Retief Goosen beat him 1 up

Shingo Katayama	T-9	$125,000.00

Round One - Beat Paul McGinley 2 & 1
Round Two - Beat Colin Montgomerie 3 & 2
Round Three - Zach Johnson beat him 4 & 3

Mike Weir	T-9	$125,000.00

Round One - Beat Stewart Cink 4 & 3
Round Two - Beat Bernhard Langer 20 holes
Round Three - Geoff Ogilvy beat him 21 holes

Phil Mickelson	T-9	$125,000.00

Round One - Beat Charles Howell III 2 up
Round Two - Beat John Daly 2 & 1
Round Three - David Howell beat him 3 & 1

Chrysler Classic of Tucson

Course: Tucson National Resort, Tucson, Ariz.

Par: 72 Yardage: 7,193

Last day of event: Sunday, February 26, 2006

Player	Place	Score	Earnings
Kirk Triplett	Win	68-71-64-63=266	$540,000.00
Jerry Kelly	2	66-68-68-65=267	$324,000.00

Player	Place	Score	Earnings
Duffy Waldorf	T-3	66-66-65-72=269	$156,000.00
Bubba Watson	T-3	67-67-65-70=269	$156,000.00
Heath Slocum	T-3	67-69-65-68=269	$156,000.00
David Branshaw	6	71-65-66-68=270	$108,000.00
Jason Gore	T-7	68-66-69-68=271	$96,750.00
Doug Barron	T-7	66-70-67-68=271	$96,750.00
Mark Wilson	T-9	64-69-67-72=272	$75,000.00
Gabriel Hjertstedt	T-9	66-71-65-70=272	$75,000.00
Bo Van Pelt	T-9	71-69-65-67=272	$75,000.00
Cameron Beckman	T-9	72-64-70-66=272	$75,000.00
Charley Hoffman	T-9	69-68-69-66=272	$75,000.00

Ford Championship at Doral

Course: Doral C.C. (Blue), Miami, Fla.
Par: 72 Yardage: 7,266
Last day of event: Sunday, March 5, 2006

Player	Place	Score	Earnings
Tiger Woods	Win	64-67-68-69=268	$990,000.00
Camilo Villegas	T-2	65-66-71-67=269	$484,000.00
David Toms	T-2	66-66-70-67=269	$484,000.00
Fredrik Jacobson	4	70-67-68-68=273	$264,000.00
Tag Ridings	T-5	68-69-66-71=274	$209,000.00
Lucas Glover	T-5	67-67-71-69=274	$209,000.00
Rich Beem	T-7	65-67-69-74=275	$160,050.00
Carlos Franco	T-7	69-67-70-69=275	$160,050.00
Ernie Els	T-7	72-65-69-69=275	$160,050.00
Jerry Kelly	T-7	69-70-68-68=275	$160,050.00
Jeff Sluman	T-7	69-68-72-66=275	$160,050.00

Honda Classic

Course: C.C. at Mirasol (Sunrise Course), Palm Beach Gardens, Fla.
Par: 72 Yardage: 7,384
Last day of event: Sunday, March 12, 2006

Player	Place	Score	Earnings
Luke Donald	Win	72-67-68-69=276	$990,000.00
Geoff Ogilvy	2	67-71-71-69=278	$594,000.00
Billy Mayfair	T-3	68-67-72-72=279	$319,000.00
David Toms	T-3	67-67-76-69=279	$319,000.00
Tom Pernice, Jr.	5	74-71-67-68=280	$220,000.00
Dudley Hart	6	69-72-71-69=281	$198,000.00
Jeff Gove	T-7	68-71-69-74=282	$171,416.66
Frank Lickliter II	T-7	71-70-70-71=282	$171,416.67
Stephen Ames	T-7	70-69-75-68=282	$171,416.67
Mathew Goggin	T-10	71-75-65-72=283	$143,000.00
D.A. Points	T-10	73-71-71-68=283	$143,000.00

Bay Hill Invitational

Course: Bay Hill Club, Orlando, Fla.
Par: 72 Yardage: 7,267
Last day of event: Sunday, March 19, 2006

Player	Place	Score	Earnings
Rod Pampling	Win	70-65-67-72=274	$990,000.00
Greg Owen	2	70-69-67-69=275	$594,000.00
Darren Clarke	3	73-70-63-70=276	$374,000.00
Robert Allenby	4	68-67-73-69=277	$264,000.00
Lee Westwood	T-5	68-71-72-67=278	$209,000.00
Ted Purdy	T-5	69-71-71-67=278	$209,000.00
Vijay Singh	7	71-71-68-69=279	$184,250.00
Tom Pernice, Jr.	T-8	68-73-68-71=280	$165,000.00
Justin Rose	T-8	70-70-71-69=280	$165,000.00
Sergio Garcia	T-10	68-69-71-73=281	$126,500.00

Player	Place	Score	Earnings
Dean Wilson	T-10	66-70-73-72=281	$126,500.00
Scott Verplank	T-10	72-69-70-70=281	$126,500.00
Joey Sindelar	T-10	70-73-69-69=281	$126,500.00
Fred Funk	T-10	69-75-68-69=281	$126,500.00

The Players Championship

Course: TPC at Sawgrass, Ponte Vedra Beach, Fla.
Par: 72 Yardage: 7,098
Last day of event: Sunday, March 26, 2006

Player	Place	Score	Earnings
Stephen Ames	Win	71-66-70-67=274	$1,440,000.00
Retief Goosen	2	69-71-71-69=280	$864,000.00
Henrik Stenson	T-3	69-71-70-73=283	$384,000.00
Jim Furyk	T-3	65-71-75-72=283	$384,000.00
Pat Perez	T-3	71-72-69-71=283	$384,000.00
Camilo Villegas	T-3	74-70-68-71=283	$384,000.00
Jose Maria Olazabal	7	68-71-74-71=284	$268,000.00
Vijay Singh	T-8	68-70-70-77=285	$208,000.00
John Rollins	T-8	68-71-72-74=285	$208,000.00
Bo Van Pelt	T-8	68-71-72-74=285	$208,000.00
Carl Pettersson	T-8	71-70-70-74=285	$208,000.00
Vaughn Taylor	T-8	73-71-68-73=285	$208,000.00
Ernie Els	T-8	72-70-72-71=285	$208,000.00

BellSouth Classic

Course: TPC at Sugarloaf, Duluth, Ga.
Par: 72 Yardage: 7,343
Last day of event: Sunday, April 2, 2006

Player	Place	Score	Earnings
Phil Mickelson	Win	63-65-67-65=260	$954,000.00
Zach Johnson	T-2	69-70-64-70=273	$466,400.00
Jose Maria Olazabal	T-2	71-64-69-69=273	$466,400.00
J.J. Henry	T-4	69-65-72-68=274	$233,200.00
Retief Goosen	T-4	69-70-69-66=274	$233,200.00
Jonathan Byrd	6	69-68-66-73=276	$190,800.00
Doug Barron	T-7	74-67-65-71=277	$165,183.33
Richard S. Johnson	T-7	73-71-66-67=277	$165,183.33
Shane Bertsch	T-7	68-69-74-66=277	$165,183.34
Steve Flesch	T-10	71-68-67-72=278	$121,900.00
Briny Baird	T-10	72-69-68-69=278	$121,900.00
Ryuji Imada	T-10	71-67-72-68=278	$121,900.00
Luke Donald	T-10	68-70-74-66=278	$121,900.00
Charley Hoffman	T-10	71-72-69-66=278	$121,900.00

Masters

Course: Augusta National G.C., Augusta, Ga.
Par: 72 Yardage: 7,445
Last day of event: Sunday, April 9, 2006

Player	Place	Score	Earnings
Phil Mickelson	Win	70-72-70-69=281	$1,260,000.00
Tim Clark	2	70-72-72-69=283	$756,000.00
Chad Campbell	T-3	71-67-75-71=284	$315,700.00
Fred Couples	T-3	71-70-72-71=284	$315,700.00
Tiger Woods	T-3	72-71-71-70=284	$315,700.00
Retief Goosen	T-3	70-73-72-69=284	$315,700.00
Jose Maria Olazabal	T-3	76-71-71-66=284	$315,700.00
Vijay Singh	T-8	67-74-73-71=285	$210,000.00
Angel Cabrera	T-8	73-74-70-68=285	$210,000.00
Stewart Cink	10	72-73-71-70=286	$189,000.00

Verizon Heritage

Course: Harbour Town G.L., Hilton Head, S.C.
Par: 71 Yardage: 6,973
Last day of event: Monday, April 17, 2006

Player	Place	Score	Earnings
Aaron Baddeley	Win	66-67-66-70=269	$954,000.00
Jim Furyk	2	64-67-68-71=270	$572,400.00
Billy Mayfair	T-3	65-69-68-69=271	$307,400.00
Vaughn Taylor	T-3	63-70-72-66=271	$307,400.00
Jerry Kelly	T-5	68-69-66-70=273	$201,400.00
Brett Quigley	T-5	68-70-68-67=273	$201,400.00
Ernie Els	T-7	71-67-65-71=274	$170,925.00
Tim Clark	T-7	72-65-68-69=274	$170,925.00
Jose Coceres	T-9	69-67-68-72=276	$148,400.00
Brian Gay	T-9	66-67-73-70=276	$148,400.00

Shell Houston Open

Course: Redstone G.C. (Tournament Course), Humble, Texas
Par: 72 Yardage: 7,457
Last day of event: Sunday, April 23, 2006

Player	Place	Score	Earnings
Stuart Appleby	Win	66-67-69-67=269	$990,000.00
Bob Estes	2	71-69-66-69=275	$594,000.00
Steve Stricker	3	72-70-68-66=276	$374,000.00
Mathias Gronberg	4	68-69-67-73=277	$264,000.00
Jerry Smith	5	67-70-69-72=278	$220,000.00
K.J. Choi	T-6	71-69-67-72=279	$172,150.00
Brett Wetterich	T-6	70-69-69-71=279	$172,150.00
J.L. Lewis	T-6	71-69-68-71=279	$172,150.00
Richard S. Johnson	T-6	72-69-67-71=279	$172,150.00
Mike Weir	T-6	71-71-70-67=279	$172,150.00

Zurich Classic of New Orleans

Course: English Turn G. & C.C., New Orleans, La.
Par: 72 Yardage: 7,078
Last day of event: Sunday, April 30, 2006

Player	Place	Score	Earnings
Chris Couch	Win	70-70-64-65=269	$1,080,000.00
Charles Howell III	T-2	70-69-66-65=270	$528,000.00
Fred Funk	T-2	70-69-69-62=270	$528,000.00
Joe Durant	T-4	68-64-73-68=273	$248,000.00
Brett Wetterich	T-4	69-65-73-66=273	$248,000.00
Stuart Appleby	T-4	65-72-72-64=273	$248,000.00
Ian Poulter	T-7	67-68-72-67=274	$180,750.00
Tim Herron	T-7	67-71-69-67=274	$180,750.00
Danny Ellis	T-7	71-69-69-65=274	$180,750.00
Lucas Glover	T-7	66-73-72-63=274	$180,750.00

Wachovia Championship

Course: Quail Hollow Club, Charlotte, N.C.
Par: 72 Yardage: 7,442
Last day of event: Sunday, May 7, 2006

Player	Place	Score	Earnings
Jim Furyk	Win	68-69-68-71=276	$1,134,000.00
Playoff: Beat Trevor Immelman with par on first extra hole			
Trevor Immelman	2	68-72-66-70=276	$680,400.00
Adam Scott	3	71-72-66-71=280	$428,400.00
Lucas Glover	T-4	69-73-67-72=281	$277,200.00
Bill Haas	T-4	68-72-71-70=281	$277,200.00
Bo Van Pelt	T-6	70-64-73-75=282	$203,962.50
Steve Lowery	T-6	73-68-69-72=282	$203,962.50
Vaughn Taylor	T-6	70-70-71-71=282	$203,962.50
Joey Sindelar	T-6	71-74-68-69=282	$203,962.50
Retief Goosen	T-10	70-71-65-77=283	$163,800.00
Geoff Ogilvy	T-10	71-71-70-71=283	$163,800.00

EDS Byron Nelson Championship

Course: TPC at Las Colinas—Home course, Cottonwood Valley Course, Irving, Texas
Home course / Par: 70 Yardage: 7,052
Last day of event: Sunday, May 14, 2006

Player	Place	Score	Earnings
Brett Wetterich	Win	66-64-70-68=268	$1,116,000.00
Trevor Immelman	2	68-67-64-70=269	$669,600.00
Adam Scott	T-3	65-65-69-71=270	$359,600.00
Omar Uresti	T-3	67-66-69-68=270	$359,600.00
Chad Campbell	5	72-65-65-69=271	$248,000.00
Luke Donald	T-6	69-66-69-68=272	$215,450.00
Shigeki Maruyama	T-6	71-68-67-66=272	$215,450.00
Charley Hoffman	T-8	70-67-65-71=273	$167,400.00
Dudley Hart	T-8	68-68-68-69=273	$167,400.00
Jason Bohn	T-8	70-68-68-67=273	$167,400.00
Rod Pampling	T-8	71-69-67-66=273	$167,400.00
Brian Davis	T-8	70-68-70-65=273	$167,400.00

Bank of America Colonial

Course: Colonial C.C., Fort Worth, Texas
Par: 70 Yardage: 7,054
Last day of event: Sunday, May 21, 2006

Player	Place	Score	Earnings
Tim Herron	Win	67-65-68-68=268	$1,080,000.00
Playoff: Beat Richard S. Johnson with birdie on second extra hole			
Richard S. Johnson	2	68-65-68-67=268	$648,000.00
Rod Pampling	3	67-63-70-70=270	$408,000.00
Peter Lonard	T-4	66-66-69-70=271	$209,571.43
Nathan Green	T-4	67-67-67-70=271	$209,571.42
Stewart Cink	T-4	64-67-72-68=271	$209,571.43
Arron Oberholser	T-4	65-68-71-67=271	$209,571.43
Brett Quigley	T-4	68-70-67-66=271	$209,571.43
Ben Crane	T-4	71-65-71-64=271	$209,571.43
Stephen Ames	T-4	65-66-77-63=271	$209,571.43

FedEx St. Jude Classic

Course: TPC at Southwind, Germantown, Tenn.
Par: 70 Yardage: 7,244
Last day of event: Sunday, May 28, 2006

Player	Place	Score	Earnings
Jeff Maggert	Win	72-66-68-65=271	$936,000.00
Tom Pernice, Jr.	2	67-68-68-71=274	$561,600.00
Kris Cox	T-3	74-67-63-72=276	$301,600.00
John Cook	T-3	69-69-67-71=276	$301,600.00
Jay Delsing	T-5	70-69-66-72=277	$182,650.00
Briny Baird	T-5	71-68-68-70=277	$182,650.00
Zach Johnson	T-5	68-71-70-68=277	$182,650.00
Daisuke Maruyama	T-5	68-73-69-67=277	$182,650.00
John Senden	9	73-65-70-70=278	$150,800.00
Ryan Palmer	T-10	69-68-69-73=279	$115,266.66
David Toms	T-10	69-67-72-71=279	$115,266.66
Tjaart van der Walt	T-10	73-70-67-69=279	$115,266.67
Brett Quigley	T-10	69-71-71-68=279	$115,266.67
Dudley Hart	T-10	74-67-70-68=279	$115,266.67
Brent Geiberger	T-10	69-73-70-67=279	$115,266.67

Memorial Tournament

Course: Muirfield Village G.C., Dubin, Ohio
Par: 72 Yardage: 7,337
Last day of event: Sunday, June 4, 2006

Player	Place	Score	Earnings
Carl Pettersson	Win	69-67-69-71=276	$1,035,000.00
Zach Johnson	T-2	70-68-70-70=278	$506,000.00
Brett Wetterich	T-2	69-69-73-67=278	$506,000.00
Phil Mickelson	T-4	69-70-70-70=279	$237,666.66
Adam Scott	T-4	71-66-73-69=279	$237,666.67
Brandt Jobe	T-4	70-68-74-67=279	$237,666.67
Woody Austin	T-7	71-69-67-73=280	$179,208.33
Trevor Immelman	T-7	72-70-69-69=280	$179,208.33
Vaughn Taylor	T-7	70-72-70-68=280	$179,208.34
Paul Azinger	10	73-71-70-67=281	$155,250.00

Barclays Classic

Course: Westchester C.C., Harrison, N.Y.
Par: 71 Yardage: 6,839
Last day of event: Sunday, June 11, 2006

Player	Place	Score	Earnings
Vijay Singh	Win	70-64-72-68=274	$1,035,000.00
Adam Scott	2	65-72-69-70=276	$621,000.00
Billy Andrade	T-3	66-70-69-72=277	$333,500.00
Brett Quigley	T-3	71-66-70-70=277	$333,500.00
Fredrik Jacobson	T-5	67-68-72-71=278	$201,968.75
Luke Donald	T-5	72-65-71-70=278	$201,968.75
Jeff Sluman	T-5	69-69-72-68=278	$201,968.75
Tom Pernice, Jr.	T-5	70-71-70-67=278	$201,968.75
Ian Poulter	T-9	72-71-65-71=279	$155,250.00
Mathew Goggin	T-9	73-68-68-70=279	$155,250.00
Jason Bohn	T-9	76-64-72-67=279	$155,250.00

U.S. Open

Course: Winged Foot G.C. (West), Mamaroneck, N.Y.
Par: 70 Yardage: 7,264
Last day of event: Sunday, June 18, 2006

Player	Place	Score	Earnings
Geoff Ogilvy	Win	71-70-72-72=285	$1,225,000.00
Phil Mickelson	T-2	70-73-69-74=286	$501,249.00
Colin Montgomerie	T-2	69-71-75-71=286	$501,249.00
Jim Furyk	T-2	70-72-74-70=286	$501,249.00
Padraig Harrington	5	73-69-74-71=287	$255,642.00
Kenneth Ferrie	T-6	71-70-71-76=288	$183,255.00
Steve Stricker	T-6	70-69-76-73=288	$183,255.00
Vijay Singh	T-6	71-74-70-73=288	$183,255.00
Mike Weir	T-6	71-74-71-72=288	$183,255.00
Nick O'Hern	T-6	75-70-74-69=288	$183,255.00
Jeff Sluman	T-6	74-73-72-69=288	$183,255.00

Booz Allen Classic

Course: TPC at Avenel, Potomac, Md.
Par: 71 Yardage: 6,987
Last day of event: Tuesday, June 27, 2006

Player	Place	Score	Earnings
Ben Curtis	Win	62-65-67-70=264	$900,000.00
Steve Stricker	T-2	68-67-66-68=269	$330,000.00
Nick O'Hern	T-2	74-64-64-67=269	$330,000.00
Padraig Harrington	T-2	70-65-68-66=269	$330,000.00
Billy Andrade	T-2	69-68-68-64=269	$330,000.00

Brett Quigley	T-6	69-63-67-71=270	$167,500.00
Jeff Gove	T-6	63-68-71-68=270	$167,500.00
Ben Crane	T-6	68-68-68-66=270	$167,500.00
Daniel Chopra	T-9	69-65-67-70=271	$140,000.00
Robert Allenby	T-9	68-68-66-69=271	$140,000.00

Buick Championship

Course: TPC at River Highlands, Cromwell, Conn.
Par: 70 Yardage: 6,820
Last day of event: Sunday, July 2, 2006

Player	Place	Score	Earnings
J.J. Henry	Win	68-68-63-67=266	$792,000.00
Ryan Moore	T-2	69-66-67-67=269	$387,200.00
Hunter Mahan	T-2	69-67-68-65=269	$387,200.00
Nathan Green	4	71-65-69-66=271	$211,200.00
Woody Austin	T-5	67-70-68-68=273	$154,550.00
Stewart Cink	T-5	69-65-72-67=273	$154,550.00
Bubba Dickerson	T-5	69-67-70-67=273	$154,550.00
Shigeki Maruyama	T-5	74-65-68-66=273	$154,550.00
Peter Lonard	T-9	65-68-70-71=274	$101,828.57
Steve Flesch	T-9	69-70-64-71=274	$101,828.57
Joe Ogilvie	T-9	72-63-69-70=274	$101,828.57
Notah Begay III	T-9	68-66-71-69=274	$101,828.57
David McKenzie	T-9	69-69-67-69=274	$101,828.57
Nick Watney	T-9	69-67-70-68=274	$101,828.57
Skip Kendall	T-9	68-67-74-65=274	$101,828.58

Cialis Western Open

Course: Cog Hill G. & C.C. (Dubsdread), Lemont, Ill.
Par: 71 Yardage: 7,326
Last day of event: Sunday, July 9, 2006

Player	Place	Score	Earnings
Trevor Immelman	Win	69-66-69-67=271	$900,000.00
Mathew Goggin	T-2	69-69-66-69=273	$440,000.00
Tiger Woods	T-2	72-67-66-68=273	$440,000.00
Vijay Singh	T-4	67-67-68-73=275	$181,250.00
Stewart Cink	T-4	71-64-69-71=275	$181,250.00
Carl Pettersson	T-4	69-70-65-71=275	$181,250.00
Jim Furyk	T-4	69-67-69-70=275	$181,250.00
Stephen Leaney	T-4	67-70-70-68=275	$181,250.00
Tim Clark	T-4	70-71-68-66=275	$181,250.00
Scott Gutschewski	T-10	70-66-69-71=276	$130,000.00
Jason Gore	T-10	70-67-69-70=276	$130,000.00

John Deere Classic

Course: TPC at Deere Run, Silvis, Ill.
Par: 71 Yardage: 7,326
Last day of event: Sunday, July 16, 2006

Player	Place	Score	Earnings
John Senden	Win	64-69-64-68=265	$720,000.00
J.P. Hayes	2	64-71-66-65=266	$432,000.00
Heath Slocum	T-3	69-65-66-68=268	$232,000.00
Alex Cejka	T-3	69-68-64-67=268	$232,000.00
B.J. Staten	T-5	66-70-66-67=269	$152,000.00
John Riegger	T-5	67-69-69-64=269	$152,000.00
Patrick Sheehan	T-7	68-66-66-70=270	$124,666.66
Billy Mayfair	T-7	70-70-63-67=270	$124,666.67
Kent Jones	T-7	71-65-68-66=270	$124,666.67
Joe Ogilvie	T-10	65-67-69-70=271	$85,714.28
Daniel Chopra	T-10	64-69-68-70=271	$85,714.28
Daisuke Maruyama	T-10	66-70-66-69=271	$85,714.28

Jason Gore	T-10	67-69-67-68=271	$85,714.29
Todd Hamilton	T-10	68-69-67-67=271	$85,714.29
Jeff Overton	T-10	68-69-68-66=271	$85,714.29
Bubba Dickerson	T-10	68-68-70-65=271	$85,714.29

British Open
Course: Royal Liverpool Golf Club, Hoylake, England
Par: 72 Yardage: 7,258
Last day of event: Sunday, July 23, 2006

Player	Place	Score	Earnings
Tiger Woods	Win	67-65-71-67=270	$1,338,480.00
Chris DiMarco	2	70-65-69-68=272	$799,370.00
Ernie Els	3	68-65-71-71=275	$511,225.00
Jim Furyk	4	68-71-66-71=276	$390,390.00
Sergio Garcia	T-5	68-71-65-73=277	$296,510.50
Hideto Tanihara	T-5	72-68-66-71=277	$296,510.50
Angel Cabrera	7	71-68-66-73=278	$237,952.00
Adam Scott	T-8	68-69-70-72=279	$177,224.64
Andres Romero	T-8	70-70-68-71=279	$177,224.64
Carl Pettersson	T-8	68-72-70-69=279	$177,224.64

B.C. Open
Course: Atunyote Golf Club, Verona, N.Y.
Par: 72 Yardage: 7,315
Last day of event: Sunday, July 23, 2006

Player	Place	Score	Earnings
John Rollins	Win	67-70-68-64=269	$540,000.00
Bob May	2	73-66-67-64=270	$324,000.00
Shigeki Maruyama	3	68-71-67-65=271	$204,000.00
David Branshaw	T-4	71-64-68-69=272	$132,000.00
Omar Uresti	T-4	67-71-70-64=272	$132,000.00
Gabriel Hjertstedt	T-6	67-67-68-71=273	$90,750.00
Daisuke Maruyama	T-6	67-67-71-68=273	$90,750.00
Matt Gogel	T-6	67-71-67-68=273	$90,750.00
Larry Mize	T-6	69-69-67-68=273	$90,750.00
Scott Gutschewski	T-6	67-71-68-67=273	$90,750.00
Nicholas Thompson	T-6	69-70-70-64=273	$90,750.00

U.S. Bank Championship in Milwaukee
Course: Brown Deer Park G.C., Milwaukee, Wis.
Par: 70 Yardage: 6,759
Last day of event: Sunday, July 30, 2006

Player	Place	Score	Earnings
Corey Pavin	Win	61-64-68-67=260	$720,000.00
Jerry Kelly	2	64-67-64-67=262	$432,000.00
Jeff Sluman	3	66-65-68-64=263	$272,000.00
D.J. Trahan	T-4	66-65-65-69=265	$176,000.00
Frank Lickliter II	T-4	66-66-64-69=265	$176,000.00
Billy Andrade	T-6	65-67-66-68=266	$134,000.00
Joey Sindelar	T-6	67-65-67-67=266	$134,000.00
Woody Austin	T-6	70-68-63-65=266	$134,000.00
Nathan Green	T-9	67-64-67-69=267	$104,000.00
K.J. Choi	T-9	67-67-69-64=267	$104,000.00
Dicky Pride	T-9	68-67-69-63=267	$104,000.00
Dean Wilson	T-9	66-70-68-63=267	$104,000.00

Buick Open
Course: Warwick Hills C.C., Grand Blanc, Mich.
Par: 72 Yardage: 7,127
Last day of event: Monday, August 7, 2006

Player	Place	Score	Earnings
Tiger Woods	Win	66-66-66-66=264	$864,000.00
Jim Furyk	2	66-68-69-64=267	$518,400.00
Joe Durant	3	65-69-67-67=268	$326,400.00
Scott Verplank	T-4	68-66-66-69=269	$198,400.00
Vaughn Taylor	T-4	67-71-63-68=269	$198,400.00
Sean O'Hair	T-4	68-68-66-67=269	$198,400.00
Brett Quigley	T-7	65-66-71-68=270	$144,600.00
Woody Austin	T-7	65-69-68-68=270	$144,600.00
Harrison Frazar	T-7	70-64-69-67=270	$144,600.00
Tom Pernice, Jr.	T-7	69-69-68-64=270	$144,600.00

The International
Course: Castle Pine G.C., Castle Rock, Colo. (Stableford format)
Par: 72 Yardage: 7,619
Last day of event: Sunday, August 13, 2006

Player	Place	Score	Earnings
Dean Wilson	Win	2-11-9-12=34	$990,000.00

Playoff: Beat Tom Lehman with birdie on second extra hole

Tom Lehman	2	5-11-8-10=34	$594,000.00
Steve Flesch	T-3	8-5-13-6=32	$319,000.00
Daisuke Maruyama	T-3	2-10-7-13=32	$319,000.00
Stewart Cink	5	11-6-8-6=31	$220,000.00
Ian Leggatt	T-6	4-13-8-5=30	$184,250.00
Jeff Brehaut	T-6	10-2-9-9=30	$184,250.00
Bubba Watson	T-6	5-7-7-11=30	$184,250.00
Nathan Green	9	7-5-9-8=29	$159,500.00
Brett Quigley	T-10	8-8-2-9=27	$137,500.00
Ernie Els	T-10	8-4-5-10=27	$137,500.00
Rod Pampling	T-10	0-10-5-12=27	$137,500.00

PGA Championship
Course: Medinah C.C. (No 3), Medinah, Ill.
Par: 72 Yardage: 7,561
Last day of event: Sunday, August 20, 2006

Player	Place	Score	Earnings
Tiger Woods	Win	69-68-65-68=270	$1,224,000.00
Shaun Micheel	2	69-70-67-69=275	$734,400.00
Luke Donald	T-3	68-68-66-74=276	$353,600.00
Sergio Garcia	T-3	69-70-67-70=276	$353,600.00
Adam Scott	T-3	71-69-69-67=276	$353,600.00
Mike Weir	6	72-67-65-73=277	$244,800.00
K.J. Choi	T-7	73-67-67-71=278	$207,787.50
Steve Stricker	T-7	72-67-70-69=278	$207,787.50
Geoff Ogilvy	T-9	69-68-68-74=279	$165,000.00
Ian Poulter	T-9	70-70-68-71=279	$165,000.00
Ryan Moore	T-9	71-72-67-69=279	$165,000.00

WGC-NEC Invitational
Course: Firestone C.C. (South), Akron, Ohio
Par: 70 Yardage: 7,360
Last day of event: Sunday, August 27, 2006

Player	Place	Score	Earnings
Tiger Woods	Win	67-64-71-68=270	$1,300,000.00

Playoff: Beat Stewart Cink with birdie on fourth extra hole

Stewart Cink	2	70-67-64-69=270	$750,000.00
Jim Furyk	3	69-65-69-68=271	$450,000.00
Davis Love III	T-4	67-65-70-71=273	$246,250.00
Paul Casey	T-4	69-69-64-71=273	$246,250.00
Lucas Glover	T-4	66-69-69-69=273	$246,250.00
Angel Cabrera	T-4	70-68-70-65=273	$246,250.00

Luke Donald	T-8	67-69-70-68=274	$152,500.00
David Toms	T-8	67-74-65-68=274	$152,500.00
Adam Scott	T-10	63-71-71-70=275	$120,000.00
J.J. Henry	T-10	70-68-68-69=275	$120,000.00
Arron Oberholser	T-10	70-71-69-65=275	$120,000.00

Reno-Tahoe Open
Course: Montreux G. & C.C., Reno, Nev.
Par: 72 Yardage: 7,472
Last day of event: Sunday, August 27, 2006

Player	Place	Score	Earnings
Will MacKenzie	Win	63-67-67-71=268	$540,000.00
Bob Estes	2	64-65-68-72=269	$324,000.00
Joe Ogilvie	3	71-68-69-62=270	$204,000.00
Daniel Chopra	4	71-67-64-69=271	$144,000.00
John Cook	T-5	66-66-69-71=272	$105,375.00
Jeff Brehaut	T-5	70-68-65-69=272	$105,375.00
Nick Watney	T-5	66-68-71-67=272	$105,375.00
Jose Coceres	T-5	72-67-67-66=272	$105,375.00
Alex Cejka	T-9	67-67-70-69=273	$84,000.00
Shigeki Maruyama	T-9	70-70-64-69=273	$84,000.00

Deutsche Bank Championship
Course: TPC of Boston, Norton, Mass.
Par: 71 Yardage: 7,415
Last day of event: Monday, September 4, 2006

Player	Place	Score	Earnings
Tiger Woods	Win	66-72-67-63=268	$990,000.00
Vijay Singh	2	70-71-61-68=270	$594,000.00
Brian Bateman	3	69-71-70-66=276	$374,000.00
Justin Rose	T-4	67-69-69-72=277	$242,000.00
Robert Allenby	T-4	70-66-73-68=277	$242,000.00
J.J. Henry	6	68-71-68-71=278	$198,000.00
Shaun Micheel	T-7	69-70-68-72=279	$160,050.00
Aaron Baddeley	T-7	67-71-71-70=279	$160,050.00
Stephen Leaney	T-7	70-71-69-69=279	$160,050.00
Steve Stricker	T-7	71-72-69-67=279	$160,050.00
Frank Lickliter II	T-7	71-72-69-67=279	$160,050.00

Canadian Open
Course: Hamilton Golf & C.C., Hamilton, Ontario, Canada
Par: 70 Yardage: 6,930
Last day of event: Sunday, September 10, 2006

Player	Place	Score	Earnings
Jim Furyk	Win	63-71-67-65=266	$900,000.00
Bart Bryant	2	69-67-64-67=267	$540,000.00
Sean O'Hair	3	65-69-66-68=268	$340,000.00
Brett Quigley	4	71-63-67-68=269	$240,000.00
Jonathan Byrd	T-5	65-68-67-70=270	$169,500.00
Trevor Immelman	T-5	68-66-66-70=270	$169,500.00
Steve Lowery	T-5	70-66-65-69=270	$169,500.00
Camilo Villegas	T-5	69-64-69-68=270	$169,500.00
Rory Sabbatini	T-5	67-69-68-66=270	$169,500.00
Steve Stricker	10	67-69-68-67=271	$135,000.00

84 Lumber Classic
Course: Nemocolin Woodlands Resort (Mystic Rock Course), Farmington, Pa.
Par: 72 Yardage: 7,550
Last day of event: Sunday, September 17, 2006

Player	Place	Score	Earnings
Ben Curtis	Win	66-69-69-70=274	$828,000.00
Charles Howell III	2	67-69-68-72=276	$496,800.00
Brett Quigley	3	69-70-68-70=277	$312,800.00
Robert Garrigus	T-4	67-70-68-73=278	$202,400.00
Ted Purdy	T-4	66-72-73-67=278	$202,400.00
Ryan Moore	T-6	68-67-71-73=279	$154,100.00
Charles Warren	T-6	70-72-66-71=279	$154,100.00
Kent Jones	T-6	69-68-75-67=279	$154,100.00
Greg Owen	T-9	69-68-68-75=280	$115,000.00
Hunter Mahan	T-9	67-71-67-75=280	$115,000.00
Steve Stricker	T-9	70-67-70-73=280	$115,000.00
Briny Baird	T-9	73-67-67-73=280	$115,000.00
Jeff Overton	T-9	72-68-71-69=280	$115,000.00

Valero Texas Open
Course: LaCantera G.C., San Antonio, Texas
Par: 70 Yardage: 6,881
Last day of event: Sunday, September 24, 2006

Player	Place	Score	Earnings
Eric Axley	Win	68-63-63-71=265	$720,000.00
Dean Wilson	T-2	66-67-66-69=268	$298,666.67
Justin Rose	T-2	64-71-65-68=268	$298,666.66
Anthony Kim	T-2	69-68-66-65=268	$298,666.67
Frank Lickliter II	T-5	67-66-65-71=269	$152,000.00
Chris Riley	T-5	70-64-64-71=269	$152,000.00
David McKenzie	7	65-68-68-69=270	$134,000.00
Charley Hoffman	T-8	66-67-67-71=271	$120,000.00
Paul Goydos	T-8	69-63-69-70=271	$120,000.00
Harrison Frazar	T-10	69-66-70-67=272	$104,000.00
Jose Coceres	T-10	68-73-68-63=272	$104,000.00

WGC-American Express Championship
Course: The Grove, Chandlers Cross, Hertfordshire, England
Par: 71 Yardage: 7,125
Last day of event: Sunday, October 1, 2006

Player	Place	Score	Earnings
Tiger Woods	Win	63-64-67-67=261	$1,300,000.00
Adam Scott	T-2	67-68-65-69=269	$610,000.00
Ian Poulter	T-2	64-71-68-66=269	$610,000.00
Jim Furyk	4	67-65-69-69=270	$345,000.00
Ernie Els	5	65-70-69-67=271	$290,000.00
Brett Wetterich	T-6	70-66-69-68=273	$216,666.67
Luke Donald	T-6	68-70-67-68=273	$216,666.66
Stuart Appleby	T-6	71-66-70-66=273	$216,666.67
Brett Quigley	T-9	70-64-67-73=274	$150,000.00
Trevor Immelman	T-9	68-68-68-70=274	$150,000.00
Thongchai Jaidee	T-9	71-67-71-65=274	$150,000.00

Southern Farm Bureau Classic
Course: Annandale G.C., Madison, Miss.
Par: 72 Yardage: 7,199
Last day of event: Sunday, October 1, 2006

Player	Place	Score	Earnings
D.J. Trahan	Win	65-68-71-71=275	$540,000.00
Playoff: Beat Joe Durant with birdie on third extra hole			
Joe Durant	2	70-65-74-66=275	$324,000.00
Lee Janzen	3	70-69-67-70=276	$204,000.00
J.P. Hayes	4	73-68-68-68=277	$144,000.00
Bo Van Pelt	T-5	69-70-70-69=278	$109,500.00
Ted Purdy	T-5	68-70-72-68=278	$109,500.00

Player	Place	Score	Earnings
Glen Day	T-5	67-72-73-66=278	$109,500.00
Nick Watney	T-8	67-71-71-70=279	$78,000.00
Robert Damron	T-8	69-69-71-70=279	$78,000.00
Troy Matteson	T-8	72-66-71-70=279	$78,000.00
Jason Gore	T-8	68-71-70-70=279	$78,000.00
Fred Funk	T-8	69-70-71-69=279	$78,000.00
Olin Browne	T-8	72-69-71-67=279	$78,000.00

Chrysler Classic of Greensboro
Course: Forest Oaks C.C., Greensboro, N.C.
Par: 72 Yardage: 7,333
Last day of event: Sunday, October 8, 2006

Player	Place	Score	Earnings
Davis Love III	Win	69-69-68-66=272	$900,000.00
Jason Bohn	2	69-69-70-66=274	$540,000.00
Steve Flesch	T-3	69-69-69-68=275	$290,000.00
Eric Axley	T-3	68-69-71-67=275	$290,000.00
Ryan Palmer	5	71-65-73-67=276	$200,000.00
Ryan Moore	T-6	67-70-71-69=277	$151,250.00
Joe Durant	T-6	67-71-70-69=277	$151,250.00
Daniel Chopra	T-6	68-74-66-69=277	$151,250.00
Lucas Glover	T-6	73-69-66-69=277	$151,250.00
Nick Watney	T-6	64-71-74-68=277	$151,250.00
Troy Matteson	T-6	71-68-70-68=277	$151,250.00

Frys.Com Open-Vegas
Course: TPC at Summerlin, TPC At The Canyons, Las Vegas, Nev.
Home course / TPC at Summerlin, Par: 72 Yardage: 7,243
Last day of event: Sunday, October 15, 2006

Player	Place	Score	Earnings
Troy Matteson	Win	67-65-64-69=265	$720,000.00
Daniel Chopra	T-2	69-67-64-66=266	$352,000.00
Ben Crane	T-2	66-71-64-65=266	$352,000.00
Frank Lickliter II	4	67-69-67-64=267	$192,000.00
Charley Hoffman	T-5	66-66-65-71=268	$152,000.00
Lee Janzen	T-5	70-66-66-66=268	$152,000.00
Tom Pernice, Jr.	T-7	66-65-70-68=269	$129,000.00
Bubba Dickerson	T-7	65-71-66-67=269	$129,000.00
Joey Sindelar	T-9	68-66-69-67=270	$112,000.00
Ron Whittaker	T-9	70-66-68-66=270	$112,000.00

FUNAI Classic at the Walt Disney World Resort
Course: Walt Disney (Magnolia, Palm), Lake Buena Vista, Fla.
Home course / Magnolia, Par: 72 Yardage: 7,516
Last day of event: Sunday, October 22, 2006

Player	Place	Score	Earnings
Joe Durant	Win	69-65-64-65=263	$828,000.00
Troy Matteson	T-2	67-65-65-70=267	$404,800.00
Frank Lickliter II	T-2	68-70-67-62=267	$404,800.00
Justin Rose	4	60-67-72-69=268	$220,800.00
Davis Love III	T-5	67-69-64-69=269	$161,575.00
Nick Watney	T-5	69-68-64-68=269	$161,575.00
Marco Dawson	T-5	67-66-69-67=269	$161,575.00
Vijay Singh	T-5	68-69-68-64=269	$161,575.00
Charles Howell III	T-9	65-70-65-70=270	$115,000.00
Heath Slocum	T-9	68-67-66-69=270	$115,000.00
Jerry Kelly	T-9	66-68-68-68=270	$115,000.00
Mark Calcavecchia	T-9	66-73-63-68=270	$115,000.00
Jesper Parnevik	T-9	68-69-68-65=270	$115,000.00

Chrysler Championship
Course: Westin Innisbrook Resort (Copperhead Course), Palm Harbor, Fla.
Par: 71 Yardage: 7,340
Last day of event: Sunday, October 29, 2006

Player	Place	Score	Earnings
K.J. Choi	Win	68-66-70-67=271	$954,000.00
Paul Goydos	T-2	68-68-69-70=275	$466,400.00
Brett Wetterich	T-2	72-70-67-66=275	$466,400.00
Jonathan Byrd	T-4	68-67-73-68=276	$233,200.00
Joe Durant	T-4	70-71-67-68=276	$233,200.00
Ernie Els	T-6	69-66-70-72=277	$177,550.00
Jesper Parnevik	T-6	72-71-68-66=277	$177,550.00
Rod Pampling	T-6	69-74-69-65=277	$177,550.00
Brian Gay	T-9	64-71-70-73=278	$148,400.00
Troy Matteson	T-9	70-72-64-72=278	$148,400.00

The Tour Championship
Course: East Lake G.C., Atlanta, Ga.
Par: 70 Yardage: 7,154
Last day of event: Sunday, November 5, 2006

Player	Place	Score	Earnings
Adam Scott	Win	69-67-67-66=269	$1,170,000.00
Jim Furyk	2	69-71-67-65=272	$730,000.00
Joe Durant	3	68-68-70-67=273	$480,000.00
Retief Goosen	4	68-71-68-67=274	$345,000.00
Trevor Immelman	T-5	73-66-69-69=277	$266,000.00
Tom Pernice, Jr.	T-5	69-72-67-69=277	$266,000.00
Luke Donald	T-5	73-67-69-68=277	$266,000.00
Vijay Singh	T-8	69-72-65-72=278	$215,000.00
Lucas Glover	T-8	73-71-66-68=278	$215,000.01
Ernie Els	T-10	71-72-66-72=281	$182,800.00
Stuart Appleby	T-10	69-70-72-70=281	$182,800.00

2007

Hoping to drum up interest in the waning weeks of the American golf season, the PGA Tour introduced the FedEx Cup Playoffs, a four-tournament stretch of limited-field events culminating in the Tour Championship and a deferred $10 million bonus to the winner of a season-long points scheme. To no one's surprise, Woods won the inaugural FedEx Cup even though he skipped the first playoff event—circumstances that exposed flaws in the system. Zach Johnson—a "normal guy" from Cedar Rapids, Iowa—won the Masters by two shots over Woods, Retief Goosen and Rory Sabbatini on an Augusta National course that measured 7,445 yards (520 yards longer than when Arnold Palmer won in 1958). The U.S. Open at Oakmont went to Angel Cabrera, a chain-smoking Argentinian who came up from the caddie yards. Cabrera posted a closing 69, then watched as Woods and Jim Furyk made valiant attempts to catch him, each coming up one shot short. Padraig Harrington became the first Irishman since Fred Daly 60 years earlier to win the British Open, closing with 67 (including double bogey at the 72nd hole) and beating Sergio Garcia (who bogeyed the 72nd) 15 to 16 in a four-hole aggregate playoff. Riding a third-round 63 and refusing to wilt in oppressive heat, Woods won the PGA Championship by two shots over Woody Austin at Southern Hills.

Mercedes Championshipss
Course: Kapalua Resort Plantation Course, Kapalua, Maui, Ha.
Par: 73 Yardage: 7,411
Last day of event: Sunday, January 7, 2007

Player	Place	Score	Earnings
Vijay Singh	Win	69-69-70-70=278	$1,100,000.00
Adam Scott	2	73-69-69-69=280	$630,000.00
Trevor Immelman	3	71-68-72-72=283	$410,000.00
Will MacKenzie	T-4	69-70-73-72=284	$260,000.00
J.B. Holmes	T-4	73-68-71-72=284	$260,000.00

Davis Love III	T-4	70-71-75-68=284	$260,000.00
Luke Donald	7	72-71-71-71=285	$193,000.00
J.J. Henry	T-8	74-73-68-71=286	$170,000.00
K.J. Choi	T-8	69-77-71-69=286	$170,000.00
David Toms	T-8	75-72-72-67=286	$170,000.00

Sony Open in Hawaii
Course: Waialae C.C., Honolulu, Ha.
Par: 70 Yardage: 7,044
Last day of event: Sunday, January 14, 2007

Player	Place	Score	Earnings
Paul Goydos	Win	66-63-70-67=266	$936,000.00
Charles Howell III	T-2	69-63-65-70=267	$457,600.00
Luke Donald	T-2	63-66-69-69=267	$457,600.00
Steve Stricker	T-4	67-67-67-70=271	$204,750.00
Jim Furyk	T-4	65-68-69-69=271	$204,750.00
K.J. Choi	T-4	64-71-68-68=271	$204,750.00
Doug LaBelle II	T-4	69-71-66-65=271	$204,750.00
Robert Allenby	T-8	67-66-70-69=272	$156,000.00
Geoff Ogilvy	T-8	67-72-69-64=272	$156,000.00
Craig Kanada	T-10	72-65-66-70=273	$130,000.00
Steve Lowery	T-10	72-67-67-67=273	$130,000.00
Pat Perez	T-10	68-70-69-66=273	$130,000.00

Bob Hope Chrysler Classic
Course: Classic Club, PGA West/Palmer, Bermuda Dunes C.C., La Quinta C.C.,
Palm Desert, Calif.
Home course / Classic Club, Par: 72 Yardage: 7,305
Last day of event: Sunday, January 21, 2007

Player	Place	Score	Earnings
Charley Hoffman	Win	66-70-68-68-71=343	$900,000.00

Playoff: Beat John Rollins with birdie on first extra hole

John Rollins	2	67-67-69-67-73=343	$540,000.00
Justin Rose	3	67-65-66-70-76=344	$340,000.00
Heath Slocum	T-4	68-68-69-68-72=345	$220,000.00
Jeff Quinney	T-4	68-69-69-66-73=345	$220,000.00
Charles Warren	T-6	71-67-67-69-72=346	$173,750.00
Cliff Kresge	T-6	72-68-68-66-72=346	$173,750.00
Mark Calcavecchia	T-8	65-70-75-68-69=347	$135,000.00
Harrison Frazar	T-8	68-71-68-69-71=347	$135,000.00
Scott Verplank	T-8	66-66-68-74-73=347	$135,000.00
Robert Allenby	T-8	63-70-70-70-74=347	$135,000.00
Dudley Hart	T-8	66-70-70-67-74=347	$135,000.00

Buick Invitational
Course: Torrey Pines (South), Torrey Pines (North), San Diego, Calif.
Home Course -Par: 72 Yardage: 7,568
Last day of event: Sunday, January 28, 2007

Player	Place	Score	Earnings
Tiger Woods	Win	66-72-69-66=273	$936,000.00
Charles Howell III	2	70-64-73-68=275	$561,600.00
Brandt Snedeker	3	61-70-74-71=276	$353,600.00
Andrew Buckle	T-4	66-71-68-72=277	$214,933.33
Mark Calcavecchia	T-4	66-74-68-69=277	$214,933.33
Bubba Watson	T-4	67-74-69-67=277	$214,933.34
Jeff Quinney	T-7	64-74-70-70=278	$167,700.00
Bart Bryant	T-7	66-73-70-69=278	$167,700.00
Charlie Wi	T-9	63-72-73-71=279	$130,000.00
Rich Beem	T-9	67-68-73-71=279	$130,000.00
Nick Watney	T-9	69-69-70-71=279	$130,000.00
Robert Allenby	T-9	70-70-71-68=279	$130,000.00
Ian Poulter	T-9	72-68-71-68=279	$130,000.00

FBR Open
Course: TPC of Scottsdale, Scottsdale, Ariz.
Par: 71 Yardage: 7,216
Last day of event: Sunday, February 4, 2007

Player	Place	Score	Earnings
Aaron Baddeley	Win	65-70-64-64=263	$1,080,000.00
John Rollins	2	65-68-68-63=264	$648,000.00
Jeff Quinney	3	66-63-68-68=265	$408,000.00
Bart Bryant	4	66-66-68-66=266	$288,000.00
Billy Mayfair	5	66-66-70-65=267	$240,000.00
Heath Slocum	6	67-68-67-66=268	$216,000.00
Vijay Singh	7	71-67-67-64=269	$201,000.00
Bubba Watson	T-8	66-67-69-68=270	$174,000.00
David Toms	T-8	65-69-68-68=270	$174,000.00
Dean Wilson	T-8	70-69-65-66=270	$174,000.00

AT&T Pebble Beach National Pro-Am
Courses: Pebble Beach G.L., Spyglass Hill G.C., Poppy Hills G.C., Pebble Beach, Calif.
Home Course/ Pebble Beach G.L., Par: 72 Yardage: 6,816
Last day of event: Sunday, February 11, 2007

Player	Place	Score	Earnings
Phil Mickelson	Win	65-67-70-66=268	$990,000.00
Kevin Sutherland	2	72-63-67-71=273	$594,000.00
John Mallinger	3	65-70-68-71=274	$374,000.00
Davis Love III	T-4	70-67-70-69=276	$242,000.00
Greg Owen	T-4	68-70-71-67=276	$242,000.00
Corey Pavin	T-6	68-72-67-70=277	$184,250.00
Jim Furyk	T-6	67-65-76-69=277	$184,250.00
Matt Kuchar	T-6	72-69-70-66=277	$184,250.00
Ryan Armour	T-9	68-71-72-67=278	$154,000.00
Ted Purdy	T-9	73-70-68-67=278	$154,000.00

Nissan Open
Course: Riviera C.C., Pacific Palisades, Calif.
Par: 71 Yardage: 7,279
Last day of event: Sunday, February 18, 2007

Player	Place	Score	Earnings
Charles Howell III	Win	69-65-69-65=268	$936,000.00

Playoff: Beat Phil Mickelson with par on third extra hole

Phil Mickelson	2	66-65-69-68=268	$561,600.00
Robert Allenby	T-3	69-66-68-68=271	$270,400.00
Jim Furyk	T-3	67-70-67-67=271	$270,400.00
Ernie Els	T-3	69-68-67-67=271	$270,400.00
Sergio Garcia	6	67-68-69-69=273	$187,200.00
Padraig Harrington	7	63-68-70-73=274	$174,200.00
Pat Perez	8	66-69-75-65=275	$161,200.00
Rory Sabbatini	T-9	69-70-67-70=276	$135,200.00
Jeff Quinney	T-9	70-70-67-69=276	$135,200.00
Rocco Mediate	T-9	71-66-71-68=276	$135,200.00
Anthony Kim	T-9	72-69-71-64=276	$135,200.00

WGC-Accenture Match Play Championship
Course: The Gallery At Dove Mountain (South Course), Marana, Ariz.
Par: 72 Yardage: 7,466
Last day of event: Sunday, February 25, 2007

Player	Place	Earnings
Henrik Stenson	Win	$1,350,000.00

Round One - Beat Zach Johnson 1 up
Round Two - Beat K.J. Choi 2 up
Round Three - Beat Aaron Baddeley 4 & 3

Quarterfinals - Beat Nick O'Hern 1 up
Semifinals - Beat Trevor Immelman 3 & 2
Finals - Beat Geoff Ogilvy 2 & 1

| Geoff Ogilvy | 2 | $800,000.00 |

Round One - Beat Steve Stricker 4 & 3
Round Two - Beat Jose Maria Olazabal 2 & 1
Round Three - Beat Niclas Fasth 2 & 1
Quarterfinals - Beat Paul Casey 5 & 4
Semifinals - Beat Chad Campbell 3 & 2
Finals - Henrik Stenson beat him 2 & 1

| Trevor Immelman | 3 | $575,000.00 |

Round One - Beat Thomas Bjorn 6 & 5
Round Two - Beat Chris DiMarco 3 & 1
Round Three - Beat Ian Poulter 2 & 1
Quarterfinals - Beat Justin Rose 5 & 4
Semifinals - Henrik Stenson beat him 3 & 2
Consolation - Beat Chad Campbell 4 & 2

| Chad Campbell | 4 | $475,000.00 |

Round One - Beat Angel Cabrera 1 up
Round Two - Beat Jim Furyk 19 holes
Round Three - Beat David Toms 1 up
Quarterfinals - Beat Stephen Ames 1 up
Semifinals - Geoff Ogilvy beat him 3 & 2
Consolation - Trevor Immelman beat him 4 & 2

| Nick O'Hern | T-5 | $260,000.00 |

Round One - Beat Lucas Glover 4 & 3
Round Two - Beat Rory Sabbatini 2 & 1
Round Three - Beat Tiger Woods 20 holes
Quarterfinals - Henrik Stenson beat him 1 up

| Justin Rose | T-5 | $260,000.00 |

Round One - Beat Michael Campbell 6 & 5
Round Two - Beat Phil Mickelson 3 & 1
Round Three - Beat Charles Howell III 3 & 2
Quarterfinals - Trevor Immelman beat him 5 & 4

| Paul Casey | T-5 | $260,000.00 |

Round One - Beat Mike Weir 1 up
Round Two - Beat Colin Montgomerie 2 & 1
Round Three - Beat Shaun Micheel 2 up
Quarterfinals - Geoff Ogilvy beat him 5 & 4

| Stephen Ames | T-5 | $260,000.00 |

Round One - Beat Robert Karlsson 2 & 1
Round Two - Beat Vijay Singh 19 holes
Round Three - Beat Stewart Cink 3 & 1
Quarterfinals - Chad Campbell beat him 1 up

| Tiger Woods | T-9 | $130,000.00 |

Round One - Beat J.J. Henry 3 & 2
Round Two - Beat Tim Clark 5 & 4
Round Three - Nick O'Hern beat him 20 holes

| Aaron Baddeley | T-9 | $130,000.00 |

Round One - Beat Shingo Katayama 1 up
Round Two - Beat Luke Donald 1 up
Round Three - Henrik Stenson beat him 4 & 3

| Niclas Fasth | T-9 | $130,000.00 |

Round One - Beat Joe Durant 1 up
Round Two - Beat Retief Goosen 1 up
Round Three - Geoff Ogilvy beat him 2 & 1

| Ian Poulter | T-9 | $130,000.00 |

Round One - Beat Bart Bryant 5 & 4
Round Two - Beat Bradley Dredge 3 & 1
Round Three - Trevor Immelman beat him 2 & 1

| Shaun Micheel | T-9 | $130,000.00 |

Round One - Beat Adam Scott 21 holes
Round Two - Beat Rod Pampling 1 up
Round Three - Paul Casey beat him 2 up

| David Toms | T-9 | $130,000.00 |

Round One - Beat Arron Oberholser 5 & 4
Round Two - Beat Ben Crane 3 & 2

Round Three - Chad Campbell beat him 1 up

| Stewart Cink | T-9 | $130,000.00 |

Round One - Beat Jeev M. Singh 3 & 2
Round Two - Beat Padraig Harrington 1 up
Round Three - Stephen Ames beat him 3 & 1

| Charles Howell III | T-9 | $130,000.00 |

Round One - Beat Stuart Appleby 4 & 3
Round Two - Beat Sergio Garcia 4 & 3
Round Three - Justin Rose beat him 3 & 2

Mayakoba Golf Classic
Course: El Camaleon, Quintana Roo,, Mexico
Par: 70 Yardage: 6,023
Last day of event: Sunday, February 25, 2007

Player	Place	Score	Earnings
Fred Funk	Win	62-69-64-71=266	$630,000.00
Playoff: Beat Jose Coceres with birdie on second extra hole			
Jose Coceres	2	67-65-65-69=266	$378,000.00
Peter Lonard	3	65-68-67-67=267	$238,000.00
Ryan Armour	4	68-65-69-66=268	$168,000.00
Bill Haas	5	66-66-70-67=269	$140,000.00
Boo Weekley	6	64-67-70-69=270	$126,000.00
Cameron Beckman	7	64-67-69-71=271	$117,250.00
Steve Marino	8	68-68-69-67=272	$108,500.00
Skip Kendall	T-9	69-69-63-72=273	$91,000.00
Gavin Coles	T-9	69-66-70-68=273	$91,000.00
Larry Mize	T-9	71-66-71-65=273	$91,000.00
Brendon de Jonge	T-9	69-71-68-65=273	$91,000.00

Honda Classic
Course: PGA National Resort (Champion Course), Palm Beach Gardens, Fla.
Par: 70 Yardage: 7,241
Last day of event: Monday, March 5, 2007

Player	Place	Score	Earnings
Mark Wilson	Win	72-66-66-71=275	$990,000.00
Playoff: Beat Jose Coceres with birdie on third extra hole (Boo Weekley and Camilo Villegas eliminated on second hole with bogeys)			
Boo Weekley	T-2	71-68-66-70=275	$410,666.67
Camilo Villegas	T-2	70-68-71-66=275	$410,666.66
Jose Coceres	T-2	69-71-69-66=275	$410,666.67
Steve Stricker	T-5	68-69-70-69=276	$200,750.00
Robert Allenby	T-5	67-68-73-68=276	$200,750.00
Tripp Isenhour	T-5	71-70-68-67=276	$200,750.00
Daniel Chopra	T-8	70-68-68-71=277	$165,000.00
Brett Wetterich	T-8	68-71-71-67=277	$165,000.00
Arron Oberholser	T-10	68-73-69-69=279	$137,500.00
Bernhard Langer	T-10	66-75-70-68=279	$137,500.00
J.P. Hayes	T-10	71-73-67-68=279	$137,500.00

PODS Championship
Course: Innisbrook Resort (Copperhead Course), Palm Harbor, Fla.
Par: 71 Yardage: 7,340
Last day of event: Sunday, March 11, 2007

Player	Place	Score	Earnings
Mark Calcavecchia	Win	75-67-62-70=274	$954,000.00
Heath Slocum	T-2	68-69-67-71=275	$466,400.00
John Senden	T-2	69-71-69-66=275	$466,400.00
Lucas Glover	T-4	72-68-67-69=276	$233,200.00
Brian Gay	T-4	69-72-66-69=276	$233,200.00
K.J. Choi	T-6	69-69-67-72=277	$184,175.00
Charles Howell III	T-6	70-74-68-65=277	$184,175.00

Player	Place	Score	Earnings
Stephen Leaney	T-8	69-67-72-70=278	$148,400.00
Ryan Moore	T-8	69-71-68-70=278	$148,400.00
J.B. Holmes	T-8	72-68-69-69=278	$148,400.00
Jonathan Byrd	T-8	69-69-72-68=278	$148,400.00

Arnold Palmer Invitational

Course: Bay Hill Club, Orlando, Fla.
Par: 70 Yardage: 7,137
Last day of event: Sunday, March 18, 2007

Player	Place	Score	Earnings
Vijay Singh	Win	70-68-67-67=272	$990,000.00
Rocco Mediate	2	66-65-76-67=274	$594,000.00
Vaughn Taylor	3	64-71-67-73=275	$374,000.00
Ben Curtis	4	68-67-69-72=276	$264,000.00
Tom Lehman	T-5	67-69-69-72=277	$200,750.00
John Rollins	T-5	69-65-72-71=277	$200,750.00
Sergio Garcia	T-5	66-69-71-71=277	$200,750.00
Luke Donald	8	68-71-70-69=278	$170,500.00
Trevor Immelman	T-9	66-70-70-73=279	$148,500.00
Jerry Kelly	T-9	67-69-70-73=279	$148,500.00
Stephen Ames	T-9	68-67-72-72=279	$148,500.00

WGC-CA Championship

Course: Doral C.C. (Blue), Miami, Fla.
Par: 72 Yardage: 7,266
Last day of event: Sunday, March 25, 2007

Player	Place	Score	Earnings
Tiger Woods	Win	71-66-68-73=278	$1,350,000.00
Brett Wetterich	2	72-70-67-71=280	$800,000.00
Sergio Garcia	T-3	71-70-71-70=282	$378,333.33
Geoff Ogilvy	T-3	72-69-71-70=282	$378,333.33
Robert Allenby	T-3	67-74-74-67=282	$378,333.34
Nick O'Hern	T-6	72-72-66-73=283	$212,500.00
Aaron Baddeley	T-6	69-71-71-72=283	$212,500.00
Niclas Fasth	T-6	72-70-70-71=283	$212,500.00
Paul Casey	T-9	76-70-66-72=284	$157,500.00
Zach Johnson	T-9	72-68-73-71=284	$157,500.00
Geoff Ogilvy	Win	65-67-68-71=271	$1,350,000.00
Jim Furyk	T-2	69-71-64-68=272	$530,000.00
Retief Goosen	T-2	71-69-64-68=272	$530,000.00
Vijay Singh	T-2	73-68-63-68=272	$530,000.00
Tiger Woods	5	67-66-72-68=273	$285,000.00
Graeme Storm	T-6	71-70-63-71=275	$198,333.33
Nick O'Hern	T-6	67-75-67-66=275	$198,333.33
Steve Stricker	T-6	71-68-73-63=275	$198,333.34
Adam Scott	T-9	67-68-69-72=276	$147,500.00
Zach Johnson	T-9	69-72-67-68=276	$147,500.00

Shell Houston Open

Course: Redstone G.C. (Tournament Course), Humble, Texas
Par: 72 Yardage: 7,457
Last day of event: Sunday, April 1, 2007

Player	Place	Score	Earnings
Adam Scott	Win	69-71-65-66=271	$990,000.00
Bubba Watson	T-2	71-67-64-72=274	$484,000.00
Stuart Appleby	T-2	66-72-67-69=274	$484,000.00
Tommy Armour III	4	68-71-70-66=275	$264,000.00
Hunter Mahan	T-5	68-71-68-69=276	$200,750.00
Anthony Kim	T-5	70-73-66-67=276	$200,750.00
Robert Garrigus	T-5	69-72-70-65=276	$200,750.00
D.J. Trahan	8	71-72-66-68=277	$170,500.00

Player	Place	Score	Earnings
Johnson Wagner	T-9	66-75-64-73=278	$137,500.00
Bob Estes	T-9	67-71-69-71=278	$137,500.00
Bernhard Langer	T-9	71-70-67-70=278	$137,500.00
Steve Stricker	T-9	68-73-68-69=278	$137,500.00
Arron Oberholser	T-9	70-71-69-68=278	$137,500.00

Masters

Course: Augusta National G.C., Augusta, Ga.
Par: 72 Yardage: 7,445
Last day of event: Sunday, April 8, 2007

Player	Place	Score	Earnings
Zach Johnson	Win	71-73-76-69=289	$130.00
Tiger Woods	T-2	73-74-72-72=291	$541,333.00
Rory Sabbatini	T-2	73-76-73-69=291	$541,333.00
Retief Goosen	T-2	76-76-70-69=291	$541,333.00
Justin Rose	T-5	69-75-75-73=292	$275,500.00
Jerry Kelly	T-5	75-69-78-70=292	$275,500.00
Stuart Appleby	T-7	75-70-73-75=293	$233,812.00
Padraig Harrington	T-7	77-68-75-73=293	$233,812.00
David Toms	9	70-78-74-72=294	$210,250.00
Vaughn Taylor	T-10	71-72-77-75=295	$181,250.00
Luke Donald	T-10	73-74-75-73=295	$181,250.00
Paul Casey	T-10	79-68-77-71=295	$181,250.00

Verizon Heritage

Course: Harbour Town G.L., Hilton Head, S.C.
Par: 71 Yardage: 6,973
Last day of event: Monday, April 16, 2007

Player	Place	Score	Earnings
Boo Weekley	Win	67-69-66-68=270	$972,000.00
Ernie Els	2	65-65-71-70=271	$583,200.00
Stephen Leaney	3	66-68-70-68=272	$367,200.00
Kevin Na	T-4	67-68-66-73=274	$237,600.00
Vaughn Taylor	T-4	71-66-67-70=274	$237,600.00
Zach Johnson	6	70-68-66-71=275	$194,400.00
Sean O'Hair	7	69-66-69-72=276	$180,900.00
Jerry Kelly	T-8	63-70-67-77=277	$162,000.00
Carl Pettersson	T-8	71-68-67-71=277	$162,000.00
Dean Wilson	T-10	69-68-68-73=278	$124,200.00
Ken Duke	T-10	71-67-67-73=278	$124,200.00
Aaron Baddeley	T-10	70-66-70-72=278	$124,200.00
Tom Pernice, Jr.	T-10	74-67-65-72=278	$124,200.00
Bo Van Pelt	T-10	71-67-70-70=278	$124,200.00

Zurich Classic of New Orleans

Course: TPC Louisiana, Avondale, La.
Par: 72 Yardage: 7,341
Last day of event: Sunday, April 22, 2007

Player	Place	Score	Earnings
Nick Watney	Win	69-67-68-69=273	$1,098,000.00
Ken Duke	2	69-71-66-70=276	$658,800.00
John Mallinger	T-3	69-70-71-67=277	$353,800.00
Anthony Kim	T-3	71-72-69-65=277	$353,800.00
Mark Calcavecchia	T-5	66-69-72-71=278	$222,650.00
Chris Stroud	T-5	68-70-71-69=278	$222,650.00
Bubba Watson	T-5	72-67-70-69=278	$222,650.00
Lucas Glover	T-8	67-69-74-69=279	$176,900.00
Bob Estes	T-8	69-71-70-69=279	$176,900.00
Alex Cejka	T-8	70-72-69-68=279	$176,900.00

EDS Byron Nelson Championship

Course: TPC at Las Colinas, Cottonwood Valley Course, Irving, Texas
Home course / TPC at Las Colinas, Par: 70 Yardage: 7,022
Last day of event: Sunday, April 29, 2007

Player	Place	Score	Earnings
Scott Verplank	Win	67-68-66-66=267	$1,134,000.00
Luke Donald	2	67-66-67-68=268	$680,400.00
Ian Poulter	T-3	70-69-65-66=270	$302,400.00
Phil Mickelson	T-3	69-70-66-65=270	$302,400.00
Jerry Kelly	T-3	69-70-67-64=270	$302,400.00
Rory Sabbatini	T-3	70-69-67-64=270	$302,400.00
Fredrik Jacobson	T-7	67-67-71-66=271	$203,175.00
Ken Duke	T-7	68-73-64-66=271	$203,175.00
Ryuji Imada	9	70-68-67-67=272	$182,700.00
Brett Wetterich	T-10	66-68-72-67=273	$157,500.00
Steve Marino	T-10	69-67-70-67=273	$157,500.00
Rod Pampling	T-10	68-70-69-66=273	$157,500.00

Wachovia Championship

Course: Quail Hollow Club, Charlotte, N.C.
Par: 72 Yardage: 7,442
Last day of event: Sunday, May 6, 2007

Player	Place	Score	Earnings
Tiger Woods	Win	70-68-68-69=275	$1,134,000.00
Steve Stricker	2	72-70-66-69=277	$680,400.00
Rory Sabbatini	T-3	70-71-64-74=279	$365,400.00
Phil Mickelson	T-3	70-71-68-70=279	$365,400.00
Stewart Cink	T-5	70-71-69-70=280	$239,400.00
Anthony Kim	T-5	72-69-69-70=280	$239,400.00
Vijay Singh	T-7	67-71-69-74=281	$196,350.00
Arron Oberholser	T-7	69-69-69-74=281	$196,350.00
Ken Duke	T-7	70-70-68-73=281	$196,350.00
John Senden	T-10	72-70-69-72=283	$151,200.00
Billy Mayfair	T-10	73-71-67-72=283	$151,200.00
Brett Quigley	T-10	70-74-69-70=283	$151,200.00
Bernhard Langer	T-10	70-73-71-69=283	$151,200.00

The Players

Course: TPC Sawgrass, Ponte Vedra Beach, Fla.
Par: 72 Yardage: 7,215
Last day of event: Sunday, May 13, 2007

Player	Place	Score	Earnings
Phil Mickelson	Win	67-72-69-69=277	$1,620,000.00
Sergio Garcia	2	73-73-67-66=279	$972,000.00
Jose Maria Olazabal	T-3	78-66-69-67=280	$522,000.00
Stewart Cink	T-3	74-69-71-66=280	$522,000.00
Jose Coceres	5	73-70-68-70=281	$360,000.00
Peter Lonard	T-6	69-72-68-73=282	$281,700.00
Jeff Quinney	T-6	71-74-64-73=282	$281,700.00
J.P. Hayes	T-6	71-73-68-70=282	$281,700.00
Adam Scott	T-6	74-71-70-67=282	$281,700.00
Robert Karlsson	T-6	77-68-71-66=282	$281,700.00

AT&T Classic

Course: TPC at Sugarloaf, Duluth, Ga.
Par: 72 Yardage: 7,343
Last day of event: Sunday, May 20, 2007

Player	Place	Score	Earnings
Zach Johnson	Win	71-66-69-67=273	$972,000.00

Playoff: Beat Ryuji Imada with birdie on first extra hole

Ryuji Imada	2	67-67-69-70=273	$583,200.00
Troy Matteson	T-3	70-64-69-73=276	$280,800.00
Camilo Villegas	T-3	70-67-68-71=276	$280,800.00
Matt Kuchar	T-3	70-72-64-70=276	$280,800.00
Steve Marino	T-6	67-71-69-70=277	$180,900.00
Bob Estes	T-6	71-69-67-70=277	$180,900.00
Chris Tidland	T-6	71-67-71-68=277	$180,900.00
Jonathan Byrd	T-9	69-72-68-69=278	$135,000.00
Robert Gamez	T-9	70-69-71-68=278	$135,000.00
Henrik Stenson	T-9	70-69-71-68=278	$135,000.00
Briny Baird	T-9	69-71-70-68=278	$135,000.00
Olin Browne	T-9	69-69-74-66=278	$135,000.00

Crowne Plaza Invitational at Colonial

Course: Colonial C.C., Fort Worth, Texas
Par: 70 Yardage: 7,054
Last day of event: Sunday, May 27, 2007

Player	Place	Score	Earnings
Rory Sabbatini	Win	70-67-62-67=266	$1,080,000.00

Playoff: Beat Jim Furyk and Bernhard Langer with birdie on first extra hole

Jim Furyk	T-2	65-66-68-67=266	$528,000.00
Bernhard Langer	T-2	65-68-66-67=266	$528,000.00
Pat Perez	4	66-67-69-66=268	$288,000.00
Tom Lehman	T-5	66-67-68-68=269	$228,000.00
Nathan Green	T-5	65-66-72-66=269	$228,000.00
Scott Verplank	T-7	70-66-63-71=270	$174,600.00
Kevin Na	T-7	63-69-70-68=270	$174,600.00
D.J. Trahan	T-7	67-67-69-67=270	$174,600.00
Jerry Kelly	T-7	70-64-69-67=270	$174,600.00
Harrison Frazar	T-7	68-67-69-66=270	$174,600.00

Memorial Tournament

Course: Muirfield Village G.C., Dubin, Ohio
Par: 72 Yardage: 7,366
Last day of event: Sunday, June 3, 2007

Player	Place	Score	Earnings
K.J. Choi	Win	69-70-67-65=271	$1,080,000.00
Ryan Moore	2	66-69-71-66=272	$648,000.00
Rod Pampling	T-3	65-68-68-72=273	$348,000.00
Kenny Perry	T-3	69-74-67-63=273	$348,000.00
Adam Scott	T-5	70-62-72-70=274	$210,750.00
Sean O'Hair	T-5	65-70-69-70=274	$210,750.00
Stewart Cink	T-5	69-71-65-69=274	$210,750.00
Fredrik Jacobson	T-5	68-68-70-68=274	$210,750.00
Aaron Baddeley	T-9	66-68-71-71=276	$168,000.00
Geoff Ogilvy	T-9	70-67-69-70=276	$168,000.00

Stanford St. Jude Classic

Course: TPC at Southwind, Germantown, Tenn.
Par: 70 Yardage: 7,239
Last day of event: Sunday, June 10, 2007

Player	Place	Score	Earnings
Woody Austin	Win	72-66-67-62=267	$1,080,000.00
Brian Davis	2	70-68-68-66=272	$648,000.00
David Toms	3	70-68-66-69=273	$408,000.00
Brian Gay	4	68-66-70-70=274	$288,000.00
Brandt Snedeker	T-5	70-68-69-68=275	$228,000.00
Dean Wilson	T-5	70-71-66-68=275	$228,000.00
Adam Scott	7	67-66-68-75=276	$201,000.00
Will MacKenzie	T-8	71-69-67-70=277	$180,000.00
Scott Verplank	T-8	69-69-70-69=277	$180,000.00

Vance Veazey	T-10	73-71-67-67=278	$156,000.00
Jeff Overton	T-10	71-71-70-66=278	$156,000.00

U.S. Open

Course: Oakmont C.C., Oakmont, Pa.
Par: 70 Yardage: 7,257
Last day of event: Sunday, June 17, 2007

Player	Place	Score	Earnings
Angel Cabrera	Win	69-71-76-69=285	$1,260,000.00
Tiger Woods	T-2	71-74-69-72=286	$611,336.00
Jim Furyk	T-2	71-75-70-70=286	$611,336.00
Niclas Fasth	4	71-71-75-70=287	$325,923.00
Bubba Watson	T-5	70-71-74-74=289	$248,948.00
David Toms	T-5	72-72-73-72=289	$248,948.00
Scott Verplank	T-7	73-71-74-72=290	$194,245.00
Jerry Kelly	T-7	74-71-73-72=290	$194,245.00
Nick Dougherty	T-7	68-77-74-71=290	$194,245.00
Justin Rose	T-10	71-71-73-76=291	$154,093.00
Stephen Ames	T-10	73-69-73-76=291	$154,093.00
Paul Casey	T-10	77-66-72-76=291	$154,093.00

Travelers Championship

Course: TPC at River Highlands, Cromwell, Conn.
Par: 70 Yardage: 6,820
Last day of event: Sunday, June 24, 2007

Player	Place	Score	Earnings
Hunter Mahan	Win	62-71-67-65=265	$1,080,000.00
Playoff: Beat Jay Williamson with birdie on first extra hole			
Jay Williamson	2	66-66-67-66=265	$648,000.00
Nick O'Hern	3	67-70-66-66=269	$408,000.00
Vijay Singh	4	68-71-66-65=270	$288,000.00
Fred Funk	5	70-65-67-69=271	$240,000.00
David Toms	T-6	67-65-69-71=272	$201,000.00
Tom Lehman	T-6	67-68-70-67=272	$201,000.00
Bo Van Pelt	T-6	73-68-67-64=272	$201,000.00
Justin Rose	T-9	69-68-68-68=273	$156,000.00
Billy Mayfair	T-9	67-72-66-68=273	$156,000.00
Kevin Na	T-9	70-67-69-67=273	$156,000.00
B.J. Staten	T-9	67-71-69-66=273	$156,000.00

Buick Open

Course: Warwick Hills C.C., Grand Blanc, Mich.
Par: 72 Yardage: 7,127
Last day of event: Sunday, July 1, 2007

Player	Place	Score	Earnings
Brian Bateman	Win	65-70-69-69=273	$882,000.00
Woody Austin	T-2	65-71-69-69=274	$365,866.66
Jason Gore	T-2	71-66-70-67=274	$365,866.67
Justin Leonard	T-2	69-72-66-67=274	$365,866.67
Scott Verplank	T-5	66-69-69-71=275	$166,110.00
Jim Furyk	T-5	66-68-71-70=275	$166,110.00
Steve Elkington	T-5	66-70-71-68=275	$166,110.00
Marco Dawson	T-5	68-71-68-68=275	$166,110.00
John Rollins	T-5	70-71-67-67=275	$166,110.00
Kenny Perry	T-10	71-63-71-71=276	$108,616.66
Fredrik Jacobson	T-10	68-70-67-71=276	$108,616.66
Lucas Glover	T-10	68-68-70-70=276	$108,616.67
Gavin Coles	T-10	68-70-68-70=276	$108,616.67
Brandt Snedeker	T-10	71-69-66-70=276	$108,616.67
Steve Marino	T-10	69-70-68-69=276	$108,616.67

AT&T National

Course: Congressional C.C. (Blue Course), Bethesda, Md.
Par: 70 Yardage: 7,255
Last day of event: Sunday, July 8, 2007

Player	Place	Score	Earnings
K.J. Choi	Win	66-67-70-68=271	$1,080,000.00
Steve Stricker	2	67-70-67-70=274	$648,000.00
Stuart Appleby	T-3	66-67-68-76=277	$312,000.00
Jim Furyk	T-3	66-74-68-69=277	$312,000.00
Pat Perez	T-3	71-70-69-67=277	$312,000.00
Tiger Woods	T-6	73-66-69-70=278	$208,500.00
Robert Allenby	T-6	70-71-69-68=278	$208,500.00
Mike Weir	T-8	72-66-67-74=279	$168,000.00
Brandt Snedeker	T-8	69-72-70-68=279	$168,000.00
Rocco Mediate	T-8	75-68-70-66=279	$168,000.00
Hunter Mahan	T-8	70-74-70-65=279	$168,000.00

John Deere Classic

Course: TPC at Deere Run, Silvis, Ill.
Par: 71 Yardage: 7,268
Last day of event: Sunday, July 15, 2007

Player	Place	Score	Earnings
Jonathan Byrd	Win	67-68-65-66=266	$738,000.00
Tim Clark	2	68-65-66-68=267	$442,800.00
Nathan Green	T-3	67-63-68-71=269	$237,800.00
Troy Matteson	T-3	69-67-67-66=269	$237,800.00
Carl Pettersson	5	67-64-71-68=270	$164,000.00
Neal Lancaster	T-6	64-68-70-69=271	$128,330.00
Jason Dufner	T-6	65-66-72-68=271	$128,330.00
Kevin Sutherland	T-6	66-67-70-68=271	$128,330.00
Jeff Gove	T-6	69-68-66-68=271	$128,330.00
Heath Slocum	T-6	70-69-67-65=271	$128,330.00

British Open

Course: Carnoustie G.C., Carnoustie, Angus, Scotland
Par: 71 Yardage: 7,421
Last day of event: Sunday, July 22, 2007

Player	Place	Score	Earnings
Padraig Harrington	Win	69-73-68-67=277	$1,542,450.00
Playoff: Won four-hole aggregate playoff (3-3-4-5=15) with Sergio Garcia (5-3-4-4=16)			
Sergio Garcia	2	65-71-68-73=277	$925,470.00
Andres Romero	3	71-70-70-67=278	$596,414.00
Ernie Els	T-4	72-70-68-69=279	$411,320.00
Richard Green	T-4	72-73-70-64=279	$411,320.00
Stewart Cink	T-6	69-73-68-70=280	$299,235.30
Hunter Mahan	T-6	73-73-69-65=280	$299,235.30
Steve Stricker	T-8	71-72-64-74=281	$194,862.85
K.J. Choi	T-8	69-69-72-71=281	$194,862.85
Mike Weir	T-8	71-68-72-70=281	$194,862.85
Ben Curtis	T-8	72-74-70-65=281	$194,862.85

U.S. Bank Championship in Milwaukee

Course: Brown Deer Park G.C., Milwaukee, Wis.
Par: 70 Yardage: 7,361
Last day of event: Sunday, July 22, 2007

Player	Place	Score	Earnings
Joe Ogilvie	Win	67-63-69-67=266	$720,000.00
Tim Herron	T-2	66-67-65-72=270	$298,666.67
Tim Clark	T-2	68-65-66-71=270	$298,666.66

Charlie Wi	T-2	70-66-66-68=270	$298,666.67
Kenny Perry	T-5	69-65-67-71=272	$140,500.00
Jeff Maggert	T-5	63-69-71-69=272	$140,500.00
Steve Flesch	T-5	69-64-71-68=272	$140,500.00
Bob Heintz	T-5	69-64-71-68=272	$140,500.00
Billy Mayfair	T-9	69-64-70-70=273	$104,000.00
Jeff Sluman	T-9	71-67-65-70=273	$104,000.00
Craig Bowden	T-9	66-67-71-69=273	$104,000.00
Mark Wilson	T-9	67-70-67-69=273	$104,000.00

Canadian Open

Course: Angus Glen Golf Club (North Course), Markham, Ontario, Canada
Par: 71 Yardage: 7,320
Last day of event: Sunday, July 29, 2007

Player	Place	Score	Earnings
Jim Furyk	Win	69-66-69-64=268	$900,000.00
Vijay Singh	2	68-65-68-68=269	$540,000.00
Ryan Palmer	T-3	67-67-71-66=271	$290,000.00
George McNeill	T-3	70-69-66-66=271	$290,000.00
Hunter Mahan	T-5	62-74-67-69=272	$190,000.00
Bob Heintz	T-5	69-69-67-67=272	$190,000.00
Steve Allan	T-7	64-68-70-71=273	$155,833.33
John Mallinger	T-7	66-66-70-71=273	$155,833.33
Brandt Snedeker	T-7	67-68-70-68=273	$155,833.34
Pat Perez	T-10	68-70-66-70=274	$115,000.00
Tom Pernice, Jr.	T-10	68-68-69-69=274	$115,000.00
Paul Gow	T-10	70-69-67-68=274	$115,000.00
Camilo Villegas	T-10	68-68-72-66=274	$115,000.00
Alex Cejka	T-10	69-70-71-64=274	$115,000.00

WGC-Bridgestone Invitational

Course: Firestone C.C. (South), Akron, Ohio
Par: 70 Yardage: 7,400
Last day of event: Sunday, August 5, 2007

Player	Place	Score	Earnings
Tiger Woods	Win	68-70-69-65=272	$1,350,000.00
Rory Sabbatini	T-2	67-67-72-74=280	$635,000.00
Justin Rose	T-2	69-72-71-68=280	$635,000.00
Chris DiMarco	T-4	69-70-72-70=281	$310,000.00
Peter Lonard	T-4	70-70-73-68=281	$310,000.00
Andres Romero	T-6	71-71-69-71=282	$202,000.00
Davis Love III	T-6	74-65-74-69=282	$202,000.00
Tim Clark	T-6	71-70-72-69=282	$202,000.00
Scott Verplank	T-9	70-68-73-72=283	$147,500.00
Justin Leonard	T-9	73-67-71-72=283	$147,500.00

Reno-Tahoe Open

Course: Montreux G. & C.C., Reno, Nev.
Par: 72 Yardage: 7,472
Last day of event: Sunday, August 5, 2007

Player	Place	Score	Earnings
Steve Flesch	Win	63-69-69-72=273	$540,000.00
Charles Warren	T-2	71-63-73-71=278	$264,000.00
Kevin Stadler	T-2	74-67-67-70=278	$264,000.00
John Merrick	T-4	65-73-68-74=280	$132,000.00
Rich Barcelo	T-4	71-72-69-68=280	$132,000.00
Steve Elkington	T-6	69-70-69-73=281	$100,500.00
Brendon de Jonge	T-6	67-70-72-72=281	$100,500.00
Shaun Micheel	T-6	68-70-71-72=281	$100,500.00
Todd Fischer	T-9	69-68-69-76=282	$81,000.00
Brian Davis	T-9	68-73-71-70=282	$81,000.00
Michael Allen	T-9	70-72-70-70=282	$81,000.00

PGA Championship

Course: Southern Hills C.C., Tulsa, Ok.
Par: 70 Yardage: 7,131
Last day of event: Sunday, August 12, 2007

Player	Place	Score	Earnings
Tiger Woods	Win	71-63-69-69=272	$1,260,000.00
Woody Austin	2	68-70-69-67=274	$756,000.00
Ernie Els	3	72-68-69-66=275	$476,000.00
John Senden	T-4	69-70-69-71=279	$308,000.00
Arron Oberholser	T-4	68-72-70-69=279	$308,000.00
Geoff Ogilvy	T-6	69-68-74-69=280	$227,500.00
Trevor Immelman	T-6	75-70-66-69=280	$227,500.00
Simon Dyson	T-6	73-71-72-64=280	$227,500.00
Scott Verplank	T-9	70-66-74-71=281	$170,333.34
Kevin Sutherland	T-9	73-69-68-71=281	$170,333.33
Boo Weekley	T-9	76-69-65-71=281	$170,333.33

Wyndham Championship

Course: Forest Oaks C.C., Greensboro, N.C.
Par: 72 Yardage: 7,333
Last day of event: Sunday, August 19, 2007

Player	Place	Score	Earnings
Brandt Snedeker	Win	70-67-66-63=266	$900,000.00
Jeff Overton	T-2	65-67-66-70=268	$373,333.33
Tim Petrovic	T-2	68-65-68-67=268	$373,333.33
Billy Mayfair	T-2	69-68-64-67=268	$373,333.34
Carl Pettersson	5	66-67-68-68=269	$200,000.00
Greg Kraft	6	66-67-71-66=270	$180,000.00
Shigeki Maruyama	T-7	66-69-67-69=271	$150,625.00
Will MacKenzie	T-7	64-71-68-68=271	$150,625.00
Jason Gore	T-7	67-68-69-67=271	$150,625.00
Kevin Stadler	T-7	68-67-70-66=271	$150,625.00

Barclays Classic (FedEx Cup Playoffs)

Course: Westchester C.C., Harrison, N.Y.
Par: 71 Yardage: 6,839
Last day of event: Sunday, August 26, 2007

Player	Place	Score	Earnings
Steve Stricker	Win	67-67-65-69=268	$1,260,000.00
K.J. Choi	2	64-66-70-70=270	$756,000.00
Rory Sabbatini	3	63-71-69-68=271	$476,000.00
Geoff Ogilvy	T-4	68-66-69-69=272	$289,333.33
Ernie Els	T-4	65-71-68-68=272	$289,333.33
Mark Calcavecchia	T-4	67-75-65-65=272	$289,333.34
Rich Beem	T-7	64-68-69-72=273	$225,750.00
Phil Mickelson	T-7	67-70-69-67=273	$225,750.00
Jerry Kelly	T-9	67-70-69-68=274	$189,000.00
Ian Poulter	T-9	70-67-70-67=274	$189,000.00
Robert Garrigus	T-9	70-70-68-66=274	$189,000.00

Deutsche Bank Championship (FexEx Cup Playoffs)

Course: TPC of Boston, Norton, Mass.
Par: 71 Yardage: 7,207
Last day of event: Monday, September 3, 2007

Player	Place	Score	Earnings
Phil Mickelson	Win	70-64-68-66=268	$1,260,000.00
Brett Wetterich	T-2	66-68-66-70=270	$522,666.67
Arron Oberholser	T-2	69-66-66-69=270	$522,666.66
Tiger Woods	T-2	72-64-67-67=270	$522,666.67
Aaron Baddeley	5	67-66-70-70=273	$280,000.00

Rory Sabbatini	T-6	68-67-70-69=274	$243,250.00
Geoff Ogilvy	T-6	70-70-67-67=274	$243,250.00
Robert Allenby	8	69-69-70-67=275	$217,000.00
Camilo Villegas	T-9	63-72-69-72=276	$175,000.00
Steve Stricker	T-9	67-69-69-71=276	$175,000.00
Troy Matteson	T-9	71-66-69-70=276	$175,000.00
Sean O'Hair	T-9	68-66-74-68=276	$175,000.00
Fredrik Jacobson	T-9	66-72-70-68=276	$175,000.00

BMW Championship (FedEx Cup Playoffs)

Course: Cog Hill G. & C.C. (Dubsdread), Lemont, Ill.
Par: 71 Yardage: 7,326
Last day of event: Sunday, September 9, 2007

Player	Place	Score	Earnings
Tiger Woods	Win	67-67-65-63=262	$1,260,000.00
Aaron Baddeley	2	68-65-65-66=264	$756,000.00
Steve Stricker	3	68-66-64-68=266	$480,000.00
Adam Scott	4	69-69-67-65=270	$340,000.00
Justin Rose	T-5	65-69-69-68=271	$270,000.00
Tim Clark	T-5	68-69-67-67=271	$270,000.00
Camilo Villegas	T-7	65-69-71-67=272	$229,000.00
Stewart Cink	T-7	66-73-68-65=272	$229,000.00
Sergio Garcia	9	68-70-69-67=274	$206,000.00
Jonathan Byrd	T-10	64-69-71-71=275	$171,000.00
Carl Pettersson	T-10	71-68-69-67=275	$171,000.00
Ian Poulter	T-10	68-72-69-66=275	$171,000.00
Rory Sabbatini	T-10	69-72-68-66=275	$171,000.00

The Tour Championship (FecEx Cup Final)

Course: East Lake G.C., Atlanta, Ga.
Par: 70 Yardage: 7,154
Last day of event: Sunday, September 16, 2007

Player	Place	Score	Earnings
Tiger Woods	Win	64-63-64-66=257	$1,260,000.00
Mark Calcavecchia	T-2	65-66-63-71=265	$619,500.00
Zach Johnson	T-2	71-66-60-68=265	$619,500.00
Sergio Garcia	4	68-64-64-70=266	$336,000.00
Hunter Mahan	T-5	65-68-65-71=269	$266,000.00
Scott Verplank	T-5	66-68-67-68=269	$266,000.00
Tim Clark	T-7	62-69-70-69=270	$231,000.00
Vijay Singh	T-7	68-68-65-69=270	$231,000.00
Rory Sabbatini	T-9	68-68-67-68=271	$204,400.00
Camilo Villegas	T-9	67-68-70-66=271	$204,400.00

Turning Stone Resort Championship

Course: Atunyote Golf Club, Verona,, N.Y.
Par: 72 Yardage: 7,482
Last day of event: Sunday, September 23, 2007

Player	Place	Score	Earnings
Steve Flesch	Win	66-65-66-73=270	$1,080,000.00
Michael Allen	2	69-67-68-68=272	$648,000.00
John Mallinger	T-3	67-70-68-68=273	$348,000.00
John Senden	T-3	66-70-70-67=273	$348,000.00
Carl Pettersson	T-5	69-66-66-73=274	$203,400.00
Parker McLachlin	T-5	70-68-65-71=274	$203,400.00
Charley Hoffman	T-5	69-65-71-69=274	$203,400.00
Mathew Goggin	T-5	66-69-70-69=274	$203,400.00
Tommy Armour III	T-5	70-68-68-68=274	$203,400.00
Charles Warren	T-10	68-65-68-74=275	$156,000.00
Bill Haas	T-10	69-66-69-71=275	$156,000.00

Viking Classic

Course: Annandale G.C., Madison, Miss.
Par: 72 Yardage: 7,199
Last day of event: Sunday, September 30, 2007

Player	Place	Score	Earnings
Chad Campbell	Win	70-72-64-69=275	$630,000.00
Johnson Wagner	2	73-65-68-70=276	$378,000.00
Bill Haas	T-3	68-67-70-72=277	$203,000.00
Boo Weekley	T-3	68-69-70-70=277	$203,000.00
David Branshaw	T-5	66-68-69-75=278	$127,750.00
Shaun Micheel	T-5	70-68-68-72=278	$127,750.00
John Senden	T-5	68-69-71-70=278	$127,750.00
Kent Jones	T-8	71-70-67-71=279	$101,500.00
Alex Cejka	T-8	69-72-68-70=279	$101,500.00
Bo Van Pelt	T-8	70-71-68-70=279	$101,500.00

Valero Texas Open

Course: LaCantera G.C., San Antonio, Texas
Par: 70 Yardage: 6,881
Last day of event: Sunday, October 7, 2007

Player	Place	Score	Earnings
Justin Leonard	Win	65-67-64-65=261	$810,000.00
Playoff: Beat Jesper Parnevik with birdie on third extra hole			
Jesper Parnevik	2	61-65-74-61=261	$486,000.00
Mathias Gronberg	T-3	65-65-65-69=264	$261,000.00
Daniel Chopra	T-3	65-69-64-66=264	$261,000.00
Heath Slocum	5	69-65-70-62=266	$180,000.00
Ryan Armour	T-6	67-67-64-69=267	$140,850.00
Chris Stroud	T-6	69-65-64-69=267	$140,850.00
Dan Forsman	T-6	65-68-67-67=267	$140,850.00
Dean Wilson	T-6	68-67-66-66=267	$140,850.00
J.J. Henry	T-6	71-65-67-64=267	$140,850.00

Frys.Com Open-Vegas

Course: TPC at Summerlin, TPC At The Canyons, Las Vegas, Nev.
Home course / TPC at Summerlin, Par: 72 Yardage: 7,243
Last day of event: Sunday, October 14, 2007

Player	Place	Score	Earnings
George McNeill	Win	66-64-67-67=264	$720,000.00
D.J. Trahan	2	65-65-72-66=268	$432,000.00
Robert Garrigus	T-3	71-63-68-70=272	$232,000.00
Cameron Beckman	T-3	65-71-68-68=272	$232,000.00
Bo Van Pelt	T-5	66-69-68-70=273	$152,000.00
Bob May	T-5	63-70-71-69=273	$152,000.00
Garrett Willis	T-7	68-62-73-71=274	$124,666.66
Mathias Gronberg	T-7	69-64-71-70=274	$124,666.67
Jason Gore	T-7	63-68-73-70=274	$124,666.67
Joe Ogilvie	T-10	71-65-71-68=275	$96,000.00
Mark Wilson	T-10	66-67-71-71=275	$96,000.00
Kent Jones	T-10	68-67-68-72=275	$96,000.00
Mike Weir	T-10	69-67-69-70=275	$96,000.00

Fry's Electronics Open

Course: Grayhawk Golf Club (Raptor Course), Scottsdale, Ariz.
Par: 70 Yardage: 7,125
Last day of event: Sunday, October 21, 2007

Player	Place	Score	Earnings
Mike Weir	Win	69-64-65-68=266	$900,000.00
Mark Hensby	2	71-61-66-69=267	$540,000.00
Billy Mayfair	3	68-66-68-68=270	$340,000.00

Carl Pettersson	T-4	67-66-64-74=271	$220,000.00
Sean O'Hair	T-4	68-66-68-69=271	$220,000.00
Ryan Moore	T-6	66-63-71-72=272	$151,250.00
Daisuke Maruyama	T-6	67-65-69-71=272	$151,250.00
Justin Leonard	T-6	68-68-65-71=272	$151,250.00
Alex Cejka	T-6	68-67-68-69=272	$151,250.00
Brian Davis	T-6	70-67-66-69=272	$151,250.00
Pat Perez	T-6	66-71-67-68=272	$151,250.00

Ginn sur Mer Classic at Tesoro

Course: Tesoro Club, Port St. Lucie,, Fl.
Par: 73 Yardage: 7,381
Last day of event: Monday, October 29, 2007

Player	Place	Score	Earnings
Daniel Chopra	Win	67-66-69-71=273	$810,000.00
Shigeki Maruyama	T-2	69-68-68-69=274	$396,000.00
Fredrik Jacobson	T-2	71-67-67-69=274	$396,000.00
Dicky Pride	4	73-70-69-64=276	$216,000.00
Sean O'Hair	T-5	68-68-69-74=279	$158,062.50
Cameron Beckman	T-5	70-70-67-72=279	$158,062.50
Charlie Wi	T-5	69-71-68-71=279	$158,062.50
Ken Duke	T-5	72-67-70-70=279	$158,062.50
Michael Sim	T-9	69-67-72-72=280	$121,500.00
Robert Garrigus	T-9	72-70-67-71=280	$121,500.00
Robert Gamez	T-9	72-71-71-66=280	$121,500.00

Children's Miracle Network Classic

Course: Walt Disney (Magnolia, Palm), Lake Buena Vista, Fla.
Home course / Magnolia, Par: 72 Yardage: 7,516
Last day of event: Sunday, November 4, 2007

Player	Place	Score	Earnings
Stephen Ames	Win	70-63-70-68=271	$828,000.00
Tim Clark	2	67-69-70-66=272	$496,800.00
Scott Verplank	T-3	66-66-71-71=274	$239,200.00
Tag Ridings	T-3	67-66-71-70=274	$239,200.00
Robert Gamez	T-3	70-69-67-68=274	$239,200.00
Justin Leonard	T-6	67-67-70-71=275	$154,100.00
Jeff Overton	T-6	67-68-69-71=275	$154,100.00
Bryce Molder	T-6	68-69-70-68=275	$154,100.00
Heath Slocum	T-9	68-68-69-71=276	$119,600.00
J.P. Hayes	T-9	65-69-72-70=276	$119,600.00
J.B. Holmes	T-9	70-66-70-70=276	$119,600.00
Nick Watney	T-9	68-68-73-67=276	$119,600.00

2008

Trevor Immelman shot 3-over-par 75 in the final round, but it was all he needed for a workmanlike 3-shot victory over Tiger Woods at the Masters. Unbeknownst to all but his inner circle, Woods was nursing a bum knee and stress fractures in his left shin. The severity of the injury couldn't be hidden as Woods limped to victory in the U.S. Open. In a riveting final round at Torrey Pines, Rocco Mediate shot even-par 71 and Woods birdied the 72nd hole to force a playoff. Woods dispatched Mediate and secured his 14th major title with a par to end an equally compelling 19-hole playoff, which Tiger had extended with birdie at the 18th. Two days later, the season deflated when Woods announced his season-ending knee surgery had been scheduled. That left the stage to Padraig Harrington, who successfully defended his British Open title and won the PGA Championship for good measure. Harrington's victory at wind-swept Royal Birkdale was by four shots over Ian Poulter. Runners-up Sergio Garcia and Ben Curtis, who each bogeyed two of the last four holes, were the victims at Oakland Hills, where Harrington posted a pair of 66s on the weekend and scored a 1-shot victory. By winning the first two playoff events, Vijay Singh took all the suspense out of a marginally tweaked FedEx Cup, having only to

show up for the Tour Championship (won by Camilo Villegas) to claim the $10 million FedEx bonus. The United States righted the Ryder Cup ship, beating Europe 16 ½ to 11 ½ at Valhalla. The total purse on the PGA Tour in 2008 was nearly $279 million. Players competed for a combined $1 million in 1958.

Mercedes Championipss

Course: Kapalua Resort Plantation Course, Kapalua, Maui, Ha.
Par: 73 Yardage: 7,411
Last day of event: Sunday, January 6, 2008

Player	Place	Score	Earnings
Daniel Chopra	Win	69-72-67-66=274	$1,100,000.00
Playoff: Beat Steve Stricker with birdie on fourth extra hole			
Steve Stricker	2	73-69-68-64=274	$630,000.00
Stephen Ames	3	72-67-70-66=275	$410,000.00
Mike Weir	4	71-67-68-70=276	$310,000.00
Nick Watney	T-5	68-72-67-71=278	$218,000.00
Jim Furyk	T-5	74-70-66-68=278	$218,000.00
Hunter Mahan	T-5	73-72-69-64=278	$218,000.00
Justin Leonard	T-8	73-68-69-69=279	$175,000.00
Charles Howell III	T-8	74-70-68-67=279	$175,000.00
Brandt Snedeker	T-10	71-69-70-70=280	$155,000.00
Mark Calcavecchia	T-10	75-66-71-68=280	$155,000.00

Sony Open in Hawaii

Course: Waialae C.C., Honolulu, Ha.
Par: 70 Yardage: 7,044
Last day of event: Sunday, January 13, 2008

Player	Place	Score	Earnings
K.J. Choi	Win	64-65-66-71=266	$954,000.00
Rory Sabbatini	2	66-69-66-68=269	$572,400.00
Jerry Kelly	3	67-67-69-67=270	$360,400.00
Kevin Na	T-4	67-64-69-72=272	$208,687.50
Steve Marino	T-4	65-67-68-72=272	$208,687.50
Pat Perez	T-4	69-66-67-70=272	$208,687.50
Steve Stricker	T-4	71-65-66-70=272	$208,687.50
Troy Matteson	T-8	69-67-65-72=273	$159,000.00
Tom Pernice, Jr.	T-8	70-67-66-70=273	$159,000.00
Chad Campbell	T-10	66-69-66-73=274	$113,571.42
Fred Funk	T-10	69-64-69-72=274	$113,571.43
Doug LaBelle II	T-10	67-69-66-72=274	$113,571.43
Heath Slocum	T-10	65-69-69-71=274	$113,571.43
Dustin Johnson	T-10	68-68-67-71=274	$113,571.43
Stephen Ames	T-10	70-68-65-71=274	$113,571.43
Parker McLachlin	T-10	73-66-65-70=274	$113,571.43

Bob Hope Chrysler Classic

Course: Classic Club, PGA West/Palmer, SilverRock G.C., La Quinta C.C., Palm Desert, Calif.
Home course / Classic Club, Par: 72 Yardage: 7,305
Last day of event: Sunday, January 20, 2008

Player	Place	Score	Earnings
D.J. Trahan	Win	67-64-68-70-65=334	$918,000.00
Justin Leonard	2	68-64-67-66-72=337	$550,800.00
Anthony Kim	T-3	69-67-67-66-69=338	$295,800.00
Kenny Perry	T-3	66-72-65-66-69=338	$295,800.00
Steve Elkington	T-5	66-68-69-67-69=339	$186,150.00
Ryan Moore	T-5	75-64-67-67-66=339	$186,150.00
Chez Reavie	T-5	69-68-67-70-65=339	$186,150.00
Boo Weekley	T-8	69-70-62-69-71=341	$142,800.00
Brett Rumford	T-8	67-68-69-67-70=341	$142,800.00
Charley Hoffman	T-8	68-72-71-63-67=341	$142,800.00
Vaughn Taylor	T-8	70-68-68-69-66=341	$142,800.00

Buick Invitational

Course: Torrey Pines (South), Torrey Pines (North), San Diego, Calif.

Home Course -Par: 72 Yardage: 7,569

Last day of event: Sunday, January 27, 2008

Player	Place	Score	Earnings
Tiger Woods	Win	67-65-66-71=269	$936,000.00
Ryuji Imada	2	69-72-69-67=277	$561,600.00
Stewart Cink	T-3	68-69-69-73=279	$301,600.00
Rory Sabbatini	T-3	67-75-70-67=279	$301,600.00
Justin Leonard	5	76-68-65-72=281	$208,000.00
Joe Durant	T-6	70-70-67-75=282	$180,700.00
Phil Mickelson	T-6	70-73-68-71=282	$180,700.00
Stuart Appleby	T-8	67-72-71-73=283	$150,800.00
John Senden	T-8	70-69-72-72=283	$150,800.00
Fred Couples	T-8	71-69-71-72=283	$150,800.00

FBR Open

Course: TPC of Scottsdale, Scottsdale, Ariz.

Par: 71 Yardage: 7,216

Last day of event: Sunday, February 3, 2008

Player	Place	Score	Earnings
J.B. Holmes	Win	68-65-66-71=270	$1,080,000.00

Playoff: Beat Phil Mickelson with birdie on first extra hole

Player	Place	Score	Earnings
Phil Mickelson	2	68-68-67-67=270	$648,000.00
Charles Warren	3	65-69-67-70=271	$408,000.00
Ben Crane	T-4	70-65-67-70=272	$226,200.00
Kevin Na	T-4	69-67-67-69=272	$226,200.00
Kevin Sutherland	T-4	65-72-66-69=272	$226,200.00
Steve Elkington	T-4	69-66-70-67=272	$226,200.00
Stuart Appleby	T-4	69-66-71-66=272	$226,200.00
Brandt Snedeker	T-9	67-69-67-70=273	$156,000.00
Bill Haas	T-9	67-68-69-69=273	$156,000.00
Mark Wilson	T-9	68-69-68-68=273	$156,000.00
Boo Weekley	T-9	68-69-69-67=273	$156,000.00

AT&T Pebble Beach National Pro-Am

Courses: Pebble Beach G.L., Spyglass Hill G.C., Poppy Hills G.C., Pebble Beach, Calif.

Home Course / Pebble Beach G.L., Par: 72 Yardage: 6,816

Last day of event: Sunday, February 10, 2008

Player	Place	Score	Earnings
Steve Lowery	Win	69-71-70-68=278	$1,080,000.00

Playoff: Beat Vijay Singh with birdie on first extra hole

Player	Place	Score	Earnings
Vijay Singh	2	70-70-67-71=278	$648,000.00
Dudley Hart	T-3	69-70-68-72=279	$312,000.00
Corey Pavin	T-3	73-69-71-66=279	$312,000.00
John Mallinger	T-3	67-74-73-65=279	$312,000.00
Jason Day	6	69-70-71-70=280	$216,000.00
Dustin Johnson	T-7	73-68-68-73=282	$193,500.00
Nicholas Thompson	T-7	69-69-74-70=282	$193,500.00
Y.E. Yang	T-9	69-73-68-73=283	$150,000.00
Tag Ridings	T-9	73-71-68-71=283	$150,000.00
Brent Geiberger	T-9	69-73-71-70=283	$150,000.00
Joe Ogilvie	T-9	74-69-70-70=283	$150,000.00
Jason Gore	T-9	70-74-69-70=283	$150,000.00

Northern Trust Open

Course: Riviera C.C., Pacific Palisades, Calif.

Par: 71 Yardage: 7,279

Last day of event: Sunday, February 17, 2008

Player	Place	Score	Earnings
Phil Mickelson	Win	68-64-70-70=272	$1,116,000.00
Jeff Quinney	2	69-67-67-71=274	$669,600.00
Padraig Harrington	T-3	69-69-71-68=277	$359,600.00
Luke Donald	T-3	68-71-70-68=277	$359,600.00
Scott Verplank	T-5	68-69-71-70=278	$235,600.00
Ryuji Imada	T-5	71-69-70-68=278	$235,600.00
Stuart Appleby	T-7	69-70-69-71=279	$186,775.00
K.J. Choi	T-7	65-73-71-70=279	$186,775.00
J.B. Holmes	T-7	74-66-69-70=279	$186,775.00
Robert Allenby	T-7	70-66-75-68=279	$186,775.00

WGC-Accenture Match Play Championship

Course: The Gallery At Dove Mountain (South Course), Marana, Ariz.

Par: 72 Yardage: 7,351

Last day of event: Sunday, February 24, 2008

Player	Place	Earnings
Tiger Woods	Win	$1,350,000.00

Round One - Beat Geoff Ogilvy 2 & 1
Round Two - Beat Lee Westwood 2 & 1
Round Three - Beat Stuart Appleby 3 & 2
Quarterfinals - Beat Vijay Singh 1 up
Semifinals - Beat Henrik Stenson 2 up
Finals - Beat Stewart Cink 8 & 7

Player	Place	Earnings
Stewart Cink	2	$800,000.00

Round One - Beat Miguel A. Jimenez 4 & 3
Round Two - Beat Padraig Harrington 2 up
Round Three - Beat Colin Montgomerie 4 & 2
Quarterfinals - Beat Angel Cabrera 3 & 2
Semifinals - Beat Justin Leonard 4 & 2
Finals - Tiger Woods beat him 8 & 7

Player	Place	Earnings
Henrik Stenson	3	$575,000.00

Round One - Beat Robert Allenby 1 up
Round Two - Beat Trevor Immelman 25 holes
Round Three - Beat Jonathan Byrd 1 up
Quarterfinals - Beat Woody Austin 2 up
Semifinals - Tiger Woods beat him 2 up
Consolation - Beat Justin Leonard 3 & 2

Player	Place	Earnings
Justin Leonard	4	$475,000.00

Round One - Beat Geoff Ogilvy 2 & 1
Round Two - Beat Lee Westwood 2 & 1
Round Three - Beat Stuart Appleby 3 & 2
Quarterfinals - Beat Vijay Singh 1 up
Semifinals - Stewart Cink beat him 4 & 2
Consolation - Henrik Stenson beat him 3 & 2

Player	Place	Earnings
K.J. Choi	T-5	$260,000.00

Round One - Beat Camilo Villegas 3 & 2
Round Two - Beat Ian Poulter 19 holes
Round Three - Beat Paul Casey 2 up
Quarterfinals - Tiger Woods beat him 3 & 2

Player	Place	Earnings
Woody Austin	T-5	$260,000.00

Round One - Beat Toru Taniguchi 6 & 5
Round Two - Beat Adam Scott 19 holes
Round Three - Beat Boo Weekley 3 & 2
Quarterfinals - Henrik Stenson beat him 2 up

Player	Place	Earnings
Vijay Singh	T-5	$260,000.00

Round One - Beat Peter Hanson 19 holes
Round Two - Beat Niclas Fasth 1 up
Round Three - Beat Rod Pampling 25 holes
Quarterfinals - Justin Leonard beat him 3 & 2

Player	Place	Earnings
Angel Cabrera	T-5	$260,000.00

Round One - Beat Anders Hansen 3 & 2
Round Two - Beat Luke Donald 2 & 1
Round Three - Beat Steve Stricker 4 & 3
Quarterfinals - Stewart Cink beat him 3 & 2

Player	Place	Earnings
Jonathan Byrd	T-9	$130,000.00

Round One - Beat Ernie Els 6 & 5
Round Two - Beat Andres Romero 6 & 4
Round Three - Henrik Stenson beat him 1 up

Boo Weekley	T-9		$130,000.00

Round One - Beat Martin Kaymer 2 & 1
Round Two - Beat Sergio Garcia 3 & 1
Round Three - Woody Austin beat him 3 & 2

Steve Stricker	T-9		$130,000.00

Round One - Beat Daniel Chopra 20 holes
Round Two - Beat Hunter Mahan 20 holes
Round Three - Angel Cabrera beat him 4 & 3

Colin Montgomerie	T-9		$130,000.00

Round One - Beat Jim Furyk 3 & 2
Round Two - Beat Charles Howell III 1 up
Round Three - Stewart Cink beat him 4 & 2

Aaron Baddeley	T-9		$130,000.00

Round One - Beat Mark Calcavecchia 4 & 2
Round Two - David Toms WD, conceded match, illness
Round Three - Tiger Woods beat him 20 holes

Paul Casey	T-9		$130,000.00

Round One - Beat Robert Karlsson 2 up
Round Two - Beat Bradley Dredge 2 & 1
Round Three - K.J. Choi beat him 2 up

Stuart Appleby	T-9		$130,000.00

Round One - Beat Tim Clark 3 & 2
Round Two - Beat Phil Mickelson 2 & 1
Round Three - Justin Leonard beat him 3 & 2

Rod Pampling	T-9		$130,000.00

Round One - Beat Justin Rose 2 & 1
Round Two - Beat Nick O'Hern 5 & 4
Round Three - Vijay Singh beat him 25 holes

Mayakoba Golf Classic
Course: El Camaleon, Playa Del Carmen,, Mexico
Par: 70 Yardage: 6,923
Last day of event: Sunday, February 24, 2008

Player	Place	Score	Earnings
Brian Gay	Win	66-67-62-69=264	$630,000.00
Steve Marino	2	67-69-64-66=266	$378,000.00
John Merrick	T-3	64-68-69-67=268	$203,000.00
Matt Kuchar	T-3	68-69-64-67=268	$203,000.00
Cliff Kresge	5	68-71-64-66=269	$140,000.00
Patrick Sheehan	6	71-67-67-65=270	$126,000.00
Peter Lonard	T-7	68-71-64-68=271	$112,875.00
Tim Petrovic	T-7	67-71-67-66=271	$112,875.00
Roland Thatcher	T-9	71-73-61-68=273	$98,000.00
Nick Flanagan	T-9	75-66-68-64=273	$98,000.00

Honda Classic
Course: PGA National Resort (Champion Course), Palm Beach Gardens, Fla.
Par: 70 Yardage: 7,158
Last day of event: Sunday, March 2, 2008

Player	Place	Score	Earnings
Ernie Els	Win	67-70-70-67=274	$990,000.00
Luke Donald	2	64-74-66-71=275	$594,000.00
Nathan Green	3	71-70-68-67=276	$374,000.00
Matt Jones	T-4	66-67-71-73=277	$227,333.33
Mark Calcavecchia	T-4	70-67-67-73=277	$227,333.33
Robert Allenby	T-4	69-68-70-70=277	$227,333.34
Brian Davis	T-7	65-67-73-73=278	$160,050.00
Michael Letzig	T-7	70-69-68-71=278	$160,050.00
John Mallinger	T-7	68-67-73-70=278	$160,050.00
Alex Cejka	T-7	69-71-68-70=278	$160,050.00
Mathew Goggin	T-7	71-70-68-69=278	$160,050.00

PODS Championship
Course: Innisbrook Resort (Copperhead Course), Palm Harbor, Fla.
Par: 71 Yardage: 7,340
Last day of event: Sunday, March 9, 2008

Player	Place	Score	Earnings
Sean O'Hair	Win	69-71-71-69=280	$954,000.00
Stewart Cink	T-2	66-73-69-74=282	$294,591.66
Billy Mayfair	T-2	68-71-71-72=282	$294,591.66
George McNeill	T-2	70-72-71-69=282	$294,591.67
Troy Matteson	T-2	70-72-71-69=282	$294,591.67
Ryuji Imada	T-2	72-70-72-68=282	$294,591.67
John Senden	T-2	67-74-74-67=282	$294,591.67
Brandt Snedeker	T-8	69-68-73-73=283	$159,000.00
Rod Pampling	T-8	70-71-73-69=283	$159,000.00
Geoff Ogilvy	T-10	69-72-69-74=284	$127,200.00
Tom Pernice, Jr.	T-10	67-73-71-73=284	$127,200.00
Stuart Appleby	T-10	66-73-74-71=284	$127,200.00
Lee Janzen	T-10	65-74-75-70=284	$127,200.00

Arnold Palmer Invitational
Course: Bay Hill Club, Orlando, Fla.
Par: 70 Yardage: 7,162
Last day of event: Sunday, March 16, 2008

Player	Place	Score	Earnings
Tiger Woods	Win	70-68-66-66=270	$1,044,000.00
Bart Bryant	2	68-68-68-67=271	$626,400.00
Vijay Singh	T-3	66-65-73-69=273	$301,600.00
Sean O'Hair	T-3	72-69-63-69=273	$301,600.00
Cliff Kresge	T-3	67-68-71-67=273	$301,600.00
Hunter Mahan	T-6	68-72-65-69=274	$201,550.00
Ken Duke	T-6	67-67-72-68=274	$201,550.00
Bubba Watson	T-8	67-69-68-72=276	$150,800.00
Tom Lehman	T-8	66-69-71-70=276	$150,800.00
Carl Pettersson	T-8	68-65-74-69=276	$150,800.00
Tom Pernice, Jr.	T-8	73-66-68-69=276	$150,800.00
Alex Cejka	T-8	67-70-71-68=276	$150,800.00
Niclas Fasth	T-8	71-66-73-66=276	$150,800.00

Puerto Rico Open
Course: Trump International Puerto Rico, Rio Grande,, Puerto Rico
Par: 72 Yardage: 7,569
Last day of event: Sunday, March 23, 2008

Player	Place	Score	Earnings
Greg Kraft	Win	69-66-69-70=274	$630,000.00
Bo Van Pelt	T-2	64-68-71-72=275	$308,000.00
Jerry Kelly	T-2	67-66-72-70=275	$308,000.00
Briny Baird	T-4	67-68-69-72=276	$154,000.00
Kevin Stadler	T-4	70-69-70-67=276	$154,000.00
Marco Dawson	T-6	68-69-69-71=277	$117,250.00
Tommy Armour III	T-6	72-67-67-71=277	$117,250.00
Tim Wilkinson	T-6	71-67-70-69=277	$117,250.00
Brenden Pappas	9	67-69-69-73=278	$101,500.00
Ted Purdy	T-10	66-68-73-73=280	$87,500.00
Larry Mize	T-10	71-68-72-69=280	$87,500.00
Steve Allan	T-10	70-70-71-69=280	$87,500.00

Zurich Classic of New Orleans

Course: TPC Louisiana, Avondale, La.
Par: 72 Yardage: 7,341
Last day of event: Sunday, March 30, 2008

Player	Place	Score	Earnings
Andres Romero	Win	73-69-65-68=275	$1,116,000.00
Peter Lonard	2	67-70-70-69=276	$669,600.00
Tim Wilkinson	3	71-68-71-67=277	$421,600.00
Woody Austin	T-4	69-71-67-71=278	$256,266.67
Nicholas Thompson	T-4	69-71-67-71=278	$256,266.66
Padraig Harrington	T-4	71-70-68-69=278	$256,266.67
John Merrick	T-7	72-67-67-73=279	$193,233.33
Tim Petrovic	T-7	74-68-66-71=279	$193,233.34
Tommy Armour III	T-7	70-68-75-66=279	$193,233.33
Marco Dawson	T-10	71-68-70-71=280	$161,200.00
Steve Elkington	T-10	68-71-72-69=280	$161,200.00

Shell Houston Open

Course: Redstone G.C. (Tournament Course), Humble, Texas
Par: 72 Yardage: 7,457
Last day of event: Sunday, April 6, 2008

Player	Place	Score	Earnings
Johnson Wagner	Win	63-69-69-71=272	$1,008,000.00
Chad Campbell	T-2	73-64-65-72=274	$492,800.00
Geoff Ogilvy	T-2	67-73-66-68=274	$492,800.00
Billy Mayfair	T-4	72-68-69-66=275	$246,400.00
Fred Couples	T-4	73-69-67-66=275	$246,400.00
Charley Hoffman	T-6	65-70-69-72=276	$194,600.00
Bob Estes	T-6	71-69-64-72=276	$194,600.00
Kevin Sutherland	T-8	70-70-71-67=278	$162,400.00
Jason Day	T-8	73-71-69-65=278	$162,400.00
Pat Perez	T-8	69-73-72-64=278	$162,400.00

Masters

Course: Augusta National G.C., Augusta, Ga.
Par: 72 Yardage: 7,445
Last day of event: Sunday, April 13, 2008

Player	Place	Score	Earnings
Trevor Immelman	Win	68-68-69-75=280	$1,350,000.00
Tiger Woods	2	72-71-68-72=283	$810,000.00
Brandt Snedeker	T-3	69-68-70-77=284	$435,000.00
Stewart Cink	T-3	72-69-71-72=284	$435,000.00
Steve Flesch	T-5	72-67-69-78=286	$273,750.00
Phil Mickelson	T-5	71-68-75-72=286	$273,750.00
Padraig Harrington	T-5	74-71-69-72=286	$273,750.00
Robert Karlsson	T-8	70-73-71-73=287	$217,500.00
Andres Romero	T-8	72-72-70-73=287	$217,500.00
Miguel-A. Jimenez	T-8	77-70-72-68=287	$217,500.00

Verizon Heritage

Course: Harbour Town G.L., Hilton Head, S.C.
Par: 71 Yardage: 6,973
Last day of event: Sunday, April 20, 2008

Player	Place	Score	Earnings
Boo Weekley	Win	69-64-65-71=269	$990,000.00
Anthony Kim	T-2	67-67-67-71=272	$484,000.00
Aaron Baddeley	T-2	69-67-67-69=272	$484,000.00
Jim Furyk	4	68-68-68-69=273	$264,000.00
Cliff Kresge	5	69-66-68-71=274	$220,000.00
Jason Bohn	6	70-66-67-72=275	$198,000.00

Lucas Glover	T-7	66-66-73-71=276	$160,050.00
Stewart Cink	T-7	67-68-70-71=276	$160,050.00
Camilo Villegas	T-7	67-71-71-67=276	$160,050.00
Matt Kuchar	T-7	71-70-68-67=276	$160,050.00
Michael Letzig	T-7	68-73-70-65=276	$160,050.00

EDS Byron Nelson Championship

Course: TPC Four Seasons Resort, Irving, Texas
Par: 70 Yardage: 7,166
Last day of event: Sunday, April 27, 2008

Player	Place	Score	Earnings
Adam Scott	Win	68-67-67-71=273	$1,152,000.00
Playoff: Beat Ryan Moore with birdie on third extra hole			
Ryan Moore	2	67-70-68-68=273	$691,200.00
Bart Bryant	3	72-66-67-72=277	$435,200.00
Mark Hensby	T-4	69-67-73-69=278	$264,533.33
Carl Pettersson	T-4	74-68-67-69=278	$264,533.33
Nicholas Thompson	T-4	69-72-70-67=278	$264,533.34
Charley Hoffman	T-7	69-68-68-74=279	$179,733.33
Kevin Sutherland	T-7	68-70-67-74=279	$179,733.33
Dudley Hart	T-7	70-70-66-73=279	$179,733.33
Brian Gay	T-7	72-67-68-72=279	$179,733.33
Roland Thatcher	T-7	69-68-72-70=279	$179,733.34
Charlie Wi	T-7	71-70-70-68=279	$179,733.34

Wachovia Championship

Course: Quail Hollow Club, Charlotte, N.C.
Par: 72 Yardage: 7,442
Last day of event: Sunday, May 4, 2008

Player	Place	Score	Earnings
Anthony Kim	Win	70-67-66-69=272	$1,152,000.00
Ben Curtis	2	69-71-72-65=277	$691,200.00
Jason Bohn	3	68-67-72-71=278	$435,200.00
Robert Allenby	4	70-70-73-66=279	$307,200.00
Heath Slocum	T-5	71-68-68-73=280	$243,200.00
Dudley Hart	T-5	71-67-70-72=280	$243,200.00
Jim Furyk	7	71-67-71-72=281	$214,400.00
Stewart Cink	T-8	73-70-65-74=282	$179,200.00
Fred Couples	T-8	72-69-69-72=282	$179,200.00
Adam Scott	T-8	72-73-66-71=282	$179,200.00
Rod Pampling	T-8	71-70-75-66=282	$179,200.00

The Players

Course: TPC Sawgrass, Ponte Vedra Beach, Fla.
Par: 72 Yardage: 7,215
Last day of event: Sunday, May 11, 2008

Player	Place	Score	Earnings
Sergio Garcia	Win	66-73-73-71=283	$1,710,000.00
Playoff: Beat Paul Goydos with par on first extra hole			
Paul Goydos	2	68-71-70-74=283	$1,026,000.00
Jeff Quinney	3	71-73-70-70=284	$646,000.00
Briny Baird	4	71-71-73-72=287	$456,000.00
Stephen Ames	5	74-68-74-72=288	$380,000.00
Tom Lehman	T-6	73-73-69-74=289	$307,562.50
Ben Crane	T-6	70-72-75-72=289	$307,562.50
Ernie Els	T-6	72-71-74-72=289	$307,562.50
Brett Quigley	T-6	70-76-72-71=289	$307,562.50
J.B. Holmes	T-10	72-72-71-75=290	$218,500.00
Greg Kraft	T-10	75-72-68-75=290	$218,500.00
Henrik Stenson	T-10	73-71-75-71=290	$218,500.00
Dean Wilson	T-10	74-72-75-69=290	$218,500.00
Chad Campbell	T-10	73-72-77-68=290	$218,500.00

AT&T Classic
Course: TPC at Sugarloaf, Duluth, Ga.
Par: 72 Yardage: 7,311
Last day of event: Sunday, May 18, 2008

Player	Place	Score	Earnings
Ryuji Imada	Win	71-69-66-67=273	$990,000.00
Playoff: Beat Kenny Perry with birdie on first extra hole			
Kenny Perry	2	66-69-69-69=273	$594,000.00
Camilo Villegas	3	68-69-71-66=274	$374,000.00
Jonathan Byrd	4	66-66-73-70=275	$264,000.00
Justin Bolli	T-5	73-66-68-69=276	$200,750.00
Parker McLachlin	T-5	66-70-73-67=276	$200,750.00
James Driscoll	T-5	71-72-66-67=276	$200,750.00
Charles Howell III	T-8	67-69-67-74=277	$165,000.00
Heath Slocum	T-8	69-68-69-71=277	$165,000.00
Ryan Palmer	10	66-69-70-73=278	$148,500.00

Crowne Plaza Invitational at Colonial
Course: Colonial C.C., Fort Worth, Texas
Par: 70 Yardage: 7,054
Last day of event: Sunday, May 25, 2008

Player	Place	Score	Earnings
Phil Mickelson	Win	65-68-65-68=266	$1,098,000.00
Rod Pampling	T-2	69-67-63-68=267	$536,800.00
Tim Clark	T-2	68-69-64-66=267	$536,800.00
Stephen Ames	4	68-67-64-70=269	$292,800.00
Ben Crane	5	68-68-67-67=270	$244,000.00
Pat Perez	6	72-68-67-65=272	$219,600.00
Geoff Ogilvy	T-7	72-64-69-68=273	$196,725.00
Jeff Quinney	T-7	71-68-66-68=273	$196,725.00
Matt Kuchar	9	70-64-71-69=274	$176,900.00
Brian Gay	T-10	69-65-69-72=275	$140,300.00
Mark Wilson	T-10	70-67-68-70=275	$140,300.00
Tommy Armour III	T-10	71-66-68-70=275	$140,300.00
Paul Goydos	T-10	68-71-66-70=275	$140,300.00
Steve Marino	T-10	68-70-71-66=275	$140,300.00

Memorial Tournament
Course: Muirfield Village G.C., Dubin, Ohio
Par: 72 Yardage: 7,366
Last day of event: Sunday, June 1, 2008

Player	Place	Score	Earnings
Kenny Perry	Win	66-71-74-69=280	$1,080,000.00
Mathew Goggin	T-2	65-72-71-74=282	$396,000.00
Jerry Kelly	T-2	66-72-73-71=282	$396,000.00
Justin Rose	T-2	68-73-70-71=282	$396,000.00
Mike Weir	T-2	71-72-68-71=282	$396,000.00
Luke Donald	T-6	68-71-74-73=286	$201,000.00
Steve Lowery	T-6	70-70-75-71=286	$201,000.00
Rocco Mediate	T-6	70-73-74-69=286	$201,000.00
Geoff Ogilvy	9	69-71-73-74=287	$174,000.00
Matt Kuchar	T-10	68-72-71-77=288	$120,666.66
Nick O'Hern	T-10	70-70-72-76=288	$120,666.66
Joe Ogilvie	T-10	69-75-71-73=288	$120,666.66
Carl Pettersson	T-10	68-75-74-71=288	$120,666.67
Robert Allenby	T-10	69-76-72-71=288	$120,666.67
Ryan Moore	T-10	73-71-75-69=288	$120,666.67
Brett Quigley	T-10	67-78-74-69=288	$120,666.67
John Mallinger	T-10	71-74-74-69=288	$120,666.67
Cliff Kresge	T-10	73-73-74-68=288	$120,666.67

Stanford St. Jude Classic
Course: TPC at Southwind, Germantown, Tenn.
Par: 70 Yardage: 7,239
Last day of event: Sunday, June 8, 2008

Player	Place	Score	Earnings
Justin Leonard	Win	68-73-67-68=276	$1,080,000.00
Playoff: Beat Trevor Immelman and Robert Allenby with birdie on second extra hole			
Trevor Immelman	T-2	74-66-67-69=276	$528,000.00
Robert Allenby	T-2	71-71-69-65=276	$528,000.00
Alex Cejka	T-4	69-69-69-70=277	$236,250.00
Boo Weekley	T-4	65-75-69-68=277	$236,250.00
Padraig Harrington	T-4	71-72-66-68=277	$236,250.00
Sergio Garcia	T-4	68-72-71-66=277	$236,250.00
Gavin Coles	T-8	73-64-70-71=278	$174,000.00
Scott Verplank	T-8	71-72-67-68=278	$174,000.00
Tom Pernice, Jr.	T-8	72-72-71-63=278	$174,000.00

U.S. Open
Course: Torrey Pines (South), San Diego,, Calif.
Par: 71 Yardage: 7,643
Last day of event: Monday, June 16, 2008

Player	Place	Score	Earnings
Tiger Woods	Win	72-68-70-73=283	$1,350,000.00
Playoff: Beat Rocco Mediate with par on19th hole (tied 18-hole playoff at 71)			
Rocco Mediate	2	69-71-72-71=283	$810,000.00
Lee Westwood	3	70-71-70-73=284	$491,995.00
D.J. Trahan	T-4	72-69-73-72=286	$307,303.00
Robert Karlsson	T-4	70-70-75-71=286	$307,303.00
Miguel-A. Jimenez	T-6	75-66-74-72=287	$220,686.00
John Merrick	T-6	73-72-71-71=287	$220,686.00
Carl Pettersson	T-6	71-71-77-68=287	$220,686.00
Geoff Ogilvy	T-9	69-73-72-74=288	$160,769.00
Camilo Villegas	T-9	73-71-71-73=288	$160,769.00
Brandt Snedeker	T-9	76-73-68-71=288	$160,769.00
Eric Axley	T-9	69-79-71-69=288	$160,769.00
Heath Slocum	T-9	75-74-74-65=288	$160,769.00

Travelers Championship
Course: TPC at River Highlands, Cromwell, Conn.
Par: 70 Yardage: 6,837
Last day of event: Sunday, June 22, 2008

Player	Place	Score	Earnings
Stewart Cink	Win	66-64-65-67=262	$1,080,000.00
Hunter Mahan	T-2	68-63-67-65=263	$528,000.00
Tommy Armour III	T-2	69-64-65-65=263	$528,000.00
Heath Slocum	4	67-66-64-67=264	$288,000.00
Vijay Singh	5	66-68-64-68=266	$240,000.00
Kenny Perry	T-6	66-67-65-69=267	$194,250.00
Brad Adamonis	T-6	64-68-68-67=267	$194,250.00
Bubba Watson	T-6	66-68-67-66=267	$194,250.00
Michael Allen	T-6	69-66-68-64=267	$194,250.00
Kevin Streelman	T-10	73-63-62-70=268	$150,000.00
Michael Letzig	T-10	68-68-63-69=268	$150,000.00
Corey Pavin	T-10	68-66-70-64=268	$150,000.00

Buick Open

Course: Warwick Hills C.C., Grand Blanc, Mich..
Par: 72 Yardage: 7,127
Last day of event: Sunday, June 29, 2008

Player	Place	Score	Earnings
Kenny Perry	Win	69-67-67-66=269	$900,000.00
Woody Austin	T-2	66-67-69-68=270	$440,000.00
Bubba Watson	T-2	67-67-68-68=270	$440,000.00
Matt Jones	T-4	70-63-71-67=271	$206,666.66
Ken Duke	T-4	69-66-69-67=271	$206,666.67
Bob Tway	T-4	68-71-67-65=271	$206,666.67
Lucas Glover	T-7	70-66-69-67=272	$161,250.00
Brian Gay	T-7	69-68-70-65=272	$161,250.00
Dudley Hart	T-9	64-68-70-71=273	$135,000.00
Fredrik Jacobson	T-9	68-66-72-67=273	$135,000.00
John Rollins	T-9	72-64-72-65=273	$135,000.00

AT&T National

Course: Congressional C.C. (Blue Course), Bethesda, Md.
Par: 70 Yardage: 7,255
Last day of event: Sunday, July 6, 2008

Player	Place	Score	Earnings
Anthony Kim	Win	67-67-69-65=268	$1,080,000.00
Fredrik Jacobson	2	67-72-66-65=270	$648,000.00
Nick O'Hern	T-3	70-65-67-69=271	$256,500.00
Tommy Armour III	T-3	67-69-66-69=271	$256,500.00
Robert Allenby	T-3	68-69-67-67=271	$256,500.00
Dean Wilson	T-3	69-70-65-67=271	$256,500.00
Jim Furyk	T-3	70-68-67-66=271	$256,500.00
Rod Pampling	T-3	66-69-71-65=271	$256,500.00
Tom Pernice, Jr.	T-9	68-63-69-72=272	$162,000.00
Jeff Overton	T-9	66-65-71-70=272	$162,000.00
Alex Cejka	T-9	67-71-68-66=272	$162,000.00

John Deere Classic

Course: TPC at Deere Run, Silvis, Ill.
Par: 71 Yardage: 7,268
Last day of event: Sunday, July 13, 2008

Player	Place	Score	Earnings
Kenny Perry	Win	65-66-67-70=268	$756,000.00

Playoff: Beat Jay Williamson and Brad Adamonis with par on first extra hole

Player	Place	Score	Earnings
Brad Adamonis	T-2	66-66-66-70=268	$369,600.00
Jay Williamson	T-2	69-68-62-69=268	$369,600.00
Eric Axley	T-4	65-66-67-71=269	$173,600.00
Will MacKenzie	T-4	65-64-70-70=269	$173,600.00
Charlie Wi	T-4	64-67-69-69=269	$173,600.00
Chad Campbell	7	67-67-67-69=270	$140,700.00
Kevin Sutherland	8	68-68-67-68=271	$130,200.00
J.P. Hayes	T-9	67-68-65-72=272	$113,400.00
Woody Austin	T-9	66-71-66-69=272	$113,400.00
Jeff Gove	T-9	66-68-70-68=272	$113,400.00

British Open

Course: Royal Birkdale G.C., Southport, Lancashire, England
Par: 70 Yardage: 7,173
Last day of event: Sunday, July 20, 2008

Player	Place	Score	Earnings
Padraig Harrington	Win	74-68-72-69=283	$1,498,875.00
Ian Poulter	2	72-71-75-69=287	$899,325.00
Greg Norman	T-3	70-70-72-77=289	$509,617.50
Henrik Stenson	T-3	76-72-70-71=289	$509,617.50
Chris Wood	T-5	75-70-73-72=290	
Jim Furyk	T-5	71-71-77-71=290	$359,730.00
Anthony Kim	T-7	72-74-71-75=292	$193,743.48
Ben Curtis	T-7	78-69-70-75=292	$193,743.48
Robert Allenby	T-7	69-73-76-74=292	$193,743.48
Steve Stricker	T-7	77-71-71-73=292	$193,743.48
Stephen Ames	T-7	73-70-78-71=292	$193,743.48
Paul Casey	T-7	78-71-73-70=292	$193,743.48
Robert Karlsson	T-7	75-73-75-69=292	$193,743.48
Ernie Els	T-7	80-69-74-69=292	$193,743.48
David Howell	T-7	76-71-78-67=292	$193,743.48

U.S. Bank Championship in Milwaukee

Course: Brown Deer Park G.C., Milwaukee, Wis.
Par: 70 Yardage: 6,759
Last day of event: Sunday, July 20, 2008

Player	Place	Score	Earnings
Richard S. Johnson	Win	63-67-70-64=264	$720,000.00
Ken Duke	2	67-65-68-65=265	$432,000.00
Chris Riley	T-3	68-66-67-66=267	$208,000.00
Chad Campbell	T-3	67-67-68-65=267	$208,000.00
Dean Wilson	T-3	65-73-64-65=267	$208,000.00
George McNeill	T-6	67-67-66-68=268	$125,200.00
Patrick Sheehan	T-6	65-68-68-67=268	$125,200.00
Joe Ogilvie	T-6	66-67-68-67=268	$125,200.00
Troy Matteson	T-6	67-65-70-66=268	$125,200.00
Kenny Perry	T-6	67-68-69-64=268	$125,200.00

RBC Canadian Open

Course: Glen Abbey G.C., Oakville, Ontario, Canada
Par: 71 Yardage: 7,222
Last day of event: Sunday, July 27, 2008

Player	Place	Score	Earnings
Chez Reavie	Win	65-64-68-70=267	$900,000.00
Billy Mayfair	2	68-66-68-68=270	$540,000.00
Steve Marino	T-3	67-67-67-70=271	$290,000.00
Sean O'Hair	T-3	65-71-67-68=271	$290,000.00
Scott McCarron	T-5	66-72-63-71=272	$182,500.00
Nicholas Thompson	T-5	67-66-70-69=272	$182,500.00
Mike Weir	T-5	65-70-68-69=272	$182,500.00
Anthony Kim	T-8	65-69-64-75=273	$145,000.00
Kevin Na	T-8	69-66-70-68=273	$145,000.00
Glen Day	T-8	71-70-64-68=273	$145,000.00

Reno-Tahoe Open

Course: Montreux G. & C.C., Reno, Nev.
Par: 72 Yardage: 7,472
Last day of event: Sunday, August 3, 2008

Player	Place	Score	Earnings
Parker McLachlin	Win	68-62-66-74=270	$540,000.00
Brian Davis	T-2	67-67-68-75=277	$264,000.00
John Rollins	T-2	70-66-70-71=277	$264,000.00
Ryan Palmer	T-4	71-66-71-70=278	$118,125.00
Harrison Frazar	T-4	67-68-74-69=278	$118,125.00
Eric Axley	T-4	72-66-71-69=278	$118,125.00
Martin Laird	T-4	73-70-69-66=278	$118,125.00
John Merrick	T-8	67-67-73-72=279	$87,000.00
Jason Gore	T-8	68-70-70-71=279	$87,000.00
Mark Wilson	T-8	74-67-71-67=279	$87,000.00

WGC-Bridgestone Invitational

Course: Firestone C.C. (South), Akron, Ohio
Par: 70 Yardage: 7,400
Last day of event: Sunday, August 3, 2008

Player	Place	Score	Earnings
Vijay Singh	Win	67-66-69-68=270	$1,350,000.00
Lee Westwood	T-2	70-65-67-69=271	$635,000.00
Stuart Appleby	T-2	70-66-67-68=271	$635,000.00
Phil Mickelson	T-4	68-66-68-70=272	$310,000.00
Retief Goosen	T-4	66-71-68-67=272	$310,000.00
Darren Clarke	T-6	70-71-65-67=273	$220,000.00
Peter Lonard	T-6	69-66-72-66=273	$220,000.00
D.J. Trahan	T-8	69-67-70-68=274	$162,500.00
Paul Casey	T-8	70-71-68-65=274	$162,500.00
Miguel-A. Jimenez	T-10	70-66-70-69=275	$133,000.00
Hunter Mahan	T-10	71-66-70-68=275	$133,000.00

PGA Championship

Course: Oakland Hills C.C., Birmingham, Mich.
Par: 70 Yardage: 7,395
Last day of event: Sunday, August 10, 2008

Player	Place	Score	Earnings
Padraig Harrington	Win	71-74-66-66=277	$1,350,000.00
Ben Curtis	T-2	73-67-68-71=279	$660,000.00
Sergio Garcia	T-2	69-73-69-68=279	$660,000.00
Henrik Stenson	T-4	71-70-68-72=281	$330,000.00
Camilo Villegas	T-4	74-72-67-68=281	$330,000.00
Steve Flesch	6	73-70-70-69=282	$270,000.00
Andres Romero	T-7	69-78-65-72=284	$231,250.00
Phil Mickelson	T-7	70-73-71-70=284	$231,250.00
Charlie Wi	T-9	70-70-71-74=285	$176,725.00
Jeev M. Singh	T-9	68-74-70-73=285	$176,725.00
Justin Rose	T-9	73-67-74-71=285	$176,725.00
Alastair Forsyth	T-9	73-72-70-70=285	$176,725.00

Wyndham Championship

Course: Sedgefield C.C., Greensboro, N.C.
Par: 70 Yardage: 7,118
Last day of event: Sunday, August 17, 2008

Player	Place	Score	Earnings
Carl Pettersson	Win	64-61-66-68=259	$918,000.00
Scott McCarron	2	65-64-64-68=261	$550,800.00
Rich Beem	3	70-67-63-63=263	$346,800.00
Martin Laird	T-4	63-74-64-63=264	$224,400.00
J.J. Henry	T-4	70-66-66-62=264	$224,400.00
Kevin Streelman	T-6	66-64-67-68=265	$170,850.00
Tim Clark	T-6	64-67-68-66=265	$170,850.00
John Senden	T-6	66-66-67-66=265	$170,850.00
Briny Baird	T-9	67-68-62-69=266	$122,400.00
Bob Sowards	T-9	65-66-68-67=266	$122,400.00
Jerry Kelly	T-9	66-65-68-67=266	$122,400.00
Michael Letzig	T-9	67-68-67-64=266	$122,400.00
Shane Bertsch	T-9	67-68-67-64=266	$122,400.00
Mark Wilson	T-9	68-67-67-64=266	$122,400.00

Barclays Classic (FedEx Cup Playoffs)

Course: Ridgewood Country Club, Paramus,, N.J.
Par: 71 Yardage: 7,319
Last day of event: Sunday, August 24, 2008

Player	Place	Score	Earnings
Vijay Singh	Win	70-70-66-70=276	$1,260,000.00

Playoff: Beat Sergio Garcia with birdie on second extra hole (Kevin Sutherland eliminated on first hole with par)

Sergio Garcia	T-2	70-67-69-70=276	$616,000.00
Kevin Sutherland	T-2	70-69-69-68=276	$616,000.00
Kevin Streelman	T-4	67-70-68-72=277	$289,333.33
Ben Curtis	T-4	71-68-70-68=277	$289,333.33
Mathew Goggin	T-4	67-74-69-67=277	$289,333.34
Paul Casey	T-7	66-71-69-72=278	$203,700.00
Mike Weir	T-7	72-67-67-72=278	$203,700.00
Martin Laird	T-7	70-69-72-67=278	$203,700.00
Justin Leonard	T-7	70-70-71-67=278	$203,700.00
Nicholas Thompson	T-7	75-68-68-67=278	$203,700.00

Deutsche Bank Championship (FedEx Cup Playoffs)

Course: TPC of Boston, Norton, Mass.
Par: 71 Yardage: 7,207
Last day of event: Monday, September 1, 2008

Player	Place	Score	Earnings
Vijay Singh	Win	64-66-69-63=262	$1,260,000.00
Mike Weir	2	61-68-67-71=267	$756,000.00
Camilo Villegas	T-3	68-66-63-73=270	$406,000.00
Ernie Els	T-3	66-65-69-70=270	$406,000.00
Sergio Garcia	T-5	67-64-68-72=271	$266,000.00
Tim Herron	T-5	72-67-67-65=271	$266,000.00
Jim Furyk	T-7	66-65-69-72=272	$218,166.66
Justin Leonard	T-7	69-70-66-67=272	$218,166.67
Chad Campbell	T-7	67-70-69-66=272	$218,166.67
Ben Crane	T-10	72-65-63-73=273	$175,000.00
Steve Marino	T-10	66-66-71-70=273	$175,000.00
Ken Duke	T-10	66-67-70-70=273	$175,000.00

BMW Championship (FedEx Cup Playoffs)

Course: Bellerive C.C., St. Louis, Mo.
Par: 70 Yardage: 7,324
Last day of event: Sunday, September 7, 2008

Player	Place	Score	Earnings
Camilo Villegas	Win	65-66-66-68=265	$1,260,000.00
Dudley Hart	2	67-69-66-65=267	$756,000.00
Jim Furyk	T-3	70-62-66-70=268	$406,000.00
Anthony Kim	T-3	68-67-66-67=268	$406,000.00
D.J. Trahan	T-5	71-63-68-67=269	$255,500.00
K.J. Choi	T-5	70-68-64-67=269	$255,500.00
Stephen Ames	T-5	68-69-66-66=269	$255,500.00
Tim Clark	T-8	67-68-66-69=270	$210,000.00
Hunter Mahan	T-8	69-67-68-66=270	$210,000.00
Aaron Baddeley	T-10	71-64-67-69=271	$175,000.00
Steve Stricker	T-10	66-71-68-66=271	$175,000.00
Fredrik Jacobson	T-10	67-67-72-65=271	$175,000.00

Viking Classic

Course: Annandale G.C., Madison, Miss.
Par: 70 Yardage: 7,199
Last day of event: Sunday, September 21, 2008

Player	Place	Score	Earnings
Will MacKenzie	Win	70-64-67-68=269	$648,000.00

Playoff: Beat Marc Turnesa with birdie on second extra hole (Brian Gay eliminated on first hole with par)

Marc Turnesa	T-2	65-68-66-70=269	$316,800.00
Brian Gay	T-2	66-68-67-68=269	$316,800.00

Casey Wittenberg	T-4	68-67-68-69=272	$148,800.00
Bill Haas	T-4	69-69-66-68=272	$148,800.00
Steve Allan	T-4	71-68-67-66=272	$148,800.00
Greg Kraft	7	68-69-68-68=273	$120,600.00
Dicky Pride	T-8	67-67-68-72=274	$97,200.00
Brad Elder	T-8	68-68-69-69=274	$97,200.00
Woody Austin	T-8	69-69-67-69=274	$97,200.00
David Toms	T-8	69-68-71-66=274	$97,200.00
Jason Gore	T-8	71-69-68-66=274	$97,200.00

The Tour Championship (FedEx Cup Final)

Course: East Lake G.C.. Atlanta, Ga.
Par: 70 Yardage: 7,304
Last day of event: Sunday, September 28, 2008

Player	Place	Score	Earnings
Camilo Villegas	Win	72-66-69-66=273	$1,260,000.00
Playoff: Beat Sergio Garcia with par on first extra hole			
Sergio Garcia	2	70-65-67-71=273	$756,000.00
Anthony Kim	T-3	64-69-72-69=274	$409,500.00
Phil Mickelson	T-3	68-68-69-69=274	$409,500.00
Ben Curtis	5	71-69-68-70=278	$280,000.00
Mike Weir	T-6	70-69-71-70=280	$238,000.00
Ernie Els	T-6	68-73-70-69=280	$238,000.00
Jim Furyk	T-6	72-70-69-69=280	$238,000.00
K.J. Choi	9	69-70-70-72=281	$210,000.00
Trevor Immelman	T-10	68-73-71-70=282	$180,040.00
Billy Mayfair	T-10	72-71-69-70=282	$180,040.00
Dudley Hart	T-10	73-69-71-69=282	$180,040.00
Stuart Appleby	T-10	72-71-70-69=282	$180,040.00
Justin Leonard	T-10	73-69-73-67=282	$180,040.00

Turning Stone Resort Championship

Course: Atunyote Golf Club, Verona,, N.Y.
Par: 72 Yardage: 7,482
Last day of event: Sunday, October 5, 2008

Player	Place	Score	Earnings
Dustin Johnson	Win	72-68-70-69=279	$1,080,000.00
Robert Allenby	2	71-68-71-70=280	$648,000.00
Charles Howell III	T-3	71-68-69-73=281	$244,714.28
Davis Love III	T-3	75-70-66-70=281	$244,714.28
Mathew Goggin	T-3	71-70-71-69=281	$244,714.29
Steve Allan	T-3	68-74-70-69=281	$244,714.29
Ryuji Imada	T-3	72-71-69-69=281	$244,714.29
Woody Austin	T-3	74-69-69-69=281	$244,714.29
Robert Garrigus	T-3	72-72-68-69=281	$244,714.28
Jeff Overton	T-10	67-69-73-73=282	$138,000.00
Charles Warren	T-10	73-71-67-71=282	$138,000.00
Pat Perez	T-10	71-72-69-70=282	$138,000.00
Joe Ogilvie	T-10	75-69-68-70=282	$138,000.00
Nick O'Hern	T-10	71-72-71-68=282	$138,000.00

Valero Texas Open

Course: LaCantera G.C., San Antonio, Texas
Par: 70 Yardage: 6,881
Last day of event: Sunday, October 12, 2008

Player	Place	Score	Earnings
Zach Johnson	Win	69-66-62-64=261	$810,000.00
Tim Wilkinson	T-2	67-69-63-64=263	$336,000.00
Mark Wilson	T-2	68-66-66-63=263	$336,000.00
Charlie Wi	T-2	67-68-67-61=263	$336,000.00
Jeff Overton	5	69-64-67-65=265	$180,000.00

Chris Stroud	T-6	66-64-69-68=267	$156,375.00
Stephen Ames	T-6	68-71-66-62=267	$156,375.00
Rory Sabbatini	T-8	67-66-63-72=268	$130,500.00
Tim Herron	T-8	65-67-67-69=268	$130,500.00
Pat Perez	T-8	71-64-68-65=268	$130,500.00

Justin Timberlake Shriners Hospitals for Children Open

Course: TPC at Summerlin, Las Vegas, Nev.
Par: 72 Yardage: 7,243
Last day of event: Sunday, October 19, 2008

Player	Place	Score	Earnings
Marc Turnesa	Win	62-64-69-68=263	$738,000.00
Matt Kuchar	2	63-63-71-67=264	$442,800.00
Michael Allen	T-3	63-69-64-70=266	$213,200.00
John Mallinger	T-3	64-64-70-68=266	$213,200.00
Chad Campbell	T-3	65-67-67-67=266	$213,200.00
Davis Love III	T-6	68-67-65-67=267	$142,475.00
Tim Herron	T-6	72-65-58-62=267	$142,475.00
Tom Pernice, Jr.	T-8	68-68-67-65=268	$123,000.00
Scott Sterling	T-8	69-65-70-64=268	$123,000.00
Chris DiMarco	T-10	69-64-63-73=269	$94,300.00
Zach Johnson	T-10	62-65-70-72=269	$94,300.00
Brad Adamonis	T-10	67-65-66-71=269	$94,300.00
Charles Howell III	T-10	67-67-69-66=269	$94,300.00
Mike Weir	T-10	69-68-66-66=269	$94,300.00

Frys.Com Open

Course: Grayhawk Golf Club (Raptor Course), Scottsdale, Ariz.
Par: 70 Yardage: 7,125
Last day of event: Sunday, October 26, 2008

Player	Place	Score	Earnings
Cameron Beckman	Win	69-66-64-63=262	$900,000.00
Playoff: Beat Kevin Sutherland with par on second extra hole			
Kevin Sutherland	2	67-66-63-66=262	$540,000.00
Mathew Goggin	3	69-63-68-63=263	$340,000.00
Arron Oberholser	T-4	65-64-71-66=266	$206,666.66
J.J. Henry	T-4	65-69-68-64=266	$206,666.67
Mike Weir	T-4	66-68-69-63=266	$206,666.67
Steve Allan	T-7	67-63-68-69=267	$150,625.00
Paul Goydos	T-7	70-62-66-69=267	$150,625.00
Michael Sim	T-7	72-63-68-64=267	$150,625.00
Pat Perez	T-7	71-66-67-63=267	$150,625.00

Ginn sur Mer Classic

Course: The Conservatory, Palm Coast, Fla.
Par: 72 Yardage: 7,663
Last day of event: Sunday, November 2, 2008

Player	Place	Score	Earnings
Ryan Palmer	Win	67-71-72-71=281	$828,000.00
Michael Letzig	T-2	65-74-70-73=282	$276,000.00
Ken Duke	T-2	70-69-72-71=282	$276,000.00
Vaughn Taylor	T-2	69-74-69-70=282	$276,000.00
Nicholas Thompson	T-2	71-70-72-69=282	$276,000.00
George McNeill	T-2	71-71-71-69=282	$276,000.00
John Huston	T-7	70-70-70-73=283	$133,860.00
Robert Allenby	T-7	68-71-73-71=283	$133,860.00
Brian Gay	T-7	72-70-72-69=283	$133,860.00
Tom Scherrer	T-7	68-76-70-69=283	$133,860.00
Troy Matteson	T-7	71-74-70-68=283	$133,860.00

Children's Miracle Network Classic
Course: Walt Disney (Magnolia, Palm), Lake Buena Vista, Fla.
Home course / Magnolia, Par: 72 Yardage: 7,516
Last Day of Event: November 9, 2008

Player	Place	Score	Earnings
Davis Love III	Win	66-69-64-64-=263	$828,000.00
Tommy Gainey	2	68-66-66-64-=264	$496,800.00
Scott Verplank	T-3	64-64-69-71-=268	$266,800.00
Steve Marino	T-3	65-66-66-71-=268	$266,800.00
Joe Durant	5	68-68-68-65-=269	$184,000.00
Scott Sterling	T-6	70-63-66-71-=270	$154,100.00
Troy Matteson	T-6	63-68-69-70-=270	$154,100.00
Kevin Streelman	T-6	64-69-69-68-=270	$154,100.00
Michael Allen	9	70-67-68-67-=272	$133,400.00
Robert Garrigus	T-10	65-67-68-73-=273	$101,966.66
Tim Petrovic	T-10	67-67-68-71-=273	$101,966.66
Tag Ridings	T-10	66-66-71-70-=273	$101,966.67
Cameron Beckman	T-10	68-68-67-70-=273	$101,966.67
Bob Estes	T-10	70-63-71-69-=273	$101,966.67
Chris Stroud	T-10	70-68-66-69-=273	$101,966.67